ASPEN PUBLISHERS

Complete Guide to Credit and Collection Law

AF722988

2009–2010 Edition

By Jay Winston and Arthur Winston

Highlights of the 2009–2010 Edition

As chief financial officers, credit managers, collection attorneys, and owners of large, medium-sized, and small businesses are well informed as to what procedures to use in the extension of credit and the practices that should be used to collect both consumer and business debts, their concern is summarized in two short sentences: "Can I do it legally?" and "Where do I find the answer?" This book is a comprehensive effort to provide answers.

The book was published in 1996 and is updated annually. This is the 13th annual edition. When the first edition was published by Prentice Hall, the book was 600 pages. Fourteen years later and 35,000 copies sold, the book has over 2,000 pages and may be the leading handbook in the industry.

The following is a summary of some of the highlights of this edition.

- *Bell v. Twombly*, a new U.S. Supreme Court decision has significantly expanded the criteria set forth in *Twombly*, a 2007 case decided by the Supreme Court which required that every claim in a complaint must be a "plausible" claim and not be based merely on conclusions that are not supported by facts. Another major element of the new case is that despite much interpretation of the extent of the *Twombly* case, which applies to an anti-trust situation, the court now stated that the concepts in *Twombly* apply to "all civil actions." Justice Kennedy has provided a clearer criteria as to how much factual information is required to defeat a motion to dismiss. (See Appendix to Chapter 7.)
- **Lender's Liability**—Pre-negotiation agreements are the instrument of choice before lenders make advances, grant loans or refinance. The sharp decrease in litigation on this topic proves the agreements are effective. (See Chapter 4.)
- **State Right of Assignment Laws**: The ACA International has provided us with a copy of the state right-of-assignment laws on a state-by-state listing which provides the section numbers and a short

Wolters Kluwer
Law & Business

summary of the right to assign claims under state law. (See Appendix to Chapter 7.)

- **Manifest Disregard of the Law**: A U.S. Supreme Court decision has fundamentally abolished this ground to vacate or modify a decision of the arbitrators. (See Chapter 5.)
- **The "Hanging Paragraph**." A look at the "hanging paragraph" in 11 U.S.C. 1325(a)(9). (See Chapter 6.)
- **Servicemembers Civil Relief Act**: A bulletin from the Comptroller of the Currency sets forth the new legal requirements to proceed against members of the armed forces. (See Appendix to Chapter 5.)
- **Telephone—Third Party Disclosure**: Sections 805(b), 806(6), and 807(11) of the Fair Debt Collection Practices Act describe specific requirements when communicating with third parties, especially by telephone. Several decisions from Florida address the issues raised in the *Foti* decision concerning the type of disclosure that must be made when leaving a message on the telephone. The appendices contain an interesting article written by Rozanne M. Anderson, Esq., a Vice President of ACA International, which cites the recent cases and submits the perspective of the ACA International. (See Chapter 15.)
- **Administrative Claims.** A closer look at the 20-day and 45-day window of opportunity on recent shipments to the bankrupt. (See Chapter 6.)
- **Legal Fees/Bankruptcy**: A recent decision has clarified the requirements to assert a claim for legal fees during a bankruptcy proceeding. (See Chapter 6.)

The following are new appendices:

- An article entitled "Foreclosing on a Mezzanine Loan Under UCC Article 9" prepared and provided by Peter E. Fisch, Steven Simkin and S.H. Spencer Compton, New York, New York. (Chapter 4.)
- State right-of-assignment laws provided by ACA International. (Chapter 7.)
- An article entitled "Voice Mail Messages in the Wake of *Foti*" provided by Rozanne M. Anderson, Esq. (The ACA International). (Chapter 15.)
- An article entitled "Pursuing U.S. Claims Against Foreign Debtors" prepared and provided by Johnathan C. Bolton of Fulbright & Jaworski L.L.P., Houston, Texas. (Chapter 4.)
- Sanctions Under Bankruptcy Act. (Chapter 7.)
- Modification of Licensing Law—Colorado. (Chapter 15.)

- Modifying or Correcting an Arbitration Award—9 USCS § 11. (Chapter 5.)
- Vacating Arbitration Award—9 USCS § 10. (Chapter 5.)
- Summary of Recent Revisions of Servicemembers Civil Relief Act issued by Office of Comptroller of the Currency (OCC Bulletin 2008-30) and Section 2203 (Housing and Economic Recovery Act). (Chapter 5.)
- Modifications of Law—Personal Information and Identity Theft—Massachusetts. (Chapter 9.)
- Confirmation of Plan—11 USC 1325 of the Bankruptcy Code. (Chapter 6.)
- Determination of Secured Claim—11 USC 506 of the Bankruptcy Code. (Chapter 6.)
- Discovery Provisions—FRCP Rule 26. (Chapter 17.)
- Identity Theft Federal Statutes. (Chapter 5.)

The purpose of this edition is to furnish users of a *Complete Guide to Credit and Collection Law* an explanation of the key laws that affect credit and collection. The information furnished has been absorbed by the authors attending financial services conferences, credit, and collection conferences, as well as auto finance and bankruptcy conferences during the year. We also subscribe to a significant number of publications in the auto finance, asset-based lending, commercial workout, and bankruptcy fields.

In addition to the American Bar Association (Consumer & Commercial Financial Services Subcommittees) and the New York, New Jersey, and Connecticut State Bar Associations, our firm is a member of several industry-wide trade associations, including: The Turnaround Management Association (TMA), The National Association of Retail Collection Attorneys (NARCA), the Commercial Law League of America (CLLA), National Association of Credit Management (NACM–Multiple chapters), the Map Attorney Program of the ACA International (formerly American Collectors Association, Inc.), and the American Bankruptcy Institute (ABI).

Our firm, Winston & Winston, P.C., New York, New York, has been for 30 years and continues to be actively engaged in the credit and collection industry. Our firm represents creditors in commercial, post-judgment enforcement, and bankruptcy litigation for banks, businesses, and financial institutions. We maintain our own network of attorneys across the country. During the year these attorneys often furnish us with information about new cases and changes in the law as well as new developments in the credit and collection industry. Lastly, we draw on our own experiences in servicing our clients and monitor decisions in the credit and collection area that are rendered during the year. Jay Winston has published many articles and presented many educational presentations over the year at various trade association conferences. Jay Winston is a certified instructor for ACA International.

Every attorney at some time will be approached to collect a debt against a business or a consumer. At the other end of the spectrum, many law firms treat credit and collection law as an area of expertise. Both must maintain access to the current developments in this area of the law, for both are subject to the Fair Debt Collection Practices Act.

Because educated individuals want to read the actual law as much as someone else's explanation and opinion of what the law means, we have included in the Appendices the actual federal law and the commentary to the federal law (which are explanations of the federal law) as well as examples of the various state laws in the more populated states and excerpts from key decisions. We also include in-depth analysis and many tables identifying the applicable laws of each state.

Our primary goal is to present a broad overview of the laws that affect the credit and collection effort, with more emphasis on the collection effort. Several chapters are exclusively devoted to the collection of debts from businesses. Most of the federal laws deal with consumer debtors. The new Bankruptcy Act is covered as well as the amendments to the Fair Credit Reporting Act. We have included over 1,000 case citations, citing mostly to the state appellate and federal cases.

The following are brief descriptions of the chapters together with some highlights:

- ***An Explanation of Legal Terminology in a Collection Case—Chapter 1*** provides an insight into the operation of the office of a collection firm. Legal terminology is defined so that the non-attorney understands the language of the attorney. An explanation of the progress of the suit and the options open to the client are presented. The design of this chapter is to enable the non-attorney to communicate more effectively with the collection attorney to collect the accounts and at the same time meticulously and carefully comply with the laws. *Chapter 1 contains an in-depth look at settlement negotiations and the contents of a settlement agreement, which incorporates a payout over time as well as a discussion of a general and mutual release.* Guidelines for testimony at a deposition and guidelines for testimony at a trial should provide some help to the individual subpoenaed as a witness. An updated analysis is provided of the treatment by the courts of claims for damages for emotional distress. Although no one likes to admit that a document has been misplaced, lost, or destroyed, the admissibility of evidence to replace lost or destroyed documents during a trial is addressed. An explanation of the various types of judgment, and the means to enforce the judgment is provided. The time restrictions for starting suit is covered.

- ***Letters and Telephone Calls—Chapter*** 2 reviews the preparation of letters and contacting the business and the consumer by telephone. The chapter covers the distinction between consumer and business debts and the interplay between collection letters and telephone calls. The four necessary steps to a successful phone call are outlined and ten frequent excuses used by businesses and consumers are listed, with the proper responses to said excuses.
- ***Legal Concepts of Business and Legal Remedies for Business Creditors—Chapters 3 and 4*** address business concepts and business remedies. We have added material on secondary liens, mezzanine financing, and inter-creditor agreements. The problems and the use of letters of credit are extensive including the "red clause" and the criteria for discrepancies. Article 2, the Sales Act as adopted in California, appears in the Appendix. The Appendices to Chapter 3 include examples of the law with regard to the Fraudulent Transfer Act, Assignment for the Benefit of Creditors, and the Mechanic's Lien Law. An interesting portion is devoted to the preparation of the credit application and how the credit application should be used in the collection effort. Another device to hold officers and directors liable is the de facto merger, where the business ceases to operate and reappears as a new business. The problems encountered in the sale of a debtor's assets and the procedures involved are addressed. *The proper approach to piercing the corporate veil is offered with criteria for supporting a suit against officers and directors of an insolvent corporation.* Chapter 4 contains in the Appendix an article on "Foreclosing on a Mezzanine Loan Under UCC Article 9."
- ***Legal Issues of Consumers—Chapter 5:*** To keep up with the times of the recent involvement of our military forces, we review the 2004 amendment entitled "The Service members Civil Relief Act," which replaced the "Soldiers and Sailors Civil Relief Act." The use of mandatory arbitration increased substantially to satisfy the desire of lenders to avoid class actions. AAA arbitration rules appear in the Appendices. *Manifest Disregard of the Law is no longer available to vacate or modify an arbitration award.* Divorces, deceased parties, jointly held property, relationships of husbands, wives and children, social security, and welfare recipients are all discussed. The ability to garnish members of the military service and the enforcement of gambling debts are also addressed, as is the use of 1099C. *Consumer attorney claims for emotional stress may have difficulty in most circuits.* The Appendices contain the statutes dealing with modifying and vacating arbitration awards.
- ***Bankruptcy—Chapter 6:*** We have reorganized and rewritten a large portion of this chapter due to the 500-page amendment entitled the

"Bankruptcy Abuse Prevention and Consumer Protection Act" (BAPCPA). Unfortunately, because of space limitations, we could not present the 500-page amendment to the Bankruptcy Act in the Appendix. The chapter is written from the perspective of the creditor. The Appendices contain some of the sections of the Code that deal with automatic stays, discharge, stay of action, and reaffirmation agreements, all of which have been modified by the new Bankruptcy Act. An old theory regarding insolvent businesses is analyzed that permits a creditor to prosecute a claim against officers, directors, principal shareholders and, in some instances, the lender. The new rights of creditors to reclaim property or receive an administrative claim may surprise some. Proof of claim 101 assists the creditor who wishes to file his or her own proof of claim with a step-by-step instruction on the proper way to prepare and to file a proof of claim. An in-depth treatment of strategy in preference litigation is included, as well as the recent *Kmart* decision affecting critical vendors and the right to pierce the corporate veil in bankruptcy is covered. The 363 sale used by many purchasers of assets carries some risks.

- *Law Firms and Collection Agencies—Chapter 7:* The statute of limitations for each state appears in a table in the Appendices. Bonding requirements for collection agencies are also listed in the Appendices. Chapter 7 itself deals primarily with selecting, working with, and monitoring outside attorneys or collection agencies, and includes *taping and monitoring telephone calls* and what to expect from international collection efforts throughout the world. We have provided a state survey of laws that affect attorneys engaged in a collection practice and a table of state right to assignment laws. The case taxing attorneys' fees is reported. The recent case which placed in issue when a contingent fee is entitled to be alleged and collected is discussed. **The rules of the game as to attorney fees in bankruptcy have changed**. The recent U.S. Supreme Court case which expanded Bell Twombly is discussed.
- *Checks, Notes, and Guarantees—Chapter 8:* The legal consequences of checks, notes, and guarantees are discussed, including certified checks, stale checks, unsigned checks, post-dated checks, stop payment checks, and bad check charges. The distinction between negotiable instruments and checks is explained. The obligations of the guarantor from a simple guarantee to a three-page small print guarantee offered by financial institutions are carefully considered. Section 3-311 covering paid-in-full checks is also explored in Chapter 7 with an in-depth Appendix prepared by Jay Winston, a co-author of this book. We have provided a summary of the Check Clearing for the 21st Century Act and have included a copy of the Act in the Appendix. Regulation E is now an Appendix. A form for using

a bank account as security for a loan provided by the American Bar Association is set forth in the Appendix.

- *Privacy—Chapter 9:* This chapter deals primarily with the Gramm-Leach-Bliley Act. Several Appendices are presented to furnish information concerning the contents of the notices and sample clauses, all provided by the Federal Trade Commission. The essentials from a collection point of view of the Health Insurance Portability and Accountability Act is offered. The issue of privacy, harassment, malicious prosecution, and abuse of process are addressed.
- ***Secured Lending: Real Estate—Mortgages and Secured Lending: Personal Property—Chapters 10 and 11*** deal with secured lending, with Chapter 10 dealing with real estate and mortgages and Chapter 11 dealing with personal property. *An extensive analysis of judicial foreclosure, non-judicial foreclosure, and deed in lieu of foreclosure are offered, together with the Real Estate Settlement Procedure Act in the Appendices. Chapter 10 is primarily devoted to the application of UCC Revised Article 9, which was finally adopted in all 50 states in 2003.* The thrust of the chapter is to distinguish the Revised Article 9 from the old Article 9 and in what respect the procedures and application of the law are different. The last state statute (New York) holding the lessor vicariously liable for damages when the lessee (short-term rental of a vehicle) suffers an accident while driving the rental vehicle has been repealed. The Appendices contain Revised Article 9 as adopted in California. The Appendices also list the places to file a financing statement under Revised Article 9.
- ***Repossession of Property—Chapter 12*** undertakes to explain the legal difficulties in repossessing personal property, principally vehicles. A commercially reasonable sale and peaceful repossession are clarified. The pre-repossession requirements and the post-repossession requirements for motor vehicles are listed by state in the Appendices. Cure notices, mailing requirements, breach of peace, and liability of lenders and lessors for a breach of peace, are reviewed.
- *Fair Credit Reporting Act—Chapter 13:* The Fair and Accurate Transaction Act of 2004 amended the Fair Credit Reporting Act. A summary of the new system of "alerts" is covered and points out the various ways that consumers may alert the credit reporting agencies if they have been a victim of, or suspect that they have been a victim of, identity theft. In the Appendix we have included a copy of the Fair Credit Reporting Act, together with the amendment, which distinguishes the deletions in the Fair Credit Reporting Act and the additions of the Fair and Accurate Transaction Act (with the permission of the ACA International). The chapter covers the permissible purposes of a consumer report (a recent case significantly limits the definition

of permissible purpose), as well as the obligations of the furnisher of information to a credit reporting agency and the necessary restrictions placed on credit reporting agencies when they receive credit information, including the changes due to the amendment. After a bankruptcy the issue of reporting is discussed.

- *What to Do When You Are Served—Chapter 14:* A summons and complaint is mailed to your business by the Secretary of State. What do you do? Hopefully, we have answered most of the questions that cross the mind of the defendant.
- *Fair Debt Collection Practices Act—Chapter 15* is devoted to the Fair Debt Collection Practices Act. The Class Action Fairness Act was enacted into law in 2005. The principle purpose of the Act was to prevent the consumer legal profession from shopping the action to a favorable state court and to a favorable judge. The Act now requires certain types of class actions to fall under the jurisdiction of the federal courts and certain types of class actions to fall under the jurisdiction of state courts. A mistake of law may now be a bona fide error. The Act also covers new methods of awarding attorneys' fees and new criteria for coupon settlements. The amendments appear in the Appendix. We have included an Appendix prepared by the ACA International which covers the consequences of issuing a 1099 and recommendations how to proceed with a 1099 so that the courts will not treat the filing of a 1099 as a discharge of the debt. An article on voice mail messages is included by Rozanne M. Anderson.
- For attorneys, in Chapter 15, an in-depth analysis and a history of meaningful involvement appears in the Appendix written by the co-author, Jay Winston, who also contributed an article on "Responding to Debt Protestors" in the Appendix. He also offers some creative and unique approaches to defending an FDCPA lawsuit. A section-by-section analysis of the Act is offered. The Fair Debt Collection Practices Act and the Staff Commentary appear in the Appendices. Validation, verification, unfair practices, overshadowing, imputed knowledge, pro se plaintiffs, attorneys' fees, deceptive and misleading conduct, the safe harbor letter, the proper amount of the debt, and current cases including the recent case requiring the creditor to investigate whether the agency is violating the law—a catch-22 situation—are discussed. Another recent decision may change the script for training debt collectors (who work the telephone calls), requiring identification of the debt collector.
- *Truth in Lending Regulation Z—Chapter 16* deals with the Truth in Lending Act and Regulation Z which are included in the Appendix. The initial disclosures, the disclosure of fees, and the recent Supreme Court decision on the right to rescission are addressed in Chapter 16

as well as the "yield spread premium." The Fair Credit Billing Act describes the rights of debtors in the billing process.

- *E-Commerce Technology—Chapter 17* is devoted to the three electronic laws: the Electronic Signature in Global and National Commerce Act (E-Sign), a federal law that has been adopted, the Uniform Electronic Transaction Act, and the Uniform Computer Information Transaction Act, which has not received a favorable response in the legislatures of the states. The chapter also covers the use of e-mail in litigation and collection as well as The National Automated Clearinghouse Network (NACHA), which is making significant progress in the electronic transfer of funds. The E-Sign Act and the Uniform Electronic Transaction Act are included in the Appendices. The Appendix contains an article entitled "Practical Strategies for Constructing Electronic Discovery Agreements."
- *Equal Credit Opportunity Act—Chapter 18:* We have provided Regulation B of the Equal Credit Opportunity Act in the Appendix. Discrimination, adverse action, the credit application are addressed. The circumstances under which the lender can obtain the guarantee of the wife for her husband's business loan are covered.
- *Skiptracing—Chapter 19* deals with locating a debtor who has disappeared.

An effort is being made to present the book as a one-stop guide to the various laws affecting credit and collection that you will refer to again and again in addressing your legal issues.

We welcome information as to new legislation, state and federal, new, significant or interesting court decisions, challenging or interesting articles, as well as suggestions for new topics or new material for the book. If mistakes are noticed, please notify us. Our address is: Winston & Winston, P.C., 295 Madison Avenue, Suite 930, New York, New York 10017, Attention: Jay Winston. Telephone: 212-532-2700; Fax: 212-532-2722; E-Mail: jwin@winstonandwinston.com, website - www.winstonandwinston.com.

10/09

For questions concerning this shipment, billing, or other customer service matters, call our Customer Service Department at 1-800-234-1660.

For toll-free ordering, please call 1-800-638-8437.

ASPEN PUBLISHERS

COMPLETE GUIDE TO

CREDIT AND COLLECTION LAW

2009–2010 EDITION

JAY WINSTON
ARTHUR WINSTON

Wolters Kluwer
Law & Business

AUSTIN BOSTON CHICAGO NEW YORK THE NETHERLANDS

Printed in the United States of America

ISBN 978-0-7355-8079-4

ISSN 1931-4639

About Wolters Kluwer Law & Business

Wolters Kluwer Law & Business is a leading provider of research information and workflow solutions in key specialty areas. The strengths of the individual brands of Aspen Publishers, CCH, Kluwer Law International and Loislaw are aligned within Wolters Kluwer Law & Business to provide comprehensive, in-depth solutions and expert-authored content for the legal, professional and education markets.

CCH was founded in 1913 and has served more than four generations of business professionals and their clients. The CCH products in the Wolters Kluwer Law & Business group are highly regarded electronic and print resources for legal, securities, antitrust and trade regulation, government contracting, banking, pension, payroll, employment and labor, and healthcare reimbursement and compliance professionals.

Aspen Publishers is a leading information provider for attorneys, business professionals and law students. Written by preeminent authorities, Aspen products offer analytical and practical information in a range of specialty practice areas from securities law and intellectual property to mergers and acquisitions and pension/benefits. Aspen's trusted legal education resources provide professors and students with high-quality, up-to-date and effective resources for successful instruction and study in all areas of the law.

Kluwer Law International supplies the global business community with comprehensive English-language international legal information. Legal practitioners, corporate counsel and business executives around the world rely on the Kluwer Law International journals, loose-leafs, books and electronic products for authoritative information in many areas of international legal practice.

Loislaw is a premier provider of digitized legal content to small law firm practitioners of various specializations. Loislaw provides attorneys with the ability to quickly and efficiently find the necessary legal information they need, when and where they need it, by facilitating access to primary law as well as state-specific law, records, forms and treatises.

Wolters Kluwer Law & Business, a unit of Wolters Kluwer, is headquartered in New York and Riverwoods, Illinois. Wolters Kluwer is a leading multinational publisher and information services company.

ASPEN PUBLISHERS SUBSCRIPTION NOTICE

This Aspen Publishers product is updated on a periodic basis with supplements to reflect important changes in the subject matter. If you purchased this product directly from Aspen Publishers, we have already recorded your subscription for the update service.

If, however, you purchased this product from a bookstore and wish to receive future updates and revised or related volumes billed separately with a 30-day examination review, please contact our Customer Service Department at 1-800-234-1660, or send your name, company name (if applicable), address, and the title of the product to:

ASPEN PUBLISHERS
7201 McKinney Circle
Frederick, MD 21704

Important Aspen Publishers Contact Information

- To order any Aspen Publishers title, go to *www.aspenpublishers.com* or call 1-800-638-8437.
- To reinstate your manual update service, call 1-800-638-8437.
- To contact Customer Care, e-mail *customer.care@aspenpublishers.com,* call 1-800-234-1660, fax 1-800-901-9075, or mail correspondence to Order Department, Aspen Publishers, PO Box 990, Frederick, MD 21705.
- To review your account history or pay an invoice online, visit *www .aspenpublishers.com/payinvoices.*

Wolters Kluwer
Law & Business

To Audrey, Liz, Rory and Zoe

ACKNOWLEDGMENTS

I would like to specifically thank the following persons and organizations for some of the appendix material appearing in the book:

1. ACA International (formerly American Collectors Association, Inc.) Minneapolis, Minnesota, for "Special Text Requirements for Collection Notices" (1/23/08) in Chapter 15; State Right of Assignment Laws in Chapter 7; Security Breach Notification Statutes by State (7/2/07) in Chapter 5; State Survey of Laws Governing Commercial Collection (12/3/07) in Chapter 4; State Statutes—Statute of Limitations (2/27/08) in Chapter 5.
2. An article entitled "Voice Mail Messages in the Wake of *Foti*" prepared by Rozanne M. Anderson, Esq. (The ACA International) in Chapter 15.
3. American Bar Association for the suggested form agreement, Deposit Account Control Agreement, to be used to grant a security interest in a deposit account at a bank in Chapter 8.
4. Mark Sidoti and Phillip Duffy, Newark, New Jersey for an article published in the New York Law Journal, New York, NY entitled "Practical Strategies for Constructing Electronic Discovery Agreements (12/3/07) in Chapter 17.
5. *The American Bank Lawyer* for a listing in Chapter 11 of the state offices where the financing statements are to be recorded under the Revised Uniform Commercial Code Section 9. *The American Bank Lawyer* newsletter is published by Texas Tech University School of Law in Lubbock, Texas.
6. John Poles of Poles, Tublin, Stratakis, Gonzalez & Weichart, LLP for an article on the Ship Mortgage Act in Chapter 12.
7. Adam Olshan Esq. of Wolpoff & Abramson, LLP, Rockville, Maryland for a State Survey of Laws Affecting Attorneys in Collection Practice in Chapter 7; reprinted with permission of his former Law Firm, Howard Lee Schiff, P.C.
8. The Commercial Law League of America for the Operative Guides for Forwarders and Receivers in Chapter 7.
9. American Arbitration Association for their Commercial Arbitration Rules in Chapter 5.
10. An article entitled "Pursuing U.S. Claims Against Foreign Debtors" prepared and provided by Johnathan C. Bolton of Fulbright & Jaworski L.L.P., Houston, Texas in Chapter 4.
11. An article entitled "Foreclosing on a Mezzanine Loan Under UCC Article 9" prepared and provided by Peter E. Fisch, Steven Simkin and S.H. Spencer Compton, New York, New York in Chapter 4.
12. Susan Grant for her special help and assistance in organizing and arranging the contents of this book.

NOTE

No attempt has been made here to review, include, or comment upon all the relevant laws and statutes. The major federal laws mentioned in the text or set forth in the appendices must be considered in light of the laws passed by each of the fifty states. Some states have passed separate laws that directly subject creditors to regulations. Other states have passed more oppressive or burdensome mirror images of the federal law.

Most of the general statements presented are representative of the laws in the majority of states, but some states have passed laws that modify or change the legal consequences of the general statement. Exceptions exist to every general statement. Therefore, a general statement should not be used to fit a particular set of circumstances until after a thorough examination of the facts and laws plus a review of the decisions of the court of the appropriate state.

Laws and statutes are continually amended, revised, and repealed and court decisions may be reversed or rendered obsolete by more recent decisions or decisions of higher courts. The limited material presented reflects what generally existed at the time this book was written. By the time this 2009-2010 edition reaches the reader, changes in the statutes and more recent cases may have affected the contents. A review of all the state laws and federal laws as well as the court decisions of the federal courts and the state courts should be performed before any decision is made with regard to any legal problem involved with the credit or collection effort. Consultation with an attorney is always recommended before proceeding.

While we attempt to cover all the major amendments to laws as well as the major decisions that affect the industry, we know that it is impossible to be comprehensive and complete. There are certainly many changes in the laws of the various states as well as decisions that we have not addressed, either because we are not aware of them or because of the limited space available.

The tables offered were prepared months or perhaps years prior to publication, and thus the information should be verified.

This book is not intended to be a substitute for consultation with an attorney. Consultation is not only recommended but encouraged. We hope that this volume provides you with additional compliance guidance in your credit and collection efforts.

SPECIAL NOTE

In this and prior editions of the book, the authors refer to the area circuit courts around the United States and sometimes refer to the judges in the 13 circuit courts.

The major circuits are the Second Circuit, Seventh Circuit, and the Ninth Circuit, and the decisions handed down by these circuits are frequently followed by the other circuits.

A listing of the states covered by each Circuit Court of Appeals follows on the next page.

First Circuit

Maine
New Hampshire
Massachusetts
Rhode Island
Puerto Rico

Second Circuit

New York
Vermont
Connecticut

Third Circuit

Pennsylvania
New Jersey
Delaware
Virgin Islands

Fourth Circuit

West Virginia
Maryland
Richmond
North Carolina
South Carolina

Fifth Circuit

Texas
Louisiana
Mississippi

Sixth Circuit

Ohio
Kentucky
Tennessee
Michigan

Seventh Circuit

Wisconsin
Illinois
Indiana

Eighth Circuit

Arkansas
Missouri
Iowa
Nebraska
South Dakota
North Dakota
Minnesota

Ninth Circuit

Washington
Oregon
Idaho
Nevada
California
Arizona
Alaska
Hawaiian Islands
Northern Mariana Islands
Guam

Tenth Circuit

Wyoming
Utah
Colorado
Kansas
Oklahoma
New Mexico

Eleventh Circuit

Alabama
Georgia
Florida

Federal Circuit

(Patent, etc.)

District of Columbia Circuit

CONTENTS

APPENDICES

CHAPTER 1

An Explanation of Legal Terminology in a Collection Case

The credit and collection manager will frequently have direct dealings with the in-house attorney or the outside counsel. A strong working knowledge of legal terminology is critical during the course of these conversations. This chapter will present an explanation of legal terminology as it affects a civil collection case against a business or a consumer.

Our firm conducts collection efforts throughout the country through our network of attorneys. We practice in the New York, New Jersey, and Connecticut courts, and primarily are exposed to the terminology commonly used in these state court systems. While the legal terms may vary from state to state, the institution of a lawsuit, the entry of a judgment, and the procedures to collect a judgment are similar in almost all of the states (with the exception of Louisiana, which still operates in some ways under the Napoleonic code).

The listings and explanations set forth here are for the purpose of furnishing general information and are not intended to be specific definitions of particular terms or a particular set of circumstances. The definitions or explanations should not be relied on as comprehensive and accurate in view of the limited space available in a book of this size. They are provided as a general overview with the understanding that each statement may have exceptions, may not be complete, and may have limitations or restrictions. For a full interpretation of any term, we recommend consulting with counsel.

JURISDICTION OF THE COURT

The "jurisdiction" of a court means the conditions and terms which must be satisfied to enable a party to commence suit or a proceeding in that particular court. Certain courts of the state, usually the lower courts, are considered "original" jurisdiction, which means that an individual or business may commence a proceeding initially in that court. Other courts are deemed to be courts of appellate jurisdiction in that the only way a proceeding can be brought into that court is to appeal a decision from a lower court. The highest courts in most states are considered appellate courts whose only function is to review appeals from the lower courts.

The courts of original jurisdiction set forth the requirements to be met before a suit is commenced. The courts are often divided into criminal courts, family courts, landlord-tenant courts, surrogate courts, small claims courts, or civil courts. In most instances, credit and collection matters are instituted in civil courts, courts of general jurisdiction or small claims courts. Equitable remedies such as rescission or unjust enrichment, or an order of seizure, are only available in certain courts. The selection of the courts depends mainly on the remedy and balance demanded in the complaint. For example, in New York City, the small claims court will only hear cases involving damages of $5,000 or less; the Civil Court in the City of New York will hear cases involving damages up to $25,000; the Supreme Court of the state will hear all cases involving damages in excess of $25,000. Only the Supreme Courts of New York are authorized to grant equitable remedies. Jurisdiction varies from state to state, from county to county as well as from city to city. Consultation with your counsel is recommended.

The Justice or Magistrate Courts are courts of original jurisdiction, and usually prohibit suits in excess of a certain amount, generally between $1,000 and $10,000. The opportunity for discovery is limited, and after the defendant interposes an answer, the court sets a date for trial. Sometimes the judge will hold a preliminary conference to settle the case. In many jurisdictions, a corporation must be represented by an attorney. Adjournments of the trial are not readily granted. The costs to commence suit are significantly less than city, town, county, or state courts. Justice and Magistrate Courts usually handle consumer disputes and problems. This is not an advantageous forum for collection cases because the plaintiff must appear in court with a witness, and, in some cases, with an attorney. These appearances are expensive if the debtor defaults, and exceed the savings in court costs. In metropolitan areas, the equivalent court is usually denoted as the "small claims court," and often holds court in the evening hours.

SELECTION OF JURISDICTION. There are various rules which determine the court used by a plaintiff in suing a defendant. If a business or individual is suing a consumer, Fair Debt Collection Practices Act (FDCPA) requires the suit against the consumer to be instituted in the county in which the consumer resides or where the transaction occurred regardless of where the business is located. One business suing another business constitutes a commercial transaction, which may be brought either where the defendant corporation is located or in the county in which the transaction took place. Where the business defendant is located outside the state, the plaintiff may commence a suit within the state if the transaction took place within the plaintiff's state, and jurisdiction is obtained under a "Long Arm" statute, which allows service on the defendant in another state. Sometimes the business agreement will identify what court should be used and what state law will govern or whether arbitration is required. In some instances, the federal court may be utilized for disputes between parties from different states.

The plaintiff certainly has a distinct advantage in instituting suit in the state in which the creditor is located. Before any creditor embarks upon this course, the creditor should examine the laws of the state in which the judgment is to be enforced to be certain that the state will docket the judgment and enable the creditor to enforce the judgment without the institution of a new suit in a distant state. For example, New York, Connecticut, and Vermont will not docket a default judgment obtained in another state. A new suit would have to be instituted in those states. If the defendant filed an appearance or answered in the action and a judgment was ultimately entered, all states give full faith and credit to the judgment.[1]

In the business environment, parties to a contract may include a "forum selection clause" wherein they have selected which state law will apply and may also select which court will have jurisdiction of any dispute. Such clauses that are contained in written agreements and signed by the parties are prima facie valid and will be enforced unless enforcement is shown by the resisting party to be "unreasonable" under the circumstances. Thus, a party may validly consent though contractual designation to be sued in the jurisdiction where he cannot be found for service of process.

Where consumers are involved, the specifics of the transaction may be covered by laws which protect the consumer and require the suit to be commenced where the transaction took place or where the consumer resides. Since this decision in 1972, many consumer laws were enacted designed to protect the consumer from unreasonable forum selection clauses.[2]

LONG-ARM JURISDICTION. Most states have what is known as the "Long-Arm Statute," which enables a plaintiff to institute a suit in the state where the plaintiff resides and to serve the defendant in a distant state.

---

[1]Fair Debt Collection Practices Act, 15 U.S.C. § 1692I(2).

[2]*M/S Bremen v. Zapata Off-Shore Company*, 407 U.S. 1 (1972).

The Long-Arm Statute varies from state to state but, in general, provides that if the transaction took place in the state where the plaintiff resides, the plaintiff may serve the defendant in a distant state and the defendant will have to appear in the state in which the plaintiff is located. Thus, if the defendant has a plant in Texas, but conducted enough business in New York to constitute a presence in New York, the state court of New York has jurisdiction and the summons and complaint may be served in Texas.

Service on the defendant is usually accomplished by forwarding the summons to a sheriff (or other authorized process server) in the county where the defendant resides; the sheriff will serve the defendant in that county. The defendant then must decide whether to defend the case or permit the case to proceed to a default judgment. In most instances the second state will give full faith and credit to a default judgment (no answer or appearance by the defendant) obtained in another state.

PRE-JUDGMENT ATTACHMENT

Pre-judgment attachment is a proceeding that enables a creditor to seize assets of the debtor simultaneously with the institution of the suit by service of a summons and complaint. This powerful remedy assures a creditor that the judgment will be paid from the assets attached. The court is allowing the creditor to seize assets, even though the debtor may have valid defenses and may be successful in dismissing the creditor's claim. During the attachment the debtor is unable to use or sell the assets attached, that is, the bank account and the real estate. If the debtor is later successful in dismissing the complaint, the creditor may be severely penalized because the debtor has been deprived of the use of assets and will undoubtedly sue the creditor for damages. For this reason, in many states a bond must be posted by the creditor, as security, usually one to two times the fair market value of the property seized. For example, if the debtor is about to buy a house and the funds for the closing are in a bank account that has been attached, the debtor cannot perform, loses the house, and forfeits the deposit.

PROPER NAME OF DEFENDANT

Suits must be instituted against the proper party whether a business or individual. If you institute suit and use the incorrect name of the individual, the judgment will be filed against the incorrect name of the individual and you will be unable to execute on the assets of the debtor. In many instances the debtor provides a social security number along with the proper name. All credit applications should contain provisions instructing the debtor to print his name on the appropriate line, instead of having the creditor ask verbally for the name and then writing it on the application. If a mistake is made in the spelling of the first or last name, a suit instituted against this incorrect name may be attacked. Credit applications should be reviewed carefully to be certain that the debtor's name is accurate. Suits are instituted against individuals by using the first and last name of the party and if a middle initial is provided, we include the middle initial to differentiate that person from other people with the same first and last name. Additional information to identify an individual is the address of the party, the social security number, and the date of birth. A post office box address is not considered adequate because a party cannot be served at a post office box. An individual is usually served at their residential address, or at his/her place of business. Sometimes individuals operate under alias names or maiden names. If the alias is known, it should be provided to the attorney to enable the process server to serve the summons and complaint on the correct person. If the defendant is operating under an alias and the process server is not aware of the alias, service of the summons of complaint may not be made.

Business. Businesses operate as sole proprietorships, partnerships, or corporations. When instituting suit against a business, we must determine whether the debtor falls within one of these three categories. Many of the states have separate requirements for institution of suit against unions, trade associations, charitable associations, and other types of entities which do not fall within the criteria of the three types of business operations.

Sole Proprietor. A sole proprietorship occurs when an individual is doing business under a trade name or its own individual name. The proper party to sue is John Jones individually and d/b/a Jones Advertising (d/b/a means "doing business as"). If we sue him individually, we would be able to reach the assets of the business of Jones Advertising (because he is personally operating under the name of Jones Advertising), plus his own personal assets. If we just sue the business, Jones Advertising Company, this would be useless because Jones Advertising Company does not exist except as a trade name.

Partnership. A partnership is similar to a sole proprietorship except instead of one person operating under a trade name, two or more people operate under a trade name (John Jones and Mary Jones d/b/a Jones Advertising). In both sole proprietorships and partnerships, the business may end in "co." or "company." A corporation can operate under a trade name such as "Jones Corp." d/b/a as "Jones Advertising."

Corporation. Corporations must be sued under their proper corporate name. In most states corporations are identified by the words and letters which are at the end of the name such as "Corp.," "Corporation," "Inc.," "Co. Inc.," "Incorporation," or "Ltd." Separate identifications are designated for professional corporations such as attorneys or accountants (in New York designated as "P.C."). The limited liability companies are now designated "LLC." (A limited liability company is a mixture of a partnership and corporation and the name usually ends in "LLC.")

The key to meeting these problems is a proper credit application. A designation should appear on the credit application as to whether the business defendant is an individual partnership, sole proprietorship, or corporation. *We recommend that a copy of the first check received from the customer be photocopied since the proper business name is on the check.* Prior to starting suit against a corporation, it is suggested that a corporate search be performed with the Secretary of State to confirm the corporate name.

For partnerships and individuals d/b/a under a trade name, the assets of the individual and partners may be reached.

COMMENCING A SUIT

Summons. In a civil action, the summons is the instrument initially served upon the defendant to commence the suit. The summons acts as a notice and identifies the court in which the action is being brought and the address of the court. The summons sets forth the time period within which the defendant must answer or the date and time that the defendant must appear in court or file an appearance. The summons also may contain other local rules, such as indicating a particular room where the defendant must appear.

Complaint. In the complaint the plaintiff recites the grounds for relief and damages from the defendant. The complaint may state a claim for breach of contract, monies loaned to the defendant and not paid, or a claim for merchandise sold to the defendant which remains unpaid. The complaint may contain several claims, that is, "causes of action" or "counts." The complaint is attached to the summons or incorporated into the summons depending upon the rules of the local court, and is usually served on the defendant along with the summons. Sometimes a summons is served and a complaint is served after the defendant appears. The defendant appears by serving a paper (Notice of Appearance) stating that the defendant appears.

In many states the complaint must be supported by a document signed by the attorney upon information and belief or by the creditor. These documents are often referred to as an affidavit, certification, or verification. These documents generally require the creditor to affirm that the balance owed to the creditor is due and owing.

Service of Papers. In most jurisdictions the plaintiff must file the summons and complaint with the court (*before service* of the summons and complaint) and pay a fee ranging from $35 to $350. (The purpose of this filing fee is to raise funds for the court.) Most statutes provide that the summons and complaint must be served within a period of time after the filing, which is 90 to 120 days. If service is not completed, a new fee must be paid. In some jurisdictions service may be first made and then the fee paid. If service is not made, no fee is paid. Upon payment of the fee, the court will issue a case number (index or docket number) to identify and create a file for the case, similar to a file number system used in most businesses. The same problems occur in court as in any business. Papers are misfiled and files are lost. Even when counsel can replace lost papers, valuable time is lost and sometimes proceedings must be repeated and started over. Summons and complaints are usually served by the Sheriff of the County. A flat fee is paid plus an additional fee based on the mileage, but process serving firms may serve in most states. In some states they must be licensed. The fee for service may range from $20 to $100 per paper. In the Justice, Magistrate and small claims court, state law allows the summons and complaint to be served by certified mail. Many states permit the use of process servers.

Service of Summons and Complaint. Although the law varies from state to state, three methods are generally available to serve a summons and complaint:

1. **Personal Service:** The individual is personally served by placing the paper in the hands of the debtor or at the feet of the debtor.
2. **Substituted Service:** This is done in several ways: by serving on a suitable person at the business or in the household; by serving a neighbor plus mailing the papers to the debtor; serving a doorman or nailing the papers to the door of the last known residence of the debtor (Nail and Mail). State laws allow one or more combinations of these procedures, and usually provide strict details as well as conditions when this type of service may be used.
3. **Service by Publication:** This type of service is used when the defendant cannot be found, but assets of the defendant (such as real estate) are located in the jurisdiction. Publication of the summons in newspapers for several weeks several times a week is generally required. Application to court to use this method is necessary. Each state has its own procedures, conditions, and time frames, but due diligence must be exercised in attempting to locate the party before publication is available. This method of service is expensive, because of the application to court and the cost of publishing notices in the newspaper.

Service on a Corporation. A corporation is usually served by personal service on an officer or managing agent of the corporation who apparently is the party in charge of the office where the corporation is located. In addition, every state has a requirement that a corporation, when filing a certificate of incorporation, designate the Secretary of State as authorized to accept service of papers for the corporation. A creditor can serve the Secretary of State's office (or the proper office designated by the state) and service would be effective. The Secretary of State mails the summons to the address designated on the certificate of incorporation; *any corporation moving to a new address should so notify the Secretary of State of the new address.*

Service on a Partnership and Limited Liability Company. The only effective way to serve a partnership is to serve one of the partners in the same way an individual is served. A limited liability company's structure is more similar to a partnership and, thus, a partner must be served.

Defective Service. Sometimes the debtor will claim improper service. The process server may have served the wrong person by personal service; the summons may have been mailed to the wrong address; the debtor may have been staying at a hotel when service is alleged to have been made at home; or the corporation may allege that the managing agent served was not a managing agent and was not authorized to accept service. The procedure is for the defendant to assert defective service in the answer, and thereafter an application to court is made by either party for a hearing to be held to determine if service was proper. If the hearing officer determines proper service was made, the application will be denied and the case will proceed. If service is held to be defective, the case will be dismissed and the creditor will be forced to start all over again (assuming the Statute of Limitations has not expired).

If the transaction is covered by the FDCPA, the creditor is required to institute suit where the consumer resides or where the transactions occurred.

ANSWERS AND DEMURRERS

An answer or demurrer is the response to the complaint and states how the defendant disputes the claim set forth in the complaint. The normal answer may contain denials of each claim made in the complaint taking the form of "deny each and every allegation of paragraph 4 of the complaint." Affirmative defenses may also be set forth, including:

1. **Statute of Limitations:** The law recognizes that a claim against another party should be resolved within a reasonable time.

Accordingly, the statute provides that a suit must be started within a certain prescribed time or else the claim is deemed abandoned. The time limits vary from state to state. One state may provide a statute of limitations of four years for goods sold and delivered while another state may provide only three years. The time limit usually starts from the time the transaction took place; so that if the merchandise was shipped in April 1998, and the Statute of Limitations was four years, a suit would have to be started by April 2002. A key issue is choice of law if the two states have different time periods.

2. **Payment:** Usually, payment must be alleged as an affirmative defense.
3. **Fraud:** Inducing the defendant to enter into the agreement by fraud usually is an affirmative defense.
4. **Lack of jurisdiction:** For example, an attack on the personal jurisdiction of the court over the defendant.
5. Failure to state a claim upon which relief can be granted.
6. **Laches:** an unreasonable delay in prosecuting.
7. **Estoppel:** Where an act of plaintiff prevents or prohibits plaintiff from instituting suit.

ESTOPPEL

Estoppel is a word of art often used by attorneys, but it does possess different meanings.

Collateral Estoppel. Once an issue has been determined by a court having jurisdiction over the matter, that resolution is conclusive in any future litigation involving the party to the prior case wherein it was decided—even if it involves a different claim. The purpose of collateral estoppel is to prevent re-litigating the same issue involving the same parties. The issues in the two separate proceedings must be the same. Collateral estoppel is normally not available if the prior judgment was entered by default, for the issue was never litigated.

Equitable Estoppel. A defensive doctrine preventing one party from taking unfair advantage of another when, through false language or conduct, the person to be estopped has induced another person to act in a certain way with the result that the other person has been injured in some way (Black's Law Dictionary, 7th Edition, 1999). This usually requires the other party to rely on the representation and prevents the party from acting against his own statement or representation. To have equitable estoppel you must have a false representation and a lack of knowledge on behalf of the other party and reliance on the representation resulting in an injury.

In Section 1-103, the Uniform Commercial Code states that unless displaced by its particular provisions, the principles of law and equity and the law of merchant and the law relative to contract, principle and agent, *estoppel*, fraud, misrepresentation, duress, coercion, mistake, bankruptcy, and other validating or invalidating cause supplement the Code's provisions.

COUNTERCLAIM—CROSS-CLAIM

Whenever a suit is started against a defendant, the defendant may assert defenses to the suit. The defendant may plead a complaint against the plaintiff on a totally separate claim that may or may not have a connection with the claim of the plaintiff. This is described as a *counterclaim.* If an attorney or doctor sues for services rendered, the defendant may counterclaim for damages for malpractice.

Response or Reply to Counterclaim. In the event the defendant asserts a counterclaim, the plaintiff has an opportunity to respond or reply to the counterclaim. This is the equivalent of an answer by the defendant to the complaint, except the plaintiff is answering the defendant's counterclaim. In some courts, if you do not file a reply or answer to the counterclaim, the defendant can obtain a default against the plaintiff on the counterclaim. In other courts, the counterclaim is assumed to be denied.

Cross-Claim. When the defendant has a claim against a third party arising out of the transaction, the defendant may cross-claim against the third-party defendant or co-defendant in the same suit (a cross-claim against an insurance company for indemnification, for example). The cross-claim is then served on the third party together with the complaint and answer. A defendant can bring a new party into the case by serving a complaint on the new party and adding the suit to the existing action.

Quantum Meruit. Often when drafting a complaint based on an oral agreement where one party has performed all the services or delivered the merchandise and the other party has not made payment, your attorney may include claims which are designed to overcome the failure to have a written agreement. Wherever an oral agreement is the basis of a lawsuit, counsel must always consider the fact that the proof and the terms of the oral agreement is a question of the credibility of your client and the defendant when they testify before the court. As a result they often use a claim for quantum meruit or an account stated.

The claim for quantum meruit is basically a claim that:

1. The plaintiff performs services for the defendant.
2. These services were accepted and the benefits of the services were used by the defendant.
3. The plaintiff expected payment for the services rendered.

This last element of expecting payment may present problems where the services rendered were not within the scope of the contract. An example would be an oral contract to paint the house, and the painter rendered additional services without an agreement and spent an hour fixing the gutters. The plaintiff may have a difficult time proving the expected compensation.

Account Stated. Another claim that may be made is one for an account stated. The account stated is often used where the parties entered an oral agreement and then bills were sent to the defendant each month or the parties entered a written contract which failed to include a description of the particular services rendered or goods that were sold. A dispute arises as to whether the plaintiff was expecting compensation.

The account stated consists of the plaintiff sending bills each month for the amount due and the defendant ignores the bills. The defendant does not send to plaintiff anything in writing that the services were inadequate, late or not done on time. If it was goods and not services, the defendant does not allege a shortage or that the goods were defective or that delivery was late. The plaintiff's claim is that the defendant said nothing despite receipt of bills each month. Counsel is attempting to offer the account stated as evidence of the fact that the defendant owes the money.

Unjust Enrichment. When all other legal and contractual claims fail, this simple allegation covers a broad brush stroke. The concept sometimes is used in conjunction with the contractual claim.

COMPULSORY ARBITRATION

In many of the metropolitan courts the judges use a system of compulsory arbitration or mediation. Discovery is usually not allowed and both parties must submit the dispute to an arbitrator or mediator (*see* Chapter 5). The difference from private arbitration is that the loser still receives the option to seek a trial in the court system, for the loser has not waived the right to trial by a judge or jury. Sometimes the loser must pay minor additional costs or expenses to exercise this right. In many courts, the loser does not have a right to new trial if they did not appear at the arbitration hearing.

DISCOVERY PROCEEDINGS

Discovery proceedings occur after an answer has been interposed by a defendant denying the allegations in the complaint. The purpose of discovery proceedings is to enable either party to a lawsuit to obtain the details of the claim or defense of the other party. By determining these details, the parties can narrow the issues and prevent surprise at the trial. Often the information obtained or furnished leads the parties to dispose of the case prior to trial.

There are five major devices used to obtain information about the other party's claim: demand for a bill of particulars, interrogatories, depositions of parties and witnesses, production of documents, and notices to admit. These pleadings can be served by either party because the defendant requests information concerning the plaintiff's claim and the plaintiff seeks information as to the defenses asserted by the defendant. If the questions are improper or the answers inadequate, the defendant must object or the plaintiff must apply to court for relief.

Demand for a Bill of Particulars. This device is not available in all states, but where available, a set of questions is submitted to the plaintiff to explain the details of the complaint. An example might be a request to set forth how plaintiff arrives at $100,000 damages for a breach of contract. A bill of particulars is similar to interrogatories, but confined to questions about the complaint and not as broad as interrogatories.

Interrogatories. Interrogatories are a set of written questions submitted to the other party who is required to answer. The questions may be broad, and may cover any question that may be asked at trial. Sometimes the questions are inappropriate, or not applicable to the claim or defense, or are too broad and too general. In this instance the party to whom the questions are addressed may apply to the court to limit or omit the particular questions. On the other hand, the responses to questions may be inadequate or omitted and the party seeking the answers may make an application to court to compel the party to answer the questions adequately. After a response to a set of interrogatories, a second set of questions may be propounded—or a third set.

Depositions of Parties and Witnesses. The defendant may seek to examine the plaintiff under oath as to the claim in the complaint, and the plaintiff may examine the defendant as to the defenses in the answer. During this deposition any question may be asked that is permitted to be asked at a trial of this matter and thus a broad interrogation may take place. The proceeding is commenced by serving a notice of an "examination before trial" (or deposition), which sets forth the day, time, and place of the examination which can take place either at an attorney's office or at the courthouse. The notice will also describe what documents, books, or records must be produced. The opposing party will appear and a court stenographer will be present to record the questions and answers.

Examinations before trial are frequently adjourned, often for 30-day periods. Thus, either side may delay the prosecution of the case by seeking several adjournments for a variety of reasons (for example, attorney is engaged at a trial, party is sick, etc.). If the opposing party is uncooperative, sometimes an application to court is necessary to compel the party to appear. Either party has a right to examine witnesses. The most common reason to examine your own witness is if the witness is located at a distant place or will be unable to travel to the location of the court where the trial is taking place.

PRODUCTION OF DOCUMENTS. Either party may require production of documents in the other party's possession which are connected with or relevant to the claim or defense. The party served with this "notice to produce" must produce the documents if they are available. If the party does not produce the documents, the other party may make an application to court to compel compliance. On the other hand, if the document request is unreasonable or has no connection with the claim or defense, the party served may then make application to court to "quash" (cancel) the notice to produce. If the documents are unavailable or lost, the party does not have to produce them. However, a miraculous discovery on the eve of trial will be treated skeptically by the court, or will be excluded by the court.

NOTICE TO ADMIT. A notice to admit is designed to save time at the trial by having the parties agree prior to the trial on certain facts or the validity of certain documents. Certain facts will be set forth for the opposing party to admit. An example would be if monies were loaned, the plaintiff asks the defendant to admit the execution of the promissory note (a copy of which is attached to the notice to admit). If the defendant executed the note, the defendant would not respond. A non-response is an admission and the note then may be offered as evidence at the trial. On the other hand, if the party denies the execution of the note, the note must be identified by a knowledgeable witness at the trial. If proving the note is expensive because money is paid to bring witnesses to attend the trial and the note is admitted as evidence, the cost and expense of offering proof at the trial are borne by the party who refused to admit the execution of the note.

ADJOURNMENTS

In depositions, interrogatories, production of documents, bills of particulars, and notices to admit, the parties to whom the papers are addressed frequently request additional time to respond or to produce a witness. These adjournments are generously allowed; for if an attorney refuses to grant the adjournment, the other party will normally apply to court and the judge will grant a reasonable adjournment. Furthermore, if plaintiff's attorney refuses a reasonable adjournment, the defendant's attorney may later refuse a reasonable adjournment to plaintiff's attorney. Nevertheless, after one or two adjournments are granted, with each one being for less time, an attorney will allow an adversary one last adjournment providing the adversary agrees not to ask for any more. Although discovery proceedings require an extensive amount of time in complicated actions because of frequent adjournments, discovery is crucial to the success or failure of a case.

MOTIONS AND APPLICATIONS

A motion or an application is a request to the judge or court to order or prohibit a particular action of the plaintiff or the defendant to dismiss the complaint or to grant judgment in favor of plaintiff. Motions and applications serve many purposes.

A. A motion to dismiss the complaint based on the fact that even if everything is true in the complaint, it does not form the basis upon which relief can be granted.
B. A motion to allow the filing of a paper notwithstanding the fact that the paper was filed late (nunc pro tunc—now for then). The party making the application will usually provide a reasonable excuse.
C. A motion by an attorney to be relieved from representing a party because the attorney feels that the relationship between the parties has deteriorated, that further representation would not be in the best interest of the client, or for the simple reason that the attorney has not been paid.
D. A motion to compel the party to answer the questions specified in the interrogatories or a motion to compel the party to appear on a given date at a given place to submit to an examination before trial.

In any motion or application to the court, the party seeking the relief must notify the other party so that the opposing party may also either consent to the relief that is being sought by defaulting (failing to appear at the designated date) or oppose the relief by submitting affidavits and documents. The court will review the application and supporting papers by both parties. The court may require the parties to appear in court on "contested" motions (where the party opposes the motion) and argue orally before the court. The party making the application must provide the opposing party usually with at least ten to fourteen days' notice before the date set in court to hear the motion. The date that is set is usually referred to as the "return date." As in discovery proceedings, the party seeking the relief may grant several adjournments to the other party before all affidavits and documents are submitted to the court so that the judge may decide the motion.

ORDER TO SHOW CAUSE. Under certain circumstances, the party cannot wait for relief for the ten to fourteen days. In that case, an "order to show cause" is used. This enables the party seeking the relief to set the return date (the day on which both parties must appear in court) within twenty-four to seventy-two hours rather than to wait seven to fourteen days. The party seeking the short return date applies to the judge *prior to giving notice to the defendant* so that the judge will review the emergency situation and approve a short two- or three-day period for the "return date." The judge must sign "the order to show cause," before it is served on the other side, usually by personal service.

SUMMARY JUDGMENT. A summary judgment is a motion (an application to court) supported by affidavits to court stating that either the plaintiff or the defendant is entitled to win the case as a matter of law *without a trial* based on the documentary evidence (such as a note or lease), testimony at a deposition, or other evidence. One party states that sufficient documentary evidence is before the court to warrant a decision in favor of that party. An application to court for a summary judgment will save the time and the expense of a trial. A summary judgment may be made either before, during, or after discovery proceedings, and will suspend the discovery proceedings pending a decision. Sometimes the discovery proceedings provide evidence and testimony to support a motion for summary judgment, and in that event the motion is made after discovery. A presentation to the court of the testimony, the answers to the interrogatories, and documentary evidence may be sufficient for the court to render a decision without a formal trial. If the facts are disputed, the court usually denies the motion for summary judgment on the grounds that a factual dispute must be resolved by a trial.

ORDER. After each application (motion) is made to court, a judge renders a decision on whether the motion is denied or granted. This decision is usually contained in an "order" signed by the judge and sent to each attorney. The winning side must serve a copy on the other side, and file an affidavit in court that service was made. This process is a "notice of entry" of the order. In federal courts the judge mails the decision to both parties. This procedure of serving a copy of the order on your adversary ensures that the losing side receives a copy of the order and causes the appeal time period to begin.

STIPULATIONS

A stipulation is an agreement entered into between the plaintiff and the defendant. A stipulation extending the time to answer is an agreement between the attorney for the plaintiff and the attorney for the defendant that the time within which the defendant must serve an answer has been extended to a certain date. A stipulation extending the time to respond to a set of interrogatories or adjourn an examination of a party is a similar document.

A stipulation can be entered to discontinue an action commenced by the plaintiff against the defendant. An action may be discontinued with prejudice "on the merits," which means that an action cannot be commenced in a new suit based on the same facts. On the other hand, an action discontinued "without prejudice" means that the action can be commenced in a new suit based upon the same set of facts. An action is discontinued "without prejudice" due to jurisdictional failure, the wrong court, wrong name, wrong summons, wrong address of the court, or reasons other than "on the merits" of the case.

CONFERENCE

Prior to a trial most state courts, federal courts, and other active courts of original jurisdiction schedule a preliminary conference. The judge, or the judge's clerk, will convene both attorneys and/or parties in a room to discuss whether the case can be settled, and the judge will often counsel both parties as to the best way to settle so the court's time is not wasted. Either side always has the option to refuse to settle, and exercise the right to a trial. In many courts the judge will hold periodical "status" conferences to monitor and control the progress of the litigation.

SETTLEMENT NEGOTIATIONS

Many books have been written about negotiating a deal and the same number of books can be written about negotiating a settlement of a debt. The key ingredients in negotiating any type of indebtedness are the same key ingredients that are self-evident in negotiating any type of a deal. Preparation, a consideration of all the facts and circumstances, and plain old-fashioned common sense are the basics.

Clients should recognize the fact that their attorneys have much more experience in negotiating a settlement, but unfortunately many clients refuse to accept this self-evident fact and persist in controlling the negotiation themselves, ignoring or disregarding the advice of their attorney. The argument most often offered is that the attorney is acting in self-interest when negotiating a settlement. If the attorney's recommended offer is not accepted, the case will ultimately be tried and the attorney will be generating fees for himself or herself. On the other side of the coin, if the attorney is handling the matter on a contingency basis, the client usually argues that the attorney is recommending a settlement for the purpose of earning the contingency fee and much more would be collected if a suit were started.

If the client seriously believes that the attorney is only interested in generating fees and that any negotiation on which the attorney embarks will be designed for this purpose, the client should immediately discharge the attorney and find another attorney to negotiate in the best interest of the client. We assure you that many attorneys successfully retain their clients by negotiating in the best interest of the client.

The important thing to remember is that the attorney is negotiating these situations on a day-to-day basis. Every negotiation of a settlement must be considered upon the facts and circumstances then and there prevailing, but there are certain recommendations that can be made that apply to every negotiation of a settlement of a debt.

A. The classic rule that must never be violated is not to "bid against yourself." For example, if you are requesting the full amount, the response should be negative to an inquiry such as "well, give me the best figure you will take" before the debtor has made any offer. The response should be that "we do not bid against ourselves." If the debtor feels that a settlement is in order, let the debtor make a reasonable offer and then consider the grounds upon which the debtor is making the reduced offer.

B. Probably the most basic reason that the debtor offers an adjustment in price or a payout plan is the fact that the debtor has financial problems. The problem is that many creditors do not seek sufficient financial information from the debtor to make a valued judgment. If it is a corporate debt, the ability to obtain financial information is only limited by time and effort. Most creditors' attorneys have financial forms to be completed by the debtor's business or request financial statements from the debtor. If the debtor claims he cannot furnish statements prepared by an accountant, the creditor should obtain the financial statements under a representation by the individual principal that the statements are true and accurate. Then the creditor can state that he relied on these financial statements to enter into the final settlement agreement with the debtor.

C. Many creditors take the position that they want the full amount and allow little room for their attorney to settle. If any leeway is allowed, it is to permit a 20 percent to 30 percent discount from the face amount. Nevertheless, this reasoning is flawed because every debt must be reviewed on a case-by-case basis. The financial problems of the debtor are extremely important in settling any debt. It is far better to retain a small cash payment than be faced with a bankruptcy petition where there has been no payment or a small payment of less than 10 percent.

D. Another factor which must be considered when demanding the full amount is that the attorney for the debtor may make the following recommendation to the debtor:

> The creditor wants the full amount or else he is going to sue. We can drag this case through the courts for at least a year and maybe longer. The worst that can happen is that if we lose the case, we will pay the full amount plus interest. In addition, we may win because the creditor is . . .

E. When dealing with a debtor asserting financial difficulties, the reasonable assumption that a creditor should make is that the debtor is not paying several other creditors as well. The number is not important. There may be only five pieces of pie to feed 10 or 15 hungry creditors. Most creditors who address the problem with information, investigation, and common sense will walk away with their hunger at least partially satisfied. The remaining creditors may go hungry for a long time and ultimately may starve.

F. The most advantageous time to commence negotiation is when the matter reaches the attorney's office. At this point, the debtor is faced with the inevitable conclusion that the debt has been referred to an attorney and that a suit is imminent. If a settlement cannot be negotiated at this point, the next best time to open negotiation is immediately after a summons and complaint is served upon the debtor and, hopefully, before an attorney is retained by the debtor.

G. While the creditor must have absolute control over the settlement negotiations, the effort must be joint and both parties must recognize the function of the other party to achieve a fair and reasonable settlement. Remember that settlements make both parties *partially unhappy.* A settlement that makes one party totally happy and the other party totally unhappy will probably never be consummated.

H. The client usually does not wish to accept the uncertainties and costs of litigation. The attorney, on the other hand, is well aware that even with a "rock solid" case, a case may be lost in litigation for any number of reasons including, but not limited to, witnesses inadvertently offering the wrong answers, documents being lost or unavailable, witnesses leaving for parts unknown or passing away, judges rendering decisions subjectively rather than objectively, decisions being reversed on appeal for technical errors during the trial, and, of course, the fact that mistakes in strategy may be made by both the client and the attorney. How many times over the past 30 years have

I seen cases that I expected to lose turn out to be winners and some cases I initially thought to be sure winners turn out to be losers? A "rock solid" case does not exist. Rock solid cases are sometimes won at summary judgments, not at trial. For this reason, most attorneys are more attuned to the settlement process than clients.

Settlement—Privilege. Federal rules of civil procedure provide that "parties may obtain discovery regarding any matter, *not privileged*, that is relevant to the claim or defense of any party." Accordingly, the right to discovery is not absolute. A strong public interest prevails in favor of secrecy of matters discussed by parties during settlement negotiations. This is true whether negotiations are done under the supervision of the court or informally between the parties. Confidential settlement negotiations are a tradition in this country and the secrecy of settlement terms is a well-established American litigation practice. The courts have recognized the existence of some doctrine of formal privilege. Case law is well established that settlement negotiations are not subject to discovery.[3]

One U.S. Circuit Court of Appeals has held that the existence of a federal settlement privilege is an open question and declined to adopt the lower courts holding that no such privilege exists nor did the Circuit Court reverse the lower court.

Many of the circuits have adopted local rules to promote and protect mediation discussions and many of the states have attempted through legislation to protect the confidentiality of settlement communications and documents that take place in the context of formal mediation proceedings. Settlement discussions that take place before the commencement of litigation are a totally different issue, and have not been resolved by the courts.

Settlement Agreement. A vast difference exists between a settlement agreement drafted prior to suit and a settlement agreement drafted after suit. As to the latter, the attorney will be drafting the settlement agreement and normally will afford the client the protections that are necessary.

Certain essential elements should be included in every settlement agreement whether before or after suit. We will use a checklist to key both the creditor and the attorney as to the elements to be included in a settlement agreement.

1. Basics—The following are basics of a settlement agreement:
   A. The complete name, title, and address of the parties signing the agreement.

[3] *In re Subpoena Duces Tecum Issued to Commodity Futures Tradition Comm'n WD Energy Serv.*, 439 F.3d 740 (D.C. Cir. 2006); *Goodyear Tire & Rubber Co. v. Chiles Power Supply, Inc.*, 332 F.3d 976 (6th Cir. 2003).

B. The account number (or the index number or case number if suit is started).

C. The terms of the settlement, including interest, costs, and when and where to be paid.

D. Where to send the check and to whom to make it payable.

2. Due date of payment—The suggested clause to use is that "payments are to reach our office by _______ (date)." Other types of phrases such as "make payment by, is due, commencing on, continue to make your payments" should not be used since they are subject to various interpretations as where or when a payment is to be made.

3. No waiver of rights as to non-signing parties—The creditor should specifically provide in the agreement that all rights against any other person who has not executed the agreement are not waived and should reserve the right against all other persons not a party to the stipulation who may be liable to the creditor.

4. Fax signatures are deemed to be originals.

5. Duration of an offer—The offer should be limited to a specific short time period and specific directions should set forth the manner in which the agreement is consummated. Suggested terms are as follows:

   A. "to accept this offer, we must receive the executed settlement agreement in our office by _______."

   B. "if payment is not received according to the arrangements set forth above, the settlement will be deemed withdrawn and shall be null and void for all purposes."

6. Prejudice—Any offer should be specifically made "without prejudice." The creditor is not acknowledging that the debt has been resolved for a lesser amount than the full amount other than for the purposes of this settlement. Furthermore, the debtor will not be able to mention this offer in any future settlement negotiations before the court. The wording might be as follows:

"This offer is made without prejudice and if the agreement is not received in our office by _______ (date), this offer will be deemed null and void and withdrawn for all purposes."

7. Admission—It is suggested that the debtor admit owing the debt plus interest, court costs and attorneys' fees before the terms of the settlement are recited. The following language might be appropriate:

"Debtor admits that she/he/they are indebted to the creditor in the sum of $ _______ (amount) plus interest at the rate of _______ percent totaling

$ _______ (amount) plus court costs of $ _______, plus attorneys fees $ _______."

8. Forbearance—In the event the settlement is made prior to suit, the consideration for the settlement is that the creditor will not institute suit on the debt as long as the debtor makes payments. Suggested language might be:

   "Creditor agrees to forbear any right to enforce its legal rights and remedies with regard to this debt as long as the debtor complies with the terms of this settlement agreement."

9. Consumer representation—The debtor often attempts to settle a debt prior to selling a home or other real estate since a judgment is a lien upon the real estate. At the closing, the purchaser will require the debtor to remove the judgment. If an offer of settlement is made many years after a judgment was entered, the debtor is likely selling real estate. Suggested language might be:

   "The debtor has not entered into any negotiations or executed any contract of sale with regard to any real estate owned by the undersigned."

   If the debtor refuses to sign, the debtor is selling real estate and you may want to reconsider the offer of settlement.

10. Address—It is suggested that any change in address must be given to the other party by certified mail.

In the event that suit has already been started and the creditor enters into a settlement, the stipulation will provide that in the event the debtor defaults in the payments set forth in the agreement, the creditor will have a right to enter a judgment against the debtor. The following are some suggestions with regard to this type of stipulation:

A. If the debtor is a consumer, a statement is necessary that he/she is not in military service.
B. The consent by the debtor to the use of affidavits or other documents for the attorney to submit to the clerk of the court to have a judgment entered, and that this is sufficient for the clerk to enter judgment.
C. What amounts will be included in the judgment including attorneys' fees and interest costs.

These suggestions are all subject to various state laws which may affect the preparation of these stipulations of settlement or the procedures for entering judgments based upon these stipulations. A review of the state law is necessary.

COURT PROCEDURES

The court systems in each state have their own different procedures and local rules with regard to the conduct of litigation. Most courts require attorneys to attend a conference for purposes of settlement before the trial. At these conferences, the judges will exert a significant amount of pressure on the attorneys to settle the case. Other judges will treat these conferences perfunctorily by asking the attorneys whether they have attempted to settle the case and, upon receiving a negative response, will set a date for trial. In federal court, the judges will set a schedule for discovery; that is, set the dates within which time interrogatories must be served and answered and depositions must be taken. Some state courts utilize the same procedures that are used in federal court.

In some state courts, the judges require their consent to adjournments in the scheduling process, whereas in most of the lower courts, adjournments can be obtained with the consent of both attorneys. Each system tends to set its own rules with regard to the procedure for the case.

The federal bankruptcy court has totally different procedures with regard to the examination of the bankrupt and the devices available to the creditors to obtain information from the bankrupt.

LOST AND DESTROYED DOCUMENTS

The Federal Rules of Evidence cover the issue of lost documents in Rule 1002, 1003, and 1004. Rule 1002 provides that you must produce the original of the document in order "[t]o prove the content of a writing, recording, or photograph is required, except as otherwise provided in these rules or by Act of Congress."

Immediately, thereafter Rule 1003 allows duplicates to be offered as evidence:

A duplicate is admissible to the same extent as an original unless:

1. A genuine question is raised as to the authenticity of the original or
2. In the circumstances it would be unfair to admit the duplicate in lieu of the original.

Accordingly, if no genuine issue exists and no other reason exists to require an original, a party offering evidence at a trial may offer a duplicate. Photocopies of checks or notes may be offered as evidence at a trial unless an objection is offered that the photocopy of the check is not a true copy of the original check. In simple terms, the party objecting must show that either the original document was tampered with and is inadmissible or must show that the copy has been tampered and does not conform to the original. Absent proof of this non-conformity, the copies will be admissible.

The courts will examine the quality of the copy and whether the copy reproduces the entire original. Language in the decisions indicates that the courts are liberal in admitting copies into evidence and leave it to a jury to determine whether the original had been tampered with or whether the copy was incomplete.

The courts will admit copies when documents are destroyed. The threshold of proof is to demonstrate that a document was burned in a fire or rendered illegible by reason of a flood from the river or from the washing machine. The general perception of the court is that if a document is destroyed because of flood or fire, the fault is not with the party who had possession of the document. Military action or the terror attack that happened on 9/11 are other examples of meeting the threshold of proof.

Rule 1004 deals directly with the issue of destroyed documents. It specifically lays out the criteria for admitting copies.

Admissibility of Other Evidence or Contents. The original is not required and other evidence of the contents of a writing, recording, or photograph is admissible if:

1. Originals lost or destroyed. All originals are lost or have been destroyed, unless the proponent lost or destroyed them in bad faith; or
2. Original not obtainable. No original can be obtained by any available judicial process or procedure; or
3. Original in possession of opponent. At a time when an original was under the control of the party against whom offered, that party was put on notice, by the pleadings or otherwise, that the contents would be a subject of proof at the hearing, and that party does not produce the original at the hearing; or
4. Collateral matters. The writing, recording, or photograph is not closely related to a controlling issue.

The basis of the above rule is that if the party offering the evidence fails to produce the original and provides a satisfactory explanation, secondary evidence or copies are admissible. The rule is not an issue of preference, for the court cannot prefer originals. If a satisfactory explanation is provided, the secondary evidence, whether it is copies or otherwise, will be admissible. If the document is in the hands of a third party, a reasonable explanation must be provided that the party used diligent efforts to require the third party to produce the original. Issuing a subpoena or using any other judicial remedy to obtain the original is enough. When offering evidence under Rule 1003, the party offering it does not have to show that the original is unavailable. A duplicate is admissible unless the presumption of admissibility is overcome. Under Rule 1004, the proponent must show that the original is unavailable, but once that showing is made, the substitute evidence need not be a copy, but may take other forms. Even a witness could testify to prove the contents of the document. Rule 1005 enables you to offer the contents of an official record or of a document authorized to be recorded or filed and may be proved by offering a copy which has to be certified by the court as correct.

In contested litigation if the other side is put on notice that the original will be required and your adversary has the original in their possession, the only way your adversary can render the copies inadmissible is by offering the original. The last paragraph of the rule deals with situations where it is immaterial whether an original or copy is being offered where the particular document is not particularly relevant to any of the issues that have to be decided by the court.

Even when the destruction of documents is done intentionally, secondary evidence still may be available. In one case, the Federal Reserve had a routine practice of destruction of old records. The court held that this routine practice did not constitute bad faith since it was done continually and routinely for some time and, accordingly, the court allowed secondary evidence to be admissible under Rule 1004.[4]

As a general rule the courts require the party submitting the copy to offer proof of good faith in that a careful search for the document has been made, sufficient evidence was offered to the court that the document was destroyed, and the document was not obtainable by any available judicial process. Little weight is allocated to the significant expense, difficulty, or time that must be expended to obtain the original document. In short, a diligent effort is required for the original to offer secondary evidence. In one case, the court admitted copies of checks as secondary evidence, but stated in a footnote that the copies should be viewed as duplicate originals under Rule 1003.[5]

Secondary evidence takes many forms and is not necessarily limited to copies. Documents normally made in the course of business would be admissible, such as if a doctor made a report on his readings of an x-ray, that report would be secondary evidence if the x-ray was not available. Electrical usage printouts could be used when the actual bills were not available. Dividend books were used to establish ownership of stock when the stock ledger book was destroyed.[6]

The defendant could not locate an x-ray taken by a doctor which he claimed had been transferred to a Kansas storage facility. The defendant successfully introduced another doctor's testimony and the written x-ray

---

[4] *United States v. Carroll*, 860 F.2d 500 (1st Cir. 1988).

[5] *United States v. Gerhart*, 538 F.2d 807 (8th Cir. 1976).

[6] *Schozer v. William Penn Life Ins. Co.*, 84 N.Y.2d 639 (N.Y. 1996); *Briar Hill Apartments Co. v. Teperman*, 165 A.D.2d 519 (1st Dep't 1991); *Seymour v. Mechanics & Metals Nat'l Bank*, 213 N.Y.S. 907 (1st Dep't 1925).

report to establish that the plaintiff's x-ray would have revealed an enlarged heart.[7]

TRIAL PREPARATION

Cases are not won at trial, but at the office. Trial preparation is the key ingredient to a successful outcome. If a case is going to trial, the client should devote the necessary time to prepare. The attorney will review the witnesses' testimony as well as the documentary evidence. Evidence that appears useless to the client may be gold to the attorney. To go to trial without seeing the original file is setting up the attorney for failure. Time and preparation are necessary. Meeting at the courthouse early in the morning to prepare a case for trial that afternoon is a disaster waiting to happen. Do not be upset at your counsel when the unexpected occurs, or the judge is unreasonable, if sufficient preparation was not performed.

TRIAL

If the parties cannot settle the case, the case will proceed to trial. Either party may serve the other party and file a *notice of trial form,* which may be slightly different in different states. Notice of trial is a written request to the clerk to issue a trial calendar number. This notice identifies the parties, the type of case and other information to enable the clerk to classify when the case will be tried and in larger jurisdictions, and what courtroom in the courthouse. In smaller jurisdictions, the clerk will notify the parties when the trial will take place. Some courts require affidavits stating that all discovery proceedings have been completed.

In the metropolitan areas the clerk issues a trial number in consecutive order, and both parties wait for the court to reach the number. A special room is designated where the clerk calls the numbers each day, each week, or each month. Both parties appear and indicate they are ready for trial. The clerk assigns a judge for the case. The attorneys then appear before the assigned judge. Both parties and the judge agree when the trial will begin. Because the judge, attorneys, and clients are often not ready on the day when the case is called, adjournments occur frequently. But the attorneys must be in court for the calendar calls, the requests for adjournments, and the decision of the judge to adjourn. Many times the judge requires both sides to be ready on a given day with the expectation that the current case before the judge will be completed; when it is not, the

---

[7]N.C. Gen. Stat. § 8-45.1; N.J.R. Evid. 801; Tex. Evid. R. 1001; *Schozer v. William Penn Life Ins. Co.,* 84 N.Y.2d 639 (N.Y. 1996); *Briar Hill Apartments Co. v. Teperman,* 165 A.D.2d 519 (1st Dep't 1991).

client's case is adjourned to another day. For this reason actual trials are expensive due to the waiting time in court. The adjournment time and waiting time for a trial are probably the best reasons to settle a case.

JUDGMENT

A judgment is the final effect of a decision on a motion addressed to the merits of a case such as a summary judgment or a verdict after a trial. A contested judgment is when the defendant appears and has answered the complaint. A default judgment is where the defendant has not appeared or answered the complaint.

A judgment of a court of record usually becomes a lien by filing papers that create a lien in the office designated by the state. In some instances, the judgment will become a lien statewide or countywide without any further filing or perfection. In some states the lien requires a specific address to become a lien that attaches to property, such as in Connecticut. In other states the lien is countywide such as in New York. In some states the lien is statewide such as in New Jersey.

Vacating a Default Judgment. Sometimes the creditor will enter a default judgment, and the creditor will then attach assets of the debtor—either a bank account, inventory, or even real estate. The debtor will claim that service was never made, and the default resulted only because the debtor never knew a suit was started. The procedure is a motion to vacate the judgment for improper service. A hearing is held. If the creditor cannot prove proper service, the judgment is vacated and the creditor must begin again. If the creditor proves proper service, the proceeding by the creditor continues with regard to the assets. In some cases the judge will vacate the judgment, based on equity and permit the debtor to defend the action. The creditor should request that the items be held as security pending the outcome of the lawsuit.

The debtor may also vacate a judgment on the grounds that the court has no jurisdiction over the debtor. For example the amount claimed exceeds the amount permitted by the court, or the corporation is located in another state and service has not been properly made. Many other reasons may be offered; and while some are valid and result in dismissal, many are frivolous and interposed by debtors merely to delay and stall the proceedings.

Declaratory Judgments. Declaratory judgments are treated in 28 U.S.C. Section 2201 and most of the states have similar statutes. The party who normally would have been the defendant in a lawsuit utilizes this procedure when the other party is threatening a suit. The party who would have been the plaintiff becomes the defendant and the party who would have been the defendant becomes the plaintiff.

The respective positions of each party is reversed. The purpose of a declaratory judgment by the party being threatened with the suit is to commence the action first with a declaratory judgment action and thus be the plaintiff rather than the defendant. The suit proceeds in the normal way. Federal Rule of Civil Procedure 611 assists the court in sorting out the procedures of evidence to resolve having the affirmative claim being offered after the opposition to the affirmative claims which might render the trial somewhat confusing.

Foreign Judgments—State. While the enforcement of foreign judgments of other states under state law varies from state to state, judgments issued by the various district courts are controlled under the Federal Rules of Civil Procedure and are consistent throughout the country. Rule 54 identifies a judgment as a decree or order from which an appeal lies. A judgment must be final to enforce same and is identified as final when set forth on a separate document and when entered pursuant to the federal rules of civil procedure. Interest on a judgment is calculated pursuant to 28 U.S.C. Section 1961, which states that interest shall be calculated at a rate equal to the coupon issue yield equivalent of the average accepted auction price for the last auction of 52-week United States treasury bills settled immediately prior to the date of the judgment. Costs may be assessed pursuant to 28 U.S.C. Section 1920.

28 U.S.C. Section 1962 states that a judgment rendered by a district court within a state shall be a lien on the property located in such state in the same manner, to the same extent and under the same conditions as a judgment of a court of that state and shall cease to be a lien in the same manner and time.

A federal court judgment may be recorded in the state court and filed in the county or city records as required by state law. As such, the judgment becomes a lien on the debtor's property only in the county where it is recorded in accordance with state law. The priority of the judgment is the same as state court judgments. In some states you may have to file or docket the judgment in the land record division to obtain the judgment lien. In short, you must comply with the state law. Once the judgment is filed in the particular county, transcripts of said judgment can be obtained to be filed in other counties in the same manner as obtaining a transcript of a state court judgment.

Circumstances may exist that the creditor may wish to record the judgment in another federal jurisdiction. Under 28 U.S.C. Section 1963, the federal registration statute, a judgment may be registered by filing a certified copy of the judgment in any other district court. Once the judgment is filed in the district court, the same procedures are used to record the judgment in the state court.

ENFORCEMENT OF A FOREIGN JUDGMENT—COUNTRY. The general premise is that the United States Court will enforce a foreign judgment based upon "comity." Comity is defined in Black's Law Dictionary, 7th Edition, as the courtesy among political entities such as nation states, and courts of different jurisdictions involving mutual recognition of legislative, executive, and judicial acts. Thus, valid judgments of foreign courts are enforceable in the United States as a matter of comity. Comity is not a statute nor is it a part of a treaty. It is one nation's intention to demonstrate mutual respect of international relations and its duty to enforce and protect the rights of its citizens in the event they have been justly or unjustly treated.

If the defendant voluntarily appeared in the foreign court and a fair and full trial was conducted under a system which provided a reasonable expectation of justice in the administration of that system and no fraud or prejudice was present in the system, nor was there any other reason why a court of this nation should not allow full faith and credit based on comity to the judgment of the foreign nation, an action may be brought on that judgment and the issues should not be tried all over again upon a mere assertion that the judgment was erroneous in law or in fact.[8]

The principal defenses that are used in opposition to a suit on a foreign judgment are (1) the lack of jurisdiction over the person or the subject matter of the suit and (2) the fact that the foreign proceedings do not comply with the concepts of due process in the United States. Due process would probably also include the fact that the proceeding must be conducted with some degree of fairness to the defendant so that the defendant is fully aware of the claim against him and has an opportunity to be heard before an impartial tribunal.

When plaintiff seeks to pursue a debtor in a foreign country with a judgment obtained in the United States, it may be more difficult than enforcing a judgment of a foreign country in the United States. In many countries no treaty has been signed between that country and the United States relating to the enforcement of a United States judgment unless a written waiver has been executed. The European countries do have a treaty amongst themselves wherein the judgments of each country are recognized in the other countries. Usually, arbitration awards are easier to enforce in another country if they are a party to the United Nations Convention on the recognition and enforcement of foreign arbitral awards (New York Convention). Currently, over 100 nations have now subscribed to the Convention.

UNIFORM ENFORCEMENT OF FOREIGN JUDGMENTS ACT. The Uniform Enforcement of Foreign Judgments Act has been passed in almost all states. The Act enables a creditor to obtain from the court in its state

---

[8] *Somportex Limited v. Philadelphia Chewing Gum*, 453 F.2d 435 (3d Cir. 1971).

either an exemplified or certified copy of the judgment. Sometimes it is referred to as an Act of Congress copy. You must present this to the court in the state in which you wish to file your judgment and where the debtor now resides. The clerk of that court must enter the judgment in the court and the clerk must thereafter mail a copy of the judgment to the last known address in that jurisdiction. The clerk also must make a note of the date of mailing of the copy. It is suggested that the counsel also mail to the debtor by certified mail a copy of the judgment in the event that the clerk has failed to mail the copy or fails to make a note of the date of mailing. Thus, the debtor cannot claim that he or she did not receive notice of the registration of the foreign judgment. The judgment creditor then must wait a period of time before issuing any execution under the judgment and the creditor must proceed in accordance with the laws of the state in which the judgment is presently filed.[9]

Recognition of certain foreign judgments is primarily dependent upon the terms of the statute which is itemized as follows:

A. Whether the foreign country's court had personal jurisdiction over the judgment debtor.
B. Whether it was an impartial tribunal utilizing procedures compatible with due process of law.
C. Whether enforcing the foreign country money judgment would be unfair, fraudulent, or violate public policy.

Generally, if the foreign country's judgment meets these criteria, it is conclusive and is entitled to recognition.

The defendants argued that the New York courts may not recognize an out-of-country judgment and may not enforce it against defendants in New York unless the defendants have an actual current presence within the state or some basis or nexus exists for New York's exercise of personal jurisdiction over the defendants. But the court stated that the issue of personal jurisdiction is not an issue before the court.

The only issue before the court is whether the foreign court had personal jurisdiction over the debtor, not whether New York presently has personal jurisdiction over the debtor. No jurisdiction or basis for proceeding against a judgment debtor need be shown before a foreign judgment will be recognized or enforced in a given state providing it has complied with the criteria set forth in the Uniform Foreign Money Judgment Recognition Act. The foreign country's court personal jurisdiction is sufficient for the statutory scheme does not contemplate a challenge to the court's exercise of personal jurisdiction over the judgment debtor in the recognition proceeding.[10]

---

[9]N.Y. CPLR Article 53 (*Uniform Foreign Money Judgment Recognition Act*).
[10]*Lenchyshyn v. Pelko Elec., Inc.*, 723 N.Y.S.2d 285 (4th Dep't 2001).

A case squarely addressed the issue of whether a plaintiff who is attempting to enforce a foreign judgment must present to the court minimum contacts supporting the original jurisdiction. The court held that the traditional minimum contacts to support personal jurisdiction over a defendant to enforce the judgment are not necessary when enforcing a foreign judgment. The court did not follow the traditional approach in requiring that the transactions that supported the foreign judgment take place in New York nor that the defendant have assets in New York or is a resident of New York. The creditor is only asking the court to perform its duty to recognize the foreign judgment and convert it into a judgment in the State of New York. A year later, the Federal Court in Ohio followed the same reasoning. So few cases are decided on this subject, it is too early to determine whether this concept will be adopted in both the state and federal courts.[11]

Exemplified Judgment/Triple Seal Judgment/Certified Copy of Judgment. If a creditor obtains a judgment in one state and the debtor travels to another state, in most instances the full faith and credit provisions follow the debtor to enforce collection of the judgment. The courts of one state must afford full faith and credit to the judgments of another state. In order that one state will recognize the judgment of another state, the courts will usually require that the creditor obtain a triple seal or exemplified copy of the judgment which can be obtained from the County Clerk or the Judgment Clerk where the particular judgment was entered. The clerk will certify in writing, affixing a corporate seal or some form of a stamp, that the particular judgment was entered and will list the name of the judgment creditor, the name of the judgment debtor, the amount of the judgment, the date the judgment was entered, the court and index number under which the judgment was entered, and a judge will certify that the judgment is valid. The creditor files this instrument in the state and county where the debtor now resides and under most statutes is entitled to enforce the judgment in the same manner as the judgment entered in the state where the debtor formerly resided.

One exception is a judgment that is obtained on default, where the debtor has neither answered the complaint nor appeared in the action. Some states (New York, Connecticut, Vermont, Massachusetts) rely on the position that a judgment of this nature should not be recognized since the debtor has neither answered nor appeared in the action and therefore has not submitted to the jurisdiction of the court. Under these circumstances, the creditor will have to institute a separate suit in a sister state on the judgment against the debtor. In these states, the courts frown on default judgments based on long-arm jurisdiction and will often vacate these

---

[11] *Pure Fishing Inc. v. Silver Star Co.*, 202 F. Supp. 2d 905 (N.D. Iowa 2002); *Lenchyshyn v. Pelko Elec., Inc.*, 723 N.Y.S.2d 285 (4th Dep't 2001).

judgments. It is strongly recommended that counsel for the creditor sue not only on the judgment but also sue the debtor on the underlying debt in the states that do not permit enforcement of a foreign judgment where the judgment was obtained by default.

ROOKER/FELDMAN DOCTRINE. Under the *Rooker/Feldman* Doctrine, lower federal courts do not have subject matter jurisdiction over certain challenges to state court judgments. Nor do federal courts have jurisdiction "over claims" that are "inextricably intertwined" with claims adjudicated in state court. A claim is "inextricably intertwined" with a state court judgment:

1. If it succeeds only to the extent that the state court wrongly decided the issues before it.
2. If the relief requested . . . would effectively reverse a state court judgment or void its rulings.
3. The doctrine only applies when the goal of the federal action is to nullify a state court judgment.[12]

A Supreme Court decision held that a suit commenced in state court does not bar a proceeding concerning the same issues in federal court providing that no judgment has been rendered against the defendant. The defendant in the state court action filed a new suit in the federal court on the same counterclaims that the defendant had used as a defense in the state court. The Supreme Court clarified the doctrine that a federal court must give full faith in credit to a state court judgment in the same manner that full faith and credit is afforded to a foreign judgment from another state as long as there was a "full opportunity to be heard before the state court." But, if the suit is pending, and judgment has not been rendered, the defendant has not had an opportunity to be heard. In the instant case, the plaintiff filed a federal court suit as insurance in the event they lost the state court suit, and the Supreme Court did not find this strategy offensive.[13]

CONFESSION OF JUDGMENT. A *confession of judgment* allows a judgment to be entered in favor of a creditor automatically when the debtor breaches the terms of the confession of judgment. The debtor normally will confess the judgment that is, admit liability for the debt, either before or

[12]*Rooker v. Fidelity Trust Co.*, 263 U.S. 413 (1923); *Resler v. Messerli & Kramer, P.A.*, 2003 U.S. Dist. LEXIS 1741 (D. Minn. 2003); *Felder v. Credit Acceptance Corp.*, 188 F.3d 1031 (8th Cir. 1999); *Canal Capital Corp. v. Valley Pride Pack Inc.*, 169 F.3d 508 (8th Cir. 1999).

[13]*Exxon Mobil Corp. v. Saudi Basic Industries Corp.*, 544 U.S. 280 (2005).

after suit is instituted. The debtor is basically waiving any right to assert any defenses to a suit to recover the debt.

A confession of judgment sometimes appears in commercial leases or loan documents. Under the Credit Practices Act, consumer credit contracts that include the use of confession of judgment involving individuals or consumers are unenforceable; some states had already prohibited them even before enactment of the Act. On the other hand, the use of confessions of judgment under business transactions, leases of real estate or property, or in lending situations with financial institutions are quite common, though varied, across the 50 states. The laws in a particular state should be examined carefully.

Any confession of judgment obtained under duress will be set aside and rendered unenforceable. To be valid, a confession of judgment must contain several important terms, including a confession as to the fact that the plaintiff's claim is valid and that the debtor consents to the entry of the judgment (filing the judgment with the clerk of the court). Naturally, the amount of the judgment and the terms of any payout plan must also be set forth. In most instances, the debtor authorizes entering the judgment (filing in court) once the attorney for the creditor files an affidavit with the court stating that the debtor breached the terms of the confession of judgment. Most states permit a confession of judgment prior to the maturity of the obligation; on the other hand, a few prohibit judgments confessed prior to maturity or before commencement of suit. In the minority states, a confession of judgment is not enforceable unless executed by the debtor after an action is instituted on the matter. In many states, once a confession of judgment is entered, to preserve the due process rights of the debtor, certain notice provisions must be complied with to enable the debtor to have an opportunity to vacate the judgment for the reasons set forth in the statute.

> ***Credit & Collection Tip:*** *Most states provide that confessions of judgment must be entered within a specified time from the date of the signing of the judgment, that is, one to three years from date of signing. Thus, confessions are not used where payouts or performance extend beyond the time limitations. Failure to enter (file the judgment with the clerk) within the prescribed time will render it void and useless. Further, many courts will docket only the original document and not a copy.*

Satisfaction of Judgment. When a judgment is paid, the debtor is entitled to have the judgment marked *"paid"* at the clerk's office where the judgment was recorded (docketed or entered). The attorney for the plaintiff prepares a document to *satisfy the judgment*, an instrument which identifies the judgment by name of plaintiff and defendant, index number, court, recites that the judgment is paid. The plaintiff files its satisfaction of judgment with the clerk of the court where the judgment is recorded.

DAMAGES

The general standard for most damages is compensatory damages. The courts recognize damages which may fairly and reasonably be considered as arising naturally from a breach of contract and any damages that may reasonably be supposed to have been in the contemplation of both parties as the probable result of a breach of contract. Some courts have placed strict interpretations on consequential damages which are permitted to be recovered in special circumstances, and usually are foreseeable.

Punitive damages are not awarded in a breach of contract case. Nevertheless, if the breach of contract is also a tort, the court may still award punitive damages. Examples of tort claims are fraud, a willful misrepresentation to induce entering a contract, or a conversion of funds or personal property. Most punitive damage awards are in tort litigation involving accidents, an intentional infliction of bodily harm, or other injuries suffered by a large number of consumers with the purpose being to deter the wrongdoer from similar conduct in the future and to deter others from engaging in such type of conduct. The courts normally do not award damages for mental distress or emotional upset in a breach of contract suit because the damages are too vague and uncertain to be considered as foreseeable by the parties to the contract. Damages for emotional stress have been awarded in FDCPA cases.

The insured party's obligation to mitigate damages is always present, but the courts only require that the party mitigating the damages use a reasonable effort. The injured party need not act if the cost of avoidance is an unreasonable expense or causes the injured party to commit a wrong by breaching other contracts to mitigate damages.

In most suits for violation of the Fair Debt Collection Practices Act or the Fair Credit Reporting Act, a claim is generally made for damages due to emotional distress. The case law on the interpretation of emotional distress is wide and varied. The circuits themselves disagree as to the necessary evidence to prove a claim of emotional distress.

In the 2nd and 3rd Circuits, the courts are liberal and will allow conclusory testimony that the victim suffered emotional distress. The victim may offer a description of the victim's feelings. A district court in the 11th Circuit added that an intentional infliction is sufficient to support a claim of emotional distress. Exactly what constitutes intentional infliction of emotional distress is another issue. A district court in California (the 9th Circuit) did not award emotional distress damages where the victim testified that she was angry and couldn't sleep and received unknown phone calls. Even within the circuits, the decisions of the district courts vary radically. Some courts require some form of corroboration of the emotional distress. The courts act on a strictly case-by-case basis and probably on a more subjective point of view than any bright line rule of law. The best response to such a situation is to examine carefully the most recent cases in the circuit from the Circuit Court of Appeals as well as the district courts.

For those members of the ACA International, the August 2008 issue of the Map Bulletin provided an in-depth look at this issue.[14]

STATUTE OF LIMITATIONS

The statute of limitations is designed to encourage a plaintiff to commence suit when the remedy becomes available so that potential and contingent suits are not indefinitely available to the creditor. The law encourages a plaintiff to commence suit as soon as practicable after plaintiff discovers the availability of a remedy. A time frame is created within which a suit must be commenced. If the suit is not commenced within this time period, it is said to be barred by the statute of limitations. In general, it is more favorable to institute suits as soon as they accrue because witnesses and evidence are readily available.

The statute of limitations varies from state to state and is not uniform. The statute of limitations is also dependent upon the legal theory sued upon. Do not assume that the legal theories are the same in every state or that the statute of limitation periods are similar. The time period may vary by a period of over ten years in some cases. Some courts hold that certain transactions are covered under a specific time period because of the nature of the transaction. For example, some states such as New Jersey hold that the Uniform Commercial Code applies to retail installment contracts for automobiles. Thus, a four-year statute of limitations applies as opposed to a six-year statute of limitations period. The statute of limitations is longer for leases than installment loans.

Certain acts suspend the statute of limitations period from expiring (that is tolling). The most common exception is a partial payment. However, in some states, such as Georgia, the act of a partial payment is insufficient. When there are two co-debtors, and one party makes a payment, does the statute toll against both debtors or only one debtor? The results can vary from state to state. Most of the statutes, or at least the decision law in the states, allow the statute to be suspended if the defendant has left the state during the period covered by the statute of limitations.

Different time periods may be applicable because it is not clear which state law applies. Some courts will hold that the contract dictates which state law is applicable, while other courts will hold that the state law in which the consumer resides controls. When there are two possible statutes of limitations that could be applied, the courts generally apply the shorter

---

[14]*Costa v. National Action Fin. Servs.*, 2007 WL 4526510 (E.D. Cal. 2007); *Carrigan v. Central Adjustment Bureau, Inc.*, 502 F. Supp. 468 (N.D. Ga. 1980); *Philbin v. Trans Union Corp.*, 101 F.3d 957 (3d Cir. 1996); *Chiverton v. Federal Fin. Group, Inc.*, 399 F. Supp. 2d 96 (D. Conn. 2005).

of the two time periods when consumers are involved. The courts are all over the place in this area of law.

In general, the statute of limitations in a contract case will run from when a breach of contract first occurred. In most situations dealing with demand notes, the time runs from when a demand is first made for payment. If the note is a time note, the demand must be made at the date of maturity of the note. With a contract of guarantee, the time frame begins to run from the time the obligation of the principal debtor first becomes due. This time frame would change radically if it was a guarantee of collection where the creditor must exhaust all remedies against the principal debtors before commencing suit against the guarantor. Notwithstanding these general statements, we must again emphasize that a review of state law is absolutely necessary.

Review of the local state statutes and judicial case law is important. Several sources are available on the Internet that describe these time periods. However, our experience has been that different sources report different time periods and are often incorrect in their assumptions. Consultation with counsel is strongly recommended.

ENFORCEMENT AND COLLECTION OF A JUDGMENT

Transcript of Judgment. A judgment is recognized in the county where it is obtained. If suit was started in the Supreme Court of Clark County, the judgment would be recognized in Clark County and would enable the sheriff to levy on the real or personal property of the defendant located in Clark County. This would apply whether the judgment was a contested judgment or a default judgment where the defendant did not appear. A transcript of judgment is a document issued under the signature of the county clerk, in the county where the judgment is entered, listing the plaintiff, the defendant, the amount of the judgment, the date it was obtained, the county in which it was obtained, and the index number issued. If the defendant owns property in another county, a transcript of judgment must be filed in the other county to conduct enforcement proceedings in that county. Thus, if the debtor had property in Cook County and judgment was entered in Clark County, a transcript of the judgment from Clark County must be filed in Cook County to proceed against property in Cook County. In some states, judgments are liens statewide, and transcripts are unnecessary.

Garnishment of Wages. After a judgment has been obtained, the creditor has a right to garnishee the salary of the debtor. To garnishee a salary means to issue a document (execution) reciting the details of the judgment to a sheriff or marshal who notifies the employer of the debtor to deduct a percentage of the wages of the debtor and send this amount to the sheriff, who deducts fees and sends the balance to the creditor. The amount permitted to be deducted from the salary is between 10 percent and 25 percent and varies from state to state. In some states, the sheriff must first notify the debtor of the fact that a garnishment will be served on the employer and allow the debtor to make voluntary payments equivalent to what would be deducted from the salary and avoid the notification to the employer. Failing this the debtor knows the employer will be notified. The Department of Education may issue an administrative wage garnishment.

The salaries of federal employees and the military are now subject to garnishment, effective in 1994. The garnishment process for federal employees is simple and similar to state garnishment proceedings. As for members of the military, the Department of Defense issued rules which are available from the Department of Defense, Finance and Accounting Service, Code L., P.O. Box 998002, Cleveland, Ohio 44119, telephone number 216-522-5301. In most states, employees of the state or city government are subject to garnishment.

Garnishment/Execution of Personal Property (Writs of Execution). Once a judgment is obtained, the creditor is entitled to garnishee or attach assets of the debtor in the hands of third parties. (To garnishee, attach, or restrain assets requires the third party to transfer the monies or properties of the debtor to the creditor.) The method used is to serve the third party with a garnishment (execution) that lists the amount of the judgment, date of entry, name of court, plaintiff and defendant, and the balance due. A prime example of third parties holding assets of the debtor is a bank account where the bank is holding money of the debtor. The garnishment is served on the bank, and monies on deposit are paid to the creditor up to the amount of the judgment. Another example would be third parties who owe money to the debtor such as a tenant owing money to the landlord (debtor) or a mortgagor owing money to the mortgagee (debtor). In each instance, a restraining notice (garnishment) served upon the tenant or the mortgagor would require payment of the monies directly to the creditor (rent due landlord, mortgage payment due mortgagee).

This powerful tool should be used where the creditor knows that monies belonging to the debtor are resting in the hands of third parties who owe money to the debtor. The procedure is simple and usually only requires service of a notice upon the third party. In some jurisdictions notice must be also sent to the debtor.

Wage executions and property executions (sometimes called a writ) are directions to a marshal or sheriff to take possession of assets of the debtor. Wage executions are more properly called "garnishees," as described previously. A property execution (writ) is an instrument delivered to the sheriff reciting the amount of the judgment, date of entry, court, plaintiff and defendant, and the location of the assets to be levied upon. In property executions the sheriff levies and executes on the assets of the debtor, sells the assets at public sale by auction, collects the proceeds from the sale, and remits the proceeds to the creditor, less any fees or expenses incurred in the process of the sale by the sheriff or the marshal. After a judgment has been obtained by a creditor, the creditor's attorney may issue an execution to the sheriff or marshal of the county in which the debtor resides or where the debtor is operating a business or has other types of assets. Real estate is heavily regulated and controlled by statute and specific requirements must be met before a judgment creditor can sell real property to satisfy a debt. The execution or garnishment is a document which directs the sheriff to collect the judgment by selling any property that the debtor may have for cash and then remitting the cash to the creditor. The sheriff usually performs this function for a fee of about 5 percent plus his expenses.

The execution contains the date the judgment was entered, the court, the index number, the amount of the judgment, the amount of interest, the location of the debtor, and, in most instances, the location of the property which the sheriff is to sell. The execution will be mailed or delivered personally to the debtor and allow the debtor a certain time period within which to voluntarily pay the judgment or arrange for an installment plan. In the event the judgment is not paid voluntarily by a specified time or arrangements are not made, the sheriff proceeds to levy on the assets (visiting the premises and identifying the assets).

The sheriff then publishes a notice of sale in the newspaper in the same geographic area as the debtor and publishes the date of sale, description of property to be sold, and other information. The judgment creditor pays in advance the fees to hold a sale, which include the cost of tagging the property, advertising in the newspaper, and conducting the auction of the property. The cost may approach several hundred dollars or substantially more, depending upon the amount of the property and whether it is real estate. On the date set for sale, an auction is conducted on all the property or specific parts of the property. If a bid of all the property is greater than the bid for the specific property, the property is sold to the party who bid for all of the property. If the bid for the specific property is greater than the bids for all of the property, the sheriff will sell the parts rather than the whole. A down payment of around 10 percent is required and the balance is due when the property is removed by the purchaser from the premises. The proceeds first are used to pay off a specific judgment and the remainder of the proceeds, if any, may be used to pay other creditors in a surplus money proceeding, which is regulated by specific state laws.

Prior to the auction the sheriff visits the debtor's place of business to conduct an inventory of any assets. The debtor may oppose this levy on the grounds that the property had been mortgaged to a bank or another secured creditor. Under these circumstances, the levy by the sheriff will be subject to the prior lien and the sheriff will have to announce at the public sale that the purchaser is buying the assets subject to the prior lien. This happens frequently with regard to automobiles or boats, which are usually subject to prior liens to a bank or a financial institution.

Information Subpoenas. In most states, after a judgment has been obtained, the creditor may serve an information subpoena or similar disclosure document upon any third party who may have information concerning the debtor or who owes the debtor any money. Landlords, telephone companies, accountants, utility companies, banks, prior owners of residences, past and present employers, and all types of third parties upon whom information subpoenas may be served. In some jurisdictions, witness information subpoenas may be served upon relatives and friends of the debtor. The information subpoena lists questions asking the third party where the debtor is residing, the name and address of the debtor's employer, and similar questions helpful to the creditor in locating assets of the debtor. With certain third parties, such as banks and telephone companies, questions are used to determine if the bank has monies on deposit or whether the debtor has a telephone deposit with the telephone company. Sometimes landlords have security deposits and are able to furnish information as to the whereabouts of the debtor, or where the debtor works. (In some states, landlord's security deposits may be exempt.)

Subpoenas. Subpoenas are documents served upon the debtor or witnesses requiring an appearance at a given time and place to be examined under oath. After a judgment is obtained, a creditor is entitled to examine the debtor under oath as to the whereabouts of any assets that the debtor may own or information where the debtor is employed. The subpoena also may be served upon a witness who may have information concerning the debtor. Such witnesses may be the debtor's spouse, relatives, or former employers. With regard to judgments against businesses, the subpoena is available to be served upon its officers, directors, or employees who have information concerning its assets.

Subpoenas—Disclosure of Client's Address. The attorney-client privilege normally does not apply when a plaintiff is seeking an address or location of the debtor. If a subpoena is served upon an attorney to disclose the whereabouts of the debtor after a judgment has already been entered, the courts have held that the attorney-client privilege is not absolute. It is intended to encourage a client's free and full disclosure of information to the client's attorney to facilitate the attorney's best advice in return. Application of the privilege is to be strictly construed to achieve its underlying purpose in light of the reason for its assertion and the attorney's ethical obligations under the unique circumstances of each case. A communication is privileged only if it is expressed by an individual acting in the capacity of a client while seeking or receiving legal advice or services from an attorney. An attorney's post-judgment disclosure of the client's whereabouts to prevent the obstruction of the collection of the court's judgment would not constitute a violation of the attorney's duty of confidentiality. The court will require the attorney to reveal the debtor's address unless it would cause him to violate his legal and ethical obligations. The court held that the attorney-client privilege does not apply under these circumstances, because the defendant's flight from enforcement of the judgment and the attorney's cooperation in withholding the whereabouts constitute a fraud upon the court.

As to post-judgment enforcement proceedings to enforce a money judgment, a party under most state laws usually may depose any person, providing the discovery is not privileged, and is relevant to the subject matter involved in the pending action.[15]

Contempt Orders. If a subpoena is served upon the debtor or a witness who does not appear, the creditor may make an application to court to punish the debtor for contempt of court. In New York this is called an "order to show cause to punish the debtor for contempt of court," or just a contempt order. In other states, relief is called a "body attachment or warrant for arrest." The creditor alleges that the debtor was served and that the debtor failed to appear. The judge will issue an order requiring the debtor to appear on a specified day at the courthouse to cure said default. The difficulty with contempt orders is that usually they must be served personally upon the debtor and if the debtor is evading service, the likelihood of success is slim. Failure to serve within the specified time requires preparing a new contempt order. If the debtor is served and does not appear, in most jurisdictions the creditor may apply to court for a warrant to arrest the debtor. This order is issued to the sheriff who arrests and produces the debtor in court to be examined under oath. After the debtor is examined, the judge usually releases the debtor.

The judges rarely incarcerate a debtor for failure to appear pursuant to a subpoena. Many sophisticated debtors will respond only to a contempt order; and some will wait for notice of an arrest order (the sheriff notifies the debtor before executing the arrest order) before submitting to an examination.

The remedy is perfectly legal, because the debtor is avoiding a court order. Nevertheless, common sense should be used when using this collection device. It may be advisable to avoid the use of said remedy if the debtor is old or infirm or is known to suffer from a medical condition. It is also recommended that other remedies be utilized first.

[15] *Horon Holding Corp. v. McKenzie*, 775 A.2d 1111 (N.J. Sup. Ct. App. Div. 2001); *Fellerman v. Bradley*, 99 N.J. 493 (1985).

Freedom of Information. Under the terms of the Freedom of Information Act, information can be obtained from federal and state governmental agencies about the debtor. For example, if the debtor is using a post office box number, a service of the proper papers upon the U.S. Postal Service will require it to furnish you with the street address of the owner of the post office box. In a new policy change this device is only available to attorneys, process servers, and plaintiffs appearing in person (*see* Chapter 19).

Skiptracing. This is a term used to locate either the residence, the place of employment, or the bank account of the debtor. Businesses in every state provide this type of service (*see* Chapter 19).

Order to Compel Payment. Sometimes a creditor obtains a judgment against a debtor who has no visible assets or stream of income. Nevertheless, the debtor appears to be living in expensive accommodations and apparently enjoying expensive means of transportation, travel, food, and other luxuries.

Most states have statutes which allow the creditor to request the court to compel the debtor to make monthly payments because the debtor is spending money which should be paid to the creditor. For example, one particular debtor was sending three children to private prep school, was renting a Cadillac, and paying several thousand dollars each month for an apartment in New York. In addition, he took a yearly vacation for two weeks to the Caribbean and maintained a membership in a country club. His source of income could not possibly cover all of these expenses. When he was examined, he testified to an income barely enough to cover the obvious living expenses. After the obvious expenses were deducted from his stream of income, the debtor had barely enough to cover food, clothing, and medical expenses for maybe a few days out of each month. After a hearing on an application to court to compel the debtor to make payments, the court directed the debtor to make a substantial payment each month.

In the event the debtor defaults on a payment plan, the creditor has the right to ask the court to punish the debtor for contempt of court. The application to court to punish for contempt is a function of the judge's discretion. Some judges fashion severe punishments, but most judges will just allow the debtor more time to make the payments or may even reduce the payments. Consultation with counsel is recommended.

ARBITRATION (See Chapter 5)

Arbitration is the method by which a plaintiff and a defendant avoid the use of the court system and agree between themselves, usually in writing, to submit their disputes to binding arbitration. An arbitration award has no legal significance unless it is confirmed by a court. The winner generally has to file an application to confirm the award within one year of the date of the award, or the award is unenforceable.

In most instances, the parties will seek an arbitration board in the state in which they are located or will use the American Arbitration Association, which will present a selection of some 20 to 25 arbitrators. The plaintiff and the defendant will each select one to three arbitrators; the association will then choose from this selection either one arbitrator who is acceptable to both parties or a panel of three arbitrators acceptable to both parties. The parties then will offer their evidence before the arbitrators who will render a decision. The main distinction in resolving a dispute by arbitration as distinguished from a lawsuit is as follows:

- In an arbitration, little discovery is available in the way of examinations of witnesses before trial, interrogatories, or production of documents. Because discovery prior to the arbitration is severely limited, the savings in legal fees are substantial.
- The rules of evidence are not as closely followed during an arbitration hearing and the arbitrator will normally listen to everything offered.
- No appeal on the merits of the case is allowed from a decision by the arbitrator. The arbitrator's decision is final unless a conflict of interest exists or one of the arbitrators acted improperly due to personal reasons. If an unfavorable decision is rendered, the losing party must live with that decision. In the court system, if a bad decision is rendered by a judge, the option to appeal to the appellate court is available. (*See* Chapter 5.)
- Arbitrations usually are arranged more quickly than are trials in the present court system.

Many written commercial agreements, purchase orders, lease agreements, and other types of complicated written contracts contain "boiler plate" terminology providing for arbitration. Attorneys often are opposed to arbitration, because of the lack of any opportunity to appeal a bad decision. On the other hand, some businessmen find arbitration exceptionally advantageous because of the speed of resolution of the dispute and the savings in legal fees. In most arbitration proceedings, both parties share the fees. (*See* Chapter 15 and Chapter 5 for use of arbitration clauses.) Some matters may only be resolved through arbitration (for example, NASDAQ matters).

GENERAL RELEASE

The general release is a statement by the creditor that releases the debtor from any and all claims the creditor may have against the debtor.

Most attorneys use the broadest release possible. However, it may not be in the best interest of the client to sign this type of release. We recommend that our client include language limiting the scope of the release. Depending upon the situation, you will need to customize the release to protect your interests. Many attorneys claim that their release is the standard release that everyone uses, but this is not the case. Forms vary from state to state and from attorney to attorney. A release is an important document and its terms are negotiable. The party executing the release should review the document carefully to determine and confirm which parties are being released and what obligations are being released.

When multiple obligors [co-signer, guarantor(s)] are involved, you should determine whether you will be settling the debt with some of the obligors or with all of the obligors. The release needs to be drafted in accordance with the intention of the parties. Sometimes the settlement agreement and release agreement are combined into one agreement and the release portion of the agreement may contradict the settlement portion of the agreement. Combination agreements must be carefully reviewed because the courts tend to resolve any ambiguity against the party who drafted the agreement.

Another situation in which releases need to be carefully reviewed involves vehicle lease agreements. The lease agreement creates both contractual liability for the lessee and tort liability. The lessor, as owner of the vehicle, is liable for any personal injuries to third parties that arise out of the use of the vehicle. If a balance is owed by the lessee after termination, as part of the settlement, auto leasing companies specifically limit their releases to contractual liability only. The lessee is required to indemnify the lessor for any liability incurred due to accidents involving third parties that took place prior to the date of the release but the claim is made after the date of the release. If the leasing company releases the lessee from all liability, including tort liability, it will lose its right to indemnification. This issue must be addressed before a motor vehicle lessor executes a general release.

A problem also occurs when the debtor has multiple obligations with the creditor. For example, the debtor has a car loan, credit card, and a mortgage with the same bank. Other examples are leases for three cars with three different leases from the same company; or when the debtor owes money to several divisions of a large multi-national corporation. In most cases the creditor representative is aware of only its department's debt. Be careful. You do not want to unintentionally release the debtor from other obligations owed to your company.

If the debtor defaults on some of the multiple obligations, the creditor should only release the debt(s) that has been settled. The release should contain limiting language that refers to the account number, invoice number, date of the loan, the collateral, and/or the docket number under which a lawsuit was commenced. Often the creditor thinks that he is settling a single debt, while the debtor is fully aware of the multiple liabilities to the creditor.

A release agreement is an enforceable agreement. Its terms are negotiable. If the terms of the release are unambiguous, a court will examine the four corners of the document, and will not consider other evidence. If the terms of the release are silent or unclear as to the dispute, the court will consider extrinsic evidence consistent with the terms of the agreement to determine the intent of the parties. The court will not consider contradictory evidence. When dealing in a commercial context by parties of roughly equivalent bargaining power, and ready access to counsel, a court is less likely to look beyond the four corners of the document. Plaintiffs should limit what you are releasing and defendants should obtain the broadest releases possible.

SUBORDINATION AGREEMENT

Often a lender wishes to extend credit to a borrower who already has a lien or a mortgage on the property which the borrower wishes to offer as collateral to the creditor. The borrower enters an agreement with the existing mortgagee so that the mortgagee will become subordinate to the new mortgage being placed on the property by the bank. For example, real estate worth $200,000 carries a $10,000 mortgage. The owner seeks a loan of $100,000. The existing mortgagee agrees to subordinate the $10,000 mortgage to the $100,000 mortgage which is being placed on the premises by the bank. Some form of consideration may be paid to the existing mortgagee, such as a prepayment or an increase in interest. As a result, the $100,000 is the first mortgage and $10,000 is the second mortgage. The agreement between the borrower and the existing mortgagee is the subordination agreement.

SURETYSHIP

A contract of suretyship is a promise made by a third person to be responsible for the debtor's obligation with some benefit to the party becoming the surety (an insurance contract). A surety in the strict sense is primarily liable for the debt of the principal. The creditor need not exhaust all remedies against the principal debtor before holding the surety responsible. A surety agreement that benefits the surety does not have to be in writing to be enforceable, whereas a contract of guarantee, where someone promises to answer for the debt of another and may be of no benefit to the guarantor, must be in writing. With a guarantee of payment, the guarantor is secondarily liable. The guarantor can only be required to pay the obligation after the principal defaults, whereas the surety is primarily liable. As to a guaranty of collection, the creditor must exhaust the remedies against the debtor before proceeding against the guarantor.

A surety may be known as a co-maker or an endorser or an accommodation party. A surety includes all types of guarantors. If the creditor received collateral from the debtor, the surety could be discharged to the extent of the impairment of said collateral. If the creditor repossessed an automobile and was negligent in storing the vehicle before the auction sale, and the car was damaged, the surety may be discharged to the extent of the damage of the collateral.

PAROL EVIDENCE RULE

Parol evidence is a rule of evidence that bestows a preferred status on final written agreements. The rule is designed to provide stability in business transactions. The rule protects the agreement from the risk of perjured testimony and the risk of uncertain testimony of a party with a "slippery" and "self-serving" memory. At trial, the rule excludes earlier oral agreements or any contemporaneous oral agreements. The basis of the rule is that these earlier agreements were not intended to survive, but to be merged into the final agreement.

The Parol Evidence Rule holds that where an agreement has been reduced to writing and is intended to be the final and complete expression of the agreement between the parties, any evidence of earlier oral or written agreements or any contemporaneous oral agreements are not admissible in a court of law to vary, add to, or contradict the terms of the written agreement.

When Does the Parol Evidence Apply? Two key issues must be addressed: First, one must determine whether the parties intended the writing to be the final written agreement. Second, one must determine whether there is partial or total integration of the prior oral or written agreements. If a court determines that only partial integration exists, the agreement may be supplemented by additional terms. Seems simple, right? Five different tests have been developed to apply this rule.

Four Corners Rule. In applying the first test, the trial judge actually examines only the written agreement and makes a determination if the agreement represents the final intent of the parties. This test is not widely accepted due to the limited information provided. The drafter of the agreement is subject to the subjective interpretation of the judge hearing the case. This test usually favors the drafter of the agreement unless the agreement is too specific or too vague. If the agreement is poorly drafted, the drafter of the agreement suffers, especially if this interpretation is beneficial to the other party. Although many creditors desire the courts to apply this test, it rarely occurs, especially in consumer credit transactions.

Any Relevant Evidence Test. The second test directs the court to seek out the actual intention of the parties to determine if the document was partially or totally integrated. Under this test, a judge would admit evidence of all relevant prior negotiations and treat the document as partially integrated. This test is increasingly applied by judges, because it permits the court wide latitude in making its determination to admit evidence, as anything may be relevant.

Collateral Contract Rule. This test is subject to two interpretations. Under one version, (A) all written agreements are deemed to be partially integrated. Additional terms in prior or contemporaneous agreements that do not contradict the writing are admissible. The key point is that the additional terms may not contradict the terms in the main agreement. Additional writings explaining the original writing would be admissible; (B) if the additional terms are covered in the original written agreement, the evidence is excluded. However, if the additional terms are not covered by the original agreement, the document is treated as partially integrated, and the additional terms are considered by the court. The test is applied only by a few courts and is open to subjective interpretation.

The Modern Test. This test holds that if the written agreement includes a merger clause, expressly and conspicuously stating that this writing is intended to be the final and complete version of the agreement, the agreement is held to be completely integrated. Only if it is obvious that the agreement is incomplete, or that the merger clause was included as a result of fraud or mistake, will a court consider additional evidence. In the absence of the merger clause, the court will examine the writing. Additional terms may be provided if the writing is obviously incomplete, or if the additional terms are of the type that would naturally appear in a separate writing.

UCC Test. The fifth test is set forth in Section 2-202 of the Uniform Commercial Code, which applies to contracts for the sale of goods. Section 2-202 states:

> Terms with respect to which the confirmatory memoranda of the parties agree or which are otherwise set forth in the writing intended by the parties as a final expression of the agreement with respect to such terms as are included therein may not be contradicted by evidence of any prior agreement or of a contemporaneous oral agreement, but may be explained or supplemented

(a) by course of dealing or usage of trade . . . or by course of performance . . . and

(b) by evidence of consistent terms unless the court finds the writing to have been intended also as a complete and exclusive statement of the terms of agreement.

The UCC test is a liberal test because evidence of a separate agreement is admissible unless the matters covered in the alleged agreement "certainly would have been included" in the writing.

Depending on which test is used, a different result may occur. Judges usually consider fairness, equity, and who benefits from the interpretation of the agreement. For example, a liberal judge is more likely to use a test that favors a consumer against a large corporation. However, in a situation between two corporations, the same test might lead to a different outcome.

This rule only prohibits the allegations from being offered into evidence. If the allegations are not in evidence, the trier of fact (jury) will never hear the evidence. In a trial by a judge, the judge makes the ruling of admissibility as well as being the trier of fact. Once the document is offered, and the judge has seen the document, the issue of admissibility may no longer be relevant.

Even if the allegedly damaging allegations are admitted into evidence, what weight the trier of the fact (judge or jury) assesses to the prior negotiations is another story. Many judges believe that the evidence should be excluded. To prevent being overturned on appeal, the judge, nevertheless, admits the documents into evidence, but then assesses little credibility to the evidence when rendering a decision. Appellate courts have discretion to determine if evidence was excluded, but rarely overrule a judge or jury on assessing the credibility of the evidence.

HEARSAY

Hearsay usually consists of testimony that is furnished by a witness who relates not what he or she knows personally but "what others have said," and which is dependent on the credibility of someone other than the testifying witness. Such testimony is inadmissible under the rules of evidence, for such statements are not made under oath and are not subject to cross-examination. The federal rules of evidence provides certain exceptions to the hearsay rule, regardless of whether the party who made the statement is not available to testify under oath and cannot be cross-examined that is deathbed declaration.[16]

[16]Black's Law Dictionary 726 (7th ed. 1999).

PREPARING FOR TRIAL—AS A WITNESS, WHAT SHOULD I DO?

When a witness prepares for trial, certain items should be reviewed to avoid awkward situations at the trial. Sometimes these issues occur because their counsel assumes that the client will bring the necessary documentation to prove the case.

1. *Be prepared and organized.* Image is everything when you are in court. Review the documentation to confirm that you understand all the numbers and references on the documents. For example, if your employer uses a trade name on the documents which is different from the plaintiff, be prepared to explain the difference.
2. *Bring a payment history.* Produce an itemized payment history. Statements showing late charges only may be viewed with skepticism by the court. Be able to explain how the balance is calculated. The method by which payments are applied varies in different parts of the country. Be prepared for cross-examination by the judge as to the *process* by which the balance of principal and interest was computed.
3. *Documentation.* Bring invoices or copies of cancelled checks to establish miscellaneous charges. If you incurred a repossession fee or a lien title search fee, bring supporting documentation.
4. *Assignments or Power of Attorney.* If you cannot prove you own the loan or are authorized to enforce the loan, you will lose.

In many cases, such as in retail installment agreements, the originating party (Seller) often assigns the matter to a finance company. The assignment is often included in the agreement. But in some cases it is a separate document. With the wave of mergers and acquisitions by national lenders, the party suing on the loan is not the originating party. Thus, it is important that the witness is prepared to describe how the loan was acquired (that is by reason of merger, acquisition, assignment) to the court. Supporting documentation should also be presented to the court.

Original documents demonstrate to the court that you are serious. A complete file serves the same purpose: to prove to the court that no one else owns the account. The witness should discuss with counsel a prepared summary of the procedure for acquiring accounts. Indirect evidence, such as a cancelled check or receipt, will help prove ownership. Be prepared to explain what steps are required before the plaintiff ever attempts to collect on the loan. Explaining the process demonstrates to the judge that you did not improperly obtain the papers.

Credit & Collection Tip: *Try to obtain an admission of plaintiff's ownership from the debtor.*

5. *Can you testify?* If you are required to testify as to procedures and practices of your employer, be certain that you were employed at the time that the relevant practices occurred.

To testify as to the procedural safeguards employed by your employer to prevent against fraud, or to establish a commercially reasonable sale, you must have been employed at the time the alleged fraud or sale occurred to be qualified to testify. You had to be there to know the practice. It cannot be based on what you have been told.

6. *No original documents available.* Some courts require original documents. If originals are not available because they were destroyed as part of your business practice, you must be prepared to testify regarding the procedures to verify the accuracy of the duplicates. You must also be prepared to explain why and when the original documents were destroyed, and why this practice is justified and a common business practice. You should also become familiar with the Uniform Electronic Document Act. Finally, note when there is an issue of fraud as to the contents of the documents, the court may insist upon originals.
7. *Review all legal documents submitted by your employer and the adversary* (that is affidavits, replies to discovery requests and depositions). You may be cross-examined as to these documents. Review the documents and exhibits for inconsistencies which may be prejudicial to your case.
8. *If the contract exists, read the document(s) carefully.* The judge or the adversary may cross-examine you as to certain portions of the agreement. If you do not understand the contract, you will appear less credible to the judge, especially if your employer drafted the clause.

Guidelines for Testimony at Deposition. Either party is entitled to examine the witness before the trial to attempt to obtain information, to narrow the client's testimony, and cause the client to commit to as many positions as possible. The general purpose is to prevent surprise at the trial, and reduce the number of issues.

Some comments as to conduct at a deposition follow:

1. The client should volunteer no information, should answer only the questions asked as briefly as possible *and should be thoroughly prepared.*
2. The reporter serves to record the testimony and at the end certifies that it is a true record of what took place at the examination before trial.
3. The testimony may be used at the trial. The procedure is for the opposing attorney to read the reporter's record of the testimony into the record at the trial.

4. If an answer to a question at the examination before trial is different from an answer to the same question at the trial, the credibility of the witness is severely impaired. The client should provide a truthful answer at the examination and the same answer at the trial.
5. The attorneys may agree prior to the examination before trial that all objections, except as to the form of the questions, are reserved for the trial. The purpose of this stipulation is to permit the examination to go forward but to enable the other side to object to the question and answer at the trial.
6. During the examination the attorney may not wish the client to respond to the question. When the attorney interrupts the question-and-answer procedure, the client should stop talking immediately and permit the attorney to speak.
7. The client should create a small pause before each answer to enable the attorney to object to that specific question. Once the question is answered by the client, it cannot be erased from the transcript.
8. An examination before trial is usually conducted in a friendly atmosphere between the attorneys. Do not be misled by this friendly atmosphere into volunteering any information or discussing with the attorney for the opposing side or the adversary any details of the case.
9. It is permissible to ask the attorney to repeat the question and to ask the court reporter to read the question back when you state that you did not understand it. This procedure should be utilized whenever appropriate.
10. If you are testifying and you have kept some notes to refresh your recollection at the examination, do not refer to those notes in the presence of the opposing attorney. The attorney for the other side is then entitled to examine all of those notes, including the notes you did not use. Furthermore, the notes can be used at the trial to cross-examine. The best course is to review these notes prior to the examination and out of the sight of the opposing attorney.
11. You will have an opportunity to review a transcript of the examination, and correct any answer—but the original answer remains.

Guidelines for Testimony at Trial.

1. The oath warrants repeating "to tell the truth, the whole truth, and nothing but the truth." Accordingly, the truth should be stated at all times. *The truth hangs together.*
2. Do not try to evaluate whether your answer is hurting your side or helping the other side. Answer the question to the best of your recollection.

3. Do not try to color or exaggerate your answer, or use intonations of indignation or sincerity, to help or hurt your side. Give your answer truthfully and in a level and sincere tone of voice.
4. Listen carefully to the questions. Remember that the other attorney is attempting to help his or her client. Failure to understand the question may produce an answer which is harmful to your side, especially since everyone else in the courtroom will have heard the question correctly. If necessary, ask that the question be repeated.
5. Do not respond quickly to a question, nor should you respond slowly to a question. The reason you do not respond quickly is to afford your attorney an opportunity to lodge an objection. If your attorney does so, do not answer the question until the Court directs you. If you answer the question slowly and spend too much time deliberating, the impression may be that you are framing or fabricating an answer.
6. The most important thing to remember when answering a question is that the answer should respond only to the question. Do not furnish information that is not sought. Furnishing additional information creates more material about which the opposing attorney will ask questions.
7. Where possible, an answer of "yes" or "no" is preferred. Nevertheless, if the answer needs an explanation, furnish the explanation.
8. If during your testimony you remember that a prior question was answered improperly, stop, state that you would like to change an answer to a prior question, and change the answer.
9. Do not memorize any answers prior to the trial. Answer the questions truthfully and to the best of your recollection.
10. If you finish an answer and the other attorney remains silent, do not continue to speak. The attorney is hoping you will offer more information.

DEMEANOR.

1. Maintain a serious attitude. Do not laugh or talk loud in the hallways, restrooms, or anywhere in the courthouse.
2. Do not try to approach or talk to any members of the jury if you should meet them in the hall or in the courtroom.
3. While testifying, direct your answers directly at the attorney or the jury. Look at them most of the time and speak to them openly and frankly as you would to any friend or neighbor. Do not cover your mouth with your hand. Do not look down at the floor. Do not gaze up at the ceiling. Do not try to look up at the judge and answer the question to the judge. The answer should be responsive to the attorney, or preferably to the jury if one is present.

4. Be polite to the attorney and to the judge. Do not be argumentative. Do not be curt or brief.
5. Do not be a conceited or a wise-guy type of witness.
6. Do not act nervous. Avoid mannerisms which will make the jury think you are scared or not telling the truth.
7. Sit upright and do not slump in the chair.
8. As a general rule, the male's attire should be a suit and tie. Women should wear a dress or suit. Conservative colors are advisable. Neatness counts in your overall appearance.

TESTIMONY—SUGGESTIONS.

1. The Court and the jury want the facts. They do not want conclusions, opinions, or what you heard other people say. Testifying as to conclusions, opinions, or what other people say normally produce objections by the other attorney.
2. Do not say "that's all that was said," "nothing else was said," or "nothing else happened." Use the words "that's all I recall," "that's all I remember," or "that's all I recollect." You may use "to the best of my recollection," or "at this time all I remember." This leaves an opening in case your recollection is refreshed in the future and you wish to add facts or certain statements.
3. Give firm answers whenever possible. If you do remember something, do not say "I think," "I believe," or "in my opinion." If you do not know something, answer "I do not know" or "I do not remember." If the other attorney is seeking minor and small details, it is best to say that you do not remember them. Of course, you should remember major points.

CONDUCT.

1. Do not ask the judge for advice or ask the judge to help you.
2. If you feel that the question is improper or you feel you should not be answering, wait for your attorney to object. If your attorney does not object, you must answer the question.
3. Do not argue with the other attorney or be flippant. It is best to respond with no side remarks, no comments, no groans, or any other physical move which would offend the attorney, the judge, or the jury.
4. Do not use your head for "yes" or "no" answers. Speak out.

FATIGUE. Fatigue always enters into cross-examination of a witness. After being on the witness stand for an hour, or being examined before trial for an hour, it is easy to become fatigued, short-tempered, and anxious for the next question to be the last. Do not lose your temper. When you become tired, and you feel you are nervous or angry or careless, be aware of these symptoms and attempt to control the fatigue. Other symptoms are crossness, nervousness, a willingness to answer any question, a desire to stand up out of your seat and walk around, a slight headache, or impatience waiting for the next question. Remember that many attorneys on cross-examinations attempt to induce this fatigue and cause you to lose your temper to provoke you into careless answers. Do not let this happen. Request a recess when fatigue is present.

Down the Garden Path. Some attorneys lead you down the garden path with trick questions that have been used many times before.

1. *Have you talked to anyone about the case?* If you say no, the jury knows lawyers always talk to their witnesses before a trial.
2. *Has your attorney told you what to say at this trial?* This is the same type of question. The answer is that the case was discussed with you and you were told to tell the truth.
3. *Are you getting paid to testify in this case?* If you are being paid, your answer should be that you are paid to compensate for your time off from work and the expenses to appear at the trial or whatever the arrangement is.
4. Often an attorney will try to narrow down "time," "days," "hours," and "approximate values":

   Q. When was the last time you saw the car before it struck your car?

   A. I don't know.

   Q. Well, was it a minute, ten seconds, five seconds, two seconds?

   A. I don't know; perhaps two seconds.

   Q. Well, you must realize that a car can travel somewhere around 60 to 80 feet in two seconds. If you saw a car 60 to 80 feet away from you, you could have certainly done something to avoid the collision.

   The same principle applies when you are recollecting a conversation that took place several years ago and the attorney asks you when the conversation took place. For example:

   Q. Was it in January, February, the first week in January, the first week in February?

   If you do not remember the exact time, and only remember that it happened during the first half of the year, the testimony is:

A. It happened during the first half of the year. I don't remember exactly when during that period of time. The same line of questioning may apply when you are asked:

Q. How many boxes did you see? Did you see ten, twenty, fifty, a hundred boxes? If you don't remember how many you saw, and all you remember is that you saw a lot of boxes, the answer should be:

A. I saw a lot of boxes. I don't remember how many there were.

5. The client should not adopt the attorney's friendly questions as the testimony or adopt a summary of the situation furnished by the attorney where it appears to be substantially correct, although not exactly correct. In short, the client should testify as to exactly what happened and not adopt any summary provided by the attorney requesting a "yes" or "no" answer, as follows:

   Q. The borrower was at your desk and signed the note.

   A. Yes.

   The attorney for the other side failed to mention that one of the defenses is that the defendant was not wearing glasses and could not read the note. The witness, on the other hand, failed to tell the defendant that the borrower spent about two minutes reading the note carefully (without glasses).

Special Testimony.

1. As a general rule, you may testify as to what you saw, heard, felt, touched, or smelled.
2. You are not permitted to testify as to opinion, conclusions, what someone said about something happening, what you believe to have happened, what you hope to happen, etc.

Telephone Conversations. There are special foundations which must be laid in order to permit a telephone conversation or a letter to be admitted as evidence.

The key to a telephone conversation is the recognition of a voice. An essential part to this is that you spoke to the party either before the telephone conversation took place, or after the telephone conversation took place, and you can state that you recognize the voice on the telephone. A series of questions might be as follows:

Q. Did you speak to John Smith before July 4th?

A. Yes.

Q. On July 4th, did you or did you not telephone him?

A. I telephoned him on July 4th.

Q. Did you dial his number?

A. Yes.

Q. Did you recognize the voice on the telephone as the voice of John Smith?

A. Yes.

Q. What did he say and what did you say?

A. He said . . .

Mailing a Letter. A similar problem may arise with regard to offering a copy of a letter as evidence.

The key to this line of questioning is that you compared the original to the copy, and that the envelope was mailed in a depository of the United States, that is a mailbox. A line of questioning might be as follows:

Q. Did you write (dictate) the letter dated July 4, 1976?

A. Yes.

Q. Did you see the original letter before it was mailed?

A. Yes.

Q. Did you compare the original with the copy?

A. Yes.

Q. Then what did you do with the letter?

A. I sealed it in an envelope, affixed postage to it and mailed it in a mailbox at Fifth Avenue and 42nd Street.

Conclusion. When you leave the witness stand, try to have a confident expression and not a downcast one. It is best not to discuss the case, and if you have been excused, you should leave the courtroom and the courthouse.

HELL OR HIGH WATER CLAUSE

Hell or high water clauses usually cause the obligation of the lessee under a finance lease to be irrevocable upon the acceptance of the goods. The doctrine applies to personal property leases which require the lessee to continue to send the payments even if the item leased is damaged, defective, or destroyed. The company who sold the item to the lessee is responsible. An example of such a clause might be as follows:

> You agree that you are unconditionally obligated to pay all the rent and other amounts due for the entire lease term even if the equipment is defective, damaged or destroyed, or if you can no longer use it. You are not entitled to reduce or set off against rental payments or other amounts due to us or to anyone to whom lessor transfers this lease, whether your claim arises out of this lease, any written or oral statement by a vendor or manufacturer, or negligence of any vendor or manufacturer or otherwise. This lease is a finance lease.

Clauses such as or similar to this one are fairly common in the commercial leasing industry and federal appellate courts usually uphold the validity of the clause.[17]

---

[17] *Wells Fargo Bank, N.A. v. BrooksAmerica Mortgage Corp.*, 419 F.3d 107 (2d Cir. 2005); *Harte-Hanks Direct Mktg./Baltimore, Inc. v. Varilease Tech. Finance Group, Inc.*, 299 F. Supp. 2d 505 (D. Md. 2004); *Great America Leasing Corp. v. Star Photo Lab Inc.*, 672 N.W.2d 502 (CA Iowa, 2003); *Gen. Electric Capital Corp. v. National Tractor Trailer School Inc.*, 667 N.Y.S.2d 614 (N.Y. 1997). *See* Hell & High Water Clause—Leases, Black's Law Dictionary (7th ed. 1999).

CHAPTER 2

Letters and Telephone Calls

COMPLIANCE WITH FAIR DEBT COLLECTION PRACTICES ACT

A debt collector who is subject to the Fair Debt Collection Practices Act (FDCPA) is faced with a wide variety of conditions, restrictions, and requirements when writing a collection letter or making a collection telephone call. The reader must review Chapter 15 to be informed as to all the requirements set forth in the FDCPA. They range from the requirements of repeating the mini-Miranda warning during each telephone call to the number of times when the telephone calls can be made and the restrictions on whom you may speak to over the telephone other than the debtor.

Creditors who deal with consumers are not subject to the FDCPA except under certain circumstances, such as misleading the consumer as to who is doing the collection or using another name to mislead the consumer. Again, the author refers the reader to Chapter 15 to review the appropriate sections of the FDCPA to be certain that the Act is not being violated.

Your author wrote a book entitled "*The Complete Guide to Tested Telephone Collection Techniques*" in 1988 and there was a short chapter in the book that dealt with compliance. The FDCPA was passed in 1979 and for the 11 years up to 1988 a few decisions were rendered each year which interpreted the Act. In any given year since 1995, there were probably more legal decisions in one year than there were in the 11 years between 1979 and 1988.

See Chapter 15 before utilizing any of the material in this chapter when making a collection telephone call to a consumer for a debt that is covered by the FDCPA.

The same advice would apply to the preparation of letters. The litigation over the FDCPA has developed into a myriad of restrictions and requirements that must be considered when preparing a letter to a consumer on a debt that is covered by the FDCPA.

CONSUMERS' DEBTS

The collection of a consumer debt for personal, family, or household purposes is covered by the FDCPA. While the Act requires an extension of credit, the courts have expanded the reach of the FDCPA with a broad brush, and almost all attempts to collect from an individual will be covered by the FDCPA including checks, rent, and foreclosing on real estate. Although creditors are generally exempt from coverage while collecting their own debts, many exceptions carved out by the statute and courts cause creditors to be subject to the Act, as well as collection agencies, debt collectors, debt purchasers, and attorneys who collect debts for others.

A careful reading of Chapter 15 and a careful review of the statute and the court decisions is strongly recommended before collecting by mail or over the telephone.

BUSINESS DEBTS

While business debts are fundamentally not covered by the FDCPA, many states and localities have enacted mirror images of the FDCPA with one major change. The Act covers collection of all consumer and business debts. The courts have also determined that a business debt is determined not by the main purpose of the product, but the use of the product. If it is used personally, it is covered by the Act.

Every state has their Unfair Trade Practices Act which prohibits business from engaging in "unfair practices." The courts often use the Act as a benchmark to define what is an "unfair practice."

Accordingly, a careful reading of Chapter 15, a review of the statute and your state unfair trade practice rule, or any statute passed by the state as well as any court decisions is strongly recommended before doing any collection by mail or over the telephone.

A WINNING COMBINATION—LETTERS AND TELEPHONE CALLS

Why the Interplay Between Letter and Telephone Is Critical to Your Collection Effort Strategy. Any general will tell you that the key to a successful military operation on land consists of air cover and tanks. For a collection manager the principle is the same: send forth a series of letters (the air cover), and follow up with the telephone call (the tanks). It is critical that you first understand the importance of the interplay between a letter and a telephone call.

PROPER CREDIT CHECKING—THE FIRST LINE OF DEFENSE

Proper credit checking will prevent a bad debt. To make such a simplistic statement begs the questions. While the first mercantile credit agency was organized in the mid-1800s, and Dun and Bradstreet is over 100 years old, the credit society in which we live did not really come into being until after World War II. Prior to that time, the principal extension of credit to the consumer was the mortgage on his home and a local charge account at the general store until next payday. However, lending for business purposes had been common much earlier. The extension of credit was both secured and unsecured, and perhaps the best example of secured lending was the 90 percent margin accounts which prevailed on Wall Street prior to the crash of 1929. Each margin account was secured by securities which were systematically sold as the prices declined, eventually triggering the worst depression our nation has ever known.

Each organization has its own forms for obtaining financial information concerning the prospective borrower. Credit procedures vary from company to company. Articles and books appear each year to guide the American businessman. Seminars flourish at luxury hotels. Credit reporting agencies, such as Experian, Equifax, and Trans Union have created huge databases on consumers. Financial information and payment experience are provided by local business and trade associations. Dun and Bradstreet is still with us.

USE AND FREQUENCY OF INVOICES AND STATEMENTS

Repeated invoices and statements to a delinquent debtor is probably the device used by most businesses to respond to a delinquent debt. The temptation to use statements is sweetened by the apparent attractiveness of the computer to print all types of messages on invoices that are delinquent.

While invoices and statements should be used, their repeated use beyond a 60-day period after the debt is due is certainly not warranted and adds nothing to the collection effort. Actually, the invoice is the mildest form of dunning, and a statement, with or without a message, is really no improvement.

HOW THE INTERPLAY BETWEEN COLLECTION LETTERS AND TELEPHONE CALLS WORKS

How to Get the Impact of Two Calls for the Price of One. When a debtor receives a letter after the telephone call, the first memory is of the prior telephone call. Accordingly, the net result is a free second telephone call. For this reason, a follow-up letter should always be mailed after a telephone call. While telephone calls may be made without the use of letters, without a letter after the telephone call, their efficiency may be reduced by as much as 20 to 30 percent. *Again, be certain to mail a letter after each telephone call.*

The Ingredients of an Effective Letter. Basically, four types of collection letters are used.

1. **Notice:** The first is the notice or reminder letter, stating that the account is past due, or a simple reminder that the customer has ignored the statement and the creditor is now requesting payment. No consequences for nonpayment are set forth in the letter.
2. **Customer Relations:** The second letter is a customer relations letter. The creditor inquires as to the reason why the debt has not been paid. The letter seeks information as to defective merchandise, late delivery, inadequate services, shortages, or any other reason that might justify nonpayment. *This is never used as a first letter unless it is combined with a first letter.*
3. **Collection Letter:** The third letter is the true collection letter. The creditor insists that the debtor pay the debt. The letter is direct and to the point.
4. **Consequence Letter:** This is the final written notice. The creditor states that some further consequence will take place if payment is not made within a prescribed period of time. The promised action usually takes the form of referral to a collection agency, or a referral to an attorney.

Three Special Keys to a Series of Letters.

1. **Series of Letters:** While there are basically only four types of collection letters, it is possible to mail a series of eight letters consisting of two notice letters, two customer relation letters, two collection letters, and two consequence letters, or any combination thereof. At the same

time, a series of only two letters may be mailed by combining the notice and customer relation letter into one letter and combining the collection and consequence letter into another letter.

2. **Special Types of Letters:** Other types of letters are appropriate to specific situations. After a message is left on the telephone, a special letter should be prepared and mailed a day or so later advising the debtor that a telephone call was made and of the fact that a debt is due, etc. Special letters should be prepared for situations where the debtor promises payment, pays on account, wants to return merchandise, or whatever other situation indicates a follow-up letter.
3. **Trick to Writing the Letter:** Consultants are paid hundreds and thousands of dollars to write a series of collection letters. In our experience the best collection letter is the one written by the owner or the collection manager, for this truly reflects the policy and attitude of the business and its owners. Letters should be integrated with telephone calls and each letter should convey the appropriate message. The letters should be reviewed by an attorney knowledgeable in this area.

FOUR GOLDEN KEYS TO AN EFFECTIVE TELEPHONE COLLECTION

Golden Key 1—Positive Identification. Always confirm that you are speaking to the correct person. For example:

1. Is this James Jones at 235 Main Street?
2. Is this the Speedy Cleaning Company on Route 66?

After you are certain you are speaking to the correct person or firm, the next step is to identify yourself.

For consumers, be certain you recite the mini-Miranda statement at the beginning of each call. (*See* Chapter 15.)

Business-to-Business Collection Calls. When calling a business, ask to speak to the owner first. If the owner is not available, ask for the bookkeeper. If the debtor is a large business, ask first to speak to the accounts payable department and then the bookkeeping department. If all of the above are not available, speak to anyone who is in charge or who is *authorized* to accept a message.

If the debtor is a corporation, speak to the following corporate officers: comptroller, financial manager, treasurer, credit manager, bookkeeper, vice-president, or the president if there is no accounts payable department.

Golden Key 2—Foundation for Demand for Payment. A telephone call is weak and ineffective without the proper foundation. A foundation consists of advising the customer of the length of the delinquency, the number of bills or invoices that were sent and ignored, the number of collection letters mailed and ignored, and any prior telephone calls made and ignored. The purpose of the foundation is to strip the customer of any defensive argument. The moment the customer realizes a creditor is dunning him or her, the first thought is to obtain some form of extension of time and avoid an immediate payment. The purpose of the foundation is to surround the customer and allow no opening for the customer to claim ignorance of the debt or the fact that the debt was delinquent. The foundation might take the following form.

1. "XYZ Corporation has sent several statements, and your bill is past due over 60 days."
2. "We have written you several letters and called you once."
3. "Your charge account is 60 days in arrears and you have ignored three letters and one telephone call."
4. "Your mortgage payment is two months in arrears, and we have sent you two delinquency notices. You are already incurring late charges."

Prior Promise to Pay. The best foundation is to cite a prior written or oral promise by the customer to pay. Ninety-five percent of the population attempts to keep their promises, and a broken promise should be utilized to its fullest extent. Imposing a feeling of guilt on a customer is the surest road to obtaining payment. Use a prior broken promise at the beginning, in the middle, and at the end of the telephone conversation, when possible. When the debtor previously promised any specific action, reference should be made to that action:

1. You promised payment.
2. You promised to return the merchandise or equipment.
3. You said you would check your records.

Do not threaten criminal action on a civil matter. Threatening criminal action on a bad check is the surest way to be sued, unless you have sufficient evidence to prove intent and a reasonable percentage of cases are referred to the police department. (*See* Chapter 8.)

Golden Key 3—Bottom Line—Demanding a Payment. When you demand payment, you should do exactly that. Do not use "please" and do not "ask" for money. Do not plead or beg for money. Even if the debtor is a person with whom a personal relationship exists, a firm demand should be made.

1. We must have full payment by Monday, May 7.
2. Your check must reach our office by Monday, May 7.
3. The last day for the April installment is Monday, May 7.

> ***Credit & Collection Tip: Name, Rank, and Serial Number.*** *You should always advise the debtor of the name, address, and ZIP code of the creditor, including to which department or person the letter and/or payment should be addressed. The debtor should be told to write this information on a piece of paper. The debtor should be told to affix the account number on the check.*

Golden Key 4—Closing Statement Must End Telephone Call. The general rule is that a closing statement must be made at the end of every telephone call. A *closing statement is a concise statement of the consequences which will take place if the debtor does not pay.* Normally, this means that the creditor will refer the claim to a collection agency for letters and telephone calls, or to an attorney for collection and institution of suit. This closing statement will be used in 90 percent of the telephone collection calls.

SOME WARNINGS ABOUT USING THREATS

Threat to Refer Claim to Collection Agency or Attorney. Section 807, Subdivision 5, of the FDCPA provides that a violation of the Act takes place where the creditor threatens to take any action which cannot be taken legally or that is not intended to be taken. It is imperative that the action threatened be taken. If referral to a collection agency or attorney is the essential ingredient of the closing statement, the creditor must refer the claim to the collection agency or attorney. Implications that action is intended although never taken can also violate this section.

Negative Closing Statement. The basic closing statement may not be suitable for all situations, and to react to the different circumstances, alternative responses are available and illustrated here.

1. **Negative Closing Statement:** This is a weaker closing statement properly used in response to a promise of immediate payment or return of the goods. "Be certain that you mail your check by Monday, May 7, so that it will not be necessary for this matter to be referred to a collection agency/attorney for further action or institution of suit." A negative closing statement is less effective, but should be used where the debtor

is expressing good faith in an effort to pay and has made a promise of some form of payment.

2. It can be argued that it is unfair to threaten to refer an account to a collection agency/attorney if the debtor has just promised payment in full. Nevertheless, some variations of the closing statement are appropriate. An example of a negative closing statement would be as follows:
   - We will hold up reviewing the account for referral to our collection agency/attorney until Monday, May 7, but no later.
   - If we do not receive your check by Monday, May 7, then we will have no alternative but to refer this matter to our collection agency/attorney, so please be sure it is mailed in time.

TEN FREQUENTLY USED EXCUSES AND HOW TO RESPOND TO THEM

Excuse 1—Promise of Future Payment. The most powerful excuse for a debtor to use is a promise of future payment. A promise to pay may not be defined technically as an excuse, but in reality, this promise buys more time and is a persuasive device to forestall any action by the creditor. How the telephone worker reacts to this offer of good faith will often determine whether payment is actually made as promised, or as more frequently happens, another telephone call becomes a necessity. Sometimes promises of payment delay further action for weeks, months, and even longer.

Always Demand Payment in Full. Always request and expect payment in full whenever the debtor promises payment. Often, the telephone worker will respond to a promise of payment by inquiring as to "how much do you intend to pay?" The response should never be a question. A request for the full amount should always be made.

Debtor: I don't have the money right now.

Creditor: But we must have payment by Monday, May 7.

Debtor: Well, maybe I can send a little.

Creditor: You don't understand. We must have payment in full by Monday, May 7.

The Right Response to Partial Payment. When the debtor responds that only a partial payment can be made, a serious attempt to obtain a commitment for the balance must be made at that time.

CREDITOR: This is Mrs. Clark concerning the balance due to Dr. Jones.

DEBTOR: Yes, I know about this, but I can't possibly pay that money now. I just do not have it.

CREDITOR: The balance is only $80 and this debt is almost four months past due, and you have made absolutely no payment on the account.

DEBTOR: Well, maybe I can send you a little and the balance in a month or so.

CREDITOR: A little is not enough.

DEBTOR: I just don't have the money right now.

CREDITOR: We must have at least half immediately.

Explaining the Installment Schedule. For the debtor who is only able to pay in installments, a weekly or monthly schedule should be worked out explaining the due dates and the amounts of each future payment. The best approach is to choose a day of each week or a date of each month, preferably the first day of each month.

Demand for a Lump Sum. When regular payments are promised in writing and the debtor has fallen behind in these obligations, the aim is to bring the loan up to date. Collection of the past due payments in one lump sum is the main objective, and then the debtor may be permitted to continue making the regular payments.

Will the Debtor Deliver on His Promise? Evaluating the credibility of the debtor's promise is significant. A promise to resume payments when the promise obviously will not be kept is certainly not the ideal situation. Intimidation may produce this promise, but the creditor must be realistic. Sometimes, a smaller payment should be considered if the amount and schedule can be maintained.

EXCUSE 2—THE DEBTOR CLAIMS PAYMENT. Whenever the debtor claims that payment was already made, the immediate response must be that "the creditor has no record of receiving payment." The reason for the careful wording of the response is to protect the creditor in the event the debtor is correct. If the office is uncertain, the follow-up response is to ask the debtor for a copy of the front and back of the check.

Never Ask for a Check Number. Never ask when the check was sent! The debtor will leave the telephone to pull out his checkbook and ruffle through the pages. After an extended period of time, the check number and date will be furnished to the creditor. Both bits of information are useless except as an indication of the debtor's sincerity. The check number contributes nothing of value.

Excuse 3—Debtor Wants Proof of Obligation. *Debtor Wants Invoice.* When a debtor requests an invoice for the first time, agree to mail it to the debtor, but always use a closing statement. The closing statement can be a weak closing statement or a negative closing statement, but always use a closing statement.

Second Request for Invoice. If a second request is made for an invoice, the debtor should be reminded that an invoice was already sent. At this point, you have been forewarned that the debtor is obviously stalling and a second invoice should not be sent. The sooner action is commenced the sooner payment will be received.

Excuse 4—Check in the Mail. How does the telephone worker respond to this statement made by the business debtor? This statement, in most instances, is a promise of payment, rather than a description of a past act. The creditor must acknowledge this fact, and treat the statement as if it was a promise of payment. Do not contradict the debtor since this serves no purpose and would probably antagonize the debtor.

Debtor: Don't worry, my bookkeeper mailed a check for $3,000 sometime last week. You know the mails are very slow during Christmas. You'll get it in a few days.

Creditor: Well, we have not received it yet.

Debtor: Look, if you don't get it by the end of the week, call me and I'll send another check.

Creditor: Sir, the bill for the desk is 60 days old. This is my second telephone call to you. We will wait two more days, but if we do not receive the check, the matter will be referred to our attorney by Friday, May 12, with instructions to start suit. We will not call you again about this.

Excuse 5—Check the Records. The debtor's assurance that he will check his records, because he has no recollection of the matter, is just another device to delay the inevitable. The debtor certainly knows that the bill or loan payment has not been made. Most businesses do not select one or two bills not to pay.

The proper response is that checking the records is unnecessary since the creditor has not received payment, and the matter is now ready to be forwarded to a collection agency or attorney.

Excuse 6—Employee Had No Authority to Order. A statement that the employee has no authority to order may have validity. If the creditor did business with the janitor, obviously a question arises as to whether the janitor has apparent authority to order industrial cleaning products, and perhaps building maintenance products such as piping, electrical wire, etc. The office manager has the apparent authority to order office supplies, and the purchasing department has the apparent authority to order all types of supplies. The purchasing department has the right to order for the entire firm, and usually relies on purchase orders. Any purchase that requires a written contract should bear the signature of an officer (*see* Chapter 3).

While the laws may vary somewhat from state to state, the basic legal principle is that the employer is responsible if the employee had apparent authority to act on behalf of the business. This apparent authority may consist of the duties generally exercised by the employee who is a purchasing manager. The title of the employee, such as a "manager" or "officer," may in itself indicate apparent authority.

Excuse 7—Employee No Longer Employed. Usually, the employer claims the merchandise was not received and that somehow the employee who left managed to remove the merchandise. The normal response should be the same as when the employer claims that the employee had no authority. The business received the product, and must pay for it. The seller will not absorb the loss due to the employee leaving.

Excuse 8—Need Proof of Delivery. Proof of delivery should not be furnished to the debtor unless the creditor sincerely believes that the merchandise may not have arrived. If the telephone call is being made after several letters, and this is the first personal contact with the debtor, the question must be asked: Why didn't the debtor respond to the letters with this claim of nondelivery? Why did the debtor wait until the telephone call to raise the issue of nondelivery? The clear inference is that this allegation is just an excuse to ask for an extension of time. It should be treated in the same manner that is extended to any other request for an extension of time.

Excuse 9—Financial Trouble. When the debtor admits that the reason for nonpayment is a lack of funds, the debtor is at this moment honest and sincere. This is the main reason for nonpayment, and all of the above excuses are only façades to cover the true reason.

At this point, the creditor is in a position to make a considered judgment as to whether the debtor is entitled to an extension of time. Converting the above excuses to the "real" reason should be the goal of the creditor. The real reason enables the creditor to obtain a fair picture of the chances of ultimately obtaining payment. This dismal picture may or may not be the catalyst for refinancing or reducing payments.

Excuse 10—The Computer Is Down. There is no reason why a check could not be written manually.

The key to an effective collection effort is:

1. Training and testing.
2. Education as to compliance laws.
3. Reliable information.
4. Periodic updates on laws and court decisions.

Probably, the most important activity is the continual monitoring of staff as to performance.

CHAPTER 3

Legal Concepts of Business

To properly extend credit and collect money from a business debtor, you must understand the structure of the debtor's business as well as the basic ingredients of a contract. Each type of business and each agreement creates different exposures to liability. This chapter will describe the various types of business organizations and the liabilities of the organization and its principals. The basic contract will be reviewed to determine if a contract actually existed.

AN INDIVIDUAL IN BUSINESS

The simplest form of doing business is an individual conducting a business under his or her own name or a trade name. An example of a trade name would be "Joe's Shoe Repair Shop." This designation could indicate either an individual or a partnership, but not a corporation. Corporations must be designated as "Corporation," "Corp.," "Inc.," "Co. Inc.," or "Ltd." (Some state laws may vary these designations.) To determine whether the business is an individual or a partnership, a search of the filing records in the county where the business is located should be performed by your attorney. A limited liability company requires the designation of "Limited Liability Company" or abbreviations "L.L.C." or "LLC."

A professional corporation (attorney) in some states is designated "p.c.," and other professionals (accountants, doctors) have other designations.

***Credit & Collection Tip:** You can include a designation on your credit application as follows:*

____ Individual ____ Partnership ____ Corporation ____ Limited Liability

The credit application should provide space for listing all the partners and all the stockholders and directors of corporations and their home addresses, telephone numbers, and social security numbers. In lieu of the stockholders and directors, you might provide for the "principals" of the corporation.

PARTNERSHIP

A partnership is a group of two or more persons who contribute capital and engage in a business enterprise. Most states have laws regulating the creation of partnerships and the liabilities of partners. The individuals are liable in the same manner as they would be if they were operating the business as a single individual. Some states require a creditor to first proceed against the assets of the partnership before proceeding against the individual partners. Partners are only taxed once.

A special type of partnership is a *limited partnership*. General partners operate the partnership, and limited partners invest money. The liability of limited partners extends only to the amount of capital contributed to the partnership, whereas general partners are liable for all of the debts of the partnership. If limited partners act as a general partner or are perceived by the creditor as a general partner, the limited partner may be liable as a general partner.

Before the states enacted statutes setting forth the exact liability of partners, the common law rule was that partners must be sued with the names of all the partners and that a suit against a partnership must name all of the partners. The state laws changed this by enacting various statutes which are now known as "common name" or "joint debtor" statutes.

A partner is always considered the agent of the partnership. Even if all the partners are not served, a judgment creditor can still proceed against the partnership assets under a common name statute (California). The judgment creditor is limited to the assets of the individual partner who is served and may not proceed against the assets of any partner who is not served.

On the other hand, we have what is known as "joint debtor" statutes (New York), which are not the same but have the same effect. Usually, they apply only to contract claims and not to tort liabilities (accidents). In "joint debtor" statutes, a plaintiff may name all of the partners but only serve some of them. With regard to the partners that have been served, no problem exists. The end result is the same because the judgment remains against the property of all the partners (partnership) and against the separate property of the defendants actually served.

The Uniform Partnership Act has been adopted in almost every state but with changes which produce either joint debtor statutes or common name statutes. Nevertheless, the Act adopted in New Jersey provides for joint and several liability for the contract obligations of the partnership but joint liability for other debts and obligations of the partnership that were not created by means of a contract. The New Jersey Act seems to place partners in a position more vulnerable than stockholders but less vulnerable than guarantors of payment. Partners were held liable for partnership contract debts, but their assets were not at risk until it was shown that the partnership could not discharge the debt. Therefore, the court held that partners are more like guarantors of collection as distinguished from guarantors of payment.

> ***Credit & Collection Tip:*** *Most states have adopted the common name statutes so suits against partners and partnerships may proceed simultaneously. Again, the particular partnership law of the particular state must be reviewed before proceeding.*

CORPORATION

A corporation is created solely by law and therefore only has the powers and the rights that the law provides. One basic right is perpetuity—the corporation can operate forever. Thus, groups of people, endlessly replacing each other, may devote themselves to a particular purpose to achieve a particular goal, as if one person had lived forever. Double taxation occurs in corporations since the corporation is taxed on income and the shareholder is taxed when a dividend is declared.

A corporation is created in three tiers. The first tier is the stockholders who contribute the money and capital by purchasing the shares of stock. This ownership share is represented by stock certificates. If it is a public corporation that has complied with the registration statutes of the state and the Securities and Exchange Commission, the stock certificates can be traded publicly either through the National Association of Security Dealers (NASD) or through one of the exchanges, such as the New York Stock Exchange. The shareholder is not personally liable for corporate debts except to the extent of the money used to purchase stock in the corporation. The only money the shareholder can lose is the money invested.

The second tier of the corporation consists of the Board of Directors, which is elected by the stockholders at an annual meeting. The Board of Directors then elects the officers of the corporation at the first meeting of the directors. Directors have a fiduciary duty to the stockholders—and, to some degree, to the creditors—to conduct the affairs of the corporation in a proper manner. Directors are not personally liable to creditors of a corporation except in unusual circumstances.

The third tier of the corporation is the officers who operate the corporation on a day-to-day basis. The officers of the corporation include the

President, Vice Presidents, Secretaries, Controllers, Treasurers, etc., who have the authority to sign checks and to execute contracts and purchase orders. Officers are not personally liable for corporate debts except in unusual circumstances.

Liabilities of Stockholders, Directors, and Officers. For a corporate debt to be valid, an officer or an authorized person (*see* section titled "Relying on Apparent Authority," in this chapter) of the corporation must execute the instrument binding the corporation. The officers, directors, and stockholders are generally not personally liable for debts of the corporation.

The officer of the corporation who signs or supervises the issuing of payroll checks may be personally liable to the Internal Revenue Service for withholding taxes if they have not been set aside and paid to the government at the same time the salary was paid to the employees. Liability for failure to collect and remit sales taxes also may apply to officers pursuant to state law. Sometimes individual business debtors rely on this liability to the IRS to support their inability to continue to pay their debts. You should verify before accepting this excuse. While the circumstances may exist, the IRS will normally allow long periods (running into years) to discharge this liability, and a thorough investigation may reveal substantial monies or income available to pay debts.

Stockholders usually do not have any liability for debts, but the directors of the corporation would probably be liable to the creditors for the declaration of an improper or illegal dividend. Directors and officers may also be liable for fraud and deceit for misrepresenting the financial status of the corporation to vendors, or in publicly owned corporations to stockholders.

In some instances, the principals of the corporation do not operate it either as a business or a corporation. Corporate books are not kept, corporate bank accounts are used for personal debts, and the individuals commingle their personal affairs under the "corporate veil." Under these circumstances, the courts have recognized a theory of law entitled "piercing the corporate veil" wherein a creditor can sue the individuals as well as the corporation and hold the individuals liable for a corporate debt because the individuals were not operating the corporation as a corporation solely for corporate purposes. (*See* section titled "Relying on Apparent Authority," in this chapter.)

> ***Credit & Collection Tip:*** *If an officer or agent of a corporation commits an act of fraud to obtain property or services from you, consult with counsel to evaluate the circumstances. If fraud, collusion, and/or conspiracy are involved in the transaction, you may be able to look to the individual officer or the agent for payment. A fraudulent application, forgery, or misrepresentations as to solvency may be sufficient grounds.*

Limited Liability Company. The limited liability company (LLC) is somewhere between a corporation and a partnership. With an LLC, individual partners have all the tax advantages of a partnership to avoid double taxation plus the limited liability of the partners similar to the stockholders in a corporation. The partners are only liable for the partnership debts up to the amount of the investment in the LLC. The LLC may or may not have the characteristic of continuity of existence, even perpetuity, depending upon the state's statute. The LLC may resemble the corporate characteristic of free transferability of the interest of a partner in a manner similar to the transfer of a stock certificate.

The four characteristics that the Internal Revenue Service (IRS) considers in taxing an LLC are:

1. the continuity of life.
2. whether the central management is an individual or a board.
3. the ability of the partners to limit their liability to the investment.
4. the extent of the transferability of the interest of the limited liability partner.

The general theory is that if the new organization lacks two of these four corporate ingredients, the IRS will tax the LLC as a partnership and not as a corporation.

The major question surrounding LLCs is whether the courts will "pierce the veil" of the LLC on the grounds that the LLC has not complied with the statute's requirements; and thus the partners are personally liable.[1]

Each state's statute is somewhat different and there are many specific requirements with which the LLC must comply before the LLC attains the status of a properly organized LLC. The LLC must operate carefully within the parameters of the partnership agreement and in compliance with the requirements of the laws of the state in which it is located. The creditor should examine the books of the LLC, the filings, as well as the day-to-day operations of the company to determine if it has complied not only with its partnership agreement, but also with the requirements set forth in the state law.

Failure to comply may expose the partners to personal liability for the debts of the partnership. Where the debt is substantial, it may be worthwhile to spend the money to search the records of the state with regard to the filings of the LLC and the operation of the LLC. Certainly, if the partners are individuals of substance and the debt is substantial, these activities may be warranted.

Almost all the states have passed laws to authorize the use of a limited liability company. The appropriate laws should be reviewed with counsel.

---

[1]*Anderson v. Stewart*, 366 Ark. 203 (Ark. 2006).

BUSINESS TRUST

In several states a *business trust* may be created to operate a business for the benefit of investors. Property is transferred to a trustee under a specified agreement which sets forth the purpose and the powers of the trustee and how the trustee is to pay the benefits. Certificates are issued to the beneficiaries according to their investment and these parties are entitled to receive any income or dividend from the trust. Although some state statutes attempt to regulate trusts, a trust is primarily regulated by the agreement that created the trust. Whereas the trust may be considered a partnership, at the same time the certificate holders (similar to shareholders of a corporation) may be relieved from any liability and only the trustee is liable for the obligations and the business dealings of the trust.

A careful examination of the trust agreement and the state law is necessary before extending credit.

RELYING ON APPARENT AUTHORITY

An agent is a party who represents a principal, and binds the principal. Businesses utilize agents for a wide variety of purposes: an officer of a corporation is the agent for the corporation; a partner is the agent for the partnership; a salesman is the agent for sales of merchandise. Individuals or businesses may also act as agents of other businesses. An attorney, accountant, stockbroker, real estate broker, or food broker, all are agents of the business.

Doing business with an agent is the same as doing business with the principal. Sometimes agents are appointed for all business transactions and other times for limited or specific transactions. When dealing with an agent, the best protection is to obtain the written authority of the agent to act on behalf of the principal, but if a written agreement cannot be obtained, you may rely on the "apparent authority" of the agent to act for the business.

The question of a valid agency will turn on this "apparent authority," and "apparent authority" comes in many different forms. The decision to start suit may depend upon whether an agency relationship has been established, or, more to the point, whether the "apparent authority" of the party is sufficient to create an agency.

Apparent authority may be utilized in three situations. First, a principal may be vicariously liable for tortuous conduct if the principal expressly or implicitly *authorized the conduct*. Second, a principal may be liable for an agent's acts under a *respondeat superior theory*, but in this instance the agent must act for the benefit of the principal within the scope of the employment. Third, a principal may be liable for an agent's tortuous conduct *if the principal cloaked the agent with apparent authority* in that the agent was held out to third parties as possessing sufficient authority to commit to the particular act in question and the victim relied upon the apparent authority.[2] Some examples follow:

1. The scope of the employee's duties may entitle a businessperson to rely on the "apparent authority" of the agent, such as dealing with the sales manager. Even if the sales manager is not an officer of the corporation or a partner, the title of sales manager is adequate "apparent authority" to bind the business to a sale of merchandise.
2. Prior dealings where past orders were accepted and delivered will support the "apparent authority." For example, the owner of a business alleges that the party who ordered the merchandise did not have the authority to order and did not bind the business to a contract. The owner states that the individual is no longer employed or was employed in such a position that the creditor had no right to rely on the employee's authority to order. The fact the party is no longer employed is not relevant. The only question is whether "apparent authority" was present, and whether prior activities enabled a reasonable businessman to rely on the representations of the employee. If the employee ordered in the past and the bills were paid, the employee has "apparent authority" to bind the business.
3. Accepting the benefits of the transaction will also support "apparent authority." For example, a bookkeeper orders merchandise. The seller (creditor) ships the merchandise directly to the customer (the employer of the bookkeeper). The customer retains the merchandise and the benefits of the transaction, but refuses to pay on the grounds the bookkeeper had no authority to order merchandise. The seller may recover for "unjust enrichment" in addition to breach of contract. If the bookkeeper had no authority, the breach of contract claim may fail, but the seller would recover for "unjust enrichment" since the buyer cannot retain the goods and not pay for them. At the same time, an argument may be offered that a bookkeeper in a small business may have "apparent authority" to order at least office supplies.
4. Officers of corporations and partners of partnerships have the authority to bind the corporation and partnership. Whether other employees or staff can do so depends upon "apparent authority."

Credit & Collection Tip: *When dealing with professional agents, such as real estate brokers, attorneys, accountants, or stockbrokers, reliance on a written agreement to establish the agency is recommended.*

---

[2] *Smith v. Sears Roebuck & Co.*, 276 F. Supp. 2d 603 (S.D. Miss. 2003).

PRINCIPAL-AGENT RELATIONSHIP

A case involving the rental of mailing lists analyzed in depth the relationship between a principal, the agent (broker), and a third party who was dealing with the agent. In that case, a list owner engaged a firm, known as a list broker, to rent mailing lists to a mailer. The agreement stated as follows:

> Greenfield Direct Response, Inc. acts only as agent to the list owner and does not guarantee payment under this order. Upon receipt of payment from the mailer who was solely responsible for payment of this order, Greenfield Direct Response, Inc. will remit to the list owner, less the standard 20% commission.

The case arose because the list broker was in bankruptcy and a bank had issued a letter of credit secured by accounts receivable. The bank believed that all this money that the list broker was collecting from mailers belonged to the list broker. The list owners contended that the list broker was merely an agent, and that all the monies (less commissions) belonged to the list owners for the rental of their lists.

The list owners took the position that the wording in the contract delineated that the broker acted only as agent for the list owner. The bank contended that the funds belonged to the broker and that the broker was not an agent because the broker was not subject to the control of the list owner, that the funds were commingled with those of other list owners, and no agency relationship existed because there was no such understanding between the parties. In addition, the contractual writing was merely "boilerplate."

The usual test of what creates an agency is whether the principal has authority to control the method or manner of accomplishing a task by the agent and whether the agent has authority to subject the principal to liability. Existence of an agency relationship is a question of fact. However, where an agency's authority has been conferred in writing and there is no dispute concerning the parties' relationship, the question becomes one of law.

The word "agent" is broader than the word "broker" and more comprehensive in its legal scope. Though every broker is in a sense an agent, every agent is not a broker. Attorneys, brokers, auctioneers, and similar persons are employed for a single transaction of agency, although as to their physical activities, they are independent contractors.

The court seemed to conclude that the broker could have been a limited agent for both the mailer and the list owner as to different tasks and responsibilities. The broker contended that it was really retained by the mailer to search for a customer list owned by the list owner which would meet the criteria of the mailer. The court emphasized the fact that if the broker held itself out to be a broker, it represented itself as an agent to someone and in the "collection" paragraph of the agreement, the broker stated that the broker was an "agent for the list owner." Thus, the broker was an agent of the list owner for purposes of collection and prompt remittance, notwithstanding whether it might have been an agent for the mailer in searching out the proper list for the mailer to use.

Extrinsic evidence to alter the terms of the contract was disallowed even though it was a "boilerplate" contract. *Whether or not it was a boilerplate contract, it was a contract.* The court dismissed the lack of control by the principal since there was no control that the principal had to exercise to be certain that the broker remitted collections for the rental of the lists. Accordingly, an agent who collects money on behalf of the principal does not become the owner of such money, and the court decided that the money belongs to the list owners and not to the creditor of the list broker.

One of the interesting aspects of this case was the distinction the court drew with another case, where the party held the funds for 60 days by agreement and the monies actually became the property of the party holding the money because he was entitled to ownership for a period of 60 days. However, in the mailing list broker case, the broker had to remit the monies immediately upon receipt.

The fact that brokers or agents sometimes act for one party for a certain part of the transaction and for the other party for a different part of the transaction will lead to different results depending upon which transaction is involved in a dispute. The method to solve this type of situation is to be certain that the contract is clear as to the responsibility of the broker or agent.[3]

The principal-agent relationship becomes relevant when a collection agency is retained and the level of control over the agency is excessive. (*See* Chapter 15.)

CONTRACTS

To understand whether a debtor is legally liable on a debt requires the creditor to understand whether a contract was actually formed, and thus would be enforceable. Whether a contract is enforceable has continually confronted the courts and the legislators. Contract law covers hundreds of pages of the UCC. In each state, hundreds of cases each year interpret the terms and conditions of a contract between two parties. Nevertheless, certain ingredients are essential to the formation of a contract. With that in mind, we will review some contract law 101.

---

[3] *Greenfield Direct Response, Inc. v. Adco List Management*, 171 B.R. 848 (Bankr. N.D. Ill. 1994).

An Offer and Acceptance. Until the two parties agree on the terms of the contract, no contract exists. For there to be a contract, an offer has to be made by the creditor and the debtor has to accept. If the debtor counteroffers with new terms, the debtor is making a new offer awaiting the acceptance by the creditor of the new terms. After agreement on the terms, a contract is formed.

A contract does not have to be in writing (for exceptions *see* section titled "Statute of Frauds"), but reducing an agreement to writing is the most desirable form of a contract because the uncertainty of the memory of either party is removed.

An offer is open for acceptance for a reasonable time or at least until it is revoked. If an offer is open for a specific time period, the offer automatically terminates at the end of that period.

Another way that a contract can be formed, despite the fact that the parties did not agree on all the terms, is by performance. If the creditor and the debtor agreed on most, but not all, the terms of the contract, and thereafter the creditor performed the contract by shipping the goods. If the debtor accepted the goods, the parties entered a contract by virtue of performance.

Agreeing on Material Terms. Every contract contains material terms and minor terms. Material terms consist of identifying the subject of the contract (e.g., building, merchandise, service, commodity), price, delivery terms, and the important ingredients necessary to complete the transaction. If the material terms of a contract are acceptable to both parties, a contract may be formed even if certain minor or trivial terms are not mentioned or agreed upon. Nevertheless, the courts lean to the concept that where a written agreement is contemplated, no contract has been entered into until the written agreement has been executed.

If partial performance by either party is added, the court is more likely to enforce the contract to the extent performed. A breach of a material term of a contract may enable the other party to refuse to perform. A breach of a minor term may not release the other party from performance, although a claim for damages may be made. Each contract is different, and what is a "material" or "minor" term is a question of fact to be decided by a judge or jury.

Consideration and Payment. Some form of consideration is generally necessary to support a contract. The most common example of consideration is the payment of money. Other forms of considerations which do not involve payment of money may be sufficient to form a binding contract. Agreeing to do something or to perform an act in return for the promise of another is consideration. The surrender of a legal right or the forbearance of a right to act, such as a right to sue, is sufficient to constitute consideration. An example is when one party agrees not to sue if the other party enters a payment arrangement or agrees to perform an act.

On the other hand, if no consideration is received, the agreement may be unenforceable. For example:

A. "Joe, you've known me for 40 years. I need about $10,000 to clear up my debts. So, instead of giving $10,000 to United Way, give me the $10,000."

J. "Allen, you have been a good friend for many years and next week I am going to give you the $10,000 you need."

Allen cannot enforce this promise for there is no "consideration" for the promise. Allen has not done anything or performed any act or service in return for the promise to give him $10,000.

The interpretation of consideration by the courts creates many exceptions to this rule. The courts enforce contracts even though no apparent consideration is present, either because the contract falls into an exception, or the circumstances of the contract present what appears to be consideration. In certain states and in certain circumstances, consideration is not necessary if the contract is entered into in writing, or if there has been partial or full performance of the contract. In the example above, if the promise to give Allen $10,000 was in writing, in certain circumstances and in some states, the contract may be binding.

Mistakes in Contract. Where both parties entered into a contract and made a mistake concerning one of the material ingredients of the contract, no offer and acceptance of the terms and conditions exists since the parties mutually misunderstood an essential element, and no "meeting of the minds" took place. An example is where the seller offers to sell a Pentium II computer but only has a Pentium I in inventory, which the seller believes is a Pentium II computer and the buyer wants to purchase a Pentium II computer. The buyer accepts the Pentium I believing it to be a Pentium II. This is considered a mutual mistake of fact, and the contract for the Pentium II computer could not be enforced.

On the other hand, if a mistake was made by one of the parties, that party cannot evade liability by alleging a mistake was made. A loan is made and the documents recite the interest at the prime rate. The borrower thought the prime rate was 6 percent when in fact it was 7 percent. This is a mistake by one party.

Where consumers are involved, the courts produce different results. The storeowner mistakenly advertises a ridiculously low price for a product, such as $30 for a camcorder on sale when $300 was meant. The storeowner argues that the consumer knew that the advertised price was a mistake and refuses to sell at that price. Some courts treat such an advertisement as an offer to negotiate, and not an offer to contract. The cases go both ways with the majority probably requiring the storeowner to honor the advertised offer.

Good Faith and Fair Dealing. The interpretation of good faith and fair dealing is vague and speculative. The courts generally examine the fact situation to determine whether the party being accused acted in such an abominable manner lacking any of the virtues of good faith and fair dealing. The number of cases are numerous. To try and define the plateau or criteria of good faith and fair dealing would be foolish other than to recite other adjectives and adverbs to describe what good faith and fair dealing actually is.

The courts are fairly clear that the obligation to exercise good faith and fair dealing does not create any additional right or obligation emanating from the contract, but the good faith may be required or inferred from duties and obligations set forth in the contract. The court will not entertain the birth of a new obligation or a new duty.[4]

NOTIFICATION OF ASSIGNMENT OF DEBT

UCC section 9-318(3) delineates the legal relationship between the account debtor and the assignee of a debt once the debtor receives notification of the assignment from the assignee. The debtor upon receipt of said notification of an assignment is duty bound to pay the assignee and not the assignor. Payment to an assignor after notification of an assignment does not relieve the account debtor of his obligation to pay the assignee unless the assignee consents to such a collection process.

> ***Credit & Collection Tip:*** *The account debtor's failure to pay the assignee after receiving due notification may afford the assignee a claim for wrongful payment.*

This situation arises when a business assigns all their accounts receivable to a factor or a finance company and the factor or finance company notifies the debtors to make payment directly to them. The UCC does not specify the exact type of notice that is to be sent, but Article I defines, "notifies" as a notice or notification to another by taking such steps as may be reasonably required to inform the other party, whether or not the party to whom notification is addressed actually comes to know about the notification. In short, the obligation is on the party giving the notice. Written notice should be sufficient and in some instances oral notice has been held sufficient if it is provided to the proper parties and can be proven in court.

Under the revised Article 9, Section 9-406 (*see* Appendix to Chapter 11), notification is ineffective if it does not reasonably identify the rights assigned. Furthermore, the debtor has a specific right to request a copy of the written assignment and if same is not forthcoming or for whatever

---

[4] *Blue Hills Office Park LLC v. J.P. Morgan Chase Bank*, 477 F. Supp. 2d 366 (D. Mass. 2007).

reason the debtor feels that the assignment is not proper, the debtor is authorized to continue to pay the original assignor.[5]

> ***Credit & Collection Tip:*** *In the event a debtor receives notification of an assignment, before the debtor makes the final decision not to pay the assignee, consultation with counsel should be had to be certain that the debtor has the right to continue to pay the assignor. In the event the debtor should pay the assignor, after proper notification of the assignment, the debtor may end up paying twice; that is, being required to pay the assignee and thereafter attempting to recover the money that was paid to assignor.*

STATUTE OF FRAUDS

Almost all states have a Statute of Frauds, which requires certain types of contracts to be in writing. A review of each state law is necessary since the laws differ from state to state. The following types of contracts usually must be in writing:

A. Contracts for sale or lease of real estate.

B. Agreements that cannot be fully performed within a period of one year from the date of the agreement.

C. A guarantee of the debt of another party.

D. Contracts for the sale of goods (not services) in excess of $500. (Revised UCC Article 2 has increased this to $5,000.)

Section 2-201 of the UCC recites certain exceptions. A contract where the goods are specifically manufactured for the buyer and are not suitable for sale to others is one exception, as well as if the goods have been received and accepted. In these instances, a failure to have a written contract cannot be asserted under the Statute of Frauds (only to the extent the contract is completed).

UCC 2-201 Subdivision 2 provides between merchants a ten-day period to object to the terms and conditions set forth in a written confirmation, which arrives after an oral contract. An oral agreement is entered into over the telephone. One of the parties confirms this oral agreement by writing to the other party, setting forth the terms of the agreement. Under the UCC, the receiving party has a ten-day period to object to these terms and conditions in the written confirmation. If no objection is made within that ten-day period, the written confirmation becomes the written contract between the parties.

---

[5]*Transcentral, Inc. v. Emery Worldwide Airlines, Inc.*, 2001 WL 1117733 (Minn. App. 2001).

Credit & Collection Tip: *If the written confirmation does not specifically agree with what the party understood over the telephone, that party has an obligation to object in writing within ten days. Failure to object may result in a binding written agreement to which the party did not agree.*

If the agreement cannot be completed by its own terms within one year, UCC 2-201 provides that you must have a written agreement. If the terms of performance are possible within one year, however unlikely or improbable that performance may be, the agreement or promise is usually not within the statute of frauds and a written agreement is not needed. Contracts that are of an indefinite time period are usually not within this provision of the statute.

Revised UCC Article 2 did not grasp the opportunity to expand this to non-merchant transactions.

Another provision in state law is that a contract must be executed by the party to be charged. Some courts add additional criteria such as identifying both contracting parties, setting forth the subject matter of the contract and the essential terms of the contract and requiring consideration to be described. The courts are still uncertain as to exactly what the criteria should be and the decisions seem to vary from state to state and from court to court even within the same state.

One case analyzed the question of an alleged contract bearing no signature of the party being charged. The court relied on the commentary to the UCC, which acknowledges that a complete signature is not necessary. It may be printed, stamped, or written and may be by initials or even by a thumbprint. It may be on a part of the document and in appropriate cases may be found in a bill head or a letterhead.[6] The court must use common sense and commercial experience in passing upon these matters. If we translate, it means that the courts must look at these situations on a case-by-case basis. Actually, the courts sometimes utilize any symbol executed or adopted by a party with the present intention to authenticate a writing. An examination of other cases will reveal the creation of other criteria to create a signature.

E-MAIL. The exchange of e-mail may create an enforceable contract, but such contract must adhere to the basic elements of contract formation. Mutual assent on all essential terms must be present.

In most instances when this issue is presented to the courts, they will normally look at it on a case-by-case basis to determine if there is a mutual intent to enter into the contract. The courts look to some form of performance by one or by the other side in reliance on the e-mails or some indication of mutual consent or intent to perform.

---

[6]*Owen v. Kroger Co.*, 936 F. Supp. 579 (S.D. Ind. 1996); *Dow Chemical Co. v. General Elec. Co.*, 2005 WL 1862418 (E.D. Mich. 2005); *Cloud Corp. v. Hasbro Inc.*, 314 F.3d 289 (7th Cir. 2002).

An e-mail is much like a contract without a signature on it. To what extent have the parties displayed an intent or some evidence of their intent to perform the contract is the final criteria.

Part Performance. If the specific transaction is listed in the Statute of Frauds of the particular state, the contract is unenforceable in the courts of that state unless it is in writing. Exceptions and defenses to the Statute of Frauds vary from state to state, but they usually include the following:

1. Part performance—a contract is not in writing, but one party has partially performed the contract with knowledge of the other party.
2. Equitable estoppel—where one party's conduct leads the other party to reasonably rely on the activity or representation of the first party and their position is changed to their detriment.

A printer enters an agreement with a customer and sends the customer a contract. The customer calls on the telephone and pressures the printer (because of prior business dealings) to run the job even though the contract was not received by the customer. The printer runs the job, and on the same day, the customer calls for a progress report. After half the job is run, the customer cancels and refuses to pay since no contract was signed. Elements of both part performance and equitable estoppel would support a suit in this instance.

OFFERS AND ACCEPTANCE—ADDITIONAL DIFFERENT TERMS

Do Not Agree. UCC Section 2-207 was an attempt to clarify the situation where a buyer submitted a written purchase order to purchase goods (with printed terms on the reverse side) and the seller then confirms the offer to purchase in writing. If the seller merely confirms the order and accepts the order on the terms submitted by the buyer, no problem would exist. What often happens is that the seller sends additional terms either separately or with the product itself (such as in the carton) and these additional terms do not match the terms of the purchase order under which the buyer intended to purchase the goods.

Under traditional contract law, an offer had to be identical for the acceptance to be effective. If any discrepancy existed between the terms of the written offer and the written acceptance, the discrepancy would be treated as a rejection of the contract.

If the parties perform the contract by having the seller ship the goods and the buyer accepts the goods and utilizes the goods, under the common law, the act of performance was an acceptance of the original offer made by the purchaser. The purchaser needed the goods and the seller refused to perform, the attitude of the courts was that no contract existed since there was no acceptance. If there was performance, as we described above on the terms of the original offer, and a dispute arose after the performance, the general perception was that a contract existed on the terms of the original offer.

Most merchants understood under the law prior to the UCC that an offer had to be accepted. If the offer was not accepted under the terms of the offer, it was now up to the other party to accept the counteroffer. That was the law until the UCC and particularly Section 2-207 was adopted. The section was designed to promote trade between merchants and was further designed to eliminate litigation over the type of terms that would and would not impact a transaction. Unfortunately, rather than clarify and make trading easier, Section 2-207 has complicated things and created more litigation. We will try to put this section in simple terms, although we doubt we will be successful.

The primary UCC section is as follows:

> UCC Section 2-207. Additional Terms in Acceptance or Confirmation.
>
> A definite and seasonable expression of acceptance or a written confirmation that is sent within a reasonable time operates as an acceptance even though it states terms additional to or different from those offered or agreed upon, unless acceptance is expressly made conditional on assent to the additional or different terms.
>
> The additional terms are to be construed as proposals for addition to the contract. Between merchants, such terms become part of the contract unless:
>
> a. the offer expressly limits acceptance to the terms of the offer;
>
> b. they materially alter it; or
>
> c. notification of objection to them has already been given or is given within a reasonable time after notice of them is received.
>
> Conduct by both parties that recognizes the existence of a contract is sufficient to establish a contract for sale although the writings of the parties do not otherwise establish a contract. In such case, the terms of the particular contract consist of those terms on which the writings of the parties agree, together with any supplementary terms incorporated under any other provisions of this Act.

Section A states that acceptance or confirmation (sent within a reasonable time) operates as an acceptance of an offer even though it states terms additional to or different from those offered or agreed upon. The section provides for one exception where the offer expressly states that acceptance is totally conditional on agreeing to the additional or different terms. In summary, additional or different terms in the acceptance still creates an acceptance unless the original offer expressly sets forth in writing that no additional or different terms will be tolerated.

The drafters understood that there were additional problems with Subdivision 1 and attempted to clarify these problems in Subdivision 2. When a contract is entered into between the parties by reason of Subdivision 1 (additional or different terms), one must now read Subdivision 2 to understand what are the terms of the contract. The additional terms are to be construed as proposals for additions to the contract in all situations unless the contract is between merchants. Thus, if the contract is between two individuals or the contract is between a merchant and an individual, the additional terms are to be construed as proposals. Between merchants, such terms become part of the contract (1) unless the offer expressly limits acceptance to the terms of the offer (and this refers to the last lines of Subdivision 1); (2) unless the additional or different terms materially alter the contract; or (3) unless notification of objection to them has already been given or is given within a reasonable time after notice of them is received.

Unless two merchants are involved, any additional or different terms are merely a proposal and do not become part of the contract unless expressly accepted by the other party to the contract. The reasoning is simple. The additional terms probably were inserted solely for the benefit of the party inserting them. For this reason, the contract between the parties is based on the offer as it was originally submitted without any additional terms and the acceptance deals with the terms of the original offer.

Click-Wrap and Shrink-Wrap. The issue of whether a consumer is subject to the terms of click-wrap or shrink-wrap is another issue. In these situations, the consumer breaks the seal on a software tape or a CD, and terms and conditions are set forth therein, or a consumer uses the Internet and when clicking onto a website, certain terms and conditions are set forth on the website. The small print usually prohibits the users from making unauthorized copies or reverse engineering the programs in the software, disclaims any warranties, and limits the liability of the operator of the website.

The courts seem to treat these contracts as offers by the seller to purchase their goods and the buyer is accepting the offer when they break the seal on the software program or on the CD. The license flashes onto the screen of the computer and, at that point, the individual buyer has a right to refuse the purchase if the terms are not acceptable and return the software. If the individual purchaser inspects the package and tries the software and then learns of the license, and had an opportunity to return the goods and did not return the goods, the court treats this as an acceptance of the contract terms. The same thing would apply to the shrink-wrap for a CD-ROM.

Merchants. Between merchants, the additional terms become effective unless three contingencies happen. The first contingency is that the additional terms will not become part of the contract if the offer expressly limits acceptance to the terms of the offer. The offer must expressly state that there will be no contract unless you accept all the terms or the specific terms set forth in this contract.

Secondly, the new proposals do not become part of the contract if they are material. The official comment to this section sets forth certain examples of typical clauses that materially alter the contract and result in surprise or hardship if incorporated without express awareness by the other party. The examples are a clause negating such standard warranties as that of merchantability or fitness for a particular purpose, a clause requiring a guarantee of 90 percent or 100 percent deliveries where the usage of the trade allows greater leeway, a clause reserving to the seller the power to cancel upon the buyer's failure to meet any invoice when due, a clause requiring that complaints be made in a time materially shorter than customary or reasonable, or inclusion of an arbitration clause. No attempt will be made to define what is and what is not a material clause. Suffice it to say that judges will go different ways on the same set of facts. Between two merchants, an additional term that is not customarily used in the industry and causes some kind of hardship or burden on the other party may well be considered a material term.

The third exception is when notification of objection has already been given or is given within a reasonable time after notice of them is received. The purchaser would therefore have a reasonable time to object to the additional terms.

As to different terms, Section 2-207 presents significant questions. An examination of Subdivision 1 of UCC 2-207 reveals a reference to both additional and different terms. Unfortunately, a reference to Subdivision 2 of UCC 2-207 deals only with additional terms and makes no reference at all to different terms. When there are different terms in the offer and in the acceptance that covered the same subject matter, the two sets of different terms cancel themselves out and the contract is deemed silent on the issue.

What the difference is between a different term and an additional term is also a fine question of law. What some courts consider a different term, other courts will consider an additional term. The general thesis is that a different term contradicts a term from the other contract. An additional term that may not affect the exact subject area may still be an additional term as well as a different term.

Considerable material has been published on these two sections of what is known as the "battle of the forms" both in legal publications and in legal decisions. For the purposes of this book, to educate the credit and collection managers, I hope that I have at least clarified (although not solved) what the problems are when you are dealing with additional or different terms—although I may have added to the confusion.[7]

---

[7]*See Ionics, Inc. v. Elwood Sensors,* 110 F.3d 184 (1st Cir. 1997).

WAIVER

An issue which arises frequently is whether a purchaser has waived a delivery date or some act of performance by virtue of conduct between the purchaser and the seller. A leading case has held that a waiver requires "reliance" under the UCC.

The Seventh Circuit case addressed a contract prohibiting oral modifications and considered whether an attempted oral modification could constitute a waiver. The court took the position that the prohibition against oral modifications would have no effect if the contract terms could be waived without a detrimental reliance. If attempted oral modifications were unenforceable but were enforced as waivers, as a matter of law oral modifications would be effective. The Seventh Circuit held that the difference between modifications and a waiver was a detrimental reliance on the said waiver.

The Eleventh Circuit took a completely opposite view and stated that the chief judge of the Seventh Circuit ignored a fundamental difference between modifications and waivers. A party who has agreed to a contract modification cannot cancel the modification without giving consideration for the cancellation whereas a party may unilaterally retract its waiver of a contract term provided reasonable notice is provided. The fact that waivers may unilaterally be retracted provides the difference. Thus, a waiver under the UCC does not require detrimental reliance.

Although the UCC does not specifically lay out the elements of the waiver, the basic elements are:

A. The existence at the time of the waiver of a right or privilege or advantage or benefit which may be waived.

B. The actual constructive knowledge thereof.

C. An intention to relinquish such right, privilege, advantage, or benefit.

Conduct may constitute a waiver of a contract term, but an implied waiver must be demonstrated by clear evidence. Waiver may be implied when a party's actions are inconsistent with the continued retention of the right.

The plaintiff was engaged to produce four assembly line processes to be used in the production of eyeglasses. While there were certain delays in performing, the parties amended the contract on two occasions to extend the delivery date and continued to cooperate in trying to complete the contract. The plaintiff paid the defendant additional monies and the plaintiff continued to perform the contract. The plaintiff finally notified the defendant that they were ready to deliver.

The court decided that the parties by their conduct had waived the delivery dates. The issue of a detrimental reliance was not reached since the waiver had met the general criteria. If the court had decided to consider the issue of detrimental reliance, the court probably would have decided that the plaintiff did rely upon the continued cooperation of the defendant, for the plaintiff would have suffered significant damages by completing this contract and having no purchaser for the product.[8]

Late Payments. Almost every seller of goods has faced the situation where the buyer continues to buy the merchandise each month paying less than the face amount of the bill or delaying payment for several months—and in the meantime pays current bills. The effect of this conduct is that the outstanding balance grows. Unfortunately, the monthly payments do not cover the prior outstanding balance.

The end result of this activity is that the seller is delivering the merchandise each month on time and the outstanding balance from the customer is growing. The customer is paying each month, but not enough. The problem for the seller is that the customer is usually a major customer and the seller does not want to lose the customer. Nevertheless, the seller has to make a decision and the UCC has a section directly targeted at this situation.

Section 2-609 states:

> A contract for sale imposes an obligation on each party that the other's expectation of receiving due performance will not be impaired. When reasonable grounds for insecurity arise with respect to the performance of either party, the other may in writing demand adequate assurance of due performance and until he receives such assurance, may, if commercially reasonable, suspend any performance for which he has not already received the agreed return.
>
> Between merchants the reasonableness of grounds for insecurity and the adequacy of any assurance offered shall be determined according to commercial standards.
>
> Acceptance of any improper delivery or payment does not prejudice the agreed party's right to demand adequate assurance of future performance.
>
> After receipt of a justified demand, failure to provide within a reasonable time not exceeding 30 days such assurance of due performance as is adequate under the circumstances of the particular case is a repudiation of the contract.

Where the customer was late on every payment, notwithstanding the fact that the contract provided that payment was due in 30 days on amounts delivered on a weekly basis, an issue arises as to whether strict compliance with the payment terms was actually waived. If so, could the seller rely on the late payments as an excuse to unilaterally repudiate the

[8] *BMC Indus. v. Barth Indus.*, 160 F.3d 1322 (11th Cir. 1998); *Wisconsin Knife Works v. National Metal Crafters*, 781 F.2d 1280 (7th Cir. 1986).

contract? To find a waiver, the party asserting the waiver must show reasonable reliance and altering his position to his detriment (damages). Furthermore, the intention to waive the contract clause must be clearly present.

USURY

Usury is charging a rate of interest in excess of the legal rate provided by the statute in the state where the law is to be enforced. Aside from certain usury laws contained in federal laws, most states have usury laws which affect the extension of credit or the lending of money. A contract may be declared unenforceable in the event it is usurious.

Although banks and credit card companies charge in excess of the rate allowed by the state, federal law permits these rates for consumer credit transactions. In some states, charging a corporation an interest rate in excess of 15 percent constitutes usury. The legal rate of interest to charge a corporation or a consumer varies from state to state. The state laws also provide a wide range of exceptions to the legal rate of interest that maybe charged a consumer or a corporation. Review the state laws for these exceptions.

If there is a violation of the usury law of a particular state, the consequences vary from state to state and may include any of the following:

A. Sometimes the creditor may lose only the amount of the interest that exceeds the legal rate of interest, and in other instances the creditor may lose the entire amount of interest.

B. Some state laws expressly provide that the creditor has no right to enforce the debt.

C. In some states, charging usurious interest may be punishable as a crime.

Penalties for a late payment are usually treated as interest and included as interest for purposes of the usury law.

EXCULPATORY CLAUSE

An exculpatory clause enables a party to a contract to escape liability for a particular act. A typical clause used is the "Act of God" phrase where one party seeks absolution from responsibility for failure to deliver merchandise on time due to an "Act of God," such as a flood, a fire, an act of war, or some other natural phenomenon.

Although such clauses are usually upheld by the courts, an exculpatory clause which permits one party to escape liability for performing an activity under the contract in a negligent way presents different problems. An example would be a printer who states that the printing firm shall not be liable for any damages due to printing errors. Courts frown on exculpatory clauses unless the words specify the exact activity that is being pardoned, such as "negligence." For instance, if the terms and conditions on the order form eliminate liability for printing errors due to "negligence," the printer has a better chance of relying on that clause in a court of law. If the clause is not specific or the word "negligence" is totally omitted, the courts usually will not enforce this type of clause, even between merchants. Where a consumer is the aggrieved party, the courts are more inclined not to enforce any type of exculpatory clause even when "negligence" is used and the specificity of the activity is present.

LIQUIDATED DAMAGE CLAUSE

A liquidated damage clause is an example of the exculpatory clause. The purpose of the liquidated damage clause is not to remove liability, but to limit the liability of one of the contracting parties. For example, a liquidated damage clause may be used in the printing contract instead of or in addition to the exculpatory clause. With regard to printing errors, the clause may provide that "the printer will only be liable to the extent of reprinting the job and will not be liable for any damages resulting from the distribution of the printed material."

The courts will usually not enforce a liquidated damage clause if the damages are reasonably ascertainable and can be determined with a degree of effort. The amount of liquidated damages must bear a reasonable relationship to the actual amount of damages sustained. The courts normally will frown on liquidated damage clauses unless they are fair and equitable to both parties and are not excessive as to amount to a penalty, which will not be allowed.

> ***Credit & Collection Tip:*** *Exculpatory clauses and liquidated damage clauses do not have to be accepted when they are contained in printed order forms or printed contracts. Printed contracts can be changed. If the clause is unreasonable, consultation with counsel is advised and the clause should be modified.*

BAILMENTS

A "bailment" is created when one party (bailor) delivers property to another party (bailee) for a specific purpose and the agreement between the parties is that the property will be returned after the purpose is accomplished. Bailments are encountered by consumers almost every day.

The shoes are delivered to the shoemaker, the dress to the cleaners, and the automobile to the mechanic. But bailments are also created in a wide number of business situations. An example would be an original document delivered for the purpose of printing several hundred copies and thereafter returned to the owner. Other examples of a bailment are delivering computer discs to a computer service bureau for the purpose of adding to a database; the delivery of property to a trucker for the purpose of transport; the delivery of securities to a transfer agent for the purpose of transferring the stock certificates to a new ownership; or delivering printed brochures and envelopes to a fulfillment house for the purpose of affixing labels, folding, inserting, and mailing the envelopes.

The basic intent of the parties is that the property is to be delivered for a specific reason and thereafter the property is to be returned to the owner or, as in the case of the envelopes, sent to the potential customers of the owner. If the recipient of the goods (bailee) is entitled to return to the party who delivers the goods anything other than the property itself, such as cash, then the transaction does not create a bailment, but may create a sale. In certain circumstances where a bailment is created, the party who receives the merchandise is entitled to a lien on the property to the extent of the services that were rendered by the party (*see* Chapter 4).

Under a bailment the bailee (the party receiving the goods for a specific purpose) has the exclusive right to possession during the bailment as long as the bailee is performing in accordance with the bailment agreement. Thus, the bailee may recover any property taken by any third party, including the bailor (if the property was taken before the end of the bailment). The bailee cannot use the property other than to perform the specific purpose.

A gratuitous bailee, such as a neighbor who collects your mail when you are away, receives no compensation. Gratuitous bailees are usually liable only for gross negligence. In normal bailments for compensation, the bailee is liable for ordinary negligence.

Special statutes control common carriers such as trucks and trains, and other statutes regulate innkeepers, such as hotels.

CONSIGNMENT

Where merchandise is delivered to a merchant by the owner and the agreement is that the merchant will sell the merchandise, but the title of the merchandise shall remain in the name of the owner, the arrangement is known as a "consignment." The merchant has no obligation to pay for the merchandise until it is sold. If the merchandise is never sold, it will be returned to the owner. If the merchant sells the merchandise, the proceeds from the sale technically could be segregated and remitted to the owner, less the commission that the merchant has earned by selling the merchandise. If the agreement between the parties is that the merchant has an obligation to pay for the merchandise, the arrangement is not a consignment, but a sale. The key ingredient of a consignment is that no obligation exists on the part of the merchant to pay.

Sometimes determining whether the actual transaction constituted a consignment or a sale is difficult. Whether the owner had the right to determine the price of the merchandise, the right to set the periods of time within which the merchant had the right to sell the merchandise, or the right to terminate the transaction at any time and require the return of the merchandise to the owner are factors which indicate that the transaction was fundamentally a consignment. The ability to set the price and to demand a return are elements of a consignment as opposed to a sale.

Even with a reservation of title to the owner, an obligation on the part of the merchant to pay for the merchandise would be an indication that the contract was a sale and not a consignment. The courts will look to all the ingredients which lead to the contract and will consider the substance of the transaction as opposed to what label is affixed.

The courts rely on the intent of the parties. Where the question of intent is involved, the decision is subject to a review of the facts of each transaction.

In one case, the court stated that "intent" is to be determined by an objective standard that considers the economic realities of the transactions rather than the actual intent of the parties. The court relied on four criteria that they felt would determine that the purpose of the transaction was to create a sale and not a consignment:

1. The setting of the resale price by the consignee.
2. Billing the consignee upon shipment.
3. Commingling of proceeds or failure to keep proper accounts by the consignee.
4. Mixing consigned goods with goods owned by the consignee.

In contrast, certain factors indicated that the parties intended a true consignment:

1. Consignor retained control over the resale price of the consigned property.
2. Possession was delivered with authority to sell only upon the consent of the consignor.
3. The consignor may recall the goods.
4. The consignee was to receive a commission and not a profit on the sale.
5. The consigned property was segregated from other property of the consignee.

6. The consignor was entitled to inspect sales records and the physical inventory of the goods in the consignee's possession.
7. Consignee has no obligation to pay for the goods unless the goods are sold.

The criteria set by the courts seem to be sound, but unfortunately, many of the courts evaluate these transactions on a case-by-case basis and try to balance these factors to arrive at what they feel is a fair and equitable decision with each court selecting one or two criteria as essential and relegating the others as immaterial.[9]

Consignment and Creditors. A consignment of goods consists of the consignor delivering the goods to the consignee for the purpose of selling the goods. The consignor still owns the goods. The rights of creditors as to consigned goods are covered in UCC 2-326, which states:

> Section 2-236: Sale on Approval and Sale or Return; Consignment Sales and Rights of Creditors.
>
> 1. Unless otherwise agreed, if delivered goods may be returned by the buyer even though they conform to the contract, the transaction is
>   a. a sale on approval if the goods are delivered primarily for use, and
>   b. a sale or return if the goods are delivered primarily for resale.
> 2. Except as provided in subsection (3), goods held on approval are not subject to the claims of the buyer's creditors until acceptance; goods held on sale or return are subject to such claims while in the buyer's possession.
> 3. Where goods are delivered to a person for sale and such a person maintains a place of business at which he deals in goods of the kind involved, under a name other than the name of the person making delivery, then with respect to claims of creditors of the person conducting the business the goods are deemed to be on sale or return. The provisions of this subsection are applicable even though an agreement purports to reserve title to the person making delivery until payment or resale or uses such words as nonconsignment or nonmemorandum. However, this subsection is not applicable if the person making delivery:
>   a. complies with an applicable law providing for a consignor's interest or the like to be evidenced by a sign, or
>   b. establishes that the person conducting the business is generally known by his creditors to be substantially engaged in selling goods of others, or

[9] *In re Oriental Rug Warehouse Club, Inc.*, 205 B.R. 407 (Bankr. D. Minn. 1997); *Underwriters at Lloyds v. Shimer (In re Ide Jewelry Co., Inc.)*, 75 B.R. 969 (Bankr. S.D.N.Y. 1987); *In re Haley and Steele Inc.*, 58 UCC Rep. Serv. 2d 394 (Mass. 2005).

   c. complies with the filing provisions of the Article on Secured Transactions (Article 9).

4. Any "or return" term of a contract for sale is to be treated as a separate contract for sale within the statute of frauds section of this Article (Section 2-201) and as contradicting the sale aspect of the contract within the provisions of this Article on parol or extrinsic evidence (Section 2-202).

Prior to the enactment of this section of the UCC, creditors of the consignee (who receives the goods on consignment) could not rely on consigned goods in possession of the consignee because the title of the consignor (who delivers the goods on consignment) was superior to the claim of the creditor. The purpose of enacting the statute is to allow a creditor to attach a lien against property of a third person, which is in the consignee's possession on consignment, and to permit the creditor to treat such property as if it were owned by the consignee *under certain circumstances*.

Subdivision 3 spells out three separate and distinct exceptions and the purpose of the exceptions is to allow the consignor to protect himself by showing that the creditor had no right to assume that the goods were owned by the consignee. If the interest of the consignor is displayed by a sign or similar means identifying the consignor's interest in the property, or if the filing provisions of the article on secured transactions that involves the filing of a financing statement is used, the consignor may protect its interest.

One issue would be the person conducting the business is generally *not* known by the creditors to be substantially engaged in selling the goods of others, but the creditor had actual knowledge that the goods were subject to a consignment. In several states, the courts have held that the creditor's actual knowledge of the consignment before becoming a creditor is sufficient to meet the requirements of the exceptions set forth in Section 2-326; and the consignor will prevail.[10]

The minority view is that the creditor's knowledge of the debtor's possession of consigned property is totally irrelevant and the consignor's interest is junior to the creditor.[11]

As a general statement, where there is no evidence that the consignee's creditors are generally aware that the consignee is engaged in selling goods on consignment, the consignor (who delivers the goods to the consignee for the purposes of selling the goods on consignment) is bound to file a

---

[10] *In re Corvette Collection of Boston Inc.*, 294 B.R. 409 (2003); *GBS Meat Industry Pty., Ltd. v. Kress-Dobkin Co.*, 474 F. Supp. 1357 (W.D. Pa. 1979); *Eurpac Service Inc. v. Republic Acceptance Corp.*, 2000 WL 1228791 (Colo. App. Aug. 31, 2000); *Belmont Int'l, Inc. v. American Int'l Shoe Co.*, 313 Ore. 112, 831 P.2d 15 (Sup. Ct. Or. 1992).

[11] *In re State Street Auto Sales, Inc.*, 81 B.R. 215 (Bankr. D. Mass. 1988).

financing statement to prevent their property from becoming subject to the claims of the consignee's creditors.

> ***Credit & Collection Tip:*** *Where the creditors of the consignee are not totally aware of the fact that the consignee sells goods on consignment, and knowledge of this by the consignor may be difficult to ascertain and difficult to prove, the best course for the consignor is to file a financing statement. If it is common in the industry and it is known to most of the firms in the industry that this particular business does accept goods on consignment, the consignor would probably not be required to file a financing statement. The best advice is when in doubt, file a financing statement.*[12]

UNITED STATES WAREHOUSE ACT

The United States Warehouse Act clarified that electronic warehouse receipts are to be treated identically as paper receipts with respect to the perfection of a security interest under state law. Congress did not intend to give electronic receipts a super priority, but merely intended for electronic receipts to be on parity with paper receipts and to be prioritized according to state law.

ESTABLISHING A POWER OF ATTORNEY

An individual is unable to be present at the time that it is necessary to enter into a contract or execute documents necessary to consummate a business transaction. In these circumstances the party executes a power of attorney in favor of another party. The power of attorney authorizes the other party to perform certain acts for the authorizing party. The language must be clear and specific.

A power of attorney normally authorizes the agent to perform all necessary acts in connection with a particular purpose, such as executing a contract between two parties, operating a business, or receiving, or transporting goods or merchandise. A general power of attorney will authorize the agent to act for the principal generally.

> ***Credit & Collection Tip:*** *Before accepting the agent's authority, be certain that the party executing the power of attorney is alive at the time the transaction takes place, for a power of attorney is automatically terminated upon the death of the principal.*

---

[12]*In re Russell*, 254 B.R. 132 (Bankr. D. Va. 2000); *South Beverly Wilshire Jewelry & Loan v. Superior Court*, 16 Cal. Rptr. 3d 710 (Cal. App. 2d Dist. 2004).

THE UNIFORM COMMERCIAL CODE

The UCC has been adopted in similar form in all 50 states of the United States. The purpose of the code was to establish in all the states the same laws which apply to negotiable paper, credit transactions, and bank and commercial businesses so that businesses can deal with their counterparts in other states based on a fairly uniform code throughout the country. Nevertheless, the code as adopted in each state is somewhat distinct from that adopted in every other state, since the legislatures of each state at the time of adoption made changes and modifications. For that reason, it is necessary to review the code with respect to the state's law that affects a particular transaction.

The code runs hundreds of pages; textbooks analyzing the code run thousands of pages; hundreds of cases are decided each year interpreting the code. Covering each section of the code in this particular book would be nearly impossible. However, the following list of sections of the UCC will give you a general awareness of the topics the code covers:

1. General Provisions
2. Sales
   —Leases (adopted by most states)
3. Commercial paper
4. Bank deposits and collection
   —Funds transfer
5. Documentary letters of credit
6. Bulk transfers
7. Warehouse receipt, bills of lading, and other documents of title
8. Investment securities
9. Secured transactions (recently revised)
10. Effective date and transition provision

In 2002, Revised Article 9 was adopted in all 50 states, and radically changed the rules affecting the filing of financing statements and enforcing security agreements (*see* Chapter 11).

UNIFORM COMMERCIAL CODE—REVISED ARTICLE 1

Article 1 of the UCC generally deals with definitions and applies to transactions covered by the UCC's other articles. The National Conferences of Commissioners on Uniform State Laws and the American Law Institute prepared the final draft of the revision to Article 1 in 2001. Many states have adopted the revisions, and other are in the process.

An important revision is the definition of "good faith" contained in the new Section 1-201, which sets forth the definitions of the various terms used throughout the code. "Good faith" is defined as follows:

> "good faith" except as otherwise provided in Chapter 5 means honesty in fact and the observance of reasonable commercial standards of fair dealing.

Under the old Uniform Commercial Code, "good faith" was defined as:

> "good faith" means honesty in fact in the conduct or transaction concerned.

The revised article combining "honesty in fact" and "reasonable commercial standards of fair dealing" should provide sufficient material for the courts to write many pages to reinterpret exactly what the meaning of "good faith" is.

A major revision is Section 1-301 enlarging the power of merchants to select the applicable law. Section 1-301 allows merchants to select the law that will govern their transaction by providing in writing in the agreement which state law will be applicable. The particular jurisdiction need not have some relationship to the particular transaction. As to consumers, the transaction has to bear a reasonable relationship to the jurisdiction designated and the consumer cannot be deprived of any laws that were passed to protect the consumer.

The laws passed in the respective states differ to a lesser or greater degree from the laws recommended by the National Conferences of Commissioners on Uniform State Laws and the American Law Institute. The ultimate goal of these two organizations is that all the states will adopt Revised Section 1 in the same form. Unfortunately, this goal is rarely achieved.

UNIFORM CUSTOMS AND PRACTICES FOR DOCUMENTARY CREDITS (UCP)

Background. Originally the Uniform Customs and Practices for Documentary Credits (UCP) was not designed or intended to be law. UCP was prepared as standard terms to apply to letters of credit. Only those parties who chose to use these standard terms by a written agreement, or by inserting a clause in the letter of credit that this letter of credit is subject to these standard terms, could actually use them. If the parties chose to use a letter of credit without utilizing the standard terms of the UCP, the UCC would apply. Unfortunately, the UCC does not set forth in detail all the obligations and procedures set forth in the UCP—and the reverse is also true.

The UCP has been almost universally adopted by the banks and is now a worldwide standard. An applicant seeking a letter of credit without utilizing the UCP would have difficulty locating a bank that would issue the letter of credit.

Imprinted on each letter of credit is a stamp or writing that the letter of credit is subject to the UCP. As a result, the UCP could be identified as law, and operates as law since the courts apply the UCP as prevailing law. If the particular issue before the court is not covered by the UCP, the court will then apply the UCC or the appropriate law of the particular country where the litigation is proceeding. In today's environment, the UCP regulates and controls the issuance of both domestic and foreign letters of credit.

Publications. The International Chamber of Commerce (ICC) publishes a pamphlet known as the Uniform Customs and Practice for Documentary Credits, which is recognized as a set of rules governing the use of documentary credit in international commerce. The ICC states that banking associations and banks in more than 100 countries and territories have adopted the most recent revision providing a working aid to bankers, lawyers, importers, exporters, and transport executives involved in international trade.

The pamphlet runs 60 pages and is divided into seven categories as follows:

A. General provisions and definitions
B. Form and notification of credits
C. Liabilities and responsibilities
D. Documents
E. Miscellaneous provisions
F. Transferable credit
G. Assignment of proceeds

The rules cover the distinctions in extending credit that are considered separate transactions from sales or other contracts as well as instructions to issue the credits and the criteria and precise manner in which the credits must be issued. A section is devoted to the form and notification of the credits, including the revocation of a credit and the liability of the issuing and confirming bank. The rule states that the letter of credit or other document should indicate whether it is revocable or irrevocable. Obligations and liabilities of the banks and distinguishing between confirming banks and issuing banks are addressed. The extent of the examination of documents is set at reasonable care in ascertaining whether or not they appear on their face to be in compliance with the terms and conditions of the credit. Documents not stipulated in the credit will not be examined by the bank.

Almost 20 pages are devoted to identifying the various types of documents, from letters of credit to marine/ocean bills of lading to air transport documents to insurance.

In most international letters of credit, the letter of credit will be subject to the terms of the UCP so that the rules of the UCP will control the operation, procedures, and transfers of the funds pursuant to the letter of credit. Even domestic letters may also operate subject to the rules of the UCP. *The document itself will bear terminology indicating the document is subject to the terms of the UCP*. In those instances where the issue is not covered by the rules, the courts apply the law of the particular country, such as in the United States, the appropriate section of the UCC which covers letters of credit.

Besides this pamphlet on the UCP, the ICC also publishes "The New ICC Guide to Documentary Credit Operations," which uses a combination of drafts, charts, and sample documents that illustrate the documentary credit process. The ICC also publishes "The New ICC Standard Documentary Credit Forms."

The United Nations Convention on Independent Guarantees and Standby Letters of Credit also may come into play. This was promulgated by UNCITRAL (United Nations Commission of International Trade Law), a trade arm of the United Nations in 1995, but it has been ratified by only a few countries.

The ICC has also published the uniform rules for demand guarantees. The commission on banking of the ICC also approved a draft form of the international standby letter of credit (in 1998), which has been published by the ICC and is available for banks to incorporate into their standby credits since 1999.

UCP—Update to UCP 600 Plus eUCP. Effective July 1, 2007, the ICC has now published UCP 600, which contains substantial changes to the existing rules. The UCP 600 has cut the number of articles down to 39 from 49 and has created new sections of "definitions," containing terms such as "honour" and "negotiation." They have also addressed the difficulty of determining a "reasonable time" with a definite number of days for examining and determining the compliance of documents. A new provision concerning addresses of the beneficiary and the applicant is included as well as an expanded discussion of exactly what is "original documents." The new UCP also has redrafted transport articles aimed at resolving confusion over the identifications of carriers and agents.

The ICC supplements to the UCP governing presentation of documents in electronic or partial electronic form are included in the new UCP 600.

Those readers who are involved in letter of credit transactions probably already have the updates and the eUCP, but for those who do not, they can be obtained from the ICC Publishing Inc., 156 5th Avenue, Suite 308, New York, New York 10010 (212) 206-1150.

LETTER OF CREDIT

When a person first encounters the transaction of a letter of credit, or arranges for the issuance of the letter of credit, or is the recipient of the letter of credit, the transaction surrounding the letter of credit may seem somewhat complex. We will attempt to furnish a basic explanation.

First, the letter of credit is a direct agreement between the issuing bank and the beneficiary (selling party) of the credit. Basically, the beneficiary of the credit is the party who is to receive payment and the bank is the party who is to issue payment to the beneficiary (seller).

Second, a separate agreement lies between the account party (buyer) and the issuing bank. The account party (purchasing party) is a debtor and owes the bank money in the event that a letter of credit is exercised.

The account party has a separate agreement with the bank, and under the terms of this agreement must pay the bank in advance or reimburse the bank for any monies paid under the letter of credit, that is, for any monies that the bank pays to the beneficiary. This agreement between the issuing bank and the account party is totally separate and distinct from the actual letter of credit, which is a separate agreement between the issuing bank and the beneficiary (seller).

Distinct and apart from the above two contracts, a separate contract exists between the beneficiary (seller) and the account party (buyer), which is the contract for the sale of the goods and the terms and conditions of payment for the goods by a letter of credit.

Three contracts exist:

1. a contract between the issuing bank and the *beneficiary (the selling party)* of the credit;
2. a contract between the issuing bank and the *account party (the purchasing party buyer)*, who is obligated to advance or to reimburse the bank for any monies paid out by the bank; and
3. the contract between the beneficiary (the selling party) and the account party (the purchasing party) who arranges for the issuance of the letter of credit.

One of the results of the above contractual relationships is that in a bankruptcy proceeding of the purchasing party, the selling party is still entitled to enforce the letter of credit because the purchasing party is neither involved in nor has any connection with the agreement between the beneficiary and the issuing bank.

The concept that each contract is separate and distinct from the other contract is most important to understand in the letter of credit transaction. Each contract is independent and can be enforced by the parties to the contract regardless of the other two contracts.

Where a seller delivers defective goods to a buyer, the buyer attempts to persuade the bank not to pay the letter of credit. Because of the separateness of the contracts, the bank is under a direct obligation to fulfill the letter of credit if the seller presents the proper documents of title to the bank. The failure of the bank to honor the said letter of credit will expose the bank to a lawsuit directly by the seller. After the bank pays the seller, the buyer may institute suit for a breach of contract or a breach of warranty (or whatever other remedies are available against the seller) for the seller's failure to deliver the merchandise as it was ordered.

Situations arise where a bank may choose to dishonor a letter of credit even on presentation of proper documents or titles. If the buyer can produce clear evidence of fraud in the underlying contract that was entered into between the buyer and seller, the bank may have a right to refuse to honor the letter of credit in a fraudulent situation. The buyer must produce convincing evidence that the entire transaction was a total fraud, for example, the shipment consists of empty cartons with no furniture in the cartons. What is more likely to happen is that the buyer would retain counsel, make an application to court, and have the court issue an injunction directing the bank not to make payment under its obligation to the seller.

If the bank does honor the letter of credit and pays the seller, the buyer may now sue the seller to recover all or part of the letter of credit proceeds from the seller. The seller cannot avail itself of the defense that a separate contract existed between the seller and the bank to defend itself against the buyer's suit, because the theory of independence is not applicable once the payment by the bank has been made. Whereas the separate contract guarantees that the money will reach the seller upon presentation of the proper documents of title, the independence theory does not affect the contract between the seller and the buyer after payment has been made by the bank. A buyer may sue the seller for a breach of contract.

In a situation where the bank honors its obligation to the seller, but the buyer does not reimburse the bank, the bank may immediately commence suit against the buyer for reimbursement. The bank also may claim to be subjugated to the seller's rights against the buyer. Accordingly, the bank would have two claims against the buyer. The first claim would be under its contract with the buyer to reimburse, and the second claim would be under the seller's contract with the buyer to be paid for the goods.

Commercial and Standby. There are two types of letters of credit. The first is the commercial letter of credit, facilitating the sale of goods and protecting a third party against the customer's default in the underlying obligation. The buyer arranges for a bank to issue a letter of credit for the benefit of the seller. The buyer is the applicant, the seller is the beneficiary, and the bank is the issuer. The letter is an undertaking by the bank to honor all drafts drawn by the seller for the purchase price as long as the drafts are accompanied by the necessary documents in the letter such as the invoice, a bill of lading, or an inspection certificate. The risk of the buyer's insolvency is shifted to the bank, as is the risk of the buyer trying to renege on the agreement. The seller receives the benefit of the bank's undertaking upon the seller complying with the documentary requirements.

The second type of letter of credit is the standby letter of credit. The standby letter of credit guarantees that the bank will honor its customer's performance of obligations in a variety of situations. For example, instead of a performance bond from a surety, an owner of real estate may require the contractor to procure a letter of credit obligating its bank to pay the owner upon presentation of a certificate of default accompanied by a draft demanding payment. The letter of credit was a standby letter of credit, which is common in the construction industry.

The nature of a standby letter of credit is that it is essentially equivalent to a loan made by the issuing bank to the applicant. Like a surety contract, the standby credit insures against the applicant's nonperformance of an obligation. Unlike a surety contract, the beneficiary of the standby letter of credit may receive its money first regardless of pending litigation with the applicant.[13]

The bankruptcy court in a recent case held that a payment made pursuant to a standby letter of credit during the 90-day preference period is not considered a preference because the security interest (i.e., the letter of credit) was established prior to the 90-day period. If no collateral was provided, the payment might be considered an indirect transfer of the debtor's assets for the creditor's benefit during the 90-day period. A careful review of the case law is suggested.[14]

A letter of credit may state that it is governed by the UCP. Unfortunately, the UCP has no provisions that cover fraud. The UCP does not specifically prohibit the defense of fraud in a transaction; but being silent on the subject, the court may use the UCC. The UCC allows the dishonor of a draft on a letter of credit when fraud is in the transaction.[15]

UCC Section 5-114 states:

1. issuer must honor a draft or demand for payment that complies with the terms of the relevant credit regardless of whether the goods or documents conform to the underlying contract for sale or other contract between the customer and the beneficiary . . .

---

[13] *Nobel Ins. Co. v. First National Bank of Brundidge*, 821 So. 2d 210 (Ala. 2001).
[14] *In re ITXS*, 318 B.R. 85 (Bankr. W.D. Pa. 2004).
[15] *Prairie State Bank v. Universal Bonding Ins. Co.*, 953 P.2d 1047 (C.A. Kan. 1998).

2. unless otherwise agreed when documents appear on the face to comply with the terms of credit but . . . there is fraud in the transaction:

> Subdivision B . . . an issuer acting in good faith may honor the draft or demand for payment despite notification from the customer of fraud, forgery, or other defect not apparent on the face of the document, but a court of appropriate jurisdiction may enjoin such honor.

A commercial letter of credit is made up of three independent contracts: one between the customer (buyer) and the issuer, one between the issuer and the beneficiary (seller), and one between the beneficiary and the customer. A standby letter of credit involves the customer (construction firm), the issuer (the bank), and the insurer beneficiary (the bonding company). Each contract is independent of the other contract, and for this reason, the courts interpret the contracts on a strict basis. Nevertheless, the UCC states that the bank may honor a letter of credit in the case of fraud and the courts interpret this to mean that the bank may also decide not to honor the letter of credit. The option is with the issuer of the letter of credit.

The fraud in the transaction must stem from the conduct of the beneficiary against the customer. The purpose of the letter of credit is to allow the beneficiary to rely thereon. Fraud in this connection is defined as "of such an egregious nature as to vitiate the entire transaction."[16]

A bank may dishonor a sight draft drawn on a letter of credit valid on its face and made in compliance with the terms of the letter of credit if it determines fraud was committed. The fraud must be of a serious nature to outweigh the public policy consideration requiring issuing banks to pay upon demand under the letter of credit if the documents submitted comply with the terms of the letter of credit. Where there is a blatant fraud being practiced, and evidence of the fraud is present, a bank can refuse to pay the letter of credit.

To what extent the customer would have to indemnify the bank is an open question, since banks recognize that if they do not pay a letter of credit when the sight draft complies strictly with the requirements of the letter of credit, a suit will be instituted and a claim may be made upon the bank not only for the funds that it refuses to pay, but for consequential damages flowing from the failure to honor the letter of credit and even punitive damages. A rare situation occurs even with fraud, when a bank refuses to honor a letter of credit. What is more likely is that the customer obtains a court order expressly enjoining the bank from paying the letter of credit. Consult with experienced counsel.

---

[16] *Fisher v. Dakota Community Bank*, 405 F. Supp. 2d 1089 (D.N.D. 2005); *Bank of Newport v. First Nat'l Bank and Trust Co. of Bismarck*, 687 F.2d 1257 (8th Cir. 1982); *KMW Intern. v. Chase Manhattan Bank*, N.A., 606 F.2d (2d Cir. 1979).

Red Clause. A red clause (because it is often printed in red) allows a beneficiary under a letter of credit to receive advances, even before shipping the merchandise, upon presentation of certain documents that include an undertaking that the normal papers would be presented later. The reason a red clause is printed in red is that it is a deviation from the normal letter of credit and it may create a dangerous problem when a party receives advances but has not produced the product ready for delivery. Red clauses are often present where there is collusion, fraud, or gross negligence between the bank and the seller, because advancing the money before shipping opens up a world of opportunity for the seller to defraud the purchaser.

The beneficiary of the letter of credit may by agreement be required to notify you before drawing upon a letter of credit. A better course of action would be to have the bank notify you of the intent to draw or prescribe a requirement in the letter of credit itself. The beneficiary will be required initially to provide the bank with prior notice (of 30 days or some other period of time) of their intent to draw on the letter of credit. Accompanying this request for a 30-day notice of intent to draw carries with it the obligation that the draw be made within the same 30 days. Having the beneficiary provide notice to you is ineffective since the bank cannot enforce the obligation. The bank will not recognize a failure of this type of notification. But if the obligation is to notify the bank, the bank can enforce the notice provision.

Silent Confirmation. The independence principle is a cornerstone of the letter of credit bank. Many courts have stated that the confirming or nominating bank (agent bank of issuing bank) owes a statutory duty only to the issuing bank and not to the issuing bank's customer. Often the customer of the issuing bank wishes to proceed against the nominating or confirming bank and the courts have held that no privity is present between the customer and the nominating or confirming bank and will not permit the beneficiary to proceed against said bank.

A silent confirmation occurs when a bank agrees to confirm a letter of credit, but the agreement to do so does not appear on the face of the letter of credit. Silent confirmations often happen when a bank is authorized but not obligated by the issuing bank to make advances against the letter of credit. Subrogation is allowed so that a customer may stand in the place of the bank and proceed against a nominating or confirming bank.[17]

Choice of Law. Under UCC 5-116(b), when a letter of credit is silent regarding a choice of law, the law where the issuing bank is located normally governs the issuing bank's liability.[18]

---

[17] *Leonard A. Feinberg, Inc. v. Central Asia Capital Corp.*, 974 F. Supp. 822 (E.D. Pa. 1997); *Tokyo Kyogo Boeki Shokai v. United States Nat'l Bank of Oregon*, 126 F.3d 1135 (9th Cir. 1997).

[18] *BM Electronic Corporations v. LaSalle Bank, N.A.*, 2006 WL 760196 (N.D. Ill. 2006).

Discrepancies. A Circuit Court of Appeals decision in the Second Circuit reemphasized the effect of having the UCP apply to a letter of credit. Section 14(c) and (d) of UCP states as follows:

> c. If the Issuing Bank determines that the documents appear on their face not to be in compliance with the terms and conditions of the Credit, it may in its sole judgment approach the Applicant for a waiver of the discrepancy(ies). This does not, however, extend the period mentioned in sub-Article 13(b).
>
> d. i. If the Issuing Bank and/or Confirming Bank, if any, or a Nominated Bank acting on their behalf, decides to refuse the documents, it must give notice to that effect by telecommunication or, if that is not possible, by other expeditious means, without delay but no later than the close of the seventh banking day following the day of receipt of the documents. Such notice shall be given to the bank from which it received the documents, or to the Beneficiary, if it received the documents directly from him.
>
> ii. Such notice must state all discrepancies in respect of which the bank refuses the documents and must also state whether it is holding the documents at the disposal of, or is returning them to, the presenter.
>
> iii. The issuing Bank and/or Confirming Bank, if any, shall then be entitled to claim from the remitting bank refund with interest, of any reimbursement which has been made to that bank.

The court stated as follows:

> Article 14 of the UCP allows an issuing bank to refuse to pay on a letter of credit if it determines that the documents appear on their face not to be in compliance with the terms and conditions of the credit (UCP Article 14(c)). The issuing bank must give notice of its refusal by telecommunication or, if that is not possible by other expeditious means, without delay but no later than the close of the seventh banking day following the day of receipt of the documents and its notice must state all discrepancies in respective which the bank refuses the documents (UCP Article 14(d)(i)(ii)). Failure to comply with Article 14 notice provisions precludes the issuing bank from claiming that the documents are not in compliance with the terms and conditions of the credit (UCP Article 14(e)). The bank failed to comply in that its first disclaimer was not sent by telecommunication and did not specify the grounds for the disclaimer. The bank was justifying its refusal based upon a fraud of the underlying transactions and that non-conforming documents were knowingly forwarded in violation of Article 13.

Article 14 of the UCP addresses the issues of banks' and beneficiaries' rights when the beneficiary's documents contain discrepancies in a payment demand. The standard of strict compliance applies to the beneficiary's duty to provide the documentation that the letter of credit requires, which means that even slight discrepancies in compliance with the terms of the letter of credit justify refusal to pay. The courts have carved a narrow exception to the standard of strict compliance for variations in documents so insignificant that said variations do not relieve the issuing bank of its obligation to pay, including a situation where a word in the document is unmistakably clear despite an obvious typographical error, or where the customer provides only five copies of the documents instead of six.

When documents containing discrepancies are presented to an issuing bank, the issuing bank must provide notice of the *refusal decision* within seven days, stating exactly what the discrepancies are and why the bank is refusing the documents. An appellate court in California took the position that the seven day period enumerated in UCP 500 sub-article 13(b) was agreed upon as a compromise, and the seven days are not a safe harbor within which the issuing bank must give notice if the reasonable time would be less than seven days, due to the type of documents submitted. In such a case the reasonable time would be less than seven days—but the court did not specifically say the number of days. If the bank doesn't provide such notice, it is precluded from claiming that the documents are not in compliance with the terms and conditions of the letter of credit. The bank must explain which discrepancies are the basis for its refusal to accept the letter of credit. Merely listing discrepancies and not distinguishing which are immaterial and which are significant is insufficient. The notice must set forth in clear language the exact grounds for refusal to accept the letter of credit. A letter listing all the discrepancies without distinguishing between the material and the immaterial would not be an adequate notice, and the issuer of the letter of credit may be liable if the documents submitted were rejected.[19]

Waiver of Discrepancies. The independence principle supports the concept that an issuing bank is not bound to accept an applicant's waiver of discrepancies. The letter of credit is a contract between the beneficiary and the issuing bank. The issuing bank will honor its payment obligations if the beneficiary strictly complies with the letter of credit. If the beneficiary's documents do not comply, the issuing bank at that point has an option to ask the buyer (who paid for the letter of credit) whether the buyer wishes to waive the discrepancies in the terms and conditions of the letter of credit.

While the established law seems to be that the bank still has the right to insist on strict compliance notwithstanding the waiver, over the years some

---

[19] *Hamilton Bank, N.A. v. Kookmin Bank*, 245 F.3d 82 (2d Cir. 2001); *Timothy W. v. Rochester, N.H., School Dist.*, 875 F.2d 954 (1st Cir. 1989); *National Union Fire Insurance Co. of Pennsylvania v. Standard Federal Bank*, 309 F. Supp. 2d 960 (E.D. Mich. 2004); *Creaciones Con Idea, S.A. de C.V. v. MashreqBank PSC*, 51 F. Supp. 2d 423 (S.D.N.Y.), *dismissed*, 75 F. Supp. 2d 279 (S.D.N.Y. 1999); *Trifinery v. Banque Paribas*, 762 F. Supp. 1119 (S.D.N.Y. 1991); *DBJJ Inc. v. National City Bank*, 123 Cal. App. 4th 330 (Cal. App. 2004).

cases have determined that the bank must comply with a waiver of discrepancies communicated to it by the buyer.

Article 14(c) of the UCP provides that if the issuing bank determines that the documents appear on their face not to be in compliance with the terms and conditions of the credit, the bank in its sole discretion may approach the applicant for a waiver of the discrepancy. The UCP does not expressly make any statement whether the bank must accept the waiver of discrepancies by the buyer. The position of most of the courts is that the bank has no obligation to accept a waiver of discrepancy and may refuse to honor the credit notwithstanding the communication of a written waiver by the buyer to the bank.

The request for a waiver does not extend the period of time set forth in Article 13(b). The bank has seven days to examine the documents and determine whether to accept or refuse the documents and to inform the party from whom it received the documents.

A case from the Fifth Circuit addressed three criteria for dishonoring a letter of credit. First, the issuing bank reviews the documents presented for discrepancies. Second, if the bank discovers a problem, a waiver may be sought from the applicant. Third, the bank may issue its notice of refusal or waive the discrepancy. This sequence under UCP 500, ensures the issuing bank's independence in making its decision while also allowing the purchaser an opportunity to waive a discrepancy, thus promoting efficiency in the field where as many as half of the demands for payment under letters of credit are discrepant. In the vast majority of cases the buyer party waives the discrepancy and authorizes payment.[20]

The bank rejected a waiver even where both the applicant for the letter of credit and the beneficiary of the letter of credit agreed to the waiver. The discrepancies were not minor and the failure to include shipping documents complying with the terms of credit was sufficient to justify dishonor. If the discrepancies were minor, the bank probably would have honored the waiver between the parties, but the court held that the bank should have the discretion to reject a waiver by the applicant even when the beneficiary agrees.[21]

> ***Credit & Collection Tip:*** *A business utilizing letters of credit should obtain the UCP. Almost all letters of credit issued by the banks, both domestic and foreign, are issued under the provisions of the UCP. Counsel for the banks are familiar with the provisions and you should also be familiar with the provisions of the UCP before you undertake the use of letters of credit.*

Confirming Bank. When a confirming bank is brought into the transaction, the issuing bank creates a contract between them wherein

---

[20] *Voest Alpine Trading U.S.A. v. Bank of China*, 288 F.3d 262 (5th Cir. 2002).

[21] *BM Electronics Corp. v. LaSalle Bank, N.A.*, 59 UCC Rep. Serv. 2d 280 (N.D. Ill. 2006).

the issuing bank will reimburse the confirming bank for any payments that the confirming bank makes to the seller. This contract is separate and distinct from the other three contracts. The confirming bank also creates a separate obligation to the seller.

Rules Governing Letter of Credit. The Uniform Customs and Practices for Documentary Credits (ICC Publication 600 or "UCP 600") should be used instead of having your letter of credit subject to the laws of the country to which you are exporting. This should be stamped or recited on the actual letter of credit in a clear and conspicuous manner. If your letter of credit does not specify some recognized international rules, it will be subject to the laws of the country of the bank which issues the letter of credit. The bank may apply laws unfamiliar to you. It is advisable to have the Uniform Customs and Practices for Documentary Credits or UCP 600 stamped or recited on all your letters of credit.

Third-Party Beneficiary. The undertaking of a letter of credit is sometimes called a "contract," but most prefer to refer to it only as a letter of credit or as an undertaking and not a contract. The courts wish to avoid contract inferences, primarily because of the third-party beneficiary status of others. In any event, the letter of credit is a unilateral undertaking with no promise by anyone other than the bank.

A third-party beneficiary is one for whose benefit a promise is made in a contract between two parties but who is not a party to the contract. A classic example is an insurance policy where a husband obtains life insurance from the insurance company. The wife is the beneficiary and can enforce the terms of the contract against the insurance company if the insurance company fails to pay, but she was not a party to the contract between the husband and the insurance company. A prime requisite to the status of a third-party beneficiary is that the two parties to the contract must have intended to benefit the third party, whose intent must be something more than a mere incidental intention. The third party would have the right to institute suit against either one of the parties to the contract in the event that the particular party failed to perform the terms of the contract, which is not the case in a letter of credit.[22]

Bankruptcy. A transfer was made to the account of the debtor, and the bank swept up the money to pay an antecedent obligation by reason of a standby letter of credit. While the bankrupt was insolvent, the transfer occurred within 90 days of the filing of the petition and the transfer allowed the bank to be paid in full although other unsecured creditors would not have received full payment in a liquidation of the bankrupt. The bankrupt acknowledged that the only purpose of the deposit (which both parties

[22] *Pere Marquette Ry. Co. v. J. F. French & Co.*, 254 U.S. 538, 41 S. Ct. 195, 65 L. Ed. 391 (1921).

knew would be swept up by the bank) was to pay the bankrupt's obligations on the letter of credit.

The bank argued that the independence principle should not be applied and the economic realty of the transaction must be examined for purposes of a preference analysis. Letters of credit are different from other financing mechanisms. As soon as the bank issued irrevocable letters in favor of the beneficiaries, it assumed the obligations of paying upon the drafts supported by documents that conform to the terms of the credit.

When the beneficiary presented its draft with conforming documents, the bank was required to pay whether or not the bankrupt paid the bank a red cent. If the bankrupt did not comply with the standby letter of credit by reimbursing the bank, the bank would have had a contract action against the bankrupt—but no defense against the beneficiary. Therefore, the moment the beneficiary presented the draft, a debt arose between the bankrupt (debtor) and the bank (creditor) in the amount of the requested draft. The bankrupt arranged for the transfer of the $31 million from the Swiss bank to its account at Bank One. Once the bankrupt placed the amount in its bank account, it authorized the bank to take that money in satisfaction of its obligations under the standby letter of credit—which the bank did.

The court affirmed the lower court's decision that the funds seized to cover the bank payments to beneficiaries were recoverable as a preference and that the bank's security interest in debtor's deposit accounts did not prevent the bankrupt from recovering the seized funds.[23]

EVERGREEN CLAUSE. An evergreen clause is defined as a term in a letter of credit providing for automatic renewal of the credit. It reflects the party's intent to make credit available for an indefinite period of time. In the instant case, the evergreen clause provided for an automatic renewal of the letter for one year from the expiration date thereof or any future expiration provided that the bank did not give 30 days' notice of nonrenewal.

The court opined if this was the sole provision, the letter was renewable on an annual basis without limit absent notification by the defendant of its intention not to renew. Nevertheless, the clause also provided that plaintiff may draw upon the credit line on or before June 2, 1993, but not beyond June 2, 1994. The letter issued June 3, 1992, expired by its terms, was subject to the evergreen renewal on June 2, 1994. Absent any action by the defendant as required by the clause, the letter was automatically renewed for a one-year term. At that point, the expiration provision became paramount as by its terms the letter expired June 2, 1994. The defendants argued that its evergreen clause prevails over its expiration provision. The court held the expiration provision cancelled out and modified the evergreen clause and the defendant was not liable past June 2, 1994.

---

[23]*In re P.A. Bergner & Co.*, 140 F.3d 1111 (7th Cir. 1998).

Common sense would probably dictate this logical conclusion, for one would not reasonably expect an automatic renewal clause to cancel an expiration date. Poor drafting has its price.[24]

Landlord Tenant. The independence principle applies to the situation where a tenant has furnished to the landlord a letter of credit as a security deposit. If the tenant files for bankruptcy, the tenant cannot prevent the landlord from receiving payment of the letter of credit from the bank. The tenant can obtain a full or partial return of the security deposit from the landlord notwithstanding the independence principle providing the tenant is entitled to the return of the money.[25]

BILL OF LADING

Similar to a letter of credit, a bill of lading is a contract that is strictly construed. Absent a valid agreement to the contrary, the carrier (the issuer of the bill of lading) is responsible for releasing the cargo only to the party who presents the original bill of lading. If instead of insisting upon the production and surrender of the bill of lading, the carrier chooses to deliver to the wrong party, the carrier is then liable for conversion and must indemnify the shipper for any loss that results.

In New York the carrier delivered the goods without obtaining surrender of the bill of lading. The party to whom the goods were delivered did not have a bill of lading and the carrier misdelivered the goods. Unless this misdelivery of the goods was caused or induced by the shipper, the carrier is liable to the shipper for conversion since delivery was made without obtaining a surrender of the bill of lading. This is a different situation from where the carrier delivered the goods without obtaining a bill of lading, but the recipient did have possession of the bill of lading.

Although this may seem like plain and simple common sense, the Federal Court in the Second Circuit cited a case in 1985 that stated "absent a valid agreement to the contrary, the carrier, the issuer of the bill of lading, is responsible for releasing the cargo only to the party who presents the original bill of lading. . . . If the carrier delivers the goods to one other than the authorized holder of the bill of lading, the carrier is liable for misdelivery."[26]

---

[24] *AXA Assurs., Inc. v. Chase Manhattan*, 339 N.J. Super. 22 (N.J. Super. Ct. App. Div. 2001).

[25] *In re Builders Transport*, 471 F.3d 1178 (11th Cir. 2006); *In re Graham Square*, 126 F.3d 823 (6th Cir. 1997).

[26] *Allied Chemical Intern. Corp. v. Companhia de Navegacao Lloyd Brasileiro*, 775 F.2d 476 (2d Cir. 1985); *Datas Industries Ltd v. OEC Freight (HK), Ltd.*, 2000 WL 1597843 (S.D.N.Y. Oct. 25, 2000).

FREIGHT FORWARDER—NVOCC

A non-vessel operating common carrier (NVOCC) normally consolidates cargo from numerous shippers into large groups for shipment by an ocean carrier. A NVOCC, as opposed to the actual ocean carrier transporting the cargo, issues a bill of lading to each shipper. If anything happens to the goods during the voyage, the NVOCC is liable to the shipper because of the issued bill of lading.

A freight forwarder simply facilitates the movement of cargo to an ocean vessel. The freight forwarder secures cargo space with a steamship company, advises on governmental licensing requirements, proper ports of exit and letter of credit intricacies, and arranges to have the cargo reach the seaboard in time to meet the designated vessel.

Freight forwarders generally make arrangements for the movement of cargo at the request of clients and are vitally different from carriers such as vessels, truckers, railroads, or warehouses, which are directly involved in transporting the cargo. Unlike a carrier, a freight forwarder does not issue a bill of lading and is therefore not liable to a shipper for any damages that occur to the goods during shipment. The freight forwarder limits its role to arranging for transportation and is not liable to the shipper if the goods are damaged en route.

WAREHOUSE LIEN

We have included in the Appendix a portion of Article 7 of the UCC entitled "Warehouse Receipts, Bills of Lading and Other Documents of Title" (Florida). The use of warehouses and warehouse receipts is quite common. Each state has passed a slightly different version of Article 7 and a careful review of the state law applicable to the warehouse transaction must be made before any steps are taken.

Under Section 7-202, a warehouse receipt does not have to be in any particular form, but there are certain terms which must be included for a document to constitute a warehouse receipt. Included among these terms are the location of the warehouse where the goods are stored, the date of issue of the receipt, the consecutive number of the receipt, a statement whether the goods received will be delivered to the bearer or to specified person, the rate of storage and handling charges, a description of the goods or the package containing the goods, the signature of the warehouseman, and other information contained in Section 7-202 of the UCC. An invoice or bill from the warehouseman, which simply itemizes the charges of the warehouseman and states the total amount due, does not qualify as a warehouse receipt.

Merely packing and loading a truck does not mean "repairing, servicing, treating, or improving personal property" within the meaning of the specific North Carolina statute.

The lesson to be learned is that whereas the state may have adopted the UCC, the state may have also passed specific laws dealing with warehouse receipts. Even though the state laws may conform closely to the UCC, variations may affect the situation.

When a firm is dealing with a warehouse situation, they should be familiar with the laws of that particular state. Needless to say, the warehouseman is familiar with the law and accordingly it is only fair that the person who deals with the warehouseman should also be familiar with the law.

CHAPTER 3
APPENDIX I

ARTICLE 2 OF THE UNIFORM COMMERCIAL CODE AS ADOPTED IN CALIFORNIA

2101. This division shall be known and may be cited as Uniform Commercial Code—Sales.

2102. Unless the context otherwise requires, this division applies to transactions in goods; it does not apply to any transaction which although in the form of an unconditional contract to sell or present sale is intended to operate only as a security transaction nor does this division impair or repeal any statute regulating sales to consumers, farmers or other specified classes of buyers.

2103. (1) In this division unless the context otherwise requires:

(a) "Buyer" means a person who buys or contracts to buy goods.

(b) (Reserved)

(c) "Receipt of goods" means taking physical possession of them.

(d) "Seller" means a person who sells or contracts to sell goods.

(2) Other definitions applying to this division or to specified chapters thereof, and the sections in which they appear are:

"Acceptance."	Section 2606.
"Banker's credit."	Section 2325.
"Between merchants."	Section 2104.
"Cancellation."	Section 2106(4).
"Commercial unit."	Section 2105.
"Confirmed credit."	Section 2325.
"Conforming to contract."	Section 2106.
"Contract for sale."	Section 2106.
"Cover."	Section 2712.
"Entrusting."	Section 2403.
"Financing agency."	Section 2104.

"Future goods."	Section 2105.
"Goods."	Section 2105.
"Identification."	Section 2501.
"Installment contract."	Section 2612.
"Letter of Credit."	Section 2325.
"Lot."	Section 2105.
"Merchant."	Section 2104.
"Overseas."	Section 2323.
"Person in position of seller."	Section 2707.
"Present sale."	Section 2106.
"Sale."	Section 2106.
"Sale on approval."	Section 2326.
"Sale or return."	Section 2326.
"Termination."	Section 2106.

(3) The following definitions in other divisions apply to this division:

"Check."	Section 3104.
"Consignee."	Section 7102.
"Consignor."	Section 7102.
"Consumer goods."	Section 9102.
"Control."	Section 7106.
"Dishonor."	Section 3502.
"Draft."	Section 3104.

(4) In addition, Division 1 (commencing with Section 1101) contains general definitions and principles of construction and interpretation applicable throughout this division.

2104. (1) "Merchant" means a person who deals in goods of the kind or otherwise by his occupation holds himself out as having knowledge or skill peculiar to the practices or goods involved in the transaction or to whom such knowledge or skill may be attributed by his employment of an agent or broker or other intermediary who by his occupation holds himself out as having such knowledge or skill.

(2) "Financing agency" means a bank, finance company, or other person who in the ordinary course of business makes advances against goods or documents of title or who by arrangement with either the seller or the buyer intervenes in ordinary course to make or collect payment due or claimed under the contract for sale, as by purchasing or paying the seller's draft or making advances against it or by merely taking it for collection whether or not documents of title accompany or are associated with the draft. "Financing agency" includes also a bank or other person who similarly intervenes between persons who are in the position of seller and buyer in respect to the goods (Section 2707).

(3) "Between merchants" means in any transaction with respect to which both parties are chargeable with the knowledge or skill of merchants.

2105. (1) "Goods" means all things (including specially manufactured goods) which are movable at the time of identification to the contract for sale other than the money in which the price is to be paid, investment securities (Division 8) and things in action. "Goods" also includes the unborn young of animals and growing crops and other identified things attached to realty as described in the section on goods to be severed from realty (Section 2107).

(2) Goods must be both existing and identified before any interest in them can pass. Goods which are not both existing and identified are "future" goods. A purported present sale of future goods or of any interest therein operates as a contract to sell.

(3) There may be a sale of a part interest in existing identified goods.

(4) An undivided share in an identified bulk of fungible goods is sufficiently identified to be sold although the quantity of the bulk is not determined. Any agreed proportion of such a bulk or any quantity thereof agreed upon by number, weight or other measure may to the extent of the seller's interest in the bulk be sold to the buyer who then becomes an owner in common.

(5) "Lot" means a parcel or a single article which is the subject matter of a separate sale or delivery, whether or not it is sufficient to perform the contract.

(6) "Commercial unit" means such a unit of goods as by commercial usage is a single whole for purposes of sale and division of which materially impairs its character or value on the market or in use. A commercial unit may be a single article (as a machine) or a set of articles (as a suite of furniture or an assortment of sizes) or a quantity (as a bale, gross, or carload) or any other unit treated in use or in the relevant market as a single whole.

2106. (1) In this division unless the context otherwise requires "contract" and "agreement" are limited to those relating to the present or future sale of goods. "Contract for sale" includes both a present sale of goods and a contract to sell goods at a future time. A "sale" consists in the passing of title from the seller to the buyer for a price (Section 2401). A "present sale" means a sale which is accomplished by the making of the contract.

(2) Goods or conduct including any part of a performance are "conforming" or conform to the contract when they are in accordance with the obligations under the contract.

(3) "Termination" occurs when either party pursuant to a power created by agreement or law puts an end to the contract otherwise than for its breach. On "termination" all obligations which are still executory on both sides are discharged but any right based on prior breach or performance survives.

(4) "Cancellation" occurs when either party puts an end to the contract for breach by the other and its effect is the same as that of "termination" except that the cancelling party also retains any remedy for breach of the whole contract or any unperformed balance.

2107. (1) A contract for the sale of minerals or the like (including oil and gas) or a structure or its materials to be removed from realty is a contract for the sale of goods within this division if they are to be severed by the seller but until severance a purported present sale thereof which is not effective as a transfer of an interest in land is effective only as a contract to sell.

(2) A contract for the sale apart from the land of growing crops or other things attached to realty and capable of severance without material harm thereto but not described in subdivision (1) or of timber to be cut is a contract for the sale of goods within this division whether the subject matter is to be severed by the buyer or by the seller even though it forms part of the realty at the time of contracting, and the parties can by identification effect a present sale before severance.

(3) The provisions of this section are subject to any third party rights provided by the law relating to realty records, and the contract for sale may be executed and recorded in the same manner as a document transferring an interest in land and shall then constitute notice to third parties of the buyer's rights under the contract for sale.

2201. (1) Except as otherwise provided in this section a contract for the sale of goods for the price of five hundred dollars ($500) or more is not enforceable by way of action or defense unless there is some writing sufficient to indicate that a contract for sale has been made between the parties and signed by the party against whom enforcement is sought or by his or her authorized agent or broker. A writing is not insufficient because it omits or incorrectly states a term agreed upon but the contract is not enforceable under this paragraph beyond the quantity of goods shown in the writing.

(2) Between merchants if within a reasonable time a writing in confirmation of the contract and sufficient against the sender is received and the party receiving it has reason to know its contents, it satisfies the requirements of subdivision (1) against the party unless written notice of objection to its contents is given within 10 days after it is received.

(3) A contract which does not satisfy the requirements of subdivision (1) but which is valid in other respects is enforceable:

(a) If the goods are to be specially manufactured for the buyer and are not suitable for sale to others in the ordinary course of the seller's business and the seller, before notice of repudiation is received and under circumstances which reasonably indicate that the goods are for the buyer, has made either a substantial beginning of their manufacture or commitments for their procurement;

(b) If the party against whom enforcement is sought admits in his or her pleading, testimony, or otherwise in court that a contract for sale was made, but the contract is not enforceable under this provision beyond the quantity of goods admitted; or

(c) With respect to goods for which payment has been made and accepted or which have been received and accepted (Section 2606).

(4) Subdivision (1) of this section does not apply to a qualified financial contract as that term is defined in paragraph (2) of subdivision (b) of Section 1624 of the Civil Code if either (a) there is, as provided in paragraph (3) of subdivision (b) of 1624 of the Civil Code, sufficient evidence to indicate

that a contract has been made or (b) the parties thereto, by means of a prior or subsequent written contract, have agreed to be bound by the terms of the qualified financial contract from the time they reach agreement (by telephone, by exchange of electronic messages, or otherwise) on those terms.

2202. Terms with respect to which the confirmatory memoranda of the parties agree or which are otherwise set forth in a writing intended by the parties as a final expression of their agreement with respect to such terms as are included therein may not be contradicted by evidence of any prior agreement or of a contemporaneous oral agreement but may be explained or supplemented

(a) By course of dealing, course of performance, or usage of trade (Section 1303); and

(b) By evidence of consistent additional terms unless the court finds the writing to have been intended also as a complete and exclusive statement of the terms of the agreement.

2204. (1) A contract for sale of goods may be made in any manner sufficient to show agreement, including conduct by both parties which recognizes the existence of such a contract.

(2) An agreement sufficient to constitute a contract for sale may be found even though the moment of its making is undetermined.

(3) Even though one or more terms are left open a contract for sale does not fail for indefiniteness if the parties have intended to make a contract and there is a reasonably certain basis for giving an appropriate remedy.

2205. (a) An offer by a merchant to buy or sell goods in a signed writing which by its terms gives assurance that it will be held open is not revocable, for lack of consideration, during the time stated or if no time is stated for a reasonable time, but in no event may such period of irrevocability exceed three months; but any such term of assurance on a form supplied by the offeree must be separately signed by the offeror.

(b) Notwithstanding subdivision (a), when a merchant renders an offer, oral or written, to supply goods to a contractor licensed pursuant to the provisions of Chapter 9 (commencing with Section 7000) of Division 3 of the Business and Professions Code or a similar contractor's licensing law of another state, and the merchant has actual or imputed knowledge that the contractor is so licensed, and that the offer will be relied upon by the contractor in the submission of its bid for a construction contract with a third party, the offer relied upon shall be irrevocable, notwithstanding lack of consideration, for 10 days after the awarding of the contract to the prime contractor, but in no event for more than 90 days after the date the bid or offer was rendered by the merchant; except that an oral bid or offer, when for a price of two thousand five hundred dollars ($2,500) or more, shall be confirmed in writing by the contractor or his or her agent within 48 hours after it is rendered. Failure by the contractor to confirm such offer in writing shall release the merchant from his or her offer. Nothing in this subdivision shall prevent a merchant from providing that the bid or offer will be held open for less than the time provided for herein.

2206. (1) Unless otherwise unambiguously indicated by the language or circumstances

(a) An offer to make a contract shall be construed as inviting acceptance in any manner and by any medium reasonable in the circumstances;

(b) An order or other offer to buy goods for prompt or current shipment shall be construed as inviting acceptance either by a prompt promise to ship or by the prompt or current shipment of conforming or non-conforming goods, but such a shipment of nonconforming goods does not constitute an acceptance if the seller seasonably notifies the buyer that the shipment is offered only as an accommodation to the buyer.

(2) Where the beginning of a requested performance is a reasonable mode of acceptance an offeror who is not notified of acceptance within a reasonable time may treat the offer as having lapsed before acceptance.

2207. (1) A definite and seasonable expression of acceptance or a written confirmation which is sent within a reasonable time operates as an acceptance even though it states terms additional to or different from those offered or agreed upon, unless acceptance is expressly made conditional on assent to the additional or different terms.

(2) The additional terms are to be construed as proposals for addition to the contract. Between merchants such terms become part of the contract unless:

(a) The offer expressly limits acceptance to the terms of the offer;

(b) They materially alter it; or

(c) Notification of objection to them has already been given or is given within a reasonable time after notice of them is received.

(3) Conduct by both parties which recognizes the existence of a contract is sufficient to establish a contract for sale although the writings of the parties do not otherwise establish a contract. In such case the terms of the particular contract consist of those terms on which the writings of the parties agree, together with any supplementary terms incorporated under any other provisions of this code.

2209. (1) An agreement modifying a contract within this division needs no consideration to be binding.

(2) A signed agreement which excludes modification or rescission except by a signed writing cannot be otherwise modified or rescinded, but except as between merchants such a requirement on a form supplied by the merchant must be separately signed by the other party.

(3) The requirements of the statute of frauds section of this division (Section 2201) must be satisfied if the contract as modified is within its provisions.

(4) Although an attempt at modification or rescission does not satisfy the requirements of subdivision (2) or (3) it can operate as a waiver.

(5) A party who has made a waiver affecting an executory portion of the contract may retract the waiver by reasonable notification received by the other party that strict performance will be required of any term waived, unless the retraction would be unjust in view of a material change of position in reliance on the waiver.

2210. (1) A party may perform his or her duty through a delegate unless otherwise agreed or unless the other party has a substantial interest in having his or her original promisor perform or control the acts required by the contract. No delegation of performance relieves the party delegating of any duty to perform or any liability for breach.

(2) Except as otherwise provided in Section 9406, unless otherwise agreed, all rights of either seller or buyer can be assigned except where the assignment would materially change the duty of the other party, or increase materially the burden or risk imposed on him or her by his or her contract, or impair materially his or her chance of obtaining return performance. A right to damages for breach of the whole contract or a right arising out of the assignor's due performance of his or her entire obligation can be assigned despite agreement otherwise.

(3) The creation, attachment, perfection, or enforcement of a security interest in the seller's interest under a contract is not a transfer that materially changes the duty of, or increases materially the burden or risk imposed on, the buyer or impairs materially the buyer's chance of obtaining return performance within the purview of subdivision (2) unless, and then only to the extent that, enforcement actually results in a delegation of material performance of the seller. Even in that event, the creation, attachment, perfection, and enforcement of the security interest remain effective, but (A) the seller is liable to the buyer for damages caused by the delegation to the extent that the damages could not reasonably be prevented by the buyer, and (B) a court having jurisdiction may grant other appropriate relief, including cancellation of the contract for sale or an injunction against enforcement of the security interest or consummation of the enforcement.

(4) Unless the circumstances indicate the contrary, a prohibition of assignment of "the contract" is to be construed as barring only the delegation to the assignee of the assignor's performance.

(5) An assignment of "the contract" or of "all my rights under the contract" or an assignment in similar general terms is an assignment of rights and, unless the language or the circumstances (as in an assignment for security) indicate the contrary, it is a delegation of performance of the duties of the assignor, and its acceptance by the assignee constitutes a promise by him or her to perform those duties. This promise is enforceable by either the assignor or the other party to the original contract.

(6) The other party may treat any assignment which delegates performance as creating reasonable grounds for insecurity and may, without prejudice to

his or her rights against the assignor, demand assurances from the assignee (Section 2609).

2301. The obligation of the seller is to transfer and deliver and that of the buyer is to accept and pay in accordance with the contract.

2303. Where this division allocates a risk or a burden as between the parties "unless otherwise agreed," the agreement may not only shift the allocation but may also divide the risk or burden.

2304. (1) The price can be made payable in money or otherwise. If it is payable in whole or in part in goods each party is a seller of the goods which he is to transfer.

(2) Even though all or part of the price is payable in an interest in realty the transfer of the goods and the seller's obligations with reference to them are subject to this division, but not the transfer of the interest in realty or the transferor's obligations in connection therewith.

2305. (1) The parties if they so intend can conclude a contract for sale even though the price is not settled. In such a case the price is a reasonable price at the time for delivery if

(a) Nothing is said as to price; or

(b) The price is left to be agreed by the parties and they fail to agree; or

(c) The price is to be fixed in terms of some agreed market or other standard as set or recorded by a third person or agency and it is not so set or recorded.

(2) A price to be fixed by the seller or by the buyer means a price for him to fix in good faith.

(3) When a price left to be fixed otherwise than by agreement of the parties fails to be fixed through fault of one party the other may at his option treat the contract as canceled or himself fix a reasonable price.

(4) Where, however, the parties intend not to be bound unless the price be fixed or agreed and it is not fixed or agreed there is no contract. In such a case the buyer must return any goods already received or if unable so to do must pay their reasonable value at the time of delivery and the seller must return any portion of the price paid on account.

2306. (1) A term which measures the quantity by the output of the seller or the requirements of the buyer means such actual output or requirements as may occur in good faith, except that no quantity unreasonably disproportionate to any stated estimate or in the absence of a stated estimate to any normal or otherwise comparable prior output or requirements may be tendered or demanded.

(2) A lawful agreement by either the seller or the buyer for exclusive dealing in the kind of goods concerned imposes unless otherwise agreed an obligation by the seller to use best efforts to supply the goods and by the buyer to use best efforts to promote their sale.

2307. Unless otherwise agreed all goods called for by a contract for sale must be tendered in a single delivery and payment is due only on such tender but where the circumstances give either party the right to make or demand delivery in lots the price if it can be apportioned may be demanded for each lot.

2308. Unless otherwise agreed

(a) The place for delivery of goods is the seller's place of business or if he has none, his residence; but

(b) In a contract for sale of identified goods which to the knowledge of the parties at the time of contracting are in some other place, that place is the place for their delivery; and

(c) Documents of title may be delivered through customary banking channels.

2309. (1) The time for shipment or delivery or any other action under a contract if not provided in this division or agreed upon shall be a reasonable time.

(2) Where the contract provides for successive performances but is indefinite in duration it is valid for a reasonable time but unless otherwise agreed may be terminated at any time by either party.

(3) Termination of a contract by one party except on the happening of an agreed event requires that reasonable notification be received by the other party and an agreement dispensing with notification is invalid if its operation would be unconscionable.

2310. Unless otherwise agreed:

(a) Payment is due at the time and place at which the buyer is to receive the goods even though the place of shipment is the place of delivery; and

(b) If the seller is authorized to send the goods he may ship them under reservation, and may tender the documents of title, but the buyer may inspect the goods after their arrival before payment is due unless such inspection is inconsistent with the terms of the contract (Section 2513); and

(c) If delivery is authorized and made by way of documents of title otherwise than by subdivision (b) then payment is due regardless of where the goods are to be received (i) at the time and place at which the buyer is to receive delivery of the tangible documents or (ii) at the time the buyer is to receive delivery of the electronic documents and at the seller's place of business or if none, the seller's residence; and

(d) Where the seller is required or authorized to ship the goods on credit, the credit period runs from the time of shipment but postdating the invoice or delaying its dispatch will correspondingly delay the starting of the credit period.

2311. (1) An agreement for sale which is otherwise sufficiently definite (subdivision (3) of Section 2204) to be a contract is not made invalid by the fact that it leaves particulars of performance to be specified by one of the parties. Any such specification must be made in good faith and within limits set by commercial reasonableness.

(2) Unless otherwise agreed specifications relating to assortment of the goods are at the buyer's option and except as otherwise provided in subdivisions (1)(c) and (3) of Section 2319, specifications or arrangements relating to shipment are at the seller's option.

(3) Where such specification would materially affect the other party's performance but is not seasonably made or where one party's co-operation is necessary to the agreed performance of the other but is not seasonably forthcoming, the other party in addition to all other remedies

(a) Is excused for any resulting delay in his own performance; and

(b) May also either proceed to perform in any reasonable manner or after the time for a material part of his own performance treat the failure to specify or to co-operate as a breach by failure to deliver or accept the goods.

2312. (1) Subject to subdivision (2) there is in a contract for sale a warranty by the seller that

(a) The title conveyed shall be good, and its transfer rightful; and

(b) The goods shall be delivered free from any security interest or other lien or encumbrance of which the buyer at the time of contracting has no knowledge.

(2) A warranty under subdivision (1) will be excluded or modified only by specific language or by circumstances which give the buyer reason to know that the person selling does not claim title in himself or that he is purporting to sell only such right or title as he or a third person may have.

(3) Unless otherwise agreed a seller who is a merchant regularly dealing in goods of the kind warrants that the goods shall be delivered free of the rightful claim of any third person by way of infringement or the like but a buyer who furnishes specifications to the seller must hold the seller harmless against any such claim which arises out of compliance with the specifications.

2313. (1) Express warranties by the seller are created as follows:

(a) Any affirmation of fact or promise made by the seller to the buyer which relates to the goods and becomes part of the basis of the bargain creates an express warranty that the goods shall conform to the affirmation or promise.

(b) Any description of the goods which is made part of the basis of the bargain creates an express warranty that the goods shall conform to the description.

(c) Any sample or model which is made part of the basis of the bargain creates an express warranty that the whole of the goods shall conform to the sample or model.

(2) It is not necessary to the creation of an express warranty that the seller use formal words such as "warrant" or "guarantee" or that he have a specific intention to make a warranty, but an affirmation merely of the value of the goods or a statement purporting to be merely the seller's opinion or commendation of the goods does not create a warranty.

2314. (1) Unless excluded or modified (Section 2316), a warranty that the goods shall be merchantable is implied in a contract for their sale if the seller is a merchant with respect to goods of that kind. Under this section the serving for value of food or drink to be consumed either on the premises or elsewhere is a sale.

(2) Goods to be merchantable must be at least such as

(a) Pass without objection in the trade under the contract description; and

(b) In the case of fungible goods, are of fair average quality within the description; and

(c) Are fit for the ordinary purposes for which such goods are used; and

(d) Run, within the variations permitted by the agreement, of even kind, quality and quantity within each unit and among all units involved; and

(e) Are adequately contained, packaged, and labeled as the agreement may require; and

(f) Conform to the promises or affirmations of fact made on the container or label if any.

(3) Unless excluded or modified (Section 2316) other implied warranties may arise from course of dealing or usage of trade.

2315. Where the seller at the time of contracting has reason to know any particular purpose for which the goods are required and that the buyer is relying on the seller's skill or judgment to select or furnish suitable goods, there is unless excluded or modified under the next section an implied warranty that the goods shall be fit for such purpose.

2316. (1) Words or conduct relevant to the creation of an express warranty and words or conduct tending to negate or limit warranty shall be construed wherever reasonable as consistent with each other; but subject to the provisions of this division on parol or extrinsic evidence (Section 2202) negation or limitation is inoperative to the extent that such construction is unreasonable.

(2) Subject to subdivision (3), to exclude or modify the implied warranty of merchantability or any part of it the language must mention merchantability and in case of a writing must be conspicuous, and to exclude or modify any implied warranty of fitness the exclusion must be by a writing and conspicuous. Language to exclude all implied warranties of fitness is sufficient if it states, for example, that "There are no warranties which extend beyond the description on the face hereof."

(3) Notwithstanding subdivision (2)

(a) Unless the circumstances indicate otherwise, all implied warranties are excluded by expressions like "as is," "with all faults" or other language which in common understanding calls the buyer's attention to the exclusion of warranties and makes plain that there is no implied warranty; and

(b) When the buyer before entering into the contract has examined the goods or the sample or model as fully as he desired or has refused to examine the goods there is no implied warranty with regard to defects which an examination ought in the circumstances to have revealed to him; and

(c) An implied warranty can also be excluded or modified by course of dealing or course of performance or usage of trade.

(4) Remedies for breach of warranty can be limited in accordance with the provisions of this division on liquidation or limitation of damages and on contractual modification of remedy (Sections 2718 and 2719).

2317. Warranties whether express or implied shall be construed as consistent with each other and as cumulative, but if such construction is unreasonable the intention of the parties shall determine which warranty is dominant. In ascertaining that intention the following rules apply:

(a) Exact or technical specifications displace an inconsistent sample or model or general language of description.

(b) A sample from an existing bulk displaces inconsistent general language of description.

(c) Express warranties displace inconsistent implied warranties other than an implied warranty of fitness for a particular purpose.

2319. (1) Unless otherwise agreed the term F.O.B. (which means "free on board") at a named place, even though used only in connection with the stated price, is a delivery term under which

(a) When the term is F.O.B. the place of shipment, the seller must at that place ship the goods in the manner provided in this division (Section 2504) and bear the expense and risk of putting them into the possession of the carrier; or

(b) When the term is F.O.B. the place of destination, the seller must at his own expense and risk transport the goods to that place and there tender delivery of them in the manner provided in this division (Section 2503);

(c) When under either (a) or (b) the term is also F.O.B. vessel, car or other vehicle, the seller must in addition at his own expense and risk load the goods on board. If the term is F.O.B. vessel the buyer must name the vessel and in an appropriate case the seller must comply with the provisions of this division on the form of bill of lading (Section 2323).

(2) Unless otherwise agreed the term F.A.S. vessel (which means "free alongside") at a named port, even though used only in connection with the stated price, is a delivery term under which the seller must

(a) At his own expense and risk deliver the goods alongside the vessel in the manner usual in that port or on a dock designated and provided by the buyer; and

(b) Obtain and tender a receipt for the goods in exchange for which the carrier is under a duty to issue a bill of lading.

(3) Unless otherwise agreed in any case falling within subdivision (1)(a) or (c) or subdivision (2) the buyer must seasonably give any needed instructions for making delivery, including when the term is F.A.S. or F.O.B. the loading berth of the vessel and in an appropriate case its name and sailing date. The seller may treat the failure of needed instructions as a failure of co-operation under this division (Section 2311). He may also at his option move the goods in any reasonable manner preparatory to delivery or shipment.

(4) Under the term F.O.B. vessel or F.A.S. unless otherwise agreed the buyer must make payment against tender of the required documents and the seller may not tender nor the buyer demand delivery of the goods in substitution for the documents.

2320. (1) The term C.I.F. means that the price includes in a lump sum the cost of the goods and the insurance and freight to the named destination. The term C. & F. or C.F. means that the price so includes cost and freight to the named destination.

(2) Unless otherwise agreed and even though used only in connection with the stated price and destination, the term C.I.F. destination or its equivalent requires the seller at his own expense and risk to

(a) Put the goods into the possession of a carrier at the port for shipment and obtain a negotiable bill or bills of lading covering the entire transportation to the named destination; and

(b) Load the goods and obtain a receipt from the carrier (which may be contained in the bill of lading) showing that the freight has been paid or provided for; and

(c) Obtain a policy or certificate of insurance, including any war risk insurance, of a kind and on terms then current at the port of shipment in the usual amount, in the currency of the contract, shown to cover the same goods covered by the bill of lading and providing for payment of loss to the order of the buyer or for the account of whom it may concern; but the seller may add to the price the amount of the premium for any such war risk insurance; and

(d) Prepare an invoice of the goods and procure any other documents required to effect shipment or to comply with the contract; and

(e) Forward and tender with commercial promptness all the documents in due form and with any indorsement necessary to perfect the buyer's rights.

(3) Unless otherwise agreed the term C. & F. or its equivalent has the same effect and imposes upon the seller the same obligations and risks as a C.I.F. term except the obligation as to insurance.

(4) Under the term C.I.F. or C. & F. unless otherwise agreed the buyer must make payment against tender of the required documents and the seller may not tender nor the buyer demand delivery of the goods in substitution for the documents.

2321. Under a contract containing a term C.I.F. or C. & F.

(1) Where the price is based on or is to be adjusted according to "net landed weights," "delivered weights," "out turn" quantity or quality or the like, unless otherwise agreed the seller must reasonably estimate the price. The payment due on tender of the documents called for by the contract is the amount so estimated, but after final adjustment of the price a settlement must be made with commercial promptness.

(2) An agreement described in subdivision (1) or any warranty of quality or condition of the goods on arrival places upon the seller the risk of ordinary deterioration, shrinkage and the like in transportation but has no effect on the place or time of identification to the contract for sale or delivery or on the passing of the risk of loss.

(3) Unless otherwise agreed where the contract provides for payment on or after arrival of the goods the seller must before payment allow such preliminary inspection as is feasible; but if the goods are lost delivery of the documents and payment are due when the goods should have arrived.

2322. (1) Unless otherwise agreed a term for delivery of goods "ex-ship" (which means from the carrying vessel) or in equivalent language is not restricted to a particular ship and requires delivery from a ship which has reached a place at the named port of destination where goods of the kind are usually discharged.

(2) Under such a term unless otherwise agreed

(a) The seller must discharge all liens arising out of the carriage and furnish the buyer with a direction which puts the carrier under a duty to deliver the goods; and

(b) The risk of loss does not pass to the buyer until the goods leave the ship's tackle or are otherwise properly unloaded.

2323. (1) Where the contract contemplates overseas shipment and contains a term C.I.F. or C. & F. or F.O.B. vessel, the seller unless otherwise agreed must obtain a negotiable bill of lading stating that the goods have been loaded on board or, in the case of a term C.I.F. or C. & F., received for shipment.

(2) Where in a case within subdivision (1) a tangible bill of lading has been issued in a set of parts, unless otherwise agreed if the documents are not to be sent from abroad the buyer may demand tender of the full set; otherwise only one part of the bill of lading need be tendered. Even if the agreement expressly requires a full set

(a) Due tender of a single part is acceptable within the provisions of this division on cure of improper delivery (subdivision (1) of Section 2508); and

(b) Even though the full set is demanded, if the documents are sent from abroad the person tendering an incomplete set may nevertheless require payment upon furnishing an indemnity which the buyer in good faith deems adequate.

(3) A shipment by water or by air or a contract contemplating such shipment is "overseas" insofar as by usage of trade or agreement it is subject to the commercial, financing or shipping practices characteristic of international deepwater commerce.

2324. Under a term "no arrival, no sale" or terms of like meaning, unless otherwise agreed,

(a) The seller must properly ship conforming goods and if they arrive by any means he must tender them on arrival but he assumes no obligation that the goods will arrive unless he has caused the nonarrival; and

(b) Where without fault of the seller the goods are in part lost or have so deteriorated as no longer to conform to the contract or arrive after the contract time, the buyer may proceed as if there had been casualty to identified goods (Section 2613).

2325. (1) Failure of the buyer seasonably to furnish an agreed letter of credit is a breach of the contract for sale.

(2) The delivery to seller of a proper letter of credit suspends the buyer's obligation to pay. If the letter of credit is dishonored, the seller may on seasonable notification to the buyer require payment directly from him.

(3) Unless otherwise agreed the term "letter of credit" or "banker's credit" in a contract for sale means an irrevocable credit issued by a financing agency of good repute and, where the shipment is overseas, of good international repute. The term "confirmed credit" means that the credit must also carry the direct obligation of such an agency which does business in the seller's financial market.

2326. (1) Unless otherwise agreed, if delivered goods may be returned by the buyer even though they conform to the contract, the transaction is

(a) A "sale on approval" if the goods are delivered primarily for use, and

(b) A "sale or return" if the goods are delivered primarily for resale.

(2) Goods held on approval are not subject to the claims of the buyer's creditors until acceptance; goods held on sale or return are subject to such claims while in the buyer's possession.

(3) Any "or return" term of a contract for sale is to be treated as a separate contract for sale within the statute of frauds section of this division (Section 2201) and as contradicting the sale aspect of the contract within the provisions of this division on parol or extrinsic evidence (Section 2202).

(4) If a person delivers or consigns for sale goods which the person used or bought for use for personal, family, or household purposes, these goods do not become the property of the deliveree or consignee unless the deliveree or consignee purchases and fully pays for the goods. Nothing in this subdivision shall prevent the deliveree or consignee from acting as the deliverer's agent to transfer title to these goods to a buyer who pays the full purchase price. Any payment received by the deliveree or consignee from a buyer of these goods, less any amount which the deliverer expressly agreed could be deducted from the payment for commissions, fees, or expenses, is the property of the deliverer and shall not be subject to the claims of the deliveree's or consignee's creditors.

2327. (1) Under sale on approval unless otherwise agreed

(a) Although the goods are identified to the contract the risk of loss and the title do not pass to the buyer until acceptance; and

(b) Use of the goods consistent with the purpose of trial is not acceptance but failure seasonably to notify the seller of election to return the goods is acceptance, and if the goods conform to the contract acceptance of any part is acceptance of the whole; and

(c) After due notification of election to return, the return is at the seller's risk and expense but a merchant buyer must follow any reasonable instructions.

(2) Under a sale or return unless otherwise agreed

(a) The option to return extends to the whole or any commercial unit of the goods while in substantially their original condition, but must be exercised seasonably; and

(b) The return is at the buyer's risk and expense.

2328. (1) In a sale by auction if goods are put up in lots each lot is the subject of a separate sale.

(2) A sale by auction is complete when the auctioneer so announces by the fall of the hammer or in other customary manner. Where a bid is made while the hammer is falling in acceptance of a prior bid the auctioneer may in his discretion reopen the bidding or declare the goods sold under the bid on which the hammer was falling.

(3) Such a sale is with reserve unless the goods are in explicit terms put up without reserve. In an auction with reserve the auctioneer may withdraw the goods at any time until he announces completion of the sale. In an auction without reserve, after the auctioneer calls for bids on an article or lot, that article or lot cannot be withdrawn unless no bid is made within a reasonable time. In either case a bidder may retract his bid until the auctioneer's announcement of completion of the sale, but a bidder's retraction does not revive any previous bid.

(4) If the auctioneer knowingly receives a bid on the seller's behalf or the seller makes or procures such a bid, and notice has not been given that liberty for

such bidding is reserved, the buyer may at his option avoid the sale or take the goods at the price of the last good faith bid prior to the completion of the sale. This subdivision shall not apply to any bid at a forced sale.

2401. Each provision of this division with regard to the rights, obligations, and remedies of the seller, the buyer, purchasers or other third parties applies irrespective of title to the goods except where the provision refers to such title. Insofar as situations are not covered by the other provisions of this division and matters concerning title become material the following rules apply:

(1) Title to goods cannot pass under a contract for sale prior to their identification to the contract (Section 2501), and unless otherwise explicitly agreed the buyer acquires by their identification a special property as limited by this code. Any retention or reservation by the seller of the title (property) in goods shipped or delivered to the buyer is limited in effect to a reservation of a security interest. Subject to these provisions and to the provisions of the division on secured transactions (Division 9), title to goods passes from the seller to the buyer in any manner and on any conditions explicitly agreed on by the parties.

(2) Unless otherwise explicitly agreed title passes to the buyer at the time and place at which the seller completes his performance with reference to the physical delivery of the goods, despite any reservation of a security interest and even though a document of title is to be delivered at a different time or place; and in particular and despite any reservation of a security interest by the bill of lading

(a) If the contract requires or authorizes the seller to send the goods to the buyer but does not require him to deliver them at destination, title passes to the buyer at the time and place of shipment; but

(b) If the contract requires delivery at destination, title passes on tender there.

(3) Unless otherwise explicitly agreed where delivery is to be made without moving the goods,

(a) If the seller is to deliver a tangible document of title, title passes at the time when and the place where he delivers such documents and if the seller is to deliver an electronic document of title, title passes when the seller delivers the document; or

(b) If the goods are at the time of contracting already identified and no documents of title are to be delivered, title passes at the time and place of contracting.

(4) A rejection or other refusal by the buyer to receive or retain the goods, whether or not justified, or a justified revocation of acceptance revests title to the goods in the seller. Such revesting occurs by operation of law and is not a "sale."

2402. (1) Except as provided in subdivisions (2) and (3), rights of unsecured creditors of the seller with respect to goods which have been identified to a contract for sale are subject to the buyer's rights to recover the goods under this division (Sections 2502 and 2716).

(2) A creditor of the seller may treat a sale or an identification of goods to a contract for sale as void if as against him or her a retention of possession by the seller is fraudulent or void under any rule of law of the state where the goods are situated, except that retention of possession in good faith and current course of trade by a merchant-seller for a commercially reasonable time after a sale or identification is not fraudulent or void.

(3) Nothing in this division shall be deemed to impair the rights of creditors of the seller:

(a) Under the provisions of the division on secured transactions (Division 9); or

(b) Where identification to the contract or delivery is made not in current course of trade but in satisfaction of or as security for a pre-existing claim for money, security, or the like and is made under circumstances which under any rule of law of the state where the goods are situated would apart from this division constitute the transaction a fraudulent transfer or voidable preference.

2403. (1) A purchaser of goods acquires all title which his transferor had or had power to transfer except that a purchaser of a limited interest acquires rights only to the extent of the interest purchased. A person with voidable title has power to transfer a good title to a good faith purchaser for value. When goods have been delivered under a transaction of purchase the purchaser has such power even though

(a) The transferor was deceived as to the identity of the purchaser, or

(b) The delivery was in exchange for a check which is later dishonored, or

(c) It was agreed that the transaction was to be a "cash sale," or

(d) The delivery was procured through fraud punishable as larcenous under the criminal law.

(2) Any entrusting of possession of goods to a merchant who deals in goods of that kind gives him power to transfer all rights of the entruster to a buyer in ordinary course of business.

(3) "Entrusting" includes any delivery and any acquiescence in retention of possession for the purpose of sale, obtaining offers to purchase, locating a buyer, or the like; regardless of any condition expressed between the parties to the delivery or acquiescence and regardless of whether the procurement of the entrusting or the possessor's disposition of the goods have been such as to be larcenous under the criminal law.

(4) The rights of other purchasers of goods and of lien creditors are governed by the divisions on secured transactions (Division 9), bulk transfers (Division 6), and documents of title (Division 7).

2501. (1) The buyer obtains a special property and an insurable interest in goods by identification of existing goods as goods to which the contract refers even though the goods so identified are nonconforming and he has an option to return or reject them. Such identification can be made at any time and in any manner explicitly agreed to by the parties. In the absence of explicit agreement identification occurs

(a) When the contract is made if it is for the sale of goods already existing and identified;

(b) If the contract is for the sale of future goods other than those described in paragraph (c), when goods are shipped, marked or otherwise designated by the seller as goods to which the contract refers;

(c) If the contract is for the sale of unborn young or future crops, when the crops are planted or otherwise become growing crops or the young are conceived.

(2) The seller retains an insurable interest in goods so long as title to or any security interest in the goods remains in him and where the identification is by the seller alone he may until default or insolvency or notification to the buyer that the identification is final substitute other goods for those identified.

(3) Nothing in this section impairs any insurable interest recognized under any other statute or rule of law.

2502. (1) Subject to subdivisions (2) and (3), and even though the goods have not been shipped, a buyer who has paid a part or all of the price of goods in which he or she has a special property under the provisions of the immediately preceding section may on making and keeping good a tender of any unpaid portion of their price recover them from the seller if either:

(a) In the case of goods bought for personal, family, or household purposes, the seller repudiates or fails to deliver as required by the contract.

(b) In all cases, the seller becomes insolvent within 10 days after receipt of the first installment on their price.

(2) The buyer's right to recover the goods under paragraph (a) of subdivision (1) vests upon acquisition of a special property, even if the seller had not then repudiated or failed to deliver.

(3) If the identification creating his or her special property has been made by the buyer, he or she acquires the right to recover the goods only if they conform to the contract for sale.

2503. (1) Tender of delivery requires that the seller put and hold conforming goods at the buyer's disposition and give the buyer any notification reasonably necessary to enable him to take delivery. The manner, time, and place for tender are determined by the agreement and this division, and in particular

(a) Tender must be at a reasonable hour, and if it is of goods they must be kept available for the period reasonably necessary to enable the buyer to take possession; but

(b) Unless otherwise agreed, the buyer must furnish facilities reasonably suited to the receipt of the goods.

(2) Where the case is within the next section respecting shipment tender requires that the seller comply with its provisions.

(3) Where the seller is required to deliver at a particular destination tender requires that he comply with subdivision (1) and also in any appropriate case tender documents as described in subdivisions (4) and (5) of this section.

(4) Where goods are in the possession of a bailee and are to be delivered without being moved

(a) Tender requires that the seller either tender a negotiable document of title covering such goods or procure acknowledgment by the bailee of the buyer's right to possession of the goods; but

(b) Tender to the buyer of a nonnegotiable document of title or of a record directing the bailee to deliver is sufficient tender unless the buyer seasonably objects, and except as otherwise provided in Division 9 (commencing with Section 9101), receipt by the bailee of notification of the buyer's rights fixes those rights as against the bailee and all third persons; but risk of loss of the goods and of any failure by the bailee to honor the nonnegotiable document of title or to obey the direction remains on the seller until the buyer has had a reasonable time to present the document or direction, and a refusal by the bailee to honor the document or to obey the direction defeats the tender.

(5) Where the contract requires the seller to deliver documents

(a) He must tender all such documents in correct form, except as provided in this division with respect to bills of lading in a set (subdivision (2) of Section 2323); and

(b) Tender through customary banking channels is sufficient and dishonor of a draft accompanying or associated with the documents constitutes nonacceptance or rejection.

2504. Where the seller is required or authorized to send the goods to the buyer and the contract does not require him to deliver them at a particular destination, then unless otherwise agreed he must (a) put the goods in the possession of such a carrier and make such a contract for their transportation as may be reasonable having regard to the nature of the goods and other circumstances of the case; and (b) obtain and promptly deliver or tender in due form any document necessary to enable the buyer to obtain possession of the goods or otherwise required by the agreement or by usage of trade; and (c) promptly notify the buyer of the shipment. Failure to notify the buyer under paragraph (c) or to make a proper contract under paragraph (a) is a ground for rejection only if material delay or loss ensues.

2505. (1) Where the seller has identified goods to the contract by or before shipment:

(a) His procurement of a negotiable bill of lading to his own order or otherwise reserves in him a security interest in the goods. His procurement of the bill to the order of a financing agency or of the buyer indicates in addition only the seller's expectation of transferring that interest to the person named.

(b) A nonnegotiable bill of lading to himself or his nominee reserves possession of the goods as security but except in a case of conditional delivery (subdivision (2) of Section 2507) a nonnegotiable bill of lading naming the buyer as consignee reserves no security interest even though the seller retains possession or control of the bill of lading.

(2) When shipment by the seller with reservation of a security interest is in violation of the contract for sale it constitutes an improper contract for transportation within the preceding section but impairs neither the rights given to the buyer by shipment and identification of the goods to the contract nor the seller's powers as a holder of a negotiable document of title.

2506. (1) A financing agency by paying or purchasing for value a draft which relates to a shipment of goods acquires to the extent of the payment or purchase and in addition to its own rights under the draft and any document of title securing it any rights of the shipper in the goods including the right to stop delivery and the shipper's right to have the draft honored by the buyer.

(2) The right to reimbursement of a financing agency which has in good faith honored or purchased the draft under commitment to or authority from the buyer is not impaired by subsequent discovery of defects with reference to any relevant document which was apparently regular.

2507. (1) Tender of delivery is a condition to the buyer's duty to accept the goods and, unless otherwise agreed, to his duty to pay for them. Tender entitles the seller to acceptance of the goods and to payment according to the contract.

(2) Where payment is due and demanded on the delivery to the buyer of goods or documents of title, his right as against the seller to retain or dispose of them is conditional upon his making the payment due.

2508. (1) Where any tender or delivery by the seller is rejected because nonconforming and the time for performance has not yet expired, the seller may seasonably notify the buyer of his intention to cure and may then within the contract time make a conforming delivery.

(2) Where the buyer rejects a nonconforming tender which the seller had reasonable grounds to believe would be acceptable with or without money allowance the seller may, if he seasonally notifies the buyer, have a further reasonable time to substitute a conforming tender.

2509. (1) Where the contract requires or authorizes the seller to ship the goods by carrier

(a) If it does not require him to deliver them at a particular destination, the risk of loss passes to the buyer when the goods are duly delivered to the carrier even though the shipment is under reservation (Section 2505); but

(b) If it does require him to deliver them at a particular destination and the goods are there duly tendered while in the possession of the carrier, the risk of loss passes to the buyer when the goods are there duly so tendered as to enable the buyer to take delivery.

(2) Where the goods are held by a bailee to be delivered without being moved, the risk of loss passes to the buyer

(a) On his receipt of possession or control of a negotiable document of title covering the goods; or

(b) On acknowledgment by the bailee of the buyer's right to possession of the goods; or

(c) After his receipt of possession or control of a nonnegotiable document of title or other direction to deliver in a record, as provided in subdivision (4)(b) of Section 2503.

(3) In any case not within subdivision (1) or (2), the risk of loss passes to the buyer on his receipt of the goods if the seller is a merchant; otherwise the risk passes to the buyer on tender of delivery.

(4) The provisions of this section are subject to contrary agreement of the parties and to the provisions of this division on sale on approval (Section 2327) and on effect of breach on risk of loss (Section 2510).

2510. (1) Where a tender or delivery of goods so fails to conform to the contract as to give a right of rejection the risk of their loss remains on the seller until cure or acceptance.

(2) Where the buyer rightfully revokes acceptance he may to the extent of any deficiency in his effective insurance coverage treat the risk of loss as having rested on the seller from the beginning.

(3) Where the buyer as to conforming goods already identified to the contract for sale repudiates or is otherwise in breach before risk of their loss has passed to him, the seller may to the extent of any deficiency in his effective insurance coverage treat the risk of loss as resting on the buyer for a commercially reasonable time.

2511. (1) Unless otherwise agreed, tender of payment is a condition to the seller's duty to tender and complete any delivery.

(2) Tender of payment is sufficient when made by any means or in any manner current in the ordinary course of business unless the seller demands payment in legal tender and gives any extension of time reasonably necessary to procure it.

(3) Subject to the provisions of this code on the effect of an instrument on an obligation (Section 3310), payment by check is conditional and is defeated as between the parties by dishonor of the check on due presentment.

2512. (1) Where the contract requires payment before inspection nonconformity of the goods does not excuse the buyer from so making payment unless (a) the nonconformity appears without inspection or (b) despite tender of the required documents the circumstances would justify injunction against honor under this code (subdivision (b) of Section 5109).

(2) Payment pursuant to subdivision (1) does not constitute an acceptance of goods or impair the buyer's right to inspect or any of his remedies.

2513. (1) Unless otherwise agreed and subject to subdivision (3), where goods are tendered or delivered or identified to the contract for sale, the buyer has a right before payment or acceptance to inspect them at any reasonable place and time and in any reasonable manner. When the seller is required or authorized to send the goods to the buyer, the inspection may be after their arrival.

(2) Expenses of inspection must be borne by the buyer but may be recovered from the seller if the goods do not conform and are rejected.

(3) Unless otherwise agreed and subject to the provisions of this division on C.I.F. contracts (subdivision (3) of Section 2321), the buyer is not entitled to inspect the goods before payment of the price when the contract provides

(a) For delivery "C.O.D." or on other like terms; or

(b) For payment against documents of title, except where such payment is due only after the goods are to become available for inspection.

(4) A place or method of inspection fixed by the parties is presumed to be exclusive but unless otherwise expressly agreed it does not postpone identification or shift the place for delivery or for passing the risk of loss. If compliance becomes impossible, inspection shall be as provided in this section unless the place or method fixed was clearly intended as an indispensable condition failure of which avoids the contract.

2514. Unless otherwise agreed documents against which a draft is drawn are to be delivered to the drawee on acceptance of the draft if it is payable more than three days after presentment; otherwise, only on payment.

2515. In furtherance of the adjustment of any claim or dispute

(a) Either party on reasonable notification to the other and for the purpose of ascertaining the facts and preserving evidence has the right to inspect, test, and sample the goods including such of them as may be in the possession or control of the other; and

(b) The parties may agree to a third party inspection or survey to determine the conformity or condition of the goods and may agree that the findings shall be binding upon them in any subsequent litigation or adjustment.

2601. Subject to the provisions of this division on breach in installment contracts (Section 2612) and unless otherwise agreed under the sections on contractual limitations of remedy (Sections 2718 and 2719), if the goods or the tender of delivery fail in any respect to conform to the contract, the buyer may

(a) Reject the whole; or

(b) Accept the whole; or

(c) Accept any commercial unit or units and reject the rest.

2602. (1) Rejection of goods must be within a reasonable time after their delivery or tender. It is ineffective unless the buyer seasonably notifies the seller.

(2) Subject to the provisions of the two following sections on rejected goods (Sections 2603 and 2604),

(a) After rejection any exercise of ownership by the buyer with respect to any commercial unit is wrongful as against the seller; and

(b) If the buyer has before rejection taken physical possession of goods in which he does not have a security interest under the provisions of this division (subdivision (3) of Section 2711), he is under a duty after rejection to hold them with reasonable care at the seller's disposition for a time sufficient to permit the seller to remove them; but

(c) The buyer has no further obligations with regard to goods rightfully rejected.

(3) The seller's rights with respect to goods wrongfully rejected are governed by the provisions of this division on seller's remedies in general (Section 2703).

2603. (1) Subject to any security interest in the buyer (subdivision (3) of Section 2711), when the seller has no agent or place of business at the market of rejection a merchant buyer is under a duty after rejection of goods in his possession or control to follow any reasonable instructions received from the seller with respect to the goods and in the absence of such instructions to make reasonable efforts to sell them for the seller's account if they are perishable or threaten to decline in value speedily. Instructions are not reasonable if on demand indemnity for expenses is not forthcoming.

(2) When the buyer sells goods under subdivision (1), he is entitled to reimbursement from the seller or out of the proceeds for reasonable expenses of caring for and selling them, and if the expenses include no selling commission then to such commission as is usual in the trade or if there is none to a reasonable sum not exceeding 10 percent on the gross proceeds.

(3) In complying with this section the buyer is held only to good faith and good faith conduct hereunder is neither acceptance nor conversion nor the basis of an action for damages.

2604. Subject to the provisions of the immediately preceding section on perishables if the seller gives no instructions within a reasonable time after notification of rejection the buyer may store the rejected goods for the seller's account or reship them to him or resell them for the seller's account with reimbursement as provided in the preceding section. Such action is not acceptance or conversion.

2605. (1) The buyer's failure to state in connection with rejection a particular defect which is ascertainable by reasonable inspection precludes him from relying on the unstated defect to justify rejection or to establish breach

(a) Where the seller could have cured it if stated seasonably; or

(b) Between merchants when the seller has after rejection made a request in writing for a full and final written statement of all defects on which the buyer proposes to rely.

(2) Payment against documents made without reservation of rights precludes recovery of the payment for defects apparent in the documents.

2606. (1) Acceptance of goods occurs when the buyer

(a) After a reasonable opportunity to inspect the goods signifies to the seller that the goods are conforming or that he will take or retain them in spite of their nonconformity; or

(b) Fails to make an effective rejection (subdivision (1) of Section 2602), but such acceptance does not occur until the buyer has had a reasonable opportunity to inspect them; or

(c) Does any act inconsistent with the seller's ownership; but if such act is wrongful as against the seller it is an acceptance only if ratified by him.

(2) Acceptance of a part of any commercial unit is acceptance of that entire unit.

2607. (1) The buyer must pay at the contract rate for any goods accepted.

(2) Acceptance of goods by the buyer precludes rejection of the goods accepted and, if made with knowledge of a nonconformity, cannot be revoked because of it unless the acceptance was on the reasonable assumption that the nonconformity would be seasonably cured. Acceptance does not of itself impair any other remedy provided by this division for nonconformity.

(3) Where a tender has been accepted:

(a) The buyer must, within a reasonable time after he or she discovers or should have discovered any breach, notify the seller of breach or be barred from any remedy; and

(b) If the claim is one for infringement or the like (subdivision (3) of Section 2312) and the buyer is sued as a result of such a breach, the buyer must so notify the seller within a reasonable time after he or she receives notice of the litigation or be barred from any remedy over for liability established by the litigation.

(4) The burden is on the buyer to establish any breach with respect to the goods accepted.

(5) Where the buyer is sued for breach of a warranty or other obligation for which his or her seller is answerable over:

(a) He or she may give the seller written notice of the litigation. If the notice states that the seller may defend and that if the seller does not do so he or she will be bound in any action against the seller by the buyer by any determination of fact common to the two litigation actions, then unless the seller after seasonable receipt of the notice does defend he or she is so bound.

(b) If the claim is one for infringement or the like (subdivision (3) of Section 2312) the original seller may demand in writing that the buyer turn over to the seller control of the litigation, including settlement, or else be barred from any remedy over and if the seller also agrees to bear all expense and to satisfy any adverse judgment, then unless the buyer after seasonable receipt of the demand does turn over control the buyer is so barred.

(6) The provisions of subdivisions (3), (4), and (5) apply to any obligation of a buyer to hold the seller harmless against infringement or the like (subdivision (3) of Section 2312).

2608. (1) The buyer may revoke his acceptance of a lot or commercial unit whose nonconformity substantially impairs its value to him if he has accepted it

(a) On the reasonable assumption that its nonconformity would be cured and it has not been seasonably cured; or

(b) Without discovery of such nonconformity if his acceptance was reasonably induced either by the difficulty of discovery before acceptance or by the seller's assurances.

(2) Revocation of acceptance must occur within a reasonable time after the buyer discovers or should have discovered the ground for it and before any substantial change in condition of the goods which is not caused by their own defects. It is not effective until the buyer notifies the seller of it.

(3) A buyer who so revokes has the same rights and duties with regard to the goods involved as if he had rejected them.

2609. (1) A contract for sale imposes an obligation on each party that the other's expectation of receiving due performance will not be impaired. When reasonable grounds for insecurity arise with respect to the performance of either party the other may in writing demand adequate assurance of due performance and until he receives such assurance may if commercially reasonable suspend any performance for which he has not already received the agreed return.

(2) Between merchants the reasonableness of grounds for insecurity and the adequacy of any assurance offered shall be determined according to commercial standards.

(3) Acceptance of any improper delivery or payment does not prejudice the aggrieved party's right to demand adequate assurance of future performance.

(4) After receipt of a justified demand failure to provide within a reasonable time not exceeding 30 days such assurance of due performance as is adequate under the circumstances of the particular case is a repudiation of the contract.

2610. When either party repudiates the contract with respect to a performance not yet due the loss of which will substantially impair the value of the contract to the other, the aggrieved party may

(a) For a commercially reasonable time await performance by the repudiating party; or

(b) Resort to any remedy for breach (Section 2703 or Section 2711), even though he has notified the repudiating party that he would await the latter's performance and has urged retraction; and

(c) In either case suspend his own performance or proceed in accordance with the provisions of this division on the seller's right to identify goods to the contract notwithstanding breach or to salvage unfinished goods (Section 2704).

2611. (1) Until the repudiating party's next performance is due he can retract his repudiation unless the aggrieved party has since the repudiation canceled or materially changed his position or otherwise indicated that he considers the repudiation final.

(2) Retraction may be by any method which clearly indicates to the aggrieved party that the repudiating party intends to perform, but must include any assurance justifiably demanded under the provisions of this division (Section 2609).

(3) Retraction reinstates the repudiating party's rights under the contract with due excuse and allowance to the aggrieved party for any delay occasioned by the repudiation.

2612. (1) An "installment contract" is one which requires or authorizes the delivery of goods in separate lots to be separately accepted, even though the contract contains a clause "each delivery is a separate contract" or its equivalent.

(2) The buyer may reject any installment which is nonconforming if the nonconformity substantially impairs the value of that installment and cannot be cured or if the nonconformity is a defect in the required documents; but if the nonconformity does not fall within subdivision (3) and the seller gives adequate assurance of its cure the buyer must accept that installment.

(3) Whenever nonconformity or default with respect to one or more installments substantially impairs the value of the whole contract there is a breach of the whole. But the aggrieved party reinstates the contract if he accepts a nonconforming installment without seasonably notifying of cancellation or if he brings an action with respect only to past installments or demands performance as to future installments.

2613. Where the contract requires for its performance goods identified when the contract is made, and the goods suffer casualty without fault of either party before the risk of loss passes to the buyer, or in a proper case under a "no arrival, no sale" term (Section 2324) then

(a) If the loss is total the contract is avoided; and

(b) If the loss is partial or the goods have so deteriorated as no longer to conform to the contract the buyer may nevertheless demand inspection and at his option either treat the contract as avoided or accept the goods with due allowance from the contract price for the deterioration or the deficiency in quantity but without further right against the seller.

2614. (1) Where without fault of either party the agreed berthing, loading, or unloading facilities fail or an agreed type of carrier becomes unavailable or the agreed manner of delivery otherwise becomes commercially impracticable but a commercially reasonable substitute is available, such substitute performance must be tendered and accepted.

(2) If the agreed means or manner of payment fails because of domestic or foreign governmental regulation, the seller may withhold or stop delivery unless the buyer provides a means or manner of payment which is commercially a substantial equivalent. If delivery has already been taken, payment by the means or in the manner provided by the regulation discharges the buyer's obligation unless the regulation is discriminatory, oppressive or predatory.

2615. Except so far as a seller may have assumed a greater obligation and subject to the preceding section on substituted performance:

(a) Delay in delivery or nondelivery in whole or in part by a seller who complies with paragraphs (b) and (c) is not a breach of his duty under a contract for sale if performance as agreed has been made impracticable by the occurrence of a contingency the nonoccurrence of which was a basic assumption on which the contract was made or by compliance in good faith with any applicable foreign or domestic governmental regulation or order whether or not it later proves to be invalid.

(b) Where the causes mentioned in paragraph (a) affect only a part of the seller's capacity to perform, he must allocate production and deliveries among his customers but may at his option include regular customers not then under contract as well as his own requirements for further manufacture. He may so allocate in any manner which is fair and reasonable.

(c) The seller must notify the buyer seasonably that there will be delay or nondelivery and, when allocation is required under paragraph (b), of the estimated quota thus made available for the buyer.

2616. (1) Where the buyer receives notification of a material or indefinite delay or an allocation justified under the preceding section he may by written notification to the seller as to any delivery concerned, and where the prospective deficiency substantially impairs the value of the whole contract under the provisions of this division relating to breach of installment contracts (Section 2612), then also as to the whole,

(a) Terminate and thereby discharge any unexecuted portion of the contract; or

(b) Modify the contract by agreeing to take his available quota in substitution.

(2) If after receipt of such notification from the seller the buyer fails so to modify the contract within a reasonable time not exceeding 30 days the contract lapses with respect to any deliveries affected.

(3) The provisions of this section may not be negated by agreement except insofar as the seller has assumed a greater obligation under the preceding section.

2701. Remedies for breach of any obligation or promise collateral or ancillary to a contract for sale are not impaired by the provisions of this division.

2702. (1) Where the seller discovers the buyer to be insolvent he may refuse delivery except for cash including payment for all goods theretofore delivered under the contract, and stop delivery under this division (Section 2705).

(2) Where the seller discovers that the buyer has received goods on credit while insolvent he may reclaim the goods upon demand made within 10 days after the receipt, but if misrepresentation of solvency has been made to the particular seller in writing within three months before delivery the 10-day limitation does not apply. Except as provided in this subdivision the seller may not base a right to reclaim goods on the buyer's fraudulent or innocent misrepresentation of solvency or of intent to pay.

(3) The seller's right to reclaim under subdivision (2) is subject to the rights of a buyer in ordinary course or other good faith purchaser under this division (Section 2403). Successful reclamation of goods excludes all other remedies with respect to them.

2703. Where the buyer wrongfully rejects or revokes acceptance of goods or fails to make a payment due on or before delivery or repudiates with respect to a part or the whole, then with respect to any goods directly affected and, if the breach is of the whole contract (Section 2612), then also with respect to the whole undelivered balance, the aggrieved seller may

(a) Withhold delivery of such goods;

(b) Stop delivery by any bailee as hereafter provided (Section 2705);

(c) Proceed under the next section respecting goods still unidentified to the contract;

(d) Resell and recover damages as hereafter provided (Section 2706);

(e) Recover damages for nonacceptance (Section 2708) or in a proper case the price (Section 2709);

(f) Cancel.

2704. (1) An aggrieved seller under the preceding section may

(a) Identify to the contract conforming goods not already identified if at the time he learned of the breach they are in his possession or control;

(b) Treat as the subject of resale goods which have demonstrably been intended for the particular contract even though those goods are unfinished.

(2) Where the goods are unfinished an aggrieved seller may in the exercise of reasonable commercial judgment for the purposes of avoiding loss and of effective realization either complete the manufacture and wholly identify the goods to the contract or cease manufacture and resell for scrap or salvage value or proceed in any other reasonable manner.

2705. (1) The seller may stop delivery of goods in the possession of a carrier or other bailee when he discovers the buyer to be insolvent (Section 2702) and may stop delivery of carload, truckload, planeload, or larger shipments of express or freight when the buyer repudiates or fails to make a payment due before delivery or if for any other reason the seller has a right to withhold or reclaim the goods.

(2) As against such buyer the seller may stop delivery until

(a) Receipt of the goods by the buyer; or

(b) Acknowledgment to the buyer by any bailee of the goods except a carrier that the bailee holds the goods for the buyer; or

(c) Such acknowledgment to the buyer by a carrier by reshipment or as a warehouse; or

(d) Negotiation to the buyer of any negotiable document of title covering the goods.

(3) To stop delivery the seller must so notify as to enable the bailee by reasonable diligence to prevent delivery of the goods.

(a) After such notification the bailee must hold and deliver the goods according to the directions of the seller but the seller is liable to the bailee for any ensuing charges or damages.

(b) If a negotiable document of title has been issued for goods the bailee is not obliged to obey a notification to stop until surrender of possession or control of the document.

(c) A carrier who has issued a nonnegotiable bill of lading is not obliged to obey a notification to stop received from a person other than the consignor.

2706. (1) Under the conditions stated in Section 2703 on seller's remedies, the seller may resell the goods concerned or the undelivered balance thereof. Where the resale is made in good faith and in a commercially reasonable manner the seller may recover the difference between the resale price and the contract price together with any incidental damages allowed under the provisions of this division (Section 2710), but less expenses saved in consequence of the buyer's breach.

(2) Except as otherwise provided in subdivision (3) or unless otherwise agreed resale may be at public or private sale including sale by way of one or more contracts to sell or of identification to an existing contract of the seller. Sale may be as a unit or in parcels and at any time and place and on any terms but every aspect of the sale including the method, manner, time, place and terms must be commercially reasonable. The resale must be reasonably identified as referring to the broken contract, but it is not

necessary that the goods be in existence or that any or all of them have been identified to the contract before the breach.

(3) Where the resale is at private sale the seller must give the buyer reasonable notification of his intention to resell.

(4) Where the resale is at public sale

(a) Only identified goods can be sold except where there is a recognized market for a public sale of futures in goods of the kind; and

(b) It must be made at a usual place or market for public sale if one is reasonably available and except in the case of goods which are perishable or threaten to decline in value speedily the seller must give the buyer reasonable notice of the time and place of the resale; and

(c) If the goods are not to be within the view of those attending the sale the notification of sale must state the place where the goods are located and provide for their reasonable inspection by prospective bidders; and

(d) The seller may buy.

(5) A purchaser who buys in good faith at a resale takes the goods free of any rights of the original buyer even though the seller fails to comply with one or more of the requirements of this section.

(6) The seller is not accountable to the buyer for any profit made on any resale. A person in the position of a seller (Section 2707) or a buyer who has rightfully rejected or justifiably revoked acceptance must account for any excess over the amount of his security interest, as hereinafter defined (subdivision (3) of Section 2711).

2707. (1) A "person in the position of a seller" includes as against a principal an agent who has paid or become responsible for the price of goods on behalf of his principal or anyone who otherwise holds a security interest or other right in goods similar to that of a seller.

(2) A person in the position of a seller may as provided in this division withhold or stop delivery (Section 2705) and resell (Section 2706) and recover incidental damages (Section 2710).

2708. (1) Subject to subdivision (2) and to the provisions of this division with respect to proof of market price (Section 2723), the measure of damages for non-acceptance or repudiation by the buyer is the difference between the market price at the time and place for tender and the unpaid contract price together with any incidental damages provided in this division (Section 2710), but less expenses saved in consequence of the buyer's breach.

(2) If the measure of damages provided in subdivision (1) is inadequate to put the seller in as good a position as performance would have done then the measure of damages is the profit (including reasonable overhead) which the seller would have made from full performance by the buyer, together with any incidental damages provided in this division (Section 2710), due allowance for costs reasonably incurred and due credit for payments or proceeds of resale.

2709. (1) When the buyer fails to pay the price as it becomes due the seller may recover, together with any incidental damages under the next section, the price

(a) Of goods accepted or of conforming goods lost or damaged within a commercially reasonable time after risk of their loss has passed to the buyer; and

(b) Of goods identified to the contract if the seller is unable after reasonable effort to resell them at a reasonable price or the circumstances reasonably indicate that such effort will be unavailing.

(2) Where the seller sues for the price he must hold for the buyer any goods which have been identified to the contract and are still in his control except that if resale becomes possible he may resell them at any time prior to the collection of the judgment. The net proceeds of any such resale must be credited to the buyer and payment of the judgment entitles him to any goods not resold.

(3) After the buyer has wrongfully rejected or revoked acceptance of the goods or has failed to make a payment due or has repudiated (Section 2610), a seller who is held not entitled to the price under this section shall nevertheless be awarded damages for nonacceptance under the preceding section.

2710. Incidental damages to an aggrieved seller include any commercially reasonable charges, expenses, or commissions incurred in stopping delivery, in the transportation, care, and custody of goods after the buyers' breach, in connection with return or resale of the goods or otherwise resulting from the breach.

2711. (1) Where the seller fails to make delivery or repudiates or the buyer rightfully rejects or justifiably revokes acceptance then with respect to any goods involved, and with respect to the whole if the breach goes to the whole contract (Section 2612), the buyer may cancel and whether or not he has done so may in addition to recovering so much of the price as has been paid

(a) "Cover" and have damages under the next section as to all the goods affected whether or not they have been identified to the contract; or

(b) Recover damages for nondelivery as provided in this division (Section 2713).

(2) Where the seller fails to deliver or repudiates the buyer may also

(a) If the goods have been identified recover them as provided in the division (Section 2502); or

(b) In a proper case obtain specific performance or replevy the goods as provided in this division (Section 2716).

(3) On rightful rejection or justifiable revocation of acceptance a buyer has a security interest in goods in his possession or control for any payments made on their price and any expenses reasonably incurred in their inspection, receipt, transportation, care, and custody and may hold such goods and resell them in like manner as an aggrieved seller (Section 2706).

2712. (1) After a breach within the preceding section the buyer may "cover" by making in good faith and without unreasonable delay any reasonable purchase of or contract to purchase goods in substitution for those due from the seller.

(2) The buyer may recover from the seller as damages the difference between the cost of cover and the contract price together with any incidental or consequential damages as hereinafter defined (Section 2715), but less expenses saved in consequence of the seller's breach.

(3) Failure of the buyer to effect cover within this section does not bar him from any other remedy.

2713. (1) Subject to the provisions of this division with respect to proof of market price (Section 2723), the measure of damages for nondelivery or repudiation by the seller is the difference between the market price at the time when the buyer learned of the breach and the contract price together with any incidental and consequential damages provided in this division (Section 2715), but less expenses saved in consequence of the seller's breach.

(2) Market price is to be determined as of the place for tender or, in cases of rejection after arrival or revocation of acceptance, as of the place of arrival.

2714. (1) Where the buyer has accepted goods and given notification (subdivision (3) of Section 2607) he or she may recover, as damages for any nonconformity of tender, the loss resulting in the ordinary course of events from the seller's breach as determined in any manner that is reasonable.

(2) The measure of damages for breach of warranty is the difference at the time and place of acceptance between the value of the goods accepted and the value they would have had if they had been as warranted, unless special circumstances show proximate damages of a different amount.

(3) In a proper case any incidental and consequential damages under Section 2715 also may be recovered.

2715. (1) Incidental damages resulting from the seller's breach include expenses reasonably incurred in inspection, receipt, transportation and care and custody of goods rightfully rejected, any commercially reasonable charges, expenses, or commissions in connection with effecting cover and any other reasonable expense incident to the delay or other breach.

(2) Consequential damages resulting from the seller's breach include

(a) Any loss resulting from general or particular requirements and needs of which the seller at the time of contracting had reason to know and which could not reasonably be prevented by cover or otherwise; and

(b) Injury to person or property proximately resulting from any breach of warranty.

2716. (1) Specific performance may be decreed where the goods are unique or in other proper circumstances.

(2) The decree for specific performance may include such terms and conditions as to payment of the price, damages, or other relief as the court may deem just.

(3) The buyer has a right of replevin for goods identified to the contract if after reasonable effort he or she is unable to effect cover for such goods or the circumstances reasonably indicate that such effort will be unavailing or if the goods have been shipped under reservation and satisfaction of the security interest in them has been made or tendered. In the case of goods bought for personal, family, or household purposes, the buyer's right of replevin vests upon acquisition of a special property, even if the seller had not then repudiated or failed to deliver.

2717. The buyer on notifying the seller of his intention to do so may deduct all or any part of the damages resulting from any breach of the contract from any part of the price still due under the same contract.

2718. (1) Damages for breach by either party may be liquidated in the agreement subject to and in compliance with Section 1671 of the Civil Code. If the agreement provides for liquidation of damages, and such provision does not comply with Section 1671 of the Civil Code, remedy may be had as provided in this division.

(2) Where the seller justifiably withholds delivery of goods because of the buyer's breach, the buyer is entitled to restitution of any amount by which the sum of his or her payments exceeds:

(a) The amount to which the seller is entitled by virtue of terms liquidating the seller's damages in accordance with subdivision (1), or

(b) In the absence of such terms, 20 percent of the value of the total performance for which the buyer is obligated under the contract or five hundred dollars ($500), whichever is smaller.

(3) The buyer's right to restitution under subdivision (2) is subject to offset to the extent that the seller establishes:

(a) A right to recover damages under the provisions of this chapter other than subdivision (1), and

(b) The amount or value of any benefits received by the buyer directly or indirectly by reason of the contract.

(4) Where a seller has received payment in goods their reasonable value or the proceeds of their resale shall be treated as payments for the purposes of subdivision (2); but if the seller has notice of the buyer's breach before reselling goods received in part performance, his or her resale is subject to the conditions laid down in this division on resale by an aggrieved seller (Section 2706).

2719. (1) Subject to the provisions of subdivisions (2) and (3) of this section and of the preceding section on liquidation and limitation of damages,

(a) The agreement may provide for remedies in addition to or in substitution for those provided in this division and may limit or alter the measure of damages recoverable under this division, as by limiting the buyer's remedies to return of the goods and repayment of the price or to repair and replacement of nonconforming goods or parts; and

(b) Resort to a remedy as provided is optional unless the remedy is expressly agreed to be exclusive, in which case it is the sole remedy.

(2) Where circumstances cause an exclusive or limited remedy to fail of its essential purpose, remedy may be had as provided in this code.

(3) Consequential damages may be limited or excluded unless the limitation or exclusion is unconscionable. Limitation of consequential damages for injury to the person in the case of consumer goods is invalid unless it is proved that the limitation is not unconscionable. Limitation of consequential damages where the loss is commercial is valid unless it is proved that the limitation is unconscionable.

2720. Unless the contrary intention clearly appears, expressions of "cancellation" or "rescission" of the contract or the like shall not be construed as a renunciation or discharge of any claim in damages for an antecedent breach.

2721. Remedies for material misrepresentation or fraud include all remedies available under this division for nonfraudulent breach. Neither rescission or a claim for rescission of the contract for sale nor rejection or return of the goods shall bar or be deemed inconsistent with a claim for damages or other remedy.

2722. Where a third party so deals with goods which have been identified to a contract for sale as to cause actionable injury to a party to that contract

(a) A right of action against the third party is in either party to the contract for sale who has title to or a security interest or a special property or an insurable interest in the goods; and if the goods have been destroyed or converted a right of action is also in the party who either bore the risk of loss under the contract for sale or has since the injury assumed that risk as against the other;

(b) If at the time of the injury the party plaintiff did not bear the risk of loss as against the other party to the contract for sale and there is no arrangement between them for disposition of the recovery, his suit or settlement is, subject to his own interest, as a fiduciary for the other party to the contract;

(c) Either party may with the consent of the other sue for the benefit of whom it may concern.

2723. (1) If an action based on anticipatory repudiation comes to trial before the time for performance with respect to some or all of the goods, any damages based on market price (Section 2708 or Section 2713) shall be determined according to the price of such goods prevailing at the time when the aggrieved party learned of the repudiation.

(2) If evidence of a price prevailing at the times or places described in this division is not readily available the price prevailing within any reasonable time before or after the time described or at any other place which in commercial judgment or under usage of trade would serve as a reasonable substitute for the one described may be used, making any proper allowance for the cost of transporting the goods to or from such other place.

(3) Evidence of a relevant price prevailing at a time or place other than the one described in this division offered by one party is not admissible unless and until he has given the other party such notice as the court finds sufficient to prevent unfair surprise.

2724. Whenever the prevailing price or value of any goods regularly bought and sold in any established commodity market is in issue, reports in official publications or trade journals or in newspapers or periodicals of general circulation published as the reports of such market shall be admissible in evidence. The circumstances of the preparation of such a report may be shown to affect its weight but not its admissibility.

2725. (1) An action for breach of any contract for sale must be commenced within four years after the cause of action has accrued. By the original agreement the parties may reduce the period of limitation to not less than one year but may not extend it.

(2) A cause of action accrues when the breach occurs, regardless of the aggrieved party's lack of knowledge of the breach. A breach of warranty occurs when tender of delivery is made, except that where a warranty explicitly extends to future performance of the goods and discovery of the breach must await the time of such performance the cause of action accrues when the breach is or should have been discovered.

(3) Where an action commenced within the time limited by subdivision (1) is so terminated as to leave available a remedy by another action for the same breach such other action may be commenced after the expiration of the time limited and within six months after the termination of the first action unless the termination resulted from voluntary discontinuance or from dismissal for failure or neglect to prosecute.

(4) This section does not alter the law on tolling of the statute of limitations nor does it apply to causes of action which have accrued before this code becomes effective.

2800. As used in this chapter "goods" means goods used or bought for use primarily for personal, family, or household purposes.

2801. In any retail sale of goods, if the manufacturer or seller of the goods issues a written warranty or guarantee as to the condition or quality of all or part of the goods which requires the buyer to complete and return any form to the manufacturer or seller as proof of the purchase of the goods, such warranty or guarantee shall not be unenforceable solely because the buyer fails to complete or return the form. This section does not relieve the buyer from proving the fact of purchase and the date thereof in any case in which such a fact is in issue.

The buyer must agree in writing to any waiver of this section for the waiver to be valid. Any waiver by the buyer of the provisions of this section which is not in writing is contrary to public policy and shall be unenforceable and void.

APPENDIX II

LETTERS OF CREDIT—ILLINOIS

ARTICLE 5
LETTER OF CREDIT

Sec. 5-101. Short title. This Article may be cited as Uniform Commercial Code—Letters of Credit.

Sec. 5-102. Definitions.

(a) In this Article:

(1) "Adviser" means a person who, at the request of the issuer, a confirmer, or another adviser, notifies or requests another adviser to notify the beneficiary that a letter of credit has been issued, confirmed, or amended.

(2) "Applicant" means a person at whose request or for whose account a letter of credit is issued. The term includes a person who requests an issuer to issue a letter of credit on behalf of another if the person making the request undertakes an obligation to reimburse the issuer.

(3) "Beneficiary" means a person who under the terms of a letter of credit is entitled to have its complying presentation honored. The term includes a person to whom drawing rights have been transferred under a transferable letter of credit.

(4) "Confirmer" means a nominated person who undertakes, at the request or with the consent of the issuer, to honor a presentation under a letter of credit issued by another.

(5) "Dishonor" of a letter of credit means failure timely to honor or to take an interim action, such as acceptance of a draft, that may be required by the letter of credit.

(6) "Document" means a draft or other demand, document of title, investment security, certificate, invoice, or other record, statement, or representation of fact, law, right, or opinion (i) which is presented in a written or other medium permitted by the letter of credit or, unless prohibited by the letter of credit, by the standard practice referred to in

Section 5-108(e) and (ii) which is capable of being examined for compliance with the terms and conditions of the letter of credit. A document may not be oral.

(7) "Good faith" means honesty in fact in the conduct or transaction concerned.

(8) "Honor" of a letter of credit means performance of the issuer's undertaking in the letter of credit to pay or deliver an item of value. Unless the letter of credit otherwise provides, "honor" occurs

(i) upon payment,

(ii) if the letter of credit provides for acceptance, upon acceptance of a draft and, at maturity, its payment, or

(iii) if the letter of credit provides for incurring a deferred obligation, upon incurring the obligation and, at maturity, its performance.

(9) "Issuer" means a bank or other person that issues a letter of credit, but does not include an individual who makes an engagement for personal, family, or household purposes.

(10) "Letter of credit" means a definite undertaking that satisfies the requirements of Section 5-104 by an issuer to a beneficiary at the request or for the account of an applicant or, in the case of a financial institution, to itself or for its own account, to honor a documentary presentation by payment or delivery of an item of value.

(11) "Nominated person" means a person whom the issuer (i) designates or authorizes to pay, accept, negotiate, or otherwise give value under a letter of credit and (ii) undertakes by agreement or custom and practice to reimburse.

(12) "Presentation" means delivery of a document to an issuer or nominated person for honor or giving of value under a letter of credit.

(13) "Presenter" means a person making a presentation as or on behalf of a beneficiary or nominated person.

(14) "Record" means information that is inscribed on a tangible medium, or that is stored in an electronic or other medium and is retrievable in perceivable form.

(15) "Successor of a beneficiary" means a person who succeeds to substantially all of the rights of a beneficiary by operation of law, including a corporation with or into which the beneficiary has been merged or consolidated, an administrator, executor, personal representative, trustee in bankruptcy, debtor in possession, liquidator, and receiver.

(b) Definitions in other Articles applying to this Article and the Sections in which they appear are:

"Accept" or "Acceptance"	Section 3-409
"Value"	Sections 3-303, 4-211

(c) Article 1 contains certain additional general definitions and principles of construction and interpretation applicable throughout this Article.

Sec. 5-103. Scope.

(a) This Article applies to letters of credit and to certain rights and obligations arising out of transactions involving letters of credit.

(b) The statement of a rule in this Article does not by itself require, imply, or negate application of the same or a different rule to a situation not provided for, or to a person not specified, in this Article.

(c) With the exception of this subsection, subsections (a) and (d), Sections 5-102(a)(9) and (10), 5-106(d), and 5-114(d), and except to the extent prohibited in Sections 1-102(3) and 5-117(d), the effect of this Article may be varied by agreement or by a provision stated or incorporated by reference in an undertaking. A term in an agreement or undertaking generally excusing liability or generally limiting remedies for failure to perform obligations is not sufficient to vary obligations prescribed by this Article.

(d) Rights and obligations of an issuer to a beneficiary or a nominated person under a letter of credit are independent of the existence, performance, or nonperformance of a contract or arrangement out of which the letter of credit arises or which underlies it, including contracts or arrangements between the issuer and the applicant and between the applicant and the beneficiary.

Sec. 5-104. Formal requirements. A letter of credit, confirmation, advice, transfer, amendment, or cancellation may be issued in any form that is a record and is authenticated (i) by a signature or (ii) in accordance with the agreement of the parties or the standard practice referred to in Section 5-108(e).

Sec. 5-105. Consideration. Consideration is not required to issue, amend, transfer, or cancel a letter of credit, advice, or confirmation.

Sec. 5-106. Issuance, amendment, cancellation, and duration.

(a) A letter of credit is issued and becomes enforceable according to its terms against the issuer when the issuer sends or otherwise transmits it to the person requested to advise or to the beneficiary. A letter of credit is revocable only if it so provides.

(b) After a letter of credit is issued, rights and obligations of a beneficiary, applicant, confirmer, and issuer are not affected by an amendment or cancellation to which that person has not consented except to the extent the letter of credit provides that it is revocable or that the issuer may amend or cancel the letter of credit without that consent.

(c) If there is no stated expiration date or other provision that determines its duration, a letter of credit expires one year after its stated date of issuance or, if none is stated, after the date on which it is issued.

(d) A letter of credit that states that it is perpetual expires 5 years after its stated date of issuance, or if none is stated, after the date on which it is issued.

Sec. 5-107. Confirmer, nominated person, and adviser.

(a) A confirmer is directly obligated on a letter of credit and has the rights and obligations of an issuer to the extent of its confirmation. The confirmer also has rights against and obligations to the issuer as if the issuer were an applicant and the confirmer had issued the letter of credit at the request and for the account of the issuer.

(b) A nominated person who is not a confirmer is not obligated to honor or otherwise give value for a presentation.

(c) A person requested to advise may decline to act as an adviser. An adviser that is not a confirmer is not obligated to honor or give value for a presentation. An adviser undertakes to the issuer and to the beneficiary accurately to advise the terms of the letter of credit, confirmation, amendment, or advice received by that person and undertakes to the beneficiary to check the apparent authenticity of the request to advise. Even if the advice is inaccurate, the letter of credit, confirmation, or amendment is enforceable as issued.

(d) A person who notifies a transferee beneficiary of the terms of a letter of credit, confirmation, amendment, or advice has the rights and obligations of an adviser under subsection (c). The terms in the notice to the transferee beneficiary may differ from the terms in any notice to the transferor beneficiary to the extent permitted by the letter of credit, confirmation, amendment, or advice received by the person who so notifies.

Sec. 5-108. Issuer's rights and obligations.

(a) Except as otherwise provided in Section 5-109, an issuer shall honor a presentation that, as determined by the standard practice referred to in subsection (e), appears on its face strictly to comply with the terms and conditions of the letter of credit. Except as otherwise provided in Section 5-113 and unless otherwise agreed with the applicant, an issuer shall dishonor a presentation that does not appear so to comply.

(b) An issuer has a reasonable time after presentation, but not beyond the end of the seventh business day of the issuer after the day of its receipt of documents:

(1) to honor,

(2) if the letter of credit provides for honor to be completed more than seven business days after presentation, to accept a draft or incur a deferred obligation, or

(3) to give notice to the presenter of discrepancies in the presentation.

(c) Except as otherwise provided in subsection (d), an issuer is precluded from asserting as a basis for dishonor any discrepancy if timely notice is not given, or any discrepancy not stated in the notice if timely notice is given.

(d) Failure to give the notice specified in subsection (b) or to mention fraud, forgery, or expiration in the notice does not preclude the issuer from asserting as a basis for dishonor fraud or forgery as described in Section 5-109(a) or expiration of the letter of credit before presentation.

(e) An issuer shall observe standard practice of financial institutions that regularly issue letters of credit. Determination of the issuer's observance of the standard practice is a matter of interpretation for the court. The court shall offer the parties a reasonable opportunity to present evidence of the standard practice.

(f) An issuer is not responsible for:

(1) the performance or nonperformance of the underlying contract, arrangement, or transaction,

(2) an act or omission of others, or

(3) observance or knowledge of the usage of a particular trade other than the standard practice referred to in subsection (e).

(g) If an undertaking constituting a letter of credit under Section 5-102(a)(10) contains nondocumentary conditions, an issuer shall disregard the non-documentary conditions and treat them as if they were not stated.

(h) An issuer that has dishonored a presentation shall return the documents or hold them at the disposal of, and send advice to that effect to, the presenter.

(i) An issuer that has honored a presentation as permitted or required by this Article:

(1) is entitled to be reimbursed by the applicant in immediately available funds not later than the date of its payment of funds;

(2) takes the documents free of claims of the beneficiary or presenter;

(3) is precluded from asserting a right of recourse on a draft under Sections 3-414 and 3-415;

(4) except as otherwise provided in Sections 5-110 and 5-117, is precluded from restitution of money paid or other value given by mistake to the extent the mistake concerns discrepancies in the documents or tender which are apparent on the face of the presentation; and

(5) is discharged to the extent of its performance under the letter of credit unless the issuer honored a presentation in which a required signature of a beneficiary was forged.

Sec. 5-109. Fraud and forgery.

(a) If a presentation is made that appears on its face strictly to comply with the terms and conditions of the letter of credit, but a required document is forged or materially fraudulent, or honor of the presentation would facilitate a material fraud by the beneficiary on the issuer or applicant:

(1) the issuer shall honor the presentation, if honor is demanded by (i) a nominated person who has given value in good faith and without notice of forgery or material fraud, (ii) a confirmer who has honored its confirmation in good faith, (iii) a holder in due course of a draft

drawn under the letter of credit which was taken after acceptance by the issuer or nominated person, or (iv) an assignee of the issuer's or nominated person's deferred obligation that was taken for value and without notice of forgery or material fraud after the obligation was incurred by the issuer or nominated person; and

(2) the issuer, acting in good faith, may honor or dishonor the presentation in any other case.

(b) If an applicant claims that a required document is forged or materially fraudulent or that honor of the presentation would facilitate a material fraud by the beneficiary on the issuer or applicant, a court of competent jurisdiction may temporarily or permanently enjoin the issuer from honoring a presentation or grant similar relief against the issuer or other persons only if the court finds that:

(1) the relief is not prohibited under the law applicable to an accepted draft or deferred obligation incurred by the issuer;

(2) a beneficiary, issuer, or nominated person who may be adversely affected is adequately protected against loss that it may suffer because the relief is granted;

(3) all of the conditions to entitle a person to the relief under the law of this State have been met; and

(4) on the basis of the information submitted to the court, the applicant is more likely than not to succeed under its claim of forgery or material fraud and the person demanding honor does not qualify for protection under subsection (a)(1).

Sec. 5-110. Warranties.

(a) If its presentation is honored, the beneficiary warrants:

(1) to the issuer, any other person to whom presentation is made, and the applicant that there is no fraud or forgery of the kind described in Section 5-109(a); and

(2) to the applicant that the drawing does not violate any agreement between the applicant and beneficiary or any other agreement intended by them to be augmented by the letter of credit.

(b) The warranties in subsection (a) are in addition to warranties arising under Articles 3, 4, 7, and 8 because of the presentation or transfer of documents covered by any of those Articles.

Sec. 5-111. Remedies.

(a) If an issuer wrongfully dishonors or repudiates its obligation to pay money under a letter of credit before presentation, the beneficiary, successor, or nominated person presenting on its own behalf may recover from the issuer the amount that is the subject of the dishonor or repudiation. If the issuer's obligation under the letter of credit is not for the payment of money, the claimant may obtain specific performance or, at the claimant's election, recover an amount equal to the value of performance from the issuer. In either case, the claimant may also recover incidental but not consequential damages. The claimant is not obligated to take action to avoid damages that might be due from the issuer under this subsection. If, although not obligated to do so, the claimant avoids damages, the claimant's recovery from the issuer must be reduced by the amount of damages avoided. The issuer has the burden of proving the amount of damages avoided. In the case of repudiation the claimant need not present any document.

(b) If an issuer wrongfully dishonors a draft or demand presented under a letter of credit or honors a draft or demand in breach of its obligation to the applicant, the applicant may recover damages resulting from the breach, including incidental but not consequential damages, less any amount saved as a result of the breach.

(c) If an adviser or nominated person other than a confirmer breaches an obligation under this Article or an issuer breaches an obligation not covered in subsection (a) or (b), a person to whom the obligation is owed may recover damages resulting from the breach, including incidental but not consequential damages, less any amount saved as a result of the breach. To the extent of the confirmation, a confirmer has the liability of an issuer specified in this subsection and subsections (a) and (b).

(d) An issuer, nominated person, or adviser who is found liable under subsection (a), (b), or (c) shall pay interest on the amount owed thereunder from the date of wrongful dishonor or other appropriate date.

(e) Reasonable attorney's fees and other expenses of litigation must be awarded to the prevailing party in an action in which a remedy is sought under this Article.

(f) Damages that would otherwise be payable by a party for breach of an obligation under this Article may be liquidated by agreement or undertaking, but only in an amount or by a formula that is reasonable in light of the harm anticipated.

Sec. 5-112. Transfer of letter of credit.

(a) Except as otherwise provided in Section 5-113, unless a letter of credit provides that it is transferable, the right of a beneficiary to draw or otherwise demand performance under a letter of credit may not be transferred.

(b) Even if a letter of credit provides that it is transferable, the issuer may refuse to recognize or carry out a transfer if:

(1) the transfer would violate applicable law; or

(2) the transferor or transferee has failed to comply with any requirement stated in the letter of credit or any other requirement relating to transfer imposed by the issuer which is within the standard practice referred to in Section 5-108(e) or is otherwise reasonable under the circumstances.

Sec. 5-113. Transfer by operation of law.

(a) A successor of a beneficiary may consent to amendments, sign and present documents, and receive payment or other items of value in the name of the beneficiary without disclosing its status as a successor.

(b) A successor of a beneficiary may consent to amendments, sign and present documents, and receive payment or other items of value in its own name as the disclosed successor of the beneficiary. Except as otherwise provided in subsection (e), an issuer shall recognize a disclosed successor of a beneficiary as beneficiary in full substitution for its predecessor upon compliance with the requirements for recognition by the issuer of a transfer of drawing rights by operation of law under the standard practice referred to in Section 5-108(e) or, in the absence of such a practice, compliance with other reasonable procedures sufficient to protect the issuer.

(c) An issuer is not obliged to determine whether a purported successor is a successor of a beneficiary or whether the signature of a purported successor is genuine or authorized.

(d) Honor of a purported successor's apparently complying presentation under subsection (a) or (b) has the consequences specified in Section 5-108(i) even if the purported successor is not the successor of a beneficiary. Documents signed in the name of the beneficiary or of a disclosed successor by a person who is neither the beneficiary nor the successor of the beneficiary are forged documents for the purposes of Section 5-109.

(e) An issuer whose rights of reimbursement are not covered by subsection (d) or substantially similar law and any confirmer or nominated person may decline to recognize a presentation under subsection (b).

(f) A beneficiary whose name is changed after the issuance of a letter of credit has the same rights and obligations as a successor of a beneficiary under this Section.

Sec. 5-114. Assignment of proceeds.

(a) In this Section, "proceeds of a letter of credit" means the cash, check, accepted draft, or other item of value paid or delivered upon honor or giving of value by the issuer or any nominated person under the letter of credit. The term does not include a beneficiary's drawing rights or documents presented by the beneficiary.

(b) A beneficiary may assign its right to part or all of the proceeds of a letter of credit. The beneficiary may do so before presentation as a present assignment of its right to receive proceeds contingent upon its compliance with the terms and conditions of the letter of credit.

(c) An issuer or nominated person need not recognize an assignment of proceeds of a letter of credit until it consents to the assignment.

(d) An issuer or nominated person has no obligation to give or withhold its consent to an assignment of proceeds of a letter of credit, but consent may not be unreasonably withheld if the assignee possesses and exhibits the letter of credit and presentation of the letter of credit is a condition to honor.

(e) Rights of a transferee beneficiary or nominated person are independent of the beneficiary's assignment of the proceeds of a letter of credit and are superior to the assignee's right to the proceeds.

(f) Neither the rights recognized by this Section between an assignee and an issuer, transferee beneficiary, or nominated person nor the issuer's or nominated person's payment of proceeds to an assignee or a third person affect the rights between the assignee and any person other than the issuer, transferee beneficiary, or nominated person. The mode of creating and perfecting a security interest in or granting an assignment of a beneficiary's rights to proceeds is governed by Article 9 or other law. Against persons other than the issuer, transferee beneficiary, or nominated person, the rights and obligations arising upon the creation of a security interest or other assignment of a beneficiary's right to proceeds and its perfection are governed by Article 9 or other law.

Sec. 5-115. Statute of limitations. An action to enforce a right or obligation arising under this Article must be commenced within one year after the expiration date of the relevant letter of credit or one year after the cause of action accrues, whichever occurs later. A cause of action accrues when the breach occurs, regardless of the aggrieved party's lack of knowledge of the breach.

Sec. 5-116. Choice of law and forum.

(a) The liability of an issuer, nominated person, or adviser for action or omission is governed by the law of the jurisdiction chosen by an agreement in the form of a record signed or otherwise authenticated by the affected parties in the manner provided in Section 5-104 or by a provision in the person's letter of credit, confirmation, or other undertaking. The jurisdiction whose law is chosen need not bear any relation to the transaction.

(b) Unless subsection (a) applies, the liability of an issuer, nominated person, or adviser for action or omission is governed by the law of the jurisdiction in which the person is located. The person is considered to be located at the address indicated in the person's undertaking. If more than one address is indicated, the person is considered to be located at the address from which the person's undertaking was issued. For the purpose of jurisdiction, choice of law, and recognition of interbranch letters of credit, but not enforcement of a judgment, all branches of a bank are considered separate juridical entities and a bank is considered to be located at the place where its relevant branch is considered to be located under this subsection.

(c) Except as otherwise provided in this subsection, the liability of an issuer, nominated person, or adviser is governed by any rules of custom or practice, such as the Uniform Customs and Practice for Documentary Credits, to which the letter of credit, confirmation, or other undertaking is expressly made subject. If (i) this Article would govern the liability of an issuer, nominated person, or adviser under subsection (a) or (b), (ii) the relevant undertaking incorporates rules of custom or practice, and (iii) there is conflict between this Article and those rules as applied to that undertaking, those rules govern except to the extent of any conflict with the nonvariable provisions specified in Section 5-103(c).

(d) If there is conflict between this Article and Article 3, 4, 4A, or 9, this Article governs.

(e) The forum for settling disputes arising out of an undertaking within this Article may be chosen in the manner and with the binding effect that governing law may be chosen in accordance with subsection (a).

Sec. 5-117. Subrogation of issuer, applicant, and nominated person.

(a) An issuer that honors a beneficiary's presentation is subrogated to the rights of the beneficiary to the same extent as if the issuer were a secondary obligor of the underlying obligation owed to the beneficiary and of the applicant to the same extent as if the issuer were the secondary obligor of the underlying obligation owed to the applicant.

(b) An applicant that reimburses an issuer is subrogated to the rights of the issuer against any beneficiary, presenter, or nominated person to the same extent as if the applicant were the secondary obligor of the obligations owed to the issuer and has the rights of subrogation of the issuer to the rights of the beneficiary stated in subsection (a).

(c) A nominated person who pays or gives value against a draft or demand presented under a letter of credit is subrogated to the rights of:

(1) the issuer against the applicant to the same extent as if the nominated person were a secondary obligor of the obligation owed to the issuer by the applicant;

(2) the beneficiary to the same extent as if the nominated person were a secondary obligor of the underlying obligation owed to the beneficiary; and

(3) the applicant to the same extent as if the nominated person were a secondary obligor of the underlying obligation owed to the applicant.

(d) Notwithstanding any agreement or term to the contrary, the rights of subrogation stated in subsections (a) and (b) do not arise until the issuer honors the letter of credit or otherwise pays and the rights in subsection (c) do not arise until the nominated person pays or otherwise gives value. Until then, the issuer, nominated person, and the applicant do not derive under this Section present or prospective rights forming the basis of a claim, defense, or excuse.

Sec. 5-118. Security interest of issuer or nominated person.

(a) An issuer or nominated person has a security interest in a document presented under a letter of credit to the extent that the issuer or nominated person honors or gives value for the presentation.

(b) So long as and to the extent that an issuer or nominated person has not been reimbursed or has not otherwise recovered the value given with respect to a security interest in a document under subsection (a), the security interest continues and is subject to Article 9, but:

(1) a security agreement is not necessary to make the security interest enforceable under Section 9-203(b)(3);

(2) if the document is presented in a medium other than a written or other tangible medium, the security interest is perfected; and

(3) if the document is presented in a written or other tangible medium and is not a certificated security, chattel paper, a document of title, an instrument, or a letter of credit, the security interest is perfected and has priority over a conflicting security interest in the document so long as the debtor does not have possession of the document.

APPENDIX III

STATUTE OF FRAUD—CALIFORNIA UCC SECTIONS 2201–2210

2201. (1) Except as otherwise provided in this section a contract for the sale of goods for the price of five hundred dollars ($500) or more is not enforceable by way of action or defense unless there is some writing sufficient to indicate that a contract for sale has been made between the parties and signed by the party against whom enforcement is sought or by his or her authorized agent or broker. A writing is not insufficient because it omits or incorrectly states a term agreed upon but the contract is not enforceable under this paragraph beyond the quantity of goods shown in the writing.

(2) Between merchants if within a reasonable time a writing in confirmation of the contract and sufficient against the sender is received and the party receiving it has reason to know its contents, it satisfies the requirements of subdivision (1) against the party unless written notice of objection to its contents is given within 10 days after it is received.

(3) A contract which does not satisfy the requirements of subdivision (1) but which is valid in other respects is enforceable:

(a) If the goods are to be specially manufactured for the buyer and are not suitable for sale to others in the ordinary course of the seller's business and the seller, before notice of repudiation is received and under circumstances which reasonably indicate that the goods are for the buyer, has made either a substantial beginning of their manufacture or commitments for their procurement;

(b) If the party against whom enforcement is sought admits in his or her pleading, testimony, or otherwise in court that a contract for sale was made, but the contract is not enforceable under this provision beyond the quantity of goods admitted; or

(c) With respect to goods for which payment has been made and accepted or which have been received and accepted (Section 2606).

(4) Subdivision (1) of this section does not apply to a qualified financial contract as that term is defined in paragraph (2) of subdivision (b) of Section 1624 of the Civil Code if either (a) there is, as provided in paragraph (3) of subdivision (b) of 1624 of the Civil Code, sufficient evidence to indicate that a

contract has been made or (b) the parties thereto, by means of a prior or subsequent written contract, have agreed to be bound by the terms of the qualified financial contract from the time they reach agreement (by telephone, by exchange of electronic messages, or otherwise) on those terms.

2202. Terms with respect to which the confirmatory memoranda of the parties agree or which are otherwise set forth in a writing intended by the parties as a final expression of their agreement with respect to such terms as are included therein may not be contradicted by evidence of any prior agreement or of a contemporaneous oral agreement but may be explained or supplemented

(a) By course of dealing, course of performance, or usage of trade (Section 1303); and

(b) By evidence of consistent additional terms unless the court finds the writing to have been intended also as a complete and exclusive statement of the terms of the agreement.

2204. (1) A contract for sale of goods may be made in any manner sufficient to show agreement, including conduct by both parties which recognizes the existence of such a contract.

(2) An agreement sufficient to constitute a contract for sale may be found even though the moment of its making is undetermined.

(3) Even though one or more terms are left open a contract for sale does not fail for indefiniteness if the parties have intended to make a contract and there is a reasonably certain basis for giving an appropriate remedy.

2205. (a) An offer by a merchant to buy or sell goods in a signed writing which by its terms gives assurance that it will be held open is not revocable, for lack of consideration, during the time stated or if no time is stated for a reasonable time, but in no event may such period of irrevocability exceed three months; but any such term of assurance on a form supplied by the offeree must be separately signed by the offeror.

(b) Notwithstanding subdivision (a), when a merchant renders an offer, oral or written, to supply goods to a contractor licensed pursuant to the provisions of Chapter 9 (commencing with Section 7000) of Division 3 of the Business and Professions Code or a similar contractor's licensing law of another state, and the merchant has actual or imputed knowledge that the contractor is so licensed, and that the offer will be relied upon by the contractor in the submission of its bid for a construction contract with a third party, the offer relied upon shall be irrevocable, notwithstanding lack of consideration, for 10 days after the awarding of the contract to the prime contractor, but in no event for more than 90 days after the date the bid or offer was rendered by the merchant; except that an oral bid or offer, when for a price of two thousand five hundred dollars ($2,500) or more, shall be confirmed in writing by the contractor or his or her agent within 48 hours after it is rendered. Failure by the contractor to confirm such offer in writing shall release the merchant from his or her offer. Nothing in this subdivision shall prevent a merchant from providing that the bid or offer will be held open for less than the time provided for herein.

2206. (1) Unless otherwise unambiguously indicated by the language or circumstances

(a) An offer to make a contract shall be construed as inviting acceptance in any manner and by any medium reasonable in the circumstances;

(b) An order or other offer to buy goods for prompt or current shipment shall be construed as inviting acceptance either by a prompt promise to ship or by the prompt or current shipment of conforming or nonconforming goods, but such a shipment of nonconforming goods does not constitute an acceptance if the seller seasonably notifies the buyer that the shipment is offered only as an accommodation to the buyer.

(2) Where the beginning of a requested performance is a reasonable mode of acceptance an offeror who is not notified of acceptance within a reasonable time may treat the offer as having lapsed before acceptance.

2207. (1) A definite and seasonable expression of acceptance or a written confirmation which is sent within a reasonable time operates as an acceptance even though it states terms additional to or different from those offered or agreed upon, unless acceptance is expressly made conditional on assent to the additional or different terms.

(2) The additional terms are to be construed as proposals for addition to the contract. Between merchants such terms become part of the contract unless:

(a) The offer expressly limits acceptance to the terms of the offer;

(b) They materially alter it; or

(c) Notification of objection to them has already been given or is given within a reasonable time after notice of them is received.

(3) Conduct by both parties which recognizes the existence of a contract is sufficient to establish a contract for sale although the writings of the parties do not otherwise establish a contract. In such case the terms of the particular contract consist of those terms on which the writings of the parties agree, together with any supplementary terms incorporated under any other provisions of this code.

2209. (1) An agreement modifying a contract within this division needs no consideration to be binding.

(2) A signed agreement which excludes modification or rescission except by a signed writing cannot be otherwise modified or rescinded, but except as between merchants such a requirement on a form supplied by the merchant must be separately signed by the other party.

(3) The requirements of the statute of frauds section of this division (Section 2201) must be satisfied if the contract as modified is within its provisions.

(4) Although an attempt at modification or rescission does not satisfy the requirements of subdivision (2) or (3) it can operate as a waiver.

(5) A party who has made a waiver affecting an executory portion of the contract may retract the waiver by reasonable notification received by the other party that strict performance will be required of any term waived, unless the retraction would be unjust in view of a material change of position in reliance on the waiver.

2210. (1) A party may perform his or her duty through a delegate unless otherwise agreed or unless the other party has a substantial interest in having his or her original promisor perform or control the acts required by the contract. No delegation of performance relieves the party delegating of any duty to perform or any liability for breach.

(2) Except as otherwise provided in Section 9406, unless otherwise agreed, all rights of either seller or buyer can be assigned except where the assignment would materially change the duty of the other party, or increase materially the burden or risk imposed on him or her by his or her contract, or impair materially his or her chance of obtaining return performance. A right to damages for breach of the whole contract or a right arising out of the assignor's due performance of his or her entire obligation can be assigned despite agreement otherwise.

(3) The creation, attachment, perfection, or enforcement of a security interest in the seller's interest under a contract is not a transfer that materially changes the duty of, or increases materially the burden or risk imposed on, the buyer or impairs materially the buyer's chance of obtaining return performance within the purview of subdivision (2) unless, and then only to the extent that, enforcement actually results in a delegation of material performance of the seller. Even in that event, the creation, attachment, perfection, and enforcement of the security interest remain effective, but (A) the seller is liable to the buyer for damages caused by the delegation to the extent that the damages could not reasonably be prevented by the buyer, and (B) a court having jurisdiction may grant other appropriate relief, including cancellation of the contract for sale or an injunction against enforcement of the security interest or consummation of the enforcement.

(4) Unless the circumstances indicate the contrary, a prohibition of assignment of "the contract" is to be construed as barring only the delegation to the assignee of the assignor's performance.

(5) An assignment of "the contract" or of "all my rights under the contract" or an assignment in similar general terms is an assignment of rights and, unless the language or the circumstances (as in an assignment for security) indicate the contrary, it is a delegation of performance of the duties of the assignor, and its acceptance by the assignee constitutes a promise by him or her to perform those duties. This promise is enforceable by either the assignor or the other party to the original contract.

(6) The other party may treat any assignment which delegates performance as creating reasonable grounds for insecurity and may, without prejudice to his or her rights against the assignor, demand assurances from the assignee (Section 2609).

APPENDIX IV

DOCUMENTS OF TITLE—FLORIDA—UNIFORM COMMERCIAL CODE: CHAPTER 677

PART I GENERAL

677.101 Short title.—Chapter 677 shall be known and may be cited as the "Uniform Commercial Code—Documents of Title."

677.102 Definitions and index of definitions.—

(1) In this chapter, unless the context otherwise requires:

(a) "Bailee" means the person who by a warehouse receipt, bill of lading or other document of title acknowledges possession of goods and contracts to deliver them.

(b) "Consignee" means the person named in a bill to whom or to whose order the bill promises delivery.

(c) "Consignor" means the person named in a bill as the person from whom the goods have been received for shipment.

(d) "Delivery order" means a written order to deliver goods directed to a warehouseman, carrier or other person who in the ordinary course of business issues warehouse receipts or bills of lading.

(e) "Document" means document of title as defined in the general definitions in chapter 671 (s. 671.201).

(f) "Goods" means all things which are treated as movable for the purposes of a contract of storage or transportation.

(g) "Issuer" means a bailee who issues a document except that in relation to an unaccepted delivery order it means the person who orders the possessor of goods to deliver. Issuer includes any person for whom an agent or employee purports to act in issuing a document if the agent or employee has real or apparent authority to issue documents, notwithstanding that the issuer received no goods or that the goods were misdescribed or that in any other respect the agent or employee violated his or her instructions.

(h) "Warehouseman" is a person engaged in the business of storing goods for hire.

(2) Other definitions applying to this chapter or to specified parts thereof, and the sections in which they appear are:

"Duly negotiate," s. 677.501.

"Person entitled under the document," s. 677.403(4).

(3) Definitions in other chapters applying to this chapter and the sections in which they appear are:

"Contract for sale," s. 672.106.

"Overseas," s. 672.323.

"Receipt" of goods, s. 672.103.

(4) In addition chapter 671 contains general definitions and principles of construction and interpretation applicable throughout this chapter.

677.103 Relation of chapter to treaty, statute, tariff, classification or regulation.— To the extent that any treaty or statute of the United States, regulatory statute of this state or tariff, classification or regulation filed or issued pursuant thereto is applicable, the provisions of this chapter are subject thereto.

677.104 Negotiable and nonnegotiable warehouse receipt, bill of lading or other document of title.—

(1) A warehouse receipt, bill of lading or other document of title is negotiable:

(a) If by its terms the goods are to be delivered to bearer or to the order of a named person; or

(b) Where recognized in overseas trade, if it runs to a named person or assigns.

(2) Any other document is nonnegotiable. A bill of lading in which it is stated that the goods are consigned to a named person is not made negotiable by

a provision that the goods are to be delivered only against a written order signed by the same or another named person.

677.105 Construction against negative implication.—The omission from either part II or part III of this chapter of a provision corresponding to a provision made in the other part does not imply that a corresponding rule of law is not applicable.

PART II WAREHOUSE RECEIPTS: SPECIAL PROVISIONS

677.201 Who may issue a warehouse receipt; storage under government bond.—

(1) A warehouse receipt may be issued by any warehouseman.

(2) Where goods including distilled spirits and agricultural commodities are stored under a statute requiring a bond against withdrawal or a license for the issuance of receipts in the nature of warehouse receipts, a receipt issued for the goods has like effect as a warehouse receipt even though issued by a person who is the owner of the goods and is not a warehouseman.

677.202 Form of warehouse receipt; essential terms; optional terms.—

(1) A warehouse receipt need not be in any particular form.

(2) Unless a warehouse receipt embodies within its written or printed terms each of the following, the warehouseman is liable for damages caused by the omission to a person injured thereby:

(a) The location of the warehouse where the goods are stored;

(b) The date of issue of the receipt;

(c) The consecutive number of the receipt;

(d) A statement whether the goods received will be delivered to the bearer, to a specified person, or to a specified person or his or her order;

(e) The rate of storage and handling charges, except that where goods are stored under a field warehousing arrangement a statement of that fact is sufficient on a nonnegotiable receipt;

(f) A description of the goods or of the packages containing them;

(g) The signature of the warehouseman, which may be made by his or her authorized agent;

(h) If the receipt is issued for goods of which the warehouseman is owner, either solely or jointly or in common with others, the fact of such ownership; and

(i) A statement of the amount of advances made and of liabilities incurred for which the warehouseman claims a lien or security interest (s. 677.209). If the precise amount of such advances made or of such liabilities incurred is, at the time of the issue of the receipt, unknown to the warehouseman or to his or her agent who issues it, a statement of the fact that advances have been made or liabilities incurred and the purpose thereof is sufficient.

(3) A warehouseman may insert in his or her receipt any other terms which are not contrary to the provisions of this code and do not impair his or her obligation of delivery (s. 677.403) or his or her duty of care (s. 677.204). Any contrary provisions shall be ineffective.

677.203 Liability of nonreceipt or misdescription.—A party to or purchaser for value in good faith of a document of title other than a bill of lading relying in either case upon the description therein of the goods may recover from the issuer damages caused by the nonreceipt or misdescription of the goods, except to the extent that the document conspicuously indicates that the issuer does not know whether any part or all of the goods in fact were received or conform to the description, as where the description is in terms of marks or labels or kind, quantity or condition, or the receipt or description is qualified by "contents, condition and quality unknown," "said to contain" or the like, if such indication be true, or the party or purchaser otherwise has notice.

677.204 Duty of care; contractual limitation of warehouseman's liability.—

(1) A warehouseman is liable for damages for loss of or injury to the goods caused by his or her failure to exercise such care in regard to them as a reasonably careful person would exercise under like circumstances but unless otherwise agreed he or she is not liable for damages which could not have been avoided by the exercise of such care.

(2) Damages may be limited by a term in the warehouse receipt or storage agreement limiting the amount of liability in case of loss or damage, and setting forth a specific liability per article or item, or value per unit of weight, beyond which the warehouseman shall not be liable; provided, however, that such liability may on written request of the bailor at the time of signing such storage agreement or within a reasonable time after receipt of the warehouse receipt be increased on part or all of the goods thereunder, in which event increased rates may be charged based on such increased valuation, but that no such increase shall be permitted contrary to a lawful limitation of liability contained in the warehouseman's tariff, if any. No such limitation is effective with respect to the warehouseman's liability for conversion to his or her own use.

(3) This section does not impair or repeal any statute which imposes a higher responsibility upon the warehouseman or invalidates contractual limitations which would be permissible under this chapter.

677.205 Title under warehouse receipt defeated in certain cases.—A buyer in the ordinary course of business of fungible goods sold and delivered by a warehouseman who is also in the business of buying and selling such goods takes free of any claim under a warehouse receipt even though it has been duly negotiated.

677.206 Termination of storage at warehouseman's option.—

(1) A warehouseman may on notifying the person on whose account the goods are held and any other person known to claim an interest in the goods require payment of any charges and removal of the goods from the warehouse at the termination of the period of storage fixed by the document, or, if no period is fixed, within a stated period not less than 30 days after the notification. If the goods are not removed before the date specified in the notification, the warehouseman may sell them in accordance with the provisions of the section on enforcement of a warehouseman's lien (s. 677.210).

(2) If a warehouseman in good faith believes that the goods are about to deteriorate or decline in value to less than the amount of his or her lien within the time prescribed in subsection (1) for notification, advertisement and sale, the warehouseman may specify in the notification any reasonable shorter time for removal of the goods and in case the goods are not removed, may sell them at public sale held not less than 1 week after a single advertisement or posting.

(3) If as a result of a quality or condition of the goods of which the warehouseman had no notice at the time of deposit the goods are a hazard to other property or to the warehouse or to persons, the warehouseman may sell the goods at public or private sale without advertisement on reasonable notification to all persons known to claim an interest in the goods. If the warehouseman after a reasonable effort is unable to sell the goods he or she may dispose of them in any lawful manner and shall incur no liability by reason of such disposition.

(4) The warehouseman must deliver the goods to any person entitled to them under this chapter upon due demand made at any time prior to sale or other disposition under this section.

(5) The warehouseman may satisfy his or her lien from the proceeds of any sale or disposition under this section but must hold the balance for delivery on the demand of any person to whom he or she would have been bound to deliver the goods.

677.207 Goods must be kept separate; fungible goods.—

(1) Unless the warehouse receipt otherwise provides, a warehouseman must keep separate the goods covered by each receipt so as to permit at all times identification and delivery of those goods except that different lots of fungible goods may be commingled.

(2) Fungible goods so commingled are owned in common by the persons entitled thereto and the warehouseman is severally liable to each owner for that owner's share. Where because of overissue a mass of fungible goods is insufficient to meet all the receipts which the warehouseman has issued against it, the persons entitled include all holders to whom overissued receipts have been duly negotiated.

677.208 Altered warehouse receipts.—Where a blank in a negotiable warehouse receipt has been filled in without authority, a purchaser for value and without notice of the want of authority may treat the insertion as authorized. Any other unauthorized alteration leaves any receipt enforceable against the issuer according to its original tenor.

677.209 Lien of warehouseman.—

(1) A warehouseman has a lien against the bailor on the goods covered by a warehouse receipt or on the proceeds thereof in his or her possession for charges for storage or transportation (including demurrage and terminal charges), insurance, labor, or charges present or future in relation to the goods, and for expenses necessary for preservation of the goods or reasonably incurred in their sale pursuant to law. If the person on whose account the goods are held is liable for like charges or expenses in relation to other goods whenever deposited and it is stated in the receipt that a lien is claimed for charges and expenses in relation to other goods, the warehouseman also has a lien against him or her for such charges and expenses whether or not the other goods have been delivered by the warehouseman. But against a person to whom a negotiable warehouse receipt is duly negotiated a warehouseman's lien is limited to charges in an amount or at a rate specified on the receipt or if no charges are so specified then to a reasonable charge for storage of the goods covered by the receipt subsequent to the date of the receipt.

(2) The warehouseman may also reserve a security interest against the bailor for a maximum amount specified on the receipt for charges other than those specified in subsection (1), such as for money advanced and interest. Such a security interest is governed by the chapter on secured transactions (chapter 679).

(3) A warehouseman's lien for charges and expenses under subsection (1) or a security interest under subsection (2) is also effective against any person who so entrusted the bailor with possession of the goods that a pledge of them by him or her to a good faith purchaser for value would have been valid but is not effective against a person as to whom the document confers no right in the goods covered by it under s. 677.503.

(4) A warehouseman loses his or her lien on any goods which he or she voluntarily delivers or which he or she unjustifiably refuses to deliver.

677.210 Enforcement of warehouseman's lien.—

(1) Except as provided in subsection (2), a warehouseman's lien may be enforced by public or private sale of the goods in block or in parcels, at any time or place and on any terms which are commercially reasonable, after notifying all persons known to claim an interest in the goods. Such notification must include a statement of the amount due, the nature of the proposed sale and the time and place of any public sale. The fact that a better price could have been obtained by a sale at a different time or in a different method from that selected by the warehouseman is not of itself sufficient to establish that the sale was not made in a commercially reasonable manner. If the warehouseman either sells the goods in the usual manner in any recognized market therefor, or if he or she sells at the price

current in such market at the time of his or her sale, or if he or she has otherwise sold in conformity with commercially reasonable practices among dealers in the type of goods sold, he or she has sold in a commercially reasonable manner. A sale of more goods than apparently necessary to be offered to ensure satisfaction of the obligation is not commercially reasonable except in cases covered by the preceding sentence.

(2) A warehouseman's lien on goods other than goods stored by a merchant in the course of his or her business may be enforced only as follows:

(a) All persons known to claim an interest in the goods must be notified.

(b) The notification must be delivered in person or sent by registered or certified letter to the last known address of any person to be notified.

(c) The notification must include an itemized statement of the claim, a description of the goods subject to the lien, a demand for payment within a specified time not less than 10 days after receipt of the notification, and a conspicuous statement that unless the claim is paid within that time the goods will be advertised for sale and sold by auction at a specified time and place.

(d) The sale must conform to the terms of the notification.

(e) The sale must be held at the nearest suitable place to that where the goods are held or stored.

(f) After the expiration of the time given in the notification, an advertisement of the sale must be published once a week for 2 weeks consecutively in a newspaper of general circulation where the sale is to be held. The advertisement must include a description of the goods, the name of the person on whose account they are being held, and the time and place of the sale. The sale must take place at least 15 days after the first publication. If there is no newspaper of general circulation where the sale is to be held, the advertisement must be posted at least 10 days before the sale in not less than 6 conspicuous places in the neighborhood of the proposed sale.

(3) Before any sale pursuant to this section any person claiming a right in the goods may pay the amount necessary to satisfy the lien and the reasonable expenses incurred under this section. In that event the goods must not be sold, but must be retained by the warehouseman subject to the terms of the receipt and this chapter.

(4) The warehouseman may buy at any public sale pursuant to this section.

(5) A purchaser in good faith of goods sold to enforce a warehouseman's lien takes the goods free of any rights of persons against whom the lien was valid, despite noncompliance by the warehouseman with the requirements of this section.

(6) The warehouseman may satisfy his or her lien from the proceeds of any sale pursuant to this section but must hold the balance, if any, for delivery on demand to any person to whom he or she would have been bound to deliver the goods.

(7) The rights provided by this section shall be in addition to all other rights allowed by law to a creditor against his or her debtor.

(8) Where a lien is on goods stored by a merchant in the course of his or her business the lien may be enforced in accordance with either subsection (1) or subsection (2).

(9) The warehouseman is liable for damages caused by failure to comply with the requirements for sale under this section and in case of willful violation is liable for conversion.

PART III BILLS OF LADING: SPECIAL PROVISIONS

677.301 Liability for nonreceipt or misdescription; "said to contain"; "shipper's load and count"; improper handling.—

(1) A consignee of a nonnegotiable bill who has given value in good faith or a holder to whom a negotiable bill has been duly negotiated relying in either case upon the description therein of the goods, or upon the date therein shown, may recover from the issuer damages caused by the misdating of the bill or the nonreceipt or misdescription of the goods, except to the extent that the document indicates that the issuer does not know whether any part or all of the goods in fact were received or conform to the description, as where the description is in terms of marks or labels or kind, quantity, or condition or the receipt or description is qualified by "contents or condition of contents of packages unknown," "said to contain," "shipper's weight, load and count" or the like, if such indication be true.

(2) When goods are loaded by an issuer who is a common carrier, the issuer must count the packages of goods if package freight and ascertain the kind and quantity if bulk freight. In such cases "shipper's weight, load and count" or other words indicating that the description was made by the shipper are ineffective except as to freight concealed by packages.

(3) When bulk freight is loaded by a shipper who makes available to the issuer adequate facilities for weighing such freight, an issuer who is a common carrier must ascertain the kind and quantity within a reasonable time after receiving the written request of the shipper to do so. In such cases "shipper's weight" or other words of like purport are ineffective.

(4) The issuer may by inserting in the bill the words "shipper's weight, load and count" or other words of like purport indicate that the goods were loaded by the shipper; and if such statement be true the issuer shall not be liable for damages caused by the improper loading. But their omission does not imply liability for such damages.

(5) The shipper shall be deemed to have guaranteed to the issuer the accuracy at the time of shipment of the description, marks, labels, number, kind, quantity, condition and weight, as furnished by him or her; and the shipper shall indemnify the issuer against damage caused by inaccuracies in such particulars. The right of the issuer to such indemnity shall in no way limit his or her responsibility and liability under the contract of carriage to any person other than the shipper.

677.302 Through bills of lading and similar documents.—

(1) The issuer of a through bill of lading or other document embodying an undertaking to be performed in part by persons acting as its agents or by connecting carriers is liable to anyone entitled to recover on the document for any breach by such other persons or by a connecting carrier of its obligation under the document but to the extent that the bill covers an undertaking to be performed overseas or in territory not contiguous to the continental United States or an undertaking including matters other than transportation this liability may be varied by agreement of the parties.

(2) Where goods covered by a through bill of lading or other document embodying an undertaking to be performed in part by persons other than the issuer are received by any such person, he or she is subject with respect to his or her own performance while the goods are in his or her possession to the obligation of the issuer. His or her obligation is discharged by delivery of the goods to another such person pursuant to the document, and does not include liability for breach by any other such persons or by the issuer.

(3) The issuer of such through bill of lading or other document shall be entitled to recover from the connecting carrier or such other person in possession of the goods when the breach of the obligation under the document occurred, the amount it may be required to pay to anyone entitled to recover on the document therefor, as may be evidenced by any receipt, judgment, or transcript thereof, and the amount of any expense reasonably incurred by it in defending any action brought by anyone entitled to recover on the document therefor.

677.303 Diversion; reconsignment; change of instructions.—

(1) Unless the bill of lading otherwise provides, the carrier may deliver the goods to a person or destination other than that stated in the bill or may otherwise dispose of the goods on instructions from:

(a) The holder of a negotiable bill; or

(b) The consignor on a nonnegotiable bill notwithstanding contrary instructions from the consignee; or

(c) The consignee on a nonnegotiable bill in the absence of contrary instructions from the consignor, if the goods have arrived at the billed destination or if the consignee is in possession of the bill; or

(d) The consignee on a nonnegotiable bill if he or she is entitled as against the consignor to dispose of them.

(2) Unless such instructions are noted on a negotiable bill of lading, a person to whom the bill is duly negotiated can hold the bailee according to the original terms.

677.304 Bills of lading in a set.—

(1) Except where customary in overseas transportation, a bill of lading must not be issued in a set of parts. The issuer is liable for damages caused by violation of this subsection.

(2) Where a bill of lading is lawfully drawn in a set of parts, each of which is numbered and expressed to be valid only if the goods have not been delivered against any other part, the whole of the parts constitutes one bill.

(3) Where a bill of lading is lawfully issued in a set of parts and different parts are negotiated to different persons, the title of the holder to whom the first due negotiation is made prevails as to both the document and the goods even though any later holder may have received the goods from the carrier in good faith and discharged the carrier's obligation by surrender of his or her part.

(4) Any person who negotiates or transfers a single part of a bill of lading drawn in a set is liable to holders of that part as if it were the whole set.

(5) The bailee is obliged to deliver in accordance with part IV of this chapter against the first presented part of a bill of lading lawfully drawn in a set. Such delivery discharges the bailee's obligation on the whole bill.

677.305 Destination bills.—

(1) Instead of issuing a bill of lading to the consignor at the place of shipment a carrier may at the request of the consignor procure the bill to be issued at destination or at any other place designated in the request.

(2) Upon request of anyone entitled as against the carrier to control the goods while in transit and on surrender of any outstanding bill of lading or other receipt covering such goods, the issuer may procure a substitute bill to be issued at any place designated in the request.

677.306 Altered bills of lading.—An unauthorized alteration or filling in of a blank in a bill of lading leaves the bill enforceable according to its original tenor.

677.307 Lien of carrier.—

(1) A carrier has a lien on the goods covered by a bill of lading for charges subsequent to the date of its receipt of the goods for storage or transportation (including demurrage and terminal charges) and for expenses necessary for preservation of the goods incident to their transportation or reasonably incurred in their sale pursuant to law. But against a purchaser for value of a negotiable bill of lading a carrier's lien is limited to charges stated in the bill or the applicable tariffs, or if no charges are stated then to a reasonable charge.

(2) A lien for charges and expenses under subsection (1) on goods which the carrier was required by law to receive for transportation is effective against the consignor or any person entitled to the goods unless the carrier had notice that the consignor lacked authority to subject the goods to such charges and expenses. Any other lien under subsection (1) is effective against the consignor and any person who permitted the bailor to have control or possession of the goods unless the carrier had notice that the bailor lacked such authority.

(3) A carrier loses his or her lien on any goods which the carrier voluntarily delivers or which he or she unjustifiably refuses to deliver.

677.308 Enforcement of carrier's lien.—

(1) A carrier's lien may be enforced by public or private sale of the goods, in block or in parcels, at any time or place and on any terms which are commercially reasonable, after notifying all persons known to claim an interest in the goods. Such notification must include a statement of the amount due, the nature of the proposed sale and the time and place of any public sale. The fact that a better price could have been obtained by a sale at a different time or in a different method from that selected by the carrier is not of itself sufficient to establish that the sale was not made in a commercially reasonable manner. If the carrier either sells the goods in the usual manner in any recognized market therefor or if he or she sells at the price current in such market at the time of his or her sale or if the carrier has otherwise sold in conformity with commercially reasonable practices among dealers in the type of goods sold he or she has sold in a commercially reasonable manner. A sale of more goods than apparently necessary to be offered to ensure satisfaction of the obligation is not commercially reasonable except in cases covered by the preceding sentence.

(2) Before any sale pursuant to this section any person claiming a right in the goods may pay the amount necessary to satisfy the lien and the reasonable expenses incurred under this section. In that event the goods must not be sold, but must be retained by the carrier subject to the terms of the bill and this chapter.

(3) The carrier may buy at any public sale pursuant to this section.

(4) A purchaser in good faith of goods sold to enforce a carrier's lien takes the goods free of any rights of persons against whom the lien was valid, despite noncompliance by the carrier with the requirements of this section.

(5) The carrier may satisfy his or her lien from the proceeds of any sale pursuant to this section but must hold the balance, if any, for delivery on demand to any person to whom the carrier would have been bound to deliver the goods.

(6) The rights provided by this section shall be in addition to all other rights allowed by law to a creditor against his or her debtor.

(7) A carrier's lien may be enforced in accordance with either subsection (1) or the procedure set forth in s. 677.210(2).

(8) The carrier is liable for damages caused by failure to comply with the requirements for sale under this section and in case of willful violation is liable for conversion.

677.309 Duty of care; contractual limitation of carrier's liability.—

(1) A carrier who issues a bill of lading whether negotiable or nonnegotiable must exercise the degree of care in relation to the goods which a reasonably careful person would exercise under like circumstances. This subsection does not repeal or change any law or rule of law which imposes liability upon a common carrier for damages not caused by its negligence.

(2) Damages may be limited by a provision that the carrier's liability shall not exceed a value stated in the document if the carrier's rates are dependent upon value and the consignor by the carrier's tariff is afforded an opportunity to declare a higher value or a value as lawfully provided in the tariff, or where no tariff is filed he or she is otherwise advised of such opportunity; but no such limitation is effective with respect to the carrier's liability for conversion to its own use.

(3) Reasonable provisions as to the time and manner of presenting claims and instituting actions based on the shipment may be included in the bill of lading or tariff.

PART IV WAREHOUSE RECEIPTS AND BILLS OF LADING: GENERAL OBLIGATIONS

677.401 Irregularities in issue of receipt or bill or conduct of issuer.—The obligations imposed by this chapter on an issuer apply to a document of title regardless of the fact that:

(1) The document may not comply with the requirements of this chapter or of any other law or regulation regarding its issue, form or content; or

(2) The issuer may have violated laws regulating the conduct of his or her business; or

(3) The goods covered by the document were owned by the bailee at the time the document was issued; or

(4) The person issuing the document does not come within the definition of warehouseman if it purports to be a warehouse receipt.

677.402 Duplicate receipt or bill; overissue.—Neither a duplicate nor any other document of title purporting to cover goods already represented by an outstanding document of the same issuer confers any right in the goods, except as provided in the case of bills in a set, overissue of documents for fungible goods and substitutes for lost, stolen or destroyed documents. But the issuer is liable for damages caused by his or her overissue or failure to identify a duplicate document as such by conspicuous notation on its face.

677.403 Obligation of warehouseman or carrier to deliver; excuse.—

(1) The bailee must deliver the goods to a person entitled under the document who complies with subsections (2) and (3), unless and to the extent that the bailee establishes any of the following:

(a) Delivery of the goods to a person whose receipt was rightful as against the claimant;

(b) Damage to or delay, loss or destruction of the goods for which the bailee is not liable, but the burden of establishing negligence in such cases when value of such damage, delay, loss, or destruction exceeds $10,000 is on the person entitled under the document;

(c) Previous sale or other disposition of the goods in lawful enforcement of a lien or on warehouseman's lawful termination of storage;

(d) The exercise by a seller of his or her right to stop delivery pursuant to the provisions of the chapter on sales (s. 672.705);

(e) A diversion, reconsignment or other disposition pursuant to the provisions of this chapter (s. 677.303) or tariff regulating such right;

(f) Release, satisfaction or any other fact affording a personal defense against the claimant;

(g) Any other lawful excuse.

(2) A person claiming goods covered by a document of title must satisfy the bailee's lien where the bailee so requests or where the bailee is prohibited by law from delivering the goods until the charges are paid.

(3) Unless the person claiming is one against whom the document confers no right under s. 677.503(1), he or she must surrender for cancellation or notation of partial deliveries any outstanding negotiable document covering the goods, and the bailee must cancel the document or conspicuously note the partial delivery thereon or be liable to any person to whom the document is duly negotiated.

(4) "Person entitled under the document" means holder in the case of a negotiable document, or the person to whom delivery is to be made by the terms of or pursuant to written instructions under a nonnegotiable document.

677.404 No liability for good faith delivery pursuant to receipt or bill.—A bailee who in good faith including observance of reasonable commercial standards has received goods and delivered or otherwise disposed of them according to the terms of the document of title or pursuant to this chapter is not liable therefor. This rule applies even though the person from whom he or she received the goods had no authority to procure the document or to dispose of the goods and even though the person to whom he or she delivered the goods had no authority to receive them.

PART V WAREHOUSE RECEIPTS AND BILLS OF LADING: NEGOTIATION AND TRANSFER

677.501 Form of negotiation and requirements of "Due negotiation."—

(1) A negotiable document of title running to the order of a named person is negotiated by the named person's indorsement and delivery. After his or her indorsement in blank or to bearer any person can negotiate it by delivery alone.

(2) (a) A negotiable document of title is also negotiated by delivery alone when by its original terms it runs to bearer.

(b) When a document running to the order of a named person is delivered to him or her the effect is the same as if the document had been negotiated.

(3) Negotiation of a negotiable document of title after it has been indorsed to a specified person requires indorsement by the special indorsee as well as delivery.

(4) A negotiable document of title is "duly negotiated" when it is negotiated in the manner stated in this section to a holder who purchases it in good faith without notice of any defense against or claim to it on the part of any person and for value, unless it is established that the negotiation is not in the regular course of business or financing or involves receiving the document in settlement or payment of a money obligation.

(5) Indorsement of a nonnegotiable document neither makes it negotiable nor adds to the transferee's rights.

(6) The naming in a negotiable bill of a person to be notified of the arrival of the goods does not limit the negotiability of the bill nor constitute notice to a purchaser thereof of any interest of such person in the goods.

677.502 Rights acquired by due negotiation.—

(1) Subject to the following section and to the provisions of s. 677.205 on fungible goods, a holder to whom a negotiable document of title has been duly negotiated acquires thereby:

(a) Title to the document;

(b) Title to the goods;

(c) All rights accruing under the law of agency or estoppel, including rights to goods delivered to the bailee after the document was issued; and

(d) The direct obligation of the issuer to hold or deliver the goods according to the terms of the document free of any defense or claim by him or her except those arising under the terms of the document or under this chapter. In the case of a delivery order the bailee's obligation accrues only upon acceptance and the obligation acquired by the holder is that the issuer and any indorser will procure the acceptance of the bailee.

(2) Subject to the following section, title and rights so acquired are not defeated by any stoppage of the goods represented by the document or by surrender of such goods by the bailee, and are not impaired even though the negotiation or any prior negotiation constituted a breach of duty or even though any person has been deprived of possession of the document by misrepresentation, fraud, accident, mistake, duress, loss, theft or conversion, or even though a previous sale or other transfer of the goods or document has been made to a third person.

677.503 Document of title to goods defeated in certain cases.—

(1) A document of title confers no right in goods against a person who before issuance of the document had a legal interest or a perfected security interest in them and who neither:

(a) Delivered or entrusted them or any document of title covering them to the bailor or the bailor's nominee with actual or apparent authority to ship, store or sell or with power to obtain delivery under this chapter (s. 677.403) or with power of disposition under this code (ss. 672.403 and 679.320) or other statute or rule of law; nor

(b) Acquiesced in the procurement by the bailor or the bailor's nominee of any document of title.

(2) Title to goods based upon an unaccepted delivery order is subject to the rights of anyone to whom a negotiable warehouse receipt or bill of lading covering the goods has been duly negotiated. Such a title may be defeated under the next section to the same extent as the rights of the issuer or a transferee from the issuer.

(3) Title to goods based upon a bill of lading issued to a freight forwarder is subject to the rights of anyone to whom a bill issued by the freight forwarder is duly negotiated; but delivery by the carrier in accordance with part IV of this chapter pursuant to its own bill of lading discharges the carrier's obligation to deliver.

677.504 Rights acquired in the absence of due negotiation; effect of diversion; seller's stoppage of delivery.—

(1) A transferee of a document, whether negotiable or nonnegotiable, to whom the document has been delivered but not duly negotiated, acquires the title and rights which his or her transferor had or had actual authority to convey.

(2) In the case of a nonnegotiable document, until but not after the bailee receives notification of the transfer, the rights of the transferee may be defeated:

(a) By those creditors of the transferor who could treat the sale as void under s. 672.402; or

(b) By a buyer from the transferor in ordinary course of business if the bailee has delivered the goods to the buyer or received notification of his or her rights; or

(c) As against the bailee by good faith dealings of the bailee with the transferor.

(3) A diversion or other change of shipping instructions by the consignor in a nonnegotiable bill of lading which causes the bailee not to deliver to the consignee defeats the consignee's title to the goods if they have been delivered to a buyer in ordinary course of business and in any event defeats the consignee's rights against the bailee.

(4) Delivery pursuant to a nonnegotiable document may be stopped by a seller under s. 672.705, and subject to the requirement of due notification there provided. A bailee honoring the seller's instructions is entitled to be indemnified by the seller against any resulting loss or expense.

677.505 Indorser not a guarantor for other parties.—The indorsement of a document of title issued by a bailee does not make the indorser liable for any default by the bailee or by previous indorsers.

677.506 Delivery without indorsement; right to compel indorsement.—The transferee of a negotiable document of title has a specifically enforceable right to have his or her transferor supply any necessary indorsement but the transfer becomes a negotiation only as of the time the indorsement is supplied.

677.507 Warranties on negotiation or transfer of receipt or bill.—Where a person negotiates or transfers a document of title for value otherwise than as a mere intermediary under the next following section, then unless otherwise agreed the person warrants to his or her immediate purchaser only in addition to any warranty made in selling the goods:

(1) That the document is genuine; and

(2) That he or she has no knowledge of any fact which would impair its validity or worth; and

(3) That his or her negotiation or transfer is rightful and fully effective with respect to the title to the document and the goods it represents.

677.508 Warranties of collecting bank as to documents.—A collecting bank or other intermediary known to be entrusted with documents on behalf of another or with collection of a draft or other claim against delivery of documents warrants by such delivery of the documents only its own good faith and authority. This rule applies even though the intermediary has purchased or made advances against the claim or draft to be collected.

677.509 Receipt or bill; when adequate compliance with commercial contract.—The question whether a document is adequate to fulfill the obligations of a contract for sale or the conditions of a credit is governed by the chapters on sales (chapter 672) and on letters of credit (chapter 675).

PART VI WAREHOUSE RECEIPTS AND BILLS OF LADING: MISCELLANEOUS PROVISIONS

677.601 Lost and missing documents.—

(1) If a document has been lost, stolen or destroyed, a court may order delivery of the goods or issuance of a substitute document and the bailee may without liability to any person comply with such order. If the document was negotiable the claimant must post security approved by the court to indemnify any person who may suffer loss as a result of nonsurrender of the document. If the document was not negotiable, such security may be required at the discretion of the court. The court may also in its discretion order payment of the bailee's reasonable costs and counsel fees.

(2) A bailee who without court order delivers goods to a person claiming under a missing negotiable document is liable to any person injured thereby, and if the delivery is not in good faith becomes liable for conversion. Delivery in good faith is not conversion if made in accordance with a filed classification or tariff or, where no classification or tariff is filed, if the claimant posts security with the bailee in an amount at least double the value of the goods at the time of posting to indemnify any person injured by the delivery who files a notice of claim within 1 year after the delivery.

677.602 Attachment of goods covered by a negotiable document.—Except where the document was originally issued upon delivery of the goods by a person who had no power to dispose of them, no lien attaches by virtue of any judicial process to goods in the possession of a bailee for which a negotiable document of title is outstanding unless the document be first surrendered to the bailee or its negotiation enjoined, and the bailee shall not be compelled to deliver the goods pursuant to process until the document is surrendered to him or her or impounded by the court. One who purchases the document for value without notice of the process or injunction takes free of the lien imposed by judicial process.

677.603 Conflicting claims; interpleader.—If more than one person claims title or possession of the goods, the bailee is excused from delivery until he or she has had a reasonable time to ascertain the validity of the adverse claims or to bring an action to compel all claimants to interplead and may compel such interpleader, either in defending an action for nondelivery of the goods, or by original action, whichever is appropriate.

CHAPTER 4

Legal Remedies for Business Creditors

While compliance by the creditor with the state and federal laws is essential to enable the creditor to take advantage of the law, sometimes the debtor uses the law to avoid payment of the debt or fails to comply. The creditor should be alert to any suspicions that the debtor has not complied with the law, is evading the intent and purpose of the law or is even engaging in actions to defraud the creditor. This chapter discusses some of the more common remedies available to business creditors and some of the alternatives offered to business debtors.

CREDIT APPLICATION—USE FOR COLLECTION

One goal of the business owner is profitability and profitability is a direct result of sales and sales are a direct result of marketing a viable product. Unfortunately, too often the issue of credit and collection is sometimes omitted and some businesses are remiss in acknowledging the fact that not all purchasers of the product or service will pay within 10 or 30 days.

Two major concerns of the businessman should be the extension of credit and the collection of the account receivable. When the sale is first made or the service first requested, the main priority is whether or not to extend credit and how much credit to extend. The credit application is probably the most important document to determine whether or not to extend credit. In addition to the credit application, a credit report, verification with the bank, verification with other references furnished by the customer, the use of credit databases, and a wide variety of other channels including financial statements, is utilized to verify the financial responsibility of the customer. Many books have been written upon the extension of credit and we will not attempt to improve upon the procedures and methods used to conduct a proper credit department.

Notwithstanding same, we would like to address the collection end of a debt and what the owner of the business can do to assist the attorney in the collection of a debt. We begin with the credit application.

Identification of Borrower. When the client wishes to institute suit against the debtor, identify the nature of the entity which is being sued. (*See* Chapter 3.) It is incumbent to place on the credit application a field where the customer can designate whether the customer is a corporation, partnership, limited liability company or partnership (LLC or LLP), or an individual doing business under a trade name. Without this information the attorney must conduct searches either with the Secretary of State, the County Clerk's Office or other state office to determine exactly how the debtor is conducting business. The attorney must be certain the correct entity is being prosecuted.

While this information is generally available in a public database, searches cost money. Delay works in favor of the debtor. We recommend that the credit application contain the name of the principal officers of the corporation, the partners of the partnership, the members of the LLC or LLP, and the principal owner of the individual who is doing business. Provide a space to obtain the home address and the home telephone number of the individual. If the debtor is out of business, we know where the principal officers reside. If we have a telephone number, we are able to contact them. This contact prior to suit sometimes saves the money of instituting suit.

With the address of the officers, service of the summons can be made on the corporation. A corporation also may be sued by service upon a Secretary of State, but this is more expensive than by serving the principal officer at the residence and delays the collection effort. To serve partnerships or individuals d/b/a, you must serve partners—you cannot serve the Secretary of State.

As to the address of the customer, consumer applications request that the borrower check whether the property is rented or owned. The same question should be addressed to a business in a credit application to indicate whether the corporation, partnership, or individual rents or owns the property located at that address. Property owned provides significant information if the customer is out of business or filed a petition bankruptcy. If it is a rental, seeking the vehicle identification number or other identification number may be helpful when the time comes to serve a summons of complaint. Some credit applications request the listing of all vehicles owned by the business as well as vehicle identification numbers. From a collection point of view, the vehicles may be traced after the customer is out of business. This trail often leads to fraudulent sales to family or friends where the proper amount has not been paid to the company that is out of business.

The lender or owner of the business might query whether they have the right to ask these questions and whether some of the questions would constitute an invasion of privacy. When a lender or owner of a business is extending credit, the owner is entitled to ask whatever questions are appropriate, providing the questions do not discriminate against race, sex, nationality, age, etc. These questions are proper and do not constitute any encroachment on the privacy of the party. The home address of the owner is important if it is a small business and even if it is a large business, the home address is helpful as is the telephone number (serving a summons and complaint on an officer where corporation is out of business).

References. Contacting the business references to obtain information about the customer will certainly assist in a credit decision. From a collection standpoint, business references are sometimes helpful, because we sometimes learn from the references that the particular borrower has organized a new business at another location under a different name.

Obtaining the name of the bank where the borrower or purchaser maintains bank accounts may be helpful with regard to extending credit. It is also helpful after a judgment has been obtained, for the judgment creditor may attach the bank account.

Sometimes the customer or borrower is a wholly owned subsidiary of another corporation and some credit applications ask the question whether the customer is a subsidiary of another company or the parent of another company and request the name and address of the other company. This information helps determine the name of the affiliated company. In certain circumstances affiliated corporations may be joined in lawsuits and be held jointly liable. If we do not know about them, the information never surfaces and the affiliated corporation is never joined in the lawsuit.

Some companies use a credit reference form in conjunction with the credit application. The credit reference form usually contains the company name, address, and a signature line at the end of the form. The party seeking credit states the following above his signature:

> the undersigned hereby authorizes the above named entity to release any and all information requested in this particular document to XYZ Company

The form also should contain the bank name, the type of account, such as checking or saving accounts, including the account number of both the checking and savings accounts. Often the business maintains more than one checking account, so space should be provided for a second checking account number.

The next portion of the form should be used for the bank to respond with an introductory statement as follows:

> The above named party is seeking credit with the XYZ Corporation. Below is the signature authorizing you to furnish the information herein requested. All information received by XYZ Corporation will be held confidential and will not be released.

The form then should seek to identify when the account was opened and closed and what the average balance was. A request also should be made with regard to whether the debtor is a borrowing account, the date when the borrowing commenced, whether it is still open, whether there is any security, and the present balance due. A request should be made for information as to whether the amount was in default, how many times or if the account is current. A line should be provided for the name and title of the party furnishing the information.

Financial Information. Some lenders or companies request financial statements or balance sheets, depending upon the nature of the credit and the amount of the credit. This information provides additional information as to the assets and liabilities of the business. When the debtor has gone into a new business, these assets may be traced to the new business and the new business may not have paid the old firm that is out of business. A suit may be started for fraud against the new business, especially when equipment vehicles and trucks are registered in the new name without appropriate payment.

A search for Uniform Commercial Code financing statements will often be conducted by the extender of credit to determine whether the debtor's assets (other than real estate) are free and clear or whether they are encumbered by liens. When a company is out of business, tracing these assets may reveal the company has paid the lien, is now the owner and the assets are located in the hands of businesses, friends, and relatives who never paid the defunct company.

Where partnerships and individuals are concerned, the assets of the individual partners may be reached. Home addresses become important since most of the time the individuals and partners own their own residences. Sometimes the credit applications require the debtor to list whether the vehicle is owned, is leased and whether it has a lien.

Some applications provide a form balance financial statement for the individual owner (or guarantor) listing all assets, liabilities, and net worth with emphasis on real estate.

Use in Bankruptcy. In adversary proceedings in bankruptcy, comparison of the financial statement with the information in the bankruptcy schedules is fatal when a creditor, and not the bankrupt, filled out the credit application in the handwriting of the creditor. *Credit applications should be completed by the individual and not by the creditor.* When creditors fill out credit applications, names are misspelled and addresses are incorrect. The customer will write the name and address accurately. The important thing to remember is that the application be legible, for many times we encounter applications which are illegible and no one requests the customer to rewrite or print the information requested. A post office box is inadequate as an address of a corporation, an individual or a partnership. A summons cannot be served upon a post office box.

Invasion of Privacy. The response of many lenders or owners of businesses is that the customers will not complete the credit application containing these questions. To some extent that is probably true. Nevertheless, most will complete the credit application and furnish the information. Failing to complete the credit application is a factor in determining whether to extend the credit being requested.

Mortgages and Financing Statement. A customer who owns real estate may have a first mortgage on the property in favor of a bank, who normally lends between 50 percent to 70 percent on commercial property. But if the property carries a second mortgage or even a third, the property may have no equity. This information should affect the extension of credit. If the customer has borrowed against furniture and equipment, inventory, or accounts receivable, a financing statement will be filed with the Clerk of the County where the corporation is located (*see* Chapter 11: Revised Article 9). This information is also helpful in arriving at a credit decision.

Title companies, service bureaus, and in some states, attorneys, conduct the search for mortgages, usually at a reasonable price. Several national companies provide searches for financing statements at prices more reasonable than mortgage searches. Consult with your attorney to locate the organization in your state. Credit applications which contain questions about the existence of mortgages and financing statements are proper.

> ***Credit & Collection Tip:*** *Information is power and information is money. The more information that you obtain about your customer and the more knowledge acquired with regard to credit results in more power acquired to collect a delinquent account.*

ASSIGNMENT FOR THE BENEFIT OF CREDITORS

An "assignment for the benefit of creditors" may be considered an alternative to bankruptcy. The debtor (assignor) transfers the property, assets, and receivables of the business to a person, usually an attorney (assignee, trustee), in trust to convert the property into cash and distribute the proceeds to the creditors of the debtor. Any surplus is returned to the debtor. Almost all states, except Connecticut, Maine, Maryland, Illinois, Nebraska, Nevada, Oregon, and Wyoming have provisions providing for an assignment for the benefit of creditors.

Usually the debtor executes a written "assignment for the benefit of creditors" in favor of a trustee. This assignment transfers to the assignee (trustee) all the assets of the business. The consent of the creditors is not required although notice to the creditors is required under the laws of most states. The assignee's duties are to distribute the assets in accordance with the provisions of the state law. The priorities of general creditors and secured creditors are specifically set forth. The duties and powers of the assignee (to sell, to settle disputes, to sue, and to liquidate the business) are set forth in the instrument of assignment or in the provisions of the state law.

After the assignee mails a notice to the creditors, a proof of claim must be filed by a creditor with the assignee within a specific time.

The assignee sells all the property, as well as any real estate, receivables, intangibles (trademark) and other assets, at the best possible price, and converts the property into cash. The assignee is authorized to pay the expenses of the sale and is entitled to retain counsel and other professionals necessary to effectuate the sale. After all the assets are sold and converted to cash, the assignee distributes the proceeds, less fees, to the creditors. Compensation of the assignee is fixed by the statute. In many states, the fee is usually 5 percent of the total value of the assets after conversion to cash.

Only the debtor may voluntarily file an assignment for the benefit of creditors. The creditor *may favor use* of this remedy because it is quick and relatively cheap compared with a bankruptcy. Unlike a bankruptcy, a creditor cannot make a debtor use this device. Also, the sale of assets should provide the maximum amount for creditors. On the other hand, the process in most states does not allow creditors to examine the debtor under oath, and little supervision is offered by the judicial system. Thus, the remedy becomes attractive to the unscrupulous debtor who sells the assets to a friend for pennies, and then sets up a new business around the corner.

But the power lies with creditors to file an involuntary petition in bankruptcy if they suspect fraud, improper transfers, or self-dealing by the debtor, notwithstanding that the debtor has filed an assignment for the benefit of creditors. An involuntary petition in bankruptcy filed by the creditors terminates the assignment for the benefit of creditors. *Therefore, if preferential payments or transfers of property to family members or other creditors for little value are suspected, a creditor should consider an involuntary petition in bankruptcy.* (*See* Chapter 6 for amendments affecting preferences.)

A distinction exists between a "common law" assignment for the benefit of creditors and a statutory assignment under the respective state law. "Common law" assignments are rarely used in today's environment primarily because the consent of all the creditors is required. A "common law" assignment usually operates under the court decisions rendered in the particular state.

Assignments in the various states range from simple types of assignments to extremely comprehensive and complex types. The statutory law as well as the case law requires that an assignment include all of the debtor's property and must be for the benefit of all the creditors. Within a period of days after the assignment, the debtor must file a copy of the schedules and if he does not file a copy of his schedules, the assignee must file schedules. The assignee's duties in many respects are similar to those of a trustee in bankruptcy. The creditors are entitled to receive ten days notice of a proposed sale of property, payment of dividends, and other proceedings under the assignment. The courts provide a wide brush to supervise the entire proceeding and creditors may seek relief in the court in the event these proceedings do not proceed in accordance with the requirements of the statute.

The question of a discharge in an assignment proceeding has been treated by the Supreme Court, which has held that a discharge of a debt is a unique feature of bankruptcy legislation, which cannot be superseded by the states. Those creditors who have actually consented to an assignment have effectively granted the debtor a discharge. In that respect, the Supreme Court has upheld the assignment statute by virtue of the fact that the consenting creditors are effectively releasing the debtor from any claims. Of course, creditors who do not consent do not discharge the debtor from the claim.

The extent of court supervision over state assignments is limited and the procedures before the court are often before different judges regarding the same assignment. The major reason that the debtors do not use state assignment is the inability to obtain a complete and valid discharge. This is an important consideration for an individual who is conducting a business although it is not particularly important with respect to a corporate debtor. Individuals rarely file assignments.

One of the major advantages of an assignment, as a benefit for creditors, is the cost factor. The assignment is less expensive than filing a petition in bankruptcy. The fee of the assignee may be a contingency fee and may be capped by the contract of assignment. In some states the court supervising the assignment must approve the fees. Similar to the bankruptcy proceeding, the assignee may require attorneys, accountants, real estate brokers, or other professionals in the liquidation of the business.

The qualifications of the assignee are extremely important. The assignee should have experience in other assignments or in bankruptcy, and be qualified to act as the equivalent of a debtor in possession and as a fiduciary for the creditors. The assignee should be bonded and preferably should have experience in the industry. A key advantage is that an assignee can be personally selected by the debtor, and an experienced assignee would not only satisfy the debtor but also the creditors. In bankruptcy the trustee is sometimes randomly picked from several potential trustees.

If you receive a notice of an assignment for the benefit of creditors, you should do the following:

1. Obtain the basic information from the court in which the proceeding has been started: the date of the filing, the index number, the list of creditors, the value of the property transferred, the name and address of the assignee, and the name and address of the attorney for the assignee, as well as the name and address of the attorney for the debtor.
2. If the creditor is a secured creditor (the debtor has executed a security agreement in favor of the creditor covering specific property such as machinery, equipment, automobiles, or trucks—*see* Chapter 11), determine the location of the property and consult with your counsel.
3. Instruct your counsel to file a proof of claim with the assignee. The proof of claim should be filed by certified mail to obtain a receipt, or enclose a postcard for the assignee to return.

Credit & Collection Tip: *Some states have repealed the statutes authorizing an assignment for the benefit of creditors based on the premise that the bankruptcy statute is a better alternative, and other states are processing bills to repeal the statute.*

ATTACHMENT

"Attachment" is a proceeding where the property, whether it is real estate, bank accounts, automobiles, or boats, of the debtor is segregated by a court order so that the debtor is unable to transfer said property until such time as the suit is finally concluded, and the property is held as security to pay any judgment rendered against the debtor.

General Attachment Statutes. In some New England states, such as Connecticut, Massachusetts, and New Hampshire, general attachment is available. The creditor prepares "a writ of attachment," listing the debtor's real property or bank accounts, and serves it on those parties in whose name the property is registered. A copy is filed with the appropriate court officer to prohibit the transfer of any real property until a hearing may be held. An option for the debtor is to obtain a bond to release the attachment. The bond stands as security for any judgment. Any judgment later obtained in these states after a writ is filed is satisfied immediately, providing enough property is attached to cover the amount of the judgment. The attaching party is usually not required to file a bond.

In the New England states, the writ of attachment is prepared by the attorney and filed with the court. The attachment in most other states requires the preparation of an extensive set of papers to warrant the attachment. In marginal cases, the attorney may not be assured of success and often the court will deny the remedy unless the party petitioning the court has clearly met the criteria for obtaining the attachment. The creditor must allege a fact situation reflecting one of the reasons mentioned above and an allegation that the creditor is likely to succeed in obtaining a judgment against the debtor.

Obviously, in those states where attachment is available, this proceeding is a substantial remedy, which should be used where the creditor can identify real estate owned by the defendant. For example, if bank accounts can be identified and a likelihood exists that a substantial amount is on deposit (not exempt), or if a defendant owns a boat or automobile with substantial equity, attachment of these assets is an ideal remedy for the creditor.

Because of due process concerns and the hardship that might be inflicted upon the debtor, most states have abolished this ideal scenario for the plaintiff.

Limited Attachment Statutes. In most states, the power to attach is limited by requiring the creditor to post a bond (usually in an amount double the value of the property attached) and by providing several restrictions before an attachment is effective. Most states allow attachment only under the following circumstances:

1. The debtor is not a resident of a state but has property within the state.
2. The debtor is a resident of the state, but has left the state and is secreting property within the state, and the creditor has identified that secreted property.
3. The debtor has left or is leaving the state and is about to remove, conceal, or dispose of property for the sole purpose of defrauding creditors.

In some states, if the claim against the debtor is based on fraud, an attachment may be available.

The creditor must post a bond in an amount up to twice the amount of the claim to protect the debtor if the creditor should not be successful. The debtor may file a counter bond to release the attachment.

To prove that the debtor is about to leave the state or has left the state while concealing property in the state is a difficult task. The remedy is seldom used except in the New England states.

> ***Credit & Collection Tip:*** *The creditor should be certain of success before attachment is used in a lawsuit. If the debtor is successful, the creditor may be liable for substantial damages, which is the reason for a bond.*

COLLATERAL MORTGAGE

A collateral mortgage indirectly secures a debt and consists of three documents. First, there is the promissory note, usually called a collateral mortgage note. Second, the collateral mortgage provides the creditor with security to enforce the collateral mortgage note. A note is executed because a mortgage is unenforceable without a corresponding note—the note is the obligation and the mortgage the security. Security without an obligation is worthless. A third contract is known as an accessory contract (collateral pledge agreement) by which a third party (individual or corporation) provides something of value to a creditor as security for the obligation of the debtor.

A collateral mortgage note standing alone is meaningless. It has no intrinsic value and evidences no debt or obligation actually owed by or to anyone. Only when viewed in the context of the entire collateral mortgage package, with all the component parts present, does the collateral mortgage take on meaning. It is not a separate enforceable instrument like other promissory notes. *Thus, the collateral mortgage does not create a personal obligation beyond the value of the mortgaged property.*

A collateral mortgage may secure "a negotiable or non-negotiable instrument or other written evidence of the debt that is issued, pledged, or otherwise used as security for another obligation." The maker of a collateral mortgage is not personally liable beyond the value of the mortgaged property when the collateral mortgage note is pledged to secure the debt of a third party, absent some additional agreement personally binding the maker of the collateral mortgage note (such as a personal guaranty of the debt).

> ***Credit & Collection Tip:*** *To avoid litigation, language should be used that the maker of the note is not personally liable under the terms of the note and the collateral mortgage and that the transaction is in the nature of a pledge.*[1]

BULK SALES

Many states have statutes compelling a debtor who wishes to sell all or most of its goods, wares, merchandise, and fixtures for an amount less than its liabilities to comply with the procedures set forth in the "bulk sales" law. The merchant must notify creditors of an intention to consummate said sale and afford the creditors an opportunity to object to the sale if fraud is detected. The Uniform Commercial Code adopted by most states controls the terms and conditions under which a merchant must effectuate a bulk sale. Sales made pursuant to an assignment for the benefit of creditors, transfers and settlements of liens or other security interests and sales by executors, administrators, receivers or trustees in bankruptcy are exempt.

---

[1] *Diamond Servs. Corp. v. Benoit*, 780 So. 2d 367 (La. 2001).

Many states have repealed their statute covering bulk sales, and other states are in the process of doing same. Consult with counsel.

The procedure used in a bulk sale is for the purchaser to require the seller (debtor) of the business to furnish a list of all the creditors. The purchaser then notifies the creditors of the date of the intended sale and whether the proceeds will be sufficient to pay all the creditors of the seller. *Creditors have a limited time to act, only ten days in some states.* The list of creditors must be available for inspection by all the creditors.

A common situation for a bulk sale arises where a debtor has borrowed money from a bank, has collaterized (mortgaged) the loan with inventory and accounts receivable, and has executed a security agreement (mortgage) on all of its equipment. The debtor becomes insolvent and at this stage obtains a purchaser for inventory, receivables, and equipment. A bulk sale is set up and a statement is made that the creditors will not be paid from the proceeds of the sale, because the inventory, accounts receivable and equipment are mortgaged to the bank. Since the bank has a prior lien, the bank will be paid first. Usually the sale of the inventory and accounts receivable rarely produces enough money to pay the bank, and *thus creditors of the seller never receive payment.*

What motivates the debtor to sell the inventory, receivables, and equipment when he or she will not receive any of the proceeds of said sale? The answer is that the principal owner of the debtor personally guarantees the corporate debt to the bank. The proceeds of the sale of all the assets are paid to the bank, reducing the balance due to the bank and reducing the personal obligation of the principal owner to the bank. In this type of situation the creditor has few options. If the sale is made to a purchaser at arm's length and a valid obligation exists with the bank, the resulting transaction leaves no assets to pay creditors.

An alternative scenario of a bulk sale is where the notice of bulk sale states that some payments will be made to the creditors. The key factors are who the purchaser is and whether the sale of the assets is an arm's-length transaction with the purchaser paying full value for the assets. If the purchaser is a new corporation organized by the principal owner of the selling corporation, sufficient reasons exist to investigate as to whether the price paid is fair and reasonable. A valid obligation may exist to the bank, but the assets of the business may be substantially greater than the bank loan. If the inventory, receivables, and equipment are valued in excess of the bank loan, the corporation does have a net worth and monies should be available to pay the creditors. The creditors should be certain that the sale of these assets is made for a fair price to an "arm's-length" purchaser (a purchaser not connected or affiliated in any way to the seller).

Sometimes a creditor learns about a bulk sale weeks or months after it has taken place, because notice has not been received. The failure to notify the creditor may have been intentional or accidental. The seller at the time of the sale may have deliberately omitted the creditor's name from the list of creditors since the debtor suspected that this creditor might have been more aggressive to investigate and review the bulk sale. On the other hand, the purchaser may have accidentally forgotten to include the name of this creditor for any number of reasons, including the fact that the purchaser was careless. The remedy available to the creditor at this stage is to move to set aside the transfer with respect to this particular debt. The procedure available to the creditor varies from state to state, and a careful reading of the state statute is necessary. This process can be costly to pursue.

Only persons with claims at the time of the bulk sale or transfer are creditors within the framework of the bulk sales law. Persons who extend credit or whose claims come into existence after the sale or transfer are not covered. Liquidated claims at the time of sale or transfer are entitled to the law's protection even though the claim or loan may not be due. In one case, a claim for future rent was beyond the scope of the bulk transfer act. Having a claim that is contingent but becomes certain upon the happening of a subsequent event or circumstance does not fall within the protection of the act. The Uniform Commercial Code does include disputed claims, but the claim must meet the other criteria of being a liquidated claim at the time of the bulk sale.

SALE OF DEBTOR'S ASSETS

After a judgment has been obtained by a creditor, the creditor may issue an execution to the sheriff of the county in which the debtor resides. The creditor is notifying the sheriff in writing of the judgment and directing the sheriff to collect the judgment by selling the property of the debtor for cash. After deducting appropriate fees (about 5 percent of the amount collected), the sheriff will remit the balance to the creditor to satisfy the judgment.

Execution. The execution contains the date the judgment was entered, the court, the docket number, the amount of the judgment, the amount of interest, the location of the debtor and, in some instances, the location of the property which the sheriff is to sell. The sheriff will mail or deliver personally the same type of information to the debtor and allow the debtor a certain period of time within which to voluntarily pay the judgment. In the event the judgment is not paid voluntarily by the specified time, the sheriff will proceed to levy on the debtor's assets (visiting the premises of the debtor and identifying the assets).[2]

---

[2]*Schlussel v. Emmanuel Roth Co.*, 270 N.J. Super. 628, 637 A.2d 944 (N.J. Super. Ct. App. Div. 1994).

Levy. Prior to the auction, the sheriff will visit the debtor at the place of business to determine the presence of any assets. On arrival the sheriff will make a levy. A levy is the tagging and identifying all of the equipment and inventory at the place of business. However, the debtor may oppose this levy on the grounds that the property has been mortgaged to a bank or another secured creditor. Under these circumstances, the levy will be subject to the prior lien and the sheriff would have to announce at the public sale that the purchaser would be buying the particular merchandise or equipment subject to the prior lien. The purchaser would have to pay off the lien before full and unencumbered title to the property could be acquired. This happens often in the situation where the sheriff levies and executes on an automobile or a boat which is subject to a prior lien to a bank.

After a levy is made, the debtor often voluntarily tries to make arrangements with the sheriff to pay off the lien. The sheriff will communicate this offer to the attorney who, in turn, will communicate the offer to the creditor. The creditor should recognize that where a payout plan is offered, and the payments are sent directly to the attorney or the creditor, the sheriff still must be paid a fee (5 percent of the amount collected in New York).

Notice of Sale. The sheriff will then publish a notice of the sale in a newspaper in the same geographic area as the debtor, and publish the date of the sale, description of property to be sold, and other pertinent information. The judgment creditor pays the fees in advance to hold a sale, which include the costs of tagging all the property, advertising in the newspaper, and auctioning the property. The cost may approach hundreds of dollars or more for personal property, and substantially more for real estate.

On the date set for the sale, the sheriff conducts an auction of all the property or specific parts of the property. If the bid for all the property is greater than the bid for the specific machinery or the specific inventory, the property will be sold to the party who bid for all of the property. Usually a down payment of 10 percent is required at the auction and the balance is due when the property is removed by the purchaser. The proceeds will then be used to pay off the specific judgment and the remainder of the proceeds will be paid to other judgment creditors. If a balance remains, the amount will be paid to the debtor. The creditor should appear at the sale to bid up the price, or if allowed, set an upset price with the auctioneer.

Friendly Purchaser. In the event the debtor has insufficient money to pay the judgment or to enter a payout plan over a period of time, the debtor will probably walk away and allow the sheriff to proceed with the sale.

Occasionally, an unscrupulous debtor arranges to have a friendly creditor sue him or her for an amount greater than is owed to the friendly creditor. The friendly creditor then obtains a judgment, engages a sheriff to execute, and arranges a sale under the judgment. The friendly creditor's judgment is larger than the value of the assets of the debtor, and the friendly creditor is the purchaser of all the assets at the sheriff's sale. The assets are sold by the friendly creditor to a new corporation organized by the debtor. The friendly creditor is the conduit to help the debtor start a new business using the assets of the old business.

When this type of situation develops, consult with an attorney because it is obvious that this "friendly" sale was held to defraud the creditors. The attorney may recommend a bankruptcy or a suit against the individual based upon fraud or other grounds.

SALE OF ASSETS BY LENDER

Often a small business, such as a restaurant, a retail store, or a service business, will need financing and will mortgage all of its assets to a bank, a financial institution, or the seller of merchandise (such as the kitchen equipment for a restaurant). For example, the owner of a restaurant purchases kitchen equipment by paying $10,000 down and the balance over three years in equal monthly payments. A trucker sells his two old trucks and uses the proceeds as a down payment on two new trucks, and agrees to pay the balance of this purchase price over four years in equal monthly payments. The owner of the restaurant and the trucker execute security agreements (mortgages) on the kitchen equipment and the trucks.

The food preparation is poor in the restaurant, and the number of customers declines. The trucking business stops since the trucker's major client terminates all shipments because of a strike. Both enterprises fail to make the required payments and decide to abandon their businesses. They surrender the collateral to the sellers who extended them credit.

The seller/lender takes possession of the kitchen equipment and the trucks and publishes a notice of sale at auction in a newspaper. A sale is held at the premises of the debtors. The sale may be attended by dealers in kitchen equipment or truck brokers, and these parties may bid at the sale. In most instances, the sellers/lenders themselves will bid up to the amount of their indebtedness, and may acquire title to the vehicles or the kitchen equipment.

One day the vendor, who sells paper products to the restaurant, telephones the restaurant and the number has been disconnected. A visit to the premises reveals that the restaurant is closed, and the landlord has put a "For Rent" sign in the window. Little can be done if it is a proper lien. While this may be a worst-case scenario where the debtor owes a substantial sum of money for paper products, almost every vendor has faced this set of circumstances at one time or another. If you haven't, consider yourself fortunate.

When the debtor surrenders the collateral (kitchen equipment or trucks), the debtor has effectively gone out of business. The lender usually must comply with state laws that require the lender to sell the collateral in a "commercially reasonable manner." A review of the revised Uniform Commercial Code Article 9 adopted in the state must be made before any sale is conducted (*see* Chapter 11).

> ***Credit & Collection Tip:*** *You can verify whether the assets are mortgaged by engaging a service organization to search the public records at the county clerk's office to determine if financing statements have been filed reflecting the existence of the liens (mortgages). If the assets are mortgaged, consider obtaining a personal guarantee before selling to the debtor. Many vendors incorporate a personal guarantee in the opening order form, and, in some cases, the guarantee form must be executed with each order.*

The creditor may decide to consult with counsel to determine if the lender complied with the applicable laws—proper notice, a commercially reasonable sale, the disposition of the monies if a third party bought at the sale, proper advertising, and other requirements familiar to counsel.

LENDER'S LIABILITY

Most of the cases under lender's liability seem to have occurred in the late 1980s and the 1990s and recently have not been the subject of major litigation. The leading case was *Citibank, N.A. v. Plapinger*[3] wherein the Court of Appeals of the State of New York held that fraud in the inducement in the execution of a guarantee by the officers of a corporation is not a valid defense in an action by the bank where the guarantees recite clearly that it is an absolute and unconditional guarantee. The guarantee also contained a clause stating that the guarantors were not entitled to rely on any oral representation that the banks were committed to extend to the corporation any additional line of credit. The disclaimer language in the guarantee was sufficient. This was not a boilerplate guarantee but a negotiated guarantee which gave some additional support to the court's decision. *Plapinger* has more or less been followed by many other courts in New York. Oral promises to extend additional credit or to perform some other financial accommodation usually have not been given credibility where the express terms of the guarantee or the contract or the loan agreement clearly contradicts such statements. Whether a mortgage was to be orally modified, a note was to be discharged orally, permanent financing was orally promised, or whether there was an oral agreement

[3]*Citibank, N.A. v. Plapinger*, 66 N.Y.2d 90 (1985).

to extend a due date, the courts generally find a reason to uphold the written agreement.

Another theory on lender's liability is economic duress. In these cases, the party seeks to avoid some type of written agreement by alleging economic duress resulting in substantial injury to the debtor. Most courts feel that the debtor has to undertake a heavy burden to prove economic duress and contracts should be declared voidable only in extreme and unusual cases. The plaintiff must show that the defendant actually caused the economic condition and except for the plaintiff's actions, the defendant would have never suffered this particular economic condition.[4]

When mortgages and security agreements are drafted, counsel usually provides for a wide variety of remedies in the event of default wherein the lender can exercise control over the borrower and its business. This exercise of control may often lead to a variety of claims by creating some form of a fiduciary duty owed not only to the entity but to the creditors of the entity.

When the debtor enters bankruptcy, the allegations are usually that the lender, by exercising the control, became the principal cause of the bankruptcy. A further issue to consider is whether the lender has now acquired the clothing of an insider together with the liability of an insider. The lender was making all the business decisions as opposed to the situation where the lender merely provided business advice with most of their interest on cash flow and on payments to be made to the lender. The latter situation does not normally produce liability. The extent to which creditors are harmed will have an impact on the lender's liability. These problems arise automatically when a mortgagee on a multi-family building takes possession under the terms of the mortgage and evicts tenants, rents to new tenants and engages in repairs and construction. The collection of rents and operation of the property creates liability.

Members of the lender are placed on the board of directors. The members of the lender serving on the board make almost all the business decisions and directs the borrower to carry out the decisions. On the other hand the lender may remain on the board of directors but only provide consultation and allow the borrower to operate the business for the benefit of the lender and other creditors.

The lender must walk a tightrope so that the exposure to liability is a bare minimum. In mortgage situations the amount involved is substantial and the lender is devoted to increasing the profitability of the borrower. When faced with this situation, the lender must be careful and consultation with experienced counsel is recommended.

To protect against lender's liability, many banks in dealing with large loans are insisting upon an initial agreement to protect the bank against

---

[4] *Bank of China v. Chan*, 937 F.2d 780 (2d Cir. 1991); *Scott v. Dime Sav. Bank*, 886 F. Supp. 1073 (S.D.N.Y. 1995); *Lee v. Wal-Mart Stores, Inc.*, 34 F.3d 285 (5th Cir. 1994); *Krivo Indus. Supply Co. v. National Distillers & Chemical Corp.*, 483 F.2d 1098 (5th Cir. 1973); *In re Olick*, 221 B.R. 146 (Bankr. E.D. Pa. 1998).

claims that the borrower relied on representations made by the bank. The allegation by the borrower is normally that the representations constituted a commitment to make the loan. The debtor was damaged when the loan was not made.

These agreements are labeled "pre-negotiation" agreements. The purpose is to avoid lender liability if the bank should decide not to grant the loan. The agreements address oral representations by any agent or employee of the bank that deal with commitments to loans, amount of loan, interest rates, and other terms of the loan. The use of these agreements has increased substantially and, in some instances, is extended to smaller loans. Perhaps this preventive step is the reason that lender liability cases have decreased substantially over the years.

The agreements are also used for refinancing or restructuring.

NEW OWNER

A creditor may contact a debtor. The conversation develops as follows:

CREDITOR: Is Charlie there?

NEW OWNER: Charlie's no longer here. We bought the business from Charlie.

CREDITOR: When did this happen? I spoke to Charlie two weeks ago.

NEW OWNER: We purchased the business as of last Monday. Charlie has left for Las Vegas.

CREDITOR: What about my debt for a thousand dollars for videotapes that I sold to Charlie?

NEW OWNER: We are not liable for Charlie's debt.

CREDITOR: What do you mean you're not liable for Charlie's debt? You have the business. You have the same phone number.

NEW OWNER: We purchased only the video tapes in the store. This is a new corporation which was formed by me. We are not liable for the debts of Charlie's corporation.

CREDITOR: But you have the same phone number and you are at the same place and using the same name.

NEW OWNER: We entered a new lease with the landlord and took Charlie's phone number and trade name.

In this instance the buyer formed a new corporation to purchase only the inventory, the video tapes. In the contract of sale executed with

Charlie's former corporation, the telephone number and the trade name also were purchased.

The purchaser rarely buys the stock of the prior corporation, but instead purchases the assets and organizes a new corporation, since the new owner does not want to be liable for the debts of the old corporation. If the purchaser acquires the stock of the prior corporation, the prior corporation continues to exist and the purchaser is liable for the debt (and no new corporation is created).

Extensive questioning as to the transfer is recommended or have your attorney contact the attorney for the purchaser.

CREDITOR: I don't understand. Was Charlie in financial trouble?

NEW OWNER: I really don't know.

CREDITOR: Did you purchase these video tapes at a sheriff's sale?

NEW OWNER: No, there was no sheriff's sale, there was no judgment. I entered into a purchase and sale contract with Charlie when I purchased the video tapes.

CREDITOR: How much did you pay for these video tapes?

NEW OWNER: I paid $23,000.

CREDITOR: What happened to the $23,000?

NEW OWNER: I really don't know what happened to the $23,000.

CREDITOR: Was this a bulk sale? Did you send out a notice to the creditors? Did you get a list of the creditors from Charlie?

NEW OWNER: No, it was not a bulk sale. I have no list of creditors from Charlie and I had no interest in whether Charlie had any creditors or not. I issued a check to him for $23,000.

CREDITOR: But these are all his assets.

NEW OWNER: I never made any inquiry as to whether it was all his assets or not. I merely issued a check for $23,000 to Charlie and Charlie turned over the entire stock of video tapes to my corporation.

CREDITOR: What's the name of your corporation?

NEW OWNER: My corporation's name is the XYZ corporation.

CREDITOR: How did you get a lease at Charlie's store? Did Charlie transfer the lease to you?

NEW OWNER: No, he did not transfer the lease to me. Charlie's lease expired about a month ago. He hadn't paid any rent and the landlord was about to evict him. I approached the landlord and entered into a new lease with the landlord. I am now occupying the premises under the lease.

CREDITOR: Why are you using Charlie's name and phone number?

NEW OWNER: I'm using Charlie's name because it was known in the neighborhood. Part of that $23,000 was for Charlie's name and some also was for the telephone number, because people would call up to see whether we had a particular movie and I thought it would be best to keep the same phone number.

CREDITOR: So all you did was enter into a new contract with Charlie for the name, the phone number, and all the video tapes.

NEW OWNER: That's right.

CREDITOR: Did you know that these were the only assets Charlie had?

NEW OWNER: I told you once and I'll tell you a second time that I made no inquiry to see whether this was all the assets or wasn't all the assets. And I think I've answered enough questions up to now.

CREDITOR: Could you please give me the name of your attorney.

NEW OWNER: My attorney's name is John Eagle at 25 Main Street, Centerville, New Jersey. His telephone number is 201-555-1234.

CREDITOR: Do you know the name of Charlie's attorney?

NEW OWNER: I think the attorney's name is Sparrow and Hawk at 15 Spring Street, Centerville, New Jersey.

CREDITOR: Do you know the telephone number?

NEW OWNER: No, I don't know the telephone number, but I suppose the number is in the book.

CREDITOR: Do you know where Charlie is conducting business now?

NEW OWNER: I don't have the foggiest idea.

CREDITOR: Thank you very much.

Credit & Collection Tip: *If assets are purchased, the next question is the disposition of the money paid for the assets. Was the money used to pay off certain creditors and not others? Were there any liens on Charlie's property? Was the money used to pay only those debts which were personally guaranteed? Was the money used to form a new corporation for the principal owner or for other personal uses such as travel, boats, entertainment, etc.? Is there really a new corporation or merely a name change? Did Charlie violate the bulk sales law? The money should be used to pay the creditors. Consultation with counsel is advised.*

RECEIVERSHIP

In some instances the debtor is depleting the assets of a business either by neglecting them or by willfully selling the assets piece by piece for less than fair market value. In most states where the creditor obtains a judgment, and in some states (e.g., Massachusetts) before suit, the creditor may make an application to court to appoint a receiver of the assets. A receivership also may be requested where the debtor owns real estate, permits the real estate to fall into disrepair, collects the rents, but fails to use the rents to maintain the property. In these instances, the mortgagee will make an application to court to appoint a receiver, but the remedy is also available to a creditor who improved the property by performing construction work, or by furnishing other equipment or services. A receiver who is appointed by the court takes possession of the real estate, collects the rents, uses the rents to maintain the property, and uses the surplus monies to pay off the creditors.

Some states allow a receiver to be appointed during a foreclosure proceeding of a multi-unit building. The application is simple, and if unopposed, usually granted quickly. The mortgagee uses the income generated from the tenants to maintain the property and to pay off debt. A review of the state law is necessary. In some states receivership is your best remedy because the state law does not provide for a sheriff's sale of the debtor's property.

RISK OF LOSS

When commercial transactions were governed by the Uniform Sales Act, the question of which party had the risk of loss when the goods were in transit, such as on a train, plane, or a truck, depended upon which party had title at the time the accident happened. If the seller had title at the time the accident happened, the seller had to bear the loss and seek reimbursement from the insurance company. If title to the goods had already passed to the buyer, the buyer assumes the risk. There were no set rules. Each case presented a specific problem and often created additional questions. The end result was confusion and a significant amount of litigation.

The Uniform Commercial Code (UCC) Sections 2-509 and 2-510 resolved many of the problems that existed under the Uniform Sales Act and Sections 2-319 and 2-320 have further resolved many of the problems by defining the term "free on board" (FOB). Section 509 states that when a contract authorizes a seller to ship by carrier, if there is no requirement in the contract to deliver the goods at a particular specified location, the buyer assumes the risk of loss at the time the goods are delivered to the carrier. If the contract does require delivery at a specific designation and the goods are delivered there, the buyer assumes the risk of loss when the goods are tendered at the specific designation. The term FOB is defined as a delivery term. When the term "FOB place of shipment" is used, the seller must ship the goods and bear the expense of putting them into the possession of the carrier. Once in the possession of the carrier, the buyer assumes the risk of loss. When the term "FOB place of destination" is used, the seller bears the expense and risk until delivery to the place of destination.

Most frequently, shipments are made FOB seller's place of business; that is, shipment contracts in which the seller agrees to make a contract for shipment and delivery of the goods into the possession of the carrier. The risk of loss passes to the buyer immediately upon delivery to the carrier. When the contract reads FOB buyer's place of business, the risk of loss does not pass to the buyer until the carrier tenders the goods to the buyer at the buyer's place of business. It is assumed that the goods are delivered in a conforming condition and that the buyer has had reasonable notice to pick up the goods.

The actual address to which the seller is to deliver the goods as set forth in the contract has no bearing and will not affect the liability of either the seller or buyer—which is solely controlled by the FOB clause. If the term says FOB seller's place of business and then designates to what address the shipment is to be made, the seller's risk of loss ends when he delivers the merchandise to the carrier. The contract terms identify who is paying the expense of shipping, but this has no effect on the liability of the parties, which is controlled by the FOB clause (nor would the fact that the seller is using his own trucks to ship the merchandise under a FOB place of shipment clause in the contract).

If there is no FOB designation in the contract, the risk of loss passes to the buyer immediately upon delivery to the carrier if no requirement is present to deliver at a particular designation. The parties may expressly provide in writing for any other terms and conditions that are contrary to the UCC and the written agreement would prevail.

SURETY—CONSTRUCTION CONTRACTS

Frequently, surety agreements are created in construction contracts where the owners of property obtain what is known as performance bonds from insurance companies. A case in New York clarified some of the issues and liabilities of the insurance company.

Contracts of surety are to be construed like other contracts, so as to give effect to the intention of the parties. Once the liability and the meaning of the language in the surety contract has been determined, the responsibility of the surety is not to be extended or enlarged by construction or implication and is "strictissimi juris," which means the courts tend to interpret surety contracts strictly within the terms of the contract in the same manner as letters of credit are interpreted.

In general, third parties such as subcontractors or co-prime contractors have no right to recover from performance bonds for a contractor/principal's breach. Where a laborer sought to recover unpaid wages from a contractor's performance bond executed by the surety solely in favor of the owner, the judge concluded that such a bond was not intended to benefit anyone other than the named beneficiary (owner). Allowing a third party to assert a claim against a performance bond would frustrate the purpose of the bond since the purpose of the bond is to benefit the beneficiary and not third parties. To allow the third party to assert a claim against the performance bond, the amount of the performance bond would be reduced and the beneficiary would suffer. The court reasoned that if third parties were allowed to assert claims against the bond, sufficient monies would not be available to complete the performance, the purpose for which the bond was intended.

Another claim in the case was that the insurance company is itself liable for the delay, because they were stepping into the shoes of the contractor. Therefore, the third party could assert a claim against the insurance company since the contractor delayed the performance and the third party suffered damages. The court interpreted the contract strictly and stated that the insurance company had really become obligated to complete the work and did not step into the shoes of the prime contractor who defaulted in the performance, but stepped into the shoes of the beneficiary (the owner) and as the beneficiary under the contract, the insurance company was completing the work. In short, the obligations of the surety bond are solely for the benefit of the beneficiary, usually the owner of the property.

Sometimes the contractor himself is the beneficiary and other times the subcontractors may be the beneficiaries under the surety agreement. A careful reading of the surety contract is essential. Problems arise when the insurance company on the surety bond is competing with a bank that has a security interest in the accounts of the contractor. The surety is completing the job and should be entitled to the progress payments. On the other hand, the bank has a right to the progress payments to discharge their indebtedness. The bank filed a financing statement whereas the surety company had no opportunity to file a financing statement under its contract to complete the construction work (except as to the heavy equipment of the contractor). Consultation with counsel is recommended.[5]

NOTICE OF DEFECT

We continue to see cases where one party to a contract has failed to provide notice of the breach of the contract to the other party. Usually, it is an obvious defect or a defect that is not discovered until a later date.

[5] *Anron Heating & Air Conditioning, Inc. v. City of New York*, Index No. 605981/97, 1998 N.Y. Misc. LEXIS 520 (Sup. Ct. New York Co. Nov. 4, 1998).

Section 2-607 states as follows:

1. the buyer must pay at the contract rate for any goods accepted.
2. acceptance of goods by the buyer precludes rejection of the goods accepted and if made with knowledge of a non-conformity cannot be revoked because of it unless the acceptance was on the reasonable assumption that the non-conformity would be seasonably cured but acceptance does not of itself impair any other remedy provided by this article for non-conformity.
3. where a tender has been accepted
   a. the buyer must within a reasonable time after he discovers or should have discovered any breach, notify the seller of breach or be barred from any remedy. . . .

The statute avers that within a reasonable time the party should notify the seller of the breach. The statute does not specify whether notice is oral, in writing, or whether you should use certified mail or overnight express. Many cases revolve around an oral notice that the other party denies receiving. Oral notice will meet the standards of this section if it is delivered within a reasonable time. The best of both worlds is to provide oral notice with a notation of whom you spoke to as well as the date and time, and to immediately mail to the seller written notice of the breach.

The written notice does not have to contain a detailed itemization of the nature of the breach nor in what respect was the particular product defective. The notice need not set forth any claim for damages, or of any threatened litigation, or of any other threat of a resort to a remedy. The notice only must inform the seller that the transaction involved a breach.

Whether the notice should be given by certified mail to establish the fact that the seller received notification of the breach or by use of an overnight express carrier where a record of delivery of the notice is available probably depends upon whether the purchaser of the product wishes to be cautious and upon the amount of the damages that the buyer will incur if the buyer is unable to prove notice to the seller.[6]

CREDITORS OF A BAILEE

In the western states, the branding of an animal creates evidence of ownership. However, a brand on livestock is only prima facie evidence of ownership and is not ownership that may not be attacked by third parties. An agreement between the parties that one party retained ownership while

[6] *Aqualon Co. v. MAC Equipment*, 149 F.3d 262 (4th Cir. 1998).

the other party became a bailee and received possession of the cattle is strong evidence that the ownership was retained in the name of the bailor.

The cattle were branded by the bailee and the creditor of the bailee of the cattle attempted to seize the cattle allegedly owned by someone other than the bailee. The mere fact that a bailee has possession of property does not mean that the creditor can attach this property, if, in fact, it is a genuine bailment. Case law indicates that a security interest of a bailee's creditor does not attach to goods that are the subject of a bailment. The new brand was that of the bailee, but older brands were on the cattle. The last brand is not necessarily automatically dispositive of ownership. Under the Wyoming statute, the brand, prima facie ownership, was subject to rebuttal. Two brands were on the cattle and both of them could be treated as evidence of prima facie ownership. A lien search under the bailee's name revealed no liens. The court ultimately held that the bailor maintained ownership of the cattle. The case also provided an analysis of the branding customs in the industry as well as the impact of separate agreements between the parties as to ownership and bailment.[7]

RECLAMATION—DISCOVERY OF BUYER'S INSOLVENCY

Reclamation under the bankruptcy law has been radically changed by the Bankruptcy Abuse Prevention and Consumer Protection Act (BAPCPA) covered in Chapter 6. This section reviews reclamation outside of the Bankruptcy statute.

The seller's remedies on discovery of a buyer's insolvency are set forth in Section 2-702 of the UCC:

1. Where the seller discovers the buyer to be insolvent, he may refuse delivery except for cash including payment for all goods theretofore delivered under the contract and stop delivery under this Article (Section 2-706).
2. Where the seller discovers that the buyer has received goods on credit while insolvent, he may reclaim the goods upon demand made within ten days after the receipt, but if misrepresentation of solvency has been made to the particular seller in writing within three months before delivery, the ten-day limitation does not apply. Except as provided in this subsection, the seller may not base a right to reclaim goods on the buyer's fraudulent or innocent misrepresentation of solvency or of intent to pay.

[7] *Estate of Harris v. Harris*, 218 F.3d 1140 (10th Cir. 2000).

3. The seller's right to reclaim under Subsection 2 is subject to the rights of a buyer in ordinary course or other good faith purchaser under this article (Section 2-403). Successful reclamation of goods excludes all other remedies with respect to them.

The theory of Subsection 2 is that any receipt of goods on credit by an insolvent buyer amounts to a misrepresentation of solvency and is fraudulent as against the particular seller. The ten-day limitation operates from the time of receipt of the goods. If a written misrepresentation is made within three months prior to delivery, the ten-day limitation is not applicable. In Subsection 3, the act states that the reclamation bars any other remedies with regard to the goods—the creditor must take the goods back and cannot sue for damages.

In general, before a reclamation can be made, the following criteria usually would apply:

1. The goods are to be sold initially on credit to the debtor.
2. Whether the debtor is insolvent rests on whether the debtor has stopped paying his debts as they become due. While a creditor may apply other definitions of insolvency, such as the balance sheet definition or the liabilities exceed the assets, the principal reason a creditor would become aware of the insolvency is because the debtor is not paying bills.
3. The statute requires a written demand. The goods must still be in the possession of the debtor when the demand is received by the debtor.
4. The debtor must purchase the goods in the ordinary course of business. If the acquisition of the goods is not in the ordinary course of business, this section would not apply.
5. If the merchandise received has already been sold by the debtor or is subject to a lien, the moment the merchandise is acquired, the seller may not be entitled to reclaim the goods. Where there is a floating lien on inventory, the courts seem to go both ways on whether the lien is superior to a claim for reclamation.

Goods in Transit. Section 2-705 of the UCC states:

1. The seller may stop delivery of goods in the possession of a carrier or other bailee when he discovers the buyer to be insolvent (Section 2-702) and may stop delivery of carload, truckload, planeload or larger shipments of express or freight when the buyer repudiates or fails to make a payment due before delivery or if for any other reason the seller has a right to withhold or reclaim the goods.
2. As against such buyer the seller may stop delivery until
   (a) receipt of the goods by the buyer; or

(b) acknowledgment to the buyer by any bailee of the goods except a carrier that the bailee holds the goods for the buyer; or

(c) such acknowledgment to the buyer by a carrier by reshipment or as warehouseman; or

(d) negotiation to the buyer of any negotiable document of title covering the goods.

3. (a) To stop delivery the seller must so notify as to enable the bailee by reasonable diligence to prevent delivery of goods.

(b) After such notification the bailee must hold and deliver the goods according to the directions of the seller but the seller is liable to the bailee for any ensuing charges or damages.

(c) If a negotiable document of title has been issued for goods, the bailee is not obliged to obey a notification to stop until surrender of the document.

(d) A carrier who has issued a non-negotiable bill of lading is not obliged to obey a notification to stop goods received from a person other than the consignor.

The court held that the carrier must deliver the goods according to the seller's directions and that the seller is always liable to the bailee (carrier) for any damages that the carrier may thereafter incur. The bailee (carrier) had no right to ask for indemnity for damages by requiring the seller to get a letter of credit to secure their indemnity. The courts made it clear that "the seller automatically undertakes the duty to indemnify when it stops delivery."[8]

In one case, the seller attempted to hold up the delivery of certain goods but in this instance the bill of lading was already delivered to the purchaser in a negotiable form. The court held that because it was a negotiable document in the hands of the purchaser, the carrier was under no obligation to stop the transit and must surrender the goods to the purchaser.[9]

MECHANIC'S LIEN

A *mechanic's lien* is an additional right available to those vendors who perform work and labor or furnish materials to repair and improve real property. Each state has passed specific laws which enable this class of vendors to file a lien on the property.

---

[8] *Siderpali, S.P.A. v. Judal Indus., Inc.*, 833 F. Supp. 1023 (S.D.N.Y. 1993).

[9] *In re Treco Steel Co., LLC*, 282 B.R. 318 (Bankr. D. Del. 2002); *Petroleum Products v. Mid-America Pipeline Co.*, 815 F. Supp. 1421 (D. Kan. 1993).

The lien form generally sets forth the value of the work, labor and materials furnished, when the work was done, the location of the property, and a description of work. The filing of the lien creates the effect of a mortgage on the property at the time of the filing of the lien. The mechanic's lien is subject to those liens and mortgages which were filed prior to the date of the lien, and is ahead and prior to those liens or mortgages filed after the date the lien was filed. The lienor (e.g., electrician, plumber, or carpenter) usually has a period of approximately three or four months after the time the work is completed to file the lien, and sometimes up to seven or eight months. (This time period may vary from state to state, depending upon the type of property affected and other circumstances.)

The debtor may make an application to court to remove the lien or the debtor may wait until the lienor commences a foreclosure suit under the lien. *Since a mechanic's lien normally expires after a certain period of time and requires renewal by the lienor, the debtor may permit the mechanic's lien to expire with the hope that the lienor will not renew the lien.*

Bond. A further device available to the debtor is to bond the lien. The debtor arranges with the insurance company to obtain a bond at least in the amount of the lien (in some states a greater amount is required). Upon receipt of said bond, counsel will make an appropriate application to court to have the lien removed and will utilize the bond to secure the lienor who filed the lien. A bond is usually used when the owner of the property is preparing to sell the property or the property is already under a contract of sale. The lienor files the mechanic's lien to exert pressure on the owner of the property to pay the bill at the closing or else the purchaser will deduct the amount of the lien from the purchase price. For this reason, the use of the bond is uniquely designed to prevent an unscrupulous lienor from interfering with the prospective sale of real estate in the event the owner disputes the amount due under the lien.

The mechanic's lien is a powerful tool protecting the construction firm that repairs or improves real estate. If the bill is not paid promptly, the recourse of the creditor is to file a lien with the county clerk in the county in which the property is located. This remedy was created by the state, and therefore each state has its own requirements and procedures with regard to filing and foreclosing a lien, and providing notice and information. A review of each state law is essential.

Hazardous Waste Removal. Black's Law Dictionary defines the term "improvement" as an addition to real property, whether permanent or not; especially, one that increases its value or utility or that enhances its appearance.[10] In most states' statutes, mechanic's liens are allowed to be filed where there has been an "improvement of real property." Nevertheless, there are variations from state to state dealing with this particular verbiage and a review of the state law is absolutely necessary before filing a mechanic's lien.

A particular statute was carefully analyzed in a Kansas case, albeit the decision left some questions. The statute read as follows:

> Any person furnishing labor, equipment, material, or supplies used or consumed for the improvement of real property, under a contract with the owner or with the trustee, agent or spouse of the owner, should have a lien upon the property for the labor, equipment, material or supplies furnished and for the cost of transporting same.

In the removal of hazardous waste material, the court reasoned that no construction was ever commenced and there were no visible or physical manifestations of the contractor's work on the property. The court acknowledged that there is no necessity for a visible effect on the real property for the activity to be lienable, as long as the services did enhance the value of the land.

Improvement of Property. After a thorough analysis, the court set down several observations concerning the definition of "improvement of real property":

1. What is or is not an improvement of real property must be based upon the circumstances of each case;
2. Improvement of the property does not require the actual construction of a physical improvement;
3. The improvement of the property need not necessarily be visible, although in most instances it is;
4. The improvement of the real property must enhance the value of the real property, although it need not enhance the selling value of the property;
5. For labor, equipment, material or supplies to be lienable items, they must be used or consumed and thus become part of the real property;
6. The nature of the activity performed is not necessarily a determining factor of whether there is an improvement of real property within the meaning of the statute; rather, the purpose of the activity is more directly concerned in the determination of whether there is an improvement of property which is thus lienable; and
7. The furnishing of labor, equipment, material or supplies used or consumed for the improvement of real property may become lienable if it

[10] Black's Law Dictionary 757 (7th ed. 1999).

is established as part of an overall plan to enhance the value of the property, its beauty or utility, or to adapt it for a new or further purpose, or if the furnishing of labor, equipment, materials, or supplies is a necessary feature of plaintiff's construction of a physical improvement to the real property.

The court decided that removal of a hazardous waste product did not qualify under this seven-pronged test and that the contractor did not have a right to file a mechanic's lien.[11]

This court emphasized the necessity to increase value. The analysis seems sound, but other courts might favor the contractor and measure the labor and material. Environmental cleanup is desirable, and penalizing a contractor may not be in the best interest of the community.

Credit & Collection Tip: *After the lien is filed, the creditor also has the option to commence a suit against the debtor for the debtor's failure to pay for services or materials, or foreclose against the property by reason of the mechanics lien.*

The most important ingredient to file a mechanic's lien is a proper description of the property. In some states, a block and lot number is sufficient. In other states, a detailed legal description of the property must be attached to the lien. In many states both are needed.

The statutes vary from state-to-state, for example, in California, 90 days to file a lien, whereas in Illinois, two years. A mechanic's lien is usually subject to a first mortgage or even a second mortgage, and therefore depending upon the amount of the lien, a foreclosure suit might not be economically worthwhile. In some states, a notice of suit must be filed with strict time frames for filing. In other states, the notice must contain where the owner resides. Some states allow the filing of a *lis pendens* similar to the one in a foreclosure suit, which provides notice that a suit is presently contemplated. Many of the statutes require you to send a certified letter to the owner of the property setting forth information concerning the lien or at least a copy of the lien itself. If an owner of the property sells the property, the purchaser will require the owner to pay off all liens. Judgment liens as well as mechanic's liens are paid at that time.

In some states, a general contractor must file a document or a notice of commencement, which provides information concerning the name of the contractor, the owner of the property and alleges if a bond or surety is provided. If the contractor does not send this notice and the contractor has started the job, *the contractor may be barred from filing a lien at a later date.* For those who are entitled to file a lien for improving property, consult with an experienced counsel in the state.

---

[11]*Haz-Mat Response, Inc. v. Certified Waste Servs. Ltd.*, 259 Kan. 166, 910 P.2d 839 (Kan. 1996); *In re 110 Church Street LLC* (Supreme Court, N.Y), N.Y.L.J., Sept. 20, 2001, at 27, col. 2.

FINANCIAL LEASE—REASONABLE TIME TO TEST TECHNOLOGY

UCC Section 2a-407 states as follows:

1. In the case of a finance lease that is not a consumer lease, the lessee's promises under the lease contract become irrevocable and independent upon the lessee's acceptance of the goods.
2. Promise that has become irrevocable and independent under subsection (1):
   a. is effective and enforceable between the parties, and by or against third parties including assignee's of the parties; and
   b. is not subject to cancellation, termination, modification, repudiation, excuse or substitution without the consent of the party to whom the promise runs.
3. This section does not affect the validity under any other law of a covenant in any lease contract making the lessee's promises irrevocable and independent upon the lessee's acceptance of the goods.

The section treats covenants in a finance lease as irrevocable and independent. The lessee looks to the supplier to perform the essential warranties. Thus, upon the lessee's acceptance of the goods, the lessee's promises to the lessor under the lease contract become irrevocable and independent. The provisions of this section remain subject to the obligations of good faith and the lessee's revocation of acceptance.

In a classic case, the defendant bought a computer and software package that would generate estimates for insurance companies. The defendant entered into a finance lease with a leasing corporation and the president signed the lease as an agent for the defendant and also signed as a personal guarantor. The finance company required the individual to sign an acceptance and acknowledgment form which stated that the equipment had been received from the supplier and was satisfactory despite the fact the defendant had not received the equipment. In fact, the defendant also made an initial lease payment.

Thereafter, the defendant received the equipment. The finance lessor contacted the defendant seeking a verbal verification that the equipment was acceptable. He was told that the equipment was received, but was not yet operational. On the second day, the finance lessor again contacted the defendant to inquire whether the system was operational and he was told that the system was working. At that point, the finance company paid the supplier. On the same day, the system crashed and all efforts failed to restore it to working order. Approximately two years later, the defendant and the individual president were sued. The plaintiff relied on Section 2(a)-407 of the UCC (*see* above).

Section 2(a)-515 of the Code provides that acceptance occurs when the lessee does any of the three things after a reasonable opportunity to inspect goods:

1. Signifies acceptance.
2. Fails to make an effective rejection.
3. Does any act that signifies acceptance.

The court emphasized that taking possession of the goods is not acceptance, signing a form written acceptance before receipt of the goods is not acceptance, nor is making a payment acceptance. The reasonable time to inspect under the UCC is an opportunity to put the product to its intended use or for testing to verify its capability to perform. The reasonable opportunity after possession to inspect and test is contemplated prior to acceptance.

Even when a lessee has signed an acceptance form acknowledging the equipment was satisfactory and in working order, no acceptance takes place until a reasonable time elapses to test the product for its intended use. When a contract requires payment prior to inspection, payment does not constitute an acceptance nor does it impair the buyer's right to inspect. Obviously, to execute these agreements prior to receiving the computer equipment, the defendant must have trusted not only the supplier, but the leasing company. The president also advised the financing company over the telephone that the software was working.

The equipment did not function properly and it was returned immediately. This case illustrates an example of how forcing a defendant to pay for equipment that is returned would be totally unfair (the president verbally stated the equipment was working, and the finance company relied on this statement *and* paid the supplier).[12]

> ***Credit & Collection Tip:*** *The moral of the story is when buying any technology, be certain that a clause is inserted in the contract which allows you a reasonable time to test the equipment.*

FINANCING BY AFFILIATED COMPANY

The seller of a product or service often provides its own credit company which finances the transaction. The finance company is operated separately and distinctly from the equipment company and enters into the financing arrangement or lease arrangement, whichever is more appropriate, with the purchaser; the equipment company furnishes the equipment

---

[12] *Colonial Pac. Leasing Corp. v. J.W.C.J.R. Corp.*, 977 P.2d 541 (Utah 1999).

and is paid by the finance company. Most of these types of credit arrangements are several pages of fine print and it is incumbent upon the buyer to be fully aware of the fine print. The disclaimers and liquidated damage clauses contained in the fine print are comprehensive and are designed primarily to protect the financing organization.

In the instance case, the court found that a particular agreement was not a consumer lease. Consumer leases are treated differently and consumers have additional protection when the product they purchase is being financed by an affiliated company. But courts are reluctant to change the terms of business agreements. This case happened in New Jersey and the court determined that the agreement was a finance lease, wherein the financial firm does not manufacture or supply the goods, but only acquires the goods or the right to possession in connection with the lease.

The portion of the disclaimer in the lease was common wherein it stated that the lessor, the credit company, shall not be deemed to have made any representation, warranty, or promise made by the seller of the product. Neither the seller nor the lessor shall act as or be deemed to be an agent of the other. The lessor shall not be bound by, or be liable for, any representation or promise made by the seller (even if the lessor is affiliated with the seller). The agreement also provided that the lessor shall have no liability to the lessee, the lessee's customers, or any third parties for any direct, indirect, special, or consequential damages arising out of the agreement. The lease provides that the agreement will not deprive the lessee of any rights it may have against any other person, that is, the seller. Most of these financing agreements specifically state that the lessee shall look solely to the seller for any or all claims, representations, and warranties relating to the equipment. If a manufacturer's warranty is available, the lessee may rely on that agreement.

The court pointed out that the finance company performed no other function and its disclaimers were prominent in the lease and the lease provided that the purchaser had a right to pursue the seller for any warranties and representations. The fact that there was a close connection between the finance company and the seller is not of itself sufficient.

Arguments might be made that the finance company was involved in the sale of the equipment or was involved in the delivery or maintenance of the equipment. But most finance companies are careful to be involved only in collecting payments, and totally remove themselves from any involvement in the sale or maintenance of the equipment.

The personal guarantee of the individual officer of the lessee was also deemed enforceable by the court. In this particular case, the telephone company was still in business and ultimately may answer for their breach of contract. The problem is that by the time the lessee takes the equipment company to court and obtains a judgment, the lessee itself may be out of business because the finance company will have repossessed all their equipment.

Credit & Collection Tip: *When entering into these types of transactions, the financial responsibility of the seller of the equipment is much more important than obtaining financing. If the seller of the equipment should file a petition in bankruptcy, the purchaser would have to seek out other firms to maintain and service the equipment. The charge for said services by third parties might be exorbitant compared to what the seller was charging. A careful reading of the finance agreement is important, but the most important ingredient is to know from whom you are purchasing the equipment and that they will stand behind the equipment.*[13]

PIERCING THE CORPORATE VEIL

Sometimes under unique circumstances, creditors may proceed on corporate obligations personally against the principals of a privately held corporation if the principals are not operating the corporation either as a business or as a corporation. They may be utilizing the corporation to pay their personal debts and the debts of their spouses, thereby commingling their personal affairs with their corporate affairs and not distinguishing one from the other. Usually, when the corporation is paying personal debts along with corporate debts, corporate books are not kept and corporate bank accounts are used for personal debt. Under these circumstances, the courts have recognized the theory of law entitled "piercing the corporate veil" wherein a creditor can sue individuals as well as the corporation and hold them liable for corporate debt.

Corporate Requirements. Corporations must be operated under the laws in the state in which they are incorporated. The corporation should deposit all checks and income in the corporate bank account and only the checks issued from the bank account should be for corporate purposes. The board of directors, which may consist only of a husband and wife, should meet periodically and the minutes of the meeting should be recorded. The stock of the corporation may be held by only one person, but that doesn't eliminate the need to have a meeting of stockholders at least once a year, to ratify the acts of the officers and to record the fact that a board of directors has been elected and is properly operating.

Liability. A close examination of the law in the respective states should be made with regard to liquidation of corporations who leave outstanding debts that were incurred prior to the time of the dissolution. Sometimes, the creditors may bring actions against the officers, directors, or even the individual stockholders of the defunct corporations on the grounds that the corporation did not properly liquidate or did not file the necessary papers for liquidation in compliance with the particular statute of

[13]*AT&T Credit Corp. v. Transglobal Telecom Alliance, Inc.*, 966 F. Supp. 299 (D.N.J. 1997).

the state. Other times, the question of fraud or misrepresentations in self dealing are involved and sometimes the assets have been diverted from the corporation into the individual hands of the directors, officers, or stockholders. In some cases, the property of the corporation may be in the hands of a third party. Consultation with experienced counsel is recommended.[14]

The purpose of a corporation is primarily to shelter the shareholders, directors, and officers from personal liability. To take advantage of this umbrella, the officers, directors, and shareholders must operate the corporate entity as a separate corporate entity for the benefit of that corporate entity. In some instances, the same shareholder controls two different corporations and dominates both corporations to the extent that the corporations, their operations, and dealings are all within the control of the one shareholder. Sometimes, one corporation will liquidate or even file bankruptcy, leaving outstanding debts and judgments. Before ceasing business or filing a petition in bankruptcy, the corporation transfers its assets to the other corporation with or without consideration. Sometimes, circumstances present themselves to allow a creditor to pierce this corporate veil and hold that the corporations are alter egos of each other and that the solvent corporation should be liable for the debts of the insolvent or bankrupt corporation.

Criteria. In recent years, suits based on piercing the corporate veil have increased and more and more creditors are recognizing that sophisticated debtors are using this corporate device to avoid payment of their debts. Piercing the corporate veil is a vague and illusory concept and applied by the courts in a discriminatory and subjective manner. It is not codified or statutory, but merely a common law creation to prevent a fraudulent use of the corporate umbrella.

When a corporate veil is pierced, the judges usually rely on various theories. The creation of the corporation is a privilege granted by the state and must not be abused. The arrangement among the corporation, the shareholders, and creditors is a contractual relationship and this contractual relationship should not be violated.

Many criteria are used to justify piercing the corporate veil.

1. Common shareholders, stockholders, and directors.
2. Does the parent corporation own all or most of the stock of the other corporation or does the individual own the stock in both corporations?

---

[14] *Kyle v. Stewart*, 360 F.2d 753 (5th Cir. 1996); *Exxon Corp. v. Fisher*, 817 F.2d 1429 (9th Cir. 1987); *In re Oakwood Homes Corp.*, 340 B.R. 510 (Bankr. D. Del. 2006); *James Rodney Moore, Sr. v. Principal Credit Corp.*, 1998 WL 378387 (N.D. Miss. Mar. 31, 1998); *Travelers Ins. Co. v. Jacob C. Mol, Inc.*, 898 F. Supp. 528 (W.D. Mich. 1995); *In re Verestar, Inc.*, 343 B.R. 444 (Bankr. S.D.N.Y. 2006); *Brunson Bonding and Ins. Agency v. Elm*, 540 So. 2d 530 (La. App. 1st Cir. 1989); *Sweeney, Cohn, Stahl & Vaccaro v. Kane*, 6 A.D.3d 72, 773 N.Y.S.2d 420 (N.Y. App. Div. 2d Dep't 2004); *In re CITX Corp., Inc.*, 2005 WL 1388963 (E.D. Pa. June 7, 2005), *aff'd*, 448 F.3d 672 (3d Cir. 2006).

3. Does the parent corporation finance a subsidiary or is the subsidiary allowed to use the line of credit of the parent?
4. Does one corporation have inadequate capital?
5. Does one corporation pay the salaries and the day-to-day expenses of the other corporation?
6. Does one corporation have no employees and no day-to-day expenses other than buying and selling merchandise at a profit?
7. Does one corporation have no assets and use its income to pay the expenses of the other corporation?
8. Does the individual treat the corporation as his own personal business, running personal expenses through the corporation?
9. Does the corporation maintain books?
10. Does one corporation fail to maintain corporate formality, such as directors' meetings, shareholders' meetings, minutes of these meetings, stock transfer books, etc.?
11. Is one corporation described by the other corporation as a department or division?
12. Do the directors and officers of one corporation take their direction from the other corporation? Did transfers of assets take place from one corporation to the other, rendering the corporation insolvent?
13. Was there extensive and pervasive control over the operation of the corporations by one individual?
14. Was there commingling of the properties or accounts of the corporation with the other corporation or with the individual?
15. Is there an absence of corporate records?
16. Is one corporation merely a façade for the personal operations of the dominant shareholder?
17. Do the financial statements of the two corporations clearly show overlapping and reliance on each other? Are the daily operations of one corporation being maintained by the other corporation?

The above listing identifies certain markers that recur regularly. Unfortunately, no standard has been established to tell you how many of these markers are necessary to induce a particular court to pierce the corporate veil nor are there any criteria to determine which markers receive heavy consideration. A review of the cases seems to indicate that each judge has his own agenda and each case seems to rest on its own set of facts.

SUBSIDIARY. Piercing the corporate veil requires a showing that the parent corporation dominates the subsidiary to such an extent that the latter is really an agent for or an instrumental part of the former, and the parent corporation used that control to commit fraud or some other wrong. A showing is usually required that the dominant party exercises complete control of the corporation with respect to the transactions, and such dominion was used to commit a fraud or wrong against the creditor which resulted in an injury to the creditor. Complete domination is the key to piercing the corporate veil when the owners use the corporation as a mere device to further their personal agenda rather than the legitimate corporate interest. It makes no difference whether the corporation had been dominated by an individual or another corporation. If the separate entity concepts are so ignored that one corporation primarily transacts the business of the dominant corporation instead of its own, it may be called the other's alter ego, and corporate form may be disregarded to achieve an equitable result.

A subsidiary to stand on its own should be properly capitalized and have its own bank accounts. The subsidiary should not commingle money with the parent and should have its own executives, a separate board of directors and use its own stationery. The issue considered by the courts is the extent of the control over the subsidiary. If the action of the parent causes the subsidiary to incur a liability, the court may hold the parent liable.

A company that is organized solely to conceal assets usually exhibits certain benchmarks. The company has no employees or perhaps one or two employees. The employees work jointly for the parent as well as the subsidiary. The company engages in the sale of the product to receive the money, but somehow fails to remit the money directly to the parent. Often the subsidiary has no stationery, pays no rent, and little or no space has been designated for occupation by the subsidiary on the parent's premise. No lease was signed between the parties. The subsidiary uses the telephone number of the parent and does not contract separately with the telephone company.

These benchmarks are the obvious ones and in many instances the sophisticated parent takes steps to create the semblance of an independent subsidiary. Nevertheless, a careful and persistent creditor may be successful in identifying that the sole and singular purpose of the subsidiary is to conceal assets.

While the majority of the courts have determined that the reverse piercing of the corporate veil is a valid cause of action, a small minority have held that it is not a proper remedy.[15]

Limited Liability Companies. While all the statutes set forth the premise that limited liability companies are to be treated as corporations in

---

[15]*Cordus v. Klummerfeld Trust*, 242 F.3d 264 (2d Cir. 2001); *American Fuel Corp. v. Utah Energy*, 122 F.3d 130 (2d Cir. 1997); *Scholes v. Lehman*, 56 F.3d 750 (7th Cir. 1995); *In re Richels*, 163 B.R. 760 (Bankr. E.D. Va. 1994); *State v. Eastern*, 647 N.Y.S.2d 904 (Sup. Ct. Albany Co. 1995).

that they shield their partners from personal liability, the statutes from state-to-state provide some assistance with regard to piercing the corporate veil. Some statutes do not address the problem at all, some statutes indirectly address the issue and a few address the issue explicitly. The explicit treatments vary from applying the test of a corporate veil to limited liability companies or stating that a partner is liable in the same way as stockholders if the corporate veil is pierced. On the other hand, many states, such as New York and Kentucky, do not address the issue at all in their limited liability statutes.

Limited liability companies are different from corporations in that the members sometimes operate the company with little formality and with little record keeping. The alter ego element usually is the main grounds for piercing the corporate veil, but distinctions are drawn between the large limited liability company and the small family-owned limited liability company. Consultation is recommended with experienced counsel.[16]

SECONDARY LIENS

The foundation of a second lien loan is that the lien attaches to the "same collateral" as the primary lien. The agreement usually provides that the first lien is paid in full before any money is paid on the second lien. This obligation is usually spelled out in what is commonly known as an "inter-creditor agreement." After a foreclosure by the first lienor or a liquidation by the bankruptcy court of the collateral, the first lienor will be paid in full before any money is distributed to the second lienor.

If the collateral is inadequate to pay the first lienor, the first and second lienor will become unsecured creditors and accordingly will share equally in any distribution in bankruptcy or absent a bankruptcy they may commence separate suits to collect the monies due to them.

Mezzanine Financing. The distinction between mezzanine financing and second lien loans is that the lender has a right to convert the debt into ownership of stock under certain terms and conditions as set forth in the inter-creditor agreements. Mezzanine loans may either be secured or unsecured.

Inter-creditor Agreements. These subordination agreements between the first and second lien holders or between the first lien holder and the mezzanine debtor set forth the agreements and obligations between the parties. The priority of the payouts, the remedies available to each, the notification provisions between them, as well as with the debtor, the right to initiate foreclosure proceedings, under what conditions

[16]Eric Fox, *Piercing the Veil of Limited Liability Companies*, 62 Geo. Wash. L. Rev. 1143 (1994).

the second lienor or mezzanine debtor may, if at all, commence suits or foreclosure proceedings, the right of the first lien holder to amend the agreements if there is such a right, and a variety of other clauses protect each party. The debtor also undertakes certain obligations with regard to each creditor including the usual waiver clauses, default clauses and specifications of remedies as well as all the fees and penalties.

Inter-creditor agreements and mezzanine financing present some distinct problems when attempting to enforce the mezzanine lending agreement as well as the inter-creditor agreements.

Some mezzanine financing may entail converting the loan to an equity interest in the corporation. A bank or a commercial finance company usually does not have any interest in owning or managing the business or the real estate, but wishes to recoup the money advanced to the debtor. The mezzanine lender will be faced with inter-creditor agreements concerning one or more prior lenders with ground leases or agreements which affect specific properties of the debtor. A careful review and examination of each separate agreement is absolutely necessary. Almost all junior financing allows the junior creditor in the event of acceleration to purchase the senior debt.

The secured secondary lien has the right to proceed under Article 9 either by strict foreclosure or by disposition at an auction. A commercially reasonable sale of the property pursuant to UCC Section 9-610 provides that the public disposition must be in a commercially reasonable manner and advance notice must be given to the interested parties and the debtor and other obligors under Sections 611 and 612. The most desired procedure is to utilize a public auction and publish the notification of the sale in a recognized newspaper.

At times, a public sale will not be appropriate for certain types of property such as a commercial finance company that deals primarily in vehicles for the disabled or where a ready market is not available to conduct a sale at a public auction. But a commercially reasonable sale must be proven. Direct marketing by mail or e-mail, advertising in trade magazines or trade journals or any other similar method should be used to reach the type of purchasers who might be interested in that particular type of property. Records should be kept of each advertisement. A direct marketing effort requires the list of names to whom the solicitations were sent. All bids should be kept. The price you ultimately receive must bear some relationship to other bids made on the property. A fact-specific inquiry could be made by the debtor attacking whether the creditor used a cost benefit analysis. The surrounding circumstances and period of time from the initial advertisement to the final disposition depend a great deal on the complexity of the property, the market conditions, the length of time before consummation and the relationship between the balance due and the estimated value of the property.

A mezzanine lender or creditor may accept the property in partial or full satisfaction under UCC Section 9-620. The debtor must consent and agree in writing under Section 620(c)(1).

Waiver of Voting Rights. As a general rule, subordinate lien creditors wish to retain their voting rights in the bankruptcy proceeding and rarely waive their voting rights or transfer their voting rights to a prior lien creditor to vote on a confirmation plan. A case in 2000 addressed this issue and held that "subordination" is a common practice which defines an act or process in which a person's rights are ranked below those of others. Such an agreement may affect priority of payment of claims in bankruptcy, but it does not allow for the transfer of voting rights from one creditor to another creditor.

A recent case in Georgia directly contradicted and concluded that the bankruptcy code does not prohibit a second lien creditor from transferring his voting rights to the primary creditor. The court chose specifically not to follow the *LaSalle* decision in Illinois in 2000.[17]

DE FACTO MERGER

The concept of "de facto merger" has been around for awhile, but recently one of the circuit courts has applied a significant restriction on the application of the doctrine.

The purchaser of a corporation's assets does not, as a result of the purchase, ordinarily become liable for the seller's debts. The amount paid for the assets ordinarily is available to satisfy those debts. So long as the buyer pays a bona fide, arm's-length price for the assets, the creditors receive a fair consideration and receive the proceeds of the sale roughly equal to the value of the purchased assets.

Only in a case where the two corporations merge to become a single entity is the successor corporation automatically liable for the debts of both predecessors for the simple reason that the merger of the two corporations consist of both predecessors.[18]

The four recognized exceptions to the rule that an asset purchaser is not liable for the seller's debts are: (1) a buyer who formally assumes a seller's debts; (2) transactions undertaken to defraud creditors; (3) a buyer who de facto merged with a seller; and (4) a buyer that is a mere continuation of the seller. The mere continuation and the "de facto merger" are so similar that they usually are considered as one exception. A de facto merger occurs when a transaction, although not a formal merger, is in substance a consolidation or merger of seller and purchaser.

To find that a de facto merger has occurred, a continuity of the selling corporation must be evident by the same management, personal assets, and physical location as well as a continuity of stockholders accomplished by

[17] *In re Aerosol Packing, LLC*, 362 B.R. (Bankr. N.D. Ga. 2006); *In re 203 North LaSalle Street Partnership*, 246 B.R. 325 (Bankr. N.D. Ill. 2000).

[18] *In re Aerosol Packaging, LLC*, 362 B.R. 43 (Bankr. N.D. Ga. 2006).

paying for the acquired corporation by purchasing shares of its stock, a dissolution of the selling corporation, and the assumption of liabilities by the purchaser.

The general thrust of the requirements is that all of the elements of a de facto merger do not have to be present to assert a de facto merger. Continuity of ownership is one of the factors often missing in prosecuting a claim. Some of the decisions follow the premise that without continuity of ownership, no de facto merger can take place.

A recent decision in the Second Circuit carries substantial weight when this court takes the position that continuity of ownership is a required element of a de facto merger. Absent continuity of ownership, no de facto merger exists. The circuit court pointed out that most of the cases which do not require continuity of ownership are in the product liability area.[19]

UNIFORM FRAUDULENT TRANSFER ACT

The Uniform Fraudulent Transfer Act is the successor act to the Uniform Fraudulent Conveyance Act. (*See* Appendix to this Chapter.) The act that is set forth in the appendix was adopted at the National Conference of Commissioners on Uniform State Laws. Nevertheless, when the act was adopted by the various states, changes and modifications in the act may have been made, and a careful review of the law in the particular state must be made.

The key section of the Uniform Fraudulent Transfer Act states that a transfer made by a debtor is fraudulent as to a creditor if the debtor made the transfer or incurred a new obligation with actual intent to hinder, delay, or defraud any creditor of the debtor, or in the alternative, without receiving a reasonably equivalent value in exchange for the transfer. A transfer is also fraudulent if the debtor intended to incur, or believed or reasonably should have believed debts would be incurred beyond the ability to pay for the debts as they became due. The statute provides 11 suggestions for determining the actual intent:

1. The transfer was to an insider.
2. The debtor retains possession or control of the property.
3. The transfer obligation was disclosed or concealed.
4. Before the transfer was made or the obligation was incurred, the debtor had been sued or threatened with a suit.

---

[19] *Cargo Partners A.G. v. Albatrans Inc.*, 352 F.3d 41 (2d Cir. 2003). *See also Smithkline Beecham Corp. v. Rohan & Hoss Co.*, 89 F.3d 154 (3d Cir. 1996); *In re Penn. Cent. Secs. Litig.*, 367 F. Supp. 1158 (E.D. Pa. 1973); *Savage Arms Inc. v. Western Auto Supply Co.*, 18 P.3d 49 (Alaska 2001); *Welco Indus. Inc. v. Applied Cos.*, 617 N.E.2d 1129 (Ohio 1993).

5. The transfer was substantially of all the debtor's assets.
6. The debtor absconded.[20]
7. The debtor removed or concealed assets.
8. The value of the consideration received by the debtor was reasonably equivalent to the value of the assets transferred or the amount of the obligation incurred.
9. The debtor was insolvent or became insolvent shortly after the transfer was made or the obligation was incurred.
10. The transfer occurred shortly before or shortly after a substantial debt was incurred.
11. The debtor transferred the essential assets of the business to a lienor who transferred the assets to an insider of the debtor.

Some of the remedies available include setting aside the transfer to satisfy the creditor's claim or an attachment using the applicable principles of equity. The court may prohibit further disposition of the property or perhaps appoint a receiver to take charge of the assets transferred.

One of the key problems faced in utilizing the remedies available under the Uniform Fraudulent Transfer Act is the question of the Statute of Limitations and the definition of a creditor.

A key feature of the Uniform Fraudulent Transfer Act is that a creditor is permitted, but not required, to maintain an action to annul a fraudulent conveyance before the debt has matured. It is no longer necessary that a creditor reduce its claim to judgment before seeking the benefit of the Uniform Fraudulent Transfer Act. The law actually gives the creditor an option. The creditor may establish its debt, whether matured or unmatured, and challenge the conveyance in a single suit or may pursue the unmatured claim to judgment, and follow it by a suit to set aside the fraudulent transfer.

The next question is the effect of the Statute of Limitations on this new option. One court opined that the date of the underlying judgment, combined with the creditor's knowledge of the transfer, were the key factors in determining when the Statute of Limitations begins to run. If the debtor chooses the old procedure, and sues upon its debt to judgment in ordinary fashion, the time for a later suit to set aside a fraudulent conveyance runs from the date of judgment. If the creditor exercises the other option and initially commences its suit to set aside the transfer, then the limitation period runs from the time when the transfer was made or the obligation was incurred, or at least from the time the transfer or obligation was or could reasonably have been discovered by the creditor.[21] (*See* Section 726.110 of the Uniform Fraudulent Transfer Act in the Appendix to this Chapter.)

---

[20] *Continental Ins. Company v. Schneider*, 2002 PA Super. 323 (Pa. Super. Ct. 2002).
[21] *Cortez v. Vogt*, 52 Cal. App. 4th 917, 60 Cal. Rptr. 2d 841 (Cal. Ct. App. 4th Dist. 1997).

BUSINESS JUDGMENT RULE

The business judgment rule is the presumption that when making a business decision not involving direct self-interest or self-dealing, corporate directors act on an informed basis in good faith and in the honest belief that their actions are in the corporation's best interest. The rule shields directors and officers from liability for unprofitable or harmful corporate transactions if the transactions were made in good faith, with due care and within the director's or officer's authority. Some of the courts have added an additional requirement that the directors and officers must make reasonable efforts to become informed about the particular transaction.[22]

CORPORATE SIGNATURE

A new amendment to revised Articles 3 and 4 of the UCC provides that a representative will not be liable if the capacity of the person (representative) signing is ambiguous, and the name of the principal is not disclosed and the representative proves by oral evidence that the parties to the agreement did not intend to make the representative personally liable. This codifies the rule using oral evidence to resolve a situation where ambiguity exists as to whether the representative has or has not signed in a representative capacity. It is best to remove ambiguity by setting forth the corporate name and the title of the officer on all instruments signed, including checks and notes.

Another danger that appears is a situation where an officer enters into an oral agreement with another party and only refers to the business under a name which does not indicate that the business is a corporation, such as referring to "ABC Restaurant" instead of "ABC Restaurant Corporation." Several courts have held that the other party was led to believe that the business was an individual or a partnership because the officer did not mention that it was a corporation or mention the full corporate name. Under those circumstances, officers may expose themselves to personal liability.

TORTUOUS INTERFERENCE

A claim for tortuous interference may lie when a person without a privilege to do so purposely causes a third party not to enter a contract with another. To establish a claim for tortuous interference, a party must show:

1. A business relationship or contract.
2. The wrongdoer's knowledge of the relationship or contract.

[22]Black's Law Dictionary 192 (7th ed. 1999).

3. The wrongdoer's intentional and improper action taken to prevent a contract formation.
4. A lack of a privilege.
5. Resulting damages.

A purposeful interference with a third party business relationship is privileged if undertaken by the defendant in good faith to protect a legally protected interest which might otherwise be impaired or destroyed.

To determine the existence of a privilege, the court will consider the nature of the conduct of the actor, the nature of the expectancy with which it's conduct interferes, the relationship between the parties, the interest sought to be advanced by the actor and the social interest in protecting the expectancy on one hand and the freedom of action on the other hand.

The key issue in most tortuous interference cases (where one party is interfering in a contract of another party) is distinguishing whether that party has a privilege.

UNJUST ENRICHMENT

Absent some kind of reliance by a creditor, one might argue that the creditor should make restitution to a person who mistakenly pays the debt of a third party (such as mistakenly paying a debt to C that was owed to C by B). The courts do not follow this reasoning principally on the theory that where the creditor may have benefited from the mistake, the creditor certainly was not enriched (and not unjustly enriched) since the creditor was receiving payment of a debt. The courts seem to be unable to identify a contractual or implied relationship that would create a duty to indemnify the third party who mistakenly paid the debt.

On the other hand, if the debtor (not the third party) mistakenly sent a check to its creditor in excess of the amount that was actually due to the creditor, a claim for unjust enrichment may lie since the creditor received money to which the creditor was not entitled. The creditor was enriched—and unjustly enriched merely by virtue of the mistake of the debtor. When a third party becomes involved, the situation is different since the creditor is not enriched upon receipt of money from someone other than the debtor which is being applied to the debt of the debtor. But if a third party mistakenly issues a check to a person to whom no money is owed, that person is enriched—and unjustly enriched—and a suit would lie for unjust enrichment.[23]

---

[23]*Greenwald v. Chase Manhattan Mortg. Co.*, 241 F.3d 76 (1st Cir. 2001).

PRIOR LIENS—DILIGENT INQUIRY

A creditor obtains a judgment against a business debtor and the individual who guaranteed the debt. The response is that all assets are pledged to the bank. The creditor's logical conclusion is that if the assets such as inventory, accounts receivable and equipment are liened, the debtor is judgment proof and a creditor cannot execute on any property. If at the same time the individual guarantor draws no salary, the creditor cannot garnish salary and the individual is judgment proof.

Nevertheless, depending upon the amount of the judgment in favor of the creditor, the creditor should consult with counsel as to "marshalling" of the assets. If the bank has a security agreement on machinery and equipment for $50,000 and the machinery and equipment is worth $100,000, $50,000 is available to satisfy the creditor. If the bank has a lien on inventory, accounts receivable and equipment totaling $100,000 and the equipment alone is valued at $100,000, the inventory and accounts receivable would be available to satisfy the creditor's lien. *Also, inquiry must be made by examining the debtor to determine the balance due to the bank, for the debtor may be paying every month. An examination after judgment should be conducted.* Obtain a list of the assets securing the bank loan and arrange for an appraisal of the assets. If the appraisal exceeds the amount of the loan, inquire as to what the assets would bring at an auction sale.

The debtor has oversecured the loan and would have significant surplus in the event the bank foreclosed. This surplus could be made available to the unsecured creditor who just obtained a judgment. The creditor, after establishing the fact that the debtor has significant equity in certain assets, could levy on the inventory or accounts receivable—leaving the equipment to secure the loan of the bank or execute on the machinery and equipment and pay the bank. Consultation with experienced counsel is recommended.

DUTY TO READ

A party who signs an instrument infers to the other party that he has read the agreement. He may not later complain that he did not read the agreement and did not understand the agreement. If an individual has the capacity to read an agreement and to understand the agreement, he cannot complain that he did not read it and did not understand it. If this was not the case, it is fairly obvious that no one can rely on a signed document if the other party can merely avoid the agreement by stating that he did not read the agreement or did not understand the agreement. The same thing would apply to the acceptance of documents such as bills of lading, passenger tickets, insurance policies, bank books, and warehouse receipts, where these documents purport to be a contract between the parties. The party accepting these documents is assenting to the terms of the contract.

The courts over the years have carefully and systematically developed a number of exceptions to this rule for consumers. If the document is not legible or not easily read, a party is not bound by the fine print, or if it were in such small type and so long and so crowded that it was physically difficult to read the document, the court could believe that no assent was present. The courts are reluctant to enforce terms of contract not sufficiently called to the attention of one party, such as printed notices on letterheads, catalogs, or tags or printed notices inside of clothing. Some courts have been reluctant to enforce clauses that are printed on the reverse side of a document unless it is clearly and conspicuously referred to on the front side of the document. Purported contracts posted on desks, walls, or other public places may also be an exception unless the particular party to the contract actually observed the particular contractual terms or because the posting was so clearly conspicuous, the party should have observed the particular contractual terms. Another exception is where a party receives a document that the party has no reason to believe contains any contractual terms. This applies to the proverbial parking receipt or the ticket that is issued when a party checks his coat at the restaurant or the ticket that he receives when he delivers a package to a parcel checkroom.

FRAUD. Fraud and mistake are another exception to the rule of duty to read. This occurs where a particular party deliberately misrepresents what the contents of a writing or an agreement are and the other party relies on that oral representation and signs without having read the document. A minority of the courts will decide that the party had no right to rely on the oral representation because he was entering into a written contract, and a reasonable man should know that the written contract merges all the oral representations into the written contract. On the other hand, the majority of the courts feels a lack of mutual agreement is present between the parties and that the party who makes the misrepresentation is guilty of fraud and cannot enforce the contract.

A misrepresentation becomes more difficult where the contract specifically states that all oral representations made prior to the contract are merged into the contract. Even here a conflict exists between the courts with some courts stating that a failure to read the integration provision in the contract which merges the oral representation into the agreement precludes that party from offering the oral representation, even though it was a fraudulent one. Perhaps the better view is that a party is bound to know the contents of the paper that is signed.

Contracts of adhesion are also exceptions to the rule. An adhesion contract is one in which an unconscionable bargain is entered into, due to a prodigious amount of bargaining power on behalf of the stronger party, which is used to the stronger party's advantage. In those cases, the contract is normally avoidable.

> ***Credit & Collection Tip:*** *The issue of whether a consumer or a business is involved is an important factor in these decisions. The courts tend to protect the consumer when the consumer is dealing with a business. The majority of the courts leave the written contract stand between two businesses on the theory that the two businesses are sophisticated enough to understand that they have to read the written agreement.*

Business. Perhaps the best advice is to read the contract. This applies even more so to contracts between two businesses, because the courts apply a strict liability test to these documents as opposed to parking tickets and coat checkroom tickets.[24]

DISCRETIONARY TRUSTS

When there is a discretionary trust, the law is clear that a creditor of a beneficiary, who was not the settlor (the individual who set up the trust and contributed to it), cannot compel the trustee to pay any part of the income derived from the principal to a creditor. However, when a person creates for his own benefit a discretionary trust, creditors can reach the maximum amount which the trustee under the terms of the trust could pay to him or apply for his benefit; even though the trustee in the exercise of his discretion wishes to pay nothing to the beneficiary or to the creditors and even though the beneficiary could not compel the trustee to pay anything.

NATIONAL REGISTRY

The National Registry is a comprehensive proprietary database of over 34 million landlord-tenant eviction court records. The organization sells information about potential residential tenants to landlords and real estate management companies, which are collected from court records. The product is used by its customers to blacklist applicants because they have been involved in litigation with landlords.

LAWS REGULATING COMMERCIAL COLLECTION

Over 20 states have already passed some form of legislation that regulates both commercial collection as well as consumer collection.

---

[24]*In re Commonwealth Sprinkler Co., Inc.*, 296 B.R. 694 (Bankr. E.D. Va. 2001).

Some states require that the commercial debt collectors be licensed and follow the same laws and regulations of consumer debt collectors.

The ACA International also provided (their FastFacts Demand Service) a listing of the regulations of those states which affect Interstate Commercial Collection. (*See* Appendix to this Chapter.)

CHAPTER 4 APPENDIX I

UNIFORM FRAUDULENT TRANSFER ACT—FLORIDA

CHAPTER 726

FRAUDULENT TRANSFERS

726.101 Short title. This act may be cited as the "Uniform Fraudulent Transfer Act."

726.102 Definitions.

(1) "Affiliate" means:

(a) A person who directly or indirectly owns, controls, or holds with power to vote, 20 percent or more of the outstanding voting securities of the debtor, other than a person who holds the securities:

1. As a fiduciary or agent without sole discretionary power to vote the securities; or

2. Solely to secure a debt, if the person has not exercised the power to vote.

(b) A corporation 20 percent or more of whose outstanding voting securities are directly or indirectly owned, controlled, or held with power to vote, by the debtor or a person who directly or indirectly owns, controls, or holds, with power to vote, 20 percent or more of the outstanding voting securities of the debtor, other than a person who holds the securities:

1. As a fiduciary or agent without sole power to vote the securities; or

2. Solely to secure a debt, if the person has not in fact exercised the power to vote.

(c) A person whose business is operated by the debtor under a lease or other agreement, or a person substantially all of whose assets are controlled by the debtor; or

(d) A person who operates the debtor's business under a lease or other agreement or controls substantially all of the debtor's assets.

(2) "Asset" means property of a debtor, but the term does not include:

(a) Property to the extent it is encumbered by a valid lien;

(b) Property to the extent it is generally exempt under nonbankruptcy law; or

(c) An interest in property held in tenancy by the entireties to the extent it is not subject to process by a creditor holding a claim against only one tenant.

(3) "Claim" means a right to payment, whether or not the right is reduced to judgment, liquidated, unliquidated, fixed, contingent, matured, unmatured, disputed, undisputed, legal, equitable, secured, or unsecured.

(4) "Creditor" means a person who has a claim.

(5) "Debt" means liability on a claim.

(6) "Debtor" means a person who is liable on a claim.

(7) "Insider" includes:

(a) If the debtor is an individual:

1. A relative of the debtor or of a general partner of the debtor;

2. A partnership in which the debtor is a general partner;

3. A general partner in a partnership described in subparagraph 2.; or

4. A corporation of which the debtor is a director, officer, or person in control;

(b) If the debtor is a corporation:

1. A director of the debtor;
2. An officer of the debtor;
3. A person in control of the debtor;
4. A partnership in which the debtor is a general partner;
5. A general partner in a partnership described in subparagraph 4.; or
6. A relative of a general partner, director, officer, or person in control of the debtor.

(c) If the debtor is a partnership:

1. A general partner in the debtor;
2. A relative of a general partner in, a general partner of, or a person in control of the debtor;
3. Another partnership in which the debtor is a general partner;
4. A general partner in a partnership described in subparagraph 3.; or
5. A person in control of the debtor.

(d) An affiliate, or an insider of an affiliate as if the affiliate were the debtor.

(e) A managing agent of the debtor.

(8) "Lien" means a charge against or an interest in property to secure payment of a debt or performance of an obligation, and includes a security interest created by agreement, a judicial lien obtained by legal or equitable process or proceedings, a common-law lien, or a statutory lien.

(9) "Person" means an individual, partnership, corporation, association, organization, government or governmental subdivision or agency, business trust, estate, trust, or any other legal or commercial entity.

(10) "Property" means anything that may be the subject of ownership.

(11) "Relative" means an individual related by consanguinity within the third degree as determined by the common law, a spouse, or an individual related to a spouse within the third degree as so determined, and includes an individual in an adoptive relationship within the third degree.

(12) "Transfer" means every mode, direct or indirect, absolute or conditional, voluntary or involuntary, of disposing of or parting with an asset or an interest in an asset, and includes payment of money, release, lease, and creation of a lien or other encumbrance.

(13) "Valid lien" means a lien that is effective against the holder of a judicial lien subsequently obtained by legal or equitable process or proceedings.

726.103 Insolvency.

(1) A debtor is insolvent if the sum of the debtor's debts is greater than all of the debtor's assets at a fair valuation.

(2) A debtor who is generally not paying his or her debts as they become due is presumed to be insolvent.

(3) A partnership is insolvent under subsection (1) if the sum of the partnership's debts is greater than the aggregate, at a fair valuation, of all of the partnership's assets and the sum of the excess of the value of each general partner's nonpartnership assets over the partner's nonpartnership debts.

(4) Assets under this section do not include property that has been transferred, concealed, or removed with intent to hinder, delay, or defraud creditors or that has been transferred in a manner making the transfer voidable under ss. 726.101-726.112.

(5) Debts under this section do not include an obligation to the extent it is secured by a valid lien on property of the debtor not included as an asset.

726.104 Value.

(1) Value is given for a transfer or an obligation if, in exchange for the transfer or obligation, property is transferred or an antecedent debt is secured or satisfied, but value does not include an unperformed promise made otherwise than in the ordinary course of the promisors business to furnish support to the debtor or another person.

(2) For the purposes of ss. 726.105(1)(b) and 726.106, a person gives a reasonably equivalent value if the person acquires an interest of the debtor in an asset pursuant to a regularly conducted, noncollusive foreclosure sale or execution of a power of sale for the acquisition or disposition of the interest of the debtor upon default under a mortgage, deed of trust, or security agreement.

(3) A transfer is made for present value if the exchange between the debtor and the transferee is intended by them to be contemporaneous and is in fact substantially contemporaneous.

726.105 Transfers fraudulent as to present and future creditors.

(1) A transfer made or obligation incurred by a debtor is fraudulent as to a creditor, whether the creditor's claim arose before or after the transfer was made or the obligation was incurred, if the debtor made the transfer or incurred the obligation:

(a) With actual intent to hinder, delay, or defraud any creditor of the debtor; or

(b) Without receiving a reasonably equivalent value in exchange for the transfer or obligation, and the debtor:

1. Was engaged or was about to engage in a business or a transaction for which the remaining assets of the debtor were unreasonably small in relation to the business or transaction; or

2. Intended to incur, or believed or reasonably should have believed that he or she would incur, debts beyond his or her ability to pay as they became due.

(2) In determining actual intent under paragraph (1)(a), consideration may be given, among other factors, to whether:

(a) transfer or obligation was to an insider.

(b) The debtor retained possession or control of the property transferred after the transfer.

(c) The transfer or obligation was disclosed or concealed.

(d) Before the transfer was made or obligation was incurred, the debtor had been sued or threatened with suit.

(e) The transfer was of substantially all the debtor's assets.

(f) The debtor absconded.

(g) The debtor removed or concealed assets.

(h) The value of the consideration received by the debtor was reasonably equivalent to the value of the asset transferred or the amount of the obligation incurred.

(i) The debtor was insolvent or became insolvent shortly after the transfer was made or the obligation was incurred.

(j) The transfer occurred shortly before or shortly after a substantial debt was incurred.

(k) The debtor transferred the essential assets of the business to a lienor who transferred the assets to an insider of the debtor.

726.106 Transfers fraudulent as to present creditors.

(1) A transfer made or obligation incurred by a debtor is fraudulent as to a creditor whose claim arose before the transfer was made or the obligation was incurred if the debtor made the transfer or incurred the obligation without receiving a reasonably equivalent value in exchange for the transfer or obligation and the debtor was insolvent at that time or the debtor became insolvent as a result of the transfer or obligation.

(2) A transfer made by a debtor is fraudulent as to a creditor whose claim arose before the transfer was made if the transfer was made to an insider for an antecedent debt, the debtor was insolvent at that time, and the insider had reasonable cause to believe that the debtor was insolvent.

726.107 When transfer made or obligation incurred.—

(1) A transfer is made:

(a) With respect to an asset that is real property other than a fixture, but including the interest of a seller or purchaser under a contract for the sale of the asset, when the transfer is so far perfected that a good faith purchaser of the asset from the debtor against whom applicable law permits the transfer to be perfected cannot acquire an interest in the asset that is superior to the interest of the transferee.

(b) With respect to an asset that is not real property or that is a fixture, when the transfer is so far perfected that a creditor on a simple contract cannot acquire a judicial lien otherwise than under ss. 726.101-726.112 that is superior to the interest of the transferee.

(2) If applicable law permits the transfer to be perfected as provided in subsection (1) and the transfer is not so perfected before the commencement of an action for relief under ss. 726.101-726.112, the transfer is deemed made immediately before the commencement of the action.

(3) If applicable law does not permit the transfer to be perfected as provided in subsection (1), the transfer is made when it becomes effective between the debtor and the transferee.

(4) A transfer is not made until the debtor has acquired rights in the asset transferred.

(5) An obligation is incurred:

(a) If oral, when it becomes effective between the parties; or

(b) If evidenced by a writing, when the writing executed by the obligor is delivered to or for the benefit of the obligee.

726.108 Remedies of creditors.

(1) In an action for relief against a transfer or obligation under ss. 726.101-726.112, a creditor, subject to the limitations in s. 726.109 may obtain:

(a) Avoidance of the transfer or obligation to the extent necessary to satisfy the creditor's claim;

(b) An attachment or other provisional remedy against the asset transferred or other property of the transferee in accordance with applicable law;

(c) Subject to applicable principles of equity and in accordance with applicable rules of civil procedure:

(1) An injunction against further disposition by the debtor or a transferee, or both, of the asset transferred or of other property;

(2) Appointment of a receiver to take charge of the asset transferred or of other property of the transferee; or

(3) Any other relief the circumstances may require.

(d) If a creditor has obtained a judgment on a claim against the debtor, the creditor, if the court so orders, may levy execution on the asset transferred or its proceeds.

726.109 Defenses, liability, and protection of transferee.

(1) A transfer or obligation is not voidable under s. 726.105(1)(a) against a person who took in good faith and for a reasonably equivalent value or against any subsequent transferee or obligee.

(2) Except as otherwise provided in this section, to the extent a transfer is voidable in an action by a creditor under s. 726.108(1)(a), the creditor may recover judgment for the value of the asset transferred, as adjusted under subsection (3), or the amount necessary to satisfy the creditor's claim, whichever is less. The judgment may be entered against:

(a) The first transferee of the asset or the person for whose benefit the transfer was made; or

(b) Any subsequent transferee other than a good faith transferee who took for value or from any subsequent transferee.

(3) If the judgment under subsection (2) is based upon the value of the asset transferred, the judgment must be for an amount equal to the value of the asset at the time of the transfer, subject to adjustment as the equities may require.

(4) Notwithstanding voidability of a transfer or an obligation under ss. 726.101-726.112, a good faith transferee or obligee is entitled, to the extent of the value given the debtor for the transfer or obligation, to:

(a) A lien on or a right to retain any interest in the asset transferred;

(b) Enforcement of any obligation incurred; or

(c) A reduction in the amount of the liability on the judgment.

(5) A transfer is not voidable under s. 726.105(1)(b) or s. 726.106 if the transfer results from:

(a) Termination of a lease upon default by the debtor when the termination is pursuant to the lease and applicable law; or

(b) Enforcement of a security interest in compliance with Article 9 of the Uniform Commercial Code.

(6) A transfer is not voidable under s. 726.106(2):

(a) To the extent the insider gave new value to or for the benefit of the debtor after the transfer was made unless the new value was secured by a valid lien;

(b) If made in the ordinary course of business or financial affairs of the debtor and the insider; or

(c) If made pursuant to a good faith effort to rehabilitate the debtor and the transfer secured present value given for that purpose as well as an antecedent debt of the debtor.

726.110 Extinguishment of cause of action. A cause of action with respect to a fraudulent transfer or obligation under ss. 726.101-726.112 is extinguished unless action is brought:

(1) Under s. 726.105(1)(a), within 4 years after the transfer was made or the obligation was incurred or, if later, within 1 year after the transfer or obligation was or could reasonably have been discovered by the claimant;

(2) Under s. 726.105(1)(b) or s. 726.106(1), within 4 years after the transfer was made or the obligation was incurred; or

(3) Under s. 726.106(2), within 1 year after the transfer was made or the obligation was incurred.

726.111 Supplementary provisions. Unless displaced by the provisions of ss. 726.101-726.112, the principles of law and equity, including the law merchant and the law relating to principal and agent, estoppel, laches, fraud, misrepresentation, duress, coercion, mistake, insolvency, or other validating or invalidating cause, supplement those provisions.

726.112 Uniformity of application and construction. Chapter 87-79, Laws of Florida, shall be applied and construed to effectuate its general purpose to make uniform the law with respect to the subject of the law among states enacting it.

726.201 Fraudulent loans void. When any loan of goods and chattels shall be pretended to have been made to any person with whom or those claiming under her or him, possession shall have remained for the space of 2 years without demand and pursued by due process of law on the part of the pretended lender, or where any reservation or limitation shall be pretended to have been made of a use or property by way of condition, reversion, remainder or otherwise in goods and chattels, and the possession thereof shall have remained in another as aforesaid, the same shall be taken, as to the creditors and purchasers of the persons aforesaid so remaining in possession, to be fraudulent within this chapter, and the absolute property shall be with the possession, unless such loan, reservation or limitation of use or property were declared by will or deed in writing proved and recorded.

APPENDIX II

SELLER'S REMEDY ON DISCOVERY OF BUYER'S INSOLVENCY—NEW YORK

Section 2-702. Seller's Remedies on Discovery of Buyer's Insolvency.

(1) Where the seller discovers the buyer to be insolvent he may refuse delivery except for cash including payment for all goods theretofore delivered under the contract, and stop delivery under this Article (Section 2-705).

(2) Where the seller discovers that the buyer has received goods on credit while insolvent he may reclaim the goods upon demand made within ten days after the receipt, but if misrepresentation of solvency has been made to the particular seller in writing within three months before delivery the ten day limitation does not apply. Except as provided in this subsection the seller may not base a right to reclaim goods on the buyer's fraudulent or innocent misrepresentation of solvency or of intent to pay.

(3) The seller's right to reclaim under subsection (2) is subject to the rights of a buyer in ordinary course or other good faith purchaser under this Article (Section 2-403). Successful reclamation of goods excludes all other remedies with respect to them.

APPENDIX III

GARAGE KEEPER'S LIEN— MASSACHUSETTS

CHAPTER 255. MORTGAGES, CONDITIONAL SALES AND PLEDGES OF PERSONAL PROPERTY, AND LIENS THEREON OTHER LIENS

Chapter 255: Section 25 Garage keepers; effects of liens on motor vehicles obtained by fraud; etc.; lien for charges reimbursed by insurance company

Section 25. Persons maintaining public garages for the storage and care of motor vehicles brought to their premises or placed in their care by or with the consent of the owners thereof and persons engaged in performing work upon or in connection with the inspection, reconditioning and repairing of motor vehicles shall have a lien upon such motor vehicles for proper charges due them for the storage, work and care of the same.

If the owner of such motor vehicle obtains possession of the same by fraud, trick or by check, draft or order upon any depository or bank which is not honored, the lien on said motor vehicle shall not be deemed to have been discharged and the lien holder may thereafter continue to enforce said lien until the proper charges due him have been paid.

In any instance where a lien arises under this section for charges due that are to be paid or reimbursed by an insurance company licensed in the commonwealth, upon written notice by the holder of such lien to the insurance company, the check or draft issued by such insurance company for such charges shall name the holder of the lien, together with the holder of a security interest as defined by Article 9 of chapter one hundred and six, as a loss payee, unless otherwise provided by law. The holder of a security interest that does not have priority over the lien established under this section shall be required to endorse any check or draft issued for payment of such charges by such insurance company over to the holder of such lien, whether or not such lien has then been released by the holder; provided, however, that the holder of a security interest other than the lien provided by this section, may, within two business days of notice of a request to endorse any such check require the owner of the vehicle to make said vehicle available for inspection at a time and place convenient to the owner and lienholder, to reinspect the repaired vehicle, and, as a prerequisite for such endorsement, the holder of such security interest may require the holder of the lien established under this section to provide it with an itemized list of repairs and other services which it certifies, in writing, have been completed or provided, and a copy of any repair certification form required by law to be provided to the insurance company.

Nothing in this section shall affect or modify the provisions of any direct payment plans implemented by an insurer pursuant to section thirty-four O of chapter ninety.

Appendix IV

ASSIGNMENT FOR BENEFIT OF CREDITORS—TENNESSEE

§ 47-13-101. Bond and oath

Every trustee or assignee to whom property exceeding the value of five hundred dollars ($500) is conveyed in trust for the benefit of creditors, sureties, or other persons, unless by them released, in writing, from the obligations hereinafter prescribed, before entering upon the discharge of such trustee's or assignee's duty, shall give bond, with two (2) or more good and sufficient sureties, or one (1) corporate surety, in an amount equal to the value of the property mentioned in the deed or assignment, payable to the state of Tennessee, conditioned for the faithful performance of all the duties imposed upon the trustee or assignee by law and by the terms of the deed or assignment, and shall take and subscribe, before the person performing the duties of the county clerk of the county in which the trustee or assignee resides, an oath to the effect that the trustee or assignee will:

(1) Honestly and faithfully execute and perform all the duties imposed upon such trustee or assignee by law and by the deed or assignment;

(2) Cause to be made a full, true, and perfect inventory of the goods, chattels, lands, or other assets, all and singular, contained in the trust deed or assignment which have or may come into the trustee's or assignee's hands or into the hands of any other person for such trustee or assignee; and

(3) Return, or cause to be filed in the office of the person performing the duties of the county clerk, a full and true account of all the sales of the effects, and of all moneys received or securities taken.

§ 47-13-102. Filing of bond and affidavit

The bond and affidavit shall be filed and preserved by the person performing the duties of the county clerk in such person's office.

§ 47-13-103. Settlement

Any trustee or assignee to whom property has been conveyed in trust for the benefit of creditors, under the provisions of this chapter, shall be required to make settlement with the person performing the duties of the county clerk of the county in which the deed of trust or assignment was made, as soon after qualification as the nature of the deed or assignment will admit, showing what funds the trustee or assignee has received, how the trustee or assignee has disposed of the trust property, what expenses the trustee or assignee has paid out, and what amount of the funds remain in the trustee's or assignee's hands for payment to beneficiaries under the deed or assignment.

§ 47-13-104. Failure or refusal to settle; citation

Should any such trustee or assignee fail or refuse to make settlement as required by the provisions of § 47-13-103, the person performing the duties of the county clerk shall be required, upon application of anyone interested in the trust property, to issue a citation to such trustee or assignee, requiring the trustee or assignee to appear before the person performing the duties of the county clerk on a given day and make settlement as required by § 47-13-103, a copy of which citation shall be served by the sheriff or any constable of the county at least five (5) days before the day appointed in the citation for such settlement or casting of account.

§ 47-13-105. Failure or refusal to settle; compelling settlement by citation

The person performing the duties of the county clerk, after the expiration of two (2) years from the qualification of such trustee or assignee, shall have power, without application from anyone interested in the trust property, to compel such trustee or assignee to make settlement by citation, as prescribed in § 47-13-104.

§ 47-13-106. Criminal liability for failure to settle

Any such trustee or assignee, who fails or refuses to settle, as above required, after such citation or notice, commits a Class A misdemeanor, and shall be liable to indictment or presentment in the same manner as administrators who fail or refuse to settle as required of them by law.

§ 47-13-107. Removal of trustee for failure to settle

(a) In addition to the foregoing penalties for failure to settle, the court having the jurisdiction of the monthly county court has the power, and it is its duty, upon application, by petition, unless satisfactory reasons be shown why the same shall not be done, to revoke the appointment of such trustee and remove the trustee, and appoint another, who shall be subject to the provisions of §§ 47-13-103–47-13-109.

(b) In all such proceedings to remove such trustee or assignee, the trustee or assignee shall have reasonable notice, not less than ten (10) days, of such application and an opportunity to defend same.

§ 47-13-108. Application of law

Nothing in §§ 47-13-103–47-13-109 shall be construed to exempt trustees or assignees from qualifying, giving bond, and returning inventories, as prescribed by law, nor shall these sections be construed to make them applicable to deeds or mortgages given purely as security for money lent or advanced, but the sections apply only to conveyances made for the benefit of creditors.

§ 47-13-109. Fees

The person performing the duties of the county clerk, and the sheriff or constable, for the services performed by them under §§ 47-13-103–47-13-108, shall be entitled to and be allowed the same fees as are allowed them by law for like services in other cases.

§ 47-13-110. Compensation

The court having the jurisdiction of the monthly county court, upon application, or the chancery court, if the trust is administered in the chancery court, may allow a trustee or assignee compensation exceeding the compensation of clerks and masters, if the character of the services rendered entitle the trustee or assignee to such compensation in the opinion of such court, but such compensation in no case shall exceed five percent (5%).

§ 47-13-111. Noncompliance by trustee—Appointment of receiver

If any trustee or assignee fails or refuses to comply with this chapter, the court having the jurisdiction of the monthly county court, upon application of any person interested, shall, in lieu of the delinquent, appoint a trustee or receiver who, upon executing the bond and taking the oath aforementioned, may execute the trust or assignment.

§ 47-13-112. Death, resignation, or removal of trustee

The chancery court or the court having the jurisdiction of the monthly county court is empowered, upon suggestion and proof of the death, resignation, or removal beyond the limits of this state, of any trustee named as such in any deed of trust conveying realty or personalty as security for the payment of debts or other obligations, to appoint and qualify a trustee in lieu of the trustee dead, resigned, or removed as aforementioned.

§ 47-13-113. Powers of successor trustee

Any trustee so appointed and qualified shall be vested with all the power and authority given in the deed of trust to the original trustee and be subject to all the conditions and limitations therein imposed upon the original trustee.

§ 47-13-114. Release of sureties

The sureties of a trustee or assignee for the benefit of creditors may be released in the manner prescribed in title 29, chapter 33.

§ 47-13-115. General Assignments—Preference of creditors

(a) Preference of creditors in general assignments of all a debtor's property for the benefit of creditors shall be illegal and voidable, and all general assignments shall operate for the benefit of all the debtor's creditors pro rata, whether all the creditors are named in the assignment or not.

(b) The insertion of a clause in the assignment giving a preference shall not render the assignment itself invalid, but the clause only shall be nugatory, and all the debtor's creditors shall share ratably in property assigned.

§ 47-13-116. General Assignments—Prior Conveyance for benefit of particular creditor

Any mortgage, deed of trust, security interest under the Uniform Commercial Code, or any other conveyance of a portion of a debtor's property for the benefit of any particular creditor or creditors, made within three (3) months preceding a general assignment and in contemplation of making a general assignment, shall be void in the event a general assignment is made within three (3) months thereafter, and the property conveyed by such conveyance shall be shared ratably by all creditors just as that embraced in general assignments.

§ 47-13-117. General Assignments—Prior judgment by confession or default

Any confession of judgment by a debtor, or permitting judgment to be taken by default, or by collusion, within three (3) months preceding a general assignment, and in contemplation of such assignment, shall be void, in the event a general assignment is made within three (3) months after the judgment.

§ 47-13-118. General Assignments—Inventory—Trustee's rights to property

The debtor making a general assignment shall annex thereto a full and complete inventory or schedule under oath of all the debtor's property of every description, and the trustee or assignee shall be entitled to any other property of the debtor not embraced in the assignment, and not exempt from execution, and also to property conveyed in violation of § 47-13-116, and to the property or its proceeds assigned to satisfy judgments rendered in violation of § 47-13-117.

§ 47-13-119. Mortgages, deed of trust or security agreements

The provisions of this chapter shall not prevent any person from making a mortgage, deed of trust, or security agreement under the Uniform Commercial Code to secure the payment for property bought or money lent, or for necessary advancements of supplies, stock, or farming implements to be made, to enable the owner of crops to make and save the same; provided, that the mortgage, deed of trust, or security agreement is executed at the time of buying the property, or borrowing the money, or making the contract for the advancements to be made, if the mortgage, deed of trust, or security agreement fixes the amount of advancement to be made under the contract.

§ 47-13-120. Times for presenting claims—Notice.

(a) A trustee under a general assignment made for the benefit of creditors shall give notice for a reasonable time by advertisement for four (4) consecutive issues in the nearest newspaper to or within the county in which the trustee is qualified, and by posting at the courthouse door of the county, for all persons having claims secured by the assignment to present the claims to the trustee, taking the trustee's receipt therefor, on or before a day fixed in such notice, which day shall not be less than twelve (12) months after the day of notice.

(b) Any claims not presented to the trustee on or before the day so fixed, or before an appropriation of the trust funds, shall be forever barred, both in law and equity.

APPENDIX V

MECHANIC'S LIEN LAW—TEXAS

§ 53.021. PERSONS ENTITLED TO LIEN.

(a) A person has a lien if:

(1) the person labors, specially fabricates material, or furnishes labor or materials for construction or repair in this state of:

(A) a house, building, or improvement;

(B) a levee or embankment to be erected for the reclamation of overflow land along a river or creek; or

(C) a railroad; and

(2) the person labors, specially fabricates the material, or furnishes the labor or materials under or by virtue of a contract with the owner or the owner's agent, trustee, receiver, contractor, or subcontractor.

(b) A person who specially fabricates material has a lien even if the material is not delivered.

(c) An architect, engineer, or surveyor who prepares a plan or plat under or by virtue of a written contract with the owner or the owner's agent, trustee, or receiver in connection with the actual or proposed design, construction, or repair of improvements on real property or the location of the boundaries of real property has a lien on the property.

(d) A person who provides labor, plant material, or other supplies for the installation of landscaping for a house, building, or improvement, including the construction of a retention pond, retaining wall, berm, irrigation system, fountain, or other similar installation, under or by virtue of a written contract with the owner or the owner's agent, trustee, or receiver has a lien on the property.

(e) A person who performs labor as part of, or who furnishes labor or materials for, the demolition of a structure on real property under or by virtue of a written contract with the owner of the property or the owner's agent, trustee, receiver, contractor, or subcontractor has a lien on the property.

§ 53.022. PROPERTY TO WHICH LIEN EXTENDS.

(a) The lien extends to the house, building, fixtures, or improvements, the land reclaimed from overflow, or the railroad and all of its properties, and to each lot of land necessarily connected or reclaimed.

(b) The lien does not extend to abutting sidewalks, streets, and utilities that are public property.

(c) A lien against land in a city, town, or village extends to each lot on which the house, building, or improvement is situated or on which the labor was performed.

(d) A lien against land not in a city, town, or village extends to not more than 50 acres on which the house, building, or improvement is situated or on which the labor was performed.

§ 53.023. PAYMENT SECURED BY LIEN.

The lien secures payment for:

(1) the labor done or material furnished for the construction or repair;

(2) the specially fabricated material, even if the material has not been delivered or incorporated into the construction or repair, less its fair salvage value; or

(3) the preparation of a plan or plat by an architect, engineer, or surveyor in accordance with Section 53.021(c).

§ 53.024. LIMITATION ON SUBCONTRACTOR'S LIEN.

The amount of a lien claimed by a subcontractor may not exceed:

(1) an amount equal to the proportion of the total subcontract price that the sum of the labor performed, materials furnished, materials specially fabricated, reasonable overhead costs incurred, and proportionate profit margin bears to the total subcontract price; minus

(2) the sum of previous payments received by the claimant on the subcontract.

§ 53.025. LIMITATION ON ORDINARY RETAINAGE LIEN.

A lien for retainage is valid only for the amount specified to be retained in the contract, including any amendments to the contract, between the claimant and the original contractor or between the claimant and a subcontractor.

§ 53.026. SHAM CONTRACT.

(a) A person who labors, specially fabricates materials, or furnishes labor or materials under a direct contractual relationship with another person is considered to be in direct contractual relationship with the owner and has a lien as an original contractor, if:

(1) the owner contracted with the other person for the construction or repair of a house, building, or improvements and the owner can effectively control that person through ownership of voting stock, interlocking directorships, or otherwise;

(2) the owner contracted with the other person for the construction or repair of a house, building, or improvements and that other person can effectively control the owner through ownership of voting stock, interlocking directorships, or otherwise; or

(3) the owner contracted with the other person for the construction or repair of a house, building, or improvements and the contract was made without good faith intention of the parties that the other person was to perform the contract.

(b) In this section, "owner" does not include a person who has or claims a security interest only.

§ 53.051. NECESSARY PROCEDURES.

To perfect the lien, a person must comply with this subchapter.

§ 53.052. FILING OF AFFIDAVIT.

(a) Except as provided by Subsection (b), the person claiming the lien must file an affidavit with the county clerk of the county in which the property is located or into which the railroad extends not later than the 15th day of the fourth calendar month after the day on which the indebtedness accrues.

(b) A person claiming a lien arising from a residential construction project must file an affidavit with the county clerk of the county in which the property is located not later than the 15th day of the third calendar month after the day on which the indebtedness accrues.

(c) The county clerk shall record the affidavit in records kept for that purpose and shall index and cross-index the affidavit in the names of the claimant, the original contractor, and the owner. Failure of the county clerk to properly record or index a filed affidavit does not invalidate the lien.

§ 53.053. ACCRUAL OF INDEBTEDNESS.

(a) For purposes of Section 53.052, indebtedness accrues on a contract under which a plan or plat is prepared, labor was performed, materials furnished, or specially fabricated materials are to be furnished in accordance with this section.

(b) Indebtedness to an original contractor accrues:

(1) on the last day of the month in which a written declaration by the original contractor or the owner is received by the other party to the original contract stating that the original contract has been terminated; or

(2) on the last day of the month in which the original contract has been completed, finally settled, or abandoned.

(c) Indebtedness to a subcontractor, or to any person not covered by Subsection (b) or (d), who has furnished labor or material to an original contractor or to another subcontractor accrues on the last day of the last month in which the labor was performed or the material furnished.

(d) Indebtedness for specially fabricated material accrues:

(1) on the last day of the last month in which materials were delivered;

(2) on the last day of the last month in which delivery of the last of the material would normally have been required at the job site; or

(3) on the last day of the month of any material breach or termination of the original contract by the owner or contractor or of the subcontract under which the specially fabricated material was furnished.

(e) A claim for retainage accrues on the last day of the month in which all work called for by the contract between the owner and the original contractor has been completed, finally settled, or abandoned.

§ 53.054. CONTENTS OF AFFIDAVIT.

(a) The affidavit must be signed by the person claiming the lien or by another person on the claimant's behalf and must contain substantially:

(1) a sworn statement of the amount of the claim;

(2) the name and last known address of the owner or reputed owner;

(3) a general statement of the kind of work done and materials furnished by the claimant and, for a claimant other than an original contractor, a statement of each month in which the work was done and materials furnished for which payment is requested;

(4) the name and last known address of the person by whom the claimant was employed or to whom the claimant furnished the materials or labor;

(5) the name and last known address of the original contractor;

(6) a description, legally sufficient for identification, of the property sought to be charged with the lien;

(7) the claimant's name, mailing address, and, if different, physical address; and

(8) for a claimant other than an original contractor, a statement identifying the date each notice of the claim was sent to the owner and the method by which the notice was sent.

(b) The claimant may attach to the affidavit a copy of any applicable written agreement or contract and a copy of each notice sent to the owner.

(c) The affidavit is not required to set forth individual items of work done or material furnished or specially fabricated. The affidavit may use any abbreviations or symbols customary in the trade.

§ 53.055. NOTICE OF FILED AFFIDAVIT.

(a) A person who files an affidavit must send a copy of the affidavit by registered or certified mail to the owner or reputed owner at the owner's last known business or residence address not later than the fifth day after the date the affidavit is filed with the county clerk.

(b) If the person is not an original contractor, the person must also send a copy of the affidavit to the original contractor at the original contractor's last known business or residence address within the same period.

APPENDIX VI

COMMERCIAL COLLECTION—STATE SURVEY OF LAWS GOVERNING COMMERCIAL COLLECTION

Fastfax

From ACA's Fastfax Service
Last Updated on August 1, 2006

Page 1 of 37
Document No. 2034

ACA
INTERNATIONAL
The Association of Credit and Collection Professionals

Now get immediate access to ACA's compliance expertise. Visit E-Compliance at ternational.org to search and access Fastfax documents and other compliance e-mail a compliance officer.

A Brief Summary of Commercial Collection Regulations

Actions taken by state legislatures in recent years have changed the number of states that regulate consumer and commercial collections. Note, however, that the states listed below may afford some exemptions depending on the type of transaction. States that require collection agencies who collect commercial debt to be licensed include:

Alabama*
Alaska
Arizona
Arkansas
Delaware
Florida
Idaho
Illinois
Indiana
Minnesota
Nebraska
Nevada
New Jersey
North Carolina
North Dakota
Oregon
Pennsylvania
South Carolina*
Tennessee
Utah
Washington
West Virginia
Wisconsin

* These states require a general business license for all businesses located within the state

This is a summary of a Fastfax developed by ACA's Compliance Department for the International Association of Commercial Collectors (IACC), which is attached below. Collectors should review both this summary and the following document and also consult with their own attorney before making business decisions. For additional information on these requirements, please see *ACA's Guide to State Collection Laws and Practices*, which is available from ACA's Member Services Department at 952.926.6547. More information about particular state licensing laws can be found in ACA's Interstate Chart which can be found on E-Compliance at www.acainternational.org.

Commercial Collections

In order to determine whether or not one needs to be licensed in a particular state in order to collect commercial debt, one must examine each state's definition of debt and debt collector. If either of these definitions includes commercial, corporate or business debts, the next step is to examine that state's licensing requirements for debt collectors. This document provides the applicable statutes regarding the definition of debt and debt collector.

This document is not a full analysis of commercial collections. One must consult with her own legal counsel in order to determine if licensing is required.

ALABAMA

Every person, firm, company, corporation or association, receiver or trustee, but not a governmental subdivision, engaged in any business, vocation, occupation, calling, or profession herein enumerated or who shall exercise any privilege hereinafter described for which a license or privilege tax is required shall first procure a state license, and a county license when so required, and shall pay for the same or shall pay for the exercise of such privilege the amounts hereinafter provided, and comply with all other provisions of this title. Ala. Code § 40-12-40 (WESTLAW through End of 2005 Reg. Sess.).

<u>Definition</u>

Each person who shall employ agents to solicit claims for collection from persons, firms, or corporations in the state shall be deemed a collection agency within the meaning of this section. This section shall not apply to any person who is excluded from the definition of the term "debt collector" under the federal Fair Debt Collection Practices Act, 15 U.S.C. § 1692a(6). Ala. Code § 4-12-80 (WESTLAW through End of 2005 Reg. Sess.).

ALASKA

<u>Definitions</u>

In this chapter,

(1) "collection agency" means a person licensed and authorized to engage in the collection agency business;

(2) "collection agency business" means the business of engaging directly or indirectly and having as a primary or secondary object, business or pursuit the solicitation of claims for collection or repossession of collateral security or the collection of claims owed or due or asserted to be owed or due to another or the repossession of collateral security;

> (A) a house, agency, firm, person, corporation or voluntary association using a name other than its own in collecting its own claims with the intention of conveying, or which tends to convey, the impression that a third party has been employed, is conducting a collection agency business within the meaning of this chapter;
>
> (B) a person who sells, attempts to sell, gives away or attempts to give away to another person, other than a licensee under this chapter a system of collection letters, demand forms or other printed matter where the name of a person other than a creditor appears in a manner to indicate that a request or demand is being made by another person, other than the creditor, for the payment of a sum due, or asserted to be due, or who solicits or accepts accounts for collection on a contingent or percentage basis or by a fee or outright purchase for collection purposes, is considered to be in the collection agency business within the meaning of this chapter;

(3) "commissioner" means the commissioner of commerce, community, and economic development;

(4) "department" means the Department of Commerce, Community, and Economic Development;

(5) "operator" means a person having managerial control of a collection agency.

Alaska Stat. §§ 08.24.380 (WESTLAW through all 2004 Sessions, Annotations through Opinions Decided as of September 17, 2004).

Exemptions
(b) This chapter['s licensing requirements] do...not apply to the following when engaged in the regular course of their respective businesses:

(1) attorneys at law;
(2) persons regularly employed on a regular wage or salary in the capacity of credit men or a similar capacity, except as an independent contractor;
(3) banks, including trust departments of banks, fiduciaries and financing and lending institutions;
(4) common carriers;
(5) title insurers and abstract companies while doing an escrow business;
(6) licensed real estate brokers;
(7) employees of licensees under this chapter;
(8) substation payment offices employed by or serving as independent contractors for public utilities.

Alaska Stat. Section 08.24.090(b)(WESTLAW through all 2004 Sessions, Annotations through Opinions Decided as of September 17, 2004).

ARIZONA
Definitions
In this chapter, unless the context otherwise requires:
1 "Claim" means an obligation for the payment of money or its equivalent and a sum or sums owed, due or asserted to be owed or due to another, for which a person is employed to demand payment and collect or enforce such payment, and includes:

(a) Obligations for the payment of money to another, in the form of conditional sales agreements, notwithstanding the personal property sold thereunder, for which payment is claimed or may be or is repossessed in lieu of payment.
(b) An obligation for the payment of money or its equivalent and a sum or sums owed, due or asserted to be owed or due which is sold or assigned to a purchaser or assignee for which either:

(i) The final payment has not been tendered to the seller or assignor.
(ii) Title has not yet passed.
(iii) The purchaser or assignee has a right of recourse against the seller or assignor.

2. "Collection agency" means:

(a) All persons engaged directly or indirectly in soliciting claims for collection or in collection of claims owed, due or asserted to be owed or due.
(b) Any person who, in the process of collecting debts occurring in the operation of his own business, uses any name other than his own which would indicate that a third person is collecting or attempting to collect such debts.

Ariz. Stat. Ann. § 32-1001(a)(1)-(2) (WESTLAW through 47th Leg., First Reg. Sess. (2005)).

A. In this chapter, unless the context otherwise requires:
1. "Claim" means an obligation for the payment of money or its equivalent and a sum or sums owed, due or asserted to be owed or due to another, for which a person is employed to demand payment and collect or enforce such payment, and includes:

(a) Obligations for the payment of money to another, in the form of conditional sales agreements, notwithstanding the personal property sold thereunder, for which payment is claimed or may be or is repossessed in lieu of payment.
(b) An obligation for the payment of money or its equivalent and a sum or sums owed, due or asserted to be owed or due which is sold or assigned to a purchaser or assignee for which either:

(i) The final payment has not been tendered to the seller or assignor.
(ii) Title has not yet passed.
(iii) The purchaser or assignee has a right of recourse against the seller or assignor.

2. "Collection agency" means:

(a) All persons engaged directly or indirectly in soliciting claims for collection or in collection of claims owed, due or asserted to be owed or due.

(b) Any person who, in the process of collecting debts occurring in the operation of his own business, uses any name other than his own which would indicate that a third person is collecting or attempting to collect such debts.

Ariz. Stat. Ann. § 32-1001(a)(1)-(2) (WESTLAW through End of 47th Leg., First Reg. Sess. (2005)).

Exemptions

A. The following persons are exempt from the provisions of this chapter when engaged in the regular course of their respective businesses but shall comply with the requirements of § 32-1051, paragraphs 2 through 7 and § 32-1055, subsection C and subsection D, paragraphs 1, 2, 3 and 5:

1. Attorneys-at-law.
2. A person regularly employed on a regular wage or salary in the capacity of credit person or a similar capacity, except as an independent contractor.
3. Banks, including trust departments of a bank, fiduciaries and financing and lending institutions.
4. Common carriers.
5. Title insurers, title insurance agents and abstract companies while doing an escrow business.
6. Licensed real estate brokers.
7. Employees of licensees under this chapter.
8. Substation payment offices employed by or serving as independent contractors or public utilities.
9. A person licensed pursuant to title 6, chapter 7.
10. A person licensed pursuant to title 6, chapter 9.
11. A person licensed pursuant to title 6, chapter 14, article 1.
12. A participant in a finance transaction in which a lender receives the right to collect commercial claims due the borrower by assignment, by purchase or by the taking of a security interest in those commercial claims.
13. An accounting, bookkeeping or billing service provider that complies with all of the following:
    (a) Does not accept accounts that are contractually past due at the time of receipt.
    (b) Does not initiate any contact with individual debtors except for the initial written notice of the amount owing and one written follow-up notice.
    (c) Does not give or send to any debtor a written communication that requests or demands payment.
    (d) Does not receive or have access to monies paid by debtors or their insurers.
    (e) All communications with the debtors are done in the name of the creditor.
14. A person collecting claims owed, due or asserted to be owed or due to a financial institution the deposits of which are insured by an agency of the federal government, or any affiliate of the financial institution, if the person is related by common ownership or affiliated by corporate control with the financial institution and collects the claims only for the financial institution or any affiliate of the financial institution.
15. A person who is licensed pursuant to title 20, chapter 2, article 3, 3.1, 3.2, 3.3 or 3.4 and who is authorized to collect premiums under an insurance policy financed by a premium finance agreement as defined in § 6-1401.

B. For the purposes of subsection A, paragraph 12 of this section:

1. A transaction shall not be deemed a finance transaction if the primary purpose is to facilitate the collection of claims.
2. "Commercial claim" does not include an account arising from the purchase of a service or product intended for personal, family or household use.

Ariz. Stat. Ann. § 32-1004(A)-(B) (WESTLAW through End of 47th Leg., First Reg. Sess. (2005)).

ARKANSAS

Definitions

As used in this chapter, unless the context otherwise requires, "collection agency" means any person who works with or employs one (1) or more other persons, or any partnership, corporation, or association which engages in the collection of delinquent accounts, bills, or other forms of indebtedness, or any person, partnership, corporation, or association using a fictitious name or any name other than their own in the collection of their own accounts receivable, or any person, partnership, corporation, or association which solicits claims for collection. Ark. Code Ann. § 17-24-101 (WESTLAW through 2005 Reg. Sess.).

Exemptions

(a) The provisions of this chapter shall not be applicable to:

(1) Regular employees of a single creditor;

(2) Banks;

(3) Trust companies;

(4) Savings and loan associations;

(5) Abstract companies doing an escrow business;

(6) Licensed real estate brokers and agents when the claims or accounts being handled by the broker or agent are related to or in connection with the broker's or agent's regular real estate business;

(7) Express and telegraph companies subject to public regulation and supervision;

(8) Attorneys at law handling claims and collections in their own names and not operating a collection agency under the management of a layman or under names other than their own;

(9) Persons, firms, corporations, or associations handling claims, accounts, or collections under an order of any court. However, child support collection agencies not operating pursuant to Title IV-D of the Social Security Act are not exempt from this chapter and shall be subject to licensure; and

(10) Any person, firm, corporation, or association which, for a valuable consideration, purchases accounts, claims, or demands of another which were not in default or delinquent at the time of acquisition and then, in such purchaser's own name, proceeds to assert or collect the accounts, claims, or demands.

(b) Nothing in §§ 17-24-301, 17-24-309, 17-24-401, or this section with respect to licensure by the State Board of Collection Agencies, or limitations of fees for collection services, shall include or be applicable to attorneys at law licensed to practice in the State of Arkansas who are engaged in rendering legal services for clients in the collection of accounts, debts, or claims, nor shall §§ 17-24-301, 17-24-309, 17-24-401, or this section amend or repeal in any way the exemptions set out in subsection (a) of this section.

(c) (1) Nothing in this chapter shall include or be applicable to the foreclosure of real property under the provisions of § 18-49-101 et seq. or § 18-50-101 et seq.

(2) Foreclosure of real property is not deemed to be debt collection as defined in the federal Fair Debt Collections Practices Act, 15 U.S.C. § 1692a(6), as in existence on January 1, 2005.

Ark. Code Ann. § 17-24-102 (WESTLAW through the 2005 Reg. Sess.).

CALIFORNIA

Definitions

(a) Definitions and rules of construction set forth in this section are applicable for the purpose of this title.

(b) The term "debt collection" means any act or practice in connection with the collection of consumer debts.

(c) The term "debt collector" means any person who, in the ordinary course of business, regularly, on behalf of himself or herself or others, engages in debt collection. The term includes any person who composes and sells, or offers to compose and sell, forms, letters, and other collection media used or intended to be used for debt collection, but does not include an attorney or counselor at law.

(d) The term "debt" means money, property or their equivalent which is due or owing or alleged to be due or owing from a natural person to another person.
(e) The term "consumer credit transaction" means a transaction between a natural person and another person in which property, services or money is acquired on credit by that natural person from such other person primarily for personal, family, or household purposes.
(f) The terms "consumer debt" and "consumer credit" mean money, property or their equivalent, due or owing or alleged to be due or owing from a natural person by reason of a consumer credit transaction.
(g) The term "person" means a natural person, partnership, corporation, limited liability company, trust, estate, cooperative, association or other similar entity.
(h) The term "debtor" means a natural person from whom a debt collector seeks to collect a consumer debt which is due and owing or alleged to be due and owing from such person.
(i) The term "creditor" means a person who extends consumer credit to a debtor.
(j) The term "consumer credit report" means any written, oral or other communication of any information by a consumer reporting agency bearing on a consumer's creditworthiness, credit standing, credit capacity, character, general reputation, personal characteristics or mode of living which is used or expected to be used or collected in whole or in part for the purpose of serving as a factor in establishing the consumer's eligibility for (1) credit or insurance to be used primarily for person, family, or household purposes, or (2) employment purposes, or (3) other purposes authorized under any applicable federal or state law or regulation. The term does not include (a) any report containing information solely as to transactions or experiences between the consumer and the person making the report; (b) any authorization or approval of a specific extension of credit directly or indirectly by the issuer of a credit card or similar device; or (c) any report in which a person who has been requested by a third party to make a specific extension of credit directly or indirectly to a consumer conveys his or her decision with respect to that request, if the third party advises the consumer of the name and address of the person to whom the request was made and such person makes the disclosures to the consumer required under any applicable federal or state law or regulation.
(k) The term "consumer reporting agency" means any person which, for monetary fees, dues, or on a cooperative nonprofit basis, regularly engages, in whole or in part, in the practice of assembling or evaluating consumer credit information or other information on consumers for the purpose of furnishing consumer credit reports to third parties, and which uses any means or facility for the purpose of preparing or furnishing consumer credit reports.
Cal. Civ. Code Ann § 1788.2 (WESTLAW through Ch. 153 of 2005 Reg. Sess. Urgency Leg. & Governor's Reorganization Plans No. 1 & 2 of 2005).

COLORADO

Definitions

(2)(a) "Collection agency" means any:

- (I) Person who engages in a business the principal purpose of which is the collection of debts; or
- (II) Person who:
  - (A) Regularly collects or attempts to collect, directly or indirectly, debts owed or due or asserted to be owed or due another;
  - (B) Takes assignment of debts for collection purposes;
  - (C) Directly or indirectly solicits for collection debts owed or due or asserted to be owed or due another;
  - (D) Collects debt for the department of personnel, but only for the purposes specified in paragraph (d) of this subsection (2);

Colo. Rev. Stat. Ann. § 12-14-103(2)(a) (WESTLAW through End of the 2005 First Reg. Sess. of the 65th Gen. Assembly).

(6) (a) "Debt" means any obligation or alleged obligation of a consumer to pay money arising out of a transaction, whether or not such obligation has been reduced to judgment.

(b) "Debt" does not include a debt for business, investment, commercial, or agricultural purposes or a debt incurred by a business.

(7) "Debt collector" means any person employed or engaged by a collection agency to perform the collection of debts owed or due or asserted to be owed or due to another, and includes any person employed by the department of personnel, or any division of said department, when collecting debts due to the state on behalf of another state agency.

Colo. Rev. Stat. Ann. § 12-14-103(6)-(7) (WESTLAW through End of the 2005 First Reg. Sess. of the 65th Gen. Assembly).

Exemptions

(2)(b) "Collection agency" does not include:

(I) Any officer or employee of a creditor while, in the name of the creditor, collecting debts for such creditor;

(II) Any person while acting as a collection agency for another person, both of whom are related by common ownership or affiliated by corporate control, if the person acting as a collection agency does so only for creditors to whom it is so related or affiliated and if the principal business of such person is not the collection of debts;

(III) Any officer or employee of the United States or any state to the extent that collecting or attempting to collect any debt is in the performance of such officer's or employee's official duties, except as otherwise provided in subsection (7) of this section;

(IV) Any person while serving or attempting to serve legal process on any other person in connection with the judicial enforcement of any debt;

(V) Any nonprofit organization which, at the request of consumers, performs bona fide consumer credit counseling and assists consumers in the liquidation of their debts by receiving payments from such consumers and distributing such amounts to creditors;

(VI) Repealed by Laws 1990, H.B.90-1005, § 27.

(VII) Any person collecting or attempting to collect any debt owed or due or asserted to be owed or due another to the extent that:

(A) Such activity is incidental to a bona fide fiduciary obligation or a bona fide escrow arrangement;

(B) Such activity concerns a debt which was extended by such person;

(C) Such activity concerns a debt which was not in default at the time it was obtained by such person; or

(D) Such activity concerns a debt obtained by such person as a secured party in a commercial credit transaction involving the creditor;

(VIII) Any person whose principal business is the making of loans or the servicing of debt not in default and who acts as a loan correspondent, or seller and servicer for the owner, or holder of a debt which is secured by a deed of trust on real property whether or not such debt is also secured by an interest in personal property.

(c) Notwithstanding the provisions of subparagraph (VII) of paragraph (b) of this subsection (2), "collection agency" includes any person who, in the process of collecting his or her own debts, uses another name which would indicate that a third person is collecting or attempting to collect such debts.

(d) For the purposes of section 12-14-108(1)(f), "collection agency" includes any person engaged in any business the principal purpose of which is the enforcement of security interests. For purposes of sections 12-14-104, 12-14-105, 12-14-106, 12-14-107, 12-14-108, and 12-14-109 only, "collection agency" includes a debt collector for the department of personnel.

(e) Notwithstanding paragraph (b) of this subsection (2), "collection agency" includes any person who engages in any of the following activities; except that such person shall be exempt from provisions of this article that concern licensing and licensees:

(I) Deleted by Laws 2000, Ch. 218, § 2, eff. July 1, 2000.

(II) Is an attorney-at-law and regularly engages in the collection or attempted collection of debts

in this state;
(III) Is a person located outside this state whose collection activities are limited to collecting debts not incurred in this state from consumers located in this state and whose collection activities are conducted by means of interstate communications, including telephone, mail, or facsimile transmission, and who is located in another state that regulates and licenses collection agencies but does not require Colorado collection agencies to obtain a license to collect debts in their state if such agencies' collection activities are limited in the same manner.

Colo. Rev. Stat. Ann. §§ 12-14-103(2)(b) (WESTLAW through End of the 2005 First Reg. Sess. of the 65th Gen. Assembly).

CONNECTICUT

Definitions

As used in sections 36a-800 to 36a-810, inclusive, unless the context otherwise requires:
(1) "Consumer collection agency" means any person engaged in the business of collecting or receiving for payment for others of any account, bill or other indebtedness from a consumer debtor or engaged in the business of collecting or receiving for payment property tax from a property tax debtor on behalf of a municipality, including any person who, by any device, subterfuge or pretense, makes a pretended purchase or takes a pretended assignment of accounts from any other person or municipality of such indebtedness for the purpose of evading the provisions of sections 36a-800 to 36a-810, inclusive. It includes persons who furnish collection systems carrying a name which simulates the name of a consumer collection agency and who supply forms or form letters to be used by the creditor, even though such forms direct the consumer debtor or property tax debtor to make payments directly to the creditor rather than to such fictitious agency. "Consumer collection agency" further includes any person who, in attempting to collect or in collecting such person's own accounts or claims from a consumer debtor, uses a fictitious name or any name other than such person's own name which would indicate to the consumer debtor that a third person is collecting or attempting to collect such account or claim.
(2) "Consumer debtor" means any natural person, not an organization, who has incurred indebtedness or owes a debt for personal, family or household purposes, including current or past due child support, or who has incurred indebtedness or owes a debt to a municipality due to a levy by such municipality of a personal property tax;
(3) "Creditor" means a person, including a municipality, that retains, hires, or engages the services of a consumer collection agency;
(4) "Municipality" means any town, city or borough, consolidated town and city, consolidated town and borough, district as defined in section 7-324 or municipal special services district established under chapter 105a;
(5) "Organization" means a corporation, partnership, association, trust or any other legal entity or an individual operating under a trade name or a name having appended to it a commercial, occupational or professional designation;
(6) "Property tax" has the meaning given to the term in section 7-560;
(7) "Property tax debtor" means any natural person or organization who has incurred indebtedness or owes a debt to a municipality due to a levy by such municipality of a property tax.

Con. Gen. Stat. Ann. § 36a-800 (WESTLAW through 2005 Jan. Reg. Sess. Leg. approved by the Gov. on or before 6-24-05).

As used in sections 36a-645 to 36a-647, inclusive, unless the context otherwise requires:
(1) "Consumer debtor" means any natural person residing in this state who owes a debt to a creditor.
(2) "Creditor" means (A) any person to whom a debt is owed by a consumer debtor and such debt results from a transaction occurring in the ordinary course of such person's business, or (B) any person to whom such debt is assigned. "Creditor" shall not include a consumer collection agency, as defined in section 36a-800, or any department or agency of the United States, this state, any other state, or any political subdivision thereof.

(3) "Debt" means an obligation or alleged obligation arising out of a transaction in which the money, property, goods or services which are the subject of the transaction are for personal, family or household purposes, whether or not such obligation has been reduced to judgment.
Con. Gen. Stat. Ann. §§ 36a-645 (WESTLAW through 2005 Jan. Reg. Sess. Leg. approved by the Gov. on or before 6-24-05).

As used in Sections 36a-809-1 to 36-809-5, inclusive, of these regulations:
(1) "Commissioner" means the commissioner of banking.
(3) "Consumer collection agency" has the same meaning as provided in Section 42-127 of the Connecticut General Statutes.
(4) "Consumer debtor" has the same meaning as provided in Section 42-127 of the Connecticut General Statutes.
(5) "Creditor" has the same meaning as provided in Section 42-127 of the Connecticut General Statutes.
(6) "Debt" means any obligation or alleged obligation of a consumer debtor to pay money arising out of a transaction in which the money, property, insurance or services which are the subject of the transaction are primarily for personal, family or household purposes, or arising out of a levy of a personal property tax by a municipality, as defined in Section 42-127 of the Connecticut General Statutes, whether or not such obligation has been reduced to judgment.
Conn. Agencies Regs. § 36a-809-3(1), (3)-(6) (WESTLAW through 2005 Jan. Reg. Sess. Leg. approved by the Gov. on or before 6-24-05).

Exemptions
"Consumer collection agency" does not include (A) an individual employed on the staff of a licensed consumer collection agency, or by a creditor who is exempt from licensing, when attempting to collect on behalf of such consumer collection agency, (B) persons not primarily engaged in the collection of debts from consumer debtors who receive funds in escrow for subsequent distribution to others, including, but not limited to, real estate brokers and lenders holding funds of borrowers for payment of taxes or insurance, (C) any public officer or a person acting under the order of any court, (D) any member of the bar of this state, and (E) a person who services loans or accounts for the owners thereof when the arrangement includes, in addition to requesting payment from delinquent consumer debtors, the providing of other services such as receipt of payment, accounting, record-keeping, data processing services and remitting, for loans or accounts which are current as well as those which are delinquent. Any person not included in the definition contained in this subsection is, for purposes of sections 36a-645 to 36a-647, inclusive, a "creditor", as defined in subdivision (3) of section 36a-645; Con. Gen. Stat. Ann. § 36a-800(1) (WESTLAW through 2005 Jan. Reg. Sess. Leg. approved by the Gov. on or before 6-24-05).

DELAWARE
Definitions
"Mercantile agency" or "collection agency" includes every person operating a business of investigation of financial ratings and credit and/or the collection of commercial accounts for other persons, except attorneys-at-law having a license to practice such profession in this State.
Del. Code Ann. tit. 30 § 2301 (a)(13) (WESTLAW through the First Reg. Sess. of the 143rd Gen. Assembly 75 Del. Laws, Ch. 60 (2005)).

DISTRICT OF COLUMBIA
Definitions
(a) This section only applies to conduct and practices in connection with collection of obligations arising from consumer credit sales, consumer leases, and direct installment loans (other than a loan directly secured on real estate or a direct motor vehicle installment loan covered by Chapter 36 of Title 28).
(b) As used in this section, the term --

(1) "claim" means any obligation or alleged obligation, arising from a consumer credit sale,

consumer lease, or direct installment loan;
(2) "debt collection" means any action, conduct or practice in connection with the solicitation of claims for collection or in connection with the collection of claims, that are owed or due, or are alleged to be owed or due, a seller or lender by a consumer; and
(3) "debt collector" means any person engaging directly or indirectly in debt collection, and includes any person who sells or offers to sell forms represented to be a collection system, device, or scheme intended or calculated to be used to collect claims.

D.C. Code Ann. § 28-3814(a)-(b)(3)(WESTLAW through May 31, 2005).

FLORIDA

Definitions

As used in this part:

(1) "Claim" or "commercial claim" means any obligation for the payment of money or its equivalent arising out of a transaction wherein credit has been offered or extended to any person, and the money, property, or service which was the subject of the transaction was primarily for commercial purposes and not primarily for personal, family, or household purposes, whether or not such obligation has been reduced to judgment. The term "claim" or "commercial claim" includes an obligation of a person who is comaker, endorser, guarantor, or surety as well as the person to whom such credit was originally extended.

(2) "Commercial collection agency" means any person engaged, as a primary or secondary business activity, in the business of soliciting commercial claims for collection or in the business of collecting commercial claims, asserted to be owed or due to another person, regardless of whether the collection efforts are directed at the primary debtor or some other source of payment.

(3) "Credit grantor" means any person or entity to whom a commercial claim is owed, due, or alleged to be owed or due, whether or not such person or entity is domiciled or doing business within this state and whether or not such commercial claim arose within this state. However, such term does not apply to any registrant under this part who has received an assignment or transfer of a commercial claim in default solely for the purpose of facilitating collection of such commercial claim for another.

(4) "Out-of-state collector" means any person or business entity engaged in the business of soliciting commercial claims for collection or of collecting commercial claims whose business activities in this state are limited to collecting commercial claims by means of interstate communications, including telephone, mail, or facsimile transmission, originating from outside this state.

Fla. Stat. Ann. § 559.543 (WESTLAW through Ch. 352 and H.J.R. No. 1723, H.J.R. 1177 and S.J.R. No. 2144 (End) of the 2005 First Reg. Sess. of the 19th Leg.).

Exemptions

(5) This section shall not apply to:

(a) A member of The Florida Bar, unless such person is primarily engaged in the collection of commercial claims. "Primarily engaged in the collection of commercial claims" means that more than one-half of the income of such person arises from the business of soliciting commercial claims for collection or collecting commercial claims.
(b) A financial institution authorized to do business in this state and any wholly owned subsidiary and affiliate thereof.
(c) A licensed real estate broker.
(d) A title insurance company authorized to do business in this state.
(e) A collection agency which is not primarily engaged in the collection of commercial claims. "Not primarily engaged in the collection of commercial claims" means that less than one-half of the collection revenue of such agency arises from the collection of commercial claims.
(f) A consumer finance company and any wholly owned subsidiary and affiliate thereof.
(g) A person licensed pursuant to chapter 520.
(h) A credit grantor.

(i) An out-of-state collector as defined in this part.

(j) An FDIC-insured institution or subsidiary or affiliate thereof.

Fla. Stat. Ann. § 559.544(5) (WESTLAW through Ch. 352 and H.J.R. No. 1723, H.J.R. 1177 and S.J.R. No. 2144 (End) of the 2005 First Reg. Sess. of the 19th Leg.).

GEORGIA

There are no statutory licensing requirements in the state of Georgia.

HAWAII

Definitions

As used in this chapter:

"Client" means a person who offered or extended credit which created a debt, or to whom a debt is owed, and who engages the professional services of a collection agency. The term does not include any person who receives an assignment or transfer of a debt in default solely for the purpose of facilitating collection of a debt for another.

"Collection agency" means any person, whether located within or outside this State, who by oneself or through others offers to undertake or holds oneself out as being able to undertake or does undertake to collect for another person, claims or money due on accounts or other forms of indebtedness for a commission, fixed fee, or a portion of the sums so collected.

"Collection agency" includes:

(1) Any person using any name other than the person's own in collecting the person's own claims with the intention of conveying, or which tends to convey the impression that a third party has been employed;

(2) Any person who, in the conduct of the person's business for a fee, regularly repossesses any merchandise or chattels for another; and

(3) Any person who regularly accepts the assignment of claims or money due on accounts or other forms of indebtedness and brings suits upon the assigned claims or money due on accounts or other forms of indebtedness in the person's own name; provided that any suits shall be initiated and prosecuted by an attorney who shall have been appointed by the assignee.

"Communication" means directly or indirectly conveying information regarding a debt to any person by any means.

"Debt" means any obligation or alleged obligation of a consumer to pay money or other forms of payment arising out of a transaction in which the money, property, insurance, or services, which are the subject of the transaction, are primarily for personal, family, or household purpose, whether or not such obligation has been reduced to judgment.

"Debtor" means any person or the person's spouse or reciprocal beneficiary, parent (if the person is a minor), guardian, executor, or administrator obligated or allegedly obligated to pay a debt.

"Principal collector" means an individual who has been designated by a collection agency to assume responsibility for the operations and activities of the agency's office in this State.

Hawaii Rev. Stat. Ann. § 443B-1 (Bender through 2004 Reg. Sess.)

As used in this chapter:

"Consumer debt" means any debt of a natural person incurred primarily for personal, family, or household purposes.

"Debt" means any obligation or alleged obligation of a person to pay money arising out of any transaction, whether or not the obligation has been reduced to judgment.

"Debt collector" means any person, who is not a collection agency, and who in the regular course of business collects or attempts to collect consumer debts owed or due or asserted to be owed or due to the collector.

"Person" means an individual, partnership, joint venture, corporation, association, business, trust, or any organized group of persons, or any combination thereof.

Hawaii Rev. Stat. Ann. § 480D-2 (Bender through 2004 Reg. Sess.)

Exemptions
"Collection agency" does not include licensed attorneys at law acting within the scope of their profession, licensed real estate brokers, and salespersons residing in this State when engaged in the regular practice o their profession, nor banks, trust companies, building and loan associations, savings and loan associations, financial services loan companies, credit unions, companies doing an escrow business, individuals regularly employed on a regular wage or salary in the capacity of credit persons or in other similar capacity for a single employer who is not a collection agency, nor any public officer or any persor acting under an order of court. Hawaii Rev. Stat. Ann. § 443B-1 (Bender through 2004 Reg. Sess.)

IDAHO

Definitions
As used in this chapter:
(1) "Agent" means any person who is compensated on a commission basis or by salary, or both, by any permittee and who either contacts debtors or creditors in connection with the collection agency business of the permittee.
(2) "Business funds" means all moneys belonging to or due the permittee in connection with the operatior of a collection agency business.
(3) "Collection agency," "collection bureau" or "collection office" shall be a person who engages in any of the activities enumerated in section 26-2223, Idaho Code.
(4) "Director" means the director of the department of finance.
(5) "Creditor" means any person who transfers to a permittee accounts due and owing for collection purposes.
(6) "Creditors' account" means all funds due and owing a creditor within the definition of this chapter.
(7) "Net collections" means all funds that are due to creditors from the permittee pursuant to the contract between the permittee and creditor, or permittee and debtor without taking into account any offset or funds due from the creditor to the permittee, because of the creditor having collected any part of the account due, plus all funds that the permittee agreed to return to debtors or that were not to be applied to debts.
(8) "Permittee" means a person who has a permit to do business as a collection agency, or debt counselor, or credit counselor in Idaho.
(9) "Person" means any permittee, agent, solicitor, individual, corporation, association, copartnership, trust, company or unincorporated organization.
(10) "Debt counselor" means any person engaged in any of the activities enumerated in subsection (6) of section 26-2223, Idaho Code.
(11) "Credit counselor" means any person engaged in any of the activities enumerated in subsection (6) oı (7) of section 26-2223, Idaho Code. No credit counselor shall be granted a permit pursuant to this chapter unless qualified as an exempt organization under section 501(c)(3) of the Internal Revenue Code.
Idaho Code Ann. § 26-2222 (WESTLAW through the 2005 Leg. Sess.).

ILLINOIS

Definitions
A person, association, partnership, corporation, or other legal entity acts as a collection agency when he or it:
(a) Engages in the business of collection for others of any account, bill or other indebtedness;
(b) Receives, by assignment or otherwise, accounts, bills, or other indebtedness from any person owning or controlling 20% or more of the business receiving the assignment, with the purpose of collecting monies due on such account, bill or other indebtedness;
(c) Sells or attempts to sell, or gives away or attempts to give away to any other person, other than one registered under this Act, any system of collection, letters, demand forms, or other printed matter where

the name of any person, other than that of the creditor, appears in such a manner as to indicate, directly or indirectly, that a request or demand is being made by any person other than the creditor for the payment of the sum or sums due or asserted to be due;
(d) Buys accounts, bills or other indebtedness with recourse and engages in collecting the same; or
(e) Uses a fictitious name in collecting its own accounts, bills, or debts with the intention of conveying to the debtor that a third party has been employed to make such collection.
225 Ill. Comp. Stat. Ann. § 425/3 (WESTLAW through P.A. 94-259 of the 2005 Reg. Sess.).

"Collection agency" or "agency" means any person, association, partnership, or corporation who, for compensation, either contingent or otherwise, or for other valuable consideration, offers services to collect an alleged delinquent debt. 225 Ill. Comp. Stat. Ann. § 425/2.02 (WESTLAW through P.A. 94-259 of the 2005 Reg. Sess.).

Exemptions
This Act does not apply to persons whose collection activities are confined to and are directly related to the operation of a business other than that of a collection agency, and specifically does not include the following:
1. Banks, including trust departments thereof, fiduciaries, and financing and lending institutions (except those who own or operate collection agencies);
2. Abstract companies doing an escrow business;
3. Real estate brokers when acting in the pursuit of their profession;
4. Public officers and judicial officers acting under order of a court;
5. Licensed attorneys at law;
6. Insurance companies;
7. Credit unions;
8. Loan and finance companies;
9. Retail stores collecting their own accounts;
10. Unit Owner's Associations established under the Condominium Property Act, and their duly authorized agents, when collecting assessments from unit owners; and
11. Any person or business under contract with a creditor to notify the creditor's debtors of a debt using only the creditor's name.
225 Ill. Comp. Stat. Ann. § 425/2.03 (WESTLAW through P.A. 94-259 of the 2005 Reg. Sess.).

INDIANA
Definitions
As used in this chapter, unless the context otherwise requires:
(a) The term "person" means any individual, firm, partnership, limited liability company, or corporation.
(b) The term "collection agency" means and includes all persons engaging directly or indirectly and as a primary or secondary object, business, or pursuit, in soliciting claims for collection, or in the collection of claims owed or due or asserted to be owed or due to another, including child support arrearages under IC 12-17-2. The term "collection agency" also means and includes, but shall not be limited to, any person who sells, furnishes, or maintains a letter or written demand service, including stickers or coupon books, designed for the purpose of making demand on any debtor on behalf of any creditor for the payment of any claim wherein the person furnishing or maintaining such letter or written demand service, including stickers or coupon books, shall sell such services for a stated amount or for a percentage of money collected whether paid to the creditor or to the collection agency, or where such services may be rendered as a part of a membership in such collection agency regardless of whether or not a separate fee or percentage is charged. The term "collection agency" shall also include, but not be limited to, any individual, firm, partnership, limited liability company, or corporation who uses a fictitious name, or any name other than the individual's or entity's name, in the collection of accounts receivable with the intention of conveying to the debtor that a third person has been employed.

(c) The term "claim" means any obligation for the payment of money or its equivalent and any sum or sums owed or due or asserted to be owed or due to another, for which any person may be employed to demand payment and to collect or enforce payment thereof. The term "claim" also includes obligations for the payment of money in the form of conditional sales agreements, notwithstanding that the personal property sold thereunder, for which payment is claimed, may be or is repossessed in lieu of payment. Ind. Code Ann. § 25-11-1-1 (WESTLAW through the 2005 First Reg. Sess.).

IOWA

Definitions

As used in this article, unless the context otherwise requires:

1. "Administrator" means the person designated in section 537.6103.
2. "Creditor", for the purposes of this article, means the person to whom a debtor is obligated, either directly or indirectly, on a debt.
3. "Debt" means an actual or alleged obligation arising out of a consumer credit transaction, consumer rental purchase agreement, or a transaction which would have been a consumer credit transaction either if a finance charge was made, if the obligation was not payable in installments, if a lease was for a term of four months or less, or if a lease was of an interest in land. A debt includes a check as defined in section 554.3104 given in a transaction in connection with a consumer rental purchase agreement, in a transaction which was a consumer credit sale or in a transaction which would have been a consumer credit sale if credit was granted and if a finance charge was made, or in a transaction regulated under chapter 533D.
4. "Debt collection" means an action, conduct or practice in soliciting debts for collection or in the collection or attempted collection of a debt.
5. "Debt collector" means a person engaging, directly or indirectly, in debt collection, whether for the person, the person's employer, or others, and includes a person who sells, or offers to sell, forms represented to be a collection system, device, or scheme, intended to be used to collect debts.
6. "Debtor", for the purposes of this article, means the person obligated.

Iowa Code Ann. § 537.7102 (WESTLAW through Acts of 2005 1st Reg. Sess.).

KANSAS

There are no statutory licensing requirements in the state of Kansas.

KENTUCKY

There are no statutory licensing requirements in the state of Kentucky.

LOUISIANA

There are no statutory licensing requirements in the state of Louisiana.

MAINE

Definitions

As used in this chapter, unless the context otherwise indicates, the following terms have the following meanings.

3. Consumer. "Consumer" means any natural person obligated or allegedly obligated to pay any debt.
4. Creditor. "Creditor" means any person who offers or extends credit creating a debt or to whom a debt is owed, but that term does not include any person to the extent that he receives an assignment or transfer of a debt in default solely for the purpose of facilitating collection of that debt for another.
5. Debt. "Debt" means any obligation or alleged obligation of a consumer to pay money arising out of a transaction in which the money, property, insurance or services that are the subject of the transaction are primarily for personal, family or household purposes, whether or not the obligation has been reduced to judgment. "Debt" includes any obligation or alleged obligation for payment of child support owed to, or owed by, a resident of this State.
6. Debt collector. "Debt collector" means any person conducting business in this State, the principal

purpose of which is the collection of any debts, or who regularly collects or attempts to collect, directly or indirectly, debts owed or due or asserted to be owed or due another. "Debt collector" includes persons who furnish collection systems carrying a name that simulates the name of a debt collector and who supply forms or form letters to be used by the creditor even though the forms direct the debtor to make payments directly to the creditor. Notwithstanding the exclusion provided by section 11003, subsection 7, "debt collector" includes any creditor who, in the process of collecting the creditor's own debts, uses any name other than the creditor's that would indicate that a 3rd person is collecting or attempting to collect these debts. For purposes of subchapter II, "debt collector" includes any attorney-at-law whose principal activities include collecting debts as an attorney on behalf of and in the name of clients. "Debt collector" also includes any person regularly engaged in the enforcement of security interests securing debts. "Debt collector" does not include any person who retrieves collateral when a consumer has voluntarily surrendered possession. A person is regularly engaged in the enforcement of security interests if that person enforced security interests more than 5 times in the previous calendar year. If a person does not meet these numerical standards for the previous calendar year, the numerical standards must be applied to the current calendar year.
Me. Rev. Stat. Ann. Tit. 32, § 11002 (5)-(6) (WESTLAW through the 2005 First Reg. Sess. of the 122nd Leg. and with emergency legislation through the 2005 First Spec. Sess. of the 122nd Leg.).

Exemptions
The term debt collector does not include:
1. Officers or employees of a creditor. Any officer or employee of a creditor while, in the name of the creditor, collecting debts for that creditor;
2. Persons related by common ownership or affiliated by corporate control. Any person while acting as a debt collector for another person, both of whom are related by common ownership or affiliated by corporate control, if the person acting as a debt collector does so only for persons to whom it is so related or affiliated and if the principal business of that person is not the collection of debts;
3. Officers or employees of the United States or any state. Any officer or employee of the United States or any state or agencies or instrumentalities of the State to the extent that collecting or attempting to collect any debt is in the performance of his official duties;
4. Persons serving legal process. Any person while serving or attempting to serve legal process on any other person in connection with the judicial enforcement of any debt;
5. Nonprofit organizations performing consumer credit counseling. Any nonprofit organization which, at the request of consumers, performs bona fide consumer credit counseling and assists consumers in the liquidation of their debts by receiving payments from those consumers and distributing those amounts to creditors;
6. Repealed. Laws 1993, c. 126, § 2.
7. Persons collecting debts owed or due to another. Any person collecting or attempting to collect any debt owed or due, or asserted to be owed or due, to another to the extent that the activity:
  A. Is incidental to a bona fide fiduciary obligation or a bona fide escrow arrangement;
  B. Concerns a debt which was originated by that person;
  C. Concerns a debt which was not in default at the time it was obtained by that person; or
  D. Concerns a debt obtained by that person as a secured party in a commercial credit transaction involving the creditor; and
8. Collection activities related to the operation of a business. Any person whose collection activities are confined to and directly related to the operation of a business other than that of a debt collector, such as, but not limited to, financial institutions regulated under Title 9-B.
Me. Rev. Stat. Ann. Tit. 32, §§ 11003 (WESTLAW through the 2005 First Reg. Sess. of the 122nd Leg. and with emergency legislation through the 2005 First Spec. Sess. of the 122nd Leg.).

MARYLAND

Definitions

(a) In this title the following words have the meanings indicated.

(c) "Collection agency" means a person who:

(1) engages directly or indirectly in the business of collecting for, or soliciting from another, a consumer claim;

(2) in collection of a consumer claim by its owner, uses a name or other artifice that indicates that another party is attempting to collect the consumer claim;

(3) gives, sells, attempts to give or sell to another, or uses, for collection of a consumer claim, a series or system of forms or letters that indicates directly or indirectly that a person other than the owner is asserting the consumer claim; or

(4) employs the services of an individual or business to solicit or sell a collection system to be used for collection of a consumer claim.

(e) "Consumer claim" means a claim that:

(1) is for money owed or said to be owed by a resident of the State; and

(2) arises from a transaction in which, for a family, household, or personal purpose, the resident sought or got credit, money, personal property, real property, or services.

Md. Code Ann. Bus. Reg. §§ 7-101(a), (c), (e) (WESTLAW through laws from the 2005 Reg. Sess. effective through July 1, 2005).

Exemptions

(b) This title does not apply to:

(1) a bank;

(2) a federal or State credit union;

(3) a mortgage lender;

(4) a person acting under an order of a court of competent jurisdiction;

(5) a licensed real estate broker, or an individual acting on behalf of the real estate broker, in the collection of rent or allied charges for property;

(6) a savings and loan association;

(7) a title company as to its escrow business;

(8) a trust company;

(9) a lawyer who is collecting a debt for a client, unless the lawyer has an employee who:

(i) is not a lawyer; and

(ii) is engaged primarily to solicit debts for collection or primarily makes contact with a debtor to collect or adjust a debt through a procedure identified with the operation of a collection agency; or

(10) a person who is collecting a debt for another person if:

(i) both persons are related by common ownership;

(ii) the person who is collecting a debt does so only for those persons to whom it is related by common ownership;

(iii) the principal business of the person who is collecting a debt is not the collection of debts; and

(iv) before collecting a debt, the person files with the Board:

1. the correct name of the person;

2. an address and telephone number of a contact person; and

3. the name of the person's resident agent.

Md. Code Ann. Bus. Reg. § 7-102(b) (WESTLAW through laws from the 2005 Reg. Sess. effective through July 1, 2005).

MASSACHUSETTS

Definitions

As used in sections 24 to 28, inclusive the following words shall have the following meanings, unless the context requires otherwise:--

"Consumer", any natural person obligated or allegedly obligated to pay any debt.
"Creditor", any person who offers or extends credit creating a debt or to whom a debt is owed, but the term shall not include a person to the extent that he receives an assignment or transfer of a debt in default solely for the purpose of facilitating collection of the debt for another.
"Debt", any obligation or alleged obligation of a consumer to pay money arising out of a transaction in which the money, property, insurance, or services which are the subject of the transaction are primarily for personal, family, or household purposes, whether or not the obligation has been reduced to judgment.
"Debt collector", any person who uses an instrumentality of interstate commerce or the mails in any business the principal purpose of which is the collection of a debt, or who regularly collects or attempts to collect, directly or indirectly, a debt owed or due or asserted to be owed or due another. Notwithstanding the exclusion provided by clause (f), debt collector shall include a creditor who, in the process of collecting his own debt, uses any name other than his own which would indicate that a third person is collecting or attempting to collect the debt. Debt collector shall also include a person who uses an instrumentality of interstate commerce or the mails in a business the principal purpose of which is the enforcement of security interests.
Mass. Gen. Laws ch. 93, § 24 (West, WESTLAW through through Ch. 79 of the 2005 1st Annual Sess.).

"Consumer" means any natural person obligated or allegedly obligated to pay any debt.
"Creditor" means any person who offers or extends credit creating a debt or to whom a debt is owed, but such term does not include any person to the extent that he receives an assignment or transfer of a debt in default solely for the purpose of facilitating collection of such debt for another.
"Debt" means any obligation or alleged obligation of a consumer to pay money arising out of a transaction in which the money, property, insurance, or services which are the subject of the transaction are primarily for personal, family, or household purposes, whether or not the obligation has been reduced to judgment.
"Debt Collector' means any person who uses an instrumentality of interstate commerce or the mails in any business the principal purpose of which is the collection of a debt, or who regularly collects or attempts to collect, directly or indirectly, a debt owed or due or asserted to be owed or due another. Notwithstanding the exclusion provided by 209 CMR 18.02: Debt Collector(f), debt collector shall include a creditor who, in the process of collecting his own debt, uses any name other than his own which would indicate that a third person is collecting or attempting to collect the debt. Debt collector shall also include a person who uses an instrumentality of interstate commerce or the mails in a business the principal purpose of which is the enforcement of security interests. Debt collector shall not include:

(a) an officer or employee of a creditor while, in the name of the creditor, collecting debts for the creditor;

(b) a person while acting as a debt collector for another person, both of whom are related by common ownership or affiliated by corporate control, if the person acting as a debt collector does so only for a person to whom it is so related or affiliated and if the principal business of the person is not the collection of a debt;

(c) an officer or employee of the United States or a state of the United States to the extent that collecting or attempting to collect a debt is in the performance of his official duty;

(d) a person while serving or attempting to serve legal process on another person in connection with the judicial enforcement of a debt;

(e) a nonprofit organization which, at the request of a consumer, performs bona fide consumer credit counseling and assists the consumer in the liquidation of debts by receiving payments from the consumer and distributing the amounts to creditors;

(f) a person collecting or attempting to collect a debt owed or due or asserted to be owed or due another to the extent the activity:

1. is incidental to a bona fide fiduciary obligation or a bona fide escrow arrangement;
2. concerns a debt which was originated by the person;
3. concerns a debt which was not in default at the time it was obtained by the person; or

4. concerns a debt obtained by the person as a secured party in a commercial credit transaction involving the creditor;

(g) attorneys-at-law collecting a debt on behalf of a client; and

(h) an agent or independent contractor employed for the purpose of collecting a charge or bill owed by a tenant to a landlord or owed by a customer to a corporation subject to the supervision of the Department of Telecommunications and Energy or the Division of Insurance insofar as the person collects charges or bills only for the landlord or supervised corporations.

Mass. Regs. Code tit. 209, § 18.02 (WESTLAW through August 26, 2005, Reg. #1033).

"Debt" means money or its equivalent which is, or is alleged to be, more than 30 days past due and owing, unless a different period is agreed to by the debtor, under a single account as a result of a purchase, lease, or loan of goods, services, or real or personal property, for personal, family or household purposes or as a result of a loan of money which is obtained for personal, family or household purposes; provided, however, that money which is, or is alleged to be, owing as a result of a loan secured by a first mortgage on real property, or in an amount in excess of $25,000, shall not be included within this definition of "debt".

"Debtor" means a natural person, or his guardian, administrator or executor, present or residing in Massachusetts who is allegedly personally liable for a debt.

Mass. Regs. Code tit. 940, § 7.03 (West, WESTLAW through August 26, 2005, Register #1033).

Exemptions

Debt collector shall not include:--

(a) an officer or employee of a creditor while, in the name of the creditor, collecting debts for the creditor;

(b) a person while acting as a debt collector for another person, both of whom are related by common ownership or affiliated by corporate control, if the person acting as a debt collector does so only for a person to whom it is so related or affiliated and if the principal business of the person is not the collection of a debt;

(c) an officer or employee of the United States or a state of the United States to the extent that collecting or attempting to collect a debt is in the performance of his official duty;

(d) a person while serving or attempting to serve legal process on another person in connection with the judicial enforcement of a debt;

(e) a nonprofit organization which, at the request of a consumer, performs bona fide consumer credit counseling and assists the consumer in the liquidation of debts by receiving payments from the consumer and distributing the amounts to creditors;

(f) a person collecting or attempting to collect a debt owed or due or asserted to be owed or due another to the extent the activity (i) is incidental to a bona fide fiduciary obligation or a bona fide escrow arrangement; (ii) concerns a debt which was originated by the person; (iii) concerns a debt which was not in default at the time it was obtained by the person; or (iv) concerns a debt obtained by the person as a secured party in a commercial credit transaction involving the creditor;

(g) attorneys-at-law collecting a debt on behalf of a client; and

(h) an agent or independent contractor employed for the purpose of collecting a charge or bill owed by a tenant to a landlord or owed by a customer to a corporation subject to the supervision of the department of telecommunications and energy or the division of insurance insofar as the person collects charges or bills only for the landlord or supervised corporations.

Mass. Gen. Laws ch. 93, § 24 (West, WESTLAW through through Ch. 79 of the 2005 1st Annual Sess.).

MICHIGAN

Definitions

As used in this article:

(a) "Claim" or "debt" means an obligation or alleged obligation for the payment of money or thing of value arising out of an expressed or implied agreement or contract for a purchase made primarily for

personal, family, or household purposes.
(b) "Collection agency" means a person directly or indirectly engaged in soliciting a claim for collection or collecting or attempting to collect a claim owed or due or asserted to be owed or due another, or repossessing or attempting to repossess a thing of value owed or due or asserted to be owed or due another arising out of an expressed or implied agreement. A collection agency shall include a person representing himself or herself as a collection or repossession agency, or a person performing the activities of a collection agency, on behalf of another, which are regulated by this act. A collection agency shall also include a person who furnishes or attempts to furnish a form or a written demand service represented to be a collection or repossession technique, device, or system to be used to collect or repossess claims, if the form contains the name of a person other than the creditor in a manner indicating that a request or demand for payment is being made by a person other than the creditor even though the form directs the debtor to make payment directly to the creditor rather than to the other person whose name appears on the form. Collection agency also includes a person who uses a fictitious name or the name of another in the collection or repossession of claims to convey to the debtor that a third person is collecting or repossessing or has been employed to collect or repossess the claim.
(e) "Creditor" or "principal" means a person who offers or extends credit creating a debt or a person to whom a debt is owed or due or asserted to be owed or due. Creditor or principal shall not include a person who receives an assignment or transfer of a debt solely for the purpose of facilitating collection of the debt for the assignor or transferor. In those instances, the assignor or transferor of the debt shall continue to be considered the creditor or the principal for purposes of this article.
(f) "Consumer" or "debtor" means a natural person obligated or allegedly obligated to pay a debt.
Mich. Stat. Ann. § 339.901(a)-(b), (e)-(f) (WESTLAW through P.A. 2005, No. 1-103).

As used in this act:
(a) "Claim" or "debt" means an obligation or alleged obligation for the payment of money or thing of value arising out of an expressed or implied agreement or contract for a purchase made primarily for personal, family, or household purposes.
(b) "Collection agency" means a person directly or indirectly engaged in soliciting a claim for collection or collecting or attempting to collect a claim owed or due or asserted to be owed or due another, or repossessing or attempting to repossess a thing of value owed or due or asserted to be owed or due another person, arising out of an expressed or implied agreement. Collection agency includes a person representing himself or herself as a collection or repossession agency or a person performing the activities of a collection agency, on behalf of another, which activities are regulated by Act No. 299 of the Public Acts of 1980, as amended, being sections 339.101 to 339.2601 of the Michigan Compiled Laws. Collection agency includes a person who furnishes or attempts to furnish a form or a written demand service represented to be a collection or repossession technique, device, or system to be used to collect or repossess claims, if the form contains the name of a person other than the creditor in a manner indicating that a request or demand for payment is being made by a person other than the creditor even though the form directs the debtor to make payment directly to the creditor rather than to the other person whose name appears on the form. Collection agency includes a person who uses a fictitious name or the name of another in the collection or repossession of claims to convey to the debtor that a third person is collecting or repossessing or has been employed to collect or repossess the claim.
(d) "Consumer" or "debtor" means a natural person obligated or allegedly obligated to pay a debt.
(e) "Creditor" or "principal" means a person who offers or extends credit creating a debt or a person to whom a debt is owed or due or asserted to be owed or due. Creditor or principal does not include a person who receives an assignment or transfer or a debt solely for the purpose of facilitating collection of the debt for the assignor or transferor. In those instances, the assignor or transferor of the debt shall continue to be considered the creditor or the principal for purposes of this act.
Mich. Stat. Ann. § 445.251 (WESTLAW through P.A. 2005, No. 1-103).

Exemptions

Collection agency does not include a person whose collection activities are confined and are directly related to the operation of a business other than that of a collection agency such as, but not limited to, the following:

(i) A regular employee when collecting amounts for 1 employer if all collection efforts are carried on in the name of the employer.

(ii) A state or nationally chartered bank when collecting its own claims.

(iii) A trust company when collecting its own claims.

(iv) A state or federally chartered savings and loan association when collecting its own claims.

(v) A state or federally chartered credit union when collecting its own claims.

(vi) A licensee under Act No. 21 of the Public Acts of 1939, as amended, being sections 493.1 to 493.26 of the Michigan Compiled Laws.

(vii) A business licensed by this state under a regulatory act in which collection activity is regulated.

(viii) An abstract company doing an escrow business.

(ix) A licensed real estate broker or salesperson if the claims being handled by the broker or salesperson are related to or in connection with his or her real estate business.

(x) A public officer or person acting under a court order.

(xi) An attorney handling claims and collections on behalf of clients and in the attorney's own name.

Mich. Stat. Ann. § 339.901(b) (WESTLAW through P.A. 2005, No. 1-103).

MINNESOTA

Definitions

The terms in this section for the purposes of sections 332.31 to 332.45 shall have the meanings given them.

Subd. 2. Person. "Person" means and includes individuals, partnerships, associations or corporations.

Subd. 3. Collection agency. "Collection agency" means and includes any person engaged in the business of collection for others any account, bill or other indebtedness except as hereinafter provided. It includes persons who furnish collection systems carrying a name which simulates the name of a collection agency and who supply forms or form letters to be used by the creditor, even though such forms direct the debtor to make payments directly to the creditor rather than to such fictitious agency.

Subds. 4, 5. Repealed by Laws 1979, c. 144, § 7.

Subd. 6. Collector. "Collector" is a person acting under the authority of a collection agency under subdivision 3, and on its behalf in the business of collection for others an account, bill, or other indebtedness except as otherwise provided in this chapter.

Subd. 7. Exempt out-of-state collection agency. "Exempt out-of-state collection agency" means a collection agency that has no physical presence in this state, that is engaged in the business of collecting claims on behalf of creditors that have no physical presence in this state, and that only conducts business within this state by means of interstate communications including telephone, mail, and facsimile transmission.

Minn. Stat. Ann. § 332.31 (WESTLAW through the laws of the 2005 Regular Session effective through June 1, 2005).

Exemptions

The term "collection agency" shall not include persons whose collection activities are confined to and are directly related to the operation of a business other than that of a collection agency such as, but not limited to banks when collecting accounts owed to the banks and when the bank will sustain any loss arising from uncollectible accounts, abstract companies doing an escrow business, real estate brokers, public officers, persons acting under order of a court, lawyers, trust companies, insurance companies, credit unions, savings associations, loan or finance companies unless they are engaged in asserting, enforcing or prosecuting unsecured claims which have been purchased from any person, firm, or association when there is recourse to the seller for all or part of the claim if the claim is not collected. Minn. Stat. Ann. § 332.32 (West, WESTLAW through End of 2001 1st Special Session).

MISSISSIPPI
There are no statutory licensing requirements in the state of Mississippi.

MISSOURI
There are no statutory licensing requirements in the state of Missouri.

MONTANA
There are no statutory licensing requirements in the state of Montana.

NEBRASKA
Definitions
For purposes of the Collection Agency Act:
(1) Board shall mean the Collection Agency Licensing Board;
(2) Collection agency shall mean and include:

(a) All persons, firms, corporations, and associations directly or indirectly engaged in soliciting, from more than one person, firm, corporation, or association, claims of any kind owed or due or asserted to be owed or due such solicited person, firm, corporation, or association, and all persons, firms, corporations, and associations directly or indirectly engaged in asserting, enforcing, or prosecuting such claims;

(b) Any person, firm, corporation, or association which, in attempting to collect or in collecting his, her, or its own accounts or claims, uses a fictitious name or any name other than his, her, or its own name which would indicate to the debtor that a third person is collecting or attempting to collect such account or claim; and

(c) Any person, firm, corporation, or association which attempts to or does give away or sell to any person, firm, corporation, or association, other than one licensed under the act, any system or series of letters or forms for use in the collection of accounts or claims which assert or indicate, directly or indirectly, that the claim or account is being asserted or collected by any other person, firm, corporation, or association other than the creditor or owner of the claim or demand; and

Neb. Rev. Stat. Ann. § 45-602(1)-(2) (WESTLAW Second Reg. Sess. of the 98th Leg. (2004)).

Exemptions
(3) Collection agency shall not mean or include (a) regular employees of a single creditor, (b) banks, (c) trust companies, (d) savings and loan associations, (e) building and loan associations, (f) abstract companies doing an escrow business, (g) duly licensed real estate brokers and agents when the claims or accounts being handled by such broker or agent are related to or are in connection with such brokers' or agents' regular real estate business, (h) express and telegraph companies subject to public regulation and supervision, (i) attorneys at law handling claims and collections in their own names and not operating a collection agency under the management of a layperson, (j) any person, firm, corporation, or association handling claims, accounts, or collections under an order or orders of any court, or (k) a person, firm, corporation, or association which, for valuable consideration, purchases accounts, claims, or demands of another and then, in such purchaser's own name, proceeds to assert or collect such accounts, claims, or demands. Neb. Rev. Stat. Ann. § 45-602(3) (WESTLAW Second Reg. Sess. of the 98th Leg. (2004)).

NEVADA

Definitions

"Claim" means any obligation for the payment of money or its equivalent that is past due. Nev. Rev. Stat. Ann. § 649.010 (WESTLAW through the 2004 21st Spec. Sess. of the 72nd Leg. and the 2004 Revisions by the Legislative Counsel Bureau).

1. "Collection agency" means all persons engaging, directly or indirectly, and as a primary or a secondary object, business or pursuit, in the collection of or in soliciting or obtaining in any manner the payment of a claim owed or due or asserted to be owed or due to another.

3. "Collection agency":

(a) Includes a community manager while engaged in the management of a common-interest community if the community manager, or any employee, agent or affiliate of the community manager, performs or offers to perform any act associated with the foreclosure of a lien pursuant to NRS 116.31162 to 116.31168, inclusive; and

(b) Does not include any other community manager while engaged in the management of a common-interest community.

4. As used in this section:

(a) "Community manager" has the meaning ascribed to it in NRS 116.023.

(b) "Unit-owners' association" has the meaning ascribed to it in NRS 116.011.

Nev. Rev. Stat. Ann. § 649.020(1), (3)-(4) (WESTLAW through the 2004 21st Spec. Sess. of the 72nd Leg. and the 2004 Revisions by the Legislative Counsel Bureau).

Exemptions

2. "Collection agency" does not include any of the following unless they are conducting collection agencies:

(a) Individuals regularly employed on a regular wage or salary, in the capacity of credit men or in other similar capacity upon the staff of employees of any person not engaged in the business of a collection agency or making or attempting to make collections as an incident to the usual practices of their primary business or profession.

(b) Banks.

(c) Nonprofit cooperative associations.

(d) Unit owners' associations and the board members, officers, employees and units' owners of those associations when acting under the authority of and in accordance with chapter 116 of NRS and the governing documents of the association, except for those community managers included within the term "collection agency" pursuant to subsection 3.

(e)Abstract companies doing an escrow business.

(f) Duly licensed real estate agents except for those real estate agents who are community managers included within the term "collection agency" pursuant to subsection 3.

(g) Attorneys and counselors at law licensed to practice in this State, so long as they are retained by their clients to collect or to solicit or obtain payment of such clients' claims in the usual course of the practice of their profession.

Nev. Rev. Stat. Ann. § 649.020(2) (WESTLAW through the 2004 21st Spec. Sess. of the 72nd Leg. and the 2004 Revisions by the Legislative Counsel Bureau).

NEW HAMPSHIRE

Definitions

In this chapter:

I. "Consumer" means a natural person who seeks or acquires, or is offered property, services or credit for personal, family or household purposes.

II. "Consumer credit transaction" means a transaction between a creditor and a consumer in which real or personal property, services, money or a form of money is acquired on credit and the consumer's obligation is payable in 4 or more installments or for which credit a finance charge is or may be imposed.

The term includes consumer credit sales, consumer loans, consumer leases of personal property and transactions pursuant to a seller or lender credit card, but shall not include leases of real property.
III. "Consumer transaction" means a transaction between a consumer and a person who sells, leases or provides property, services or credit to consumers. The term shall not include leases of real property.
IV. "Creditor" means a person who in the ordinary course of business engages in consumer credit transactions with consumers.
V. "Credit" means the right granted by a person to a consumer to defer payment of a debt, to incur debt and defer its payment, or purchase property or services and defer payment therefor.
VI. "Debt" means any obligation or alleged obligation arising out of a consumer transaction.
VII. "Debtor" means a person who owes or allegedly owes an obligation arising out of a consumer transaction.
VIII. "Debt collector" means:

(a) Any person who by any direct or indirect action, conduct or practice enforces or attempts to enforce an obligation that is owed or due, or alleged to be owed or due, by a consumer as a result of a consumer credit transaction; or

(b) Any person who, for any fee, commission or charge other than wages or salary, engages in any direct or indirect action, conduct or practice to enforce or attempt to enforce an obligation that is owed or due, or alleged to be owed or due, by a consumer as a result of a consumer transaction; or

(c) Any person who, pursuant to an assignment, sale or transfer of a claim against a consumer, engages in any direct or indirect action, conduct or practice to enforce an obligation that is owed or due, or alleged to be owed or due, by a consumer as a result of a consumer transaction.

IX. "Finance charge" means a charge such as interest, fees, service charges, discounts and other charges associated with the extension of credit.
X. "Person" means an individual, corporation, trust, partnership, incorporated or unincorporated association or any other legal entity.
N.H. Rev. Stat. Ann. §§ 358-C:1(WESTLAW through End of 2004 Reg. Sess.).

NEW JERSEY

Definitions:

No person shall conduct a collection agency, collection bureau or collection office in this state, or engage therein in the business of collecting or receiving payment for others of any account, bill or other indebtedness, or engage therein in the business of soliciting the right to collect or receive payment for another of any account, bill or other indebtedness, or advertise for or solicit in print the right to collect or receive payment for another of any account, bill or other indebtedness, unless such person, or the person for whom he may be acting as agent has on file with the secretary of state sufficient bond as hereinafter specified. N.J. Stat. Ann. § 45:18-1 (WESTLAW through L .2005, c. 1 to 144).

NEW MEXICO

Definitions

As used in the Collection Agency Regulatory Act:
C. "collection agency" means any person engaging in business for the purpose of collecting or attempting to collect, directly or indirectly, debts owed or due or asserted to be owed or due another, where such person is so engaged by two or more creditors. The term also includes any creditor who, in the process of collecting his own debts, uses any name other than his own which would indicate that a third person is collecting or attempting to collect such debts.
F. "debt" means any obligation or alleged obligation of a debtor to pay money arising out of a transaction in which the money, property, insurance or services which are the subject of the transaction are primarily for personal, family or household purposes, whether or not such obligation has been reduced to judgment;
G. "debt collector" means a collection agency, a repossessor, a manager, a solicitor and any attorney-at-law collecting a debt as an attorney on behalf of and in the name of a client;

H. "debtor" means any natural person obligated or allegedly obligated to pay any debt;
M. "solicitor" means a natural person who, through lawful means, communicates with debtors or solicits the payment of debts for a collection agency licensee by the use of telephone, personal contact, letters or other methods of collection conducted from and within the licensee's office.
N.M. Stat. Ann. Ann. § 61-18A-(C), (F)-(H), (M) (WESTLAW through Ch. 351 (End) of the First Reg. Sess. of the 47th Leg. (2005) (including Constitutional Amendments 1 and 2))

Exemptions
The term "collection agency" does not include:
(1) any officer or employee of a creditor while, in the name of the creditor, collecting debts for such creditor;
(2) any person while collecting debts for another person, both of whom are related by common ownership or affiliated by corporate control, if the person collects debts only for persons to whom it is so related or affiliated and if the principal business of such person is not the collection of debts;
(3) any officer or employee of the United States, any state or any political subdivision thereof to the extent that collecting or attempting to collect any debt is in the performance of his official duties;
(4) any person while serving or attempting to serve legal process on any other person in connection with the judicial enforcement of any debt;
(5) any nonprofit organization which, at the request of debtors, performs bona fide consumer credit counseling and assists debtors in the liquidation of their debts by receiving payments from such debtors and distributing such amounts to creditors;
(6) any attorney-at-law collecting a debt as an attorney on behalf of and in the name of a client; and
(7) any person collecting or attempting to collect any debt owed or due or asserted to be owed or due to another to the extent such activity:
  (a) is incidental to a bona fide fiduciary obligation or a bona fide escrow arrangement;
  (b) concerns a debt which was originated by such person;
  (c) concerns a debt which was not in default at the time it was obtained by such person; or
  (d) concerns a debt obtained by such person as a secured party in a commercial credit transaction involving the creditor;

N.M. Stat. Ann. Ann. § 61-18A-(C) (WESTLAW through Ch. 351 (End) of the First Reg. Sess. of the 47th Leg. (2005) (including Constitutional Amendments 1 and 2)).

NEW YORK
Definitions
As used in this article, unless the context or subject matter otherwise requires:
1. "Consumer claim" means any obligation of a natural person for the payment of money or its equivalent which is or is alleged to be in default and which arises out of a transaction wherein credit has been offered or extended to a natural person, and the money, property or service which was the subject of the transaction was primarily for personal, family or household purposes. The term included an obligation of a natural person who is a co-maker, endorser, guarantor or surety as well as the natural person to whom such credit was originally extended.
2. "Debtor" means any natural person who owes or who is asserted to owe a consumer claim.
N.Y. Bus. Corp. Law § 600(1)-(2) (WESTLAW through L. 2005, ch. 328 (except for chs. 1 to 3, 105, 110, 149, 161, 214, 239, 243, 262, 284 and 316).

New York City
Definitions
a. "Debt collection agency" shall mean a person engaged in business the principal purpose of which is to regularly collect or attempt to collect debts owed or due or asserted to be owed or due to another.
c. The term "consumer" means any natural person obligated or allegedly obligated to pay any debt.
d. The term "debt" means any obligation or alleged obligation of a consumer to pay money arising out of

a transaction in which the money, property, insurance, or services which are the subject of the transaction are primarily for personal, family, or household purposes, whether or not such obligation has been reduced to judgment, or any obligation or alleged obligation arising out of a judgment or valid agreement for the payment of child support.
New York City, N.Y., Code § 20-489(a), (c)-(d) (WESTLAW through Local Law 51 of 2004 and Chs. 1-755 of the Laws of New York for 2004).

Exemptions
The term "Debt collection agency" does not include:
(1) any officer of employee of a creditor while, in the name of the creditor, collecting debts for such creditor;
(2) any officer or employee of a debt collection agency;
(3) any person while acting as a debt collection agency for another person, both of whom are related by common ownership or affiliated by corporate control, if the person acting as a debt collection agency does so only for persons to whom it is so related or affiliated and if the principal business of such person is not the collection of debts;
(4) any person while serving or attempting to serve legal process on any other person in connection with the judicial enforcement of any debt;
(5) any attorney-at-law collecting a debt as an attorney on behalf of and in the name of a client;
(6) any person employed by a utility regulated under the provisions of the public service law, acting for such utility;
(7) any person collecting or attempting to collect any debt owed or due or asserted to be owed or due another to the extent such activity (i) is incidental to a bona fide fiduciary obligation or a bona fide escrow agreement; (ii) concerns a debt which was originated by such person; (iii) concerns a debt which was not in default at the time it was obtained by such person as a secured party in a commercial credit transaction involving the creditor;
(8) any officer or employee of the United States, any state thereof or any political subdivision of any state to the extent that collecting or attempting to collect any debt owed is in the performance of his or her official duties;
(9) any non-profit organization which, at the request of consumers, performs bona fide consumer credit counseling and assists customers in the liquidation of their debts by receiving payments from such customers and distributing such amounts to creditors.
New York City, N.Y., Code § 20-489(a) (WESTLAW through Local Law 51 of 2004 and Chs. 1-755 of the Laws of New York for 2004).

NORTH CAROLINA
Definitions
As used in this Part, the following terms have the meanings specified:
(1) "Collection agency" means a collection agency as defined in G.S. 58-70-15 which engages, directly or indirectly, in debt collection from a consumer.
(2) "Consumer" means an individual, aggregation of individuals, corporation, company, association, or partnership that has incurred a debt or alleged debt.
(3) "Debt" means any obligation owed or due or alleged to be owed or due from a consumer.
N.C. Gen. Stat. § 58-70-90 (WESTLAW through S.L. 2005-154 of the 2005 Reg. Sess.).

(a) "Collection agency" means a person directly or indirectly engaged in soliciting, from more than one person delinquent claims of any kind owed or due or asserted to be owed or due the solicited person and all persons directly or indirectly engaged in the asserting, enforcing or prosecuting of those claims.
(b) "Collection agency" includes:

> (1) Any person that procures a listing of delinquent debtors from any creditor and that sells the listing or otherwise receives any fee or benefit from collections made on the listing; and

(2) Any person that attempts to or does transfer or sell to any person not holding the permit prescribed by this Article any system or series of letters or forms for use in the collection of delinquent accounts or claims which by direct assertion or by implication indicate that the claim or account is being asserted or collected by any person, firm, corporation, or association other than the creditor or owner of the claim or demand; and
(3) An in-house collection agency, whereby a person, firm, corporation, or association sets up a collection service for his or its own business and the agency has a name other than that of the business.
N.C. Gen. Stat. § 58-70-15(a)-(b) (WESTLAW through S.L. 2005-154 of the 2005 Reg. Sess.).

The following words and terms as used in this Article shall be construed as follows:
(1) "Consumer" means any natural person who has incurred a debt or alleged debt for personal, family, household or agricultural purposes.
(2) "Debt" means any obligation owed or due or alleged to be owed or due from a consumer.
(3) "Debt collector" means any person engaging, directly or indirectly, in debt collection from a consumer except those persons subject to the provisions of Article 70, Chapter 58 of the General Statutes.
N.C. Gen. Stat. § 75-50 (WESTLAW through S.L. 2005-154 of the 2005 Reg. Sess.).

Exemptions
(c) "Collection agency" does not mean:
(1) Regular employees of a single creditor;
(2) Banks, trust companies, or bank-owned, controlled or related firms, corporations or associations engaged in accounting, bookkeeping or data processing services where a primary component of such services is the rendering of statements of accounts and bookkeeping services for creditors;
(3) Mortgage banking companies;
(4) Savings and loan associations;
(5) Building and loan associations;
(6) Duly licensed real estate brokers and agents when the claims or accounts being handled by the broker or agent are related to or are in connection with the broker's or agent's regular real estate business;
(7) Express, telephone and telegraph companies subject to public regulation and supervision;
(8) Attorneys-at-law handling claims and collections in their own name and not operating a collection agency under the management of a layman;
(9) Any person, firm, corporation or association handling claims, accounts or collections under an order or orders of any court;
(10) A person, firm, corporation or association which, for valuable consideration purchases accounts, claims, or demands of another, which such accounts, claims, or demands of another are not delinquent at the time of such purchase, and then, in its own name, proceeds to assert or collect the accounts, claims or demands;
(11) Any person attempting to collect or collecting claims, in that person's name, of a business or businesses owned wholly or substantially by that person;
(12) Any nonprofit tax exempt corporation organized for the purpose of providing mediation or other dispute resolution services; and
(13) The designated representatives of programs as defined by G.S. 110-129 (5).
N.C. Gen. Stat. § 58-70-15(c) (WESTLAW through S.L. 2005-154 of the 2005 Reg. Sess.).

NORTH DAKOTA
Except as otherwise herein provided, no person other than a collection agency licensed and authorized under this chapter may advertise or solicit either in print, by letter, in person, or otherwise, the right to collect or receive payment of any claim for another or sell or give away collection letters as demand

forms in the state of North Dakota. As used in this chapter, the term "collection agency" does not include attorneys at law who are licensed to practice in the state of North Dakota, licensed real estate brokers, banks, trust companies, building and loan associations, credit unions, agencies of a state or of the federal government, abstract companies doing an escrow business, creditors collecting their own debts, individuals or firms who purchase or take accounts receivable for collateral purposes, individuals employed in the capacity of creditman upon the staff of an employer not engaged in the business of a collection agency, or any public officer, receiver, or trustee acting under the order of a court. A person may not be considered to be engaged in collection activity within this state if that person's activities are limited to collecting debts from debtors located in this state by means of interstate communications, including telephone, mail, or facsimile transmission from the person's location in another state if the person is licensed and bonded in that state and the state has enacted similar legislation. N.D. Cent. Code §13-05-02 (WESTLAW through 2003 Gen. and Spec. Sess.).

OHIO

Definitions

(A)(1) As used in this section, "collection agency" means any person who, for compensation, contingent or otherwise, or for other valuable consideration, offers services to collect an alleged debt asserted to be owed to another. Ohio Stat. Ann. § 1319.12(A)(1) (WESTLAW through 2005 File 36 of the 126th GA (2005-2006) apv. by 8/26/05, and filed with the Secretary of State by 8/26/05).

As used in sections 1345.01 to 1345.13 of the Revised Code:

(A) "Consumer transaction" means a sale, lease, assignment, award by chance, or other transfer of an item of goods, a service, a franchise, or an intangible, to an individual for purposes that are primarily personal, family, or household, or solicitation to supply any of these things. "Consumer transaction" does not include transactions between persons, defined in sections 4905.03 and 5725.01 of the Revised Code, and their customers; transactions between certified public accountants or public accountants and their clients; transactions between attorneys, physicians, or dentists and their clients or patients; and transactions between veterinarians and their patients that pertain to medical treatment but not ancillary services.

(D) "Consumer" means a person who engages in a consumer transaction with a supplier.

Ohio Stat. Ann. § 1345.01(A), (D) (WESTLAW through 2005 File 36 of the 126th GA (2005-2006) apv. by 8/26/05, and filed with the Secretary of State by 8/26/05).

Exemptions

(2) "Collection agency" does not mean a person whose collection activities are confined to and directly related to the operation of another business, including, but not limited to, the following:

(a) Any bank, including the trust department of a bank, trust company, savings and loan association, savings bank, credit union, or fiduciary as defined in section 1339.03 of the Revised Code, except those that own or operate a collection agency;

(b) Any real estate broker or real estate salesperson, as defined in section 4735.01 of the Revised Code;

(c) Any retail seller collecting its own accounts;

(d) Any insurance company authorized to do business in this state under Title XXXIX of the Revised Code or a health insuring corporation authorized to operate in this state under Chapter 1751. of the Revised Code;

(e) Any public officer or judicial officer acting under order of a court;

(f) Any licensee as defined either in section 1321.01 or 1321.71 of the Revised Code, or any registrant as defined in section 1321.51 of the Revised Code;

(g) Any public utility;

(h) Any person registered to sell interment rights under section 4767.031 of the Revised Code.

Ohio Stat. Ann. § 1319.12(A)(2) (WESTLAW through 2005 File 36 of the 126th GA (2005-2006) apv. by 8/26/05, and filed with the Secretary of State by 8/26/05).

OKLAHOMA

There are no statutory licensing requirements in the state of Oklahoma.

OREGON

Definitions

(1) As used in subsection (2) of this section:

(a) "Consumer" means a natural person who purchases or acquires property, services or credit for personal, family or household purposes.

(b) "Consumer transaction" means a transaction between a consumer and a person who sells, leases or provides property, services or credit to consumers.

(c) "Commercial creditor" means a person who in the ordinary course of business engages in consumer transactions.

(d) "Credit" means the right granted by a creditor to a consumer to defer payment of a debt, to incur a debt and defer its payment, or to purchase or acquire property or services and defer payment therefor.

(e) "Debt" means any obligation or alleged obligation arising out of a consumer transaction.

(f) "Debtor" means a consumer who owes or allegedly owes an obligation arising out of a consumer transaction.

(g) "Debt collector" means any person who by any direct or indirect action, conduct or practice, enforces or attempts to enforce an obligation that is owed or due to any commercial creditor, or alleged to be owed or due to any commercial creditor, by a consumer as a result of a consumer transaction.

(h) "Person" means an individual, corporation, trust, partnership, incorporated or unincorporated association or any other legal entity.

Or. Rev. Stat. § 646.639(1)(WESTLAW through End of the 2003 Reg. Sess.).

As used in ORS 697.005 to 697.095:

(1)(a) "Collection agency" means:

(A) Any person directly or indirectly engaged in soliciting claims for collection, or collecting or attempting to collect claims owed, due or asserted to be owed or due to another person or to a public body;

(B) Any person who directly or indirectly furnishes, attempts to furnish, sells or offers to sell forms represented to be a collection system even though the forms direct the debtor to make payment to the creditor and even though the forms may be or are actually used by the creditor in the creditor's own name;

(C) Any person who in attempting to collect or in collecting the person's own claim uses a fictitious name or any name other than the person's own that indicates to the debtor that a third person is collecting or attempting to collect the claim;

(D) Any person in the business of engaging in the solicitation of the right to repossess or in the repossession of collateral security due or asserted to be due to another person; or

(E) Any person who in the collection of claims from another person:

(i) Uses any name other than the name regularly used in the conduct of the business out of which the claim arose; and

(ii) Engages in any action or conduct that tends to convey the impression that a third party has been employed or engaged to collect the claim.

(2) "Collection system" means a scheme intended or calculated to be used to collect claims sent, prepared or delivered by:

(a) A person who in collecting or attempting to collect the person's own claim uses a fictitious name or any name other than the person's own that indicates to the debtor that a third person is collecting or attempting to collect the claim; or

(b) A person directly or indirectly engaged in soliciting claims for collection, or collecting or attempting to collect claims owed or due or asserted to be owed or due another person.

(3) "Claim" means any obligation for the payment of money or thing of value arising out of any agreement or contract, express or implied.

(4) "Client" or "customer" means any person authorizing or employing a collection agency to collect a claim.

(5) "Debtor" means any person owing or alleged to owe a claim.

(6) "Debts incurred outside this state" means any action or proceeding that:

(a) Arises out of a promise, made anywhere to the plaintiff or a third party for the plaintiff's benefit, by the defendant to perform services outside of this state or to pay for services to be performed outside of this state by the plaintiff;

(b) Arises out of services actually performed for the plaintiff by the defendant outside of this state or services actually performed for the defendant by the plaintiff outside of this state, if the performance outside of this state was authorized or ratified by the defendant;

(c) Arises out of a promise, made anywhere to the plaintiff or a third party for the plaintiff's benefit, by the defendant to deliver or receive outside of this state or to send from outside of this state goods, documents of title or other things of value;

(d) Relates to goods, documents of title or other things of value sent from outside of this state by the defendant to the plaintiff or a third person on the plaintiff's order or direction;

(e) Relates to goods, documents of title or other things of value actually received outside of this state by the plaintiff from the defendant or by the defendant from the plaintiff, without regard to where delivery to carrier occurred; or

(f) Where jurisdiction at the time the debt was incurred was outside of this state.

(9) "Out-of-state collection agency" means a collection agency located outside of this state whose activities within this state are limited to collecting debts incurred outside of this state from debtors located in this state. As used in this subsection, "collecting debts" means collecting by means of interstate communications, including telephone, mail or facsimile transmission from the collection agency location in another state on behalf of clients located outside of this state.

Or. Rev. Stat. § 697.005(1)(a), (2)-(6), (9) (WESTLAW through End of the 2003 Reg. Sess.).

Exemptions

(b) "Collection agency" does not include:

(A) Any individual engaged in soliciting claims for collection, or collecting or attempting to collect claims on behalf of a registrant under ORS 697.005 to 697.095, if the individual is an employee of the registrant;

(B) Any individual collecting or attempting to collect claims for not more than three employers, if all collection efforts are carried on in the name of the employer and the individual is an employee of the employer;

(C) Any person who prepares or mails monthly or periodic statements of accounts due on behalf of another person if all payments are made to that other person and no other collection efforts are made by the person preparing the statements of accounts;

(D) Any attorney-at-law rendering services in the performance of the duties of an attorney-at-law;

(E) Any licensed certified public accountant or public accountant rendering services in the performance of the duties of a licensed certified public accountant or public accountant;

(F) Any bank, mutual savings bank, consumer finance company, trust company, savings and loan association, credit union or debt consolidation agency;

(G) Any real estate licensee or escrow agent licensed under the provisions of ORS chapter 696, as to any collection or billing activity involving a real estate transaction or collection escrow transaction of the licensee or escrow agent;

(H) Any individual regularly employed as a credit person or in a similar capacity by one person, firm or corporation that is not a collection agency as defined in this section;

(I) Any public officer or any person acting under order of any court;
(J) Any person acting as a property manager in collecting or billing for rent, fees, deposits or other sums due landlords of managed units;
(K) Any person while the person is providing billing services. A person is providing billing services for the purposes of this subparagraph if the person engages, directly or indirectly, in the business or pursuit of collection of claims for other persons, whether in the other person's name or any other name, by any means that:
(i) Is an accounting procedure, preparation of mail billing or any other means intended to accelerate cash flow to the other person's bank account or to any separate trust account; and
(ii) Does not include any personal contact or contact by telephone with the person from whom the claim is sought to be collected;
(L) Any person while the person is providing factoring services. A person is providing factoring services for the purposes of this subparagraph if the person engages, directly or indirectly, in the business or pursuit of:
(i) Lending or advancing money to commercial clients on the security of merchandise or accounts receivable and then enforcing collection actions or procedures on such accounts; or
(ii) Soliciting or collecting on accounts that have been purchased from commercial clients under an agreement whether or not the agreement:
(I) Allows recourse against the commercial client;
(II) Requires the commercial client to provide any form of guarantee of payment of the purchased account; or
(III) Requires the commercial client to establish or maintain a reserve account in any form;
(M) Any individual employed by another person who operates as a collection agency if the person does not operate as a collection agency independent of that employment;
(N) Any mortgage banker as defined in ORS 59.840;
(O) Any public utility, as defined in ORS 757.005, any telecommunications utility, as defined in ORS 759.005, any people's utility district, as defined in ORS 261.010, and any cooperative corporation engaged in furnishing electric or communication service to consumers;
(P) Any public body or any individual collecting or attempting to collect claims owed, due or asserted to be owed or due to any public body, if the individual is an employee of the public body; or
(Q) Any person for whom the Director of the Department of Consumer and Business Services determines by order or by rule that the protection of the public health, safety and welfare does not require registration with the department as a collection agency.

Or. Rev. Stat. §§ 697.005(1)(b). (WESTLAW through End of the 2003 Reg. Sess.).

PENNSYLVANIA

Definitions

(h) Definitions.--As used in this section the following words and phrases shall have the meanings given to them in this subsection:

"Claim." Includes any claim, demand, account, note, or any other chose in action or liability of any kind whatsoever.

"Collection agency." A person, other than an attorney at law duly admitted to practice in any court of record in this Commonwealth, who, as a business, enforces, collects, settles, adjusts, or compromises claims, or holds himself out, or offers, as a business, to enforce, collect, settle, adjust, or compromise claims.

"Creditor." Includes a person having or asserting such a claim.

"Debtor." Includes any person against whom a claim is asserted.

Pa. Cons. Stat. Ann. § 7311 (h) (WESTLAW through Act 2005-2).

RHODE ISLAND

There are no statutory licensing requirements in the state of Rhode Island.

SOUTH CAROLINA

Definitions

In addition to definitions appearing in subsequent articles, in this title:

(10) "Consumer" means the buyer, lessee, or debtor to whom credit is extended in a consumer credit transaction. In addition, for purposes of Chapters 10, 11, 13, and 15 of this title, as well as Sections 37-5-108, 37-6-108, 37-6-117(i), and 37-6-118, the term also includes:

> (1) a natural person who is a purchaser or lessee or prospective purchaser or lessee in any transaction arising out of the production, promotion, sale, or lease of consumer goods or services; or
>
> (2) a natural person who is the object of a solicitation or offer relating to a contest, game, or prize offer subject to Chapter 15.

(11) "Consumer credit transaction" means a consumer credit sale (§ 37-2-104) or consumer loan (§ 37-3-104) or a refinancing or consolidation thereof, a consumer lease (§ 37-2-106), or a consumer rental-purchase agreement (§ 37-2-701).

(14) "Debtor" means any person who is an obligor in a credit transaction, including any cosigner, comaker, guarantor, endorsee or surety, and the assignee of any obligor, and also includes any person who agrees to assume the payment of a credit obligation.

(28) "Debt collector" means any person who collects, attempts to collect, directly or indirectly, debts due or asserted to be owed or due another. The term also includes a creditor who collects, attempts to collect, directly or indirectly, his own debts.

S.C. Code Ann. § 37-1-301 (10)-(11), (14), (28) (WESTLAW through End of 2004 Reg. Sess.).

SOUTH DAKOTA

There are no statutory licensing requirements in the state of South Dakota.

TENNESSEE

Definitions

As used in this chapter, unless the context otherwise requires:

(3) "Collection service" means any person who, directly or indirectly, for a fee, commission, or other compensation, offers to a client or prospective client the service of collecting, or purchasing for collection, accounts, bills, notes or other indebtedness due such client for various debtors. "Collection service" includes, but is not limited to:

> (A) Any deputy sheriff, constable or other individual who, in the course of that person's duties, accepts any compensation other than that fixed by statute in connection with the collection of an account;
>
> (B) Any person who, in the process of collecting that person's own accounts, uses or causes to be used any fictitious name which would indicate to the debtor that a third party is handling the accounts;
>
> (C) Any person who offers for sale, gives away, or uses any letter or form designed for use in the collection of accounts which deceives the receiver into believing that an account is in the hands of a third party, even though the letter or form may instruct the debtor to pay directly to the debtor's creditor; and
>
> (D) Any person who engages in the solicitation of claims in this state for purchase or collection;

Tenn. Code Ann. § 62-20-102(3) (WESTLAW through laws from 2005 First Reg. Sess. eff. through June 30, 2005).

Whether a debt buyer is acting as a "collection service" as defined in § 62- 20-102(13), depends upon whether the debt buyer is buying the accounts to collect on the debts (for which it would be required to obtain a license) or whether the debt buyer is simply engaging in the purchase of factored accounts receivable, whereby it may not need a license. If the accounts being purchased have not reached maturity at the time of purchase, no debt collection service license would be required. [Possible Debt Buyer and Debts Not In Default Exemption] Op.Atty.Gen. No. 97-131, Sept. 23, 1997.

Exemptions
(a) The provisions of this chapter shall not apply to:

(1) Any person handling claims, accounts or collections under order of any court;

(2) Attorneys at law; or

(3) Any person engaged in the collection of indebtedness incurred in the normal course of business, or the business of a parent, subsidiary, or affiliated firm or corporation; however, no person who is or represents such person to be a collection service is exempt from this chapter.

(b) Nothing contained within this chapter shall be construed to require an individual or business entity, which collects only the individual's or its own unpaid accounts, to submit to licensure or regulation by the collection service board.
Tenn. Code Ann. § 62-20-103 (WESTLAW through laws from 2005 First Reg. Sess. eff. through June 30, 2005).

TEXAS
Definitions
In this chapter:
(1) "Consumer" means an individual who has a consumer debt.
(2) "Consumer debt" means an obligation, or an alleged obligation, primarily for personal, family, or household purposes and arising from a transaction or alleged transaction.
(3) "Creditor" means a party, other than a consumer, to a transaction or alleged transaction involving one or more consumers.
(4) "Credit bureau" means a person who, for compensation, gathers, records, and disseminates information relating to the creditworthiness, financial responsibility, and paying habits of, and similar information regarding, a person for the purpose of furnishing that information to another person.
(5) "Debt collection" means an action, conduct, or practice in collecting, or in soliciting for collection, consumer debts that are due or alleged to be due a creditor.
(6) "Debt collector" means a person who directly or indirectly engages in debt collection and includes a person who sells or offers to sell forms represented to be a collection system, device, or scheme intended to be used to collect consumer debts.
(7) "Third-party debt collector" means a debt collector, as defined by 15 U.S.C. Section 1692a(6), but does not include an attorney collecting a debt as an attorney on behalf of and in the name of a client unless the attorney has nonattorney employees who:

(A) are regularly engaged to solicit debts for collection; or

(B) regularly make contact with debtors for the purpose of collection or adjustment of debts.

Tex. Fin. Code Ann. § 392.001 (WESTLAW through Chs effective immediately through Ch. 290 of the 2005 Reg. Sess. of the 79th Leg.).

UTAH
Definitions
No person shall conduct a collection agency, collection bureau, or collection office in this state, or engage in this state in the business of soliciting the right to collect or receive payment for another of any account, bill, or other indebtedness, or advertise for or solicit in print the right to collect or receive payment for another of any account, bill, or other indebtedness, unless at the time of conducting the collection agency, collection bureau, collection office, or collection business, or of advertising or soliciting, that person or

the person for whom he may be acting as agent, is registered with the Division of Corporations and Commercial Code and has on file a good and sufficient bond as hereinafter specified. Utah Code Ann. § 12-1-1 (WESTLAW through the End of 2005 First Spec. Sess.).

Exemptions
This title shall not apply to an attorney at law duly authorized to practice in this state, to a national bank, or to any bank or trust company duly incorporated under the laws of this state. Utah Code Ann. § 12-1-7 (WESTLAW through End of 2005 First Spec. Sess.).

VERMONT
There are no statutory licensing requirements in the state of Vermont.

VIRGINIA
There are no statutory licensing requirements in the state of Virginia.

WASHINGTON
Definitions
Unless a different meaning is plainly required by the context, the following words and phrases as hereinafter used in this chapter shall have the following meanings:
(1) "Person" includes individual, firm, partnership, trust, joint venture, association, or corporation.
(2) "Collection agency" means and includes:

> (a) Any person directly or indirectly engaged in soliciting claims for collection, or collecting or attempting to collect claims owed or due or asserted to be owed or due another person;
> (b) Any person who directly or indirectly furnishes or attempts to furnish, sells, or offers to sell forms represented to be a collection system or scheme intended or calculated to be used to collect claims even though the forms direct the debtor to make payment to the creditor and even though the forms may be or are actually used by the creditor himself or herself in his or her own name;
> (c) Any person who in attempting to collect or in collecting his or her own claim uses a fictitious name or any name other than his or her own which would indicate to the debtor that a third person is collecting or attempting to collect such claim.

(4) "Out-of-state collection agency" means a person whose activities within this state are limited to collecting debts from debtors located in this state by means of interstate communications, including telephone, mail, or facsimile transmission, from the person's location in another state on behalf of clients located outside of this state, but does not include any person who is excluded from the definition of the term "debt collector" under the federal fair debt collection practices act (15 U.S.C. Sec. 1692a(6)).
(5) "Claim" means any obligation for the payment of money or thing of value arising out of any agreement or contract, express or implied.
(11) "Debtor" means any person owing or alleged to owe a claim.
(12) "Commercial claim" means any obligation for payment of money or thing of value arising out of any agreement or contract, express or implied, where the transaction which is the subject of the agreement or contract is not primarily for personal, family, or household purposes.
Wash. Rev. Code Ann. § 19.16.100(1)-(2), (4)-(5), (11)-(12) (WESTLAW through 2005 legislation effective through July 1, 2005).

Exemptions
(3) "Collection agency" does not mean and does not include:

> (a) Any individual engaged in soliciting claims for collection, or collecting or attempting to collect claims on behalf of a licensee under this chapter, if said individual is an employee of the licensee;
> (b) Any individual collecting or attempting to collect claims for not more than one employer, if all the collection efforts are carried on in the name of the employer and if the individual is an

employee of the employer;

(c) Any person whose collection activities are carried on in his, her, or its true name and are confined and are directly related to the operation of a business other than that of a collection agency, such as but not limited to: Trust companies; savings and loan associations; building and loan associations; abstract companies doing an escrow business; real estate brokers; property management companies collecting assessments, charges, or fines on behalf of condominium unit owners associations, associations of apartment owners, or homeowners' associations; public officers acting in their official capacities; persons acting under court order; lawyers; insurance companies; credit unions; loan or finance companies; mortgage banks; and banks;

(d) Any person who on behalf of another person prepares or mails monthly or periodic statements of accounts due if all payments are made to that other person and no other collection efforts are made by the person preparing the statements of account;

(e) An "out-of-state collection agency" as defined in this chapter; or

(f) Any person while acting as a debt collector for another person, both of whom are related by common ownership or affiliated by corporate control, if the person acting as a debt collector does so only for persons to whom it is so related or affiliated and if the principal business of the person is not the collection of debts.

Wash. Rev. Code Ann. § 19.16.100(3) (WESTLAW through 2005 legislation effective through July 1, 2005).

WEST VIRGINIA

The following words and terms shall be construed as follows:

(a) "Claim" means any obligation for the payment of money due or asserted to be due to another person, firm, corporation or association.

(b) "Collection agency" means and includes all persons, firms, corporations and associations: (1) Directly or indirectly engaged in the business of soliciting from or collecting for others any account, bill or indebtedness originally due or asserted to be owed or due another and all persons, firms, corporations and associations directly or indirectly engaged in asserting, enforcing or prosecuting those claims; (2) which, in attempting to collect or in collecting his or her or its own accounts or claims uses a fictitious name or names other than his or her or its own name; (3) which attempts to or does give away or sell to others any system or series of letters or forms for use in the collection of accounts or claims which assert or indicate directly or indirectly that the claims or accounts are being asserted or collected by any person, firm, corporation or association other than the creditor or owner of the claim or account; or (4) directly or indirectly engaged in the business of soliciting, or who holds himself or herself out as engaged in the business of soliciting, debts of any kind owed or due, or asserted to be owed or due, to any solicited person, firm, corporation or association for fee, commission or other compensation.

W. Va. Code Ann. § 47-16-2(b) (WESTLAW through End of 2005 Third Ex. Sess.).

Exemptions

The term "collection agency" shall not mean or include:

(1) Regular employees of a single creditor or of a collection agency licensed hereunder;

(2) banks;

(3) trust companies;

(4) savings and loan associations;

(5) building and loan associations;

(6) industrial loan companies;

(7) small loan companies;

(8) abstract companies doing an escrow business;

(9) duly licensed real estate brokers or agents when the claims or accounts being handled by such broker or agent are related to or in connection with such brokers' or agents' regular real estate business;

(10) express and telegraph companies subject to public regulation and supervision;
(11) attorneys-at-law handling claims and collections in their own names and not operating a collection agency under the management of a layman;
(12) any person, firm, corporation or association acting under the order of any court of competent jurisdiction; or
(13) any person collecting a debt owed to another person only where:

> (A) Both persons are related by wholly-owned, common ownership or affiliated by wholly-owned corporate control;
> (B) the person collecting the debt acts only on behalf of persons related as described in paragraph (A) of this subdivision; and
> (C) debt collection is not the principal business of the person collecting the debt.

W. Va. Code Ann. § 47-16-2(b) (WESTLAW through End of 2005 Third Ex. Sess.).

WISCONSIN
Definitions
(1) "Claim" means any obligation or alleged obligation arising from a consumer transaction, including a transaction that is primarily for an agricultural purpose.
(2) "Debt collection" means any action, conduct or practice of soliciting claims for collection or in the collection of claims owed or due or alleged to be owed or due a merchant by a customer.
(3) "Debt collector" means any person engaging, directly or indirectly, in debt collection, and includes any person who sells, or offers to sell, forms represented to be a collection system, device or scheme, intended or calculated to be used to collect claims. The term does not include a printing company engaging in the printing and sale of forms.
Wis. Stat. Ann. 427.103 (WESTLAW through 2005 Act 21, published 7/22/05).

(1) Definitions. The following terms, as used in this section, shall have the meaning stated, unless the context requires a different meaning:

> (a) A "collection agency," for purposes of the state's licensing requirements, is defined as any person engaging in the business of collecting or receiving for payment for others of any account, bill or other indebtedness. It shall not include attorneys at law authorized to practice in this state and resident herein, banks, express companies, state savings banks, state savings and loan associations, insurers and their agents, trust companies, district attorneys acting under s. 971.41, persons contracting with district attorneys under s. 971.41(5), real estate brokers, and real estate salespersons.
> (b) "Collector" or "solicitor" means any person employed by a collection agency to collect or receive payment or to solicit the receiving or collecting of payment for others of any account, bill or other indebtedness outside of the office.

Wis. Stat. Ann. § 218.04(1)(a)-(b) (WESTLAW through 2005 Act 21, published 7/22/05).

Exemptions
(4) The following persons shall not be subject to this section solely by reason of their debt collection activities unless they are licensed debt collectors under s. 218.04:

> (a) Attorneys authorized to practice law in this state or professional service corporations composed of licensed attorneys formed pursuant to ss. 180.1901 to 180.1921;
> (b) Duly licensed real estate brokers and real estate salespersons; and
> (c) Duly licensed insurance companies subject to the supervision of the office of the commissioner of insurance.

(5) No person is subject to this section solely by reason of offering the discount described in s. 422.201(8).
Wis. Stat. Ann. § 426.201(1), (4) (West, WESTLAW through 2001 Act 43, published 2/15/02.)

WYOMING

Definitions

(a) As used in this act:

(ii) "Business debt" means the obligation arising from a credit transaction between business or commercial enterprises for goods or services used or to be used primarily in a commercial or business enterprise and not for personal, family or household purposes;

(iii) "Collection agency" means any person who:

(A) Engages in any business, the purpose of which is the collection of any debts for Wyoming creditors;

(B) Regularly collects or attempts to collect for Wyoming creditors, directly or indirectly, debts owed or due or asserted to be owed or due another;

(C) Takes assignment of debts for the purpose of collecting such debts;

(D) Directly or indirectly, solicits for collection debts owed or due or asserted to be owed or due a Wyoming creditor;

(E) Uses a fictitious name or any name other than their own name in the collection of their own accounts receivable; or

(F) Collects debts incurred in this state from debtors located in this state by means of interstate communications, including telephone, mail or facsimile or any other electronic method, from the debt collector's location in another state.

(v) "Consumer" means any natural person obligated or allegedly obligated to pay any debt;

(vii) "Debt" means any obligation or alleged obligation of a consumer to pay money arising out of a transaction in which the money, property, insurance or services which are the subject of the transaction are primarily for personal, family or household purposes, whether or not the obligation has been reduced to judgment;

(viii) "Debt collector" means any person employed or engaged by a collection agency to perform the collection of debts owed or due or asserted to be owed or due to another, including any owner or shareholder of the collection agency business who engages in the collection of debts;

Wyoming Stat. Ann. § 33-11-101(a)(ii)-(viii) (WESTLAW through the 2004 Spec. Sess. (57th Leg.))

Exemptions

(b) The term "collection agency" does not include:

(i) Any officer or employee of a creditor while collecting debts for and in the name of the creditor;

(ii) Any officer or employee of the United States or of any state, to the extent that collecting or attempting to collect a debt is in the performance of his official duties;

(iii) Any person while serving or attempting to serve legal process on another person in connection with the judicial enforcement of any debt;

(iv) Any person whose principal business is the making of loans or the servicing of debt, and who acts as a loan correspondent, seller or servicing agent for the owner or holder of a debt which is secured by a mortgage on real property, whether or not the debt is also secured by an interest in personal property;

(v) Any person whose collection activities are carried on in the true name of the creditor, and are confined to the operation of a business other than a collection agency, including but not limited to banks, trust companies, savings and loan associations, abstract companies doing an escrow business, real estate brokers, attorneys, insurance companies, credit unions or loan or finance companies;

(vi) Any person whose business is the servicing of credit card debt;

(vii) Any person engaged solely in the collection of one (1) or more business debts; or

(viii) Any licensed attorney acting in an attorney-client relationship with the creditor, and who conducts the collection in the true name of the client.

Wyoming Stat. Ann. § 33-11-101(b) (WESTLAW through the 2004 Spec. Sess. (57th Leg.)).

ACA International, P.O. Box 390106, Minneapolis, MN 55439-0106
Phone +1(952) 926-6547 Fax (952) 926-1624
Web http://www.acainternational.org

APPENDIX VII

FORECLOSING ON A MEZZANINE LOAN UNDER UCC ARTICLE 9

By Peter E. Fisch, Steven Simkin and S.H. Spencer Compton*

As structured real estate finance has matured over the past several years, the requirements of the rating agencies (principally motivated by bankruptcy concerns) and the realities of the secondary market have greatly increased the use of mezzanine loans, which have largely replaced second mortgages in real estate finance.

This evolution has continued to the point where more sophisticated real estate financings are structured with multiple tiers of mezzanine loans held by disparate lenders with preferences for different risk positions in the capital structure, with each tier sometimes carved into separate pari passu notes, or into an A/B or A/B/C note structure that creates subordination within a mezzanine loan tier.

The repayment obligation of the mezzanine borrower (usually a direct or indirect parent of the property owner) is typically secured by a perfected security interest in the equity interests owned by such borrower in the property owner under Article 9 of the Uniform Commercial Code (UCC).

This article will focus on the remedies of a mezzanine lender under Article 9.

INTERCREDITOR ARRANGEMENTS

As real estate markets head into a downturn, mezzanine lenders, in prior loss position relative to mortgage lenders, will increasingly find themselves with borrowers in distress or default. Undoubtedly, a mezzanine lender will be constrained to act by

---

*Peter E. Fisch and Steven Simkin are partners in the real estate department of Paul, Weiss, Rifkind, Wharton & Garrison, LLP, and Spencer Compton is a Senior Vice President and Special Counsel of First American Title Insurance Company. Emily J. Carey, an associate at Paul, Weiss, assisted in the preparation of this article. The authors wish to acknowledge the invaluable contribution of James D. Prendergast, Senior Vice President and General Counsel of the UCC Division of First American Title Insurance Company.

virtue of intercreditor arrangements with the mortgage lender and any senior mezzanine lenders; but after navigating those constraints, a mezzanine lender may have to contemplate enforcement of its remedies against its collateral. Article 9 allows enforcement of a mezzanine lender's remedies through a foreclosure of the equity interest regardless of whether the lender's security interest is in (1) investment property, as either non-certificated or certificated securities, perfected by filing, possession or control under Article 9 or (2) a "general intangible" perfected only by filing under Article 9, though a secured lender will have more leverage if it holds a certificated interest.[25]

Before entering into substantive discussions with the debtor, a mezzanine lender should obtain a "pre-negotiation" or "standstill" agreement to protect against potential reliance claims the debtor might interpose should the workout negotiations or other discussions fail and foreclosure be the only course of action. If the debtor "opted into" Article 8, it is important to locate the share certificate or understand the control agreement.

A mezzanine lender exercising remedies must also be cognizant of any transfer taxes that may arise on account of a transfer in foreclosure (or in lieu thereof). Reviewing the relevant transaction documents may also disclose curable problems, such as the failure to obtain a necessary endorsement to a certificated security, that might be remedied while the parties are still talking.

In planning post-default strategies, the secured party must understand the nature of the debtor's problems that led to the default, as well as the secured party's endgame. The endgame may depend on whether the secured party is a "loan to own" investor who acquired the mezzanine debt (perhaps after default) to acquire control over the real estate, or an institutional lender that may not have the interest or the capacity to own and manage the real estate and whose primary goal is to recoup as much of its investment as the asset will bear.

No step is more critical than to understand the impact that a foreclosure transfer will have on the various rights and interests underlying the mezzanine loan collateral, including the mortgage loan and any senior mezzanine loans, ground leases or material contracts pertaining to the underlying property. Any intercreditor agreements will provide the most significant input into the timing and nature of remedies.

Using the Cure Rights

The mezzanine lender's best strategy may be to use the cure rights in the intercreditor agreement to stave off a foreclosure action by the senior lender(s). One option provided to each junior mezzanine lender in the standard intercreditor

[25] Article 9 governs the perfection of security interests, and Article 9 refers a secured party to Article 8 in order to determine how perfection is accomplished for both certificated and uncertificated securities where the pledged entity has opted into Article 8. In general, the lender will want to qualify as a "protected purchaser" under Article 8 of the UCC in order to cut off all adverse claims in the pledged equity collateral. For further discussion, see James D. Prendergast and Keith Pearson, *How to Perfect Equity Collateral Under Article 8*, 20 No. 6 Practical Real Estate Lawyer 33 (2004).

agreement, in the event the mortgage loan is accelerated, foreclosed or becomes "specially serviced," is the right to purchase at par each position senior to it.[26]

Once a secured party has accelerated its loan (or upon maturity of the loan), three remedies are available: (1) common law remedies through the courts; (2) foreclosure by disposition of collateral under Article 9; and (3) strict foreclosure under Article 9. Common law remedies would entail maintaining an action to enforce the note, obtaining a judgment, and enforcing the judgment by executing on the collateral and the other assets of the borrower (subject to any nonrecourse provisions). However, such a path is likely to be significantly more costly and time-consuming than Article 9 remedies.

Exercise of remedies under Article 9 does not require resort to the courts or the entry of a judgment on the note, though the collateral disposition process under Article 9 allows the debtor and other parties entitled to notice the opportunity to bring an action in the courts on legal or equitable grounds to contest the secured party's exercise of remedies. Once in receipt of a foreclosure notice, debtors may also interpose lender liability claims against the secured party which can create a drag on the process, whether or not they have merit, and as a last resort, file bankruptcy to take advantage of the automatic stay.

Disposition of Collateral

Article 9 provides that a disposition of collateral can be accomplished by either a "public disposition" or a "private disposition." "Although the term is not defined . . . a 'public disposition' is one at which the price is determined after the public has had a meaningful opportunity for competitive bidding. 'Meaningful opportunity' is meant to imply that some form of advertisement or public notice must precede the sale . . . and that the public must have access to the sale. . . ."[27] Any advertisement for the sale of collateral at a public sale should be calculated to maximize public participation. UCC § 9-610(b) provides that a public disposition must be a "commercially reasonable" disposition with advance notice under §§ 9-611 and 9-612 to the debtor, any secondary obligor and, depending on the facts of the loan transaction, certain additional parties.[28]

The forms of notice set forth in UCC § 9-613 should be used, as there is likely little benefit to any creativity by the mezzanine lender in this exercise. UCC § 9-612(b) provides a 10-day "safe harbor" for notice of public dispositions, which the Official Comment to § 9-612 states is intended only to be a "safe harbor" and not a minimum requirement. However, in the real estate financing arena, as discussed below, the process to prepare for the sale and market the interests will usually result in a notice period far in excess of the safe harbor.

[26]The industry standard intercreditor agreement can be found at http://www.cmbs.org/WorkArea/showcontent.aspx?id=10064.

[27]Official Comment 7 to UCC § 9-610.

[28]A UCC Foreclosure Notice Insurance Policy, certifying the identities of security interest holders and lien holders of record, will soon be available from First American Title Insurance Company.

While the disposition may be either private or public, a secured party may only purchase collateral at a private disposition "if the collateral is a kind that is customarily sold on a recognized market or the subject of widely distributed standard price quotations."[29] The sale of collateral consisting of privately held, limited liability company or partnership interests or shares of stock in a closely held corporation should therefore be sold at a public disposition unless the collateral falls into the description above or the secured party has no intention of purchasing it. Where a secured party is pursuing a "loan to own" strategy, a public disposition is clearly preferred, unless the debtor is amenable to strict foreclosure.

Both public and private dispositions must, in all aspects, be "commercially reasonable." A rule of thumb for a secured party is to market the security as a non-foreclosing seller might market the underlying property—if possible, structure the public notice and the disposition to comply with exemptions from securities laws, advertise in a way calculated to reach the highest number of likely buyers[30] (such advertisement should put forth all information typically given in similar advertisements), provide sufficient diligence materials and time to allow potential buyers to review those materials, and minimize restrictions on the sale of or future rights attaching to the collateral (which may require obtaining various consents under the mortgages or intercreditor or entity agreements).

Diligence materials should include many of the materials that a buyer of a commercial property would require, such as information pertaining to the mortgage and other senior loans, a rent roll, title report, survey and structural and environmental assessments, to the extent available and subject to any confidentiality restrictions in the loan documents or the intercreditor agreement. A foreclosing mezzanine lender should consider retaining a local third-party broker or auctioneer experienced in selling property similar to the underlying real estate to handle the marketing of the interest.

In addition, the location and manner of the sale should also be appropriate. In the case of a sale of privately held, limited liability company or partnership interests or shares of stock in a closely held corporation, this may mean in an electronic forum, or in the major city nearest the underlying real property interests. The commercial reasonableness of each of these steps is a fact-specific inquiry, and depends on a cost/benefit analysis and the surrounding circumstances (for example, a reasonable period of time from the initial advertisement of the disposition and the disposition itself may depend on, inter alia, market conditions, the complexity of the documentation relating to the underlying assets and how long it would take a typical buyer to obtain financing).

The secured party can exercise some discretion in setting the terms of the sale and assessing the bona fides and qualification of any bidder, and reject a higher bid on that basis (such discretion must, of course, be exercised in a commercially reasonable manner). An unscrupulous debtor could easily send an unqualified bidder to the sale without any real intention of completing a transaction in order to buy more time.

---

[29]UCC § 9-610 (c).

[30]*See Ford & Vlahos v. ITT Commercial Finance Corp.*, 8 Cal. 4th 1220 (1994).

Whether the collateral is a "security" under federal and/or state securities laws is a threshold issue when contemplating acceleration and/or foreclosure. Securities laws prohibit the offering and public sale of unregistered securities. Conducting a foreclosure sale that is sufficiently public to be "commercially reasonable" without crossing the line into a public offering of unregistered securities can be challenging. Comment 8 to § 9-610 advises: "Although a 'public' disposition of securities under this Article may implicate the registration requirements of the Securities Act of 1933, it need not do so. A disposition that qualifies for a 'private placement' exemption under the Securities Act of 1933 nevertheless may constitute a 'public' disposition within the meaning of this section."[31]

Commercial Reasonableness

As with all other aspects of an Article 9 foreclosure sale, commercial reasonableness is the standard by which the eventual sale price is judged (not the "shocks the conscience" standard applied to mortgage foreclosures). "The fact that a greater amount could have been obtained by a collection, enforcement, disposition, or acceptance at a different time or in a different method from that selected by the secured party is not itself sufficient to preclude the secured party from establishing that the collection, enforcement, disposition or acceptance was made in a commercially reasonable manner."[32] Because the Article 9 definition of a commercially reasonable sale is vague and because a judgment as to whether or not a sale was reasonable will frequently turn on the circumstances of a particular case, many courts have held this to be a question of fact with the burden of proof on the secured party.

The third remedy available to a foreclosing mezzanine lender is strict foreclosure, in which the secured party retains the debtor's collateral in full or partial satisfaction of the secured debt. UCC § 9-620 expressly permits "acceptance in satisfaction" for all types of collateral, and that such satisfaction can be "full or partial." Where the secured party seeks *partial* satisfaction, the debtor must affirmatively consent to the proposed acceptance of collateral as provided in § 9-620 (c)(1) "in a record authenticated after default." A debtor's consent to acceptance of the secured party's proposal in full satisfaction of the debt may be passive (e.g., where the secured party sends a proposal to the debtor and does not receive an objection within 20 days).[33] Without such consent or lack of objection, strict foreclosure is not an available remedy.

While strict foreclosure may be desirable, as it is a streamlined process that eliminates the need for a sale or other disposition and is certainly a preferred outcome for a "loan to own" strategy, the practical difficulty is that in most cases a debtor has little incentive not to raise an objection for strategic reasons. The presence of appropriate non-recourse carveouts in the mezzanine loan documents, and a guaranty of those carveouts by the principals of the borrower, are likely to be effective in

---

[31]For a comprehensive discussion of this issue, see Lynn A. Soukup, *Securities Law and the UCC: When Godzilla Meets Bambi*, 38 UCC L.J. 1 Art. 1 (2005).

[32]UCC § 9 627(a).

[33]UCC § 9-620(c)(2)(C).

conforming a borrower's actions in the face of a strict foreclosure to the economic realities of the situation.[34] In other cases, unpalatable as it may be for a secured party, it may make sense to compensate the debtor to incentivize cooperation.

Other Considerations

There are usually contractual limitations on the transfer of membership or limited partnership interests in the mezzanine loan borrower arising out of one or more of (i) the underlying mortgage or deed of trust, (ii) the intercreditor agreement and/or (iii) the borrower's operating agreement or limited partnership agreement.

One of the most significant restrictions on the transfer of mezzanine collateral is a limitation under the intercreditor agreement that such transfers must be to a "Qualified Transferee," an entity generally defined in the operative document as either the mezzanine lender itself or an institutional investor meeting certain requirements.[35] This significantly restricts the potential universe of purchasers at a foreclosure sale, and the process of "qualifying" the winning bidder may inject uncertainty surrounding the ability of a buyer to close and, at a minimum, may delay the closing.

Additionally, without any necessary consents from other partners or members, the successful purchaser at a foreclosure sale cannot succeed to the rights or powers of a partner or member and is only entitled to receive proceeds and distributions.

In cases in which the mezzanine lender is the beneficiary of a pledge of all of the equity interests in the subject pledged entity, this issue does not arise.

In other cases, though, the lack of rights as a partner or member will seriously inhibit the purchaser's ability to enforce payment of distributions, deny such purchaser access to books and records, and undermine a claim by such purchaser for breach of fiduciary duty; moreover, the lack of a voting interest impairs the value of the collateral in a foreclosure sale.

When documenting a mezzanine loan which is secured only by a partial interest in a pledged entity, it is important to obtain a recognition agreement or other consent to admission into the pledged entity from the other partners or members.

Complexities may arise due to the "carving up" of the capital structure. Many mezzanine loans are originated as part of a mortgage/mezzanine structure in the CMBS market, with the originator selling off certain pieces and keeping others. Often, the servicing or collateral agency rights for each tier of indebtedness are

---

[34] *See* John C. Murray, *Carveouts to Nonrecourse Loans: They Mean What They Say!*, 19 No. 3 Prac. Real Est. Law. 19 (2003).

[35] *See* the form intercreditor agreement (http://www.cmbs.org/WorkArea/showcontent.aspx?id=10064), at page 6. The institutional investor would need to meet a negotiated assets management threshold, be a '33 Act "qualified institutional buyer" or meet certain other related requirements.

retained in the originator or its successor, who also may have significant exposure in one or more of the tiers of indebtedness.

In a distress situation, this can create significant conflicts of interest between a servicer/collateral agent that also holds an interest in a mortgage or mezzanine tranche and another holder of an interest in a mezzanine tranche. This conflict may impede the exercise of remedies by a mezzanine lender.

For example, if the servicer/collateral agent or holder of a mortgage loan also holds a blocking or controlling interest in a mezzanine tranche, and such party is in negotiations with the borrower to grant concessions under a matured or defaulted loan, that party can effectively block the exercise of remedies by the mezzanine tranche or provide any necessary consent on behalf of the mezzanine tranche, even if it is against the interests of the other holders of that tranche to do so, on the basis that such party's interest as mortgage lender is better served by making the concessions.

Regardless of its interests, the servicer/collateral agent has fiduciary obligations to its principal, the mezzanine holder, under general principles of agency law. The relevant agreements may contain express waivers of such fiduciary obligations, though it is not clear to what extent any such waivers would be enforced by a court. A prudent mezzanine lender will fight the inclusion of any waivers of fiduciary duty with vigor. In the event any conflict becomes apparent, the mezzanine lender must also put the servicer/collateral agent on notice of the conflict of interest, underscoring the fiduciary obligations of the servicer/collateral agent.

Conclusion

Foreclosure of a mezzanine loan under Article 9 offers many benefits to a secured party, chief among them the streamlined process that generally achieves the desired result both faster and more economically than a mortgage foreclosure. A foreclosing mezzanine lender should make sure that at each point in the foreclosure process its actions are carefully considered to minimize the chance of a challenge for lack of commercial reasonableness. The secured party who has followed the recommendations of Moody's Investors Service in structuring and documenting the mezzanine loan at the outset will be in the best position to negotiate a satisfying outcome in a distressed loan situation.[36]

One final note: A mezzanine lender must also be careful what it wishes for. Once the foreclosure is completed, the mezzanine lender may find itself in the unfamiliar situation, for which it may be ill-equipped, of having to operate the property and deal with the various competing property interests. Moreover, once the mezzanine lender takes control of the pledged entity, various claims against the distressed entity may only begin to come out of the woodwork.

---

[36]*See* Daniel B. Rubock, *Moody's Investors Service, Inc., US CMBS and CRE CDO: Moody's Approach to Rating Commercial Real Estate Mezzanine Loans* 3 (2007). Moody's recommends a pledge of 100% of the equity, opting into Article 8, certificating the equity, filing a financing statement, control of the ability to opt out through hardwire or proxy and the purchase of UCC insurance.

APPENDIX VIII

Bulletin

Pursuing U.S. Claims Against Foreign Debtors

BY JOHNATHAN C. BOLTON, SENIOR ASSOCIATE, FULBRIGHT & JAWORSKI L.L.P.

To pursue a claim against a foreign debtor, a creditor must follow the laws and rules of the jurisdiction in which the debtor's insolvency case is pending to register its claim in a timely manner.

But what if a creditor holds an unliquidated tort claim under U.S. law and the foreign debtor already has obtained an order enjoining U.S. creditors from pursuing pre-petition claims against the foreign debtor through an ancillary proceeding in the United States? Will a U.S. Bankruptcy Court allow the tort claim to be litigated to a final judgment in a U.S. court so that the claim in the foreign insolvency court can be liquidated?

Two recent cases from the Southern District of New York addressed this issue.

Osanitsch v. Marcolni PLC

In the first case, *Osanitsch v. Marcolni PLC (In re Marconi PLC)*, 363 B.R. 361, *2 (S.D.N.Y. 2007), a former executive of a British debtor's U.S. subsidiary sued the British parent company and its U.S. subsidiary, asserting unpaid severance benefits. By the time the suit was filed, the British company already had filed for bankruptcy protection in the U.K. and entered into a Scheme of Arrangement that was approved by the High Court in London in April 2003.[1]

In addition, the British debtor's court-appointed representatives commenced an ancillary proceeding in U.S. Bankruptcy Court for the Southern District of New York under former Section 304 of the Bankruptcy Code. The Bankruptcy Court entered an order on May 14, 2003, that recognized and gave full force and effect to the Scheme of Arrangement, deemed the British debtor discharged, and enjoined its creditors from "commencing or continuing any action or other proceeding…against it." See *id.*

> Bringing an ancillary proceeding in the United States does not necessarily give U.S. courts jurisdiction over claims against a foreign debtor.

Unaware of the Section 304 order, Osanitsch filed suit against the British debtor, its U.S. subsidiary, and others in California state court, alleging fraud and breach of contract. The British debtor removed the case to U.S. District Court in California. Osanitsch filed a motion to remand the case, and the British debtor filed a motion to dismiss the suit based on the Section 304 order. The District Court "denied Osanitsch's motion to remand and dismissed the case [without prejudice], finding it barred by the [New York] Bankruptcy Court's injunction." Osanitsch appealed the District Court's dismissal to the 9th U.S. Circuit Court of Appeals.

In the meantime, Osanitsch commenced an adversary proceeding in U.S. Bankruptcy Court in New York, where the Section 304 ancillary case was pending, essentially repeating the claims he had asserted in the California suit. Osanitsch alleged that the New York court had jurisdiction over his adversary complaint because, among other things, it "is arising in the debtor's case number 03-B-11949 pursuant to Section 304 of the Bankruptcy Code." *Id.*

The British debtor filed a motion to dismiss the case, which the Bankruptcy Court converted to a motion for summary judgment. The court then granted summary judgment, finding that it lacked jurisdiction over the adversary complaint. See id. at *4. On appeal, the U.S. District Court in New York affirmed, explaining:

> Section 304…does not permit the filing by domestic creditors of adversary proceedings to establish claims against a foreign bankrupt. Indeed, its very purpose is to centralize such proceedings (where the bankruptcy court determines that such centralization is appropriate) in the foreign court administering the bankruptcy. Id. at *11.

The District Court also found that Osanitsch's damage claims did not "arise in" the case because it "raises no claims created by or unique to bankruptcy law, but rather ordinary tort and contract claims arising under the common law of California." The District Court ruled that the Bankruptcy Court was correct in holding that it lacked jurisdiction over the plaintiff's complaint, "at least to the extent that it seeks a judgment for damages." Id. at *13, *16.

LEGAL BULLETIN

However, the District Court also treated Osanitsch's request in his complaint that his claims "be permitted to proceed to resolution by final judgment in an appropriate forum" as a motion to modify the Section 304 order, and it found that the Bankruptcy Court had jurisdiction to do so if it chose. Id. at *17. The District Court remanded the case to the Bankruptcy Court to address Osanitsch's application for an amendment or modification of the injunction but cautioned that "however the Bankruptcy Court disposes of Osanitsch's request, its ruling will be an exercise of discretion on the merits." Id. at *20.

The important lesson of *Osanitsch* is that bringing an ancillary proceeding in the United States does not necessarily give U.S. courts jurisdiction over claims against a foreign debtor. To pursue a U.S. claim against a foreign debtor, a creditor may have to seek modification of a Bankruptcy Court's Section 304 (or now Chapter 15) injunction and persuade the court that it should be permitted to pursue its claim in U.S. courts.

In re Parmalat Securities Litigation

The second case involving claims against a foreign debtor was *In re Parmalat Securities Litigation*, 2007 U.S. Dist. LEXIS 46955 (S.D.N.Y. June 28, 2007), which was decided in June by U.S. District Court Judge Lewis Kaplan. Some plaintiffs were allowed to pursue U.S. securities fraud claims against foreign debtors — despite a Section 304 order prohibiting suits against those debtors — based on the terms of the plan approved in the foreign proceeding.

In *Parmalat*, several Italian entities, collectively known as Old Parmalat, filed for bankruptcy protection in Parma, Italy, in December 2003.[2] An "extraordinary administrator" was appointed in the case in accordance with Italian law.

Immediately after the bankruptcy filing, several investors in Old Parmalat filed actions in the United States that alleged violations of U.S. securities laws by Old Parmalat's officers, directors, auditors, and others. The cases were consolidated into one purported class action.

The extraordinary administrator filed three separate lawsuits in the United States against certain banks and accounting firms, alleging that those entities committed fraud against Old Parmalat and its investors. It also filed a Section 304 ancillary proceeding in U.S. Bankruptcy Court for the Southern District of New York and obtained an order barring all U.S. actions against Old Parmalat.

Certain defendants in the recovery actions moved to withdraw the reference of the Section 304 proceeding so that they could adequately defend themselves. The Bankruptcy Court modified the Section 304 order to permit discovery against the foreign debtors, to allow the defendants to assert compulsory counterclaims, and to allow a third-party complaint by Grant Thornton International in the securities fraud action against New Parmalat.

In July 2004, the extraordinary administrator proposed a restructuring plan in the Parma Court that called for the formation of a "*concordato*," the purpose of which was to enable the continued operation of the foreign debtors while creating a vehicle to discharge claims of unsecured creditors. The *concordato* was approved by a majority of the creditors and approved by the Italian Court on October 1, 2005.

The *concordato* created a new entity referred to as New Parmalat to act as a vehicle to carry out the purposes of the reorganization. New Parmalat succeeded to the assets of Old Parmalat and assumed all of the debts of those entities. The restructuring plan discharged creditor claims by allocating to each an approved amount of stock in New Parmalat according to certain "recovery ratios" set forth in the plan. Certain plaintiffs in the securities fraud action filed claims in the Parma Court and received shares in New Pamalat.

After the *concordato* was approved and New Parmalat was formed, plaintiffs in the securities fraud action in the United States sought to add New Parmalat as a defendant in their case. They argued *inter alia* that New Parmalat was liable as a successor to Old Parmalat for violations of Sections 10(b) and 10b-5 of the Securities and Exchange Act of 1934. The plaintiffs wisely informed the New York Bankruptcy Court that "in asserting the claims against New Parmalat in the United States, they seek only to liquidate their claims here. They represent that they will seek to enforce any judgment only in the Parma Court." See *id.* at *11. The Bankruptcy Court granted the motion on July 21, 2006.

New Parmalat moved to dismiss the plaintiffs' claims against it on three grounds, arguing that:

- New Parmalat could not be liable as a successor to Old Parmalat because it did not assume Old Parmalat's liabilities.
- The two-year statue of limitations on the plaintiffs' securities fraud claim had run.
- The doctrine of *res judicata* barred relitigation of the issues asserted in the Parma Court.

The U.S. District Court in New York did not find any of these grounds to be persuasive. On the first issue, the court found that because the parties did not indicate that Italian law differed from New York law on successor liability, New York successor liability law applied and the plain language of the *concordato* provided that New Parmalat expressly agreed to assume "[a]ll debts" of Old Parmalat. See *id.* at *15 n. 38.

On the second issue, the District Court found that equitable tolling applied to the fraud claims because although the plaintiffs had been enjoined from pursuing their claims against Old Parmalat by the Section 304 order, that order did not protect it from suit after New Parmalat was formed under the *concordato*.

The District Court also found that the plaintiffs' efforts to amend their suit to add New Parmalat were sufficiently diligent. Further, the court found that "extraordinary circumstances" were present due to the pendency of the Section 304 order, which enjoined the plaintiffs from seeking relief in the United States against Old Parmalat, and thus limitations were tolled.

On the final issue, the District Court rejected New Parmalat's argument that the bondholders' fraud claims were barred because they "could have been brought" in the Parma Court but were not. *Id.* at *28. The court found that the claims submitted by the bondholders to the Parma Court "arose out of different transactions" than the claims in the securities fraud action. *Id.* at *34.

The District Court found that *res judicata* did not apply to bar the fraud claims of the plaintiffs (who were also bondholders of Old Parmalat) because the proofs of claim they filed in the Parma Court differed sufficiently from the fraud claims asserted in the securities fraud action. The court explained:

LEGAL BULLETIN

The court concluded that the interests of comity and the just treatment of claim holders would be served by **allowing the claims to go forward** in the District Court.

"The proofs of claim that the [b]ondholders submitted in the Parma Court identified only the type, face value, interest rate, and guarantor of each note the [b]ondholders owned....Here, by contrast, the bondholders seek to recover damages allegedly caused by Old Parmalat's fraud — that is, the losses they suffered due to the decline in value of their securities as a result of the alleged fraud." *Id.* at *26.

Similarly, the court found that the fraud claims asserted by certain other (non-bondholder) plaintiffs in the securities fraud action were not precluded by *res judicata*. Even though they were excluded by the Parma Court, that ruling was part of a "summary, administrative proceeding" under Italian law that was not based on discovery and could "be reversed by a court following a full review of the evidence and legal argument." *Id.* at *35.

The District Court found that although it is "long...held that the pendency of an appeal ordinarily does not suspend the preclusive effect of an otherwise final judgment...there is an exception for situations in which the appeal actually involves a trial *de novo*." *Id.* at *37. The court added that even though it was not dismissing the claims, "[t]his may mean, of course, that [the plaintiffs] will end up [litigating their] claims simultaneously in this [c]ourt and in Italy." *Id.* at *38.

Finally, the court refused requests by the extraordinary administrator and New Parmalat to modify the Section 304 order to add protection for New Parmalat. It found that Grant Thornton's third-party complaint already had made New Parmalat a party before the New York court to litigate the issue of its relative fault in the fraud alleged in the securities fraud action, and:

> "[T]he Italian courts therefore would benefit from having New Parmalat's liability determined alongside that of other alleged perpetrators of the fraud, 'as opposed to being confronted...with the need...to relitigate the Securities Fraud Action in Italy for the purpose of determining... [New Parmalat's fault] under the complex and, to Italian courts, unfamiliar federal securities laws." *Id.* at *44-*45.

The court concluded that the interests of comity and the just treatment of claim holders would be served by allowing the claims to go forward in the District Court because the plaintiffs sought only to liquidate their claims in the New York Court but would seek to enforce their judgments in Italy. "It will be up to the Italian courts to decide whether a . . . judgment rendered [against New Parmalat] should be recognized at all, and if so, its consequences in the bankruptcy proceedings." *Id.* at *45.

The important lesson of *Parmalat* is to keep in mind that, even though a U.S. court may allow a creditor to litigate and liquidate its claims against a foreign debtor in the United States, that does not mean that the insolvency forum in the other country will actually recognize or honor that judgment against the debtor.

[1] Osanitsch apparently submitted a claim under the Scheme of Arrangement, which was rejected by the scheme supervisors on the basis of a release signed by Osanitsch when he left his job. See *id.* at *20 n. 15.

[2] The Italian Ministry of Productive Activities issued an emergency decree, later ratified by the Italian Parliament, called the Marzano Law, which amended and supplemented existing Italian bankruptcy law applicable to large companies with substantial debt, including granting new powers to the extraordinary administrator (akin to a U.S. bankruptcy trustee) to propose a plan for restructuring.

Johnathon C. Bolton is a senior associate in the Houston office of Fulbright & Jaworski L.L.P. His practice centers on U.S. and international bankruptcy and cross-border insolvency matters. He can be reached at (713) 651-5151 or jbolton@fulbright.com.

CHAPTER 5

Legal Issues of Consumers

The clichéd phrase that used to permeate our society was "buyer beware." But during the 1970s the phrase gradually changed to "seller beware." At the same time, the federal and state governments enacted significant legislation designed to protect the consumer from abusive and coercive credit and collection practices. In today's environment, the emphasis is on the protection of the privacy of the consumer (*see* Chapter 9). In either case, the creditor must be careful to review these laws before proceeding with the collection effort. In this chapter, we will attempt to provide information concerning consumer exemptions, remedies, and laws that may affect the collection effort.

EXEMPTIONS

The federal government and the state authorities, always sympathetic to the impoverished citizen, have slowly and deliberately passed laws to protect the essential property of every citizen. An "exemption" means that this essential property may not be taken from the consumer before a lawsuit, during a lawsuit, or after a judgment has been obtained against the consumer. The Fair Debt Collection Practices Act provides in Section 807, Subdivision 5, that:

> a debt collector may not use any false, deceptive or misleading representations or means in connection with the collection of any debt. Without

> limiting the general application of the foregoing, the following conduct is a violation of this debt . . . the threat to take any action that cannot legally be taken or that is not intended to be taken.

Thus, the creditor may not take or threaten to take property that is "exempt." The particular assets may be cash, personal property, real estate, or a stream of income from a particular source such as wages, dividends, or interest income.

> ***Credit & Collection Tip:*** *A frustrated telephone collector may easily violate this section of the act. Threats to take possession of jewelry, clothes, or farm animals are obvious violations. But a threat to attach alimony payments or social security, or suggesting to the consumer that the social security must be used to pay the debt suffices as a violation.*

Household furniture is an example of "exempt" property. A prohibited telephone conversation would be as follows:

DEBT COLLECTOR: Is Mrs. Smith there?

DEBTOR: This is Mrs. Smith.

DEBT COLLECTOR: This is the ABC Finance Company and I am calling about your loan. You haven't made any payments for the last three months. This is an attempt to collect a debt and any information obtained will be used for that purpose.

DEBTOR: What are you talking about? I'm not behind three months; I'm only behind one month.

DEBT COLLECTOR: Mrs. Smith, you are behind three months and it is going on four months. You were supposed to bring your loan up to date last time I spoke to you. You were three payments in arrears and you only made two payments at that time, so even then you were over a month behind and now in three days you are going to be three months behind.

DEBTOR: I'm out of work right now and there is just nothing I can do to make payment. You will have to do whatever you want to do.

DEBT COLLECTOR: Mrs. Smith, you wouldn't want us to take all your furniture and your bed and your chairs, would you? If you don't pay your bill, that's what may happen.

Since household furnishings are exempt, the debt collector has no right to threaten to remove them. If the property was not exempt, the debt collector would have to make a statement that suit would be started first.

The federal law sets forth a list of exemptions and each of the 50 states has its own specified list. If the exemption in a particular state is broader or larger than the federal exemption, the consumer will be able to take advantage of the state exemption.

Federal Exemptions. Under the federal laws, several exemptions are well-known and recognized in the credit field.

1. When garnishing a salary, the federal law (as well as most state laws) allows the creditor to attach only a small percent of the salary of the individual. The amount depends upon the state law.
2. Retirement income is exempt under the Employee Retirement Income Security Act (ERISA) 29 U.S.C. Section 1056(D).
3. Veterans benefits are exempt under 38 U.S.C. Section 30101(A).
4. Social security payments are exempt under 42 U.S.C. Section 407(A).
5. Civil Service Retirement Benefits are exempt under 5 U.S.C. Section 8346(A).
6. Railroad Retirement Act annuities and pensions are exempt under 45 U.S.C. Section 231, subdivision M(A).
7. Payments under the Longshoreman and Harbor Workers Compensation Act 33 U.S.C. Section 916 are exempt.

These exemptions are in addition to, and are to be distinguished from, the exemptions under the federal bankruptcy law, which are applicable only in a bankruptcy filing.

State Exemptions. Under the various state laws, a broad range of income and assets is exempt from execution. Examples of the types of exemptions are:

A. Alimony and support payments.
B. Appliances.
C. Cemetery plots.
D. Community property.
E. Homestead exemption. This is an exemption for the home occupied by the consumer. Each state protects the home of the resident in varying degrees, usually measured in dollars ranging from $5,000 to $10,000 in such states as New York or up to $1 million in Florida. In a foreclosure or bankruptcy, the amount set by the state is exempt, and may not be reached by the creditor conducting the sale. If real

property (the principal residence) is sold at foreclosure and money is realized in excess of the amount of the mortgages, that money must be paid over to the owner of the property in an amount equal to the state or federal exemption. (*See* this chapter for new federal exemptions which in some circumstance preempts state law.)

F. Disability benefits.

G. Farm animals and feed.

H. Financial aid to students.

I. Household furnishings.

J. Insurance proceeds.

K. Jewelry.

L. Livestock.

M. Pension plans—in most states.

N. Personal effects—in most states a provision allows for an exemption for personal effects.

O. Public employee retirement benefits, vacation credits, or other benefits.

P. Rental security deposits.

Q. Welfare benefits.

R. Unemployment benefits and contributions.

S. Wearing apparel.

T. Workman's compensation.

U. Wrongful death damages.

The list is far from inclusive, but the general area of exemptions is obvious. The lawmakers are primarily interested in protecting the debtor's household furniture and personal effects, and the stream of income from pension, retirement, and other payments which are necessary for the maintenance of the consumer.[1]

> ***Credit & Collection Tip:*** *IRA and Keogh plans are not exempt under the federal law or under many state laws where they can be attached, but this is changing in many states.*

Whether an exemption under the federal law will be recognized by the state has led to court decisions interpreting the preemption motivation of Congress. In some instances, the states have held that the federal

[1]California Exemptions Section Code of Civil Procedure, Section 703.010 et seq.; Illinois Code of Civil Procedure, Section 735 ILCS 5/12-1001 et seq.; New York exemptions of certain insurance and annuity contracts, Insurance Law Section 3212, New York C.P.L.R. Section 5205 et seq.

exemption does not preempt the laws of the state, whereas in most instances the federal law explicitly preempts the state law.[2]

Some of the district courts look upon the Fair Debt Collection Practices Act as a strict liability statute. Under these circumstances, debt collectors may be acting at their own peril in any effort to persuade debtors to utilize exempt income or exempt property. A sample conversation might go as follows:

DEBT COLLECTOR: This mortgage is almost six months in arrears.

DEBTOR: I've been out of work for the last six months and I have been unable to make the payments. As a matter of fact, my wife and I had to go on welfare.

DEBT COLLECTOR: How much do you receive each month from welfare?

DEBTOR: We get food stamps and we receive $125 a week.

DEBT COLLECTOR: So, basically, you are getting $125 a week.

DEBTOR: Yeah, but I need the money for my wife and children and there's just no money to make the payments on this loan.

DEBT COLLECTOR: Maybe you can squeeze out a $25 payment to us once a month in order to keep this loan open, so I don't have to take any action under the judgment I have.

DEBTOR: You mean to tell me you can take my welfare benefits away?

DEBT COLLECTOR: I didn't say that exactly. I just want you to make a $25 payment.

DEBTOR: In the last letter you sent to me, you said you can levy on all my assets. Does that mean that the sheriff can take my welfare benefits to pay the debt?

DEBT COLLECTOR: I didn't say that exactly.

DEBTOR: You did say it in the letter. Isn't it a fact that you can't take my welfare benefits?

The use of a letter threatening a levy on the assets of a consumer may create an embarrassing situation. Sometimes collection letters are written with broad strokes and tend to include general terms referring to property and income. The letter must not mislead the consumer into believing that any exempt income or property can be subject to execution under the judgment.

Credit & Collection Tip: *The sophisticated consumer is fully aware of how inexpensive it is to purchase the equipment to record a telephone conversation.*

---

[2]*Lanier Collection Agency & Service v. Mackey*, 256 Ga. 499, 350 S.E.2d 439 (Ga. 1986).

Homestead Exemption. In one case, the husband and wife used two residences as their homestead. The bank claimed that there was only one homestead available, but the court held that the correct test for a homestead is whether a debtor uses a residence as a home.

The case leads one to the impression that the court was really stretching to provide two homesteads for the husband and wife, notwithstanding the state statute, which seemed to restrict holding two homesteads.

In Massachusetts, the consumer debtor alleged that he was entitled to claim both his $300,000 exemption as a disabled person pursuant to Massachusetts General Laws Annotated CH.188 Section 1a and the $300,000 exemption of his non-debtor spouse under Section B. The $600,000 exemption would avoid entirely the lien on the property.

The court noted that the statute stated that the exemption may be acquired by an owner or owner of the homes or one or all who rightfully possess the premises and who occupy the home as a principal residence. While acknowledging that Massachusetts laws have construed the state homestead exemptions liberally in favor of debtors, the wording of the statute unequivocally allows one exemption. When the wife exercised her exemption, it was the only exemption available for the benefit of the family. The court felt that reaching any other conclusion would effectively produce an unreasonable result.[3]

Real Property Lien. With regard to real property liens, Florida has unlimited exemptions if it is the primary residence of the debtor (*see* below). Kansas and Texas also have unlimited exemptions, with Texas having some significant exemptions. These exemptions do not apply if it is the debtor's secondary residence. Other states have exemptions which are measured in dollars and a review of the state law is necessary.

Florida Exemptions. Some creditors are intimidated by the exemption laws in Florida, Texas, and one or two other states. When a debtor moves to one of those states, the creditor may abandon any attempt to collect a debt and refuse to spend money to collect the debt because of the exemption laws.

In Florida, the exemption laws date back to 1868, when the state constitution was enacted and the homestead was originally restricted to the heads of household. Considerable litigation revolved around the question of whether or not a particular debtor qualified as head of the household. In 1985, the exemption was amended to apply to any person keeping a household of half an acre within a municipality or 160 acres outside a municipality. Thus, any person who owns a home of any value on 160 acres of land outside a municipality would be entitled to the exemption

[3]*Garran v. SMS Financial v. LLC*, 338 F.3d 1 (1st Cir. 2003); *Beal Bank v. Siems*, 2003 WL 22299351 (Iowa 2003).

even if the home is valued at over $1 million. If the husband and wife maintain separate residences, both parties may enjoy a homestead exemption under Florida law. Wages of a Florida resident are also exempt, as are bank accounts, but if both husband and wife work and live in the same household, the wages of only one spouse are exempt.

Florida has thus become a magnet for people seeking to avoid paying their debts, but sometimes they find that the homestead exemption is not available. The Florida courts insist that the party's legal residence be in Florida to take advantage of the exemption, and they require some form of corroboration of the intent of the party. Merely stating what your intent is without substantiation is not sufficient.

The Florida courts will consider where the party is employed, where he or she is registered to vote, the address on the driver's license and the address on the federal income tax return. People who visit Florida are not necessarily entitled to the benefits of the exemption. The debtor must intend to use Florida as a residence and must be present in Florida on a continuing basis. The fact that the debtor is present in the state for a period of time without any intention of remaining is usually insufficient. The debtor must offer some evidence of the intention to reside in Florida, at least in the foreseeable future.[4]

The above analysis applies to a greater or lesser degree to the other states which are favorable to debtors, such as Texas, North Carolina, South Carolina, and Pennsylvania, in which creditors are prohibited from garnishing salaries of debtors.

If the amount is substantial, the creditor should not abandon pursuing a debtor in a "debtor's state," but should determine whether the debtor still maintains personal and business ties within the original state. If that is the fact, counsel may be able to pursue the debtor in both states.

> ***Credit & Collection Tip:*** *In recent years, our experience has found that recording judgment liens from other states under full faith and credit is worthwhile, especially in Florida. With interest rates low, and parties refinancing, our firm has seen many loans paid so that the debtor could refinance the mortgage at a lower rate. It may be worthwhile to consider this procedure depending on the debtor's financial position.*

While the courts in Florida have always upheld the homestead exemption, they have also said that the homestead exemption should not be liberally construed to make it an instrument of fraud or an imposition upon creditors. On the other hand, in 1992, the state sought a civil forfeiture of the defendant's residence following a conviction on one count of racketeering in violation of the Florida Racketeer Influenced and Corrupt Organization

---

[4]*In re Cooke*, 412 So. 2d 340 (Fla. 1982) (tourist or temporary residence not entitled to exemption); *Judd v. Schooley*, 158 So. 2d 514 (Fla. 1963) (separate residence); *Bloomfield v. City of St. Petersburg Beach*, 82 So. 2d 364 (Fla. 1955) (intention).

Act and 15 counts of bookmaking.[5] The state said that the homestead was used in the course of racketeering. The court prohibited the forfeiture of the homestead.

CREDIT PRACTICES ACT

The Credit Practices Act was enacted by the Federal Trade Commission to prohibit creditors from using certain contract provisions that the Commission found to be unfair to consumers. In addition, the Act requires creditors to inform consumers who co-sign obligations about their liability if the borrower fails to pay the obligation. Finally, the rule sets certain restrictions on assessing late charges.

The Credit Practices Act prohibits creditors from including the following provisions in any consumer credit contract.

Confession of Judgment. Confessions of judgment, or "cognovit" notes, are agreements wherein the debtor is obligated to make payment. These notes authorize the creditor to appear in court and confess judgment on behalf of the debtor in the event the payment schedule is breached or the agreed payment is not made when due. A confession of judgment allows a judgment to be entered in favor of the creditor automatically when the debtor is in breach of the contract. "Automatically" means that the creditor does not usually have to appear in court and in some states is allowed to submit an affidavit in lieu of that appearance. Based upon this affidavit by the attorney that the debtor has not made payments as agreed in the confession of judgment, the clerk of the court will enter the judgment without any further court proceedings (such as allowing the debtor to appear and contest the entry of judgment). The Credit Practices Act prohibits creditors from using a confession of judgment provision in a consumer credit contract. (This is still permitted in commercial transactions.)

Waiver of Exemption. Some consumer credit contracts previously contained a waiver of exemption provision which permitted creditors to seize specific property even if the property was exempt under state law. Such provisions are expressly prohibited.

Assignment of Wages. In some states, consumers were permitted to assign their wages, or a part of their wages, to creditors in the event of a default under an obligation, such as a loan or a purchase of goods on time. The problem with this device is that the debtor lost a portion of the salary without notice and without being able to assert any defense. Over the past 20 years, most states have prohibited this practice by passing specific laws.

---

[5]*Butter Worth v. Caggione*, 605 So. 2d 56 (Fla. 1992).

Under the rule, such an assignment of wages is expressly prohibited. The only way a creditor is entitled to a portion of a consumer's salary is to institute a suit, obtain a judgment, and issue a garnishment to the sheriff.

Security Agreement—Household Goods. The rule provides that a creditor is prohibited from obtaining a security agreement on household goods whether or not the household goods are exempt under state law. Certain personal property such as works of art, electronic entertainment equipment, and other items acquired such as antiques and jewelry (except wedding rings) as well as pianos, musical instruments, boats, snowmobiles, bicycles, cameras, and similar items may be offered to creditors as security under a security agreement to secure the loan.

Co-Signer. The rule requires a co-signer of a loan to be specifically informed of the potential liability before signing the obligation of the debt. A specific written statement must be included in the loan document in which the liability of the co-signer is specifically described. The law sets forth the wording of the document and informs the co-signer that the debt must be paid directly to the creditor if the borrower does not pay, and that the creditor may proceed against the co-signer without proceeding against the borrower. The co-signer must also be informed that if the debt should be in default, the default and loan will become a part of the credit record of the co-signer. The state may provide for a different notice, which must be included in addition to the notice under the Credit Practices Act. The law also requires that the notice be in the same language as the agreement to which it applies so that if the agreement is in Spanish, the notice must be in Spanish.

A co-signer is different from a co-buyer, co-borrower, or co-applicant, because a co-signer receives no tangible benefits from the agreement, but usually undertakes the liability as a favor to the principal debtor who would not otherwise qualify for credit. On the other hand, co-buyers, co-borrowers, or co-applicants do receive certain benefits. They are not considered co-signers under the rule and are not entitled to the required notice.

Late Fees. "Pyramiding of late charges" occurs when one payment is made after its due date and a late fee is assessed, but not paid promptly. All future payments are considered delinquent even though they are paid in full within the required time period. As a result, late fees are assessed on all future payments. This particular practice is now prohibited.

GARNISHMENT AND HOMESTEAD EXEMPTION

The Consumer Credit Protection Act limits the maximum amount that can be garnished to 30 times the minimum wage. The great majority of states have an exemption of either 30 or 40 times the federal minimum wage, and most states also permit 75 percent of net weekly take-home pay as an exemption, whichever amount is greater. Florida, North Carolina, Pennsylvania, and Texas completely exempt the wages of the heads of household from any form of garnishment, although North Carolina and Pennsylvania legislatures are reviewing these exemptions. Some of the other states have fairly liberal exemption laws such as:

A. Connecticut—75 percent of the weekly wages (but only one debtor can be garnished at a time).
B. Missouri—90 percent for the head of a family.
C. Illinois—85 percent of weekly disposable earnings or an amount by which such earnings exceed 40 times the minimum wage.

Some states allow only a minimum percentage of the salary to be garnished, such as 15 percent in Illinois, and only 10 percent in Missouri and New York.

Florida has a $500-a-week exemption for heads of household, but not for their spouses. Alaska has an exemption of 65 times the state minimum wage for heads of household. South Dakota has an exemption of 80 percent or 40 times the minimum wage plus $25 for each dependent. The garnishee in Wisconsin is also 80 percent exempt.

With regard to homestead exemptions for the household residence of the debtor and family, only Connecticut, Delaware, Maryland, New Jersey, Pennsylvania, and the District of Columbia do not provide for some sort of exemption. The most favorable state is Florida, which allows an exemption up to 160 acres and no minimum dollar amount. A debtor could purchase a residence for a million dollars and every dollar of it would be exempt. Massachusetts allows for $300,000 for a principal family residence, but the exemption is not available for debts arising after the purchase of the homestead or for support payments for spouses or children. Arizona is also liberal in allowing $100,000 as an exemption on a personal residence. Many of the states make distinctions between heads of households as opposed to individuals and do not exempt the personal residence where the debts involve child support or alimony. (Subject to new law—*see* this chapter.)

Homestead exemptions can be lost in the event the debtor is operating a business on the property or the debtor continually rents out the property and does not occupy it. If the debtor conveyed the residence to a corporation, he would lose the exemption even though the debtor owned all the stock in the corporation. This is sometimes done to avoid usury laws.[6]

Credit & Collection Tip: *These exemptions are to be distinguished from exemptions under the Federal Bankruptcy Law, which is only applicable in the event of a bankruptcy filing.*

---

[6]*In re Perry*, 345 F.3d 303 (5th Cir. 2003).

Direct Deposit and Garnishment. While some states prohibit wage garnishing, they do not prohibit execution on a debtor's bank account. What happens when a debtor has a direct deposit account? This situation enables a creditor to obtain an entire paycheck or even two payments before the debtor can notify his employer. In some states, it is not considered wage garnishment and you can take all non-exempt monies in the account. In other states, the courts consider it a wage garnishment and the creditor is only entitled to a percentage of the wage check proportioned to the statutory scheme. (The hold must be reduced to that balance or it could constitute a violation of the exemption.)

Welfare Recipients. Welfare income is exempt from attachment, and therefore cannot be attached even if the welfare check is deposited in a bank account. If the creditor attaches the bank account, the consumer may assert that the monies attached are the proceeds from a welfare check and, the court would order the creditor to release the account.

Welfare recipients can be sued for a just debt and a judgment can be obtained against them. A welfare recipient is still liable for the debt notwithstanding that he or she is receiving welfare payments. When the recipient returns to the workforce, welfare payments cease and the wages can be garnished. If the debtor owns a car, a boat, or other assets from more prosperous times, they may be attached providing no exemption exists under federal or state law.

Social Security. As with welfare, social security is also exempt under state law. Social security recipients are not prohibited from receiving a certain limited amount of income which can be from a job, from consulting, or from doing part-time work as an independent contractor. While social security may be exempt from execution, the other stream of income or other assets acquired when the consumer worked may be subject to levy or execution, depending upon the nature of the income and assets. A telephone conversation with the debtor may proceed as follows:

Creditor: Your credit card account is past due almost five months and we must have some form of payment arrangement.

Debtor: I just retired and right now I'm on social security so you can do what you want.

Creditor: How much social security do you receive a month?

Debtor: My social security is about $1,500 a month.

Creditor: Do you earn or receive any other income outside of your social security?

DEBTOR: I told you I receive social security and what I do otherwise is none of your business.

CREDITOR: You didn't answer the question as to whether you receive any additional income. Do you hold a part-time job?

The debtor may be earning or receiving other income (such as holding a part-time job). Social security is intended to replace earnings lost because of the retirement of the wage earner. Any income received from savings, investments, or insurance, which may be substantial, will not affect the monthly benefits. However, certain social security recipients work. Once the debtor reaches the age of 62, he or she may earn any amount and still collect social security. Social security is an indication of age, but not necessarily ability to pay.

Credit & Collection Tip: *When the party acknowledges receiving social security, this should be the beginning, not the end, of the telephone conversation. The creditor should then inquire as to what the personal assets are and whether the debtor has any other income.*

FEDERAL GARNISHMENT. Under the federal garnishment law, the wages of federal employees or members of the military may be garnished. A judgment must be obtained in the state and county in which the debtor works and service must be made on the payroll office in the location where the debtor works. If the debtor resides in one state and works in a second state, suit must first be instituted in the state in which the debtor resides. Notwithstanding the federal garnishment, Pennsylvania, Texas, Florida (head of household), South Carolina, and North Carolina still prohibit garnishment.

Another important part of the law is that federal garnishments are available for any judgments which have been entered in the past, prior to the enactment of the law. Therefore, if you do have old judgments against federal government employees, you should reactivate them and utilize this law.

The law permits the creditor to deduct up to 25 percent of the debtor's wages unless state law provides for a lesser amount, which is the case in many states. The creditor must only provide a copy of judgment, and the amount of interest set forth in the judgment can be collected. (In the initial rules, suit had to be instituted separately for the interest.) If the commander determines that the debtor's absence was due to exigencies of military duty, the rule provides a right of appeal.

A garnishment may be denied because of a prior garnishment which is using the maximum deductions. The state laws provide that the garnishments line up. As soon as one is paid, the next in line begins to operate.

RESPONSIBILITY OF PARENTS

The position of most states is that necessities for children are the responsibility of the parents. Unless the parents are divorced, separated, or living apart, both parents are jointly liable for the debts of the children, and each parent is liable individually for the debts of the children.

> ***Credit & Collection Tip:*** *Submit to the parent an agreement acknowledging liability. Several gray areas exist in which a product or service may or may not be a necessity.*

The parent who has custody of the child is normally liable for the necessities of that child which consist of food, lodging, medical, educational, and clothing needs. Necessities do not include luxury items and probably not educational items purchased by the child which are partly educational and partly for amusement, such as videocassettes, which are marginally educational.

Clothing, shoes, medical supplies, doctor's bills, prescriptions, school supplies, and similar items would fall under the classification of "necessities." Bicycles, athletic equipment, records, audio CDs, videotapes, audiotapes, toys, video games, and other items for entertainment or amusement would not.

A child may disaffirm a contract entered into while he or she was under the age of 18. Sometimes the merchandise is designed for children under the age of 18, and the order form bears only the child's signature. In these instances, the creditor cannot proceed against the child or parent, but may only request that the parents pay the debt. Any letters or communications must be addressed to the parents of the child and should clearly and conspicuously state that parents have no obligation to pay the child's debt. Most reputable law firms and collection agencies include this wording in their collection letters and in their telephone calls:

DEBT COLLECTOR: May I speak to the parents of Robert Arnold Smith?

MOTHER: Yes, this is his mother.

DEBT COLLECTOR: We sent Robert a set of videotapes on dinosaurs and reptiles, and we have not received payment for those tapes.

MOTHER: He did order them, but we didn't even know about him ordering them. He should know better than to order that kind of material.

DEBT COLLECTOR: He did receive the tapes and I assume that he used them.

MOTHER: He looked at them once and one of the tapes got broken. I don't even know where they are anymore. I don't think I have any obligation to pay for the tapes. You should not have accepted an order from a child.

DEBT COLLECTOR: But the child did accept the tapes and he did use the tapes and therefore he is responsible to pay for the tapes.

MOTHER: I'm sorry. He may have used the tapes. I don't know whether he is responsible for payment. I don't even know if he understands at the age of twelve years old that he has to pay. If you speak to my husband, he'll tell you that none of the children knows the value of a dollar.

DEBT COLLECTOR: I don't know whether your son knows the value of a dollar, but the tapes were sent and the price was $49.95 and we must insist upon payment.

MOTHER: Well, you can insist upon payment, but I don't think that I have any obligation to pay for this debt.

The debt collector avoided communicating to the consumer that she actually had no obligation to pay the debt, but inferred that the child did. Both of these failures would probably constitute a violation of the Fair Debt Collection Practices Act. The debt collector has misrepresented to the debtor that both mother and child may be obligated for this debt. The child has an absolute right to disaffirm the contract and the parent is not responsible for the child's debt except to the extent of food, lodging, and necessities. A tape on the lifestyle of dinosaurs and reptiles does not fall under the heading of necessities, and whether it is educational may be debatable. On the other hand, if the parent made the purchase and signed the document or personally ordered the merchandise, the parent would be liable. The problem arises only when the child makes the purchase.

A review of the state law is necessary.

HUSBANDS AND WIVES—NECESSITIES. Under common law, a married woman's legal identity merged with that of her husband, a condition known as coverture. The wife was unable to own any property, she could not enter into contracts, nor did anyone extend credit to her. A married woman was dependent upon her husband for maintenance and support and, as a result, he was under a duty to provide his wife with food, clothing, and shelter, as well as medical services. The doctrine of necessities mitigated the possible effects of coverture in the event the husband failed to fulfill his support obligation. Therefore, her husband was liable to any third party for any necessities that the third party creditor provided to the wife. Because the duty of this support was unique to the husband's obligation, and because coverture restricted the wife's access to the economic realm of credit, the doctrine normally did not impose a similar liability upon married women.

The wife's "necessities" are more limited in scope than are those of a child. The wife's necessities certainly include food, clothing, lodging, and medical expenses and probably exclude education, entertainment, amusement, and athletics. If the husband makes the purchase for the wife, the husband is liable whether or not it is a necessity. On the other hand, if the wife makes the purchase, the husband is liable only for a necessity.

While the general law is that the husband is liable for the necessities of the wife, the law in the various states is a mixture and is changing on a day-to-day basis.

A case in Florida held that the husband was no longer liable for the wife's necessities. The court acknowledged the fact that the disability of coverture was basically abrogated and that the responsibilities between husband and wife in many instances are now reciprocal obligations.[7] The courts in other states have split on this question of necessities, which is treated differently both from a statutory viewpoint and as to the way the courts evaluate the obligation.[8]

The court pointed out that some states have abrogated the doctrine entirely, leaving to the legislature the final decision, such as in Alabama, Maryland, and Virginia. Other states have extended the common-law doctrine to apply reciprocally, so that the husband is liable for the wife's necessities and the wife is liable for the husband's necessities, such as in Indiana, Kansas, New Jersey, North Carolina, Rhode Island, and South Carolina. Two states, Oklahoma and Kentucky, have codified the doctrine in its original common-law form requiring the husband to be liable for the wife, but the wife is not liable for the husband. Minnesota recently altered the common-law "doctrine of necessities" and limited the ability of creditors and collectors to hold a spouse liable for the debts of the other spouse.

If the spouses are living together, they are jointly and severally liable for necessary household articles and supplies furnished to and used by the family. Either spouse is allowed to close a credit card account for the other's unsecured consumer line of credit on which both spouses are liable if they give a written notice to the creditor. North Dakota imposes joint and several liability for debts incurred by either spouse for the necessities of food, clothing, fuel and shelter, but expressly excludes medical care. A review of the state law is essential before proceeding against either a husband or wife based on the theory of necessities; the law on this subject is changing radically state by state, year to year.

---

[7] *Connor v. Southwest Florida Regional Medical Center, Inc.*, 668 So. 2d 175 (Fla. 1995).

[8] *Connor*, 668 So. 2d 175 (Fla. 1995).

The wife may not be liable even if she executes an instrument as a guarantor or co-signer for the husband's obligations under circumstances when the bank is not relying on her financial condition to extend the credit to the husband (*see* Chapter 18). A decision in 1998 held that a retail installment contract which contained an arbitration clause was enforceable even if only the husband signed it and the wife did not sign it.[9]

Jointly Held Property. When a young couple purchases their first home, the title is normally transferred to both the husband and the wife. Usually the designation on the deed is "joint tenants with right of survivorship" or words of similar import. The legal effect of such a transfer of title to a husband and wife is that if one of the spouses dies, the surviving spouse acquires title to the property free and clear of any claims or judgments against the deceased spouse.

The net effect of joint ownership is that most creditors do not execute on a judgment against jointly owned property. In the event a creditor obtains a judgment against the husband, the recourse of the creditor is to sell the husband's interest at a sheriff's sale and use the proceeds to satisfy the judgment. The creditor—wearing a different robe—becomes a buyer at the sale, and thus becomes the owner of the husband's interest. Whatever was paid at the sale is used to pay the judgment, similar to moving money from one pocket to the other pocket: the creditor bids $1,000 at the sale; the sheriff deducts the fees for the sale and remits $900 to the creditor to pay the judgment.

The creditor now is a joint owner with the wife. The creditor cannot evict either the husband or wife, but must wait to see which spouse survives. If the husband dies first, the creditor has no claim against the wife and the wife becomes the owner of the property free of any claims of the creditor. However, if the wife dies first, the creditor becomes the owner of the property.

The better course for the creditor is to have the judgment recorded as a lien against the real estate and hope that a time will come when the husband and wife will sell their home. The lien will remain on record for many years, depending upon state law. At the time of the sale, any purchaser of the property will require the husband and wife to discharge the debt, since the purchaser does not want to own the property with a lien in favor of a judgment creditor.

The same rules apply to personal property owned jointly between a husband and wife, such as a joint checking account or joint ownership of a

---

[9] *Nationwide of Bryan Inc. d/b/a Nationwide Housing Systems Inc. v. Daryll D. Dyer & Sherry Dyer*, 968 S.W.2d 518 (S.W. App. 1998).

boat. In each of these instances, the disadvantaged judgment creditor must wait to determine who the survivor is.

> ***Credit & Collection Tip:*** *The creditor receives a telephone call from the judgment debtor who has not been heard from for several years. The judgment debtor will probably offer a settlement of substantially less than the face amount of the judgment. In most instances, when a judgment debtor makes a telephone call to the creditor after many years, the judgment debtor probably owns real estate and is attempting to sell the property, but the purchaser wants the debtor to discharge the judgment lien. In many instances, the judgment creditor may not have known that the debtor owned real estate, but the attorney took the precaution of filing the judgment as a lien against real property. Consider this before you settle.*

Sometimes property is owned by a husband and wife as "tenants in common." Property may be held in this way by any two persons who do not have to be husband and wife. The distinction between "tenants in common" and "joint tenants with the right of survivorship" is that tenants in common own a separate undivided one-half of the property. The undivided one-half would be subject to execution by the creditor. The creditor who obtains a judgment may hold a sheriff's sale and cause the one-half interest in the property to be sold at public sale. In the event there is no purchaser at the sale, the judgment creditor could purchase the interest and thus become the one-half owner with the other tenant in common. The distinct advantage is that the creditor may then either seek to partition the property or apply to court for an order directing the entire property to be sold, and the creditor/owner would be entitled to one-half of the sale price less expenses.

Tenancy by the entirety is unique to married couples. Each tenant of the tenancy by the entirety owns all of the property and thus the surviving tenant by the entirety does not acquire the tenant's interest in real property because he/she already owned the entirety. The interest of the party who is deceased merely disappears from the record and with it all liens and claims against the interest of the deceased party in the property.

A joint tenancy is somewhere in between a tenancy in common and tenancy by the entirety. A joint tenancy is composed of two persons not married. The joint tenant owns all of the property but at the same time may convey or sell the interest in the property or leave the property by last will. Title will vest in the surviving tenant at the moment of the decease of the other tenant, free of any liens or claims against the deceased tenant.

Joint tenancies and tenancies by the entirety can be attacked when a real property conveyance is made with no consideration by one of the joint tenants to the tenants by the entirety or the joint tenants. If the debtor has been rendered insolvent, in many of the states a creditor can proceed to set aside the conveyance as fraudulent with respect to the creditors. The timing of the transfer by the debtor to the debtor and his wife is most important.

The transfer must take place after the loan was granted and usually after the loan is in default. If a transfer is made while payments are current, the additional burden of proving that the debtor was insolvent at the time will have to be overcome.

COMMUNITY PROPERTY. There are eight states which still enforce community property laws: Arizona, California, Idaho, Louisiana, Nevada, New Mexico, Texas, and Washington. The law of community property allocates any property acquired after the marriage to each party on a 50-50 basis. Marriage is similar to a partnership and any property acquired after the marriage should be equally divided between the husband and wife. The heir of the husband and wife will receive the share that the husband and wife are entitled to from the property acquired after marriage.

If properties were acquired before the marriage, and were owned separately by the wife, the creditor may treat them as belonging to the wife and said properties may be used as collateral for a loan without the other spouse's signature or consent. When the wife and husband conduct a business, in some states the income and profits from that business will belong to the individual who is conducting the business, whereas in other states it may become part of the community property.

The laws of the community property states are different in many respects with regard to creditors. For example, in some states community property may be subject to execution even if the debt was incurred solely by one spouse. In other states, the result is almost the opposite. In some states, the husband may incur the debt for the total community property and in other states only the husband and wife jointly may incur debt for the community property. In some states, clear distinctions are drawn if the indebtedness is secured by the residence. A careful review of the laws of the community property states must be made before extending credit or using collection efforts against the community property.

DIVORCE. Parties engaged in obtaining a divorce frequently stop paying their debts until the divorce proceedings are finalized either by written agreement or court order. If the only wage earner is the husband, the wife must look to him for payment of debts and the husband may deliberately withhold payment as a negotiating tool. Lawyers tend to thrive on these situations, and creditors are then faced with the unusual situation where money is available, but debts are not paid.

A hypothetical telephone conversation:

CREDITOR: We have sent you several notices and we still have not received any payment.

DEBTOR: I'm divorcing my husband and he is going to pay all my debts.

CREDITOR: When will he start making the payments?

DEBTOR: I don't know exactly when. My attorneys are fighting with his attorneys and we're still arguing over the house and the BMW and the dog and tickets to the U.S. Open, but I think we should have everything settled pretty quickly.

CREDITOR: What do you mean pretty quickly?

DEBTOR: I really don't know. Pretty quickly. As soon as it's settled, my husband said that he will continue to pay the balance on my credit card. If you want, I can give you my husband's name and the address at which he is now living, but it's a hotel and I think he will be checking out shortly.

The first important consideration is that the debt is based on the wife's credit card and therefore the wife is primarily liable. While the husband may also be liable, the wife is primarily liable for payment since she obligated herself to pay the debt and is over the age of 18. The creditor's approach is that the wife is liable for the debt, and suit may be instituted against her. The creditor has no interest in the negotiations between the husband and the wife, and is not bound by them, even though circumstances exist under which the husband may be liable for payment of the debt by reason of a necessity furnished to the wife.

After the couple separates, the husband is usually not responsible for the debts incurred by the wife for luxury items and, in some instances under state laws, for necessities. A review of the state laws is absolutely necessary.

Sometimes a husband will publish advertisements to notify creditors not to extend further credit to his wife. In some states, such a notice can relieve the husband of future liability.

> ***Credit & Collection Tip:*** *Divorce negotiations can drag on indefinitely and wives are often overly optimistic about the obligations to be undertaken by their husbands to pay off their debts. Where the wife is primarily or jointly liable, the creditor should rely on the wife's ability to repay the debt, and proceed quickly to obtain a judgment, as other creditors are doing the same thing. A judgment creditor is in a better bargaining position since the debt cannot be disputed. Many joint debts are paid pursuant to divorce agreements.*

DECEASED PERSONS. The first notification that the debtor has died usually happens during a collection telephone call to the debtor's number. The response is frequently that since the relative has passed away, the family does not want to be bothered by any collection calls. The fact that a party died does not render the debt uncollectible, although some difficulties are present.

A major problem is property owned jointly between the husband and the wife. If a husband and a wife jointly own a private home, the property will pass to the surviving spouse automatically and the deceased party will have no further interest. A creditor cannot proceed against the house owned by the surviving spouse for any debt of the deceased spouse. The same rule applies to bank accounts which are held jointly between a husband and wife. Upon presentation of a death certificate to the bank, the money is transferred into the surviving spouse's name and the creditor will be unable to attach or levy on the account.

Where the property is held in the individual name of the debtor (which is most cases), papers must be filed with the proper Surrogate Court (probate court) to commence a "probate" proceeding to distribute the property to beneficiaries. A "probate" is a proceeding where the administrator (appointed by the court where no will was executed) or executor (named by the deceased in the will) of the estate collects all the assets of the deceased, pays all the debts, deducts the expenses of administration and distributes the balance to the beneficiaries under the will, or if there is no will, according to the state law. Creditors are allowed to assert in the probate proceedings their claims for any debts owed to the creditor by the deceased party. The normal method is to inquire whether a probate proceeding (estate) has been filed. The information needed is the name of the court in which the estate has been filed and the index number of the filing. The names and addresses of the executor or administrator of the estate and the attorney for the executor or administrator are helpful.

A typical conversation follows:

CREDITOR: May I please speak to Mrs. Smith?

DEBTOR: Mrs. Smith just passed away two days ago.

CREDITOR: To whom am I speaking?

DEBTOR: This is her daughter.

CREDITOR: I'm sorry to hear that. I will call in a few weeks.

DEBTOR: Thank you very much. Goodbye.

At this particular time it would be futile to try to determine whether the decedent has property and whether the beneficiaries are filing an estate. The procedures to probate a will (file an estate) are usually delayed for several weeks to months after the date of death. The follow-up conversation:

CREDITOR: This is Mr. Grant from the XYZ department store and I'm calling about the open charge account bill of Mrs. Ann Smith.

DEBTOR: Mrs. Smith died.

CREDITOR: When did she die?

DEBTOR: She died about two months ago.

CREDITOR: Has someone retained an attorney to handle her affairs?

DEBTOR: Yes, we've retained an attorney. What's this about?

CREDITOR: This is about a debt owed to the XYZ department store. She had a charge account here and there's a balance of $550 still open. We'd like to know the name of the attorney handling the estate.

DEBTOR: The attorney is John Mitchell at 14 Main Street, Centerville. Telephone number 555-1212.

CREDITOR: Tell me, have probate papers been filed?

DEBTOR: Yes, we did sign some papers to file them in court.

CREDITOR: Could you tell me what court that is?

DEBTOR: Probate court of the County of Centerville.

CREDITOR: Do you know the index number?

DEBTOR: No, the attorney would probably know that.

CREDITOR: Who's the executor of the estate?

DEBTOR: My sister and I.

CREDITOR: What's your name and address?

DEBTOR: I told you that my name is Frank Smith and my sister is Marilyn Smith. Speak to our attorney.

CREDITOR: Thank you very much. I will get in touch with your attorney.

At this stage of the proceedings, obtain from the attorney the proper index number and name of the estate under which the papers have been filed so that a proof of claim can be filed. A proof of claim may be furnished by the attorney for the executor for the estate or may be obtained from a stationery store or from the court itself. Consult with counsel to file the proper papers.

If efforts to contact survivors prove futile, your attorney may search the record of the Surrogate Court where the debtor died to determine if the debtor has filed an estate.

Probate proceedings are only necessary where property is in the name of the deceased and must be transferred to a beneficiary. In many cases the assets of the deceased were transferred prior to death, and thus the deceased has no assets at the time of death. In other cases the only assets are jointly owned with a spouse or relative, such as the house or bank account, and in such case the property is transferred to the survivor without a probate proceeding. If no probate proceeding is filed with the court, and the creditor suspects the debtor had assets at his death or knows of assets of the deceased, consult with counsel for remedies are available.

If assets of the deceased were transferred or delivered to an heir without probate and were not jointly held with right of survivorship (stamp or coin collections, paintings, tools, and equipment), the creditor should consult counsel to file a probate of the estate to recover these items which may be sold to pay debts. The laws vary from state to state.

Before filing a proof of claim, a review of the state law on the contents of the proof of claim, the procedure, and the time limitation to file should be conducted. All of these requirements vary from state to state. In some states, a proof of claim must be filed in four months or less. Failure to file timely forfeits all rights against the estate.

UNIFORM PROBATE CODE

Most claims against deceased parties survive the death of the deceased party and a suit normally may be instituted against the executor or the administrator of the estate. One of the primary functions of the executor/administrator is to pay any debts of the estate. If the assets are insufficient to pay the claim, the Uniform Probate Code, which has been adopted in many states with some variations, provides for priority setting forth the order in which the debts should be paid:

1. Funeral expenses
2. Debts and taxes deferred under federal law
3. Medical expenses of the deceased's last illness
4. Claims deferred under other state laws
5. Other claims

At one time, administrators or executors were empowered to prefer one creditor over another creditor within each class, but under the present Uniform Probate Code, each member of each class must receive an equal prorata share.

The Uniform Probate Code typically bars all claims unless presented within four months after the date of first publication of the notice to creditors. The Code provides that the administrator or executor must publish notice of debt in certain publications and notices of claims of debt owing to a creditor must be presented within a stated period of time. The particular period of time and the procedure for publishing a notice is governed by state law and a review of the particular statute is absolutely necessary. If a claim is not presented within the specified period of time in those states that have "non-claim" statutes, then the creditor is barred from asserting a claim against the estate. This presents problems because not every creditor is aware that the debtor is deceased and not every creditor sees the notice of publication of the deceased (public figures excepted).

If the personal representative (executor or administrator) knows of the claim, it would appear reasonable that the personal representative should make some effort to notify the creditor. In many states, if the executor or administrator knows of the claim but complies with the terms of the statute and the creditor does not file within the required time, the claim may be barred. On the other hand, creditors have attacked successfully the unreasonableness of this statute and some courts adopt the attitude that notice by publication is sufficient only for creditors who are not reasonably ascertainable. Some creditors have successfully asserted claims against the executors and the distributees where an executor fails to notify ascertainable creditors.[10]

If a suit is pending at the time of death against the deceased, some conflict arises as to whether a presentation of a claim is or is not necessary. The best advice is to file your claim. If the executor or administrator disallows a claim and notifies the creditor that the estate will not pay that claim, the creditor usually has a specified time within which to bring proceedings against the representative of the estate. *Needless to say, the statutes from state to state vary considerably in time periods and requirements. Consultation with counsel is recommended.*

CREDIT CARD ORDERS—FRAUD

Notwithstanding the recent national do-not-call list and the Telephone Consumer Protection Act, a merchant will still take an order over the telephone for which a customer will use a credit card. In order to control fraud, certain procedures should be followed.

A. Always obtain:
   1. the name and address of the purchaser,
   2. the card number and the name of the credit card,
   3. the expiration date of the credit card and the security code,
   4. the name and address of the issuing bank, and
   5. the telephone number of the customer.
B. If an individual is ordering, obtain a home telephone number and, if necessary, an office or work telephone number.
C. If a company is placing the order, obtain its telephone number and the home address of the individual placing the order.

[10] *Tulsa Professional Collection Services, Inc. v. Pope*, 485 U.S. 478, 108 S. Ct. 1340 (1998).

D. Obtain the source code, if used. In direct marketing the source code is on the mailing label and identifies the specific mailing.

E. If the merchandise is unique to an advertisement over radio or TV, ask when the offer was made or when the TV advertisement was seen.

Asking the home address of a business employee who is placing an order for merchandise over the telephone, where the individual is acting on behalf of the business, is a reasonable request before the creditor extends credit. The purpose of asking questions is to smoke out credit card fraud or a stolen credit card. The more questions asked, the more likely a stolen credit card or a credit card fraud will be identified. If the customer has problems in answering the questions or refuses to answer, the creditor may decide to withhold shipment. The above questions may be expanded depending upon how much time the merchant allocates to the credit checking process which is usually a function of the amount of the order.

The merchant could call the telephone number furnished to verify if the individual is there or whether the company is a viable business. Such a call may furnish more significant information than verifying a bank account or obtaining a credit report on a business.

An example of a telephone conversation:

CREDITOR: Can I help you?

DEBTOR: Yes, I would like to order some office equipment from your catalog. I need two boxes of fine point pens, and a box of computer paper, a magnifying glass, a ruler, and a box of tape.

CREDITOR: Is this your first time ordering from our company?

DEBTOR: Yes, it is.

CREDITOR: How do you intend to pay for this?

DEBTOR: A credit card.

CREDITOR: Do you have a business corporate card by American Express or Diner's Club?

DEBTOR: No, I'm using my boss's Visa Card.

CREDITOR: What is your name?

DEBTOR: My name is Mary Jones.

CREDITOR: The items you wanted are two boxes of fine point pens, product number 5749; a magnifying glass, product number 9485; a ruler, product number 3968; a box of tape, product number 3958; and a box of computer paper, product number 3963.

DEBTOR: Yes, those are the items and product numbers.

CREDITOR: Do you wish to order anything else?

DEBTOR: No, just those things.

CREDITOR: What is the name and address of the company?

DEBTOR: The Smith Plumbing Supply Company and the address is 420 Main Street, Centerville.

CREDITOR: Do you want the merchandise shipped to that address?

DEBTOR: Yes.

CREDITOR: Is there any room number or floor number?

DEBTOR: No.

CREDITOR: What is your job there?

DEBTOR: I am the bookkeeper.

CREDITOR: What is the name of the principal owner?

DEBTOR: Charlie Smith.

CREDITOR: How long have you been working there?

DEBTOR: Why is that any of your business?

CREDITOR: You are placing an order for Mr. Smith and we would like to know how long you have been working there.

DEBTOR: I've been working here about a year or so.

CREDITOR: What is your home address?

DEBTOR: I don't have to give you my home address.

CREDITOR: You're placing an order and we would like to verify who you are and that you are the bookkeeper. We will call back at another time to verify this order. Do you have an objection to that?

DEBTOR: I don't have an objection to that. I gave the name and address of the firm. You haven't even asked for the credit card number.

CREDITOR: Yes, I do want Mr. Smith's credit card number.

DEBTOR: The card is a Visa Card. The number is 1111-3333-6666-1212.

CREDITOR: What are the expiration date and the security code?

DEBTOR: The date is December of 2006 and the code is 5555.

CREDITOR: Issuing bank?

DEBTOR: Citibank.

CREDITOR: Can you tell me how long Mr. Smith has been in business?

DEBTOR: About ten years or so.

CREDITOR: How many people does he employ?

DEBTOR: I guess about 5 or 6 people.

CREDITOR: I'm just trying to get information concerning your employer so that we can approve shipping the merchandise.

DEBTOR: Do you need any more information?

CREDITOR: No, that will be good for now. Thank you.

The creditor probably was suspicious about the nature of the order for the business. Each item was small and could be used by an individual at home as opposed to a business. Only one of the products was ordered—either one box of computer paper or one roll of tape. Usually several rolls of tape are ordered for a business. The bookkeeper's reluctance to answer the questions and her uncertainty about the size of the business also might lead the creditor to be suspicious. The next step would be for the creditor to make a call back to the debtor and attempt to contact Mr. Smith himself.

When a credit card is offered for payment of merchandise, the merchant should not accept the order simply based on the fact that the credit card company has advised the merchant that the card number represents a valid account and that the customer has not used up the credit line. The merchant has no assurance that the party placing the order is the same person who actually owns the credit card. The mere fact that the credit card company has approved the account only assures the merchant that a valid account is under that name and card number, but it does not assure that the party signing the credit card slip or furnishing a credit card number over the telephone is the person entitled to use the credit card.

USE OF CREDIT CARD BY COLLECTION AGENCIES. Collection agencies and attorneys sometimes offer to the consumer the option to utilize payment by credit card. The credit card company wishes the option only to be afforded to those debtors who are current on their debts. Once the account is referred to a collection agency or an attorney for collection, the debtor is now delinquent and the credit card company does not want to have a charge being made by a debtor who has already defaulted in the payment of a debt. As a result, collection agencies and attorneys cannot process credit card charges directly, and the only way collection agencies or attorneys can utilize the credit card option is either:

1. Forward the credit card charge to their client and then the client processes it through their normal channels, or
2. Process the credit card charge through a third-party agency which processes credit charges for a fee.

The option most often used by attorneys or collection agencies that are offering this to the debtor is to forward the charge directly to the client and the client thereafter processes the charge. The agency or the attorney may be violating the FDCPA, which states that they cannot add any incidental charges unless those charges were created in the agreement creating the debt or permitted by law.

Pre-Approved Credit Card. When there is a pre-approved credit card, the issuer of the pre-approved card assumes the risk of nonpayment at least for several months after the credit card is issued. The theory is that the defendant did not make any representations to the credit card company about credit worthiness because no representation was made. The card was solely issued upon information gathered by the agent of the credit card company who did the screening and collected the information about the debtor. No information was furnished by the debtor. Thus, no inferred intention or implied promise emanated from the debtor regarding the intention to repay the credit card debt.

The turning point in the case was whether a pre-approved credit card is relevant as to whether the creditor's reliance was justifiable. Credit card use is not the acceptance of the credit card. Whereas each credit card use inherently carries with it a promise to pay the debt, no representation was offered in accepting the card. Therefore, no grounds were present to object to the discharge in bankruptcy of the credit card debt.

The case was ultimately remanded to review each representation made by the debtor to determine whether it was knowingly false and whether the creditor justifiably relied.[11]

Charge Backs. "Charge backs" occur when the customer claims that the merchandise was returned, was never delivered, or for some reason the customer refuses to accept the charge. Normally, the merchant will accept a reasonable amount of charge backs from customers without questioning their bank. Sometimes the merchant agreement states charge backs cannot be disputed if the customer ordered by phone or not on site and the merchant may have to absorb a substantial loss. Nevertheless, when the charge back is not warranted, the merchant is urged to persuade its bank to return the charge to the cardholder bank. Frequently, the merchant will ask its bank not to accept the charge back for 60 days to enable the merchant to collect and submit documentation to its bank. The bank sends this documentation to the cardholder's bank showing that the merchandise was delivered to the customer, that the customer signed for the merchandise, and that the customer retained the merchandise for a month or longer. Based on this set of circumstances or other

---

[11]*AT&T Universal Card Service v. Mercer*, 246 F.3d 391 (5th Cir. 2001).

convincing documentation, the cardholder's bank should charge the cardholder's account. The cardholder may then assert a claim directly against the merchant.

CREDIT CARD AGREEMENT—APPLICATION

The credit card agreement or the application for the credit card often is not available during a trial. If the credit card was issued with these documents and the cardholder was approved to use the card, the court will normally accept as evidence that the agreement was executed. The mailing of monthly statements or a file history indicating some form of contact with the debtor is helpful.[12]

MERCHANT AGREEMENT

To utilize Visa or MasterCard, a merchant enters into an agreement with its bank—not with Visa or MasterCard. Each bank prepares a separate agreement with the merchant who accepts its Visa and MasterCard and each agreement prepared by the bank is different from any other agreement. A standard agreement does not really exist, although Visa and MasterCard do require certain terms and conditions. The legal liabilities of the merchant and the cardholder are controlled by the written agreements and should be reviewed by an attorney prior to execution.[13] Remember that agreements are negotiable if the terms and conditions are not satisfactory to the merchant. Said terms and conditions may be compromised, modified, and adjusted providing the bank wants the business of the merchant. If the bank is independent and not anxious for the business, the agreement will be presented as a "fait accompli" and the bank will accept no changes.

SERVICEMEMBERS CIVIL RELIEF ACT OF 2003 (SCRA)

The Servicemembers Civil Relief Act (SCRA) of 2003 amends and at the same time replaces the Soldiers and Sailors Relief Act (SSCRA) of 1940, which had updated a version of the Act of 1918. An additional Act dealing with soldiers is the Uniform Services Employment and Re-Employment Act (USERRA) of 1994.

---

[12] *Davis v. Discover Bank*, 627 S.E.2d 819 (Ga. App. 2006).

[13] *American Express Co. v. Geller*, 343 N.Y.S.2d 644 (1973); *Franklin National Bank v. Kass*, 19 Misc. 2d 280 (1959).

The prime purpose of the SCRA is to protect servicepersons from litigation and the institution of suits while they are in military service. The USERRA deals primarily with the employment and reemployment of military personnel. The SCRA of 2003 was a revision of the SSCRA and adopted verbatim many of the provisions of the SSCRA with several significant changes as follows:

1. The right to reduce the interest on credit to 6 percent remains and the only requirement for the service member to obtain this reduction is a copy of the military order and the date of induction is effective as of the date of the military order inducting him into service.
2. The automatic 90-day stay applies to any civil action or proceeding in which the defendant is in military service or is within 90 days after termination of or release from military service and has received notice of the action of the proceeding. The court may on its own motion and shall upon application stay any action for not less than 90 days. A service member also may apply for an additional stay when it appears that the service member is unavailable to prosecute or defend the action.
3. The SSCRA required an affidavit to be submitted with the default judgment that the defendant is not in military service, but unfortunately the act provided no penalties in the event the plaintiff fails to comply. Under the SCRA of 2003, the affidavit is required. The act provides for a criminal penalty in the event a false affidavit is submitted. The court must appoint a guardian *ad litem* to represent the defendant before a judgment may be entered. If the service member does not receive a notice, the court must give at least a 90-day stay.
4. A service member may not be evicted when the monthly rent is less than $2,465 based on year 2004 figures. The court has significant latitude with regard to granting stays of 90 days. A person who knowingly takes part in an eviction or distress shall be fined and may be imprisoned for not more than one year or both. This penalty also applies to a person who knowingly resumes possession of property by repossession while the service member is still in military service. If a default is entered against an applicable military defendant, the defendant may apply to set aside the default within 60 days after the end of their applicable military service and the judgment may be reopened upon application to the court. If the serviceman wishes to terminate the lease, he must provide written notice to the landlord and the effective date of termination is 30 days after the first date on which the next rental payment is due for a lease that provides for monthly rent payments. The termination date starts the period of time for the return of any advance rental payments which is 30 days after the termination date.

5. A mortgagee cannot foreclose on a mortgage which was originated prior to the service member entering military service without an order of the court. The court also has power to stay the proceeding or to make whatever adjustment seems appropriate.
6. With regard to vehicles, pre-service vehicle agreements may be terminated if the service member is assigned for more than 180 days outside the continental United States. To properly terminate a lease of a vehicle, the service member must provide to the lender written notice, a copy of their transfer orders and actually return the vehicle within 15 days of the delivery of the written notice. At that particular time, the lease is ended and the serviceman has no further liability. This applies to either a personal lease or a business lease.
7. The dependants of the service member may make application to the court for protection and obtain stays even though the service member is not a party to the action.
8. After a service member enters military service, a contract by the service member for the purchase of real or personal property, including a motor vehicle or the lease or bailment of property, may not be rescinded or terminated for a breach of terms of the contract occurring before or during the person's military service nor may the property be repossessed for such breach without a court order.

A copy of Section 101-308 from the SCRA covering the general provisions and general relief as well as specific provisions which apply to rent, installment contracts, mortgage liens, assignment and leases are contained in Appendix to this chapter.

It should be noted that several states, such as Georgia, South Carolina, and Ohio, have passed laws which provide additional protection to those in military service. The telephone numbers to obtain the status of a member of the Armed Services is 1-800-346-3374 for Army, Air Force, and Navy, and 1-800-594-8302 for the Marines.

Section 2203 of the Housing and Economic Recovery Act of 2008, PUB.L.110-289, 122 Stat. 2654 (2008) has provided additional protection to servicemembers by extending the period during which a creditor may not charge interest in excess of 6 percent in connection with obligations and liabilities consisting of a mortgage, trust or other security in the nature of a mortgage. The revisions also extend the periods during which a creditor is restricted from enforcing, or foreclosing upon, credit obligations of a servicemember on real and personal property. The revisions were effective as of July 30, 2008.

A servicemember must provide the creditor written notice and a copy of the servicemember's military orders to receive the interest rate reduction to 6 percent. This reduction to 6 percent is forgiving of any excess charge over 6 percent and remains in effect throughout the term of the service.

Residential and motor vehicle leases by servicemembers are covered. A residential lease may be terminated if the servicemember either enters into military service or executes the lease while in military service, but subsequently receives an order for a permanent change of station or for a deployment of at least 90 days. The Act covers the issue of eviction and in some instances permits the servicemember to waive certain rights, except the waiver must be in writing and must be executed during or after the servicemember's period of military service. A summary issued by the Controller of Currency is in the Appendix to this chapter.

Forms can be obtained from the Defense Finance and Accounting Service and the request should be for the form "Involuntary Allotment Application, DD Form 2635." The branch of service and the social security number are required. The current duty station and address of the military member should be furnished. The garnishment is sent to:

Defense Finance and Accounting Service

Cleveland Center, Code L

P.O. Box 998002

Cleveland, Ohio 44199-8002

If the military member is attached to the Coast Guard, the garnishment should be sent to:

Coast Guard Pay and Personnel Center (LGL)

444 S.E. Quincy Street

Topeka, Kansas 66683-3591

RENT-TO-OWN TRANSACTIONS

Rent-to-own agreements are common among consumers who cannot afford to buy on credit. In most of these transactions, the customer pays in advance to rent the items, usually on a weekly or a monthly basis. At the end of each week or the end of each month, the customer renews the rental for a new period of time, and, of course, pays the rental fee in advance. Many states regulate this type of transaction.

The courts have not been sympathetic to the owners of the rent-to-own businesses. In several recent cases, they have decided there was noncompliance with the particular statute in the state, or the rent-to-own was a consumer-credit transaction which failed to comply with the state's laws. Rent-to-own businesses must be careful with their compliance if their intention is to repossess the equipment.

GAMBLING DEBTS

At one time the collection of a gambling debt presented severe problems in many states as legalized gambling was confined to the state of Nevada. When New Jersey entered the arena, followed by American Indian tribes across the country, the treatment of gambling debts radically changed.

Collecting gambling debts today is probably easier than it was in the past, but really not that much easier, as many problems and pitfalls exist. The courts favor the consumer and seem to look for some reason to find a gambling debt unenforceable. Many states will look to the state in which the debt was incurred to see whether the debt was enforceable. Sometimes the creditor will sue in the state in which the debt was incurred and then attempt to sue on the judgment in another state, on the theory that the other state will give full faith and credit to the judgment that was acquired in the state where the gambling debt was incurred, as most states do. In a few states (for example, New York) a new suit would have to be started on a default judgment and the court might review whether a gambling debt was enforceable in the state where the consumer resides.

Gambling debts have also presented problems in the bankruptcy courts when the consumer used a credit card. The credit grantor has objected to the discharge of the credit card debt on the grounds that the consumer (gambler) used a credit card to gamble and did not intend to repay the debt. The courts seem to shrug off this argument by stating that the gambler always intends to pay back a debt because the gambler intends to win. In one case where the debtor used his credit card over a period of six months and did make some payments on the credit card, the court denied the credit grantor's claim that the debt should be non-dischargeable. Timing of the cash advances and the facts of each case are important to the bankruptcy judge. Only clear abuses should be pursued.

Indian Reservations. With regard to debts incurred on American Indian reservations, one must look to the Indian Gaming Regulatory Act.[14] The act requires a compact (agreement) between the reservation and the state which will determine the enforceability of gambling debts. Sometimes these agreements contain provisions about the extension of credit to persons who gamble. The question of whether an acceptance of a check from a resident of the hotel is "per se" an extension of credit for the purpose of gambling merely because the hotel has a casino is a question of fact to be decided by the court. In many of the compacts, the casinos are not allowed to extend credit for the sole purpose of gambling.[15]

---

[14]IGRA (Indian Gaming Regulatory Act), 25 U.S.C. §§ 2701-21 (1988).

[15]*In re Anastas*, 947 F.3d 1280 (9th Cir. 1996); *CBA Credit Services of N.D. v. Azar*, 551 N.W.2d 787 (N.D. 1996).

TOTTEN TRUST

A Totten Trust arises when an individual deposits money in a bank account in trust for a beneficiary with the intent that money will pass to the beneficiary upon the death of the individual. The Totten Trust is recognized in most states. A cardinal characteristic of a Totten (or tentative) Trust is that while it is effective as a testamentary device upon the death of a depositor, the monies on deposit can be withdrawn by the depositor and are within reach of creditors during the debtor's lifetime.[16]

WITNESS PROTECTION PROGRAM

The Federal Witness Protection Program is mentioned frequently on television police programs such as "Law & Order." The program is designed to protect witnesses against bodily harm from organized crime (or even unorganized crime), so that the witness will not be injured and, furthermore, to set an example so that future witnesses may testify freely without risk of harm. Many of the witnesses in the program have a record of prior violations of law.

If such a person is indebted to a creditor, the debt is going to be extremely difficult to collect in view of the fact that the witness has assumed a totally different identity. Nevertheless, the U.S. Code provides that the Attorney General shall make reasonable efforts to serve a copy of process (summons of complaint) upon any person in the program. After service, the Attorney General will notify the plaintiff whether the particular process has been served. If a judgment is entered against the debtor, the Attorney General will make reasonable efforts to find out whether the witness actually complied with the judgment and may take certain actions to persuade the person to comply with the judgment. Payment will usually be made through the Attorney General's office and not directly to the creditor.

If the witness refuses to pay, and has the ability to pay, the Attorney General may at that point, upon request, disclose the identity and location of the debtor to the creditor. Before this would be done, the Attorney General would have to consider the danger of physical harm to the particular individual and would probably do a balancing of the equity depending upon the ability of the witness to pay, the risk that the witness would entail if his identity was disclosed, and other factors.

---

[16] *In re Totten*, 179 N.Y. 112, 71 N.E. 748 (1904); *Seymour v. Seymour*, 85 So. 2d 726 (Fla. 1956).

ARBITRATION

The issue of whether a creditor is entitled to arbitration has been confronting the courts for the past several years and the decisions being rendered have not been consistent. The arbitration clauses are being used more frequently in today's environment for the purpose of avoiding class action suits and many corporations that sell to consumers are inserting in the agreement with the consumer that "any disputes must be resolved by arbitration." The courts favor arbitration since it means one more case that does not have to work its way through the overcrowded judicial system.

The creditors who lend the money to the consumers or the sellers who sell their merchandise to the consumers have passed the stage of using a simple "right to arbitrate clause," but are including in the arbitration clause terms and conditions that are forcing the courts to find the arbitration clauses unenforceable. An example is the arbitration clause that requires the debtor to arbitrate in a particular jurisdiction that may be thousands of miles from where the debtor resides or the debtor is required to absorb all of the costs and expenses of the arbitration or even half the expenses of the arbitration, where those expenses are extremely oppressive and unreasonable in relation to the amount in dispute.

Strict Interpretation. The Federal Arbitration Act specifically states that an arbitration shall proceed "in the manner provided for in such agreement." Once the court has determined that it is satisfied as to the agreement for arbitration, the court shall make an order directing the parties to proceed to arbitration "in accordance with the terms of the agreement."

The Circuit Court of Appeals in the Seventh Circuit has held that the Federal Arbitration Act requires that the courts enforce the arbitration agreement according to its terms. The court acknowledged that the terms could conceivably allow a class action, but in the particular case a provision for a class action was not in the agreement and no express term in the agreement provided for class arbitration. Accordingly, *absent any express provision in the agreement providing for a class arbitration*, the courts do not have the authority to reform the agreement and order an arbitration panel to hear claims on a class basis pursuant to Rule 23.[17]

Considerable litigation on this point has taken place, but the large majority of the cases, with the exception of isolated cases under state law, prohibit arbitration of class claims even when they are brought under the Truth and Lending Act or the Fair Debt Collection Practices Act, both of which acts expressly allow class action proceedings.

---

[17] *Champ v. Siegel Trading Co.*, 55 F.3d 269 (7th Cir. 1995).

The great majority of the courts seem to have approved the bank's right to include a mandatory arbitration clause in the credit card agreement and will enforce the arbitration clause as to any future disputes.

One of the major problems is whether one party to an agreement has the right to alter the agreement without the consent of the other party. Whereas the federal courts are favorable to arbitration agreements under the Federal Arbitration Act, consumer attorneys have been attacking the arbitration agreements as oppressive and unconscionable on a wide variety of grounds. Undoubtedly, the retroactivity of some of these "legal notices" will also be attacked.

The courts have found both technical and factual reasons not to enforce the change of terms notification, but in most cases the courts favor arbitration.

Prohibition Against Review. The Second Circuit considered a case where the arbitration agreement insulated the award from judicial review. The court held that a prohibition against review by the court is unenforceable; and a federal court can review the award.[18]

Material Alteration. The Second Circuit has taken the position that an arbitration clause in a contract is not necessarily a material alteration of the contract—even if it was inserted on an invoice and the other party was not aware of it. Judge Miner went to great efforts to analyze the appropriate statutory section under the Uniform Commercial Code.[19]

A court in New York overruled a prior decision which held that an arbitration clause in an invoice constitutes a material alteration that would result in surprise or hardship if incorporated without the express awareness of the buyer. The court extensively discussed trade usage, the official comments to New York, UCC 2-207 and analyzed prior cases. The court found no hardship and thus the arbitration clause stands in a commercial business transaction.

An examination of the cases will reveal that the courts seem to go both ways on this particular point.[20]

Waiver by Litigation. The court was extremely suspect when the litigation continued through discovery and class certification before the insurance company moved to compel arbitration. The trial court ruled that the defendants had waived their right to compel arbitration because the defendants had substantially invoked the litigation process and had substantially prejudiced the party opposing arbitration. Whether a party's

[18] *Hoeft v. MUL Group Inc.*, Docket #02-9155, 2d Cir., Sept. 3, 2003 (N.Y.L.J. Sept. 15, 2003, Pg. 18).

[19] UCC § 2-207.

[20] *Aceros v. Prefabricados, S.A. v. Treadearbed Inc.*, 282 F.3d 92 (2d Cir. 2002); *J.J.'s Mae, Inc. v. H. Warshaw & Sons, Inc.*, 717 N.Y.S.2d 37 (1st Dept. 2000).

participation in an action amounts to an enforceable waiver of its right to arbitrate depends on whether the participation bespeaks an intention to abandon the right in favor of the judicial process; and, if so, whether the opposing party would be prejudiced by a subsequent order requiring it to submit to arbitration. The test apparently has two prongs, substantial participation and the possibility of prejudice. This theory is rarely considered by the courts primarily because the party entitled to arbitration usually makes the motion immediately after the suit is instituted.[21]

By Agreement. The arbitration issue continues before the courts with some courts finding the arbitration clauses unconscionable and others choosing to enforce them. The trend seems to be that arbitration clauses will be enforced unless flagrant abuse exists in the transaction.[22]

In the case before the Supreme Court of Kentucky, the court examined an arbitration provision which was contained in the contract in bold letters as follows:

> the parties voluntarily and knowingly waive any right they have to a jury trial either pursuant to arbitration under this clause or pursuant to a court action by you (as provided herein).

In addition to that bold clause, the contract also provided that "all disputes, claims or controversies arising from or relating to this contract of the parties thereto shall be resolved by binding arbitration by one arbitrator selected by you (seller/assignee) with my (buyers) consent." The creditor reserved an option to use judicial or non-judicial relief to enforce the security agreement relating to the manufactured home to enforce the monetary obligations or to foreclose on the manufactured home.

The Kentucky court held that a fundamental rule of contract law holds that absent fraud in the inducement, a written agreement duly executed by the party, who had an opportunity to read it, will be enforced according to its terms. The doctrine of unconscionability has developed as a narrow exception. This doctrine of unconscionability is only directed against one-sided oppressive and grossly unfair contracts, and not against contracts of uneven bargaining power or even a simple, old-fashioned bad bargain. An unconscionable contract is characterized as one which no man except under a delusion would make on the one hand and which no fair and honest man would accept on the other hand. The cases are usually addressed on a case-by-case basis.

The issue of an adhesion contract may rest on the grounds that the clause was not concealed or disguised within the forms. Its provisions were clearly stated so that purchasers of ordinary experience and education are

---

[21] *Voyager Life Ins. Co. v. Hughes*, 841 So. 2d 1216 (Ala. 2001).
[22] *In re Lynn Fin. Servs.*, 257 S.W.3d 228 (Tex. 2008).

able to understand the general import. Its effect is not to alter the principal bargain in an extreme or surprising way.

It appears that the key to survival of an arbitration clause is in the drafting of the arbitration agreement. The agreement should be drawn fairly to the consumer paying particular attention to be certain that the consumer is aware of the rights being waived. The defense of arbitration should be asserted in the answer to the complaint and the motion to compel arbitration should be immediately made.

The case in Kentucky analyzed the pros and cons of an arbitration agreement and cited many cases in favor of arbitration and opposed to arbitration. In the event the creditor is faced with an attack on an arbitration agreement, the cases cited are recommended reading.[23]

Class Actions. The use of an arbitration clause has increased radically over the years in the area of credit cards and other transactions with consumers. One of the major reasons for the use of arbitration clauses is to prevent consumer attorneys from instituting class actions. When an arbitration clause is used in a retail installment contract or in a lease or other credit agreement, the scope of the arbitration will be limited to the individual transaction with that individual consumer, and thus in the event of a violation of the FDCPA, FCRA, ECOA, or TILA, the violation would be limited to that individual consumer and no class action could be asserted by a consumer attorney. An arbitration is quicker and cheaper for both parties; and the disadvantage of not being able to appeal a bad decision by the arbitrator is overcome by the benefit to the creditor in that the creditor is not being faced with the threat of class action.[24]

The issue of whether an arbitration is unconscionable in an arbitration agreement that involves a consumer such as in a credit card obligation has given rise to a conflict in the courts. In the Eleventh and Fourth Circuits, the courts have found that agreements barring class actions are permissible and are not unconscionable and may be enforced. Nevertheless, several state courts have found the prohibition unconscionable and have permitted the assertion of a class action.[25]

The Supreme Court agreed to review a decision which upheld a class-wide *arbitration* award against Green Tree Financial Corp. The South Carolina Supreme Court ruled that class-wide arbitration could be ordered even if the arbitration agreement was silent as to class actions. *The*

---

[23]*Bowen v. First Family Fin. Servs.*, 233 F.3d 1331 (11th Cir. 2000); *Am. Gen. Fin., Inc. v. Morton*, 812 So. 2d 282 (Ala. 2001); *Conseco Fin. Servicing Corp. v. Wilder*, 47 S.W.3d 335 (Ky. Ct. App. 2001); *Tillman v. Commercial Credit Loan, Inc.*, 362 N.C. 93 (N.C. 2008).

[24]*Nationwide of Bryan, Inc. v. Dyer*, 969 S.W.2d 518 (Tex. App. 1998) (consumer identity fraud).

[25]*Snowden v. Checkpoint Check Cashing*, 290 F.3d 631 (4th Cir. 2002); *Randolph v. Green Tree Financial Corp.*, 244 F.3d 814 (11th Cir. 2001); *Leonard v. Terminix International Co.*, 854 So. 2d 529 (Ala. 2002); *Mandel v. Household Bank*, 105 Cal. App. 4th (Cal. App. 4th Dist. 2003); *Lowden v. T-Mobile USA, Inc.*, 512 F.3d 1213 (9th Cir. 2008).

Supreme Court held that where an arbitration agreement is silent, arbitrators, not the judges, will decide whether an agreement permits classwide arbitration.[26]

On the other hand, a California decision held that the California Consumer Legal Remedies Act provides an anti-waiver provision that provides *any waiver by a consumer of the provisions of this title is contrary to public policy* and shall be unenforceable and void. Furthermore, under the California Business and Professional Code, Section 1770, any consumer who suffers damages may bring a class action. Under the Code, the courts have found that placing unlawful or unenforceable terms in form contracts constitute unfair business practices. The court ultimately held that a clause designed to avoid class actions is illegal and unconscionable under California law.

California possesses a wide variety of statutes to protect the consumer from unfair and unconscionable practices. It is questionable whether this would stand up in other states, which have not passed such strong legislation.[27]

In a 2003 case from the liberal 7th Circuit, the court considered the question of whether an arbitration agreement which prohibits class actions is unconscionable as a matter of Illinois law. The court recognized a split amongst the states and that case law supported both parties' arguments, but ultimately concluded that the "no class action" provision was not so one-sided or oppressive as to render the agreement unconscionable. Most of the circuit courts have enforced arbitration agreements which contain "no class action" clauses with the exception of the Ninth Circuit, and a few states have declared such arbitration agreements unenforceable or unconscionable such as Pennsylvania and California. A careful examination of the cases is necessary since some of the agreements contain other provisions that were unconscionable, which may have influenced the decisions.[28]

Drafting. The issue of drafting an arbitration clause has now become a significant problem, because creditors recognize that at some point in time, their mandatory arbitration clauses will be tested before a tribunal. The major issue to address is the extent and the content of the disclosure to the consumer. The costs to the consumer, the geographical considerations, the distance to be traveled by the consumer, the controlling law, and a variety of other criteria must be thoroughly evaluated. Some courts are favorable to arbitrations and most of these items present no problems. Other courts are favorable to the consumer and will apply the law on a strict liability basis, carefully examining each clause of the arbitration agreement. Some liberal judges find a technical violation that enables them to render the entire arbitration agreement invalid.

---

[26]*Greentree Financial Corp. v. Bazzle*, 2003 WL 21433403; Brooks R. Burdette and Michael Schwartz, *Employment Law* (N.Y.L.J. July 30, 2003, Pg. 5).

[27]*Ting v. AT&T*, 182 F. Supp. 2d 902 (2002).

[28]*Rosen v. SCIL, LLC*, 799 N.E. 2d 488 (Ill. Ct. App. 2003).

The notification to the consumer and the actual agreement of arbitration must be carefully drawn under the supervision of an attorney who is experienced in this area. The pitfalls are numerous and the numbers of cases that have found unusual and unique reasons to deny arbitration are many. The broadest possible terms should be used to protect against the widest area of liability. Ambiguity in the arbitration agreement will certainly be decided against the creditor. Full disclosure of all the rights that the consumer has in a court proceeding should be clearly and conspicuously disclosed to the consumer. The consumer must be told that these rights will be forfeited in an arbitration.

Many lawyers suggest a wide variety of clauses to be included in arbitration agreements so that they will be upheld by the courts. Among the recommendations are the following:

- Be certain that the costs to be incurred by the consumer to conduct the arbitration are reasonable.
- Provide for more than minimal discovery during an arbitration.
- Require a written award.
- Allow the arbitrator the right to award injunctive or punitive relief.
- Do not make the consumer travel too far to attend the arbitration.
- Disclose all the rights the consumer is forfeiting—class action, jury trial, appeal.

In some instances suggestions are being made to specifically have the consumer waive a class action.

As a general statement, the Federal Arbitration Act has expanded to include the commerce clause so that it affects the state courts and supersedes inconsistent state laws and statutes. A lender would not have to comply with the state law, but may rely on the Federal Arbitration Act in the states where they do business. Most states encourage arbitration, but a few states (in particular, Alabama) do not favor arbitration. Many states set criteria to be met for the arbitration clause to be enforceable.

Insert Notices. A credit card issuer may add an arbitration clause to a credit card agreement by means of mailing an insert statement to the consumer notifying the consumer that in the future he or she will be subject to arbitration with regard to any future charges on the credit card.

The court did not accept the argument of the plaintiff that the bank could not change an agreement unilaterally without obtaining the consent of the defendant. The debtor claimed that he did not read the notification, but the court acknowledged that agreements are binding whether or not the recipient reads them. In a prior agreement with the debtor, the bank had reserved its right to send an insert to the customer notifying him that any future disputes will be resolved through arbitration. Several other federal courts have adopted similar postures.[29]

A case in California held that the bank did not have an unequivocal right to deny the consumer a right to a jury trial and that the arbitration clause did not become part of the credit card agreement and could not be enforced against the cardholder. Because the bank did not deal with the question of dispute resolution in the original cardholder agreement with the consumer, the court indicated that the bank did not have the right to change the terms of the cardholder agreement to now include a specific method of arbitration as the means to resolve a dispute between the parties.[30]

A few courts have held that if the agreement with the debtor is silent as to arbitration, the creditor cannot send an insert notice to compel the debtor to arbitrate because this would constitute a new term to the agreement and not an amendment to the agreement.

A case in New York emphasized the Delaware Statute, which expressly permitted a bank at any time or from time to time to amend such agreement in any respect, whether or not the amendment or the subject of the amendment was originally contemplated or addressed by the parties or is integral to the relationship between the parties. The statute went on to say that, without limiting the foregoing, such amendment may change terms by the addition of "new terms" or by the deletion or modification of existing terms, whether relating to plan benefits or features, the manner for amending the terms of the agreement, arbitration or other alternative dispute resolution mechanism or other matters of any kind whatsoever.

While this is a liberal statute designed to enable the creditor to amend that agreement at any time, it is interesting that the case took place in the Southern District of New York, in a state that is consumer-oriented. The court applied the law of Delaware since the lower court judge determined that this issue was decided in prior litigation and the credit card agreement expressly provided that Delaware law would be applicable. However, between the lines, federal judges frequently look favorably on permitting arbitration.[31]

The courts are split as to the ability of credit card issuers to change the terms of a credit card agreement by inserting an arbitration clause. Some authorizing cases seem to rely on a provision in the original agreement for the right to change the agreement by inserting an arbitration clause and

---

[29] *Cappalli v. Nat'l Bank of the Great Lakes*, 281 F.3d 219 (3d Cir. 2001).

[30] *Taylor v. First North American National Bank*, 325 F. Supp. 2d 1304 (M.D. Ala. 2004); *Jaimez v. MBNA America Bank, N.A.*, 2006 U.S. Dist. LEXIS 7526 (D. Kan. February 27, 2006); *Bill Heard Chevrolet Corp. v. Robert Wilson*, 877 So. 2d 15 (Fla. App. 2004); *Badie v. Bank of America*, 67 Cal. App. 4th 779, 79 Cal. Rptr. 2d 272 (Cal. Ct. App. 1st Dist. 1998).

[31] *Kurz v. Chase Manhattan Bank USA, N.A.*, 319 F. Supp. 2d 457 (S.D.N.Y. 2004); *Tsadilas v. Providian National Banks*, 786 N.Y.S.2d 478 (2004).

other cases rely on statutory authority to change an arbitration clause. The conflict between the courts is splintered with each relying on a somewhat different fact basis and ultimately this issue will probably reach the Supreme Court.[32]

On the other hand, the courts take the position that where the credit card did not have any reference to an arbitration agreement in the initial agreement, the creditor has no right to send an insert notice to add an arbitration agreement or to amend an arbitration agreement.

When the credit card agreement reserves the right to insert an arbitration clause in the credit card agreement, the courts tend to permit the addition of the arbitration agreement. But a credit card agreement totally silent has been distinguished by several courts, notwithstanding the fact that this distinction seems more technical than substantive.[33]

Review of Arbitrator. When our firm handles an arbitration, the first item we impress upon our client is that, under normal circumstances, no appeal is available from the decision of the arbitrator. An appeal cannot be taken to a state appellate court or a federal appellate court. Nevertheless, exceptions are available to review an arbitrator's decision or even to remove an arbitrator during arbitration proceedings.

Because of the limited possibility of review by the federal courts of an arbitration award, the parties to an arbitration often provide by agreement for an expanded review of the award and the arbitration proceeding depending upon the wording in the agreement. Sometimes, the parties agree that the review of the arbitration award should be narrower than the limited review that the federal courts afford. The state courts even provide a more restrictive review than the federal courts. As often happens, the circuits offer differing application of these clauses that are set forth in written agreements. Actually, one court has suggested that an arbitration agreement may contain wording which will eliminate any type of review by either a federal or state court.

Unlike arbitration, judicial review is not a creation of contract and the authority of a federal court to review an arbitration award does not derive from a private agreement.

Once an arbitration award is rendered, the prevailing party can seek to have that award confirmed by the courts and, having done so, can evoke the coercive power of the state to enforce it in the same manner as it could a court judgment. Because the successful party may obtain a judgment which

---

[32]*Hughes v. All Tell Corp.*, 2004 U.S. Dist. LEXIS 20705 (D.C. N.D. Fla. 2004).

[33]*Discover Bank v. Shea*, 827 A. 2d 358 (N.J. Sup. Ct. 2001) (adding an arbitration clause where the cardholder agreement was silent); *Fields v. Howe*, 2002 W.L. 418011 (S.D. Ind. 2002) (An Ohio statute specifically authorized the addition of an arbitration clause); *Badie v. Bank of America*, 79 Cal. Rptr. 273 (Cal. Dist. Ct. of App. 1998) (where a change of terms provision was contained and the agreement was silent as to arbitration, the court did not permit it).

affords him the remedy set forth in the statutes to enforce that judgment, federal courts have a duty to ensure that the arbitration award satisfies certain minimum standards. Congress imposed limited, but critical, safeguards into this process by which an arbitration award became a court judgment. Congress also barred federal courts from confirming awards tainted by partiality, procedural fairness, corruption, or other similar misconduct.

Agreements which tend to limit, expand, or eliminate judicial review are generally not enforceable and the courts will have their say with regard to whether an arbitration award can be confirmed and converted into a judgment to be enforced by the creditor. These two recent decisions to some extent overrule some prior decisions, which upheld the enforceability of such clauses. With these two recent Circuit Court of Appeals decisions, it seems unlikely that the prior cases will prevail in other circuits.[34]

Vacation of Award. The Federal Arbitration Act sets forth the circumstances under which an award may be vacated upon the application of any party to the arbitration.

The statute states as follows:

a. In any of the following cases the United States court in and for the district wherein the award was made may make an order vacating the award upon the application of any party to the arbitration—
    1. where the award was procured by corruption, fraud, or undue means;
    2. where there was evident partiality or corruption in the arbitrators, or either of them;
    3. where the arbitrators were guilty of misconduct in refusing to postpone the hearing, upon sufficient cause shown, or in refusing to hear evidence pertinent and material to the controversy; or of any other misbehavior by which the rights of any party have been prejudiced; or
    4. where the arbitrators exceeded their powers, or so imperfectly executed them that a mutual, final, and definite award upon the subject matter submitted was not made.

b. If an award is vacated and the time within which the agreement required the award to be made has not expired, the court may, in its discretion, direct a rehearing by the arbitrators.

c. The United States district court for the district wherein an award was made that was issued pursuant to section 580 of Title 5 may make an

---

[34] *Kyosenna Corp. v. Prudential Trade Services*, 341 F.3d 987 (9th Cir. 2003); *Hoeft, III v. MVL Group, Inc.*, 2003 WL 22048228 (2d Cir. 2003).

order vacating the award upon the application of a person, other than a party to the arbitration, who is adversely affected or aggrieved by the award, if the use of arbitration or the award is clearly inconsistent with the factors set forth in section 572 of Title 5.

Manifest Disregard. A case in the U.S. Supreme Court in 2008 has now effectively revoked the right to set aside an arbitration award for a "manifest disregard" of the law. The court addressed the *Wilco* decision in 1953 that stated expandable judicial review authority had been accepted as the law. The language in *Wilco* arguably favoring "manifest disregard" did not go as far as to require it and was overruled by the *Rodriquez* decision in 1989.

The plaintiff sought a general review of the arbitrator's legal errors and substantiated the request with the argument that a review of a legal error should prevail simply because the whole concept of arbitration is a creature of contract.

The Supreme Court acknowledged that many features of arbitration are controlled by contract including the way arbitrators are chosen, what their qualifications should be, which issues are arbitrable, along with procedures and choice of substantive law. Unfortunately, the Federal Arbitration Act does not have text to enforce a contract to expand judicial review following the arbitration. In simple language, 9 U.S.C.S 10(a) and 11 are exclusive.

The argument offered against eliminating manifest disregard of the law is that people would be discouraged from utilizing arbitration and place an additional burden on the court. The exclusivity reading of the statute is more of a threat to the popularity of arbitrators or to that of the courts. The text of the statute controls.

The conflict that existed in the courts as to the manifest disregard of the law extended to finding that an erroneous interpretation of the law would not necessarily subject an arbitration of law to reversal. An obvious disregard of a major principle of accepted law might constitute the manifest disregard needed to modify a decision of the arbitrators. Prior decisions of the Supreme Court have reiterated that a party that submits to arbitration may obtain relief in federal court only in unusual circumstances and in the past has allowed modification of awards where a manifest disregard of the law existed.

Manifest disregard doctrine as defined in *Black's Law Dictionary*, 7th Edition, is the principle that an arbitration award will be vacated if the arbitrator knows the applicable law and deliberately chooses to disregard it. An award will not be vacated for a mere error in misunderstanding of the law. The word "disregard" technically means to take no notice of, to leave out of consideration, to ignore, to overlook or to fail to observe (*American Heritage Dictionary*). In the past, the fact that an arbitration award incorrectly interprets a law does not necessarily mean it is "manifestly disregarded." The arbitrator merely made a legal mistake. To disregard the law, one must be conscious of the law and deliberately ignore it. The record must show that arbitrators knew the law and expressly disregarded it.

The Supreme Court decision in 2008 has probably put to bed all the scholarly analysis of what a manifest disregard of the law means. The grounds for modifying an arbitration award are stated in text in Section 9 U.S.C.S. 10(a) and 11 and said sections are exclusive.

Notwithstanding the Supreme Court decision, the conflict over manifest disregard still remains. Many of the courts have found some reason to apply the manifest disregard concept since the *Hall* decision. In most cases they disregard *Hall* or find some other reason to ignore *Hall*, such as relying on the old theory that the contract of arbitration allows the review.

On the other side of the coin, many courts have categorically and unequivocally upheld the *Hall* decision and refuse to apply any element of the "manifest disregard" of the law.[35]

Removal of Arbitrator. The Federal Arbitration Act allows a court to vacate an arbitration, but the Act contains no language allowing the court to remove an arbitrator during the proceedings even if the facts presented would allow the court to judicially review an award or vacate an award. The language of the Act is unambiguous. Only after an award has been made by the arbitrators can a party seek to attack the arbitrators by moving to vacate, modify, or correct the award. A district court is without authority to review the validity of an arbitrator's ruling prior to the making of an award. Where an arbitrator makes an interim ruling that does not to purport to resolve finally the issues submitted to them, judicial review is unavailable.[36]

Removal of an arbitrator during the proceeding is an unusual event and the courts rarely will make an exception to this general rule. If both parties agree to the removal of the arbitrator, the arbitration may be terminated at that point.

Arbitrability. The question of whether the parties have submitted a particular dispute to arbitration, i.e., the question of "arbitrability," is an issue for judicial determination unless the parties clearly and unmistakenly

---

[35]*Merrill Lynch, Pierce, Fenner & Smith v. Bobker*, 808 F.2d 930 (2d Cir. 1986); *Hall Street Associates, LLC v. Mattel Inc.*, 128 S. Ct. 1396 (2008); *Wilko v. Swan*, 436 U.S. 427 (1953); *Rodriguez de Quijas v. Shearson/American Express, Inc.*, 490 U.S. 477 (1989); *Dean Witter Reynolds, Inc. v. Byrd*, 470 U.S. 213 (1985); *Fitzgerald v. H & R Block Financial Advisors, Inc.*, 2008 WL 2397636 (E.D. Mich. 2008); *Wood v. Penntex Resources LP*, 2008 WL 2609319 (S.D. Tex. 2008); *First Options of Chicago v. Kaplan*, 115 S. Ct. 1920 (1995); *Wilko v. Swan*, 74 S. Ct. 182 (1953); *Montes v. Shearson Lehman Bros.*, 128 F.3d 1456 (11th Cir. 1997); *Merrill Lynch v. Bobker*, 808 F.2d 930 (2d Cir. 1986).

[36]*Howsom v. Dean Witter*, 123 S. Ct. 588 (2002); *Michaels v. Mariforum Shipping S.A.*, 624 F.2d 411 (2d Cir. 1980).

provide otherwise. Nevertheless, the presumption is that an arbitrator should decide allegations of waiver, delay or defense to arbitrability. Under the Federal Arbitration Act an arbitrator shall decide whether a condition precedent to arbitrability has been fulfilled. In the absence of an agreement to the contrary, issues of substantive arbitrability are for a court to decide. Issues of procedural arbitrability, i.e., whether prerequisites, such as time limits, notices, laches, estoppel, and other conditions precedent to an obligation to arbitrate have been met, are for the arbitrators to decide.

NON-SIGNATORY TO AN ARBITRATION AGREEMENT. Although some conflicts exist, a non-signatory to an arbitration agreement can be compelled to arbitrate. Whether a court should decide if a non-signatory should be bound by the arbitration, or the arbitrators should decide whether they should have jurisdiction of the arbitration, seems to be favoring the arbitrators in recent cases.[37]

While the Eleventh Circuit recently agreed that a non-signatory may be compelled to arbitrate, another issue is whether a non-signatory can initiate arbitration proceedings. Conflict does exist, but the trend seems to be, at least in certain cases, to allow a non-party to initiate arbitration where the scope of the arbitration clause is "sufficiently broad" to permit non-signatories to invoke the clause. At least the courts have narrowed the basis of the decision to the wording in the arbitration clause.

RECENT LAW. The litigation concerning arbitration continues each year. The split between the courts seems to increase, rather than decrease. The only recommendation is to carefully review both the state and circuit cases.

ADDITIONAL CHARGES—UNIFORM CONSUMER CREDIT CODE

The Uniform Consumer Credit Code provides that any agreement with respect to a consumer credit sale may not provide for any charges as a result of a default by the buyer other than authorized by the act. A provision in violation of this section is unenforceable. The Consumer Credit Code has been adopted in several western states.

---

[37]*Thomson-CSF, S.A. v. American Arbitration Association*, 64 F.3d 773 (2d Cir. 1995); *Masefield AG v. Colonial Oil Industries, Inc.*, 2005 U.S. Dist. LEXIS 6737 (S.D.N.Y. April 18, 2005); *Blinco v. Green Tree Servicing, LLC*, 400 F.3d 1308 (11th Cir. 2005); *Sherer v. Green Tree Servicing, LLC*, 548 F.3d 379 (5th Cir. 2008); *Bridas S.A.P.I.C. v. Government of Turkmenistan*, 345 F.3d 347 (5th Cir. 2003).

PREDICTIVE DIALERS—ABANDONMENT

A predictive dialer is designed to automatically dial numbers and obtain a live person on the phone for the debt collector. The predictive dialer discards busy signals and disconnected numbers or wrong numbers and offers the debt collector a live debtor on the other end of the telephone line. To furnish this live debtor to the debt collector, the predictive dialer will dial more than enough telephone numbers to ensure that debt collectors are speaking to a live debtor and not spending the time dialing or redialing, etc.

The net result is that the predictive dialer will dial 10 to 20 percent more debtors than necessary to keep 20 to 30 debt collectors busy. Sometimes, when the predictive dialer dials the additional debtors, the additional debtors are not needed and the first 20 debtors contacted will be delivered to the 20 debt collectors. Thus, no live operator is available to speak to the extra live debtors. If a live debt collector does not pick up, the call to that particular debtor within a prescribed number of seconds is abandoned—resulting in what is known as an "abandoned call," which is usually between 3 to 5 percent of all calls.

The abandoned call has found a home amongst some of the consumer attorneys. The theory is that an abandoned call made to a live debtor, who may be a mother or a housewife, may cause that person to worry about stalking or, in the alternative, robbery where the caller is trying to determine whether someone is home to either rob the premises or kidnap the children. The largest percentage of abandoned calls are wrong numbers.

Early in 2005, the Federal Trade Commission released a rulemaking proposal to revise its regulation of the telemarketing industry. In that proposal was the use of predictive dialers and one of the issues was "abandoned calls."

Several states, such as New York, have new legislation concerning predictive dialers and this may be one of the new crusades to protect consumers.

OBLIGATION OF HOSPITAL TO BILL INSURERS

Several inquiries have been made to our office whether a hospital has an obligation to submit the claim to an insurance company. In some states statutes may require the hospital to bill workman's compensation or even the insurance company in a motor vehicle accident. In most instances, none of the papers that a patient signs when entering a hospital contains any obligation upon the hospital to bill the insurance company. Most hospitals do have agreements with the major HMOs. The terms of the contract between the HMO and the hospital may include requirements regarding billing, although the requirements vary from HMO to HMO and from hospital to hospital.

PAYDAY LENDING

Payday lenders across the country continue to make short-term loans to consumers at high interest rates. Many states do not have limitations on rates that lenders can earn on small loans (New Hampshire, Wisconsin, Illinois, New Mexico, Idaho, Washington, and North Dakota).

A number of states prohibit payday lending (most in the northeast from Maine down to South Carolina, Georgia, Alabama, Indiana, Michigan, South Dakota, Texas, Arizona, and Alaska). The remaining states, by and large, have laws that permit payday lending. In some of the states that prohibit payday lending, the lenders have formed relationships with the national banks and other financial institutions because these institutions have federal preemption authority to enable them to operate under federal laws and not the state laws that prohibit the practice.

Several bills have been recently introduced in Congress to regulate the abuses of payday lending, including the usurious rates of interest, as well as prohibiting the relationships between the federally-chartered financial institutions and payday lenders.

Predatory Lending. Predatory lending are loans to consumers with high fees or other oppressive and burdensome terms. Several states have enacted anti-predatory lending laws (including California, Georgia, North Carolina, New York, New Jersey, New Mexico, Arkansas, Illinois, Nevada and Massachusetts). These laws tend to define a predatory loan as a high-cost loan. Once it is defined as a high-cost loan, the restrictions and requirements are triggered. The law is primarily targeted at subprime lenders who take advantage of the poor borrower who may not be adequately represented by counsel.

CANCELLATION OF DEBT—FORM 1099-C

If a federal agency, financial institution, credit or finance company, or credit card company cancels or forgives a debt of $600 or more, they are obligated to forward to the debtor a form 1099-C. When a debt of $600 or more is cancelled, the debtor must report on Schedule F of the federal income tax return the cancelled amount of the debt since it is income for the purposes of income tax.

The American Collectors International in their *Fast Facts* states unequivocally that "there is nothing in the IRS Code, regulations or guidelines that prohibit attempts to collect a debt after filing a Form 1099-C." A creditor should file an amended 1099-C if the debtor pays the debt after receiving the Form 1099-C. Creditors and debt collectors may continue collection activity after a Form 1099-C has been filed, but an amended form should be filed with the IRS and sent to the debtor to correct the prior discharge of the debt.[38]

While an earlier case has held that it is inequitable to allow a creditor to institute a legal action to collect a debt after it has issued an IRS Form 1099-C to the debtor when the form indicates to the debtor that creditor has discharged the debt, the better decisions seem to hold that until the creditor corrects or withdraws the 1099-C that it mistakenly filed against the debtor, a creditor cannot enforce its claim against the debtor.

A Court of Appeals case in California also addressed the problem and stated that the original Form 1099-C, standing alone, should not result in the automatic extinguishments of the obligation. The court further emphasized that the original tax Form 1099-C is not a release, for a release must be clear, explicit and comprehensible. The court felt that the original Form 1099-C hardly meets these requirements and further stated that a Form 1099-C is an IRS reporting document that does not contain the word "release."

While some of the courts are somewhat reluctant to come to the conclusion that a 1099-C is unequivocally not a discharge of a debt, the courts seems to be leaning strongly in that direction. Before any collection activity is commenced against the debtor, including letters, telephone calls, and certainly institution of suit, the creditor should file a corrected return stating that the original 1099-C was filed either in error or whatever other explanation the creditor wishes to furnish to the IRS. At the same time notify the debtor. The obvious purpose of this notification to the debtor and to the IRS is to protect the debtor from paying additional taxes on a debt.[39]

The ACA International reports that most debt purchasers will no longer be required to file a Form 1099-C because payment was not made on a debt within 36 months. If a different triggering event happens, a debt purchaser is still required to file a Form 1099-C. The new regulations are effective as of November 10, 2008. Contained in the regulations are eight triggering events which must occur for an entity to be required to file a Form 1099-C (the 36-month rule is one of the triggering events when the creditor has not received payment of a debt within a 36-month period).

---

[38]*In re Crosby*, 261 B.R. 470 (Bankr. D. Kan. 2001); *International Commercial Bank of China v. L&L, Inc.*, 2005 U.S. Dist. LEXIS 6737 (March 16, 2005); *Franklin Credit Management Corp. v. Nicholas*, 2001 Conn. Super. LEXIS 1908 (Conn. Super. Ct. July 12, 2001); *Hathaway v. Tompkins*, 2005 NY Slip Op 25160 (2005).

[39]*Hathaway v. Tompkins*, 8 Misc.3d 260, 794 N.Y.S.2d 899 (Seneca Co. 2005).

IDENTITY THEFT

Identity theft is occurring more frequently than ever before. A social security number and a name and address provide all the information necessary for someone to assume your identity. Articles in the newspapers and magazines recommend that social security numbers not be offered over the telephone or even in person unless it is absolutely necessary. Furnishing your social security number with your address is an invitation to disaster.

The Circuit Court of Appeals addressed this issue of identity theft wherein the court recognized that in many ways persons are required to make their social security numbers available so that they are no longer private or confidential, but open to scrutiny and copying. An application for credit is a perfect example where a social security number becomes available together with your address. The date of your birth or the first name of your parent is used for confirming identification. Thus, one who has access to a credit application has the opportunity to steal your identity.

In a recent case, the impostor was a receptionist in a doctor's office and copied the information that a patient supplied to the doctor. The impostor then applied for credit to four companies subscribing to TRW credit reports. The impostor used the social security number of the plaintiff, but her own address and own telephone number. The only misinformation was the use of the social security number and the date of birth. In each instance, TRW responded to the credit inquiry by treating the application as made by the plaintiff and added the three inquiries to plaintiff's files.

In one case where the credit was approved, the account became delinquent and therefore was referred to a collection agency. The plaintiff became aware of the impostor when she sought to refinance her home and the financing institution saw the report which combined information from TRW and two other reporting agencies. Now aware of the fraud, the consumer contacted TRW and requested deletion from her file. TRW complied and thereafter a suit was filed alleging that TRW furnished credit reports without reasonable grounds for believing that she was the consumer whom the credit applications involved, and that TRW had not maintained reasonable procedures required by that statute to assure maximum possible accuracy of the information concerning the individual about whom the report relates.[40] Under Section 607(b) the FCRA provides that whenever a consumer reporting agency prepares a consumer report, it shall follow reasonable procedures to assure maximum possible accuracy of the information. The court, after listening to arguments, decided it was a question for the jury whether identity theft had become common enough for it to be reasonable for a credit reporting agency to disclose credit information "merely because the last name matches a social security number on the

[40] *Andrews v. TRW, Inc.*, 255 F.3d 1063 (9th Cir. 2000).

file." The reasonableness of TRW's responses should be assessed by a jury with reference to the information TRW had indicating that the impostor was not the plaintiff. TRW argued that people do use nicknames and change addresses, but the plaintiff argued "how many people misspell their first name" (in this case, one of the applications had a misspelled first name).

The jury would have to determine whether it is reasonable that a social security number trumps all other information of dissimilarity between the plaintiff and an impostor. A sidelight to the cause of action was that the lower court decided that the statute of limitations runs from the time the credit company issued the reports and the appellate court held that the statute of limitations of two years runs from the time of discovery of the fraud and not when the credit reports were issued.

As the databases increase and the opportunities increase, the instances of identity theft will probably increase in direct ratio and the litigation covering identity theft will also increase.

FACTA has addressed the problem by providing the consumer a method to alert the credit reporting agencies. (*See* "FACTA—Identity Theft," following.)

The Federal Trade Commission has passed some regulations which are often called the "red flag rules" which became mandatory by November 1, 2008. The rules are directed at financial institutions such as state or national banks, state or federal savings and loan associations, a mutual savings bank, a state or federal credit union and any other person who directly or indirectly holds a transaction account.

A transaction account is a depositor account in which the depositor is permitted to make withdrawals by negotiable or transfer instruments, payment orders, withdrawal, telephone transfers or other similar transaction for the purpose of making payments or transfers to third person. This includes demand deposits, negotiable order of withdrawal accounts, savings account subject to automatic transfers and shared draft accounts.

ACA, in the Map Bulletin of October 2008, has provided a comprehensive summary of the "red flag rules," which is available to members.[41]

FACTA—IDENTITY THEFT. Section 605a (new) provides consumers with three types of alerts which may be placed in their credit file at the consumer's request by contacting the credit reporting agency. The three alerts are as follows:

Initial Alert. This alert notifies the prospective user of a consumer report that the consumer has been or is about to become a victim of fraud or a related crime including identity theft. The request may be made by the consumer or someone acting on his behalf.

[41]Theft Red Flags under the Fair and Accurate Credit Transaction Act of 2003, 72 F. Reg. 63772-74 (Nov. 9, 2007) (to be codified at 16 C.F.R. pt. 681.2).

The credit reporting agency must include the fraud alert in the file of the consumer and provide the fraud alert with any credit score generated in using that file for a period of not less than 90 days from the date of such request. The consumer or the representative has the right to terminate said alert. The credit reporting agency also has an obligation to report the fraud alert to other consumer reporting agencies and to provide consumers a form to complete with regard to their claim of identity theft or fraud.

The consumer reporting agency is also obliged to provide the consumer with a free copy of his or her entire consumer file. The file should include: all the information in the consumer's file at the time of the request; the source of the information; the names of the parties that have obtained a copy of the consumer's report; the dates, original payees, and amounts of any checks included in the file that have led to an adverse characterization of the consumer; and a record of all inquiries of the past year. This report must be furnished within three business days after a request by the consumer.

Extended Alert. The consumer may request an extended alert. The agency shall then include a fraud alert in the file of the consumer and provide that alert with any credit score generated during the seven-year period beginning on the date of such request unless it is terminated by the consumer. The credit reporting agency will exclude the consumer from any list prepared by the credit reporting agency for a third-party offer of credit or insurance as part of a marketing initiative unless the consumer expressly permits this. The credit reporting agency must notify the other reporting agencies.

Access to Free Reports. As part of the extended alert, the credit reporting agency shall disclose to the consumer that the consumer may request two free copies of his file during the 12-month period beginning on the date on which the identity or fraud alert was included in his file.

Active Duty Alert. Upon the request of a consumer who is on *active military duty*, the credit reporting agency shall include an active duty alert in the consumer's file for a period of not less than 12 months, or such longer period as the commission shall determine unless the consumer requests that such fraud alert be removed before the end of such period. Beginning on the date of such request, the agency shall exclude the active duty military consumer from any list of consumers prepared by the credit reporting agency for any third party for the purposes of marketing, credit, or insurance. The consumer may terminate this action. The credit reporting agency shall also notify the other credit reporting agencies.

Notification to Furnisher of Information. The credit reporting agency shall then notify the furnisher of information identified by the consumer (which information was incorrectly associated with the consumer) that the information may be a result of identity theft and that an identity theft has been reported. Further, the agency shall notify the furnisher of information that a block has been requested and provide the dates of the block.

A consumer reporting agency may decline to block or rescind any block if the agency determines that the information was blocked in error, was requested by the consumer in error, or if the consumer actually obtained possession of goods, services, or money as a result of a blocked transaction. If the credit reporting agency takes such action, they shall promptly notify the consumer.

Consumers are also able to dispute incorrect information on their credit report directly with the data furnisher. Upon receipt of the notification from the consumer, the data furnisher is now required to investigate and review the information provided by the consumer. Prior thereto, the furnisher of the information only had to conduct the investigation if he or she received notification from the credit reporting agency.[42] After the investigation, the furnisher of the information must report the results of the investigation to the credit bureaus within 30 days. Data furnishers also must have in place procedures to prevent reporting the same information a second time.

The responsibility for determining the date of delinquency is on the original creditor who granted the credit. In the event the existing creditor does not have information available from the original credit grantor, the existing creditor has to use reasonably diligent procedures for determining the date of the delinquency. If this change in the law improves the reporting of the date of delinquency, the debt buyers will receive the benefit when purchasing delinquent accounts, for they will be able to put a more accurate value on the account.[43]

SECURITY BREACH NOTIFICATION STATUTES

The Security Breach Notification Statutes enacted in the various states usually cover any person or business which owns or controls computerized data that may include private information. The statutes require a business or person to disclose any breach of the security of that system following the discovery or notification of the breach of the security of the system where private information was acquired by a person who did not have valid authorization. The disclosure must be made within a certain time frame or as quickly as possible and without unreasonable delay. The statutes vary from state to state. Several states have already enacted a statute including the major states such as California, Florida, New Jersey, New York, North Carolina, Pennsylvania, Tennessee, and Texas. Other states are considering

---

[42] *Elmore v. North Fork Bancorporation*, 325 F. Supp. 2d 336 (S.D.N.Y. 2004). *See also Perry v. First Nat'l Bank*, 459 F.3d 816 (7th Cir. 2006); *Cole v. U.S. Capital Inc.*, 389 F.3d 719 (7th Cir. 2004); *McDonald v. Nelnet, Inc.*, 477 F. Supp. 2d 1010 (E.D. Mo. 2007).

[43] *Regatos v. North Fork Bank*, 257 F. Supp. 2d 632 (S.D.N.Y. 2002).

similar bills and even some of the states are revising their bills to have a more effective statute. (*See* Appendix.)[44]

A recent case addressed the issue of a breach in a secured list of clients which was ultimately downloaded and the party then sold the information to a marketing company who in turn used the names and addresses to advertise by use of a direct mail program. The court stated that the plaintiff did not offer evidence of any injury.

In many of these security breach notification instances, the proof of an injury to a class consisting of the names and addresses that were released presents significant difficulties under the class action statute. In most instances the great majority of the names and addresses suffered no injury and those that may have been contacted would still have difficulty proving that they were injured if the names and addresses are used solely for marketing.[45]

Several class actions have been instituted under the statute, but the plaintiffs have not faired particularly well and in one case the plaintiff voluntarily agreed to dismiss the complaint. The courts are not satisfied that the plaintiffs suffered any injury without some evidence that the security breach caused damages to the plaintiffs. Even if some type of injury was absorbed, such as an identity theft, unauthorized use of the credit card, or release of credit information, some type of causal connection must exist between the security breach and the damages sustained. While the class consist of individuals whose non-personal information was accessed as a result of the security breach, connecting the injuries to the breach is difficult.

An increased risk of identity theft is not necessarily sufficient for damages since the legal system does not usually award damages based on a possible future injury. The injury actually has to occur. Some relationship must exist between the act and the damage sustained. The use of a monitoring service has not received favorable treatment by the courts.[46]

SECURED CLAIMS—ATTORNEY FEES

The court will usually allow reasonable attorney fees under Section 506(b) with respect to a mortgage secured by property, the value of which is greater than the amount of the claim. Interest on such claim and any reasonable fees costs or charges provided for under the agreement or state statute are also allowed.

---

[44]Patricia Covington et al., Recent Developments Affecting Privacy in 2007, *Business Lawyer*, Feb. 2008, pg. 639-640.

[45]*Bell v. Acxiom Corp.*, 2006 WL 2850042 (E.D. Ark. Oct. 3, 2006).

[46]*Bell v. Acxiom Corp.*, 2006 WL 2850042 (E.D. Ark. Oct. 3, 2006); *Forbes v. Wells Fargo Bank, N.A.*, 420 F. Supp. 2d 1018 (D. Minn. 2006); *Key v. DSW Inc.*, 454 F. Supp. 2d 684 (S.D. Ohio 2006).

Bankruptcy Chapter 11 Section 1322(b)(2) affords to a petitioner submitting a plan a right to modify the rights of holders of secured claims, other than a claim secured by a security interest in real property that is the debtor's principle residence (subject to Section 1322(e)). The interplay of these statutes appears to indicate that Section 506(b) does not really apply to post-confirmation fees and costs or charges, but does apply to pre-confirmation fees and charges where the property is secured by the debtor's principal residence. (*See* Chapter 6.)

OUTRAGEOUS CONDUCT

While the facts and circumstances of this case were unusual, it illustrates the exposure of creditors in attempting to collect their debts directly from the debtors—and step over the line of common sense.

The wife committed credit card fraud by obtaining credit cards in the name of her husband not only from Discover but from other credit card companies. The husband asserted that Discover was on notice of his wife's fragile mental status and crossed the line between excessive but permissible pressure tactics and outrageous conduct intended to cause harm.

Discover argued that the debtor had actually committed credit card fraud. By unlawfully submitting her husband's personal information over the internet to obtain a credit card, threatening criminal action was justified.

The court acknowledged that Discover was owed the debt, but plaintiff was not necessarily criminally libel for credit card fraud. Accordingly, the claim for outrageous conduct is sufficient based on Discover's threats of criminal prosecution for failure to pay a civil debt and threatening the plaintiff with jail. The husband contended his wife committed suicide as a direct result of the pressure exerted by Discover.

The general rule is that a creditor has a right to urge payment of a just debt and to threaten to resort to proper legal procedure to enforce the obligation. The use of improper methods to collect the debt may be the basis for the maintenance of an action for mental or emotion distress.

The court stretched a bit and stated that a wife's insertion of her husband's name and social security number to obtain a credit card, even if she does so without his permission, is not necessarily fraud. Most of the claims of the plaintiff for wrongful death, fraud, civil extortion, violations of the Fair Debt Collection Practices Act, credit defamation and violation of the Truth in Lending Act were dismissed, but the court did leave open the intentional infliction of the emotional distress claim for further proceedings.

The moral of the story and the reason for its inclusion in the book is to point out that a debt collector does not at any time know exactly the circumstances or the physical and mental condition of the party who is on the other side of the telephone. The threat of criminal prosecution, putting someone in jail or stating that somebody will come "visit" them at the house (all of which took place in this case) are wrought with danger even if the defendant had legally the right to make such statements. In this case, the wife committed suicide and left a note stating that the pressures exerted upon her were too much.[47]

---

[47] *MacDermid v. Discover Fin. Servs.*, 488 F.3d 721 (6th Cir. 2007).

CHAPTER 5 APPENDIX I

COMMERCIAL ARBITRATION RULES OF THE AMERICAN ARBITRATION ASSOCIATION*

Commercial Arbitration Rules and Mediation PROCEDURES (Including Procedures for Large, Complex Commercial Disputes) Amended and Effective September 1, 2007

IMPORTANT NOTICE

These rules and any amendment of them shall apply in the form in effect at the time the administrative filing requirements are met for a demand for arbitration or submission agreement received by the AAA. To ensure that you have the most current information, see our Web Site at www.adr.org.

INTRODUCTION

Each year, many millions of business transactions take place. Occasionally, disagreements develop over these business transactions. Many of these disputes are resolved by arbitration, the voluntary submission of a dispute to an impartial person or persons for final and binding determination. Arbitration has proven to be an effective way to resolve these disputes privately, promptly, and economically.

The American Arbitration Association (AAA), a not-for-profit, public service organization, offers a broad range of dispute resolution services to business executives, attorneys, individuals, trade associations, unions, management, consumers, families, communities, and all levels of government. Services are available through AAA headquarters in New York and through offices located in major cities throughout the United States. Hearings may be held at locations convenient for the parties and are not limited to cities with AAA offices. In addition, the AAA serves as a center for education and training, issues specialized publications, and conducts research on all forms of out-of-court dispute settlement.

---

*Reprinted with permission of the American Association.

Standard Arbitration Clause

The parties can provide for arbitration of future disputes by inserting the following clause into their contracts:

> *Any controversy or claim arising out of or relating to this contract, or the breach thereof, shall be settled by arbitration administered by the American Arbitration Association under its Commercial Arbitration Rules, and judgment on the award rendered by the arbitrator(s) may be entered in any court having jurisdiction thereof.*

Arbitration of existing disputes may be accomplished by use of the following:

> *We, the undersigned parties, hereby agree to submit to arbitration administered by the American Arbitration Association under its Commercial Arbitration Rules the following controversy: (describe briefly) We further agree that the above controversy be submitted to (one) (three) arbitrator(s). We further agree that we will faithfully observe this agreement and the rules, that we will abide by and perform any award rendered by the arbitrator(s), and that a judgment of any court having jurisdiction may be entered on the award.*

In transactions likely to require emergency interim relief, the parties may wish to add to their clause the following language:

> *The parties also agree that the AAA Optional Rules for Emergency Measures of Protection shall apply to the proceedings.*

These Optional Rules may be found below.

The services of the AAA are generally concluded with the transmittal of the award. Although there is voluntary compliance with the majority of awards, judgment on the award can be entered in a court having appropriate jurisdiction if necessary.

Administrative Fees

The AAA charges a filing fee based on the amount of the claim or counterclaim. This fee information, which is included with these rules, allows the parties to exercise control over their administrative fees. The employee under certain circumstances can obtain a hardship status or meet the criteria of a promulgated plan employment agreement and avoid the obligation to split the fees of the arbitrator.

The fees cover AAA administrative services; they do not cover arbitrator compensation or expenses, if any, reporting services, or any post-award charges incurred by the parties in enforcing the award.

Mediation

The parties might wish to submit their dispute to mediation prior to arbitration. In mediation, the neutral mediator assists the parties in reaching a settlement but does not have the authority to make a binding decision or award. Mediation is administered by the AAA in accordance with its Commercial Mediation

Procedures. There is no additional administrative fee where parties to a pending arbitration attempt to mediate their dispute under the AAA's auspices.

If the parties want to adopt mediation as a part of their contractual dispute settlement procedure, they can insert the following mediation clause into their contract in conjunction with a standard arbitration provision:

> *If a dispute arises out of or relates to this contract, or the breach thereof, and if the dispute cannot be settled through negotiation, the parties agree first to try in good faith to settle the dispute by mediation administered by the American Arbitration Association under its Commercial Mediation Procedures before resorting to arbitration, litigation, or some other dispute resolution procedure.*

If the parties want to use a mediator to resolve an existing dispute, they can enter into the following submission:

> *The parties hereby submit the following dispute to mediation administered by the American Arbitration Association under its Commercial Mediation Procedures. (The clause may also provide for the qualifications of the mediator(s), method of payment, locale of meetings, and any other item of concern to the parties.)*

Large, Complex Cases

Unless the parties agree otherwise, the procedures for Large, Complex Commercial Disputes, which appear in this pamphlet, will be applied to all cases administered by the AAA under the Commercial Arbitration Rules in which the disclosed claim or counterclaim of any party is at least $500,000 exclusive of claimed interest, arbitration fees and costs.

The key features of these procedures include:

- a highly qualified, trained Roster of Neutrals;
- a mandatory preliminary hearing with the arbitrators, which may be conducted by teleconference;
- broad arbitrator authority to order and control discovery, including depositions;
- presumption that hearings will proceed on a consecutive or block basis.

COMMERCIAL MEDIATION PROCEDURES

M-1. Agreement of Parties

Whenever, by stipulation or in their contract, the parties have provided for mediation or conciliation of existing or future disputes under the auspices of the American Arbitration Association (AAA) or under these procedures, the parties and their representatives, unless agreed otherwise in writing, shall be deemed to have made these procedural guidelines, as amended and in effect as of the date of filing of a request for mediation, a part of their agreement and designate the AAA as the administrator of their mediation.

The parties by mutual agreement may vary any part of these procedures including, but not limited to, agreeing to conduct the mediation via telephone or other electronic or technical means.

M-2. Initiation of Mediation

Any party or parties to a dispute may initiate mediation under the AAA's auspices by making a request for mediation to any of the AAA's regional offices or case management centers via telephone, email, regular mail or fax.

Requests for mediation may also be filed online via WebFile at www.adr.org.

The party initiating the mediation shall simultaneously notify the other party or parties of the request. The initiating party shall provide the following information to the AAA and the other party or parties as applicable:

i. A copy of the mediation provision of the parties' contract or the parties' stipulation to mediate.
ii. The names, regular mail addresses, email addresses, and telephone numbers of all parties to the dispute and representatives, if any, in the mediation.
iii. A brief statement of the nature of the dispute and the relief requested.
iv. Any specific qualifications the mediator should possess.

Where there is no preexisting stipulation or contract by which the parties have provided for mediation of existing or future disputes under the auspices of the AAA, a party may request the AAA to invite another party to participate in "mediation by voluntary submission." Upon receipt of such a request, the AAA will contact the other party or parties involved in the dispute and attempt to obtain a submission to mediation.

M-3. Representation

Subject to any applicable law, any party may be represented by persons of the party's choice. The names and addresses of such persons shall be communicated in writing to all parties and to the AAA.

M-4. Appointment of the Mediator

Parties may search the online profiles of the AAA's Panel of Mediators at www.aaamediation.com in an effort to agree on a mediator. If the parties have not agreed to the appointment of a mediator and have not provided any other method of appointment, the mediator shall be appointed in the following manner:

i. Upon receipt of a request for mediation, the AAA will send to each party a list of mediators from the AAA's Panel of Mediators. The parties are encouraged to agree to a mediator from the submitted list and to advise the AAA of their agreement.

ii. If the parties are unable to agree upon a mediator, each party shall strike unacceptable names from the list, number the remaining names in order of preference, and return the list to the AAA. If a party does not return the list within the time specified, all mediators on the list shall be deemed acceptable. From among the mediators who have been mutually approved by the parties, and in accordance with the designated order of mutual preference, the AAA shall invite a mediator to serve.

iii. If the parties fail to agree on any of the mediators listed, or if acceptable mediators are unable to serve, or if for any other reason the appointment cannot be made from the submitted list, the AAA shall have the authority to make the appointment from among other members of the Panel of Mediators without the submission of additional lists.

M-5. Mediator's Impartiality and Duty to Disclose

AAA mediators are required to abide by the Model Standards of Conduct for Mediators in effect at the time a mediator is appointed to a case. Where there is a conflict between the Model Standards and any provision of these Mediation Procedures, these Mediation Procedures shall govern. The Standards require mediators to (i) decline a mediation if the mediator cannot conduct it in an impartial manner, and (ii) disclose, as soon as practicable, all actual and potential conflicts of interest that are reasonably known to the mediator and could reasonably be seen as raising a question about the mediator's impartiality.

Prior to accepting an appointment, AAA mediators are required to make a reasonable inquiry to determine whether there are any facts that a reasonable individual would consider likely to create a potential or actual conflict of interest for the mediator. AAA mediators are required to disclose any circumstance likely to create a presumption of bias or prevent a resolution of the parties' dispute within the time-frame desired by the parties. Upon receipt of such disclosures, the AAA shall immediately communicate the disclosures to the parties for their comments.

The parties may, upon receiving disclosure of actual or potential conflicts of interest of the mediator, waive such conflicts and proceed with the mediation. In the event that a party disagrees as to whether the mediator shall serve, or in the event that the mediator's conflict of interest might reasonably be viewed as undermining the integrity of the mediation, the mediator shall be replaced.

M-6. Vacancies

If any mediator shall become unwilling or unable to serve, the AAA will appoint another mediator, unless the parties agree otherwise, in accordance with section M-4.

M-7. Duties and Responsibilities of the Mediator

i. The mediator shall conduct the mediation based on the principle of party self-determination. Self-determination is the act of coming to a voluntary, uncoerced decision in which each party makes free and informed choices as to process and outcome.

ii. The mediator is authorized to conduct separate or ex parte meetings and other communications with the parties and/or their representatives, before, during, and after any scheduled mediation conference. Such communications may be conducted via telephone, in writing, via email, online, in person or otherwise.

iii. The parties are encouraged to exchange all documents pertinent to the relief requested. The mediator may request the exchange of memoranda on issues, including the underlying interests and the history of the parties' negotiations. Information that a party wishes to keep confidential may be sent to the mediator, as necessary, in a separate communication with the mediator.

iv. The mediator does not have the authority to impose a settlement on the parties but will attempt to help them reach a satisfactory resolution of their dispute. Subject to the discretion of the mediator, the mediator may make oral or written recommendations for settlement to a party privately or, if the parties agree, to all parties jointly.

v. In the event a complete settlement of all or some issues in dispute is not achieved within the scheduled mediation session(s), the mediator may continue to communicate with the parties, for a period of time, in an ongoing effort to facilitate a complete settlement.

vi. The mediator is not a legal representative of any party and has no fiduciary duty to any party.

M-8. Responsibilities of the Parties

The parties shall ensure that appropriate representatives of each party, having authority to consummate a settlement, attend the mediation conference.

Prior to and during the scheduled mediation conference session(s) the parties and their representatives shall, as appropriate to each party's circumstances, exercise their best efforts to prepare for and engage in a meaningful and productive mediation.

M-9. Privacy

Mediation sessions and related mediation communications are private proceedings. The parties and their representatives may attend mediation sessions. Other persons may attend only with the permission of the parties and with the consent of the mediator.

M-10. Confidentiality

Subject to applicable law or the parties' agreement, confidential information disclosed to a mediator by the parties or by other participants (witnesses) in the course of the mediation shall not be divulged by the mediator. The mediator shall maintain the confidentiality of all information obtained in the mediation, and all records, reports, or other documents received by a mediator while serving in that capacity shall be confidential.

The mediator shall not be compelled to divulge such records or to testify in regard to the mediation in any adversary proceeding or judicial forum.

The parties shall maintain the confidentiality of the mediation and shall not rely on, or introduce as evidence in any arbitral, judicial, or other proceeding the following, unless agreed to by the parties or required by applicable law:

i. Views expressed or suggestions made by a party or other participant with respect to a possible settlement of the dispute;
ii. Admissions made by a party or other participant in the course of the mediation proceedings;
iii. Proposals made or views expressed by the mediator; or
iv. The fact that a party had or had not indicated willingness to accept a proposal for settlement made by the mediator.

M-11. No Stenographic Record

There shall be no stenographic record of the mediation process.

M-12. Termination of Mediation

The mediation shall be terminated:

i. By the execution of a settlement agreement by the parties; or
ii. By a written or verbal declaration of the mediator to the effect that further efforts at mediation would not contribute to a resolution of the parties' dispute; or
iii. By a written or verbal declaration of all parties to the effect that the mediation proceedings are terminated; or
iv. When there has been no communication between the mediator and any party or party's representative for 21 days following the conclusion of the mediation conference.

M-13. Exclusion of Liability

Neither the AAA nor any mediator is a necessary party in judicial proceedings relating to the mediation. Neither the AAA nor any mediator shall be liable to any party for any error, act or omission in connection with any mediation conducted under these procedures.

M-14. Interpretation and Application of Procedures

The mediator shall interpret and apply these procedures insofar as they relate to the mediator's duties and responsibilities. All other procedures shall be interpreted and applied by the AAA.

M-15. Deposits

Unless otherwise directed by the mediator, the AAA will require the parties to deposit in advance of the mediation conference such sums of money as it, in consultation with the mediator, deems necessary to cover the costs and expenses of the mediation and shall render an accounting to the parties and return any unexpended balance at the conclusion of the mediation.

M-16. Expenses

All expenses of the mediation, including required traveling and other expenses or charges of the mediator, shall be borne equally by the parties unless they agree otherwise. The expenses of participants for either side shall be paid by the party requesting the attendance of such participants.

M-17. Cost of the Mediation

There is no filing fee to initiate a mediation or a fee to request the AAA to invite parties to mediate.

The cost of mediation is based on the hourly mediation rate published on the mediator's AAA profile. This rate covers both mediator compensation and an allocated portion for the AAA's services. There is a four-hour minimum charge for a mediation conference. Expenses referenced in Section M-16 may also apply.

If a matter submitted for mediation is withdrawn or cancelled or results in a settlement after the agreement to mediate is filed but prior to the mediation conference, the cost is $250 plus any mediator time and charges incurred.

The parties will be billed equally for all costs unless they agree otherwise.

If you have questions about mediation costs or services visit our website at www.adr.org or contact your local AAA office.

Conference Room Rental

The costs described above do not include the use of AAA conference rooms. Conference rooms are available on a rental basis. Please contact your local AAA office for availability and rates.

COMMERCIAL ARBITRATION RULES

R-1. Agreement of Parties*†

(a) The parties shall be deemed to have made these rules a part of their arbitration agreement whenever they have provided for arbitration by the American Arbitration Association (hereinafter AAA) under its Commercial Arbitration Rules or for arbitration by the AAA of a domestic commercial dispute without specifying particular rules. These rules and any amendment of them shall apply in the form in effect at the time the administrative requirements are met for a demand for arbitration or submission agreement received by the AAA. The parties, by written agreement, may vary the procedures set forth in these rules. After appointment of the arbitrator, such modifications may be made only with the consent of the arbitrator.

(b) Unless the parties or the AAA determines otherwise, the Expedited Procedures shall apply in any case in which no disclosed claim or counterclaim exceeds $75,000, exclusive of interest and arbitration fees and costs. Parties may also agree to use these procedures in larger cases. Unless the parties agree otherwise, these procedures will not apply in cases involving more than two parties. The Expedited Procedures shall be applied as described in Sections E-1 through E-10 of these rules, in addition to any other portion of these rules that is not in conflict with the Expedited Procedures.

(c) Unless the parties agree otherwise, the Procedures for Large, Complex Commercial Disputes shall apply to all cases in which the disclosed claim or counterclaim of any party is at least $500,000, exclusive of claimed interest, arbitration fees and costs. Parties may also agree to use the Procedures in cases involving claims or counterclaims under $500,000, or in nonmonetary cases. The Procedures for Large, Complex Commercial Disputes shall be applied as described in Sections L-1 through L-4 of these rules, in addition to any other portion of these rules that is not in conflict with the Procedures for Large, Complex Commercial Disputes.

(d) All other cases shall be administered in accordance with Sections R-1 through R-54 of these rules.

---

*The AAA applies the *Supplementary Procedures for Consumer-Related Disputes* to arbitration clauses in agreements between individual consumers and businesses where the business has a standardized, systematic application of arbitration clauses with customers and where the terms and conditions of the purchase of standardized, consumable goods or services are non-negotiable or primarily non-negotiable in most or all of its terms, conditions, features, or choices. The product or service must be for personal or household use. The AAA will have the discretion to apply or not to apply the Supplementary Procedures and the parties will be able to bring any disputes concerning the application or non-application to the attention of the arbitrator. Consumers are not prohibited from seeking relief in a small claims court for disputes or claims within the scope of its jurisdiction, even in consumer arbitration cases filed by the business.

†A dispute arising out of an employer promulgated plan will be administered under the AAA's National Rules for the Resolution of Employment Disputes.

R-2. AAA and Delegation of Duties

When parties agree to arbitrate under these rules, or when they provide for arbitration by the AAA and an arbitration is initiated under these rules, they thereby authorize the AAA to administer the arbitration. The authority and duties of the AAA are prescribed in the agreement of the parties and in these rules, and may be carried out through such of the AAA's representatives as it may direct. The AAA may, in its discretion, assign the administration of an arbitration to any of its offices.

R-3. National Roster of Arbitrators

The AAA shall establish and maintain a National Roster of Commercial Arbitrators ("National Roster") and shall appoint arbitrators as provided in these rules. The term "arbitrator" in these rules refers to the arbitration panel, constituted for a particular case, whether composed of one or more arbitrators, or to an individual arbitrator, as the context requires.

R-4. Initiation under an Arbitration Provision in a Contract

(a) Arbitration under an arbitration provision in a contract shall be initiated in the following manner:

   (i) The initiating party (the "claimant") shall, within the time period, if any, specified in the contract(s), give to the other party (the "respondent") written notice of its intention to arbitrate (the "demand"), which demand shall contain a statement setting forth the nature of the dispute, the names and addresses of all other parties, the amount involved, if any, the remedy sought, and the hearing locale requested.

   (ii) The claimant shall file at any office of the AAA two copies of the demand and two copies of the arbitration provisions of the contract, together with the appropriate filing fee as provided in the schedule included with these rules.

   (iii) The AAA shall confirm notice of such filing to the parties.

(b) A respondent may file an answering statement in duplicate with the AAA within 15 days after confirmation of notice of filing of the demand is sent by the AAA. The respondent shall, at the time of any such filing, send a copy of the answering statement to the claimant. If a counterclaim is asserted, it shall contain a statement setting forth the nature of the counterclaim, the amount involved, if any, and the remedy sought. If a counterclaim is made, the party making the counterclaim shall forward to the AAA with the answering statement the appropriate fee provided in the schedule included with these rules.

(c) If no answering statement is filed within the stated time, respondent will be deemed to deny the claim. Failure to file an answering statement shall not operate to delay the arbitration.

(d) When filing any statement pursuant to this section, the parties are encouraged to provide descriptions of their claims in sufficient detail to make the circumstances of the dispute clear to the arbitrator.

R-5. Initiation under a Submission

Parties to any existing dispute may commence an arbitration under these rules by filing at any office of the AAA two copies of a written submission to arbitrate under these rules, signed by the parties. It shall contain a statement of the nature of the dispute, the names and addresses of all parties, any claims and counterclaims, the amount involved, if any, the remedy sought, and the hearing locale requested, together with the appropriate filing fee as provided in the schedule included with these rules. Unless the parties state otherwise in the submission, all claims and counterclaims will be deemed to be denied by the other party.

R-6. Changes of Claim

After filing of a claim, if either party desires to make any new or different claim or counterclaim, it shall be made in writing and filed with the AAA. The party asserting such a claim or counterclaim shall provide a copy to the other party, who shall have 15 days from the date of such transmission within which to file an answering statement with the AAA. After the arbitrator is appointed, however, no new or different claim may be submitted except with the arbitrator's consent.

R-7. Jurisdiction

(a) The arbitrator shall have the power to rule on his or her own jurisdiction, including any objections with respect to the existence, scope or validity of the arbitration agreement.

(b) The arbitrator shall have the power to determine the existence or validity of a contract of which an arbitration clause forms a part. Such an arbitration clause shall be treated as an agreement independent of the other terms of the contract. A decision by the arbitrator that the contract is null and void shall not for that reason alone render invalid the arbitration clause.

(c) A party must object to the jurisdiction of the arbitrator or to the arbitrability of a claim or counterclaim no later than the filing of the answering statement to the claim or counterclaim that gives rise to the objection. The arbitrator may rule on such objections as a preliminary matter or as part of the final award.

R-8. Mediation

At any stage of the proceedings, the parties may agree to conduct a mediation conference under the Commercial Mediation Procedures in order to facilitate settlement. The mediator shall not be an arbitrator appointed to the case. Where the parties to a pending arbitration agree to mediate under the AAA's rules, no additional administrative fee is required to initiate the mediation.

R-9. Administrative Conference

At the request of any party or upon the AAA's own initiative, the AAA may conduct an administrative conference, in person or by telephone, with the parties and/or their representatives. The conference may address such issues as arbitrator selection, potential mediation of the dispute, potential exchange of information, a timetable for hearings and any other administrative matters.

R-10. Fixing of Locale

The parties may mutually agree on the locale where the arbitration is to be held. If any party requests that the hearing be held in a specific locale and the other party files no objection thereto within 15 days after notice of the request has been sent to it by the AAA, the locale shall be the one requested. If a party objects to the locale requested by the other party, the AAA shall have the power to determine the locale, and its decision shall be final and binding.

R-11. Appointment from National Roster

If the parties have not appointed an arbitrator and have not provided any other method of appointment, the arbitrator shall be appointed in the following manner:

(a) Immediately after the filing of the submission or the answering statement or the expiration of the time within which the answering statement is to be filed, the AAA shall send simultaneously to each party to the dispute an identical list of 10 (unless the AAA decides that a different number is appropriate) names of persons chosen from the National Roster. The parties are encouraged to agree to an arbitrator from the submitted list and to advise the AAA of their agreement.

(b) If the parties are unable to agree upon an arbitrator, each party to the dispute shall have 15 days from the transmittal date in which to strike names objected to, number the remaining names in order of preference, and return the list to the AAA. If a party does not return the list within the time specified, all persons named therein shall be deemed acceptable. From among the persons who have been approved on both lists, and in accordance with the designated order of mutual preference, the AAA shall invite the acceptance of an arbitrator to serve. If the parties fail to agree on any of the persons named, or if acceptable arbitrators are unable to act, or if for any other reason the appointment cannot be made from the submitted lists, the AAA shall have the power to make the appointment from among other members of the National Roster without the submission of additional lists.

(c) Unless the parties agree otherwise when there are two or more claimants or two or more respondents, the AAA may appoint all the arbitrators.

R-12. Direct Appointment by a Party

(a) If the agreement of the parties names an arbitrator or specifies a method of appointing an arbitrator, that designation or method shall be followed.

The notice of appointment, with the name and address of the arbitrator, shall be filed with the AAA by the appointing party. Upon the request of any appointing party, the AAA shall submit a list of members of the National Roster from which the party may, if it so desires, make the appointment.

(b) Where the parties have agreed that each party is to name one arbitrator, the arbitrators so named must meet the standards of Section R-17 with respect to impartiality and independence unless the parties have specifically agreed pursuant to Section R-17(a) that the party-appointed arbitrators are to be non-neutral and need not meet those standards.

(c) If the agreement specifies a period of time within which an arbitrator shall be appointed and any party fails to make the appointment within that period, the AAA shall make the appointment.

(d) If no period of time is specified in the agreement, the AAA shall notify the party to make the appointment. If within 15 days after such notice has been sent, an arbitrator has not been appointed by a party, the AAA shall make the appointment.

R-13. Appointment of Chairperson by Party-Appointed Arbitrators or Parties

(a) If, pursuant to Section R-12, either the parties have directly appointed arbitrators, or the arbitrators have been appointed by the AAA, and the parties have authorized them to appoint a chairperson within a specified time and no appointment is made within that time or any agreed extension, the AAA may appoint the chairperson.

(b) If no period of time is specified for appointment of the chairperson and the party-appointed arbitrators or the parties do not make the appointment within 15 days from the date of the appointment of the last party-appointed arbitrator, the AAA may appoint the chairperson.

(c) If the parties have agreed that their party-appointed arbitrators shall appoint the chairperson from the National Roster, the AAA shall furnish to the party-appointed arbitrators, in the manner provided in Section R-11, a list selected from the National Roster, and the appointment of the chairperson shall be made as provided in that Section.

R-14. Nationality of Arbitrator

Where the parties are nationals of different countries, the AAA, at the request of any party or on its own initiative, may appoint as arbitrator a national of a country other than that of any of the parties. The request must be made before the time set for the appointment of the arbitrator as agreed by the parties or set by these rules.

R-15. Number of Arbitrators

If the arbitration agreement does not specify the number of arbitrators, the dispute shall be heard and determined by one arbitrator, unless the AAA, in its discretion, directs that three arbitrators be appointed. A party may request three arbitrators in the demand or answer, which request the AAA will consider in exercising its discretion regarding the number of arbitrators appointed to the dispute.

R-16. Disclosure

(a) Any person appointed or to be appointed as an arbitrator shall disclose to the AAA any circumstance likely to give rise to justifiable doubt as to the arbitrator's impartiality or independence, including any bias or any financial or personal interest in the result of the arbitration or any past or present relationship with the parties or their representatives. Such obligation shall remain in effect throughout the arbitration.

(b) Upon receipt of such information from the arbitrator or another source, the AAA shall communicate the information to the parties and, if it deems it appropriate to do so, to the arbitrator and others.

(c) In order to encourage disclosure by arbitrators, disclosure of information pursuant to this Section R-16 is not to be construed as an indication that the arbitrator considers that the disclosed circumstance is likely to affect impartiality or independence.

R-17. Disqualification of Arbitrator

(a) Any arbitrator shall be impartial and independent and shall perform his or her duties with diligence and in good faith, and shall be subject to disqualification for

  (i) partiality or lack of independence,

  (ii) inability or refusal to perform his or her duties with diligence and in good faith, and

  (iii) any grounds for disqualification provided by applicable law. The parties may agree in writing, however, that arbitrators directly appointed by a party pursuant to Section R-12 shall be nonneutral, in which case such arbitrators need not be impartial or independent and shall not be subject to disqualification for partiality or lack of independence.

(b) Upon objection of a party to the continued service of an arbitrator, or on its own initiative, the AAA shall determine whether the arbitrator should be disqualified under the grounds set out above, and shall inform the parties of its decision, which decision shall be conclusive.

R-18. Communication with Arbitrator

(a) No party and no one acting on behalf of any party shall communicate ex parte with an arbitrator or a candidate for arbitrator concerning the arbitration, except that a party, or someone acting on behalf of a party, may communicate ex parte with a candidate for direct appointment pursuant to Section R-12 in order to advise the candidate of the general nature of the controversy and of the anticipated proceedings and to discuss the candidate's qualifications, availability, or independence in relation to the parties or to discuss the suitability of candidates for selection as a third arbitrator where the parties or party-designated arbitrators are to participate in that selection.

(b) Section R-18(a) does not apply to arbitrators directly appointed by the parties who, pursuant to Section R-17(a), the parties have agreed in writing are non-neutral. Where the parties have so agreed under Section R-17(a), the AAA shall as an administrative practice suggest to the parties that they agree further that Section R-18(a) should nonetheless apply prospectively.

R-19. Vacancies

(a) If for any reason an arbitrator is unable to perform the duties of the office, the AAA may, on proof satisfactory to it, declare the office vacant. Vacancies shall be filled in accordance with the applicable provisions of these rules.

(b) In the event of a vacancy in a panel of neutral arbitrators after the hearings have commenced, the remaining arbitrator or arbitrators may continue with the hearing and determination of the controversy, unless the parties agree otherwise.

(c) In the event of the appointment of a substitute arbitrator, the panel of arbitrators shall determine in its sole discretion whether it is necessary to repeat all or part of any prior hearings.

R-20. Preliminary Hearing

(a) At the request of any party or at the discretion of the arbitrator or the AAA, the arbitrator may schedule as soon as practicable a preliminary hearing with the parties and/or their representatives. The preliminary hearing may be conducted by telephone at the arbitrator's discretion.

(b) During the preliminary hearing, the parties and the arbitrator should discuss the future conduct of the case, including clarification of the issues and claims, a schedule for the hearings and any other preliminary matters.

R-21. Exchange of Information

(a) At the request of any party or at the discretion of the arbitrator, consistent with the expedited nature of arbitration, the arbitrator may direct
   (i) the production of documents and other information, and
   (ii) the identification of any witnesses to be called.

(b) At least five business days prior to the hearing, the parties shall exchange copies of all exhibits they intend to submit at the hearing.

(c) The arbitrator is authorized to resolve any disputes concerning the exchange of information.

R-22. Date, Time, and Place of Hearing

The arbitrator shall set the date, time, and place for each hearing. The parties shall respond to requests for hearing dates in a timely manner, be cooperative in scheduling the earliest practicable date, and adhere to the established hearing schedule. The AAA shall send a notice of hearing to the parties at least 10 days in advance of the hearing date, unless otherwise agreed by the parties.

R-23. Attendance at Hearings

The arbitrator and the AAA shall maintain the privacy of the hearings unless the law provides to the contrary. Any person having a direct interest in the arbitration is entitled to attend hearings. The arbitrator shall otherwise have the power to require the exclusion of any witness, other than a party or other essential person, during the testimony of any other witness. It shall be discretionary with the arbitrator to determine the propriety of the attendance of any other person other than a party and its representatives.

R-24. Representation

Any party may be represented by counsel or other authorized representative. A party intending to be so represented shall notify the other party and the AAA of the name and address of the representative at least three days prior to the date set for the hearing at which that person is first to appear. When such a representative initiates an arbitration or responds for a party, notice is deemed to have been given.

R-25. Oaths

Before proceeding with the first hearing, each arbitrator may take an oath of office and, if required by law, shall do so. The arbitrator may require witnesses to testify under oath administered by any duly qualified person and, if it is required by law or requested by any party, shall do so.

R-26. Stenographic Record

Any party desiring a stenographic record shall make arrangements directly with a stenographer and shall notify the other parties of these arrangements at least three days in advance of the hearing. The requesting party or parties shall pay the cost of the record. If the transcript is agreed by the parties, or determined by the arbitrator to be the official record of the proceeding, it must be provided to the arbitrator and made available to the other parties for inspection, at a date, time, and place determined by the arbitrator.

R-27. Interpreters

Any party wishing an interpreter shall make all arrangements directly with the interpreter and shall assume the costs of the service.

R-28. Postponements

The arbitrator may postpone any hearing upon agreement of the parties, upon request of a party for good cause shown, or upon the arbitrator's own initiative.

R-29. Arbitration in the Absence of a Party or Representative

Unless the law provides to the contrary, the arbitration may proceed in the absence of any party or representative who, after due notice, fails to be present or fails to obtain a postponement. An award shall not be made solely on the default of a party. The arbitrator shall require the party who is present to submit such evidence as the arbitrator may require for the making of an award.

R-30. Conduct of Proceedings

(a) The claimant shall present evidence to support its claim. The respondent shall then present evidence to support its defense. Witnesses for each party shall also submit to questions from the arbitrator and the adverse party. The arbitrator has the discretion to vary this procedure, provided that the parties are treated with equality and that each party has the right to be heard and is given a fair opportunity to present its case.

(b) The arbitrator, exercising his or her discretion, shall conduct the proceedings with a view to expediting the resolution of the dispute and may direct the order of proof, bifurcate proceedings and direct the parties to focus their presentations on issues the decision of which could dispose of all or part of the case.

(c) The parties may agree to waive oral hearings in any case.

R-31. Evidence

(a) The parties may offer such evidence as is relevant and material to the dispute and shall produce such evidence as the arbitrator may deem necessary to an understanding and determination of the dispute. Conformity to legal rules of evidence shall not be necessary. All evidence shall be taken in the presence of all of the arbitrators and all of the parties, except where any of the parties is absent, in default or has waived the right to be present.

(b) The arbitrator shall determine the admissibility, relevance, and materiality of the evidence offered and may exclude evidence deemed by the arbitrator to be cumulative or irrelevant.

(c) The arbitrator shall take into account applicable principles of legal privilege, such as those involving the confidentiality of communications between a lawyer and client.

(d) An arbitrator or other person authorized by law to subpoena witnesses or documents may do so upon the request of any party or independently.

R-32. Evidence by Affidavit and Post-hearing Filing of Documents or Other Evidence

(a) The arbitrator may receive and consider the evidence of witnesses by declaration or affidavit, but shall give it only such weight as the arbitrator deems it entitled to after consideration of any objection made to its admission.

(b) If the parties agree or the arbitrator directs that documents or other evidence be submitted to the arbitrator after the hearing, the documents or other evidence shall be filed with the AAA for transmission to the arbitrator. All parties shall be afforded an opportunity to examine and respond to such documents or other evidence.

R-33. Inspection or Investigation

An arbitrator finding it necessary to make an inspection or investigation in connection with the arbitration shall direct the AAA to so advise the parties. The arbitrator shall set the date and time and the AAA shall notify the parties. Any party who so desires may be present at such an inspection or investigation. In the event that one or all parties are not present at the inspection or investigation, the arbitrator shall make an oral or written report to the parties and afford them an opportunity to comment.

R-34. Interim Measures**

(a) The arbitrator may take whatever interim measures he or she deems necessary, including injunctive relief and measures for the protection or conservation of property and disposition of perishable goods.

(b) Such interim measures may take the form of an interim award, and the arbitrator may require security for the costs of such measures.

(c) A request for interim measures addressed by a party to a judicial authority shall not be deemed incompatible with the agreement to arbitrate or a waiver of the right to arbitrate.

R-35. Closing of Hearing

The arbitrator shall specifically inquire of all parties whether they have any further proofs to offer or witnesses to be heard. Upon receiving negative replies or if satisfied that the record is complete, the arbitrator shall declare the hearing closed. If briefs are to be filed, the hearing shall be declared closed as of the final date set by the arbitrator for the receipt of briefs. If documents are to be filed as provided in Section R-32 and the date set for their receipt is later than that set for the receipt of briefs, the later date shall be the closing date of the hearing. The time limit within which the arbitrator is required to make the award shall commence, in the absence of other agreements by the parties, upon the closing of the hearing.

**The Optional Rules may be found below.

R-36. Reopening of Hearing

The hearing may be reopened on the arbitrator's initiative, or upon application of a party, at any time before the award is made. If reopening the hearing would prevent the making of the award within the specific time agreed on by the parties in the contract(s) out of which the controversy has arisen, the matter may not be reopened unless the parties agree on an extension of time. When no specific date is fixed in the contract, the arbitrator may reopen the hearing and shall have 30 days from the closing of the reopened hearing within which to make an award.

R-37. Waiver of Rules

Any party who proceeds with the arbitration after knowledge that any provision or requirement of these rules has not been complied with and who fails to state an objection in writing shall be deemed to have waived the right to object.

R-38. Extensions of Time

The parties may modify any period of time by mutual agreement. The AAA or the arbitrator may for good cause extend any period of time established by these rules, except the time for making the award. The AAA shall notify the parties of any extension.

R-39. Serving of Notice

(a) Any papers, notices, or process necessary or proper for the initiation or continuation of an arbitration under these rules, for any court action in connection therewith, or for the entry of judgment on any award made under these rules may be served on a party by mail addressed to the party, or its representative at the last known address or by personal service, in or outside the state where the arbitration is to be held, provided that reasonable opportunity to be heard with regard to the dispute is or has been granted to the party.

(b) The AAA, the arbitrator and the parties may also use overnight delivery or electronic facsimile transmission (fax), to give the notices required by these rules. Where all parties and the arbitrator agree, notices may be transmitted by electronic mail (E-mail), or other methods of communication.

(c) Unless otherwise instructed by the AAA or by the arbitrator, any documents submitted by any party to the AAA or to the arbitrator shall simultaneously be provided to the other party or parties to the arbitration.

R-40. Majority Decision

When the panel consists of more than one arbitrator, unless required by law or by the arbitration agreement, a majority of the arbitrators must make all decisions.

R-41. Time of Award

The award shall be made promptly by the arbitrator and, unless otherwise agreed by the parties or specified by law, no later than 30 days from the date of closing the hearing, or, if oral hearings have been waived, from the date of the AAA's transmittal of the final statements and proofs to the arbitrator.

R-42. Form of Award

(a) Any award shall be in writing and signed by a majority of the arbitrators. It shall be executed in the manner required by law.

(b) The arbitrator need not render a reasoned award unless the parties request such an award in writing prior to appointment of the arbitrator or unless the arbitrator determines that a reasoned award is appropriate.

R-43. Scope of Award

(a) The arbitrator may grant any remedy or relief that the arbitrator deems just and equitable and within the scope of the agreement of the parties, including, but not limited to, specific performance of a contract.

(b) In addition to a final award, the arbitrator may make other decisions, including interim, interlocutory, or partial rulings, orders, and awards. In any interim, interlocutory, or partial award, the arbitrator may assess and apportion the fees, expenses, and compensation related to such award as the arbitrator determines is appropriate.

(c) In the final award, the arbitrator shall assess the fees, expenses, and compensation provided in Sections R-49, R-50, and R-51. The arbitrator may apportion such fees, expenses, and compensation among the parties in such amounts as the arbitrator determines is appropriate.

(d) The award of the arbitrator(s) may include:

  (i) interest at such rate and from such date as the arbitrator(s) may deem appropriate; and

  (ii) an award of attorneys' fees if all parties have requested such an award or it is authorized by law or their arbitration agreement.

R-44. Award upon Settlement

If the parties settle their dispute during the course of the arbitration and if the parties so request, the arbitrator may set forth the terms of the settlement in a "consent award." A consent award must include an allocation of arbitration costs, including administrative fees and expenses as well as arbitrator fees and expenses.

R-45. Delivery of Award to Parties

Parties shall accept as notice and delivery of the award the placing of the award or a true copy thereof in the mail addressed to the parties or their representatives at the last known addresses, personal or electronic service of the award, or the filing of the award in any other manner that is permitted by law.

R-46. Modification of Award

Within 20 days after the transmittal of an award, any party, upon notice to the other parties, may request the arbitrator, through the AAA, to correct any clerical, typographical, or computational errors in the award. The arbitrator is not empowered to redetermine the merits of any claim already decided. The other parties shall be given 10 days to respond to the request. The arbitrator shall dispose of the request within 20 days after transmittal by the AAA to the arbitrator of the request and any response thereto.

R-47. Release of Documents for Judicial Proceedings

The AAA shall, upon the written request of a party, furnish to the party, at the party's expense, certified copies of any papers in the AAA's possession that may be required in judicial proceedings relating to the arbitration.

R-48. Applications to Court and Exclusion of Liability

(a) No judicial proceeding by a party relating to the subject matter of the arbitration shall be deemed a waiver of the party's right to arbitrate.

(b) Neither the AAA nor any arbitrator in a proceeding under these rules is a necessary or proper party in judicial proceedings relating to the arbitration.

(c) Parties to an arbitration under these rules shall be deemed to have consented that judgment upon the arbitration award may be entered in any federal or state court having jurisdiction thereof.

(d) Parties to an arbitration under these rules shall be deemed to have consented that neither the AAA nor any arbitrator shall be liable to any party in any action for damages or injunctive relief for any act or omission in connection with any arbitration under these rules.

R-49. Administrative Fees

As a not-for-profit organization, the AAA shall prescribe an initial filing fee and a case service fee to compensate it for the cost of providing administrative services. The fees in effect when the fee or charge is incurred shall be applicable. The filing fee shall be advanced by the party or parties making a claim or counterclaim, subject to final apportionment by the arbitrator in the award. The AAA may, in the event of extreme hardship on the part of any party, defer or reduce the administrative fees.

R-50. Expenses

The expenses of witnesses for either side shall be paid by the party producing such witnesses. All other expenses of the arbitration, including required travel and other expenses of the arbitrator, AAA representatives, and any witness and the cost of any proof produced at the direct request of the arbitrator, shall be borne equally by the parties, unless they agree otherwise or unless the arbitrator in the award assesses such expenses or any part thereof against any specified party or parties.

R-51. Neutral Arbitrator's Compensation

(a) Arbitrators shall be compensated at a rate consistent with the arbitrator's stated rate of compensation.

(b) If there is disagreement concerning the terms of compensation, an appropriate rate shall be established with the arbitrator by the AAA and confirmed to the parties.

(c) Any arrangement for the compensation of a neutral arbitrator shall be made through the AAA and not directly between the parties and the arbitrator.

R-52. Deposits

The AAA may require the parties to deposit in advance of any hearings such sums of money as it deems necessary to cover the expense of the arbitration, including the arbitrator's fee, if any, and shall render an accounting to the parties and return any unexpended balance at the conclusion of the case.

R-53. Interpretation and Application of Rules

The arbitrator shall interpret and apply these rules insofar as they relate to the arbitrator's powers and duties. When there is more than one arbitrator and a difference arises among them concerning the meaning or application of these rules, it shall be decided by a majority vote. If that is not possible, either an arbitrator or a party may refer the question to the AAA for final decision. All other rules shall be interpreted and applied by the AAA.

R-54. Suspension for Nonpayment

If arbitrator compensation or administrative charges have not been paid in full, the AAA may so inform the parties in order that one of them may advance the required payment. If such payments are not made, the arbitrator may order the suspension or termination of the proceedings. If no arbitrator has yet been appointed, the AAA may suspend the proceedings.

EXPEDITED PROCEDURES

E-1. Limitation on Extensions

Except in extraordinary circumstances, the AAA or the arbitrator may grant a party no more than one seven-day extension of time to respond to the demand for arbitration or counterclaim as provided in Section R-4.

E-2. Changes of Claim or Counterclaim

A claim or counterclaim may be increased in amount, or a new or different claim or counterclaim added, upon the agreement of the other party, or the consent of the arbitrator. After the arbitrator is appointed, however, no new or different claim or counterclaim may be submitted except with the arbitrator's consent. If an increased claim or counterclaim exceeds $75,000, the case will be administered under the regular procedures unless all parties and the arbitrator agree that the case may continue to be processed under the Expedited Procedures.

E-3. Serving of Notices

In addition to notice provided by Section R-39(b), the parties shall also accept notice by telephone. Telephonic notices by the AAA shall subsequently be confirmed in writing to the parties. Should there be a failure to confirm in writing any such oral notice, the proceeding shall nevertheless be valid if notice has, in fact, been given by telephone.

E-4. Appointment and Qualifications of Arbitrator

(a) The AAA shall simultaneously submit to each party an identical list of five proposed arbitrators drawn from its National Roster from which one arbitrator shall be appointed.

(b) The parties are encouraged to agree to an arbitrator from this list and to advise the AAA of their agreement. If the parties are unable to agree upon an arbitrator, each party may strike two names from the list and return it to the AAA within seven days from the date of the AAA's mailing to the parties. If for any reason the appointment of an arbitrator cannot be made from the list, the AAA may make the appointment from other members of the panel without the submission of additional lists.

(c) The parties will be given notice by the AAA of the appointment of the arbitrator, who shall be subject to disqualification for the reasons specified in Section R-17. The parties shall notify the AAA within seven days of any objection to the arbitrator appointed. Any such objection shall be for cause and shall be confirmed in writing to the AAA with a copy to the other party or parties.

E-5. Exchange of Exhibits

At least two business days prior to the hearing, the parties shall exchange copies of all exhibits they intend to submit at the hearing. The arbitrator shall resolve disputes concerning the exchange of exhibits.

E-6. Proceedings on Documents

Where no party's claim exceeds $10,000, exclusive of interest and arbitration costs, and other cases in which the parties agree, the dispute shall be resolved by submission of documents, unless any party requests an oral hearing, or the arbitrator determines that an oral hearing is necessary. The arbitrator shall establish a fair and equitable procedure for the submission of documents.

E-7. Date, Time, and Place of Hearing

In cases in which a hearing is to be held, the arbitrator shall set the date, time, and place of the hearing, to be scheduled to take place within 30 days of confirmation of the arbitrator's appointment. The AAA will notify the parties in advance of the hearing date.

E-8. The Hearing

(a) Generally, the hearing shall not exceed one day. Each party shall have equal opportunity to submit its proofs and complete its case. The arbitrator shall determine the order of the hearing, and may require further submission of documents within two days after the hearing. For good cause shown, the arbitrator may schedule additional hearings within seven business days after the initial day of hearings.

(b) Generally, there will be no stenographic record. Any party desiring a stenographic record may arrange for one pursuant to the provisions of Section R-26.

E-9. Time of Award

Unless otherwise agreed by the parties, the award shall be rendered not later than 14 days from the date of the closing of the hearing or, if oral hearings have been waived, from the date of the AAA's transmittal of the final statements and proofs to the arbitrator.

E-10. Arbitrator's Compensation

Arbitrators will receive compensation at a rate to be suggested by the AAA regional office.

PROCEDURES FOR LARGE, COMPLEX COMMERCIAL DISPUTES

L-1. Administrative Conference

Prior to the dissemination of a list of potential arbitrators, the AAA shall, unless the parties agree otherwise, conduct an administrative conference with the parties and/or their attorneys or other representatives by conference call. The conference will take place within 14 days after the commencement of the arbitration. In the event the parties are unable to agree on a mutually acceptable time for the conference, the AAA may contact the parties individually to discuss the issues contemplated herein. Such administrative conference shall be conducted for the following purposes and for such additional purposes as the parties or the AAA may deem appropriate:

(a) to obtain additional information about the nature and magnitude of the dispute and the anticipated length of hearing and scheduling;

(b) to discuss the views of the parties about the technical and other qualifications of the arbitrators;

(c) to obtain conflicts statements from the parties; and

(d) to consider, with the parties, whether mediation or other non-adjudicative methods of dispute resolution might be appropriate.

L-2. Arbitrators

(a) Large, Complex Commercial Cases shall be heard and determined by either one or three arbitrators, as may be agreed upon by the parties. If the parties are unable to agree upon the number of arbitrators and a claim or counterclaim involves at least $1,000,000, then three arbitrator(s) shall hear and determine the case. If the parties are unable to agree on the number of arbitrators and each claim and counterclaim is less than $1,000,000, then one arbitrator shall hear and determine the case.

(b) The AAA shall appoint arbitrator(s) as agreed by the parties. If they are unable to agree on a method of appointment, the AAA shall appoint arbitrators from the Large, Complex Commercial Case Panel, in the manner provided in the Regular Commercial Arbitration Rules. Absent agreement of the parties, the arbitrator(s) shall not have served as the mediator in the mediation phase of the instant proceeding.

L-3. Preliminary Hearing

As promptly as practicable after the selection of the arbitrator(s), a preliminary hearing shall be held among the parties and/or their attorneys or other representatives and the arbitrator(s). Unless the parties agree otherwise, the preliminary hearing will be conducted by telephone conference call rather than in person. At the preliminary hearing the matters to be considered shall include, without limitation:

(a) service of a detailed statement of claims, damages and defenses, a statement of the issues asserted by each party and positions with respect thereto, and any legal authorities the parties may wish to bring to the attention of the arbitrator(s);

(b) stipulations to uncontested facts;

(c) the extent to which discovery shall be conducted;

(d) exchange and premarking of those documents which each party believes may be offered at the hearing;

(e) the identification and availability of witnesses, including experts, and such matters with respect to witnesses including their biographies and expected testimony as may be appropriate;

(f) whether, and the extent to which, any sworn statements and/or depositions may be introduced;

(g) the extent to which hearings will proceed on consecutive days;

(h) whether a stenographic or other official record of the proceedings shall be maintained;

(i) the possibility of utilizing mediation or other non-adjudicative methods of dispute resolution; and

(j) the procedure for the issuance of subpoenas.

By agreement of the parties and/or order of the arbitrator(s), the pre-hearing activities and the hearing procedures that will govern the arbitration will be memorialized in a Scheduling and Procedure Order.

L-4. Management of Proceedings

(a) Arbitrator(s) shall take such steps as they may deem necessary or desirable to avoid delay and to achieve a just, speedy and cost-effective resolution of Large, Complex Commercial Cases.

(b) Parties shall cooperate in the exchange of documents, exhibits and information within such party's control if the arbitrator(s) consider such production to be consistent with the goal of achieving a just, speedy and cost-effective resolution of a Large, Complex Commercial Case.

(c) The parties may conduct such discovery as may be agreed to by all the parties provided, however, that the arbitrator(s) may place such limitations on the conduct of such discovery as the arbitrator(s) shall deem appropriate. If the parties cannot agree on production of documents and other information, the arbitrator(s), consistent with the expedited nature of arbitration, may establish the extent of the discovery.

(d) At the discretion of the arbitrator(s), upon good cause shown and consistent with the expedited nature of arbitration, the arbitrator(s) may order depositions of, or the propounding of interrogatories to, such persons who may possess information determined by the arbitrator(s) to be necessary to determination of the matter.

(e) The parties shall exchange copies of all exhibits they intend to submit at the hearing 10 business days prior to the hearing unless the arbitrator(s) determine otherwise.

(f) The exchange of information pursuant to this rule, as agreed by the parties and/or directed by the arbitrator(s), shall be included within the Scheduling and Procedure Order.

(g) The arbitrator is authorized to resolve any disputes concerning the exchange of information.

(h) Generally hearings will be scheduled on consecutive days or in blocks of consecutive days in order to maximize efficiency and minimize costs.

OPTIONAL RULES FOR EMERGENCY MEASURES OF PROTECTION

O-1. Applicability

Where parties by special agreement or in their arbitration clause have adopted these rules for emergency measures of protection, a party in need of emergency relief prior to the constitution of the panel shall notify the AAA and all other parties in writing of the nature of the relief sought and the reasons why such relief is required on an emergency basis. The application shall also set forth the reasons why the party is entitled to such relief. Such notice may be given by facsimile transmission, or other reliable means, but must include a statement certifying that all other parties have been notified or an explanation of the steps taken in good faith to notify other parties.

O-2. Appointment of Emergency Arbitrator

Within one business day of receipt of notice as provided in Section O-1, the AAA shall appoint a single emergency arbitrator from a special AAA panel of emergency arbitrators designated to rule on emergency applications. The emergency arbitrator shall immediately disclose any circumstance likely, on the basis of the facts disclosed in the application, to affect such arbitrator's impartiality or independence. Any challenge to the appointment of the emergency arbitrator must be made within one business day of the communication by the AAA to the parties of the appointment of the emergency arbitrator and the circumstances disclosed.

O-3. Schedule

The emergency arbitrator shall as soon as possible, but in any event within two business days of appointment, establish a schedule for consideration of the application for emergency relief. Such schedule shall provide a reasonable opportunity to all parties to be heard, but may provide for proceeding by telephone conference or on written submissions as alternatives to a formal hearing.

O-4. Interim Award

If after consideration the emergency arbitrator is satisfied that the party seeking the emergency relief has shown that immediate and irreparable loss or damage will result in the absence of emergency relief, and that such party is entitled to such relief, the emergency arbitrator may enter an interim award granting the relief and stating the reasons therefore.

O-5. Constitution of the Panel

Any application to modify an interim award of emergency relief must be based on changed circumstances and may be made to the emergency arbitrator until the panel is constituted; thereafter such a request shall be addressed to the panel. The emergency arbitrator shall have no further power to act after the panel is constituted unless the parties agree that the emergency arbitrator is named as a member of the panel.

O-6. Security

Any interim award of emergency relief may be conditioned on provision by the party seeking such relief of appropriate security.

O-7. Special Master

A request for interim measures addressed by a party to a judicial authority shall not be deemed incompatible with the agreement to arbitrate or a waiver of the right to arbitrate. If the AAA is directed by a judicial authority to nominate a special master to consider and report on an application for emergency relief, the AAA shall proceed as provided in Section O-1 of this article and the references to the emergency arbitrator shall be read to mean the special master, except that the special master shall issue a report rather than an interim award.

O-8. Costs

The costs associated with applications for emergency relief shall initially be apportioned by the emergency arbitrator or special master, subject to the power of the panel to determine finally the apportionment of such costs.

ADMINISTRATIVE FEES

The administrative fees of the AAA are based on the amount of the claim or counterclaim. Arbitrator compensation is not included in this schedule. Unless the parties agree otherwise, arbitrator compensation and administrative fees are subject to allocation by the arbitrator in the award.

In an effort to make arbitration costs reasonable for consumers, the AAA has a separate fee schedule for consumer-related disputes. Please refer to Section C-8 of the *Supplementary Procedures for Consumer-Related Disputes* when filing a consumer-related claim.

The AAA applies the *Supplementary Procedures for Consumer-Related Disputes* to arbitration clauses in agreements between individual consumers and businesses where the business has a standardized, systematic application of arbitration clauses with customers and where the terms and conditions of the purchase of standardized, consumable goods or services are non-negotiable or primarily non-negotiable in most or all of its terms, conditions, features, or choices. The product or service must be for personal or household use. The AAA will have the discretion to apply or not to apply the Supplementary Procedures and the parties will be able to bring any disputes concerning the application or non-application to the attention of the arbitrator. Consumers are not prohibited from seeking relief in a small claims court for disputes or claims within the scope of its jurisdiction, even in consumer arbitration cases filed by the business.

Fees

An initial filing fee is payable in full by a filing party when a claim, counterclaim or additional claim is filed. A case service fee will be incurred for all cases that proceed to their first hearing. This fee will be payable in advance at the time that the first hearing is scheduled. This fee will be refunded at the conclusion of the case if no hearings have occurred. However, if the Association is not notified at least 24 hours before the time of the scheduled hearing, the case service fee will remain due and will not be refunded.

These fees will be billed in accordance with the following schedule:

Amount of Claim	Initial Filing Fee	Case Service Fee
Above $0 to $10,000	$ 750	$ 200
Above $10,000 to $75,000	$ 950	$ 300
Above $75,000 to $150,000	$ 1,800	$ 750
Above $150,000 to $300,000	$ 2,750	$1,250
Above $300,000 to $500,000	$ 4,250	$1,750
Above $500,000 to $1,000,000	$ 6,000	$2,500
Above $1,000,000 to $5,000,000	$ 8,000	$3,250
Above $5,000,000 to $10,000,000	$10,000	$4,000
Above $10,000,000	*	*
Non-monetary Claims**	$ 3,250	$1,250

**This fee is applicable only when a claim or counterclaim is not for a monetary amount. Where a monetary claim amount is not known, parties will be required to state a range of claims or be subject to the highest possible filing fee.

Fee Schedule for Claims in Excess of $10 Million.

The following is the fee schedule for use in disputes involving claims in excess of $10 million. If you have any questions, please consult your local AAA office or case management center.

Claim Size	Fee	Case Service Fee
$10 million and above	Base fee of $12,500 plus .01% of the amount of claim above $10 million.	$6,000
	Filing fees capped at $65,000	

Fees are subject to increase if the amount of a claim or counterclaim is modified after the initial filing date. Fees are subject to decrease if the amount of a claim or counterclaim is modified before the first hearing.

The minimum fees for any case having three or more arbitrators are $2,750 for the filing fee, plus a $1,250 case service fee. Expedited Procedures are applied in any case where no disclosed claim or counterclaim exceeds $75,000, exclusive of interest and arbitration costs.

Parties on cases held in abeyance for one year by agreement, will be assessed an annual abeyance fee of $300. If a party refuses to pay the assessed fee, the other party or parties may pay the entire fee on behalf of all parties, otherwise the matter will be closed.

Refund Schedule

The AAA offers a refund schedule on filing fees. For cases with claims up to $75,000, a minimum filing fee of $300 will not be refunded. For all other cases, a minimum fee of $500 will not be refunded. Subject to the minimum fee requirements, refunds will be calculated as follows:

- 100% of the filing fee, above the minimum fee, will be refunded if the case is settled or withdrawn within five calendar days of filing.
- 50% of the filing fee will be refunded if the case is settled or withdrawn between six and 30 calendar days of filing.
- 25% of the filing fee will be refunded if the case is settled or withdrawn between 31 and 60 calendar days of filing.

No refund will be made once an arbitrator has been appointed (this includes one arbitrator on a three-arbitrator panel). No refunds will be granted on awarded cases.

Note: the date of receipt of the demand for arbitration with the AAA will be used to calculate refunds of filing fees for both claims and counterclaims.

Hearing Room Rental

The fees described above do not cover the rental of hearing rooms, which are available on a rental basis. Check with the AAA for availability and rates.

AAA235

APPENDIX II

MODIFYING OR CORRECTING AN ARBITRATION AWARD

9 USCS § 11

U.S. Code collection

§ 11. Same; modification or correction; grounds; order

In either of the following cases the United States court in and for the district wherein the award was made may make an order modifying or correcting the award upon the application of any party to the arbitration—

(a) Where there was an evident material miscalculation of figures or an evident material mistake in the description of any person, thing, or property referred to in the award.

(b) Where the arbitrators have awarded upon a matter not submitted to them, unless it is a matter not affecting the merits of the decision upon the matter submitted.

(c) Where the award is imperfect in matter of form not affecting the merits of the controversy.

The order may modify and correct the award, so as to effect the intent thereof and promote justice between the parties.

APPENDIX III

VACATING ARBITRATION AWARD

9 USCS § 10

U.S. Code collection

§ 10. Same; vacation; grounds; rehearing

(a) In any of the following cases the United States court in and for the district wherein the award was made may make an order vacating the award upon the application of any party to the arbitration—

(1) where the award was procured by corruption, fraud, or undue means;

(2) where there was evident partiality or corruption in the arbitrators, or either of them;

(3) where the arbitrators were guilty of misconduct in refusing to postpone the hearing, upon sufficient cause shown, or in refusing to hear evidence pertinent and material to the controversy; or of any other misbehavior by which the rights of any party have been prejudiced; or

(4) where the arbitrators exceeded their powers, or so imperfectly executed them that a mutual, final, and definite award upon the subject matter submitted was not made.

(b) If an award is vacated and the time within which the agreement required the award to be made has not expired, the court may, in its discretion, direct a rehearing by the arbitrators.

(c) The United States district court for the district wherein an award was made that was issued pursuant to section 580 of title 5 may make an order vacating the award upon the application of a person, other than a party to the arbitration, who is adversely affected or aggrieved by the award, if the use of arbitration or the award is clearly inconsistent with the factors set forth in section 572 of title 5.

Appendix IV

SUMMARY OF RECENT REVISIONS OF SERVICEMEMBERS CIVIL RELIEF ACT ISSUED BY OFFICE OF COMPTROLLER OF THE CURRENCY (OCC BULLETIN 2008–30) AND SECTION 2203 (HOUSING AND ECONOMIC RECOVERY ACT)

OCC 2008-30

OCC BULLETIN

Comptroller of the Currency
Administrator of National Banks

Subject: **Servicemembers Civil Relief Act** Description: **Legal Requirements**

Date: October 24, 2008

TO: Chief Executive Officers and Compliance Officers of All National Banks, Department and Division Heads, and All Examining Personnel

Background

The Servicemembers Civil Relief Act (SCRA) (codified at 50 USC App. 501 *et seq.*) seeks to strengthen the national defense by providing, among other things, for interest rate adjustments on certain debts and for temporary suspension of legal proceedings that may adversely affect the rights of servicemembers during their military service. Section 2203 of the Housing and Economic Recovery Act of 2008 (HERA), Pub. L. 110-289, 122 Stat. 2654 (2008), revised certain provisions of the SCRA. The revisions provide additional protections to servicemembers by extending the period during which a creditor may not charge interest in excess of six percent per year in connection with obligations and liabilities consisting of a mortgage, trust deed, or other security in the nature of a mortgage. The revisions also extend the periods during which a creditor is restricted from enforcing, or foreclosing upon, such credit obligations on real or personal property owned by a servicemember. The revisions became effective upon enactment on July 30, 2008.

This bulletin provides general information about the provisions of the SCRA that are most likely to affect national banks, including the recent revisions to SCRA. This guidance supersedes OCC Advisory Letter 2004-8 (Servicemembers Civil Relief Act), June 18, 2004.

Rate of Interest

The SCRA requires creditors to forgive (not merely defer) interest in excess of six percent per year on any obligation or liability, such as debts (including credit card and other open-end debts), incurred by a servicemember *before* the servicemember entered military service. The SCRA requires that the reduced interest rate must continue throughout the period of military service. In the case of credit obligations secured by a mortgage, trust deed, or other security in the nature of a mortgage, the SCRA, as amended by HERA, provides that the reduced interest rate will apply during the period of military service and one year thereafter.

Thus, a servicemember is entitled to have the interest rate on any debt outstanding as of the date of entry into military service reduced to six percent. This rate stays in effect throughout the term of service and, in the case of an obligation secured by a mortgage, trust deed, or other security in the nature of a mortgage, until one year after the end of such service.

The SCRA's interest rate limitation also applies to debts jointly incurred by the servicemember and the servicemember's spouse that were entered into prior to the servicemember's military service. The SCRA defines "interest" to include "service charges, renewal charges, fees, or any other charges (except bona fide insurance)" related to the debt. To prevent the acceleration of principal repayment, the SCRA also provides that creditors must reduce any periodic payments due under the debt to reflect the amount of forgiven interest.

The SCRA provides that the servicemember must give the creditor written notice and a copy of the servicemember's military orders to receive the interest rate reduction. The notice must be provided to the creditor no later than 180 days after the servicemember's termination or release from military service, and the creditor must then apply the interest rate reduction effective as of the date the servicemember was called to military service.

When a servicemember provides notice after commencement of service, but within the time period described above, the creditor also must account for any interest payments that have been made in excess of the six percent rate during the period in which the reduced rate applies. Any such excess payments should be provided to the servicemember as a refund, applied toward future monthly payments, or applied toward principal curtailment. If feasible, the servicemember should be given an opportunity to direct how such funds should be applied.

The reduced interest rate provision applies unless a court finds that the ability of the servicemember to pay interest on the debt at a higher rate is not materially affected by the servicemember's military service. In such cases, the court may grant a creditor relief from the interest rate limitations of the SCRA. The SCRA does not provide a mechanism outside of a petition by the creditor to an appropriate court for such relief.

Mortgages and Trust Deeds

The SCRA contains special rules regarding debts secured by a mortgage, trust deed, or other security in the nature of a mortgage on real or personal property owned by a servicemember. As revised by HERA, the SCRA prohibits, with limited exceptions, the sale, foreclosure, or seizure of property, based on a breach of such a secured obligation, during the period of the servicemember's military service, or within nine months after the end of the period of military service. A related provision applies to any legal action to enforce such an obligation. A court may, after a hearing and on its own motion, and shall, upon application by a servicemember whose ability to comply with the obligation is materially affected by military service, stay the proceedings or adjust the obligation to preserve the interests of all parties. In such cases, the SCRA, as amended by HERA, permits such action during the period of military service or within nine months after the end of service. These provisions apply only to obligations that originated prior to the servicemember's military service, and for which the servicemember is still obligated.

The HERA amendments extended, on a temporary basis, the period after the end of military service during which these foreclosure prohibition and stay of proceedings provisions apply from 90 days to nine months. This extension ends on December 31, 2010. On January 1, 2011, the period after the end of a servicemember's military service during which a creditor may not sell, foreclose, or seize property based on a breach of a mortgage, trust deed, or other security in the nature of a mortgage on real or personal property owned by a servicemember, or a court may stay proceedings enforcing such obligations will again be 90 days.

Installment Contracts and Leases

The SCRA addresses installment contracts by servicemembers for the purchase, lease, or bailment of real or personal property (including motor vehicles) in which the servicemember has paid a deposit or installment on the contract *before* entry into military service. The SCRA provides that the other party may not rescind or terminate the contract after the servicemember's entry into service for any breach of the contract by the servicemember that occurred *before or during* the period of military service. Moreover, the property may not be repossessed for such a breach without a court order.

The SCRA contains specific provisions relating to the termination of residential and motor vehicle leases by servicemembers. The SCRA generally allows a servicemember to terminate a residential lease if the servicemember either (1) enters into military service after executing the lease, or (2) executes the lease while in military service but subsequently receive orders for a permanent change of station or for a deployment of at least 90 days. Motor vehicle leases generally may be terminated if the servicemember either (1) after executing the lease, enters into military service under a call or order for a specified term of at least 180 days, or (2) executes the lease while in military service but subsequently receives orders for a permanent change of station outside of the continental United States or for a deployment of at least 180 days.

Eviction

Except by court order, a servicemember, or the dependents of a servicemember, may not be evicted, during a period of military service of the servicemember, from premises that are occupied or intended to be occupied primarily as a residence, and for which the monthly rent does not exceed an amount that is published annually in the *Federal Register* by the Department of Defense.

Exercise of Rights

The fact that a servicemember applies for or is granted temporary relief from his or her obligations and liabilities pursuant to the SCRA may not itself (without regard to other considerations) be the basis for any of the following:

- A determination by a lender or other person that the servicemember is unable to pay the obligation or liability in accordance with its terms;
- A creditor's denial or revocation of credit, change in terms of an existing credit arrangement, or refusal to grant credit in substantially the amount or on substantially the terms requested;
- An adverse report related to the creditworthiness of the servicemember by or to a

credit bureau;
- An annotation in the servicemember's record by a creditor or credit bureau identifying the servicemember as a member of the National Guard or a reserve component;
- A refusal by an insurer to insure the servicemember; or
- A change in the terms offered or conditions required for the issuance of insurance.

Waiver of Rights

A servicemember may waive any of the rights and protections provided by the SCRA. For the following types of actions, a waiver must be in writing:

- The modification, termination, or cancellation of:
    - A contract, lease, or bailment; or
    - An obligation secured by a mortgage, trust, deed, lien, or other security in the nature of a mortgage;
- The repossession, retention, foreclosure, sale, forfeiture, or taking possession of property that:
    - Is security for any obligation; or
    - Was purchased or received under a contract, lease, or bailment.

In such cases, the written waiver agreement is effective only if it is executed during or after the servicemember's period of military service. The written agreement must specify the legal instrument to which the waiver applies.

Business or Trade Obligations

If any trade or business of a servicemember has an obligation or liability for which the servicemember is personally liable, the assets of the servicemember not held in connection with the trade or business may not be used to satisfy the obligation or liability during the servicemember's military service. Upon application of the holder of the obligation or liability, a court may grant relief from this SCRA servicemember protection for equitable and other reasons.

Dependents and Persons Secondarily Liable

Many of the benefits accorded to servicemembers by the SCRA relating to financial obligations may be extended to dependents of servicemembers if the dependents apply to a court for such protection. Dependents are entitled to these protections if the ability of the dependent to comply with the terms of the obligation is materially affected by the servicemember's military service. Additionally, certain provisions of the SCRA may apply, if so ordered by a court, to other persons who are primarily or secondarily liable on obligations of servicemembers.

Additional provisions of the SCRA may apply to an individual bank's operations or its customers' circumstances. The OCC, therefore, encourages national banks to seek the advice of bank counsel to resolve any disputes that arise over claims for relief and to ensure the institution's compliance with the SCRA. Banks should monitor their portfolios and the performance of loans affected by the SCRA to adjust loan loss allowances accordingly.

If you have any questions regarding this bulletin, please contact the appropriate supervisory office, the Community and Consumer Law Division at (202) 874-5750, or the Compliance Policy Division at (202) 874-4428.

/signed/

Ann F. Jaedicke
Deputy Comptroller for Compliance Policy

APPENDIX V

DEBT ELIMINATION SCAM PUBLISHED BY THE BOARD OF GOVERNORS OF THE FEDERAL RESERVE SYSTEM DIVISION OF BANKING SUPERVISION AND REGULATION JANUARY 28, 2004

Board staff has become aware of various illegal schemes being offered to the public that purport to eliminate outstanding debt through the use of specially prepared documents. The organizers of these schemes concoct specious legal documents based on the borrower's debt, which are then presented to the borrower's bank, mortgage company, finance company, or other lending institution in an attempt to satisfy the debt.[1] The scams are reminiscent of the tax protesters' tax invasion schemes seen throughout the 1990s.

The purported legal documents used in the current scams include fake financial instruments that claim to eliminate the borrower's debt obligation.[2] The instruments usually question the authenticity of financial obligations, and often refer to a specific government agency (such as the Federal Reserve) in an attempt to support their claims. Some of the literature seen by Board staff questions the legitimacy of the Federal Reserve and the validity of United States currency. The literature may selectively cite from passages of government publications, statements by politicians, constitutional provisions, court decisions, various statutes, and private newsletters to support claims and to ultimately conclude that a specific government agency sanctions these debt elimination programs. For example, some of the

---

[1]Lending institutions and insurance companies offer various products or include various terms in loan documents that have the effect of paying off loans (or deferring loan payments for certain periods of time) in the event, for example, of a borrower's death, loss of employment, or other significant personal life changes. These are legitimate products and should not be confused with the false promises to eliminate a borrower's debt upon the presentation of fraudulent documents that are the subject of his alert.

[2]The documents have variously been titled: Declaration of Voidance, Bond for Discharge of Debt, and Redemption Certificate.

documents specifically refer to the elimination of debt through the use of a "Federal Reserve approved" procedure.

Debt elimination programs that claim Federal Reserve approval or acquiescence and the satisfaction of legitimate debts through the presentation of suspicious documents are totally bogus. The Federal Reserve does not approve and is in no way involved in any program aimed at eliminating anyone's debt obligations.

These schemes are proliferating on the Internet, and the organizers are charging borrowers substantial up-front fees and commissions based on the total amount of debt that can be forgiven.[3] Members of the public are being harmed as borrowers generally pay significant amounts of money without eliminating or reducing their overall debt obligations—which of course is not in fact possible through any of these programs. Also, the cessation of legitimate loan payments increases the risk of a foreclosure or other legal action being taken against the borrower, and in additional could negatively affect a borrower's credit rating. Financial institutions may find that the use of the specious documents complicates the collection process, and may at least temporarily prevent any final action against the consumer.

Examiners and banking organizations should be cognizant of these scams, and the public should avoid becoming involved with them. Bank holding companies and state member banks should modify their policies and procedures as needed to ensure that staff involved in any way in a lending function is able to identify and respond appropriately to these current schemes. If an institution supervised by the Federal Reserve is presented with fraudulent documents as described in this SR letter, the institution is expected to file a Suspicious Activity Report (SAR) in accordance with the Board's suspicious activity reporting rules. The banking organization must also retain the written materials associated with the purported debt elimination scheme as supporting documentation to the SAR, as required by the Board's SAR rules.[4]

Reserve Banks are asked to distribute this SR letter to domestic and foreign banking organizations supervised by the Federal Reserve in their districts. Questions regarding apparent fraudulent debt elimination schemes can be directed to Leonard Zawistowski, Senior Special Investigator, at (202)452-6488.

Richard Spillenkothen

Director

---

[3]Federal Reserve staff has seen advertised up-front fees as high as $2,500. Some programs also require the up-front payment of an amount equal to 15 percent of a borrower's total debt obligations.

[4]Refer to 12 CFR 208.62. The SAR rules can be found on the web at: http://a257.g.akamaitech.net/7/257/2422/14mar20010800/edocket.access.gpo.gov/cfr2003/pdf/12cfr208.62.pdf.

APPENDIX VI

EXCERPTS FROM THE SERVICE MEMBERS CIVIL RELIEF ACT OF 2003

Excerpts from
The Soldiers' and Sailors' Civil Relief Act of 1940
As Amended as of December 19, 2003

PUBLIC LAW 108-189—DEC. 19, 2003
Public Law 108-189
108th Congress

An Act
To restate, clarify, and revise the Soldiers' and Sailors' Civil Relief Act of 1940.

Be it enacted by the Senate and House of Representatives of the United States of America in Congress assembled,

SECTION 1. RESTATEMENT OF ACT.
The Soldiers' and Sailors' Civil Relief Act of 1940 (50 U.S.C. App. 501 *et seq.*) is amended to read as follows:

SECTION 1. SHORT TITLE; TABLE OF CONTENTS.
(a) SHORT TITLE.—This Act may be cited as the "Servicemembers Civil Relief Act".
(b) TABLE OF CONTENTS.—The table of contents of this Act is as follows:

SEC. 2. PURPOSE.

The purposes of this Act are—

(1) to provide for, strengthen, and expedite the national defense through protection extended by this Act to servicemembers of the United States to enable such persons to devote their entire energy to the defense needs of the Nation; and

(2) to provide for the temporary suspension of judicial and administrative proceedings and transactions that may adversely affect the civil rights of servicemembers during their military service.

TITLE I—GENERAL PROVISIONS

SEC. 101. DEFINITIONS.

For the purposes of this Act:

(1) SERVICEMEMBER.—The term "servicemember" means a member of the uniformed services, as that term is defined in section 101(a)(5) of title 10, United States Code.

(2) MILITARY SERVICE.—The term "military service" means—

(A) in the case of a servicemember who is a member of the Army, Navy, Air Force, Marine Corps, or Coast Guard—

(i) active duty, as defined in section 101(d)(1) of title 10, United States Code, and

(ii) in the case of a member of the National Guard, includes service under a call to active service authorized by the President or the Secretary of Defense for a period of more than 30 consecutive days under section 502(f) of title 32, United States Code, for purposes of responding to a national emergency declared by the President and supported by Federal funds;

(B) in the case of a servicemember who is a commissioned officer of the Public Health Service or the National Oceanic and Atmospheric Administration, active service; and

(C) any period during which a servicemember is absent from duty on account of sickness, wounds, leave, or other lawful cause.

(3) PERIOD OF MILITARY SERVICE.—The term "period of military service" means the period beginning on the date on which a servicemember enters military service and ending on the date on which the servicemember is released from military service or dies while in military service.

(4) DEPENDENT.—The term "dependent," with respect to a servicemember, means—

(A) the servicemember's spouse;

(B) the servicemember's child (as defined in section 101(4) of title 38, United States Code); or

(C) an individual for whom the servicemember provided more than one-half of the individual's support for 180 days immediately preceding an application for relief under this Act.

(5) COURT.—The term "court" means a court or an administrative agency of the United States or of any State (including any political subdivision of a State), whether or not a court or administrative agency of record.

(6) STATE.—The term "State" includes—

(A) a commonwealth, territory, or possession of the United States; and

(B) the District of Columbia.

(7) SECRETARY CONCERNED.—The term "Secretary concerned"—

(A) with respect to a member of the armed forces, has the meaning given that term in section 101(a)(9) of title 10, United States Code;

(B) with respect to a commissioned officer of the Public Health Service, means the Secretary of Health and Human Services; and

(C) with respect to a commissioned officer of the National Oceanic and Atmospheric Administration, means the Secretary of Commerce.

(8) MOTOR VEHICLE.—The term "motor vehicle" has the meaning given that term in section 30102(a)(6) of title 49, United States Code.

SEC. 102. JURISDICTION AND APPLICABILITY OF ACT.

(a) JURISDICTION.—This Act applies to—

(1) the United States;

(2) each of the States, including the political subdivisions thereof; and

(3) all territory subject to the jurisdiction of the United States.

(b) APPLICABILITY TO PROCEEDINGS.—This Act applies to any judicial or administrative proceeding commenced in any court or agency in any jurisdiction subject to this Act. This Act does not apply to criminal proceedings.
(c) COURT IN WHICH APPLICATION MAY BE MADE.—When under this Act any application is required to be made to a court in which no proceeding has already been commenced with respect to the matter, such application may be made to any court which would otherwise have jurisdiction over the matter.

SEC. 103. PROTECTION OF PERSONS SECONDARILY LIABLE.
(a) EXTENSION OF PROTECTION WHEN ACTIONS STAYED, POSTPONED, OR SUSPENDED.—Whenever pursuant to this Act a court stays, postpones, or suspends (1) the enforcement of an obligation or liability, (2) the prosecution of a suit or proceeding, (3) the entry or enforcement of an order, writ, judgment, or decree, or (4) the performance of any other act, the court may likewise grant such a stay, postponement, or suspension to a surety, guarantor, endorser, accommodation maker, comaker, or other person who is or may be primarily or secondarily subject to the obligation or liability the performance or enforcement of which is stayed, postponed, or suspended.
(b) VACATION OR SET-ASIDE OF JUDGMENTS.—When a judgment or decree is vacated or set aside, in whole or in part, pursuant to this Act, the court may also set aside or vacate, as the case may be, the judgment or decree as to a surety, guarantor, endorser, accommodation maker, comaker, or other person who is or may be primarily or secondarily liable on the contract or liability for the enforcement of the judgment or decree.
(c) BAIL BOND NOT TO BE ENFORCED DURING PERIOD OF MILITARY SERVICE.—A court may not enforce a bail bond during the period of military service of the principal on the bond when military service prevents the surety from obtaining the attendance of the principal. The court may discharge the surety and exonerate the bail, in accordance with principles of equity and justice, during or after the period of military service of the principal.
(d) WAIVER OF RIGHTS.—

(1) WAIVERS NOT PRECLUDED.—This Act does not prevent a waiver in writing by a surety, guarantor, endorser, accommodation maker, comaker, or other person (whether primarily or secondarily liable on an obligation or liability) of the protections provided under subsections (a) and (b). Any such waiver is effective only if it is executed as an instrument separate from the obligation or liability with respect to which it applies.

(2) WAIVER INVALIDATED UPON ENTRANCE TO MILITARY SERVICE.—If a waiver under paragraph (1) is executed by an individual who after the execution of the waiver enters military service, or by a dependent of an individual who after the execution of the waiver enters military service, the waiver is not valid after the beginning of the period of such military service unless the waiver was executed by such individual or dependent during the period specified in section 106.

SEC. 104. EXTENSION OF PROTECTIONS TO CITIZENS SERVING WITH ALLIED FORCES.
A citizen of the United States who is serving with the forces of a nation with which the United States is allied in the prosecution of a war or military action is entitled to

the relief and protections provided under this Act if that service with the allied force is similar to military service as defined in this Act. The relief and protections provided to such citizen shall terminate on the date of discharge or release from such service.

SEC. 105. NOTIFICATION OF BENEFITS.
The Secretary concerned shall ensure that notice of the benefits accorded by this Act is provided in writing to persons in military service and to persons entering military service.

SEC. 106. EXTENSION OF RIGHTS AND PROTECTIONS TO RESERVES ORDERED TO REPORT FOR MILITARY SERVICE AND TO PERSONS ORDERED TO REPORT FOR INDUCTION.
(a) RESERVES ORDERED TO REPORT FOR MILITARY SERVICE.—A member of a reserve component who is ordered to report for military service is entitled to the rights and protections of this title and titles II and III during the period beginning on the date of the member's receipt of the order and ending on the date on which the member reports for military service (or, if the order is revoked before the member so reports, or the date on which the order is revoked).
(b) PERSONS ORDERED TO REPORT FOR INDUCTION.—A person who has been ordered to report for induction under the Military Selective Service Act (50 U.S.C. App. 451 et seq.) is entitled to the rights and protections provided a servicemember under this title and titles II and III during the period beginning on the date of receipt of the order for induction and ending on the date on which the person reports for induction (or, if the order to report for induction is revoked before the date on which the person reports for induction, on the date on which the order is revoked).

SEC. 107. WAIVER OF RIGHTS PURSUANT TO WRITTEN AGREEMENT.
(a) IN GENERAL.—A servicemember may waive any of the rights and protections provided by this Act. In the case of a waiver that permits an action described in subsection (b), the waiver is effective only if made pursuant to a written agreement of the parties that is executed during or after the servicemember's period of military service. The written agreement shall specify the legal instrument to which the waiver applies and, if the servicemember is not a party to that instrument, the servicemember concerned.
(b) ACTIONS REQUIRING WAIVERS IN WRITING.—The requirement in subsection (a) for a written waiver applies to the following:

(1) The modification, termination, or cancellation of—

(A) a contract, lease, or bailment; or

(B) an obligation secured by a mortgage, trust, deed, lien, or other security in the nature of a mortgage.

(2) The repossession, retention, foreclosure, sale, forfeiture, or taking possession of property that—

(A) is security for any obligation; or

(B) was purchased or received under a contract, lease, or bailment.

(c) COVERAGE OF PERIODS AFTER ORDERS RECEIVED.—For the purposes of this section—

(1) a person to whom section 106 applies shall be considered to be a servicemember; and

(2) the period with respect to such a person specified in subsection (a) or (b), as the case may be, of section 106 shall be considered to be a period of military service.

SEC. 108. EXERCISE OF RIGHTS UNDER ACT NOT TO AFFECT CERTAIN FUTURE FINANCIAL TRANSACTIONS.

Application by a servicemember for, or receipt by a servicemember of, a stay, postponement, or suspension pursuant to this Act in the payment of a tax, fine, penalty, insurance premium, or other civil obligation or liability of that servicemember shall not itself (without regard to other considerations) provide the basis for any of the following:

(1) A determination by a lender or other person that the servicemember is unable to pay the civil obligation or liability in accordance with its terms.

(2) With respect to a credit transaction between a creditor and the servicemember—

(A) a denial or revocation of credit by the creditor;

(B) a change by the creditor in the terms of an existing credit arrangement; or

(C) a refusal by the creditor to grant credit to the servicemember in substantially the amount or on substantially the terms requested.

(3) An adverse report relating to the creditworthiness of the servicemember by or to a person engaged in the practice of assembling or evaluating consumer credit information.

(4) A refusal by an insurer to insure the servicemember.

(5) An annotation in a servicemember's record by a creditor or a person engaged in the practice of assembling or evaluating consumer credit information, identifying the servicemember as a member of the National Guard or a reserve component.

(6) A change in the terms offered or conditions required for the issuance of insurance.

SEC. 109. LEGAL REPRESENTATIVES.

(a) REPRESENTATIVE.—A legal representative of a servicemember for purposes of this Act is either of the following:

(1) An attorney acting on the behalf of a servicemember.

(2) An individual possessing a power of attorney.

(b) APPLICATION.—Whenever the term "servicemember" is used in this Act, such term shall be treated as including a reference to a legal representative of the servicemember.

TITLE II—GENERAL RELIEF

SEC. 201. PROTECTION OF SERVICEMEMBERS AGAINST DEFAULT JUDGMENTS.

(a) APPLICABILITY OF SECTION.—This section applies to any civil action or proceeding in which the defendant does not make an appearance.

(b) AFFIDAVIT REQUIREMENT.—

(1) PLAINTIFF TO FILE AFFIDAVIT.—In any action or proceeding covered by this section, the court, before entering judgment for the plaintiff, shall require the plaintiff to file with the court an affidavit—

(A) stating whether or not the defendant is in military service and showing necessary facts to support the affidavit; or

(B) if the plaintiff is unable to determine whether or not the defendant is in military service, stating that the plaintiff is unable to determine whether or not the defendant is in military service.

(2) APPOINTMENT OF ATTORNEY TO REPRESENT DEFENDANT IN MILITARY SERVICE.—If in an action covered by this section it appears that the defendant is in military service, the court may not enter a judgment until after the court appoints an attorney to represent the defendant. If an attorney appointed under this section to represent a servicemember cannot locate the servicemember, actions by the attorney in the case shall not waive any defense of the servicemember or otherwise bind the servicemember.

(3) DEFENDANT'S MILITARY STATUS NOT ASCERTAINED BY AFFIDAVIT.—If based upon the affidavits filed in such an action, the court is unable to determine whether the defendant is in military service, the court, before entering judgment, may require the plaintiff to file a bond in an amount approved by the court. If the defendant is later found to be in military service, the bond shall be available to indemnify the defendant against any loss or damage the defendant may suffer by reason of any judgment for the plaintiff against the defendant, should the judgment be set aside in whole or in part. The bond shall remain in effect until expiration of the time for appeal and setting aside of a judgment under applicable Federal or State law or regulation or under any applicable ordinance of a political subdivision of a State. The court may issue such orders or enter such judgments as the court determines necessary to protect the rights of the defendant under this Act.

(4) SATISFACTION OF REQUIREMENT FOR AFFIDAVIT.—The requirement for an affidavit under paragraph (1) may be satisfied by a statement, declaration, verification, or certificate, in writing, subscribed and certified or declared to be true under penalty of perjury.

(c) PENALTY FOR MAKING OR USING FALSE AFFIDAVIT.—A person who makes or uses an affidavit permitted under subsection (b) (or a statement, declaration, verification, or certificate as authorized under subsection (b)(4)) knowing it to be false, shall be fined as provided in title 18, United States Code, or imprisoned for not more than one year, or both.

(d) STAY OF PROCEEDINGS.—In an action covered by this section in which the defendant is in military service, the court shall grant a stay of proceedings for a minimum period of 90 days under this subsection upon application of counsel, or on the court's own motion, if the court determines that—

(1) there may be a defense to the action and a defense cannot be presented without the presence of the defendant; or

(2) after due diligence, counsel has been unable to contact the defendant or otherwise determine if a meritorious defense exists.

(e) INAPPLICABILITY OF SECTION 202 PROCEDURES.—A stay of proceedings under subsection (d) shall not be controlled by procedures or requirements under section 202.

(f) SECTION 202 PROTECTION.—If a servicemember who is a defendant in an action covered by this section receives actual notice of the action, the servicemember may request a stay of proceeding under section 202.

(g) VACATION OR SETTING ASIDE OF DEFAULT JUDGMENTS.—

(1) AUTHORITY FOR COURT TO VACATE OR SET ASIDE JUDGMENT.—If a default judgment is entered in an action covered by this section against a servicemember during the servicemember's period of military service (or within 60 days after termination of or release from such military service), the court entering the judgment shall, upon application by or on behalf of the servicemember, reopen the judgment for the purpose of allowing the servicemember to defend the action if it appears that—

(A) the servicemember was materially affected by reason of that military service in making a defense to the action; and

(B) the servicemember has a meritorious or legal defense to the action or some part of it.

(2) TIME FOR FILING APPLICATION.—An application under this subsection must be filed not later than 90 days after the date of the termination of or release from military service.

(h) PROTECTION OF BONA FIDE PURCHASER.—If a court vacates, sets aside, or reverses a default judgment against a servicemember and the vacating, setting aside, or reversing is because of a provision of this Act, that action shall not impair a right or title acquired by a bona fide purchaser for value under the default judgment.

SEC. 202. STAY OF PROCEEDINGS WHEN SERVICEMEMBER HAS NOTICE.

(a) APPLICABILITY OF SECTION.—This section applies to any civil action or proceeding in which the defendant at the time of filing an application under this section—

(1) is in military service or is within 90 days after termination of or release from military service; and

(2) has received notice of the action or proceeding.

(b) STAY OF PROCEEDINGS.—

(1) AUTHORITY FOR STAY.—At any stage before final judgment in a civil action or proceeding in which a servicemember described in subsection (a) is a party, the court may on its own motion and shall, upon application by the servicemember, stay the action for a period of not less than 90 days, if the conditions in paragraph (2) are met.

(2) CONDITIONS FOR STAY.—An application for a stay under paragraph (1) shall include the following:

(A) A letter or other communication setting forth facts stating the manner in which current military duty requirements materially affect the servicemember's ability to appear and stating a date when the servicemember will be available to appear.

(B) A letter or other communication from the servicemember's commanding officer stating that the servicemember's current military duty prevents appearance and that military leave is not authorized for the servicemember at the time of the letter.

(c) APPLICATION NOT A WAIVER OF DEFENSES.—An application for a stay under this section does not constitute an appearance for jurisdictional purposes and does not constitute a waiver of any substantive or procedural defense (including a defense relating to lack of personal jurisdiction).

(d) ADDITIONAL STAY.—

(1) APPLICATION.—A servicemember who is granted a stay of a civil action or proceeding under subsection (b) may apply for an additional stay based on continuing material affect of military duty on the servicemember's ability to appear. Such an application may be made by the servicemember at the time of the initial application under subsection (b) or when it appears that the servicemember is unavailable to prosecute or defend the action. The same information required under subsection (b)(2) shall be included in an application under this subsection.

(2) APPOINTMENT OF COUNSEL WHEN ADDITIONAL STAY REFUSED.—If the court refuses to grant an additional stay of proceedings under paragraph (1), the court shall appoint counsel to represent the servicemember in the action or proceeding.

(e) COORDINATION WITH SECTION 201.—A servicemember who applies for a stay under this section and is unsuccessful may not seek the protections afforded by section 201.

(f) INAPPLICABILITY TO SECTION 301.—The protections of this section do not apply to section 301.

SEC. 203. FINES AND PENALTIES UNDER CONTRACTS.

(a) PROHIBITION OF PENALTIES.—When an action for compliance with the terms of a contract is stayed pursuant to this Act, a penalty shall not accrue for failure to comply with the terms of the contract during the period of the stay.

(b) REDUCTION OR WAIVER OF FINES OR PENALTIES.—If a servicemember fails to perform an obligation arising under a contract and a penalty is incurred arising from that nonperformance, a court may reduce or waive the fine or penalty if—

(1) the servicemember was in military service at the time the fine or penalty was incurred; and

(2) the ability of the servicemember to perform the obligation was materially affected by such military service.

SEC. 204. STAY OR VACATION OF EXECUTION OF JUDGMENTS, ATTACHMENTS, AND GARNISHMENTS.

(a) COURT ACTION UPON MATERIAL AFFECT DETERMINATION.—If a servicemember, in the opinion of the court, is materially affected by reason of military service in complying with a court judgment or order, the court may on its own motion and shall on application by the servicemember—

(1) stay the execution of any judgment or order entered against the servicemember; and

(2) vacate or stay an attachment or garnishment of property, money, or debts in the possession of the servicemember or a third party, whether before or after judgment.

(b) APPLICABILITY.—This section applies to an action or proceeding commenced in a court against a servicemember before or during the period of the servicemember's military service or within 90 days after such service terminates.

SEC. 205. DURATION AND TERM OF STAYS; CODEFENDANTS NOT IN SERVICE.

(a) PERIOD OF STAY.—A stay of an action, proceeding, attachment, or execution made pursuant to the provisions of this Act by a court may be ordered for the period of military service and 90 days thereafter, or for any part of that period. The court may set the terms and amounts for such installment payments as is considered reasonable by the court.

(b) CODEFENDANTS.—If the servicemember is a codefendant with others who are not in military service and who are not entitled to the relief and protections provided under this Act, the plaintiff may proceed against those other defendants with the approval of the court.

(c) INAPPLICABILITY OF SECTION.—This section does not apply to sections 202 and 701.

SEC. 206. STATUTE OF LIMITATIONS.

(a) TOLLING OF STATUTES OF LIMITATION DURING MILITARY SERVICE.—The period of a servicemember's military service may not be included in computing any period limited by law, regulation, or order for the bringing of any action or proceeding in a court, or in any board, bureau, commission, department, or other agency of a State (or political subdivision of a State) or the United States by or against the servicemember or the servicemember's heirs, executors, administrators, or assigns.

(b) REDEMPTION OF REAL PROPERTY.—A period of military service may not be included in computing any period provided by law for the redemption of real property sold or forfeited to enforce an obligation, tax, or assessment.

(c) INAPPLICABILITY TO INTERNAL REVENUE LAWS.—This section does not apply to any period of limitation prescribed by or under the internal revenue laws of the United States.

SEC. 207. MAXIMUM RATE OF INTEREST ON DEBTS INCURRED BEFORE MILITARY SERVICE.

(a) INTEREST RATE LIMITATION.—

(1) LIMITATION TO 6 PERCENT.—An obligation or liability bearing interest at a rate in excess of 6 percent per year that is incurred by a servicemember, or the servicemember and the servicemember's spouse jointly, before the servicemember enters military service shall not bear interest at a rate in excess of 6 percent per year during the period of military service.

(2) FORGIVENESS OF INTEREST IN EXCESS OF 6 PERCENT.—Interest at a rate in excess of 6 percent per year that would otherwise be incurred but for the prohibition in paragraph (1) is forgiven.

(3) PREVENTION OF ACCELERATION OF PRINCIPAL.—The amount of any periodic payment due from a servicemember under the terms of the instrument that created an obligation or liability covered by this section shall be reduced by the amount of the interest forgiven under paragraph (2) that is allocable to the period for which such payment is made.

(b) IMPLEMENTATION OF LIMITATION.—

(1) WRITTEN NOTICE TO CREDITOR.—In order for an obligation or liability of a servicemember to be subject to the interest rate limitation in subsection (a), the servicemember shall provide to the creditor written notice and a copy of the military orders calling the servicemember to military service and any orders further extending military service, not later than 180 days after the date of the servicemember's termination or release from military service.

(2) LIMITATION EFFECTIVE AS OF DATE OF ORDER TO ACTIVE DUTY.—Upon receipt of written notice and a copy of orders calling a servicemember to military service, the creditor shall treat the debt in accordance with subsection (a), effective as of the date on which the servicemember is called to military service.

(c) CREDITOR PROTECTION.—A court may grant a creditor relief from the limitations of this section if, in the opinion of the court, the ability of the servicemember to pay interest upon the obligation or liability at a rate in excess of 6 percent per year is not materially affected by reason of the servicemember's military service.

(d) INTEREST.—As used in this section, the term "interest" includes service charges, renewal charges, fees, or any other charges (except bona fide insurance) with respect to an obligation or liability.

TITLE III—RENT, INSTALLMENT CONTRACTS, MORTGAGES, LIENS, ASSIGNMENT, LEASES

SEC. 301. EVICTIONS AND DISTRESS.

(a) COURT-ORDERED EVICTION.—

(1) IN GENERAL.—Except by court order, a landlord (or another person with paramount title) may not—

(A) evict a servicemember, or the dependents of a servicemember, during a period of military service of the servicemember, from premises—

(i) that are occupied or intended to be occupied primarily as a residence; and

(ii) for which the monthly rent does not exceed $2,400, as adjusted under paragraph (2) for years after 2003; or

(B) subject such premises to a distress during the period of military service.

(2) HOUSING PRICE INFLATION ADJUSTMENT.—(A) For calendar years beginning with 2004, the amount in effect under paragraph (1)(A)(ii) shall be increased by the housing price inflation adjustment for the calendar year involved.

(B) For purposes of this paragraph—

(i) The housing price inflation adjustment for any calendar year is the percentage change (if any) by which—

(I) the CPI housing component for November of the preceding calendar year, exceeds

(II) the CPI housing component for November of 1984.

(ii) The term "CPI housing component" means the index published by the Bureau of Labor Statistics of the Department of Labor known as the Consumer Price Index, All Urban Consumers, Rent of Primary Residence, U.S. City Average.

(3) PUBLICATION OF HOUSING PRICE INFLATION ADJUSTMENT.— The Secretary of Defense shall cause to be published in the Federal Register each year the amount in effect under paragraph (1)(A)(ii) for that year following the housing price inflation adjustment for that year pursuant to paragraph (2). Such publication shall be made for a year not later than 60 days after such adjustment is made for that year.

(b) STAY OF EXECUTION.—

(1) COURT AUTHORITY.—Upon an application for eviction or distress with respect to premises covered by this section, the court may on its own motion and shall, if a request is made by or on behalf of a servicemember whose ability to pay the agreed rent is materially affected by military service—

(A) stay the proceedings for a period of 90 days, unless in the opinion of the court, justice and equity require a longer or shorter period of time; or

(B) adjust the obligation under the lease to preserve the interests of all parties.

(2) RELIEF TO LANDLORD.—If a stay is granted under paragraph (1), the court may grant to the landlord (or other person with paramount title) such relief as equity may require.

(c) PENALTIES.—

(1) MISDEMEANOR.—Except as provided in subsection (a), a person who knowingly takes part in an eviction or distress described in subsection (a), or who knowingly attempts to do so, shall be fined as provided in title 18, United States Code, or imprisoned for not more than one year, or both.

(2) PRESERVATION OF OTHER REMEDIES AND RIGHTS.—The remedies and rights provided under this section are in addition to and do not preclude any remedy for wrongful conversion (or wrongful eviction) otherwise available under the law to the person claiming relief under this section, including any award for consequential and punitive damages.

(d) RENT ALLOTMENT FROM PAY OF SERVICEMEMBER.—To the extent required by a court order related to property which is the subject of a court action under this section, the Secretary concerned shall make an allotment from the pay of a servicemember to satisfy the terms of such order, except that any such allotment shall be subject to regulations prescribed by the Secretary concerned establishing the maximum amount of pay of servicemembers that may be allotted under this subsection.

(e) LIMITATION OF APPLICABILITY.—Section 202 is not applicable to this section.

SEC. 302. PROTECTION UNDER INSTALLMENT CONTRACTS FOR PURCHASE OR LEASE.

(a) PROTECTION UPON BREACH OF CONTRACT.—

(1) PROTECTION AFTER ENTERING MILITARY SERVICE.—After a servicemember enters military service, a contract by the servicemember for—

(A) the purchase of real or personal property (including a motor vehicle); or

(B) the lease or bailment of such property, may not be rescinded or terminated for a breach of terms of the contract occurring before or during that person's military service, nor may the property be repossessed for such breach without a court order.

(2) APPLICABILITY.—This section applies only to a contract for which a deposit or installment has been paid by the servicemember before the servicemember enters military service.

(b) PENALTIES.—

(1) MISDEMEANOR.—A person who knowingly resumes possession of property in violation of subsection (a), or in violation of section 107 of this Act, or who knowingly attempts to do so, shall be fined as provided in title 18, United States Code, or imprisoned for not more than one year, or both.

(2) PRESERVATION OF OTHER REMEDIES AND RIGHTS.—The remedies and rights provided under this section are in addition to and do not preclude any remedy for wrongful conversion otherwise available under law to the person claiming relief under this section, including any award for consequential and punitive damages.

(c) AUTHORITY OF COURT.—In a hearing based on this section, the court—

(1) may order repayment to the servicemember of all or part of the prior installments or deposits as a condition of terminating the contract and resuming possession of the property;

(2) may, on its own motion, and shall on application by a servicemember when the servicemember's ability to comply with the contract is materially affected by military service, stay the proceedings for a period of time as, in the opinion of the court, justice and equity require; or

(3) may make other disposition as is equitable to preserve the interests of all parties.

SEC. 303. MORTGAGES AND TRUST DEEDS.

(a) MORTGAGE AS SECURITY.—This section applies only to an obligation on real or personal property owned by a servicemember that—

(1) originated before the period of the servicemember's military service and for which the servicemember is still obligated; and

(2) is secured by a mortgage, trust deed, or other security in the nature of a mortgage.

(b) STAY OF PROCEEDINGS AND ADJUSTMENT OF OBLIGATION.—In an action filed during, or within 90 days after, a servicemember's period of military service to enforce an obligation described in subsection (a), the court may after a hearing and on its own motion and shall upon application by a servicemember when the servicemember's ability to comply with the obligation is materially affected by military service—

(1) stay the proceedings for a period of time as justice and equity require, or

(2) adjust the obligation to preserve the interests of all parties.

(c) SALE OR FORECLOSURE.—A sale, foreclosure, or seizure of property for a breach of an obligation described in subsection (a) shall not be valid if made during, or within 90 days after, the period of the servicemember's military service except—

(1) upon a court order granted before such sale, foreclosure, or seizure with a return made and approved by the court; or

(2) if made pursuant to an agreement as provided in section 107.

(d) PENALTIES.—

(1) MISDEMEANOR.—A person who knowingly makes or causes to be made a sale, foreclosure, or seizure of property that is prohibited by subsection (c), or who knowingly attempts to do so, shall be fined as provided in title 18, United States Code, or imprisoned for not more than one year, or both.

(2) PRESERVATION OF OTHER REMEDIES.—The remedies and rights provided under this section are in addition to and do not preclude any remedy for wrongful conversion otherwise available under law to the person claiming relief under this section, including consequential and punitive damages.

SEC. 304. SETTLEMENT OF STAYED CASES RELATING TO PERSONAL PROPERTY.

(a) APPRAISAL OF PROPERTY.—When a stay is granted pursuant to this Act in a proceeding to foreclose a mortgage on or to repossess personal property, or to rescind or terminate a contract for the purchase of personal property, the court may appoint three disinterested parties to appraise the property.

(b) EQUITY PAYMENT.—Based on the appraisal, and if undue hardship to the servicemember's dependents will not result, the court may order that the amount of the servicemember's equity in the property be paid to the servicemember, or the servicemember's dependents, as a condition of foreclosing the mortgage, repossessing the property, or rescinding or terminating the contract.

SEC. 305. TERMINATION OF RESIDENTIAL OR MOTOR VEHICLE LEASES.

(a) TERMINATION BY LESSEE.—The lessee on a lease described in subsection (b) may, at the lessee's option, terminate the lease at any time after—

(1) the lessee's entry into military service; or

(2) the date of the lessee's military orders described in paragraph (1)(B) or (2)(B) of subsection (b), as the case may be.

(b) COVERED LEASES.—This section applies to the following leases:

(1) LEASES OF PREMISES.—A lease of premises occupied, or intended to be occupied, by a servicemember or a servicemember's dependents for a residential, professional, business, agricultural, or similar purpose if—

(A) the lease is executed by or on behalf of a person who thereafter and during the term of the lease enters military service; or

(B) the servicemember, while in military service, executes the lease and thereafter receives military orders for a permanent change of station or to deploy with a military unit for a period of not less than 90 days.

(2) LEASES OF MOTOR VEHICLES.—A lease of a motor vehicle used, or intended to be used, by a servicemember or a servicemember's dependents for personal or business transportation if—

(A) the lease is executed by or on behalf of a person who thereafter and during the term of the lease enters military service under a call or order specifying a period of not less than 180 days (or who enters military service under a call or order specifying a period of 180 days or less and who, without a break in service, receives orders extending the period of military service to a period of not less than 180 days); or

(B) the servicemember, while in military service, executes the lease and thereafter receives military orders for a permanent change of station outside of the continental United States or to deploy with a military unit for a period of not less than 180 days.

(c) MANNER OF TERMINATION.—

(1) IN GENERAL.—Termination of a lease under subsection (a) is made—

(A) by delivery by the lessee of written notice of such termination, and a copy of the servicemember's military orders, to the lessor (or the lessor's grantee), or to the lessor's agent (or the agent's grantee); and

(B) in the case of a lease of a motor vehicle, by return of the motor vehicle by the lessee to the lessor (or the lessor's grantee), or to the lessor's agent (or the agent's grantee), not later than 15 days after the date of the delivery of written notice under subparagraph (A).

(2) DELIVERY OF NOTICE.—Delivery of notice under paragraph (1)(A) may be accomplished—

(A) by hand delivery;

(B) by private business carrier; or

(C) by placing the written notice in an envelope with sufficient postage and with return receipt requested, and addressed as designated by the lessor (or the lessor's grantee) or to the lessor's agent (or the agent's grantee), and depositing the written notice in the United States mails.

(d) EFFECTIVE DATE OF LEASE TERMINATION.—

(1) LEASE OF PREMISES.—In the case of a lease described in subsection (b)(1) that provides for monthly payment of rent, termination of the lease under subsection (a) is effective 30 days after the first date on which the next rental payment is due and payable after the date on which the notice under subsection (c) is delivered. In the case of any other lease described in subsection (b)(1), termination of the lease under subsection (a) is effective on the last day of the month following the month in which the notice is delivered.

(2) LEASE OF MOTOR VEHICLES.—In the case of a lease described in subsection (b)(2), termination of the lease under subsection (a) is effective on the day on which the requirements of subsection (c) are met for such termination.

(e) ARREARAGES AND OTHER OBLIGATIONS AND LIABILITIES.—Rents or lease amounts unpaid for the period preceding the effective date of the lease termination shall be paid on a prorated basis. In the case of the lease of a motor vehicle, the lessor may not impose an early termination charge, but any taxes, summonses, and title and registration fees and any other obligation and liability of the lessee in accordance with the terms of the lease, including reasonable charges to the lessee for excess wear, use and mileage, that are due and unpaid at the time of termination of the lease shall be paid by the lessee.

(f) RENT PAID IN ADVANCE.—Rents or lease amounts paid in advance for a period after the effective date of the termination of the lease shall be refunded to the lessee by the lessor (or the lessor's assignee or the assignee's agent) within 30 days of the effective date of the termination of the lease.

(g) RELIEF TO LESSOR.—Upon application by the lessor to a court before the termination date provided in the written notice, relief granted by this section to a servicemember may be modified as justice and equity require.

(h) PENALTIES.—

(1) MISDEMEANOR.—Any person who knowingly seizes, holds, or detains the personal effects, security deposit, or other property of a servicemember or a servicemember's dependent who lawfully terminates a lease covered by this section, or who knowingly interferes with the removal of such property from premises covered by such lease, for the purpose of subjecting or attempting to subject any of such property to a claim for rent accruing subsequent to the date of termination of such lease, or attempts to do so, shall be fined as provided in title 18, United States Code, or imprisoned for not more than one year, or both.

(2) PRESERVATION OF OTHER REMEDIES.—The remedy and rights provided under this section are in addition to and do not preclude any remedy for wrongful conversion otherwise available under law to the person claiming relief under this section, including any award for consequential or punitive damages.

SEC. 306. PROTECTION OF LIFE INSURANCE POLICY.

(a) ASSIGNMENT OF POLICY PROTECTED.—If a life insurance policy on the life of a servicemember is assigned before military service to secure the payment of an obligation, the assignee of the policy (except the insurer in connection with a policy loan) may not exercise, during a period of military service of the servicemember or within one year thereafter, any right or option obtained under the assignment without a court order.

(b) EXCEPTION.—The prohibition in subsection (a) shall not apply—

(1) if the assignee has the written consent of the insured made during the period described in subsection (a);

(2) when the premiums on the policy are due and unpaid; or

(3) upon the death of the insured.

(c) ORDER REFUSED BECAUSE OF MATERIAL AFFECT.—A court which receives an application for an order required under subsection (a) may refuse to grant such order if the court determines the ability of the servicemember to comply with the terms of the obligation is materially affected by military service.

(d) TREATMENT OF GUARANTEED PREMIUMS.—For purposes of this subsection, premiums guaranteed under the provisions of title IV of this Act shall not be considered due and unpaid.

(e) PENALTIES.—

(1) MISDEMEANOR.—A person who knowingly takes an action contrary to this section, or attempts to do so, shall be fined as provided in title 18, United States Code, or imprisoned for not more than one year, or both.

(2) PRESERVATION OF OTHER REMEDIES.—The remedy and rights provided under this section are in addition to and do not preclude any remedy for wrongful conversion otherwise available under law to the person claiming relief under this section, including any consequential or punitive damages.

SEC. 307. ENFORCEMENT OF STORAGE LIENS.

(a) LIENS.—

(1) LIMITATION ON FORECLOSURE OR ENFORCEMENT.—A person holding a lien on the property or effects of a servicemember may not, during any period of military service of the servicemember and for 90 days thereafter, foreclose or enforce any lien on such property or effects without a court order granted before foreclosure or enforcement.

(2) LIEN DEFINED.—For the purposes of paragraph (1), the term "lien" includes a lien for storage, repair, or cleaning of the property or effects of a servicemember or a lien on such property or effects for any other reason.

(b) STAY OF PROCEEDINGS.—In a proceeding to foreclose or enforce a lien subject to this section, the court may on its own motion, and shall if requested by a servicemember whose ability to comply with the obligation resulting in the proceeding is materially affected by military service—

(1) stay the proceeding for a period of time as justice and equity require; or

(2) adjust the obligation to preserve the interests of all parties.

The provisions of this subsection do not affect the scope of section 303.

(c) PENALTIES.—

(1) MISDEMEANOR.—A person who knowingly takes an action contrary to this section, or attempts to do so, shall be fined as provided in title 18, United States Code, or imprisoned for not more than one year, or both.

(2) PRESERVATION OF OTHER REMEDIES.—The remedy and rights provided under this section are in addition to and do not preclude any remedy for wrongful conversion otherwise available under law to the person claiming relief under this section, including any consequential or punitive damages.

SEC. 308. EXTENSION OF PROTECTIONS TO DEPENDENTS.

Upon application to a court, a dependent of a servicemember is entitled to the protections of this title if the dependent's ability to comply with a lease, contract, bailment, or other obligation is materially affected by reason of the servicemember's military service.

APPENDIX VII

HOMESTEAD EXEMPTION—FLORIDA

EXCERPTS FROM THE CONSTITUTION OF THE STATE OF FLORIDA

4. Homestead; exemptions.

(a) There shall be exempt from forced sale under process of any court, and no judgment, decree or execution shall be a lien thereon, except for the payment of taxes and assessments thereon, obligations contracted for the purchase, improvement or repair thereof, or obligations contracted for house, field or other labor performed on the realty, the following property owned by a natural person:

(1) a homestead, if located outside a municipality, to the extent of one hundred sixty acres of contiguous land and improvements thereon, which shall not be reduced without the owner's consent by reason of subsequent inclusion in a municipality; or if located within a municipality, to the extent of one-half acre of contiguous land, upon which the exemption shall be limited to the residence of the owner or the owner's family;

(2) personal property to the value of one thousand dollars.

(b) These exemptions shall inure to the surviving spouse or heirs of the owner.

(c) The homestead shall not be subject to devise if the owner is survived by spouse or minor child, except the homestead may be devised to the owner's spouse if there be no minor child. The owner of homestead real estate, joined by the spouse if married, may alienate the homestead by mortgage, sale or gift and, if married, may by deed transfer the title to an estate by the entirety with the spouse. If the owner or spouse is incompetent, the method of alienation or encumbrance shall be as provided by law.

Appendix VIII

IDENTITY THEFT FEDERAL STATUTES

§ **1028**. Fraud and related activity in connection with identification documents, authentication features, and information

(a) Whoever, in a circumstance described in subsection (c) of this section—

(1) knowingly and without lawful authority produces an identification document, authentication feature, or a false identification document;

(2) knowingly transfers an identification document, authentication feature, or a false identification document knowing that such document or feature was stolen or produced without lawful authority;

(3) knowingly possesses with intent to use unlawfully or transfer unlawfully five or more identification documents (other than those issued lawfully for the use of the possessor), authentication features, or false identification documents;

(4) knowingly possesses an identification document (other than one issued lawfully for the use of the possessor), authentication feature, or a false identification document, with the intent such document or feature be used to defraud the United States;

(5) knowingly produces, transfers, or possesses a document-making implement or authentication feature with the intent such document-making implement or authentication feature will be used in the production of a false identification document or another document-making implement or authentication feature which will be so used;

(6) knowingly possesses an identification document or authentication feature that is or appears to be an identification document or authentication feature of the United States or a sponsoring entity of an event designated as a special event of national significance which is stolen or produced without lawful authority knowing that such document or feature was stolen or produced without such authority;

(7) knowingly transfers, possesses, or uses, without lawful authority, a means of identification of another person with the intent to commit, or to aid or abet, or in connection with, any unlawful activity that

constitutes a violation of Federal law, or that constitutes a felony under any applicable State or local law; or

(8) knowingly traffics in false or actual authentication features for use in false identification documents, document-making implements, or means of identification; shall be punished as provided in subsection (b) of this section.

(b) The punishment for an offense under subsection (a) of this section is—

(1) except as provided in paragraphs (3) and (4), a fine under this title or imprisonment for not more than 15 years, or both, if the offense is—

(A) the production or transfer of an identification document, authentication feature, or false identification document that is or appears to be—

(i) an identification document or authentication feature issued by or under the authority of the United States; or

(ii) a birth certificate, or a driver's license or personal identification card;

(B) the production or transfer of more than five identification documents, authentication features, or false identification documents;

(C) an offense under paragraph (5) of such subsection; or

(D) an offense under paragraph (7) of such subsection that involves the transfer, possession, or use of 1 or more means of identification if, as a result of the offense, any individual committing the offense obtains anything of value aggregating $1,000 or more during any 1-year period;

(2) except as provided in paragraphs (3) and (4), a fine under this title or imprisonment for not more than 5 years, or both, if the offense is—

(A) any other production, transfer, or use of a means of identification, an identification document,[1] authentication feature, or a false identification document; or

(B) an offense under paragraph (3) or (7) of such subsection;

(3) a fine under this title or imprisonment for not more than 20 years, or both, if the offense is committed—

(A) to facilitate a drug trafficking crime (as defined in section 929 (a)(2));

(B) in connection with a crime of violence (as defined in section 924 (c)(3)); or

(C) after a prior conviction under this section becomes final;

(4) a fine under this title or imprisonment for not more than 30 years, or both, if the offense is committed to facilitate an act of domestic terrorism (as defined under section 2331 (5) of this title) or an act of international terrorism (as defined in section 2331 (1) of this title);

(5) in the case of any offense under subsection (a), forfeiture to the United States of any personal property used or intended to be used to commit the offense; and

(6) a fine under this title or imprisonment for not more than one year, or both, in any other case.

(c) The circumstance referred to in subsection (a) of this section is that—

(1) the identification document, authentication feature, or false identification document is or appears to be issued by or under the authority of the United States or a sponsoring entity of an event designated as a special event of national significance or the document-making implement is designed or suited for making such an identification document, authentication feature, or false identification document;

(2) the offense is an offense under subsection (a)(4) of this section; or

(3) either—

(A) the production, transfer, possession, or use prohibited by this section is in or affects interstate or foreign commerce, including the transfer of a document by electronic means; or

(B) the means of identification, identification document, false identification document, or document-making implement is transported in the mail in the course of the production, transfer, possession, or use prohibited by this section.

(d) In this section and section 1028A—

(1) the term "authentication feature" means any hologram, watermark, certification, symbol, code, image, sequence of numbers or letters, or other feature that either individually or in combination with another feature is used by the issuing authority on an identification document, document-making implement, or means of identification to determine if the document is counterfeit, altered, or otherwise falsified;

(2) the term "document-making implement" means any implement, impression, template, computer file, computer disc, electronic device, or computer hardware or software, that is specifically configured or primarily used for making an identification document, a false identification document, or another document-making implement;

(3) the term "identification document" means a document made or issued by or under the authority of the United States Government, a State, political subdivision of a State, a sponsoring entity of an event designated as a special event of national significance, a foreign government, political subdivision of a foreign government, an international governmental or an international quasi-governmental organization which, when completed with information concerning a particular individual, is of a type intended or commonly accepted for the purpose of identification of individuals;

(4) the term "false identification document" means a document of a type intended or commonly accepted for the purposes of identification of individuals that—

(A) is not issued by or under the authority of a governmental entity or was issued under the authority of a governmental entity but was subsequently altered for purposes of deceit; and

(B) appears to be issued by or under the authority of the United States Government, a State, a political subdivision of a State, a sponsoring entity of an event designated by the President as a special event of national significance, a foreign government, a political subdivision of a foreign government, or an international governmental or quasi-governmental organization;

(5) the term "false authentication feature" means an authentication feature that—

(A) is genuine in origin, but, without the authorization of the issuing authority, has been tampered with or altered for purposes of deceit;

(B) is genuine, but has been distributed, or is intended for distribution, without the authorization of the issuing authority and not in connection with a lawfully made identification document, document-making implement, or means of identification to which such authentication feature is intended to be affixed or embedded by the respective issuing authority; or

(C) appears to be genuine, but is not;

(6) the term "issuing authority"—

(A) means any governmental entity or agency that is authorized to issue identification documents, means of identification, or authentication features; and

(B) includes the United States Government, a State, a political subdivision of a State, a sponsoring entity of an event designated by the President as a special event of national significance, a foreign government, a political subdivision of a foreign government, or an international government or quasi-governmental organization;

(7) the term "means of identification" means any name or number that may be used, alone or in conjunction with any other information, to identify a specific individual, including any—

(A) name, social security number, date of birth, official State or government issued driver's license or identification number, alien registration number, government passport number, employer or taxpayer identification number;

(B) unique biometric data, such as fingerprint, voice print, retina or iris image, or other unique physical representation;

(C) unique electronic identification number, address, or routing code; or

(D) telecommunication identifying information or access device (as defined in section 1029 (e));

(8) the term "personal identification card" means an identification document issued by a State or local government solely for the purpose of identification;

(9) the term "produce" includes alter, authenticate, or assemble;

(10) the term "transfer" includes selecting an identification document, false identification document, or document-making implement and placing or directing the placement of such identification document, false identification document, or document-making implement on an online location where it is available to others;

(11) the term "State" includes any State of the United States, the District of Columbia, the Commonwealth of Puerto Rico, and any other commonwealth, possession, or territory of the United States; and

(12) the term "traffic" means—

(A) to transport, transfer, or otherwise dispose of, to another, as consideration for anything of value; or

(B) to make or obtain control of with intent to so transport, transfer, or otherwise dispose of.

(e) This section does not prohibit any lawfully authorized investigative, protective, or intelligence activity of a law enforcement agency of the United States, a State, or a political subdivision of a State, or of an intelligence agency of the United States, or any activity authorized under chapter 224 of this title.

(f) Attempt and Conspiracy.—Any person who attempts or conspires to commit any offense under this section shall be subject to the same penalties as those prescribed for the offense, the commission of which was the object of the attempt or conspiracy.

(g) Forfeiture Procedures.—The forfeiture of property under this section, including any seizure and disposition of the property and any related judicial or administrative proceeding, shall be governed by the provisions of section 413 (other than subsection (d) of that section) of the Comprehensive Drug Abuse Prevention and Control Act of 1970 (21 U.S.C. 853).

(h) Forfeiture; Disposition.—In the circumstance in which any person is convicted of a violation of subsection (a), the court shall order, in addition to the penalty prescribed, the forfeiture and destruction or other disposition of all illicit authentication features, identification documents, document-making implements, or means of identification.

(i) Rule of Construction.—For purpose of subsection (a)(7), a single identification document or false identification document that contains 1 or more means of identification shall be construed to be 1 means of identification.

APPENDIX IX

INSTRUCTIONS FOR COMPLETING THE ID THEFT AFFIDAVIT

Instructions for Completing the ID Theft Affidavit

To make certain that you do not become responsible for any debts incurred by an identity thief, you must prove to each of the companies where accounts were opened or used in your name that you didn't create the debt.

A group of credit grantors, consumer advocates, and attorneys at the Federal Trade Commission (FTC) developed an ID Theft Affidavit to make it easier for fraud victims to report information. While many companies accept this affidavit, others require that you submit more or different forms. Before you send the affidavit, contact each company to find out if they accept it.

It will be necessary to provide the information in this affidavit anywhere a **new** account was opened in your name. The information will enable the companies to investigate the fraud and decide the outcome of your claim. If someone made unauthorized charges to an **existing** account, call the company for instructions.

This affidavit has two parts:

- **Part One** — the ID Theft Affidavit — is where you report general information about yourself and the theft.
- **Part Two** — the Fraudulent Account Statement — is where you describe the fraudulent account(s) opened in your name. Use a separate Fraudulent Account Statement for each company you need to write to.

When you send the affidavit to the companies, attach copies (NOT originals) of any supporting documents (for example, driver's license or police report). Before submitting your affidavit, review the disputed account(s) with family members or friends who may have information about the account(s) or access to them.

Complete this affidavit as soon as possible. Many creditors ask that you send it within two weeks. Delays on your part could slow the investigation.

Be as accurate and complete as possible. You may choose not to provide some of the information requested. However, incorrect or incomplete information will slow the process of investigating your claim and absolving the debt. Print clearly.

When you have finished completing the affidavit, mail a copy to each creditor, bank, or company that provided the thief with the unauthorized credit, goods, or services you describe. Attach a copy of the Fraudulent Account Statement with information only on accounts opened at the institution to which you are sending the packet, as well as any other supporting documentation you are able to provide.

Send the appropriate documents to each company by certified mail, return receipt requested, so you can prove that it was received. The companies will review your claim and send you a written response telling you the outcome of their investigation. Keep a copy of everything you submit.

If you are unable to complete the affidavit, a legal guardian or someone with power of attorney may complete it for you. Except as noted, the information you provide will be used only by the company to process your affidavit, investigate the events you report, and help stop further fraud. If this affidavit is requested in a lawsuit, the company might have to provide it to the requesting party. Completing this affidavit does not guarantee that the identity thief will be prosecuted or that the debt will be cleared.

DO NOT SEND AFFIDAVIT TO THE FTC OR ANY OTHER GOVERNMENT AGENCY

If you haven't already done so, report the fraud to the following organizations:

1. Any one of the nationwide consumer reporting companies to place a fraud alert on your credit report. Fraud alerts can help prevent an identity thief from opening any more accounts in your name. The company you call is required to contact the other two, which will place an alert on their versions of your report, too.

   - **Equifax:** 1-800-525-6285; www.equifax.com
   - **Experian:** 1-888-EXPERIAN (397-3742); www.experian.com
   - **TransUnion:** 1-800-680-7289; www.transunion.com

   In addition to placing the fraud alert, the three consumer reporting companies will send you free copies of your credit reports, and, if you ask, they will display only the last four digits of your Social Security number on your credit reports.

2. The security or fraud department of each company where you know, or believe, accounts have been tampered with or opened fraudulently. Close the accounts. Follow up in writing, and include copies (NOT originals) of supporting documents. *It's important to notify credit card companies and banks in writing.* Send your letters by certified mail, return receipt requested, so you can document what the company received and when. Keep a file of your correspondence and enclosures.

   When you open new accounts, use new Personal Identification Numbers (PINs) and passwords. Avoid using easily available information like your mother's maiden name, your birth date, the last four digits of your Social Security number or your phone number, or a series of consecutive numbers.

3. Your local police or the police in the community where the identity theft took place to file a report. Get a copy of the police report or, at the very least, the number of the report. It can help you deal with creditors who need proof of the crime. If the police are reluctant to take your report, ask to file a "Miscellaneous Incidents" report, or try another jurisdiction, like your state police. You also can check with your state Attorney General's office to find out if state law requires the police to take reports for identity theft. Check the Blue Pages of your telephone directory for the phone number or check www.naag.org for a list of state Attorneys General.

4. The Federal Trade Commission. By sharing your identity theft complaint with the FTC, you will provide important information that can help law enforcement officials across the nation track down identity thieves and stop them. The FTC also can refer victims' complaints to other government agencies and companies for further action, as well as investigate companies for violations of laws that the FTC enforces.

   You can file a complaint online at **www.consumer.gov/idtheft**. If you don't have Internet access, call the FTC's Identity Theft Hotline, toll-free: 1-877-IDTHEFT (438-4338); TTY: 1-866-653-4261; or write: Identity Theft Clearinghouse, Federal Trade Commission, 600 Pennsylvania Avenue, NW, Washington, DC 20580.

DO NOT SEND AFFIDAVIT TO THE FTC OR ANY OTHER GOVERNMENT AGENCY

Name ______________________________ *Phone number* ____________________ *Page 1*

ID Theft Affidavit

Victim Information

(1) My full legal name is ____
(First) (Middle) (Last) (Jr., Sr., III)

(2) (If different from above) When the events described in this affidavit took place, I was known as

____
(First) (Middle) (Last) (Jr., Sr., III)

(3) My date of birth is ____________________
(day/month/year)

(4) My Social Security number is ______________________________

(5) My driver's license or identification card state and number are ________________________

(6) My current address is ____

City ________________________ State ______________ Zip Code ____________

(7) I have lived at this address since ____________________
(month/year)

(8) (If different from above) When the events described in this affidavit took place, my address was

____

City ________________________ State ______________ Zip Code ____________

(9) I lived at the address in Item 8 from __________ until __________
(month/year) (month/year)

(10) My daytime telephone number is (____)____________________

My evening telephone number is (____)____________________

DO NOT SEND AFFIDAVIT TO THE FTC OR ANY OTHER GOVERNMENT AGENCY

Name ______________________________ *Phone number* ____________________ *Page 2*

How the Fraud Occurred

Check all that apply for items 11 - 17:

(11) ☐ I did not authorize anyone to use my name or personal information to seek the money, credit, loans, goods or services described in this report.

(12) ☐ I did not receive any benefit, money, goods or services as a result of the events described in this report.

(13) ☐ My identification documents (for example, credit cards; birth certificate; driver's license; Social Security card; etc.) were ☐ stolen ☐ lost on or about ______________.
(day/month/year)

(14) ☐ To the best of my knowledge and belief, the following person(s) used my information (for example, my name, address, date of birth, existing account numbers, Social Security number, mother's maiden name, etc.) or identification documents to get money, credit, loans, goods or services without my knowledge or authorization:

Name (if known)	Name (if known)
Address (if known)	Address (if known)
Phone number(s) (if known)	Phone number(s) (if known)
Additional information (if known)	Additional information (if known)

(15) ☐ I do NOT know who used my information or identification documents to get money, credit, loans, goods or services without my knowledge or authorization.

(16) ☐ Additional comments: (For example, description of the fraud, which documents or information were used or how the identity thief gained access to your information.)

____

____

____

____

____

(Attach additional pages as necessary.)

DO NOT SEND AFFIDAVIT TO THE FTC OR ANY OTHER GOVERNMENT AGENCY

Name ______________________ *Phone number* ______________________ *Page 3*

Victim's Law Enforcement Actions

(17) (check one) I ❑ am ❑ am not willing to assist in the prosecution of the person(s) who committed this fraud.

(18) (check one) I ❑ am ❑ am not authorizing the release of this information to law enforcement for the purpose of assisting them in the investigation and prosecution of the person(s) who committed this fraud.

(19) (check all that apply) I ❑ have ❑ have not reported the events described in this affidavit to the police or other law enforcement agency. The police ❑ did ❑ did not write a report. *In the event you have contacted the police or other law enforcement agency, please complete the following:*

(Agency #1)	(Officer/Agency personnel taking report)
(Date of report)	(Report number, if any)
(Phone number)	(email address, if any)
(Agency #2)	(Officer/Agency personnel taking report)
(Date of report)	(Report number, if any)
(Phone number)	(email address, if any)

Documentation Checklist

Please indicate the supporting documentation you are able to provide to the companies you plan to notify. Attach copies (NOT originals) to the affidavit before sending it to the companies.

(20) ❑ A copy of a valid government-issued photo-identification card (for example, your driver's license, state-issued ID card or your passport). If you are under 16 and don't have a photo-ID, you may submit a copy of your birth certificate or a copy of your official school records showing your enrollment and place of residence.

(21) ❑ Proof of residency during the time the disputed bill occurred, the loan was made or the other event took place (for example, a rental/lease agreement in your name, a copy of a utility bill or a copy of an insurance bill).

DO NOT SEND AFFIDAVIT TO THE FTC OR ANY OTHER GOVERNMENT AGENCY

Name __________________________________ *Phone number* ______________________ *Page 4*

(22) ❑ A copy of the report you filed with the police or sheriff's department. If you are unable to obtain a report or report number from the police, please indicate that in Item 19. Some companies only need the report number, not a copy of the report. You may want to check with each company.

Signature

I certify that, to the best of my knowledge and belief, all the information on and attached to this affidavit is true, correct, and complete and made in good faith. I also understand that is affidavit or the information it contains may be made available to federal, state, and/or local law enforcement agencies for such action within their jurisdiction as they deem appropriate. I understand that knowingly making any false or fraudulent statement or representation to the government may constitute a violation of 18 U.S.C. §1001 or other federal, state, or local criminal statutes, and may result in imposition of a fine or imprisonment or both.

______________________________ ______________________________

(signature) (date signed)

____

(Notary)

[Check with each company. Creditors sometimes require notarization. If they do not, please have one witness (non-relative) sign below that you completed and signed this affidavit.]

Witness:

______________________________ ______________________________

(signature) (printed name)

______________________________ ______________________________

(date) (telephone number)

DO NOT SEND AFFIDAVIT TO THE FTC OR ANY OTHER GOVERNMENT AGENCY

APPENDIX X

FRAUDULENT ACCOUNT STATEMENT

Name ______________________ *Phone number* ______________________ *Page 5*

Fraudulent Account Statement

Completing this Statement

- Make as many copies of this page as you need. **Complete a separate page for each company you're notifying and only send it to that company.** Include a copy of your signed affidavit.
- List only the account(s) you're disputing with the company receiving this form. **See the example below.**
- If a collection agency sent you a statement, letter or notice about the fraudulent account, attach a copy of that document (**NOT** the original).

I declare (check all that apply):

❏ As a result of the event(s) described in the ID Theft Affidavit, the following account(s) was/were opened at your company in my name without my knowledge, permission or authorization using my personal information or identifying documents:

Creditor Name/Address *(the company that opened the account or provided the goods or services)*	**Account Number**	**Type of unauthorized credit/goods/services provided by creditor** *(if known)*	**Date issued or opened** *(if known)*	**Amount/Value provided** *(the amount charged or the cost of the goods/services)*
Example Example National Bank 22 Main Street Columbus, Ohio 22722	01234567-89	auto loan	01/05/2002	$25,500.00

❏ During the time of the accounts described above, I had the following account open with your company:

Billing name ______________________

Billing address ______________________

Account number ______________________

DO NOT SEND AFFIDAVIT TO THE FTC OR ANY OTHER GOVERNMENT AGENCY

APPENDIX XI

CREDIT PRACTICES AMENDMENT (16 CFR PART 444)

Table of Contents

Sec.

444.1 Definitions.

(a) Lender. A person who engages in the business of lending money to consumers within the jurisdiction of the Federal Trade Commission.

(b) Retail installment seller. A person who sells goods or services to consumers on a deferred payment basis or pursuant to a lease-purchase arrangement within the jurisdiction of the Federal Trade Commission.

(c) Person. An individual, corporation, or other business organization.

(d) Consumer. A natural person who seeks or acquires goods, services, or money for personal, family, or household use.

(e) Obligation. An agreement between a consumer and a lender or retail installment seller.

(f) Creditor. A lender or a retail installment seller.

(g) Debt. Money that is due or alleged to be due from one to another.

(h) Earnings. Compensation paid or payable to an individual or for his or her account for personal services rendered or to be rendered by him or her, whether denominated as wages, salary, commission, bonus, or otherwise, including periodic payments pursuant to a pension, retirement, or disability program.

(i) Household goods. Clothing, furniture, appliances, one radio and one television, linens, china, crockery, kitchenware, and personal effects (including wedding rings) of the consumer and his or her dependents, provided that the following are not included within the scope of the term household goods:

(1) Works of art;

(2) Electronic entertainment equipment (except one television and one radio);

(3) Items acquired as antiques; and

(4) Jewelry (except wedding rings).

(j) Antique. Any item over one hundred years of age, including such items that have been repaired or renovated without changing their original form or character.

(k) Cosigner. A natural person who renders himself or herself liable for the obligation of another person without compensation. The term shall include any person whose signature is requested as a condition to granting credit to another person, or as a condition for forbearance on collection of another person's obligation that is in default. The term shall not include a spouse whose signature is required on a credit obligation to perfect a security interest pursuant to State law. A person who does not receive goods, services, or money in return for a credit obligation does not receive compensation within the meaning of this definition. A person is a cosigner within the meaning of this definition whether or not he or she is designated as such on a credit obligation.

444.2 Unfair credit practices.

(a) In connection with the extension of credit to consumers in or affecting commerce, as commerce is defined in the Federal Trade Commission Act, it is an unfair act or practice within the meaning of Section 5 of that Act for a lender or retail installment seller directly or indirectly to take or receive from a consumer an obligation that:

(1) Constitutes or contains a cognovit or confession of judgment (for purposes other than executory process in the State of Louisiana), warrant of attorney, or other waiver of the right to notice and the opportunity to be heard in the event of suit or process thereon.

(2) Constitutes or contains an executory waiver or a limitation of exemption from attachment, execution, or other process on real or personal property held, owned by, or due to the consumer, unless the waiver applies solely to property subject to a security interest executed in connection with the obligation.

(3) Constitutes or contains an assignment of wages or other earnings unless:

(i) The assignment by its terms is revocable at the will of the debtor, or

(ii) The assignment is a payroll deduction plan or preauthorized payment plan, commencing at the time of the transaction, in which the consumer authorizes a series of wage deductions as a method of making each payment, or

(iii) The assignment applies only to wages or other earnings already earned at the time of the assignment.

(4) Constitutes or contains a nonpossessory security interest in household goods other than a purchase money security interest.

(b) [Reserved]

444.3 Unfair or deceptive cosigner practices.

(a) In connection with the extension of credit to consumers in or affecting commerce, as commerce is defined in the Federal Trade Commission Act, it is:

(1) A deceptive act or practice within the meaning of section 5 of that Act for a lender or retail installment seller, directly or indirectly, to misrepresent the nature or extent of cosigner liability to any person.

(2) An unfair act or practice within the meaning of section 5 of that Act for a lender or retail installment seller, directly or indirectly, to obligate a cosigner unless the cosigner is informed prior to becoming obligated, which in the case of open end credit shall mean prior to the time that the agreement creating the cosigner's liability for future charges is executed, of the nature of his or her liability as cosigner.

(b) Any lender or retail installment seller who complies with the preventive requirements in paragraph (c) of this section does not violate paragraph (a) of this section.

(c) To prevent these unfair or deceptive acts or practices, a disclosure, consisting of a separate document that shall contain the following statement and no other, shall be given to the cosigner prior to becoming obligated, which in the case of open end credit shall mean prior to the time that the agreement creating the cosigner's liability for future charges is executed.

NOTICE TO COSIGNER

You are being asked to guarantee this debt. Think carefully before you do. If the borrower doesn't pay the debt, you will have to. Be sure you can afford to pay if you have to, and that you want to accept this responsibility.

You may have to pay up to the full amount of the debt if the borrower does not pay. You may also have to pay late fees or collection costs, which increase this amount.

The creditor can collect this debt from you without first trying to collect from the borrower. The creditor can use the same collection methods against you that can be used against the borrower, such as suing you, garnishing your wages, etc. If this debt is ever in default, that fact may become a part of your credit record.

This notice is not the contract that makes you liable for the debt.

444.4 Late charges.

(a) In connection with collecting a debt arising out of an extension of credit to a consumer in or affecting commerce, as commerce is defined in the Federal Trade Commission Act, it is an unfair act or practice within the meaning of section 5 of that Act for a creditor, directly or indirectly, to levy or collect any delinquency charge on a payment, which payment is otherwise a full payment for the applicable period and is paid on its due date or within an applicable grace period, when the only delinquency is attributable to late fee(s) or delinquency charge(s) assessed on earlier installment(s).

(b) For purposes of this section, collecting a debt means any activity other than the use of judicial process that is intended to bring about or does bring about repayment of all or part of a consumer debt.

444.5 State exemptions.

(a) If, upon application to the Federal Trade Commission by an appropriate State agency, the Federal Trade Commission determines that:

(1) There is a State requirement or prohibition in effect that applies to any transaction to which a provision of this rule applies; and

(2) The State requirement or prohibition affords a level of protection to consumers that is substantially equivalent to, or greater than, the protection afforded by this rule;

Then that provision of the rule will not be in effect in that State to the extent specified by the Federal Trade Commission in its determination, for as long as the State administers and enforces the State requirement or prohibition effectively.

APPENDIX XII

STATUTES OF LIMITATION

Fast Facts

ACA INTERNATIONAL
The Association of Credit and Collection Professionals

From ACA's Fast Facts Service *Page 1 of 33*
Last Updated on January 9, 2006 *Document No. 1122*

Now get immediate access to ACA's compliance expertise. Visit E-Compliance at http://www.acainternational.org to search and access Fast Facts documents and other compliance information or to e-mail a compliance officer.

Statutes of Limitation

* Updated Louisiana statute of limitations.
* Updated Rhode Island statute of limitations.
* Updated Virgin Island statute of limitations.

The applicability of statutes of limitation vary from state-to-state and from case to case depending on the cause of action in the lawsuit. We have listed a few general statutes of limitation here. They are provided for information only. **Check with your own attorney to determine which, if any, are applicable to a given action.**

Alabama

Contracts 10 years. Actions founded upon any contract or writing **under seal** must be commenced within 10 years. Ala. Code § 6-2-33(1) (WESTLAW through End of 2001 Reg. Session).

Contracts 6 years. Actions founded on promises in writing **not under seal** must be commenced within six years. Ala. Code § 6-2-34(4) (WESTLAW through End of 2001 Reg. Session).

Contracts 6 years. Actions upon any **simple contract** or specialty not specifically enumerated in this section must be commenced within six years. Ala. Code § 6-2-34(9) (WESTLAW through End of 2001 Reg. Session).

Judgments - Domestic

Of record 20 years. Within 20 years, actions upon a judgment or decree of any court of this state, of the United States or of any state or territory of the United States must be commenced. Ala. Code § 6-2-32 (WESTLAW through End of 2001 Reg. Session).

Alaska

Contracts Unless the action is commenced within three (3) years, a person may not bring an action upon a contract or liability, express or implied, except as provided in Alaska Stat. § 09.10.040, or as otherwise provided by law, or, except if the provisions of this section are waived by contract. Alaska Stat. § 09.10.053 (Lexis, WESTLAW through 2001 1st Special Session of the Twenty-Second Legislature).

An action may not be brought upon a **sealed instrument**, unless the action is commenced within 10 years. Alaska Stat. § 09.10.040(a) (Lexis, WESTLAW through 2001 1st Special Session of the Twenty-Second Legislature).

Judgments – Domestic - A person may not bring an action upon a judgment or decree of a court of the

United States, or of a state or territory within the United States, unless the action is commenced within 10 years. Alaska Stat. § 09.10.040(a) (Lexis, WESTLAW through 2001 1st Special Session of the Twenty-Second Legislature).

No acknowledgment or promise is sufficient evidence of a new or continuing contract to take the case out of the operation of this chapter unless the acknowledgment or promise is contained in writing, signed by the party to be charged, and, as to instruments affecting real estate, acknowledged and recorded in the office of the recorder of the district where the original contract was filed or recorded. This section does not alter the effect of any payment of principal or interest. Alaska Stat. § 09.10.200 (Lexis, WESTLAW through 2001 1st Special Session of the Twenty-Second Legislature).

When a past due payment of principal or interest is made upon any evidence of indebtedness, the running of the time within which an action may be commenced starts from the time the last payment is made. Alaska Stat. § 09.10.210 (Lexis, WESTLAW through 2001 1st Special Session of the Twenty-Second Legislature).

Arizona

In-State Contract

An action for debt where indebtedness is evidenced by or founded upon a contract **in writing** executed within Arizona shall be commenced and prosecuted within six (6) years after the cause of action accrues and not afterward. Ariz. Rev. Stat. Ann. § 12-548 (West, WESTLAW through End of 45th Leg., 2nd Reg. Session and 5th Special Session 2002).

Out-of-State Contract/Foreign Judgment

There shall be commenced and prosecuted within four (4) years after the cause of action accrues, and not afterward, the following actions:

(1) For the penalty or for damages on the penal cause of a bond to convey real property.

(2) By one partner against his co-partner for a settlement of the partnership account, or upon mutual and current accounts concerning the trade of merchandise between merchant and merchant, their factors or agents, and the cause of action shall be considered as having accrued upon a cessation of the dealing in which they were interested together.

(3) Upon a judgment or decree of a court rendered without the state, or upon an instrument in writing executed without the state. This does not apply to a judgment for support and to associated costs and attorney fees.

(4) An action arising under the provisions of title 47, chapter 2, for breach of any contract of sale, which action shall be governed by § 47-2725, notwithstanding any other provision of this section or of § 12-543 or § 12-548.

Ariz. Rev. Stat. Ann. § 12-544 (West, WESTLAW through End of 45th Leg., 2nd Reg. Session and 5th Special Session 2002).

Oral Contract

There shall be commenced and prosecuted within three (3) years after the cause of action accrues, and not afterward, the following actions:

(1) For debt where the indebtedness is not evidenced by a contract in writing.

(2) Upon stated or open accounts other than such mutual and current accounts as concern the trade of merchandise between merchant and merchant, their factors or agents, but no item of a stated or open account shall be barred so long as any item thereof has been incurred within three years immediately prior to the bringing of an action thereon.

(3) For relief on the ground of fraud or mistake, which cause of action shall not be deemed to have accrued until the discovery by the aggrieved party of the facts constituting the fraud or mistake.

Ariz. Rev. Stat. Ann. § 12-543 (West, WESTLAW through End of 45th Leg., 2nd Reg. Session and 5th Special Session 2002).

Arkansas

Contracts

The following actions shall be commenced within three (3) years after the cause of action accrues: (1) All actions founded upon any contract, obligation, or liability not under seal and **not in writing**, excepting such as are brought upon the judgment or decree of some court of record of the United States or of this or some other state; …(3) All actions founded on any contract or liability, expressed or implied… Ark. Code Ann. §§ 16-56-105(1), (3) (WESTLAW through End of 2001 Regular Session)

(a) Actions to enforce **written obligations**, duties, or rights, except those to which § 4-4-111 is applicable, shall be commenced within five (5) years after the cause of action shall accrue.

(b) However, partial payment or written acknowledgement of default shall toll this statute of limitations. Ark. Code Ann. § 16-56-111 (WESTLAW through End of 2001 Regular Session).

An action to enforce an obligation, duty, or right arising under Title 4, Chapter 4 [governing liability of a bank for action or non-action with respect to an item handled by it for purposes of presentment, payment, or collection] must be commenced within three (3) years after the cause of action accrues. Ark. Code Ann. § 4-4-111 (WESTLAW through End of 2001 Regular Session).

Judgments -

Actions on all judgments and decrees shall be commenced within ten (10) years after cause of action shall accrue, and not afterward. Ark. Code Ann. § 16-56-114 (WESTLAW through End of 2001 Regular Session).

California

Contracts

2 years **(oral)** Cal. Civ. Proc. § 339(1) (West, WESTLAW through 1st Ex. Sess. and urgency legislation through ch. 109 of the 2001 Reg. Sess. and ch. 13 of the 2001 1st Ex. Session).

4 years **(written)** Cal. Civ. Proc. § 337(1) (West, WESTLAW through 1st Ex. Sess. and urgency legislation through ch. 109 of the 2001 Reg. Sess. and ch. 13 of the 2001 1st Ex. Session).

Judgments - Domestic

10 years Cal. Civ. Proc. § 337.5(3) (West, WESTLAW through 1st Ex. Sess. and urgency legislation through ch. 109 of the 2001 Reg. Sess. and ch. 13 of the 2001 1st Ex. Session).

Colorado

Contracts

3 years, except as provided:
(1) The following civil actions, regardless of the theory upon which suit is brought, or against whom suit is brought, shall be commenced within three years after the cause of action accrues, and not thereafter:
(a) All contract actions, including personal contracts and actions under the "Uniform Commercial Code," except as otherwise provided in section 13-80-103.5;
(k) All actions accruing outside this state if the limitation of actions of the place where the cause of action accrued is greater than that of this state.
Colo. Rev. Stat. Ann. § 13-80-101(1)(a), (k) (West, WESTLAW through Second Reg. Sess. of the Sixty-Third Gen. Assembly (2002)).

General limitation of actions - six years.

(1) The following actions shall be commenced within six years after the cause of action accrues, and not thereafter:

(a) All actions to recover a liquidated debt or an unliquidated, determinable amount of money due to the person bringing the action, all actions for the enforcement of rights set forth in any instrument securing the payment of or evidencing any debt, and all actions of replevin to recover the possession of personal property encumbered under any instrument securing any debt; except that actions to recover pursuant to section 38-35-124.5(3), C.R.S. [*ed. note*: involving closing and settlement services for real estate transactions], shall be commenced within one year.

(b) All actions for arrears of rent;

(c) All actions brought under section 13-21-109 [*ed. note*: recovery of damages for checks, drafts, or orders not paid upon presentment], except actions brought under section 13-21-109(2) [*ed. note*: cases in which notice of nonpayment on presentment has been given];

(d) All actions by the public employees' retirement association to collect unpaid contributions from employers for persons who are not members or inactive members at the time the association first notifies an employer of its claim for unpaid contributions. This paragraph (d) shall apply to causes of action as provided in section 24-51-402(2) [*ed. note*: payment of public employees' retirement association benefits], C.R.S.

(e) All actions brought for restitution and civil penalties pursuant to section 26-4-1104, C.R.S. [*ed. note*: involving civil penalties for false Medicaid claims].

Colo. Rev. Stat. Ann. § 13-80-103.5 (West, WESTLAW through Second Reg. Sess. of the Sixty-Third Gen. Assembly (2002)), *amended by* 2002 Colo. Legis. Serv. Ch. 315 (S.B. 161).

Judgments -
6 years (if judgment entered in county court on or after July 1, 1981) Colo. Rev. Stat. Ann. § 13-52-102(2)(b)(I) [see statute below].

20 years (if judgment entered before July 1, 1981) Colo. Rev. Stat. Ann. § 13-52-102(2)(a) [see statute below].

Property subject to execution – lien – real estate
(1) All goods and chattels, lands, tenements, and real estate of every person against whom any judgment is obtained in any court of record in this state, either at law or in equity, or against whom any foreign judgment is filed with the clerk of any court of this state in accordance with the provisions of the "Uniform Enforcement of Foreign Judgments Act" pursuant to article 53 of this title, which judgment, in either case, is for any debt, damages, costs, or other sum of money are liable to be sold on execution to be issued upon such judgment. A transcript of the judgment record of such judgment, certified by the clerk of such court, may be recorded in any county; and from the time of recording such transcript, and not before, the judgment shall become a lien upon all the real estate, not exempt from execution in the county where such transcript of judgment is recorded, owned by such judgment debtor or which such judgment debtor may afterwards acquire in such county, until such lien expires. The lien of such judgment shall expire six years after the entry of judgment unless, prior to the expiration of such six-year period, such judgment is revived as provided by law and a transcript of the judgment record of such revived judgment, certified by the clerk of the court in which such revived judgment was entered, is recorded in the same county in which the transcript of the original judgment was recorded, in which event the lien shall continue for six years from the entry of the revived judgment. A lien may be obtained with respect to a revived judgment in the same manner as an original judgment and the lien of a revived judgment may be continued in the same manner as the lien of an original judgment. The lien of any judgment shall expire if the judgment is satisfied or considered as satisfied as provided in this section. The lien created by recording a notice of lien of a judgment for child support or maintenance or arrears thereof or child support debt pursuant to section 14-10-122, C.R.S., shall be governed by such section. The lien created by recording a transcript of an order for restitution pursuant to section 16-18.5-104(5)(a), C.R.S., shall be governed by article 18.5 of title 16, C.R.S.

(2)(a) Except as provided in paragraph (b) of this subsection (2), execution may issue on any judgment described in subsection (1) of this section to enforce the same at any time within twenty years from the entry

thereof, but not afterwards, unless revived as provided by law, and, after twenty years from the entry of final judgment in any court of this state, the judgment shall be considered as satisfied in full, unless so revived.

(b)(I) With respect to judgments entered in county courts on or after July 1, 1981, the time limitation within which execution may issue is six years from the entry thereof, but not afterwards, unless revived as provided by law, and, after six years from the entry of final judgment in any county court of this state, the judgment shall be considered as satisfied in full, unless so revived.

(II) The twenty year limitation contained in paragraph (a) of this subsection (2) shall not apply to judgments entered for restitution pursuant to article 18.5 of title 16, C.R.S. Execution may issue on judgments for restitution at any time until paid in full.

Colo. Rev. Stat. Ann. § 13-52-102(1)-(2) (West, WESTLAW through Second Reg. Sess. of the Sixty-Third Gen. Assembly (2002)).

Connecticut

Contracts 3 years **(oral)** Conn. Gen. Stat. Ann. § 52-581(a) (West, WESTLAW current with amendments received through 1-1-01).

6 years **(written)** (Conn. Gen. Stat. Ann. § 52-576(a) (West, WESTLAW through Gen. St., Rev. to 1-1-01).

Judgments - Domestic Of Record No execution to enforce a judgment for money damages rendered in any court of this state may be issued after the expiration of twenty years (20) from the date the judgment was entered and no action based upon such a judgment may be instituted after the expiration of twenty-five (25) years from the date the judgment was entered. Conn. Gen. Stat. Ann. § 52-598(a) (West, WESTLAW current with amendments received through 1-1-01).

No execution to enforce a judgment for money damages rendered in a small claims session may be issued after the expiration of ten (10) years from the date the judgment was entered, and no action based upon any such judgment may be instituted after the expiration of fifteen (15) years from the date the judgment was entered. Conn. Gen. Stat. Ann. § 52-598(b) (West, WESTLAW current with amendments received through 1-1-01).

Delaware

Contracts 3 years (Oral, not under seal)

[N]o action to recover a debt not evidenced by a record or by an instrument under seal, no action based on a detailed statement of mutual demands in the nature of debit and credit between parties arising out of contractual or fiduciary relations, no action based on a promise, no action based on a statute, and no action to recover damages caused by an injury unaccompanied with force or resulting indirectly from the act of the defendant shall be brought after the expiration of 3 years from the accruing of the cause of such action; subject, however, to the provisions of §§ 8108-8110, 8119 and 8127 of this title. Del. Code Ann. tit. 10, § 8106 (WESTLAW through 2001 Reg. Session).

Bills and notes - 6 years

When a cause of action arises from a promissory note, bill of exchange, or an acknowledgment under the hand of the party of a subsisting demand, the action may be commenced at any time within 6 years from the accruing of such cause of action. Del. Code Ann. tit. 10, § 8109 (WESTLAW through 2001 Reg. Session).

Judgments -
Domestic 5 years
An execution may be issued upon a judgment in a civil action at any time within 5 years from the time when such judgment was entered or rendered, or from the time when such judgment became due; or to collect any instalment of a judgment within 5 years from the time when such instalment fell due. This section shall only apply to cases when no execution has been previously issued to collect such judgment or instalment, and to cases where one or more have been issued for such purposed, and it appears by the return of the officer that such judgment or instalment, as the case may be, has not been paid or satisfied. As to all other cases the law shall remain unaffected. Del. Code Ann. tit. 10 § 5072(a) (WESTLAW through 2001 Reg. Session).

Foreign – Filing and statute:
A copy of any foreign judgment authenticated in accordance with an act of Congress, or the statutes of this State, may be filed in the office of any Prothonotary of this State. The Prothonotary shall treat the foreign judgment in the same manner as a judgment of the Superior Court of this State. A judgment so filed has the same effect and is subject to the same procedures, defenses and proceedings for reopening, vacating or staying, as a judgment of the Superior Court of this State and may be enforced or satisfied in like manner. Del. Code Ann. tit. 10, § 4782 (WESTLAW through 2001 Reg. Session).

District of Columbia

Except as otherwise specifically provides by law, actions for the following purposes may not be brought after the expiration of the period specified below from the time the right to maintain the action accrues:...
(6) on an **executor's or administrator's bond** – 5 years; on any **other bond or single bill, covenant, or other instrument under seal** – 12 years;
(7) on a **simple contract, express or implied** – 3 years...
This section does not apply to actions for breach of contracts for sale governed by §28:2-725, nor to actions brought by the District of Columbia government. D.C. Code Ann. § 12-301 (WESTLAW through October 2, 2001).

In an action upon a **simple contract**, an **acknowledgement**, or **promise, by words only** is not sufficient evidence of an new or continuing contract whereby to take the case out of the operation of the statute of limitations or to deprive a party of the benefit thereof unless the acknowledgement, or promise, is in writing, signed by the party chargeable thereby. This section does not alter or take away, or lessen the effect of a payment of principal or interest made by any person. In actions against two or more joint contractors, or executors, or administrators, if it appears at the trial, or otherwise, that the plaintiff, though barred by the statute of limitations as to one or more of the defendants, is nevertheless entitled to recover against any other defendant by virtue of a new acknowledgement, or promise, or otherwise, judgment may be given for the plaintiff as to that defendant. **An indorsement or memorandum of a payment written or made upon a promissory note, bill of exchange, or other writing,** by or on behalf of the party to whom the payment is to be made, is not sufficient proof of the payment so as to take the case out of the operation of the statute of limitations. D.C. Code Ann. § 28-3504 (WESTLAW through October 2, 2001).

Judgments -
(a) Except as provided by subsection (b) of this section, every final judgment or final decree for the payment of money rendered in the –
  (1) United States District Court for the District of Columbia; or
  (2) Superior Court for the District of Columbia, when filed and recorded in the office of the Recorder of Deeds of the District of Columbia,
Is enforceable, by execution issued thereon, for the period of twelve (12) years only from the date when an execution might first be issued thereon, or from the date of the last order of revival thereof. The time during which the judgment creditor is stayed from enforcing the judgment, by written agreement filed in the case, or other order, or by the operation of an appeal, may not be computed as a part of the period within which the judgment is enforceable by execution.

(b) At the expiration of the twelve-year period provided by subsection (a) of this section, the judgment or decree shall cease to have any operation or effect. Thereafter, except in the case of a proceeding that may be then pending for the enforcement of the judgment or decree, action may not be brought on, nor may it be revived, and execution may not issue on it. D.C. Code Ann. § 15-101 (WESTLAW through October 2, 2001).

An order of revival issued upon a judgment or decree during the period of twelve years from the rendition or from the date of an order reviving the judgment or decree, extends the effect and operation of the judgment or decree with the lien thereby created and all the remedies for its enforcement for the period of twelve years from the date of the order. D.C. Code Ann. § 15-103 (WESTLAW through October 2, 2001).

Florida

Contracts – oral: 4 years
A legal or equitable action on a contract, obligation, or liability not founded on a written instrument, including an action for the sale and delivery of goods, wares, and merchandise, and on store accounts. Fla. Stat. Ann. § 95.11(3)(k) (West, WESTLAW through End of 2001 1st Reg. Session).

Contracts – written: 5 years
A legal or equitable action on a contract, obligation, or liability founded on a written instrument, except for an action to enforce a claim against a payment bond, which shall be governed by the applicable provisions of §§ 255.05(2)(a)2 and 713.23(1)(e). Fla. Stat. Ann. § 95.11(2)(b) (West, WESTLAW through End of 2001 1st Reg. Session).

Judgments -
Domestic
Of Record 20 years

An action on a judgment or decree of a court of record in this state. Fla. Stat. Ann. § 95.11(1) (West, WESTLAW through End of 2001 1st Reg. Session).

Judgments -
Foreign or
Not of Record 5 years
An action on a judgment or decree of any court, not of record, of this state or any court of the United States, any other state or territory in the United States, or a foreign country. Fla. Stat. Ann. § 95.11(2)(a) (West, WESTLAW through End of 2001 1st Reg. Session).

Georgia

Oral Contracts
All actions upon open account, or for the breach of any contract not under the hand of the party sought to be charged, or upon any implied promise or undertaking shall be brought within 4 years after the right of action accrues. However, this Code section shall not apply to actions for the breach of contracts for the sale of goods under Article 2 of Title 11. Ga. Code Ann. § 9-3-25 (WESTLAW through 2002 Reg. Session of the General Assembly).

All other actions upon contracts express or implied not otherwise provided for shall be brought within 4 years from the accrual of the right of action. However, this Code shall not apply to actions for the breach of contracts for the sale of goods under Article 2 of Title 11. Ga. Code Ann. § 9-3-26 (WESTLAW through 2002 Reg. Session of the General Assembly).

Written Contracts

All actions upon simple contracts in writing shall be brought within 6 years after the same become due and payable. However, this Code section shall not apply to actions for the breach of contracts for the sale of goods under Article 2 of Title 11 or to negotiable instruments under Article 3 of Title 11. Ga. Code Ann. § 9-3-24 (WESTLAW through 2002 Reg. Session of the General Assembly).

Sealed Instruments

Actions upon bonds or other instruments under seal shall be brought within 20 years after the right of action has accrued. No instrument shall be considered under seal unless so recited in the body of the instrument. Ga. Code Ann. § 9-3-23 (WESTLAW through 2002 Reg. Session of the General Assembly).

Judgments

A judgment shall become dormant and shall not be enforced when 7 years shall elapse after the rendition of the judgment before execution is issued thereon and is entered on the general execution docket of the county in which the judgment was rendered. Ga. Code Ann. § 9-12-60(a)(1) (WESTLAW through 2002 Reg. Session of the General Assembly).

Guam

Contracts

Within three (3) years -- (7) An action upon a contract, obligation or liability not founded an instrument in writing, other than that mentioned in Subdivision (2) of § 11303 of this Title; or an action founded upon a contract, obligation or liability, evidenced by a certificate, or abstract or guaranty of title of real property or by a policy of title insurance; shall not be deemed to have accrued until the aggrieved party has discovered the loss or damage. 7 Guam Code Ann. § 11305 (WESTLAW through P.L. 26-116 (2002)).

Within four (4) years --

(1) An action upon any contract, obligation or liability founded an instrument in writing.

(2) An action to recover (1) upon a book account whether consisting of one (1) or more entries; (2) upon an account stated based upon an account in writing, but the acknowledgment of the account stated need not be in writing; (3) a balance due upon a mutual, open and current account, provided, however, that where an account stated is based upon an account of one (1) item, the time shall begin to run from the date of said item, and where an account stated is based upon an account of more than one (1) item, the time shall begin to run from the date of the last item.

(3) An action based upon rescission of a contract. The time begins to run from the date upon which occurred the facts that the aggrieved party claims permits him to rescind the contract. Where the ground for rescission is fraud or mistake, the time does not begin to run until the aggrieved party discovers the facts constituting the fraud or mistake. Where the ground for rescission is misrepresentation relating to an offer to insure or an application to obtain insurance, the time does not begin to run until the representation becomes false. 7 Guam Code Ann. § 11303 (WESTLAW through P.L. 26-116 (2002)).

The term book account means a statement which constitutes the principal record of one (1) or more transactions between a debtor and a creditor arising out of a contract or some fiduciary relation, and which shows the debits and credits in connection therewith, and against whom and in favor of whom entries are made, is entered in the regular course of business as conducted by the creditor or fiduciary, and is kept in a reasonably permanent form and manner and is (1) in a bound book, or (2) on a sheet or sheets fastened in a book or to a backing but detachable therefrom, or (3) on a card or cards of a permanent character or is kept in any reasonably permanent form and manner. 7 Guam Code Ann. § 11304 (WESTLAW through P.L. 26-116 (2002)).

Judgments

Within five (5) years --

1. An action upon a judgment or decree of any court of the United States or of any state within the United States.

7 Guam Code Ann. § 11302 (WESTLAW through P.L. 26-116 (2002)).

Hawaii

Contracts

The following actions shall be commenced within six (6) years next after the cause of action accrued, and not after:

(1) Actions for the recovery of any debt founded upon contract, obligation, or liability, excepting such as are brought upon the judgment or decree of a court; excepting further that actions for the recovery of any contract, obligation or liability made pursuant to chapter 577A shall be governed by chapter 577A;

(2) Actions for taking or detaining any goods or chattels, including actions in the nature of replevin.

Haw. Rev. Stat. Ann. §§ 657-1(1), (3) (Lexis, WESTLAW through 2001 Third Special Session of the Twenty-First Legislature).

Judgments -

Unless an extension is granted, every judgment and decree of any court of the State shall be presumed to be paid and discharged at the expiration of ten (10) years after the judgment or decree was rendered. No action shall be commenced after the expiration of ten years from the date a judgment or decree was rendered or extended. No extension of a judgment or decree shall be granted unless the extension is sought within ten years of the date the original judgment or decree was rendered. A court shall not extend any judgment or decree beyond twenty years from the date of the original judgment or decree. No extension shall be granted without notice and the filing of a non-hearing motion or a hearing motion to extend the life of the judgment or decree.

Haw. Rev. Stat. Ann. § 657-5 (Lexis, WESTLAW through 2001 Third Special Session of the Twenty-First Legislature).

The following actions shall be commenced within six (6) years next after the cause of action accrued, and not after:

(1) Actions upon judgments or decrees rendered in any court not of record in the State, or subject to section 657-9, in any court of record in any foreign jurisdiction.

Haw. Rev. Stat. Ann. § 657-1(2) (Lexis, WESTLAW through 2001 Third Special Session of the Twenty-First Legislature).

Idaho

Contracts

Within 4 years: Oral

An action upon a contract, obligation or liability not founded upon an instrument of writing. Idaho Code § 5-217 (Lexis, WESTLAW through 2002 Cumulative Supplement (2nd Reg. Session of the 56th Legislature)).

Within 5 years: Written

An action upon any contract, obligation or liability founded upon an instrument in writing. The limitations prescribed by this section shall never apply to actions in the name or for the benefit of the state and shall never be asserted nor interposed as a defense to any action in the name or for the benefit of the state although such limitations may have become fully operative as a defense prior to the adoption of this amendment."

Idaho Code Ann. § 5-216 (Lexis, WESTLAW through 2002 Cumulative Supplement (2nd Reg. Session of the 56th Legislature)).

Judgments – 6 years.

"Within six (6) years:

1. An action upon a judgment or decree of any court of the United States, or of any state or territory within the United States.

2. An action for mesne profits of real property." ***[Editor's Note: Mesne profits are profits of an estate received in wrongful possession between two dates.]*** Idaho Code Ann. § 5-215 (Lexis, WESTLAW through 2002 Cumulative Supplement (2nd Reg. Session of the 56th Legislature)).

Tolling of Statutes
Where a judgment is made payable in installments, the statute of limitations applies to each installment separately, and does not begin to run on any installment until it is due.
Simonton v. Simonton, 193 P. 386 (Idaho 1920).

Acknowledgment or new promise -- Effect on operation of statute – Effect of partial payment:
No acknowledgment or promise is sufficient evidence of a new or continuing contract by which to take the case out of the operation of this chapter, unless the same is contained in some writing, signed by the party to be charged thereby; but any payment of principal or interest is equivalent to a new promise in writing, duly signed, to pay the residue of the debt. Idaho Code Ann. § 5-238 (Lexis, WESTLAW through 2002 Cumulative Supplement (2nd Reg. Session of the 56th Legislature)).

Statute of limitations can be extended by an obligor who makes a partial payment after a note is due. Such a partial payment is equivalent to a new promise by an obligor to pay a debt. *Thomson v. Sunny Ridge Village P'ship*, 796 P.2d 539, 540 (Idaho Ct. App. 1990).

Partial payment by one of several debtors only binds the person making the payment and does not operate to take the debt out of the statute of limitations with regard to any other debtor. *Id at 541.*

Illinois

Oral Contracts
Except as provided in Section 2-725 of the "Uniform Commercial Code", approved July 31, 1961, as amended, and Section 11-13 of "The Illinois Public Aid Code", approved April 11, 1967, as amended, actions on unwritten contracts, expressed or implied, or on awards of arbitration, or to recover damages for an injury done to property, real or personal, or to recover the possession of personal property or damages for the detention or conversion thereof, and all civil actions not otherwise provided for, shall be commenced within 5 years next after the cause of action accrued. 735 Ill. Comp. Stat. 5/13-205 (West, WESTLAW through P.A. 92-650, 92-652 through 92-700 of the 2002 Reg. Session of the 92nd Gen. Assembly).

Written Contracts
Except as provided in Section 2-725 of the "Uniform Commercial Code", actions on bonds, promissory notes, bills of exchange, written leases, written contracts, or other evidences of indebtedness in writing, shall be commenced within 10 years next after the cause of action accrued; but if any payment or new promise to pay has been made, in writing, on any bond, note, bill, lease, contract, or other written evidence of indebtedness, within or after the period of 10 years, then an action may be commenced thereon at any time within 10 years after the time of such payment or promise to pay. For purposes of this Section, with regard to promissory notes dated on or after the effective date of this amendatory Act of 1997, a cause of action on a promissory note payable at a definite date accrues on the due date or date stated in the promissory note or the date upon which the promissory note is accelerated. With respect to a demand promissory note dated on or after the effective date of this amendatory Act of 1997, if a demand for payment is made to the maker of the demand promissory note, an action to enforce the obligation of a party to pay the demand promissory note must be commenced within 10 years after the demand. An action to enforce a demand promissory note is barred if neither principal nor interest on the demand promissory note has been paid for a continuous period of 10 years and no demand for payment has been made to the maker during that period. 735 Ill. Comp. Stat. 5/13-206 (West, WESTLAW through P.A. 92-650, 92-652 through 92-700 of the 2002 Reg. Session of the 92nd Gen. Assembly).

Judgments

Judgments in a circuit court may be revived as provided by Section 2-1601 of this Act, within 20 years next after the date of such judgment and not after; and the provisions of Section 13-217 of this Act shall apply also to this Section. 735 Ill. Comp. Stat. 5/13-218 (West, WESTLAW through P.A. 92-650, 92-652 through 92-700 of the 2002 Reg. Session of the 92nd Gen. Assembly).

Indiana

Contracts 6 years (**oral**)

The following actions must be commenced within six (6) years after the cause of action accrues:

1. Actions on accounts and contracts not in writing.
2. Actions for use, rents, and profits of real property.
3. Actions for injuries to property other than personal property, damages for detention of personal property and for recovering possession of personal property.
4. Actions for relief against frauds.

Ind. Code Ann § 34-11-2-7 (West, WESTLAW through End of 2001 1st Regular Session).

6 years (**written contract for payment of money**)

An action upon promissory notes, bills of exchange or other written contracts for the payment of money executed after August 31, 1982, must be commenced within six (6) years after the cause of action accrues. An action upon promissory notes, bills of exchange, and other written contracts for the payment of money executed on or after September 19, 1881, and before September 1, 1982, must be commenced with ten (10) years after the cause of action accrues. Ind. Code Ann. § 34-11-2-9 (West, WESTLAW through End of 2001 1st Regular Session).

10 years (**written contract other than for payment of money**)

An action upon contracts in writing other than those for the payment of money, and including all mortgages other than chattel mortgages, deeds of trust, judgments of courts of record, and for the recovery of the possession of real estate, must be commenced within ten (10) years after the cause of action accrues. However, an action upon contracts in writing other than those for the payment of money entered into before September 1, 1982, including chattel mortgages, deeds of trust, judgments of courts of record, and for the recovery of the possession of real estate, must be commenced within twenty (20) years after the cause of action accrues. Ind. Code Ann. § 34-11-2-11 (West, WESTLAW through End of 2001 1st Regular Session).

Judgments - Of record:

20 years. Every judgment and decree of any court of record of the United States, of Indiana, or of any other state shall be considered satisfied after the expiration of twenty (20) years. Ind. Code Ann. § 34-11-2-12 (West, WESTLAW through End of 2001 1st Regular Session).

Iowa

Contracts

Oral

Actions on oral contracts must be brought within five years. Iowa Code Ann. § 614.1(4) (West, WESTLAW through end of 2001 2nd Ex. Session).

Written

Actions on written contracts must be brought within ten (10) years. Iowa Code Ann. § 614.1(5) (West, WESTLAW through end of 2001 2nd Ex. Session).

Judgments

Of Courts Not of Record

Actions on judgment of courts not of record must be brought within ten (10) years. Iowa Code Ann. § 614.1(5) (West, WESTLAW through end of 2001 2nd Ex. Session).

Of Courts of Record
Actions founded on a judgment of a court of record, whether of this or of any other of the United States, or of the federal courts of the United States, must be brought within twenty (20) years. Iowa Code Ann. § 614.1(6) (West, WESTLAW through end of 2001 2nd Ex. Session).

Kansas

Contracts
3 years all actions upon contracts, obligations or liabilities expressed or implied but not in writing. Kan. Stat. Ann. § 60-512(1) (WESTLAW through End of 2000 Reg. Session).

5 years an action upon any agreement, contract or promise in writing. Kan. Stat. Ann. § 60-511(1) (WESTLAW through End of 2000 Reg. Session).

(a) In any case founded on contract, when any part of the principal or interest shall have been paid, or an acknowledgment of an existing liability, debt or claim, or any promise to pay the same, shall have been made, an action may be brought in such case within the period prescribed for the same, after such payment, acknowledgment or promise; but such acknowledgment or promise must be in writing, signed by the party to be charged thereby.
(b) If there be two or more joint contractors, no one of whom is entitled to act as the agent of the others, no such joint contractor shall lose the benefit of the statute of limitations so as to be chargeable by reason of any acknowledgment, promise or payment made by any other or others of them, unless done with the knowledge and consent of, or satisfied [ratified] by the joint contractor sought to be charged. Kan. Stat. Ann. § 60-520 (WESTLAW through End of 2000 Reg. Session).

Judgments -
Domestic
Of Record Renewal affidavit or execution keeps judgment alive every five (5) years. Kan. Stat. Ann. § 60-2403(a)(1) (WESTLAW through End of 2000 Reg. Session).

Kentucky

Contracts

5 years after the cause of action accrued **(oral, express or implied)** Ky. Rev. Stat. Ann. § 413.120(1) (West, WESTLAW through End of 2001 Reg. Session).

15 years after the cause of action first accrued **(written)** Ky. Rev. Stat. Ann. § 413.090(2) (West, WESTLAW through End of 2001 Reg. Session).

Parties may contract for a shorter limitation period:
"It is now well settled law in this state that parties, dealing at arm's length, may contract for a limitation shorter than that provided by statute, so long as the period provided for is a reasonable one." *Prewitt v. Supreme Council of Royal Arcanum*, 194 S.W.2d 633, 635 (Ky. 1946).

An action on a merchant's account for goods sold and delivered, or any article charged in such store account must commence within 5 years from January 1 next succeeding the respective dates of the delivery of the several articles charged in the account. Judgment shall be rendered for no more than the amount of articles actually charged or delivered within five (5) years preceding that in which the action was brought... Ky. Rev. Stat. Ann. §§ 413.120(10), 413.130 (West, WESTLAW through End of 2001 Reg. Session).

Judgments -
Domestic 15 years after the cause of action first accrued. Ky. Rev. Stat. Ann. § 413.090(1) (West, WESTLAW through End of 2001 Reg. Session).

Foreign 15 years after the cause of action first accrued. Ky. Rev. Stat. Ann. § 413.090(1) (West, WESTLAW through End of 2001 Reg. Session).

Louisiana

The following actions are subject to a liberative prescription of three (3) years:

(1) An action for the recovery of compensation for services rendered, including payment of salaries, wages, commissions, tuition fees, professional fees, fees and emoluments of public officials, fright, passage, money, lodging, and board;

(2) An action for arrearages of rent and annuities;

(3) An action on money lent...

La. Civ. Code Ann. Art. 3494 (West, WESTLAW through all 2001 Regular and Second Extraordinary Session Acts).

Unless otherwise provided by legislation, a personal claim is subject to a liberative prescription of ten years. La. Civ. Code Ann. Art. 3499 (WESTLAW through 2005 Reg. Sess.).

Actions on **instruments**, whether negotiable or not, and on **promissory notes**, whether negotiable or not, are subject to a liberative prescription of five (5) years. This prescription commences to run from the day payment is exigible. La. Civ. Code Ann. Art. 3498 (West, WESTLAW through all 2001 Regular and Second Extraordinary Session Acts).

A money judgment rendered by a trial court of this state is prescribed by the lapse of ten (10) years from its signing if no appeal has been taken, or, if an appeal has been taken, it is prescribed by the lapse of ten (10) years from the time the judgment becomes final.

An action to enforce **a money judgment** rendered by a court of another state or a possession of the United States, or of a foreign country, is barred by the lapse of ten (10) years from its rendition; but such a judgment is not enforceable in this state if it is prescribed, barred by the statute of limitations, or is otherwise unenforceable under the laws of the jurisdiction in which it was rendered.

Any party having an interest in a **money judgment** may have it revived before it prescribes, as provided in Article 2031 of the Code of Civil Procedure. A judgment so revived is subject to the prescription provided by the first paragraph of this Article. An interested party may have a money judgment rendered by a court of this state revived as often as he may desire.
La. Civil Code Ann. art. 3501 (West, WESTLAW through all 2001 Regular and Second Extraordinary Session Acts).

Maine

Contracts

All civil actions shall be commenced within 6 years after the cause of action accrues and not afterwards, except actions on a judgment or decree of any court of record of the United States, or of any state or of a justice of the peace in Maine, and except as otherwise specially provided. Me. Rev. Stat. Ann. tit. 14, § 752 (West, WESTLAW through 2001 1st Reg. Session of 120th Leg.).

Contracts Under Seal

Personal actions on contracts or liabilities under seal, promissory notes signed in the presence of an attesting witness or on the bills, notes or other evidences of debt issued by a bank shall be commenced within 20 years after the cause of action accrues. Me. Rev. Stat. Ann. tit. 14, § 751 (West, WESTLAW through 2001 1st Reg. Session of 120th Leg.).

Judgments
Every judgment and decree of any court of record of the United States, or of any state, or justice of the peace in this State shall be presumed to be paid and satisfied at the end of 20 years after any duty or obligations accrued by virtue of such judgment or decree. Me. Rev. Stat. Ann. tit. 14, § 864 (West, WESTLAW through 2001 1st Reg. Session of 120th Leg.).

Maryland

Contracts – Three Year Limitation
A civil action at law shall be filed within three (3) years from the date it accrues unless another provision of the Code provides a different period of time within which an action shall be commenced. Md. Code Ann., Cts. & Jud. Pro. § 5-101 (West, WESTLAW through end of 2002 Reg. Session).

Action on Specialties – Twelve Year Limitation
An action on one of the following specialties shall be filed within 12 years after the cause of action accrues, or within 12 years from the date of the death of the last to die of the principal debtor or creditor, whichever is sooner:

(1) Promissory note or other instrument under seal;
(2) Bond except a public officer's bond;
(3) Judgment;
(4) Recognizance;
(5) Contract under seal; or
(6) Any other specialty.

Md. Code Ann., Cts. & Jud. Pro. § 5-102(5) (West, WESTLAW through end of 2002 Reg. Session).

Massachusetts

Contracts
Actions of contract, other than those to recover for personal injuries, founded upon contracts or liabilities, express or implied, except actions limited by section one or actions upon judgments or decrees of courts of record of the United States or of this or of any other state of the United States, shall, except as otherwise provided, be commenced only within six (6) years next after the cause of action accrues. Mass. Gen. Laws Ann. ch. 260, § 2 (West, WESTLAW through Ch. 353 of the 2002 2nd Annual Session).

Contracts Under Seal
The following actions shall be commenced only within twenty (20) years next after the cause of action accrues:

(1) Actions upon contracts under seal.
(2) Actions upon bills, notes or other evidences of indebtedness issued by a bank.
(3) Actions upon promissory notes signed in the presence of an attesting witness, if brought by the original payee or by his executor or administrator.
(4) Actions upon contracts not limited by the following section or by any other law.
(5) Actions under section thirty-two of chapter one hundred and twenty-three to recover for the support of inmates in state institutions.

Mass. Gen. Laws Ann. ch. 260, § 1 (West, WESTLAW through Ch. 353 of the 2002 2nd Annual Session).

Contracts for Sale
An action for breach of any contract for sale must be commenced within four (20) years after the cause of action has accrued. By the original agreement the parties may reduce the period of limitation to not less than one year but may not extend it. Mass. Gen. Laws Ann. ch. 106, § 2-725(1) (West, WESTLAW through Ch.353 of the 2002 2nd Annual Session).

Judgments
A judgment or decree of a court of record of the United States or of any state thereof shall be presumed to be paid and satisfied at the expiration of twenty (20) years after it was rendered. Mass. Gen. Laws Ann. ch. 260, § 20 (West, WESTLAW through Ch. 353 of the 2002 2nd Annual Session).

Michigan

Contracts 6 years.
The period of limitations is 6 years for all other actions to recover damages or sums due for breach of contract. Mich. Comp. Laws Ann. § 600.5807(8) (West, WESTLAW through P.A. 2002, No. 100 of the 2002 Reg. Session).

Judgments -
Of Record 10 years.
Except as provided in subsection (4) [actions under the support and parenting time enforcement act], the period of limitations is 10 years for an action founded upon a judgment or decree rendered in a court of record in this state, or in a court of record of the United States or of another state of the United States, from the time of the rendition of the judgment or decree. Mich. Comp. Laws Ann. § 600.5809(3) (West, WESTLAW through 2002, No. 100 of the 2002 Reg. Session).

Not of Record 6 years.
The period of limitations is 6 years for an action founded upon a judgment or decree rendered in a court not of record of this sate, or of another state, from the time of the rendition of the judgment or decree. ***[Editor's note: the statute states that a judgment entered in the small claims division of the district court is not a judgment of a court of record.]*** Mich. Comp. Laws Ann. § 600.5813(3) (West, WESTLAW through P.A. 2002, No. 100 of the 2002 Reg. Session).

Minnesota

Contracts
Except where the Uniform Commercial Code otherwise prescribes, the following actions shall be commenced within six (6) years:

(1) Upon contract or other obligation, express or implied, as to which no other limitation is expressly prescribed;
(2) Upon a liability created by statute, other than those arising upon a penalty or forfeiture or where a shorter period is provided by section 541.07;
(3) For trespass upon real estate;
(4) For taking, detaining, or injuring personal property, including actions for the specific recovery thereof;
(5) For criminal conversation, or for any other injury to the person or rights of another, not arising on contract, and not hereinafter enumerated;
(6) For relief on the ground of fraud, in which case the cause of action shall not be deemed to have accrued until the discovery by the aggrieved party of the facts constituting the fraud;
(7) To enforce a trust or compel a trustee to account, where the trustee has neglected to discharge the trust, or claims to have fully performed it, or has repudiated the trust relation;
(8) Against sureties upon the official bond of any public officer, whether of the state or of any county, town, school district, or a municipality therein; in which case the limitation shall not begin to run until the term of such officer for which the bond was given shall have expired;
(9) For damages caused by a dam, used for commercial purposes; or
(10) For assault, battery, false imprisonment, or other tort, resulting in personal injury, in the conduct that gives rise to the cause of action also constitutes domestic abuse as defined in section 518B.01.

Minn. Stat. § 541.05(1) (West, WESTLAW through End of 2001 First Special Session).

Contracts for Sale
An action for breach of any contract for sale must be commenced within four years after the cause of action has accrued. By the original agreement the parties may reduce the period of limitation to not less than one year but may not extend it. Minn. Stat. § 336.2-725(1) (West, WESTLAW through End of 2001 First Special Session).

Judgments
No action shall be maintained upon a judgment or decree of a court of the United States, or of any state or territory thereof, unless begun within ten (10) years after the entry of such judgment. Minn. Stat. § 541.04 (West, WESTLAW through End of 2001 First Special Session).

Mississippi

(1) The completion of the period of limitation prescribed to bar any action, shall defeat and extinguish the right as well as the remedy. However, the former legal obligation shall be a sufficient consideration to uphold a new promise based thereon.
Miss. Code Ann. § 15-1-3 (West, WESTLAW through End of 2004 Reg. and 1st Extra Session).

(2) In any case founded on a debt, when any part of the debt shall have been paid, or an acknowledgment of an existing liability, debt or claim, or any promise to pay the same shall have been made, the statute of limitations not having run, an action may be brought in such case within the period prescribed for the same, with the said period to begin after such payment, acknowledgment or promise. [**Ed. Note:** The effective date for subsection 2 is July 1, 2005.] Miss. Code Ann. § 15-1-3 (West, WESTLAW through End of 2004 3rd Extra Session).

[**Ed. Note**: Miss.Code Ann. § 15-1-51 and Miss. Const. Art. 4, § 104 provide that the statute of limitations in civil cases does not run against the state, its political subdivisions, or municipal corporations thereof. However, Miss. Code Ann. § 15-1-3 still applies with respect to private debts.]

See Parish v. Frazier, 195 F.3d 761, 764 (5th Cir. 1999). The court held that "because the debt was owed to a governmental entity, the statute of limitations did not run, and the debt remains due and payable under Miss.Code Ann. § 15-1-51. As such, the suit by [the collection agency] against Parish was not time barred. [The collection agency] did not violate the FDCPA on this basis."

Contracts

3 years **(oral)**
Except as otherwise provided in the Uniform Commercial Code, actions on an open account or account stated not acknowledged in writing, signed by the debtor, and on any unwritten contract, express or implied, shall be commenced within three (3) years next after the cause of such action accrued, and not after, except that an action based on an unwritten contract of employment shall be commenced within one (1) year next after the cause of such action accrued, and not after. Miss. Code Ann. § 15-1-29 (West, WESTLAW through End of 2001 2nd Ex. Session).

3 years **(written)**
Miss. Code Ann. § 15-1-49 (West, WESTLAW through End of 2001 2nd Ex Session).

6 years **(sale of goods)**
Miss. Code Ann. § 75-2-725(1) (West, WESTLAW through End of 2000 3rd Extra Session).

Judgments - Domestic
Of Record 7 years
Miss. Code Ann. § 15-1-43 (West, WESTLAW through End of 2001 2nd Extra Session).

Not of Record 3 years
Miss. Code Ann. § 15-1-49 (West, WESTLAW through End of 2001 2nd Extra Session).

__Missouri__

Contracts
10 years **(written, whether sealed or unsealed)** Mo. Ann. Stat. § 516.110(1) (West, WESTLAW through End of 2001 1st Reg. Sess. and 1st Extra Sess. of the 91st Gen. Assembly).

5 years **(oral)** Mo. Ann. Stat. § 516.120(1) (West, WESTLAW through End of 2001 1st Reg. Sess. and 1st Extra Sess. of the 91st Gen. Assembly).

Judgments – Domestic
Of Record 10 years Mo. Ann. Stat. § 516.350(1) (West, WESTLAW through End of 2001 1st Reg. Sess. and 1st Extra Sess. of the 91st Gen. Assembly).

Not of Record 5 years Mo. Ann. Stat. § 516.120(1) (West, WESTLAW through End of 2001 1st Reg. Sess. and 1st Extra Sess. of the 91st Gen. Assembly).

__Montana__

Contracts
5 years **(oral)**
Mont. Code Ann. § 27-2-202(2) (West, WESTLAW through 2000 Special Session).
8 years **(written)**
Mont. Code Ann. § 27-2-202(1) (West, WESTLAW through 2000 Special Session).

Judgments -
Domestic 10 years
Mont. Code Ann. §§ 27-2-201(1), (2) (West, WESTLAW through 2000 Special Session, *as amended by* Ch. 515, H.B. No. 496, Regular Session of the 57th Legislature).

__Nebraska__

Contracts
An action upon a contract, **not in writing**, expressed or implied, or an action upon liability created by statute, other than a forfeiture or a penalty, can only be brought within four (4) years. Neb. Rev. Stat. Ann. § 25-206 (WESTLAW through End of 2001 First Special Session).

(1) Except as provided in subsection (2) of this section, an action upon a specialty, or any agreement, contract, or promise **in writing**, or foreign judgment, can only be brought within five (5) years. No action at law or equity may be brought or maintained attacking the validity or enforceability of or to rescind or declare void and uncollectible any written contract entered into pursuant to, in compliance with, or in reliance on, a statute of the State of Nebraska which has been or hereafter is held to be unconstitutional by the Supreme Court of Nebraska where such holding is the basis for such action, unless such action be brought or maintained within one year from the effective date of such decision. The provisions hereof shall not operate to extend the time in which to bring any action or to revive any action now barred by reason of the operation of any previously existing limitation provision.

(2) An action to recover collateral (a) the possession and ownership of which a debtor has in any manner transferred to another person and (b) which was used as security for payment pursuant to an agreement, contract, or promise in writing which covers farm products as described in Nebraska Statute section 9-102, Uniform Commercial Code, or farm products which become inventory of a person engaged in farming, shall

be brought within eighteen (18) months from the date possession and ownership of such collateral was transferred.
Neb. Rev. Stat. Ann. § 25-205 (WESTLAW through End of 2001 First Special Session).

In any cause founded on contract, when any part of the principal or interest shall have been voluntarily paid, or an acknowledgment of an existing liability, debt or claim, or any promise to pay the same shall have been made in writing, an action may be brought in such case within the period prescribed for the same, after such payment, acknowledgment or promise; PROVIDED, that the provisions of this section shall not be applicable to real estate mortgages which have become barred under the provisions of Nebraska Statute section 25-202 as against subsequent encumbrances and purchasers for value. Neb. Rev. Stat. Ann. § 25-216 (WESTLAW through End of 2001 First Special Session).

Judgments -
If execution is not sued out within five (5) years after the date of entry of any judgment that now is or may hereafter be rendered in any court of record in this state, or if five (5) years have intervened between the date of the last execution issued on such judgment and the time of suing out another writ of execution thereon, such judgment, and all taxable costs in the action in which such judgment was obtained, shall become dormant and shall cease to operate as a lien on the estate of the judgment debtor. Neb. Rev. Stat. Ann. § 25-1515 (WESTLAW through End of 2001 First Special Session).

Nevada

Written Contracts 6 years
Nev. Rev. Stat. 11.190(1)(b) (WESTLAW through 2001 Reg. Session and 17th and 18th Special Sessions of the 71st Leg.).

Oral Contracts 4 years
Nev. Rev. Stat. 11.190(2)(c) (WESTLAW through 2001 Reg. Session and 17th and 18th Special Sessions of the 71st Leg.).

Judgments 6 years
Nev. Rev. Stat. 11.190(1)(a) (WESTLAW through 2001 Reg. Session and 17th and 18th Special Sessions of the 71st Leg.).

New Hampshire

Contracts 3 years
Except as otherwise provided by law, all personal actions, except actions for slander or libel, may be brought only within 3 years of the act or omission complained of, except that when the injury and its causal relationship to the act or omission were not discovered and could not reasonably have been discovered at the time of the act or omission, the action shall be commenced within 3 years of the time the plaintiff discovers, or in the exercise of reasonable diligence should have discovered, the injury and its causal relationship to the act or omission complained of. N.H. Rev. Stat. Ann. § 508:4 (WESTLAW through End of 2002 Reg. Session).

20 years **(under seal)**
Actions of debt upon... contracts under seal may be brought within 20 years after the cause of action accrued, and not afterward. N.H. Rev. Stat. Ann. § 508:5 (WESTLAW through End of 2002 Reg. Session).

Judgments 20 years.
Actions of debt upon judgments... may be brought within 20 years after the cause of action accrued, and not afterward. N.H. Rev. Stat. Ann. § 508:5 (WESTLAW through End of 2002 Reg. Session).

<u>New Jersey</u>

Contracts

Every action at law… for recovery upon a contractual claim or liability, express or implied, not under seal,… shall be commenced within 6 years next after the cause of any such action shall have accrued. This section shall not apply to any action for breach of any contract for sale governed by section 12A:2-725 of the New Jersey Statutes. N.J. Stat. Ann. § 2A:14-1 (West, WESTLAW through L.2001, c. 457).

Every action at law for rent or arrears of rent, founded upon a lease under seal, every action at law upon a single or penal bill under seal for the payment of money only, upon an obligation under seal conditioned for the payment of money only, upon a recognizance or upon an award under the hands and seals of arbitrators for the payment of money only, shall be commenced within 16 years next after the cause of action shall have accrued. If, however, any payment is made on any such lease, specialty, recognizance, or award within or after such period of 16 years, an action thereon may be commenced within 16 years next after such payment, and not thereafter.

This section shall not apply to any action for breach of any contract for sale governed by section 12A:2-725. This section shall also not apply to any action founded upon an instrument under seal brought by a merchant or bank, finance company, or other financial institution. Any such action shall be commenced within 6 years next after the cause of any such action shall have accrued. N.J. Stat. Ann. § 2A:14-4 (West, WESTLAW through L.2000, c. 457).

Judgments

An action to enforce an obligation, duty, or right arising under the Uniform Commercial Code, Bank Deposits and Collections chapter must be commenced within three (3) years after the cause of action accrues. N.J. Stat. Ann. § 12A:4-111 (West, WESTLAW through L.2001, c. 457).

A judgment in any court of record in this state may be revived by proper proceedings or an action at law may be commenced thereon within 20 years next after the date thereof, but not thereafter. An action may be commenced on a judgment obtained in any other state or country within 20 years next after the date thereof or within the period in which a like action might be brought thereon in that state or country, whichever period is shorter, but not thereafter. N.J. Stat. Ann. § 2A:14-5 (West, WESTLAW through L.2001, c.457).

<u>New Mexico</u>

Oral Contracts

Actions founded upon accounts and unwritten contracts; those brought for injuries to property or for the conversion of personal property or for relief upon the ground of fraud, and all other actions not herein otherwise provided for and specified within four (4) years. N.M. Stat. Ann. § 37-1-4 (WESTLAW through 2002 2nd Reg. Session of the 45th Leg.).

Written Contracts and Judgment Not of Record

Actions founded upon any bond, promissory note, bill of exchange or other contract in writing, or upon any judgment of any court not of record, within six (6) years. N.M. Stat. Ann. § 37-1-3(A) (WESTLAW through 2002 2nd Reg. Session of the 45th Leg.).

Judgments of Record

Actions founded upon any judgment of any court of the state may be brought within fourteen (14) years from the date of the judgment, and not afterward. Actions founded upon any judgment of any court of record of any other state or territory of the United States, or of the federal courts, may be brought within the applicable period of limitation within that jurisdiction, not to exceed fourteen (14) years from the date of the judgment, and not afterward. N.M. Stat. Ann. § 37-1-2 (WESTLAW through 2002 2nd Reg. Session of the 45th Leg.).

<u>**New York**</u>

Contracts 6 years (see below)

Actions to be commenced within six (6) years: where not otherwise provided for; on contract; on sealed instrument; on bond or note, and mortgage upon real property; by state based on misappropriation of public property; based on mistake; by corporation against director, officer or stockholder; based on fraud:
The following actions must be commenced within six years:
1. an action for which no limitation is specifically prescribed by law;
2. an action upon a contractual obligation or liability, express or implied, except as provided in section two hundred thirteen-a of this article or article 2 of the uniform commercial code or article 36-B of the general business law;
3. an action upon a sealed instrument;
4. an action upon a bond or note, the payment of which is secured by a mortgage upon real property, or upon a bond or note and mortgage so secured, or upon a mortgage of real property, or any interest therein;
5. an action by the state based upon the spoliation or other misappropriation of public property; the time within which the action must be commenced shall be computed from discovery by the state of the facts relied upon;
6. an action based upon mistake;
7. an action by or on behalf of a corporation against a present or former director, officer or stockholder for an accounting, or to procure a judgment on the ground of fraud, or to enforce a liability, penalty or forfeiture, or to recover damages for waste or for an injury to property or for an accounting in conjunction therewith.
8. an action based upon fraud; the time within which the action must be commenced shall be computed from the time the plaintiff or the person under whom he claims discovered the fraud, or could with reasonable diligence have discovered it.
N.Y. C.P.L.R. § 213 (West, WESTLAW through L. 2002, chs. 1, 5 to 591 and 598 to 601).

Breach of contract for sale 4 years

An action for breach of any contract for sale must be commenced within four (4) years after the cause of action has accrued. By the original agreement the parties may reduce the period of limitation to not less than one year but may not extend it. N.Y. U.C.C. § 2-725(1) (West, WESTLAW through L. 2002, chs. 1, 5 to 591 and 598 to 601).

Judgments

Domestic 20 years

Actions to be commenced within twenty (20) years
On a money judgment. A money judgment is presumed to be paid and satisfied after the expiration of twenty years from the time when the party recovering it was first entitled to enforce it. This presumption is conclusive, except as against a person who within the twenty years acknowledges an indebtedness, or makes a payment, of all or part of the amount recovered by the judgment, or his heir or personal representative, or a person whom he otherwise represents. Such an acknowledgment must be in writing and signed by the person to be charged. Property acquired by an enforcement order or by levy upon an execution is a payment, unless the person to be charged shows that it did not include property claimed by him. If such an acknowledgment or payment is made, the judgment is conclusively presumed to be paid and satisfied as against any person after the expiration of twenty years after the last acknowledgment or payment made by him. The presumption created by this subdivision may be availed of under an allegation that the action was not commenced within the time limited. N.Y. C.P.L.R § 211(b) (West, WESTLAW through L. 2002, chs. 1, 5 to 591 and 598 to 601).

<u>**North Carolina**</u>

Contracts

Three Year Limitation
Within three (3) years an action –

(1) Upon a contract, obligation or liability arising out of a contract, express or implied, except those mentioned in the preceding sections or in G.S. 1-53(1).
(1a) Upon the official bond of a public officer.
(2) Upon a liability created by statute, either state or federal, unless some other time is mentioned in the statute creating it.
(3) For trespass upon real property. When the trespass is a continuing one, the action shall be commenced within three years from the original trespass, and not thereafter.
(4) For taking, detaining, converting or injuring any goods or chattels, including action for their specific recovery.
(5) For criminal conversation, or for any other injury to the person or rights of another, not arising on contract and not hereafter enumerated.
(6) Against the sureties of any executor, administrator, collector or guardian on the official bond of their principal; within three years after the breach thereof complained of.
(7) Against bail; within three years after judgment against the principal; but bail may discharge himself by a surrender of the principal, at any time before final judgment against the bail.
(8) For fees due to a clerk, sheriff or other officer, by the judgment of a court; within three years from the rendition of the judgment, or the issuing of the last execution thereon.
(9) For relief on the ground of fraud or mistake; the cause of action shall not be deemed to have accrued until the discovery by the aggrieved party of the facts constituting the fraud or mistake.
(10) Repealed by Session Laws 1977, c. 886, s. 1.
(11) For the recovery of any amount under and by virtue of the provisions of the Fair Labor Standards Act of 1938 and amendments thereto, said act being an act of Congress.
(12) Upon a claim for loss covered by an insurance policy which is subject to the three-year limitation contained in lines 158 through 161 of the Standard Fire Insurance Policy for North Carolina, G.S. 58-44-15(c).
(13) Against a public officer, for a trespass, under color of his office.
(14) An action under Chapter 75B of the General Statutes, the action in regard to a continuing violation accrues at the time of the latest violation.
(15) For the recovery of taxes paid as provided in G.S. 105-267 and G.S. 105-381.
(16) Unless otherwise provided by statute, for personal injury or physical damage to claimant's property, the cause of action, except in causes of actions referred to in G.S. 1-15(c), shall not accrue until bodily harm to the claimant or physical damage to his property becomes apparent or ought reasonably to have become apparent to the claimant, whichever event first occurs. Provided that no cause of action shall accrue more than 10 years from the last act or omission of the defendant giving rise to the cause of action.
(17) Against a public utility, electric or telephone membership corporation, or a municipality for damages or for compensation for right-of-way or use of any lands for a utility service line or lines to serve one or more customers or members unless an inverse condemnation action or proceeding is commenced within three years after the utility service line has been constructed or by October 1, 1984, whichever is later.
(18) Against any registered land surveyor as defined in G.S. 89C-3(9) or any person acting under his supervision and control for physical damage or economic or monetary loss due to negligence or a deficiency in the performance of surveying or platting as defined in G.S. 1-47(6).
(19) For assault, battery, or false imprisonment.

N.C. Gen. Stat. § 1-52 (West, WESTLAW through S.L. 20002-113 of the 2002 Reg. and Ex. Sessions).

Judgments
Ten Year Limitation
Within ten (10) years an action –

(1) Upon a judgment or decree of any court of the United States, or of any state or territory thereof, from the date of its rendition. No such action may be brought more than once, or have the effect to continue the lien of the original judgment.

(1a) Upon a judgment rendered by a justice of the peace, from its date.

(2) Upon a sealed instrument or an instrument of conveyance of an interest in real property, against the principal thereto. Provided, however, that if action on an instrument is filed, the defendant or defendants in such action may file a counterclaim arising out of the same transaction or transactions as are the subject of plaintiff's claim, although a shorter statute of limitations would otherwise apply to defendant's counterclaim. Such counterclaim may be filed against such parties as provided in G.S. 1A-1, Rules of Civil Procedure.

(3) For the foreclosure of a mortgage, or deed in trust for creditors with a power of sale, or real property, where the mortgagor or grantor has been in possession of the property, within ten years after the forfeiture of the mortgage, or after the power of sale became absolute, or within ten (10) years after the last payment on the same.

(4) For the redemption of a mortgage, where the mortgagee has been in possession, or for a residuary interest under a deed in trust for creditors, where the trustee or those holding under him has been in possession, within ten years after the right of action accrued.

(5) Repealed by Laws 1959, c. 879, s. 2.

(6)a. Against any registered land surveyor as defined in G.S. 89C-3(9) or any person acting under his supervision and control for physical damage or for economic or monetary loss de to negligence or a deficiency in the performance of surveying or platting, within 10 years after the last act or omission giving rise to the cause of action.

(6)b. For purposes of this subdivision, "surveying and platting" means boundary surveys, topographical surveys, surveys of property lines, and any other measurement or surveying of real property and the consequent graphic representation thereof.

(6)c. The limitation prescribed by this subdivision shall apply to the exclusion of G.S. 1-15(c) and G.S. 1-52(16).

N.C. Gen. Stat. § 1-47(1) (West, WESTLAW through S.L. 2002-113 of the 2002 Reg. and Ex. Sessions).

North Dakota

Contracts

An action upon a contract, obligation, or liability, express or implied, subject to the provisions of sections 28-01-15 and sections 41-02-104, must be commenced within six (6) years after the claim for relief has accrued. N.D. Cent. Code § 28-01-16(1) (Lexis, WESTLAW through End of 2001 Regular Session).

An action for breach of any contract for sale must be commenced within four (4) years after the claim for relief has accrued. By the original agreement the parties may reduce the period of limitation to not less than one year but may not extend it. N.D. Cent. Code § 41-02-104 (Lexis, WESTLAW through End of 2001 Regular Session)

Judgments

An action upon a judgment or decree of any court of the United States or of any state or territory within the United States must be commenced within ten (10) years after the claim for relief has accrued. N.D. Cent. Code § 28-01-15(1) (Lexis, WESTLAW through End of 2001 Regular Session).

Ohio

Contracts

An action upon a contract **not in writing**, express or implied, or upon a liability created by statute other than a forfeiture or penalty, shall be brought within 6 years after the cause thereof accrued. Ohio Rev. Code Ann. § 2305.07 (West, WESTLAW through 124th GA, Files 1 to 83, apv. 1/4/02).

An action upon a specialty or an agreement, contract or promise **in writing** shall be brought within 15 years after the cause thereof accrued. Ohio Rev. Code Ann. § 2305.06 (West, WESTLAW through 124th GA, Files 1 to 83, apv. 1/4/02).

An action for breach of any **contract for sale** must be commenced within 4 years after the cause of action has accrued. By the original agreement the parties may reduce the period of limitation to not less than one year but may not extend it. Ohio Rev. Code Ann. § 1302.98(A) (West, WESTLAW through 124th GA, Files 1 to 83, apv. 1/4/02).

If payment has been made upon any demand founded on a contract, or a written acknowledgement thereof, or a promise to pay it has been made and signed by the party to be charged, an action may be brought thereon within the time limited by sections 2305.06 and 2305.07 of the Revised Code, after such payment, acknowledgement, or promise. Ohio Rev. Code Ann. § 2305.08 (West, WESTLAW through 124th GA, Files 1 to 83, apv. 1/4/02).

Judgments
Domestic Revived within 21 years Ohio Rev. Code Ann. § 2325.18 (West, WESTLAW through 124th GA, Files 1 to 83, apv. 1/4/02).

Oklahoma

Contracts

3 years (**oral**) Okla. Stat. tit. 12, § 95 (West, WESTLAW through 2001 1st Ex. Session).
5 years (**written**) Okla. Stat. tit. 12, § 95 (West, WESTLAW through 2001 1st Ex. Session).

Judgments
Domestic Kept alive by renewal, execution or garnishment summons every five (5) years (does not apply to child support) Okla. Stat. Ann. tit. 12, §§ 735 B, C (West, WESTLAW through Chapter 9 of 2000 1st Extra Session).

Debts:
A statute of limitations does not discharge a debt or extinguish the cause of action on the debt, but only acts as a bar to an otherwise valid cause of action. *Apache Lanes, Inc. v. National Educators Life Ins. Co. of Okla.*, 529 P.2d 984 (1974).

Oregon

Contracts An action upon a contract or liability, express or implied, excepting those mentioned in Oregon Revised Statutes sections 12.070, 12.110 and 12.135 and except as otherwise provided in Oregon Revised Statutes section 72.7250; shall be commenced within six (6) years. Or. Rev. Stat. § 12.080 (WESTLAW through End of 2001 Reg. Sess. and 2001 Cumulative Supplement).

An action for breach of any contract for sale must be commenced within four (4) years after the cause of action has accrued. By the original agreement the parties may reduce the period of limitation to not less than one (1) year but may not extend it. Or. Rev. Stat. § 72.7250(1) (WESTLAW through End of 2001 Reg. Sess. and 2001 Cumulative Supplement).

Judgments
(1) An action upon a judgment or decree of any court of the United States, or of any state or territory within the United States; or

(2) An action upon a sealed instrument entered into before August 13, 1965,
shall be commenced within 10 years.
Or. Rev. Stat. § 12.070 (WESTLAW through End of 2001 Reg. Sess. and 2001 Cumulative Supplement).

Pennsylvania

Contracts

Four year limitation

(a) General rule. Except as provided for in subsection (b) [relating to identity theft], the following actions and proceedings must be commenced within four (4) years:

(1) An action upon a contract, under seal or otherwise, for the sale, construction or furnishing of tangible personal property or fixtures.
(2) Any action subject to 13 Pa. C.S. § 2775 (relating to statute of limitations in contracts for sale).
(3) An action upon an express contract not founded upon an instrument in writing.
(4) An action upon a contract implied in law, except an action subject to another limitation specified in this subchapter.
(5) An action upon a judgment or decree of any court of the United States or of any state.
(6) An action upon any official bond of a public official, officer or employee.
(7) An action upon a negotiable or nonnegotiable bond, note or other similar instrument in writing. Where such an instrument is payable upon demand, the time within which an action on it must be commenced shall be computed from the later of either demand or any payment of principal of or interest on the instrument.
(8) An action upon a contact, obligation or liability founded upon a writing not specified in paragraph (7), under seal or otherwise, except an action subject to another limitation specified in this subchapter.

42 Pa. Cons. Stat. Ann. § 5525(a) (West, WESTLAW through Act 2002-39), *amended by* 2002 Pa. Legis. Serv. Act 2002-62 (H.B. 1546) (West, WESTLAW through 185th Reg. Sess. of the Gen. Assembly).

Any civil action or proceeding which is neither subject to another limitation specified in this subchapter nor excluded from the application of a period of limitation by section 5531 (relating to no limitation) must be commenced within six (6) years. 42 Pa. Cons. Stat. Ann. § 5527 (West, WESTLAW through Act 2002-39).

20 years **(written, under seal)**

(a) Execution against personal property - An execution against personal property must be issued within 20 years after the entry of the judgment upon which the execution is to be issued.

(b) Instruments under seal—

(1) Notwithstanding section 5525(7) (relating to four year limitation), an action upon an instrument in writing under seal must be commenced within 20 years.

(2) This subsection shall expire on June 27, 2018.

42 Pa. Cons. Stat. Ann. § 5529 (West, WESTLAW through Act 2002-39).

Judgments

Four year limitation

The following actions must be commenced within four years: An action upon a judgment or decree of any court of the United States or of any state. 42 Pa. Cons. Stat. Ann. § 5525(a) (West, WESTLAW through Act 2002-39), *amended by* 2002 Pa. Legis. Serv. Act 2002-62 (H.B. 1546) (West, WESTLAW through 185th Reg. Sess. of the Gen. Assembly).

Puerto Rico

Editor's Note: Please consult with a Spanish-speaking attorney. Pay particular attention to 10 L.P.R.A. § 1908 and 31 L.P.R.A. § 5294.

§ 518 Statute of limitations

(a) Except as provided in subsection (e) of this section, an action to enforce the obligation of a party to pay a note payable at a definite time must be commenced within three (3) years after the due date or dates stated in the note or, if a due date is accelerated, within three (3) years after the accelerated due date.

(b) Except as provided in subsection (d) or (e) of this section, if demand for payment is made to the maker of a note payable on demand, an action to enforce the obligation of a party to pay the note must be commenced within three (3) years after the demand. If no demand for payment is made to the maker, an action to enforce the note is barred if neither principal nor interest on the note has been paid for a continuous period of five (5) years.

(c) Except as provided in subsection (d) of this section, an action to enforce the obligation of a party to an unaccepted draft to pay the draft must be commenced within five (5) years after dishonor of the draft or ten (10) years after the date of the draft, whichever period expires first.

(d) An action to enforce the obligation of the acceptor of a certified check or the issuer of a teller's check, cashier's check, or traveler's check must be commenced within three (3) years after demand for payment is made to the acceptor or issuer, as the case may be.

(e) An action to enforce the obligation of a party to a certificate of deposit to pay the instrument must be commenced within three (3) years after demand for payment is made to the maker, but if the instrument states a due date and the maker is not required to pay before that date, the three (3) year period begins when a demand for payment is in effect and the due date has passed.

(f) An action to enforce the obligation of a party to pay an accepted draft, other than a certified check, must be commenced: (i) within three (3) years after the due date or dates stated in the draft or acceptance if the obligation of the acceptor is payable at a definite time, or (ii) within three (3) years after the date of the acceptance if the obligation of the acceptor is payable on demand.

(g) Unless governed by other law regarding claims for indemnity or contribution, an action: (i) for conversion of an instrument, for money had and received, or like action based on conversion, (ii) for breach of warranty, or (iii) to enforce an obligation, duty, or right arising under §§ 501-755 of this title and not governed by this section must be commenced within three (3) years after the cause of action accrues.

(h) Notwithstanding anything to the contrary herein, an action to enforce the obligation of a party to pay a note secured by a real estate mortgage should be commenced within the period of time provided by § 5294 of Title 31 for the exercise of a mortgage action.

(i) The statute of limitations shall be interrupted by suit or any judicial proceeding brought against the debtor, by the acknowledgment of the obligations, or by the renewal of the instrument on which the right of the creditor is based. The statute of limitations shall be considered uninterrupted by a judicial proceeding if the plaintiff should withdraw it, or the case should go by default or the complaint be dismissed. The period of the statute of limitations shall begin to be counted again, in case of the acknowledgment of the obligations, from the day P.R. Laws Ann. tit. 19, § 518 (Lexis, WESTLAW through Dec. 1999).

Rhode Island

Contracts/Judgments

The following actions shall be commenced and sued within twenty (20) years next after the cause of action shall accrue and not after: actions on contracts or liabilities under seal; and actions on judgments or decrees of any court of record of the United States, or of any state.
R.I. Gen. Laws § 9-1-17 (Lexis, WESTLAW through 2001 Reg. Session)

South Carolina

Contracts

3 years. S.C. Code Ann. § 15-3-530(1) (WESTLAW through End of 2001 Reg. Session).
Editor's Note: S.C. Code Ann. § 15-3-530(1) provides a statute of limitations for three years for "an action upon a contract, obligation, or liability, expressed or implied, excepting those provided for in Section 15-3-520."

Except as otherwise specially provided, all civil actions shall be commenced within ten (10) years next after the cause of action shall accrue, and not after.
R.I. Gen. Laws § 9-1-13(a) (WESTLAW through January 2004 Sess.).

Judgments - Domestic

10 years. S.C. Code Ann. § 15-3-600 (WESTLAW through End of 2001 Reg. Session).

South Dakota

Contracts

An action upon a contract, obligation, or liability, express or implied 6 years (except those mentioned in sections 15-2-6 to 15-2-8, inclusive, and subdivisions 15-2-15(3) and (4)). S.D. Codified Laws § 15-2-13(1) (WESTLAW through 76th Legislative Assembly (2001)).

An action upon a sealed instrument, except a real estate mortgage 20 years. S.D. Codified Laws § 15-2-6(2) (WESTLAW through 76th Legislative Assembly (2001)).

Judgments

An action upon a judgment or decree of any court of this state 20 years. S.D. Codified Laws § 15-2-6(1) (WESTLAW through 76th Legislative Assembly (2001)).

An action upon a judgment or decree of any court of the United States, or any state or territory other than this state within the United States 10 years. S.D. Codified Laws § 15-2-8(1) (WESTLAW through 76th Legislative Assembly (2001)).

An action for relief not otherwise provided for 10 years. S.D. Codified Laws § 15-2-8(4) (WESTLAW through 76th Legislative Assembly (2001)).

Tennessee

Contracts 6 years.

(a) The following actions shall be commenced within six (6) years after the cause of action accrued:

(1) Actions for the use and occupation of land and for rent;

(2) Actions against the sureties of guardians, executors and administrators, sheriffs, clerks, and other public officers, for nonfeasance, misfeasance, and malfeasance in office; and

(3) Actions on contracts not otherwise expressly provided for.

(b) The cause of action on title insurance policies, guaranteeing title to real estate, shall accrue on the date the loss or damage insured or guaranteed against is sustained.

(c) The cause of action on demand notes shall be commenced within ten (10) years after the cause of action accrued.

Tenn. Code Ann. § 28-3-109 (West, WESTLAW through 2002 Second Reg. Session).

Open accounts

Merchants; open accounts

The limitations provided in this chapter do not apply to such actions as concern the trade of merchandise between merchant and merchant, their agents and factors, while the accounts between them are current. Tenn. Code Ann. § 28-3-111 (West, WESTLAW through 2002 Second Reg. Session).

Judgments – of record

Domestic or foreign 10 years.

The following actions shall be commenced within ten (10) years after the cause of action accrued:

(1) Actions against guardians, executors, administrators, sheriffs, clerks, and other public officers on their bonds;

(2) Actions on judgments and decrees of courts of record of this or any other state or government; and

(3) All other cases not expressly provided for.

Tenn. Code Ann. § 28-3-110 (West, WESTLAW through 2002 Second Reg. Session).

Texas

Contracts

4 years (contract for sale)

An action for breach of any contract for sale must be commenced within four (4) years after the cause of action has accrued. By the original agreement the parties may reduce the period of limitation to not less than one year but may not extend it. Tex. Bus. & Com. Code Ann. § 2.725(a) (West, WESTLAW through End of 2001 Regular Session)

4 years (debt)
A person must bring suit on the following actions not later than four (4) years after the day the cause of action accrues… debt.
Tex. Civ. Prac. & Rem. Code Ann. § 16.004(3) (West, WESTLAW through End of 2001 Regular Session)

Judgments - Domestic
Of Record 10 years. If a writ of execution is not issued within 10 years after the rendition of a judgment of a court of record or a justice court, the judgment is dormant and execution may not be issued on the judgment unless it is revived. Tex. Prac. & Rem. Code Ann. § 34.001(a) (West, WESTLAW through End of 2001 Reg. Session).

A dormant judgment may be revived by scire facias [***ed. note:*** a legal proceeding instituted by a judicial writ founded upon some matter of record and requiring the party proceeded against to show cause why the record should not be enforced (as by revival of the judgment), annulled, or vacated] or by an action of debt brought not later than the second anniversary of the date that the judgment becomes dormant. Tex. Prac. & Rem. Code Ann. § 31.006 (West, WESTLAW through End of 2001 Reg. Session).

Utah

Contracts
An action may be brought within four (4) years upon a contract, obligation, or liability **not founded upon an instrument in writing**; also on an open account for goods, wares, and merchandise, and for any article charged on a store account; also on an open account for work, labor or services rendered, or materials furnished; provided, that action in all of the foregoing cases may be commenced at any time within four (4) years after the last charge is made or the last payment is received. Utah Code Ann. § 78-12-25(1) (Lexis, WESTLAW through 2001 Supplement (2001 First Special Session)).

An action may be brought within six (6) years upon any contract, obligation, or liability founded upon an instrument **in writing**, except those mentioned in Section 78-12-22. Utah Code Ann. § 78-12-23(2) (Lexis, WESTLAW through 2001 Supplement (2001 First Special Session)).

Judgments
An action may be brought within eight (8) years upon a judgment or decree of any court of the United State, or of any state or territory within the United States. Utah Code Ann. § 78-12-22 (Lexis, WESTLAW through 2001 Supplement (2001 First Special Session)).

Vermont

Contracts
A civil action, except one brought upon the judgment or decree of a court of record of the United States or of this or some other state, and except as otherwise provided, shall be commenced within six (6) years after the cause of action accrues and not thereafter. Vt. Stat. Ann. tit. 12, § 511 (WESTLAW through end of 1999 Adjourned Session (2001 Regular Session)).

An action brought on a promissory note signed in the presence of an attesting witness shall be commenced within fourteen years after the cause of action accrues, and not after. Vt. Stat. Ann. tit. 12, § 508 (WESTLAW through end of 1999 Adjourned Session (2001 Regular Session)).

Judgments -
Actions on judgments and actions for the renewal or revival of judgments shall be brought within eight (8) years after the rendition of the judgment, and not after. Vt. Stat. Ann. tit. 12, § 506 (WESTLAW through end of 1999 Adjourned Session (2001 Regular Session)).

Virginia

Contracts
Actions founded upon a contract, other than actions on a judgment or decree, shall be brought within the following number of years next after the cause of action shall have accrued:

(1) In actions or upon a recognizance, except recognizance of bail in a civil suit, within ten (10) years; and in actions or motions upon a recognizance of bail in a civil suit, within three (3) years, omitting from the computation of such three years such time as the right to sue out such execution shall have been suspended by injunction, supersedes or other process;

(2) In actions on any contract which is not otherwise specified and which is in writing and signed by the party to be charged thereby, or by his agent, within five (5) years whether such writing be under seal or not;

(3) In actions by a partner against another for settlement of the partnership account or in actions upon accounts concerning the trade of merchandise between merchant and merchant, their factors, or servants, within five (5) years from the cessation of the dealings in which they are interested together;

(4) In actions upon any unwritten contract, express or implied, within three (3) years.

Va. Code Ann. § 8.01-246(4) (West, WESTLAW through End of 2002 Reg. Session).

Judgments
No execution shall be issued and no action brought on a judgment, including a judgment in favor of the Commonwealth, after twenty (20) years from the date of such judgment, unless the period is extended as provided in this section. Va. Code Ann. § 8.01-251(A) (West, WESTLAW through End of 2002 Reg. Session).

District Court Judgments
For judgments entered in a general district court on or after January 1, 1985, no execution shall be issued or action brought on such judgment, including a judgment in favor of the Commonwealth, after ten (10) years from the date of such judgment except as provided in § 16.1-69.55(B)(4). Va. Code Ann. § 16.1-94.1 (West, WESTLAW through End of 2002 Reg. Session).

Virgin Islands

Contracts 4 years.

(1) An action for breach of any contract for sale must be commenced within four years after the cause of action has accrued. By the original agreement the parties may reduce the period of limitation to not less than one year but may not extend it.
(2) A cause of action accrues when the breach occurs, regardless of the aggrieved party's lack of knowledge of the breach. A breach of warranty occurs when tender of delivery is made, except that where a warranty explicitly extends to future performance of the goods and discovery of the breach must await the time of such performance the cause of action accrues when the breach is or should have been discovered.
(3) Where an action commenced within the time limited by subsection (1) is so terminated as to leave available a remedy by another action for the same breach such other action may be commenced after the

expiration of the time limited and within six months after the termination of the first action unless the termination resulted from voluntary discontinuance or from dismissal for failure or neglect to prosecute.
(4) This section does not alter the law on tolling of the statute of limitations nor does it apply to causes of action which have accrued before this title becomes effective.
11(A) V.I. Code Ann. § 2-725 (WESTLAW through Act 6503 of the 2002 Session).

Express or Implied Contracts 6 years.

Civil actions shall only be commenced within the periods prescribed below after the cause of action shall have accrued, except when, in special cases, a different limitation is prescribed by statute:
Six years --
(A) An action upon a contract or liability, express or implied, excepting those mentioned in paragraph (1)(C) of this section.
5 V.I. Code Ann. § 31(3)(A) (WESTLAW through Acts 6644 through 6725 of the 2004 Reg. Sess.).

Sealed instrument 20 years.

Civil actions shall only be commenced within the periods prescribed below after the cause of action shall have accrued, except when, in special cases, a different limitation is prescribed by statute:
(1) Twenty years--
(C) An action upon a sealed instrument.
5 V.I. Code Ann. § 31(1)B) (WESTLAW through Act 6503 of the 2002 Session).

Negotiable Instruments
(a) Except as provided in subsection (e), an action to enforce the obligation of a party to pay a note payable at a definite time must be commenced within six years after the due date or dates stated in the note or, if a due date is accelerated, within six years after the accelerated due date.
(b) Except as provided in subsection (d) or (e), if demand for payment is made to the maker of a note payable on demand, an action to enforce the obligation of a party to pay the note must be commenced within six years after the demand. If no demand for payment is made to the maker, an action to enforce the note is barred if neither principal nor interest on the note has been paid for a continuous period of 10 years.
(c) Except as provided in subsection (d), an action to enforce the obligation of a party to an unaccepted draft to pay the draft must be commenced within three years after dishonor of the draft or 10 years after the date of the draft, whichever period expires first.
(d) An action to enforce the obligation of the acceptor of a certified check or the issuer of a teller's check, cashier's check, or traveler's check must be commenced within three years after demand for payment is made to the acceptor or issuer, as the case may be.
(e) An action to enforce the obligation of a party to a certificate of deposit to pay the instrument must be commenced within six years after demand for payment is made to the maker, but if the instrument states a due date and the maker is not required to pay before that date, the six-year period begins when a demand for payment is in effect and the due date has passed.
(f) An action to enforce the obligation of a party to pay an accepted draft, other than a certified check, must be commenced (i) within six years after the due date or dates stated in the draft or acceptance if the obligation of the acceptor is payable at a definite time, or (ii) within six years after the date of the acceptance if the obligation of the acceptor is payable on demand.
(g) Unless governed by other law regarding claims for indemnity or contribution, an action (i) for conversion of an instrument, for money had and received, or like action based on conversion, (ii) for breach of warranty, or (iii) to enforce an obligation, duty, or right arising under this Article and not governed by this section must be commenced within three years after the cause of action accrues.
11(A) V.I. Code Ann. § 3-118 (WESTLAW through Act 6503 of the 2002 Session).

Judgments 20 years.
Civil actions shall only be commenced within the periods prescribed below after the cause of action shall have accrued, except when, in special cases, a different limitation is prescribed by statute:

(1) Twenty (20) years--
An action upon a judgment or decree of any court of the United States, or of any state, Commonwealth, or Territory within the United States.
5 V.I. Code Ann. § 31(1)(B) (WESTLAW through Act 6503 of the 2002 Session).

Washington

Contracts

3 years **(oral)**. Except as provided in RCW 4.16.040(2) (below), an action upon a contract or liability, express or implied, which is not in writing, and does not arise out of any written instrument. Wash. Rev. Code Ann. § 4.16.080(3) (West, WESTLAW through Chap. 3 of 2002 Reg. Session).

6 years **(written)**

The following actions shall be commenced within six (6) years:

(1) An action upon a contract in writing, or liability express or implied arising out of a written agreement.
(2) An action upon an account receivable incurred in the ordinary course of business.
(3) An action for the rents and profits or for the use and occupation of real estate.

Wash. Rev. Code Ann. § 4.16.040 (West, WESTLAW through Chap. 3 of 2002 Reg. Session).

Judgments -
Domestic 10 years

(1) Except as provided in subsections (2) and (3) of this section, after the expiration of ten (10) years from the date of the entry of any judgment heretofore or hereafter rendered in this state, it shall cease to be a lien or charge against the estate or person of the judgment debtor. No suit, action or other proceeding shall ever be had on any judgment rendered in this state by which the lien shall be extended or continued in force for any greater or longer period than ten (10) years.
(2) An underlying judgment or judgment lien entered after the effective date of this act for accrued child support shall continue in force for ten (10) years after the eighteenth birthday of the youngest child named in the order for whom support is ordered. All judgments entered after the effective date of this act shall contain the birth date of the youngest child for whom support is ordered.
(3) A lien based upon an underlying judgment continues in force for an additional ten (10) year period if the period of execution for the underlying judgment is extended under RCW 6.17.020.

Wash. Rev. Code Ann. § 4.56.210(1) (West, WESTLAW through Chap. 3 of 2002 Reg. Session).

West Virginia

Contracts

10 years **(written, under seal)**. W. Va. Code § 55-2-6 (West, WESTLAW through 2002 First Ex. Session).

5 years **(oral)**. W. Va. Code § 55-2-6 (WESTLAW through 2002 First Ex. Session).

10 years **(written)**. W. Va. Code § 55-2-6 (WESTLAW through 2002 First Ex. Session).

Actions to recover on award or contract other than judgment or recognizance

Every action to recover money, which is founded upon an award, or on any contract other than a judgment or recognizance, shall be brought within the following number of years next after the right to bring the same shall have accrued, that is to say: If the case be upon an indemnifying bond taken under any statute, or upon a bond of an executor, administrator or guardian, curator, committee, sheriff or deputy sheriff, clerk or deputy clerk, or any other fiduciary or public officer, within ten (10) years; if it be upon any other contract in writing under seal, within ten years; if it be upon an award, or upon a contract in writing, signed by the party to be charged thereby, or by his agent, but not under seal, within ten (10) years; and if it be upon any other contract, express or implied, within five years, unless it be an action by one party against his copartner for a settlement of the partnership accounts, or upon accounts concerning the trade or merchandise between merchant and merchant, their factors or servants, where the action of account would lie, in either of which cases the action may be brought until the expiration of five (5) years from a cessation of the dealings in which they are interested together, but not after. W Va. Code Ann. § 55-2-6 (West, WESTLAW through 2002 First Ex. Session).

Judgments -
Domestic 10 years. W. Va. Code § 38-3-18 (West, WESTLAW through 2002 First Ex. Session).

Limitations on enforcement of judgments

On a judgment, execution may be issued within ten years after the date thereof. Where execution issues within ten years as aforesaid, other executions may be issued on such judgment within ten years from the return day of the last execution issued thereon, on which there is no return by an officer or which has been returned unsatisfied. An action, suit or scire facias may be brought upon a judgment where there has been a change of parties by death or otherwise at any time within ten years next after the date of the judgment; or within ten years from the return day of the last execution issued thereon on which there is no return by an officer or which has been returned unsatisfied. But if such action, suit or scire facias be against the personal representative of a decedent, it shall be brought within five years from the qualification of such representative. W. Va. Code Ann. § 38-3-18 (West, WESTLAW through 2002 First Ex. Session).

Tolling of Statute/Reviving of Barred Debt

Acknowledgment by new promise

If any person against whom the right shall have so accrued on an award, or on any such contract, shall by writing signed by him or his agent promise payment of money on such award or contract, the person to whom the right shall have so accrued may maintain an action or suit for the moneys so promised within such number of years after such promise as it might originally have been maintained within upon the award or contract, and the plaintiff may either sue on such a promise, or on the original cause of action, and in the latter case, in answer to a plea under the sixth section, may, by way of replication, state such promise, and that such action was brought within such number of years thereafter; but no promise, except by writing as aforesaid, shall take any case out of the operation of the said sixth section, or deprive any party of the benefit thereof. An acknowledgment in writing as aforesaid, from which a promise of payment may be implied, shall be deemed to be such promise within the meaning of this section. W. Va. Code Ann. § 55-2-8 (West, WESTLAW through 2002 First Ex. Session).

"The fact that the statute of limitations has run on a debt does not extinguish that debt. [citations omitted] It merely bars recovery thereof. The effect of a new promise to pay, or a written acknowledgment from which a promise to pay may be implied, is to revive the period of limitation of the original obligation, and the new period of limitation begins to run from the date of the subsequent promise or acknowledgment. *State ex rel. Battle v. Demkovich*, 136 S.E.2d 895, 899 (W. Va. 1964).

"The rule in most jurisdictions is that partial payment on a debt may start the statute of limitations running anew where the payment is made voluntarily by a debtor under circumstances that warrant a clear inference that the debtor recognizes the whole debt to be subsisting and demonstrates his willingness or obligation to pay the balance of the debt. [citations omitted]

As a corollary, if a debtor restricts or qualifies his partial payment in some manner which indicates an intention not to pay the balance of the debt, then the statute of limitations will not be tolled. [citations omitted] Finally, the burden of proof rests on the creditor to demonstrate that the statute of limitations has been renewed by partial payment." *Greer Limestone Co. v. Nestor*, 332 S.E.2d 589, 596 (W.Va. 1985).

Wisconsin

Contracts 6 years (**contract, obligation or liability, express or implied**)
Wis. Stat. Ann. § 893.43 (West, WESTLAW through 2001 Act 43, published 2/15/02).

10 years (**personal actions on any contract not limited by this chapter or any other law of this state**)
Wis. Stat. Ann. § 893.50 (West, WESTLAW through 2001 Act 43, published 2/15/02).

Judgments - Domestic
Of Record 20 years Wis. Stat. Ann. § 893.40 (West, WESTLAW through 2001 Act 43, published 2/15/02).

Not of Record 6 years. Wis. Stat. Ann. § 893.42 (West, WESTLAW through 2001 Act 43, published 2/15/02).

Ed. note: Wisconsin follows the minority rule, holding that expiration of the statute of limitations extinguishes the right as well as the remedy. A recent unpublished case, *Klewer v. Cavalry Investments, LLC*, No. 01-C-541-S, 2002 U.S. Dist. LEXIS 1778 at *6-*8 (W.D. Wis. Jan. 30, 2002), reaffirmed this rule. *Klewer* cites both *First Nat. Bank of Madison v. Kolbeck*, 19 N.W.2d 908, 909 (Wis. 1945) and Wis. Stat. Ann. § 893.05 (West, WESTLAW through 2001 Act 43, published 2/15/02) for this proposition.

The *Klewer* court held that attempting to collect a time-barred debt via collection letter violates the Fair Debt Collection Practices Act § 807(2)(A) (§1692e(2)(A)), finding that when the statute of limitations expired the creditor could no longer claim that the money was owed. 2002 U.S. Dist. LEXIS 1778, at *8. Thus, making such a claim misrepresented the legal status of the debt. *Id.* This interpretation bars debt buyers and collectors from attempting to collect debts upon which the statute of limitations has expired, and most likely bars them from credit reporting such accounts.

Wis. Stat. Ann. § 893.05 states, "When the period within which an action may be commenced on a Wisconsin cause of action has expired, the right is extinguished as well as the remedy." The annotation to the statute notes that it is a codification of Wisconsin case law. Actions in equity are not so barred, however. *Elkhorn Area School Dist. v. East Troy Community School Dist.* 377 N.W.2d 627, 630 (Wis. Ct. App. 1985).

Wyoming

Contracts
8 years (**oral**)
Wyo. Stat. Ann. § 1-3-105 (WESTLAW through End of 2001 Regular Session).

10 years (**written**)
Wyo. Stat. Ann. § 1-3-105 (WESTLAW through End of 2001 Regular Session).

Judgments
No action shall be brought to revive a judgment after ten (10) years after it becomes dormant, unless the party entitled to bring the action was: (i) a minor or subject to any other legal disability at the time the judgment became dormant, in which case the action may be brought within fifteen (15) years after the disability has ceased; or (ii) A party in a child support proceeding, in which case the action shall be

brought within twenty-one (21) years.
Wyo. Stat. Ann. § 1-16-503 (WESTLAW through Wyoming 2004 Budget Session of the 57th Legislature).

ACA International, P.O. Box 390106, Minneapolis, MN 55439-0106
Phone +1(952) 926-6547 Fax (952) 926-1624 E-mail compliance@aca.international.org
Web http://www.acainternational.org

CHAPTER 6

Bankruptcy

The Bankruptcy Law of 1898 was the first law to allow a business to file a petition in bankruptcy to discharge debts. Consumers were not included because credit was rarely extended to them. The law was modified over the years to expand the relief (some might contend too much relief) of the bankruptcy law to consumers. The Bankruptcy Abuse Prevention and Consumer Protection Act passed at the end of 2005.

BANKRUPTCY ABUSE PREVENTION AND CONSUMER PROTECTION ACT OF 2005

The Bankruptcy Abuse Prevention and Consumer Protection Act of 2005 (hereinafter referred to as "BAPCPA" or the "ACT") became effective on October 17, 2005. Most of the media attention has been directed at the changes in the law that seriously affect the consumers ability to file a bankruptcy and to obtain a discharge. Changes that impact a Chapter 11 debtor as well as the creditors of the business debtor are just as significant and even more so in some instances.

The Act has favored creditors at the expense of the debtor. Business creditors of business bankruptcies have received considerable additional protections, principally in the perfection, preference, reclamation, and lease area. As to the consumers, the burden appears to be oppressive and the Act will discourage some consumers from using the bankruptcy law. In some respects the law is similar to Medicaid where you have to divest yourself of most of the assets before you may take advantage of the benefit. In this instance, your earnings must be less than the mean average of the particular state. Because of certain time requirements and black and white approaches in some of the statutory language, the law may deprive the judges of the discretion that they once enjoyed to provide the bankrupt with a fresh start.

The 500 pages of revisions to the Act will provide substantial material until the courts and the legal profession finally grasp all the nuances in those pages.

Because the revisions are massive, the last 3 years have provided ample material for the courts to interpret the new act. The courts appear to be favoring the consumer who filed. As to the bankrupt consumers, the jury is still out.

We have reorganized the chapter under new headings and subheadings so the reader will have a more comprehensive exposure to the old and new law.

A copy of the new bankruptcy code can be obtained from the American Bar Association Section of Business Law. The address is: Book Publishing, American Bar Association, 321 North Clark Street, Chicago, Illinois 60610.

What is set forth here are the highlights only. The Act is 500 pages, a book in itself. The reader must realize that we are dealing with the highlights, and not all 500 pages of the Act.

PROOF OF CLAIM

Filing a Proof of Claim. Rule 3002 of the Bankruptcy Code states that a proof of claim shall be filed with the clerk in the district where the case is pending. In a Chapter 7, Chapter 12, or a Chapter 13 proceeding, the proof of claim must be filed within 90 days after the first date set for the meeting of creditors. The deadline is always based on the first meeting of the creditors, not any subsequent or adjourned meetings. One exception to this is when assets are discovered after the bankruptcy, and the creditors are notified of the deadline for filing claims.

When filing claims, request that the clerk stamp a copy of the proof of claim and return it to you. The best approach is to furnish the bankruptcy clerk an additional copy of your proof of claim and to request the bankruptcy clerk to stamp on the additional copy the fact that the claim was received and filed. Provide a self-addressed stamped envelope. If you fail to obtain a return of your stamped copy within 15 to 20 days, refile the proof of claim. The initial proof of claim should be filed within 30 days after the first meeting of creditors to allow sufficient time for the bankruptcy clerk to stamp the proof of claim and return same to you, and to refile the claim if you do not receive your stamped copy.

Today, most bankruptcy courts are accessible electronically and the option is available to access the docket of the bankruptcy court electronically to see whether your proof of claim has been filed.

In a Chapter 7 proceeding under Rule 726(a)(3), a proof of claim which has been filed past the deadline is satisfied after other unsecured claims, which have been properly filed or are paid in full. The bankruptcy court does not disallow the claim for failure to file within the specified time, but states that the claim should be subordinate to other timely filed claims.

We recommend clients file a proof of claim notwithstanding whether or not the debtor has listed your claim in the schedules filed with the petition. One reason is that the amount may not be mentioned in the schedules or the amount listed in the schedule is different from the amount owing to the creditor. The bankrupt amended the schedules and omitted the name of the creditor. The creditor never filed a proof of claim and will not share in the distribution.

Where a distribution will not be made to unsecured creditors, the original notice sent to creditors notifying the creditor of the bankruptcy will contain a statement that creditors need not file a proof of claim at that time and that if assets are discovered, a distribution may be made to creditors. The creditor will have 90 days from the mailing of the notice to file a proof of claim. *File a proof of claim.* Creditors have moved and they did not receive the subsequent notice and did not share in the distribution.

Under Chapter 11, if the claim is listed as undisputed, liquidated and not contingent, the option is available to the creditor not to file a proof of claim. *Again, file a proof of claim.*

When filing a proof of claim, the bankruptcy court requires you to file the documents to support the proof of claim. *Do not file originals.*

> ***Credit & Collection Tip:*** *Always file a proof of claim whether a secured proof of claim or an unsecured claim, or even if the court says no proof of claim is necessary at this time.*

Completing a Proof of Claim. A proof-of-claim form is sometimes furnished by the court, or it may be obtained in a stationery store that stocks legal forms. (A sample form is provided in the Appendix to this chapter.) A summary of the basic information that a bankruptcy proof of claim requires is furnished. We recommend that if you complete a proof of claim, the document should be reviewed by competent counsel. Some courts have revised the forms.

1. At the top of the form insert the proper bankruptcy court, corresponding to the name appearing on the notice of bankruptcy.
2. The case number (or the index number) must correspond to the case number on the notice of bankruptcy. (The number appears with the year '99-0000 or 0000-99.)
3. The debtor's name, which corresponds to the name on the notice of bankruptcy, is usually inserted in the rectangular outlined box.

4. The first blank is the identification of whether an individual, a partnership, or a corporation is filing a proof of claim.
5. If a corporation is filing a proof of claim, list the name and the title of the officer. If a partnership, list the name of the partner.
6. Under certain circumstances, an agent may file a proof of claim. (Consult with counsel.)
7. The total amount of the claim must be inserted.
8. The basis of the claim is described by answering the question which asks for the "consideration of the debt." "Merchandise shipped," "monies loaned," or "services rendered" are appropriate responses. Attach invoices, the note or check evidencing the monies loaned, or a bill describing the services rendered.
9. If the claim is based on a written agreement, attach a copy of the agreement.
10. If the claim is founded on an open account, set forth the invoices or the bill for services rendered as specified above.
11. A statement must be made that a judgment has been rendered for the amount due or that no judgment has been rendered for the amount due.
12. An allegation must be set forth as to any payments made and credited and deducted from the amount due.
13. A statement must be made that the claim is not subject to any set-off, offset, or counterclaim, and if so, describe the nature of the claim, that is, the debtor is claiming defective merchandise or claiming 54 cartons were never received.
14. A secured claim must be *designated as a secured claim* and a copy of the documents supporting the secured claim must be attached, including evidence of perfection of the lien, i.e., UCC financing statement and the security agreement or the real estate mortgage.
15. A general unsecured claim must be so designated. If priority or secured claims are filed, consult with an attorney. *In the event your claim is not listed as secured, its secured status may be lost and the claim will be treated as unsecured.*
16. Whenever a proof of claim is forwarded to the bankruptcy court, use certified mail or a postcard should be enclosed identifying the case by name and case number to be acknowledged by the bankruptcy clerk and thereafter retained as evidence the proof of claim was properly filed on a specific date.
17. On the reverse side of the bankruptcy form, the instructions to Bankrutpcy Form 10 in subsection c, refers to a "claim based on writing" and states as follows: "when a claim, or an interest in property of the debtor securing the claim, is based on writing, the original

or duplicate shall be filed with the proof of claim. If the writing has been lost or destroyed, a statement of the circumstances of the loss or destruction shall be filed with the claim."

Generally, if it's a commercial claim, a creditor should file at the minimum a statement itemizing each invoice showing how the amount was determined. In the event interest, late fees, or other items are charged to the debtor, a copy of the agreement authorizing the charges should be added. If there are only a few invoices, it is suggested to attach the invoices to the statement. If there are several hundred invoices, this form authorizes the debtor to substitute a summary of debt (which would be the statement of account).

As to credit cards, a recent case held that the account summaries that are usually attached to the proof claim are insufficient. The proof of claim must have attached the agreement governing the account which sets forth the terms of the account as well as the interest and other fees. Whether this decision will be adopted by other courts is unknown since the bankruptcy court rules specifically allow a claimant to substitute a summary of the debt in lieu of the substantial documentation that may be necessary in credit card debt. The court does not want detailed information about purchases, finance charges, and interest. In two decisions in Washington, the court explained the requirements for a valid summary as to the "amount of a debt" i.e., the name and account number of the debtor. The documentation should be in a form of a business record or some other reliable form. Finally, the document must itemize interest and fees, if any.[1]

Chapter 7. A proof of claim must be filed within 90 days after the first meeting of creditors. Emphasis is on the *first* meeting of creditors and not the last meeting of creditors (which is the marker for objections to discharge).[2] All proofs of claim are deemed valid unless the trustee or debtor files an objection to the claim.[3]

Chapter 11. In all Chapter 11 reorganization cases creditors should file proofs of claim.[4] The time within which a proof of claim must be filed (bar-date) is set by the court and is printed on the notice of bankruptcy. If a claim is properly listed in the schedule by the debtor and is not disputed, the claim will be recognized and will receive a full distribution, even if the creditor does not file a proof of claim. Some creditors examine the schedules, and if the schedules list the creditor, no proof of claim need be filed.

---

[1]*In re Vann*, 321 B.R. 734 (Bankr. W.D. Wash. 2005); *In re Schraner*, 321 B.R. 738 (Bankr. W.D. Wash. 2005); *In re Henry*, 311 B.R. 813 (Bankr. W.D. Wash. 2004).

[2]Bankruptcy Rule 3002(c).

[3]Bankruptcy Rule 3077.

[4]11 U.S.C. § 501.

The possibility is always present that the claim is listed improperly, is not recognized, will become lost, or, for any number of reasons, will not be paid.

> ***Credit & Collection Tip:*** *We recommend that every creditor should file a proof of claim in a Chapter 11 proceeding even if the creditor is properly listed in the schedules.*

Chapter 13. Under a Chapter 13 proceeding, a creditor must file a proof of claim to share in any distribution. The notice of bankruptcy provides a "bar-date" by which time the proof of claim must be filed. Under certain circumstances, both in Chapter 11 and Chapter 13 proceedings, the bar-date may be modified by court order in response to an application to the court to permit a creditor to file a late proof of claim. These circumstances are extremely rare, especially with consumers, for the court rarely grants leave to extend the time.

Late Proof of Claim. A considerable amount of case law has developed regarding the efforts of those creditors who fail to file a timely proof of claim to correct and cure this failure and ultimately file a valid proof of claim. The main ingredient that creditors use is excusable neglect and sometimes the neglect of the attorney and the main reason is that the proof of claim was lost in the mail.

The usual procedure is that the creditor alleges that an "informal proof of claim" was filed within the specified time limits and that the informal "proof of claim" was later amended with a conventional filing and that this conventional filing in turn relates back to the date of the "informal proof of claim." The question is whether the informal proof of claim could possibly qualify as a proof of claim under the Bankruptcy Code.

Such informal proofs of claim may include letters to the attorney for the estate, letters to the trustee, participation in the proceedings, seeking a relief from stay without making any effort to file a proof of claim, participating in some particular proceeding in the bankruptcy court, or any other activity which falls within the activities mentioned. This method of curing a failure to file a proof of claim is somewhat different from the basic application to court to file a late proof of claim due to excusable neglect. Consult with counsel.

The courts use a test of excusable neglect which includes several criteria.

1. The danger of prejudice to the debtor.
2. The length of the delay and its potential impact on judicial proceedings.
3. The reason for the delay including whether it was within the reasonable control of the movant.

4. Whether the movant acted in good faith.[5]
5. Whether the attorney had actual knowledge of the date of the filing by virtue of filing other proofs of claim for other creditors.
6. Whether the attorney attempted to confirm that the proof of claim was timely filed by failing to make a follow-up call or including a stamped self-addressed envelope or a certified mail receipt.
7. A larger claim is more apt to be denied an extension since it will have a greater affect on the bankrupt rather than a smaller claim.

As to the production of supporting documentation, a recent circuit court case took the "exclusive view" and held that supporting documentation that was not provided is not grounds to disallow the proof of claim. The court held that 11 U.S.C. § 502(b) provided an exclusive list of reasons why a claim should be dismissed. Technical defects in a proof of claim are not grounds for objections. The "non-exclusive views," which are shared by some of the other circuits, hold that the factors listed in Section 502(b) are not the only grounds to dismiss a creditor's claim and that the court may look for other grounds.[6]

Attorneys' Fees. Under certain circumstances attorneys will undertake to file proofs of claim on behalf of their clients and will charge a fee for same. In the event the fee is to become part of the proof of claim, the attorney must disclose the fee so that the bankrupt knows that the fee is part of a secured or unsecured claim. Secondly, the fee should be included in the arrearages claim portion of the debt so that the debtor can pay the fee through his or her plan as allowed under Chapter 13.[7]

CORE PROCEEDINGS

The Bankruptcy Code identifies two types of proceedings that affect its jurisdiction. Core proceedings are those connected to the administration of the bankruptcy and basically involve the rights, obligations, and the remedies that are created under the bankruptcy code, such as setting aside preferential transfers, dischargeability, and other proceedings which are indigenous to the bankruptcy procedure. In such proceedings the bankruptcy court, as opposed to another court, conducts the trial or hearing and enters the judgment.

---

[5] *Pioneer Inv. Servs. Co. v. Brunswick Assocs. Ltd. P'ship*, 507 U.S. 380 (1993); *In re Enron*, 419 F.3d 115 (2d Cir. 2005).

[6] *B-Line, LLC v. Kirkland (In re Kirkland)*, 379 B.R. 341 (B.A.P. 10th Cir. 2007); *In re Dove-Nation*, 318 B.R. 147 (B.A.P. 8th Cir. 2007).

[7] *In re Catherine D. Slick*, 2002 Bankr. LEXIS 772 (S.D. Ala. 2002).

Non-core proceedings or related proceedings involve a claim that *will* affect the administration of the debtor's estate, *but does not arise* under the bankruptcy law and could be adjudicated in a court other than the bankruptcy court. Non-core proceedings usually are adjudicated in the district courts unless the bankrupt and the other party consents to the jurisdiction of the bankruptcy court or unless the district court decides to refer the matter to the bankruptcy court. (*See* Chapter 15.)

A recent case addressed the issue of whether an FDCPA claim is a "core proceeding" which may be addressed in the bankruptcy court. Conflict exists over this issue. The bankruptcy court in Virginia took the position that the trustee could reopen a bankruptcy and they would determine the FDCPA claim.[8] An appellate court, when squarely faced with the issue, might well conclude that the bankruptcy court lacks subject matter jurisdiction to consider the FDCPA claim.

VOLUNTARY PETITION

The debtor may file a petition at any time by alleging the inability to pay debts as they mature. A filing fee is required, and upon acceptance by the clerk, all proceedings against the debtor must cease and desist. This right is also afforded to businesses, but most businesses do not file a bankruptcy petition if they are going out of business. On the other hand, if the business wishes to reorganize and continue to operate, the debtor may take advantage of Chapter 11 of the bankruptcy laws.

INVOLUNTARY PETITION

Section 303 of the Bankruptcy Act provides that "an involuntary action may be commenced only under Chapter 7 or Chapter 11 and only against the person, or a corporation that is not a money, business or commercial corporation, or that may be a debtor under the chapter under which such case is commenced."

An involuntary case must be commenced:

1. By three or more entities each of which is either a holder of a claim against such person that is not contingent as to liability or the subject of a bona fide dispute.
2. Such non-contingent, undisputed claims must aggregate at least $12,300 more than the value of any lien on property of the debtor.

---

[8] *In re Burgess*, 2007 Bankr. LEXIS 142 (Bankr. E.D. Va. Jan. 12, 2007).

3. If fewer than 12 such holders (excluding any employee or insider of such person and any transferee of a transfer that is voidable under Section 544, 545, 547, 549 or 724) then by one or more such holders that hold in the aggregate at least $12,300 of such claims.

An involuntary petition filed by a single creditor is not an action that most attorneys would recommend. The courts view them as a dispute between two parties which belongs in the federal or state court. The claims tend to be dismissed if any bona fide dispute as to liability or to the amount is present. The mere filing of a counterclaim in litigation in a state or federal court which hasn't been dismissed by the court would probably support a dismissal in the bankruptcy court.

If the bankrupt debtor chooses to contest the involuntary petition, the creditor would have to prove non-payment of his debts as they become due. Other than disputed debts, the court may review the picture of the liabilities of the debtor as to the amount of the debt, the fact that the party filing the involuntary petition may be the only debtor that is not being paid, whether the debtor is still in business and his business is solvent and other factors indicating that the matter does not belong in the bankruptcy court.

The creditor filing the petition is subject to damage claims by the bankrupt debtor to reimburse the debtor for the damage to his reputation and other damages sustained due to the petition being filed. Punitive damages and attorney fees are an option for the bankrupt debtor as well as any damages sustained in objecting to the bankruptcy.

The damage claim could increase substantially if the court determines that the creditor was acting in bad faith with full knowledge that the debtor was meeting all of his other obligations except the one obligation due to the petitioning creditor.

An involuntary may be commenced either under Chapter 7 or Chapter 11, but may not be commenced under Chapter 9, 12, or Chapter 13. A trustee may be appointed before the order of relief to preserve the assets or prevent loss of estate property. An application to restrict the ability of the debtor to dispose of any property may also be made.

The case may only be dismissed after a hearing and after notice to all the creditors. If you are able to settle with the bankrupt, the notice should contain the terms of the settlement. If it is a favorable settlement, you probably will receive objections from other creditors who have received no monies at all. You must provide notice to all the bankrupt's creditors, which may be difficult since you may not know all the creditors and the bankrupt may not wish to provide that information.

U.S. TRUSTEE

A trustee in a bankruptcy proceeding under Chapter 7, 11, or 13 is appointed to collect the assets of the bankrupt, convert them to cash, and distribute the monies to the creditors.[9] The trustee acts as a fiduciary for the benefit of all creditors, secured, or unsecured. The trustee has the right to employ attorneys, accountants, and other professionals and do whatever is needed to preserve and protect the assets of the estate. The trustee is empowered to sue on behalf of the bankrupt estate or to avoid certain liens or preferences which affect the debtor estate. In addition, the trustee may accept or reject contracts, such as leases, which bind the debtor. The trustee may continue to operate the business if appointed by the court to succeed a debtor in possession. Normally, a trustee does not actively run a business on a day-to-day basis, but supervises the running of a business through the debtor in possession or, if a large corporation, through the board of directors.

CREDITOR'S COMMITTEE

A new section has been added to the bankruptcy code which states as follows:

> Section 1102(b)(3)(A) provides as follows:
> "A committee appointed under subsection (a) shall—

A. provide access information to creditors who—
   i. hold claims of the kind representing by the committee; and
   ii. are not appointed to the committee
B. Soliciting and receive comments from the creditors described in subparagraph A; and
C. Be subject to a court order that compels any additional report or disclosure to be made to the creditors described in subparagraph A.

The code does not define the information that the committee must provide and no indication of what information is privileged or should be privileged is offered. Another issue is the confidentiality of this financial information and whether the debtor may not want his creditors to have this information.

Under the prior Act, the U.S. trustee appointed a creditor's committee consisting of the largest creditors. The new Act has added an option that the U.S. trustee may increase the number of members of a committee to include

[9] 11 U.S.C. § 704.

a small business creditor if the proposed creditor has the same type of claims similar to the others on the committee and the claim is a large claim in comparison to the small business creditor's annual income. The Act also states that the Committee must provide information and report to the creditors of the kind that are on the Committee, but not appointed to the Committee, and to receive comments from these similar creditors.

The U.S. trustee is required to create a creditor's committee consisting of the seven largest unsecured creditors.[10] The trustee contacts the 20 largest unsecured creditors from the list filed in the petition for bankruptcy. If the largest creditors do not serve, other creditors will be selected. A large creditor located geographically convenient to court should consider serving on the creditor's committee, if economically feasible. The committee represents all creditors rather than any particular class of creditors and sets its own schedule as to meetings and procedures for voting. The Bankruptcy Act allows the committee to retain professionals such as attorneys, accountants, appraisers, and other types of industry experts needed to achieve their objectives. The creditor's committee will receive the reports concerning the debtor's operation when they are filed. The reports and its experience in the industry enable the committee to review the operation of the business as to salaries, shipments of goods, payments of liabilities, purchases of inventory, payments to insiders, salaries, and to embark on any appropriate action. (11 U.S.C. § 1104).

The individual members of the creditor's committee usually are not liable for payment of the professional fees since these fees come from the debtor in possession. In some instances, the creditor's committee may guarantee to the professionals the payment of their fees.

The creditor's committee will designate certain duties of investigation to specific members, so that all devote an equal amount of time to learning about the operation of the debtor's business. The members of the committee will have available the periodical reports furnished to the trustee and will be able to monitor the progress of the debtor in possession in fulfilling a plan of reorganization and, ultimately, coming out of a Chapter 11 bankruptcy. (11 U.S.C. § 1103).

Whether to Serve on Creditor's Committee. If the creditor is one of the seven largest unsecured creditors, it probably is advisable to serve on the creditor's committee since this creditor has a substantial amount at stake. The proposed plans may offer from 10 percent to 20 percent to 50 percent payment of debts over a period of time, significant dollars to a large creditor. By serving on the creditor's committee, the creditor is receiving information as to the operation of the debtor and may be offering input with regard to a proposed plan. The committee, if necessary,

---

[10] 11 U.S.C. § 1102(b)(1).

may make an appropriate request to the court for the appointment of a trustee to operate the business in the event the debtor in possession is not properly operating the business. The committee may pursue fraudulent or preferential transfers and furnish this information to the trustee to act upon or actively defend against an improperly filed security interest.

The creditor's committee and the bankrupt become partners in the quest for salvage of the debtor's business. Suggestions as to financing become an all-important function of the committee. Members of the creditor's committee monitor the pulse of the Chapter 11 bankruptcy and must consider the probability of any plan being viable. A good creditor's committee is of invaluable assistance to the debtor. The creditor's committee works closely with the members of the secured class to reassure them as to the viability of a reorganization to avoid the dismantling of the business.

Separate committees for other holders of claims such as secured parties and pension claimants may also be formed under the Bankruptcy Act under to the discretion of the court.

The most potent weapon of the creditor's committee is to gather organized support or opposition to the Chapter 11 plan. Thus, the debtor is careful to cultivate the committee and be as cooperative as possible.

Providing Information. The new Act does not define the information that an official creditors' committee provides to its constituency or state the manner of delivery. A recent case indicated that the committee was not required to divulge confidential, proprietory or non-public information concerning the debtor or any other information where the effect of such disclosure would constitute a waiver of the attorney/client or other privilege of the committee.

The code has long contained requirements for bankruptcy trustees to furnish such information concerning the estate and the estate's administration as is requested by a party in interest. A trustee should point to a countervailing fiduciary duty to protect creditors in the estate from a particular harm, the performance of which is more important than avoiding the harm resulting from withholding the information in question.

A trustee's duty is fairly extensive and the burden is on the trustee to provide the requested information to parties of interest. The responsibilities have been interpreted broadly and a trustee may encounter difficulties in refusing a request unless an application is made to the court for an order to the contrary.

The obligation to provide information is not unlimited. A trustee may always obtain a protective order against disclosure if disclosure would result in waiver of a privilege or the information sought is proprietary and confidential. The main grounds for a protective order is a countervailing fiduciary duty to protect the creditors and the estate from harm. If the order is used to gain an advantage over the party seeking the information, the order should be denied.

The committee is not required to provide to each creditor all the data that it receives in the course of performing its duties. The committee should furnish a fair presentation of the status. The committee owes a duty to the debtor's unsecured creditors as well as to their secured creditors.

A decision provides the equivalent of an outline of what the duties of the creditors committee are when providing information.[11] Several paragraphs are devoted to confidential information and how to handle creditor information requests, as well as responses to information requests for access to confidential information and the release of confidential information to third parties. We are including in the Appendix a copy of the Southern District of New York decision (*In re Refco*).

Converting Chapters 13 and 11 to Chapter 7. After notice and hearing, any creditor may request that the Chapter 11 reorganization be converted to a Chapter 7 liquidation for the following reasons.[12]

- The creditor operates the business with continuing losses and no likelihood of rehabilitation is evident.
- An inability to effectuate a plan.
- An unreasonable delay takes place in effectuating a plan, which may prejudice creditors.

The individual petitioner may also have option to convert a 13 filing to a 7 filing, to convert a 13 filing to an 11 filing, and certainly to convert an 11 filing to a 7 filing. A debtor may not be eligible for a Chapter 13 because the debts exceed one million dollars under Section 109(e) or sufficient regular income is not available to meet the criteria of a Chapter 13. An advantage of a Chapter 11 is that the debtor may seek to continue to operate his business as a debtor in possession and may want more time to file a plan than Chapter 13 provides.

The option to convert must be in good faith and all disclosures must be properly made within the time frame set forth. Any move by the debtor to convert will receive significant review by the trustee. The trustee may move to dismiss the bankruptcy without help from any of the creditors. Furnishing information to the trustee and keeping in contact with the trustee is always advisable. *As we have said, read the plan carefully.*

As to dismissal, normally a Chapter 11 debtor has no right to seek to dismiss the filing of a petition under a Chapter 11.

---

[11] *In re Refco Inc.*, 336 B.R. 187 (Bankr. S.D.N.Y. 2006). *See Garner v. Wolfburger*, 401 U.S. 974 (1971).

[12] 11 U.S.C. § 1112(b).

BANKRUPTCY NOTICE

The first notification of a bankruptcy to a creditor is in the form of a computer-generated printed notice from the bankruptcy court. This notice provides the following information:

A. Name and the location of the bankruptcy court, and the case number.
B. The name and address of the debtor.
C. The date that the petition was filed and whether it has been filed under Chapter 7, 11, or 13.
D. The date and time of the first meeting of creditors.
E. A statement that suits and proceedings against the bankrupt are stayed preventing creditors from commencing or continuing suits in state or federal courts and compelling creditors to assert their claims in the bankruptcy court, a more favorable arena for the bankrupt.
F. The last date for filing of objections is usually set forth in the notice, or in a Chapter 7 proceeding within 60 days after the date set for the first meeting of creditors.
G. The names, addresses, and telephone numbers of the attorney for the debtor and of the trustee as well as the name of the bankruptcy judge.
H. Some notices specify that the bankruptcy is listed as a "no asset" case and a proof of claim need not be filed. If assets are located by the trustee, a new notice will be sent enabling the creditor to file a proof of claim.
I. The total amount of assets and liabilities may be listed.

Response to Notice. When a creditor receives the bankruptcy notice, the avenues to be considered are the following:

A. If the claim of the creditor is too small to justify spending the time and effort to file a proof of claim, the creditor may ignore the notice of bankruptcy.
B. The creditor may prepare and file a proof of claim with the bankruptcy court.
C. Consultation with an attorney is recommended if:
    1. the creditor is a secured creditor and wishes to remove the automatic stay of proceedings to enable the creditor to repossess and reclaim the property covered by a secured lien, or seek from the bankrupt a reaffirmation ("Reaffirmation," below) of the indebtedness;
    2. the claim is large;
    3. the claim is complicated;

4. the creditor suspects fraud or preferences (see "Preferences," below) and is considering objecting to the discharge;
5. the security that the creditor holds is subject to rapid devaluation;
6. the creditor is uncertain as to which way to proceed.

The question of notification of the filing of a bankruptcy petition is governed by certain rules of which many creditors are unaware. *The automatic stay is effective even if the creditor is not aware of the filing of the bankruptcy and receives no notification of the bankruptcy if the creditor proceeds to recover collateral under a lien.*

If an employee or agent of the creditor has received notice, notice to one office is sufficient notice to the creditor even if the creditor has a multitude of offices. Many courts have stated that the creditor has a duty to inquire before proceeding if the creditor has reason to believe that the debtor may have filed a petition in bankruptcy or even contemplates filing a petition in bankruptcy. (*See* BAPCPA.)

> ***Credit & Collection Tip:*** *If a creditor hires an outside attorney or collection agency, notice to that attorney or the agency may in fact be notice to the creditor even where the agency or attorney failed to notify the creditor that they received the bankruptcy notice. If a creditor directs an agency to return a case, the creditor should notify the debtor that the case has been returned and provide the address of the creditor to which notices should be sent. Otherwise, the bankruptcy notice may notify the agency or the attorney and the agency or attorney may fail to notify the creditor because they are no longer actively handling the case. A letter to the agency advising them to forward all bankruptcy notices to the creditor, or to the new attorney is suggested.*

IGNORING BANKRUPTCY NOTICES. We have chosen to put this heading immediately after filing a proof of claim, because if the creditor is filing their own proof of claim, then hopefully they will pay attention to the heading of this paragraph.

Bankruptcy notices should never be ignored. If you have not retained an attorney to handle the bankruptcy matter, the creditor must carefully review each bankruptcy notice. With regard to Chapter 11 reorganizations and occasionally Chapter 7 liquidations, significant dividends may be paid to creditors. In Chapter 13, the debtor is attempting to pay his or her debts over a period of time. The failure to make these payments may result in a dismissal of the Chapter 13, or a conversion to Chapter 7, which is liquidation. Certain discharges of student loans are prohibited by the bankruptcy code for the law provides that student loans are never discharged except in extenuating circumstances (*see* "STUDENT LOANS," below).

With respect to a plan that includes a discharge of a student loan, the courts generally state that the plan is enforceable after confirmation even though the plan may constitute a violation of the Bankruptcy Code. The theory is that *the creditor had notice of the plan,* failed to object to the plan or failed to appeal the confirmation order, and thus the creditor is bound. The creditor may object to the confirmed plan and may ask the bankruptcy court to correct the situation by making application to the court.

> ***Credit & Collection Tip:*** *The only purpose of this paragraph is to impress upon the creditor that he must monitor all bankruptcy proceedings and particularly all the plans containing disclosure statements and a subsequent discharge of the debtors. Read all notices thoroughly and carefully. Needless to say, when you read a bankruptcy notice that you do not understand, consult with counsel.*[13]

FIRST MEETING OF CREDITORS

Once it has been determined that a petition of bankruptcy was filed, a creditor must be concerned with the following:

A. Filing a proof of claim.

B. Deciding whether to attend the first meeting of creditors (341 hearing).

C. Retaining an attorney to handle the proceedings before the bankruptcy court.

D. Deciding whether you as a creditor will take an active interest in the bankruptcy proceeding whether by objection, removal of automatic stay, or merely attending the 341 hearing.

E. Whether to serve on the creditor's committee.

The first meeting of creditors is usually scheduled about four to five weeks after the petition is filed. The first notice to the creditor contains the date when the first meeting of creditors will be held. The purpose of the first meeting of creditors is to question and examine the debtor with regard to any information that the creditor wishes to obtain which deals with the filing of the petition in bankruptcy. An individual who is not a partnership or a corporation may appear without an attorney and ask the bankrupt questions. Partnerships and corporations are required to have an attorney represent them before the bankruptcy court.

The Bankruptcy Act permits any party in interest to examine the bankrupt. The examination may relate to any acts, conduct, or property that affect the liabilities and financial conditions of the debtor or to any

---

[13] *In re Pardee,* 218 B.R. 916 (B.A.P. 9th Cir. 1998); *In re Ruehle,* 296 B.R. 146 (Bankr. N.D. Ohio 2003).

matter which may affect the administration of the debtor's estate or the debtor's right to a discharge. The examination may relate to the operation of any business and the desirability of its continuance, the source of any money or property acquired or to be acquired by the debtor for purposes of consummating a plan and the consideration offered.

But what is more important, the examination may concern any matter relevant to the filing of the petition, the operation of the business, or to the formulation of the plan. This is a broad stroke to enable a creditor to examine the debtor. The first meeting of creditors is an important meeting in a bankruptcy proceeding and if a creditor has any reservations or suspicions, the creditor should be present to question the debtor.

The clerk of the bankruptcy court as well as the attorney for the bankrupt must provide notice to the creditors of any significant occurrence that develops in a bankruptcy hearing. The bankrupt must also notify the creditors in the event the bankrupt is objecting to their claims or attacking a properly secured lien on property. For this reason all bankruptcy notices should be read carefully and the creditor should be careful to peruse the notice to be certain of the time frames within which responses must be given.

Credit & Collection Tip: *It is recommended that you use an attorney if any proceedings are to be conducted before the bankruptcy court. The proceedings are complicated and are not the same type of proceedings that take place in other courts. Failure to meet time periods can cause a creditor to lose fundamental rights.*

Credit & Collection Tip: *If you wish to know whether a petition in bankruptcy has been filed, you may call the bankruptcy court and ask the clerk.*

BANKRUPTCY SCHEDULES

When a business files a bankruptcy petition, the Bankruptcy Code requires a schedule of all their assets and liabilities and a complete statement of their financial condition. They also must file a listing of both their contingent and their fixed liabilities. On the asset side they must list all their assets, the real estate they own as well as their machinery, equipment, and vehicles and indicate whether any of these fixed assets have been furnished as security for loans. The schedules are detailed and are organized as responses to 20 searching questions involving the bankrupt's past and present financial operation.

A creditor may secure a copy of these schedules for a nominal fee by contacting the clerk at the Bankruptcy Court. The simplest way to do this is to mail a request for the schedule to the clerk (call first to inquire about the fee). Within a short time you will receive the information. If the court is nearby, you may obtain a copy right away or you have your attorney obtain a copy of the schedules for you. Some of the bankruptcy courts are online.

EXEMPTIONS

Under the federal bankruptcy law certain assets in bankruptcy, which are deemed to be necessary for sustenance and living, may be exempt from the reach of creditors:

- As to homestead exemptions, *see* BAPCPA.
- An amount not to exceed $7,500 in cash or personal property, if the debtor is not using the homestead exemption. In a joint petition this amount doubles where both spouses own the property.
- A motor vehicle whose equity does not exceed $2,400.
- A grub stake consisting of any property or cash value which does not exceed $400.
- Any number of household items, each of whose value does not exceed $400. Some states limit the total amount claimed, i.e., Texas has a $30,000 limit.
- Jewelry not exceeding $1,000 in value.
- Other specific exemptions, such as tools of trade for carpenters, electricians, or plumbers, professional books, etc., up to $1,500 in value.
- Life insurance up to $8,000 in value.
- Personal injury exemption $15,000 (recovery for injuries sustained in an accident).
- Certain pension payments and government payments.

In most instances, the exemptions allowed under state law are more generous than those under federal law. The bankrupt debtor may select the more generous exemptions provided under state law. A review of the state law where the bankrupt resides is recommended.

CONVERTING NON-EXEMPT TO EXEMPT PROPERTY

Most of the circuits are in agreement that the conversion of non-exempt property to exempt property for the purpose of placing property out of the reach of creditors, without more, will not deprive the debtor of the exemption to which he otherwise would be entitled. Nevertheless, debtors may be denied discharge if they converted property with intent to hinder, delay or defraud a creditor within one year after the date of filing of the petition. The issue is whether intent to defraud could be proven. The courts look for specific indicia of fraud and an actual intent to defraud.

The mere desire to convert assets into exempt forms by itself alone does not constitute intent to defraud. The cases usually are fact specific and the activity in each situation must be viewed individually before a determination can be made as to the intent to defraud. Unfortunately, substantial conflict prevails among the courts concerning what is and what is not an actual intent to defraud creditors. The courts need extrinsic evidence to support a fraudulent intent. Converting non-exempt into exempt is not enough.

In one particular case, the debtor paid off most of their mortgage with the money they had in the savings accounts. They did this even though one was unemployed and it was questionable whether they could live on the income of the other party. The court held that this was just a conversion with no intent to defraud.

It is difficult to reconcile the cases on this issue. Where one court will find no intent to defraud, another court will find the intent and will set aside the transfers. One can say that it depends upon the perspective of the judge or perhaps upon the conduct of the bankrupt or even on the performance of the attorney for the bankrupt.[14]

CHAPTER 7 LIQUIDATION

There are four principal chapters (7, 9, 11, and 13) under which a person or business may file a bankruptcy petition. Chapter 9 deals with municipalities and will not be discussed.

Most cases that are filed in court are usually filed under Chapter 7, known as straight bankruptcy. These are asset or no-asset cases. Chapter 7 may be used by individuals, corporations, partnerships, and associations. An individual may only file this type of bankruptcy every six years. The purpose of Chapter 7 is to collect all the assets of the debtor, sell these assets, and convert them into cash. The filing of a sworn petition in bankruptcy listing the assets and liabilities of the debtor commences the Chapter 7. After the trustee deducts the expenses of selling the assets, the fees due to the trustees and other professional administrative expenses, the remaining money is distributed to the creditors. Significant changes for consumers have been made by the new Act.

The original notice to creditors advising them of Chapter 7 bankruptcy sets forth a date for a first meeting of creditors. This meeting may be adjourned by the trustee upon application of the debtor or the creditors. In the event the debtor fails to appear at the meeting, the trustee may move the court to dismiss the bankruptcy.

At the first meeting of creditors, the debtor must bring all financial records and submit to an examination under oath by the trustee, or any other interested party, as to the particulars of the petition. The trustee, if

[14]*Carey v. Marine Midland Bus. Loans*, 938 F.2d 1073 (10th Cir. 1991).

notified of some problem, that is, the existence of a home that is not listed, will request the debtor to furnish documentation prior to the hearing. A creditor should immediately communicate with the trustee any suspicions concerning the activities of the debtor.

Once the trustee finishes the examination of the debtor, which may continue through several adjournments (continuations), any interested party may examine the debtor. During the examination, if the debtor is not responsive to a question, the trustee may order the debtor to produce additional documentation to answer the question at a subsequent hearing.

This examination, if properly conducted, can be the basis of an objection by the trustee or a creditor to the bankruptcy petition.

CHAPTER 11

Reorganization. A corporation or person can file a Chapter 11 bankruptcy, known as a reorganization. Reorganization can either be commenced voluntarily or involuntarily.[15] The debtor continues to operate the business as a "debtor in possession" as long as: (1) the debtor runs the business in good faith, and (2) the debtor accounts to the court for all business transactions. Failure to do either of the above may result in the court appointing a trustee to operate the business, or in the alternative, a possible dismissal of the action.

During the reorganization, the debtor may sell assets "in the ordinary course of business" and need not obtain approval from the court.[16] If assets are not sold in the ordinary course of business, or if a large portion of or substantially all the assets are sold, whether or not in the ordinary course of business, approval of the court must be obtained. The debtor must keep adequate financial records, which are to be submitted to the trustee on a monthly basis.

While it is axiomatic to remind a creditor to read a plan of reorganization, most creditors who receive a Chapter 11 plan of reorganization normally do not pay attention to the plan unless the obligation is significant. To motivate a creditor to read the plan, one has only to read two cases. The court held that the liability of another party for a debt is not affected by the discharge of the debtor, but at the same time a guarantor could be discharged as an integral part of any reorganization plan.[17] (*See* BAPCPA.)

Credit & Collection Tip: *It is possible for a plan of reorganization to contain a provision discharging a guarantor.*

---

[15] 11 U.S.C. § 301; 11 U.S.C. § 303.

[16] 11 U.S.C. § 363(c)(1).

[17] *Republic Supply Co. v. Shoaf*, 815 F.2d 1046 (5th Cir. 1987); *Michigan Nat'l Bank v. Laskowski*, 580 N.W.2d 8 (Mich. Ct. App. 1998).

Thus, if the bankrupt debtor failed in his plan of reorganization and ultimately had to be liquidated under Chapter 7, the creditor still would not be able to proceed against the guarantor if the bankrupt debtor was discharged under the plan of reorganization. Consult an attorney. (*See* BAPCPA.)

Plan of Payment. The debtor is required to offer a plan of payment to the creditors. This plan will apply separately to each classification of claimants (creditors), such as administrative (priority) claimants, secured creditors, or unsecured creditors.

Priority creditors are those who sell or service the bankrupt after the filing. When the debtor continues to do business after the bankruptcy filing and vendors continue to sell goods or render services to the bankrupt business, these creditors are treated as priority administrative claims. If no priority existed, no vendor would sell to a business operating under the bankruptcy act.

Secured creditors are usually financial institutions and banks which have mortgages on real estate and security agreements on automobiles, boats, machinery, and equipment or accounts receivable and inventory. Secured creditors may seek a removal of the stay of proceedings so that they can take possession of their collateral. (*See* "Automatic Stay," below.) Unsecured creditors are those claimants which became creditors prior to the filing of the petition but have no security, such as merchandise suppliers and those who render services such as programmers, consultants, or brokers.

Each class of creditor must vote on the approval of the payment plan to the extent that the plan affects those creditors. The plan will be approved by the court if each classification of creditor receives an amount similar or equal to what the creditor would have received in a Chapter 7 proceeding. Accordingly, the bankruptcy court is protecting each creditor to the extent of money that a creditor would receive if the assets of the bankrupt were liquidated and were sold at an auction proceeding. Thus, the total amount of the payment plan in reorganization must equal or exceed the amount that could be realized in liquidation (Chapter 7). The bankruptcy judge has the authority to override a negative vote of any particular class of creditors upon showing the totality of the plan is fair to the majority of creditors. This procedure is known as a "cramdown."

A careful examination of the plan should determine whether the debtor is able to perform the plan, and has enough income to meet the payments to the Trustee, to meet payments to be made outside the plan to the mortgagee or other secured creditors and to have enough money left to maintain the lifestyle of the bankrupt. If the creditor has reservations, he should consult with experienced counsel to objecting the plan.

Leases. Under the new law a 120-day period is allowed to the bankrupt to either reject or accept a lease, and the court is allowed to grant one 90-day extension of the 120 deadline to assume or reject the lease of business property, a total of 210 days. The landlord must consent to a further extension. This limited window enables the landlord to know when to begin to lease the property. If the bankrupt assumes the lease, the landlord will receive rent. As to those bankrupts who have retail outlets or numerous properties, this short time frame may cause serious problems in resolving the question of whether to assume or reject the lease.

A case in the bankruptcy court in South Carolina addressed the issue of the 120-day deadline.[18] Prior to the act, the 4th Circuit Court of Appeals was split on whether the court could grant an extension beyond the deadline to assume or reject the lease. The Fourth Circuit after passage of the new Act identified the deadline as a statutorily mandated deadline. The district court was in harmony with the bankruptcy court in denying the extension.

Small Business Provisions. A small business seeking reorganization is defined as having unsecured or secured debt that does not exceed $2 million dollars, and no creditors' committee is formed. The court is recommending an official form for a disclosure statement as well as a form for a plan of reorganization for small business debtors. The Act requires a small business to file periodic financial informations, reports on compliance with all applicable bankruptcy laws, and include timely file its tax returns and other government filings and reports.

The duties of a small business are extensive under the new Act:

A. Filing a balance sheet, statement of operations, cash flow, and federal income tax return with the petition.
B. All schedules and statements of financial affairs must be timely filed unless the court grants extensions.
C. Maintain insurance that is customary in the industry.
D. Complete access to the premises, books, and records by the trustee.

The small business must attend all the meetings scheduled by the court including scheduling conferences, meetings of creditors, as well as the initial interview. Separate requirements are added if the small business is a serial filer, A thorough review of the statute is mandatory.

Utility Payments. Under current law in a Chapter 11 proceeding, the court must assure payment to a utility. The court was allowed to review the fact that no security was pledged to the utility company prior to the bankruptcy petition, the past payment for utility services in a timely

---

[18] *In re Tubular Tech.*, LLC, 362 B.R. 243, *motion and stay denied by* 348 B.R. 699 (Bankr. D.S.C. 2006).

manner before the date of petition, or the availability of an administrative expense priority. Under the new Act, the debtor must furnish a cash deposit, a letter of credit, a bond to secure payment, a prepayment, or other form of security that the utility company approves. In short, any security other than the equivalent of cash or a bond does not have to be accepted by the utility company. Furthermore, this arrangement with the utility company must be consummated within 30 days after the filing of the petition.

Prepackaged Plans. Solicitations of acceptances for a prepackaged plan has received assistance from the new Act in that dissident creditors will be unable to stop the solicitation by permitting the solicitation to continue after filing of a petition as long as the solicitation is started before the filing and the solicitation complies with the securities law. Creditors wishing to stop a prepackaged plan will have to file their involuntary petition before the solicitation begins. Other pressure by suits or otherwise on the debtor to file a voluntary plan will not stop a prepackaged plan.

Conversion or Dismissal from Chapter 11. 11 U.S.C. 1112 covers this area and significant changes have been made. The section runs almost 2 pages and lays out the requirements to convert a Chapter 11 to a Chapter 7 or a Chapter 11 to a Chapter 13. Cause must be established to convert. The definition of what the word "cause" includes consist of 16 separate and distinct criteria. Rather than repeat, a copy of the section is in the Appendix to this chapter.

The Act also provides that conversion shall not be granted absent unusual circumstances specifically identified by the court that establishes:

1. If such relief is not in the best interest of the creditors and the estate;
2. If there is a reasonable likelihood that a plan will be confirmed within a time frame established;
3. The grounds for granting such relief include an act or admission of the debtor for which exists reasonable justification or that would be cured within a reasonable time.

The section leaves the judge to decide whether a conversion or dismissal is appropriate and the guidelines allow the judge much more discretion than was available before.

Investment Advisors—Conflict of Interest. The Act also deletes investment banker from those persons whose conflict of interest made them ineligible to advise the bankrupt debtor. Even if they previously underwrote the failed company's securities, banks may now compete with other firms as restructuring advisors.

Cash Collateral. Section 363(c)(2) states as follows:

A. The trustee may not use, sell, or lease cash collateral under paragraph 1 of this subsection unless:

(1) each entity that has an interest in such cash collateral consents

(2) the court, after notice and a hearing, authorizes such use, sale, or lease in accordance with the provisions of this section.

The definition of "cash collateral" is that which is readily converted into cash, such as inventory and accounts receivable. Inventory is sold and the bankrupt has obtained cash, or accounts receivable have been collected and converted into cash. The court takes the position that before the bankrupt can utilize this cash in a Chapter 11 proceeding to continue to operate the business, the bankrupt has two options: either obtain the consent of the secured creditor or obtain a hearing before the court on notice to the secured creditor. No other option exists. If the cash is utilized without obtaining consent and without a hearing, the bankrupt has violated Section 363(c)(2).

The bankrupt will contact the secured creditor or, in the alternative, will send out a notice for a hearing before the court. The creditor at that point can negotiate for adequate protection payments or some other adequate form of security so that the secured creditor will be protected. If the secured creditor and the debtor cannot reach an agreement, the court will design a solution usually not as favorable to the secured creditor as a negotiated agreement.

A secured creditor should take action where a creditor has a lien that can be converted into cash. The creditor should negotiate directly with the bankrupt to arrange for adequate security in the event the bankrupt intends to use the cash to operate the business. On the other hand, the secured creditor may take the position that the Chapter 11 will not succeed and on proper grounds may oppose any use of the cash collateral.[19]

What occasionally happens is that the bankrupt utilizes the cash collateral without consent of the secured creditor or without serving a notice of a hearing. Several cases have addressed this issue and all of them seem to agree that a remedy should be afforded to the creditor. They do not agree on the type of remedy, since the statute is silent as to an available remedy where the bankrupt fails to comply with Section 363(c)(2).

In the event the cash collateral is used without the consent of the secured creditor or without a hearing, the court will craft some type of remedy such as a replacement lien or a payment plan or hold an officer of the debtor, or perhaps the trustee, liable. One court did not agree with holding the trustee liable, but the court acknowledged that where the debtor misused the cash collateral, a fair and just remedy must be available

[19] *Harvis Trien & Beck, P.C. v. Federal Home Loan Mortg. Corp.*, 153 F.3d 61 (2d Cir. 1998).

to the creditor. The courts do not imply or infer consent of the creditor—the consent must be in writing.

At this point of the bankruptcy proceeding, whatever remedy is developed by the court will not be adequate to satisfy the secured party. It is recommended that the secured party act quickly when cash collateral is involved.[20]

> ***Credit & Collection Tip:*** *If the secured party is of the opinion that the cash collateral will not be used in the business, the secured party should take some affirmative action to bring this fact to the attention of the court and seek protection immediately. Waiting for a bankrupt to act may result in serious harm. In addition, the secured party will be faced with Section 552(a), which denies a security interest in after-acquired inventory.*

CRITICAL VENDORS. In Chapter 11 reorganizations, the prime purpose is not only to satisfy the creditors with a reasonable distribution, but to continue the operation of the business and come out of the bankruptcy as an operating business.

The doctrine of necessity involves the payment of pre-petition debts to vendors who are critical to the operation and to the continuation of the operation of the business and to the debtor's survival. The grounds to pay a pre-petition creditor is usually based on the critical needs of the debtor, either because the particular vendor is the only source of the particular product that is essential to the debtor's business or that the vendor provides essential goods and services to the debtor which are necessary for the continuation of the business. Where the debtor is the sole customer of the vendor, the debtor may offer the fact that the vendor will be unable to continue in business unless payment is received.[21]

Critical vendors include those vendors that are necessary not only for the continuation of the business, but also for certain services which are essential to the operation of the business. These essential services include, for example, payment on insurance coverage, payments on leases or liens on personal property, such as automobiles, copy machines, computer equipment, which are probably just as essential to the operation of the business as a delivery of goods, or merchandise by the business itself.

The availability of other vendors who could provide the same product is a consideration in approving a critical vendor. When the critical vendor motion is made by the debtor, creditors should be careful to be certain that the vendor is named in the motion. A motion that may deal with a group of creditors without naming them may present problems at a later date. The debtor on the other hand will probably request authorization to make payments, but not a direction to continue payments, so that at a future date the debtor may be in a position to terminate his relationship with the vendor.

---

[20] *Cargocaire Eng'g Corp., v. Dwyer (In re Gemel Int'l)*, 190 B.R. 4 (Bankr. D. Mass. 1995); *Freightliner Market Dev. Corp. v. Silver Wheel Freightlines, Inc.*, 823 F.2d 362 (9th Cir. 1987).

[21] Section 105(a).

The creditor should consider that if there is a conversion to a Chapter 7, the issue of preferences may arise.

While the doctrine of necessity has become somewhat standardized and cash collateral motions as well as motions to pay critical vendors have been routinely granted in the bankruptcy courts, a recent decision in the Seventh Circuit has thrown a cloud over whether or not payments to critical vendors is or is not allowed under Section 105(a). The court first addressed Section 105(a) which states as follows:

> The court may issue any order, process or judgment that is necessary or appropriate to carry out the provisions of this title. No provision of this title providing for the raising of an issue by a party in interest shall be construed to preclude the court from, sua sponte taking any action or making any determination necessary or appropriate to enforce or implement court orders or rules, or to prevent an abuse of process.

K-Mart relied on the doctrine of necessity when electing to pay their critical vendors. This doctrine of necessity was developed in railroad reorganizations as justification for payment of pre-petition debts paid under duress to secure continued supplies or services essential to the operation of a railroad. As a result, the doctrine of necessity has been applied to the payment of pre-petition creditors' claims in Chapter 11 proceedings. No statutory authority exists for said concept. Where many of the district courts do favor payment to critical vendors, several circuit courts have held the opposite including the Fourth, Fifth, and Ninth Circuits. The Seventh Circuit court chose to agree with these circuits and held that the bankruptcy courts do not have either statutory or equitable power to authorize pre-plan payment of pre-petition unsecured claims.

Most of the cases addressing or applying the doctrine of necessity dealt with confirming bankruptcy plans of reorganization. In the instant K-Mart plan, the plan of reorganization has not yet been confirmed. The court suggested that the monies may be returned. K-Mart argued that undoing the bankruptcy orders would paralyze K-Mart by forcing it to undergo the huge task of immediately commencing thousands of law suits to collect millions of dollars from thousands of vendors.[22]

Single Asset Real Estate (SARE). Single Asset Real Estate (SARE) is defined in the bankruptcy law as:

1. Property constituting a single project;
2. As a project other than residential real property with fewer than four residential units;

---

[22]*Chiasson v. J. Louis Matherne & Assoc.*, 4 F.3d 1329 (5th Cir. 1993); *Official Comm. of Equity Sec. Holders v. Mabel*, 832 F.2d 299 (4th Cir. 1987); *In re B&W Enters., Inc.*, 713 F.2d 534 (9th Cir. 1983); *Capital Factors, Inc. v. K-Mart Corp.*, 285 F. Supp. 2d 200 (N.D. Ill. 2003).

3. Property which generates substantially all the gross income of a debtor;
4. Property not owned by a family farmer;
5. Property on which no substantial business is being conducted by a debtor other than the business of operating the real property and the activities incidental thereto.

Prior to the new bankruptcy law the requirement that the debtor have aggregate non-contingent liquidated secured debt in an amount of no more than $4 million has been eliminated. If the debtor is generating other income from the operation of the real property other than rent, the property will not be covered by the statute. Case law has held that debtors who are operating several properties may still qualify as a SARE since the court may decide that the properties were a single project.

The new Act also clarifies the fact that the rent or other income generated before, on or after the date of the commencement of the case by and from a project may be used to pay to the creditors in the sole discretion of the debtor, notwithstanding Section 363 (c)(2). The SARE debtor may now prevent a foreclosure providing payments are made equal to the applicable non-default contract rate of interest on the value of the creditor's interest in the project. *The elimination of the $4 million cap now brings under the umbrella of the statute properties in which the debt may exceed or be substantially more than $4 million, and large entities will be subject to this time frame spelled out in the statutory scheme.* The plan of reorganization must be filed within 90 days. While the court might extend this period of time, the opportunity for a secured creditor to object to any further extension will afford them a better bargaining position.[23]

Substantive Consolidation. The doctrine of substantive consolidation to some degree is similar to a de facto merger except that the doctrine is generally applied in the bankruptcy environment of a Chapter 11. It has been said that substantive consolidation "merges the assets and liability of the debtor's entities into a unitary debtor's estate to which all holders are allowed to assert claims." A creditor treats substantive consolidation as a device to enhance its position by corralling unencumbered assets of other related entities.[24]

Section 11-23(a)(5)(C) is the basis for a substantive consolidation in that it refers to a merger or consolidation of the debtor with one or more persons.

Developed during the 1940s, the concept of substantive consolidation is where a trustee was able to consolidate the assets of a bankrupt

---

[23] *In re McGreals*, 201 B.R. 736 (Bankr. E.D. Pa. 1996).

[24] *In re Stone & Webster*, 286 B.R. 532 (Bankr. D. Del. 2002); Theory and Practice, a Guide to Reorganization, Paragraph 24.01 (4th ed. 1994).

individual debtor with a corporation to whom he had fraudulently transferred substantial assets, notwithstanding the fact that corporation had creditors who were harmed by this "pooling of the assets." The doctrine reappeared sometime in the 80s and 90s when the courts developed the concept that the benefits of consolidation might exceed the harm to creditors of the companies being consolidated.[25]

From fraudulent conveyances between individual and corporations to the use of the alter ego concept, the courts appear to examine whether the corporation was really acting as a single operation rather than being separate entities. The two corporations were so entangled and entwined that the only conclusion is that they are really one and the same. These conclusions have the elements of a de facto merger between the corporations.

In a Chapter 11 proceeding, the merging of two corporations in bankruptcy will seriously affect the creditors of the corporation that was not in bankruptcy and favor the creditors in bankruptcy. If the creditors who are not in bankruptcy were not a party to this so called substantive consolidation, the issue is that the creditors of the non-bankrupt corporation should not be sacrificed for the benefit of the creditors of the bankrupt corporation. This concept may receive future development and hopefully the courts will treat these situations on a case-by-case basis so that no harm will come to the innocent creditor unless the corporation was aiding and assisting the bankrupt to evade or defraud the creditors of the bankrupt.

Retiree Benefits. The new Act also prohibits debtors in Chapter 11 from modifying retiree benefits and health plans that are post retirement without complying with a lengthy negotiation process such as a corporation might do when dealing with a union under a collective bargaining agreement. The key ingredient is that the debtor must convince the court that the modifications sought are necessary to permit the reorganization to be successful (Section 1114).

Key Employee Retention Programs—KERP. The new Act does not permit the payment to any "insider" as defined in Section 101(31) to induce the insider to remain employed by the debtor unless the individual not only is essential to the retention of business, but also has an offer from another business at the same or greater rate of compensation (Section 503). The compensation offered may not exceed *ten times the mean of payments* made to non-insiders (employees), and if no such payments were made, compensation cannot exceed 25 percent of any transfer made to the insider in the prior year. In short, the amount cannot exceed ten times the bonus or cannot exceed ten times what the employees receive in bonuses or compensation (the multiple of ten also applies to severance pay). The purpose of the amendment is to regulate or prohibit excessive bonuses and

[25] *In re Giller*, 962 F.2d 796 (8th Cir. 1992).

severance packages to executives, but the net effect is that executives will find a competing job offer at the same or higher salary. The logical conclusion is that if higher pay is offered at a solvent firm, the insider or officer may or should accept that job.

This new language does not mention incentive based compensation. The issue arose as to whether incentive plans would continue to be evaluated under the business judgment rule. In a recent hearing in the District of Delaware, Chief U.S. Bankruptcy Court Judge Mary F. Walrath considered a proposal by the bankrupt that would pay two members of management hired before the date of the bankruptcy petition under terms that paid incentive pay based on a percentage of the sales generated by each party.[26] The bankrupt already received an offer for all the assets and the purpose of the incentive pay was to obtain a price greater than the bid already delivered.

The court took the position the limitations were catchall provisions for all transfers made outside the ordinary course of business. If this was a sale in the ordinary course of business, the court would accept the agreement. If the agreement is other than a retention or severance plan, the business judgment standard will apply in the same manner as in the past subject to the new restrictions that set forth in the statute.

In another case four incentive plans covering different levels of management were based on triggering events involving performance metrics, including the adjusted enterprise value and the successful confirmation of a plan of reorganization.

363 Sale. Prior to this decision, in *Channel Outdoor Inc. v. Knupfer*, rather than have a foreclosure, lenders often opted for a 363 sale for the purpose of disposing of the property free and clear of all liens.

11 U.S.C. § 363 provides the certainty of the sale. The section prescribed the finality, because an appeal could not be made unless the sale or lease were stayed by the court pending the appeal.

The lender contends that Section 363 deprives the court of the ability to affect the sale. The debtor did not obtain a stay pending appeal and the bankruptcy court made findings that the lender acted in good faith. These facts reinforce the court's decision not to tamper with the transfer, but the sale involved lien stripping. An arm's-length buyer did not purchase at the sale because a credit bid by a secured party was made at the sale.

From that point forward the court embarked on an "in depth" analysis of Section 363. Two major issues confronted the court. One is that the senior secured party was stripping the lien of the junior creditor and the second was that a credit bid was made by the senior secured party rather than by an arm's-length purchaser.

The court finally held that the 363(m) was moot as to the appeal of the validity of the sale, but was not equitably moot with respect to the lien

---

[26]*In re Nobex Corp.*, 2006 Bankr. LEXIS 417 (Bankr. D. Del. Jan. 19, 2006).

stripping. The appellate court reversed that part of the bankruptcy court's order that the sale was free and clear of the junior lien under Section 363(f)(5). The case was remanded for further proceedings to permit the parties to identify a qualifying proceeding under non-bankruptcy law (if one exists) that would enable them to strip the junior lienor's lien and cause the sale of the property to be free and clear under Section 363(f)(5).[27]

CHAPTER 13

Several changes will apply to a Chapter 13 proceeding including some changes in the strip down of purchase money security interest and the valuation of certain claims as well as the payments made before and after a confirmation. The new Act revises the length of the plan which must be a minimum of five years if payment in full is not made. Chapter 13 plans which pay 100 percent of unsecured claims may be shorter than the five-year period. The filing requirements and the timing of the confirmation hearing are also revised.

The type of debts that cannot be discharged in Chapter 13 include fraud and fraudulent statements, unscheduled debts, domestic support, student loans, drunk driving accidents, criminal fines, and fines for willful and malicious injuries.

CRAMDOWN PROVISIONS

The cram down was created to enable debtors to retain property while only paying the present value of the collateral. If the loan was for the sum of $10,000, but the car was only worth $5,000, the court would cramdown the $5,000 amount and the debtor would only have to pay the sum of $5,000 in a Chapter 13 proceeding. The same thing would apply to a mortgage for $200,000 where the property was only worth $150,000. The debtor would only be required to make payments on the $150,000. The exception to the rule in the new statute prohibits a cramdown if certain criteria are met.

A. The debt must be a purchase money security interest. The debt must be incurred within a 910-day period preceding the date of the filing;
B. The collateral must consist of a motor vehicle or anything else of value;
C. The debt must be incurred during the one-year period preceding that filing; and
D. The debt must be acquired for the personal use of the debtor.

---

[27] *In re PW*, LLC, 391 B.R. 25 (B.A.P. 9th Cir. 2008).

Debtor attorneys may allege that the car is for a business use or that someone else drove the car. A business use must appear as a deduction on the tax return. Variations in measurement might affect the 910-day period. The statute is drafted in a fairly black and white manner and the debtor's attorney may have a difficult time avoiding the consequences of the wording.

Automobiles which were purchased within two and a half years of filing a petition are immune from cramdown, and other collateral of value purchased within one year of filing a petition are also immune from the cramdown.

Those who are presently financing their car will be unable to strip down the amount of their payments to equal the present value of the car at the time of the filing of the bankruptcy petition if the above criteria are met, but will be required to make the payments based upon the original purchase price less any payments already made. In the past, if the car was purchased for $15,000, and $3,000 was paid, leaving a balance of $12,000, but the car was only valued at $8,000, the debtor would only have to pay $8,000. Under the new law, the debtor would have to pay $12,000.

> ***Credit & Collection Tip:*** *If a creditor does not object to a plan, the creditor is deemed to have accepted the plan. Sometimes the debtor offers a cramdown in the plan even though the debtor may not be entitled to the cramdown. The trustee should not accept the plan, but sometimes a trustee does not object. Creditors must read the plan to avoid surprises.*

FORMULA INTEREST IN CRAMDOWN. A total value of future payments to be made as of the effective date of a Chapter 13 plan to discharge a secured loan must not be less than the allowed amount of the secured claim. In the *Rash* decision referred to above, the Supreme Court decided that the replacement value is the correct value to use for the collateral in a secured claim and addressed the issue of what rate of interest must be paid on a secured claim during which the debtor would be making payments under a payment plan in a Chapter 13. The court commented in a footnote that a creditor's secured interest should be valued from the debtor's, rather than the creditor's perspective.[28]

Under a Chapter 13, a debtor's proposed debt adjustment plan must provide each allowed secured creditor both a lien securing the claim and a promise of future disbursements, the total value of which as of the plan date is not less than the claim's allowed amount. When such a plan provides for installment payments, the installment must be calibrated to insure that the creditor receives payments whose total present value equals or exceeds that of the allowed claim.

---

[28]*Associates Commercial v. Rash*, 520 U.S. 953 (1997).

In the instant case, the secured claim had a value of $4,000 and the petitioner proposed the debtor adjustment plan would pay an annual interest rate of 9.5 percent on the respondent's secured claim. This prime plus or formula rate was reached by augmenting the national prime rate of 8 percent to account for the nonpayment risk posed by a borrower in petitioner's financial position. The bankruptcy court overruled respondent's objection that it was entitled to a contract interest rate of 21 percent.

Thereafter, the district court reversed and stated that the creditor was entitled to the 21 percent interest. The basis of the 21 percent interest rate was that if the creditor had foreclosed and obtained $4,000 in proceeds, they would be entitled to the amount of interest they would have received if they had invested that $4,000 in a similar risk to a similar debtor. The creditor stated that they would have charged 21 percent interest on this sub-prime loan extended to the debtor.

The Circuit Court of Appeals said the creditor should be entitled to the interest rate on a new loan, and the interest rate should be based on the rate that the creditor would charge to a debtor who is similarly situated, although not necessarily in bankruptcy. Under this guideline, the 21 percent interest rate would not apply. One of the judges in the Seventh Circuit offered a fourth theory. The court should arbitrarily determine what interest rate the creditor would be entitled to replace the $4,000 it would not receive on the foreclosure.

The Supreme Court adopted the formula approach as the proper solution to this problem. Because bankrupt debtors typically pose a greater risk of nonpayment than solvent commercial borrowers, the approach requires a bankruptcy court to adjust the prime rate accordingly. The size of the risk adjustment depends on such factors as the circumstances of the estate, the nature of the security, and the duration and feasibility of the reorganization plan. The court must therefore hold a hearing at which the debtor and any creditors may present evidence about the appropriate risk adjustment. Starting with a concededly low estimate and adjusting upward places the evidentiary burden squarely on the creditors who are likely to have access to any information absent from the debtor's filing. The court stated that, unlike the coerced loan, the formula approach entails a straightforward, familiar, and objective inquiry and minimizes the need for potentially costly additional evidentiary proceedings. The resulting "prime plus" rate of interest depends only on the state of financial markets, the circumstances of the bankruptcy estate, and the characteristics of the loan, not on the creditor's circumstances or its prior interactions with the debtor. The court stated that the prime plus or formula rate best comports with the purposes of the Bankruptcy Code.[29]

---

[29]*Till v. SCS Credit Corp.*, 541 U.S. 465 (2004); *In re Prussia Assocs.*, 322 B.R. 572 (Bankr. E.D. Pa. 2005); *Bank of Montreal v. Official Committee of Unsecured Creditors*, 420 F.3d 559 (6th Cir. 2005).

REAFFIRMATION

The requirements for reaffirmation of a debt are substantially the same as the amendments passed several years ago. The debtor must disclose the income and actual current monthly expenses as well as the amount available to pay the debt before the reaffirmation is approved. The creditors are now allowed to receive payments prior to the filing of a reaffirmation agreement and under agreements which the creditor believes are in good faith.

Contact After Bankruptcy. A case from the Appellate Panel in the Ninth Circuit addressed the issue of contacting a debtor after a discharge in bankruptcy where the debtor retained the collateral but did not reaffirm the debt. The creditor made no threats other than to assert its right to repossess the vehicle if payments were not timely made. The creditor never threatened to sue the debtor personally. The creditor continued calling, notwithstanding the debtor's demand that the creditor stop calling her. The creditor maintained that as long as the debtor had its car, the creditor had the right to call her regarding her voluntary payments if she is past due. (*See* BAPCPA.)

The court stated clearly that "a phone call is not a per se violation" under Section 524(a)(2). Under this discharge injunction an *unsecured* creditor has no right to any of the debtor's property post-discharge to satisfy a discharged debt. A discharge extinguishes only the personal liability of the debtor. A secured creditor's rights to proceed against the collateral survives the bankruptcy.

Where the bankrupt neither surrenders the collateral at the time of bankruptcy nor redeems the collateral or reaffirms the debt and the bankrupt retains the collateral and makes the monthly payments (known as a "ride through"), this arrangement creates a new agreement between the debtor and the creditor. The debtor is not personally liable on any deficiency that may arise because the underlying debt creating the liability has been discharged. The creditor's sole recourse is to repossess or foreclose on the property.

Requests for payment are not barred, absent coercion or harassment by the creditor. Either written or oral communications with the debtor are allowed, providing no threat to sue the debtor is made or claim that the debtor is personally liable. Contact is considered unavoidable between them and phone calls to collect payments in a "ride through" jurisdiction are not per se improper collection activities.[30]

Accordingly the Ninth Circuit Court has held that a post-petition agreement to repay a discharged debt is not a valid reaffirmation

[30]*Garske v. Arcadia Fin., Ltd.*, 287 B.R. 537 (B.A.P. 9th Cir. 2002); *Ramirez v. GMC*, 280 B.R. 252 (Bankr. C.D. Cal. 2002); *Henry v. Assocs. Home Equity Servs.*, 266 B.R. 457 (Bankr. C.D. Cal. 2001).

agreement under Section 524(c) if the consideration offered by the debtor is the repayment of the discharged debt.[31] Since the consideration for the release was repayment of the discharged debt, the agreement amounted to an attempted reaffirmation. If it is a reaffirmation, it must be completed prior to the discharge in bankruptcy.

Secured and Unsecured Linkage. The bankrupt offered to reaffirm the mortgage on their residence. The creditor had an unsecured loan and insisted that the bankrupt reaffirm the unsecured loan as well as the secured loan. The attorney for the bankrupt refused to support the reaffirmation agreement.[32]

The First Circuit Court of Appeals decided that the reaffirmation of a secured debt conditioned on the reaffirmation of an unsecured debt is not a per se violation of the automatic stay. Linking the two debts together does not force a debtor to reaffirm unsecured obligations. Reaffirmation agreements are agreements on consent. The debtor does not have to reaffirm either the secured debt or the unsecured debt. If the debtor wishes to reaffirm the debt on his home, the debtor has to negotiate with the mortgagee. If part of the negotiation is that the mortgagee wants the unsecured debt reaffirmed, the debtor's only option is to come to terms with the mortgagee. This reasoning may not be followed in other circuits.[33]

While it is perfectly acceptable for a secured creditor to enter into an agreement to reaffirm a secured claim, it is unacceptable for the creditor to predicate the entering of the reaffirmation on the secured claim as a condition to collect a separate unsecured claim. The court held that said action was a violation of the automatic stay.[34]

Letter to the Debtor. An attorney for a debtor argued strenuously that mailing a copy of a letter seeking reaffirmation to a debtor who is represented by an attorney in a bankruptcy proceeding is prohibited. The court relied on Section 524(c)(3)(A), which requires an attorney to declare in an affidavit that the debtor's consent to a reaffirmation agreement was "fully informed and voluntary" and in this case the Illinois Rule of Professional Conduct requires an attorney to keep the client reasonably informed about the status of the matter. The court felt that sending a copy of a letter directly to the debtor was not improper as long as it was not inherently coercive or threatening. The court left open the possibility that if the party writing the letter was a debt collector, there might be a violation of

[31] *In re Bennett*, 298 F.3d 1059 (9th Cir. 2002). *See Hibernia Nat'l Bank v. Taylor*, 901 So. 2d 574 (La. App. 2005).

[32] *In re Jacobs*, 321 B.R. 451 (Bankr. N.D. Ohio 2004).

[33] *In re Stephan and Lynn M. Jamo*, No. 01-9010 (1st Cir. Mar. 26, 2002); *Green v. National Cash Register*, 15 B.R. 75 (Bankr. S.D. Ohio 1981).

[34] *In re Casenova*, 306 B.R. 367 (Bankr. M.D. Fla. 2004); *In re Jacobs*, 321 B.R. 451 (Bankr. N.D. Ohio 2004); *Jamo v. Katahdin Fed. Credit Union*, 253 B.R. 115 (Bankr. D. Me. 2000).

the Fair Debt Collection Practices Act since the debt collector may not communicate with the consumer without the consumer's permission if the debt collector knows the consumer is represented by an attorney with respect to such debt and has knowledge of, or can readily ascertain such an attorney's name and address. Sears was not a debt collector in the sense that they were collecting debts of others. The letter was held not to violate the automatic stay provisions nor does the Bankruptcy Code require as a matter of law that the creditor refrain from copying the debtor on correspondence to the debtor's attorney.[35]

A bankruptcy court held that Ohio, which prohibits *direct* solicitation in an attempt to collect debts of debtors known to be represented by attorneys, does prevent creditors from seeking reaffirmation agreements under the bankruptcy code by communicating directly with the debtor. The determination was that seeking a reaffirmation agreement was the equivalent of an attempt to collect the debt and thus did fall within the Ohio code. Whether this preemption would be recognized by the federal courts has not been tested, *but it points out a sound reason why a review of the particular state law must be made in all instances.*[36]

A letter offering the debtor an opportunity to reaffirm a debt has been accepted by the courts, as long as the letter is non-threatening and does not appear to coerce the debtor into executing the reaffirmation agreement.[37]

The concept that an offer of reaffirmation violates the automatic stay has been generally rejected by the courts. If this proposition was considered, the whole concept of offering debtors reaffirmation agreements would be undermined; for the opportunity to communicate with the debtor would be terminated. If such was the case, no purpose would exist for Congress to enact the particular sections of the bankruptcy law which enable debtors to reaffirm their debt.

In a recent amendment to the Bankruptcy Code, the procedure is as follows:

1. Offers the debtor an opportunity to rescind the reaffirmation agreement.
2. Requires an attorney's affidavit that the debtor is fully informed about all rights concerning the reaffirmation agreement.
3. The debtor must be told that there is no obligation to reaffirm.
4. The debtor must execute the reaffirmation voluntarily.
5. The agreement must not impose upon the debtor an undue burden or hardship. In general, the attorneys will not allow their clients to reaffirm a debt unless they have a job or some other obvious source of income which will enable the debtor to make the required payments.

---

[35]*In re Duke*, 7 F.3d 43 (7th Cir. 1996).

[36]*Greenwood Trust v. Smith*, 212 B.R. 599 (B.A.P. 8th Cir. 1997); *In re Jacobs*, 321 B.R. 451 (Bankr. N.D. Ohio 2004).

[37]*In re Jacobs*, 321 B.R. 451 (Bankr. N.D. Ohio 2004); *In re Hazzard*, No. 94 B 18893, 1995 WL 110588 (Bankr. N.D. Ill. Feb. 10, 1995); *In re Jefferson*, 144 B.R. 620 (Bankr. D.R.I. 1992).

All of these protections being afforded to the debtor would be useless if at the same time the courts interfered with the communication between the creditor and the debtor. The purpose is to require creditors to clearly disclose that the debtor has the option to exercise the right to reaffirm voluntarily and that no language is contained in the letter which might coerce the debtor or mislead the debtor into entering the reaffirmation agreement.

CHAPTER 13

Wage Earner. Any individual who is a non-corporate business, with regular income whose unsecured debt does not exceed $250,000, and secured debt does not exceed $350,000, may use Chapter 13 to file a voluntary bankruptcy petition. This section covers sole proprietors as well as partnerships, but is known as a "wage earner" bankruptcy.

Filing the Petition. Filing can be either individual or joint with a spouse.[38] The filing of a Chapter 13 petition operates as a stay of action not only against the debtor who files the petition but also against co-debtors or guarantors on consumer loans during the pendency of the bankruptcy so long as the debt is to be paid in full.[39] Nevertheless, a guarantor of a commercial or business debt remains liable for the debt during payment in a Chapter 13 or a Chapter 11. A trustee is appointed to collect the funds from the debtor and to file a plan for repayment of the debts within 15 days after the filing of the petition or such extension as the court allows. Only the Chapter 13 debtor, not the creditors, has a right to file this plan. The plan must provide for all future earnings to be subject to the supervision and control of the trustee and must provide for full payment of all secured claims.

Creditors. Unsecured creditors are only required to be paid an amount equal to or exceeding the amount the creditor would have received if a Chapter 7 bankruptcy had been filed. Upon completion of payments, where less than the full amount of debts is paid, the debtor receives a discharge as to the balance not paid under the plan. If the debtor fails to make the payments, the trustee or the creditors may apply to court for an order to convert the bankruptcy to a Chapter 7 or Chapter 11.

A Chapter 13 plan is voluntary, for a debtor cannot be forced into a repayment plan by creditors. In Chapter 13, the real and personal property of the bankrupt is protected from being sold for the benefit of the creditors by the debtor paying the debts or a portion of them over a period of time.

---

[38] 11 U.S.C. § 302(a).
[39] 11 U.S.C. § 1301.

The secured creditor must accept the plan, but retains a lien subject to the automatic stay which prevents the secured creditor from reclaiming or selling the property. The secured creditor recovers the full value of the claim by virtue of the plan. The debtor may surrender the property securing the debt to the secured creditor. The secured creditor then may sell the security after receiving relief from the automatic stay and become an unsecured creditor as to any balance due.

PAYMENT. Payment under the plan must begin within 30 days after the initial filing unless that time is extended by the court. To share in any distribution, the creditor, whether secured or unsecured, must file a proof of claim before the specified deadline which is set forth in the original notice of bankruptcy.

The Bankruptcy Reform Act now allows the debtor to protect the personal residence by filing a Chapter 13 up until an actual foreclosure sale (even though a judgment of foreclosure was already entered).

Section 1322(b)(2) of the Bankruptcy Code states as follows:

> the plan (debtor's plan of payment in Chapter 13) may modify the rights of holders of secured claims, other than a claim secured by a security interest in real property that is the debtor's principal residence or of holders of unsecured claims or leave unaffected the rights of holders of any class of claims.

OMITTED CREDITORS. Creditors who file late or tardy claims in Chapter 7 cases are subject to the language set forth in Sections 501, 507, and 726 of the Bankruptcy Code which specify the order of payment and the status of late or tardy claim. In Chapter 11 cases, the bar-dates are established by order of the court rather than by any language in the Bankruptcy Code.

The courts are in agreement that extending a bar-date in a Chapter 13 case is not authorized by the code or the rules. The courts even have been precluded from utilizing equitable reasons to extend the dates beyond those permitted by the rule. The lack of code provisions or rules applicable to Chapter 13 cases has resulted in a split of authority as to the proper means to remedy the problem of an omitted Chapter 13 creditor. The majority hold that the debtor, no matter how innocent, must be denied a discharge of the omitted creditor's indebtedness. A few cases emphasize the due process ramifications of the debtor's omissions of a creditor, and hold that the proper solution, irrespective of the apparent immutability of the bar-date, is to extend the bar-date for the omitted creditor. Nevertheless, most of the courts agree that extending the bar date in a Chapter 13 is not authorized by the code or the rules. A resolution which awards a windfall to the omitted creditor, to the possible detriment of not only a debtor, but of other creditors, is not very satisfying.[40] (*See* BAPCPA.)

PREFERENCES

Protecting Against Preferences. If you are careful when dealing with a delinquent debtor, you may be able to avoid reading the rest of this subject. The simplest answer is to be paid when the goods are delivered. Unfortunately, the simplest answer is often not achieved.

If you do have outstanding invoices and the debtor pays you on a current invoice within the 30-day period that your invoice provides, the best answer is to apply it to the 30-day invoice and not to the oldest invoice. The customer should not be allowed to indicate to which invoice the payment should be applied. Changing the method of payment from a check to a certified check or cash or even a wire transfer might remove the ordinary course of business defense where the normal course of payment is a "garden variety" check. Letters of credit are helpful since the money is already set aside and allocated. The customer has already paid the bank.

Guarantees at the beginning of the transaction with the customer, or even if the guarantee is furnished along the way after the customer becomes delinquent, should be handled under the supervision of counsel so that the proper protection against preferences can be set forth in the guarantee.

While taking all of these precautions will not furnish assurance that a preference will not be asserted, it should help in the negotiations. If settlement cannot be achieved, the suggestions offered might be useful in the ensuing litigation.

Payment to Non-Insider. In 1994, Section 550(c) of the code modified this decision to the extent that a transfer to a non-insider that benefits an insider may not be recovered from the non-insider creditor. Unfortunately, many courts still allow the trustee to recover from the non-insider. The Act also restricts any transfers or the creation of any debt to an insider that is outside the normal course of business and not justified by the circumstance of the case, which includes any transfers to officers, managers, or consultants hired after the date of the commencement of the bankruptcy proceeding.

The Act now states clearly in Section 547(i) that if the trustee avoids a transfer made between 90 days and one year before the date of the filing of the petition by the debtor to an entity that is not an insider for the benefit of the creditor, such transfer shall be considered to be avoided only with

[40] *In re Morris and Johnnee Fugate*, 286 B.R. 778 (N.D. Cal. 2002); *In re Kristiniak*, 208 B.R. 132 (E.D. Pa. 1997); *In re Cole*, 146 B.R. 837 (D. Cal. 1992).

respect to the insider and not with respect to the creditor. In short, in normal circumstances where the payment was made to a bank, the trustee cannot recover the payment from the bank, but may recover the payment from the insider who was the principal (and guarantor) of the corporation.

Ordinary Course of Business. Prior to the Act, when a creditor was sued for a preference, the defense available was that payment was made within the ordinary course of business and in addition, was made in accordance with the custom in the industry. The first defense was usually readily available to the defendant creditor since officers or employees of the corporation could testify that in dealing with this customer, the customer normally made late payments and normally was delinquent in their account. To prove custom in the industry is somewhat more difficult since an expert may be needed and the defense is vulnerable to an attack that the dealings with the bankrupt were not customary. Under the new Act, the creditor has to prove that the debt was incurred in the ordinary course of business "*or*" in the alternative according to the custom in the industry. In most instances, the creditor will use "in the ordinary course of business" and will not venture into the caldron of "custom in the industry."[41]

This case addressed the issue favorably of whether industry standards could be used regardless of whether the transaction was in the ordinary course of business between the debtor and the creditor. If this is followed by other courts, the creditor will be able to select whichever criteria are more favorable.

Minimum Amount and Jurisdiction. The Act provides that a transfer may not be avoided as a preference if the aggregate value of the property is less than $5,000. Thus, all preference actions under the Act will start at $5,001. The attorney for the trustee may still send a demand letter for an amount under $5,000. The creditor should immediately consult with counsel.

An action by a trustee against a trade creditor for a sum less than $10,000 must be started in a district court where the trade creditor is located. The $10,000 threshold only applies to a trade debt of a non-insider for a non-consumer debt. The Act has also clarified the definition of transfer to mean the creation of a lien, or the retention of title as a security interest or the foreclosure of the debtor's equity of redemption.

With regard to consumers, a trustee must proceed in the district court in which the defendant resides if the claim is less than $15,000. The prior law set the limit at $5,000. A consumer now will be able to litigate such a claim in his own district rather than in a faraway court.

---

[41] *In re National Gas Distributors, LLC*, 346 B.R. 394 (Bankr. E.D.N.C. 2006).

Definition of Preference. In the past five years, a cottage industry of "preference attorneys" has been born. The preference claims of a Chapter 11 business debtor are offered to law firms on a bid basis. A contingency fee is charged depending upon the amount the law firm collects. The normal procedure is a shotgun approach where the law firm will mail form letters asserting a claim for a preference on a payment that was made during the 90-day period prior to filing. (*See* BAPCPA.)

Two rules should be observed when one of these letters is received:

A. *Never pay the amount requested upon receipt of the first letter.*
B. *Do not ignore or forget about the letter, thinking it must be a mistake and it will go away.*

If you pay the amount without investigating your liability, you are probably paying too much. If you ignore it or forget about it, several months later you will undoubtedly receive a summons and complaint from the trustee for the amount of the payment.

A preferential transfer under the Bankruptcy Code requires the following specified elements. If these elements are present when a transfer is made by the bankrupt to a creditor, the trustee will have the power to avoid the preference and require the creditor to reimburse the estate of the bankrupt the amount of the transfer to the creditor. The six elements are as follows:

1. A transfer of an interest in the debtor's of property,
2. For the benefit of the creditor,
3. On account of an antecedent debt,
4. Which transaction took place while the debtor was insolvent,
5. Within 90 days before the date of filing, and
6. Enabling the creditor to receive more than such creditor would have received in a Chapter 7 liquidation of the estate.

The elements described appear to be simple and straightforward and a businessman should be able to quickly determine whether the monies received from the bankrupt qualify for a preference. What appears to be is not necessarily what is. The interpretations of those statements and the exceptions which have been carved out by the courts for several different reasons treat what often appears to be a preference as not a preference.

The attorneys for the trustee or the trustee are willing to settle preferences. A creditor who pays the full amount of a preference without consulting with an attorney experienced in the field will certainly qualify for the expression "when you represent yourself, you have a fool for a client." The interpretation of the six elements together with the exceptions that have been shaped by the judicial system plus the general reluctance, because they are so busy, of the trustees to litigate preferences provide an opportunity to oppose, or at least to radically reduce, the preference. We will consider how the court has interpreted the above elements and will discuss some exceptions to the preferential transfers.

TRANSFER. A transfer must take place. A transfer is generally interpreted in broad terms and covers both a voluntary or involuntary transfer of property to a creditor. The granting of a mortgage, the execution and perfection of a security interest all would constitute transfers, but the transfer must be of the debtor's property. No preference takes place when the debtor pays a debt from funds that is not the property of the debtor, but the property of a third party. Funds in escrow or funds that have been deposited for a letter of credit are not property of the bankrupt.

DATE OF TRANSFER. As a general rule a transfer occurs on a date that the creditor receives the property. Where there is a lien involved, the transfer will take place when the real estate mortgage is recorded. In the event it is a security agreement, the transfer will take place on the date it is perfected.

The use of checks sometimes presents problems. The choice is between when the check is delivered, mailed, received, or when its clears. The courts are somewhat in conflict. The general resolution seems to be that the transfer takes place on the date that the bank actually pays the check by deducting the money from the debtor's account.

FOR THE BENEFIT OF THE CREDITOR. A transfer of property to someone who is not a creditor cannot constitute an avoidable preference. An example is a contemporaneous exchange of property for money. A transfer is not being made to a creditor, but to a vendor who is transferring property to the bankrupt. The creditors of the bankrupt's estate are receiving equivalent property for the transfer of the cash.

The courts define the term creditor in broad terms. Where a debtor transferred property to his wife who immediately mortgaged the property to a creditor, the mortgage was treated as being made directly from the debtor to the creditor. The court requires that the property received in a contemporaneous exchange be reasonably equivalent in value to the amount that was paid to the vendor. Some cases hold that the amount transferred does not necessarily have to be equal in value.

ANTECEDENT DEBT. Where new value is received in exchange for cash, no antecedent debt exists and thus the estate is not diminished because of the transaction. An installment loan is not considered a new debt when each installment becomes due, for the debt is deemed to have been incurred on the date of the original loan and periodic payments made within a 90-day preference period may be avoided as preferences.

The debtor must be insolvent at the time of the transfer. The requirement of insolvency is a second reason why the time of transfer is so important. Under the Bankruptcy Code a presumption of insolvency exists within 90 days of the filing of the petition to assist the trustee in achieving the purpose of treating all creditors equally. The debtor is presumed to have been insolvent on and during the 90 days immediately preceding the date of filing the petition. The obligation of the creditor is to offer some evidence to rebut this presumption of insolvency. Once there is evidence offered, the trustee must prove the insolvency of the bankrupt at the time of the transfer.

If it is a public company, the 10Q's and 8K's financials filed quarterly with the Securities and Exchange Commission as well as the interim changes of financial condition which are periodically filed by the public companies will reveal whether or not the debtor was or was not solvent at the time of the transfer. If the debtor is a private company, the production of financial statements, bank statements, monthly profit and loss statements will be helpful in determining the solvency of the debtor within 90 days of the filing of the petition.

The 90-day period applies to creditors and does not apply to insiders. With regard to controlling shareholders, directors, family or other insiders, the period of time is one year prior to the date of filing the bankruptcy instead of 90 days. An insider is defined as an officer, director, partner, person in control, or relatives of the aforesaid. It may also extend to those who control by virtue of a close relationship wherein significant influence can be exercised.

Diminution of an Estate. As a general rule the courts tend to look at whether property transferred to a debtor within the 90-day period is a preference by applying the "diminution" of an estate doctrine, that is, where the transfer diminishes the fund to which creditors of the same class may be entitled for payment of the monies owed to such creditors to such an extent that other creditors will not obtain as great a percentage as the preferred creditor, the transfer is avoidable.

The trustee must establish that the transfer to the creditor would have been more than the creditor would have received had the creditor filed a proof of claim in bankruptcy under liquidation pursuant to Chapter 7. When computing this amount that the creditor would have received, the court will treat the amount of the alleged preference as if it had not been transferred. If the creditor would have received the full amount of the debt in a bankruptcy proceeding, the transfer to the creditor could not be considered a preference. Where a creditor is fully secured by equipment, automobile, or otherwise and a payment is made to the secured creditor, this would not be considered a preference since the creditor will be able to satisfy the full debt from the security—assuming that the security is sufficient to satisfy the debt.

Ordinary Course of Business. "Ordinary course of business" exception is probably the one most used by creditors. It requires that payment of a debt be done in the ordinary course of business of the debtor and according to the custom in the industry. (*See* Appendices.) The new Act mitigates the standards that must be met and allows a defense of ordinary course of business or custom in the industry.

Payment must be made in the customary manner of conducting normal business. If the customer must pay bills on terms of 90 days, then the bill would not be considered an antecedent debt and the payment is not a preference if it was consistently paid within 90 days. If the contract is actually entered into for payment to be made within 30 days, and the parties continually ignore the 30-day period and begin to make payment after 60 days, these circumstances may or may not be a defense of the ordinary course of business since the parties were not complying with the original credit terms.

In addition, the creditor must offer evidence that the manner of payments is customary in the industry. While the "ordinary course of business" may be satisfied by using an employee of the creditor as a witness, the additional test may require a witness who has knowledge and experience in the industry, which means an expert or close to it. Fortunately, BAPCPA eliminates both tests and substituted the word "or" for "and" so *that the creditor has the option of using the "ordinary course of business" or the "custom in the industry."* The choice probably will be the "ordinary course of business."

Late payments between parties may be the custom and may be ordinary and consistent with prior practice. Nevertheless, the courts seem to examine whether the payments during the preference period fall within the normal range of lateness. The factors the courts consider are as follows:

1. The length of time the parties were engaged in the transactions at issue,
2. Whether the amount of form of tender differ from past practices,
3. Whether the debtor or creditor engage in any unusual collection or payment activity,
4. Whether the creditor took advantage of the debtor's deteriorating financial condition, and
5. Whether there a contract provision stating that no waiver occurs.

A payment history is a sufficient and guiding factor. Other factors may be considered according to their appropriate weight under the circumstances.[42] A recent case in the Eastern District of New York provides a good discussion of the "ordinary course of business."[43]

Earmarking Doctrine. The Earmarking Doctrine is applicable to situations where a creditor either pays monies to the bankrupt that is specifically earmarked to be paid to an antecedent creditor and are paid by the bankrupt to the old creditor or the new creditor pays the monies directly to the old creditor without any intervention by the bankrupt, but for the benefit of the bankrupt. This type of a situation does not result in any loss to the bankrupt's estate and the monies paid to the old creditor do not constitute a preference nor may the transfer be set aside as a preference.

The Earmarking Doctrine applies where the guarantor paid to the creditor the money owed by the debtor. The courts reject the claim that such a payment is an avoidable transfer. The rationale to justify this is that no preferential transfer had occurred, because the transfer consisted of new property, not the debtor's property and no diminution to the debtor's estate resulted because the transaction merely substitutes one creditor for another.

New Value. Section 547—subdivision c(3) states as follows:

> The trustee may not avoid under this section a transfer
>
> 3. that creates a security interest in property acquired by the debtor
>   - (A) to the extent such security interest secures new value that was
>   - (i) given at or after the signing of a security agreement that contains a description of such property as collateral;
>   - (ii) given by or on behalf of the secured party under such agreement;
>   - (iii) given to enable the debtor to acquire such property; and
>   - (iv) in fact used by the debtor to acquire such property; and
>   - (B) that is perfected on or before 20 days after the debtor receives possession of such property;

The new value defense was designed to apply to revolving credit arrangements and was intended to allow creditors to continue with the

---

[42] *Klevin v. Household Bank F.S.B.*, 334 F.3d 638 (7th Cir. 2003); *In re Grand Chevrolet, Inc.*, 257 F.3d 728 (9th Cir. 1994); *Laclede Steel Co. v. Concast Canada, Inc.*, 271 B.R. 127 (B.A.P. 8th Cir. 2002); *In re Global Tissue, LLC*, 302 B.R. 808 (D. Del. 2003); *In re Ameriserve Food Distribution Inc. et al.*, 41 Bankr. Ct. Dec. 208 (D. Del. 2003).

[43] *Gold Force Int'l Ltd. v. Official Comm. of Unsecured Creditors of Cyberrebate Inc.*, 2004 U.S. Dist. LEXIS 2089 (E.D.N.Y. Feb. 10, 2004).

revolving credit agreement in reliance on prior payments. Otherwise, anyone who extended revolving credit would be exposed to a preference action because of payments during the 90-day period. The creditor has to furnish new value after the alleged preferential transfer. The new value normally should be unsecured so that the estate of the bankrupt is not diminished. If the new value should be secured and the security agreement cannot be avoided, new value has not been given since the transfer has been totally secured.

The Third and the Seventh Circuits now require that new value must remain unpaid while the Fifth and Ninth Circuits have taken the opposite position. The other circuits have not addressed the issue, at least not at the Circuit Court of Appeals level.[44]

The contemporaneous exchange, where both the payment and the delivery of the goods were substantially contemporaneous, protects the creditor under the ordinary course of business defense. Contemporaneous exchange covers the creditor shipping the goods because the debtor agreed to make payment shortly thereafter. The "shortly thereafter" refers to the check in the mail or received within a few days after the shipment.

Secured Liens. Secured liens granted to creditors for new advances, extensions of credit or loans are not considered preferences. This exception is targeted at sellers of goods or banks that extend credit to purchase property that becomes security for the extension of credit.

Statutory liens such as those of garage keepers, mechanics, and landlords are liens created under state law to provide protection for certain types of creditors and may only be avoided in bankruptcy under unusual circumstances by the trustee. Normally, the liens cannot be attacked as a preference.

With regard to consumers, if the total value of the property involved in the transfer is less than $600, the trustee cannot avoid the transfer.

Section 546(b)(2) requires a lien preservation notice be filed that the holder of the mechanic's lien will perfect and enforce his lien against the real property which was improved. A preservation notice must be filed with the bankruptcy court and served on the trustee in bankruptcy in a Chapter 7 case. If it is a Chapter 11, service must be made upon the debtor in possession prior to the time of the state law deadline set for commencing an action to enforce the lien rights.

Section 546(b)(2) is as follows:

(2) If—

(a) a law described in Paragraph (1) requires seizure of such property or commencement of an action to accomplish such perfection, or

---

[44]*In re IRFM*, 65 F.3d 778 (9th Cir. 1995); *In re Toyota of Jefferson Inc.*, 14 F.3d 1088 (5th Cir. 1994); *In re New York Shoes Inc.*, 880 F.2d 679 (3d Cir. 1989); *Matter of Prescott*, 805 F.2d 719 (7th Cir. 1986).

maintenance or continuation of perfection of an interest in property; and

(b) such property has not been seized or such action has not been commenced before the date of the filing of the petition; such interest in such property shall be perfected, or perfection of such interest shall be maintained or continued, by giving notice within the time fixed by such law for such seizure or such commencement.

Strategy in Preference Litigation. When responding to a complaint, examine *all* the defenses to a preference including a contemporaneous exchange, subsequent new value, the earmarking doctrine, as well as the ordinary course of business. A careful examination of other preference defenses should also be reviewed.

When asserting an ordinary course of business defense, analyze the payment history over the past several years to establish what the elapsed time is between invoice date and check clearance date. The items needed are the invoice number, the date of the invoice, the date the check actually cleared, and the elapsed time between the date the check clears and the invoice date. A review of the elapsed time is made to determine whether other invoices had the same comparable elapsed time as the invoices and checks supporting the preferences the trustee is claiming. At this point, you should submit a settlement letter to the trustee detailing specifically your reasons for offering a settlement and why you believe that either a preference did not take place or why the settlement offer should be accepted by the trustee. The analysis of the elapsed time should be attached to the settlement letter.

With regard to ordinary course of business in the industry, an examination of industry standards should be made and the trustee should be made aware of the fact that you have testimony available from representatives of the defendant as well as independent expert testimony to prove industry standards. Do not overlook trade associations or firms that compete with the creditor. Trade associations may provide you with the expert testimony that you require. Credit personnel from firms in the same business as the creditor also may be of help. Always demand a jury. (*See* Appendix to this chapter.)

The solvency or insolvency of the debtor at the time of the preference should be investigated as well as the power of the party or the trustee to assert a claim for a preference which must be by order of the court. *Be certain you obtain a copy of the order.*

Try to determine whether the trustee is performing a "shotgun approach" (usually in large bankruptcies), where every payment is attacked that the bankrupt made during the 90-day period in the hope that a certain amount will settle. If a shotgun approach is being used and the attorney for the trustee has fifty or hundreds of preferences on the table, the attorney for the trustee is only planning on litigating a few of the cases and hopes that all the rest will settle for either greater or lesser amounts. Don't be too generous with your offers and don't be anxious. Be patient. Sometimes an effort will be made to resolve the preferences by arbitration with both parties bearing the costs. Such a tactic should be treated skeptically.

Insider Preferences. An "insider" is defined as a spouse, child, parent, relative, or partner of the debtor. Transfers to insiders up to a year prior to filing a petition may be set aside. The "insider preference" extends to insiders who guarantee corporate debts, and in anticipation of bankruptcy, cause the corporation to pay the corporate debt to the bank. The guarantor wants the corporation to pay the debt since the personal liability of the guarantor is being reduced with each payment to the bank. The insider's liability on the guarantee is reduced to the detriment of the other general creditors who have not received a personal guarantee. The trustee may proceed to recover the payments to the banks, who are usually the beneficiaries of such an arrangement. This right of recapture by the trustee was modified by the Bankruptcy Reform Act. Where the loan repayment to the bank is made by one other than an insider, the payments may not be subject to recapture. (*See* Appendices of new Act as to insiders.) (*See* BAPCPA.)

The above are the principal highlights of some of the defenses that may be asserted against a preference. Consultation with experienced counsel is recommended.

Assumption of Lease or Contract. What may properly be called another defense to a preference is the assumption of a lease or a contract where a payment to the creditor was made within the 90-day period. *The 7th Circuit has decided that Section 365 of the Bankruptcy Code requires that the trustee guarantee payment of all amounts owing to the non-debtor contracting party*. If there is an assumption, the trustee does not have the right to attack any prior payment since it requires payment of "all" monies due to the other party to the executory contract or to the landlord when the lease is assumed.[45]

Assumption of Leases—Contracts. When a party assumes a lease or an executory contract, this should be asserted as a defense against any preference payment made under that contract or under the lease. From a creditor's point of view, a defense should always be alleged and let the burden rest on the debtor or trustee to attack the defense to a preference.[46]

---

[45] *In re Superior Toy & Mfg. Co., Inc.*, 78 F 3d 1169 (7th Cir. 1996); *In re Dehon, Inc.*, 352 B.R. 546 (Bankr. D. Mass. 2006).

[46] *In re Philip Services*, 284 B.R. 541 (Bankr. D. Del. 2002).

State Preference Laws. California and several other states have laws which permit an assignee for the benefit of creditors to prosecute a claim for a preference. The Ninth Circuit ruled that the bankruptcy code preempts the exercise of state preference avoidance powers since they do not afford the protection that the bankruptcy court provides. In a bankruptcy court an appointed trustee has the power to avoid and recover a preference and the trustee is not selected by the debtor, as is the case under the states' statutes.[47]

Tips to the Creditor—Preference Claims. The following are some suggestions to the creditor when a letter is received from the bankrupt's attorney alleging a preference claim.

1. Do not disregard the demand letter. The claim will not go away despite the fact that you have received payment for services or goods and no complaint was ever made by the debtor.
2. The creditor should have their attorney acknowledge receipt of the claim and send a letter to the attorney requesting a copy of all the cancelled checks including front and back, wire transfers, etc. which are the basis of the claim. At the same time a request for a detailed explanation of the basis of the claim should be made. You may or may not receive a proper response to this question.
3. Conduct a thorough examination of your business dealings with regard to the following:
    a. A complete payment history of all payments received, dates of payments, all invoices sent and dates of invoices at least a year before the commencement of the 90-day preference period and during the preference period.
    b. Credit applications, any financial information furnished including profit and loss statements and balance sheets.
    c. All correspondence, notations of phone calls, e-mails sent and received.
4. Consult with counsel who will respond to the demand letter made by the debtor and request copies of all checks that are the basis of the preference claim including the front and back of the checks or proof of wire transfers or other payment instruments.
5. Upon receipt of same, make sure that all the alleged payments have been made.
6. Consult with counsel as to the expiration of the Statute of Limitations and the minimum amount that can be asserted as a claim.

---

[47] *Sherwood Partners, Inc. v. Lycos, Inc.*, 394 F.3d 1198 (9th Cir. 2005).

7. While a creditor may wish to negotiate a settlement without the benefit of counsel, your author recommends that you consult with your attorney and discuss the defenses available and allow your counsel to negotiate the settlement.
8. If you receive a summons of complaint, do not personally attempt to obtain an extension or to settle the case. Consult with counsel immediately.

CONSUMER BANKRUPTCY

The 2005 Act does not fundamentally change or modify the existing Bankruptcy Act as to consumers, but instead increases the procedures, requirements, counseling, and a wide variety of other obstacles placed upon the consumer designed to create additional burdens for the consumer to file the petition and obtain a discharge.

One important revision is that a debtor who has the ability to repay a debt over a period of time is now compelled to do same if he meets certain criteria. While most of the revisions do not affect the creditors, the attorneys for the debtors as well as the trustees will find several additional obligations to investigate the financial condition of the particular debtor.

MEANS TESTING. Section 707(b)(1) provides that any creditor may make a motion to dismiss a bankruptcy if it finds that granting relief would be an abuse of the provisions of this chapter. The court shall presume that an abuse exists if the debtor's current monthly income meets or exceeds the median family income for a family of the debtor's size residing in the applicable state. The median family income is defined in a new section, Section 101(39(a)), which contains the information reported by the Bureau of Census in the most recent year adjusted by the consumer price index. If the current monthly income is less than this median income, a creditor may not make a motion to dismiss the bankruptcy under Chapter 7.

The definition of current monthly income is covered in Section 101 (10(a)). The section defines monthly incomes as income from all sources, without regard to whether such income is taxable income, derived from a six-month period ending on the last day of the calendar month immediately preceding the date of commencement of the case. It includes any amount paid by any entity on a regular basis for household expenses of the debtor or the debtor's dependents, but excludes benefits received under social security, payments to victims of war crimes or crimes against humanity, and payments to victims of international terrorism or domestic terrorism.

Unfortunately, what will be left to interpretation by the court is the issue of whether the debtor lost his or her job during the six-month period, received promotions, or collected overtime plus several other factors.

Under Section 521(i) if an individual debtor in a voluntary Chapter 7 or 13 fails to file tax returns, copies of all payment advices from the employer received within 60 days before filing, statements of the amount of the monthly net income, showing how the amount was calculated, anticipated increases in income or expenditures over the 12-month period prior to filing the petition, within 45 days after filing the petition, the case must be dismissed. To extend this time, the debtor must make a motion before the court.

Individuals will find it difficult to file if the income of the consumer is greater than the median income for the particular state. In such a case, the bankrupt must utilize Chapter 13, which does not include what some critics characterize as oppressive burdens. The debtor will have to pay off some portion of the debt over at least five years. Certain expenses, such as paying for a car or a vacation home, may be deducted to come under the median income. Those who earn more than the median income will have to pay at least $6,000 over five years to seek protection under Chapter 13.

To qualify for a Chapter 7 bankruptcy to discharge all debts and not be required to pay a portion of the debts, the debtor's income would have to be less than the median household income for the particular state in which the debtor resides. The median incomes for the various states are significantly different. For example, the median income in California was approximately $48,000 while the median income in Florida was approximately $38,000. Judges will have some discretion to waive this requirement in cases of undue hardship.

The court cost for filing a Chapter 7 bankruptcy is now substantially larger than it was. Several bankruptcy attorneys have indicated that because of the complications in the filing, not only in Chapter 7 but the more complicated Chapter 13, legal fees may increase significantly due to the additional paperwork. Credit counseling will be required before a debtor will be able to emerge from bankruptcy.

MEANS TESTING—INVOLUNTARY PETITION. In a Chapter 7 bankruptcy if the bankrupt debtor's income exceeds the average income in the particular state, the bankruptcy may be dismissed. But does the section cover the situation where an involuntary petition is filed against the debtor? In this instance, the debtor does not file the petition, but the creditors file the petition. How the courts handle this issue will be interesting. The court could utilize Section 707(a) which allows the court to dismiss a case for cause, but the court may find that somewhat different than being unable to meet the criteria for means testing.

EVIDENCE OF COMPLIANCE WITH MEANS TESTING. The debtor will be required to provide a copy of the debtor's last year federal income tax return to the trustee within a week before the 341 hearing. The trustee will then be required to review this document along with the schedules and the other information concerning the current monthly income to determine whether any abuses have taken place and will determine whether the debtor's case would be presumed to be an abuse. Such statement will have to be filed and sent to all creditors.

Expenses. After the monthly income is determined, the debtor's monthly expenses shall be the amount specified under the national standards and local standards and the debtor's actual monthly expenses which are necessary expenses promulgated by the Internal Revenue Service in the area in which the debtor resides. The standards, national throughout the country except for Alaska and Hawaii, are based on family size and gross monthly income for a family of four with monthly income of $3,000. The national standard is $990 per month. An additional expense is allowed for food and clothing. Several other expenses are available such as home energy costs and a monthly payment for secured debt, mortgages, etc. Transportation costs for ownership of a car, payments for alimony, dependent care for the elderly, education for handicapped, union dues, disability insurance, health savings accounts, education allowances for each child, life insurance, etc. are all deductible. The parameters for interpretation of the criteria are broad. The bankrupt debtors with an income in excess of the median income will do their best to manipulate the expense factor so that they will fall below the median income. The whole areas of dependent care and education as well as some of the other items of expenses are open to vast differences depending upon the perspective of the creditor, the debtor, and the trustee.[48]

Bad Faith. The trustee at this point will determine whether the debtor filed the petition in bad faith or whether substantial abuse is present. This is somewhat of a subjective decision by the trustee. On the other hand, the trustee will have significant documents available to substantiate the decision. The trustee will have the opportunity to question the debtor as to any activity that transpired immediately preceding the bankruptcy and as to any practices that could be considered bad faith for the sole purpose of meeting the alleged criteria of the means testing or which may have affected his ability to repay the debts. The trustee will have to examine carefully the current monthly income and how the debtor arrived at the current monthly income. The *annualized* current monthly income then must be determined. The final current monthly income, after the expenses are deducted, is compared with the median income for that particular state. One important factor under the Act seems to be that the debtor has to provide documentation and detailed explanations of the current monthly income and the monthly expenses.

---

[48]*Babin v. Wilson (In re Wilson)*, 383 B.R. 729 (B.A.P. 8th Cir. 2008).

Presumption of Abuse. The debtor has an opportunity to rebut any presumption of abuse offered by the trustee. A change of circumstances may have occurred where the debtor's current monthly income radically changed such as if he was discharged from work, suffered a serious illness or even was a member of the National Guard and was called for duty.

The whole concept of means testing also contains time frames and the areas of disagreement between the creditors and the debtor are wide open. If the debtor's current average monthly income exceeds the means income of the particular state, a repayment plan is required of the debtor which will pay the debt of the creditor. Failure to meet the means test only prohibits the debtor from filing a Chapter 7. To convert the Chapter 7 filing into a Chapter 11 or a Chapter 13 requires the consent of the debtor. If the debtor does not consent and does not meet the threshold of the means testing, the Chapter 7 will be dismissed and the creditor may proceed with his remedies against the debtor as if no bankruptcy has been filed. *The importance of documenting current monthly income to be less than the means for the particular state is probably the most important test that the debtor will have to meet.*

Luxury Debts. The eligibility of discharge for luxury debts incurred within 90 days of bankruptcy has been reduced to $500 and cash advances greater than $750 obtained prior to 70 days before the filing also are ineligible for discharge. The prior law provided for $1,150 for debts incurred for luxury goods and cash advances within 60 days of filing.

Time Frames for Confirmation. An effort has been made to accelerate the submission and confirmation of the plan. A confirmation must occur between 20 and 45 days after the creditors meeting and plan payments must begin within 30 days.

Financial Management. The debtor will have to attend an instructional course concerning personal and financial management by a nonprofit budget and credit counseling agency that has been approved by a U.S. trustee. The debtor must undergo credit counseling within 180 days prior to the time of the filing of the petition to be eligible to file a bankruptcy petition.

Fraudulent Transfers. Section 522(o) deals with reducing the exemption in the following way:

For purposes of subsection (b) 3 A and notwithstanding Subsection (a) the value of an interest in

1. Real or personal property that the debtor or the dependant of the debtor uses as a residence
2. A cooperative that owns property that the debtor or dependant of the debtor uses as a residence
3. A burial plot for the debtor or a dependant of the debtor

4. Real or personal property that the debtor or dependant of the debtor claims as a homestead shall be reduced to the extent that such value is attributable to any portion of any property that the debtor disposed of in the ten year period ending on the date of the filing of the petition with the intent to hinder, delay or defraud a creditor and that the debtor could not exempt or that the portion that the debtor could not exempt, under Subsection (b), if on such date the debtor had held the property so disposed of.

The above new section permits the creditor to look back up to ten years prior to the date of the petition for a fraudulent transfer of assets. Prior to the law many of the states permitted the transfer of non-exempt funds out of the reach of creditors and into an exempt homestead. Some of the laws even extended to allowing such a fraudulent transfer up until the time that the debtor filed the petition in bankruptcy. Well-established case law clarifies exactly what the creditor must prove to support a fraudulent transfer.

A creditor whose claim arose after the time that the transfer took place may be able to proceed under this particular section. The huge impact of this statute will not be felt until it has been thoroughly interpreted by the bankruptcy courts.

> ***Credit & Collection Tip:*** *The creditor must realize that any recovery under this section benefits all unsecured creditors. The issue before the creditor is whether the cost and expense of pursuing this collection procedure would convert enough exempt property into non-exempt property to produce a significant distribution to each creditor. A thorough review of the bankrupt estate is recommended before any effort in this direction is developed.*

EVICTION

The landlord is permitted to continue with an eviction proceeding providing a judgment of possession was obtained prior to the petition being filed, even though he has not received actual possession. The law now allows eviction proceedings to proceed because of the illegal use of controlled substances providing it was commenced before the filing of the bankruptcy and the illegal use occurred within 30 days before the bankruptcy filing. If the landlord is unable to offer evidence of same, an application to court will be required.

REDEMPTION

In an effort to comply with the case law, the courts have held that redemption requires full payment of a secured claim. With regard to the value of the personal property securing the claim, a new provision replaces the old provision that the value of the collateral for purposes of the redemption should be measured by what the creditor would receive upon repossession. Under the new law in a Chapter 7, the value will be based on the cost to the debtor of replacing the property without deduction for cost or sale or marketing. If the property was acquired for personal, family or household purposes, it will be the retail price for property of similar age and condition (Section 506).

Ride Through Provisions. The debtor will be required to elect whether he intends to surrender the property, redeem the property, or reaffirm the property which is covered by a security agreement or mortgage. A common practice has been for the debtor not to choose any of said elections and to continue payments during the bankruptcy proceeding without complying with this section of the bankruptcy law. The advantage to the bankrupt was that no personal liability attached if the vehicle was not properly maintained. If the debtor stopped paying, the vehicle was surrendered—period. Under the new law, the debtor must elect and no opportunity is available to "ride through." The debtor must choose one of the above three options.

Section 362(h) is a new section which deals with the area of redeeming, reaffirming, or surrendering collateral. The statute provides that if the debtor fails to file a statement of intention that he will redeem, reaffirm or surrender the collateral within 30 days after the filing of the petition, the stay will terminate with regard to the collateral and the collateral will no longer be considered property of the estate.

If the debtor files his statement of intention within the 30-day period, but fails to properly select one of the three choices (redeem, reaffirm or surrender), the stay will also terminate. The statement of intention must precisely elect one of these three options. A failure to elect the options or the use other terminology such as "he intends to sell the car" terminates the stay.

If the debtor does file a proper statement within the 30 days electing the option to either redeem, reaffirm or surrender, but fails to take the actions specified in the statement within the 30 days after the date set for the first meeting of creditors, under Section 341(a), the stay will terminate.

Under Section 362(h)(2), the court allows on motion of the trustee, after a notice and hearing, to provide, if the personal property is of a consequential value or benefit to the estate, appropriate adequate protection of the creditor's interest. In the event said motion is not granted, the stay will terminate at the conclusion of the hearing on the motion.

This new change must be read in conjunction with Section 521(a)(6). The courts are going to have to reconcile some of the statutory language in 362(h) with the language in 521 by virtue of certain conflicts. The courts have yet to address these issues (at least at this writing). Read both statutes carefully and examine the contradictions between them.[49]

Reduction of Claim of Creditor. A creditor may be exposed to having his claim reduced if the creditor refused to negotiate a reasonable prepayment schedule proposed by an "approved non-profit budget and credit counseling agency." When the offer provides a payment of at least 60 percent of the debt within the time frame when the loan is due, or a reasonable extension was offered, the court may reduce the claim in the bankruptcy proceeding. This applies only to offers made within 60 days of the date of the petition.

Exemption of IRA Accounts. In 2005, the Supreme Court ruled that an IRA is exempt property from the bankruptcy estate under Section 522(d)(10)(e) of Bankruptcy Code (11 USC Section 522(d)(10)(e)).[50]

Section 11 U.S.C. 522(d)(10)(e) provides as follows:

> (10) the debtor's right to receive
>
> (e) a payment under a stock bonus, pension, profit sharing, annuity, or similar plan or contract on account of illness, disability, death, age, or length of service to the extent reasonably necessary for the support of the debtor and any dependent of the debtor unless
>
> (i) such plan or contract was established by or under the auspices of an insider that employed the debtor at the time the debtor's right under such plan or contract arose
>
> (ii) such payment is on account of age or length of service
>
> (iii) . . . .

No-Asset Case. An issue often arises where a debtor in a Chapter 7 no-asset, no-bar-date bankruptcy proceeding fails to list a claim on its schedule of creditors and the bankruptcy case is closed. Is the debt discharged pursuant to 11 U.S.C. Section 727(b) and Section 523(a)(3) or must the debtor apply to the bankruptcy court for an order reopening the closed proceeding to add the omitted creditor for the purpose of discharging the claim?

As a general rule, the courts are inclined to hold that in a no-asset, no-bar-date case, dischargeability is unaffected by scheduling. After a case is closed, the debt in question is either discharged or excepted from discharge based on Sections 523(a)(3) and 727(b). Therefore, the filing of a motion to reopen is not necessary to discharge the debt if the statutory exceptions to discharge do not apply. Section 727(b) states: except as provided in

---

[49] *In re Boring*, 346 B.R. 178 (Bankr. N.D. W. Va. 2006).

[50] *Rousey v. Jacoway*, 544 U.S. 320 (2005).

Section 523 of this title, a discharge under subsection (a) of this section discharges the debtor *from all debts* that arose before the date of the order for relief under this chapter.

Courts have observed that the operative word in this section is *all*. Section 727 does not create an exception for unlisted or unscheduled debts except those subject to Section 523. Debts listed in Section 523 describe debts which arise from intentional torts such as fraud. They include debts incurred by false pretenses, false representation, actual fraud, defalcation while acting as a fiduciary, and for willful and malicious injury.

Most creditors claim the fundamental right enjoyed in bankruptcy to file a proof of claim, because filing a claim is obviously necessary to participate in a distribution. In a case where there are no assets to distribute, the right to file a proof of claim is a hollow one. An omitted creditor, who would not have received anything even if he had been originally scheduled, has not been harmed by omission from the bankrupt schedules and the lack of notice to file a proof of claim. Thus, in a no asset Chapter 7 case where a no bar-date has been set, no purpose is served by reopening a case to add an omitted creditor to the bankrupt schedule. If it was an asset case and a failure to schedule the debt, no right to reopen and add the creditor is afforded and the debt is not discharged.[51]

As to omitted creditors in Chapter 13 cases, the courts seem to be agreeing that a debtor cannot force an omitted creditor to participate in a plan to which it had no opportunity to object.[52]

Pre-Petition Counseling. The new statute compels debtors to undergo credit counseling within 180-days before filing for bankruptcy. The credit counseling must be with an entity that has been approved by the courts. This obligation is mandatory under the statute. Most judges are dismissing the bankruptcy when the bankrupt has not produced proof of the credit counseling.

Two options were open: either obtain the credit counseling or upon your failure, the bankruptcy will be dismissed.[53] One judge in the Northern District in New York adopted a third option wherein the petition was dismissed so that the trustee receives the dismissal sought and the debtor retains the full benefit of the automatic stay.[54] This solution is the latest attempt by the judiciary to rewrite the new law. Other judges have stricken the petition on the theory that the debtor was not eligible to file the petition in the first place, with the same result as where the petition is dismissed.

Another problem with the mandatory credit counseling is an involuntary bankruptcy. The involuntary bankruptcy against an individual does

---

[51] *Beezley v. California Land Title Co.*, 994 F.2d 1433 (9th Cir. 1993).

[52] *In re Morris and Johnnee Fugate*, 286 B.R. 778 (N.D. Cal. 2002).

[53] *In re Salazar*, 339 B.R. 622 (D.C. S.D. Houston Div. Texas 2006); *In re Brown*, 342 B.R. 248 (D.C. Md. 2006).

[54] *In re Brickey*, 363 B.R. 59 (Bankr. N.D.N.Y. 2007).

not provide the time for credit counseling since the creditors probably will not be able to persuade the debtor to obtain credit counseling. It will be interesting to see how the courts treat this situation. Is the debtor eligible, will the court waive the credit counseling, or will the court dismiss—or find another road to travel such as extending the time frame.

HOMESTEAD EXEMPTIONS. While Florida is the outstanding example of a homestead exemption where an individual can purchase a house for several million dollars and the home is exempt from creditors when the debtor files a bankruptcy petition, several other states have unlimited homestead exemptions such as Texas, Iowa, Kansas, and South Dakota. In most of these states, the exemption applies both to a judgment lien as well as to a forced sale. A creditor cannot enforce a lien on the property due to the exemption. Other states have high homestead exemptions, but they are less restrictive and in most instances are limited in amount.

The 2005 Act Section 522(p)(1) limits the bankrupt to a $125,000 exemption. Section 522 deals with exemptions and runs more than six pages with three pages of new material or revisions of old material. Debtors may only use state exemptions if they have lived in the state for 730 days (two years) before filing a petition. If the debtor did not live in one place for two years prior to the petition filing, the debtor must use the place where domiciled in single state for 180 days preceding the 730 days (Section 522(6)(3)). If the debtor doesn't qualify, the federal exemption of $125,000 is available. Any addition to the value that was added over the past ten years cannot be exempted. Any exemption equity acquired within 1215 days (three years) preceding the petition cannot be added to a $125,000 exemption regardless of the state exemption (Section 522(p)).

Some states like Florida, Iowa, Kansas, South Dakota, and Texas have no cap on the value of a homestead exemption that may be exempt under state law. In most of these so-called debtor havens, the debtors will purchase an expensive house for the sole purpose of exempting it in a future bankruptcy filing.

Under Section 522 a bankruptcy debtor has the option of electing either the federal exemption provided in the bankruptcy code or the exemption available to them under state law unless the state has passed a law that prohibits such election. Almost two-thirds of the states have opted out of the federal exemption and do not permit such an election. A recent case held that the newly enacted $125,000 limitation only applied in states where the debtor could elect either the federal or the state exemption and it is not applicable in those states that have opted out from the federal exemption.

Only two states that have not opted out of the federal exemptions provide homestead exemptions in excess of the $125,000; that is, Texas with an unlimited homestead for the family and Minnesota with a $200,000 maximum homestead. The remaining states which have unlimited values for homestead exemptions, that is: Florida, Iowa, Kansas, South Dakota, and rural property in Oklahoma have all opted out.

Certainly this issue will probably end up in the appellate court sooner rather than later, but for the time being, the Florida, Iowa, Kansas, and South Dakota exemptions will probably still be applicable until such time as the issue reaches an appellate court or Congress passes a corrective law.[55]

The *McNab* decision analyzed the statute to determine whether it applied in Arizona. Like Florida, Arizona is a state which allows a homestead exemption in excess of $125,000 and is an "out" state, i.e. a state like Florida in which debtors must use the Florida exemption in a bankruptcy case.

The result of this conclusion would mean that the federal law would only be applicable in two states (Texas and Minnesota) which allow debtors to choose between federal and state exemptions. A Florida court strongly disagreed with the result and simply stated "the canons of statutory construction permit the court to consider legislative intent in these circumstances." When the intent of Congress is considered, the statute was intended to apply in all states, including Florida which allows homestead exemptions in excess of $125,000. In Florida, the state exemption is applicable, at least until another decision.[56]

Florida has increased the exemptions on personal property by the sum of $4,000 plus the $1,000 that already exists under Florida Statutes Section 222.25(4). A husband and wife may file a petition jointly, and an exemption of $10,000 in personal property is available.

A debtor will not be permitted to use the Homestead Exemption rather than the federal exemption if the court determined after notice of a hearing that the debtor has been convicted for a felony, the filing of a case was an abuse of the provisions of the bankruptcy Act, the debtor owes a debt arising from any violation of the federal or state securities law or regulation, or through manipulation in a fiduciary capacity in connection with a purchase or sale of any security.

Filing the Petition. The bankruptcy attorneys are unhappy because of new obligations to a client who retains them to file a petition in bankruptcy. The attorney must sign the petition and certify that he has conducted a reasonable investigation into the documentation and the reasons that the debtor offers to substantiate the grounds to file a petition.

The Act specifically does not define what a reasonable investigation is. A starting point for a reasonable investigation would probably include a title search, judgment search, tax lien search, mortgage search, and

---

[55]*In re McNabb*, 326 B.R. 785 (Bankr. D. Ariz. 2005). Fla. Stat. § 222.20.

[56]*In re Kaplan*, 331 B.R. 483 (Bankr. S.D. Fla. 2005).

certainly a UCC search to determine if security agreements are on file. The Act allows an award of costs and fees to a trustee if a Chapter 7 violation is revealed under Section 911. The costs and fees are the responsibility of the attorney, not the debtor. Section 707 is silent as to sanctions, but nevertheless allows the trustee to assess civil penalties against the attorney, payable to the trustee or the bankruptcy administrator, for a violation of the bankruptcy rules. This violation is similar to the Federal Rules of Civil Procedure, Rule 11, which states the signature of a debtor's attorney constitutes a certification that the attorney performed an investigation.

The attorney must have good reason to believe that the debtor's current monthly income after deduction of all expenses does not exceed the median income for the state. The fees for filing an individual petition have increased substantially ranging as high as low four figures. The retainer agreement must advise the debtor that a petition may be filed without the services of an attorney which may encourage individuals to file a petition without the benefit of counsel.

Notices to Creditors. Section 342 covers the issue of notice to creditors by the debtor and describes in detail those circumstances under which the debtor will and will not become liable for incorrect notices and spells out the rights of the creditors. The creditor also has a right to designate to the trustee, court, or the debtor where notices should be sent to this particular creditor. If the debtor does not send the notice to the proper address, the creditor may not be liable for a violation of the automatic stay.

AUTOMATIC STAY

Section 362(a) of the Bankruptcy Code states that a petition filed under the Bankruptcy Code operates to stay:

(1) the commencement or continuation, including the issuance or employment of process, of a judicial, administrative, or other action or proceeding against the debtor that was or could have been commenced before the commencement of the case under this title, or to recover a claim against the debtor that arose before the commencement of the case under this title;

(2) the enforcement, against the debtor or against property of the estate, of a judgment obtained before the commencement of the case under this title;

(3) any act to obtain possession of property of the estate or of property from the estate or to exercise control over property of the estate;

(4) any act to create, perfect, or enforce any lien against property of the estate;

(5) any act to create, perfect, or enforce against property of the debtor any lien to the extent that such lien secures a claim that arose before the commencement of the case under this title;

(6) any act to collect, assess, or recover a claim against the debtor that arose before the commencement of the case under this title;

(7) the setoff of any debt owing to the debtor that arose before the commencement of the case under this title against any claim against the debtor; and

(8) the commencement or continuation of a proceeding before the United States Tax Court concerning a corporate debtor's tax liability for a taxable period the bankruptcy court may determine or concerning the tax liability of a debtor who is an individual for a taxable period ending before the date of the order for relief under this title.

The new Act has made some changes favorable to creditors. The automatic stay is not applicable when a landlord has already obtained a judgment prior to the filing of a petition or in the event that an eviction is based on an endangerment of the leased property due to illegal use of controlled substances. The automatic stay also may be terminated if the debtor has not exercised the right, either to reaffirm, redeem in full at time of redemption, or surrender the collateral within 30–45 days of the first day set for the meeting of the creditors (Section 362(b)). The automatic stay will end in 30 days if the debtor files a new petition within one year of the prior bankruptcy (Section 362(c)(3)(4)). Section 362(b) sets forth two pages (28 subheadings) of which more than half are new which sets forth situations in which a stay is not applicable.

Commencement or Continuing Suit. The first section deals with the fact that a creditor is prohibited from beginning any suit or continuing to prosecute a suit against the debtor that was commenced before the filing of the petition, or to recover a claim against the debtor that arose before the filing of a petition. This includes any type of proceeding whether judicial, administrative, or an arbitration proceeding. It applies only to the creditor's activity against the entity or individual that files the petition. If an action is pending against one of several defendants, the stay only prevents the continuation against the one defendant who filed the petition.

Post Judgment. The second section deals with the enforcement of a judgment obtained before the petition was filed, either against the debtor personally or against property of the debtor's estate. The creditor cannot proceed with any levy, execution, or any other proceeding after judgment to collect or satisfy the pre-bankruptcy judgment.

Obtain Possession. The third section is one of the most important targets of the automatic stay in that it prohibits any effort to obtain possession or exercise control over any property of the debtor. The property of the debtor includes the debtor's legal and equitable interest in any property in which the debtor has an interest as of the date of the petition. The courts tend to look at this section with a broad brush and have applied this automatic stay to prevent the cancellation of licenses, commencement of a personal injury action against the debtor's insurer, the cancellation of insurance policies, the unilateral termination of contracts by non-debtor parties, and other similar types of actions by creditors designed to either protect the creditor's interest or in some manner coerce the debtor.

What Is Property of the Estate? Property of the estate includes anything that the debtor controls or possesses whether the debtor may or may not have valid title to the property. The most comprehensive part of the automatic stay is that part which prohibits any attempt to collect or recover on any claim against the bankrupt that arose prior to the filing of the petition in bankruptcy. The creditor cannot coerce a debtor to pay an obligation, encourage the debtor to pay an obligation, or even tempt the debtor to pay an obligation after the petition was filed concerning a claim that arose prior to the petition.

Coercion—Duress. A classic situation might be where the creditor refused to sell goods to the debtor in Chapter 11 on a cash basis when his sole purpose was to persuade the debtor to pay a debt that was incurred prior to the bankruptcy. A similar situation is where a college denied an individual a transcript of grades, in the hope that it would persuade the student to pay a debt that was incurred to the college prior to the bankruptcy.

The scenarios are endless and only limited by the creativity of the creditor, but the major thrust of the courts is to impress upon the creditor that no effort should be made to collect that debt whether by coercion, duress, offering a carrot or a stick, leading the debtor down the garden path or committing some other action, the sole purpose of which is directly or indirectly to force the debtor into a position where he has to pay the debt that was incurred prior to bankruptcy.

The concept that no effort should be made by duress or coercion extends even to the situation where you may do something that is lawful, but it is unlawful to use the threat to extort money from the bankrupt. For example, you may threaten a licensed professional with filing a complaint to cancel the professional's license, but you cannot communicate that to the bankrupt for the purpose of forcing the bankrupt to settle a claim of the creditor. You may file the complaint with the licensing board, but you cannot use the threat to extort a settlement.

Work Performed Prior to Bankruptcy. The stay also prevents the filing of any lien on work that was completed prior to the bankruptcy, such as a mechanics lien wherein the work was performed prior to the petition or a situation where the security agreement is being used to secure a claim that was incurred before the commencement of the bankruptcy case.

Set-Off Prior to Bankruptcy. The creditor cannot set off a debt owed to the debtor against the debtor's liability to the creditor. In simple terms, if the creditor owes the debtor $500 and the debtor owes the creditor $500, he cannot offset mutual debts. The creditor still owes the debtor the full $500, whereas the debt from the bankrupt to the creditor of $500 will be paid according to the direction of the bankruptcy court depending upon the amount of money available for all the creditors. The courts in some instances have carved out certain exceptions to this rule.

Exceptions to the Automatic Stay. There are various exceptions to the automatic stay and creditors should be aware of what these exceptions are. Bankruptcy laws do not shield the bankrupt from being prosecuted criminally. Collection of alimony, maintenance, and support is not affected by the automatic stay unless it is coming from the property of the estate. Normally, these claims are not discharged by the bankruptcy. The automatic stay does not affect certain governmental actions concerning the health and welfare of the population such as enforcing injunctions, judgments, or prosecuting actions for violations of various laws. Certain exceptions to the automatic stay deal with commodity transactions and with certain swap agreements that take place in the financial markets. Tax deficiencies may not be affected by the automatic stay and under certain conditions in non-residential real estate transactions, the automatic stay may be disregarded as eviction was in process against a business tenant. Other exceptions to the automatic stay are indigenous to certain industries and certain types of transactions. (*See* BAPCPA.)

Notwithstanding these certain specific exceptions to the automatic stay, the courts tend to treat the automatic stay liberally. Even these exceptions that are noted may be stayed if the proper application to court is made seeking such relief.

Knowledge of the Bankruptcy. A duty rests upon a creditor to comply with the automatic stay if the creditor has knowledge of the bankruptcy proceeding, even though written notice in the mail was not received. The estimate is that 1 percent of all first-class mail is not delivered, so a one-percent chance exists that the bankruptcy notice was not received. If word of mouth or other communication apprises the creditor of the bankruptcy, and the creditor proceeds notwithstanding this knowledge, violation of the provisions of the automatic stay may take place.[57] Often the creditor has knowledge of the bankruptcy. But when the account is referred to the debt collector, the creditor fails to notify the debt collector of the bankruptcy. While knowledge may be imputed to agents, debt collectors are independent contractors and such knowledge by the creditor is not imputed to the debt collector. If the debt collector has knowledge of the bankruptcy, the debt collector must comply with the automatic stay.[58]

The court case addressed a mistake by the bank in threatening a repossession when at the same time they were offering to refinance the debt. The bank immediately sent a letter of apology but the debtor commenced a suit. The court reasoned that this was an innocent clerical error, a simple mistake and therefore not a willful violation. A stay violation that is not willful does not warrant sanctions by the bankruptcy court. If a willful violation of the stay occurs, the party may recover actual damages including costs, attorneys' fees, and punitive damages.[59]

Notice to Junior Lienor. An additional duty is set forth to notify junior lienors when the property is sold. No precedent imposed a legal duty on a superior lienor to provide notice to the junior lienor when the senior lienor was seeking removal of the automatic stay in a bankruptcy proceeding. The junior lienor will receive notice of a subsequent sale.[60]

Notice of Sale After Removal of Automatic Stay. The creditor instructs their attorney to remove the automatic stay on a vehicle upon which they had a security interest. The attorney makes the necessary application to remove the stay. The attorney notifies the client creditor that the stay has been removed.

The creditor must recognize that the sale has to be conducted in accordance with the terms and conditions of the security agreement and the provisions of the statute of the state. Ergo, if there is a requirement that a notice of sale is to be delivered to the debtor or to any guarantors, the creditor must comply with that notice requirement. If the creditor should fail to deliver this notice, the creditor may forfeit any claim for deficiency, depending upon the provisions contained in the statute. The courts recognize that notice may be dispensed with if the collateral is perishable, or if its value threatens to decline speedily, or if it is customarily sold in a recognized market. This exception does not apply to machinery, vehicles, or other types of fixed assets.[61]

---

[57]*Randolph J.M.B. v. IMBS Inc.*, 368 F.3d 726 (7th Cir. 2004); *In re Bush*, 166 B.R. 69 (Bankr. W.D. Va. 1994), *rev'd*, 166 B.R. 34 (W.D. Va. 1994).

[58]*Randolph v. IMBS, Inc.*, 368 F.3d 726 (7th Cir. 2004).

[59]*In re Peterson*, 297 B.R. 467 (Bankr. W.D.N.C. 2003).

[60]*TMS Mortgage, Inc. v. Golias*, 102 S.W.3d 768 (Tx. Ct. App. 2003).

[61]*Diamond Bank v. Carter (In re Carter)*, 203 B.R. 697 (Bankr. W.D. Mo. 1996); *Motors Acceptance Corp. v. Rozier*, 597 S.E.2d 367 (Ga. 2004).

Waiver—Ipso Facto. An "ipso facto" clause is a term of an agreement that states that in the event of insolvency or a filing of a petition in bankruptcy, the bankrupt debtor waives certain specific rights of the debtor in bankruptcy or insolvency. These rights may include the prohibition set forth under the automatic stay or the provisions which are the criteria for determining what is property of the bankrupt estate.

Abundant case law has found such types of agreements to be unenforceable when they apply to executory contracts and leases under Section 365(e)(1) of the Bankruptcy Code. Nevertheless, most of the courts declare the "ipso facto" unenforceable not only in leases or security agreements, but in all types of agreements.

Rule 365(e)(1) states as follows:

> Notwithstanding a provision in an executory contract or unexpired lease, or an applicable law, an executory contract or unexpired lease of the debtor may not be terminated or modified and any right or obligation under such contract or lease may not be terminated or modified at any time after the commencement of the case solely because of a provision in such contract or lease that is conditioned on Paragraph (A) the insolvency or financial condition of the debtor at any time before the closing of the case; Paragraph (B) the commencement of a case under this title; Paragraph (C) the appointment of or taking possession by trustee in a case under this title or a custodian before such commencement.

Sometimes creditors make an effort to avoid this section and create what is known as "remote entities." The lender either creates a new entity that controls the borrower or modifies the structure of the borrower to achieve the purpose of the "ipso facto" clause. The debtor or the remote entity requires the consent of all the directors on the board in order for either the debtor or the remote entity to file a petition in bankruptcy. The debtor's corporation or the remote entity will at the same time enter an agreement that the lender shall be entitled to a sufficient number of seats on the board of directors. This arrangement will assure the creditor that the debtor or the remote entity will not file a petition in bankruptcy except on the consent of the creditor.

Unfortunately, such an agreement raises the issue of the fiduciary obligation of the directors appointed by the creditor. These directors must conduct themselves as representing all the stockholders and not just one specific lender. Sometimes the directors that have been appointed resign when faced with these problems. Another problem is that an involuntary petition may be filed against the debtor or the remote entity which will not require the consent of the board of directors.

Waiving Protection of Automatic Stay. While a waiver of the protection afforded by the automatic stay is not automatically enforceable, such waivers are not per se enforceable. The court further finds that in deciding whether relief from a stay should be granted based on such waivers, the following factors must be considered:

1. The sophistication of the party making the waiver;
2. The consideration for the waiver including the creditor's risk and the length of time the waiver covers;
3. Whether other parties are affected including unsecured creditors and junior lien holders;
4. The feasibility of the debtor's plan;
5. Whether there is evidence that the waiver was obtained by coercion, fraud, or mutual mistake of material facts;
6. Whether enforcing the agreement will further the legitimate public policy of encouraging out of court restructurings and settlements;
7. Whether a likelihood of reorganization prevails;
8. The extent to which the creditor would be otherwise prejudiced if the waiver is not enforced;
9. The proximity and time between the date of the waiver and the date of the bankruptcy filing and whether a compelling change in circumstances existed during that time; and
10. Whether the debtor has equity in the property and the creditor is otherwise entitled to relief from the stay under Section 362(d).[62]

As a general rule, pre-bankruptcy waivers entered into by the lender or a junior creditor cannot overrule a provision of the bankruptcy code. The courts have prohibited waivers of automatic stays, and prohibitions against filing a petition for relief under the bankruptcy code. Where the waiver only involves the rights of two parties (the lender and the junior creditor), the courts tend to permit the exercise of said waiver.

The courts seem to allow the right of the lender to file documents and claims on behalf of a junior creditor, and also to vote or consent in any proceeding with regard to the documents or the claims.[63] These rights are not waivers in the strict sense since the senior and junior creditor share the same interest to a limited degree.

The bankruptcy permitted its senior lender to confirm a plan of reorganization on behalf of the junior lender, absent showing that the agreement was unenforceable. In this instance, the senior lender voted a junior lender's interest even though the voting of the interest involved more than the two creditors. Some courts will not permit the senior lender

---

[62]*In re Frye*, 320 B.R. 786 (Bankr. D. Vt. 2005); *In re Atrium High Point Ltd. P'ship*, 189 B.R. 599 (Bankr. M.D.N.C. 1995).

[63]*See In re 230 N. LaSalle St. P'ship*, 246 B.R. 325 (Bankr. N.D. Ill. 2000); *In re Inter Urban Broadcasting of Cincinnati, Inc.*, 1994 WL 646176 (E.D. La. Nov. 16, 1994).

to vote on the junior lender's right to vote on a plan of reorganization and this case agreed.

SERIAL BANKRUPTCY

Under Section 362(c)(3), if a single or joint case is filed by or against any debtor wherein the case was pending within the preceding year but was dismissed (other than a case re-filed under another chapter other than Chapter 7 after dismissal) the stay with respect to that action shall terminate on the 30th day after the filing of the latest case. The section also provides that the court may have a hearing to extend the stay under certain circumstances providing that the party who filed the petition in the latter case filed in good faith as to the creditors to be stayed.

Under Section 362(c)(4)(A)(i), the act provides that if there are two or more single or joint cases pending within the previous year, but were dismissed, the automatic stay shall not go into effect upon the filing of the later case (subject to Section 707(b)). Several pages of requirements, restrictions and exceptions to the suspension of the automatic stay must be reviewed. Consultation with experienced counsel is recommended.

Bankruptcy attorneys are moving for an extension of the automatic stay beyond the 30-day limitation period. The court observes a distinction that the limitation period only applies to "debts" or "property" of the debtor, but does not apply to "property of the estate" as long as the subject property remains "property" of the estate. The stay remains in effect until a dismissal or discharge of the bankruptcy. A creditor cannot take any action without a successful motion to remove the stay. Whether other courts will follow is questionable.[64] Other courts have found problems with this section and other different interpretations will occur.

As to the timely filing of the statement of intention, the debtor must comply with the statement of intention within 30 days after the first date set for a meeting of creditors. Although many of the time limits in the bankruptcy law require compliance after the date of the last meeting of creditors, this time limit specifically states that the compliance must be *within the 30 days after the first date* of the meeting of creditors. The statute would not apply if the debtor offered to reaffirm the debt under the original contract terms and the creditor rejected the reaffirmation or if the court did not approve the reaffirmation agreement.[65]

The courts are also becoming generous with regard to the debtor who fails to obtain credit counseling before filing the petition. One court strikes the petition, but does not dismiss the case. Another court requires a suit by the creditor prior to the petition, because the statute refers to the word

---

[64] *In re Paschal*, 337 B.R. 274 (Bankr. E.D.N.C. 2006).

[65] *In re Hinson*, 352 B.R. 48 (Bankr. E.D.N.C. 2006).

"actions taken." If no suit (action) was commenced, the stay remains in effect until the creditor makes the motion to remove the stay.[66]

SECURED CREDITOR

Security Interest Perfection. The date of perfection for a security agreement is generally extended from 10 to 30 days and the transfer will then occur at the time of the transfer between a debtor and a creditor (*see* 547(e)) if perfection occurs within the 30 days. A careful reading of Section 547(e) is recommended for the determination of the date of transfer. If a transfer is not perfected within the 30-day period, then a transfer (for the purposes of determining the date) occurs before the date of the commencement of the bankruptcy case or the transfer is deemed to be made when the perfection takes place.

Valuation of Security. Chapter 13 of the Bankruptcy Court permits a debtor to retain the use and possession of property while paying creditors out of future earnings. The property that most consumers want to retain is their automobile or their home, which are usually subject to a security agreement or mortgage. The Chapter 13 plan may state that the creditor retains the lien on the automobile and the debtor continues to make payments equal to the "present value" of the automobile.

The courts have variously considered the "present value" to be retail value, the replacement value, the fair market value, or the wholesale value. Some courts have used the replacement value on the theory that the debtor is continuing to use the car, whereas other courts have emphasized the wholesale value. If the creditor recovered the car, the car would be sold and the wholesale value would be the closest to what the creditor would recover. The Fifth Circuit has chosen the foreclosure value of the car, which probably is somewhat less than the wholesale value of the car (which was adopted by the Sixth Circuit Court of Appeals).[67]

The differences between the circuits were partially resolved by the Supreme Court identifying the proper value to be applied to secured property which the debtor retains in a Chapter 13 case. The appropriate value to use when a Chapter 13 debtor elects to retain the property is the "replacement" value. The definition of replacement value offered by the Supreme Court was "the price a willing buyer in the debtor's trade, business or situation would pay a willing seller to obtain a property of like age and condition." Section 506, Subdivision (A) of the Bankruptcy Code was the

---

[66] *In re Brown*, 342 B.R. 248 (Bankr. D. Md. 2006).

[67] *In re Trimble*, 50 F.3d 530 (9th Cir. 1995); *Matter of Rash*, 90 F.3d 1036 (5th Cir. 1996); *In re Hoskins*, 102 F.3d 311 (7th Cir. 1996); *General Motors Acceptance Corp. v. Jones*, 999 F.2d 63 (3d Cir. 1993).

basis of this decision, such value shall be determined in light of the purpose of the valuation and of the proposed disposition or use of such property.

Replacement Value of Security. The Supreme Court decided that if the debtor retained the property, the creditor could not possibly foreclose on the property and sell it in a commercially reasonable sale. Therefore, the foreclosure value of the property would certainly be inappropriate. Since the debtor intended to use the property to generate a stream of income, the actual use, rather than a foreclosure sale that will never take place, is the proper guide under a prescription hinged to the property's "disposition or use." The theory of some of the circuits to allow a different valuation based on the facts and circumstances of each case was also rejected. The Court also rejected the idea of averaging a replacement value and a foreclosure value and arriving at some figure in between. Unfortunately, the Court did not identify exactly what "the replacement value" actually is and it appears that this will be left to further litigation. The replacement value could mean the retail value or wholesale value or even some other value depending upon the type of the debtor, the nature of the property and the use to which the property will ultimately be applied.

This particular theory probably will be applied to Chapter 11 as well as Chapter 7 bankruptcies. Unfortunately, litigation over a more refined definition of "replacement value" will probably continue.[68]

Pre-Petition Repossession. When you have the control over "property of a bankrupt" prior to bankruptcy, the party exercising control has an obligation to deliver the property to the trustee in bankruptcy, but conflicts exist among the circuits as to the application of the automatic stay.

Some of the circuits feel that a party in possession of the property should immediately deliver that property to the trustee (*see* above). Other circuits state that a creditor, before he surrenders the property to the trustee, should be entitled to require adequate protection of the collateral as a pre-condition to the debtor's use of the collateral. The delivery of the property to the trustee should be made after notice of a hearing and subject to the court establishing conditions for adequate protection such as insurance and a safe and secure place for the property.

A repossession of a vehicle took place two days before the debtor filed a Chapter 13. The bank received notice from the bankruptcy court about ten days later, but misplaced the bankruptcy notice. About seven days later the vehicle was sold at auction. The bankrupt sought damages for the violation of the automatic stay. The bankruptcy judge determined the vehicle was not property of the estate. It was the interest of the debtor in the vehicle and the right to redeem the vehicle that was the property of the estate.

---

[68] *Associates Commercial Corp. v. Rash*, 117 S. Ct. 1879, 138 L. Ed. 2d 694 (1997).

Other courts have also taken this position and the general theory is that if the repossession takes place before the petition in bankruptcy is filed, the bankrupt can only claim the property as property of the estate if some affirmative action in the bankruptcy court is made to direct the creditor to turn the vehicle over to the estate of the bankrupt.

On the other hand, some courts take the position that the obligation is on the creditor to surrender the vehicle to the estate notwithstanding whether the vehicle has insurance or whether the creditor has adequate security. This position seems to be a minority view.[69]

AUTOMOBILE—CROSS COLLATERAL. The credit union provided in their auto financing agreement that the automobile which secured the car loan also secured the credit card which was issued to the bankrupt. The debtor paid his car loan. Notwithstanding same, the credit union repossessed the car since the bankrupt had not paid the credit card.

When the debtor learned of this, the debtor immediately filed a petition in bankruptcy. The credit union asserted that they should be classified as a secured creditor and alleged that the security agreement clearly stated that the auto was security for all loans. The security agreement thus covered the Visa debt.

The bankruptcy court in California candidly admitted that they leaned toward determining what the intent of the party is rather than the language in the security agreement. The bankrupt stated that he did not know that this clause was contained in a security agreement. The court applied the "relationship of loans" and "reliance on the security" doctrines which are used by other courts in this type of case. The court decided that the car loan and the credit card debt were totally unrelated except for the fact that they were consumer debts and they were extended to the same debtor. Many other courts have found the same class of debts sufficiently related to meet the "relationship of loans" test.

The second test of reliance on the security also failed, because no evidence was presented that the credit union issued the credit card in reliance on the auto loan secured by Buick. The credit union testified that they verified the bankrupt's good credit and issued the card. The court concluded it was an adhesion contract where the credit union had superior bargaining power. The motion for relief from the stay or for adequate protection was denied.

The use of cross-collateralization clauses in lending situations with consumers must be treated carefully to be certain they meet the several criteria used by the courts examining these cross-collateralization clauses. In most instances the debtor did not read the clause and was not aware of the clause, nor did the lender explain the clause or make any effort to emphasize the clause. It probably would be helpful if the security

---

[69] *In re Nelson Alberto*, 3.00-C.V.-1791 (N.D.N.Y 2002).

agreement set forth in bold language the cross-collateralization clause or have the cross-collateralization clause in a separate box initialed or signed by the debtor. The "relationship test" and the "reliance of the security test" are devices the courts use to avoid enforcing cross-collateralization clauses, even if bold print is used and even if the debtor could not avoid reading the clause.

> ***Credit & Collection Tip:*** *If the creditor sets forth in bold language the cross-collateralization clause that the loans are related and that the creditor is relying on the security to create the new loan and the security is necessary for the new loan, the cross-collateralization clause has a better chance to withstand the efforts of the courts to declare them unenforceable. Careful drafting of the agreement is necessary, and facts, documents, and conduct must support the agreement.*[70]

Strip Down. A "strip down" occurs when the balance on a mortgage ($71,000) is reduced to the market value of the security (home—$23,500). Section 506 of the Bankruptcy Code provides as follows:

Determination of Secured Status 11 U.S.C. 506:

- (1) an allowed claim of a creditor secured by a lien on property in which the estate has an interest, or that is subject to set off under Section 563 of this title, is a secured claim to the extent of the value of such creditor's interest in the estate's interest in such property, or to the extent of the amount subject to set off, as the case may be, and is an unsecured claim to the extent that the value of such creditor's interest or the amount so subject to set off is less than the amount of such allowed claim. Such value shall be determined in light of the purpose of the valuation and of the proposed disposition or use of such property, and in conjunction with any hearing on such disposition or use, or on a plan affecting such creditor's interest.
- If the debtor is an individual debtor in a case under Chapter 7 or 13, such value with respect to personal property securing an allowed claim shall be determined based on the replacement value of such property as of the date of the filing of the petition without deduction for costs or sale or marketing. With respect to property acquired for personal, family or household purposes, replacement value shall mean the price a retail merchant would charge for property of that kind considering the age and condition of the property at the time value is determined.

(b) . . .

---

[70]*In re Kim*, 256 B.R. 793 (Bankr. S.D. Cal. 2000).

Section 506(a)(2) has been added as a result of the conflict amongst the courts with regard to valuation in a "strip down." A recent case addressed Section 506 (a) which allows the bifurcation of a claim of a secured creditor into two claims—a secured claim for the actual value of the collateral as of the petition date and unsecured claim representing the difference between the actual value and the amount owed on the collateral under the loan agreement.[71] A secured creditor's lien position under the contract is an amount capped at the actual value. The debtor pays the secured claim under the plan and pays a small percentage based on the debtor's disposable income of the unsecured claim, along with the other unsecured creditor's claims. The procedure is commonly known as the "cram down" option of a plan confirmation, which may be enforced over a claim holder's objections. This option usually results in a small amount being paid above the secured claim amount. The case provides a thorough picture of the "strip down" and the interplay between other sections of the new act as well as addressing the appropriate interest rate.

The Supreme Court considered the application by a debtor to "strip down" the lenders' secured claim of $71,000 to the home's reduced value of $23,500. The Supreme Court prohibited this option under Section 506 by stating that Chapter 13 prohibits the debtor from reducing an unsecured homestead mortgage to the fair market value of the mortgage residence. The Supreme Court recognized that claims in bankruptcy could be broken down between secured and unsecured parts. Section 1322(b)(2) protected the unsecured components of a partially secured claim. Unfortunately, the Supreme Court did not decide whether its holding should be extended to wholly unsecured homestead mortgages.[72]

This issue has divided the bankruptcy courts as well as the district courts. The majority view seems to follow the reasoning that the antimodification provisions protect only the under-secured and not the wholly unsecured homestead lenders. Under this theory, if the mortgage was $50,000 and the security was worthless, the claim would automatically become an unsecured claim rather than a secured claim. The minority view takes the opposite position. The fact that a claim is under-secured does not mean that the mortgagee is limited by the valuation of its secured claim. The emphasis in this type of reasoning is on the homestead lender rather than on the value of the collateral that shields the claim from modification. If it is a homestead lender, the secured mortgage is protected just as if the collateral was of some value. The Circuit Court of Appeals of the Eleventh Circuit has provided an in-depth analysis of this issue and sided with the majority opinion.[73]

---

[71] *In re Fleming*, 339 B.R. 716 (Bankr. E.D. Mo. 2006).
[72] *Nobelman v. American Savings Bank*, 508 U.S. 324 (1993).
[73] *Tanner v. FirstPlus Fin., Inc. (In re Tanner)*, 217 F.3d 1357 (11th Cir. 2000).

Student Loans. Federal Student Loans are usually granted through federal agencies. The availability to students of financial assistance can either be funneled through the educational facility itself or directly from the government. The educational facility may finance and include loans for tuition, room and board, and other receivables such as parking, student health charges, etc. The two federal agencies that grant loans are the Department of Education which operates under Title 4 and the Department of Health and Human Services which operates programs under Title 7. The Department of Education offers the following types of federal family educational loans:

1. Federal Direct Student Loan, which provides funds to a bank which in turn lends the money to the school under a specific program which allows specific rates and beneficial terms for the school.
2. The Federal Perkins Loan is a separate program that requires the educational institution to match a certain portion of the federal funds (10% to 25%) when granting the loan to the students so that the federal government is not granting the full 100% of the loan.

The Department of Health and Human Services primarily provides financial assistance to students entering the field of medicine and includes the primary care loan, the nursing student loan, and the health professional student loans.

The Department of Health and Human Services provides student loans for the most needy disadvantaged students who will be unable to attend college without assistance. Some of the federal loans permit students to defer or even cancel repayment of the loan if they enter certain careers such as law enforcement or the military. The financial aid package covers a situation where the student is not only offered a loan, but offered a grant for which the student qualifies, and only a portion of said grant needs to be repaid.

From a collection point of view, debt collectors usually are not allowed to contact parents with regard to the collection of student loans and this applies to the credit grantor who approved the loan. The prohibition even extends to responding to the inquiries made by parents.

In 1998, the statute of limitations on government insured student loans was removed and thus does not bar the collection of a government insured student loan.

In bankruptcy, the chances of discharging a student loan is remote since the test used by the court is "undue hardships," and the bankruptcy courts are reluctant to find most "undue hardship" insufficient to discharge a student loan (*see* Chapter 6—Non-Dischargeability—Student Loans).[74]

---

[74]The Collector—Published by ACA International, March 2006, pg. 47, *Higher Ed 101* by Amelia Anderson.

DEFICIENCY—SECURED VEHICLE DEBT—HANGING PARAGRAPH

A Louisiana District Court recently reviewed in depth the case law applicable when a debtor surrenders a vehicle within the 910 days within filing the petition and where the Chapter 11 plan does not bar a creditor from pursuing an unsecured deficiency claim against the debtor if the agreement and state law allow a deficiency claim.

The court referred to the hanging paragraph in 11 U.S.C. 1325(a)(9) which converts a claim secured by a motor vehicle acquired by the debtor for personal use during the 910-day period preceding the bankruptcy to a secured claim that must be paid under the plan. The amendment prevents a debtor from stripping down a lien on a vehicle acquired during the period.

The court reviewed decisions in the Sixth, Seventh, Eighth, and Tenth Circuits, all of which addressed this problem. The analysis applies to Chapter 11 and 13 debtors who surrender a 910 vehicle through a plan. The creditor still has a right to assert a deficiency claim when authorized by state law. The Sixth Circuit addressed the position that Congress only intended that the hanging paragraph prevent debtors from cramming down debt when they elect to retain collateral. No legislative history suggests that car lenders and lien holders should be negatively impacted by the hanging paragraph in situations where the debtor elects to surrender the collateral.[75]

The hanging paragraph limits the availability of bifurcation into a secured and unsecured debt by adding an "unnumbered" or "hanging" paragraph to the end of the Section.

The court emphasized the hanging paragraph is not ambiguous. Section 506(a), shall not apply to a 910 claim. The language of this paragraph does not differentiate between claims against debtors who chose to retain collateral pursuant to 1325(a)(5)(B) and those who opt for surrender pursuant to 1325(a)(5)(C). If Congress intended for the limitation of the hanging paragraph to apply alone rather than as a whole, it could have drafted such a limitation into the language of the statute. Courts must presume that Congress said what it meant and meant what it said. *The court concluded a 910-day claim is not subject to bifurcation whether or not the debtor chooses to retain collateral or surrender collateral.*[76]

---

[75] *In re Horrobin*, 391 B.R. 573 (Bankr. M.D. La. 2008); *In re Wright*, 492 F.3d 829 (7th Cir. 2007); *In re Song*, 519 F.3d 288 (6th Cir. 2008); *Capital One Auto Finance v. Osborne*, 515 F.3d 817 (8th Cir. 2008); *In re Ballard*, 526 F.3d 634 (10th Cir. 2008).

[76] *In re Carter*, 2008 WL 410275 (M.D. Ga. 2008).

RECLAMATION

Several general situations are presented wherein a creditor may reclaim property.[77] The new Act has made significant changes in reclamation.

A. If the seller discovers the buyer to be insolvent.
B. If the seller discovers that the buyer has received the goods on credit and the buyer was insolvent at the time the goods were received, the seller may reclaim the goods.
C. If the buyer pays for the goods with a check and the check is ultimately dishonored, the seller may reclaim the goods.
D. If the seller delivers the goods to a carrier and discovers that the debtor is insolvent, the seller may reclaim the goods. Section 2-705 deals with the stoppage of delivery in transit in possession of a carrier.

Section 2-702 of the Uniform Commercial Code covers subdivision A & B set forth above.

1. When the seller discovers the buyer to be insolvent, he may refuse delivery except for cash including payment for all goods theretofore delivered under the contract and stop delivery under this article (Section 2-705).
2. Where the seller discovers that the buyer has received goods on credit while insolvent, he may reclaim the goods upon demand made within 10 days after the buyer's receipt. If misrepresentation of solvency has been made to the particular seller in writing within 3 months before delivery, the 10-day limitation does not apply. Except as provided in this subsection, the seller may not base a right to reclaim goods on the buyer's fraudulent or innocent misrepresentation of solvency or of intent to pay. (Revised UCC Article 2 changes this to "reasonable time" but contradicts 11 USC 546I.)
3. The seller's right to reclaim under subsection 2 is subject to the rights of a buyer in ordinary course or other good faith purchaser under this article (Section 2-403). Successful reclamation of goods excludes all other remedies with respect to them.

The theory of subsection 2 is that any receipt of goods on credit by an insolvent buyer amounts to a misrepresentation of solvency and is fraudulent as against the particular seller. The ten-day limitation starts from the time of the receipt of the goods and normally excludes the day that the merchandise is actually received. If a written misrepresentation of solvency is dated within three months prior to the delivery and addressed to seller, the ten-day limitation is not applicable.

---

[77] 11 U.S.C. § 546(c).

Subsection 3 of the act states that the reclamation bars any other remedies with regards to the goods—the creditor must take the goods back and cannot sue for damages.

Under Section 2-507 of the UCC, subsection 2 states as follows:

> "where payment is due and demanded on the delivery to the buyer of goods or documents of title, his right as against the seller to retain or dispose of them is conditional upon his making the payment due."

Accordingly, under UCC Section 2-507, 2-511 and 2-546I of the Bankruptcy Code, the creditor would have a right to reclaim goods where the merchandise was delivered against payment by cash or check and buyer was insolvent.

Notice. Under Section 2-546(c) of the Bankruptcy Code, the seller has a right to reclaim goods if the debtor has received such goods while insolvent and they were sold to the debtor in the ordinary course of such seller's business. The seller may not reclaim the goods unless such seller demands in writing reclamation of such goods within 10 days after receipt of such goods by the debtor.

State Action. Once the debtor has received notice and is obviously uncooperative, an immediate decision must be made as to whether a reclamation proceeding should be commenced in state court. The important part of the state action is to obtain a temporary restraining order so that the debtor does not use, transfer or dispose of the merchandise that belongs to the creditor. If this proceeding precipitates an immediate bankruptcy, the creditor may proceed in the bankruptcy court for a reclamation. On the other hand, the bankruptcy court does have the right to deny reclamation even if the creditor can prove his right to reclamation on condition that the court awards a priority claim or in the alternative secures the claim with a lien. The bankruptcy court at their option may grant a partial return of goods, or grant a lien on the property of the creditor or perhaps on other property.

Considerations Before Reclamation. Before a reclamation can be made, the following suggestions may be helpful:

1. The goods have to be sold initially on credit to the debtor.
2. The principal reason a debtor would become aware of the insolvency is because the debtor is not paying his bills, but this inability to pay the bills is not sufficient to prove insolvency. The courts tend to look at a balance sheet definition of insolvency wherein the liabilities must exceed the assets. A minority of the courts adopts the failure to pay the debts as they become due. Information as to whether the debtor is

insolvent at the time the creditor seeks to reclaim the goods can be established by a careful examination of the bankruptcy schedules together with an examination of prior financials of the bankrupt.

3. If the bankrupt is a public corporation, the monthly public filings of financial statements and other financial information are available. Credit reports might be another source of information as to whether the debtor was insolvent.
4. Most courts require a written communication and the Bankruptcy Code specifically states that it must be a 10-day written communication. Certified mail or overnight express probably would be adequate. 11 U.S.C. Section 546I.
5. Reference should be made in the letter to Section 2-702 if that is the section you are proceeding under. Specifically identify all the merchandise and goods that were sold, preferably by enclosing the invoices initially sent to the debtor. The letter should contain a notification to the bankrupt that the merchandise must be protected, segregated, and maintained by the debtor until such time as the goods are reclaimed.
6. The goods must be identifiable and cannot be the type of goods that are easily commingled or that may lose their identity once they are in the possession of the debtor. For example, the debtor buys peanuts from several suppliers and customarily stores them by commingling them with peanuts from other suppliers. Another example might be where a buyer uses wool yarn to knit sweaters on a loom in conjunction with other materials that are used to produce the sweater.
7. The goods must still be in the possession of the debtor when the demand is received by the debtor. If the debtor has sold the goods, a reclamation action will not be successful.
8. The debtor must purchase the goods in the ordinary course of business. If it is not the ordinary course of business for the seller to sell the goods, the goods would not qualify for a reclamation proceeding.
9. If the merchandise received is subject to a lien the moment the merchandise is acquired, the seller may not be entitled to reclaim the goods. If the automobiles are sold to a dealer and the bank has a floating lien on the inventory of the dealer, the inventory may not qualify to be reclaimed since it is subject to a lien. A lien on inventory of a retail store also may preclude a claim for reclamation. The courts seem to go both ways on whether or not a lien is superior to a claim for reclamation.
10. If the creditor should be aware that the debtor is insolvent at the time the goods are sold to the debtor, some courts take the position that this knowledge by the creditor does not entitle him to reclaim the goods because of this knowledge.

11. If you fail to give written notice under Section 2-546I, you will have no right to assert a reclamation in bankruptcy. The Official Creditors Committee owes a fiduciary duty towards the creditors of the bankrupt estate. The creditor asserting a reclamation claim may have difficulty being appointed to the Official Creditors Committee since his interest, at least to the extent of the property covered by the reclamation claim, is opposed to that of the Official Creditors Committee.

Consultation with an experienced counsel is certainly recommended before any demand for a reclamation is made. Slight variations in the statutes and the interpretations of the particular sections by the courts vary from state to state.

Reclamation Time Requirements. Several changes have been made to protect the seller's rights to reclaim goods sold to the insolvent debtor after the seller sends a written demand for reclamation.

Under the Uniform Commercial Code (UCC) Section 702 the demand must be made within ten days after the buyer's receipt of the goods. The Act now provides that the demand may be made no later than 45 days from the debtor's receipt of the goods or no later than 20 days after the filing of the bankruptcy case if the 45-day period expires after the commencement of the bankruptcy case. The ten-day period after receipt of goods has now been extended to 45 days and the 20-day period after the receipt of goods is now measured by the 20-day period after the petition is filed providing the 45 days have expired. A prior security interest on such goods will prevail over a seller's reclamation rights.

If a seller sells and delivers goods to the debtor in the ordinary course of business within 20 days prior to filing of the petition, the seller may apply to the court for an administrative claim for the goods sold. The purpose is to provide the seller with an administrative claim to avoid the burden of reclamation proceedings. But if the secured claims are more than the assets of the debtor, this modification is of little help to the seller.

> ***Credit & Collection Tip:*** *The new bankruptcy law supersedes any state laws. The reliance upon state reclamation statutes will not be recognized by the bankruptcy court.*

Reclamation—"Did the Seller's Rights Improve?" The major changes in the reclamation law have dealt with timing. No changes were made as to whether the seller is entitled to reclamation against the secured party. At the time of the passing of BAPCA, a conflict arose with regard to two cases. A pre-petition lender had a security interest in the debtor's pre-petition inventory and financing was arranged for the post-petition debtor in possession (Phar-Mor). *The security interest in the assets was not transferred to the debtor in possession lender* and the pre-petition lender released its security interest upon payment. The court held that because the pre-petition lender had released their security interest so that the prior lien was released, reclamation was available to the sellers to assert the full value of their reclamation claims.[78]

Another case in 2003 had substantially the same fact situation where the pre-petition prior lender was paid in full and released the security interest and a new security interest was issued by the lender to the debtor in possession. In this situation, the reclamation claims were subject to the security interest of the new lender to the debtor in possession. The reason offered by the court was that the pre-petitioned lender had sold its pre-petition security interest to the new lender to the debtor in possession and the proceeds of the reclaimed goods had been applied toward payment of the pre-petition lien. The creditors' reclamation claims were of no value.[79]

In 2007, a case in the Southern District of New York followed the reasoning in the *Dairy Mart* case, which also was a New York case in the Southern District. The *Dana* court analyzed both the *Phar-Mor* case and the *Dairy Mart* case and basically rejected the *Phar-Mor* reasoning and provided that the new security interest would prevail.[80]

A case in Delaware addressed the issue where the pre-petition lien was not satisfied and the pre-petition lien was superior to the reclamation claims. The court concluded if the secured lien was released, the post-petition secured creditor would still prevail over the reclaiming creditors.[81]

A seller attempting to reclaim goods in a bankruptcy case still has to face the claims of the lenders and their secured interest under state law. While federal law may preempt state law, up to now most of the decisions are upholding the claims of the secured post-petition lenders.

Administrative Claims. Section 503 provides that all administrative expense claims as identified in said section must be paid at the time of confirmation. Administrative claims enjoy a preference in the bankruptcy procedure since the claims are paid before payments are made pursuant to the approved plan in Chapters 11 and 13.

Where goods are delivered during the 20-day period before the petition date, the creditor may file a motion not only to have its claim allowed, but also to be treated as an administrative claim (20-day claim). The 20-day claim cannot be asserted by filing a proof of claim in bankruptcy. The creditor must make a motion to allow the claim as an administrative claim and be paid as an administrative claim. Such a motion is a small price for the privilege of being paid before the unsecured claims.

---

[78] *In re Phar-Mor, Inc.*, 301 B.R. 482 (Bankr. N.D. Ohio 2003).
[79] *In re Dairy Mart Convenience Stores, Inc.*, 302 B.R. 128 (Bankr. S.D.N.Y. 2003).
[80] *In re Dana Corp.*, 367 B.R. 409 (Bankr. S.D.N.Y. 2007).
[81] *In re Incredible Auto Sales, LLC*, 2007 WL 927615 (Bankr. D. Mont. Mar. 26, 2007).

Section 503(b) states as follows:

> After notice and hearing, there shall be allowed administrative expenses, other than claims allowed under Section 502(f) of this title, including . . .
>
> (9) The value of any goods received by the debtor within 20-days before the date of commencement of a case under this title in which the goods have been sold to the debtor in the ordinary course of such debtor's business.

As to Section 546(c) which deals with the power to reclaim goods, the new law states as follows:

> (c)(1) Except as provided in subsection (d) of this section and in Section 507(c), and subject to the prior rights of a holder of a security interest in such goods or the proceeds thereof, the rights and the powers of the trustee under Section 544(a), 545, 547 and 549 are subject to the right of a seller of goods that has sold goods to the debtor, in the ordinary course of such seller's business, to reclaim such goods if the debtor has received such goods while insolvent, within 45-days before the date of commencement of a case under the title, *but such seller may not reclaim such goods unless such seller demands in writing reclamation of such goods*
>
> (A) not later than 45 days after the date of receipt of such goods by the debtor; or
>
> (B) not later than 20 days after the date of commencement of the case, if the 45-day period expires after the commencement of the case.
>
> (c)(2) If a seller of goods fails to provide notice in the manner described in paragraph (1), the seller still may assert the rights contained in section 503(b)(9).

If you had sold goods to the debtor and you did not meet the criteria of the law as to the 45-day notice, a claim still may be asserted under 503(b)(9) with regard to an administrative claim if the goods were delivered to the debtor within 20 days before the bankruptcy in the ordinary course of business.

An important section is 503(b)(9) which states that a creditor will be allowed an administrative expense claim for:

> "the value of any goods received by the debtor within 20 days before the date of commencement of a case under this title in which the goods have been sold to the debtor in the ordinary course of such debtor's business."

Electricity is usually provided 20 days prior to the commencement of every case. Some cases indicate that electricity is a commercial product or a manufactured product and thus qualifies as goods under the terminology of Section 503(b)(9). The opposing argument is that electricity is a service and not goods. Many cases support this posture. A recent case in Kentucky stated that electricity was not goods, but a service using the test that goods are movable.[82]

Section 503(c) deals with those administrative claims which will not be paid including claims payable to an insider. When dealing with persons essential to the survival of the business, the amount of the transfer or obligation incurred must not be greater than an amount equal to ten times the amount of a similar kind paid to a non-management employee (Section 503(c)(C)(i)). A severance payment to an insider is not allowed unless the payment is part of a program generally applicable to all full-time employees and not greater than ten times the amount of the mean severance pay paid to non-management employees during the calendar year in which the payment is made (Section 503(c)(2)(B)).

The last paragraph of Section 503 sets forth the criteria for treating other transfers or obligations as administrative claims outside the ordinary course of business. Transfers made to or obligations incurred for the benefit of officers, managers or consultants hired after the date of the filing of the petition will not receive an administrative claim (Section 503(c)(3)).

DISCHARGE IN BANKRUPTCY

A discharge in bankruptcy does not extinguish debts. The purpose of the discharge is to prevent any creditor from further efforts to collect the debt. The debt basically remains and the only affect of the discharge is to prevent the creditor from making any effort to collect the debt. An issue often arises as to whether merely reporting the debt to a credit bureau is a violation of the discharge in bankruptcy.

The pertinent section of the bankruptcy law states clearly that a discharge in a case under this title operates as an injunction against the commencement or continuation of an action, the employment of process, or an act to collect, recover, or offset any such debt as a personal liability of the debtor whether or not the discharge of such debt is waived. Actually, it is a permanent injunction against any activity to collect the debt.[83]

See Chapter 15, under the heading "Credit Reporting—After Discharge" as to whether reporting the debt is equivalent to an activity to collect the debt.

---

[82]*In re Samaritan Alliance, LLC*, 2008 Bankr. LEXIS 1830 (Bankr. E.D. Ky. 2008); *Bryant v. Tri-County Elec. Membership Corp.*, 844 F. Supp. 347 (W.D. Ky. 1994); *Encogen Four Partners, L.P. v. Niagara Mohawk Power Corp.*, 914 F. Supp. 57 (S.D.N.Y. 1996); *Enron Power Mktg. v. Nev. Power Co.*, 2004 U.S. Dist. LEXIS 20351 (S.D.N.Y. 2004).

[83]*In re Irby*, 337 B.R. 293 (Bankr. N.D. Ohio 2005); *In re Goodfellow*, 298 B.R. 358 (Bankr. N.D. Iowa 2003).

Objection to Discharge. Rule 727 covers the situations under which the court shall grant a discharge to an individual debtor. The exceptions are:

1. Where the debtor intends to hinder, delay, or defraud a creditor or an officer of the bankruptcy estate charged with custody of the property.
2. Where the debtor has transferred, removed, destroyed, mutilated, or concealed or has permitted same to be done as to property of the debtor within one year before the date of filing of the petition or even after the date of the petition.

The Section also covers the situation where the debtor has concealed, destroyed, mutilated, or failed to keep or preserve any recorded information, including books, documents, records, and papers from which the debtor's financial condition or business transactions may be ascertained unless such failure was justified under all the circumstances of the case then and there prevailing. This section continues on for three pages and covers situations such as:

- The debtor made a false oath.
- The debtor offered, received, or attempted to obtain money or property or promise of money for forbearing to act.
- The debtor has failed to explain a loss of assets or a deficiency of assets to meet the debtor's liability.
- The debtor refused to obey a lawful order.

The above are probably the major reasons that discharges are denied to individual debtors. This section covers a wide area of other acts that the debtor committed or omitted to act, all of which could result in the denial of a debtor's discharge in bankruptcy.

Rule 727 (objecting to the discharge of the debtor) is often considered in conjunction with Section 523 of the Code which covers an issue of exceptions to discharge. The creditor often wishes to object to the discharge of a particular debt (Section 523) as opposed to objecting to the discharge of the debtor with regard to the petition that was filed in bankruptcy (Section 727).

Section 523 states that a discharge under 727 does not discharge an individual debtor from any debt for money, property, services or an extension, renewal or refinancing of credit to the extent that said debt was obtained by false pretenses, a false representation or an actual fraud. This normally refers to the financial statement in writing furnished to a lender which must meet the following tests:

- A materially false financial statement.
- Respecting the debtor's or an insider's financial condition.

- On which a creditor relies.
- That the debtor caused to be made or published with the intent to deceive and;
- The transaction dealt with a consumer debt owed to a single creditor aggregating more than $500 for luxury goods or services incurred by
    a. An individual debtor within 90 days before the order for relief are presumed to be non-dischargeable;
    b. That such cash advances aggregating more than $750 that are extensions of consumer credit under an open-end credit plan obtained by an individual debtor on or within 70 days before the order for relief are presumed to be non-dischargeable.

Section 523 uses three more pages and sets forth various other situations which are exceptions to a discharge, although the ones just mentioned are the most frequent grounds that creditors use.

The creditor must be aware of the fact that under 727(a) an objection to discharge must be filed within 60 days of the initial creditors meeting. A creditor may move during the original 60 days period for an extension under Bankruptcy Rule 4004(a)(b). Some courts have held that this deadline is an inflexible and mandatory rule, not subject to a court's discretion. Bankruptcy Rule 4003(b) requires an objection to a debtor's claim of exemption be lodged within 30 days after the initial creditors meeting is concluded and no exception to this 30-day rule is recognized. Even though these short limitations lead to harsh results in certain cases, the courts have observed that the bankruptcy bar and the enforcement by the courts result in finality to bankruptcy proceedings.

Credit & Collection Tip: *Creditors must be aware of the fact that a failure to file within said timeframes or a failure to obtain extensions will effectively prohibit a motion to deny the discharge.*[84]

A creditor and debtor will often attempt to settle an objection either under 727(a) or 523(a). Bankruptcy courts are concerned that no consideration is involved in the dismissal of a 727 action. Since discharges are a statutory right, the exchange of a quid pro quo is not acceptable and not a proper subject for negotiation.[85]

Several bankruptcy courts have held that when a creditor commences an adversary proceeding, the creditor becomes a trustee in that the proceeding benefits all the creditors.

When the original party bringing the objection to discharge declines to proceed and enters some form of a settlement agreement with the debtor,

---

[84]*Taylor v. Freeland & Kronz*, 503 U.S. 638 (1992); *In re Chalasani*, 92 F.3d 1300 (2d Cir. 1996).
[85]*In re Moore*, 50 B.R. 661 (Bankr. E.D. Tenn. 1985).

the courts tend to prevent fraudulent debtors from using the courts to escape the consequences of their action. The remedy is to allow other creditors or the trustee to intervene or be substituted for the original complaining creditor to prosecute the 727 objection to discharge. Those creditors who did not commence the 727 objection within the 60-day limit are permitted to continue the timely action even though the 60-day limit has expired.[86]

While some courts follow the above theory, other courts will not permit the settlement and dismissal of the objection to discharge and will refuse to allow another creditor to be substituted as the claimant for the party who initially asserted the objection to the discharge.[87]

> ***Credit & Collection Tip:*** *The time period is relatively short and a creditor must act quickly to assert a claim that a debt is non-dischargeable. If the creditor fails to meet the time limitation, the debt will be discharged since the courts are reluctant to allow a creditor to cure this default. Immediate consultation with counsel is recommended.*

Non-Dischargeable Debts. The Bankruptcy Code provides for certain types of debts to be non-dischargeable in bankruptcy. These debts are not affected by the bankruptcy, and survive. The debts include:

1. Most taxes.
2. Debts which were created by the debtor practicing fraud or misrepresentation by use of a false financial statement upon which the creditor relied.
3. Unscheduled debts. If the bankrupt did not list the debt in the bankruptcy petition, the debt will not be discharged. The courts have held that if the creditor knew about the bankruptcy, or received some notice of the bankruptcy in sufficient time to file a proof of claim, the debt may be discharged (but there are exceptions).
4. Any debt which is a result of embezzlement or larceny.
5. Alimony, maintenance, and support.
6. Obligations to pay fines (such as traffic fines).
7. Student loans.
8. Debts as a result of drunk driving.
9. Debts due to willful, intentional, and malicious injury.
10. Funds which have been borrowed for the purpose of paying non-dischargeable federal tax liabilities. The practice of borrowing money to pay back taxes, and then listing the debt in bankruptcy and discharging the debt to the lender, while not that common, was frequent

---

[86]*In re Nicolosi*, 86 B.R. 882 (Bankr. W.D. La. 1988).
[87]*In re Chalasani*, 92 F.3d 1300 (2d Cir. 1996).

enough for the Internal Revenue Service to persuade Congress to close the loophole. The benefit is to the lender, and now the debt will not be discharged.

Under Section 523(a)(2)(A) of the Bankruptcy Code, a debt for money, credit, property, or services will not be discharged in bankruptcy if it is obtained by false pretenses, false representation, or actual fraud by means of a statement respecting the debtor's financial condition. The question before the court was whether the debt fell under this section of the statute when he charged against his credit card, was unable to pay the credit card bill and was seeking a discharge in bankruptcy of the credit card debt. The creditor, of course, was claiming that the debtor was charging a debt fraudulently knowing that he would be unable to pay it. The court held that the creditor must show actual fraud, that is, the debtor did not intend to repay the charges at the time the charges were made. The debtor relied on a test described in *In re Dougherty*,[88] which consisted of various factors of circumstantial evidence which are considered in determining the debtor's intent. These factors are as follows:

1. The length of time between the charges made and the filing of the bankruptcy.
2. Whether or not an attorney has been consulted concerning the filing of the bankruptcy before the charges were made.
3. The number of charges made.
4. The amount of the charges.
5. Financial condition of the debtor at the time the charges were made.
6. Whether the charges were above the credit limit.
7. Whether the debtor made multiple charges on the same day.
8. Whether or not the debtor was employed.
9. The debtor's prospects for employment.
10. The financial sophistication of the debtor.
11. Whether there was a sudden change in the debtor's buying habits.
12. Whether the purchases were made for luxuries or necessaries.

The court found this test was the preferable approach to determining whether a debt will be non-dischargeable under Section 523(a)(2)(A) and the court applied this analysis.[89]

A major classification of debts that are non-dischargeable includes a false financial statement in writing with regard to the financial condition of

[88] *In re Dougherty*, 84 B.R. 653 (B.A.P. 9th Cir. 1988).
[89] *Matter of Janecek*, 183 B.R. 571 (Bankr. D. Neb. 1995).

the debtor used to induce the creditor to extend credit and upon which the creditor relied.

The courts are uncomfortable with this question of reliance. Since the bankruptcy judges' major duty is to discharge a debtor, they seek reasons to have a debt discharged, notwithstanding the claim that the creditor relied on the misrepresentation. If the misrepresentation covered a minor asset of the debtor, the court might say that the creditor relied on the major assets of the debtor and the misrepresentation was immaterial.

Actual fraud by the debtor may be committed by a false representation, by a false pretense, or by some other act of conduct which constitutes the fraud, even without a written statement. The fraud category rests on the fact that a creditor is extending credit based upon misrepresentation of the debtor, whether in a credit application or in any other form of communication. The false representation may be oral as opposed to the use of a written financial statement.

The one area where credit card companies have run into severe problems is where they have issued unsolicited pre-approved credit cards. The credit is extended based on a credit scoring system or other type of screening, but with no investigation of the financial status of the debtor. The courts do not look favorably upon the creditor who cannot provide information about the debtor's assets and liabilities to justify reliance upon the representations made by the debtor on the credit card application.[90] In one case the debtor had received a pre-approved credit card while the debtor's bankruptcy was actually proceeding.[91]

Increasing the limit of the debtor on a credit card without an investigation regarding the financial condition of the debtor may also be considered by the court when proceeding with a non-dischargeability action.[92]

The Second Circuit is becoming more cognizant of the substantial abuse that takes place in the bankruptcy courts when they allowed both the trustee and the creditor to participate in the process of objecting to the discharge of a debtor who was a living example of abuse of the statute. The lifestyle of the debtor included over $50,000 a year to send children to private school, but at the same time the debtor was filing a petition in bankruptcy. They had an income of over $400,000. Eventually, the pendulum does swing.[93] Consultation with counsel is advised as to other non-dischargeable debts.

NON-DISCHARGEABLE LOAN—FINANCIAL STATEMENT. When lending and financial institutions extend credit to businesses and request the owner of the business to guarantee the loan, the normal procedure requires the guarantor to provide a financial statement. The financial

---

[90]*Household Credit Servs., Inc. v. Walters*, 208 B.R. 651 (Bankr. W.D. La. 1997).

[91]*In re Hunter*, 210 B.R. 212 (Bankr. M.D. Fla. 1997).

[92]*In re Sziel*, 206 B.R. 490 (Bankr. N.D. Ill. 1997).

[93]*In re Robert N. and Karen E. Cornfeld*, 164 F.3d 778 (2d Cir. 1999).

statement form furnished by the lending institution usually includes a detailed listing of all assets and liabilities, including a statement as to what the annual income is both from salary as well as passive income from bank accounts, CDs, dividends on stock, and interest on bonds or other types of income-producing assets. The financial statement usually will contain statements as to cash in the bank, value of real estate, vehicles, stock ownership, as well as a listing of liabilities including mortgages, security agreements, taxes, and other debts.

When the debtor files a bankruptcy petition, the debtor must furnish in the bankruptcy schedules the income and monthly expenses and must list the value of any real estate, stocks, bonds, and other types of assets.

When comparing the financial statement furnished to the lending institution with the financial information furnished in the bankruptcy schedules, the creditor may find a wide discrepancy in some of the figures, especially in the amount of income received and the value of real estate or stocks and bonds. A principal reason contributing to this is that at the time the debtor is seeking to borrow, the debtor is probably presenting the *best case* scenario to the bank and at the time of filing the petition in bankruptcy, the debtor is probably presenting the *worst case* scenario. The discrepancies may be substantial and present an opportunity for the creditor to file an adversary proceeding under Section 523 that the debt in bankruptcy should not be discharged for the reasons set forth under Section 523(a)(2) as follows.

The debtor must use a statement in writing that is materially false. If large differences between the financial statement and the schedules in bankruptcy are present, those discrepancies would probably satisfy the requirement that the statement is materially false. The creditor must rely on the statement. If the false statement is of a minor nature or involved an item which would not reasonably have affected the decision of the creditor, the courts tend to frown upon technical or minor discrepancies. If it was substantial, the creditor still would have to prove reliance. The intent to deceive aspect of the statement is satisfied by virtue of the fact that the debtor was seeking a loan and deceived the creditor to obtain the loan.

The loan document should state that the creditor is relying upon the financial information set forth in the financial statement. It would be helpful to set forth clear language that the borrower understands that the debtor is relying on the information furnished. The courts try to determine whether the creditor actually did rely on the misrepresentation in the financial statement. If income was represented to be $200,000 and the income in the schedules is listed as $20,000, this may be sufficient unless an explanation can be provided. If the debtor owned several hundred thousand dollars in real estate, the court might determine that the creditor was relying on the real estate for a $50,000 loan rather than on the income of the debtor.

A careful evaluation must be made of the bankruptcy schedules and a careful comparison must be made with the financial statement. A decision must be made whether to file an adversary objection to assert the debt is non-dischargeable.

> ***Credit & Collection Tip:*** *Filing these adversary proceedings with a meritorious claim usually produces offers of settlement by the guarantor. Our office has been engaged in these types of proceedings for many years and we can testify to the fact that the efforts expended are usually rewarded.*

NON-DISCHARGEABILITY—STUDENT LOANS. Student loans as a rule may not be discharged unless the court determines that payment of the loan will impose "undue hardship" on the debtor or the debtor's dependents.

A student loan may be discharged in bankruptcy through use of a Chapter 13 plan which specifically states the terms under which the student loan will be paid, and contains the magic language that allows a student loan to be discharged pursuant to 11 U.S.C. Section 523(a)(8)(B).

Courts have exercised wide discretion in determining on a case-by-case basis when repayment of the loan will impose an undue hardship. Different standards and factors have been used in making these determinations and, as a general rule, the standards are expressed in general terms. Some bankruptcy courts will state that a filing of undue hardship requires the presence of unique or extraordinary circumstances which render it unlikely that the debtor would ever be able to honor his obligations. Other courts have used a four-point test in determining whether there is undue hardship by considering:

1. the accumulated wealth of the debtor;
2. the debtor's chance of retaining steady employment;
3. the amount the debtor will need to maintain a minimum living standard; and
4. whether there would be anything left to make payments on the student loan without reducing what is needed for living expenses.

Other courts require good faith for a finding of undue hardship. Still other bankruptcy courts have used a test of two factors:

1. if the dominant purpose of the bankruptcy was to escape a student loan, and
2. whether the education obtained through the loan had enhanced the debtor's earning capacity.

The courts accept that they must make a yes or no decision whereas in many instances, the debtor can pay some of the student loan, but not necessarily all of the student loan. The debtor can pay some amount monthly and the court is examining some way to recover monies on the student loan and at the same time, permit the debtor to carry on with his life. A solution presented by the Tenth Circuit in this matter is not unusual and may be adopted by other courts; the leading case is from the Second Circuit.[94]

The Third Circuit has now joined the Second, Sixth, and Seventh Circuits in stating that a student loan cannot be discharged in a Chapter 7 proceeding unless repaying it will cause "undue hardship." In the instant case the debtor was seeking a discharge of a student loan of $30,000 because he was only making $27,000 a year. Mere financial sacrifice was not sufficient and apparently the only way the court might discharge the loan is if the burden of paying the loan would cause the bankrupt to fall below the minimum standard of living. This would apply even if the debtor had a Chapter 13 plan confirmed which included the discharge of the student loan and was not objected to by any creditor.[95]

The end result is that it is probably more difficult than before to obtain a discharge utilizing the hardship route. The Ninth Circuit has also joined in accepting the *Brunner* Test for discharge of student loans.[96]

The statute of limitations on government-insured student loans was removed in 1998. The new law became effective on October 7, 1998.

Settlement of Fraud Claims. Little difference is present where litigation ends in a settlement as opposed to a judgment. An issue arises when a debt incurred pursuant to a settlement agreement is non-dischargeable in bankruptcy. Reducing a fraud claim to settlement does not change the nature of the debt for dischargeability purposes. The determination of whether a debt arises out of fraud may take place in the bankruptcy court since the fullest possible inquiry was intended to ensure that all debts arising out of fraud are excepted from discharge—no matter what form they may take.[97]

CHAPTER 15

Chapter 15 replaces Section 304 that deals with cross border insolvency cases and covers the access of foreign representatives and creditors to the court. Foreign creditors are not necessarily subject to the jurisdiction of the U.S. courts in the event access is sought under Chapter 15. The court

---

[94] *In re Timothy Gerard O'Hearn*, 339 F.3d 559 (7th Cir. 2003); *Brunner v. New York State Higher Educ. Servs. Corp.*, 831 F.2d 395 (2d Cir. 1987); *Andersen v. HEAF (In re Doreen & Anderson)*, 215 B.R. 792 (D. Kan. 1998).

[95] *Whelton v. Educational Credit Mgmt. Corp.*, 432 F.3d 150 (2d Cir. 2005).

[96] *In re Cox*, 338 F.3d 1238 (11th Cir. 2003).

[97] *Archer v. Warner*, 538 U.S. 314 (2003); *In re Detrano*, 326 F.3d 319 (2d Cir. 2003).

has the right to extend the time to file a proof of claim if the court feels that the creditor's request was reasonable under the circumstances. *Most of the material in the chapter is brand new and does not revise any other sections.*

FEES TO BANKRUPTCY ATTORNEYS—BOARD CERTIFICATION

The new Act permits bankruptcy judges to consider whether the lawyer has met the objective standards to become board certified by the American Board of Certification when awarding fees. The judges must consider "whether the person is board certified or otherwise has demonstrated skill and expertise in the bankruptcy field." The purpose is to encourage attorneys to take the American Board of Certification Examinations so that the court will not penalize them in the awarding of fees.

Attorneys' Fees Disclosure. The crux of the controversy was whether the bank can charge attorneys' fees to debtor's accounts any time during a bankruptcy. The bank had outsourced its bankruptcy function of filing proof of claims to outside law firms. Outside law firms charge a fee for the service. The fee is posted to the debtor's accounts, but the fees are never disclosed to the debtor during the bankruptcy case.

The Ninth Circuit held that an attorney's fee for filing a proof of claim must be disclosed so that the debtor knows the fee is part of the secured claim. Secondly, the fee must be included in the arrearage claim portion of the debt so that the debtor can pay the fee through his or her plan as allowed.

If the fee is not listed, the debtor does not know it exists. If the debtor does not know it exists, it cannot be part of the secured claim and cannot be collected. If a creditor fails to disclose those charges, they cannot be added later. The bank has no choice. If the fee is not disclosed, the fee is discharged.[98]

> ***Credit & Collection Tip:*** *The reasoning would appear to apply to any other fees, charges, or expenses which are not disclosed in the proof of claim.*

Not only pre-petition attorneys' fees but post-petition fees also must be disclosed so that sufficient notice is available of all fees to place a debtor and all interested parties on notice that a fee has been charged.

Post-Petition Attorney Fees of Unsecured Creditors. Since 1991 the claim of attorneys for unsecured creditors post-petition attorney

[98] *Harris v. First Union Mortg. Corp.*, 2002 Bankr. LEXIS 771 (Bankr. S.D. Ala. 2002); *Powe v. Chrysler Fin. Corp., L.L.C.*, 278 B.R. 539 (Bankr. S.D. Ala. 2002).

fees was not permitted if the attorney was litigating issues involving contract enforcement questions instead of issues peculiar to the federal bankruptcy law. This rule was known as the Fabian Rule by virtue of the case decided in 1991 in the Ninth Circuit.

The U.S. Supreme Court reversed the Fabian Rule and stated in unequivocal terms that denial of certain categories of fee requests was not supported by either statutory or applicable state law.

The U.S. Supreme Court was asked to consider whether the federal bankruptcy law precludes an unsecured creditor from recovering attorney fees authorized by a pre-petition contract during post-petition litigation. The Fabian case had held that such fees are categorically prohibited—even when the contractual allocation of the attorney fees would be enforceable under applicable non-bankruptcy law—to the extent the litigation involves issues other than federal bankruptcy law. The court could not find any subsection of Section 502(b) that would require the disallowance of such a claim for fees. *A claim should be allowed unless it is unenforceable against the debtor under any agreement or applicable law.*

The court stated in essence that where a party objects to a claim, the claim must be allowed under the nine exceptions in Section 502(b) which has not been changed by the recent Bankruptcy Abuse Prevention and Consumer Protection Act (BAPCPA). The Supreme Court emphasized they were not interested in developing a federal common law and where the dispute can be resolved by state law, state law should prevail.

The Supreme Court is applying the state law to the agreements made in written contracts which award attorney fees to creditors.[99]

FRAUD

The bankruptcy statute expressly prohibits the discharge of a debt that was obtained by false pretenses, false representation, or actual fraud (other than a statement respecting the debtor's financial condition). As to a misrepresentation of the debtor's or insider's financial condition, the debtor may be prohibited from obtaining a discharge as to the respective debt, but the debtor still may obtain a discharge for the entire bankruptcy. In order to prevail, the creditor must prove that:

1. the debtor made a representation at a time that the debtor knew the representation was false;
2. the debtor made the representation deliberately and intentionally with the intention and purpose of deceiving the creditor;

---

[99]*In re Fabian*, 951 F.2d 1149 (9th Cir. 1991); *Travelers Casualty & Surety Co. of America v. Pacific Gas & Electric Co.*, 549 U.S. 443 (2007).

3. the creditor justifiably relied on such representation;
4. the creditor sustained the loss and damage as the proximate result of the representation being made.

Actual fraud by definition consists of any deceit, artifice, trick, or design involving direct and active operation of the mind used to circumvent and cheat another—something said, done, or admitted with the design of perpetrating a deceit or a deception. A silence regarding a material fact may constitute a false representation actionable under this section.

The intent element does not require a finding of malice or personal ill will: all it requires is a showing of intent to induce the creditor to rely and act on the misrepresentation in question.

Because direct proof of intent (the debtor's state of mind) is nearly impossible to obtain, the creditor may present evidence of the surrounding circumstances from which intent may be inferred. Intent to deceive will be inferred where a debtor makes false representation and the debtor knows or should know that the statement will induce another to act. Justifiable reliance on the part of the plaintiff claiming to have been defrauded must be proved.

A person is justified in relying on a representation of fact even though he may have ascertained the falsity of the representation had he made an investigation. If a person sells land and represents that it is free of encumbrances and the buyer relied on this statement, notwithstanding the buyer could have walked across the street to the office of the register of deeds and easily learned of an unsatisfied mortgage, justifiable reliance is present. Contributory negligence is no bar to a recovery because fraudulent representation is an intentional tort. On the other hand, a creditor cannot recover if he blindly relies upon a misrepresentation, the falsity of which would be obvious to him if he had utilized the opportunity to make a cursory examination or investigation.[100]

GARNISHMENT

An issue is whether you are allowed to garnish the wages of a debtor who is still repaying his debt under a Chapter 13 bankruptcy, even though the debt for which the creditor is collecting is a post-petition debt. Section 1306 covers the situation when property of the estate includes earnings from services performed by the debtor after the commencement of the case, but before the case is dismissed or converted to a Chapter 7. Under those circumstances, the earnings are considered property of the estate and

[100] *In re SaMala*, 295 B.R. 380 (Bankr. D.N.M. 2003); *Leverett v. Oligschlaeger (In re Oligschlaeger)*, 239 B.R. 553 (Bankr. W.D. Mo. 1999).

the only method of garnishment is to obtain a removal of the stay by making an application to the bankruptcy court.

PRIVATE RIGHT OF ACTION

Section 524 states that the discharge operates as an injunction prohibiting the collection or recovering of any debt that was listed in the bankruptcy. More and more debtors are instituting suits because they claim that their rights were violated under Section 524 of the Bankruptcy Code. The debtors are commencing suits based upon the failure to comply with the reaffirmation requirements.

A few courts have found that a private right of action exists under Section 524, but the vast majority of the courts have held that no such private right of action exists. The principal reasoning is that when Congress intends that a private action would exist, they expressly specified that a private action would exist in the Bankruptcy Code, such as in Section 362, which states clearly that an individual injured by any violation of the provisions of Section 362 ("automatic stay") may recover actual damages including costs, and also may recover punitive damages. Nevertheless, under Section 524, which is the discharge section, no such private right of action is specified.[101]

A few decisions in California have asserted that the debtor does have a private right of action under Section 524 for violation of the discharge injunction, but recent decisions in California have gone the other way.[102]

Several cases deal with the failure to file reaffirmation agreements and on balance it seems that the decisions were favorable. In the First Circuit in Massachusetts, where the *Sears* case was originally instituted, the court held that the failure to file a reaffirmation agreement may be enforced through the contempt powers of the bankruptcy courts by virtue of Section 105 (the proceeding is confined to the bankruptcy court). The case did not address the issue of a private right of action.

Judge Posner in the Seventh Circuit agreed with the First Circuit, but stated that no private right of action arises by virtue of failure to file the reaffirmation agreement and that the contempt powers of the bankruptcy court is the remedy for this type of a violation.

The Sixth Circuit stated that Section 524 of the Bankruptcy Code does not provide a private right of action.[103]

---

[101]*Costa v. Welch*, 173 B.R. 954 (Bankr. E.D. Cal. 1999); *Bessette v. Avco Fin. Servs.*, 240 B.R. 147 (D.R.I. 1999).

[102]*Ramirez v. GMAC*, 2000 U.S. Dist. LEXIS 14700 (C.D. Cal. Mar.29, 2000); *Molloy v. Primus Auto. Fin. Servs.*, 247 B.R. 804 (C.D. Cal. 2000).

[103]*Cox v. Zale Delaware, Inc.*, 239 F.3d 910 (7th Cir. 2001); *Pertuso v. Ford Motor Credit Co.*, 233 F.3d 417 (6th Cir. 2000); *Bessette v. Avco Fin. Servs.*, 230 F.3d 439 (1st Cir. 2000).

MONITORING LIEN IN BANKRUPTCY

The well-known statement that "liens pass through bankruptcy unaffected" is far too broad for creditors, for liens may be affected by the bankruptcy proceeding, especially where creditors participate in the bankruptcy proceedings. The normal rule, where a debtor plan under Chapter 13 does not expressly preserve a secured creditor's lien, is that the confirmation of the plan acts to extinguish the lien provided that:

1. The secured creditor participated in the debtor's case by filing a proof of claim.
2. The property was either dealt with or provided for by the plan.

It is necessary for a creditor to file a proof of claim. The problem is that once a creditor files a proof of claim, most creditors do not follow the bankruptcy if the amount involved is not significant upon the premise that the bankruptcy court will protect the creditor and that their lien will pass through the bankruptcy court proceeding.

The creditor's property must be dealt with or provided for in the Chapter 13 plan itself. *If the plan does not provide for the secured status, the lien is lost*. Before a plan can be confirmed, the bankruptcy court normally holds a hearing on the confirmation of the debtor's plan and the creditor has an opportunity to object to the confirmation. If the creditor does not object, the plan will be confirmed.[104]

RIGHT OF SET-OFF

The question of whether a bank can set off a deposit made by a bankrupt prior to bankruptcy against a loan incurred by the bankrupt has created conflict among the district courts leading to the Supreme Court of the United States finally resolving the question.

The right of set-off entitles persons who owe each other money to apply their mutual debts against each other, thereby avoiding the absurdity of making A pay B when B also owes A. In simpler terms, if Smith owed Jones money and Jones owed Smith money, they offset the money against each other rather than have Smith pay Jones and then Jones pay Smith. Under the Bankruptcy Code, no specific provision governs whether a creditor has a right of set-off. Section 553(a) provides that whatever rights to a set-off that exist under state law are preserved under the federal law in bankruptcy.

---

[104] *In re Siemers*, 205 B.R. 583 (Bankr. D. Minn. 1997).

Monies on deposit in a bank account are technically a loan by the depositor to the bank, and the bank must repay this loan on demand less any expenses assessed by the bank. The bank occasionally seeks to offset these monies in the bank account against an actual loan made by the bank to the depositor. If no right of set-off by the bank existed, and the monies on deposit were turned over to the trustee in bankruptcy, the bankrupt depositor might repay the loan over a three-year period of time under Chapter 13. On the other hand, if the proceeding was in Chapter 7 with no right of set-off, the bank will pay the monies on deposit to the Trustee and will receive only whatever distribution the other unsecured creditors receive (usually 10 cents or less on the dollar). In many consumer bankruptcies no distribution is made and even where assets are available, the distribution is usually minimal. The right of set-off is a significant advantage to the bank where money is on deposit in the checking account of the bankrupt and an outstanding loan of the bankrupt is in default. But the question arises as to whether this right of set-off violates the automatic stay of all proceedings which affects every creditor after bankruptcy is filed.

In the case that came before the Supreme Court, the results were diametrically opposite each step of the way. The bankruptcy court originally ruled that the bank's "administrative hold" (where the bank put a hold on the bank account but did not transfer any monies to the bank) on the monies on deposit in the bankrupt's account amounted to a set-off and violated the automatic stay. The bank was then sanctioned. After this sanctioning, the bank released the "administrative hold" and immediately made an application for removal of the stay in the bankruptcy court. The bankruptcy court authorized the bank to set off the respondent's remaining checking account balance against the unpaid loan since the court took the position that the creditor was proceeding in the bankruptcy court and therefore was entitled to a removal of the stay, whereas before, the creditor moved unilaterally without the approval of the bankruptcy court.

The problem with this favorable decision by the bankruptcy court was that the respondent had reduced the checking account balance to zero, so at this point there was nothing to set off. The horse had left the barn.

The district court then rendered a decision diametrically opposed to the bankruptcy court and reversed the judgment by holding that the original administrative hold was not a violation. Unfortunately, this decision did not help. The matter then went to the Court of Appeals, which reversed and agreed with the bankruptcy court. The administrative hold was an exercise of the right of set-off and violated the automatic stay. From the Circuit Court of Appeals, the matter went directly to the Supreme Court of the United States.

The Supreme Court held that the action of the bank was not a set-off because the bank did not purport permanently to reduce respondent's account balance by the amount of the defaulted loan. The bank only put an administrative hold on the account so that the monies could be later withdrawn from the bank account and, therefore, the monies still remained on deposit to the credit of the bankrupt. The court identified a requirement of intent with regard to a set-off that is followed by the majority of jurisdictions, and held that a set-off has not occurred until three steps have been taken:

1. A decision to effectuate a set-off.
2. Some action accomplishing the set-off.
3. A recording of the set-off.

The court held that by using an administrative hold, the bank did not meet this test and, therefore, the automatic stay was not violated.

This reasoning might be applied to any monies on deposit with a creditor, such as a lease of equipment, or a lease of real estate, office space or residential apartment space, or any type of storage situation, or circumstances where a deposit of money is left with the creditor for a specific purpose. Creditors should consult with counsel.[105]

A recent case in the Second Circuit clarified the above ruling of the Supreme Court. In this instance a credit union placed an administrative hold on the account of a bankrupt. Neither the bankrupt nor the credit union took any action for almost four months. The bankruptcy judge held that this freeze was a willful violation and awarded the bankrupt $500 for attorneys' fees. The credit union appealed and shortly thereafter the Supreme Court handed down the decision on *Strumpf* dealing with set-offs. Finally, the district court agreed with the bankruptcy court and rejected the credit union's position finding a distinct difference between the *Strumpf* case and the instance case.[106]

In *Strumpf*, the administrative hold was on the bank account for only five days whereas here it was maintained for almost two months, not exactly a freeze of a temporary nature as happened in the Supreme Court decision. Actually, the court commented that nothing probably would have happened, for the freeze would have remained indefinitely unless the bankrupt made the motion to remove the freeze—thus, an extended hold was the equivalent of a set-off.

EXTENDING CREDIT TO THE BANKRUPT

Under Section 364 of the United States Bankruptcy Code, lending institutions may offer to finance debtors who are operating under Chapter 11. With post-petition financing, the lending institution arranges to have its

[105]*Citizens Bank of Maryland v. Strumpf*, 116 S. Ct. 286, 33 L. Ed. 2d 258 (1995).
[106]*Town of Hempstead Employees F.C.U. v. Wicks*, 215 B.R. 316 (Bankr. E.D.N.Y. 1997).

claims treated as administrative expenses, or to receive priority over any and all administrative expenses, or to have its claims secured by a super priority or equal lien on the property. This priority can only be granted to a lending institution or a credit grantor after a notice and hearing before the court.

The presumption is that this particular credit is being extended outside the ordinary course of business and all interested parties must have notice. A formal hearing must be held as to the rights that are to be afforded the lending institution.

The bankruptcy court allows the debtor in possession, after notice and a hearing before the court, to do the following:

1. obtain unsecured credit as an administrative expense;
2. obtain secured credit which will have priority over any and all administrative expenses;
3. obtain credit or incur debt secured by a lien on the property.

In some instances, this type of lending will have priority, under what is called "super priority," over other expenses and other claims and, in effect, will change the order of priorities. With regard to any change of priorities or any super priority liens, court approval is absolutely necessary.

Where unsecured credit is extended to a Chapter 11 debtor "in the ordinary course of business," court approval is usually not necessary for the debt to be treated as an administrative expense. Whether a transaction is in the ordinary course of business depends upon the nature of the relationship between the creditor and the bankrupt. Before one extends credit to a Chapter 11 bankrupt, consultation with counsel should be made to be certain that the transaction meets the criteria of credit extended in the ordinary course of business. Consideration should be given to whether other creditors feel that the transaction is made within the ordinary course of business and also whether other businesses enter into this same type of transaction and consider same in the "ordinary course of business." If significant credit is being extended to the Chapter 11 bankrupt, and the creditor wishes to adequately protect itself, consult with counsel before the extension of credit.

While certain transactions clearly are or are not in the ordinary course of business, the gray area may present problems. The question of whether the transaction is in the "ordinary course of the business" has perplexed the courts and leaves two types of definitions of the "ordinary course of business." The first test is the most simplistic in that the transaction is an ordinary one and is performed in the operation of the debtor's business. The creditors normally will not expect to receive any notice and will not expect to have an opportunity to object because the creditors recognize that the debtor in possession has been authorized to operate its business.

If the transaction is unusual or out of the ordinary, the creditors will expect to receive notice of the particular transaction. The courts will compare what transactions the debtor entered into before the bankruptcy and what transactions are taking place after the bankruptcy. The criteria of the general test may be the "creditors' expectations" as to what ordinary business normally will be.

The second test requires the transaction be ordinary for the particular business and be the type of transaction engaged in by other similar businesses.

If the creditor meets either one of the above tests and satisfies the court that the financing is in the ordinary course of business, the creditor is entitled to treat the debt as an administrative expense. If the debt was incurred in the ordinary course of business, no notice or hearing is necessary to treat the claim as an administrative expense.

Nevertheless, any post-petition financing that produces any doubt as to whether the creditor is operating in the ordinary course of business with the debtor in possession should be examined carefully before the transaction is completed. Consult with counsel to be assured that you are operating within the ordinary course of business. Otherwise, your claim may not be treated as an administrative expense and the creditor will not have the protection afforded by the Bankruptcy Code.

> ***Credit & Collection Tip:*** *The creditor usually learns about a super priority financing in a notice from the Bankruptcy Court. Do not discard the notice seeking approval of post-petition financing. Such financing could destroy a valid secured claim. Consult with counsel.*

SELLING YOUR BANKRUPTCY CLAIM

Occasionally, a large nationally known corporation will file a Chapter 11. Many creditors owe money to the bankrupt corporation. A cottage industry of organizations evaluates these large bankruptcies and make estimates on what the distribution will be. Based on their investigation and analysis and the fact that the list of creditors is available to them, these organizations offer to purchase the bankruptcy claim of the creditor at a discounted value based upon what they determine the distribution will be.

The organization offers cash immediately, which becomes attractive because the creditor recognizes that the distribution may not be made for many months or sometimes years later. When the creditor receives an offer, the credit manager or collection manager is faced with a difficult decision. Sometimes the decision is not difficult in the event the creditor is in need of money at that particular time. The credit manager or the owner has a motive to accept the offer immediately. Those businesses that are financially solvent can wait for a distribution. The issue being faced by that manager or owner is "how do I make an informed decision?"

Many years ago it was difficult, since information was not available. In today's environment a significant amount of information is available to assist the creditor. The Internet has created many services to provide you with the documents that have been filed in the bankruptcy proceeding which afford significant information about the bankrupt. If the company is a publicly owned company and listed on one of the exchanges, services are available which provide the financial information required to be filed with the Securities and Exchange Commission. Credit reports can be ordered on businesses; and databases provide information as to real estate owned, liens, and mortgages.

An obvious conclusion is that if the party offering to purchase the discount feels the claim is worth 10 cents on the dollar, a likelihood exists (perhaps even a certainty) that the party making the offer expects to receive a distribution larger than the amount being offered to you. Sometimes acceptance of the discount is indicated. The key is obtaining as much information as you can before you make a decision. The extent of the effort to obtain information will probably be determined by the amount of claim. If the amount is relatively small, the best decision would probably be to wait for a distribution.

> ***Credit & Collection Tip:*** *If the amount is large, consult with your legal counsel to obtain as much information as possible. Make sure you are not subject to any preference claims. The offer is usually conditioned on the fact no preference claim will be made by the trustee.*

The agreement should be reviewed by competent bankruptcy counsel. *A proof of claim should be filed, notwithstanding the intent to sell the claim.* The purchaser is buying the claim on the premise that the debt owed is a valid claim that will be recognized by the bankrupt debtor. The agreement provides certain protections for the purchaser in the event that the trustee commences a proceeding to expunge the claim or reduce the amount of the claim. Before selling, consider whether the trustee may have a preference claim by virtue of a payment by the debtor within 90 days of the bankruptcy petition. The purchaser will insert protective language. Researching the bankruptcy is important. The Internet provides several sources of information. At the beginning of the bankruptcy less information is available and any decision made to sell will be based primarily on the creditor's judgment.

The filed schedules of assets and liabilities, income, etc. are available online through Pacer, which can be obtained through your counsel. The buyer has done an evaluation of the bankruptcy filings, and has researched the latest news as well as any financial data that may be on file if it is a publicly traded organization. The creditor is playing in the buyer's ballpark.

The first offer you receive is an invitation and if the buyer is serious, the offer will probably be improved. But a decision to sell should not be based on the price since the offer will increase if the offer is rejected.

Emphasizing that experienced counsel should review the agreement is warranted. The final agreements presented by the buyer are complicated and designed entirely to protect the buyer in the same manner that a promissory note is prepared by the bank to protect the bank.

The principal problems are if the claim is objected to or a trustee moves to expunge the claim or the claim is disallowed. Do you have the right to defend, is a court order required or merely an objection, what are the obligations of the buyer to notify you and if the claim is disallowed and how much will the seller be obligated to repay the buyer plus interest?

The bottom line is to retain experienced counsel before you sell a significant claim. If the claim is a small claim, the recommendation is still to retain counsel to review the agreement.

An effort should be made to confirm that your purchaser is one of the major players in this area and be certain that the purchaser is not stigmatized by a questionable reputation. The best source of this information as a starting point is the bankruptcy attorney that you retain to review the agreement.

U.S. TRUSTEE LIABILITY

The trustee and an assistant enjoy quasi-judicial immunity from liability. This quasi-judicial immunity sometimes is extended to non-judicial officers if they are performing official duties comparable to judges, such as exercising discretion in resolving disputes or in scheduling a hearing. Only when the judgment of an official other than a judge involves the exercise of discretionary judgment does quasi-judicial immunity apply.[107]

IPSO FACTO CLAUSE—WAIVER

Contracts and leases or any other type of agreement which requires the payment of money may contain an "ipso facto" clause. An "ipso facto" clause states that a default or a breach of the agreement takes place

[107]*In re Cherry Barbara Costello*, 298 F.3d 940 (9th Cir. 2002).

immediately upon the filing of a bankruptcy petition. The lease would be terminated, the contract would be breached, and the security agreement or mortgage would be in default.

The Bankruptcy Code has expressly addressed this issue by stating that an executory contract or unexpired lease may not be terminated or modified, notwithstanding any provision in an executory contract or an unexpired lease, solely because of a provision that such contract or lease is conditioned on the insolvency or financial condition of the debtor, before such filing of a bankruptcy petition or the appointment or taking possession by a trustee under the Bankruptcy Code.[108]

Any attempt to create a default or breach in a written agreement because of a filing of a petition would be declared invalid and unenforceable by the court.

Efforts have been made to evade the intent and purpose of this particular provision of the Bankruptcy Code, but the courts seem to see through the deception. One of the techniques is to empower a creditor to appoint sufficient directors who would vote against any filing of a petition in bankruptcy and block the filing of the petition. Sometimes a new entity is created which has complete control over the borrowing party or the lessee, and the board of directors of the new entity is controlled by the landlord or the creditor. These attempts have failed since the courts have taken the position that directors owe a duty not only to the corporation, but a duty to the creditors of the corporation. These techniques do not prohibit a third party from filing an involuntary petition in bankruptcy.[109]

MONEY JUDGMENTS

The bankruptcy courts are divided as to whether the bankruptcy court may enter a judgment notwithstanding it has jurisdiction to enter an appropriate judgment under 28 U.S.C. Section 157(b), which states, "bankruptcy judges may hear and determine all cases under Title 11 and all core proceedings arising under Title 11 . . . and may enter appropriate orders and judgments."

Despite this power to enter appropriate judgments, a split is present between the bankruptcy courts as to whether money judgments may be entered after a determination is made that an obligation is excepted from discharge. A careful review of the particular cases in the particular circuit is recommended before making a decision.

---

[108]11 U.S.C. § 365e(1).

[109]*In re National Hydro Vac. Industry Servs.*, 262 B.R. 781 (Bankr. E.D. Ark. 2001); *In re Kingston Square Assocs.*, 214 B.R. 713 (S.D.N.Y. 1997).

INSUFFICIENT FUNDS—CHECK RETURNED

The Supreme Court has stated that depositing checks that were not supported by sufficient funds does not involve issuing a false statement, principally because a check is not a factual assertion—it is merely an unconditional promise or order to pay a sum certain of money.

A Supreme Court criminal case stated that a check is not a factual assertion and therefore cannot be characterized as "true" or "false." To interpret the criminal statute as meaning that a drawer of a check has made a "false statement" whenever he has insufficient funds in the account at the moment the check is presented would "slight" the wording the statute.

This case has been relied on by many other courts to allow a discharge where a bankrupt has issued checks that were returned unpaid.[110]

The bank check served only to direct the drawer to cause the bank to pay the face amount to the bearer while committing petitioner to make good the obligation if the bank dishonored the draft. Each check did not make any representation as to the state of the bank balance of the issuer of the check. The maker of the check merely states that upon dishonor of the draft or notice of dishonor or protest, he will pay the amount of the draft to the holder of the check. The court dismissed the argument that a representation is present that funds are sufficient to cover the face value of the check. Unfortunately, this particular case involved a criminal prosecution wherein the government was attempting to prove that the defendant made a "false statement."

The majority of the courts adopts this presumption and grant a discharge in bankruptcy even though debtor issued checks that were not paid.[111]

CREDIT CARD PAYMENT

In a recent case, the debtor paid an antecedent debt to a creditor by means of his credit card. The trustee claimed that the debtor's use of the credit card was a transfer of "an interest of the debtor in property."[112]

The Bankruptcy Code does not define the term "interest of the debtor in property," but the Supreme Court has interpreted this term to coincide with the definition of property of the estate which includes all legal and equitable interest of the debtor in property as of the commencement of the case. If the debtor transfers property that would have been available for

[110]*Williams v. United States*, 458 U.S. 279 (1982).

[111]*In re Miller*, 310 B.R. 185 (Bankr. C.D. Cal. 2004); *In re Beza*, 310 B.R. 432 (Bankr. W.D. Mo. 2004).

[112]*In re Perry*, 343 B.R. 685 (Bankr. D. Utah 2005).

distribution to the creditors, it would be property of the estate. If the property would not have reduced the cash available for distribution, such as the extension of credit on the credit card in this instance, creditors of an estate cannot force a debtor to use credit to create liquidity available for distribution. Credit on its own serves no immediate benefit to the estate of the bankrupt. Accordingly, the court held that payment to the antecedent creditor does not constitute property of the estate in which the debtor has an interest.

FDCPA CLAIM IN BANKRUPTCY

The Ninth Circuit has stated that if a creditor is in contempt of a discharge injunction, a claim under the FDCPA would not be available in addition to relief under the bankruptcy code.[113]

On the other hand, the Seventh Circuit found a way to keep the FDCPA claim alive.[114] The bankruptcy code and the FDCPA do not meet the narrow criteria for one federal statute's implied repeal of another. The bankruptcy code does not repeal that portion of the FDCPA and therefore a claim would be entertained under the FDCPA in the Seventh Circuit (not the bankruptcy court).

Two more cases on the same subject were decided in the Sixth Circuit and both traveled down different roads.[115] One case has held that an irreconcilable conflict does not exist between the bankruptcy code and the FDCPA and no legislative intent has been identified showing that the bankruptcy code preempts the FDCPA. The bankruptcy court did not dismiss the FDCPA claim.

The next case in 2006 in Michigan held that applying the FDCPA to bankruptcy proofs of claim could discourage creditors from filing claims and encourage debtors to ignore the procedural safeguards within the bankruptcy code, such as the right to object to a proof of claim and to seek sanctions against creditors who violate provisions within the bankruptcy code, in favor of the FDCPA.[116] The practice of debtors deliberately bypassing the bankruptcy codes objection process in favor of alternative litigation would undermine the entire bankruptcy system.

New matters commenced in those Circuits which have not addressed this problem will probably result in a toss of the coin until the Supreme Court or another Circuit Court of Appeals considers the issue.

---

[113]*Walls v. Wells Fargo Bank, N.A.*, 276 F.3d 502 (9th Cir. 2002).
[114]*Randolph v. IMBS, Inc.*, 368 F.3d 726 (7th Cir. 2004).
[115]*In re Gunter*, 334 B.R. 900 (Bankr. S.D. Ohio 2005).
[116]*In re Rice-Etherly*, 336 B.R. 308 (Bankr. E.D. Mich. 2006).

PIERCING THE CORPORATE VEIL

We have devoted space to piercing the corporate veil and deepening insolvency in Chapter 4. The same opportunity may arise if the corporate debtor files a bankruptcy, and the reason for the bankruptcy is because of the fraud practiced by either the shareholders, directors, or officers. If the fraud affects all the creditors, the suit to proceed against the individuals inures to the benefit of the trustee so that all the creditors will share. If the fraud practiced is personal in nature to one particular creditor, that creditor pleading sufficient personal injuries may be able to divert the claim from the trustee and assert the claim on behalf of the individual creditor.

DEEPENING INSOLVENCY

While debtors were not too successful in relying on the concept of lender's liability, the tort of deepening insolvency has been sufficiently litigated to attract the attention of the secured financial institutions that extend credit.

A few cases in the 1980s and 1990s flirted with the concept, but did not identify it as a companion to lenders liability, nor was the terminology "deepening insolvency" frequently mentioned in the legal publications. A major case in the bankruptcy courts of Delaware, *In re Exide Technologies, Inc.*, has brought to the table this developing doctrine of deepening insolvency. The courts seem to be accepting a definition of deepening insolvency, which was first set forth in a Third Circuit decision in 2001 and described the idea as "injury to the debtors corporate property from the fraudulent expansion of corporate debt and prolongation of corporate life."[117]

A recent case in Pennsylvania limited the decision in *Lafferty* to a requirement that only fraudulent conduct will suffice to support a deepening insolvency claim under Pennsylvania law.[118] The court stated:

> we know no reason to extend the scope of deepening insolvency beyond Lafferty's limited holding (fraudulent conduct). To that end we hold that a claim of negligence cannot sustain a deepening insolvency cause of action.

---

[117] *In re Exide Technologies*, 299 B.R. 732 (Bankr. Del. 2003). *See also In re CitX Corp. Inc.*, 448 F. 3d 672 (3d Cir. 2006); *Official Comm. of Unsecured Creditors v. R.F. Lafferty & Co., Inc.*, 267 F. 3d 340 (3d Cir. 2001); *In re Oakwood Homes Corp.*, 340 B.R. 510 (Bankr. D. Del. 2006); *Trenwick Am. Litig. Trust v. Ernst & Young, L.L.P.*, 906 A. 2d 168 (Del. Ch. 2006).

[118] *In re CitX Corp., Inc.*, 2005 WL 1388963 (E.D. Pa. June 7, 2005), *aff'd*, 448 F.3d 672 (3d Cir. 2006).

In a later case which interpreted *Lafferty*, the judge held that the plaintiff must prove all 5 of the typical elements of fraud under the applicable state laws. Notwithstanding that the five elements are somewhat different in the various states, the five elements that were described were "a representation of material fact, falsity, scienter, reliance and injury."[119]

At the same time, both the Pennsylvania court and the most recent decision in Delaware indicated that deepening insolvency would not support a tort like negligence or even a tort such as malpractice. Fraudulent conduct is the essential element of deepening insolvency. Shortly after the *CitX* opinion, a bankruptcy court in New York cited *CitX* as a basis for dismissing a claim of deepening insolvency.[120]

In several instances, "deepening insolvency" has been utilized in the environment of the bankruptcy courts where auditors have negligently or intentionally issued false financial statements, or where an insurer was allowed to continue business while the officers and directors diverted monies and assets into their own pockets.[121]

The major defense that directors assert to deepening insolvency is the business judgment rule, which generally protects directors by granting deference to their decisions so long as the directors use due diligence that a reasonable director would exercise before rendering a decision. The Model Business Corporation Act in Section 8.30(a)(2002) states that a director shall discharge his duties as a director (1) in good faith; (2) with the care that an ordinary prudent person in a like position would exercise under similar circumstances; and (3) in a manner he reasonably believes to be in the best interest of the corporation.

The function of the "business judgment rule" is significant in that the rule requires that the directors of a corporation act on an informed basis, in good faith and with the honest belief that the action taken was in the best interest of the company. Absent an abuse of discretion, the decision is usually respected by the court. The burden is on the party challenging the decision to establish facts rebutting the presumption.

The protection can only be claimed by disinterested directors who otherwise meet the test of the business judgment rule. The test declares that directors may not appear on both sides of a transaction nor expect to derive any personal financial benefit from it in the sense of self dealing, as opposed to a benefit for the corporation or all stockholders generally. Furthermore, to invoke the rules' protection, directors have a duty to inform themselves, prior to making a business decision, of all material

---

[119] *In re Oakwood Homes Corp.*, 340 B.R. 510 (Bankr. D. Del. 2006).

[120] *In re Verestar, Inc.*, 343 B.R. 444 (Bankr. S.D.N.Y. 2006); *In re CitX Corp., Inc.*, 2005 WL 1388963 (E.D. Pa. June 7, 2005), *aff'd*, 448 F.3d 672 (3d Cir. 2006).

[121] *In re Flagship Healthcare*, 269 B.R. 721 (Bankr. S.D. Fla. 2001); *Gouiran Holdings Inc. v. DeSantis*, 165 B.R. 104 (E.D.N.Y. 1994); *Corcoran v. Frank B. Hall*, 155 A.D.2d 314 (N.Y. App. Div. 1st Dep't 1989).

information reasonably available to them. Having become so informed, they must then act with the requisite care in the discharge of their duties.[122]

The theory essentially states that a defendant's conduct which conceals a company's insolvency by fraud or negligence and prolongs the continuation of a business, when the business is insolvent, and increases the debt and the exposure of losses to the creditors, exposes the culpable party to liability. The liability certainly extends to officers and directors as well as to attorneys, accountants, and other professionals if they are aiding and abetting the concealment of the insolvency from the creditors. The exposure of financial institutions, lenders, and particularly secured lenders, to liability was identified in the *Exide* case.

A syndication of banks extended over $600 million in credit to Exide. As time went on, the losses at Exide were running over $100 million. The syndicate at that particular time made an additional loan of several million dollars to finance an acquisition of a competitor. In consideration of the additional extension of credit, Exide provided substantial additional collateral and personal guarantees that the court determined were more valuable than the consideration provided for the acquisition. It appeared that the lenders actually encouraged and promoted this acquisition to obtain this additional collateral.

The major issue is whether the claim for deepening insolvency would be recognized. The court responded in the affirmative. The complaint alleged that the corporation was insolvent and market conditions were continuing to decline. The debtors were facing future economic uncertainty, allowing the lenders to acquire overwhelming economic leverage resulting in a de facto control over Exide. The lenders received collateral pledges and guarantees far in excess of the value of the new credit provided. The chief financial officer was replaced. The debtor made payment or reimbursement to the professionals of the lenders for significant fees. The complaint also alleged that the lenders knowingly participated in all of these transactions for the sole purpose of continuing the life of the corporation, notwithstanding that the lenders knew that the corporation was insolvent. The transaction was designed solely to acquire additional collateral.

The moral of the story is that lenders must be cognizant of their exposure to the tort of deepening insolvency in the event they delay either foreclosing on their collateral, or what is more important, extending additional credit to the debtor in consideration of receiving additional collateral. One of the important ingredients in the case was that the lenders appeared to be exercising control over the borrower. A significant point was made of the replacement of the CFO. Before any extension of credit should be made, the lender should obtain detailed financial statements, budgets, and financial projections that the company is solvent and can continue to operate.

---

[122] *Aronson v. Lewis*, 473 A.2d 805 (Del. 1984).

The collateral obtained should not exceed the loan. Finally, a diligent inquiry and review that the debtor is solvent and will continue to be solvent should be conducted.

A development of the doctrine of "deepening insolvency" moved a few steps backward in the last year. The first case in New York, while recognizing that the doctrine is still in existence, limited the doctrine to the extent that before a recovery under deepening insolvency will be available, some kind of tort such as fraud or other wrong or some other type of obligation or duty not only continued to prolong the debtor's life but also increased the indebtedness of the debtor during said prolongation.[123]

A Delaware state court, not a federal court, has made it even more difficult to assert a claim of deepening insolvency.[124] Most of the major corporations are organized in Delaware. A business failure does not mean that a plaintiff can assert claims against the directors, officers and advisers on the scene by alleging their business strategy did not pan out. If a simple failure supported claims, this deterrent to healthy risk taken by businesses would undermine the potential of capitalist endeavors. The law does not oblige directors of an insolvent corporation to cause the liquidation of the corporation. A member of a board of directors who embarks upon a strategy to save an insolvent company is not necessarily the guarantor of that strategy. For many years, Delaware has been the choice of the officers and directors to incorporate, primarily because of the friendliness of the courts to the same officers and directors.

When we add the above several recent decisions, we are not at all sure that the concept of deepening insolvency is surviving the restrictions and tests that have been created by several courts. The courts seem to feel that other remedies are available. Deepening insolvency is just another name for some other remedy.

Fraud or some form of a tort which has the ingredient of a breach of a fiduciary duty, a fraudulent conveyance or some other misrepresentation for a deceptive act may constitute together a fraud upon a third party. The third party relies upon the said deceptive act or fraud since otherwise he should not be instituting the suit. The advice is to plead the deepening insolvency and the fraudulent conveyance as alternative causes of action, at least in those states that allow it. By the time the next edition of the book rolls around, some decisions may totally abolish the concept of deepening insolvency.[125]

---

[123] *In re Global Serv. Group, LLC*, 316 B.R. 451 (Bankr. S.D.N.Y. 2004).

[124] *Trenwick Am. Litig. Trust v. Ernst & Young, LLP*, 906 A.2d 168 (Del. Ch. 2006).

[125] *Fehribach v. Ernst & Young LLP*, 493 F.3d 905 (7th Cir. 2007); *In re Parmalat Secs. Litig.*, 501 F. Supp. 2d 560 (S.D.N.Y. 2007); *In re Amcast Indus. Corp.*, 365 B.R. 91 (Bankr. S.D. Ohio 2007).

CHARITABLE CONTRIBUTIONS

As a result of the new act, those debtors who are above the median income may not deduct from their income the actual expenses. Rather, they must use the specific standardized dollar amounts listed in an IRS publication.

The trustee took the position that the debtor's deduction for charitable contributions in calculating disposable income under the means test is not permissible as it is not an allowed expense under the Internal Revenue Manual Section 5.15.1.10, entitled "Other Expenses." Under these rules the trustee held that "tithing" is not allowed. One attorney for the debtor had to go all the way to Arkansas to find another judge who disagreed.[126]

PACER—ACCESS TO ELECTRONIC RECORDS OF THE BANKRUPTCY COURTS

A company known as "Pacer" provides for a fee access to the court's electronic records. They will provide the docket sheets and copies of filed pleadings as well as the bankruptcy schedules which include the liabilities and assets as well as income of the bankrupt. Pacer is located at 7550 Interstate Highway #10 West, Suite 600, San Antonio, Texas 78229; Telephone Number: 1-800-676-6856.

BAD FAITH

Bad faith frequently comes up in the bankruptcy court when describing either the debtor or the creditor. When speaking of the debtor and whether a petition has been filed in bad faith, many of the courts use "an improper use" test which "finds bad faith when a petitioning creditor uses involuntary bankruptcy procedures in an attempt to obtain a disproportionate advantage for itself, rather than protect against other creditors obtaining disproportionate advantages, particularly when the petitioner could have advanced its own interests in a different forum."

"Improper purpose" has been defined by the courts as bad faith if the filing of the petition was motivated by ill will, malice or a desire to embarrass or harass the alleged debtor. Another line of cases examines what a reasonable person would have believed and the test basically becomes an

---

[126] *See In re Diagostino*, 347 B.R. 116 (Bankr. N.D.N.Y. 2006); *In re Petty*, 338 B.R. 805 (Bankr. E.D. Ark. 2006).

objective evaluation. Other courts have utilized the language in Rule 9011(b) which states as follows:

Representations to the court:

(b) "by presenting to the court (whether by signing, filing, submitting, or later advocating) a petition, pleading, written notice or other paper an attorney or unrepresented party are certifying that to the best of the person's knowledge, information, and belief, formed after an inquiry reasonable under the circumstances,

1. It is not being presented for any improper purpose such as to harass or to cause unnecessary delay or needless increase in the cost of litigation;
2. The claims, defenses, and other legal contentions therein are warranted by existing law or by a nonfrivolous argument for the extension, modification, or reversal of existing law or the establishment of new law;
3. The allegation and other factual contentions have evidentiary support or, if specifically so identified a likely to have evidentiary support after a reasonable opportunity for further investigation or discovery; and
4. The denials of factual contentions are warranted on the evidence or if specifically so identified, are reasonably based on a lack of information or belief.

Where doubt is present, a thorough examination of the case law in the circuit should be conducted to identify which theory the bankruptcy courts are using. A thorough examination of Rule 9011(b) is warranted since said rule is available to any court to use at any time, notwithstanding the theory being promulgated by other case law.[127]

[127] *In re Better Care*, 97 B.R. 405 (Bankr. N.D. Ill. 1989); *In re Camelot, Inc.*, 25 B.R. 861 (Bankr. E.D. Tenn. 1982); *In re Fox Island Square Partnership*, 106 B.R. 962 (Bankr. N.D. Ill. 1989); *In re Bayshore Wire Products Corp.*, 209 F.3d 100 (2d Cir. 2000).

CHAPTER 6
APPENDIX I

PROOF OF CLAIM FORM

B 10 (Official Form 10) (04/07)

UNITED STATES BANKRUPTCY COURT WESTERN DISTRICT OF WISCONSIN

PROOF OF CLAIM

Name of Debtor

Case Number

NOTE: This form should not be used to make a claim for an administrative expense arising after the commencement of the case. A "request" for payment of an administrative expense may be filed pursuant to 11 U.S.C. § 503.

Name of Creditor (The person or other entity to whom the debtor owes money or property):

□ Check box if you are aware that anyone else has filed a proof of claim relating to your claim. Attach copy of statement giving particulars.

Name and address where notices should be sent:

□ Check box if you have never received any notices from the bankruptcy court in this case.

□ Check box if the address differs from the address on the envelope sent to you by the court.

Telephone number:

THIS SPACE IS FOR COURT USE ONLY

Last four digits of account or other number by which creditor identifies debtor:

Check here if this claim □ replaces □ amends a previously filed claim, dated:________________

1. **Basis for Claim**
□ Goods sold
□ Services performed
□ Money loaned
□ Personal injury/wrongful death
□ Taxes
□ Retiree benefits as defined in 11 U.S.C. § 1114(a)
□ Other________________________
□ Wages, salaries, and compensation (fill out below)
Last four digits of your SS #:____
Unpaid compensation for services performed
From ____________ to ____________
(date) (date)

2. **Date debt was incurred:**

3. **If court judgment, date obtained:**

4. **Classification of Claim.** Check the appropriate box or boxes that best describe your claim and state the amount of the claim at the time the case was filed. See reverse side for important explanations.

Unsecured Nonpriority Claim $____________________

□ Check this box if: a) there is no collateral or lien securing your claim, or b) your claim exceeds the value of the property securing it, or c) none or only part of your claim is entitled to priority.

Unsecured Priority Claim

□ Check this box if you have an unsecured claim, all or part of which is entitled to priority.

Amount entitled to priority $____________________

Specify the priority of the claim:

□ Domestic support obligations under 11 U.S.C. § 507(a)(1)(A) or (a)(1)(B).

□ Wages, salaries, or commissions (up to $10,950),* earned within 180 days before filing of the bankruptcy petition or cessation of the debtor's business, whichever is earlier - 11 U.S.C. § 507(a)(4).

□ Contributions to an employee benefit plan - 11 U.S.C. § 507(a)(5).

Secured Claim

□ Check this box if your claim is secured by collateral (including a right of setoff).

Brief Description of Collateral:
□ Real Estate □ Other________________
□ Motor Vehicle

Value of Collateral: $________________

Amount of arrearage and other charges at time case filed included in secured claim, if any: $________________

□ Up to $2,425* of deposits toward purchase, lease, or rental of property or services for personal, family, or household use - 11 U.S.C. § 507(a)(7).

□ Taxes or penalties owed to governmental units - 11 U.S.C. § 507(a)(8).

□ Other - Specify applicable paragraph of 11 U.S.C. § 507(a)(___).

**Amounts are subject to adjustment on 4/1/10 and every 3 years thereafter with respect to cases commenced on or after the date of adjustment.*

5. **Total Amount of Claim at Time Case Filed:** $__________ __________ __________ __________
(unsecured) (secured) (priority) (total)

□ Check this box if claim includes interest or other charges in addition to the principal amount of the claim. Attach itemized statement of all interest or additional charges.

6. **Credits:** The amount of all payments on this claim has been credited and deducted for the purpose of making this proof of claim.

7. **Supporting Documents:** *Attach copies of supporting documents,* such as promissory notes, purchase orders, invoices, itemized statements of running accounts, contracts, court judgments, mortgages, security agreements, and evidence of perfection of lien. DO NOT SEND ORIGINAL DOCUMENTS. If the documents are not available, explain. If the documents are voluminous, attach a summary.

8. **Date-Stamped Copy:** To receive an acknowledgment of the filing of your claim, enclose a stamped, self-addressed envelope and copy of this proof of claim.

THIS SPACE IS FOR COURT USE ONLY

All copies should be submitted on single sided 8 1/2 by 11 paper.

Date

Sign and print the name and title, if any, of the creditor or other person authorized to file this claim (attach copy of power of attorney, if any):

Penalty for presenting fraudulent claim: Fine of up to $500,000 or imprisonment for up to 5 years, or both. 18 U.S.C. §§ 152 and 3571.

APPENDIX II

INSTRUCTIONS FOR PROOF OF CLAIM FORM

B 10 (Official Form 10) (04/07)

INSTRUCTIONS FOR PROOF OF CLAIM FORM

The instructions and definitions below are general explanations of the law. In particular types of cases or circumstances, such as bankruptcy cases that are not filed voluntarily by a debtor, there may be exceptions to these general rules.

----- DEFINITIONS -----

Debtor

The person, corporation, or other entity that has filed a bankruptcy case is called the debtor.

Creditor

A creditor is any person, corporation, or other entity to whom the debtor owed a debt on the date that the bankruptcy case was filed.

Proof of Claim

A form telling the bankruptcy court how much the debtor owed a creditor at the time the bankruptcy case was filed (the amount of the creditor's claim). This form must be filed with the clerk of the bankruptcy court where the bankruptcy case was filed.

Secured Claim

A claim is a secured claim to the extent that the creditor has a lien on property of the debtor (collateral) that gives the creditor the right to be paid from that property before creditors who do not have liens on the property.

Examples of liens are a mortgage on real estate and a security interest in a car, truck, boat, television set, or other item of property. A lien may have been obtained through a court proceeding before the bankruptcy case began; in some states a court judgment is a lien. In addition, to the extent a creditor also owes money to the debtor (has a right of setoff), the creditor's claim may be a secured claim. (See also *Unsecured Claim.*)

Unsecured Claim

If a claim is not a secured claim it is an unsecured claim. A claim may be partly secured and partly unsecured if the property on which a creditor has a lien is not worth enough to pay the creditor in full.

Unsecured Priority Claim

Certain types of unsecured claims are given priority, so they are to be paid in bankruptcy cases before most other unsecured claims (if there is sufficient money or property available to pay these claims). The most common types of priority claims are listed on the proof of claim form. Unsecured claims that are not specifically given priority status by the bankruptcy laws are classified as *Unsecured Nonpriority Claims.*

Items to be completed in Proof of Claim form (if not already filled in)

Court, Name of Debtor, and Case Number:
Fill in the name of the federal judicial district where the bankruptcy case was filed (for example, Central District of California), the name of the debtor in the bankruptcy case, and the bankruptcy case number. If you received a notice of the case from the court, all of this information is near the top of the notice.

Information about Creditor:
Complete the section giving the name, address, and telephone number of the creditor to whom the debtor owes money or property, and the debtor's account number, if any. If anyone else has already filed a proof of claim relating to this debt, if you never received notices from the bankruptcy court about this case, if your address differs from that to which the court sent notice, or if this proof of claim replaces or changes a proof of claim that was already filed, check the appropriate box on the form.

1. **Basis for Claim:**
   Check the type of debt for which the proof of claim is being filed. If the type of debt is not listed, check "Other" and briefly describe the type of debt. If you were an employee of the debtor, fill in the last four digits of your social security number and the dates of work for which you were not paid.

2. **Date Debt Incurred:**
   Fill in the date when the debt first was owed by the debtor.

3. **Court Judgments:**
   If you have a court judgment for this debt, state the date the court entered the judgment.

4. **Classification of Claim:**
   Secured Claim:
   Check the appropriate place if the claim is a secured claim. You must state the type and value of property that is collateral for the claim, attach copies of the documentation of your lien, and state the amount past due on the claim as of the date the bankruptcy case was filed. A claim may be partly secured and partly unsecured. (See DEFINITIONS, above).

   Unsecured Priority Claim:
   Check the appropriate place if you have an unsecured priority claim, and state the amount entitled to priority. (See DEFINITIONS, above). A claim may be partly priority and partly nonpriority if, for example, the claim is for more than the amount given priority by the law. Check the appropriate place to specify the type of priority claim.

   Unsecured Nonpriority Claim:
   Check the appropriate place if you have an unsecured nonpriority claim, sometimes referred to as a "general unsecured claim." (See DEFINITIONS, above.) If your claim is partly secured and partly unsecured, state here the amount that is unsecured. If part of your claim is entitled to priority, state here the amount **not** entitled to priority.

5. **Total Amount of Claim at Time Case Filed:**
   Fill in the total amount of the entire claim. If interest or other charges in addition to the principal amount of the claim are included, check the appropriate place on the form and attach an itemization of the interest and charges.

6. **Credits:**
   By signing this proof of claim, you are stating under oath that in calculating the amount of your claim you have given the debtor credit for all payments received from the debtor.

7. **Supporting Documents:**
   You must attach to this proof of claim form copies of documents that show the debtor owes the debt claimed or, if the documents are too lengthy, a summary of those documents. If documents are not available, you must attach an explanation of why they are not available.

APPENDIX III

EXCERPTS FROM BANKRUPTCY CODE—AUTOMATIC STAY

TITLE 11. BANKRUPTCY UNITED STATES CODE

Chapter 3. Case Administration

Subchapter III. Administration

11 USC § 362. Automatic stay

(a) Except as provided in subsection (b) of this section, a petition filed under section 301, 302, or 303 of this title, or an application filed under section 5(a)(3) of the Securities Investor Protection Act of 1970, operates as a stay, applicable to all entities, of—

(1) the commencement or continuation, including the issuance or employment of process, of a judicial, administrative, or other action or proceeding against the debtor that was or could have been commenced before the commencement of the case under this title, or to recover a claim against the debtor that arose before the commencement of the case under this title;

(2) the enforcement, against the debtor or against property of the estate, of a judgment obtained before the commencement of the case under this title;

(3) any act to obtain possession of property of the estate or of property from the estate or to exercise control over property of the estate;

(4) any act to create, perfect, or enforce any lien against property of the estate;

(5) any act to create, perfect, or enforce against property of the debtor any lien to the extent that such lien secures a claim that arose before the commencement of the case under this title;

(6) any act to collect, assess, or recover a claim against the debtor that arose before the commencement of the case under this title;

(7) the setoff of any debt owing to the debtor that arose before the commencement of the case under this title against any claim against the debtor; and

(8) the commencement or continuation of a proceeding before the United States Tax Court concerning a corporate debtor's tax liability for a taxable period the bankruptcy court may determine or concerning the tax liability of a debtor who is an individual for a taxable period ending before the date of the order for relief under this title.

(b) The filing of a petition under section 301, 302, or 303 of this title, or of an application under section 5(a)(3) of the Securities Investor Protection Act of 1970, does not operate as a stay—

(1) under subsection (a) of this section, of the commencement or continuation of a criminal action or proceeding against the debtor;

(2) under subsection (a)—

(A) of the commencement or continuation of a civil action or proceeding—

(i) for the establishment of paternity;

(ii) for the establishment or modification of an order for domestic support obligations;

(iii) concerning child custody or visitation;

(iv) for the dissolution of a marriage, except to the extent that such proceeding seeks to determine the division of property that is property of the estate; or

(v) regarding domestic violence;

(B) of the collection of a domestic support obligation from property that is not property of the estate;

(C) with respect to the withholding of income that is property of the estate or property of the debtor for payment of a domestic support obligation under a judicial or administrative order or a statute;

(D) of the withholding, suspension, or restriction of a driver's license, a professional or occupational license, or a recreational license, under State law, as specified in section 466(a)(16) of the Social Security Act;

(E) of the reporting of overdue support owed by a parent to any consumer reporting agency as specified in section 466(a)(7) of the Social Security Act;

(F) of the interception of a tax refund, as specified in sections 464 and 466(a)(3) of the Social Security Act or under an analogous State law; or

(G) of the enforcement of a medical obligation, as specified under title IV of the Social Security Act;

(3) under subsection (a) of this section, of any act to perfect, or to maintain or continue the perfection of, an interest in property to the extent that the trustee's rights and powers are subject to such perfection under section 546(b) of this title or to the extent that such act is accomplished within the period provided under section 547(e)(2)(A) of this title;

(4) under paragraph (1), (2), (3), or (6) of subsection (a) of this section, of the commencement or continuation of an action or proceeding by a governmental unit or any organization exercising authority under the Convention on the Prohibition of the Development, Production, Stockpiling and Use of Chemical Weapons and on Their Destruction, opened for signature on January 13, 1993, to enforce such governmental unit's or organization's police and regulatory power, including the enforcement of a judgment other than a money judgment, obtained in an action or proceeding by the governmental unit to enforce such governmental unit's or organization's police or regulatory power;

[(5) Repealed. Pub. L. 105-277, div. I, title VI, § 603(1), Oct. 21, 1998, 112 [(5) Stat. 2681-866;]

(6) under subsection (a) of this section, of the setoff by a commodity broker, forward contract merchant, stockbroker, financial institution, financial participant, or securities clearing agency of any mutual debt and claim under or in connection with commodity contracts, as defined in section 761 of this title, forward contracts, or securities contracts, as defined in section 741 of this title, that constitutes the setoff of a claim against the debtor for a margin payment, as defined in section 101, 741, or 761 of this title, or settlement payment, as defined in section 101 or 741 of this title, arising out of commodity contracts, forward contracts, or securities contracts against cash, securities, or other property held by, pledged to, under the control of, or due from such commodity broker, forward contract merchant, stockbroker, financial institution, financial participant, or securities clearing agency to margin, guarantee, secure, or settle commodity contracts, forward contracts, or securities contracts;

(7) under subsection (a) of this section, of the setoff by a repo participant or financial participant, of any mutual debt and claim under or in connection with repurchase agreements that constitutes the setoff of a claim against the debtor for a margin payment, as defined in section 741, or 761 of this title, or settlement payment, as defined in section 741 of this title, arising out of repurchase agreements against cash, securities, or other property held by, pledged to, under the control of, or due from such repo participant or financial participant to margin, guarantee, secure or settle repurchase agreements;

(8) under subsection (a) of this section, of the commencement of any action by the Secretary of Housing and Urban Development to foreclose a mortgage or deed of trust in any case in which the mortgage or

deed of trust held by the Secretary is insured or was formerly insured under the National Housing Act and covers property, or combinations of property, consisting of five or more living units;

(9) under subsection (a), of—

(A) an audit by a governmental unit to determine tax liability;

(B) the issuance to the debtor by a governmental unit of a notice of tax deficiency;

(C) a demand for tax returns; or

(D) the making of an assessment for any tax and issuance of a notice and demand for payment of such an assessment (but any tax lien that would otherwise attach to property of the estate by reason of such an assessment shall not take effect unless such tax is a debt of the debtor that will not be discharged in the case and such property or its proceeds are transferred out of the estate to, or otherwise revested in, the debtor).

(10) under subsection (a) of this section, of any act by a lessor to the debtor under a lease of nonresidential real property that has terminated by the expiration of the stated term of the lease before the commencement of or during a case under this title to obtain possession of such property;

(11) under subsection (a) of this section, of the presentment of a negotiable instrument and the giving of notice of and protesting dishonor of such an instrument;

(12) under subsection (a) of this section, after the date which is 90 days after the filing of such petition, of the commencement or continuation, and conclusion to the entry of final judgment, of an action which involves a debtor subject to reorganization pursuant to chapter 11 of this title and which was brought by the Secretary of Transportation under section 31325 of title 46 (including distribution of any proceeds of sale) to foreclose a preferred ship or fleet mortgage, or a security interest in or relating to a vessel or vessel under construction, held by the Secretary of Transportation under section 207 or title XI of the Merchant Marine Act, 1936, or under applicable State law;

(13) under subsection (a) of this section, after the date which is 90 days after the filing of such petition, of the commencement or continuation, and conclusion to the entry of final judgment, of an action which involves a debtor subject to reorganization pursuant to chapter 11 of this title and which was brought by the Secretary of Commerce under section 31325 of title 46 (including distribution of any proceeds of sale) to foreclose a preferred ship or fleet mortgage in a vessel or a mortgage, deed of trust, or other security interest in a fishing facility held by the Secretary of Commerce under section 207 or title XI of the Merchant Marine Act, 1936;

(14) under subsection (a) of this section, of any action by an accrediting agency regarding the accreditation status of the debtor as an educational institution;

(15) under subsection (a) of this section, of any action by a State licensing body regarding the licensure of the debtor as an educational institution;

(16) under subsection (a) of this section, of any action by a guaranty agency, as defined in section 435(j) of the Higher Education Act of 1965 or the Secretary of Education regarding the eligibility of the debtor to participate in programs authorized under such Act;

(17) under subsection (a), of the setoff by a swap participant or financial participant of a mutual debt and claim under or in connection with one or more swap agreements that constitutes the setoff of a claim against the debtor for any payment or other transfer of property due from the debtor under or in connection with any swap agreement against any payment due to the debtor from the swap participant or financial participant under or in connection with any swap agreement or against cash, securities, or other property held by, pledged to, under the control of, or due from such swap participant or financial participant to margin, guarantee, secure, or settle any swap agreement;

(18) under subsection (a) of the creation or perfection of a statutory lien for an ad valorem property tax, or a special tax or special assessment on real property whether or not ad valorem, imposed by a governmental unit, if such tax or assessment comes due after the date of the filing of the petition;

(19) under subsection (a), of withholding of income from a debtor's wages and collection of amounts withheld, under the debtor's agreement authorizing that withholding and collection for the benefit of a pension, profit-sharing, stock bonus, or other plan established under section 401, 403, 408, 408A, 414, 457, or 501(c) of the Internal Revenue Code of 1986, that is sponsored by the employer of the debtor, or an affiliate, successor, or predecessor of such employer—

(A) to the extent that the amounts withheld and collected are used solely for payments relating to a loan from a plan under section 408(b)(1) of the Employee Retirement Income Security Act of 1974 or is subject to section 72(p) of the Internal Revenue Code of 1986; or

(B) a loan from a thrift savings plan permitted under subchapter III of chapter 84 of title 5, that satisfies the requirements of section 8433(g) of such title;

but nothing in this paragraph may be construed to provide that any loan made under a governmental plan under section 414(d), or a contract or account under section 403(b), of the Internal Revenue Code of 1986 constitutes a claim or a debt under this title;

(20) under subsection (a), of any act to enforce any lien against or security interest in real property following entry of the order under subsection (d)(4) as to such real property in any prior case under this title, for a period of 2 years after the date of the entry of such an order, except that

the debtor, in a subsequent case under this title, may move for relief from such order based upon changed circumstances or for other good cause shown, after notice and a hearing;

(21) under subsection (a), of any act to enforce any lien against or security interest in real property—

(A) if the debtor is ineligible under section 109(g) to be a debtor in a case under this title; or

(B) if the case under this title was filed in violation of a bankruptcy court order in a prior case under this title prohibiting the debtor from being a debtor in another case under this title;

(22) subject to subsection (l), under subsection (a)(3), of the continuation of any eviction, unlawful detainer action, or similar proceeding by a lessor against a debtor involving residential property in which the debtor resides as a tenant under a lease or rental agreement and with respect to which the lessor has obtained before the date of the filing of the bankruptcy petition, a judgment for possession of such property against the debtor;

(23) subject to subsection (m), under subsection (a)(3), of an eviction action that seeks possession of the residential property in which the debtor resides as a tenant under a lease or rental agreement based on endangerment of such property or the illegal use of controlled substances on such property, but only if the lessor files with the court, and serves upon the debtor, a certification under penalty of perjury that such an eviction action has been filed, or that the debtor, during the 30-day period preceding the date of the filing of the certification, has endangered property or illegally used or allowed to be used a controlled substance on the property;

(24) under subsection (a), of any transfer that is not avoidable under section 544 and that is not avoidable under section 549;

(25) under subsection (a), of—

(A) the commencement or continuation of an investigation or action by a securities self regulatory organization to enforce such organization's regulatory power;

(B) the enforcement of an order or decision, other than for monetary sanctions, obtained in an action by such securities self regulatory organization to enforce such organization's regulatory power; or

(C) any act taken by such securities self-regulatory organization to delist, delete, or refuse to permit quotation of any stock that does not meet applicable regulatory requirements;

(26) under subsection (a), of the setoff under applicable nonbankruptcy law of an income tax refund, by a governmental unit, with respect to a taxable period that ended before the date of the order for relief against an income tax liability for a taxable period that also ended before the date of the order for relief, except that in any case in which the setoff of an income tax refund is not permitted under

applicable nonbankruptcy law because of a pending action to determine the amount or legality of a tax liability, the governmental unit may hold the refund pending the resolution of the action, unless the court, on the motion of the trustee and after notice and a hearing, grants the taxing authority adequate protection (within the meaning of section 361) for the secured claim of such authority in the setoff under section 506(a);

(27) under subsection (a), of the setoff by a master netting agreement participant of a mutual debt and claim under or in connection with one or more master netting agreements or any contract or agreement subject to such agreements that constitutes the setoff of a claim against the debtor for any payment or other transfer of property due from the debtor under or in connection with such agreements or any contract or agreement subject to such agreements against any payment due to the debtor from such master netting agreement participant under or in connection with such agreements or any contract or agreement subject to such agreements or against cash, securities, or other property held by, pledged to, under the control of, or due from such master netting agreement participant to margin, guarantee, secure, or settle such agreements or any contract or agreement subject to such agreements, to the extent that such participant is eligible to exercise such offset rights under paragraph (6), (7), or (17) for each individual contract covered by the master netting agreement in issue; and

(28) under subsection (a), of the exclusion by the Secretary of Health and Human Services of the debtor from participation in the Medicare program or any other Federal health care program (as defined in section 1128B(f) of the Social Security Act pursuant to title XI or XVIII of such Act).

The provisions of paragraphs (12) and (13) of this subsection shall apply with respect to any such petition filed on or before December 31, 1989.

(c) Except as provided in subsections (d), (e), (f), and (h) of this section—

(1) the stay of an act against property of the estate under subsection (a) of this section continues until such property is no longer property of the estate;

(2) the stay of any other act under subsection (a) of this section continues until the earliest of—

(A) the time the case is closed;

(B) the time the case is dismissed; or

(C) if the case is a case under chapter 7 of this title concerning an individual or a case under chapter 9, 11, 12, or 13 of this title, the time a discharge is granted or denied;

(3) if a single or joint case is filed by or against debtor who is an individual in a case under chapter 7, 11, or 13, and if a single or joint case of the debtor was pending within the preceding 1-year period but was

dismissed, other than a case refiled under a chapter other than chapter 7 after dismissal under section 707(b)—

(A) the stay under subsection (a) with respect to any action taken with respect to a debt or property securing such debt or with respect to any lease shall terminate with respect to the debtor on the 30th day after the filing of the later case;

(B) on the motion of a party in interest for continuation of the automatic stay and upon notice and a hearing, the court may extend the stay in particular cases as to any or all creditors (subject to such conditions or limitations as the court may then impose) after notice and a hearing completed before the expiration of the 30-day period only if the party in interest demonstrates that the filing of the later case is in good faith as to the creditors to be stayed; and

(C) for purposes of subparagraph (B), a case is presumptively filed not in good faith (but such presumption may be rebutted by clear and convincing evidence to the contrary)—

(i) as to all creditors, if—

(I) more than 1 previous case under any of chapters 7, 11, and 13 in which the individual was a debtor was pending within the preceding 1-year period;

(II) a previous case under any of chapters 7, 11, and 13 in which the individual was a debtor was dismissed within such 1-year period, after the debtor failed to—

(aa) file or amend the petition or other documents as required by this title or the court without substantial excuse (but mere inadvertence or negligence shall not be a substantial excuse unless the dismissal was caused by the negligence of the debtor's attorney);

(bb) provide adequate protection as ordered by the court; or

(cc) perform the terms of a plan confirmed by the court; or

(III) there has not been a substantial change in the financial or personal affairs of the debtor since the dismissal of the next most previous case under chapter 7, 11, or 13 or any other reason to conclude that the later case will be concluded—

(aa) if a case under chapter 7, with a discharge; or

(bb) if a case under chapter 11 or 13, with a confirmed plan that will be

(cc) fully performed; and

(ii) as to any creditor that commenced an action under subsection (d) in a previous case in which the individual was a debtor if, as of the date of dismissal of such case, that action was still pending or had been resolved by terminating, conditioning, or limiting the stay as to actions of such creditor; and

(4)(A)

(i) if a single or joint case is filed by or against a debtor who is an individual under this title, and if 2 or more single or joint cases of the debtor were pending within the previous year but were dismissed, other than a case refiled under section 707(b), the stay under subsection (a) shall not go into effect upon the filing of the later case; and

(ii) on request of a party in interest, the court shall promptly enter an order confirming that no stay is in effect;

(B) if, within 30 days after the filing of the later case, a party in interest requests the court may order the stay to take effect in the case as to any or all creditors (subject to such conditions or limitations as the court may impose), after notice and a hearing, only if the party in interest demonstrates that the filing of the later case is in good faith as to the creditors to be stayed;

(C) a stay imposed under subparagraph shall be effective on the date of the entry of the order allowing the stay to go into effect; and

(D) for purposes of subparagraph, a case is presumptively filed not in good faith (but such presumption may be rebutted by clear and convincing evidence to the contrary)—

(i) as to all creditors if—

(I) 2 or more previous cases under this title in which the individual was a debtor were pending within the 1-year period;

(II) a previous case under this title in which the individual was a debtor was dismissed within the time period stated in this paragraph after the debtor failed to file or amend the petition or other documents as required by this title or the court without substantial excuse (but mere inadvertence or negligence shall not be substantial excuse unless the dismissal was caused by the negligence of the debtor's attorney), failed to provide adequate protection as ordered by the court, or failed to perform the terms of a plan confirmed by the court; or

(III) there has not been a substantial change in the financial or personal affairs of the debtor since the dismissal of the next most previous case under this title, or any other reason to conclude that the later case will not be concluded, if a case under chapter 7, with a discharge, and if a case under chapter 11 or 13, with a confirmed plan that will be fully performed; or

(ii) as to any creditor that commenced an action under subsection (d) in a previous case in which the individual was a debtor if, as of the date of dismissal of such case, such action was still pending or had been resolved by terminating, conditioning, or limiting the stay as to such action of such creditor.

(d) On request of a party in interest and after notice and a hearing, the court shall grant relief from the stay provided under subsection (a) of this section, such as by terminating, annulling, modifying, or conditioning such stay—

(1) for cause, including the lack of adequate protection of an interest in property of such party in interest;

(2) with respect to a stay of an act against property under subsection (a) of this section, if—

(A) the debtor does not have an equity in such property; and

(B) such property is not necessary to an effective reorganization;

(3) with respect to a stay of an act against single asset real estate under subsection (a), by a creditor whose claim is secured by an interest in such real estate, unless, not later than the date that is 90 days after the entry of the order for relief (or such later date as the court may determine for cause by order entered within that 90-day period) or 30 days after the court determines that the debtor is subject to this paragraph, whichever is later—

(A) the debtor has filed a plan of reorganization that has a reasonable possibility of being confirmed within a reasonable time; or

(B) the debtor has commenced monthly payments that—

(i) may, in the debtor's sole discretion, notwithstanding section 363(c)(2), be made from rents or other income generated before, on, or after the date of the commencement of the case by or from the property to each creditor whose claim is secured by such real estate (other than a claim secured by a judgment lien or by an unmatured statutory lien); and

(ii) are in an amount equal to interest at the then applicable nondefault contract rate of interest on the value of the creditor's interest in the real estate; or

(4) with respect to a stay of an act against real property under subsection (a), by a creditor whose claim is secured by an interest in such real property, if the court finds that the filing of the petition was part of a scheme to delay, hinder, and defraud creditors that involved either—

(A) transfer of all or part ownership of, or other interest in, such real property without the consent of the secured creditor or court approval; or

(B) multiple bankruptcy filings affecting such real property.

If recorded in compliance with applicable State laws governing notices of interests or liens in real property, an order entered under paragraph (4) shall be binding in any other case under this title purporting to affect such real property filed not later than 2 years after the date of the entry of such order by the court, except that a debtor in a subsequent case under this title may move for relief from such order based upon changed circumstances or for good cause shown, after notice and a hearing. Any Federal, State, or local governmental unit that accepts notices of interests or liens in real property shall accept any certified copy of an order described in this subsection for indexing and recording.

(e) (1) Thirty days after a request under subsection (d) of this section for relief from the stay of any act against property of the estate under subsection (a) of this section, such stay is terminated with respect to the party in interest making such request, unless the court, after notice and a hearing, orders such stay continued in effect pending the conclusion of, or as a result of, a final hearing and determination under subsection (d) of this section. A hearing under this subsection may be a preliminary hearing, or may be consolidated with the final hearing under subsection (d) of this section. The court shall order such stay continued in effect pending the conclusion of the final hearing under subsection (d) of this section if there is a reasonable likelihood that the party opposing relief from such stay will prevail at the conclusion of such final hearing. If the hearing under this subsection is a preliminary hearing, then such final hearing shall be concluded not later than thirty days after the conclusion of such preliminary hearing, unless the 30-day period is extended with the consent of the parties in interest or for a specific time which the court finds is required by compelling circumstances.

(2) Notwithstanding paragraph (1), in a case under chapter 7, 11, or 13 in which the debtor is an individual, the stay under subsection (a) shall terminate on the date that is 60 days after a request is made by a party in interest under subsection (d), unless—

(A) a final decision is rendered by the court during the 60-day period beginning on the date of the request; or

(B) such 60-day period is extended—

(i) by agreement of all parties in interest; or

(ii) by the court for such specific period of time as the court finds is required for good cause, as described in findings made by the court.

(f) Upon request of a party in interest, the court, with or without a hearing, shall grant such relief from the stay provided under subsection (a) of this section as is necessary to prevent irreparable damage to the interest of an entity in property, if such interest will suffer such damage before there is an opportunity for notice and a hearing under subsection (d) or (e) of this section.

(g) In any hearing under subsection (d) or (e) of this section concerning relief from the stay of any act under subsection (a) of this section—

(1) the party requesting such relief has the burden of proof on the issue of the debtor's equity in property; and

(2) the party opposing such relief has the burden of proof on all other issues.

(h) (1) In a case in which the debtor is an individual, the stay provided by subsection (a) is terminated with respect to personal property of the estate or of the debtor securing in whole or in part a claim, or subject to an unexpired lease, and such personal property shall no longer be property of the estate if the debtor fails within the applicable time set by section 521(a)(2)—

(A) to file timely any statement of intention required under section 521(a)(2) with respect to such personal property or to indicate in such statement that the debtor will either surrender such personal property or retain it and, if retaining such personal property, either redeem such personal property pursuant to section 722, enter into an agreement of the kind specified in section 524(c) applicable to the debt secured by such personal property, or assume such unexpired lease pursuant to section 365(p) if the trustee does not do so, as applicable; and

(B) to take timely the action specified in such statement, as it may be amended before expiration of the period for taking action, unless such statement specifies the debtor's intention to reaffirm such debt on the original contract terms and the creditor refuses to agree to the reaffirmation on such terms.

(2) Paragraph (1) does not apply if the court determines, on the motion of the trustee filed before the expiration of the applicable time set by section 521(a)(2), after notice and a hearing, that such personal property is of consequential value or benefit to the estate, and orders appropriate adequate protection of the creditor's interest, and orders the debtor to deliver any collateral in the debtor's possession to the trustee. If the court does not so determine, the stay provided by subsection (a) shall terminate upon the conclusion of the hearing on the motion.

(i) If a case commenced under chapter 7, 11, or 13 is dismissed due to the creation of a debt repayment plan, for purposes of subsection (c)(3), any subsequent case commenced by the debtor under any such chapter shall not be presumed to be filed not in good faith.

(j) On request of a party in interest, the court shall issue an order under subsection (c) confirming that the automatic stay has been terminated.

(k) (1) Except as provided in paragraph (2), an individual injured by any willful violation of a stay provided by this section shall recover actual damages, including costs and attorneys' fees, and, in appropriate circumstances, may recover punitive damages.

(2) If such violation is based on an action taken by an entity in the good faith belief that subsection (h) applies to the debtor, the recovery under

paragraph (1) of this subsection against such entity shall be limited to actual damages.

(l) (1) Except as otherwise provided in this subsection, subsection (b)(22) shall apply on the date that is 30 days after the date on which the bankruptcy petition is filed, if the debtor files with the petition and serves upon the lessor a certification under penalty of perjury that—

(A) under nonbankruptcy law applicable in the jurisdiction, there are circumstances under which the debtor would be permitted to cure the entire monetary default that gave rise to the judgment for possession, after that judgment for possession was entered; and

(B) the debtor (or an adult dependent of the debtor) has deposited with the clerk of the court, any rent that would become due during the 30-day period after the filing of the bankruptcy petition.

(2) If, within the 30-day period after the filing of the bankruptcy petition, the debtor (or an adult dependent of the debtor) complies with paragraph (1) and files with the court and serves upon the lessor a further certification under penalty of perjury that the debtor (or an adult dependent of the debtor) has cured, under nonbankrupcty law applicable in the jurisdiction, the entire monetary default that gave rise to the judgment under which possession is sought by the lessor, subsection (b)(22) shall not apply, unless ordered to apply by the court under paragraph (3).

(3) (A) If the lessor files an objection to any certification filed by the debtor under paragraph (1) or (2), and serves such objection upon the debtor, the court shall hold a hearing within 10 days after the filing and service of such objection to determine if the certification filed by the debtor under paragraph (1) or (2) is true.

(B) If the court upholds the objection of the lessor filed under subparagraph (A)—

(i) subsection (b)(22) shall apply immediately and relief from the stay provided under subsection (a)(3) shall not be required to enable the lessor to complete the process to recover full possession of the property; and

(ii) the clerk of the court shall immediately serve upon the lessor and the debtor a certified copy of the court's order upholding the lessor's objection.

(4) If a debtor, in accordance with paragraph (5), indicates on the petition that there was a judgment for possession of the residential rental property in which the debtor resides and does not file a certification under paragraph (1) or (2)—

(A) subsection (b)(22) shall apply immediately upon failure to file such certification, and relief from the stay provided under subsection (a)(3) shall not be required to enable the lessor to complete the process to recover full possession of the property; and

(B) the clerk of the court shall immediately serve upon the lessor and the debtor a certified copy of the docket indicating the absence of a filed certification and the applicability of the exception to the stay under subsection (b)(22).

(5) (A) Where a judgment for possession of residential property in which the debtor resides as a tenant under a lease or rental agreement has been obtained by the lessor, the debtor shall so indicate on the bankruptcy petition and shall provide the name and address of the lessor that obtained that pre-petition judgment on the petition and on any certification filed under this subsection.

(B) The form of certification filed with the petition, as specified in this subsection, shall provide for the debtor to certify, and the debtor shall certify—

(i) whether a judgment for possession of residential rental housing in which the debtor resides has been obtained against the debtor before the date of the filing of the petition; and

(ii) whether the debtor is claiming under paragraph (1) that under nonbankruptcy law applicable in the jurisdiction, there are circumstances under which the debtor would be permitted to cure the entire monetary default that gave rise to the judgment for possession, after that judgment of possession was entered, and has made the appropriate deposit with the court.

(C) The standard forms (electronic and otherwise) used in a bankruptcy proceeding shall be amended to reflect the requirements of this subsection.

(D) The clerk of the court shall arrange for the prompt transmittal of the rent deposited in accordance with paragraph (1)(B) to the lessor.

(m)(1) Except as otherwise provided in this subsection, subsection (b)(23) shall apply on the date that is 15 days after the date on which the lessor files and serves a certification described in subsection (b)(23).

(2) (A) If the debtor files with the court an objection to the truth or legal sufficiency of the certification described in subsection (b)(23) and serves such objection upon the lessor, subsection (b)(23) shall not apply, unless ordered to apply by the court under this subsection.

(B) If the debtor files and serves the objection under subparagraph (A), the court shall hold a hearing within 10 days after the filing and service of such objection to determine if the situation giving rise to the lessor's certification under paragraph (1) existed or has been remedied.

(C) If the debtor can demonstrate to the satisfaction of the court that the situation giving rise to the lessor's certification under paragraph (1) did not exist or has been remedied, the stay provided under subsection (a)(3) shall remain in effect until the termination of the stay under this section.

(D) If the debtor cannot demonstrate to the satisfaction of the court that the situation giving rise to the lessor's certification under paragraph (1) did not exist or has been remedied—

(i) relief from the stay provided under subsection (a)(3) shall not be required to enable the lessor to proceed with the eviction; and

(ii) the clerk of the court shall immediately serve upon the lessor and the debtor a certified copy of the court's order upholding the lessor's certification.

(3) If the debtor fails to file, within 15 days, an objection under paragraph (2)(A)—

(A) subsection (b)(23) shall apply immediately upon such failure and relief from the stay provided under subsection (a)(3) shall not be required to enable the lessor to complete the process to recover full possession of the property; and

(B) the clerk of the court shall immediately serve upon the lessor and the debtor a certified copy of the docket indicating such failure.

(n) (1) Except as provided in paragraph (2), subsection (a) does not apply in a case in which the debtor—

(A) is a debtor in a small business case pending at the time the petition is filed;

(B) was a debtor in a small business case that was dismissed for any reason by an order that became final in the 2-year period ending on the date of the order for relief entered with respect to the petition;

(C) was a debtor in a small business case in which a plan was confirmed in the 2-year period ending on the date of the order for relief entered with respect to the petition; or

(D) is an entity that has acquired substantially all of the assets or business of a small business debtor described in subparagraph (A), (B), or (C), unless such entity establishes by a preponderance of the evidence that such entity acquired substantially all of the assets or business of such small business debtor in good faith and not for the purpose of evading this paragraph.

(2) Paragraph (1) does not apply—

(A) to an involuntary case involving no collusion by the debtor with creditors; or

(B) to the filing of a petition if—

(i) the debtor proves by a preponderance of the evidence that the filing of the petition resulted from circumstances beyond the control of the debtor not foreseeable at the time the case then pending was filed; and

(ii) it is more likely than not that the court will confirm a feasible plan, but not a liquidating plan, within a reasonable period of time.

(o) The exercise of rights not subject to the stay arising under subsection (a) pursuant to paragraph (6), (7), (17), or (27) of subsection (b) shall not be stayed by any order of a court or administrative agency in any proceeding under this title.

APPENDIX IV

EXCERPTS FROM BANKRUPTCY CODE—DISCHARGE

11 USC § 727. Discharge

(a) The court shall grant the debtor a discharge, unless—

(1) the debtor is not an individual;

(2) the debtor, with intent to hinder, delay, or defraud a creditor or an officer of the estate charged with custody of property under this title, has transferred, removed, destroyed, mutilated, or concealed, or has permitted to be transferred, removed, destroyed, mutilated, or concealed—

(A) property of the debtor, within one year before the date of the filing of the petition; or

(B) property of the estate, after the date of the filing of the petition;

(3) the debtor has concealed, destroyed, mutilated, falsified, or failed to keep or preserve any recorded information, including books, documents, records, and papers, from which the debtor's financial condition or business transactions might be ascertained, unless such act or failure to act was justified under all of the circumstances of the case;

(4) the debtor knowingly and fraudulently, in or in connection with the case—

(A) made a false oath or account;

(B) presented or used a false claim;

(C) gave, offered, received, or attempted to obtain money, property, or advantage, or a promise of money, property, or advantage, for acting or forbearing to act; or

(D) withheld from an officer of the estate entitled to possession under this title, any recorded information, including books, documents, records, and papers, relating to the debtor's property or financial affairs;

(5) the debtor has failed to explain satisfactorily, before determination of denial of discharge under this paragraph, any loss of assets or deficiency of assets to meet the debtor's liabilities;

(6) the debtor has refused, in the case—

(A) to obey any lawful order of the court, other than an order to respond to a material question or to testify;

(B) on the ground of privilege against self-incrimination, to respond to a material question approved by the court or to testify, after the debtor has been granted immunity with respect to the matter concerning which such privilege was invoked; or

(C) on a ground other than the properly invoked privilege against self-incrimination, to respond to a material question approved by the court or to testify;

(7) the debtor has committed any act specified in paragraph (2), (3), (4), (5), or (6) of this subsection, on or within one year before the date of the filing of the petition, or during the case, in connection with another case, under this title or under the Bankruptcy Act, concerning an insider;

(8) the debtor has been granted a discharge under this section, under section 1141 of this title, or under section 14, 371, or 476 of the Bankruptcy Act, in a case commenced within 8 years before the date of the filing of the petition;

(9) the debtor has been granted a discharge under section 1228 or 1328 of this title, or under section 660 or 661 of the Bankruptcy Act, in a case commenced within six years before the date of the filing of the petition, unless payments under the plan in such case totaled at least—

(A) 100 percent of the allowed unsecured claims in such case; or

(i) 70 percent of such claims; and

(ii) the plan was proposed by the debtor in good faith, and was the debtor's best effort;

(10) the court approves a written waiver of discharge executed by the debtor after the order for relief under this chapter;

(11) after filing the petition, the debtor failed to complete an instructional course concerning personal financial management described in section 111, except that this paragraph shall not apply with respect to a debtor who is a person described in section 109(h)(4) or who resides in a district for which the United States trustee (or the bankruptcy administrator, if any) determines that the approved instructional courses are not adequate to service the additional individuals who would otherwise be required to complete such instructional courses under this section (The United States trustee (or the bankruptcy administrator, if any) who makes a determination described

in this paragraph shall review such determination not later than 1 year after the date of such determination, and not less frequently than annually thereafter.); or

(12) the court after notice and a hearing held not more than 10 days before the date of the entry of the order granting the discharge finds that there is reasonable cause to believe that—

(A) section 522(q)(1) may be applicable to the debtor; and

(B) there is pending any proceeding in which the debtor may be found guilty of a felony of the kind described in section 522(q)(1)(A) or liable for a debt of the kind described in section 522(q)(1)(B).

(b) Except as provided in section 523 of this title, a discharge under subsection (a) of this section discharges the debtor from all debts that arose before the date of the order for relief under this chapter, and any liability on a claim that is determined under section 502 of this title as if such claim had arisen before the commencement of the case, whether or not a proof of claim based on any such debt or liability is filed under section 501 of this title, and whether or not a claim based on any such debt or liability is allowed under section 502 of this title.

(c) (1) The trustee, a creditor, or the United States trustee may object to the granting of a discharge under subsection (a) of this section.

(2) On request of a party in interest, the court may order the trustee to examine the acts and conduct of the debtor to determine whether a ground exists for denial of discharge.

(d) On request of the trustee, a creditor, or the United States trustee, and after notice and a hearing, the court shall revoke a discharge granted under subsection (a) of this section if—

(1) such discharge was obtained through the fraud of the debtor, and the requesting party did not know of such fraud until after the granting of such discharge;

(2) the debtor acquired property that is property of the estate, or became entitled to acquire property that would be property of the estate, and knowingly and fraudulently failed to report the acquisition of or entitlement to such property, or to deliver or surrender such property to the trustee;

(3) the debtor committed an act specified in subsection (a)(6) of this section; or

(4) the debtor has failed to explain satisfactorily—

(A) a material misstatement in an audit referred to in section 586(f) of title 28; or

(B) a failure to make available for inspection all necessary accounts, papers, documents, financial records, files, and all other papers, things, or property belonging to the debtor that are requested for an audit referred to in section 586(f) of title 28.

(e) The trustee, a creditor, or the United States trustee may request a revocation of a discharge—

(1) under subsection (d)(1) of this section within one year after such discharge is granted; or

(2) under subsection (d)(2) or (d)(3) of this section before the later of—

(A) one year after the granting of such discharge; and

(B) the date the case is closed.

APPENDIX V

EXCERPTS FROM BANKRUPTCY CODE—PREFERENCES

11 USC § 547. Preferences

(a) In this section—

(1) "inventory" means personal property leased or furnished, held for sale or lease, or to be furnished under a contract for service, raw materials, work in process, or materials used or consumed in a business, including farm products such as crops or livestock, held for sale or lease;

(2) "new value" means money or money's worth in goods, services, or new credit, or release by a transferee of property previously transferred to such transferee in a transaction that is neither void nor voidable by the debtor or the trustee under any applicable law, including proceeds of such property, but does not include an obligation substituted for an existing obligation;

(3) "receivable" means right to payment, whether or not such right has been earned by performance; and

(4) a debt for a tax is incurred on the day when such tax is last payable without penalty, including any extension.

(b) Except as provided in subsections (c) and (i) of this section, the trustee may avoid any transfer of an interest of the debtor in property—

(1) to or for the benefit of a creditor;

(2) for or on account of an antecedent debt owed by the debtor before such transfer was made;

(3) made while the debtor was insolvent;

(4) made—

(A) on or within 90 days before the date of the filing of the petition; or

(B) between ninety days and one year before the date of the filing of the petition, if such creditor at the time of such transfer was an insider; and

(5) that enables such creditor to receive more than such creditor would receive if—

(A) the case were a case under chapter 7 of this title;

(B) the transfer had not been made; and

(C) such creditor received payment of such debt to the extent provided by the provisions of this title.

(c) The trustee may not avoid under this section a transfer—

(1) to the extent that such transfer was—

(A) intended by the debtor and the creditor to or for whose benefit such transfer was made to be a contemporaneous exchange for new value given to the debtor; and

(B) in fact a substantially contemporaneous exchange;

(2) to the extent that such transfer was in payment of a debt incurred by the debtor in the ordinary course of business or financial affairs of the debtor and the transferee, and such transfer was—

(A) made in the ordinary course of business or financial affairs of the debtor and the transferee; or

(B) made according to ordinary business terms;

(3) that creates a security interest in property acquired by the debtor—

(A) to the extent such security interest secures new value that was—

(i) given at or after the signing of a security agreement that contains a description of such property as collateral;

(ii) given by or on behalf of the secured party under such agreement;

(iii) given to enable the debtor to acquire such property; and

(iv) in fact used by the debtor to acquire such property; and

(B) that is perfected on or before 30 days after the debtor receives possession of such property;

(4) to or for the benefit of a creditor, to the extent that, after such transfer, such creditor gave new value to or for the benefit of the debtor—

(A) not secured by an otherwise unavoidable security interest; and

(B) on account of which new value the debtor did not make an otherwise unavoidable transfer to or for the benefit of such creditor;

(5) that creates a perfected security interest in inventory or a receivable or the proceeds of either, except to the extent that the aggregate of all such transfers to the transferee caused a reduction, as of the date of the filing of the petition and to the prejudice of other creditors holding unsecured

claims, of any amount by which the debt secured by such security interest exceeded the value of all security interests for such debt on the later of—

(A) (i) with respect to a transfer to which subsection (b)(4)(A) of this section applies, 90 days before the date of the filing of the petition; or

(ii) with respect to a transfer to which subsection (b)(4)(B) of this section applies, one year before the date of the filing of the petition; or

(B) the date on which new value was first given under the security agreement creating such security interest;

(6) that is the fixing of a statutory lien that is not avoidable under section 545 of this title;

(7) to the extent such transfer was a bona fide payment of a debt for a domestic support obligation;

(8) if, in a case filed by an individual debtor whose debts are primarily consumer debts, the aggregate value of all property that constitutes or is affected by such transfer is less than $600; or

(9) if, in a case filed by a debtor whose debts are not primarily consumer debts, the aggregate value of all property that constitutes or is affected by such transfer is less than $5,000 [$5,000 (added by BAPCPA 10-17-05) effective 4-1-04. Adjusted every three years by section 104.].

(d) The trustee may avoid a transfer of an interest in property of the debtor transferred to or for the benefit of a surety to secure reimbursement of such a surety that furnished a bond or other obligation to dissolve a judicial lien that would have been avoidable by the trustee under subsection (b) of this section. The liability of such surety under such bond or obligation shall be discharged to the extent of the value of such property recovered by the trustee or the amount paid to the trustee.

(e) (1) For the purposes of this section—

(A) a transfer of real property other than fixtures, but including the interest of a seller or purchaser under a contract for the sale of real property, is perfected when a bona fide purchaser of such property from the debtor against whom applicable law permits such transfer to be perfected cannot acquire an interest that is superior to the interest of the transferee; and

(B) a transfer of a fixture or property other than real property is perfected when a creditor on a simple contract cannot acquire a judicial lien that is superior to the interest of the transferee.

(2) For the purposes of this section, except as provided in paragraph (3) of this subsection, a transfer is made—

(A) at the time such transfer takes effect between the transferor and the transferee, if such transfer is perfected at, or within 30 days after, such time, except as provided in subsection (c)(3)(B);

(B) at the time such transfer is perfected, if such transfer is perfected after such 30 days; or

(C) immediately before the date of the filing of the petition, if such transfer is not perfected at the later of—

(i) the commencement of the case; or

(ii) 30 days after such transfer takes effect between the transferor and the transferee.

(3) For the purposes of this section, a transfer is not made until the debtor has acquired rights in the property transferred.

(f) For the purposes of this section, the debtor is presumed to have been insolvent on and during the 90 days immediately preceding the date of the filing of the petition.

(g) For the purposes of this section, the trustee has the burden of proving the avoidability of a transfer under subsection (b) of this section, and the creditor or party in interest against whom recovery or avoidance is sought has the burden of proving the nonavoidability of a transfer under subsection (c) of this section.

(h) The trustee may not avoid a transfer if such transfer was made as a part of an alternative repayment schedule between the debtor and any creditor of the debtor created by an approved nonprofit budget and credit counseling agency.

(i) If the trustee avoids under subsection (b) a transfer made between 90 days and 1 year before the date of the filing of the petition, by the debtor to an entity that is not an insider for the benefit of a creditor that is an insider, such transfer shall be considered to be avoided under this section only with respect to the creditor that is an insider.

APPENDIX VI

REAFFIRMATION AGREEMENT

Form 240A - Reaffirmation Agreement (1/07)

☐ **Presumption of Undue Hardship**
☐ **No Presumption of Undue Hardship**
(Check box as directed in Part D: Debtor's Statement in Support of Reaffirmation Agreement.)

UNITED STATES BANKRUPTCY COURT
____________________District of____________________

In re ______________________________, Debtor

Case No.____________________
Chapter__________________

REAFFIRMATION AGREEMENT

[Indicate all documents included in this filing by checking each applicable box.]

☐ Part A: Disclosures, Instructions, and Notice to Debtor (pages 1 - 5)

☐ Part B: Reaffirmation Agreement

☐ Part C: Certification by Debtor's Attorney

☐ Part D: Debtor's Statement in Support of Reaffirmation Agreement

☐ Part E: Motion for Court Approval

*[**Note:** Complete Part E only if debtor was not represented by an attorney during the course of negotiating this agreement. **Note also:** If you complete Part E, you must prepare and file Form 240B - Order on Reaffirmation Agreement.]*

Name of Creditor:____

☐ *[Check this box if]* Creditor is a Credit Union as defined in §19(b)(1)(a)(iv) of the Federal Reserve Act

PART A: DISCLOSURE STATEMENT, INSTRUCTIONS AND NOTICE TO DEBTOR

1. DISCLOSURE STATEMENT

Before Agreeing to Reaffirm a Debt, Review These Important Disclosures:

SUMMARY OF REAFFIRMATION AGREEMENT

This Summary is made pursuant to the requirements of the Bankruptcy Code.

AMOUNT REAFFIRMED

The amount of debt you have agreed to reaffirm: $__________________

The amount of debt you have agreed to reaffirm includes all fees and costs (if any) that have accrued as of the date of this disclosure. Your credit agreement may obligate you to pay additional amounts which may come due after the date of this disclosure. Consult your credit agreement.

Form 240A - Reaffirmation Agreement (Cont.) **2**

ANNUAL PERCENTAGE RATE

[The annual percentage rate can be disclosed in different ways, depending on the type of debt.]

a. If the debt is an extension of "credit" under an "open end credit plan," as those terms are defined in § 103 of the Truth in Lending Act, such as a credit card, the creditor may disclose the annual percentage rate shown in (i) below or, to the extent this rate is not readily available or not applicable, the simple interest rate shown in (ii) below, or both.

(i) The Annual Percentage Rate disclosed, or that would have been disclosed, to the debtor in the most recent periodic statement prior to entering into the reaffirmation agreement described in Part B below or, if no such periodic statement was given to the debtor during the prior six months, the annual percentage rate as it would have been so disclosed at the time of the disclosure statement: ______%.

--- *And/Or* ---

(ii) The simple interest rate applicable to the amount reaffirmed as of the date this disclosure statement is given to the debtor: __________%. If different simple interest rates apply to different balances included in the amount reaffirmed, the amount of each balance and the rate applicable to it are:

$ _________ @ _________%;
$_________ @ _________%;
$_________ @ _________%.

b. If the debt is an extension of credit other than under than an open end credit plan, the creditor may disclose the annual percentage rate shown in (I) below, or, to the extent this rate is not readily available or not applicable, the simple interest rate shown in (ii) below, or both.

(i) The Annual Percentage Rate under §128(a)(4) of the Truth in Lending Act, as disclosed to the debtor in the most recent disclosure statement given to the debtor prior to entering into the reaffirmation agreement with respect to the debt or, if no such disclosure statement was given to the debtor, the annual percentage rate as it would have been so disclosed: _________%.

--- And/Or ---

(ii) The simple interest rate applicable to the amount reaffirmed as of the date this disclosure statement is given to the debtor: __________%. If different simple interest rates apply to different balances included in the amount reaffirmed,

Form 240A - Reaffirmation Agreement (Cont.) 3

the amount of each balance and the rate applicable to it are:
$ _________ @ _________%;
$_________ @ _________%;
$_________ @ _________%.

c. If the underlying debt transaction was disclosed as a variable rate transaction on the most recent disclosure given under the Truth in Lending Act:

The interest rate on your loan may be a variable interest rate which changes from time to time, so that the annual percentage rate disclosed here may be higher or lower.

d. If the reaffirmed debt is secured by a security interest or lien, which has not been waived or determined to be void by a final order of the court, the following items or types of items of the debtor's goods or property remain subject to such security interest or lien in connection with the debt or debts being reaffirmed in the reaffirmation agreement described in Part B.

Item or Type of Item	Original Purchase Price or Original Amount of Loan

Optional---At the election of the creditor, a repayment schedule using one or a combination of the following may be provided:

Repayment Schedule:

Your first payment in the amount of $___________ is due on _________(date), but the future payment amount may be different. Consult your reaffirmation agreement or credit agreement, as applicable.

— Or —

Your payment schedule will be: _________(number) payments in the amount of $___________ each, payable (monthly, annually, weekly, etc.) on the __________ (day) of each ____________ (week, month, etc.), unless altered later by mutual agreement in writing.

— Or —

A reasonably specific description of the debtor's repayment obligations to the extent known by the creditor or creditor's representative.

Form 240A - Reaffirmation Agreement (Cont.) 4

2. INSTRUCTIONS AND NOTICE TO DEBTOR

Reaffirming a debt is a serious financial decision. The law requires you to take certain steps to make sure the decision is in your best interest. If these steps are not completed, the reaffirmation agreement is not effective, even though you have signed it.

1. Read the disclosures in this Part A carefully. Consider the decision to reaffirm carefully. Then, if you want to reaffirm, sign the reaffirmation agreement in Part B (or you may use a separate agreement you and your creditor agree on).

2. Complete and sign Part D and be sure you can afford to make the payments you are agreeing to make and have received a copy of the disclosure statement and a completed and signed reaffirmation agreement.

3. If you were represented by an attorney during the negotiation of your reaffirmation agreement, the attorney must have signed the certification in Part C.

4. If you were not represented by an attorney during the negotiation of your reaffirmation agreement, you must have completed and signed Part E.

5. The original of this disclosure must be filed with the court by you or your creditor. If a separate reaffirmation agreement (other than the one in Part B) has been signed, it must be attached.

6. If the creditor is not a Credit Union and you were represented by an attorney during the negotiation of your reaffirmation agreement, your reaffirmation agreement becomes effective upon filing with the court unless the reaffirmation is presumed to be an undue hardship as explained in Part D. If the creditor is a Credit Union and you were represented by an attorney during the negotiation of your reaffirmation agreement, your reaffirmation agreement becomes effective upon filing with the court.

7. If you were not represented by an attorney during the negotiation of your reaffirmation agreement, it will not be effective unless the court approves it. The court will notify you and the creditor of the hearing on your reaffirmation agreement. You must attend this hearing in bankruptcy court where the judge will review your reaffirmation agreement. The bankruptcy court must approve your reaffirmation agreement as consistent with your best interests, except that no court approval is required if your reaffirmation agreement is for a consumer debt secured by a mortgage, deed of trust, security deed, or other lien on your real property, like your home.

Form 240A - Reaffirmation Agreement (Cont.) 5

YOUR RIGHT TO RESCIND (CANCEL) YOUR REAFFIRMATION AGREEMENT

You may rescind (cancel) your reaffirmation agreement at any time before the bankruptcy court enters a discharge order, or before the expiration of the 60-day period that begins on the date your reaffirmation agreement is filed with the court, whichever occurs later. To rescind (cancel) your reaffirmation agreement, you must notify the creditor that your reaffirmation agreement is rescinded (or canceled).

Frequently Asked Questions:

What are your obligations if you reaffirm the debt? A reaffirmed debt remains your personal legal obligation. It is not discharged in your bankruptcy case. That means that if you default on your reaffirmed debt after your bankruptcy case is over, your creditor may be able to take your property or your wages. Otherwise, your obligations will be determined by the reaffirmation agreement which may have changed the terms of the original agreement. For example, if you are reaffirming an open end credit agreement, the creditor may be permitted by that agreement or applicable law to change the terms of that agreement in the future under certain conditions.

Are you required to enter into a reaffirmation agreement by any law? No, you are not required to reaffirm a debt by any law. Only agree to reaffirm a debt if it is in your best interest. Be sure you can afford the payments you agree to make.

What if your creditor has a security interest or lien? Your bankruptcy discharge does not eliminate any lien on your property. A ''lien'' is often referred to as a security interest, deed of trust, mortgage or security deed. Even if you do not reaffirm and your personal liability on the debt is discharged, because of the lien your creditor may still have the right to take the security property if you do not pay the debt or default on it. If the lien is on an item of personal property that is exempt under your State's law or that the trustee has abandoned, you may be able to redeem the item rather than reaffirm the debt. To redeem, you make a single payment to the creditor equal to the current value of the security property, as agreed by the parties or determined by the court.

> **NOTE:** When this disclosure refers to what a creditor ''may'' do, it does not use the word "may'' to give the creditor specific permission. The word ''may'' is used to tell you what might occur if the law permits the creditor to take the action. If you have questions about your reaffirming a debt or what the law requires, consult with the attorney who helped you negotiate this agreement reaffirming a debt. If you don't have an attorney helping you, the judge will explain the effect of your reaffirming a debt when the hearing on the reaffirmation agreement is held.

Form 240A - Reaffirmation Agreement (Cont.) **6**

PART B: REAFFIRMATION AGREEMENT.

I (we) agree to reaffirm the debts arising under the credit agreement described below.

1. Brief description of credit agreement:

2. Description of any changes to the credit agreement made as part of this reaffirmation agreement:

SIGNATURE(S):

Borrower:	Accepted by creditor:
______________________________	______________________________
(Print Name)	(Printed Name of Creditor)
______________________________	______________________________
(Signature)	(Address of Creditor)
Date: ________________	______________________________
	(Signature)
Co-borrower, if also reaffirming these debts:	______________________________
______________________________	
(Print Name)	(Printed Name and Title of Individual Signing for Creditor)
______________________________	
(Signature)	Date of creditor acceptance:
Date: ________________	________________________

Form 240A - Reaffirmation Agreement (Cont.) 7

PART C: CERTIFICATION BY DEBTOR'S ATTORNEY (IF ANY).

[To be filed only if the attorney represented the debtor during the course of negotiating this agreement.]

I hereby certify that (1) this agreement represents a fully informed and voluntary agreement by the debtor; (2) this agreement does not impose an undue hardship on the debtor or any dependent of the debtor; and (3) I have fully advised the debtor of the legal effect and consequences of this agreement and any default under this agreement.

☐ *[Check box, if applicable and the creditor is not a Credit Union.]* A presumption of undue hardship has been established with respect to this agreement. In my opinion, however, the debtor is able to make the required payment.

Printed Name of Debtor's Attorney: ______________________________

Signature of Debtor's Attorney: ______________________________

Date: ______________

Form 240A - Reaffirmation Agreement (Cont.) **8**
PART D: DEBTOR'S STATEMENT IN SUPPORT OF REAFFIRMATION AGREEMENT

*[Read and complete sections 1 and 2, **OR**, if the creditor is a Credit Union and the debtor is represented by an attorney, read section 3. Sign the appropriate signature line(s) and date your signature. If you complete sections 1 and 2 **and** your income less monthly expenses does not leave enough to make the payments under this reaffirmation agreement, check the box at the top of page 1 indicating "Presumption of Undue Hardship." Otherwise, check the box at the top of page 1 indicating "No Presumption of Undue Hardship"]*

1. I believe this reaffirmation agreement will not impose an undue hardship on my dependents or me. I can afford to make the payments on the reaffirmed debt because my monthly income (take home pay plus any other income received) is $________, and my actual current monthly expenses including monthly payments on post-bankruptcy debt and other reaffirmation agreements total $________, leaving $________ to make the required payments on this reaffirmed debt.

I understand that if my income less my monthly expenses does not leave enough to make the payments, this reaffirmation agreement is presumed to be an undue hardship on me and must be reviewed by the court. However, this presumption may be overcome if I explain to the satisfaction of the court how I can afford to make the payments here: ____________
____
____.

(Use an additional page if needed for a full explanation.)

2. I received a copy of the Reaffirmation Disclosure Statement in Part A and a completed and signed reaffirmation agreement.

Signed: ___________________________________
(Debtor)

____
(Joint Debtor, if any)

Date: __________________

— Or —

[If the creditor is a Credit Union and the debtor is represented by an attorney]

3. I believe this reaffirmation agreement is in my financial interest. I can afford to make the payments on the reaffirmed debt. I received a copy of the Reaffirmation Disclosure Statement in Part A and a completed and signed reaffirmation agreement.

Signed: ___________________________________
(Debtor)

____
(Joint Debtor, if any)

Date: __________________

Form 240A - Reaffirmation Agreement (Cont.) 9

PART E: MOTION FOR COURT APPROVAL
[To be completed and filed only if the debtor is not represented by an attorney during the course of negotiating this agreement.]

MOTION FOR COURT APPROVAL OF REAFFIRMATION AGREEMENT

I (we), the debtor(s), affirm the following to be true and correct:

I am not represented by an attorney in connection with this reaffirmation agreement.

I believe this reaffirmation agreement is in my best interest based on the income and expenses I have disclosed in my Statement in Support of this reaffirmation agreement, and because (provide any additional relevant reasons the court should consider):

Therefore, I ask the court for an order approving this reaffirmation agreement under the following provisions (*check all applicable boxes)*:

☐ 11 U.S.C. § 524(c)(6) (debtor is not represented by an attorney during the course of the negotiation of the reaffirmation agreement)

☐ 11 U.S.C. § 524(m) (presumption of undue hardship has arisen because monthly expenses exceed monthly income)

Signed:______________________________
(Debtor)

____
(Joint Debtor, if any)

Date: __________________

APPENDIX VII

EXCERPTS FROM BANKRUPTCY REFORM ACT—STAY OF ACTION AGAINST CO-DEBTOR (UNDER CHAPTER 13)

11 USC § 1301. Stay of action against codebtor

(a) Except as provided in subsections (b) and (c) of this section, after the order for relief under this chapter, a creditor may not act, or commence or continue any civil action, to collect all or any part of a consumer debt of the debtor from any individual that is liable on such debt with the debtor, or that secured such debt, unless—

(1) such individual became liable on or secured such debt in the ordinary course of such individual's business; or

(2) the case is closed, dismissed, or converted to a case under chapter 7 or 11 of this title.

(b) A creditor may present a negotiable instrument, and may give notice of dishonor of such an instrument.

(c) On request of a party in interest and after notice and a hearing, the court shall grant relief from the stay provided by subsection (a) of this section with respect to a creditor, to the extent that—

(1) as between the debtor and the individual protected under subsection (a) of this section, such individual received the consideration for the claim held by such creditor;

(2) the plan filed by the debtor proposes not to pay such claim; or

(3) such creditor's interest would be irreparably harmed by continuation of such stay.

(d) Twenty days after the filing of a request under subsection (c)(2) of this section for relief from the stay provided by subsection (a) of this section, such stay is terminated with respect to the party in interest making such request, unless the debtor or any individual that is liable on such debt with the debtor files and serves upon such party in interest a written objection to the taking of the proposed action.

APPENDIX VIII

TELEPHONE NUMBERS OF THE BANKRUPTCY COURTS[1]

(*) Designates VCIS Access

Court	Telephone
Alabama	334-441-5637*
Alaska	907-271-2658*
Arizona-Phoenix	602-640-5820* 602-640-5800
Arizona-Tucson	520-620-7475* 520-620-7500
Arizona-Yuma	520-783-0288*
Arkansas	501-918-5555*
California-Fresno	916-498-5583* 559-498-7217
California-Los Angeles	213-894-3118 213-894-4111*
California-Modcsto	209-521-5160* 800-736-0158*
California-Oakland	800-570-9819* 415-434-8103*
California-Riverside	909-774-1150*
California-Sacramento	916-498-5583* 916-930-4400*
California-San Bernadino	909-774-1150*
California-San Diego	619-557-6521*
California-San Francisco	415-705-3200 800-570-9819*
California-San Jose	408-535-5118 888-457-0604*
California-Santa Ana	714-338-5401* 714-836-2993
California-Santa Barbara	805-884-4805*
California-San Fernando	818-587-2936* 818-587-2900*
California-Santa Rosa	888-457-0604* 707-525-8520
California-Woodland Hills	818-587-2963*
Colorado	303-844-0267*
Connecticut	203-240-3345*
Delaware	888-667-5530
Florida-Orlando	407-648-6800 305-536-5979
Georgia-Middle	912-752-8183*
Georgia-Northern	404-730-2866 404-730-2877*

[1]Reprinted with permission of Frank Bouche and Linda Hunt.

Georgia-Southern	912-650-4100*
Hawaii	808-522-8122*
Idaho-Boise	208-334-9386* 208-334-1074 208-334-9464
Idaho-Coeur D'Alene	208-664-4925
Idaho-Pocatello	208-478-4123 208-334-9386
Illinois-Central	207-492-4550* 800-827-9005*
Illinois-Chicago	888-232-6814*
Illinois-Southern	618-482-9365* 800-726-5622
Indiana-Northern	800-755-8393* 219-236-8247 219-236-8814*
Indiana-Terre Haute	812-238-1550
Iowa-Cedar Rapids	800-249-9859* 319-286-2200
Iowa-Des Moines	888-219-5534* 515-284-9859*
Kansas	316-269-6668* 800-827-9028*
Kentucky-Eastern	606-233-2657* 800-998-2657*
Kentucky-Western	502-625-7391
Louisiana-Middle	225-389-0211*
Louisiana-Eastern	504-589-7878*
Louisiana-Western	308-676-4267 800-326-4026*
Maine	207-780-3755*
Maryland	410-962-0733*
Michigan-Eastern-Detroit	877-422-3066*
Michigan-Eastern-Bay City	517-894-8840
Michigan-Eastern-Flint	810-235-4126
Michigan-Middle-Ft. Myers	813-332-3937
Michigan-Western-Grand Rapids	616-456-2075*
Michigan-Western-Marquette	906-226-2117
Minnesota	800-959-9002*
Mississippi-Northern	601-369-8147*
Mississippi-Southern	800-293-2723*
Mississippi-Jackson	800-601-8859*
Mississippi-Biloxi	800-293-2723* 228-432-5542
Montana-Butte	888-879-0071* 406-782-3354
Nebraska-Lincoln	402-437-5100
Nevada-Las Vegas	800-294-6920* 702-388-6708* 702-388-6257
Nevada-Reno	800-294-6920* 775-784-5559
New Hampshire	603-666-7424*
New Jersey	973-645-6045*
New Mexico-Albuquerque	888-435-7822* 505-348-2444* 505-348-2500
New York-Eastern	708-852-5726*
New York-Northern	800-206-1952*
New York-Western	800-776-9578*
North Carolina-Eastern	888-847-9138*
North Carolina-Middle	910-333-5532*
North Carolina-Western	701-350-7500*
North Dakota	701-239-5641*
Ohio-Northern	800-898-6899*
Ohio-Southern-Dayton	937-225-2544*
Ohio-Southern-Columbus	513-225-2562*
Ohio-Western	800-726-1004*
Oklahoma-Western	405-231-5141 405-231-4768*
Oklahoma-Eastern	918-756-8617*
Oregon-Eugene	800-726-2227* 541-465-6448

Oregon-Portland	800-726-2227* 503-326-2249* 503-326-2231
Pennsylvania-Pittsburgh	412-355-3210* 412-644-4060
Pennsylvania-Eastern	215-597-2244*
Rhode Island	401-528-4476*
S. Carolina	800-669-8767*
S. Dakota	605-330-4559*
Tennessee-Eastern	800-767-1512
Tennessee-Western	901-544-4325*
Texas-Amarillo	888-436-7477* 512-916-5237
Texas-Beaumont	409-389-2617
Texas-Corpus Christi	800-745-4459* 512-888-3484
Texas-Dallas	800-886-9008* 214-753-2128* 214-753-2000
Texas-El Paso	888-436-7477* 915-779-7362
Texas-Fort Worth	817-978-3802
Texas-Houston	800-745-4459* 713-250-5049*
Texas-Lubbock	806-472-5000
Texas-Midland	888-436-7477*
Texas-Plano	800-466-1694* 972-509-1240
Texas-San Antonio	888-436-7477* 210-229-4023* 210-472-6720
Texas-Eastern	800-466-1694
Texas-Northern	800-886-9008
Texas-Southern	800-745-4459
Texas-Western	888-436-7477
Utah-Salt Lake City	800-733-6740* 801-524-3107* 801-524-5157
Vermont	802-474-7627*
Virginia	800-326-5879*
Washington-Seattle	206-553-8543* 206-553-7545
Washington-Spokane	509-353-2404*
Washington-Tacoma	888-409-4662
Washington D.C.	202-273-0048*
W. Virginia-Northern	253-596-6310*
W. Virginia-Southern	304-347-5337*
Wisconsin-Eastern	414-297-3582*
Wisconsin-Western	800-743-8247*
Wyoming-Cheyenne	888-804-5537* 307-772-2191

APPENDIX IX

IN RE REFCO INC.

UNITED STATES BANKRUPTCY COURT
SOUTHERN DISTRICT OF NEW YORK

In re:	:	Chapter 11
REFCO INC., et al.,	:	Case No. 05-60006 (RDD)
Debtors	:	(Jointly Administered)

Appearances:

MILBANK, TWEED, HADLEY & McCLOY, by Luc. A. Despins, Esq., for the Official Committee of Unsecured Creditors of Refco Inc. and affiliated debtors.

STROOCK, STROOCK & LAVAN LLP, by Michael J. Sage, for the *Ad Hoc* Committee of Senior Subordinated Noteholders

MEMORANDUM OF DECISION ON OFFICIAL COMMITTEE'S MOTION FOR AN ORDER REGARDING ACCESS TO INFORMATION UNDER 11 U.S.C. § 1102(b)(3)(A)

ROBERT D. DRAIN, United States Bankruptcy Judge:

Soon after its appointment, the Official Committee of Unsecured Creditors (the "Committee") filed a motion to clarify its obligation under section 1102(b)(3)(A) of the Bankruptcy Code to provide unsecured creditors who are not members of the Committee with access to information. Recently enacted as part of the Bankruptcy Abuse Prevention and Consumer Protection Act of 2005, Pub. L. No. 109-08, 119 Stat. 23 (2005) ("BAPCPA"), section 1102(b)(3) states:

> A committee appointed under subsection (a) shall – (A) provide access to information for creditors who – (i) hold claims of the kind represented by that committee; and (ii) are not appointed to the committee; and (B) solicit and receive comments from the creditors described in subparagraph (A); and (C) be subject to a court order that compels any additional report or disclosure to be made to the creditors described in subparagraph (A).

11 U.S.C. § 1102(b)(3).

BAPCPA does not define the "information" that section 1102(b)(3)(A) requires an official creditors' committee to make available to its constituency (for example, whether it includes information obtained in confidence) or state how it is to be delivered (for example, whether to all unsecured creditors at once, or upon individual creditors' demand), but its language permits a broad construction.[1] The Committee's motion was based on the fear that section 1102(b)(3)(A) might be interpreted to impose an obligation contrary to other applicable laws and the Committee's fiduciary duties and hamper the Committee's performance under section 1103 of the Bankruptcy Code.

Notwithstanding the possibility of such a broad construction, the Court's first inclination, particularly given the review process contemplated by section 1102(b)(3)(C), the absence from the statute of any adverse consequences for an initial failure to comply, and the qualified immunity accorded official committees and their professionals,[2] was to deny the motion as not raising a case or controversy. Until a creditor contended that the Committee was being too stingy with information, the Committee could be left to make reasonable efforts to provide access to relevant information consistent with its resources and any conflicting duties.

This is, however, a large and rapidly moving case, and meaningful information may become stale before the completion of litigation over whether and how

---

[1] The legislative history of section 1102(b)(3) does not provide meaningful guidance regarding the type of information to which access must be given, the manner in which it should be communicated or whether an official creditors' committee faces any sanction, other than being subject to a court order compelling the provision of additional information, if the committee's view of the proper scope and means of delivering access to information is too narrow. The House Report states merely, "Section 405(b) requires the committee to give creditors having claims of the kind represented by the committee access to information. In addition, the committee must solicit and receive comments from these creditors and, pursuant to court order, make additional reports or disclosures available to them." H.R. Rep. No. 109-31, 109th Cong., 1st Sess. 87 (2005).

[2] *See In re PWS Holding Corp.*, 228 F.3d 224, 246 (3d Cir. 2000); *Pan Am Corp. v. Delta Air Lines, Inc.*, 175 B.R. 438, 514 (S.D.N.Y. 1994).

it should be provided. Moreover, it appears that the Committee's motion did not arise in a vacuum; unsecured creditors apparently were pressing for information in ways that raised issues neither expressly addressed by the statute nor, given the section's recent enactment, the case law. Under the circumstances, therefore, the Committee's request to establish parameters for the provision of information under section 1102(b)(3)(A) of the Bankruptcy Code was appropriate, although, as the law develops, the need for comfort orders should end.

Background

Refco, Inc. ("Refco") and its direct and indirect subsidiaries were providers of execution and clearing services for exchange-traded derivatives and prime brokerage services in the fixed income and foreign exchange markets. In 2004, they were the largest providers of customer transaction volume to the Chicago Mercantile Exchange, the largest derivatives exchange in the United States.

On October 10, 2005, Refco disclosed that an entity owned by Refco's CEO and Chairman, Phillip R. Bennett, owed Refco entities approximately $430 million, and soon Mr. Bennett was arrested and charged with various crimes, including securities fraud in connection with Refco's initial public offering, which had occurred only two months earlier.[3] This news precipitated a crisis of customer confidence in Refco and its various subsidiaries, which in turn led Refco to impose a moratorium on withdrawals from its largest unregulated subsidiary, Refco Capital Management, Inc. ("RCM"), and the filing of voluntary chapter 11 petitions on October 17, 2005 by Refco, RCM and twenty-two related entities.

---

[3] In addition to Refco's publicly held stock, Refco and several of its subsidiaries have issued or guarantied a large amount of public debt.

Under a new Chief Executive Officer, Refco immediately sought to sell its largest asset, its regulated futures business, on an expedited basis to prevent further erosion of value and satisfy regulators. At the same time, Refco pursued the sale of other substantial assets and attempted to address the demands of numerous RCM customers to the immediate return of money and securities in which they claimed an interest, while other parties in interest contended that such property was, instead, property of RCM's chapter 11 estate, available to pay all unsecured creditors.

The Committee was appointed on October 28, 2005 and promptly turned its attention to these pressing issues, working closely with the Debtors and their professionals -- particularly on the proposed sales of the regulated futures business and other assets, which involved the exchange of significant confidential information regarding the businesses proposed to be sold, strategies for negotiating with competing bidders and the evaluation of competing bids. In large part because of this cooperative approach, the regulated futures business was successfully sold. On its own, but with information provided by the Debtors, the Committee also analyzed the issues raised by RCM's customers' claims to money and securities. And it also began to investigate the events that precipitated the chapter 11 filings, which entailed a more circumspect approach to information-sharing with the Debtors and others (indeed, the Court granted the Committee's motion for discovery under Bankruptcy Rule 2004 only after the imposition of certain confidentiality requirements in the light of, among other things, an ongoing criminal investigation).

Thus, in the early days of the chapter 11 cases the Committee was engaged in tasks that required it to exchange confidential information with the Debtors and other parties, develop factual and legal analyses of significant inter-creditor issues, and pursue an investigation on a confidential basis. The Committee believed that the premature, unguarded or selective disclosure of information obtained in performing these tasks not only could jeopardize the Committee's desired result in each instance, but also might violate the securities laws (given Refco's public stock and debt) or violate a Court order (in the case of information obtained pursuant to the Rule 2004 order).

It is not particularly surprising, then, that the Committee moved three days after its appointment for approval of a protocol for complying with section 1102(b)(3)(A). On an interim basis it sought an order providing that it was not required in the first instance to divulge any (i) confidential, proprietary, non-public information concerning the Debtors or (ii) any other information if the effect of such disclosure would constitute a waiver of the attorney-client or other privilege of the Committee. With minor changes, the Court entered the interim order, which also required the Debtors to assist the Committee by identifying the proprietary or non-public nature of any information given to the Committee, pending a final hearing.

The Committee's motion received one response, by an *ad hoc* committee of holders of approximately $487 million of senior subordinated notes and bank debt. The *ad hoc* committee's primary objections focused on the circumstances under which the Committee could be forced to provide access to confidential information if the requesting party was prepared to agree to certain confidentiality constraints, as well as on the Committee's proposed schedule for resolving disputes regarding whether particular information should be disclosed. Without accusing the Committee of any dereliction of duty, the *ad hoc* committee asserted that because the interests of the *ad hoc* committee were under-represented on the Committee, the Committee might not use certain information (for example, information related to the RCM customer dispute) in an even-handed way.

With additional input by Refco and the United States Trustee, however, the objection was ultimately resolved by the final form of Order Regarding Creditor Access to Information, which is attached as Exhibit A.

Discussion

Notwithstanding the statute's ambiguity and unhelpful legislative history, there are sources for construing the Committee's obligation to provide "access to information" under Bankruptcy Code section 1102(b)(3)(A). First, the Code has long contained a similar requirement for bankruptcy trustees. Bankruptcy Code section 704(7), which applies under 11 U.S.C. §§ 1106(a)(1) and 1107(a) to chapter 11 trustees and debtors in possession, respectively, states that a "trustee shall . . . unless the court orders otherwise, furnish such information concerning the estate and the estate's administration as is requested by a party in interest."

The facial differences between Bankruptcy Code sections 704(7) and 1102(b)(3) do not appear to be material. Under section 704(7), information shall be furnished only upon a party's request, whereas section 1102(b)(3)(A) may envision a committee's volunteering information or at least establishing a mechanism for unsecured creditors to obtain it. Arguably the right to court review also is more explicit in section 704(7) than in section 1102(b)(3)(C). On the other hand, each section contemplates that the bankruptcy court shall resolve disputes over whether information should be shared. Once that fact is recognized, the two provisions do not differ in practical terms, as long as court resolution is sought on a timely basis. (For the same reason, a committee's good faith decision not to volunteer information under section 1102(b)(3)(A) also may not be of practical consequence: ultimately the issue would come down to the Court's decision whether to compel the information's release under section 1102(b)(3)(C)). In addition, the information to be provided under section 704(7) is limited to "information concerning the estate and the estate's administration," while section 1102(b)(3)(A) refers perhaps more broadly to "information." However, the Code's definition of "estate" is itself so broad[4] that it is hard to see how section 704(7)'s requirement generally would be any more limited in practical terms that section 1102(b)(3)(A)'s reference to "information."[5] Thus cases construing section 704(7) may be applied by analogy to section 1102(b)(3).

Authorities interpreting Bankruptcy Code section 704(7) stand for three propositions relevant to the scope of a committee's obligation under section 1102(b)(3). First, a trustee's duty under section 704(7)

> is fairly extensive, as § 704(7) places the burden of providing requested information on the trustee, and reflects the overriding duty to keep parties in interest informed. Courts have interpreted the trustee's responsibilities broadly, making a request for information difficult for the trustee to avoid, in the absence of a court order to the contrary.

Pineiro v. Pension Benefit Guaranty Corporation, 318 F. Supp. 2d 67, 102 (S.D.N.Y. 2003) (internal citations and quotations omitted). *See also In re Robert Landau Assocs., Inc.*, 50 B.R. 670, 677 (Bankr. S.D.N.Y. 1985) ("The policy of open inspection, established in the Code itself through section 704(7) and F.R.B.P. 5005 and 5007, is

---

[4] *See* 11 U.S.C. § 541(a).

[5] *But see In re Walters*, 136 B.R. 256, 258 (Bankr. C.D. Cal. 1992), in which the court found that information pertaining to the trustee's investigation of claims against debtor's wife was not covered by the plain meaning of section 704(7), because, after the estate's claims against the wife were settled, such information did not relate to the status of the trustee's pursuit or administration of estate property.

fundamental to the operation of the bankruptcy system and is the best means of avoiding any suggestion of impropriety that might or could be raised.") (internal citation and quotation omitted); *In re Sports Accessories, Inc.*, 34 B.R. 80, 82 (Bankr. D. Md. 1983) (discussing importance of trustee's duty to disclose).

Second, the duty to provide information under section 704(7) is not unlimited, however, as is made clear by the section's introductory clause. *Robert Landau*, 50 B.R. at 675; *Speleos v. McCarthy*, 201 B.R. 325, 328 (D. D.C. 1996). In particular, a trustee may obtain a protective order against disclosure of information under section 704(7) if disclosure would result in waiver the attorney-client privilege, *In re Lee Way Holding Co.*, 120 B.R. 881, 908 (Bankr. S.D. Ohio 1990), or of information that is proprietary and confidential. *In re Grabill Corp.*, 109 B.R. 329, 333 (N.D. Ill. 1989); *see also* 6 *Collier on Bankruptcy* ¶ 704.11 (15th ed. 2005), at 704-23 (noting that section 107 of the Bankruptcy Code must also be kept in mind when considering a trustee's duty to furnish information).[6]

Third, a trustee's right to a protective order under section 704(7) is informed by the trustee's fiduciary duties, because the requirement to disclose information under section 704(7) derives from a trustee's fiduciary duty to creditors and the estate. *In re Scott*, 172 F.3d 959, 967 (7th Cir. 1999); *In re Modern Office Supply, Inc.*, 28 B.R. 943, 944 (Bankr. W.D. Okla. 1983). If the request for such an order is not also in furtherance of those duties, but is, rather, designed to obtain an undue advantage over a party in interest, it should be denied. *Robert Landau*, 50 B.R. at 677. To override

[6] Bankruptcy Code section 107(a) provides for public access to all papers filed in a bankruptcy case, but subjects such access to the right to obtain an order preventing the disclosure of trade secrets, confidential research, development, or commercial information; protecting a person with respect to disclosure of scandalous or defamatory matter; and protecting individuals from disclosure of means of identification that would create undue risk of identity theft or other unlawful injury. 11 U.S.C. § 107(b), (c).

the duty to disclose, a trustee should point to a countervailing fiduciary duty, such as to protect creditors and the estate from a particular harm, whose performance is more important than avoiding the harm resulting from withholding the information in question. *See generally Garner v. Wolfinbarger*, 430 F.2d 1093, 1103-04 (5th Cir. 1970), *cert. denied*, 401 U.S. 974 (1971) (attorney-client privilege may be asserted by corporation against those for whom it acts as fiduciary, subject to right of such beneficiaries to show cause why it should not be invoked in the particular instance).

Each of these aspects of section 704(7) should also apply to a creditor's committee's analogous obligation to provide access to information under Bankruptcy Code section 1102(b)(3)(A).

There also were provisions similar to section 1102(b)(3)(A) under the Bankruptcy Act of 1898. Section 339(1) of the Act listed the functions that a creditors committee appointed under Chapter XI could perform, including "(d) to report to the creditors from time to time concerning the progress of the proceeding;" and under Bankruptcy Act Rule 11-29, which was derived from section 339(1) of the Act, 14 *Collier on Bankruptcy* ¶ 11-29.02 (14th ed. 1982) at 11-29-3, one of the functions of an official committee was to "advise the creditors of its recommendations with respect to the proposed plan [and] report to the creditors concerning the progress of the case. . . ." Bankruptcy Act Rule 11-29(a).

The case law and commentary concerning this information-provision role is very scant. One court, however, construed Bankruptcy Act Rule 11-29(a) in affirming a bankruptcy court's confirmation of a Chapter XI plan over the objection that acceptances of the plan were not solicited in good faith. *In re Gilchrist Co.*, 410 F. Supp.

circulated a letter recommending the plan, it had improperly kept creditors in the dark about several material facts, such as the debtor's receipt of a tax abatement and rent reduction, the existence of additional proofs of claim and potential fraudulent transfer recoveries, and the opposition of four members of the creditors committee to the plan followed by two members' resignation. *Id.* at 1076-77. The court determined, however, expressly notwithstanding Rule 11-29(a), that "It is clear that the Creditors' Committee is not required to forward to each creditor all of the raw data it receives and considers in the process of carrying out its duties." *Id.* at 1078. Instead, the committee had to provide "a fair presentation of the status of the Debtor." *Id.* Finding no support for the appellants' argument that the committee had made material omissions or otherwise acted improperly, such as acting collusively with the debtor, the court found that the plan was solicited and accepted in good faith. *Id.*

The *Gilchrist* court's statement that a committee should not have to "forward all of the raw data it receives and considers," as if it were a virtual information bank for its constituents, would appear to apply with equal logic to Bankruptcy Code section 1102(b)(3)(A), although courts may differ about what constitutes a material development in the case and, therefore, a material disclosure omission in the context of a committee solicitation letter or otherwise.

Last, the proper scope of section 1102(b)(3)(A) may be analyzed in the light of the duties and functions of a creditors committee under the Bankruptcy Code and by analogy to several pre-BAPCPA decisions that have considered committee confidentiality restrictions in the context of such duties and functions.

"An official committee of creditors plays a pivotal role in the bankruptcy process. The function of an official creditors committee is to aid, assist and monitor the debtor to ensure that the unsecured creditors' views are heard and their interests promoted and protected." *Pan Am Corp. v. Delta Airlines, Inc.*, 175 B.R. 438, 514 (S.D.N.Y. 1994) (citations omitted). Official committees have diverse duties: they are the primary negotiating bodies for a chapter 11 plan; they also provide supervision of the debtor and execute an oversight function; they may investigate the debtor's assets and affairs; and they may perform such other services as are in the interest of the unsecured creditor body. *Johns-Manville Sales Corp. v. Doan* (*In re Johns-Manville Corp.*), 26 B.R. 919, 925 (Bankr. S.D.N.Y. 1983); *see also* 11 U.S.C. §§ 1103(c) (stating tasks an official committee may undertake) and 1109(b) (stating that an official creditors committee "may raise and may appear and be heard on any issue" in a chapter 11 case).[7] Broadly speaking,

> The creditors' committee is not merely a conduit through whom the debtor speaks to and negotiates with creditors generally. On the contrary, it is purposely intended to represent the necessarily different interests and concerns of the creditors it represents. It must necessarily be adversarial in a sense, though its relation with the debtor may be supportive and friendly. There is simply no other entity established by the Code to guard those interests. The committee as the sum of its members is not intended to be merely an arbiter but a partisan which will aid, assist, and monitor the debtor pursuant to its own self-interest.

In re Daig Corp., 17 B.R. 41, 43 (Bankr. D. Minn. 1981).

---

[7] Because any transaction not in the ordinary course of the debtor's business requires notice and the opportunity for a hearing, 11 U.S.C. § 363(b), an official committee may consider and challenge virtually everything important that a debtor undertakes. Under section 1109(b), official committees have the right to intervene in adversary proceedings. *Term Loan Holder Comm. v. Ozer Group, L.L.C.* (*In re Caldor Corp.*), 303 F.3d 161, 175 (2d Cir. 2002); *Adelphia Communications Corp. v. Rigis* (*In re Adelphia Communications Corp.*), 285 B.R. 848, 850-51 (Bankr. S.D.N.Y. 2002)

It is well recognized that, to fulfill these roles, the members of an official committee owe a fiduciary duty to their constituents -- in the case of an official creditors committee, to all of the debtor's unsecured creditors. *The Bohack Corp. v. Gulf & Western Indus., Inc.* (*In re Bohack Corp.*), 607 F.2d 258, 262 n. 4 (2d Cir. 1979); *see also Pan Am*, 175 B.R. at 514; *Rickel & Associates v. Smith* (*In re Rickel & Associates*), 272 B.R. 74, 99 (Bankr. S.D.N.Y. 2002); *Johns-Manville,* 26 B.R. at 925 (noting, "In the case of reorganization committees, these fiduciary duties are crucial because of the importance of committees.").

In addition, under certain circumstances, an official creditors committee may be authorized by the bankruptcy court to act not only on behalf of the unsecured creditor body but also as a fiduciary on behalf of the debtor's estate. *Commodore Int'l Ltd. v Gould* (*In re Commodore Int'l Ltd.*), 262 F.3d 96, 100 (2d Cir. 2001) (authorizing official committee to pursue fraudulent transfer avoidance litigation for the benefit of the chapter 11 estate).

It is important to keep these functions in mind when sorting out the circumstances under which a creditors committee should not be required to make information available to its constituents. For example, in performing its oversight and negotiation function, a committee acts as the voice of all of the unsecured creditors, many of whom lack the resources to speak for themselves and all of whom benefit from the representative role played by the committee. *See* 4 *Norton Bankr. L. & Prac.* § 78.1 (2d ed. 2004). This means that committee members should and will receive commercially sensitive or proprietary information from the debtor and other parties (including each other, because plan negotiations are as often conducted between unsecured creditor groups as between the unsecured creditors and the debtor), often in the context of settlement discussions. It has frequently been held that committee members' fiduciary duties of loyalty and care to the unsecured creditor body require such information to be held in confidence. Otherwise, communications between the committee and third parties and among committee members themselves would be improperly curtailed, or the debtor might be harmed with a resulting decline in the creditors' recovery. *See In re Swolksy*, 55 B.R. 144, 146 (Bankr. N.D. Ohio 1985); *In re Johns-Manville*, 26 B.R. at 926; *Daig*, 17 B.R. at 42; *see also* 7 *Collier on Bankruptcy* ¶ 1103.05[2][a] at 1103-30.

When the debtor has public stock or debt, moreover, the securities laws may preclude the debtor from disclosing material non-public information on a selective basis to committee members absent a binding confidentiality agreement. *See, e.g.*, SEC Regulation FD (17 C.F.R. § 243.100). In addition, a committee's selective disclosure of material non-public information that it has developed on its own (including the results of inter-creditor negotiations and its own investigations) may raise similar issues, although the underlying concern would not be a breach of the securities laws as much as a breach of members' fiduciary duties of loyalty and care to all unsecured creditors by profiting from, or enabling selected creditors to profit from, non-public information obtained as a result of committee membership. *See In re Federated Dep't Stores*, 1991 WL 79143 (Bankr. S.D. Ohio 1991) (recognizing ability of creditors committee members to trade in the debtor's securities, subject to applicable securities laws, *provided* that such members institute procedures for screening personnel engaged in trading from personnel involved in committee work); *see also In re Spiegel*, 292 B.R. 748, 750-51 (Bankr. S.D.N.Y. 2003), in which the court discussed its concerns regarding committee members' trading in the debtor's securities even if information blocking procedures were to be adopted. If a committee member's use of non-public information for trading without an appropriate information wall breaches its fiduciary duties of care and loyalty to unsecured creditors, one can readily see the mischief that might arise by construing section 1102(b)(3) to require the unfettered release of such information to other, perhaps friendly, parties who are engaged in such trading, particularly given today's enormous market in distressed debt securities and claims.[8] The selective possession of material information can equate to very large swings in value and, therefore, creditors may seek such information not for legitimate purposes related to their position in the case but, rather, to obtain an unfair trading edge.

Maintaining the parties' reasonable expectations of confidentiality, therefore, is often critical to a committee's performance of its oversight and negotiation functions, compliance with applicable securities laws, and the proper exercise of committee members' fiduciary duties.

Maintaining confidentiality against unsecured creditors generally also may be necessary to preserve a committee's attorney-client privilege. That privilege clearly can be enforced against those who are not represented by the committee or who are standing in an adversarial relationship to the unsecured creditors as a group. *In re Subpoena Duces Tecum*, 978 F.2d 1159, 1161 (9th Cir. 1992); *In re Baldwin-United Corp.*, 38 B.R. 802, 804-5 (Bankr. S.D. Ohio 1984); 7 *Collier on Bankruptcy* ¶ 1103.03[8] at 1103-17 ("When a committee is engaged in litigation with a third party, there is no doubt that the attorney-client privilege is applicable to shield communications

---

[8] *See* Drain and Schwartz, *Are Bankruptcy Claims Subject to the Federal Securities Laws?*, 10 AM. BANKR. INST. L. REV. 569, 569 n. 1 (2002) (noting reasonableness of multi-billion dollar estimates of distressed debt market).

between the committee and its counsel relating to the litigation. The privilege ought also to be available for communications relating to strategy in the case *vis-à-vis* the debtor and third parties. This should be particularly so for strategy and negotiations over the plan of reorganization.").[9] Thus, one should proceed cautiously concerning the disclosure of information that could reasonably have the effect of waiving the attorney-client or other privilege (for example when the committee has been given standing to pursue a claim on behalf of the debtor's estate, including against an unsecured creditor, or is conducting an investigation that might give rise to such a claim, or the information relates to ongoing negotiations with a third party), notwithstanding Bankruptcy Code section 1102(b)(3).

On the other hand, although a committee's assent to a plan or a transaction does not bind its members, let alone its constituents, *see generally* 7 *Collier on Bankruptcy* ¶ 1103.05[1][d][i] at 1103-26; *see also In re Armstrong World Indus., Inc.*, 2005 U.S. App. LEXIS 28897 (3d Cir. 2005), the importance of a committee's recommendations should require a committee to remain in touch with its constituents to determine their reasonable views.

How should a committee balance the foregoing tension, however – that is, the committee's need to preserve access to sensitive information (which usually is the only information of any value to unsecured creditors, whether for legitimate or illegitimate purposes), to protect the attorney-client privilege, and to comply with the securities laws, on the one hand, against the right of unsecured creditors to be informed

---

[9] Even *In re Christian Life Center, First Assembly of God*, 16 B.R. 35, 37 (Bankr. N.D. Cal. 1981), which the Ninth Circuit in *In re Subpoena Duces Tecum*, 978 F.2d at 1161, found to have unduly limited a committee's attorney-client privilege, suggested that a committee has an attorney-client privilege when the committee has the power to act, or is acting in the guise of a trustee.

of material developments in the case before they are presented with what in practical terms may be a *fait accompli*, on the other?

In Refco's case, as set forth in the order attached as Exhibit A hereto, the balance has been achieved by not requiring in the first instance -- that is, without further court order -- the Committee's disclosure of information (a) that could reasonably be determined to be confidential and non-public or proprietary, (b) the disclosure of which could reasonably be determined to result in a general waiver of the attorney-client or other applicable privilege, or (c) whose disclosure could reasonably be determined to violate an agreement, order or law, including applicable securities laws. Because many, if not all, of the adverse consequences of releasing certain information discussed above may be acceptably reduced or eliminated by the requesting party's agreement to be bound by confidentiality and/or trading constraints, however, the order further provides that the Committee shall take into account the requesting party's willingness to agree to such constraints when the Committee determines whether to release otherwise protected information. Consistent with Code section 1102(b)(3)(C), the order also contemplates that the Court will promptly decide disputes over the provision of such information if they are not resolved by the parties.[10]

Except with respect to the foregoing protected information, the order contemplates the Committee's proactive provision of specified types of information on a website.[11] Finally, recognizing the policy behind the qualified immunity given to

---

[10] The schedule specified in the order for the resolution of such disputes was driven by the large size of these cases, the large number of unsecured creditors and, particularly in the early days of these cases, the intense demands on the time and resources of the Committee and its professionals.

[11] Obviously, this may not be justified in a smaller case.

members of an official creditors committee and the committee's professionals,[12] the order provides for exculpation of such parties coextensive with such immunity.

Of course, those seeking protected information under the attached order are free to raise any argument to show that the Committee's need to protect specified information is not outweighed by the creditor's legitimate need to receive it. For example, the balance described above depends in large measure upon the assumption that the Committee is adequately representative of the unsecured creditors and functioning properly.[13]

Conclusion

For the foregoing reasons, the Committee's motion is granted to the extent provided in the order attached hereto as Exhibit A.

Dated: New York, New York
January 20, 2006

/s/ Robert D. Drain
United States Bankruptcy Judge

---

[12] *Supra*, note 2.

[13] In an analogous context, courts have declined to apply the attorney-client privilege against a committee's own constituents' assertion that committee members or professionals have breached their fiduciary duties to them. *See, e.g., In re Fibremark, Inc.*, 330 B.R. 480, 498 n. 6 (Bankr. D. Vt. 2005) (noting that while "(a) attorney-client privilege is available to a creditors committee in a chapter 11 case, … (b) that privilege may not be asserted as a shield to protect against disclosure of fraud or other misconduct on the part of the committee or its attorneys); *In re Baldwin-United Corp.*, 38 B.R. 802, 805 (Bankr. Ohio 1984); *see also In re Christian Life Center, First Assembly of God*, 16 B.R. 35, 37-38 (Bankr. C.D. Cal. 1981); 7 *Collier on Bankruptcy* ¶ 1103.03[8] ("Committee members have a fiduciary responsibility to their constituency and should not use the attorney-client privilege to shield themselves in litigation from the people they are supposed to be representing."). However, before opening wide the gates to such information, it should be kept in mind that (a) a committee member's fiduciary duties do not preclude it from representing its own interests, provided that in so doing it does not abuse its position on the committee at the expense of the creditor class, *In re Rickel & Associates, Inc.*, 272, B.R. 74, 100 (Bankr. S.D.N.Y. 2002), and (b) resolving intercreditor disputes is one of an official committee's primary functions, which may require committee professionals and members to share the differing views of various unsecured creditor groups with a reasonable expectation of confidentiality.

EXHIBIT A

UNITED STATES BANKRUPTCY COURT
SOUTHERN DISTRICT OF NEW YORK

In re:	Chapter 11
REFCO INC., et al.,	Case No. 05-60006 (RDD)
Debtors.	(Jointly Administered)

ORDER REGARDING CREDITOR ACCESS TO INFORMATION PURSUANT TO 11 U.S.C. §§ 105(a), 1102(b)(3) AND 1103(c)

Upon the motion, dated November 1, 2005 (the "Motion"), filed by the Official Committee of Unsecured Creditors of Refco Inc., et al. (the "Committee"), pursuant to sections 105(a), 1102(b)(3) and 1103(c) of title 11 of the United States Code, 11 U.S.C. §§ 101 et seq. (as amended, the "Bankruptcy Code"), for an order clarifying the Committee's requirement to provide access to information *nunc pro tunc* to October 28, 2005, the date the Committee was appointed; and upon the order to show cause, dated November 1, 2005, provisionally granting the relief requested in the Motion until the Court further clarifies the requirements under section 1102(b)(3)(A) of the Bankruptcy Code or the Committee establishes an acceptable information sharing protocol, and requiring that all interested parties show cause by filing and serving an objection setting forth why the Motion and the relief requested therein should not be entered on a final basis; and the Court having held a hearing on the Motion on December 8, 2005 (the "Hearing") and having considered the Committee's proposed protocol, the objection thereto by the Ad Hoc Committee of Senior Subordinated Noteholders, the statement of the United States Trustee, and the record of the Hearing, the Committee having revised the proposed protocol in the light of the foregoing; and after due deliberation and sufficient cause appearing therefor,

IT IS HEREBY FOUND AND DETERMINED THAT:[1a]

A. Jurisdiction and Venue; Core Proceeding. The Court has jurisdiction to grant the relief provided for herein pursuant to 28 U.S.C. §§ 157 and 1334. This matter constitutes a core proceeding within the meaning of 28 U.S.C. § 157(b). Venue of this chapter 11 case and the Motion is proper under 28 U.S.C. §§ 1408 and 1409(a).

B. Statutory Predicates. The statutory predicates for the relief sought in the Motion are sections 105(a), 1102(b)(3) and 1103 of the Bankruptcy Code.

C. Adequacy of Notice. Notice of the Motion was timely, adequate, proper and sufficient and constituted the best notice practicable under the particular circumstances, and no other or further notice of the Motion is required.

D. Memorandum of Law Waiver. The requirements of Rule 9013-1(b) of the Local Rules are waived.

E. Opportunity to be Heard. A reasonable opportunity to object or be heard with respect to the Motion and the relief requested therein and granted in this Order has been afforded.

NOW THEREFORE, IT IS HEREBY ORDERED, ADJUDGED, AND DECREED THAT:

1. All objections to the Motion or the relief requested therein that have not been withdrawn, waived, or settled, including all reservations of rights included

[1a] Findings of fact shall be construed as conclusions of law and conclusions of law shall be construed as findings of fact, as appropriate.

therein, which are not otherwise resolved in this Order, are overruled on the merits.

2. The Motion is granted to the extent provided herein.
3. Access To Creditor Information. In satisfaction of the Committee's obligations to provide access to information for creditors ("Creditor Information Protocol") in accordance with section 1102(b)(3)(A) and (B) of the Bankruptcy Code, the Committee shall, until the earliest to occur of dissolution of the Committee, dismissal, or conversion of these chapter 11 cases, and a further order of the Court:
   - (a) Establish and maintain an Internet-accessed website (the "Committee Website") that provides, without limitation:
     - (1) general information concerning the chapter 11 cases of Refco Inc. and its affiliated debtors (collectively, the "Debtors"), including, case dockets, access to docket filings, and general information concerning significant parties in the cases;
     - (2) monthly Committee written reports summarizing recent proceedings, events and public financial information;
     - (3) highlights of significant events in the cases;
     - (4) a calendar with upcoming significant events in the cases;
     - (5) access to the claims docket as and when established by the Debtors or any claim agent retained in the cases;
     - (6) a general overview of the chapter 11 process;

conduct, assets, liabilities and financial condition of the Debtors, the operation of the Debtors' business and the desirability of the continuance of such business, or any other matter relevant to these cases or to the formulation of one or more chapter 11 plans (including any and all confidential, proprietary, or other nonpublic materials of the Committee) whether provided (voluntarily or involuntarily) by or on behalf of the Debtors or by any third party or prepared by or for the Committee (collectively, the "Confidential Information") or (ii) any other information if the effect of such disclosure would constitute a general waiver of the attorney-client, work-product, or other applicable privilege possessed by the Committee.

5. Any information received (formally or informally) by the Committee from any Entity in connection with an examination pursuant to Rule 2004 of the Federal Rules of Bankruptcy Procedure or in connection with any formal or informal discovery in any contested matter, adversary proceeding or other litigation shall not be governed by the terms of this Order but, rather, by any order governing such discovery.

6. The Debtors shall assist the Committee in identifying any Confidential Information concerning the Debtors that is provided by the Debtors or their agents or professionals, or by any third party, to the Committee, its agents and professionals.

7. Creditor Information Requests. If a creditor (the "Requesting Creditor") submits a written request (including on the Committee Website or by electronic mail) (the "Information Request") for the Committee to disclose information, the Committee

shall as soon as practicable, but no more than twenty (20) days[1b] after receipt of the Information Request, provide a response to the Information Request (including on the Committee Website) (the "Response"), including providing access to the information requested or the reasons the Information Request cannot be complied with. If the Response is to deny the Request because the Committee believes the Information Request implicates Confidential Information that need not be disclosed pursuant to the terms of this Order or otherwise under 11 U.S.C. § 1102 (b)(3)(A), or that the Information Request is unduly burdensome, the Requesting Creditor may, after a good faith effort to meet and confer with an authorized representative of the Committee regarding the Information Request and the Response, seek to compel such disclosure for cause pursuant to a motion. Such motion shall be served and the hearing on such motion shall be noticed and scheduled pursuant to the Case Management Order. The Committee shall not object to any Requesting Creditor's request to participate in any such hearing by telephone conference. Nothing herein shall be deemed to preclude the Requesting Creditor from requesting (or the Committee objecting to such request) that the Committee provide the Requesting Creditor a log or other index of any information specifically responsive to the Requesting Creditor's request that the Committee deems to be Confidential Information or protected by the attorney/client, work product, or any other privilege. Furthermore, nothing herein shall be deemed to preclude the Requesting Creditor from requesting that the Court conduct an *in camera* review of any information specifically responsive to

[1b] This shall read ten (10) days on or after January 31, 2006.

the Requesting Creditor's request that the Committee claims is Confidential Information or subject to the attorney/client, work product, or other privilege.

8. In its Response to an Information Request for access to Confidential Information, the Committee shall consider whether (a) the Requesting Creditor is willing to agree to reasonable confidentiality and trading restrictions with respect to such Confidential Information and represents that such trading restrictions and any information-screening process complies with applicable securities laws; and (b) under the particular facts, such agreement and any information-screening process that it implements will reasonably protect the confidentiality of such information; provided, however, that if the Committee elects to provide access to Confidential Information on the basis of such confidentiality and trading restrictions, the Committee shall have no responsibility for the Requesting Creditor's compliance with, or liability for violation of, applicable securities or other laws. Any disputes with respect to this paragraph shall be resolved as provided in the preceding paragraph, and, to the extent applicable, the next paragraph.

9. Release of Confidential Information of Third Parties. In addition, if the Information Request implicates Confidential Information of the Debtors (or any other Entity) and the Committee agrees that such request should be satisfied, or if the Committee on its own wishes to disclose such Confidential Information to creditors, the Committee may demand (the "Demand") for the benefit of the Debtors' creditors: (a) if the Confidential Information is information of the Debtors, by submitting a written request, each captioned as a "Committee Information Demand," to Skadden, Arps, Slate, Meagher & Flom LLP, counsel

for the Debtors, Four Times Square, New York, New York 10036 (Attention: J. Gregory Milmoe, Esq. (gmilmoe@skadden.com) and Sally McDonald Henry, Esq. (shenry@skadden.com)) ("Debtors' Counsel"), stating that such information will be disclosed in the manner described in the Demand unless the Debtors object to such Demand on or before fifteen (15) days after the service of such Demand; and, after the lodging of such an objection, the Committee, the Requesting Creditor and the Debtors may schedule a hearing with the Court pursuant to the Case Management Order seeking a ruling with respect to the Demand under 11 U.S.C. § 704(a)(7); and (b) if the Confidential Information is information of another Entity, by submitting a written request to such Entity and its counsel of record, with a copy to Debtors' Counsel, stating that such information will be disclosed in the manner described in the Demand unless such Entity objects to such Demand on or before fifteen (15) days after the service of such Demand; and, after the lodging of such an objection, the Committee, the Requesting Creditor, such Entity and the Debtors may schedule a hearing with the Court pursuant to the Case Management Order seeking a ruling with respect to the Demand.

10. Nothing in this Order requires the Committee to provide access to information or solicit comments from any Entity that has not demonstrated to the satisfaction of the Committee, in its sole discretion, or to the Court, that it holds claims of the kind described in section 1102(b)(3) of the Bankruptcy Code.

11. Exculpation. None of the Debtors, the Committee and any of their respective directors, officers, employees, members, attorneys, consultants, advisors and

agents (acting in such capacity) (collectively, the "Exculpated Parties"), shall have or incur any liability to any Entity (including the Debtors and their affiliates) for any act taken or omitted to be taken in connection with the preparation, dissemination, or implementation of the Creditor Information Protocol, the Committee Website and other information to be provided pursuant to section 1102(b)(3) of the Bankruptcy Code; provided, however, that the foregoing shall not affect the liability of any Exculpated Party protected pursuant to this paragraph 11 that otherwise would result from any such act or omission to the extent that such act or omission is determined in a final non-appealable order to have constituted a breach of fiduciary duty, gross negligence, or willful misconduct, including, without limitation, fraud and criminal misconduct, or the breach of any confidentiality agreement or Order. Without limiting the foregoing, the exculpation provided in this paragraph shall be coextensive with any Exculpated Party's qualified immunity under applicable law.

12. This Order shall be effective as of January 3, 2006, however, the terms of this Order shall apply to all information governed by this Order, including information in the Committee's possession prior to January 3, 2006.

13. This Order shall be binding in all respects upon the Debtors and any successors thereto.

Dated: New York, New York
December 23, 2005

/s/ Robert D. Drain
HONORABLE ROBERT D. DRAIN
UNITED STATES BANKRUPTCY COURT

APPENDIX X

REDEMPTION, SURRENDER OR REAFFIRMATION

Section 11 U.S.C. 521(a)(6) the debtor shall file:

6. in a case under chapter 7 of this title (11 U.S.C.S. 701) in which the debtor is an individual, not retain possession of personal property as to which a creditor has an allowed claim for the purchase price secured in whole or in part by an interest in such personal property unless the debtor, not later than 45 days after the first meeting of creditors under section 341(a), either—

   (A) enters into an agreement with the creditor pursuant to section 524(c) with respect to the claim secured by such property; or

   (B) redeems such property from the security interest pursuant to section 722.

   If the debtor fails to so act within the 45-day period referred to in paragraph (6), the stay under section 362(a) is terminated with respect to the personal property of the estate or of the debtor which is affected, such property shall no longer be property of the estate, and the creditor may take whatever action as to such property as is permitted by applicable nonbankruptcy law, unless the court determines on the motion of the trustee filed before the expiration of such 45-day period, and after notice and a hearing, that such property is of consequential value or benefit to the estate, orders appropriate adequate protection of the creditor's interest, and orders the debtor to deliver any collateral in the debtor's possession to the trustee; and

7. . . .

APPENDIX XI

CONVERSION OR DISMISSAL— 11 U.S.C. § 1112

(a) The debtor may convert a case under this chapter to a case under chapter 7 of this title unless—

(1) the debtor is not a debtor in possession;

(2) the case originally was commenced as an involuntary case under this chapter; or

(3) the case was converted to a case under this chapter other than on the debtor's request.

(b) Except as provided in paragraph (2) of this subsection, subsection (c) of this section, and section 1104(a)(3), on request of a party in interest, and after notice and a hearing, absent unusual circumstances specifically identified by the court that establish that the requested conversion or dismissal is not in the best interests of creditors and the estate, the court shall convert a case under this chapter to a case under chapter 7 or dismiss a case under this chapter, whichever is in the best interests of creditors and the estate, if the movant establishes cause.

(1) The relief provided in paragraph (1) shall not be granted absent unusual circumstances specifically identified by the court that establish that such relief is not in the best interests of creditors and the estate, if the debtor or another party in interest objects and establishes that—

(A) there is a reasonable likelihood that a plan will be confirmed within the timeframes established in sections 1121(e) and 1129(e) of this title, or if such sections do not apply, within a reasonable period of time; and

(B) the grounds for granting such relief include an act or omission of the debtor other than under paragraph (4)(A)—

(i) for which there exists a reasonable justification for the act or omission; and

(ii) that will be cured within a reasonable period of time fixed by the court.

(2) The court shall commence the hearing on a motion under this subsection not later than 30 days after filing of the motion, and shall decide the motion not later than 15 days after commencement of such hearing, unless the movant expressly consents to a continuance for a specific period of time or compelling circumstances prevent the court from meeting the time limits established by this paragraph.

(3) For purposes of this subsection, the term "cause" includes—

(A) substantial or continuing loss to or diminution of the estate and the absence of a reasonable likelihood of rehabilitation;

(B) gross mismanagement of the estate;

(C) failure to maintain appropriate insurance that poses a risk to the estate or to the public;

(D) unauthorized use of cash collateral substantially harmful to 1 or more creditors;

(E) failure to comply with an order of the court;

(F) unexcused failure to satisfy timely any filing or reporting requirement established by this title or by any rule applicable to a case under this chapter;

(G) failure to attend the meeting of creditors convened under section 341(a) or an examination ordered under rule 2004 of the Federal Rules of Bankruptcy Procedure without good cause shown by the debtor;

(H) failure timely to provide information or attend meetings reasonably requested by the United States trustee (or the bankruptcy administrator, if any);

(I) failure to timely pay taxes owed after the date of the order for relief or to file tax returns due after the date of the order for relief;

(J) failure to file a disclosure statement, or to file or confirm a plan, within the time fixed by this title or by order of the court;

(K) failure to pay any fees or charges required under chapter 123 of title 28;

(L) revocation of an order of confirmation under section 1144;

(M) inability to effectuate substantial consummation of a confirmed plan;

(N) material default by the debtor with respect to a confirmed plan;

(O) termination of a confirmed plan by reason of the occurrence of a condition specified in the plan; and

(P) failure of the debtor to pay any domestic support obligation that first becomes payable after the date of the filing of the petition.

(c) The court may not convert a case under this chapter to a case under chapter 7 of this title if the debtor is a farmer or a corporation that is not a moneyed, business, or commercial corporation, unless the debtor requests such conversion.

(d) The court may convert a case under this chapter to a case under chapter 12 or 13 of this title only if—

(1) the debtor requests such conversion;

(2) the debtor has not been discharged under section 1141(d) of this title; and

(3) if the debtor requests conversion to chapter 12 of this title, such conversion is equitable.

(e) Except as provided in subsections (c) and (f), the court, on request of the United States trustee, may convert a case under this chapter to a case under chapter 7 of this title or may dismiss a case under this chapter, whichever is in the best interest of creditors and the estate if the debtor in a voluntary case fails to file, within fifteen days after the filing of the petition commencing such case or such additional time as the court may allow, the information required by paragraph (1) of section 521, including a list containing the names and addresses of the holders of the twenty largest unsecured claims (or of all unsecured claims if there are fewer than twenty unsecured claims), and the approximate dollar amounts of each of such claims.

(f) Notwithstanding any other provision of this section, a case may not be converted to a case under another chapter of this title unless the debtor may be a debtor under such chapter.

APPENDIX XII

DETERMINATION OF SECURED CLAIM

11 USC 506—Bankruptcy Code

§ 506. Determination of secured status

(a) (1) An allowed claim of a creditor secured by a lien on property in which the estate has an interest, or that is subject to setoff under section 553 of this title, is a secured claim to the extent of the value of such creditor's interest in the estate's interest in such property, or to the extent of the amount subject to setoff, as the case may be, and is an unsecured claim to the extent that the value of such creditor's interest or the amount so subject to setoff is less than the amount of such allowed claim. Such value shall be determined in light of the purpose of the valuation and of the proposed disposition or use of such property, and in conjunction with any hearing on such disposition or use or on a plan affecting such creditor's interest.

(2) If the debtor is an individual in a case under chapter 7 or 13, such value with respect to personal property securing an allowed claim shall be determined based on the replacement value of such property as of the date of the filing of the petition without deduction for costs of sale or marketing. With respect to property acquired for personal, family, or household purposes, replacement value shall mean the price a retail merchant would charge for property of that kind considering the age and condition of the property at the time value is determined.

(b) To the extent that an allowed secured claim is secured by property the value of which, after any recovery under subsection (c) of this section, is greater than the amount of such claim, there shall be allowed to the holder of such claim, interest on such claim, and any reasonable fees, costs, or charges provided for under the agreement or State statute under which such claim arose.

(c) The trustee may recover from property securing an allowed secured claim the reasonable, necessary costs and expenses of preserving, or disposing of, such property to the extent of any benefit to the holder of such claim, including the payment of all ad valorem property taxes with respect to the property.

(d) To the extent that a lien secures a claim against the debtor that is not an allowed secured claim, such lien is void, unless—

(1) such claim was disallowed only under section 502(b)(5) or 502(e) of this title; or

(2) such claim is not an allowed secured claim due only to the failure of any entity to file a proof of such claim under section 501 of this title.

APPENDIX XIII

CONFIRMATION OF PLAN

11 USC 1325—Bankruptcy Code

§ 1325. Confirmation of plan

(a) Except as provided in subsection (b), the court shall confirm a plan if—

(1) The plan complies with the provisions of this chapter and with the other applicable provisions of this title;

(2) any fee, charge, or amount required under chapter 123 of title 28, or by the plan, to be paid before confirmation, has been paid;

(3) the plan has been proposed in good faith and not by any means forbidden by law;

(4) the value, as of the effective date of the plan, of property to be distributed under the plan on account of each allowed unsecured claim is not less than the amount that would be paid on such claim if the estate of the debtor were liquidated under chapter 7 of this title on such date;

(5) with respect to each allowed secured claim provided for by the plan—

(A) the holder of such claim has accepted the plan;

(B) (i) the plan provides that—

(I) the holder of such claim retain the lien securing such claim until the earlier of—

(aa) the payment of the underlying debt determined under nonbankruptcy law; or

(bb) discharge under section 1328; and

(II) if the case under this chapter is dismissed or converted without completion of the plan, such lien shall also be retained by such holder to the extent recognized by applicable nonbankruptcy law;

(ii) the value, as of the effective date of the plan, of property to be distributed under the plan on account of such claim is not less than the allowed amount of such claim; and

(iii) if—

(I) property to be distributed pursuant to this subsection is in the form of periodic payments, such payments shall be in equal monthly amounts; and

(II) the holder of the claim is secured by personal property, the amount of such payments shall not be less than an amount sufficient to provide to the holder of such claim adequate protection during the period of the plan; or

(C) the debtor surrenders the property securing such claim to such holder;

(6) the debtor will be able to make all payments under the plan and to comply with the plan;

(7) the action of the debtor in filing the petition was in good faith;

(8) the debtor has paid all amounts that are required to be paid under a domestic support obligation and that first become payable after the date of the filing of the petition if the debtor is required by a judicial or administrative order, or by statute, to pay such domestic support obligation; and

(9) the debtor has filed all applicable Federal, State, and local tax returns as required by section 1308.

For purposes of paragraph (5), section 506 shall not apply to a claim described in that paragraph if the creditor has a purchase money security interest securing the debt that is the subject of the claim, the debt was incurred within the 910-day preceding the date of the filing of the petition, and the collateral for that debt consists of a motor vehicle (as defined in section 30102 of title 49) acquired for the personal use of the debtor, or if collateral for that debt consists of any other thing of value, if the debt was incurred during the 1-year period preceding that filing.

(b) (1) If the trustee or the holder of an allowed unsecured claim objects to the confirmation of the plan, then the court may not approve the plan unless, as of the effective date of the plan—

(A) the value of the property to be distributed under the plan on account of such claim is not less than the amount of such claim; or

(B) the plan provides that all of the debtor's projected disposable income to be received in the applicable commitment period beginning on the date that the first payment is due under the plan will be applied to make payments to unsecured creditors under the plan.

(2) For purposes of this subsection, the term "disposable income" means current monthly income received by the debtor (other than child support payments, foster care payments, or disability payments for a

dependent child made in accordance with applicable nonbankruptcy law to the extent reasonably necessary to be expended for such child) less amounts reasonably necessary to be expended—

(A) (i) for the maintenance or support of the debtor or a dependent of the debtor, or for a domestic support obligation, that first becomes payable after the date the petition is filed; and

(ii) for charitable contributions (that meet the definition of "charitable contribution" under section 548 (d)(3) [1] to a qualified religious or charitable entity or organization (as defined in section 548 (d)(4)) in an amount not to exceed 15 percent of gross income of the debtor for the year in which the contributions are made; and

(B) if the debtor is engaged in business, for the payment of expenditures necessary for the continuation, preservation, and operation of such business.

(3) Amounts reasonably necessary to be expended under paragraph (2), other than subparagraph (A)(ii) of paragraph (2), shall be determined in accordance with subparagraphs (A) and (B) of section 707(b)(2), if the debtor has current monthly income, when multiplied by 12, greater than—

(A) in the case of a debtor in a household of 1 person, the median family income of the applicable State for 1 earner;

(B) in the case of a debtor in a household of 2, 3, or 4 individuals, the highest median family income of the applicable State for a family of the same number or fewer individuals; or

(C) in the case of a debtor in a household exceeding 4 individuals, the highest median family income of the applicable State for a family of 4 or fewer individuals, plus $525 per month for each individual in excess of 4.

(4) For purposes of this subsection, the "applicable commitment period"—

(A) subject to subparagraph (B), shall be—

(i) 3 years; or

(ii) not less than 5 years, if the current monthly income of the debtor and the debtor's spouse combined, when multiplied by 12, is not less than—

(I) in the case of a debtor in a household of 1 person, the median family income of the applicable State for 1 earner;

(II) in the case of a debtor in a household of 2, 3, or 4 individuals, the highest median family income of the applicable State for a family of the same number or fewer individuals; or

(III) in the case of a debtor in a household exceeding 4 individuals, the highest median family income of the applicable State for a family of 4 or fewer individuals, plus $525 per month for each individual in excess of 4; and

(B) may be less than 3 or 5 years, whichever is applicable under subparagraph (A), but only if the plan provides for payment in full of all allowed unsecured claims over a shorter period.

(C) After confirmation of a plan, the court may order any entity from whom the debtor receives income to pay all or any part of such income to the trustee.

[1] So in original. Probably should be followed by a second closing parenthesis.

CHAPTER 7

Law Firms and Collection Agencies

Every credit or collection manager at some point must deal with an outside attorney or a collection agency. To my knowledge, no "How to Books" on the accepted way to monitor or to retain a collection agency or attorney are on the market. This chapter is devoted to the legal problems that are encountered, as well as the criteria for selecting and the methods of monitoring an outside collection agency or attorney.

SELECTION OF AN ATTORNEY OR AGENCY

Four good reasons exist for using an attorney or collection agency after the creditor has exhausted the collection effort.

1. Statistics have demonstrated that engaging a new entity involved in the collection of a debt often dramatically improves the results. This is known as "transferring" the collection effort to a third party.
2. The collection agency and attorney provide trained and sophisticated collectors to continue the collection activity.
3. The attorney, in addition to engaging in the activities of a collection agency, is empowered to institute suit against the debtor.
4. And the major reason, is that the creditor cannot collect the debt, and will have to absorb the loss by charging off the indebtedness as a bad debt.

Reputation. The principal reason to engage a particular attorney or agency is reputation. The best source of such information is a personal recommendation from another firm that has been exposed to the agency or attorney. A recommendation that a business has utilized the services over a long period of time and obtained good results both from collection and reporting aspects should be considered. Nevertheless, a creditor should not act without inquiry. The fact that the agency or attorney has satisfied one creditor does not mean it will satisfy you, and the fact that it has performed well for one year is no assurance it will perform well next year. The attorney or agency not only must collect money and furnish reports, but also must meet the following qualifications:

1. It must belong to trade associations that provide the current laws and court cases to enable the attorney or collection agency to comply with same.
2. At least as to collection agencies, it must be licensed in the states which require licensing (32 states) and must carry errors-and-omission insurance.
3. It must have procedures in place to protect the creditor from exposure to suits for violation of the Fair Debt Collection Practices Act (FDCPA) and the unfair trade practices law that have been passed in most of the states. Agencies should be bonded so that assurance exists that the client can recover money. Various trade associations or law lists will bond collection agencies for this purpose.
4. The attorney must carry malpractice insurance. A recommendation is an excellent place to start, but only the first step in a multi-step process.
5. The issues of privacy, security, and compliance with the law must be addressed.
6. The number of years in business is significant for both collection agencies and law firms. If the debt collector does not turn over the money promptly to clients or uses abusive tactics which resulted in lawsuits, the law firm or the collection agency will not remain in the industry too long. The client must recognize that when the law firm or the agency is sued for a violation of the Fair Debt Collection Practices Act, the Fair Credit Reporting Act or the Truth in Lending Act, a likelihood exists that the client will also be sued.
7. A review of the reporting techniques used will determine whether you will be satisfied with the extent of the information being furnished. While you can examine the reports that they have furnished to other clients, you are unable to examine how frequently and how regularly they submit the reports and *the quality and reliability of the report.* Obtaining references will help but be certain that the reference you

wish to utilize is a firm of similar size to your own and recognize that the agency knows the reference will recommend the agency.

8. The geographical area is important. If your customer base is local, a local firm would be suitable. If your customer base is national, the collection agency will either have offices that are based in other states or will have a relationship with other agencies. If you are dealing with a law firm, the law firm has several options. A network of referral attorneys is suitable for a national client. For special cases attorneys can be admitted to the local federal or state court for that particular case. In many instances the firm practices in surrounding states, maintains offices in some of the larger states or is affiliated with firms in the other states.

Financial Responsibility. A representation should be obtained that no judgments are outstanding against the attorney or agency. Inquiry may be made as to whether any suits for violation of the FDCPA were instituted and, if successful, was the problem corrected.

Collection agencies and attorneys borrow from lending institutions, and their assets consist primarily of cash in the bank and office equipment. The liabilities should be nominal. Unfortunately, some law firms and agencies are heavy borrowers and they sometimes fail to remit escrow money to the client. Caution by the creditor in this area may avoid grief in the future. The creditor should periodically audit the agency or law firm for performance.

Insurance. You should ask both a law firm and a collection agency about the type of insurance carried and the extent of coverage. In today's litigious environment, insurance in the sum of $1 million is a necessity.

Attorneys. Attorneys are covered by malpractice insurance, which insures them primarily against negligent acts performed in the course of representing clients. The coverage normally ranges from one hundred thousand dollars to several million dollars. Many law firms operate "naked," that is, without insurance. In some states, the percentage "naked" is substantial. A request for a copy of the malpractice policy is common, and is recommended. The policy will provide the coverage, the deductible, premium, and expiration date. Copies of new policies should be requested each year.

Some states (for example, New York) maintain a fund which is specifically earmarked to protect against an attorney stealing monies that were entrusted to the attorney on behalf of the client. In some states, attorneys pay an annual fee to support this fund. Accordingly, if monies are not remitted to the client, the client may have a claim upon this fund for reimbursement. Consult with an attorney.

Collection Agencies. Collection agencies carry errors-and-omission policies which are similar to those carried by a business. These policies cover the collection agency if an error or omission is made and the agency becomes liable to one of its customers, or to one of its delinquent debtors. Some of these policies insure the agency against violation of the Fair Debt Collection Practices Act.

A large number of states require agencies to be licensed to conduct business within the state. As part of the licensing process, the state requires the agency to post a bond and have an office in the state. The amount of the bond varies from state to state and may be a fixed amount, or a fixed amount per office in the state, or an amount that is a function either of the number of employees or of the gross billing. The purpose of the bond is to ensure that the agency remits to the client the monies collected from the debtors and, upon a failure to remit, the client may proceed against the insurance company that issued the bond.

References. Requesting three to seven references is appropriate. You should avoid those references which have a close personal relationship to the collector, because the reference will be biased. Select references in the same field and choose at least three from the ten provided. The location of the reference should also be considered. One located across the street from the agency may have a different perspective than the one located several hundred miles away.

While contacting the individual named is a reasonable starting point, contacting the clerical staff or other staff members of the reference may produce an unbiased and different perspective. Remember that the firm is providing the ten best clients as references and the likelihood is that the principal of the agency or the partner of the law firm has a personal relationship with the individual furnished as a reference. While this is not meant to imply that information provided will be inaccurate, the reference will probably be biased. The following are suggested inquiries:

1. How often is a report furnished?
2. What is the content of the report furnished?
3. Are monies remitted each month at the same time?
4. Are telephone calls returned promptly?
5. Is the client communication with one party or several parties?
6. In the event the party designated to deal with your firm is absent, is there an alternate who is knowledgeable?
7. Have complaints from debtors about the law firm or agency been made to the reference?
8. Such inquiries may lead to other questions, and the creditor will undoubtedly think of additional inquiries. The more inquiries made, the more information will be provided.

MONITORING

The First Referral. Whether a creditor continues to use an agency or attorney will often depend upon the first referral of a claim or claims. Many creditors decide that if the first claim is not immediately collected, they will seek another firm. Often the money is not collected immediately, and the creditor ceases to refer business.

Sometimes the creditor will forward old accounts that have been worked on by another firm to determine whether the new agency or attorney can produce results. This philosophy is not fair. A collector may do an excellent job and still collect no money because the accounts were worked on by a prior firm and often the accounts are not only old, but no efforts to collect have been made for a long time. Even when new accounts are referred, the possibility exists that the first few will not be collected. When the first few accounts are collected, the creditor is impressed and often will forward more work. This approach is flawed, since a combination of fresh accounts and a little luck may have prevailed. The attorney or agency should be monitored to confirm the necessary number of letters and the contacts by telephone, and a reasonable test should cover a period of three to six months. If only a few accounts are referred each year, the creditor should examine the reports carefully to be certain the accounts are processed quickly and thoroughly. If the job is being done right, the collectible money will be recovered.

Reports. Agencies and attorneys provide a wide variety of reports to their clients. Some of these are statistical reports which show the number of cases referred, the amount referred, and the total collected on liquidation reports by month. Others will be detailed case histories of exactly what the collection activity produced on a particular case. The former is usually provided for a large number of cases of relatively small amounts, while the latter is provided for an individual case of a large amount, usually commercial matters. Initially, after retaining an agency or attorney, the client should insist upon reports within the first 30 to 60 days and monthly or bimonthly thereafter. Some creditors do not pay attention to the reports, arguing that their only interest is the amount collected, but reports are essential to monitor the progress and the fact that the agency or attorney is devoting attention to the collection effort.

The type of report furnished is significant if it provides information not already available. A descriptive report of procedures is helpful. Reports using standardized codes can be meaningless because active accounts generate telephone activity or correspondence. It is far better to obtain descriptive reports that tell a story and explain the progress of the case.

Statistical reports are easily manipulated to show favorable results. One report may deduct bankrupt debtors or out-of-business debtors from the total amount referred, thereby increasing the percentage collected.

Another report may not include in the total amount referred those debtors who returned the goods or who were issued a credit because goods were defective or undelivered. Some reports treat returned merchandise as a paid account, while others do not. You must use your own figures, and apply them equally to all outside attorneys and agencies, and not rely on percentages furnished by the law firms or agencies.

TESTING

An important consideration is to test the collection agency or law firm fairly, allowing for a sufficient period of time to fully evaluate performance. Two qualifying firms should receive an equal number of accounts over a given period of time with the same type of account, with same average balances, same aging, same geographical area, and from the same department or source. If the debtors are businesses as opposed to retailers, the business debtors should be in the same industry and should have other similarities such as size, product line, etc. With regard to business accounts, a random selection probably will satisfy these criteria.

When considering the performance of two firms, the reporting qualities should be integrated as well as the communication and support between the firm and the creditor. In general, the agency or law firm which performs better will usually provide the better communication, the better reporting, the better support, the better performance, and generate the fewest complaints.

LICENSING

All states require attorneys to be licensed and a large number of states require collection agencies to be licensed.

Collection Agencies. The great majority of the states have laws that affect collection agencies and more than half have specific laws requiring out-of-state collection agencies to be licensed, registered, or bonded if the agency should do business in that state. Some states impose specific requirements for licensing and do not provide exemptions: Alaska, Arizona, Arkansas, Connecticut, Hawaii, Louisiana, Maine, Maryland, Massachusetts, and Minnesota. Other states are "open" to out-of-state collectors as they impose no licensing requirements: Alabama, California, Georgia, Iowa (if collections exceed $25,000), Kansas, Kentucky, Missouri, Montana, New Hampshire, Ohio, Oklahoma, Pennsylvania, Rhode Island, South Carolina, South Dakota, Vermont, and Virginia. Nevertheless, other provisions of the laws in these states may prohibit certain practices. Many states require collection agencies to be licensed if they are collecting for an in-state creditor or soliciting business. These states may have no specific licensing requirements, but may have a bond and registration requirement.

The U.S. Postal Service does forward letters addressed to a consumer from one state to another state. In the event the agency is not licensed in the other state, the collection agency may be faced with specific problems. It is recommended to include on the envelope underneath the agency's return address, "ADDRESS CORRECTION REQUESTED. DO NOT FORWARD." In such a case, the post office will return the letter to the sender and avoid any potential problems with state licensing laws in the event the letter should be forwarded to a state where the agency is not licensed.

Because most collection agencies conduct business across the entire country in this fluid economy, many conduct business without licenses in the states requiring them. Most national agencies are licensed, but some regional agencies do not wish to absorb the licensing expense in a state where little business is conducted. Inquire whether the agency is licensed in the states requiring licenses, and ask for proof.

The collection laws in the various states impose certain burdens upon collection agencies with regard to a large variety of their activities. Some state laws require the collection agency to have an actual office within the state, while other states require that any monies collected from a consumer within the state must be kept in bank accounts in the state. Other states require that the agency keep books and records in the state where the debtor resides and maintain all their records with regard to the collection of the debts in that state. These types of requirements are burdensome and oppressive to small agencies with but one office. The agency may collect only one or two debts in another state in a period of six months or a year. Considerable litigation concerning this particular problem has taken place. The national association of collection agencies, the American Collectors Association (ACA), has been active in trying to modify and reduce the burdensome requirements of these particular laws. Ask for copies of the statutes and proof of compliance.

Attorneys. Attorneys have to be licensed in the state where their practice is conducted. The attorney must meet the qualifications of the state bar association, and is formally admitted to practice by a court of the state. Attorneys do not have to qualify in other states to engage in collection activities in those states, except in Connecticut which requires attorneys engaged in collecting consumer accounts to register in the same manner as collection agencies. Texas has licensing laws and requires a bond and Florida has certain requirements and fees.

Most states feel that regulation by the state bar association where the attorney is located is adequate. An attorney is permitted to engage in collection activities by writing letters and making telephone calls to a debtor located in a different state, but some states require the attorney to be licensed as a debt collector in the same manner as an agency (Connecticut).

An attorney cannot practice in the courts of another state and should not consult or advise a client concerning the laws of the other state unless admitted to practice in that state. When a client forwards a claim for suit in another state, a local attorney is retained to institute suit. In FDCPA defense matters, our office retains local counsel, but we make application to court to be admitted for the particular case and conduct the litigation from our office in New York, leaving to local counsel routine appearances in court.

TRADE ASSOCIATIONS

A key question to ask is "Does the collection agency or the attorney belong to a trade association?" In today's legal environment, keeping abreast of the current laws is essential to the operation of a collection agency or a law firm engaged in collection. Aside from policy statements released by the Federal Trade Commission and changes in federal and state laws, both state and federal courts are rendering decisions daily which affect the collection process. Many collection agencies and law firms do not have the staff or the funds to monitor the changing legal atmosphere. The alternative is a trade association which maintains a legal staff whose sole function is to oversee the legal environment and to communicate to its members any changes affecting the collection process.

Inquiry may be made to the association to determine whether the collection agency or attorney is a member in good standing. Of the 6,000 collection agencies in the United States, many belong to regional or national associations, but a large number do not belong to any trade association. There are two major trade associations for collection agencies: The American Collectors Association (ACA), 4040 West 70th Street, Minneapolis, Minnesota 55435, and the Associated Credit Bureau, P.O. Box 21300, Houston, Texas 77218.

Law firms belong to state bar associations and/or to the American Bar Association, 750 N. Lake Shore Dr., Chicago, Illinois 60611. In addition, the law firm may be a member of citywide associations in the major cities, such as Association of the Bar of the City of New York, 42 W. 44th St., New York, NY 10036.

Attorneys and collection agencies belong to the Commercial Law League of America at 222 West Adam Street, Chicago, Illinois, 60606-5278. This association is devoted to commercial matters only, and the association subscribes to the triad philosophy. The collection agency represents the client and then retains the attorney. The attorney deals with the collection agency, not the client. The Commercial Law League provides guidelines for the relationship between forwarder and receiver of a claim.

The National Association of Retail Collection Attorneys (NARCA), 1515 North Warson Road, St. Louis, MO 63132, provides a listing of attorneys who engage in the collection of consumer accounts. This association subscribes to the philosophy that attorneys may deal directly with the client.

The American Bankruptcy Institute, 44 Canal Center Plaza, Suite 404, Alexandria, VA 22314-5192 publishes a monthly journal for the insolvency professional and enjoys a large membership of bankruptcy attorneys.

The purchasers of debts have their own association. The Debt Buyers' Association is located at 10444 Pioneer, Santa Fe Springs, CA 90670.

The Turnaround Management Association, 100 South Wacker Drive, Suite 850, Chicago, IL 60606 is active in restructuring financially troubled businesses.

All of these associations arrange conferences to update their members on the current law, to train their members, and to encourage networking. Most associations issue a magazine or newsletter to inform the members of new laws, court decisions, administrative agency decisions, and other events which affect the industry. Our firm belongs to six trade associations.

ADVANTAGES OF ATTORNEYS AND COLLECTION AGENCIES

Over the years many of the large credit card companies expanded, absorbed small credit card issuers, or merged with other credit card issuers. Also, Visa and MasterCard entered the arena. Now a significant number of companies that issue credit cards operate on a national basis. Some major credit unions also operate on a national basis. These institutions refer claims to either regional or national collection agencies across the country, and the collection agencies, in turn, refer these matters to attorneys locally to institute suit.

Collection agencies promoted the idea that creditors should refer all accounts to collection agencies and that if the agency was unable to collect the delinquent account, the collection agency would refer the matter to an attorney. Several law firms list published national lists of attorneys and provided these lists to the collection agencies. The collection agencies selected attorneys from these national lists and forwarded the claims to the attorney operating an office closest to where the debtor's business or the consumer was located. (Examples of these lists of attorneys appear in the Appendix to this chapter.) The three-way arrangement consisted of permitting the collection agencies to deal directly with the creditors, the law lists publishing the list of attorneys to be selected for referrals, and the attorneys receiving the claims from the collection agencies. While this arrangement was originally applied almost totally to commercial claims, as the credit card industry grew the majority of collection agencies also engaged in collecting debts from consumers.

The targets of the membership promotion of NARCA were law firms engaged in consumer collection. The major purpose of NARCA was to promote the concept that creditors could deal directly with attorneys without using the collection agency as an intermediary, and that attorneys could write dunning letters and make telephone calls as effectively as, if not better than, the collection agencies. Creditors understood that the collection agencies could do only two things: write letters and make telephone calls. Collection agencies could not institute suit without retaining an attorney. On the other hand, if a claim was referred to an attorney directly, the law firm could write letters, make telephone calls, and furthermore institute suit. Another marketing tool of the collection agency was that the agency paid the upfront costs ($100–$300) to the attorney to start suit, whereas the client must pay the costs if an attorney was retained directly. But to enable the agency to do this, the agency usually charged a higher fee than the attorney and usually started fewer suits than the client would start—two reasons why the benefit disappeared.

The effective collection of debts is dependent upon many factors and the collection agencies had several points in their favor. First, many large collection agencies across the country have staffs in excess of 100 people, and in a few instances, as many as 1,000 or more employees, and could service the large credit grantor. Second, many collection agencies have sophisticated computer programs to enable them to monitor a large volume of accounts. Third, the major weapon of the collection agencies and their clients as to consumer debtors is reporting the consumer to a credit reporting agency, which impacts the consumer's ability to obtain credit. While consumers may be wary of suits by attorneys, they are also apprehensive about their credit profile.

One prime advantage of using an attorney is the availability of legal consultation on problems in the collection effort. Prevention in today's environment may avoid a costly lawsuit.

Since agencies use profiling, they exclude certain states, area codes, or zip codes so no collection effort, letter, or telephone call, is made on a particular debt. Because most law firms are not as sophisticated, such profiling usually is not used to reduce costs.

The law firms involved in collections are mostly small; only a few have a support staff of over 100 persons. One of the major elements that limited the use of attorneys was the fact that attorneys could only institute suit in the state in which they were admitted to the bar. Since most attorneys were only admitted to the bar in the state in which their office was located, they could not cross state lines to institute suit, but were forced to retain attorneys in the state in which the debtor resided.

Attorney Networks. From this creation of the new trade association developed the idea of an attorney network for consumer and credit card claims. In essence, a network of attorneys consisted of attorneys located in each state banding together in a loosely knit affiliation which promoted their services to the large credit card grantors in the country.

To my knowledge, approximately three or four networks operate across the country, and each one of them uses one or more attorneys in each state. Separate and distinct requirements are set forth for each network for law firms to become members. The attorneys may pay initiation dues, annual dues, transmission fees, dues per case received, or a percentage of each fee that is collected. Some of the networks transmit claims electronically. The idea is that the network centralizes the distribution of the cases as well as the status reporting from each member law firm. The network combines the status reports from all the member attorney firms into one combined report. Whereas the networks are suitable for national credit grantors, some regional credit grantors are also using the networks in their regional area. Our firm has maintained one of these networks for over thirty years, but our network attorneys pay no dues or similar charges.

AGREEMENTS WITH LAW FIRMS OR AGENCIES

Most financial institutions and large corporations require the agency or law firm to execute a written agreement setting forth the terms and conditions under which the accounts are being referred. These agreements range from a few pages to as many as 40 pages in length. The agreements cover:

- the fees paid to the agency or law firm
- the procedure of account referral
- the requirement to hold monies in escrow in special trust accounts
- the procedures for remitting money to the client
- the conditions of termination
- the terms of withdrawal of an account
- indemnification of the client
- insurance coverage
- licensing compliance
- appropriate clauses with attorneys so that attorneys may comply with the doctrine of "meaningful involvement" (*see* Appendix to Chapter 15) in consumer collection
- status reporting
- reporting payments
- compliance with laws
- right to audit
- fees
- other boilerplate clauses indigenous to all contracts.

For a skeleton outline of such a contract *see* Appendix to this chapter.

Most contracts provide that the agency or law firm comply with all laws and regulations. The agency or law firm must maintain a record of every payment received and the amount of the fees deducted. The right to audit and inspect records with or without notice should also be included. Collection agencies cannot start lawsuits, but they do retain or employ attorneys to start suit. Agreements should cover the criteria under which a suit may be initiated, the payment of costs, disbursements, and the control over the conduct of the litigation. For appeals, separate provisions allow the attorney to perform services on a specified hourly rate rather than on a contingency basis. Contracts provide for termination upon 30-day written notice and for the return of all cases to the client. Copies of judgments should be furnished to the client. An optional clause is whether the attorney should file proof of claim in all bankruptcies or only in those cases exceeding certain amounts. If counterclaims are asserted in a litigation matter, the client must be notified immediately, and furnished with a copy of the papers served upon the attorney. Where counterclaims are interposed, the attorney charges an hourly fee (as opposed to a contingency fee under which the claim is being handled) to defend the counterclaim.

The procedures in settlements should include the discretion of the attorney to settle and the procedure for oral or written approval from the client. At the time of signing the contract, attorneys usually submit copies of their malpractice insurance, and collection agencies provide evidence of the bonding by the various states, as well as copies of the errors-and-omissions policies.

A key clause in all contracts is an agreement by the collection agency or law firm indemnifying the creditor against negligent acts as well mutual agreement and for creditor indemnification. Accordingly, if a suit is instituted against the creditor by reason of the negligent conduct of the agency or law firm, the agreement indemnifies the creditor for costs and expenses in defending the suit and the amount of any judgment awarded against the creditor. A clause requiring the client to advise the attorney of any bankruptcy notice on the account should be inserted, as well as requiring the client to notify the attorney or agency if an attorney is representing the debtor.

WITHDRAWAL OF CLAIM

A claim may always be withdrawn from a collection agency or a law firm. If the withdrawal is because the agency or law firm did not collect enough money or did not collect it quickly enough, the creditor may be liable for fees for services. Work and effort has been expended in the collection of this account, and the agency or attorney is entitled to be paid for these services, since the creditor is abrogating the right to continue the collection effort. If the account is referred to another collection agency and the claim is collected, the first collector is entitled to a portion of the fee. Collection agencies often refuse to return an account unless the creditor agrees to pay a fee in the event the account is ultimately collected. But if the account is active, or litigation has been started, and the claim is withdrawn from the attorney, the attorney will usually charge an hourly fee for the services already rendered.

Many large corporations and financial institutions retain a collection agency or law firm for primary work, when the account is referred for the first time for outside collection. After a period of time, the creditor withdraws the account and refers it to a secondary agency or law firm. The theory behind this transfer is that debtors respond positively when a new collector is involved, and perhaps the new collector uses an initial extra effort. Statistics show that secondary firms often collect money that primary agencies were unable to collect. The creditor should not transfer the account unless a written agreement is executed by the primary firm waiving any further fees. Accounts that are paying currently or are active usually are not recalled since the agency or attorney would be entitled to a fee upon collection.

If no written agreement exists, the creditor and the agency or law firm may agree on a fixed amount as a full settlement for the withdrawal of one or more claims. This is a negotiable figure and the amount is a function of past and future business and other circumstances prevailing at the time of the withdrawal.

ASSIGNMENT OF CLAIM

In some states a non-resident cannot sue or a bond must be posted; in other states a non-resident individual or corporation may be required to pay in advance the court costs that may be awarded to the defendant-debtor in the event the debtor wins the case (costs may amount from a few dollars up to several hundred dollars, depending upon the amount of the suit). In addition, some collection agencies wish to proceed in their own name to facilitate the prosecution of the case. The device used is "an assignment of claim" by the creditor to the collection agency.

The assignment is a short agreement between the creditor and the collection agency assigning the debt to the collection agency for prosecution or for suit. The agency proceeds in its name against the debtor, identifying itself as the assignee of the creditor.

Most claims are not assigned to collection agencies since the relevant problems are encountered in only a few states.

REFERRAL TO ATTORNEYS

After letters and telephone calls are made, collection agencies often refer claims to outside attorneys locally and across the country. (Some large collection agencies employ full-time attorneys on their staff.)

Collection agencies seem to acknowledge that outside attorneys may collect monies by dunning or suit that the agencies themselves are unable to collect. Agencies use their own staff attorneys or outside affiliated attorneys to write letters and contact the debtor by telephone. Statistics show that attorneys' letters and phone calls are successful in generating more collections. For this reason attorneys often argue that creditors should use an attorney initially instead of a collection agency.

Law firms will institute suit after unsuccessful letters and telephone calls and will refer matters to local attorneys across the country to institute suit if the debtor is out of state. As noted before, several organizations provide national lists of collection attorneys. These law firms will accept claims from collection agencies as well as from other attorneys, and from creditors. A creditor may require a written suit authorization setting forth the anticipated costs to start suit before suit is instituted.

SUIT FEES

A suit fee is a fee the local attorney requests in advance of the institution of a suit in addition to the contingency fee. The fee enables the attorney to institute the suit, prosecute the claim, and, if necessary, conduct a trial without any additional payment. Suit must be started to earn a suit fee. If suit is not started, the local attorney must return the suit fee. Preparation of a summons and complaint and delivering same to the sheriff or process server for service is commencement of the suit even if the sheriff or process server does not serve the summons and complaint.

Over the past several years, the fees to institute suit that are paid by out-of-state attorneys have significantly changed. The normal suit fee that most local attorneys charged was approximately 10 percent of the face amount of the claim. The percentage usually declines to 7 percent as the amount increases and to as little as 5 percent on large claims. The minimum suit fee that almost all local attorneys requested was approximately $100 and, in some instances, the suit fees on large claims ranged as high as $1,000 to $2,500 or more.

A non-contingent suit fee means that the attorney retains the suit fee even if the claim is not collected. A contingent suit fee is earned only if collection of the debt is made.

The local attorney contemplates that only a small portion of the suits will be contested. If the local attorney collects suit fees on every case, the one case that becomes complex will be paid for by the other suit fees. The suit fee is usually non-contingent and will not be returned.

Some attorneys request an additional contingent suit fee payable in the event the attorney is successful in collecting after suit. The contingent suit fee may range from 5 percent to 10 percent in addition to the non-contingent suit fee, both of which are in addition to the contingent fees.

In recent years, many creditors have taken the position that they do not want to pay a suit fee in advance to institute suit against a consumer. The forwarders prefer a straight contingent fee payable on collection of the claim by the attorney. This contingent fee covers the entire collection process from initiation of suit through trial. The pressure is on the attorney to produce collection. The creditor only pays a fee if collection is effected. A general trend in the industry today is that consumer claims are being forwarded on a straight contingency basis. The drawback in this arrangement is that the fee charged by the local attorney is more than would be charged with an advance suit fee. The local attorney is earning significantly more, but only if collection is made.

In today's environment, creditors with consumer claims usually do not pay suit fees and prefer not to pay suit fees on commercial claims. Costs must be advanced to the local attorney whether on a contingent basis or on a suit fee plus contingent basis. If a counterclaim is asserted, the local attorney normally requests an hourly fee to defend the counterclaim.

COURT COSTS

Court costs have increased dramatically over the last year. Court costs usually range from $35 to $500 depending upon the amount of the claim. The average filing fee in court is around $150 to $200. However, in recent years, the filing fees have increased substantially, approaching $300 or more in some instances. The attorney must also pay the process server or sheriff to serve the summons and complaint, usually from $30 to $100 or more depending on the location of the defendant and difficulty of service. Unfortunately, some attorneys request court costs not only to cover the minimum costs, but the maximum costs that may be needed, which include "anticipated costs"; that is, costs that may or may not be needed. Necessary costs include service and filing a summons and complaint. Anticipated costs include skiptracing, judgment, property executions, garnishees, and other expenses of enforcing the judgment. If the case is contested, the cost of depositions (stenographic minutes at about $4.00 to $7.00 per page), filing papers, fees for filing motions (New York), and other expenses are included in "anticipated costs." In these cases, court costs are negotiable when "anticipated costs" are requested.

In most states the sheriff serves the summons and complaint, and fees are fixed by law. These expenses are the primary reason for the court costs, although the attorney may use the advance costs to engage a service bureau to conduct a search to determine the proper name of the corporation, to locate a debtor, or to skiptrace, if authorized. The court costs and disbursements may also include the use of faxes, messenger services, or other office expenses. Court costs must be returned if not expended.

CONTINGENT FEES

Contingent fees that collection agencies charge may range from as low as 10 to 15 percent to as high as 50 percent. In general, commercial claims warrant fees between 15 and 33 percent and retail claims warrant fees between 25 and 50 percent.

At one time, attorneys used Commercial Law League rates for commercial collections, but these rates were abolished for antitrust reasons. Nevertheless, today many attorneys use the same rates, since they appear to be fair and equitable.

If a commercial claim is sent to an attorney by a collection agency under CLLA rate or law firm (because the debtor is located in another part of the country), the fees for the receiving attorney may be as follows:

- 331/3 percent of the first $75.
- 25 percent of excess over $75 to $300.
- 18 percent of excess over $300 to $2,000.
- 13 percent of excess over $2,000.

The forwarder (the collection agency or law firm) adds "approximately" 50 percent or less to the receiver's fee (33 percent plus 16 percent = 50 percent) so that the client pays as follows:

- 50 percent of the first $75.
- 33 percent of excess over $75 to $300.
- 27 percent of excess over $300 to $2,000.
- 20 percent of excess over $2,000.

In addition to the above fees, the client pays a 5 to 10 percent suit fee to commence suit plus the court costs.

> ***Credit & Collection Tip:*** *The least expensive is not always the best; the quality, effort, and experience of the attorney to produce the best result should be the prime consideration.*

RECOUPMENT OF COLLECTION COSTS

Many extensions of credit contracts (credit cards, installment vehicle contracts) contain clauses that the debtor must pay reasonable attorneys' fees if the matter is turned over to the attorney plus all collection costs. Sometimes the collection costs are measured in percentages such as 15 percent collection costs or 35 percent or sometimes as high as 40 percent collection costs. Some of the cases now have been looking at the issue of whether the collection agencies or attorney have to justify this fixed percentage and prove to the court that they actually incurred expenses in collection equal to the amount of the percentage of the unpaid balance that is specified in the agreement.[1]

COLLECTION OF DEBT BY CREDITOR

The collection of a debt is due to the joint effort of both the client and the agency or attorney. The agency or attorney earns a contingent fee even if the settlement is made with the client. The fact that the client is the last person to contact the debtor, or that payment is made directly to the client, is not material. Whether a client expends more time than the attorney to negotiate a settlement is also not material.

> ***Credit & Collection Tip:*** *The client is still liable for the contingent fee once the agency or the attorney has been retained and contact with the debtor by the agency or law firm by mail or telephone has been consummated.*

TRUST ACCOUNT

The agency or law firm must maintain a separate trust account for the monies collected from the debtor. If the checks are deposited, as is generally the case, the contingency fee is deducted before the monies are transmitted to the client.

REMITTANCE OF MONIES

Many states have enacted laws regarding the method in which collection agencies handle the collection of monies and the manner in which they

---

[1] *Hagan v. Mrs. Assocs.*, 2001 U.S. Dist. LEXIS 6789 (E.D. La. May 15, 2001); *Kojetin v. C.U. Recovery, Inc.*, 1999 U.S. Dist. LEXIS 10930 (D. Minn. Mar. 29, 1999); *Patzka v. Viterbro College*, 917 F. Supp. 654 (W.D. Wis. 1996).

remit the monies to the clients. The American Collectors Association lists 12 states which have laws that directly affect the handling of funds on behalf of clients and the remittance of said funds to the clients. A copy of these state laws can be obtained from the American Collectors Association at 4040 West 70th Street, Minneapolis, Minnesota 55435 (612) 926-6547.

ONE OR TWO COLLECTION AGENCIES OR ATTORNEYS?

Many creditors, if they are large enough, believe that they should always utilize at least two or three collection agencies or law firms to encourage competition and to compare results to determine who performs best. Other creditors conclude it is difficult enough to find a single good collection agency or law firm, much less several, and would rather use only one. Both arguments have merit and each creditor has to decide which road to travel.

ADVERTISING

Until recently, collection agencies were much more successful than attorneys in marketing their services to credit grantors primarily because attorneys were prohibited from advertising or soliciting. Only in the past decade have the barriers to advertising by lawyers been eliminated, and now law firms actively advertise and compete with the collection agencies. Ten years ago the National Association of Retail Collection Attorneys (NARCA) was organized for the purpose of presenting to credit grantors the concept that law firms were able to collect debts, and the creditors could use attorneys for initial collection efforts of letters and telephone calls.

PORTFOLIO PURCHASES

The Attorney General of Tennessee has taken the position that the purchasers of delinquent accounts are subject to the state's licensing requirement since it is a collection service which requires licensing in the event you collect an account for a fee, commission, or other compensation. It would appear that anyone who purchases portfolio accounts who intends to locate in Tennessee should investigate whether they fall within the definitions set forth by the office of the Attorney General, and if appropriate, obtain a license. Several other states are actively considering labeling debt buyers as debt collectors.

INTERNATIONAL COLLECTIONS

Doing business outside the United States presents a mixed bag when retaining attorneys. Our office handles a significant number of claims that are referred overseas and results depend upon not only the attorneys that we retain, but also upon the country in which the debtor resides.

Canada. In Canada outside of Quebec, most attorneys do not work on a contingency basis. However when a relationship is built up with the attorney, the flat fees or hourly charges will be close to what the contingency fee might be. On the other hand, the attorneys do require fees up front to institute suit. Quebec attorneys are permitted to handle matters on contingency, although some attorneys will ask for an hourly fee. The major problem in Quebec is the language, because documents have to be translated into French, although a witness may testify in English.

France. Notwithstanding that Quebec follows the French law, in France the attorneys do not work on a contingency basis. Developing a relationship with the law firm is recommended. The system recognizes that lawyers must have a fee to institute suit which must not be contingent on collection. This might be compared to the suit fee that we use in the United States, with some of the fee contingent on actual collection. In France there are different types of lawyers with different legal qualifications and the fees for the more qualified attorneys are much higher than for the less qualified attorneys.

Germany. Germany is one of the countries where contingency fees are totally prohibited. They have special fees for special procedures and, in general, the fees are constructed in such a way that they escalate with the amount of the indebtedness.

Italy. In Italy, contingency fees are also prohibited, but fees are usually set by the system or by the court which bear some relationship to the amount involved and the quantity of the work.

Turkey. Prior to institution of suit or any court action, the fees are on a contingency. In the event the collection is not effectuated, no fee is charged. Once court action is commenced, advance fees are required commensurate with the services to be rendered as well as to the amount involved. When a judgment is obtained, the law does provide significant remedies for the enforcement of the judgment.

Greece. Prior to the use of the court system, attorneys are available on a straight contingency basis. Once court action becomes necessary, the fee usually becomes a combination of fees for services rendered and a contingency fee. The fees for services rendered may be commensurate not only with these services but also with the amount involved. On large balances, the matter can drag on for a long time, but the law contains provisions to enforce the judgment.

ENGLAND. In England, contingency fees are not permitted, but the fees charged usually bear a strong relationship to the amount involved and the work that is necessary to collect the debt. A distinction in British law is that the loser pays the costs and normally the successful party may recover 40 to 60 percent of the attorney's fees in addition to the costs and damages awarded. If you are not a resident of England or your business is not located in England, the court might require you to post security for costs. This power is discretionary and the burden is usually upon the defendant to prove the estimated cost of defending the action. The court often will make interim awards of the security for cost as the trial progresses. The decision of the judge is often a function of the merits of the case and the issue of whether the plaintiff has assets in the country.

RUSSIA. At one time Russian attorneys would usually not accept a case before they review all the papers, receive their retainer and have investigated the party they are suing. Times are changing in Russia. The banking system and the court system seem to be improving and hopefully this will have an effect on the attorneys.

BRAZIL. In Brazil, you must furnish a power of attorney and you have to have an official certified translation of your documents before any proceeding can be started. The fees are more or less negotiated, although you can work out a combination of fees plus a contingency.

MEXICO AND CENTRAL AMERICA. Mexico allows the attorneys to charge either a contingency fee or an hourly rate. The problem in Mexico is that the legal system operates well in the major cities, but in the smaller cities, towns, or villages it depends a great deal on the extent of the attorney's relationship with the persons in the governmental structure. With regard to some of the countries in Central America, the results depend upon the attorney that you retain. The legal systems and the enforcement and collection of judgments are speculative at best.

MONITORING TELEPHONE CALLS

Federal laws govern telephone calls. Telemarketing is the targeting of a select group of prospects on the telephone through the use of a sales force that utilizes a prepared script to market a designated product. Telepromotion is the persuasion of consumers through advertising to call a 900 number that provides some form of information for entertainment. These two methods of marketing have gained the attention of regulators because of their potential for abuse.

The employer is subject to federal law that allows employers to monitor its employees (sales force) by using a monitoring device installed by a local utility company (U.S.C. Section 2510(5)(a) and Section 2511). Employers, on the other hand, must do the monitoring in the normal course of business and the monitoring must normally be limited in time and in scope and furthermore must not be used to intrude upon the privacy of an employee.[2]

Most employers notify their employees that their conversations will be taped and that they will cease taping or monitoring at such time as the employee is not engaged in a call in the course of business. Employers have the employees execute written agreements wherein the employee is advised of the monitoring or taping program.

> ***Credit & Collection Tip:*** *A carefully drafted manual should be provided for the individuals conducting the monitoring or taping with express instructions as to the time and scope of the taping, as well as procedures to use when encountering conversations on the telephone of a personal nature.*

State Laws. Because states provide their own additional restrictions, a review of the state laws that deal with monitoring and taping a telephone conversation by an employer should be conducted. Informed consent of the employee is specified in many of the state laws and specifically is directed at notifying the employee and requiring the employer to obtain consent of the employee in writing. Many of the state laws are even more restrictively drawn, addressing the issues of the type of interception, the times when the interception will be done, when the interception will be terminated, and the manner of interception. Many employers will engage in a meeting with the employees so that the employees have the opportunity to ask questions concerning the monitoring or taping of the conversation. Sometimes, the monitoring and taping notification will be posted on a bulletin board in clear and conspicuous language so that a new employee has easy access if an employee is hired without being notified of the taping program or without being required to execute a written agreement. Not all the states have major restrictions, but many of the state laws have nuances that should be reviewed.

State Laws as to Consent. Eleven states have laws requiring disclosure to employees when their phone calls are being monitored: California, Delaware, Florida, Georgia, Illinois, Massachusetts, Michigan, Montana, New Hampshire, Pennsylvania, and Washington. Many employers utilize a beep tone to identify the fact that employees are being

---

[2]*Briggs v. American Air Filter*, 630 F.2d 414 (5th Cir. 1980); *James v. Newspaper Agency Corp.*, 591 F.2d 579 (10th Cir. 1979); *United States v. Harper*, 493 F.3d 346 (10th Cir. 1974).

monitored prior to the act of monitoring. This requirement is not present in all the state laws and is not present in the federal law. The statute in the State of Montana actually requires the consent of the customer to the monitoring and when the telephone beeps, the employee must notify the customer that the conversation is being monitored. The Massachusetts statute is similar to the Montana statute.

Taping Telephone Calls. To tape a telephone call from individual to individual requires a minimum amount of electronic equipment. In many of the new telephone systems that are sold with voice mail and electronic message receipt, you merely have to push a button on the system to record the conversation. The conversation is then recorded on your voice mail and you can record that voice mail conversation to a tape recorder.[3]

It probably would be permissible to monitor or tape an employee's telephone conversation, providing a reasonable purpose existed to tape the conversation even without the consent or notification or a written agreement with the employee. One set of circumstances was where a supervisor felt that the employee was collaborating with a competitor to divulge some trade secrets. The court did hold that this taping was an act in the normal course of business and was permissible.

Federal law allows the taping of a telephone conversation with the consent of either party. Accordingly, one of the parties may be the party who initiates the telephone call and the other party is the party who receives the telephone call. Under federal law, the party who makes the telephone call may tape the conversation without the consent of the individual who receives the call. President Nixon taped many telephone calls in his Oval Office both on the telephone and of those parties that were present in the office. The only one who consented to the taping was the President. None of the people who received the phone calls or who made the phone calls to the President or who were visitors to the Oval Office consented to the taping.

The great majority of the states allow taping of telephone calls with the consent of one party.

> ***Credit & Collection Tip:*** *A group of states requires the consent of both parties. They include California, Delaware, Florida, Georgia, Illinois, Maryland, Massachusetts, Michigan, Montana, New Hampshire, Pennsylvania, and Washington. A review of the state law is absolutely necessary before taping.*

Taping Telephone Conversations—Attorneys. Certain bar associations (such as in New York) are in conflict over the question of whether an attorney may or may not tape a telephone conversation with

---

[3] *State v. Nova*, 361 So. 2d 411 (Fla. 1978).

a third party or with his client. The New York County Bar Association stated that if an attorney does not obtain the consent of the other party, the taping, whether it is of a third party or the client, would not be considered a breach of ethics. On the other hand, the New York State Bar Association unequivocally states that taping a telephone conversation is a violation of the ethics of the bar of the State of New York.

The American Bar Association in 2002 issued a formal opinion, 01-422, that obtaining consent is not necessary if the laws of the jurisdiction permit it where the taping of the telephone conversation took place.

The issue of whether to tape or not to tape a telephone conversation usually rests with the attorney. While each attorney must necessarily abide by the laws of the particular state in which they were admitted to practice law, the fact remains that almost two-thirds of the states allow taping of a conversation without the consent of the other party and only about a dozen require the consent of both parties. The attorney has the additional obligation of complying with the ethical rules set down by their respective state bar association as well as the rules set by the American Bar Association. The issue actually rests with the attorney whether or not to tape a telephone conversation depending upon the necessity and the importance of having a record of that telephone conversation. The admissibility of that taped conversation at a trial, notwithstanding the fact that it may have violated the ethics of a bar association, is also an issue that has not been completely resolved.

A case addressed the situation where a financial institution called clients in California and recorded the telephone conversation. Georgia permits the recording of a telephone conversation whereas California insists upon the consent of all parties. The California Supreme Court decided that the court must consider which jurisdictional interest would be more severely affected if its laws were not applied.

In this instance, Georgia's residents would not be harmed but in fact would receive additional protection, whereas California residents may suffer damages by reason of not being protected. California law applied.

The state laws on monitoring and taping telephone conversations vary from state to state. Before undertaking to tape telephone conversations or use them in litigation, the author recommends consultation with experienced counsel.

INADVERTENT DISCLOSURE OF CONFIDENTIAL MATERIALS

The American Bar Association appears to have treated confidentiality as more important than zealous advocacy. Accordingly, the ABA Ethics OP. 92-368 (1992) provides that when an attorney receives documents that he recognizes as clearly covered by an attorney-client privilege and where it is vividly obvious that the said documents were not intended to be delivered to the receiving lawyer, the lawyer has an obligation not only to *not examine* the documents, but also *to return the documents* from where they came. If there are instructions, such as in an e-mail, which clearly indicate that the party received them in error and directing the party to return them, the lawyer should abide by these instructions. The ABA and various other bar associations take the position that, even in those situations where conduct or circumstances present themselves which are specifically not covered by any of the codes of professional responsibility of either the ABA or the state in which the lawyer is practicing, *failure to cover the situation in the ethics guidelines does not mean that it is permitted and not prohibited*. The code of professional responsibility requires that even in these circumstances the attorney is to promote public confidence in the integrity and ethics of the legal profession.[4]

COUNTY ATTORNEYS AND SHERIFFS

In some states, the county attorney, district attorney, or even the sheriff is allowed to write letters to collect checks. Usually the law provides that they are entitled to a fee. Where an outside contractor had a contract with the State of Michigan to collect dishonored checks, the court held that they must comply with the Fair Debt Collection Practices Act.

Their notices violated the Act because their statements concerning violations of criminal law and arrest were not merely statements of a debt collector, but were clothed in the authorization of the sheriff's department. The notice instructed the check writer to report to the sheriff's office for an interview about the check complaint and the notices were sent on sheriff's department letterhead omitting any reference to the outside contractor. The notice conveyed the impression that they were authorized and sent by the sheriff's department without any inference in the letter that the party actually collecting was an outside contractor for the county.[5]

RETAINERS—ATTORNEYS

The classic retainer is payment to an attorney before the attorney renders any services. Even if the attorney doesn't render any services, the attorney is entitled to keep the money since he earned the money

---

[4]*Victor Stanley, Inc. v. Creative Pipe, Inc.*, 250 F.R.D. 251 (D. Md. 2008); *Hobson v. Mayor of Baltimore*, 232 F.R.D. 228 (D. Md. 2005).

[5]*Gradisher v. Check Enforcement Unit, Inc.*, 210 F. Supp. 2d 907 (W.D. Mich. 2002).

when it was paid to him. A *special* retainer may fall under either of the following headings:

1. A security retainer arises when monies are paid to the attorney and this money is retained by the attorney as security for payment for services to be rendered. If the services rendered by the attorney do not utilize all the money, the balance of the security advance will be returned to the client.
2. The advance fee retainer covers the situation where the client pays in advance for the services that are to be rendered by the attorney. This is somewhat similar to the security agreement except under the security arrangement the monies belong to the client and under the advance fee arrangement the monies belong to the attorney.
3. The Evergreen retainer is given to the attorney usually in a bankruptcy situation, where the attorney retains the monies but the final fee has to be approved by the bankruptcy court. Evergreen retainers are normally allowed in Chapter 11 proceedings.

TAX ON ATTORNEYS' FEES

The United States Supreme Court held that the contingent fee portions of settlements in law suits and awards are taxable to the client even if the money is paid directly to the attorney. In anticipation of this decision, Congress recently passed a provision allowing taxpayers who are successful in employment, whistle blowing, and civil rights litigation not to treat attorneys' fees and court costs as taxable income. This new legislation follows similar legislation for personal injury cases.

In commercial litigation the settlements may have to include the taxes that the plaintiffs will have to pay and thus may be a stumbling point in arriving at settlements. From a credit and collection point of view, it seems that recoveries under the Fair Debt Collection Practices Act, Fair Credit Reporting Act, the Truth in Lending Act, and the Equal Credit and Opportunity Act will be taxed to the consumer bringing the suit. An interesting issue is whether consumer attorneys will be forced to make this disclosure before they accept the retainer.[6]

PRETEXTING

The House passed bill 409-0 in April of 2006. Finally, in December of 2006, the Senate passed a bill which set a fine of up to $500,000 plus imprisonment up to ten years for misleading telephone companies into disclosing

[6] *Commissioner of Internal Revenue v. Banks*, 543 U.S. 426 (2005).

the calling records of individuals. Anyone who sells or buys phone records knowing the lists were obtained through deceptive means is subject to this law. The catalyst for this type of legislation was the Hewlett Packard fiasco where the chairwoman's authorized investigation into the source of various leaks to the media ultimately led to the board of directors.

ATTORNEYS AFFIDAVIT NOT PROTECTED BY IMMUNITY

A recent decision addressed the issue of whether an attorney's affidavit should receive absolute immunity for the statements made in an affidavit. The court set forth the Supreme Court precedent as follows:

1. A private witness testifying at trial is absolutely immune for her testimony.
2. A private witness testifying at a grand jury is absolutely immune for her testimony.
3. A private witness testifying as a complaining witness has no immunity for her testimony.

The court identified the defendant as a complaining witness. The Supreme Court has ruled "although public prosecutors and judges were accorded absolute immunity at common law, such protection does not extend to complaining witnesses, who, like respondents, set the wheels of government in motion by instigated a legal action."

In the instant case, the defendant attorney instigated the legal action of garnishment and set the wheels of government in motion. The attorney swore to the truth of a certain set of facts, i.e., the attorney had a reasonable belief that the target property of the garnishment was non-exempt. The plaintiff's bank account was attached.

The court did make a distinction between adversarial affidavits and exparte affidavits citing several cases in the Ninth Circuit. The court determined that this type of affidavit to attach a bank account which has non-exempt property would fall under an exparte action. Absolute immunity is only afforded where the particular affidavit or pleading is confined to an adversarial judicial proceeding.

Many of the states require an affidavit at the time a garnishment is issued that the affirmant had a reasonable basis to believe that the property was non-exempt or at least was subject to garnishment. The non-exempt property happened to be the social security benefits of the debtor and no other garnishable funds were in the bank account—although the case is not clear on this point.

Some of the states, such as New York, have issued specific requirements to be met before issuing a restraining order to attach a bank account. In the past representation of a reasonable basis to attach was not necessary. Future case law will determine the effect this will have on attaching bank accounts since it is difficult to determine whether the party's bank account consists of social security benefits or pension benefits or any other property that is exempt from attachment. Whereas social security benefits only apply to those who are 65 and older, the bank account may contain other exempt property. The court did not address the issue of whether a combination of exempt property and non-exempt property is in the account.

The bank account contained only social security benefits for the debtor and his wife's short term disability benefits. No non-exempt monies were in the account. The plaintiff contended that the defendant did not conduct a debtor's examination prior to the attachment as to whether plaintiff possessed non-exempt assets and thus had no basis for believing that the bank account contained non-exempt assets. The debtor was over the age of 65 and the wife was on disability.[7]

ABUSE OF PROCESS

Abuse of process consists of a wrongful initiation of a lawsuit, whether a criminal suit or a civil suit. The main ingredient of an abuse of process lawsuit is that an ulterior purpose is alleged other than the purpose set forth in the lawsuit. A willful and intentional act is an essential ingredient to support the suit. In the alternative, a negligent, reckless, or wanton act may be considered willful where the defendant knew or should have anticipated the results of the action. The aggrieved party must have suffered mental anguish or mental distress.

MALICIOUS PROSECUTION

Malicious prosecution requires a suit to be started in either a civil or criminal court which is terminated in favor of the aggrieved party. The suit may be willful, intentional, or malicious. Reckless negligence is also equal to an intentional suit, but the aggrieved party must suffer mental distress or mental anguish or actual damages.

A consumer and a consumer attorney were sued for malicious prosecution. In this particular action, the attorney and the consumer abandoned the action for a violation of the FDCPA against an attorney after it was started. The attorney that was being sued then commenced a suit for malicious prosecution against the consumer and her attorney. The case was

---

[7]*Briscoe v. LaHue*, 460 U.S. 325 (1983); *Todd v. Weltman, Weinberg & Reis Co., L.P.A.*, 434 F.3d 432 (6th Cir. 2006); *Keko v. Hingle*, 318 F.3d 639 (9th Cir. 2003); *Cruz v. Kauai County*, 279 F.3d 1064 (9th Cir. 2002); *Burns v. County of King*, 883 F.2d 819 (9th Cir. 1989).

dismissed in the lower court on the grounds that the FDCPA basically preempted a malicious prosecution suit under state law. The consumer and her attorney were relying on the preemption clauses contained in the FDCPA. The appellate court pointed out that this preemption clause only applies if the state court laws are less restrictive than the federal laws. The court then ruled: "We cannot conclude that Congress intended to pre-empt the state law claim seeking compensation for malicious prosecution under the FDCPA."

The court also went on to address the attorney for the consumer and stated: "It is inappropriate to bring an action for a technical violation of the act for the purpose of obtaining the mandatory award of attorney's fees as provided under the act."

The case illustrates that the defendants in FDCPA claims are becoming more aggressive in prosecuting the growing number of attorneys who bring these suits for technical violations. Judges often refer to claims as purely "technical violations" and are becoming less and less favorable to the consumer when the consumer has suffered no damages. If malicious prosecution suits become more prevalent, this alone may become a deterrent to consumer attorneys so that future suits will be brought only for violations that cause injury and harm to the consumer.[8]

Any suit started after a claim of forgery (even without an affidavit of forgery by the debtor) without a handwriting expert's opinion or an in-depth investigation places the creditor at risk in the event the creditor loses the suit.[9]

DISTINCTION BETWEEN ABUSE OF PROCESS AND MALICIOUS PROSECUTION

Actions based on abuse of process and malicious prosecution are often joined in the same suit. The distinction between them is shadowy. The major area of concern is using a criminal process in an effort to collect a civil debt. This will often support an action for an abuse of process since an ulterior motive existed, especially if the criminal proceeding is discontinued immediately upon payment of the debt. Whether the debt is collected is not important. The key ingredient is that the criminal process is used for an ulterior purpose. A criminal prosecution on a bad check where the creditor does not appear to testify is strong evidence that the purpose of the prosecution was to collect the debt, not to press criminal charges.[10]

Attachment is available in various states prior to suit. If the attachment is obtained and the suit is continued, no problem exists (*see* Chapter 4). If the purpose of the attachment is to coerce the debtor to continue to make

---

[8] *Ziobron v. Crawford*, 667 N.E.2d 202 (Ind. Ct. App. 1996).

[9] *Leak v. Avco Fin. Servs.*, 646 So. 2d 642 (Ala. 1994).

[10] *Zablonsky v. Perkins*, 187 A.2d 314, 230 Md. 365 (1962) (criminal process issued but money not received); *Gore v. Gorman's Inc.*, 143 F. Supp. 9 (1956) (suit to collect a debt discharged in bankruptcy).

payments, to furnish security for the debt, or to guarantee the liability of a corporate debt, the creditor is exposed to an abuse of process suit if the attachment is released after the creditor's goal is achieved.

Another area of danger is starting suit against a party with no liability. An example is where a suit is instituted against a corporation and the directors of the corporation. The debt is obviously a corporate debt, and the directors are not liable. The directors are joined as co-conspirators for the purpose of intimidating and coercing the Board of Directors to vote to settle the claim which will terminate the personal suit against the directors. This type of suit is a prime example of an ulterior purpose.

A malicious prosecution requires more elements than an abuse of process suit. The process of a malicious prosecution suit is where a creditor brings action to collect a debt, but no real foundation exists for the suit. Negligence is not available as a defense against a malicious prosecution suit. A suit to collect a debt already discharged in bankruptcy is malicious prosecution, just as a suit against a person who has already paid the debt. Sometimes a suit is instituted carelessly against a party with the same name as the true debtor, who never executed a note or had any business relationship at all with the creditor. This type of suit still may constitute malicious prosecution even though the creditor was only negligent. The question is whether the negligence was so reckless as to amount to a willful act.

DEFAMATION

Defamation is a false statement about a person's reputation. Slander is oral defamation with publication to some third party (a third party hears the slanderous statement). Libel is written or printed defamation and includes publication in all media of a permanent nature such as drawings, printings, newspapers, magazines, advertisements, etc. Truth is a defense to defamation.

Certain types of defamations are treated as libel or slander "per se," which means the words themselves are so defamatory that the plaintiff does not have to suffer damages to recover. If a defamation is not "per se," the plaintiff must prove damages. A letter to a third party characterizing one as the "worse kind of crook" is libel "per se." Falsely charging someone in business with being insolvent or bankrupt may be libel "per se" since the credit of a person in business is essential to its operation.

FTC REGULATION OF ATTORNEYS

The FTC made an effort to regulate attorneys under Gramm-Leach-Bliley. The New York State Bar Association and American Bar Association were successful in persuading the court that a lawyer is not a financial institution. Attorneys are not subject to the federal privacy provision of the Act requiring financial institutions to send annual privacy disclosure notices to their clients.[11]

It should come as no surprise that some of the attorneys general in the various states review the complaints filed by consumers against attorneys or law firms. The information is forwarded directly to the grievance committee of the respective state.

BELL v. TWOMBLY MOTION TO DISMISS

The Supreme Court, in its infinite wisdom, has overruled a 50-year-old doctrine that "a complaint should not be dismissed for failure to state a claim unless it appears *beyond doubt* that the plaintiff can prove no set of facts in support of his claim which would entitle him to relief."[12]

The new decision stated "asking for a plausible ground to infer an agreement does not impose a probability or requirement in the pleading stage; it simply calls for enough facts to raise a reasonable expectation that discovery will reveal evidence of an illegal agreement."[13]

The court was applying a heightened pleading standard, but only enough facts to state a claim to relief that is *plausible* on its face. The key word in the decision seems to be "plausible." The media has reported that over 1,300 decisions have cited this decision within a few months after the decision. The Second Circuit spent some time analyzing the Supreme Court decision and observed that "considerable uncertainty concerning the standard for assessing the adequacy of pleadings has been created by the Supreme Court's decision."[14] Considering the number of cases that have cited *Bell v. Twombly*, many of them have varying definitions of what the word "plausible" means. Many motions to dismiss were made after the decision was rendered. By the time of the next edition of this book comes out, hopefully the circuit courts will have reached consensus on what "plausible" really means.[15]

The case is over a year old and it seems that almost every federal court has addressed this Supreme Court case. Several of the cited cases refer to prior decisions.[16]

---

[11]*American Bar Ass'n v. Federal Trade Comm'n*, 430 F.3d 457 (D.C. Cir. 2005).

[12]*Conley v. Gibson*, 355 U.S. 41 (1957).

[13]*Bell Atlantic Corp. v. Twombly*, 127 S. Ct. 1955 (2007).

[14]*Iqbal v. Hasty*, 490 F.3d 143 (2d Cir. 2007). *See also Tellabs, Inc. v. Makor Issues & Rights, Ltd.*, 127 S. Ct. 2499 (2007).

[15]*Goldstein v. Pataki*, 516 F.2d 50 (2d Cir. 2008); *Wilkerson v. New Media Technology Charter School Inc.*, 522 F.3d 315 (3d Cir. 2008); *Limestone Development Corp. v. Village of Lemont, Ill.*, 520 F.3d 797 (7th Cir. 2008); *Kendall v. Visa U.S.A., Inc.*, 518 F.3d 1042 (9th Cir. 2008); *Davis v. Coca-Cola Bottling Co. Consol.*, 516 F.3d 955 (11th Cir. 2008).

[16]*John D. Ashcroft, Former Attorney General v. Javid Iqbal*, 556 U.S. (May 18, 2009). Case No. 07-1015.

TWOMBLY IS EXPANDED

The last sentence in the above paragraph unfortunately created many different interpretations of the word "plausible." The U.S. Supreme Court found it necessary to provide some additional explanation to the definition of "plausible."

Federal Rule of Civil Procedure 8(a)(2) requires a short and plain statement of the claim showing that the pleader is entitled to relief. *Twombly* does not require detailed factual allegations. A pleading that offers labels and conclusions or a formulaic recitations of the elements of a cause of action will not do. The complaint must state a claim that is "plausible" on its face and this standard is not akin to a probability requirement, but asks for more than sheer possibility that a defendant has acted unlawfully.

That a court must "accept as true all the allegations contained in a complaint" is inapplicable to legal conclusions. Recitals of the elements of a cause of action supported by mere conclusory statements do not suffice. FRCP Rule 8 does not unlock the doors of discovery for a plaintiff armed with nothing more than conclusions.

A plausible claim for relief will certainly survive a motion to dismiss. If the court only infers the mere possibility of misconduct, the pleader is not entitled to relief. Pleadings that are no more than conclusions are not entitled to the assumption of truth. While pleadings may provide the framework of a complaint, they must be supported by factual allegations. If they are supported by factual allegations, their veracity will be accepted and then the court will make a determination as to whether they are plausible on their face to support a claim for relief.

The court also addressed the issue argued by the respondents in the Supreme Court case that *Twombly* should be limited to pleadings made in the context of an anti-trust dispute and not expanded to other types of actions. Justice Kennedy expressly stated the following:

> "Our decision in *Twombly* expounded the pleading standard for 'all civil actions' and it applies to anti-trust and discrimination suits alike."

WEBSITE DANGERS

Attorneys often do not consider a problem with websites. A disclaimer should appear on the website that no attorney/client privilege may be created without an express agreement in writing by the party and the law firm.

The situation may arise that a third party communicates with the website and a response provided by the attorney may conceivably create not only an attorney/client relationship, but also an attorney/client privilege. A similar situation occurs where a client communicates with the website and the circumstances create a conflict between the attorney and some third party. Careful disclaimer language should be contained in the website to control and limit the attorney/client privilege or such communications between the third party and the website. Responding to inquiries should be limited and carefully considered despite the potential opportunity to develop a new client.

Websites also are multiple jurisdictional and communications may originate in other states as well as in other countries. Problems may arise with regard to subjecting the attorney to the laws of the particular state where the third party is located. Providing advice on the laws of other states to third parties where the attorney is unauthorized to practice law presents problems. All of these issues are beyond the scope of this book, but the author wishes to make counsel aware of the potential risks involved.

RIGHT TO ASSIGN

Many states allow an assignment of a claim to a collection agency, but some states require the party in interest to sue. (See Appendix for listing of State Right-of-Assignment Laws provided by ACA International.)

CHAPTER 7
APPENDIX I

ATTORNEY/CLIENT AGREEMENT

AGREEMENT dated ____________ day of ____________, 20__ between [the firm] located at [address], [town] [zip code] (hereinafter referred to as the attorney), and ____________ referred to as the client.
The parties hereunto agree as follows:

1. REFERRAL OF ACCOUNTS—The client from time to time may refer to the attorney delinquent accounts for collection and the attorney shall attempt to collect those accounts in accordance with the terms of this agreement.
2. CONFLICT OF INTEREST—The attorney shall not accept any accounts which by so doing may create a conflict of interest under the rules of ethics of the Bar Association of the State of New York.
3. WARRANTY OF THE ATTORNEY—The attorney represents and warrants that it has a license to practice law under the State of New York and Connecticut and our network attorney has a license to practice in the state where the network attorney is located. Our firm and our network attorneys have complied with all laws to enable them to perform the obligations which they undertake in this agreement.
   A. The attorney agrees that during the terms of this agreement, the attorney will strictly comply with all applicable, federal, state and all local statutes, rules, regulations and ordinances, including, without limitation, the Federal Fair Debt Collection Practices Act, the Federal Credit Reporting Act, Equal Credit Opportunity Act, and any other laws directly or indirectly affecting the collection process.
   B. The attorney will use its best efforts to collect any and all amounts due with regard to the accounts herein referred.
   C. The attorney shall not threaten suit or institute suit on any of the accounts unless expressly authorized by the client in writing.
4. PAYMENTS—The attorney shall place in its special trust account any and all funds collected by the attorney. The attorney shall remit to the client the amount collected less any fees or expenses incurred in the collection effort.
   A. The attorney shall maintain complete records of all payments, disbursements, and fees charged to the client.

B. During the last week of the month following the month in which payment is received, all funds collected by the attorney shall be remitted to the client.

C. Each remittance hereunder shall be accompanied by a detailed statement setting forth the fees, expenses, and disbursements.

5. INDEMNIFICATION—The attorney shall indemnify and hold harmless the client from and against any and all claims, suits, actions, debts, damages, costs, charges, and expenses, including court costs and reasonable attorney's fees and against all liabilities, loss and damages of any nature, that the client shall or may at any time sustain which arise solely from the failure of the attorneys to perform its obligation under these agreements due to negligence. The client indemnifies the attorney in the same manner.

6. MALPRACTICE INSURANCE—The attorney shall carry a policy of malpractice insurance with a recognized carrier in the amount of one million dollars. The attorney upon request shall furnish the client a copy of the current cover page setting forth the amount of coverage of the insurance policy and other information concerning the insurance coverage upon request.

7. OBLIGATIONS OF THE CLIENT—The client shall provide copies of all documentation and information relating to the accounts referred to the attorney. This information and documentation shall be sufficient for the attorney to validate the debt and to provide information as required under the Fair Debt Collection Practices Act.

   A. Client shall advise attorney whether such an account has been previously placed for collection with another collection agency or attorney.

   B. Client shall promptly furnish written notice to the attorney of any payments that they receive on any account which has been referred to the attorney.

8. TERMINATION—This agreement may be terminated by either party on 30 days prior written notice by either party giving written notice of same to other party. At such time, the attorney shall continue to pursue collection efforts on those accounts that were heretofore referred to him. Nevertheless, in the event that the attorney fails to perform his obligation under this contract by failure to vigorously and diligently perform collection efforts on those accounts, the client shall have a right to immediately demand that the attorney return all the accounts to the client and the attorney shall waive all of his rights to receive compensation on the accounts returned to the client. Before the files are returned to the client, the client shall pay all outstanding fees and expenses to the attorney.

9. FEES—The fee arrangement between the attorney and the client is as follows:

10. INDEPENDENT CONTRACTOR—This agreement creates no relationship such as a joint venture, partnership, association, or employment between the client and the attorney, but rather the attorney shall at all times act as and be an independent contractor. Nothing in this agreement constitutes or authorizes the attorney to bind the client to any obligation or assume or create

any responsibility for or on behalf of the client for or to any third party except upon the client's prior approval. Attorney is an independent contractor and shall not represent any third party that is an agent of the client.

11. MODIFICATION AND MERGER—This agreement constitutes the entire agreement of the parties and all other oral representations or agreements are hereby merged herein. This agreement may only be amended in writing executed by both parties.
12. NOTICES—Any written notices or writings concerning this agreement may be delivered either personally or by certified mail to the address at the beginning of this agreement or to such other address as may be given by written notice to the other party.
13. LAWS—This agreement shall be construed or interpreted in accordance with the laws of the State of [name]. If any part of this agreement shall be held void or unenforceable, the remaining portions of this agreement shall remain valid and enforceable.
14. BINDING—This agreement is binding upon the successors and assigns of the respective parties.

IN WITNESS WHEREOF, the parties have hereunto set their hand and seal the day and year written above.

BY: [THE FIRM]

____

BY: BY:

____

APPENDIX II

STATE SURVEY OF LAWS AFFECTING ATTORNEYS IN COLLECTION PRACTICE*

This survey will examine each state relevant to statutory law and in some cases, ensuing regulations and common law, that affect collection attorneys, collection agencies and original creditor in-house collectors. This survey is provided for ***informational purposes only*** and collection attorney, agency, and/or creditor collectors should consult house counsel or a local attorney before making any strategic business decisions regarding state law compliance. ***This information is not intended to be legal advice.*** There is not space to list each law specifically. This survey will generally identify the states that possess substantive collection laws (for attorneys, agencies, and/or creditor collectors) as well as the states that require an out-of-state attorney or agency to obtain a collection license or bond.

Additionally, most states possess some form of unfair trade practices statute that generally proscribe abusive business practices and would therefore protect consumers regarding the unfair collection practices of attorneys, agencies, and original creditors.

Alabama
Collection attorneys:
No local law on point.

Collection agencies:
Ala. Code § 40-12-80 requires collection agencies to pay a license tax.

Creditor collectors:
No local law on point.

Alaska
Collection attorneys:
Attorneys are exempt from the license and bond requirements when collection conduct is part of the attorney's regular course of business. A.S.08.24.090(b)(1).

*Prepared by Adam Olshan, Esquire of Wolpoff & Abramson, LLP. Reprinted with the permission of his former firm, Law Offices Howard Lee Schiff, PC.

Collection agencies:
Alaska requires that both the collection agency and the individual operators obtain local licenses pursuant to A.S. 08.24.130. Agencies are also required to maintain a bond. A.S. 08.24.150(a).

Creditor collectors:
Creditors that are not engaged in the collection or repossession business would not appear to be "collection agencies."

Arizona
Collection attorneys:
Attorneys are exempt from the state's license statute if they are acting, "in the regular course of their business" when contacting AZ consumers. A.R.S. § 32-1004(A)(1). Collection attorneys must, however, comply with the substantive requirements of A.R.S. § 32-1051(3)-(8) and A.R.S. § 32-1055(c) and (d)(1), (2), (4) and (6).

Collection agencies: Defined in 32-1001(A)(1), AZ requires the agency to obtain both a license (A.R.S. section 32-1021(A)) and a $10,000-$35,000 bond (A.R.S. section 32-1022). Out-of-state agencies may obtain a license R20-1502(b). The statute goes on to impose substantive collection restrictions on the collection agency.

Creditor collectors: A.R.S. section 32-1001A 2(b) treats creditors like governed "collection agencies" when the creditor uses a different name while collecting its own debts.

Arkansas
Collection attorneys:
Attorneys handling claims and collections in their own name and not operating a collection agency under the management of a layman, or under names other than their own, are not governed by the state statute. Ark. Code Ann. § 17-24-102. In addition, Ark. Code Ann. § 17-24-102(b) in a separate statute, states that attorneys who are licensed to practice in Arkansas and engaged to render legal services for clients in the collection of accounts, will be exempt from the collection agency licensing provisions.

Collection agencies:
Arkansas requires the agency to obtain both a license (Ark. Code Ann § 17-24-301) and a $10,000-$25,000 bond (Ark. Code Ann. § 17-24-306(a)). The statute goes on to impose substantive collection restrictions on the collection agency that are more restrictive than the FDCPA in some instances.

Creditor collectors:
Creditor collectors will generally be exempted from this statute unless they use a "fictitious" name while collecting their debts. Ark. Code Ann. § 17-24-101.

California
Collection attorneys:
Under California Business & Professional Code § 6077.5, an attorney, and his or her employees who are employed primarily to assist with the collection of

consumer debt, as defined by Cal. Civ. Code § 1788.2, must comply with specified statutory restrictions that are similar to the FDCPA. Attorneys are exempt from the RFDCPA.

Collection agencies:
Rosenthal Fair Debt Collection Practices Act (RFDCPA) has a broad definition of "debt collector." While CA does not require that a license or a bond be obtained, it will impose limitations on collectors beyond the FDCPA (*see* Cal. Civ. Code § 1788 et seq.).

Creditor collectors:
The RFDCPA defines "debt collector" to include a creditor who engages in debt collection, "on behalf of himself or herself" and as such, creditor collectors must comply with this statute.

Colorado
Collection attorneys:
While attorneys are generally exempt from the CFDCPA's licensing requirement, a 1995 amendment brought attorneys under the Act's substantive restrictions if the attorney, "regularly engage[s] in the collection or attempted collection of debts in Colorado." Col. Rev. Stat. Ann. § 12-14-103(2)(e)(II).

Collection agencies:
Agencies must obtain both a license, Col Rev. Stat. Ann. § 12-14-115, and a bond, Col. Rev. Stat. Ann. § 12-14-124(1), pursuant to the CFDCPA. Additionally, agencies, like attorneys, must comply with the Act's substantive collection restrictions that are in some instances more restrictive than the FDCPA.

Creditor collectors:
The term "collection agency" does not extend to creditors that collect debts under their own name Col. Rev. Stat. Ann. § 12-14-103(2)(b)(1).

Connecticut
Collection attorneys:
Out-of-state attorneys may need to obtain a license (and post the requisite $5000 bond) pursuant to CGS section 36a-800(1)(D) prior to communicating with Connecticut consumer debtors unless counsel can legitimately claim that they are not "engaged in the business of collecting or receiving for payment of others any account, bill or other indebtedness from a consumer debtor." Licensed attorneys will be considered to be a "collection agency" that must comply with the collection agency statute's substantive requirements. Local attorneys are exempt from this statute.

Collection agencies:
The Connecticut Consumer Collection Agency Act (CGS section 36a-800 et seq.) requires that the "collection agency obtain both a license, CGS 36a-801 and a bond, CGS 36a-802." Additionally, the statute requires that the licensee comply with substantive requirements that are more restrictive than the FDCPA.

Creditor collectors:
The Connecticut Creditor Collector Practices Act (CGS section 36a-645 et seq.) establishes substantive requirements that govern consumer creditor collections. Also, creditor collectors must comply with CGS 36a-800, if using a name other than their own. While this statute and its ensuing regulations mirror the FDCPA in many aspects, the regulations do contain several restrictions beyond the FDCPA.

Delaware

Collection attorneys:
Unless licensed to practice law in DE, the collection attorney is not exempt from the definition of a DE "collection agency." Del. Code Ann. Tit. 30. § 2301(a)(13).

Collection agencies:
The "collection agency" is required to obtain an annual license pursuant to statute. Del. Code Ann tit. 30, § 2301.

Creditor collectors:
No DE law on point.

District of Columbia

Collection attorneys:
D.C. Code 28 § 3814 broadly defines "debt collector" as anyone attempting to collect a debt. No distinction is made between collection attorneys, agencies, and creditor collectors. As "debt collector," the collection attorney must comply with substantive compliance requirements that are more restrictive than the FDCPA.

Collection agencies:
Like the collection attorney, the collection agency must comply with the Code's substantive requirements (D.C. Code 28 § 3814). The D.C. Code does not require the "debt collector" to obtain a license.

Creditor collectors:
Like the collection attorney, the creditor collector must comply with the Code's substantive requirements (D.C. Code 28 § 3814).

Florida

Collection attorneys:
Members of the Florida bar are exempt, in some instances, from The Florida Commercial Act's licensing requirement, and not exempt in other instances. (Fla. Stat. Ann. § 559.544(5)(a)). Out-of-state attorneys are not exempt from the licensing requirement pursuant to the FL statute (Fla. Stat. Ann. § 559.553(4)(b)). Substantive provisions will apply to licensees.

Collection agencies:
Agencies must obtain a license pursuant to Fla. Stat. Ann. § 559.553(2). The substantive requirements closely resemble the FDCPA provisions in all but a few instances. Fla. Stat. Ann. § 559.715 and § 559.72.

Creditor collectors:
The statute exempts original creditors from the term "debt collector" unless the creditor uses any name other than its own name that would indicate that a third person is attempting to collect such debts. Fla. Stat. Ann. § 559.553(4)(a).

Georgia
Collection attorneys:
No GA law on point.

Collection agencies:
No license is required but a bond is, 10-6100. Collection agencies must comply with substantive provisions that are partially more restrictive than the FDCPA.

Creditor collectors:
No GA law on point.

Hawaii
Collection attorneys:
When "operating within the scope of their profession," attorneys are exempt from the state's collection agency licensing statute. Hi. Rev. Stat. Ann. § 443B-1.

Collection agencies:
Agencies must obtain both a license and bond unless they demonstrate that they are so regulated by another state. Hi. Rev. Stat. Ann. 443B *et seq.* Out-of-state collection agencies are exempt from licensing and bond requirements if they can meet certain requirements. Hi. Rev. Stat. Ann. 443B-3.5. The agency must comply with substantive requirements that are in some cases more restrictive than the FDCPA.

Creditor collectors:
The collection practices statute governs creditor collectors that use a name other than their own name when collecting their own claims. Hi. Rev. Stat. Ann. Sec. 480D-2.

Idaho
Collection attorneys:
Out-of-state attorneys not licensed to practice in Idaho, and whose client is not an exempt "regulated lender" (28-41-301(37)) will be subject to the statute's license and bond requirements. Idaho Code § 26-2239(1).

Collection agencies:
The agency must obtain both a license, § 26-2223, and a bond, § 26-2232 pursuant to the statute. Out of state collection agents are allowed if they comply with § 26-2250.

Creditor collectors:
The collection practices statute governs creditor collectors that use a name other than their own name when collecting their own claims. Idaho Code § 26-2223(5).

Illinois

Collection attorneys:

Licensed attorneys at law are exempt from the statute's "collection agency" provisions, yet it is unclear whether "licensed" refers to an IL-specific license or a license in any state. The attorney will lose the exempt status if she or he engages in "flat-rating" practices where the attorney's letterhead is sold to an agency. 225 ILCS 425/2.03(5).

Collection agencies:

The agency must obtain both a license and a bond pursuant to the statute.

Creditor collectors:

Creditors will generally be exempt from the collection agency statute unless the creditor acts like a collection agency or unless it uses fictitious names to collect its own debt. 225 ILCS 425/3(e).

Indiana

Collection attorneys:

No IN law on point, as all attorneys are exempt from the IN statute. Ind. Code Ann. § 25-11-1-2(a).

Collection agencies:

The agency must obtain both a license and a bond pursuant to the statute. Ind. Code Ann. § 25-11-1-3.

Creditor collectors:

Creditors will likely be exempt from the collection statute (i.e., the creditor is not collecting debts for "another") unless the creditor collector uses a name other than its own name while collecting its own debts.

Iowa

Collection attorneys:

Since the Iowa Debt Collection Practices Act does not include a list of exempt persons, it is clear that the statute applies to collection attorneys, agencies, and creditor collectors alike. "Debt collectors" will be required to obtain a license in certain instances (§ 537.6201(2) and § 537.6203). Additionally, the Iowa statute imposes substantive requirements on such "debt collectors."

Collection agencies:

See above for "collection attorneys."

Creditor collectors:

See above for "collection attorneys."

Kansas

Collection attorneys:

No KS law on point.

Collection agencies:
The state does not require a license or bond but may require certificates of authority in some instances.

Creditor collectors:
No KS law on point.

Kentucky
Collection attorneys:
No KY law on point.

Collection agencies:
As long as the agency is paid by the creditor, and not by the debtor, the agency will not be governed by any KY-specific laws.

Creditor collectors:
No KY law on point.

Louisiana
Collection attorneys:
Louisiana Collection Agency Regulation Act was repealed in 2003 No. 638 § 1.

Collection agencies:
No on point statutes. See Collection Attorneys.

Creditor collectors:
No on point statutes. See Collection Attorneys.

Maine
Collection attorneys:
Attorneys will be subject to the substantive provisions of the Maine Fair Debt Collection Practices Act and not the statute's license and bond provisions. 32 Me. Rev. Stat. Ann. § 11002(6).

Collection agencies:
The agency must obtain both a license and a bond pursuant to the statute. 32 Me. Rev. Stat. Ann. § 11002(2). The agency must also comply with the statute's substantive provisions, which are similar to the FDCPA requirements.

Creditor collectors:
Creditors will generally be exempt from the collection agency statute unless the creditor acts like a collection agency or unless it uses fictitious names to collect its own debt. 32 Me. Rev. Stat. Ann. § 11002(6). However, the state's Consumer Credit Code does impose certain substantive obligations on creditor collectors where the creditor seeks to enforce rights created from the consumer credit transaction. 9-A Me. Rev. Stat. Ann. Sec. 5-102.

Maryland

Collection attorneys:

Attorneys are subject to the Maryland Consumer Debt Collection Act regarding nine specific substantive prohibitions (Md. Ann. Code § 14-201) as well as the Collection Agencies Licensing Act where the attorney employs lay staff to act like a collection agency (Md. Ann. Code § 7-102(9)).

Collection agencies:

The agency must obtain both a license and a bond pursuant to the statute. Md. Ann. Code § 7-301 and § 7-304. The agency must also comply with the state's substantive requirements regarding collection activities. Md. Ann. Code § 14-201 *et seq.*

Creditor collectors:

Like attorneys, creditor collectors are governed by the Maryland Consumer Debt Collection Act and thus must comply with the nine specific requirements. (Md. Ann. Code § 14-201 *et seq.*).

Massachusetts

Collection attorneys:

Out-of-state attorneys, not licensed in MA, should comply with the MA Agency statute that requires a license, when collecting debts in MA. Mass. Gen. Laws Ann. Ch. 93, § 24.

Collection agencies:

The agency must obtain both a license and a bond pursuant to the statute. Mass. Gen. Laws Ann. Ch. 93 § 24. The agency must also comply with the state's substantive requirements regarding collection activities.

Creditor collectors:

While the original creditor that collects in its own name will be exempt from the Agency Licensing statute, the same creditor will be subject to the MA Debt Collection regulations that list a host of substantive requirements. 940 C.M.R. 7.00 *et seq.*

Michigan

Collection attorneys:

Attorneys and creditor collectors are both governed by the state's Collection Practices Act (MCL 445.251 et seq.). This statute governs substantive areas that generally resemble the types of conduct proscribed by the FDCPA. Attorneys are exempt from the licensing statute MCL § 339.901(b)(xi).

Collection agencies:

The agency must obtain both a license and a bond pursuant to the statute. MCL 339.904. The agency must also comply with the state's substantive requirements regarding collection activities. MCL 445.251 *et seq.*

Creditor collectors:
Attorneys and creditor collectors are both governed by the state's Collection Practices Act. MCL 445.251 *et seq.* This statute governs substantive areas that generally resemble the types of conduct proscribed by the FDCPA.

Minnesota
Collection attorneys:
The statute's definition of "collection agency" specifically states that the term does not include "lawyers." MSA § 332.32.

Collection agencies:
The agency must obtain both a license and a bond pursuant to the statute. MSA § 332.33.

Creditor collectors:
An original creditor that collects debts using its own name will not be a "collection agency" under the statute. MSA § 332.32.

Mississippi
Collection attorneys:
No local law on point. Attorneys must comply with Miss. Code Ann. § 97-29-45 per the below discussion.

Collection agencies:
While Miss. Code Ann. § 97-29-45 will govern debt collectors who attempt to collect debts through telephone calls. This section identifies various types of proscribed calls. The state does not require a license or bond but does require certificates of authority in some instances.

Creditor collectors:
No local law on point.

Missouri
Collection attorneys:
Out-of-state attorneys, not licensed to practice in Missouri, are governed by the state's debt adjustment laws and thus must exercise caution when settling debtor accounts. Mo. Rev. Stat. § 425.040(1).

Collection agencies:
The state does not require a license or bond but may require certificates of authority in some instances.

Creditor collectors:
Creditor collectors may adjust debts unless the debtor pays any part of the cost of the transaction. Mo. Rev. Stat. § 425.040(4).

Montana

Collection attorneys:
Out-of-state attorneys, not licensed to practice in Montana, are governed by the state's debt adjustment laws and thus must exercise caution when settling debtor accounts. Montana Code 31-3-201. In state attorneys are exempt. Montanta Code 31-3-203(1).

Collection agencies:
The state does not require a license or bond but may require certificates of authority in some instances.

Creditor collectors:
Creditor collectors may adjust debts unless the debtor pays any part of the cost of the transaction. Montana Code, Title 31.

Nebraska

Collection attorneys:
The Collection Agency Act exempts attorneys from the definition of a "collection agency." Neb. Rev. Stat. § 45-602(3)(a).

Collection agencies:
The agency must obtain both a license (Neb. Rev. Stat. § 45-606), and a bond (Nev. Rev. Stat. § 45-608) pursuant to the statute. The agency must also comply with the state's substantive requirements regarding collection activities.

Creditor collectors:
Creditors will generally be exempt from the collection agency statute unless the creditor uses fictitious names to collect its own debt. Neb. Rev. Stat. § 45-602(2)(b).

Nevada

Collection attorneys:
NV attorneys will be exempt from the collection agency licensing statute unless the NV attorney receives placements in a manner other than the traditional manner of placements with a lawyer. Nev. Rev. Stat. § 649.020(2)(f). Out-of-state attorneys are not exempt from the definition of a "collection agency" but will likely be exempt from the license requirement pursuant to Nev. Rev. Stat. § 649.075. Communications with NV debtors is limited to contact through interstate commerce.

Collection agencies:
The agency must obtain both a license and a bond pursuant to the statute. Nev. Rev. Stats. § 649.075 and § 649.105. The agency must also comply with the state's substantive requirements regarding collection activities.

Creditor collectors:
Since the creditor is not collecting for "another," the creditor collector is likely exempted from this statute. Nev. Rev. Stat. § 649.020(2)(a).

New Hampshire

Collection attorneys:

Attorneys are subject to the state's substantive collection laws pursuant to the statute's broad definition of a "debt collector." N.H. Rev. Stat. Ann. § 358-C:1(VIII).

Collection agencies:

The state does not require a license or bond but does require certificates of authority in some instances. Furthermore, the agency must comply with the state's substantive collection requirements. N.H. Rev. Stat. Ann. § 358-C:1 *et seq.*

Creditor collectors:

Like collection attorneys, consumer creditors will generally need to comply with the statute's substantive requirements pursuant to N.H. Rev. Stat. Ann. § 358-C:1(VIII)(a).

New Jersey

Collection attorneys:

Out-of-state collection attorneys are not exempt from the state's bonding requirement. N.J. Rev. Stat. § 45:18-6.

Collection agencies:

Collection agencies must obtain a bond prior to communicating with debtors who reside in NJ. N.J. Rev. Stat. § 45:18-1.

Creditor collectors:

Since the creditor is not collecting for "others," the creditor collector is likely exempted from this statute. N.J. Rev. Stat. § 45:18-1.

New Mexico

Collection attorneys:

Attorneys are exempt from the "collection agency" definition. N.M. Stat. Ann. § 61-18A-2(C)(6).

Collection agencies:

The agency must obtain both a license and a bond pursuant to the statute. N.M. Stat. Ann. § 61-18A-7. The agency must also comply with the state's substantive requirements regarding collection activities.

Creditor collectors:

Creditors will generally be exempt from the collection agency statute unless the creditor uses fictitious names to collect its own debt. N.M. Stat. Ann. § 61-18A-2(C).

New York

Collection attorneys:

Attorneys attempting to collect debts from NY debtors will be governed by the NY General Business Law—Debt Collection Procedures Act and Regulation 10 of the NYC Consumer Protection Law. In both cases, the laws generally mirror the FDCPA in several regards. N.Y. Gen. Bus. § 600(2).

Collection agencies:
The NY statute contains no license or bond requirements, however NYC requires agencies to obtain a license, and the City of Buffalo requires agencies to obtain both a license and a bond.

Creditor collectors:
Like collection attorneys, creditor collectors will be governed by NY's substantive law as well as the NYC regulation. N.Y. Gen. Bus. § 600(3) and Article 6 of the NYC Debt Collection Procedures Act and Regulation.

North Carolina

Collection attorneys:
Attorneys attempting to collect in NC are covered by Art. 2, Ch. 75. There is neither a license nor bond requirement and attorneys are generally exempt from the statute's substantive requirements. G.S. § 58-70-15. Attorneys should review ensuing regulations regarding substantive requirements that must be followed.

Collection agencies:
The agency must obtain both a license and a bond pursuant to the statute. The agency must also comply with the state's substantive requirements regarding collection activities.

Creditor collectors:
The "Prohibited Acts by Debt Collectors" statute prohibits abusive collection activity by creditor collectors. G.S. § 58-70-15. Additionally, the creditor collection should review the ensuing regulations.

North Dakota

Collection attorneys:
Attorneys are exempt from both the definition of a "collection agency" and a "debt collector." N.D. Cent. Code § 13-05-02 and Reg. § 13-05-02-01(3), respectively.

Collection agencies:
The agency must obtain both a license and a bond pursuant to the statute. N.D. Cent. Code § 13-05-02 and § 13-05-04. The agency must also comply with the state's substantive requirements regarding collection activities.

Creditor collectors:
Original creditors are exempt from the definition of a "collection agency." N.D. Cent. Code § 13-05-02 and Reg. § 13-05-02-01(3).

Ohio

Collection attorneys:
Ohio has statutory language that addresses third party debt collection and it appears that the statute exempts attorneys from the definition of a "collection agency." Ohio Rev. Code Ann. § 1319.12.

Collection agencies:
The state does not require a license or bond, but does require certificates of authority in some instances. Ohio does have a substantive collection statute which governs the practices of collection agencies and these requirements are in some instances more restrictive than the FDCPA. 1319.12.

Creditor collectors:
Creditors will generally be exempt from the collection agency statute unless the creditor uses fictitious names to collect its own debt. Ohio Rev. Code Ann. § 1319.12(A)(2)(c).

Oklahoma
Collection attorneys:
No local law on point.

Collection agencies:
No local law on point.

Creditor collectors:
No local law on point.

Oregon
Collection attorneys:
Attorneys are subject to the requirements of the Oregon Unfair Debt Collection Practices Act. ORS 646.639. This statute requires that collection attorneys comply with various substantive provisions. Attorneys are, however, exempt from the statute's definition of "collection agency." ORS 697.005(1)(b)(D).

Collection agencies:
The agency must obtain both a license, ORS 697.015, and a bond, ORS 697.031(2)(a), pursuant to the statute. Out of state collection agencies are, in some instances, exempt from the licensing and bond requirements. ORS 697.038(4) *et seq.* The agency must also comply with the statutes' substantive requirements.

Creditor collectors:
Creditors will generally be exempt from the collection agency statute unless the creditor uses a fictitious or affiliate name to collect its own debt. ORS 697.005(1)(a)(E).

Pennsylvania
Collection attorneys:
The Fair Credit Extension Uniformity Act (FCEUA) specifically applies to attorney debt collectors and requires that attorney collectors comply with FDCPA-like provisions. Pa. Stat. Ann. Tit. 73, § 2270.3(3). In state attorneys are exempt from the collection agencies statute. Pa. Stat. Ann. Tit. 18 § 7311.

Collection agencies:
The state does not require a license or bond but may require certificates of authority in some instances. The state's collection statutes do require that the agencies comply with substantive provisions. Pa. Stat. Ann. Tit. 73 § 2270.1-§ 2270.6

Creditor collectors:
While creditor collectors are generally subject to the FCEAU, they will be exempt from the statute's FDCPA-like requirements unless the creditor uses a fictitious name to collect its own debt. Pa. Stat. Ann. Tit. 73, § 2270.04(b).

Rhode Island
Collection attorneys:
No local law on point.

Collection agencies:
The state does not require a license or bond but may require certificates of authority in some instances.

Creditor collectors:
No local law on point.

South Carolina
Collection attorneys:
The SC Consumer Protection statute states that "debt collectors" shall not use "unconscionable" conduct to collect debts. The definition of "debt collector" is broad and while collection attorneys will need to comply with the substantive language, the statute contains no license or bond requirements. S.C. Code Ann. § 37-5-108(2) and (3).

Collection agencies:
The state does not require a license or bond but may require certificates of authority in some instances. The agency must also comply with the state's substantive requirements regarding collection activities. S.C. Code Ann. § 37-5-108.

Creditor collectors:
Like collection attorneys, creditor collectors will be subject to the expansive statutory definition of "debt collector" and thus must comply with the substantive requirements.

South Dakota
Collection attorneys:
No local law on point. However, attorneys should review SDCL 16-18-2 regarding the unauthorized practice of law before contacting local debtors if the attorney is not licensed to practice in SD.

Collection agencies:
The state does not require a license or bond but may require certificates of authority in some instances.

Creditor collectors:
No local law on point.

Tennessee
Collection attorneys:
Collection attorneys are exempt from the TN Collection Services Act. Tenn. Code Ann. § 62-20-103(2).
OAG opinion 00-105: A company owned and operated by licensed attorneys operates as a "collection service" under § 62-20-103(3). The attorney exemption is applicable only to attorneys who seek to collect the debts owing to their clients who have retained them as attorneys.

Collection agencies:
The agency must obtain both a license and a bond pursuant to the statute. Tenn. Code Ann. § 62-20-105(a). The agency must also comply with the state's substantive requirements regarding collection activities.

Creditor collectors:
Creditors will generally be exempt from the collection agency statute unless the creditor uses fictitious names to collect its own debt. Tenn. Code Ann. § 62-20-102(3)(B).

Texas
Collection attorneys:
The Texas Debt Collection Practices Act applies to anyone, including collection attorneys, attempting to collect a consumer debt in TX. Tex. Fin. Code Ann. § 392.001(6). Attorneys must obtain a bond pursuant to Tex. Fin. Code Ann. § 392.101 prior to collecting from TX consumers. Additionally, collection attorneys must comply with substantive requirements pursuant to the statute. Tex. Fin. Code Ann. § 392.301 *et seq.*

Collection agencies:
The agency must also obtain a bond pursuant to the statute as well as comply with the substantive compliance requirements. Tex. Fin. Code Ann. § 392.101.

Creditor collectors:
Creditors are subject to the definition of a "debt collector" pursuant to this statute and thus must fully comply with the statute. Tex. Fin. Code Ann. § 392.001(6). Such exposure has been well documented by the local TX courts.

Utah
Collection attorneys:
Out-of-state collection attorneys are not exempt from the Utah statute and thus must obtain a bond pursuant to the UT statute. Utah Code Ann. § 12-1-7.

Collection agencies:
Agencies must obtain a bond to collect debts in UT. Utah Code Ann. § 12-1-1.

Creditor collectors:
National banks, as well as local banks and trust companies incorporated under UT law, are exempt from the bond requirement. It is unclear how the bond requirement will apply to creditor collectors who are not cleanly exempt from the requirement. Utah Code Ann. § 12-1-7.

Vermont
Collection attorneys:
Pursuant to the VT Consumer Fraud statute, the Attorney General has enacted rules that regulate the collection attorney. These rules closely follow the FDCPA and attorneys should review this law prior to collecting in VT. 9 V.S.A. § 2453(c) and CF 104.01 *et seq.* (*see* § 104.04(b) that requires a Miranda-like statement in all written communications with debtors).

Collection agencies:
Although VT does not require the agency to obtain a license or bond, agencies are subject to the Vermont Consumer Fraud statute when collecting debts.

Creditor collectors:
Like collection attorneys and agencies, creditor collectors must comply with the statute and the ensuing regulations while collecting both consumer and commercial debt in VT. CF 104.07(1).

Virginia
Collection attorneys:
No local law on point.

Collection agencies:
The state does not require a license or bond but may require certificates of authority in some instances.

Creditor collectors:
No local law on point.

Washington
Collection attorneys:
Attorneys collecting debts for a client are not considered to be a "collection agency" if their collection activities are "carried on in their true name" and are "confined and directly related to the operation of a business other than that of a collection agency." Wash. Rev. Code Ann. § 19.16.100(3)(c). As such, it appears that collection attorneys are exempt from the statute's requirements.

Collection agencies:
Agencies must obtain both a license and bond pursuant to the statute as well as comply with the statute's substantive requirements.

Creditor collectors:
Creditors will generally be exempt from the collection agency statute unless the creditor uses fictitious names to collect its own debt. Wash. Rev. Code Ann. § 19.16.100(2)(c).

West Virginia
Collection attorneys:
Out-of-state collection attorneys are not prohibited by the WV Consumer Credit and Protection Act from sending collection letters to WV debtors pursuant to local caselaw (*Chevy Chase Bank v. McCamant*, 512 S.E.2d 217 (W.Va. 1998)). However, attorneys should review this statute as it does not exempt the lawyer from the definition of a "debt collector." (W. Va. Code § 47-16-2(b)). As such, the attorney should comply with the statute's substantive requirements. Attorneys are exempt from the definition of "collection agencies" pursuant to the Collection Agency Act.

Collection agencies:
Agencies must obtain both a license and bond pursuant to the Collection Agency Act as well as comply with the statute's substantive requirements. W.Va. Code § 47-16-4.

Creditor collectors:
Like attorneys, creditor collectors are exempt from the definition of "collection agency" pursuant to the Collection Agency Act as long as they do not collect under a fictitious name. W. Va. Code § 47-16-2(b). However, like attorneys, the creditor collector is subject to the substantive collection requirements pursuant to the WV Consumer Credit and Protection Act.

Wisconsin
Collection attorneys:
Attorneys who both reside in WI and who are licensed to practice law in WI will be exempt from the WI Collection Agencies Act. Wis. Stat. Ann. § 218.04(1)(a). However, those attorneys that are exempt from the Collection Agencies Act are still considered "debt collectors" and, therefore, must comply with the statute's substantive requirements. Wis. Stat. Ann. § 427.101 *et seq.*

If an attorney is not exempt from the statute, the attorney must obtain a license prior to communicating with Wisconsin debtors as well as comply with the statute's substantive requirements.

Collection agencies:
Agencies must obtain both a license and bond pursuant to the Collection Agency Act as well as comply with the statute's substantive requirements.

Creditor collectors:
Creditors will be exempt from the definition of a "collection agency" under the WI Collection Agencies Act if they are collecting for themselves, and thus do not need to obtain a license. However, the creditor collector will be subject to the substantive requirements pursuant to the Debt Collection Act. Wis. Stat. Ann. § 218.04(1)(a).

Wyoming
Collection attorneys:
The Wyoming Collection Agencies Act exempts "licensed attorneys acting in an attorney-client relationship with the creditor." Wyo. Stat. § 33-11-101(b)(viii). It is unclear whether an out-of-state licensed attorney will be covered by this statute. If governed by this statute, the attorney would need to obtain a license and bond as well as comply with substantive requirements more restrictive than the FDCPA.

Collection agencies:
Agencies must obtain both a license and bond pursuant to the Collection Agency Act as well as comply with the statute's substantive requirements. In some instances, the WY statute is more restrictive that the FDCPA regarding substantive requirements. Wyo. Stat. § 33-11-101 *et seq.*

Creditor collectors:
Creditors may be exempt from the WY statute if they are owed a debt and if their principal office is located in WY. Wyo. Stat. § 33-11-101(a)(vi)(B). Otherwise, the creditor collector may be governed by the Collection Agencies Act.

APPENDIX III

NEW JERSEY COLLECTION AGENCY LAW

45:18-1. Collection agencies to file bond
No person shall conduct a collection agency, collection bureau or collection office in this state, or engage therein in the business of collecting or receiving payment for others of any account, bill or other indebtedness, or engage therein in the business of soliciting the right to collect or receive payment for another of any account, bill or other indebtedness, or advertise for or solicit in print the right to collect or receive payment for another of any account, bill or other indebtedness, unless such person, or the person for whom he may be acting as agent has on file with the secretary of state sufficient bond as hereinafter specified.

45:18-2. Amount, term, and provisions of bond; renewal; limitation of actions
The bond shall be in the sum of five thousand dollars and shall provide that the person giving the same shall, upon written demand, pay and turn over to or for the person for whom any account, bill or other indebtedness is taken for collection the proceeds thereof in accordance with the terms of the agreement upon which such account, bill or other indebtedness was received for collection. The board

shall be in such form and shall contain such further provisions and conditions as the Secretary of State deems necessary or proper for the protection of the persons for whom the accounts, bills or other indebtedness are taken for collection, and shall be for the term of one year from its date and must be renewed annually. No action on the bond shall be begun after two years from the expiration thereof.

45:18-3. Execution and approval of bond; sureties
The bond mentioned in sections 45:18-1 and 45:18-2 of this Title shall be executed by the person filing the same to the State of New Jersey for the use of any party aggrieved with sufficient surety, to be furnished by any company or corporation authorized to transact such business in this State. The said bond shall be examined and approved by the Attorney General and thereafter accepted and filed with the Secretary of State; provided, however, that cash may be accepted in lieu of sureties; and provided, further, that no such bond with individual sureties thereon may be approved, accepted or filed.

45:18-4. Record of bonds; filing fee
The Secretary of State shall keep a record of such bonds, with the names, places of residence and places of business of the principals and sureties, and the name of the officer before whom the bond was executed or acknowledged, and the record shall be open to public inspection. There shall be paid a filing fee of $25.00 to the Secretary of State for the filing of each bond.

45:18-5. Penalty
Any person, member of a partnership or officer of an association or corporation who fails to comply with any of the provisions of this chapter shall be subject to a fine of not more than five hundred dollars or to imprisonment for not more than three months, or both.

45:18-6. Exemptions
This chapter shall not apply to an attorney at law duly authorized to practice in this state, a national bank, or any bank or trust company duly incorporated under the laws of this state.

45:18-6.1. Discontinuance of operation; filing of notice
Any person who shall discontinue the operation of a collection agency, collection bureau, or collection office in this State pursuant to the chapter hereby supplemented shall file with the Secretary of State a notice of such discontinuance.

APPENDIX IV

COLORADO COLLECTION AGENCY LAW

CHAPTER 287

PROFESSIONS AND OCCUPATIONS

HOUSE BILL 03-1219 [Digest]

BY REPRESENTATIVE(S) Hall, Fritz, Hoppe, Larson, McCluskey, White, Williams T., Frangas, and Stengel;
also SENATOR(S) Johnson S., Jones, Kester, and Sandoval.

AN ACT

CONCERNING THE REGULATION OF COLLECTION AGENCIES, AND, IN CONNECTION THEREWITH, CONTINUING THE COLLECTION AGENCY BOARD.

Be it enacted by the General Assembly of the State of Colorado:

§ 12-14-103. Definitions

(2) (d) For the purposes of section 12-14-108(1)(f), (d) "collection agency" includes any person engaged in any business the principal purpose of which is the enforcement of security interests. For purposes of sections 12-14-104, 12-14-105, 12-14-106, 12-14-107, 12-14-108, and 12-14-109 only, "collection agency" includes a debt collector for the department of personnel.

(e) Notwithstanding paragraph (b) of this subsection (2), "collection agency" includes any person who engages in any of the following activities; except that such person shall be exempt from provisions of this article that concern licensing and licensees:

(I) Deleted by Laws 2000, Ch. 218, § 2, eff. July 1, 2000.

(II) Is an attorney-at-law and regularly engages in the collection or attempted collection of debts in this state;

(III) Is a person located outside this state whose collection activities are limited to collecting debts not incurred in this state from consumers located in this state and whose collection activities are conducted by means of interstate communications, including telephone, mail, or facsimile transmission, and who is located in another state that regulates and licenses collection agencies but does not require Colorado collection agencies to obtain a license to collect debts in their state if such agencies' collection activities are limited in the same manner.

Laws 2003, Ch. 287, § 1 in par. (2)(d) in the second sentence deleted "but not for purposes of section 12-14-109(1)(g)," preceding "collection agency", and in subpars. (2)(e)(II) and (2)(e)(III) deleted "except that such person shall also be exempt from section 12-14-109(1)(f) and (1)(g)" at the end.

§ 12-14-105. Communication in connection with debt collection. (1) (b) If the debt collector or collection agency knows the consumer is represented by an attorney with respect to such debt and has knowledge of, or can readily ascertain, such attorney's name and address, unless the attorney fails to respond within a reasonable period of time to a communication from the debt collector or collection agency or unless the attorney consents to direct communication with the consumer; or

(3) (a) If a consumer notifies a debt collector or collection agency in writing (a) that the consumer refuses to pay a debt or that the consumer wishes the debt collector or collection agency to cease further communication with the consumer, the debt collector or collection agency shall not communicate further with the consumer with respect to such debt, except to:

(I) Advise the consumer that the debt collector's or collection agency's further efforts are being terminated;

(II) Notify the consumer that the collection agency or creditor may invoke specified remedies that are ordinarily invoked by such collection agency or creditor; or

(III) Notify the consumer that the collection agency or creditor intends to invoke a specified remedy.

(b) If such notice from the consumer is made by mail, notification shall be complete upon receipt.

(c) In its initial written communication to a consumer, a collection agency shall include the following statement: "FOR INFORMATION ABOUT THE COLORADO FAIR DEBT COLLECTION PRACTICES ACT, SEE WWW.AGO.STATE.CO.US/CADC/CADCMAIN.CFM. If such notification is placed on the back of the written communication, there shall be a statement on the front notifying the consumer of such fact.

(d) Deleted by Laws 2003, Ch. 287, § 2, eff. May 21, 2003.

Laws 2003, Ch. 287, § 2 in par. (1)(b) deleted "not less than thirty days," preceding "to a communication", and rewrote subsec. (3), which read:

"(3) (a) If a consumer notifies a debt collector or collection agency in" (3) (a) writing that:

"(I) The consumer wishes the collection agency to cease contact by telephone at the consumer's residence or place of employment, then no such further contact by telephone shall be made;

"(II) The consumer refuses to pay a debt or the consumer wishes the collection agency to cease further communication with the consumer, then the debt collector or collection agency shall not communicate further with the consumer with respect to such debt, except for a written communication:

"(A) To advise the consumer that the collection agency's further efforts are being terminated;

"(B) To notify the consumer that the collection agency or creditor may invoke specified remedies which are ordinarily invoked by such collection agency or creditor; or

"(C) Where applicable, to notify the consumer that the collection agency or creditor intends to invoke a specified remedy permitted by law.

"(b) If such notice from the consumer is made by mail, notification shall be complete upon receipt.

"(c) In its initial written communication to a consumer, a collection agency shall include notification of the consumer's rights under this subsection (3). If such notification is placed on the back of the written communication, there shall be a statement on the front notifying the consumer of such fact.

"(d) If a consumer orally informs a debt collector or collection agency of any of the matters specified in paragraph (a) of this subsection (3), the debt collector or collection agency shall advise the consumer that such communication must be made in writing."

Laws 2006, Ch. 308, § 18, in par. (3)(c), deleted "WWW.AGO.STATE.CO.US/CAB.HTM." following "SEE".

12-14-107. False or misleading representations. (1) A debt collector or collection agency shall not use any false, deceptive, or misleading representation or means in connection with the collection of any debt, including, but not limited to, the following conduct:

(1) Except as otherwise provided for communications to acquire location information under section 12-14-104, the failure to disclose clearly, in the initial written communication made to collect a debt or obtain information about a consumer and also, if the initial communication with the consumer is oral,

in the initial oral communication, that the debt collector or collection agency is attempting to collect a debt and that any information obtained will be used for that purpose, and, in subsequent communications, that the communication is from a debt collector or collection agency; except that this paragraph (l) shall not apply to a formal pleading made in connection with a legal action;

Laws 2003, Ch. 287, § 3 in subsec. (l) inserted "and also, if the initial communication with the consumer is oral, in the initial oral communication", inserted "and, in subsequent communications, that the communication is from a debt collector or collection agency; except that this paragraph" and inserted "shall not apply to a formal pleading made in connection with a legal action";

§ 12-14-109. Validation of debts. (1) Within five days after the initial communication with a consumer in connection with the collection of any debt, a debt collector or collection agency shall, unless the following information is contained in the initial communication or the consumer has paid the debt, send the consumer a written notice with the disclosures specified in paragraphs (a) to (e) of this subsection (1). If such disclosures are placed on the back of the notice, the front of the notice shall contain a statement notifying consumers of that fact. Such disclosures shall state:

(f) Deleted by Laws 2003, Ch. 287, § 3, eff. May 21, 2003.

(g) Deleted by Laws 2003, Ch. 287, § 3, eff. May 21, 2003.

Laws 2003, Ch. 287, § 4 in subsec. (1) in the introductory paragraph deleted "written" preceding "communication" and substituted "paragraphs (a) to (e)" for "paragraphs (a) to (g)", and deleted pars. (1)(f) and (1)(g), which read:

"(f) That collection agencies are licensed by the collection agency board. The address of the board shall also be disclosed. If, however, the debt collector is a person employed by the department of personnel for the purpose of collecting debts due to the state on behalf of another state agency, the disclosure required under this paragraph (f) shall state that the activities of such debt collector are subject to sections 12-14-104 to 12-14-109, Colorado Revised Statutes, as contained in the "Colorado Fair Debt Collection Practices Act", that complaints may be filed with the executive director of the department of personnel, and that disciplinary actions will be subject to the rules and regulations of the state personnel system."

"(g) That consumers shall not send payments to the collection agency board."

§ 12-14-111. Legal actions by collection agencies. (1) Any debt collector or collection agency who brings any legal action on a debt against any consumer shall:

(a) In the case of an action to enforce an interest in real property securing the consumer's obligation, bring such action only in a judicial district or similar legal entity in which such real property is located; or

(b) In the case of an action not described in paragraph (a) of this subsection (1), bring such action only in the judicial district or similar legal entity in which:

(I) Such consumer signed the contract sued upon;

(II) Such consumer resides at the commencement of the action; or

(III) Such action may be brought pursuant to article 13 or 13.5 of title 26, C.R.S., section 14-14-104, C.R.S., or article 4 or 6 of title 19, C.R.S., if the action is by a private collection agency acting on behalf of a delegate child support enforcement unit.

Laws 2003, Ch. 287, § 5 in subsec. (1) in the introductory paragraph substituted a colon for "comply with all provisions of law concerning the location at which such action may be brought", and added paras. (1)(a) and (1)(b).

§ 12-14-113. Civil liability. (1) In addition to administrative enforcement pursuant to section 12-14-114 and subject to section 12-14-134 and the limitations provided by subsection (9) of this section, and except as otherwise provided by this section, any debt collector or collection agency who fails to comply with any provision of this article or private child support collector, as defined in section 12-14.1-102(9), who fails to comply with any provision of this article or article 14.1 of this title, with respect to a consumer is liable to such consumer in an amount equal to the sum of:

(3) A debt collector, private child support collector, as defined in section 12-14.1-102(9), or collection agency may not be held liable in any action brought pursuant to the provisions of this article if the debt collector or collection agency shows by a preponderance of evidence that the violation was not intentional or grossly negligent and which violation resulted from a bona fide error, notwithstanding the maintenance of procedures reasonably adapted to avoid any such error.

(8) It shall be an affirmative defense to any action based upon failure of a debt collector, private child support collector, as defined in section 12-14.1-102(9), or collection agency to comply with this section that the debt collector or collection agency believed, in good faith, that the debtor was other than a natural person.

(9) There shall be no private cause of action under this section for any alleged violation of section 12-14-128(4)(a). Violations of section 12-14-128(4)(a) may be prosecuted only through administrative enforcement pursuant to section 12-14-114.

Laws 2003, Ch. 287, § 6 in subsec. (1) in the introductory paragraph inserted "and the limitations provided by subsection (9) of this section", and added subsecs. (8) and (9).

Laws 2006, Ch. 112, § 2, in the introductory portion of subsec. (1), inserted "or private child support collector, as defined in section 12-14.1-102(9), who fails to comply with any provision of this article or article 14.1 of this title," and in subsecs. (3) and (8), inserted "private child support collector, as defined in section 12-14.1-102(9)".

§ 12-14-116. Collection agency board—created. (1) For the purpose of carrying out the provisions of this article, the governor shall appoint five members to the collection agency board, which board is hereby created. The members of the board serving on July 1, 2003, shall continue to serve their appointed terms, and their successors shall be appointed for three-year terms. Upon the death, resignation, or removal of any member of the board, the governor shall appoint a member to fill the unexpired term. Any member of the board may be removed by the governor for misconduct, neglect of duty, or incompetence. No member may serve more than two consecutive terms without first a lapse of at least one term before being appointed to any additional terms.

Laws 2003, Ch. 287, § 7 in subsec. (1) substituted "2003" for "1985" and added "without first a lapse of at least one term before being appointed to any additional terms" at the end.

§ 12-14-119. Collection agency license—requirements—application—fee—expiration. (4) When the administrator approves the application, the applicant shall pay a nonrefundable license fee in an amount to be determined by the administrator in consultation with the board.

(5) The administrator shall establish procedures for the maintenance of license lists and the establishment of initial and renewal license fees and schedules. The administrator may change the renewal date of any license issued pursuant to this article to the end that approximately the same number of licenses are scheduled for renewal in each month of the year. Where any renewal date is so changed, the fee for the license shall be proportionately increased or decreased, as the case may be. Every licensee shall pay the administrator a license fee to be determined and collected pursuant to section 12-14-121 and subsection (4) of this section, and shall obtain a license certificate for the current license period. Notwithstanding any other provision of this section, a licensee, at any time, may voluntarily surrender the license to the administrator to be cancelled, but such surrender shall not affect the licensee's liability for violations of this article that occurred prior to the date of surrender.

(6) Deleted by Laws 2003, Ch. 287, § 8, eff. May 21, 2003.

Laws 2003, Ch. 287, § 8 in subsec. (4) inserted "administrator in consultation with the", rewrote subsec. (5), and deleted subsec. (6). Prior thereto, subsecs. (5) and (6) read:

"(5) Each license issued pursuant to this section shall expire on July 1 of each year; except that a licensee, at any time, may voluntarily surrender the license to the administrator to be cancelled, but such surrender shall not affect the licensee's liability for violations of this article that occurred prior to the date of surrender."

"(6) If an application is approved between January 1 and June 30 in any year, the license fee for the remainder of that licensing year shall be one-half the license fee determined by the board."

12-14-121. Collection agency license—renewals. Each licensee shall make an application to renew its license in the form and manner prescribed by the administrator. The application shall be accompanied by a nonrefundable renewal fee in an amount determined by the administrator in consultation with the board.
Laws 2003, Ch. 287, § 9 rewrote the section, which formerly read:

"(1) Each licensee shall make an application to renew its license on or before June 15 of each year. Said application shall be in the form and manner prescribed by the administrator and shall be accompanied by a nonrefundable renewal fee in an amount determined by the board.

"(2) If the application is not postmarked on or before June 15, a penalty fee of twenty-five dollars per day shall be assessed and added to the license fee. No license shall be renewed until the total fee is paid.

"(3) If a licensee fails to submit an application or any part of the total fee on or before July 15 of each year, the license shall automatically expire and an application for a new license must be submitted.

"(4) If a licensee submits an application and the total fee on or before July 15 of the renewal year, the licensee may continue to operate as a collection agency until the renewal application is approved or denied."

§ 12-14-130. Complaint—investigations—powers of the board—sanctions. (2) For reasonable cause, the board may, on its own motion, conduct an investigation of the conduct of any person concerning compliance with this article.

(4) In any proceeding held under this section, the board may accept as prima facie evidence of grounds for disciplinary or adverse action any disciplinary or adverse action taken against a licensee, the licensee's principals, debt collector, solicitor, or collections manager by another jurisdiction that issues professional, occupational, or business licenses, if the conduct which prompted the disciplinary or adverse action by that jurisdiction would be grounds for disciplinary action under this section.

(5) For reasonable cause, the board, or someone designated by it for such purpose, has the right, during normal business hours without resort to subpoena, to examine the books, records, and files of any licensee. If the books, records, and files are located outside Colorado, the licensee shall bear all expenses in making them available to the board or its designee.

(6) For reasonable cause, the board may require the making and filing, by any (a) licensee, at any time, of a written, verified statement of the licensee's assets and liabilities, including, if requested, a detailed statement of amounts due claimants. The board may also require an audited statement when cause has been shown that an audited statement is needed.

Laws 2003, Ch. 287, § 10 in subsecs. (2) and (5) and par. (6)(a) inserted "For reasonable cause," at the beginning.

Laws 2004, Ch. 316, § 30, in subsec. (4), substituted "principals" for "principles".

§ 12-14-136. Disposition of fees and fines. (2) All fines collected pursuant to this article, including but not limited to fines collected pursuant to section 12-14-130, shall be collected by the administrator and transmitted to the state treasurer, who shall credit the same to the general fund.

Laws 2003, Ch. 287, § 11 in subsec. (2) substituted "general fund" for "collection agency cash fund, created in subsection (1) of this section".

§ 12-14-137. Termination of board. The collection agency board shall be terminated July 1, 2008. Prior to such termination, the board shall be reviewed as provided in section 24-34-104, C.R.S.

Laws 2003, Ch. 287, § 12 substituted "2008" for "2003".

§ 24-34-104. General assembly review of regulatory agencies and functions for termination, continuation, or reestablishment. (32.5) The following agencies, functions, or both, shall terminate on July 1, 2003:

(f) Repealed by Laws 2003, ch. 287, § 13, eff. May 21, 2003.

(39) (b) The following agencies, functions, or both, shall terminate on July 1, 2008:

(XVIII) The regulation of collection agencies pursuant to article 14 of title 12, C.R.S.;
Laws 2003, Ch. 287, § 13, repealed par. (32.5)(f), which read:

"(f) The collection agency board created in section 12-14-116, C.R.S.;"

Capital letters indicate new material added to existing statutes; dashes through words indicate deletions from existing statutes and such material not part of act.

APPENDIX V

OPERATIVE GUIDES FOR FORWARDERS AND RECEIVERS ADOPTED BY THE COMMERCIAL LAW LEAGUE OF AMERICA*

Index

---

*Reprinted with the permission of the Commercial Law League of America.

ENABLING RESOLUTIONS ADOPTED BY THE BOARD OF GOVERNORS OF THE COMMERCIAL LAW LEAGUE OF AMERICA ON JULY 6, 1974

RESOLVED, That all provisions of any prior "Operative Resolutions" of The Commercial Law League of America are hereby repealed and made void; and

FURTHER RESOLVED, That the following "Operative Guides for Forwarders and Receivers" are hereby adopted by the Commercial Law League of America. These Guides shall be mandatory, unless expressly excluded or modified by the parties in writing, for all forwarders (agencies or attorneys) and receivers (attorneys) in the handling of claims as these terms are defined herein. The Guides are incorporated by reference in the written authorization and forwarding contract between the forwarder and receiver, and shall be subject to the disciplinary provisions of the Constitution of the Commercial Law League of America upon the filing of a complaint; and

FURTHER RESOLVED, That the "Declaration of Fair Practices of Collection Agencies" as approved by the National Conference of Lawyers and Collection Agencies February 18, 1963, as same may from time to time be amended, is incorporated herein by reference; and

FURTHER RESOLVED, That it is not the intent of the Commercial Law League of America to adopt any Guide which may be or become inconsistent with the Code of Professional Responsibility of the American Bar Association or any Code of Conduct or law in any state or locality applying to forwarders and receivers subjected to jurisdiction therein; any Guide that is or becomes inconsistent shall be deemed inoperative.

Part I—Definitions

1.1 Claim. A claim is either commercial or retail.

   a. A Commercial Claim is a claim which arises from an obligation to pay for goods sold or leased, services rendered, or monies loaned for use, in the conduct of a business or profession. An "average" commercial claim may be defined for general purposes as $2,000.

   b. A Retail Claim is a claim which arises from any obligation of a consumer to pay money arising out of a transaction in which the goods, money, financing, lease, property, insurance, or services rendered are the subject of a transaction which is primarily for personal, family, or household purposes.

   c. All other claims that are not covered under 1.1(b) are considered commercial claims under 1.1(a).

1.2 Agency. An agency is a collection agency to which claims are referred for collection by creditors.

1.3 Forwarder. A forwarder is a person who, or an entity which, as the agent of the creditor, refers claims to attorneys for collection. A forwarder may be an attorney, a collection agency, a credit bureau, a credit insurance company, or any other entity which acts on behalf of the creditor as its agent, in the referral of claims for collection.

1.4 Receiver. A receiver is an attorney to whom an account is referred for collection by a forwarder, and who is thereby employed, as attorney for the creditor, to collect the same. Upon acceptance of the claim for collection, the full attorney-client relationship exists between the receiver and the creditor.

1.5 Law List. A law list is a publication which lists the names and addresses of receiving attorneys and law firms.

1.6 Commission. A commission is the compensation payable by a creditor and earned by a receiver for his services in effecting collection of a claim, in whole or in part, and is normally contingent and computed as a percentage of the sum collected.

1.7 Forwarding Contract. A forwarding contract is the agreement entered into between the creditor (or the forwarder as the agent of the creditor and with the creditor's consent) and the receiver, specifying among other things the commission agreed upon between the receiver and the creditor as the receiver's compensation for effecting collection, in whole or in part, of a claim.

1.8 Suit Fee. A suit fee is a fee payable to the receiver in addition to the commission, for legal services rendered by the receiver for the creditor involving court action in connection with the prosecution of a claim.

1.9 Cost Advance. A cost advance is a sum of money advanced by the creditor to the receiver, as a fund from which court costs are to be expended.

1.10 Retainer. A retainer is a sum of money paid in advance to retain the services of an attorney, and should be taken into account in determining the ultimate fee to be charged for services rendered and results obtained.

Part II—General Provisions

2.1 A forwarder, when so authorized by the creditor as his principal, may act for the creditor in the forwarding of claims, and when so acting is performing a service for the creditor separate and apart from the service performed by the receiving attorney, for which service the forwarder is entitled to be separately compensated by the creditor, the amount thereof being a matter of contract between the forwarder as agent and the creditor as principal.

2.2 Under no circumstances shall the forwarder receive a share of the compensation of the receiver; except that where the forwarder is an attorney primarily engaged in the private practice of law and there is an actual division of the work and responsibility between the attorney forwarder and the receiver, the compensation may be divided between them in proportion to the effort expended and responsibility assumed by each.

2.3 These guides are intended to apply in the absence of specific agreement to the contrary, but nothing contained herein shall prevent the parties from making an agreement at variance with these guides so long as such agreement is consistent with the enabling Resolutions.

2.4 Violation of these guides by a member of the League, or violation by a member of any agreement between the parties which supercedes or which further explains these Operative Guides, shall upon the filing of a complaint subject such member to disciplinary proceedings under Article Xl of the Constitution of the League.

Part III—Contractual Compensation

A. Commissions

3.1 Unless otherwise expressly agreed, commissions are contingent on the recovery of money or property. Upon request by the receiver prior to acceptance of the forwarding contract, the forwarder should promptly supply information on the total compensation being charged to the creditor on a specific claim. If a forwarder requests a receiver to charge a contingent commission lower than the receiver's regular commission, the forwarder should disclose to the receiver in its forwarding contract the total compensation the forwarder is charging the creditor on that claim.

3.2 In all cases where terms are stated in a forwarding contract, such terms control. However:

a. A mere statement by the receiver that he will not handle the claim except upon other terms will not establish his right to compensation other than as offered in the original forwarding contract.

b. A receiver objecting to the terms as set forth in the forwarding contract should either return the claim or withhold taking action on the claim until satisfactory arrangements are made with respect to compensation. The terms of the original forwarding contract shall prevail notwithstanding the fact that the receiver has performed services in connection with the claim, unless and until the terms are changed by agreement or acquiescence.

c. A forwarder shall be deemed to have acquiesced in the terms proposed by the receiver where the forwarder subsequently instructs the receiver to proceed, without making reference to the receiver's counter-proposal. A forwarder's mere request for a status report, however, shall not be construed as an instruction to proceed.

3.3 When a claim is collected in installments, the contractual commission rate shall apply to the aggregate of the installments collected, and not to each installment individually. In the event the forwarding contract provides for a declining percentage rate, the higher rate may be taken on the first installments collected, with adjustments to be made in accordance with the forwarding contract, to the end that the total commission on the aggregate of all installments collected shall not exceed the total commissions permitted upon such aggregate by the forwarding contract.

3.4 In situations where the receiver may obtain amicable agreement for the debtor to make payments over an extended period of time, the receiver can give the creditor the option to (a) pay a higher contingent fee without suit or (b) litigate, giving requirements for suit including suit fees and court costs.

3.5 Where the time elapsed from the creditor's original due date on any claim is greater than one year at the time it is placed with the forwarder, and the forwarder is receiving a commission rate higher than its commission on claims less than one year old, the receiver should be entitled to additional commission.

3.6 In cases where a collection results from the filing of a claim in probate, or in bankruptcy, receivership, assignment, or other insolvency or kindred proceedings:

a. The mere filing of a claim in said proceedings and the receiving and remitting of a dividend or dividends thereon entitles the receiver to commissions in accordance with the forwarding contract, and

b. The aggregate of all dividends received from such proceeding, together with the aggregate of all collections prior to the institution of such proceeding, shall be treated as a single recovery for the purposes of applying a commission rate in accordance with the forwarding contract, and

c. The mere appearance of the receiver before the court or any officer thereof to represent such claim, there being no contest as to its validity, shall not entitle the receiver to any additional compensation; but if the receiver, in order to establish a claim filed in any of said proceedings, is obliged to serve notices, examine witnesses, or to take other comparable steps to obtain allowance or to insure payment of the claim, or if the exigencies of the situation make it immediately necessary to perform legal services to protect the creditor's interests, the receiver shall be entitled to a reasonable fee in addition to the commissions provided for in the forwarding contract, as provided in guide 6.1.

3.7 When a claim is paid by the debtor, directly to the creditor or the forwarder, after it has arrived at the office of the receiver:

a. The receiver is entitled to commissions in accordance with the forwarding contract, if payment was made by the debtor after demand was made by the receiver. The mere technical failure of a receiver immediately to acknowledge receipt of a claim shall not operate to deprive him of his right to compensation at the agreed rate, provided he actually made demand for payment (*see* guide 7.1f).

b. The receiver is entitled to no compensation if payment was made by the debtor before the receiver made demand on the debtor or otherwise worked on the claim, provided notice of such direct payment is furnished the receiver by the creditor or the forwarder before work is begun or demand is made (*see* guides 3.9b and 7.1f).

3.8 Without limiting the rights set forth in guide 3.6, the receiver is entitled to full compensation in accordance with the forwarding contract in each of the following situations:

a. Where the receiver receives the claim and does work on it, and the debtor subsequently pays the amount of the claim to another person who had previously been employed to collect the claim.

b. Where the claim is in the hands of the receiver and either the creditor or the forwarder intervenes for the purpose of accepting a postdated check or a promissory note, or an acceptance or other instrument from the debtor, thereupon withdrawing the claim from the hands of the receiver; and the commission shall be computed upon the face amount of the instrument so taken, and shall be payable to the receiver in full upon the taking of the instrument, the same as if money had been collected.

c. Where the receiver settles the claim by taking such an instrument from the debtor, provided that such settlement is authorized or ratified by the creditor. In such event:

   (1) If the instrument remains in the hands of the receiver until maturity and collection, the receiver shall be entitled to compensation only upon the money actually collected and only when collected, but

   (2) If the creditor or forwarder demands possession of the instrument, the receiver is at once entitled to full compensation computed on the face amount of the instrument, the same as if money had been collected. In the event the instrument is not paid at maturity and is returned to the receiver for collection, the employment to collect the same is a new employment, and (a) in the event of a failure to collect, the receiver shall not be required to refund the commissions previously earned, or (b) in the event of a full or partial collection, the receiver shall be entitled to full commissions computed on the amount collected, irrespective of the commission previously earned on the taking of the instrument.

d. Where a claim or judgment is compromised upon the advice or with the approval, tacit or expressed, of the receiver; but in such event, the receiver's compensation shall be computed only upon the amount actually recovered and not upon the original debt.

3.9 If portions of a claim are sent to the receiver at intervals without notice to the effect that other portions are to follow, and

a. If settlement is reached before the other portion or portions are forwarded, or

b. If the receiver is required to render separate services on the portion or portions subsequently forwarded, the subsequent forwarding shall constitute a new and separate employment. But if no settlement is reached and no separate services are required by reason of the delay, the subsequent portions shall merely increase the amount of the original claim, and the entire employment will be deemed a single employment.

3.10 A receiver is not entitled to commission in any of the following situations:

a. Where the receiver returns the claim as Uncollectible, or where it has been properly withdrawn from his hands, and the debtor subsequently makes payment in full or in part to the creditor, to the forwarder, or to a subsequent receiver.

b. Where a claim is paid or settled after it arrives at the office of the receiver but before the receiver has performed any services in connection with the claim, provided the receiver is notified by the forwarder or the creditor of the payment or the settlement before work is done on the claim.

c. When the receiver reports a claim to be uncollectible without suit and the creditor chooses not to sue, and the claim is returned to the forwarder, except as provided in guide 7.1g.

B. Interest, Costs, Attorney Fees, Etc.

4.1 Interest collected on an account or judgment is the property of the creditor, and the collection of interest must be disclosed by the receiver to the forwarder. Interest collected should be added to the principal collected for the purpose of computing the commission. However, where not in violation of the law of the forum, where monies are collected in excess of the principal, said excess shall first be allocated as a recovery of court costs, and only when costs have been recovered in full shall additional monies collected be deemed interest and subject to commission.

4.2 Court costs expended in connection with litigation and subsequently recovered from the debtor may not be added to the principal in computing the commission, and the creditor is entitled to a full return of the money advanced by him for costs when such money is collected from the debtor as part of the judgment.

4.3 Where, under local law, a plaintiff is awarded a sum in addition to his damages and costs (which sum is variously known as statutory costs, taxed fees, taxed cost, or the like), said additional sum shall be deemed to be the property of the creditor and shall be treated, for purposes of computing commissions, the same as interest, unless prohibited by law. If so prohibited, the receiver shall retain the amount so awarded and collected as his own, by way of his suit fee or on account of his suit fee, and shall compute his commission upon the collection of principal and interest only, so that the receiver will not be paid twice for his court services, once by the statutory recovery and once by the creditor.

4.4 Unless otherwise agreed upon by and between the forwarder and receiver, because an attorneys' fee clause in a contract or note is intended to reimburse the holder for expenses incurred in the collection thereof, any such attorneys' fee collected in addition to principal and interest, where no suit has been filed, shall be deemed to be the property of the creditor and shall be treated for purposes of computing commissions, the same as interest, unless prohibited by law. If so prohibited, the receiver shall retain the same as his own, and shall compute his commission upon the collection of principal and interest only, and shall deduct the amount so retained from the commission computed in accordance with the commission contract.

4.5 Sums awarded by a court or arbitrator for contempt for failure to appear; failure to proceed; failure to comply with an order of the court; false or frivolous pleadings; or the like; and intended to compensate the receiving attorney, shall belong to the attorney.

4.6 In all instances of recovery pursuant to Sections 4.3 and 4.4 herein above, it shall be the obligation of the receiving attorney to disclose said recovery to the forwarder and to inform the forwarder of the specific local law which prohibits said recovery from being deemed the property of the creditor.

C. Suits and Suit Fees

5.1 The mere forwarding of a claim for collection does not warrant the commencement of suit, nor does the mere employment to collect a claim imply any authority to sue. No suit shall be commenced by any receiver unless he shall have authority from the creditor, or from the forwarder to do so.

5.2 The amount of the suit fee is a matter of contract between the receiver and the creditor, as is the question of whether the suit fee is to be contingent or non-contingent, or partly contingent and partly non-contingent. A suit fee, if earned, is payable in addition to commissions. It belongs exclusively to the receiver unless there is a division of service and responsibility between the receiver and an attorney forwarder (*see* guide 5.5). The suit fee agreement preferably should be entered into before suit is commenced, and the fee should be commensurate with the services rendered, the amount involved, and the results accomplished.

5.3 The mere authorization to commence suit does not entitle the receiver to charge a suit fee, and a suit fee is not earned until suit has actually been commenced by the filing of the requisite papers in court or by their delivery, as the practice may be, to a process server, constable, or other properly constituted authority, for service on the defendant. The mere preparation for suit is not sufficient to justify the charging of a suit fee, but neither is it actually necessary to serve the defendant or recover a judgment against him. When a suit fee arrangement contemplates that it shall be fully contingent, then the suit fee arrangement may be greater than one that is fully non-contingent. When a suit fee arrangement contemplates that it shall be partly contingent and partly non-contingent, then the suit fee arrangement may be less than one that is fully contingent but more than one that is fully non-contingent.

5.4 When the suit fee arrangement contemplates that the suit fee will be computed as a percentage of the recovery, the percentage shall be computed on the gross amount collected by the receiver, not including the court costs expended and recovered from the defendant. When the suit fee and court costs arrangement contemplates the creditor advancing a portion or all thereof, the forwarder is obligated to forward to the attorney all of such costs and fees received from the creditor.

5.5 A suit fee, being compensation for legal services rendered, may not be divided between the receiver and any other person except members of his law firm; provided, that if the forwarder is also an attorney primarily engaged in the practice of law, and if there is a division of both the work and the responsibility between the attorney forwarder and the receiver, the fee may be divided between them in proportion to the efforts expended and responsibility assumed by each.

Part IV—Non-Contractual Compensation

A. Compensation in Addition to the Contract

6.1 In addition to the commissions agreed upon between the creditor (or the forwarder as agent of the creditor) and the receiver, the receiver shall be entitled to reasonable compensation in the following situations:

a. Where the receiver, in order to establish a claim filed in probate, bankruptcy, receivership, or other insolvency or other kindred proceedings, is obliged to serve notices, examine witnesses, or to take other steps in an attempt to obtain allowance or to insure payment of the claim (aside from the mere filing thereof).

b. When the exigencies of any situation make it immediately necessary to perform on behalf of the creditor legal services which would normally not be anticipated.

c. When a claim has been put into litigation and it is necessary for the receiver to attend a trial or arbitration hearing, the receiver may charge a reasonable trial fee in addition to his or her normal suit fee if notice of the possibility of such additional fee has been given in the suit fee requirements letter.

6.2 In all cases in which a claim has been forwarded to a receiver, if payment is not received after initial demand by the receiver, the receiver may request in advance a reasonable non-contingent administrative fee.

6.3 In all cases calling for additional compensation as set forth in guides 6.1 and 6.2, the receiver shall promptly advise the creditor or forwarder as agent of the creditor as to the necessity for additional compensation.

B. Reasonable Compensation as a Substitute for Contractual Compensation

7.1 Normally, the compensation to be paid to the receiver is a matter of contract between the creditor and the receiver, but it is recognized that situations arise in good faith which are not covered by the forwarding contract and which alter the circumstances; thereby requiring a different compensation basis. In such situations, the receiver shall be reasonably compensated for the work and services actually performed, and where appropriate, for the expenses incurred. Some of such situations are described as follows:

a. Where goods or property are taken in settlement, rather than money. If this situation is not covered by the forwarding contract, the receiver's compensation shall be an amount to be determined by the reasonable worth of the services rendered, viewed from the standpoint of the work done, the amount involved, the character of the employment, and the results accomplished, whether such amount is greater or lesser than the amount as measured by the forwarding contract.

b. Where goods or property are taken in partial settlement, and money is also taken in partial settlement. In this situation, the forwarding contract controls the compensation earned upon the recovery of the money, and guide 7.1a above controls the compensation earned upon the property taken.

c. Where a claim is met by a debtor's claim of prior payment, offset, counterclaim, or other similar defense, or is barred by the statute of limitations, and the receiver accepts the claim without notice of the defense and learns of the defense only in the course of his work, and where the defense is a valid one and is either accepted as valid by the creditor or is ruled valid in litigation. In this situation, the receiver is entitled to a reasonable fee on the amount so disallowed, in addition to his contract compensation on any remaining balance actually collected. But if the claim was forwarded with notice of the defense, the receiver shall not be entitled to any non-contractual compensation on the portion disallowed by reason of such defense.

d. Where a claim is disputed and the dispute is known to either the creditor or the forwarder but is not disclosed to the receiver at the time of his employment. In this situation, the receiver shall be entitled to reasonable compensation for services performed and expenses incurred by him in endeavoring to collect such claim in the event he is, by reason of such dispute, unsuccessful in the collection thereof.

e. When either the creditor or the forwarder shall improperly interfere with the efforts of the receiver and thereby prevent collection. In this situation, the receiver shall be entitled to reasonable compensation for services rendered.

f. Where a claim is paid directly to the creditor or the forwarder. In this situation, it is the duty of the forwarder to notify the receiver immediately of the fact of payment, and

   (1) Where payment is made prior to the arrival of the claim in the office of the receiver, and

      (a) Where such notice is given, the receiver shall be entitled to no compensation, but

      (b) Where notice is not immediately given the receiver, and he does work on the claim or incurs expense before notice is received, he is entitled to reasonable compensation for work performed and expense incurred.

   (2) Where payment is made after arrival of the claim in the office of the receiver, and

      (a) Where such notice is given before receiver has done any work on the claim, the receiver is entitled to no compensation, but

      (b) Where such notice is given after the receiver has started work on the claim or has incurred expense, the receiver is entitled to reasonable compensation for work performed and expense incurred, and

      (c) Where such notice is not given until after the receiver has made a demand on the debtor, the receiver is entitled to full compensation as measured by the forwarding contract.

Where the fact of payment does not become immediately known to the forwarder through the neglect of the creditor, thereby preventing the forwarder from giving immediate notice to the receiver, this guide 7.1f shall remain applicable and fully effective.

a. Where the arrangement under which the claim was referred authorized the commencement of suit, and the receiver performed services in reliance upon the creditor's good faith in that regard, and subsequently the creditor chooses not to sue. In this situation, the receiver shall be entitled to reasonable compensation for services rendered.

7.2 Because the placement of a claim with a receiver on a contingent basis vests the receiver with an interest in the claim to the extent of his contingent commission, the withdrawal of a claim for any reason (including a desire to file the claim directly in any probate, bankruptcy, receivership, insolvency or other kindred proceedings) except fault on the part of the receiver, shall entitle the receiver to reasonable compensation for services rendered.

7.3 When a claim is sent to a receiver by mistake of either the creditor or the forwarder, and the mistake or fact of prior payment has been learned by the receiver in the course of his work and by him brought to the attention of either the creditor or the forwarder, the receiver is entitled to reasonable compensation for his services.

7.4 When any neglect or failure to act on the part of a creditor or forwarder, including but not limited to, the failure to give timely notice of payments received from or settlements made with a debtor, which neglect or failure results in the receiver being compelled to do work which otherwise could have been avoided and for which he will not be otherwise compensated, the receiver is entitled to reasonable compensation for services rendered.

7.5 Where suit is authorized and all requisite papers have been prepared, and the creditor fails to cooperate with the receiver, the receiver is entitled to reasonable compensation for his services.

7.6 Where suit is authorized and commenced, and the creditor fails to furnish the receiver with the evidence or testimony to substantiate the claim, or to comply with orders of the court, which failure results in the dismissal of the case or in a judgment adverse to the creditor, the receiver is entitled to reasonable compensation for his services.

7.7 Where a creditor employs two or more receivers in the same or different towns to handle the same matter, and fails to inform each of them of the dual representation, and where either of them collects the claim in whole or in part, the other is entitled to reasonable compensation for his services.

Part V—Court Costs and Expenses

8.1 Money advanced for court costs is a fund to be drawn upon for the purpose of paying court costs, and should be accounted for at the conclusion of the receiver's employment.

8.2 Except in cases of emergency, where the interests of the creditor might be prejudiced by delay, it shall be the duty of the receiver to consult the creditor, or the forwarder as agent of the creditor, before incurring any items of expense.

8.3 Money expended in service of process or endeavoring to serve process on defendants where suit is authorized is a legitimate expense that the creditor must pay.

Part VI—Duties

A. Of Receivers

9.1 A receiver shall acknowledge receipt of a claim promptly unless otherwise instructed.

9.2 If a receiver finds it impossible or impractical to handle a claim personally, it shall be his duty promptly to return the same, rather than to transfer the claim to any other party for attention. This provision, however, shall not be interpreted as prohibiting the delegation of authority by the receiver to associates, employees, or clerks in his office.

9.3 A receiver shall report the fact that a claim is being collected in installments, and shall remit within a reasonable time any money so collected.

9.4 A receiver shall promptly return all papers and/or remit all moneys collected and unexpended costs on claims that have been withdrawn because of the receiver's neglect or inability to handle the same.

9.5 Where a receiver is called upon to remit the proceeds of a collection to different and conflicting parties, he shall impound the money with some responsible depository, and shall then notify the conflicting parties that it will not be released until he is assured by both parties, by stipulation or otherwise, that the dispute has been completely adjusted.

9.6 A receiver shall account for and remit on:

a. Principal

b. Costs which are not commissionable

c. Interest

d. Statutory fees (where permitted)

e. Contractual fees (where permitted)

9.7 To minimize receiver costs of handling small claims, a receiver can be expected to make demand on the debtor in an effort to obtain payment; but the receiver need report only every 90 days unless:

a. Documentation is needed

b. Payment is made

c. Merchandise is offered for return

d. Account is closed or

e. Requested by forwarder

9.8 To minimize receiver reporting, it is recommended that, on claims in litigation, a receiver

a. Confirm that suit is filed

b. Report each significant development or event in the course of the litigation and

c. Give realistic file datings based on local procedure

B. Of Forwarders

11.1 In an effort to minimize receiver requests for information and documentation, every claim forwarded to a receiver should be accompanied by the following where available:

a. Information

1. Creditor's full name and address
2. Debtor's legal name, legal composition, and address, including the name and address of any guarantor
3. Amount due, principal and interest
4. Debtor's contact and phone number
5. Nature of creditor's business
6. Details of any dispute and creditor's response with copies of memos and correspondence

b. Documentation

1. Credit agreement
2. Contracts, leases, personal guarantees, promissory notes, and NSF checks
3. Purchase orders, delivery receipts, invoices, and statements of account
4. Security agreement (with copy of any financing statements)

c. Credit information

1. Credit application
2. Financial statements
3. Credit reports
4. Debtor banking information
5. Real estate owned
6. Place of employment
7. Social security number or employer ID number
8. Vehicle identification number

11.2 The forwarder should disclose to the creditor the receiver's contingent fee requirements. Where practical:

a. A copy of the receiver's letter stating suit fee and cost request should be sent to the creditor with the request that the creditor make its check for such fee and costs payable to the receiver and

b. Contingent and non-contingent fee requests by a receiver should be acknowledged by the creditor.

11.3 It shall be the duty of the forwarder to provide relevant information on any of the following matters to the receiver at the time of forwarding:

a. When the forwarder knows or suspects that a forwarded claim is other than a commercial claim;

b. When the forwarder knows of any dispute on the claim;

c. When the forwarder has knowledge that creditor will not authorize suit or provide witnesses or has other restrictions on suit.

Part VII—Restrictions

A. Upon Receivers

11.1 No receiver shall retain an item of business if he cannot handle it properly for any reason; except that, if the reason is an apparent conflict of interest, the receiver shall place the creditor or forwarder in full possession of all the facts or shall return the claim at once.

11.2 No receiver, having taken property or money from a debtor as settlement of a claim, may, in a controversy arising with the creditor or forwarder regarding his compensation, return the property or money to the debtor. Once the property or money is taken and received as payment of the claim, the property or money is in the constructive possession of the creditor and may not be returned without his authority.

11.3 No receiver shall charge and retain in one case the fees or costs claimed in another, where there is no authority to do so.

11.4 No receiver shall incur any item of expense, chargeable to the creditor, without the creditor's consent, except in cases of emergency where the interests of the creditor are likely to be prejudiced by delay.

11.5 No receiver may institute a suit or compromise a claim without authority of the creditor, either given directly by the creditor or by the forwarder as his agent.

11.6 A receiver having voluntarily relinquished an account should not, after giving notice to that effect to the forwarder as agent for the creditor, accept payment from the debtor; and the receiver shall not be entitled to any commissions on any payments which he does accept.

B. Upon Forwarders

12.1 No forwarder shall withdraw a claim from a receiver in the absence of fault on the part of the receiver, without compensating the receiver in accordance with guide 7.2.

12.2 No forwarder shall send any claim to a receiver on condition that it be handled without charge. No forwarder shall induce a receiving attorney to accept a lower contingent fee by a false representation that the total percentage charged the creditor will be reduced by at least that percent.

12.3 No forwarder shall use the name of an attorney in the assertion of rights against a third party.

12.4 No forwarder shall intentionally mail or deliver envelopes to a debtor containing a letter or a letter copy purporting to be written to an attorney, either authorizing or instructing action by the attorney against the debtor, for the purpose of deceiving the debtor into thinking that the attorney has been so authorized or instructed.

12.5 No forwarder shall use a form of notice which purports to be a summons or other writ issued by a court, for the purpose of deceiving the debtor into believing that legal action has been actually commenced, or that the communication is a court notice.

12.6 No forwarder shall place a claim with a receiver without disclosing, if such be the fact, that the claim has previously been forwarded to and worked on by another receiver.

12.7 No forwarder shall request an attorney to incur the cost of litigation without an express agreement for reimbursement by the creditor.

12.8 No forwarder shall attach more than one law list coupon to any item placed with a receiver, nor send bonding coupons to more than one law list on a single item placed with a receiver.

12.9 No forwarder shall place a claim with a receiver reserving the right to withdraw the same without payment of compensation in the event of any insolvency proceedings concerning the debtor. (*See* guide 7.2.)

12.10 No forwarder shall himself file one or more claims in bankruptcy or other insolvency proceedings, and send one or more claims to a receiver, for the purpose of obtaining status reports from the receiver as to the progress of the proceeding.

12.11 Subject to guide 3.2, no forwarder shall discourage a receiver from requesting a higher commission than set forth in the forwarding contract and shall not view adversely any receiver who makes such a request.

Part VIII—Arbitration

13.1 Any dispute between a forwarder and a receiver may be resolved by arbitration. In any dispute between two or more League members involving a forwarding contract, the League members are presumed to have submitted to the jurisdiction of the Committee on Arbitration, Grievances, and Objections to Membership of the Commercial Law League of America for resolution of the dispute unless all League members involved in the dispute agree otherwise or the forwarding contract specifically states otherwise. Arbitration shall be in accordance with the rules of procedure from time to time adopted by the Committee and approved by the Board of Governors pursuant to authority granted by the Constitution of the Commercial Law League of America.

APPENDIX VI

EXCERPT FROM *BELL ATLANTIC CORP. v. TWOMBLY*

[4] [5] [6] The inadequacy of showing parallel conduct or interdependence, without more, mirrors the ambiguity of the behavior: consistent with conspiracy, but just as much in line with a wide swath of rational and competitive business strategy unilaterally prompted by common perceptions of the market. See, *e.g.*, AEI-Brookings Joint Center for Regulatory Studies, Epstein, Motions to Dismiss Antitrust Cases: Separating Fact from Fantasy, Related Publication 06-08, pp. 3-4 (2006) (discussing problem of "false positives" in § 1 suits). Accordingly, we have previously hedged against false inferences from identical behavior at a number of points in the trial sequence. An antitrust conspiracy plaintiff with evidence showing nothing beyond parallel conduct is not entitled to a directed verdict, see *Theatre Enterprises, supra;* proof of a § 1 conspiracy must include evidence tending to exclude the possibility of independent action, see *Monsanto Co. v. Spray-Rite Service Corp.*, 465 U.S. 752, 104 S.Ct. 1464, 79 L.Ed.2d 775 (1984); and at the summary judgment stage a § 1 plaintiff's offer of conspiracy evidence must tend to rule out the possibility that the defendants were acting independently, see *Matsushita Elec. Industrial Co. v. Zenith Radio Corp.*, 475 U.S. 574, 106 S.Ct. 1348, 89 L.Ed.2d 538 (1986).

B

[7] [8] [9] This case presents the antecedent question of what a plaintiff must plead in order to state a claim under § 1 of the Sherman Act. Federal Rule of Civil Procedure 8(a)(2) requires only "a short and plain statement of the claim showing that the pleader is entitled to relief," in order to "give the defendant fair notice of what the ... claim is and the grounds upon which it rests," *Conley v. Gibson*, 355 U.S. 41, 47, 78 S.Ct. 99, 2 L.Ed.2d 80 (1957). While a complaint attacked by a Rule 12(b)(6) motion to dismiss does not need detailed factual allegations, *ibid.*; *Sanjuan v. American Bd. of Psychiatry and Neurology, Inc.*, 40 F.3d 247, 251 (C.A.7 1994), a plaintiff's obligation to provide the ***1965** "grounds" of his "entitle[ment] to relief" requires more than labels and conclusions, and a formulaic recitation of the elements of a cause of action will not do, see *Papasan v. Allain*, 478 U.S. 265, 286, 106 S.Ct. 2932, 92 L.Ed.2d 209 (1986) (on a motion to dismiss, courts "are not bound to accept as true a legal conclusion couched as a factual allegation"). Factual allegations must be enough to raise a right to relief above the speculative level, see 5 C. Wright & A. Miller, Federal Practice and Procedure § 1216, pp. 235-236 (3d ed.2004) (hereinafter Wright & Miller) ("[T]he pleading must contain something more ... than ... a statement of facts that merely creates a suspicion [of] a legally cognizable right of action"),[FN3] on the assumption that all the allegations in the complaint are true (even if doubtful in fact), see, *e.g.*, *Swierkiewicz v. Sorema N. A.*, 534 U.S. 506, 508, n. 1, 122 S.Ct. 992, 152 L.Ed.2d 1 (2002); *Neitzke v. Williams*, 490 U.S. 319, 327, 109 S.Ct. 1827, 104 L.Ed.2d 338 (1989) (" Rule 12(b)(6) does not countenance ... dismissals based on a judge's disbelief of a complaint's factual allegations"); *Scheuer v. Rhodes*, 416 U.S. 232, 236, 94 S.Ct. 1683, 40 L.Ed.2d 90 (1974) (a well-pleaded complaint may proceed even if it appears "that a recovery is very remote and unlikely").

FN3. The dissent greatly oversimplifies matters by suggesting that the Federal Rules somehow dispensed with the pleading of facts altogether. See *post*, at 1979 (opinion of STEVENS, J.) (pleading standard of Federal Rules "does not require, or even invite, the pleading of facts"). While, for most types of cases, the Federal Rules eliminated the cumbersome requirement that a claimant "set out *in detail* the facts upon which he bases his claim," Conley v. Gibson, 355 U.S. 41, 47, 78 S.Ct. 99, 2 L.Ed.2d 80 (1957) (emphasis added), Rule 8(a)(2) still requires a "showing," rather than a blanket assertion, of entitlement to relief. Without some factual allegation in the complaint, it is hard to see how a claimant could satisfy the requirement of providing not only "fair notice" of the nature of the claim, but also "grounds" on which the claim rests. See 5 Wright & Miller § 1202, at 94, 95 (Rule 8(a) "contemplate[s] the statement of circumstances, occurrences, and events in support of the claim presented" and does not authorize a pleader's "bare averment that he wants relief and is entitled to it").

[10] [11] [12] [13] In applying these general standards to a § 1 claim, we hold that stating such a claim requires a complaint with enough factual matter (taken as true) to suggest that an agreement was made. Asking for plausible grounds to infer an agreement does not impose a probability requirement at the pleading stage; it simply calls for enough fact to raise a reasonable expectation that discovery will reveal evidence of illegal agreement.[FN4] And, of course, a well-pleaded complaint may proceed even if it strikes a savvy judge that actual proof of those facts is improbable, and "that a recovery is very remote and unlikely." *Ibid.* In identifying facts that are suggestive enough to render a § 1 conspiracy plausible, we have the benefit ***1966** of the prior rulings and considered views of leading commentators, already quoted, that lawful parallel conduct fails to bespeak unlawful agreement. It makes sense to say, therefore, that an allegation of parallel conduct and a bare assertion of conspiracy will not suffice. Without more, parallel conduct does not suggest conspiracy, and a conclusory allegation of agreement at some unidentified point does not supply facts adequate to show illegality. Hence, when allegations of parallel conduct are set out in order to make a § 1 claim, they must be placed in a context that raises a suggestion of a preceding agreement, not merely parallel conduct that could just as well be independent action.

FN4. Commentators have offered several examples of parallel conduct allegations that would state a § 1 claim under this standard. See, *e.g.,* 6 Areeda & Hovenkamp ¶ 1425, at 167-185 (discussing "parallel behavior that would probably not result from chance, coincidence, independent responses to common stimuli, or mere interdependence unaided by an advance understanding among the parties"); Blechman, Conscious Parallelism, Signalling and Facilitating Devices: The Problem of Tacit Collusion Under the Antitrust Laws, 24 N.Y.L. S. L.Rev. 881, 899 (1979) (describing "conduct [that] indicates the sort of restricted freedom of action and sense of obligation that one generally associates with agreement"). The parties in this case agree that "complex and historically unprecedented changes in pricing structure made at the very same time by multiple competitors, and made for no other discernible reason" would support a plausible inference of conspiracy. Brief for Respondents 37; see also Reply Brief for Petitioners 12.

The need at the pleading stage for allegations plausibly suggesting (not merely consistent with) agreement reflects the threshold requirement of Rule 8(a)(2) that the "plain statement" possess enough heft to "sho[w] that the pleader is entitled to relief." A statement of parallel conduct, even conduct consciously undertaken, needs some setting suggesting the agreement necessary to make out a § 1 claim; without that further circumstance pointing toward a meeting of the minds, an account of a defendant's commercial efforts stays in neutral territory. An allegation of parallel conduct is thus much like a naked assertion of conspiracy in a § 1 complaint: it gets the complaint close to stating a claim, but without some further factual enhancement it stops short of the line between possibility and plausibility of "entitle[ment] to relief." Cf. *DM Research, Inc. v. College of Am. Pathologists,* 170 F.3d 53, 56 (C.A.1 1999) ("[T]erms like 'conspiracy,' or even 'agreement,' are border-line: they might well be sufficient in conjunction with a more specific allegation-for example, identifying a written agreement or even a basis for inferring a tacit agreement, ... but a court is not required to accept such terms as a sufficient basis for a complaint").[FN5]

FN5. The border in *DM Research* was the line between the conclusory and the factual. Here it lies between the factually neutral and the factually suggestive. Each must be crossed to enter the realm of plausible liability.

We alluded to the practical significance of the Rule 8 entitlement requirement in *Dura Pharmaceuticals, Inc. v. Broudo*, 544 U.S. 336, 125 S.Ct. 1627, 161 L.Ed.2d 577 (2005), when we explained that something beyond the mere possibility of loss causation must be alleged, lest a plaintiff with " 'a largely groundless claim' " be allowed to " 'take up the time of a number of other people, with the right to do so representing an *in terrorem* increment of the settlement value.' " *Id.*, at 347, 125 S.Ct. 1627 (quoting *Blue Chip Stamps v. Manor Drug Stores*, 421 U.S. 723, 741, 95 S.Ct. 1917, 44 L.Ed.2d 539 (1975)). So, when the allegations in a complaint, however true, could not raise a claim of entitlement to relief, " 'this basic deficiency should ... be exposed at the point of minimum expenditure of time and money by the parties and the court.' " 5 Wright & Miller § 1216, at 233-234 (quoting *Daves v. Hawaiian Dredging Co.*, 114 F.Supp. 643, 645 (D.Hawai *1953*) *); see also* Dura, supra, *at 346, 125 S.Ct. 1627;* Asahi Glass Co. v. Pentech Pharmaceuticals, Inc ., *289 F.Supp.2d 986, 995 (N.D.Ill.2003) (Posner, J., sitting by designation) ("[S]ome threshold of plausibility must be crossed at the outset before a patent antitrust case should be permitted to go into its inevitably costly and protracted discovery phase").*

Thus, it is one thing to be cautious before dismissing an antitrust complaint in advance of discovery, cf. ***1967** *Poller v. Columbia Broadcasting System, Inc.*, 368 U.S. 464, 473, 82 S.Ct. 486, 7 L.Ed.2d 458 (1962), but quite another to forget that proceeding to antitrust discovery can be expensive. As we indicated over 20 years ago in *Associated Gen. Contractors of Cal., Inc. v. Carpenters*, 459 U.S. 519, 528, n. 17, 103 S.Ct. 897, 74 L.Ed.2d 723 (1983), "a district court must retain the power to insist upon some specificity in pleading before allowing a potentially massive factual controversy to proceed." See also *Car Carriers, Inc. v. Ford Motor Co.*, 745 F.2d 1101, 1106 (C.A.7 1984) ("[T]he costs of modern federal antitrust litigation and the increasing caseload of the federal courts counsel against sending the parties into discovery when there is no reasonable likelihood that the plaintiffs can construct a claim from the events related in the complaint"); Note, Modeling the Effect of One-Way Fee Shifting on Discovery Abuse in Private Antitrust Litigation, 78 N.Y. & U. L.Rev. 1887, 1898-1899 (2003) (discussing the unusually high cost of discovery in antitrust cases); Manual for Complex Litigation, Fourth, § 30, p. 519 (2004) (describing extensive scope of discovery in antitrust cases); Memorandum from Paul V. Niemeyer, Chair, Advisory Committee on Civil Rules, to Hon. Anthony J. Scirica, Chair, Committee on Rules of Practice and Procedure (May 11, 1999), 192 F.R.D. 354, 357 (2000) (reporting that discovery accounts for as much as 90 percent of litigation costs when discovery is actively employed). That potential expense is obvious enough in the present case: plaintiffs represent a putative class of at least 90 percent of all subscribers to local telephone or high-speed Internet service in the continental United States, in an action against America's largest telecommunications firms (with many thousands of employees generating reams and gigabytes of business records) for unspecified (if any) instances of antitrust violations that allegedly occurred over a period of seven years.

It is no answer to say that a claim just shy of a plausible entitlement to relief can, if groundless, be weeded out early in the discovery process through "careful case management," *post* at 1975, given the common lament that the success of judicial supervisión in checking discovery abuse has been on the modest side. See, *e.g.*,

Easterbrook, Discovery as Abuse, 69 B.U.L.Rev. 635, 638 (1989) ("Judges can do little about impositional discovery when parties control the legal claims to be presented and conduct the discovery themselves"). And it is self-evident that the problem of discovery abuse cannot be solved by "careful scrutiny of evidence at the summary judgment stage," much less "lucid instructions to juries," *post,* at 1975; the threat of discovery expense will push cost-conscious defendants to settle even anemic cases before reaching those proceedings. Probably, then, it is only by taking care to require allegations that reach the level suggesting conspiracy that we can hope to avoid the potentially enormous expense of discovery in cases with no " 'reasonably founded hope that the [discovery] process will reveal relevant evidence' " to support a § 1 claim. *Dura,* 544 U.S., at 347, 125 S.Ct. 1627 (quoting *Blue Chip Stamps, supra,* at 741, 95 S.Ct. 1917; alteration in *Dura*).FN6

FN6. The dissent takes heart in the reassurances of plaintiffs' counsel that discovery would be " ' "phased" ' " and "limited to the existence of the alleged conspiracy and class certification." *Post,* at ----24. But determining whether some illegal agreement may have taken place between unspecified persons at different ILECs (each a multibillion dollar corporation with legions of management level employees) at some point over seven years is a sprawling, costly, and hugely time-consuming undertaking not easily susceptible to the kind of line drawing and case management that the dissent envisions. Perhaps the best answer to the dissent's optimism that antitrust discovery is open to effective judicial control is a more extensive quotation of the authority just cited, a judge with a background in antitrust law. Given the system that we have, the hope of effective judicial supervision is slim: "The timing is all wrong. The plaintiff files a sketchy complaint (the Rules of Civil Procedure discourage fulsome documents), and discovery is launched. A judicial officer does not know the details of the case the parties will present and in theory *cannot* know the details. Discovery is used to find the details. The judicial officer always knows less than the parties, and the parties themselves may not know very well where they are going or what they expect to find. A magistrate supervising discovery does not-cannot-know the expected productivity of a given request, because the nature of the requester's claim and the contents of the files (or head) of the adverse party are unknown. Judicial officers cannot measure the costs and benefits to the requester and so cannot isolate impositional requests. Requesters have no reason to disclose their own estimates because they gain from imposing costs on rivals (and may lose from an improvement in accuracy). The portions of the Rules of Civil Procedure calling on judges to trim back excessive demands, therefore, have been, and are doomed to be, hollow. We cannot prevent what we cannot detect; we cannot detect what we cannot define; we cannot define 'abusive' discovery except in theory, because in practice we lack essential information." Easterbrook, Discovery as Abuse, 69 B.U.L.Rev. 635, 638-639 (1989).

***1968** [14] Plaintiffs do not, of course, dispute the requirement of plausibility and the need for something more than merely parallel behavior explained in *Theatre Enterprises, Monsanto,* and *Matsushita,* and their main argument against the plausibility standard at the pleading stage is its ostensible conflict with an early statement of ours construing Rule 8. Justice Black's opinion for the Court in *Conley v. Gibson* spoke not only of the need for fair notice of the grounds for entitlement to relief but of "the accepted rule that a complaint should not be dismissed for failure to state a claim unless it appears beyond doubt that the plaintiff can prove no set of facts in support of his claim which would entitle him to relief." 355 U.S., at 45-46, 78 S.Ct. 99. This "no set of facts" language can be read in isolation as saying that any statement revealing the theory of the claim will suffice unless its factual impossibility may be shown from the face of the pleadings; and the Court of Appeals appears to have read *Conley* in some such way when formulating its understanding of the proper pleading standard, see 425 F.3d, at 106, 114 (invoking *Conley's* "no set of facts" language in describing the standard for dismissal).FN7

APPENDIX VII

STATE RIGHT-OF-ASSIGNMENT LAWS PROVIDED BY ACA INTERNATIONAL

Fastfax

ACA INTERNATIONAL
The Association of Credit and Collection Professionals

From ACA's Fastfax Service ***Page 1 of 22***

Last Updated on August 9, 2006 *Document No. 2028*

Now get immediate access to ACA's compliance expertise. Visit E-Compliance at http://www.acainternational.org to search and access Fastfax documents and other compliance information or to e-mail a compliance officer.

* Updated Louisiana & Pennsylvania

* Updated Louisiana & Pennsylvania

State Right-of-Assignment Laws

Many state statutes specifically provide for the "assignment" of debts from the original creditor to a third-party debt collector. The usual intention is to allow the collector to lawfully pursue the claim against the consumer in the name of the debt collector. As well, the collector may be able to consolidate into one legal action, when legally appropriate, several debts owed by a single consumer. This makes a lawsuit more economically feasible than would be the case if individual small debts must each be pursued separately. These agencies can also legally inform consumers that they will be taking legal action if in fact they have the authority and intent to do so.

Although many states' statutes provide for assignment of debts to collectors, a careful analysis of contractual arrangements and actual practices must be undertaken to assure that the statutes are being properly complied with and that the agency is not engaging in the unauthorized practice of law as that is defined in the individual states.

The following document indicates the states in which the right of assignment is allowed, by legislative enactment or court decisions. In states that are labeled "undetermined," the regulatory authorities disagree about whether collection agencies are allowed to sue in their own names.

Alabama

Real Party in Interest:

Every action shall be prosecuted in the name of the real party in interest. An executor, administrator, guardian, bailee, trustee of an express trust, a party with whom or in whose name a contract has been made for the benefit of another, or a party authorized by statute may sue may sue in that person's own name without joining the party for whose benefit the action is brought. No action shall be dismissed on the ground that it is not prosecuted in the name of the real party in interest until a reasonable time has been allowed after objection for ratification of commencement of the action by, or joinder or substitution of, the real party in interest; and such ratification, joinder or substitution shall have the same effect as if the action had been commenced in the name of the real party in interest. Ala. R. Civ. Proc. 17 (WESTLAW through amendments received May 1, 2005).

Alaska

This state currently does not have a specific assignment statute.

A collection agency is not entitled to maintain a suit or action involving the collection of money on behalf of its customers in a court of this state without alleging and proving that it is licensed and has procured a bond, as provided in this chapter. A copy of the collection agency license, certified by the department to be a true and correct copy is prima facie evidence of the licensing and bonding of the collection agency for the term expressed in the copy of the license. Alaska Stat. § 08.24.300 (WESTLAW through all 2004 Sess.).

Arizona

The Arizona Court of Appeals held that collection agencies could bring suit in their own name on assigned claims under the laws regulating collection agencies in Arizona (A.R.S. §§ 32-1001–32-1057). The court determined the collection agency was the "real party in interest" for purposes of Rule 17(a) of the Arizona Rules of Civil Procedure. *See Cruz v. Lusk Collection Agency*, 580 P.2d 1210, 1214 (Ariz. App. 1978).

Every action shall be prosecuted in the name of the real party in interest. An executor, administrator, guardian, bailee, trustee of an express trust, a party with whom or in whose name a contract has been made for the benefit of another, or a party authorized by statute may sue in that person's own name without joining the party for whose benefit the action is brought; and when a statute of the state so provides, an action for the use or benefit of another shall be brought in the name of the State of Arizona. No action shall be dismissed on the ground that it is not prosecuted in the name of the real party in interest until a reasonable time has been allowed after objection for ratification of commencement of the action by, or joinder or substitution of, the real party in interest; and such ratification, joinder or substitution shall have the same effect as if the action had been commenced in the name of the real party in interest. Ariz. Rules Civ. Proc. Rule 17(a) (WESTLAW through amendments received June 15, 2005).

Arkansas

(a) When the assignment is not authorized by statute, the assignor must be a party as plaintiff or defendant.

(b) Where the right of the plaintiff is transferred or assigned during the pendency of the action, it may be continued in his name, or the court may allow the person to whom the transfer or assignment is made to be substituted in the action, proper orders being made as to security for the costs.

Ark Code. § 16-61-112 (WESTLAW through 2003 Extraordinary Sess. and the Nov. 2, 2004, General Election, and including Revisor Changes received through Mar. 2005).

California

State case law holds that a collection agency, when it obtains an absolute assignment of a creditor's claim, is the real party in interest and may sue to collect the debt if it appears by a licensed attorney. *LeDoux v. Credit Research Corp.*, 52 Cal. App. 3d 451, 455 (1975) (quoting *Cohn v. Thompson*, 16 P.2d 364 (Cal. App. Supp. 1932)).

Statutory law states that no claim shall be filed or maintained in small claims court by the assignee of the claim. Cal. Civ. Proc. § 116.420(a) (WESTLAW through Ch. 71 of 2005 Reg. Sess. urgency legislation (except Ch. 48) and Governor's Reorganization Plans Nos. 1 & 2 of 2005).

No debt collector shall collect or attempt to collect a consumer debt by means of any communication by a licensed collection agency to a debtor demanding money unless the claim is actually assigned to the collection agency. Cal. Civ. Code § 1788.13(l) (WESTLAW through Ch. 71 of 2005 Reg. Sess. urgency legislation (except Ch. 48) and Governor's Reorganization Plans Nos. 1 & 2 of 2005).

Colorado

"Creditor" means any person who offers or extends credit creating a debt or to which a debt is owed, but such term does not include any person to the extent such person receives an assignment or transfer of a debt in default solely for the purpose of facilitating collection of such debt for another. Colo. Rev. Stat. Ann. § 12-14-103(5) (WESTLAW through First Reg. Sess. of 65th General Assembly).

Legal actions by debt collectors

(1) Any debt collector or collection agency who brings any legal action on a debt against any consumer shall:

(a) In the case of an action to enforce an interest in real property securing the consumer's obligation, bring such action only in a judicial district or similar legal entity in which such real property is located; or

(b) In the case of an action not described in paragraph (a) of this subsection (1), bring such action only in the judicial district or similar legal entity in which:

(I) Such consumer signed the contract sued upon;

(II) Such consumer resides at the commencement of the action; or

(III) Such action may be brought pursuant to article 13 or 13.5 of title 26, C.R.S., section 14-14-104, C.R.S., or article 4 or 6 of title 19, C.R.S., if the action is by a private collection agency acting on behalf of a delegate child support enforcement unit. Colo. Rev. Stat. Ann. § 12-14-111 (WESTLAW through Chapter 190 and 261 of the First Reg. Sess. of the Sixty-Firth Gen. Assembly).
Editor's note: This section precludes suits by unlicensed agencies. *See Commercial Serv. of Perry, Inc. v. Fitzgerald*, 856 P.2d 58, 62 (Colo. Ct. App. 1993).

State statute and state case law allows licensed collection agencies to take accounts from creditors on assignment and, represented by an attorney, to bring legal action on those accounts in their own name. *Thibodeaux v. Creditors Services, Inc.*, 551 P.2d 714 (Colo. 1976).

A licensee may solicit claims for collection and take assignments and pursue the collection thereof subject to the provisions of law concerning the unauthorized practice of law. Colo. Rev. Stat. Ann. § 12-14-128(3) (WESTLAW through Ch. 190 and Ch. 261 of First Reg. Sess. of the 65th Gen. Assembly (2005)).

Connecticut

No consumer collection agency shall: furnish legal advice or perform legal services or represent that it is competent to do so, or institute judicial proceedings on behalf of others; communicate with consumer debtors or property tax debtors in the name of an attorney or upon the stationery of an attorney, or prepare any forms or instruments which only attorneys are authorized to prepare; purchase or receive assignments of claims for the purpose of collection or institute suit thereon in any court; assume authority on behalf of a creditor to employ or terminate the services of an attorney unless such creditor has authorized such agency in writing to act as such creditor's agent in the selection of an attorney to collect the creditor's accounts. Conn. Gen. Stat. Ann. §§ 36a-805(a)(1)–(4) (WESTLAW through 2005 Jan. Reg. Sess. legislation approved by the Gov. on or before 6-24-05).

In Small Claims Court, the word "representative" shall not mean a consumer collection agency as defined in chapter 669 of the General Statutes or an individual acting pursuant to a power of attorney. Conn. R. Super. Ct. Civ. § 24-6(a) (WESTLAW current with amendments received through 3-15-2005).

Delaware

A person to whom a contract, express or implied, has been transferred or assigned, either in accordance with a statute or with the common law, may sue thereon in his or her own name. Del. Code Ann. tit. 10, § 3902 (WESTLAW through First Reg. Sess. of the 143rd Gen. Assembly).

Ed. note: Collectors should exercise caution when attempting take assignment of debts in Sussex County. Sussex County judges have ruled that collectors are not allowed to combine separate hospital bills in one lawsuit. Please consult your attorney for advice on the matter.

District of Columbia

An obligee named in a bond or obligation under seal for the payment of money may assign it in writing and the assignee may maintain an action thereon in his own name. D.C. Code Ann. § 28-2302 (WESTLAW through May 31, 2005).

An owner of a non-negotiable written agreement for the payment of money, including a nonnegotiable bill of exchange and a promissory note, or for the delivery of personal property, an open account, debt, and demand of a liquidated character, except a claim against the United States or the salary of a public officer, may assign it in writing, and the assignee may maintain an action thereon in his own name. D.C. Code Ann. § 28-2303 (WESTLAW through May 31, 2005).

No debt collector shall take or accept for assignment any of the following: (1) an assignment of any claim for attorney's fees which have not been lawfully provided for in the writing evidencing the obligation; or (2) an assignment for collection of any claim upon which suit has been filed or judgment obtained, without the debt collector first making a reasonable effort to contact the attorney representing the consumer. D.C. Code Ann. § 28-3814(i) (WESTLAW through May 31, 2005).

See also J.H. Marshall & Assoc., Inc. v. Burleson, 313 A.2d 587 (D.C. 1973)

Florida

This part does not prohibit the assignment, by a creditor, of the right to bill and collect a consumer debt. However, the assignee must give the debtor written notice of such assignment within 30 days after the assignment. The assignee is a real party in interest and may bring an action in a court of competent jurisdiction to collect a debt that has been assigned to such assignee and is in default. Fla. Stat. Ann. § 559.715 (WESTLAW through Chapters in effect from the 2005 First Reg. Sess. of the 19th Legislature.).

Georgia

No debt collector shall solicit assignments of claims for the purpose of suit or at the instigation of an attorney. Nor shall any debt collector institute judicial proceedings on behalf of other persons except on an assigned claim. Ga. Comp. R. & Regs. r. 120-1-14-.19(b), (c) (WESTLAW through June 30, 2005).

Guam

The debtor is authorized to pay the original lender until he receives notification of transfer of rights to payment pursuant to a consumer loan and that payment is to be made to the transferee of the rights. A notification which does not reasonably identify the rights transferred is ineffective. If requested by the debtor, the transferee must seasonably furnish reasonable proof that the transfer has been made and unless he does so the debtor may pay the original lender. 14 Guam Code Ann. § 3406 (WESTLAW through P.L. 28-037 (2005)).

This Article (§ 3406) does not apply to loans in which the principal is Twenty-Five Thousand Dollars ($25,000.00) or more. 14 Guam Code Ann. § 3401 (WESTLAW through P.L. 28-037 (2005)).

(1) With respect to a consumer credit sale or lease, other than a sale or lease primarily for an agricultural purpose, an agreement by the buyer or lessee not to assert against a transferee a claim or defense arising out of the sale or lease is enforceable only by a transferee not related to the seller or lessor who acquires the buyer's or lessee's contract in good faith and for value, who gives the buyer or lessee notice of the transfer as provided in this section and who, within six months after the mailing of the notice of transfer, receives no written notice of the facts giving rise to the buyer's or lessee's claim or defense. The notice of transfer shall be in writing and addressed to the buyer or lessee at his address as stated in the contract, identify the contract, describe the goods or services, state the name and address of the transferee, the amount payable by the buyer or lessee and the number, amounts and due dates of the installments, and contain a conspicuous notice to the buyer or lessee that he has six months within which to notify the transferee in writing of any complaints, claims or defenses he may have against the seller or lessor and that if written notification of the complaints, claims or defenses is not given within the six-month period, the transferee will have the right to enforce the contract free of any claims or defenses the buyer or lessee may have against the seller or lessor.

(2) A transferee does not acquire a buyer's or lessee's contract in good faith within the meaning of subsection (1) if the transferee has knowledge or, from his course of dealing with the seller or lessor or his records, notice of substantial complaints by other buyers or lessees of the seller's or lessor's failure or refusal to perform his contracts with them and of the seller's or lessor's failure to remedy his defaults within a reasonable time after the transferee notifies him of the complaints. 14 Guam Code Ann. § 2404 (WESTLAW through P.L. 23-037 (2005)).

Article 2404 does not apply: (a) to sales in which the amount financed is Twenty-Five Thousand Dollars ($25,000.00) or more or to leases in which the amount payable under the lease is Twenty-Five Thousand Dollars ($25,000.00) or more. 14 Guam Code Ann. § 2401 (WESTLAW through P.L. 28-037 (2005)).

Small Claims Court

No claim shall be filed or presented in small claims court by the assignee of such claim, unless assignee is an attorney admitted to practice law in Guam and the assignor is not a resident of Guam. 7 Guam Civ. P. Code § App. A, Rule 92 (WEST-LAW through P.L. 28-037 (2005)).

Hawaii

"Collection agency" includes: (3) Any person who regularly accepts the assignment of claims or money due on accounts or other forms of indebtedness and brings suit upon the assigned claims or money due on accounts or other forms of indebtedness in the person's own name; provided that any suits shall be initiated and prosecuted by an attorney who shall have been appointed by the assignee. Haw. Rev. Stat. Ann. § 443B-1(3) (WESTLAW through 2004 Reg. Sess.).

Idaho

State law allows a creditor the assignment of rights to payment on a debt to a collection agency in any regulated consumer credit transaction. The creditor must provide the debtor with a written notice that the assignment has been made. The agency that is assigned an account must also furnish reasonable proof the assignment has been made. A debtor may pay the original creditor unless that proof is provided to the debtor. *See Idaho Code § 28-43-202* (WESTLAW through 2005 Legislative Sess.).

Champerty

Every attorney, public officer or licensed collector, who, either directly or indirectly, buys or is interested in buying any evidence of debt or thing in action, with intent to bring suit thereon, is guilty of a misdemeanor. Idaho Code § 18-1003 (Lexis, WESTLAW through 2005 Legislative Sess.). However, the taking of an interest in an obligation for the purpose of collecting on the debt is not a violation of this section of the law. *See Garren v. Saccomanno*, 385 P.2d 396 (1963); *Interstate Credit League v. Widdison*, 297 P. 1106 (1931); *Merchants Protective Association v. Jacobsen*, 127 P. 315 (1912).

Illinois

An account may be assigned to a collection agency for collection with title passing to the collection agency to enable collection of the account in the agency's name as assignee for the creditor provided:

(1) The assignment is manifested by a written agreement, separate from and in addition to any document intended for the purpose of listing a debt with a collection agency. The document manifesting the assignment shall specifically state and include:

   a. the effective date of the assignment; and

   b. the consideration for the assignment.

(2) The consideration for the assignment may be paid or given either before or after the effective date of the assignment. The consideration may be contingent upon the settlement or outcome of litigation and if the claim being assigned has been listed with the collection agency as an account for collection, the consideration for assignment may be the same as the fee for collection.

(3) All assignments shall be voluntary and properly executed and acknowledged by the corporate authority or individual transferring title to the collection agency before any action can be taken in the name of the collection agency.

(4) No assignment shall be required by any agreement to list a debt with a collection agency as an account for collection.

(5) No litigation shall commence in the name of the licensee as plaintiff unless:

a. there is an assignment of the account that satisfies the requirements of this Section and

b. the licensee is represented by a licensed attorney at law.

(6) If a collection agency takes assignments of accounts from 2 or more creditors against the same debtor and commences litigation against that debtor in a single action, in the name of the collection agency, then

a. the complaint must be stated in separate counts for each assignment and

b. the debtor has an absolute right to have any count severed from the rest of the action. 225 Ill. Comp. Stat. 425/8b (West, WESTLAW through P.A. 94-89 of the 2005 Reg. Sess.).

Indiana

(a) A person who is licensed under this chapter may, for the purpose of acting as an agent for collection:

(1) receive another person's accounts, bills, or other evidence of indebtedness;

(2) be the assignee of another person's accounts, bills, or other evidence of indebtedness; and

(3) at the direction of an assignor or assignors:

(A) employ an attorney to represent an assignee in the filing of an action to collect a debt in the county of preferred venue for the action as set forth in Rule 75 of the Indiana Rules of Trial; and

(B) advance court costs for the filing of an action to collect a debt.

(b) For purposes of filing one (1) action, an assignee may consolidate:

(1) assigned claims against an individual debtor; or

(2) assigned claims against joint debtors.

(c) An action in which claims are consolidated under subsection (b) must be filed in the county of preferred venue as to all alleged debtors for the action as set forth in Rule 75 of the Indiana Rules of Trial Procedure.

(d) If an assignee files an action in a county other than the county of preferred venue as to all alleged debtors, the court upon motion shall order:

(1) the action transferred to the county of preferred venue; and

(2) the assignee to reimburse the person or persons against whom the action is filed for attorney's fees necessitated for correction of the preferred venue. Ind. Code Ann. § 25-11-1-13 (WESTLAW through 2005 Public Laws approved and effective through May 3, 2005).

Iowa

Bonds, due bills, and all instruments used to establish a promise by a maker to pay another are assignable to a collection agency. The assignee collection agency has the right to bring action in its own name on the assignments. The assignments are subject to any defense or counterclaim which the maker or debtor had against an assignor of the instrument before notice of the assignment. Iowa Code Ann. § 539.1 (WESTLAW through Acts of 2005 First Reg. Sess.).

In 2001, the Iowa Supreme Court interpreted "assignment" to include only a true assignment, defined as "a transfer or making over to another the whole of any property, real or personal, in possession or in action, or of any estate or right therein." An agreement between a collection agency and a creditor that purported to be an assignment, in which the creditor retained an interest in the underlying debt and received the proceeds of any recovery less a fixed sum for the collection agency, was not a true assignment. Thus, the collection agency engaged in the unauthorized practice of law when it instituted and maintained legal action to recover the debt. *Iowa Sup. Ct. Comm'n on Unauthorized Practice of Law v. A-1 Assoc.*, 623 N.W.2d 803, 808 (Iowa 2001).

Kansas

If any person, firm or corporation sells or assigns an account to any person or collecting agency, that person, firm or corporation or their assignees shall not have or be entitled to the benefits of wage garnishment. The provision of this subsection shall not apply to the following: . . . . Kan. Stat. Ann. § 60-2310(d) (WESTLAW through 2004 Reg. Sess.). (*Editor's Note:* This statute applies to garnishment of assigned accounts).

(a) Every action shall be prosecuted in the name of the real party in interest; but an executor, administrator, guardian, conservator, trustee of an express trust, receiver, a party with whom or in whose name a contract has been made for the benefit of another, or a party authorized by statute may sue in the party's own name without joining the party for whose benefit the action is brought. When a statute so provides, an action for the use or benefit of another shall be brought in the name of the state of Kansas. No action shall be dismissed on the ground that it is not prosecuted in the name of the real party in interest until a reasonable time has been allowed after objection for ratification of commencement of the action by, or joinder or substitution of, the real party in interest; and such ratification, joinder or substitution shall have the same effect as if the action had been commenced in the name of the real party in interest.

(b) Whenever a cause of action has accrued under or by virtue of the laws of any other state or territory, such cause of action may be sued upon in any of the courts of this state by the person or persons who are authorized to bring and maintain an action thereon in the state or territory where the same arose. When the law of the state or territory where a cause of action for death arose authorizes said action to be prosecuted by an administrator or executor, then said action may also be maintained in any of the courts of this state by an administrator or executor appointed under the laws of the state of Kansas.

(c) Whenever a minor or incapacitated person has a representative, such as a general guardian, committee, conservator, or other like fiduciary, the representative may sue or defend on behalf of the minor or incapacitated person. If a minor or incapacitated person does not have a duly appointed representative the minor or incapacitated person may sue by the minor or

> incapacitated person's next friend or by a guardian ad litem. The court shall appoint a guardian ad litem for a minor or incapacitated person not otherwise represented in an action or shall make such other order as it deems proper for the protection of the minor or incapacitated person.

Kan. Stat. Ann. § 60-217 (WESTLAW through 2004 Reg. Sess.).

Kentucky

Every action shall be prosecuted in the name of the real party in interest, but a personal representative, guardian, curator, committee of a person of unsound mind, trustee of an express trust, a person with whom or in whose name a contract is made for the benefit of another, a county, municipal corporation, public board or other such body, a receiver appointed by a court, the assignee or trustee of a bankrupt, an assignee for the benefit of creditors, or a person expressly authorized by statute to do so, may bring an action without joining the party or parties for whose benefit it is prosecuted. Nothing herein, however, shall abrogate or take away an individual's right to sue. Ky. R. Civ. P. § 17.01 (West, WESTLAW through 5/15/05).

In 1939, the Kentucky Court of Appeals (then the highest state court) cited *Cohn v. Thompson*, 16 P.2d 364 (Cal. App. Dep't Super. Ct. 1932) with approval, summarizing it as follows: "Collection agent who was not an attorney was held not to be engaged in the 'practice of law' where a claim was assigned to him under an agreement that, if he could not collect the claim without suit, he was to hire an attorney at his expense and sue in his own name, and, if the collection was made, he was to remit the balance to the assignor, after deducting costs and a percentage for his services." *Mutual Bankers Corp. v. Covington Bros. and Co.*, 125 S.W.2d 202, 205 (Ky. 1939).

Small Claims Court—Actions Prohibited

(1) The appearance of an attorney at law on behalf of any party is permitted but not required.

(2) No party may file an assigned claim or a class action in the division.

(3) No person, firm, partnership, association, or corporation engaged, either primarily or secondarily, in the business of lending money at interest, nor any collection agency or collection agent, may bring an action in the division in furtherance of their business.

(4) Notwithstanding any other provision of this section, an executor or administrator of a decedent's estate, a guardian, a trustee or a conservator may be a party in the division.

Ky. Rev. Stat. Ann. § 24A.240 (WESTLAW through End of 2004 First Extraordinary Sess.).

Louisiana

C. In any suit brought by a collection agency or debt collector to collect a debt acquired from a client or customer via assignment, an agreement in writing by the such collector to expend time, effort, money, or other resources in pursuit of such debt, and to pay the credit grantor a net percentage of the amount collected on the debt shall be deemed a valid and enforceable assignment pursuant to this Section, and all other applicable laws of Louisiana.

D. When such collector attempts the collection of a debt owed a credit grantor, the representation of the credit grantor by such collector shall in all instances be deemed as an assignment and authorization for the purpose of allowing such collector to bring legal action to collect the debt. When such legal action is brought through an attorney licensed to practice law by the Supreme Court of Louisiana it shall not be a violation of any state law, rule, or regulation including but not limited to R.S. 37:212.

E. In any suit brought by a collection agency or debt collection to collect the debt of a client or customer, the formal assignment of the debt to such collector shall be presumed valid if a copy of the assignment is filed in court with the petition. If the defendant fails to object to the validity of the assignment prior to the filing of an answer, then the assignment shall be conclusively presumed valid.

F. Subsections C and D of this Section shall apply in all instances whether or not the debt is assigned for valuable consideration; whether or not the services performed by the attorney were for the collector alone; whether or not the collector hired the attorney; and whether or not the collector's fees are contingent upon the amount collected by the attorney. La. Rev. Stat. Ann. § 9:3534.1 (West, WESTLAW through all 2006 First Extraordinary and Regular Session Acts).

A purported assignment of a debt from a creditor to a collection agency, which did not require the collection agency to make any payment unless it was successful in its efforts to collect the debt, in which case the collection agency would pay 50% of any amount recovered, did not convey any ownership interest of the creditor's right to the debt to the collection agency such as might permit the collection agency to sue in its own right. The plain language of the agreement did not manifest an intent to transfer ownership of the debt from the creditor to the collection agency. In the agreement, the collection agency agreed to hold the creditor harmless from any liability for any violations of fair collection practices. If the creditor had sold its rights in the debt to the collection agency, the creditor would have no liability for any fault or negligence in the collection agency's efforts to collect. The collection agency also agreed to pay all costs in connection with the collection of the debt. If the collection agency had a valid assignment of the debt, logically it would be the collection agency's responsibility to pay for the collection of the debt. This purported assignment did not transfer ownership of the debt from the creditor to the collection agency. The collection agency's act of filing suit constituted the practice of law. Since the collection agency was not licensed to practice law in Louisiana, the filing of the suit by the collection agency to enforce the rights of the creditor constituted the unauthorized practice of law. As such, the contract between the creditor and the collection agency violated Revised Statute section 37:213 and was absolutely null and without effect. *Alco Collections, Inc. v. Poirier*, 680 So. 2d 735 (La. Ct. App. 1996).

Maine

Undetermined under state statutes or state case law.

Maryland

If a surety in any bond or other obligation for the payment of money or a promissory note, or the endorser of a protested draft, pays or tenders the money due on it in full, he is entitled to an assignment of it and, by virtue of the assignment, may maintain an action in his name against the principal debtor.

Md. Code Ann., Com. Law § 15-401 (WESTLAW through ch. 17 of the 2005 Reg. Sess.).

(a) Subject to the provisions of subsection (d) of this section, the assignee of a bond or other obligation under seal which was assigned to the assignor's signature and seal, may maintain an action in his name against the obligor named in the bond or other obligation.

(b) Except as provided in subsection (c) of this section, if the assignee cannot recover the debt from the obligor because the obligor is unable to pay or cannot be found, or for any other reason the assignee may maintain an action against the oblige, unless the assignee is a surety in the bond or other obligation.

(c) If because of negligence or default of the assignee, he cannot recover the debt from the obligor, the assignee may not maintain an action against the obligee.

(d) An action may not be maintained by the assignee against the obligor unless the obligee certifies before a notary public, in writing on the bond or other obligation, that at the time of the assignment the obligor still owed the amount for which the action is filed.

Md. Code Ann., Com Law § 15-402 (WESTLAW through ch. 17 of the 2005 Reg. Sess.).

Massachusetts

A collection agency shall not institute judicial proceedings on behalf of others. Mass. Regs. Code tit. 209, § 18.17(12)(a) (WESTLAW through July 29, 2005).

Michigan

"Creditor" or "principal" means a person who offers or extends credit creating a debt or a person to whom a debt is owed or due or asserted to be owed or due. **Creditor or principal shall not include a person who receives an assignment or transfer of a debt solely for the purpose of facilitating collection of the debt for the assignor or transferor.** In those instances, the assignor or transferor of the debt shall continue to be considered the creditor or the principal for purposes of this article. Mich. Comp. Laws Ann.§ 339.901(e) (WESTLAW through P.A. 2005, No. 1-70) (emphasis added).

A licensee shall not commit any of the following acts: Soliciting, purchasing, or receiving an assignment of a claim for the sole purpose of instituting an action on the claim in court. Mich. Comp. Laws Ann. § 339.915a(f) (WESTLAW through P.A. 2005, No. 1-70).

Engaging in the business of representing the interests of assignors and controlling the proceedings to be taken in suits on assigned claims in which assignors retain an interest is engaging in the practice of law. When this is done by one not licensed as an attorney, it constitutes the unauthorized practice of law whether done by him in person or through his agent, regardless of whether the later be a layman or a licensed attorney. *Bar County Bar Ass'n v. Fin. Sys. of Bay City*, 76 N.W.2d 23, 29 (Mich. 1956).

Minnesota

(a) Assignee's rights subject to terms, claims, and defenses; exceptions. Unless an account debtor has made an enforceable agreement not to assert defenses or claims, and subject to subsections (b) through (e), the rights of an assignee are subject to:

(1) all terms of the agreement between the account debtor and the assignor and any defense or claim in recoupment arising from the transaction that gave rise to the contract; and

(2) any other defense or claim of the account debtor against the assignor which accrues before the account debtor receives a notification of the assignment authenticated by the assignor or the assignee.

(b) Account debtor's claim reduces the amount owed to assignee. Subject to subsection (c) and otherwise provided in subsection (d), the claim of an account debtor against an assignor may be asserted against an assignee under subsection (a) only to reduce the amount the account debtor owes.

(c) Rule for individual under other law. This section is subject to law other than this article which establishes a different rule for an account debtor who is an individual and who incurred the obligation primarily for personal, family, or household purposes.

(d) Omission of required statement in consumer transaction. In a consumer transaction, if a record evidences the account debtor's obligation, law other than this article requires that the record include a statement to the effect that the account debtor's recovery against an assignee with respect to claims and defenses against the assignor may not exceed amounts paid by the account debtor under the record, and the record does not include such a statement, the extent to which a claim of an account debtor against the assignor may be asserted against an assignee is determined as if the record included such a statement.

(e) In applicability to health-care-insurance receivable. This section does not apply to an assignment of a health-care-insurance receivable.

Minn. Stat. § 336.9-404 (WESTLAW through 2005 1st Spec. Sess.).

Mississippi

Collectors may take assignment and bring action in their own name. The assignment must be made in writing. If an action has been started by the original party, the court may allow the person to whom the assignment has been made to be substituted for the original plaintiff. Miss. Code Ann. § 11-7-3 (WESTLAW through End of 2005 Reg. and First Extraordinary Sess.).

Missouri

Collection agencies may take assignment of claims in their own name as real parties in interest for the purpose of billing and collection and bringing suit in their own and the claimant's names thereon, provided that no suit authorized by this section may be instituted on behalf of a collection agency in any court unless the collection agency appears by a duly authorized and licensed attorney at law. Upon good cause being shown, a court may sever any actions brought under this section. Mo. Ann. Stat. § 425.300 (West, WESTLAW through the 93rd General Assembly (2005)).

Montana

Based on state case law, collection agencies may bring action on accounts in their own name. "It is well settled that an assignment for collection, without any consideration being paid by the assignee, vests the legal title in the assignee, which is sufficient to enable him to recover, although the assignor retains an equitable interest in the thing assigned." *Rae v. Cameron*, 114 P.2d 1060, 1068 (Mont. 1941).

Nebraska

"It is now settled . . . that if the assignment, whether written or verbal, of anything in action is absolute in its terms, so that by virtue thereof the entire apparent legal title vests in the assignee, any contemporaneous collateral agreement by virtue of which he is to receive a part only of the proceeds, 'and is to account to the assignor or other person for the residue, or even is to thus account for the whole proceeds, or by virtue of which the absolute transfer is made conditional upon the fact of recovery, or by which his title is in any other similar manner partial or conditional,' does not render him any the less the real party in interest; he is entitled to sue in his own name, whatever collateral arrangements have been made between him and the assignor respecting the proceeds. The debtor is completely protected by the assignment, and cannot be exposed to a second action brought by any of the parties, either the assignor or other, to whom the assignee is bound to account." *Archer v. Musick*, 25 N.W.2d 908, 913 (Neb. 1947).

Nothing in the Collection Agency Act shall be construed to authorize or permit the holder of a license or the holder of a solicitor's certificate, as provided for in the act, to engage in the practice of law. Neb Rev. Stat. Ann. § 45-622 (WESTLAW through Second Reg. Sess. of the 98th Legislature (2004)).

Nevada

Any creditor may, without the consent of the debtor, transfer all or any part of his rights against the debtor to any third party. The assignee is entitled by virtue of an assignment or transfer to sue in his own name as a real party in interest. This section does not preclude a contract between the parties prohibiting the assignment or transfer of the creditor's rights against the debtor to a third party. Nev. Rev. Stat. § 100.075 (WESTLAW through the 2004 21st Special Sess. of the 72nd Legislature).

A collection agency, or its managers, agents, or employees shall not, assign or transfer any claim or account upon termination or abandonment of its collection business unless prior written consent by the customer is given for the assignment or transfer. The written consent must contain an agreement with the customer as to all terms and conditions of the assignment or transfer, including the name and address of the intended assignee. Prior written consent of the Commissioner must also be obtained for any bulk assignment or transfer of claims or accounts, and any assignment or transfer may be regulated and made subject to such limitations or conditions as the Commissioner by regulation may reasonably prescribe. Nev. Rev. Stat. § 649.375(3) (WESTLAW through the 2004 21st Special Sess. of the 72nd Legislature).

New Hampshire

Collection agencies may not take assignment and bring an action in their own name.

New Jersey

All contracts for the sale and conveyance of real estate, all judgments and decrees recovered in any of the courts of this state or of the United States or in any of the courts of any other state of the United States and all choses in action arising on contract shall be assignable, and the assignee may sue thereon in his own name. In such an action, the person sued shall be allowed, not only all set-offs, discounts and defenses he has against the assignee, but also all set-offs, discounts and defenses he had against the assignor before notice of such assignment was given to him. The assignment of a sealed instrument by writing not under seal shall be as valid as if under seal.

The assignee for a valuable consideration of any chose in action may, although the assignor is dead, sue for and recover the same in his own name. The person sued in any such action shall be allowed not only all set-offs, discounts and defenses he has against the assignee, but also all set-offs, discounts and defenses he had against the assignor or his representatives before notice of such assignment was given to him. Security interests in commercial tort claims may be created, attached, perfected and enforced in accordance with Chapter 9 of Title 12A of the New Jersey Statutes (12A:9-101 et seq.). N.J. Stat. Ann. § 2A:25-1 (WESTLAW through L.2005, c. 1-104).

New Mexico

Collection agencies may take assignment of claims in their own name as real parties in interest for the purpose of billing, collection and bringing suit in their own name. No suit may be brought by a collection agency in any court unless the agency is represented by a duly authorized and licensed attorney. In any action, the court may authorize payment of reasonable attorney fees and costs to the prevailing party. N.M. Stat. Ann. § 61-18A-26 (WESTLAW through End of First Reg. Sess. of the 47th Legislature (2005)).

The New Mexico Rules of Court allow collection agencies to take assignment of claims in their own names and bring suit. When an agency brings an action, which can be done only in either magistrate or metropolitan court, the agency must be represented by a licensed attorney. N.M. Rules of Court, Rule 1-107(D), Rule 2-107(D) and Rule 3-107(D) (WESTLAW through May 15, 2002).

New York

Purchase of claims by corporations or collection agencies:

No person or co-partnership, engaged directly or indirectly in the business of collection and adjustment of claims, and no corporation or association, directly or indirectly, itself or by or through its officers, agents or employees, shall solicit, buy or take an assignment of, or be in any manner interested in buying or taking an assignment of a bond, promissory note, bill of exchange, book debt, or other thing in action, or any claim or demand, with the intent and for the purpose of bringing an action or proceeding thereon; provided however, that bills receivable, notes receivable, bills of exchange, judgments or other things in action may be solicited, bought, or assignment thereof taken, from any executor, administrator, assignee for the benefit of creditors, trustee or receiver in bankruptcy, or any other person or persons in charge of the administration, settlement or compromise of any estate, through court actions, proceedings or otherwise. Nothing herein contained shall affect any assignment heretofore or hereafter taken by any moneyed corporation authorized to do business in the state of New York or its nominee pursuant to a subrogation agreement or a salvage operation, or by any corporation organized for religious, benevolent or charitable purposes.

Any corporation or association violating the provisions of this section shall be liable to a fine of not more than five thousand dollars; any person or co-partnership, violating the provisions of this section, and any officer, trustee, director, agent or employee of any person, co-partnership, corporation or association violating this section who, directly or indirectly, engages or assists in such violation, is guilty of a misdemeanor. N.Y. Judiciary Law § 489 (WESTLAW current through L. 2005).

North Carolina

Neither a collection agency nor any representative thereof who is not a duly licensed attorney shall engage in the practice of law. As used in this section, "practice of law" includes the preparation of warrants or subpoenas. A collection agency's representative is prohibited from appearing in court on behalf of a creditor except as required by court order or subpoena, and except to submit and explain claims in bankruptcy court. N.C. Gen Stat. § 58-70-120 (WESTLAW through S.L. 2005-100 of the 2005 Reg. Sess.).

Unauthorized Practice of Law
State law makes it unlawful for any person other than an attorney duly licensed to practice law, or any corporation, firm, or association other than a law firm, to appear for another:

- in any bankruptcy or insolvency proceeding;
- in any action or proceeding for or growing out of the appointment of a receiver;
- in any matter involving an assignment for the benefit of creditors; or
- to present or vote any claim of another, whether the claim is under assignment or transfer of the claim.

N.C. Gen. Stat. § 84-9 (WESTLAW through S.L. 2005-100 of the 2005 Reg. Sess.).

North Dakota
A right arising out of an obligation is the property of the person to whom it is due and may be transferred as such. N.D. Cent. Code § 9-11-01 (WESTLAW through 2003 Gen. and Spec. Sess.).

No debt collector may:

1. Perform legal services, furnish legal advice, or falsely represent, directly or by implication, that the debt collector is an attorney.
2. Solicit assignments of claims for the purpose of suit or at the instigation of an attorney.
3. Institute judicial proceedings on behalf of other persons except on an assigned claim.
4. Communicate with debtors in the name of an attorney or upon stationery or other written matter bearing an attorney's name.
5. Make any demand for or payment of money constituting a share of compensation for services performed or to be performed by an attorney in collecting a claim . . .

N.D. Admin. Code §§ 13-04-02-04(1)–(5) (WESTLAW through Supplement 313 (July 1, 2005)).

Ohio
(A) Two or more creditors of a debtor or co-debtors may join their respective claims together for the purpose of commencing litigation against the debtor or co-debtors.

(B) If a debtor or co-debtor raises a good faith dispute concerning any accounts, bills, or other evidences of indebtedness that have been joined together for litigation pursuant to this section, the court shall separate the disputed account, bill, or other evidence of indebtedness from the action and hear the disputed account, bill, or other evidence of indebtedness on its own merits in a separate action. The court shall charge the filing fee of the separate action to the losing party. Ohio Rev. Code Ann. § 1319.11 (WESTLAW through 2005 File 27 of the 126th GA (2005-2006), apv. by 6-29-05).

(A)(1) As used in this section, "collection agency" means any person who, for compensation, contingent or otherwise, or for other valuable consideration, offers services to collect an alleged debt asserted to be owed to another.

(B) A collection agency with a place of business in this state may take assignment of another person's accounts, bills, or other evidences of indebtedness in its own name for the purpose of billing, collecting, or filing suit in its own name as the real party in interest.

(C) No collection agency shall commence litigation for the collection of an assigned account, bill, or other evidence of indebtedness unless it has taken the assignment in accordance with all of the following requirements:

(1) The assignment was voluntary, properly executed, and acknowledged by the person transferring title to the collection agency.

(2) The collection agency did not require the assignment as a condition to listing the account, bill, or other evidence of indebtedness with the collection agency for collection.

(3) The assignment was manifested by a written agreement separate from and in addition to any document intended for the purpose of listing the account, bill, or other evidence of indebtedness with the collection agency. The written agreement shall state the effective date of the assignment and the consideration paid or given, if any, for the assignment and shall expressly authorize the collection agency to refer the assigned account, bill, or other evidence of indebtedness to an attorney admitted to the practice of law in this state for the commencement of litigation. The written agreement also shall disclose that the collection agency may consolidate, for purposes of filing an action, the assigned account, bill, or other evidence of indebtedness with those of other creditors against an individual debtor or co-debtors.

(4) Upon the effective date of the assignment to the collection agency, the creditor's account maintained by the collection agency in connection with the assigned account, bill, or other evidence of indebtedness was canceled.

(D) A collection agency shall commence litigation for the collection of an assigned account, bill, or other evidence of indebtedness in a court of competent jurisdiction located in the county in which the debtor resides, or in the case of co-debtors, a county in which at least one of the co-debtors resides.

(E) No collection agency shall commence any litigation authorized by this section unless the agency appears by an attorney admitted to the practice of law in this state. . . .

(G) Nothing in this section relieves a collection agency from complying with the "Fair Debt Collection Practices Act," 91 Stat. 874 (1977), 15 U.S.C. 1692, as amended, or deprives any debtor of the right to assert defenses as provided in section 1317.031 of the Revised Code and 16 C.F.R. 433, as amended.

(H) For purposes of filing an action, a collection agency that has taken an assignment or assignments pursuant to this section may consolidate the assigned accounts, bills, or other evidences of indebtedness of one or more creditors against an individual debtor or co-debtors. Each separate assigned account, bill, or evidence of indebtedness must be separately identified and pled in any consolidated action authorized by this section. If a debtor or co-debtor raises a good faith dispute concerning any account, bill, or other evidence of indebtedness, the court shall separate each disputed account, bill, or other evidence of indebtedness from the action and hear the disputed account, bill, or other evidence of indebtedness on its own merits in a separate action. The court shall charge the filing fee of the separate action to the losing party. Ohio Rev. Code Ann. § 1319.12 (WESTLAW through 2005 File 27 of the 126th GA (2005-2006), apv. by 6-29-05).

Oklahoma

No action may be brought under the small claims procedure by any collection agency, collection agent, or assignee of a claim, except that an action may be brought against an insurer or third-party administrator by a health care provider as that term is defined in Section 6552 of Title 36 of the Oklahoma Statutes, who is an assignee of benefits available under an accident and health insurance policy, trust, plan or contract. Okla. Stat. Tit. 12, § 1751 (WESTLAW through 2005 First Reg. Sess.).

Debt purchasers are prohibited from bringing an action in small claims court to collect on purchased contracts, notes or accounts. 18 Okla. Op. Att'y Gen. No. 86-55, 1986 WL 235103 (Okl. A.G. Oct. 6, 1986).

Oregon

(1) A registered collection agency has a property right in any claim or account assigned to the agency in writing for collection. Except as may be otherwise provided in writing between the assignor of the claim or account and the registered collection agency, the registered collection agency as assignee of the claim or account, in its own name, may:

   (a) Collect the claim or account;

   (b) Compromise or accept a settlement of an account;

   (c) Bring and maintain a civil suit or action to recover the amount owing from the claim or account; and

   (d) With prior written approval of the assignor, transfer or forward the claim or account to another collection agency for collection.

(2) Except as may be otherwise provided in writing between the assignor of the claim or account and the registered collection agency, the assignor may withdraw the claim or account from the agency at any time without condition or charge.

(3) Notwithstanding ORS 9.160 and 9.320, in any action in the small claims department of a circuit court or justice court a registered collection agency may appear as a party without appearance by attorney for the purpose of recovering the amount owing on a claim or account assigned to the agency

in writing for collection. The provisions of this subsection apply to any supplementary proceeding in aid of execution after entry of a judgment in the small claims department.

(4) No collection agency is entitled to bring or maintain any civil suit or action involving the collection of a claim or account on behalf of its customers in any courts of this state without alleging and proving that it is duly registered under Oregon Revised Statutes sections 697.015 and 697.031. A registration certificate or a certification of registration by the Director of the Department of Consumer and Business Services for any designated time period shall be received by the court as prima facie evidence of the collection agency's registration for the time period designated.

Or. Rev. Stat. § 697.045 (WESTLAW through End of 2003 Reg. Sess.).

Any bona fide assignment of a chose in action by way of sale or pledge made in writing for a good, valuable and adequate consideration is deemed completed at the time the writing is executed by the assignor and takes effect at the time of execution according to the terms of the writing without the giving of notice to the debtor therein mentioned unless such notice is required by statute; but if notice is not given to a debtor, and such debtor, without knowledge of the assignment pays or discharges in whole or in part the obligation of the debtor to the assignor or to any subsequent assignee of the chose in action who has given notice, such payment constitutes a discharge of the debtor to the extent thereof without prejudice to any right or remedy between the several assignees. Or. Rev. Stat. § 80.010 (WESTLAW through End of 2003 Reg. Sess.).

In the case of an assignment of a thing in action, an action or suit by the assignee is without prejudice to any setoff or other defense existing at the time of, or before notice of the assignment; but this section does not apply to a negotiable instrument transferred in good faith and upon good consideration before due. Or. Rev. Stat. § 80.020 (WESTLAW through End of 2003 Reg. Sess.).

Pennsylvania

(a) Assignments of claims—It is lawful for a collection agency, for the purpose of collecting or enforcing the payment thereof, to take an assignment of any such claim from a creditor, if all of the following apply:

(a) The assignment between the creditors and collection agency is in writing.

(b) The original agreement between the creditor and debtor does not prohibit assignments.

(c) The collection agency complies with the act of December 17, 1968 (P.L. 1224, No. 387), known as the Unfair Trade Practices and Consumer Protection Law, [73 P.S. § 201-1 et seq.] and with the regulations promulgated under this act.

18 Pa. Cons. Stat. § 7311(a) (West, WESTLAW through Act 2002-39).

It is unlawful for a collection agency to appear for or represent a creditor in any manner whatsoever, but a collection agency, pursuant to subsection (a) [above], may bring legal action on claims assigned to it . . . if the agency appears by an attorney. 18 Pa. Cons. Stat. Ann. § 7311(b) (West, WESTLAW through Act 2002-39).

Puerto Rico

A debtor who may have consented to the assignment of rights made by a creditor in favor of a third person, cannot oppose, against the assignee, the compensation which should pertain to him against the assignor.

If the creditor gave him notice of the assignment and the debtor did not consent thereto, he may oppose compensation for prior debts, but not for subsequent ones.

If the assignment is made without knowledge of the debtor, he may oppose compensation for prior credits, and for subsequent ones, until he should have been informed of the assignment. 31 P.R. Laws Ann. § 3224 (WESTLAW through December 2002).

Editor's Note: 10 P.R. Laws Ann. §§ 551-560 and 10 P.R. Laws Ann. §§ 582-583, regarding the assignment of accounts, were repealed (effective 120 days after Sept. 19, 1996).

Rhode Island

The assignee of a nonnegotiable chose in action which has been assigned in writing may maintain an action thereon in his or her own name, but subject to all defenses and rights of counterclaim, recoupment, or setoff to which the defendant would have been entitled had the action been brought in the name of the assignor. R.I. Gen. Laws § 9-2-8 (WESTLAW through Jan. 2004 Sess.).

South Carolina

There is no right of assignment in the state of South Carolina.

South Dakota

(Editor's Note: This state currently does not have a specific assignment statute.) An assignment for the benefit of creditors must be in writing, subscribed by the assignor, or by his agent thereto authorized by writing. It must be acknowledged or proved and certified, in the mode prescribed by this code for recording transfers of real property and recorded as required by § 54-9-8. Unless such provisions are complied with, an assignment for the benefit of creditors is void against every creditor of the assignor not assenting thereto. S.D. Codified Laws § 54-9-2 (WESTLAW through End of 2005 Reg. Sess. and Supreme Court Rule 05-10).

Every action shall be prosecuted in the name of the real party in interest. A personal representative, guardian, conservator, bailee, trustee of an express trust, a party with whom or in whose name a contract has been made for the benefit of another, or a party authorized by statute may sue in his own name without joining with him the party for whose benefit the action is brought; and when a statute of the state so provides, an action for the use or benefit of another shall be brought in the name of the state. No action shall be dismissed on the ground that it is not prosecuted in the name of the real party in interest until a reasonable time has been allowed after objection for ratification of commencement of the action by, or joinder or substitution of, the real party in interest; and such ratification, joinder, or substitution shall have the same effect as if the action had been commenced in the name of the real party in interest. S.D. R. Civ. P. § 15-6-17(a) (WESTLAW through End of 2005 Reg. Sess. and Supreme Court Rule 05-10).

Tennessee

Assignment of indebtedness (Effective date: July 1, 2004)

(a) A collection service holding a valid license under this chapter may take assignment of accounts, bills, notes or other indebtedness held by another person or entity, for the purpose of billing, collecting or filing suit in the collection service licensee's own name, as the real party in interest, if all the following requirements have been met:

(1) The assignment was voluntary, properly executed, and acknowledged by the person or entity making the assignment to the collection service licensee;

(2) The original agreement between the creditor and the debtor does not prohibit assignments;

(3) The assignment was manifested by a written agreement stating the effective date of the assignment and the consideration paid or given, if any, for the assignment. The written agreement must also disclose that the collection service licensee may, for purposes of litigation, consolidate the assigned account, bill, note or other indebtedness with those of other creditors against the individual debtor or codebtors; and

(4) A collection service licensee bringing suit in its own name as an assignee may submit an affidavit of sworn account that has been executed under oath by the assigning party or by a person qualified to execute a sworn account pursuant to § 24-5-107(a). A copy of the sworn account shall be filed with the court for service upon the debtor.

(b) A collection service licensee may commence litigation for the collection of an assigned account, bill, note or other indebtedness in a court of competent jurisdiction located in any of the following counties:

(1) The county in which the debtor signed the account, bill, note or other indebtedness sued upon;

(2) In the case of consolidated accounts that all arose from the same county, the county in which all of the consolidated accounts, bills, notes or other indebtednesses arose; or

(3) The county in which the debtor resides at the commencement of the action.

(c) No collection service licensee shall commence any litigation authorized by this section, unless the collection service licensee appears by an attorney admitted to practice law in the state of Tennessee.

(d) (1) For purposes of commencing litigation, a collection service licensee that has taken an assignment or assignments pursuant to this section may consolidate the assigned accounts, bills, notes or other indebtedness of one or more creditors against one individual debtor or co-debtors, in one case. Each assigned account, bill, note or indebtedness must be separately identified and pled in any consolidated action authorized by this section. The individual amount of each account, bill, note or other indebtedness that forms the basis for any consolidated action shall not exceed two hundred dollars ($200) each, as identified and pled by the collection service licensee, exclusive of court costs, attorney fees and interest that may have accrued before the filing of the consolidated action. The aggregate amount of consolidated accounts, bills, notes and other indebtedness in any one case shall not exceed five hundred dollars ($500), as identified and pled by the collection service licensee, exclusive of court costs, attorney fees and interest that may have accrued before the filing of the consolidated action. Court costs shall be assessed to the losing party. Interest and attorney fees and reimbursable expenses shall be assessed against the losing party, if provided in any of the consolidated accounts, bills, notes or other indebtedness, or as otherwise permitted or required by law.

(2) If a debtor or co-debtor files a sworn denial or otherwise raises a dispute concerning any account, bill, note or other evidence of indebtedness, the court shall dismiss the account, bill, note or other evidence of indebtedness, without prejudice. The collection service licensee may bring a separate case for any such disputed account, bill, note or other evidence of indebtedness within one (1) year of dismissal; provided, however, that the disputed account, bill, note or other evidence of indebtedness cannot be consolidated with any other account, bill, note or other evidence of indebtedness.

(3) For any account on which an affidavit of sworn account is filed pursuant to § 24-5-107(a), a separate affidavit shall be filed for each account in a consolidated action.

(e) Nothing in this section relieves a collection service licensee from complying with the "Fair Debt Collection Practices Act," 15 U.S.C. § 1692, as amended, or deprives any debtor of the right to assert defenses as provided in that act.

(f) On the face of any warrant or other pleading filed in any consolidated action, or in an attachment thereto, the collection service licensee shall state the order in which the creditor intends to apply payments received on any judgment obtained in the consolidated action. The collection service licensee shall also state that payments will be applied as stated unless the debtor instructs otherwise in writing or the court orders otherwise.

Tenn. Code Ann. § 62-20-127 (WESTLAW through 2005 First Reg. Sess.).

Assignment of bonds, bills or notes; prosecution of suit by assignee:

Bonds with collateral conditions, bills or notes for specific articles or the performance of any duty, nonnegotiable notes for money and accepted orders shall be assignable, and suit may be prosecuted by the assignee in the assignee's own name. Tenn. Code Ann. § 47-50-102 (WESTLAW through 2005 First Reg. Sess.).

A collection agency engages in the unlawful practice of law when it solicits or accepts claims or debts for collection by assignment or any other form of contract under which payment to the assignor is dependant on collection from the debtor and which authorizes the enforcement of collection by suit brought in the name of either party by the collection agency or an attorney to be paid by the agency. *State v. James Sanford Agency*, 69 S.W. 2d 895, 899 (Tenn. 1934).

A collection agency may not institute or maintain legal or equitable actions for others, whether by its own agents or attorneys or those specially employed by it for that purpose. *Id.*

A collection agency may not collect sums against debtors as attorney's fees on notes authorizing such judgment except when such judgment is its bona fide property and is not rendered on a claim in its hands for collection by assignment or otherwise. *Id.*

Texas
Undetermined under state statutes or state case law.

Utah
Any collector having complied with the provisions of this chapter, may receive accounts, bills or other indebtedness, take assignments for the purpose of collections, and at the direction of the assignor bring suit as assignee, provided however, that all accounts shall be within the statute of limitations as provided by law. All legal processes, pleadings, and court representations shall be prepared and conducted by a duly licensed attorney, and a copy of summons and complaint, in all cases, shall be served on defendants. Utah Code. Ann. § 12-1-8 (WESTLAW through End of 2005 First Spec. Sess.).

Vermont
(a) Every action shall be prosecuted in the name of the real party in interest. An executor, administrator, guardian, bailee, trustee of an express trust, a party with whom or in whose name a contract has been made for the benefit of another, or a party authorized by statute may sue in that person's own name without joining the party for whose benefit the action is brought; and when a statute so provides, an action for the use or benefit of another shall be brought in the name of the State of Vermont. An insurer who has paid all or part of a loss may sue in the name of the assured to whose rights it is subrogated. No action shall be dismissed on the ground that it is not prosecuted in the name of the real party in interest until a reasonable time has been allowed after objection for ratification of commencement of the action by, or joinder or substitution of, the real party in interest; and such ratification, joinder, or substitution shall have the same effect as if the action had been commenced in the name of the real party in interest. Vt. R. Civ. Pro. R. 17 (WESTLAW current with amendments received through 2-15-2005).

The practice of law by any debt collector, not a licensed attorney, in the collection or enforcement of debts arising out of consumer transactions constitutes an unfair and deceptive trade act and practice in commerce under Vermont Statute title 9, section 2453(a).

Such unfair and deceptive acts include (but shall not be limited to) the following:

(a) Performance of legal services, provision of legal advice or making of a false representation or false implication that any person is an attorney;

(b) Any communication with a debtor in the name of an attorney or upon stationery or other written matter bearing an attorney's name.

Vt. Code R. 104.06 (Weil, WESTLAW through June 2005 (Issue no. 188)).

<u>Virgin Islands</u>

Discharge of account debtor; notification of assignment identification and proof of assignment; restrictions on assignment of accounts, chattel paper, payment intangibles and promissory notes ineffective:

(a) Discharge of account debtor; effect of notification. Subject to subsections (b) through (i), an account debtor on an account, chattel paper, or a payment intangible may discharge its obligation by paying the assignor until, but not after, the account debtor receives a notification, authenticated by the assignor or the assignee, that the amount due or to become due has been assigned and that payment is to be made to the assignee. After receipt of the notification, the account debtor may discharge its obligation by paying the assignee and may not discharge the obligation by paying the assignor.

(b) When notification ineffective. Subject to subsection (h), notification is ineffective under subsection (a):

(1) if it does not reasonably identify the rights assigned;

(2) to the extent that an agreement between an account debtor and a seller of a payment intangible limits the account debtor's duty to pay a person other than the seller and the limitation is effective under law other than this article; or

(3) at the option of an account debtor, if the notification notifies the account debtor to make less than the full amount of any installment or other periodic payment to the assignee, even if:

(A) only a portion of the account, chattel paper, or payment intangible has been assigned to that assignee;

(B) a portion has been assigned to another assignee; or

(C) the account debtor knows that the assignment to that assignee is limited.

(c) Proof of assignment. Subject to subsection (h), if requested by the account debtor, an assignee shall seasonably farnish reasonable proof that the assignment has been made. Unless the assignee complies, the account debtor may discharge its obligation by paying the assignor, even if the account debtor has received a notification under subsection (a).

(d) Term restricting assignment generally ineffective. Except as otherwise provided in subsection (e) and Sections 2A-303 and 9-407, and subject to subsection (h), a term in an agreement between an account debtor and an assignor or in a promissory note is ineffective to the extent that it:

(1) prohibits, restricts, or requires the consent of the account debtor or person obligated on the promissory note to the assignment or transfer

of, or the creation, attachment, perfection, or enforcement of a security interest in, the account, chattel paper, payment intangible, or promissory note; or

(2) provides that the assignment or transfer or the creation, attachment, perfection, or enforcement of the security interest may give rise to a default, breach, right of recoupment, claim, defense, termination, right of termination, or remedy under the account, chattel paper, payment intangible, or promissory note.

(e) Inapplicability of subsection (d) to certain sales. Subsection (d) does not apply to the sale of a payment intangible or promissory note.

(f) Legal restrictions on assignment generally ineffective. Except as otherwise provided in Sections 2A-303 and 9-407 and subject to subsections (h) and (i), a rule of law, statute, or regulation that prohibits, restricts, or requires the consent of a government, governmental body or official, or account debtor to the assignment or transfer of, or creation of a security interest in, an account or chattel paper is ineffective to the extent that the rule of law, statute, or regulation:

(1) prohibits, restricts, or requires the consent of the government, governmental body or official, or account debtor to the assignment or transfer of, or the creation, attachment, perfection, or enforcement of a security interest in the account or chattel paper; or

(2) provides that the assignment or transfer or the creation, attachment, perfection, or enforcement of the security interest may give rise to a default, breach, right of recoupment, claim, defense, termination, right of termination, or remedy under the account or chattel paper.

(g) Subsection (b)(3) not waivable. Subject to subsection (h), an account debtor may not waive or vary its option under subsection (b)(3).

(h) Rule for individual under other law. This section is subject to law other than this article which establishes a different rule for an account debtor who is an individual and who incurred the obligation primarily for personal, family, or household purposes.

(i) Inapplicability to health-care-insurance receivable. This section does not apply to an assignment of a health-care-insurance receivable.

(j) Section prevails over specified inconsistent law. This section prevails over any inconsistent provisions of an existing or future statute, rule or regulation of this State unless the provision is contained in a statute of this State, refers expressly to this section and states that the provision prevails over this section.

11A V.I. Code Ann. § 9-406 (WESTLAW through Acts 6644 through 6725 of the 2004 Reg. Sess.).

Virginia

The assignee or beneficial owner of any bond, note, writing or other chose in action, not negotiable may maintain thereon in his own name any action which the original obligee, payee, or contracting party might have brought, but shall allow all just discounts, not only against himself but against such obligee, payee, or contracting party, before the defendant had notice of the assignment or transfer by such obligee, payee, or contracting party, and shall also allow all such discounts against any intermediate assignor or transferor, the right to which was acquired on the faith of the assignment or transfer to him and before the defendant had notice of the assignment or transfer by such assignor or transferor to another. Va. Code Ann. § 8.01-13 (WESTLAW through End of 2005 Reg. Sess.).

Washington

Any assignee or assignees of any judgment, bond, specialty, book account, or other chose in action, for the payment of money, by assignment in writing, signed by the person authorized to make the same, may, by virtue of such assignment, sue and maintain an action or actions in his or her name, against the obligor or obligors, debtor or debtors, named in such judgment, bond, specialty, book account, or other chose in action, notwithstanding the assignor may have an interest in the thing assigned: PROVIDED, That any debtor may plead in defense as many defenses, counterclaims and offsets, whether they be such as have heretofore been denominated legal or equitable, or both, if held by him against the original owner, against the debt assigned, save that no counterclaim or offset shall be pleaded against negotiable paper assigned before due, and where the holder thereof has purchased the same in good faith and for value, and is the owner of all interest therein. Wash. Rev. Code Ann. § 4.08.080 (WESTLAW through 2005 Legislation effective through July 1, 2005).

Licensing prerequisite to suit:
No collection agency or out-of-state collection agency may bring or maintain an action in any court of this state involving the collection of a claim of any third party without alleging and proving that he or it is duly licensed under this chapter and has satisfied the bonding requirements hereof, if applicable: PROVIDED, That in any case where judgment is to be entered by default, it shall not be necessary for the collection agency or out-of-state collection agency to prove such matters. A copy of the current collection agency license, certified by the director to be a true and correct copy of the original, shall be prima facie evidence of the licensing and bonding of such collection agency as required by this chapter. Wash. Rev. Code Ann. § 19.16.260 (WESTLAW through 2005 Legislation effective through July 1, 2005).

Presumption of validity of assignment:
In any action brought by licensee to collect the claim of his or its customer, the assignment of the claim to licensee by his or its customer shall be conclusively presumed valid, if the assignment is filed in court with the complaint, unless objection is made thereto by the debtor in a written answer or in writing five days or more prior to trial. Wash. Rev. Code Ann. § 19.16.270 (WESTLAW through 2005 Legislation effective through July 1, 2005).

West Virginia

The assignee of any bond, note, account, or writing, not negotiable, or other chose in action arising out of contract or injury to personal or real property, may maintain thereupon any action in his own name, without the addition of "assignee," which the original obligee, promisee, payee, contracting party, or owner of such chose in action might have brought; but shall allow all just defenses and setoffs, not only against himself, but against the assignor, before the defendant had notice of the assignment. In every such action the plaintiff may unite claims payable to him individually with those payable to him as such assignee, provided it be otherwise proper to join them. But nothing in this section shall be construed to make assignable any right of action not otherwise assignable. W. Va. Code § 55-8-9 (WESTLAW through End of 2005 Third Ex. Sess.).

A consumer is authorized to pay the original creditor until he receives notification of assignment of rights to payment pursuant to a consumer credit sale, consumer lease or a consumer loan and that payment is to be made to the assignee. A notification which does not reasonably identify the rights assigned is ineffective. If requested by the consumer, the assignee must seasonably furnish reasonable proof that the assignment has been made and unless he does so the consumer may pay the original creditor. W. Va. Code § 46A-2-113 (WESTLAW through End of 2005 Third Ex. Sess.).

Wisconsin

Consolidation of accounts:

(a) A licensee may, after receiving authorization from a creditor, consolidate the creditor's account or accounts relating to a particular debtor with those of any other creditor or creditors relating to that debtor and may cause an action to be brought on behalf of the creditor or creditors. All of the following apply to any action caused to be brought by a licensee on behalf of a creditor or creditors under this subsection:

1. The summons and complaint shall be prepared by an attorney or at the direction of an attorney.
2. The name or names of the creditor or creditors shall appear in the pleadings and in the caption of the case as the real party or parties in interest and the licensee's name shall not appear in the caption or pleadings.
3. The creditor or creditors in each instance shall be given the opportunity either to select an attorney to commence the action or to designate, as a part of the authorization process, the collection agency as the agent of the creditor or creditors to retain an attorney and forward the claim or claims to the attorney on behalf of the creditor or creditors.

(b) In any action caused to be brought by a licensee under this subsection, the licensee shall not appear on behalf of any creditor or creditors before any court, including the clerk of any small claims court in an action on the debt or in garnishment proceedings, except when called as a witness by the plaintiff's attorney in open court.

Wis. Stat. Ann. § 218.04(9j) (WESTLAW through 2005 Act 12, published 6/15/05).

Effective Date: Oct. 1, 2006

(1) Except as set forth in sub. (2), no collector or other employee of a licensee may in attempting to collect an account, engage in the practice of law. This includes but is not limited to the preparation of a summons or complaint or the appearance on behalf of any creditor, except when called as a witness by the plaintiff's attorney in open court, before any court including the clerk of any small claims court in an action on the debt or in garnishment proceedings. It is not considered the practice of law for an employee of a licensee to prepare a summons or complaint under the direction of an attorney which will subsequently be signed and filed by the plaintiff's attorney. This section does not prohibit the appearance of an owner or officer of a licensed collection agency in court for the purpose of obtaining judgment on a debt owed to the licensee directly.

(2) Sub. (1) does not apply to an attorney who is an employee of the collection agency.

Wis. Admin. Code § DFI-Bkg 74.15 (2006).

Wyoming

No licensee, under the terms of this act, shall render legal services or advertise directly or indirectly, that it will render legal services, but any licensee can solicit claims exclusively for the purpose of collection, take assignments thereof for the purpose of collection by suit or otherwise, and for such purpose, shall be deemed to be the real party in interest in any suit brought upon such assigned claim. Wyo. Stat. Ann. § 33-11-114 (WESTLAW through the 2004 Spec. Sess. (57th Legislature).

ACA International, P.O. Box 390106, Minneapolis, MN 55439-0106
Phone +1(952) 926-6547 Fax (952) 926-1624
E-mail compliance@acainternational.org
Web http://www.acainternational.org

APPENDIX VIII

SANCTIONS UNDER BANKRUPTCY ACT

Federal Rules of Bankruptcy Procedure § 9011

Rule 9011. Signing of Papers; Representations to the Court; Sanctions; Verification and Copies of Papers

(a) Signing of papers.
Every petition, pleading, written motion, and other paper, except a list, schedule, or statement, or amendments thereto, shall be signed by at least one attorney of record in the attorney's individual name. A party who is not represented by an attorney shall sign all papers. Each paper shall state the signer's address and telephone number, if any. An unsigned paper shall be stricken unless omission of the signature is corrected promptly after being called to the attention of the attorney or party.

(b) Representations to the court.
By presenting to the court (whether by signing, filing, submitting, or later advocating) a petition, pleading, written motion, or other paper, an attorney or unrepresented party is certifying that to the best of the person's knowledge, information, and belief, formed after an inquiry reasonable under the circumstances,—

(1) it is not being presented for any improper purpose, such as to harass or to cause unnecessary delay or needless increase in the cost of litigation;

(2) the claims, defenses, and other legal contentions therein are warranted by existing law or by a nonfrivolous argument for the extension, modification, or reversal of existing law or the establishment of new law;

(3) the allegations and other factual contentions have evidentiary support or, if specifically so identified, are likely to have evidentiary support after a reasonable opportunity for further investigation or discovery; and

(4) the denials of factual contentions are warranted on the evidence or, if specifically so identified, are reasonably based on a lack of information or belief.

(c) Sanctions.

If, after notice and a reasonable opportunity to respond, the court determines that subdivision (b) has been violated, the court may, subject to the conditions stated below, impose an appropriate sanction upon the attorneys, law firms, or parties that have violated subdivision (b) or are responsible for the violation.

(1) How initiated.

(A) By motion. A motion for sanctions under this rule shall be made separately from other motions or requests and shall describe the specific conduct alleged to violate subdivision (b). It shall be served as provided in Rule 7004. The motion for sanctions may not be filed with or presented to the court unless, within 21 days after service of the motion (or such other period as the court may prescribe), the challenged paper, claim, defense, contention, allegation, or denial is not withdrawn or appropriately corrected, except that this limitation shall not apply if the conduct alleged is the filing of a petition in violation of subdivision (b). If warranted, the court may award to the party prevailing on the motion the reasonable expenses and attorney's fees incurred in presenting or opposing the motion. Absent exceptional circumstances, a law firm shall be held jointly responsible for violations committed by its partners, associates, and employees.

(B) On court's initiative. On its own initiative, the court may enter an order describing the specific conduct that appears to violate subdivision (b) and directing an attorney, law firm, or party to show cause why it has not violated subdivision (b) with respect thereto.

(2) Nature of sanction; limitations.

A sanction imposed for violation of this rule shall be limited to what is sufficient to deter repetition of such conduct or comparable conduct by others similarly situated. Subject to the limitations in subparagraphs (A) and (B), the sanction may consist of, or include, directives of a nonmonetary nature, an order to pay a penalty into court, or, if imposed on motion and warranted for effective deterrence, an order directing payment to the movant of some or all of the reasonable attorneys' fees and other expenses incurred as a direct result of the violation.

(A) Monetary sanctions may not be awarded against a represented party for a violation of subdivision (b)(2).

(B) Monetary sanctions may not be awarded on the court's initiative unless the court issues its order to show cause before a voluntary dismissal or settlement of the claims made by or against the party which is, or whose attorneys are, to be sanctioned.

(3) Order. When imposing sanctions, the court shall describe the conduct determined to constitute a violation of this rule and explain the basis for the sanction imposed.

(d) Inapplicability to discovery.

Subdivisions (a) through (c) of this rule do not apply to disclosures and discovery requests, responses, objections, and motions that are subject to the provisions of Rules 7026 through 7037.

(e) Verification.

Except as otherwise specifically provided by these rules, papers filed in a case under the Code need not be verified. Whenever verification is required by these rules, an unsworn declaration as provided in 28 U.S.C. § 1746 satisfies the requirement of verification.

(f) Copies of signed or verified papers.

When these rules require copies of a signed or verified paper, it shall suffice if the original is signed or verified and the copies are conformed to the original.

CHAPTER 8

Checks, Notes, and Guarantees

As a general rule, a deposit made in a bank creates a creditor and debtor relationship. Title to the deposit is transferred to the bank. The bank undertakes an obligation to the depositor as the creditor to pay the checks or any other instruments in accordance with their depositor's instructions.

A deposit is generally presumed to be a "general deposit" in that title to the deposit passes to the bank who owes money to the depositor. As to a special deposit deposited for a specific purpose which the bank agrees to accept as a special deposit, the bank becomes a trustee and holds the money in a fiduciary capacity.

As to a general deposit, if the depositor is a borrower from the bank, the depositor and the bank are mutually indebted. If the depositor's debt to the bank has matured, the bank may exercise its right of "set-off." The bank may apply the deposit or such portion as may be necessary to the payment of the debt.[1]

CHECKS

Bounced Checks—Criminal Intent. "Issuing a check that bounces is a crime." This statement is partially true. Some background is necessary.

[1] *Sterling Sav. Bank v. Air Wisconsin Airlines Corp.*, 492 F. Supp. 2d 1256 (E.D. Wash. 2007).

In the 1930s, the con artist would enter a small town and issue checks to many of the merchants. Before the checks were cashed, the con man had crossed the state border, leaving the helpless merchants holding the worthless checks. The criminal "bad checks" laws were born.

These laws generally provide that a party who issues a check, knowing that the check will not be paid, may be subject to a fine and imprisonment. The key ingredient of all crimes is the element of "intent" and this crime is no different. The party must know that the check will not be paid. When creditors receive bad checks, "reasonable" explanations are offered to show the debtor did not know that the check would not be paid.

A. There was a mistake in addition. The calculator the bank gave me for opening the account was broken.
B. My dog chewed up the bank statement, and I thought money was in the account.
C. My spouse switched the money to another account without telling me.
D. The bank should have called me and told me I didn't have money.
E. I pay the bills, my wife deposits the money. Unfortunately, she left, took the car, the money, and the children, and left me with the mortgage and the bills.
F. The president of the corporation opened a new account without telling the bookkeeper, his wife.
G. The computer shows a balance in the account. We are doing it manually now.
H. The bookkeeper left on vacation, but it doesn't look like she will return. We are reviewing our bank statements now.
I. I do not know how to add!

The explanations are infinite, depending only on the creativity and resourcefulness of the debtor. Proving that a consumer or business debtor issued a check knowing the check would not be paid is difficult, if not impossible—with certain exceptions.

Threatening a debtor with criminal prosecution would be unwise unless you are certain that the consumer is committing a fraud. When a check has been returned, do not use innuendoes or inferences, such as:

1. "There are serious consequences for issuing a bad check."
2. "I am sure you are aware that issuing a check which is returned is much more serious than just owing money."

Do not use any flagrant or obvious threats such as:

A. "If you don't pay the balance on the check, you're going to end up in jail."

B. "I'm going to see the district attorney and have you arrested."

C. "I will prosecute you criminally unless you pay this check in ten days."

If you have evidence from information obtained from other sources that the debtor had no intention of paying the check and that the debtor intended a fraud at the time the check was issued, review with counsel whether this debtor may be prosecuted criminally. If the debtor had issued returned checks to other creditors and is engaging in a pattern of fraud, the matter should be reviewed with counsel.

Creditors attempt to enlist the aid of a county, district, or city attorney to help on the theory that the bad-check issuer may be guilty of a crime pursuant to the state laws. In most instances, the creditor withdraws the charges after an offer of payment. For this reason, county or city attorneys do not assist the creditor who is referring the check for the sole purpose of collecting the monies and not for prosecuting a crime. A few states and jurisdictions do allow government attorneys to engage in the collection of checks and debts for creditors, although many bar associations and debt collectors oppose this activity.

On the other hand, an issuer of many bad checks to many creditors, or someone with an unsavory reputation issuing a bad check for a large amount may persuade the county, district, or city attorney to actively prosecute. In the course of the prosecution, restitution may be made, and the creditor will have the best of both worlds. If the check was sent through the mail, consulting with the postal inspector is recommended.

Review of Bank Statement. Section 4-406 of the Uniform Commercial Code (UCC) deals with the customer's duty to discover and report an unauthorized signature or alteration.

A prerequisite to the application of this statute is that the bank must make available to a customer a statement of account showing payments of items and provide information sufficient to allow the customer to reasonably identify the items paid. The section further states that when the bank sends such a statement, the customer must exercise reasonable promptness in examining the statement to determine whether any payment was not authorized because of the alteration of an item or because a signature on behalf of the customer was not authorized. The customer must promptly notify the bank of these facts. The statute also notes that the reasonable period of time may not exceed 30 days to examine the item or statement of account and notify the bank. The statute is equally applicable to businesses and individuals.

A court dealt with the issue of whether the statute covered a lack of a required signature as opposed to an unauthorized signature. The bank account required two signatures and the defendant argued that this was not covered in the statute since the statute only dealt with unauthorized signatures. The court did not agree that a signature of an organization is unauthorized if one of the required signatures is lacking.

It is worth repeating Section 4-406(c) as follows:

> If a bank sends or makes available a statement of account or items pursuant to subsection (a) the customer must exercise reasonable promptness in examining the statement or the items to determine whether any payment was not authorized because of an alteration of an item or because a purported signature by and on behalf of the customer was not authorized . . . the customer must promptly notify the bank of the facts.

In addition, another subsection of Section 4-406 states as follows:

> Without regard to care or lack of care of either the customer or the bank, a customer who does not within one year after the statement or items are made available to the customer discover and report the customer's unauthorized signature or any alteration on the item is precluded from asserting against the bank the unauthorized signature of alteration.

Notwithstanding these clear and unequivocal obligations of the customer to review the bank statement, the number of cases where customers sue the banks for an unauthorized signature continue from year to year. As to the first requirement, the bank must make the payment in good faith. A negligent act does not constitute bad faith. The second requirement contains no obligation of good faith and the bank's statutory right after one year is absolute.[2]

> ***Credit & Collection Tip:*** *One cannot emphasize enough the fact that bank statements must be reviewed and examined as soon as they are received. Failure to follow this course of action will lead either to losses or expensive litigation—and usually unsuccessful litigation.*

An effort by the bank to reduce the time frame within which the depositor must review the bank statement was put in issue in New York—involving a $600,000 withdrawal from the customer's account on fraudulent electronic (fax) signatures. The local bank decided to reduce the period of time to review the bank statement and notify the bank of any discrepancies from the one-year statutory period to 15 days in their deposit agreement. In addition, the time period would start from the date of the statement, not from the time the depositor received the statement.

In this particular instance, the bank was authorized by the depositor to withhold sending its regular statements until the depositor asked for them.

---

[2] *Falk v. N. Trust Co.*, 763 N.E.2d 380 (Ill. App. Ct. 2001); *Dow City Cemetery Ass'n v. Defiance State Bank*, 596 N.W.2d 77 (Iowa 1999).

Finally, the depositor notified the bank well before the expiration of the one-year period provided for in the statute, but certainly well after the fifteen (15) day period that he was allowed in the deposit agreement.

The court came down hard and stated that permitting a bank to vary the notice by agreement would reduce the effectiveness of the statute's one-year period. While this decision may be comforting to some depositors who are lazy about reviewing their bank statements, one might say that an individual who has $600,000 on deposit in his account may have contributed to the negligence in authorizing the bank to withhold sending regular bank statements to him each month until he asked.

Statutory Costs and Treble Damages. Many states allow the holder of a returned check to recover the costs and expenses incurred in collecting the check and to recover double and treble damages if the terms and conditions of the statute are met. In recovering double and treble damages, the statutes provide specific notice requirements, forms, and procedures to provide an opportunity for the issuer to pay the check. A review of the state law where the check is enforced is essential before any proceeding is commenced. These statutes are to be distinguished from those authorizing the collection of bank charges for returning bad checks.

Collecting Bad Check Charges. The Fair Debt Collection Practices Act (FDCPA) allows a creditor to charge a fee for the returned check if the right to collect is set forth in the agreement creating the debt or, in the alternative, if it is permitted by law. In many states, some provision is made for charging a debtor in the event a check is returned. The statutes vary from state to state. Some are extremely burdensome, whereas others do allow a creditor to charge a reasonable charge for a bad check merely by making a demand on the debtor and thereafter suing for the amount.

Some states allow a creditor to charge at least $10 for a returned check without any notice or other requirement. Many states allow the creditor to pass on to the debtor the actual charge that the creditor incurs with the proviso that the charge does not exceed a specific amount.

Other states have set the maximum amount that may be charged, while other states require a specific type of notice to the debtor. In most states a specific notice mailed to the debtor within a specified time is usually required and, in many instances, the notice must be mailed by certified or registered mail. Certified or registered mail adds a prohibitive cost if the check is for a small amount.

Some of these states permit a fixed fee of $15 to $20, or 5 percent of the face amount of the check, as a charge. Others permit charges of up to $100 and some provide for treble damages. Many states have separate provisions applying specifically to retail stores. If the retail outlet clearly and conspicuously displays the charge in the store, the creditor may collect fees ranging from a few dollars to treble damages on each check. A current examination of the state law must be conducted by counsel.

Collecting bad check charges where the debtors are within one state is feasible, since the creditor is regulated only by that state's statute. To collect bad check charges on a national basis would require familiarity with the law of each state and would require the collection procedure to conform with the statute in the debtor's resident state. A national program by the creditor to collect bad check charges in every state would be difficult to institute and would probably not be cost effective because the average fees recovered on the returned check would be approximately $15 to $20. The cost of certified mail required in many of the state statutes decreases the net return on collecting bad check fees. The cost of preparing the specific notices required for each state, and maintaining an up-to-date library of the notices together with secretarial or computer time to prepare each notice will decrease the return and may be prohibitive unless on a volume basis.

Some collection agencies market their services on the grounds that they can collect the fees for a returned check on a national basis. The theory offered is that the agency is complying with the laws in the state where the agency or creditor is located, and that is sufficient. The flaw in this reasoning is that the FDCPA prohibits any charge unless permitted by law. But suit must be started in the county where the debtor resides. If the bad check charge is not permitted by law in the county where the debtor resides, the debtor is not liable. Thus, threatening to collect the charge is threatening that which cannot be legally collected by suit, which constitutes a violation of the Act.

A debt collector may not use unfair or unconscionable means to collect or attempt to collect the debt. Without limiting the general application of the foregoing, the following conduct is a violation of section 1692e:

> (1) The collection of any amount (including any interest, fee, charge, or expense incidental to the principal obligation) unless such amount is expressly authorized by the agreement creating the debt or permitted by law. . . .

The commentary to the Debt Collection Practices Act expressly states that "bad checks handling charges" come within the purview of this section. Accordingly, the collection of a "bad check handling charge" must be expressly authorized by the agreement creating the debt or permitted by law. Appropriate terminology must appear in the order form, or the agreement between the consumer and the creditor, authorizing the collection of a fee in the event that the check is returned, or a clear and conspicuous display must appear at a retail store.

A California case addressed the question of whether a state must expressly authorize bad check fees or whether the burden is on the plaintiff to demonstrate that state law prohibits the particular claims.[3] The court did not adopt the defendant's theory that any charges not prohibited by law are necessarily permitted. Accordingly, an express statute must specifically authorize bad check charges for a creditor to assess said charges. The other alternative is that the obligation to pay bad check charges is contained in the agreement creating the debt, as specified in the FDCPA.

In the case, the question was whether the posting of notices in the store created an agreement between the creditor and the check-writing consumer. The retail store alleged that it was the intention of the merchant that the notice affixed to the cash register would alert customers to the fees that would be charged if the check did not clear. The store stated that the notice of the fee for a bad check was intended to make the sale subject to these terms.

The court stated that there was absolutely no evidence that the customer saw the signs or intended to accept the offer. Nevertheless, rather than deny summary judgment, the court stated that it would be a question of fact to be decided at a trial to determine whether a contract actually had been entered into between the customers and the retail store. Eight states (Delaware, Maine, Massachusetts, New Jersey, New Mexico, Oklahoma, Pennsylvania, and Vermont) do not have any law which deals with a service charge for returned checks (this may have changed by the time this edition is published). Consultation with counsel is suggested to review the case law in the state to determine if the courts have promulgated any new criteria for service charges.

While this was not an important expense in the past, the recent efforts of banks to charge for all services has resulted in bank charges for returned checks ranging from $5 to $25 or more.

Post-Dated Checks and Preauthorized Transfers. A post-dated check is a promise to pay an amount of money on a specified day in the future. Issuing a post-dated check which is returned unpaid creates no presumption of fraud or intent to defraud the creditor. A post-dated check is a reasonable expectation that the maker will have funds available on a specified future date. Since the event is in the future, the maker of the check cannot know at the time of issuance that the check will or will not be paid.

California has held that a post-dated check that is returned unpaid is within the operation of the fraud statute and that "it is, nevertheless a check."[4] Illinois allows no distinction between a check and a check that is post-dated.[5]

Conflict exists between the states as to whether a post-dated check can be the subject of a criminal statute. The general theory is that any criminal statute usually requires intent on the part of the perpetrator and relates back to a false pretense, and a false pretense under a criminal statute relates

---

[3]*Newman v. Checkwrite California, Inc.*, 912 F. Supp. 1354 (E.D. Cal. 1995).

[4]*Wright v. The Bank of America*, 176 Cal. App. 2d 176, 1 Cal. Rptr. 202 (1959); *People v. Percuwitz*, 163 Cal. 636 (Cal. 1912).

[5]82 Bus. L.J. 347.

to a past existing fact. Even though a promisor has at the time no intention of keeping the promise, such a pretense requires intent to come within the criminal statute, principally because it is a promise of a future act. Certainly, a post-dated check is a promise of a future act.

In most of the early rubber check statutes, the legislatures required the element of intent in order to support a criminal prosecution. For example, the New Jersey statute does not require intent to defraud. Even though the defendant did not intend to actively defraud the party to whom he issued the check, the fact that he had knowledge that the check would not be honored at the time that it was presented is apparently sufficient and may be described as the equivalent of the "intent" to defraud to support a criminal prosecution, at least in New Jersey.[6]

The conflict between the various states ends with many state courts holding that a post-dated check cannot be the subject of any criminal statute, and other state courts taking a great deal of effort to spell out a situation where the action of the debtor was sufficient to meet the criteria of the criminal statute. In some instances, the courts rely on the fact that the statutes themselves are worded differently, and therefore provide different avenues for the courts to follow. Needless to say, a reading of the state's statute and a review of the court decisions is not only recommended, but absolutely necessary before any step is taken with regard to prosecuting a debtor for issuing a post-dated check that has not been paid.

Massachusetts prohibits a collection agency from demanding from a debtor a post-dated check. Massachusetts may be the only state with such a prohibition.[7]

FDCPA Section 808(2) prohibits debt collectors from accepting a consumer check which is postdated more than 5 days unless such person is notified in writing when the check will be deposited and this notification must take place not more than 10 nor less than 3 business days prior to said deposit.

Pre-authorized drafts sent on the same day are probably not considered a check. If a series of pre-authorized drafts are printed, they might be treated as post-dated checks under the Fair Debt Collection Practices Act. Prior to depositing a check, the holder of the post-dated check or the pre-authorized check must have authorization from the issuer. The burden of proof is on the party depositing the check. Evidence needs to be offered that the notification was sent to the maker of the check. If a series of transactions are performed in accordance with the automated clearing house (ACH rules), and the transactions are electronic transfers which occur under the rules of ACH, 12 C.F.R. 205.10(b) states that authorization from the party who approved and authorized the electronic transfer is needed.

---

[6] *State v. Kelm*, 289 N.J. Super. 55, 672 A.2d 1261 (N.J. Super. Ct. App. Div.), *cert. denied*, 146 N.J. 68, 679 A.2d 655 (N.J. 1996).

[7] 209 Mass. Code Regs. 18.2.1.

The above statute covers the requirements that financial institution must meet when accepting written authorization for pre-authorized transfers from the consumer account and should be reviewed carefully.

Gambling Markers. An interesting analysis was offered in a case in a California bankruptcy court as to markers issued by the bankrupt to the casino. The casino argued that the markers should be nondischargeable. The court determined that a casino marker is a type of a check drawn on the customer's bank account designated in the instrument and is subject to the laws governing checks. Accordingly, the court, in dealing with the nondischargeability of the marker, was also dealing with the nondischargeability of a check.

To issue a marker to the casino, the customer must make an application for credit to the casino. The casino conducts a credit check and verifies that the customer has funds in one or more bank accounts to cover the credit requested. The casino approves the credit request after obtaining the bank account information and the customer signs and delivers a marker (a type of check) to the casino to draw money against the bank account and purchase gambling chips to use in casino games. Ultimately, the final marker that the debtor executed was returned unpaid, and, thereafter, the debtor filed a bankruptcy petition.

Since the marker check is not barred by the hearsay rule, the marker is admissible as evidence in the same manner as a check is admissible as evidence since both documents are self-authenticating. If either a check or marker is alleged in a complaint, it is deemed to be admitted unless specifically denied in the pleadings. The presentation of a check does not involve the making of a false statement nor does the presentation of a marker involve the making of a false statement. Without an actual false statement, no representation is made that the check is good or that the marker will be good.

At one time, the UCC did state that the drawer engages that, upon dishonor of the draft, the amount of the draft will be paid. The Revised UCC now provides only that, if an unaccepted check is dishonored at the bank, the drawer is obliged to pay it according to its terms at the time it was issued. The obligation is simply statutory and involves no representation, promise, or engagement. Delivering a check or marker simply does not constitute a representation. If the mere presentation of the marker or check included implied representations, they would constitute hearsay and would require a separate exception to the hearsay rule.

One court offered its analysis by considering false pretenses, intent to deceive, justifiable reliance, and a nondisclosure of financial information in connection with the presentation of a check.[8]

[8]*Mandalay Resort Group v. Miller*, 310 B.R. 185 (Bankr. C.D. Cal. 2004).

STOP PAYMENT. The issuer of a check may direct a bank not to pay a check. Verbal communications to a bank are valid, but written communications are a better means of notifying the bank. Generally, oral communication to a bank to stop payment on a check obligates the bank to keep the stop payment in effect for a period of a week, unless properly followed by a written communication which usually compels the bank to keep the stop payment in effect for six months as provided in the UCC. After the six-month period, it appears that the bank would not be liable if the check was presented for payment. The maker of the check may argue that the bank was negligent for paying the check due to the stale date on the check.[9]

Certified mail should be used, or deliver the notice personally and obtain an initialed receipt of said notice. The written communication should be clear and definitive as to the identification of the exact check and should include a notation of the dates of both the notice and the check, the check number, the amount, the name of the drawer, and the name of the payee, as well as any other pertinent information.

STALE CHECK. The court was faced with a situation where a stale check was paid after the debtor had delivered a stop payment order to the bank. A stop payment order is valid for six months. The check was paid three weeks after the six-month period ended. Section 4-404 of the UCC provides as follows:

A bank is under no obligation to a customer having a checking account to pay a check (other than a certified check) which is presented more than six months after its date, but it may charge its customer's account for a payment made thereafter in good faith.

The court pointed out that the UCC expressly permits payment of stale checks if payment is made in good faith. In this particular instance, the check was stale only by three weeks. The term "good faith" is defined as "honesty in fact in the conduct or transaction." Good faith is a subjective test requiring an evaluation of the honesty of the bank's intent, rather than its diligence. Indeed, a bank could act in good faith and still not follow accepted banking procedures. In the particular case, the court pointed out that the plaintiff was unable to produce any evidence to demonstrate that the bank had noted the stale date or the existence of an expired stop payment order. Furthermore, plaintiff has been unable to raise a question of fact disputing the bank's allegation that its review of the check was limited to signature verification because of its practices of signature verifications on all checks over $50,000.

The general posture of the courts when dealing with payment of stale checks probably follows this particular case, for imposing an obligation on the banks to review the date on each check would be an insurmountable and unfair burden. The plaintiff has to go far beyond the fact that a stale

---

[9] *R.P.M. Pizza Inc. v. Bank One Cambridge*, 869 F. Supp. 517 (E.D. Mich. 1994).

check was paid to hold the bank liable. Sometimes, a separate claim for negligence or failure to use normal banking procedures may be asserted.[10]

Certified Checks and Cashier's Checks. Certified checks and money orders are types of instruments which are used frequently in purchasing homes or securities and in other business transactions where the payee of the check wants assurance that the check will not be returned unpaid. At a real estate closing, the seller requires certified checks or bank checks. The perception is that a certified check or a bank check is as good as cash. Unfortunately, this is not true. A certified check can be stopped by the maker of the check if a bond is obtained to indemnify the bank against any claim that may be made against the bank. The premium may be substantial, since the amount of the bond may be double the amount or more of the check.

Money orders are checks issued by private institutions after receiving a cash payment in person. The money order is made payable to the person designated by the party paying for the money order, and it is used to send money through the mail rather than cash. The same scenario would apply to stopping payment of a money order issued by American Express or any company which issues money orders, although arguments may be offered that it is closer to a bank check than a certified check.

A cashier's check is a check issued by the bank and signed by a bank officer drawn on the capital assets of the bank. If the bank refuses to pay the check, the payee of the check would look to the assets of the bank for payment. If the bank issues a check on behalf of a depositor after receiving payment from the depositor, the bank would consider the check similar to a certified check and would not stop payment unless the depositor produced a sufficient indemnification bond. Several court decisions have held that a cashier's check is the equivalent of cash and thus cannot be stopped, even with an indemnification bond.

The liability of the bank to follow instructions is a function of the banking law of the particular state. If the bank should pay the check despite the stop payment instructions, consultation with an attorney is recommended. Some states, such as Arizona, California, Florida, Nevada, and Utah, have special laws affecting stop orders.

Some courts will allow the bank to stop payment on a cashier's check if it was procured by fraud, since to honor the check would only assist in the fraudulent transaction. In this situation, the check should still be in the hands of the original payee. On the other hand, if the check was negotiated to a holder in due course, the bank could not refuse to pay the check. The issues of reliance by the payee when he received the check or whether the payee has really changed a position in reliance on the check seem to be

---

[10] *R.P.M. Pizza, Inc. v. Bank One Cambridge*, 869 F. Supp. 517 (E.D. Mich. 1994).

factors that the courts consider in determining whether they are going to allow the bank to stop payment of the cashier's check.[11]

The payee must realize that certified checks, cashier's checks, and money orders are rarely returned unpaid, and only in unusual circumstances would someone incur the expense to arrange for an indemnification bond.

Credit & Collection Tip: *While deposits are guaranteed by the Federal Deposit Insurance Corporation, certified checks and cashier's checks are not.*

A minority of courts have concluded that cashier's checks should be treated as ordinary negotiable instruments (Maryland, Nebraska, Connecticut, Delaware, and Louisiana). In these instances, the reliance is on the UCC provision governing the liability of obligors on most ordinary checks. On the other hand, the majority of the courts have adopted the "cash equivalent," whereby cashier's checks are treated as equivalent to cash. The bank becomes the guarantor of the value of the check and budgets its resources for the payment of the amount. To allow the bank to stop payment on such an instrument would be inconsistent with a representation it made when issuing the check. Accordingly, the court adopted a theory that the bank may refuse to honor a stop payment on a cashier's check because the check itself is accepted by the bank upon the issuance of the check. The case provides an in-depth analysis of this topic, with many citations.[12]

Unsigned Check. A check that is unsigned may be deposited by the recipient by endorsing on the reverse side of the check the payee's signature and guaranteeing the signature of the maker of the check to the bank in writing on the reverse side of the check. When the check is presented to the maker's bank, the bank accepts the check and transfers the funds. The maker who receives the debit on the bank statement will not contact the bank since he or she believed the check was signed. The maker who did not sign the check deliberately will contact the bank which, in turn, will contact the depositor's bank and assert no signature. The bank will charge the depositor's account and the depositor will be in no worse or better position than if the check was returned to the maker for signature. The only expense incurred is the charge of the bank for returning the check.

Credit & Collection Tip: *If the unsigned check is returned by mail to the debtor for signature, the debtor may never sign the check and send it back to the creditor. Sometimes the debtor does not sign the check intentionally as a ploy to stall for time. For this reason, we recommend guaranteeing the signature and depositing the check, as described above.*

---

[11] *Associated Carriages, Inc. v. International Bank of Commerce*, 37 S.W.3d 69 (Tex. Ct. App. 4th Dist. 2000); *Parks v. Commerce Bank*, 377 N.J. Super. 378 (App. Div. 2005).

[12] *Weldon v. Trust Co. Bank of Columbus*, 499 S.E.2d 293 (Ga. App. 1998).

Alternate Payees. A check made payable in the alternative to one of several payees is covered by the UCC Section 3-110(d). It states that such a check payable to two or more persons alternatively is payable to any of them and may be negotiated, discharged, or enforced by any or all of them in possession of the instrument. If an instrument is payable to two or more persons not alternatively, it is payable to all of them and may be negotiated, discharged or enforced only by all of them. If the instrument is ambiguous as to whether it is payable to the persons alternatively or otherwise, the instrument is payable to all persons alternatively. If a check is payable to two or more people in the alternative and contains one unauthorized signature, is the check valid bearing only one valid endorsement? Despite a forgery of one payee's endorsement, one valid endorsement is sufficient to negotiate a check even if the check is payable in the alternative or if it is ambiguous as to whether it is payable jointly or in the alternative.[13]

Attachment of Checking Accounts. In the event a judgment is entered against a corporation, a partnership, or an individual, the creditor has the right to issue a restraining notice or "garnishment," which will attach a bank account up to or double the amount of the judgment. In today's computerized environment, restraining notices are easy to prepare and serve on a bank. In the major metropolitan areas, the money center banks or the large regional banks maintain numerous branches. The restraining notice may be served on only one branch and it will affect all the branches. For example, if half a dozen restraining notices are issued in a major city, such as New York, Los Angeles, or Chicago, to the major banks in the city, they may cover hundreds of branches. Thus, the restraining notice is effective and the business, as well as the individual, must be aware that once a judgment is entered, the bank account is vulnerable to execution by the creditor.

One of the problems in attaching a bank account after a judgment is that the debtor will assert:

1. that the account is jointly held with another party;
2. that the monies do not belong to the depositor and that it is being held for someone else;
3. that the account is a direct deposit account that receives salary checks.

In reverse order, if it is a salary check, and the state law only permits a certain percentage of salary to be levied upon (such as in New York, where the limitation is 10%), then the creditor would be entitled to 10 percent of that salary check and would not be entitled to levy on the entire amount in

---

[13]*Coregis Ins. Co. v. Fleet Nat'l Bank*, 793 A.2d 244 (Conn. 2002); *S.R. Simplot Inc. v. Knight*, 988 P.2d 955 (Wash. 1999); *Pelican Nat'l Bank v. Provident Bank of Maryland*, 849 A.2d 475 (Md. 2004); *L.B. Smith, Inc. v. Bankers Trust Co. Western N.Y.*, 55 N.Y.2d 942 (1982).

the account. An examination of the bank statement should be made to verify that only salary checks are deposited.

If it is money that the debtor claims belongs to someone else (such as his mother, sister, spouse, etc.), the attorney for the creditor should obtain sufficient documentation to establish that it is not the debtor's money. The burden of proof, of course, is upon the debtor, and if he cannot produce sufficient documentation, the creditor should make a motion in court to obtain the full amount.

If it is a joint account, the account should be labeled jointly between the husband and the wife. Under those circumstances, levy on half of the account and leave the other half of the account for the other party. If it is a joint account with right of survivorship, the debtor may argue successfully that you would have to wait to see who survives before executing on the monies in the account. If the wife survived, the creditor would not be entitled to any monies in the account and if the debtor survived, the creditor would be entitled to the full amount in the account. In most instances, in our practice, a settlement is made around 50 percent of the account.

The most dangerous aspect of attaching bank accounts is attaching a bank account with the wrong name, a typographical error in the account number, or some other clerical error that ends up attaching the wrong account. The attorney for the creditor should act rapidly to remove the attachment because the creditor may be liable for damages that the account holder would sustain by reason of the account being attached inadvertently. Often, the error is caused by the bank. The bank should also act quickly to remove the attachment. The problem is not serious if the attachment is only on the bank account for a day or two and the amount attached is not a large amount, but when the attachment remains for weeks or months, the damages could be significant.

The use of restraining notices has been radically changed by new laws in New York City, requiring notices, warnings, and information to be furnished to judgment debtors. Other states or cities may copy the procedures.

COMMERCIAL BAD FAITH

To hold a bank liable for fraud committed by a third party usually requires proof that the bank had full knowledge of the fraud, participated in the fraud, and benefited from the fraud. The fact that the bank knowingly or recklessly disregarded several "badges of fraud," including irregularities in the opening of the accounts and in the documents being submitted for the wire transfer, and knowing that the employee who handled the transaction lived on the same block as the party who committed the fraud, and the rejection of wire transfers should have alerted the bank, are insufficient allegations to create an inference that the bank knew of or participated in the fraud.

A claim for commercial bad faith may arise if a plaintiff alleges facts that the principals of the bank were actual participants in the unlawful activity. Despite the fact several red flags were flying that should have alerted the bank to a fraud, or at least prompted the bank to investigate, and even though the bank acted negligently with regard to its conduct, allegations that a bank disregarded suspicious circumstances that may have induced the prudent banker to inquire do not suffice to state a claim for commercial bad faith. The bank's actions may be negligent and even grossly negligent, but this does not sufficiently allege the actual knowledge or the participation in the fraudulent action that supports a claim for commercial bad faith.

JOINT ACCOUNT—OVERDRAFT

The UCC states that a person is not liable for the amount of an overdraft if the customer neither signed the item nor received the proceeds of the item. The Official Commentary Subsection B adopts the view that if there is more than one customer who can draw on an account, the nonsigning customer is not liable for an overdraft unless that person benefits from the proceeds of the item.

Section 4-401 applies to the relationship between the payor bank and its customer. Joint ownership usually means that either owner can sign checks and both may be liable. Where the joint ownership is between a husband and wife, one spouse would be liable even though the other spouse signed the checks. In the event of a divorce of separation, the parties should close out joint checking accounts immediately. If one party maintained the joint checking account and made the deposits in the joint checking account and issued the checks on the joint checking account without the consent or knowledge of the other party, case law is uneven as to whether the other party would be liable.

The obligation of the nonsigning party of the check is uncertain where the nonsigning party has no knowledge that the other party is signing the check and probably receives no benefit or consideration from the transaction. Under these circumstances, when a suit is instituted against a nonsigner, the debt collector or the creditor can expect vigorous opposition, especially if the check is for a large amount.

> ***Credit & Collection Tip:*** *Whenever considering the institution of suit upon a check from a joint account against the nonsigner of the check, the amount should be large enough to warrant litigation. The second step is to determine the case law within the state. If these results are affirmative, the third question is whether the nonsigner received any benefits.*[14]

---

[14]*Heard v. Bonneville Billing and Collections*, 216 F.3d 1087 (10th Cir. 2000).

FORGED ENDORSEMENT

Signatures on checks and notes are not often forged, but if you deal with enough checks and notes, a signature does get forged. When an endorsement is forged on a check, a general rule applies shifting the risk of loss either upon the drawee bank for improper payment over a forged endorsement or to the drawer of the check when the fictitious payee exception applies. The official comment adopts the principle that the risk of loss for fraudulent endorsements by employees who are entrusted with responsibility for checks falls on the employer rather than the bank that takes the check or pays it, if the bank was not negligent in the transaction. The section is based on the belief that the employer is in a better position to avoid the loss by using care in choosing employees, in supervising them, and in adopting other measures to prevent forged endorsements on instruments payable to the employer or fraud in the issuance of instruments in the name of the employer. If the bank failed to exercise ordinary care, Subsection B allows the employer to shift the loss to the bank to the extent of the bank's failure to exercise ordinary care.

In the official comment to the statute, several examples are afforded concerning forged checks. A janitor finds a check and forges the employer's name on the check, cashes the check, and absconds with the money. In this case, the employer was not necessarily negligent unless the bank can show that the employer left the check negligently around for the janitor to find.

A second example is where the treasurer of a corporation, who is authorized to write the checks on behalf of the corporation, issues the check to himself and signs the check as an authorized officer of the corporation. The check is not forged although it was not authorized since no money was owed to the treasurer. Under these circumstances, the corporation is bound to pay the check.

A bookkeeper steals a check payable to the employer and forges the employer's endorsement. The check is deposited to the employee's account and honored. The endorsement is effective as the employer's endorsement because the employee was a bookkeeper and she was entrusted with the check for bookkeeping purposes. The employer is liable.

One should remember that UCC Section 4-406 penalizes the customer who waits to report a forgery more than one year after the customer receives a bank statement. After the one-year period expires, the customer is barred from recovering against the bank.[15]

A bank normally undertakes the risk of a maker's signature being unauthorized unless the person actually presenting the check has knowledge

---

[15]*Chester Township Board of Trustees v. Bank One, N.A.*, 2007 WL 1881311 (Ohio App. 11th Dist. 2007).

that the signature of the maker of the check is unauthorized. The bank is presumed to know the signature of the drawer. If the bank pays a forged check to a holder, the bank will not be entitled to recover the money where a fraud was practiced upon the maker.[16]

In the Appendix to this chapter, you will find UCC Article 3, Sections 3-403-407, which deals with unauthorized signatures, fictitious payees, and employer's responsibility for fraudulent endorsements and forged signatures or alterations of instruments.[17]

BANKS—LIABILITY FOR OPERATIONAL ERRORS

A recent decision out of a district court in California discussed the liability of the bank for wrongfully cashing checks without proper signatures, the obligation of the bank as a fiduciary, an error made in communication between the bank and depositor and various other types of errors that commonly can be made in the operation of any business.

The case summarizes the available remedies against the bank and the application of the Uniform Commercial Code to some of the banking laws. The case is decided under California law, but many of the statements cross state lines. The issue of liability as a fiduciary as opposed to the tort of negligent misrepresentation is discussed at length. The case is a good beginning point in the event the bank has made an error.[18]

DEMAND DRAFT

A demand draft arises in a situation where the debtor does not actually sign the check. The creditor affixes a legend of some kind to the signature line that states the check has been authorized by the maker (drawer). This is often used in situations where the debtor authorizes telephonically, or in some other manner, a credit card company or a creditor to create a demand draft upon the debtor's account.

Demand drafts are often addressed as a "pre-authorized draft" or a "check by telephone." A demand draft is actually created on actual paper and in most instances the creditor provides a printed form that will recite that it is a demand draft. The creditor signs the draft through the use of his signature and by marking his signature the "authorized signature."

---

[16]*Clear World Eng'g Ltd. v. Midamerica Bank FSB*, 793 N.E.2d 110 (Ill. App. Ct. 2003).
[17]*Guardian Life Ins. Co. of Am. v. Chemical Bank*, 727 N.E.2d 111 (N.Y. 2000).
[18]*Holcomb v. Wells Fargo Bank, N.A.*, 155 Cal. App. 4th 490 (Cal. App. 4th Dist. 2007).

The New York statute states as follows:

Signature by Authorized Representative

1. A signature may be made by an agent or other representative, and its authority to make it may be established as in other cases of representation. No particular form of appointment is necessary to establish such authority.
2. An authorized representative who signs his own name to an instrument.
   (a) is personally obligated if the instrument neither names the person represented nor shows that the representative signed in a representative capacity.
   (b) except as otherwise established between the immediate parties, is personally obligated if the instrument names the person represented but does not show that the representative signed in a representative capacity, or if the instrument does not name the person represented but does show that the representative signed in a representative capacity.
3. Except as otherwise established in the name of an organization preceded or followed by the name and office of an authorized individual is a signature made in a representative capacity.

The creditor must use due diligence to confirm the identity of the consumer as well as the fact that the consumer is actually authenticating the signature to be signed by the "authorized representative." The most common manner of authentication is by previous transaction history. For transactions that occur over the internet, with old customers, passwords and pin numbers may be used. The legal requirements seem to be that the whole transaction must be handled in a commercially reasonable manner.

Verification of the authorization to create the demand draft can be done by requiring the consumer to provide written authorization by fax or to record the telephone call with a witness on the other side with full disclosure to the consumer that you are recording the phone call and that another party is listening to the statement by the consumer authorizing you to create the draft.

Several companies that provide this kind of service also provide the equipment to print the demand draft. Before any creditor embarks upon this program, consultation with counsel is recommended to be certain that all the required steps in a "commercially reasonable manner" are performed.

If the demand draft is unauthorized, the collecting bank, which created the draft, is liable in the event the bank has knowledge. When the check is sent to the payor bank, the payor bank can look to the depository bank (collecting bank) for payment if said bank had knowledge that the check was unauthorized, but if the depository (collecting bank) does not have knowledge, the payor bank is liable. (UCC 4-208.)

Where the document does not bear a handwritten signature purporting to be the signature of the drawer, the revised UCC Articles 3 and 4 indicate from their commentary that they are reversing the premise that the payor bank should be liable for these unauthorized demand drafts where the collecting bank had no knowledge of the unauthorized draft. The reasoning is that the collecting bank is in a better position to monitor and control this type of fraud more effectively as opposed to the paying bank. As of this writing, only one state, Minnesota, has adopted Article 3 and the author does not know of any decisions which have addressed these new warranties in Articles 3 and 4 of the UCC. (Revised UCC 3-103.)

INTEREST AND USURY—USURY SAVINGS CLAUSE

Many federal institutions are governed by federal laws which regulate the amount of interest they can charge. The Small Business Investment Act describes specific criteria under which the Small Business Administration lends money and sets forth certain maximum rates that are allowed to be charged by the Small Business Administration.

Most states have a maximum rate of interest which may be charged on loans. Different maximum rates may be set for individuals and corporations. In addition, the law provides for a lower legal rate of interest after a judgment is obtained. For example, in New York the legal rate allowed to be charged to a corporation is 25 percent. After a judgment is entered against the corporation, the legal rate which the creditor may charge the corporate debtor is only 9 percent. Under this set of circumstances, a debtor who has no defense to a suit may find it useful to permit a creditor to enter judgment quickly to reduce the rate of interest that the creditor may charge, rather than delay the suit by interposing frivolous defenses.

Several years ago the banks were successful in establishing that they can export interest rates from their home state to those credit card customers who are living in different states, even though the interest rate in their home state was prohibited by law in the state in which the credit card customer resided. Late charges also were treated as interest. For this reason many of the banks position their credit card operations in states which are favorable to the banks and enable them to charge higher rates than are allowed in the other states of the country.

The Monetary Control Act sets forth certain provisions which remove some federal institutions from regulation by the state. Under certain circumstances, the states may override this insulation. State-chartered banks and federal banks also may be insulated against the usury statute of the state, due to the application of federal laws to banks. In most states, laws are specifically applied to the rates of interest and other charges that a state bank may impose.

When one charges a rate in excess of the amount allowed by state law, the rate is deemed to be usurious. Nevertheless, determining whether a rate is usurious or is not usurious is complex and confusing. The rates of interest allowed by the various states vary so substantially that one cannot begin to speak about these rates until the law of each state is examined and a table is constructed as to what restrictions are set forth in each state. The penalties for violations of a statute also differ significantly from state to state:

1. The creditor loses the difference of the interest rate charge which is in excess of the rate allowed.
2. That the creditor not only loses the interest in excess of the rate allowed but loses the entire interest.
3. The creditor may forfeit a sum of money double the amount of the interest charge.
4. In some states, the lender may be unable to enforce the entire debt merely because interest in excess of the permitted rate was charged.
5. In some states, the charging of a usurious rate of interest may actually be a criminal offense ranging from a misdemeanor to a felony.

When the rate of interest is the maximum rate allowed under a particular statute, and then other charges are added by virtue of other transactions or other activities by the debtor the lender always runs the risk of being targeted with a charge of usury. The other charges may be treated as interest.[19]

Many contracts contain what is commonly known as a "usury savings clause." These clauses basically state something along the following terms:

> Notwithstanding anything contained herein in the contract, in no event shall the aggregate of any interest charged plus any other amounts charged which are deemed interest, exceed the maximum amount of interest which could lawfully be charged. If any amount of interest taken or received by the creditor shall be in excess of the maximum amount of interest which could lawfully be collected, then the excess shall be deemed to have been a result of a mathematical error and shall be refunded promptly to the debtor.

A clause such as this normally will not help if the creditor intended to charge usurious rates, such as where the allowable legal rate of interest was 9 percent and the promissory note provided for an interest rate of 14 percent.

A different result follows when the claim of the debtor rests upon the fact that the interest or other charges become usurious after a default in the terms of payment. The note provides for late charges per diem together with an interest rate, which together are in excess of a usurious rate. If there is a

[19] *Sunburst Bank v. Keith*, 648 So. 2d 1147 (Miss. 1995).

default in payment, this is not necessarily a usurious rate of interest providing a usury savings clause is present. A usury savings clause may not rescue a transaction that is necessarily usurious by its explicit terms, but on the other hand it may rescue the collection of usurious interest that is contingent solely on making late payments and the extent of the tardiness of those payments. The court pointed out that the late charges would not necessarily create a usurious rate of interest unless the delinquency was significant. The court did conclude that the occurrence of the contingency, the late payments, would not necessarily have resulted in usurious interest. The debtor would have to be late on numerous monthly payments before the interest generated by the late charges would have been usurious. Under those circumstances, at least in this case, the court held that the late payment provisions were not usurious and were saved by the usury savings clause.[20]

Another problem in usurious contracts is determining whether or not the particular transaction constitutes a loan or constitutes some other type of transaction. If the transaction is not a loan, the question of usury does not come into play. A loan is a contract whereby one party transfers to the other a sum of money which the other agrees to pay absolutely together with such additional sums as may be agreed upon for the use of the money. The furnishing of merchandise or services does not impact the usury laws.

A late penalty charge imposed on a condominium association was considered to be neither a loan nor a forbearance or any kind of retention of money and accordingly, no "lending relationship" was contemplated by the statute in Connecticut. The court concluded that the late charge did not fall within any of the statutory definitions of interest and was not interest as a matter of law. The assessments under various fees and charges claimed to be excessive were not subject to the provisions of the state usury laws.[21]

Many businesses charge 18 percent per annum or 1.5 percent per month on delinquent accounts and often this additional charge for delinquent accounts could exceed the usurious rate either in the state in which the business resides or in the state where the customer resides. The problem arises as to which state law would apply, which is a function of whether you are attempting to enforce the debt in the state where the customer resides or in the state where the seller resides. Where the provisions for interest are included in the original agreement, the seller should not be faced with this problem unless the state statute provides for a limitation on the interest charged to corporations or businesses. In some states, the legal rate of interest for corporations is much higher than the individual rate, and lenders will require the individual to form a corporation.

The best place for such a provision is in a clear and conspicuous format in the credit application and the guarantee. The good news is

[20] *Parhms v. B&B Ventures, Inc.*, 938 S.W.2d 199 (Tex. Ct. App. 14th Dist. 1997).

[21] *Mountain View Condo. Ass'n of Vernon, Conn., Inc. v. Rumford Assoc., IV*, No. CV 94556935, 1997 WL 120254 (Conn. Super. Ct. Mar. 4, 1997).

that the majority of the states, although not an overwhelming majority, take the position that an increased rate of interest which may be usurious is really not usurious because it basically is avoidable by the borrower paying on time. The minority states do not follow this theory, with some cases depending upon whether the judge feels the increased rate of interest is fair or unfair. It is recommended that your credit applications and the charging of interest be reviewed by counsel.

A Court of Appeals case in Texas addressed this issue and stated flatly that asserting the defense of a usury savings clause will not be enforced if a contract is usurious by its explicit terms.[22] This reasoning prevents a creditor from freely contracting for usurious interest knowing that for the few debtors who do complain, the creditor will escape a penalty by simply referring to a boilerplate savings clause and refunding the usurious amount. Frankly, the court was right on target.

NEGOTIABLE INSTRUMENTS

We start with a promise to pay a debt which reads as follows:

> I, Mary Jones, hereby acknowledge that I owe John Smith One thousand dollars and promise to pay to John Smith One thousand dollars by June 1, 1996. Signature *Mary Jones*

John Smith decides to sell that obligation of Mary Jones to his uncle (Harry Adams) for $900, because he cannot wait until June 1 for payment. Mary Jones does not pay the debt by June 1 and, ultimately, the uncle sues Mary Jones in court. Mary Jones asserts the defense that John Smith coerced her under duress to sign her signature since she received only $750 and not $1,000.

This type of agreement is described as an "IOU" or a "marker." The defense of duress that Mary Jones is asserting is a valid defense against both John Smith (the assignor), who did the actual coercion, and his uncle (the assignee), who purchased the note from John Smith, but was not aware of the coercion and duress. The purchaser of the note (the uncle) is subject to the defenses to which John Smith is subject. This fair result preserves the defenses of Mary Jones against the person to whom John Smith transferred the note. This is identified as a non-negotiable agreement to pay a payee (Smith), and the note was assigned by the assignor (payee) to an assignee (uncle).

On the other hand, a negotiable instrument would produce an entirely different result. A negotiable instrument states:

> I agree to *pay to the order* of John Smith One thousand dollars on the 1st day of June, 1996. *MARY JONES*

---

[22] *Kaplan v. Tiffany Dev. Corp.*, 2001 WL 846070 (Tex. Ct. App. 2001).

The magic words are "pay to the order of," which means that the maker agrees to pay $1,000 to John Smith, or to anyone that John Smith should "order" or designate as the person to receive a negotiation (purchase or transfer) of the note. The purchase of the note for $900 by the uncle from John Smith is defined as a negotiation; and because of those magic words, the legal consequences change radically. When the uncle tries to enforce the note, the defense of duress would not be available to Mary Jones. The third party (uncle) purchases the note for the $900 free of any defenses that the maker of the note (Mary Jones) may assert against the payee (John Smith). This purchase is accomplished by John Smith writing his name on the reverse side of the note. To continue the negotiable characteristics of the note, in favor of the uncle, the magic words "pay to the order" of the "uncle" would precede the signature of John Smith.

The inscription on the reverse side would appear as follows:

> Pay to the order of Harry Adams.
> Signature *John Smith*

The uncle is described as a "holder in due course," which means he owns the note and is not concerned with the defenses of the maker.

The reason for this result is to promote the negotiability (sale or transfer) of notes so that the purchaser of the note will not be concerned with any defenses of the maker of the note. The UCC states that not only must the words "pay to the order" be used, but the following requirements must also be met:

1. The party to whom the note is negotiated (sold) must have good title to the instrument in that the prior selling party had good title (the note was not stolen by John Smith, the payee).
2. The signature on the note must be genuine. If the signature was forged, Mary Jones would not be liable.
3. No material alteration of the note has occurred (no erasures or alterations of amounts or other material terms).
4. The party to whom the note is negotiated (the uncle) does not have any knowledge of any defect in the note in that he knew of any material alteration, forgery, fraud, duress, or any other defense. If the uncle knows of Mary's defense at the time the note was sold to him, the uncle is not "a holder in due course."

Other circumstances must be met to support a negotiable instrument:

- The note or check must be in writing.
- The note or check must be payable either on demand or on some fixed day or time.

- The note or check may be payable to the order of a named person (John Smith), but may also be payable to the order of the "bearer." Instead of inserting the name of John Smith, the word "bearer" is inserted. A "bearer" instrument is freely transferable, and anyone who comes into possession is the owner of the note (except if stolen).

The note or check must be in writing and usually must be payable in cash or the equivalent.

One court held that where the note and a separate agreement entitled the party to be repaid in the form of common shares of stock, the court decided that the note was not negotiable.[23]

Promissory Notes. A promissory note (a negotiable instrument) is often used in business transactions when a business debtor wishes to pay the debt over a period of time. The use of post-dated checks is not desirable since suit cannot be instituted on all post-dated checks until each check is presented for payment and is returned unpaid. If six post-dated checks were delivered to the creditor, and the first check was returned unpaid, suit would lie on that one check, not the remaining five checks. A second suit may be instituted after the next check is returned unpaid. The solution is a series of six promissory notes containing a provision enabling the creditor to accelerate all six notes in the event one of the notes is returned unpaid.

Although promissory notes and checks are both negotiable instruments, substantial distinctions exist between them:

A. Promissory notes may provide for acceleration so that the entire balance will be due upon a default in payment of one note.
B. Promissory notes may provide for reasonable attorney fees or a fixed amount of attorney fees if the note is referred to an attorney for collection.
C. Promissory notes can be drafted in some states with a power of attorney permitting the holder of the note to enter a judgment in a commercial transaction in the event of the default of one note. This is the equivalent of a confession of judgment and is known as a "cognovit" note (under the Credit Practice Act, not enforceable as to consumers).
D. Promissory notes may contain a variety of terms and conditions which may consume several pages, such as a note prepared by a bank or a financial institution. The note may provide for payment of interest calculated in a number of different ways, the requirement of security to ensure the payment of the note, provisions covering

[23] *Gem Global Yield Fund v. Surgilight, Inc.*, 2006 WL 2389345 (S.D.N.Y. 2006).

bankruptcy as a default, creating a default by failing to meet other obligations to the creditor, efforts by other creditors against the borrower creating a default, and other acts constituting a default under the note other than nonpayment. The note may allow recovery if in the judgment of the creditor the collateral is deemed inadequate to secure the bank. The note may provide for reimbursement to the creditor of all costs and expenses incurred in the granting of the loan or the recovery of the loan, including the cost of attorney fees. The note allows the creditor to assign and transfer the debt. The terms and conditions of the note are unlimited and usually drafted with precision to protect the creditor.

E. Promissory notes are negotiable instruments and may provide for a waiver of defenses and rights in certain circumstances. An example is a waiver of a jury trial and an agreement that the laws of a specific state will control the transaction (usually the state where the lender is located).

Trade Acceptance. A trade acceptance is the equivalent of a promissory note drawn by one businessperson upon another businessperson and issued for the payment of goods. While there is no prescribed form, the trade acceptance is similar to and operates generally as a promissory note.

LOST NOTES—ENFORCEMENT

All of us at one time or another have misplaced papers for an extended length of time and we do not wish to admit that the papers are lost. Under the UCC Section 3-309, a person is entitled to recover on a lost note. The section states as follows:

a. a person not in possession of an instrument is entitled to enforce the instrument if (i) the person was in possession of the instrument and entitled to enforce it when loss of possession occurred, (ii) the loss of possession was not the result of a transfer by the person or a lawful seizure, (iii) the person cannot reasonably obtain possession of the instrument because the instrument was destroyed, its whereabouts cannot be determined, or it is in the wrongful possession of an unknown person or a person that cannot be found or is not amenable to service of process.

b. a person seeking enforcement of an instrument under subsection (a) must prove the terms of the instrument and the person's right to enforce the instrument. If that proof is made, Section 3-308 applies to the case as if the person seeking enforcement had produced the instrument. The court may not enter judgment in favor of the person

> seeking enforcement unless it finds that the person required to pay the instrument is "adequately protected" against loss that might occur by reason of a claim by another person to enforce the instrument. Adequate protection may be provided by any reasonable means.

The section replaced an older section in the UCC wherein the owner of a lost instrument rather than the person in the possession of the instrument at the time of loss was entitled to enforce it.

The "adequate protection" wording is a flexible concept. A holder in due course may make demand for payment, if the instrument was payable to bearer when it was lost or stolen. If the instrument was payable to the person who lost the instrument and that person did not endorse the instrument, no other person could be a valid holder in due course. Under a recent case, the Federal Deposit Insurance Corporation (FDIC) sold a note after it was lost and issued an affidavit of a lost note to the plaintiff who sought to enforce the note. The defendants argued that plaintiff was not the party in possession at time of loss and could not utilize the revised UCC section. The court used the strict interpretation and stated "the plain language of the provision mandates that the plaintiff suing on the note must meet two tests, not just one: it must have been both in possession of the note when it was lost and entitled to enforce the note when it was lost." Under that theory, the plaintiff would not have been able to enforce the note.

Nevertheless in the instant case, the plaintiff was successful because a provision in the guarantee executed by the defendant stated "any invalidity, irregularity, or enforceability of the obligation was hereby waived." This, or words of similar import, is a common clause in many guarantees. In the guarantees used by creditors that are only a few lines or are contained in credit applications or parts of other documents, where the president is guaranteeing the payment of the corporation's debt, this type of clause does not appear. Whether this reasoning would be successful in other jurisdictions is questionable, since the initial note is not enforceable under the UCC and if such is the case, the court stretched when they created a new life and a new obligation by virtue of the guarantee (when the original obligation was unenforceable).[24] (*See* Chapter 1, "Lost and Destroyed Documents.")

GUARANTEES

An individual or a corporation may guarantee the debt of another party. A guarantee must be in writing, since an oral guarantee is unenforceable. The written guarantee must be clear and must specify exactly what is being guaranteed, that is, the payment of a debt, the performance of a contract.

[24] *Dennis Joslin Co. v. Robinson Broad. Corp.*, 977 F. Supp. 491 (D.D.C. 1997).

The more specific a guarantee is, the better the chance it will be enforceable. Guarantees can cover many pages, and may provide for the waiver of defenses, a provision that the guarantee continues indefinitely to cover future advances to the corporation, the conditions under which the guarantee may be enforced, and a wide variety of clauses favorable to the person enforcing the guarantee.

> ***Credit & Collection Tip:*** *Be certain that the guarantee is dated, that it identifies the place where the guarantee is being executed, the amount being guaranteed, the party's debt that is being guaranteed, and when the guarantee begins to operate.*

CORPORATE GUARANTEE. Guarantees by corporations should be reviewed carefully since the by-laws of many corporations do not permit the execution of guarantees. Corporations in certain states need some form of consideration or benefit or payment to the corporation to be liable on a guarantee. A resolution of the board of directors is usually requested by the lender, stating that the board of directors has authorized this guarantee and, if possible, designating specifically the benefit or the consideration the corporation receives. Even in those states where consideration is not required, obtaining a corporate resolution of the board of directors is still the best practice.

CREDIT APPLICATION. Guarantees are frequently used in conjunction with credit applications by printing a guarantee on the reverse side or on the bottom of a credit application for execution by the individual officer of the corporation, the principal owner of the stock of the corporation, or a partner of the partnership. If properly drawn and clearly and conspicuously labeled, the guarantee is enforceable.

HUSBAND AND WIFE. A financial institution seeks the guarantee of the husband and wife as a condition of extending credit to the husband's business. If the financial institution is not relying upon the credit of the spouse, under the Equal Credit Opportunity Act, the guarantee of the spouse may be unenforceable (*see* Chapter 18). A review of that law and the relevant court decisions is recommended.

ELEMENTS OF GUARANTEES. How often have credit grantors heard the following pleas of lack of knowledge or understanding: "I was not aware that I signed a guarantee." "I did not understand what I was signing." "I cannot read English." "I was told that it was only a credit application." A classic example of a problem with a guarantee occurred in a case in Nevada.[25] The president in his corporate capacity signed a document

[25]*Pentax Corp. v. Boyd*, 111 Nev. 1296, 904 P.2d 1024 (Nev. 1995).

entitled "Credit Application and Renewal." The document listed the corporation as the customer and the president as owner/president. On the reverse side of this credit application was a document entitled "guarantee," which stated that the president unconditionally guaranteed current or future indebtedness for which the customer was obligated to the plaintiff. The guarantee included terms which allowed the plaintiff to release or surrender the security without the consent of a guarantor. The president admitted signing the guarantee although there were a few blank spaces in the guarantee for the date and the name of the customer.

The president contended no relationship was formed because the plaintiff used a credit application rather than an application for an open account and no underlying contractual relationship existed. The president was not even aware that he signed as a guarantor. The plaintiff said that the president was told that his signature on the guarantee would expedite the approval of credit (and the guarantee probably did expedite approval).

The above set of circumstances is a classic example of what often happens in the business environment.

Parties may be held liable for contracts they did not read. Since the president was a merchant and the one-page guarantee was conspicuously labeled, his failure to read the guarantee is not relevant; and the guarantee is enforceable.

Certain essential elements make a guarantee binding and enforceable:

1. the name of the guarantor
2. the name of the party whose debts are being guaranteed
3. the terms and conditions of the guarantee
4. the interest of property affected
5. the consideration to be paid.

Several writings together may supply an essential term which may be missing and may be construed together to supply the essential terms *if there is a reference in one document to another document*. Where more than one writing is used, there is an "internal reference" to describe the requisite nexus between the writings. The credit application and the guarantee construed together clearly refer to the same transaction and the customer's name on the credit application is the same customer referenced in the guarantee. The blank spaces in the guarantee did not render it indefinite, as long as the intent of the parties was readily ascertainable. Oral evidence is allowed to explain the information that should have been entered in the blank spaces.

While this is a classic example of a guarantor claiming that he did not read the guarantee and that blank spaces should void the guarantee, the lesson learned is that a guarantee should be carefully completed and reviewed so that the lender has the proper documentation in the event of a problem at a later date. As to the defense that the guarantor did not read or understand the guarantee or thought it was a different type of agreement, a risk is always present where the guarantor is representing himself and no attorney is present. The guarantee should be conspicuously labeled a guarantee of the debt of a corporation and the print setting forth the guarantee should be clear, conspicuous, readable, and understandable by the guarantor. Including the five requirements listed in this Nevada case is also helpful.

FRAUD. Usually, a fraudulent act to induce an individual to execute a guarantee will allow a guarantor to avoid his obligation. Where the guarantee is absolute, unconditional, and irrevocable, a court may take the position that fraud in the inducement of a guarantee of the corporate officer of a corporation's indebtedness is not a defense to an action on the guarantee.[26]

BANK GUARANTEES. While many credit applications provide for a guarantee by principal owners of a corporation, these guarantees are usually simple, direct, and primarily state that the principal guarantees all the debts of the corporation to the seller. On the other hand, the situation is quite different where the principal owners or officers execute a written guarantee in favor of a lending institution.

Depending upon the policy of the institution extending the credit, the written guarantee may consist of only a few lines, but in most instances the guarantee consists of several paragraphs that primarily provide for waivers of defenses that could be asserted by the guarantor. Guarantees provided by the large financial institutions and banks sometimes run one to two pages of small print and cover every conceivable waiver of defense that may be asserted by the guarantor. The guarantee allows the lender to enter into any type or form of modification or agreement with the primary borrower without affecting the liability of the guarantor.

The comprehensive guarantee of all liability drafted by the major financial institutions sets forth virtually everything you can possibly squeeze into a guarantee. The guarantee provides for an "absolute and unconditional guarantee" for the prompt payment of all claims of every nature and description that the lender may have against a corporate borrower. The key words to which a guarantor must be alert are the time frames that affect the guarantee. The most comprehensive terminology is "debts now existing or thereafter incurred" by the corporation. This terminology covers the situation where the guarantor has left the services of the corporation either by retirement, buy out, or otherwise, and is still liable for future loans or advances to the corporation that are unpaid.

---

[26]*Citibank, N.A. v. Plapinger*, 66 N.Y.2d 90, 485 N.E.2d 974, 495 N.Y.S.2d 309 (1985).

Lending institutions also provide for a right to set off monies on deposit or any assets in the possession of the bank against any liabilities of the borrower. Usually, this can be done without any notice to the guarantor. The ability of the lender to continue to finance the borrower without being restricted by the state laws that afford protection to the guarantor is essential to these types of agreement. The lender is most concerned with any activity the borrower may engage in which renews, extends, modifies, accelerates, compromises, or settles any of the obligations of the borrower and the lender does not want to be concerned with notifying the guarantor each time.

Many state laws require a lender to notify the guarantor if any collateral is sold. Court decisions provide that when there are modifications of agreements, guarantors are usually released unless they are notified of the modification. As a result, these comprehensive guarantee agreements provide a waiver by the guarantor of these defenses that he may assert under the law. Some states do provide that certain waivers are ineffective: for example, an obligation on the part of the lender to use reasonable care in the custody and preservation of any collateral. State laws usually do not permit the guarantor to waive notice of sale of the collateral.

The default provisions of guarantees may be extremely comprehensive. A default in any obligation by the corporation to the bank would constitute a default of the primary obligation. If a business happens to be a partnership, the death of the partner usually constitutes a default. Insolvency, assignment for the benefit to creditors, or a bankruptcy may terminate the agreement. Some agreements provide that even the failure to furnish financial information or to permit inspection of the books would constitute a default under the borrower's agreement with the bank. If such a default occurs by virtue of any of these activities, the guarantor would still become liable.

A default might also occur in the event enforcement proceedings proceed under any judgment that had been entered against the borrower. Interestingly, some guarantees provide that in the event of default, the financial institution can call upon the guarantor to assemble the collateral and make it available to the bank. The bank may then proceed with the sale. State laws may prohibit, regulate, or otherwise affect many of these obligations in the guarantee. Sometimes the obligation has more than one guarantor. The lending institution provides that it may terminate or revoke the other guarantee without terminating and revoking the guarantee of the party against whom it is proceeding. While this may seem unfair, the guarantor against whom the bank proceeds still has a right against the co-guarantor since it is the bank that has released and terminated the obligation to the bank.

The bank cannot release the obligation of its co-guarantors. It is possible that an agreement provided that a new instrument of guarantee executed in favor of a financial institution would not necessarily terminate the old instrument of guarantee unless it was expressly provided for in the new instrument of guarantee. This could be misleading to a guarantor asked to execute a new guarantee, since it would be reasonable to assume the new guarantee is instead of the old guarantee. Nevertheless, this type of clause in the old guarantee would have to be considered by the courts.

Guarantees may be terminated by the guarantor, and most agreements provide that the termination agreement must be in writing. The guarantor should send a notice of termination by certified mail. The notice of termination would not apply retroactively to any obligations that exist as of the date of termination, but would apply to any new obligations incurred by the corporation after the date of notice of termination. The notice should be worded carefully and reviewed by counsel.

Guarantees provide for the jurisdiction in which a suit must be started and the guarantor waives any defenses as to jurisdiction. The agreement provides that the guarantor waives a jury trial and in some instances the guarantor agrees to service by mail of process (service of a summons of complaint) rather than by personal service, the accepted method—a dangerous clause from a guarantor's point of view, especially if the summons of complaint is lost in the mail.

Attorneys' fees are also usually provided if the matter is referred to an attorney for collection and range anywhere from 15 percent to 25 percent depending upon the state where the transaction took place. Waiving any defense of the statute of limitations is also included, as well as an agreement that a particular state law will govern the interpretation of the guarantee.

The above are some of the highlights of a financial institution instrument of guarantee and no effort is made to cover each and every sentence in the guarantee since many of these guarantees can run several pages of fine print. If a guarantee is executed, read carefully and consult with experienced counsel.

Since the guarantees are usually executed when the financial institution is advancing monies and since the same financial institution usually states up front that it will not make any changes in its printed forms, one might ask, "Why review the guarantee or consult with counsel, since the bank will not make changes?" All of these so-called printed forms are drafted by other attorneys. Banks do make changes in their printed form if a good reason is furnished. Having been house counsel for a bank in my earlier years, I can testify to the fact that banks will make changes in their printed forms. Nothing is sacred about a printed form other than the fact that the bank took the effort to have the agreement drafted by their counsel and printed because of continued use. Since many guarantors execute personal guarantees for corporate debts which far exceed their personal liabilities, I still recommend that counsel review the guarantee carefully to be certain that the client understands all the terms.

Corporate Officers Guarantee—Resignation. Litigation keeps continuing in situations where an officer has guaranteed a loan and terminates his relationship with the corporation either by resigning or being discharged. The officer is still liable on the guarantee. Notification to the bank or the creditor that he has ended his relationship with the corporation does not relieve the guarantor of liability. The guarantee has no bearing on the status of his relationship with the corporation. He must obtain a release from the bank or the creditor. The guarantee would remain even if the corporation filed a bankruptcy petition or went out of business. A third party assuming performance of the guarantee merely adds another person to the guarantee, but does not release the original party who executed the guarantee until such time as the creditor releases that party.[27]

Guarantee of Payment of Money or Performance. Where a guarantee consists of both monetary and nonmonetary obligations, in that the defendant is guaranteeing performance or some other action that is not of a monetary nature, the creditor should divide the document into two separate guarantees rather than setting forth the obligations within the four corners of one guarantee. If one guarantee is being used, the terms of the guarantee should expressly state that the guarantee is an instrument for the payment of money *only* as to that portion of the guarantee that deals with money. This eliminates some problems if the guarantee reached litigation and the dispute dealt with what performance was required of the guarantor.

Guarantee of Payment or Guarantee of Collection. A guarantee of payment requires the guarantor to pay the indebtedness upon the happening of a default by the primary debtor. A guarantee of collection can only be enforced in the event the lender has made attempts to obtain payment from the debtor. In most instances, guarantees will not identify whether they are guarantees of payment or guarantees of collection. The court will review the terms of the guarantee to determine the intent of the parties.

Considerable litigation results from this distinction. Most guarantors will contend that the guarantee is one of collection, since lenders engage in diligent efforts to collect the debt from the primary borrower before commencing action against the guarantor.

Since most lenders want a guarantee of payment, it is important when drafting the guarantee that the proper wording is used.

---

[27] *Wing-It Delivery Servs., Inc. v. Virgin Islands Cmty. Bank,* No. 2000/176, 2005 U.S. Dist. LEXIS 14061 (D.C.V.I. June 24, 2005).

Credit & Collection Tip: *Consultation with an attorney is recommended with regard to the preparation and drafting of any guarantee, not only to be certain it is a guarantee of payment but also to include other appropriate terminology which will protect the lender.*

GUARANTEE—SEPARATE AGREEMENT. Often a guarantor will defend liability on the grounds that the debt against the principal debtor is void. If the principal's debt is not valid, any claim against the guarantor should be invalid.

The guarantee agreement executed by the guarantor usually contains some clause that provides that the guarantee is a continuing, absolute, and unconditional guarantee of payment regardless if the principal's debt is held to be invalid or unenforceable. In one case, the original obligation was found unenforceable because of certain omissions and irregularities in the agreements executed by the principal.

The court stressed that an agreement of guarantee is a separate agreement from the principal's obligation. As a separate agreement, the liability of the guarantor may be lesser or even greater than the liability of the principal. In another case, the principal's debt was released by the creditor, but the creditor still proceeded against the guarantor.

Agreements of guarantee used by institutions are comprehensive. Before execution, consultation with counsel is recommended and counsel should not be the same counsel who is representing the principal. In plain and simple terms, the guarantor should understand what the obligations are and exactly what the agreement provides.[28]

IMPAIRMENT OF CAPITAL. A secured party has an obligation to the guarantor not to impair the collateral. The secured party must be certain that a proper lien is filed so that the collateral can be repossessed and the collateral will maintain the value, reasonable wear and tear excepted. Since the collateral at most times is in the possession of the debtor, these obligations on behalf of the secured party come into play only with regard to perfecting the lien and after a repossession covering the time period necessary to effectuate a sale of the property.

Section 3-605(e) of the UCC states as follows:

> if the obligation of a party to pay an instrument is secured by an interest in collateral and a person entitled to enforce the instrument impairs the value of the interest in the collateral, the obligation of an endorser or accommodation party having a right of recourse against the obligor is discharged to the extent of the impairment.

---

[28] *Ursa Minor Ltd. v. Aon Fin. Prods.*, 2000 U.S. Dist. LEXIS 10166 (S.D.N.Y. July 20, 2000); *Manufacturers Hanover Trust Co. v. Green*, 95 A.D.2d 737, 464 N.Y.S.2d 474 (N.Y.A.D. 1st Dep't 1983).

The theory is that if the lender obtains payment from the guarantor, the guarantor becomes subjugated to the lender's security interest in the collateral. If the value of the collateral is impaired because of the conduct of the secured party, the guarantor is discharged to the extent of the impairment. If the impairment is total, the discharge of the guarantor may be total.

This situation arises in the event that the secured party does not properly perfect the security interest and induces the guarantor to execute the instrument of guarantee relying on the fact that the collateral will discharge the indebtedness or most of the indebtedness. If a third party intervenes and exercises his right to the collateral so that the secured party cannot repossess the collateral and sell it and use the proceeds to discharge the indebtedness, the guarantor would be discharged to the extent of the value of the collateral. If the secured party took possession of the collateral and did not promptly arrange a sale and the collateral deteriorated or was placed in an unsecure location where it was easily stolen or removed, the same result would follow. Examples of impairment of capital would be:

1. Where a lender fails to file a continuation statement after five years with the County Clerk's Office and the lien of the lender becomes subordinate to some third parties.
2. In the event the lender fails to properly maintain the security in a warehouse.
3. After repossession, allows the security to be damaged through negligence.

Because of this, many agreements provide for a waiver of the defense of impairment of capital and will state substantially as follows:

> the obligation of the undersigned shall not be released or discharged by reason of the fact that a valid lien on the collateral may not be conveyed or created by reason of the fact that the collateral may be subject to equities or defenses or claims in favor of others or may be invalid or defective or may have deteriorated etc.

Some states have statutes prohibiting the waiver of a guarantor's right to challenge the commercial reasonableness of a sale, but most states do not prohibit a guarantor from waiving the impairment of collateral defense. The original debtor and the original secured party must act prudently with regard to collateral since the destruction of the collateral will certainly impact the obligation of the guarantor.

Available Impairment Defenses. A case reiterated the principle that a guarantor in some states is treated just as a debtor and stands in the shoes of a debtor. Where notice to the debtor is required before collateral is sold, the courts will often take the position that notice to the guarantor must also be furnished.

The bank had a perfected security interest in the assets of a corporation, in which debt was guaranteed by the defendants. The corporation thereafter executed a subordinate security interest on the same property to a third party. The bank failed to file a continuation statement. The corporation filed a petition in bankruptcy and the third party asserted that its subordinate lien had become the primary lien. The defendants executed new guarantees after the fact without being told by the bank that the collateral had been "impaired" by the failure of the bank to file the continuation statement.

The Court of Appeals of Indiana applied the Indiana common-law rule.[29] When a creditor unjustifiably impairs collateral securing a debt, the independent, absolute, continuing guarantors should be discharged to the extent the creditor has impaired the right to the collateral. The case was appealed to the Supreme Court of Indiana on the question that the guarantee was not a negotiable instrument, and thus not covered by the UCC.

Another case addressed the issue of impairment of capital by virtue of the attorney being sued for malpractice for failure to file a continuation statement to preserve the priority of the security interest in the personal property pledged to the client.[30]

The sellers, husband and wife, financed the debtors' purchase of the business and accepted a security agreement and financing statement on the business. When the debtors defaulted on the notes, the seller no longer had a priority interest in the debtors' assets because of the failure of their attorney to file the continuation statement. The sellers never sought recovery against the debtors, because they argued that the debtors, as accommodation makers, were entitled to the defense of impairment of collateral and thus had no liability on the promissory note.

The court held that the question of whether a party is an accommodation maker or a principal obligor in an instrument is a question of intent. An accommodation party is one who signs the instrument in any capacity for the purpose of lending his name to another party. An accommodation party is a surety and guarantees that in the event of default, the accommodation party will be liable. The husband and wife who were the purchasers of the business signed the notes as co-makers and the purpose of the notes was to make each of them liable personally for the obligations of the corporation of which they were the principals. Neither the language of the promissory note nor any extrinsic evidence suggests that the makers signed as surety guarantors or in any other form of accommodation status. The only reasonable inference to be drawn from the record is that they were

---

[29] *Farmers Loan and Trust Co. v. Letsinger*, 635 N.E.2d 194 (Ind. Ct. App. 1994).

[30] *Borley Storage & Transfer Co., Inc. v. Whitted*, 271 Neb. 84, 710 N.W.2d 71 (2006).

principal obligors of the note, not accommodation parties, and as principals of the notes could not have asserted an impairment of collateral defense to a claim on the note. The court properly held that the sellers should have proceeded against the two makers of the notes to determine whether they could collect the debt from the two makers of the notes before they proceeded against the attorney for malpractice.

The court held that a guarantor who satisfies the principal debtor's obligation to a creditor generally *steps into the shoes of the debtor*, becoming subjugated to the creditor's claim and entitled to have the collateral as security for the debt. When a creditor unjustifiably impairs the right to the collateral securing a guaranteed loan, it impairs the guarantor's collateral, which recourse the guarantor would have understood itself to have at the time of contracting to guarantee the principal's debt. Whenever you are dealing with guarantors and you wish to preserve your rights against the guarantor, a creditor should be certain that the guarantor is treated as the equivalent of the debtor with regard to notice, protection of collateral, and any other requirements under the law, and review the law of the particular state as to the status of the guarantor.[31]

When a guarantee is executed after the note has been executed and is entered into independently of the transaction which created the note or obligation, the guarantor's promise must be supported by consideration distinct from that of the primary debt. If the promise of the guarantor is made contemporary to the promise of the primary debtor, the consideration which supports the primary debtor's promise also supports that of the guarantor.

A promise to become a surety on the debt of another is sufficient consideration for the debt if the promise is made at, or before, the time the debt is created.[32]

LIABILITY ON SIGNING CHECKS

In the corporate environment, owners, officers, managers, and authorized parties execute checks. On the signature line, the title of the party signing the checks should be clearly printed. The corporate name should be printed immediately above the signature, although printing the name at the top of the check is usually sufficient. The reason the title of the party should be printed on the check is because case law has indicated that if an individual signs a check without a proper corporate identification, a possibility exists in certain states that the individual could be liable personally, even though the check was executed in the corporate capacity. In most states

[31] *Farmers Loan and Trust Co. v. Letsinger*, 635 N.E.2d 194 (Ind. Ct. App. 1994).
[32] *First Commerce Bank v. J.V. 3, Inc.*, 165 S.W.3d 366 (Tex. App. 2004).

either the title or the corporate name on the check should be sufficient, but for adequate protection, both the title and the corporate name should be clear and conspicuous.

Ordinary Care—Facsimile Signatures. Often a corporation wishes to use facsimile signatures on its checks. The normal procedure is to enter into an agreement with the bank, which provides that the bank has the authority to pay money against the facsimile signature. The language in these agreements varies, but in one case in Florida the agreement provided that the bank could pay any check when "bearing or purporting to bear" the facsimile signature. The plaintiff contended that the phrase was not a risk-shifting clause and served only to allow the bank to pay checks with facsimile signatures that have some technical defect in the ink such as smudges or a smear. The court disagreed in that the word "purport" covered the situation of a forgery which by its definition "purports to bear" a facsimile signature. On that ground alone, the court held that the agreement was "risk shifting." The issuer of the check would bear the loss.

The agreement with the bank was not treated as an exculpatory clause since it was recognized that the bank did have a duty to exercise ordinary care. The bank does have a statutory duty of good faith and ordinary care and the plaintiff had a right to conduct depositions and other discovery to ascertain whether the bank acted with ordinary care.

Ordinary care in the banking environment does not necessarily mean that the bank should have examined the check for the forgery. Under many circumstances, the bank never looks at the signature line of a check and the failure to look at the signature line of the check or to examine the signature line would not necessarily be a lack of ordinary care, providing the bank was acting in a customary manner in the banking industry. If the banks actually reviewed (check by check) the signature line on each check, the entire banking system would probably come to a halt. The bank itself makes the decision which checks are examined, considering the cost of reviewing the checks and the general damages they might incur by paying forged checks due to a failure to review the checks. The statutory definition of ordinary care would probably relieve the bank of any liability in most cases for losses from forgeries of the original signatures of the drawer.[33]

PAID-IN-FULL CHECKS FOR LESSER AMOUNT

A debtor disputes a debt with a creditor and offers a check for a lesser amount in full settlement of the debt. The creditor receives the check and, at

---

[33]*Arkwright Mut. Ins. Co. v. Nations Bank, N.A.*, 212 F.3d 1224 (11th Cir. 2000).

that point, must make a decision whether to deposit the check and accept the settlement, or to return the check and continue to prosecute a claim for the full balance due. If the claim is a bona fide disputed claim and the creditor accepts the check, then the creditor is precluded from instituting any further suit for the balance.

The legal terminology for the above transaction would be "an accord and satisfaction," that is, a compromise which pays the debt in full. Until recently, this doctrine was almost universally accepted as the majority position throughout the United States. Nevertheless, the "common law" doctrine ("common law" means the law inherited from England, which was not written into statute law but resulted from court decisions and common sense) is no longer the majority view.

Under the common law, the creditor has two options: reject the offer or cash the check. The full settlement check constitutes an offer and when the creditor cashes the "full payment" check concerning a bona fide dispute of an unliquidated or disputed claim, the debtor is released from any further legal obligation under the common law. A creditor cannot avoid an accord and satisfaction by reciting a reservation of rights on the reverse side of the check, or by crossing out the "paid-in-full" language on the check.

A number of states, including New York, Ohio, South Dakota, and West Virginia, have rejected this position. These courts hold that the common-law rule places the creditor in a disadvantageous position and permits the debtor to practice extortion. Offering a check for less than the contract amount, but "in full settlement," allegedly inflicts an exquisite form of commercial torture on the creditor. These state courts have held that Section 1-207 of the UCC permits the creditor to cash a check and avoid an accord of satisfaction, if the creditor makes an explicit reservation of rights by writing on the reverse side of the check such words as "without prejudice," "under protest," or words of similar import. The courts adopted this theory based upon a literal interpretation of UCC Section 1-207. No meeting of the minds takes place and the result appears to be unfair when the debtor intends merely to offer the check on condition that the creditor accept it as full payment for the disputed debt. In summary these states allow a creditor to accept the check as part payment of the debt and to proceed with suit for the balance due, notwithstanding the fact that this is not the intent or wish of the debtor. If a letter accompanies the check spelling out the conditions of the offer of settlement, the creditor may still deposit the check and sue for the balance (New York).

When a check for a lesser amount marked "paid-in-full" is submitted to a creditor and the debt is not disputed, deposit of the check by the creditor will not discharge the debt. But what happens if the debtor claims that the account was disputed and someone else in the corporation knew about the dispute? This situation often arises where a debtor mails a check to a large corporation and the department receiving the check is different from the department which charged the debtor.

This dilemma is addressed by UCC Section 3-311, which clearly states that a debtor cannot use a paid-in-full check to discharge a claim if:

1. the payee is an organization;
2. if the organization has communicated to the other party that an offer of full payment is to be sent to a particular person, office, or place;
3. the check was not received by the designated person, office, or place.

The "paid-in-full" check is treated as a partial payment and not an offer to settle unless it meets the above requirements. This rule is not absolute because the debt will be settled if the recipient of the check had knowledge of the dispute.

The purpose of the section is to prevent an accord and satisfaction from taking place when a check is sent to an automated collection center or a large corporation and is cashed without inspection. In the commercial world, hundreds of thousands of checks are processed daily by merchants and corporations. These parties are neither equipped, nor economically positioned, to inspect every check for the purpose of avoiding an inadvertent accord and satisfaction. The section thus prevents a clever debtor from pulling a fast one by slipping a full settlement check through the system to pay less than the full amount on a disputed debt.

One may revoke an accord and satisfaction within 90 days by fully repaying the amount received. Some of the states have modified Section 3-311 and have either excluded certain parts of the statute or have included additional wording.

Section 3-311 of the UCC, designed to solve the problem of UCC 2-207 (which allows a recipient to deposit a check marked "paid in full," utilizing the magic words in the UCC and suing for the balance), has now been passed in 47 of 50 states. Only New York, Rhode Island, and South Carolina have not passed the law. In fact, we are now beginning to see some litigation over the new section and a recent case in Connecticut pinpointed the efforts of a plaintiff's attorney, who altered a check by obliterating the language on the reverse side indicating that the check was to be treated as payment in full. The court properly held that under Section 3-311 in Connecticut, the cashing of the check qualifies as an accord and satisfaction and the effort to obliterate the paid-in-full language and use the magic words of Section 3-311 was ineffective. A copy of Connecticut General Statutes Section 42A-3-311 appears in the Appendix to this chapter.

STATUTE OF LIMITATIONS

The statute of limitations in many states is suspended if service of a summons and complaint cannot be effected upon the defendant within the state. Some states even allow the tolling of the statute if the plaintiff is an infant or incompetent, or is in prison. In addition, many claims are not discovered due to fraud, misrepresentation, or concealment until a period of time after the actual transaction. In those instances, the statute usually runs from the time of the discovery of the claim.

In most states the statute distinguishes between promissory notes and similar obligations in contract. In Georgia, Connecticut, Delaware, and Alaska, for example, the statute of limitations on a promissory note is usually six years. In Idaho, Kansas, and Oklahoma the statute is only five years and on the other hand in North Carolina and the District of Columbia just three years.

On open accounts the statute can range from as little as three to as long as eight years. For example, the three-year statute on a sales contract is applicable in Arkansas, Arizona, Mississippi, Virginia, Washington, and South Carolina, and there is a four-year statute in Georgia, Florida, and California, with a six-year statute in Massachusetts, Michigan, and New Jersey.

In most states time frames for ordinary contracts are different from those for judgments in courts of record. The statute in ordinary contracts can range from three to ten years while judgments in courts of records can range from four to twenty years. You must review the state law to determine the time period that applies to the transaction, not only as to how long the period is but also for what restrictions and requirements must be met in order for a defendant to assert the statute of limitations.

The defense of the statute of limitations usually must be pleaded by the defendant affirmatively (expressly setting forth the defense in the answer to the complaint), and if it is not pleaded affirmatively, the statute is considered to be waived and the plaintiff may then proceed to obtain a judgment notwithstanding the fact that the statute has run. For this reason, many suits are started even though the statute has already run, for defendants sometimes fail to assert the defense in their answer.

In consumer debts that are barred by the statute of limitations, most courts say threatening or starting suit on a time-barred date is a violation of the FDCPA (*see* Chapter 15).

Default and Acceleration. An issue often associated with notes is: "When does the statute of limitations begin to commence?" Does a statute begin with the date of default? Does it begin on the date of notice of default or finally does it begin at the date of maturity of the note?

A case discussed this issue where a note was executed and payable in annual installments over a 20-year period.[34] The court rejected the argument that the statute of limitations runs from the date of the first default. In this particular case, the notes contained an acceleration clause and an

[34] *Pan Am. Life Ins. Co. v. Invex Holdings N.V.* 1996 WL 73 4692 (N.D. Ill. 1996).

option was available to the creditor to accelerate all the payments so that the entire debt would automatically become due. The exercise of an option to accelerate must be clear and unequivocal as to the holder's intentions so that the debtor knows the option has been exercised. Acceleration is seldom implied and courts usually require that an acceleration be exercised in a manner so clear that it leaves no doubt as to the lender's intention and no doubt that the borrower is fully apprised that the option has been exercised. The debtor should not casually or by implication of some kind be stripped of the right to bring delinquent payments current or the requirement that the debtor immediately pay the entire debt.

The court dismissed the defendant's contention that the statute of limitations should not commence to run until the maturity date of the promissory note in question. Under those circumstances, despite continual annual defaults over a period of many years, the failure to pay at the maturity date would first present the accrual of a cause of action on behalf of the creditor. Such reasoning would prohibit the creditor from instituting suit until the maturity date even though the debtor may have defaulted many, many years prior thereto. The court acknowledged that this makes no sense.

The court finally concluded that where a note provides for repayment in installments, each installment is a distinct cause of action and the statute of limitations begins to run against each installment from the time it matures or becomes due. The statute of limitations on the entire debt does not begin to run until the holder elects to declare the balance due and owing under the acceleration clause.

> ***Credit & Collection Tip:*** *The statute of limitations runs from the date each installment becomes due and the debtor defaults on that particular installment. If the creditor chooses to accelerate, the statute of limitations runs from notice to the debtor of the acceleration.*

Part Payment. The general consensus is when a debtor makes a payment on a particular loan, the statute of limitations runs from the date of said payment. The key words are "makes a payment on that loan." On the other hand, the debtor may make a payment, but not designate whether the payment is the payment on that particular loan, is a payment on another loan, or is a payment for some other purpose. Part payment, to have the effect of starting the statute of limitations running again from the beginning, must show evidence that the payment was for an admitted debt accompanied by circumstances amounting to an absolute and unqualified acknowledgment by the debtor of more being due, from which a promise may be inferred to pay the remainder. Where there is more than one debt, part payment is insufficient if the payment is not accompanied by an indication of which debt is being paid. Where a debtor makes a part payment accompanied by a letter stating that the part payment is dependent on certain conditions set forth being met, the payment may not be an unequivocal promise to pay.[35]

Date of Measurement. Litigation continues on the question of what date measures the expiration of the statute of limitations. If payment is made by the debtor with a clear indication that the debtor intends to resume payments, the statute of limitations will run from this new date of payment. If payment is made by the debtor and the debtor specifically instructs the creditor to apply the payment to a specific loan and not the loan in question, the extension of the statute of limitations extends to the loan on which the payment was credited.

If the debtor made the payment and at the same time stated in a covering letter that this payment represented the only monies due to the creditor, but not the full amount, the payment would not extend the statute of limitations since no promise is made by the debtor to continue to make payments. *A payment extends the statute of limitations if coupled with a promise to continue to make payments.* Along the same lines, if the payment is made by a third party, such as a mother or an insurance company or any entity other than the debtor (including a corporation owned by the debtor), the statute of limitations probably would not be extended.

MUTUAL MISTAKE

Encoding errors by banks are common where a deposit by one customer is inadvertently credited to another customer's account because the wrong numbers are entered into the computer. The customer realizes the balance in the bank account unexpectedly has substantially increased by virtue of a mysterious deposit. The customer immediately withdraws the money from the bank account.

Shortly thereafter, the bank writes a letter to the customer to return the money and, of course, the customer has spent all the money by either repaying an indebtedness or making a handsome gift to a fiancée or, as happened in one case, the payee used the funds to operate a law practice, claiming reliance on the bank's mistake. The payee relied on a case where the customer used the money for the daily essentials of life and was not forced to repay the money to the bank. The courts in most of these cases hold that a mutual mistake occurred and the customer cannot be unjustly enriched.[36]

Mistakes in payments occur quite frequently in the medical area where an insurance company pays a hospital by mistake. The insurance company attempts to obtain a return of the payment—but usually fails. First, the

---

[35] *Schlefer v. Schloss*, N.Y.L.J., Supreme Court (New York, Dec. 27, 2001, Pg. 18).
[36] *Bank One Trust Co. v. LaCour*, 721 N.E.2d 491 (Ohio Ct. App. Franklin Co. 1999).

hospital is an innocent third-party creditor and is not unjustly enriched since the hospital is receiving payment for services already performed. Second, usually the hospital did not induce the mistake in payment, did not ask the insurance company to make the payment and no representation was made to the insurance company. Finally, the hospital may assert a material change in their position in accepting payment by not pursuing other payment options such as attempting to sue the patient. In this case, the insurance company may pursue the patient for unjust enrichment.[37]

In another case the lender surrendered the note marked "paid" and also delivered the certificate of title to the borrower with the lien released.[38] Notwithstanding, $20,000 was still due on the loan.

The bank claimed that the surrender of the note as well as the personal loan agreement marked "paid" was totally due to inadvertence and/or mistake. The witness for the bank was accepted by the court as credible. The appellate court in Ohio upheld the decision. The appellate courts do not as a rule question the credibility of a witness in a lower court since the court defers to the trier of fact. The court emphasized that the record contained sufficient, competent, credible evidence to support the trial courts judgment. Whether other courts would agree is questionable.

CHECK CLEARING FOR THE 21st CENTURY ACT ("CHECK 21 ACT")

The Check Clearing for the 21st Century Act was signed on October 28, 2003, and became effective on October 28, 2004. The Act is targeted at eliminating the use of paper checks between the bank and the depositor, but also between the banks themselves. If the banks can present their checks for payment electronically, it will save a huge amount of money in transporting the physical checks from bank to bank and the time for clearance of the checks should be compressed significantly. The banks also have the opportunity to send a substitute check or send electronically the information relating to the original check. Some banks are sending copies of the check to the depositors.

This Act allows the bank to electronically process all checks by converting them into digital copies. Today the physical checks are actually delivered across the country to the various banks represented by the electronic numbers at the bottom of the check. Airplanes, trucks, and trains are utilized in delivering the checks from one bank to another bank or through the Federal Reserve Bank. In certain areas, if the checks are drawn on banks

---

[37] *Trustmark Life Ins. Co. v. Univ. of Chicago Hosps.*, 207 F.3d 876 (7th Cir. 2000); *Nat'l Ben. Admrs., Inc. v. Mississippi Method. Hosp.*, 748 F. Supp. 459 (S.D. Miss. 1990); *Lincoln Nat'l Life Ins. Co. v. Brown Sch., Inc.*, 757 S.W.2d 411 (Tex. App. 1988).

[38] *Huntington Nat'l Bank v. Mark*, 2004 WL 1627029 (Ohio App. 4th Dist., July 14, 2004).

within the local area, the check could conceivably clear within a day or two. On the other hand, with checks drawn on banks out-of-state, the normal processing time can be anywhere from three to five days. When you add the time it takes the bank to process the check and deliver notice through the mail advising that the check deposited was returned unpaid, the time from beginning to end could run as many as seven to eight days or even longer.

Electronic Checking. With electronic checking, the bank will be able to deduct the amount on the same day that you issued the check to the party who receives the check, that is, the payee of the check. Thus, when you leave a check at your doctor's office for your co-pay, the doctor can present that check at the bank the same day, and it will be electronically presented to your bank on the same day, and your account will be deducted on the same day. This will enable those who receive your check to obtain payment immediately so that they, in turn, may utilize the money to pay other creditors. The issuer or the maker of the check will not have the advantage of the "float running from two to ten days."

The issuer of the check will be required to pay that check within the same day and certainly within 48 hours whether the check is drawn on a local bank or on an out-of-state bank. With electronic transmission, the distance between the banks becomes infinitesimal and the trains, trucks, and airplanes do not need to move the checks from one financial institution to another. Banks will not need the paper checks to return to the issuer of the check, and as a result, most of the checks will probably be destroyed.

Electronic Copy of Check. If a depositor needs a copy of the check to prove payment to a third party who claims the check was not received, the bank will be authorized to make what is known as a "substitute check" from the image of the check that is made electronically. The substitute check will say "this is a legal copy of your check, you can use it the same way you would use the original check." Those who issue a check may be tempted to make a copy of the check before they issue it to possess some evidence that the check was issued to the third party. The substitute check will bear all endorsements applied by any parties that previously handled the check, whether in electronic form or in the form of the original paper check or a substitute check. The bank will also identify itself as a reconverting bank on any substitute check for which the bank is reconverting the check to paper. A substitute check is the legal equivalent of the original check for all purposes including any provision of any federal or state law.[39]

---

[39]12 U.S.C. §§ 5004-5005. *See Borley Storage & Transfer Co., Inc. v. Whitted*, 271 Neb. 84, 710 N.W.2d 71 (2006).

COMPARATIVE NEGLIGENCE. Interestingly, the statute contains comparative negligence provisions which state that if a person incurs any damages that resulted from the negligence or failure to act in good faith, the amount of any liability due to that person shall be reduced in proportion to the amount of negligence or bad faith attributable to that person. Notwithstanding same, this subsection does not reduce the rights of the consumer or any other person under the UCC or other applicable provision of the federal or state law.[40]

TIME LIMIT TO ASSERT CLAIM. The statute provides that the consumer must submit a claim within a 40-day period under 12 U.S.C. Section 5006. If the consumer is delayed due to extenuating circumstances such as travel or illness, the 40-day period may be extended by a reasonable amount of time. 12 U.S.C. Section 5006 sets forth in detail the procedure for the expedited recredit to consumers, the procedure for consumers to present claims, the availability of recredits, and the necessary notice to the consumers. A careful review is necessary.

SUBSTITUTE CHECK. The substitute check must include the magnetic ink character recognition line (MICR line). All checks are eligible to become substitute checks. The financial institution upon request for the original has a right to provide the substitute check to the customer.

VOLUNTARY COMPLIANCE. The statute is not mandatory and it expects that presenting checks electronically will develop slowly over time as the banks become aware of the costs and savings that are available by using electronic presentation. The reason why the option is with the bank is that the Federal Reserve realized that many small banks do not have the technology nor the funds to implement this electronic presentation of checks.

Several different views exist as to whether or not this act is helpful or harmful. Substantial sums of money may be saved, but on the other hand the bank will not have the opportunity to accommodate those depositors who wish to take advantage of the time differential between when they issue the check and when the check ultimately reaches the bank. On the other hand, attorneys have raised the issue of whether the use of the substitute checks will be sufficient to establish that a signature was forged or that the amount in the check was altered. The experts that render these opinions would not be able to examine the pressure and the other nuances that identify a forgery or a material alteration of a document. The American Banking Association contends that it will eliminate check fraud by increasing the speed of payment. Perhaps forgers will have less chance to disappear.

The banks will probably receive many requests to return substitute checks each month with the bank statement. Whether the banks will charge

---

[40]12 U.S.C. § 5009.

additional fees to generate the substitute checks is something that has not been addressed. The question has always been when electronic checking will come into being, not whether it will come into being. Fortunately, it will probably develop initially in a rather slow manner, but once the major banks start utilizing it, the smaller banks will necessarily follow.

The effect on the collections industry will probably be an increase in return checks, since those debtors who are already strapped for funds and utilizing the float will probably be the most frequent offenders when the new system is instituted. Collection agencies and collection attorneys will probably see a substantial increase in returned checks. Both the agency and the attorney will also be able to determine in a day or so whether the check has been returned or whether it has been paid instead of having to wait the two to five or possibly eight or nine days to be certain that the check has cleared and has been paid.

With every two steps forward, we experience one step backward, but we all must acknowledge that electronic presentment is now here and the future is that checks will be presented within a 24-hour time frame.

The major purpose of the Check 21 Act is to save money. The Federal Reserve Bank has almost 200 flights everyday during the week for the sole purpose of transporting checks. If these flights can be eliminated by the electronic transfer of monies, without using paper, the savings will be substantial. The second big cost-saving factor is the ability of the banks to eliminate the mailing of the checks to the depositor. The cost saving, aside from postage, will be substantial. A copy of the Act is in the Appendix to this chapter.[41]

WIRE TRANSFERS

When a customer receives notification identifying a payment order, the customer is precluded from asserting that the bank is not entitled to retain the payment unless the customer notifies the bank of the customer's objection to the payment within one year after the notification was received by the customer.

In the instance of a wire transfer, a district court set forth an in-depth analysis and came to the final conclusion that this one-year period cannot be compressed into less than a one-year period by an agreement between the bank and its customer. The parties could have reduced the time period to 15 days in which the customer is precluded from asserting that the bank is not entitled to retain the payment. The court held that the time period may not be shortened by any agreement between the parties and that the one-year period shall apply.[42]

---

[41] 12 U.S.C. §§ 5001-5018.

[42] *Regatos v. Northfork Bank*, 257 F. Supp. 2d 632 (S.D.N.Y. 2002).

PAYMENT WHEN CHECK RECEIVED

Payment in the form of a check should be credited to the debtor's account at the time it is received. When a check is delivered to an individual, the money is deemed to be received when the check is delivered and not when the check is cashed. With regard to garnishment funds, a debtor should be credited with payment as of the date that the garnished funds were available.[43]

CONTROL DEPOSIT ACCOUNT

UCC 9-104 provides as follows:
A secured party has control of a deposit account if

1. The secured party is the bank with which deposit account is maintained.
2. The debtor, secured party, and the bank have agreed in an authenticated record that the bank will comply with instructions originated by the secured party directing disposition of the funds in the deposit account without further consent by the debtor or
3. The secured party becomes the bank's customer with respect to the deposit account.

A bank in which a deposit account is maintained may exercise any right of recoupment against a secured party that holds a security interest in the deposit account except in those cases where the secured party actually becomes the bank's customer with respect to the deposit account.

Another exception would be a situation where the bank, the customer and a secured party entered into an agreement where they recognize the secured interest as prior to the bank's interest.

As a general rule general deposit account proceeds are treated as property of the bank. The account balance represents the bank's indebtedness to the depositor. When a deposit is made in a bank, the depositor and the bank are creating a lender and borrower relationship. The bank is agreeing to disburse the money pursuant to the instructions of the depositor. The money on deposit is treated as property of the bank and the bank owes the depositor the money.

An action for setoff against the bank should be treated as a breach of a contract as opposed to a conversion. A conversion against the bank arises out of a debtor/creditor relationship between the bank and the depositor. The essential element of conversion is an absence of consent and since the

[43]*Asch v. Teller Levit & Silvertrust P.C.*, 2003 U.S. Dist. LEXIS 16747 (N.D. Ill. Sept. 23, 2003).

depositor has consented to placing the money within the control of the bank, a conversion would not lie.[44]

UCC 9-342 states as follows:

> This article does not require a bank to enter into an agreement of the kind described in Section 9-104(a)(2) even if its customer so requested or directs. A bank that has entered into such an agreement is not required to confirm the existence of the agreement to another person unless requested to do so by its customer.

The purpose of this section as stated in the Official Comment was to protect banks from the need to enter into agreements against their will and from the need to respond to inquiries from persons other than their customers.

Banks must affirmatively consent to a control arrangement between the depositor and the secured party before they can be required to acknowledge that the deposit account is to be provided as security to the secured party. As a result of this ability to refuse to enter into this agreement, the banks are in a position to dictate the terms of the agreement as well as the fees. Creditors may refuse to extend credit if the terms of the agreement are burdensome. A joint task force of the American Bar Association was organized in 2004 to provide a form deposit control agreement. This model form is in the Appendix to this chapter.

For those who wish to use this type of a transaction, we recommend that you review an excellent article in the New York Law Journal in April 6, 2006, by Alan M. Christenfeld and Shephard W. Melzer and also to review the "Initial Report of the Joint Task Force on Deposit Control Agreements," ABA section of the Business Law dated February 13, 2006, which appeared in the Business Lawyer, Volume 61, February, 2006.

When a company decides to utilize wire transfers, the company is usually confronted with a standard boilerplate agreement that the bank asks the company to execute.

The UCC article that covers wire transfers is UCC 4(A). The Business Law section of the American Bar Association recently published a new "Model Funds Transfer Services Agreement" to assist those using wire transfers through the intricacies of Article 4(A) and to help in any negotiation over these boilerplate agreements that the banks are utilizing. The proposed agreement of the American Bar Association may be ordered from the Service Center, American Bar Association, 750 M. Lakeshore Drive, Chicago, Illinois 60611. The cost is about $40 for members.

---

[44] *Pioneer Comm. Funding Corp. v. American Fin. Mortg. Corp.*, 855 A.2d 818 (Pa. 2004).

CHAPTER 8
APPENDIX I

VARIABLE INTEREST TIME NOTE UNSECURED

On the ________ day of ____________________ 20 ________ , for value received, the undersigned hereby promises to pay to the order of ________________________________ at its office at ________________ ________________________N.Y. ("the holder") ________________ ________________DOLLARS.

With interest payable on ______________________________ and the last day of each ____________________________ thereafter at a variable per annum rate as follows: __________ % above the rate of ________ announced to be in effect from time to time for prime domestic commercial loans of 90-day maturities, adjusted as of the date of each such change, but in no event higher than the maximum permitted under applicable law. Interest on any past due amount, whether at the due date thereof or by acceleration, shall be paid at a rate of one percent per annum in excess of the above-stated interest rate but in no event in excess of the maximum legal rate of interest permitted under applicable law for individuals or above the maximum rate a corporation may assert as a defense of usury.

In the event of default in payment of any liability (direct or contingent) to the holder hereof (however acquired), complete and partial suspension or liquidation of business, calling of a meeting of creditors, assignment for the benefit of creditors, dissolution, bulk sale or notice thereof, any mortgage, pledge of or creation of a security interest in any assets without consent of the holder of this note, insolvency of any kind, attachment, distraint, levy, execution, judgment, death, dissolution, merger, consolidation or reorganization of Obligor, tax assessment by the United States or any sate, application for or appointment of a receiver, filing of a voluntary or involuntary petition under any provision of the Bankruptcy Act or amendments thereto, of, by or against any Obligor, (which term shall include each of the undersigned and each endorser or guarantor hereof) or any property or rights of any Obligor, failure of any Obligor, on request, to furnish any financial information, or to permit inspection of any books or records, if any warranty, representation of statement of any Obligor in any application, statement to or agreement with the holder in connection with this note or to induce the holder to make a loan to the Obligor proves to have been false in any material respect when made or furnished, any change in, or discovery with regard to, the condition or affairs of any Obligor which, in the holder's opinion, increases its credit risk, or if the holder for any other reasons deems itself insecure, this note and all other liabilities (direct or contingent) of any Obligor to the holder (however acquired), shall become absolute, due and payable, without demand or notice notwithstanding anything to the contrary contained herein or in any other instrument. In addition to any other rights of holder, under applicable law, the holder shall have a lien on, and a security interest in, the deposit balances of any Obligor, and may at any time, without notice, apply the same to this note or such other liabilities, whether due or not. If an attorney is used to enforce or collect this note, Obligor shall be obligated to pay, in addition, reasonable attorney's fees. Each Obligor waives trial by jury and the right to interpose any counterclaims or setoffs of any kind in any litigation relating to this note or any of such other liabilities. The undersigned shall be jointly and severally liable hereon.

Failure or delay of the holder to enforce any provisions of this note shall not be deemed a waiver of any such provision, nor shall the holder be estopped from enforcing any such provision at a later time. Any waiver of any provision hereof must be in writing. Acceptance of any payments shall not waive or affect prior demand or acceleration of liabilities, and each such payment shall be applied first to the payment of accrued interest and interest.

The provisions of this note shall be construed and interpreted and all rights and obligations hereunder determined in accordance with the laws of the State of New York.

X ____________________________

Note No. ________________ Address ____________________

(VARIABLE INTEREST TIME NOTE UNSECURED) ____________________________

Address ____________________

03 1170* (1-82)

APPENDIX II

GUARANTY

(insert Date)	______________________________, New York, 20 ________ Location
(insert name, place of business and; if a corporation, State of incorporations)	WHEREAS ___________, (hereinafter called the "Borrower"), desires to transact business with and to obtain credit or a continuation of credit or other financial accommodations from ____
	WHEREAS, the Bank is unwilling to extend or continue credit to or other financial accommodations to the Borrower, unless it receives the following guaranty of the undersigned;

NOW, THEREFORE, in consideration of the premises and of other good and valuable consideration and in order to induce the Bank from time to time, in its discretion, to extend or continue credit or other financial accommodations to the Borrower, the undersigned hereby guarantees, absolutely and unconditionally, to the Bank the payment of all liabilities of the Borrower to the Bank of whatever nature, whether now existing or hereafter incurred, whether created directly or acquired by the Bank by assignment or otherwise, whether matured or unmatured and whether absolute or contingent (all of which are hereinafter collectively referred to as the "Liabilities of the Borrower").

In order to further secure the payment of the Liabilities of the Borrower, the undersigned does hereby give Bank a continuing lien and right of setoff for the amount of the Liabilities of the Borrower upon any and all moneys, securities and any and all other property of the undersigned and the proceeds thereof, now or hereafter actually or constructively held or received by or in transit in any manner to or from the Bank, ____, or any other affiliate of the Bank from or for the undersigned, whether for safekeeping, custody, pledge, transmission, collection or otherwise or coming into the possession of the Bank, or any other affiliate of the Bank in any way, or placed in any safe deposit box leased by the Bank, or any other affiliate of the Bank to the undersigned. The Bank is also given a continuing lien and right of setoff for the amount of said Liabilities of the Borrower upon any and all deposits (general and special) and credits of, or for the benefit of the undersigned with, and any and all claims of the undersigned against, the Bank, or any other affiliate of the Bank at any time existing, and the Bank is hereby authorized at any time or times, without prior notice, to apply such deposits or credits, or any part thereof, to such Liabilities of the Borrower, and although said Liabilities of the Borrower may be contingent or unmatured, and whether the collateral security therefore is deemed adequate or not. The undersigned authorizes Bank to deliver a copy of this Guaranty to others as written notification of the undersigned's transfer of a security interest in the collateral described herein to the Bank.

The undersigned agrees that, with or without notice or demand, the undersigned shall reimburse the Bank for all the Bank's expenses (including reasonable fees of counsel for the Bank, who may be employees thereof) incurred in connection with any of the Liabilities of the Borrower or the collection thereof.

This guaranty is a continuing guaranty and shall remain in full force and effect irrespective of any interruptions in the business relations of the Borrower with the Bank; provided, however, that the undersigned may by notice in writing, delivered personally or received by certified mail, return receipt requested, addressed to the Bank's office at ______________________________ ____________________, terminate this guaranty with respect to all Liabilities of the Borrower incurred or contracted by the Borrower or acquired by the Bank after the date on which such notice is so delivered or received.

All moneys available to the Bank for application in payment or reduction of the Liabilities of the Borrower may be applied by the Bank in such manner and in such amounts and at such time or times as it may see fit to the payment or reduction of such of the Liabilities of the Borrower as the Bank may elect.

The undersigned hereby waives (a) notice of appearance of this guaranty and of extensions of credit or other financial accommodations by the Bank to the Borrower; (b) presentment and demand for payment of any of the Liabilities of the Borrower; (c) protest and notice of dishonor or default to the undersigned or to any other party with respect to any of the Liabilities of the Borrower; (d) all other notices to which the undersigned may otherwise be entitled; and (e) any demand for payment hereunder.

All liabilities of the undersigned to the Bank hereunder or otherwise, whether or not then due or absolute or contingent, shall without notice or demand become due and payable immediately upon the occurrence of any default or event of default with respect to any Liabilities of the Borrower (or the occurrence of any other event which results in acceleration of the maturity of any thereof) or the occurrence of any default hereunder. This is a guaranty of payment and not of collection and the undersigned further waives any right to require that any action be brought against the Borrower or any other person or to require that resort be had to any security or to any balance of any deposit account or credit on the books of the Bank in favor of the Borrower or any other person.

The undersigned hereby consents that from time to time, before or after any default by the Borrower or any notice of termination hereof, with or without further notice to or assent from the undersigned, any security at any time held by or available to the Bank for any obligation of the Borrower, or any security at any time held by or available to the Bank for any obligation of any other person secondarily or otherwise liable for any of the Liabilities of the Borrower, may be exchanged, surrendered or released and any obligation of the Borrower, or of any such other person, may be changed, altered, renewed, extended, continued, surrendered, compromised, waived, discharged or released in whole or in part (including without limitation any such event resulting from any insolvency, bankruptcy, reorganization or other similar proceeding affecting the Borrower or its assets) or any default with respect thereto waived, and the Bank may fail to set off and may release, in whole or in part, any balance of any deposit account or credit on its books in favor of the Borrower, or of any such other person, and may extend further credit in any manner whatsoever to the Borrower, and generally deal or take action or no action with regard to the Borrower or any such security or other person as the Bank may see fit; and the undersigned shall remain bound under this guaranty notwithstanding any such exchange, surrender, release, change, alteration, renewal, extension, continuance, compromise, waiver, discharge, inaction, extension of further credit or other dealing.

The obligations of the undersigned are absolute and unconditional and are valid irrespective of any other agreement or circumstance which might otherwise constitute a defense to the obligations hereunder or to the obligations of others related thereto and the undersigned irrevocably waives the right to assert defenses, setoffs and counterclaims in any litigation relating to this guaranty and the Liabilities of the Borrower. This guaranty sets forth the entire understanding of the parties, and the undersigned acknowledges that no oral or other agreements, conditions, promises, understandings, representations, or warranties exist in regard to the obligations hereunder, except those specifically set forth herein.

The undersigned irrevocably waives and shall not seek to enforce or collect upon any rights which it now has or may acquire against the Borrower, either by way of subrogation, indemnity, reimbursement or contribution, or any other similar right, for any amount paid under this guaranty or by way of any other obligations whatsoever of the Borrower to the undersigned. In the event either a petition is filed under the Bankruptcy Code in regard to the Borrower or an action or proceeding is commenced for the benefit of the creditors of the Borrower, this agreement shall at all times thereafter remain effective in regard to any payments or other transfers of assets to the Bank received from or on behalf of the Borrower prior to notice of termination of this guaranty and which are or may be held voidable or otherwise subject to recission or return on the grounds of preference, fraudulent conveyance or otherwise, whether or not the Liabilities of the Borrower have been paid in full.

Each reference herein to the Bank shall be deemed to include its successors and assigns, in whose favor the provisions of this guaranty shall also insure. Each reference herein to the undersigned shall be deemed to include the heirs, executors, administrators, legal representatives, successors and assigns of the undersigned, all of whom shall be bound by the provisions of this guaranty.

The term "undersigned" as used herein shall, if this instrument is signed by more than one party, mean the "undersigned and each of them" and each undertaking herein contained shall be their joint and several undertaking, provided, however, that in the next succeeding paragraph hereof the term "undersigned" shall mean the "undersigned or any of them." If any party hereto shall be a partnership, the agreements and obligations on the part of the undersigned herein contained shall remain in force and applicable against the partnership and all of its partners notwithstanding any changes in the individuals composing the partnership (or any release of one or more partners) and the term "undersigned" shall include any altered or successive partnership but the predecessor partnerships and their partners shall not thereby be released from any obligation or liability.

No delay on the part of the Bank in exercising any rights hereunder or failure to exercise the same shall operate as a waiver of such rights; no notice to or demand on the undersigned shall be deemed to be a waiver of the obligation of the undersigned or of the right of the Bank to take further action without notice or demand as provided herein; nor in any event shall any modification or waiver of the provisions of this guaranty be effective unless in writing signed by an authorized officer of the Bank nor shall any such waiver be applicable except in the specific instance for which given.

This guaranty is, and shall be deemed to be, a contract entered into under and pursuant to the laws of ______________________________ and shall be in all respects governed, construed, applied and enforced in accordance with the laws of said State; and no defense given or allowed by the laws of any other State or Country shall be interposed in any action hereon unless such defense is also given or allowed by the laws of the ______________________ ____________.

The undersigned hereby unconditionally WAIVES ANY RIGHT TO JURY TRIAL in connection with actions by or against the Bank arising out of or in connection with the Liabilities of the Borrower and this guaranty.

If partnership, name of partnership and signature of general partner(s) must appear.	Individual or Partnership	Corporation
	____________________	____________________
	Name of Guarantor (Type or Print)	Name of Guarantor (Type or Print)
	____________________	____________________
	____________________	By: ________________
	____________________	____________________
	Address	____________________
	____________________	Title ______________
		CORPORATE SEAL

Individual Acknowledgment

STATE OF

SS:

COUNTY OF

On the __________ day of ______________________, 20 _________, before me personally came ____, to me known to be the individual described in and who executed the foregoing instrument and he/she acknowledged to me that he/she executed the same.

______________________________, Notary Public

My commission expires:

Corporate Acknowledgment

STATE OF
SS:
COUNTY OF

On the __________ day of ________________________, 20 ________ , before me personally came ________________________________ ________________________________, to me known, who, being by me duly sworn, did depose and say that he/she is ________________________ __________ of ______________________________, the corporation described in and which executed the above instrument, that he/she knows the seal of said corporation; that the seal affixed to said instrument is such corporate seal; that it was so affixed by order of the board of directors of said corporation, and that he/she signed his name thereto by like order.

________________________________, Notary Public

My commission expires:

Partnership Acknowledgment

STATE OF
SS:
COUNTY OF

On the __________ day of ________________________, 20 ________, before me personally came __________, to me known to be the individual described in and who executed the foregoing instrument and he/she a Partnership, as his/her act and deed.

________________________________, Notary Public

My commission expires:

APPENDIX III

CHECK CLEARING FOR THE 21st CENTURY ACT

Public Law 108–100
108th Congress
An Act
To facilitate check truncation by authorizing substitute checks, to foster innovation in the check collection system without mandating receipt of checks in electronic form, and to improve the overall efficiency of the Nation's payments system, and for other purposes.

Be it enacted by the Senate and House of Representatives of the United States of America in Congress assembled,

SECTION 1. SHORT TITLE; TABLE OF CONTENTS.

(a) SHORT TITLE.—This Act may be cited as the "Check Clearing for the 21st Century Act" or the "Check 21 Act."

(b) TABLE OF CONTENTS.—The table of contents of this Act is as follows:

SEC. 2. FINDINGS; PURPOSES.

(a) FINDINGS.—The Congress finds as follows:

(1) In the Expedited Funds Availability Act, enacted on August 10, 1987, the Congress directed the Board of Governors of the Federal Reserve System to consider establishing regulations requiring Federal reserve banks and depository institutions to provide for check truncation, in order to improve the check processing system.

(2) In that same Act, the Congress—

(A) provided the Board of Governors of the Federal Reserve System with full authority to regulate all aspects of the payment system, including the receipt, payment, collection, and clearing of checks, and related functions of the payment system pertaining to checks; and

(B) directed that the exercise of such authority by the Board superseded any State law, including the Uniform Commercial Code, as in effect in any State.

(3) Check truncation is no less desirable in 2003 for both financial service customers and the financial services industry, to reduce costs, improve efficiency in check collections, and expedite funds availability for customers than it was over 15 years ago when Congress first directed the Board to consider establishing such a process.

(b) PURPOSES.—The purposes of this Act are as follows:

(1) To facilitate check truncation by authorizing substitute checks.

(2) To foster innovation in the check collection system without mandating receipt of checks in electronic form.

(3) To improve the overall efficiency of the Nation's payments system.

SEC. 3. DEFINITIONS.

For purposes of this Act, the following definitions shall apply:

(1) ACCOUNT.—The term "account" means a deposit account at a bank.

(2) BANK.—The term "bank" means any person that is located in a State and engaged in the business of banking and includes—

(A) any depository institution (as defined in section 19(b)(1)(A) of the Federal Reserve Act);

(B) any Federal reserve bank;

(C) any Federal home loan bank; or

(D) to the extent it acts as a payor—

(i) the Treasury of the United States;

(ii) the United States Postal Service;

(iii) a State government; or

(iv) a unit of general local government (as defined in section 602(24) of the Expedited Funds Availability Act).

(3) BANKING TERMS.—

(A) COLLECTING BANK.—The term "collecting bank" means any bank handling a check for collection except the paying bank.

(B) DEPOSITARY BANK.—The term "depositary bank" means—

(i) the first bank to which a check is transferred, even if such bank is also the paying bank or the payee; or

(ii) a bank to which a check is transferred for deposit in an account at such bank, even if the check is physically received and indorsed first by another bank.

(C) PAYING BANK.—The term "paying bank" means—

(i) the bank by which a check is payable, unless the check is payable at or through another bank and is sent to the other bank for payment or collection; or

(ii) the bank at or through which a check is payable and to which the check is sent for payment or collection.

(D) RETURNING BANK.—

(i) IN GENERAL.—The term "returning bank" means a bank (other than the paying or depositary bank) handling a returned check or notice in lieu of return.

(ii) TREATMENT AS COLLECTING BANK.—No provision of this Act shall be construed as affecting the treatment of a returning bank as a collecting bank for purposes of section 4–202(b) of the Uniform Commercial Code.

(4) BOARD.—The term "Board" means the Board of Governors of the Federal Reserve System.

(5) BUSINESS DAY.—The term "business day" has the same meaning as in section 602(3) of the Expedited Funds Availability Act.

(6) CHECK.—The term "check"—

(A) means a draft, payable on demand and drawn on or payable through or at an office of a bank, whether or not negotiable, that is handled for forward collection or return, including a substitute check and a travelers check; and

(B) does not include a noncash item or an item payable in a medium other than United States dollars.

(7) CONSUMER.—The term "consumer" means an individual who—

(A) with respect to a check handled for forward collection, draws the check on a consumer account; or

(B) with respect to a check handled for return, deposits the check into, or cashes the check against, a consumer account.

(8) CONSUMER ACCOUNT.—The term "consumer account" has the same meaning as in section 602(10) of the Expedited Funds Availability Act.

(9) CUSTOMER.—The term "customer" means a person having an account with a bank.

(10) FORWARD COLLECTION.—The term "forward collection" means the transfer by a bank of a check to a collecting bank for settlement or the paying bank for payment.

(11) INDEMNIFYING BANK.—The term "indemnifying bank" means a bank that is providing an indemnity under section 6 with respect to a substitute check.

(12) MICR LINE.—The terms "MICR line" and "magnetic ink character recognition line" mean the numbers, which may include the bank routing number, account number, check number, check amount, and other information, that are printed near the bottom of a check in magnetic ink in accordance with generally applicable industry standards.

(13) NONCASH ITEM.—The term "noncash item" has the same meaning as in section 602(14) of the Expedited Funds Availability Act.

(14) PERSON.—The term "person" means a natural person, corporation, unincorporated company, partnership, government unit or instrumentality, trust, or any other entity or organization.

(15) RECONVERTING BANK.—The term "reconverting bank" means—

(A) the bank that creates a substitute check; or

(B) if a substitute check is created by a person other than a bank, the first bank that transfers or presents such substitute check.

(16) SUBSTITUTE CHECK.—The term "substitute check" means a paper reproduction of the original check that—

(A) contains an image of the front and back of the original check;

(B) bears a MICR line containing all the information appearing on the MICR line of the original check, except as provided under generally applicable industry standards for substitute checks to facilitate the processing of substitute checks;

(C) conforms, in paper stock, dimension, and otherwise, with generally applicable industry standards for substitute checks; and

(D) is suitable for automated processing in the same manner as the original check.

(17) STATE.—The term "State" has the same meaning as in section 3(a) of the Federal Deposit Insurance Act.

(18) TRUNCATE.—The term "truncate" means to remove an original paper check from the check collection or return process and send to a recipient, in lieu of such original paper check, a substitute check or, by agreement, information relating to the original check (including data taken from the MICR line of the original check or an electronic image of the original check), whether with or without subsequent delivery of the original paper check.

(19) UNIFORM COMMERCIAL CODE.—The term "Uniform Commercial Code" means the Uniform Commercial Code in effect in a State.

(20) OTHER TERMS.—Unless the context requires otherwise, the terms not defined in this section shall have the same meanings as in the Uniform Commercial Code.

SEC. 4. GENERAL PROVISIONS GOVERNING SUBSTITUTE CHECKS.

(a) NO AGREEMENT REQUIRED.—A person may deposit, present, or send for collection or return a substitute check without an agreement with the recipient, so long as a bank has made the warranties in section 5 with respect to such substitute check.

(b) LEGAL EQUIVALENCE.—A substitute check shall be the legal equivalent of the original check for all purposes, including any provision of any Federal or State law, and for all persons if the substitute check—

(1) accurately represents all of the information on the front and back of the original check as of the time the original check was truncated; and

(2) bears the legend: "This is a legal copy of your check. You can use it the same way you would use the original check."

(c) ENDORSEMENTS.—A bank shall ensure that the substitute check for which the bank is the reconverting bank bears all endorsements applied by parties that previously handled the check (whether in electronic form or in the form of the original paper check or a substitute check) for forward collection or return.

(d) IDENTIFICATION OF RECONVERTING BANK.—A bank shall identify itself as a reconverting bank on any substitute check for which the bank is a reconverting bank so as to preserve any previous reconverting bank identifications in conformance with generally applicable industry standards.

(e) APPLICABLE LAW.—A substitute check that is the legal equivalent of the original check under subsection (b) shall be subject to any provision, including any provision relating to the protection of customers, of part 229 of title 12 of the Code of Federal Regulations, the Uniform Commercial Code, and any other applicable Federal or State law as if such substitute check were the original check, to the extent such provision of law is not inconsistent with this Act.

SEC. 5. SUBSTITUTE CHECK WARRANTIES.

A bank that transfers, presents, or returns a substitute check and receives consideration for the check warrants, as a matter of law, to the transferee, any subsequent collecting or returning bank, the depositary bank, the drawee, the drawer, the payee, the depositor, and any endorser (regardless of whether the warrantee receives the substitute check or another paper or electronic form of the substitute check or original check) that—

(1) the substitute check meets all the requirements for legal equivalence under section 4(b); and

(2) no depositary bank, drawee, drawer, or endorser will receive presentment or return of the substitute check, the original check, or a copy or other paper or electronic version of the substitute check or original check such that the bank, drawee, drawer, or endorser will be asked to make a payment based on a check that the bank, drawee, drawer, or endorser has already paid.

SEC. 6. INDEMNITY.

(a) INDEMNITY.—A reconverting bank and each bank that subsequently transfers, presents, or returns a substitute check in any electronic or paper form, and receives consideration for such transfer, presentment, or return shall indemnify the transferee, any subsequent collecting or returning bank, the depositary bank, the drawee, the drawer, the payee, the depositor, and any endorser, up to the amount described in subsections (b) and (c), as applicable, to the extent of any loss incurred by any recipient of a substitute check if that loss occurred due to the receipt of a substitute check instead of the original check.

(b) INDEMNITY AMOUNT.—

(1) AMOUNT IN EVENT OF BREACH OF WARRANTY.—The amount of the indemnity under subsection (a) shall be the amount of any loss (including costs and reasonable attorney's fees and other expenses of representation) proximately caused by a breach of a warranty provided under section 5.

(2) AMOUNT IN ABSENCE OF BREACH OF WARRANTY.—In the absence of a breach of a warranty provided under section 5, the amount of the indemnity under subsection (a) shall be the sum of—

(A) the amount of any loss, up to the amount of the substitute check; and

(B) interest and expenses (including costs and reasonable attorney's fees and other expenses of representation).

(c) COMPARATIVE NEGLIGENCE.—

(1) IN GENERAL.—If a loss described in subsection (a) results in whole or in part from the negligence or failure to act in good faith on the part of an indemnified party, then that party's indemnification under this section shall be reduced in proportion to the amount of negligence or bad faith attributable to that party.

(2) RULE OF CONSTRUCTION.—Nothing in this subsection reduces the rights of a consumer or any other person under the Uniform Commercial Code or other applicable provision of Federal or State law.

(d) EFFECT OF PRODUCING ORIGINAL CHECK OR COPY.—

(1) IN GENERAL.—If the indemnifying bank produces the original check or a copy of the original check (including an image or a substitute check) that accurately represents all of the information on the front and back of the original check (as of the time the original check was truncated) or is otherwise sufficient to determine whether or not a claim is valid, the indemnifying bank shall—

(A) be liable under this section only for losses covered by the indemnity that are incurred up to the time that the original check or copy is provided to the indemnified party; and

(B) have a right to the return of any funds it has paid under the indemnity in excess of those losses.

(2) COORDINATION OF INDEMNITY WITH IMPLIED WARRANTY.—The production of the original check, a substitute check, or a copy under paragraph (1) by an indemnifying bank shall not absolve the bank from any liability on a warranty established under this Act or any other provision of law.

(e) SUBROGATION OF RIGHTS.—

(1) IN GENERAL.—Each indemnifying bank shall be subrogated to the rights of any indemnified party to the extent of the indemnity.

(2) RECOVERY UNDER WARRANTY.—A bank that indemnifies a party under this section may attempt to recover from another party based on a warranty or other claim.

(3) DUTY OF INDEMNIFIED PARTY.—Each indemnified party shall have a duty to comply with all reasonable requests for assistance from an indemnifying bank in connection with any claim the indemnifying bank brings against a warrantor or other party related to a check that forms the basis for the indemnification.

SEC. 7. EXPEDITED RECREDIT FOR CONSUMERS.

(a) RECREDIT CLAIMS.—

(1) IN GENERAL.—A consumer may make a claim for expedited recredit from the bank that holds the account of the consumer with respect to a substitute check, if the consumer asserts in good faith that—

(A) the bank charged the consumer's account for a substitute check that was provided to the consumer;

(B) either—

(i) the check was not properly charged to the consumer's account; or

(ii) the consumer has a warranty claim with respect to such substitute check;

(C) the consumer suffered a resulting loss; and

(D) the production of the original check or a better copy of the original check is necessary to determine the validity of any claim described in subparagraph (B).

(2) 40-DAY PERIOD.—Any claim under paragraph (1) with respect to a consumer account may be submitted by a consumer before the end of the 40-day period beginning on the later of—

(A) the date on which the financial institution mails or delivers, by a means agreed to by the consumer, the periodic statement of account for such account which contains information concerning the transaction giving rise to the claim; or

(B) the date on which the substitute check is made available to the consumer.

(3) EXTENSION UNDER EXTENUATING CIRCUMSTANCES.—If the ability of the consumer to submit the claim within the 40-day period under paragraph (2) is delayed due to extenuating circumstances, including extended travel or the illness of the consumer, the 40-day period shall be extended by a reasonable amount of time.

(b) PROCEDURES FOR CLAIMS.—

(1) IN GENERAL.—To make a claim for an expedited recredit under subsection (a) with respect to a substitute check, the consumer shall provide to the bank that holds the account of such consumer—

(A) a description of the claim, including an explanation of—

(i) why the substitute check was not properly charged to the consumer's account; or

(ii) the warranty claim with respect to such check;

(B) a statement that the consumer suffered a loss and an estimate of the amount of the loss;

(C) the reason why production of the original check or a better copy of the original check is necessary to determine the validity of the charge to the consumer's account or the warranty claim; and

(D) sufficient information to identify the substitute check and to investigate the claim.

(2) CLAIM IN WRITING.—

(A) IN GENERAL.—The bank holding the consumer account that is the subject of a claim by the consumer under subsection (a) may, in the discretion of the bank, require the consumer to submit the information required under paragraph (1) in writing.

(B) MEANS OF SUBMISSION.—A bank that requires a submission of information under subparagraph (A) may permit the consumer to make the submission electronically, if the consumer has agreed to communicate with the bank in that manner.

(c) RECREDIT TO CONSUMER.—

(1) CONDITIONS FOR RECREDIT.—The bank shall recredit a consumer account in accordance with paragraph (2) for the amount of a substitute check that was charged against the consumer account if—

(A) a consumer submits a claim to the bank with respect to that substitute check that meets the requirement of subsection (b); and

(B) the bank has not—

(i) provided to the consumer—

(I) the original check; or

(II) a copy of the original check (including an image or a substitute check) that accurately represents all of the information on the front and back of the original check, as of the time at which the original check was truncated; and

(ii) demonstrated to the consumer that the substitute check was properly charged to the consumer account.

(2) TIMING OF RECREDIT.—

(A) IN GENERAL.—The bank shall recredit the consumer's account for the amount described in paragraph (1) no later than the end of the business day following the business day on which the bank determines the consumer's claim is valid.

(B) RECREDIT PENDING INVESTIGATION.—If the bank has not yet determined that the consumer's claim is valid before the end of the 10th business day after the business day on which the consumer submitted the claim, the bank shall recredit the consumer's account for—

(i) the lesser of the amount of the substitute check that was charged against the consumer account, or $2,500, together with interest if the account is an interest-bearing account, no later than the end of such 10th business day; and

(ii) the remaining amount of the substitute check that was charged against the consumer account, if any, together with interest if the account is an interest bearing account, not later than the 45th calendar day following the business day on which the consumer submits the claim.

(d) AVAILABILITY OF RECREDIT.—

(1) NEXT BUSINESS DAY AVAILABILITY.—Except as provided in paragraph (2), a bank that provides a recredit to a consumer account under subsection (c) shall make the recredited funds available for withdrawal by the consumer by the start of the next business day after the business day on which the bank recredits the consumer's account under subsection (c).

(2) SAFEGUARD EXCEPTIONS.—A bank may delay availability to a consumer of a recredit provided under subsection (c)(2)(B)(i) until the start of either the business day following the business day on which the bank determines that the consumer's claim is valid or the 45th calendar day following the business day on which the consumer submits a claim for such recredit in accordance with subsection (b), whichever is earlier, in any of the following circumstances:

(A) NEW ACCOUNTS.—The claim is made during the 30-day period beginning on the business day the consumer account was established.

(B) REPEATED OVERDRAFTS.—Without regard to the charge that is the subject of the claim for which the recredit was made—

(i) on 6 or more business days during the 6-month period ending on the date on which the consumer submits the claim, the balance in the consumer account was negative or would have become negative if checks or other charges to the account had been paid; or

(ii) on 2 or more business days during such 6-month period, the balance in the consumer account was negative or would have become negative in the amount of $5,000 or more if checks or other charges to the account had been paid.

(C) PREVENTION OF FRAUD LOSSES.—The bank has reasonable cause to believe that the claim is fraudulent, based on facts (other than the fact that the check in question or the consumer is of a particular class) that would cause a well-grounded belief in the mind of a reasonable person that the claim is fraudulent.

(3) OVERDRAFT FEES.—No bank that, in accordance with paragraph (2), delays the availability of a recredit under subsection (c) to any consumer account may impose any overdraft fees with respect to drafts drawn by the consumer on such recredited amount before the end of the 5-day period beginning on the date notice of the delay in the availability of such amount is sent by the bank to the consumer.

(e) REVERSAL OF RECREDIT.—A bank may reverse a recredit to a consumer account if the bank—

(1) determines that a substitute check for which the bank recredited a consumer account under subsection (c) was in fact properly charged to the consumer account; and

(2) notifies the consumer in accordance with subsection (f)(3).

(f) NOTICE TO CONSUMER.—

(1) NOTICE IF CONSUMER CLAIM NOT VALID.—If a bank determines that a substitute check subject to the consumer's claim was in fact properly charged to the consumer's account, the bank shall send to the consumer, no later than the business day following the business day on which the bank makes a determination—

(A) the original check or a copy of the original check (including an image or a substitute check) that—

(i) accurately represents all of the information on the front and back of the original check (as of the time the original check was truncated); or

(ii) is otherwise sufficient to determine whether or not the consumer's claim is valid; and

(B) an explanation of the basis for the determination by the bank that the substitute check was properly charged, including a statement that the consumer may request copies of any information or documents on which the bank relied in making the determination.

(2) NOTICE OF RECREDIT.—If a bank recredits a consumer account under subsection (c), the bank shall send to the consumer, no later than the business day following the business day on which the bank makes the recredit, a notice of—

(A) the amount of the recredit; and

(B) the date the recredited funds will be available for withdrawal.

(3) NOTICE OF REVERSAL OF RECREDIT.—In addition to the notice required under paragraph (1), if a bank reverses a recredited amount under subsection (e), the bank shall send to the consumer, no later than the business day following the business day on which the bank reverses the recredit, a notice of—

(A) the amount of the reversal; and

(B) the date the recredit was reversed.

(4) MODE OF DELIVERY.—A notice described in this subsection shall be delivered by United States mail or by any other means through which the consumer has agreed to receive account information.

(g) OTHER CLAIMS NOT AFFECTED.—Providing a recredit in accordance with this section shall not absolve the bank from liability for a claim made under any other law, such as a claim for wrongful dishonor under the Uniform Commercial Code, or from liability for additional damages under section 6 or 10.

(h) CLARIFICATION CONCERNING CONSUMER POSSESSION.—A consumer who was provided a substitute check may make a claim for an expedited recredit under this section with regard to a transaction involving the substitute check whether or not the consumer is in possession of the substitute check.

(i) SCOPE OF APPLICATION.—This section shall only apply to customers who are consumers.

SEC. 8. EXPEDITED RECREDIT PROCEDURES FOR BANKS.

(a) RECREDIT CLAIMS.—

(1) IN GENERAL.—A bank may make a claim against an indemnifying bank for expedited recredit for which that bank is indemnified if—

(A) the claimant bank (or a bank that the claimant bank has indemnified) has received a claim for expedited recredit from a consumer under section 7 with respect to a substitute check or would have been subject to such a claim had the consumer's account been charged;

(B) the claimant bank has suffered a resulting loss or is obligated to recredit a consumer account under section 7 with respect to such substitute check; and

(C) production of the original check, another substitute check, or a better copy of the original check is necessary to determine the validity of the charge to the customer account or any warranty claim connected with such substitute check.

(2) 120-DAY PERIOD.—Any claim under paragraph (1) may be submitted by the claimant bank to an indemnifying bank before the end of the 120-day period beginning on the date of the transaction that gave rise to the claim.

(b) PROCEDURES FOR CLAIMS.—

(1) IN GENERAL.—To make a claim under subsection (a) for an expedited recredit relating to a substitute check, the claimant bank shall send to the indemnifying bank—

(A) a description of—

(i) the claim, including an explanation of why the substitute check cannot be properly charged to the consumer account; or

(ii) the warranty claim;

(B) a statement that the claimant bank has suffered a loss or is obligated to recredit the consumer's account under section 7, together with an estimate of the amount of the loss or recredit;

(C) the reason why production of the original check, another substitute check, or a better copy of the original check is necessary to determine the validity of the charge to the consumer account or the warranty claim; and

(D) information sufficient for the indemnifying bank to identify the substitute check and to investigate the claim.

(2) REQUIREMENTS RELATING TO COPIES OF SUBSTITUTE CHECKS.—If the information submitted by a claimant bank pursuant to paragraph (1) in connection with a claim for an expedited recredit includes a copy of any substitute check for which any such claim is made, the claimant bank shall take reasonable steps to ensure that any such copy cannot be—

(A) mistaken for the legal equivalent of the check under section 4(b); or

(B) sent or handled by any bank, including the indemnifying bank, as a forward collection or returned check.

(3) CLAIM IN WRITING.—

(A) IN GENERAL.—An indemnifying bank may, in the discretion of the bank, require the claimant bank to submit the information required by paragraph (1) in writing, including a copy of the written or electronically submitted claim, if any, that the consumer provided in accordance with section 7(b).

(B) MEANS OF SUBMISSION.—An indemnifying bank that requires a submission of information under subparagraph (A) may permit the claimant bank to make the submission electronically, if the claimant bank has agreed to communicate with the indemnifying bank in that manner.

(c) RECREDIT BY INDEMNIFYING BANK.—

(1) PROMPT ACTION REQUIRED.—No later than 10 business days after the business day on which an indemnifying bank receives a claim under subsection (a) from a claimant bank with respect to a substitute check, the indemnifying bank shall—

(A) provide, to the claimant bank, the original check (with respect to such substitute check) or a copy of the original check (including an image or a substitute check) that—

(i) accurately represents all of the information on the front and back of the original check (as of the time the original check was truncated); or

(ii) is otherwise sufficient to determine the bank's claim is not valid; and

(B) recredit the claimant bank for the amount of the claim up to the amount of the substitute check, plus interest if applicable; or

(C) provide information to the claimant bank as to why the indemnifying bank is not obligated to comply with subparagraph (A) or (B).

(2) RECREDIT DOES NOT ABROGATE OTHER LIABILITIES.—Providing a recredit under this subsection to a claimant bank with respect to a substitute check shall not absolve the indemnifying bank from liability for claims brought under any other law or from additional damages under section 6 or 10 with respect to such check.

(3) REFUND TO INDEMNIFYING BANK.—If a claimant bank reverses, in accordance with section 7(e), a recredit previously made to a consumer account under section 7(c), or otherwise receives a credit or recredit with regard to such

substitute check, the claimant bank shall promptly refund to any indemnifying bank any amount previously advanced by the indemnifying bank in connection with such substitute check.

(d) PRODUCTION OF ORIGINAL CHECK OR A SUFFICIENT COPY GOVERNED BY SECTION 6(d).—If the indemnifying bank provides the claimant bank with the original check or a copy of the original check (including an image or a substitute check) under subsection (c)(1)(A), section 6(d) shall govern any right of the indemnifying bank to any repayment of any funds the indemnifying bank has recredited to the claimant bank pursuant to subsection (c).

SEC. 9. DELAYS IN AN EMERGENCY.

A delay by a bank beyond the time limits prescribed or permitted by this Act shall be excused if the delay is caused by interruption of communication or computer facilities, suspension of payments by another bank, war, emergency conditions, failure of equipment, or other circumstances beyond the control of a bank and if the bank uses such diligence as the circumstances require.

SEC. 10. MEASURE OF DAMAGES.

(a) LIABILITY.—

(1) IN GENERAL.—Except as provided in section 6, any person who, in connection with a substitute check, breaches any warranty under this Act or fails to comply with any requirement imposed by, or regulation prescribed pursuant to, this Act with respect to any other person shall be liable to such person in an amount equal to the sum of—

(A) the lesser of—

(i) the amount of the loss suffered by the other person as a result of the breach or failure; or

(ii) the amount of the substitute check; and

(B) interest and expenses (including costs and reasonable attorney's fees and other expenses of representation) related to the substitute check.

(2) OFFSET OF RECREDITS.—The amount of damages any person receives under paragraph (1), if any, shall be reduced by the amount, if any, that the claimant receives and retains as a recredit under section 7 or 8.

(b) COMPARATIVE NEGLIGENCE.—

(1) IN GENERAL.—If a person incurs damages that resulted in whole or in part from the negligence or failure of that person to act in good faith, then the amount of any liability due to that person under subsection (a) shall be reduced in proportion to the amount of negligence or bad faith attributable to that person.

(2) RULE OF CONSTRUCTION.—Nothing in this subsection reduces the rights of a consumer or any other person under the Uniform Commercial Code or other applicable provision of Federal or State law.

SEC. 11. STATUTE OF LIMITATIONS AND NOTICE OF CLAIM.

(a) ACTIONS UNDER THIS ACT.—

(1) IN GENERAL.—An action to enforce a claim under this Act may be brought in any United States district court, or in any other court of competent

jurisdiction, before the end of the 1-year period beginning on the date the cause of action accrues.

(2) ACCRUAL.—A cause of action accrues as of the date the injured party first learns, or by which such person reasonably should have learned of, the facts and circumstances giving rise to the cause of action.

(b) DISCHARGE OF CLAIMS.—Except as provided in subsection (c), unless a person gives notice of a claim to the indemnifying or warranting bank within 30 days after the person has reason to know of the claim and the identity of the indemnifying or warranting bank, the indemnifying or warranting bank is discharged from liability in an action to enforce a claim under this Act to the extent of any loss caused by the delay in giving notice of the claim.

(c) NOTICE OF CLAIM BY CONSUMER.—A timely claim by a consumer under section 7 for expedited recredit constitutes timely notice of a claim by the consumer for purposes of subsection (b).

SEC. 12. CONSUMER AWARENESS.

(a) IN GENERAL.—Each bank shall provide, in accordance with subsection (b), a brief notice about substitute checks that describes—

(1) how a substitute check is the legal equivalent of an original check for all purposes, including any provision of any Federal or State law, and for all persons, if the substitute check—

(A) accurately represents all of the information on the front and back of the original check as of the time at which the original check was truncated; and

(B) bears the legend: "This is a legal copy of your check. You can use it in the same way you would use the original check."; and

(2) the consumer recredit rights established under section 7 when a consumer believes in good faith that a substitute check was not properly charged to the account of the consumer.

(b) DISTRIBUTION.—

(1) EXISTING CUSTOMERS.—With respect to consumers who are customers of a bank on the effective date of this Act and who receive original checks or substitute checks, a bank shall provide the notice described in subsection (a) to each such consumer no later than the first regularly scheduled communication with the consumer after the effective date of this Act.

(2) NEW ACCOUNT HOLDERS.—A bank shall provide the notice described in subsection (a) to each consumer who will receive original checks or substitute checks, other than existing customers referred to in paragraph (1), at the time at which the customer relationship is initiated.

(3) MODE OF DELIVERY.—A bank may send the notices required by this subsection by United States mail or by any other means through which the consumer has agreed to receive account information.

(4) CONSUMERS WHO REQUEST COPIES OF CHECKS.—Notice shall be provided to each consumer of the bank that requests a copy of a check and receives a substitute check, at the time of the request.

(c) MODEL LANGUAGE.—

(1) IN GENERAL.—Before the end of the 9-month period beginning on the date of the enactment of this Act, the Board shall publish model forms and clauses that a bank may use to describe each of the elements required by subsection (a).

(2) SAFE HARBOR.—

(A) IN GENERAL.—A bank shall be treated as being in compliance with the requirements of subsection (a) if the bank's substitute check notice uses a model form or clause published by the Board and such model form or clause accurately describes the bank's policies and practices.

(B) DELETION OR REARRANGEMENT.—A bank may delete any information in the model form or clause that is not required by this Act or rearrange the format.

(3) USE OF MODEL LANGUAGE NOT REQUIRED.—This section shall not be construed as requiring any bank to use a model form or clause that the Board prepares under this subsection.

SEC. 13. EFFECT ON OTHER LAW.
This Act shall supersede any provision of Federal or State law, including the Uniform Commercial Code, that is inconsistent with this Act, but only to the extent of the inconsistency.

SEC. 14. VARIATION BY AGREEMENT.
(a) SECTION 8.—Any provision of section 8 may be varied by agreement of the banks involved.
(b) NO OTHER PROVISIONS MAY BE VARIED.—Except as provided in subsection (a), no provision of this Act may be varied by agreement of any person or persons.

SEC. 15. REGULATIONS.
The Board may prescribe such regulations as the Board determines to be necessary to implement, prevent circumvention or evasion of, or facilitate compliance with the provisions of this Act.

SEC. 16. STUDY AND REPORT ON FUNDS AVAILABILITY.
(a) STUDY.—In order to evaluate the implementation and the impact of this Act, the Board shall conduct a study of—

(1) the percentage of total checks cleared in which the paper check is not returned to the paying bank;

(2) the extent to which banks make funds available to consumers for local and nonlocal checks prior to the expiration of maximum hold periods;

(3) the length of time within which depositary banks learn of the nonpayment of local and nonlocal checks;

(4) the increase or decrease in check-related losses over the study period; and

(5) the appropriateness of the time periods and amount limits applicable under sections 603 and 604 of the Expedited Funds Availability Act, as in effect on the date of enactment of this Act.

(b) REPORT TO CONGRESS.—Before the end of the 30-month period beginning on the effective date of this Act, the Board shall submit a report to the Congress containing the results of the study conducted under this section, together with recommendations for legislative action.

SEC. 17. STATISTICAL REPORTING OF COSTS AND REVENUES FOR TRANSPORTING CHECKS BETWEEN RESERVE BANKS.

In the annual report prepared by the Board for the first full calendar year after the date of enactment of this Act and in each of the 9 subsequent annual reports by the Board, the Board shall include the amount of operating costs attributable to, and an estimate of the Federal Reserve banks' imputed revenues derived from, the transportation of commercial checks between Federal Reserve bank check processing centers.

SEC. 18. EVALUATION AND REPORT BY THE COMPTROLLER GENERAL.

(a) STUDY.—During the 5-year period beginning on the date of the enactment of this Act, the Comptroller General of the United States shall evaluate the implementation and administration of this Act, including—

(1) an estimate of the gains in economic efficiency made possible from check truncation;

(2) an evaluation of the benefits accruing to consumers and financial institutions from reduced transportation costs, longer hours for accepting deposits for credit within 1 business day, the impact of fraud losses, and an estimate of consumers' share of the total benefits derived from this Act; and

(3) an assessment of consumer acceptance of the check truncation process resulting from this Act, as well as any new costs incurred by consumers who had their original checks returned with their regular monthly statements prior to the date of enactment of this Act.

(b) REPORT TO CONGRESS.—Before the end of the 5-year period referred to in subsection (a), the Comptroller General shall submit a report to the Congress containing the findings and conclusions of the Comptroller General in connection with the evaluation conducted pursuant to subsection (a), together with such recommendations for legislative and administrative action as the Comptroller General may determine to be appropriate.

SEC. 19. DEPOSITARY SERVICES EFFICIENCY AND COST REDUCTION.

(a) FINDINGS.—The Congress finds as follows:

(1) The Secretary of the Treasury has long compensated financial institutions for various critical depositary and financial agency services provided for or on behalf of the United States by—

(A) placing large balances, commonly referred to as "compensating balances," on deposit at such institutions; and

(B) using imputed interest on such funds to offset charges for the various depositary and financial agency services provided to or on behalf of the Government.

(2) As a result of sharp declines in interest rates over the last few years to record low levels, or the public debt outstanding reaching the statutory debt limit, the Department of the Treasury often has had to dramatically increase or decrease the size of the compensating balances on deposit at these financial institutions.

(3) The fluctuation of the compensating balances, and the necessary pledging of collateral by financial institutions to secure the value of compensating balances placed with those institutions, have created unintended financial

uncertainty for the Secretary of the Treasury and for the management by financial institutions of their cash and securities.

(4) It is imperative that the process for providing financial services to the Government be transparent, and provide the information necessary for the Congress to effectively exercise its appropriation and oversight responsibilities.

(5) The use of direct payment for services rendered would strengthen cash and debt management responsibilities of the Secretary of the Treasury because the Secretary would no longer need to dramatically increase or decrease the level of such balances when interest rates fluctuate sharply or when the public debt outstanding reaches the statutory debt limit.

(6) An alternative to the use of compensating balances, such as direct payments to financial institutions, would ensure that payments to financial institutions for the services they provide would be made in a more predictable manner and could result in cost savings.

(7) Limiting the use of compensating balances could result in a more direct and cost-efficient method of obtaining those services currently provided under compensating balance arrangements.

(8) A transition from the use of compensating balances to another compensation method must be carefully managed to prevent higher-than-necessary transitional costs and enable participating financial institutions to modify their planned investment of cash and securities.

(b) AUTHORIZATION OF APPROPRIATIONS FOR SERVICES RENDERED BY DEPOSITARIES AND FINANCIAL AGENCIES OF THE UNITED STATES.—There are authorized to be appropriated for fiscal years beginning after fiscal year 2003 to the Secretary of the Treasury such sums as may be necessary for reimbursing financial institutions in their capacity as depositaries and financial agents of the United States for all services required or directed by the Secretary of the Treasury, or a designee of the Secretary, to be performed by such financial institutions on behalf of the Secretary of the Treasury or another Federal agency, including services rendered before fiscal year 2004.

(c) ORDERLY TRANSITION.—

(1) IN GENERAL.—As appropriations authorized in subsection (b) become available, the Secretary of the Treasury shall promptly begin the process of phasing in the use of the appropriations to pay financial institutions serving as depositaries and financial agents of the United States, and transitioning from the use of compensating balances to fund these services.

(2) POST-TRANSITION USE LIMITED TO EXTRAORDINARY CIRCUMSTANCES.—

(A) IN GENERAL.—Following the transition to the use of the appropriations authorized in subsection (b), the Secretary of the Treasury may use the compensating balances to pay financial institutions serving as depositaries and financial agents of the United States only in extraordinary situations where the Secretary determines that they are needed to ensure the fiscal operations of the Government continue to function in an efficient and effective manner.

(B) REPORT.—Any use of compensating balances pursuant to subparagraph (A) shall promptly be reported by the Secretary of the Treasury to the Committee on Financial Services of the House of Representatives and the Committee on Banking, Housing, and Urban Affairs of the Senate.

(3) REQUIREMENTS FOR ORDERLY TRANSITION.—In transitioning to the use of the appropriations authorized in subsection (b), the Secretary of the Treasury shall take such steps as may be appropriate to—

(A) prevent abrupt financial disruption to the functions of the Department of the Treasury or to the participating financial institutions; and

(B) maintain adequate accounting and management controls to ensure that payments to financial institutions for their banking services provided to the Government as depositaries and financial agents are accurate and that the arrangements last no longer than is necessary.

(4) REPORTS REQUIRED.—

(A) ANNUAL REPORT.—

(i) IN GENERAL.—For each fiscal year, the Secretary of the Treasury shall submit a report to the Congress on the use of compensating balances and on the use of appropriations authorized in subsection (b) during that fiscal year.

(ii) INCLUSION IN BUDGET.—The report required under clause (i) may be submitted as part of the budget submitted by the President under section 1105 of title 31, United States Code, for the following fiscal year and, if so, the report shall be submitted concurrently to the Committee on Financial Services of the House of Representatives and the Committee on Banking, Housing, and Urban Affairs of the Senate.

(B) FINAL REPORT FOLLOWING TRANSITION.—

(i) IN GENERAL.—Following completion of the transition from the use of compensating balances to the use of the appropriations authorized in subsection (b) to pay financial institutions for their services as depositaries and financial agents of the United States, the Secretary of the Treasury shall submit a report on the transition to the Committee on Financial Services of the House of Representatives and the Committee on Banking, Housing, and Urban Affairs of the Senate.

(ii) CONTENTS OF REPORT.—The report submitted under clause (i) shall include a detailed analysis of—

(I) the cost of transition;

(II) the direct costs of the services being paid from the appropriations authorized in subsection (b); and

(III) the benefits realized from the use of direct payment for such services, rather than the use of compensating balance arrangements.

(d) TECHNICAL AMENDMENT.—The second undesignated paragraph of section 16 of the Federal Reserve Act (12 U.S.C. 412) is amended—

(1) in the third sentence, by inserting "or any other asset of a Federal reserve bank" before the period at the end; and

(2) in the last sentence, by inserting "or are otherwise held by or on behalf of" after "in the vaults of."

(e) EFFECTIVE DATE.—Notwithstanding section 20, this section shall take effect on the date of the enactment of this Act.

SEC. 20. EFFECTIVE DATE.

This Act shall take effect at the end of the 12-month period beginning on the date of the enactment of this Act, except as otherwise specifically provided in this Act.

APPENDIX IV

ACCORD AND SATISFACTION (SECTION 42A-3-311)—CONNECTICUT

Sec. 42a-3-311. Accord and satisfaction by use of instrument.

(a) If a person against whom a claim is asserted proves that (i) that person in good faith tendered an instrument to the claimant as full satisfaction of the claim, (ii) the amount of the claim was unliquidated or subject to a bona fide dispute, and (iii) the claimant obtained payment of the instrument, the following subsections apply.

(b) Unless subsection (c) applies, the claim is discharged if the person against whom the claim is asserted proves that the instrument or an accompanying written communication contained a conspicuous statement to the effect that the instrument was tendered as full satisfaction of the claim.

(c) Subject to subsection (d), a claim is not discharged under subsection (b) if either of the following applies:

(1) The claimant, if an organization, proves that (i) within a reasonable time before the tender, the claimant sent a conspicuous statement to the person against whom the claim is asserted that communications concerning disputed debts, including an instrument tendered as full satisfaction of a debt, are to be sent to a designated person, office, or place, and (ii) the instrument or accompanying communication was not received by that designated person, office, or place.

(2) The claimant, whether or not an organization, proves that within ninety days after payment of the instrument, the claimant tendered repayment of the amount of the instrument to the person against whom the claim is asserted. This paragraph does not apply if the claimant is an organization that sent a statement complying with paragraph (1)(i).

(d) A claim is discharged if the person against whom the claim is asserted proves that within a reasonable time before collection of the instrument was initiated, the claimant, or an agent of the claimant having direct responsibility with respect to the disputed obligation, knew that the instrument was tendered in full satisfaction of the claim.

APPENDIX V

DISHONORED CHECK (SECTION 5-328)—NEW YORK

New York General Obligation Law Chapter 24a, Article 5, Title 3

§ 5-328. Processing fee by holder dishonored of check.

1. As used in this section the following terms shall have the following meanings:
   a. "Holder of a check" means the holder or its assignee, representative or any other person retained by the holder to seek collection of the face value of a dishonored check.
   b. "Dishonored check" means a check, draft or like instrument drawn on a bank or depository institution as full or partial payment for an unpaid balance on an account, or for other extensions of credit or payments of money in connection with a consumer transaction, which is not paid or is dishonored or is returned by such institution due to insufficient funds or other cause not attributable to the holder.
   c. "Consumer transaction" means a transaction in which a natural person is extended credit for, or purchases or leases, personal property, money or services primarily for personal, family or household purposes.
   d. "Account" means a loan account, a retail credit account or an obligation under a retail lease agreement, retail installment contract or retail installment obligation or a retail installment credit agreement, as defined in sections three hundred one, three hundred thirty-one and four hundred one of the personal property law.
2. Notwithstanding the provisions of any law:
   a. The holder of a dishonored check given in payment for a consumer transaction or an account may collect from, charge, or add to the outstanding balance of the account of, the person from whom such check was received or to whom such credit was extended, a dishonored check charge of not more than the lesser of the amount agreed upon, if contracted for, or twenty dollars.

b. A dishonored check charge shall not be deemed a credit service charge, interest or an incident to or a condition to the extension of credit, for any purpose of law.

3. Notwithstanding any other provision of law, any person to whom a check, draft or like instrument, other than a money order, bank cashier's check or certified check, is tendered for any transaction, other than a consumer transaction, may, if such instrument is dishonored charge or collect from the maker or drawer the amount of twenty dollars for the return of such unpaid or dishonored instrument.

Appendix VI

AMENDMENT TO REGULATION E

§ 205.3 Coverage.

(a) *General.* This part applies to any electronic fund transfer that authorizes a financial institution to debit or credit a consumer's account. Generally, this part applies to financial institutions. For purposes of §§ 205.3(b)(2), and (b)(3), 205.10(b), (d), and (e) and 205.13, this part applies to any person.

(b) *Electronic fund transfer—*

(1) *Definition.* The term electronic fund transfer means any transfer of funds that is initiated through an electronic terminal, telephone, computer, or magnetic tape for the purpose of ordering, instructing, or authorizing a financial institution to debit or credit a consumer's account. The term includes, but is not limited to—

(i) Point-of-sale transfers;

(ii) Automated teller machine transfers;

(iii) Direct deposits or withdrawals of funds;

(iv) Transfers initiated by telephone; and

(v) Transfers resulting from debit card transactions, whether or not initiated through an electronic terminal.

(2) *Electronic fund transfer using information from a check.*

(i) This part applies where a check, draft, or similar paper instrument is used as a source of information to initiate a one-time electronic fund transfer from a consumer's account. The consumer must authorize the transfer.

(ii) The person initiating an electronic fund transfer using the consumer's check as a source of information for the transfer must provide a notice that the transaction will or may be processed as an electronic fund transfer, and obtain a consumer's authorization for each transfer. A consumer authorizes a one-time electronic fund transfer (in providing a check to a merchant or other payee for the MICR encoding, that is, the routing number of the financial institution, the consumer's account number and the serial number) when the consumer receives notice and goes forward with the underlying transaction. For point-of-sale transfers, the notice must be posted in a prominent and conspicuous location, and a copy thereof, or a substantially similar notice, must be provided to the consumer at the time of the transaction.

(iii) The person that initiates an electronic fund transfer using the consumer's check as a source of information for the transfer shall also provide a notice to the consumer at the same time it provides the notice required under paragraph (b)(2)(ii) that when a check is used to initiate an electronic fund transfer, funds may be debited from the consumer's account as soon as the same-day payment is received, and, as applicable, that the consumer's check will not be returned by the financial institution holding the consumer's account. For point-of-sale transfers, the person initiating the transfer may post the notice required in this paragraph (b)(2)(iii) in a prominent and conspicuous location and need not include this notice on the copy of the notice given to the consumer under paragraph (b)(2)(ii). The requirements in this paragraph (b)(2)(iii) shall remain in effect until December 31, 2009.

(iv) A person may provide notices that are substantially similar to those set forth in Appendix A–6 to comply with the requirements of this paragraph (b)(2).

(3) *Collection of returned item fees via electronic fund transfer.*

(i) *General.* The person initiating an electronic fund transfer to collect a fee for the return of an electronic fund transfer or a check that is unpaid, including due to insufficient or uncollected funds in the consumer's account, must obtain the consumer's authorization for each transfer. A consumer authorizes a one-time electronic fund transfer from his or her account to pay the fee for the returned item or transfer if the person collecting the fee provides notice to the consumer stating that the person may electronically collect the fee, and the consumer goes forward with the underlying transaction. The notice must state that the fee will be collected by means of an electronic fund transfer from the consumer's account if the payment is returned unpaid and must disclose the dollar amount of the fee. If the fee may vary due to the amount of the transaction or due to other factors, then, except as otherwise provided in paragraph (b)(3)(ii) of this section, the person collecting the fee may disclose, in place of the dollar amount of the fee, an explanation of how the fee will be determined.

(ii) *Point-of-sale transactions.* If a fee for an electronic fund transfer or check returned unpaid may be collected electronically in connection with a point-of-sale transaction, the person initiating an electronic fund transfer to collect the fee must post the notice described in paragraph (b)(3)(i) of this section in a prominent and conspicuous location. The person also must either provide the consumer with a copy of the posted notice (or a substantially similar notice) at the time of the transaction, or mail the copy (or a substantially similar notice) to the consumer's address as soon as reasonably practicable after the person initiates the electronic fund transfer to collect the fee. If the amount of the fee may vary due to the amount of the transaction or due to other factors, the posted notice may explain how the fee will be determined, but the notice provided to the consumer must state the dollar amount of the fee if the amount can be calculated at the time the notice is provided or mailed to the consumer.

(iii) *Delayed compliance date for fee disclosure.* Through December 31, 2007, the notice required to be provided to consumers under paragraph (b)(3)(ii) of this section in connection with a point-of-sale transaction, whether given to the consumer at the time of the transaction or subsequently mailed to the consumer, need not include either the dollar amount of any fee collected electronically for a check or electronic fund transfer returned unpaid or an explanation of how the amount of the fee will be determined.

(c) *Exclusions from coverage.* The term electronic fund transfer does not include:

(1) *Checks.* Any transfer of funds originated by check, draft, or similar paper instrument; or any payment made by check, draft, or similar paper instrument at an electronic terminal.

(2) *Check guarantee or authorization.* Any transfer of funds that guarantees payment or authorizes acceptance of a check, draft, or similar paper instrument but that does not directly result in a debit or credit to a consumer's account.

(3) *Wire or other similar transfers.* Any transfer of funds through Fedwire or through a similar wire transfer system that is used primarily for transfers between financial institutions or between businesses.

(4) *Securities and commodities transfers.* Any transfer of funds the primary purpose of which is the purchase or sale of a security or commodity, if the security or commodity is:

(i) Regulated by the Securities and Exchange Commission or the Commodity Futures Trading Commission;

(ii) Purchased or sold through a broker-dealer regulated by the Securities and Exchange Commission or through a futures commission merchant regulated by the Commodity Futures Trading Commission; or

(iii) Held in book-entry form by a Federal Reserve Bank or federal agency.

(5) *Automatic transfers by account-holding institution.* Any transfer of funds under an agreement between a consumer and a financial institution which provides that the institution will initiate individual transfers without a specific request from the consumer:

(i) Between a consumer's accounts within the financial institution;

(ii) From a consumer's account to an account of a member of the consumer's family held in the same financial institution; or

(iii) Between a consumer's account and an account of the financial institution, except that these transfers remain subject to § 205.10(e) regarding compulsory use and sections 915 and 916 of the act regarding civil and criminal liability.

(6) *Telephone-initiated transfers.* Any transfer of funds that:

(i) Is initiated by a telephone communication between a consumer and a financial institution making the transfer; and

(ii) Does not take place under a telephone bill-payment or other written plan in which periodic or recurring transfers are contemplated.

(7) *Small institutions.* Any preauthorized transfer to or from an account if the assets of the account-holding financial institution were $100 million or less on the preceding December 31. If assets of the account-holding institution subsequently exceed $100 million, the institution's exemption for preauthorized transfers terminates one year from the end of the calendar year in which the assets exceed $100 million. Preauthorized transfers exempt under this paragraph (c)(7) remain subject to § 205.10(e) regarding compulsory use and sections 915 and 916 of the act regarding civil and criminal liability.

[Codified to 12 C.F.R. § 205.3]

[Section 205.3 amended at 44 Fed. Reg. 59470, October 15, 1979, effective November 15, 1979; 45 Fed. Reg. 66347, October 6, 1980; 46 Fed. Reg. 2973, January 13, 1981, effective January 15, 1981; 46 Fed. Reg. 9920, January 30, 1981, effective January 29, 1981; 47 Fed. Reg. 44713, October 12, 1982; 61 Fed. Reg. 19669, May 2, 1996; 71 Fed. Reg. 1659, January 10, 2006, effective February 9, 2006, mandatory compliance date is January 1, 2007; 71 Fed. Reg. 51456, August 30, 2006, effective July 1, 2006; 71 Fed. Reg. 69437, December 1, 2006, effective January 1, 2007]

APPENDIX VII

DEPOSIT ACCOUNT CONTROL AGREEMENT AND GENERAL TERMS–AMERICAN BAR ASSOCIATION

DEPOSIT ACCOUNT CONTROL AGREEMENT

version 1 dated February 13, 2006

available from the American Bar Association's Business Law Section at http://www.abanet.org/dch/committee.cfm?com=CL710060[1]

Executed and Delivered as of _______ __, 20__

PARTIES

This Agreement is among the persons signing this Agreement as the "*Secured Party*", the "*Debtor*" and the "*Bank*".

BACKGROUND

The Debtor is the Bank's customer with respect to one or more demand deposit accounts identified by the account numbers specified below (individually and collectively, as re-numbered and including any funds in the account or accounts, the "*Deposit Account*"). The Debtor has granted the Secured Party a security interest in the Deposit Account. The Debtor is requesting that the Bank enter into this Agreement. The Bank is willing to do so upon the terms contained in this Agreement.

This Agreement includes the General Terms, the Specific Terms and the Exhibit, each as defined or referred to below.

AGREEMENTS

A. GENERAL TERMS. This Agreement is subject to the General Terms for Deposit Account Control Agreement version 1 dated February 13, 2006, developed by a special task force of the American Bar Association's Business Law Section and available from the Business Law Section at http://www.abanet.org/dch/committee.cfm?com=CL710060 (the "*General Terms*"). The General Terms are incorporated in this Agreement by reference and without modification except as may be provided in Section 10 of the Specific Terms.

---

[1] This document is a model form produced by the Joint Task Force on Deposit Account Control Agreements of the Business Law Section of the American Bar Association. The provisions of the form have not been approved by the House of Delegates or Board of Governors of the American Bar Association and, accordingly, should not be construed as representing the policy of the American Bar Association.

B. SPECIFIC TERMS. The following terms (the "*Specific Terms*") complete, supplement or modify the General Terms:

1. Deposit Account *(see "Background" above)*. The following account or accounts comprise the Deposit Account [*list by account number*]:

____

2. Business Day *(see definition of "Business Day" in Section 1 of the General Terms)*:

A day will not be considered as a "Business Day" if commercial banks in the following city or cities are closed on that day: ______________________. If the preceding sentence is not completed, no additional days are excluded from the definition of "Business Day".

3. Outside Time *(see definition of "Outside Time" in Section 1 of the General Terms)*:

If the Outside Time is to be based on a period of less than two Business Days, the following is the earlier period:______________________. If an earlier period is not inserted in the preceding sentence, then the Outside Time will be based on two Business Days.

4. Disposition of less than all or multi-disposition of funds *(see Section 4(a)(ii)(E) of the General Terms)*:

The following is any computation or formula by which a Disposition Instruction originated by the Secured Party may provide for a disposition of less than all of the funds in the Deposit Account and whether there may be multiple recipients of the funds:

____

____

____.

If the preceding paragraph is not completed to permit a disposition of less than all of the funds in the Deposit Account, then a Disposition Instruction originated by the Secured Party must be for a disposition of all of the funds. If the preceding paragraph is not completed to permit a disposition of the funds in the Deposit Account to multiple recipients, then a Disposition Instruction originated by the Secured Party must require that the funds be sent to a single recipient.

5. Reimbursement Claim Period *(see Section 6(b) of the General Terms)*:

The number of days following the termination of the Agreement in which a reimbursement claim must be made against the Secured Party under Section 6(b) of the General Terms is ________. If a number is not inserted in the preceding sentence, the number is 90.

6. Electronic Records *(see definition of "writing" in Section 1 of the General Terms)*:

Checking this line ___ means that the parties permit a writing to include an electronic record and permit communications by email. Otherwise, the parties do not permit a writing to include an electronic record and do not permit communications by email.

7. Governing Law *(see Section 13(a) of the General Terms)*:

The jurisdiction whose law governs this Agreement is ______________________________. If a jurisdiction is not inserted in the preceding sentence, the jurisdiction will be determined by applicable law.

8. Bank's Jurisdiction for UCC Purposes *(see Section 13(b) of the General Terms)*:

The Bank's jurisdiction for purposes of part 3 of UCC Article 9 is ______________________________. If the Bank's jurisdiction for such purposes is not inserted in the preceding sentence, the Bank's jurisdiction for such purposes will be determined by applicable law.

9. Delivery of Executed Copy *(see Part D)*:

Checking this line ___ means that the delivery of an executed copy of this Agreement may be made by electronic transmission in addition to a transmission by facsimile. Otherwise, delivery of an executed copy of this Agreement may not be made by a form of electronic transmission other than facsimile.

10. Additional Provisions *(see Section 12(b) of the General Terms)*:

The following provisions modify or supplement the General Terms:

If no provisions are inserted above in this Section 10, then there are no modifications to or supplements of the General Terms.

C. EXHIBIT. The parties have completed and attach hereto the Exhibit to be used as the form of the Initial Instruction. [*Note to person completing this Agreement: the Exhibit requires the designation of the person or persons or department at the Bank to receive the Initial Instruction. See Note 1 to the Exhibit.*]

D. SINGLE AGREEMENT; COUNTERPARTS. The General Terms, the Specific Terms and the Exhibit shall be read and construed together with the other provisions of this Agreement as a single agreement. Delivery of executed copies of this Agreement may be made by facsimile or, if so permitted in Section 9 of Part B, by another form of electronic transmission. This Agreement may be executed in counterparts, each of which shall constitute an original and all of which collectively shall constitute a single agreement.

[remainder of page intentionally left blank]

SIGNATURES

Debtor:

____

By:__________________________
Name:
Title:
Address:

Attention:
Telephone Number (for information only):
Facsimile Number:
Electronic mail address (if Section 6 of Part B permits):

Secured Party:

____

By:__________________________
Name:
Title:
Address:

Attention:
Telephone Number (for information only):
Facsimile Number:
Electronic mail address (if Section 6 of Part B permits):

Bank:

____

By:________________________________
Name:
Title:
Address:

Attention:
Telephone Number (for information only):
Facsimile Number:
Electronic mail address (if Section 6 of Part B permits):

Exhibit

[LETTERHEAD OF THE SECURED PARTY]

DEPOSIT ACCOUNT CONTROL AGREEMENT

INITIAL INSTRUCTION

[Date]

____
[Name of Bank]
____
____
[Address of Bank]

Attention: ____
[Person or Persons or Department] *[See Note 1 below]*

Ladies and Gentlemen:

This is the Initial Instruction as defined in the Deposit Account Control Agreement dated _______ __, 20__, among you, us and [Debtor] (the "*Debtor*") (as currently in effect , the "*Control Agreement*"). A copy of the Control Agreement as fully executed is attached. Capitalized terms used in this Initial Instruction have the meanings given them in the Control Agreement

This Initial Instruction directs the Bank no longer to comply with the Debtor's Disposition Instructions.

[As an included Disposition Instruction, we direct you to send the funds in the Deposit Account to us by the method and at the address indicated below. We recognize that, as a condition to your complying with this Disposition Instruction and to the extent that we have not already done so, we must provide to you evidence reasonably required by you as to the authority of the person giving this Disposition Instruction to act for us. We also recognize that your obligation to comply with this Disposition Instruction is subject to the other provisions of Section 4(a)(ii) of the General Terms. *[See Note 2 below]*

Funds transfer instructions:

Receiving bank: __________________________________.

ABA routing number for domestic wire:______________________.

ABA routing number for ACH transaction:____________________.

International: Swift Code No. __________________________.

Reference details:____________________________________.]

Very truly yours,

[SECURED PARTY]

By:____________________

Title:__________________

Notes to the person completing this form of Initial Instruction:

1. The "attention" line should be completed with particular care. Until the Initial Instruction is actually received by the person or persons or department at the Bank designated in the "attention" line, the time period by which the Bank must comply with the Initial Instruction will not commence. Accordingly, it is advisable to provide in the "attention" line a specific department or specific officer or officers at the Bank by title rather than by name. If an individual at the Bank is to be designated by title or even by name, it is advisable that one or more additional individuals at the Bank be designated as alternatives to receive the Initial Instruction if the first individual is not available.

2. The bracketed language relating to a Disposition Instruction (including funds transfer instructions) is optional. Not including this language does not preclude the Secured Party from subsequently giving a Disposition Instruction.

General Terms for the Deposit Account Control Agreement

1. Definitions and Rules of Interpretation. In this Agreement (a) terms defined in the UCC and not otherwise defined in this Agreement have the same meanings in this Agreement as in the UCC, (b) the rules of interpretation in Article 1 of the UCC apply to the interpretation of this Agreement and (c) the term "or" is not exclusive. Unless otherwise stated, section references are to sections of these General Terms. In addition, the following terms in this Agreement have the following meanings or interpretations:

This *"Agreement"* means the Deposit Account Control Agreement dated the Agreement Date among the Secured Party, the Debtor and the Bank. The Deposit Account Control Agreement includes these General Terms (incorporated by reference), the Specific Terms and the Exhibit read and construed together as a single agreement.

"Agreement Date" means the date set forth at the beginning of this Agreement as the date as of which this Agreement was executed and delivered by the parties.

An *"address"* includes the person or persons or department of the Bank on an "attention" line.

"Bank" means the organization signing this Agreement as the Bank.

"Business Day" means:

(i) for communications to the Bank, a day other than a day (A) that is not a "business day" as defined in Federal Reserve Board Regulation CC, 12 CFR Part 229, (B) on which the office, branch or department of the Bank specified as the Bank's address in the Exhibit is closed, or (C) on which commercial banks are closed in the city or cities set forth in the Specific Terms; and

(ii) for communications to any other party, a day, other than a Saturday or Sunday, on which the other party is open for business at the location to which the communication is sent.

"Claim" means a claim, loss, cost or expense, and includes out-of-pocket or allocable internal legal fees and expenses incurred in bringing or defending a claim.

A *"communication"* includes the Initial Instruction, a Disposition Instruction or a notice.

"Debtor" means the person signing this Agreement as the Debtor.

"Deposit Account" has the meaning set forth in the "Background" of this Agreement. The Deposit Account is identified in Section 1 of the Specific Terms.

"Deposit-related Agreements" means, collectively, the deposit account agreement and any other agreements between the Bank and the Debtor governing the Deposit Account and any cash management or similar services provided by the Bank to the Debtor in connection with the Deposit Account.

"Disposition Instruction" means an instruction to the Bank directing the disposition of the funds in the Deposit Account.

"Exhibit" means the Exhibit referred to in Part C of and attached to this Agreement as the form to be used as the Initial Instruction.

"Initial Instruction" means the first instruction to the Bank originated by the Secured Party directing that the Bank no longer comply with the Debtor's Disposition Instructions. The Initial Instruction may also contain a Disposition Instruction originated by the Secured Party.

"Order or Process" means an order, judgment, decree or injunction, or a garnishment, restraining notice or other legal process, directing, or prohibiting or otherwise restricting, the disposition of the funds in the Deposit Account.

"Outside Time" means, unless an earlier Outside Time is stated in the Specific Terms, the opening of business on the second Business Day after the Business Day on which the Initial Instruction in substantially the form of the Exhibit is actually received at the address for the Bank specified in the Exhibit. If the Initial Instruction is actually received at that address after 12:00 noon, local time, at that address, then in determining the Outside Time, the Initial Instruction will be considered to have been actually received on the following Business Day.

"Secured Party" means the person signing this Agreement as the Secured Party, whether the person is acting in a representative capacity or otherwise.

"Specific Terms" means the terms contained in Part B of this Agreement.

"UCC" means the Uniform Commercial Code of the jurisdiction whose law governs this Agreement or, if relevant to any matter other than the meaning of a defined term, the Uniform Commercial Code of the jurisdiction whose law applies to the matter under the choice of law rules of the jurisdiction whose law governs this Agreement.

A *"writing"* means a tangible writing, including a facsimile and, if the Specific Terms permit, an electronic record; *"written"* refers to a communication in the form of a writing.

2. The Debtor's Dealings with the Deposit Account.

(a) Except as provided in Section 2(b), the Bank may comply with the Debtor's Disposition Instructions in accordance with the Deposit-related Agreements.

(b) The Bank will not comply with the Debtor's Disposition Instructions after the Outside Time. In its discretion the Bank may cease complying with the Debtor's Disposition Instructions at an earlier time as permitted by Section 4(a)(iv).

3. The Secured Party's Right to Give Instructions as to the Deposit Account. The Bank will comply with the Initial Instruction, and with any Disposition Instructions originated by the Secured Party, in each case (i) without the Debtor's further consent, and (ii) even if following the instruction results in the dishonoring by the Bank of items presented for payment from the Deposit Account or the Bank otherwise not complying with the Debtor's Disposition Instructions. The Initial Instruction may not be rescinded or otherwise modified without the Bank's consent.

4. Exculpation of the Bank.

(a) Notwithstanding the Bank's agreements in Sections 2 and 3, the Bank will not be liable to any other party for:

(i) either failing to follow an Initial Instruction that (A) is not in the form of the Exhibit, (B) does not specify the address to which the Initial Instruction was to have been sent, (C) is not otherwise completed, or (D) does not have attached to it a copy of this Agreement as fully executed or, as a result of any such defect in the Initial Instruction, continuing to comply with the Debtor's Disposition Instructions;

(ii) failing to follow a Disposition Instruction originated by the Secured Party (A) before the Outside Time, (B) that requires the disposition of the funds in the Deposit Account by a method not available to the Debtor under the Deposit-related Agreements, (C) that the Bank determines would result in the Bank's failing to comply with a statute, rule or regulation, or an Order or Process, binding upon the Bank, (D) that requires the disposition of funds that are not immediately available in the Deposit Account, (E) that, unless otherwise set forth in the Specific Terms, directs the disposition of less than all the funds in the Deposit Account or directs that the funds be sent to more than one recipient, or (F) for which the Bank has not received evidence reasonably required by the Bank as to the authority of the person giving the Disposition Instruction to act for the Secured Party;

(iii) complying with the Debtor's Disposition Instructions, or otherwise completing a transaction involving the Deposit Account, that the Bank or an affiliate had started to process before the Outside Time; or

(iv) after the Bank becomes aware that the Secured Party has sent the Initial Instruction, but before the Outside Time, complying with the Initial Instruction or a Disposition Instruction originated by the Secured Party, notwithstanding any fact or circumstance and even if the Initial Instruction (A) has not been actually received at the address specified in the Exhibit, (B) fails to have attached to it a copy of this Agreement as fully executed, or (C) is not completed or otherwise fails to be in the form of Initial Instruction set forth on the Exhibit.

(b) The Bank will not be liable to any other party for:

(i) wrongful dishonor of any item as a result of the Bank following the Initial Instruction or any Disposition Instruction originated by the Secured Party,

(ii) failing to comply or delaying in complying with the Initial Instruction, any Disposition Instruction or any provision of this Agreement due to a computer malfunction, interruption of communication facilities, labor difficulties, act of God, war, terrorist attack, or other cause, in each case beyond the Bank's reasonable control,

(iii) any other Claim, except to the extent directly caused by the Bank's gross negligence or willful misconduct, or

(iv) any indirect, special, consequential or punitive damages.

(c) The Bank will have no fiduciary duties under this Agreement to any other party, whether as trustee, agent, bailee or otherwise. The Bank will have no duties to the Secured Party except as expressly set forth in this Agreement. The Bank will have no duty to inquire into or determine the existence or enforceability of the Debtor's obligations to the Secured Party or whether, under any separate agreement between the Debtor and the Secured Party, the Debtor's obligations to the Secured Party are in default, the Debtor may originate a Disposition Instruction or the Secured Party may originate the Initial Instruction or any Disposition Instruction.

5. The Bank's Recourse to the Deposit Account.

(a) Except for amounts referred to in Section 5(b), the Bank (i) subordinates any security interest, lien or other encumbrance against the Deposit Account to the Secured Party's security interest and (ii) will not exercise any right of recoupment, setoff or debit against the Deposit Account. This subordination will not apply to any security interest that the Bank has in an item under UCC Article 4 as a collecting bank.

(b) Notwithstanding Section 5(a), and regardless of any agreement of the Debtor to compensate the Bank by means of balances in the Deposit Account, the Bank may charge the Deposit Account, to the extent permitted by any of the Deposit-related Agreements or applicable law, for:

(i) the face amount of a check, draft, money order, instrument, wire transfer of funds, automated clearing house entry, credit from a merchant card transaction, other electronic transfer of funds or other item (A) deposited in or credited to the Deposit Account, whether before or after the Agreement Date, and returned unpaid or otherwise uncollected or subject to an adjustment entry, whether for insufficient funds or for any other reason and without regard to the timeliness of the return or adjustment or the occurrence or timeliness of any other person's notice of nonpayment or adjustment, (B) subject to a claim against the Bank for breach of transfer, presentment, encoding, retention or other warranty under Federal Reserve Regulations or Operating Circulars, clearing house rules, the UCC or other applicable law, or (C) for a merchant card transaction, against which a contractual demand for chargeback has been made;

(ii) normal service charges or fees payable to the Bank in connection with the Deposit Account or any related services;

(iii) any adjustments or corrections of any posting or encoding errors; and

(iv) reimbursements for out-of-pocket or allocable internal legal fees and expenses in connection with the negotiation, administration or enforcement of this Agreement by the Bank.

6. Indemnification and Reimbursement.

(a) The Debtor indemnifies the Bank against all Claims incurred, sustained or payable by the Bank arising out of this Agreement except to the extent directly caused by the Bank's gross negligence or willful misconduct.

(b) The Secured Party agrees to reimburse the Bank for any charge against the Deposit Account under Section 5(b) for which there were insufficient funds in the Deposit Account to satisfy the charge. Such reimbursement will be limited to the aggregate amount transferred from the Deposit Account as a result of the Bank's acting upon Disposition Instructions originated by the Secured Party or pursuant to Section 9(b). Any demand by the Bank for reimbursement must be made within the number of days after the termination of this Agreement set forth in the Specific Terms. The Bank may not make a Claim for reimbursement under this subsection unless (i) the Debtor fails to satisfy the Claim within 15 days after the Bank makes a demand on the Debtor under Section 6(a) or (ii) the Bank is enjoined, stayed or prohibited by operation of law from making the demand on the Debtor.

(c) The Secured Party's reimbursement obligations under Section 6(b) will not apply to (i) a charge for reimbursement of or indemnification for any out-of-pocket or allocable internal legal fees and expenses incurred by the Bank in connection with any claim or defense by the Bank against the Secured Party relating to this Agreement or (ii) the amount of any loss incurred by the Bank to the extent directly caused by the Bank's gross negligence or willful misconduct. If the Bank satisfies any Claim against the Debtor referred to in the foregoing clause (i) by charging the Deposit Account, the amount of the Secured Party's maximum liability for reimbursement obligations under Section 6(b) will be reduced by the amount of the Claim so satisfied.

(d) If the Secured Party fails to reimburse the Bank for any amount under Section 6(b), the Secured Party will pay the Bank's out-of-pocket or allocable internal legal fees and expenses in collecting from the Secured Party the amount payable.

(e) The Secured Party indemnifies the Bank against all other Claims incurred, sustained or payable by the Bank arising from the Bank following an Initial Instruction or a Disposition Instruction originated by the Secured Party, or from the Bank's remittance of funds pursuant to Section 9(b), except to the extent directly caused by the Bank's gross negligence or willful misconduct.

7. Representations and Warranties; Agreements with Other Persons. The Bank represents and warrants to the Secured Party that the Bank (i) is an organization engaged in the business of banking, (ii) maintains the Deposit Account as a demand deposit account or accounts in the ordinary course of the Bank's business and (iii) has not entered into any currently effective agreement with any person under which the Bank may be obligated to comply with Disposition Instructions originated by a person other than the Debtor or the Secured Party. The Bank will not enter into any agreement with any person under which the Bank may be obligated to comply with Disposition Instructions originated by a person other than the Debtor or the Secured Party.

8. Deposit Account Information. If the Secured Party so requests, to the extent that the Bank has the operational ability to do so, the Bank will provide to the Secured Party, whether by Internet access or otherwise, a copy of each periodic account statement relating to the Deposit Account ordinarily furnished by the Bank to the Debtor. The Bank's liability for failing to provide the account statement will not exceed the Bank's cost of providing the statement. The Debtor authorizes the Bank to provide to the Secured Party, whether by Internet access or otherwise, any other information concerning the Deposit Account that the Bank may agree to provide to the Secured Party at the Secured Party's request.

9. Termination; Closure of the Deposit Account.

(a) Neither the Debtor nor the Bank will close the Deposit Account prior to termination of this Agreement. This Agreement may not be terminated by the Debtor except by a notice to the Bank given jointly by the other parties. This Agreement may be terminated (i) by the Secured Party at any time by notice to the other parties and (ii) by the Bank (A) immediately upon notice to the other parties if the Bank becomes obligated to terminate this Agreement or to close the Deposit Account under any statute, rule or regulation, or any Order or Process, binding upon the Bank, (B) upon five Business Days' notice to the other parties if any other party is in material breach of any of the Deposit-related Agreements or this Agreement, and (C) otherwise upon 30 days' notice to the other parties.

(b) If the Bank terminates this Agreement pursuant to clause (A) of Section 9(a)(ii), the Bank will remit any funds in the Deposit Account on the date of termination (i) at the direction of the Secured Party if the direction is received by the Bank prior to the date of termination of this Agreement or (ii) if no such direction is received by the Bank prior to such date, by check mailed to the address of the Secured Party for receiving communications under this Agreement. If the Bank terminates this Agreement pursuant to clause (B) or (C) of Section 9(a)(ii), the Bank will remit any funds in the Deposit Account on the date of termination at the direction of the Secured Party only if the direction is received by the Bank prior to the date of termination of this Agreement. Any obligation of the Bank to remit any funds to or at the direction of the Secured Party under this subsection is subject to clauses (B) through (F) of Section 4(a)(ii).

(c) Except as provided in Section 9(b) and in any event if the Secured Party has communicated to the Bank that the Secured Party does not wish to receive or direct the disposition of the funds, the Secured Party will not receive from the Bank any remittance of funds from the Deposit Account upon termination of this Agreement by the Bank.

(d) The termination of this Agreement will not affect any rights created or obligations incurred under this Agreement before the termination. Sections 4 and 6 will survive the termination of this Agreement for actions taken or omitted before the termination. Sections 9(b) and (c) will survive the termination of this Agreement, and Section 5 will survive the termination of this Agreement solely for any funds to be remitted to or at the direction of the Secured Party pursuant to Section 9(b).

10. Communications.

(a) All communications under this Agreement must be in writing and must be delivered by hand or overnight courier service, mailed by certified or registered mail, or sent by facsimile to the party addressee. If the Specific Terms permit a writing to include an electronic record, a communication, other than the Initial Instruction, may be sent by email.

(b) For a communication under this Agreement to be effective, it must be received (i) for the Initial Instruction, at the Bank's address specified on the Exhibit and (ii) in all other cases, at the party's address indicated below the party's signature to this Agreement, in each case subject to any change in address provided in Section 10(c). Receipt of the Initial Instruction does not occur until it is received by the person or persons or department specified on the "attention" line on the Exhibit. If more than one person is specified, receipt occurs when the Initial Instruction is received by one of the persons.

(c) The Bank may communicate to the Secured Party changes in the address for the Initial Instruction, and any party may communicate to the other parties changes in its address for communications under this Agreement.

11. Successors and Transferees.

(a) This Agreement will inure to the benefit of, and be binding upon, the parties and their respective successors and other transferees permitted under this Section. Except as provided in this Section, a voluntary transfer of a party's rights or duties under this Agreement without the written consent of the other parties will be void.

(b) The Bank may transfer its rights and duties under this Agreement to a transferee to which, by contract or operation of law, the Bank transfers substantially all of its rights and duties under the Deposit-related Agreements.

(c) The Secured Party may transfer its rights and duties under this Agreement to (i) a transferee to which, by contract or operation of law, the Secured Party transfers substantially all of its rights and duties under the financing or other arrangements between the Secured Party and the Debtor for which the Deposit Account acts as collateral security or (ii) if the Secured Party is acting as a trustee, indenture trustee, agent, collateral agent, or other representative in whose favor a security interest is created or provided for, a transferee that is a successor trustee, indenture trustee, agent, collateral agent, or other representative.

(d) No transfer under this Section will be binding upon a non-transferring party until the transferring party or the transferee notifies the non-transferring parties of the transfer in a writing signed by the transferee that identifies the transferee, gives the transferee's address for communications under this Agreement, and states that the transferee is a successor of the transferor or other transferee permitted under this Section and is entitled to the benefit of the transferring party's rights and has assumed all of the transferring party's duties under this Agreement.

(e) A non-transferring party need not request proof of any transfer or that the transferee is a successor of the transferor or other transferee permitted by this Section. If requested by a non-transferring party, however, the transferring party or the transferee will provide reasonable proof thereof. If the Bank or the Secured Party, as a non-transferring party, requests such proof, then the effectiveness of the notification of transfer as to the non-transferring party will be suspended until the proof is provided.

(f) When a transfer becomes binding on the non-transferring parties, the transferring party will not be entitled to exercise any rights, and will be relieved of its obligations, accruing under this Agreement from and after that time. Those rights may be exercised and those obligations will be incurred by the transferee.

(g) The provisions of subsections (d) and (e) requiring notification for a transfer to be binding on the non-transferring parties and suspending the effectiveness of the notification of transfer until reasonable proof of the transfer has been provided do not apply to the Bank as the transferring party if the transfer is by operation of law and by operation of the law (i) the transferee succeeds to all or substantially all of the rights and becomes generally bound by all of the duties of the Bank, including the Bank's duties under this Agreement, and (ii) the Bank ceases to exist.

12. Entire Agreement; Relation to Other Agreements.

(a) This Agreement constitutes the entire agreement of the parties, and supersedes all previous and contemporaneous negotiations, understandings and agreements, with respect to its subject matter, all of which have become merged and finally integrated into this Agreement.

(b) If a term in the Specific Terms conflicts with a term of this Agreement not in the Specific Terms, the term in the Specific Terms controls.

(c) If this Agreement conflicts with any of the Deposit-related Agreements, this Agreement will control. However, this Agreement will not (i) derogate from any Claim or defense that the Bank may have against the Debtor under any of the Deposit-related Agreements or (ii) create any third party beneficiary rights under any of the Deposit-related Agreements in favor of the Secured Party.

(d) This Agreement does not amend or otherwise modify any of the agreements between the Debtor and the Secured Party or provide any rights for the Debtor to originate a Disposition Instruction in contravention of any agreement between the Debtor and the Secured Party.

13. Governing Law, Depositary Bank's Jurisdiction and Waiver of Jury Trial.

(a) Except as otherwise required by Article 9 of the UCC, this Agreement will be governed by the law of that jurisdiction set forth in the Specific Terms without giving effect to any choice of law rule that would require the application of the law of another jurisdiction.

(b) If the Specific Terms are completed expressly to designate the Bank's jurisdiction for purposes of part 3 of Article 9 of the UCC, then the Deposit-related Agreements are amended to provide that for those purposes that jurisdiction is the Bank's jurisdiction so designated.

(c) **To the extent permitted by applicable law, each party waives all rights to trial by jury in any action, claim or proceeding (including any counterclaim) of any type arising out of or directly or indirectly relating to this Agreement.**

14. Miscellaneous.

(a) No amendment to this Agreement will be binding on any party unless it is in writing and signed by all of the parties. Any provision of this Agreement benefiting a party may be waived only by a writing signed by that party.

(b) If a provision of this Agreement is held invalid or unenforceable in any respect, the validity or enforceability of the remaining provisions will not in any way be affected, it being understood that the invalidity or unenforceability of an affected provision in a particular jurisdiction will not in and of itself affect the validity or enforceability of the provision in any other jurisdiction.

CHAPTER 9

Privacy

GRAMM-LEACH-BLILEY ACT (GLB)

On November 12, 1999, President Clinton signed into law the Gramm-Leach-Bliley Act (GLB), running about 400 or more pages, which imposed an array of new requirements on financial institutions with respect to customer privacy.

The Act applies to any institution whose business engages in any activity that is financial in nature or incidental to a financial activity. Anyone actually engaged in this activity would be covered by the Act. The Act also covers activities that are now authorized for financial holding companies, which may cover such diverse activities as travel agencies. The Act applies to nonpublic information. The financial institution must provide to the consumer clear and conspicuous disclosures concerning the privacy of the consumer, including its policies and practices on disclosing to affiliates, on protecting the information, and on disclosing information of customers who are no longer customers. The consumer has an opportunity to opt out of sharing the financial information. The institution must make clear and conspicuous disclosure to the consumer of what information may be disclosed to third parties and how the consumer can contact the financial institution to opt out of said disclosure.

One cannot use false pretenses to obtain information maintained by or for a financial institution. The Act provides for criminal penalties. Under the new law, any person, including an attorney or a debt collector, could be fined substantial amounts or be imprisoned for contacting a financial institution to obtain financial information about a consumer under false pretenses.

The definition of a financial institution is broad and includes any loan or finance company, any credit card issuer, a debt buyer, an operator of a credit card system, and any consumer reporting agency that compiles and maintains files on consumers on a nationwide basis (Section 603(p) of the Consumer Credit Protection Act). By including credit reporting agencies within the definition of the financial institution, persons who obtain credit reports must be careful that they do so only for permissible purposes.

Customers do not have any rights under the statute to bring lawsuits, but the Federal Trade Commission (FTC) and the Federal Bank Regulatory Agency are designated as the agencies to enforce the Act.

A state law will prevail only to the extent that state authority is not inconsistent with the Act. If the state provides greater protection for the consumer, it is not deemed to be inconsistent. At least in this area, the banks were successful in not providing a private right of action to consumers and to consumer attorneys. (We have included the text of the Final Rule on Standards for Safeguarding Customer Information, issued by the FTC, as required by Section 501(b) of the GLB in the Appendix.)

Financial institutions must provide notice to existing customers so that they may opt out of sharing financial information. A consumer is anyone who obtains a financial product or a service, whereas a customer is someone who has a customer relationship with the financial institution. This means the customer is either depositing money with the bank or is investing or has already obtained some form of credit from the institution.

In the privacy area, the Act generally states that financial institutions are required to provide their customers the right to opt out of having information shared with third parties, but expressly allowing the banks to share information with their affiliates. The financial institutions must establish clear policies as to the use of customer data, both at the time of establishing a customer relationship and yearly thereafter.

A privacy notice must be provided by the institution at the time of establishing any type of customer relationship prior to sharing any nonpublic information with nonaffiliated third parties. This notice must be provided at least once during every 12-month period. The opt-out notice must contain a description of: (1) nonpublic information that is disclosed to affiliates and nonaffiliated parties; (2) categories of parties to whom the information will be disclosed; and (3) policies regarding confidentiality and security of nonpublic personal information. These notices must be provided before any sharing of the information and this sharing will be performed unless the customer opts out. A reasonable means of opting out must be provided, such as a reply form or a toll-free number. The consumer must be provided a 30-day window to opt out, but an opt-out received after the reasonable time will stop all future disclosures.

The FTC provided some examples of covered financial institutions, including the following:

1. A retailer that extends credit by issuing its own credit card.
2. A real estate appraiser.
3. A business that wires money to consumers.
4. A check cashing business.
5. A mortgage broker.
6. A travel agency that operates with financial services.
7. A real estate settlement service.
8. An investment adviser.
9. A consumer credit counseling agency.

The definition of financial institutions covers a wide array of activities. Financial activities that would be covered might include some of the following—being a mortgage broker or servicing loans, leasing real property, or even leasing personal property such as copy machines, dealing in underwriting or in any type of stock or securities, providing any type of financial investment advice, doing any type of lending, exchanging or investing for other people, guaranteeing checks, providing any type of consulting or counseling activities, selling money orders, saving bonds or travel checks, providing financial data or processing, acting in any manner as a fiduciary which involves either advice or handling of monies for others.

Nonpublic Personal Information. Nonpublic information (NPI) is the main privacy ingredient which is being regulated by the GLB. Nonpublic information is information that is *personally identifiable financial information* not publicly available and consumer lists that use *personally identifiable financial information* that is not publicly available.

Personally identifiable financial information consists of the following:

1. Information a consumer provides on a credit application.
2. Account balance, payment history, credit or debit card information.
3. The fact that a person is or has been a customer or obtained a financial product or service.
4. Any information about a consumer which discloses the person has been your customer.
5. Any information that a consumer provides you or your agent while collecting on or servicing a credit account.
6. Information obtained from an Internet cookie or from a consumer report.

Consumer lists that are derived using personally identifiable information that is not publicly available, such as:

1. The list is derived from information obtained in the extension of credit.
2. The list is derived from information provided in connection with a bank account.
3. The list is derived from an Internet cookie or a credit bureau.

Publicly available information is information that you have a reasonable basis to believe is lawfully made available to the general public from:

1. Federal, state, or local government records.
2. Widely distributed media such as telephone books and newspapers.
3. Disclosure to the general public required by federal or state local law such as Uniform Commercial Code (UCC) 1 financing statements, judgments, and professional licenses.

Financial services or products means any product or service that a financial holding company could offer by engaging in an activity that is financial in nature or incidental to such financial activity. Financial services include a request for an application from the consumer for a financial product or service.

1. A retailer is not a financial institution if its only means of extending credit are occasional layaway and deferred payment plans or accepting payment by means of credit cards issued by others.
2. A retailer is not a financial institution because it accepts payments in the form of cash, checks, or credit cards that it did not issue.
3. A merchant is not a financial institution because it allows an individual to run up a tab.

If you intend to disclose nonpublic information to nonaffiliated third parties (except for the accepted disclosures), state that fact and the following:

1. The categories of nonpublic personal information that you collect.
2. Policies and practices with respect to protecting the confidentiality and security of nonpublic information.
3. If disclosures are made to nonaffiliated third parties subject to exceptions, state that you disclose nonpublic information to third parties authorized under the law. Describing the exception is not necessary.

Nonpublic Information Notice. The following should be set forth in the notice to consumers:

1. Information supplied by consumer.
2. Information about the transaction from you or an affiliate.
3. Information about the consumer's transaction with nonaffiliated third parties.
4. Information from a consumer reporting agency.
5. If the disclosure is made of less than all nonpublic information, provide a few examples to illustrate the types of nonpublic information you do disclose.
6. If the disclosure of all information collected is made, reserve the right to do same, and set this forth in your disclosure.

Joint Marketers. The following is appropriate for the notice:

1. State whether the third party is:
   (a) a service provider that performs marketing services on your behalf;
   (b) or on behalf of you and another financial institution; or
   (c) a financial institution with whom you have a joint marketing agreement.
2. List the categories of nonpublic information you disclose. The same criteria are applicable.

Opt-Out. The Act allows the consumer to prevent your disclosure of nonpublic information to nonaffiliated third parties by opting out. You are required to provide a notice of opt-out and the reasonable means to exercise the right. Adequate notice is as follows:

1. Describe all the categories of nonpublic information you disclose.
2. Describe all the categories of nonaffiliated third parties to whom you disclose.
3. State the consumer can opt out.
4. State the financial services or products to which opt-out applies.
5. Provide prominent check-off boxes on relevant forms with the opt-out notice.
6. Include a reply form that states the address to where it would be sent; or
7. Provide an electronic means if the consumer agrees or a toll-free number.

JOINT RELATIONSHIPS. As to joint accounts, to allow one to opt out of a joint account relationship, the following may be applicable:

1. Explain how you opt out of joint relationships.
2. Provide a single opt-out or an opt-out to either one.
3. Treat one opt-out as applying to all or just to the person requesting the opt-out.
4. Allow a single opt-out on behalf of all.
5. Require all persons to opt out for an opt-out to be effective.
6. Send a single opt-out notice to one party's address that accepts an opt-out direction from either John or Mary.
7. Treat an opt-out direction by either John or Mary as applying to the entire account. If so, and John opts out, require Mary to opt out as well before implementing John's opt-out directions.
8. Permit John and Mary to make different opt-out directions. If you do so,
   - (a) permit John and Mary to opt out for each other;
   - (b) if both opt out, you must permit both to notify you in a single response such as on a form or through a telephone call; or
   - (c) if John opts out and Mary does not, you may only disclose non-public information about Mary but not about John and not about Mary and John jointly.

Once a party has opted out, the opt-out remains in effect until the consumer revokes it in writing or electronically or establishes a new customer relationship with you.

FINANCIAL PRODUCT OR SERVICE. Financial product or service means any product or service that a financial company could offer by engaging in an activity that is financial in nature or incidental to such financial activity under the Bank Holding Act of 1956. A financial service may include the evaluation of information that you collect in connection with the request or an application from a consumer for a financial product or service.

CONSUMER/CUSTOMER. If you are a financial institution and offering a financial product or service, GLB will apply to a relationship with a consumer or with a customer. An individual who obtained a financial product or service for personal, family, or household purposes is a consumer. A customer is a consumer who has a customer relationship with you. The obligations to consumers are different from the obligations to customer relationships.

Nonaffiliated Third Party. A nonaffiliated third party means any person except:

A. Your affiliate.
B. A person employed jointly by you and any company that is not your affiliate (but a nonaffiliated third party includes the other company that jointly employs the person).

An affiliate means any company that controls, is controlled by or is under common control with another company.

Unreasonable Means of Communication. Unreasonable means of communication covers the following:

A. The only means is for the consumer to write a letter.
B. If a subsequent notice states that the only means is for the consumer to use the check-off boxes provided with the initial notice.
C. Provide only an electronic means if the consumer agrees or a toll-free number.

Debt Purchasers. When a financial institution is engaged in marketing their loan portfolios to debt purchasers, the transaction may be subject to the opt-out provisions in GLB. If personal identifiable information is part of the review process by the debt purchaser, the financial institution may be forced to provide the individual with the right to opt out. Also, GLB does exclude a proposed or actual securitization, secondary market sale, or similar transaction related to a transaction of the consumer.

Exemption. Under GLB, the FTC Commentary includes "collection agency, credit bureau."[1] At the same time, the FTC states that a consumer has a customer relationship with a debt collector that purchases an account from the original creditor, but does not have this relationship with a debt collector that simply attempts to collect amounts owed to the creditor.[2]

This issue will probably be visited by the FTC again and by the courts, before it is resolved.

Social Security Numbers. Congress passed an act to include the social security number within the GLB. Specifically, the bill stated that notwithstanding any other provision of the Act, no financial institution may sell or purchase a social security number or a social security account number in a manner that violates the regulations. In essence, a social security number is financial information. Some agencies of the state and federal

---

[1]16 C.F.R. § 65, p. 33,647.
[2]16 C.F.R. § 65, p. 11,176.

government only require the last 4 digits of the social security number, but this protection is expanding slowly both in this government and in the private sector.[3]

Account and Social Security Number. Several interagency guidance interpretive letters are available concerning the GLB Regulation B prohibition on disclosing account numbers to nonaffiliated third parties. The letters were issued by the office of the Controller of Currency, the Federal Reserve Board, and the Federal Deposit Insurance Company, and are available at *http://www.occ.treas.gov/foia/int910.pdf.*

Credit Reporting Agency. A credit reporting agency is covered by the regulations of the FTC under the GLB.[4]

HEALTH INSURANCE PORTABILITY AND ACCOUNTABILITY ACT (HIPAA)

The Health Insurance Portability and Accountability Act (HIPAA) was passed in 1996 and on December 20, 2000, the privacy requirement rules were released by the U.S. Department of Health and Human Services. The Act will have a significant impact upon business associates of healthcare organizations, which include collection agencies and attorneys. The new regulations provide consumers with new rights to control the release of their medical information, including advance consent for most disclosures of health information, the right to obtain documentation of disclosures, and the right to an explanation of the privacy rights and how this information is being used.

The final regulations deal directly with the procedures for releasing medical information. Patients are provided new rights to access their medical records and to know to whom the medical records were released. The disclosure of any medical records is restricted on a need-to-know basis and only for the purpose intended. New criminal and civil sanctions for violations of the rules now apply.

A valid business associate (collection agency or law firm) contract should include the use to which the medical information is intended and how the medical information will be protected from use other than its intended purpose. The healthcare provider should have the right to terminate the contract if there is a violation of the contract. The business associate should not disclose any medical information other than is permitted or required by the contract and use adequate protection to prevent the disclosure of the information to third parties. The business associate should be

---

[3]Bus. Law., Feb. 2008, p. 645.

[4]*Trans Union v. F.T.C.*, CV 02087 (D.C. Cir. 2002). *See also Business Lawyer*, Feb. 2008, p. 644.

required to notify the healthcare provider of a violation of the contract. The medical information released should be available by the healthcare organization to the patient upon request.

The business associate also should organize its records so that the medical information is available to the Secretary of the Department of Health and Human Services, in the event it should be required to demonstrate that the healthcare provider has been complying with HIPAA.

In the event the debtor requests verification information and disclosure of the medical services rendered, the debt collector should insist upon a request for verification information in writing. The documentation that should be furnished should clarify the amount of the debt and identify the proper creditor. If the debtor should request a copy of the billing statement, this request should be fulfilled only if made in writing. The debt collector should request that the debtor specify the time period and the nature of the services rendered. If the healthcare provider should request a written consent, which does occur, the debt collector should obtain the form of the consent from the healthcare provider and furnish it to the debtor to execute.

A written agreement should be entered into between the agency or law firm and the healthcare provider concerning their responsibilities under HIPAA.

A careful reading of the law is necessary and consultation with counsel is in order.

Protected Health Information. Sometimes an affidavit must be filed concerning accounts receivable of a hospital or a copy of an itemized medical bill must be furnished to court. Often this is required when entering a default judgment. The issue is whether you can disclose this medical information; that is, protected health information including an itemized bill when filing a lawsuit. If the state law requires a copy of the itemized bill be attached to a complaint or requires the itemized bill be attached to an affidavit, the party must comply.

On the other hand, if the itemized bill is sought by the defendant by either a notice to produce or a demand for a bill of particulars or some other discovery process, communication may be had with counsel for the defendant with regard to the treatment of this protected health information.

> ***Credit & Collection Tip:*** *If any use of protected health information or disclosure of protected health information occurs by reason of some other law or is required by law, the party must comply with that law.*

Private Right of Action. HIPAA does not provide a private right of action for a consumer if there is a violation of HIPAA, but does name the Secretary of Health and Human Services Office of Civil Rights as the designated party to enforce the Act. While individuals may not have a private right of action, they may file a complaint with the Secretary of Health and

Human Services, Office of Civil Rights. The Office of Civil Rights website is helpful and can be found at *http://www.hhs.gov/ocr/hipaa.*

Criminal Penalties. Criminal violations are punishable by fines up to $250,000 or imprisonment to a maximum of 10 years or both. Noncompliant entities are subject to civil monetary penalties ranging from $100 to $25,000 depending upon the extent of noncompliance which applies when a covered entity wrongfully and knowingly discloses health information in violation of the privacy regulations.

Business Associate. The privacy standard applies to any treatment, payment and healthcare operation including billing, claims management and healthcare data processing. Business associates are not responsible for obtaining the patient's consent. If the healthcare client is sending information in connection with the pursuit of payment, the agency or attorney is safe in assuming that the provider has obtained consent from the patient for all activities related to treatment, payment and healthcare operation (TPO). Special limitations should be specified in a clear and conspicuous manner to the business associate. Special limitations should not be buried in the fine print, the computer printout or other material, but should be presented in the cover sheet in bold print.

> ***Credit & Collection Tip:*** *The business associate should confirm in writing with the client that the client has obtained the consent and that all special limitations are in bold print.*

The business associate agreement should itemize the internal procedures being utilized. The client must agree to accept this itemization as compliance with HIPAA. The business associate also must contract with its vendors so that they will comply with the contract between the business associate and the client. Specific written assurances must be obtained from the vendors that they agree to comply with all the requirements set forth in the contract with the client.

The contract will usually provide that health information disclosed will be held to a minimum, that is, that you allow the minimum disclosure necessary to achieve your business purpose. The disclosure should be made only to "need to know" employees. Written agreements should be executed with all vendors, including vendors who access the office and who may inadvertently view the medical information. An explanation of internal procedures, restrictions and other steps implemented to ensure confidentiality must be provided to the staff. Written acknowledgment is required that staff is aware of all limitations of access. Some staff members are barred access and others have limited access.

The two major ingredients are training and a paper trail. Training sessions should be instituted wherein the staff is advised of the regulations of HIPAA and the degree to which the business associates must comply with these regulations. Attendance at the meetings is to be recorded and a record maintained that staff understood the training sessions by signing acknowledgments.

The paper trail is evidence of the effort of the business associate to comply with the regulations as laid out under HIPAA.

Privacy rules are published at 45 CFR, Section 160, and 45 CFR, Section 164.

Access to Computer. The business associate's computer system should contain a password to access the data so that other members of the staff (such as a receptionist or file clerk) not involved in servicing this healthcare provider will not have access to the information on the computer. Efforts must be made to segregate the files by use of separate file cabinets, separate rooms, and marking the files by color or otherwise. Notification to the rest of the staff and acknowledgment of the awareness of these privacy concerns is appropriate.

Verification. Special attention should be devoted to verification requests by debtors under HIPAA. Special letters and procedures should be prepared so that all requests from the debtor are consented to in writing by the debtor. Create a specific internal step-by-step procedure when responding to a verification request or when furnishing medical records to the patient. A checklist and a fixed procedure should be used.

Covered Entities. The law states that where the vendor converts standard and nonstandard data for covered entities (hospitals), they are defined as a clearinghouse and qualify as a covered entity just as a hospital is a covered entity. A collection agency has several vendors who may have access to the personal health information, such as printing companies, fulfillment companies, letter shops, and other businesses that enable the business associate to mail letters and notices to the debtors.

On the other side of the spectrum are the vendors who service the equipment in the office of the business associate, which include programmers, software and hardware service organizations, and other service organizations that have access to the office, the computers, and the files, that is, service people for copy machines, printers, fax machines, and telephones. A standard contract may be prepared.

The business associate must recognize that HIPAA not only covers information received from hospitals, but also covers medical and dental offices, radiology laboratories, pharmacies, including any type of retail store that provides pharmaceutical services, plus all other types of businesses that provide medical information, such as stores that specialize in surgical appliances or wheelchairs. The regulation might even apply to the plumbing supply house that provides special equipment for the bathroom for the disabled.

> ***Credit & Collection Tip:*** *If you are doing outsourcing for the hospital or the medical client, the obligations increase substantially and your status as a business associate may reach a level which might conceivably make you a covered entity under HIPAA. If the level of involvement is such that you are a covered entity, all the obligations set forth under HIPAA (and not just the obligations of a business associate) must be addressed.*

Disclosure to Another Client. An issue has been raised as to whether information obtained from a client under HIPAA with regard to a debt owed to that client can be utilized to collect the debt due to another client from the same debtor. At this time, no case law is out there to answer the question.

Under most business associate agreements, a requirement is usually present that the information be accessed only on a need-to-know basis and based on this premise alone, the information from the client could not be used for the collection of a debt against the same debtor for another client. On the other hand, it seems unreasonable to conclude that the drafters of HIPAA intended to prohibit the sale of medical accounts receivable.

> ***Credit & Collection Tip:*** *If the information is available from other sources, one could argue that this information is readily available from credit reports or databases. Order a credit report or conduct a database search and hopefully the same information will surface.*

GLB AND HIPAA—PRIVACY POLICIES

After a privacy program is implemented, the program needs to be continually reexamined and reevaluated to be certain that what has been implemented actually works. Documentation of the policies and updating are extremely important and are necessary to address employee turnover as well as vendor turnover.

CONTACTING MILITARY BASES

Many books on collection recommend that creditors or debt collectors contact the commanding officer of military personnel who are in debt to urge the soldier to pay the outstanding debt. The commanding officer is under no obligation and has no legal authority to require a member of the armed services to pay a debt. The question of contacting a third party may be a violation of the Fair Debt Collection Practices Act (FDCPA) prohibiting such communication as to collection agencies and attorneys. Certainly advising the commanding officer that the debtor is delinquent in the payment of the debt may affect a decision of the commanding officer in granting promotions. While some creditors and debt collectors still engage in this practice, we do not recommend its use.[5] Creditors may continue this procedure on the theory they are not subject to the Act, but the danger is self-evident. (*See* Chapter 15.)

Privacy. The founding fathers made no provision for "privacy" under the Constitution. The right to privacy began with an article published in 1890 in the Harvard Law Review by Samuel D. Warren and Louis D. Brandeis (who later became a Supreme Court Justice) in which they set forth that a person has a right to be left alone and to conduct activities without outside interference by other persons unless the outside interference is necessary in the interest of public welfare.[6] A broad definition of the invasion of privacy is the unreasonable intrusion into one's personal life either by exploiting the person's name and background or using one's personal affairs for the purpose of humiliation, coercion, or shame. If the ultimate purpose is to cause the debtor to pay the debt, the creditor will find it difficult to argue a reasonable intrusion. In fact, today's society does not provide aid and assistance to the debt collector.

Invasion of Privacy. The invasion of privacy concept has breathed life into new legal remedies for the consumer. The impact of the word "abuse" on our society is not lost on the sophisticated debtor. If we add to this brew the fact that the courts award damages for emotional stress, a dormant area of the law has now gained the attention of credit and collection managers. Harassment, intimidation, abuse of process, and defamation practiced by the collectors may expose the creditor, collection agency, or law firm to liability. The application of this doctrine varies from state to state. Some states use a broad brush and others a limited scope.

The courts award damages for mental anguish, emotional suffering, and what may be called "general personal distress." If a physical injury is committed, the general personal distress is usually a result of the physical injury. Even where no personal injury is sustained, such as in cases of fraud or coercion, the court may award damages for emotional distress.

The word "harassment" is defined as "distress," "torment," "irritation," "depression," etc. The words used to define "intimidation" are "scare," "fright," "terror," and "fear." Harassment and intimidation

---

[5] *Holloway v. Davis*, 208 So. 2d 794, 44 Ala. App. 346 (Ct. App. Ala. 1967), *La Salle Extension Univ. v. Fogerty*, 253 N.W. 424 (Neb. 1934); *Keating v. Conviser*, 246 N.Y. 632 (N.Y. 1922).

[6] Harv. L. Rev. 193 (1890).

together, usually presumed to be intentional by the very nature of the act, will produce a situation where the debtor may be substantially damaged.

No set definition can determine whether an act constitutes harassment or intimidation. The definitions of both terms as they apply to the collection process are more a question of degree than a question of a finite act. In many instances, harassment and intimidation are self-fulfilling: if the debtor suffers emotional distress or some measurable damages, then the activity must "per se" constitute harassment or intimidation. The courts employ self-serving terms such as "unreasonable" and "abusive," which are subject to diverse interpretations by different courts. Numerous telephone calls to the debtor may be oppressive under one set of circumstances and be totally warranted under another. A telephone call at night may be reasonable in one case and unreasonable in another.

Willful Act. The courts sometimes distinguish between the action being intentional and willful, as opposed to being negligent. If the act is negligent, the court will not afford relief to the consumer. A debt collector is not liable if there is a preponderance of evidence that the violation was not intentional and resulted solely from a bona-fide error, and the debt collector maintained procedures reasonably adopted to avoid such error. Negligence by itself may be a good defense to a harassment and abuse charge, providing proper procedures and a compliance manual are in place and the incident was solely isolated. Nevertheless, the courts may state that if the negligence is so reckless that a reasonable person should have anticipated the result, the negligent action becomes a willful and intentional act. At what point the negligent act becomes an intentional act is difficult to identify. If the court can find that the offender knew or, with reasonable care, should have known that the actions harass, oppress, and abuse a debtor, a strong likelihood exists that the court will find that harassment existed.

TRUTH AS DEFENSE

Truth is not a defense in an action for the invasion of privacy. Whereas it may be a defense in defamation or libel, truthful statements about the personal life may be actionable if the said truthful statements are improperly used. While the debtor may be a "deadbeat" and owe many creditors, using the term to a neighbor may be an invasion of privacy. Truthful statements used purely for the purpose of humiliating, coercing, or shaming a party may support a suit for invasion of privacy. If the information disseminated is false, grounds for a suit for libel and slander in addition to one for invasion of privacy may lie.

PRIVACY—SOCIAL SECURITY NUMBER

In 2003, Bankruptcy Rules 105, 107, and 2002 were amended to include certain official forms. The rules require the bankrupt to file a full social security number, but the full number will only be available to the clerk and will not be available to the public either through paper or electronic access. Only the last four numbers of the social security number will be available for electronic or paper access. The full social security number will be included on the 341 Notice to Creditors.

RECKLESS NEGLIGENCE

Malice is not an ingredient that must be established to prove an invasion of privacy. At the same time, negligence is not a defense to an invasion of privacy. Where a defendant alleges the defense of negligence, the defendant may be faced with the same problems that appear in a harassment and abuse case. If the negligence is so reckless and wanton that the creditor should have anticipated the results, or if the creditor knew or should have known that the activity would constitute an invasion of privacy, the courts will state that the reckless negligent act was tantamount to an intentional and willful act.[7]

DATA SECURITY BREACH

This issue of notification to consumers in the event of a data breach has apparently had an impact upon the legislature in Washington. At the present time, the Direct Marketing Association reports four bills that the direct marketing association considers important and is monitoring with regard to this problem before the Senate Commerce Committee, the Senate Judiciary Committee, House Financial Services Committee, and the House Energy and Commerce Committee. A bill regulating a data security breach on a national scale and requiring notification to consumers will certainly emerge from Congress within the next year or so. Some of the bills are broad enough to involve not only the breach notification, but will also affect information brokers such as persons who rent, sell or exchange personal information to third-party noncustomers. This certainly would include the list brokers who rent and exchange the lists of the direct marketers.

---

[7] *Mason v. Williams Disc. Ctr., Inc.*, 639 S.W.2d 836 (Mo. Ct. App. 1982) (posting a list of debtors' names in view of customers stating that the plaintiff was a bad credit risk); *Santiesteban v. Goodyear Tire & Rubber Co.*, 306 F.2d 9 (5th Cir. 1962) (repossessing a set of tires in view of third parties may be deemed an invasion of privacy).

Notwithstanding the activity within Congress, various states have passed their own security breach notification laws with the first state being California. In addition, Arkansas, Indiana, Florida, and Georgia have all passed their own specific state laws, and other state legislatives have similar bills before them. We have added an Appendix consisting of the state notification laws.

A new California law states that consumers must actively provide permission to have their financial information shared with outside companies. It also gives the option to consumers to prevent the sharing of the information with affiliates or subsidiaries of the companies.

But the heart of the law is the fact that companies must provide notice to the consumer of any breach of security following a discovery of the notice of the breach in the security of any data or database. The disclosure must be made to any resident of California whose information may have been accessed by an unauthorized person.

The law also applies to companies inside California as well as outside of California as long as they maintain a database or information on California residents.[8] Many other states have adopted similar laws.

SAFEGUARDING CUSTOMER INFORMATION—FINAL RULE

The standards for safeguarding customer information were initially published in May 2002 and became effective on May 23, 2003. Most collection agencies felt they were not subject to this rule since, although collection agencies were deemed financial institutions, they were not required to comply with many of the sections of the GLB. The principal exception was that they did not have to send out a privacy notice for any opt-out requirements providing they were conducting normal collection activity to collect debts for others.

The safeguard rule sets forth the rules and regulations for financial institutions that collect personal information from their own customers. It also covers financial institutions that receive customer information from other institutions and accordingly, many more financial institutions are included, such as collection agencies and other firms that simply receive customer information from other institutions. A copy of the "Standards for Safeguarding Customer Information: Final Rule" is in the Appendix to this chapter.

The FTC's position is that the safeguarding of information is not necessarily a privacy problem, but more in the nature of a security situation.

---

[8]Kelly D. Talcott, *Stolen Identities: State Law Affects All Businesses With Californians in Databases*, N.Y.L.J., Aug. 26, 2003, p. 5; Jennifer Lee, *California Law Provides More Financial Privacy*, N.Y. Times, Aug. 28, 2003, p. A24.

The rule requires that procedures be in place to protect information and to design and employ safeguards to protect the information. The employer must monitor the procedures and measures that are in place on an ongoing basis. A careful reading of the rule is recommended.[9]

FDCPA—HIPAA CONFLICT

To some degree a conflict is present between the FDCPA and HIPAA. The FDCPA allows communication to a spouse concerning a debt. Nevertheless, HIPAA prohibits a disclosure to a parent or spouse of health information for payment purposes and under Section 164.522(a) an individual has the right to request restrictions as to the disclosure of health information for payment. Actually, the FDCPA's regulation is permissive only and thus no requirement must be met on the part of the debt collector to reveal the information to the spouse. HIPAA does restrict certain disclosure of health information for payment, and other restrictions in HIPAA prohibit disclosure of health information. When confronted with this situation, the health information should not be disclosed, which would comply not only with HIPAA but with the FDCPA.

MODIFICATIONS OF LAW—PROTECTION OF PERSONAL INFORMATION AND IDENTITY THEFT—MASSACHUSETTS

The Massachusetts Office of Consumer Affairs and Business Regulations (OCABR) passed a comprehensive regulation governing personal information in relation to their identity theft laws. Personal information includes the social security number or any other financial credit or debit account number and it applies to personal information whether it is by electronic, paper, visual or audio. The law also applies to almost any entity which licenses or stores personal information in the State of Massachusetts. The law includes a listing of what the company must do to comply. A copy of the regulations are effective January 1, 2009 and are available on the OCABR website (OCBRAMA) *http://www.mass.gov/?pageID=ocahomepage&L=1&L0=Home&sid=Eoca.*

[9]Safeguarding Rule, 14 C.F.R. Part 314.

CHAPTER 9 APPENDIX I

GRAMM-LEACH-BLILEY ACT—STANDARDS FOR SAFEGUARDING CUSTOMER INFORMATION—FINAL RULE—FEDERAL TRADE COMMISSION

Federal Register

Thursday,
May 23, 2002

Part VII

Federal Trade Commission

16 CFR Part 314
Standards for Safeguarding Customer Information; Final Rule

FEDERAL TRADE COMMISSION

16 CFR Part 314

RIN 3084 AA87

Standards for Safeguarding Customer Information

AGENCY: Federal Trade Commission.

ACTION: Final rule.

SUMMARY: The Federal Trade Commission ("FTC" or "Commission") is issuing a final Safeguards Rule, as required by section 501(b) of the Gramm-Leach-Bliley Act ("G–L–B Act" or "Act"), to establish standards relating to administrative, technical and physical information safeguards for financial institutions subject to the Commission's jurisdiction. As required by section 501(b), the standards are intended to: Ensure the security and confidentiality of customer records and information; protect against any anticipated threats or hazards to the security or integrity of such records; and protect against unauthorized access to or use of such records or information that could result in substantial harm or inconvenience to any customer.

EFFECTIVE DATE: This rule is effective on May 23, 2003.

FOR FURTHER INFORMATION CONTACT: Laura D. Berger, Attorney, Division of Financial Practices, (202) 326–3224.

SUPPLEMENTARY INFORMATION: The contents of this preamble are listed in the following outline:

A. Background
B. Overview of Comments Received
C. Section-by-Section Analysis
D. Paperwork Reduction Act
E. Regulatory Flexibility Act

Section A. Background

On November 12, 1999, President Clinton signed the G–L–B Act (Pub. L. 106–102) into law. The purpose of the Act was to reform and modernize the banking industry by eliminating existing barriers between banking and commerce. The Act permits banks to engage in a broad range of activities, including insurance and securities brokering, with new affiliated entities. Subtitle A of Title V of the Act, captioned "Disclosure of Nonpublic Personal Information," limits the instances in which a financial institution may disclose nonpublic personal information about a consumer to nonaffiliated third parties, and requires a financial institution to disclose certain privacy policies and practices with respect to its information sharing with both affiliates and nonaffiliated third parties. On May 12, 2000, the Commission issued a final rule, Privacy of Consumer Financial Information, 16 CFR part 313, which implemented Subtitle A as it relates to these requirements (hereinafter "Privacy Rule").[1] The Privacy Rule took effect on November 13, 2000, and full compliance was required on or before July 1, 2001.

Subtitle A of Title V also requires the Commission and other federal agencies to establish standards for financial institutions relating to administrative, technical, and physical safeguards for certain information.[2] *See* 15 U.S.C. 6801(b), 6805(b)(2). As described in the Act, the objectives of these standards are to: (1) Ensure the security and confidentiality of customer records and information; (2) protect against any anticipated threats or hazards to the security or integrity of such records; and (3) protect against unauthorized access to or use of such records or information which could result in substantial harm or inconvenience to any customer. *See* 15 U.S.C. 6801(b)(1)–(3). The Act does not require all of the agencies to coordinate in developing their safeguards standards, and does not impose a deadline to establish them.[3] Although the Act permits most of the agencies to develop their safeguards standards by issuing guidelines, it requires the SEC and the Commission to proceed by rule.[4]

On September 7, 2000, the Commission issued for publication in the **Federal Register** a Advanced Notice of Proposed Rulemaking ("the ANPR") on the scope and potential requirements of a Safeguards Rule for the financial institutions subject to its jurisdiction.[5] The Commission received thirty comments in response to the ANPR. Based on these comments, as well as the safeguards standards already issued by the other GLB agencies, the Commission issued a Notice of Proposed Rulemaking respecting Standards for Safeguarding Customer Information ("the proposal" or "the Proposed Rule") on August 7, 2001.[6] In response to the proposal, the Commission received forty-four comments from a variety of interested parties. The Commission now issues a final rule governing the safeguarding of customer records and information for the financial institutions subject to its jurisdiction ("Safeguards Rule").

Like the proposal, the Final Rule requires each financial institution to develop a written information security program that is appropriate to its size and complexity, the nature and scope of its activities, and the sensitivity of the customer information at issue. As described below, each information security program must include certain basic elements to ensure that it addresses the relevant aspects of a financial institution's operations and that it keeps pace with developments that may have a material impact on its safeguards. In developing the Final Rule, the Commission carefully weighed the comments, including concerns expressed about the ability of smaller and less sophisticated financial institutions to meet the Rule's requirements. It also sought to ensure that the Rule mirrored the requirements of the guidelines already established by the NCUA and the other banking agencies (collectively, "the Banking Agency Guidelines"),[7] with adjustments as needed to clarify the Rule's scope and accommodate the diverse range of entities covered by the Commission's Rule. The Commission believes that the Final Rule strikes an appropriate balance between allowing flexibility to financial institutions and establishing standards for safeguarding customer information that are consistent with the Act's goals. As described below, the Commission will issue educational materials in connection with the Rule in order to assist businesses—and in particular, small entities—to comply with its requirements without imposing undue burdens.

---

[1] The rule was published in the **Federal Register** at 65 FR 33646 (May 24, 2000).

[2] The other agencies responsible for establishing safeguards standards are: the Office of the Comptroller of the Currency ("OCC"); the Board of Governors of the Federal Reserve System ("Board"); the Federal Deposit Insurance Corporation ("FDIC"); the Office of Thrift Supervision ("OTS"); the National Credit Union Administration ("NCUA"); the Secretary of the Treasury ("Treasury"); and the Securities and Exchange Commission ("SEC").

[3] By contrast, section 504 of the Act required the Agencies to work together to issue consistent and comparable rules to implement the Act's privacy provisions.

[4] The NCUA and the remaining banking agencies—the OCC, the Board, the FDIC, and OTS—have already issued final guidelines that are substantively identical. 66 FR 8152 (Jan. 30, 2001); 66 FR 8616 (Feb. 1, 2001). The SEC also adopted a final safeguards rule as part of its Privacy of Consumer Financial Information Final Rule (hereinafter "SEC rule"). *See www.sec.gov/rules/final/34-42974.htm* (June 29, 2000).

[5] 65 FR 54186.

[6] 66 FR 41162. In addition to considering the Banking Agency Guidelines, the Commission also considered the Final Report that was issued by the Federal Trade Commission Advisory Committee on Online Access and Security on May 15, 2000 ("Advisory Committee's Report" or "ACR"). Although the Advisory Committee's Report addressed security only in the online context, the Commission believes that its principles have general relevance to information safeguards.

[7] *See supra* n.4.

Section B. Overview of Comments Received

The comments received were submitted by a variety of interested parties:[8] twenty-eight were from trade or other associations or companies related to financial or Internet-related services;[9] six were from corporations or associations related to higher education or the funding of student loans;[10] five were from individuals;[11] three were from information security companies;[12] two were from consumer reporting agencies;[13] and one was from a non-profit association of consumer agencies.[14]

The majority of commenters supported the proposal overall, citing its flexibility[15] and similarity to the Banking Agency Guidelines.[16] However, as discussed below, commenters expressed different views on issues concerning the Rule's scope—in particular, whether financial institutions should be responsible for the safeguards of their affiliates and service providers and whether the Rule should apply to a financial institution that has no customer relationship but receives customer information from another financial institution. In addition, a number of commenters asked that compliance with alternative standards be deemed compliance with the Rule and/or sought to exclude certain entities from the Rule's definition of "service provider." Finally, numerous commenters urged that the Commission provide guidance to businesses—particularly smaller businesses—on how to comply with the Rule without incurring undue expense.[17] As discussed in detail below, comments on all of these issues were instrumental in shaping the Final Rule.

Additional comments, and the Commission's responses thereto, are discussed in the following Section-by-Section analysis.

Section C. Section-by-Section Analysis

Consistent with the proposal, the Safeguards Rule will be part 314 of 16 CFR, to be entitled "Standards for Safeguarding Customer Information." This Part will follow the Privacy Rule, which is contained in part 313 of 16 CFR. The following is a section-by-section analysis of the Final Rule.

Section 314.1: Purpose and Scope

Paragraph 314.1(a) states that the Rule is intended to establish standards for financial institutions to develop, implement and maintain administrative, technical, and physical safeguards to protect the security, confidentiality, and integrity of customer information. This paragraph also states the statutory authority for the proposed Rule. No comments addressed this provision, and the Commission has made no changes to it.

Paragraph 314.1(b) sets forth the scope of the Rule, which applies to the handling of customer information by all financial institutions over which the FTC has jurisdiction. Because, as noted below, "financial institution" is defined as it is in section 509(3)(A) of the Act and the Privacy Rule, the Rule covers a wide range of entities, including: non-depository lenders; consumer reporting agencies; debt collectors; data processors; courier services; retailers that extend credit by issuing credit cards to consumers; personal property or real estate appraisers; check-cashing businesses; mortgage brokers, and any other entity that meets this definition.[18] Consistent with the proposal, the Safeguards Rule covers any financial institution that is handling "customer information"—*i.e.*, not only financial institutions that collect nonpublic personal information from their own customers, but also financial institutions that receive customer information from other financial institutions.

Comments were split on whether the Rule should apply to customer information that a financial institution receives from another financial institution. A number of commenters agreed that such recipients should be required to maintain safeguards, citing the added protections provided by this requirement.[19] However, one of these commenters expressed concern that a recipient financial institution could be subject to multiple safeguards standards or even required to prepare multiple written safeguards plans if that financial institution also acts as a service provider or is subject to other laws, such as the Fair Credit Reporting Act, that impose confidentiality requirements.[20] In addition, some commenters opposed covering recipients on the grounds that such coverage is: (1) Beyond the intent of section 501(a), which refers to a financial institution's obligation to "its customers;" (2) unnecessary in light of the Rule's separate treatment of service providers and affiliates; and/or (3) too burdensome.[21]

After considering the comments, the Commission has determined that covering recipient financial institutions is consistent with the purpose and language of the Act. The Commission believes that imposing safeguards obligations as to customer information that a financial institution receives about another institution's customers is the most reasonable reading of the statutory language and clearly furthers the express congressional policy to

---

[8] These comments are available on the Commission's Web site, at www.ftc.gov.

[9] ACA International ("ACA"); America's Community Bankers ("ACB"); Associated Credit Bureaus, now renamed the Consumer Data Industry Association ("CDIA"); BITS/Financial Services Roundtable ("BITS"); Commerce Bankshares, Inc.; Credit Union Nat'l Ass'n ("CUNA"); Council of Ins. Agents and Brokers; Debt Buyers Ass'n ("DBA"); Ernst & Young LLP ("Ernst & Young"); Financial Planning Ass'n ("FPA"); Household Finance Corporation ("Household"); Independent Community Bankers of America ("ICB"); Independent Ins. Agents of America ("Indep. Ins. Agents"); Intuit Inc. ("Intuit"); Information Technology Ass'n of America ("ITAA"); MasterCard International ("MasterCard"); Nat'l Ass'n of Indep. Insurers ("NAII"); Nat'l Ass'n of Mutual Ins. Cos. ("NAMIC"); Nat'l Automotive Dealers Ass'n ("NADA"); Nat'l Retail Federation ("NRF"); Navy Federal Credit Union ("NFCU"); Nat'l Indep. Automobile Dealers Ass'n ("NIADA"); Navy Federal Financial Group ("NFFG"); North American Securities Administrators Ass'n, Inc. ("NASAA"); Ohio Credit Union League ("OCUL"); Oracle Corporation ("Oracle"); Software & Information Industry Ass'n ("SIIA"); Visa USA, Inc. ("Visa").

[10] American Council on Education ("ACE"); Education Finance Council and the National Council of Higher Education Loan Programs; Nat'l Council of Higher Educ. Loan Programs, Inc.; USA Education, Inc. & Student Loan Marketing Ass'n (collectively "Sallie Mae"); Texas Guaranteed Student Loan Corp. ("TGSL"); United Student Aid Funds, Inc. ("USA Funds").

[11] Forest Landreth ("Landreth"); Lou Larson ("Larson"); Sheila Musgrove ("Musgrove"); David Paas ("Paas"); Norman Post ("Post").

[12] Portogo, Inc. ("Portogo"); Tiger Testing; VeriSign, Inc. ("VeriSign").

[13] Equifax, Inc ("Equifax"); Experian Information Solutions, Inc. ("Experian").

[14] Nat'l Ass'n of Consumer Agency Administrators ("NACAA").

[15] *See, e.g.*, Household at 1; Intuit at 2; ITAA at 1; NRF at 2; Sallie Mae at 2; SIIA at 3; TGSL at 1; Verisign at 2.

[16] See, e.g., Visa at 1.

[17] *See, e.g.*, ICB at 2; Musgrove at 2; NADA at 2; NIADA at 9; Paas at 4–6.

[18] Under section 313.3(k)(1) of the Privacy Rule, "financial institution" means: any institution the business of which is engaging in financial activities as described in section 4(k) of the Bank Holding Company Act of 1956 (12 U.S.C. 1843(k)). An institution that is significantly engaged in financial activities is a financial institution.

Additional examples of financial institutions are provided in section 313.3(k)(2) of the Privacy Rule.

[19] See, e.g., Equifax at 1–2; Intuit at 2; NIADA at 2; TGSL at 1.

[20] Equifax at 2.

[21] See, e.g., ACA at 2–3; CDIA at 3; Experian at 2; Mastercard at 2–3; NAMIC at 2–3; NRF at 3. In addition, one comment stated that numerous financial institutions that do not have customer relationships of their own could be swept into the Rule in this fashion (Visa at 4). Although no commenters identified the types of financial institutions that are likely to be so affected, the Commission envisions that such entities could include consumer reporting agencies, debt collectors, independent check cashers, automated teller machine operators, and other businesses that obtain customer information from other financial institutions to process customer data, facilitate customer transactions, or carry out transactions in a consumer context.

respect the privacy of these customers and to protect the security and confidentiality of their nonpublic personal information. Covering recipients will ensure that all financial institutions over which the Commission has jurisdiction safeguard customer information and that such safeguards are not lost merely because information is shared with a third-party financial institution.[22] The Commission also believes that the Rule's provisions for affiliates and service providers, discussed below, are not sufficient to address circumstances where information is transferred to another financial institution in the absence of a service or affiliate relationship, such as for use in debt collection or consumer reporting. Without imposing safeguards in such cases, customer information would be insufficiently protected and Congressional intent to safeguard such information would be undermined. Finally, the flexible requirements of the Rule—which allow the safeguards to vary according to the size and complexity of a financial institution, the nature and scope of its activities, and the sensitivity of any customer information at issue—permit entities to develop safeguards appropriate to their operations and should minimize any burdens on recipient entities.

Nevertheless, the Commission recognizes that financial institutions covered by its Rule also may simultaneously be subject to the Rule's requirements for service providers or affiliates.[23] For example, check printers, data processors, and real property appraisers that receive customer information as service providers for a financial institution will also be directly subject to the rule because they are themselves financial institutions.[24] However, the obligations the Rule creates for financial institutions are entirely consistent with the standard it requires them to impose on their affiliate or service provider, so that each entity ultimately is required to maintain safeguards that are appropriate in light of the relevant circumstances. Thus, a financial institution that develops an information safeguards program according to the Rule will not be faced with additional or conflicting requirements merely because it also received customer information as an affiliate or service provider.

As under the proposal, the Safeguards Rule does not cover recipients of customer information that are not financial institutions, and are also neither affiliates nor service providers as defined by the Rule. However, the Commission encourages each financial institution to take reasonable steps to assure itself that any third party to which it discloses customer information has safeguards that are adequate to fulfill any representations made by the financial institution regarding the security of customer information or the manner in which it is handled by third parties.[25]

In addition, as under the proposal, the Safeguards Rule only applies to information about a consumer who is a "customer" of a financial institution within the meaning of the Rule.[26] This approach is consistent with the Banking Agency Guidelines and the majority of comments that addressed this issue.[27] Although the Commission believes that limiting the Rule to information about customers is warranted by the plain language of section 501 of the Act, the Commission notes, as it did in the proposal, that protecting information about consumers may be a part of providing reasonable safeguards to "customer information" where the two types of information cannot be segregated reliably. Further, consistent with its mandate under section 5 of the FTC Act, the Commission expects that, as with customers, any information that a financial institution provides to a consumer will be accurate concerning the extent to which safeguards apply to them. Finally, the Commission expects that each financial institution will have in place at least the administrative or other safeguards necessary to honor any "opt-out" requests made by consumers under the Privacy Rule.

Other comments on the Rule's scope urged that compliance with various alternative standards should constitute compliance with the Safeguards Rule. Several such commenters urged that the Rule permit compliance with another agency's safeguards standard in lieu of the FTC's. Specifically, commenters urged that: (1) Compliance with the SEC's rule constitute compliance with the FTC Rule, so that state investment advisors covered by the FTC Rule would be subject to the same standards as federal investment advisors, which are subject to the SEC's jurisdiction;[28] (2) non-federally-insured credit unions be permitted to comply with the NCUA's guidelines instead of the FTC's Rule, so that they would be subject to the same standards as federally-insured credit unions, which are under the NCUA's jurisdiction;[29] and (3) compliance with the Banking Agency Guidelines[30] be deemed compliance for service providers that may be engaged by banks as well as by entities under the FTC's jurisdiction. In addition, other commenters requested that compliance with other laws be deemed compliance with the Rule, such as the Fair Credit Reporting Act ("FCRA");[31] the Health Insurance Portability and Accountability Act ("HIPAA");[32] and the Fair Debt Collection Practices Act ("FDCPA").[33]

As discussed above in connection with recipient financial institutions and others, the Commission does not intend to impose undue burdens on entities that already are subject to comparable safeguards requirements. In particular, the Commission envisions that any entity that can demonstrate compliance with the Banking Agency Guidelines (including the substantively identical NCUA Guidelines) will also satisfy the Rule. With respect to other rules and laws that may contain some safeguards, the Commission notes that the adoption of safeguards in furtherance of such rules or laws will be weighted heavily in assessing compliance with the Rule. However, because such other rules and laws do not necessarily provide comparable protections in terms of the safeguards mandated, data covered, and range of circumstances to which protections apply, compliance with such standards will not automatically ensure compliance with the Rule. For example, an entity's compliance with the FCRA, which limits the purposes for which certain financial information may be disclosed, will not guarantee that an

[22] Under the Act, the Commission has jurisdiction over "any other financial institution or other person that is not subject to the jurisdiction of any agency or authority." 15 U.S.C. Section 6805(7). Thus, the Commission does not have jurisdiction over any financial institution that is subject to another Agency's authority by the Act, including national banks, bank holding companies and savings associations the deposits of which are insured by the FDIC. *See id.* at Section 6805(a)(1)–(6).

[23] As discussed below, the FTC Rule requires financial institutions to ensure the safeguards of their affiliates and take steps to oversee their service providers' safeguards. *See* sections 314.2(b) and 314.4(d), below. What safeguards would be appropriate for an affiliate or service provider depends on the facts and circumstances, just as it would for a financial institution that is directly covered by the Rule.

[24] It should be noted that this potential overlap exists for all financial institutions that are affiliates or service providers of other financial institutions, not just recipient entities.

[25] Misrepresentations regarding these issues could violate the Privacy Rule and Section 5 of the FTC Act.

[26] The Rule incorporates the definition of "customer" set forth in section 313(h) of the Privacy Rule. *See* section 314.2(a).

[27] *See, e.g.*, ACA at 4; DBA at 1; Mastercard at 1–2; *but see* Intuit at 3–4; NACAA at 1.

[28] NASAA at 2.

[29] CUNA at 1; OCUL at 3.

[30] Indep. Ins. Agents at 2.

[31] CDIA at 2–3; NIADA at 3.

[32] NIADA at 3.

[33] ACA at 4–5.

entity has adopted a comprehensive information security plan as described in the Rule.

Section 314.2: Definitions

This section defines terms used in the Safeguards Rule. As under the proposal, paragraph (a) makes clear that, unless otherwise stated, terms used in the Safeguards Rule bear the same meaning as in the Commission's Privacy Rule. The remaining paragraphs (b)-(d) of this section define the terms "customer information," "information security program," and "service provider," respectively.

In addressing this section generally, several commenters expressed concern that the definitions would be confusing to the extent that they differ from those set forth in the Privacy Rule or the Banking Agency Guidelines.[34] In response, the Commission notes that, the terms used in the Rule are consistent with those used in the Privacy Rule, and differ from those used in the Guidelines only as needed to clarify the Rule's scope and make its terms more understandable and appropriate to the diverse range of non-bank financial institutions subject to the Commission's jurisdiction. Thus, as described below, the Rule defines "customer information" to include information handled by affiliates. Similarly, the Rule omits definitions found in the Guidelines, such as "Board of Directors" or "subsidiary," that are not universally applicable to entities that will be subject to the Rule.

Proposed paragraph (b) defined "customer information" as any record containing nonpublic personal information, as defined in paragraph 313.3(n) of the Privacy Rule, about a customer of a financial institution, whether in paper, electronic, or other form, that is handled or maintained by or on behalf of a financial institution or its affiliates." Thus, to the extent that a financial institution shares customer information with its affiliates, the proposal required it to ensure that the affiliates maintain appropriate safeguards for the customer information at issue.

Commenters expressed varying views on whether a financial institution should be responsible for its affiliates' safeguards. Some commenters agreed that customer information held by affiliates should be protected by the Rule.[35] However, some commenters requested that affiliates that are financial institutions subject to the jurisdiction of another agency be permitted to comply with the safeguards standards of that agency in lieu of the Commission's Rule.[36] Finally, several commenters stated that the Rule should not cover affiliates at all because (1) the Act was not meant to cover any entity that is not a financial institution and some affiliates may not be financial institutions[37] or (2) the fact that the Act permits financial institutions to disclose nonpublic personal information to affiliates without providing any notice or opt out indicates that no affiliates were intended to be covered by the Act's safeguards provisions.[38]

The Commission agrees that section 501 of the Act focuses on the obligations of financial institutions. It also notes, however, that the purpose of the Act is to protect customer information, and that such information easily may be shared with companies that are affiliated and under common control with such financial institutions. Therefore, the Rule imposes obligations only on financial institutions, but gives them duties with respect to customer information shared with their affiliates. The Commission does not believe that the unrestricted sharing that the Act permits among affiliates—including affiliates that are not financial institutions—shows an intent to exclude affiliates from safeguards obligations. To the contrary, the free sharing the Act permits among affiliates warrants a coordinated and consistent approach to security. The Commission notes, however, that the duty to ensure appropriate safeguards by affiliates arises only if a financial institution shares customer information with its affiliates; therefore this obligation can, and need only be, addressed as part of such sharing arrangements. In addition, the flexible standards of the Rule permit entities to develop safeguards appropriate to their operations and the sensitivity of the information at issue and should therefore minimize burdens on affiliates. Finally, as noted above, the Commission agrees that compliance with the Banking Agency Guidelines should satisfy the safeguards standards under the Commission's Rule. Therefore, any financial institution that can demonstrate its compliance with the Guidelines will not be subject to additional requirements merely because it is an affiliate of a financial institution that is covered by the Rule.

Proposed paragraph (c) defined "information security program" as "the administrative, technical, or physical safeguards" that a financial institution uses "to access, collect, process, store, use, transmit, dispose of, or otherwise handle customer information." This definition is virtually identical to the Banking Agency Guidelines' definition of "customer information systems." *See* Banking Agency Guidelines, section I.C.2.d. Few comments were received on this definition. In response to one commenter who urged that this term should better describe all of the ways that "customer information" can be provided to others, the Commission has added the words "distribute" and "protect" to this definition.[39] At the same time, the Commission notes that the words "otherwise handle" are intended to cover other ways that customer information is dealt with that are not specifically mentioned in the definition. Thus, the definition is adopted with only the minor changes noted above.

Proposed paragraph (d) defined the term "service provider" to mean "any person or entity that receives, maintains, processes, or otherwise is permitted access to customer information through its provision of services directly to a financial institution that is subject to the rule." This definition is virtually identical to the definition set forth in the Banking Agency Guidelines. *See* Banking Agency Guidelines, section I.C.2.e. Several commenters urged that this definition be amended to exclude particular entities from the definition of service providers, namely: (1) Accountants and auditors[40] (2) financial institutions that also provide services to banks, and are subject to examination under the Bank Service Company Act (BSCA);[41] (3) any service provider that is also an affiliate of a financial institution;[42] and (4) any service provider that receives information under the Privacy Rule's general exceptions in Sections 313.14 and 313.15, and is therefore permitted access to nonpublic personal information without need for a specific agreement concerning its reuse and redisclosure.[43]

The Commission notes that the Banking Agency Guidelines do not contain exceptions to the definition of service provider. Thus, some of the recommended exceptions could result

[34] *See, e.g.*, Intuit at 4; NADA at 2; NIADA at 2, 4.

[35] Equifax at 2–4; Household at 1–2; NACAA at 1; NIADA at 4; SIIA at 2. *See also* NCHELP at 1.

[36] *See, e.g.*, Household at 1–2; NCHELP at 2; OCUL at 2; USA Funds at 1. *See also* Equifax at 2.

[37] Mastercard at 4–5. *See also* NRF at 4.

[38] NAMIC at 5–6.

[39] Equifax at 4.

[40] Ernst & Young at 1–2.

[41] Visa at 4.

[42] NIADA at 5.

[43] NIADA at 6 (but stating that the Rule's obligations for service providers are for the most part consistent with the Privacy Rule).

entity has adopted a comprehensive information security plan as described in the Rule.

Section 314.2: Definitions

This section defines terms used in the Safeguards Rule. As under the proposal, paragraph (a) makes clear that, unless otherwise stated, terms used in the Safeguards Rule bear the same meaning as in the Commission's Privacy Rule. The remaining paragraphs (b)-(d) of this section define the terms "customer information," "information security program," and "service provider," respectively.

In addressing this section generally, several commenters expressed concern that the definitions would be confusing to the extent that they differ from those set forth in the Privacy Rule or the Banking Agency Guidelines.[34] In response, the Commission notes that, the terms used in the Rule are consistent with those used in the Privacy Rule, and differ from those used in the Guidelines only as needed to clarify the Rule's scope and make its terms more understandable and appropriate to the diverse range of non-bank financial institutions subject to the Commission's jurisdiction. Thus, as described below, the Rule defines "customer information" to include information handled by affiliates. Similarly, the Rule omits definitions found in the Guidelines, such as "Board of Directors" or "subsidiary," that are not universally applicable to entities that will be subject to the Rule.

Proposed paragraph (b) defined "customer information" as any record containing nonpublic personal information, as defined in paragraph 313.3(n) of the Privacy Rule, about a customer of a financial institution, whether in paper, electronic, or other form, that is handled or maintained by or on behalf of a financial institution or its affiliates." Thus, to the extent that a financial institution shares customer information with its affiliates, the proposal required it to ensure that the affiliates maintain appropriate safeguards for the customer information at issue.

Commenters expressed varying views on whether a financial institution should be responsible for its affiliates' safeguards. Some commenters agreed that customer information held by affiliates should be protected by the Rule.[35] However, some commenters requested that affiliates that are financial institutions subject to the jurisdiction of another agency be permitted to comply with the safeguards standards of that agency in lieu of the Commission's Rule.[36] Finally, several commenters stated that the Rule should not cover affiliates at all because (1) the Act was not meant to cover any entity that is not a financial institution and some affiliates may not be financial institutions [37] or (2) the fact that the Act permits financial institutions to disclose nonpublic personal information to affiliates without providing any notice or opt out indicates that no affiliates were intended to be covered by the Act's safeguards provisions.[38]

The Commission agrees that section 501 of the Act focuses on the obligations of financial institutions. It also notes, however, that the purpose of the Act is to protect customer information, and that such information easily may be shared with companies that are affiliated and under common control with such financial institutions. Therefore, the Rule imposes obligations only on financial institutions, but gives them duties with respect to customer information shared with their affiliates. The Commission does not believe that the unrestricted sharing that the Act permits among affiliates—including affiliates that are not financial institutions—shows an intent to exclude affiliates from safeguards obligations. To the contrary, the free sharing the Act permits among affiliates warrants a coordinated and consistent approach to security. The Commission notes, however, that the duty to ensure appropriate safeguards by affiliates arises only if a financial institution shares customer information with its affiliates; therefore this obligation can, and need only be, addressed as part of such sharing arrangements. In addition, the flexible standards of the Rule permit entities to develop safeguards appropriate to their operations and the sensitivity of the information at issue and should therefore minimize burdens on affiliates. Finally, as noted above, the Commission agrees that compliance with the Banking Agency Guidelines should satisfy the safeguards standards under the Commission's Rule. Therefore, any financial institution that can demonstrate its compliance with the Guidelines will not be subject to additional requirements merely because it is an affiliate of a financial institution that is covered by the Rule.

Proposed paragraph (c) defined "information security program" as "the administrative, technical, or physical safeguards" that a financial institution uses "to access, collect, process, store, use, transmit, dispose of, or otherwise handle customer information." This definition is virtually identical to the Banking Agency Guidelines' definition of "customer information systems." *See* Banking Agency Guidelines, section I.C.2.d. Few comments were received on this definition. In response to one commenter who urged that this term should better describe all of the ways that "customer information" can be provided to others, the Commission has added the words "distribute" and "protect" to this definition.[39] At the same time, the Commission notes that the words "otherwise handle" are intended to cover other ways that customer information is dealt with that are not specifically mentioned in the definition. Thus, the definition is adopted with only the minor changes noted above.

Proposed paragraph (d) defined the term "service provider" to mean "any person or entity that receives, maintains, processes, or otherwise is permitted access to customer information through its provision of services directly to a financial institution that is subject to the rule." This definition is virtually identical to the definition set forth in the Banking Agency Guidelines. *See* Banking Agency Guidelines, section I.C.2.e. Several commenters urged that this definition be amended to exclude particular entities from the definition of service providers, namely: (1) Accountants and auditors [40] (2) financial institutions that also provide services to banks, and are subject to examination under the Bank Service Company Act (BSCA);[41] (3) any service provider that is also an affiliate of a financial institution;[42] and (4) any service provider that receives information under the Privacy Rule's general exceptions in Sections 313.14 and 313.15, and is therefore permitted access to nonpublic personal information without need for a specific agreement concerning its reuse and redisclosure.[43]

The Commission notes that the Banking Agency Guidelines do not contain exceptions to the definition of service provider. Thus, some of the recommended exceptions could result

[34] *See, e.g.*, Intuit at 4; NADA at 2; NIADA at 2, 4.

[35] Equifax at 2–4; Household at 1–2; NACAA at 1; NIADA at 4; SIIA at 2. *See also* NCHELP at 1.

[36] *See, e.g.*, Household at 1–2; NCHELP at 2; OCUL at 2; USA Funds at 1. *See also* Equifax at 2.

[37] Mastercard at 4–5. *See also* NRF at 4.

[38] NAMIC at 5–6.

[39] Equifax at 4.

[40] Ernst & Young at 1–2.

[41] Visa at 4.

[42] NIADA at 5.

[43] NIADA at 6 (but stating that the Rule's obligations for service providers are for the most part consistent with the Privacy Rule).

requirement that each institution involve and report to its Board of Directors (*see* 66 FR 41166, *citing* Paragraphs III.A. and III.F., respectively), but allows designation of any employee or employees to better accommodate entities that are not controlled by Boards of Directors. Nearly all commenters on this paragraph expressed support, noting the importance of establishing a point of contact and citing the provision's flexibility.[53] However, some commenters requested minor changes, namely: (1) That the Rule state that a financial institution need not designate an employee for each of its subsidiaries; (2) that the words "as appropriate" be added to the requirement; and (3) that the Rule make clear that financial institutions may outsource safeguards procedures.[54] By contrast, one commenter opposed requiring financial institutions to designate any individual employee(s), based on a concern that customers might attempt to hold such designee(s) individually liable for any breach of security that occurs.[55]

The Commission recognizes the importance of reserving to financial institutions the flexibility to select and designate the employee(s) that are needed to ensure accountability and achieve adequate safeguards. The Commission is particularly concerned that small institutions not be burdened disproportionately by this paragraph (or by other requirements) of the Rule. For these reasons, the paragraph allows each financial institution to determine which employee(s) to designate, including whether to designate additional employees to handle different subsidiaries. Further, there is nothing in the Rule to prevent a financial institution from outsourcing safeguards functions as appropriate, provided that at least one of its own employees is designated to see that such functions are properly carried out. At the same time, the Commission declines to add the words "as appropriate" to this paragraph because such language would only repeat the Rule's overarching requirement that each financial institution develop, implement and maintain "appropriate" safeguards. Lastly, the Commission notes that this Rule does not address or alter traditional principles of corporate liability and, therefore, should neither create nor limit individual liability for a financial institution's designated employee(s). Thus, paragraph (a) is adopted as proposed.

2. Paragraph (b)

Proposed paragraph (b) required each financial institution to "identify reasonably foreseeable internal and external risks to the security, confidentiality, and integrity of customer information that could result in the unauthorized disclosure, misuse, alteration, destruction or other compromise of such information, and assess the sufficiency of any safeguards in place to control these risks." The proposal further required each financial institution to consider risks in each area of its operations, including three areas that the Commission believes are particularly relevant to information security: (1) Employee training and management; (2) information systems, including information processing, storage, transmission and disposal; and (3) detecting, preventing and responding to attacks, intrusions, or other systems failures. This paragraph is similar to the Banking Agency Guidelines requirement to assess risks.[56]

Commenters who addressed the issue generally supported including a risk assessment requirement within the Rule.[57] Some of these commenters supported the paragraph as proposed, stating that its benefits are appropriate relative to its burdens, and that it provides the proper level of guidance on how risk assessment should be carried out.[58] Commenters that supported the paragraph's general description of the types of risks to be considered—including the proposed areas of operation—emphasized that the threats to information security are ever changing, and therefore can only be described in general terms.[59] By contrast, other commenters urged that the paragraph be made more specific in a variety of ways, namely by: (1) Defining specific categories of threats and hazards, such as "risks to physical security;" (2) including more concrete and extensive guidance on how small businesses might perform the required assessment; or (3) including a procedure by which the FTC will conduct reviews or audits of the security practices of financial institutions under its jurisdiction.[60]

The Commission notes the importance of providing guidance to financial institutions, particularly small businesses, on how to comply with this and other aspects of the Rule. The Commission therefore intends to issue educational materials to help businesses identify risks and comply with the various other provisions of the Rule. Because of the ever-changing nature of the relevant risks, however, the Commission does not find it appropriate to delineate risks more specifically within the Rule. In addition, to retain appropriate flexibility, the Commission will rely on its discretion in enforcing the Rule, and not describe any particular schedule or methods for enforcement.[61] At the same time, the Commission has amended slightly the areas of operation, in order to better describe the activities that financial institutions should consider in developing, implementing and maintaining their information security programs. Specifically, the Commission has added (1) the item "network and software design" to the examples of information systems a financial institution should examine; and (2) the term "detecting" to the requirement that each financial institution consider means of "preventing and responding" to attacks, intrusions and other systems failures. In all other respects, paragraph (b) is adopted as proposed.

3. Paragraph (c)

Proposed paragraph (c) required each financial institution to "design and implement information safeguards to control the risks [identified] through risk assessment, and regularly test or otherwise monitor the effectiveness of the safeguards' key controls, systems, and procedures." The proposal further required each financial institution to consider its areas of operation in fulfilling this requirement. As with proposed paragraph (b), above, commenters generally supported this provision, citing its flexibility and the appropriateness of its benefits relative to its burdens.[62] However, one commenter

---

[53] *See, e.g.*, Intuit at 4; Mastercard at 6–7; NACAA at 1–2; NCHELP at 3; Sallie Mae at 3; SIIA at 2; Visa at 2.

[54] Sallie Mae at 3; Equifax at 6; NRF at 5, respectively.

[55] NIADA at 6.

[56] *See* Banking Agency Guidelines, Paragraph III. B.

[57] *See, e.g.*, Equifax at 7; Intuit at 5; Mastercard at 7; NASAA at 2; NCHELP at 3; Portugo at 1; SIAA at 4; VeriSign at 1.

[58] *See, e.g.*, Intuit at 5; Mastercard at 7; SIAA at 2.

[59] Oracle at 2; Mastercard at 7.

[60] NACAA comment on the ANPR, at 2; Pans at 3; Musgrove at 2, respectively.

[61] By contrast to the Banking Agencies, the Commission is not authorized to conduct regular audits and review of entities under its jurisdiction.

[62] Intuit at 5; NCHELP at 4; SIIA at 2. In addition, as elsewhere, commenters urged that the paragraph include more guidance, so that businesses—particularly smaller entities, such as sole proprietorships—will better understand what safeguards are sufficient to comply with the Rule. *See* NIADA at 7–8; Pans at 4–5. As discussed above, the Commission agrees that educating businesses

Continued

asked that the provision be revised to require only such safeguards as are "commercially reasonable,"[63] while another urged that the paragraph require each financial institution to keep specific written records of its particular safeguards procedures, such as its employee training activities and records retention schedules, to demonstrate compliance with the Rule.[64]

The Commission recognizes that each financial institution must focus its limited resources on addressing those risks that are most relevant to its operations. However, because the Rule already contains flexible standards that take a variety of factors into account, the Commission does not believe it is necessary or appropriate to revise the Rule to require only such safeguards as are "commercially reasonable." At the same time, to preserve flexibility and minimize burdens, the Commission declines to revise this paragraph to require that financial institutions document specific aspects of their risk control activities. For these reasons, paragraph (c) is adopted as proposed.

4. Paragraph (d)

Proposed paragraph (d) required each financial institution to oversee its service providers by selecting and retaining service providers that are "capable of maintaining appropriate safeguards" for the customer information at issue (paragraph (d)(1)), and requiring its service providers by contract to "implement and maintain such safeguards" (paragraph(d)(2)). For the reasons discussed below, paragraph (d)(1) is revised slightly, while paragraph (d)(2) is adopted as proposed.

Commenters supported requiring oversight of service providers' safeguards by financial institutions, particularly when, as one coalition of financial services organizations noted, the financial services industry increasingly relies on third parties to support core functions and online delivery.[65] However, in commenting on proposed paragraph (d)(1), some commenters expressed concern about the ability of businesses—particularly smaller entities—to evaluate a service provider's capabilities.[66] At the same time, other commenters supported adding to the Rule various standards for financial institutions to use in selecting service providers, specifically: (1) That financial institutions have "reason to believe" their service providers are capable of maintaining appropriate safeguards;[67] (2) that they use a "due diligence" review, as under the Banking Agency guidelines;[68] or (3) that they select service providers that are "capable of maintaining appropriate safeguards."[69]

The Commission agrees that businesses cannot be expected to perform unlimited evaluation of their service providers' capabilities. Thus, the Commission has amended the provision to state that each financial institution must "take reasonable steps" to select and retain appropriate service providers. This added language more closely parallels the Banking Agency Guidelines, as well as the Rule's requirement to assess risks that are "reasonably foreseeable." The steps that are reasonable under the Rule will depend upon the circumstances and the relationship between the financial institution and the service provider in question. At a minimum, the Commission envisions that each financial institution will (1) take reasonable steps to assure itself that its current and potential service providers maintain sufficient procedures to detect and respond to security breaches, and (2) maintain reasonable procedures to discover and respond to widely-known security failures by its current and potential service providers.

Proposed paragraph (d)(2) required financial institutions to enter into contracts that require service providers to implement and maintain appropriate safeguards. Most comments that addressed this requirement supported it.[70] Nevertheless, as discussed above, some commenters urged that certain service providers be exempt from the Rule, or be permitted to comply with the safeguards standards of another agency, such as their own functional regulator in the case of financial institution service providers. These comments already have been addressed above. In addition, two commenters urged that the Rule give examples of appropriate language or specifically require the inclusion of certain clauses in the contract,[71] while other commenters stated that no such specifications are needed or desirable.[72] The Commission believes that financial institutions are well positioned to develop and implement appropriate contracts with their service providers. Further, keeping the contract provision flexible should allow financial institutions and their service providers to develop arrangements that do not impose undue or conflicting burdens on service providers that may be subject to other standards and/or agreements concerning safeguards. Therefore, the Commission declines to include specific contract language within the Rule. However, the Commission intends to provide education for businesses on how to comply with the Rule, and will include general guidance concerning oversight of service providers as part of this effort. For these reasons, paragraph (d)(2) is adopted as proposed.

5. Paragraph (e)

Proposed paragraph (e) required each financial institution to "evaluate and adjust [its] information security program in light of any material changes to [its] business that may affect [its] safeguards." The preamble to the proposed section offered examples of such material changes, namely changes in technology; changes to its operations or business arrangements, such as mergers and acquisitions, alliances and joint ventures, outsourcing arrangements, or changes to the services provided; new or emerging internal or external threats to information security; or any other circumstances that give it reason to know that its information security program is vulnerable to attack or compromise. *See* 66 FR 41167. Several commenters supported this requirement as proposed.[73] However, a few commenters recommended certain revisions to the paragraph's description of the types of changes that may warrant evaluation and adjustment of an entity's safeguards. Specifically, one commenter urged that although changes in the sensitivity of customer information or the nature of any threats will warrant evaluation, changes to a business's internal organization may be irrelevant to its safeguards, and therefore should not necessitate a review.[74] Similarly, another commenter urged that the paragraph be revised to require that a financial institution "take reasonable steps so that the information security

---

and others is critical to achieving the Rule's objectives, and plans to issue educational materials in connection with the Rule.

[63] Equifax at 8.

[64] Musgrove at 2.

[65] BITS at 1. *See also* CDIA at 6; ITAA at 3; VeriSign at 2 (Rule appropriately places on financial institutions the burden to select appropriate service providers).

[66] Paus at 5. *See also* NRF at 5 (expressing concern that Rule could make financial institutions strictly liable for safeguards breaches by their service providers).

[67] NRF at 5; TGSL at 2.

[68] Household at 1; ICBA at 1; NIADA at 6.

[69] Mastercard at 7.

[70] Equifax at 8; Indep. Ins. Agents 3; Intuit at 5; Mastercard at 7; NACAA at 2; NCHELP at 4; Navy Federal Financial Group at 1–2; NIADA at 7; Sallie Mae at 3; SIIA at 2.

[71] NADA at 3; Navy Federal Financial Group at 1–2.

[72] Intuit at 5; Sallie Mae at 3.

[73] NACAA at 2; NCHELP at 5; SIIA at 2.

[74] Intuit at 6.

program continues to be appropriate" for the financial institution.[75]

Consistent with the intent of the Proposed Rule, as well as the concerns reflected in these comments, the Commission believes that the bases for a financial institution to adjust its information security program will vary depending on the circumstances and may include a wide range of factors. Accordingly, paragraph (e) has been amended to more clearly reflect the fact-specific nature of the inquiry and to better encompass the broad range of factors that a financial institution should consider. Under the revised paragraph, each financial institution must evaluate and adjust its information security program "in light of the results of the testing and monitoring required by paragraph (c); any material changes to [its] operations or business arrangements; or any other circumstances that you know or have reason to know may have a material impact on [its] information security program." The Commission believes that the Rule allows a financial institution sufficient flexibility as to how to adjust its safeguards, and therefore finds it unnecessary to limit the responsibility of financial institutions to taking "reasonable steps" to make any adjustments. Thus, paragraph (e) is adopted with the changes noted above.

Section 314.5: Effective Date

Proposed section 314.5 required each financial institution covered by the Rule to implement an information security program not later than one year from the date on which a Final Rule is issued. In addition, the proposal requested comment on whether the Rule should contain a transition period to allow the continuation of existing contracts with service providers, even if the contracts would not satisfy the Rule's requirements.

Many commenters supported as adequate an effective date of one year from the date on which the Final Rule is issued.[76] A few commenters urged that a longer time be given, such as 18 months,[77] or that an additional year be allowed for businesses—particularly small entities—to comply.[78] In addition, all commenters who addressed the issue urged that the Rule allow a transition period for service provider contracts.[79] Most of these commenters requested that financial institutions be given two years to make service provider contracts comply,[80] while a few commenters sought a slightly longer time.[81]

Consistent with the majority of comments, the Rule will take effect one year from the date on which the Final Rule is published in the **Federal Register**, except that there will be a transition rule for contracts between financial institutions and nonaffiliated third party service providers. Under the transition Rule, set forth in section 314.5(b) of the Rule, financial institutions will be given an additional year to bring these service provider contracts into compliance with the Rule, as long as the contract was in place 30 days after the date on which the Final Rule is published in the **Federal Register**. The transition rule parallels the two-year grandfathering of service contracts that was permitted under both the Privacy Rule and the Banking Agency Guidelines. The Commission believes that the effective date and transition rule will provide businesses appropriate flexibility in complying with the Rule.

Section D. Paperwork Reduction Act

The Paperwork Reduction Act ("PRA"), 44 U.S.C. Chapter 35, requires federal agencies to seek and obtain OMB approval before undertaking a collection of information directed to ten or more persons. 44 U.S.C. 3502(3)(a)(i). Under the PRA, a rule creates a "collection of information" where ten or more persons are asked to report, provide, disclose, or record information" in response to "identical questions." *See* 44 U.S.C. 3502(3)(A). Applying these standards, the Rule does not constitute a "collection of information." The Rule calls upon affected financial institutions to develop or strengthen their information security programs in order to provide reasonable safeguards. Under the Rule, each financial institution's safeguards will vary according to its size and complexity, the nature and scope of its activities, and the sensitivity of the information involved. For example, a financial institution with numerous employees would develop and implement employee training and management procedures beyond those that would be appropriate or reasonable for a sole proprietorship, such as an individual tax preparer or mortgage broker. Similarly, a financial institution that shares customer information with numerous affiliates would need to take steps to ensure that such information remains protected, while a financial institution with no affiliates would not need to address this issue. Thus, although each financial institution must summarize its compliance efforts in one or more written documents, the discretionary balancing of factors and circumstances that the Rule allows—including the myriad operational differences among businesses that it contemplated—does not require entities to answer "identical questions," and therefore does not trigger the PRA's requirements. *See* "The Paperwork Reduction Act of 1995: Implementing Guidance for OMB Review of Agency Information Collection," Office of Information and Regulatory Affairs, OMB (August 16, 1999), at 20–21.

Section E. Regulatory Flexibility Act

In its ANPR, the Commission stated its belief that, under the Regulatory Flexibility Act ("RFA"), 5 U.S.C. 604(a), it was not required to issue an Initial Regulatory Flexibility Analysis ("IRFA") because the Commission did not expect that the Proposed Rule would have a significant economic impact on a substantial number of small entities within the meaning of the Act. *See* 66 FR at 41167. The Commission nonetheless issued an IRFA with the Proposed Rule in order to inquire into the possible impact of the Proposed Rule on small entities, and to provide information to small businesses, as well as other businesses, on how to implement the Rule. *Id.*

Although the Commission specifically sought comment on the costs to small entities of complying with the Rule, no commenters provided specific cost information. Some commenters generally praised the proposal's flexibility[82] or noted that given its flexible standards, it was appropriate for the Rule to apply equally to businesses of all sizes.[83] However, other commenters suggested that small entities may be disproportionately burdened by the Rule because they lack expertise (relative to larger entities) in developing, implementing and maintaining the required safeguards.[84] In light of these comments, the Commission has carefully considered whether to certify that the Rule will not have a significant impact on a

[75] Equifax at 9.

[76] *See, e.g.*, Equifax at 10; Intuit at 6; Mastercard at 8; NIADA at 8; OCUL at 3; Sallie Mae at 3; SIIA at 2; USA Funds at 1–2.

[77] NADA at 2–3; NIADA at 8. *See also* NFFG at 2 (2 years).

[78] ACA at 6–7.

[79] *See, e.g.*, CDIA at 5; NIADA at 8; OCUL at 3; SIIA at 2; TGSL at 2; Visa at 5.

[80] *See, e.g.*, Equifax at 10; NRF at 5; NFFG at 2; OCUL at 3.

[81] Sallie Mae at 3; Visa at 5.

[82] *See, e.g.*, Household at 1; SIIA at 1; TGSL at 1; VeriSign at 1.

[83] Intuit at 2; NASAA at 2.

[84] *See, e.g.*, NADA at 2; NIADA at 9; Musgrove at 2 (stating that small financial institutions may need to hire outside consultants to comply with Rule).

substantial number of small entities. The Commission continues to believe that the Rule's impact will not be substantial in the case of most small entities. However, the Commission cannot quantify the impact the Rule will have on such entities. Therefore, in the interest of thoroughness, the Commission has prepared the following Final Regulatory Flexibility Analysis ("FRFA") with this Final Rule. 5 U.S.C. 605.

1. Succinct Statement of the Need for, and Objectives of, the Rule

The Final Rule is necessary in order to implement section 501(b) of the G–L–B Act, which requires the FTC to establish standards for financial institutions subject to its jurisdiction relating to administrative, technical, and physical standards. According to section 501(b), these standards must: (1) Insure the security and confidentiality of customer records and information; (2) protect against any anticipated threats or hazards to the security or integrity of such records; and (3) protect against unauthorized access to or use of such records or information which could result in substantial harm or inconvenience to any customer. These objectives have been discussed above in the statement of basis and purpose for the Final Rule.

2. Summary of the Significant Issues Raised by the Public Comments in Response to the IRFA; Summary of the Assessment of the Agency of Such Issues; and Statement of Any Changes Made in the Rule as a Result of Such Comments

As stated above, no comments were received concerning specific costs that will be imposed on small entities by the Rule. However, some commenters stated that the Rule and/or certain of its requirements would impose high costs on businesses, including small entities.[85] In addition, as stated, a few commenters suggested that small entities may be disproportionately burdened by the Rule because they lack expertise (relative to larger entities) in developing, implementing and maintaining the required safeguards.[86] Finally, as stated above, many commenters urged that the Commission provide guidance on how to comply with the Rule to assist entities—particularly smaller businesses—to comply without incurring undue expense.[87] In addition, some commenters specifically requested guidance on how to assess risks as required by section 314.4(b);[88] develop, implement and maintain safeguards as required by section 314.4(c);[89] and oversee service providers as required by section 314.4(d).

The Commission took comments respecting the Rule's impact on small entities into account by designing flexible safeguards standards (section 313.3(a)). Similarly, the Commission took smaller entities into account in allowing each financial institution to decide for itself what employees to designate to handle safeguards (section 314.4(a)), in order to give businesses, particularly smaller entities, flexibility in complying with the Rule. Lastly, because some commenters expressed concern about the ability of businesses—particularly smaller entities—to evaluate a service provider's capabilities,[90] the Commission amended the relevant paragraph to state that each financial institution must "take reasonable steps" to select and retain appropriate service providers.

In addition to the above changes, the Commission has taken into account those comments that stated the importance of educating businesses and others on how to implement and maintain information safeguards. The Commission agrees that such education is critical to achieving the Rule's objectives and to minimizing burdens on businesses. Thus, as stated in the Rule's preamble, the Commission plans to provide educational materials on or near the date on which compliance is required. As part of this effort, the Commission intends to perform outreach to inform small entities, such as individual tax preparers or other sole proprietors, of the Rule and its requirements.

In addition to the forthcoming educational materials, the Commission has given guidance in the Rule and its Preamble that is intended to assist businesses, particularly small entities, to comply with the Rule. Specifically, as discussed above, the Commission has included within the Rule a brief description of those areas of a business' operations that the Commission believes are most relevant to information security: (1) Employee training and management; (2) information systems, including network and software design, as well as information processing, storage, transmission and disposal; and (3) detecting, preventing and responding to attacks, intrusions, or other systems failures. *See* section 314.3(b).

3. Description and Estimate of the Number of Small Entities to Which the Rule Will Apply or an Explanation of Why No Such Estimate Is Available

As previously discussed in the IRFA accompanying the Proposed Rule, it is difficult to estimate accurately the number of small entities that are financial institutions subject to the Rule. The definition of "financial institution," as under the Privacy Rule, includes any institution the business of which is engaging in a financial activity, as described in section 4(k) of the Bank Holding Company Act, which incorporates by reference the activities listed in 12 CFR 225.28 and 12 CFR 211.5(d), consolidated in 12 CFR 225.86. *See* 65 FR 14433 (Mar. 17, 2000).

The G–L–B Act does not specify the categories of financial institutions subject to the Commission's jurisdiction; rather, section 505(a)(5) vests the Commission with enforcement authority with respect to "any other financial institution or other person that is not subject to the jurisdiction of any [other] agency or authority [charged with enforcing the statute]." Financial institutions covered by the Rule will include many of the same lenders, financial advisors, loan brokers and servicers, collection agencies, financial advisors, tax preparers, real estate settlement services, and others that are subject to the Privacy Rule. Many of these financial institutions will not be subject to the Safeguards Rule to the extent that they do not have any "customer information" within the meaning of the Safeguards Rule. The Commission did not receive comments that helped it to identify in any comprehensive manner the small entities that will be affected by the rule. However, one commenter, the National Association of Automobile Dealers Association ("NADA") submitted 1999 data showing that, at that time, 5,292 franchised new automobile dealers had 30 or fewer employees; 1,706 had 20 or fewer employees; and 575 had 10 or fewer employees.[91] In addition, the Commission is aware that many small businesses, such as individual tax preparers or mortgage brokers, will be covered by the Rule.

---

[85] FPA at 3; Paas at 2; *see also* OCUL (stating that the NCUA's safeguards rule is very burdensome for credit unions); Post at 1 (stating that Privacy Rule is very burdensome).

[86] *See supra* n. 81.

[87] *See, e.g.*, ICB at 2; Musgrove at 2; NADA at 2; NIADA at 9; Paas at 4–6.

[88] Paas at 3.

[89] *See* NIADA at 7; Paas at 4–5.

[90] Paas at 5; *see also* NRF at 5 (expressing concern that Rule could make financial institutions strictly liable for safeguards breaches by their service providers).

[91] NADA at 1.

4. Description of the Projected Reporting, Recordkeeping and Other Compliance Requirements of the Rule, Including an Estimate of the Classes of Small Entities That Will Be Subject to the Requirement and the Type of Professional Skills Necessary for Preparation of the Report or Record

As explained in the Commission's IRFA and the Paperwork Reduction Act discussion that appears elsewhere in this document, the Safeguards Rule does not impose any specific reporting or recordkeeping requirements. Accordingly, compliance with the Rule does not entail expenditures for particular types of professional skills that might be needed for the preparation of such reports or records.

The Rule, however, requires each covered institution to develop a written information security program covering customer information that is appropriate to its size and complexity, the nature and scope of its activities, and the sensitivity of the customer information at issue. The institution must designate an employee or employees to coordinate its safeguards, identify reasonably foreseeable risks and assess the effectiveness of any existing safeguards for controlling these risks; design and implement a safeguards program and regularly monitor its effectiveness; require service providers (by contract) to implement appropriate safeguards for the customer information at issue; and evaluate and adjust its program to material changes that may affect its safeguards, such as new or emerging threats to information security. As discussed above, these requirements will apply to institutions of all sizes that are subject to the FTC's jurisdiction pursuant to the Rule, including small entities, although the Commission did not receive comments that would enable a reliable estimate of the number of such small entities.

In light of concerns that compliance with these requirements might require the use of professional consulting skills that could be costly, the Commission, as explained in its IRFA, fashioned the Rule's requirements to be as flexible as possible consistent with the purposes of the G–L–B Act, so that entities subject to the Rule, including small entities, could simplify their information security program to the same extent that their overall operations are simplified. Furthermore, the Commission invited comments on the costs of establishing and operating an information security program for such entities, particularly any costs stemming from the proposed requirements to: (1) Regularly test or otherwise monitor the effectiveness of the safeguards' key controls, systems, and procedures, and (2) develop a comprehensive information security program in written form. In response to comments that raised concerns that many businesses would not possess the required resources or expertise to fulfill the Rule's requirements, the Commission notes that the Rule is not intended to require that entities hire outside experts or consultants in order to comply. Further, the Commission has noted that it intends to provide educational materials that will assist such entities in compliance. In addition, in response to concerns that the preparation of a written plan could be burdensome, the Commission amended this requirement slightly to emphasize the flexibility of the writing requirement and make clear that the writing need not be contained in a single document.

5. Description of the Steps the Agency Has Taken To Minimize the Significant Economic Impact on Small Entities, Consistent with the Stated Objectives of Applicable Statutes, Including a Statement of the Factual, Policy, and Legal Reasons for Selecting the Alternative Adopted in the Final Rule and Why Each of the Other Significant Alternatives to the Rule Considered by the Agency That Affect the Impact on Small Entities Was Rejected

The G–L–B Act requires the FTC to issue a rule that establishes standards for safeguarding customer information. The G–L–B Act requires that standards be developed for institutions of all sizes. Therefore, the Rule applies equally to entities with assets of $100 million or less, and not just to larger entities.

As previously noted, the Commission does not believe the Safeguards Rule imposes a significant economic impact on a substantial number of small entities. Nonetheless, to the extent that small entities are subject to the Rule, it imposes flexible standards that allow each institution to develop an information security program that is appropriate to its size and the nature of its operations. In this way, the impact of the Rule on small entities and any other entities subject to the Rule is no greater than necessary to effectuate the purposes and objectives of the G–L–B Act, which requires that the Commission adopt a rule specifying procedures sufficient to safeguard the privacy of customer information protected under the Act. To the extent that commenters suggested alternative regulatory approaches—such as that compliance with alternative standards be deemed compliance with the Rule—that could affect the Rule's impact on small entities, those comments and the Commission's responses are discussed above in the statement of basis and purpose for the Final Rule.

List of Subjects for 16 CFR Part 314

Consumer protection, Credit, Data protection, Privacy, Trade practices.

Final Rule

For the reasons set forth in the preamble, the Federal Trade Commission amends 16 CFR chapter I, subchapter C, by adding a new part 314 to read as follows:

PART 314—STANDARDS FOR SAFEGUARDING CUSTOMER INFORMATION

Sec.

314.1 Purpose and scope.
314.2 Definitions.
314.3 Standards for safeguarding customer information.
314.4 Elements.
314.5 Effective date.

Authority: 15 U.S.C. 6801(b), 6805(b)(2).

§ 314.1 Purpose and scope.

(a) *Purpose.* This part, which implements sections 501 and 505(b)(2) of the Gramm-Leach-Bliley Act, sets forth standards for developing, implementing, and maintaining reasonable administrative, technical, and physical safeguards to protect the security, confidentiality, and integrity of customer information.

(b) *Scope.* This part applies to the handling of customer information by all financial institutions over which the Federal Trade Commission ("FTC" or "Commission") has jurisdiction. This part refers to such entities as "you." This part applies to all customer information in your possession, regardless of whether such information pertains to individuals with whom you have a customer relationship, or pertains to the customers of other financial institutions that have provided such information to you.

§ 314.2 Definitions.

(a) *In general.* Except as modified by this part or unless the context otherwise requires, the terms used in this part have the same meaning as set forth in the Commission's rule governing the Privacy of Consumer Financial Information, 16 CFR part 313.

(b) *Customer information* means any record containing nonpublic personal information as defined in 16 CFR 313.3(n), about a customer of a financial institution, whether in paper, electronic, or other form, that is handled or maintained by or on behalf of you or your affiliates.

(c) *Information security program* means the administrative, technical, or physical safeguards you use to access, collect, distribute, process, protect, store, use, transmit, dispose of, or otherwise handle customer information.

(d) *Service provider* means any person or entity that receives, maintains, processes, or otherwise is permitted access to customer information through its provision of services directly to a financial institution that is subject to this part.

§ 314.3 Standards for safeguarding customer information.

(a) *Information security program.* You shall develop, implement, and maintain a comprehensive information security program that is written in one or more readily accessible parts and contains administrative, technical, and physical safeguards that are appropriate to your size and complexity, the nature and scope of your activities, and the sensitivity of any customer information at issue. Such safeguards shall include the elements set forth in § 314.4 and shall be reasonably designed to achieve the objectives of this part, as set forth in paragraph (b) of this section.

(b) *Objectives.* The objectives of section 501(b) of the Act, and of this part, are to:

(1) Insure the security and confidentiality of customer information;

(2) Protect against any anticipated threats or hazards to the security or integrity of such information; and

(3) Protect against unauthorized access to or use of such information that could result in substantial harm or inconvenience to any customer.

§ 314.4 Elements.

In order to develop, implement, and maintain your information security program, you shall:

(a) Designate an employee or employees to coordinate your information security program.

(b) Identify reasonably foreseeable internal and external risks to the security, confidentiality, and integrity of customer information that could result in the unauthorized disclosure, misuse, alteration, destruction or other compromise of such information, and assess the sufficiency of any safeguards in place to control these risks. At a minimum, such a risk assessment should include consideration of risks in each relevant area of your operations, including:

(1) Employee training and management;

(2) Information systems, including network and software design, as well as information processing, storage, transmission and disposal; and

(3) Detecting, preventing and responding to attacks, intrusions, or other systems failures.

(c) Design and implement information safeguards to control the risks you identify through risk assessment, and regularly test or otherwise monitor the effectiveness of the safeguards' key controls, systems, and procedures.

(d) Oversee service providers, by:

(1) Taking reasonable steps to select and retain service providers that are capable of maintaining appropriate safeguards for the customer information at issue; and

(2) Requiring your service providers by contract to implement and maintain such safeguards.

(e) Evaluate and adjust your information security program in light of the results of the testing and monitoring required by paragraph (c) of this section; any material changes to your operations or business arrangements; or any other circumstances that you know or have reason to know may have a material impact on your information security program.

§ 314.5 Effective date.

(a) Each financial institution subject to the Commission's jurisdiction must implement an information security program pursuant to this part no later than May 23, 2003.

(b) Two-year grandfathering of service contracts. Until May 24, 2004, a contract you have entered into with a nonaffiliated third party to perform services for you or functions on your behalf satisfies the provisions of § 314.4(d), even if the contract does not include a requirement that the service provider maintain appropriate safeguards, as long as you entered into the contract not later than June 24, 2002.

By direction of the Commission.

Donald S. Clark,

Secretary.

[FR Doc. 02–12952 Filed 5–22–02; 8:45 am]

BILLING CODE 6750–01–P

APPENDIX II

GRAMM-LEACH-BLILEY ACT—CONTENTS OF NOTICES

CONTENTS OF ALL NOTICES

(1) The categories of nonpublic personal information that you collect;

(2) The categories of nonpublic personal information that you disclose;

(3) The categories of affiliates and nonaffiliated third parties to whom you disclose NPI, other than those parties to excepted by GLB;

(4) The categories on NPI about your former customers that you disclose and the categories of affiliates and nonaffiliated third parties to whom you disclose NPI about your former customers, other than those parties to whom you disclose information that are excepted by GLB;

(5) If you disclose NPI to a nonaffiliated third party with whom you engage in joint marketing or services where GLB excepts opt out (and no other exception applies under GLB) a separate statement of the categories of information you disclose and the categories of third parties with whom you have contracted;

(6) An explanation of the consumer's right to opt out of the disclosure of NPI to nonaffiliated third parties, including the method(s) by which the consumer may exercise that right at that time;

(7) Any disclosures that you make under section 603(d)(2)(A)(iii) of the Fair Credit Reporting Act (15 U.S.C. 1681a(d)(2)(A)(iii)) (that is, notices regarding the ability to opt out of disclosures of information among affiliates);

(8) Your policies and practices with respect to protecting the confidentiality and security of NPI; and

(9) If you make disclosures to nonaffiliated third parties subject to exceptions, you must state that you disclose NPI to third parties as authorized under law, but you do not have to describe the exceptions.

APPENDIX III

GRAMM-LEACH-BLILEY ACT—SAMPLE CLAUSES—FEDERAL TRADE COMMISSION

16 C.F.R. Pt. 313, App. A

CODE OF FEDERAL REGULATIONS
TITLE 16—COMMERICAL PRACTICES
CHAPTER I—FEDERAL TRADE COMMISSION
SUBCHAPTER C—REGULATIONS UNDER SPECIFIC ACTS OF CONGRESS
PART 313—PRIVACY OF CONSUMER FINANCIAL INFORMATION

Appendix A to Part 313—Sample Clauses

Financial institutions, including a group of financial holding company affiliates that use a common privacy notice, may use the following sample clauses, if the clause is accurate for each institution that uses the notice. (Note that disclosure of certain information, such as assets and income, and information from a consumer reporting agency, may give rise to obligations under the Fair Credit Reporting Act, such as a requirement to permit a consumer to opt out of disclosures to affiliates or designation as a consumer reporting agency if disclosures are made to nonaffiliated third parties.)

A-1—CATEGORIES OF INFORMATION YOU COLLECT (ALL INSTITUTIONS)

You may use this clause, as applicable, to meet the requirement of § 313.6(a)(1) to describe the categories of nonpublic personal information you collect.

Sample Clause A-1

We collect nonpublic personal information about you from the following sources:

- Information we receive from you on applications or other forms;

- Information about your transactions with us, our affiliates, or others; and
- Information we receive from a consumer reporting agency.

A-2—CATEGORIES OF INFORMATION YOU DISCLOSE (INSTITUTIONS THAT DISCLOSE OUTSIDE OF THE EXCEPTIONS)

You may use one of these clauses, as applicable, to meet the requirement of § 313.6(a)(2) to describe the categories of nonpublic personal information you disclose. You may use these clauses if you disclose nonpublic personal information other than as permitted by the exceptions in §§ 313.13, 313.14, and 313.15.

Sample Clause A-2, Alternative 1

We may disclose the following kinds of nonpublic personal information about you:

- Information we receive from you on applications or other forms, such as [provide illustrative examples, such as "your name, address, social security number, assets, and income"];
- Information about your transactions with us, our affiliates, or others, such as [provide illustrative examples, such as "your account balance, payment history, parties to transactions, and credit card usage"]; and
- Information we receive from a consumer reporting agency, such as [provide illustrative examples, such as "your creditworthiness and credit history"].

Sample Clause A-2, Alternative 2

We may disclose all of the information that we collect, as described [describe location in the notice, such as "above" or "below"].

A-3—CATEGORIES OF INFORMATION YOU DISCLOSE AND PARTIES TO WHOM YOU DISCLOSE (INSTITUTIONS THAT DO NOT DISCLOSE OUTSIDE OF THE EXCEPTIONS)

You may use this clause, as applicable, to meet the requirements of §§ 313.6(a)(2), (3), and (4) to describe the categories of nonpublic personal information about customers and former customers that you disclose and the categories of affiliates and nonaffiliated third parties to whom you disclose. You may use this clause if you do not disclose nonpublic personal information to any party, other than as permitted by the exceptions in §§ 313.14 and 313.15.

Sample Clause A-3

We do not disclose any nonpublic personal information about our customers or former customers to anyone, except as permitted by law.

A-4—CATEGORIES OF PARTIES TO WHOM YOU DISCLOSE (INSTITUTIONS THAT DISCLOSE OUTSIDE OF THE EXCEPTIONS)

You may use this clause, as applicable, to meet the requirement of § 313.6(a)(3) to describe the categories of affiliates and nonaffiliated third parties to whom you disclose nonpublic personal information. You may use this clause if you disclose nonpublic personal information other than as permitted by the exceptions in §§ 313.13, 313.14, and 313.15, as well as when permitted by the exceptions in §§ 313.14 and 313.15.

Sample Clause A-4

We may disclose nonpublic personal information about you to the following types of third parties:

- Financial service providers, such as [provide illustrative examples, such as "mortgage bankers, securities broker-dealers, and insurance agents"];
- Non-financial companies, such as [provide illustrative examples, such as "retailers, direct marketers, airlines, and publishers"]; and
- Others, such as [provide illustrative examples, such as "non-profit organizations"].

We may also disclose nonpublic personal information about you to non-affiliated third parties as permitted by law.

A-5—SERVICE PROVIDER/JOINT MARKETING EXCEPTION

You may use one of these clauses, as applicable, to meet the requirements of § 313.6(a)(5) related to the exception for service providers and joint marketers in § 313.13. If you disclose nonpublic personal information under this exception, you must describe the categories of nonpublic personal information you disclose and the categories of third parties with whom you have contracted.

Sample Clause A-5, Alternative 1

We may disclose the following information to companies that perform marketing services on our behalf or to other financial institutions with whom we have joint marketing agreements:

- Information we receive from you on applications or other forms, such as [provide illustrative examples, such as "your name, address, social security number, assets, and income"];
- Information about your transactions with us, our affiliates, or others, such as [provide illustrative examples, such as "your account balance, payment history, parties to transactions, and credit card usage"]; and
- Information we receive from a consumer reporting agency, such as [provide illustrative examples, such as "your creditworthiness and credit history"].

Sample Clause A-5, Alternative 2

We may disclose all of the information we collect, as described [describe location in the notice, such as "above" or "below"] to companies that perform marketing services on our behalf or to other financial institutions with whom we have joint marketing agreements.

A-6—EXPLANATION OF OPT OUT RIGHT (INSTITUTIONS THAT DISCLOSE OUTSIDE OF THE EXCEPTIONS)

You may use this clause, as applicable, to meet the requirement of § 313.6(a)(6) to provide an explanation of the consumer's right to opt out of the disclosure of nonpublic personal information to nonaffiliated third parties, including the method(s) by which the consumer may exercise that right. You may use this clause if you disclose nonpublic personal information other than as permitted by the exceptions in §§ 313.13, 313.14, and 313.15.

Sample Clause A-6

If you prefer that we not disclose nonpublic personal information about you to nonaffiliated third parties, you may opt out of those disclosures, that is, you may direct us not to make those disclosures (other than disclosures permitted by law). If you wish to opt out of disclosures to nonaffiliated third parties, you may [describe a reasonable means of opting out, such as "call the following toll-free number: (insert number)"].

A-7—CONFIDENTIALITY AND SECURITY (ALL INSTITUTIONS)

You may use this clause, as applicable, to meet the requirement of § 313.6(a)(8) to describe your policies and practices with respect to protecting the confidentiality and security of nonpublic personal information.

Sample Clause A-7

We restrict access to nonpublic personal information about you to [provide an appropriate description, such as "those employees who need to know that information to provide products or services to you"]. We maintain physical, electronic, and procedural safeguards that comply with federal regulations to guard your nonpublic personal information.

APPENDIX IV

MODIFICATION OF LAW—PERSONAL INFORMATION AND IDENTITY THEFT—MASSACHUSETTS

201 CMR: OFFICE OF CONSUMER AFFAIRS AND BUSINESS REGULATION

201 CMR 17.00: STANDARDS FOR THE PROTECTION OF PERSONAL INFORMATION OF RESIDENTS OF THE COMMONWEALTH

Section

17.01: Purpose and Scope

(1) Purpose. 201 CMR 17.00 implements the provisions of M.G.L. c. 93H relative to the standards to be met by persons who own, license, store or maintain personal information about a resident of the Commonwealth of Massachusetts. 201 CMR 17.00 establishes minimum standards to be met in connection with the safeguarding of personal information contained in both paper and electronic records. Further purposes are to:

(a) ensure the security and confidentiality of such information in a manner consistent with industry standards;

(b) protect against anticipated threats or hazards to the security or integrity of such information; and

(c) protect against unauthorized access to or use of such information in a manner that creates a substantial risk of identity theft or fraud against such residents.

(2) Scope. The provisions of 201 CMR 17.00 applies to all persons who own, license, store or maintain personal information about a resident of the Commonwealth.

17.02: Definitions

The following words as used in 201 CMR 17.00 shall, unless the context requires otherwise, have the following meanings:

Breach of Security, the unauthorized acquisition or unauthorized use of unencrypted data or, encrypted electronic data and the confidential process or key that is capable of compromising the security, confidentiality, or integrity of personal information, maintained by a person or agency that creates a substantial risk of identity theft or fraud against a resident of the commonwealth. A good faith but unauthorized acquisition of personal information by a person or agency, or employee or agent thereof, for the lawful purposes of such person or agency, is not a breach of security unless the personal information is used in an unauthorized manner or subject to further unauthorized disclosure.

Electronic, relating to technology having electrical, digital, magnetic, wireless, optical, electromagnetic or similar capabilities.

Encrypted, the transformation of data through the use of an algorithmic process, or an alternative method at least as secure, into a form in which meaning cannot be assigned without the use of a confidential process or key, unless further defined by regulation by the Office of Consumer Affairs and Business Regulation.

Person, a natural person, corporation, association, partnership or other legal entity, other than an agency, executive office, department, board, commission, bureau, division or authority of the Commonwealth, or any of its branches, or any political subdivision thereof.

Personal Information, a Massachusetts resident's first name and last name or first initial and last name in combination with any one or more of the following data elements that relate to such resident:

(a) Social Security number;

(b) driver's license number or state-issued identification card number; or

201 CMR: OFFICE OF CONSUMER AFFAIRS AND BUSINESS REGULATION

17.02: continued

(c) financial account number, or credit or debit card number, with or without any required security code, access code, personal identification number or password, that would permit access to a resident's financial account; provided, however, that Personal Information shall not include information that is lawfully obtained from publicly available information, or from federal, state or local government records lawfully made available to the general public.

Record or Records, any material upon which written, drawn, spoken, visual, or electromagnetic information or images are recorded or preserved, regardless of physical form or characteristics.

17.03: Duty to Protect and Standards for Protecting Personal Information

(1) Every person who owns, licenses, stores or maintains personal information about a resident of the Commonwealth shall develop, implement, maintain and monitor a comprehensive, written information security program applicable to any records containing such personal information. Such comprehensive information security program shall be reasonably consistent with industry standards, and shall contain administrative, technical, and physical safeguards to ensure the security and confidentiality of such records. Moreover, the safeguards contained in such program must be consistent with the safeguards for protection of personal information and information of a similar character set forth in any state or federal regulations by which the person who owns, licenses, stores or maintains such information may be regulated.

(2) Whether the comprehensive information security program is in compliance with 201 CMR 17.00 for the protection of personal information, whether pursuant to 201 CMR 17.03 or 17.04, shall be evaluated taking into account:

(a) the size, scope and type of business of the person obligated to safeguard the personal information under such comprehensive information security program;
(b) the amount of resources available to such person;
(c) the amount of stored data; and
(d) the need for security and confidentiality of both consumer and employee information.

(3) Without limiting the generality of the foregoing, every comprehensive information security program shall include, but not be limited to:

(a) Designating one or more employees to maintain the comprehensive information security program;
(b) Identifying and assessing reasonably foreseeable internal and external risks to the security, confidentiality, and/or integrity of any electronic, paper or other records containing personal information, and evaluating and improving, where necessary, the effectiveness of the current safeguards for limiting such risks, including but not limited to:
1. ongoing employee (including temporary and contract employee) training;
2. employee compliance with policies and procedures; and
3. means for detecting and preventing security system failures.
(c) Developing security policies for employees that take into account whether and how employees should be allowed to keep, access and transport records containing personal information outside of business premises.
(d) Imposing disciplinary measures for violations of the comprehensive information security program rules.
(e) Preventing terminated employees from accessing records containing personal information by immediately terminating their physical and electronic access to such records, including deactivating their passwords and user names.
(f) Taking all reasonable steps to verify that any third-party service provider with access to personal information has the capacity to protect such personal information in the manner provided for in 201 CMR 17.00; and taking all reasonable steps to ensure that such third party service provider is applying to such personal information protective security measures at least as stringent as those required to be applied to personal information under 201 CMR 17.00.

17.03: continued

(g) Limiting the amount of personal information collected to that reasonably necessary to accomplish the legitimate purpose for which it is collected; limiting the time such information is retained to that reasonably necessary to accomplish such purpose; and limiting access to those persons who are reasonably required to know such information in order to accomplish such purpose or to comply with state or federal record retention requirements.
(h) Identifying paper, electronic and other records, computing systems, and storage media, including laptops and portable devices used to store personal information, to determine which records contain personal information, except where the comprehensive information security program provides for the handling of all records as if they all contained personal information.
(i) Reasonable restrictions upon physical access to records containing personal information, including a written procedure that sets forth the manner in which physical access to such records is restricted; and storage of such records and data in locked facilities, storage areas or containers.
(j) Regular monitoring to ensure that the comprehensive information security program is operating in a manner reasonably calculated to prevent unauthorized access to or unauthorized use of personal information; and upgrading information safeguards as necessary to limit risks.
(k) Reviewing the scope of the security measures at least annually or whenever there is a material change in business practices that may reasonably implicate the security or integrity of records containing personal information.
(l) Documenting responsive actions taken in connection with any incident involving a breach of security, and mandatory post-incident review of events and actions taken, if any, to make changes in business practices relating to protection of personal information.

17.04: Computer System Security Requirements

Every person who owns, licenses, stores or maintains personal information about a resident of the Commonwealth and electronically stores or transmits such information shall include in its written, comprehensive information security program the establishment and maintenance of a security system covering its computers, including any wireless system, that, at a minimum, shall have the following elements:

(1) Secure user authentication protocols including:
(a) control of user IDs and other identifiers;
(b) a reasonably secure method of assigning and selecting passwords, or use of unique identifier technologies, such as biometrics or token devices;
(c) control of data security passwords to ensure that such passwords are kept in a location and/or format that does not compromise the security of the data they protect;
(d) restricting access to active users and active user accounts only; and
(e) blocking access to user identification after multiple unsuccessful attempts to gain access or the limitation placed on access for the particular system;

(2) Secure access control measures that:
(a) restrict access to records and files containing personal information to those who need such information to perform their job duties; and
(b) assign unique identifications plus passwords, which are not vendor supplied default passwords, to each person with computer access, that are reasonably designed to maintain the integrity of the security of the access controls;

(3) To the extent technically feasible, encryption of all transmitted records and files containing personal information that will travel across public networks, and encryption of all data containing personal information to be transmitted wirelessly.

(4) Reasonable monitoring of systems, for unauthorized use of or access to personal information;

17.04: continued

(5) Encryption of all personal information stored on laptops or other portable devices;

(6) For files containing personal information on a system that is connected to the Internet, there must be reasonably up-to-date firewall protection and operating system security patches, reasonably designed to maintain the integrity of the personal information.

(7) Reasonably up-to-date versions of system security agent software which must include malware protection and reasonably up-to-date patches and virus definitions, or a version of such software that can still be supported with up-to-date patches and virus definitions, and is set to receive the most current security updates on a regular basis.

(8) Education and training of employees on the proper use of the computer security system and the importance of personal information security.

17.05: Compliance Deadline

Every person who owns, licenses, stores or maintains personal information about a resident of the Commonwealth shall, unless otherwise expressly provided in 201 CMR 17.00, be in full compliance with 201 CMR 17.00 on or before January 1, 2010.

REGULATORY AUTHORITY

201 CMR 17.00: M.G.L. c. 93H.

CHAPTER 10

Secured Lending: Real Estate—Mortgages

New York State law will be utilized primarily in this chapter since that is where we primarily practice. The principles enunciated are substantially similar in most other states, but review of the law where the property is located is *absolutely necessary* since some states are title states as opposed to mortgage states. Despite a few decisions to the contrary, lawyers who engage regularly in foreclosure practice are construed to be debt collectors and subject to the Fair Debt Collection Practices Act.[1]

MORTGAGES

In most states a mortgage is a lien on real estate, land and/or building, furnished by one party to another party to be used as security for the repayment of money. The mortgagee (the lending institution) holds a mortgage lien on the property, but does not own the property nor does the mortgagee have any right to possession of the property until such time as the mortgage is foreclosed and sold at a foreclosure sale to the mortgagee. In some states, the borrower transfers the property in trust to the lender, and the instrument is designated a *deed of trust.* In title states, a mortgage is executed in favor of the lending party, creating a lien on the property while the title remains with the mortgagor. The differences

[1] *Blum v. Fisher & Fisher, P.C.*, 961 F. Supp. 1218 (N.D. Ill. 1997).

between a "deed of trust" and a "mortgage" are not significant. For our purposes we will consider only the mortgage.

A mortgage is treated as a conveyance of property and, as such, it must meet the criteria set forth in the Statute of Frauds (the state laws requiring certain transactions to be in writing to be enforceable). A mortgage must be in writing and must be signed by the mortgagor or his/her agent, acting pursuant to written authority. A mortgage recites the amount of the indebtedness for which the property is being offered as security, a detailed description of the property, usually by a "metes and bounds" description (describing the property by terminal points, angles, distances, and compass directions), and the terms and conditions under which the parties are to operate under the terms of the mortgage. The mortgage also recites the obligation of the mortgagor (debtor) to pay the mortgage, the taxes and other charges against the property, as well as to maintain the property, and its operation. In addition, the mortgage recites the rights of the mortgagee (lending institution), including the right to act in the event of a default, the right to take possession of the property upon default, the right to make an application to the court for the appointment of a receiver (one who preserves the property during a foreclosure proceeding), and the right to pay taxes and insurance for the benefit of the mortgagor and to operate the property in the event of a foreclosure.

A "mortgage note" or bond is a separate instrument and is essential to enforce the mortgage. The note recites the indebtedness, the terms of payment, the interest rate, the place of payment, and the terms and conditions under which the note must be paid. If the terms of the note and the mortgage conflict, the terms of the note control. A mortgage without a note may be unenforceable unless it is a collateral mortgage with a separate collateral agreement.

A statute of limitations may affect the note and destroys any judicial remedy, but does not bar a mortgage foreclosure because the statute does not destroy the debt, but merely bars the remedy. As a result mortgage foreclosure actions are not barred by the statute of limitations.[2]

PURCHASE MONEY MORTGAGE

"A purchase money mortgage" is usually a loan advance that is allied with the debtor's purchase of the collateral. This may apply both to a motor vehicle, cattle, other personal property or to real estate. The timing of the loan does not necessarily determine whether the creditor receives a purchase money security interest in the collateral. *The key consideration is whether the loan enabled the debtor to acquire an interest in the collateral whether real estate or personal property.*

---

[2]*Federal Deposit Ins. Corp. v. Owen*, 88 Conn. App. 806 (App. Ct. Conn. 2005).

In one situation the time period ranged from the day that a borrower received the cattle until 18 days after receiving the cattle before the purchaser signed a loan certificate. The loans were closely allied to the purchase transaction and were deemed a purchase money mortgage. UCC 9-103 does not contain a requirement that the debtor receive the loan proceeds before purchasing the collateral. "Rather the key consideration is whether the loan enables the debtor to acquire rights in the collateral."

Subject to other requirements under UCC 9, a purchase money mortgage where the loan is used to purchase real estate or goods that secure the advance made by the lender, enables the lender to assert priority over other conflicting security interests. The priority also extends to the proceeds of the sale of the said collateral.[3]

RECORDING

Mortgages usually are recorded after execution in the Office of the County Clerk, the register, the recorder of deeds, or a similar county office where the property is located. The recording of the mortgage acts as constructive notice to the entire world that the owner has a lien on the property. The owner of the property may execute a number of mortgages whose priority is established by chronological date when the mortgage is recorded in the county clerk's office. The date of the recording establishes priority, with the mortgage first recorded having priority over a mortgage or lien recorded after that date. A mortgage recorded on January 1, 2003 would be subordinate to a mortgage recorded on January 1, 2002. Thus, the importance of filing the mortgage instrument immediately is paramount. At the time of the mortgage closing, the mortgage is immediately delivered to a representative of the title company or attorney who, either on the same day or the next day, will deliver it to the proper office for recording.

TITLE SEARCH

After the mortgage commitment is delivered, but before the mortgage documents are executed, a title search is conducted, either by a title company or by an attorney, depending upon the state. A title search is a summary of the "chain of title" (transfer of property from one person to another), as well as liens, taxes, mortgages, and covenants (agreements restricting or affecting use) that affect the property, listed in chronological order. The purpose of the title search is to determine that the seller has good

---

[3]*First National Bank in Munday v. Lubbock Feeders L.P.*, 183 S.W.3d 875 (Tex. Ct. App.—Eastland 2006).

title to sell, the number of liens against the property, the number of claims against the property, and whether the property is encumbered by any restrictions in prior deeds. The title search will reveal prior mortgages that the debtor has executed. The date of the mortgage and the original amount of the mortgage will be revealed, but the present balance due will not be disclosed by a title search; for this information, contacting the mortgagee (usually the bank) is necessary.

The title search reveals whether the debtor has paid the taxes and whether any taxes are unpaid and open. Unpaid taxes become liens against the property after a certain period of time, depending upon the state or county. Once this happens, the lien becomes the equivalent of a mortgage in the same manner as the mortgage becomes a lien against the property. Judgment liens, mechanics' liens, bankruptcies, UCC financing statements that affect real property and other encumbrances will also appear in the search, since these parties may be made a party to the action.

In addition to determining the number of claims against the property, the lender also wants to determine whether the owner has a clear title to the property as described in the mortgage. Prior deeds may have been recorded which set forth restrictive covenants, restrictions, or easements on the property. An easement is a right of an adjourning property owner to pass over the property of the debtor under certain terms and conditions, or to have a right of way over the property either by use of a road or pathway or even the use of the property itself. Covenants which pass with the land may affect the use of the land, the type of buildings which may be built on the land, or other restrictions as to use of the land, which may have been set forth by the prior owner of the property (such as limiting housing to one-family homes, restrictions on height of building, or use as a slaughterhouse). The lender will have to make a decision on whether the particular covenant or easement affects the value of the property sufficiently to refuse to extend credit. Toxic waste and environmental considerations may also be indirectly revealed by title searches when, for example, a prior owner was a gas station or chemical plant.

ASSIGNMENT OF MORTGAGE

A mortgage and note may be transferred from one lending institution to another by use of an assignment: an agreement between two parties transferring the ownership of a mortgage and note from one mortgagee to a new mortgagee. The assignment of mortgage identifies the mortgage and the property covered under the mortgage as well as the name and address of the mortgagor and enough information to leave no doubt as to which mortgage is being assigned. The assignment is recorded in the same manner as a mortgage by filing the assignment in the county where the property is located.

The purchaser of a mortgage by assignment takes the assignment subject to any existing defenses or claims in favor of the mortgagor. In some instances, the mortgagor will execute an "estoppel certificate" which asserts that the mortgagor has no defense or offsets to the mortgage.

FORBEARANCE AGREEMENT

A forbearance agreement is often utilized to settle a foreclosure action. While variations from state to state control the procedure of the foreclosure, certain elements of the forbearance agreement are unique to the foreclosure action.

A forbearance agreement constitutes a settlement of the foreclosure action. Such agreement terminates all the claims of the parties made in the action and the agreement becomes enforceable as a contract binding on all parties. The foreclosure action remains pending during the life of the forbearance agreement. While the foreclosure action remains dormant, the forbearance agreement settles the matter.

New York requires the forbearance agreement to be filed with the court. While it may, by its terms, relieve the foreclosing party of notifying or reserving the borrower to reinstate the foreclosure proceeding, in New York the foreclosing party must notify the court that the settlement is recorded.

A New York case made several suggestions with regard to the contents of a forbearance agreement which might be applicable in other states. The following were suggested:

1. The foreclosure action will not be terminated or cancelled, but will be postponed provided no default occurs under the agreement.
2. If you fail to comply with each and all of the terms and conditions of the agreement, the agreement may terminate immediately and automatically without further notice to you and the forbearance agreement shall be of no further force and affect. All amounts that are owing under your loan shall become immediately due and payable.
3. If a default occurs in the forbearance agreement, the foreclosing party may commence foreclosure proceedings or continue an existing foreclosure action, as the case may be, or take such other action as is permitted by law.
4. The acceptance of any payments from you which, individually or collectively, are less than the total amount due to payoff your loan shall in no way prevent the foreclosing party from commencing a new foreclosure action or continuing with a foreclosure action or require the foreclosing party to notify you of your default, reaccelerate your loan or issue any notice or recommence any process prior to proceeding with the foreclosure action.

The lender must recognize that a provision in the forbearance agreement concerning waiver of notice by the borrower may not be upheld in many states and that it should be drafted carefully in accordance with case law in the particular state.

The above are merely suggestions of certain clauses that may be appropriate to add to a forbearance agreement providing a state law does not prohibit the clause or a waiver of a right.[4]

JUDGMENT

A judgment creditor who has entered a judgment against the mortgagor and docketed (filed) the judgment with the county clerk where the property is located (*see* Chapter 1) has the same rights as a mortgagee and will have priority over any subsequent mortgages or liens, whether or not they are recorded. The docketing of the judgment in the county clerk's office where the debtor resides is important, but the creditor may not know where property owned by the debtor is located. Sometimes the debtor cannot be located, and the creditor will docket the judgment with the county clerks of several surrounding counties. The law as to the reach of a docketed (filed) judgment varies from state to state. In certain states the judgment lien covers the whole state and when the debtor attempts to sell a residence, the docketed judgment appears in the title search conducted by the buyer. Any purchaser of the property will usually require that the judgment be satisfied. If the judgment is not satisfied, it remains a lien on the property. Consult with counsel.

SALE BY MORTGAGOR

When a mortgagor sells the property to a new owner, the new owner must purchase the property subject to the terms of the mortgage. The original owner of the property remains liable on the mortgage. The new owner will usually agree to assume the payment of the mortgage, and in that instance the new owner becomes the primary obligor and the original owner of the property is liable secondarily.

When interest rates were high, banks provided that any transfer of property matured the mortgage so that the new owner would have to pay the mortgage and obtain a new mortgage at a higher interest rate (or modify the existing mortgage at a higher interest rate). In today's interest market, the acceleration clause, known as "due on sale," is less frequently used.

---

[4] *Deutsche Bank Nat'l Trust Co. v. Williams*, 842 N.Y.S.2d 338 (N.Y. Sup. Ct. 2007).

MORTGAGOR'S OBLIGATIONS

The mortgagor has an obligation not to impair the value of the property during the term of the mortgage and, in general, to maintain the property. However, in many cases, the mortgagor does not maintain and repair the property during foreclosure proceedings. Often, by the time the foreclosure is completed, the amount of money necessary to repair the home or building may be substantial.

USURY

Usury is a defense available to the mortgagor in a foreclosure action. Usury is the charging of interest in excess of that allowed by law. The penalties for usury will vary from the loss of the interest to the loss of the principal in some states. In a few states, usury is a criminal offense (*see* Chapter 8).

FUTURE ADVANCES

A mortgage may be used to secure future advances of money. Such a mortgage is valid and may be enforced according to its terms. A mortgage also may be used to secure the debts of another party or to secure a guarantee of another party.

EQUITABLE MORTGAGE

If a security transaction concerning real property does not satisfy the formal requirement of a mortgage (such as not being in writing or not being a proper mortgage or deed in trust), "an equitable mortgage" may be created. An equitable mortgage may or may not have rights with regard to the property, depending upon the circumstances and conditions prevailing at the time it was created, and depending upon the intent of the parties. If the written instrument lacks the essential features of a mortgage, the courts may find that an equitable mortgage exists when the circumstances and other transactions reflect the intent of the parties to create a mortgage.

REAL ESTATE SETTLEMENT PROCEDURES ACT

The Real Estate Settlement Procedures Act, commonly referred to as RESPA, became effective June 20, 1975, to provide consumers with more information as to the settlement costs when purchasing or transferring a residence as a result of a loan from a bank and, at the same time, to prohibit excessive settlement charges. Regulation X defined the settlement process of a transfer of a residential home from one consumer to another.

The law was amended the same year it took effect (1975), in response to an enormous number of complaints about the vague and inflexible provisions causing significant delays in the settlement procedure. Regulation X was modified substantially as to the restrictions on the closing process, but the provisions affecting abusive settlement charges were not altered. The amendment took effect January 2, 1976.

RESPA covers the normal real estate transaction involving a federal mortgage loan. The federal mortgage loan covers almost all mortgage loans since not only are loans from federal agencies covered but also any loan from a bank which is insured by the Federal Deposit Insurance Corporation (FDIC) or the Federal Savings and Loan Insurance Corporation.[5] The loan must be secured by a first lien on the residence, and must be used to finance the purchase or transfer of the residence.[6] A home improvement loan, construction loan, permanent loan, or refinancing made after the acquisition of the property is not covered by the Act.[7]

Not later than three days after the lender receives an application for credit from a consumer, the lender must furnish to the consumer a Special Information Booklet[8] prepared by the Housing and Urban Development Corporation (HUD). It sets forth the consumer's rights and obligations when the consumer is obtaining a mortgage loan from a bank.

The lending bank at this point must provide a "good faith estimate" of the charges that will be incurred by the consumer, based on the bank's past experience, who the providers of the services are if the bank requires these providers (such as law firms, title companies), the fact that the estimate is based on the charges of the provider of the service, and the business relationship between the provider and the bank.

The charges for which a "good faith estimate" must be furnished include fees for origination, appraisal, inspection, insurance premium, title search, attorney, recording, transfer tax, and others set forth in the regulation.[9]

At the closing, HUD Form 1 must be used by the attorney, title company or other person conducting the closing process. This statement recites a summary of the transaction, including the price, taxes, deposit, adjustments in price, payments, advances, reserves, charges for services, recording and transfer fees, and a detailed breakdown of exactly what took place at the closing.

---

[5]Reg. X. Sec. 3500.5(c)(1).
[6]Reg. X. Sec. 3500.5(b)(2).
[7]Reg. X. Sec. 3500.5(d)(2)(5).
[8]Reg. X. Sec. 3500.6.
[9]Reg. X. Sec. 3500.7(c).

YIELD SPREAD PREMIUMS

The Real Estate Settlement Procedures Act of 1974 (RESPA) prohibits the payment to a mortgage broker of kickbacks for referral of prospects to lenders seeking a federally backed mortgage.

Section 8 of RESPA prohibits:

> any person from giving and any person from accepting any fee, kickback, or other thing of value pursuant to any agreement or understanding that business shall be referred to any person.

The law does provide for an exemption if the payments are compensation for goods or facilities actually furnished or for services actually performed. The test set by HUD (Department of Housing and Urban Development) on March 1, 1999 basically consists of a two-pronged criteria:

> Were the goods or facilities actually furnished or services actually performed for the total compensation and if they were actually performed, were they reasonably related to the value of the goods and services or facilities furnished.

About two years prior to the issuance of the March 1, 1999 policy statement, the leading case on the subject set forth slightly different criteria to determine a violation.[10] In the *Culpepper* case, if the fee is tied to the goods, facilities, or services purchased and only after it passes this test, may you determine if the amount is reasonable.

In the *Culpepper* decision the broker was paid for an above par loan and it was held that the yield spread premium did not constitute a reasonable payment for goods or for services and did not fall within any of the exceptions. The court felt that the broker spent the same amount of time and the same quality and quantity of services whether it originated an above-par loan, a par loan, or below-par loan, and was only paid the additional fee when they generated an above-par loan. On a motion for a rehearing before the Eleventh Circuit, the Circuit Court of Appeals left open the fact that a lender might prove as a defense that a yield spread premium may be a legitimate payment for brokerage services. The court flatly rejected that a yield spread premium is illegal per se.

This test was set forth in the lower court and then the Eleventh Circuit vacated the lower court's denial of the class action claims and the motion for class certification and also decided to apply the HUD test. The case was remanded back to the district court. Several other cases in Alabama, Minnesota, and New York have also dealt with this particular problem.

---

[10] *Culpepper v. Inland Mortgage Co.*, 132 F.3d 692 (11th Cir. 1998).

Prior to the issuance of the HUD Policy Statement in March 1999, the minority of the courts applied the test used in *Culpepper,* while the majority of courts leaned toward the test which ultimately became the policy statement of HUD. The core of the policy statement is as follows:

A. Goods or facilities must actually be furnished or services actually performed for the total compensation paid.
B. The total compensation must be reasonably related to the value of the goods or facilities that were actually furnished or services that were actually performed.

So long as the total compensation is justified, it is irrelevant whether all or part of the compensation is calculated with reference to the interest rate and whether the components are paid entirely by the borrower, entirely by the lender, or partially by the lender and partially by the borrower. The HUD policy statement adopts the Independent Banker's Association of America letter in restating the list of 14 services that must be performed by a mortgage broker in connection with the origination of the loan. Sufficient origination work must be performed and at least five additional services identified. The reasonableness of the compensation uses a market value test in the policy statement. Payments to the broker must be no greater than the amount normally charged for similar services, goods, or facilities.

The violation causing the most litigation is the situation where a mortgage broker refers a prospect and earns a fee if the rate of interest is higher than the lender required (yield spread premium). This additional fee is paid because the rate of interest that the borrower is paying is higher than the rate of interest that the lender advised the broker would be the minimum required. Whether the fee falls within the *Culpepper* test or the HUD test is still an open question, depending upon the facts and circumstances of each particular case. At the time of this writing, it still has not been resolved. Up to this point, the courts have interpreted the statute with a narrow approach. Whether added fees are illegal kickbacks or whether they are connected to the volume or the value of the business referred is still an open issue.[11]

The Ninth Circuit added their voice to the issue of a yield spread premium. The yield spread premium is calculated by the extent to which the borrower's interest rate is above what the lender sought. Sometimes it will be what the broker's services are worth, but only by chance. Unfortunately, the yield spread premium does not measure the value of the services.

---

[11]*McCrillis v. WMC Mortg. Corp.,* 133 F. Supp. 2d 470 (S.D. Miss. 2000); *Dujanovic v. MortgageAmerica, Inc.,* 185 F.R.D. 660 (N.D. Ala. 1999); *Golon v. Ohio Sav. Bank,* 1999 WL 965593 (N.D. Ill. Mar. 26, 1999); *Schmitz v. Aegis Mortgage Corp.,* 48 F. Supp. 2d 877 (D. Minn. 1999); *Brancheau v. Residential Mortg.,* 187 F.R.D. 591 (D. Minn. 1999).

The higher the interest rate the broker's client pays, the bigger the yield spread premium.

Congress prohibited kickbacks whether or not it was good economics. The Ninth Circuit decided that deference is due to the HUD policy statements. The HUD test focuses on whether compensation is reasonably related to the services provided and this is consistent with the general attempt of Congress in enacting RESPA to foster home ownership. The HUD statement is construed as prohibiting payments for nothing other than the referral of business.

Section 8(b) of the HUD policy statement prohibits any fee in excess of the reasonable value of goods and services provided or the services actually performed. The Ninth Circuit emphasized that the total compensation, which includes the fees paid by the borrower and any yield spread premium paid by the lender, must be reasonable. Total compensation to the broker must be reasonably related to the total value of goods or facilities provided or services performed. Payments must be commensurate with the amount normally charged for similar services in similar transactions in similar markets.[12]

Several other cases have been decided with regard to overcharges that did not involve the third-party fee splitting element of RESPA. So far, the courts seem to be in agreement that overcharges that are not brought about by fee splitting are not a prohibitive practice.

The Chicago Title Company collected fees from plaintiff in its capacity as a title company and retained the overcharges in that same capacity. The court acknowledged unearned fees were a windfall, but did not violate RESPA Section 8(b). The court did not recognize the County Recorder as a third party for the purposes of RESPA Section 8(b) because there was no involvement in the unearned fees.

The plain language of Section 8(b) does not apply to every overcharge for a real estate settlement service. Section 8(b) is not a broad price control provision. It only prohibits overcharges when a portion or percentage of the overcharge is kicked back to or "split" with a third party. Compensating a third party for services actually performed without giving the third party a portion, split or percentage of the overcharge does not violate Section 8(b). Congress was clearly aiming at a sharing arrangement rather than a unilateral overcharge.[13]

---

[12]*Lane v. Residential Funding Corp.*, 323 F.3d 739 (9th Cir. 2003); *Schuetz v. Banc One Mortg. Corp.*, 292 F.3d 1004 (9th Cir. 2002).

[13]*Haug v. Bank of America*, 317 F.3d 832 (8th Cir. 2003); *Boulware v. Crossland Mortg. Corp.*, 291 F.3d 261 (4th Cir. 2002); *Echevarria v. Chicago Title & Trust Co.*, 256 F.3d 623 (7th Cir. 2001); *Barnett v. Chicago Title Ins.*, 2008 WL 3411684 (E.D. Pa. 2008).

FORECLOSURE

A foreclosure action is the right of the mortgagee, after the debtor fails to pay as agreed, to exercise the right under the mortgage to recover the property to satisfy the debt. Each state has detailed statutes governing the foreclosure procedure, and a thorough knowledge of the law by an attorney is necessary to undertake a foreclosure.

Judicial foreclosure is a procedure available in all states where the mortgagee commences a suit to foreclose a real estate mortgage. In most states you have a choice of a judicial foreclosure as distinguished from a non-judicial foreclosure.

Judicial Foreclosure. Judicial foreclosure is a procedure available in all states wherein the mortgagor commences a suit to foreclose a real estate mortgage. The foreclosure procedure is heavily regulated by each state. In most states, a choice is available of judicial foreclosure, as distinguished from non-judicial foreclosure.

In judicial foreclosure a suit has to be commenced against the debtor in the same manner as any suit is instituted. The procedure varies from state to state; but, in general, before a judgment can be entered, procedures in many states have to be undertaken by the court to determine that no hardship will be inflicted upon the debtor and, in some instances, a person appointed by the court reviews the entire foreclosure proceeding to determine that it was properly performed and to determine that the amount claimed to be due is accurate. If a judgment of foreclosure is obtained, the creditor may hold a public sale after publication in the newspaper and, after the sale and application to the court, proceed against the debtor for the deficiency, if there is a deficiency. The procedures are enumerated in the statutes in the various states and require meticulous compliance. In a few states, this procedure can be accomplished within 60 to 90 days. In most states the uncontested procedure takes at least six to eight months and, in some states the procedure can run from a year to a year and a half to even two years or more before the creditor can obtain title to the property and obtain a deficiency judgment. If the foreclosure is contested, no estimate of the length of time to complete should be made.

> ***Credit & Collection Tip:*** *The United States has 120 days to redeem the property if a federal tax lien or other lien arising under the Internal Revenue Code is being cut off by the foreclosure action. The 120 days' redemption usually runs from the date of sale. As to a judicial foreclosure, the 120 days' redemption usually runs from the auction date.*

Non-Judicial Foreclosure. The non-judicial foreclosure is available in approximately 35 states and is heavily regulated, with the procedure carefully enumerated in the statutes of the respective states. The procedure requires sending out notices of a proposed sale by personally serving this information upon any person who has an interest in the property and publishing the sale over a period of weeks prior to the sale so that a public sale may be held. A deficiency can be obtained against the debtor if the property does not bring sufficient monies. In California, a foreclosing party is not entitled to a deficiency judgment.

The advantage of a non-judicial sale is that usually it can be accomplished in a speedier time frame than the judicial foreclosure, from 60 to 120 days on average, although some states may still take as long as a year.

DEED IN LIEU OF FORECLOSURE

In order to avoid a judicial foreclosure or a non-judicial foreclosure, sometimes a creditor will accept a deed offered by the debtor in lieu of proceeding with the foreclosure. The debtor executes a deed in the same manner as an owner would to a purchaser and the lender becomes the owner of the property. The debtor may feel the property is worth more than the mortgage and may offer to sell the property to the mortgagee in consideration of a certain amount above the mortgage. The normal situation is where the value of the property is somewhat less than the balance due on the mortgage and the creditor accepts the deed and waives any further proceeding against the debtor. One of the strong motivating forces of a deed in lieu of foreclosure is the desire of the borrower to avoid the stigma of a foreclosure proceeding.

The lender must understand that the offering of a deed in lieu of foreclosure is not a defense to the lender's foreclosure action. If the lender believes the property is worth substantially less than the mortgage, the lender would be advised to institute a foreclosure action and obtain a deficiency judgment against the debtor—assuming the debtor possesses assets in addition to the property in question.

The courts do not look kindly on deeds in lieu of foreclosure since they feel that somehow the lender has coerced the debtor into transferring the property for an amount less than the value of the property. The lender and the borrower are not in equal bargaining positions and, if this is the case, the borrower at a later date might pursue a suit to set aside the transfer.

Obtaining a title insurance policy is absolutely essential because the lender must treat this deed in lieu of foreclosure in the same way that any buyer would treat the purchase of any property and review all the potential liens or potential claims against the property.

Fraudulent Transfer. Another problem with the deed in lieu of foreclosure is that the courts sometimes feel the lender is somehow persuading the debtor to execute the deed. The conveyance may be a fraudulent transfer or a transfer without adequate consideration, because the lender enjoyed an unconscionable advantage over the borrower.

If a transfer is made without adequate consideration, the borrower at a later date may move to set aside the transfer. If the debtor files a bankruptcy petition, the lender is faced with some additional problems when accepting a deed in lieu of foreclosure. Any transfer made by the bankrupt within 90 days prior to the filing of a bankruptcy petition or within one year of the filing, if the transfer is made to an insider (relative or owner), may be set aside. A transfer made for an inadequate consideration may be considered a fraudulent transfer and is subject to being set aside by the trustee in bankruptcy. Fraudulent transfers may be set aside if they are made within a year prior to the filing of a bankruptcy petition and, in some states, the statute of limitations for a fraudulent transfer exceeds the one-year period set forth in the bankruptcy court.

Appraisal. The lender can exercise caution to overcome some of these risks of a deed in lieu of foreclosure. The first and probably the most important is to obtain an independent appraisal of the property to establish that the fair market value of the property is equal to or less than the amount of the mortgage debt. Most problems arise because an appraisal has not been made and the debtor claims that the value of the property was greater than the amount of the mortgage and the debtor was coerced or unduly influenced into executing the deed. The independent appraisal can be used if the debtor files a bankruptcy and the trustee asserts a fraudulent transfer or a transfer made without adequate consideration. The risk of a trustee asserting a preference with regard to the transfer will remain in any deed in lieu of the foreclosure, where the debtor is threatening to file a bankruptcy petition or the financial condition of the debtor indicates that a bankruptcy petition is imminent.

As a normal course of doing business, a title company usually will not issue a title policy unless the independent appraisal shows that the value of the property is somewhat below the amount of the debt. The title policy issued to the lender is a policy that was issued to protect a mortgagee. When the lender accepts a deed in lieu of foreclosure, the lender should obtain an owner's policy, as opposed to a lender's policy. The title insurance company may want to approve the independent appraisal or may want to conduct the appraisal themselves before issuing a policy.

No Interest in Property. The lender should not permit the borrower to have any further interest in the property, such as any option to purchase, a right of first refusal when the lender sells, or any type of a lease. The risk is that the court might interpret such relationships between the lender and the borrower as creating a mortgage in lieu of a transfer of property. If the courts identify a mortgage, the lender would be in the same place he was before and would be faced with a judicial or non-judicial foreclosure, rather than a deed in lieu of foreclosure. The lender also must treat this deed in lieu of foreclosure in the same way that one would treat the purchase of any property, and review all other liens or potential claims against the property.

Merger of Title. Where the same person owns a mortgage and the property, the mortgage merges into the title and disappears. This concept is disadvantageous to the lender, for if the transfer to the lender should ever be set aside, the lender wants to maintain the mortgage. Accordingly, the lender will usually set forth in their agreements with the debtor that the mortgage shall remain alive and the mortgage will maintain its priority over any other liens that were filed after the date of the original mortgage. To keep the mortgage alive, the debt must be kept alive in the same manner and the settlement agreement between the parties must establish that the debt is to remain alive to support the fact that the mortgage will remain alive. This is usually solved by the lender agreeing not to sue the debtor on the debt, in exchange for the deed in lieu of foreclosure providing that the transfer is never set aside, and providing that the debtor does not file a petition in bankruptcy.

This section touches only the highlights of a deed in lieu of foreclosure. Considering a deed in lieu of foreclosure requires the balancing of various choices to be made, and consultation with an experienced attorney is recommended.

FRAUDULENT CONVEYANCE

Many articles state that the backbone of the country, from a capitalistic point of view, is the small business which has less than 25 or 50 employees. This small business can range from the retail store to the plumbing and heating service company to the professional attorney or accountant. Unfortunately, not all entrepreneurs are successful. Many businesses do fail and the owners of the business often have guaranteed loans to banks and financial institutions which are unpaid.

The debtor has an option to enter a payment arrangement with the creditor or, as an alternative, file bankruptcy. A third option is to render his/herself judgment-proof. The third option often is attractive except in the situation where the debtor owns the family residence or owns the family residence jointly with his wife. The debtor husband tidies up his affairs by closing his bank accounts, selling his stock and securities and depositing the cash in his wife's account, and cashing his payroll check so no monies are on deposit in the bank account. Finally, the debtor husband must face the fact that he is the owner of the family residence. The final step to render him judgment-proof would be to transfer his interest in the family residence to his wife, whether he owns the family residence solely himself or jointly with his wife.

A transfer by one spouse to the other spouse presents an opportunity for creditors to examine the transaction to determine whether it can be set aside. Almost all the states have statutes which prohibit what is known as fraudulent transfers of property, including real estate, for no payment or consideration. These statutes substantially state that any conveyance or transfer of property that will render the party insolvent is fraudulent as to any creditors, without regard to the intent of the particular party, providing of course that the transfer is made without a fair consideration.

To determine if a transfer was actually made by the debtor to the wife or some third party, the creditor must conduct a title search either by using a title company or an attorney. The transfer is a matter of record in the county clerk's office or register's office of the particular county. An examination of the deed will often reveal the amount of the consideration. In many states the custom is not to state the consideration in the deed and place a nominal consideration such as $10. Nevertheless, many states require tax stamps to be affixed to the deed before filing to indicate the amount of consideration, and the tax stamps are usually a percentage of the actual consideration. Thus, a little reverse mathematics determines the price.

Creditors should act quickly to set aside a transfer because of the statute of limitations in each state. A fraudulent transfer is controlled by each state's statute of limitations that covers fraud. Some statutes run from the date that the fraud should have been discovered and other statutes run from the date of the conveyance. If the creditor commences the suit after the statute of limitations has expired, the court will dismiss the suit and the creditor will leave empty-handed.

Credit & Collection Tip: *If a creditor suspects a transfer by the debtor is fraudulent, the creditor should consult immediately with counsel to determine what the statute of limitations is in the state in which the property is located and act accordingly.*

FORECLOSURE PROCEDURE

Answer. Most foreclosure proceedings proceed to judgment without the owner or any of the defendants interposing an answer. If they do interpose an answer, the case, as with any other lawsuit, will proceed with discovery, including interrogatories and depositions, and will be disposed of by a summary judgment or will reach a trial.

Acceleration. Acceleration of the mortgage is the right of the mortgagee to declare the entire balance due after a default by the debtor in paying the agreed upon monthly payment. In most cases, because a foreclosure proceeding is expensive, acceleration is only used against a chronic defaulter, where the value of the property reasonably exceeds the balance due on the mortgage plus the legal fees and expenses of foreclosure and sale. The right to accelerate is usually provided in the mortgage agreement. Before a foreclosure suit is commenced, a letter reciting the exercise of the acceleration should be sent to the debtor or, if not, *an allegation of acceleration should be included in the complaint.*

NOTICE. After a lending institution decides to foreclose, the matter is referred to inside or outside counsel to commence the foreclosure proceedings and to comply with any notice requirements in the mortgage and with the Fair Debt Collection Practices Act. If the debtor is a consumer, the first step is usually a letter from counsel advising the debtor that if payment is not made, a foreclosure proceeding will be started.

SUBORDINATE CLAIMANTS. The method of eliminating all encumbrances subordinate to the mortgage is to join all these claimants as defendants in the lawsuit. A title search is performed to identify subordinate mortgages, judgments docketed in the county clerk's office, tax liens both state and federal, and any other persons who may have a claim against the property. The title search identifies to counsel the names of those parties to be joined as defendants to bar those claimants from asserting any claim against the property. If those parties who have a claim against the property are not joined, the interest of the claimant is not cut off and the claimant still has a claim against the property even after a foreclosure sale, and transfer to a purchaser.

TENANTS. Counsel joins "John Doe" as defendant(s) to cover those parties who may be occupying the said property by virtue of leases, other agreements, or by being trespassers. This "John Doe" covers the situation where the mortgagee does not know whether tenants exist or who they are. Most leases provide that the lease is subject to the mortgage. The purchaser at the foreclosure sale has the option to evict the tenants or the owner at the end of the foreclosure. On the other hand, the purchaser may deem it economical to continue the leases. But tenants or persons occupying the premises that are not served with the foreclosure summons and complaint are not affected by the foreclosure action.

SUIT ON DEBT. The mortgagee has a right to either sue on the mortgage debt or commence a foreclosure proceeding. Once a suit is brought on the debt, some states provide that the mortgagee cannot start a foreclosure proceeding until a judgment is obtained on the debt and the judgment remains unpaid. For this reason, lenders choose to foreclose the mortgage and not sue on the debt. In addition, a docketed judgment takes its place in priority at the date when the judgment is filed. A foreclosure proceeding relies on the date when the mortgage was recorded, which was probably five to thirty years prior to the foreclosure. The mortgage takes its place in the chain of title on the date it is recorded, whereas the judgment does not take its place until it is docketed in the proper office.

Personal Service. Serving the summons and complaint for foreclosure by "personal" service on the mortgagor is important in foreclosure actions. The lender is concerned that the title company will issue a clean title after the sale without any exceptions. Where service of the summons and complaint has been made by means other than personal delivery on the owner of the property, the title companies review the situation, because the mortgagor served by substituted service is more likely to claim he or she was not properly served with the summons and complaint and will question the jurisdictional grounds of the foreclosure action. Defective service on the mortgagor (owner) could invalidate the foreclosure.

If the owner does not occupy the residence, a greater likelihood exists for improper service. For this reason, counsel will attempt to effectuate personal service of the summons and complaint on the debtor even though this is more difficult and may delay commencement of suit.

Referee's Report. If no answer is interposed, and the defendants default or a trial results in a decision for the mortgagee, the next step in the proceeding in some states, such as New York, is to request the court to appoint a referee to compute the amount due and to submit a report to the court on the foreclosure. The report usually encompasses a review of all the papers on file, a summary of what transpired during the proceeding and the amount due. Other states omit this procedure, or use a procedure not as extensive as in New York.

Judgment. After the report is submitted by the referee to the court, the plaintiff finally submits judgment to the court ordering a judicial sale of the property. The judgment requires the plaintiff to advertise the sale in a newspaper pursuant to the requirements of the state statute.

Sale. At a time and place set forth in the newspaper advertisement, the sheriff will conduct the sale and open the bidding at a public auction. The mortgagee is entitled to bid at the sale for the property being foreclosed and thus become the owner of the property.

Title at Sale. The purchaser acquires title to the property at the foreclosure sale free of the claims of the subordinate mortgages, liens, judgments, and claimants and the title reverts to the date of the mortgage. A prior mortgage lien or judgment lien recorded prior to the foreclosed mortgage will survive the sale and remain a lien on the property. The payments of the prior mortgage must be kept up-to-date or the prior mortgagee may commence a separate foreclosure action.

Surplus Money Proceedings. If the sale is for a price in excess of the balance due on the mortgage, surplus money proceedings follow. The surplus money is paid into court, and the monies are paid to the other creditors who file claims. Payment is made in order of priority. If monies are left after payment of lien creditors, they are paid to the mortgagor (owner).

Mortgage Deficiency. If the amount accepted by the sheriff at the sale is insufficient to pay off the mortgage, the balance due is the deficiency amount for which the mortgagor (owner) of the property, and anyone who assumes the mortgage, may still be liable. Many times no one appears at the auction sale to bid for the foreclosed property, and the lending institution purchases the property at the sale for a nominal amount. In this instance, the deficiency is substantial, since the nominal amount bid by the lender is credited to the balance due on the lender's mortgage. (Actually, the amount bid is deducted from the mortgage balance.) Some states prohibit the lender from bidding a nominal amount and require that the fair market value of the property be credited to the balance due on the mortgage, whereas other states allow the lender to credit the actual bid at the sale.

The question of recovering a deficiency judgment against the debtor is controlled by the statutes of the respective states and strict compliance is essential to insure the right to proceed against the debtor for the deficiency amount. In some states the procedure is complex, and consultation with experienced counsel is recommended. For example, in New Jersey, a separate suit must be started on the note to obtain a deficiency judgment whereas in New York the suit for the deficiency may be included in the foreclosure action, and after the judgment of foreclosure is obtained, a motion for a deficiency is made within a specific period of time.[14]

Right of Redemption. In some states, the debtor enjoys a right of redemption prior to the sale or even as long as two years after the sale. The debtor may redeem the property by payment of the sale price established at the foreclosure sale within a certain period of time, as set forth in the respective state's statute. The redemption right was designed to deter low bids at a foreclosure sale. In those states where a right of redemption is allowed, some statutes allow the mortgagee to extinguish this right of redemption by agreement in the mortgage document.

---

[14] *First Union Nat'l Bank v. Penn Salem Marina, Inc.*, 383 N.J. Super. 562 (N.J. Super. Ct. App. Div. 2006).

DEFAULT INTEREST RATE

The terms of the mortgage note provided that the following categories or damages would be included in the event of default:

A. default interest
B. prepayment premium
C. late charges

The policy of some lending institutions is to include in the mortgage provisions that require the payment of oppressive interest rates in the event of default as well as a prepayment premium in the event a party pays the mortgage before it is due. The court in *First Union* explained that a default interest rate is presumptively reasonable and it is the defendants who have the burden of proving it is unreasonable. Liquidated damage provisions in a *commercial contract* between sophisticated parties are presumptively reasonable and the party who challenges the clause bears the burden of proving its unreasonableness (a commercial property).

The defendant argued that the default interest rate amounted to a penalty and bore no relationship to the damages that the bank sustained by the reason of the foreclosure or the fact that the loan was in default for a period of time. In this case, the default interest was over $400,000. The defendant offered no evidence that a default rate of interest based on a floating rate and the other based on a fixed rate is anything other than an accepted commercial practice intended to be a reasonable estimate of the potential cost of administering a defaulted loan and the potential difference between the contract interest rate and the rate the bank might pay to secure a commercial loan replacing the lost funds.

The defendant with some evidence of fraud or duress might attack the default rate of interest, but since the defendant offered no such evidence to overcome the presumptive reasonableness of the agreed upon provision, the court concluded that the default interest rate was proper.

The defendant also argued that the default interest rate and the default prepayment premium were duplicative and that the bank should not be entitled to both penalties. A prepayment premium is not a different form of interest. A prepayment premium was defined by a New Jersey case in 1962 as a sum exacted for the company for the use of plaintiff's money (that is, interest). The court held that other courts have found that a prepayment premium is not interest because it is not compensation for the use of money, but a charge for the option or privilege of prepayment. The rationale for enforcing prepayment premiums rests on the recognition that such premiums serve as compensation to the lender for the losses incurred by the lender when it received prepayment of its loan earlier than originally planned.

As in the default interest rate, the burden of proof to show that this clause constitutes an unenforceable penalty rests on the defendants. Since no evidence was produced that they lacked an opportunity to bargain over this clause, and the financial sophistication and experience of the defendant, the prepayment premium was nothing more than a common practice in a competitive industry. This case was in a commercial setting. The analysis in a consumer environment may be different, although default interest rates are used frequently by lenders in consumer loans.[15]

Another case disallowed 14.72 percent of default rate of interest where the regular rate of interest is 9.72 percent. There were also late charges of over $17,000. The court took a strong position and asserted that collecting a default rate of interest is the same as the late charge and since they have already collected a late charge, the default rate of interest is unacceptable.

The borrower claimed that the prepayment was not voluntary since the debt was accelerated and therefore the prepayment premium was involuntary. The court did not address this issue and allowed the prepayment premium principally because the debtor never raised it before and the court would not consider it.

This case was in the bankruptcy court in Illinois, a fairly liberal circuit. Some courts have taken the position the reasonable default rate of interest is 2 percent above the base rate that was being charged. A case in Connecticut recently approved an 18 percent default interest rate. The bankruptcy courts are even more protective of the debtor.[16]

Notwithstanding the difficulties encountered by using a default rate of interest, a creditor brought a suit in a liberal state (New York) where the default interest was charged at the rate of 31.240% for purchases and 56.148% for advances. The plaintiff made their argument that the state in which they were incorporated, South Dakota, has no law regulating or prohibiting the charging of interest. The major mistake was believing that the bank will be allowed to collect 56% on a consumer loan in the State of New York.

To quote the judge, "common sense and reasonable persons" would have understood that a suit such as this would "shock the conscience of the court and violate the public policy of New York law." Frankly, the result might have been the same whether it was a liberal or a conservative state.[17]

---

[15]*Emigrant Mortg. Co. v. D'Agostino*, 896 A.2d 814 (Conn. App. Ct. 2006); *Money Life Ins. Co. v. Paramus Parkway*, 364 N.J. Super. 92 (N.J. Super. Ct. App Div. 2003).

[16]*In re AE Hotel Venture*, 321 B.R. 209 (Bankr. N.D. Ill. 2005); *Emigrant Mortg. Co. v. D'Agostino*, 896 A.2d 814 (Conn. App. Ct. 2006).

[17]*Citibank, N.A. v. Mahmoud*, *N.Y. Law Journal*, 6/11/08, Pg. 35, N.Y. Supreme Court, Richmond County.

MORTGAGE ELECTRONIC REGISTRATION SYSTEM

The Mortgage Electronic Registration System (MERS) operates a National Electronic Registration System for residential mortgages and related instruments. The lenders are primarily the banks who subscribe to the Mortgage Electronic Registration System and designate MERS as their nominee or the mortgagee of record for the purpose of recording MERS instruments where the subject real property is located. The MERS instruments are registered in a central database which tracks all future transfers of the beneficial ownership interest and servicing rights amongst MERS members. MERS states that they have recorded more than 4 million MERS instruments in more than 3,000 counties in all 50 states.

A case in New York addressed an informal Attorney General opinion which concluded that the county clerk had a statutory duty to record MERS instruments if they were duly acknowledged and accompanied by the proper fee.[18] The county clerk should list the MERS instruments in the county's alphabetical indexes under the names of the actual lenders.

A neighboring county clerk, relying on the Attorney General's informal opinion, announced that they would no longer accept MERS instruments which listed MERS as the mortgagee or nominee of record unless MERS was, in fact, the actual mortgagee. The case involved whether or not the preliminary injunction to maintain the status quo should be maintained, and the court answered in the affirmative. The court decided that MERS demonstrated a reasonable probability of success on the merits of their claim to compel the county clerk to perform his ministerial duty.

MARKUPS

Section 8(b) of RESPA provides as follows:

> No person shall give and no person shall accept any portion, split or percentage of any charge made or received for the rendering of a real estate settlement service in connection with the transaction involving a federally related mortgage loan other than for services actually performed.

A conflict has arisen over the use of the word "and" in the first five (5) words of the statute. Some courts have taken the position that it requires a "third party" to the transaction whereas other courts have taken the position that any type of markup is a violation of RESPA. The Fourth, Seventh, and Eighth Circuits generally have held that markups do not constitute a "split of

---

[18]*Merscorp, Inc. v. Romaine*, 743 N.Y.S.2d 562 (N.Y. App. Div. 2d Dep't 2002).

fees" or "unearned fees."[19] Those courts accept that the statute is merely an anti-kickback provision that unambiguously requires at least two parties to share a settlement fee in order to violate the statute. They rely on the argument that where the language of a statute is unambiguous, the statute should be enforced as written unless a clear legislative intent to the contrary is shown. If the intent of the statute is clear, the judicial inquiry ends.

Another distinction was made in that a "markup" refers to the greater price defendant charged plaintiff for the credit report without providing any additional service than that which the defendant paid to the third party vendor. In contrast, an "overcharge" refers to "services" provided by the lender itself, but charged to consumers seeking home mortgages for substantially more than the providers cost. The policy statement issued by HUD states that nothing is more common than for professionals to re-price the incidental charges that they incur on behalf of their clients.

The Second, Third, and Eleventh Circuits choose to read the statute in a different way.[20] The statute should be separated into two parts stating:

1. No person shall give any portion, split, or percentage of any charge
2. No person shall accept any portion, split, or percentage of any charge.
3. Adding a portion of a charge is prohibited whether or not there is a culpable acceptor and accepting a portion of a charge is prohibited regardless of whether there is a culpable giver.

The most recent case in this conflict out the District Court in Ohio followed the reasoning in the Fourth, Seventh, and Eighth Circuits and followed the interpretation that the statute requires a third party and therefore a markup is not a violation of RESPA.[21]

Sometime in the future this matter will reach the Supreme Court for resolution.

PREDATORY LENDING

Many legislatures are now considering predatory lending bills that are similar to the bills passed in California, New York, New Jersey, Georgia,

---

[19]*See Haug v. Bank of Am., N.A.*, 317 F.3d 832 (8th Cir. 2003); *Boulware v. Crossland Mortg. Corp.*, 291 F.3d 261 (4th Cir. 2002); *Krzalic v. Republic Title Co.*, 314 F.3d 875 (7th Cir. 2002); *Echevarria v. Chi. Title & Trust Co.*, 256 F.3d 623 (7th Cir. 2001).

[20]*See Santiago v. GMAC Mortg. Group, Inc.*, 417 F.3d 384 (3d Cir. 2005); *Kruse v. Wells Fargo Home Mortg., Inc.*, 383 F.3d 49 (2d Cir. 2004); *Sosa v. Chase Manhattan Mortg. Corp.*, 348 F.3d 979 (11th Cir. 2003).

[21]*Morrison v. Brookstone Mortg. Co., Inc.*, 2006 U.S. Dist. LEXIS 73389 (S.D. Ohio Sept. 29, 2006).

New Mexico, and Arkansas. While the laws may differ in some respects, the basic initiative is to put a stop to high-cost home loans.

Some of the provisions of the New York and Georgia Acts are the following:

A. Limiting the charges for a mortgage on one- to four-family houses occupied as a principal residence.
B. The interest cannot exceed eight points above the yield of treasury securities and total points cannot exceed 5 percent.
C. If a provision is present for default interest, more than two payments cannot be deducted.
D. Mandatory arbitration is prohibited.
E. The lender must consider the ability of the borrower to pay.
F. Financing.
G. No additional points or additional fees can be charged.

While some of these requirements may seem reasonable, some will present serious problems and litigation will probably follow. In a foreclosure proceeding, it is simple for a debtor to assert that the lender knew that he was unable to make the payments. While the debtor may not succeed, the foreclosure may drag through the courts. It will be interesting to see whether other states will be more careful in their drafting or whether they will adopt the broad spectrum of requirements set forth in the New York and Georgia law. The heart of the new law is a provision allowing borrowers to sue the assignees of the predatory lenders—usually the investment firms who buy the loans and consolidate them into financial pools for sale in a secondary market. The risk is that the rating agencies may refuse to rate the creditworthiness of the mortgage pools organized by the investment firms, and predatory lending would dry up. No firms would purchase the loans resulting in an absence of a secondary market. Other states have promulgated regulations on predatory lending, but the regulations are not as severe or comprehensive as the laws in the above six states.

OVERSECURED CLAIMS—INTEREST AND PREPAYMENT

The U.S. Code Section 506b states as follows:

> to the extent that an allowed secured claim is secured by property, the value of which, after any recovery under subsection (c) of this section, is greater than the amount of such claim, there shall be allowed to the holder of such

claim, interest on such claim and any reasonable fees, costs, or charges provided for under the agreement under which such claim arose.

A Supreme Court case set forth that secured creditors, both consensual and non-consensual, are entitled to post-petition interest, but other reasonable fees, costs and other charges will only be added to a secured claim to the extent they are both reasonable and are provided for in the agreement between the debtor and the creditor.

Most mortgages contain a default rate of interest and accordingly, since this is provided for in the mortgage document, the default rate of interest would be included in the proof of claim for an over secured creditor. The default must have taken place before the petition was filed. If the default was not present at the time of the filing of the petition, the creditor would only be allowed the interest rate that was charged before a default took place. The courts are also not in full agreement as to what a reasonable default rate of interest is and they will certainly examine the default rate of interest to see whether it is equivalent to a liquidated damage clause. A conflict arises over late fees since some cases have disallowed the late fees where the creditor claims a default rate of interest. Attorney fees are always reviewed for reasonableness.

As to prepayment premiums, the courts generally hold that the mortgage must set forth the terms and conditions under which a prepayment can be made. Most states adhere to the concept that no penalty will attach to a prepayment unless the mortgage or note expressly restricts prepayment, prohibits prepayment or requires additional fees in the event of prepayment.[22]

SINGLE PURPOSE ENTITIES

Single Purpose Entities (SPEs) are a creation of a necessity. Lenders try to prevent real estate collateral from being included in a bankruptcy that is solely due to the failure of the operation of the business of the owner.

A separate corporation is organized to own the real estate and the loan is made to the separate corporation. To file a bankruptcy petition, the board of directors is required to have an unanimous vote and one of the directors must be a director who has no relationship or obligations to either the lender or the borrower. This director will be acting in the interest of the creditors as well as the stockholders and the corporation that owns the real estate.

---

[22]*In re AE Hotel Venture*, 321 B.R. 209 (Bankr. N.D. Ill. 2005); *In re Kroh Bros. Dev. Co.*, 88 B.R. 997 (Bankr. W.D. Mo. 1988); *In re Vest Assocs.*, 217 B.R. 696 (Bankr. S.D.N.Y. 1998); *Russo Enters., Inc. v Citibank, N.A.*, 266 A.D.2d 528 (2d Dep't 1999).

To effectively separate the SPE from the business and the assets of the owner of the property, commingling and guaranteeing or incurring debt must be carefully addressed by the directors. Unanimous consent of the board is necessary for any type of liquidation or merger or engaging in any business outside of the operation of the real estate. While separate corporations are utilized primarily for SPEs, a recent trend has developed to utilize limited liability companies.

TITLE POLICY

Illinois provided the classic case involving a title company and the property owner.[23] The title company provided a title search and an insurance policy was issued to the property owner. Several years later the owner found that the title insurance policy did not disclose a restrictive covenant which prohibited the property from being used for commercial purposes. The property owner discovered this after he had commenced building for commercial purposes.

The court pointed out initially that the mortgage was refinanced and the payoff amount released the mortgagee and thus the title company's liability under the policy of title insurance was terminated.

The additional issue before the court is whether the title company was subject to liability for negligent misrepresentation when they issued the title insurance policy without disclosing that this restrictive covenant against commercial property was present.

The general rule is that a party cannot recover for solely economic loss under the tort theories of strict liability or negligent and innocent misrepresentation. The only exceptions to this rule are if the plaintiff sustained damages consisting of personal injury or property damage resulting from a sudden or dangerous occurrence, where the plaintiff's damages are proximately caused by a defendant's intentional false representation, or finally where the plaintiff's damages are caused by a negligent misrepresentation by a defendant in the business of supplying information for the guidance of others in their business transactions.

The last exception was the basis of plaintiff's case, but the court rejected the fact that the title company is in the business of supplying information for the guidance of others. If the information provided is just incidental to the sale of the product, providing inaccurate information does not create liability.

An amicus curiae brief of a trade association stated the title company is not one who provides an abstract of title. The title company is in the business of issuing a title commitment to provide a listing of defects, liens and encumbrances affecting the property. A title commitment is simply a

---

[23]*First Midwest Bank, N.A. v. Stewart Title Guar. Co.*, 218 Ill. 2d 326, 843 N.E.2d 327 (2006).

promise to insure a particular state of title. To the extent the title commitment contains information concerning the title, such information is submitted to provide notice of the limitations to the risk that the title insurer is willing to insure. The purpose of the title commitment is set forth in the terms of the issuing policy of title insurance and the purpose of the policy of title insurance is to insure against the risk of undiscovered defects, liens and encumbrances. The court held that the title company was not providing information for the guidance of others and negligent misrepresentation cannot support an economic loss.

In the instant case, the title agreement was terminated because the mortgage was paid off and the bank in this instance was seeking a recovery based solely upon negligent misrepresentation. If the mortgage was not paid, the result may have been different.

RIGHT TO OBTAIN AN ASSIGNMENT OF A MORTGAGE

The lender was charging the borrower a fee of 1 percent for a $51 million dollar mortgage to satisfy a request for an assignment of mortgage rather than a satisfaction of a mortgage. A lengthy decision held that the parties are bound by their contract, which did not provide for any additional fee for an assignment. The judge also mentioned that custom and usage of the trade indicates lenders will provide an assignment of a mortgage upon payment of a reasonable preparation fee. Borrowers should be careful to expressly provide in the mortgage that the lender will furnish an assignment of a mortgage for a reasonable preparation fee.[24]

REFINANCING—RIGHT TO RESCIND

A majority of the cases permit a borrower to rescind a transaction even when the transaction consists of a refinancing of the mortgage. A small minority of cases have taken the opposite view.

Regulation C says that the right to rescind shall expire:

1. Three years after consummation.;
2. Upon transfer of all the consumer's interest in the property.
3. Upon sale of the property, whichever comes first.

---

[24]*767 Third Ave., LLC v. Orix Capital Markets, LLC*, 6 Misc. 3d 1019(A), 800 N.Y.S.2d 357 (Misc. Ct. N.Y. Co. 2005).

The legislation does not address the act of refinancing an existing loan, nor does it state that such an act of refinancing cuts off the right of rescission. The sale of the property cuts off the right to rescind. Congress did not provide that a refinancing would produce the same result.

When the bank fails to disclose adequately the terms of the loan, the three day right of rescission becomes a three year right of rescission. The courts have reiterated that the Truth and Lending Act is to be favorably construed towards borrowers.[25]

FORECLOSURES—HIGH-COST MORTGAGES AND SUB-PRIME MORTGAGES

As a result of our economic problems, the decline of housing prices and an increase in foreclosures, almost 36 states have passed some form of statutory law that deals with sub-prime and high-cost mortgages. By the time this edition is printed, other states will have taken steps to assist the delinquent homeowner. The courts at the same time have been aware of the problems faced by the homeowners attempting to meet their payments, and the bankruptcy courts have been added as a method of assistance. Unfortunately, the courts are not always distinguishing sub-prime and high-cost mortgages from well-secured mortgages.

Even minor violations in the original loan documents or discrepancies and overcharges in the servicing of the mortgages now become material issues during the foreclosure process. The judge and the clerk are alert to search for some way to aid the desperate property owner. Defenses, in the past ignored, are now finding favorable treatment. Even in the non-judicial foreclosure states, the homeowners are seeking court relief for violations which in the past were addressed as technical or minor. The Truth In Lending Act, the Equal Credit Opportunity Act, the Fair Credit Reporting Act, and the Fair Debt Collection Practices Act are frequently appearing in the foreclosure process.

In the past, mortgages were packaged, sold, and resold. Rarely did a problem arise in a foreclosure action. Today, the courts are insisting *upon documentary evidence of every assignment* to be certain that the party starting the foreclosure action has possession of the hard copy evidence to prove the plaintiff was the actual owner *at the time suit was instituted.* In today's environment a purchaser of mortgages must pay more attention to documentation. While many courts still follow prior decisions, some judges use unique forms of reasoning to justify favoring the consumer.

The bankruptcy situation is now more difficult as the number of serial filers multiply. Some law firms on the day before, on the day of the sale or

[25] *See Barrett v. J.P. Morgan Chase*, 445 F.3d 874 (6th Cir. 2006); *King v. California*, 7847 F.2d 9110 (9th Cir. 1986); *MacIntosh v. Erwin Union Bank & Trust Co.*, 215 F.R.D. 26 (D. Mass. 2003).

just before the sale are checking the bankruptcy court to be certain that the borrower has not filed bankruptcy.

MORTGAGE—FIRE INSURANCE

The normal protection against fire with regard to the property is to be the named beneficiary in the fire insurance policy obtained by the borrower. This type of relationship is a third-party beneficiary relationship and creates a separate contract between the insurance company and the mortgagee.

Failing to file a proof of loss after a fire or other catastrophe usually will not constitute a breach of the policy as to the mortgagee under the provisions of the standard insurance policy. The standard policy, nonetheless, usually requires the insured to notify the insurance company of any specific conditions, such as the property being vacant and not occupied if the mortgagor knows of these circumstances.

Suits instituted to recover insurance proceeds by the owner of the property must include the mortgagee as a named defendant by virtue of the mortgagee being named as a beneficiary under the policy.

CHAPTER 10
APPENDIX I

REAL ESTATE SETTLEMENT PROCEDURES ACT—(24 CFR PART 3500)—FINAL RULE—DEPARTMENT OF HOUSING AND URBAN DEVELOPMENT

Federal Register

Thursday,
October 18, 2001

Part V

Department of Housing and Urban Development

24 CFR Part 3500

Real Estate Settlement Procedures Act Statement of Policy 2001–1: Clarification of Statement of Policy 1999–1 Regarding Lender Payments to Mortgage Brokers, and Guidance Concerning Unearned Fees Under Section 8(b); Final Rule

53052 Federal Register / Vol. 66, No. 202 / Thursday, October 18, 2001 / Rules and Regulations

DEPARTMENT OF HOUSING AND URBAN DEVELOPMENT

24 CFR Part 3500

[Docket No. FR-4714-N-01]

RIN 2502-AH74

Real Estate Settlement Procedures Act Statement of Policy 2001-1: Clarification of Statement of Policy 1999-1 Regarding Lender Payments to Mortgage Brokers, and Guidance Concerning Unearned Fees Under Section 8(b)

AGENCY: Office of the Assistant Secretary for Housing-Federal Housing Commissioner, HUD.

ACTION: Statement of Policy 2001-1.

SUMMARY: This Statement of Policy is being issued to eliminate any ambiguity concerning the Department's position with respect to those lender payments to mortgage brokers characterized as yield spread premiums and to overcharges by settlement service providers as a result of questions raised by two recent court decisions, *Culpepper* v. *Irwin Mortgage Corp.* and *Echevarria* v. *Chicago Title and Trust Co.*, respectively. In issuing this Statement of Policy, the Department clarifies its interpretation of Section 8 of the Real Estate Settlement Procedures Act (RESPA) in Statement of Policy 1999-1 Regarding Lender Payments to Mortgage Brokers (the 1999 Statement of Policy), and reiterates its long-standing interpretation of Section 8(b)'s prohibitions. *Culpepper* v. *Irwin Mortgage Corp.* involved the payment of yield spread premiums from lenders to mortgage brokers. *Echevarria* v. *Chicago Title and Trust Co.* involved the applicability of Section 8(b) to a settlement service provider that overcharged a borrower for the service of another settlement service provider, and then retained the amount of the overcharge.

Today's Statement of Policy reiterates the Department's position that yield spread premiums are not per se legal or illegal, and clarifies the test for the legality of such payments set forth in HUD's 1999 Statement of Policy. As stated there, HUD's position that lender payments to mortgage brokers are not illegal per se does not imply, however, that yield spread premiums are legal in individual cases or classes of transactions. The legality of yield spread premiums turns on the application of HUD's test in the 1999 Statement of Policy as clarified today.

The Department also reiterates its long-standing position that it may violate Section 8(b) and HUD's implementing regulations: (1) For two or more persons to split a fee for settlement services, any portion of which is unearned; or (2) for one settlement service provider to mark-up the cost of the services performed or goods provided by another settlement service provider without providing additional actual, necessary, and distinct services, goods, or facilities to justify the additional charge; or (3) for one settlement service provider to charge the consumer a fee where no, nominal, or duplicative work is done, or the fee is in excess of the reasonable value of goods or facilities provided or the services actually performed.

This Statement of Policy also reiterates the importance of disclosure so that borrowers can choose the best loan for themselves, and it describes disclosures HUD considers best practices. The Secretary is also announcing that he intends to make full use of his regulatory authority to establish clear requirements for disclosure of mortgage broker fees and to improve the settlement process for lenders, mortgage brokers, and consumers.

EFFECTIVE DATE: October 18, 2001.

FOR FURTHER INFORMATION CONTACT: Ivy M. Jackson, Acting Director, RESPA/ILS Division, Room 9156, U.S. Department of Housing and Urban Development, 451 Seventh Street, SW., Washington, DC 20410; telephone (202) 708-0502, or (for legal questions) Kenneth A. Markison, Assistant General Counsel for GSE/RESPA, Room 9262, Department of Housing and Urban Development, Washington, DC 20410; telephone (202) 708-3137 (these are not toll-free numbers). Persons who have difficulty hearing or speaking may access this number via TTY by calling the toll-free Federal Information Relay Service at (800) 877-8339.

SUPPLEMENTARY INFORMATION:

General Background

The Department is issuing this Statement of Policy in accordance with 5 U.S.C. 552 as a formal pronouncement of its interpretation of relevant statutory and regulatory provisions. Section 19(a) (12 U.S.C. 2617(a)) of the Real Estate Settlement Procedures Act of 1974 (12 U.S.C. 2601-2617) (RESPA) specifically authorizes the Secretary "to prescribe such rules and regulations [and] to make such interpretations * * * as may be necessary to achieve the purposes of [RESPA]."

Section 8(a) of RESPA prohibits any person from giving and any person from accepting "any fee, kickback, or thing of value pursuant to an agreement or understanding, oral or otherwise" that real estate settlement service business shall be referred to any person. *See* 12 U.S.C. 2607(a). Section 8(b) prohibits anyone from giving or accepting "any portion, split, or percentage of any charge made or received for the rendering of a real estate settlement service * * * other than for services actually performed." 12 U.S.C. 2607(b). Section 8(c) of RESPA provides, "Nothing in [Section 8] shall be construed as prohibiting * * * (2) the payment to any person of a bona fide salary or compensation or other payment for goods or facilities actually furnished or for services actually performed * * *" 12 U.S.C. 2607(c)(2). RESPA also requires the disclosure of settlement costs to consumers at the time of or soon after a borrower applies for a loan and again at the time of real estate settlement. 12 U.S.C. 2603-4. RESPA's requirements apply to transactions involving a "federally related mortgage loan" as that term is defined at 12 U.S.C. 2602(1).

I. Lender Payments to Mortgage Brokers

The Conference Report on the Department's 1999 Appropriations Act directed HUD to address the issue of lender payments to mortgage brokers under RESPA. The Conference Report stated that "Congress never intended payments by lenders to mortgage brokers for goods or facilities actually furnished or for services actually performed to be violations of [Sections 8](a) or (b) [12 U.S.C. sec. 2607] in its enactment of RESPA." H. Rep. 105-769, at 260. As also directed by Congress, HUD worked with industry groups, federal agencies, consumer groups and other interested parties in collectively producing the 1999 Statement of Policy issued on March 1, 1999, 64 FR 10080. Interested members of the public are urged to consult the 1999 Statement of Policy for a more detailed discussion of the background on lender payments to brokers addressed in today's Statement.

HUD's 1999 Statement of Policy established a two-part test for determining the legality of lender payments to mortgage brokers for table funded transactions and intermediary transactions under RESPA: (1) Whether goods or facilities were actually furnished or services were actually performed for the compensation paid and; (2) whether the payments are reasonably related to the value of the goods or facilities that were actually furnished or services that were actually performed. In applying this test, HUD believes that total compensation should be scrutinized to assure that it is reasonably related to the goods, facilities, or services furnished or performed to determine whether it is legal under RESPA. In the determination of whether payments from lenders to mortgage brokers are permissible under Section 8 of RESPA, the threshold question is whether there were goods or facilities actually furnished or services actually performed for the total compensation paid to the mortgage broker. Where a lender payment to a mortgage broker comprises a portion of total broker compensation, the amount of the payment is not, under the HUD test, scrutinized separately and apart from total broker compensation.

Since HUD issued its 1999 Statement of Policy, most courts have held that yield spread premiums from lenders to mortgage brokers are legal provided that such payments meet the test for legality articulated in the 1999 Statement of Policy and otherwise comport with RESPA. However, in a recent decision, *Culpepper v. Irwin Mortgage Corp.*, 253 F.3d 1324 (11th Cir. 2001), the Court of Appeals for the Eleventh Circuit upheld certification of a class in a case alleging that yield spread premiums violated Section 8 of RESPA where the defendant lender, pursuant to a prior understanding with mortgage brokers, paid yield spread premiums to the brokers based solely on the brokers' delivery of above par interest rate loans. The court concluded that a jury could find that yield spread premiums were illegal kickbacks or referral fees under RESPA where the lender's payments were based exclusively on interest rate differentials reflected on rate sheets, and the lender had no knowledge of what services, if any, the broker performed. The court described HUD's 1999 Statement of Policy as "ambiguous." *Id.* at 1327. Accordingly, and because courts have now rendered conflicting decisions, HUD has an obligation to clarify its position and issues this Statement today to provide such clarification and certainty to lenders, brokers, and consumers.

Because this clarification focuses on the legality of lender payments to mortgage brokers in transactions subject to RESPA, the coverage of this statement is restricted to payments to mortgage brokers in table funded and intermediary broker transactions. Lender payments to mortgage brokers where mortgage brokers initially fund the loan and then sell the loan after settlement are outside the coverage of this statement as exempt from RESPA under the secondary market exception.

II. Disclosure

Besides establishing the two-part test for determining the legality of yield spread premiums, the 1999 Statement of Policy discussed the importance of disclosure in permitting borrowers to choose the best loan for themselves. The mortgage transaction is complicated, and most people engage in such transactions relatively infrequently, compared to the other purchases they make. In some instances, borrowers have paid very large origination costs, either up front fees, yield spread premiums, or both, which they might have been able to avoid with timely disclosure. Timely disclosure would permit them to shop for preferable origination costs and mortgage terms and to agree to those costs and terms that meet their needs. The Department therefore is issuing a clarification of the importance of disclosure, with a description of disclosures that it considers to be best practices.

In this Statement of Policy, the Secretary is announcing that he intends to make full use of his regulatory authority as expeditiously as possible to provide clear requirements and guidance prospectively regarding disclosure of mortgage broker fees and, more broadly, to improve the mortgage settlement process so that homebuyers and homeowners are better served. Pending the promulgation of such a rule, the Secretary asks the industry to adopt new disclosure requirements to promote competition and to better serve consumers.

III. Unearned Fees

The 1999 Statement of Policy also touched upon another area of recurring questions under Section 8 of RESPA: the legality of payments that are in excess of the reasonable value of the goods or facilities provided or services performed. See 64 FR 10082–3.

Since RESPA was enacted, HUD has consistently interpreted Section 8(b) and HUD's RESPA regulations to prohibit settlement service providers from charging unearned fees, as occurred in *Echevarria v. Chicago Title & Trust Co.*, 256 F.3d 623 (7th Cir. 2001). Such an interpretation is consistent with Congress's finding, when enacting RESPA, that consumers need protection from unnecessarily high settlement costs. Through this Statement of Policy, HUD makes clear that Section 8(b) prohibits any person from giving or accepting any fees other than payments for goods and facilities provided or services actually performed. Payments that are unearned fees occur in, but are not limited to, cases where: (1) Two or more persons split a fee for settlement services, any portion of which is unearned; or (2) one settlement service provider marks-up the cost of the services performed or goods provided by another settlement service provider without providing additional actual, necessary, and distinct services, goods, or facilities to justify the additional charge; or (3) one settlement service provider charges the consumer a fee where no, nominal, or duplicative work is done, or the fee is in excess of the reasonable value of goods or facilities provided or the services actually performed.

In a July 5, 2001 decision, the Court of Appeals for the Seventh Circuit concluded that unearned fees must be passed from one settlement provider to another in order for such fees to violate Section 8(b). Accordingly, the court held that a settlement service provider did not violate Section 8(b) when, in billing a borrower, it added an overcharge to another provider's fees and retained the additional charge without providing any additional goods, facilities or services. *Echevarria v. Chicago Title & Trust Co.* Other courts have held that two or more parties must split or share a fee in order for a violation of Section 8(b) to occur. Still other courts have stated, however, that a single provider can violate Section 8(b). Because the courts are now divided, HUD is issuing this Statement of Policy to reiterate its interpretation of Section 8(b).

The Court of Appeals for the Seventh Circuit rendered its conclusion in *Echevarria* "absent a formal commitment by HUD to an opposing position. * * *" *Id.* at 630. In issuing this Statement of Policy pursuant to Section 19(a), HUD reiterates its position on unearned fees under Section 8(b) of RESPA, which HUD regards as long standing.

IV. Statement of Policy 2001–1

To give guidance to interested members of the real estate settlement industry and the general public on the application of RESPA and its implementing regulations, the Secretary hereby issues the following Statement of Policy. The interpretations embodied in this Statement of Policy are issued pursuant to Section 19(a) of RESPA, 12 U.S.C. 2617(a).

Part A. Mortgage Broker Fees

Yield Spread Premiums

One of the primary barriers to homeownership and homeowners' ability to refinance and lower their housing costs is the up front cash needed to obtain a mortgage. The closing costs and origination fees associated with a mortgage loan are a significant component of these up front cash requirements. Borrowers may choose to pay these fees out of pocket, or to pay the origination fees, and possibly all the closing fees, by financing them; *i.e.*, adding the amount of such fees to the principal balance of their mortgage loan. The latter approach, however, is not available to those whose loan-to-value ratio has already reached the maximum permitted by the lender. For those without the available cash, who are at the maximum loan-to-value ratio, or who simply choose to do so, there is a third option. This third option is a yield spread premium.

Yield spread premiums permit homebuyers to pay some or all of the up front settlement costs over the life of the mortgage through a higher interest rate. Because the mortgage carries a higher interest rate, the lender is able to sell it to an investor at a higher price. In turn, the lender pays the broker an amount reflective of this price difference. The payment allows the broker to recoup the up front costs incurred on the borrower's behalf in originating the loan. Payments from lenders to brokers based on the rates of borrowers' loans are characterized as "indirect" fees and are referred to as yield spread premiums.[1]

A yield spread premium is calculated based upon the difference between the interest rate at which the broker originates the loan and the par, or market, rate offered by a lender. The Department believes, and industry and consumers agree, that a yield spread premium can be a useful means to pay some or all of a borrower's settlement costs. In these cases, lender payments reduce the up front cash requirements to borrowers. In some cases, borrowers are able to obtain loans without paying any up front cash for the services required in connection with the origination of the loan. Instead, the fees for these services are financed through a higher interest rate on the loan. The yield spread premium thus can be a legitimate tool to assist the borrower. The availability of this option fosters homeownership.

HUD has recognized the utility of yield spread premiums in regulations issued prior to the 1999 Statement of Policy. In a final rule concerning "Deregulation of Mortgagor Income Requirements," HUD indicated that up front costs could be lowered by yield spread premiums.54 FR 38646 (September 20, 1989).

In a 1992 rule concerning RESPA, HUD specifically listed yield spread premiums as an example of fees that must be disclosed. The example was codified as Illustrations of Requirements of RESPA, Fact Situations 5 and 13 in Appendix B to 24 CFR part 3500. (See also Instructions at Appendix A to 24 CFR part 3500 for Completing HUD–1 and HUD–1A Settlement Statements.) HUD did not by these examples mean that yield spread premiums were *per se* legal, but HUD also did not mean that yield spread premiums were *per se* illegal.

HUD also recognizes, however, that in some cases less scrupulous brokers and lenders take advantage of the complexity of the settlement transaction and use yield spread premiums as a way to enhance the profitability of mortgage transactions without offering the borrower lower up front fees. In these cases, yield spread premiums serve to increase the borrower's interest rate and the broker's overall compensation, without lowering up front cash requirements for the borrower. As set forth in this Statement of Policy, such uses of yield spread premiums may result in total compensation in excess of what is reasonably related to the total value of the origination services provided by the broker, and fail to comply with the second part of HUD's two-part test as enunciated in the 1999 Statement of Policy, and with Section 8.

The 1999 Statement of Policy's Test for Legality

The Department restates its position that yield spread premiums are not per se illegal. HUD also reiterates that this statement "does not imply * * * that yield spread premiums are legal in individual cases or classes of transactions." 64 FR 10084. The legality of any yield spread premium can only be evaluated in the context of the test HUD established and the specific factual circumstances applicable to each transaction in which a yield spread premium is used.

The 1999 Statement of Policy established a two-part test for determining whether lender payments to mortgage brokers are legal under RESPA. In applying Section 8 and HUD's regulations, the 1999 Statement of Policy stated:

> In transactions where lenders make payments to mortgage brokers, HUD does not consider such payments (*i.e.*, yield spread premiums or any other class of named payments) to be illegal *per se*. HUD does not view the name of the payment as the appropriate issue under RESPA. HUD's position that lender payments to mortgage brokers are not illegal *per se* does not imply, however, that yield spread premiums are legal in individual cases or classes of transactions. The fees in cases and classes of transactions are illegal if they violate the prohibitions of Section 8 of RESPA.
>
> In determining whether a payment from a lender to a mortgage broker is permissible under Section 8 of RESPA, the first question is whether goods or facilities were actually furnished or services were actually performed for the compensation paid. The fact that goods or facilities have been actually furnished or that services have been actually performed by the mortgage broker does not by itself make the payment legal. The second question is whether the payments are reasonably related to the value of the goods or facilities that were actually furnished or services that were actually performed.
>
> In applying this test, HUD believes that total compensation should be scrutinized to assure that it is reasonably related to goods, facilities, or services furnished or performed to determine whether it is legal under RESPA. Total compensation to a broker includes direct origination and other fees paid by the borrower, indirect fees, including those that are derived from the interest rate paid by the borrower, or a combination of some or all. The Department considers that higher interest rates alone cannot justify higher total fees to mortgage brokers. All fees will be scrutinized as part of total compensation to determine that total compensation is reasonably related to the goods or facilities actually furnished or services actually performed. HUD believes that total compensation should be carefully considered in relation to price structures and practices in similar transactions and in similar markets. 64 FR 10084.

Culpepper

The need for further clarification of HUD's position, as set forth in the 1999 Statement of Policy, on the treatment of lender payments to mortgage brokers under Section 8 of RESPA (12 U.S.C. 2607), is evident from the recent decision of the Court of Appeals for the Eleventh Circuit in *Culpepper*.

In upholding class certification in *Culpepper*, the court only applied the first part of the HUD test, and then further narrowed its examination of whether the lender's yield spread payments were "for services" by focusing exclusively on the presumed intent of the lender in making the payments. The crux of the court's decision is that Section 8 liability for the payment of unlawful referral fees could be established under the first part of the HUD test alone, based on the facts that the lender's payments to mortgage brokers were calculated solely on the difference between the par interest rate and the higher rate at which the mortgage brokers delivered loans, and that the lender had no knowledge of what services, if any, the brokers had performed.

HUD was not a party to the case and disagrees with the judicial interpretation regarding Section 8 of

[1] Indirect fees from lenders are also known as "back funded payments," "overages," or "servicing release premiums."

Federal Register / Vol. 66, No. 202 / Thursday, October 18, 2001 / Rules and Regulations 53055

RESPA and the 1999 Statement of Policy.

Clarification of the HUD Test

It is HUD's position that where compensable services are performed, the 1999 Statement of Policy requires application of both parts of the HUD test before a determination can be made regarding the legality of a lender payment to a mortgage broker.

1. *The First Part of the HUD Test:* Under the first part of HUD's test, the total compensation to a mortgage broker, of which a yield spread premium may be a component or the entire amount, must be for goods or facilities provided or services performed. HUD's position is that in order to discern whether a yield spread premium was for goods, facilities or services under the first part of the HUD test, it is necessary to look at each transaction individually, including examining all of the goods or facilities provided or services performed by the broker in the transaction, whether the goods, facilities or services are paid for by the borrower, the lender, or partly by both.

It is HUD's position that neither Section 8(a) of RESPA nor the 1999 Statement of Policy supports the conclusion that a yield spread premium can be presumed to be a referral fee based solely upon the fact that the lender pays the broker a yield spread premium that is based upon a rate sheet, or because the lender does not have specific knowledge of what services the broker has performed. HUD considers the latter situation to be rare. The common industry practice is that lenders follow underwriting standards that demand a review of originations and that therefore lenders typically know that brokers have performed the services required to meet those standards.

Yield spread premiums are by definition derived from the interest rate. HUD believes that a rate sheet is merely a mechanism for displaying the yield spread premium, and does not indicate whether a particular yield spread premium is a payment for goods and facilities actually furnished or services actually performed under the HUD test. Whether or not a yield spread premium is legal or illegal cannot be determined by the use of a rate sheet, but by how HUD's test applies to the transaction involved.

Section 8 prohibits the giving and accepting of fees, kickbacks, or things of value for the referral of settlement services and also unearned fees. It is therefore prudent for a lender to take action so as to ensure that brokers are performing compensable services and receiving only compensation that, in total, is reasonable for those services provided. As stated, however, in the 1999 Statement of Policy:

> The Department recognizes that some of the goods or facilities actually furnished or services actually performed by the broker in originating a loan are "for" the lender and other goods or facilities actually furnished or services actually performed are "for" the borrower. HUD does not believe that it is necessary or even feasible to identify or allocate which facilities, goods or services are performed or provided for the lender, for the borrower, or as a function of State or Federal law. All services, goods and facilities inure to the benefit of both the borrower and the lender in the sense that they make the loan transaction possible. * * * 64 FR 10086.

The 1999 Statement of Policy provided a list of compensable loan origination services originally developed by HUD in a response to an inquiry from the Independent Bankers Association of America (IBAA), which HUD considers relevant in evaluating mortgage broker services. In analyzing each transaction to determine if services are performed HUD believes the 1999 Statement of Policy should be used as a guide. As stated there, the IBAA list is not exhaustive, and while technology is changing the process of performing settlement services, HUD believes that the list is still a generally accurate description of settlement services. Compensation for these services may be paid either by the borrower or by the lender, or partly by both. Compensable services for the first part of the test do not include referrals or no, nominal, or duplicative work.

2. *Reasonableness of Broker Fees:* The second part of HUD's test requires that total compensation to the mortgage broker be reasonably related to the total set of goods or facilities actually furnished or services performed.

The 1999 Statement of Policy said in part:

> The Department considers that higher interest rates alone cannot justify higher total fees to mortgage brokers. All fees will be scrutinized as part of total compensation to determine that total compensation is reasonably related to the goods or facilities actually furnished or services actually performed. 64 FR 10084.

Accordingly, the Department believes that the second part of the test is applied by determining whether a mortgage broker's total compensation is reasonable. Total compensation includes fees paid by a borrower and any yield spread premium paid by a lender, not simply the yield spread premium alone. Yield spread premiums serve to allow the borrower a lower up front cash payment in return for a higher interest rate, while allowing the broker to recoup the total costs of originating the loan. Total compensation to the broker must be reasonably related to the total value of goods or facilities provided or services performed by the broker. Simply delivering a loan with a higher interest rate is not a compensable service. The Department affirms the 1999 Statement of Policy's position on this matter for purposes of RESPA enforcement.

The 1999 Statement also said:

> In analyzing whether a particular payment or fee bears a reasonable relationship to the value of the goods or facilities actually furnished or services actually performed, HUD believes that payments must be commensurate with the amount normally charged for similar services, goods or facilities. This analysis requires careful consideration of fees paid in relation to price structures and practices in similar transactions and in similar markets. If the payment or a portion thereof bears no reasonable relationship to the market value of the goods, facilities or services provided, the excess over the market rate may be used as evidence of a compensated referral or an unearned fee in violation of Section 8(a) or (b) of RESPA. 64 FR 10086.

The 1999 Statement of Policy also stated:

> The level of services mortgage brokers provide in particular transactions depends on the level of difficulty involved in qualifying applicants for particular loan programs. For example, applicants have differences in credit ratings, employment status, levels of debt, or experience that will translate into various degrees of effort required for processing a loan. Also, the mortgage broker may be required to perform various levels of services under different servicing or processing arrangements with wholesale lenders. 64 FR 10081.

In evaluating mortgage broker fees for enforcement purposes, HUD will consider these factors as relevant in assessing the reasonableness of mortgage broker compensation, as well as comparing total compensation for loans of similar size and similar characteristics within similar geographic markets.

Also, while the Department continues to believe that comparison to prices in similar markets is generally a key factor in determining whether a mortgage broker's total compensation is reasonable, it is also true that in less competitive markets comparisons to the prices charged by other similarly situated providers may not, standing alone, provide a useful measure. As a general principle, HUD believes that in evaluating the reasonableness of broker compensation in less competitive markets, consideration of price structures from a wider range of

53056 Federal Register / Vol. 66, No. 202 / Thursday, October 18, 2001 / Rules and Regulations

providers may be warranted to reach a meaningful conclusion.

Part B. Providing Meaningful Information to Borrowers

In addition to addressing the legality of yield spread premiums in the 1999 Statement of Policy, HUD emphasized the importance of disclosing broker fees, including yield spread premiums.

There is no requirement under existing law that consumers be fully informed of the broker's services and compensation prior to the GFE. Nevertheless, HUD believes that the broker should provide the consumer with information about the broker's services and compensation, and agreement by the consumer to the arrangement should occur as early as possible in the process. 64 FR 10087.

HUD continues to believe that disclosure is extremely important, and that many of the concerns expressed by borrowers over yield spread premiums can be addressed by disclosing yield spread premiums, borrower compensation to the broker, and the terms of the mortgage loan, so that the borrower may evaluate and choose among alternative loan options.

In the 1999 Statement of Policy, HUD stated:

* * * HUD believes that for the market to work effectively, borrowers should be afforded a meaningful opportunity to select the most appropriate product and determine what price they are willing to pay for the loan based on disclosures which provide clear and understandable information.

The Department reiterates its long-standing view that disclosure alone does not make illegal fees legal under RESPA. On the other hand, while under current law, pre-application disclosure to the consumer is not required, HUD believes that fuller information provided at the earliest possible moment in the shopping process would increase consumer satisfaction and reduce the possibility of misunderstanding. 64 FR 10087.

HUD currently requires the disclosure of yield spread premiums on the Good Faith Estimate and the HUD–1. The 1999 Statement of Policy said:

The Department has always indicated that any fees charged in settlement transactions should be clearly disclosed so that the consumer can understand the nature and recipient of the payment. Code-like abbreviations like 'YSP to DBG, POC', for instance, have been noted. [Footnote omitted.] Also the Department has seen examples on the GFE and/or the settlement statement where the identity and/or purposes of the fees are not clearly disclosed.

The Department considers unclear and confusing disclosures to be contrary to the statute's and the regulation's purposes of making RESPA-covered transactions understandable to the consumer. At a minimum, all fees to the mortgage broker are to be clearly labeled and properly estimated on the GFE. On the settlement statement, the name of the recipient of the fee (in this case, the mortgage broker) is to be clearly labeled and listed, and the fee received from a lender is to be clearly labeled and listed in the interest of clarity. 64 FR 10086–10087.

While the disclosure on the GFE and HUD–1 is required, the Department is aware and has stated that the current GFE/HUD–1 disclosure framework is often insufficient to adequately inform consumers about yield spread premiums and other lender paid fees to brokers. Under the current rules, the GFE need not be provided until after the consumer has applied for a mortgage and may have paid a significant fee, and the HUD–1 is only given at closing. Because of this, HUD has in recent years sought to foster a more consumer beneficial approach to disclosure regarding yield spread premiums through successive rulemaking efforts. This history is discussed more fully in the 1999 Statement of Policy.[2]

Representatives of the mortgage industry have said that since the 1999 Statement of Policy, many brokers provide borrowers a disclosure describing the function of mortgage brokers and stating that a mortgage broker may receive a fee in the transaction from the lender. While the 1999 Statement of Policy commended the National Association of Mortgage Brokers and the Mortgage Bankers Association of America for strongly suggesting such a disclosure to their respective memberships, the Statement of Policy added:

Although this statement of policy does not mandate disclosures beyond those currently required by RESPA and Regulation X, the most effective approach to disclosure would allow a prospective borrower to properly evaluate the nature of the services and all costs for a broker transaction, and to agree to such services and costs before applying for a loan. Under such an approach, the broker would make the borrower aware of whether the broker is or is not serving as the consumer's agent to shop for a loan, and the total compensation to be paid to the mortgage broker, including the amounts of each of the fees making up the compensation. 64 FR 10087.

In HUD's view, meaningful disclosure includes many types of information: what services a mortgage broker will perform, the amount of the broker's total compensation for performing those services (including any yield spread premium paid by the lender), and whether or not the broker has an agency or fiduciary relationship with the borrower. The disclosure should also make the borrower aware that he or she may pay higher up front costs for a mortgage with a lower interest rate, or conversely pay a higher interest rate in return for lower up front costs, and should identify the specific trade-off between the amount of the increase in the borrower's monthly payment (and also the increase in the interest rate) and the amount by which up front costs are reduced. HUD believes that disclosure of this information, and written acknowledgment by the borrower that he or she has received the information, should be provided early in the transaction. Such disclosure facilitates comparison shopping by the borrower, to choose the best combination of up front costs and mortgage terms from his or her individual standpoint. HUD regards full disclosure and written acknowledgment by the borrower, at the earliest possible time, as a best practice.

Yield spread premiums are currently required to be listed in the "800" series of the HUD–1 form, listing "Items Payable in Connection with Loan." This existing practice, however, does not disclose the purpose of the yield spread premium, which is to lower up front cost to borrowers. To achieve this end it has been suggested to the Department that the yield spread premium should be reported as a credit to the borrower in the "200" series, among the "Amounts Paid by or in Behalf of Borrowers." The homebuyer or homeowner could then see that the yield spread premium is reducing closing costs, and also see the extent of the reduction.

HUD believes that improved early disclosure regarding mortgage broker compensation and the entry of yield spread premiums as credits to borrowers on the GFE and the HUD–1 settlement statement are both useful and complementary forms of disclosure. The Department believes that used together these methods of disclosure offer greater assurance that lender payments to mortgage brokers serve borrowers' best interests.

While the 1999 Policy Statement and IV. Part A. of this Statement only cover certain lender payments to mortgage brokers, as described above, HUD also believes that similar information on the trade-off between lower up front costs and higher interest rates and monthly payments should be disclosed to borrowers on all mortgage loan originations, not merely those originated by brokers. HUD is aware that while yield spread premiums are not used in loans originated by lenders, lenders are able to offer loans with low or no up

[2] In both the HUD/Federal Reserve Board Report on RESPA/TILA Reform, 1998, and the HUD/Treasury Report on Curbing Predatory Home Mortgage Lending, 2000, the agencies recommended earlier disclosures to facilitate shopping and lower settlement costs.

Federal Register / Vol. 66, No. 202 / Thursday, October 18, 2001 / Rules and Regulations 53057

front costs required at closing by charging higher interest rates and recouping the costs by selling the loans into the secondary market for a price representing the difference between the interest rate on the loan and the par, or market, interest rate. Sale of such a loan achieves the same purpose as the yield spread premium does on a loan originated by a broker. The Department strongly believes that all lenders and brokers should provide the level of consumer disclosure that the purposes of RESPA intend and that fair business practices demand. As indicated in the 1999 Statement of Policy, HUD emphasizes that fuller information provided as early as possible in the shopping process would increase consumer satisfaction and reduce the possibility of misunderstanding. In the future, full and early disclosures are factors that the Department would weigh favorably in exercising its enforcement discretion in cases involving mortgage broker fees. Nevertheless, the Department also again makes clear that disclosure alone does not make illegal fees legal under RESPA. The Department will scrutinize all relevant information in making enforcement decisions, including whether transactions evidence practices that may be illegal.

Part C. Section 8(b) Unearned Fees

A. Background

RESPA was enacted in 1974 to provide consumers "greater and more timely information on the nature of the costs of the [real estate] settlement process" and to protect consumers from "unnecessarily high settlement charges caused by certain abusive practices * * *" 12 U.S.C. 2601.

Since RESPA was enacted, HUD has interpreted Section 8(b) as prohibiting any person from giving or accepting any unearned fees, i.e., charges or payments for real estate settlement services other than for goods or facilities provided or services performed. Payments that are unearned fees for settlement services occur in, but are not limited to, cases where: (1) Two or more persons split a fee for settlement services, any portion of which is unearned; or (2) one settlement service provider marks-up the cost of the services performed or goods provided by another settlement service provider without providing additional actual, necessary, and distinct services, goods, or facilities to justify the additional charge; or (3) one settlement service provider charges the consumer a fee where no, nominal, or duplicative work is done, or the fee is in excess of the reasonable value of goods or facilities provided or the services actually performed.

In the first situation, two settlement service providers split or share a fee charged to a consumer and at least part, if not all, of at least one provider's share of the fee is unearned. In the second situation, a settlement service provider charges a fee to a consumer for another provider's services that is higher than the actual price of such services, and keeps the difference without performing any actual, necessary, and distinct services to justify the additional charge. In the third situation, one settlement service provider charges a fee to a consumer where no work is done or the fee exceeds the reasonable value of the services performed by that provider, and for this reason the fee or any portion thereof for which services are not performed is unearned.

HUD regards all of these situations as legally indistinguishable, in that they involve payments for settlement services where all or a portion of the fees are unearned and, thus, are violative of the statute. HUD, therefore, specifically interprets Section 8(b) as not being limited to situations where at least two persons split or share an unearned fee for the provision to be violated.

As already indicated in this Statement of Policy, meaningful disclosure of all charges and fees is essential under RESPA. Such disclosures help protect consumers from paying unearned or duplicate fees. However, as noted above, in the 1999 Statement of Policy the Department reiterated "its long-standing view that disclosure alone does not make illegal fees legal under RESPA." 64 FR 10087.

B. HUD's Guidance and Regulations

HUD guidance and regulations have consistently interpreted Section 8 as prohibiting all unearned fees. In 1976, HUD issued a Settlement Costs Booklet that provided that "[i] t is also illegal to charge or accept a fee or part of a fee where no service has actually been performed." 41 FR 20289 (May 17, 1976). Between 1976 and 1992, HUD indicated in informal opinions that unearned fees occur where there are excessive fees charged, regardless of the number of settlement service providers involved.[3]

In the preamble to HUD's 1992 final rule revising Regulation X (57 FR 49600 (November 2, 1992)), HUD stated: "Section 8 of RESPA (12 U.S.C. 2607) prohibits kickbacks for referral of business incident to or part of a settlement service and also prohibits the splitting of a charge for a settlement service, other than for services actually performed (i.e., no payment of unearned fees)." 57 FR 49600 (November 2, 1992).

HUD's regulations, published on November 2, 1992, implement Section 8(b). Section 3500.14(c)[4] provides:

> No person shall give and no person shall accept any portion, split, or percentage of any charge made or received for the rendering of a settlement service in connection with a transaction involving a federally-related mortgage loan other than for services actually performed. A charge by a person for which no or nominal services are performed or for which duplicative fees are charged is an unearned fee and violates this Section. The source of the payment does not determine whether or not a service is compensable. Nor may the prohibitions of this part be avoided by creating an arrangement wherein the purchaser of services splits the fee.

24 CFR 3500.14(g)(2) states in part:

> The Department may investigate high prices to see if they are the result of a referral fee or a split of a fee. If the payment of a thing of value bears no reasonable relationship to the market value of the goods or services provided, then the excess is not for services or goods actually performed or provided. These facts may be used as evidence of a violation of Section 8 and may serve as a basis for a RESPA investigation. High prices standing alone are not proof of a RESPA violation.

24 CFR 3500.14(g)(3) provides in part:

> When a person in a position to refer settlement service business * * * receives a payment for providing additional settlement services as part of a real estate transaction, such payment must be for services that are actual, necessary and distinct from the primary services provided by such person.

---

[3] See e.g., Old Informal Opinion [6], August 16, 1976 and Old Informal Opinion [65], April 4, 1980; Barron and Berenson, *Federal Regulation of Real Estate and Mortgage Lending*, (4th Ed. 1998). On November 2, 1992 (57 F.R. 49600), when HUD issued revisions to its RESPA regulations, it withdrew all of its informal counsel opinions and staff interpretations issued before that date. The 1992 rule provided, however, that courts and administrative agencies could use HUD's previous opinions to determine the validity of conduct occurring under the previous version of Regulation X. See 24 CFR 3500.4(c).

[4] The heading to 24 CFR 3500.14 is titled "Prohibition against kickbacks and unearned fees." However, the heading of subsection (c) is titled "split of charges," and the preamble to the November 1992 rule states "[s]ection 8 of RESPA (12 U.S.C. 2607) prohibits kickbacks for referral of business incident to or part of a settlement service and also prohibits the splitting of a charge for a settlement service, other than for services actually performed (i.e., no payment of unearned fees)." 57 FR 49600 (November 2, 1992). The rule headings and preamble text are a generalized description of Section 8 that is more developed in the actual regulation text. As discussed in Section D of this Statement of Policy, HUD believes that the actual text of the rules, as amended in 1992, makes clear that Section 8(b)'s prohibitions against unearned fees apply even when only one settlement service provider is involved.

53058 Federal Register / Vol. 66, No. 202 / Thursday, October 18, 2001 / Rules and Regulations

In Appendix B to the HUD RESPA regulations, HUD provides illustrations of the requirements of RESPA. Comment 3 states in part:

> The payment of a commission or portion of the * * * premium * * * or receipt of a portion of the payment * * * where no substantial services are being performed * * * is a violation of Section 8 of RESPA. It makes no difference whether the payment comes from [the settlement service provider] or the purchaser. The amount of the payment must bear a reasonable relationship to the services rendered. Here [the real estate broker in the example] is being compensated for a referral of business to [the title company].

In 1996, in the preamble to the final rule on the Withdrawal of Employer/Employee and Computer Loan Origination Systems Exemptions[5] (61 FR 29238 (June 7, 1996)), HUD reiterated its interpretation of Section 8(b) of RESPA as follows.

> HUD believes that Section 8(b) of the statute and the legislative history make clear that no person is allowed to receive 'any portion' of charges for settlement services, except for services actually performed. The provisions of Section 8(b) could apply in a number of situations: (1) where one settlement service provider receives an unearned fee from another provider; (2) where one settlement service provider charges the consumer for third-party services and retains an unearned fee from the payment received; or (3) where one settlement service provider accepts a portion of a charge (including 100% of the charge) for other than services actually performed. The interpretation urged [by the commenters to the proposed rule published on July 21, 1994], that a single settlement service provider can charge unearned or excessive fees so long as the fees are not shared with another, is an unnecessarily restrictive interpretation of a statute designed to reduce unnecessary costs to consumers. The Secretary, charged by statute with interpreting RESPA, interprets Section 8(b) to mean that two persons are not required for the provision to be violated. 61 FR 29249.

The latest revision to the Settlement Costs Booklet for consumers, issued in 1997, also provides "[i]t is also illegal for anyone to accept a fee or part of a fee for services if that person has not actually performed settlement services for the fee." 62 FR 31998 (June 11, 1997).

Further, HUD has provided information to the public and the mortgage industry in the "Frequently Asked Questions" section of its RESPA Web site, located at *<http://www.hud.gov/fha/sfh/res/resindus.html>*. Question 25 states:

> Can a lender collect from the borrower an appraisal fee of $200, listing the fee as such on the HUD–1, yet pay an independent appraiser $175 and collect the $25 difference?

The answer reads:

> No, the lender may only collect $175 as the actual charge. It is a violation of Section 8(b) for any person to accept a split of a fee where services are not performed.

In 1999, by letter submitted at the request of the Superior Court of California, Los Angeles County, in the case of *Brown v. Washington Mutual Bank* (Case No. BC192874), HUD provided the following response to a specific question posed by the court on lender "markups" of another settlement service provider's fees:

> A lender that purchases third party vendor services for purposes of closing a federally related mortgage loan may not, under RESPA, mark up the third party vendor fees for purposes of making a profit. HUD has consistently advised that where lenders or others charge consumers marked-up prices for services performed by the third party providers without performing additional services, such charges constitute "splits of fees" or "unearned fees" in violation of Section 8(b) of RESPA.

HUD noted in its letter to the court that the response reflected the Department's long-standing position.

C. Recent Cases

Notwithstanding HUD's regulations and other guidance, the Court of Appeals for the Seventh Circuit held, in *Echevarria v. Chicago Title and Trust Co.*, 256 F.3d 623 (7th Cir. 2001), that Section 8(b) was not violated where a title company, without performing any additional services, charged the plaintiffs more money than was required by the recorder's office to record a deed and the title company then retained the difference. The court reasoned that plaintiffs "failed to plead facts tending to show that Chicago Title illegally shared fees with the Cook County Recorder. The Cook County Recorder received no more than its regular recording fees and it did not give to or arrange for Chicago Title to receive an unearned portion of these fees. The County Recorder has not engaged in the third party involvement necessary to state a claim under [RESPA § 8(b)]." Id. at 626. The court in essence concluded that unearned fees must be passed from one settlement provider to another in order for such fees to violate Section 8(b).

Earlier, in *Willis v. Quality Mortgage USA, Inc.*, 5 F. Supp. 2d 1306 (M.D. Ala. 1998), cited by the Seventh Circuit in support of its conclusion, the district court concluded that 24 CFR 3500.14(c), "[w]hen read as a whole," prohibits payments for which no services are performed "only if those payments are split with another party." Id. at 1309. The *Willis* court held that there must be a split of a charge between a settlement service provider and a third party to establish a violation Section 8(b). The court also concluded that 24 CFR 3500.14(g)(3) only applied when there was a payment from a lender to a broker, or vice versa. The payment from a borrower to a mortgage lender could not be the basis for a violation of 24 CFR 3500.14(g)(3) and Section 8(b).

HUD was not a party to the cases and disagrees with these judicial interpretations of Section 8(b) which it regards as inconsistent with HUD's regulations and HUD's long-standing interpretations of Section 8(b).

D. Unearned Fees Under Section 8(b)

This Statement of Policy reaffirms HUD's existing, long-standing interpretation of Section 8(b) of RESPA. Sections 8(a) and (b) of RESPA contain distinct prohibitions. Section 8(a) prohibits the giving or acceptance of any payment pursuant to an agreement or understanding for the referral of settlement service business involving a federally related mortgage loan; it is intended to eliminate kickbacks or compensated referral arrangements among settlement service providers. Section 8(b) prohibits the giving or accepting of any portion, split, or percentage of any charge other than for goods or facilities provided or services performed; it is intended to eliminate unearned fees. Such fees are contrary to the Congressional finding when enacting RESPA that consumers need protection from unnecessarily high settlement charges. 12 U.S.C. 2601(a).

It is HUD's position that Section 8(b) proscribes the acceptance of any portion or part of a charge other than for services actually performed. Inasmuch as Section 8(b)'s proscription against "any portion, split, or percentage" of an unearned charge for settlement services is written in the disjunctive, the prohibition is not limited to a split. In HUD's view, Section 8(b) forbids the paying or accepting of any portion or percentage of a settlement service—including up to 100%—that is unearned, whether the entire charge is divided or split among more than one person or entity or is retained by a single person. Simply put, given that Section 8(b) proscribes unearned portions or percentages as well as splits, HUD does not regard the provision as restricting only fee splitting among settlement service providers. Further, since Section 8(b) on its face prohibits

[5] This final rule was delayed by legislation, but the Department implemented portions of the final rule that were not affected by the legislative delay on November 15, 1996. 61 FR 58472 (November 15, 1996).

Federal Register / Vol. 66, No. 202 / Thursday, October 18, 2001 / Rules and Regulations 53059

the giving or accepting of an unearned fee by any person, and 24 CFR 3500.14(c) speaks of a charge by "a person," it is also incorrect to conclude that the Section 8(b) proscription covers only payments or charges among settlement service providers.[6]

A settlement service provider may not levy an additional charge upon a borrower for another settlement service provider's services without providing additional services that are bona fide and justify the increased charge. Accordingly, a settlement service provider may not mark-up the cost of another provider's services without providing additional settlement services; such payment must be for services that are actual, necessary and distinct services provided to justify the charge. 24 CFR 3500.14(g)(3).[7] The HUD regulation implementing Section 8(b) states: "[a] charge by a person for which no or nominal services are performed or for which duplicative fees are charged is an unearned fee and violates this Section." 24 CFR 3500.14 (c).

The regulations also make clear that a charge by a single service provider where little or no services are performed is an unearned fee that is prohibited by the statute. 24 CFR 3000.14(c). A single service provider is also prohibited from charging a duplicative fee. Further, a single service provider cannot serve in two capacities, e.g., a title agent and closing attorney, and be paid twice for the same service. The fee the service provider would be receiving in this case is duplicative under 24 CFR 3000.14(c) and not necessary and distinct under 24 CFR 3000.14(g)(3). Clearly, in all of these instances, the source of the payment—whether from consumers, other settlement service providers, or other third parties—is not relevant in determining whether the fee is earned or unearned because ultimately, all settlement payments come directly or indirectly from the consumer. See 24 CFR 3500.14(c). Therefore, a single settlement service provider violates Section 8(b) whenever it receives an unearned fee.

A single service provider also may be liable under Section 8(b) when it charges a fee that exceeds the reasonable value of goods, facilities, or services provided. HUD's regulations as noted state: "If the payment of a thing of value bears no relationship to the goods or services provided, then the excess is not for services or goods actually performed or provided." 24 CFR 3500.14(g)(2). Section 8(c)(2) only allows "the payment to any person of a bona fide salary or compensation or other payment for goods or facilities actually furnished or services actually performed," i.e., permitting only that compensation which is reasonably related to the goods or facilities provided or services performed. Compensation that is unreasonable is unearned under Section 8(b) and is not bona fide under Section 8(c)(2).

The Secretary, therefore, interprets Section 8(b) of RESPA to prohibit all unearned fees, including, but not limited to, cases where: (1) Two or more persons split a fee for settlement services, any portion of which is unearned; or (2) one settlement service provider marks-up the cost of the services performed or goods provided by another settlement service provider without providing additional actual, necessary, and distinct services, goods, or facilities to justify the additional charge; or (3) one service provider charges the consumer a fee where no, nominal, or duplicative work is done, or the fee is in excess of the reasonable value of goods or facilities provided or the services actually performed.

V. Executive Order 12866, Regulatory Planning and Review

The Office of Management and Budget (OMB) has reviewed this Statement of Policy in accordance with Executive Order 12866, (captioned "Regulatory Planning and Review"). OMB determined that this Statement of Policy is a "significant regulatory action" as defined in Section 3(f) of the Order (although not an economically significant regulatory action under the Order). Any changes to the Statement of Policy resulting from this review are available for public inspection between 7:30 a.m. and 5:30 p.m. weekdays in the Office of the Rules Docket Clerk.

Dated: October 15, 2001.

John C. Weicher,

Assistant Secretary for Housing-Federal Housing Commissioner.

[FR Doc. 01–26321 Filed 10–15–01; 4:51 pm]

BILLING CODE 4210–27–P

[6] HUD is, of course, unlikely to direct any enforcement actions against consumers for the payment of unearned fees, because a consumer's intent is to make payment for services, not an unearned fee.

[7] HUD notes that some lenders have charged an additional fee merely for "reviewing" another settlement service provider's services. HUD does not regard such "review" as constituting an actual, necessary, or distinct additional service permissible under HUD's regulations.

CHAPTER 11

Secured Lending—Personal Property

A lending institution may use a wide variety of methods to secure a loan, including accounts receivable inventory, warehousing receipts, or security agreements covering vehicles, boats, machinery, equipment, etc. The use of these devices may be supervised by an attorney, but in most instances by the lending officer completing form agreements in accordance with the instruction of the attorneys unless the amount is significant. The legal proceedings to enforce the security agreement are left entirely to the attorney. Rarely does a credit and collection manager become involved in this process.

The credit and collection manager is deeply involved in negotiating with the debtor when the debtor is in default, and is continually communicating with the attorney in the enforcement process of the security agreement. In this chapter, the rights and obligations under a security agreement will be explained so that a credit and collection manager and counsel may communicate more effectively regarding the enforcement of security agreements.

REVISED ARTICLE 9

The Revised Article 9 has now been adopted in 50 states. The effective date of Revised Article 9 varies from state to state. We have included in the Appendix to this chapter the Revised Article 9 adopted in California, which is representative of the Article 9 passed in the other states.

Each state has made minor, and in a few instances, major changes in Article 9. Before you embark on any security transaction, consult with experienced counsel to be certain that you are complying with the law of the state where the security agreement is being enforced.

We provide here an overview of Article 9 and present in detail some of the problems with regard to preparation of a financing statement and some of the transition problems. We also cover some of the sections that deal with notification of disposition of collateral and the actual disposition of collateral.

For those who are heavily involved in obtaining and enforcing security agreements, you must already have a copy of Article 9 with the comments as well as an explanation, comparison, checklist, and other things which have been provided in a new book, entitled The New Article 9, Uniform Commercial Code (UCC), published by the American Bar Association. For those of you who do not have this book, we strongly recommend that you obtain it from the American Bar Association by calling 1-800-285-2221. They also have a smaller edition, entitled The Portable UCC, which may be slipped into a briefcase. Some state bar associations are offering other publications.

Of the 28 provisions of Revised Article 9's Part 6 (Enforcement), which covers the sections from 600 through 628, several are brand new and do not resemble similar sections in Old Article 9. Many of the other sections have been revised and the revisions in some of the sections are substantial. *Since Old Article 9 will apply to all existing finance statements, security agreements, and litigation prior to Revised Article 9*, we will present the law as it existed as well as set forth the changes. Since many sections of Revised Article 9 are the same as Old Article 9, much of the case law is still applicable to Revised Article 9.

GOODS OR SERVICES

Under UCC 2-102, the UCC applies only to transactions in goods. Under Section 2-105, "goods" means all things which are movable. The concept is movability, not the existence of the goods. If the goods are not movable, they are considered to be real estate or fixtures attached to the real estate. Goods also include unborn young animals and growing crops and, other identified things attached to real estate (review UCC Section 107 covering goods severed from realty).

An issue often arises as to whether a contract is predominately for the sale of goods or for the sale of services. As a question of law, the "predominate factor" test is used in deciding whether the essence of the contract is primarily a sale of goods or providing services. If it is a sale of goods, the UCC will govern. This issue is often litigated when the existence of the alleged agreement or terms are in dispute. The UCC contains "gap" filling provisions to address these issues and permit the enforcement of the agreement. If it is for services, the UCC will not be applied. Where goods and services are both involved, the decision rests on whether the services are incidental to the goods or the goods are merely incidental to the services. Price allocation between the goods and labor is usually not a consideration in determining the predominate factor. The rendition of substantial amounts of labor does not necessarily exclude the transaction from the coverage of the UCC.[1]

DURATION

A financing statement is effective for a period of five years. A continuation statement can be filed to extend the period for an additional five years, providing the continuation statement is filed not less than six months prior to the expiration of the first period.

CONTINUATION STATEMENT

A continuation statement filed before the six-month period is not timely and cannot have the continuing effectiveness of the original financing statement. Filing a few days before the six-month period is not substantial compliance and does not cure an untimely filing. The continuation statement must be filed within that six-month period before the financing statement expires and not one day prior to it.[2] Filing the continuation properly extends the initial filing for an additional five years (Revised UCC 9-515).

The number of filings that occur on the last day of the five-year period lead to significant litigation over the measurement of the five-year period. Despite a six-month window within which to file a continuation statement, the tendency of a portion of the population to do things at the last minute apparently applies equally to the filing of financing statements.

The measurement of the five-year period is not a bright line and that's what causes the litigation. Many states have time computation statutes that refer to a particular act that must be done within a specific period of time. The time computation statute identifies the first day of the act as well as the last day of the act and usually explicit exclusions of certain days and inclusions of certain days are contained in the statute. If you are one of the many who decide to file on what you believe is the last day of the five-year period, review the time computation statute in the particular state. Your author

---

[1] *Kietzer v. Land O'Lakes*, 2002 WL 233746 (Minn. App. Feb. 19, 2002).

[2] *NBD Bank, N.A. v. Timberjack, Inc.*, 208 Mich. App. 153, 527 N.W.2d 50 (Mich. Ct. App. 1995).

cannot provide assurance that a time computation statute exists in every state and, in those states where a statute does not exist, you must review the case law of the state to find the correct last day. The lesson: File at least a week prior to the end of the five-year period—or even a month before.[3]

SECURITY AGREEMENT—FINANCING STATEMENT

The security agreement is the basic agreement creating the secured interest of the creditor in the property. It identifies the personal property which is covered and is being used as collateral for the loan, the amount of the loan, the terms of the loan, the interest charged, the terms of the repayment, any late charges, and attorneys' fees. The agreement also will include obligations of the debtor to maintain the personal property, to obtain insurance, or to otherwise protect the property. Provisions in favor of the creditor generally deal with the acts of default which accelerate the balance due, the terms and conditions under which the creditor can repossess the collateral, the notices which have to be given, the charges that the debtor must pay, and any other waivers of rights by the debtor, such as a waiver to a jury trial. If the collateral should be crops or fixtures, a description of the real estate where the crops or fixtures are located will be included.

The description is sufficient if it reasonably identifies the collateral intended by the parties. After-acquired property (property acquired after the date of execution of the security agreement) may be covered, except with regard to consumer goods, unless they are acquired within ten days (Revised Article 9-204).

One of the questions often raised is whether a financing statement alone is sufficient to create a security agreement. Most states hold that the execution of a financing statement is not the execution of a security agreement. Perhaps this goes to the ancient theory that a mortgage without a note is insufficient since a mortgage alone is not an obligation, but merely the collateral for the obligation. In this particular instance, the financing statement will merely be the recording device and the security agreement will be the collateral. The great majority of the courts adhere to the rule that a financing statement alone is not sufficient to create a security.

Creditors continually litigate the question of whether a financing statement can act as a security agreement without the magic words that there is a grant of a security interest. A financing statement does not have these magic words. A case decided that financing statements with

---

[3] *Bank of Holden v. Bank of Warrensburg*, 15 S.W.3d 75 (Mo. Ct. App. 2000).

a description of collateral together with invoices from the creditor without a security agreement did not create a valid security interest in goods.[4]

Most security agreements require blank spaces to be completed. The collateral must be identified with model and serial numbers and a description of the property mortgaged. The security agreements are drafted by the lenders (banks) with attention to the rights of the secured party, since the security agreement is designed to benefit the secured party and is used repeatedly. For this reason, secured parties will rarely change the printed portions of the agreement without consulting with counsel. Nevertheless, a printed agreement may be changed if the circumstances so warrant. Sometimes, under unique circumstances, the secured party should consult with counsel to determine if a change sought by the borrowing party is warranted. If the agreement should have an ambiguity, the law will interpret the ambiguity least favorably to the drafter of the agreement (the bank).

Writing Requirement. Only a writing creates a security interest. The Statute of Frauds requires a writing for certain types of transactions, such as real estate transactions, an individual guaranty, or a sale of goods in excess of $500 (to be changed by Revised Article 2).

The writing must show some intent to create a security interest. If the writing does not really meet the test of whether or not the parties intend to grant a security interest, the courts may refer the matter to a factual inquiry as to whether or not this is what the parties intended.

When an agreement does not meet the criteria for a security interest, the creditor often tries to utilize all kinds of documents to create the security agreement since the UCC does not require any particular language to create a security interest. Creditors alleging that a bill of sale, a promissory note or collateral papers are sufficient to establish security interests face the courts on a continual basis. Minutes of meetings of the Board of Directors have been used in conjunction with bills of sale and notes to create a security interest. Needless to say, the states go different ways.

Some state courts want a clear intent set forth in the security agreement, evidencing a right to create a security interest, and will pay little attention to collateral documents. A review of the particular state law is absolutely necessary when confronted with this issue.

Description of Property. A security agreement must "reasonably identify what is described." A copy of a security agreement should be sufficient as a financing statement if it contains the same information that a financing statement is required to contain and is also signed by the debtor. On the other hand, a copy of a financing statement will not suffice to be a security agreement. A description in the financing statement may be used to support a security agreement where a description is absent.

---

[4]*In re Arctic Air, Inc.*, 202 B.R. 533 (Bankr. D.R.I. 1996).

Nevertheless, a description in the financing statement cannot enlarge a description in the security agreement.[5]

Major problems can develop when lenders try to protect themselves by using such terms as "All the equipment set forth in Schedule A" and Schedule A is missing or Schedule A is blank, or Schedule A does not list the debtor's equipment. Such a situation would be litigated as to whether there was an intent to furnish all debtor's equipment as collateral, only a part thereof, or perhaps just two machines. The question of identification may be left to oral evidence where no description was set forth.

The major question is whether to use a broad description to include as much property as possible or a narrow specific description and identify each item of property. The latter is probably the better option.

Another problem arises with the phrase "All the debtor's equipment located at 15 Main Street," a specific address which happens to be the defendant's only store. The debtor may subsequently open a new store and move some of the equipment to that store.

The creditor must realize that the description of the property in the security agreement is not a simple clause to prepare. *Consult with counsel before the preparation and drafting of a security agreement.*

AFTER-ACQUIRED PROPERTY. The use of the phrase "after-acquired equipment" also presents problems and is the subject of considerable litigation. The purpose of this clause is to have the security agreement cover property which is acquired after the execution of the security agreement.

After-acquired property interest is not, by virtue of that fact alone, security for a pre-existing claim (a prior debt secured by the security agreement). The problem arises often in the bankruptcy code, which makes certain transfers for antecedent debts voidable as preferences. If the secured party pays new value and the after-acquired property is given as security in the ordinary course of the debtor's business, the after-acquired property may avoid the problem of the preference. Despite the considerable litigation over the use of this terminology, lawyers and creditors continue to use it as often as possible, for it is an added protection if enforceable.

Article 9 of the UCC and some state laws prohibit after-acquired property clauses in security agreements to enable a creditor to obtain a lien on property which is later acquired by a consumer. Revised *Article 9-204 makes ineffective an after-acquired clause as to consumer goods acquired more than ten days after the secured party gives value, except as accessions.*

SIGNATURES. The code requires the debtor to sign the security agreement. It has been held that a typewritten name is sufficient if oral testimony

---

[5]UCC § 9-324; UCC § 9-327; *Zink v. Vanmiddlesworth*, 300 B.R. 394 (N.D.N.Y. 2003); *Compass Bank v. Kone*, 134 P.3d 500 (Colo. App. 2006); *Dickason v. Marine Nat. Bank of Naples, N.A.*, 898 So. 2d 1170 (Fla. Dist. Ct. App. 2d Dist. 2005).

is received showing the intent of the parties. Courts have held that in certain states it is not necessary that the corporate name or the proper partnership name of the debtor be on the agreement as long as it was the principal who signed. Other courts disagree and require the proper business name, as well as the individual's name. Nevertheless, to avoid litigation, the best advice is to have the principal debtor sign the agreement or an officer with authority of the debtor corporation.

PLEDGE

A pledge of security is where the collateral or personal property is actually transferred physically to the creditor and retained by the creditor until the debtor repays the loan (for example, pawning a watch at a pawn shop). In this case, no filing is necessary.

PRIORITIES

The filing of financing statements is similar to the filing of mortgages in that the financing statement which is filed first in time is prior to a second financing statement that is executed later and filed at a later date. The second financing statement filed would have an interest in the personal property subordinate to the first financing statement. However, exceptions exist for a purchase money security interest in inventory and equipment.

The priorities of a purchase money mortgage are covered in UCC 9-324, which is a rewrite of the old Section 9-312, together with its titles, headings, and many more subdivisions. The commentary is helpful in understanding the rewrite. A careful review of the UCC 9-324 through 9-327 is recommended.

PERFECTION

A security agreement "attaches" when it is enforceable. Enforceable means when value is given, the debtor has a right to the collateral and the power to transfer it. In addition, the debtor has authenticated the agreement (signed) and a description of the property is set forth.

Perfection takes place when a financing statement is filed. Sections 9-310 to 9-316 cover agricultural liens, property subject to statute and certificate of title states (9-311), chattel paper documents, deposit accounts, letter of credit (9-312), and delivery of collateral (9-313). Revised Sections 9-314, 315, and 316 cover perfection by control, rights on disposition of collateral and to proceeds, and continued perfection following a change in the law (where property moves from state to state, a four-month window is available).

LEASES OR SECURITY AGREEMENT

Any financing transaction may be a security interest if the purpose was to create one. If the parties intended to have a security agreement but labeled the transaction a lease, the lease will be treated as a security agreement subject to the provisions of Article 9. Some states, under a new section in the UCC, provide that: (1) if the lessee can return the goods and end the lease, or (2) if the goods have some economic life at the end of the lease, the arrangement is a true lease. A lease of personal property to a consumer which provides that the lessee may purchase the property at the end of the lease for a nominal consideration may convert that lease to a security agreement to be governed by Article 9. Other circumstances are considered by the courts to determine whether the lease was intended as a security agreement.

A lease is not intended to be a security interest. The case law covering the question of whether a transaction is a lease or a security interest is substantial. If the transaction is truly a lease, no financing statement need be filed and, therefore, no notice need be delivered to third parties. If the transaction is not a lease but a security interest, and the lessor did not file a financing statement, third parties take priority over this creditor when the creditor attempts to assert a claim to the collateral.

By failing to file the financing statement, the creditor has what is known as an "unperfected security interest" and may lose priority to other creditors, such as trustees in bankruptcy or creditors who have perfected security interests. Creditors often attempt to formulate a lease instead of a security interest to avoid the filing requirements under the Code. Tax reasons and considerations in marketing the product may also dictate why a lease may be more advantageous than a security interest.

The main danger in treating a transaction as a lease when it is a security interest is that if the debtor seeks bankruptcy protection, the trustee may have a prior claim to the collateral because of failure to file a financing statement. The other danger is that the debtor may use the leased property as collateral in another transaction and the new creditor perfects a security interest by filing a financing statement. In either instance, the initial creditor may lose any claim to the leased property, if in fact it was a security interest.

The courts continually refer to what is known as "A True Lease" as opposed to a security agreement. The judicial system has devoted pages and pages of criteria describing what is and what is not a true lease. Each time parties fashion a new plan to evade the law, the courts are put to the test of creating new criteria.

Lease cases in 2005 revisited the issue of whether the option price is so small that the lessee was economically compelled to exercise the option, or in more simple words, would be foolish not to exercise the option. In these circumstances, the lease is often treated as a security agreement. The earlier cases generally addressed the intent of the parties and when a minimal price was at the end of the lease to exercise the option to buy, the courts concluded that the intent was to have a security agreement. The recent cases reach the same result. The decisions rest not on intent, but on whether an economically meaningful price to the leased equipment is present at the end of the term so that the lessee has a true option to buy or surrender.

To create a true lease, the lessor must fundamentally expect at the time the lease was made that the vehicle or equipment will be returned to the lessor and at that time will have a residual value that can been realized by the lessor. The important factor is whether the lessor intends to deliver to the lessee the total control and ownership for the entire life of the product so that the product is never returned to the lessor or the lessee is to receive a product of established value at the end of the lease. If the lessee receives the product at the end of the lease, a sale is made whether or not the product has a value.

The UCC provides that it is a security agreement where the lessee has an option to become the owner of the goods for no additional consideration or nominal additional consideration upon compliance with the lease agreement. As a result of the UCC, the leases were no longer drafted with the one-dollar and other valuable consideration which allowed the lessee to purchase the vehicle or the equipment. If the consideration is nominal or if it is less than the lessee's reasonably predictable cost of performing under the lease agreement, the option would normally be exercised. Other examples are where the debtor is economically forced to purchase the equipment at the expiration of the lease such as if replacing the equipment would cost more than exercising the option or returning the equipment would be an excessive cost.[6]

The basic section of the UCC defining a lease is Section 1-201(37), which sets forth (in a page and a half) twelve criteria as to whether a transaction creates a lease or security interest. A new Section 1-201(37) revises those criteria. In addition, under Section 2A of the Code, which deals directly with consumer leases, one might find some additional distinctions set forth with regard to leases and security interests.

When drafting, perhaps the best advice is to file a financing statement whether the creditor believes it is a lease or a security interest. Unfortunately, strong reasons sometimes are present to avoid filing a financing statement and to construct the transaction as a lease. The creditor's attorney usually will advise the creditor of the calculated risk when embarking on a course

---

[6]*In re Grubb Constr. Co.*, 319 B.R. 698 (Bankr. M.D. Fla. 2005); *In re Fleming Companies*, 308 B.R. 693, 694 (Bankr. D. Del. 2004).

of casting a transaction as a lease when in fact it is not a true lease, but really a security interest. The risk is simple, that is, loss of collateral and treatment as an unsecured creditor in bankruptcy or a legal battle with other creditors who have perfected their security interests in the same collateral.

A recent scholarly opinion addressed the issue of whether a lease is a true lease or whether it is a security interest. The court addressed the revised Section UCC 1-201(37) (also in some states I-203) and spent 30 pages analyzing the problem, with numerous citations—must reading for any creditor drafting a new lease.[7]

LIABILITY OF LESSOR. The efforts of the lessee to assert claims against the leasing company continue and in some instances they become successful. In a New Jersey case the warranty was clearly for manufacturing defects. The court held that the warranty claim may be raised if there is sufficiently close relationship between the car dealer, the manufacturer and the lessor, which was the case in this particular instance. What happened was the leasing company created the lease form and authorized personnel employed by the dealership to execute the leases. The leasing company was very much involved in the operation of the dealership in closing the leases.[8]

LEASE—NOTICE OF TERMINATION. The issue is whether the transaction was a lease or a security interest. The lease was for a term of five years. The lessee was not required to renew the lease or purchase the equipment and the lessee did not have the option to renew the lease or purchase the property at the end of the term for a nominal consideration. Because of these factors the court held the lease outside the definition of a secured transaction.

The case addressed the issue of notice of termination. The vehicle was repossessed prior to the bankruptcy and the notice dated pre-petition was received by the debtor's post-petition. The notice stated that "the vehicle has been repossessed due to a default in the contract or an early termination." The debtor claimed that this was not a definitive notice that the defendant had terminated the lease. The court held the defendant was not required to provide the debtor with a notice of termination. A creditor is only required to provide notice if so stated in the lease agreement.

Article 2A, Section 502 which states as follows:

> [e]xcept as otherwise provided in this article or the lease agreement, the lessor or lessee in default under the lease contract is not entitled to notice of default or notice of enforcement from the other party to the lease agreement.

---

[7] *In re Grubbs Constr. Co.*, 319 B.R. 698 (Bankr. M.D. Fla. 2005).

[8] *Mercedes Benz Credit Corp. v. Lotito*, 306 N.J. Super. 25, 703 A.2d 288 (N.J. Super. Ct. App. Div. 1997).

Revised Article 9 does require notice of disposition if the transaction is a security interest, but under Article 2A notice of default or of enforcement of the lease is not required.[9]

Security Deposit. The conflict amongst the states with regard to whether a security deposit on a lease does or does not constitute collateral under the UCC has produced different results in different states. The majority of the states seem to feel that a security deposit does not create a security interest wherein the debtor would be entitled to an increase in profits of said collateral. If the deposit is treated as collateral, the debtor would be entitled to the interest that was earned on the security deposit.

The court in Wisconsin, addressing the issue as a case of first impression, cited several cases from other jurisdictions which determined that no security interest existed because no intent was specifically expressed in the language of the lease.[10] The Alabama case applied a two-part test to whether a security interest had been created in the context of a security deposit.[11] First, did the language embody in the writing objectively indicate that the parties intended to create or provide for a security interest? Second, did the parties actually intend to create a security interest?

In an Ohio case, the courts flatly stated that a security deposit does not create a security interest because a conclusion to the contrary contradicts the common law principle that a security deposit creates only a debt.[12]

By virtue of the debtor/creditor relationship, no requirement is present to pay interest on the contract and the debtor would not be entitled to receive interest on the security deposit.[13] On the other hand, some states have passed specific statutes requiring interest to be paid on security deposits.

Leasing Legislation. Many of the states are now adopting leasing laws which do require certain mandatory disclosures to the consumer. Many of the large leasing firms are already beginning to disclose much of the information.

In most instances, these leasing laws are more restrictive than the federal laws and a review of each state's leasing law is absolutely necessary. The New York law and the other state laws are principally designed to supplement the provisions of the Federal Consumer Leasing Act (*see* Appendix to this chapter). For example, the New York law includes a provision similar to that contained in the trade regulation rule concerning the preservation of consumer's claims and defenses wherein the consumer's rights are

---

[9] *Lamar v. Mitsubishi Motors Credit of Am., Inc.*, 249 B.R. 822 (Bankr. S.D. Ga. 2000).

[10] *Doe v. GMAC*, 635 N.W.2d 7 (Wis. Ct. App. 2001).

[11] *Yeager v. GMAC*, 719 So. 2d 210 (Ala. 1998).

[12] *Dolan v. GMAC*, 137 Ohio App. 3d 668 (2000).

[13] *Demitropoulos v. Bank One Milwaukee*, 924 F. Supp. 924 (N.D. Ill. 1996); *Rosen v. PRIMUS Auto. Fin. Servs.*, 618 N.W.2d 606 (Minn. Ct. App. 2000).

not cut off in the event the loans are negotiated to a third party. The New York law also provides certain reinstatement rights to cure defaults solely caused by failure to make a timely payment. Nevertheless, the holder has certain remedies during this period in which the borrower can cure the default. The holder must also deliver a notice of intention to sell the vehicle at early termination and the vehicle must be sold under a commercially reasonable sale. A careful review of the leasing law of New York is necessary in the event vehicles are to be leased to consumers in New York.

> ***Credit & Collection Tip:*** *The same careful review should be applied to the leasing law of each state where the lessor is leasing vehicles.*

Revised Article 9 also provides for the electronic filing across the states and uniform procedures and forms for all states.

Leasing and Rental Companies—Vicarious Liability. Most of the dealers in New York State have been reluctant to lease vehicles in the state because of the vicarious liability when one of the lessees or renters are in an accident with a pedestrian or vehicle due to the negligence of the driver. Most of the states across the country have removed this vicarious liability for leased or rent vehicles.

The Transportation Equity Act of 2005 preempted all state laws and effectively removed vicarious liability for those engaged in vehicle leasing and renting. After this law was passed, the vehicle leasing companies began to return to New York to engage in the leasing business.

Fortunately, the Appellate Division of the Supreme Court of the State of New York held in plain and unequivocable terms that actions against rental and leasing companies based solely on vicarious liability may no longer be maintained and thus reversed a lower court ruling to the contrary. Needless to say numerous amicus curiae were filed by a wide variety of automobile dealers, associations, financial institutions, truck renting and leasing associations, and rental agencies, etc., all of which were pleased with the decision.[14]

A case in New York specifically states that a loaner vehicle without charge is not a rental vehicle and does not fall under the Graves Amendment with regard to the exemption of vicarious liability.

The driver has no protection if an accident occurs with a loaner vehicle. The loaning of a vehicle has no effect whatsoever on the market for leased or rental vehicles nor does it contribute in any way to the problems Congress addressed with the Graves Amendment.[15]

---

[14]*Graham v. Dunkley*, 50 A.D.3d 55 (N.Y. App. Div. 2d Dep't 2008).

[15]*Zizersky v. Life Quality Motor Sales Inc.*, 866 N.Y.S.2d 501 (Sup. Ct. 2008).

REVISED ARTICLE 9—SCOPE OF COVERAGE

Section 9-109, Subdivision D, lists 13 items to which Article 9 does not apply. Section A sets forth the general scope of the article. This new Section 9-109 is a combination of the old Sections 9-102 and 9-104. It would be well to review this article before embarking on new transactions. Payment intangibles and promissory notes are within the scope of the article. When dealing with a sale of an account, chattel paper, promissory note, or payment intangible, the article now includes a sale of the right in this type of receivable, such as a sale of a participation interest. The term also includes the sale of an enforcement right.

The article now applies to every type of a consignment whereas the old article included many but not all "true" consignments, such as bailments. Under the Old Article 9, the creditors of a consignee did not have to perfect the consignment providing the consignee creditors generally knew that the debtor dealt in consigned goods. Under the Revised Article 9, they must file a financing statement. Prior Section 9-104 excluded transfers by governmental debtors. The exclusion now applies to a security interest created by a state, foreign country, or a governmental unit (defined in Section 9-102 as "a subdivision, agency, department, county, parish, municipality or other unit of the government of the United States, a state or a foreign country . . ."). Whereas Article 9 does narrow the broad exclusion of interest in an insurance policy, it now expressly covers assignments by or to a healthcare provider or healthcare insurance receivables.

Section 9-109(d)(10) states that Article 9 does not apply to recoupment or set-off rights except as to deposit amounts. A new section 9-340 regulates the effectiveness of a setoff against a deposit account that stands as collateral. Section 9-404 affords the obligor on an account, chattel paper, or general intangible the right to raise claims and defenses against an assignee (secured party). Subsection B-12 somewhat narrows the broad exclusion of transfers of a tort claim in that it now applies only to assignments of commercial tort claims as well as to a security interest in tort claims that constitute proceeds of other collateral (e.g., a right to payment for negligence destruction of the debtor's inventory).

Deposit accounts may now be taken as original collateral under this article unless it is a consumer transaction.

If your particular transaction is not covered or is excluded by Section 9-109, the legal results of your transaction would be vastly different. For that reason alone, it is recommended that before one becomes involved in any UCC security interest, spend a few minutes reviewing Section 9-109 to be certain the transaction does not fall either under the scope of the article or in the inapplicability of the article.

Civil Aircraft liens on aircraft are to be filed with the Federal Aviation Administration pursuant to 49 U.S.C. Section 44-107(a)(1) and (a)(2). If the aircraft is whole and intact at the time the security interest was granted, the filing must be with the Federal Aviation Administration (FAA). On the other hand, if the party dealt in aircraft parts, the proper place for filing on aircraft parts would be covered by UCC Section 9.[16]

> ***Credit & Collection Tip:*** *Some states follow this section and other states exclude some of the exclusions or either add to or exclude some of the wording in the coverage. The various enactments of the statute by the various states deviate in many ways from the recommended text promulgated by the National Conference of Commissioners on Uniform State Laws. These deviations sometimes can present problems when the laws of two states affect the same transaction.*

The "financing statement" includes the name and address of the secured party, the debtor, the date, description of the personal property, and what type of agreement is being filed: security agreement, assignment, termination, continuation, etc. As a rule, the security agreement need not be filed with the financing statement, although it may be filed.

Certain states use a certificate of title for automobiles, and liens are recited on the title. Filing a financing statement is unnecessary in those states that use the title system, which requires separate procedures for filing and protecting the lien.

The rules for the financing statement have been radically changed. Under the existing Rule 9, there are about ten states which still require dual filing: (1) filing with the secretary of state and (2) where the goods are located or where the debtor is located. Under the new rule we have a one single filing rule that requires the filing of only one financing statement in a state office, such as the secretary of state or a designated clerk of the state. The creditor does not have to concern himself with the location of the collateral nor the requirement to file in the county where the collateral or debtor is located. The obligation is to file the financing statement in the state where the debtor is incorporated, registered, or organized; or if the debtor is an individual, where the debtor has a legal residence. There are no dual filings. If it is a real estate related transaction, the perfection of the filing is where the mortgage is properly filed, indexed, or recorded. The revised law provides that a filing against a foreign debtor is to be done in Washington, D.C. The advantage of this unified rule is that where a security interest covers goods located in many jurisdictions, only one filing is necessary.

A corporation is a registered organization of a state if it is organized under the laws of the state and is treated as being located in that state. Where the corporation is organized can be determined with certainty and will eliminate a determination of which law applies where a corporation has many offices across many states. Financing statements will be filed in the state where the corporation is organized or where the debtor resides, notwithstanding where the collateral is located. Where the corporation has

[16] *In re AV Central Inc.*, 289 B.R. 170 (D. Kan. 2003).

more than one office in the same state, the creditor need not determine which is the chief executive office, but merely has to file in the state in which the debtor is registered (organized).

The rules for transition to the new provisions provide that a financing statement perfected prior to the enactment of the new law will remain effective at least for an additional year.

One obligation of a creditor will be to conduct searches in possibly two states. Because the revision provides for a possibly different place to file the financing statement, the creditor, during this period of transition, will have to search in the jurisdictions where the financing statement would be filed under the Old Article 9, as well as in the jurisdictions in which the financing statement would be filed under the Revised Article 9. The creditor will have to furnish the necessary information concerning the debtor so that the searching organization will be able to conduct the searches in the proper states to identify any prior liens on the collateral.

If a creditor desires to file a continuation statement during the transition period, the continuation statement has to be filed under the Revised Article 9 as if it was an initial financing statement together with certain information concerning the old financing. The old six-month window to file the continuation statement before the expiration of the five-year period for filing a financing statement disappears and the new continuation statement may be filed at any time before the expiration of the old financing statement as a new financing statement in the proper jurisdiction under the new law. This may be done before the Revised Article 9 becomes effective, although not before it is passed by the respective state legislatures to be effective law. Taking action before the revised law becomes effective in your respective state should only be done after consultation with counsel. Filing a continuation statement should be carefully considered to be certain that it is timely and properly filed.

Perfection Before Effective Date. If you are perfected by a means other than filing when the date of the revised UCC becomes effective in your state, you remain perfected for one year. If you want to continue, you must perfect under Revised Article 9 before the year expires.

Collateral Expansion. Certain transactions now require a financing statement where one was not required under the Old Article 9. The Revised Article 9 has expanded the collateral that can be accepted, such as license fees, credit card receivables, franchise fees, healthcare insurance receivables, deposit accounts, lottery winnings, and even commercial tort claims. Some of these were listed as general intangibles under the Old Article 9, but now are considered to be "accounts." The creditor will have to *change the description in these financing statements from "general intangibles" to "accounts" to have a proper collateral description* in the financing statement.

Contents of Financing Statement. The simple requirements for an effective financing statement are:

A. The debtor's name.
B. The name of a secured party or representative of the secured party.
C. An indication of the collateral.

The former Section 9-402 required the debtor's signature to appear on the financing statement, but the Revised Article 9 contains no signature requirement. The elimination of the signature facilitates paperless filing. The fact an authenticating symbol is not contained in the public record does not mean that all filings are authorized. Section 9-509(a) entitles a person to file an initial financing statement, an amendment that adds collateral and an amendment that adds a debtor only if the debtor authorizes the filing. Section 9-509(d) entitles a person other than the debtor to file a termination statement only if the debtor authorizes the filing. Thus, a filing is legally effective only if it is authorized.

Section 9-503 provides that the financing statement must include the name of the debtor indicated on the public record of the debtor's jurisdiction of organization showing the debtor to have been properly organized. Under Section 9-102 "registered organization" means an organization created under the laws of a single state or the United States. The state must maintain a public record showing the organization to have been organized.

The creditor must use the correct name of the corporation. Before executing the financing statement it may be necessary to see the stamped receipt from the Secretary of State on the certificate of incorporation to confirm the correct name of the corporation. The same procedure would apply to limited partnerships and limited liability companies. A decedent's estate must contain the name of decedent and indicate that the debtor is an estate. If the debtor is a trust or a trustee acting with respect to property held in trust, the financing statement must provide the correct name specified for the trust in its organization documents. If no name is specified, provide the name of the settlor and additional information sufficient to distinguish the debtor from other trusts having one or more of the same settlors. The debtor's name must reveal that the debtor is a trust or is a trustee acting with respect to property held in trust.

A filing is not rendered ineffective by the absence of a trade name or other name. *At the same time, a financing statement that provides only the debtor's trade name and does not provide the name of the debtor is ineffective.* As in the old law, a financing statement may provide the name of more than one debtor and secured party. The failure to indicate the representative capacity of a secured party does not affect the sufficiency of the financing statement.

Filing Financing Statements. Evidence of past acts determines whether a person has the requisite authority to file a record under

Section 9-502. Debtor's authentication of a security agreement is convincing evidence of the authorization to file a filing statement covering the same collateral as described in a security agreement. The secured party does not really have to obtain a separate authorization.

The creditor must have the authority to file the financing statement on behalf of the debtor, but this does not have to appear on the financing statement itself. National forms of the financing statement will be accepted in every state and no longer will we use separate forms for each state. The revised article permits generic descriptions in the financing statement such as "all assets," but at the same time, the security agreement has to be more specific than "all assets" or "all personal property."

The law has taken away the powers of the clerks to reject the financing statement in the event that, in their opinion, the information contained in the financing statement contains a legal deficiency. A filing officer may not refuse to file a financing statement if the collateral is missing. The amendment specifically states the limited grounds that the filing officer can use to reject a financing statement.

An unauthorized filing may give rise to civil or criminal liabilities under other laws. The important thing to remember is that *the filing office is neither obligated nor permitted to inquire into issues of authorization.* Under Sections 9-518 and 9-509, a person may add to the public record a statement that the financing statement was indexed under the person's name wrongfully.

Partial and Full Satisfaction. Old Section 9-505 applied to both partial and full satisfaction of the obligation. Nevertheless, under the new UCC Section 9-620, the consumer must consent to an acceptance of collateral in partial satisfaction of the obligation and the acceptance is effective only if the consumer agrees to the terms of the acceptance in a record authenticated after default. Thus, a partial satisfaction requires consent of the consumer in a record authenticated after default. A careful reading of Revised 9-620 (which is a strict foreclosure) is recommended, for numerous requirements are set forth which were not present in the old Article. Some of these requirements do not apply to business debtors.

Authentication. Under Section 9-102, "authenticate" means "to sign" or "to execute or otherwise adopt a symbol, or encrypt or similarly process a record in whole or in part, with the present intent of the authenticating person to identify the person and adopt or accept a record." In Black's Law Dictionary, "authenticate" is defined as "to sign before a notary public or other public official." Having the consent notarized is suggested since accepting the consent with only the debtor's signature under circumstances wherein you retain the collateral may allow the debtor to assert additional defenses due to a change of mind at a later date.

Notice. Before disposing of collateral, if the collateral is other than consumer goods, the creditor must notify the debtor, any secondary obligor, and any other person from whom a secured party has received, before the notification date, a notification of a claim of an interest in the collateral. Other secured parties are entitled to notice where a security interest indexed under the debtor's name by a financing statement filed in the proper office. Each party must receive at least ten days' notice.[17] The former Section 9-504 did not require notice of a sale to a junior lienor unless the secured party has received (before sending his notification to the debtor or before the debtor's renunciation of right) written notice of a claim of an interest in the collateral.

Both Old and Revised Article 9 require that notice be reasonable. Nevertheless, Revised Article 9 now sets forth that a notification must be sent within a reasonable time and does not define what a reasonable time is—except Revised Article 9 states that in a commercial transaction, the timing of the notice is a reasonable time if it was sent at least ten days before the time of the disposition stated in the notification to the parties as required in Section 9-611 (*see* preceding sections). The section also excludes the requirement of notification if the collateral is perishable or threatens to decline rapidly in value or if it is of type customarily sold on a recognized market.

The creditor must realize that this ten-day notification requirement does not apply to consumers and consumers must receive notification within a reasonable time. Case law has in some instances established a reasonable time under the Old Article 9. The courts may be reluctant to change that reasonable time.

The best course of action is to follow the definition of reasonable under the case law under the Old Article 9. The courts may choose to utilize the ten-day notification to be minimum notice with consumers although the definition of a reasonable time under the Old Article 9 is that the consumers must have sufficient time to allow them to protect their interest in the disposition of the collateral. Natural disasters or emergencies affecting the debtor affect what is a reasonable time.

Notice—Safe Harbor Procedure. Under the same section, the statute seems to lay out a safe harbor to protect the secured party if he complies with Section 9-611(e). The foreclosing party is allowed to comply with the notification if the notification is provided no later than 20 days or earlier than 30 days before the notification date to the proper public filing office requesting financing statements indexed under the debtor's name. After this, and before the notification date, the foreclosing party will have complied with the notification, if the foreclosing party:

1. Sent authenticated notification of disposition to each secured party named in that response and who's financing statement covered the collateral.
2. If he did not receive a response to the request for the information.

[17]UCC § 9-611 (2000).

This apparently is an umbrella that is provided to the creditor so that if he receives no response from the public filing office, the third party who also has a lien has no remedy against the foreclosing party. If the foreclosing party receives notice from the secured party the foreclosing party must give notice of sale.

This section requires the request to the clerk's office for information to be performed in a "commercially reasonable manner," but no definition is offered as to what is "commercially reasonable." What if the foreclosing party seeks the information, and the clerk sends the information by mail or fax, but the foreclosing party never receives the information. This "safe harbor" may not be a "harbor," and certainly may not be "safe."

An oral notification of the sale will not satisfy the statutory requirements because it must be an authenticated record. Under the Old Article 9 cases held that an oral notification was sufficient. Revised Sections 9-613 and 9-614 set forth the contents of the notification and provide a form for the notification of disposition of collateral. Section 9-614 provides the contents and form of notification before disposition of collateral with regard to consumer goods and notice of a plan to sell the property including a distinction between a public disposition and a private disposition. (*See* section on Procedure for Disposition of Collateral.)

Failure to Comply. Old Section 9-507 (dealing with notification) states that if the disposition of the property occurred and the creditor did not comply "with this part" of the article, the debtor or any person entitled to notification or whose security interest has been made known to the secured party *has a right to recover any loss covered by the failure to comply.* If the collateral is a consumer debt, the debtor has a further right to recover an amount not less than the credit service charge plus 10 percent of the principal amount of the debt or the time price differential plus 10 percent of the cash price.

Revised Section 9-625 covers remedies when secured parties fail to comply with the article. This section does not confine the failure to comply "with this part" of the article, *but refers to the full Revised Article 9. It states that a person is liable for damages in the amount of any loss caused by a failure to comply with this article.*

Subsection C refers to consumer goods transactions, and allows a recovery of not less than the credit service charge plus 10 percent of the principal amount of the obligation or the time price differential plus 10 percent of the cash price. The debtor is also entitled, when the deficiency is eliminated, to recover damages in the event a surplus is not created by reason of the secured party failing to comply with Section 9-626, which covers the issue of deficiency or surplus.

The debtor is entitled to recover $500 plus any other damages for failure to comply with Section 9-625(b) and the following sections:

1. Section 9-208, which deals with the duties of a secured party having control of the collateral.

2. Section 9-209, which deals with an account debtor who has been notified of an assignment which requires the secured party to send within ten days an authenticated record that releases the account debtor from any further obligation to the secured party.
3. Section 9-509(a), which deals with parties entitled to file a record.
4. Section 9-513, which deals with requiring the secured party to file and send a termination statement.
5. Section 9-616, which deals with the calculation of the surplus or deficiency after a disposition of collateral.

Section 9-628 relieves the secured party of liability when he does not know that a person is a debtor or obligor, the identity of the person or how to communicate with the person.

Notice—Disposition of Collateral. The creditor must send to the debtor and any secondary obligor a reasonable authenticated notification of the disposition (Section 9-611). The secured party must notify:

1. The debtor;
2. Secondary obligor;
3. If the collateral is other than consumer goods, any other person from which the secured party has received before the notification date an authenticated notification of a claim of an interest in the collateral.

A careful reading of Section 9-611 is suggested since much of the section is brand new, and the statute provides forms.

Section 9-611 also provides:

> (E) Compliance with subsection (c)(3)(B). A secured party complies with the requirement for notification prescribed by subsection (c)(3)(B) if:
>
> 1. Not later than 20 days or earlier than 30 days before the notification date, the secured party requests, in a commercially reasonable manner, information concerning financing statements indexed under the debtor's name in the office indicated in subsection (c)(3)(B)
> 2. Before the notification date, the secured party
>   A. did not receive a response to the request for information or
>   B. received a response to the request for information and sent an authenticated notification of disposition to each secured party or other lienholder named in that response whose financing statement covered the collateral.

Compliance with Subdivision (E) is referred to as a "safe harbor" for protection in the event of delays that may occur when receiving information from a public filing office. If at least 20 but not more than 30 days before sending notification to the debtor, order the search and send notification to all secured parties and other lienholders. Thus, a secured party who is entitled to notification, but was not listed in the report that you obtained from the proper filing office, will have no remedy against the foreclosing secured party who does not send the notification.

Accounts Receivable. Under the Revised Article 9, old Section 9-502 is recodified at 9-607, which provides as follows:

> 9-607(c) Commercially Reasonable Collection and Enforcement
>
> A secured party shall proceed in a commercially reasonable manner if the secured party:
>
> 1. undertakes to collect from or enforce an obligation of an account debtor or other person obligated on collateral, and
> 2. is entitled to charge back uncollected collateral or otherwise to full or limited recourse against the debtor as secondary obligor.

Old Section 9-504(3) now becomes Section 9-610(b), which provides:

> Commercially Reasonable Dispositions: Every aspect of a disposition of collateral including the method, manner, time, place, and other terms must be commercially reasonable. If commercially reasonable, a secured party may dispose of collateral by public or private proceedings, by one or more contracts, as a unit or in parcels, and at any time and place and on any terms.

A court in New York acknowledged that independent research has not found a single case applying the commercially reasonable standard to the collection of accounts receivable where the secured party was not afforded the right or took no responsibility to be the exclusive collector. Thus, the court concluded that commercial reasonableness presupposes possession and control over collection of the accounts receivable and/or justifiable reliance by the debtor on the creditor's collection effort.[18]

The few cases that have applied the commercially reasonable standard in the accounts receivable context usually involves debtors who by virtue of operation of a bankruptcy plan or other agreement deliver control of the receivables to the secured creditor. Commercial reasonableness is not defined under the revised Section 9 and the court concluded that the test of commercial reasonableness hinges on the totality of the circumstances,

---

[18] *FDIC v. Wrapwell Corp.*, 2002 U.S. Dist. LEXIS 76 (S.D.N.Y. Jan. 2, 2002).

including the good faith efforts of the creditor. Once commercial reasonableness is raised, the burden is on the creditor to establish the commercial reasonableness of its action.

As pointed out elsewhere, the failure to utilize commercial reasonableness does not affect liability but only reduces the amount of the deficiency. In this situation, the secured party had not taken control of the accounts to prevent the guarantor of the account from using efforts to collect the accounts. The court granted summary judgment in favor of the secured party.

Rights and Obligations of Assignee. The revised Section 9-404 spells out the rights acquired by an assignee. As in the Old Article 9, an assignee accepts an assignment subject to defenses and claims of an account debtor accrued before the account debtor is notified of the assignment. The revised Section 9-404 now limits the claim that the account debtor may assert against an assignee *only to reduce the amount the account debtor owes.* The account debtor may not proceed against the assignee in excess of the claim against the assignor.

Revised 9-404 states that the rights set forth in this section are subject to other laws establishing special rules for consumer account debtors. The assignee is subject to the "holder in due course rule" contained in Federal Trade Commission Rule 433 (16 C.F.R. Part 433).

Revised Section 9-406 is similar to the old law. The debtor has a right to pay the assignor until such time as the debtor receives an appropriate notification. Once the debtor receives the notification, the debtor cannot discharge its obligation by payment to the assignor. Payment to the assignor before notification or payment to the assignee after notification discharges the obligation. If requested by the debtor, the assignee must furnish proof that the assignment has been made. If the assignee fails to comply to furnish proof of the assignment, the debtor may discharge the obligation by paying the assignor even if the account debtor has received notification.

The official comment states that an effective notification must be *authenticated.* This requirement normally could be satisfied by sending notification on the notifying person's letterhead or on a form on which the notifying person's name appears. In each case, the printed name would be a symbol adopted by the notifying party for the purpose of identifying the person and adopting the notification as required under Section 9-102 which defines "authenticate." It also requires a reasonable identification of the rights that have been assigned, but it leaves to the creditor to determine what is reasonable. On the other hand, the debtor may notify the assignee as to the reasons for disregarding the notifications and in what respect the notification is defective.

The prohibition of an assignment of an account by an agreement between the debtor and the assignor continues in revised Section 9-406.

Anti-assignment clauses are ineffective and do not prohibit the assignment from taking effect between the parties. The prohibitive assignment does not constitute a default under the agreement between the debtor and the assignor. Again, the rules of the section are subject to other laws establishing special rules for consumers.

Multi-State Transactions. Revised Sections 9-301, 9-303, 9-316, and 9-337 deal with perfection of security interest in multiple state transactions. These sections cover all the situations where a vehicle is in one state and the lien is in another state, what the obligations are between the parties with regard to a creditor perfecting the lien and with regard to the debtor obtaining a certificate of title in the state to which the vehicle has been removed. The situation often arises where the creditor has perfected his security interest in one state where the vehicle was at the time of perfection. Thereafter, the debtor has moved the vehicle to another state and for whatever reason has failed to obtain the certificate of title required in the other state or failed to note the lien of the creditor on the certificate of title.

Termination Statement. Any person may file a termination statement if the secured party fails to comply with its obligation to file a termination statement or send one to the debtor.

Deficiency—Compliance with UCC. Revised Section 9-626 (which is brand new) deals with the amount of a deficiency in transactions *other than consumer transactions, leaving to the courts to apply established approaches (Revised UCC 9-626(b)).* Under Section 9-626(a)(i) a secured party need not prove compliance relating to collection, enforcement, and disposition or acceptance of the collateral unless the debtor or the guarantor places the compliance question in issue. Accordingly, the secured party does not have to prove compliance with Section 9-600 et seq. to enforce the deficiency after the debtor has defaulted. If compliance is placed in issue by the debtor, the secured party has the burden of establishing compliance *with all the requirements* and rules dealing with the collection, enforcement, disposition, or acceptance of the collateral. This certainly would include a commercially reasonable sale as well as the other sections in Section 9-600 et seq.

In the past, if the secured party failed to comply with the UCC in repossessing, storing, and selling the vehicle, the courts were in conflict as to what the secured party could recover on a deficiency. Some courts promulgated a rule of "absolute bar," which prohibited the secured party from collecting any deficiency if there was any noncompliance with the UCC. Other courts allowed the debtor to interpose a counterclaim for damages against the claim for a deficiency to the extent that the debtor could prove damages. A fair majority of the courts seem to favor what became known as "a rebuttable presumption," which partially adopted the absolute bar theory but allowed the secured party to prove that the debtor did not suffer damages equal to the deficiency. The secured party could prove that the damages by virtue of the noncompliance were minor and the deficiency amount should be reduced by the amount.

Revised Article 9 adopts the "rebuttable presumption rule." Section 9-626(a)(4) states that the amount the debtor is entitled to is equal to the total of the obligation plus expenses and attorney fees—thus the damages may be equal to the deficiency. The secured party would be prohibited from collecting any deficiency. The "rebuttable presumption" theory would allow the secured party to prove that the debtor suffered a lesser amount of damages. The secured party would be entitled to a deficiency reduced by the debtor's damages due to the noncompliance of the secured party.

The first case in a lower court in New York addressed the portion of UCC 9-626(b), which leaves to the courts the issue of applying established approaches to consumer transactions.[19] The New York court adopted the "absolute bar rule" for the reason that it has not been legislatively displaced by Revised Article 9, and precluded the creditor from recovering a deficiency from the debtor. The lower court followed the New York State Law Revision Committee comments that accompany Revised Article 9, which stated only that "with respect to consumer defaults, Revised Article 9 makes no recommendations whatsoever, leaving the courts free to shape a remedy as is appropriate in each case." Other courts follow this reasoning. The prior procedure as to consumer transaction will continue despite the change in Revised Article 9 that applies to commercial transactions.

DEFICIENCY—EXPLANATION. Under Section 9-616, the creditor is obligated to provide an explanation of the calculation of any surplus or any deficiency. This obligation is primarily limited to consumer goods, for the statute contains no duty in a commercial transaction to provide the calculation of surplus or deficiency. No time requirement is specified within which the creditor must provide the explanation of surplus or deficiency, but the explanation must be furnished. The statute requires the creditor to furnish the explanation after the disposition and before or when the lender accounts to the debtor and pays him any surplus or in the event the lender makes any written demand on the debtor for payment of any deficiency. The debtor has a right to request an explanation. The request may not be oral. It must be sent after the disposition of the collateral. If a request is received by the creditor, the creditor must furnish the explanation within 14 days after receipt.

---

[19] *Coxall v. Clover Commercial Corp.*, 781 N.Y.S.2d 567 (N.Y. Civ. Ct. 2004).

Section 616(c) requires that the creditor provide the following information:

1. The aggregate amount of the obligations including unearned interest or credit service charges to the amount of proceeds of the disposition of the collateral.
2. The amount of proceeds.
3. The aggregate amount of the obligations after deducting the amount of the proceeds.
4. The amount in aggregate of expenses including the retaking, holding, preparing for disposition, processing, and disposing of the collateral and any attorneys' fees secured by the collateral which are known to the secured party and relate to the disposition.
5. The amount of any credits including rebates of interest or credit service charges.
6. The amount of surplus or deficiency.

The statute does not require any particular phrasing of the explanation. The explanation may contain minor errors if they are not seriously misleading. A debtor is entitled to one request without charge, but in the event he makes another request, the creditor may charge a fee not exceeding $25.

Foreclosure Under UCC. Under Revised Article 9-609 the secured party has a right to take possession of the collateral after default similar to the provisions in the old law. The party still may proceed without judicial process to repossess property, providing no breach of peace is committed. Although it was hoped that the revised article would provide more help to the secured party as to exactly what a "breach of peace" is, the statute offers no more help than the old law and leaves the issue to the various state courts. However, in the Official Comment, the following statement is offered:

> in considering whether a secured party has engaged in the breach of peace, however, courts should hold the secured party responsible for the actions of others taken on the secured party's behalf, including independent contractors engaged by the secured party to take possession of collateral.

A conflict is present amongst the states on this issue, and hopefully the courts will not adopt this reasoning.

> ***Credit & Collection Tip:*** *If the creditor is in a state which adopts this reasoning, the creditor must be careful in the selection of the repossession agent. The retention document should contain specific instructions to refrain from committing a breach of peace, and an obligation to indemnify creditor for the actions and conduct of the repossession agent if the creditor should be sued by reason of said conduct. This presupposes selection of a financially responsible repossession agent. (See Chapter 12.)*

Commercially Reasonable. When disposing of collateral, a few uneducated creditors may overlook their duty to engage in a commercially reasonable sale. This section states that a creditor "may sell, lease, or otherwise dispose of any or all of the collateral in its then condition or following any commercially reasonable preparation or processing."

While this section appears to make the preparation of a collateral for disposition optional, a number of courts have held that failure to do so was commercially unreasonable. These courts justified their position on the grounds of a cost-benefit analysis. If minor preparation substantially increases market value, it is commercially reasonable to perform this preparation. Thus, the secured party must act in good faith and in a commercially reasonable manner.

While no specific time limit is set forth within which an item must be disposed, a prolonged interval between repossession and sale raises the inference of commercial unreasonableness. The burden of proof shifts to the secured party to establish that its actions were commercially reasonable. If the delay is excessive, some courts bar the creditor from recovering a deficiency. This result is especially true when the creditor accrues excessive storage charges. The courts feel that the debtor should not be penalized if the loss of value of the property is due to the negligence of the creditor. Commercial reasonableness can be established through comparisons with industry standards and with prior sales conducted by the creditor. The code sets forth three standards for courts to determine whether the sale was performed in a commercially reasonable manner (Old Articles 9-504 and 507, Revised Article 9-627):

A sale in the usual manner in a recognized market is commercially reasonable.

A sale at a price current in a recognized market at the time of sale, regardless of how the sale was completed, is commercially reasonable.

Disposing of a collateral in conformity with reasonable commercial practices among dealers in the type of property sold is commercially reasonable.

The fact that the creditor may have obtained a higher price by selling the collateral at a different time or by using a different method is not sufficient by itself to establish that the sale was defective.

Creditors must use common sense to minimize the deficiency. Laziness and negligence by the creditors are primary grounds for a court to hold a sale commercially unreasonable. The following are examples of commercially unreasonable sales:

- If creditors in the industry utilize a public sale to dispose of collateral, a private sale at a below-average price may be improper.

- Selling the collateral to a friend at an arbitrary price would be unreasonable.
- After attempting to sell the collateral privately, failing to notify previous bidders of a future public auction is unreasonable. Always obtain the name and address of all who are present at the auction.

Choosing an inconvenient location or an unusual time to sell property may be unreasonable.

> ***Credit & Collection Tip:*** *If the first sale was called off, or delayed, always invite the bidders from the first auction to the second auction. Failure to do so is damaging to the creditor's case, especially if the bids at the original sale were higher than at the second sale.*

With regard to the actual disposition of the collateral, the revised statute follows the old statute and the case law but provides no help in the definition of "commercially reasonable." The method, manner, time, place, and other terms of the sale must be "commercially reasonable." If it is commercially reasonable, the secured party, as in the old statute, may dispose of the property by public or private sale and at any time and place and on any terms.

Subsection A of Section 9-610 refers to the fact that the sale of the collateral may be made in its present conditions or following any commercially reasonable preparation or processing. The secured party may sell the property in "its then condition" some of the time, but perhaps not all of the time. The Official Comment states "a secured party may not dispose of collateral" in its "then condition" when, taking into account the costs and probable benefits of preparation or processing and the fact that the secured party would be advancing the costs at its risk. The secured party may purchase collateral at a public disposition which has always been the case and at a private disposition if the collateral is of a kind that is customarily sold on a recognized market or the subject of a widely distributed standard quotation (New York Stock Exchange, etc.).

Purchase of Collateral—Good Faith. Under the former Article 9, a distinction arose in the liability of a purchaser at a public sale and a private sale. In a public sale, the purchaser's rights were not affected by the secured party's noncompliance if the purchaser did not know of any defects and no collusion existed between the purchaser and the secured party. If there was a private sale, the purchaser only had to act in good faith. Under Revised Article 9, in all dispositions, whether public or private, a purchaser's rights are not affected by the secured party's noncompliance if the purchaser acted in good faith.

Section 9-617 states:

> a transferee that acts in good faith takes free of the rights in interest described in Subsection A(a) even if the secured party fails to comply with this article or the requirements of any judicial proceeding.

Waiver. The law has always permitted the parties to determine by agreement the standards measuring the rights of a debtor or an obligor and the duties of a secured party if the standards are not unreasonable. The secured parties used their bargaining positions in many instances to obtain the consent of the debtor to certain conduct in the repossession of a car. Often, the conduct that the debtor consented to constituted a breach of peace. Under Section 9-603, the Revised Article 9 expressly excludes entering into any agreement that consents to conduct which amounts to a breach of peace. If a breach of peace takes place, a written agreement cannot erase the breach of peace.

Section 9-602 expressly states that the debtor may not waive or vary the rules stated in the following situations:

1. The right to a response to a request for accounting concerning a list of collateral and a statement of account.
2. The right to have the secured party conduct in a commercially reasonable manner the sale of any property.
3. The right to a calculation of a deficiency or surplus when a disposition is made by the secured party, a person related to the secured party, or a secondary obligor.
4. The restrictions on the secured party with regard to the use and operation of the collateral by the secured party.
5. The duty to apply non-cash proceeds in a commercially reasonable manner.[20]

Goods or Services. When a contract contains a mix of sales and services, the UCC applies if the sale of goods is the dominant factor or the essence of the transaction. The majority of the jurisdictions have concluded that distributorship agreements are subject to the UCC.[21]

Assignment of Security Agreement. A secured lender may assign his or her rights in the security agreement to a purchaser. A secured party may release a part or portion of the collateral from the security agreement by executing a partial release of collateral and filing the agreement with the financing statement.

Revised Section 9-514 of the UCC provides that a secured party *may* assign all or part of his rights under a financing statement by filing same in the place where the original financing statement was filed. A separate

---

[20] U.C.C. § 9-602 (2000).

[21] *L&M Enters., Inc. v. BEI Sensors & Sys. Co.*, 231 F.3d 1284 (10th Cir. 2000); *Continental Casing Corp. v. Siderca Corp.*, 38 S.W.3d 782 (Tex. App. 2001), *aff'd*, *Monarch Beverage Co. v. Tyfield Importers, Inc.*, 823 F.2d 1187 (7th Cir. 1987).

written statement of assignment must be signed by the secured party of record setting forth:

1. The name of the secured party of record and the debtor.
2. The file number and date of filing of the financing statement.
3. The name and address of the assignee.
4. A description of the collateral assigned.

This section does not require an assignee to file a financing statement. The section provides an option to the assignee to file the financing statement.

Old Section 9-302 (Revised Sections 309-310) of the UCC provides if a secured party assigns a perfected security interest, no filing under this article is required to continue the perfected status of the security interest against creditors of and transferees from the original debtor. Thus, an assignee is not required to file a financing statement and his failure to file a financing statement does not affect the perfected status of the security interest.

Old Section 9-405 (Revised 9-318(2)) was a permissive device whereby a secured party who has assigned all or part of his interest may have the assignment noted of record so that inquiries concerning the transaction would be addressed not to the original secured creditor but to the assignee. After a secured party has assigned his rights of record, the assignee becomes the secured party of record and may file a continuation statement under old Section 9-403 (Revised 9-206), a termination statement under old Section 9-404 (Revised 9-318(1)) or a statement of release under Section 9-406.

> ***Credit & Collection Tip:*** *The aforementioned should certainly persuade a secured lender to familiarize himself with the Revised Article 9—not just a brief review. We have instructed our clients to carefully read the Revised Article 9, section by section, paragraph by paragraph, to make notes and to prepare checklists with regard to their procedures in granting secured loans to both businesses and consumers as well as checklists for repossession and sale of personal property. The article is very different than what we have been dealing with for so many years and requires a significant amount of attention to the details.*

Seriously Misleading Terms. Section 9-503 of the Revised Uniform Commercial Code provides as follows:

> a. Sufficiency of Debtor's Name. A financing statement sufficiently provides the name of the debtor
>
> (1) if the debtor is a registered organization, only if the financing statement provides the name of the debtor indicated on the public record of the debtor's jurisdiction of organization which shows the debtor to have been organized. . . .

Section 9-506 deals with the effects of errors and omissions and states as follows:

> (a) Minor Errors and Omissions. A financing statement substantially satisfying the requirement of this part is effective, even if it has minor errors or omissions, unless the errors or omissions make the financing statement seriously misleading.
>
> (b) Financing Statement Seriously Misleading. Except as otherwise provided in subsection (c), a financing statement that fails sufficiently to provide the name of the debtor in accordance with Section 9-503 is seriously misleading.
>
> (c) Financing Statement Not Seriously Misleading. If a search of the records of the filing office under the debtor's correct name, using the filing office's standard search logic, if any, would disclose a financing statement that fails sufficiently to provide the name of the debtor in accordance with Section 9-503(a), the name provided does not make the financing statement seriously misleading.
>
> (d) Debtor's Correct Name. For the purposes of Section 9-508(b) the "debtor's correct name" in subsection (c) means the correct name of the new debtor.

The Revised Article 9 has changed the definition of "seriously misleading" by using the terminology of the filing office, "standard search logic." The test now is that a name is seriously misleading if it cannot be found by the "standard search logic" employed by the filing office. At the time Revised Article 9 was passed, not all of the filing offices in the various states had a standard search logic, but one can find the "standard search logic" by examining "International Association of Commercial Administrators (IACA)," a website entitled www.iaca.org/node/46 and a link to the home page of IACA (www.krahmer.net).

A scholarly case in Kansas provided an excellent analysis of the application of the filing office's "standard search logic."[22] A financing statement that fails sufficiently to provide the name of the debtor is seriously misleading. A misspelled name of the debtor may not be seriously misleading providing a search of the records of the filing office under the debtor's correct name, using the filing office's "standard search logic," would disclose a financing statement.

If a search under the debtor's correct name using the "standard search logic" did not disclose the financing statement with the debtor's misspelled name, the financing statement would be seriously misleading.

---

[22] *Pankratz Implement Co. v. Citizens Nat'l Bank*, 102 P.3d 1165 (Kan. Ct. App. 2005), *aff'd*, 130 P.3d 57 (Kan. 2006); *see Receivable Purchasing Co. Inc. v. R&R Directional Drilling, LLC*, 588 S.E.2d 831 (Ga. Ct. App. 2003); *Peoples Bank v. Bryan Bros. Cattle Co.*, 504 F.3d 549 (5th Cir. 2007).

An argument was made that a search conducted on the Internet would have revealed the misspelling. The court emphasized that the misspelling must be recognized in the "standard search logic" used in the particular state (Kansas) and only that search determines whether a name is seriously misleading. The search by using the "standard search logic" did not disclose the financing statement using the misspelled name of the debtor. This was the final and complete criteria that the court used to make a decision. If a search under the debtor's correct name discloses the financing statement filed with a minor error, then the minor error does not make the financing statement misleading.

The case also reviews some of the prior cases which addressed the issue.

Section 9-507 states that a name change in the debtor by means of an acquisition or merger will be effective on the date of the change plus collateral acquired for four months thereafter. The financing statement would not be effective to perfect a security interest in collateral acquired by the debtor more than four months after the change unless an amendment to the financing statement renders the financing statement not seriously misleading and is filed within four months after the change.

The net effect of the section is that inquiry must be made either through credit reports or otherwise to determine whether a change of name has taken place in the prior four months and upon making said determination, searches must be made not only in the current name but also in the prior names.[23]

The same rule would apply to a situation where a new debtor has acquired rights in the collateral which results in a financing statement that is seriously misleading under UCC 9-506.[24]

A case in Florida addressed the issue where the financing statement listed the "John Beam Farms Inc." instead of the debtor's actual corporate name, "John Beam Farm of Homestead, Inc." The trustee conducted a search of the registries online database using the debtor's correct name. The search yielded no matches. The court acknowledged that if a search by the use of the correct name revealed the incorrect name, the financing statement would be effective because it would have provided the notice necessary using the standard search logic. If the financing statement under the user's correct name does not produce the financing statement using the debtor's incorrect name, the financing statement is ineffective.

If the incorrect name produced the existence of the correct name, a lawsuit probably would never have occurred.[25]

---

[23]UCC § 9-507.
[24]UCC § 9-508.
[25]*In re John's Bean Farm of Homestead, Inc.*, 378 B.R. 385 (Bankr. S.D. Fla. 2007).

Out-of-Country Debtors. As to foreign debtors, UCC 9-307(c) states in substance that the act would apply only if a "debtor's residence, place of business or chief executive office, as applicable, is located in a jurisdiction whose law generally requires information concerning the existence of a non-possessory security interest to be made generally available in filing, recording or registration system as a condition or result of a security interest obtaining priority over the rights of a lien creditor with respect to the collateral."

This is the equivalence test requirement. The UCC is stating that the United States meets this test. If the foreign country meets this test, you must do your filing there. If the country doesn't meet this test, the secured party need only file in the District of Columbia.

FUTURE ADVANCES

Section 923 sets forth a variety of rules which deal with the issue of the priority of future advances. The issue of priority does not seem to rest on the time frame when a future advance is made. A secured creditor will maintain his priority with regard to any collateral which has been pledged for the future advance. A careful reading of the statute and the commentary to the statute is recommended with emphasis on subdivision 4 of the Official Comment.[26]

JUDICIAL FORECLOSURE

The Revised Article 9-601 does make a significant change when a secured party reduces a claim to judgment based on a security interest. Under the prior law, the lien dates back only to the perfection date. The new law states that the judgment relates back to the earlier of (1) the date of perfection of the security interest or agricultural lien; (2) the date of filing a financing statement covering the collateral; or (3) any dates specified in a statute under which the agricultural lien was created.[27]

COOPERATIVE AND CONDOMINIUM

The distinction between cooperatives and condominiums is significant. A condominium is an estate in real property consisting of an undivided ownership interest in a portion of a parcel of real property together

[26] UCC § 9-323.
[27] UCC § 9-601.

with a separate ownership interest in another portion of the same parcel. Condominium ownership is a merger of two estates in land into one: the ownership of an apartment or unit in a condominium project and a tenancy in common ownership interest with other co-owners in the common elements of that unit. The condominium is real property and a creditor to recover this property must conduct a foreclosure proceeding under the state law that covers real property. The owner of the condominium is entitled to all the notices and all the provisions that protect the owner of a private residence with regard to the commencement and the prosecution of a foreclosure action. A time share may be a condominium.

A cooperative is organized for the purpose of rendering some type of service to shareholders or members who own and control it. Cooperative apartments are usually dwelling units in a multi-dwelling complex. Each member has an interest in the entire complex and a lease of its own property (apartment), although members do not own the apartments as is the case with a condominium. The ownership of the co-op is organized in corporate form and is treated as a corporation and the members of the co-op only receive certificates of stock as indicia of their ownership as well as a lease on the apartment. The relationship between the tenant-shareholder and the co-op owner is largely determined by reviewing the lease, the certificate of incorporation, the stock offering prospectus, the stock subscription agreement, financial statements, bylaws, rules, and regulations, and all the other documents that pertain to the occupation of an apartment.[28]

To recover a cooperative apartment, a creditor must proceed (unless the state law indicates otherwise) under Section 9 of the UCC which deals with personal property. The owner of the co-op apartment is entitled to all the notices and protection afforded under this particular section of the UCC. Cooperative ownership is considered personal property because the interest is represented by a lease and a stock certificate; whereas condominium ownership is considered an estate in real property, and the condominium owner is the owner of the property in the same way that a party owns a private residence.[29]

The owner of the condominium is the fee owner of the apartment and a portion of the common areas. The legal status is in the nature of ownership of real estate, and a condominium is treated as real property. A deed or mortgage is used to transfer ownership in the same manner as real estate is transferred or mortgaged.

A cooperative apartment involves two types of relationships, both of them not in the nature of ownership in real estate. The first relationship is that of a stockholder in a corporation and the second relationship is that of a lessee who enjoys a lease relationship with the parent corporation (the cooperative).

---

[28] *L&M Enters., Inc. v. BEI Sensors & Sys. Co.*, 231 F.3d 1284 (10th Cir. 2000); *Monarch Beverage Co. v. Tyfield Importers, Inc.*, 823 F.2d 1187 (7th Cir. 1987); *Continental Casing Corp. v. Siderca Corp.*, 38 S.W.3d 782 (Tex. App. 2001).

[29] *In re Pandeff*, 201 B.R. 865 (Bankr. S.D.N.Y. 1996).

Cooperative ownership is treated as personal property. When a lease terminates, the tenant would normally owe to the landlord the rent up until the time the lease was terminated, the use and occupancy after the lease was terminated during the time that the tenant still remained in the apartment and finally, a clause in the lease that would require the tenant to pay to the landlord the balance of the rent required under the lease after subtracting any rent that the landlord collected from renting the premises during the term of the lease. The normal cooperative relationship involves the long-term lease together with stock ownership in the corporation. The party who is the lessee and the owner of the stock must be one and the same party.

The stock normally cannot be sold or transferred without the consent of the cooperative board and, at the same time, the lessee cannot sub-lease the premises without the consent of the cooperative board. If a cooperative board is to terminate a lease and evict a tenant for non-payment, usually the agreement permits the board to cancel the stock certificates and issue a new stock certificate to whomsoever the board decides to lease the premises, and to issue a new certificate to this party as well as a new lease.

Some courts have rejected this particular posture and do not allow the cooperative board to cancel the stock and issue a new stock certificate when the lease is terminated. The reverse situation also can come into play where the owner of the stock certificate dies and leaves the stock to an heir who is not suitable to the board. Some leases provide that the lease would terminate and automatically come to an end.[30]

A sale of a cooperative apartment is, in reality, a sale of the stock of the cooperative apartment and has nothing to do with the leasehold interest. The rights of a cooperative tenant flow from stock ownership and not from the proprietary lease which merely creates a landlord-and-tenant relationship between the cooperative corporation and the stockholder.[31]

Cooperative Apartments—Security Interests. Article 9 of the UCC covers the obtaining of security interests in cooperatives. The use of financing statements and security agreements is the appropriate method under the UCC. The tenant grants to the secured lender a security interest in the right, title, and interest to the shares of stock in the co-op, and the agreement includes pledging the leasehold interest as security. The secured lender and the cooperative corporation usually execute what is known as a "recognition agreement" where each party recognizes and acknowledges the rights of the other party.

Foreclosing on a cooperative is covered in Revised Article 9 and is similar to a foreclosure on a vehicle—the debtor (if a consumer) must receive the required notice under the Fair Debt Collection Practices Act,

---

[30] *United States v. 110-118 Riverside Tenants Corp.*, 886 F.2d 514 (2d Cir. 1998).

[31] *State Tax Comm'n v. Shor*, 378 N.Y.S.2d 222 (N.Y. Sup. Ct. N.Y. Co. 1975), *aff'd*, 385 N.Y.S.2d 290 (N.Y. App. Div. 1st Dep't 1976), *aff'd*, 371 N.E.2d 523 (1977).

and be afforded an opportunity to dispute the debt. After the 30-day period a notice of sale is prepared to conform to the requirements of Revised Article 9. A search is conducted to determine the parties who will receive the notice of sale. An auctioneer is retained and a sale is conducted to conform to Revised Article 9.[32]

MOBILE HOMES

Obtaining a security interest on a mobile home presents unique problems. The courts do not always agree on whether a mobile home is or is not a fixture attached to the land or is part of the land.

Many states have specific laws dealing with mobile homes. When the creditor files an application for a mobile home title, a certificate of title notation showing its lien may be required. If a mobile home is transported from one state to another, Section 9-103 of the Revised UCC would apply covering multi-state certificate of title problems.

Where a mobile home is placed on a part of land, the issue is whether it is a fixture or whether it is part of the real estate. If the debtor actually owns the real estate underneath the mobile home and the intent is to place the mobile home on the property permanently to be his home, this would be no different than any other home located on a piece of real estate with both the home and the real estate owned by the debtor, and no filing under the UCC would be necessary. Under those circumstances a mobile home is not considered a fixture. The home is part of the real estate covered by a real estate mortgage.

Unfortunately, not all the courts agree on this particular concept and some courts consider a mobile home a fixture if:

1. It is annexed to the realty.
2. Its adaptation or application to the realty is being used appropriately.
3. No intention is exhibited that the home is a permanent accession to the realty.

A fixture may qualify as a consumer good under old Section 9-109 (Revised 9-102).

A recent case addressed this issue in Pennsylvania and set forth certain criteria.[33] The court first distinguished three classes of mobile homes.

A. Those homes which are manifestly furniture as distinguished from improvements and not particularly fitted to the property with which they are used. These homes usually remain personalty.

---

[32]*Cavollero v. Shapiro & Kreisman*, 933 F. Supp. 1148 (E.D.N.Y. 1996).
[33]*In re Nowlin*, 321 B.R. 678 (Bankr. E.D. Pa. 2005).

B. Homes annexed to the property that cannot be removed without material injury to the real estate or to themselves. These homes remain realty, even in the face of an expressed intention that they should be considered personalty.

C. Some mobile homes although physically connected with the real estate are so affixed as to be removable without destroying or materially injuring the chattels themselves or the property to which they are annexed. These homes become part of the reality or remain personalty, depending upon the intention of the parties at the time of the annexations. In this class fall such chattels as boilers, and machinery affixed for the use of an owner or a tenant but readily removable.

When a mobile home falls within the third category, the court examines the intent of the parties, and the "facts and circumstances" of each case. The "facts and circumstances" to be considered are the following:

A. Whether the mobile home and the lot are owned by the same party.
B. Whether the mobile home is permanently attached to the land.
C. The method by which the mobile home is attached to the land.
D. The length of time that the mobile home has been attached to the land.
E. The relative ease of moving the mobile home from the land.
F. Whether the mobile home can be removed from the land without damaging the land.
G. Whether the mobile home is necessary or essential to the real property.
H. The conduct of the owner and whether evidence is present of an intent to permanently attach the mobile home.

When mobile homes are in the dealer's possession, they usually are treated as part of the stock of the dealer and any financing would have to be done under the UCC to protect the creditor's interest from a real estate mortgage on the property. A mobile home is a fixture or part of the real estate and the creditor should be wary of specific state statutes which may require an application for a certificate of title notation. An application for a certificate of title notation may be in addition to the filing requirements under the UCC or relying on a real estate mortgage if the property is owned by the debtor and the intent is to place the mobile home on the property permanently.

Similar problems exist with regard to prefabricated buildings and other types of construction. The creditor should be skeptical of protecting its interest in a mobile home with only a real estate mortgage in the event the mobile home is moved to another state. A filing would give the creditor protection under old Section 9-103 dealing with multi-state certificate of title problems, but review Revised UCC 9-301, 303, 304, 305, 306, 307, 316, and 337.

> ***Credit & Collection Tip:*** *Before embarking on any financing in a particular state, a careful review should be conducted of the state law and the court decisions. If there is no specific state law, the cautious creditor may file the mortgage as a real estate mortgage and at the same time perfect a security interest on the mobile home under the UCC.*[34]

DRAGNET CLAUSE—RELATEDNESS RULE

A "dragnet clause" provides that the collateral described in a security agreement secures any new advances, extension, renewals, or refinancing. It may secure any other amounts that the debtor may owe to their lender now or in the future.[35]

The "relatedness rule" serves to limit the application of a future advance clause to those advances that are of the same class as the primary transaction. The "relatedness rule" developed prior to the enactment of the UCC and was a reflection of the disfavor with which the courts viewed dragnet clauses in security agreements, notwithstanding the fact they were common. This device is abused when a lender, relying on a broadly drafted clause, seeks to bring within the shelter of his security arrangements claims against the debtor that are unrelated to the financing that was contemplated by the parties. The courts have regularly curbed such abuses no matter how well the clause is drafted, for the future advances to be covered must be of the same class as the primary obligation or so related to it that the consent of the debtor to its inclusion may be inferred.

One particular court has set down four tests to be applied in the application of the relatedness rule.

1. Whether the indebtedness allegedly covered by the mortgage containing said dragnet clause is specifically intentional.
2. Whether the other indebtedness allegedly covered is of the same class as the debt referenced in the mortgage.
3. Whether the indebtedness was intended to be separately secured.
4. Whether the mortgagee relied on the dragnet clause in making further loans.

Under these tests, it would seem that any future advance must be used for the same purpose as the original advance. The debtor should have some knowledge of the presence of the dragnet clauses, although some courts feel this is cured by the mere execution of the security agreement. As to the question of the lender relying on the dragnet clause, this particular test is not an essential ingredient in most decisions.

---

[34] *In re Kroskie*, 258 B.R. 676 (Bankr. W.D. Mich. 2001).

[35] *Brockbank v. Best Capital Corp.*, 341 S.C. 372, 534 S.E.2d 688 (S.C. Sup. Ct. 2000).

The same class test is also applied rather differently by various courts. Some courts will treat loans of a business nature as the same class. Loans to satisfy an overdraft business checking account were not related to a prior loan. As courts do not generally approve of dragnet clauses, whether or not the court will uphold the terms in the security agreement or the mortgage agreement appears to be decided more on a case-by-case basis than by any fixed precedent. While the reasons for enforcing or for not enforcing the dragnet clause vary from state to state and from court to court, most of the courts pay lip service to the relatedness rule in holding some relationship must exist between the original indebtedness and the future advance and some inferred consent by the debtor. Both issues are subjective, and no black-and-white line is drawn.

SECURITY INTEREST—COPYRIGHT

Computer programs, articles, books, or any other items which are a subject for copyright may be offered as security for an extension of credit. Intellectual property such as trademarks or patents would fall under this category.

The proper place to file a secured interest is in the copyright office because the federal government has provided a national registration and specifies the place of filing for perfecting a security interest in a copyright. Not all of the federal courts agree with this position and some of them take the position that a security interest may be recorded in the United States copyright office but does not have to be recorded in the United States Copyright Office if the creditor properly filed the security interest in the appropriate state office in accordance with state laws. The recommendation of most attorneys is to file in the United States Copyright Office and in the proper offices in the state. File in both places.[36]

Trademark. The Lanham Act governs trademarks. Its provisions on the transfer of interest in a trademark states in a relevant part:

> a registered mark or mark for which application to register has been filed shall be assignable with the good will of the business in which the mark was used, or with that part of the good will of the business connected with the use of and symbolized by the mark . . . an assignment shall be void as against any subsequent purchaser for a valuable consideration without notice, unless it is recorded in the patent and trademark office within three months after the date thereof or prior to such subsequent purchase.

The Lanham Act does not define the word "assignment." The few courts that have addressed the problem have indicated that the Act does

[36] *Peregrine Entm't, Ltd. v. Capital Fed. S & L Assoc. of Denver*, 116 B.R. 194 (C.D. Cal. 1990).

not preempt the UCC's filing requirement and that the perfection of a security interest in a trademark is governed by Article 9. A filing with the patent office of a financing statement and security agreement would not be sufficient to protect the secured party.[37]

PATENTS. The issue before the court is whether a security interest in a patent is perfected if filed with a patent office or whether a filing must take place under the UCC to protect the patent from a claim of the trustee in bankruptcy. The major issue is whether the federal statute has preempted state law. If the Patent Act does not preempt state law, the court must look to the UCC.[38]

The UCC will not apply to security interest to the extent that a federal statute regulates the rights of the parties and third parties. If that exclusion does apply, Article 9 filing requirements do not apply to transactions wherein a federal statute that provides for national registration of a "security interest" or specifies a place for filing a security interest that is different from the place designated in Article 9.

The Patent Act provides that an interest in a patent is assignable and an assignment is void against the subsequent purchaser or mortgagee without notice of the assignment unless the assignment has been recorded in the patent office.

The court held that a security interest is not an assignment, grant, or conveyance of a patent and the omission of the words security interest should be contrasted with other federal statutes that expressly include security, interest, and liens within their scope.

Thus, the Patent Act does not preempt state law and Article 9 of the UCC controls the perfection of security interest in a patent. The best advice to the creditor would be to file a security interest in a patent not only in the state under the UCC but also with the patent office itself. As a practical matter, the patent office records a security interest on a discretionary basis and such recording does not provide constructive notice.[39]

> ***Credit & Collection Tip:*** *As stated before, the best of both worlds is to file liens on patents, copyrights, and trademarks both under the UCC and at the same time in the copyright and patent office.*

PURCHASE MONEY SECURITY INTEREST. The Revised Article 9 continues the priority of a purchase money security interest over a prior perfected security interest except for some additional conditions. The purchase money security interest must be perfected within 20 days after the debtor

---

[37] 15 U.S.C. § 1051; *Trimarchi & Personal Dating Services v. Together Dev. Corp.*, 255 B.R. 606 (Mass. Dist. Ct. 2000); *In re Roman Cleanser Co.*, 43 B.R. 940 (Bankr. E.D. Mich. 1984), *aff'd*, 802 F.2d 207 (6th Cir. 1986).

[38] *In re Coldwave Systems, LLC*, 368 B.R. 91 (Bankr. D. Mass. 2007).

[39] *In re Cybernetic Servs.*, 239 B.R. 917 (B.A.P. 9th Cir. 1999).

receives possession of the collateral (Section 9-324(a)). If the collateral must be inventoried, the secured party is under an obligation to forward an authenticated notification to the holders of any prior conflicting interest, which means that the purchase money secured creditor must run a search before he accepts a purchase money security interest. Said notice is effective for a period of five years under Section 9-324(b).[40]

A case in New York held that a refinancing does not create a purchase security interest and a secured claim is not entitled to the exception against cramdown and bifurcation provided for in the Bankruptcy Act (Section 1325(a)(9)). In this instance, the trade-in vehicle with negative equity was used as part of a replacement vehicle purchase.[41]

ACCOUNTS RECEIVABLE—FINANCING—FACTORING

One form of accounts receivable financing is known as factoring arrangements which are common in the textile industry and other industries. The factor (finance company) purchases the account receivable from the debtor corporation and assumes all the credit risk. The factor buys the account under an agreement that does not provide for any recourse or charge back against the debtor corporation if the account proves uncollectible. The factor will purchase the account for a percentage less than the face amount of the account receivable and in essence becomes the owner of the account. This fee represents the compensation for the factor assuming all the risks of collection. Under such an arrangement, neither the debtor corporation nor any of its creditors have any legitimate concern with any disposition that the factor may make of the accounts receivable. The factor is under no obligation to furnish the debtor corporation with a notice of sale or disposition of the said accounts receivable, because the factor is the owner.

Under another form of accounts receivable financing, the finance company (as distinguished from a factor) does not assume the credit risk, but still receives an assignment of the accounts receivable and advances money to a debtor corporation (usually 2/3 to 4/5 of the face amount of the invoice). The finance corporation retains a right of full or limited recourse, or charge back to the debtor corporation (or any guarantors) for any accounts that are uncollectible. Any disposition of the accounts receivable by the finance company under the terms of their agreement requires the finance company to provide notice to the debtor corporation or the guarantor, for such disposition may increase a deficiency claim or reduce a possible surplus to which the debtor corporation may be liable or entitled.[42]

---

[40] UCC § 9-324.

[41] *In re Peaslee*, 358 B.R. 545 (Bankr. W.D.N.Y. 2006).

[42] *Al Gailani v. Riyad Bank Houston Agency*, 22 S.W.3d 560 (Tex. App. 2000).

TITLE LENDING

Sub-prime lending is a common term in the industry where auto finance companies extend credit to consumers who have poor credit ratings. Title lending practiced in many states is somewhat different. The consumer is seeking a small loan, usually less than $1,000. The title lender cuts a check for a one-month loan with interest ranging as high as 20 percent per month, which would be 240 percent per year. The consumer then transfers title of the car to the lender and the lender usually insists upon a separate set of keys to the car so that they do not have to incur the expense of a tow job when time for repossession comes. As a rule, the lender will probably extend credit of no more than half the value of the car. In most instances, the car is valued at no more than $1,000 to $2,000.

While title lending is in the nature of a pawn operation, no federal regulation is in place to monitor this type of lending. Regulation emanates from the states. Sixteen states have regulated or prohibit this type of lending. The statutes vary from state to state from providing maximum loan amounts to caps on interest and/or other costs as well as additional disclosure requirements.

The states that do regulate title loans as of 2008 are as follows:[43]

Alabama	Kentucky	New Hampshire
Arizona	Minnesota	Oregon
Florida	Mississippi	South Carolina
Georgia	Missouri	Tennessee
Idaho	Montana	Utah
Illinois	Nevada	

Some of the states regulate or prohibit this type of lending, but in many states the lenders are successful in promoting favorable state legislation or the states themselves do not pay too much attention to enforcing their usury laws. In Florida, because the title lenders are classified as pawn shops, they do not have to return to the borrowers the excess of the sales price if the vehicle exceeds the unpaid loan balance. Some states, such as Georgia and Tennessee, have passed legislation favorable to title lenders. Regulation of title lending is through state laws and a careful examination of the state law is recommended. The UCC would still cover repossessions.

[43]Bus. Law., Feb. 2008, p. 598.

MORTGAGE—REAL AND PERSONAL PROPERTY

An issue often comes up when the creditor is foreclosing under a real estate mortgage and the mortgage covers both real property and personal property.

The Court of Appeals in Indiana answered the question in simple terms.[44] Under the Indiana code, when a mortgage covers both real and personal property, the secured party may proceed in two ways. It may proceed as to the personal property under the UCC or it may proceed as to both the real and personal property in accordance with its rights and remedies with respect to the real property. The UCC does not apply if the secured party elects to proceed in the latter manner. Unfortunately, different results occur in other states.

COLLECTION BY CREDITOR AGAINST THIRD PARTIES

Section 9-607 expands somewhat the right of a creditor to collect against third parties who have an obligation to the debtor. The claims might include a breach of warranty claim arising out of a defect in the equipment that is the collateral and even for an injunction against infringement of a patent that is collateral.

The creditor may also proceed against the guarantors or any other third party which may be obligated to render some type of performance such as a vendor who has entered into a contract to repair the equipment but who has failed to live up to his contract.[45]

TRANSFER OF RECORD OR TITLE

Section 9-619 provides a broader right to the creditor to obtain title after a default. It identifies a transfer statement as a record authenticated by a secured party that states as follows:

1. The debtor has defaulted in connection with an obligation secured by a specified collateral.
2. The secured party has exercised its post default remedies with respect to the collateral.

[44] *Art County Squire v. Inland Mortg. Co.*, 745 N.E.2d 885 (Ind. Ct. App. 2001).
[45] UCC § 9-607.

3. That, by reason of the exercise, a transferee has acquired the rights of the debtor in the collateral.
4. The name and address of the secured party, debtor, and transferee.

A transfer statement entitles the transferee to the transfer of record of all rights of the debtor in the collateral specified in the statement in any official filing, recording, registration, or certificate of title system covering the collateral . . .

The official filing office must accept the transfer and properly amend its record, and if applicable issue a new certificate of title in the name of the transferee. The official filing officer has no discretion to refuse this transfer statement providing it has complied with Section 9-619.[46]

COMMERCIAL TORT CLAIMS

Section 9-109(d)(12) specifically prevents a lender from obtaining a security interest in a personal injury claim of a consumer. On the other hand, this section allows a security interest on a commercial tort claim, which means that a lender may take a security interest in a commercial tort claim which arises out of a business or a profession.[47]

TAX REFUNDS AND TAX LIENS

A tax refund can be defined as a general intangible. The lender might feel that under the Revised Article 9 that the general intangible is subject to a lien by filing a financing statement. Nevertheless, where the tax refund is from the United States government, tax refunds are subject to the requirements of the Federal Assignment of Claims Act. Other ways may be available to obtain a lien on a tax refund by exercising some type of control over a debtor's bank account. Consultation with experienced counsel is recommended.

With regard to tax liens, the law is clear that tax liens will take priority over a security agreement that was properly filed in the event any advances are made by the lender after notice of the filing of the lien or within 45 days following such filing, whichever occurs earlier. If the lender is dealing with a borrower who is having financial problems, and is continuing to advance monies on inventory, construction loans, etc. the lender must be cognizant of these tax liens. If only a few advances are made over the year, a lien search should be conducted before any advance. If the monies are being

---

[46]UCC § 9-619.
[47]UCC § 9-109(d)(12).

advanced on a regular basis, a lien search should be conducted at least every 45 days to be certain no intervening tax liens have been filed.[48]

ENFORCEMENT OF A JUDGMENT

To obtain a lien on real property, the creditor must record or perfect a judgment according to rules under a particular state law. In some cases the lien only applies to a specific piece of property. In other cases, the lien can be either statewide or countywide. In this situation the lien is a floating lien and attaches to any property owned in part by the judgment debtor. In many states, if the debtor later purchases property, the lien will attach to the new property. Most title search companies are aware of this situation and will report same in their title searches as the prior judgment lien will be superior to a consensual lien.

The real estate lien law varies substantially from state to state and sometimes by the type of court. For example, in New York, a Supreme Court judgment is an automatic lien on property in the county in which the suit was started. However, if the lawsuit was commenced in a City, Civil, District, or other lower court, a transcript of judgment must be obtained and filed with the clerk of the county in which the lawsuit was filed. In Connecticut, the lien only applies to a specific piece of property. Meanwhile, in New Jersey, the lien is statewide and the judgment must be filed in only one location.

AGRICULTURE BUSINESS LIENS—PERISHABLE AGRICULTURAL COMMODITIES AND PACKERS ACT (PACA), PACKERS AND STOCKYARDS ACT (PSA)

The PACA provides that perishable agricultural commodities received by a buyer and all inventories, food, or other products derived from perishable agricultural commodities as well as any receivables or proceeds from the sale must be held by the buyer for the benefit of any unpaid suppliers or sellers of such commodities or any agents in the transaction until full payment owing to them in connection with the transaction has been received. A produce seller must send a written notice of its intent to do so within 30 days after the payment deadline set by the regulations of the Secretary of Agriculture and such other deadline as the parties may agree to in a signed writing. *The most important feature of PACA is that the lien is superior to a secured creditor under the UCC even though the secured creditor has*

[48]ICR Section 6321, 6323; 31 U.S.C. § 3727.

perfected his security interest and is also superior to a claim of a trustee in bankruptcy. The trust for the benefit for the unpaid suppliers or sellers actually is created upon the sale to the buyer and might be called a "floating trust" which means that the unpaid seller is not required to trace the produce into any particular inventory even if the proceeds are a sale of the produce. A copy of the statute is in the Appendix.[49]

In a similar fashion, the PSA provides that all livestock purchased by a packer in cash sales and all proceeds from meat and meat food products, and livestock products shall be held by the packer in trust for the benefit of unpaid sellers of such livestock until full payment has been made. *Similar to the PACA, the trust is superior to a secured creditor's lien arising under the UCC.* The trust in both Acts is superior in the same manner to any claims made by the bankruptcy trustee. The seller must give written notice to a buyer within 30 days of the final date set for making payment and must file that notice with the Secretary of Agriculture.[50]

Many states provide protection to sub-contractors by requiring general contractors to hold funds in trust for the benefit of sub-contractors and suppliers. Sub-contractors then must hold the funds in trust for their own supplier and sub–sub-contractors.

Joint check agreements have been treated by some courts as trust funds whereas other courts consider them a contractual relationship. These agreements are similar to the agriculture and stockyard agreements in that the results from the labor or materials supplied by the beneficiary are to be held in trust for the beneficiary and usually take priority in bankruptcy, since they do not become part of the bankruptcy estate and the debtor will be unable to grant a security interest in a trust fund.

CERTIFICATES OF ORIGIN

The use of the certificates of origin was analyzed in depth. The bank, a floor plan lender, provided financing to an auto dealership to purchase vehicles. The bank received a security interest in the dealership's motor vehicle inventory and any proceeds from the inventory. The bank perfected the security interest by filing a UCC 1 financing statement.

A credit union provided funding for three vehicles to customers of a dealership and filed a security agreement to perfect its security interest. The bank discovered that the dealership had been selling vehicles out of trust to consumers without remitting the proceeds to the bank. The bank

---

[49]Perishable Agricultural Commodities Act, 7 U.S.C. § 499(a), (b), (e) (2000).
[50]Packers and Stockyard Act, 7 U.S.C. § 196(b)-(c) (2000).

never received the proceeds for the three disputed vehicles sold by the dealership. The bank retained possession of the certificate of origin until the credit union signed a stipulation to release the titles to the customers to enable them to register the vehicle with the state. The bank sent a letter to the credit union for the return of the certificate of origin, stating that its only intention in delivering them to the credit union was to facilitate registration by the party who had paid for the vehicle and had obtained financing through the credit union. The credit union refused to return the certificate stating that they had received them for value.

The bank sued the credit union alleging conversion of the vehicle titles and seeking recovery of the proceeds received by the credit union. The lower court held that neither the purchasers of the vehicles nor the credit union could acquire an interest in the title until the titles were delivered to either of them and that neither could qualify as buyers in the ordinary course of business under UCC 9-320.

The appellate court acknowledged that a security interest continues in collateral notwithstanding the sale, exchange or other disposition unless the disposition was authorized by the secured party in the security agreement or otherwise.[51] The lien also continues in any identifiable proceeds including collections received by the debtor dealership. Whereas the credit union did make the loan to the customers and filed their financing statements a year after the bank perfected its security interest, the dealership failed to make the required remittances of the proceeds to the bank and the bank refused to surrender the certificates of origin. The credit union received the titles only when the bank surrendered the certificates for the benefit of the credit union's customers to register the vehicles under a stipulation of agreement with the bank.

The mistake was that the bank authorized the disposition of the collateral without informing the buyers that the bank was reserving a right to the collateral if the dealership did not make the required payments. Thus, the bank lost its security interest in that collateral and the credit union's interest in the vehicles prevails. The credit union received an enforceable right to its security interest in the vehicles as a purchaser of value. The definitions of "purchase" and "purchaser" as set forth in the UCC are sufficiently broad to encompass the dealer as a lender who takes a security interest in goods as security for its loans. Arguments could be made that the stipulation releasing the certificates of origin specifically required the return of the certificates, but the court refused to accept this interpretation. Perhaps another court will.

---

[51] *Valley Bank & Trust Co. v. Holyoke Cmty. Fed. Credit Union*, 121 P.3d 358 (Colo. Ct. App. 2005).

CHAPTER 11
APPENDIX I

REVISED ARTICLE 9 OF THE UNIFORM COMMERCIAL CODE—CALIFORNIA

9101. This division may be cited as the Uniform Commercial Code—Secured Transactions.

§ 9102. (a) In this division:

(1) "Accession" means goods that are physically united with other goods in such a manner that the identity of the original goods is not lost.

(2) "Account," except as used in "account for," means a right to payment of a monetary obligation, whether or not earned by performance, (i) for property that has been or is to be sold, leased, licensed, assigned, or otherwise disposed of, (ii) for services rendered or to be rendered, (iii) for a policy of insurance issued or to be issued, (iv) for a secondary obligation incurred or to be incurred, (v) for energy provided or to be provided, (vi) for the use or hire of a vessel under a charter or other contract, (vii) arising out of the use of a credit or charge card or information contained on or for use with the card, or (viii) as winnings in a lottery or other game of chance operated or sponsored by a state, governmental unit of a state, or person licensed or authorized to operate the game by a state or governmental unit of a state. The term includes health care insurance receivables. The term does not include (i) rights to payment evidenced by chattel paper or an instrument, (ii) commercial tort claims, (iii) deposit accounts, (iv) investment property, (v) letter-of-credit rights or letters of credit, or (vi) rights to payment for money or funds advanced or sold, other than rights arising out of the use of a credit or charge card or information contained on or for use with the card.

(3) "Account debtor" means a person obligated on an account, chattel paper, or general intangible. The term does not include persons obligated to pay a negotiable instrument, even if the instrument constitutes part of chattel paper.

(4) "Accounting," except as used in "accounting for," means a record that is all of the following:

(A) Authenticated by a secured party.

(B) Indicating the aggregate unpaid secured obligations as of a date not more than 35 days earlier or 35 days later than the date of the record.

(C) Identifying the components of the obligations in reasonable detail.

(5) "Agricultural lien" means an interest in farm products that meets all of the following conditions:

(A) It secures payment or performance of an obligation for either of the following:

(i) Goods or services furnished in connection with a debtor's farming operation.

(ii) Rent on real property leased by a debtor in connection with its farming operation.

(B) It is created by statute in favor of a person that does either of the following:

(i) In the ordinary course of its business furnished goods or services to a debtor in connection with a debtor's farming operation.

(ii) Leased real property to a debtor in connection with the debtor's farming operation.

(C) Its effectiveness does not depend on the person's possession of the personal property.

(6) "As-extracted collateral" means either of the following:

(A) Oil, gas, or other minerals that are subject to a security interest that does both of the following:

(i) Is created by a debtor having an interest in the minerals before extraction.

(ii) Attaches to the minerals as extracted.

(B) Accounts arising out of the sale at the wellhead or minehead of oil, gas, or other minerals in which the debtor had an interest before extraction.

(7) "Authenticate" means to do either of the following:

(A) To sign.

(B) To execute or otherwise adopt a symbol, or encrypt or similarly process a record in whole or in part, with the present intent of the authenticating person to identify the person and adopt or accept a record.

(8) "Bank" means an organization that is engaged in the business of banking. The term includes savings banks, savings and loan associations, credit unions, and trust companies.

(9) "Cash proceeds" means proceeds that are money, checks, deposit accounts, or the like.

(10) "Certificate of title" means a certificate of title with respect to which a statute provides for the security interest in question to be indicated on the certificate as a condition or result of the security interest's obtaining priority over the rights of a lien creditor with respect to the collateral.

(11) "Chattel paper" means a record or records that evidence both a monetary obligation and a security interest in specific goods, a security interest in specific goods and software used in the goods, a security interest in specific goods and license of software used in the goods, a lease of specific goods, or a lease of specific goods and license of software used in the goods. In this paragraph, "monetary obligation" means a monetary obligation secured by the goods or owed under a lease of the goods and includes a monetary obligation with respect to software used in the goods. The term does not include (i) charters or other contracts involving the use or hire of a vessel or (ii) records that evidence a right to payment arising out of the use of a credit or charge card or information contained on or for use with the card. If a transaction is evidenced by records that include an instrument or series of instruments, the group of records taken together constitutes chattel paper.

(12) "Collateral" means the property subject to a security interest or agricultural lien. The term includes all of the following:

(A) Proceeds to which a security interest attaches.

(B) Accounts, chattel paper, payment intangibles, and promissory notes that have been sold.

(C) Goods that are the subject of a consignment.

(13) "Commercial tort claim" means a claim arising in tort with respect to which either of the following conditions is satisfied:

(A) The claimant is an organization.

(B) The claimant is an individual and both of the following conditions are satisfied regarding the claim:

(i) It arose in the course of the claimant's business or profession.

(ii) It does not include damages arising out of personal injury to or the death of an individual.

(14) "Commodity account" means an account maintained by a commodity intermediary in which a commodity contract is carried for a commodity customer.

(15) "Commodity contract" means a commodity futures contract, an option on a commodity futures contract, a commodity option, or another contract if the contract or option is either of the following:

(A) Traded on or subject to the rules of a board of trade that has been designated as a contract market for such a contract pursuant to federal commodities laws.

(B) Traded on a foreign commodity board of trade, exchange, or market, and is carried on the books of a commodity intermediary for a commodity customer.

(16) "Commodity customer" means a person for which a commodity intermediary carries a commodity contract on its books.

(17) "Commodity intermediary" means a person that is either of the following:

(A) Is registered as a futures commission merchant under federal commodities law.

(B) In the ordinary course of its business provides clearance or settlement services for a board of trade that has been designated as a contract market pursuant to federal commodities law.

(18) "Communicate" means to do any of the following:

(A) To send a written or other tangible record.

(B) To transmit a record by any means agreed upon by the persons sending and receiving the record.

(C) In the case of transmission of a record to or by a filing office, to transmit a record by any means prescribed by filing-office rule.

(19) "Consignee" means a merchant to which goods are delivered in a consignment.

(20) "Consignment" means a transaction, regardless of its form, in which a person delivers goods to a merchant for the purpose of sale and all of the following conditions are satisfied:

(A) The merchant satisfies all of the following conditions:

(i) He or she deals in goods of that kind under a name other than the name of the person making delivery.

(ii) He or she is not an auctioneer.

(iii) He or she is not generally known by its creditors to be substantially engaged in selling the goods of others.

(B) With respect to each delivery, the aggregate value of the goods is one thousand dollars ($1,000) or more at the time of delivery.

(C) The goods are not consumer goods immediately before delivery.

(D) The transaction does not create a security interest that secures an obligation.

(21) "Consignor" means a person that delivers goods to a consignee in a consignment.

(22) "Consumer debtor" means a debtor in a consumer transaction.

(23) "Consumer goods" means goods that are used or bought for use primarily for personal, family, or household purposes.

(24) "Consumer-goods transaction" means a consumer transaction in which both of the following conditions are satisfied:

(A) An individual incurs an obligation primarily for personal, family, or household purposes.

(B) A security interest in consumer goods secures the obligation.

(25) "Consumer obligor" means an obligor who is an individual and who incurred the obligation as part of a transaction entered into primarily for personal, family, or household purposes.

(26) "Consumer transaction" means a transaction in which (i) an individual incurs an obligation primarily for personal, family, or household purposes, (ii) a security interest secures the obligation, and (iii) the collateral is held or acquired primarily for personal, family, or household purposes. The term includes consumer-goods transactions.

(27) "Continuation statement" means an amendment of a financing statement which does both of the following:

(A) Identifies, by its file number, the initial financing statement to which it relates.

(B) Indicates that it is a continuation statement for, or that it is filed to continue the effectiveness of, the identified financing statement.

(28) "Debtor" means any of the following:

(A) A person having an interest, other than a security interest or other lien, in the collateral, whether or not the person is an obligor.

(B) A seller of accounts, chattel paper, payment intangibles, or promissory notes.

(C) A consignee.

(29) "Deposit account" means a demand, time, savings, passbook, or similar account maintained with a bank. The term does not include investment property or accounts evidenced by an instrument.

(30) "Document" means a document of title or a receipt of the type described in subdivision (b) of Section 7201.

(31) "Electronic chattel paper" means chattel paper evidenced by a record or records consisting of information stored in an electronic medium.

(32) "Encumbrance" means a right, other than an ownership interest, in real property. The term includes mortgages and other liens on real property.

(33) "Equipment" means goods other than inventory, farm products, or consumer goods.

(34) "Farm products" means goods, other than standing timber, with respect to which the debtor is engaged in a farming operation and which are any of the following:

(A) Crops grown, growing, or to be grown, including both of the following:

(i) Crops produced on trees, vines, and bushes.

(ii) Aquatic goods produced in aquacultural operations.

(B) Livestock, born or unborn, including aquatic goods produced in aquacultural operations.

(C) Supplies used or produced in a farming operation.

(D) Products of crops or livestock in their unmanufactured states.

(35) "Farming operation" means raising, cultivating, propagating, fattening, grazing, or any other farming, livestock, or aquacultural operation.

(36) "File number" means the number assigned to an initial financing statement pursuant to subdivision (a) of Section 9519.

(37) "Filing office" means an office designated in Section 9501 as the place to file a financing statement.

(38) "Filing-office rule" means a rule adopted pursuant to Section 9526.

(39) "Financing statement" means a record or records composed of an initial financing statement and any filed record relating to the initial financing statement.

(40) "Fixture filing" means the filing of a financing statement covering goods that are or are to become fixtures and satisfying subdivisions (a) and (b) of Section 9502. The term includes the filing of a financing statement covering goods of a transmitting utility which are or are to become fixtures.

(41) "Fixtures" means goods that have become so related to particular real property that an interest in them arises under real property law.

(42) "General intangible" means any personal property, including things in action, other than accounts, chattel paper, commercial tort claims, deposit accounts, documents, goods, instruments, investment property, letter-of-credit rights, letters of credit, money, and oil, gas, or other minerals before extraction. The term includes payment intangibles and software.

(43) (Reserved).

(44) "Goods" means all things that are movable when a security interest attaches. The term includes (i) fixtures, (ii) standing timber that is to be cut and removed under a conveyance or contract for sale, (iii) the unborn young of animals, (iv) crops grown, growing, or to be grown, even if the crops are produced on trees, vines, or bushes, and (v) manufactured homes. The term also includes a computer program embedded in goods and any supporting information provided in connection with a transaction relating to the program if (i) the program is associated with the goods in such a manner that it customarily is considered part of the goods, or (ii) by becoming the owner of the goods, a person acquires a right to use the program in connection with the goods. The term does not include a computer program embedded in goods that consist solely of the medium in which the program is embedded. The term also does not include accounts, chattel paper, commercial tort claims, deposit accounts, documents, general intangibles, instruments, investment property, letter-of-credit rights, letters of credit, money, or oil, gas, or other minerals before extraction.

(45) "Governmental unit" means a subdivision, agency, department, county, parish, municipality, or other unit of the government of the United States, a state, or a foreign country. The term includes an organization having a separate corporate existence if the organization is eligible to issue debt on

which interest is exempt from income taxation under the laws of the United States.

(46) "Health care insurance receivable" means an interest in or claim under a policy of insurance which is a right to payment of a monetary obligation for health care goods or services provided or to be provided.

(47) "Instrument" means a negotiable instrument or any other writing that evidences a right to the payment of a monetary obligation, is not itself a security agreement or lease, and is of a type that in ordinary course of business is transferred by delivery with any necessary indorsement or assignment. The term does not include (i) investment property, (ii) letters of credit, or (iii) writings that evidence a right to payment arising out of the use of a credit or charge card or information contained on or for use with the card.

(48) "Inventory" means goods, other than farm products, which are any of the following:

(A) Leased by a person as lessor.

(B) Held by a person for sale or lease or to be furnished under a contract of service.

(C) Furnished by a person under a contract of service.

(D) Consist of raw materials, work in process, or materials used or consumed in a business.

(49) "Investment property" means a security, whether certificated or uncertificated, security entitlement, securities account, commodity contract, or commodity account.

(50) "Jurisdiction of organization," with respect to a registered organization, means the jurisdiction under whose law the organization is organized.

(51) "Letter-of-credit right" means a right to payment or performance under a letter of credit, whether or not the beneficiary has demanded or is at the time entitled to demand payment or performance. The term does not include the right of a beneficiary to demand payment or performance under a letter of credit.

(52) (A) "Lien creditor" means any of the following:

(i) A creditor that has acquired a lien on the property involved by attachment, levy, or the like.

(ii) An assignee for benefit of creditors from the time of assignment.

(iii) A trustee in bankruptcy from the date of the filing of the petition.

(iv) A receiver in equity from the time of appointment.

(B) "Lien creditor" does not include a creditor who by filing a notice with the Secretary of State has acquired only an attachment or judgment lien on personal property, or both.

(53) "Manufactured home" means a structure, transportable in one or more sections, which, in the traveling mode, is eight body-feet or more in width or 40 body-feet or more in length, or, when erected on site, is

320 or more square feet, and which is built on a permanent chassis and designed to be used as a dwelling with or without a permanent foundation when connected to the required utilities, and includes the plumbing, heating, air-conditioning, and electrical systems contained therein. The term includes any structure that meets all of the requirements of this paragraph except the size requirements and with respect to which the manufacturer voluntarily files a certification required by the United States Secretary of Housing and Urban Development and complies with the standards established under Title 42 of the United States Code.

(54) "Manufactured home transaction" means a secured transaction that satisfies either of the following:

(A) It creates a purchase money security interest in a manufactured home, other than a manufactured home held as inventory.

(B) It is a secured transaction in which a manufactured home, other than a manufactured home held as inventory, is the primary collateral.

(55) "Mortgage" means a consensual interest in real property, including fixtures, which secures payment or performance of an obligation.

(56) "New debtor" means a person that becomes bound as debtor under subdivision (d) of Section 9203 by a security agreement previously entered into by another person.

(57) "New value" means (i) money, (ii) money's worth in property, services, or new credit, or (iii) release by a transferee of an interest in property previously transferred to the transferee. The term does not include an obligation substituted for another obligation.

(58) "Noncash proceeds" means proceeds other than cash proceeds.

(59) "Obligor" means a person that, with respect to an obligation secured by a security interest in or an agricultural lien on the collateral, (i) owes payment or other performance of the obligation, (ii) has provided property other than the collateral to secure payment or other performance of the obligation, or (iii) is otherwise accountable in whole or in part for payment or other performance of the obligation. The term does not include issuers or nominated persons under a letter of credit.

(60) "Original debtor," except as used in subdivision (c) of Section 9310, means a person that, as debtor, entered into a security agreement to which a new debtor has become bound under subdivision (d) of Section 9203.

(61) "Payment intangible" means a general intangible under which the account debtor's principal obligation is a monetary obligation.

(62) "Person related to," with respect to an individual, means any of the following:

(A) The spouse of the individual.

(B) A brother, brother-in-law, sister, or sister-in-law of the individual.

(C) An ancestor or lineal descendant of the individual or the individual's spouse.

(D) Any other relative, by blood or marriage, of the individual or the individual's spouse who shares the same home with the individual.

(63) "Person related to," with respect to an organization, means any of the following:

(A) A person directly or indirectly controlling, controlled by, or under common control with the organization.

(B) An officer or director of, or a person performing similar functions with respect to, the organization.

(C) An officer or director of, or a person performing similar functions with respect to, a person described in subparagraph (A).

(D) The spouse of an individual described in subparagraph (A), (B), or (C).

(E) An individual who is related by blood or marriage to an individual described in subparagraph (A), (B), (C), or (D) and shares the same home with the individual.

(64) "Proceeds," except as used in subdivision (b) of Section 9609, means any of the following property:

(A) Whatever is acquired upon the sale, lease, license, exchange, or other disposition of collateral.

(B) Whatever is collected on, or distributed on account of, collateral.

(C) Rights arising out of collateral.

(D) To the extent of the value of collateral, claims arising out of the loss, nonconformity, or interference with the use of, defects or infringement of rights in, or damage to, the collateral.

(E) To the extent of the value of collateral and to the extent payable to the debtor or the secured party, insurance payable by reason of the loss or nonconformity of, defects or infringement of rights in, or damage to, the collateral.

(65) "Promissory note" means an instrument that evidences a promise to pay a monetary obligation, does not evidence an order to pay, and does not contain an acknowledgment by a bank that the bank has received for deposit a sum of money or funds.

(66) "Proposal" means a record authenticated by a secured party that includes the terms on which the secured party is willing to accept collateral in full or partial satisfaction of the obligation it secures pursuant to Sections 9620, 9621, and 9622.

(67) "Public finance transaction" means a secured transaction in connection with which all of the following conditions are satisfied:

(A) Debt securities are issued.

(B) All or a portion of the securities issued have an initial stated maturity of at least 20 years.

(C) The debtor, obligor, secured party, account debtor or other person obligated on collateral, assignor or assignee of a secured obligation, or assignor or assignee of a security interest is a state or a governmental unit of a state.

(68) "Pursuant to commitment," with respect to an advance made or other value given by a secured party, means pursuant to the secured party's obligation, whether or not a subsequent event of default or other event not within the secured party's control has relieved or may relieve the secured party from its obligation.

(69) "Record," except as used in "for record," "of record," "record or legal title," and "record owner," means information that is inscribed on a tangible medium or which is stored in an electronic or other medium and is retrievable in perceivable form.

(70) "Registered organization" means an organization organized solely under the law of a single state or the United States and as to which the state or the United States must maintain a public record showing the organization to have been organized.

(71) "Secondary obligor" means an obligor to the extent that either of the following conditions are satisfied:

(A) The obligor's obligation is secondary.

(B) The obligor has a right of recourse with respect to an obligation secured by collateral against the debtor, another obligor, or property of either.

(72) "Secured party" means any of the following:

(A) A person in whose favor a security interest is created or provided for under a security agreement, whether or not any obligation to be secured is outstanding.

(B) A person that holds an agricultural lien.

(C) A consignor.

(D) A person to which accounts, chattel paper, payment intangibles, or promissory notes have been sold.

(E) A trustee, indenture trustee, agent, collateral agent, or other representative in whose favor a security interest or agricultural lien is created or provided for.

(F) A person that holds a security interest arising under Section 2401, 2505, 4210, or 5118, or under subdivision (3) of Section 2711 or subdivision (5) of Section 10508.

(73) "Security agreement" means an agreement that creates or provides for a security interest.

(74) "Send," in connection with a record or notification, means to do either of the following:

(A) To deposit in the mail, deliver for transmission, or transmit by any other usual means of communication, with postage or cost of transmission provided for, addressed to any address reasonable under the circumstances.

(B) To cause the record or notification to be received within the time that it would have been received if properly sent under subparagraph (A).

(75) "Software" means a computer program and any supporting information provided in connection with a transaction relating to the program. The term does not include a computer program that is included in the definition of goods.

(76) "State" means a state of the United States, the District of Columbia, Puerto Rico, the United States Virgin Islands, or any territory or insular possession subject to the jurisdiction of the United States.

(77) "Supporting obligation" means a letter-of-credit right or secondary obligation that supports the payment or performance of an account, chattel paper, document, general intangible, instrument, or investment property.

(78) "Tangible chattel paper" means chattel paper evidenced by a record or records consisting of information that is inscribed on a tangible medium.

(79) "Termination statement" means an amendment of a financing statement that does both of the following:

(A) Identifies, by its file number, the initial financing statement to which it relates.

(B) Indicates either that it is a termination statement or that the identified financing statement is no longer effective.

(80) "Transmitting utility" means a person primarily engaged in the business of any of the following:

(A) Operating a railroad, subway, street railway, or trolley bus.

(B) Transmitting communications electrically, electromagnetically, or by light.

(C) Transmitting goods by pipeline or sewer.

(D) Transmitting or producing and transmitting electricity, steam, gas, or water.

(b) The following definitions in other divisions apply to this division:

"Applicant"	Section 5102.
"Beneficiary"	Section 5102.
"Broker"	Section 8102.
"Certificated security"	Section 8102.
"Check"	Section 3104.
"Clearing corporation"	Section 8102.
"Contract for sale"	Section 2106.
"Control"	Section 7106.
"Customer"	Section 4104.
"Entitlement holder"	Section 8102.
"Financial asset"	Section 8102.
"Holder in due course"	Section 3302.
"Issuer" (with respect to a letter of credit or letter-of-credit right)	Section 5102.

"Issuer" (with respect to a security)	Section 8201.
"Issuer" (with respect to documents of title)	Section 7102.
"Lease"	Section 10103.
"Lease agreement"	Section 10103.
"Lease contract"	Section 10103.
"Leasehold interest"	Section 10103.
"Lessee"	Section 10103.
"Lessee in ordinary course of business"	Section 10103.
"Lessor"	Section 10103.
"Lessor's residual interest"	Section 10103.
"Letter of credit"	Section 5102.
"Merchant"	Section 2104.
"Negotiable instrument"	Section 3104.
"Nominated person"	Section 5102.
"Note"	Section 3104.
"Proceeds of a letter of credit"	Section 5114.
"Prove"	Section 3103.
"Sale"	Section 2106.
"Securities account"	Section 8501.
"Securities intermediary"	Section 8102.
"Security"	Section 8102.
"Security certificate"	Section 8102.
"Security entitlement"	Section 8102.
"Uncertificated security"	Section 8102.

(c) Division 1 (commencing with Section 1101) contains general definitions and principles of construction and interpretation applicable throughout this division.

9103.

(a) In this section:

(1) "Purchase money collateral" means goods or software that secures a purchase money obligation incurred with respect to that collateral.

(2) "Purchase money obligation" means an obligation of an obligor incurred as all or part of the price of the collateral or for value given to enable the debtor to acquire rights in or the use of the collateral if the value is in fact so used.

(b) A security interest in goods is a purchase money security interest as follows:

(1) To the extent that the goods are purchase money collateral with respect to that security interest.

(2) If the security interest is in inventory that is or was purchase money collateral, also to the extent that the security interest secures a purchase money obligation incurred with respect to other inventory in which the secured party holds or held a purchase money security interest.

(3) Also to the extent that the security interest secures a purchase money obligation incurred with respect to software in which the secured party holds or held a purchase money security interest.

(c) A security interest in software is a purchase money security interest to the extent that the security interest also secures a purchase money obligation incurred with respect to goods in which the secured party holds or held a purchase money security interest if both of the following conditions are satisfied:

(1) The debtor acquired its interest in the software in an integrated transaction in which it acquired an interest in the goods.

(2) The debtor acquired its interest in the software for the principal purpose of using the software in the goods.

(d) The security interest of a consignor in goods that are the subject of a consignment is a purchase money security interest in inventory.

(e) In a transaction other than a consumer-goods transaction, if the extent to which a security interest is a purchase money security interest depends on the application of a payment to a particular obligation, the payment must be applied as follows:

(1) In accordance with any reasonable method of application to which the parties agree.

(2) In the absence of the parties' agreement to a reasonable method, in accordance with any intention of the obligor manifested at or before the time of payment.

(3) In the absence of an agreement to a reasonable method and a timely manifestation of the obligor's intention, in the following order:

(A) To obligations that are not secured.

(B) If more than one obligation is secured, to obligations secured by purchase money security interests in the order in which those obligations were incurred.

(f) In a transaction other than a consumer-goods transaction, a purchase money security interest does not lose its status as such, even if any of the following conditions are satisfied:

(1) The purchase money collateral also secures an obligation that is not a purchase money obligation.

(2) Collateral that is not purchase money collateral also secures the purchase money obligation.

(3) The purchase money obligation has been renewed, refinanced, consolidated, or restructured.

(g) In a transaction other than a consumer-goods transaction, a secured party claiming a purchase money security interest has the burden of establishing the extent to which the security interest is a purchase money security interest.

(h) The limitation of the rules in subdivisions (e), (f), and (g) to transactions other than consumer-goods transactions is intended to leave to the court the determination of the proper rules in consumer-goods transactions. The court may not infer from that limitation the nature of the proper rule in consumer-goods transactions and may continue to apply established approaches.

9104.

(a) A secured party has control of a deposit account if any of the following conditions is satisfied:

(1) The secured party is the bank with which the deposit account is maintained.

(2) The debtor, secured party, and bank have agreed in an authenticated record that the bank will comply with instructions originated by the secured party directing disposition of the funds in the deposit account without further consent by the debtor.

(3) The secured party becomes the bank's customer with respect to the deposit account.

(b) A secured party that has satisfied subdivision (a) has control, even if the debtor retains the right to direct the disposition of funds from the deposit account.

9105. A secured party has control of electronic chattel paper if the record or records comprising the chattel paper are created, stored, and assigned in such a manner that each of the following conditions is satisfied:

(1) A single authoritative copy of the record or records exists which is unique, identifiable, and, except as otherwise provided in paragraphs (4), (5), and (6), unalterable.

(2) The authoritative copy identifies the secured party as the assignee of the record or records.

(3) The authoritative copy is communicated to and maintained by the secured party or its designated custodian.

(4) Copies or revisions that add or change an identified assignee of the authoritative copy can be made only with the participation of the secured party.

(5) Each copy of the authoritative copy and any copy of a copy is readily identifiable as a copy that is not the authoritative copy.

(6) Any revision of the authoritative copy is readily identifiable as an authorized or unauthorized revision.

9106.

(a) A person has control of a certificated security, uncertificated security, or security entitlement as provided in Section 8106.

(b) A secured party has control of a commodity contract if either of the following conditions is satisfied:

(1) The secured party is the commodity intermediary with which the commodity contract is carried.

(2) The commodity customer, secured party, and commodity intermediary have agreed that the commodity intermediary will apply any value distributed on account of the commodity contract as directed by the secured party without further consent by the commodity customer.

(c) A secured party having control of all security entitlements or commodity contracts carried in a securities account or commodity account has control over the securities account or commodity account.

9107. A secured party has control of a letter-of-credit right to the extent of any right to payment or performance by the issuer or any nominated person if the issuer or nominated person has consented to an assignment of proceeds of the letter of credit under subdivision (c) of Section 5114 or otherwise applicable law or practice.

9108.

(a) Except as otherwise provided in subdivisions (c), (d), and (e), a description of personal or real property is sufficient, whether or not it is specific, if it reasonably identifies what is described.

(b) Except as otherwise provided in subdivision (d), a description of collateral reasonably identifies the collateral if it identifies the collateral by any of the following:

(1) Specific listing.

(2) Category.

(3) Except as otherwise provided in subdivision (e), a type of collateral defined in this code.

(4) Quantity.

(5) Computational or allocational formula, or procedure.

(6) Except as otherwise provided in subdivision (c), any other method, if the identity of the collateral is objectively determinable.

(c) A description of collateral as "all the debtor's assets" or "all the debtor's personal property," or using words of similar import does not reasonably identify the collateral.

(d) Except as otherwise provided in subdivision (e), a description of a security entitlement, securities account, or commodity account is sufficient if it describes either of the following:

(1) The collateral by those terms or as investment property.

(2) The underlying financial asset or commodity contract.

(e) A description only by type of collateral defined in this code is an insufficient description of either of the following:

(1) A commercial tort claim.

(2) In a consumer transaction, consumer goods, a security entitlement, a securities account, or a commodity account.

(f) A description of investment property collateral also shall meet the applicable requirements of Section 1799.103 of the Civil Code. A description of consumer goods also shall meet the applicable requirements of Section 1799.100 of the Civil Code.

§ 9109.

(a) Except as otherwise provided in subdivisions (c) and (d), this division applies to each of the following:

(1) A transaction, regardless of its form, that creates a security interest in personal property or fixtures by contract.

(2) An agricultural lien.

(3) A sale of accounts, chattel paper, payment intangibles, or promissory notes.

(4) A consignment.

(5) A security interest arising under Section 2401 or 2505, or under subdivision (3) of Section 2711, or subdivision (5) of Section 10508, as provided in Section 9110.

(6) A security interest arising under Section 4210 or 5118.

(b) The application of this division to a security interest in a secured obligation is not affected by the fact that the obligation is itself secured by a transaction or interest to which this division does not apply.

(c) This division does not apply to the extent that either of the following conditions is satisfied:

(1) A statute, regulation, or treaty of the United States preempts this division.

(2) The rights of a transferee beneficiary or nominated person under a letter of credit are independent and superior under Section 5114.

(d) This division does not apply to any of the following:

(1) A landlord's lien, other than an agricultural lien.

(2) A lien, other than an agricultural lien, given by statute or other rule of law for services or materials, but Section 9333 applies with respect to priority of the lien.

(3) An assignment of a claim for wages, salary, or other compensation of an employee.

(4) A sale of accounts, chattel paper, payment intangibles, or promissory notes as part of a sale of the business out of which they arose.

(5) An assignment of accounts, chattel paper, payment intangibles, or promissory notes which is for the purpose of collection only.

(6) An assignment of a right to payment under a contract to an assignee that is also obligated to perform under the contract.

(7) An assignment of a single account, payment intangible, or promissory note to an assignee in full or partial satisfaction of a preexisting indebtedness.

(8) Any loan made by an insurance company pursuant to the provisions of a policy or contract issued by it and upon the sole security of the policy or contract.

(9) An assignment of a right represented by a judgment, other than a judgment taken on a right to payment that was collateral.

(10) A right of recoupment or setoff, provided that both of the following sections apply:

(A) Section 9340 applies with respect to the effectiveness of rights of recoupment or setoff against deposit accounts.

(B) Section 9404 applies with respect to defenses or claims of an account debtor.

(11) The creation or transfer of an interest in or lien on real property, including a lease or rents thereunder, except to the extent that provision is made for each of the following:

(A) Liens on real property in Sections 9203 and 9308.

(B) Fixtures in Section 9334.

(C) Fixture filings in Sections 9501, 9502, 9512, 9516, and 9519.

(D) Security agreements covering personal and real property in Section 9604.

(12) An assignment of a claim arising in tort, other than a commercial tort claim, but Sections 9315 and 9322 apply with respect to proceeds and priorities in proceeds.

(13) An assignment of a deposit account in a consumer transaction, but Sections 9315 and 9322 apply with respect to proceeds and priorities in proceeds.

(14) Any security interest created by the assignment of the benefits of any public construction contract under the Improvement Act of 1911 (Division 7 (commencing with Section 5000) of the Streets and Highways Code).

(15) Transition property, as defined in Section 840 of the Public Utilities Code, except to the extent that the provisions of this division are referred to in Article 5.5 (commencing with Section 840) of Chapter 4 of Part 1 of Division 1 of the Public Utilities Code, and recovery property, as defined in Section 848 of the Public Utilities Code, except to the extent that the provisions of this division are referred to in Article 5.6 (commencing with Section 848) of Chapter 4 of Part 1 of Division 1 of the Public Utilities Code.

(16) A claim or right of an employee or employee's dependents to receive workers' compensation under Division 1 (commencing with Section 50) or Division 4 (commencing with Section 3200) of the Labor Code.

(17) A transfer by a government or governmental unit.

9110. A security interest arising under Section 2401 or 2505, or under subdivision (3) of Section 2711, or subdivision (e) of Section 10508 is subject to this division.

However, until the debtor obtains possession of the goods, all of the following apply:

1. The security interest is enforceable, even if paragraph (3) of subdivision (b) of Section 9203 has not been satisfied.
2. Filing is not required to perfect the security interest.
3. The rights of the secured party after default by the debtor are governed by Division 2 (commencing with Section 2101) or Division 10 (commencing with Section 10101).
4. The security interest has priority over a conflicting security interest created by the debtor.

9201.

(a) Except as otherwise provided in this code, a security agreement is effective according to its terms between the parties, against purchasers of the collateral, and against creditors.

(b) A transaction subject to this division is subject to any applicable rule of law which establishes a different rule for consumers; to Chapter 5 (commencing with Section 17200) of Part 2 of Division 7 of the Business and Professions Code; Chapter 1 (commencing with Section 17500) of Part 3 of Division 7 of the Business and Professions Code; the Retail Installment Sales Act, Chapter 1 (commencing with Section 1801) of Title 2 of Part 4 of Division 3 of the Civil Code; the Automobile Sales Finance Act, Chapter 2b (commencing with Section 2981) of Title 14 of Part 4 of Division 3 of the Civil Code; Part 4 (commencing with Section 1738) of Division 3 of the Civil Code, with respect to the applicable provisions of Titles 1 (commencing with Section 1738), 1.3 (commencing with Section 1747), 1.3A (commencing with Section 1748.10), 1.3B (commencing with Section 1748.20), 1.4 (commencing with Section 1749), 1.5 (commencing with Section 1750), 1.6 (commencing with Section 1785.1), 1.61 (commencing with Section 1785.41), 1.6A (commencing with Section 1786), 1.6B (commencing with Section 1787.1), 1.6C (commencing with Section 1788), 1.6D (commencing with Section 1789), 1.6E (commencing with Section 1789.10), 1.6F (commencing with Section 1789.30), 1.7 (commencing with Section 1790), 1.8 (commencing with Section 1798), 1.83 (commencing with Section 1799.5), 1.84 (commencing with Section 1799.8), 1.85 (commencing with Section 1799.90), 1.86 (commencing with Section 1799.200), 2 (commencing with Section 1801), 2.4 (commencing with Section 1812.50), 2.5 (commencing with Section 1812.80), 2.6 (commencing with Section 1812.100), 2.7 (commencing with Section 1812.200), 2.8 (commencing with Section 1812.300), 2.9 (commencing with Section 1812.400), 2.95 (commencing with Section 1812.600), 2.96 (commencing with Section 1812.620), 3 (commencing with Section 1813), 4 (commencing with Section 1884), and 14 (commencing with Section 2872); the Industrial Loan Law, Division 7 (commencing with Section 18000) of the Financial Code; the Pawnbroker Law, Division 8 (commencing with Section 21000) of the Financial Code; the California Finance Lenders Law, Division 9 (commencing with Section 22000) of the Financial Code; and the

Mobilehomes-Manufactured Housing Act of 1980, Part 2 (commencing with Section 18000) of Division 13 of the Health and Safety Code; and to any applicable consumer protection statute, regulation, or law.

(c) In case of conflict between this division and a rule of law, statute, or regulation described in subdivision (b), the rule of law, statute, or regulation controls. Failure to comply with a statute or regulation described in subdivision (b) has only the effect the statute or regulation specifies.

(d) This division does not do either of the following:

(1) Validate any rate, charge, agreement, or practice that violates a rule of law, statute, or regulation described in subdivision (b).

(2) Extend the application of the rule of law, statute, or regulation to a transaction not otherwise subject to it.

9202. Except as otherwise provided with respect to consignments or sales of accounts, chattel paper, payment intangibles, or promissory notes, the provisions of this article with regard to rights and obligations apply whether title to collateral is in the secured party or the debtor.

9203.

(a) A security interest attaches to collateral when it becomes enforceable against the debtor with respect to the collateral, unless an agreement expressly postpones the time of attachment.

(b) Except as otherwise provided in subdivisions (c) to (i), inclusive, a security interest is enforceable against the debtor and third parties with respect to the collateral only if each of the following conditions is satisfied:

(1) Value has been given.

(2) The debtor has rights in the collateral or the power to transfer rights in the collateral to a secured party.

(3) One of the following conditions is met:

(A) The debtor has authenticated a security agreement that provides a description of the collateral and, if the security interest covers timber to be cut, a description of the land concerned.

(B) The collateral is not a certificated security and is in the possession of the secured party under Section 9313 pursuant to the debtor's security agreement.

(C) The collateral is a certificated security in registered form and the security certificate has been delivered to the secured party under Section 8301 pursuant to the debtor's security agreement.

(D) The collateral is deposit accounts, electronic chattel paper, investment property, or letter-of-credit rights, and the secured party has control under Section 9104, 9105, 9106, or 9107 pursuant to the debtor's security agreement.

(c) Subdivision (b) is subject to Section 4210 on the security interest of a collecting bank, Section 5118 on the security interest of a letter-of-credit issuer or nominated person, Section 9110 on a security interest arising under Division 2 (commencing with Section 2101) or Division 10 (commencing with Section 10101), and Section 9206 on security interests in investment property.

(d) A person becomes bound as debtor by a security agreement entered into by another person if, by operation of law other than this division or by contract, either of the following conditions is satisfied:

(1) The security agreement becomes effective to create a security interest in the person's property.

(2) The person becomes generally obligated for the obligations of the other person, including the obligation secured under the security agreement, and acquires or succeeds to all or substantially all of the assets of the other person.

(e) If a new debtor becomes bound as debtor by a security agreement entered into by another person both of the following apply:

(1) The agreement satisfies paragraph (3) of subdivision (b) with respect to existing or after-acquired property of the new debtor to the extent the property is described in the agreement.

(2) Another agreement is not necessary to make a security interest in the property enforceable.

(f) The attachment of a security interest in collateral gives the secured party the rights to proceeds provided by Section 9315 and is also attachment of a security interest in a supporting obligation for the collateral.

(g) The attachment of a security interest in a right to payment or performance secured by a security interest, or other lien on personal or real property is also attachment of a security interest in the security interest, mortgage, or other lien.

(h) The attachment of a security interest in a securities account is also attachment of a security interest in the security entitlements carried in the securities account.

(i) The attachment of a security interest in a commodity account is also attachment of a security interest in the commodity contracts carried in the commodity account.

9204.

(a) Except as otherwise provided in subdivision (b), a security agreement may create or provide for a security interest in after-acquired collateral.

(b) A security interest does not attach under a term constituting an after-acquired property clause to either of the following:

(1) Consumer goods, other than an accession when given as additional security, unless the debtor acquires rights in them within 10 days after the secured party gives value.

(2) A commercial tort claim.

(c) A security agreement may provide that collateral secures, or that accounts, chattel paper, payment intangibles, or promissory notes are sold in connection with, future advances or other value, whether or not the advances or value are given pursuant to commitment.

9205.

(a) A security interest is not invalid or fraudulent against creditors solely because either of the following applies:

(1) The debtor has the right or ability to do any of the following:

(A) Use, commingle, or dispose of all or part of the collateral, including returned or repossessed goods.

(B) Collect, compromise, enforce, or otherwise deal with collateral.

(C) Accept the return of collateral or make repossessions.

(D) Use, commingle, or dispose of proceeds.

(2) The secured party fails to require the debtor to account for proceeds or replace collateral.

(b) This section does not relax the requirements of possession if attachment, perfection, or enforcement of a security interest depends upon possession of the collateral by the secured party.

9206.

(a) A security interest in favor of a securities intermediary attaches to a person's security entitlement if both of the following conditions are satisfied:

(1) The person buys a financial asset through the securities intermediary in a transaction in which the person is obligated to pay the purchase price to the securities intermediary at the time of the purchase.

(2) The securities intermediary credits the financial asset to the buyer's securities account before the buyer pays the securities intermediary.

(b) The security interest described in subdivision (a) secures the person's obligation to pay for the financial asset.

(c) A security interest in favor of a person that delivers a certificated security or other financial asset represented by a writing attaches to the security or other financial asset if both of the following conditions are satisfied:

(1) The security or other financial asset satisfies both of the following:

(A) In the ordinary course of business it is transferred by delivery with any necessary endorsement or assignment.

(B) It is delivered under an agreement between persons in the business of dealing with those securities or financial assets.

(2) The agreement calls for delivery against payment.

(d) The security interest described in subdivision (c) secures the obligation to make payment for the delivery.

9207.

(a) Except as otherwise provided in subdivision (d), a secured party shall use reasonable care in the custody and preservation of collateral in the secured party's possession. In the case of chattel paper or an instrument, reasonable care includes taking necessary steps to preserve rights against prior parties unless otherwise agreed.

(b) Except as otherwise provided in subdivision (d), if a secured party has possession of collateral all of the following apply:

(1) Reasonable expenses, including the cost of insurance and payment of taxes or other charges, incurred in the custody, preservation, use, or operation of the collateral are chargeable to the debtor and are secured by the collateral.

(2) The risk of accidental loss or damage is on the debtor to the extent of a deficiency in any effective insurance coverage.

(3) The secured party shall keep the collateral identifiable, but fungible collateral may be commingled.

(4) The secured party may use or operate the collateral for any of the following purposes:

(A) For the purpose of preserving the collateral or its value.

(B) As permitted by an order of a court having competent jurisdiction.

(C) Except in the case of consumer goods, in the manner and to the extent agreed by the debtor.

(c) Except as otherwise provided in subdivision (d), a secured party having possession of collateral or control of collateral under Section 9104, 9105, 9106, or 9107 may or shall, as the case may be, do all of the following:

(1) May hold as additional security any proceeds, except money or funds, received from the collateral.

(2) Shall apply money or funds received from the collateral to reduce the secured obligation, unless remitted to the debtor.

(3) May create a security interest in the collateral.

(d) If the secured party is a buyer of accounts, chattel paper, payment intangibles, or promissory notes or a consignor both of the following apply:

(1) Subdivision (a) does not apply unless the secured party is entitled under an agreement to either of the following:

(A) To charge back uncollected collateral.

(B) Otherwise to full or limited recourse against the debtor or a secondary obligor based on the nonpayment or other default of an account debtor or other obligor on the collateral.

(2) Subdivisions (b) and (c) do not apply.

§ 9208.

(a) This section applies to cases in which there is no outstanding secured obligation and the secured party is not committed to make advances, incur obligations, or otherwise give value.

(b) Within 10 days after receiving an authenticated demand by the debtor, all of the following apply:

(1) A secured party having control of a deposit account under paragraph (2) of subdivision (a) of Section 9104 shall send to the bank with which the deposit account is maintained an authenticated statement that releases the bank from any further obligation to comply with instructions originated by the secured party.

(2) A secured party having control of a deposit account under paragraph (3) of subdivision (a) of Section 9104 shall do either of the following:

(A) Pay the debtor the balance on deposit in the deposit account.

(B) Transfer the balance on deposit into a deposit account in the debtor's name.

(3) A secured party, other than a buyer, having control of electronic chattel paper under Section 9105 shall do all of the following:

(A) Communicate the authoritative copy of the electronic chattel paper to the debtor or its designated custodian.

(B) If the debtor designates a custodian that is the designated custodian with which the authoritative copy of the electronic chattel paper is maintained for the secured party, communicate to the custodian an authenticated record releasing the designated custodian from any further obligation to comply with instructions originated by the secured party and instructing the custodian to comply with instructions originated by the debtor.

(C) Take appropriate action to enable the debtor or its designated custodian to make copies of or revisions to the authoritative copy which add or change an identified assignee of the authoritative copy without the consent of the secured party.

(4) A secured party having control of investment property under paragraph (2) of subdivision (d) of Section 8106 or under subdivision (b) of Section 9106 shall send to the securities intermediary or commodity intermediary with which the security entitlement or commodity contract is maintained an authenticated record that releases the securities intermediary or commodity intermediary from any further obligation to comply with entitlement orders or directions originated by the secured party.

(5) A secured party having control of a letter-of-credit right under Section 9107 shall send to each person having an unfulfilled obligation to pay or deliver proceeds of the letter of credit to the secured party an authenticated release from any further obligation to pay or deliver proceeds of the letter of credit to the secured party.

(6) A secured party having control of an electronic document under Section 7106 shall:

(A) give control of the electronic document to the debtor or its designated custodian;

(B) if the debtor designates a custodian that is the designated custodian with which the authoritative copy of the electronic document is maintained for the secured party, communicate to the custodian an authenticated record releasing the designated custodian from any further obligation to comply with instructions originated by the secured party and instructing the custodian to comply with instructions originated by the debtor; and

(C) take appropriate action to enable the debtor or its designated custodian to make copies of or revisions to the authoritative copy which add or change an identified assignee of the authoritative copy without the consent of the secured party.

9209.

(a) Except as otherwise provided in subdivision (c), this section applies if both of the following conditions are satisfied:

(1) There is no outstanding secured obligation.

(2) The secured party is not committed to make advances, incur obligations, or otherwise give value.

(b) Within 10 days after receiving an authenticated demand by the debtor, a secured party shall send to an account debtor that has received notification of an assignment to the secured party as assignee under subdivision (a) of Section 9406 an authenticated record that releases the account debtor from any further obligation to the secured party.

(c) This section does not apply to an assignment constituting the sale of an account, chattel paper, or payment intangible.

9210.

(a) In this section:

(1) "Request" means a record of a type described in paragraph (2), (3), or (4).

(2) "Request for an accounting" means a record authenticated by a debtor requesting that the recipient provide an accounting of the unpaid obligations secured by collateral and reasonably identifying the transaction or relationship that is the subject of the request.

(3) "Request regarding a list of collateral" means a record authenticated by a debtor requesting that the recipient approve or correct a list of what the debtor believes to be the collateral securing an obligation and reasonably identifying the transaction or relationship that is the subject of the request.

(4) "Request regarding a statement of account" means a record authenticated by a debtor requesting that the recipient approve or correct a statement indicating what the debtor believes to be the aggregate amount of unpaid obligations secured by collateral as of a specified date and reasonably identifying the transaction, or relationship that is the subject of the request.

(b) Subject to subdivisions (c), (d), (e), and (f), a secured party, other than a buyer of accounts, chattel paper, payment intangibles, or promissory notes or a consignor, shall comply with a request within 14 days after receipt as follows:

(1) In the case of a request for an accounting, by authenticating, and sending to the debtor an accounting.

(2) In the case of a request regarding a list of collateral or a request regarding a statement of account, by authenticating, and sending to the debtor an approval or correction.

(c) A secured party that claims a security interest in all of a particular type of collateral owned by the debtor may comply with a request regarding a list of collateral by sending to the debtor an authenticated record including a statement to that effect within 14 days after receipt.

(d) A person that receives a request regarding a list of collateral, claims no interest in the collateral when it receives the request, and claimed an interest in the collateral at an earlier time shall comply with the request within 14 days after receipt by sending to the debtor an authenticated record that contains both of the following:

(1) It disclaims any interest in the collateral.

(2) If known to the recipient, it provides the name and mailing address of any assignee of or successor to the recipient's interest in the collateral.

(e) A person that receives a request for an accounting or a request regarding a statement of account, claims no interest in the obligations when it receives the request, and claimed an interest in the obligations at an earlier time shall comply with the request within 14 days after receipt by sending to the debtor an authenticated record that contains both of the following:

(1) It disclaims any interest in the obligations.

(2) If known to the recipient, it provides the name and mailing address of any assignee of or successor to the recipient's interest in the obligations.

(f) A debtor is entitled without charge to one response to a request under this section during any six-month period. The secured party may require payment of a charge not exceeding twenty-five dollars ($25) for each additional response.

9301. Except as otherwise provided in Sections 9303-9306, inclusive, the following rules determine the law governing perfection, the effect of perfection or nonperfection, and the priority of a security interest in collateral:

(1) Except as otherwise provided in this section, while a debtor is located in a jurisdiction, the local law of that jurisdiction governs perfection, the effect of perfection or nonperfection, and the priority of a security interest in collateral.

(2) While collateral is located in a jurisdiction, the local law of that jurisdiction governs perfection, the effect of perfection or nonperfection, and the priority of a possessory security interest in that collateral.

(3) Except as otherwise provided in paragraph (4), while negotiable documents, goods, instruments, money, or tangible chattel paper is

located in a jurisdiction, the local law of that jurisdiction governs all of the following:

(A) Perfection of a security interest in the goods by filing a fixture filing.

(B) Perfection of a security interest in timber to be cut.

(C) The effect of perfection or nonperfection and the priority of a nonpossessory security interest in the collateral.

(4) The local law of the jurisdiction in which the wellhead or minehead is located governs perfection, the effect of perfection or nonperfection, and the priority of a security interest in as-extracted collateral.

9302. While farm products are located in a jurisdiction, the local law of that jurisdiction governs perfection, the effect of perfection or nonperfection, and the priority of an agricultural lien on the farm products.

9303.

(a) This section applies to goods covered by a certificate of title, even if there is no other relationship between the jurisdiction under whose certificate of title the goods are covered and the goods or the debtor.

(b) Goods become covered by a certificate of title when a valid application for the certificate of title and the applicable fee are delivered to the appropriate authority. Goods cease to be covered by a certificate of title at the earlier of the time the certificate of title ceases to be effective under the law of the issuing jurisdiction or the time the goods become covered subsequently by a certificate of title issued by another jurisdiction.

(c) The local law of the jurisdiction under whose certificate of title the goods are covered governs perfection, the effect of perfection or nonperfection, and the priority of a security interest in goods covered by a certificate of title from the time the goods become covered by the certificate of title until the goods cease to be covered by the certificate of title.

9304.

(a) The local law of a bank's jurisdiction governs perfection, the effect of perfection or nonperfection, and the priority of a security interest in a deposit account maintained with that bank.

(b) The following rules determine a bank's jurisdiction for purposes of this chapter:

(1) If an agreement between the bank and the debtor governing the deposit account expressly provides that a particular jurisdiction is the bank's jurisdiction for purposes of this chapter, this division, or this code, that jurisdiction is the bank's jurisdiction.

(2) If paragraph (1) does not apply and an agreement between the bank and its customer governing the deposit account expressly provides that the agreement is governed by the law of a particular jurisdiction, that jurisdiction is the bank's jurisdiction.

(3) If neither paragraph (1) nor paragraph (2) applies and an agreement between the bank and its customer governing the deposit account expressly provides that the deposit account is maintained at an office in a particular jurisdiction, that jurisdiction is the bank's jurisdiction.

(4) If none of the preceding paragraphs applies, the bank's jurisdiction is the jurisdiction in which the office identified in an account statement as the office serving the customer's account is located.

(5) If none of the preceding paragraphs applies, the bank's jurisdiction is the jurisdiction in which the chief executive office of the bank is located.

9305.

(a) Except as otherwise provided in subdivision (c), the following rules apply:

(1) While a security certificate is located in a jurisdiction, the local law of that jurisdiction governs perfection, the effect of perfection or nonperfection, and the priority of a security interest in the certificated security represented thereby.

(2) The local law of the issuer's jurisdiction as specified in subdivision (d) of Section 8110 governs perfection, the effect of perfection or nonperfection, and the priority of a security interest in an uncertificated security.

(3) The local law of the securities intermediary's jurisdiction as specified in subdivision (e) of Section 8110 governs perfection, the effect of perfection or nonperfection, and the priority of a security interest in a security entitlement or securities account.

(4) The local law of the commodity intermediary's jurisdiction governs perfection, the effect of perfection or nonperfection, and the priority of a security interest in a commodity contract or commodity account.

(b) The following rules determine a commodity intermediary's jurisdiction for purposes of this chapter:

(1) If an agreement between the commodity intermediary and commodity customer governing the commodity account expressly provides that a particular jurisdiction is the commodity intermediary's jurisdiction for purposes of this chapter, this division, or this code, that jurisdiction is the commodity intermediary's jurisdiction.

(2) If paragraph (1) does not apply and an agreement between the commodity intermediary and commodity customer governing the commodity account expressly provides that the agreement is governed by the law of a particular jurisdiction, that jurisdiction is the commodity intermediary's jurisdiction.

(3) If neither paragraph (1) nor paragraph (2) applies and an agreement between the commodity intermediary and commodity customer governing the commodity account expressly provides that the commodity account is maintained at an office in a particular jurisdiction, that jurisdiction is the commodity intermediary's jurisdiction.

(4) If none of the preceding paragraphs applies, the commodity intermediary's jurisdiction is the jurisdiction in which the office identified in an account statement as the office serving the commodity customer's account is located.

(5) If none of the preceding paragraphs applies, the commodity intermediary's jurisdiction is the jurisdiction in which the chief executive office of the commodity intermediary is located.

(c) The local law of the jurisdiction in which the debtor is located governs all of the following:

(1) Perfection of a security interest in investment property by filing.

(2) Automatic perfection of a security interest in investment property created by a broker or securities intermediary.

(3) Automatic perfection of a security interest in a commodity contract or commodity account created by a commodity intermediary.

9306.

(a) Subject to subdivision (c), the local law of the issuer's jurisdiction or a nominated person's jurisdiction governs perfection, the effect of perfection or nonperfection, and the priority of a security interest in a letter-of-credit right if the issuer's jurisdiction or nominated person's jurisdiction is a state.

(b) For purposes of this chapter, an issuer's jurisdiction, or nominated person's jurisdiction is the jurisdiction whose law governs the liability of the issuer or nominated person with respect to the letter-of-credit right as provided in Section 5116.

(c) This section does not apply to a security interest that is perfected only under subdivision (d) of Section 9308.

9307.

(a) In this section, "place of business" means a place where a debtor conducts its affairs.

(b) Except as otherwise provided in this section, the following rules determine a debtor's location:

(1) A debtor who is an individual is located at the individual's principal residence.

(2) A debtor that is an organization and has only one place of business is located at its place of business.

(3) A debtor that is an organization and has more than one place of business is located at its chief executive office.

(c) Subdivision (b) applies only if a debtor's residence, place of business, or chief executive office, as applicable, is located in a jurisdiction whose law generally requires information concerning the existence of a nonpossessory security interest to be made generally available in a filing, recording, or registration system as a condition or result of the security interest's obtaining priority over the rights of a lien creditor with respect to the collateral. If subdivision (b) does not apply, the debtor is located in the District of Columbia.

(d) A person that ceases to exist, have a residence, or have a place of business continues to be located in the jurisdiction specified by subdivisions (b) and (c).

(e) A registered organization that is organized under the law of a state is located in that state.

(f) Except as otherwise provided in subdivision (i), a registered organization that is organized under the law of the United States and a branch or agency of a bank that is not organized under the law of the United States or a state are located in any of the following jurisdictions:

(1) In the state that the law of the United States designates, if the law designates a state of location.

(2) In the state that the registered organization, branch, or agency designates, if the law of the United States authorizes the registered organization, branch, or agency to designate its state of location.

(3) In the District of Columbia, if neither paragraph (1) nor paragraph (2) applies.

(g) A registered organization continues to be located in the jurisdiction specified by subdivision (e) or (f) notwithstanding either of the following:

(1) The suspension, revocation, forfeiture, or lapse of the registered organization's status as such in its jurisdiction of organization.

(2) The dissolution, winding up, or cancellation of the existence of the registered organization.

(h) The United States is located in the District of Columbia.

(i) A branch or agency of a bank that is not organized under the law of the United States or a state is located in the state in which the branch or agency is licensed, if all branches and agencies of the bank are licensed in only one state.

(j) A foreign air carrier under the Federal Aviation Act of 1958, as amended, is located at the designated office of the agent upon which service of process may be made on behalf of the carrier.

(k) This section applies only for purposes of this chapter.

9308.

(a) Except as otherwise provided in this section and in Section 9309, a security interest is perfected if it has attached and all of the applicable requirements for perfection in Sections 9310-9316, inclusive, have been satisfied. A security interest is perfected when it attaches if the applicable requirements are satisfied before the security interest attaches.

(b) An agricultural lien is perfected if it has become effective and all of the applicable requirements for perfection in Section 9310 have been satisfied.

An agricultural lien is perfected when it becomes effective if the applicable requirements are satisfied before the agricultural lien becomes effective.

(c) A security interest or agricultural lien is perfected continuously if it is originally perfected by one method under this division and is later perfected by another method under this division, without an intermediate period when it was unperfected.

(d) Perfection of a security interest in collateral also perfects a security interest in a supporting obligation for the collateral.

(e) Perfection of a security interest in a right to payment or performance also perfects a security interest in a security interest, mortgage, or other lien on personal or real property securing the right.

(f) Perfection of a security interest in a securities account also perfects a security interest in the security entitlements carried in the securities account.

(g) Perfection of a security interest in a commodity account also perfects a security interest in the commodity contracts carried in the commodity account.

§ 9309.

The following security interests are perfected when they attach:

(1) A purchase money security interest in consumer goods, except as otherwise provided in subdivision (b) of Section 9311 with respect to consumer goods that are subject to a statute or treaty described in subdivision (a) of Section 9311.

(2) An assignment of accounts or payment intangibles which does not by itself or in conjunction with other assignments to the same assignee transfer a significant part of the assignor's outstanding accounts or payment intangibles.

(3) A sale of a payment intangible.

(4) A sale of a promissory note.

(5) A security interest created by the assignment of a health care insurance receivable to the provider of the health care goods or services.

(6) A security interest arising under Section 2401 or 2505, under subdivision (3) of Section 2711, or under subdivision (5) of Section 10508, until the debtor obtains possession of the collateral.

(7) A security interest of a collecting bank arising under Section 4210.

(8) A security interest of an issuer or nominated person arising under Section 5118.

(9) A security interest arising in the delivery of a financial asset under subdivision (c) of Section 9206.

(10) A security interest in investment property created by a broker or securities intermediary.

(11) A security interest in a commodity contract or a commodity account created by a commodity intermediary.

(12) An assignment for the benefit of all creditors of the transferor and subsequent transfers by the assignee thereunder.

(13) A security interest created by an assignment of a beneficial interest in a decedent's estate.

(14) A sale by an individual of an account that is a right to payment of winnings in a lottery or other game of chance.

9310.

(a) Except as otherwise provided in subdivision (b) and in subdivision (b) of Section 9312, a financing statement must be filed to perfect all security interests and agricultural liens.

(b) The filing of a financing statement is not necessary to perfect a security interest that satisfies any of the following conditions:

(1) It is perfected under subdivision (d), (e), (f), or (g) of Section 9308.

(2) It is perfected under Section 9309 when it attaches.

(3) It is a security interest in property subject to a statute, regulation, or treaty described in subdivision (a) of Section 9311.

(4) It is a security interest in goods in possession of a bailee which is perfected under paragraph (1) or (2) of subdivision (d) of Section 9312.

(5) It is a security interest in certificated securities, documents, goods, or instruments which is perfected without filing or possession under subdivision (e), (f), or (g) of Section 9312.

(6) It is a security interest in collateral in the secured party's possession under Section 9313.

(7) It is a security interest in a certificated security which is perfected by delivery of the security certificate to the secured party under Section 9313.

(8) It is a security interest in deposit accounts, electronic chattel paper, investment property, or letter-of-credit rights which is perfected by control under Section 9314.

(9) It is a security interest in proceeds which is perfected under Section 9315.

(10) It is perfected under Section 9316.

(11) It is a security interest in, or claim in or under, any policy of insurance including unearned premiums which is perfected by written notice to the insurer under paragraph (4) of subdivision (b) of Section 9312.

(c) If a secured party assigns a perfected security interest or agricultural lien, a filing under this division is not required to continue the perfected status of the security interest against creditors of and transferees from the original debtor.

9311.

(a) Except as otherwise provided in subdivision (d), the filing of a financing statement is not necessary or effective to perfect a security interest in property subject to any of the following:

(1) A statute, regulation, or treaty of the United States whose requirements for a security interest's obtaining priority over the rights of a lien creditor with respect to the property preempt subdivision (a) of Section 9310.

(2)(A) The provisions of the Vehicle Code which require registration of a vehicle or boat.

(B) The provisions of the Health and Safety Code which require registration of a mobilehome or commercial coach, except that during any period in which collateral is inventory, the filing provisions of Chapter 5 (commencing with Section 9501) apply to a security interest in that collateral.

(C) The provisions of the Health and Safety Code which require registration of all interests in approved air contaminant emission reductions (Sections 40709-40713, inclusive, of the Health and Safety Code).

(3) A certificate of title statute of another jurisdiction which provides for a security interest to be indicated on the certificate as a condition or result of the security interest's obtaining priority over the rights of a lien creditor with respect to the property.

(b) Compliance with the requirements of a statute, regulation, or treaty described in subdivision (a) for obtaining priority over the rights of a lien creditor is equivalent to the filing of a financing statement under this division. Except as otherwise provided in subdivision (d), in Section 9313, and in subdivisions (d) and (e) of Section 9316 for goods covered by a certificate of title, a security interest in property subject to a statute, regulation, or treaty described in subdivision (a) may be perfected only by compliance with those requirements, and a security interest so perfected remains perfected notwithstanding a change in the use or transfer of possession of the collateral.

(c) Except as otherwise provided in subdivision (d) and in subdivisions (d) and (e) of Section 9316, duration and renewal of perfection of a security interest perfected by compliance with the requirements prescribed by a statute, regulation, or treaty described in subdivision (a) are governed by the statute, regulation, or treaty. In other respects, the security interest is subject to this division.

(d) During any period in which collateral subject to a statute specified in paragraph (2) of subdivision (a) is inventory held for sale or lease by a person or leased by that person as lessor and that person is in the business of selling goods of that kind, this section does not apply to a security interest in that collateral created by that person.

9312.

(a) A security interest in chattel paper, negotiable documents, instruments, or investment property may be perfected by filing.

(b) Except as otherwise provided in subdivisions (c) and (d) of Section 9315 for proceeds, all of the following apply:

(1) A security interest in a deposit account may be perfected only by control under Section 9314.

(2) Except as otherwise provided in subdivision (d) of Section 9308, a security interest in a letter-of-credit right may be perfected only by control under Section 9314.

(3) A security interest in money may be perfected only by the secured party's taking possession under Section 9313.

(4) A security interest in, or claim in or under, any policy of insurance, including unearned premiums, may be perfected only by giving written notice of the security interest or claim to the insurer. This paragraph does not apply to a health care insurance receivable. A security interest in a health care insurance receivable may be perfected only as otherwise provided in this division.

(c) While goods are in the possession of a bailee that has issued a negotiable document covering the goods both of the following apply:

(1) A security interest in the goods may be perfected by perfecting a security interest in the document.

(2) A security interest perfected in the document has priority over any security interest that becomes perfected in the goods by another method during that time.

(d) While goods are in the possession of a bailee that has issued a nonnegotiable document covering the goods, a security interest in the goods may be perfected by any of the following methods:

(1) Issuance of a document in the name of the secured party.

(2) The bailee's receipt of notification of the secured party's interest.

(3) Filing as to the goods.

(e) A security interest in certificated securities, negotiable documents, or instruments is perfected without filing or the taking of possession for a period of 20 days from the time it attaches to the extent that it arises for new value given under an authenticated security agreement.

(f) A perfected security interest in a negotiable document or goods in possession of a bailee, other than one that has issued a negotiable document for the goods, remains perfected for 20 days without filing if the secured party makes available to the debtor the goods or documents representing the goods for the purpose of either of the following:

(1) Ultimate sale or exchange.

(2) Loading, unloading, storing, shipping, transshipping, manufacturing, processing, or otherwise dealing with them in a manner preliminary to their sale or exchange.

(g) A perfected security interest in a certificated security or instrument remains perfected for 20 days without filing if the secured party delivers the security certificate or instrument to the debtor for the purpose of either of the following:

(1) Ultimate sale or exchange.

(2) Presentation, collection, enforcement, renewal, or registration of transfer.

(h) After the 20-day period specified in subdivision (e), (f), or (g) expires, perfection depends upon compliance with this division.

9313.

(a) Except as otherwise provided in subdivision (b), a secured party may perfect a security interest in negotiable documents, goods, instruments, money, or tangible chattel paper by taking possession of the collateral. A secured party may perfect a security interest in certificated securities by taking delivery of the certificated securities under Section 8301.

(b) With respect to goods covered by a certificate of title issued by this state, a secured party may perfect a security interest in the goods by taking possession of the goods only in the circumstances described in subdivision (d) of Section 9316.

(c) With respect to collateral other than certificated securities and goods covered by a document, a secured party takes possession of collateral in the possession of a person other than the debtor, the secured party, or a lessee of the collateral from the debtor in the ordinary course of the debtor's business, when either of the following conditions is satisfied:

(1) The person in possession authenticates a record acknowledging that it holds possession of the collateral for the secured party's benefit.

(2) The person takes possession of the collateral after having authenticated a record acknowledging that it will hold possession of collateral for the secured party's benefit.

(d) If perfection of a security interest depends upon possession of the collateral by a secured party, perfection occurs no earlier than the time the secured party takes possession and continues only while the secured party retains possession.

(e) A security interest in a certificated security in registered form is perfected by delivery when delivery of the certificated security occurs under Section 8301 and remains perfected by delivery until the debtor obtains possession of the security certificate.

(f) A person in possession of collateral is not required to acknowledge that it holds possession for a secured party's benefit.

(g) If a person acknowledges that it holds possession for the secured party's benefit both of the following apply:

(1) The acknowledgment is effective under subdivision (c) or under subdivision (a) of Section 8301, even if the acknowledgment violates the rights of a debtor.

(2) Unless the person otherwise agrees or law other than this division otherwise provides, the person does not owe any duty to the secured

party and is not required to confirm the acknowledgment to another person.

(h) A secured party having possession of collateral does not relinquish possession by delivering the collateral to a person other than the debtor or a lessee of the collateral from the debtor in the ordinary course of the debtor's business if the person was instructed before the delivery or is instructed contemporaneously with the delivery to do either of the following:

(1) To hold possession of the collateral for the secured party's benefit.

(2) To redeliver the collateral to the secured party.

(i) A secured party does not relinquish possession, even if a delivery under subdivision (h) violates the rights of a debtor. A person to which collateral is delivered under subdivision (h) does not owe any duty to the secured party and is not required to confirm the delivery to another person unless the person otherwise agrees or law other than this division otherwise provides.

§ 9314.

(a) A security interest in investment property, deposit accounts, letter-of-credit rights, electronic chattel paper, or electronic documents may be perfected by control of the collateral under Section 7106, 9104, 9105, 9106, or 9107.

(b) A security interest in deposit accounts, electronic chattel paper, letter-of-credit rights, or electronic documents is perfected by control under Section 7106, 9104, 9105, or 9107 when the secured party obtains control and remains perfected by control only while the secured party retains control.

(c) A security interest in investment property is perfected by control under Section 9106 from the time the secured party obtains control and remains perfected by control until both of the following conditions are satisfied:

(1) The secured party does not have control.

(2) One of the following occurs:

(A) If the collateral is a certificated security, the debtor has or acquires possession of the security certificate.

(B) If the collateral is an uncertificated security, the issuer has registered or registers the debtor as the registered owner.

(C) If the collateral is a security entitlement, the debtor is or becomes the entitlement holder.

9315.

(a) Except as otherwise provided in this division and in subdivision (2) of Section 2403, both of the following apply:

(1) A security interest or agricultural lien continues in collateral notwithstanding sale, lease, license, exchange, or other disposition thereof unless the secured party authorized the disposition free of the security interest or agricultural lien.

(2) A security interest attaches to any identifiable proceeds of collateral.

(b) Proceeds that are commingled with other property are identifiable proceeds as follows:

(1) If the proceeds are goods, to the extent provided by Section 9336.

(2) If the proceeds are not goods, to the extent that the secured party identifies the proceeds by a method of tracing, including application of equitable principles, that is permitted under law other than this division with respect to commingled property of the type involved.

(c) A security interest in proceeds is a perfected security interest if the security interest in the original collateral was perfected.

(d) A perfected security interest in proceeds becomes unperfected on the 21st day after the security interest attaches to the proceeds unless any of the following conditions is satisfied:

(1) All of the following are satisfied:

(A) A filed financing statement covers the original collateral.

(B) The proceeds are collateral in which a security interest may be perfected by filing in the office in which the financing statement has been filed.

(C) The proceeds are not acquired with cash proceeds.

(2) The proceeds are identifiable cash proceeds.

(3) The security interest in the proceeds is perfected other than under subdivision (c) when the security interest attaches to the proceeds or within 20 days thereafter.

(e) If a filed financing statement covers the original collateral, a security interest in proceeds which remains perfected under paragraph (1) of subdivision (d) becomes unperfected at the later of either of the following:

(1) When the effectiveness of the filed financing statement lapses under Section 9515 or is terminated under Section 9513.

(2) The 21st day after the security interest attaches to the proceeds.

(f) Cash proceeds retain their character as cash proceeds while in the possession of a levying officer pursuant to Title 6.5 (commencing with Section 481.010) or Title 9 (commencing with Section 680.010) of Part 2 of the Code of Civil Procedure.

9316.

(a) A security interest perfected pursuant to the law of the jurisdiction designated in subdivision (1) of Section 9301 or in subdivision (c) of Section 9305 remains perfected until the earliest of any of the following:

(1) The time perfection would have ceased under the law of that jurisdiction.

(2) The expiration of four months after a change of the debtor's location to another jurisdiction.

(3) The expiration of one year after a transfer of collateral to a person that thereby becomes a debtor and is located in another jurisdiction.

(b) If a security interest described in subdivision (a) becomes perfected under the law of the other jurisdiction before the earliest time or event described in that subdivision, it remains perfected thereafter. If the security interest does not become perfected under the law of the other jurisdiction before the earliest time or event, it becomes unperfected and is deemed never to have been perfected as against a purchaser of the collateral for value.

(c) A possessory security interest in collateral, other than goods covered by a certificate of title and as-extracted collateral consisting of goods, remains continuously perfected if all of the following conditions are satisfied:

(1) The collateral is located in one jurisdiction and subject to a security interest perfected under the law of that jurisdiction.

(2) Thereafter the collateral is brought into another jurisdiction.

(3) Upon entry into the other jurisdiction, the security interest is perfected under the law of the other jurisdiction.

(d) Except as otherwise provided in subdivision (e), a security interest in goods covered by a certificate of title which is perfected by any method under the law of another jurisdiction when the goods become covered by a certificate of title from this state remains perfected until the security interest would have become unperfected under the law of the other jurisdiction had the goods not become so covered.

(e) A security interest described in subdivision (d) becomes unperfected as against a purchaser of the goods for value and is deemed never to have been perfected as against a purchaser of the goods for value if the applicable requirements for perfection under subdivision (b) of Section 9311 or under Section 9313 are not satisfied before the earlier of either of the following:

(1) The time the security interest would have become unperfected under the law of the other jurisdiction had the goods not become covered by a certificate of title from this state.

(2) The expiration of four months after the goods had become so covered.

(f) A security interest in deposit accounts, letter-of-credit rights, or investment property which is perfected under the law of the bank's jurisdiction, the issuer's jurisdiction, a nominated person's jurisdiction, the securities intermediary's jurisdiction, or the commodity intermediary's jurisdiction, as applicable, remains perfected until the earlier of the following:

(1) The time the security interest would have become unperfected under the law of that jurisdiction.

(2) The expiration of four months after a change of the applicable jurisdiction to another jurisdiction.

(g) If a security interest described in subdivision (f) becomes perfected under the law of the other jurisdiction before the earlier of the time or the end of the period described in that subdivision, it remains perfected thereafter. If the security interest does not become perfected under the law of the other jurisdiction before the earlier of that time or the end of that period, it becomes unperfected and is deemed never to have been perfected as against a purchaser of the collateral for value.

9317.

(a) A security interest or agricultural lien is subordinate to the rights of both of the following:

(1) A person entitled to priority under Section 9322.

(2) Except as otherwise provided in subdivision (e), a person that becomes a lien creditor before the earlier of the time the security interest or agricultural lien is perfected, or one of the conditions specified in paragraph (3) of subdivision (b) of Section 9203 is met and a financing statement covering the collateral is filed.

(b) Except as otherwise provided in subdivision (e), a buyer, other than a secured party, of tangible chattel paper, documents, goods, instruments, or a security certificate takes free of a security interest or agricultural lien if the buyer gives value and receives delivery of the collateral without knowledge of the security interest or agricultural lien and before it is perfected.

(c) Except as otherwise provided in subdivision (e), a lessee of goods takes free of a security interest or agricultural lien if the lessee gives value and receives delivery of the collateral without knowledge of the security interest or agricultural lien and before it is perfected.

(d) A licensee of a general intangible or a buyer, other than a secured party, of accounts, electronic chattel paper, general intangibles, or investment property other than a certificated security takes free of a security interest if the licensee or buyer gives value without knowledge of the security interest and before it is perfected.

(e) Except as otherwise provided in Sections 9320 and 9321, if a person files a financing statement with respect to a purchase money security interest before or within 20 days after the debtor receives delivery of the collateral, the security interest takes priority over the rights of a buyer, lessee, or lien creditor which arise between the time the security interest attaches and the time of filing.

9318.

(a) A debtor that has sold an account, chattel paper, payment intangible, or promissory note does not retain a legal or equitable interest in the collateral sold.

(b) For purposes of determining the rights of creditors of, and purchasers for value of an account or chattel paper from, a debtor that has sold an account or chattel paper, while the buyer's security interest is unperfected, the debtor is deemed to have rights and title to the account or chattel paper identical to those the debtor sold.

9319.

(a) Except as otherwise provided in subdivision (b), for purposes of determining the rights of creditors of, and purchasers for value of goods from, a consignee, while the goods are in the possession of the consignee, the consignee is deemed to have rights and title to the goods identical to those the consignor had or had power to transfer.

(b) For purposes of determining the rights of a creditor of a consignee, law other than this division determines the rights and title of a consignee while goods are in the consignee's possession if, under this chapter, a perfected security interest held by the consignor would have priority over the rights of the creditor.

9320.

(a) Except as otherwise provided in subdivision (e), a buyer in ordinary course of business takes free of a security interest created by the buyer's seller, even if the security interest is perfected and the buyer knows of its existence.

(b) Except as otherwise provided in subdivision (e), a buyer of goods from a person who used or bought the goods for use primarily for personal, family, or household purposes takes free of a security interest, even if perfected, if all of the following conditions are satisfied:

(1) The buyer buys without knowledge of the security interest.

(2) The buyer buys for value.

(3) The buyer buys primarily for the buyer's personal, family, or household purposes.

(4) The buyer buys before the filing of a financing statement covering the goods.

(c) To the extent that it affects the priority of a security interest over a buyer of goods under subdivision (b), the period of effectiveness of a filing made in the jurisdiction in which the seller is located is governed by subdivisions (a) and (b) of Section 9316.

(d) A buyer in ordinary course of business buying oil, gas, or other minerals at the wellhead or minehead or after extraction takes free of an interest arising out of an encumbrance.

(e) Subdivisions (a) and (b) do not affect a security interest in goods in the possession of the secured party under Section 9313.

§ 9321.

(a) In this section, "licensee in ordinary course of business" means a person that becomes a licensee of a general intangible in good faith, without knowledge that the license violates the rights of another person in the general intangible, and in the ordinary course from a person in the business of licensing general intangibles of that kind. A person becomes a licensee in the ordinary course if the license to the person comports with the usual or customary practices in the kind of business in which the licensor is engaged or with the licensor's own usual or customary practices.

(b) A licensee in ordinary course of business takes its rights under a nonexclusive license free of a security interest in the general intangible created by the licensor, even if the security interest is perfected and the licensee knows of its existence.

(c) A lessee in ordinary course of business takes its leasehold interest free of a security interest in the goods created by the lessor, even if the security interest is perfected and the lessee knows of its existence.

(d) This section shall remain in effect only until January 1, 2010, and as of that date is repealed, unless a later enacted statute, that is enacted before January 1, 2010, deletes or extends that date.

§ 9321.

(a) A lessee in ordinary course of business takes its leasehold interest free of a security interest in the goods created by the lessor, even if the security interest is perfected and the lessee knows of its existence.

(b) This section shall become operative on January 1, 2010.

9322.

(a) Except as otherwise provided in this section, priority among conflicting security interests and agricultural liens in the same collateral is determined according to the following rules:

(1) Conflicting perfected security interests and agricultural liens rank according to priority in time of filing or perfection. Priority dates from the earlier of the time a filing covering the collateral is first made or the security interest or agricultural lien is first perfected, if there is no period thereafter when there is neither filing nor perfection.

(2) A perfected security interest or agricultural lien has priority over a conflicting unperfected security interest or agricultural lien.

(3) The first security interest or agricultural lien to attach or become effective has priority if conflicting security interests and agricultural liens are unperfected.

(b) For the purposes of paragraph (1) of subdivision (a), the following rules apply:

(1) The time of filing or perfection as to a security interest in collateral is also the time of filing or perfection as to a security interest in proceeds.

(2) The time of filing or perfection as to a security interest in collateral supported by a supporting obligation is also the time of filing or perfection as to a security interest in the supporting obligation.

(c) Except as otherwise provided in subdivision (f), a security interest in collateral which qualifies for priority over a conflicting security interest under Section 9327, 9328, 9329, 9330, or 9331 also has priority over a conflicting security interest in both of the following:

(1) Any supporting obligation for the collateral.

(2) Proceeds of the collateral if all of the following conditions are satisfied:

(A) The security interest in proceeds is perfected.

(B) The proceeds are cash proceeds or of the same type as the collateral.

(C) In the case of proceeds that are proceeds of proceeds, all intervening proceeds are cash proceeds, proceeds of the same type as the collateral, or an account relating to the collateral.

(d) Subject to subdivision (e) and except as otherwise provided in subdivision (f), if a security interest in chattel paper, deposit accounts, negotiable documents, instruments, investment property, or letter-of-credit rights is perfected by a method other than filing, conflicting perfected security interests in proceeds of the collateral rank according to priority in time of filing.

(e) Subdivision (d) applies only if the proceeds of the collateral are not cash proceeds, chattel paper, negotiable documents, instruments, investment property, or letter-of-credit rights.

(f) Subdivisions (a) to (e), inclusive, are subject to all of the following:

(1) Subdivision (g) and the other provisions of this chapter.

(2) Section 4210 with respect to a security interest of a collecting bank.

(3) Section 5118 with respect to a security interest of an issuer or nominated person.

(4) Section 9110 with respect to a security interest arising under Division 2 (commencing with Section 2101) or Division 10 (commencing with Section 10101).

(g) A perfected agricultural lien on collateral has priority over a conflicting security interest in or agricultural lien on the same collateral if the statute creating the agricultural lien so provides.

9323.

(a) Except as otherwise provided in subdivision (c), for purposes of determining the priority of a perfected security interest under paragraph (1) of subdivision (a) of Section 9322, perfection of the security interest dates from the time an advance is made to the extent that the security interest secures an advance that satisfies both of the following conditions:

(1) It is made while the security interest is perfected only under either of the following:

(A) Under Section 9309 when it attaches.

(B) Temporarily under subdivision (e), (f), or (g) of Section 9312.

(2) It is not made pursuant to a commitment entered into before or while the security interest is perfected by a method other than under Section 9309 or under subdivision (e), (f), or (g) of Section 9312.

(b) Except as otherwise provided in subdivision (c), a security interest is subordinate to the rights of a person who becomes a lien creditor to the extent that the security interest secures an advance made more than 45 days after the person becomes a lien creditor unless either of the following conditions is satisfied:

(1) The advance is made without knowledge of the lien.

(2) The advance is made pursuant to a commitment entered into without knowledge of the lien.

(c) Subdivisions (a) and (b) do not apply to a security interest held by a secured party who is a buyer of accounts, chattel paper, payment intangibles, or promissory notes or a consignor.

(d) Except as otherwise provided in subdivision (e), a buyer of goods other than a buyer in the ordinary course of business takes free of a security interest to the extent that it secures advances made after the earlier of the following:

(1) The time the secured party acquires knowledge of the buyer's purchase.

(2) Forty-five days after the purchase.

(e) Subdivision (d) does not apply if the advance is made pursuant to a commitment entered into without knowledge of the buyer's purchase and before the expiration of the 45-day period.

(f) Except as otherwise provided in subdivision (g), a lessee of goods, other than a lessee in the ordinary course of business, takes the leasehold interest free of a security interest to the extent that it secures advances made after the earlier of either of the following:

(3) The time the secured party acquires knowledge of the lease.

(4) Forty-five days after the lease contract becomes enforceable.

(g) Subdivision (f) does not apply if the advance is made pursuant to a commitment entered into without knowledge of the lease and before the expiration of the 45-day period.

9324.

(a) Except as otherwise provided in subdivision (g), a perfected purchase money security interest in goods other than inventory or livestock has priority over a conflicting security interest in the same goods, and, except as otherwise provided in Section 9327, a perfected security interest in its identifiable proceeds also has priority, if the purchase money security interest is perfected when the debtor receives possession of the collateral or within 20 days thereafter.

(b) Subject to subdivision (c) and except as otherwise provided in subdivision (g), a perfected purchase money security interest in inventory has priority over a conflicting security interest in the same inventory, has priority over a conflicting security interest in chattel paper or an instrument constituting proceeds of the inventory and in proceeds of the chattel paper, if so provided in Section 9330, and, except as otherwise provided in Section 9327, also has priority in identifiable cash proceeds of the inventory to the extent the identifiable cash proceeds are received on or before the delivery of the inventory to a buyer, if all of the following conditions are satisfied:

(1) The purchase money security interest is perfected when the debtor receives possession of the inventory.

(2) The purchase money secured party sends an authenticated notification to the holder of the conflicting security interest.

(3) The holder of the conflicting security interest receives the notification within five years before the debtor receives possession of the inventory.

(4) The notification states that the person sending the notification has or expects to acquire a purchase money security interest in inventory of the debtor and describes the inventory.

(c) Paragraphs (2) to (4), inclusive, of subdivision (b) apply only if the holder of the conflicting security interest had filed a financing statement covering the same types of inventory as follows:

(1) If the purchase money security interest is perfected by filing, before the date of the filing.

(2) If the purchase money security interest is temporarily perfected without filing or possession under subdivision (f) of Section 9312, before the beginning of the 20-day period thereunder.

(d) Subject to subdivision (e) and except as otherwise provided in subdivision (g), a perfected purchase money security interest in livestock that are farm products has priority over a conflicting security interest in the same livestock, and, except as otherwise provided in Section 9327, a perfected security interest in their identifiable proceeds and identifiable products in their unmanufactured states also has priority, if all of the following conditions are satisfied:

(1) The purchase money security interest is perfected when the debtor receives possession of the livestock.

(2) The purchase money secured party sends an authenticated notification to the holder of the conflicting security interest.

(3) The holder of the conflicting security interest receives the notification within six months before the debtor receives possession of the livestock.

(4) The notification states that the person sending the notification has or expects to acquire a purchase money security interest in livestock of the debtor and describes the livestock.

(e) Paragraphs (2) to (4), inclusive, of subdivision (d) apply only if the holder of the conflicting security interest had filed a financing statement covering the same types of livestock as follows:

(1) If the purchase money security interest is perfected by filing, before the date of the filing.

(2) If the purchase money security interest is temporarily perfected without filing or possession under subdivision (f) of Section 9312, before the beginning of the 20-day period thereunder.

(f) Except as otherwise provided in subdivision (g), a perfected purchase money security interest in software has priority over a conflicting security interest in the same collateral, and, except as otherwise provided in Section 9327, a perfected security interest in its identifiable proceeds also has priority, to the extent that the purchase money security interest in the goods in which the software was acquired for use has priority in the goods and proceeds of the goods under this section.

(g) If more than one security interest qualifies for priority in the same collateral under subdivision (a), (b), (d), or (f), the following rules apply:

(1) A security interest securing an obligation incurred as all or part of the price of the collateral has priority over a security interest securing an obligation incurred for value given to enable the debtor to acquire rights in, or the use of, collateral.

(2) In all other cases, subdivision (a) of Section 9322 applies to the qualifying security interests.

9325.

(a) Except as otherwise provided in subdivision (b), a security interest created by a debtor is subordinate to a security interest in the same collateral created by another person if all of the following apply:

(1) The debtor acquired the collateral subject to the security interest created by the other person.

(2) The security interest created by the other person was perfected when the debtor acquired the collateral.

(3) There is no period thereafter when the security interest is unperfected.

(b) Subdivision (a) subordinates a security interest only if either of the following conditions is satisfied:

(1) The security interest otherwise would have priority solely under subdivision (a) of Section 9322 or under Section 9324.

(2) The security interest arose solely under subdivision (3) of Section 2711 or subdivision (5) of Section 10508.

9326.

(a) Subject to subdivision (b), a security interest created by a new debtor which is perfected by a filed financing statement that is effective solely under Section 9508 in collateral in which a new debtor has or acquires rights is subordinate to a security interest in the same collateral which is perfected other than by a filed financing statement that is effective solely under Section 9508.

(b) The other provisions of this chapter determine the priority among conflicting security interests in the same collateral perfected by filed financing statements that are effective solely under Section 9508. However, if the security agreements to which a new debtor became bound as debtor were not entered into by the same original debtor, the conflicting security interests rank according to priority in time of the new debtor's having become bound.

9327. The following rules govern priority among conflicting security interests in the same deposit account:

(1) A security interest held by a secured party having control of the deposit account under Section 9104 has priority over a conflicting security interest held by a secured party that does not have control.

(2) Except as otherwise provided in subdivisions (3) and (4), security interests perfected by control under Section 9314 rank according to priority in time of obtaining control.

(3) Except as otherwise provided in subdivision (4), a security interest held by the bank with which the deposit account is maintained has priority over a conflicting security interest held by another secured party.

(4) A security interest perfected by control under paragraph (3) of subdivision (a) of Section 9104 has priority over a security interest held by the bank with which the deposit account is maintained.

9328. The following rules govern priority among conflicting security interests in the same investment property:

(1) A security interest held by a secured party having control of investment property under Section 9106 has priority over a security interest held by a secured party that does not have control of the investment property.

(2) Except as otherwise provided in subdivisions (3) and (4), conflicting security interests held by secured parties each of which has control under Section 9106 rank according to priority in time of one of the following:

(A) If the collateral is a security, obtaining control.

(B) If the collateral is a security entitlement carried in a securities account and if the secured party obtained control under paragraph (1) of subdivision (d) of Section 8106, the secured party's becoming the person for which the securities account is maintained.

(C) If the collateral is a security entitlement carried in a securities account and if the secured party obtained control under paragraph (2) of subdivision (d) of Section 8106, the securities intermediary's agreement to comply with the secured party's entitlement orders with respect to security entitlements carried, or to be carried, in the securities account.

(D) If the collateral is a security entitlement carried in a securities account and if the secured party obtained control through another person under paragraph (3) of subdivision (d) of Section 8106, the time on which priority would be based under this paragraph if the other person were the secured party.

(E) If the collateral is a commodity contract carried with a commodity intermediary, the satisfaction of the requirement for control specified in paragraph (2) of subdivision (b) of Section 9106 with respect to commodity contracts carried, or to be carried, with the commodity intermediary.

(3) A security interest held by a securities intermediary in a security entitlement or a securities account maintained with the securities intermediary has priority over a conflicting security interest held by another secured party.

(4) A security interest held by a commodity intermediary in a commodity contract or a commodity account maintained with the commodity intermediary has priority over a conflicting security interest held by another secured party.

(5) A security interest in a certificated security in registered form which is perfected by taking delivery under subdivision (a) of Section 9313 and not by control under Section 9314 has priority over a conflicting security interest perfected by a method other than control.

(6) Conflicting security interests created by a broker, securities intermediary, or commodity intermediary which are perfected without control under Section 9106 rank equally.

(7) In all other cases, priority among conflicting security interests in investment property is governed by Sections 9322 and 9323.

9329. The following rules govern priority among conflicting security interests in the same letter-of-credit right:

(1) A security interest held by a secured party having control of the letter-of-credit right under Section 9107 has priority to the extent of its control over a conflicting security interest held by a secured party that does not have control.

(2) Security interests perfected by control under Section 9314 rank according to priority in time of obtaining control.

9330.

(a) A purchaser of chattel paper has priority over a security interest in the chattel paper which is claimed merely as proceeds of inventory subject to a security interest if both of the following conditions are satisfied:

(1) In good faith and in the ordinary course of the purchaser's business, the purchaser gives new value and takes possession of the chattel paper or obtains control of the chattel paper under Section 9105.

(2) The chattel paper does not indicate that it has been assigned to an identified assignee other than the purchaser.

(b) A purchaser of chattel paper has priority over a security interest in the chattel paper which is claimed other than merely as proceeds of inventory subject to a security interest if the purchaser gives new value and takes possession of the chattel paper or obtains control of the chattel paper under Section 9105 in good faith, in the ordinary course of the purchaser's business, and without knowledge that the purchase violates the rights of the secured party.

(c) Except as otherwise provided in Section 9327, a purchaser having priority in chattel paper under subdivision (a) or (b) also has priority in proceeds of the chattel paper to the extent that either of the following applies:

(1) Section 9322 provides for priority in the proceeds.

(2) The proceeds consist of the specific goods covered by the chattel paper or cash proceeds of the specific goods, even if the purchaser's security interest in the proceeds is unperfected.

(d) Except as otherwise provided in subdivision (a) of Section 9331, a purchaser of an instrument has priority over a security interest in the instrument perfected by a method other than possession if the purchaser gives value and takes possession of the instrument in good faith and without knowledge that the purchase violates the rights of the secured party.

(e) For purposes of subdivisions (a) and (b), the holder of a purchase money security interest in inventory gives new value for chattel paper constituting proceeds of the inventory.

(f) For purposes of subdivisions (b) and (d), if chattel paper or an instrument indicates that it has been assigned to an identified secured party other than the purchaser, a purchaser of the chattel paper or instrument has knowledge that the purchase violates the rights of the secured party.

9331.

(a) This division does not limit the rights of a holder in due course of a negotiable instrument, a holder to which a negotiable document of title has been duly negotiated, or a protected purchaser of a security. These holders or purchasers take priority over an earlier security interest, even if perfected, to the extent provided in Division 3 (commencing with Section 3101), Division 7 (commencing with Section 7101), and Division 8 (commencing with Section 8101).

(b) This division does not limit the rights of or impose liability on a person to the extent that the person is protected against the assertion of a claim under Division 8 (commencing with Section 8101).

(c) Filing under this division does not constitute notice of a claim or defense to the holders, purchasers, or persons described in subdivisions (a) and (b).

9332.

(a) A transferee of money takes the money free of a security interest unless the transferee acts in collusion with the debtor in violating the rights of the secured party.

(b) A transferee of funds from a deposit account takes the funds free of a security interest in the deposit account unless the transferee acts in collusion with the debtor in violating the rights of the secured party.

9333.

(a) In this section, "possessory lien" means an interest, other than a security interest or an agricultural lien which satisfies all of the following conditions:

(1) It secures payment or performance of an obligation for services or materials furnished with respect to goods by a person in the ordinary course of the person's business.

(2) It is created by statute or rule of law in favor of the person.

(3) Its effectiveness depends on the person's possession of the goods.

(b) A possessory lien on goods has priority over a security interest in the goods unless the lien is created by a statute that expressly provides otherwise.

9334.

(a) A security interest under this division may be created in goods that are fixtures or may continue in goods that become fixtures. A security interest does not exist under this division in ordinary building materials incorporated into an improvement on land.

(b) This division does not prevent creation of an encumbrance upon fixtures under real property law.

(c) In cases not governed by subdivisions (d) to (h), inclusive, a security interest in fixtures is subordinate to a conflicting interest of an encumbrancer or owner of the related real property other than the debtor.

(d) Except as otherwise provided in subdivision (h), a perfected security interest in fixtures has priority over a conflicting interest of an encumbrancer or owner of the real property if the debtor has an interest of record in or is in possession of the real property and all of the following conditions are satisfied:

(1) The security interest is a purchase money security interest.

(2) The interest of the encumbrancer or owner arises before the goods become fixtures.

(3) The security interest is perfected by a fixture filing before the goods become fixtures or within 20 days thereafter.

(e) A perfected security interest in fixtures has priority over a conflicting interest of an encumbrancer or owner of the real property if any of the following conditions is satisfied:

(1) The debtor has an interest of record in the real property or is in possession of the real property and both of the following conditions are satisfied:

(A) The security interest is perfected by a fixture filing before the interest of the encumbrancer or owner is of record.

(B) The security interest has priority over any conflicting interest of a predecessor in title of the encumbrancer or owner.

(2) The fixtures are readily removable factory or office machines or readily removable replacements of domestic appliances that are consumer goods.

(3) The conflicting interest is a lien on the real property obtained by legal or equitable proceedings after the security interest was perfected by any method permitted by this division.

(4) The security interest is both of the following:

(C) Created in a manufactured home in a manufactured home transaction.

(D) Perfected pursuant to a statute described in paragraph (2) of subdivision (a) of Section 9311.

(f) A security interest in fixtures, whether or not perfected, has priority over a conflicting interest of an encumbrancer or owner of the real property if either of the following conditions is satisfied:

(1) The encumbrancer or owner has, in an authenticated record, consented to the security interest, or disclaimed an interest in the goods as fixtures.

(2) The debtor has a right to remove the goods as against the encumbrancer or owner.

(g) The priority of the security interest under paragraph (2) of subdivision (f) continues for a reasonable time if the debtor's right to remove the goods as against the encumbrancer or owner terminates.

(h) A mortgage is a construction mortgage to the extent that it secures an obligation incurred for the construction of an improvement on land, including the acquisition cost of the land, if a recorded record of the mortgage so indicates. Except as otherwise provided in subdivisions (e) and (f), a security interest in fixtures is subordinate to a construction mortgage if a record of the mortgage is recorded before the goods become fixtures and the goods become fixtures before the completion of the construction. A mortgage has this priority to the same extent as a construction mortgage to the extent that it is given to refinance a construction mortgage.

(i) A perfected security interest in crops growing on real property has priority over a conflicting interest of an encumbrancer or owner of the real property if the debtor has an interest of record in, or is in possession of, the real property.

9335.

(a) A security interest may be created in an accession and continues in collateral that becomes an accession.

(b) If a security interest is perfected when the collateral becomes an accession, the security interest remains perfected in the collateral.

(c) Except as otherwise provided in subdivision (d), the other provisions of this chapter determine the priority of a security interest in an accession.

(d) A security interest in an accession is subordinate to a security interest in the whole which is perfected by compliance with the requirements of a certificate of title statute under subdivision (b) of Section 9311.

(e) After default, subject to Chapter 6 (commencing with subdivision 9601), a secured party may remove an accession from other goods if the security interest in the accession has priority over the claims of every person having an interest in the whole.

(f) A secured party that removes an accession from other goods under subdivision (e) shall promptly reimburse any holder of a security interest or other lien on, or owner of, the whole or of the other goods, other than the debtor, for the cost of repair of any physical injury to the whole or the other goods. The secured party need not reimburse the holder or owner for any diminution in value of the whole or the other goods caused by the absence of the accession removed or by any necessity for replacing it. A person entitled to reimbursement may refuse permission to remove until the secured party gives adequate assurance for the performance of the obligation to reimburse.

9336.

(a) In this section, "commingled goods" means goods that are physically united with other goods in such a manner that their identity is lost in a product or mass.

(b) A security interest does not exist in commingled goods as such. However, a security interest may attach to a product or mass that results when goods become commingled goods.

(c) If collateral becomes commingled goods, a security interest attaches to the product or mass.

(d) If a security interest in collateral is perfected before the collateral becomes commingled goods, the security interest that attaches to the product or mass under subdivision (c) is perfected.

(e) Except as otherwise provided in subdivision (f), the other provisions of this chapter determine the priority of a security interest that attaches to the product or mass under subdivision (c).

(f) If more than one security interest attaches to the product or mass under subdivision (c), the following rules determine priority:

(1) A security interest that is perfected under subdivision (d) has priority over a security interest that is unperfected at the time the collateral becomes commingled goods.

(2) If more than one security interest is perfected under subdivision (d), the security interests rank equally in proportion to the value of the collateral at the time it became commingled goods.

9337. If, while a security interest in goods is perfected by any method under the law of another jurisdiction, this state issues a certificate of title that does not show that the goods are subject to the security interest or contain a statement that they may be subject to security interests not shown on the certificate both of the following apply:

(1) A buyer of the goods, other than a person in the business of selling goods of that kind, takes free of the security interest if the buyer gives value and receives delivery of the goods after issuance of the certificate and without knowledge of the security interest.

(2) The security interest is subordinate to a conflicting security interest in the goods that attaches, and is perfected under subdivision (b) of Section 9311, after issuance of the certificate and without the conflicting secured party's knowledge of the security interest.

9338. If a security interest or agricultural lien is perfected by a filed financing statement providing information described in paragraph (5) of subdivision (b) of Section 9516 which is incorrect at the time the financing statement is filed both of the following apply:

(1) The security interest or agricultural lien is subordinate to a conflicting perfected security interest in the collateral to the extent that the holder of the conflicting security interest gives value in reasonable reliance upon the incorrect information.

(2) A purchaser, other than a secured party, of the collateral takes free of the security interest or agricultural lien to the extent that, in reasonable reliance upon the incorrect information, the purchaser gives value and, in the case of chattel paper, documents, goods, instruments, or a security certificate, receives delivery of the collateral.

9339. This division does not preclude subordination by agreement by a person entitled to priority.

9340.

(a) Except as otherwise provided in subdivision (c), a bank with which a deposit account is maintained may exercise any right of recoupment or setoff against a secured party that holds a security interest in the deposit account.

(b) Except as otherwise provided in subdivision (c), the application of this division to a security interest in a deposit account does not affect a right of recoupment or setoff of the secured party as to a deposit account maintained with the secured party.

(c) The exercise by a bank of a setoff against a deposit account is ineffective against a secured party that holds a security interest in the deposit account which is perfected by control under paragraph (3) of subdivision (a) of Section 9104, if the setoff is based on a claim against the debtor.

9341. Except as otherwise provided in subdivision (c) of Section 9340, and unless the bank otherwise agrees in an authenticated record, a bank's rights, and duties with respect to a deposit account maintained with the bank are not terminated, suspended, or modified by any of the following:

(1) The creation, attachment, or perfection of a security interest in the deposit account.

(2) The bank's knowledge of the security interest.

(3) The bank's receipt of instructions from the secured party.

9342. This division does not require a bank to enter into an agreement of the kind described in paragraph (2) of subdivision (a) of Section 9104, even if its customer so requests or directs. A bank that has entered into such an agreement is not required to confirm the existence of the agreement to another person unless requested to do so by its customer.

9401.

(a) Except as otherwise provided in subdivision (b) and in Sections 9406, 9407, 9408, and 9409, whether a debtor's rights in collateral may be voluntarily or involuntarily transferred is governed by law other than this division.

(b) An agreement between the debtor and secured party which prohibits a transfer of the debtor's rights in collateral or makes the transfer a default does not prevent the transfer from taking effect.

9402. The existence of a security interest, agricultural lien, or authority given to a debtor to dispose of or use collateral, without more, does not subject a secured party to liability in contract or tort for the debtor's acts or omissions.

9403.

(a) In this section, "value" has the meaning provided in subdivision (a) of Section 3303.

(b) Except as otherwise provided in this section, an agreement between an account debtor and an assignor not to assert against an assignee any claim or defense that the account debtor may have against the assignor is enforceable by an assignee that takes an assignment that satisfies all of the following conditions:

(1) It is taken for value.

(2) It is taken in good faith.

(3) It is taken without notice of a claim of a property or possessory right to the property assigned.

(4) It is taken without notice of a defense or claim in recoupment of the type that may be asserted against a person entitled to enforce a negotiable instrument under subdivision (a) of Section 3305.

(c) Subdivision (b) does not apply to defenses of a type that may be asserted against a holder in due course of a negotiable instrument under subdivision (b) of Section 3305.

(d) In a consumer transaction, if a record evidences the account debtor's obligation, law other than this division requires that the record include a statement to the effect that the rights of an assignee are subject to claims or defenses that the account debtor could assert against the original obligee, and the record does not include such a statement, then both of the following apply:

(1) The record has the same effect as if the record included such a statement.

(2) The account debtor may assert against an assignee those claims and defenses that would have been available if the record included such a statement.

(e) This section is subject to law other than this division which establishes a different rule for an account debtor who is an individual and who incurred the obligation primarily for personal, family, or household purposes.

(f) Except as otherwise provided in subdivision (d), this section does not displace law other than this division which gives effect to an agreement by an account debtor not to assert a claim or defense against an assignee.

9404.

(a) Unless an account debtor has made an enforceable agreement not to assert defenses or claims, and subject to subdivisions (b) to (e), inclusive, the rights of an assignee are subject to both of the following:

(1) All terms of the agreement between the account debtor and assignor, and any defense or claim in recoupment arising from the transaction that gave rise to the contract.

(2) Any other defense or claim of the account debtor against the assignor which accrues before the account debtor receives a notification of the assignment authenticated by the assignor or the assignee.

(b) Subject to subdivision (c) and except as otherwise provided in subdivision (d), the claim of an account debtor against an assignor may be asserted against an assignee under subdivision (a) only to reduce the amount the account debtor owes.

(c) This section is subject to law other than this division which establishes a different rule for an account debtor who is an individual and who incurred the obligation primarily for personal, family, or household purposes.

(d) In a consumer transaction, if a record evidences the account debtor's obligation, law other than this division requires that the record include a statement to the effect that the account debtor's recovery against an assignee with respect to claims and defenses against the assignor may not exceed amounts paid by the account debtor under the record, and the record does not include such a statement, the extent to which a claim of an account debtor against the assignor may be asserted against an assignee is determined as if the record included such a statement.

(e) This section does not apply to an assignment of a health care insurance receivable.

9405.

(a) A modification of or substitution for an assigned contract is effective against an assignee if made in good faith. The assignee acquires corresponding rights under the modified or substituted contract. The assignment may provide that the modification or substitution is a breach of contract by the assignor. This subdivision is subject to subdivisions (b) to (d), inclusive.

(b) Subdivision (a) applies to the extent that either of the following apply:

(1) The right to payment or a part thereof under an assigned contract has not been fully earned by performance.

(2) The right to payment or a part thereof has been fully earned by performance and the account debtor has not received notification of the assignment under subdivision (a) of Section 9406.

(c) This section is subject to law other than this division which establishes a different rule for an account debtor who is an individual and who incurred the obligation primarily for personal, family, or household purposes.

(d) This section does not apply to an assignment of a health care insurance receivable.

9406.

(a) Subject to subdivisions (b) to (i), inclusive, an account debtor on an account, chattel paper, or a payment intangible may discharge its obligation by paying the assignor until, but not after, the account debtor receives a notification, authenticated by the assignor or the assignee, that the amount due or to become due has been assigned and that payment is to be made to the assignee. After receipt of the notification, the account debtor may discharge its obligation by paying the assignee and may not discharge the obligation by paying the assignor.

(b) Subject to subdivision (h), notification is ineffective under subdivision (a) as follows:

(1) If it does not reasonably identify the rights assigned.

(2) To the extent that an agreement between an account debtor and a seller of a payment intangible limits the account debtor's duty to pay a person other than the seller and the limitation is effective under law other than this division.

(3) At the option of an account debtor, if the notification notifies the account debtor to make less than the full amount of any installment or other periodic payment to the assignee, even if any of the following conditions is satisfied:

(A) Only a portion of the account, chattel paper, or payment intangible has been assigned to that assignee.

(B) A portion has been assigned to another assignee.

(C) The account debtor knows that the assignment to that assignee is limited.

(c) Subject to subdivision (h), if requested by the account debtor, an assignee shall seasonably furnish reasonable proof that the assignment has been made. Unless the assignee complies, the account debtor may discharge its obligation by paying the assignor, even if the account debtor has received a notification under subdivision (a).

(d) Except as otherwise provided in subdivision (e) and in Sections 9407 and 10303, and subject to subdivision (h), a term in an agreement between an account debtor and an assignor or in a promissory note is ineffective to the extent that it does either of the following:

(1) Prohibits, restricts, or requires the consent of the account debtor or person obligated on the promissory note to the assignment or transfer of, or the creation, attachment, perfection, or enforcement of a security interest in, the account, chattel paper, payment intangible, or promissory note.

(2) Provides that the assignment or transfer or the creation, attachment, perfection, or enforcement of the security interest may give rise to a default, breach, right of recoupment, claim, defense, termination, right of termination, or remedy under the account, chattel paper, payment intangible, or promissory note.

(e) Subdivision (d) does not apply to the sale of a payment intangible or promissory note.

(f) Except as otherwise provided in Sections 9407 and 10303, and subject to subdivisions (h) and (i), a rule of law, statute, or regulation, that prohibits, restricts, or requires the consent of a government, governmental body or official, or account debtor to the assignment or transfer of, or creation of a security interest in, an account or chattel paper is ineffective to the extent that the rule of law, statute, or regulation does either of the following:

(1) Prohibits, restricts, or requires the consent of the government, governmental body or official, or account debtor to the assignment or transfer of, or the creation, attachment, perfection, or enforcement of a security interest in, the account or chattel paper.

(2) Provides that the assignment or transfer or the creation, attachment, perfection, or enforcement of the security interest may give rise to a default, breach, right of recoupment, claim, defense, termination, right of termination, or remedy under the account or chattel paper.

(g) Subject to subdivision (h), an account debtor may not waive or vary its option under paragraph (3) of subdivision (b).

(h) This section is subject to law other than this division which establishes a different rule for an account debtor who is an individual and who incurred the obligation primarily for personal, family, or household purposes.

(i) This section does not apply to an assignment of a health care insurance receivable.

(j) Subdivision (f) does not apply to an assignment or transfer of, or the creation, attachment, perfection, or enforcement of a security interest in, a claim or right to receive compensation for injuries or sickness as described in paragraph (1) or (2) of subdivision (a) of Section 104 of Title 26 of the United States Code, as amended, or a claim or right to receive benefits under a special needs trust as described in paragraph (4) of subdivision (d) of Section 1396p of Title 42 of the United States Code, as amended, to the extent that subdivision (f) is inconsistent with those laws.

9407.

(a) Except as otherwise provided in subdivision (b), a term in a lease agreement is ineffective to the extent that it does either of the following:

(1) Prohibits, restricts, or requires the consent of a party to the lease to the assignment or transfer of, or the creation, attachment, perfection, or enforcement of a security interest in, an interest of a party under the lease contract or in the lessor's residual interest in the goods.

(2) Provides that the assignment or transfer or the creation, attachment, perfection, or enforcement of the security interest may give rise to a default, breach, right of recoupment, claim, defense, termination, right of termination, or remedy under the lease.

(b) Except as otherwise provided in subdivision (g) of Section 10303, a term described in paragraph (2) of subdivision (a) is effective to the extent that there is either of the following:

(1) A transfer by the lessee of the lessee's right of possession or use of the goods in violation of the term.

(2) A delegation of a material performance of either party to the lease contract in violation of the term.

(c) The creation, attachment, perfection, or enforcement of a security interest in the lessor's interest under the lease contract or the lessor's residual interest in the goods is not a transfer that materially impairs the lessee's prospect of obtaining return performance or materially changes the duty of or materially increases the burden or risk imposed on the lessee within the purview of subdivision (d) of Section 10303 unless, and then only to the extent that, enforcement actually results in a delegation of material performance of the lessor.

§ 9408.

(a) Except as otherwise provided in subdivision (b), a term in a promissory note or in an agreement between an account debtor and a debtor that relates to a health care insurance receivable or a general intangible, including a contract, permit, license, or franchise, and which term prohibits, restricts, or requires the consent of the person obligated on the promissory note or the account debtor to, the assignment or transfer of, or the creation, attachment, or perfection of a security interest in, the promissory note, health care insurance receivable, or general intangible, is ineffective to the extent that the term does, or would do, either of the following:

(1) It would impair the creation, attachment, or perfection of a security interest.

(2) It provides that the assignment or transfer or the creation, attachment, or perfection of the security interest may give rise to a default, breach, right of recoupment, claim, defense, termination, right of termination, or remedy under the promissory note, health care insurance receivable, or general intangible.

(b) Subdivision (a) applies to a security interest in a payment intangible or promissory note only if the security interest arises out of a sale of the payment intangible or promissory note.

(c) A rule of law, statute, or regulation that prohibits, restricts, or requires the consent of a government, governmental body or official, person obligated on a promissory note, or account debtor to the assignment or transfer of, or the creation of a security interest in, a promissory note, health care insurance receivable, or general intangible, including a contract, permit, license, or franchise between an account debtor and a debtor, is ineffective to the extent that the rule of law, statute, or regulation does, or would do, either of the following:

(1) It would impair the creation, attachment, or perfection of a security interest.

(2) It provides that the assignment or transfer or the creation, attachment, or perfection of the security interest may give rise to a default, breach, right of recoupment, claim, defense, termination, right of termination, or remedy under the promissory note, health care insurance receivable, or general intangible.

(d) To the extent that a term in a promissory note or in an agreement between an account debtor and a debtor that relates to a health care insurance receivable or general intangible or a rule of law, statute, or regulation described in subdivision (c) would be effective under law other than this division but is ineffective under subdivision (a) or (c), the creation, attachment, or perfection of a security interest in the promissory note, health care insurance receivable, or general intangible is subject to all of the following rules:

(1) It is not enforceable against the person obligated on the promissory note or the account debtor.

(2) It does not impose a duty or obligation on the person obligated on the promissory note or the account debtor.

(3) It does not require the person obligated on the promissory note or the account debtor to recognize the security interest, pay or render performance to the secured party, or accept payment or performance from the secured party.

(4) It does not entitle the secured party to use or assign the debtor's rights under the promissory note, health care insurance receivable, or general intangible, including any related information or materials furnished to the debtor in the transaction giving rise to the promissory note, health care insurance receivable, or general intangible.

(5) It does not entitle the secured party to use, assign, possess, or have access to any trade secrets or confidential information of the person obligated on the promissory note or the account debtor.

(6) It does not entitle the secured party to enforce the security interest in the promissory note, health care insurance receivable, or general intangible.

(e) Subdivision (c) does not apply to an assignment or transfer of, or the creation, attachment, perfection, or enforcement of a security interest in, a claim or right to receive compensation for injuries or sickness as described in paragraph (1) or (2) of subdivision (a) of Section 104 of Title 26 of the United States Code, as amended, or a claim or right to receive benefits under a special needs trust as described in paragraph (4) of subdivision (d) of Section 1396p of Title 42 of the United States Code, as amended, to the extent that subdivision (c) is inconsistent with those laws.

9409.

(a) A term in a letter of credit or a rule of law, statute, regulation, custom, or practice applicable to the letter of credit which prohibits, restricts, or requires the consent of an applicant, issuer, or nominated person to a beneficiary's assignment of or creation of a security interest in a letter-of-credit right is ineffective to the extent that the term or rule of law, statute, regulation, custom, or practice does, or would do, either of the following:

(1) It would impair the creation, attachment, or perfection of a security interest in the letter-of-credit right.

(2) It provides that the assignment or the creation, attachment, or perfection of the security interest may give rise to a default, breach, right of

recoupment, claim, defense, termination, right of termination, or remedy under the letter-of-credit right.

(b) To the extent that a term in a letter of credit is ineffective under subdivision (a) but would be effective under law other than this division or a custom, or practice applicable to the letter of credit, to the transfer of a right to draw or otherwise demand performance under the letter of credit, or to the assignment of a right to proceeds of the letter of credit, all of the following rules apply with respect to the creation, attachment, or perfection of a security interest in the letter-of-credit right:

(1) It is not enforceable against the applicant, issuer, nominated person, or transferee beneficiary.

(2) It imposes no duties or obligations on the applicant, issuer, nominated person, or transferee beneficiary.

(3) It does not require the applicant, issuer, nominated person, or transferee beneficiary to recognize the security interest, pay or render performance to the secured party, or accept payment or other performance from the secured party.

9501.

(a) Except as otherwise provided in subdivision (b), if the local law of this state governs perfection of a security interest or agricultural lien, the office in which to file a financing statement to perfect the security interest or agricultural lien is either of the following:

(1) The office designated for the filing or recording of a record of a mortgage on the related real property, if either of the following conditions is satisfied:

(A) The collateral is as-extracted collateral or timber to be cut.

(B) The financing statement is filed as a fixture filing and the collateral is goods that are or are to become fixtures.

(2) The office of the Secretary of State in all other cases, including a case in which the collateral is goods that are or are to become fixtures and the financing statement is not filed as a fixture filing.

(b) The office in which to file a financing statement to perfect a security interest in collateral, including fixtures, of a transmitting utility is the office of the Secretary of State. The financing statement also constitutes a fixture filing as to the collateral indicated in the financing statement which is or is to become fixtures.

9502.

(a) Subject to subdivision (b), a financing statement is sufficient only if it satisfies all of the following conditions:

(1) It provides the name of the debtor.

(2) It provides the name of the secured party or a representative of the secured party.

(3) It indicates the collateral covered by the financing statement.

(b) Except as otherwise provided in subdivision (b) of Section 9501, to be sufficient, a financing statement that covers as-extracted collateral or timber to be cut, or which is filed as a fixture filing and covers goods that are or are to become fixtures, must satisfy subdivision (a) and also satisfy all of the following conditions:

(1) Indicate that it covers this type of collateral.

(2) Indicate that it is to be recorded in the real property records.

(3) Provide a description of the real property to which the collateral is related sufficient to give constructive notice of a mortgage under the law of this state if the description were contained in a record of the mortgage of the real property.

(4) If the debtor does not have an interest of record in the real property, provide the name of a record owner.

(c) A record of a mortgage is effective, from the date of recording, as a financing statement filed as a fixture filing, or as a financing statement covering as-extracted collateral or timber to be cut only if all of the following conditions are satisfied:

(1) The record indicates the goods or accounts that it covers.

(2) The goods are or are to become fixtures related to the real property described in the record or the collateral is related to the real property described in the record and is as-extracted collateral or timber to be cut.

(3) The record satisfies the requirements for a financing statement in this section other than an indication that it is to be filed in the real property records.

(4) The record is duly recorded.

(d) A financing statement may be filed before a security agreement is made or a security interest otherwise attaches.

9503.

(a) A financing statement sufficiently provides the name of the debtor only if it does so in accordance with the following rules:

(1) If the debtor is a registered organization, only if the financing statement provides the name of the debtor indicated on the public record of the debtor's jurisdiction of organization which shows the debtor to have been organized.

(2) If the debtor is a decedent's estate, only if the financing statement provides the name of the decedent and indicates that the debtor is an estate.

(3) If the debtor is a trust or a trustee acting with respect to property held in trust, only if the financing statement satisfies both of the following conditions:

(A) It provides the name specified for the trust in its organic documents or, if no name is specified, provides the name of the settlor, and additional information sufficient to distinguish the debtor from other trusts having one or more of the same settlors.

(B) It indicates, in the debtor's name or otherwise, that the debtor is a trust or is a trustee acting with respect to property held in trust.

(4) In other cases, according to the following rules:

(A) If the debtor has a name, only if it provides the individual or organizational name of the debtor.

(B) If the debtor does not have a name, only if it provides the names of the partners, members, associates, or other persons comprising the debtor.

(b) A financing statement that provides the name of the debtor in accordance with subdivision (a) is not rendered ineffective by the absence of either of the following:

(1) A trade name or other name of the debtor.

(2) Unless required under subparagraph (B) of paragraph (4) of subdivision (a), names of partners, members, associates, or other persons comprising the debtor.

(c) A financing statement that provides only the debtor's trade name does not sufficiently provide the name of the debtor.

(d) Failure to indicate the representative capacity of a secured party or representative of a secured party does not affect the sufficiency of a financing statement.

(e) A financing statement may provide the name of more than one debtor and the name of more than one secured party.

9504. A financing statement sufficiently indicates the collateral that it covers if the financing statement provides either of the following:

(1) A description of the collateral pursuant to Section 9108.

(2) An indication that the financing statement covers all assets or all personal property.

9505.

(a) A consignor, lessor, or other bailor of goods, a licensor, or a buyer of a payment intangible or promissory note may file a financing statement, or may comply with a statute or treaty described in subdivision (a) of Section 9311, using the terms "consignor," "consignee," "lessor," "lessee," "bailor," "bailee," "licensor," "licensee," "owner," "registered owner," "buyer," "seller," or words of similar import, instead of the terms "secured party" and "debtor."

(b) This chapter applies to the filing of a financing statement under subdivision (a) and, as appropriate, to compliance that is equivalent to filing a financing statement under subdivision (b) of Section 9311, but the filing or compliance is not of itself a factor in determining whether the collateral secures an obligation. If it is determined for another reason that the collateral secures an obligation, a security interest held by the consignor, lessor, bailor, licensor, owner, or buyer which attaches to the collateral is perfected by the filing or compliance.

9506.

(a) A financing statement substantially satisfying the requirements of this part is effective, even if it has minor errors or omissions, unless the errors or omissions make the financing statement seriously misleading.

(b) Except as otherwise provided in subdivision (c), a financing statement that fails sufficiently to provide the name of the debtor in accordance with subdivision (a) of Section 9503 is seriously misleading.

(c) If a search of the records of the filing office under the debtor's correct name, using the filing office's standard search logic, if any, would disclose a financing statement that fails sufficiently to provide the name of the debtor in accordance with subdivision (a) of Section 9503, the name provided does not make the financing statement seriously misleading.

(d) For purposes of subdivision (b) of Section 9508, the "debtor's correct name" in subdivision (c) means the correct name of the new debtor.

9507.

(a) A filed financing statement remains effective with respect to collateral that is sold, exchanged, leased, licensed, or otherwise disposed of and in which a security interest or agricultural lien continues, even if the secured party knows of or consents to the disposition.

(b) Except as otherwise provided in subdivision (c) and in Section 9508, a financing statement is not rendered ineffective if, after the financing statement is filed, the information provided in the financing statement becomes seriously misleading under Section 9506.

(c) If a debtor so changes its name that a filed financing statement becomes seriously misleading under Section 9506, the following rules apply:

(1) The financing statement is effective to perfect a security interest in collateral acquired by the debtor before, or within four months after, the change.

(2) The financing statement is not effective to perfect a security interest in collateral acquired by the debtor more than four months after the change, unless an amendment to the financing statement which renders the financing statement not seriously misleading is filed within four months after the change.

9508.

(a) Except as otherwise provided in this section, a filed financing statement naming an original debtor is effective to perfect a security interest in collateral in which a new debtor has or acquires rights to the extent that the financing statement would have been effective had the original debtor acquired rights in the collateral.

(b) If the difference between the name of the original debtor and that of the new debtor causes a filed financing statement that is effective under subdivision (a) to be seriously misleading under Section 9506, the following rules apply:

(1) The financing statement is effective to perfect a security interest in collateral acquired by the new debtor before, and within four months after, the new debtor becomes bound under subdivision (d) of Section 9203.

(2) The financing statement is not effective to perfect a security interest in collateral acquired by the new debtor more than four months after the new debtor becomes bound under subdivision (d) of Section 9203 unless an initial financing statement providing the name of the new debtor is filed before the expiration of that time.

(c) This section does not apply to collateral as to which a filed financing statement remains effective against the new debtor under subdivision (a) of Section 9507.

9509.

(a) A person may file an initial financing statement, an amendment that adds collateral covered by a financing statement, or an amendment that adds a debtor to a financing statement only if either of the following conditions is satisfied:

(1) The debtor authorizes the filing in an authenticated record or pursuant to subdivision (b) or (c).

(2) The person holds an agricultural lien that has become effective at the time of filing and the financing statement covers only collateral in which the person holds an agricultural lien.

(b) By authenticating or becoming bound as debtor by a security agreement, a debtor, or new debtor authorizes the filing of an initial financing statement, and an amendment, covering both of the following:

(1) The collateral described in the security agreement.

(2) Property that becomes collateral under paragraph (2) of subdivision (a) of Section 9315, whether or not the security agreement expressly covers proceeds.

(c) By acquiring collateral in which a security interest or agricultural lien continues under paragraph (1) of subdivision (a) of Section 9315, a debtor authorizes the filing of an initial financing statement, and an amendment, covering the collateral, and property that becomes collateral under paragraph (2) of subdivision (a) of Section 9315.

(d) A person may file an amendment other than an amendment that adds collateral covered by a financing statement or an amendment that adds a debtor to a financing statement only if either of the following conditions is satisfied:

(1) The secured party of record authorizes the filing.

(2) The amendment is a termination statement for a financing statement as to which the secured party of record has failed to file or send a

termination statement as required by subdivision (a) or (c) of Section 9513, the debtor authorizes the filing, and the termination statement indicates that the debtor authorized it to be filed.

(e) If there is more than one secured party of record for a financing statement, each secured party of record may authorize the filing of an amendment under subdivision (d).

9510.

(a) A filed record is effective only to the extent that it was filed by a person that may file it under Section 9509.

(b) A record authorized by one secured party of record does not affect the financing statement with respect to another secured party of record.

(c) A continuation statement that is not filed within the six-month period prescribed by subdivision (d) of Section 9515 is ineffective.

9511.

(a) A secured party of record with respect to a financing statement is a person whose name is provided as the name of the secured party or a representative of the secured party in an initial financing statement that has been filed. If an initial financing statement is filed under subdivision (a) of Section 9514, the assignee named in the initial financing statement is the secured party of record with respect to the financing statement.

(b) If an amendment of a financing statement which provides the name of a person as a secured party or a representative of a secured party is filed, the person named in the amendment is a secured party of record. If an amendment is filed under subdivision (b) of Section 9514, the assignee named in the amendment is a secured party of record.

(c) A person remains a secured party of record until the filing of an amendment of the financing statement which deletes the person.

9512.

(a) Subject to Section 9509, a person may add or delete collateral covered by, continue, or terminate the effectiveness of, or, subject to subdivision (e), otherwise amend the information provided in, a financing statement by filing an amendment that does both of the following:

  (1) Identifies, by its file number, the initial financing statement to which the amendment relates.

  (2) If the amendment relates to an initial financing statement filed or recorded in a filing office described in paragraph (1) of subdivision (a) of Section 9501, provides the date that the initial financing statement was filed or recorded and the information specified in subdivision (b) of Section 9502.

(b) Except as otherwise provided in Section 9515, the filing of an amendment does not extend the period of effectiveness of the financing statement.

(c) A financing statement that is amended by an amendment that adds collateral is effective as to the added collateral only from the date of the filing of the amendment.

(d) A financing statement that is amended by an amendment that adds a debtor is effective as to the added debtor only from the date of the filing of the amendment.

(e) An amendment is ineffective to the extent that it does either of the following:

(1) It purports to delete all debtors and fails to provide the name of a debtor to be covered by the financing statement.

(2) It purports to delete all secured parties of record and fails to provide the name of a new secured party of record.

9513.

(a) A secured party shall cause the secured party of record for a financing statement to file a termination statement for the financing statement if the financing statement covers consumer goods and either of the following conditions is satisfied:

(1) There is no obligation secured by the collateral covered by the financing statement and no commitment to make an advance, incur an obligation, or otherwise give value.

(2) The debtor did not authorize the filing of the initial financing statement.

(b) To comply with subdivision (a), a secured party shall cause the secured party of record to file the termination statement in accordance with either of the following rules:

(1) Within one month after there is no obligation secured by the collateral covered by the financing statement and no commitment to make an advance, incur an obligation, or otherwise give value.

(2) If earlier, within 20 days after the secured party receives an authenticated demand from a debtor.

(c) In cases not governed by subdivision (a), within 20 days after a secured party receives an authenticated demand from a debtor, the secured party shall cause the secured party of record for a financing statement to send to the debtor a termination statement for the financing statement or file the termination statement in the filing office if any of the following conditions is satisfied:

(1) Except in the case of a financing statement covering accounts or chattel paper that has been sold, or goods that are the subject of a consignment, there is no obligation secured by the collateral covered by the financing statement and no commitment to make an advance, incur an obligation, or otherwise give value.

(2) The financing statement covers accounts or chattel paper that has been sold but as to which the account debtor, or other person obligated has discharged its obligation.

(3) The financing statement covers goods that were the subject of a consignment to the debtor but are not in the debtor's possession.

(4) The debtor did not authorize the filing of the initial financing statement.

(d) Except as otherwise provided in Section 9510, upon the filing of a termination statement with the filing office, the financing statement to which the termination statement relates ceases to be effective. Except as otherwise provided in Section 9510, for purposes of subdivision (g) of Section 9519, subdivision (a) of Section 9522, and subdivision (c) of Section 9523, the filing with the filing office of a termination statement relating to a financing statement that indicates that the debtor is a transmitting utility also causes the effectiveness of the financing statement to lapse.

9514.

(a) Except as otherwise provided in subdivision (c), an initial financing statement may reflect an assignment of all of the secured party's power to authorize an amendment to the financing statement by providing the name and mailing address of the assignee as the name and address of the secured party.

(b) Except as otherwise provided in subdivision (c), a secured party of record may assign all or part of its power to authorize an amendment to a financing statement by filing in the filing office an amendment of the financing statement which does all of the following:

(1) Identifies, by its file number, the initial financing statement to which it relates.

(2) Provides the name of the assignor.

(3) Provides the name and mailing address of the assignee.

(c) An assignment of record of a security interest in a fixture covered by a record of a mortgage which is effective as a financing statement filed as a fixture filing under subdivision (c) of Section 9502 may be made only by an assignment of record of the mortgage in the manner provided by law of this state other than the Uniform Commercial Code.

9515.

(a) Except as otherwise provided in subdivisions (b), (e), (f), and (g), a filed financing statement is effective for a period of five years after the date of filing.

(b) Except as otherwise provided in subdivisions (e), (f), and (g), an initial financing statement filed in connection with a public finance transaction or manufactured home transaction is effective for a period of 30 years after the date of filing if it indicates that it is filed in connection with a public finance transaction or manufactured home transaction.

(c) The effectiveness of a filed financing statement lapses on the expiration of the period of its effectiveness unless before the lapse a continuation statement is filed pursuant to subdivision (d). Upon lapse, a financing statement ceases to be effective and any security interest, or agricultural lien that was perfected by the financing statement becomes unperfected, unless the security interest is perfected otherwise. If the security interest or agricultural lien becomes unperfected upon lapse, it is deemed never to have been perfected as against a purchaser of the collateral for value.

(d) A continuation statement may be filed only within six months before the expiration of the five-year period specified in subdivision (a) or the 30-year period specified in subdivision (b), whichever is applicable.

(e) Except as otherwise provided in Section 9510, upon timely filing of a continuation statement, the effectiveness of the initial financing statement continues for a period of five years commencing on the day on which the financing statement would have become ineffective in the absence of the filing. Upon the expiration of the five-year period, the financing statement lapses in the same manner as provided in subdivision (c), unless, before the lapse, another continuation statement is filed pursuant to subdivision (d). Succeeding continuation statements may be filed in the same manner to continue the effectiveness of the initial financing statement.

(f) If a debtor is a transmitting utility and a filed financing statement so indicates, the financing statement is effective until a termination statement is filed.

(g) A record of a mortgage that is effective as a financing statement filed as a fixture filing under subdivision (c) of Section 9502 remains effective as a financing statement filed as a fixture filing until the mortgage is released or satisfied of record, or its effectiveness otherwise terminates as to the real property.

9516.

(a) Except as otherwise provided in subdivision (b), communication of a record to a filing office and tender of the filing fee or acceptance of the record by the filing office constitutes filing.

(b) Filing does not occur with respect to a record that a filing office refuses to accept because of any of the following:

(1) The record is not communicated by a method or medium of communication authorized by the filing office.

(2) An amount equal to or greater than the applicable filing fee is not tendered.

(3) The filing office is unable to index the record because of any of the following:

(A) In the case of an initial financing statement, the record does not provide a name for the debtor.

(B) In the case of an amendment or correction statement, either of the following applies with respect to the record:

(i) It does not identify the initial financing statement as required by Section 9512 or 9518, as applicable.

(ii) It identifies an initial financing statement whose effectiveness has lapsed under Section 9515.

(C) In the case of an initial financing statement that provides the name of a debtor identified as an individual or an amendment that provides a name of a debtor identified as an individual which was not previously provided in the financing statement to which the record relates, the record does not identify the debtor's last name.

(D) In the case of a record filed or recorded in the filing office described in paragraph (1) of subdivision (a) of Section 9501, the record does not provide a sufficient description of the real property to which it relates.

(4) In the case of an initial financing statement or an amendment that adds a secured party of record, the record does not provide a name, and mailing address for the secured party of record.

(5) In the case of an initial financing statement or an amendment that provides a name of a debtor which was not previously provided in the financing statement to which the amendment relates, the record does not do any of the following:

(A) Provide a mailing address for the debtor.

(B) Indicate whether the debtor is an individual or an organization.

(C) If the financing statement indicates that the debtor is an organization, provide any of the following:

(i) A type of organization for the debtor.

(ii) A jurisdiction of organization for the debtor.

(iii) An organizational identification number for the debtor or indicate that the debtor has none.

(6) In the case of an assignment reflected in an initial financing statement under subdivision (a) of Section 9514 or an amendment filed under subdivision (b) of Section 9514, the record does not provide a name and mailing address for the assignee.

(7) In the case of a continuation statement, the record is not filed within the six-month period prescribed by subdivision (d) of Section 9515.

(c) For purposes of subdivision (b), both of the following rules apply:

(1) A record does not provide information if the filing office is unable to read or decipher the information.

(2) A record that does not indicate that it is an amendment or identify an initial financing statement to which it relates, as required by Section 9512, 9514, or 9518, is an initial financing statement.

(d) A record that is communicated to the filing office with tender of the filing fee, but which the filing office refuses to accept for a reason other than one set forth in subdivision (b), is effective as a filed record except as against a purchaser of the collateral which gives value in reasonable reliance upon the absence of the record from the files.

9517. The failure of the filing office to index a record correctly does not affect the effectiveness of the filed record.

9518.

(a) A person may file in the filing office a correction statement with respect to a record indexed there under the person's name if the person believes that the record is inaccurate or was wrongfully filed.

(b) A correction statement must do all of the following:

(1) Identify the record to which it relates by both of the following:

(A) The file number assigned to the initial financing statement to which the record relates.

(B) If the correction statement relates to a record filed or recorded in a filing office described in paragraph (1) of subdivision (a) of Section 9501, the date that the initial financing statement was filed or recorded, and the information specified in subdivision (b) of Section 9502.

(2) Indicate that it is a correction statement.

(3) Provide the basis for the person's belief that the record is inaccurate and indicate the manner in which the person believes the record should be amended to cure any inaccuracy or provide the basis for the person's belief that the record was wrongfully filed.

(c) The filing of a correction statement does not affect the effectiveness of an initial financing statement or other filed record.

9519.

(a) For each record filed in a filing office, the filing office shall do all of the following:

(1) Assign a unique number to the filed record.

(2) Create a record that bears the number assigned to the filed record and the date, and time of filing.

(3) Maintain the filed record for public inspection.

(4) Index the filed record in accordance with subdivisions (c), (d), and (e).

(b) Except as otherwise provided in subdivision (i), a file number assigned after January 1, 2002, must include a digit that:

(1) Is mathematically derived from or related to the other digits of the file number.

(2) Aids the filing office in determining whether a number communicated as the file number includes a single-digit or transpositional error.

(c) Except as otherwise provided in subdivisions (d) and (e), the filing office shall do both of the following:

(1) Index an initial financing statement according to the name of the debtor and index all filed records relating to the initial financing statement in a manner that associates with one another an initial financing statement and all filed records relating to the initial financing statement.

(2) Index a record that provides a name of a debtor which was not previously provided in the financing statement to which the record relates also according to the name that was not previously provided.

(d) If a financing statement is filed as a fixture filing or covers as-extracted collateral or timber to be cut, it must be recorded, and the filing office shall index it in accordance with both of the following rules:

(1) Under the names of the debtor and of each owner of record shown on the financing statement as if they were the mortgagors under a mortgage of the real property described.

(2) To the extent that the law of this state provides for indexing of records of mortgages under the name of the mortgagee, under the name of the secured party as if the secured party were the mortgagee thereunder, or, if indexing is by description, as if the financing statement were a record of a mortgage of the real property described.

(e) If a financing statement is filed as a fixture filing or covers as-extracted collateral or timber to be cut, the filing office shall index an assignment filed under subdivision (a) of Section 9514 or an amendment filed under subdivision (b) of Section 9514 in accordance with both of the following rules:

(1) Under the name of the assignor as grantor.

(2) To the extent that the law of this state provides for indexing a record of the assignment of a mortgage under the name of the assignee, under the name of the assignee.

(f) The filing office shall maintain a capability to do both of the following:

(1) Retrieve a record by the name of the debtor and by either of the following:

(A) If the filing office is described in paragraph (1) of subdivision (a) of Section 9501, by the file number assigned to the initial financing statement to which the record relates and the date that the record was filed or recorded.

(B) If the filing office is described in paragraph (2) of subdivision (a) of Section 9501, by the file number assigned to the initial financing statement to which the record relates.

(2) Associate and retrieve with one another an initial financing statement and each filed record relating to the initial financing statement.

(g) The filing office may not remove a debtor's name from the index until one year after the effectiveness of a financing statement naming the debtor lapses under Section 9515 with respect to all secured parties of record.

(h) Except as otherwise provided in subdivision (i), the filing office shall perform the acts required by subdivisions (a) to (e), inclusive, at the time and in the manner prescribed by filing-office rule, but not later than two business days after the filing office receives the record in question.

(i) Subdivisions (b) and (h) do not apply to a filing office described in paragraph (1) of subdivision (a) of Section 9501.

9520.

(a) A filing office shall refuse to accept a record for filing for a reason set forth in subdivision (b) of Section 9516 and may refuse to accept a record for filing only for a reason set forth in subdivision (b) of Section 9516.

(b) If a filing office refuses to accept a record for filing, it shall communicate to the person that presented the record the fact of and reason for the refusal, and the date and time the record would have been filed had the filing office accepted it. The communication shall be made at the time and in the manner prescribed by filing-office rule, but in the case of a filing office described in paragraph (2) of subdivision (a) of Section 9501, in no event more than two business days after the filing office receives the record.

(c) A filed financing statement satisfying subdivisions (a) and (b) of Section 9502 is effective, even if the filing office is required to refuse to accept it for filing under subdivision (a). However, Section 9338 applies to a filed financing statement providing information described in paragraph (5) of subdivision (b) of Section 9516 which is incorrect at the time the financing statement is filed.

(d) If a record communicated to a filing office provides information that relates to more than one debtor, this chapter applies as to each debtor separately.

9521.

(a) A filing office that accepts written records may not refuse to accept a written initial financing statement in the following form and format except for a reason set forth in subdivision (b) of Section 9516:

(b) A filing office that accepts written records may not refuse to accept a written record in the following form and format except for a reason set forth in subdivision (b) of Section 9516:

9522.

(a) The filing office shall maintain a record of the information provided in a filed financing statement for at least one year after the effectiveness of the financing statement has lapsed under Section 9515 with respect to all secured parties of record. The record shall be retrievable by using the name of the debtor and either of the following:

(1) If the record was filed or recorded in a filing office described in paragraph (1) of subdivision (a) of Section 9501, by using the file number assigned to the initial financing statement to which the record relates and the date the record was filed or recorded.

(2) If the record was filed in a filing office described in paragraph (2) of subdivision (a) of Section 9501, by using the file number assigned to the initial financing statement to which the record relates.

(b) Except to the extent that a statute governing disposition of public records provides otherwise, the filing office immediately may destroy any written record evidencing a financing statement. However, if the filing office destroys a written record, it shall maintain another record of the financing statement which complies with subdivision (a).

9523.

(a) If a person that files a written record requests an acknowledgment of the filing, the filing office shall send to the person an image of the record showing the number assigned to the record pursuant to paragraph (1) of subdivision (a) of Section 9519 and the date and time of the filing of the record. However, if the person furnishes a copy of the record to the filing office, the filing office may instead do both of the following:

(1) Note upon the copy the number assigned to the record pursuant to paragraph (1) of subdivision (a) of Section 9519 and the date and time of the filing of the record.

(2) Send the copy to the person.

(b) If a person files a record other than a written record, the filing office shall communicate to the person an acknowledgment that provides all of the following information:

(1) The information in the record.

(2) The number assigned to the record pursuant to paragraph (1) of subdivision (a) of Section 9519.

(3) The date and time of the filing of the record.

(c) The filing office shall communicate or otherwise make available in a record all of the following information to any person that requests it:

(1) Whether there is on file on a date and time specified by the filing office, but not a date earlier than three business days before the filing office receives the request, any financing statement that satisfies all of the following conditions:

(A) It designates a particular debtor or, if the request so states, designates a particular debtor at the address specified in the request.

(B) It has not lapsed under Section 9515 with respect to all secured parties of record.

(C) If the request so states, it has lapsed under Section 9515 and a record of which is maintained by the filing office under subdivision (a) of Section 9522.

(2) The date and time of filing of each financing statement.

(3) The information provided in each financing statement.

(d) In complying with its duty under subdivision (c), the filing office may communicate information in any medium. However, if requested, the filing office shall communicate information by issuing its written certificate.

(e) The filing office described in paragraph (2) of subdivision (a) of Section 9501 shall perform the acts required by subdivisions (a) to (d), inclusive, at the time, and in the manner prescribed by filing-office rule, but not later than two business days after the filing office receives the request.

(f) At least weekly, the filing office described in paragraph (2) of subdivision (a) of Section 9501 shall offer to sell or license to the public on a nonexclusive basis, in bulk, copies of all records filed in it under this chapter, in every medium from time to time available to the filing office.

9524. Delay by the filing office beyond a time limit prescribed by this chapter is excused if both of the following conditions are satisfied:

(1) The delay is caused by interruption of communication or computer facilities, war, emergency conditions, failure of equipment, or other circumstances beyond control of the filing office.

(2) The filing office exercises reasonable diligence under the circumstances.

9525.

(a) Except as otherwise provided in subdivision (d), the fee for filing and indexing a record under this chapter is set forth in subdivisions (a), (b), and (c) of Section 12194 of the Government Code.

(b) The number of names required to be indexed does not affect the amount of the fee in subdivision (a).

(c) The fee for responding to a request for information from the filing office, including for issuing a certificate showing whether there is on file any financing statement naming a particular debtor, is as follows:

(1) Ten dollars ($10) if the request is communicated in writing.

(2) Five dollars ($5) if the request is communicated by another medium authorized by a rule adopted by the filing office.

(d) This section does not require a fee with respect to a record of a mortgage which is effective as a financing statement filed as a fixture filing or as a financing statement covering as-extracted collateral or timber to be cut under subdivision (c) of Section 9502.

However, the recording and satisfaction fees that otherwise would be applicable to the record of the mortgage apply.

9526.

(a) The Secretary of State shall adopt and publish rules to implement this division. The filing-office rules shall be consistent with this division.

(b) To keep the filing-office rules and practices of the filing office in harmony with the rules and practices of filing offices in other jurisdictions that enact substantially this chapter, and to keep the technology used by the filing office compatible with the technology used by filing offices in other jurisdictions that enact substantially this chapter, the Secretary of State, so far as is consistent with the purposes, policies, and provisions of this division, in adopting, amending, and repealing filing-office rules, shall do all of the following:

(1) Consult with filing offices in other jurisdictions that enact substantially this chapter.

(2) Consult the most recent version of the Model Rules promulgated by the International Association of Corporate Administrators or any successor organization.

(3) Take into consideration the rules and practices of, and the technology used by, filing offices in other jurisdictions that enact substantially this chapter.

9526.5.

(a) For purposes of this section, the following terms have the following meanings:

(1) "Official filing" means the permanent archival filing of all instruments, papers, records, and attachments as accepted for filing by a filing office.

(2) "Public filing" means a filing that is an exact copy of an official filing except that any social security number contained in the copied filing is truncated. The public filing shall have the same legal force and effect as the official filing.

(3) "Truncate" means to redact at least the first five digits of a social security number.

(4) "Truncated social security number" means a social security number that displays no more than the last four digits of the number.

(b) For every filing containing an untruncated social security number filed before August 1, 2007, a filing office shall create a public filing.

(c) A filing office shall post a notice on its Web site informing filers not to include social security numbers in any portion of their filings. A filing office's online filing system shall not contain a field requesting a social security number.

(d) Beginning August 1, 2007, for every filing containing an untruncated social security number filed by means other than the filing office's Web site, a filing office shall create a public filing.

(e) When a public filing version of an official filing exists, both of the following shall apply:

(1) Upon a request for inspection, copying, or any other public disclosure of an official filing that is not exempt from disclosure, a filing office shall make available only the public filing version of that filing.

(2) A filing office shall publicly disclose an official filing only in response to a subpoena or order of a court of competent jurisdiction.

(3) Nothing in this article shall be construed to restrict, delay, or modify access to any official filing, or modify any existing agreements regarding access to any official filing, prior to the creation and availability of a public filing version of that official filing.

(f) A filing office shall be deemed to be in compliance with the requirements of this section and shall not be liable for failure to truncate a social security number if he or she uses due diligence to locate social security numbers in official records and truncate the social security numbers in the public filing version of those official filings. The use of an automated program with a high rate of accuracy shall be deemed to be due diligence.

(g) In the event that a filing office fails to truncate a social security number contained in a record pursuant to subdivision (b) or (d), any person may request that the filing office truncate the social security number contained in that record. Notwithstanding that a filing office may be deemed to be in compliance with this section pursuant to subdivision (f), a filing office that receives a request that identifies the exact location of an untruncated social security number that is required to be truncated pursuant to subdivision (b) or (d) within a specifically identified record, shall truncate that number within 10 business days of receiving the request. The public filing with the truncated social security number shall replace the record with the untruncated number.

(h) The Secretary of State shall not produce or make available financing statements in the form and format described in Section 9521 that provide a space identified for the disclosure of the social security number of an individual.

(i) The Secretary of State shall produce and make available financing statements in the form and format described in Section 9521, except that the financing statements shall not provide a space identified for the disclosure of the social security number of an individual.

(j) The provisions of this section shall not apply to a county recorder.

9527. The Secretary of State shall report annually on or before January 31 to the Legislature on the operation of the filing office. The report must contain a statement of the extent to which both of the following apply:

(1) The filing-office rules are not in harmony with the rules of filing offices in other jurisdictions that enact substantially this chapter and the reasons for these variations.

(2) The filing-office rules are not in harmony with the most recent version of the Model Rules promulgated by the International Association of Corporate Administrators, or any successor organization, and the reasons for these variations.

9528. Upon the request of any person, the Secretary of State shall issue a combined certificate showing the information as to financing statements as specified in Section 9523, the information as to state tax liens as specified in Section 7226 of the Government Code, the information as to attachment liens as specified in Sections 488.375 and 488.405 of the Code of Civil Procedure, the information as to judgment liens as specified in Section 697.580 of the Code of Civil Procedure, and the information as to federal liens as specified in Section 2103 of the Code of Civil Procedure.

9601.

(a) After default, a secured party has the rights provided in this chapter and, except as otherwise provided in Section 9602, those rights provided by agreement of the parties. A secured party may do both of the following:

(1) Reduce a claim to judgment, foreclose, or otherwise enforce the claim, security interest, or agricultural lien by any available judicial procedure.

(2) If the collateral is documents, proceed either as to the documents or as to the goods they cover.

(b) A secured party in possession of collateral or control of collateral under Section 7106, 9104, 9105, 9106, or 9107 has the rights and duties provided in Section 9207.

(c) The rights under subdivisions (a) and (b) are cumulative and may be exercised simultaneously.

(d) Except as otherwise provided in subdivision (g) and in Section 9605, after default, a debtor and an obligor have the rights provided in this chapter and by agreement of the parties.

(e) If a secured party has reduced its claim to judgment, the lien of any levy that may be made upon the collateral by virtue of an execution based upon the judgment relates back to the earliest of any of the following:

(1) The date of perfection of the security interest or agricultural lien in the collateral.

(2) The date of filing a financing statement covering the collateral.

(3) Any date specified in a statute under which the agricultural lien was created.

(f) A sale pursuant to an execution is a foreclosure of the security interest or agricultural lien by judicial procedure within the meaning of this section. A secured party may purchase at the sale and thereafter hold the collateral free of any other requirements of this division.

(g) Except as otherwise provided in subdivision (c) of Section 9607, this part imposes no duties upon a secured party that is a consignor or is a buyer of accounts, chattel paper, payment intangibles, or promissory notes.

9602. Except as otherwise provided in Section 9624, to the extent that they give rights to a debtor or obligor, and impose duties on a secured party, the debtor or obligor may not waive, or vary the rules stated in the following listed sections:

(1) Subparagraph (C) of paragraph (4) of subdivision (b) of Section 9207, which deals with use and operation of the collateral by the secured party.

(2) Section 9210, which deals with requests for an accounting and requests concerning a list of collateral and statement of account.

(3) Subdivision (c) of Section 9607, which deals with collection and enforcement of collateral.

(4) Subdivision (a) of Section 9608 and subdivision (c) of Section 9615 to the extent that they deal with application or payment of noncash proceeds of collection, enforcement, or disposition.

(5) Subdivision (a) of Section 9608 and subdivision (d) of Section 9615 to the extent that they require accounting for or payment of surplus proceeds of collateral.

(6) Section 9609 to the extent that it imposes upon a secured party that takes possession of collateral without judicial process the duty to do so without breach of the peace.

(7) Subdivision (b) of Section 9610, and Sections 9611, 9613, and 9614 which deal with disposition of collateral.

(8) Subdivision (f) of Section 9615, which deals with calculation of a deficiency or surplus when a disposition is made to the secured party, a person related to the secured party, or a secondary obligor.

(9) Section 9616, which deals with explanation of the calculation of a surplus or deficiency.

(10) Section 9620, 9621, and 9622, which deal with acceptance of collateral in satisfaction of obligation.

(11) Section 9623, which deals with redemption of collateral.

(12) Section 9624, which deals with permissible waivers.

(13) Sections 9625 and 9626, which deal with the existence of a deficiency and with the secured party's liability for failure to comply with this division.

9603.

(a) The parties may determine by agreement the standards measuring the fulfillment of the rights of a debtor or obligor and the duties of a secured party under a rule stated in Section 9602 if the standards are not manifestly unreasonable.

(b) Subdivision (a) does not apply to the duty under Section 9609 to refrain from breaching the peace.

9604.

(a) If an obligation secured by a security interest in personal property or fixtures is also secured by an interest in real property or an estate therein:

(1) The secured party may do any of the following:

(A) Proceed, in any sequence, (i) in accordance with the secured party's rights and remedies in respect of real property as to the real property security, and (ii) in accordance with this chapter as to the personal property or fixtures.

(B) Proceed in any sequence, as to both, some, or all of the real property and some or all of the personal property or fixtures in accordance with the secured party's rights and remedies in respect of the real property, by including the portion of the personal property, or fixtures selected by the secured party in the judicial or nonjudicial foreclosure of the real property in accordance with the procedures applicable to real property. In proceeding under this subparagraph, (i) no provision of this chapter other than this subparagraph, subparagraph (C) of paragraph (4), and paragraphs (7) and (8) shall apply to any aspect of the foreclosure; (ii) a power of sale under the deed of trust or mortgage shall be exercisable with respect to both the real property and the personal property or fixtures being sold; and (iii) the sale may be conducted by the mortgagee under the mortgage or by the trustee under the deed of trust. The secured party shall not be deemed to have elected irrevocably to proceed as to both real property and personal property or fixtures as provided in this subparagraph with respect to any particular property, unless and until that particular property actually has been disposed of pursuant to a unified sale (judicial or nonjudicial) conducted in accordance with the procedures applicable to real property, and then only as to the property so sold.

(C) Proceed, in any sequence, as to part of the personal property, or fixtures as provided in subparagraph (A), and as to other of the personal property or fixtures as provided in subparagraph (B).

(2) Except as otherwise provided in paragraph (3), provisions and limitations

(A) of any law respecting real property and obligations secured by an interest in real property or an estate therein, including, but not limited to, Section 726 of the Code of Civil Procedure, provisions regarding acceleration or reinstatement of obligations secured by an interest in real property or an estate therein, prohibitions against deficiency judgments, limitations on deficiency judgments based on the value of the collateral, limitations on the right to proceed as to collateral, and requirements that a creditor resort either first or at all to its security, do not in any way apply to either (i) any personal property or fixtures other than personal property or fixtures as to which the secured party has proceeded or is proceeding under subparagraph (B) of paragraph (1), or (ii) the obligation.

(B) Pursuant to, but without limiting subparagraph (A), in the event that an obligation secured by personal property, or fixtures would otherwise become unenforceable by reason of Section 726 of the Code of Civil Procedure or any requirement that a creditor resort first to its security, then, notwithstanding that section or any similar requirement, the obligation shall nevertheless remain enforceable to the full extent necessary to permit a secured party to proceed against personal property, or fixtures securing the obligation in accordance with the secured party's rights, and remedies as permitted under this chapter.

(3) (A) Paragraph (2) does not limit the application of Section 580b of the Code (A) of Civil Procedure.

(B) If the secured party commences an action, as defined in Section 22 of the Code of Civil Procedure, and the action seeks a monetary judgment on the debt, paragraph (2) does not prevent the assertion by the debtor or an obligor of any right to require the inclusion in the action of any interest in real property or an estate therein securing the debt. If a monetary judgment on the debt is entered in the action, paragraph (2) does not prevent the assertion by the debtor or an obligor of the subsequent unenforceability of the encumbrance on any interest in real property or an estate therein securing the debt and not included in the action.

(C) Nothing in paragraph (2) shall be construed to excuse compliance with Section 2924c of the Civil Code as a prerequisite to the sale of real property, but that section has no application to the right of a secured party to proceed as to personal property or fixtures except, and then only to the extent that, the secured party is proceeding as to personal property or fixtures in a unified sale as provided in subparagraph (B) of paragraph (1).

(D) Paragraph (2) does not deprive the debtor of the protection of Section 580d of the Code of Civil Procedure against a deficiency judgment following a sale of the real property collateral pursuant to a power of sale in a deed of trust or mortgage.

(E) Paragraph (2) shall not affect, nor shall it determine the applicability, or inapplicability of, any law respecting real property or obligations secured in whole or in part by real property with respect to a loan or a credit sale made to any individual primarily for personal, family, or household purposes.

(F) Paragraph (2) does not deprive the debtor or an obligor of the protection of Section 580a of the Code of Civil Procedure following a sale of real property collateral.

(G) If the secured party violates any statute or rule of law that requires a creditor who holds an obligation secured by an interest in real property or an estate therein to resort first to its security before resorting to any property of the debtor that does not secure the obligation, paragraph (2) does not prevent the assertion by the debtor or an obligor of any right to require correction of the violation, any right of the secured party to correct the violation, or the assertion by the debtor or an obligor of the subsequent unenforceability of the encumbrance on any interest in real property or an estate therein securing the obligation, or the assertion by the debtor or an obligor of the subsequent unenforceability of the obligation except to the extent that the obligation is preserved by subparagraph (B) of paragraph (2).

(4) If the secured party realizes proceeds from the disposition of collateral that is personal property or fixtures, the following provisions shall apply:

(A) The disposition of the collateral, the realization of the proceeds, the application of the proceeds, or any one or more of the foregoing shall not operate to cure any nonmonetary default.

(B) The disposition of the collateral, the realization of the proceeds, the application of the proceeds, or any one or more of the foregoing shall not operate to cure any monetary default (although the application of the proceeds shall, to the extent of those proceeds, satisfy the secured obligation) so as to affect in any way the secured party's rights, and remedies under this chapter with respect to any remaining personal property or fixtures collateral.

(C) All proceeds so realized shall be applied by the secured party to the secured obligation in accordance with the agreement of the parties and applicable law.

(5) An action by the secured party utilizing any available judicial procedure shall in no way be affected by omission of a prayer for a monetary judgment on the debt. Notwithstanding Section 726 of the Code of Civil Procedure, any prohibition against splitting causes of action, or any other statute or rule of law, a judicial action which neither seeks nor results in a monetary judgment on the debt shall not preclude a subsequent action seeking a monetary judgment on the debt or any other relief.

(6) As used in this subdivision, "monetary judgment on the debt" means a judgment for the recovery from the debtor of all or part of the principal amount of the secured obligation, including, for purposes of this subdivision, contractual interest thereon. "Monetary judgment on the debt" does not include a judgment which provides only for other relief (whether or not that other relief is secured by the collateral), such as one or more forms of nonmonetary relief, and monetary relief ancillary to any of the foregoing, such as attorneys' fees, and costs incurred in seeking the relief.

(7) If a secured party fails to comply with the procedures applicable to real property in proceeding as to both real and personal property under subparagraph (B) of paragraph (1), a purchaser for value of any interest in the real property at judicial or nonjudicial foreclosure proceedings conducted pursuant to subparagraph (B) of paragraph (1) takes that interest free from any claim or interest of another person, or any defect in title, based upon that noncompliance, unless:

(A) The purchaser is the secured party and the failure to comply with this chapter occurred other than in good faith; or

(B) The purchaser is other than the secured party and at the time of sale of the real property at that foreclosure the purchaser had knowledge of the failure to comply with this chapter and that the noncompliance occurred other than in good faith.

Even if the purchaser at the foreclosure sale does not take his or her interest free of claims, interests, or title defects based upon that noncompliance with this chapter, a subsequent purchaser for value who acquires an interest in that real property from the purchaser at that foreclosure takes that interest free from any claim or interest of another person, or any defect in title, based upon that noncompliance, unless at the time of acquiring the interest the subsequent purchaser has knowledge of the failure to comply with this chapter, and that the noncompliance occurred other than in good faith.

(8) If a secured party proceeds by way of a unified sale under subparagraph (B) of paragraph (1), then, for purposes of applying Section 580a or subdivision (b) of Section 726 of the Code of Civil Procedure to any such unified sale, the personal property, or fixtures included in the unified sale shall be deemed to be included in the "real property or other interest sold," as that term is used in Section 580a or subdivision (b) of Section 726 of the Code of Civil Procedure.

9605. A secured party does not owe a duty based on its status as secured party to either of the following persons:

(1) To a person that is a debtor or obligor, unless the secured party knows all of the following:

(A) That the person is a debtor or obligor.

(B) The identity of the person.

(C) How to communicate with the person.

(2) To a secured party or lienholder that has filed a financing statement against a person, unless the secured party knows both of the following:

(A) That the person is a debtor.

(B) The identity of the person.

9606. For purposes of this chapter, a default occurs in connection with an agricultural lien at the time the secured party becomes entitled to enforce the lien in accordance with the statute under which it was created.

9607.

(a) If so agreed, and in any event after default, a secured party may do all of the following:

(1) Notify an account debtor or other person obligated on collateral to make payment or otherwise render performance to or for the benefit of the secured party.

(2) Take any proceeds to which the secured party is entitled under Section 9315.

(3) Enforce the obligations of an account debtor or other person obligated on collateral and exercise the rights of the debtor with respect to the obligation of the account debtor or other person obligated on collateral to make payment or otherwise render performance to the debtor, and with respect to any property that secures the obligations of the account debtor or other person obligated on the collateral.

(4) If it holds a security interest in a deposit account perfected by control under paragraph (1) of subdivision (a) of Section 9104, apply the balance of the deposit account to the obligation secured by the deposit account.

(5) If it holds a security interest in a deposit account perfected by control under paragraph (2) or (3) of subdivision (a) of Section 9104, instruct the bank to pay the balance of the deposit account to or for the benefit of the secured party.

(b) If necessary to enable a secured party to exercise under paragraph (3) of subdivision (a) the right of a debtor to enforce a mortgage nonjudicially, the secured party may record in the office in which a record of the mortgage is recorded both of the following:

(1) A copy of the security agreement that creates or provides for a security interest in the obligation secured by the mortgage.

(2) The secured party's sworn affidavit in recordable form stating both of the following:

(A) That a default has occurred.

(B) That the secured party is entitled to enforce the mortgage nonjudicially.

(c) A secured party shall proceed in a commercially reasonable manner if both of the following apply with respect to the secured party:

(1) It undertakes to collect from or enforce an obligation of an account debtor or other person obligated on collateral.

(2) It is entitled to charge back uncollected collateral or otherwise to full or limited recourse against the debtor or a secondary obligor.

(d) A secured party may deduct from the collections made pursuant to subdivision (c) reasonable expenses of collection, and enforcement, including reasonable attorney's fees and legal expenses incurred by the secured party.

(e) This section does not determine whether an account debtor, bank, or other person obligated on collateral owes a duty to a secured party.

9608.

(a) If a security interest or agricultural lien secures payment or performance of an obligation, the following rules apply:

(1) A secured party shall apply or pay over for application the cash proceeds of collection or enforcement under Section 9607 in the following order to:

(A) The reasonable expenses of collection and enforcement and to the extent provided for by agreement and not prohibited by law, reasonable attorney's fees, and legal expenses incurred by the secured party.

(B) The satisfaction of obligations secured by the security interest or agricultural lien under which the collection or enforcement is made.

(C) The satisfaction of obligations secured by any subordinate security interest in or other lien on the collateral subject to the security interest or agricultural lien under which the collection or enforcement is made if the secured party receives an authenticated demand for proceeds before distribution of the proceeds is completed.

(2) If requested by a secured party, a holder of a subordinate security interest, or other lien shall furnish reasonable proof of the interest or lien within a reasonable time. Unless the holder complies, the secured party need not comply with the holder's demand under subparagraph (C) of paragraph (1).

(3) A secured party need not apply or pay over for application noncash proceeds of collection and enforcement under Section 9607 unless the

failure to do so would be commercially unreasonable. A secured party that applies or pays over for application noncash proceeds shall do so in a commercially reasonable manner.

(4) A secured party shall account to and pay a debtor for any surplus, and except as otherwise provided in subdivision (b) of Section 9626, the obligor is liable for any deficiency.

(b) If the underlying transaction is a sale of accounts, chattel paper, payment intangibles, or promissory notes, the debtor is not entitled to any surplus, and the obligor is not liable for any deficiency. Subdivision (b) of Section 701.040 of the Code of Civil Procedure relating to the payment of proceeds applies only if the security agreement provides that the debtor is entitled to any surplus.

9609.

(a) After default, a secured party may do both of the following:

(1) Take possession of the collateral.

(2) Without removal, render equipment unusable, and dispose of collateral on a debtor's premises under Section 9610.

(b) A secured party may proceed under subdivision (a) in either of the following ways:

(1) Pursuant to judicial process.

(2) Without judicial process, if it proceeds without breach of the peace.

(c) If so agreed, and in any event after default, a secured party may require the debtor to assemble the collateral, and make it available to the secured party at a place to be designated by the secured party which is reasonably convenient to both parties.

9610.

(a) After default, a secured party may sell, lease, license, or otherwise dispose of any or all of the collateral in its present condition or following any commercially reasonable preparation or processing.

(b) Every aspect of a disposition of collateral, including the method, manner, time, place, and other terms, must be commercially reasonable. If commercially reasonable, a secured party may dispose of collateral by public or private proceedings, by one or more contracts, as a unit or in parcels, and at any time and place and on any terms.

(c) A secured party may purchase collateral at either of the following:

(1) At a public disposition.

(2) At a private disposition only if the collateral is of a kind that is customarily sold on a recognized market or the subject of widely distributed standard price quotations.

(d) A contract for sale, lease, license, or other disposition includes the warranties relating to title, possession, quiet enjoyment, and the like which by operation of law accompany a voluntary disposition of property of the kind subject to the contract.

(e) A secured party may disclaim or modify warranties under subdivision (d) in either of the following ways:

(1) In a manner that would be effective to disclaim or modify the warranties in a voluntary disposition of property of the kind subject to the contract of disposition.

(2) By communicating to the purchaser a record evidencing the contract for disposition and including an express disclaimer or modification of the warranties.

(f) A record is sufficient to disclaim warranties under subdivision (e) if it indicates "There is no warranty relating to title, possession, quiet enjoyment, or the like in this disposition" or uses words of similar import.

9611.

(a) In this section, "notification date" means the earlier of the date on which:

(1) A secured party sends to the debtor and any secondary obligor an authenticated notification of disposition.

(2) The debtor and any secondary obligor waive the right to notification.

(b) Except as otherwise provided in subdivision (d), a secured party that disposes of collateral under Section 9610 shall send to the persons specified in subdivision (c) a reasonable authenticated notification of disposition.

(c) To comply with subdivision (b), the secured party shall send an authenticated notification of disposition to all of the following persons:

(1) The debtor.

(2) Any secondary obligor.

(3) If the collateral is other than consumer goods to both of the following persons:

(A) Any other person from which the secured party has received, before the notification date, an authenticated notification of a claim of an interest in the collateral.

(B) Any other secured party or lienholder that, 10 days before the notification date, held a security interest in, or other lien on the collateral perfected by the filing of a financing statement with respect to which all of the following apply:

(i) It identified the collateral.

(ii) It was indexed under the debtor's name as of that date.

(iii) It was filed in the office in which to file a financing statement against the debtor covering the collateral as of that date.

(C) Any other secured party that, 10 days before the notification date, held a security interest in the collateral perfected by compliance with a statute, regulation, or treaty described in subdivision (a) of Section 9311.

(d) Subdivision (b) does not apply if the collateral is perishable or threatens to decline speedily in value or is of a type customarily sold on a recognized market.

(e) A secured party complies with the requirement for notification prescribed in subparagraph (B) of paragraph (3) of subsection (c) if it satisfies both of the following conditions:

(1) Not later than 20 days or earlier than 30 days before the notification date, the secured party requests, in a commercially reasonable manner, information concerning financing statements indexed under the debtor's name in the office indicated in subparagraph (B) of paragraph (3) of subdivision (c).

(2) Before the notification date, the secured party either:

(A) Did not receive a response to the request for information.

(B) Received a response to the request for information and sent an authenticated notification of disposition to each secured party or other lienholder named in that response whose financing statement covered the collateral.

9612.

(a) Except as otherwise provided in subdivision (b), whether a notification is sent within a reasonable time is a question of fact.

(b) In a transaction other than a consumer transaction, a notification of disposition sent after default and 10 days, or more before the earliest time of disposition set forth in the notification is sent within a reasonable time before the disposition.

9613. Except in a consumer-goods transaction, the following rules apply:

(1) The contents of a notification of disposition are sufficient if the notification does all of the following:

(A) It describes the debtor and the secured party.

(B) It describes the collateral that is the subject of the intended disposition.

(C) It states the method of intended disposition.

(D) It states that the debtor is entitled to an accounting of the unpaid indebtedness and states the charge, if any, for an accounting.

(E) It states the time and place of a public disposition or the time after which any other disposition is to be made.

(2) Whether the contents of a notification that lacks any of the information specified in paragraph (1) are nevertheless sufficient is a question of fact.

(3) The contents of a notification providing substantially the information specified in paragraph (1) are sufficient, even if the notification includes either of the following:

(A) Information not specified by that paragraph.

(B) Minor errors that are not seriously misleading.

(4) A particular phrasing of the notification is not required.

(5) The following form of notification and the form appearing in subdivision (3) of Section 9614, when completed, each provides sufficient information:

NOTIFICATION OF DISPOSITION OF COLLATERAL

To: ____

(Name of debtor, obligor, or other person to which the notification is sent)

From: ______________________________________

(Name, address, and telephone number of secured party)

Name of Debtor(s): ______________________________________

____

(Include only if debtor(s) are not an addressee)

(For a public disposition:)

We will sell (or lease or license, as applicable) the ______________________

(describe collateral)

(to the highest qualified bidder in public as follows:)

Day and Date: ______________________

Time: ______________________

Place: ______________________

(For a private disposition:)

We will sell (or license, as applicable) the ______________________

(describe collateral)

privately sometime after ______________________

(day and date)

You are entitled to an accounting of the unpaid indebtedness secured by the property that we intend to sell (or lease or license, as applicable) (for a charge of $ __________).

You may request an accounting by calling us at ______________________

(telephone number)

9614. In a consumer-goods transaction, the following rules apply:

(1) A notification of disposition must provide all of the following information:

(A) The information specified in subdivision (1) of Section 9613.

(B) A description of any liability for a deficiency of the person to which the notification is sent.

(C) A telephone number from which the amount that must be paid to the secured party to redeem the collateral under Section 9623 is available.

(D) A telephone number or mailing address from which additional information concerning the disposition and the obligation secured is available.

(2) A particular phrasing of the notification is not required.

(3) The following form of notification, when completed, provides sufficient information:

(Name and address of secured party)

(Date)

NOTICE OF OUR PLAN TO SELL PROPERTY

(Name and address of any obligor who is also a debtor)

Subject:

(Identification of Transaction)

We have your ______________________, because you broke promises in our
(describe collateral)
agreement.

(For a public disposition:)

We will sell ______________________________________, at public sale.
(describe collateral)

A sale could include a ease or license. The sale will be held as follows:

Day and Date: ____________________

Time: ____________________

Place: ____________________

You may attend the sale and bring bidders if you want.

(For a public disposition pursuant to Section 9614(7)(A) or (7)(B)):

We will sell ______________________________________
(describe type of motor vehicle)

beginning on __________________ by offering it for retail sale or lease to the
(date)

general public through (select the applicable provision):

(A) Name of dealer ______________________________

Address of dealer ______________________________

You may inspect the motor vehicle and encourage people to purchase or lease it.

(or)

(B) Advertising it for sale to the general public to be purchased from

____
(name of secured creditor)

at ______________________________
(address where vehicle is to be sold)

You may inspect the motor vehicle and encourage people to purchase or lease it.

(For a private disposition:)

We will sell ______________ at private sale sometime
(describe collateral)

after ______________________________
(date)

A sale could include a lease or license.

The money that we get from the sale (after paying our costs) will reduce the amount you owe. If we get less money than you
owe, you ______________________________
(will or will not, as applicable)

still owe us the difference. If we get more money than you owe, you will get the extra money, unless we must pay it to someone else.

You can get the property back at any time before we sell it by paying us the full amount you owe (not just the past due payments), including our expenses. To learn the exact amount you must pay, call us at ______________
(telephone number)

If you want us to explain to you in writing how we have figured the amount that you owe us, you may call us at ______________ (or write us at
(telephone number)

______________________________)
(secured party's address)

and request a written explanation. (We will charge you $ ________ for the explanation if we sent you another written explanation of the amount you owe us within the last six months.)

If you need more information about the sale call us at ______________
(telephone number)

(or write us at ______________________________).
(secured party's address)

We are sending this notice to the following other people who have an interest in

______________________ or who owe money under your
(describe collateral)

agreement:

____
(Names of all other debtors and obligors, if any)

(4) A notification in the form of subdivision (3) is sufficient, even if additional information appears at the end of the form.

(5) A notification in the form of subdivision (3) is sufficient, even if it includes errors in information not required by subdivision (1), unless the error is misleading with respect to rights arising under this division.

(6) If a notification under this section is not in the form of subdivision (3), law other than this division determines the effect of including information not required by subdivision (1).

(7) If the collateral is a motor vehicle, a public disposition includes, but is not limited to, the following defined categories:

(A) Retail disposition by a retail seller of motor vehicles who offers the collateral for sale or lease to the general public in the same manner as goods that the seller disposes of on the seller's own behalf.

(B) Retail disposition made subsequent to advertising in a publication with a recognized ability to attract retail motor vehicle buyers and lessees and in a manner designed to reach the retail buying and leasing public for vehicles of that type and condition.

(8) For dispositions under subparagraphs (A) and (B) of paragraph (7), the secured creditor shall ensure that the consumer has reasonable access to the motor vehicle in question in order to be able to exercise the right to inspect the motor vehicle.

(9) Nothing in this section shall be construed to alter or disturb any right to inspect a consumer good prior to sale under existing law.

9615.

(a) A secured party shall apply or pay over for application the cash proceeds of disposition under Section 9610 in the following order to each of the following:

(1) The reasonable expenses of retaking, holding, preparing for disposition, processing, and disposing, and, to the extent provided for by agreement and not prohibited by law, reasonable attorney's fees, and legal expenses incurred by the secured party.

(2) The satisfaction of obligations secured by the security interest or agricultural lien under which the disposition is made.

(3) The satisfaction of obligations secured by any subordinate security interest in or other subordinate lien on the collateral and to the satisfaction of any subordinate attachment lien or execution lien pursuant to subdivision (b) of Section 701.040 of the Code of Civil Procedure if both of the following conditions are satisfied:

(A) The secured party receives from the holder of the subordinate security interest or other lien an authenticated demand for proceeds or notice of the levy of attachment or execution before distribution of the proceeds is completed.

(B) In a case in which a consignor has an interest in the collateral, the subordinate security interest, or other lien is senior to the interest of the consignor.

(4) A secured party that is a consignor of the collateral if the secured party receives from the consignor an authenticated demand for proceeds before distribution of the proceeds is completed.

(b) If requested by a secured party, a holder of a subordinate security interest, or other lien shall furnish reasonable proof of the interest or lien within a reasonable time. Unless the holder does so, the secured party need not comply with the holder's demand under paragraph (3) of subdivision (a).

(c) A secured party need not apply or pay over for application noncash proceeds of disposition under Section 9610 unless the failure to do so would be commercially unreasonable. A secured party that applies or pays over for application noncash proceeds shall do so in a commercially reasonable manner.

(d) If the security interest under which a disposition is made secures payment or performance of an obligation, after making the payments, and applications required by subdivision (a) and permitted by subdivision (c), both of the following apply:

(1) Unless paragraph (4) of subdivision (a) requires the secured party to apply or pay over cash proceeds to a consignor, the secured party shall account to, and pay a debtor for any surplus except as provided in Section 701.040 of the Code of Civil Procedure.

(2) Subject to subdivision (b) of Section 9626, the obligor is liable for any deficiency.

(e) If the underlying transaction is a sale of accounts, chattel paper, (1) payment intangibles, or promissory notes, both of the following apply:

(1) The debtor is not entitled to any surplus.

(A) The obligor is not liable for any deficiency.

(2) Subdivision (b) of Section 701.040 of the Code of Civil Procedure relating to the payment of proceeds and the liability of the secured party applies only if the security agreement provides that the debtor is entitled to any surplus.

(f) The surplus or deficiency following a disposition is calculated based on the amount of proceeds that would have been realized in a disposition complying with this chapter to a transferee other than the secured party, a person related to the secured party, or a secondary obligor if both of the following apply:

(1) The transferee in the disposition is the secured party, a person related to the secured party, or a secondary obligor.

(2) The amount of proceeds of the disposition is significantly below the range of proceeds that a complying disposition to a person other than the secured party, a person related to the secured party, or a secondary obligor would have brought.

(g) The following rules apply with respect to a secured party that receives cash proceeds of a disposition in good faith and without knowledge that the receipt violates the rights of the holder of a security interest or other lien that is not subordinate to the security interest or agricultural lien under which the disposition is made:

(1) The secured party takes the cash proceeds free of the security interest or other lien.

(2) The secured party is not obligated to apply the proceeds of the disposition to the satisfaction of obligations secured by the security interest or other lien.

(3) The secured party is not obligated to account to or pay the holder of the security interest or other lien for any surplus.

9616.

(a) In this section:

(1) "Explanation" means a writing that contains all of the following:

(A) States the amount of the surplus or deficiency.

(B) Provides an explanation in accordance with subdivision (c) of how the secured party calculated the surplus or deficiency.

(C) States, if applicable, that future debits, credits, charges, including additional credit service charges or interest, rebates, and expenses may affect the amount of the surplus or deficiency.

(D) Provides a telephone number or mailing address from which additional information concerning the transaction is available.

(2) "Request" means a record that is all of the following:

(A) Authenticated by a debtor or consumer obligor.

(B) Requesting that the recipient provide an explanation.

(C) Sent after disposition of the collateral under Section 9610.

(b) In a consumer-goods transaction in which the debtor is entitled to a surplus or a consumer obligor is liable for a deficiency under Section 9615, the secured party shall do either of the following:

(1) Send an explanation to the debtor or consumer obligor, as applicable, after the disposition, and in accordance with both of the following:

(A) Before or when the secured party accounts to the debtor and pays any surplus or first makes written demand on the consumer obligor after the disposition for payment of the deficiency.

(B) Within 14 days after receipt of a request.

(2) In the case of a consumer obligor who is liable for a deficiency, within 14 days after receipt of a request, send to the consumer obligor a record waiving the secured party's right to a deficiency.

(c) To comply with subparagraph (B) of paragraph (1) of subdivision (a), a writing must provide the following information in the following order:

(1) The aggregate amount of obligations secured by the security interest under which the disposition was made, and if the amount reflects a rebate of unearned interest or credit service charge, an indication of

that fact, calculated as of a specified date in accordance with either of the following:

(A) If the secured party takes or receives possession of the collateral after default, not more than 35 days before the secured party takes, or receives possession.

(B) If the secured party takes or receives possession of the collateral before default or does not take possession of the collateral, not more than 35 days before the disposition.

(2) The amount of proceeds of the disposition.

(3) The aggregate amount of the obligations after deducting the amount of proceeds.

(4) The amount, in the aggregate or by type, and types of expenses, including expenses of retaking, holding, preparing for disposition, processing, and disposing of the collateral, and attorney's fees secured by the collateral, which are known to the secured party and relate to the current disposition.

(5) The amount, in the aggregate, or by type, and types of credits, including rebates of interest or credit service charges, to which the obligor is known to be entitled, and which are not reflected in the amount in paragraph (1).

(6) The amount of the surplus or deficiency.

(d) A particular phrasing of the explanation is not required. An explanation complying substantially with the requirements of subdivision (a) is sufficient, even if it includes minor errors that are not seriously misleading.

(e) A debtor or consumer obligor is entitled without charge to one response to a request under this section during any six-month period in which the secured party did not send to the debtor or consumer obligor an explanation pursuant to paragraph (1) of subdivision (b). The secured party may require payment of a charge not exceeding twenty-five dollars ($25) for each additional response.

9617.

(a) A secured party's disposition of collateral after default does all of the following:

(1) Transfers to a transferee for value all of the debtor's rights in the collateral.

(2) Discharges the security interest under which the disposition is made.

(3) Discharges any subordinate security interest or other subordinate lien.

(b) A transferee that acts in good faith takes free of the rights and interests described in subdivision (a), even if the secured party fails to comply with this division, or the requirements of any judicial proceeding.

(c) If a transferee does not take free of the rights and interests described in subdivision (a), the transferee takes the collateral subject to all of the following:

(1) The debtor's rights in the collateral.

(2) The security interest or agricultural lien under which the disposition is made.

(3) Any other security interest or other lien.

9618.

(a) A secondary obligor acquires the rights and becomes obligated to perform the duties of the secured party after any of the following occurs:

(1) The secondary obligor receives an assignment of a secured obligation from the secured party.

(2) The secondary obligor receives a transfer of collateral from the secured party and agrees to accept the rights and assume the duties of the secured party.

(3) The secondary obligor is subrogated to the rights of a secured party with respect to collateral.

(b) Both of the following rules apply with respect to an assignment, transfer, or subrogation described in subdivision (a):

(1) It is not a disposition of collateral under Section 9610.

(2) It relieves the secured party of further duties under this division.

9619.

(a) In this section, "transfer statement" means a record authenticated by a secured party stating all of the following:

(1) That the debtor has defaulted in connection with an obligation secured by specified collateral.

(2) That the secured party has exercised its postdefault remedies with respect to the collateral.

(3) That, by reason of the exercise, a transferee has acquired the rights of the debtor in the collateral.

(4) The name and mailing address of the secured party, debtor, and transferee.

(b) A transfer statement entitles the transferee to the transfer of record of all rights of the debtor in the collateral specified in the statement in any official filing, recording, registration, or certificate of title system covering the collateral. If a transfer statement is presented with the applicable fee and request form to the official or office responsible for maintaining the system, the official, or office shall do all of the following:

(1) Accept the transfer statement.

(2) Promptly amend its records to reflect the transfer.

(3) If applicable, issue a new appropriate certificate of title in the name of the transferee.

(c) A transfer of the record or legal title to collateral to a secured party under subdivision (b) or otherwise is not of itself a disposition of collateral under this division and does not of itself relieve the secured party of its duties under this division.

9620.

(a) Except as otherwise provided in subdivision (g), a secured party may accept collateral in full, or partial satisfaction of the obligation it secures only if all of the following conditions are satisfied:

(1) The debtor consents to the acceptance under subdivision (c).

(2) The secured party does not receive, within the time set forth in subdivision (d), a notification of objection to the proposal authenticated by either of the following:

(A) A person to which the secured party was required to send a proposal under Section 9621.

(B) Any other person, other than the debtor, holding an interest in the collateral subordinate to the security interest that is the subject of the proposal.

(3) If the collateral is consumer goods, the collateral is not in the possession of the debtor when the debtor consents to the acceptance.

(4) Subdivision (e) does not require the secured party to dispose of the collateral or the debtor waives the requirement pursuant to Section 9624.

(b) A purported or apparent acceptance of collateral under this section is ineffective unless both of the following conditions are satisfied:

(1) The secured party consents to the acceptance in an authenticated record or sends a proposal to the debtor.

(2) The conditions of subdivision (a) are met.

(c) For purposes of this section both of the following rules apply:

(1) A debtor consents to an acceptance of collateral in partial satisfaction of the obligation it secures only if the debtor agrees to the terms of the acceptance in a record authenticated after default.

(2) A debtor consents to an acceptance of collateral in full satisfaction of the obligation it secures only if the debtor agrees to the terms of the acceptance in a record authenticated after default or the secured party does all of the following:

(A) Sends to the debtor after default a proposal that is unconditional or subject only to a condition that collateral not in the possession of the secured party be preserved or maintained.

(B) In the proposal, proposes to accept collateral in full satisfaction of the obligation it secures.

(C) Does not receive a notification of objection authenticated by the debtor within 20 days after the proposal is sent.

(d) To be effective under paragraph (2) of subdivision (a), a notification of objection must be received by the secured party as follows:

(1) In the case of a person to which the proposal was sent pursuant to Section 9621, within 20 days after notification was sent to that person.

(2) In other cases, in accordance with either of the following:

(A) Within 20 days after the last notification was sent pursuant to Section 9621.

(B) If a notification was not sent, before the debtor consents to the acceptance under subdivision (c).

(e) A secured party that has taken possession of collateral shall dispose of the collateral pursuant to Section 9610 within the time specified in subdivision (f) if either of the following conditions has been satisfied:

(1) Sixty percent of the cash price has been paid in the case of a purchase money security interest in consumer goods.

(2) Sixty percent of the principal amount of the obligation secured has been paid in the case of a nonpurchase money security interest in consumer goods.

(f) To comply with subdivision (e), the secured party shall dispose of the collateral within either of the following time periods:

(1) Within 90 days after taking possession.

(2) Within any longer period to which the debtor and all secondary obligors have agreed in an agreement to that effect entered into and authenticated after default.

(g) In a consumer transaction, a secured party may not accept collateral in partial satisfaction of the obligation it secures.

9621.

(a) A secured party that desires to accept collateral in full or partial satisfaction of the obligation it secures shall send its proposal to all of the following persons:

(1) Any person from which the secured party has received, before the debtor consented to the acceptance, an authenticated notification of a claim of an interest in the collateral.

(2) Any other secured party or lienholder that, 10 days before the debtor consented to the acceptance, held a security interest in, or other lien on the collateral perfected by the filing of a financing statement that satisfied all of the following conditions:

(A) It identified the collateral.

(B) It was indexed under the debtor's name as of that date.

(C) It was filed in the office or offices in which to file a financing statement against the debtor covering the collateral as of that date.

(3) Any other secured party that, 10 days before the debtor consented to the acceptance, held a security interest in the collateral perfected by

compliance with a statute, regulation, or treaty described in subdivision (a) of Section 9311.

(b) A secured party that desires to accept collateral in partial satisfaction of the obligation it secures shall send its proposal to any secondary obligor in addition to the persons described in subdivision (a).

9622.

(a) A secured party's acceptance of collateral in full or partial satisfaction of the obligation it secures does all of the following:

(1) It discharges the obligation to the extent consented to by the debtor.

(2) It transfers to the secured party all of a debtor's rights in the collateral.

(3) It discharges the security interest or agricultural lien that is the subject of the debtor's consent and any subordinate security interest or other subordinate lien.

(4) It terminates any other subordinate interest.

(b) A subordinate interest is discharged or terminated under subdivision (a), even if the secured party fails to comply with this division.

9623.

(a) A debtor, any secondary obligor, or any other secured party or lienholder may redeem collateral.

(b) To redeem collateral, a person shall tender both of the following:

(1) Fulfillment of all obligations secured by the collateral.

(2) The reasonable expenses and attorney's fees described in paragraph (1) of subdivision (a) of Section 9615.

(c) A redemption may occur at any time before a secured party has done any of the following:

(1) Collected collateral under Section 9607.

(2) Disposed of collateral or entered into a contract for its disposition under Section 9610.

(3) Accepted collateral in full or partial satisfaction of the obligation it secures under Section 9622.

9624.

(a) A debtor or secondary obligor may waive the right to notification of disposition of collateral under Section 9611 only by an agreement to that effect entered into and authenticated after default.

(b) A debtor may waive the right to require disposition of collateral under subdivision (e) of Section 9620 only by an agreement to that effect entered into and authenticated after default.

(c) Except in a consumer-goods transaction, a debtor or secondary obligor may waive the right to redeem collateral under Section 9623 only by an agreement to that effect entered into, and authenticated after default.

9625.

(a) If it is established that a secured party is not proceeding in accordance with this division, a court may order or restrain collection, enforcement, or disposition of collateral on appropriate terms and conditions.

(b) Subject to subdivisions (c), (d), and (f), a person is liable for damages in the amount of any loss caused by a failure to comply with this division. Loss caused by a failure to comply may include loss resulting from the debtor's inability to obtain, or increased costs of, alternative financing.

(c) Except as otherwise provided in Section 9628, a person that, at the time of the failure, was a debtor, was an obligor, or held a security interest in or other lien on the collateral may recover damages under subdivision (b) for its loss.

(d) A debtor whose deficiency is eliminated under Section 9626 may recover damages for the loss of any surplus. However, in a transaction other than a consumer transaction, a debtor or secondary obligor whose deficiency is eliminated or reduced under Section 9626 may not otherwise recover under subdivision (b) for noncompliance with the provisions of this chapter relating to collection, enforcement, disposition, or acceptance.

(e) In addition to any damages recoverable under subdivision (b), the debtor, consumer obligor, or person named as a debtor in a filed record, as applicable, may recover five hundred dollars ($500) in each case from any of the following persons:

(1) A person that fails to comply with Section 9208.

(2) A person that fails to comply with Section 9209.

(3) A person that files a record that the person is not entitled to file under subdivision (a) of Section 9509.

(4) A person that fails to cause the secured party of record to file or send a termination statement as required by subdivision (a) or (c) of Section 9513.

(5) A person that fails to comply with paragraph (1) of subdivision (b) of Section 9616 and whose failure is part of a pattern, or consistent with a practice, of noncompliance.

(6) A person that fails to comply with paragraph (2) of subdivision (b) of Section 9616.

(f) A debtor or consumer obligor may recover damages under subdivision (b) and, in addition, five hundred dollars ($500) in each case from a person that, without reasonable cause, fails to comply with a request under Section 9210. A recipient of a request under Section 9210 which never claimed an interest in the collateral or obligations that are the subject of a request under that section has a reasonable excuse for failure to comply with the request within the meaning of this subdivision.

(g) If a secured party fails to comply with a request regarding a list of collateral or a statement of account under Section 9210, the secured party may claim a security interest only as shown in the list or statement included in the request as against a person that is reasonably misled by the failure.

9626.

(a) In an action arising from a transaction, other than a consumer transaction, in which the amount of a deficiency or surplus is in issue, the following rules apply:

(1) A secured party need not prove compliance with the provisions of this chapter relating to collection, enforcement, disposition, or acceptance unless the debtor or a secondary obligor places the secured party's compliance in issue.

(2) If the secured party's compliance is placed in issue, the secured party has the burden of establishing that the collection, enforcement, disposition, or acceptance was conducted in accordance with this chapter.

(3) Except as otherwise provided in Section 9628, if a secured party fails to prove that the collection, enforcement, disposition, or acceptance was conducted in accordance with the provisions of this chapter relating to collection, enforcement, disposition, or acceptance, the liability of a debtor or a secondary obligor for a deficiency is limited to an amount by which the sum of the secured obligation, expenses, and attorney's fees exceeds the greater of either of the following:

(A) The proceeds of the collection, enforcement, disposition, or acceptance.

(B) The amount of proceeds that would have been realized had the noncomplying secured party proceeded in accordance with the provisions of this chapter relating to collection, enforcement, disposition, or acceptance.

(4) For purposes of subparagraph (B) of paragraph (3), the amount of proceeds that would have been realized is equal to the sum of the secured obligation, expenses, and attorney's fees unless the secured party proves that the amount is less than that sum.

(5) If a deficiency or surplus is calculated under subdivision (f) of Section 9615, the debtor or obligor has the burden of establishing that the amount of proceeds of the disposition is significantly below the range of prices that a complying disposition to a person other than the secured party, a person related to the secured party, or a secondary obligor would have brought.

(b) In a consumer transaction, the following rules apply:

(1) In an action in which a deficiency or a surplus is an issue:

(A) A secured party has the burden of proving compliance with the provisions of this chapter relating to collection, enforcement, disposition, and acceptance whether or not the debtor or a secondary obligor places the secured party's compliance in issue.

(B) If a deficiency or surplus is calculated under subdivision (f) of Section 9615, the secured party has the burden of establishing that the amount of proceeds of the disposition is not significantly below the range of prices that a complying disposition to a person other than the secured party, a person related to the secured party, or a secondary obligor would have brought.

(2) The debtor or any secondary obligor is liable for any deficiency only if all of the following conditions are met:

(A) It is not otherwise agreed or otherwise provided in the Retail Installment Sales Act (Chapter 1 (commencing with Section 1801), Title 2, Part 4, Division 3, Civil Code), and, in particular, Section 1812.5 of the Civil Code or any other statute.

(B) The debtor and obligor were given notice, in accordance with Sections 9611, 9612, and 9613, or Section 9614, as applicable, of the disposition of the collateral.

(C) The collection, enforcement, disposition, and acceptance by the secured party were conducted in good faith and in a commercially reasonable manner.

(3) Upon entry of a final judgment that the debtor or obligor is not liable for a deficiency by reason of paragraph (2) or subdivision (f) of Section 9615, the secured party may neither obtain a deficiency judgment nor retain a security interest in any other collateral of the debtor or obligor that secured the indebtedness for which the debtor or obligor is no longer liable.

(4) If, subsequent to a disposition that does not satisfy any one or more of the conditions set forth in paragraph (2), or subsequent to a disposition that is subject to subdivision (f) of Section 9615, the secured party disposes pursuant to this section of other collateral securing the same indebtedness, the debtor or obligor may, to the extent he or she is no longer liable for a deficiency judgment by reason of paragraph (2) or subdivision (f) of Section 9615, recover the proceeds realized from the subsequent dispositions, as well as any damages to which the debtor may be entitled if the subsequent disposition is itself noncomplying or otherwise wrongful.

(5) Nothing herein shall deprive the debtor of any right to recover damages from the secured party under subdivision (b) of Section 9625, or to offset any such damages against any claim by the secured party for a deficiency, or of any right or remedy to which the debtor may be entitled under any other law. A debtor or obligor in a consumer transaction shall not have any damages owed to it reduced by the amount of any deficiency that would have resulted had the disposition of the collateral by the secured party been conducted in conformity with this division.

(6) The secured party shall account to the debtor for any surplus, except as provided in Section 701.040 of the Code of Civil Procedure.

9627.

(a) The fact that a greater amount could have been obtained by a collection, enforcement, disposition, or acceptance at a different time or in a different method from that selected by the secured party is not of itself sufficient to preclude the secured party from establishing that the collection, enforcement, disposition, or acceptance was made in a commercially reasonable manner.

(b) A disposition of collateral is made in a commercially reasonable manner if the disposition satisfies any of the following conditions:

(1) It is made in the usual manner on any recognized market.

(2) It is made at the price current in any recognized market at the time of the disposition.

(3) It is made otherwise in conformity with reasonable commercial practices among dealers in the type of property that was the subject of the disposition.

(c) A collection, enforcement, disposition, or acceptance is commercially reasonable if it has been approved in or by any of the following:

(1) In a judicial proceeding.

(2) By a bona fide creditors' committee.

(3) By a representative of creditors.

(4) By an assignee for the benefit of creditors.

(d) Approval under subdivision (c) need not be obtained, and lack of approval does not mean that the collection, enforcement, disposition, or acceptance is not commercially reasonable.

9628.

(a) Unless a secured party knows that a person is a debtor or obligor, knows the identity of the person, and knows how to communicate with the person, both of the following rules apply:

(1) The secured party is not liable to the person, or to a secured party or lienholder that has filed a financing statement against the person, for failure to comply with this division.

(2) The secured party's failure to comply with this division does not affect the liability of the person for a deficiency.

(b) A secured party is not liable because of its status as secured party to either of the following persons:

(1) To a person that is a debtor or obligor, unless the secured party knows all of the following:

(A) That the person is a debtor or obligor.

(B) The identity of the person.

(C) How to communicate with the person.

(2) To a secured party or lienholder that has filed a financing statement against a person, unless the secured party knows both of the following:

(A) That the person is a debtor.

(B) The identity of the person.

(c) A secured party is not liable to any person, and a person's liability for a deficiency is not affected, because of any act or omission arising out of the secured party's reasonable belief that a transaction is not a consumer-goods transaction or a consumer transaction or that goods are not consumer goods, if the secured party's belief is based on its reasonable reliance on either of the following representations:

(1) A debtor's representation concerning the purpose for which collateral was to be used, acquired, or held.

(2) An obligor's representation concerning the purpose for which a secured obligation was incurred.

(d) A secured party is not liable under paragraph (2) of subdivision (c) of Section 9625 more than once with respect to any one secured obligation.

9629. No renunciation or modification by the debtor of any of his or her rights under this chapter as to consumer goods shall be valid or enforceable unless the renunciation or modification is in consideration of a waiver by the secured party of any right to a deficiency on the debt.

9701. This division shall become operative on July 1, 2001.

9702.

(a) Except as otherwise provided in this chapter, this division applies to a transaction or lien within its scope, even if the transaction or lien was entered into or created before this division takes effect.

(b) Except as otherwise provided in subdivision (c) and in Sections 9703 to 9709, inclusive, both of the following rules apply:

(1) Transactions and liens that were not governed by former Division 9, were validly entered into or created before July 1, 2001, and would be subject to this act if they had been entered into or created after July 1, 2001, and the rights, duties, and interests flowing from those transactions and liens remain valid after July 1, 2001.

(2) The transactions and liens may be terminated, completed, consummated, and enforced as required or permitted by this division or by the law that otherwise would apply if this division had not taken effect.

(c) This division does not affect an action, case, or proceeding commenced before July 1, 2001.

9703.

(a) A security interest that is enforceable immediately before July 1, 2001, and would have priority over the rights of a person that becomes a lien creditor at that time is a perfected security interest under this division if, on July 1, 2001, the applicable requirements for enforceability and perfection under this division are satisfied without further action.

(b) Except as otherwise provided in Section 9705, if, immediately before July 1, 2001, a security interest is enforceable and would have priority over the rights of a person that becomes a lien creditor at that time, but the applicable requirements for enforceability or perfection under this division are not satisfied on July 1, 2001, when all of the following rules apply with respect to the security interest:

(1) It is a perfected security interest until July 1, 2002.

(2) It remains enforceable thereafter only if the security interest becomes enforceable under Section 9203 before July 1, 2002.

(3) It remains perfected thereafter only if the applicable requirements for perfection under this division are satisfied before July 1, 2002.

9704. All of the following rules apply with respect to a security interest that is enforceable immediately before July 1, 2001, but which would be subordinate to the rights of a person that becomes a lien creditor at that time:

(1) It remains an enforceable security interest until July 1, 2002.

(2) It remains enforceable thereafter if the security interest becomes enforceable under Section 9203 on July 1, 2001, or on July 1, 2002.

(3) It becomes perfected in either of the following ways:

(A) Without further action, on July 1, 2001, if the applicable requirements for perfection under this division are satisfied on or before that time.

(B) When the applicable requirements for perfection are satisfied if the requirements are satisfied after that time.

9705.

(a) If action, other than the filing of a financing statement, is taken before July 1, 2001, and the action would have resulted in priority of a security interest over the rights of a person that becomes a lien creditor had the security interest become enforceable before July 1, 2001, the action is effective to perfect a security interest that attaches under this division on or before July 1, 2002. An attached security interest becomes unperfected on July 1, 2002, unless the security interest becomes a perfected security interest under this division before that date.

(b) The filing of a financing statement before July 1, 2001, is effective to perfect a security interest to the extent the filing would satisfy the applicable requirements for perfection under this division.

(c) This division does not render ineffective an effective financing statement that, before July 1, 2001, is filed and satisfies the applicable requirements for perfection under the law of the jurisdiction governing perfection as provided in former Section 9103. However, except as otherwise provided in subdivisions (d) and (e) and in Section 9706, the financing statement ceases to be effective at the earlier of either of the following:

(1) The time the financing statement would have ceased to be effective under the law of the jurisdiction in which it is filed.

(2) June 30, 2006.

(d) The filing of a continuation statement after July 1, 2001, does not continue the effectiveness of the financing statement filed before July 1, 2001. However, upon the timely filing of a continuation statement after July 1,

2001, and in accordance with the law of the jurisdiction governing perfection as provided in Chapter 3 (commencing with Section 9301), the effectiveness of a financing statement filed in the same office in that jurisdiction before July 1, 2001, continues for the period provided by the law of that jurisdiction.

(e) Paragraph (2) of subdivision (c) applies to a financing statement that, before July 1, 2001, is filed against a transmitting utility and satisfies the applicable requirements for perfection under the law of the jurisdiction governing perfection as provided in former Section 9103 only to the extent that Chapter 3 (commencing with Section 9301) provides that the law of a jurisdiction other than the jurisdiction in which the financing statement is filed governs perfection of a security interest in collateral covered by the financing statement.

(f) A financing statement that includes a financing statement filed before July 1, 2001, and a continuation statement filed after July 1, 2001, is effective only to the extent that it satisfies the requirements of Chapter 5 (commencing with Section 9501) for an initial financing statement.

9706.

(a) The filing of an initial financing statement in the office specified in Section 9501 continues the effectiveness of a financing statement filed before July 1, 2001, if all of the following conditions are satisfied:

(1) The filing of an initial financing statement in that office would be effective to perfect a security interest under this division.

(2) The pre-effective-date financing statement was filed in an office in another state or another office in this state.

(3) The initial financing statement satisfies subdivision (c).

(b) The filing of an initial financing statement under subdivision (a) continues the effectiveness of the pre-effective-date financing statement for the following periods:

(1) If the initial financing statement is filed before July 1, 2001, for the period provided in former Section 9403 with respect to a financing statement.

(2) If the initial financing statement is filed after July 1, 2001, for the period provided in Section 9515 with respect to an initial financing statement.

(c) To be effective for purposes of subdivision (a), an initial financing statement must do all of the following:

(1) Satisfy the requirements of Chapter 5 (commencing with Section 9501) for an initial financing statement.

(2) Identify the pre-effective-date financing statement by indicating the office in which the financing statement was filed and providing the dates of filing and file numbers, if any, of the financing statement and of the most recent continuation statement filed with respect to the financing statement.

(3) Indicate that the pre-effective-date financing statement remains effective.

9707.

(a) In this section, "pre-effective-date financing statement" means a financing statement filed before the date that this section becomes operative.

(b) After the date this section becomes operative, a person may add or delete collateral covered by, continue or terminate the effectiveness of, or otherwise amend the information provided in, a pre-effective-date financing statement only in accordance with the law of the jurisdiction governing perfection as provided in Chapter 3 (commencing with Section 9301). However, the effectiveness of a pre-effective-date financing statement also may be terminated in accordance with the law of the jurisdiction in which the financing statement is filed.

(c) Except as otherwise provided by subdivision (d), if the law of this state governs perfection of a security interest, the information in a pre-effective-date financing statement may be amended after the date this section becomes operative only if any of the following occur:

(1) The pre-effective-date financing statement and an amendment are filed in the office specified in Section 9501.

(2) An amendment is filed in the office specified in Section 9501 concurrently with, or after the filing in that office of, an initial financing statement that satisfies subdivision (c) of Section 9706.

(3) An initial financing statement that provides the information as amended and satisfies subdivision (c) of Section 9706 is filed in the office specified in Section 9501.

(d) If the law of this state governs perfection of a security interest, the effectiveness of a pre-effective-date financing statement may be continued only under subdivisions (d) and (f) of Section 9705 or Section 9706.

(e) Whether or not the law of this state governs the perfection of a security interest, the effectiveness of a pre-effective-date financing statement filed in this state may be terminated after the date that this section becomes operative by filing a termination statement in the office in which the pre-effective-date financing statement is filed, unless an initial filing statement that satisfies subdivision (c) of Section 9706 has been filed in the office specified by the law of the jurisdiction governing perfection as provided in Chapter 3 (commencing with Section 9301) as the office in which to file a financing statement.

9708. A person may file an initial financing statement or a continuation statement under this chapter if both of the following conditions are satisfied:

(1) The secured party of record authorizes the filing.

(2) The filing is necessary under this chapter to do either of the following:

(A) To continue the effectiveness of a financing statement filed before July 1, 2001.

(B) To perfect or continue the perfection of a security interest.

9709.

(a) This division determines priority of conflicting claims to collateral. However, if the relative priorities of the claims were established before July 1, 2001, former Division 9 (commencing with Section 9101) determines priority.

(b) For purposes of subdivision (a) of Section 9322, the priority of a security interest that becomes enforceable under Section 9203 dates from July 1, 2001, if the security interest is perfected under this division by the filing of a financing statement before July 1, 2001, which would not have been effective to perfect the security interest under former Division 9 (commencing with Section 9101). This subdivision does not apply to conflicting security interests each of which is perfected by the filing of such a financing statement.

APPENDIX II

FILING PLACES FOR UCC FINANCING STATEMENT UNDER REVISED ARTICLE 9—PREPARED BY AMERICAN BANK LAWYER*

Alabama (Rev. 9 effective Jan. 1, 2002)
UCC Division
Secretary of State
P.O. Box 5616
Montgomery, AL 36103-5616
(334) 242-5231

Alaska: UCC Central File Systems Office
Dept. of Natural Resources
550 West 7th Ave, Suite 1200-A
Anchorage, AK 99503
(907) 269-8899

Arizona: UCC Division
Secretary of State
State Capitol, West Wing, 7th Flr
Phoenix, AZ 85007
(602) 542-7386

Arkansas: UCC Division
Secretary of State
501 Woodlane, Suite 310
Little Rock, AR 72201
(501) 682-5078 or (888) 233-0325

California: UCC Division
Secretary of State
P.O. Box 942835
Sacramento, CA 94235-0001
(916) 653-3516

Colorado: UCC Division
Secretary of State
1560 Broadway, Ste 200
Denver, CO 80202
(303) 894-2200 x343 FAX (303) 894-2242

Connecticut (Rev. 9 effective Oct. 1, 2001)
UCC Division
Secretary of State
P.O. Box 15470
30 Trinity Street
Hartford, CT 06106
(860) 509-6004 FAX (860) 509-6068

Delaware: UCC Division
Secretary of State
P.O. Box 793
Dover, DE 19903
(302) 739-3077

*Reprinted with permission of American Bank Lawyer

District of Columbia: UCC Recorder
District of Columbia Recorder of Deeds
515 D. Street N.W.
Washington, D.C. 20001
(202) 727-5374 FAX (202) 727-9629

Florida (Rev. 9 effective Jan. 1, 2002)
UCC Division
Secretary of State
P.O. Box 5588
Tallahasssee, FL
(850) 487-6055

Georgia: Secretary of State
Trademark Division
2 Martin Luther King
Room 315, W Tower
Atlanta, GA 30334
(404) 656-2861

Hawaii: UCC Division
Bureau of Conveyances
P.O. Box 2867
Honolulu, HI 96803
(808) 587-0154

Idaho: UCC Division
Secretary of State
P.O. Box 83720
Boise, ID 83720-0080
(208) 334-3191 FAX (208) 334-2847

Illinois: Business Services
Secretary of State
501 S. Second Street, Ste 328
Springfield, IL 62756
(217) 782-6961

Indiana: UCC Division
Secretary of State
302 West Washington St.
Room E-018
Indianapolis, IN 46204
(317) 232-6576

Iowa: Business Services Division
Secretary of State
2nd Floor, Hoover Bldg
1305 East Walnut
Des Moines, IA 50319
(515) 281-5204

Kansas: UCC Division
Secretary of State
First Floor, Memorial Hall
120 SW 10th Ave
Topeka, KS 66612-1594
(785) 296-4564 FAX (785) 296-3659

Kentucky: UCC Division
Secretary of State
Room 86, State Capitol
P.O. Box 1470
Frankfort, KY 40602-1470
(502) 564-3490 FAX (502) 564-5687

Louisiana: UCC Records
Secretary of State
P.O. Box 94125
Baton Rouge, LA 70804-9125
(800) 256-3758 or (225) 342-0316

Maine: UCC Filing Section
Secretary of State
101 State House Station
Augusta, ME 04333-0101
(207) 287-4177

Maryland: UCC Division
Dept of Assessments & Taxation
301 West Preston St.
Baltimore, MD 21201
(410) 767-1340

Massachusetts: Massachusetts Corporation Division
Secretary of the Commonwealth
One Ashburton Place, Room 1711
Boston, MA 02108
(617) 727-2860

Michigan: UCC Division
Department of State
P.O. Box 30197
Lansing, Michigan 48909-7697
(517) 322-1144

Minnesota: UCC Division
Secretary of State
180 State Office Bldg
100 Constitution Avenue
St. Paul, MN 55155
(651) 296-2803 or (877) 551-6767

Mississippi: (Rev. 9 effective Jan. 1, 2002)
UCC Division
Secretary of State
P.O. Box 136
Jackson, MS 39205-0136
(601) 359-1350

Missouri: UCC Division
Secretary of State
P.O. Box 1159
Jefferson City, MO 65102
(573) 751-2360

Montana: Business Services Bureau
Secretary of State
P.O. Box 202801
Helena, MT 59620-2801
(406) 444-3665

Nebraska: UCC Division
Secretary of State
P.O. Box 95104
Lincoln, NE 68509
(402) 471-4080

Nevada: UCC Department
Secretary of State
Capitol Complex
Carson City, NV 89710
(775) 684-5708

New Hampshire: UCC Section
Secretary of State
107 North Main Street, Room 204
State House
Concord, NH 03301
(603) 271-3276 or (603) 271-3277

New Jersey: Department of New Jersey Treasury
Office of the Treasurer
Division of Revenue—UCC
P.O. Box 303
Trenton, NJ 08625
(609) 530-6426

New Mexico: UCC Division
Secretary of State
State Capitol Bldg, Rm 420
Santa Fe, NM 87503
(505) 827-3610

New York: UCC Division
Department of State
41 State Street
Albany, NY 12231
(518) 474-4763

North Carolina: UCC Division
Secretary of State
300 North Salisbury St, #302
Raleigh, NC 27603-5909
(919) 733-4205

North Dakota: UCC Division
Secretary of State
600 E. Boulevard Ave, 1st Floor
Bismarck, ND 58505-0500
(800) 352-0867 x8-3662

Ohio: UCC Division, 14th Floor
Secretary of State
30 E. Broad Street
State Office Tower
Columbus, OH 43215
(614) 466-3623

Oklahoma: UCC Recorder
Oklahoma County Clerk
320 R.S. Kerr Ave
County Office Bldg, Room 105
Oklahoma City, OK 73102
(405) 713-1522

Oregon: Corporate Division
Secretary of State
Public Service Bldg, Ste 151
Salem, OR 97310
(503) 986-2200 FAX (503) 373-1166

Pennsylvania: UCC Division
Department of State
P.O. Box 8721
Harrisburg, PA 17105-8721
(717) 787-1057

Rhode Island: UCC Division
Secretary of State
100 North Main Street
Providence, RI 02903
(401) 222-2249

South Carolina: UCC Division
Secretary of State
P.O. Box 11350
Columbia, SC 29211
(803) 734-2175

South Dakota: UCC Division
Secretary of State
500 East Capitol
Pierre, SD 57501-5077
(605) 773-4422

Tennessee: State of Tennessee
Department of State
Division of Business Services
UCC Section
312 Eighth Ave. North, 6th Floor
Nashville, TN 37243
(615) 741-3276

Texas: UCC Section
Secretary of State
P.O. Box 13193
Austin, TX 78711-3193
(512) 475-2705

Utah: Department of Commerce
UCC Division
160 East 300 South, Box 146705
Salt Lake City, UT 84114-6705
(801) 530-6025 FAX (801) 530-6438

Vermont: UCC Division
Secretary of State
81 River Street, Drawer 09
Montpelier, VT 05609
(802) 828-2386

Virginia: UCC Division—Office of the Clerk
State Corporation Commission
P.O. Box 1197
Richmond, VA 23218
(804) 371-9733

Washington: UCC Division
Department of Licensing
P.O. Box 9660
Olympia, WA 98507-9660
(360) 753-2523

West Virginia: UCC Division
Secretary of State
Bldg. 1, Room 145W
1900 Kanawha Blvd East
Charleston, WV 25305-0440
(304) 558-6000

Wisconsin: Department of Financial Institutions, CCS/UCC
P.O. Box 7847
Madison, WI 53707-7847
(608) 261-9555

Wyoming: UCC Division
Secretary of State
The Capitol
Cheyenne, WY 82002-0020
(307) 777-5372

Virgin Islands: (Rev. 9 effective April 1, 2002)
The Office of the Lt. Governor
18 Kongens Gade
Charlotte Amalie, V.I. 00802
(340) 774-2991 or 773-6449

APPENDIX III

REGULATION M—CONSUMER LEASING

Part 213—Consumer Leasing (Regulation M)

Sec.

Sec. 213.1 Authority, scope, purpose, and enforcement.

(a) *Authority*. The regulation in this part, known as Regulation M, is issued by the Board of Governors of the Federal Reserve System to implement the consumer leasing provisions of the Truth in Lending Act, which is Title I of the Consumer Credit Protection Act, as amended (15 U.S.C. Protection Act), as amended (15 U.S.C. 1601 et seq.). Information collection requirements contained in this regulation have been approved by the Office of

Management and Budget under the provisions of 44 U.S.C. 3501 et seq. and have been assigned OMB control number 7100-0202.

(b) *Scope and purpose*. This part applies to all persons that are lessors of personal property under consumer leases as those terms are defined in Sec. 213.2(e)(1) and (h). The purpose of this part is:

(1) To ensure that lessees of personal property receive meaningful disclosures that enable them to compare lease terms with other leases and, where appropriate, with credit transactions;

(2) To limit the amount of balloon payments in consumer lease transactions; and

(3) To provide for the accurate disclosure of lease terms in advertising.

(c) *Enforcement and liability*. Section 108 of the act contains the administrative enforcement provisions. Sections 112, 130, 131, and 185 of the act contain the liability provisions for failing to comply with the requirements of the act and this part.

Sec. 213.2 Definitions.

For the purposes of this part, the following definitions apply:

(a) *Act* means the Truth in Lending Act (15 U.S.C. 1601 et seq.) and the Consumer Leasing Act is chapter 5 of the Truth in Lending Act.

(b) *Advertisement* means a commercial message in any medium that directly or indirectly promotes a consumer lease transaction.

(c) *Board* refers to the Board of Governors of the Federal Reserve System.

(d) *Closed-end lease* means a consumer lease other than an open-end lease as defined in this section.

(e) (1) *Consumer lease* means a contract in the form of a bailment or lease for the use of personal property by a natural person primarily for personal, family, or household purposes, for a period exceeding four months and for a total contractual obligation not exceeding $25,000, whether or not the lessee has the option to purchase or otherwise become the owner of the property at the expiration of the lease. Unless the context indicates otherwise, in this part "lease" means "consumer lease."

(2) The term does not include a lease that meets the definition of a credit sale in Regulation Z (12 CFR 226.2(a)). It also does not include a lease for agricultural, business, or commercial purposes or a lease made to an organization.

(3) This part does not apply to a lease transaction of personal property which is incident to the lease of real property and which provides that:

(i) The lessee has no liability for the value of the personal property at the end of the lease term except for abnormal wear and tear; and

(ii) The lessee has no option to purchase the leased property.

(f) *Gross capitalized cost* means the amount agreed upon by the lessor and the lessee as the value of the leased property and any items that are capitalized or amortized during the lease term, including but not limited to taxes, insurance, service agreements, and any outstanding prior credit or lease balance. Capitalized cost reduction means the total amount of any rebate, cash payment, net trade-in allowance, and noncash credit that reduces the gross capitalized cost. The adjusted capitalized cost equals the gross capitalized cost less the capitalized cost reduction, and is the amount used by the lessor in calculating the base periodic payment.

(g) *Lessee* means a natural person who enters into or is offered a consumer lease.

(h) *Lessor* means a person who regularly leases, offers to lease, or arranges for the lease of personal property under a consumer lease. A person who has leased, offered, or arranged to lease personal property more than five times in the preceding calendar year or more than five times in the current calendar year is subject to the act and this part.

(i) *Open-end lease* means a consumer lease in which the lessee's liability at the end of the lease term is based on the difference between the residual value of the leased property and its realized value.

(j) *Organization* means a corporation, trust, estate, partnership, cooperative, association, or government entity or instrumentality.

(k) *Person* means a natural person or an organization.

(l) *Personal property* means any property that is not real property under the law of the state where the property is located at the time it is offered or made available for lease.

(m) *Realized value* means:

(i) The price received by the lessor for the leased property at disposition;

(ii) The highest offer for disposition of the leased property; or

(iii) The fair market value of the leased property at the end of the lease term.

(n) *Residual value* means the value of the leased property at the end of the lease term, as estimated or assigned at consummation by the lessor, used in calculating the base periodic payment.

(o) *Security interest and security* mean any interest in property that secures the payment or performance of an obligation.

(p) *State* means any state, the District of Columbia, the Commonwealth of Puerto Rico, and any territory or possession of the United States.

§ 213.3 General disclosure requirements.

(a) *General requirements.* A lessor shall make the disclosures required by § 213.4, as applicable. The disclosures shall be made clearly and conspicuously in writing in a form the consumer may keep, in accordance with this section. The disclosures required by this part may be provided to the lessee in electronic form, subject to compliance with the consumer consent and other applicable provisions of the Electronic Signatures in Global and National Commerce Act (E-Sign Act) (15 U.S.C. § 7001 et seq.). For an advertisement accessed by the consumer in electronic form, the disclosures required by § 213.7 may be provided to the consumer in electronic form in the advertisement, without regard to the consumer consent or other provisions of the E-Sign Act.

(1) *Form of disclosures.* The disclosures required by § 213.4 shall be given to the lessee together in a dated statement that identifies the lessor and the lessee; the disclosures may be made either in a separate statement that identifies the consumer lease transaction or in the contract or other document evidencing the lease. Alternatively, the disclosures required to be segregated from other information under paragraph (a)(2) of this section may be provided in a separate dated statement that identifies the lease, and the other required disclosures may be provided in the lease contract or other document evidencing the lease. In a lease of multiple items, the property description required by § 213.4(a) may be given in a separate statement that is incorporated by reference in the disclosure statement required by this paragraph.

(2) *Segregation of certain disclosures.* The following disclosures shall be segregated from other information and shall contain only directly related information: §§ 213.4(b) through (f), (g)(2), (h)(3), (i)(1), (j), and (m)(1). The headings, content, and format for the disclosures referred to in this paragraph (a)(2) shall be provided in a manner substantially similar to the applicable model form in appendix A of this part.

(3) *Timing of disclosures.* A lessor shall provide the disclosures to the lessee prior to the consummation of a consumer lease.

(4) *Language of disclosures.* The disclosures required by § 213.4 may be made in a language other than English provided that they are made available in English upon the lessee's request.

(5) *Electronic communication.* For rules governing the electronic delivery of disclosures, including a definition of electronic communication, see § 213.6.

(b) *Additional information; nonsegregated disclosures.* Additional information may be provided with any disclosure not listed in paragraph (a)(2) of this section, but it shall not be stated, used, or placed so as to mislead or confuse the lessee or contradict, obscure, or detract attention from any disclosure required by this part.

(c) *Multiple lessors or lessees.* When a transaction involves more than one lessor, the disclosures required by this part may be made by one lessor on behalf of all the lessors. When a lease involves more than one lessee, the lessor may provide the disclosures to any lessee who is primarily liable on the lease.

(d) *Use of estimates.* If an amount or other item needed to comply with a required disclosure is unknown or unavailable after reasonable efforts have been made to ascertain the information, the lessor may use a reasonable estimate that is based on the best information available to the lessor, is clearly identified as an estimate, and is not used to circumvent or evade any disclosures required by this part.

(e) *Effect of subsequent occurrence.* If a required disclosure becomes inaccurate because of an event occurring after consummation, the inaccuracy is not a violation of this part.

(f) *Minor variations.* A lessor may disregard the effects of the following in making disclosures:

(1) That payments must be collected in whole cents;

(2) That dates of scheduled payments may be different because a scheduled date is not a business day;

(3) That months have different numbers of days; and

(4) That February 29 occurs in a leap year.

Sec. 213.4 Content of disclosures.

For any consumer lease subject to this part, the lessor shall disclose the following information, as applicable:

(a) *Description of property.* A brief description of the leased property sufficient to identify the property to the lessee and lessor.

(b) *Amount due at lease signing or delivery.* The total amount to be paid prior to or at consummation or by delivery, if delivery occurs after consummation, using the term "amount due at lease signing or delivery." The lessor shall itemize each component by type and amount, including any refundable security deposit, advance monthly or other periodic payment, and capitalized cost reduction; and in motor-vehicle leases, shall itemize how the amount due will be paid, by type and amount, including any net trade-in allowance, rebates, noncash credits, and cash payments in a format substantially similar to the model forms in appendix A of this part.

(c) *Payment schedule and total amount of periodic payments.* The number, amount, and due dates or periods of payments scheduled under the lease, and the total amount of the periodic payments.

(d) *Other charges.* The total amount of other charges payable to the lessor, itemized by type and amount, that are not included in the periodic payments. Such charges include the amount of any liability the lease imposes upon the lessee at the end of the lease term; the potential difference between the residual and realized values referred to in paragraph (k) of this section is excluded.

(e) *Total of payments.* The total of payments, with a description such as "the amount you will have paid by the end of the lease." This amount is the sum of the amount due at lease signing (less any refundable amounts), the total amount of periodic payments (less any portion of the periodic payment paid at lease signing), and other charges under paragraphs (b), (c), and (d) of this section. In an open-end lease, a description such as "you will owe an additional amount if the actual value of the vehicle is less than the residual value" shall accompany the disclosure.

(f) *Payment calculation.* In a motor-vehicle lease, a mathematical progression of how the scheduled periodic payment is derived, in a format substantially similar to the applicable model form in appendix A of this part, which shall contain the following:

(1) *Gross capitalized cost.* The gross capitalized cost, including a disclosure of the agreed-upon value of the vehicle, a description such as "the agreed-upon value of the vehicle [state the amount] and any items you pay for over the lease term (such as service contracts, insurance, and any outstanding prior credit or lease balance)," and a statement of the lessee's option to receive a separate written itemization of the gross capitalized cost. If requested by the lessee, the itemization shall be provided before consummation.

(2) *Capitalized cost reduction.* The capitalized cost reduction, with a description such as "the amount of any net trade-in allowance, rebate, noncash credit, or cash you pay that reduces the gross capitalized cost."

(3) *Adjusted capitalized cost.* The adjusted capitalized cost, with a description such as "the amount used in calculating your base [periodic] payment."

(4) *Residual value.* The residual value, with a description such as "the value of the vehicle at the end of the lease used in calculating your base [periodic] payment."

(5) *Depreciation and any amortized amounts.* The depreciation and any amortized amounts, which is the difference between the adjusted capitalized cost and the residual value, with a description such as "the amount charged for the vehicle's decline in value through normal use and for any other items paid over the lease term."

(6) *Rent charge.* The rent charge, with a description such as "the amount charged in addition to the depreciation and any amortized amounts." This amount is the difference between the total of the base periodic payments over the lease term minus the depreciation and any amortized amounts.

(7) *Total of base periodic payments.* The total of base periodic payments with a description such as "depreciation and any amortized amounts plus the rent charge."

(8) *Lease payments.* The lease payments with a description such as "the number of payments in your lease."

(9) *Base periodic payment.* The total of the base periodic payments divided by the number of payment periods in the lease.

(10) *Itemization of other charges.* An itemization of any other charges that are part of the periodic payment.

(11) *Total periodic payment.* The sum of the base periodic payment and any other charges that are part of the periodic payment.

(g) *Early termination.*

(1) *Conditions and disclosure of charges.* A statement of the conditions under which the lessee or lessor may terminate the lease prior to the end of the lease term; and the amount or a description of the method for

determining the amount of any penalty or other charge for early termination, which must be reasonable.

(2) *Early-termination notice.* In a motor-vehicle lease, a notice substantially similar to the following: "Early Termination. You may have to pay a substantial charge if you end this lease early. The charge may be up to several thousand dollars. The actual charge will depend on when the lease is terminated. The earlier you end the lease, the greater this charge is likely to be."

(h) *Maintenance responsibilities.* The following provisions are required:

(1) *Statement of responsibilities.* A statement specifying whether the lessor or the lessee is responsible for maintaining or servicing the leased property, together with a brief description of the responsibility;

(2) *Wear and use standard.* A statement of the lessor's standards for wear and use (if any), which must be reasonable; and

(3) *Notice of wear and use standard.* In a motor-vehicle lease, a notice regarding wear and use substantially similar to the following: "Excessive Wear and Use. You may be charged for excessive wear based on our standards for normal use." The notice shall also specify the amount or method for determining any charge for excess mileage.

(i) *Purchase option.* A statement of whether or not the lessee has the option to purchase the leased property, and:

(1) *End of lease term.* If at the end of the lease term, the purchase price; and

(2) *During lease term.* If prior to the end of the lease term, the purchase price or the method for determining the price and when the lessee may exercise this option.

(j) *Statement referencing nonsegregated disclosures.* A statement that the lessee should refer to the lease documents for additional information on early termination, purchase options and maintenance responsibilities, warranties, late and default charges, insurance, and any security interests, if applicable.

(k) *Liability between residual and realized values.* A statement of the lessee's liability, if any, at early termination or at the end of the lease term for the difference between the residual value of the leased property and its realized value.

(l) *Right of appraisal.* If the lessee's liability at early termination or at the end of the lease term is based on the realized value of the leased property, a statement that the lessee may obtain, at the lessee's expense, a professional appraisal by an independent third party (agreed to by the lessee and the lessor) of the value that could be realized at sale of the leased property. The appraisal shall be final and binding on the parties.

(m) *Liability at end of lease term based on residual value.* If the lessee is liable at the end of the lease term for the difference between the residual value of the leased property and its realized value:

(1) *Rent and other charges.* The rent and other charges, paid by the lessee and required by the lessor as an incident to the lease transaction, with a

description such as "the total amount of rent and other charges imposed in connection with your lease [state the amount]."

(2) *Excess liability.* A statement about a rebuttable presumption that, at the end of the lease term, the residual value of the leased property is unreasonable and not in good faith to the extent that the residual value exceeds the realized value by more than three times the base monthly payment (or more than three times the average payment allocable to a monthly period, if the lease calls for periodic payments other than monthly); and that the lessor cannot collect the excess amount unless the lessor brings a successful court action and pays the lessee's reasonable attorney's fees, or unless the excess of the residual value over the realized value is due to unreasonable or excessive wear or use of the leased property (in which case the rebuttable presumption does not apply).

(3) *Mutually agreeable final adjustment.* A statement that the lessee and lessor are permitted, after termination of the lease, to make any mutually agreeable final adjustment regarding excess liability.

(n) *Fees and taxes.* The total dollar amount for all official and license fees, registration, title, or taxes required to be paid in connection with the lease.

(o) *Insurance.* A brief identification of insurance in connection with the lease including:

(1) *Through the lessor.* If the insurance is provided by or paid through the lessor, the types and amounts of coverage and the cost to the lessee; or

(2) *Through a third party.* If the lessee must obtain the insurance, the types and amounts of coverage required of the lessee.

(p) *Warranties or guarantees.* A statement identifying all express warranties and guarantees from the manufacturer or lessor with respect to the leased property that apply to the lessee.

(q) *Penalties and other charges for delinquency.* The amount or the method of determining the amount of any penalty or other charge for delinquency, default, or late payments, which must be reasonable.

(r) *Security interest.* A description of any security interest, other than a security deposit disclosed under paragraph (b) of this section, held or to be retained by the lessor; and a clear identification of the property to which the security interest relates.

(s) *Limitations on rate information.* If a lessor provides a percentage rate in an advertisement or in documents evidencing the lease transaction, a notice stating that "this percentage may not measure the overall cost of financing this lease" shall accompany the rate disclosure. The lessor shall not use the term "annual percentage rate," "annual lease rate," or any equivalent term.

(t) *Non-motor vehicle open-end leases.* Non-motor vehicle open-end leases remain subject to section 182(10) of the act regarding end of term liability.

Sec. 213.5 Renegotiations, extensions, and assumptions.

(a) *Renegotiation.* A renegotiation occurs when a consumer lease subject to this part is satisfied and replaced by a new lease undertaken by the same consumer. A renegotiation requires new disclosures, except as provided in paragraph (d) of this section.

(b) *Extension.* An extension is a continuation, agreed to by the lessor and the lessee, of an existing consumer lease beyond the originally scheduled end of the lease term, except when the continuation is the result of a renegotiation. An extension that exceeds six months requires new disclosures, except as provided in paragraph (d) of this section.

(c) *Assumption.* New disclosures are not required when a consumer lease is assumed by another person, whether or not the lessor charges an assumption fee.

(d) *Exceptions.* New disclosures are not required for the following, even if they meet the definition of a renegotiation or an extension:

(1) A reduction in the rent charge;

(2) The deferment of one or more payments, whether or not a fee is charged;

(3) The extension of a lease for not more than six months on a month-to-month basis or otherwise;

(4) A substitution of leased property with property that has a substantially equivalent or greater economic value, provided no other lease terms are changed;

(5) The addition, deletion, or substitution of leased property in a multiple item lease, provided the average periodic payment does not change by more than 25 percent; or

(6) An agreement resulting from a court proceeding.

Sec. 213.6 Electronic communication.

(a) *Definition.* "Electronic communication" means a message transmitted electronically between a lessor and a lessee in a format that allows visual text to be displayed on equipment, for example, a personal computer monitor.

(b) *General rule.* In accordance with the Electronic Signatures in Global and National Commerce Act (the E-Sign Act) (15 U.S.C. 7001 et seq.) and the rules of this part, a lessor may provide by electronic communication any disclosure required by this part to be in writing.

(c) *When consent is required.* Under the E-Sign Act, a lessor is required to obtain a lessee's affirmative consent when providing disclosures related to a transaction. For purposes of this requirement, the disclosures required under Sec. 213.7 are deemed not to be related to a transaction.

(d) *Address or location to receive electronic communication.* A lessor that uses electronic communication to provide disclosures required by this part shall:

(1) Send the disclosure to the consumer's electronic address; or

(2) Make the disclosure available at another location such as a web site; and

(i) Alert the lessee of the disclosure's availability by sending a notice to the consumer's electronic address (or to a postal address, at the lessor's option). The notice shall identify the transaction involved and the address of the Internet web site or other location where the disclosure is available; and

(ii) Make the disclosure available for at least 90 days from the date the disclosure first becomes available or from the date of the notice alerting the lessee of the disclosure, whichever comes later.

(3) Exceptions. A lessor need not comply with paragraph (d)(2)(i) and (ii) of this section for the disclosures required under Sec. 213.7.

(e) *Redelivery.* When a disclosure provided by electronic communication is returned to a lessor undelivered, the lessor shall take reasonable steps to attempt redelivery using information in its files.

Sec. 213.7 Advertising.

(a) *General rule.* An advertisement for a consumer lease may state that a specific lease of property at specific amounts or terms is available only if the lessor usually and customarily leases or will lease the property at those amounts or terms.

(b) *Clear and conspicuous standard.* Disclosures required by this section shall be made clearly and conspicuously.

(1) *Amount due at lease signing or delivery.* Except for the statement of a periodic payment, any affirmative or negative reference to a charge that is a part of the disclosure required under paragraph (d)(2)(ii) of this section shall not be more prominent than that disclosure.

(2) *Advertisement of a lease rate.* If a lessor provides a percentage rate in an advertisement, the rate shall not be more prominent than any of the disclosures in Sec. 213.4, with the exception of the notice in Sec. 213.4(s) required to accompany the rate; and the lessor shall not use the term "annual percentage rate," "annual lease rate," or equivalent term.

(c) *Catalogs and multipage advertisements.* A catalog or other multipage advertisement that provides a table or schedule of the required disclosures shall be considered a single advertisement if, for lease terms that appear without all the required disclosures, the advertisement refers to the page or pages on which the table or schedule appears.

(d) *Advertisement of terms that require additional disclosure.*

(1) Triggering terms. An advertisement that states any of the following items shall contain the disclosures required by paragraph (d)(2) of this section, except as provided in paragraphs (e) and (f) of this section:

(i) The amount of any payment; or

(ii) A statement of any capitalized cost reduction or other payment (or that no payment is required) prior to or at consummation or by delivery, if delivery occurs after consummation.

(2) Additional terms. An advertisement stating any item listed in paragraph (d)(1) of this section shall also state the following items:

(i) That the transaction advertised is a lease;

(ii) The total amount due prior to or at consummation or by delivery, if delivery occurs after consummation;

(iii) The number, amounts, and due dates or periods of scheduled payments under the lease;

(iv) A statement of whether or not a security deposit is required; and

(v) A statement that an extra charge may be imposed at the end of the lease term where the lessee's liability (if any) is based on the difference between the residual value of the leased property and its realized value at the end of the lease term.

(e) *Alternative disclosures—merchandise tags.* A merchandise tag stating any item listed in paragraph (d)(1) of this section may comply with paragraph (d)(2) of this section by referring to a sign or display prominently posted in the lessor's place of business that contains a table or schedule of the required disclosures.

(f) *Alternative disclosures—television or radio advertisements.*

(1) *Toll-free number or print advertisement.* An advertisement made through television or radio stating any item listed in paragraph (d)(1) of this section complies with paragraph (d)(2) of this section if the advertisement states the items listed in paragraphs (d)(2)(i) through (iii) of this section, and:

(i) Lists a toll-free telephone number along with a reference that such number may be used by consumers to obtain the information required by paragraph (d)(2) of this section; or

(ii) Directs the consumer to a written advertisement in a publication of general circulation in the community served by the media station, including the name and the date of the publication, with a statement that information required by paragraph (d)(2) of this section is included in the advertisement. The written advertisement shall be published beginning at least three days before and ending at least ten days after the broadcast.

(2) Establishment of toll-free number.

(i) The toll-free telephone number shall be available for no fewer than ten days, beginning on the date of the broadcast.

(ii) The lessor shall provide the information required by paragraph (d)(2) of this section orally, or in writing upon request.

Sec. 213.8 Record retention.

A lessor shall retain evidence of compliance with the requirements imposed by this part, other than the advertising requirements under Sec. 213.7, for a period of not less than two years after the date the disclosures are required to be made or an action is required to be taken.

Sec. 213.9 Relation to state laws.

(a) *Inconsistent state law.* A state law that is inconsistent with the requirements of the act and this part is preempted to the extent of the inconsistency. If a lessor cannot comply with a state law without violating a provision of this part, the state law is inconsistent within the meaning of section 186(a) of the act and is preempted, unless the state law gives greater protection and benefit to the consumer. A state, through an official having primary enforcement or interpretative responsibilities for the state consumer leasing law, may apply to the Board for a preemption determination.

(b) *Exemptions.*

(1) *Application.* A state may apply to the Board for an exemption from the requirements of the act and this part for any class of lease transactions within the state. The Board will grant such an exemption if the Board determines that:

(i) The class of leasing transactions is subject to state law requirements substantially similar to the act and this part or that lessees are afforded greater protection under state law; and

(ii) There is adequate provision for state enforcement.

(2) *Enforcement and liability.* After an exemption has been granted, the requirements of the applicable state law (except for additional requirements not imposed by federal law) will constitute the requirements of the act and this part. No exemption will extend to the civil liability provisions of sections 130, 131, and 185 of the act.

Appendix A to Part 213—Model Forms
A-1 Model Open-End or Finance Vehicle Lease Disclosures
A-2 Model Closed-End or Net Vehicle Lease Disclosures
A-3 Model Furniture Lease Disclosures

Appendix B to Part 213—Federal Enforcement Agencies
The following list indicates which federal agency enforces Regulation M (12 CFR Part 213) for particular classes of business. Any questions concerning compliance by a particular business should be directed to the appropriate enforcement agency. Terms that are not defined in the Federal Deposit Insurance Act (12 U.S.C. 1813(s)) shall have the meaning given to them in the International Banking Act of 1978 (12 U.S.C. 3101).

(1) *National banks and federal branches and federal agencies of foreign banks*
District office of the Office of the Comptroller of the Currency for the district in which the institution is located.

(2) *State member banks, branches and agencies of foreign banks (other than federal branches, federal agencies, and insured state branches of foreign banks), commercial lending companies owned or controlled by foreign banks, and organizations operating under section 25 or 25A of the Federal Reserve Act*
Federal Reserve Bank serving the District in which the institution is located.

(3) *Nonmember insured banks and insured state branches of foreign banks*
Federal Deposit Insurance Corporation Regional Director for the region in which the institution is located.

(4) *Savings institutions insured under the Savings Association Insurance*
Fund of the FDIC and federally chartered savings banks insured under the Bank Insurance Fund of the FDIC (but not including state-chartered savings banks insured under the Bank Insurance Fund)
Office of Thrift Supervision regional director for the region in which the institution is located.

(5) *Federal credit unions*
Regional office of the National Credit Union Administration serving the area in which the federal credit union is located.

(6) *Air carriers*
Assistant General Counsel for Aviation Enforcement and Proceedings, Department of Transportation, 400 Seventh Street, S.W., Washington, DC 20590

(7) *Those subject to Packers and Stockyards Act*
Nearest Packers and Stockyards Administration area supervisor.

(8) *Federal Land Banks, Federal Land Bank Associations, Federal Intermediate Credit Banks, and Production Credit Associations*
Farm Credit Administration, 490 L'Enfant Plaza, S.W., Washington, DC 20578

(9) *All other lessors (lessors operating on a local or regional basis should use the address of the FTC regional office in which they operate)*
Division of Credit Practices, Bureau of Consumer Protection, Federal Trade Commission, Washington, DC 20580

Appendix C to Part 213—Issuance of Staff Interpretations

Officials in the Board's Division of Consumer and Community Affairs are authorized to issue official staff interpretations of this Regulation M (12 CFR Part 213). These interpretations provide the formal protection afforded under section 130(f) of the act. Except in unusual circumstances, interpretations will not be issued separately but will be incorporated in an official commentary to Regulation M (Supplement I of this part), which will be amended periodically. No staff interpretations will be issued approving lessor's forms, statements, or calculation tools or methods.

APPENDIX IV

CONSUMER LEASE DISCLOSURES

TITLE 15. COMMERCE AND TRADE

CHAPTER 41. CONSUMER CREDIT PROTECTION—CONSUMER CREDIT COST DISCLOSURE—CONSUMER LEASES

Sec. 1667. Definitions

For purposes of this part

(1) The term "consumer lease" means a contract in the form of a lease or bailment for the use of personal property by a natural person for a period of time exceeding four months, and for a total contractual obligation not exceeding $25,000, primarily for personal, family, or household purposes, whether or not the lessee has the option to purchase or otherwise become the owner of the property at the expiration of the lease, except that such term shall not include any credit sale as defined in section 1602(g) of this title. Such term does not include a lease for agricultural, business, or commercial purposes, or to a government or governmental agency or instrumentality, or to an organization.

(2) The term "lessee" means a natural person who leases or is offered a consumer lease.

(3) The term "lessor" means a person who is regularly engaged in leasing, offering to lease, or arranging to lease under a consumer lease.

(4) The term "personal property" means any property which is not real property under the laws of the State where situated at the time offered or otherwise made available for lease.

(5) The terms "security" and "security interest" mean any interest in property which secures payment or performance of an obligation.

Sec. 1667a. Consumer lease disclosures

Each lessor shall give a lessee prior to the consummation of the lease a dated written statement on which the lessor and lessee are identified setting out accurately and in a clear and conspicuous manner the following information with respect to that lease, as applicable:

(1) A brief description or identification of the leased property;

(2) The amount of any payment by the lessee required at the inception of the lease;

(3) The amount paid or payable by the lessee for official fees, registration, certificate of title, or license fees or taxes;

(4) The amount of other charges payable by the lessee not included in the periodic payments, a description of the charges and that the lessee shall be liable for the differential, if any, between the anticipated fair market value of the leased property and its appraised actual value at the termination of the lease, if the lessee has such liability;

(5) A statement of the amount or method of determining the amount of any liabilities the lease imposes upon the lessee at the end of the term and whether or not the lessee has the option to purchase the leased property and at what price and time;

(6) A statement identifying all express warranties and guarantees made by the manufacturer or lessor with respect to the leased property, and identifying the party responsible for maintaining or servicing the leased property together with a description of the responsibility;

(7) A brief description of insurance provided or paid for by the lessor or required of the lessee, including the types and amounts of the coverages and costs;

(8) A description of any security interest held or to be retained by the lessor in connection with the lease and a clear identification of the property to which the security interest relates;

(9) The number, amount, and due dates or periods of payments under the lease and the total amount of such periodic payments;

(10) Where the lease provides that the lessee shall be liable for the anticipated fair market value of the property on expiration of the lease, the fair market value of the property at the inception of the lease, the aggregate cost of the lease on expiration, and the differential between them; and

(11) A statement of the conditions under which the lessee or lessor may terminate the lease prior to the end of the term and the amount or method of determining any penalty or other charge for delinquency, default, late payments, or early termination.

The disclosures required under this section may be made in the lease contract to be signed by the lessee. The Board may provide by regulation that any portion of the information required to be disclosed under this section may be given in the form of estimates where the lessor is not in a position to know exact information.

Sec. 1667b. Lessee's liability on expiration or termination of lease

(a) Estimated residual value of property as basis; presumptions; action by lessor for excess liability; mutually agreeable final adjustment. Where the lessee's liability on expiration of a consumer lease is based on the estimated residual value of the property such estimated residual value shall be a reasonable approximation of the anticipated actual fair market value of the property on lease expiration. There shall be a rebuttable presumption that the estimated residual value is unreasonable to the extent that the estimated residual value exceeds the actual residual value by more than three times the average payment allocable to a monthly period under the lease. In addition, where the lessee has such liability on expiration of a consumer lease there shall be a rebuttable presumption that the lessor's estimated residual value is not in good faith to the extent that the estimated residual value exceeds the actual residual value by more than three times the average payment allocable to a monthly period under the lease and such lessor shall not collect from the lessee the amount of such excess liability on expiration of a consumer lease unless the lessor brings a successful action with respect to such excess liability. In all actions, the lessor shall pay the lessee's reasonable attorney's fees. The presumptions stated in this section shall not apply to the extent the excess of estimated over actual residual value is due to physical damage to the property beyond reasonable wear and use, or to excessive use, and the lease may set standards for such wear and use if such standards are not unreasonable. Nothing in this subsection shall preclude the right of a willing lessee to make any mutually agreeable final adjustment with respect to such excess residual liability, provided such an agreement is reached after termination of the lease.

(b) Penalties and charges for delinquency, default, or early termination. Penalties or other charges for delinquency, default, or early termination may be specified in the lease but only at an amount which is reasonable in the light of the anticipated or actual harm caused by the delinquency, default, or early termination, the difficulties of proof of loss, and the inconvenience or nonfeasibility of otherwise obtaining an adequate remedy.

(c) Independent professional appraisal of residual value of property at termination of lease; finality. If a lease has a residual value provision at the termination of the lease, the lessee may obtain at his expense, a professional appraisal of the leased property by an independent third party agreed to by both parties. Such appraisal shall be final and binding on the parties.

Sec. 1667c. Consumer lease advertising; liability of advertising media

(a) In general. If an advertisement for a consumer lease includes a statement of the amount of any payment or a statement that any or no initial payment is required, the advertisement shall clearly and conspicuously state, as applicable:

(1) the transaction advertised is a lease;

(2) the total amount of any initial payments required on or before consummation of the lease or delivery of the property, whichever is later;

(3) that a security deposit is required;

(4) the number, amount, and timing of scheduled payments; and

(5) with respect to a lease in which the liability of the consumer at the end of the lease term is based on the anticipated residual value of the property, that an extra charge may be imposed at the end of the lease term.

(b) Advertising medium not liable. No owner or employee of any entity that serves as a medium in which an advertisement appears or through which an advertisement is disseminated, shall be liable under this section.

(c) Radio advertisements

(1) In general. An advertisement by radio broadcast to aid, promote, or assist, directly or indirectly, any consumer lease shall be deemed to be in compliance with the requirements of subsection (a) of this section if such advertisement clearly and conspicuously

(A) states the information required by paragraphs (1) and (2) of subsection (a) of this section;

(B) states the number, amounts, due dates or periods of scheduled payments, and the total of such payments under the lease;

(C) includes

(i) a referral to

(I) a toll-free telephone number established in accordance with paragraph (2) that may be used by consumers to obtain the information required under subsection (a) of this section; or

(II) a written advertisement that

appears in a publication in general circulation in the community served (aa) by the radio station on which such advertisement is broadcast during the period beginning 3 days before any such broadcast and ending 10 days after such broadcast; and

includes the information required to be disclosed under subsection (a)(bb) of this section; and

(ii) the name and dates of any publication referred to in clause (i)(II); and

(D) includes any other information which the Board determines necessary to carry out this part.

(2) Establishment of toll-free number

(A) In general. In the case of a radio broadcast advertisement described in paragraph (1) that includes a referral to a toll-free telephone number, the lessor who offers the consumer lease shall

(i) establish such a toll-free telephone number not later than the date on which the advertisement including the referral is broadcast;

(ii) maintain such telephone number for a period of not less than 10 days, beginning on the date of any such broadcast; and

(iii) provide the information required under subsection (a) of this section with respect to the lease to any person who calls such number.

(B) Form of information. The information required to be provided under subparagraph (A)(iii) shall be provided verbally or, if requested by the consumer, in written form.

(3) No effect on other law. Nothing in this subsection shall affect the requirements of Federal law as such requirements apply to advertisement by any medium other than radio broadcast.

Sec. 1667d. Civil liability of lessors

(a) Grounds for maintenance of action. Any lessor who fails to comply with any requirement imposed under section 1667a or 1667b of this title with respect to any person is liable to such person as provided in section 1640 of this title.

(b) Additional grounds for maintenance of action; "creditor" defined. Any lessor who fails to comply with any requirement imposed under section 1667c of this title with respect to any person who suffers actual damage from the violation is liable to such person as provided in section 1640 of this title. For the purposes of this section, the term "creditor" as used in sections 1640 and 1641 of this title shall include a lessor as defined in this part.

(c) Jurisdiction of courts; time limitation. Notwithstanding section 1640(e) of this title, any action under this section may be brought in any United States district court or in any other court of competent jurisdiction. Such actions alleging a failure to disclose or otherwise comply with the requirements of this part shall be brought within one year of the termination of the lease agreement.

Sec. 1667e. Applicability of State laws; exemptions by Board from leasing requirements

(a) This part does not annul, alter, affect, or exempt any person subject to the provisions of this part from complying with, the laws of any State with respect to consumer leases, except to the extent that those laws are inconsistent with any provision of this part, and then only to the extent of the inconsistency. The Board is authorized to determine whether such inconsistencies exist. The Board may not determine that any State law is inconsistent with any provision of this part if the Board determines that such law gives greater protection and benefit to the consumer.

(b) The Board shall by regulation exempt from the requirements of this part any class of lease transactions within any State if it determines that under the law of that State that class of transactions is subject to requirements substantially similar to those imposed under this part or that such law gives greater protection and benefit to the consumer, and that there is adequate provision for enforcement.

Sec. 1667f. Regulations

(a) Regulations authorized

(1) In general. The Board shall prescribe regulations to update and clarify the requirements and definitions applicable to lease disclosures and

contracts, and any other issues specifically related to consumer leasing, to the extent that the Board determines such action to be necessary

(A) to carry out this part;

(B) to prevent any circumvention of this part; or

(C) to facilitate compliance with the requirements of this part.

(2) Classifications, adjustments. Any regulations prescribed under paragraph (1) may contain classifications and differentiations, and may provide for adjustments and exceptions for any class of transactions, as the Board considers appropriate.

(b) Model disclosure

(1) Publication. The Board shall establish and publish model disclosure forms to facilitate compliance with the disclosure requirements of this part and to aid the consumer in understanding the transaction to which the subject disclosure form relates.

(2) Use of automated equipment. In establishing model forms under this subsection, the Board shall consider the use by lessors of data processing or similar automated equipment.

(3) Use optional. A lessor may utilize a model disclosure form established by the Board under this subsection for purposes of compliance with this part, at the discretion of the lessor.

(4) Effect of use. Any lessor who properly uses the material aspects of any model disclosure form established by the Board under this subsection shall be deemed to be in compliance with the disclosure requirements to which the form relates.

Description of Leased Property				
Year	Make	Model	Body Style	Vehicle ID #

Description of Leased Property				
Year	Make	Model	Body Style	Vehicle ID #

CHAPTER 12

Repossession of Property

UNIFORM COMMERCIAL CODE

Every state has adopted the UCC. Most states have made some changes when adopting Revised Article 9, and a review of the state law with counsel is recommended. (*See* Chapter 11.)

The UCC applies to liens created with the consent of both parties. Liens also may be created by statute, such as mechanic's liens and garage keeper's liens (third parties who improve property). The security agreement is identified as "the agreement between the consumer and the lender which creates the lien under the Uniform Commercial Code." In the security agreement presented to consumers by financial institutions, the consumer identifies the property securing the lien, the terms of repayment, charges, and other expenses. The agreement also defines the conditions under which the consumer will maintain the vehicle or boat, what constitutes a default under the agreement, what happens when the default takes place under the agreement, the rights of the secured party with regard to repossessing the property, the terms of crediting the payments, the conditions of the sale, and the allocation of the proceeds from the sale.

If the agreement covers both real and personal property, the secured party may proceed under the UCC as to the personal property, or may proceed under state law to foreclose the mortgage as to both the real and personal property.

REPOSSESSION

Repossession of Property. While the general law of repossession is covered under the Uniform Commercial Code (UCC), Revised Article 9, the repossession of property is primarily restricted and controlled by the written installment contracts and consumer credit contracts. Since most repossessions involve consumers, consumer protection laws must be considered, including the Bankruptcy Code, Truth in Lending Act, Equal Credit Opportunity Act, and the Fair Debt Collection Practices Act, in addition to the replevin laws of the respective states. Compliance with the laws that affect the extension of credit is required, as well as elimination of deceptive and abusive collection practices in the repossession of a vehicle, boat, or machinery and equipment.

Certificate of Title—Due Process. Some state statutes do not require that any special notice be given to the debtor before the creditor obtains title to the vehicle after repossession. Under the statute in Ohio, the debtor was neither entitled to notice of the transfer of the repossession title nor was he entitled to a hearing. The court held that allowing the secured party to obtain a repossession title without notice to the debtor and without a hearing violates the due process provisions of the U.S. Constitution.[1]

In another case involving a certificate of title state, a company financed the sales of vehicles from a dealer to several consumers, but the consumers were not able to obtain a certificate of title since the bank, which did "floor plan financing" for the dealer, held all the certificates of titles to all of the automobiles.[2] The financer of the individual cars to the consumers had notice of the security interest of the bank, but argued that the consumers were buyers in the ordinary course of business, whose purchases extinguished the floor plan security interest of the bank. The court disagreed. No legal sales were made to the purported buyers and thus they could not be considered buyers in the ordinary course of business. To have a legal sale, the buyer would have to receive title as required under the Certificate of Title Act of Texas.

In the third case involving a certificate of title, Florida had specific legislation addressing ownership and title.[3] A person acquiring a motor vehicle shall not acquire marketable title to the vehicle until he or she is issued a certificate of title to the motor vehicle. No court shall recognize the right, title, claim, or interest of any person in and to any motor vehicle sold, disposed of, mortgaged, or encumbered unless evidenced by a certificate title duly issued to that person in accordance with the provisions of the chapter. The court emphasized that title is not transferred to a creditor immediately on repossession. The creditor must present satisfactory proof in the form of an affidavit that the creditor is entitled to ownership and possession of the car. The creditor must pay a fee, must provide a lien holder 15 days' notice prior to requesting a certificate of title, and the former owner, such as the debtor in this case, has the ability to file a written

---

[1]*Leslie v. Lacy*, 91 F. Supp. 2d 1182 (S.D. Ohio 2000).
[2]*Bank One Tex. N.A. v. Arcade Fin. Ltd.*, 219 F.3d 494 (5th Cir. 2000).
[3]*In re Chiodo*, 250 B.R. 407 (Bankr. D. Fla. 2000).

protest to the issuance of a certificate of title. If a written protest is filed, a further ten-day period is required. Only after all of these conditions are met is a creditor with a repossessed vehicle able to obtain a new certificate of title and conclude a sale of the auto.

When Title Passes. Prior to the UCC, the common law set forth that when property was repossessed by a creditor, title normally passed directly to the creditor. The common law was radically changed by the UCC and now when collateral is repossessed, title still remains in the debtor's name until there is some formal disposition by the creditor such as a sale of the property.

Old Article 9-207 states as follows:

1. A secured party must use reasonable care in the custody and preservation of collateral in his possession.
2. In the case of an instrument or chattel paper, reasonable care includes taking the necessary steps to preserve rights against prior parties unless otherwise agreed.
3. A secured party is liable for any loss caused by his failure to meet any obligations imposed by the preceding subsection but does not lose his security interest.

Revised Article 9-207 expands and clarifies Old Article 9-207 to include the risks, duties, and rights of the secured party in possession.

A creditor cannot at the same time be the owner and have obligations to the debtor after repossession of the property. If the creditor is the owner of the property, a creditor has no obligations to the debtor. The creditor has no right to increase the amount of the debt as the owner of the property.

If the secured party was the owner of the property, no liability exists for any losses by virtue of the failure to exercise reasonable care in the custody of the property. The debtor also has the right to redeem the property. This right to redeem is consistent with the right of ownership. (Revised Article 9-623.)

> ***Credit & Collection Tip:*** *Any activity by the creditor which is not consistent with the concept that the secured party is merely a caretaker and a custodian for the property until the property is finally placed at public or private sale may expose the creditor to liability.*

Threat to Repossess. Threatening to repossess a vehicle from a consumer where no immediate intention to repossess is present may be a violation of the Fair Debt Collection Practices Act. A creditor must do whatever is threatened.[4] A threat to repossess should only be used

---

[4]15 U.S.C. § 1692(e).

where the immediate intent is to retain a repossession firm to repossess the vehicle. Threatening to repossess when only one payment is past due, and the normal custom is to repossess if three or four payments are late, may expose the creditor to liability under the Fair Debt Collection Practices Act.

Police Officer. Sometimes the repossessing party will ask for the assistance of a police officer whose presence, carrying a weapon, may be considered the use of force, because the consumer is not likely to resist. If the officer is a sheriff pursuant to a court order, no problem is present.

As long as no police officer or court officer is present, and no deception is used that a court officer is enforcing the law, the secured party is permitted to use deceptive practices in some jurisdictions,[5] but violation of the Fair Debt Collection Practices Act must be considered.

Statute of Limitations—Extensions. UCC Article 9 does not provide for any statute of limitations, although UCC Article 2-725 does provide for a four-year limitation for breach of a contract of sale. As a general rule the courts look to state legislation for purposes of determining which statute of limitations applies to the repossession of vehicles. It may be shortened by agreement, but no shorter than one year.

Where a creditor has repossessed a motor vehicle or other collateral and disposed of the collateral by either private or public sale, does the statute of limitations run from the date of the sale? Property of the debtor was being sold to which the debtor would be entitled to possession if not for the lien. A strong argument could be made that the payment was made by the debtor. Whether a strong argument could be made that the debtor promised to continue to make payments is questionable.

Waiver of Notice. The provisions of most security agreements contain a waiver of notice by the debtor that the creditor will accelerate the debt and a waiver of notice that the creditor will repossess the automobile or boat. *While some courts enforce this waiver, many courts find these waiver provisions against public policy and refuse to enforce them.*[6]

Right to Cure Default. The right to accelerate the loan is a serious hardship for the consumer, and many statutes and the courts find reasons to shelter the consumer from this acceleration clause, which declares the entire debt due if there is a default in one payment. Some federal statutes, and many states have "right to cure" provisions which provide that the secured party must send a notice to the consumer to allow the consumer time within which to cure the default of one payment

---

[5] *Ford Motor Credit Co. v. Cole*, 503 S.W.2d 853 (Tex. Civ. App. 1973).

[6] *Fontaine v. Industrial Nat'l Bank of Rhode Island*, 298 A.2d 521 (R.I. 1973).

so that the loan will not accelerate. Depending upon the type of loan, the secured party should review the appropriate law.

Most states do not interfere with the terms of the security agreement enabling the secured party to repossess the car peacefully without notice to the debtor. Connecticut and Massachusetts, under certain circumstances, require creditors to notify the debtors before repossession.[7] Louisiana and Wisconsin prohibit peaceful repossession.[8]

Maine's Consumer Credit Codes regulate all consumer credit transactions (secured and unsecured). If a debtor defaults by failing to make payment within ten days of the due date, prior to enforcing any contractual remedies, M.R.S.A. Sections 5-510 and 5-511 require that a debtor be sent a written notice to cure including accelerating the balance due or retaking possession of the secured property. A creditor must issue a 14-day written notice of default, which must describe the alleged default and allow the borrower the right to cure. The notice must include the name and telephone number of the creditor, the amount of payment to cure the default, and the last date payment must be made. Notice may be sent by regular or certified mail. The 14-day time period does not begin until the consumer actually receives the notice. If the notice is sent by ordinary first-class mail, the date of receipt is determined by the date the consumer receives the mail. If a post office certificate is obtained, the date of receipt by the consumer will be judicially presumed to occur on the third calendar day after mailing.[9]

Using certified mail may not be the best way to proceed. If notice is sent by certified mail, return receipt requested, the date of receipt is determined by the date the consumer signs for the receipt, or the last date that delivery was attempted on unclaimed certified mail. The problem is that it may be difficult to determine the date of receipt unless the debtor completes the return receipt. Thus, a creditor may need to wait as long as four or five weeks to establish that the notice has been received so that the 14-day cure period may begin to run. If the debtor claims he did not receive the notice, the burden of proof is on the creditor to establish that notice was received. The recommended procedure is to mail by first-class mail and obtain a post office certificate of mailing. Without proof of compliance, a lawful act, such as peaceful possession, could be immediately transformed into a wrongful conversion and could expose the creditor to liability under state as well as federal laws.

The creditor is not required by statute to send an additional notice if the debtor should default again within one year. But it is important that proof of this notice be maintained with the same diligence that is accorded to the original agreement. If the original notice is lost or if no notice was

---

[7]Conn. Gen. Stat. § 42-98B; Mass. Gen. Laws ch. 255B, § 20A(b).
[8]Wis. Stat. § 425.206; LSA-C.C.P. art. 34501.
[9]*Griffin v. Chrysler Credit Corp.*, 553 A.2d 653 (Me. 1989).

sent, on the second default it is advisable to send another notice. A party who is purchasing paper in the State of Maine should obtain affidavits from the original creditor stating that the original creditor has complied with Maine statutory requirements for debtors residing in Maine. The affidavit should recite that the original creditor issued a proper statutory notice to cure and that the debtor failed to cure the default.

The above furnishes a summary of some of the problems that will be faced in other states and why it is necessary that an in-depth review be made of each state's statute, and consultation with experienced counsel is recommended.

Service Members Civil Relief Act. Under the Service Members Civil Relief Act of 2003, significant protection is afforded military personnel from peaceful repossession. The act expressly refers to debts that are incurred prior to the time that the consumer entered military service. If the individual is stationed permanently on a post, a court proceeding should be used instead of peaceful repossession. (*See* Chapter 5.)

Late Payments—Waiver. Despite the fact that the statute is clear that whenever the debtor is in default, the creditor has a right to take possession of the collateral as long as the taking of possession is done without a breach of the peace, the creditor must examine the words introducing the paragraph, "unless otherwise agreed." Many courts have held that where a secured creditor routinely accepts the debtor's delinquent payments, the creditor is waiving strict compliance with the parties' contractual requirement to make payments on time (the parties have otherwise agreed as to a payment schedule).

The courts have held that acceptance of late payments constitutes a waiver of strict compliance with the contract terms specifying when payment should be made. In most of these instances, the cases have dealt with individual consumers who have purchased cars on an installment basis and the debtor is no more than one, two, or maybe three months in arrears and the arrears usually have been continuous.

A secured party, not insisting upon strict compliance in the past, and before embarking upon a course of action to declare a default and effect a repossession, *should deliver notice to the debtor that strict compliance with the terms of contract will be demanded henceforth if repossession is to be avoided.*

In an Arkansas case, the debtor made only one timely payment of the fourteen monthly payments required; thirteen late payments were made ranging from a few days to more than 30 days delinquent from the due date required under the agreement. The court emphasized that the bank could reinstate its right to repossess by delivering written notice to the debtor stating that thereafter strict compliance was to be expected.

It is recommended that certified or registered mail be used when sending such a written notice, for it will be necessary to prove notice.

Failure to prove notice to the debtor may expose the creditor to significant damages for repossessing the secured property, since such repossession may constitute a conversion of property.[10]

> ***Credit & Collection Tip:*** *Fill out the receipt for certified mailing. Do not merely staple it to a default letter. By completing the form, it becomes a business record and is admissible as evidence. A blank form stamped as a receipt is susceptible to attack as unreliable.*

Property Taken with Repossessed Vehicle. Any personal property contained in the repossessed vehicle should be returned forthwith to the consumer. A problem arises when the consumer alleges that property was left in the vehicle, but the property is no longer there. Among those who are involved in repossession of vehicles, the frequency within which golf clubs, sporting equipment, and carpenter tools are left in the trunk of the car bears no relationship to the number of golfers, athletes or carpenters.

Since the secured party is responsible for the activities of the party who repossesses, careful and exacting procedures have been orchestrated to take inventory of the personal property contained in the repossessed vehicle, especially a boat or a motor home. If the property is damaged or lost by reason of the repossession, the debtor is entitled to damages, including damages for loss of use in the case of tools used in a trade. *Such procedures to protect against this type of claim should include the use of independent witnesses, videotapes, and photographs.*

Peaceful Possession. Most security agreements provide that the secured party may acquire peaceful possession of property. The consumer often voluntarily surrenders the property. Voluntary surrender does not afford the secured party a right to violate the terms of the security agreement. The consumer has the right to require strict compliance with the terms of the security agreement.

A repossession must not constitute a breach of peace. Deceptive practices and threats to take security sometimes may constitute a breach of peace. Certainly physical force is prohibited. Any type of contact with the debtor would probably fall into that category while intimidation by use of threatening instruments, etc., would definitely constitute physical force.[11]

Damaging the person's property during the act of repossession is physical force if the property damaged is not the property sought to be

---

[10] *Mercedes-Benz Credit Corp. v. Morgan*, 850 S.W.2d 297 (Ark. 1993). *See also Kelly Tractor Co. v. R.J. Canfield Contracting, Inc.*, 579 So. 2d 261 (Fla. Dist. Ct. App. 4th Dist. 1991); *Ford Motor Credit Co. v. Waters*, 273 So. 2d 96 (Fla. Dist. Ct. App. 1973).

[11] *Griffith v. Valley of Sun*, 613 P.2d 1283 (Ariz. Ct. App. 1980); *Harris Truck & Trailer v. Foote*, 436 S.W.2d 460 (Tenn. Ct. App. 1968).

repossessed. Any activity indicating the consumer objects to the repossession, whether this activity is engaged in by the consumer, members of the family, or even neighbors, is evidence that the repossession is not proceeding peacefully. The best repossession is when neither the consumer nor anyone who knows the consumer, such as a friend or relative, is present during the act of repossession. A breach of peace is rare where a car is repossessed on the street or in a public parking lot.

The question of consent arose where the creditor repossessed a computer system by entering the office of the debtor. The plaintiff entered the business premises and handed the employee, who was the only party present on the premises, a set of papers representing a lawsuit, that she was the guarantor of the obligation, that certain equipment was security for the obligation, and that she was removing that equipment. There was conflicting testimony as to whether the employee told her not to take the equipment or whether the employee told her that she doesn't blame her and that the employee would do the same thing.

The defendant asserted that no matter what the employee said, the employee had no authority to consent to the removal, because he was not a management employee. The plaintiff should have been aware of this, because she had been his supervisor before she was discharged. The plaintiff, on the other hand, argued that the employee had apparent authority.

A breach of peace did not occur because the consent of the debtor is not required for repossession of the collateral by the creditor nor is a debtor entitled to a hearing before the creditor repossesses the collateral. A creditor should not enter or attempt to enter any private structure to repossess the collateral without the express consent of the person in charge or a court order. The consent of the debtor to enter the premises to repossess must be voluntarily and freely given. The plaintiff used no force or threats to take the computer system and other records out of the office. All that is necessary is consent by the person in charge for the plaintiff to enter the offices to repossess the collateral. The front door was open and not locked, and only one employee was present, which automatically made him the person in charge. At no point did the employee of the defendant object to the presence of the plaintiff on the premises.

If a person entered a house with the consent of the owner of the house and then proceeded to engage in a repossession of a lawnmower or a snow blower, and the owner verbally objected to the repossession, it is doubtful whether the court would follow this case. A different result might take place if the same type of conduct was performed in a private residential house where the actual owner was present.[12]

In Minnesota, the court took a somewhat different position on what constitutes a breach of peace. When the debtor specifically objects to

---

[12]*Rainwater v. Rx Medical Servs. Corp.*, 30 UCC Rep. Serv. 2d 983, 1995 WL 907888 (E.D. Cal. 1995).

repossession, the debtor revokes any implied right previously granted to the creditors to enter the debtor's property without consent. But even if the debtor revokes consent to repossession, that revocation applied to defendant's right to enter plaintiff's property. The objection was not an absolute revocation of the right to repossess. Plaintiff may have denied defendant the right to enter their residence or garage to repossess the car, but this does not prohibit the repossession of the car from a parking lot or a public street. The court also decided that a debtor who assaults a repossession agent in lawful possession of collateral cannot regain legitimate possession of the collateral.[13]

A debtor in Illinois attempted to claim a breach of peace after debtor wrote a letter to the repo agent stating his objection to the repossession of the car and that the creditor could not resort to self-help tactics without causing a breach of peace. The court summarily disposed of this by stating that the mere recitation in a letter of an objection to repossession does not amount to a breach of peace upon repossession.

Once a repossession agent has gained sufficient domination over collateral, which amounts to control, the repossession has been completed. Once the creditor's agent had control of the car, the repossession was complete and the car buyer's violence could not dispossess the creditor of its right to possession. The tow truck was backed up to the Tahoe, the Tahoe was hooked to the tow truck, and the Tahoe's rear wheels were lifted off the ground before any contact was had with the debtor. This was sufficient for a completed repossession.[14]

The case also addressed the issue that a secured party's authority to take possession of collateral after default carries with it the privilege to enter another's land for the purpose of taking possession of the collateral if the entry is reasonably necessary to take possession. The entry was not a trespass nor was there any evidence that the repossessor had any contact with the debtor before the wheels were lifted from the ground.

The *Thompson* case also stated that the repossession of the automobile from a driveway, absent other circumstances such as the debtor's objection, does not constitute a breach of peace, notwithstanding the driveway may be technically part of the debtor's premises. Entry into the debtor's residence in the absence of the debtor is a breach of peace, but when you move away from the residence itself to the yard, the driveway, and finally the public street, the debtor's argument for a breach of peace becomes progressively more tenuous.

> ***Credit & Collection Tip:*** *A breach of peace is defined as conduct that invites or is likely to invite immediate public turbulence, or that leads to or is likely to lead to an*

---

[13]*James v. Ford Motor Credit Co.*, 842 F. Supp. 1202 (D. Minn. 1994).

[14]*Thompson v. First State Bank of Fertile*, 709 N.W.2d 307 (Minn. Ct. App. 2006). *See also James v. Ford Motor Credit Co.*, 842 F. Supp. 1202 (D. Minn. 1994).

immediate loss of public order and tranquility. The courts have treated verbal words or physical conduct which indicates the debtor's objection to repossession as a breach of peace.[15]

Duty to Repossess. The debtor offered to surrender the car and the bank said it would retrieve the vehicle itself. The debtor was not to deliver the car to them. The bank never recovered the vehicle and the vehicle sat for 13 months. The debtor moved away and the bank merged with another institution. The successor bank repossessed the car.

A secured creditor is not required to repossess on default. The creditor may refuse surrender and sue for the debt. However, if the creditor chooses to repossess, the provisions of the statutes prevail and the creditor is required both *before and after* default to use reasonable care in the custody and preservation of the collateral. The determination of who has possession of the collateral is a question of fact and strict physical possession is not required. The secured party must merely have constructive possession of the collateral, which includes the right to control the goods even though physical possession belongs to another.

Whereas the UCC does not state time limits for a secured party to take possession of collateral or to proceed with the sale following the taking of possession, the creditor allowed the car to sit idly for over 13 months after default. The policy of the code is to protect the rights of both the debtor and the creditor while maximizing the recovery. The secured party cannot wait an inordinate period and then elect to repossess and thereafter sue for deficiency which partially may have been caused by the creditor. This was an unreasonable disposition of the collateral.[16]

GMAC was faced with a situation where a vehicle plummeted in value to such an extent that it needed to be towed to a junkyard. The junkyard declined to accept it, absent a release of the lien in favor of GMAC. GMAC determined, based on the precipitous drop in the vehicle's worth to repossess and resell the vehicle, was not cost effective. Thus, the vehicle could not be junked unless GMAC released the lien.

The court found that GMAC's refusal to release its lien was objectively coercive since it already announced that it did not intend to repossess the surrendered vehicle. GMAC expressly conditioned the release of the lien upon the agreement to repay the balance in full. The court held GMAC's pronouncement amounted to a demand for a reaffirmation which obviously never purported to comply with the stringent anti-coercion requirements of the Bankruptcy Code.

The debtor was confronted with the prospect of retaining indefinite possession of a worthless vehicle unless they paid GMAC the balance.

---

[15]*In re Rutherford*, 329 B.R. 886 (Bankr. N.D. Ga. 2005); *Valentino v. Glendale Nissan, Inc.*, 740 N.E.2d 538 (Ill. App. Ct. 2000).

[16]*Nationsbank v. Clegg*, 29 UCC Rep. Serv. 2d 1366, 1996 WL 165513 (Tenn. Ct. App. Apr. 10, 1996).

The practical effect was the elimination of the so-called surrender option. The court reasoned that since the vehicle had no value, no reason existed for the lien. The bankruptcy court is supposed to provide a debtor a fresh start, free from coercive reaffirmation demands. The creditor must waive the effect of its lien so that the debtor is able to dispose of the collateral. This case was referred to the bankruptcy court to determine whether GMAC violated the discharge injunction prior to determining damages for a violation of the discharge injunction (the coercive demand for a reaffirmation agreement).[17]

REPLEVIN

In the event that the secured party cannot obtain peaceful possession of the vehicle, the right to use the remedy of replevin, known also as "claim and delivery" and "sequestration" in other states, is available. An application to court must be supported by an affidavit stating that peaceful possession is unavailable and the consumer has not surrendered the vehicle and is still in possession of the property. This application is processed usually after notice to the debtor to allow opposition to the application and to set forth why the secured party should not be entitled to repossess the vehicle. In most states the secured party is required to state in the affidavit the value of the vehicle and to post a bond in an amount double the value of the vehicle.

Replevin actions should be pursued to a final judgment. Most secured creditors use public auctions where many lenders sell the automobiles at one centralized location and dispose of the collateral quickly, before obtaining a final judgment. If the replevin action is pursued to final judgment, the final judgment ratifies and approves the sale of the vehicle. If a final judgment is not obtained, the consumer's attorney may be entitled to actual or punitive damages in a conversion action or a similar proceeding *for selling the vehicle without a judgment.*

Replevin should be used only when the creditor knows where the property is, such as an auto in a repair shop or a boat docked at a marina. The creditor must recognize that debtors may, and often do, move the property before the sheriff arrives (garaged vehicles can be moved quickly).

REPOSSESSION AND TERMINATION OF LEASE

One day after the vehicle was repossessed, the debtor filed a petition in bankruptcy under Chapter 13. Under the Chapter 13 proceeding the

---

[17] *In re Pratt*, 462 F.3d 14 (1st Cir. 2006).

debtor sought to voluntarily pay any arrearages, to assume the lease, and to continue to make payments outside of the plan of the Chapter 13 proceeding. The case allowed the debtor to pay pre-petition arrearages during a bankruptcy proceeding.[18] The court held that the lease terminated at the time of repossession, because the terms of the lease explicitly set forth "this lease will terminate upon the return of the vehicle to the lessor." The lease also set forth that "if you are in default, Ford Credit may cancel the lease, take back the vehicle."

The debtor's lease was terminated by the repossession *prior to the filing of the petition* as provided in the agreement. In the other cases where the bankruptcy court allowed the assumption of pre-petition arrearages, the vehicle was still in the possession of the debtor and not in the possession of the creditor.[19]

> ***Credit & Collection Tip:*** *Agreements should be carefully prepared for they are usually strictly construed by the courts.*

Notice to Terminate the Lease. Many of the states structure their statutes to require the creditor to send a notice to the debtor to terminate a lease. Some creditors feel that repossession of the vehicle is sufficient notice to the debtor of termination. The repossession sends a message to the debtor that the lease is terminated. The repossession is not termination of the lease if a statute requires the creditor to provide notice of cancellation and affords the debtor a period of time to cure the default.

The repossession took place prior to the bankruptcy. The statute, the Consumer Leasing Act, required mailing a defaulting lessee a notice of cancellation to terminate the lease. Where the lease contained no notice provisions, or if the notice provisions were in contradiction of the Consumer Leasing Act, the Consumer Leasing Act would prevail.

> ***Credit & Collection Tip:*** *Most leases contain a clause that repossession constitutes termination of the lease. If this contradicts the terms of the statute or the Consumer Leasing Act, repossession will not achieve that purpose.*[20]

PRE- AND POST-BANKRUPTCY REPOSSESSIONS

A repossession that occurs after the bankruptcy petition has been filed is considered a post-petition repossession. If the creditor has knowledge of the bankruptcy, the repossession would constitute a violation of the automatic stay contained in Section 362.

---

[18] *General Motors Acceptance Corp. v. D. Lawrence*, 11 B.R. 44 (Bankr. N.D. Ga. 1981).
[19] *In the Matter of Mayhall*, 200 B.R. 241 (Bankr. N.D. Ala. 1996).
[20] *Carmichael v. Nissan Motor Acceptance Corp.*, No. 01-15302 (11th Cir. 2002).

Not all post-petition repossessions result in damage awards. Where a creditor has received notice or has become aware of the pending bankruptcy proceeding, the creditor has a duty to make inquiry. If a repossession occurs after the petition is filed, but at a time prior to the creditor being informed of the filing (either by receipt of the notice from the court or notice by the debtor's counsel), the repossession would be void; but the creditor would not be liable for damages for the act of the repossession since no actual notice was received of the pendency of the bankruptcy case. It is not a willful violation and these instances have been described as technical or inadvertent. A creditor has an affirmative duty to undo any post-petition repossession immediately upon being notified of the pendency of the bankruptcy case even in the absence of any court order. Failure to do so will subject the creditor to damages. Some repossessions occur pre-petition and the question is whether retention of collateral post-petition, which was lawfully repossessed pre-petition, constitutes a willful violation of the automatic stay. It is undisputed that property repossessed pre-petition, but not disposed of, remains the property of the estate of the bankrupt and cannot be disposed of post-petition without a court order.

The narrow focus whether a creditor holding collateral repossessed pre-petition has an affirmative duty to turn its collateral over to the debtor and risk damages, or whether the creditor has the right to hold the collateral pending a hearing. The issue is whether the creditor must make an immediate application for a hearing or whether the creditor can wait until the debtor makes an application for an adversary proceeding to recover the collateral from the creditor. Cases go both ways on this subject with the majority favoring the creditor being required to make an application to the court to remove the stay. If the customer demands the return of the car, recent cases suggest that the creditor has to return the collateral or immediately seek an ex parte order for adequate protection or risk sanctions and attorney fees. The elements that seem to cause the conflict are contained in Section 542:

(a) Except as provided in subsection (c) or (d) of this section, an entity, other than a custodian, in possession, custody, or control, during the case, of property that the trustee may use, sell, or lease under section 363 of this title, or that the debtor may exempt under section 522 of this title, shall deliver to the trustee, and account for such property or the value of such property, unless such property is of inconsequential value or benefit to the estate.

(b) Except as provided in subsection (c) or (d) of this section, an entity that owes a debt that is property of the estate and that is matured, payable on demand, or payable on order, shall pay such debt to, or on the order of, the trustee, except to the extent that such debt may be offset under section 553 of this title against a claim against the debtor.

(c) Except as provided in section 362(a)(7) of this title, an entity that has neither actual notice nor actual knowledge of the commencement of the case concerning the debtor may transfer property of the estate, or pay a debt owing to the debtor, in good faith and other than in the manner specified in subsection (d) of this section, to an entity other than the trustee, with the same effect as to the entity making such transfer or payment as if the case under this title concerning the debtor had not been commenced.

The courts read the section as providing that an entity in possession of estate property shall deliver it to the trustee and this supports an automatic turnover duty with respect to any property repossessed pre-petition. On the other hand, the creditor is entitled to adequate protection of the creditor's interest as a precondition to the debtor's use of the property. The situation arises where the debtor may not even want the return of the property.

A case in Georgia provided an excellent analysis of this situation and finally decided that no obligation rests on the creditor to make an application for the hearing, leaving the burden upon the debtor to make an application for a hearing to return the vehicle, although the case may be in the minority.[21]

Credit & Collection Tip: *The best advice is to make the application to court to remove the stay.*

Reaffirmation. The debtor's reaffirmation of the agreement with the creditor removes the agreement from the jurisdiction of the Bankruptcy Court. The debtor is obligated to continue any obligation after discharge. Reaffirmation agreements must be made in writing and filed *prior to discharge* and may be required to be submitted for approval to the bankruptcy court (*see* Chapter 6).

In some states, if the secured party continues to accept payments beyond the date of discharge of the bankruptcy, *without a reaffirmation* of the debt, the secured party is abandoning all rights to obtain a deficiency and may only resort to the vehicle or boat in the event of a default. To protect the right to collect a deficiency from the bankruptcy even where the debtor continues to pay currently, the creditor has two options: reaffirmation or application for removal of stay. Failure to obtain reaffirmation, but continuing the acceptance of payments during and after the bankruptcy discharge, will effectively discharge the bankrupt from any liability for a deficiency balance. However, if the Chapter 13 plan provides for 100 percent repayment, the court may not grant relief of stay if debtor is current. The court is rewriting the lease (*see* Chapter 6).

---

[21] *Brown v. Joe Addison, Inc.* (*In re Brown*), 210 B.R. 878 (Bankr. S.D. Ga. 1997).

THIRD-PARTY LIEN—REPAIR SHOP

Garage Keeper's Liens. In many states, the law allows a garage keeper to assert a lien on an automobile, boat, or similar vehicle for repairs completed. This lien, in some states, may cover storage charges for the vehicles. The garage keeper may exercise the lien by selling the vehicle to satisfy the bill for repairs and storage, but must notify the owner of the vehicle of the proposed sale. The garage keeper's lien is also a creation of the state and its procedures and requirements are specific to each state.

In New York, the garage keeper's superior lien is a specific one, attaching only to the motor vehicle that is subject to the unpaid charges. The garage keeper must establish:

1. a bailment of the motor vehicle (delivered for repairs, and to be returned);
2. that it has performed garage services or stored the vehicle with the vehicle owner's consent;
3. that there was an agreed price or, if no agreement as to price has been reached, that the charges are reasonable for the services supplied; and
4. that the garage is a duly registered motor vehicle repair shop, as required under state law.

The garage keeper must notify the owner of the lien on the vehicle by mailing a copy of the lien under the specific terms of the statute. Upon receipt of the notice of lien, the debtor has a right to contest the lien providing appropriate action is taken within a fixed period of time. If the debtor does not contest the lienor's storage charges, the garage keeper (without making application to the court in some states) may then sell the vehicle to satisfy the bill for repairs and storage.

In situations where the vehicle or the boat is secured by either a mortgage or a lease, the rights of the garage keeper as opposed to the rights of the secured party come into conflict. In some states, the owner of the vehicle must consent to the repairs or storage. If the vehicle is leased, consent of the owner/lessor (financial institution) is required. If the vehicle is mortgaged, the owner of the vehicle would be the debtor who has the power to consent to the repairs and storage.

The garage keeper's lien, like the mechanic's lien, is a creation of statute and a careful reading of the statute must be made to determine the rights of the garage keeper. Some states do not allow the garage keeper to assert a lien for storage or for towing.

The lien is a powerful weapon. In most states, the vehicle may be sold to satisfy the charges. The paperwork is minimal for the garage keeper. For the owner of the vehicle (which may be the leasing company) to stop the sale, an attorney will have to be retained and an application to court is required. If a credit grantor is faced with such a situation, consultation with counsel is recommended not only to analyze the statute, but also to review the case law of the particular state as to its application to the garage keeper's lien.[22]

Storage Charges. The towing and storage charges may or may not be added to the repair bill depending upon the state statute, or depending upon how the courts in the state treat them. Storage and towing charges, because they do not enhance the value of the property, should not be entitled to protection unless specified by statute.[23] A lien is not created if the repair facility initially provided a warranty on the vehicle.

Consent of Owner. The consent of the owner of the vehicle is necessary for the repairman to assert the lien. In a security agreement, the lender loans money in return for a security interest in the boat or vehicle, and the borrower is the owner. In a lease agreement, the owner of the vehicle is the financial institution (bank) and not the party who is leasing and operating the vehicle. The party operating the vehicle has the apparent authority of ownership, and thus when the vehicle is delivered to the repair shop, the repair shop has the right to rely upon this "apparent authority" that the party who delivered the vehicle is the owner. Some cases have held, however, that the financial institution is not liable for repairs where consent has not been obtained. Whether all courts will agree with this conclusion is questionable, since an unfair and unjust result is produced with respect to repair shops. Under this ruling, the repair shop has the added obligation to determine whether the party is leasing the car and then to obtain the consent of the financial institution.[24]

Excessive Charges. Where the repair shop charges an excessive amount, the lien may be forfeited under certain special circumstances. Nevertheless, this minority decision has little support. An unreasonable charge can cancel the lien. If the repairman acts in good faith, the lien survives.

REDEMPTION

At any time before the secured party has sold or disposed of the collateral or entered into a contract for its disposition, the debtor or any other secured party has an unqualified right to redeem the collateral.

[22]*National Union Fire Ins. Co. of Pitt. v. Eland Motor Car Co., Inc.*, 87 N.Y.2d 1002, 665 N.E.2d 656, 642 N.Y.S.2d 855 (1996).

[23]*Central Trust v. Dan's Marina*, 858 S.W.2d 211 (Ky. Ct. App. 1993).

[24]*Lacomini v. Liberty Mut. Ins. Co.*, 497 A.2d 854 (N.H. 1985); *Joy Oil Company v. Freuhauf Trailer*, 29 N.W.2d 691 (Mich. 1947).

This can be done by fulfilling all the obligations of the lease or security agreement, and by paying the balance due as well as the expenses reasonably incurred by the secured party in retaking, holding, and preparing the security for resale.[25] This is an unqualified right of the consumer to redeem prior to the sale of the vehicle. No notice to the consumer of this right to redeem is necessary, but if an improper notice is sent to the consumer contradicting this unqualified right to redeem before the sale of the property, the secured party may be exposed to liability for damages.

SALE OF PROPERTY

The secured party after default may sell, lease, or otherwise dispose of any or all of the collateral in its present condition. The proceeds are applied to the reasonable expenses of retaking, holding, and preparing the collateral for sale or lease, and the satisfaction of any indebtedness secured by a subordinate security interest in the collateral. Disposition may be by public or private sale. Most financial institutions sell the property at public auction or private auction of dealers, in a commercially reasonable manner, and properly advertise the sale of the vehicle. Special auctions are conducted in which the financial institutions participate. Before a private sale is made, consultation with counsel is recommended to be certain you have complied with state law and Revised Article 9 of the UCC (*see* Chapter 11).[26]

STRICT FORECLOSURE

Strict foreclosure occurs when the secured party retains the vehicle in full satisfaction of the obligation. This is seldom done in today's economic environment, since the vehicle is usually worth less than the balance due. Careful review of the statutory requirements and the court decisions is recommended in the event the secured party engages in this type of foreclosure.

SHIP MORTGAGE ACT

The Ship Mortgage Act is a Federal Act designed for a speedy and uniform practice of foreclosure on boats and ships in the federal court, instead of leaving the mortgagee to the distinct and different procedures

[25]UCC § 9-506.
[26]UCC § 9-504.

of the courts of the various states. The purpose of the Act was to encourage institutions to extend credit to owners of boats and ships. The Ship Mortgage Act sets forth certain restrictions and conditions for the boats and ships to qualify for filing under the Act.

Several courts have interpreted the Act to mean that in the event the mortgage on a boat is filed under the Ship Mortgage Act, the Act is the sole and exclusive remedy available to foreclose a mortgage on a boat or ship. If the mortgage is within the Act, the position is that no suit to foreclose may be maintained in a state court.[27] Several other cases support this concept that the Ship Mortgage Act is the exclusive remedy to foreclose a mortgage, and the Act forms a comprehensive scheme for ship foreclosures "leaving no room for the operation of *state law.*"

The weight seems to be shifting to the concept that the Ship Mortgage Act and the Judicial Sales Act are mere alternatives to the procedures afforded by the state to foreclose on a boat. Where the secured lender has not only obtained a preferred mortgage under the Ship Mortgage Act, but also has obtained an installment security agreement under the state law, New York has followed the majority view and stated that the financial institution can proceed under state law to foreclose.[28]

The majority view contradicts this exclusive jurisdiction of the Ship Mortgage Act and holds that a defaulted ship mortgagee may either utilize the Ship Mortgage Act or resort to state law to repossess and sell the vessel either with or without the aid of court. The mortgagee may thus resort to the guidelines of state law to privately foreclose on mortgages under the Act.[29]

Consultation with experienced counsel is recommended.

A recent case, in the bankruptcy court in Delaware, discussed in depth the priority of maritime claims with respect to a ship mortgage.[30]

An article on creditor's remedies under the maritime law and the Ship Mortgage Act appears in the Appendix to this chapter.

INDIAN TRIBES—REPOSSESSING VEHICLES

There are about 500 nationally recognized Indian tribes in the United States. As a general rule, the tribes usually enter into a compact (agreement) with the particular state in which they reside. When dealing with the tribes, a vendor may not have the benefit of the state or federal laws since the tribes have jurisdiction over commerce dealing with the tribe. Some of them

---

[27] *Bank of Am. Nat'l Trust & Sav. v. Fogle*, 637 F. Supp. 305 (N.D. Colo. 1985).
[28] *Chemical Bank v. Barkan 8841-91* (N.Y. Sup. Ct., July 23, 1992, unreported).
[29] *First Fed. Sav. F.S.B. v. M/Y Sweet Retreat*, 844 F. Supp. 99 (D.R.I. 1994).
[30] *In re Muma Serv., Inc.*, 322 B.R. 541 (Bankr. D. Del. 2005).

adopt portions of the state law, such as the UCC, whereas others maintain their own rules for filing and enforcing security agreements.

Most tribes, if not all, will require you to proceed through the tribal system to obtain authority to repossess a vehicle within the jurisdiction of the tribal counsel. Sending a firm to repossess a vehicle on tribal land is not the answer. When dealing with one of the Indian tribes, the best course of action is to contact the tribal counsel or the legal department of the tribe to find out what laws are in place and whether they have their own laws with regard to security interests and enforcement or whether they defer to the state laws (which does happen in some instances). Obtaining a copy of the agreement with the state is helpful, but this may not contain the laws that the tribe has enacted regarding security interests and the enforcement of same. Consult with experienced counsel.

TRIBAL EXHAUSTION DOCTRINE

The Supreme Court established this doctrine in 1985 wherein federal courts may determine whether a tribal court has exceeded its lawful jurisdiction, because the extent of tribal sovereignty is a matter of federal law. The Supreme Court held that as long as the action is not patently violative of express jurisdictional prohibition, the first examination of tribal court jurisdiction should take place in the tribal court rather than in the federal court. Justice in the federal court will be served by allowing a full record to be developed in the tribal court before either the merits or any question concerning appropriate relief is addressed. The risk of a procedural nightmare will be minimized if the federal court stays its hand until after the tribal court has had a full opportunity to determine its own jurisdiction and to rectify any errors it may have made. The Supreme Court expanded the doctrine to diversity cases.[31]

SELECTION OF REPOSSESSION SERVICE PROVIDER

Creditors must accept that they could be held liable for the activities of the firm that they retained to repossess vehicles, boats, or equipment. Repossession firms must be geographically located near the property that they intend to repossess. Many of them will cover a large area and in some cases, an entire state, and promote themselves with offices across the state. Sometimes these so-called offices across the state are only

[31]*Iowa Mut. Ins., Co. v. LaPlante*, 480 U.S. 9 (1987); *Nat'l Farmers Union Ins. Cos. v. Crow Tribe*, 471 U.S. 845 (1985); *Bank One N.A. v. Shumaker*, 281 F.3d 507 (5th Cir. 2002).

affiliations and the contractor that you have engaged is in turn retaining another contractor to do the actual work. In many, if not most of the states, a creditor is liable in the event that the repossession firm commits a breach of the peace. The exact definition of what a breach of peace is or is not requires a careful examination of the case law of the particular state in which the property is being repossessed. Principally, a breach of peace normally takes place with a repossession of the vehicle. When contact of some nature between the repossession firm and the debtor occurs during the actual act of repossession either physically or orally at the time the repossession is made, the repossession firm should back off and try another time. The temptation is to continue with the repossession. At this point the debtor is entitled not only to claim physical injury, but also emotional and mental anxiety. The courts do award damages for these questionable conditions in some of the states. The normal defense to a breach of peace against a creditor is that the repossession firm is an independent contractor, and as an independent contractor, the creditor is not liable for the conduct of the independent contractor. Only the repossession firm is liable for its own conduct. While a few states have adopted that theory, most states will find the creditor liable.

In Black's Law Dictionary, the definition of breach of peace is "the criminal offense of creating a public disturbance or engaging in disorderly conduct, particularly by making an unnecessary or distracting noise." Aside from the criminal offense, a civil breach of peace is "creating any kind of disturbance or engaging in conduct which creates a disturbance." If the debtor is not present at the time of the repossession or within sight of the repossession, a breach of peace should not take place. The problem arises whenever the debtor is somewhere in the vicinity of the breach of peace. The debtor is doing everything in his power, whether it be oral communication or any other activity, to interfere with or hinder the repossession of the vehicle.

The debtor may refuse to leave the vehicle, may jump inside the vehicle during the repossession, or in some instances vocalize in a high-pitched voice to such a degree as to create a disturbance in the vicinity of where the repossession is being conducted. No set rules exist, other than common sense. The repossessor cannot use the services of a policeman or a governmental official to assist him in the repossession since this would constitute intimidation and coercion.

Another problem in repossessing an automobile is entry onto the premises of the debtor. Any type of entry, whether cutting a chain to a gate or opening a garage door, presents a question of trespassing on private property as well as a breach of peace. Sometimes repossession firms see the vehicle sitting on a driveway on the private property of the debtor. The temptation is strong where observation suggests that the debtor is not present on the premises or in the vicinity. The courts are in agreement that *any entry onto private property* is fraught with danger.

The purpose of this discussion is so that the creditor understands that selecting a repossession firm is as important as selecting a collection agency or attorney. Each of them plays their part in the collection effort. Normally, the creditor selects the repossession firm and often does not devote the time or interest in the selection process, since creditors are under the misapprehension that the conduct of the independent contractor does not present a problem of liability for the creditor.

The following are some suggestions when engaging the services of a repossession firm:

(1) Background checks should be made both civilly and criminally.
(2) The repossession firm should also be conducting background checks on their employees to be certain that none of them have a criminal record.
(3) A judgment or litigation search might be made with respect to the background of the repossession firm. This may help the creditor in some states with regard to showing due diligence. A financial statement should be obtained to determine whether the firm is solvent in the event the claim is made against the firm and the creditor. If it is a one-man operation, insurance should be considered.
(4) Insurance is available to repossession firms. The creditor should obtain a copy of the insurance policy or a copy of the covering sheet of the insurance policy which indicates the amount of coverage, the name of the policy, and the period of the policy. At the same time, the creditor should request that the repossession firm have the creditor named as an additional insured party under the policy. Obtaining this kind of protection usually is a function of the amount of business between the repossession firm and the creditor.
(5) Creditors should investigate whether they can obtain insurance themselves or consult with their own insurance broker to determine whether any of their existing policies provide this kind of coverage.
(6) A written agreement between the repossession firm and the creditor, whether in the form of a formal agreement or a letter agreement, is certainly recommended. The general purpose of the agreement is for the repossession firm to indemnify the creditor in the event any suit should be started against the creditor for damages by reason of any activity or conduct of the repossession firm.
(7) We recommend inquiring whether the agents who actually do the repossession carry a gun or any other type of weapon. If so, continue your search for another agent.

Another consideration should be whether the repossession company is forwarding the repossession to another company within their state. If such is the case, the same procedure should be applied to the repossession company actually handling the repossession. The due diligence just performed on the company retained will have no bearing if the retained company farms out the repossession to another company. The fact you may have remedies against the company you retained will not help if the company that actually does the repossession violates the law.

If the repossession firm is financially solvent or maintains adequate insurance, an indemnity agreement carefully drawn by competent counsel should afford substantial protection to the creditor. In some indemnity agreements, the creditor spells out exactly in detail the limitations on the repossession firm and specifies not only what may be prohibited in repossessing an automobile, but also specifically what is allowed in repossessing an automobile.

Laws vary significantly from state to state. In some states, a court order is required before the repossession can take place, while other states permit repossession on the instructions of the creditor. Some states have specific laws that the car cannot be removed from a garage even if the garage door is wide open and the car is beckoning to be removed. Other states have laws concerning hot-wiring the cars or the use of duplicate keys. Interestingly, Florida requires repossessing firms to attend classes to learn what the state law is and to learn how to handle a situation when the debtor is present during the attempt to repossess.

Reporting a Car as Stolen. One of the most dangerous aspects of repossessing a car is when the repossessor is unable to locate the car and provides information as to the efforts expended and time spent trying to repossess the car. The temptation might be to report the car to the police department as stolen—a step that requires serious consideration. Once the car is reported as stolen, the police will seek to apprehend the debtor as a criminal when they locate the car and the debtor is driving. The problem is even more serious in the event some third party is driving the car with the permission of the debtor.

> ***Credit & Collection Tip:*** *Before any such action is taken, conduct a thorough investigation to confirm the car was stolen, to the extent of attempting to speak to the debtor. Before such action is taken, consultation with an experienced and competent counsel is recommended. The damages that may be sustained may be substantial if the car was not stolen, and the debtor was merely trying to avoid repossession.*

LIABILITY OF CREDITORS FOR REPOSSESSION

In a case in Mississippi, a judge stated that where the service performed entails the commission of some illegal, dangerous, or tortuous act (wrongful act), the principal and the independent contractor both play an integral part and are thus proximate causes of whatever harm ensues. Where some serious harm can be reasonably anticipated, such as in the performance of a repossession, the creditor cannot allege a defense that the act causing the harm was solely committed by the repossession firm. Repossessing an automobile is considered a dangerous and tortuous act. A violation of the law by the repossession firm may place liability for said tortuous act upon the creditor who authorized the repossession.

The repossession firm was hitching a van to the wrecker and starting to remove it when the plaintiff awakened and went outside to see what was going on. The plaintiff observed a man attaching the van to a truck by way of a "quick snap harness" and the plaintiff began to yell. In pursuing the truck and the van, the plaintiff fell into a ditch and was injured and taken to the hospital. The plaintiff served a complaint upon the repossession firm and the defendant, who authorized the repossession, predicated upon the use of unnecessary force and a breach of peace.

The decision to repossess the van in the early morning hours by use of a "quick snatch harness" and to remove the van without the knowledge of the plaintiff was deliberate and intentional and was guaranteed to generate fright or anger in the event it was discovered. The action was fraught with the peril of provoking a breach of peace of the most serious kind. The moment the repossession was discovered and the plaintiff attempted to resist the repossession, this terminated the repossession firm's right to continue because in so doing they were causing a breach of peace. Since they did not cease the repossession, they had no legal authority and a tort was committed in continuing over the protest of the plaintiff.

Where the work or service to be performed entails the possibility of the commission of some illegal, dangerous, or tortuous act, both *the lender and the independent contractor* (repossession firm) play an integral part and are both causes of whatever harm ensues. Holding the lender liable for the work of an independent contractor is usually only applicable to work which of itself involves risk of harm to others. If a crime or some tort can be reasonably anticipated in its performance, the defense that the act causing the harm was committed by the repossession firm and not the firm that employed the repossession firm will not carry much weight.[32]

LEASED CARS—MAGNUSON-MOSS WARRANTY

The Magnuson-Moss Warranty Act is a disclosure act that requires a seller of a car to offer a refund or a replacement in the event the seller is unable to live up to the warranty. The Court of Appeals of New York took the position that the Magnuson-Moss Warranty Act does not apply to leased cars, although it does apply to cars that are sold. This issue has

[32]*Rainwater v. Rx Medical Servs. Corp.*, 30 UCC Rep. Serv. 2d 983, 1995 WL 907888 (E.D. Cal. 1995).

created a dichotomy amongst the states and New York seems to be adding its voice to the very unpopular view that a brand new leased car will not be covered by the Magnuson-Moss Warranty Act. The rationalization is that Congress specifically excluded the leasing of the vehicle from the Act and the New Car Lemon Law of the State of New York, General Business Law, 198A, substantially affords the consumer the same remedies as the Magnuson-Moss Warranty Act. Some other state laws protect the lessee, but in several states the lessee has no protection.[33]

[33] *DiCintio v. DaimlerChrysler Corp.*, 2002 N.Y. LEXIS 153 (2002).

CHAPTER 12 APPENDIX I

MARITIME LIENS AND SHIP MORTGAGES

The extension of credit in maritime transactions is separate and distinct from its land based non-maritime counterpart. Maritime credit and security is often thought as an area which is rare, remote and uncommon in our traditional commercial intercourse. This exclusionary mindset often marginalizes maritime credit matters and frequently causes commercial lenders to overlook an extensive source of lucrative credit business, albeit with a unique and somewhat complex package of legal problems. Those who are about to extend credit in a maritime transaction should consult with qualified legal practitioners.

The United States consists of approximately 50,000 miles of coast and river navigable waters which manifests the magnitude of potential admiralty jurisdiction within the United States alone. Add to this the fact that the bulk of the earth is covered by water and it must be concluded that the potential for admiralty jurisdiction through the transportation of passengers and cargo on these navigable waters is of great magnitude.

Admiralty Jurisdiction in the United States

(a) State courts have general jurisdiction; they have jurisdiction over any subject matter except matters on which original jurisdiction is exclusively reserved to the federal district courts.

(b) Matters exclusively reserved to the federal court include admiralty, *in rem* actions, i.e., limitation of liability, foreclosure of ship preferred mortgages, federal forfeiture and bankruptcy.

State courts have concurrent jurisdiction in most maritime subject matters not involving *in rem* subject matters.

Admiralty jurisdiction in the United States is broader than that of England. The United States recognizes jurisdiction over maritime activities occurring on all waters, whether or not connected with the sea, which are used or capable of being used for interstate or foreign commerce.[34] The reference to "maritime" in

[34]Compare a land locked lake, totally within one state, which is generally considered not to give rise to admiralty jurisdiction—no interstate element.

Article III, Section 2 has been interpreted to limit the power of the court to matters arising out of navigation of vessels or maritime commerce.

Maritime Liens are the Preferred Security Instruments Sought by Maritime Creditors.[35]

A maritime lien is often referred to as an indelible lien which travels with the vessel; it is informal and temporary and lasts only until payment is made or security provided. The maritime lien, without notice of the lien, may be good against a *bona fide* purchaser for value (which has caused the lien to be called "a secret lien"[36]). The foregoing notwithstanding, when a vessel is sold at a judicial sale (in an *in rem* action in a federal court, sitting in admiralty), all liens are expunged from the vessel and the buyer acquires the vessel free and clear of all liens and encumbrances. Private sales, by contrast, do not cleanse the vessel's title. Consequently, an uninformed buyer may buy a vessel subject to undisclosed, unrecorded (or secret) liens.

A maritime lien substantially differs from a commercial land lien in that it is a non-possessory property right of a non-owner in a vessel and the vessel's earned freight, cargo or other maritime property. The lien holder has a right in admiralty courts to have the vessel and the vessel's property sold and the proceeds distributed to the lien holders to satisfy an *in rem* debt of the vessel and its property.

To have a maritime lien against a vessel requires it be in navigation. No lien may attach to a vessel permanently removed from navigation, such as a ship under construction. Similarly, a sunken vessel is not subject to a maritime lien.[37]

Maritime liens arise out of contract, tort or statute. The purpose of a maritime lien is to encourage suppliers to provide services to vessels away from their home ports based solely on the credit of the vessels to continue the vessels in navigation.[38]

---

[35]*See* Volume 4, Benedict on Admiralty, 7th ed., Chapters II through V (nature of maritime liens, source of maritime liens, priorities of maritime liens, discharge of maritime liens).

[36]Many times the lien is not recorded.

[37]Once a sunken vessel is raised, it can be subject to arrest for a maritime lien.

[38]Historically, from their invention to the present day, vessels (be they lake, river or ocean-going), have been man's primary vehicle of trade and transport. As such, there is a universal desire that such movement be uninterrupted. Indeed, man's very survival on this earth is dependent upon international commerce. Thus, should any of the lien laws, as applied to vessels in trade, appear overly harsh towards the lending party, reflect on the impact of stopping a petroleum super-tanker's trade in supplying trucks, cars, planes and power plants with fuel, or that of stopping a bulk carrier of grain and its impact on consumers of bread and other staples. The goal of the law is not to strip the lender of its protections, but rather to make sure that the vessel's movement is unimpeded while the lender pursues other avenues of enforcement.

Some Examples of Maritime Liens:[39]

(A) Personal injuries and death of seaman claims, passenger and invitee claims for unseaworthiness of the vessel.[40]

(B) Collision liabilities, including injuries to other vessels and cargo and persons on the other vessel.

(C) Maintenance and cure,[41] failure to pay seaman's wages, liability for cargo damage.[42]

(D) Salvage services.

- (i) Salvage is defined as the compensation allowed to persons whose assistance saved the ship or cargo in whole or in part from an impending peril of the sea or recovery of property from actual loss.
- (ii) Necessary elements to qualify as salvage:
  - (a) Maritime peril impacting on property to be rescued.
  - (b) Volunteer service not owed to the property as a matter of duty.
  - (c) Success in saving the property or part of it from the impending peril.
- (iii) Pure Salvage.[43]
- (iv) Contract Salvage.[44]
- (v) Salvor[45] has no property or possessory interest in the property saved. The rescued property must be taken to a safe port and returned to owner.[46]

(E) General average contributions.[47]

- (i) If there is a sacrifice to save the venture, all elements of the venture must contribute to the sacrificed element.
- (ii) In order to qualify as general average, the elements are as follows:
  - (a) A common danger (imminent peril).
  - (b) Sacrifice of a particular portion of the venture to save the whole.
  - (c) Attempt to avoid the imminent common peril must be successful.

(F) Repairs to vessels.

(G) Insurance premiums.

(H) Liens by subrogation.

(I) Examples of Statutory Maritime Liens: Ship's Mortgage Act, Limitation of Owner's Liability Act.

(J) Contract liens for necessaries.

---

[39]General Maritime Law and 46 U.S.C. § 31342 and 46 U.S.C. § 31301.
[40]Jones Act claims are not included.
[41]The obligation to maintain the injured seaman until he reaches maximum cure.
[42]Must be physical damage to cargo.
[43]Without prior agreement.
[44]Contract salvage by prior agreement generally entered into on a no cure no pay basis.
[45]Performer of salvage services.
[46]Subject to the salvor's maritime lien.
[47]Legal roots in ancient Rhodian law.

There are foundational differences between land liens and maritime liens, while space restrictions in this treatise do not permit a complete comparison, the main difference between the liens (which is not readily understood by creditors who lend money or services to non-maritime borrowers), is the priority among competing liens. Priority regarding competing land liens is generally considered to be "first in time—first in right." Priority regarding competing maritime liens, with certain exceptions, is considered to be "last in time—first in right."

Enforcement of Maritime Liens in the United States

Maritime liens are exclusively enforced in the United States by U.S. federal courts sitting in admiralty. The controlling rules are found in the Federal Rules of Civil Procedure (Supplemental Rules for Certain Admiralty and Maritime Claims, Rules A through F).[48]

Arrest vs. Attachment:

To avoid confusion, a distinction must be recognized between an "arrest" and an "attachment" of a vessel. A distinction must also be recognized between the entire universe of maritime disputes against persons or corporate defendants, *in personam*, and disputes and liens specifically against a vessel, *in rem*. The enforcement in the United States of *in rem* maritime liens against a vessel is within the exclusive jurisdiction of the United States federal courts; however, some non-maritime lien disputes may be brought either in United States state or federal courts.[49]

Maritime disputes which do not qualify as maritime liens, as discussed *supra*, may be brought in either a United States state or federal court in conjunction with the "attachment" of a vessel (which is the property of a person or corporate entity being sued, *in personam*). The "attached" vessel is not being specifically sued as an offending party, but rather is being "attached" to create jurisdiction over a defendant or to create security for an anticipated judgment over a defendant (*quasi in rem*).

It should be noted that an "arrest" of a vessel *in rem* in a federal court which ultimately results in the United States Marshal's judicial sale of that vessel conveys title of that vessel free and clear of all liens and encumbrances. By comparison, a judicial sale emanating from an "attachment" proceeding causes only a mere change of the vessel owner's interest in the vessel with the vessel remaining subject to all pre-judgment liens and encumbrances.

---

[48] Rule A (scope of Rules); Rule B (*in personam* actions, attachment and garnishment); Rule C (actions *in rem*); Rule D (possessory, petitory and partition actions); Rule E (actions *in rem* and *quasi in rem*) and Rule F (limitation of liability).

[49] State-owned vessels are immune from arrest. *See* U.S. Foreign Sovereign Immunities Act of 1976, 28 U.S.C. §§ 1601-1611, as amended 1994.

Ship Mortgages.[50]

Pursuant to the pre-1920 General Maritime Law of the United States, a mortgage on a vessel was not a maritime contract. Consequently, a maritime lien was not created by a mortgage on the vessel.

To create a legal environment which would encourage investment in ships, Congress legislated the Ship Mortgage Act of 1920 which created the preferred mortgage subject to foreclosure *in rem* by a federal court sitting in admiralty.[51,52]

Commencing with the Vessels Sales and Mortgage Recording Act of 1850, American ship mortgage legislation has been continually repealed, amended and recodified to correct real or perceived problems. The historical evolution of legislation has developed a plethora of confusion and complexities, resulting in complicated litigation regarding the enforcement of ship mortgages and priorities of competing maritime liens.

Priority of Fund Distribution Among Competing Maritime Liens After Judicial Sale of Arrested Vessel

Once a vessel is sold at auction and confirmed to the highest bidder, the distribution of the proceeds of the auction generally follow a certain order of priority. In United States federal courts the order of priority generally is as follows:[53]

(A) Court administrative costs and Marshal's fees.

(B) Preferred maritime liens (wages of crew, general average, salvage, including contract salvage, maritime tort).

(C) Maritime liens arising by contract which arose prior to the recording and endorsement of a preferred mortgage.

(D) A lien created by a preferred mortgage on a United States documented vessel, or a foreign vessel guaranteed under Title XI of the Merchant Marine Act, 1936.

(E) Maritime liens for repairs, supplies, towage, drydock repairs or other necessaries furnished to a foreign vessel in the United States.

(F) Lien of preferred ship mortgage on foreign vessels.

(G) Maritime liens for cargo claims and other contract liens, *i.e.*, repairs, supplies, towage and other necessaries provided outside the United States.

(H) Non-maritime liens.

The complexity and confusion of the subject of maritime liens, ship mortgages and priorities of competing maritime liens is enough of a problem when

---

[50]*See* Title 46 U.S.C.A., Chapter 25.

[51]For enforcement of ship mortgages, *see* Volume 2, Benedict on Admiralty, 7th ed., Chapter VI, Section 70.f.

[52]*See* Foreclosure Complaint Forms, Volume 4, Benedict on Admiralty, 7th ed., Forms Nos. 1-472 through 1-478.

[53]Title 46 U.S.C.A., Chapters 301 and 313 (Title 46, Section 31326).

dealing with United States maritime liens on documented domestic vessels. However, that complexity and confusion is multiplied several fold when one deals with foreign ship mortgages, foreign maritime liens seeking enforcement in foreign courts or vice versa. Given the concomitant "international" nature of vessels plying global trade, maritime liens, ship mortgages and priorities of liens has become a highly specialized area. It is strongly recommended that when a creditor is confronted with a ship mortgage or a maritime lien that creditor seek the assistance of an experienced maritime lawyer.

Chapter 13

Fair Credit Reporting Act

The use of credit reporting agencies blossomed in the 1960s when a large number of local and national credit reporting agencies entered the arena to feast on the credit boom. They furnished information to just about anyone who asked and was willing to pay a fee. The information being provided to these agencies was accepted and recorded by many with little regard for accuracy and completeness. The reporting agencies were growing at such a phenomenal rate that they found it difficult to respond to consumers' requests concerning mistakes and inaccurate information, and in many instances some of the smaller agencies totally ignored the consumer. Blatant mistakes occurred where a consumer's credit was ruined because the name was similar to that of another consumer. Most states were not too concerned with the consumer, and little state regulation was enacted in this area, especially in those states where the major reporting agencies employed a large staff. Congress sought to correct the problem in the 1970s and created stringent requirements for the credit reporting agencies.

The FCRA, effective in 1971, achieved two goals. First, the Act enabled consumers to obtain information from credit reporting agencies. Second, the Act compelled the reporting agencies, and those supplying the agencies with information, to comply with certain procedures and regulations regarding the availability of information about the consumer. *The Act applies only to consumer credit transactions; it does not apply to commercial credit transactions or commercial agencies which distribute information to businesses.*

CONSUMER REPORT

A consumer report is any written, oral, or other communication of any information by a consumer reporting agency consisting of the following seven characteristics about a consumer:[1]

1. Creditworthiness.
2. Credit standing.
3. Credit capacity.
4. Character.
5. General reputation.
6. Personal characteristics.
7. Mode of living.

A consumer report must be used primarily for personal, family, household, or employment purposes and utilized in whole or in part to establish a consumer's eligibility for credit or insurance.

A report of owners of motor vehicles, which lists the names of creditworthy individuals, is a consumer report, while a report limited solely to the consumers' names and addresses is not a consumer report, since no other information is disclosed. A telephone directory is not considered a consumer report nor is a list of names of persons with a checking account, since the mere fact that the party has a checking account is not evidence of creditworthiness. Trade directories of attorneys, insurance agencies, or accountants are not consumer reports.

Reports to determine whether the financial worth of a prospective defendant in a lawsuit is substantial enough to justify instituting a suit are not permitted, and a consumer report may not be obtained for use in discrediting a witness at a trial. Neither of the aforementioned reports is used to determine the creditworthiness of a consumer.

Collection agencies and creditors become consumer reporting agencies if they regularly furnish information beyond the transaction or experience with the consumer to third parties to use in connection with another consumer transaction.

CONSUMER REPORTING AGENCY

A consumer reporting agency is a firm that receives compensation on a cooperative non-profit basis and regularly engages in whole or in part in

---

[1] 16 C.F.R. § 603; 15 U.S.C. § 1681a(d); *Hoke v. Retail Credit Corp*, 521 F.2d 1079 (4th Cir. 1975), *cert. denied*, 423 U.S. 1087 (1976).

the practice of assembling or evaluating information on consumers for the purpose of furnishing said report to their customers. A creditor providing information to the credit bureau for a fee does not become a consumer reporting agency.

PERMISSIBLE PURPOSES

Consumer Report. A consumer report may be issued only for permissible purposes. The concept of "legitimate business need" has been broadly interpreted, but the Act addressed specifically the definition of a "legitimate business need." In Section 4(F) the permissible purpose requires a legitimate business need for the information in connection with a business transaction that is initiated by the consumer or to review an account to determine whether the consumer continues to meet the terms of the account.

Under the old FCRA we had three decisions dealing with obtaining a credit report. In the Eighth Circuit, the court held that you could not obtain a credit report for purposes of extracting a settlement from an insurance carrier in a malpractice case. The court zeroed in on the fact that the credit report was obtained for commercial or professional use and not in connection with the consumer transaction.[2]

In a case in the Eleventh Circuit, the court held there was no permissible purpose for obtaining a credit report by a party who made a claim under his policy even where the insurance company felt that the claim asserted might have been fraudulent. The insurance company argued that the credit report was not in a sense a "consumer report." The court felt that the report was a "consumer report" because the agency expected the report to be used for a permissible purpose and collected the information to satisfy what it thought was a permissible request.[3]

The Internal Revenue Service inquired whether they could obtain a report on the spouse of a taxpayer in a community property state where the taxpayer owed money to the Internal Revenue Service, and the Federal Commission responded that there was no permissible purpose if the spouse herself is not personally liable for the tax.[4]

The creditor entered a judgment against a corporation. When they were unable to collect from the corporation, the attorney ordered a consumer credit report on the sole shareholder and her husband. The creditor argued that obtaining the credit report assisted them in collecting the judgment. The approach failed because the FCRA requires a permissible purpose relating to a consumer relationship between the party requesting

[2]*Bakker v. McKinnon*, 152 F.3d 1007 (8th Cir. 1998).
[3]*Yang v. Government Employee's Ins.*, 146 F.3d 1320 (11th Cir. 1998).
[4]Bauchner, FTC Informal Staff Letter, Aug. 5, 1998.

the report and the subject of the report, regarding credit, insurance, and employment. No consumer relationship existed.[5]

A case in the Seventh Circuit addressed the issue of whether a lender may order a credit report on a rental installment contract that was consummated with the automobile dealer, and would thereafter be assigned to the lender who finances the transaction. The consumer did not know that the bank would request a credit report. The judge took the posture that while it may be a better practice for car dealers explicitly to inform their customers that unknown third-party lenders may request their customers' credit reports, we are not convinced that a failure to do so violates the FCRA as it now is written. A third party cannot troll for reports nor can they request a report on a whim. A direct link must exist between the consumer's search for credit and the bank's credit report request. If the connection between a consumer search and a bank's request is clear, the request will not infringe upon the consumer's privacy interest.

In this instance the bank ordered the plaintiff's credit report only because the plaintiff sought financing for their new car. The line of causation was direct and thus the request was properly made. Other courts might take a different tact and probably the way to address this situation is to provide in the retail installment contract that the consumer expressly consents to the lender financing the installment contract ordering a credit report. The wording might be more extensive to cover third-party purchases of the retail installment contract, such as debt buyers down the road a year or two.

> ***Credit & Collection Tip:*** *A carefully worded retail installment contract is much more desirable than to become involved in another litigated case, even though the creditor may be successful in the litigation.*[6]

A case has spelled out a distinction that many have ignored. The relevant statutory text, slightly reorganized, is as follows:

> Any consumer reporting agency may furnish a consumer report to a person which it has reason to believe intends to use the information
>
> 1. in connection with a credit transaction involving the consumer on whom the information is to be furnished and
> 2. involving the
>   a. extension of credit to or
>   b. review or collection of an account of the consumer.

---

[5] *Bakker v. McKinnon*, 152 F.3d 1007 (8th Cir. 1998); *Sather v. Weintraut*, 2003 U.S. Dist. LEXIS 12435 (D. Minn. July 10, 2003); *James v. Interstate Credit and Collection, Inc.*, 2005 U.S. Dist. LEXIS 33576 (E.D. Pa. Apr. 28, 2005).

[6] *Stergiopoulos v. First Midwest Bankcorp. Inc.*, 427 F.3d 1043 (7th Cir. 2005).

The court was didactic in pointing out that many have ignored the critical fact that the statute uses the conjunctive word "and." The collection of an account or a debt must bear a connection to a credit transaction. If a collection of a debt from a consumer does not bear a connection to a credit transaction, a permissible purpose does not exist. An excerpt from the decision rendered in the District Court of the Northern District of Illinois in February 2007 is included in an Appendix to this chapter.[7]

In a case from the Ninth Circuit, the debtor incurred the charge by virtue of his vehicle being towed, and impounded and sold. The sale price was insufficient to pay the outstanding debt and the account was turned over to a collection agency. The consumer did not voluntarily seek credit because the debt arose as a result of the consumer's vehicle being impounded. The court read the statute literally with the word "and" requiring an extension of credit to support the collection of the debt to authorize a permissible purpose.

A Circuit Court of Appeals case from the Ninth Circuit carries significant weight with the rest of the circuits. More cases will address the issue. The court held that *collection by itself is not a permissible purpose* to obtain a consumer credit report. The debt must be an extension of credit offered by the lender and accepted by the consumer—notwithstanding the word "or" preceding the phrase "review or collection of an account of consumer."[8]

Employer. The issue frequently arises as to whether an employer is liable for the acts of an employee who orders a credit report without a permissible purpose. The theory behind such liability would be the apparent authority of the employee to order the credit report electronically through the use of the computer provided by the employer on the premises of the employer.

A number of cases have applied this apparent authority theory, which is often referred to as the *respondeat superior doctrine*, on a strict liability basis, concluding that strict liability would be consistent with the FCRA's underlying deterrent purpose—because employers are in a better position to protect consumers by use of internal safeguards.

Some courts take the position that employers are in no better position than credit reporting agencies and have no greater duty under the terms of the Act to protect consumers by the use of internal safeguards. Employees should not be subjected to a greater standard of liability than the credit reporting agencies which the FCRA regulates. The FCRA is devoid of any provision which imposes on a user or a subscriber a duty to employ adequate and necessary procedures, or impose strict liability on the employer, nor does language in the FCRA create a duty to prevent willful violations since it has expressly placed that responsibility with the credit reporting

[7]*Miller v. Trans Union LLC*, CIV. No. 06 C 2883 (N.D. Ill. Feb. 28, 2007).
[8]*Pintos v. Pacific Creditors Ass'n*, 504 F.3d 792 (9th Cir. 2007).

agencies. Only if the employer receives a benefit does a basis for liability exist. Without benefits, the employer should escape liability. *Notwithstanding same, the majority of the courts consistently apply strict liability to employers.*[9]

Rental Collections. The Federal Trade Commission's (FTC) position has always been that collecting on a consumer lease on premises is not a credit transaction. A landlord would be unable to obtain a credit report since it is not a permissible purpose. One case has contradicted the FTC's position. The Circuit Court of Appeals in the Sixth Circuit has held that collection on money due on residential premises is a permissible purpose.[10]

Credit Reports on Business—Before Trial. A report that is not a consumer report does not become a consumer report just because it is used for a permissible purpose. Credit reports on businesses, such as a D&B Report, are not consumer reports.[11] A report to determine the credit eligibility of a business is not a consumer report even if it contains information on individuals.[12]

A reporting agency is allowed to furnish identifying information and other limited information concerning consumers to a governmental agency providing a permissible purpose exists.

A Sixth Circuit court held that drawing a credit report in preparation for a trial is not a permissible purpose within the FCRA.

Investigative Reports. An investigative report is one in which the consumer's character, general reputation, personal characteristics, or mode of living is determined through personal interviews with neighbors and friends or associates of the consumer.[13] Insurance companies and employers use this type of report. The information is gathered by use of the telephone or by sending a representative to the neighborhood of the consumer. The agency must disclose in writing that the report is being prepared and that the consumer is entitled to certain information.

The disclosure that an investigative report may be made must be mailed to the consumer not later than three days after the report is first requested by the client. Such disclosure is not necessary if the report is being used for employment purposes. Thus, a person or business requesting an investigative

---

[9]*Jones v. Federated Fin. Reserve Corp.*, 144 F.3d 961 (8th Cir. 1998); *Grab v. The American Lawyers Co.*, CIV. No. 05-00812 JMS/KSC (D.Haw. Mar. 19, 2007); *Kodrick v. Ferguson*, 54 F. Supp. 2d 788 (N.D. Ill. 1999); *Smith v. Sears Roebuck & Co.*, 276 F. Supp. 2d 603 (S.D. Miss. 2003); *Myers v. Bennett Law Offices*, 238 F. Supp. 2d 1196 (D. Nev. 2002).

[10]*Lusk v. TRW Inc.*, 173 F.3d 429 (6th Cir. 1999).

[11]*Levy v. Boron Oil Co.*, 419 F. Supp. 1240 (W.D. Penn. 1976).

[12]*Wrigley v. Dun & Bradstreet, Inc.*, 375 F. Supp. 969 (N.D. Ga. 1974).

[13]16 C.F.R. § 606.

report must recognize that the consumer will be notified by the reporting agency, unless the report is for employment purposes.

Upon written request by the consumer after receiving the above disclosure, any person or business that procures an investigative report must furnish a complete and accurate disclosure of the nature and the scope of the investigation requested. This written disclosure must be mailed no later than five days after the date of the request from the consumer.

STATUTE OF LIMITATIONS

In 2001, the U.S. Supreme Court and Justice Ginsberg considered the issue of whether Section 618 of the FCRA should apply the "discovery rule" to measuring the statute of limitations. Under the FCRA, any action to enforce liability must be brought within two years. As a rule, if the law states that the "statute of limitations is two years," the time runs from the discovery of the violation. But if the law is read strictly, the time runs from the date the violation actually took place.

The plaintiff contended that the generally applicable two-year statute of limitations commences to run only upon discovery of the alleged violations of the Act.

Justice Ginsberg stated that the discovery rule does not apply to Section 618 of the FCRA, and interpreted strictly the language of the statute which states as follows:

> . . . within 2 years from the date on which the liability arises . . .

The statute begins to run from the date of the violation unless the defendant has materially and willfully misrepresented any information required to be disclosed to an individual under the Act and the information so misrepresented is material to the establishment of the defendant's liability to the individual, and then the "discovery rule" applies.[14]

RECORD KEEPING

A consumer reporting agency is not obligated to convey a consumer's dispute statement in the same identical form so long as it is a clear and accurate codification or summary of the statement. In this instance, the consumer reporting agency altered the capitalization, punctuation, and

---

[14]*TRW v. Andrews*, 534 U.S. 19 (2001).

paragraph arrangement of a consumer statement.[15] With regard to keeping records, the FCRA is silent on this issue, but consumer reporting agencies must note that the FCRA imposes a two-year statute of limitations from the date of violation. This is more than the one-year statute that applies to the **Fair Debt Collection Practices Act** (FDCPA).

OBSOLETE INFORMATION

A consumer reporting agency may not issue or include in its report:[16]

1. Bankruptcies older than ten years.
2. Suits and judgments older than seven years or past the statute of limitations, whichever is longer.
3. Unpaid taxes and tax liens older than seven years.
4. Accounts placed for collection or charged to profit which antedates the report by more than seven years.
5. Records of arrest, indictment, or conviction of a crime older than seven years.
6. Any adverse information which antedates the report by more than seven years.

The amendment attempted to clarify when the seven-year period commences and states as follows:

> the seven-year period referred to in paragraphs 4(6) of Subsection A shall begin, with respect to any delinquent account that is placed for collection (internally or by referral to a third party, whichever is early) charged to profit or loss, or subjected to any single action, upon the expiration of the 180-day period beginning on the day of the commencement of the delinquency which immediately precede the collection activity, charged to profit or loss or similar action.

This seems to say that the seven-year period begins when the delinquent account is placed with a collection agency or a law firm when it is sent to a collection department in the creditor's organization, whichever occurs earlier. It also can commence if it is charged to profit or loss or subject to any similar action.

---

[15] Edwards, FTC Informal Staff Letter, July 15, 1998. *See Duncan v. Handmaker, Middletown and Reutlinger*, 149 F.3d 424 (6th Cir. 1998).

[16] 16 C.F.R. § 605.

COMPLIANCE PROCEDURES

The credit reporting agency must use due diligence to require prospective users of the information to certify the specific purpose for which the information is being sought. The information may not be used for any other purpose.[17]

The party requesting information does not have to provide certification for each name if the purpose is the same for all requests. A single certification that the information will be used for the proper purpose is sufficient to support many requests.[18]

An agency must use reasonable procedures to assure the greatest possible accuracy of the information. No specific guidelines or definitions are provided for "reasonable procedures." Cases have gone both ways on the extent of the due diligence that the agency must expend to obtain the information. To show that the credit reporting agency did not use due diligence, the consumer must prove both the inaccuracy of the information and that the credit reporting agency was not acting reasonably in obtaining the information. Due to continuous litigation in this area, specific criteria are difficult to provide since different courts considering similar facts arrive at different conclusions. In a recent case, the double reporting of a debt to a credit bureau where there was no dispute over the accuracy of the information reported is not a violation of the FDCPA.[19]

An agency is obligated to correct inaccurate information supplied by third parties. The extent of this obligation is uncertain and probably rests on the facts and circumstances of each case. Some courts hold that there is no obligation to investigate information supplied by creditors. But knowledge by an agency that the information is incorrect may provide a different result. Of course, if the final report is accurate, then the procedure used to produce the report is reasonable.[20]

If a married consumer's file does not designate whether the information belongs to either the joint or the individual credit of the two spouses, the reporting agency must honor a request by the consumer to segregate the information and report only the information that applies to one of the respective spouses.

A creditor must notify a credit reporting agency when a past due account has been paid or discharged in bankruptcy. The reporting agency is not in violation if the account is not marked "paid," if it was not informed by the creditor of the payment or discharge in bankruptcy.

---

[17] *Bryant v. TRW Inc.*, 487 F. Supp. 1234 (E.D. Mich. 1980).
[18] 16 C.F.R. § 607.
[19] *Kohut v. Trans Union, LLC*, No. 04-C-2854 (N.D. Ill. 2004).
[20] *McPhee v. Chilton Corp.*, 468 F. Supp. 494 (D. Conn. 1978).

AFFILIATE SHARING

The new Section 624 restricts the ability of an affiliate to share information that it has received with another affiliate by imposing an opt-out notice requirement. The company must clearly and conspicuously disclose to the consumer that information received from an affiliate is being used. The consumer must receive an opportunity to opt out, but this opt-out provision is only good for five years beginning on the date when the election is received unless the consumer subsequently revokes the opt-out. The opt-out notice may be combined with other required disclosures including those required by the Gramm-Leach-Bliley Act.

DISCLOSURE TO CONSUMER

Every reporting agency, upon request of the consumer and with proper identification, shall disclose accurately the nature and substance of the information on file at the time of the request. The source of the information need not be disclosed.[21]

The agency must disclose the name of any employer that has received a report within two years or any report that has been issued within one year. The reporting agency must furnish to the consumer the identity of any firm that has received a pre-screen list which contains the consumer's name.

The consumer may appear in person or make a written request with proper identification. The agency may disclose by mail, by telephone, or in person, if requested by the consumer. The consumer may have a third party present when making such a request.

PRIVATE RIGHT OF ACTION—FURNISHERS

Section 623 of the FCRA is entitled the "Responsibilities of Furnishers of Information to Consumer Reporting Agencies" and it itemizes the duties of furnishers of information to provide accurate information, to update and correct the information, and what information must be furnished upon notice of dispute.

The key paragraphs are Subdivision 623(b), (c) and (d), which deal with enforcement. Subsection 623(a) shall be enforced exclusively under Section 621 by the federal agencies and the state officials identified in Section 621. If the furnisher of information furnishes inaccurate information to a consumer reporting agency under Subdivision (a) of Section 623, only the agencies of the state and federal government can enforce

[21] 16 C.F.R. § 609.

Subdivision (a). *No private right of action exists in favor of a consumer to institute a suit against a furnisher of inaccurate information to a consumer reporting agency for violation of that section.* Subdivision (c) of Section 623 states that "Sections 616 and 617 do not apply to any failure to comply with Subsection (a) (except as provided in Section 621(c)(1)(B)). Sections 616 and 617 deal with the civil liability for willful noncompliance and civil liability for negligent compliance."

The statute states that these two sections (616 and 617) do not apply for failure to comply with Subsection (a) (the duty of furnisher of information is to provide accurate information or update information). Thus, a consumer will not be able to institute a suit against the furnisher of information who fails to provide accurate information under the Act. Section 621(c)(1)(B) enables the chief law enforcement officer of a state or an official or agency designated by the state to bring an action on behalf of the residents of the state to recover damages for this type of a violation.

Under both sections (616 and 617), if a furnisher of information fails to provide accurate information or fails to update the information, a consumer cannot institute a suit against that furnisher of information for either willful failure or negligent failure to either report accurate information or *correct and update the information.*[22]

The third duty of furnishers of information under Section 623 is to perform certain duties after receiving notice of dispute. In particular, Section 623(b) states that furnishers of information, *upon notice of dispute* with regard to completeness or accuracy of any information provided by a person to a consumer reporting agency, the person shall conduct an investigation, review all relevant information, report the results to the consumer reporting agency, and if the investigation finds that the information is incomplete or inaccurate, report those results to all other consumer reporting agencies to which the person furnished the information and compile and maintain files on consumers on a nationwide basis.

A cause of action under Section 1681s-2(a) of the FCRA must be commenced by a governmental agency or official and cannot be instituted by the consumer.[23]

As to 15 U.S.C. Section 1681s-2(b), the consumer may pursue claims for willful or negligent noncompliance and have a private right of action under Section 1681s-2(b) providing plaintiff shows that the furnisher

---

[22]*Perry v. First Nat'l Bank*, 459 F.3d 816 (7th Cir. 2006); *Johnson v. Wells Fargo Home Mortgage, Inc.*, 2007 U.S. Dist. LEXIS 79989 (D. Nev. Oct. 29, 2007).

[23]*Nelson v. Chase Manhattan Mortgage Corp.*, 282 F.3d 1057, 1059 (9th Cir. 2002); *Prakash v. Homecoming Fin.*, 2006 U.S. Dist. LEXIS 62911 (E.D.N.Y. Sept. 5, 2006); *Kane v. Guar. Residential Lending Inc.*, 2005 WL 1153623 (E.D.N.Y. May 9, 2005); *Aklagi v. Nationscredit Fin. Servs. Corp.*, 196 F. Supp. 2d 1186, 1192 (D. Kan. 2002); *Redhead v. Winston & Winston, P.C.*, 2002 WL 31106934 (S.D.N.Y. Sept. 20, 2002); *Miller v. Trans Union LLC*, 2007 U.S. Dist. LEXIS 14315 (N.D. Ill. 2007).

received notice from a consumer reporting agency that the credit information is disputed.[24]

Subdivision 2 sets forth a deadline as set forth in Section 611(A) for performing said investigation. Section 611 provides for a 30-day period and allows for a 15-day extension under certain conditions with certain limitations. If the furnisher of information under this paragraph violates the statute, no saving clause in the statute prevents a consumer from instituting suit for the violation. Thus, under Section (b), a consumer may institute a suit for a violation of the provisions after notice of dispute.[25] The Ninth Circuit addressed this issue and the results were both good and bad. The court held that Subdivision (a) (the duty to provide information and the duty to correct and update information) does not provide a private cause of action. The reason behind this is that Subdivision (c) specifically provides no private right of action is afforded for either willful noncompliance or negligent noncompliance. To enforce Subsection (a) rests entirely with the federal agencies and state officials identified under the Act.

> ***Credit & Collection Tip:*** *The duty to furnish the information and the duty to correct and update the information does not afford a consumer a private right of action to sue the furnisher in the event of noncompliance with the Act.*

The bad news is that a private right of action exists for a consumer to enforce the section when furnishers receive *notice of dispute.*

Another case in Maryland relied on a Fourth Circuit case which allowed consumers to have a private action against the furnisher of information, but consumers were required to first file their dispute with the credit reporting agency. If the consumer does not file his report with the credit reporting agency, the consumer has no right to start a suit directly against the furnisher of information. The act of reporting the dispute to the reporting agency, who in turn will report the dispute to the furnisher of information, will allow an opportunity to the furnisher of the information to make an investigation.[26]

---

[24] *Young v. Equifax Credit InfoServices*, 290 F.3d 631, 639-640 (5th Cir. 2002); *Nelson v. Chase Manhattan Mortgage Corp.*, 282 F.3d 1057, 1059 (9th Cir. 2002); *Aklagi v. Nationscredit Fin. Servs. Corp.*, 196 F. Supp. 2d 1186, 1192 (D. Kan. 2002); *Weseman v. Wells Fargo Home Mortg., Inc.*, 2008 WL 542961 (D. Or. Feb. 22, 2008); *Scott v. Amex/Centurion S & T*, 2001 WL 1645362 (N.D. Tex. Dec. 18, 2001); *Hasvold v. First USA Bank, N.A.*, 194 F. Supp. 2d 1228, 1234 (D. Wyo. 2002).

[25] *Mandlay v. Bank One Dayton*, 2000 U.S. Dist. LEXIS 16269 (Ariz. 2000).

[26] *Beattie v. Nations Credit Fin. Servs. Corp.*, No. 02-1744, 69 Fed. Appx. 585 (4th Cir. 2003); *Akalwodi v. Risk Mgmt. Alternatives, Inc.*, 336 F. Supp. 2d 492 (D. Md. 2004); *Whisenant v. 1st Nat'l Bank & Trust Co.*, 258 F. Supp. 2d 1312 (N.D. Okla. 2003); *Liceaga v. Debt Recovery Solutions, LLC*, 169 Cal. App. 4th 901 (Cal. Ct. App. 2008).

JURISDICTION

Another case in the Circuit Court of Appeals of the Ninth Circuit held that the jurisdiction and venue in a FCRA case is determined by the residence of the consumer. The appellate court disagreed with the district court's conclusion that the injury occurred where one would access the credit reports. The injury was suffered in the state where the plaintiff resided and that is where jurisdiction lies.[27]

CIVIL LIABILITY

The amended Act has expanded the liability of a consumer reporting agency in Section 616 (15 USC 1681(n)) and Section 617 (1681)(o):

SECTION 616. CIVIL LIABILITY FOR WILLFUL NONCOMPLIANCE

a. *In general.* Any person who willfully fails to comply with any requirement imposed under this title with respect to any consumer is liable to that consumer in an amount equal to the sum of
   1. (A) any actual damages sustained by the consumer as a result of the failure or damages of not less than $100 and not more than $1,000; or
      (B) in the case of liability of a natural person for obtaining a consumer report under false pretenses or knowingly without permissible purpose, actual damages sustained by the consumer as a result of the failure or $1,000, whichever is greater;
   2. such amount of punitive damages as the court may allow; and
   3. in the case of any successful action to enforce any liability under this section, the costs of the action together with reasonable attorney's fees as determined by the court.

b. *Civil liability for knowing noncompliance.* Any person who obtains a consumer report from a consumer reporting agency under false pretenses or knowingly without a permissible purpose shall be liable to the consumer reporting agency for actual damages sustained by the consumer reporting agency or $1,000, whichever is greater.

c. *Attorney's fees.* Upon a finding by the court that an unsuccessful pleading, motion, or other paper filed in connection with an action under this section was filed in bad faith or for purposes of harassment,

---

[27] *Myers v. Bennett Law Offices*, 238 F.3d 1068 (9th Cir. 2001); *Bakker v. McKinnon*, 152 F.3d 1007 (8th Cir. 1998).

the court shall award to the prevailing party attorney's fees reasonable in relation to the work expended in responding to the pleading, motion, or other paper.

Section 617. Civil Liability for Negligent Noncompliance

a. *In general.* Any person who is negligent in failing to comply with any requirement imposed under this title with respect to any consumer is liable to that consumer in an amount equal to the sum of
   1. any actual damages sustained by the consumer as a result of the failure;
   2. in the case of any successful action to enforce any liability under this section, the costs of the action together with reasonable attorney's fees as determined by the court.

b. *Attorney's fees.* On a finding by the court that an unsuccessful pleading, motion, or other paper filed in connection with an action under this section was filed in bad faith or for purposes of harassment, the court shall award to the prevailing party attorney's fees reasonable in relation to the work expended in responding to the pleading, motion, or other paper.

Prior to the amendment, the wording in Section 616(a) consisted of "any consumer reporting agency or user of the information" which is now changed to "any person who willfully fails to comply with any requirement imposed under this title with respect to any consumer is liable to that consumer in an amount equal to the sum of . . . ." Prior to the amendment, the liability for a violation was the actual damages sustained by the consumer. The amended law repeals "the actual damages" and states that the amount will be not less than $100 and not more than $1,000. The same change is carried over in Section 617, where any consumer reporting agency or user of the information is replaced by "any person." [Section 617(a).] This section deals with negligent noncompliance. The Act also includes attorneys' fees.

Another issue of liability arises from the fact that an employee might obtain a report without a permissible purpose and the issue is whether the employer is liable under an agency relationship based on apparent authority. The best protection against this problem is to train your employees properly and be certain that the party who is in charge of obtaining the report is fully aware of the consequences of obtaining a report without a permissible purpose.

Consumer reporting agencies have a duty to conduct a reasonable investigation into any item that a consumer disputes. The agency has an additional duty to go beyond the creditor's response to a disputed item and to conduct a reasonable investigation, but only under limited circumstances.

The Seventh Circuit has held that such a heightened duty to conduct an additional reasonable investigation only occurs when a consumer alerts an agency to the possibility that the source may be unreliable or the agency itself knows or should know that the source is unreliable and the cost of verifying the accuracy of the source does not outweigh the possible harm to the consumer from the inaccuracy.[28]

The court held that the credit reporting agency was entitled to rely on the integrity of the supplier of the information since the supplier had been a reliable supplier for over ten years. The credit reporting agency communicated the dispute repeatedly to the supplier providing additional information each time and the supplier reaffirmed the accuracy of the account information. Under these circumstances, the court held that the credit reporting agency was not liable.

> ***Credit & Collection Tip:*** *When preparing an employment contract (or even as a supplement to an employment application after the party is hired) or, in the alternative, an employer handbook, set forth the conditions and the procedures to be used to order a credit report. The manual and training may assist you in the event there should be suits for violations.*

TARGET MARKETING LISTS—PRESCREENING

The pertinent section in the FCRA that deals with prescreening is Section 1615(d) (15 U.S.C. 1681(m)) as follows:

a. Duties of users making written credit or insurance solicitation on the basis of information contained in consumer files:

    1. *In general.* Any person who uses a consumer report on any consumer in connection with any credit or insurance transaction that is not initiated by the consumer, that is provided to that person under Section 604(c)(1)(B)(1681b) shall provide with each written solicitation made to the consumer regarding the transaction a clear and conspicuous statement that

        A. information contained in the consumer's consumer report was used in connection with the transaction;
        B. the consumer received the offer of credit or insurance because the consumer satisfied the criteria for creditworthiness or insurability under which the consumer was selected for the offer;

[28]*Henson v. CSC Credit Serv.*, 29 F.3d 290 (7th Cir. 1994); *Stevenson v. TRW Inc.*, 987 F.2d 288 (5th Cir. 1993); *Pinner v. Schmidt*, 805 F.2d 1258 (5th Cir. 1986); *Morris v. Trans Union LLC*, 420 F. Supp. 2d 733 (S.D. Tex. 2006).

C. if applicable, the credit or insurance may not be extended if, after the consumer responds to the offer, the consumer does not meet the criteria used to select the consumer for the offer or any applicable criteria bearing on credit worthiness or insurability or does not furnish any required collateral;
D. the consumer has a right to prohibit information contained in the consumer's file with any consumer reporting agency from being used in connection with any credit or insurance transaction that is not initiated by the consumer; and
E. the consumer may exercise the right referred to in subparagraph (D) by notifying a notification system established under Section (604)(e) (§ 1681b).

2. *Disclosure of address and telephone number.* A statement under paragraph (1) shall include the address and toll-free telephone number of the appropriate notification system established under Section 604(e) (§ 1681b).
3. *Maintaining criteria on file.* A person who makes an offer of credit or insurance to a consumer under a credit or insurance transaction described in paragraph (1) shall remain on file the criteria used to select the consumer to receive the offer, all criteria bearing on creditworthiness or insurability, as applicable, that are the basis for determining whether or not to extend credit or insurance pursuant to the offer, and any requirement for the furnishing of collateral as a condition of the extension of credit or insurance, until the expiration of the 3-year period beginning on the date on which the offer is made to the consumer.
4. *Authority of federal agencies regarding unfair or deceptive acts or practices not affected.* This section is not intended to affect the authority of any Federal or State agency to enforce a prohibition against unfair or deceptive acts or practices, including the making of false or misleading statements in connection with a credit or insurance transaction that is not initiated by the consumer.

The amended FCRA looks favorably upon those parties who use prescreening.

The Act requires the marketer to provide the consumer with each written solicitation a clear and conspicuous statement that the information contained in the consumer's report was used in connection with the transaction, and that the consumer received the offer of credit because the consumer satisfied the criteria of creditworthiness. The consumer must be advised that the consumer was selected for the offer because certain criteria were met.

Prior to the amendments, the marketer had to make the offer of credit to the consumer unless there was a significant change of circumstances which was defined in a limited and narrow way. The amendment provides in Subsection (1)(C) that the credit may be withdrawn after the consumer responds to the offer, or there is a change of circumstances wherein the consumer does not meet the criteria that was used to select the consumer or in the alternative does not furnish the required collateral. At the same time in Subdivision (3), the marketer must maintain on file for three years after the offer the criteria used to select the consumer and any or all criteria bearing on the creditworthiness of the consumer which is the basis for determining whether or not to extend credit, as well as the requirements for furnishing of the collateral.

Under Subdivision (2) the consumer must be provided a statement that must have the address and toll-free telephone number of the appropriate notification system provided in Section 604(e). The section provides that a consumer may elect to have his name and address excluded from any list provided by a consumer reporting agency in connection with an extension of credit that is not initiated by the consumer, by notifying the agency that the consumer does not consent to any use of a consumer report in connection with any credit transaction that is not initiated by the consumer (prescreening).

The consumer must be notified of the fact that the credit may be denied because of a change in circumstances wherein the consumer does not meet the criteria.

Prescreeners may receive only the name and address of the consumer, and any other information must be used solely for the purpose of verifying the consumer's identity.

In the event the offer is withdrawn, the provisions of Section 615 (15 U.S.C. § 1681(n)(a)(b)) would apply in that the prescreener would be required to deliver notice of the adverse action and would necessarily have to comply with all the terms and conditions that apply to adverse action under the Act. Any withdrawal of the offer must occur between prescreen and acceptance of the offer. Once the offer is accepted, the offer must be fulfilled.

Examples of circumstances that may permit the offer to be terminated include foreclosure of a residence, bankruptcy filing, or entry of a judgment or a lien—providing these items were included in the original criteria to determine who would be selected for the offer. Banks who extend credit to the consumer by prescreening may review the consumer's response form to determine whether the consumer still meets the criteria. The bank may also verify other information to determine if the consumer still meets the criteria, and if the consumer does not, the offer may be withdrawn.

Names and Addresses. The Federal Trade Commission found that using a target marketing list of names and addresses is not an authorized use of a consumer report, and ordered target marketers to stop marketing these lists to direct marketing firms. The case went up to the D.C. Circuit, which agreed with the Federal Trade Commission that selling these types of lists for marketing purposes violated FCRA. Nevertheless, the circuit court did not agree with the Federal Trade Commission in holding that the lists were consumer reports. TransUnion petitioned the Supreme Court for review and the Supreme Court denied certiorari. As a result, it appears that credit reporting agencies will be unable to rent target marketing lists.[29]

DATA FURNISHERS—DUTIES

When a consumer initiates a dispute directly with the data furnisher, the data furnisher will be required to take specific steps to respond to said dispute.

Review all the information provided by the consumer. Respond to the consumer within the allocated time frame. The time frame is usually 30 days, unless the consumer provides additional information after the start of the investigation. The time frame is then extended to 45 days.

If the data furnisher finds the information is inaccurate, it is under an obligation to notify the reporting agency and at the same time provide the reporting agency with accurate information to correct the inaccurate information.

Data furnishers are not required to investigate frivolous or irrelevant disputes. If the consumer fails to provide sufficient information or the data furnisher determines that the debtor has submitted the same information before to the data furnisher or to the credit reporting agency, the data furnisher has already complied with the consumer's request in response to the prior claim by the consumer.

After the investigation is completed, the data furnisher must modify the item of information to correct the error, delete the information in the consumer report, or block the reporting of said item of information. The data furnisher also must notify each credit reporting agency to which it reported the item of information and advise them that the information was incorrect. The data furnisher also must notify the consumer.[30]

E-OSCAR

E-OSCAR is a web-based metro two system that allows responses to consumer credit disputes by the entities which report to the credit

---

[29] *Trans Union v. FTC*, 536 U.S. 915 (2002); *Trans Union Corp. v. FTC*, 245 F.3d 809 (D.C. Cir. 2001); *Bruce v. Keybank Nat'l Ass'n*, 2006 U.S. Dist. LEXIS 30267 (N.D. Ind. May 15, 2006); *Barnette v. Brook Rd., Inc.*, 429 F. Supp. 2d. 741 (E.D. Va. 2006). *See* 15 U.S.C. § 1681.

[30] *Elmore v. North Fork Bancorporation*, 325 F. Supp. 2d 336 (S.D.N.Y. 2004).

reporting agency. Both the consumer reporting agency and the data furnisher utilize the automatic compliance system to report.

A. ACDV stands for an Automatic Credit Dispute Verification which is sent by the credit reporting agency to the data furnisher on behalf of the consumer after the credit reporting agency receives notification of a dispute from the consumer.
B. ACDV is also the investigation response wherein the data furnisher reports to the credit reporting agency (CRA).
C. AUD stands for an Automated Universal Data form provided by the data furnisher to process "out of cycle" modifications and updates and are sent to the credit reporting agency to whom the data furnisher is reporting.

The E-OSCAR stores data for 120 days from the date that the initial ACDV is entered by the data furnisher. After 120 days the history is purged.

The ACDV and the AUD history show records of every transaction that took place with regard to the disputes. A record should be kept of all modifications to the credit report.

PATRIOT ACT

The Office of Foreign Assets Control within the United States Treasury Department maintains a "specially designated national list" (SDN list) of drug traffickers and terrorists. Under the Patriot Act, American businesses are required to take reasonable measures to ensure that they are not doing business with or extending credit to anyone on the SDN list. Trans Union for an additional fee will notify the client as to whether the person whose credit is being investigated is named on the SDN list.

Trans Union was requested to provide information concerning a particular name and reported that the name did match someone on the SDN list, notwithstanding the name was only similar. Trans Union upon further investigation would have determined that it was not the same person. As a result of this misinformation, a jury awarded damages of $50,000 and punitive damages of $750,000. The court found that the defendant acted negligently and not willfully in furnishing this information.

The moral of the story is that when dealing with this situation, tread carefully and be certain that the information furnished or received is accurate.[31]

---

[31] *Cortez v. Trans Union, LLC*, 2007 U.S. Dist. LEXIS 68074 (E.D. Pa. 2007).

WILLFUL NONCOMPLIANCE FCRA AMENDMENT

The Credit and Debit Card Receipt Clarification Act of 2007 amended the Fair Credit Reporting Act by providing a brand new definition of willful noncompliance that primarily dealt with the printing of a credit or debit card expiration dates on a consumer receipt.

Section 616 of the FCRA provided as follows:

> (d) clarification of willful noncompliance
>
> —for the purposes of this section, any person who printed an expiration date on any receipt provided to a consumer cardholder at a point of sale or transaction between December 4, 2004 and the date of enactment of this subsection, but otherwise complied with the requirements of Section 05(g) for such receipt shall not be in willful noncompliance for Section 5(g) by reason of printing such expiration date on the receipt.

Many merchants were sued because they felt that truncating the account number down to the last five digits was sufficient even though they allegedly failed to remove the expiration date of the credit card. This act was a willful violation of the FCRA even if the account number was properly truncated.

From December 4, 2004, to June 30, 2008, the merchant is not guilty of willful noncompliance as long as the account number is truncated. After June 30, 2008, the truncation is noncompliance unless the merchant truncates the credit card number and *omits the expiration date on a receipt provided to the cardholder.*

CHAPTER 13
APPENDIX I

TEXT OF THE FAIR CREDIT REPORTING ACT (15 U.S.C. §§ 1681–1681V) AS AMENDED BY THE FAIR AND ACCURATE CREDIT TRANSACTIONS ACT OF 2003 (PUBLIC LAW NO. 108-159)*

As a service to its members, the legal staff of ACA International has prepared the following revised text of the Fair Credit Reporting Act (FCRA), 15 U.S.C. § 1681 et seq., as recently amended by the Fair and Accurate Credit Transactions Act of 2003 (Public Law 108-159). This information is part of ACA's commitment to fostering and ensuring compliance with federal laws that apply to credit and collections.

This version includes the text of the Act as it appeared in 2002 and the recent 2003 amendments. New language is shown in small capital letters, which are red. Deleted language has been struck through. Effective dates, which vary per new provision, are shown in the left hand margin. These dates are provisional and may change subject to rulemaking by the Federal Trade Commission.

TABLE OF CONTENTS

---

*Reprinted with the permission of ACA International.

§ 601. Short title

This title may be cited as the "Fair Credit Reporting Act."

§ 602. Congressional findings and statement of purpose [15 U.S.C. § 1681]

(a) *Accuracy and fairness of credit reporting.* The Congress makes the following findings:

(1) The banking system is dependent upon fair and accurate credit reporting. Inaccurate credit reports directly impair the efficiency of the banking system, and unfair credit reporting methods undermine the public confidence which is essential to the continued functioning of the banking system.

(2) An elaborate mechanism has been developed for investigating and evaluating the credit worthiness, credit standing, credit capacity, character, and general reputation of consumers.

(3) Consumer reporting agencies have assumed a vital role in assembling and evaluating consumer credit and other information on consumers.

(4) There is a need to insure that consumer reporting agencies exercise their grave responsibilities with fairness, impartiality, and a respect for the consumer's right to privacy.

(b) *Reasonable procedures.* It is the purpose of this title to require that consumer reporting agencies adopt reasonable procedures for meeting the needs of commerce for consumer credit, personnel, insurance, and other information in a manner which is fair and equitable to the consumer, with regard to the confidentiality, accuracy, relevancy, and proper utilization of such information in accordance with the requirements of this title.

§ 603. Definitions; rules of construction [15 U.S.C. § 1681a]

(a) Definitions and rules of construction set forth in this section are applicable for the purposes of this title.

(b) The term "person" means any individual, partnership, corporation, trust, estate, cooperative, association, government or governmental subdivision or agency, or other entity.

(c) The term "consumer" means an individual.

(d) Consumer Report

(1) *In general.* The term "consumer report" means any written, oral, or other communication of any information by a consumer reporting agency bearing on a consumer's credit worthiness, credit standing, credit capacity, character, general reputation, personal characteristics, or mode of living which is used or expected to be used or collected in whole or in part for the purpose of serving as a factor in establishing the consumer's eligibility for

(A) credit or insurance to be used primarily for personal, family, or household purposes;

(B) employment purposes; or

(C) any other purpose authorized under section 604 [§ 1681b].

(2) *Exclusions.* Except as provided in paragraph (3), the term "consumer report" does not include

(A) subject to section 624, any

(i) report containing information solely as to transactions or experiences between the consumer and the person making the report;

(ii) communication of that information among persons related by common ownership or affiliated by corporate control; or

(iii) communication of other information among persons related by common ownership or affiliated by corporate control, if it is clearly and conspicuously disclosed to the consumer that the information may be communicated among such persons and the consumer is given the opportunity, before the time that the information is initially communicated, to direct that such information not be communicated among such persons;

(B) any authorization or approval of a specific extension of credit directly or indirectly by the issuer of a credit card or similar device;

(C) any report in which a person who has been requested by a third party to make a specific extension of credit directly or indirectly to a consumer conveys his or her decision with respect to such request, if the third party advises the consumer of the name and address of the person to whom the request was made, and such person makes the disclosures to the consumer required under section 615 [§ 1681m]; or

(D) a communication described in subsection (o) or (x).

(3) *Restriction on sharing of medical information.* Except for information or any communication of information disclosed as provided in section 604(g)(3), the exclusions in paragraph (2) shall not apply with respect to information disclosed to any person related by common ownership or affiliated by corporate control, if the information is—

(A) medical information;

(B) an individualized list or description based on the payment transactions of the consumer for medical products or services; or

(C) an aggregate list of identified consumers based on payment transactions for medical products or services.

(e) The term "investigative consumer report" means a consumer report or portion thereof in which information on a consumer's character, general reputation, personal characteristics, or mode of living is obtained through personal interviews with neighbors, friends, or associates of the consumer reported on or with others with whom he is acquainted or who may have knowledge concerning any such items of information. However, such information shall not include specific factual information on a consumer's credit record obtained directly from a creditor of the consumer or from a consumer reporting agency when such information was obtained directly from a creditor of the consumer or from the consumer.

(f) The term "consumer reporting agency" means any person which, for monetary fees, dues, or on a cooperative nonprofit basis, regularly engages in whole or in part in the practice of assembling or evaluating consumer credit information or other information on consumers for the purpose of furnishing consumer reports to third parties, and which uses any means or facility of interstate commerce for the purpose of preparing or furnishing consumer reports.

(g) The term "file," when used in connection with information on any consumer, means all of the information on that consumer recorded and retained by a consumer reporting agency regardless of how the information is stored.

(h) The term "employment purposes" when used in connection with a consumer report means a report used for the purpose of evaluating a consumer for employment, promotion, reassignment or retention as an employee.

(i) The term "medical information"—

(1) means information or data, whether oral or recorded, in any form or medium, created by or derived from a health care provider or the consumer, that relates to—

(A) the past, present, or future physical, mental, or behavioral health or condition of an individual;

(B) the provision of health care to an individual; or

(C) the payment for the provision of health care to an individual.

(2) does not include the age or gender of a consumer, demographic information about the consumer, including a consumer's residence address or e-mail address, or any other information about a consumer that does not relate to the physical, mental, or behavioral health or condition of a consumer, including the existence or value of any insurance policy.

(j) Definitions Relating to Child Support Obligations

(1) The "overdue support" has the meaning given to such term in section 666(e) of title 42 [Social Security Act, 42 U.S.C. § 666(e)].

(2) The term "State or local child support enforcement agency" means a State or local agency which administers a State or local program for establishing and enforcing child support obligations.

(k) Adverse Action

(1) *Actions included.* The term "adverse action"

(A) has the same meaning as in section 701(d)(6) of the Equal Credit Opportunity Act; and

(B) means

(i) a denial or cancellation of, an increase in any charge for, or a reduction or other adverse or unfavorable change in the terms of coverage or amount of, any insurance, existing or applied for, in connection with the underwriting of insurance;

(ii) a denial of employment or any other decision for employment purposes that adversely affects any current or prospective employee;

(iii) a denial or cancellation of, an increase in any charge for, or any other adverse or unfavorable change in the terms of, any license or benefit described in section 604(a)(3)(D) [§ 1681b]; and

(iv) an action taken or determination that is

(I) made in connection with an application that was made by, or a transaction that was initiated by, any consumer, or in connection with a review of an account under section 604(a)(3)(F)(ii)[§ 1681b]; and

(II) adverse to the interests of the consumer.

(2) *Applicable findings, decisions, commentary, and orders.* For purposes of any determination of whether an action is an adverse action under paragraph (1)(A), all appropriate final findings, decisions, commentary, and orders issued under section 701(d)(6) of the Equal Credit Opportunity Act by the Board of Governors of the Federal Reserve System or any court shall apply.

(*l*) The term "firm offer of credit or insurance" means any offer of credit or insurance to a consumer that will be honored if the consumer is determined, based on information in a consumer report on the consumer, to meet the specific criteria used to select the consumer for the offer, except that the offer may be further conditioned on one or more of the following:

(1) The consumer being determined, based on information in the consumer's application for the credit or insurance, to meet specific criteria bearing on credit worthiness or insurability, as applicable, that are established

(A) before selection of the consumer for the offer; and

(B) for the purpose of determining whether to extend credit or insurance pursuant to the offer.

(2) Verification

(A) that the consumer continues to meet the specific criteria used to select the consumer for the offer, by using information in a consumer report on the consumer, information in the consumer's application for the credit or insurance, or other information bearing on the creditworthiness or insurability of the consumer; or

(B) of the information in the consumer's application for the credit or insurance, to determine that the consumer meets the specific criteria bearing on credit worthiness or insurability.

(3) The consumer furnishing any collateral that is a requirement for the extension of the credit or insurance that was.

(A) established before selection of the consumer for the offer of credit or insurance; and

(B) disclosed to the consumer in the offer of credit or insurance.

(m) The term "credit or insurance transaction that is not initiated by the consumer" does not include the use of a consumer report by a person with which the consumer has an account or insurance policy, for purposes of

(1) reviewing the account or insurance policy; or

(2) collecting the account.

(n) The term "State" means any State, the Commonwealth of Puerto Rico, the District of Columbia, and any territory or possession of the United States.

(o) *Excluded communications.* A communication is described in this subsection if it is a Communication

(1) that, but for subsection (d)(2)(D), would be an investigative consumer report;

(2) that is made to a prospective employer for the purpose of

(A) procuring an employee for the employer; or

(B) procuring an opportunity for a natural person to work for the employer;

(3) that is made by a person who regularly performs such procurement;

(4) that is not used by any person for any purpose other than a purpose described in subparagraph (A) or (B) of paragraph (2); and

(5) with respect to which

(A) the consumer who is the subject of the communication

(i) consents orally or in writing to the nature and scope of the communication, before the collection of any information for the purpose of making the communication;

(ii) consents orally or in writing to the making of the communication to a prospective employer, before the making of the communication; and

(iii) in the case of consent under clause (i) or (ii) given orally, is provided written confirmation of that consent by the person making the communication, not later than 3 business days after the receipt of the consent by that person;

(B) the person who makes the communication does not, for the purpose of making the communication, make any inquiry that if made by a prospective employer of the consumer who is the subject of the communication would violate any applicable Federal or State equal employment opportunity law or regulation; and

(C) the person who makes the communication

(i) discloses in writing to the consumer who is the subject of the communication, not later than 5 business days after receiving any request from the consumer for such disclosure, the nature and substance of all information in the consumer's file at the time of the request, except that the sources of any information that is acquired solely for use in making the communication and is actually used for no other purpose, need not be disclosed other than under appropriate discovery procedures in any court of competent jurisdiction in which an action is brought; and

(ii) notifies the consumer who is the subject of the communication, in writing, of the consumer's right to request the information described in clause (i).

(p) The term "consumer reporting agency that compiles and maintains files on consumers on a nationwide basis" means a consumer reporting agency that regularly engages in the practice of assembling or evaluating, and maintaining, for the purpose of furnishing consumer reports to third parties bearing on a consumer's credit worthiness, credit standing, or credit capacity, each of the following regarding consumers residing nationwide:

(1) Public record information.

(2) Credit account information from persons who furnish that information regularly and in the ordinary course of business.

(q) Definitions relating to fraud alerts.

(1) The term "active duty military consumer" means a consumer in military service who—

(A) is on active duty (as defined in section 101(d)(1) of title 10, United States Code) or is a reservist performing duty under a call or order to active duty under a provision of law referred to in section 101(a)(13) of title 10, United States Code; and

(B) is assigned to service away from the usual duty station of the consumer.

(2) The terms "fraud alert" and "active duty alert" mean a statement in the file of a consumer that

(A) notifies all prospective users of a consumer report relating to the consumer that the consumer may be a victim of fraud, including identity theft, or is an active duty military consumer, as applicable; and

(B) is presented in a manner that facilitates a clear and conspicuous view of the statement described in subparagraph (A) by any person requesting such consumer report.

(3) The term "identity theft" means a fraud committed using the identifying information of another person, subject to such further definition as the Commission may prescribe, by regulation.

(4) The term "identity theft report" has the meaning given that term by rule of the Commission, and means, at a minimum, a report—

(A) that alleges an identity theft;

(B) that is a copy of an official, valid report filed by a consumer with an appropriate Federal, State, or local law enforcement agency, including the United States Postal Inspection Service, or such other government agency deemed appropriate by the Commission; and

(C) the filing of which subjects the person filing the report to criminal penalties relating to the filing of false information if, in fact, the information in the report is false.

(5) The term "new credit plan" means a new account under an open end credit plan (as defined in section 103(i) of the Truth in Lending Act) or a new credit transaction not under an open end credit plan.

(r) Credit and Debit Related Terms

(1) The term "card issuer" means—

(A) a credit card issuer, in the case of a credit card; and

(B) a debit card issuer, in the case of a debit card.

(2) The term "credit card" has the same meaning as in section 103 of the Truth in Lending Act.

(3) The term "debit card" means any card issued by a financial institution to a consumer for use in initiating an electronic fund transfer from the account of the consumer at such financial institution, for the purpose of transferring money between accounts or obtaining money, property, labor, or services.

(4) The terms "account" and "electronic fund transfer" have the same meanings as in section 903 of the Electronic Fund Transfer Act.

(5) The terms "credit" and "creditor" have the same meanings as in section 702 of the Equal Credit Opportunity Act.

(s) The term "Federal banking agency" has the same meaning as in section 3 of the Federal Deposit Insurance Act.

(t) The term "financial institution" means a State or National bank, a State or Federal savings and loan association, a mutual savings bank, a State or Federal credit union, or any other person that, directly or indirectly, holds a transaction account (as defined in section 19(b) of the Federal Reserve Act) belonging to a consumer.

(u) The term "reseller" means a consumer reporting agency that—

(1) assembles and merges information contained in the database of another consumer reporting agency or multiple consumer reporting agencies concerning any consumer for purposes of furnishing such information to any third party, to the extent of such activities; and

(2) does not maintain a database of the assembled or merged information from which new consumer reports are produced.

(v) The term "Commission" means the Federal Trade Commission.

(w) The term "nationwide specialty consumer reporting agency" means a consumer reporting agency that compiles and maintains files on consumers on a nationwide basis relating to—

(1) medical records or payments;

(2) residential or tenant history;

(3) check writing history;

(4) employment history; or

(5) insurance claims.

(x) Exclusion of Certain Communications for Employee Investigations

(1) A communication is described in this subsection if—

(A) but for subsection (d)(2)(D), the communication would be a consumer report;

(B) the communication is made to an employer in connection with an investigation of—

(i) suspected misconduct relating to employment; or

(ii) compliance with Federal, State, or local laws and regulations, the rules of a self-regulatory organization, or any preexisting written policies of the employer;

(C) the communication is not made for the purpose of investigating a consumer's credit worthiness, credit standing, or credit capacity; and

(D) the communication is not provided to any person except—

(i) to the employer or an agent of the employer;

(ii) to any Federal or State officer, agency, or department, or any officer, agency, or department of a unit of general local government;

(iii) to any self-regulatory organization with regulatory authority over the activities of the employer or employee;

(iv) as otherwise required by law; or

(v) pursuant to section 608.

(2) *Subsequent disclosure.* After taking any adverse action based in whole or in part on a communication described in paragraph (1), the employer shall disclose to the consumer a summary containing the nature and substance of the communication upon which the adverse action is based, except that the sources of information acquired solely for use in preparing what would be but for subsection (d)(2)(D) an investigative consumer report need not be disclosed.

(3) For purposes of this subsection, the term "self-regulatory organization" includes any self-regulatory organization (as defined in section 3(a)(26) of the Securities Exchange Act of 1934), any entity established under title I of the Sarbanes-Oxley Act of 2002, any board of trade designated by the Commodity Futures Trading Commission, and any futures association registered with such Commission.

§ 604. Permissible purposes of consumer reports [15 U.S.C. § 1681b]

(a) *In general.* Subject to subsection (c), any consumer reporting agency may furnish a consumer report under the following circumstances and no other:

(1) In response to the order of a court having jurisdiction to issue such an order, or a subpoena issued in connection with proceedings before a Federal grand jury.

(2) In accordance with the written instructions of the consumer to whom it relates.

(3) To a person which it has reason to believe

(A) intends to use the information in connection with a credit transaction involving the consumer on whom the information is to be furnished and involving the extension of credit to, or review or collection of an account of, the consumer; or

(B) intends to use the information for employment purposes; or

(C) intends to use the information in connection with the underwriting of insurance involving the consumer; or

(D) intends to use the information in connection with a determination of the consumer's eligibility for a license or other benefit granted by a governmental instrumentality required by law to consider an applicant's financial responsibility or status; or

(E) intends to use the information, as a potential investor or servicer, or current insurer, in connection with a valuation of, or an assessment of the credit or prepayment risks associated with, an existing credit obligation; or

(F) otherwise has a legitimate business need for the information

(i) in connection with a business transaction that is initiated by the consumer; or

(ii) to review an account to determine whether the consumer continues to meet the terms of the account.

(4) In response to a request by the head of a State or local child support enforcement agency (or a State or local government official authorized by the head of such an agency), if the person making the request certifies to the consumer reporting agency that

(A) the consumer report is needed for the purpose of establishing an individual's capacity to make child support payments or determining the appropriate level of such payments;

(B) the paternity of the consumer for the child to which the obligation relates has been established or acknowledged by the consumer in accordance with State laws under which the obligation arises (if required by those laws);

(C) the person has provided at least 10 days' prior notice to the consumer whose report is requested, by certified or registered mail to the last known address of the consumer, that the report will be requested; and

(D) the consumer report will be kept confidential, will be used solely for a purpose described in subparagraph (A), and will not be used in connection with any other civil, administrative, or criminal proceeding, or for any other purpose.

(5) To an agency administering a State plan under Section 454 of the Social Security Act (42 U.S.C. § 654) for use to set an initial or modified child support award.

(6) To the Federal Deposit Insurance Corporation or the National Credit Union Administration as part of its preparation for its appointment or as

part of its exercise of powers, as conservator, receiver, or liquidating agent for an insured depository institution or insured credit union under the Federal Deposit Insurance Act or the Federal Credit Union Act, or other applicable Federal or State law, or in connection with the resolution or liquidation of a failed or failing insured depository institution or insured credit union, as applicable.

(b) Conditions for Furnishing and Using Consumer Reports for Employment Purposes.

(1) *Certification from user.* A consumer reporting agency may furnish a consumer report for employment purposes only if

(A) the person who obtains such report from the agency certifies to the agency that

(i) the person has complied with paragraph (2) with respect to the consumer report, and the person will comply with paragraph (3) with respect to the consumer report if paragraph (3) becomes applicable; and

(ii) information from the consumer report will not be used in violation of any applicable Federal or State equal employment opportunity law or regulation; and

(B) the consumer reporting agency provides with the report, or has previously provided, a summary of the consumer's rights under this title, as prescribed by the Federal Trade Commission under section 609(c)(3) [§ 1681g].

(2) Disclosure to Consumer.

(A) *In general.* Except as provided in subparagraph (B), a person may not procure a consumer report, or cause a consumer report to be procured, for employment purposes with respect to any consumer, unless—

(i) a clear and conspicuous disclosure has been made in writing to the consumer at any time before the report is procured or caused to be procured, in a document that consists solely of the disclosure, that a consumer report may be obtained for employment purposes; and

(ii) the consumer has authorized in writing (which authorization may be made on the document referred to in clause (i)) the procurement of the report by that person.

(B) *Application by mail, telephone, computer, or other similar means.* If a consumer described in subparagraph (C) applies for employment by mail, telephone, computer, or other similar means, at any time before a consumer report is procured or caused to be procured in connection with that application—

(i) the person who procures the consumer report on the consumer for employment purposes shall provide to the consumer, by oral, written, or electronic means, notice that a consumer report may be obtained for employment purposes, and a summary of the consumer's rights under section 615(a)(3); and

(ii) the consumer shall have consented, orally, in writing, or electronically to the procurement of the report by that person.

(C) *Scope.* Subparagraph (B) shall apply to a person procuring a consumer report on a consumer in connection with the consumer's application for employment only if—

(i) the consumer is applying for a position over which the Secretary of Transportation has the power to establish qualifications and maximum hours of service pursuant to the provisions of section 31502 of title 49, or a position subject to safety regulation by a State transportation agency; and

(ii) as of the time at which the person procures the report or causes the report to be procured the only interaction between the consumer and the person in connection with that employment application has been by mail, telephone, computer, or other similar means.

(3) Conditions on use for adverse actions.

(A) *In general.* Except as provided in subparagraph (B), in using a consumer report for employment purposes, before taking any adverse action based in whole or in part on the report, the person intending to take such adverse action shall provide to the consumer to whom the report relates—

(i) a copy of the report; and

(ii) a description in writing of the rights of the consumer under this title, as prescribed by the Federal Trade Commission under section 609(c)(3).[1]

(B) Application by mail, telephone, computer, or other similar means.

(i) If a consumer described in subparagraph (C) applies for employment by mail, telephone, computer, or other similar means, and if a person who has procured a consumer report on the consumer for employment purposes takes adverse action on the employment

[1]The references in Sections 604(b)(3)(A) and 604(b)(3)(B) should be to Section 609(c)**(1)**, not (c)(3) that no longer exists as the result of Congress' re-organization of Section 609(c) in 2003 (FACT Act).

application based in whole or in part on the report, then the person must provide to the consumer to whom the report relates, in lieu of the notices required under subparagraph (A) of this section and under section 615(a), within 3 business days of taking such action, an oral, written or electronic notification—

(I) that adverse action has been taken based in whole or in part on a consumer report received from a consumer reporting agency;

(II) of the name, address and telephone number of the consumer reporting agency that furnished the consumer report (including a toll-free telephone number established by the agency if the agency compiles and maintains files on consumers on a nationwide basis);

(III) that the consumer reporting agency did not make the decision to take the adverse action and is unable to provide to the consumer the specific reasons why the adverse action was taken; and

(IV) that the consumer may, upon providing proper identification, request a free copy of a report and may dispute with the consumer reporting agency the accuracy or completeness of any information in a report.

(ii) If, under clause (B)(i)(IV), the consumer requests a copy of a consumer report from the person who procured the report, then, within 3 business days of receiving the consumer's request, together with proper identification, the person must send or provide to the consumer a copy of a report and a copy of the consumer's rights as prescribed by the Federal Trade Commission under section 609(c)(3).

(C) *Scope.* Subparagraph (B) shall apply to a person procuring a consumer report on a consumer in connection with the consumer's application for employment only if—

(i) the consumer is applying for a position over which the Secretary of Transportation has the power to establish qualifications and maximum hours of service pursuant to the provisions of section 31502 of title 49, or a position subject to safety regulation by a State transportation agency; and

(ii) as of the time at which the person procures the report or causes the report to be procured the only interaction between the consumer and the person in connection with that employment application has been by mail, telephone, computer, or other similar means.

(4) Exception for national security investigations.

(A) *In general.* In the case of an agency or department of the United States Government which seeks to obtain and use a consumer report for employment purposes, paragraph (3) shall not apply to any adverse action by such agency or department which is based in part on such consumer report, if the head of such agency or department makes a written finding that—

(i) the consumer report is relevant to a national security investigation of such agency or department;

(ii) the investigation is within the jurisdiction of such agency or department;

(iii) there is reason to believe that compliance with paragraph (3) will–

(I) endanger the life or physical safety of any person;

(II) result in flight from prosecution;

(III) result in the destruction of, or tampering with, evidence relevant to the investigation;

(IV) result in the intimidation of a potential witness relevant to the investigation;

(V) result in the compromise of classified information; or

(VI) otherwise seriously jeopardize or unduly delay the investigation or another official proceeding.

(B) *Notification of consumer upon conclusion of investigation.* Upon the conclusion of a national security investigation described in subparagraph (A), or upon the determination that the exception under subparagraph (A) is no longer required for the reasons set forth in such subparagraph, the official exercising the authority in such subparagraph shall provide to the consumer who is the subject of the consumer report with regard to which such finding was made—

(i) a copy of such consumer report with any classified information redacted as necessary;

(ii) notice of any adverse action which is based, in part, on the consumer report; and

(iii) the identification with reasonable specificity of the nature of the investigation for which the consumer report was sought.

(C) *Delegation by head of agency or department.* For purposes of subparagraphs (A) and (B), the head of any agency or department of the United States Government may delegate his or her authorities under this paragraph to an official of such agency or department who has personnel security responsibilities and is a member of the Senior Executive Service or equivalent civilian or military rank.

(D) *Report to the Congress.* Not later than January 31 of each year, the head of each agency and department of the United States Government that exercised authority under this paragraph during the preceding year shall submit a report to the Congress on the number of times the department or agency exercised such authority during the year.

(E) *Definitions.* For purposes of this paragraph, the following definitions shall apply:

(i) The term "classified information" means information that is protected from unauthorized disclosure under Executive Order No. 12958 or successor orders.

(ii) The term "national security investigation" means any official inquiry by an agency or department of the United States Government to determine the eligibility of a consumer to receive access or continued access to classified information or to determine whether classified information has been lost or compromised.

(c) Furnishing reports in connection with credit or insurance transactions that are not initiated by the consumer.

(1) *In general.* A consumer reporting agency may furnish a consumer report relating to any consumer pursuant to subparagraph (A) or (C) of subsection (a)(3) in connection with any credit or insurance transaction that is not initiated by the consumer only if

(A) the consumer authorizes the agency to provide such report to such person; or

(B) (i) the transaction consists of a firm offer of credit or insurance;

(ii) the consumer reporting agency has complied with subsection (e); and

(iii) there is not in effect an election by the consumer, made in accordance with subsection (e), to have the consumer's name and address excluded from lists of names provided by the agency pursuant to this paragraph.

(2) *Limits on information received under paragraph (1)(B).* A person may receive pursuant to paragraph (1)(B) only

(A) the name and address of a consumer;

(B) an identifier that is not unique to the consumer and that is used by the person solely for the purpose of verifying the identity of the consumer; and

(C) other information pertaining to a consumer that does not identify the relationship or experience of the consumer with respect to a particular creditor or other entity.

(3) *Information regarding inquiries.* Except as provided in section 609(a)(5) [§ 1681g], a consumer reporting agency shall not furnish to any person a record of inquiries in connection with a credit or insurance transaction that is not initiated by a consumer.

(d) Reserved.

(e) Election of consumer to be excluded from lists.

(1) *In general.* A consumer may elect to have the consumer's name and address excluded from any list provided by a consumer reporting agency under subsection (c)(1)(B) in connection with a credit or insurance transaction that is not initiated by the consumer, by notifying the agency in accordance with paragraph (2) that the consumer does not consent to any use of a consumer report relating to the consumer in connection with any credit or insurance transaction that is not initiated by the consumer.

(2) *Manner of notification.* A consumer shall notify a consumer reporting agency under paragraph (1)

(A) through the notification system maintained by the agency under paragraph (5); or

(B) by submitting to the agency a signed notice of election form issued by the agency for purposes of this subparagraph.

(3) *Response of agency after notification through system.* Upon receipt of notification of the election of a consumer under paragraph (1) through the notification system maintained by the agency under paragraph (5), a consumer reporting agency shall

(A) inform the consumer that the election is effective only for the 5-year period following the election if the consumer does not submit to the agency a signed notice of election form issued by the agency for purposes of paragraph (2)(B); and

(B) provide to the consumer a notice of election form, if requested by the consumer, not later than 5 business days after receipt of the notification of the election through the system established under paragraph (5), in the case of a request made at the time the consumer provides notification through the system.

(4) *Effectiveness of election.* An election of a consumer under paragraph (1)

(A) shall be effective with respect to a consumer reporting agency beginning 5 business days after the date on which the consumer notifies the agency in accordance with paragraph (2);

(B) shall be effective with respect to a consumer reporting agency

(i) subject to subparagraph (C), during the 5-year period beginning 5 business days after the date on which the consumer notifies the agency of the election, in the case of an election for which a consumer notifies the agency only in accordance with paragraph (2)(A); or

(ii) until the consumer notifies the agency under subparagraph (C), in the case of an election for which a consumer notifies the agency in accordance with paragraph (2)(B);

(C) shall not be effective after the date on which the consumer notifies the agency, through the notification system established by the agency under paragraph (5), that the election is no longer effective; and

(D) shall be effective with respect to each affiliate of the agency.

(5) Notification System

(A) *In general.* Each consumer reporting agency that, under subsection (c)(1)(B), furnishes a consumer report in connection with a credit or insurance transaction that is not initiated by a consumer, shall

(i) establish and maintain a notification system, including a toll-free telephone number, which permits any consumer whose consumer report is maintained by the agency to notify the agency, with appropriate identification, of the consumer's election to have the consumer's name and address excluded from any such list of names and addresses provided by the agency for such a transaction; and

(ii) publish by not later than 365 days after the date of enactment of the Consumer Credit Reporting Reform Act of 1996, and not less than annually thereafter, in a publication of general circulation in the area served by the agency

(I) a notification that information in consumer files maintained by the agency may be used in connection with such transactions; and

(II) the address and toll-free telephone number for consumers to use to notify the agency of the consumer's election under clause (I).

(B) *Establishment and maintenance as compliance.* Establishment and maintenance of a notification system (including a toll-free telephone number) and publication by a consumer reporting agency on the agency's own behalf and on behalf of any of its affiliates in accordance with this paragraph is deemed to be compliance with this paragraph by each of those affiliates.

(6) *Notification system by agencies that operate nationwide.* Each consumer reporting agency that compiles and maintains files on consumers on a

nationwide basis shall establish and maintain a notification system for purposes of paragraph (5) jointly with other such consumer reporting agencies.

(f) *Certain use or obtaining of information prohibited.* A person shall not use or obtain a consumer report for any purpose unless

(1) the consumer report is obtained for a purpose for which the consumer report is authorized to be furnished under this section; and

(2) the purpose is certified in accordance with section 607 [§ 1681e] by a prospective user of the report through a general or specific certification.

(g) Protection of Medical Information

(1) *Limitation on consumer reporting agencies.* A consumer reporting agency shall not furnish for employment purposes, or in connection with a credit or insurance transaction, a consumer report that contains medical information (other than medical contact information treated in the manner required under section 605(a)(6)) about a consumer, unless—

(A) if furnished in connection with an insurance transaction, the consumer affirmatively consents to the furnishing of the report;

(B) if furnished for employment purposes or in connection with a credit transaction—

(i) the information to be furnished is relevant to process or effect the employment or credit transaction; and

(ii) the consumer provides specific written consent for the furnishing of the report that describes in clear and conspicuous language the use for which the information will be furnished; or

(C) the information to be furnished pertains solely to transactions, accounts, or balances relating to debts arising from the receipt of medical services, products, or devises, where such information, other than account status or amounts, is restricted or reported using codes that do not identify, or do not provide information sufficient to infer, the specific provider or the nature of such services, products, or devices, as provided in section 605(a)(6).

(2) *Limitation on creditors.* Except as permitted pursuant to paragraph (3)(C) or regulations prescribed under paragraph (5)(A), a creditor shall not obtain or use medical information (other than medical contact information treated in the manner required under section 605(a)(6)) pertaining to a consumer in connection with any determination of the consumer's eligibility, or continued eligibility, for credit.

(3) *Actions authorized by federal law, insurance activities and regulatory determinations.* Section 603(d)(3) shall not be construed so as to treat information or

any communication of information as a consumer report if the information or communication is disclosed—

(A) in connection with the business of insurance or annuities, including the activities described in section 18B of the model Privacy of Consumer Financial and Health Information Regulation issued by the National Association of Insurance Commissioners (as in effect on January 1, 2003);

(B) for any purpose permitted without authorization under the Standards for Individually Identifiable Health Information promulgated by the Department of Health and Human Services pursuant to the Health Insurance Portability and Accountability Act of 1996, or referred to under section 1179 of such Act, or described in section 502(e) of Public Law 106-102; or

(C) as otherwise determined to be necessary and appropriate, by regulation or order and subject to paragraph (6), by the Commission, any Federal banking agency or the National Credit Union Administration (with respect to any financial institution subject to the jurisdiction of such agency or Administration under paragraph (1), (2), or (3) of section 621(b), or the applicable State insurance authority (with respect to any person engaged in providing insurance or annuities).

(4) *Limitation on redisclosure of medical information.* Any person that receives medical information pursuant to paragraph (1) or (3) shall not disclose such information to any other person, except as necessary to carry out the purpose for which the information was initially disclosed, or as otherwise permitted by statute, regulation, or order.

(5) Regulations and Effective Date for Paragraph (2)

(A) *Regulations required.* Each Federal banking agency and the National Credit Union Administration shall, subject to paragraph (6) and after notice and opportunity for comment, prescribe regulations that permit transactions under paragraph (2) that are determined to be necessary and appropriate to protect legitimate operational, transactional, risk, consumer, and other needs (and which shall include permitting actions necessary for administrative verification purposes), consistent with the intent of paragraph (2) to restrict the use of medical information for inappropriate purposes.

(B) *Final regulations required.* The Federal banking agencies and the National Credit Union Administration shall issue the regulations required under subparagraph (A) in final form before the end of the 6-month period beginning on the date of enactment of the Fair and Accurate Credit Transactions Act of 2003.

(6) *Coordination with other laws.* No provision of this subsection shall be construed as altering, affecting, or superseding the applicability of any other provision of Federal law relating to medical confidentiality.

§ 605. Requirements relating to information contained in consumer reports [15 U.S.C. § 1681c]

(a) *Information excluded from consumer reports.* Except as authorized under subsection (b) of this section, no consumer reporting agency may make any consumer report containing any of the following items of information:

(1) Cases under title 11 [United States Code] or under the Bankruptcy Act that, from the date of entry of the order for relief or the date of adjudication, as the case may be, antedate the report by more than 10 years.

(2) Civil suits, civil judgments, and records of arrest that from date of entry, antedate the report by more than seven years or until the governing statute of limitations has expired, whichever is the longer period.

(3) Paid tax liens which, from date of payment, antedate the report by more than seven years.

(4) Accounts placed for collection or charged to profit and loss which antedate the report by more than seven years.[2]

(5) Any other adverse item of information, other than records of convictions of crimes which antedates the report by more than seven years.

(6) The name, address, and telephone number of any medical information furnisher that has notified the agency of its status, unless—

(A) such name, address, and telephone number are restricted or reported using codes that do not identify, or provide information sufficient to infer, the specific provider or the nature of such services, products, or devices to a person other than the consumer; or

(B) the report is being provided to an insurance company for a purpose relating to engaging in the business of insurance other than property and casualty insurance.

(b) *Exempted cases.* The provisions of paragraphs (1) through (5) of subsection (a) of this section are not applicable in the case of any consumer credit report to be used in connection with

(1) a credit transaction involving, or which may reasonably be expected to involve, a principal amount of $150,000 or more;

(2) the underwriting of life insurance involving, or which may reasonably be expected to involve, a face amount of $150,000 or more; or

---

[2]The reporting periods have been lengthened for certain adverse information pertaining to U.S. Government insured or guaranteed student loans, or pertaining to national direct student loans. See sections 430A(f) and 463(c)(3) of the Higher Education Act of 1965, 20 U.S.C. 1080a(f) and 20 U.S.C. 1087cc(c)(3), respectively.

(3) the employment of any individual at an annual salary which equals, or which may reasonably be expected to equal $75,000, or more.

(c) Running of Reporting Period

(1) *In general.* The 7-year period referred to in paragraphs (4) and (6)[3] of subsection (a) shall begin, with respect to any delinquent account that is placed for collection(internally or by referral to a third party, whichever is earlier), charged to profit and loss, or subjected to any similar action, upon the expiration of the 180-day period beginning on the date of the commencement of the delinquency which immediately preceded the collection activity, charge to profit and loss, or similar action.

(2) *Effective date.* Paragraph (1) shall apply only to items of information added to the file of a consumer on or after the date that is 455 days after the date of enactment of the Consumer Credit Reporting Reform Act of 1996.

(d) Information Required to Be Disclosed

(1) *Title 11 information.* Any consumer reporting agency that furnishes a consumer report that contains information regarding any case involving the consumer that arises under title 11, United States Code, shall include in the report an identification of the chapter of such title 11 under which such case arises if provided by the source of the information. If any case arising or filed under title 11, United States Code, is withdrawn by the consumer before a final judgment, the consumer reporting agency shall include in the report that such case or filing was withdrawn upon receipt of documentation certifying such withdrawal.

(2) *Key factor in credit score information.* Any consumer reporting agency that furnishes a consumer report that contains any credit score or any other risk score or predictor on any consumer shall include in the report a clear and conspicuous statement that a key factor (as defined in section 609(f)(2)(B)) that adversely affected such score or predictor was the number of enquiries, if such a predictor was in fact a key factor that adversely affected such score. This paragraph shall not apply to a check services company, acting as such, which issues authorizations for the purpose of approving or processing negotiable instruments, electronic fund transfers, or similar methods of payments, but only to the extent that such company is engaged in such activities.

(e) *Indication of closure of account by consumer.* If a consumer reporting agency is notified pursuant to section 623(a)(4) [§ 1681s-2] that a credit account of a consumer was voluntarily closed by the consumer, the agency shall indicate that fact in any consumer report that includes information related to the account.

---

[3]This provision, added in September 1996, should read "paragraphs (4) and *(5)* . . . ." Prior Section 605(a)(6) was amended and re-designated as Section 605(a)(5) in November 1998. The current Section 605(a)(6), added in December 2003 and now containing no reference to any 7-year period, is obviously inapplicable.

(f) *Indication of dispute by consumer.* If a consumer reporting agency is notified pursuant to section 623(a)(3) [§ 1681s-2] that information regarding a consumer who was furnished to the agency is disputed by the consumer, the agency shall indicate that fact in each consumer report that includes the disputed information.

(g) Truncation of Credit Card and Debit Card Numbers

(1) *In general.* Except as otherwise provided in this subsection, no person that accepts credit cards or debit cards for the transaction of business shall print more than the last 5 digits of the card number or the expiration date upon any receipt provided to the cardholder at the point of the sale or transaction.

(2) *Limitation.* This subsection shall apply only to receipts that are electronically printed, and shall not apply to transactions in which the sole means of recording a credit card or debit card account number is by handwriting or by an imprint or copy of the card.

(3) *Effective date.* This subsection shall become effective—

(A) 3 years after the date of enactment of this subsection, with respect to any cash register or other machine or device that electronically prints receipts for credit card or debit card transactions that is in use before January 1, 2005; and

(B) 1 year after the date of enactment of this subsection, with respect to any cash register or other machine or device that electronically prints receipts for credit card or debit card transactions that is first put into use on or after January 1, 2005.

(h) Notice of Discrepancy in Address

(1) *In general.* If a person has requested a consumer report relating to a consumer from a consumer reporting agency described in section 603(p), the request includes an address for the consumer that substantially differs from the addresses in the file of the consumer, and the agency provides a consumer report in response to the request, the consumer reporting agency shall notify the requester of the existence of the discrepancy.

(2) Regulations

(A) *Regulations required.* The Federal banking agencies, the National Credit Union Administration, and the Commission shall jointly, with respect to the entities that are subject to their respective enforcement authority under section 621, prescribe regulations providing guidance regarding reasonable policies and procedures that a user of a consumer report should employ when such user has received a notice of discrepancy under paragraph (1).

(B) *Policies and procedures to be included.* The regulations prescribed under subparagraph (A) shall describe reasonable policies and procedures for use by a user of a consumer report—

(i) to form a reasonable belief that the user knows the identity of the person to whom the consumer report pertains; and

(ii) if the user establishes a continuing relationship with the consumer, and the user regularly and in the ordinary course of business furnishes information to the consumer reporting agency from which the notice of discrepancy pertaining to the consumer was obtained, to reconcile the address of the consumer with the consumer reporting agency by furnishing such address to such consumer reporting agency as part of information regularly furnished by the user for the period in which the relationship is established.

§ 605A. Identity theft prevention; fraud alerts and active duty alerts [15 U.S.C. § 1681c-1]

(a) One-call Fraud Alerts

(1) *Initial alerts.* Upon the direct request of a consumer, or an individual acting on behalf of or as a personal representative of a consumer, who asserts in good faith a suspicion that the consumer has been or is about to become a victim of fraud or related crime, including identity theft, a consumer reporting agency described in section 603(p) that maintains a file on the consumer and has received appropriate proof of the identity of the requester shall—

(A) include a fraud alert in the file of that consumer, and also provide that alert along with any credit score generated in using that file, for a period of not less than 90 days, beginning on the date of such request, unless the consumer or such representative requests that such fraud alert be removed before the end of such period, and the agency has received appropriate proof of the identity of the requester for such purpose; and

(B) refer the information regarding the fraud alert under this paragraph to each of the other consumer reporting agencies described in section 603(p), in accordance with procedures developed under section 621(f).

(2) *Access to free reports.* In any case in which a consumer reporting agency includes a fraud alert in the file of a consumer pursuant to this subsection, the consumer reporting agency shall—

(A) disclose to the consumer that the consumer may request a free copy of the file of the consumer pursuant to section 612(d); and

(B) provide to the consumer all disclosures required to be made under section 609, without charge to the consumer, not later than 3 business days after any request described in subparagraph (A).

(b) Extended Alerts

(1) *In general.* Upon the direct request of a consumer, or an individual acting on behalf of or as a personal representative of a consumer, who submits an identity theft report to a consumer reporting agency described in section 603(p) that maintains a file on the consumer, if the agency has received appropriate proof of the identity of the requester, the agency shall—

(A) include a fraud alert in the file of that consumer, and also provide that alert along with any credit score generated in using that file, during the 7-year period beginning on the date of such request, unless the consumer or such representative requests that such fraud alert be removed before the end of such period and the agency has received appropriate proof of the identity of the requester for such purpose;

(B) during the 5-year period beginning on the date of such request, exclude the consumer from any list of consumers prepared by the consumer reporting agency and provided to any third party to offer credit or insurance to the consumer as part of a transaction that was not initiated by the consumer, unless the consumer or such representative requests that such exclusion be rescinded before the end of such period; and

(C) refer the information regarding the extended fraud alert under this paragraph to each of the other consumer reporting agencies described in section 603(p), in accordance with procedures developed under section 621(f).

(2) *Access to free reports.* In any case in which a consumer reporting agency includes a fraud alert in the file of a consumer pursuant to this subsection, the consumer reporting agency shall—

(A) disclose to the consumer that the consumer may request 2 free copies of the file of the consumer pursuant to section 612(d) during the 12-month period beginning on the date on which the fraud alert was included in the file; and

(B) provide to the consumer all disclosures required to be made under section 609, without charge to the consumer, not later than 3 business days after any request described in subparagraph (A).

(c) *Active duty alerts.* Upon the direct request of an active duty military consumer, or an individual acting on behalf of or as a personal representative of an active duty military consumer, a consumer reporting agency described in section 603(p) that maintains a file on the active duty military consumer and has received appropriate proof of the identity of the requester shall—

(1) include an active duty alert in the file of that active duty military consumer, and also provide that alert along with any credit score generated in using that file, during a period of not less than 12 months, or such longer

period as the Commission shall determine, by regulation, beginning on the date of the request, unless the active duty military consumer or such representative requests that such fraud alert be removed before the end of such period, and the agency has received appropriate proof of the identity of the requester for such purpose;

(2) during the 2-year period beginning on the date of such request, exclude the active duty military consumer from any list of consumers prepared by the consumer reporting agency and provided to any third party to offer credit or insurance to the consumer as part of a transaction that was not initiated by the consumer, unless the consumer requests that such exclusion be rescinded before the end of such period; and

(3) refer the information regarding the active duty alert to each of the other consumer reporting agencies described in section 603(p), in accordance with procedures developed under section 621(f).

(d) *Procedures.* Each consumer reporting agency described in section 603(p) shall establish policies and procedures to comply with this section, including procedures that inform consumers of the availability of initial, extended, and active duty alerts and procedures that allow consumers and active duty military consumers to request initial, extended, or active duty alerts (as applicable) in a simple and easy manner, including by telephone.

(e) *Referrals of alerts.* Each consumer reporting agency described in section 603(p) that receives a referral of a fraud alert or active duty alert from another consumer reporting agency pursuant to this section shall, as though the agency received the request from the consumer directly, follow the procedures required under—

(1) paragraphs (1)(A) and (2) of subsection (a), in the case of a referral under subsection (a)(1)(B);

(2) paragraphs (1)(A), (1)(B), and (2) of subsection (b), in the case of a referral under subsection (b)(1)(C); and

(3) paragraphs (1) and (2) of subsection (c), in the case of a referral under subsection(c)(3).

(f) *Duty of reseller to reconvey alert.* A reseller shall include in its report any fraud alert or active duty alert placed in the file of a consumer pursuant to this section by another consumer reporting agency.

(g) *Duty of other consumer reporting agencies to provide contact information.* If a consumer contacts any consumer reporting agency that is not described in section 603(p) to communicate a suspicion that the consumer has been or is about to become a victim of fraud or related crime, including identity theft, the agency shall provide information to the consumer on how to contact the Commission and the consumer reporting agencies described in section 603(p) to obtain more detailed information and request alerts under this section.

(h) Limitations on Use of Information for Credit Extensions

(1) Requirements for initial and active duty alerts—

(A) *Notification.* Each initial fraud alert and active duty alert under this section shall include information that notifies all prospective users of a consumer report on the consumer to which the alert relates that the consumer does not authorize the establishment of any new credit plan or extension of credit, other than under an open-end credit plan (as defined in section 103(i)), in the name of the consumer, or issuance of an additional card on an existing credit account requested by a consumer, or any increase in credit limit on an existing credit account requested by a consumer, except in accordance with subparagraph (B).

(B) Limitation on Users

(i) *In general.* No prospective user of a consumer report that includes an initial fraud alert or an active duty alert in accordance with this section may establish a new credit plan or extension of credit, other than under an open-end credit plan (as defined in section 103(i)), in the name of the consumer, or issue an additional card on an existing credit account requested by a consumer, or grant any increase in credit limit on an existing credit account requested by a consumer, unless the user utilizes reasonable policies and procedures to form a reasonable belief that the user knows the identity of the person making the request.

(ii) *Verification.* If a consumer requesting the alert has specified a telephone number to be used for identity verification purposes, before authorizing any new credit plan or extension described in clause (i) in the name of such consumer, a user of such consumer report shall contact the consumer using that telephone number or take reasonable steps to verify the consumer's identity and confirm that the application for a new credit plan is not the result of identity theft.

(2) Requirements for Extended Alerts

(A) *Notification.* Each extended alert under this section shall include information that provides all prospective users of a consumer report relating to a consumer with—

(i) notification that the consumer does not authorize the establishment of any new credit plan or extension of credit described in clause (i), other than under an open-end credit plan (as defined in section 103(i)), in the name of the consumer, or issuance of an additional card on an existing credit account requested by a consumer, or any increase in credit limit on an existing credit account requested by a consumer, except in accordance with subparagraph (B); and

(ii) a telephone number or other reasonable contact method designated by the consumer.

(B) *Limitation on users.* No prospective user of a consumer report or of a credit score generated using the information in the file of a consumer that includes an extended fraud alert in accordance with this section may establish a new credit plan or extension of credit, other than under an open-end credit plan (as defined in section 103(i)), in the name of the consumer, or issue an additional card on an existing credit account requested by a consumer, or any increase in credit limit on an existing credit account requested by a consumer, unless the user contacts the consumer in person or using the contact method described in subparagraph (A)(ii) to confirm that the application for a new credit plan or increase in credit limit, or request for an additional card is not the result of identity theft.

§ 605B. Block of information resulting from identity theft [15 U.S.C. § 1681c-2]

(a) *Block.* Except as otherwise provided in this section, a consumer reporting agency shall block the reporting of any information in the file of a consumer that the consumer identifies as information that resulted from an alleged identity theft, not later than 4 business days after the date of receipt by such agency of—

(1) appropriate proof of the identity of the consumer;

(2) a copy of an identity theft report;

(3) the identification of such information by the consumer; and

(4) a statement by the consumer that the information is not information relating to any transaction by the consumer.

(b) *Notification.* A consumer reporting agency shall promptly notify the furnisher of information identified by the consumer under subsection (a)—

(1) that the information may be a result of identity theft;

(2) that an identity theft report has been filed;

(3) that a block has been requested under this section; and

(4) of the effective dates of the block.

(c) Authority to Decline or Rescind

(1) *In general.* A consumer reporting agency may decline to block, or may rescind any block, of information relating to a consumer under this section, if the consumer reporting agency reasonably determines that—

(A) the information was blocked in error or a block was requested by the consumer in error;

(B) the information was blocked, or a block was requested by the consumer, on the basis of a material misrepresentation of fact by the consumer relevant to the request to block; or

(C) the consumer obtained possession of goods, services, or money as a result of the blocked transaction or transactions.

(2) *Notification to consumer.* If a block of information is declined or rescinded under this subsection, the affected consumer shall be notified promptly, in the same manner as consumers are notified of the reinsertion of information under section 611(a)(5)(B).

(3) *Significance of block.* For purposes of this subsection, if a consumer reporting agency rescinds a block, the presence of information in the file of a consumer prior to the blocking of such information is not evidence of whether the consumer knew or should have known that the consumer obtained possession of any goods, services, or money as a result of the block.

(d) Exception for Resellers

(1) *No reseller file.* This section shall not apply to a consumer reporting agency, if the consumer reporting agency—

(A) is a reseller;

(B) is not, at the time of the request of the consumer under subsection (a), otherwise furnishing or reselling a consumer report concerning the information identified by the consumer; and

(C) informs the consumer, by any means, that the consumer may report the identity theft to the Commission to obtain consumer information regarding identity theft.

(2) *Reseller with file.* The sole obligation of the consumer reporting agency under this section, with regard to any request of a consumer under this section, shall be to block the consumer report maintained by the consumer reporting agency from any subsequent use, if—

(A) the consumer, in accordance with the provisions of subsection (a), identifies, to a consumer reporting agency, information in the file of the consumer that resulted from identity theft; and

(B) the consumer reporting agency is a reseller of the identified information.

(3) *Notice.* In carrying out its obligation under paragraph (2), the reseller shall promptly provide a notice to the consumer of the decision to block the file. Such notice shall contain the name, address, and telephone number of each consumer reporting agency from which the consumer information was obtained for resale.

(e) *Exception for verification companies.* The provisions of this section do not apply to a check services company, acting as such, which issues authorizations for the purpose of approvingor processing negotiable instruments, electronic fund transfers, or similar methods of payments, except that, beginning 4 business days after receipt of information described in paragraphs (1) through (3) of subsection (a), a check services company shall not report to a national consumer reporting agency described in section 603(p), any information identified in the subject identity theft report as resulting from identity theft.

(f) *Access to blocked information by law enforcement agencies.* No provision of this section shall be construed as requiring a consumer reporting agency to prevent a Federal, State, or local law enforcement agency from accessing blocked information in a consumer file to which the agency could otherwise obtain access under this title.

§ 606. Disclosure of investigative consumer reports [15 U.S.C. § 1681d]

(a) *Disclosure of fact of preparation.* A person may not procure or cause to be prepared an investigative consumer report on any consumer unless

> (1) it is clearly and accurately disclosed to the consumer that an investigative consumer report including information as to his character, general reputation, personal characteristics and mode of living, whichever are applicable, may be made, and such disclosure
>
> > (A) is made in a writing mailed, or otherwise delivered, to the consumer, not later than three days after the date on which the report was first requested, and
> >
> > (B) includes a statement informing the consumer of his right to request the additional disclosures provided for under subsection (b) of this section and the written summary of the rights of the consumer prepared pursuant to section 609(c) [§ 1681g]; and
>
> (2) the person certifies or has certified to the consumer reporting agency that
>
> > (A) the person has made the disclosures to the consumer required by paragraph (1); and
> >
> > (B) the person will comply with subsection (b).

(b) *Disclosure on request of nature and scope of investigation.* Any person who procures or causes to be prepared an investigative consumer report on any consumer shall, upon written request made by the consumer within a reasonable period of time after the receipt by him of the disclosure required by subsection (a)(1) of this section, make a complete and accurate disclosure of the nature and scope of the investigation requested. This disclosure shall be made in a writing mailed, or otherwise delivered, to the consumer not later than five days after the date on which the request for such disclosure was received from the consumer or such report was first requested, whichever is the later.

(c) *Limitation on liability upon showing of reasonable procedures for compliance with provisions.* No person may be held liable for any violation of subsection (a) or (b) of this section if he shows by a preponderance of the evidence that at the time of the violation he maintained reasonable procedures to assure compliance with subsection (a) or (b) of this section.

(d) Prohibitions

(1) *Certification.* A consumer reporting agency shall not prepare or furnish investigative consumer report unless the agency has received a certification under subsection (a)(2) from the person who requested the report.

(2) *Inquiries.* A consumer reporting agency shall not make an inquiry for the purpose of preparing an investigative consumer report on a consumer for employment purposes if the making of the inquiry by an employer or prospective employer of the consumer would violate any applicable Federal or State equal employment opportunity law or regulation.

(3) *Certain public record information.* Except as otherwise provided in section 613 [§ 1681k], a consumer reporting agency shall not furnish an investigative consumer report that includes information that is a matter of public record and that relates to an arrest, indictment, conviction, civil judicial action, tax lien, or outstanding judgment, unless the agency has verified the accuracy of the information during the 30-day period ending on the date on which the report is furnished.

(4) *Certain adverse information.* A consumer reporting agency shall not prepare or furnish an investigative consumer report on a consumer that contains information that is adverse to the interest of the consumer and that is obtained through a personal interview with a neighbor, friend, or associate of the consumer or with another person with whom the consumer is acquainted or who has knowledge of such item of information, unless

(A) the agency has followed reasonable procedures to obtain confirmation of the information, from an additional source that has independent and direct knowledge of the information; or

(B) the person interviewed is the best possible source of the information.

§ 607. Compliance procedures [15 U.S.C. § 1681e]

(a) *Identity and purposes of credit users.* Every consumer reporting agency shall maintain reasonable procedures designed to avoid violations of section 605 [§ 1681c] and to limit the furnishing of consumer reports to the purposes listed under section 604 [§ 1681b] of this title. These procedures shall require that prospective users of the information identify themselves, certify the purposes for which the information is sought, and certify that the information will be used for no other purpose. Every consumer reporting agency shall make a reasonable effort to verify the identity of a new prospective user and the uses certified by such prospective user prior to furnishing such user a consumer report. No consumer reporting agency may furnish a consumer report to any person if it has reasonable grounds for believing that the consumer report will not be used for a purpose listed in section 604 [§ 1681b] of this title.

(b) *Accuracy of report.* Whenever a consumer reporting agency prepares a consumer report it shall follow reasonable procedures to assure maximum possible accuracy of the information concerning the individual about whom the report relates.

(c) *Disclosure of consumer reports by users allowed.* A consumer reporting agency may not prohibit a user of a consumer report furnished by the agency on a consumer from disclosing the contents of the report to the consumer, if adverse action against the consumer has been taken by the user based in whole or in part on the report.

(d) Notice to Users and Furnishers of Information

(1) *Notice requirement.* A consumer reporting agency shall provide to any person

(A) who regularly and in the ordinary course of business furnishes information to the agency with respect to any consumer; or

(B) to whom a consumer report is provided by the agency;

a notice of such person's responsibilities under this title.

(2) *Content of notice.* The Federal Trade Commission shall prescribe the content of notices under paragraph (1), and a consumer reporting agency shall be in compliance with this subsection if it provides a notice under paragraph (1) that is substantially similar to the Federal Trade Commission prescription under this paragraph.

(e) Procurement of Consumer Report for Resale

(1) *Disclosure.* A person may not procure a consumer report for purposes of reselling the report (or any information in the report) unless the person discloses to the consumer reporting agency that originally furnishes the report

(A) the identity of the end-user of the report (or information); and

(B) each permissible purpose under section 604 [§ 1681b] for which the report is furnished to the end-user of the report (or information).

(2) *Responsibilities of procurers for resale.* A person who procures a consumer report for purposes of reselling the report (or any information in the report) shall

(A) establish and comply with reasonable procedures designed to ensure that the report (or information) is resold by the person only for a purpose for which the report may be furnished under section 604 [§ 1681b], including by requiring that each person to which the report (or information) is resold and that resells or provides the report (or information) to any other person

(i) identifies each end user of the resold report (or information);

(ii) certifies each purpose for which the report (or information) will be used; and

(iii) certifies that the report (or information) will be used for no other purpose; and

(B) before reselling the report, make reasonable efforts to verify the identifications and certifications made under subparagraph (A).

(3) *Resale of consumer report to a federal agency or department.* Notwithstanding paragraph (1) or (2), a person who procures a consumer report for purposes of reselling the report (or any information in the report) shall not disclose the identity of the end-user of the report under paragraph (1) or (2) if—

(A) the end user is an agency or department of the United States Government which procures the report from the person for purposes of determining the eligibility of the consumer concerned to receive access or continued access to classified information (as defined in section 604(b)(4)(E)(i)); and

(B) the agency or department certifies in writing to the person reselling the report that nondisclosure is necessary to protect classified information or the safety of persons employed by or contracting with, or undergoing investigation for work or contracting with the agency or department.

§ 608. Disclosures to governmental agencies [15 U.S.C. § 1681f]

Notwithstanding the provisions of section 604 [§ 1681b] of this title, a consumer reporting agency may furnish identifying information respecting any consumer, limited to his name, address, former addresses, places of employment, or former places of employment, to a governmental agency.

§ 609. Disclosures to consumers [15 U.S.C. § 1681g]

(a) *Information on file; sources; report recipients.* Every consumer reporting agency shall, upon request, and subject to 610(a)(1) [§ 1681h], clearly and accurately disclose to the consumer:

(1) All information in the consumer's file at the time of the request except that—

(A) if the consumer to whom the file relates requests that the first 5 digits of the social security number (or similar identification number) of the consumer not be included in the disclosure and the consumer reporting agency has received appropriate proof of the identity of the requester, the consumer reporting agency shall so truncate such number in such disclosure; and

(B) nothing in this paragraph shall be construed to require a consumer reporting agency to disclose to a consumer any information concerning credit scores or any other risk scores or predictors relating to the consumer.

(2) The sources of the information; except that the sources of information acquired solely for use in preparing an investigative consumer report and actually use for no other purpose need not be disclosed: Provided, That in the event an action is brought under this title, such sources shall be available to the plaintiff under appropriate discovery procedures in the court in which the action is brought.

(3) (A) Identification of each person (including each end-user identified under section 607(e)(1) [§ 1681e]) that procured a consumer report

(i) for employment purposes, during the 2-year period preceding the date on which the request is made; or

(ii) for any other purpose, during the 1-year period preceding the date on which the request is made.

(B) An identification of a person under subparagraph (A) shall include

(i) the name of the person or, if applicable, the trade name (written in full) under which such person conducts business; and

(ii) upon request of the consumer, the address and telephone number of the person.

(C) Subparagraph (A) does not apply if—

(i) the end user is an agency or department of the United States Government that procures the report from the person for purposes of determining the eligibility of the consumer to whom the report relates to receive access or continued access to classified information (as defined in section 604(b)(4)(E)(i)); and

(ii) the head of the agency or department makes a written finding as prescribed under section 604(b)(4)(A).

(4) The dates, original payees, and amounts of any checks upon which is based any adverse characterization of the consumer, included in the file at the time of the disclosure.

(5) A record of all inquiries received by the agency during the 1-year period preceding the request that identified the consumer in connection with a credit or insurance transaction that was not initiated by the consumer.

(6) If the consumer requests the credit file and not the credit score, a statement that the consumer may request and obtain a credit score.

(b) *Exempt information*. The requirements of subsection (a) of this section respecting the disclosure of sources of information and the recipients of consumer reports do not apply to information received or consumer reports furnished prior to the effective date of this title except to the extent that the matter involved is contained in the files of the consumer reporting agency on that date.

(c) Summary of Rights to Obtain and Dispute Information in Consumer Reports and to Obtain Credit Scores

(1) Commission Summary of Rights Required

(A) *In general*. The Commission shall prepare a model summary of the rights of consumers under this title.

(B) *Content of summary*. The summary of rights prepared under subparagraph (A) shall include a description of—

(i) the right of a consumer to obtain a copy of a consumer report under subsection (a) from each consumer reporting agency;

(ii) the frequency and circumstances under which a consumer is entitled to receive a consumer report without charge under section 612;

(iii) the right of a consumer to dispute information in the file of the consumer under section 611;

(iv) the right of a consumer to obtain a credit score from a consumer reporting agency, and a description of how to obtain a credit score;

(v) the method by which a consumer can contact, and obtain a consumer report from, a consumer reporting agency without charge, as provided in the regulations of the Commission prescribed under section 211(c) of the Fair and Accurate Credit Transactions Act of 2003; and

(vi) the method by which a consumer can contact, and obtain a consumer report from, a consumer reporting agency described in section 603(w), as provided in the regulations of the Commission prescribed under section 612(a)(1)(C).

(C) *Availability of summary of rights*. The Commission shall—

(i) actively publicize the availability of the summary of rights prepared under this paragraph;

(ii) conspicuously post on its Internet website the availability of such summary of rights; and

(iii) promptly make such summary of rights available to consumers, on request.

(2) *Summary of rights required to be included with agency disclosures.* A consumer reporting agency shall provide to a consumer, with each written disclosure by the agency to the consumer under this section—

(A) the summary of rights prepared by the Commission under paragraph (1);

(B) in the case of a consumer reporting agency described in section 603(p), a toll-free telephone number established by the agency, at which personnel are accessible to consumers during normal business hours;

(C) a list of all Federal agencies responsible for enforcing any provision of this title, and the address and any appropriate phone number of each such agency, in a form that will assist the consumer in selecting the appropriate agency;

(D) a statement that the consumer may have additional rights under State law, and that the consumer may wish to contact a State or local consumer protection agency or a State attorney general (or the equivalent thereof) to learn of those rights; and

(E) a statement that a consumer reporting agency is not required to remove accurate derogatory information from the file of a consumer, unless the information is outdated under section 605 or cannot be verified.

(d) Summary of Rights of Identity Theft Victims

(1) *In general.* The Commission, in consultation with the Federal banking agencies and the National Credit Union Administration, shall prepare a model summary of the rights of consumers under this title with respect to the procedures for remedying the effects of fraud or identity theft involving credit, an electronic fund transfer, or an account or transaction at or with a financial institution or other creditor.

(2) *Summary of rights and contact information.* Beginning 60 days after the date on which the model summary of rights is prescribed in final form by the Commission pursuant to paragraph (1), if any consumer contacts a consumer reporting agency and expresses a belief that the consumer is a victim of fraud or identity theft involving credit, an electronic fund transfer, or an account or transaction at or with a financial institution or other creditor, the consumer reporting agency shall, in addition to any other action that the agency may take, provide the consumer with a summary of rights that contains all of the information required by the Commission under paragraph (1), and information on how to contact the Commission to obtain more detailed information.

(e) Information Available to Victims

(1) *In general.* For the purpose of documenting fraudulent transactions resulting from identity theft, not later than 30 days after the date of receipt of a request from a victim in accordance with paragraph (3), and subject to verification of the identity of the victim and the claim of identity theft in accordance with paragraph (2), a business entity that has provided credit to, provided for consideration products, goods, or services to, accepted payment from, or otherwise entered into a commercial transaction for consideration with, a person who has allegedly made unauthorized use of the means of identification of the victim, shall provide a copy of application and business transaction records in the control of the business entity, whether maintained by the business entity or by another person on behalf of the business entity, evidencing any transaction alleged to be a result of identity theft to—

(A) the victim;

(B) any Federal, State, or local government law enforcement agency or officer specified by the victim in such a request; or

(C) any law enforcement agency investigating the identity theft and authorized by the victim to take receipt of records provided under this subsection.

(2) *Verification of identity and claim.* Before a business entity provides any information under paragraph (1), unless the business entity, at its discretion, otherwise has a high degree of confidence that it knows the identity of the victim making a request under paragraph (1), the victim shall provide to the business entity—

(A) as proof of positive identification of the victim, at the election of the business entity—

(i) the presentation of a government-issued identification card;

(ii) personally identifying information of the same type as was provided to the business entity by the unauthorized person; or

(iii) personally identifying information that the business entity typically requests from new applicants or for new transactions, at the time of the victim's request for information, including any documentation described in clauses (i) and (ii); and

(B) as proof of a claim of identity theft, at the election of the business entity—

(i) a copy of a police report evidencing the claim of the victim of identity theft; and

(ii) a properly completed—

(I) copy of a standardized affidavit of identity theft developed and made available by the Commission; or

(II) an affidavit of fact that is acceptable to the business entity for that purpose.

(3) *Procedures.* The request of a victim under paragraph (1) shall—

(A) be in writing;

(B) be mailed to an address specified by the business entity, if any; and

(C) if asked by the business entity, include relevant information about any transaction alleged to be a result of identity theft to facilitate compliance with this section including—

(i) if known by the victim (or if readily obtainable by the victim), the date of the application or transaction; and

(ii) if known by the victim (or if readily obtainable by the victim), any other identifying information such as an account or transaction number.

(4) *No charge to victim.* Information required to be provided under paragraph (1) shall be so provided without charge.

(5) *Authority to decline to provide information.* A business entity may decline to provide information under paragraph (1) if, in the exercise of good faith, the business entity determines that—

(A) this subsection does not require disclosure of the information;

(B) after reviewing the information provided pursuant to paragraph (2), the business entity does not have a high degree of confidence in knowing the true identity of the individual requesting the information;

(C) the request for the information is based on a misrepresentation of fact by the individual requesting the information relevant to the request for information; or

(D) the information requested is Internet navigational data or similar information about a person's visit to a website or online service.

(6) *Limitation on liability.* Except as provided in section 621, sections 616 and 617 do not apply to any violation of this subsection.

(7) *Limitation on civil liability.* No business entity may be held civilly liable under any provision of Federal, State, or other law for disclosure, made in good faith pursuant to this subsection.

(8) *No new recordkeeping obligation.* Nothing in this subsection creates an obligation on the part of a business entity to obtain, retain, or maintain information or records that are not otherwise required to be obtained, retained, or maintained in the ordinary course of its business or under other applicable law.

(9) Rule of Construction

(A) *In general.* No provision of subtitle A of title V of Public Law 106-102, prohibiting the disclosure of financial information by a business entity to third parties shall be used to deny disclosure of information to the victim under this subsection.

(B) *Limitation.* Except as provided in subparagraph (A), nothing in this subsection permits a business entity to disclose information, including information to law enforcement under subparagraphs (B) and (C) of paragraph (1), that the business entity is otherwise prohibited from disclosing under any other applicable provision of Federal or State law.

(10) *Affirmative defense.* In any civil action brought to enforce this subsection, it is an affirmative defense (which the defendant must establish by a preponderance of the evidence) for a business entity to file an affidavit or answer stating that—

(A) the business entity has made a reasonably diligent search of its available business records; and

(B) the records requested under this subsection do not exist or are not reasonably available.

(11) *Definition of victim.* For purposes of this subsection, the term "victim" means a consumer whose means of identification or financial information has been used or transferred (or has been alleged to have been used or transferred) without the authority of that consumer, with the intent to commit, or to aid or abet, an identity theft or a similar crime.

(12) *Effective date.* This subsection shall become effective 180 days after the date of enactment of this subsection.

(13) *Effectiveness study.* Not later than 18 months after the date of enactment of this subsection, the Comptroller General of the United States shall submit a report to Congress assessing the effectiveness of this provision.

(f) Disclosure of Credit Scores

(1) *In general.* Upon the request of a consumer for a credit score, a consumer reporting agency shall supply to the consumer a statement indicating that the information and credit scoring model may be different than the credit score that may be used by the lender, and a notice which shall include—

(A) the current credit score of the consumer or the most recent credit score of the consumer that was previously calculated by the credit reporting agency for a purpose related to the extension of credit;

(B) the range of possible credit scores under the model used;

(C) all of the key factors that adversely affected the credit score of the consumer in the model used, the total number of which shall not exceed 4, subject to paragraph (9);

(D) the date on which the credit score was created; and

(E) the name of the person or entity that provided the credit score or credit file upon which the credit score was created.

(2) *Definitions.* For purposes of this subsection, the following definitions shall apply:

(A) The term "credit score"—

(i) means a numerical value or a categorization derived from a statistical tool or modeling system used by a person who makes or arranges a loan to predict the likelihood of certain credit behaviors, including default (and the numerical value or the categorization derived from such analysis may also be referred to as a "risk predictor" or "risk score"); and

(ii) does not include—

(I) any mortgage score or rating of an automated underwriting system that considers one or more factors in addition to credit information, including the loan to value ratio, the amount of down payment, or the financial assets of a consumer; or

(II) any other elements of the underwriting process or underwriting decision.

(B) The term "key factors" means all relevant elements or reasons adversely affecting the credit score for the particular individual, listed in the order of their importance based on their effect on the credit score.

(3) *Time frame and manner of disclosure.* The information required by this subsection shall be provided in the same time frame and manner as the information described in subsection (a).

(4) *Applicability to certain uses.* This subsection shall not be construed so as to compel a consumer reporting agency to develop or disclose a score if the agency does not—

(A) distribute scores that are used in connection with residential real property loans; or

(B) develop scores that assist credit providers in understanding the general credit behavior of a consumer and predicting the future credit behavior of the consumer.

(5) Applicability to credit scores developed by another person.

(A) *In general.* This subsection shall not be construed to require a consumer reporting agency that distributes credit scores developed by another person or entity to provide a further explanation of them, or to process a dispute arising pursuant to section 611, except that the consumer reporting agency shall provide the consumer with the name and address and website for contacting the person or entity who developed the score or developed the methodology of the score.

(B) *Exception.* This paragraph shall not apply to a consumer reporting agency that develops or modifies scores that are developed by another person or entity.

(6) *Maintenance of credit scores not required.* This subsection shall not be construed to require a consumer reporting agency to maintain credit scores in its files.

(7) *Compliance in certain cases.* In complying with this subsection, a consumer reporting agency shall—

(A) supply the consumer with a credit score that is derived from a credit scoring model that is widely distributed to users by that consumer reporting agency in connection with residential real property loans or with a credit score that assists the consumer in understanding the credit scoring assessment of the credit behavior of the consumer and predictions about the future credit behavior of the consumer; and

(B) a statement indicating that the information and credit scoring model may be different than that used by the lender.

(8) *Fair and reasonable fee.* A consumer reporting agency may charge a fair and reasonable fee, as determined by the Commission, for providing the information required under this subsection.

(9) *Use of enquiries as a key factor.* If a key factor that adversely affects the credit score of a consumer consists of the number of enquiries made with respect to a consumer report, that factor shall be included in the disclosure pursuant to paragraph (1)(C) without regard to the numerical limitation in such paragraph.

(g) Disclosure of Credit Scores by Certain Mortgage Lenders

(1) *In general.* Any person who makes or arranges loans and who uses a consumer credit score, as defined in subsection (f), in connection with an application initiated or sought by a consumer for a closed end loan or the establishment of an open end loan for a consumer purpose that is secured by 1 to 4 units of residential real property (hereafter in this subsection referred

to as the "lender") shall provide the following to the consumer as soon as reasonably practicable:

(A) Information Required under Subsection (f)

(i) *In general.* A copy of the information identified in subsection (f) that was obtained from a consumer reporting agency or was developed and used by the user of the information.

(ii) *Notice under subparagraph (D).* In addition to the information provided to it by a third party that provided the credit score or scores, a lender is only required to provide the notice contained in subparagraph (D).

(B) Disclosures in Case of Automated Underwriting System

(i) *In general.* If a person that is subject to this subsection uses an automated underwriting system to underwrite a loan, that person may satisfy the obligation to provide a credit score by disclosing a credit score and associated key factors supplied by a consumer reporting agency.

(ii) *Numerical credit score.* However, if a numerical credit score is generated by an automated underwriting system used by an enterprise, and that score is disclosed to the person, the score shall be disclosed to the consumer consistent with subparagraph (C).

(iii) *Enterprise defined.* For purposes of this subparagraph, the term "enterprise" has the same meaning as in paragraph (6) of section 1303 of the Federal Housing Enterprises Financial Safety and Soundness Act of 1992.

(C) *Disclosures of credit scores not obtained from a consumer reporting agency.* A person that is subject to the provisions of this subsection and that uses a credit score, other than a credit score provided by a consumer reporting agency, may satisfy the obligation to provide a credit score by disclosing a credit score and associated key factors supplied by a consumer reporting agency.

(D) *Notice to home loan applicants.* A copy of the following notice, which shall include the name, address, and telephone number of each consumer reporting agency providing a credit score that was used:

"Notice To The Home Loan Applicant

"In connection with your application for a home loan, the lender must disclose to you the score that a consumer reporting agency distributed to users and the lender used in connection with your home loan, and the key factors affecting your credit scores.

"The credit score is a computer generated summary calculated at the time of the request and based on information that a consumer reporting agency or lender has on file.

The scores are based on data about your credit history and payment patterns. Credit scores are important because they are used to assist the lender in determining whether you will obtain a loan. They may also be used to determine what interest rate you may be offered on the mortgage. Credit scores can change over time, depending on your conduct, how your credit history and payment patterns change, and how credit scoring technologies change.

"Because the score is based on information in your credit history, it is very important that you review the credit-related information that is being furnished to make sure it is accurate. Credit records may vary from one company to another.

"If you have questions about your credit score or the credit information that is furnished to you, contact the consumer reporting agency at the address and telephone number provided with this notice, or contact the lender, if the lender developed or generated the credit score. The consumer reporting agency plays no part in the decision to take any action on the loan application and is unable to provide you with specific reasons for the decision on a loan application.

"If you have questions concerning the terms of the loan, contact the lender."

(E) *Actions not required under this subsection.* This subsection shall not require any person to—

(i) explain the information provided pursuant to subsection (f);

(ii) disclose any information other than a credit score or key factors, as defined in subsection (f);

(iii) disclose any credit score or related information obtained by the user after a loan has closed;

(iv) provide more than 1 disclosure per loan transaction; or

(v) provide the disclosure required by this subsection when another person has made the disclosure to the consumer for that loan transaction.

(F) No Obligation for Content

(i) *In general.* The obligation of any person pursuant to this subsection shall be limited solely to providing a copy of the information that was received from the consumer reporting agency.

(ii) *Limit on liability.* No person has liability under this subsection for the content of that information or for the omission of any information within the report provided by the consumer reporting agency.

(G) *Person defined as excluding enterprise.* As used in this subsection, the term "person" does not include an enterprise (as defined in paragraph (6) of section 1303 of the Federal Housing Enterprises Financial Safety and Soundness Act of 1992).

(2) Prohibition on Disclosure Clauses Null and Void

(A) *In general.* Any provision in a contract that prohibits the disclosure of a credit score by a person who makes or arranges loans or a consumer reporting agency is void.

(B) *No liability for disclosure under this subsection*—A lender shall not have liability under any contractual provision for disclosure of a credit score pursuant to this subsection.

§ 610. Conditions and form of disclosure to consumers [15 U.S.C. § 1681h]

(a) In general.

(1) Proper identification. A consumer reporting agency shall require, as a condition of making the disclosures required under section 609 [§ 1681g], that the consumer furnish proper identification.

(2) Disclosure in writing. Except as provided in subsection (b), the disclosures required to be made under section 609 [§ 1681g] shall be provided under that section in writing.

(b) Other forms of disclosure.

(1) In general. If authorized by a consumer, a consumer reporting agency may make the disclosures required under 609 [§ 1681g]

(A) other than in writing; and

(B) in such form as may be

(i) specified by the consumer in accordance with paragraph (2); and

(ii) available from the agency.

(2) Form. A consumer may specify pursuant to paragraph (1) that disclosures under section 609 [§ 1681g] shall be made

(A) in person, upon the appearance of the consumer at the place of business of the consumer reporting agency where disclosures are regularly provided, during normal business hours, and on reasonable notice;

(B) by telephone, if the consumer has made a written request for disclosure by telephone;

(C) by electronic means, if available from the agency; or

(D) by any other reasonable means that is available from the agency.

(c) Trained personnel. Any consumer reporting agency shall provide trained personnel to explain to the consumer any information furnished to him pursuant to section 609 [§ 1681g] of this title.

(d) Persons accompanying consumer. The consumer shall be permitted to be accompanied by one other person of his choosing, who shall furnish reasonable identification. A consumer reporting agency may require the consumer to furnish a written statement granting permission to the consumer reporting agency to discuss the consumer's file in such person's presence.

(e) Limitation of liability. Except as provided in sections 616 and 617 [§§ 1681n and 1681o] of this title, no consumer may bring any action or proceeding in the nature of defamation, invasion of privacy, or negligence with respect to the reporting of information against any consumer reporting agency, any user of information, or any person who furnishes information to a consumer reporting agency, based on information disclosed pursuant to section 609, 610, or 615 [§§ 1681g, 1681h, or1681m] of this title or based on information disclosed by a user of a consumer report to or for a consumer against whom the user has taken adverse action, based in whole or in part on the report, except as to false information furnished with malice or willful intent to injure such consumer.

§ 611. Procedure in case of disputed accuracy [15 U.S.C. § 1681i]

(a) Reinvestigations of disputed information.

(1) Reinvestigation required.

(A) In general. If the completeness or accuracy of any item of information contained in a consumer's file at a consumer reporting agency is disputed by the consumer and the consumer notifies the agency directly of such dispute, the agency shall reinvestigate free of charge and record the current status of the disputed information, or delete the item from the file in accordance with paragraph (5), before the end of the 30-day period beginning on the date on which the agency receives the notice of the dispute from the consumer.

(B) Extension of period to reinvestigate. Except as provided in subparagraph (C), the 30-day period described in subparagraph (A) may be extended for not more than 15 additional days if the consumer reporting agency receives information from the consumer during that 30-day period that is relevant to the reinvestigation.

(C) Limitations on extension of period to reinvestigate. Subparagraph (B) shall not apply to any reinvestigation in which, during the 30-day period described in subparagraph (A), the information that is the subject of the reinvestigation is found to be inaccurate or incomplete or the consumer reporting agency determines that the information cannot be verified.

(2) Prompt notice of dispute to furnisher of information.

(A) In general. Before the expiration of the 5-business-day period beginning on the date on which a consumer reporting agency receives notice of a dispute from any consumer in accordance with paragraph (1), the agency shall provide notification of the dispute to any person who provided any item of information in dispute, at the address and in the manner established with the person. The notice shall include all relevant information regarding the dispute that the agency has received from the consumer.

(B) Provision of other information from consumer. The consumer reporting agency shall promptly provide to the person who provided the information in dispute all relevant information regarding the dispute that is received by the agency from the consumer after the period referred to in subparagraph (A) and before the end of the period referred to in paragraph (1)(A).

(3) Determination that dispute is frivolous or irrelevant.

(A) In general. Notwithstanding paragraph (1), a consumer reporting agency may terminate a reinvestigation of information disputed by a consumer under that paragraph if the agency reasonably determines that the dispute by the consumer is frivolous or irrelevant, including by reason of a failure by a consumer to provide sufficient information to investigate the disputed information.

(B) Notice of determination. Upon making any determination in accordance with subparagraph (A) that a dispute is frivolous or irrelevant, a consumer reporting agency shall notify the consumer of such determination not later than 5 business days after making such determination, by mail or, if authorized by the consumer for that purpose, by any other means available to the agency.

(C) Contents of notice. A notice under subparagraph (B) shall include

(i) the reasons for the determination under subparagraph (A); and

(ii) identification of any information required to investigate the disputed information, which may consist of a standardized form describing the general nature of such information.

(4) Consideration of consumer information. In conducting any reinvestigation under paragraph (1) with respect to disputed information in the file of any consumer, the consumer reporting agency shall review and consider all relevant information submitted by the consumer in the period described in paragraph (1)(A) with respect to such disputed information.

(5) Treatment of inaccurate or unverifiable information.

(A) In general. If, after any reinvestigation under paragraph (1) of any information disputed by a consumer, an item of the information is found to be inaccurate or incomplete or cannot be verified, the consumer reporting agency shall promptly delete that item of information from the consumer's file or modify that item of information, as appropriate, based on the results of the reinvestigation.

(B) Requirements relating to reinsertion of previously deleted material.

(i) Certification of accuracy of information. If any information is deleted from a consumer's file pursuant to subparagraph (A), the information may not be reinserted in the file by the consumer reporting agency unless the person who furnishes the information certifies that the information is complete and accurate.

(ii) Notice to consumer. If any information that has been deleted from a consumer's file pursuant to subparagraph (A) is reinserted in the file, the consumer reporting agency shall notify the consumer of the reinsertion in writing not later than 5 business days after the reinsertion or, if authorized by the consumer for that purpose, by any other means available to the agency.

(iii) Additional information. As part of, or in addition to, the notice under clause (ii), a consumer reporting agency shall provide to a consumer in writing not later than 5 business days after the date of the reinsertion

(I) a statement that the disputed information has been reinserted;

(II) the business name and address of any furnisher of information contacted and the telephone number of such furnisher, if reasonably available, or of any furnisher of information that contacted the consumer reporting agency, in connection with the reinsertion of such information; and

(III) a notice that the consumer has the right to add a statement to the consumer's file disputing the accuracy or completeness of the disputed information.

(C) Procedures to prevent reappearance. A consumer reporting agency shall maintain reasonable procedures designed to prevent the reappearance in a consumer's file, and in consumer reports on the consumer, of information that is deleted pursuant to this paragraph (other than information that is reinserted in accordance with subparagraph (B)(i)).

(D) Automated reinvestigation system. Any consumer reporting agency that compiles and maintains files on consumers on a nationwide basis shall implement an automated system through which furnishers of information to that consumer reporting agency may report the results of a reinvestigation that finds incomplete or inaccurate information in a consumer's file to other such consumer reporting agencies.

(6) Notice of results of reinvestigation.

(A) In general. A consumer reporting agency shall provide written notice to a consumer of the results of a reinvestigation under this subsection not later than 5 business days after the completion of the reinvestigation, by mail or, if authorized by the consumer for that purpose, by other means available to the agency.

(B) Contents. As part of, or in addition to, the notice under subparagraph (A), a consumer reporting agency shall provide to a consumer in writing before the expiration of the 5-day period referred to in subparagraph (A)

(i) a statement that the reinvestigation is completed;

(ii) a consumer report that is based upon the consumer's file as that file is revised as a result of the reinvestigation;

(iii) a notice that, if requested by the consumer, a description of the procedure used to determine the accuracy and completeness of the information shall be provided to the consumer by the agency, including the business name and address of any furnisher of information contacted in connection with such information and the telephone number of such furnisher, if reasonably available;

(iv) a notice that the consumer has the right to add a statement to the consumer's file disputing the accuracy or completeness of the information; and

(v) a notice that the consumer has the right to request under subsection (d) that the consumer reporting agency furnish notifications under that subsection.

(7) Description of reinvestigation procedure. A consumer reporting agency shall provide to a consumer a description referred to in paragraph (6)(B)(iii) by not later than 15 days after receiving a request from the consumer for that description.

(8) Expedited dispute resolution. If a dispute regarding an item of information in a consumer's file at a consumer reporting agency is resolved in accordance with paragraph (5)(A) by the deletion of the disputed information by not later than 3 business days after the date on which the agency receives notice of the dispute from the consumer in accordance with paragraph (1)(A), then the agency shall not be required to comply with paragraphs (2), (6), and (7) with respect to that dispute if the agency

(A) provides prompt notice of the deletion to the consumer by telephone; The Federal Trade Commission increased the maximum allowable charge to $9.00, effective January 1, (continued . . .)

(B) includes in that notice, or in a written notice that accompanies a confirmation and consumer report provided in accordance with subparagraph (C), a statement of the consumer's right to request under subsection (d) that the agency furnish notifications under that subsection; and

(C) provides written confirmation of the deletion and a copy of a consumer report on the consumer that is based on the consumer's file after the deletion, not later than 5 business days after making the deletion.

(b) Statement of dispute. If the reinvestigation does not resolve the dispute, the consumer may file a brief statement setting forth the nature of the dispute. The consumer reporting agency may limit such statements to not more than one hundred words if it provides the consumer with assistance in writing a clear summary of the dispute.

(c) Notification of consumer dispute in subsequent consumer reports. Whenever a statement of a dispute is filed, unless there is reasonable grounds to believe that it is frivolous or irrelevant, the consumer reporting agency shall, in any subsequent consumer report containing the information in question, clearly note that it is disputed by the consumer and provide either the consumer's statement or a clear and accurate codification or summary thereof.

(d) Notification of deletion of disputed information. Following any deletion of information which is found to be inaccurate or whose accuracy can no longer be verified or any notation as to disputed information, the consumer reporting agency shall, at the request of the consumer, furnish notification that the item has been deleted or the statement, codification or summary pursuant to subsection (b) or (c) of this section to any person specifically designated by the consumer who has within two years prior thereto received a consumer report for employment purposes, or within six months prior thereto received a consumer report for any other purpose, which contained the deleted or disputed information.

§ 612. Charges for certain disclosures [15 U.S.C. § 1681j]

(a) Reasonable charges allowed for certain disclosures.

(1) In general. Except as provided in subsections (b), (c), and (d), a consumer reporting agency may impose a reasonable charge on a consumer

(A) for making a disclosure to the consumer pursuant to section 609 [§ 1681g], which charge

(i) shall not exceed $8; and (. . . continued) 2002. 66 Fed. Reg. 63545 (Dec. 7, 2001).

(ii) shall be indicated to the consumer before making the disclosure; And

(B) for furnishing, pursuant to 611(d) [§ 1681i], following a reinvestigation under section 611(a) [§ 1681i], a statement, codification, or summary to a person designated by the consumer under that section after the 30-day period beginning on the date of notification of the consumer under paragraph (6) or (8) of section 611(a) [§ 1681i] with respect to the reinvestigation, which charge

(i) shall not exceed the charge that the agency would impose on each designated recipient for a consumer report; and

(ii) shall be indicated to the consumer before furnishing such information.

(2) Modification of amount. The Federal Trade Commission shall increase the amount referred to in paragraph (1)(A)(I) on January 1 of each year, based proportionally on changes in the Consumer Price Index, with fractional changes rounded to the nearest fifty cents.

(b) Free disclosure after adverse notice to consumer. Each consumer reporting agency that maintains a file on a consumer shall make all disclosures pursuant to section 609 [§ 1681g] without charge to the consumer if, not later than 60 days after receipt by such consumer of a notification pursuant to section 615 [§ 1681m], or of a notification from a debt collection agency affiliated with that consumer reporting agency stating that the consumer's credit rating may be or has been adversely affected, the consumer makes a request under section 609 [§ 1681g].

(c) Free disclosure under certain other circumstances. Upon the request of the consumer, a consumer reporting agency shall make all disclosures pursuant to section 609 [§ 1681g] once during any 12-month period without charge to that consumer if the consumer certifies in writing that the consumer

(1) is unemployed and intends to apply for employment in the 60-day period beginning on the date on which the certification is made;

(2) is a recipient of public welfare assistance; or

(3) has reason to believe that the file on the consumer at the agency contains inaccurate information due to fraud.

(d) Other charges prohibited. A consumer reporting agency shall not impose any charge on a consumer for providing any notification required by this title or making any disclosure required by this title, except as authorized by subsection (a).

§ 613. Public record information for employment purposes [15 U.S.C. § 1681k]

(a) In general. A consumer reporting agency which furnishes a consumer report for employment purposes and which for that purpose compiles and reports items of information on consumers which are matters of public record and are likely to have an adverse effect upon a consumer's ability to obtain employment shall

(1) at the time such public record information is reported to the user of such consumer report, notify the consumer of the fact that public record information is being reported by the consumer reporting agency, together with

the name and address of the person to whom such information is being reported; or

(2) maintain strict procedures designed to insure that whenever public record information which is likely to have an adverse effect on a consumer's ability to obtain employment is reported it is complete and up to date. For purposes of this paragraph, items of public record relating to arrests, indictments, convictions, suits, tax liens, and outstanding judgments shall be considered up to date if the current public record status of the item at the time of the report is reported.

(b) Exemption for national security investigations. Subsection (a) does not apply in the case of an agency or department of the United States Government that seeks to obtain and use a consumer report for employment purposes, if the head of the agency or department makes a written finding as prescribed under section 604(b)(4)(A).

§ 614. Restrictions on investigative consumer reports [15 U.S.C. § 1681*l*]

Whenever a consumer reporting agency prepares an investigative consumer report, no adverse information in the consumer report (other than information which is a matter of public record) may be included in a subsequent consumer report unless such adverse information has been verified in the process of making such subsequent consumer report, or the adverse information was received within the three-month period preceding the date the subsequent report is furnished.

§ 615. Requirements on users of consumer reports [15 U.S.C. § 1681m]

(a) Duties of users taking adverse actions on the basis of information contained in consumer reports. If any person takes any adverse action with respect to any consumer that is based in whole or in part on any information contained in a consumer report, the person shall

(1) provide oral, written, or electronic notice of the adverse action to the consumer;

(2) provide to the consumer orally, in writing, or electronically

(A) the name, address, and telephone number of the consumer reporting agency (including a toll-free telephone number established by the agency if the agency compiles and maintains files on consumers on a nationwide basis) that furnished the report to the person; and

(B) a statement that the consumer reporting agency did not make the decision to take the adverse action and is unable to provide the consumer the specific reasons why the adverse action was taken; and

(3) provide to the consumer an oral, written, or electronic notice of the consumer's right

(A) to obtain, under section 612 [§ 1681j], a free copy of a consumer report on the consumer from the consumer reporting agency referred to in paragraph (2), which notice shall include an indication of the 60-day period under that section for obtaining such a copy; and

(B) to dispute, under section 611 [§ 1681i], with a consumer reporting agency the accuracy or completeness of any information in a consumer report furnished by the agency.

(b) Adverse action based on information obtained from third parties other than consumer reporting agencies.

(1) In general. Whenever credit for personal, family, or household purposes involving a consumer is denied or the charge for such credit is increased either wholly or partly because of information obtained from a person other than a consumer reporting agency bearing upon the consumer's creditworthiness, credit standing, credit capacity, character, general reputation, personal characteristics, or mode of living, the user of such information shall, within a reasonable period of time, upon the consumer's written request for the reasons for such adverse action received within sixty days after learning of such adverse action, disclose the nature of the information to the consumer. The user of such information shall clearly and accurately disclose to the consumer his right to make such written request at the time such adverse action is communicated to the consumer.

(2) Duties of person taking certain actions based on information provided by affiliate.

(A) Duties, generally. If a person takes an action described in subparagraph (B) with respect to a consumer, based in whole or in part on information described in subparagraph (C), the person shall

(i) notify the consumer of the action, including a statement that the consumer may obtain the information in accordance with clause (ii); and

(ii) upon a written request from the consumer received within 60 days after transmittal of the notice required by clause (I), disclose to the consumer the nature of the information upon which the action is based by not later than 30 days after receipt of the request.

(B) Action described. An action referred to in subparagraph (A) is an adverse action described in section 603(k)(1)(A) [§ 1681a], taken in connection with a transaction initiated by the consumer, or any adverse action described in clause (i) or (ii) of section 603(k)(1)(B) [§ 1681a].

(C) Information described. Information referred to in subparagraph (A)

(i) except as provided in clause (ii), is information that

(I) is furnished to the person taking the action by a person related by common ownership or affiliated by common corporate control to the person taking the action; and

(II) bears on the credit worthiness, credit standing, credit capacity, character, general reputation, personal characteristics, or mode of living of the consumer; and

(ii) does not include

(I) information solely as to transactions or experiences between the consumer and the person furnishing the information; or

(II) information in a consumer report.

(c) Reasonable procedures to assure compliance. No person shall be held liable for any violation of this section if he shows by a preponderance of the evidence that at the time of the alleged violation he maintained reasonable procedures to assure compliance with the provisions of this section.

(d) Duties of users making written credit or insurance solicitations on the basis of information contained in consumer files.

(1) In general. Any person who uses a consumer report on any consumer in connection with any credit or insurance transaction that is not initiated by the consumer, that is provided to that person under section 604(c)(1)(B) [§ 1681b], shall provide with each written solicitation made to the consumer regarding the transaction a clear and conspicuous statement that

(A) information contained in the consumer's consumer report was used in connection with the transaction;

(B) the consumer received the offer of credit or insurance because the consumer satisfied the criteria for credit worthiness or insurability under which the consumer was selected for the offer;

(C) if applicable, the credit or insurance may not be extended if, after the consumer responds to the offer, the consumer does not meet the criteria used to select the consumer for the offer or any applicable criteria bearing on credit worthiness or insurability or does not furnish any required collateral;

(D) the consumer has a right to prohibit information contained in the consumer's file with any consumer reporting agency from being used in connection with any credit or insurance transaction that is not initiated by the consumer; and

(E) the consumer may exercise the right referred to in subparagraph (D) by notifying a notification system established under section 604(e) [§ 1681b].

(2) Disclosure of address and telephone number. A statement under paragraph (1) shall include the address and toll-free telephone number of the appropriate notification system established under section 604(e) [§ 1681b].

(3) Maintaining criteria on file. A person who makes an offer of credit or insurance to a consumer under a credit or insurance transaction described in paragraph (1) shall maintain on file the criteria used to select the consumer to receive the offer, all criteria bearing on credit worthiness or insurability, as applicable, that are the basis for determining whether or not to extend credit or insurance pursuant to the offer, and any requirement for the furnishing of collateral as a condition of the extension of credit or insurance, until the expiration of the 3-year period beginning on the date on which the offer is made to the consumer.

(4) Authority of federal agencies regarding unfair or deceptive acts or practices not affected. This section is not intended to affect the authority of any Federal or State agency to enforce a prohibition against unfair or deceptive acts or practices, including the making of false or misleading statements in connection with a credit or insurance transaction that is not initiated by the consumer.

§ 616. Civil liability for willful noncompliance [15 U.S.C. § 1681n]

(a) In general. Any person who willfully fails to comply with any requirement imposed under this title with respect to any consumer is liable to that consumer in an amount equal to the sum of

(1) (A) any actual damages sustained by the consumer as a result of the failure or damages of not less than $100 and not more than $1,000; or

(B) in the case of liability of a natural person for obtaining a consumer report under false pretenses or knowingly without a permissible purpose, actual damages sustained by the consumer as a result of the failure or $1,000, whichever is greater;

(2) such amount of punitive damages as the court may allow; and

(3) in the case of any successful action to enforce any liability under this section, the costs of the action together with reasonable attorney's fees as determined by the court.

(b) Civil liability for knowing noncompliance. Any person who obtains a consumer report from a consumer reporting agency under false pretenses or knowingly without a permissible purpose shall be liable to the consumer reporting agency for actual damages sustained by the consumer reporting agency or $1,000, whichever is greater.

(c) Attorney's fees. Upon a finding by the court that an unsuccessful pleading, motion, or other paper filed in connection with an action under this section was filed in bad faith or for purposes of harassment, the court shall award to the prevailing party attorney's fees reasonable in relation to the work expended in responding to the pleading, motion, or other paper.

§ 617. Civil liability for negligent noncompliance [15 U.S.C. § 1681o]

(a) In general. Any person who is negligent in failing to comply with any requirement imposed under this title with respect to any consumer is liable to that consumer in an amount equal to the sum of

> (1) any actual damages sustained by the consumer as a result of the failure;
>
> (2) in the case of any successful action to enforce any liability under this section, the costs of the action together with reasonable attorney's fees as determined by the court.

(b) Attorney's fees. On a finding by the court that an unsuccessful pleading, motion, or other paper filed in connection with an action under this section was filed in bad faith or for purposes of harassment, the court shall award to the prevailing party attorney's fees reasonable in relation to the work expended in responding to the pleading, motion, or other paper.

§ 618. Jurisdiction of courts; limitation of actions [15 U.S.C. § 1681p]

An action to enforce any liability created under this title may be brought in any appropriate United States district court without regard to the amount in controversy, or in any other court of competent jurisdiction, within two years from the date on which the liability arises, except that where a defendant has materially and willfully misrepresented any information required under this title to be disclosed to an individual and the information so misrepresented is material to the establishment of the defendant's liability to that individual under this title, the action may be brought at any time within two years after discovery by the individual of the misrepresentation.

§ 619. Obtaining information under false pretenses [15 U.S.C. § 1681q]

Any person who knowingly and willfully obtains information on a consumer from a consumer reporting agency under false pretenses shall be fined under title 18, United States Code, imprisoned for not more than 2 years, or both.

§ 620. Unauthorized disclosures by officers or employees [15 U.S.C. § 1681r]

Any officer or employee of a consumer reporting agency who knowingly and willfully provides information concerning an individual from the agency's files to a person not authorized to receive that information shall be fined under title 18, United States Code, imprisoned for not more than 2 years, or both.

§ 621. Administrative enforcement [15 U.S.C. § 1681s]

(a) (1) Enforcement by Federal Trade Commission. Compliance with the requirements imposed under this title shall be enforced under the Federal Trade Commission Act [15 U.S.C. §§ 41 et seq.] by the Federal Trade Commission with respect to consumer reporting agencies and all other persons subject thereto, except to the extent that enforcement of the requirements imposed under this title is specifically committed to some other government agency under subsection (b) hereof. For the purpose of the exercise by the Federal Trade Commission of its functions and powers under the Federal Trade Commission Act, a violation of any requirement or prohibition imposed under this title shall constitute an unfair or deceptive act or practice in commerce in violation of section 5(a) of the Federal Trade Commission Act [15 U.S.C. § 45(a)] and shall be subject to enforcement by the Federal Trade Commission under section 5(b) thereof [15 U.S.C. § 45(b)] with respect to any consumer reporting agency or person subject to enforcement by the Federal Trade Commission pursuant to this subsection, irrespective of whether that person is engaged in commerce or meets any other jurisdictional tests in the Federal Trade Commission Act. The Federal Trade Commission shall have such procedural, investigative, and enforcement powers, including the power to issue procedural rules in enforcing compliance with the requirements imposed under this title and to require the filing of reports, the production of documents, and the appearance of witnesses as though the applicable terms and conditions of the Federal Trade Commission Act were part of this title. Any person violating any of the provisions of this title shall be subject to the penalties and entitled to the privileges and immunities provided in the Federal Trade Commission Act as though the applicable terms and provisions thereof were part of this title.

(2) (A) In the event of a knowing violation, which constitutes a pattern or practice of violations of this title, the Commission may commence a civil action to recover a civil penalty in a district court of the United States against any person that violates this title. In such action, such person shall be liable for a civil penalty of not more than $2,500 per violation.

(B) In determining the amount of a civil penalty under subparagraph (A), the court shall take into account the degree of culpability, any history of prior such conduct, ability to pay, effect on ability to continue to do business, and such other matters as justice may require.

(3) Notwithstanding paragraph (2), a court may not impose any civil penalty on a person for a violation of section 623(a)(1) [§ 1681s-2] unless the person has been enjoined from committing the violation, or ordered not to commit the violation, in an action or proceeding brought by or on behalf of the Federal Trade Commission, and has violated the injunction or order, and the court may not impose any civil penalty for any violation occurring before the date of the violation of the injunction or order.

(b) Enforcement by other agencies. Compliance with the requirements imposed under this title with respect to consumer reporting agencies, persons who use consumer reports from such agencies, persons who furnish information to such agencies, and users of information that are subject to subsection (d) of section 615 [§ 1681m] shall be enforced under (1) section 8 of the Federal Deposit Insurance Act [12 U.S.C. § 1818], in the case of

(A) national banks, and Federal branches and Federal agencies of foreign banks, by the Office of the Comptroller of the Currency;

(B) member banks of the Federal Reserve System (other than national banks), branches and agencies of foreign banks (other than Federal branches, Federal agencies, and insured State branches of foreign banks), commercial lending companies owned or controlled by foreign banks, and organizations operating under section 25 or 25(a) [25A] of the Federal Reserve Act [12 U.S.C. §§ 601 et seq., §§ 611 et seq.], by the Board of Governors of the Federal Reserve System; and

(C) banks insured by the Federal Deposit Insurance Corporation (other than members of the Federal Reserve System) and insured State branches of foreign banks, by the Board of Directors of the Federal Deposit Insurance Corporation;

(2) section 8 of the Federal Deposit Insurance Act [12 U.S.C. § 1818], by the Director of the Office of Thrift Supervision, in the case of a savings association the deposits of which are insured by the Federal Deposit Insurance Corporation;

(3) the Federal Credit Union Act [12 U.S.C. §§ 1751 et seq.], by the Administrator of the National Credit Union Administration [National Credit Union Administration Board] with respect to any Federal credit union;

(4) subtitle IV of title 49 [49 U.S.C. §§ 10101 et seq.], by the Secretary of Transportation, with respect to all carriers subject to the jurisdiction of the Surface Transportation Board;

(5) the Federal Aviation Act of 1958 [49 U.S.C. Appx. §§ 1301 et seq.], by the Secretary of Transportation with respect to any air carrier or foreign air carrier subject to that Act [49 U.S.C. Appx. §§ 1301 et seq.]; and

(6) the Packers and Stockyards Act, 1921 [7 U.S.C. §§ 181 et seq.] (except as provided in section 406 of that Act [7 U.S.C. §§ 226 and 227]), by the

Secretary of Agriculture with respect to any activities subject to that Act. The terms used in paragraph (1) that are not defined in this title or otherwise defined in section 3(s) of the Federal Deposit Insurance Act (12 U.S.C. § 1813(s)) shall have the meaning given to them in section 1(b) of the International Banking Act of 1978 (12 U.S.C. § 3101).

(c) State action for violations.

(1) Authority of states. In addition to such other remedies as are provided under State law, if the chief law enforcement officer of a State, or an official or agency designated by a State, has reason to believe that any person has violated or is violating this title, the State

(A) may bring an action to enjoin such violation in any appropriate United States district court or in any other court of competent jurisdiction;

(B) subject to paragraph (5), may bring an action on behalf of the residents of the State to recover

(i) damages for which the person is liable to such residents under sections 616 and 617 [§§ 1681n and 1681o] as a result of the violation;

(ii) in the case of a violation of section 623(a) [§ 1681s-2], damages for which the person would, but for section 623(c) [§ 1681s-2], be liable to such residents as a result of the violation; or

(iii) damages of not more than $1,000 for each willful or negligent violation; and

(C) in the case of any successful action under subparagraph (A) or (B), shall be awarded the costs of the action and reasonable attorney fees as determined by the court.

(2) Rights of federal regulators. The State shall serve prior written notice of any action under paragraph (1) upon the Federal Trade Commission or the appropriate Federal regulator determined under subsection (b) and provide the Commission or appropriate Federal regulator with a copy of its complaint, except in any case in which such prior notice is not feasible, in which case the State shall serve such notice immediately upon instituting such action. The Federal Trade Commission or appropriate Federal regulator shall have the right

(A) to intervene in the action;

(B) upon so intervening, to be heard on all matters arising therein;

(C) to remove the action to the appropriate United States district court; and

(D) to file petitions for appeal.

(3) Investigatory powers. For purposes of bringing any action under this subsection, nothing in this subsection shall prevent the chief law enforcement officer, or an official or agency designated by a State, from exercising the powers conferred on the chief law enforcement officer or such official by the laws of such State to conduct investigations or to administer oaths or affirmations or to compel the attendance of witnesses or the production of documentary and other evidence.

(4) Limitation on state action while federal action pending. If the Federal Trade Commission or the appropriate Federal regulator has instituted a civil action or an administrative action under section 8 of the Federal Deposit Insurance Act for a violation of this title, no State may, during the pendency of such action, bring an action under this section against any defendant named in the complaint of the Commission or the appropriate Federal regulator for any violation of this title that is alleged in that complaint.

(5) Limitations on state actions for violation of section 623(a)(1) [§ 1681s-2].

(A) Violation of injunction required. A State may not bring an action against a person under paragraph (1)(B) for a violation of section 623(a)(1) [§ 1681s-2], unless

(i) the person has been enjoined from committing the violation, in an action brought by the State under paragraph (1)(A); and

(ii) the person has violated the injunction.

(B) Limitation on damages recoverable. In an action against a person under paragraph (1)(B) for a violation of section 623(a)(1) [§ 1681s-2], a State may not recover any damages incurred before the date of the violation of an injunction on which the action is based.

(d) Enforcement under other authority. For the purpose of the exercise by any agency referred to in subsection (b) of this section of its powers under any Act referred to in that subsection, a violation of any requirement imposed under this title shall be deemed to be a violation of a requirement imposed under that Act. In addition to its powers under any provision of law specifically referred to in subsection (b) of this section, each of the agencies referred to in that subsection may exercise, for the purpose of enforcing compliance with any requirement imposed under this title any other authority conferred on it by law.

(e) Regulatory authority.

(1) The Federal banking agencies referred to in paragraphs (1) and (2) of subsection (b) shall jointly prescribe such regulations as necessary to carry out the purposes of this Act with respect to any persons identified under paragraphs (1) and (2) of subsection (b), and the Board of Governors of the Federal Reserve System shall have authority to prescribe regulations consistent with such joint regulations with respect to bank holding companies

and affiliates (other than depository institutions and consumer reporting agencies) of such holding companies.

(2) The Board of the National Credit Union Administration shall prescribe such regulations as necessary to carry out the purposes of this Act with respect to any persons identified under paragraph (3) of subsection (b).

§ 622. Information on overdue child support obligations [15 U.S.C. § 1681s-1]

Notwithstanding any other provision of this title, a consumer reporting agency shall include in any consumer report furnished by the agency in accordance with section 604 [§ 1681b] of this title, any information on the failure of the consumer to pay overdue support which

(1) is provided

(A) to the consumer reporting agency by a State or local child support enforcement agency; or

(B) to the consumer reporting agency and verified by any local, State, or Federal government agency; and

(2) antedates the report by 7 years or less.

§ 623. Responsibilities of furnishers of information to consumer reporting agencies

(a) Duty of Furnishers of Information to Provide Accurate Information.

(1) Prohibition

(A) *Reporting information with actual knowledge of errors.* A person shall not furnish any information relating to a consumer to any consumer reporting agency if the person knows or has reasonable cause to believe that the information is inaccurate.

(B) *Reporting information after notice and confirmation of errors.* A person shall not furnish information relating to a consumer to any consumer reporting agency if

(i) the person has been notified by the consumer, at the address specified by the person for such notices, that specific information is inaccurate; and

(ii) the information is, in fact, inaccurate.

(C) *No address requirement.* A person who clearly and conspicuously specifies to the consumer an address for notices referred to in subparagraph (B) shall not be subject to subparagraph (A); however, nothing in subparagraph (B) shall require a person to specify such an address.

(D) *Definition.* For purposes of subparagraph (A), the term "reasonable cause to believe that the information is inaccurate" means having specific knowledge, other than solely allegations by the consumer, that would cause a reasonable person to have substantial doubts about the accuracy of the information.

(2) *Duty to correct and update information.* A person who

(A) regularly and in the ordinary course of business furnishes information to one or more consumer reporting agencies about the person's transactions or experiences with any consumer; and

(B) has furnished to a consumer reporting agency information that the person determines is not complete or accurate, shall promptly notify the consumer reporting agency of that determination and provide to the agency any corrections to that information, or any additional information, that is necessary to make the information provided by the person to the agency complete and accurate, and shall not thereafter furnish to the agency any of the information that remains not complete or accurate.

(3) *Duty to provide notice of dispute.* If the completeness or accuracy of any information furnished by any person to any consumer reporting agency is disputed to such person by a consumer, the person may not furnish the information to any consumer reporting agency without notice that such information is disputed by the consumer.

(4) *Duty to provide notice of closed accounts.* A person who regularly and in the ordinary course of business furnishes information to a consumer reporting agency regarding a consumer who has a credit account with that person shall notify the agency of the voluntary closure of the account by the consumer, in information regularly furnished for the period in which the account is closed.

(5) Duty to Provide Notice of Delinquency of Accounts

(A) *In general.* A person who furnishes information to a consumer reporting agency regarding a delinquent account being placed for collection, charged to profit or loss, or subjected to any similar action shall, not later than 90 days after furnishing the information, notify the agency of the date of delinquency on the account, which shall be the month and year of the commencement of the delinquency on the account that immediately preceded the action.

(B) *Rule of construction.* For purposes of this paragraph only, and provided that the consumer does not dispute the information, a person that furnishes information on a delinquent account that is placed for collection, charged for profit or loss, or subjected to any similar action, complies with this paragraph, if—

(i) the person reports the same date of delinquency as that provided by the creditor to which the account was owed at the time at which the commencement of the delinquency occurred, if the creditor previously reported that date of delinquency to a consumer reporting agency;

(ii) the creditor did not previously report the date of delinquency to a consumer reporting agency, and the person establishes and follows reasonable procedures to obtain the date of delinquency from the creditor or another reliable source and reports that date to a consumer reporting agency as the date of delinquency; or

(iii) the creditor did not previously report the date of delinquency to a consumer reporting agency and the date of delinquency cannot be reasonably obtained as provided in clause (ii), the person establishes and follows reasonable procedures to ensure the date reported as the date of delinquency precedes the date on which the account is placed for collection, charged to profit or loss, or subjected to any similar action, and reports such date to the credit reporting agency.

(6) Duties of Furnishers Upon Notice of Identity Theft-Related Information

(A) *Reasonable procedures.* A person that furnishes information to any consumer reporting agency shall have in place reasonable procedures to respond to any notification that it receives from a consumer reporting agency under section 605B relating to information resulting from identity theft, to prevent that person from refurnishing such blocked information.

(B) *Information alleged to result from identity theft.* If a consumer submits an identity theft report to a person who furnishes information to a consumer reporting agency at the address specified by that person for receiving such reports stating that information maintained by such person that purports to relate to the consumer resulted from identity theft, the person may not furnish such information that purports to relate to the consumer to any consumer reporting agency, unless the person subsequently knows or is informed by the consumer that the information is correct.

(7) Negative Information

(A) Notice to Consumer Required

(i) *In general.* If any financial institution that extends credit and regularly and in the ordinary course of business furnishes information to a consumer reporting agency described in section 603(p) furnishes negative information to such an agency regarding credit extended to a customer, the financial institution shall provide a notice of such furnishing of negative information, in writing, to the customer.

(ii) *Notice effective for subsequent submissions.* After providing such notice, the financial institution may submit additional negative information to a consumer reporting agency described in section 603(p) with respect to the same transaction, extension of credit, account, or customer without providing additional notice to the customer.

(B) Time of Notice

(i) *In general.* The notice required under subparagraph (A) shall be provided to the customer prior to, or no later than 30 days after, furnishing the negative information to a consumer reporting agency described in section 603(p).

(ii) *Coordination with new account disclosures.* If the notice is provided to the customer prior to furnishing the negative information to a consumer reporting agency, the notice may not be included in the initial disclosures provided under section 127(a) of the Truth in Lending Act.

(C) *Coordination with other disclosures.* The notice required under subparagraph (A)—

(i) may be included on or with any notice of default, any billing statement, or any other materials provided to the customer; and

(ii) must be clear and conspicuous.

(D) Model Disclosure

(i) *Duty of board to prepare.* The Board shall prescribe a brief model disclosure a financial institution may use to comply with subparagraph (A), which shall not exceed 30 words.

(ii) *Use of model not required.* No provision of this paragraph shall be construed as requiring a financial institution to use any such model form prescribed by the Board.

(iii) *Compliance using model.* A financial institution shall be deemed to be in compliance with subparagraph (A) if the financial institution uses any such model form prescribed by the Board, or the financial institution uses any such model form and rearranges its format.

(E) *Use of notice without submitting negative information.* No provision of this paragraph shall be construed as requiring a financial institution that has provided a customer with a notice described in subparagraph (A) to furnish negative information about the customer to a consumer reporting agency.

(F) *Safe harbor.* A financial institution shall not be liable for failure to perform the duties required by this paragraph if, at the time of the failure, the financial institution maintained reasonable policies and procedures to comply with this paragraph or the financial institution reasonably believed that the institution is prohibited, by law, from contacting the consumer.

(G) *Definitions.* For purposes of this paragraph, the following definitions shall apply:

(i) The term "negative information" means information concerning a customer's delinquencies, late payments, insolvency, or any form of default.

(ii) The terms "customer" and "financial institution" have the same meanings as in section 509 Public Law 106-102.

(8) Ability of Consumer to Dispute Information Directly with Furnisher

(A) *In general.* The Federal banking agencies, the National Credit Union Administration, and the Commission shall jointly prescribe regulations that shall identify the circumstances under which a furnisher shall be required to reinvestigate a dispute concerning the accuracy of information contained in a consumer report on the consumer, based on a direct request of a consumer.

(B) *Considerations.* In prescribing regulations under subparagraph (A), the agencies shall weigh—

(i) the benefits to consumers with the costs on furnishers and the credit reporting system;

(ii) the impact on the overall accuracy and integrity of consumer reports of any such requirements;

(iii) whether direct contact by the consumer with the furnisher would likely result in the most expeditious resolution of any such dispute; and

(iv) the potential impact on the credit reporting process if credit repair organizations, as defined in section 403(3) [15 U.S.C. § 1679a(3)], including entities that would be a credit repair organization, but for section 403(3)(B)(i), are able to circumvent the prohibition in subparagraph (G).

(C) *Applicability.* Subparagraphs (D) through (G) shall apply in any circumstance identified under the regulations promulgated under subparagraph (A).

(D) *Submitting a notice of dispute.* A consumer who seeks to dispute the accuracy of information shall provide a dispute notice directly to such person at the address specified by the person for such notices that—

(i) identifies the specific information that is being disputed;

(ii) explains the basis for the dispute; and

(iii) includes all supporting documentation required by the furnisher to substantiate the basis of the dispute.

(E) *Duty of person after receiving notice of dispute.* After receiving a notice of dispute from a consumer pursuant to subparagraph (D), the person that provided the information in dispute to a consumer reporting agency shall—

(i) conduct an investigation with respect to the disputed information;

(ii) review all relevant information provided by the consumer with the notice;

(iii) complete such person's investigation of the dispute and report the results of the investigation to the consumer before the expiration of the period under section 611(a)(1) within which a consumer reporting agency would be required to complete its action if the consumer had elected to dispute the information under that section; and

(iv) if the investigation finds that the information reported was inaccurate, promptly notify each consumer reporting agency to which the person furnished the inaccurate information of that determination and provide to the agency any correction to that information that is necessary to make the information provided by the person accurate.

(F) Frivolous or Irrelevant Dispute

(i) *In general.* This paragraph shall not apply if the person receiving a notice of a dispute from a consumer reasonably determines that the dispute is frivolous or irrelevant, including—

(I) by reason of the failure of a consumer to provide sufficient information to investigate the disputed information; or

(II) the submission by a consumer of a dispute that is substantially the same as a dispute previously submitted by or for the consumer, either directly to the person or through a consumer reporting agency under subsection (b), with respect to which the person has already performed the person's duties under this paragraph or subsection (b), as applicable.

(ii) *Notice of determination.* Upon making any determination under clause

(I) that a dispute is frivolous or irrelevant, the person shall notify the consumer of such determination not later than 5 business days after making such determination, by mail or, if authorized by the consumer for that purpose, by any other means available to the person.

(iii) *Contents of notice.* A notice under clause (ii) shall include—

(I) the reasons for the determination under clause (i); and

(II) identification of any information required to investigate the disputed information, which may consist of a standardized form describing the general nature of such information.

(G) *Exclusion of credit repair organizations.* This paragraph shall not apply if the notice of the dispute is submitted by, is prepared on behalf of the consumer by, or is submitted on a form supplied to the consumer by, a credit repair organization, as defined in section 403(3), or an entity that would be a credit repair organization, but for section 403(3)(B)(i).

(9) *Duty to provide notice of status as medical information furnisher.* A person whose primary business is providing medical services, products, or devices, or the person's agent or assignee, who furnishes information to a consumer reporting agency on a consumer shall be considered a medical information furnisher for purposes of this title, and shall notify the agency of such status.

(b) Duties of Furnishers of Information upon Notice of Dispute

(1) *In general.* After receiving notice pursuant to section 611(a)(2) of a dispute with regard to the completeness or accuracy of any information provided by a person to a consumer reporting agency, the person shall

(A) conduct an investigation with respect to the disputed information;

(B) review all relevant information provided by the consumer reporting agency pursuant to section 611(a)(2);

(C) report the results of the investigation to the consumer reporting agency;

(D) if the investigation finds that the information is incomplete or inaccurate, report those results to all other consumer reporting agencies to which the person furnished the information and that compile and maintain files on consumers on a nationwide basis; and

(E) if an item of information disputed by a consumer is found to be inaccurate or incomplete or cannot be verified after any reinvestigation under paragraph (1), for purposes of reporting to a consumer reporting agency only, as appropriate, based on the results of the reinvestigation promptly–

(i) modify that item of information;

(ii) delete that item of information; or

(iii) permanently block the reporting of that item of information.

(2) *Deadline.* A person shall complete all investigations, reviews, and reports required under paragraph (1) regarding information provided by the person to a consumer reporting agency, before the expiration of the period under section 611(a)(1) within which the consumer reporting agency is required to complete actions required by that section regarding that information.

(c) *Limitation on liability.* Except as provided in section 621(c)(1)(B), sections 616 and 617 do not apply to any violation of—

(1) subsection (a) of this section, including any regulations issued thereunder;

(2) subsection (e) of this section, except that nothing in this paragraph shall limit, expand, or otherwise affect liability under section 616 or 617, as applicable, for violations of subsection (b) of this section; or

(3) subsection (e) of section 615.

(d) *Limitation on enforcement.* The provisions of law described in paragraphs (1) through (3) of subsection (c) (other than with respect to the exception described in paragraph (2) of subsection (c)) shall be enforced exclusively as provided under section 621 by the Federal agencies and officials and the State officials identified in section 621.

(e) Accuracy Guidelines and Regulations Required

(1) *Guidelines.* The Federal banking agencies, the National Credit Union Administration, and the Commission shall, with respect to the entities that are subject to their respective enforcement authority under section 621, and in coordination as described in paragraph (2)—

(A) establish and maintain guidelines for use by each person that furnishes information to a consumer reporting agency regarding the accuracy and integrity of the information relating to consumers that such entities furnish to consumer reporting agencies, and update such guidelines as often as necessary; and

(B) prescribe regulations requiring each person that furnishes information to a consumer reporting agency to establish reasonable policies and procedures for implementing the guidelines established pursuant to subparagraph (A).

(2) *Coordination.* Each agency required to prescribe regulations under paragraph (1) shall consult and coordinate with each other such agency so that, to the extent possible, the regulations prescribed by each such entity are consistent and comparable with the regulations prescribed by each other such agency.

(3) *Criteria.* In developing the guidelines required by paragraph (1)(A), the agencies described in paragraph (1) shall—

(A) identify patterns, practices, and specific forms of activity that can compromise the accuracy and integrity of information furnished to consumer reporting agencies;

(B) review the methods (including technological means) used to furnish information relating to consumers to consumer reporting agencies;

(C) determine whether persons that furnish information to consumer reporting agencies maintain and enforce policies to assure the accuracy and integrity of information furnished to consumer reporting agencies; and

(D) examine the policies and processes that persons that furnish information to consumer reporting agencies employ to conduct reinvestigations and correct inaccurate information relating to consumers that has been furnished to consumer reporting agencies.

§ 624. Affiliate sharing

(a) Special Rule for Solicitation for Purposes of Marketing

(1) *Notice.* Any person that receives from another person related to it by common ownership or affiliated by corporate control a communication of information that would be a consumer report, but for clauses (i), (ii), and (iii) of section 603(d)(2)(A), may not use the information to make a solicitation for marketing purposes to a consumer about its products or services, unless—

(A) it is clearly and conspicuously disclosed to the consumer that the information may be communicated among such persons for purposes of making such solicitations to the consumer; and

(B) the consumer is provided an opportunity and a simple method to prohibit the making of such solicitations to the consumer by such person.

(2) Consumer Choice

(A) *In general.* The notice required under paragraph (1) shall allow the consumer the opportunity to prohibit all solicitations referred to in such paragraph, and may allow the consumer to choose from different options when electing to prohibit the sending of such solicitations, including options regarding the types of entities and information covered, and which methods of delivering solicitations the consumer elects to prohibit.

(B) *Format.* Notwithstanding subparagraph (A), the notice required under paragraph (1) shall be clear, conspicuous, and concise, and any method provided under paragraph (1)(B) shall be simple. The regulations prescribed to implement this section shall provide specific guidance regarding how to comply with such standards.

(3) Duration

(A) *In general.* The election of a consumer pursuant to paragraph (1)(B) to prohibit the making of solicitations shall be effective for at least 5 years, beginning on the date on which the person receives the election of the consumer, unless the consumer requests that such election be revoked.

(B) *Notice upon expiration of effective period.* At such time as the election of a consumer pursuant to paragraph (1)(B) is no longer effective, a person may not use information that the person receives in the manner described in paragraph (1) to make any solicitation for marketing purposes to the consumer, unless the consumer receives a notice and an opportunity, using a simple method, to extend the opt-out for another period of at least 5 years, pursuant to the procedures described in paragraph (1).

(4) *Scope.* This section shall not apply to a person–

(A) using information to make a solicitation for marketing purposes to a consumer with whom the person has a pre-existing business relationship;

(B) using information to facilitate communications to an individual for whose benefit the person provides employee benefit or other services pursuant to a contract with an employer related to and arising out of the current employment relationship or status of the individual as a participant or beneficiary of an employee benefit plan;

(C) using information to perform services on behalf of another person related by common ownership or affiliated by corporate control, except that this subparagraph shall not be construed as permitting a person to send solicitations on behalf of another person, if such other person would not be permitted to send the solicitation on its own behalf as a result of the election of the consumer to prohibit solicitations under paragraph (1)(B);

(D) using information in response to a communication initiated by the consumer;

(E) using information in response to solicitations authorized or requested by the consumer; or

(F) if compliance with this section by that person would prevent compliance by that person with any provision of State insurance laws pertaining to unfair discrimination in any State in which the person is lawfully doing business.

(5) *No retroactivity.* This subsection shall not prohibit the use of information to send a solicitation to a consumer if such information was received prior to the date on which persons are required to comply with regulations implementing this subsection.

(b) *Notice for other purposes permissible.* A notice or other disclosure under this section may be coordinated and consolidated with any other notice required to be issued under any other provision of law by a person that is subject to this section, and a notice or other disclosure that is equivalent to the notice required by subsection (a), and that is provided by a person described in subsection (a) to a consumer together with disclosures required by any other provision of law, shall satisfy the requirements of subsection (a).

(c) *User requirements.* Requirements with respect to the use by a person of information received from another person related to it by common ownership or affiliated by corporate control, such as the requirements of this section, constitute requirements with respect to the exchange of information among persons affiliated by common ownership or common corporate control, within the meaning of section 625(b)(2).

(d) *Definitions.* For purposes of this section, the following definitions shall apply:

(1) The term "pre-existing business relationship" means a relationship between a person, or a person's licensed agent, and a consumer, based on—

(A) a financial contract between a person and a consumer which is in force;

(B) the purchase, rental, or lease by the consumer of that person's goods or services, or a financial transaction (including holding an active account or a policy in force or having another continuing relationship) between the consumer and that person during the 18-month period immediately preceding the date on which the consumer is sent a solicitation covered by this section;

(C) an inquiry or application by the consumer regarding a product or service offered by that person, during the 3-month period immediately preceding the date on which the consumer is sent a solicitation covered by this section; or

(D) any other pre-existing customer relationship defined in the regulations implementing this section.

(2) The term "solicitation" means the marketing of a product or service initiated by a person to a particular consumer that is based on an exchange of information described in subsection (a), and is intended to encourage the consumer to purchase such product or service, but does not include communications that are directed at the general public or determined not to be a solicitation by the regulations prescribed under this section.

§ 625. Relation to State laws

(a) *In general.* Except as provided in subsections (b) and (c), this title does not annul, alter, affect, or exempt any person subject to the provisions of this title from complying with the laws of any State with respect to the collection, distribution, or use of any information on consumers, or for the prevention or mitigation of identity theft, except to the extent that those laws are inconsistent with any provision of this title, and then only to the extent of the inconsistency.

(b) *General exceptions.* No requirement or prohibition may be imposed under the laws of any State

(1) with respect to any subject matter regulated under

(A) subsection (c) or (e) of section 604, relating to the prescreening of consumer reports;

(B) section 611, relating to the time by which a consumer reporting agency must take any action, including the provision of notification to a consumer or other person, in any procedure related to the disputed accuracy of information in a consumer's file, except that this subparagraph shall not apply to any State law in effect on the date of enactment of the Consumer Credit Reporting Reform Act of 1996;

(C) subsections (a) and (b) of section 615, relating to the duties of a person who takes any adverse action with respect to a consumer;

(D) section 615(d), relating to the duties of persons who use a consumer report of a consumer in connection with any credit or insurance transaction that is not initiated by the consumer and that consists of a firm offer of credit or insurance;

(E) section 605, relating to information contained in consumer reports, except that this subparagraph shall not apply to any State law in effect on the date of enactment of the Consumer Credit Reporting Reform Act of 1996;

(F) section 623, relating to the responsibilities of persons who furnish information to consumer reporting agencies, except that this paragraph shall not apply

(i) with respect to section 54A(a) of chapter 93 of the Massachusetts Annotated Laws (as in effect on the date of enactment of the Consumer Credit Reporting Reform Act of 1996); or

(ii) with respect to section 1785.25(a) of the California Civil Code (as in effect on the date of enactment of the Consumer Credit Reporting Reform Act of 1996);

(G) section 609(e), relating to information available to victims under section 609(e);

(H) section 624, relating to the exchange and use of information to make a solicitation for marketing purposes; or

(I) section 615(h), relating to the duties of users of consumer reports to provide notice with respect to terms in certain credit transactions;

(2) with respect to the exchange of information among persons affiliated by common ownership or common corporate control, except that this paragraph shall not apply with respect to subsection (a) or (c)(1) of section 2480e of title 9, Vermont Statutes Annotated (as in effect on the date of enactment of the Consumer Credit Reporting Reform Act of 1996);

(3) with respect to the disclosures required to be made under subsection (c), (d), (e), or (g) of section 609, or subsection (f) of section 609 relating to the disclosure of credit scores for credit granting purposes, except that this paragraph—

(A) shall not apply with respect to sections 1785.10, 1785.16, and 1785.20.2 of the California Civil Code (as in effect on the date of enactment of the Fair and Accurate Credit Transactions Act of 2003) and section 1785.15 through section 1785.15.2 of such Code (as in effect on such date);

(B) shall not apply with respect to sections 5-3-106(2) and 212-14.3-104.3 of the Colorado Revised Statutes (as in effect on the date of enactment of the Fair and Accurate Credit Transactions Act of 2003); and

(C) shall not be construed as limiting, annulling, affecting, or superseding any provision of the laws of any State regulating the use in an insurance activity, or regulating disclosures concerning such use, of a credit-based insurance score of a consumer by any person engaged in the business of insurance;

(4) with respect to the frequency of any disclosure under section 612(a), except that this paragraph shall not apply—

(A) with respect to section 12-14.3-105(1)(d) of the Colorado Revised Statutes (as in effect on the date of enactment of the Fair and Accurate Credit Transactions Act of 2003);

(B) with respect to section 10-1-393(29)(C) of the Georgia Code (as in effect on the date of enactment of the Fair and Accurate Credit Transactions Act of 2003);

(C) with respect to section 1316.2 of title 10 of the Maine Revised Statutes (as in effect on the date of enactment of the Fair and Accurate Credit Transactions Act of 2003);

(D) with respect to sections 14-1209(a)(1) and 14-1209(b)(1)(i) of the Commercial Law Article of the Code of Maryland (as in effect on the date of enactment of the Fair and Accurate Credit Transactions Act of 2003);

(E) with respect to section 59(d) and section 59(e) of chapter 93 of the General Laws of Massachusetts (as in effect on the date of enactment of the Fair and Accurate Credit Transactions Act of 2003);

(F) with respect to section 56:11-37.10(a)(1) of the New Jersey Revised Statutes (as in effect on the date of enactment of the Fair and Accurate Credit Transactions Act of 2003); or

(G) with respect to section 2480c(a)(1) of title 9 of the Vermont Statutes Annotated (as in effect on the date of enactment of the Fair and Accurate Credit Transactions Act of 2003); or

(5) with respect to the conduct required by the specific provisions of—

(A) section 605(g);

(B) section 605A;

(C) section 605B;

(D) section 609(a)(1)(A);

(E) section 612(a);

(F) subsections (e), (f), and (g) of section 615;

(G) section 621(f);

(H) section 623(a)(6); or

(I) section 628.

(c) *Definition of firm offer of credit or insurance.* Notwithstanding any definition of the term "firm offer of credit or insurance" (or any equivalent term) under the laws of any State, the definition of that term contained in section 603(*l*) shall be construed to apply in the enforcement and interpretation of the laws of any State governing consumer reports.

(d) *Limitations.* Subsections (b) and (c) do not affect any settlement, agreement, or consent judgment between any State Attorney General and any consumer reporting agency in effect on the date of enactment of the Consumer Credit Reporting Reform Act of 1996.

§ 626. Disclosures to FBI for counterintelligence purposes

(a) *Identity of financial institutions.* Notwithstanding section 604 or any other provision of this title, a consumer reporting agency shall furnish to the Federal Bureau of Investigation the names and addresses of all financial institutions (as that term is defined in section 1101 of the Right to Financial Privacy Act of 1978 [12 U.S.C. § 3401]) at which a consumer maintains or has maintained an account, to the extent that information is in the files of the agency, when presented with a written request for that information, signed by the Director of the Federal Bureau of Investigation, or the Director's designee in a position not lower than Deputy Assistant Director at Bureau headquarters or a Special Agent in Charge of a Bureau field office designated by the Director, which certifies compliance with this section. The Director or the Director's designee may make such a certification only if the Director or the Director's designee has determined in writing, that such information is sought for the conduct of an authorized investigation to protect against international terrorism or clandestine intelligence activities, provided that such an investigation of a United States person is not conducted solely upon the basis of activities protected by the first amendment to the Constitution of the United States.

(b) *Identifying information.* Notwithstanding the provisions of section 604 or any other provision of this title, a consumer reporting agency shall furnish identifying information respecting a consumer, limited to name, address, former addresses, places of employment, or former places of employment, to the Federal Bureau of Investigation when presented with a written request, signed by the Director or the Director's designee, which certifies compliance with this subsection. The Director or the Director's designee in a position not lower than Deputy Assistant Director at Bureau headquarters or a Special Agent in Charge of a Bureau field office designated by the Director may make such a certification only if the Director or the Director's designee has determined in writing that such information is sought for the conduct of an authorized investigation to protect against international terrorism or clandestine intelligence activities, provided that such an investigation of a United States person is not conducted solely upon the basis of activities protected by the first amendment to the Constitution of the United States.

(c) *Court order for disclosure of consumer reports.* Notwithstanding section 604 or any other provision of this title, if requested in writing by the Director of the Federal Bureau of Investigation, or a designee of the Director in a position not lower than Deputy Assistant Director at Bureau headquarters or a Special Agent in Charge of a Bureau field office designated by the Director, a court may issue an order ex parte directing a consumer reporting agency to furnish a consumer report to the Federal Bureau of Investigation, upon a showing in camera that the consumer report is sought for the conduct of an authorized investigation to protect against international terrorism or clandestine intelligence activities, provided that such an investigation of a United States person is not conducted solely upon the basis of activities protected by the first amendment to the Constitution of the United States. The terms of an order issued under this subsection shall not disclose that the order is issued for purposes of a counterintelligence investigation.

(d) *Confidentiality.* No consumer reporting agency or officer, employee, or agent of a consumer reporting agency shall disclose to any person, other than those officers, employees, or agents of a consumer reporting agency necessary to fulfill the requirement to disclose information to the Federal Bureau of Investigation under this section, that the Federal Bureau of Investigation has sought or obtained the identity of financial institutions or a consumer report respecting any consumer under subsection (a), (b), or (c), and no consumer reporting agency or officer, employee, or agent of a consumer reporting agency shall include in any consumer report any information that would indicate that the Federal Bureau of Investigation has sought or obtained such information or a consumer report.

(e) *Payment of fees.* The Federal Bureau of Investigation shall, subject to the availability of appropriations, pay to the consumer reporting agency assembling or providing report or information in accordance with procedures established under this section a fee for reimbursement for such costs as are reasonably necessary and which have been directly incurred in searching, reproducing, or transporting books, papers, records, or other data required or requested to be produced under this section.

(f) *Limit on dissemination.* The Federal Bureau of Investigation may not disseminate information obtained pursuant to this section outside of the Federal Bureau of Investigation, except to other Federal agencies as may be necessary for the approval or conduct of a foreign counterintelligence investigation, or, where the information concerns a person subject to the Uniform Code of Military Justice, to appropriate investigative authorities within the military department concerned as may be necessary for the conduct of a joint foreign counterintelligence investigation.

(g) *Rules of construction.* Nothing in this section shall be construed to prohibit information from being furnished by the Federal Bureau of Investigation pursuant to a subpoena or court order, in connection with a judicial or administrative proceeding to enforce the provisions of this Act. Nothing in this section shall be construed to authorize or permit the withholding of information from the Congress.

(h) *Reports to Congress.* On a semiannual basis, the Attorney General shall fully inform the Permanent Select Committee on Intelligence and the Committee on Banking, Finance and Urban Affairs of the House of Representatives, and the Select Committee on Intelligence and the Committee on Banking, Housing, and Urban Affairs of the Senate concerning all requests made pursuant to subsections (a), (b), and (c).

(i) *Damages.* Any agency or department of the United States obtaining or disclosing any consumer reports, records, or information contained therein in violation of this section is liable to the consumer to whom such consumer reports, records, or information relate in an amount equal to the sum of

> (1) $100, without regard to the volume of consumer reports, records, or information involved;
>
> (2) any actual damages sustained by the consumer as a result of the disclosure;
>
> (3) if the violation is found to have been willful or intentional, such punitive damages as a court may allow; and
>
> (4) in the case of any successful action to enforce liability under this subsection, the costs of the action, together with reasonable attorney fees, as determined by the court.

(j) *Disciplinary actions for violations.* If a court determines that any agency or department of the United States has violated any provision of this section and the court finds that the circumstances surrounding the violation raise questions of whether or not an officer or employee of the agency or department acted willfully or intentionally with respect to the violation, the agency or department shall promptly initiate a proceeding to determine whether or not disciplinary action is warranted against the officer or employee who was responsible for the violation.

(k) *Good-faith exception.* Notwithstanding any other provision of this title, any consumer reporting agency or agent or employee thereof making disclosure of consumer reports or identifying information pursuant to this subsection in good-faith reliance upon a certification of the Federal Bureau of Investigation pursuant to provisions of this section shall not be liable to any person for such disclosure under this title, the constitution of any State, or any law or regulation of any State or any political subdivision of any State.

(l) *Limitation of remedies.* Notwithstanding any other provision of this title, the remedies and sanctions set forth in this section shall be the only judicial remedies and sanctions for violation of this section.

(m) *Injunctive relief.* In addition to any other remedy contained in this section, injunctive relief shall be available to require compliance with the procedures of this section. In the event of any successful action under this subsection, costs together with reasonable attorney fees, as determined by the court, may be recovered.

§ 627. Disclosures to governmental agencies for counterterrorism purposes

(a) *Disclosure.* Notwithstanding section 604 or any other provision of this title, a consumer reporting agency shall furnish a consumer report of a consumer and all other information in a consumer's file to a government agency authorized to conduct investigations of, or intelligence or counterintelligence activities or analysis related to, international terrorism when presented with a written certification by such government agency that such information is necessary for the agency's conduct or such investigation, activity or analysis.

(b) *Form of certification.* The certification described in subsection (a) shall be signed by a supervisory official designated by the head of a Federal agency or an officer of a Federal agency whose appointment to office is required to be made by the President, by and with the advice and consent of the Senate.

(c) *Confidentiality.* No consumer reporting agency, or officer, employee, or agent of such consumer reporting agency, shall disclose to any person, or specify in any consumer report, that a government agency has sought or obtained access to information under subsection (a).

(d) *Rule of construction.* Nothing in section 626 shall be construed to limit the authority of the Director of the Federal Bureau of Investigation under this section.

(e) *Safe harbor.* Notwithstanding any other provision of this title, any consumer reporting agency or agent or employee thereof making disclosure of consumer reports or other information pursuant to this section in good-faith reliance upon a certification of a governmental agency pursuant to the provisions of this section shall not be liable to any person for such disclosure under this subchapter, the constitution of any State, or any law or regulation of any State or any political subdivision of any State.

§ 628. Disposal of records

(a) Regulations

(1) *In general.* Not later than 1 year after the date of enactment of this section, the Federal banking agencies, the National Credit Union Administration, and the Commission with respect to the entities that are subject to their respective enforcement authority under section 621, and the Securities and Exchange Commission, and in coordination as described in paragraph (2), shall issue final regulations requiring any person that maintains or otherwise possesses consumer information, or any compilation of consumer information, derived from consumer reports for a business purpose to properly dispose of any such information or compilation.

(2) *Coordination.* Each agency required to prescribe regulations under paragraph (1) shall—

(A) consult and coordinate with each other such agency so that, to the extent possible, the regulations prescribed by each such agency are consistent and comparable with the regulations by each such other agency; and

(B) ensure that such regulations are consistent with the requirements and regulations issued pursuant to Public Law 106-102 and other provisions of Federal law.

(3) *Exemption authority.* In issuing regulations under this section, the Federal banking agencies, the National Credit Union Administration, the Commission, and the Securities and Exchange Commission may exempt any person or class of persons from application of those regulations, as such agency deems appropriate to carry out the purpose of this section.

(b) *Rule of construction.* Nothing in this section shall be construed—

(1) to require a person to maintain or destroy any record pertaining to a consumer that is not imposed under other law; or

(2) to alter or affect any requirement imposed under any other provision of law to maintain or destroy such a record.

§ 629. Corporate and technological circumvention prohibited

The Commission shall prescribe regulations, to become effective not later than 90 days after the date of enactment of this section, to prevent a consumer reporting agency from circumventing or evading treatment as a consumer reporting agency described in section 603(p) for purposes of this title, including—

(1) by means of a corporate reorganization or restructuring, including a merger, acquisition, dissolution, divestiture, or asset sale of a consumer reporting agency; or

(2) by maintaining or merging public record and credit account information in a manner that is substantially equivalent to that described in paragraphs (1) and (2) of section 603(p), in the manner described in section 603(p).

APPENDIX II

FEDERAL TRADE COMMISSION FACTS FOR BUSINESS—WHAT INFORMATION PROVIDERS NEED TO KNOW

CREDIT REPORTS: WHAT INFORMATION PROVIDERS NEED TO KNOW

The Fair Credit Reporting Act (FCRA) is designed to protect the privacy of credit report information and to guarantee that information supplied by consumer reporting agencies (CRAs) is as accurate as possible. If you provide information to a CRA, such as a credit bureau, be aware that amendments to the law spell out new legal obligations. These amendments were effective September 30, 1997.

DOES THE FCRA AFFECT ME?

If you report information about consumers to a CRA, you are considered a "furnisher" of information under the FCRA. CRAs include many types of databases—credit bureaus, tenant screening companies, check verification services, and medical information services—that collect information to help businesses evaluate consumers. If you provide information to a CRA regularly, the FCRA requires that the CRA send you a notice of your responsibilities.

WHAT ARE MY RESPONSIBILITIES?

The responsibilities of information providers are found in Section 623 of the FCRA, 15 U.S.C. § 1681s-2, and are explained here. Items 2 and 5 apply only to furnishers who provide information to CRAs "regularly and in the ordinary course of their business." All information providers must comply with the other responsibilities.

1. General Prohibition on Reporting Inaccurate Information—Section 623(a)(1)(A) and Section 623(a)(1)(C).

You may not furnish information that you know—or consciously avoid knowing—is inaccurate. If you "clearly and conspicuously" provide consumers with an address for dispute notices, you are exempt from this obligation but subject to the duties discussed in Item 3.

What does "clear and conspicuous" mean? Reasonably easy to read and understand. For example, a notice buried in a mailing is not clear or conspicuous.

2. Correcting and Updating Information—Section 623(a)(2).

If you discover you've supplied one or more CRAs with incomplete or inaccurate information, you must correct it, resubmit to each CRA, and report only the correct information in the future.

3. Responsibilities After Notice of a Consumer Dispute from a Consumer—Sections 623(a)(1)(B) and 623(a)(3).

If a consumer writes to the address you specify for disputes to challenge the accuracy of any information you furnished, and if the information is, in fact, inaccurate, you must report only the correct information to CRAs in the future. If you are a regular furnisher, you also will have to satisfy the duties in Item 2.

Once a consumer has given notice that he or she disputes information, you may not give that information to any CRA without also telling the CRA that the information is in dispute.

4. Responsibilities After Receiving Notice from a Consumer Reporting Agency—Section 623(b).

If a CRA notifies you that a consumer disputes information you provided:

- You must investigate the dispute and review all relevant information provided by the CRA about the dispute.
- You must report your findings to the CRA.
- If your investigation shows the information to be incomplete or inaccurate, you must provide corrected information to all national CRAs that received the information.
- You should complete these steps within the time period that the FCRA sets out for the CRA to resolve the—normally 30 days after receipt of a dispute notice from the consumer. If the consumer provides additional relevant information during the 30-day period, the CRA has 15 days more. The CRA must give you all relevant information that it gets within five business days of receipt, and must promptly give you additional relevant information provided from the consumer. If you do not investigate and respond

within the specified time periods, the CRA must delete the disputed information from its files.

5. Reporting Voluntary Account Closings—Section 623(A)(4).

You must notify CRAs when consumers voluntarily close credit accounts. This is important because some information users may interpret a closed account as an indicator of bad credit unless it is clearly disclosed that the consumer—not the creditor—closed the account.

6. Reporting Delinquencies—Section 623(A)(5).

If you report information about a delinquent account that's placed for collection, charged to profit or loss, or subject to any similar action, you must, within 90 days after you report the information, notify the CRA of the month and the year of the commencement of the delinquency that immediately preceded your action. This will ensure that CRAs use the correct date when computing how long derogatory information can be kept in a consumer's file.

How do you report accounts that you have charged off or placed for collection? For example:

- *A consumer becomes delinquent on March 15, 1998. The creditor places the account for collection on October 1, 1998.*

In this case, the delinquency began on March 15, 1998. The date that the creditor places the account for collection has no significance for calculating how long the account can stay on the consumer's credit report. In this case, the date that must be reported to CRAs within 90 days after you first report the collection action is "March 1998."

- *A consumer falls behind on monthly payments in January 1998, brings the account current in June 1998, pays on time and in full every month through October 1998, and thereafter makes no payments. The creditor charges off the account in December 1999.*

In this case, the most recent delinquency began when the consumer failed to make the payment due in November 1998. The earlier delinquency is irrelevant. The creditor must report the November 1998 date within 90 days of reporting the charge-off. For example, if the creditor charges off the account in December 1999, and reports this charge-off on December 31, 1999, the creditor must provide the month and year of the delinquency (i.e., "November 1998") within 90 days of December 31, 1999.

- *A consumer's account becomes delinquent on December 15, 1997. The account is first placed for collection on April 1, 1998. Collection is not successful. The merchant places the account with a second collection agency on June 1, 2003.*

The date of the delinquency for reporting purposes is "December 1997." Repeatedly placing an account for collection does not change the date that the delinquency began.

- *A consumer's credit account becomes delinquent on April 15, 1998. The consumer makes partial payments for the next five months but never brings the account current. The merchant places the account for collection in May of 1999.*

Since the account was never brought current during the period that partial payments were made, the delinquency that immediately preceded the collection commenced in April 1998 when the consumer first became delinquent.

FOR MORE INFORMATION

The FTC works for the consumer to prevent fraudulent, deceptive and unfair business practices in the marketplace and to provide information to help consumers spot, stop and avoid them. To file a complaint or to get free information on consumer issues, visit www.ftc.gov or call toll-free, 1-877-FTC-HELP (1-877-382-4357); TTY: 1-866-653-4261. The FTC enters Internet, telemarketing, identity theft and other fraud-related complaints into Consumer Sentinel, a secure, online database available to hundreds of civil and criminal law enforcement agencies in the United States and abroad.

APPENDIX III

FEDERAL TRADE COMMISSION FACTS FOR BUSINESS—WHAT EMPLOYERS NEED TO KNOW

USING CONSUMER REPORTS: WHAT EMPLOYERS NEED TO KNOW

Your advertisement for cashiers nets 100 applications. You want credit reports on each applicant. You plan to eliminate those with poor credit histories. What are your obligations?

You are considering a number of your long-term employees for major promotions. Can you check their credit reports to ensure that only financially responsible individuals are considered?

A job candidate has authorized you to obtain a credit report. The applicant has a poor credit history. Although the credit history is considered a negative factor, it's the applicant's lack of relevant experience that's more important to you. You turn down the application. What procedures must you follow?

As an employer, you may use consumer reports when you hire new employees and when you evaluate employees for promotion, reassignment, and retention—as long as you comply with the Fair Credit Reporting Act (FCRA). Sections 604, 606, and 615 of the FCRA spell out your responsibilities when using consumer reports for employment purposes.

The FCRA is designed primarily to protect the privacy of consumer report information and to guarantee that the information supplied by consumer reporting agencies is as accurate as possible. Amendments to the FCRA—which went into effect September 30, 1997—significantly increase the legal obligations of employers who use consumer reports. Congress expanded employer responsibilities because of concern that inaccurate or incomplete consumer reports could cause applicants to be denied jobs or cause employees to be denied promotions unjustly. The amendments ensure (1) that individuals are aware that consumer reports may be used for employment purposes and agree to such use, and (2) that individuals are notified promptly if information in a consumer report may result in a negative employment decision.

WHAT IS A CONSUMER REPORT?

A consumer report contains information about your personal and credit characteristics, character, general reputation, and lifestyle. To be covered by the FCRA, a report must be prepared by a consumer reporting agency (CRA)—a business that assembles such reports for other businesses.

Employers often do background checks on applicants and get consumer reports during their employment. Some employers only want an applicant's or employee's credit payment records; others want driving records and criminal histories. For sensitive positions, it's not unusual for employers to order investigative consumer reports—reports that include interviews with an applicant's or employee's friends, neighbors, and associates. All of these types of reports are consumer reports if they are obtained from a CRA.

Applicants are often asked to give references. Whether verifying such references is covered by the FCRA depends on who does the verification. A reference verified by the employer is not covered by the Act; a reference verified by an employment or reference checking agency (or other CRA) is covered. Section 603(o) provides special procedures for reference checking; otherwise, checking references may constitute an investigative consumer report subject to additional FCRA requirements.

KEY PROVISIONS OF THE FCRA AMENDMENTS

Written Notice and Authorization. Before you can get a consumer report for employment purposes, you must notify the individual in writing—a document consisting solely of this notice—that a report may be used. You also must get the person's written authorization before you ask a CRA for the report. (Special procedures apply to the trucking industry.)

Adverse Action Procedures. If you rely on a consumer report for an "adverse action"—denying a job application, reassigning or terminating an employee, or denying a promotion—be aware that:

Step 1: **Before** you take the adverse action, you must give the individual a **pre-adverse action disclosure** that includes a copy of the individual's consumer report and a copy of "A Summary of Your Rights Under the Fair Credit Reporting Act"—a document prescribed by the Federal Trade Commission. The CRA that furnishes the individual's report will give you the summary of consumer rights.

Step 2: **After** you've taken an adverse action, you must give the individual notice—orally, in writing, or electronically—that the action has been taken in an **adverse action notice**. It must include:

- the name, address, and phone number of the CRA that supplied the report;
- a statement that the CRA that supplied the report did not make the decision to take the adverse action and cannot give specific reasons for it; and
- a notice of the individual's right to dispute the accuracy or completeness of any information the agency furnished, and his or her right to an additional free consumer report from the agency upon request within 60 days.

Certifications to Consumer Reporting Agencies. Before giving you an individual's consumer report, the CRA will require you to certify that you are in compliance with the FCRA and that you will not misuse any information in the report in violation of federal or state equal employment opportunity laws or regulations.

In 1998, Congress amended the FCRA to provide special procedures for mail, telephone, or electronic employment applications in the trucking industry. Employers do not need to make written disclosures and obtain written permission in the case of applicants who will be subject to state or federal regulation as truckers. Finally, no pre-adverse action disclosure or Section 615(a) disclosure is required. Instead, the employer must, within three days of the decision, provide an oral, written, or electronic adverse action disclosure consisting of: (1) a statement that an adverse action has been taken based on a consumer report; (2) the name, address, and telephone number of the CRA; (3) a statement that the CRA did not make the decision; and (4) a statement that the consumer may obtain a copy of the actual report from the employer if he or she provides identification.

IN PRACTICE . . .

- You advertise vacancies for cashiers and receive 100 applications. You want just credit reports on each applicant because you plan to eliminate those with poor credit histories. What are your obligations?

You can get credit reports—one type of consumer report—if you notify each applicant in writing that a credit report may be requested and if you receive the applicant's written consent. Before you reject an applicant based on credit report information, you must make a pre-adverse action disclosure that includes a copy of the credit report and the summary of consumer rights under the FCRA. Once you've rejected an applicant, you must provide an adverse action notice if credit report information affected your decision.

- You are considering a number of your long-term employees for a major promotion. You want to check their consumer reports to ensure that only responsible individuals are considered for the position. What are your obligations?

You cannot get consumer reports unless the employees have been notified that reports may be obtained and have given their written permission. If the employees gave you written permission in the past, you need only make sure that the employees receive or have received a "separate document" notice that reports may be obtained during the course of their employment—no more notice or permission is required. If your employees have not received notice and given you permission, you must notify the employees and get their written permission before you get their reports.

In each case where information in the report influences your decision to deny promotion, you must provide the employee with a **pre-adverse action disclosure**. The employee also must receive an **adverse action notice** once you have selected another individual for the job.

- A job applicant gives you the okay to get a consumer report. Although the credit history is poor and that's a negative factor, the applicant's lack of relevant experience carries more weight in your decision not to hire. What's your responsibility?

In any case where information in a consumer report is a factor in your decision—even if the report information is not a major consideration—you must follow the procedures mandated by the FCRA. In this case, you would be required to provide the applicant a pre-adverse action disclosure before you reject his or her application. When you formally reject the applicant, you would be required to provide an adverse action notice.

- The applicants for a sensitive financial position have authorized you to obtain credit reports. You reject one applicant, whose credit report shows a debt load that may be too high for the proposed salary, even though the report shows a good repayment history. You turn down another, whose credit report shows only one credit account, because you want someone who has shown more financial responsibility. Are you obliged to provide any notices to these applicants?

Both applicants are entitled to a pre-adverse action disclosure and an adverse action notice. If any information in the credit report influences an adverse decision, the applicant is entitled to the notices—even when the information isn't negative.

NON-COMPLIANCE

There are legal consequences for employers who fail to get an applicant's permission before requesting a consumer report or who fail to provide pre-adverse action disclosures and adverse action notices to unsuccessful job applicants. The FCRA allows individuals to sue employers for damages in federal court. A person who successfully sues is entitled to recover court costs and reasonable legal fees. The law also allows individuals to seek punitive damages for deliberate violations. In addition, the Federal Trade Commission, other federal agencies, and the states may sue employers for noncompliance and obtain civil penalties.

The National Small Business Ombudsman and 10 Regional Fairness Boards collect comments from small businesses about federal compliance and enforcement activities. Each year, the Ombudsman evaluates the conduct of these activities and rates each agency's responsiveness to small businesses. Small businesses can comment to the Ombudsman without fear of reprisal. To comment, call toll-free 1-888-REGFAIR (1-888-734-3247) or go to www.sba.gov/ombudsman.

FOR MORE INFORMATION

The FTC works for the consumer to prevent fraudulent, deceptive and unfair business practices in the marketplace and to provide information to help consumers spot, stop and avoid them. To file a complaint or to get free information on consumer issues, visit www.ftc.gov or call toll-free, 1-877-FTC-HELP (1-877-382-4357); TTY: 1-866-653-4261. The FTC enters Internet, telemarketing, identity theft and other fraud-related complaints into Consumer Sentinel, a secure, online database available to hundreds of civil and criminal law enforcement agencies in the U.S. and abroad.

APPENDIX IV

PERMISSIBLE PURPOSE

EXCERPT FROM MILLER v. TRANS UNION LLC

CIV NO 06 C 2883 (N.D. Ill 2/28/07)

Case 1:06-cv-02883 Document 90 Filed 02/28/2007 Page 9 of 16

-9-

This section only provides a remedy for consumer reporting agencies, not for persons whose reports were obtained under false pretenses or without a permissible purpose. See Grismore v. United Recovery Sys., L.P., No. CV-05-2094-PHX-JAT, 2006 WL 2246359, at *4 (D. Ariz. Aug. 3, 2006).

Section 1681o(a) provides, in relevant part, that "[a]ny person who is negligent in failing to comply with any requirement imposed under this subchapter with respect to any consumer is liable to that consumer" for actual damages and reasonable attorney's fees. 15 U.S.C. § 1681o(a). "Negligent" is accorded its ordinary meaning-"a failure to exercise reasonable care." Crabill v. Trans Union, L.L.C., 259 F.3d 662, 664 (7th Cir. 2001).

Supportkids's Cross-Motion for Summary Judgment

Supportkids's cross-motion for summary judgment will be denied. To begin with, § 1681b(a)(3)(A) requires a nexus to a credit transaction, and, as the following analysis will show, there is no credit transaction here. The relevant statutory text, slightly reorganized, is as follows:

> [A]ny consumer reporting agency may furnish a consumer report . . . [t]o a person which it has reason to believe intends to use the information
> (1) in connection with a credit transaction involving the consumer on whom the information is to be furnished and
> (2) involving the
> (a) extension of credit to or
> (b) review or collection of an account of the consumer.

15 U.S.C. § 1681b(a)(3)(A) (emphasis added). Clearly, the

-10-

requirement that the agency have reason to believe the person requesting the report intends to use it "in connection with a credit transaction involving the consumer" applies to <u>both</u> of the permissible purposes, the "extension of credit" and the "review or collection of an account."

Supportkids's reply brief argues that "FCRA states a consumer report can be provided to anyone to whom the consumer reporting agency has reason to believe is involved in a credit transaction with the consumer or who is involved in the review or the collection of an account of, the consumer." (Def. Reply S.J. at 4.) But the argument fails because it ignores the critical fact that the statute uses the conjunctive word "and."

Supportkids cites no authority for its view that the collection of an account or debt need not bear a nexus to a credit transaction. Even the FTC, the proponent of the "judgment creditor theory," does not doubt that § 1681b(a)(3)(A) requires a nexus to a credit transaction. <u>See</u> Federal Trade Commission, <u>FCRA Staff Opinion: Brinckerhoff-Long</u>, July 6, 2000 (available at http://www.ftc.gov/os/statutes/fcra/long.htm) (last visited February 27, 2007) ("Section [1681b(a)(3)(A)] applies only to the review or collection of a <u>credit</u> account, as well as to an extension of credit to a consumer.").

Supportkids's proposed interpretation of § 1681b(a)(3)(A) is infirm for the additional reason that it would reduce the privacy

-11-

protections intended for persons who do not voluntarily enter into a credit transaction. Under Supportkids's view, a person requesting a credit report for the purpose of extending credit must satisfy the requirements of "in connection with a credit transaction" and "involving the extension of credit to the consumer." But a person requesting a credit report for the purposes of review or collection of an account need not establish that the consumer engaged in a credit transaction; the person requesting the report need only show the request to be in connection with an effort to collect a debt. The Seventh Circuit's teachings on "permissible purpose" indicate that individuals who do not consent to a transaction deserve greater, not lesser, privacy protections under FCRA. See, e.g., Cole v. U.S. Capital, Inc., 389 F.3d 719, 725 (7th Cir. 2004) ("Many of the enumerated permissible purposes set forth in § 1681b are transactions initiated by the consumer; these purposes therefore do not create significant privacy concerns"); accord Stergiopoulos v. First Midwest Bancorp., Inc., 427 F.3d 1043, 1047 (7th Cir. 2005) ("An entity may rely on subparagraph (3)(A) only if the consumer initiates the transaction. A third party cannot troll for reports, nor can it request a report on a whim. Rather, there must be a direct link between a consumer's search for credit and the bank's credit report request. If the connection between a consumer's search and a bank's request is clear, it is unlikely that the request will infringe the

-12-

consumer's privacy interests, for it will 'involve' the plaintiff directly.") (citing Cole, 389 F.3d at 725).

Prior Interpretations of "Credit Transaction" Were Superseded by 2003 Statutory Amendments

Supportkids's claim that it had a permissible purpose is based on two sources of authority—the FTC's non-binding "FCRA Commentary" and non-binding case law from other jurisdictions. (Def. Mem. S.J. at 4-7.) The FTC's "FCRA Commentary" reiterates the agency's "judgment creditor theory," which states that a person attempting to collect a judgment has a permissible purpose to access a consumer report. 16 C.F.R. pt. 600, App. (1993). When the FTC developed its theory, the FCRA did not define the terms "credit" or "creditor." In the absence of a statutory definition of "credit" or "credit transaction," the theory was not patently unreasonable; to the contrary, a number of courts explicitly adopted the FTC's non-binding position. See, e.g., Baker v. Bronx-Westchester Investigations, Inc., 850 F. Supp. 260, 264 (S.D.N.Y. 1994); Hasbun v. County of Los Angeles, 323 F.3d 801 (9th Cir. 2003). But the FTC's "FCRA Commentary" and the judicial opinions endorsing the FTC's position are no longer persuasive because they do not take into account the December 2003 amendments to FCRA. The statutory definition of "credit" demands that a "creditor" grant rights to a "debtor" to defer payment of a "debt" or to incur debts and to defer payment of those debts. 15 U.S.C. § 1691a(d).

APPENDIX V

SECURITY BREACH NOTIFICATION

The following is a table of relevant state statutes on security breaches. If the state does not provide statutory instruction, you may wish to look to a neighboring state to develop polices and procedures to handle a security breach. Further, this issue is pending in many current state legislative sessions, and thus, law may later be codified on the subject. Therefore, it is of the utmost importance to stay current on these developments as they occur.

Alabama	No provision in state law.
Alaska	No provision in state law.
Arizona (*Editor's Note: This section was updated by S.B. 1042 & signed into law on 4/7/07).*	Ariz. Rev. Stat. Ann. § 44-7501 (West, WESTLAW through End of 47th Leg., 2nd Reg. Sess. (2006)).
Arkansas	Ark. Code Ann. §§ 4-110-101 to -180 (West, WESTLAW through End of 2006 Leg.).
California	Cal. Civ. Code § 1798.29 (West, WESTLAW through Ch. 3 of 2007 Reg. Sess. Urgency Leg.).
Colorado	Colo. Rev. Stat. Ann. § 6-1-716 (West, WESTLAW through End of 2006 1st Extraordinary Sess. of the 65th Gen. Assembly (2006)).
Connecticut	Conn. Gen. Stat. Ann. § 36a-701b (West, WESTLAW through Gen. St., Rev. to 01-01-2007).
Delaware	Del. Code Ann. tit. 6, §§ 12B-101 to -104 (West, WESTLAW through 76 Laws 2007, Ch. 3).
District of Columbia	No provision in D.C. law.
Florida	Fla. Stat. Ann. § 817.5681 (West, WESTLAW through 2007 1st Reg. Sess. of the 20th Leg. through March 12, 2007).
Georgia	Ga. Code Ann. §§ 10-1-910 to -912 (West, WESTLAW through end of 2006 Reg. Sess.).
Hawaii	Haw. Rev. Stat. § 487N-2 (West, WESTLAW through all 2006 Leg.).
Idaho	Idaho Code Ann. §§ 28-51-104 to -107 (West, WESTLAW through all 2007 laws of the 1st Reg. Sess. of 59th Leg.).
Illinois	815 Ill. Comp. Stat. Ann. 530/1 to /30 (West, WESTLAW through P.A. 94-1113 of the 2006 Reg. Sess.).
Indiana	Ind. Code Ann. §§ 24-4.9-1-1 to 24-4.9-5-1 (West, WESTLAW through 2006 Public laws approved and effective through the 2006 Reg. Sess.).
Iowa	No provision in state law.
Kansas	Kan. Stat. Ann. §§ 50-7a01, 50-7a02 (West, WESTLAW through End of 2006 Reg. Sess.).
Kentucky	No provision in state law.
Louisiana	La. Rev. Stat. Ann. §§ 51:3071-:3077 (West, WESTLAW through 2006 1st Extraordinary, Reg. & 2nd Extraordinary Sess. Acts).
Maine	Me. Rev. Stat. Ann. tit. 10, §§ 1346-1350A (West, WESTLAW through 2006 2nd Reg. Sess. of the 122nd Leg.).

Maryland	No provision in state law.
Massachusetts	No provision in state law.
Michigan (*Editor's Note: This section becomes effective 7/02/07*).	Mich. Comp. Laws Ann. § 445.72 (West, WESTLAW through P.A. 2007, No. 5).
Minnesota	Minn. Stat. Ann. § 325E.61 (West, WESTLAW current with laws of the 2007 Reg. Sess. effective through 04/01/07).
Mississippi	No provision in state law.
Missouri	No provision in state law.
Montana	Mont. Code Ann. §§ 30–14–1701 to –1705 (West, WESTLAW through 2005 Reg. Sess. of the 59th Leg. & Dec. 2005 Special Sess.).
Nebraska	Neb. Rev. Stat. §§ 87–801 to –807 (West, WESTLAW through 2nd Reg. Sess. of the 99th Leg. (2006)).
Nevada	Nev. Rev. Stat. §§ 603A.010–.040, .100, .200–.220, .900–.920 (West, WESTLAW through 2005 73rd Reg. Sess. & 22nd Special Sess. of the Nev. Leg.).
New Hampshire	N.H. Rev. Stat. Ann. §§ 359–C:19–C:21 (West, WESTLAW through end of 2006 Reg. Sess.).
New Jersey	N.J. Stat. Ann. § 56:8–163 (West, WESTLAW through L.2006, c. 103 (End) & L.2007, c. 60 & J.R. No. 4).
New Mexico	No provision in state law.
New York	N.Y. Gen. Bus. Law § 899–aa (McKinney through L.2007, ch. 13).
North Carolina	N.C. Gen. Stat. Ann. § 75–65 (West, WESTLAW through S.L. 2006–264; End of the 2006 Reg. Sess.).
North Dakota	N.D. Cent. Code §§ 51–30–01 to –07 (West, WESTLAW through 2005 Reg. Sess.).
Ohio	Ohio Rev. Code Ann. § 1349.19 (West, WESTLAW through 2007 File 1 of the 127th GA (2007–2008)).
Oklahoma (*Editor's Note: applies to governmental agencies only)*	Okla. Stat. tit. 74, § 3113.1 (West, WESTLAW through Ch.1 of the 1st Reg. Sess. of the 51st Leg. (2007)).
Oregon	No provision in state law.
Pennsylvania	73 Pa. Stat. Ann. § 2303 (West, WESTLAW through Reg. Sess. Act 2006–151 & 2005–2006 1st Sp. Sess. Act 1).
Rhode Island	R.I. Gen. Laws §§ 11–49.2–1 to –7 (West, WESTLAW through all 2006 Leg.).
South Carolina	No provision in state law.
South Dakota	No provision in state law.
Tennessee	Tenn. Code Ann. § 47–18–2107 (West, WESTLAW through end of 2006 2nd Reg. Sess.).
Texas	Tex. Bus. & Com. Code Ann. §§ 48.001–.103 (Vernon through end of 2006 3rd Called Sess. of the 79th Leg.).
Utah	Utah Code Ann. §§ 13–44–101 to –102, –201 to –202, –301 (West, WESTLAW through end of 2006 Leg.).

Vermont	Vt. Stat. Ann. tit. 9, §§ 2430–2435 (West, WESTLAW through 1st Sess. of the 68th Biennial Sess. (2005)).
Virginia	No provision in state law.
Washington	Wash. Rev. Code Ann. § 19.255.010 (West, WESTLAW through 2007 leg. effective through 03/25/07).
West Virginia	No provision in state law.
Wisconsin	Wis. Stat. Ann. § 895.507 (West, WESTLAW through 2007 Act 5, published 03/30/2007).
Wyoming (*Editor's Note: This section becomes effective 7/01/07*).	Wyo. Stat. Ann. § 40-12-502 (West, WESTLAW through 2007 Gen. Sess.).

1 Tenn. Code Ann. § 47-18-2107(a)(1) (West, WESTLAW through end of 2006 2nd Reg. Sess.).

2 *Id.*

3 Cal. Civ. Code § 1798.29(a) (West, WESTLAW through Ch. 2 of 2007 Reg. Sess. Urgency Leg.).

4 N.D. Cent. Code § 51-30-02 (West, WESTLAW through 2005 Reg. Sess.).

5 Cal. Civ. Code § 1798.3(a) (West, WESTLAW through Ch. 2 of 2007 Reg. Sess. Urgency Leg.).

6 Ark. Code Ann. § 4-110-105(a)(2) (West, WESTLAW through End of 2006 Leg.).

7 Ga. Code Ann. § 10-1-912(c) (West, WESTLAW through end of 2006 Reg. Sess.).

8 15 U.S.C. § 7001 (West, WESTLAW through P.L. 110-16, approved 03-28-07).

9 Ariz. Rev. Stat. Ann. § 44-7501(D)(3) (West, WESTLAW through End of 47th Leg., 2nd Reg. Sess. (2006)).

10 Haw. Rev. Stat. § 487N-2(e)(4) (West, WESTLAW through all 2006 Leg.).

11 Minn. Stat. Ann. § 325E.61(g)(3) (West, WESTLAW current with laws of the 2007 Reg. Sess. effective through 04/01/07).

12 Nev. Rev. Stat. § 603A.220(6) (West, WESTLAW through 2005 73rd Reg. Sess. & 22nd Special Sess. of the Nev. Leg.).

13 Colo. Rev. Stat. Ann. § 6-1-716(2)(d) (West, WESTLAW through End of 2006 1st Extraordinary Sess. of the 65th Gen. Assembly (2006)).

14 Ind. Code Ann. § 24-4.9-3-1(b) (West, WESTLAW through 2006 Public laws approved and effective through the 2006 Reg. Sess.).

15 Kan. Stat. Ann. § 50-7a02(d) (West, WESTLAW through End of 2006 Reg. Sess.).

16 La. Rev. Stat. Ann. § 51:3074(G) (West, WESTLAW through 2006 1st Extraordinary, Reg. & 2nd Extraordinary Sess. Acts).

CHAPTER 14

What to Do When You Are Served

Most creditors understand the litigation process from the eye of the plaintiff. However, they fail to understand their duties and obligations when they are the defendant. Understanding the process will reduce stress and headaches, as well as save attorneys' fees. In this chapter we will explain the process from the view of the defendant: What should I do? When should I do it? A better understanding of the process will lead to a quicker resolution.

THE BASICS

A lawsuit is usually commenced by service of a summons or a summons and complaint. A summons is merely notice of the action. A complaint is a document that sets forth why you can be sued and why the plaintiff is suing you. The complaint (usually in numbered paragraphs) will set forth the following:

1. Why this court can rule on this type of matter (subject matter jurisdiction).
2. Why this court can hold the defendant accountable/liable (personal jurisdiction).
3. A claim for relief:
    - (a) Defendant owed plaintiff a duty;
    - (b) Defendant breached the duty;
    - (c) A breach caused damages or strict liability due to breach; and
    - (d) Damages.

SUMMONS AND COMPLAINT—WHO WILL SERVE YOU

Service of the litigation papers must comply with the law of the court in which the action is started. If a lawsuit in commenced in a New York State court and the debtor lives in Florida, New York state law applies to service of the legal papers (often called service of process).

In the various state courts, these legal papers can be served upon the debtor by several different methods:

1. A private process server;
2. State Marshal or Sheriff;
3. An officer of the court by certified return receipt or registered mail; or
4. By the plaintiff by certified mail return receipt.

In federal court or bankruptcy court, a lawsuit may be commenced by:

1. Federal Marshal;
2. Private process server;
3. Mail, and the defendant accepts service.

The Federal Rules of Civil Procedure provide for an easy method of service of process. The plaintiff mails a copy of the summons and complaint. The defendant has the option to accept the papers or ignore them (reject service). This option is often used when the papers arrive close to the end of the time period in which the lawsuit can be served (statute of limitations period). If you refuse to accept service by mail, and service is later completed through a Federal Marshal or private process server, the plaintiff can apply to the court to order defendant to pay the costs of service. If service is by mail, we recommend you consult with counsel before you decide to reject or accept service.

Petition. In some proceedings, a summons and complaint is not used. For example, in some proceedings a "notice of petition" and "verified petition" is used. In other cases, you may only receive a "notice of motion" or "show cause" motion.

Read the papers carefully as they will notify you as to:

1. How much time you have to answer or oppose the papers;
2. Where to send your answer, appearance, or opposition papers;
3. In what form the papers need to be mailed.

METHOD OF SERVICE

The method of service is determined by the state law where the suit is instituted, or by the federal law if suit is commenced in federal court.

(1) In hand delivery

  (a) Hostile service: When the defendant refuses to accept the papers, the papers are dropped at their feet and left in their view.

(2) At your usual place of abode—left in the mail box or attached to the door.

(3) Suitable age and discretion—left with an adult at the location in which the defendant resides.

  (a) Sometimes an additional mailing to your address is required under state law.

(4) Nail and mail—attach to the door of your residence and mail to the same address within a certain time period.

(5) Certified mail—returned receipt requested (for example: small claims court, town court, justice court, or certain proceedings in courts of record).

(6) Service by publication (by court order)—when other means are unsuccessful, publication in a newspaper selected by the judge; usually requires 2 to 5 publications about one to three weeks apart depending upon the type of suit.

(7) Secretary of State (for corporations)—who serves the authorized agent of the corporation by mail—usually registered or certified to the address of the corporation on file with the Secretary of State, which was furnished to the Secretary of State at the time of the filing of the papers to organize a corporation.

(8) In certain circumstances when the defendant is out of the states and services by other methods cannot be made, some courts in some states will entertain an application for an alternate method i.e., internet.

If the corporation has relocated and changed their address, the Secretary of State will mail the summons to the old address and the corporation will not receive it. The courts hold the service is good, and the plaintiff may enter a judgment. Only in rare instances will the court set aside service on the Secretary of State. *The corporation has a continuing obligation to notify the Secretary of State of any change of address. (New York). In many states if the corporate license lapses, owners may be personally liable.*

Time to Respond Once Served. The time to file an answer or appearance in the action varies from state to state. In most cases, it is stated on the legal papers. The time period may differ due to the method of service utilized. This time period is often between 20-45 days. In special proceedings, the time period may only be 24-72 hours, but the papers served will specify the time period.

WHAT DO I DO WHEN I AM SERVED?

1) **Address the matter.** Do not put the matter aside. Many clients incur unnecessary attorneys' fees by avoiding the problem.
2) **Insurance carrier notification.** If you carry insurance that covers the claim, and intend to use your insurance, notify your carrier immediately and send them a copy of the summons and complaint.
3) **Determine the date of service and make a record or notation on the papers.**
4) **Determine the date to appear, answer, or otherwise move** (example: motion to dismiss) and record that date.
5) **Obtain in writing an adjournment of your time to answer, appear, or otherwise move, but first consult with counsel.**
6) **Investigate your adversary**—Learn as much as you can: to be an effective negotiator you must know your adversary.
7) **Create a file of all relevant documents**—Confirm your employees' home addresses in case they leave the company during the lawsuit. If a former employee disappears, so could your defense.

You should hire an attorney to obtain an extension to answer. In most states, and federal court, the plaintiff will grant an adjournment (14-30 days) automatically. In some states, the debtor has an automatic right to the extension. Consultation with an attorney is recommended to confirm that you are not waiving any defenses or incorrectly consenting to jurisdiction of the court.

In some states, an oral adjournment is not enforceable. The court will only accept adjournments confirmed in writing. Some plaintiff's counsel orally agree to an adjournment to settle the matter. If you refuse to pay the money demanded, the adjournment may be refused. The plaintiff's counsel alleges that the matter was postponed only to pay them and no formal adjournment was granted. While this tactic is sometimes used, the federal courts do not usually favor it. Federal judges may award sanctions against a plaintiff's attorney who does not honor an oral request for an adjournment. State courts will favor the local player.

Credit & Collection Tip: *Retain an attorney to obtain the adjournment inwriting. It is cheaper than retaining an attorney to vacate a default judgment entered against you.*

FDCPA, FCRA, TILA SUITS

These suits usually allege statutory violations and actual damages. A large portion of these lawsuits are commenced by a small number of law firms throughout the country. Most of these suits are commenced in relatively liberal jurisdictions. If you are wrong, the case should be settled. If you are right, settlement should not be offered since you only encourage the attorney to sue again, right or wrong.

Risk management practices:

1. Establish a training manual for your staff.
2. Establish procedures to prevent mistakes.
3. Avoid "cute" letters—do not use a letter you would be embarrassed to show to a liberal judge.
4. Limit the versions of the initial demand letter used. (Multiple versions increase the chances of the incorrect letter being used.)
5. Do not demand immediate payment in any letter during the first 30 days.
6. Join an association and their list serve.
   a. American Collector's Association International (ACA International)
   b. National Association of Retail Collection Attorneys (NARCA)
7. Establish a procedure to address "cease and desist" debtors and bankruptcy matters.
8. Test your staff by having a friend make dummy calls to your office to evaluate their actions.

Addressing a potential lawsuit from a plaintiff's attorney:

1. Take the letter seriously;
2. Do your research immediately—settle the losers, fight the winners;
3. *Notify your insurance carrier—delaying too long may cause you to lose coverage, but consult with counsel as to your exposure—is it less or greater than your deductible.*
4. *Investigate your adversary*—(What is his/her modus operandi?) Learn as much as you can.

To be an effective negotiator you must know your adversary:

1. Does the attorney file class actions?
2. Is s/he a player or merely a relative of the debtor?
3. Does the attorney use the initial negotiation process to run-up attorney's fees?
4. Is s/he a "turncoat"—a former creditor's attorney?
5. Will the attorney pursue a frivolous claim because they believe your insurance company will ultimately pay a "settlement bounty"?
6. Acquire all documents to defend the case as soon as possible:
   a. For example, a copy of the demand letter and documentation supporting the claim to help your attorney;
   b. Be involved in the case. Teach your attorney about your business practices—it is important. Most defense counsel have limited knowledge of the basics (for example, how automatic/computerized the process is).

Run a bankruptcy search on the debtor:

1. If a bankruptcy was filed, the claim belongs to the trustee;
2. If trustee abandoned the claim, the debtor may have committed a fraud for failing to disclose the value of an asset to the estate or the debtor may have believed the claim had little or no merit.

Replying to the initial "extortion" letter:

1. Do not ignore the letter, as the consumer attorney will treat this inaction as a sign of weakness. (Many lawsuits are commenced just before the statute of limitations expires.)
2. *If you are right, prove it now. While more time consuming, it will be cheaper than defending the matter later.*
   a. If you have case law to support the position, have your attorney provide a detailed letter explaining why their position is flawed and why you will fight to the end.
   b. If you can establish that the matter is a non-FDCPA claim, send the documentation to the attorney as soon as possible (that is, commercial matter, a tort claim)
   c. Most defense attorneys discourage forwarding documentation to the plaintiff's counsel. The attorney prefers not to provide evidence that may hurt your case. However, if the item is clearly discoverable and helps your case, let your adversary see it.

d. Make all firm offers in writing; oral offers may never reach the client of plaintiff's attorney.

Defensive Negotiation. Stay involved in the litigation. Your input may reduce your defense costs. Collection attorneys are efficient negotiators. Defense attorneys and insurance defense attorneys may be efficient litigators, but their lack of experience in the collection industry may affect their negotiation tactics. Negotiations drag on longer than expected. Provide defense counsel with your experience as we often do when retained to consult with insurance defense attorneys.

Chapter 15

Fair Debt Collection Practices Act

The Fair Debt Collection Practices Act (FDCPA) is the most important federal legislation affecting the collection industry. Prior to its enactment, no federal law on debt collection existed, although several federal agencies regulated isolated activities. For example, the Postal Service relies on the mail fraud extortion statute which requires "intent" and which is difficult to prove for the "garden variety" unethical debt collection practice. The Federal Communications Commission provisions against phone harassment also required intent, making them difficult to enforce. The Federal Trade Commission's (FTC), which regulates the FDCPA, powers are limited by their other functions and the size of their staff.

As the extension of credit and the credit card industry grew after World War II, the abuses of the collection industry grew proportionally and became a frequent subject for the media. The complaints against collection agencies grew exponentially as a function of the huge increase in extending credit and issuing credit cards. Calling on Sundays, leaving messages with neighbors, threatening to send "collectors" to the debtor's house, adding charges without notifying the debtor, and being nasty on the telephone are just a few examples of the numerous abuses, which were infinite and only limited by the collector's creativity. The stage was set for federal entry into the area; and the FDCPA was passed in 1977, *by an overwhelming majority of one vote, and became effective on March 30, 1978.*

At the time of enactment, only 37 states had laws regulating abuses of collection activity. But most of these states provided few remedies for the individual consumer and many of the laws were inadequate to achieve the purpose for which they were designed.[1] States covering about 40 million consumers had no collection laws. Furthermore, even if each of the states had a proper law addressing the problem of debt collection, the states could not regulate interstate debt collection practices, including letters and the technology available to make interstate collection calls.

The Act applied only to those who collect the debt of another, and thus was aimed primarily at collection agencies, but in 1986 an amendment was passed to include attorneys. Creditors who collect their own debts generally are exempt from the Act.

RECENT AMENDMENTS TO FDCPA

Congress completed action on the Financial Service Regulatory Relief Act of 2006, S.2856 which included three amendments to the Fair Debt Collection Practices Act. The American Collectors International has been lobbying for these amendments for many years and finally were successful.

Amendment 1 addresses the issue that a "formal pleading" is not an initial communication under the FDCPA. Accordingly, a validation notice disclosure is not required to be attached to the summons and complaint.

Amendment 2 addresses the issue of state statutes triggering compliance with the FDCPA when the statute requires a notice or form to be sent by the debt collector. The amendment specifically states that the regulations and rules which do not request payment of a debt are not deemed to be communications in connection with debt collection. Examples are situations where an agency fulfills the privacy notice under the Gramm-Leach-Bliley Act, or is required to send the consumer an Internal Revenue Code 1099C or is complying with the breach notification statutes that have been passed in many of the states.

Finally, the amendment states that the debt collector has a right to collect the debt within the 30-day validation period which overruled a minority of court decisions in liberal states holding otherwise. A copy of the amendment is set forth in the Appendix to this chapter.

CREDITOR COMPLIANCE

Our firm, as well as most attorneys, recommends that creditors comply with the principles of the Act, wherever applicable, notwithstanding the fact that creditors are not subject to the Act. The Act has established the standard for determining and identifying whether an activity is an abusive collection practice. For example, a creditor in a business-to-business

---

[1] Alabama, Delaware, Georgia, Kansas, Kentucky, Mississippi, Missouri, Montana, Ohio, Oklahoma, Rhode Island, South Carolina, and South Dakota.

transaction makes the following comments to the owner of another business who owes him money:

CREDITOR: Charlie, I know it's midnight, but you've owed me this debt for almost 12 months, so why shouldn't I call you at 12 o'clock? If you had paid the debt, it would not be necessary for me to call you.

DEBTOR: Look, I've had a bad year. I've told you a dozen times before that I don't have the money, but as soon as I do have it, I will try to send you some money each month. Will you please let me get some sleep so I can get up tomorrow?

CREDITOR: Charlie, be sure to get some sleep because tomorrow night I'm going to call you at 1 o'clock, and the next night I'm going to call you at 2 o'clock, and the night after that I'm going to call you at 3 o'clock until I receive some payment on this debt.

Most state laws prohibit "abusive or unconscionable collection practices" and creditors as well as collection agencies and attorneys are subject to these state laws. The court will examine the FDCPA to determine whether the creditor's practice is identified as a violation. If the activity does qualify as a violation, the court will probably decide that an abusive or unconscionable practice took place under state law. The procedure of the court is to use the FDCPA as the standard to measure the abusive collection activity and then apply the general terms of the state law to the activity. Since the practice described above is a violation under the Act, the court would determine that the violation must necessarily qualify as an abusive or unconscionable practice under the state law. The suit would be commenced under state law, but the court would apply the standards set by the FDCPA to determine if state law should apply to the creditor. For this reason, creditors should comply with the provisions of the Act. The result is equitable, since creditors should not be allowed to engage in deceptive or abusive collection practices that are clearly violations of the FDCPA.

A listing presented several years ago by the American Collection International highlighted 22 states where creditors are subject to some or all of the collection laws that apply to collection agencies and attorneys.

THE STATES ARE AS FOLLOWS:

California
Colorado
Connecticut
District of Columbia
Florida
Hawaii
lowa
Michigan
New Hampshire

New York (New York City and Buffalo)
North Carolina
Oregon
Pennsylvania
South Carolina
Louisiana
Maine
Maryland
Massachusetts
Texas
Vermont
West Virginia
Wisconsin

In the last few years, the above list of states may have expanded, or the laws in these states may have been amended.

Since a creditor collects debts for itself, himself, or herself, and not for another party, a creditor is exempt from the Act. The Act excludes any officer or employee of a creditor, affiliated corporations, any officer or employee of the United States or any state, process servers, and nonprofit organizations.

In certain circumstances a creditor may become subject to the Act, such as where the creditor uses a name other than their own. Where the creditor controls the agency or law firm to such a degree that the debt collector is performing routine acts under the control of the creditor, the creditor is thus collecting under a name other than their own, and thus is violating the Act.[2]

ATTORNEY COVERAGE

In July 1986, the Act was amended to cover all attorneys who collect debts. Initially, the Commission's position was that only attorneys regularly engaged in collecting a debt were subject to the Act.

The Act specifically covers attorneys who engage in the same activities as collection agencies, including such activities as sending demand letters or using the telephone to demand payment from the debtor.

Attorneys thought that a legal practice limited to legal activities such as filing and prosecuting lawsuits is not subject to the Act.[3] Then, one of the federal circuit courts chose to disagree with the prevailing view,[4] and was quickly followed by another federal court decision which decided the Act contained no attorney exemption and refused to create an exemption for purely legal activities. On April 18, 1995, the Supreme Court of the United States held that lawyers engaged in consumer debt collection litigation must comply with the FDCPA.

---

[2] *Nielsen v. Dickerson*, 1999 U.S. Dist LEXIS 13931 (N.D. Ill. Sept. 8, 1999).

[3] *National Union Buyer Ins. Co. v. Hartel*, 741 F. Supp. (S.D.N.Y. 1990); *Fireman's Ins. Co. v. Keating*, 753 F. Supp. 1137 (S.D.N.Y. 1990); *Green v. Hocking*, 792 F. Supp. 1064 (E.D. Mich. 1992).

[4] *Heintz v. Jenkins*, 514 U.S. 291 (1995); *Sayyed v. Wolpoff & Abramson*, 485 F.3d 226 (4th Cir. 2007); *Fox v. Citicorp Credit Servs.*, 15 F.3d 1507 (9th Cir. 1994).

The reasoning was that attorneys who institute suit meet the definition of a "debt collector" as one regularly engaged in the collection of or attempt to collect consumer debts. The Supreme Court also stated that when Congress repealed the exemption, no effort was made to confine the repeal to those activities prior to suit. Ergo, Congress repealed the exemption in its entirety and intended to require litigation activities to be covered by the Act.

ATTORNEYS

Since attorneys became subject to the FDCPA, law firms who are not primarily engaged in debt collections have from time to time alleged that they are not debt collectors since they are not regularly engaged in the collection of debts. Prior to the time that attorneys became subject to the Act, this defense carried substantial weight and was successful in many cases where the collection practice was minimum. Since 1987 when attorneys became subject to the Act, the attorneys became subject to Section 15 USC, Section 1692, Subdivision A(6) which define debt collectors as:

> any person who uses any instrumentality of interstate commerce or the mails in any business the principal purpose of which is the collection of any debts, or who regularly collects or attempts to collect, directly or indirectly, debts owed or due or asserted to be owed or due another.

The Supreme Court of the United States held that the Act applies to attorneys who "regularly" engage in consumer debt collection activities even when that activity consists of litigation.[5] In determining whether activity constitutes "regular" debt collection, courts have considered different criteria, including the sheer volume of the law firm's practice devoted to debt collections;[6] the number of debt collection cases filed as a percentage of all cases filed;[7] and the percentage of the practice.[8]

The Second Circuit case clarified the issue of when an attorney is subject to the FDCPA. The Second Circuit stated, "the FDCPA establishes two alternative predicates for debt collectors' status":

1. Engaging in such activity as the principle purpose of the entity's business.
2. "Regularly" engaging in such activity.

---

[5]*Heintz v. Jenkins*, 514 U.S. 291 (1995).

[6]*Nance v. Petty Livingston, Dawson and Devenina*, 881 F. Supp. 223 (W.D. Va. 1994).

[7]*Crossley v. Lieberman*, 868 F.2d 566 (3d Cir. 1989).

[8]*Cacace v. Lucas*, 775 F. Supp. 502 (D. Conn. 1990). *See Newman v. Boehm Pearlstein & Bright Ltd.*, 119 F.3d 477 (7th Cir. 1997); *Thies v. Law Offices of William Wymun*, 969 F. Supp. 604 (S.D. Cal. 1997).

The defendant's business did not principally involve debt collection. The percentage of resources dedicated to and revenues derived from debt collection work or marketing itself as a debt collector was of particular importance as to whether this was the principle business of the defendant.

The Second Circuit emphasized that the decision below should have focused on the issue of "regularity" of defendant's debt collection activity rather than principally on the percentage or proportion of its business devoted to debt collection. The Circuit Court of Appeals stated that whether a lawyer or law firm regularly engages in debt collection must be assessed on a case-by-case basis. The important facts to consider are as follows:

1. The absolute number of debt collection communications issued and/ or collection related litigation matters pursued over the relevant periods.
2. The frequency of such communications and/or litigation activity, including whether any patterns of such activity, are discernable.
3. Whether the entity has personnel specifically assigned to work on debt collection activity.
4. Whether the entity has systems or contractors in place to facilitate such activity.
5. Whether the activity is undertaken in connection with an ongoing client relationship with entities that have retained the lawyer or firm to assist in the collection of outstanding consumer debt obligations.
6. Whether the law practice seeks debt collection business by marketing itself as having debt collection expertise may also be considered.

The defendant's law firm issued over 145 thirty-day notices within a 12-month period, a repetitive pattern of issuing multiple notices each month. It had an ongoing relationship with a client since the firm regularly was issuing eviction notices to tenants. Collection notices were three-day notices pursuant to the real property law which are needed before a tenant may be evicted for nonpayment of rent. In essence, an individual may regularly render debt collection services, even if these services are not a principle purpose of the business and even if the volume of the person's debt collection services only amount to a small fraction (even if its only 1% of the business) of the total business activity—*providing the activity is conducted regularly.*

Another factor in the case was that the defendant had a system in place for preparing and issuing notices. Tenant arrears information was relayed to outside computer services which generated the notices. A paralegal was assigned to review the notices for consistency and accuracy and the notices ultimately were sent to a process server for service on the tenants.

The decision with one broad stroke may have included a wide variety of law firms who have only one of their partners regularly engaged in debt collection. The other attorneys in the firm may be exposed to the coverage of the FDCPA even though they may be only handling one or two claims a year and may not meet the criteria set forth in this decision. The court has substantially expanded the coverage of the FDCPA to a broad spectrum of law firms where the debt collection practice may represent as little as 1 percent of the total practice or even less.

It is a toss-up whether the conservative Circuits will follow this, although the more liberal circuits, such as the Seventh and Ninth Circuits, probably will embrace this new doctrine.[9]

COMMENTARY

The FTC issued a commentary on the FDCPA on December 13, 1988, which superseded all previously issued staff interpretations of the Act (*see* Appendix to this chapter). The purpose of the commentary was to clarify and modify these interpretations. Commentaries are not a trade regulation rule or a formal agency action, and are not binding on the Commission, the public, or the courts. A commentary by the FTC is similar to a textbook explanation of its interpretation of law. Even though they are not binding, the commentaries present the position and attitude of the Commission and often determine whether it will prosecute a violation of the Act. The FTC also issues opinion letters upon request for same, but these also are not binding on the Commission, the public, or the court.

FINDINGS AND PURPOSE

The findings and the purpose of the FDCPA is to eliminate abusive, deceptive, and unfair debt collection practices.

DEFINITIONS

Communication is defined as conveying information regarding a debt to any person through any type of medium, which includes all letters, faxes, telephone conversations, and probably e-mail. It expressly excludes the institution of suit and other contact during the course of the suit which is not a collection activity.

---

[9] *Goldstein v. Hutton, Ingram, Yuzak, Gaines, Carroll & Bertoletti*, 374 F.3d 56 (2d Cir. 2004); *Cashman v. Ricigliano, Jr.*, 2004 U.S. Dist. LEXIS 17027 (D.C., Aug. 25, 2004).

A *debt* is an obligation to pay money arising out of a transaction in which the money, property, insurance, or service is primarily used for personal, family, or household purposes. Under the terms of this Section, a commercial or business transaction is exempt from the Act. This would apply even if an individual is operating the business in his own name, such as "Thomas O'Reilly doing business individually as (d/b/a) O'Reilly's Restaurant."[10]

CONSUMER DEBT

Several court decisions have held that whether the loan is for a personal, family, or household use does not depend upon the intent of the seller, the nature of the product, or for what purpose the product itself was intended. *The courts look solely to the purpose for which the consumer uses the product.* A product designed for a business and intended to be sold to a business can be used for a personal purpose; and if it is used for a personal, family, or household purpose, the transaction is subject to the FDCPA. An example might be the publishing of a book of higher mathematics used solely for nuclear physics. Nevertheless, if this particular book is used by a student to learn nuclear physics, it now becomes a consumer item used for a consumer purpose notwithstanding that the book was published for graduate nuclear scientists and is not sold to universities or schools for educational purposes.

From out of nowhere the District Court in Virginia decided that even though the plaintiff applied for a "corporate card," she did not incur the debt until it was used for her personal purposes.[11] The approach of the courts is to examine exclusively the purpose for which the consumer uses the product. The debt was personal the moment it was incurred. The FDCPA's definition of debt includes "any obligation arising out of a transaction" where the subject of the transaction is "primarily for personal, family or household purposes." While plaintiff may have violated the terms of the "corporate" credit card agreement by incurring personal debt, that fact, even if true, cannot change the character of the debt and remove it from the jurisdiction of the FDCPA.[12]

The prevalent position is that the nature of the debt is determined at the time the obligation is created.

The account opened in the name of the business was used for personal purposes on many different occasions including gas, groceries, meals and other personal items. The court, in their infinite wisdom, declined to render a decision and stated that because the characterization of the debt

---

[10] *F.T.C. v. Check Investors, Inc.*, 502 F.3d 159 (3d Cir. 2007).

[11] *Peck v. Warden*, 2007 U.S. Dist. LEXIS 5450 (E.D. Va. Jan. 23, 2007).

[12] *Perk v. Worden*, 475 F. Supp. 2d 565 (E.D. Va. 2007).

determines whether the debt falls under the FDCPA, a jury, and not a court, must make the determination.

The case was in Houston, Texas. The motions by both sides for a summary judgment were denied. The courts often will stretch to find a way to declare the debt a consumer debt covered by the FDCPA. The label placed on the debt initially by the creditor is not material. The label on the bank account was a business account, but the court left the door open to declare it a consumer debt.[13]

TRANSACTIONS SUBJECT TO THE FDCPA

Many cases have held that child support payments are not considered "debts" under the FDCPA.[14] Subrogation claims are usually not subject to the FDCPA, but the Fifth Circuit held that subrogation claims do constitute debts for the purposes of the FDCPA.[15]

Assessments that are owing and due to a condominium association are classified as a debt. The transaction was the consumer's purchase of a condominium, which included obligations to comply with the rules and regulations of the condominium and was for a consumer purpose.

On the other hand, the courts seem to go in different directions, depending on how they look at the fees and the purpose to which the fees are allocated. Your authors find it difficult to identify a majority and minority view.[16]

The courts are split on the issue of whether a foreclosure action is or is not a collection of a debt against a consumer. Where coverage under the FDCPA is not found, the courts accept the argument that the foreclosing party is seeking only the return of the property and is not seeking any claim against the individual debtor. Where the courts state that the debt is covered by the FDCPA, the courts seem to distinguish that some judicial foreclosures include a judgment on the note and therefore if the creditor is seeking a judgment against the individual on a note, the FDCPA should apply. Carefully review case law in the state.

The recommendation is to give the debtor the 30-day notice before a foreclosure suit is instituted.[17]

The commentary to the FDCPA provides that the word "debt" does not include unpaid taxes, fines, tort claims, since none of these are incurred

---

[13] *Hetherington v. Allied Int'l Credit Corp.*, 2008 U.S. Dist. LEXIS 55169 (S.D. Tex. 2008).

[14] *Campbell v. Baldwin*, 90 F. Supp. 2d 754 (E.D. Tex. 2000). *See Reno v. Supportkids, Inc.*, Civ. No. 01-233 (D.C. Minn. 2004).

[15] *Hamilton v. United Health Care*, 61 Fed. Appx. 123; 2003 U.S. App. LEXIS 2940 (5th Cir. 2003); *Vasquez v. Allstate Ins. Co.*, 937 F. Supp. 773 (N.D. Ill. 1996).

[16] *Albanese v. Portnoff Law Assocs., Ltd.*, 301 F. Supp. 2d 389 (E.D. Pa. 2004).

[17] *McDaniel v. Smith and Assocs.*, No. CIV. A 03-2210-GTV (D. Kan. July 1, 2004); *Hulse v. Ocwen Federal Bank, FSB*, 195 F. Supp. 2d 1188 (D. Or. 2002).

from a transaction involving the purchase of property or services for personal, family or household purposes.

One case addressed the issue that the FDCPA does not apply to fines for parking violations. The decision was primarily because both plaintiff and the court cited no cases supporting this contention.

Library fines are also not debts since it is not an extension of credit. Taxes are usually not extensions of credit or debts.[18]

SUBROGATION CLAIMS

Two circuit courts have addressed the issue of whether a subrogation claim is covered by the FDCPA. In one instance, the Fifth Circuit Court of Appeals decided that a claim arising out of an accident is a tort claim. The FDCPA is not applicable. A consumer claim must involve some kind of business dealing or consensual obligation and not a damage obligation thrust upon one as a result of no more than their own negligence. The FDCPA language regulates consumer transactions and not obligations that arise out of tort.

On the other hand, the Fifth Circuit held that the business relationships and contracts were consumer transactions and the FDCPA applied. While the fact situations in both cases are somewhat different, each court seemed to travel down a different road.[19]

LOCATION INFORMATION

Contacting third parties presented unique problems for the FTC. Certainly debt collectors are interested in locating debtors, but, at the same time, they should not be permitted to disclose to a third party that the consumer is in debt. Debt collectors frequently threaten to reveal to neighbors, local grocery stores, banks, rotary clubs, etc., the financial condition of the consumer. One of the major purposes of the Act was to discourage any such action by the debt collector. Nevertheless, the drafters acknowledged that the debt collector is entitled to contact third parties to locate the debtor.

The result was a compromise. When communicating with a third party to locate a consumer, the debt collector must identify himself and state that "we are confirming or correcting location information" concerning the consumer and only *if expressly requested* identify the debt collector. While this may appear to make no sense, the drafters of the Act

---

[18] *Beggs v. Rossi*, 145 F.3d 511 (2d Cir. 1998); *Staub v. Harris*, 626 F.2d 275 (3d Cir. 1980); *Rector v. City and County of Denver*, 122 P.3d 1010 (Colo. App. 2005).

[19] *Hamilton v. United Healthcare of Louisiana, Inc.*, 310 F.3d 385 (5th Cir. 2002); *Hawthorne v. Mac Adjustment Inc.*, 140 F.3d 1367 (11th Cir. 1998).

finally settled on this procedure to balance the interests of the consumer and the debt collector.

The debt collector should not refer to the debt and is allowed only a single contact with a particular third party. The debt collector is not allowed to communicate by postcard or indicate by letterhead that the agency is in the collection business. The conversation may be as follows:

THIRD PARTY: Hello.

CREDITOR: Good morning. My name is Jerry Ford. And I'm trying to confirm the address of Phillip Johnson. We had him located at 430 Oak Road, Spring Grove, but we are told that he has moved. We are wondering whether you know whether he is still at that address.

THIRD PARTY: Wait a minute. What's your name?

CREDITOR: My name is Jerry Ford.

THIRD PARTY: And you want to know about Phil Johnson? Why do you want to know about him? Why are you trying to find out about him?

CREDITOR: We're trying to confirm if he's still living in Spring Grove or whether you know where he's moved to.

THIRD PARTY: I want to know why you want to know. Who are you?

CREDITOR: My name is Jerry Ford, and I'm just trying to find out where Phil Johnson is living.

THIRD PARTY: Look, what is the purpose of this call? And why do you want to know where Phil Johnson lives? I want to know who you are.

CREDITOR: My name is Jerry Ford, and I am employed by the ABC Collection Agency, and we are trying to locate Philip Johnson.

THIRD PARTY: Then you're trying to locate him to collect some money. Is that what the story is?

CREDITOR: Can you give me any information about where he is located?

THIRD PARTY: I haven't spoken to Phil Johnson in about three months and even if I did know, I probably wouldn't give you any information. But how did you get my name?

CREDITOR: Philip Johnson gave your name and address as a reference on his credit application.

THIRD PARTY: I guess I can't stop him from that, but I don't know where he is. By the way, how much money does he owe you?

CREDITOR: I can't tell you anything further.

THIRD PARTY: Then I guess you'll have to try to get some information from someone else. Goodbye.

CREDITOR: Goodbye.

The debt collector did furnish the name of the employer, but refused to reveal any further information. A debt collector may not use any name in correspondence with the third party if that name suggests the conducting of a collection business. On the other hand, if the name of the agency does not indicate a collection agency, the debt collector may use the letterhead (Jones Management Corp.) to seek location information. The Act specifically says that the name cannot contain the word "debt," "collector," or "collection." The word "credit" probably also should be classified with these words, even though not specifically mentioned in the Act.

Credit & Collection Tip: *The mini-Miranda statement should start each consumer collection call: this is an attempt to collect a debt. Any information obtained will be used for that purpose. (15 U.S.C. 1692(e)).*

CONTACTING CREDITORS TO FILE BANKRUPTCY

Revealing financial information to another creditor of the consumer is not permitted under the FDCPA. Under the bankruptcy law, three creditors are necessary to file an involuntary petition in bankruptcy against the debtor. If the creditor intends to contact other creditors to form a group to file an involuntary petition in bankruptcy, the conversations with the other creditors may be dangerous since financial information is being exchanged and disclosed to third parties. If the involuntary petition in bankruptcy is actually filed, the risk is minimal; but if no petition in bankruptcy is filed, the risk of violating the FDCPA increases significantly.

The better course is to consult with an experienced attorney to speak to either the other creditors or their attorneys.

COMMUNICATION WITH CONSUMERS AND THIRD PARTIES

CONTACT WITH CONSUMER. The Act limits any communication concerning the debt to the consumer or the spouse of the consumer. Communicating with any third parties about the debt of the consumer is prohibited. Always ask the party what the relationship is to the debtor before leaving a message. Do not speak to children, grandchildren, mother, grandmother, brother, sister, uncle, aunt, cousin, or any other relative. Furthermore, do not communicate with housekeepers, babysitters of the children, nurses caring for the spouse, girl friends or boy friends, significant others, roommates, tenants or subtenants, or any other third party. Certainly, never leave a message with an itinerant who happens to pick up the telephone, such as the plumber, electrician, gardener, delivery boy, meter reader, painter, TV or appliance repairman, priest or rabbi, or any other third party.

Exceptions to this rule include the debtor's attorney, consumer reporting agency (if permitted by the Fair Credit Reporting Act), the creditor, the attorney for the creditor, or the attorney for the debt collector. The creditor may discuss the case with the debtor's attorney. The matter may be reported to a credit reporting agency.

Consider the following telephone conversation:

THIRD PARTY: Hello.

CREDITOR: This is Jerry Ford. Can I please speak to Phil Johnson?

THIRD PARTY: Phillip isn't in right now, but he will be back in several hours. Can I take a message for him?

CREDITOR: Who is this?

THIRD PARTY: I'm his mother.

CREDITOR: Will you please leave a message for him to call Jerry Ford at this telephone number—(800) 555-1212?

THIRD PARTY: Jerry Ford. Aren't you with the ABC Collection Agency? This is the money that he owes on his Honda Accord, and he's about three months behind?

CREDITOR: Ma'am, would you please just leave a message for him.

THIRD PARTY: Look, I know all about this loan because I'm the one who makes the payments. And the reason we're behind is that he's been sick for the last three weeks, and he hasn't received a paycheck. As soon as he receives his next paycheck, we're going to send you the payment.

CREDITOR: Ma'am, I really can't talk about the debt.

THIRD PARTY: My son and I live here alone and I take care of all the finances. I pay the rent and the telephone bills and, believe me, I am well aware of this debt and I do want to pay it. I don't want you to take any action because I want you to understand that I intend to pay the debt. Now exactly what was the purpose of this phone call?

CREDITOR: All right. I'm here to tell you that unless we get the payment within the next ten days, we will have no alternative but to send it to our repossession firm to repossess the car because we cannot continue to carry this as an open account for more than three months.

THIRD PARTY: I don't know whether I can make it within the next ten days. But I'm certain I'll be able to pick up at least two payments by the end of the month. Could you possibly give me to the end of the month?

CREDITOR: The end of the month is almost three weeks away. But, if you make a promise that we will have the check by the 30th of January and not a day later, then I will put this on "hold" until the 30th of January. But we must have the check in our office by the 30th of January, not in the mail by that date.

THIRD PARTY: Please, we need the car very badly, and I will make certain that we will have at least two payments in the mail by the 28th so you will definitely have it on the 30th of the month. Please wait until the 30th of the month.

CREDITOR: All right Ma'am. We'll wait until the 30th of the month.

THIRD PARTY: Thank you very much. I will get the check in by that time. I appreciate your extending the time until the 30th.

CREDITOR: All right Ma'am. Goodbye.

THIRD PARTY: Goodbye.

Despite the mother taking care of all the finances and being familiar with the debt, the debt collector violated the Act by communicating information about the debt to the mother. The debt collector should have terminated the conversation and waited until the consumer returned the call. If the consumer failed to call, the debt collector should have contacted the consumer at a different time.[20]

TIME AND PLACE OF CONTACT. Contact cannot be made at any unusual time or place or at a place known to be inconvenient to the consumer. The usual convenient time for contact is between 8:00 a.m. and 9:00 p.m. If the collector does not have information to the contrary, a call on a Sunday is not illegal per se. However, to support a call on Sunday, several efforts should have been made during the week to contact the consumer.

---

[20] *Beasley v. Collection Training Institute*, 1999 WL 675196 (N.D. Ill. Aug. 17, 1999); *Masuda v. Thomas Richards & Co.*, 759 F. Supp. 1456 (C.D. Cal. 1991).

Contacting Debtors at Place of Employment. If the debt collector knows or has reason to know that the consumer's employer prohibits communication, no communication should be attempted. Furthermore, if a call is made at the consumer's place of employment, care should be exercised that the debtor is not being overheard by fellow employees and that it is a suitable time to speak. The telephone conversation might develop as follows:

CREDITOR: Can you talk to me now?

DEBTOR: Yeah, I guess so.

CREDITOR: Does your boss allow personal calls?

DEBTOR: Yeah.

CREDITOR: Are you in a private place where no one can hear what we say?

DEBTOR: Yeah, I guess so.

CREDITOR: Do you have the time to speak to me now or are you busy with your job? Do you want me to call you at another time or at home tonight?

DEBTOR: I guess we can talk now.

The questions as to personal calls, privacy, and non-interference with the job are designed to limit exposure. If the debtor requested no further calls at work, comply with the request. Notwithstanding such preparation, in today's environment, contact with the consumer debtor at the place of employment should be made only as a last resort. Such efforts are fraught with danger.

Many states have restrictions imposed upon collection agencies with regard to contacting debtors at their places of business. Some states even have additional restrictions imposed on contacting the debtor in general.

Massachusetts is probably the most burdensome in that it prohibits placing a telephone call to the debtor's place of employment if the debtor has made a written or oral request that such telephone calls not be made, provided that any oral requests shall be valid for only ten days unless the debtor provides a written confirmation postmarked or delivered within seven days of such request. The Massachusetts statute also requires a written notice to be sent to the debtor within 30 days after the first communication to a debtor at a place of employment. In addition, the statute prohibits any debtor communication in excess of two in each seven-day period at a debtor's residence and two calls in each 30-day period other than at the debtor's residence for each debt.

Washington also states that a communication to a debtor at a place of employment more than one time in a single week may constitute harassment. Maine and Connecticut prohibit contacting the consumer at the place of employment if the collection agency knows or has reason to know that the consumer's employer prohibits the consumer from receiving a communication. Arizona and Arkansas prohibit contact at a place of employment without first attempting to contact the debtor at the place of residence.[21]

Restrictions on Collection Activity. Minnesota and Wisconsin prohibit the debt collector from enlisting the aid of a neighbor or third party to request the debtor to contact the collection agency. New Hampshire has rather extensive restrictions including permitting debt collectors to send a single letter to the place of employment if they have been unable to locate the debtor and permitting a phone call to the debtor if they are unable to contact the debtor at the residence. Oregon and Pennsylvania statutes deal with the frequency of contact at the place of employment or at the residence. The following are pertinent sections for some states. Other states may have similar statutes. (The following list of statutes was prepared several years ago. Consult with counsel for the latest updates.)

Arizona, Administrative Code Banking Department Title 4, Chapter 4, Section R4-4-1512.

Arkansas, Statute Ann. Section 17-21-307.

Colorado, Revised Statute Section 12-14-105.

Connecticut, Rules and Regulations of the Banking Commissioner Concerning Collection Agencies 42-131d-3a.

Maine, Revised Statute Section 11012(1).

Massachusetts, 209 CMR 18.15(1).

Minnesota, Section 332-37.

New Hampshire, Revised Statute Annotated Section 358-c3.

Oregon, Rev. Stat. Section 646.639.

Pennsylvania, Section 303.4.

Washington, RCW Section 19-16.250.

Wisconsin, Section 74.14.

---

[21] *Fashakin v. Nextell Communications*, 2006 WL 1875341 (E.D.N.Y. 2006); *Option One Mortgage Corp. v. Massanet*, 2009 WL 380734 (Sup. Ct. 2009).

Contacting Attorneys. If a consumer debtor is represented by an attorney, contact must be made with the attorney. Usually, one learns that the client is represented by an attorney from the client, a telephone call, or letter from the consumer. The attorney must be representing the consumer with regard to the particular debt.

What can be done if the attorney fails to respond to a letter or telephone call? The commentary to the Debt Collection Practices Act does not seem to answer this question. The American Collectors Association, at least with regard to *commercial* matters, has taken the position that if the attorney does not respond within 14 days, then the debt collector may once again contact the debtor. It would appear that resumption of contact directly with the consumer should be allowed after a reasonable time has elapsed and after a reasonable effort (two letters or two telephone calls seems appropriate) to contact the attorney. Thus, after at least two efforts (by letter or telephone) and a reasonable wait (two weeks), contacting the consumer again is the next logical step.

> ***Credit & Collection Tip:*** *Be certain that the client knows to notify you that an attorney is representing the debtor when the case is initially referred. A letter to the client requiring this notification is appropriate and may provide a bona fide error defense.*

Most of the cases have stated that the Fair Debt Collection Practices Act is not applicable to communications between a debt collector and the attorney for the consumer, but a few cases have held a claim for relief may exist. The cases deal with intentional misrepresentation that would apply to the debtor or debtor's attorney. Some of the consumer attorneys have been successful in continuing to attack the majority of the cases. The best recommendation is to comply with the FDCPA and be careful not to violate the FDCPA when communicating with the attorney for the consumer debtor.[22]

STATUTE OF LIMITATIONS—TIME-BARRED DEBT

The Eighth Circuit has added its pronouncement to several cases which have held that no violation of the Act occurs in the absence of an

---

[22]*In re Holloway*, 337 B.R. 6 (Bankr. D. Mass 2006); *Diesi v. Shapiro*, 330 F. Supp. 2d 1002 (C.D. Ill. 2004); *Tromba v. M.R.S. Assocs., Inc.*, 323 F. Supp. 2d 424 (E.D.N.Y. 2004). *See Heintz v. Jenkins*, 514 U.S. 291 (1995); *Sayyed v. Wolpoff & Abramson*, 485 F.3d 226 (4th Cir. 2007); *Guerrero v. RJM Acquisitions LLC*, 499 F.3d 926 (9th Cir. 2007); *Guerrero v. RJM Acquisitions LLC*, 499 F.3d 926 (9th Cir. 2007).

express threat of litigation when a creditor attempts to collect on a time-barred debt.[23]

It appears that if no legal action is taken or even threatened, the statute of limitations does not eliminate the debt; it limits the judicial remedies available. In the absence of a threat of litigation or actual litigation, no violation of the FDCPA occurs when a debt collector attempts to collect a potentially time-barred debt that is otherwise valid.[24]

Notwithstanding the fact that in most states the expiration of the statute of limitations does not extinguish the debt, in Wisconsin once the statute of limitations has expired, no further efforts to collect the debt may be attempted. Whether this eliminates the debt is questionable. The Wisconsin statute states when a period within which an action may be commenced on a Wisconsin cause of action has expired, the debt (right) is extinguished as well as the remedy. Mississippi has a somewhat similar statute which reads as follows:

> The completion of the period of limitations prescribed to bar any action, shall defeat and extinguish the right as well as the remedy.

While your author does not know of any other states that contains similar wording, the Statute of Limitations should be reviewed in the pertinent state by any creditor, debt collector or debt buyer before they use their efforts to collect on time-barred debts. When defending the cases, argue that the statute of limitations is an affirmative defense like waiver and estoppel and plaintiff's duty is not to raise defenses for the defendant. The FDCPA does not alter the normal rules of litigation which is an adversarial process.

> ***Credit & Collection Tip:*** *If the debtor voluntarily offers to pay, the creditor could accept the monies either as a repayment of the debt or as a gift.*[25]

---

[23]*Kimber v. Fed. Fin. Corp.*, 668 F. Supp. 1480 (M.D. Ala. 1987) (the court held that the debt collector's filing of a lawsuit on an apparently time-barred debt, without having first determined after a reasonable inquiry that the limitation period had been tolled, was a violation of the FDCPA); *Beattie v. D.M. Collections Inc.*, 754 F. Supp. 383, 393 (D. Del. 1991) (threat of lawsuit, which debt collector knows or should know is time barred, is violation of FDCPA); *Aronson v. Commercial Fin. Serv.*, 1997 WL 1038818 (W.D. Pa. Dec. 22, 1997) (no FDCPA violation where no lawsuit threatened and language of letters track language of statute); *Shorty v. Capital One Bank*, 90 F. Supp. 2d 1330, 1332 (D. N.M. 2000) (no FDCPA violation where no lawsuit or further "collection action" threatened); *Johnson v. Capital One*, 2000 WL 1279661 (W.D. Tex. May 17, 2000) (no violation of the FDCPA where creditor only expressed intent to pursue lawful collection attempts).

[24]*Freyermuth v. Credit Bureau Servs.*, 248 F.3d 767 (8th Cir. 2001).

[25]*Baptist v. Global Holding & Inv. Co., LLC*, 2007 WL 1989450 (E.D.N.Y. July 9, 2007); *Klewer v. Cavalry Investments LLC*, 2002 U.S. Dist. LEXIS 1778 (W.D. Wis. Jan. 30, 2002) (unpublished); *Maryland Casualty Co. v. Beleznay*, 14 N.W.2d 177 (Wis. 1944).

Statute of Limitations—Discovery Rule. A case emphasized that the one-year statute of limitations provided for in the FDCPA runs from the date of the violation and not from the date of discovery of the violation.

A state court must apply the statute of limitations provided by federal law when enforcing a federal claim. The instant case concerned a violation of the FDCPA. A discovery rule (where the statute of limitations runs from the discovery of the violation) is read into statute of limitations governing federal claims in the absence of a contrary directive from Congress.

The most common type of action in which federal courts apply a discovery rule is where Congress did not provide a statute of limitations at all, so that the federal court is required to engraft the discovery rule onto the most appropriate state statute. A discovery rule postpones the date of the wrong until the time when the wrong is discovered.

The court stated that the discovery rule should not be read into the one-year statute of limitations provided by the FDCPA. Since the FDCPA states that the action must be brought within *one year from the date on which the violation occurs*, the court interpreted this language as a clear directive from Congress that courts are not to engraft the discovery doctrine onto the statute of limitations.[26]

On the other hand, the Ninth Circuit adopted a discovery rule, although the case was reversed on appeal.[27] Section 1681(P) of the Fair Credit Reporting Act set forth specific exceptions, and the statute was treated strictly so that the discovery rule did not apply. A case in California provided an extensive analysis of the one-year statute of limitations.[28]

ANSWERING MACHINES

Communicating with the telephone or telegraph company is not a third-party contact since the business purpose of these communication companies is to transmit messages. Leaving a message with an answering service falls under the same category. The commentary states:

> A debt collector may contact the employee of a telephone or telegraph company to contact the consumer without violating the prohibition on communication to third parties, if the only information furnished is that necessary to enable the collector to transmit the message to or make the contact with the consumer.

---

[26] *Holder v. GMC*, 189 Misc. 2d 297 (N.Y. Sup. Ct. 2001); *Shivone v. Washington Mutual Bank, F.a.*, 2008 WL 3154688 (E.D. Pa. 2008).

[27] *Andrews v. TRW, Inc.*, 225 F.3d 1063 (9th Cir. 2000).

[28] *Joseph v. MacIntyre Cos., LLC*, 281 F. Supp. 2d 1156 (N.D. Cal. 2003).

CEASING COMMUNICATIONS

If the consumer advises the creditor by written notice that he or she does not want to receive any further collection efforts, no further communication with the debtor is allowed except:

1. to advise the consumer that the debt collector's further efforts are being terminated;
2. to notify the consumer that the debt collector or creditor may use specific remedies which are ordinarily invoked (such as institution of suit, repossession of auto);
3. where applicable, to notify the consumer that the debt collector intends to invoke a specific remedy.

The response to a cease communication notice from the consumer must not include a demand for payment and must be limited to the three exceptions above. Any further communication other than above violates the FDCPA.

HARASSMENT AND ABUSE

This Section of the Act prohibits any conduct which harasses, oppresses, or abuses the debtor in connection with the collection of a debt. Despite considerable progress over the last 20 years, some agencies still engage in these tactics because of lack of knowledge or care. This Section provides that "without limiting the general application of the foregoing, the following conduct is a violation of the Section. . . ." Thus, any activity which harasses, oppresses, or abuses a debtor will be a violation of the Act, notwithstanding that the conduct is not expressly included in the six subdivisions of this Section.

Threat of Violence. The use of or threat to use violence or other criminal means to harm the physical person, reputation, or property of any person is prohibited. A lengthy series of questions or comments to the consumer without giving the consumer a chance to reply may constitute an abuse. Such statements as: "We're not playing around here—we can play tough" or "We're going to send somebody to collect for us one way or the other" are classic examples of threats of violence.[29]

Obscene Language. The use of obscene or profane language, the natural consequence of which is to abuse the hearer or reader, is prohibited.

---

[29] *Baker v. G.C. Servs.*, 677 F.2d 775 (1982).

Religious slurs, profanity, obscenity, calling the consumer a liar or a deadbeat, and the use of racial or sexual epithets are examples of this.[30]

Publication of List of Debtors. Publication of a list of consumers who refuse to pay debts is prohibited. Exchanging lists of "deadbeats" with other creditors would fall within the prohibitions of this Section. To maintain a list of delinquent accounts and distribute that list of accounts to members of an association would require complying with the Fair Credit Reporting Act (*see* Chapter 13). Associations should not maintain lists of delinquent consumers despite the fact their members often suggest the potential benefits of such a list.

Advertising Debt. The advertisement for sale of a debt to coerce payment of the debt or shaming a consumer by publicizing the debt to neighbors, friends, or local shopkeepers is not permitted.

Repeating Telephone Calls. Subsection 806(5) of the FDCPA prohibits a debt collector from causing a telephone to ring when engaging any person in telephone conversation repeatedly or continuously with intent to annoy, abuse, or harass the person at the call number. The question often asked is: how many telephone calls are you allowed to make to the debtor? Although several states, such as California and Texas, have laws similar to the FDCPA, apparently no state really sets forth the number of calls. Where a large number of telephone calls at various times of the day and night are used, the calls are abusive and constitute harassment. Unfortunately, the case law is no help to determine how many telephone calls "you could get away with" without violating the statute. Some of the statutes set forth requirements before you can contact a debtor at a place of business (Massachusetts).

The problem has progressed because more consumers are using "caller ID" where they identify the incoming number and refuse to accept calls without the incoming number.

We do not believe that it is possible to place a number on what is and what is not harassment. We think a violation of FDCPA will be determined not only by the number of calls, but also by when the calls are made, over how long a period they are made, and what is said on the telephone calls. All these ingredients contribute to a violation of Section 806(5).

One phone call each week at 3:00 a.m. in the morning certainly is abusive whereas one phone call at 3:00 p.m. in the afternoon every three days might not be considered repetitious. Your authors do not think that a court will offer an answer to this question nor is the question susceptible of an answer. The issue is good judgment—and that is a question of fact.

---

[30] *Jeter v. Credit Bureau*, 760 F.2d 1168 (1985).

One hundred telephone calls within 3 months and no return calls is probably too much because it is clear that debtor doesn't want to call you back.

TELEPHONE RESTRICTIONS—STATE LAWS. Many states have more restrictive requirements when making telephone calls to debtors. Some examples of those requirements are as follows:

A. New York—New York City has passed a mirror image of the FDCPA and has included in the Act business debts as well as consumer debts. New York City law requires the debt collector to include in all communications with the debtor that the communications are being used to collect a debt or to obtain information that will be used for that purpose. *New York City also provides that communicating with the consumer more than twice during a seven-day period is excessively frequent.* This is a private right of action.

B. Connecticut—A debtor may not contact a consumer at his place of employment if he has reason to know that the employer prohibits such communication. With regard to all communications, a debt collector must disclose that the communication is an attempt to collect a debt and that any information obtained will be used for that purpose.

C. Massachusetts—When making a telephone call, a debt collector must disclose the name of the agency and the personal name of the individual making the communication as well as the agency's telephone number and office hours.

D. Minnesota—A collection agency shall not imply or suggest in any communication with the debtor that healthcare services will be withheld in any emergency situation.

The American Collectors Association has compiled a book entitled *ACA's Guide to State Collection Laws and Practices* (2000 Edition). For information concerning other states that have such laws, you may obtain this book from the American Collectors Association at the following address: 4040 W. 70th Street, Minneapolis, MN 55435 (952-928-8000).[31]

IDENTIFYING TELEPHONE COLLECTORS. The placement of telephone calls without meaningful disclosure of the caller's identity is prohibited. The debt collector must identify himself or herself to the consumer directly and must comply with the identification requirement (*see* Location Information) if the contact is for the purpose of location information.

---

[31] *McGrady v. Nissan Motor Acceptance Corp.*, 40 F. Supp. 2d 1232 (M.D. Ala. 1998); *Joseph v. J.J. MacIntyre Cos.*, 238 F. Supp. 2d 1158 (N.D. Cal. 2002); *Bingham v. Collection Bureau Inc.*, 505 F. Supp. 864 (D.N.D. 1981); *U.S. v. Central Adjustment Bureau*, 667 F. Supp. 370 (N.D. Tex. 1986), *aff'd*, 823 F.2d 880 (5th Cir. 1981).

Alias. Courts have generally held that an alias is permitted providing identification is available of the name used by the alias and it is traceable to one individual. The same requirements should apply to using an alias on a letter as well as a telephone call. The alias should belong to a real person and should be identifiable.[32] Review of the state law is strongly suggested.

Personal Comments or Inquiries. Warnings of a personal nature, for example, that the debtor should not have had children if he/she could not afford children, or inquiries about personal possessions, such as jewelry,[33] are prohibited.

False or Misleading Representations. Prior to the passage of the FDCPA, using the following script to locate a debtor was not uncommon:

Third Party: Hello?

Attorney: Good morning, sir. This is the firm of Johnson and Ford. To whom am I speaking?

Third Party: Who is this calling?

Attorney: This is the firm of Johnson and Ford, and my name is Jerry Ford. We are the attorneys for Mary Baker, who is the grandmother of Robert Higgins.

Third Party: Robert Higgins?

Attorney: Yes, sir, Robert Higgins. We are trying to locate Mr. Higgins. His grandmother died about five months ago and we have a bequest in the will. We can't give you the exact amount, but it's over five figures—at least ten thousand dollars. We have been trying to locate Mr. Higgins, so we could give him this money.

Third Party: His grandmother left him over ten thousand dollars? I can't believe that.

Attorney: Well, you can believe it, sir. If you want, we'll be glad to give you our name and address, and we'll be glad to verify it to you either in writing or otherwise. All we're trying to do is locate him.

Third Party: How did you get my name?

---

[32] *Johnson v. NCB Collection Servs.*, 779 F. Supp. 1298 (D. Conn. 1992); *Supan v. Medical Bureau Economics, Inc.*, 785 F. Supp. 304 (D. Conn. 1991).

[33] *Johnson v. NCB Collection Servs.*, 779 F. Supp. 1298 (D. Conn. 1992); *Supan v. Medical Bureau Economics, Inc.*, 785 F. Supp. 304 (D. Conn. 1991).

ATTORNEY: Your name was furnished to us by one of her nurses who told us that you were a friend of Mr. Higgins. It was difficult locating you, but because there was so much money involved, we made a very determined effort. We have contacted several other people with the same name as you, but none of them knew Mr. Higgins. Do you know Mr. Higgins?

THIRD PARTY: Yes, I know Mr. Higgins.

ATTORNEY: Do you know where we can locate Mr. Higgins?

THIRD PARTY: Yes, I know where you can locate him. I'm not so sure I should tell you because he owes a lot of people a lot of money.

ATTORNEY: We're not trying to collect money from him. We're trying to give money to him.

THIRD PARTY: Actually, he recently moved to Florida and he's living there under one of his relative's names. He's living in a house down there with his relatives.

ATTORNEY: Oh, is that right? Do you know if he's working? Maybe we can reach him at his job.

THIRD PARTY: Yes. He works for the city bus company down there in the repair and maintenance garage.

ATTORNEY: I'm sure he'll be happy to receive this money.

THIRD PARTY: Yes, I'm certain he will.

ATTORNEY: Can you give me his address in Florida?

THIRD PARTY: Yes, he lives on Main Street in Ocala.

ATTORNEY: Do you have his phone number?

THIRD PARTY: It's (305) 555-1212.

ATTORNEY: Thank you very much. We're going to get in touch with him immediately to let him know about the good news.

The result of a juicy carrot at the end of the stick sometimes produces unique results in locating a debtor who has left for parts unknown. Another misleading device used was as follows:

THIRD PARTY: Hello.

DEBT COLLECTOR: Is this Marie Baker?

THIRD PARTY: Who is this?

DEBT COLLECTOR: This is the emergency room at the Meadowville Hospital. Your mother just got admitted to the hospital, but don't worry, she's okay. She's going to be fine. There's just a little minor thing that has to be taken care of, but we have to get the consent of your father. So could you please tell me quickly where I can reach your father at his work?

THIRD PARTY: At his work?

DEBT COLLECTOR: Do you know where he works?

THIRD PARTY: Are you sure my mother's all right?

DEBT COLLECTOR: Yes, your mother's okay. She's going to be fine. It's nothing serious. The important thing is to let us get in touch with your father.

THIRD PARTY: Okay, my dad works at the ABC Roofing Company on the edge of town on Green Street. I'm not sure of the address.

DEBT COLLECTOR: The ABC Roofing Company.

THIRD PARTY: Yes, that's right.

The debt collector was able to locate where the consumer worked, but unfortunately the child had an uncomfortable afternoon until the mother or father returned to the house. Few laws regulated this type of deception during the 1950s, 1960s, and 1970s. Sometimes these deceptions were targeted at locating bank accounts, automobiles, or luxury boats, or the names of stockbrokers or financial consultants who may have had assets of the debtor.

This Section of the Act prohibits any false, deceptive, or misleading representation to collect a debt. The Section lists 16 prohibited activities, but at the same time states that the 16 prohibitions are merely examples of what cannot be done, and thus a debt collector will not be able to use any type of false, deceptive, or misleading representation to collect a debt.

Most of the prohibitions are standard and obvious, whereas others consist of an effort to evade the intent and purpose of the Act.

DEBT AFFILIATED WITH GOVERNMENT. The false representation that a debt is vouched for, bonded by, or affiliated with the United States or any state, including the use of any badge, uniform, or facsimile, is a violation.

MISREPRESENTATION OF AMOUNT OF DEBT. The false representation of the character, amount, or legal status of any debt is prohibited. It was common to state that $425 was due, when in fact only $25 was due. The idea was to prompt a telephone call from the debtor. The debt collector would acknowledge the mistake and then continue to press the debtor for the collection of the $25.

Amount of Debt. Judge Posner in the Seventh Circuit rendered a decision which essentially defines what the words "amount of debt" means. Several courts have already followed this precedent.

The dunning letter said that the unpaid principal balance of the loan was $178,844.65 and that this amount does not include accrued but unpaid interest, unpaid late charges, escrow advances, or other charges for preservation and protection of the lenders interest in the property as authorized by the loan agreement. The letter went on to say that the amount to reinstate the loan or pay off the loan changes on a daily basis, but you may call the office for a complete reinstatement and payoff figure.

In an unequivocal statement, the court said that this statement does not comply with the FDCPA. The unpaid principal balance is not the debt. It is only part of a debt. The statute requires a statement of a debt and it is not satisfied by listing a phone number to call to request the total amount of the debt.

The statute requires that the letter state the total amount due, interest and other charges as well as principal—on the date that the dunning letter was sent. The chief judge referred to the fact that he had fashioned a safe harbor formula for complying with another provision of the statute—the preparation of a claim letter (except for the fact that the letter basically did not comply with FDCPA and has not been accepted by any of the other circuits). The court stated that the following statement satisfies the debt collector's duty to state the amount of the debt in cases where the amount varies from day to day:

> as of the date of this letter, you owe $___ (the exact amount due) because of interest, late charges and other charges that may vary from day to day the amount due on the day you pay may be greater. Hence, if you pay the amount shown above, an adjustment may be necessary after we receive your check, in which event we will inform you before depositing the check for collection. For further information write the undersigned or call 1-800-. . . .

A debt collector who uses this form, at least in the Seventh Circuit, will not violate the "amount of the debt" provision provided that the information furnished is accurate and is not obscured by adding other information.

Accordingly, at least in the Seventh Circuit, when you state the amount of debt, include the interest and other charges as well as the principal. Some case law holds the letter need not break down the other charges for the information of the consumer if it is a credit card debt. The interest and late charges have to be determined as of the date that appears on the letter.[34] One court has held that a specific date can be used.

---

[34]*Miller v. McCalla, Raymer, Padrick, Cobb, Nicholas, and Clark*, 2000 U.S. App. LEXIS 18232 (7th Cir. July 26, 2000); *Williams v. OSI Educational Servs., Inc.*, 505 F.3d 675 (7th Cir. 2007); *Schletz v. Academy Collection Serv., Inc.*, 2003 U.S. Dist. LEXIS 8527 (N.D. Ill. May 13, 2003).

A letter in a case in Minnesota stated that the "amount referred was $44.11." The court held that this did not state the amount of the debt, but merely stated the amount that was referred. In this particular instance, the amount of the debt was $24.11 and there was a $20 check charge. Notwithstanding the fact that the debtor paid the debt, the court quipped that an unsophisticated consumer should not be required to consult a dictionary to determine that "amount referred" really means the debt owed.[35]

We have another case from the Seventh Circuit which found a creditor liable for a violation of the FDCPA by virtue of the description of the amount of the debt. The notice described the amount of the claimed debt as "remaining principal balance $1,050 plus reasonable attorney fees as permitted by law and costs if allowed by the court."

The amount of attorneys' fees and the court costs had not yet been awarded. The amounts should have been separated from the amount of the debt. Stating the amount of the debt is designed to inform the debtor of what the current obligation is, not what the final worst case scenario could be.

Since the debtor could not be liable for the court costs or attorneys' fees until a judgment was rendered, costs and attorneys' fees are not the remaining balance. The judge apparently concluded the debtor could not read English since the letter stated the "attorney fees permitted by law" and "costs if allowed by the court." While nothing out of the Seventh Circuit surprises the authors, we do share the frustration of the creditor.[36]

Unfortunately, the Second Circuit in 2003 followed the Seventh Circuit decision and creditors will have to include interest or other charges itemizing the debt.[37]

Use of "Plaintiff" and "Defendant." Wording in the collection letter of "plaintiff v. defendant" where no suit has been started constitutes a misrepresentation under the Act, just as a letter threatening to garnishee the salary is a misrepresentation. If no judgment has been entered, do not use "v." or "vs.".

Prelegal Department. The FTC frowns on using a "prelegal department" heading on a letter unless a prelegal department is organized within the collection agency or law firm. Distinguishing a "prelegal department" from a "collection department" or a "legal department" is difficult,

---

[35]*McDowall v. Leschack P. Grodensky*, 279 F. Supp. 2d 197 (S.D.N.Y. 2003); *Armstrong v. The Rose Law Firm*, No. CIV. 00-2287 MJD/SRN (D. Minn. Mar. 25, 2002.

[36]*Fields v. Wilber Law Firm, P.C.*, 383 F.3d 562 (7th Cir. 2004); *Singer v. Pierce & Assocs., P.C.*, 383 F.3d 596 (7th Cir. 2004); *Veach v. Sheeks*, 316 F.3d 690 (7th Cir. 2003).

[37]*McDowall v. Leschak and Grodensky*, 276 F. Supp. 2d 434 (S.D.N.Y. 2003)); *Rosenau v. Unifund Corp.*, 539 F.3d 218 (3d Cir. 2008).

and special divisions of authority and activity would have to be designated. The recommendation is not to use such terminology.[38]

Misrepresenting Use of Attorney. Where a party is not an attorney, the representation that an individual is an attorney or that any communication is from an attorney is false. A creditor should not use an attorney's name in a collection effort when the attorney has not authorized the use of the name and is not supervising the collection effort (*see* Appendix to this chapter). A collection agency should not use the CEO to falsely imply his involvement in the case as that would be a violation.

Threat of Arrest. A statement that nonpayment of the debt may result in the arrest or imprisonment of any person or the seizure, garnishee, attachment, or sale of any property or wages is unlawful and a threat that the debt collector intends to take such action is a false representation.

Threatening to put the debtor in jail if the debt is not paid is expressly prohibited. In the Middle Ages, debtors were imprisoned if they were unable to pay their debts. The only way the debtor could leave prison was to persuade a friend or relative to pay the debt, and then the debtor would pay the debt to the friend or relative (usually by working off the debt over many years). Today, the alternative to "debtor's prison" is bankruptcy.[39]

Criminal Penalties for Issuing a Bad Check. Most states provide criminal penalties if an individual *intentionally* issues a check that is returned unpaid. Since many consumers are aware of this law, some debt collectors threaten to arrest a debtor if a check has been returned unpaid (*see* Chapter 8). The Act expressly prohibits such gross deception unless the debtor committed a crime and the debt collector intends to prosecute that crime (*see* Chapter 8).

Threatening Action that Is Not Intended. The threat to take any action that cannot legally be taken or is not intended to be taken is the most important of the 16 examples of prohibited activities and produces the most problems for creditor and debt collector. The area covered is comprehensive: Every firm must be careful not to be entrapped by the pitfalls of this subdivision.

Threatening to report a returned check to the police department is a violation unless the intent is to prosecute criminally, and the check actually is reported to the police department. The same rules apply to a threat to report a debt to a credit bureau.

---

[38] *Wallace v. Winston & Morrone, P.C.*, 95-C-354-C USDC (W.D. Wis. Oct. 30, 1996).
[39] *Goins v. JBC Assocs., P.C.*, 2004 U.S. Dist. LEXIS 18413 (D. Conn. Sept. 3, 2004).

In a recent case the court held that a deception in the letter which creates a threat to take action that cannot be legally taken is also a violation.[40]

The commentary states that "a debt collector may state that certain action is possible, if it is true that such action is legal and is frequently taken by the collector or creditor with respect to similar debts; however, if the debt collector has reason to know there are facts that make the action unlikely in the particular case, a statement that the action was possible would be misleading."

The same reasoning applies to a threat that legal action has been recommended and will be taken when no such recommendation was made. To support a recommendation for suit, evidence must exist that the creditor will act on the recommendation at least some of the time. Lack of intent may be inferred when the amount of the debt is so small that the action is not economical or at least when the debt collector is unable to take the action because the creditor has not authorized the action. Threatening suit within a certain period of time or threatening immediate referral to an outside collection agency is deceptive unless the time frames are met. For example, threatening a referral in two weeks and actually referring it two months later misleads the consumer as to urgency. If the claim is never referred to an agency, a misrepresentation is also committed.

Least Sophisticated Consumer. In situations where the courts try to determine whether the consumer is being misled or deceived by a threat of suit or some other action, the courts use the test of "the least sophisticated consumer." The courts try to protect those "debtors on the low side of reasonable capacity who read a given notice or hear a given statement and read into the message oppressiveness, falsehood or threat."[41]

Transfer of Debt. The false representation that a sale or transfer of a debt shall cause the consumer to lose a defense is prohibited. Under the Credit Practices Act, and under many state laws, the sale of a debt will not cut off the defenses of the consumer and the consumer may still allege those defenses in a suit by the purchaser of the debt. This section applies to an assignment of the creditor's claim to a collection agency (*see* Chapter 5).

False Credit Information. To communicate or threaten to communicate to any person credit information, which is known or which should be known to be false is a violation. Failure to communicate to a credit reporting agency that a debt is disputed may also be a violation (*see* Chapter 13).

---

[40] *In re Cambron*, 379 B.R. 371 (Bankr. M.D. Ala. 2007).

[41] *Jeter v. Credit Bureau*, 760 F.2d 1168 (11th Cir. 1985); *Bingham v. Collection Bureau Inc.*, 505 F. Supp. 864 (D.N.D. 1981).

Simulated Legal Process. This section is targeted at simulated legal process where the documents sent to the consumer imply a summons and complaint, or other official document, and is not a summons and complaint.

Deceit to Collect Debt. The use of any false representation or deceptive means to collect or attempt to collect any debt, or to obtain any information concerning a consumer, is expressly prohibited. *This is the most comprehensive subdivision of the section and is a "catchall" to cover any misrepresentation, the nature and purpose of which is to deceive the debtor.* If a facsimile of a Western Union telegram is used as a collection letter, a misrepresentation occurs because the consumer is deceived into believing a sense of urgency exists. A statement in the letter that "a failure to respond is an admission of liability" is a deception.

A statement in the letter requesting information about the assets and wages of the debtor implies that the debtor's assets and wages may be in jeopardy. Testimony that the purpose of the language was to attempt to obtain information on the debtors, reasoning the debtors who are employed and have assets are more likely to pay their debt, was found to be deceptive by the court. The court found the communication misleading because the debtor would conclude that his wages and property were in jeopardy and that he was being coerced into paying the debt.[42]

Credit & Collection Tip: *Any deception or misrepresentation is covered by this general section.*

Mini-Miranda Warning. This section requires a disclosure in *all communications* of the following phrase: "This is an attempt to collect the debt and any information will be used for that purpose" (mini-Miranda warning). This would apply to both *oral* and *written* communication. *The disclosure must be in all communications including telephone calls, face-to-face meetings, letters, balance letters, explanatory letters, or other communications between the consumer and the debt collector.* The print should be legible and at least as large as the typewritten portion of the letter. There are some state statutes that require the disclosure statement to be in at least 10-point type.

The FTC commentary states that this mini-Miranda phrase must be in the first communication with the debtor, but not in subsequent communications. Nevertheless, several federal courts have disagreed with the FTC and require that this warning be in all communications, both oral and written. (One federal court agrees with the FTC.) (See *Credit & Collection Tip:* below).

---

[42]*In re Cambron*, 379 B.R. 371 (Bankr. M.D. Ala. 2007).

An amendment to the FDCPA reads as follows:

> The failure to disclose in the initial written communication with the consumer, and, in addition, if the initial communication with the consumer is oral, in that initial oral communication, that the debt collector is attempting to collect a debt and that any further information obtained will be used for that purpose and the failure to disclose in subsequent communications that *the communication is from a debt collector*, except that this paragraph shall not apply to a formal pleading made in connection with a legal action. (Emphasis added.)

After the first communication, whether it is oral or in writing, the mini-Miranda warning is not required. The major advantage for collection agencies is that no mini-Miranda warning is required after the first letter if the letterhead of the collection agency sets forth sufficient wording to indicate that the sender of the letter is a collection agency. If the letterhead of the collection agency refers to the fact that it is a collection agency, such as "ABC Collection Agency," this new statement will not be necessary in subsequent letters since the consumer knows who the sender of the letter is. If the name of the collection agency does not contain the necessary words to indicate to the debtor that the communication is from a debt collector, the collection agency will have to include in the body of the letter or at some other conspicuous place the statement that "This communication is from a debt collector."

With regard to law firms, the FTC has taken the position that the letterhead of an attorney is not sufficient to communicate to a debtor that the communication is from a debt collector. Therefore, on each subsequent written or oral communication, the attorney will have to include either a written statement or an oral statement that "This communication is from a debt collector."

> ***Credit & Collection Tip:*** *A problem also arises with omitting the mini-Miranda warning in all subsequent communications since many states still require the mini-Miranda warning in each communication. They include Colorado, Connecticut, District of Columbia, Hawaii, Idaho, Iowa, Maine, Michigan, North Carolina, Oregon, and Texas. Each of the states requires some form of the mini-Miranda warning in either the initial written communication or in oral communications, or sets forth other specified requirements. An examination of each state law should be made before the elimination of the mini-Miranda warning. As a result of these requirements by the various states, most law firms and many of the collection agencies are still including the mini-Miranda warning in all communications, both oral and written, until such time as the states begin to repeal the requirement. The best approach for communication after the first communication is to use both the Mini-Miranda warning and the new statement required by the 1996 amendment in all contacts with the debtor.*

A case in the Tenth Circuit addressing the question of a communication to the attorney for the debtor held that failure to include a mini-Miranda warning is not a violation of the Act when there is no evidence that the collection agency was attempting to mislead the attorney, and when it was fairly clear to the attorney from all the facts of the communication (and in this case, oral) that the collection agency was trying to collect a debt.[43] But your author still recommends inclusion of the warning despite some recent cases which follow this reasoning.

As the consumer attorneys fail in one area of the law, they rise again and attack another technical violation of the FDCPA. In a recent case in 2007 a claim was made that the debt collector did not expressly identify himself as a debt collector during the message. The defendants on the other hand contended that a debt collector is only required to identify himself when the debt collector "initiates" the telephone call, not when the debt collector receives the call.[44]

A recent case six months later stated that the *Biggs* case failed to consider Congress's intent that calls for a broad construction of the FDCPA in favor of the consumer. In *Biggs* the court held that plaintiff's answering machine may be considered an indirect communication. The *Biggs* court felt that the "words" in the voice mail determines whether it conveyed information regarding the debt which would bring it within the statutory definition of "communication." The court in the *Rameriz* case relied on the broad interpretation in favor of the consumer.[45]

The Fair Debt Collection Practices Act does state that the debt collector must disclose that he is attempting to collect a debt and failing to disclose in subsequent communications that the communication is from a debt collector is a violation of the statute.

The defendant argued that the plaintiff knew he was a debt collector because plaintiff called the debt collector up with the telephone number of the debt collector. The court came to a conclusion that the particular message in question conveyed no information regarding a debt and was not covered by the FDCPA.

We have always maintained that in all communications you should utilize the mini-Miranda warning (this is an attempt to collect a debt) and identify yourself as a debt collector. That will prevent future lawsuits. The plaintiff submitted some persuasive arguments and this fact situation will be presented again to the court.

> ***Credit & Collection Tip:*** *While another court may render a different decision, the FDCPA states that the debt collector must identify himself in all communications with the debtor, whether oral, in writing or otherwise.*

---

[43] *Dikeman v. National Educators, Inc.*, 81 F.3d 949 (10th Cir. 1996). *See Biggs v. Credit Collections, Inc.*, 2007 U.S. Dist. LEXIS 84793 (W.D. Okla. Nov. 15, 2007).

[44] *Biggs v. Credit Collections Inc.*, 2007 WL 4034997 (W.D. Okla. Nov. 15, 2007).

[45] *Ramirez v. Apex Financial Management, LLC*, 567 F. Supp. 2d 1035 (N.D. Ill. 2008).

Use of Form of Governmental Communications. Using return addresses and the form or shape of envelopes indicating that the communication is being mailed from a governmental office, when such is not the case, is prohibited under the Section.

Use of Another Name. A debt collector must use the same name consistently when dealing with the consumer. The use of any business, company, or organization name other than the true name of the debt collector's business, company, or organization is prohibited. This section is not only directed at a debt collector, but is also targeted at the creditor.

A creditor may not use any name that would falsely imply that a third party is involved in the collection. If the creditor creates a collection agency which is a shell with no assets and no employees, but maintains an address different from the creditor, the consumer is misled to believe another firm is collecting other than the creditor. If a collection agency is controlled by the creditor as to staff, procedure, and contents, the agency becomes an alter ego of the creditor and the creditor is using someone else's name to collect the debt.

MATERIALITY

The court stated we do not see any reason why materiality should not equally be required in an action based on Section 1692e. The statute is designed to provide information that helps consumers to choose intelligently, and by definition immaterial information neither contributes to that objective if the statement is correct nor undermines it if the statement is incorrect.

The court also stated that "if a statement would not mislead the unsophisticated consumer, it does not violate (Act)—even if it is false in some technical sense." A statement cannot mislead unless it is material, so a false but a non-material statement is not actionable.[46]

MISREPRESENTING LEGAL DOCUMENTS

Debtor: I just received some papers left at the door. Your name was on them.

Creditor: You can ignore them. Now, about the debt.

---

[46] *Hahn v. Triumph Partnership*, 557 F.3d 755 (7th Cir. 2009); *Carter v. United States*, 530 U.S. 255 (2000).

The false representation or implication that documents are *not* legal process or do not require action by the consumer, where the consumer was lead to believe that a summons and complaint was not served (when, in fact, the consumer was served), and, therefore, no defense or answer was required is prohibited.

ATTORNEY'S LETTERHEAD

Two cases in the Seventh Circuit resulted in decisions that a lawyer's letterhead does not carry an implicit threat of suit. The court categorically stated that

> This argument is equally frivolous. If this statement were true, every collection letter from an attorney would be subject to an FDCPA action in order to determine whether the attorney actually intended to take legal action at the time the initial validation notice was sent. Clearly, this was not the intent of Congress when it enacted FDCPA.[47]

Your author's firm was the defendant in one case.

MEANINGFUL INVOLVEMENT—COLLECTION AGENCY

Two cases were decided a few months apart. The first case set forth in detail what participation by a collection agency is necessary so that a creditor shall not be deemed to be the actual debt collector and, therefore, subject to liability. The court specified the following situations as evidence that the agency is not meaningfully involved:

1. The collection agency is a mere mailing service or performs only ministerial functions.
2. The letter states that if the debtor does not pay, the debt will be referred for collection.
3. The collection agency is paid merely for sending letters rather than a percentage of debts collected.
4. The collection agency does not receive any payments or forwards all payments to the creditor.

---

[47] *Sturdevant v. Thomas E. Jolas, P.C.*, 942 F. Supp. 426 (W.D. Wis. 1996). *Wallace v. Winston & Morrone, P.C.*, 95-C-354-C USDC (W.D. Wis. Oct. 30, 1996).

5. If the debtor fails to respond to the letters, the collection agency has no further contact with the debtor, or the creditor decides whether to pursue collection.
6. The collection agency does not receive the files of the debtor.
7. The collection agency never discusses with the creditor the collection process or what steps should be taken with certain debtors.
8. The collection agency cannot initiate phone calls to the debtor.
9. Correspondence received by the collection agency is forwarded to the creditor.
10. The collection agency has no authority to negotiate collection of the debts.
11. The letters do not state the collection agency's address or phone number.
12. The letter directs questions or payments to the creditor.
13. The creditor has substantial control over the content of the letters.

On the other hand, the court laid out the evidence that indicates a creditor is not acting as a debt collector:

1. The collection agency provides traditional debt collection services for the creditor, such as direct contact with debtors, locating debtors' assets, and referrals to collection attorneys.
2. Accounts remain with the collection agency if the debtor does not pay after the receipt of a letter.
3. The collection agency has authority to decide to pursue debts that remain unpaid after letters are sent.
4. The collection agency provides follow-up services.
5. The creditor pays only for successful collection efforts.
6. The creditor exercises only limited control over the collection agency.
7. The collection agency retains information about the debtors.
8. The letter states the collection agency's telephone number and address.
9. The collection agency drafts the letters.
10. The collection agency collects debts for others.
11. The collection agency answers debtors' inquiries.
12. The collection agency recommends how to pursue debtors.

The court, after examining what the creditor did in the particular case, held that the creditor is solely a creditor and not subject to the liability of the FDCPA. It is interesting that the courts laid out 13 items that show that the creditor is participating in the collection of the debt and 12 items that show that the creditor is not participating in the collection of the debt. Unfortunately, the court has not set forth any black-and-white numerical formula for determining whether or not a creditor is liable under the FDCPA. When a court sets forth formula criteria to make a determination, other judges latch onto these simple formulas but often apply them in different ways. What is important about this case is that the judge then considered eight different activities of the collection agency and made a decision, based on these eight activities, that the creditor was not liable.

In the second case involving the same hospital, the court found that the hospital was not a debt collector and liable under the FDCPA. This case was decided only three months after the prior case in 1999. The judge in this case cited the criteria that were used in the prior case and stated candidly that he was persuaded by the prior judge's reasoning and, for the same reason, he decided that the hospital creditor was not liable. Now we have two cases that have utilized these criteria set forth by Judge Norgel and we have a feeling that these criteria will receive attention in other cases. We therefore recommend to creditors in the Seventh Circuit that they read these criteria carefully.[48]

From the Seventh Circuit, a comforting decision was rendered by Chief Judge Posner of the Circuit Court of Appeals. This decision by Judge Posner and the wording of the decision is probably the most comforting decision that your author has read in the past ten years, especially out of the Seventh Circuit. One must remember that the Seventh Circuit has always been the most liberal circuit. More decisions come out of the western district and the northern district of the Seventh Circuit than any other districts in the country on FDCPA, and a disproportionate number have been favorable to consumers. The author recommends the decision to any agency faced with a lawsuit on these grounds.[49]

The *Martsolf* decision in 2008 and the *Hammer* decision in 2009 indicate the trend in two recent meaningful involvement cases, one in Pennsylvania and one in California.[50]

ATTORNEY. Meaningful involvement means that a consumer is entitled to believe an attorney is personally involved in the collection of the debt. The representation that an individual is an attorney or that any communication is from an attorney is false. A creditor should not use an attorney's name in a collection effort where the attorney is not authorized and is not supervising the collection effort. The pertinent section of the FDCPA is

---

[48] *Morency v. Evanston Northwestern Healthcare Corp.*, No. 98 C 8436, 1999 WL 754713 (N.D. Ill. Sept. 14, 1999); *Larson v. Evanston Northwestern Healthcare Corp.*, No. 98 C 0005, 1999 WL 518901 (N.D. Ill. July 19, 1999).

[49] *White v. Goodman*, No. 98-4180, 98-4328, 98-4329 CA (7th Cir. Jan. 11, 2000).

[50] *Martsolf v. JBC Legal Group, P.C.*, 2008 U.S. Dist. LEXIS 6876 (M.D. Pa. Jan. 30, 2008); *Palmer and Hammer v. Stassinos*, 2009 U.S. Dist. LEXIS 4265 (N.D. Cal. 2009).

as follows (*see* in-depth analysis article and update by Jay Winston in Appendix VI to this chapter):

> Section 807—A debt collector may not use any false, deceptive, or misleading representation or means in connection with the collection of any debt.
>
> Without limiting the general application of the foregoing, the following conduct is a violation of this section:
>
> 1. . . .
> 2. . . .
> 3. the false representation or implication that any individual is an attorney or that any communication is from an attorney;
>
> 10. the use of any false representation of deceptive means to collect or attempt to collect any debt or to obtain information concerning a consumer.

Subdivision 10 is a catchall phrase of Section 807 entitled "False and Misleading Representations." If a misrepresentation is made to a consumer, a violation of the Act takes place. This concept has developed over the years primarily from the first major case that was decided by the Second Circuit Court of Appeals in 1993. Thereafter a few short years later, in 1996, the Seventh Circuit followed the Second Circuit's decision. From these two decisions, the concept of "meaningful involvement" was born. From 1996 until 2002, most of the other decisions were devoted to interpreting the two Circuit Court of Appeals decisions in the Second and Seventh Circuits. In 2002, the Seventh Circuit addressed the issue again, actually twice, and fully expanded their view of conducting mass mailings by collection attorneys. The Second Circuit in 2003 boarded the train and made it even more difficult for attorneys to conduct mass mailings. The article was updated by a second article in 2006. (*See* Appendix to this chapter.)

> ***Credit & Collection Tip:*** *One of the co-authors, Jay Winston, has written an extensive analysis of the doctrine of "meaningful involvement," which appears in an Appendix to this chapter. He offers some unique and creative approaches to defending an FDCPA lawsuit based on a failure of an attorney being meaningfully involved and cites many of the pertinent cases mentioned.*

Disavowment. In *Pujol vs. Universal Fidelity Corporation,*[51] and *Greco v. Trauner, Cohen & Thomas LLP et al.,*[52] two Second Circuit district court judges held that attorneys who *disavowed* any review of the account did not violate the FDCPA.

---

[51]2004 U.S. Dist. LEXIS 10556 (E.D. June 9, 2004); *Gonzalez v. Kay*, 2008 WL 2405978 (S.D. Tex. 2008).

[52]03-CV-6352 (W.D. July 12, 2004) [Unpublished].

In the letter stated in pertinent part:

> Do not consider this letter a notification of intent to sue, since I do not have the legal authority to sue. I have not, nor will I, review each detail of your account status, unless you so request.

In *Greco*, the letter stated in pertinent part:

> At this time, no attorney with this firm has personally reviewed the particular circumstances of your account.

In granting summary judgment in favor of the defendant, the judges cited *Clomon v. Jackson*[53] and found no violation *because there was no affirmative misrepresentation.*

The reader should remember that *Clomon v. Jackson* involved a situation in which a collection agency prepared and mailed over 1 million letters a year with the letterhead of a part-time attorney. *The attorney's role was symbolic as he merely lent his name to the collection agency that controlled the entire process.* Preparing the form of the letter was insufficient. The *Clomon* court considered two issues. First, that he "played virtually no day-to-day role in the debt collection process."[54] Second, a violation occurred because the attorney affirmatively represented his personal involvement in the text of the letters, when none existed.

[T]he use of an attorney's signature on a collection letter [in connection with the text] implies that the letter is "from" the attorney who signed it; it implies, in other words, that the attorney directly controlled or supervised the process through which the letter was sent.[55]

Clomon did not ban mass mailings.[56] The court held that an attorney cannot affirmatively mislead a consumer into believing that he or she is involved in the process, and then delegate the collection process to a third party (that is, collection agency). The violation was not the mass mailing, but a mass mailing of an affirmatively deceptive letter.[57] The court was deeply concerned about the "absent attorney" situation, who delegates his decision-making authority to the staff of another corporation citing, *The Complete Guide to Credit and Collection Law 2004 Edition* (Aspen Publishers 2004).

---

[53] 988 F.2d 1314 (2d Cir. 1993).

[54] *Clomon*, 988 F.2d 1314, 1320.

[55] 988 F.2d. 1314, 1321.

[56] *Clomon v. Jackson*, 988 F.2d 1314 (2d Cir. 1993). The decision followed the same proposition and ruled that when an attorney implies in the text of the letter, attorney review, the attorneys need to be personally involved, need to supervise and control the collection process on a day-to-day basis, utilize non-legal staff, and rely on the recommendation of others. *See Stinson v. Asset Acceptance, LLC*, 2006 U.S. Dist. LEXIS 42266 (E.D. Va. June 12, 2006), *vacated*, 2006 U.S. Dist. LEXIS 58865 (E.D. Va. July 17, 2006).

[57] Many consumer attorneys allege that the acts stated by the court (i.e., reviewing the file, determining who should be sent letters, etc.) were a specific list of requirements. This conclusion is incorrect. When defending these cases, attorneys should quote the above paragraph, and include the decision as an exhibit to demonstrate that the judge was showing what was not done, as opposed to what was required to be performed.

The judges in *Pujol & Greco* avoided the meaningful involvement analysis, by relying on the phrase from *Clomon* "in absence language to the contrary." Consequently, in *Pujol & Greco*, there was no violation, because there was no affirmative misrepresentation. They affirmatively disavowed involvement and that ended the court's analysis. These two decisions adhere to the proposition that the judges carefully examine the text of the letter, base their decisions on the text of the letters, and look for affirmative misrepresentations, as opposed to silent omissions.

> ***Credit & Collection Tip:*** *For those readers more interested in this issue, they can review our 18-page detailed analysis on how to defend meaningful involvement lawsuits (See Appendix to this chapter).*

A recent case in Ohio is a pleasure to read, but whether any other courts will follow the case, even in Ohio, is questionable.[58]

Two recent cases in 2007 in the Eastern District of Pennsylvania illustrate that the judicial system is not sure which road to travel on the issue of meaningful involvement.[59] Statements in both letters set forth that the corporate officers named in the letters were not personally involved with the collection activity of the specific accounts. One case held that the names, as well as the titles of the officers, were enough to indicate that the officers were meaningfully involved in the collection effort. How the court came to this conclusion in view of the statement that the corporate officer had not reviewed the account (and therefore were not meaningfully involved) is difficult to understand. Another case in Pennsylvania stated that the typewritten signature of an officer violates the Fair Debt Collection Practices Act and basically drew the opposite conclusion.

Fortunately, several cases seem to support the use of disclaimer language in a letter stating that the typewritten name of an attorney does not necessarily mean he was meaningfully involved if he specifically states in the letter that *he has not reviewed the account.* Hopefully, this is a renegade case which will not be followed elsewhere.

Fortunately, some judges do recognize the difference between officers of collection agencies and attorneys. At least the Third Circuit stated that the officers are not attorneys.

The court stated: "Analogizing senior executives to lawyers, as the district court did, was not appropriate. Corporate executives have no more direct access to legal proceedings than other laymen."[60]

---

[58]*Kistner v. Law Offices of Michael B. Margelefsky, LLC*, 2007 U.S. Dist. LEXIS 1925 (N.D. Ohio Jan. 10, 2007).

[59]*Womack v. National Action Fin. Servs.*, 2007 WL 2155669 (E.D. Pa. July 25, 2007); *Campuzano-Burgos v. Midland Credit Mgmt.*, 497 F. Supp. 2d 660 (E.D. Pa. 2007); *Kistner v. Law Offices of Michael P. Margelefsky*, 518 F.3d 433 (6th Cir. 2008).

[60]*Womack v. National Action Fin. Servs.*, 2007 WL 2155669 (E.D. Pa. 2007); *Crossly v. Lieberman*, 818 F.2d 566 (3d Cir. 1989).

The state has given lawyers certain privileges such as the ability to file a lawsuit not available to lay debt collectors. Debtors react more quickly to an attorney's communication because they believe that "a real lawyer, acting like a lawyer usually acts, directly controls or supervises the process through which such a letter was sent."[61]

UNFAIR PRACTICES

A debt collector may not use unfair or unconscionable means to collect or attempt to collect a debt. The FTC has provided eight examples of unfair or unconscionable means to collect a debt, but other acts may qualify for inclusion. The Commission has defined an unfair debt practice as one that causes injury to the consumer that is (*see* Appendix to this chapter—Commentary):

A. substantial;
B. not outweighed by countervailing benefits to consumers or competition; and
C. not reasonably avoidable by the consumer.

The following are some examples of unfair or unconscionable methods of collecting a debt.

Collection of Charges. The collection of any incidental charges to the collection of a debt is prohibited unless said amount is expressly authorized by the agreement creating the debt or permitted by law. This prohibition includes the collection of late charges, interest charges, finance charges, or service charges, unless they are expressly set forth in the agreement that created a debt. In a loan situation, the agreement creating a debt would be the originating loan document. In the purchase of goods at a retail store, the charges are to be displayed at the point of purchase. If the goods are purchased by direct mail, the charges would have to be displayed in the order form contained in the catalog or the promotional direct marketing piece. If the purchase is made by telephone, the charges are to be disclosed over the telephone at the same time the purchase is made.

Bad Check Charges. Prior to the enactment of the FDCPA, creditors commonly charged the consumer the fee the bank charged the creditor when the consumer's check was returned unpaid. Such a charge is prohibited under this section, unless it is clearly specified at the time of purchase

[61] *Avila v. Rubin*, 84 F.3d 222 (7th Cir. 1996); *Campuzano-Burgos v. Midland Credit Mgmt.*, 550 F.3d 294 (3d Cir. 2008).

that there will be a charge in the event that a check is returned unpaid or permitted by law.[62]

In some states, bad check charges are allowed by state law. If it is not authorized by state law, the charge cannot be collected unless contained in the agreement creating the debt.

Excessive charges of any type are unconscionable and cannot be collected notwithstanding a written agreement to pay these charges. If "reasonable attorneys' fees" are used, the fees must be reasonable and must be determined by the law of the state in which the contract is entered or is enforced. If bad check charges are allowed, the charges must comply with the law. Shipping and handling charges may not be excessive. Restocking charges must be reasonable.

Service charges. The FDCPA prohibits a debt collector from collecting any service charge unless such amount is expressly authorized by the agreement creating the debt or permitted by law. This case took place in Connecticut and ultimately ended up as a jury trial and was appealed to the Circuit Court of Appeals of the Second Circuit after the jury found for the check guarantee firm because the charge to the jury was improper.

The magic words were "otherwise resulting from the breach." The court held the statute permitted Equifax to impose its service charge pursuant to its agreement with the merchant. The service charge is for incidental damages to the extent that it offsets the collection expenses arising from the dishonored check and the $20 charge could be deemed to be commercially reasonable by the jury.[63]

Credit Card Payments. Some collection agencies and attorneys have offered consumers the right to make their payment by use of a credit card rather than the use of a check or cash. Certain risks are present in offering a credit card option to consumers by collection agencies or attorneys.

As a general rule, the banks which are licensed by Visa and MasterCard are prohibited or discouraged from entering into merchant agreements with firms which collect delinquent accounts. The Visa and MasterCard agreements generally provide that the bank must enter into an agreement with the party selling the product or offering the service. The collection agency or attorney offers this option and then sends the authorization directly to the client and the client processes the payment through their agreement with the bank. A further option to the collection agency or attorney is to process the payment through one of the third party agencies who process credit card charges for a fee for those businesses which are unable to persuade a bank to enter into an agreement with them because of

---

[62] *West v. Costen*, 558 F. Supp. 564 (W.D. Va. 1983).

[63] *Tuttle v. Equifax Check Servs.*, 190 F.3d 9 (2d Cir. 1999).

financial problems or other business reasons. For example, banks are reluctant to enter into merchant agreements with recently organized direct marketing firms who are selling by telemarketing or catalogs.

Permitting the consumer to use a credit card is merely substituting one debt for another debt and the substituted debt carries interest and other charges which were not incurred in the original sale of the product or service. This additional charge violates the FDCPA section prohibiting any additional charges except in the agreement creating the debt.

The American Collectors Association reported a decision in the Sixth Circuit Court of Appeals which upheld a collection agency's practice of accepting payment by credit card, even where the collection agency required the consumer to pay the 5 percent transaction fee associated with such payment, on the theory that the debtor had the option.[64] But the decision leaves some unanswered questions on this uncomfortable practice, which may be tested in the courts again.

Another risk is that the bank, when it becomes aware that these charges are being processed by the collection agency or attorney, will declare it to be a violation of the original agreement between the bank and the merchant. If the merchant is a substantial customer, it is unlikely that the bank will declare the agreement null and void for a breach of contract, but a new customer may encounter problems.

A similar situation occurs where the collection agency uses check-by-phone. Most check-by-phone operators charge a transaction fee. Some collection agencies pass this transaction fee on to the customer and add it to the balance due. In some instances, the charge is under a dollar and in other instances it may be several dollars. This is similar to the transfer of a balance to a credit card where an additional charge is imposed on the debtor which was not in the original agreement creating the debt. On the other hand with check-by-phone, the debtor has no choice but to pay the additional transaction charge.

In the course of research for one of our cases, we found an unpublished case addressing the issue of whether accepting a credit card transaction to pay a debt is a FDCPA violation. Our case was in direct contradiction of *Lee v. Maine Accounts.* The activities of the collection agency were false and misleading since no authority was granted by Visa or Master Card to engage in the transaction and a fee for the transaction was unfair and unconscionable. Unfortunately, both cases are unpublished decisions and we still do not have a published case upon which to rely. Another question left open is whether the transaction is a violation of the Unfair Practices Acts of the states.[65]

---

[64]*Lee v. Main Accounts*, 125 F.3d 855 (6th Cir. 1997); *Miller v. Credit Collection Serv.*, 49 Fed. R. Serv. 3d 1243 (S.D. Ohio Sept. 18, 2000).

[65]*Miller v. Credit & Collection Serv.*, 49 Fed. R. Serv. 3d 1243 (S.D. Ohio Sept. 18, 2000).

Credit & Collection Tip: *Until there is a definitive decision in this area, any debt collector who is pursuing these types of practices is running the risk of testing the water and having the court decide a case of first impression.*

POST-DATED CHECKS. Creditors sometimes accept post-dated checks, that is, checks that are dated at some future date, and thus cannot be deposited until said date. An example would be a debtor who owes $400 and offers the creditor four checks for $100, each dated one month apart starting on January 1 and ending on April 1 to pay the debt in full. (*See* Chapter 8.)

The acceptance from any person of a check post-dated by more than five days is not allowed unless such person is notified in writing of the intent to deposit such check. If a check is post-dated more than five days, the debt collector must give the consumer notice by mail in writing of the debt collector's intention to deposit the checks at least three and not more than ten days prior to such deposit.

This section applies only to debts covered by the FDCPA (*see* Appendix to this chapter). Absent a state law, business checks do not have this limitation.

Since a bank will refuse to accept a check for deposit prior to its date, threatening to deposit or depositing a post-dated check prior to the date is an unfair practice.

STOP PAYMENT. In a case in the Seventh Circuit, the court held that there is no authority in the statute for a collection agency to charge a consumer a fee on a check upon which payment was stopped. Many states' statutes allow fees for checks that are returned for insufficient funds or uncollected funds but there is no provision for the situation where the check is marked "payment stopped." Since there was no authority for such a fee, charging such a fee violates the FDCPA.[66]

The Tenth Circuit Court of Appeals has now held that the payment obligations arising from bounced checks constitute a debt within the meaning of the FDCPA and any collection effort on a bad check is covered by the FDCPA.[67]

TELEPHONE CHARGES. The true purposes of a communication may not be concealed so that the consumer will incur a telephone or telegram charge. A debt collector may not call the consumer collect or ask a consumer to return the call long distance without first disclosing its identity and the purpose of the call. A collection call to a cell phone may also be a violation since the debtor may be incurring charges, although the authors know of no case addressing this point.

---

[66]*Ozkaya v. Telecheck Servs., Inc.*, 982 F. Supp. 578 (N.D. Ill. 1997).
[67]*Snow v. Riddle*, 143 F.3d 1350 (10th Cir. 1998).

Threatening to Take Property of Debtor—Secured Creditor. Section 808(b) of the Act states that the following is a violation:

Taking or threatening to take any nonjudicial action to effect dispossession or disablement of property is prohibited if:

A. there is no present right to possession of the property claimed as collateral through an enforceable security interest;

B. there is no present intention to take possession of the property; or

C. the property is exempt by law from such dispossession or disablement.

The FDCPA includes secured parties whose principal business is enforcing security interests *only for purposes of this subdivision.* The purpose of this section is to prevent someone from threatening to take possession of the property if there is:

A. no right to possession;

B. no present intention to take possession of the property;

C. the property is exempt by law.

The secured party, such as a bank, who has a lien on a boat or an automobile, cannot threaten to take possession unless it has a legal right to take possession, a present intent to take possession, and a valid security agreement.

Postcard. Communicating with the debtor by postcard is a violation of the Act because a postcard can be read by anyone. The use of a fax machine would depend upon whether other parties have access, but since the creditor does not know if a third party has access, its use is not recommended. E-mail presents other problems, and its use is also not recommended (*see* Chapter 17).

Envelopes. This subsection prohibits any writing other than the debt collector's name and address on the envelope unless the business name does not indicate a debt collection business. A debt collector may not use "debt" or "collector" or any other word that indicates the debt collection business. A transparent or window envelope is a violation if the collection notice is seen through the window or the transparency and several cases have been decided favorably to the consumer. "Personal or Confidential" on the envelope is permissible if sent to the home address of the consumer.[68] It is not permissible to use an envelope that contains "final demand for payment" in large print on the outside of the envelope.[69]

---

[68] *Masuda v. Thomas Richards and Co.*, 759 F. Supp. 1456 (C.D. Cal. 1991).

[69] *Kleczy v. First Federal Credit Control Inc.*, 486 N.E.2d 204 (Ohio Ct. App. 1984).

VALIDATION OF DEBT

Within five days of the first communication, the consumer must be given a written notice, if not provided in the original communication, containing the amount of the debt and the name of the creditor along with a statement that the debt will be assumed to be valid unless the consumer disputes it within 30 days. No requirements are set forth as to the form of the notice providing all the information is furnished. Subdivision b of the Act requires that if the consumer disputes the debt, the collector must cease collection efforts until the debt is verified and a response to the consumer is mailed. Failure by the consumer to dispute the debt may not be interpreted by a court as an admission of liability.

As a general rule, a debt collector does not need to establish that a validation notice was actually received by the debtor and a mere denial by the debtor that they did not receive the letter is insufficient as a matter of law to rebut the overall presumption of receipt.

> ***Credit & Collection Tip:*** *A suggestion might be that any letters that contain the validation notice and are returned as undeliverable should be retained in the file. In the event litigation develops, the letter marked undeliverable may be used.*[70]

Some attorneys have speculated that the amendments were not properly drafted and may expose the debt collector to additional liability.

The amendment that "a communication in the form of a formal pleading in a civil action shall not be treated as an initial communication for purposes of Subsection (a)" is offered as an example. The federal rules of civil procedure define pleadings as a complaint, an answer, or a reply to a counterclaim. It does not define "formal" pleading. The "formal" pleading term could limit the definition to just a complaint and that an answer or a reply to a counterclaim would not be considered a "formal" pleading. A motion or a petition may not be technically a "formal" pleading. If you commence the action with a petition rather than a complaint, the validation notice would have to be furnished within five days of service of the papers to be on the safe side.

Interestingly, a consumer contacting the attorney to settle the case conceivably could start the five day period running to send the validation notice.

> ***Credit & Collection Tip:*** *Send the 30-day letter reciting the validation word for word from the statute and do not serve the debtor until after 35th/36th day after mailing the letter to allow the consumer that 30-day period after he receives the letter. If the consumer does not receive the letter, it will be returned to you by the post office,*

---

[70] *Kimber v. Federal Fin. Corp.*, 668 F. Supp. 1480 (1987).

usually within the 36-day period. At that time confirm whether you have the proper address.

The validation notice (Section 809 of the FDCPA) must be included in the initial communication with the debtor. The mini-Miranda Warning (Section 807(11)) must be also included in the initial communication, and should be used in every communication with the debtor, whether by letter or telephone call, because many of the states require it in all communications (FDCPA only requires it in the initial written communication).

> ***Credit & Collection Tip:*** *The best advice is to consult with counsel before preparing boilerplate letters and before training staff with regard to telephone calls. Be certain that the attorney you retain is experienced in this area of the law.*

Disputed Debt. The defendant sent plaintiff a collection letter. The plaintiff disputed the validity of the debt, but *did not follow the statutory debt validation procedure set forth in the collection letter.* Instead, she filed a lawsuit alleging a violation of the FDCPA and relied solely on her allegation that the collection letter falsely stated that the debt was in arrears.

Plaintiff's reliance is not based on the failure to report the debt as disputed, because the defendant unilaterally determined that the plaintiff failed to establish the merits of her dispute. Plaintiff did not even allege that the defendant failed to notify the credit reporting agency that she made a payment or that it falsely reported the debt under a different entity name. Absent proof that the defendant reported plaintiff's debt to the credit bureau, no violation of the FDCPA occurred. The defendant did not have a duty to report the debt to the credit bureau or to report the dispute to the credit bureau.[71]

Summons as Communication. The validation notice does not prohibit collection activities during the 30-day period unless the debtor disputes the debt. Even after the debtor disputes the debt, the statute allows the debt collector to continue collection activities after mailing verification of the debt or a copy of the judgment, or the name and address of the original creditor, if the consumer requests it. The recent amendment now allows collection activity during the 30-day period (*see* Appendix to this chapter) without violating the right to dispute the debt, or requests for the name and address of the original creditor, and further that said activity or communication does not overshadow or be inconsistent with the disclosure to dispute the debt or request name and address of original creditor.

---

[71] *Showalter v. Asset Acceptance LLC*, 2007 U.S. Dist. LEXIS 78763 (E.D. Mich. Aug. 19, 2007).

Credit & Collection Tip: *The courts seem to say that no or little action should be taken during the 30-day period and the interpretation by the courts seem to be stretched to allowing the debtor a 30-day free grace period.*

Suit during the 30-day period is not a violation of the Act. The more recent decisions are allowing the debtor to dun during the 30-day period, providing the second letter is more in the nature of a reminder than a contradiction or overshadowing of the 30-day period to dispute the debt. How to carefully word the letter to avoid a violation is another situation. One case in the Sixth Circuit which allowed such a reminder letter may be worth mentioning. The second collection letter read as follows:

> Fourteen days have passed since Computer Credit's last communication with you and your seriously delinquent balance with the Miami Valley Hospital still remains unpaid. In the absence of a valid reason for nonpayment, this debt must be paid. If we are not notified that your debt has been paid before April 4, 1996 and if this debt is not disputed, we shall advise you of our final position regarding the status of your account.[72]

IMMEDIATE COLLECTION

The Second Circuit reversed a district court case which held in favor of the collection agency. The collection agency stated in its letter that it would place an account for "immediate collection" and that payment within ten days would prevent "the posting" of unpaid collections to debtor's credit record. A letter mailed 20 days later urged "payment in full" within five days.

The district court was liberal in granting summary judgment in favor of the collection agency, alleging that there was no "threatening contradiction" and that overshadowing did not take place because of the fact that the validation notice was not overshadowed by what was printed on the front side of the letter.

The Second Circuit, notorious for applying the Fair Debt Collections Practices Act on a strict liability basis, reversed and stated that conflicting statements existed in the letter and that the threat to "post" the debtor's payments was sufficient overshadowing.[73]

A recent case out of the Fifth Circuit held that markings on the outside of an envelope consisting of "priority letters" do not violate the FDCPA. They adopted the commentary of the FDCPA, which stated as follows:

> Under Harmless Words or Symbols: A debt collector does not violate this section by using an envelope with words or notations that do not suggest

---

[72] *Vega v. McKay*, 351 F.3d 1334 (11th Cir. 2003); *Smith v. Computer Credit Inc.*, 167 F.3d 1052 (6th Cir. 1999); *McKnight v. Benetez*, 176 F. Supp. 2d 1301 (M.D. Fla. 2001).

[73] *Russell v. Equifax*, A.R.S., 74 F.3d 30 (2d Cir. 1996).

> the purpose of the communication. For example, a collector may communicate via an actual telegram or similar service that uses a Western Union (or other provider) logo and the word telegram (or similar word) on the envelope, or a letter with the word "personal" or "confidential" on the envelope.

Although the court adopted the FTC Commentary's approach, it may be well to remind the reader that Commentary by the FTC is not binding on a court of law.[74]

CONTRADICTING 30-DAY PERIOD

Such phrases in the letter as "immediate full payment," "now," and "phone us today" have been held to contradict the 30-day period to dispute the debt, and constitute a violation of the Act.[75] A threat to sue if payment is not received in ten days also was deemed a violation.[76] The common thread in the decisions seems to be prohibiting (rather than limiting) the right to demand payment or threatening to sue before the expiration of the 30-day period.

> ***Credit & Collection Tip:*** *As a result, many collection agencies and law firms are conservatively writing a vanilla pure and simple non-threatening letter and taking no additional action during the 30-day period.*

Some cases have held that the type size of the validation notice must be the same type size as in the typewritten portion of the letter. If the letter should contain only capitalization, and the mini-Miranda warning and the validation are printed in small case print, the court may conclude that no notice existed since the notice was "overshadowed" by the general impression of the letter. Placing the disclosure and the validation notice on the reverse side compels the use of the phrase "see reverse side" on the front side of the letter and may cause overshadowing. Whether using the three words "see reverse side" is clear and conspicuous enough to advise the consumer that the reverse side will set forth the rights under the FDCPA has been questioned by various judges.[77] A clear and conspicuous "see reverse side" seems to satisfy the courts.

---

[74] *Goswami v. American Collections Enterprises, Inc.*, 377 F.3d 488 (5th Cir. 2004).
[75] *Miller v. Payco General American Credits, Inc.*, 943 F.2d 482 (4th Cir. 1991).
[76] *Graziano v. Harrison*, 950 F.2d 107 (3d Cir. 1991).
[77] *Anthes v. Transworld Systems, Inc.*, 765 F. Supp. 162 (D. Del. 1991); *Higgins v. Capitol Credit Servs., Inc.*, 762 F. Supp. 1128 (D. Del. 1991); *Riviera v. MAB Collections, Inc.*, 682 F. Supp. 174 (W.D.N.Y. 1988).

The court held that a statement that "prompt payment is requested" is not a violation of the FDCPA since the statement did not convey a threat that would induce the plaintiff to ignore his rights. The court held that the payment "did not contradict the admonition that the debtor had 30 days to contest the validity of the debt." Secondly, no threat was made to encourage the debtor to waive this right.[78]

Whether other courts will follow this Circuit Court of Appeals decision from the Ninth Circuit has not been determined. The Seventh and Second Circuits disagree.[79]

Sometimes consumers immediately, on receipt of a letter, institute legal action based on a claim that the debt is invalid or that the debt collector is threatening to commence a suit on an invalid obligation. The sounder approach is that a consumer alleging that the debt referenced in a collection letter is not valid must follow the clear and orderly procedures set forth in the FDCPA before a suit may be instituted. The purpose of the required language in the letter is to enable the debt collector to investigate and verify the debt. If the debt collector finds that the debt is invalid, the debtor will be notified the debt is not a valid debt, which will terminate the proceedings. This is the sole and solitary purpose of the validation notice.[80]

Another case in the District Court in New York put an unusual spin on this problem.[81] The court took the attitude that the mandatory wording at the bottom, that is, this is an attempt to collect a debt, turns the letter into a debt collection letter absent a disclaimer and therefore the debt collector is attempting to collect a debt. If the debt is invalid, a violation occurs because the debt collector is attempting to collect the debt.

The debt collector argued that he was merely seeking information from the plaintiff, but the court felt that it was odd that the defendants would go out of their way to comply with the FDCPA only to argue that the FDCPA does not apply when they are faced with litigation. The emphasis was on the plain language that the communication was from a debt collector and "an attempt to collect the debt." The court emphasized that this type of language coupled with the balance due on the debt clearly seeks payment of a debt owed by the debtor.

Since both cases came from district courts in the Eastern District of New York, the conflict is obvious. At least the other districts have a choice which case to follow and hopefully a circuit court will resolve the issue in favor of the more recent decision. The purpose of the statute was to enable

---

[78] *Renick v. Dun & Bradstreet Receivable Mgmt.*, 2002 WL 992490 (9th Cir. May 16, 2002).
[79] *Evory v. RJM Acquisitions Funding, LLC*, 505 F.3d 769 (7th Cir. 2007).
[80] *Healy v. Jzanus, Ltd.*, 2002 U.S. Dist. LEXIS 23417 (E.D.N.Y. Nov. 20, 2002).
[81] *Elane v. The Revenue Maximazation Group, Inc.*, 233 F. Supp. 2d 996 (E.D.N.Y. 2003).

the debt collector to double-check the information he received when a debtor disputes the debt.

ADDITIONAL STATE REQUIREMENTS

CALIFORNIA. California is now a state of over 30 million residents and recently elected a well-known actor as its governor. Any law that is passed by California cannot be ignored. Effective July 1, 2004, the following language was necessary to include in the first communication with the debtor to comply with the California Rosenthal FDCPA:

> As required by law, you are hereby notified that a negative credit agency report reflecting on your credit report may be submitted to a credit reporting agency if you fail to fulfill the terms of your credit obligations. The state Rosenthal Fair Debt Collection Practices Act and the federal Fair Debt Collection Practices Act require that, except under unusual circumstances, collectors may not contact you before 8 a.m. or after 9 p.m. They may not harass you by using threats of violence or arrest or by using obscene language. Collectors may not use false or misleading statements or call you at work if they know or have reason to know that you may not receive personal calls at work. For the most part, collectors may not tell another person, other than your attorney or spouse, about your debt. Collectors may contact another person to confirm your location or enforce a judgment. For more information about debt collection activities, you may contact the Federal Trade Commission at 1-877-FTC-HELP or www.ftc.gov.[82]

A new amendment effective January, 2007, requires hospitals to include the following text with the Rosenthal Notice in California when collecting their own debt. The notice must also be provided by parties collecting debt on behalf of a hospital or parties to whom the hospital has sold the debt. The notice must only be provided in the initial communication. The notice is as follows:

"Non-profit credit counseling services may be available in the area."[83]

COLORADO. Colorado requires that in the initial communication to the debtor, the following statement in capital letters must be included in the letter, "FOR INFORMATION ABOUT THE COLORADO FAIR DEBT COLLECTION PRACTICES ACT, SEE WWW.AGOSTATE.CO.US/CADC/CADCMAIN.CFM."

The website of Colorado must be monitored to be certain no change in the address of the website has occurred. The office in Colorado must be

---

[82] *Joseph v. J. J. MacIntyre Cos., L.L.C.*, 281 F. Supp. 2d 1156 (N.D. Cal. 2003).
[83] Cal. Civ. Code § 1812.700-702.

listed and a toll-free number must be maintained. A collection manager is still required to be employed by a collection agency.

Under a new law effective July 2, 2008, the following statement also must be included, "A consumer has the right to request in writing that a debt collector or collection agency cease further communication with the consumer. A written request to cease communication will not prohibit the debt collector or the collection agency from taking any other action authorized by law to collect the debt."

The notice should be on the front side of the letter but may be on the back side providing a statement appears on the front side that further information is on the backside of the letter. This notification should be in capital letters even though the statute does not require same. Limited liability companies must notify the state of any change in ownership. (*See* website below.)

Those who collect in Colorado should be aware of their specific requirements for debt collectors. Effective November, 2008, Colorado added some changes as to the use of a toll-free number. A copy of the new rules are available on the Colorado Attorney General's Collection Agencies and Debt Collection web site.

New York. The council members of the City of New York passed a local law to amend the administrative code of the City of New York. Section 20-489 of the Code has been amended to include debt buyers as debt collectors. By their definition a debt buyer is one who seeks to collect such debt either directly or through the services of another, by including but not limited to, initiating or using legal processes or other means to collect or attempt to collect such debt.

The term does not include any attorney at law except an attorney at law for a law firm or part thereof who regularly engages in activities traditionally performed by debt collectors, including but not limited to, contacting a debtor through the mail or via telephone with the purpose of collecting a debt or other activities as determined by the rule of the Commissioner. *Thus any attorney who writes a demand letter would become a debt collector if the debt is covered by the Fair Debt Collection Practices Act.*

A debt collector agency shall, in any permitted communication with the consumer provide, a call-back number to a phone that is answered by a natural person, the name of the agency, the originating creditor of the debt, the name of the person to call back, and the amount of the debt at the time of the communication. The debt collector must also confirm in writing within five business days any debt payments, schedule or settlement agreement reached regarding the debt.

Section 420-493(2) of the administrative code prohibits an attempt to collect or contact a consumer after such consumer requests verification for such debt until such agency furnishes such consumer written documentation identifying the creditor who originated the debt and then itemizing the principal balance of the debt that remains or is alleged to remain due and all other charges that are due or alleged to be due.

The new law also prohibits contacting a consumer seeking to collect a debt as to which the statute of limitations for initiating legal action has expired, unless the debt collector first provides the consumer such information about the consumer's legal rights as the Commissioner prescribes by rule.

Any person found guilty of violating any provision of the subchapter shall be punished with the provisions of Chapter 1 of this title and shall be subject to a penalty of not less than $700 nor more than $1,000 *for each violation* provided, however, that any such person found guilty of having acted as a debt collection agency in violation of Section 20-490 of this subchapter shall be subject to an additional penalty of $100 for each instance in which contact is made with the consumer in violation of such section.

The above local law is applicable to the geographic area of the five boroughs of the City of New York and the law will not take effect until 120 days after it is enacted.

SUMMONS—VALIDATION NOTICE

The amendment to the FDCPA in 2006 states that a communication in the form of a formal pleading in a civil action is not an actual communication for purposes of Sec. 809(a) of the FDCPA, which requires a validation notice for an initial communication. Thus, a validation notice is no longer needed. (*See* Appendix to this chapter.)

VERIFICATION

If the debt collector intends to take no further action, it seems that the debt collector may ignore a request for verification. Accordingly, it appears that if the debt collector receives a written request for verification, and wishes to continue pursuing the debtor further, it will have to provide the verification. On the other hand, if the debt collector should decide not to engage in any further collection activity, and return the case to the client, the verification request does not have to be honored, but a recent case held that the obligation to verify is not extinguished.[84] Nevertheless,

---

[84] *Smith v. Transworld Sys., Inc.*, 953 F.2d 1025 (6th Cir. 1992); *Powell v. J.J. MacIntyre Co. Inc.*, 2003 U.S. Dist. LEXIS 24699 (D. Haw. Oct. 16, 2003), *reh'g denied*, 2004 U.S. Dist. LEXIS 2811 (D. Haw. Jan. 23, 2004); *Jang v. A.M. Miller and Assoc., Inc.*, No. 95 C 4919, 1996 WL 5435096 (N.D. Ill. July 31, 1996).

the client cannot merely send the case to another agency or law firm without first providing verification.

Representation by Attorney. Our firm frequently receives inquiries as to whether a validation notice should be included in a letter to an attorney when the law firm or the collection agency is notified by the client that the debtor is represented by an attorney. It is suggested to send the validation notice to the counsel rather than to the consumer.

> ***Credit & Collection Tip:*** *A statement in the letter that you have been advised that the attorney is representing the consumer and the debt is covered by the FDCPA should be sufficient, but the best advice is also to include the validation notice and the mini-Miranda warning.*[85]

Extensive Request for Information. Often the verification request is extensive: the number of employees, the location, how many delinquent accounts per year, the name of all employees in the collection department, names of all officers and directors, the salary of employees, and whatever else comes to their mind. Usually, they ask for similar information from the law firm. Often a request is made for a payment history, the balance due, as well as a copy of the collection history. How does one respond?

Verification of a debt only requires that the debt collector obtain a written statement that the amount being demanded is what the creditor is claiming is owed. The debt collector is not required to keep detailed files of the alleged debt. *Verification is only intended to eliminate the problem of the debt collectors dunning the wrong person or attempting to collect debts which the consumer had already paid.* The accounts statement, which consisted of a computer printout, is sufficient to inform the debtor of the services provided, the date on which the charges were incurred and the amount of the debt. The court held that nothing more was required.[86]

Response—Oral or in Writing. Section 1692g(a)(3) of the Act clearly does not require any communication in writing. Even if this statement is merely an oral communication, the debt will be assumed to be valid. The paragraph makes no assumption about what happens if the debtor does not dispute the debt within the 30 days. The only obligation of the debt collector is the assumption that the debt is valid. On the other hand, subdivisions 4 and 5 clearly state that the communication must be in writing or "a written request." Thus, subdivisions 4 and 5 do not begin to

---

[85]*Blum v. Fisher & Fisher, P.C.*, 961 F. Supp. 1218 (N.D. Ill. 1997).

[86]*Chaudhry v. Gallerizzo*, 174 F.3d 394 (4th Cir. 1999); *Azar v. Hayter*, 874 F. Supp. 1314, *aff'd*, 66 F.3d 342 (11th Cir. 1995); *Graziano v. Harrison*, 950 F.2d 107 (3d Cir. 1991); *Stonehart v. Rosenthal*, 2001 U.S. Dist. LEXIS 11566 (S.D.N.Y. Aug. 13, 2001).

operate until there is something in writing. Some letters omitted the requirement in Section 4 that the consumer must notify the debt collector in writing. Strangely, the courts have held this as a technical violation of the Act, even though the consumer is being afforded a broader opportunity to obtain verification of the debt without any communication in writing or without a written request. In one case, the court said that failure to include the writing requirement was a violation because the defendant cannot alter or restructure the statutory provisions. The court went on to state that the contents of the debtor's letter could not override the language in the statute and the debt collector could totally ignore his obligation in the letter to send a verification without a writing and still enforce the terms of the statute. While this seems to be stretching to protect the consumer, it is another example of what was affectionately referred to as "strict liability" of the FDCPA.

On the other hand, Sections 3 and 4 were properly set forth in the letter but were set forth in reverse order. The plaintiff in this instance argued that the particular provisions be set forth in the same order as they are set forth in Section 809. At least in this case the court took the attitude that this was not a material misrepresentation to the unsophisticated debtor and that the debtor was not misled by this reversal.[87]

The collection agency reported the debtor to a credit reporting agency because there was no notification by the consumer in writing. The consumer did notify the collection agency orally over the telephone and the collection agency admitted that they had knowledge because of this oral communication. The judge in this suit held that the true test of determining if the debt collector falsely reported a consumer debt to the credit reporting agency was whether the collection agency knew or should have known that the debt was disputed and did not depend upon when or how the agency acquired the knowledge. Again, the court ignored the "strict liability" approach to the statute and applied plain and simple common sense.[88] Unfortunately, all the courts do not apply the Act this rationally and when the court decides to hold the collection agency liable, the court will often become technical and apply the Act in an exacting manner.

Mirror Image of Statute. A recent case stated clearly that there was no authority directly supporting the idea that you must use the language of the statute on a word-for-word basis. The important ingredient is to convey the intended message required by the statute.

Credit & Collection Tip: *Your author strongly recommends that you use the language of the statute word-for-word. Perhaps the suit will never be instituted.*

---

[87] *Goldberg v. Winston*, 1997 WL 139526 (S.D.N.Y. Mar. 25, 1997).

[88] *Kartovich v. Winston*, 96-e-0893S USDC (W.D. Wis. Feb. 19, 1997) (unpublished decision).

A creditor has an obligation to report a debt as disputed if it has been reported to a credit reporting agency and the same rules apply to a collection agency. If the debtor disputes the debt orally and does not dispute it in writing, that is sufficient notification to the debt collector to require him to report the debt as disputed to any credit reporting agency to which he had previously reported the debt. Many collection agencies and debt collectors as well as creditors may have operated on the thesis that they did not report the debt as disputed unless they received a notification from the consumer in writing. The Circuit Court of Appeals has clearly stated that an oral dispute requires the debt collector to act.[89]

MULTIPLE DEBTS

This section requires the debt collector to apply payments received in accordance with the consumer's direction. Payment for a new purchase should not be applied to an old debt. The debt collector must apply a payment exactly as the debtor directs. Creditors should also comply with this section.

Paid in Full Debts. A California District Court held that "when a debt is extinguished there is no debt and there can be no debt collection." They refer to several appellate cases in the Third, Fourth, and Seventh Circuits as well as in the Eleventh Circuit.[90]

WHERE TO INSTITUTE SUIT

A suit that affects an interest in real property must be started in the judicial district in which the property is located. *For suits other than those affecting real property (which covers most suits), the action must be brought in the judicial district in which the consumer signed the contract or in which the consumer resides at the commencement of the action.*

RIGHT OF ASSIGNMENT

The American Collectors Association has reported that 25 states have enacted "right of assignment" laws with more states considering adopting

[89] *Brady v. Credit Recovery*, 160 F.3d 64 (1st Cir. 1998).

[90] *Winter v. I.C. Systems Inc.*, 543 F. Supp. 2d 1210 (S.D. Cal. 2008); *Posso v. Asta Funding Inc.*, 2007 WL 3374400 (N.D. Ill. 2007); *Zimmerman v. HBO Affiliate*, 834 F.2d 1163 (3d Cir. 1987); *Brown v. Budget Rent-A-Car*, 119 F.3d 922 (11th Cir. 1997); *Mabe v. G.C. Servs.*, 32 F.3d 86 (4th Cir. 1994).

laws to allow assignment. Twelve states have expressly prohibited this practice by either a statute or court decision.

The right of assignment gives the creditor the ability to assign the claim to a collection agency which enables the collection agency to file suit in its own name instead of the client's name. This enables many claims against one debtor to be coordinated into one suit, but unfortunately presents serious problems when a contest develops on one claim and not other claims. The division of funds when collection occurs may also become a problem unless resolved prior to handling.

PRO SE PLAINTIFFS

Often consumer attorneys institute suit for violations of FDCPA in their own names, since the attorneys themselves actually received the letter or telephone call, and included in the complaint is a claim for attorney's fees. Several cases have held that where the plaintiff appears "pro se" (for himself/herself), the plaintiff is not entitled to attorney's fees since the plaintiff is a consumer not represented by an attorney and thus not incurring the cost of an attorney.[91]

DECEPTIVE FORMS

Designing or furnishing forms knowing they are deceptive or will be used to deceive the consumer into believing that someone other than the creditor is participating in the collection of the debt is expressly forbidden. Prior to the Act, the practice of selling to creditors form letters with the letterhead of a collection agency was common where the agency was not involved in the collection process and was not participating in the collection of the debt.

Some debt collectors will prepare and mail a letter on behalf of a creditor for a fixed fee per letter. An argument may be made that the creditor is attempting to persuade the consumer that the debt collector is participating in the collection of the debt when the only interest of the debt collector is the fixed fee. Is collecting a fixed fee (called flat rating in the industry) sufficient participation? The commentary states that a debt collector is not violating this section if a flat fee is charged per letter providing the performance of other tasks associated with collection, such as handling verification requests, negotiating payment arrangements, and keeping individual records shows evidence *of participation* in the collection of the debt. If the debt collector merely received the mail, and delivered it to the

[91] *Benson v. Hafif*, 114 F.3d 1193 (9th Cir. 1997).

creditor unopened, a violation may exist. To comply with this section, the mail must be opened and reviewed by the debt collector. The debt collector must negotiate payment arrangements, verify the debts, respond where appropriate and keep records (*but see* "Meaningful Involvement—Debt Collector").

Use of Inside Counsel. The Act specifically states that if a creditor uses any name other than its own, which would indicate that a third person is collecting or attempting to collect a debt, the creditor shall become subject to the Act. This section is thus also targeted at creditors who use their inside counsel to write collection letters to the consumer to indicate an independent attorney is being paid to collect the account. On the other hand, if the letter bore the same address as the creditor and stated at the bottom of the letter that the attorney was employed by the creditor or was house counsel, the creditor would not be using a name other than her own and no deception would be practiced upon the debtor. Of course, the impact of the collection letter would be decreased.

Credit managers know that transferring a debt to an outside collection agency, and especially to an attorney, increases the collection percentages. Creditors in the past created bogus collection agencies with addresses across the street. The creditor would write the letter using the bogus collection agency letterhead. The mail would be picked up and answered by employees of the creditor, and all payments are processed by employees of the creditor. The collection agency would have no employees, no staff, and no life of its own. This section of the Act was designed specifically to address and correct this problem of deceiving the consumer into believing an outside third party is collecting the debt.

Many businesses use their inside house counsel to send collection letters. The following are some guidelines, but reliance on these guidelines is no assurance of compliance since the case law is sparse on this subject. Compliance with "meaningful involvement" as set forth in the *Clomon* and *Avila* cases may also be suggested (*see* Appendix to this chapter):

A. The ethics committees of most state bar associations usually require an attorney to have control over any matter referred to the attorney and to have sufficient information to determine the validity of any claim made by a client. Under those circumstances, the attorney should review a listing of all the debts for which letters are sent and should be able to verify, supervise, and control all the activities which the office conducts on a day-to-day basis, and thus be "meaningfully involved."

B. If the counsel is an inside attorney employed by the creditor full time, the address on the stationery should be the address where the office is, i.e. the same address as the creditor. An attorney who is employed by a creditor is not shielded from personal liability when acting as a debt collector.[92]

Inside counsel should be identified as "house counsel" to be certain the consumer is not led to believe the attorney is outside counsel.

Credit & Collection Tip: *A creditor is exposed to two distinctly different risks by the operation of this section. First, if the creditor violates the law by using letters prepared by a debt collector who is not participating in the collection of the debt, the creditor immediately becomes subject to the FDCPA; and second, by virtue of subdivision b, the creditor is in violation of the Act if the creditor deceives the consumer into believing someone other than the creditor is collecting the debt—when such is not the case.*

DAMAGES

The Act imposes civil liability for actual damages and statutory damages up to $1,000. Attorneys' fees are recoverable for the successful party. A district court decision held that a debtor may collect only $1,000 in each suit, not for each violation.[93] Most federal courts have followed this decision. The Act permits actions to be brought in federal or state courts within one year of the violation. Class action status is available, and in such event the damages will not exceed the lesser of $500,000 or 1 percent of the net worth of the debt collector (*see* "Class Actions").

Under the Rosenthal Act in California, damages may be awarded if the violations were committed willfully and knowingly. Plaintiff may recover from each debt collector up to $1,000 in statutory damages (plus $1,000 for the action under the FDCPA).[94]

BONA FIDE ERROR—RELIANCE ON CLIENT INFORMATION

The debt collector may avoid liability if it can prove that it was an unintentional act and resulted from a bona fide error. Under those circumstances a debt collector can allege that if a violation did occur, it was an isolated violation and an unintentional act over which the debt collector had no control. The key to this defense is maintaining a procedure manual and monitoring the staff. One district court judge said it all: "I find

[92]*Dorsey v. Morgan*, 760 F. Supp. 509 (D. Md. 1991).

[93]*Goodman v. Peoples Bank*, 2006 U.S. App. LEXIS 31555 (3d Cir. Nov. 26, 2006); *Wright v. Fin. Serv. of Norwalk, Inc.*, 996 F.2d 820 (6th Cir. 1993).

[94]*Lowe v. Elite Recovery Solutions L.P.*, 2008 U.S. Dist. LEXIS 8353 (E.D. Cal. 2008).

generally that a program of constant on-the-job training, coupled with telephonic monitoring, supervision, and reference to a standardized manual is a procedure reasonably adopted to avoid violation of the Act." Nevertheless, this defense was only applied to clerical errors.

The Tenth Circuit joined a growing minority of courts reaching the conclusion that a bona fide error defense is not restricted to clerical errors, but may be based on errors in legal judgment. The attorney must prove by a preponderance of the evidence that the violation of the FDCPA was unintentional and resulted from a bona fide error and occurred in spite of procedures reasonably adapted to avoid any such error. The case provides citations for the majority and minority across the country.

In one of the minority cases, the court relied on the words of the statute which does not limit defense to clerical errors and actually refers to any "error" that is "bona fide." No legislative history supports the idea that Congress intended this broad language to mean anything other than what it says. The Senate report stated "a debt collector has no liability, however, if he violates the Act in any manner, including with regard to the act's coverage, when such violation is unintentional and occurred despite procedures to avoid such violations." Absent a clearer indication that the Congress meant to limit the defense to clerical errors, the unambiguous language of the statute agrees with the legislative history.

Your author wholeheartedly endorses this interpretation of the statute.[95]

A debt collector may rely on the information their clients provide and the FDCPA does not require them to conduct their own investigation into the amount or validity of the underlying loan.

In this case, the debtor apparently borrowed from the bank on his home in Maine, but the document supporting the loan was identified in several places as a commercial note. The attorney had a right to rely on this information from the client.[96]

Section 1692(k) subdivision C states as follows:

> a debt collector may not be held liable in any action brought under this subchapter if the debt collector shows by a preponderance of the evidence that the violation was not intentional and resulted from a bona fide error notwithstanding the maintenance of procedures reasonably adapted to avoid any such error.

As a rule, the courts set forth three criteria in determining a bona fide error defense. The defendant must prove that it was an unintentional error,

---

[95]*Smith v. TransWorld*, 953 F.2d 1025 (6th Cir. 1992); *Jermain v. Carlisle, McNellie, Rini, Kramer & Ulrich, et al.*, 502 F. Supp. 2d 686 (N.D. Ohio 2007); *Massa v. L.C. Systems, Inc.*, 2008 U.S. Dist. LEXIS 13191 (S.D. Ind. 2008).

[96]*Gardner v. First Am. Title Ins. Co.*, 2003 U.S. Dist. LEXIS 1815 (D. Minn. Jan. 27, 2003).

a bona fide error and the maintenance of procedures reasonably adapted to avoid the violation.

The issue presented on many occasions is whether the bona fide error defense can apply to a mistake of law as well as clerical errors. Two circuits have already determined that the bona fide error defense is only limited to clerical errors. Accordingly, the split on the issue leaves the majority concluding that the defense is limited to clerical errors and cannot protect mistakes of law, notwithstanding a growing minority of courts that have expanded the bona fide error defense to include mistakes of law. *The Truth in Lending Act expressly states that an error in legal judgment as to a person's obligations is not a bona fide error. The FDCPA lacks a similar provision.*

We have a new case to add to a growing number of courts that have opined that the provisions of 15 U.S.C. Section 1692(k)(c) are not limited to clerical mistakes but extend to mistakes of law in asserting a bona fide error defense under the FDCPA.[97]

"Not intentional" in the FDCPA seems to mean that there was no intent to violate the law even though there was an intent to take the action that was actually taken. Thus, if a suit is started on a letter that violates the law, no question exists that there was an intent to prepare the letter. The issue before the court is the intent to violate the law.[98]

Notwithstanding a few decisions that have applied the bona fide error defense, the number of cases are few. Reliance on prevention rather than this defense is strongly recommended.

A discussion of what the courts will recognize to satisfy the "maintenance of procedures reasonable adapted to avoid any such error" is provided in several cases. In one case, the court mentioned that the staff of the agency periodically attended seminars which provided training to aid them in complying with the FDCPA. The employees were also provided with various editions of the FDCPA manual and a three-page memorandum explaining the FDCPA. The agency required a 5″ × 8″ card with the mini-Miranda language placed on every telephone and the card also instructed the debt collector to use the language when introducing themselves in conducting any form of collection business. In one case, the debt collector instructed its clients in writing to submit only those charges to which they were legally entitled and also advised clients to seek legal advice before adding unauthorized fees. Memos were issued to their staff to reinforce this message. In another case, the debt collector required the client to verify under oath that each of the charges were true and correct.

---

[97] *McCorriston v. L.W.T. Inc.*, 536 F. Supp. 2d 1268 (M.D. Fla. 2008).

[98] *Nance v. Ulferts & Herbach*, 282 F. Supp. 2d 912 (N.D. Ind. 2003). *See Johnson v. Riddle*, 443 F.3d 723 (10th Cir. 2006); *Jerman v. Carlisle McNellie, Rini, Kramer & Ulrich LPA.*, 538 F.3d 469 (6th Cir. 2008); *Nielsen v. Dickerson*, 207 F.3d 623 (7th Cir. 2002); *Pipiles v. Credit Bureau of Lockport, Inc.*, 886 F.2d 22 (2d Cir. 1989); *Vanelli v. Reynolds School Dist. No. 7*, 667 F.2d 773 (9th Cir. 1982).

The devices used to avoid violations of the Act are only limited by the creativity of the debt collector. It might be beneficial to institute procedures that are not only effective in avoiding errors, but also will be effective when presenting the procedure to the courts as a procedure reasonably adapted to avoid such an error. We also recommend that the retainer agreement contain the following representations:

A. Client represent that the original amount, balance due, and all the charges are true and correct and that the client is legally entitled to the balance due.
B. The balance due does not include any unauthorized fees or charges in violation of any laws.
C. Client shall properly furnish written notice to the attorney if any payment received directly by the client on any account which has been referred to this office.
D. Client promptly will notify the debt collector where the debtor has been represented by an attorney or that the debtor has notified the client that the debtor is represented by an attorney.
E. Client promptly will advise the debt collector if the debtor has already filed a petition in bankruptcy. If the client should later become aware of any bankruptcy, they will promptly notify the debt collector.[99]

Sending a letter to a debtor demanding payment on a debt after the debtor has filed a petition in bankruptcy is a common error that debt collectors and attorneys encounter. Often, the notification of the bankruptcy never comes to the attention of the client either in sufficient time or through channels wherein the attorney or the debt collector is advised by their client that the debtor is in bankruptcy. Sometimes the client never receives the notice since 1 percent of all first-class mail is never delivered.

Many of the courts treat the FDCPA as a strict liability statute. If you contact the debtor to collect a debt after the debtor has filed a petition in bankruptcy, a violation immediately occurs. The only defense to this violation is a bona fide error defense.

A case set forth certain criteria to meet the threshold of successfully asserting that defense. Some of the suggestions are not commonly adopted by debt collectors or law offices.

A. No written agreement or any type of understanding was entered into with the creditor and client where the client was instructed not to send the debt collectors accounts upon which bankruptcy petitions have been filed.

---

[99] *Jenkins v. Heintz*, 124 F.3d 824 (7th Cir. 1997); *Jenkins v. Union Corp.*, 999 F. Supp. 1120 (N.D. Ill. 1998); *Beattie v. D.M. Collections Inc.*, 754 F. Supp. 383 (D. Del. 1991).

B. No written agreement or signed agreement was evident that the creditor would immediately contact the debt collector if a bankrupt account erroneously slipped through its process.

C. Reliance on the client not to send accounts which had filed bankruptcy petitions was not reasonable nor was it a procedure reasonably adopted to avoid violating the FDCPA.

D. The fact that employees have been trained not to contact debtors in bankruptcy and to react to a notice in bankruptcy by ceasing collection efforts is insufficient, as a matter of law.

The court referred to several other cases which included periodic seminars, training manuals, and memorandums delineating its FDCPA policy, and posting cards on the telephone citing language required by the FDCPA. The use of an auditing agency to insure compliance with FDCPA requirements was mentioned.

The judge analyzed many of the decisions which treated various criteria of what does and what does not constitute compliance with a bona fide error defense. For anyone that has problem with a violation of the FDCPA, the decision is recommended reading.[100]

IMPUTING KNOWLEDGE—COLLECTION AGENCY

When a debt collector contacts the debtor represented by an attorney directly and the debt collector has not been advised by the creditor that the debtor was represented by an attorney, has the debt collector violated the Act? A client recently queried on whether the same rules would apply if a prior collection agency handled the account and knew that the attorney represented the debtor, but when the account was referred to the present collection agency, that information was not disclosed.

The best advice for a debt collector and the law firm is to notify the client in writing that the law requires the creditor to notify the debt collector. Section 1692c(a)(2) states that if the debt collector knows the consumer is represented by an attorney with respect to such debt, and has knowledge of *or can readily ascertain* such attorney's name and address, a debt collector may not communicate with a consumer in connection with the collection of any debt. When the present collection agency took over the accounts from the prior collection agency, the present collection agency should inquire both orally and in writing of the prior agency of any instance where a debtor is represented by an attorney.

If a creditor has an obligation when turning over a file to convey all the material facts regarding the claim, it would seem that a prior collection

[100] *Turner v. JVDB & Assocs.*, 318 F. Supp. 2d 681 (N.D. Ill. 2004).

agency has an obligation to convey all the material facts to the new collection agency concerning the particular claim against the debtor.

Another case stated that knowledge will be imputed where the debt collector does not inquire or has no procedure in place to determine whether the debtor is represented by counsel. Conversely, knowledge will not be imputed where the debt collector does have a procedure in place or did make inquiry (was able to ascertain) as to whether the debtor was represented by counsel.[101]

The Eighth Circuit Court of Appeals has contributed to the resolution of the issue of imputing knowledge to the attorney.[102] The theory of implied knowledge contradicts established agency law, which dictates that while the knowledge of the agent is imputed to the principal, the converse is not true. While an agent's knowledge is imputed to the principal due to the identity of interest that is presumed when an agent acts within the scope of agency relation, this rule does not operate in the converse and the agent cannot be imputed with the information which its principal has failed to provide.

Section 1692 (c) states as follows:

> "without the prior consent of the consumer given directly to the debt collector or the express permission of a court of competent jurisdiction, a debt collector may not communicate with a consumer in connection with the collection of any debt.
>
> . . .
>
> If the debt collector knows the consumer is represented by an attorney with respect to such debt and has knowledge of, or can readily ascertain, such attorney's name and address, unless the attorney fails to respond within a reasonable period of time to a communication from the debt collector or unless the attorney consents to direct communication with the consumer."

In the *Micare*[103] case, the court held that a creditor's knowledge could be imputed to the debt collector where the creditor knew of the plaintiff's representation prior to transferring the file to the collector. The reasoning behind the *Micare* decision was that although the FDC Commentary states that knowledge will not automatically be imputed to the debt collector, it does not state that such knowledge cannot be imputed.

---

[101]*Turner v. JVDB Assoc.*, 211 F. Supp. 2d 1108 (N.D. Ill. 2002); *Micare v. Foster & Garbus*, 132 F. Supp. 2d 77 (N.D.N.Y. 2001); *Powers v. Professional Credit Serv.*, 107 F. Supp. 166 (N.D.N.Y. 2000).

[102]*Schmitt v. FMA Alliance*, 398 F.3d 995 (8th Cir. 2005); *Powers v. Professional Credit Servs.*, 107 F. Supp. 2d 166 (N.D.N.Y. 2000).

[103]*Micare v. Foster & Garbus*, 132 F. Supp. 2d 77 (N.D.N.Y. 2001). *See Randolf v. IMBS Inc.*, 368 F.3d 726 (7th Cir. 2004); *Crouch v. J.J. Marshall & Assocs., Inc.*, 2007 U.S. Dist. LEXIS 79607 (W.D. Mich. Oct. 27, 2007); *Powers v. Professional Credit Servs., Inc.*, 107 F. Supp. 2d 166 (N.D.N.Y. 2000); *Carroll v. FIA Card Servs.*, 2008 Bankr. LEXIS 3688 (N.D. W.Va. 2008).

The Eighth Circuit forcefully declined to follow either *Powers* or *Micare* and stated that they will not embrace the FDCPA as a special exception to the general agency rule. First, no textual basis appears within the statute to suggest that an exception to such a well settled rule was intended, and second, a distinction between creditors and debt collectors is fundamental to the FDCPA which does not regulate creditors activities all. Thus, we have no authority to place a duty upon the creditor even if the FDCPA creates an exception allowing a principal's knowledge to be imputed to the agent under narrow circumstances.

No clear line is drawn as to whether the relationship between a creditor and its debt collector is one of principal-agent. Some courts have held that debt collectors are merely independent contractors. Hopefully this issue will be resolved either by amending the law or forcing a case up to the Supreme Court.

> ***Credit & Collection Tip:*** *A debt collector and a law firm should notify the client in writing that the law requires the creditor to notify the debt collector if the debtor is represented by an attorney.*

If the debt collector knows that a consumer is represented by the attorney, the letter must be directed to the attorney rather than the consumer. The letter must contain the validation notice according to the Seventh Circuit.

The same court held that a representation by a debt collector that would be unlikely to deceive a "competent" lawyer, even if the attorney is not a specialist in consumer debt law, should not be actionable. The court has changed the standard for determining whether a deceptive act practiced on an attorney constitutes a violation of the FDCPA. The standard will be determined in future cases.

ATTORNEYS' FEES

Several decisions have been rendered making it more difficult for consumer attorneys to obtain large awards for attorneys' fees and statutory damages. In a California decision, the court identified three factors: "The frequency and persistence of the debt collector's non-compliance, the nature of such non-compliance, and the extent to which non-compliance was intentional." The court awarded only $700 in statutory damages.[104]

---

[104]*Meszaros v. United Collection Corp.*, No. C-95-4634 THE, 1996 WL 346872 (N.D. Cal. June 14, 1996). *See also Purnell v. Kovitz Shifrin & Watzman*, No. 95-C-2554, 1996 WL 521401 (N.D. Ill. Sept. 11, 1996); *Beckham v. Midwest Billing Serv. Inc.*, 95-C-915-C (W.D. Wis. Oct. 29, 1996); *Shifflet v. Accelerated RecoverySys., Inc.*, No. CIV A. 95-00070-C, 1996 WL 335379 (W.D. Va. May 23, 1996).

Defendants in these types of cases should not settle in the $1,000 to $3,000 range after receiving a letter or a summons and complaint from the consumer attorney. Such a settlement only rewards the consumer attorney by paying an hourly rate of somewhere between $750 and $1,000 per hour. This type of settlement encourages the consumer attorney to write more letters and serve more summonses. On the other hand, if more collection agencies and attorneys contest these suits for technical violations, the consumer attorneys may be forced to seek their livelihood from other areas. Where the law firm or collection agency is wrong, money should be offered, but should not exceed the value of the actual time that the consumer's attorney devoted to preparing the letter or complaint. If there is a technical violation, the same reasoning should be used. If the consumer attorney institutes suit on a technical violation, an offer of judgment might succeed in significantly limiting the statutory damages and the attorneys' fees to a figure less than any settlement offer the consumer attorney would accept.

A defendant should not measure the settlement offer against the total exposure to attorneys' fees for its own attorney, the attorneys' fees for plaintiff's attorney, and the damages under the FDCPA. A defendant can always justify a settlement to the consumer comparing the settlement offer with this contingent liability. But in view of the many decisions rendered in favor of the defendant collection agencies and law firms, measuring a settlement offer on this theory only rewards the consumer attorney and at the same time encourages the attorney to assert more groundless claims. Defendants should realize that the proper approach is to contest FDCPA claims where appropriate and make the consumer attorneys work for their fees. The awards to plaintiffs in many instances are significantly less than $1,000, and the awards for attorney fees are consistently being reduced. In some cases, no amount was awarded for technical violations. Unless the violation is clear and is of the type to cause actual damage, consider all the alternatives before embarking on the settlement road.

An interesting analysis by a Florida court of the factors applicable to fee awards under federal statute was provided.[105] The court listed 12 items that have to be considered:

1. The time and labor required.
2. The novelty and difficulty of the legal questions.
3. The skills required to perform the legal services properly.
4. The preclusion of other employment by the attorney due to acceptance of the case.
5. The customary fee for similar work in the community.
6. Whether the fee is fixed or contingent.

---

[105]*Martinez v. Law Offices of David J. Stern, P.A.*, 266 B.R. 523 (Bankr. S.D. Fla. 2001).

7. Time limitations imposed by the client or the circumstances.
8. The amount involved and the results obtained.
9. The experience, reputation, and ability of the attorney.
10. The undesirability of the case.
11. The nature and length of the professional relationship with the client.
12. Awards in similar cases.

Two other cases in the Eleventh and the Fifth Circuits also contributed to this list of factors to be considered when determining whether a consumer attorney is entitled to a fee.[106]

A favorable decision to law firms and collection agencies was made by the Court of Appeals for the Fifth Circuit when it considered the question of whether to award attorneys' fees after a technical violation of the FDCPA with no award of actual damages. The court zeroed in on the wording in the FDCPA which requires a "successful" action to support an award of attorneys' fees.

The court reasoned that a violation is not "successful" if the plaintiff is unable to prove actual damages. This interpretation of the statute requires plaintiffs to seek more than technical violations before bringing suit. The court felt that this will deter suits brought only as a means of generating attorney's fees.

The court went on to state that the FDCPA will still punish errant debt collectors. The law mandates that the debt collector not only compensate the debtor fully for any monetary damages, emotional stress, or other injury that the debtor can prove the debt collector caused, but also allows the courts to assess punitive damages and requires the debt collector to pay the plaintiff's attorney's fees in addition to its own. Congress considered the risk of such punishment adequate to deter debt collectors from intentionally violating the Act.[107]

Successful Party—Right to Attorneys' Fees—Catalyst Theory. In the past, most circuits had recognized the catalyst theory which awarded attorney fees to the prevailing party even though the suit was moot. Chief Justice Rehnquist pointed out that a "prevailing party" is a legal term of art and Black's Law Dictionary, Seventh Edition (1999), defines a prevailing party as a party in whose favor a judgment is rendered, regardless of the amount of damages awarded. He also equivocated a prevailing party the same as a "successful party." The Supreme Court has found that Congress intended to permit an interim award of

---

[106]*Norman v. Hous. Auth. of Montgomery*, 836 F.2d 1292 (11th Cir. 1988); *Johnson v. Georgia Highway Express, Inc.*, 488 F.2d 914 (5th Cir. 1974); *Kapoo v. Rosenthal*, 269 F. Supp. 2d 408 (S.D.N.Y. 2003).

[107]*Johnson v. Eaton*, 80 F.3d 148 (5th Cir. 1996).

counsel fees only when a party has prevailed on the merits of at least some of the claims. A plaintiff must receive at least some relief before it can be said to prevail. Even nominal damages are sufficient. Settlement agreements enforced through a consent decree may serve as the basis for an award of attorneys' fees.

The court stated that given the clear meaning of "prevailing party" in the fee-shifting statutes, Congress has not extended any authority to the judiciary to allow counsel fees as cost or otherwise whenever the courts might deem them warranted. The court therefore held the "catalyst theory" as a nonpermissible basis for the award of attorney fees under the Fair Housing Amendments Act (FHAA).

From the above case, we move to the Federal Credit Reporting Act and a case in the Seventh Circuit rendered by Judges Posner, Easterbrook, and Williams, with the decision written by Judge Posner.[108] In this case, the plaintiff Jerry had a brother whose first name was John and their social security numbers differed by one number (829). As a result, Trans Union on several occasions furnished credit reports on John when it had been requested for information on Jerry. As a result, Jerry was denied credit several times. He complained, and Trans Union then began adding at the end of its credit reports the notation "do not confuse with brother John __." Only one creditor who denied credit to Jerry ever received a report that mistakenly attributed information about John to Jerry. The reason for the problem was that Trans Union's computer treated requests for a credit report on Jerry as a request for a credit report also on John. If any of these creditors missed the notation and erroneously supposed that both reports pertained to Jerry, the mistake was the creditors.

Jerry was unable to offer evidence that he was denied credit after receiving a report on him. The court held that without a causal relationship between the violation of the statute and the loss of credit, a plaintiff cannot obtain an award of actual damages. He has not sustained any injury or any damages or any harm to his credit and thus he is unable to collect actual damages. He is seeking attorneys' fees and costs as well as punitive damages and compensatory damages, all of which are statute authorized remedies—but no actual damage.

At this point, the Circuit Court of the Seventh Circuit moved from the Fair Credit Reporting Act to the Truth in Lending and the FDCPA and cited the similarity in statutes in the three acts stating that the three statutes related to the recovery of attorney fees are virtually identical. The court held that proof of liability without damages does not entitle the plaintiff to an award of costs and attorney fees in the absence of bad conduct by the plaintiff or other unusual circumstances.

---

[108] *Crabil v. TransUnion*, 259 F.3d 662 (7th Cir. 2001). *See also Buchannon Ford & Care Home, Inc. v. West Virginia Dep't of Health and Human Res.*, 121 S. Ct. 1835 (2001); *Johnson v. Eaton*, 80 F.3d 148 (5th Cir. 1996).

The catalyst theory holds that a plaintiff who fails to secure a "judicially sanctioned action" still will be entitled to attorneys' fees if he had caused a change in the conduct of the defendant, but has not prevailed in the action for purposes of fee shifting because the claim has become moot. Judge Posner held that a causal relation must be present between the violation of the statute and the loss of credit or some other harm. Without these ingredients the petitioner cannot obtain an award of actual damages. He even suggested that the same logic should be applied to other consumer protection statutes, referring specifically to the Truth in Lending Act and the FDCPA. Without a claim for actual damages, no controversy exists between the parties. The Constitution requires that a controversy exist between two parties from different states for the federal court to have jurisdiction under Article 3. A lack of injury and damage to the plaintiff provides no jurisdictional basis for the lawsuit and, therefore, no grounds for attorneys' fees.

Since many FDCPA suits allege a technical violation and no actual damage or injury is sustained by the plaintiff, these two cases provide a defense where no defense was present before. With the "catalyst theory" rejected, the fact that a defendant changes his conduct provides no basis for attorney fees. Furthermore, the federal courts who have defined "successful" under the catalyst theory to support attorneys' fees are now effectively overruled.

Credit & Collection Tip: *If your case does not involve actual damages, or if the damages are of a technical nature and a change in conduct will cure the violation, consult with experienced counsel and review these cases carefully.*

When a statute allows attorneys' fees, the party seeking to collect the attorneys' fees must proceed through the court to be awarded the attorneys' fees. The attorney is not entitled to attorneys' fees until a judgment is actually entered awarding attorneys' fees. Thus, attorneys' fees are not proper in the initial communication to the debtor. Nevertheless, the courts seem to be in agreement that these situations do not apply to where the party explicitly agrees to the attorneys' fees in a written contract, such as in a mortgage or a retail installment contract. The attorney had the contractual right to bill plaintiff a reasonable amount without having to obtain court approval. The reason behind this is that many times the attorney in a mortgage situation will expend significant services in negotiating a settlement or entering into a forbearance agreement and all for the purpose of resolving the issue of payment without a lawsuit. No court has been involved in the negotiations. If the mortgagee's attorney had to initiate a legal proceeding to obtain a court approval, the mortgagor would become liable for additional fees as well as the cost of that proceeding.[109]

---

[109] *Whaley v. Shapiro*, 2003 WL 22232911 (N.D. Ill. Mar. 16, 2004); *Porter v. Fairbanks Capital Corp.*, 2003 WL 21210115 (N.D. Ill. May 20, 2003).

Excessive Collection Fees. Wisconsin law expressly prohibits the attachment of collection fees to consumer debts even if the fee is separately negotiated. The Wisconsin statute provides that:

> no term of a writing evidencing a consumer credit transaction may provide for any charge as a result of default by the customer other than reasonable expenses incurred in the disposition of collateral and such other charges as are specifically authorized by Chapters 421 to 427.[110]

The Wisconsin statute 422.411(1) states that no term of a writing may provide for the payment by the customer of attorney's fees and the Wisconsin statute 422.202 specifically states "additional charges" does not list collection fees as a permissible fee a creditor may charge in connection with the consumer transaction. In addition, the Wisconsin Consumer Act requires that when a creditor and a customer establishes an open end credit account, the interest rate and all charges and fees that might be levied on the account must be disclosed to the consumer on the face of the writing evidencing the transaction before the transaction is consummated.[111]

On the other hand, each state seems to approach abusive collection fees in a different manner, although all of them agree that excessive fees should not be permitted, but the Wisconsin statute is probably the most favorable to consumers. Indiana states that a contingent fee can never be implied, but must be expressly contracted for between the attorney and his client. A contingency fee not reduced to writing may not be enforceable in Indiana. Even if the debtor agreed to pay reasonable costs of collecting the amounts due, a charge of 50 percent would probably be excessive under Indiana law.

In Indiana, the court held that if the fees charged were unrelated to fees actually paid or incurred by the agency, the plaintiff could be entitled to relief on her statutory claim of deception. The collection fee sought must be the actual amounts paid out or incurred by the agency.[112]

In Illinois, the argument that the debtor agreed to pay reasonable costs of collecting the amount due in writing is not sufficient since credit related charges may only consist of reasonable attorney fees and expenses arising from the disposition of the collateral.[113]

In Minnesota, reasonable fees are limited to collection costs up to the date of judgment and do not allow any after the date of judgment. The Minnesota court held that collection costs must relate to the costs that are incident to the collection and are basically only out-of-pocket expenses.

---

[110] Wis. Stat. § 422.413(1).

[111] *Patzka v. Viterbo Coll.*, 917 F. Supp. 654 (W.D. Wis. 1996).

[112] *Adair v. Sabharwal*, 2002 U.S. Dist. LEXIS 19023 (S.D. Ind. Aug. 16, 2002).

[113] *Thompson v. Doctors and Merchants Credit Serv.*, 2002 U.S. Dist. LEXIS 24325 (N.D. Ill. Dec. 18, 2002).

A percentage charge for collection services that only had a tangential relationship to the actual cost of collection violated the FDCPA.[114]

Some courts even hold these types of agreements where the attorneys' fees bear no relationship to the actual out-of-pocket expenses to be void on grounds of public policy. The review of the case law of the particular state is absolutely essential. Although most states do agree that excessive collection fees will not be tolerated, unless they bear a strong relationship to the out-of-pocket expenses and charges, many of the states have their own particular nuances in treating collection fees. For example, to enter a default judgment in New York City, the courts in most cases will only award attorneys' fees after an attorney has testified in court and has furnished evidence of the hours spent. This trip to court with waiting time may range from two to six hours. Thus, in New York City, attorney fees on small balances are usually waived by the plaintiff. Although we do not know of a case on the point in New York City, to reimburse a collection agency would probably be subject to the same criteria.

On the other hand, a foreclosure case was dismissed after the debtor paid reasonable attorneys' fees to avoid foreclosure and the debtor started a class action suit against the law firm on the grounds that the attorney had no right to the fees. The court stated that if the right to attorneys' fees was in the contract, the attorney is entitled to the fees. It is not uncommon for a mortgagor to fall behind, for the mortgagee to engage an attorney to obtain collection or initiate foreclosure proceedings, and for the mortgagor's attorney to seek and obtain a payoff letter which contains reasonable attorneys fees as authorized by the mortgage documents, and finally to resolve the matter by payment. No court has been involved. The attorney is entitled to the fees since a contractual right allowed the attorney to bill the debtor a reasonable amount without having first to obtain court approval.[115]

OFFER OF JUDGMENT—RULE 68

If a suit is commenced by an individual (not a class action), the amount of recovery is limited to actual damages plus additional damages not exceeding $1,000—as determined by the court. If there are no actual damages, the limit of damage is $1,000. After suit is started, the defendant has available the offer of judgment, which is an offer to pay an amount of money.

The major problem for the defendant in an individual suit is that the plaintiff's attorney is generating attorneys' fees which the defendant will

---

[114]*Kojetin v. C.U. Recovery Inc.*, 1999 U.S. Dist. LEXIS 1745 (D. Minn. Feb. 17, 1999).

[115]*Gonzalez v. Gonzalez*, 2004 U.S. Dist. LEXIS 5463 (N.D. Ill. Mar. 30, 2004); *Whaley v. Shapiro & Kreisnan LLC*, 2003 U.S. Dist. LEXIS 16982 (7th Cir. Sept. 15, 2003); *Blue Hills Office Park LLC v. J.P. Morgan Chase Bank*, 477 F. Supp. 2d 366 (D. Mass. 2007).

have to pay; and the longer the defendant contests the case, the greater the attorneys' fees of the plaintiff's attorney. An offer of judgment at the beginning of the suit may influence the judge when awarding the attorneys' fees at the conclusion of the suit if the plaintiff rejects the offer of judgment and recovers the same or less than the offer of judgment. Thus, an offer of judgment of $1,000 plus enough attorneys' fees to cover the professional services already performed may stop the incurring of charges for attorneys' fees to which the plaintiff's attorney will be entitled.

After a suit has been started, if an offer of judgment is made, the debtor is required to respond within 10 days. The defendant may make a motion to dismiss under Rule 12b(1) where an offer to the plaintiff of complete relief has not been responded to by the defendant. Such offer mooted the case.

These circumstances envision that the offer of judgment is complete relief so that the plaintiff is receiving all the damages sought in the complaint, i.e. statutory damages, plus cost of filing the suit, plus attorneys' fees.[116]

Surprisingly, a case in Michigan awarded $38,215 as reasonable attorneys' fees and $1,403.85 as reasonable costs against the plaintiff. The plaintiff was awarded zero damages on one cause of action and on the other cause of action presented with a valid bona fide error defense. While the numbers are unusual, the plaintiff probably will be unable to pay the judgment.

This should not deter the use of an offer of judgment since some courts have awarded judgment against the attorney and not the individual plaintiff. Where actual damages are sought by the plaintiff, the recommendation is to make the offer of judgment after discovery so that you can determine exactly what the actual damages are before submitting your offer of judgment.[117]

CLASS ACTIONS

The most disturbing development under the FDCPA is the significant increase in the number of class actions, although the Class Action Fairness Act of 2003 has reduced to some degree the number of suits (*see* Appendix to this chapter), one of the reasons is a publication by the National Consumer Law Center (funded by the government), the purpose of which is to teach consumer attorneys how to and when to institute class action suits. The book includes text, forms for complaints and pleadings, and checklists, as well as case citations.

---

[116]*French v. Corporate Receivables Inc.*, 489 F.3d 402 (1st Cir. 2007); *Goodmann v. People's Bank*, 209 Fed. Appx. 111 (3d Cir. 2006); *Frascogna v. Security Check, LLC*, 2009 WL 57102 (S.D. Miss. 2009); *Pietrowski v. Merchants and Medical Credit Corp.*, 2008 WL 2942214 (E.D. Mich. 2008); *Streeter v. Office of Douglas R. Burgess*, 2008 WL 508456 (M.D. Ala. 2008).

[117]*Pietrowski v. Merchants and Medical Credit Corp.*, 2008 WL 2942214 (E.D. Mich. 2008).

The maximum damages recoverable in a class action under the FDCPA are 1 percent of the net worth of the debt collector or $500,000, whichever amount is lesser plus the attorneys' fees of plaintiff's counsel, which is probably the principal motivation.[118] The FCRA has no limitation.

If there are actual damages in the class action and the number in the class is large, the amount of damages may be significant. For this reason, the plaintiff's attorney will seek to sue the major collection agencies and the major law firms on the theory that 1 percent of their net worth will be a significant amount. The plaintiff's attorney also attempts to sue the principal of the collection agency or the senior partners of the law firm and join them individually in the lawsuit on the theory that the owners of the law firm or the collection agency also have significant net worth.

A class action is really composed of two elements: a motion to certify the class and the action to prove a violation of the FDCPA with regard to the class. A separate suit against the defendant is asserted on behalf of the individual plaintiff.

In some instances, the defendant collection agency or law firm will seek to involve their insurance company in the defense of the lawsuit. The exposure under a class action suit could be significant, depending upon the number included in the class, the liability and the complexity of the lawsuit. The exposure in a class action suit is limited to $500,000 or 1 percent of net worth plus attorney's fees, but the Act does not limit the amount of attorneys' fees that the plaintiff's attorney seeks to recover, which may be substantial.

The same letter containing the same violation sent to a large number of debtors presents an ideal situation for a plaintiff to assert a class action. Nevertheless, consumer attorneys are faced with certain problems in having a class action certified.

De Minimis Recovery. A major defense to class certification is probably the de minimis recovery of the class members in a class action for violation of the FDCPA. In most instances, the amount of recovery available to the class members is limited by the statutory maximum amount of recovery set at 1 percent of net worth of the debt collector.

For example, assume that the defendant has a net worth of $1,000,000, and the class consists of 1,000. If you multiply the net worth by 1 percent, the defendant is liable for the sum of $10,000. The defendant may argue that to recover $10 per class member ($10,000 divided by 1,000) is not in the best interest of the class member. If the class member instituted a suit individually under the FDCPA, the individual could recover at least $1,000 in statutory damages (plus actual damages, if any) as opposed to recovering only $10 as a member of the class. The class action statute allows a member of the class to be removed from the class so that it can assert its own private

[118] 15 U.S.C. § 1692G(a)2(B).

action and the defendant will argue that most of the members of the class would recover more if they remove themselves from the class than if they remain members of the class.

While some courts have taken judicial notice of this argument and have denied class certification, most courts have examined this de minimis argument from an entirely different perspective. The courts acknowledge that members of a class would only receive $10 per individual but the members of the class would probably not institute a suit individually. Furthermore, the purpose of the Act is to deter harassment and unconscionable and deceptive activities of the debt collector and the use of a class action achieves that purpose even though each member of the class would receive only $10.

The federal courts in many cases have been generous in awarding attorneys' fees to the attorneys for the plaintiffs. If the plaintiffs are successful in certifying the class and obtaining an award for the members of the class of a de minimis amount, the defendants are still subject to an award for attorneys' fees. In many of these cases, considerable discovery involving interrogatories, depositions, and motions of both parties take place.

The Seventh Circuit stated that a de minimis recovery does not automatically bar a class action.[119] This doctrine at the core of the class action mechanism is that smaller recoveries do not provide the incentive for an individual to bring an action prosecuting his or her right. A class action solves this problem. Nevertheless, when the defendant claims a negative net worth or no net worth, the class would recover no monies. The plaintiff usually contends that the defendants are misrepresenting their net worth. The posture of the liberal courts is to certify the class. If the debtor does have a negative net worth or no net worth, the class is decertified later.

Numerosity. A court is entitled to make a commonsense assumption to support a finding of numerosity. But the defendant's attorney must realize *that the plaintiff must provide some evidence as to the size of the class.* Plaintiff cannot speculate as to the size of the class.

Often plaintiffs cannot determine the number of letters that a law firm or collection agency is mailing. The major caution to defendant's counsel is not to provide information as to the volume of letters in affidavits in opposition to the motion for class certification. We have seen instances where the defendant has denied the huge volume, but admitted a lesser volume or in some instances estimated the volume within a particular state. Any one of these admissions is sufficient to overcome the plaintiff's failure to provide a reasonable estimate of the number of the class members.

---

[119]*Mace v. VonRue Credit Corp.*, 1097 F.3d 338 (7th Cir. 1997). *See Caulton v. Merchants Credit—Guide Co.*, 2007 U.S. Dist. LEXIS 12577 (N.D. Ill. Feb. 22, 2007); *Jones v. CBE Group, Inc.*, 215 F.R.D. 1558 (D. Minn. 2003); *Sonmore v. Checklight Recovery Serv.*, 206 F.R.D. 257 (D. Minn. 2001).

Credit & Collection Tip: *If the class certification does not take place until after discovery, defendant's counsel must be careful in the preparation of his witnesses so that they are not aiding and abetting the plaintiff.*[120]

Bankruptcy. The issue of class actions in bankruptcy arose with the failure of Sears Roebuck to file reaffirmation agreements. The Sears case was finally settled for over a $100 million. The failure to file the reaffirmation was not only peculiar to Sears, but a number of other creditors and their law firms engaged in this practice. When subsequent suits were started, the issue raised was whether the bankruptcy court could entertain the Fair Debt Collection Practices suit and, secondly, whether the bankruptcy court could certify a class. Most of the bankruptcy courts took the position that if the claim was a federally created bankruptcy issue, such as for violations of the failure to file reaffirmations, violations of the automatic stay, or a violation of the discharge injunction, the bankruptcy court may exercise jurisdiction over a class action suit since these were core proceedings under the bankruptcy code. A core proceeding is defined as a proceeding involving claims that substantially affect the debtor/creditor relationship in bankruptcy, such as an action to recover a preferential transfer or a reaffirmation agreement.[121]

If the violation does not arise in connection with a core proceeding, such as overshadowing of the validation notice in a collection letter or a violation of the Truth in Lending Act, the courts will not grant jurisdiction. These claims are not core proceedings and are not under the jurisdiction of the bankruptcy court. As to whether the debtor could proceed with a nationwide class action in the bankruptcy court, a split exists between the circuits. A review of the case law in the circuit is recommended.[122]

Rule 68—Class Certification Offer of Judgment. A defendant made a Rule 68 offer prior to class certification. Interestingly, the court framed the issue as follows:

> . . . May Fleet "pick off" Bond's individual claims to avoid a class action, when Bond did not have a reasonable opportunity to move for class certification.

Mooting plaintiff's claims before certification has the potential for abuse by defendants if simple offers can moot a representative's standing. To adopt such a position would render the class action mechanism a nullity, because a defendant could tender an offer of judgment to each named

---

[120]*Weiss v. Fein, Such, Kahn & Shepard, P.C.*, 2002 U.S. Dist. LEXIS 4783 (S.D.N.Y. May 21, 2002); *Narwich v. Wexler*, 901 F. Supp. 1275 (N.D. Ill. 1995); *De Flumer v. Overton*, 176 F.R.D. 55 (N.D.N.Y. 1997).

[121]Black's Law Dictionary (7th ed. 1999).

[122]*In re Noletto*, 244 B.R. 845 (Bankr. S.D. Ala. 2000); *In re Williams*, 244 B.R. 858 (S.D. Ga. 2000).

plaintiff prior to any motion for class certification being filed and, thus, would frustrate the object of a class action. The court stated that if a class action device is to work, the courts must have a reasonable opportunity to consider and decide motions for class certification.

In distinguishing the major case that took an opposite position, the court noted that the plaintiffs in that case failed to move for class certification for over 17 months after filing the complaint. In the present case, the plaintiff did not even have an opportunity to file such a motion since the defendant tendered the offer of judgment a mere six days after filing the complaint.

The court finished the discussion by summing up the posture of the defendant as follows:

> this rule protects a class representative's responsibility to the putative class members from being terminated by a defendant's attempt to pay off the representative's claims.

The issue before many of the courts was whether a class action can be dismissed when the defendant makes a Rule 68 offer of judgment of the maximum relief available. The offer of judgment usually occurs in those instances where the plaintiff does not ask for actual damages, but only statutory damages and the defendant offers a $1,000 plus attorneys' fees.

In *Ambalu v. Rosenblatt*,[123] the plaintiff did not move for class certification until 17 months after the complaint was actually filed. In other cases, the offer of judgment was made almost immediately after the complaint was served and in some instances before the plaintiff had a chance to move for class certification. The fact that the plaintiff in *Ambalu* waited 17 months has been mentioned in several of the other cases for the purpose of distinguishing *Ambalu* from those cases that support the premise. An offer of judgment made prior to a certification of class does not make the suit "moot" since "moot" should only take place where the court has denied class certification and the offer of judgment satisfies the demand for injuries and costs of the suit. But a court in the Second Circuit relied on the reasoning in the *Ambalu* decision and provided a second case that stated when an offer of judgment is made plus attorneys' fees and costs, any further proceeding is moot since the plaintiff has already received everything he possibly could receive.[124]

A conflict exists between the courts with regard to whether an offer of judgment can be made before a class action is certified. The general perception that an offer of judgment used to "pick off" a named plaintiff to

---

[123]*Ambalu v. Rosenblatt*, 194 F.R.D. 451 (E.D.N.Y. 2000).

[124]*Tratt v. Retrieval Masters Credit Bureau, Inc.*, 2001 U.S. Dist. LEXIS 22401 (E.D.N.Y. May 23, 2001).

avoid the consequences of a class action before the plaintiff has moved to certify a class will not be sanctioned by the courts. The courts rely on the "relating back" rule wherein the class will be certified and will relate back to the institution of the suit which is before an offer of judgment can be made.[125]

CERTIFICATION OF CLASS—EXAMINATION OF MERITS. The Second Circuit, to a limited degree, expanded the ability of the court to examine the merits of the case with regard the certification of a class action under Rule 23. The Circuit Court of Appeals stated that "no basis for thinking that a specific Rule 23 requirement need not be fully established just because it concerns or even overlaps with an aspect of the merits" and went on to state "that all of the evidence must be assessed as with any other threshold issue." The exact extent of the examination of the merits and its effect upon an application for class certification is still somewhat hazy, but moving in the direction of allowing the court to examine the merits if in some way the review is necessary to evaluate whether the class should be certified under Rule 23.[126]

BUSINESS V. CONSUMER. Under the FDCPA, many of the class actions that are instituted are intertwined with business debts. A prime example would be credit cards where the debtor may be charging business debts as well as consumer debts. Another example may be business books used for a personal basis, such as a business book on ROI (return on investment) utilized to enable a consumer to obtain a position with a corporation. In general, the courts attempt to separate the consumer from the business and will grant the certification of the class for those consumers who utilize the product for a personal purpose.

The case law on the matter is separated only by the facts of each case and the way each judge addresses the particular issue. By virtue of this, some of the cases are in conflict with each other, but in the majority of instances the class is certified as to the consumer portion.[127]

INFLATED FEES. For those collection agencies and attorneys who inflate the expenses they incur, the court certified a class of those consumers which were affected by said increase. The decision is devoted

---

[125] *Bond v. Fleet Bank (RI), N.A.*, 2002 U.S. Dist. LEXIS 4131 (D. R.I. Feb. 21, 2002); *Shaake v. Risk Mgmt. Alternatives, Inc.*, 203 F.R.D. 108 (S.D.N.Y. 2001); *Wilner v. OSI Collection Servs.*, 198 F.R.D. 393 (S.D.N.Y. 2001); *Ambalu v. Rosenblatt*, 194 F.R.D. 451 (E.D.N.Y. 2000); *Littledove v. JBC Assocs.*, 2000 U.S. Dist. LEXIS 18490 (E.D. Cal. Dec. 21, 2000); *Lomas v. Emergency Medical Billing, LLC*, 2008 WL 4056789 (D. Utah 2008).

[126] *Eisen v. Carlisle and Jacquelin*, 417 U.S. 156 (1974); *In re Initial Public Offering Sec. Litig.*, 471 F.3d 24 (2d Cir. 2006); *Grider v. Keystone Health Plan Central, Inc.*, 2006 WL 3825178 (E.D. Pa. Dec. 20, 2006); *Sazabo v. Bridgeport*, 199 F.R.D. 280 (N.D. Ind. 2001).

[127] *Ballard v. Equifax Check Servs., Inc.*, 186 F.R.D. 589 (E.D. Cal. 1999); *Benios v. Sprint Corp.*, 1998 U.S. Dist. LEXIS 6579 (E.D.N.Y. Mar. 16, 1998).

primarily to the class certification, but it seems clear that the court has accepted the fact that any increase in an expense incurred constitutes a violation of the FDCPA. In this case, it was an increase in process service fees. Charging a fee where no expense has been incurred would probably fall within the parameter of this case.[128]

Rule 23 Amendment. An amendment of the Federal Rules of Civil Procedure covered Rule 23 class actions. Rule 23(g) directs the court to approve class counsel and includes the criteria for approval and that counsel must be appointed when the class is certified. The rule also now requires attorneys' fees awarded in a class action to be reasonable, but no guidelines as to reasonableness have been set forth, although it is suggested that fees may be a function not only of the amount recovered but also of the number of class members.

Notices sent to absent class members must be in easily understandable English. The amendment also spells out what some courts have been considering for some time. The court may conduct a discovery into the "merits" while considering class certification and the rule also provides class members a second opportunity to opt out by allowing the court to refuse to approve any settlement agreement unless it provides this option.

Net Worth. We finally received a decision which defined the net worth of the defendant. The FDCPA provides for damages in a class action up to 1 percent of the defendant corporation's net worth. The plaintiff argued that the net worth did not include goodwill and that the financial statement grossly understated the true value. In most instances, the net worth of collection agencies and law firms usually consist of the office equipment and the computer equipment in the office and often the computers, copy machines, printers, etc. are leased instead of being owned. Furthermore in small businesses, the principals tend to take out the profits either in salary or otherwise. In the particular case at hand, the defendants argued strenuously that the plaintiffs are entitled only to the net worth as measured and computed by the balance sheet. The court decided that Congress offered a simple, expedient process of determining damages by means of examining the financial statements, which most businesses maintain. The court decided that to require the parties to spend thousands of dollars in expert fees just to help the court decide the appropriate recovery amount for the plaintiff would not be in the best interest of all parties. Therefore, the financial statement furnished by the defendant was the measurement for determining the net worth.[129]

---

[128]*Clark v. Bonded Adjustment Co.*, 2002 U.S. Dist. LEXIS 723 (E.D. Wash. Jan. 8, 2002).

[129]*Sanders v. Jackson C.A.*, 33 F. Supp. 2d 693 (7th Cir. 1998); *Continental Webb Press Inc. v. NRLB*, 767 F.2d 321 (7th Cir. 1984).

But in another case the court pointed out that the FDCPA does not define net worth and that the plain meaning of the term means the amount of assets less the liabilities. The court ruled out book value, because it does not include intangible assets such as patents, trademarks, goodwill, and organizational costs. Ultimately, this issue may reach a Circuit Court of Appeals and considering the uneven approach of this decision, the author makes no predictions.[130]

Trustee as Class Representative. A Circuit Court of Appeals case in the Seventh Circuit held that a trustee in bankruptcy cannot be the class representative in a class action.[131]

Bill Stuffer—Unconscionability. The owner of a credit card brought a class action against a bank alleging that late fees were charged because the payments were posted several days late. Some time before the suit was commenced, the bank amended the credit card agreement by adding terms and conditions that prohibited the use of class actions. The amendment to the credit card agreement was sent to the consumer as a "bill stuffer" together with the monthly bill. The cardholder alleged that the "no class action" provision was unconscionable.

The North Dakota Supreme Court discussed the unconscionability from both a procedural and a substantive aspect.[132] The court stated that the requirement that unconscionability be both procedural and substantive has been adopted by some of the courts. Procedural unconscionability focuses upon the formation of a contract and the fairness of the bargaining process including such factors as inequality of bargaining power, oppression and unfair surprise. As a result, courts generally find unconscionability in consumer transactions rather than in purely commercial transactions.

The court emphasized that it has been suggested that a finding only of procedural abuse inherent in the formation process must be coupled as well with substantive abuse, such as an unfair or unreasonably harsh contractual term which benefits the drafting party at the other parties expense. Another way of viewing the problem is a contract of adhesion does not of itself render the contract unconscionable. Unfortunately, the distinction between procedural and substantive abuse is somewhat difficult to distinguish. Overwhelming bargaining strength or use of fine print or incomprehensible legalese may reflect procedural unfairness in that it takes advantage of or surprises the victim. Yet the terms contained in the

---

[130]*Scott v. Universal Fidelity Corp.*, 42 F. Supp. 2d 837 (N.D. Ill. 1999).

[131]*Dechert v. Cadle, Co.*, 333 F.3d 801 (7th Cir. 2003); *Griffith v. Javitch, Block & Rathbone, LLP*, 2007 U.S. Dist. LEXIS 5496 (S.D. Ohio Jan. 16, 2007).

[132]*Strand v. U.S. Bank Nat. Assn. ND*, 693 N.W.2d 918 (N.D. Sup. Ct. 2005). *See Luna v. Household Fin. Corp. III*, 236 F. Supp. 2d 1166 (W.D. Wash. 2002); *Maxwell v Fidelity Fin. Serv.*, 184 Ariz. 82, 907 P.2d 51 (Ariz. 1995); Gillman v. Chase Manhattan Bank, N.A., 73 N.Y.2d 1, 537 N.Y.S.2d 787 (N.Y. 1988).

resulting contract, whether in fine print or otherwise, would hardly be of concern unless they were substantially harmful to the non-drafting party. Unreasonable substantive unconscionability may be sufficient in itself even though procedural unconscionability is not.

The issue of unconscionability is a contractual question of law for the court to decide and depends upon the factual circumstances of the case. The determination of unconscionability is fact specific. Courts generally consider each claim on case by case basis. While some courts do hold that a showing of either procedural or substantive unconscionability is sufficient to invalidate a contract, other courts declare that procedural unconscionability by itself is not enough.

The more conservative courts seem to require both the procedural and the substantive to reach a finding of unconscionability whereas the more liberal courts tend to rely primarily on either one and it usually is a consumer who is affected.

CLASS ACTION FAIRNESS ACT OF 2005

The Republicans and in particular President Bush, have been promoting legislation to regulate class action litigation to eliminate some of the abuses that have developed over the past years. The Senate passed the Act 72 to 26 followed by the House where the vote was 279 to 149 and the President has signed the legislation.

The Act addresses some of the problems of inflated attorneys' fees, the power of the federal court to acquire jurisdiction over certain types of class actions, some of the abuses in the class actions, and coupon settlements in class actions where the members of the class receive a pittance and the fees to the attorneys are astronomical. A copy of the Act appears in the Appendix to this chapter.

Federal courts will have original jurisdiction over class action lawsuits in which the matter in controversy exceeds the sum or value of $5 million, includes 100 or more putative class members and any member of a class of plaintiffs is a citizen of a different state from any defendant. The $75,000 jurisdictional requirement of the federal court is not required for each class member.

The Act carves out certain exceptions for suits against home state "primary defendants." Specifically, if two-thirds of the putative class members are citizens of the defendant's home state, federal jurisdiction will not be applicable. If less than two-thirds, but greater than one-third of the class members are citizens of the defendant's home state, the federal court has the discretion to accept or refuse jurisdiction pursuant to certain factors which are used to determine the need for federal jurisdiction. If less than one-third of the class members are citizens of defendant's home state, federal jurisdiction is proper because the case predominately involves interstate commerce and the interest of justice is served. This exception also requires that the injuries of each defendant be incurred in the state where the action was filed and no other class action asserting the same or similar allegations has been filed during the proceeding three years. The Act also permits aggregation of the class damages and has destroyed the requirement that there must be complete diversity for federal cases.

A federal court may not decline jurisdiction where one-third or fewer of the proposed members are citizens of the state in which the action was filed by the plaintiff and at the same time must decline to exercise jurisdiction if more than two-thirds of class members are citizens of the state in which the action was originally filed.

If a proposed settlement in a Class Action provides for the recovery of coupons to class members, the portion of any attorney fees awarded to class counsel shall be based on the value to class members of the coupons that are actually redeemed. Those coupons not redeemed will have no effect on the attorney fees.

The attorney fees award shall be based upon the amount of time class counsel reasonably expended working on the action. Any attorneys' fees shall be subject to approval of the court and shall include an appropriate fee, if any, for obtaining equitable relief including an injunction. The court will have the discretion to use a lodestar with the multiplying method of determining attorneys' fees.

In a proposed settlement where members would receive coupons, the court may only approve the proposed settlement after a hearing to determine whether the settlement is fair, reasonable, and adequate for class members. The court also in its discretion may require that a proposed settlement agreement provide for the distribution of a portion of the value of an unclaimed coupon to one or more charitable governmental organizations as agreed to by the parties. The Court may also approve a settlement where a class member is obligated to pay class counsel more than he or she receives under a settlement only upon a written finding that the nonmonetary benefits to the class members substantially outweigh the monetary loss.

The determination of the percentage of class members that are citizens of a foreign state certainly will present problems since the class will probably have unnamed individuals and the court will be forced to make a determination of the likely number and the location of the class members. The issue of primary defendants or at least one defendant as a real defendant who contributed to the alleged harm will also require the attention of the court.

Not later than ten days after a proposed settlement of a class action is filed in court, the defendant who is participating in the settlement shall serve upon the appropriate state official of each state (where a class member resides) and the appropriate federal official a notice of a proposed settlement consisting of a copy of the complaint and any materials filed with the complaint and any amended complaints together with notice of scheduled hearings in the class action, the proposed or final class action settlement, any settlement or other agreement made between class counsel and counsel for the defendant and any final judgment or notice of dismissal. In addition, the names of the class members who reside in each state and the estimated proportionate shares of the claims of such members to the entire settlement. As a further protection, the Court may not approve a proposed settlement except within a period time of *90 days after service of the settlement upon the appropriate state official.*

This period of time will enable the State Attorney General to review the documents and intervene in the class action. More important the Attorney General may examine the facts of the case. The fact that the defendant is making a payment in the class action may lead to a further investigation by the Attorney General's office to determine whether said violations amounted to not only a civil claim, but also to a criminal claim. The Attorney General's office will have the benefit of the entire proceeding to evaluate the seriousness of the violations. Perhaps the defendants before they make a payment on a class action will seek prior approval from the Attorney General's office. *The possibility of investigations and criminal suits by the states or even the Federal Government under the enforcement statutes is a consideration each defendant will face before reaching a settlement agreement, and will certainly impact the conduct of the attorney in representing the defendant.*

Mass Actions. Some states do not have statutory law which specifically covers class actions, but defines a "mass action" as civil actions in which 100 or more plaintiffs bring suit for damages that involve common questions of law and fact. "Mass actions" are similar to class actions. The Act states that where citizenship of only one class member differs from the citizenship of the defendant, these mass actions are also subject to the jurisdiction of the federal court. A major restriction is that individual plaintiffs in a mass action must each have a claim of at least $75,000. This requirement is needed to meet the general requirement of jurisdiction of the federal court.

Appeal. Prior to the Act, when an action was remanded to a state court by the federal court, in most instances, the appeal was denied. Under the new Act, the appeal is expressly permitted of an order denying or granting remand in any case to which the Act expressly applies. The party is entitled to a decision from the Court of Appeals within 60 days.

Issues and Questions. Several unanswered questions in the Act require interpretation by the court, particularly the area where the Court of

Appeals has discretion to review an order granting or denying remand. The statute provides no indication of what the criteria should be. At the same time, the courts will probably have to determine whether federal jurisdiction actually was mandatory or in fact was merely discretionary, and then they will interpret the limits of the discretion to be used by the courts. The words of art, "primary defendants," still must be defined with a higher degree of certainty.

Prior to the Act, the hurdles to overcome transfer of a case from a state court to a federal court were substantial, even in the situation where the majority of the plaintiffs resided outside the jurisdiction of the court. The new Act will deter the forum shopping that has been engaged in by plaintiff's lawyers seeking the states, the particular courts, and the particular judges who are friendly to the certification of the classes.

An interesting outcome of the Act is the requirement that federal and state regulators must be notified whenever a settlement is pending. The state official may decide to review the settlement more carefully than the defendants may expect. The result might be a full-blown investigation by a federal or state official into the business practices of the defendant to determine whether the corporate defendant or its officers or directors have violated any particular law, the possibility of which may impact settlement negotiations. The general thrust of the Act is that the federal courts, as opposed to the state courts, will be less likely to certify classes. If that is the case, then class actions will decrease. The ingenuity of the trial lawyers should not be discounted and it appears that the Act leaves many loopholes in this attempt at regulation.

TRANSFER OF LOAN PORTFOLIOS

The purchase of loan portfolios is common in today's banking and institutional environment. When the loan portfolio is bought for servicing and collecting and the accounts are not in default, the creditor is collecting for its own account and is not subject to the FDCPA. If the great majority of the loans are in default or if the entire portfolio of loans is in default, the creditor is subject to the provisions of the Act. The question left unanswered is what percentage of default turns the loan portfolio into a defaulted loan portfolio.

The normal loan portfolio at the original lending institution contains 2 percent to 5 percent of defaulted loans. Suppose half of that loan portfolio was sold and the remaining half of the loan portfolio included all the defaulted loans, so that the defaulted loans approach 10 percent. Would that turn the remaining half of the loan portfolio into a defaulted loan portfolio, so that a purchaser would be subject to the provisions of the Act? We do not know of any case that has addressed this problem.

EVICTION NOTICE

In the United States District Court of the Southern District, a decision was rendered that a three-day eviction notice required under New York State law was a violation of the FDCPA, since it was a communication relating to a debt and failed to conform to the Act because it did not contain a validation notice or the mini-Miranda warning.[133] In a subsequent opinion regarding a certification for an interlocutory appeal, the judge acknowledged the fact that there is a conflict between the circuits as to whether an obligation must involve the deferral of a payment to constitute a debt within the meaning of the FDCPA. Rent is payable in advance and to pay rent is not one involving deferral of a payment.

The court took judicial notice of the position of the FTC that a notice "required by law as a prerequisite to enforce the contractual obligation between creditor and debtor, by judicial or non-judicial legal process" is not a communication within the meaning of the FDCPA. The three-day notice at issue was required by Section 711 of the New York Real Property Actions and Procedure Law as a prerequisite to the institution of summary proceedings for nonpayment. The judge acknowledged that if the court adopted the FTC's view, the complaint would have been dismissed. After acknowledging that the attorneys would probably not wait 30 days to commence eviction proceedings and acknowledging further that the landlord clients would probably sign the eviction notices themselves, the major concern for prompt review seems to be that the attorneys representing tenants on nonpayment proceedings are seeking to use these alleged violations of the FDCPA to seek dismissal of otherwise meritorious petitions.

The judge allowed the appeal, and the Circuit Court of Appeals affirmed. In New York, creditors, not debt collectors, are sending the three-day notice.

RECOMMENDED LETTER

In the Seventh Circuit Court of Appeals, Chief Judge Posner set forth in the opinion a letter which declared it to be "safe" from violation of the FDCPA if used within the jurisdiction of the Seventh Circuit (Indiana, Illinois, and Wisconsin).[134] The court said that they were "simply trying to provide some guidance on how to comply with it" (FDCPA). The letter reads as follows:

> Dear (Consumer),
>
> I have been retained by Medicard Services to collect from you the entire balance which as of September 25, 1995 was $1656.90,

---

[133] *Romea v. Heilberger & Assocs.*, 988 F. Supp. 712 (S.D.N.Y. 1997), *aff'd*, 163 F.3d 111 (7th Cir. 1998).

[134] *Bartlett v. Heibl*, 128 F.3d 497 (7th Cir. 1997).

that you owe Medicard Services on your MasterCard account #5414701617068749.

If you want to resolve this matter without a lawsuit, you must, within one week of the date of this letter, either pay Medicard $316 against the balance that you owe (unless you paid it since your last statement) or call Medicard at 1-800-221-5920 Ext. 6130 and work out arrangements of payment. If you do neither of these things I will be entitled to file a lawsuit against you, for the collection of this debt when the week is over.

Federal Law gives you thirty days after you receive this letter to dispute the validity of the debt or any part of it. If you don't dispute within that period, I'll assume that it's valid. If you do dispute it—by notifying me in writing to that effect—I will, as required by the law, obtain and mail to you proof of the debt. And if, within the same period, you request in writing the name and address of your original creditor, if the original creditor is different from the current creditor (Medicard Services) I will furnish you with that information too.

The law does not require me to wait until the end of the thirty day period before suing you to collect this debt. If, however you request proof of the debt or the name and address of the original creditor within the thirty day period that begins with your receipt of this letter, the law requires me to suspend my efforts (through litigation or otherwise) to collect the debt until I mail the requested information to you.

Sincerely,

(Collection Attorney)

Debt collectors may have serious problems in other circuits with the letter.

Certainly, questions of overshadowing appear in the letter because of the suit threat during the 30-day period and there is some confusion in the letter as to the requirement of a notification in writing. The author does not recommend the use of this type of a letter in any of the circuits other than the Seventh. Some of the other possible violations of the FDCPA include the following:

1. The fact that the letter did not include a mini-Miranda warning as required under Section 807(11).
2. The fact that payment was demanded within one week instead of 30 days.
3. The 30-day validation notice was somewhat confusing and an unsophisticated debtor might be led to believe that to dispute the validity of the debt adequately under the law, the debt must be disputed in writing.
4. The fact the debtor was to pay the client or contact the client might mean the debt collector may not be "meaningfully involved—more serious for the attorney than the collection agency."

LICENSING OF ATTORNEYS

Connecticut is fundamentally the only state that actually enforces a law requiring attorneys to register with the Banking Commissioner and to be licensed. It requires a bond to be posted and significant information to be filed with the state. Connecticut also requires you to deposit all collections in Connecticut banks. The National Association of Retail Collection Attorneys in one of its recent articles offered that several other states may require attorneys collecting debts across state lines to obtain a license or bond. The main problem with some of these state laws is that the statute refers to a "debt collector" rather than to a collection agency. Thus, wherever the words "debt collector" or words of similar import are mentioned, the statute may be applicable to an attorney who collects debts. On the other hand, most of these state statutes have exemptions for certain types of debts, exemptions for out-of-state attorneys, and other provisions that may exempt the attorney from complying with the requirements of the statute. Whether or not the statute covers attorneys, the authors acknowledge that none of the other states are actively enforcing these statutes against out-of-state attorneys. Nevertheless, this could change and it is recommended to review the state law carefully.

Out-of-state attorneys must tread lightly in Connecticut because there are two court decisions, one stating that an out-of-state attorney must be licensed and the second stating that, if an out-of-state attorney is not licensed, then the out-of-state attorney automatically violates the FDCPA.[135] In the case against Wolff (the Banking Commissioner), your author represented the plaintiffs, attorneys, and members of the National Association of Retail Collection Attorneys (NARCA).

On the other hand, we now have several decisions by other circuits that a failure to be licensed is not per se a violation of the FDCPA unless there is some other activity that actually violates the Act. (*See* Licensing.) The failure to license alone is not sufficient to constitute a violation of the Act. Since these decisions, consumer attorneys are not so quick to institute suits where there is a failure to be licensed. In Connecticut, the story is totally different and consumer attorneys are alert to an attorney who collects in Connecticut without being registered.

Although the author has not reviewed all of these statutes, the National Association of Retail Collection Attorneys newsletter recommends that attorneys should review:

Colorado (Colo. Rev. Stat. Sec. 12-14-103(e)); (Amended 7/1/08);
Connecticut (Conn. Gen. Stat. Sec. 42-127a(a); Conn. Credit Collection Act, 5-36-4851);

[135] *Gaetano v. Payco*, 774 F. Supp. 1404 (D. Conn. 1990); *Sharinn & Lipshie P.C. et al. v. Brian Wolff*, No. 3:95 CV 00265 (U.S.D.C. Conn. May 21, 1995).

Florida	(Fla. Stat. Ann. Chp. 559.55);
Hawaii	(Revised Statutes 480D, 443-B)
Indiana	(Ind. Code Sec. 26-2201);
Maine	(Me. Rev. Stat. Ann. 32 Sec. 11001);
Massachusetts	(Mass. Gen. L. c. 93 Sec. 24);
Maryland	(Md. Code Ann. BR 7-101);
Nevada	(Nev. Rev. Stat. Sec. 649.005);
Washington	(Wash. Rev. Code Sec. 19.16);
Wisconsin	(Wis. Stat. Ann. Sec. 218.04);
West Virginia	(W. Va. Code Sec. 46A-2-101);
Wyoming	(Wyo. Stat. Sec. 33-11-101).

In an unpublished opinion, the Ninth Circuit Court of Appeals in California decided that the mere fact that a collection agency failed to be licensed in the state is not sufficient to constitute a violation of the FDCPA, unless the particular activities in the complaint actually did violate the FDCPA separate and apart from the licensing statute. The judges considered the Commerce Clause of the U.S. Constitution and discussed the economic protection engaged in by the State of Nevada which was designed to benefit in-state economic interests by burdening out-of-state competition, and cited a Supreme Court case, *New Energy Company v. Linebach.*[136] The particular statute even prohibited all contacts by an unlicensed agency.[137]

This court seems to follow a prior Circuit Court of Appeals case in California which held that the court must first determine if it was a prohibited activity under the FDCPA and clearly stated that collection practices by an unlicensed agency were not of themselves a violation of the FDCPA.[138] These cases in the Circuit Court of Appeals in California fly in the face of the Connecticut case which was decided in 1990 and held that a violation of the state licensing law does create a violation of the FDCPA.[139]

A case out of West Virginia produced a startling result in that the court ignored the literal reading of the statute.[140] The statute read that a debt collector shall not engage in conduct deemed to be the practice of law unless he is licensed as an attorney in the State of West Virginia. In short, the statute effectively prevented out-of-state attorneys from sending letters to consumers in the State of West Virginia. The court stated that the statute was not designed to regulate the practice of law nor increase the business for West Virginia attorneys and refused to believe that the

---

[136]486 U.S. 269 (1988). *See Edwards v. Powell, Rogers & Speaks Inc.*, 207 U.S. Dist. LEXIS 52625 (W.D. Pa. July 20, 2007).

[137]*Codar, Inc. v. State of Ariz.*, 95 F.3d 1156 (9th Cir. 1996).

[138]*Wade v. Regional Credit Ass'n*, 87 F.3d 1098 (9th Cir. 1996).

[139]*Gaetano v. Payco of Wis., Inc.*, 774 F. Supp. 1404 (D. Conn. 1990). *See Pescatrice v. Elite Recovery Serv. Inc.*, 2007 U.S. Dist. LEXIS 29616 (S.D. Fla. Apr. 27, 2007).

[140]*Chevy Chase Bank v. William C. McCamant*, 512 S.E.2d 217 (W. Va. 1998). *See Ferguson v. Credit Mgmt.*, 140 F. Supp. 2d 1293 (D. M.D. Fla. 2001); *Sambor v. Omnia Credit Servs. Inc.*, 183 F. Supp. 2d 1234 (D. Haw. 2002).

legislature intended to limit out-of-state attorneys' ability to mail correspondence on behalf of a client that was directed to a West Virginia consumer.

AFFILIATED COMPANY LIABILITY

Hospitals have been involved in several suits where they have affiliated collection agencies which are 100 percent controlled by the hospital. Under the FDCPA, the consumer argues that the hospital controls the agency and misleads the consumer. A corporation may use a corporate affiliate to collect the corporation's debts using the corporate affiliate's names. In some instances, the situation operates in inverse order where the subsidiary refers its accounts to the parent and the parent collects its debts. With regard to the latter situation, a corporation may use a corporate affiliate to collect the corporation's debts using the corporate affiliate's name. Where the parent owned 100 percent of the subsidiary and was collecting the subsidiary's debt, the parent qualifies for the exception of the definition of debt collector. The parent was only collecting debts for the subsidiary and other related entities owned by the parent. The parent's principal business was not necessarily debt collection. If the affiliation is not clearly spelled out, the parent could be liable on the basis of designing, compiling, or furnishing forms, knowing such a form would be used to create the false belief in a consumer that a person other than a creditor is participating in the collection of the debt as set forth in Section 1692J(a).[141]

Where the creditor has set up an affiliated collection agency, the question revolves around whether the agency is collecting debts for other third parties or just for the creditor. In all these situations, the creditor is also faced with the issue of whether the creditor is maintaining control over the operations of the agency. This is often an issue of fact, although stock ownership of the agency usually is not a factor nor is the fact that individuals from the creditor serve on the board of directors of the agency. Nevertheless, the courts are not in agreement on this particular issue and sometimes the court will look at a violation of the Section 1692J(a) of the FDCPA rather than look at the question of affiliation. Citicorp was using a wholly owned subsidiary and sent a letter under the name of the subsidiary. Despite the fact that Citicorp stated in the letter that the subsidiary was a unit of CRS (Citicorp Retail Services), the appellate court held that the designation that it was a unit of CRS may not have necessarily been enough to inform an unsophisticated consumer. In this instance, the court did not agree with

---

[141] *Taylor v. Rollins*, 1998 WL 164890 (N.D. Ill. Mar. 30, 1998); *Aubert v. American General Fin.*, 137 F.3d 976 (7th Cir. 1998); *Wells v. McDonough NPC*, 1999 WL 162796 (N.D. Sept. 29, 1999); *Hannison v. NBD*, 968 F. Supp. 837 (E.D.N.Y. 1997).

the court in *Taylor v. Rollins*,[142] which stated that if the principal business was not debt collection and it only provided services for related entities, it could not be in violation of the FDCPA.[143]

The Seventh Circuit Court of Appeals has extended this doctrine into the area of timeshares where the timeshare owner has used another entity to collect the debt.[144] The debtor bought a timeshare at Fairfield Resorts Inc. who assigned the account to Cendant Timeshare Resort Group—Consumer Finance Inc., which in small type declared it to be a division of CTRG Consumer Finance—not a separate entity but a division of CTRG. CTRG stood for the Cendant Timeshare Resort Group, the actual creditor. Unfortunately, the letter stated that "Fairfield Communities Inc. had referred the account to us for collection" and identified Fairfield Communities as the creditor, when in fact Cendant Timeshare Resort Group was the creditor. This was confusion.

The fact that Cendant used CTRG (Consumer Finance) in the letter does not cure the fact that the letterhead bore the name of Resorts Financial Services as the creditor (a name debtor had never encountered before), which was a division of Cendant Resort Financial Services. The court relied on the Citicorp case, wherein Citicorp did not appear in the letter and the letter was from Citicorp Retail Services, the creditor.

Even though a copy of the contract was attached which recited that Fairfield Resorts was the creditor, it did not help to imply that Resorts Financial Services or CTRG was the creditor. The dunning letter appeared to be from a third party. Cendant, as the true letter's author, must be treated as the debt collector under Section 1692(a)(6).

BANKRUPTCY INQUIRY

The letter in question stated as follows:

> This office has been notified that a possible bankruptcy has been filed. We have not yet received the bankruptcy information. Please provide the information in the spaces below and return it as soon as possible. Thank you for your assistance.

The remaining part of the letter contained the name and address and telephone number of the attorney and provided spaces for the debtor to insert the case number, the chapter, his intentions, and the date of filing.

---

[142] 1998 WL 164890 (N.D. Ill. Mar. 30, 1998).

[143] *Nichols v. Washington Mut. Bank*, 2007 U.S. Dist. LEXIS 85936 (E.D.N.Y. Nov. 21, 2007); *McQuire v. Citicorp Retail Servs.*, 147 F.3d 232 (2d Cir. 1998); *Singleton v. Montgomery Ward Credit Corp.*, 2000 U.S. Dist. LEXIS 17963 (N.D. Ill. Dec. 6, 2000).

[144] *Catencamp v. Cendant Timeshare Resort Group—Consumer Fin., Inc.*, 417 F.3d 780 (7th Cir. 2006). *See also Maguire v. Citicorp Retail Serv., Inc.*, 147 F.3d 232 (2d Cir. 1998).

The letter was signed by a bankruptcy paralegal. The letter did not contain any validation notice nor did it contain the mini-Miranda warning.

The court held that the letter was not on its face a demand for payment. It does not ask for payment or even indicate how much is owed. It does seek information. The Seventh Circuit Court of Appeals stated that demands that consist simply of non-coercive offers to enter into debt reaffirmation agreements do not violate the FDCPA. The court followed this reasoning by stating that the letter was not the initial communication with the consumer in connection with collection of the debt. The court offered the obvious conclusion: "simple prudence should thus impel a debt collector who thinks the debtor may have filed for a bankruptcy to try to verify this before sending her a dunning letter."[145]

DISCOUNT FOR THE CONSUMER

It seems hard to understand that a consumer would institute a suit against the debt collector because the debt collector offered him a discount if he paid the debt within 30 days. Nevertheless, in today's environment anything is possible and a suit was instituted based upon the fact a discount was offered.

The debt collector's letter did not state that immediate payment was due nor did the discount offer state that the plaintiff must pay the debt in less than 30 days. The debt collector's discount offer extended an incentive for debtors to pay their account. The fact that the discount offer expires before the 30-day validation period does not provide evidence of overshadowing. The court held that if a debtor chooses to reject the discount offer, at worst he or she would be liable for the original amount of the debt. Consequently, the court concluded that the least sophisticated consumer would not construe the debt collector's discount offer as overshadowing or contradicting the validation notice.[146]

FDCPA AS A DEFENSE

A claim under the FDCPA by the debtor usually cannot be inserted as a defense to a suit by the creditor for the collection of a debt. The plaintiff/creditor is not a debt collector since the creditor is maintaining the action in the creditor's own name to collect the debt. The creditor is exempt and not subject to the FDCPA's requirements unless the creditor is acting as a debt collector.[147]

---

[145] *Buckley v. Bass Assocs.*, 249 F.3d 678 (7th Cir. 2001).
[146] *Harrison v. NBD, Inc.*, 968 F. Supp. 837 (E.D.N.Y. 1997).
[147] *United Companies Lending Corp. v. Candela*, 740 N.Y.S.2d 543 (4th Dep't 2000).

FAILURE TO VERIFY BANKRUPTCY

In this case, the mistake was that the debt collector sent a claim letter to a debtor who had been discharged in bankruptcy. The plaintiff claimed that the debt collector did not use due diligence to determine whether the debtor had or had not filed the bankruptcy. The court did not accept this argument, but did acknowledge that the debt collector's procedures admittedly caused it to send dunning letters. The issue was whether the procedures they followed, that is, reliance on the client—creditor not to refer debtors who are in bankruptcy plus an immediate cessation of collection efforts once it learned of the bankruptcy filing—were reasonable. The court acknowledged that they were reasonable. But a recent case from the Seventh Circuit seemed to say that the same set of facts is a prima facie violation of the FDCPA unless the debt collector is successful in asserting a bona fide error defense.[148]

CELL PHONES

The ACA International requested the Federal Communications Commission to clarify its position with regard to the ban that appears to exist under the Telephone Consumer Protection Act. Calls to a cell phone using automatic dialing constitute a violation of the TCPA as well as a violation of the Fair Debt Collection Practices Act.

The Telephone Consumer Protection Act states that it is unlawful to make any type of call, collection or otherwise, using an automatic telephone dialing system or an artificial or pre-recorded voice to any telephone number in which the called party is being charged for the call *without the prior written express consent of the calling party.* This statement effectively prohibits a collection call unless the debt collector obtains the express consent of the party who is the registered owner of the cell phone and the telephone number.

The Federal Communication Commission (FCC) identified two requirements in order for a cell phone call to be acceptable. The first was that the cell phone number had to be furnished to the creditor and the second was that the number must be provided at the time that the transaction consummated created the debt. At the same time, the FCC requires the number must be provided to the creditor granting the extension of credit. The question is open as to whether a caller id device utilized to record a cell phone number constitutes consent.

---

[148]*Turner v. J.V.D.B. & Assocs.* No. 02-3511 (7th Cir. June 4, 2003); *Hyman v. Tate,* 2003 U.S. Dist. LEXIS 4822 (N.D. Ill. Mar. 24, 2003).

Your author feels at this time a creditor should be extremely careful in utilizing either one of those options to obtain consent until the issues have been addressed by a court.

> ***Credit & Collection Tip:*** *One creditor would be unable to transfer this "consent" to another creditor.*

> ***Credit & Collection Tip:*** *Procedures should be instituted so that debt collectors will determine whether the numbers furnished are cell phone numbers or land lines. Credit applications should be modified to provide for a land line and a separate space for a cell phone. Specify that the cell phone number is provided "during the transaction." If the cell phone was furnished either before the transaction or some time after the transaction, the cell phone number should not be used.*

The FCC response is limited. The only comfort is that an express written consent on the credit application is adequate. Obtaining the cell phone number in any other way is questionable. The creditor must remember that the courts have no obligation to follow the interpretation provided by the FCC. In many, many instances the courts do not follow or cite to the administrative agencies.

The pertinent section of the FDCPA which would cover the use of cell phone numbers is Section 808 (5) which provides as follows:

> A debt collector may not engage in any conduct the natural consequence of which is to harass, oppress, or abuse any person in connection with the collection of a debt. Without limiting the general application of the foregoing, the following conduct is a violation of this section:
>
> (5) Causing charges to be made to any person for communications by concealment of the true propose of the communication. Such charges include, but are not limited to, collect telephone calls and telegram fees.

The debt collector or creditor must realize that the debtor may revoke this expressed consent at any time. The revocation should be acknowledged and no further calls should be made to the cell phone.

TELEPHONE CONSUMER PROTECTION ACT

The Telephone Consumer Protection Act (TCPA) contains certain provisions which are applicable to the collection effort.

The regulations prohibit the use of auto dialers and predictive dialers or the use of an artificial prerecorded voice to contact 911 numbers or any other type of emergency line of a hospital or similar facility such as a health center, poison control center, any law enforcement agency, nursing home, elderly home, or any number in which the consumer is charged for the call. Cell phones are excluded. This would directly apply to a debt collection call.

The only exceptions to this particular rule are if you have express consent of the party to whom you are making the call or if the call is made for an emergency reason.

The FTC *has issued a report that collection calls are not governed by the TCPA.* An express exemption from the TCPA's prohibition for debt collection calls is unnecessary, because such calls are adequately covered by other exemptions such as commercial calls which do not transmit an unsolicited advertisement. Whether the call is placed by or on behalf of the creditor, prerecorded debt collection calls should be exempt from the prohibition of such calls since they are calls from a party with whom the consumer has an established business relationship.

The prerecorded message calls will not apply to debt collection calls because they are not auto-dialed using a random or sequential number generator and are not subject to the identification requirements for prerecorded messages. In the event conflicts exist between the two statutes, compliance with both statutes is possible through the use of live calls. The comments by the FTC are not binding upon the judicial system and many times the courts will disagree with the comments of governmental agencies. A careful review of the requirements of the Telephone Consumer Protection Act is recommended as well as consultation with counsel.

The FCC recently responded to a petition filed by ACA International requesting the FCC to explain the Telephone Consumer Protection Act as it applied to auto-dialed and pre-recorded messages to wireless numbers.

The FCC stated that such messages do not apply to creditors and debt collectors when initiating such calls to wireless numbers when they are manually placing a call. Auto-dialed and pre-recorded messages to wireless numbers are also permitted as long as the consumer provides express consent. Express consent can be obtained by the debtor releasing their wireless number to the calling party and the consent does not have to be in writing. If you wish a copy, members may contact ACA International (ACA—(952) 928-8000).

ONE-TIME OFFER OF SETTLEMENT

Several cases were faced with a letter that purportedly offered to settle a debt at a discount and stated that it was a one-time offer of a limited duration. The letters were considered deceptive and a violation of the FDCPA where a new offer was made at a later date which was either the same offer or a better offer of settlement. The use of such discounts to dispose of outstanding balances is common in the industry. In view of these recent decisions, it might be better if a statement is set forth in the letter that "the same offer or a different offer may be made by the client at some later date," or words of similar import.[149]

Notwithstanding same, the judge in the federal district court in Illinois chose to disagree with these decisions and decided that a settlement offering a discount within a limited time, but does not explicitly or implicitly indicate that no other will be made, passes muster even though at a future date more favorable terms are offered.

DEBT BUYERS CHARGING INTEREST

As a general rule, a debt buyer who purchases an account is treated as an assignee of the originator of the account and may charge the same interest rate as charged by the assignor. If the assignor was a bank, the bank would be charging a rate specifically allowed under the banking laws. Since the debt buyer is not a bank, absent the assignment, the debt buyer would subject himself to the usury laws if he charged the same interest rate as the bank charged. Nevertheless, a recent case has held that the debt buyer stands in the shoes of the bank and charging the same interest as the bank charges does not violate the state usury law.[150]

MEASURING 30-DAY PERIOD

The debtor has 30 days from receipt of the letter to dispute the debt. Under the strict liability of the FDCPA, a creditor must add two or three days for mailing to allow for the debtor to receive the mail and must add another two to five days for the creditor to receive back the notice disputing the debt.

LIABILITY OF CREDITOR FOR DEBT COLLECTOR

The main thrust of a creditor when hiring a collection agency or a law firm is the recommendation received, the contingency fee charged, whether the agency is equipped to handle the volume of accounts (unless it is just one or two accounts), or the experience of the agency in the industry.

---

[149] *Hancock v. Receivables Mgmt. Solutions, Inc.*, 2006 WL 1525723 (N.D. Cal. May 30, 2006); *Gully v. Arrow Fin. Servs.*, 2006 WL 3486815 (N.D. Ill. Dec. 1, 2006); *Gully v. Van Ru Credit Corp.*, 381 F. Supp. 2d 766 (N.D. Ill. 2005); *Pleasant v. Risk Mgmt. Alternatives Inc.*, 2003 U.S. Dist. LEXIS 890 (N.D. Ill. Jan. 22, 2003); *Jones v. Risk Mgmt. Alternatives Inc.*, 2003 U.S. Dist. LEXIS 12017 (N.D. Ill. July 9, 2003); *King v. Arrow Fin. Servs. LLC*, 2003 U.S. Dist. LEXIS 13259 (E.D. Pa. July 31, 2003).

[150] *Olvera v. Blitt & Gaines, P.C.*, 421 F.3d 285 (7th Cir. 2005).

A case in the Eastern District of New York adds a new element to the relationship between the creditor and the collection agency and at the same time to a creditor and a law firm.[151] Fortunately, the court did not make a determination that the creditor was liable for the acts of the collection agency. Unfortunately, the court did take the position that if certain facts were evident, the creditor would be liable under this new doctrine for the acts of the collection agency where the agency violated the FDCPA, notwithstanding that the creditor had no control or involvement with the collection agency.

A creditor always was liable for the activities of the collection agency which violated the FDCPA if the creditor exercised a certain degree of control over the collection agency wherein the collection agency was only an alter ego of the creditor. In these instances several of the employees of the creditor were involved or actively involved in the operation of the agency and the agency occupied space on the premises of the creditor. Other indicia of control were present which established a principal-agent relationship. The principal was vicariously liable for the acts of the agents which were done in the normal course of business and pursuant to the business purpose agreed upon between the parties. If the creditor stands in a principal-agent relationship with the debt collection firm it hires, the creditor may be held liable for the negligent acts of the collection agency via the principal of vicarious liability. As a general rule if the creditor hires the debt collection firm as an independent contractor and exercises no such control, it would generally not be liable for their negligence subject to several exceptions.

First, the control factor is a crucial element of an agency relationship where the agency acts subject to the principal's direction and control. The court stated that the absence of an agency relationship between the creditor and its collection firm does not preclude the possibility that the creditor can be directly liable to the consumer for negligence. An employer can be held liable for the negligence of an independent contractor in New York and other states where the negligence of the creditor is present in selecting, instructing, or supervising the contractor. This is a form of direct liability because it concerns the employer's liability for its own acts or omissions rather than its vicarious liability for the acts and omissions of the debt collection firm. The necessity is that the consumer must satisfy the elements of negligence wherein the creditor will be held liable for its negligence in the selection, instruction, or supervision of the debt collection firm.

Judge Seybert carried this theory further when they said that a credit card issuer owes a "duty of care" to its debtors because other courts in the circuit have held that banks owe a duty of care to its customers: defining

---

[151] *Colorado Capital v. Owens*, 227 F.R.D. 181 (E.D.N.Y. 2005). *See Becker v. Poling Transportation Corp.*, 356 F.3d 381 (2d Cir. 2004).

duty as a relationship between two parties such that society imposes an obligation on one to protect the other from an unreasonable risk of harm. Noting that nothing contrary to public policy precludes the court from holding that credit card issuers should exercise care in the selection of supplies to perform services. It was a short step to mention that a creditor card issuer should not be able to escape liability if they hired a debt collection firm that used hit men or torturous means to collect debts from its customers. From here, the next step was shorter by concluding that creditors should be able to foresee that the debt collection firm might resort to impermissible or illegal conduct to collect the debt. The "duty of care" extends to using due diligence to be certain that the debt collector does not use impermissible or illegal conduct to collect the debts that is: violating the FDCPA.

To establish a claim for negligence against a party, the victim must establish that the act was the cause of the injury. An intervening act by a third party, such as a collection agency, does not break the cause or connection between the defendant's negligence and the plaintiff's injury. Many cases have held that if an intervening act was a foreseeable consequence of the defendant's negligence, the defendant will be held liable.

The case was decided in March of 2005 and so far our research shows no subsequent cases adopted this doctrine. Thus, this doctrine can be easily expanded to the debt buyers who purchase paper and are unable to provide the debtors with the information concerning the loan such as payment history. Is it a violation of the law to dun a debtor for payment on a loan where the payment history, the application for the credit, the information as to the computation of interest and late charges, or even the note are not available? Is there a legal obligation under state or federal law that the debt buyer who now becomes a creditor should have this information available for the debtor before he can insist upon payment from the debtor?

The court also failed to make any suggestion as to what criteria should be used when selecting a debt collector or an attorney. We have provided in Chapter 7 several suggestions about procedures to engage in prior to selecting a debt collector or an attorney. These suggestions were made in the context of selecting the best agency to perform the services for the creditor and not for the purposes of avoiding a suit for negligence in the selection of an agency. What the court had in mind as steps to protect the creditor from this type of a lawsuit is unknown. As to the question of the creditor providing instruction to the debt collection agency, the issue is whether the instruction to the debt collector and any action taken to be certain the instruction is followed by the debt collector will constitute control of the debt collector to the extent that the creditor is supervising the debt collection firm and the operation of their business. This may amount to a principal-agent relationship and, therefore, the creditor will be liable on a principal-agent basis and vicariously liable. A catch-22 situation is where efforts to comply with the court's ruling may lead to liability under a different theory.

Your author feels that this is a "bad decision" and the best result would be for another court not to follow the decision or have a circuit court overturn the decision. Nevertheless, at this time apparently no additional case has cited this case or overruled it. Thus, creditors must consider this case in their dealings with debt collection firms.

LIABILITY OF OFFICERS OF AGENCIES AND LAW FIRMS

A split of authority exists over the issue of whether officers, shareholders or employees collecting debts within a corporate form may be held liable under the FDCPA without piercing the corporate veil. Several district courts have held that a shareholder, officer, or employee who was personally involved in the debt collection effort may be personally liable as a debt collector without piercing the corporate veil. A case in Utah has held that the firm's sole attorney, developer, author of the letters utilized by the firm and supervisor of the firm's collection activities was regularly engaged directly or indirectly in the collection of debts and, thus, may be held personally liable.[152]

In a generic sense, an individual who authorizes the letters and supervises the activity and is a sole attorney in a debt collection firm is necessarily a debt collector. In the Eastern District of California, the party who was involved in the day-to-day operation, including training and managing the employees and supervising the review of all accounts, was directly involved in the collection of the debts and thus could be liable.[153]

In another case in the Eastern District of Pennsylvania, the courts stated that the individuals who exercised control over the affairs of the business may be held liable under the FDCPA for the business actions.[154]

Notwithstanding these district court cases, the Seventh Circuit in a decision written by Judge Posner held that the extensive control exercised by an officer or shareholder is irrelevant to determine the liability under the FDCPA, since such individuals do not become debt collectors simply by working for or owning stock in a debt collection company. Thus, the Act does not contemplate personal liability for shareholders or employees of

[152] *Brumbelow v. Law Offices of Bennett and Deloney*, P.C., 372 F. Supp. 2d 615 (D. Utah 2005); *Ditty v. Checkrite, LTD., Inc.*, 973 F. Supp. 1320 (D. Utah 1997); *Baker v. Allstate Fin. Servs.*, 554 F. Supp. 2d 945 (D. Minn. 2008).

[153] *Newman v. Checkrite California, Inc.*, 912 F. Supp. 1354 (E.D. Cal. 1995).

[154] *Piper v. Portnoff Law Assocs.*, 274 F. Supp. 2d 681 (E.D. Pa. 2003).

debt collection companies who act on behalf of these companies except perhaps in limited instances where the corporate veil is pierced. Judge Posner postured that the FDCPA had utilized the principle of "vicarious liability" so that the debt collection company answers for its employees on violations of the statute.[155]

A case examined this entire conflict and sided with most of the courts in holding that officers and employees of a debt collector, whether an attorney or a collection agency, could be held liable without piercing the corporate veil if they are either directly involved in the violation or if they manage, control, and supervise the operation of the debt collection business.[156]

CONVENIENCE FEES

An advisory opinion of the Attorney General of the State of Colorado called attention to the collection agencies in the State of Colorado that Section 1692(f)(1) of the Fair Debt Collection Practices Act states as follows:

> "a debt collector or collection agency shall not use any unfair, unconscionable means to collect or attempt to collect any debt." Without limiting the general application of the foregoing, the following conduct is a violation of the Section:
>
> (1) the collection of any amount including any interest fee, charge or expense incidental to the principle obligation, unless such amount is expressly authorized by the agreement creating the debt or permitted by law.

The Attorney General mentioned the fact that many agencies are charging fees when consumers make payments by credit card, telephone, or electronic check, check-by-phone or debit card. These convenience fees are incidental to the principal obligation and an agency may not demand, collect or attempt to collect a payment convenience fee for any particular payment method unless the underlying agreement creating the debt expressly provides for such fees or if they are expressly permitted by law.

The Attorney General stated that his review of the Colorado laws does not reveal any law that expressly permits the addition of payment convenience fees. Merchants also may not impose surcharges for accepting payments by credit card pursuant to Section 5-2-212(1) C.R.S. This advisory opinion is confined only to those agencies that are subject to the jurisdiction of the State of Colorado.

---

[155] *Pettir v. Retrieval Masters Creditors Bureau, Inc.* 211 F.3d 1057 (7th Cir. 2000).

[156] *Schutz v. Arrow Fin. Servs.*, 465 F. Supp. 2d 872 (N.D. Ill. 2006).

Agencies should make a thorough investigation of the statutory scheme in their own state to verify whether these fees are permitted. A failure to make such an investigation may expose the agency or law firm to suits for violation of the FDCPA.

LEAVING TELEPHONE MESSAGE—NEW RESTRICTIONS

Perhaps the major case that affected the FDCPA during the year occurred in New York in the Southern District decided by Judge Karas. The case addressed the issue of leaving a message and whether this message was a communication that required disclosure that this communication is an attempt to collect a debt, etc.[157]

The defendant left a pre-recorded message on the telephone that stated as follows:

> Good day, we are calling from NCO Financial Systems regarding a personal business matter that requires your immediate attention. Please call back 1-800-555-1212. Once again, please call back toll-free 1-800-555-1212. This is not a solicitation.

The plaintiff argued that this was a violation of the 1692(a)(2) which reads as follows:

> "the term "communication" means the conveying of information regarding a debt directly or indirectly to any person through any medium."

In order to have violated the FDCPA, a debt collector must issue a communication within the meaning of the Act, for if the contact with the debtor is not a communication, the Act does not apply. Telephone communications as well as written communications are both covered by the Act.

The defendant argued that the message as left is not a communication because it does not "convey any information" regarding the debt. It simply requests a return call regarding an important business matter.

The court emphasized that the FDCPA defines communication broadly as the conveying of information regarding a debt directly or indirectly to any person citing a Circuit Court of Appeals case in the Second Circuit holding that notice demanding payment of rent arrearages or

[157]*Foti v. NCO Fin. Sys., Inc.*, 424 F. Supp. 2d 643 (S.D.N.Y. 2006). *See also Leyse v. Corporate Collection Servs.*, 03CV8401 (S.D.N.Y. Sept. 6, 2006); *Joseph v. J.J. Mac Intyre Cos., LLC*, 281 F. Supp. 2d 1156 (N.D. Cal 2003).

surrender of rented premises was a communication within the meaning of the FDCPA.

One other court outside of the Second Circuit has already rejected such a claim that telephone calls such as this one are not a communication. The California court stated that while the message may not technically mention specific information about the debt, the nature of the call was part of a procedure to collect the debt and merely the first step designed to communicate with the plaintiff about the debt.[158] The information provided to the debtor stated that it required immediate attention and provided a specific number to call. The obvious purpose of the message was to provide this debtor with enough information to entice a return call. The court stated "it is difficult to imagine how the voice mail message is not a communication under the FDCPA." In substance, the court said that the phone call was related to the debt and was covered by the FDCPA.

The defendant argued for a "catch-22" since defendant was protecting plaintiff because of the danger of having a third party hear the message. The Act prohibits debt collectors from contacting third parties under Section 1692(c)(b). The court dismissed this argument summarily without providing any basic reasons other than the fact that it was Congress' clear intent to combat widespread abuse in debt collection practices and that NCO's argument is essentially based on the assumption that it is somehow entitled to have pre-recorded messages.

Two cases now agree, one in the Ninth Circuit and one in the Second Circuit. It is likely that the Seventh Circuit, which is also liberal, will follow the Second Circuit. With three major circuits adopting this theory, the odds rise significantly in favor that courts in the other circuits will follow.

The net result is that debt collectors have to address the issue of leaving telephone messages without identifying that they are a debt collector. The first option is to identify on the pre-recorded message that you are a debt collector. Most agencies and law firms recognize this will discourage debtors from returning the call.

The second answer is not to leave any message at all if the debtor does not answer the telephone—unfortunately a waste of time. The third response is not to make the telephone call—not really a solution. This decision will have significant impact on the collection effort.

Another decision states that failure to disclose your identity in subsequent communications (beyond the first communication) that the communication is from a debt collector is a violation of the FDCPA. The second communication may be a telephone call. The new case took less than half of page to follow both the *Foti* case and the *Hossinzadeh* case as to the requirements of leaving a voice mail message.[159]

---

[158]*Hosseinzadeh v. M.R.S. Assoc., Inc.*, 387 F. Supp. 2d 1104 (C.D. Cal. 2005).

[159]*Stinson v. Asset Acceptance, LLC*, 2006 U.S. Dist. LEXIS 42266 (E.D. Va. June 12, 2006), *vacated*, 2006 U.S. Dist. LEXIS 58865 (E.D. Va. July 17, 2006). *See also Belin v. Litton Loan Servicing, LP*, 2006 WL 1992410 (M.D. Fla. July 14, 2006).

We have another recent case in Florida which held that messages left on answering machines that did not directly convey information of the debt was still a communication under the FDCPA. The message conveyed information about a debt indirectly, since the purpose of the message is to persuade the debtor to return the call to discuss the debt. This new revolutionary concept may well become the accepted law across the country.[160]

An article in the Nova Law Review published by the Nova Southeastern University, Volume 32, No. 1, contains an in-depth analysis of the problems created by the *Foti* decision. The article also suggests available defenses, some of which might be helpful if they were tested before the court.

FICTITIOUS NAME—TELEPHONE CALL

A district court in Minnesota addressed the specific situation where a fictitious name was left on a caller ID identification device.[161] Despite all the arguments of the defendant and the case law which allows the use of an alias, the court decided that the fictitious name was a deception because "no meaningful disclosure" was made. The defendant argued that the text available on a caller identification device is insufficient to make a "meaningful disclosure." The defendant also argued that a debt collector would violate the "meaningful disclosure" requirement if they called an individual who had neither an answering machine nor a caller identification device. The defendant made a final argument that disclosure was made when the debtor returned the call. The court rejected each argument and held that the defendant failed to meaningfully disclose their identity by using a fictitious name.

CREDIT REPORTING—AFTER DISCHARGE

Several lawsuits considered that a pre-petition debt should have been reported by the creditor to a credit reporting agency as discharged with a balance of zero to indicate that the debt no longer exists.

The discharge in bankruptcy does not eliminate the debt. The debt remains. The debtor still has a personal obligation to pay the debt, but the discharge eliminates the debtor's personal liability to pay the debt. The discharge in bankruptcy obliterates the remedy, but does not extinguish the debt.

A creditor cannot violate the discharge injunction by failing to report the debt as cancelled. The debt itself remains, although the remedy disappears. The discharge injunction is limited solely to a debtor's personal liability, but a

[160] *Belin v. Litton Loan Servicing, LP*, 2006 WL 1992410 (M.D. Fla. July 14, 2006).

[161] *Knoll v. IntelliRisk Mgmt. Corp.*, 2006 WL 2974190 (D. Minn. Oct. 16, 2006).

creditor's in rem interest in a debtor's property will pass through bankruptcy as a legally enforceable interest, notwithstanding that the exercise of that interest will operate to deprive the debtor of their interest in the property and notwithstanding that the in rem interest was incidental to the debt creating the debtor's personal liability. Claims by a creditor against the debtor's co-obligor, guarantors and sureties remain enforceable.

As to reporting a discharged debt, if the reporting was undertaken for the specific purpose of coercing the debtor into paying the debt, a violation could be established, but the act itself does not violate the injunction. If the creditor couples this reporting with another action undertaken by the creditor to recover the debt, the creditor may be liable for violating the discharge injunction.[162]

Amending or correcting a debt status once it has been discharged would certainly fall under the heading of reporting a debt and is permissible if the purpose was not to collect the debt.

Bankruptcy information may be reported for up to 10 years.

Interestingly, the FCC stated that calls placed by a third party collector on behalf of a creditor are treated as if the creditor placed the call. While this may be comforting to the agency since they are treated as an agent of the creditor, the issue arises as to whether a suit could be started against the creditor as the principal authorizing the placement of the calls and incurring liability.

VIOLATION AFTER PAYMENT

At least two courts have addressed the issue in the past year concerning a violation of the FDCPA which occurred after the debt was paid in full. Both courts agreed that the collection process terminated when the consumer paid the debt. Once a debt is extinguished, no debt exists and no attempt to collect the debt can be made. The activity of the debt collector, whether or not improper, is not deemed to be in connection to a present debt collection proceeding. No violation occurred.[163]

CALLER ID

The plaintiff relied on a case in Minnesota from 2006. The plaintiff told the debt collector not to call him anymore. Despite the instructions the debt

[162] *In re Rusell*, 378 B.R. 735 (Bankr. E.D.N.Y. 2007); *In re Davis*, 2007 WL 1080143 (Bankr. W.D. Tex. June 26, 2007); *In re Irby*, 337 B.R. 293 (Bankr. N.D. Ohio 2005); *In re Goodfellow*, 298 B.R. 358 (Bankr. N.D. Iowa 2003); *In re Keene Corp.*, 162 B.R. 935 (Bankr. S.D.N.Y. 1994).

[163] *Winter v. I.C. System Inc.*, 543 F. Supp. 2d 1210 (S.D. Cal. 2008); *Posso v. Asta Funding Inc.*, 2007 WL 3374400 (N.D. Ill. Nov. 9, 2007).</FN>

collector did call him. The calls were placed from a telephone which registered as "Jennifer Smith" on the plaintiff's caller id device. The court held that the debt collector had improperly used a name other than its "true name" in violation of the Act causing the false name to appear on the caller id of the plaintiff.

Relying on this case the plaintiff in a 2007 case from Michigan was faced with a caller id displaying the word "unavailable" rather than the defendant's telephone number. The Michigan court traveled a different road by stating that the word "unavailable" was entirely accurate. The defendant acted to make its telephone number unavailable to the caller id device of the individuals it telephoned. Such was accurately communicated to the plaintiff when the caller id device displayed the word "unavailable." The court found "nothing false or deceptive" about defendant's actions, for the plaintiff could choose whether or not to answer his telephone.

While the Minnesota case stated that a debt collector cannot contact an individual using a telephone that causes false information to appear in the individual's id device, the allegations by the plaintiff in the Michigan case that the communication of accurate information constitutes false or deceptive behavior is not acceptable.

The Michigan court also found that simply blocking a telephone number as a matter of law is not unfair or unconscionable. The Michigan court also considered the issue of the Hosseinzadeh's "meaningful disclosure." Each telephone call does not necessarily apply to a caller id because the FDCPA was enacted before the advent of caller id. The court noted that, while Congress could amend the FDCPA to require debt collectors to meaningfully identify themselves via caller id devices, Congress has not done so and the FDCPA, as presently written, requires no such disclosure.[164]

[164]*Glover v. Client Servs., Inc.*, 2007 U.S. Dist. LEXIS 73604 (W.D. Mich. Oct. 2, 2007); *Knoll v. Intellirisk Mgmt., Corp.*, 2006 WL 2974190 (D. Minn. Oct. 16, 2006).

CHAPTER 15 APPENDIX I

FAIR DEBT COLLECTION PRACTICES ACT

As Amended by Public Law 104-208, 110 Stat. 3009 (Sept. 30, 1996)

To amend the Consumer Credit Protection Act to prohibit abusive practices by debt collectors.

Be it enacted by the Senate and House of Representatives of the United States of America in Congress assembled, That the Consumer Credit Protection Act (15 U.S.C. 1601 et seq.) is amended by adding at the end thereof the following new title:

TITLE VIII—DEBT COLLECTION PRACTICES

§ 801. Short title

This title may be cited as the "Fair Debt Collection Practices Act."

§ 802. Congressional findings and declaration of purpose

(a) There is abundant evidence of the use of abusive, deceptive, and unfair debt collection practices by many debt collectors. Abusive debt collection practices contribute to the number of personal bankruptcies, to marital instability, to the loss of jobs, and to invasions of individual privacy.

(b) Existing laws and procedures for redressing these injuries are inadequate to protect consumers.

(c) Means other than misrepresentation or other abusive debt collection practices are available for the effective collection of debts.

(d) Abusive debt collection practices are carried on to a substantial extent in interstate commerce and through means and instrumentalities of such commerce. Even where abusive debt collection practices are purely intrastate in character, they nevertheless directly affect interstate commerce.

(e) It is the purpose of this title to eliminate abusive debt collection practices by debt collectors, to insure that those debt collectors who refrain from using abusive debt collection practices are not competitively disadvantaged, and to promote consistent State action to protect consumers against debt collection abuses.

§ 803. Definitions

As used in this title—

(1) The term "Commission" means the Federal Trade Commission.

(2) The term "communication" means the conveying of information regarding a debt directly or indirectly to any person through any medium.

(3) The term "consumer" means any natural person obligated or allegedly obligated to pay any debt.

(4) The term "creditor" means any person who offers or extends credit creating a debt or to whom a debt is owed, but such term does not include any person to the extent that he receives an assignment or transfer of a debt in default solely for the purpose of facilitating collection of such debt for another.

(5) The term "debt" means any obligation or alleged obligation of a consumer to pay money arising out of a transaction in which the money, property, insurance or services which are the subject of the transaction are primarily for personal, family, or household purposes, whether or not such obligation has been reduced to judgment.

(6) The term "debt collector" means any person who uses any instrumentality of interstate commerce or the mails in any business the principal purpose of which is the collection of any debts, or who regularly collects or attempts to collect, directly or indirectly, debts owed or due or asserted to be owed or due another. Notwithstanding the exclusion provided by clause (F) of the

last sentence of this paragraph, the term includes any creditor who, in the process of collecting his own debts, uses any name other than his own which would indicate that a third person is collecting or attempting to collect such debts. For the purpose of section 808(6), such term also includes any person who uses any instrumentality of interstate commerce or the mails in any business the principal purpose of which is the enforcement of security interests. The term does not include—

(A) any officer or employee of a creditor while, in the name of the creditor, collecting debts for such creditor;

(B) any person while acting as a debt collector for another person, both of whom are related by common ownership or affiliated by corporate control, if the person acting as a debt collector does so only for persons to whom it is so related or affiliated and if the principal business of such person is not the collection of debts;

(C) any officer or employee of the United States or any State to the extent that collecting or attempting to collect any debt is in the performance of his official duties;

(D) any person while serving or attempting to serve legal process on any other person in connection with the judicial enforcement of any debt;

(E) any nonprofit organization which, at the request of consumers, performs bona fide consumer credit counseling and assists consumers in the liquidation of their debts by receiving payments from such consumers and distributing such amounts to creditors; and

(F) any person collecting or attempting to collect any debt owed or due or asserted to be owed or due another to the extent such activity

(i) is incidental to a bona fide fiduciary obligation or a bona fide escrow arrangement;

(ii) concerns a debt which was originated by such person;

(iii) concerns a debt which was not in default at the time it was obtained by such person; or

(iv) concerns a debt obtained by such person as a secured party in a commercial credit transaction involving the creditor.

(7) The term "location information" means a consumer's place of abode and his telephone number at such place, or his place of employment.

(8) The term "State" means any State, territory, or possession of the United States, the District of Columbia, the Commonwealth of Puerto Rico, or any political subdivision of any of the foregoing.

§ 804. Acquisition of location information

Any debt collector communicating with any person other than the consumer for the purpose of acquiring location information about the consumer shall—

(1) identify himself, state that he is confirming or correcting location information concerning the consumer, and, only if expressly requested, identify his employer;

(2) not state that such consumer owes any debt;

(3) not communicate with any such person more than once unless requested to do so by such person or unless the debt collector reasonably believes that the earlier response of such person is erroneous or incomplete and that such person now has correct or complete location information;

(4) not communicate by post card;

(5) not use any language or symbol on any envelope or in the contents of any communication effected by the mails or telegram that indicates that the debt collector is in the debt collection business or that the communication relates to the collection of a debt; and

(6) after the debt collector knows the consumer is represented by an attorney with regard to the subject debt and has knowledge of, or can readily ascertain, such attorney's name and address, not communicate with any person other than that attorney, unless the attorney fails to respond within a reasonable period of time to the communication from the debt collector.

§ 805. Communication in connection with debt collection

(a) COMMUNICATION WITH THE CONSUMER GENERALLY. Without the prior consent of the consumer given directly to the debt collector or the express permission of a court of competent jurisdiction, a debt collector may not communicate with a consumer in connection with the collection of any debt—

(1) at any unusual time or place or a time or place known or which should be known to be inconvenient to the consumer. In the absence of knowledge of circumstances to the contrary, a debt collector shall assume that the convenient time for communicating with a consumer is after 8 o'clock antimeridian and before 9 o'clock postmeridian, local time at the consumer's location;

(2) if the debt collector knows the consumer is represented by an attorney with respect to such debt and has knowledge of, or can readily ascertain, such attorney's name and address, unless the attorney fails to respond within a reasonable period of time to a communication from the debt collector or unless the attorney consents to direct communication with the consumer; or

(3) at the consumer's place of employment if the debt collector knows or has reason to know that the consumer's employer prohibits the consumer from receiving such communication.

(b) COMMUNICATION WITH THIRD PARTIES. Except as provided in section 804, without the prior consent of the consumer given directly to the debt collector, or the express permission of a court of competent jurisdiction, or as reasonably necessary to effectuate a postjudgment judicial remedy, a debt collector may not communicate, in connection with the collection of any debt, with any person other than a consumer, his attorney, a consumer reporting agency if otherwise permitted by law, the creditor, the attorney of the creditor, or the attorney of the debt collector.

(c) CEASING COMMUNICATION. If a consumer notifies a debt collector in writing that the consumer refuses to pay a debt or that the consumer wishes the debt collector to cease further communication with the consumer, the debt collector shall not communicate further with the consumer with respect to such debt, except—

   (1) to advise the consumer that the debt collector's further efforts are being terminated;

   (2) to notify the consumer that the debt collector or creditor may invoke specified remedies which are ordinarily invoked by such debt collector or creditor; or

   (3) where applicable, to notify the consumer that the debt collector or creditor intends to invoke a specified remedy.

   If such notice from the consumer is made by mail, notification shall be complete upon receipt.

(d) For the purpose of this section, the term "consumer" includes the consumer's spouse, parent (if the consumer is a minor), guardian, executor, or administrator.

§ 806. Harassment or abuse

A debt collector may not engage in any conduct the natural consequence of which is to harass, oppress, or abuse any person in connection with the collection of a debt. Without limiting the general application of the foregoing, the following conduct is a violation of this section:

(1) The use or threat of use of violence or other criminal means to harm the physical person, reputation, or property of any person.

(2) The use of obscene or profane language or language the natural consequence of which is to abuse the hearer or reader.

(3) The publication of a list of consumers who allegedly refuse to pay debts, except to a consumer reporting agency or to persons meeting the requirements of section 603(f) or 604(3) of this Act.[1]

(4) The advertisement for sale of any debt to coerce payment of the debt.

(5) Causing a telephone to ring or engaging any person in telephone conversation repeatedly or continuously with intent to annoy, abuse, or harass any person at the called number.

(6) Except as provided in section 804, the placement of telephone calls without meaningful disclosure of the caller's identity.

§ 807. False or misleading representations

A debt collector may not use any false, deceptive, or misleading representation or means in connection with the collection of any debt. Without limiting the

---

[1]Section 604(3) has been renumbered as Section 604(a)(3).

general application of the foregoing, the following conduct is a violation of this section:

(1) The false representation or implication that the debt collector is vouched for, bonded by, or affiliated with the United States or any State, including the use of any badge, uniform, or facsimile thereof.

(2) The false representation of—

(A) the character, amount, or legal status of any debt; or

(B) any services rendered or compensation which may be lawfully received by any debt collector for the collection of a debt.

(3) The false representation or implication that any individual is an attorney or that any communication is from an attorney.

(4) The representation or implication that nonpayment of any debt will result in the arrest or imprisonment of any person or the seizure, garnishment, attachment, or sale of any property or wages of any person unless such action is lawful and the debt collector or creditor intends to take such action.

(5) The threat to take any action that cannot legally be taken or that is not intended to be taken.

(6) The false representation or implication that a sale, referral, or other transfer of any interest in a debt shall cause the consumer to—

(A) lose any claim or defense to payment of the debt; or

(B) become subject to any practice prohibited by this title.

(7) The false representation or implication that the consumer committed any crime or other conduct in order to disgrace the consumer.

(8) Communicating or threatening to communicate to any person credit information which is known or which should be known to be false, including the failure to communicate that a disputed debt is disputed.

(9) The use or distribution of any written communication which simulates or is falsely represented to be a document authorized, issued, or approved by any court, official, or agency of the United States or any State, or which creates a false impression as to its source, authorization, or approval.

(10) The use of any false representation or deceptive means to collect or attempt to collect any debt or to obtain information concerning a consumer.

(11) The failure to disclose in the initial written communication with the consumer and, in addition, if the initial communication with the consumer is oral, in that initial oral communication, that the debt collector is attempting to collect a debt and that any information obtained will be used for that purpose, and the failure to disclose in subsequent communications that the communication is from a debt collector, except that this paragraph shall not apply to a formal pleading made in connection with a legal action.

(12) The false representation or implication that accounts have been turned over to innocent purchasers for value.

(13) The false representation or implication that documents are legal process.

(14) The use of any business, company, or organization name other than the true name of the debt collector's business, company, or organization.

(15) The false representation or implication that documents are not legal process forms or do not require action by the consumer.

(16) The false representation or implication that a debt collector operates or is employed by a consumer reporting agency as defined by section 603(f) of this Act.

§ 808. Unfair practices

A debt collector may not use unfair or unconscionable means to collect or attempt to collect any debt. Without limiting the general application of the foregoing, the following conduct is a violation of this section:

(1) The collection of any amount (including any interest, fee, charge, or expense incidental to the principal obligation) unless such amount is expressly authorized by the agreement creating the debt or permitted by law.

(2) The acceptance by a debt collector from any person of a check or other payment instrument postdated by more than five days unless such person is notified in writing of the debt collector's intent to deposit such check or instrument not more than ten nor less than three business days prior to such deposit.

(3) The solicitation by a debt collector of any postdated check or other postdated payment instrument for the purpose of threatening or instituting criminal prosecution.

(4) Depositing or threatening to deposit any postdated check or other postdated payment instrument prior to the date on such check or instrument.

(5) Causing charges to be made to any person for communications by concealment of the true propose of the communication. Such charges include, but are not limited to, collect telephone calls and telegram fees.

(6) Taking or threatening to take any nonjudicial action to effect dispossession or disablement of property if—

   (A) there is no present right to possession of the property claimed as collateral through an enforceable security interest;

   (B) there is no present intention to take possession of the property; or

   (C) the property is exempt by law from such dispossession or disablement.

(7) Communicating with a consumer regarding a debt by post card.

(8) Using any language or symbol, other than the debt collector's address, on any envelope when communicating with a consumer by use of the mails or by telegram, except that a debt collector may use his business name if such name does not indicate that he is in the debt collection business.

§ 809. Validation of debts

(a) Within five days after the initial communication with a consumer in connection with the collection of any debt, a debt collector shall, unless the following information is contained in the initial communication or the consumer has paid the debt, send the consumer a written notice containing—

(1) the amount of the debt;

(2) the name of the creditor to whom the debt is owed;

(3) a statement that unless the consumer, within thirty days after receipt of the notice, disputes the validity of the debt, or any portion thereof, the debt will be assumed to be valid by the debt collector;

(4) a statement that if the consumer notifies the debt collector in writing within the thirty-day period that the debt, or any portion thereof, is disputed, the debt collector will obtain verification of the debt or a copy of a judgment against the consumer and a copy of such verification or judgment will be mailed to the consumer by the debt collector; and

(5) a statement that, upon the consumer's written request within the thirty-day period, the debt collector will provide the consumer with the name and address of the original creditor, if different from the current creditor.

(b) If the consumer notifies the debt collector in writing within the thirty-day period described in subsection (a) that the debt, or any portion thereof, is disputed, or that the consumer requests the name and address of the original creditor, the debt collector shall cease collection of the debt, or any disputed portion thereof, until the debt collector obtains verification of the debt or any copy of a judgment, or the name and address of the original creditor, and a copy of such verification or judgment, or name and address of the original creditor, is mailed to the consumer by the debt collector. Collection activities and communications that do not otherwise violate this title may continue during the 30-day period referred to in subsection (a) unless the consumer has notified the debt collector in writing that the debt, or any portion of the debt, is disputed or that the consumer requests the name and address of the original creditor. Any collection activities and communication during the 30-day period may not overshadow or be inconsistent with the disclosure of the consumer's right to dispute the debt or request the name and address of the original creditor.

(c) The failure of a consumer to dispute the validity of a debt under this section may not be construed by any court as an admission of liability by the consumer.

(d) A communication in the form of a formal pleading in a civil action shall not be treated as an initial communication for purposes of subsection (a).

(e) The sending or delivery of any form or notice which does not relate to the collection of a debt and is expressly required by the Internal Revenue Code of 1986, title V of Gramm-Leach-Bliley Act, or any provision of Federal or State law relating to notice of data security breach or privacy, or any regulation prescribed under any such provision of law, shall not be treated as an initial communication in connection with debt collection for purposes of this section.

§ 810. Multiple debts

If any consumer owes multiple debts and makes any single payment to any debt collector with respect to such debts, such debt collector may not apply such payment to any debt which is disputed by the consumer and, where applicable, shall apply such payment in accordance with the consumer's directions.

§ 811. Legal actions by debt collectors

(a) Any debt collector who brings any legal action on a debt against any consumer shall—

(1) in the case of an action to enforce an interest in real property securing the consumer's obligation, bring such action only in a judicial district or similar legal entity in which such real property is located; or

(2) in the case of an action not described in paragraph (1), bring such action only in the judicial district or similar legal entity—

(A) in which such consumer signed the contract sued upon; or

(B) in which such consumer resides at the commencement of the action.

(b) Nothing in this title shall be construed to authorize the bringing of legal actions by debt collectors.

§ 812. Furnishing certain deceptive forms

(a) It is unlawful to design, compile, and furnish any form knowing that such form would be used to create the false belief in a consumer that a person other than the creditor of such consumer is participating in the collection of or in an attempt to collect a debt such consumer allegedly owes such creditor, when in fact such person is not so participating.

(b) Any person who violates this section shall be liable to the same extent and in the same manner as a debt collector is liable under section 813 for failure to comply with a provision of this title.

§ 813. Civil liability

(a) Except as otherwise provided by this section, any debt collector who fails to comply with any provision of this title with respect to any person is liable to such person in an amount equal to the sum of—

(1) any actual damage sustained by such person as a result of such failure;

(2) (A) in the case of any action by an individual, such additional damages as the court may allow, but not exceeding $1,000; or

(B) in the case of a class action,

(i) such amount for each named plaintiff as could be recovered under subparagraph (A), and

(ii) such amount as the court may allow for all other class members, without regard to a minimum individual recovery, not to exceed the lesser of $500,000 or 1 per centum of the net worth of the debt collector; and

(3) in the case of any successful action to enforce the foregoing liability, the costs of the action, together with a reasonable attorney's fee as determined by the court. On a finding by the court that an action under this section was brought in bad faith and for the purpose of harassment, the court may award to the defendant attorney's fees reasonable in relation to the work expended and costs.

(b) In determining the amount of liability in any action under subsection (a), the court shall consider, among other relevant factors—

(1) in any individual action under subsection (a)(2)(A), the frequency and persistence of noncompliance by the debt collector, the nature of such noncompliance, and the extent to which such noncompliance was intentional; or

(2) in any class action under subsection (a)(2)(B), the frequency and persistence of noncompliance by the debt collector, the nature of such noncompliance, the resources of the debt collector, the number of persons adversely affected, and the extent to which the debt collector's noncompliance was intentional.

(c) A debt collector may not be held liable in any action brought under this title if the debt collector shows by a preponderance of evidence that the violation was not intentional and resulted from a bona fide error notwithstanding the maintenance of procedures reasonably adapted to avoid any such error.

(d) An action to enforce any liability created by this title may be brought in any appropriate United States district court without regard to the amount in controversy, or in any other court of competent jurisdiction, within one year from the date on which the violation occurs.

(e) No provision of this section imposing any liability shall apply to any act done or omitted in good faith in conformity with any advisory opinion of the Commission, notwithstanding that after such act or omission has occurred, such opinion is amended, rescinded, or determined by judicial or other authority to be invalid for any reason.

§ 814. Administrative enforcement

(a) Compliance with this title shall be enforced by the Commission, except to the extent that enforcement of the requirements imposed under this title is specifically committed to another agency under subsection (b). For purpose of the exercise by the Commission of its functions and powers under the Federal Trade Commission Act, a violation of this title shall be deemed an unfair or deceptive act or practice in violation of that Act. All of the functions and powers of the Commission under the Federal Trade Commission Act are available to the Commission to enforce compliance by any person with this title, irrespective of whether that person is engaged in commerce or meets any other jurisdictional tests in the Federal Trade Commission Act, including the power to enforce the provisions of this title in the same manner as if the violation had been a violation of a Federal Trade Commission trade regulation rule.

(b) Compliance with any requirements imposed under this title shall be enforced under—

(1) section 8 of the Federal Deposit Insurance Act, in the case of—

(A) national banks, by the Comptroller of the Currency;

(B) member banks of the Federal Reserve System (other than national banks), by the Federal Reserve Board; and

(C) banks the deposits or accounts of which are insured by the Federal Deposit Insurance Corporation (other than members of the Federal Reserve System), by the Board of Directors of the Federal Deposit Insurance Corporation;

(2) section 5(d) of the Home Owners Loan Act of 1933, section 407 of the National Housing Act, and sections 6(i) and 17 of the Federal Home Loan Bank Act, by the Federal Home Loan Bank Board (acting directing or through the Federal Savings and Loan Insurance Corporation), in the case of any institution subject to any of those provisions;

(3) the Federal Credit Union Act, by the Administrator of the National Credit Union Administration with respect to any Federal credit union;

(4) subtitle IV of Title 49, by the Interstate Commerce Commission with respect to any common carrier subject to such subtitle;

(5) the Federal Aviation Act of 1958, by the Secretary of Transportation with respect to any air carrier or any foreign air carrier subject to that Act; and

(6) the Packers and Stockyards Act, 1921 (except as provided in section 406 of that Act), by the Secretary of Agriculture with respect to any activities subject to that Act.

(c) For the purpose of the exercise by any agency referred to in subsection (b) of its powers under any Act referred to in that subsection, a violation of any requirement imposed under this title shall be deemed to be a violation of a requirement imposed under that Act. In addition to its powers under any provision of law specifically referred to in subsection (b), each of the agencies referred to in that subsection may exercise, for the purpose of enforcing compliance with any requirement imposed under this title any other authority conferred on it by law, except as provided in subsection (d).

(d) Neither the Commission nor any other agency referred to in subsection (b) may promulgate trade regulation rules or other regulations with respect to the collection of debts by debt collectors as defined in this title.

§ 815. Reports to Congress by the Commission

(a) Not later than one year after the effective date of this title and at one-year intervals thereafter, the Commission shall make reports to the Congress concerning the administration of its functions under this title, including such recommendations as the Commission deems necessary or appropriate. In addition, each report of the Commission shall include its assessment of the extent to which compliance with this title is being achieved and a summary of the enforcement actions taken by the Commission under section 814 of this title.

(b) In the exercise of its functions under this title, the Commission may obtain upon request the views of any other Federal agency which exercises enforcement functions under section 814 of this title.

§ 816. Relation to State laws

This title does not annul, alter, or affect, or exempt any person subject to the provisions of this title from complying with the laws of any State with respect to debt collection practices, except to the extent that those laws are inconsistent with any provision of this title, and then only to the extent of the inconsistency. For purposes of this section, a State law is not inconsistent with this title if the protection such law affords any consumer is greater than the protection provided by this title.

§ 817. Exemption for State regulation

The Commission shall by regulation exempt from the requirements of this title any class of debt collection practices within any State if the Commission determines that under the law of that State that class of debt collection practices is subject to requirements substantially similar to those imposed by this title, and that there is adequate provision for enforcement.

§ 818. Exception for certain bad check enforcement programs operated by private entities

(a) In General.—

(1) TREATMENT OF CERTAIN PRIVATE ENTITIES.—Subject to paragraph (2), a private entity shall be excluded from the definition of a debt collector, pursuant to the exception provided in section 803(6), with respect to the operation by the entity of a program described in paragraph (2)(A) under a contract described in paragraph (2)(B).

(2) CONDITIONS OF APPLICABILITY.—Paragraph (1) shall apply if—

(A) a State or district attorney establishes, within the jurisdiction of such State or district attorney and with respect to alleged bad check violations that do not involve a check described in subsection (b), a pretrial diversion program for alleged bad check offenders who agree to participate voluntarily in such program to avoid criminal prosecution;

(B) a private entity, that is subject to an administrative support services contract with a State or district attorney and operates under the direction, supervision, and control of such State or district attorney, operates the pretrial diversion program described in subparagraph (A); and

(C) in the course of performing duties delegated to it by a State or district attorney under the contract, the private entity referred to in subparagraph (B)—

(i) complies with the penal laws of the State;

(ii) conforms with the terms of the contract and directives of the State or district attorney;

(iii) does not exercise independent prosecutorial discretion;

(iv) contacts any alleged offender referred to in subparagraph (A) for purposes of participating in a program referred to in such paragraph—

(I) only as a result of any determination by the State or district attorney that probable cause of a bad check violation under State penal law exists, and that contact with the alleged offender for purposes of participation in the program is appropriate; and

(II) the alleged offender has failed to pay the bad check after demand for payment, pursuant to State law, is made for payment of the check amount;

(v) includes as part of an initial written communication with an alleged offender a clear and conspicuous statement that—

(I) the alleged offender may dispute the validity of any alleged bad check violation;

(II) where the alleged offender knows, or has reasonable cause to believe, that the alleged bad check violation is the result of theft or forgery of the check, identity theft, or other fraud that is not the result of the conduct of the alleged offender, the alleged offender may file a crime report with the appropriate law enforcement agency; and

(III) if the alleged offender notifies the private entity or the district attorney in writing, not later than 30 days after being contacted for the first time pursuant to clause (iv), that there is a dispute pursuant to this subsection, before further restitution efforts are pursued, the district attorney or an employee of the district attorney authorized to make such a determination makes a determination that there is probable cause to believe that a crime has been committed; and

(vi) charges only fees in connection with services under the contract that have been authorized by the contract with the State or district attorney.

(b) Certain Checks Excluded.—A check is described in this subsection if the check involves, or is subsequently found to involve—

(1) a postdated check presented in connection with a pay-day loan, or other similar transaction, where the payee of the check knew that the issuer had insufficient funds at the time the check was made, drawn, or delivered;

(2) a stop payment order where the issuer acted in good faith and with reasonable cause in stopping payment on the check;

(3) a check dishonored because of an adjustment to the issuer's account by the financial institution holding such account without providing notice to the person at the time the check was made, drawn, or delivered;

(4) a check for partial payment of a debt where the payee had previously accepted partial payment for such debt;

(5) a check issued by a person who was not competent, or was not of legal age, to enter into a legal contractual obligation at the time the check was made, drawn, or delivered; or

(6) a check issued to pay an obligation arising from a transaction that was illegal in the jurisdiction of the State or district attorney at the time the check was made, drawn, or delivered.

(c) Definitions.—For purposes of this section, the following definitions shall apply:

(1) STATE OR DISTRICT ATTORNEY.—The term "State or district attorney" means the chief elected or appointed prosecuting attorney in a district, county (as defined in section 2 of title 1, United States Code), municipality, or comparable jurisdiction, including State attorneys general who act as chief elected or appointed prosecuting attorneys in a district, county (as so defined), municipality or comparable jurisdiction, who may be referred to by a variety of titles such as district attorneys, prosecuting attorneys, commonwealth's attorneys, solicitors, county attorneys, and state's attorneys, and who are responsible for the prosecution of State crimes and violations of jurisdiction-specific local ordinances.

(2) CHECK.—The term "check" has the same meaning as in section 3(6) of the Check Clearing for the 21st Century Act.

(3) BAD CHECK VIOLATION.—The term "bad check violation" means a violation of the applicable State criminal law relating to the writing of dishonored checks.

§ 819. Effective date

This title takes effect upon the expiration of six months after the date of its enactment, but section 809 shall apply only with respect to debts for which the initial attempt to collect occurs after such effective date.

APPENDIX II

FTC STAFF COMMENTARY—FAIR DEBT COLLECTION PRACTICES ACT

STATEMENTS OF GENERAL POLICY OR INTERPRETATION STAFF COMMENTARY ON THE FAIR DEBT COLLECTION PRACTICES ACT

AGENCY: Federal Trade Commission.

ACTION: Publication of staff commentary.

SUMMARY: The Commission staff is issuing its Commentary on the Fair Debt Collection Practices Act that will supersede all previously issued staff interpretations of the Act. The purpose of the Commentary is to clarify and codify these interpretations.

DATE: December 13, 1988.

ADDRESS: Federal Trade Commission, Washington, DC 20580.

SUPPLEMENTARY INFORMATION: On March 7, 1986, the staff of the Federal Trade Commission ("staff" or "FTC staff") published its proposed Staff Commentary on the Fair Debt Collection Practices Act ("FDCPA") in the Federal Register (51 FR 8019). That notice set forth the text of the proposed Commentary, along with (1) the staff's rationale for issuing the Commentary and (2) a list of the principal areas where it varied in appreciable measure from the informal opinions previously offered by the FTC staff. That notice also briefly described the FDCPA, the Commission's role in enforcing the statute, and the FTC staff's interest in improving the present method of providing advice by making informal staff letters available to the public. It explained that the staff viewed the publication of the Commentary as an opportunity to provide a more comprehensive vehicle for providing staff opinions concerning the FDCPA, and to revise previous advice that the staff had come to believe was inconsistent or inaccurate. Both the notice dated March 7, 1986, and the introduction to the proposed Commentary specified that it does not have the force of a trade regulation rule or formal agency action, and that it is not binding on the Commission or the public.

The notice in the Federal Register dated March 7, 1986, stated that the FTC staff would accept public comments on the proposed Commentary to aid in preparation of the final product. Three trade associations, six corporations, the consumer protection division of the offices of three state Attorneys General, one state regulatory agency, one national consumer organization, two local consumer groups, and two law firms responded to this invitation. Although the notice stated the FTC staff was requesting comments until May 6, 1986, all comments were taken into account in preparing the Commentary, even those received after that date.

On July 9, 1986, four months after publication of the proposed Commentary, the President signed into law a bill (Pub. L. 99-3610) repealing former section 803(6)(F), which had exempted "any attorney-at-law collecting a debt as an attorney on behalf of and in the name of a client." The FTC staff has responded to a large number of inquiries from attorneys seeking its views on how the FDCPA applies to their practices. Therefore, the staff has added comments in appropriate locations to reflect the advice it has provided to attorneys on these issues.

This notice (1) summarizes comments received from the public in response to the FTC staff's 1986 publication of the Fair Debt Collection Practices Act Commentary in "proposed" form, (2) highlights the major areas where the staff revised the Commentary based on those comments or refused to do so, and (3) outlines the major issues added to the Commentary, reflecting written advice which the staff has provided to attorneys following repeal of the "attorney-at-law collecting a debt" exemption in July 1986.

In this notice, the word "comment" refers to an opinion set forth in the Commentary by the staff, "public commenter" refers to a party that submitted views on the proposed Commentary following its publication in the Federal Register, and "public comments" refers to those views.

Principal Revisions to Commentary Based on Public Comments

Generally, the FTC staff found the public comments helpful in preparing the final version of the Commentary, although not all the proposals were adopted. Most of the public comments were aimed at clarifying the staff's intent. The redraft adopted these suggestions where it appeared that they resulted in an appreciable improvement. The overwhelming majority of the revisions the FTC staff made in the Commentary involved only minor changes (adding a word or parenthetical phrase or making some minor editorial change), and were designed to clarify points or to avoid possible unintended inferences. However, besides the addition of comments relating to attorney debt collectors, there were some changes of a substantive nature that were made based on public comments. This section highlights the most significant of the clarifications and revisions that were made based on public comments.

1. Location information (Section 804(1,5))

The FTC staff has made adjustments to two comments to acknowledge that a debt collector who is seeking location information by mail may identify his employer when expressly asked to do so. The staff added parenthetical references to comment #4 to section 804, and to comment #4 to section 807(14), which discusses section 804(1) and (5) under the heading "relation to other sections."

One public commenter pointed out that if the person from whom the location information is sought replies by expressly requesting the name of the employer of the individual debt collector who sent the letter, sections 804(1) and 804(5) may appear to place conflicting obligations on the debt collection firm. On the one hand, section 804(1) requires a debt collector employee, in communications seeking location information, to "identify his employer" if "expressly requested." Yet section 804(5) generally prohibits a debt collector from using "any language or symbol on any envelope or in the contents of any communication effected by the mails or telegram that indicates that the debt collector is in the debt collection business or that the communication relates to the collection of a debt."

The FTC staff believes a proper interpretation of the FDCPA is to read section 804(1) as controlling this situation, because it specifically addresses the situation in which an individual expressly requests the name of the debt collection firm. In that case, we believe that the debt collection firm must reveal its identity in order to acquire location information. The comments bearing on this issue have therefore been changed to reflect that position.

2. Contact limited to consumer's attorney (Section 805(a))

Public commenters argued forcefully that comment #3, stating that a debt collector could not communicate with a consumer who stated that an attorney would represent him with respect to all future debts, would place an unreasonable burden on the debt collector. They reported that the standard operating procedure for many debt collectors is to close the consumer's file once a debt is collected or efforts to collect it cease. Should a second debt from the same consumer be assigned to the debt collector, therefore, the collector might be unaware of the previous file on that debtor and would not know whether the consumer was represented by an attorney with respect to all future debts. These commenters contend that the only way a debt collector could comply with our proposed interpretation would be to check every new debtor file against the closed files to determine whether (1) the collector had ever previously contacted that debtor, (2) the debtor had previously been represented by an attorney, and (3) the debtor had given the collector a blanket notice of legal representation. They suggested instead that, when contacted about a subsequent debt, the consumer should simply inform the debt collector that he is still represented by an attorney and that the debt collector should contact the attorney.

The FTC staff now believes that the portion of comment #3 in the proposed Commentary regarding future representation is simply not supported by the statute, or envisioned by its legislative history. Furthermore, it could easily be the case that the attorney in fact no longer represents the consumer. Accordingly, the staff has modified the second paragraph of comment #3 to section 805(a) to replace the broad reference to "all current and future debts" with the more appropriate "other debts."

3. Consumer consent to third-party contacts (Section 805(b))

The statement in comment #1 that consumers consent to third-party contacts "may be presumed from circumstances" has been deleted. One public commenter expressed concern that this formulation might open the door to overreaching by debt collectors. The deleted phrase was not necessary to the point involved—that consent need not necessarily be in writing—which is better made by providing a clear example of such consent.

4. Lists of debtors (Section 806(3))

One public commenter noted that this section of the proposed Commentary did not completely reflect the FDCPA's reference to sections of the Fair Credit Reporting Act. The description has been amended and a comment has been added to reflect that relationship, in accord with a prior staff opinion on the section and a Commission interpretation on the FCRA.

5. Statement by debt collector of possible action (Section 807(5))

A revision was made to correct the Commentary's inadvertent reference to the *creditor*, rather than to the *debt collector*, in comment #3 to this section. Comment #3 concerns statements by the debt collector about action that is unlikely to be taken in a particular case. Obviously, as several public commenters pointed out, the creditor's knowledge that action is unlikely is not automatically imputed to the debt collector.

6. Documents deceptive as to authorship (Section 807(9))

An appropriate clause has been added to the description and to comment #1, to give a more complete discussion of this section than in the proposed Commentary, which focused only on documents that fraudulently appear to be government documents. One public commenter correctly pointed out that the statute covers a much wider range of deceptive practices as to the source of the document.

7. Letters marked "personal" or "confidential" (Section 808(8))

Comment #3 to this section has been expanded to assert that use of the term "Personal" or "Confidential," as well as the word "Telegram" or the like, does not violate this section.

One public commenter stated that debt collectors use designations of this sort to protect the consumer's privacy by attempting to ensure that the envelope is not opened by unauthorized persons, and argued that such terms are essentially part of the letter's address.

The FTC staff agrees that the proposed change is logical. The staff has already recognized that a rigid, literal approach to section 808(8) would lead to absurd results (i.e., taken literally, it would prohibit showing any part of the consumer's address on the envelope). The legislative purpose was to prohibit a debt collector from using symbols or language on envelopes that would reveal that the contents pertain to debt collection—not to totally bar the use of harmless words or symbols on an envelope. Indeed, it was for this reason that comment #3 to this section of the proposed Commentary (in accord with prior informal staff advice) explicitly recognized that the term "Telegram" or similar designation on an envelope does not violate this section.

8. Waiver of venue provision (Section 811)

Numerous public commenters objected to comment #1 to this section, indicating a fear that the staff's interpretation would lead to a flood of waiver provisions hidden in the fine print of consumer credit contracts. Although the FTC staff believes that these parties misread the comment, which clearly stated that any waiver "must be provided to the debt collector," the comment has been expanded to be even more explicit on the point.

Significant Public Comments Not Adopted

There were several areas in which public commenters suggested changes in the Commentary that were not adopted. This section discusses the most significant of those proposals, and sets forth the staff's principal reasons for maintaining its position.

1. Contacts in which the collector does not mention the debt (Sections 803(2), 805(a), 805(c))

Several public commenters contended that the FTC staff's treatment of certain contacts consumers as violations of the FDCPA was incorrect because the contacts did not involve a "communication" under the definition provided in section 803(2), which refers to "conveying of information regarding a debt directly or indirectly to any person." These commenters argued that contacts that do not explicitly refer to the debt are not "communications" and, hence, do not violate any provision where that term is used.

The FTC staff continues to believe that some contacts with consumers can violate section 805(a) or section 805(c) because they at least "indirectly" refer to the debt, even if the obligation isn't specifically mentioned. For example, there is no doubt that a debt collector who has previously contacted a consumer about a debt violates section 805(a) if he calls the consumer at 3 AM and says only "Hi, this is Joe, I haven't forgotten you"—the words may not refer to the debt, but the consumer will know from previous collection efforts by "Joe" what the call is about. The words "or indirectly" in the definition make it clear that Congress intended a commonsense approach to this situation. Furthermore, the word "communication" (or variations thereof) is used six times in section 804, which authorizes the seeking of location information from third parties with the general requirement that the debt will not be disclosed to such parties, demonstrating that this term was not intended to be limited throughout the statute to acts that specifically refer to the debt, regardless of the definition set forth in section 803(2).

2. Definition of "location information" (Section 803(7))

Public commenters made varying suggestions that would effectively amend the section's definition of "location information"—i.e., "a consumer's place of abode and his telephone number at such place, or his place of employment." One public commenter expressed the view that a debt collector was somehow limited by this language to obtaining only one of the three enumerated items (home address or home phone or work address), while others suggested that we interpret the definition to include a fourth item (work phone). Because no public commenter provided a convincing rationale for its position, and because the FTC staff believes that the definition is clear, both suggestions were declined.

3. Use of "copy of a judgment" in notice (Section 807(2)(A))

Some public commenters criticized the staff's statement in comment #3 to section 807(2) that the validation notice provided by a debt collector to comply with section 809(a)(4) may use the phrase "copy of a judgment" even where no judgment exists. Staff had previously advised in informal opinion letters that the use of those words violated section 807(2)(A) because they suggested that a judgment existed when it did not. Because the practical effect of these interpretations was to make verbatim use of the statutory language of section 809(a)(4) a violation of section 807(2)(A), they were rejected by the leading court decision and by the staff in the proposed Commentary. The FTC staff continues to believe its reasons for revising prior staff opinions (discussed in item 5 of the notice in the Federal Register dated March 7, 1986) are well-founded, and thus it has adhered to that position.

One public commenter suggested that we might also permit the phrase "copy of the judgment" as well. Because the phrase used in section 809(a)(4) is "copy of a judgment" (emphasis added) and this language led to the staff's current interpretation, the Commentary has not been revised on this point.

4. False allegations of fraud (Section 807(7))

Some public commenters contended that the language of this section, which outlaws the "false representation or implication that the consumer committed any crime or other conduct in order to disgrace the consumer" (emphasis added) demonstrates that specific intent is essential to a violation. The FTC staff agrees that some element of intent is involved, but believes that an intent to disgrace can be inferred from the nature of the acts the consumer is being accused of—fraud (comment 1) or crime (comment 2). Therefore, the comments on this section have not been changed.

5. Disclosure of debt collection purpose (Section 807(11))

Several public commenters questioned the staff's refusal to construe section 807(11) as requiring debt collectors to disclose the purpose of each and every written and oral contact, pointing out that court decisions have gone both ways on the issue. The staff's position, reflected in the Commission's Sixth and Seventh Annual Reports to Congress—that such disclosures need not be made where they are obvious or have already been made—has not changed, and the comments provide no new argument for revising that view.

Other public commenters asked the staff to retract the comment stating that a debt collector may not send a note saying only "please call me right away" to a consumer whom the collector has not previously contacted. They argued that such a note could not violate this section because it made no reference to the debt and therefore was not a "communication," as defined in section 803(2). Because the staff believes that (1) the intent of section 807(11) was to require that debt collectors' purposes be known to parties they contact, and (2) the use of the term "communication" in other sections of the FDCPA shows that its construction is not always limited to the definition set forth in section 803(2), this comment was retained.

6. Elements of unfairness (Section 808)

Some public commenters criticized comment #2, which concerns general violations of this section of the FDCPA, for construing the term "unfair" in the same way as the Commission has construed it under section 5 of the FTC Act. They argued that the comment would, in effect, repeal some of the subsections of section 808 because the proscribed conduct would not cause the type of injury required, or would not be considered unfair based on a cost/benefit analysis. Because the location of the comment—under section 808 *generally*, as opposed to any of its subsections—makes it clear that the staff did not intend to negate any of the eight types of conduct specified by Congress to be a violation of this provision in subsections (1) through (8), the staff retained this comment.

Other public commenters asked that comment #2 be expanded to state that section 808 does not cover inadvertent acts or any act that was reasonably calculated to collect the debt. Because this comment was meant simply to reflect the FTC staff's view that the Commission's approach to "unfair practices" (as reflected in its treatment of that concept in section 5 of the FTC Act) is applicable in analyzing general violations of section 808, comment #2 has not been substantially revised.

7. Details of validation notices (Section 809(a))

Some public commenters objected to the staff's view that section 809(a) imposes no requirements as to form, sequence, location, or type size of the notice (comment 3); to our reasons for reversing prior informal opinions to the contrary (item 10 in the March 7, 1986 notice in the Federal Register); and to our view that the notice may be provided orally (comment 5). However, the public commenters provided no new analysis to change the staff's reading of the section. Therefore, the Commentary has not been changed on this point.

8. Proper forum for suit on an oral contract (Section 811(a)(2))

One public commenter suggested deletion of comment 4 to section 811. Section 811(a)(2) clearly states that there are only two districts where suit may be brought by a debt collector on a debt—where the consumer "signed the contract sued upon" and where the consumer "resides at the commencement of the action." The staff decided to retain the comment, which simply notes the obvious fact that if there is only an oral agreement (which by definition can not be "signed"), suit may only be brought where the consumer resides.

9. Miscellaneous requests for added comments

Some public commenters made a number of suggestions that the FTC staff establish new principles in the Commentary.

Although not all of the proposals were without merit, the staff believes it is unwise to add major new sections to the final version of the Commentary to address issues that have never been the subject of staff correspondence.

New Comments Based on Recent Staff Letters to Attorneys

The staff has added comments to reflect the large volume of written advice it has provided to attorneys following repeal of the "attorney-at-law" exemption in July 1986.

This section synthesizes the conclusions reached in the most significant additions made to the Commentary based on this recent correspondence.

1. Coverage (Sections 803(2, 5, 6), 811)

Attorneys or law firms that engage in traditional debt collection activities (sending dunning letters, making collection calls to consumers) are covered by the FDCPA, but those whose practice is limited to legal activities are not covered.

Similarly, filing or service of a complaint or other legal paper (or transmission of a notice that is a legal prerequisite to enforcement of a debt) is not a "communication" covered by the FDCPA, but traditional collection efforts are covered.

A student loan is a "debt" covered by the FDCPA; however, alimony, tort claims, and non-pecuniary obligations are not covered.

A salaried attorney who collects debts on behalf of, and in the name of, his creditor employer, and a state educational agency that collects student loans, are exempt from coverage by the FDCPA.

Debt collectors (including attorney debt collectors) are subject to the venue limitations of the FDCPA.

2. Communications by debt collectors (Sections 805(b), 806(3-4))

An attorney debt collector, who represents either (1) a creditor or (2) a debt collector that previously tried to collect an account, may report his collection efforts to the debt collector. An attorney may communicate with a witness in a lawsuit that has been filed.

A debt collect or may provide a list of consumers, against whom judgments have been entered, to an investigator in order to locate such individuals. A debt collector may place a public notice required by law as a prerequisite to enforcing the debt.

3. Dispute and verification (Section 809)

An attorney debt collector must provide the required validation notice, even if a previous debt collector (or the creditor) has given such notice. A debt collector does not comply with the obligation to verify the debt simply by including proof with the first communication to the consumer.

An attorney debt collector may take legal action within 30 days of sending the required validation notice, regardless of whether the consumer disputes the debt; if the consumer disputes the debt, the attorney may still take legal action but must cease other collection efforts (e.g., letters or calls to the consumer) until verification is obtained and mailed to the consumer.

4. Permissible forum to enforce a judgment on a debt (Section 811)

If a judgment has been obtained from a forum that satisfies the requirements of this section, a debt collector may bring suit to enforce it in another jurisdiction.

By direction of the Commission.
Donald S. Clark,
Secretary.

Federal Trade Commission Staff Commentary on the Fair Debt Collection Practices Act

Introduction

This Commentary is the vehicle by which the staff of the Federal Trade Commission publishes its interpretations of the Fair Debt Collection Practices Act (FDCPA). It is a guideline intended to clarify the staff interpretations of the statute, but does not have the force or effect of statutory provisions. It is not a formal trade regulation rule or advisory opinion of the Commission, and thus is not binding on the Commission or the public.

The Commentary is based primarily on issues discussed in informal staff letters responding to public requests for interpretations and on the Commission's enforcement program, subsequent to the FDCPA's enactment. It is intended to synthesize staff views on important issues and to give clear advice where inconsistencies have been discovered among staff letters. In some cases, reflection on the issues posed or relevant court decisions have resulted in a different interpretation from that expressed by the staff in those informal letters. Therefore, the Commentary supersedes the staff views expressed in such correspondence.

In many cases several different sections or subsections of the FDCPA may apply to a given factual situation. This results from the effort by Congress in drafting the FDCPA to be both explicit and comprehensive, in order to limit the opportunities for debt collectors to evade the underlying legislative intention. Although it may be of only technical interest whether a given act violates one, two, or three sections of the FDCPA, the Commentary frequently provides cross references to other applicable sections so that it may serve as a more comprehensive guide for its users. The Commentary attempts to discuss the more common overlapping references, usually under the heading "Relation to other sections," and deals with issues raised by each factual situation under the section or subsection that the staff deems most directly applicable to it.

The Commentary will be revised and updated by the staff as needed, based on the experience of the Commission in responding to public inquiries about, and enforcing, the FDCPA. The Commission welcomes input from interested industry, consumer, and other public parties on the Commentary and on issues discussed in it.

The staff will continue to respond to requests for informal interpretations. Updates of the Commentary will consider and, where appropriate, incorporate issues raised in correspondence and other public contacts, as well as the Commission's enforcement efforts. Therefore, a party who is interested in raising an issue for inclusion in future editions of the Commentary does not need to make any formal submission or request to that effect.

The Commentary should be used in conjunction with the statute. The abbreviated description of each section or subsection in the Commentary is designed only as a preamble to discussion of issues pertaining to each section and is not intended as a substitute for the statutory text.

The Commentary should not be considered as a reflection of all court rulings under the FDCPA. For example, on some issues judicial interpretations of the statute vary depending on the jurisdiction, with the result that the staff's enforcement position can not be in accord with all decided cases.

Section 801—Short Title

Section 801 names the statute the "Fair Debt Collection Practices Act."

The Fair Debt Collection Practices Act (FDCPA) is Title VIII of the Consumer Credit Protection Act, which also includes other federal statutes relating to consumer credit, such as the Truth in Lending Act (Title I), the Fair Credit Reporting Act (Title VI), and the Equal Credit Opportunity Act (Title VII).

Section 802—Findings And Purpose

Section 802 recites the Congressional findings that serve as the basis for the legislation.

Section 803—Definitions

Section 803(1) defines "Commission" as the Federal Trade Commission.

1. General. The definition includes only the Federal Trade Commission, not necessarily the staff acting on its behalf.

Section 803(2) defines "communication" as the "conveying of information regarding a debt directly or indirectly to any person through any medium."

1. General. The definition includes oral and written transmission of messages which refer to a debt.

2. Exclusions. The term does not include formal legal action (e.g., filing of a lawsuit or other petition/pleadings with a court; service of a complaint or other legal papers in connection with a lawsuit, or activities directly related to such service). Similarly, it does not include a notice that is required by law as a prerequisite to enforcing a contractual obligation between creditor and debtor, by judicial or nonjudicial legal process. The term does not include situations in which the debt collector does not convey information regarding the debt, such as:

A request to a third party for a consumer to return a telephone call to the debt collector, if the debt collector does not refer to the debt or the caller's status as (or affiliation with) a debt collector.

A request to a third party for information about the consumer's assets, if the debt collector does not reveal the existence of a debt.

A request to a third party in connection with litigation (e.g., requesting a third party to complete a military affidavit that must be filed as a prerequisite to enforcing a default judgment, if the debt collector does not reveal the existence of the debt).

Section 803(3) defines "consumer" as "any natural person obligated or allegedly obligated to pay any debt."

1. General. The definition includes only a "natural person" and not an artificial person such as a corporation or other entity created by statute.

Section 803(4) defines "creditor" as "any person who offers or extends credit creating a debt or to whom a debt is owed." However, the definition excludes a party who "receives an assignment or transfer of a debt in default solely for the purpose of facilitating collection of such debt for another."

1. General. The definition includes the party that actually extended credit or became the obligee on an account in the normal course of business, and excludes a party that was assigned a delinquent debt only for collection purposes.

Section 803(5) defines "debt" as a consumer's "obligation . . . to pay money arising out of a transaction in which the money, property, insurance, or services (being purchased) are primarily for personal, family, or household purposes. . . ."

1. Examples. The term includes:

Overdue obligations such as medical bills that were originally payable in full within a certain time period (e.g., 30 days).

A dishonored check that was tendered in payment for goods or services acquired or used primarily for personal, family, or household purposes.

A student loan, because the consumer is purchasing "services" (education) for personal use.

2. *Exclusions.* The term does not include:

Unpaid taxes, fines, alimony, or tort claims, because they are not debts incurred from a "transaction (involving purchase of) property . . . or services . . . for personal, family or household purposes."

A credit card that a cardholder retains after the card issuer has demanded its return. The cardholder's account balance is the debt.

A non-pecuniary obligation of the consumer such as the responsibility to maintain adequate insurance on the collateral, because it does not involve an "obligation . . . to pay money."

Section 803(6) defines "debt collector" as a party "who uses any instrumentality of interstate commerce or the mails in . . . collection of . . . debts owed . . . another."

1. *Examples.* The term includes:

Employees of a debt collection business, including a corporation, partnership, or other entity whose business is the collection of debts owed another.

A firm that regularly collects overdue rent on behalf of real estate owners, or periodic assessments on behalf of condominium associations, because it "regularly collects . . . debts owed or due another."

A party based in the United States who collects debts owed by consumers residing outside the United States, because he "uses . . . the mails" in the collection business. The residence of the debtor is irrelevant.

A firm that collects debts in its own name for a creditor solely by mechanical techniques, such as (1) placing phone calls with pre-recorded messages and recording consumer responses, or (2) making computer-generated mailings.

An attorney or law firm whose efforts to collect consumer debts on behalf of its clients regularly include activities traditionally associated with debt collection, such as sending demand letters (dunning notices) or making collection telephone calls to the consumer. However, an attorney is not considered to be a debt collector simply because he responds to an inquiry from the consumer following the filing of a lawsuit.

2. *Exclusions.* The term does not include:

Any person who collects debts (or attempts to do so) only in isolated instances, because the definition includes only those who "regularly" collect debts.

A credit card issuer that collects its cardholder's account, even when the account is based upon purchases from participating merchants, because the issuer is collecting its own debts, not those "owed or due another."

An attorney whose practice is limited to legal activities (e.g., the filing and prosecution of lawsuits to reduce debts to judgment).

3. *Application of definition to creditor using another name.* Creditors are generally excluded from the definition of "debt collector" to the extent that they collect their own debts in their own name. However, the term specifically applies to "any creditor who, in the process of collecting his own debts, uses any name other than his own which would indicate that a third person is" involved in the collection.

A creditor is a debt collector for purposes of this act if:

He uses a name other than his own to collect his debts, including a fictitious name. His salaried attorney employees who collect debts use stationery that indicates that attorneys are employed by someone other than the creditor or are independent or separate from the creditor (e.g., ABC Corp. sends collection letters on stationery of "John Jones, Attorney-at-Law").

He regularly collects debts for another creditor; however, he is a debt collector only for purposes of collecting these debts, not when he collects his own debt in his own name.

The creditor's collection division or related corporate collector is not clearly designated as being affiliated with the creditor; however, the creditor is not a debt collector if the creditor's correspondence is clearly labeled as being from the "collection unit of the (creditor's name)," since the creditor is not using a "name other than his own" in that instance.

Relation to other sections. A creditor who is covered by the FDCPA because he uses a "name other than his own" also may violate section 807(14), which prohibits using a false business name. When he falsely uses an attorney's name, he violates section 807(3).

4. Specific exemptions from definition of debt collector.

(a) *Creditor employees.* Section 803(6)(A) provides that "debt collector" does not include "any officer or employee of a creditor while, in the name of the creditor, collecting debts for such creditor."

The exemption includes a collection agency employee, who works for a creditor to collect in the creditor's name at the creditor's office under the creditor's supervision, because he has become the *de facto* employee of the creditor.

The exemption includes a creditor's salaried attorney (or other) employee who collects debts on behalf of, and in the name of, that creditor.

The exemption does not include a creditor's former employee who continues to collect accounts on the creditor's behalf, if he acts under his own name rather than the creditor's.

(b) *Creditor-controlled collector.* Section 803(6)(B) provides that "debt collector" does not include a party collecting for another, where they are both "related by common ownership or affiliated by corporate control, if the (party collects) only for persons to whom it is so related or affiliated and if the principal business of such person is not the collection of debts."

The exemption applies where the collector and creditor have "common ownership or . . . corporate control." For example, a company is exempt when it attempts to collect debts of another company after the two entities have merged.

The exemption does not apply to a party related to a creditor if it also collects debts for others in addition to the related creditors.

(c) *State and federal officials.* Section 803(6)(C) provides that "debt collector" does not include any state or federal employee "to the extent that collecting or attempting to collect any debt is in the performance of his official duties."

The exemption applies only to such governmental employees in the performance of their "official duties" and, therefore, does not apply to an attorney employed by a county government who also collects bad checks for local merchants where that activity is outside his official duties.

The exemption includes a state educational agency that is engaged in the collection of student loans.

(d) *Process servers.* Section 803(6)(D) provides that "debt collector" does not include "any person while serving or attempting to serve legal process on any other person in connection with the judicial enforcement of any debt."

The exemption covers marshals, sheriffs, and any other process servers while conducting their normal duties relating to serving legal papers.

(e) *Non-profit counselors.* Section 803(6)(E) provides that "debt collector" does not include "any nonprofit organization which, at the request of consumers, performs bona fide consumer credit counseling and assists consumers in the liquidation of their debts by receiving payments from such consumers and distributing such amounts to creditors."

This exemption applies only to non-profit organizations; it does not apply to for-profit credit counseling services that accept fees from debtors and regularly transmit such funds to creditors.

(f) *Miscellaneous.* Section 803(6)(F) provides that "debt collector" does not include collection activity by a party about a debt that "(i) is incidental to a bona fide fiduciary obligation or . . . escrow arrangement; (ii) . . . was originated by such person; (iii) . . . was not in default at the time it was obtained by such person; or (iv) [was] obtained by such person as a secured party in a commercial credit transaction involving the creditor."

The exemption (i) for bona fide fiduciary obligations or escrow arrangements applies to entities such as trust departments of banks, and escrow companies. It does not include a party who is named as a debtor's trustee solely for the purpose of conducting a foreclosure sale (i.e., exercising a power of sale in the event of default on a loan).

The exemption (ii) for a party that originated the debt applies to the original creditor collecting his own debts in his own name. It also applies when a creditor assigns a debt originally owed to him, but retains the authority to collect the obligation on behalf of the assignee to whom the debt becomes owed. For example, the exemption applies to a creditor who makes a mortgage or school loan and continues to handle the account after assigning it to a third party. However, it does not apply to a party that takes assignment of retail installment contracts from the original creditor and then reassigns them to another creditor but continues to collect the debt arising from the contracts, because the debt was not "originated by" the collector/first assignee.

The exception (iii) for debts not in default when obtained applies to parties such as mortgage service companies whose business is servicing current accounts.

The exemption (iv) for a secured party in a commercial transaction applies to a commercial lender who acquires a consumer account that was used as collateral, following default on a loan from the commercial lender to the original creditor.

(g) *Attorneys.* A provision of the FDCPA, as enacted in 1977 (former section 803(6)(F)), providing that "debt collector" does not include "any attorney-at-law collecting a debt as an attorney on behalf of and in the name of a client," was repealed by Pub. L. 99-361, which became effective in July 1986. Therefore, an attorney who meets the definition set forth in section 803(6) is now covered by the FDCPA.

Section 803(7) defines "location information" as "a consumer's place of abode and his telephone number at such place, or his place of employment."

This definition includes only residence, home phone number, and place of employment. It does not cover work phone numbers, names of supervisors and their telephone numbers, salaries or dates of paydays.

Section 803(8) defines "state" as "any State, territory, or possession of the United States, the District of Columbia, the Commonwealth of Puerto Rico, or any political subdivision of any of the foregoing."

Section 804—Acquisition Of Location Information

Section 804 requires a debt collector, when communicating with third parties for the purpose of acquiring information about the consumer's location to (1) "identify himself, state that he is confirming or correcting location information concerning the consumer, and, only if expressly requested, identify his employer"; (2) not refer to the debt, (3) usually make only a single contact with each third party, (4) not communicate by post card, (5) not indicate the collection nature of his business purpose in any written communication, and (6) limit communications to the consumer's attorney, where the collector knows of the attorney, unless the attorney fails to respond to the communication.

1. General. Although the FDCPA generally protects the consumer's privacy by limiting debt collector communications about personal affairs to third parties, it recognizes the need for some third-party contact by collectors to seek the whereabouts of the consumer.

2. Identification of debt collector (Section 804(1)). An individual employed by a debt collector seeking location information must identify himself, but must not identify his employer unless asked. When asked, however, he must give the true and full name of the employer, to comply with this provision and avoid a violation of section 807(14). An individual debt collector may use an alias if it is used consistently and if it does not interfere with another party's ability to identify him (e.g., the true identity can be ascertained by the employer).

3. Referral to debt (Section 804(2)). A debt collector may not refer to the consumer's debt in any third-party communication seeking location information, including those with other creditors.

4. Reference to debt collector's business (Section 804(5)). A debt collector may not use his actual name in his letterhead or elsewhere in a written communication seeking location information, if the name indicates collection activity (such as a name containing the word "debt," "collector," or "collection"), except when the person contacted has expressly requested that the debt collector identify himself.

5. Communication with consumer's attorney (Section 804(6)). Once a debt collector learns a consumer is represented by an attorney in connection with the debt, he must confine his request for location information to the attorney. (*See also* comments on section 805(a)(2).)

Section 805—Communication In Connection With Debt Collection

Section 805(a)—*Communication with the consumer.* Unless the consumer has consented or a court order permits, a debt collector may not communicate with a consumer to collect a debt (1) at any time or place which is unusual or known to be inconvenient to the consumer (8AM-9PM is presumed to be convenient), (2) where he knows the consumer is represented by an attorney with respect to the debt, unless the attorney fails to respond to the communication in a reasonable time period, or (3) at work if he knows the consumer's employer prohibits such contacts.

1. Scope. For purposes of this section, the term "communicate" is given its commonly accepted meaning. Thus, the section applies to contacts with the consumer related to the collection of the debt, whether or not the debt is specifically mentioned.

2. Inconvenient or unusual times or places (Section 805(a)(1)). A debt collector may not call the consumer at any time, or on any particular day, if he has credible information (from the consumer or elsewhere) that it is inconvenient. If the debt collector does not have such information, a call on Sunday is not per se illegal.

3. Consumer represented by attorney (Section 805(a)(2)). If a debt collector learns that a consumer is represented by an attorney in connection with the debt, even if not formally notified of this fact, the debt collector must contact only the attorney and must not contact the consumer.

A debt collector who knows a consumer is represented by counsel with respect to a debt is not required to assume similar representation on other debts; however, if a consumer notifies the debt collector that the attorney has been retained to represent him for other debts placed with the debt collector, the debt collector must deal only with that attorney with respect to such debts.

The creditor's knowledge that the consumer has an attorney is not automatically imputed to the debt collector.

4. Calls at work (Section 805(a)(3)). A debt collector may not call the consumer at work if he has reason to know the employer forbids such communication (e.g., if the consumer has so informed the debt collector).

Section 805(b)—Communication with third parties. Unless the consumer consents, or a court order or section 804 permits, "or as reasonably necessary to effectuate a postjudgment judicial remedy," a debt collector "may not communicate, in connection with the collection of any debt, with any person other than the consumer, his attorney, a consumer reporting agency if otherwise permitted by law, the creditor, the attorney of the creditor, or the attorney of the debt collector."

1. Consumer consent to the third-party contact. The consumer's consent need not be in writing. For example, if a third party volunteers that a consumer has authorized him to pay the consumer's account, the debt collector may normally presume the consumer's consent, and may accept the payment and provide a receipt to the party that makes the payment. However, consent may not be inferred only from a consumer's inaction when the debt collector requests such consent.

2. Location information. Although a debt collector's search for information concerning the consumer's location (provided in section 804) is expressly excepted from the ban on third-party contacts, a debt collector may not call third parties under the pretense of gaining information already in his possession.

3. Incidental contacts with telephone operator or telegraph clerk. A debt collector may contact an employee of a telephone or telegraph company in order to contact the consumer, without violating the prohibition on communication to third parties, if the only information given is that necessary to enable the collector to transmit the message to, or make the contact with, the consumer.

4. Accessibility by third party. A debt collector may not send a written message that is easily accessible to third parties. For example, he may not use a computerized billing statement that can be seen on the envelope itself.

A debt collector may use an "in care of" letter only if the consumer lives at, or accepts mail at, the other party's address.

A debt collector does not violate this provision when an eavesdropper overhears a conversation with the consumer, unless the debt collector has reason to anticipate the conversation will be overhead.

5. Non-excepted parties. A debt collector may discuss the debt only with the parties specified in this section (consumer, creditor, a party's attorney, or credit bureau). For example, unless the consumer has authorized the communication, a collector may not discuss the debt (such as a dishonored check) with a bank, or make a report on a consumer to a non-profit counseling service.

6. Judicial remedy. The words "as reasonably necessary to effectuate a postjudgment judicial remedy" mean a communication necessary for execution or enforcement of the remedy. A debt collector may not send a copy of the judgment to an employer, except as part of a formal service of papers to achieve a garnishment or other remedy.

7. Audits or inquiries. A debt collector may disclose his files to a government official or an auditor, to respond to an inquiry or conduct an audit, because the disclosure would not be "in connection with the collection of any debt."

8. Communications by attorney debt collectors. An attorney who represents either a creditor or debt collector that has previously tried to collect an account may communicate his efforts to collect the account to the debt collector. Because the section permits a debt collector to communicate with "the attorney of the creditor, or the attorney of the debt collector," communications between these parties (even if the attorney is also a debt collector) are not forbidden.

An attorney may communicate with a potential witness in connection with a lawsuit he has filed (e.g., in order to establish the existence of a debt), because the section was not intended to prohibit communications by attorneys that are necessary to conduct lawsuits on behalf of their clients.

Section 805(c)—Ceasing communication. Once a debt collector receives written notice from a consumer that he or she refuses to pay the debt or wants the collector to stop further collection efforts, the debt collector must cease any further communication with the consumer except "(1) to advise the consumer that the debt collector's further efforts are being terminated; (2) to notify the consumer that the debt collector or creditor may invoke specified remedies which are ordinarily invoked by such debt collector or creditor; or (3) where applicable, to notify the consumer that the debt collector or creditor intends to invoke a specified remedy."

1. *Scope.* For purposes of this section, the term "communicate" is given its commonly accepted meaning. Thus, the section applies to any contact with the consumer related to the collection of the debt, whether or not the debt is specifically mentioned.

2. *Request for payment.* A debt collector's response to a "cease communication" notice from the consumer may not include a demand for payment, but is limited to the three statutory exceptions.

Section 805(d)—"consumer" definition. For section 805 purposes, the term "consumer" includes the "consumer's spouse, parent (if the consumer is a minor), guardian, executor, or administrator."

1. *Broad "consumer" definition.* Because of the broad statutory definition of "consumer" for the purposes of this section, many of its protections extend to parties close to the consumer. For example, the debt collector may not call the consumer's spouse at a time or place known to be inconvenient to the spouse. Conversely, he may call the spouse (guardian, executor, etc.) at any time or place that would be in accord with the limitations of section 805(a).

Section 806—Harassment Or Abuse

Section 806 prohibits a debt collector from any conduct that would "Harass, oppress, or abuse any person in connection with the collection of a debt." It provides six examples of harassment or abuse.

1. *Scope.* Prohibited actions are not limited to the six subsections listed as examples of activities that violate this provision.

2. *Unnecessary calls to third parties.* A debt collector may not leave telephone messages with neighbors when the debt collector knows the consumer's name and telephone number and could have reached him directly.

3. *Multiple contacts with consumer.* A debt collector may not engage in repeated personal contacts with a consumer with such frequency as to harass him. Subsection (5) deals specifically with harassment by multiple phone calls.

4. *Abusive conduct.* A debt collector may not pose a lengthy series of questions or comments to the consumer without giving the consumer a chance to reply. Subsection (2) deals specifically with harassment involving obscene, profane, or abusive language.

Section 806(1) prohibits the "use or threat of use of violence or other criminal means to harm . . . any person."

1. *Implied threat.* A debt collector may violate this section by an implied threat of violence. For example, a debt collector may not pressure a consumer with statements such as "We're not playing around here—we can play tough" or "We're going to send somebody to collect for us one way or the other."

Section 806(2) prohibits the use of obscene, profane, or abusive language.

1. *Abusive language.* Abusive language includes religious slurs, profanity, obscenity, calling the consumer a liar or a deadbeat, and the use of racial or sexual epithets.

Section 806(3) prohibits the "publication of a list of consumers who allegedly refuse to pay debts," except to report the items to a "consumer reporting agency," as defined in the Fair Credit Reporting Act or to a party otherwise authorized to receive it under that Act.

Section 806(4) prohibits the "advertisement for sale of any debt to coerce payment of the debt."

1. *Shaming prohibited.* These provisions are designed to prohibit debt collectors from "shaming" a customer into payment, by publicizing the debt.

2. *Exchange of lists.* Debt collectors may not exchange lists of consumers who allegedly refuse to pay their debts.

3. *Information to creditor subscribers.* A debt collector may not distribute a list of alleged debtors to its creditor subscribers.

4. *Coded lists.* A debt collector that publishes a list of consumers who have had bad debts, coded to avoid generally disclosing the consumer's identity (e g , showing only the driver's license number and first three letters of each consumer's name) does not violate this provision, because such publication is permitted under the Fair Credit Reporting Act.

5. *List for use by investigator.* A debt collector does not violate these provisions by providing a list of consumers against whom judgments have been entered to a private investigator in order to locate such individuals, because section 805(b) specifically permits contacts "reasonably necessary to effectuate a post-judgment judicial remedy."

6. *Public notice required by law.* A debt collector does not violate these provisions by providing public notices that are required by law as a prerequisite to enforcement of a security interest in connection with a debt.

Section 806(5) prohibits contacting the consumer by telephone "repeatedly or continuously with intent to annoy, abuse, or harass any person at the called number."

1. *Multiple phone calls.* "Continuously" means making a series of telephone calls, one right after the other. "Repeatedly" means calling with excessive frequency under the circumstances.

Section 806(6) prohibits, except where section 804 applies, "the placement of telephone calls without meaningful disclosure of the caller's identity."

1. *Aliases.* A debt collector employee's use of an alias that permits identification of the debt collector (i.e., where he uses the alias consistently, and his true identity can be ascertained by the employer) constitutes a "meaningful disclosure of the caller's identity."

2. *Identification of caller.* An individual debt collector must disclose his employer's identity, when discussing the debt on the telephone with consumers or third parties permitted by section 805(b).

3. *Relation to other sections.* A debt collector who uses a false business name in a phone call to conceal his identity violates section 807(14), as well as this section.

Section 807—False Or Misleading Representations

Section 807 prohibits a debt collector from using any "false, deceptive, or misleading representation or means in connection with the collection of any debt." It provides sixteen examples of false or misleading representations.

1. *Scope.* Prohibited actions are not limited to the sixteen subsections listed as examples of activities that violate this provision. In addition, section 807(10), which prohibits the "use of any false representation or deceptive means" by a debt collector, is particularly broad and encompasses virtually every violation, including those not covered by the other subsections.

Section 807(1) prohibits "the false representation or implication that the debt collector is vouched for, bonded by, or affiliated with the United States or any State . . ."

1. *Symbol on dunning notice.* A debt collector may not use a symbol in correspondence that makes him appear to be a government official. For example, a collection letter depicting a police badge, a judge, or the scales of justice, normally violates this section.

Section 807(2) prohibits falsely representing either "(A) the character, amount, or legal status of any debt; or (B) any services rendered or compensation which may be lawfully received by" the collector.

1. *Legal status of debt.* A debt collector may not falsely imply that legal action has begun.

2. *Amount of debt.* A debt collector may not claim an amount more than actually owed, or falsely assert that the debt has matured or that it is immediately due and payable, when it is not.

3. *Judgment.* When a debt collector provides the validation notice required by section 809(a)(4), the notice may include the words "copy of a judgment" whether or not a judgment exists, because section 809(a)(4) provides for a statement including these words. Compliance with section 809(a)(4) in this manner will not be considered a violation of section 807(2)(A).

Section 807(3) prohibits falsely representing or implying that "any individual is an attorney or that any communication is from an attorney."

1. *Form of legal correspondence.* A debt collector may not send a collection letter from a "Pre-Legal Department," where no legal department exists. An attorney may use a computer service to send letters on his own behalf, but a debt collector may not send a computer-generated letter deceptively using an attorney's name.

2. *Named individual.* A debt collector may not falsely represent that a person named in a letter is his attorney.

3. *Relation to other sections.* If a creditor falsely uses an attorney's name rather than his own in his collection communications, he both loses his exemption from the FDCPA's definition of "debt collector" (Section 803(6)) and violates this provision.

Section 807(4) prohibits falsely representing or implying to the consumer that nonpayment "will result in the arrest or imprisonment of any person or the seizure, garnishment, attachment, or sale of any property or wages of any person . . ."

Section 807(5) prohibits the "threat to take any action that cannot legally be taken or that is not intended to be taken."

1. *Debt collector's statement of his own definite action.* A debt collector may not state that he will take any action unless he intends to take the action when the statement is made, or ordinarily takes the action in similar circumstances.

2. *Debt collector's statement of definite action by third party.* A debt collector may not state that a third party will take any action unless he has reason to believe, at the time the statement is made, that such action will be taken.

3. *Statement of possible action.* A debt collector may not state or imply that he or any third party may take any action unless such action is legal and there is a reasonable likelihood, at the time the statement is made, that such action will be taken. A debt collector may state that certain action is possible, if it is true that such action is legal and is frequently taken by the collector or creditor with respect to similar debts; however, if the debt collector has reason to know there are facts that make the action unlikely in the particular case, a statement that the action was possible would be misleading.

4. *Threat of criminal action.* A debt collector may not threaten to report a dishonored check or other fact to the police, unless he actually intends to take this action.

5. *Threat of attachment.* A debt collector may not threaten to attach a consumer's tax refund, when he has no authority to do so.

6. *Threat of legal or other action.* Section 807(5) refers not only to a false threat of legal action, but also a false threat by a debt collector that he will report a debt to a credit bureau, assess a collection fee, or undertake any other action if the debt is not paid. A debt collector may also not misrepresent the imminence of such action.

A debt collector's implication, as well as a direct statement, of planned legal action may be an unlawful deception. For example, reference to an attorney or to legal proceedings may mislead the debtor as to the likelihood or imminence of legal action.

A debt collector's statement that legal action has been recommended is a representation that legal action may be taken, since such a recommendation implies that the creditor will act on it at least some of the time.

Lack of intent may be inferred when the amount of the debt is so small as to make the action totally unfeasible or when the debt collector is unable to take the action because the creditor has not authorized him to do so.

7. *Illegality of threatened act.* A debt collector may not threaten that he will illegally contact an employer, or other third party, or take some other "action that cannot legally be taken" (such as advising the creditor to sue where such advice would violate state rules governing the unauthorized practice of law). If state law forbids a debt collector from suing in his own name (or from doing so without first obtaining a formal assignment and that has not been done), the debt collector may not represent that he will sue in that state.

Section 807(6) prohibits falsely representing or implying that a transfer of the debt will cause the consumer to (A) lose any claim or defense, or (B) become subject to any practice prohibited by the FDCPA.

1. *Referral to creditor.* A debt collector may not falsely state that the consumer's account will be referred back to the original creditor, who would take action the FDCPA prohibits the debt collector to take.

Section 807(7) prohibits falsely representing or implying that the "consumer committed any crime or other conduct in order to disgrace the consumer."

1. *False allegation of fraud.* A debt collector may not falsely allege that the consumer has committed fraud.

2. *Misrepresentation of criminal law.* A debt collector may not make a misleading statement of law, falsely implying that the consumer has committed a crime, or mischaracterize what constitutes an offense by misstating or omitting significant elements of the offense. For example, a debt collector may not tell the consumer that he has committed a crime by issuing a check that is dishonored, when the statute applies only where there is a "scheme to defraud."

Section 807(8) prohibits "Communicating or threatening to communicate to any person [false] credit information . . . , including the failure to communicate that a disputed debt is disputed."

1. *Disputed debt.* If a debt collector knows that a debt is disputed by the consumer, either from receipt of written notice (section 809) or other means, and reports it to a credit bureau, he must report it as disputed.

2. *Post-report dispute.* When a debt collector learns of a dispute after reporting the debt to a credit bureau, the dispute need not also be reported.

Section 807(9) prohibits the use of any document designed to falsely imply that it issued from a state or federal source, or "which creates a false impression as to its source, authorization, or approval."

1. *Relation to other sections.* Most of the violations of this section involve simulated legal process, which is more specifically covered by section 807(13). However, this subsection is broader in that it also covers documents that fraudulently appear to be official government documents, or otherwise mislead the recipient as to their authorship.

Section 807(10) prohibits the "use of any false representation or deceptive means to collect or attempt to collect any debt or to obtain information concerning a consumer."

1. *Relation to other sections.* The prohibition is so comprehensive that violation of any part of section 807 will usually also violate subsection (10). Actions that violate more specific provisions are discussed in those sections.

2. *Communication format.* A debt collector may not communicate by a format or envelope that misrepresents the nature, purpose, or urgency of the message. It is a violation to send any communication that conveys to the consumer a false sense of urgency. However, it is usually permissible to send a letter generated by a

machine, such as a computer or other printing device. A bona fide contest entry form, which provides a clearly optional location to enter employment information, enclosed with request for payment, is not deceptive.

3. False statement or implications. A debt collector may not falsely state or imply that a consumer is required to assign his wages to his creditor when he is not, that the debt collector has counseled the creditor to sue when he has not, that adverse credit information has been entered on the consumer's credit record when it has not, that the entire amount is due when it is not, or that he cannot accept partial payments when in fact he is authorized to accept them.

4. Misrepresentation of law. A debt collector may not mislead the consumer as to the legal consequences of the consumer's actions (e.g., by falsely implying that a failure to respond is an admission of liability).

A debt collector may not state that federal law requires a notice of the debt collector's intent to contact third parties.

5. Misleading letterhead. A debt collector's employee who is an attorney may not use "attorney-at-law" stationery without referring to his employer, so as to falsely imply to the consumer that the debt collector had retained a private attorney to bring suit on the account.

Section 807(11) requires the debt collector to "disclose clearly in all communications made to collect a debt or to obtain information about a consumer, that the debt collector is attempting to collect a debt and that any information obtained will be used for that purpose," except where section 804 provides otherwise.

1. Oral communications. A debt collector must make the required disclosures in both oral and written communications.

2. Disclosure to consumers. When a debt collector contacts a consumer and clearly discloses that he is seeking payment of a debt, he need not state that all information will be used to collect a debt, since that should be apparent to the consumer. The debt collector need not repeat the required disclosure in subsequent contacts.

A debt collector may not send the consumer a note saying only "please call me right away" unless there has been prior contact between the parties and the collector is thus known to the consumer.

3. Disclosures to third parties. Except when seeking location information, the debt collector must state in the first communication with a third party that he is attempting to collect the debt and that information will be used for that purpose, but need not do so in subsequent communications with that party.

Section 807(12) prohibits falsely representing or implying that "accounts have been turned over to innocent purchasers for value."

1. Relation to other sections. Section 807(6)(A) prohibits a false statement or implication that threatening to affect the consumer's rights may be affected by transferring the account; this subsection forbids falsely stating or implying that a transfer to certain parties has occurred.

Section 807(13) prohibits falsely representing or implying that "documents are legal process."

1. *Simulated legal process.* A debt collector may not send written communications that deceptively resemble legal process forms. He may not send a form or a dunning letter that, taken as a whole, appears to simulate legal process. However, one legal phrase (such as "notice of legal action" or "show just cause why") alone will not result in a violation of this section unless it contributes to an erroneous impression that the document is a legal form.

Section 807(14) prohibits the "use of any business, company, or organization name other than the [collector's] true name."

1. *Permissible business name.* A debt collector may use a name that does not misrepresent his identity or deceive the consumer. Thus, a collector may use its full business name, the name under which it usually transacts business, or a commonly used acronym. When the collector uses multiple names in its various affairs, it does not violate this subsection if it consistently uses the same name when dealing with a particular consumer.

2. *Creditor misrepresentation of identity.* A creditor may not use any name that would falsely imply that a third party is involved in the collection. The in-house collection unit of "ABC Corp." may use the name "ABC Collection Division," but not the name "XYZ Collection Agency" or some other unrelated name.

A creditor violates this section if he uses the name of a collection bureau as a conduit for a collection process that the creditor controls in collecting his own accounts. Similarly, a creditor may not use a fictitious name or letterhead, or a "post office box address" name that implies someone else is collecting his debts.

A creditor does not violate this provision where an affiliated (and differently named) debt collector undertakes collection activity, if the debt collector does business separately from the creditor (e.g., where the debt collector in fact has other clients that he treats similarly to the creditor, has his own employees, deals at arm's length with the creditor, and controls the process himself).

3. *All collection activities covered.* A debt collection business must use its real business name, commonly used name, or acronym in both written and oral communications.

4. *Relation to other sections.* If a creditor uses a false business name, he both loses his exemption from the FDCPA's definition of "debt collector" (section 803(6)) and violates this provision. If a debt collector falsely uses the name of an attorney rather than his true business name, he violates section 807(3) as well as this section. When a debt collector uses a false business name in a phone call, he violates section 806(6) as well as this section.

When using the mails to obtain location information, a debt collector may not (unless expressly requested by the recipient to identify the firm) use a name that indicates he is in the debt collection business, or he will violate section 804(5). When a debt collector's employee who is seeking location information replies to an inquiry about his employer's identity under section 804(1), he must give the true name of his employer.

Section 807(15) prohibits falsely representing or implying that documents are not legal process forms or do not require action by the consumer.

1. *Disguised legal process.* A debt collector may not deceive a consumer into failing to respond to legal process by concealing the import of the papers, thereby subjecting the consumer to a default judgment.

Section 807(16) prohibits falsely representing or implying that a debt collector operates or is employed by a "consumer reporting agency" as defined in the Fair Credit Reporting Act.

1. *Dual agencies.* The FDCPA does not prohibit a debt collector from operating a consumer reporting agency.

2. *Misleading names.* Only a bona fide consumer reporting agency may use names such as "Credit Bureau," "Credit Bureau Collection Agency," "General Credit Control," "Credit Bureau Rating, Inc.," or "National Debtors Rating." A debt collector's disclaimer in the text of a letter that the debt collector is not affiliated with (or employed by) a consumer reporting agency will not necessarily avoid a violation if the collector uses a name that indicates otherwise.

3. *Factual issue.* Whether a debt collector that has called itself a credit bureau actually qualifies as such is a factual issue, to be decided according to the debt collector's actual operation.

Section 808—Unfair Practices

Section 808 prohibits a debt collector from using "unfair or unconscionable means" in his debt collection activity. It provides eight examples of unfair practices.

1. *Scope.* Prohibited actions are not limited to the eight subsections listed as examples of activities that violate this provision.

2. *Elements of unfairness.* A debt collector's act in collecting a debt may be "unfair" if it causes injury to the consumer that is (1) substantial, (2) not outweighed by countervailing benefits to consumers or competition, and (3) not reasonably avoidable by the consumer.

Section 808(1) prohibits collecting any amount unless the amount is expressly authorized by the agreement creating the debt or is permitted by law.

1. *Kinds of amounts covered.* For purposes of this section, "amount" includes not only the debt, but also any incidental charges, such as collection [*53 Fed. Reg. 50108*] charges, interest, service charges, late fees, and bad check handling charges.

2. *Legality of charges.* A debt collector may attempt to collect a fee or charge in addition to the debt if either (a) the charge is expressly provided for in the contract creating the debt and the charge is not prohibited by state law, or (b) the contract is silent but the charge is otherwise expressly permitted by state law. Conversely, a debt collector may not collect an additional amount if either (a) state law expressly prohibits collection of the amount or (b) the contract does not provide for collection of the amount and state law is silent.

3. *Legality of fee under state law.* If state law permits collection of reasonable fees, the reasonableness (and consequential legality) of these fees is determined by state law.

4. *Agreement not in writing.* A debt collector may establish an "agreement" without a written contract. For example, he may collect a service charge on a dishonored check based on a posted sign on the merchant's premises allowing such a charge, if he can demonstrate that the consumer knew of the charge.

Section 808(2) prohibits accepting a check postdated by more than five days unless timely written notice is given to the consumer prior to deposit.

Section 808(3) prohibits soliciting any postdated check for purposes of threatening or instituting criminal prosecution.

Section 808(4) prohibits depositing a postdated check prior to its date.

1. *Postdated checks.* These provisions do not totally prohibit debt collectors from accepting postdated checks from consumers, but rather prohibit debt collectors from misusing such instruments.

Section 808(5) prohibits causing any person to incur telephone or telegram charges by concealing the true purpose of the communication.

1. *Long distance calls to the debt collector.* A debt collector may not call the consumer collect or ask a consumer to call him long distance without disclosing the debt collector's identity and the communication's purpose.

2. *Relation to other section.* A debt collector who conceals his purpose in asking consumers to call long distance may also violate section 807(11), which requires the debt collector to disclose his purpose in some communications.

Section 808(6) prohibits taking nonjudicial action to enforce a security interest on property, or threatening to do so, where (A) there is not present right to the collateral, (B) there is no present intent to exercise such rights, or (C) the property is exempt by law.

1. *Security enforcers.* Because the FDCPA's definition of "debt collection" includes parties whose principal business is enforcing security interests only for section 808(6) purposes, such parties (if they do not otherwise fall within the definition) are subject only to this provision and not to the rest of the FDCPA.

Section 808(7) prohibits "Communicating with a consumer regarding a debt by post card."

1. *Debt.* A debt collector does not violate this section if he sends a post card to a consumer that does not communicate the existence of the debt. However, if he had not previously disclosed that he is attempting to collect a debt, he would violate section 807(11), which requires this disclosure.

Section 808(8) prohibits showing anything other than the debt collector's address, on any envelope in any written communication to the consumer, except that a debt collector may use his business name if it does not indicate that he is in the debt collection business.

1. *Business names prohibited on envelopes.* A debt collector may not put on his envelope any business name with "debt" or "collector" in it, or any other name that indicates he is in the debt collection business. A debt collector may not use the American Collectors Association logo on an envelope.

2. *Collector's name.* Whether a debt collector/consumer reporting agency's use of his own "credit bureau" or other name indicates that he is in the collection business, and thus violates the section, is a factual issue to be determined in each individual case.

3. *Harmless words or symbols.* A debt collector does not violate this section by using an envelope printed with words or notations that do not suggest the purpose of the communication. For example, a collector may communicate via an actual telegram or similar service that uses a Western Union (or other provider) logo and the word "telegram" (or similar word) on the envelope, or a letter with the word "Personal" or "Confidential" on the envelope.

4. *Transparent envelopes.* A debt collector may not use a transparent envelope, which reveals language or symbols indicating his debt collection business, because it is the equivalent of putting information on an envelope.

Section 809—Validation Of Debts

Section 809(a) requires a collector, within 5 days of the first communication, to provide the consumer a written notice (if not provided in that communication) containing (1) the amount of the debt and (2) the name of the creditor, along with a statement that he will (3) assume the debt's validity unless the consumer disputes it within 30 days, (4) send a verification or copy of the judgment if the consumer timely disputes the debt, and (5) identify the original creditor upon written request.

1. *Who must provide notice.* If the employer debt collection agency gives the required notice, employee debt collectors need not also provide it. A debt collector's agent may give the notice, as long as it is clear that the information is being provided on behalf of the debt collector.

2. *Single notice required.* The debt collector is not required to provide more than one notice for each debt. A notice need not offer to identify the original creditor unless the name and address of the original creditor are different from the current creditor.

3. *Form of notices.* The FDCPA imposes no requirements as to the form, sequence, location, or typesize of the notice. However, an illegible notice does not comply with this provision.

4. *Alternate terminology.* A debt collector may condense and combine the required disclosures, as long as he provides all required information.

5. *Oral notice.* If a debt collector's first communication with the consumer is oral, he may make the disclosures orally at that time in which case he need not send a written notice.

6. *Legal action.* A debt collector's institution of formal legal action against a consumer (including the filing of a complaint or service of legal papers by an attorney in connection with a lawsuit to collect a debt) or transmission of a notice to a consumer that is required by law as a prerequisite to enforcing a contractual obligation is not a "communication in connection with collection of any debt," and thus does not confer section 809 notice-and-validation rights on the consumer.

7. Collection activities by attorneys. An attorney who regularly attempts to collect debts by means other than litigation, such as writing the consumer demand letters (dunning notices) or calling the consumer on the phone about the obligation (except in response to a consumer's call to him after suit has been commenced), must provide the required notice, even if a previous debt collector (or creditor) has given such a notice.

8. Effect of including proof with first notice. A debt collector must verify a disputed debt even if he has included proof of the debt with the first communication, because the section is intended to assist the consumer when a debt collector inadvertently contacts the wrong consumer at the start of his collection efforts.

Section 809(b) requires that, if the consumer disputes the debt or requests identification of the original creditor in writing, the collector must cease collection efforts until he verifies the debt and mails a response. Section 809(c) states that a consumer's failure to dispute the validity of a debt under this section may not be interpreted by a court as an admission of liability.

1. Pre-notice collection. A debt collector need not cease normal collection activities within the consumer's 30-day period to give notice of a dispute until he receives a notice from the consumer. An attorney debt collector may take legal action within 30 days of sending the notice, regardless of whether the consumer disputes the debt. If the consumer disputes the debt, the attorney may still take legal action but must cease collection efforts until verification is obtained and mailed to the consumer.

A debt collector may report a debt to a credit bureau within the 30-day notice period, before he receives a request for validation or a dispute notice from the consumer.

Section 810—Multiple Debts

Section 810 provides: "If any consumer owes multiple debts and makes any single payment to any debt collector with respect to such debts, such debt collector may not apply such payment to any debt which is disputed by the consumer and, where applicable, shall apply such payment in accordance with the consumer's directions."

Section 811—Legal Actions By Debt Collectors

Section 811 provides that a debt collector may sue a consumer only in the judicial district where the consumer resides or signed the contract sued upon, except that an action to enforce a security interest in real property which secures the obligation must be brought where the property is located.

1. Waiver. Any waiver by the consumer must be provided directly to the debt collector (not to the creditor in the contract establishing the debt), because the forum restriction applies to actions brought by the debt collector.

2. Multiple defendants. Since a debt collector may sue only where the consumer (1) lives or (2) signed the contract, the collector may not join an ex-husband as a defendant to a suit against the ex-wife in the district of her residence, unless he also lives there or signed the contract there. The existence of community property at her residence that is available to pay his debts does not alter the forum limitations on individual consumers.

3. *Real estate security.* A debt collector may sue based on the location of a consumer's real property only when he seeks to enforce an interest in such property that secures the debts.

4. *Services without written contract.* Where services were provided pursuant to an oral agreement, the debt collector may sue only where the consumer resides. He may not sue where services were performed (if that is different from the consumer's residence), because that is not included as permissible forum location by this provision.

5. *Enforcement of judgments.* If a judgment is obtained in a forum that satisfies the requirements of this section, it may be enforced in another jurisdiction, because the consumer previously has had the opportunity to defend the original action in a convenient forum.

6. *Scope.* This provision applies to lawsuits brought by a debt collector, including an attorney debt collector, when the debt collector is acting on his own behalf or on behalf of his client.

Section 812—Furnishing Certain Deceptive Forms

Section 812 prohibits any party from designing and furnishing forms, knowing they are or will be used to deceive a consumer to believe that someone other than his creditor is collecting the debt, and imposes FDCPA civil liability on parties who supply such forms.

1. *Practice prohibited.* This section prohibits the practice of selling to creditors dunning letters that falsely imply that a debt collector is participating in collection of the debt, when in fact only the creditor is collecting.

2. *Coverage.* This section applies to anyone who designs, complies, or furnishes the forms prohibited by this section.

3. *Pre-collection letters.* A form seller may not furnish a creditor with (1) a letter on a collector's letterhead to be used when the collector is not involved in collecting the creditor's debts, or (2) a letter indicating "copy to (the collector)" if the collector is not participating in collecting the creditor's debt. A form seller may not avoid liability by including a statement in the text of a form letter that the sender has not yet been assigned the account for collection, if the communication as a whole, using the collector's letterhead, represents otherwise.

4. *Knowledge required.* A party does not violate this provision unless he knows or should have known that his form letter will be used to mislead consumers into believing that someone other than the creditor is involved in collecting the debt.

5. *Participation by debt collector.* A debt collector that uses letters as his only collection tool does not violate this section, merely because he charges a flat rate per letter, if he is meaningfully "participating in the collection of a debt." The consumer is not misled in such cases, as he would be in the case of a party who supplied the creditor with form letters and provided little or no additional service

in the collection process. The performance of other tasks associated with collection (e.g., handling verification requests, negotiating payment arrangements, keeping individual records) is evidence that such a party is "participating in the collection."

Section 813—Civil Liability

Section 813 (A) imposes civil liability in the form of (1) actual damages, (2) discretionary penalties, and (3) costs and attorney's fees; (B) discusses relevant factors a court should consider in assessing damages; (C) exculpates a collector who maintains reasonable procedures from liability for an unintentional error; (D) permits actions to be brought in federal or state courts within one year from the violation; and (E) shields a defendant who relies on an advisory opinion of the Commission.

1. *Employee liability.* Since the employees of a debt collection agency are "debt collectors," they are liable for violations to the same extent as the agency.

2. *Damages.* The courts have awarded "actual damages" for FDCPA violations that were not just out-of-pocket expenses, but included damages for personal humiliation, embarrassment, mental anguish, or emotional distress.

3. *Application of statute of limitations period.* The section's one-year statute of limitations applies only to private lawsuits, not to actions brought by a government agency.

4. *Advisory opinions.* A party may act in reliance on a formal advisory opinion of the Commission pursuant to 16 CFR 1.1-1.4, without risk of civil liability. This protection does not extend to reliance on this Commentary or other informal staff interpretations.

Section 814—Administrative Enforcement

Section 814 provides that the principal federal enforcement agency for the FDCPA is the Federal Trade Commission, but assigns enforcement power to other authorities empowered by certain federal statutes to regulate financial, agricultural, and transportation activities, where FDCPA violations relate to acts subject to those laws.

Section 815—Reports To Congress By Commission

Section 815 requires the Commission to submit an annual report to Congress which discusses its enforcement and other activities administering the FDCPA, assesses the degree of compliance, and makes recommendations.

Section 816—Relations To State Laws

Section 816 provides that the FDCPA pre-empts state laws only to the extent that those laws are inconsistent with any provision of the FDCPA, and then only to the extent of the inconsistency. A state law is not inconsistent if it gives consumers greater protection than the FDCPA.

1. *Inconsistent laws.* Where a state law provides protection to the consumer equal to, or greater than, the FDCPA, it is not pre-empted by the federal statute.

Section 817—Exemption For State Regulation

Section 817 orders the Commission to exempt any class of debt collection practices from the FDCPA within any state if it determines that state laws regulating those practices are substantially similar to the FDCPA, and contain adequate provision for enforcement.

1. *State exemptions.* A state with a debt collection law may apply to the Commission for an exemption. The Commission must grant the exemption if the state's law is substantially similar to the FDCPA, and there is adequate provision for enforcement. The Commission has published procedures for processing such applications (16 CFR 901).

Section 818—Effective Date

Section 818 provides that the FDCPA took effect six months from the date of its enactment.

1. *Key dates.* The FDCPA was approved September 20, 1977, and became effective March 20, 1978. [FR Doc. 88-28573 Filed 12-12-88; 8:45 am]

APPENDIX III

SPECIAL STATE TEXT REQUIREMENTS FOR COLLECTION NOTICES

Prepared By ACA's Compliance Division*

What follows is a listing of state statutes for those states that have special text requirements for collection notices. Please note that this document does not contain information on any statutory requirements regarding the collection of checks. For information regarding the collection of checks, please refer to the Internet & Check Services Program (ICSP) *Statutory Penalties Guide*. This information is based upon research completed by ACA's Compliance Division, and, while care has been taken to research the laws as carefully as possible, the Association will not be responsible for omissions. This information is not intended as legal advice and should not be used as such. Before acting on the information contained within this document, please discuss the issues raised with your own legal counsel.

ARIZONA

A collection agency must provide the debtor with: the name of the creditor; the time and place the debt was created; the merchandise, services, or other items of value underlying the debt; and the date the account was referred to the collection agency. A debtor has the right of access to the collection agency's books and records regarding the debt. Copies of any relevant documents about the debt must be provided to the debtor at no cost. Ariz. Admin. Code R20-4-1514 (WESTLAW through June 30, 2002).

Each collection agency shall at all times in its contacts with its debtors, whether such contacts are written or oral, represent itself as a collection agency. It shall not represent, either directly or indirectly, that it is a credit-reporting agency or credit bureau when it is not such an entity, nor shall it represent, either directly or indirectly, that it is a law enforcement agency or a law firm. Ariz. Admin. Code R20-4-1507 (WESTLAW through June 30, 2002).

A collection agency shall not inform a debtor that by failing to contact the agency, the debtor has waived any right of defense, or that the collection agency may circumvent the legal process or misrepresent to the debtor any of the remedies available to the collection agency. Ariz. Admin. Code R20-4-1510 (WESTLAW through June 30, 2002).

ARKANSAS

When an agency communicates with a debtor, the agency must disclose, in a written or telephone communication, the specific reason for the communication, the name of the creditor, the registered name of the agency, the date of communication in written communication, and in oral communication, the identity of the collector making the contact. Code Ark. R. 031 00 001 § XIV(b) (Weil Publishing, WESTLAW through September 2002 (Issue 27)).

A collection agency shall use only the agency name or tradestyle exactly as it appears on the agency's license issued by the State Board in all communication, (e.g., ABC Collection Agency cannot use a name such as ABC Acceptance Company) except for skiptracing and envelopes. Code Ark. R. 031 00 001 § XIV(a) (Weil Publishing, WESTLAW through September 2002 (Issue 27)).

CALIFORNIA

No debt collector shall collect or attempt to collect a consumer debt by communicating with the debtor by means of a written communication that displays or conveys any information about the consumer debt or the debtor other than the name, address and telephone number of the debtor and the debt collector and which is intended both to be seen by any other person and also to embarrass the debtor. Cal. Civ. Code § 1788.12(d) (West, WESTLAW through 1st Ex. Sess. and urgency legislation through ch. 109 of the 2001 Reg. Sess. and ch. 13 of the 2001 1st Ex. Session).

In connection with any consumer credit existing or requested to be extended to a person, such person shall within a reasonable time notify the creditor or prospective creditor of any change in such person's name, address, or employment. Each [of these responsibilities] shall apply only if and after the creditor clearly and conspicuously in writing discloses such responsibility to such person. Cal. Civ. Code § 1788.21 (West, WESTLAW through 1st Ex. Sess. and urgency legislation through ch. 109 of the 2001 Reg. Sess. and ch. 13 of the 2001 1st Ex. Session).

Duties of debtor disclosure by creditor of debtor's responsibility:

(a) In connection with any consumer credit extended to a person under an account:

   (1) No person shall attempt to consummate any consumer credit transaction thereunder knowing that credit privileges under the account have been terminated or suspended.

   (2) Each such person shall notify the creditor by telephone, letter, or any other reasonable means that unauthorized use of the account has occurred or may occur as a result of loss or theft of a credit card, or other instrument identifying the account, within a reasonable time after

such person's discovery thereof, and shall reasonably assist the creditor in determining the facts and circumstances relating to any unauthorized use of the account.

(b) Each responsibility set forth in subdivision (a) shall apply only if and after the creditor clearly and conspicuously in writing discloses such responsibility to such person.

Cal. Civ. Code § 1788.22(a)(2) (West, WESTLAW through 1st Ex. Sess. and urgency legislation through ch. 109 of the 2001 Reg. Sess. and ch. 13 of the 2001 1st Ex. Session).

No debt collector shall collect or attempt to collect a consumer debt by obtaining an affirmation from a debtor who has been adjudicated a bankrupt, of a consumer debt which has been discharged in bankruptcy, without clearly and conspicuously disclosing to the debtor, in writing, at the time such affirmation is sought, the fact that the debtor is not legally obligated to make such affirmation. Cal. Civ. Code § 1788.14(a) (West, WESTLAW through 1st Ex. Sess. and urgency legislation through ch. 109 of the 2001 Reg. Sess. and ch. 13 of the 2001 1st Ex. Session).

Negative credit information; notice to consumer:

(b) A creditor [which includes an agent or assignee of a creditor, including an agent engaged in administering or collecting the creditor's accounts] may submit negative credit information concerning a consumer to a consumer credit reporting agency, only if the creditor notifies the consumer affected. After providing this notice, a creditor may submit additional information to a credit reporting agency respecting the same transaction or extension of credit that gave rise to the original negative credit information without providing additional notice.

(c) The notice shall be in writing and shall be delivered in person or mailed first class, postage prepaid, to the party's last known address, prior to or within 30 days after the transmission of the negative credit information.

1. The notice may be part of any notice of default, billing statement, or other correspondence, and may be included as preprinted or standard form language in any of these from the creditor to the consumer.
2. The notice is sufficient if it is in substantially the following form: "As required by law, you are hereby notified that a negative credit report reflecting on your credit record may be submitted to a credit reporting agency if you fail to fulfill the terms of your credit obligations."

Cal. Civ. Code § 1785.26(b)-(c). (West, WESTLAW through 1st Ex. Sess. and urgency legislation through ch. 109 of the 2001 Reg. Sess. and ch. 13 of the 2001 1st Ex. Session).

Prohibited actions with respect to social security numbers; application and exceptions

(a) A person or entity, not including a state or local agency, shall not do any of the following:

(1) Publicly post or publicly display in any manner an individual's social security number. "Publicly post" or "publicly display" means to intentionally communicate or otherwise make available to the general public.

(2) Print an individual's social security number on any card required for the individual to access products or services provided by the person or entity.

(3) Require an individual to transmit his or her social security number over the Internet unless the connection is secure or the social security number is encrypted.

(4) Require an individual to use his or her social security number to access an Internet Web site, unless a password or unique personal identification number or other authentication device is also required to access the Web site.

(5) Print an individual's social security number on any materials that are mailed to the individual, unless state or federal law requires the social security number to be on the document to be mailed. Notwithstanding this provision, applications and forms sent by mail may include social security numbers.

(b) Except as provided in subdivision (c), subdivision (a) applies only to the use of social security numbers on or after July 1, 2002.

(c) Except as provided in subdivision (f), a person or entity, not including a state or local agency, that has used, prior to July 1, 2002, an individual's social security number in a manner inconsistent with subdivision (a), may continue using that individual's social security number in that manner on or after July 1, 2002, if all of the following conditions are met:

(1) The use of the social security number is continuous. If the use is stopped for any reason, subdivision (a) shall apply.

(2) The individual is provided an annual disclosure, commencing in the year 2002, that informs the individual that he or she has the right to stop the use of his or her social security number in a manner prohibited by subdivision (a).

(3) A written request by an individual to stop the use of his or her social security number in a manner prohibited by subdivision (a) shall be implemented within 30 days of the receipt of the request. There shall be no fee or charge for implementing the request.

(4) A person or entity, not including a state or local agency, shall not deny services to an individual because the individual makes a written request pursuant to this subdivision.

(d) This section does not prevent the collection, use, or release of a social security number as required by state or federal law or the use of a social security number for internal verification or administrative purposes.

(e) This section does not apply to documents that are recorded or required to be open to the public pursuant to Chapter 3.5 (commencing with Section 6250), Chapter 14 (commencing with Section 7150) or Chapter 14.5

(commencing with Section 7220) of Division 7 of Title 1 of, or Chapter 9 (commencing with Section 54950) of Part 1 of Division 2 of Title 5 of, the Government Code. This section does not apply to records that are required by statute, case law, or California Rule of Court, to be made available to the public by entities provided for in Article VI of the California Constitution.

(f) (1) In the case of a health care service plan, a provider of health care, an insurer or a pharmacy benefits manager, or a contractor as defined in Section 56.05, this section shall become operative in the following manner:

(A) On or before January 1, 2003, the entities listed in paragraph (1) of subdivision (f) shall comply with paragraphs (1), (3), (4), and (5) of subdivision (a) as these requirements pertain to individual policyholders.

(B) On or before January 1, 2004, the entities listed in paragraph (1) of subdivision (f) shall comply with paragraphs (1) to (5), inclusive, of subdivision (a) as these requirements pertain to new individual policyholders and new employer groups issued on or after January 1, 2004.

(C) On or before July 1, 2004, the entities listed in paragraph (1) of subdivision (f) shall comply with paragraphs (1) to (5), inclusive, of subdivision (a) for all policyholders and for all enrollees of the Healthy Families and Medi-Cal programs, except that individual and employer group policyholders in existence prior to January 1, 2004, shall comply upon their renewal date, but no later than July 1, 2005.

(2) A health care service plan, a provider of health care, an insurer or a pharmacy benefits manager, or a contractor shall make reasonable efforts to cooperate, through systems testing and other means, to ensure that the requirements of this article are implemented on or before the dates specified in this section.

(3) Notwithstanding paragraph (2), the Director of the Department of Managed Health Care, pursuant to the authority granted under Section 1346 of the Health and Safety Code, or the Insurance Commissioner, pursuant to the authority granted under Section 12921 of the Insurance Code, and upon a determination of good cause, may grant extensions not to exceed six months for compliance by health care service plans and insurers with the requirements of this section when requested by the health care service plan or insurer. Any extension granted shall apply to the health care service plan or insurer's affected providers, pharmacy benefits manager, and contractors.

(g) If a federal law takes effect requiring the United States Department of Health and Human Services to establish a national unique patient health identifier program, a provider of health care, a health care service plan, a licensed health care professional, or a contractor, as those terms are defined in Section 56.05, that complies with the federal law shall be deemed in compliance with this section.

Cal. Civ. Code § 1798.85 (West, WESTLAW through ch. 190 of 2002 Reg. Sess. urgency legislation & ch. 3 of 3rd Ex. Sess. & March 5, 2002 election).

COLORADO

Required disclosures

(1) Within five days after the initial communication with a consumer in connection with the collection of any debt, a debt collector or collection agency shall, unless the following information is contained in the initial communication or the consumer has paid the debt, send the consumer a written notice with the disclosures specified in paragraphs (a) to (e) of this subsection (1). Such disclosures shall state:

(a) The amount of the debt;

(b) The name of the creditor to whom the debt is owed;

(c) That, unless the consumer, within thirty days after receipt of the notice, disputes the validity of the debt, or any portion thereof, the debt will be assumed to be valid by the debt collector or collection agency;

(d) That, if the consumer notifies the debt collector or collection agency in writing within the thirty-day period that the debt, or any portion thereof, is disputed, the debt collector or collection agency will obtain verification of the debt or a copy of a judgment against the consumer and a copy of such verification or judgment will be mailed to the consumer by the debt collector or collection agency;

(e) That upon the consumer's written request within the thirty-day period, the debt collector or collection agency will provide the consumer with the name and address of the original creditor, if different from the current creditor;

Colo. Rev. Stat. Ann. § 12-14-109 (West, WESTLAW through 2003 Co. 1st Reg. Sess. of the 64th Gen. Assembly).

Every collection notice mailed or delivered by a licensee must contain the collection agency's name, mailing address, and telephone number. The collection agency's address may not be printed on the same line listing the Collection Agency Board's current address required by § 12-14-109(1)(f) of the validation of debts notice nor only on any portion of the collection notice designed to be returned to the agency with the consumer's communication or payment. 4 Colo. Code Regs. § 903-1, Rule 2.01(2) (WESTLAW through May 2002).

Notice of rights

(a) If a consumer notifies a debt collector or collection agency in writing that the consumer refuses to pay a debt or that the consumer wishes the debt collector or collection agency to cease further communication with the consumer, the debt collector or collection agency shall not communicate further with the consumer with respect to such debt, except to:

(I) Advise the consumer that the debt collector's or collection agency's further efforts are being terminated;

(II) Notify the consumer that the collection agency or creditor may invoke specified remedies that are ordinarily invoked by such collection agency or creditor, or

(III) Notify the consumer that the collection agency or creditor intends to invoke a specified remedy.

(b) If such notice from the consumer is made by mail, notification shall be complete upon receipt.

(c) In its initial written communication to a consumer, a collection agency shall include the following statement: "FOR INFORMATION ABOUT THE COLORADO FAIR DEBT COLLECTION PRACTICES ACT, SEE WWW.AGO.STATE.CO.US/CAB.HTM." If such notification is placed on the back of the written communication, there shall be a statement on the front notifying the consumer of such fact.

Colo. Rev. Stat. Ann. § 12-14-105(3) (West, WESTLAW through 2003 Co. 1st Reg. Sess. of the 64th Gen. Assembly).

If any required disclosures are on the back of the required validation notice, the front of the notice shall contain a statement notifying consumers of that fact. Colo. Rev. Stat. Ann. § 12-14-109(1) (West, WESTLAW through Second Reg. Sess. of the Sixty-Third Gen. Assemble (2002)).

The consumer rights information required to be in the initial written communication and the validation of debts notice may be printed on two (2) separate pages provided that the first page contains language referring the consumer to the second page and the two (2) pages are attached together. 4 Colo. Code Regs. § 903-1, Rule 2.01(1) (WESTLAW through May 2002).

CONNECTICUT

Itemized Debt and Other Charges

Within five days after the initial communication with a consumer debtor in connection with the collection of any debt, a consumer collection agency shall, unless the following information is contained in the initial communication or the consumer has paid the debt, send the consumer a written notice containing:

- the amount of the debt;
- the name of the creditor to whom the debt is owed;
- a statement that unless the consumer, within thirty days after receipt of the notice, disputes the validity of the debt, or any portion thereof, the debt will be assumed to be valid by the consumer collection agency;
- a statement that if the consumer notifies the consumer collection agency in writing within the thirty-day period that the debt, or any portion thereof, is

disputed, the consumer collection agency will obtain verification of the debt or a copy of a judgment against the consumer and a copy of such verification or judgment will be mailed to the consumer by the consumer collection agency; and

- a statement that, upon the consumer's written request within the thirty-day period, the consumer collection agency will provide the consumer with the name and address of the original creditor, if different from the current creditor.

Conn. Agencies Regs. § 36a-809-3(h)(1) (WESTLAW current with material published in Conn. L. J. through 10/9/01).

Use Licensed Agency Name Only

No person, licensed to act within this state as a consumer collection agency shall do so under any other name or at any other place of business than that named in the license. Conn. Gen. Stat. § 36a-801(c) (West, WESTLAW through Gen. St., Rev. to 1-1-01) *as amended by* 2001 Conn. Legis. Serv. P.A. 01-207 (S.H.B. 6701) (West, WESTLAW through Jan. 2001 Reg. Sess. of the General Assembly).

The use of any business, company, or organization name other than the true name of the consumer collection agency's business, company, or organization is prohibited as a false, deceptive or misleading representation. Conn. Agencies Regs. § 36a-809-3(f)(14) (WESTLAW current with material published in Conn. L. J. through 10/9/01).

Special Text or Address Requirements

No consumer collection agency shall: communicate with consumer debtors or property tax debtors in the name of an attorney or upon the stationery of an attorney, or prepare any forms or instruments which only attorneys are authorized to prepare; use or attempt to use or make reference to the term "bonded by the state of Connecticut," "bonded" or "bonded collection agency" or any combination of such terms or words, except that the word "bonded" may be used on the stationary of any such agency in type not larger than twelve point. Conn. Gen. Stat. Ann. §§ 36a-805(a)(2), (14) (West, WESTLAW through 2002 February Regular and May 9 Special Sessions).

A consumer collection agency shall not use any language or symbol, other than the consumer collection agency's address, on any envelope when communicating with a consumer by use of the mails or by telegram, except that a consumer collection agency may use its business name if such name does not indicate that it is in the debt collection business. Conn. Agencies Regs., § 36a-809-3(g)(8) (WESTLAW current with material published in Conn. L. J. through 10/9/01).

Hospital bed funds (alterations effective Oct. 1, 2003)

(a) As used in this section, (1) "hospital bed fund" means any gift of money, stock, bonds, financial instruments or other property made by any donor for the purpose of establishing a fund to provide medical care, including, but not limited to, inpatient or outpatient care, to patients at a hospital.

A hospital bed fund may be established by inter vivos gift, bequest, subscription, solicitation, dedication or any other means; (2) "hospital" means hospital as defined in section 19a-490; (3) "collection agent" means any person, either employed by or under contract to, a hospital, who is engaged in the business of collecting payment from consumers for medical services provided by the hospital, and includes, but is not limited to, attorneys performing debt collection activities.

(b) (1) Each hospital which holds or administers one or more hospital bed funds shall post or cause to be posted in a conspicuous public place in each patient admitting location, including, but not limited to, the admissions office, emergency room, social services department and patient accounts or billing office, information in English and Spanish regarding the availability of its hospital bed funds, in plain language in a forty-eight to seventy-two point type size. Such information shall include: (A) Notification of the existence of hospital bed funds and the hospital's program to administer them and (B) the person to contact for application information.

(2) Each hospital which has a hospital bed fund shall train staff, including but not limited to, hospital social workers, discharge planners and billing personnel concerning the existence of such fund, the eligibility requirements and the procedures for application.

(c) Each hospital which holds or administers one or more hospital bed funds shall make available in a place and manner allowing individual members of the public to easily obtain it, a one page summary in English and Spanish describing hospital bed funds and how to apply for them. The summary shall also describe any other free or reduced cost policies for the indigent as reported by the hospital to the Office of Health Care Access pursuant to section 19a-649, as amended by this act, and shall clearly distinguish hospital bed funds from other sources of financial assistance. The summary shall include notification that the patient is entitled to reapply upon rejection, and that additional funds may become available on an annual basis. The summary shall be available in the patient admissions office, emergency room, social services department and patient accounts or billing office, and from any collection agent. If during the admission process or during its review of the financial resources of the patient, the hospital reasonably believes the patient will have limited funds to pay for any portion of the patient's hospitalization not covered by insurance, the hospital shall provide the summary to each such patient.

(d) Each hospital which holds or administers one or more hospital bed funds shall require its collection agents to include a summary as provided in subsection (c) of this section in all bills and collection notices sent by such collection agents.

(e) Applicants for assistance from hospital bed funds shall be notified in writing of any award or any rejection and the reason for such rejection. Patients who cannot pay any outstanding medical bill at the hospital shall be allowed to apply or reapply for hospital bed funds.

(f) Each hospital which holds or administers one or more hospital bed funds shall maintain and annually compile, at the end of the fiscal year of the hospital, the following information: (1) The number of applications for hospital bed funds; (2) the number of patients receiving hospital bed fund grants and the actual dollar amounts provided to each patient from such fund; (3) the fair market value of the principal of each individual hospital bed fund, or the principal attributable to each bed fund if held in a pooled investment; (4) the total earnings for each hospital bed fund or the earnings attributable to each hospital bed fund; (5) the dollar amount of earnings reinvested as principal if any; and (6) the dollar amount of earnings available for patient care. The information compiled pursuant to this subsection shall be permanently retained by the hospital and made available to the Office of Health Care Access upon request.

Conn. Gen. Stat. Ann. § 19a-509b (West, WESTLAW through 2003 Jan. Reg. Sess. of the G.A.) (emphasis added).

Collections by hospitals from uninsured patients (alterations effective Oct. 1, 2003)

(a) As used in this section:

(1) "Cost of providing services" means a hospital's published charges at the time of billing, multiplied by the hospital's most recent relationship of costs to charges as taken from the hospital's most recently available annual financial filing with the Office of Health Care Access.

(2) "Hospital" means an institution licensed by the Department of Public Health as a short-term general hospital.

(3) "Poverty income guidelines" means the poverty income guidelines issued from time to time by the United States Department of Health and Human Services.

(4) "Uninsured patient" means any person who is liable for one or more hospital charges whose income is at or below two hundred fifty per cent of the poverty income guidelines who (A) has applied and been denied eligibility for any medical or health care coverage provided under the general assistance program or the Medicaid program due to failure to satisfy income or other eligibility requirements, and (B) is not eligible for coverage for hospital services under the Medicare or CHAMPUS programs, or under any Medicaid or health insurance program of any other nation, state, territory or commonwealth, or under any other governmental or privately sponsored health or accident insurance or benefit program including, but not limited to, workers' compensation and awards, settlements or judgments arising from claims, suits or proceedings involving motor vehicle accidents or alleged negligence.

(b) No hospital that has provided health care services to an uninsured patient may collect from the uninsured patient more than the cost of providing services.

(c) Each collection agent, as defined in section 19a-509b, as amended by this act, engaged in collecting a debt from a patient arising from services provided at a hospital shall provide written notice to such patient as to whether the hospital deems the patient an insured patient or an uninsured patient as defined in subsection (a) of this section and the reasons for such determination.

If, at any point in the debt collection process, whether before or after the entry of judgment, a hospital, a consumer collection agency acting on behalf of the hospital, an attorney representing the hospital or any employee or agent of the hospital becomes aware that a debtor from whom the hospital is seeking payment for services rendered receives information that the debtor is eligible for hospital bed funds, free or reduced price hospital services, or any other program which would result in the elimination of liability for the debt or reduction in the amount of such liability, the hospital, collection agency, attorney, employee or agent shall promptly discontinue collection efforts and refer the collection file to the hospital for determination of such eligibility. The collection effort shall not resume until such determination is made.

Conn. Gen. Stat. Ann. § 19a-673 (West, WESTLAW through 2003 Jan. Reg. Sess. of the G.A.) (emphasis added).

Ed. note: Please see 2003 Conn. Legis. Serv. P.A. 03-266 (S.S.B. 568)(WEST) for further information on hospital debt collection practices and executing judgments for debt arising from services provided at a hospital. The amended laws may be found at *http://www.cga.state.ct.us/2003/act/Pa/2003PA-00266-R00SB-00568-PA.htm.*

Include Consumer Rights/Warnings

The failure to disclose clearly, in all communications made to collect a debt or to obtain information about a consumer, that the consumer collection agency is attempting to collect a debt and that any information obtained will be used for that purpose is a false, deceptive or misleading representation, except when a consumer collection agency is communicating with any person other than the consumer for the purposes of acquiring location information about the consumer. Conn. Agencies Regs. § 36a-809-3(f)(11) (WESTLAW current with material published in Conn. L. J. through 10/9/01).

DISTRICT OF COLUMBIA

No debt collector shall use any fraudulent, deceptive, or misleading representation or means to collect or attempt to collect claims or to obtain information concerning consumers in any of the following ways: (4) the failure to clearly disclose the name and full business address of the person to whom the claim has been assigned for collection, or to whom the claim is owed, at the time of making any demand for money. D.C. Code Ann. § 28-3814(f)(4) (WESTLAW through October 2, 2001).

Use Licensed Agency Name Only

No debt collector shall use any fraudulent, deceptive, or misleading representation or means to collect or attempt to collect claims or to obtain information concerning consumers in any of the following ways: (1) the use of any company name, which engaged in debt collection, other than the debt collector's true company name. D.C. Code Ann. § 28-3814(f)(1) (WESTLAW through October 2, 2001).

Special Text or Address Requirements

No debt collector shall unreasonably publicize information relating to any alleged indebtedness or debtor in any of the following ways: (4) the use of any form of communication to the consumer, which ordinarily may be seen by any other persons, that displays or conveys any information about the alleged claim other than the name, address, and phone number of the debt collector. D.C. Code Ann. § 28-3814(e)(4) (WESTLAW through October 2, 2001).

No debt collector shall use any fraudulent, deceptive, or misleading representation or means to collect or attempt to collect claims or to obtain information concerning consumers in any of the following ways: (2) the failure to clearly disclose in all written communications made to collect or attempt to collect a claim or to obtain or attempt to obtain information about a consumer, that the debt collector is attempting to collect a claim and that any information obtained will be used for that purpose. D.C. Code Ann. § 28-3814(f)(2) (WESTLAW through October 2, 2001).

No debt collector shall use any fraudulent, deceptive, or misleading representation or means to collect or attempt to collect claims or to obtain information concerning consumers in any of the following ways: (4) the failure to clearly disclose the name and full business address of the person to whom the claim has been assigned for collection, or to whom the claim is owed, at the time of making any demand for money. D.C. Code Ann. § 28-3814(f)(4) (WESTLAW through October 2, 2001).

No person engaged in the business of collecting or aiding in the collection of private debts or obligations, or engaged in furnishing private police, investigation, or other private detective services, shall use as part of the name of such business, or employ in any communication, correspondence, notice, advertisement, circular, or other writing or publication, the words "District of Columbia," "District," the initials "D.C.," or any emblem or insignia utilizing any of the said terms as part of its design, in such manner as reasonably to convey the impression or belief that such business is a department, agency, bureau, or instrumentality of the municipal government of the District of Columbia or in any manner represents the District of Columbia. As used in this section and § 223402, the word "person" means and includes individuals, associations, partnerships, and corporations. D.C. Code Ann. § 22-3401 (WESTLAW through October 2, 2001).

Include Consumer Rights/Warnings

Creditors shall provide consumers with the "right to cure" a defaulted account. See D.C. Code Ann. § 28-3812 (WESTLAW through October 2, 2001).

Use of Alias—Registration or Forbidden

No debt collector shall use any fraudulent, deceptive, or misleading representation or means to collect or attempt to collect claims or to obtain information concerning consumers in any of the following ways: (1) the use of any company name, which engaged in debt collection, other than the debt collector's true company name. D.C. Code Ann. § 28-3814(f)(1) (WESTLAW through October 2, 2001).

FLORIDA

In collecting consumer debts, no person shall mail any communication to a debtor in an envelope or postcard with words typed, written, or printed on the outside of the envelope or postcard calculated to embarrass the debtor. An example of this would be an envelope addressed to "Deadbeat, Jane Doe" or "Deadbeat, John Doe." Fla. Stat. Ann. § 559.72(16)(West, WESTLAW through End of 2001 1st Reg. Session).

In collecting consumer debts, no person shall refuse to provide adequate identification of herself or himself or her or his employer or other entity whom she or he represents when requested to do so by a debtor from whom she or he is collecting or attempting to collect a consumer debt. Fla. Stat. Ann. § 559.72(15) (West, WESTLAW through End of 2001 1st Reg. Session).

GEORGIA

In all communications to collect a claim or attempt to obtain information about a consumer, a debt collector must clearly disclose that the debt collector is attempting to collect a claim and any information obtained will be for that purpose. Ga. Comp. R. & Regs. r. 120-1-14-.23(b) (West, WESTLAW current through Apr. 30, 2001).

Disclosure of Business Name

When making any demand for money, a debt collector must clearly disclose to a debtor the name and full business address of the person to whom the claim has been assigned for collection or to whom the claim is owed. Ga. Comp. R. & Regs. r. 120-1-14-.23(d) (West, WESTLAW current through Apr. 30, 2001).

Use of Alias—Registration or Forbidden

No debt collector, while engaged in debt collection, shall use any name other than the debt collector's true name. Ga. Comp. R. & Regs. r. 120-1-14-.23(a) (West, WESTLAW current through Apr. 30, 2001).

GUAM

Include Consumer Rights/Warnings Notice of Transfer

The buyer or lessee is authorized to pay the seller or lessor until the buyer or lessee receives notification of transfer of the rights to payment pursuant to a consumer credit sale or consumer lease and that payment is to be made to the transferee. A notification which does not reasonably identify the rights transferred is ineffective. If requested by the buyer or lessee, the transferee must seasonably furnish reasonable proof that the transfer has been made and unless he does so the buyer or lessee may pay the seller or lessor. 14 Guam Code Ann. § 2412 (WESTLAW through P.L. 26-116 (2002)).

The debtor is authorized to pay the original lender until he receives notification of transfer of rights to payment pursuant to a consumer loan and that payment is to be made to the transferee of the rights. A notification which does not reasonably identify the rights transferred is ineffective. If requested by the debtor, the transferee must seasonably furnish reasonable proof that the transfer has been made and unless he does so the debtor may pay the original lender.

14 Guam Code Ann. § 3406 (WESTLAW through P.L. 26-116 (2002)).

This Article (§ 3406) does not apply to loans in which the principal is Twenty-Five Thousand Dollars ($25,000.00) or more. 14 Guam Code Ann. § 3401 (WESTLAW through P.L. 26-116 (2002)).

HAWAII

Use Licensed Agency Name Only

No collection agency shall use any fraudulent, deceptive, or misleading representation or means to collect, or attempt to collect, claims or to obtain information concerning a debtor or alleged debtor, including any conduct which is described as follows: (1) The use of any company name while engaged in the collection of claims other than the true name of the collection agency. Haw. Rev. Stat. Ann. § 443B-18(1) (LEXIS, WESTLAW through 2001 Third Special Session of the Twenty-First Legislature).

Special Text Requirement

No collection agency shall use any fraudulent, deceptive, or misleading representation or means to collect, or attempt to collect, claims or to obtain information concerning a debtor or alleged debtor, including any conduct which is described as follows: (2) The failure to disclose clearly:

(A) In the initial written and initial oral communication made to collect, or attempt to collect, a claim or to obtain, or attempt to obtain, information about a debtor or alleged debtor that the collection agency is attempting to collect a claim and that any information obtained will be used for that purpose; and

(B) In subsequent communications that the communication is from a debt collector.

Haw. Rev. Stat. Ann. § 443B-18(2) (LEXIS, WESTLAW through 2001 Third Special Session of the Twenty-First Legislature).

No collection agency shall use any fraudulent, deceptive, or misleading representation or means to collect, or attempt to collect, claims or to obtain information concerning a debtor or alleged debtor, including any conduct which is described as follows:

(4) The failure to disclose clearly the name and full business address of the person to whom the claim has been assigned for collection or to whom the claim is owed at the time of making any demand for money;

(5) The use or distribution or sale of any written communication which simulates or is falsely represented to be a document authorized, issued, or approved by a court, an official, or any other legally constituted or authorized authority, or which creates a false impression about its source, authorization or approval.

Haw. Rev. Stat. Ann. §§ 443B-18(4), (6) (LEXIS, WESTLAW through 2001 Third Special Session of the Twenty-First Legislature).

IDAHO

In any and every instance where the permittee has a managerial or financial interest in the creditor, or where the creditor has a managerial or financial interest in the permittee, disclosure of such interest must be made on each and every contact with a debtor in seeking to make a collection of any account, claim, or other indebtedness where such interest or relationship exists between creditor and permittee. Idaho Code Ann. § 26-2229A(2) (LEXIS, WESTLAW through 2002 Cumulative Supplement, 2nd Reg. Session of the 56th Legislature).

(4) No person shall sell, distribute or make use of collection letters, demand forms or other printed matter which are made similar to or resemble governmental forms or documents, or legal forms used in civil or criminal proceedings. Idaho Code Ann. § 26-2229A(4) (LEXIS, WESTLAW through 2002 Cumulative Supplement, 2nd Reg. Session of the 56th Legislature).

(5) No person shall use any trade name, address, insignia, picture, emblem or any other means which creates any impression that such person is connected with or is an agency of government. Idaho Code Ann. § 26-2229A(5) (LEXIS, WESTLAW through 2002 Cumulative Supplement, 2nd Reg. Session of the 56th Legislature).

If the person designated by the permittee to be responsible for business carried on at the office is not normally available in the Idaho office, then the permittee's collection activities with debtors must begin with a written notice to each debtor setting forth a mailing address and toll-free telephone number whereby a debtor may contact the designated responsible person during normal business hours. Idaho Code Ann. § 26-2223A (LEXIS, WESTLAW through 2002 Cumulative Supplement, 2nd Reg. Session of the 56th Legislature).

ILLINOIS

It is an unlawful practice for a debt collector to conduct business while using a name other than its own as shown on its license or any other legally authorized name. 225 Ill. Comp. Stat. 425/9(a)(7) (West, WESTLAW through P.A. 92-650, 92-652 through 92-700 of the 2002 Reg. Session of the 92nd Gen. Assembly).

When an agency communicates with a debtor, the agency must state in a written or telephone communication the specific reason for the communication, the name of the creditor, the registered name of the agency, the date of communication in written communication; and in oral communication, the identity of the collector making the contact. Ill. Admin. Code tit. 68, § 1210.60(b) (WESTLAW through Aug. 9, 2002).

It is an unlawful practice for a debt collector to fail to disclose, at the time of making any demand for payment, the name of the person to whom the claim is owed and at the request of the debtor, the address where payment is to be made and the address of the person to whom the claim is owed. 225 Ill. Comp. Stat. 425/9(a)(25)

(West, WESTLAW through P.A. 92-650, 92-652 through 92-700 of the 2002 Reg. Session of the 92nd Gen. Assembly).

IOWA

A debt collector must disclose in the initial written or oral communication with the debtor that the debt collector is attempting to collect a debt and that information obtained will be used for that purpose. In subsequent communications, the debt collector must disclose that the communication is from a debt collector. This requirement does not apply to a formal pleading or to communications issued directly by a bank or savings and loan association. Iowa Code Ann. § 537.7103(4)(b) (West, WESTLAW through end of 2001 2nd Ex. Session).

Disclose Identity of Assignee

A debt collector must clearly disclose the name and full business address of the person to whom the claim has been assigned at the time of making a demand for money. Iowa Code Ann. § 537.7103(4)(d) (West, WESTLAW through end of 2001 2nd Ex. Session).

Form of Communication

A debt collector shall not use a form of communication to the debtor (except a telegram, an original notice or other court process, or an envelope displaying only the name and address of a debtor and the return address of the debt collector) intended or so designed as to display or convey information about the debt to another person other than the name, address, and phone number of the debt collector. Iowa Code Ann. § 537.7103(3)(c) (West, WESTLAW through end of 2001 2nd Ex. Session).

KANSAS

A person may not procure or cause to be prepared an investigative consumer report on any consumer unless (1) it is clearly and accurately disclosed to the consumer that an investigative consumer report including information as to the consumer's character, general reputation, personal characteristics, and mode of living, whichever are applicable, may be made, and such disclosure (A) is made in a writing mailed, or otherwise delivered, to the consumer, not later than three days after the date on which the report was first requested, and (B) includes a statement informing the consumer of the right to request the additional disclosures provided for under subsection (b) of this section; or (2) the report is to be used for employment purposes for which the consumer has not specifically applied.

(b) Any person who procures or causes to be prepared an investigative consumer report on any consumer shall, upon written request made by the consumer within a reasonable period of time after the receipt by him or her of the disclosure required by subsection (a)(1) of this section, make a complete and accurate disclosure of the nature and scope of the investigation requested. This disclosure shall be made in a writing mailed, or otherwise delivered, to the consumer not later than five (5) days after the date on which the request for such disclosure was received from the consumer or such report was first requested, whichever is the later.

(c) No person may be held liable for any violation of subsection (a) or (b) of this section if that person shows by a preponderance of the evidence that at the time of the violation the person maintained reasonable procedures to assure compliance with subsection (a) or (b). Kan. Stat. Ann. § 50-705 (WESTLAW through End of 2000 Reg. Session).

MAINE

Within five days of the initial communication with a debtor about a debt, unless the following information is contained in the initial communication, a collection agency shall send a written notice to the consumer showing:

(1) The amount of the debt;

(2) The name of the creditor to whom the debt is owed;

(3) A statement that unless the consumer, within 30 days after receipt of the notice, disputes the validity of the debt, the debt will be assumed to be valid by the debt collector;

(4) A statement that if the consumer notifies the debt collector in writing within the 30-day period that the debt, or any portion of the debt, is disputed, the debt collector will obtain verification of the debt or a copy of a judgment against the consumer and a copy of the verification or judgment will be mailed to the consumer by the debt collector; and

(5) A statement that, upon the consumer's written request within the 30-day period, the debt collector will provide the consumer with the name and address of the original creditor, if different from the current creditor.

Me. Rev. Stat. Ann. tit. 32, § 11014(1) (West, WESTLAW through 2001 1st Reg. Session of 120th Leg.).

Use Street Address/Telephone Number

A licensed collection agency is required to disclose the telephone number of its licensed location on the letterhead of all communications sent to Maine debtors. Code Me. R. 02-030 Ch.300, § 2(C)(4) (WESTLAW through Aug. 2002).

Use Licensed Agency Name Only

A collection agency shall not use any business, company, or organization name other than the true name of the collection agency in connection with the collection of any debt. Me. Rev. Stat. Ann. tit. 32, § 11013(2)(N) (West, WESTLAW through 2001 1st Reg. Session of 120th Leg.).

False Affiliation with United States

A debt collector may not make the false representation or implication that the debt collector is vouched for, bonded by or affiliated with the United States or any state, including the use of any badge, uniform, seal, insignia or facsimile.

Me. Rev. Stat. Ann. tit. 32, § 11013(2)(A) ((West, WESTLAW through 2001 1st Reg. Session of 120th Leg.).

A debt collector must disclose in the initial written or oral communication with the consumer that the debt collector is attempting to collect a debt and that any information obtained will be used for that purpose. A debt collector must disclose in subsequent communications that the communication is from a debt collector. This requirement does not apply to a formal pleading made in connection with a legal action. Me. Rev. Stat. Ann. tit. 32, § 11013(2)(K-1) (West, WESTLAW through 2001 1st Reg. Session of 120th Leg.).

Use of False Name

A debt collector may not use the name of any business, company or organization other than the true name of the debt collector's business, company or organization. Me. Rev. Stat. Ann. tit. 32, § 11013(2)(N) (West, WESTLAW through 2001 1st Reg. Session of 120th Leg.).

Communicate by Postcard

A debt collector may not communicate with a consumer regarding a debt by postcard. Me. Rev. Stat. Ann. tit. 32, § 11013(3)(G) (West, WESTLAW through 2001 1st Reg. Session of 120th Leg.).

Improper Use of Language on Envelope

A debt collector may not use any language or symbol, other than the debt collector's address, on any envelope when communicating with a consumer by use of the mails or by telegram, except that a debt collector may use his business name if that name does not indicate that he is in the debt collection business. Me. Rev. Stat. Ann. tit. 32, § 11013(3)(H) (West, WESTLAW through 2001 1st Reg. Session of 120th Leg.).

Threaten Legal Action in Own Name

A debt collector may not threaten to bring legal action in its own name or instituting suits on behalf of others or furnishing legal advice. Me. Rev. Stat. Ann. tit. 32, § 11013(3)(N) (West, WESTLAW through 2001 1st Reg. Session of 120th Leg.).

Hours of Operation

A licensed collection agency shall be available a minimum of 20 hours a week with sufficient personnel to provide information, personally or telephonically concerning a debtor's accounts. Such hours of operation must appear in all communications sent to Maine debtors. Code Me. R.02-030 Ch. 300, § 2(C)(3) (WESTLAW through Aug. 2002).

MASSACHUSETTS

Itemized Debt and Other Charges

It shall constitute an unfair or deceptive act or practice for a collection agency to omit to disclose to a debtor in writing, by delivering or mailing, within five days after the first contact by the collection agency with a debtor, the following information:

(1) The name and mailing address of the collection agency and proper identification of the creditor or the assignee of the creditor on whose behalf the collection agency is communicating;

(2) Identification of the debt;

(3) A brief description of the nature of the default;

(4) A statement of the action required to cure the default; and

(5) The name, address, and telephone number of the person to be contacted for additional information concerning the debt and default.

Mass. Regs. Code tit. 209, § 18.19 (WESTLAW through Aug. 30, 2002, Reg. #955).

Use Street Address/Telephone Number

An envelope sent through the mails to a consumer debtor by a collection agency engaged in the collection of debt of consumer debtors shall not contain as part of a return address the name of the collection agency or any signification that the communication is related to a debt allegedly overdue. A communication in an envelope to a debtor by a collection agency shall disclose the business address of the agency as stated on the license. A collection agency engaged in the collection of debt of consumer debtors shall disclose its telephone number on all communication to the consumer debtor. Mass. Regs. Code tit. 209, § 18.13 (WESTLAW through Aug. 30, 2002, Reg. #955).

Use Licensed Agency Name Only

In communicating with debtors, the collection agency shall use only the exact name in which the Commissioner has granted the license. Mass. Regs. Code tit. 209, § 18.13 (WESTLAW through Aug. 30, 2002, Reg. #955).

In communicating with debtors, the collection agency shall use only the exact name in which the Commissioner has granted the license. Mass. Regs. Code tit. 209, § 18.13 (WESTLAW through Aug. 30, 2002, Reg. #955).

Telephone Number/Office Hours

A collection agency engaged in the collection of debt of consumer debtors shall disclose its telephone number and office hours on all communication to the consumer debtor. Mass. Regs. Code tit. 209, § 18.13 (WESTLAW through Aug. 30, 2002, Reg. #955).

Use of Alias—Registration or Forbidden

A person communicating with a debtor may use a personal name other than their own, provided they use only one such personal name at all times and a mechanism is established by the collection agency to identify the person using such a name. The collection agency or creditor is required to submit a list of all personal names, with the persons using the names, to the Commissioner. Mass. Regs. Code tit. 209,

§ 18.15(1)(d) (WESTLAW through Aug. 30, 2002, Reg. #955); Mass. Regs. Code tit. 940, § 7.04(1)(d) (WESTLAW through Aug. 30, 2002, Reg. #955).

Required Notice

Unless a debtor has requested, in writing, that a collection agency or creditor not contact them at their place of employment, a collection agency or creditor must send the debtor the following notice in writing within 30 days after the first communication to a debtor at his place of employment regarding any debt, provided that a copy of the notice shall be sent every six months thereafter so long as collection activity by the collection agency or creditor on the debt continues:

NOTICE OF IMPORTANT RIGHTS

YOU HAVE THE RIGHT TO MAKE A WRITTEN OR ORAL REQUEST THAT TELEPHONE CALLS REGARDING YOUR DEBT NOT BE MADE TO YOU AT YOUR PLACE OF EMPLOYMENT. ANY SUCH ORAL REQUEST WILL BE VALID FOR ONLY TEN DAYS UNLESS YOU PROVIDE WRITTEN CONFIRMATION OF THE REQUEST POSTMARKED OR DELIVERED WITHIN SEVEN DAYS OF SUCH REQUEST. YOU MAY TERMINATE THIS REQUEST BY WRITING TO THE COLLECTION AGENCY.

Mass. Regs. Code tit. 209, § 18.15(1)(i) (WESTLAW through Aug. 30, 2002, Reg. #955); Mass. Regs. Code tit. 940, § 7.04(1)(i) (WESTLAW through Aug. 30, 2002, Reg. #955).

MICHIGAN

Notice of debt; dispute and verification of debt amount

(1) Within 5 days after the initial communication with a consumer in connection with a collection of a debt, a collection agency shall send the consumer, unless the following information is contained in the initial communication or the consumer has paid the debt, a written notice containing all of the following information:

  (a) The amount of the debt owed.

  (b) The date the communication was sent to the debtor.

  (c) The name of the creditor to whom the debt is owed.

  (d) A statement specifying that unless the consumer, within 30 days after receipt of this notice, disputes the validity of the debt, or a portion of the debt, the debt will be assumed to be valid.

  (e) A statement specifying that, if the consumer notifies the collection agency in writing within 30 days after receipt of this notice, that the debt, or any portion of the debt, is disputed, the collection agency shall obtain verification of the debt or a copy of a judgment against the consumer and that a copy of the verification or judgment shall be mailed to the consumer by the collection agency.

(2) If the consumer notifies the collection agency in writing, within 30 days after receiving the written notice, that the debt, or any portion of the debt, is

disputed, collection of the debt or any disputed portion of the debt shall cease until the collection agency obtains verification of the debt and a copy of the verification or judgment is mailed to the consumer by the collection agency. Verification of the debt or any disputed portion of the debt shall include the number and amount of previously made payments and the name and address of the original creditor, if different from the current creditor, or a copy of the judgment against the debtor.

(3) The failure of a consumer to dispute the validity of a debt under this section shall not be construed as an admission of liability by the consumer.

Mich. Comp. Laws Ann. § 339.918 (West, WESTLAW through P.A. 2002, No. 100 of the 2002 Reg. Session).

Use Licensed Agency Name Only

A licensee shall not commit any of the following acts: Identifying the collection agency other than by the name appearing on the license. Mich. Comp. Laws Ann. § 339.915a(n) (West, WESTLAW through P.A. 2002, No. 100 of the 2002 Reg. Session).

Use of Alias—Registration or Forbidden

A licensee shall not commit any of the following acts: Permitting an employee to use a name other than the employee's own name or the assumed name registered by the licensee with the department in the collection of a debt. Mich. Comp. Laws Ann. § 339.915a(o) (West, WESTLAW through P.A. 2002, No. 100 of the 2002 Reg. Session).

Restrictions on Communication with Debtors

A licensee shall not commit 1 or more of the following acts:

(a) Communicating with a debtor in a misleading or deceptive manner, such as using the stationery of an attorney or the stationery of a credit bureau unless it is disclosed that it is the collection department of the credit bureau.

(b) Using a method contrary to a postal law or regulation to collect an account.

Mich. Comp. Laws Ann. §§ 339.915(a), (p) (West, WESTLAW through P.A. 2002, No. 100 of the 2002 Reg. Session).

Prohibited Acts

A licensee shall not commit any of the following acts:

(a) Listing the name of an attorney in a written or oral communication, collection letter, or publication.

(k) Failing to give a debtor a written receipt for cash payment, or other payment when specifically requested, showing the amount of money received and the debt to which it was applied and the name of the specific account receiving the money.

Mich. Comp. Laws Ann. §§ 339.915a(a), (k) (West, WESTLAW through P.A. 2002, No. 100 of the 2002 Reg. Session).

MINNESOTA

Use Licensed Agency Name Only

No collection agency or collector, when attempting to collect a debt, shall fail to provide the debtor with the full name of the collection agency as it appears on its license. Minn. Stat. § 332.37(16) (West, WESTLAW through End of 2001 First Special Session).

No collection agency or collector shall operate under a name or in a manner which implies that the agency is a branch of or associated with any department of federal, state, county or local government or an agency thereof. Minn. Stat. § 332.37(9) (West, WESTLAW through End of 2001 First Special Session); Minn. R. 2870.3900 (WESTLAW through Oct. 29, 2001).

Special Text or Address Requirements

No collection agency or collector, when initially contacting a Minnesota debtor by mail, shall fail to include a disclosure on the contact notice, in a type size or font which is equal to or larger than the largest other type of type size or font used in the rest of the notice. The disclosure must state: "This collection agency is licensed by the Minnesota Department of Commerce." Minn. Stat. § 332.37(21) (West, WESTLAW through End of 2001 First Special Session).

Implication of Withholding Health Care Services

No collection agency or collector shall, in collection letters of publication, or in any communication, oral or written, imply or suggest that health care services will be withheld in an emergency situation. Minn. Stat. § 332.37(14) (West, WESTLAW through End of 2001 First Special Session).

Violation of Minnesota Law

No collection agency or collectors shall use or threaten to use methods of collection which violate Minnesota law. Minn. Stat. § 332.37(3) (West, WESTLAW through End of 2001 First Special Session).

Violation of the FDCPA

No collection agency or collectors shall violate any provisions of the Fair Debt Collection Practices Act of 1977 while attempting to collect on any account, bill or other indebtedness. Minn. Stat. § 332.37(12) (West, WESTLAW through End of 2001 First Special Session).

NEW HAMPSHIRE

Prohibited Acts

For the purposes of this chapter, any debt collection or attempt to collect a debt shall be deemed unfair, deceptive or unreasonable if the debt collector:

I. Communicates or attempts to communicate with the debtor, orally or in writing:

(d) Using any written communication which fails to clearly identify the name of the debt collector, the name of the person (as defined in

> RSA 358-C:1, X) for whom the debt collector is attempting to collect the debt, and the debt collector's business address (the foregoing shall not require the name or address of the debt collector or the person for whom the debt collector is attempting to collect the debt to be printed on any envelope containing a communication) . . .

N.H. Rev. Stat. Ann. § 358-C:3(I)(d) (WESTLAW through End of 2002 Reg. Session).

NEW YORK

(Including the Cities of Buffalo and New York City) Special Text or Address Requirement Use Licensed Agency Name Only

New York City

A debt collector, in connection with the collection of a debt, shall not make any false, deceptive, or misleading representation. Such representations include the use of any business, company, or organization name other than the true name of the debt collector's business, company, or organization, unless the general public knows the debt collector's business, company or organization by another name and to use the true name would be confusing. New York City, N.Y., Rules, Tit. 6, § 5-77(d)(13) (WESTLAW through June 30, 2002).

A debt collector may not use any unfair or unconscionable means to collect or attempt to collect a debt, including:

(5) after institution of debt collection procedures, when communicating with a consumer by use of the mails or telegram, using any language or symbol other than the debt collector's address on any envelope, or using any language or symbol that indicates the debt collector is in the debt collection business or that the communication relates to the collection of a debt on a postcard, except that a debt collector may use his or her business name or the name of a department within his or her organization as long as any name used does not connote debt collection; or

(6) after institution of debt collection procedures, communicating with a consumer regarding a debt without identifying himself or herself and his or her employer or communicating in writing with a consumer regarding a debt without identifying himself or herself by name and address and in accordance with s 5-77(e)(5) *[ed. note: directly above]*

New York City, N.Y., Rules, Tit. 6, § 5-77(e)(5)-(6) (WESTLAW through June 30, 2002).

New York City
License Number in Advertisements and Other Printed Matter:

Any advertisement, letterhead, receipt or other printed matter of a licensee must contain the license number assigned to the licensee by the New York City Department of Consumer Affairs. The license number must be clearly identified as a New York City Department of Consumer Affairs license number and must be disclosed and disseminated in a lawful manner. Any telephone listing consisting solely of the name, address, and telephone number of the licensee need not specify the licensee's license number.

Licensees holding licenses for more than one location must also include their respective license number(s) clearly identified as New York City Department of Consumer Affairs license number(s) on all correspondence and other printed matter which contains or makes reference to one or more of such licensees' licensed location(s).

New York City, N.Y., Rules, Tit. 6, § 1-05 (WESTLAW through June 30, 2002).

Include Consumer Rights/Warnings
New York City
Mini-Miranda requirement

A debt collector, in connection with the collection of a debt, shall not make any false, deceptive, or misleading representation. Such representations include, except as otherwise provided under s 5-77(a) ***[ed. note: acquisition of location information]*** and except for any communication which is required by law or chosen from among alternatives of which one is required by law, the failure to **disclose clearly in all communications** made to collect a debt or to obtain information about a consumer, that the **debt collector is attempting to collect a debt and that any information obtained will be used for that purpose**. New York City, N.Y., Rules, Tit. 6, § 5-77(d)(15) (WESTLAW through June 30, 2002).

NORTH CAROLINA

Use Street Address and Permit Number

All collection agencies licensed to do the business of a collection agency in North Carolina must include the permit number and the true name and address of such collection agency in all correspondence with debtors. N.C. Gen. Stat. § 58-70-50 (West, WESTLAW through the 2003 Reg. Sess.).

Communicate in Own Name

A collection agency must communicate with the consumer in the name of the person making the communication, the collection agency and the person or business on whose behalf the collection agency is acting or to whom the debt is owed. N.C. Gen. Stat. § 58-70-110(1) (West, WESTLAW through S.L. 2002-113 of the 2002 Reg. and Ex. Sessions).

Disclose Purpose is to Collect Debt

Failing to disclose in the initial written communication with the consumer and, in addition, if the initial communication with the consumer is oral, in that initial oral communication, that the debt collector is attempting to collect a debt and that any information obtained will be used for that purpose, and the failure to disclose in subsequent communications that the communication is from a debt collector; provided, however, that this subdivision does not apply to a formal pleading made in connection with legal action. N.C. Gen. Stat. § 58-70-110(2) (West, WESTLAW through the 2003 Reg. Session).

NORTH DAKOTA

Use Licensed Agency Name Only

No debt collector may use any fraudulent, deceptive, or misleading representation or means to collect or attempt to collect claims or to obtain information concerning consumers. Without limiting the general application of the foregoing, no debt collector may:

1. Use any name while engaged in the collection of claims other than the debt collector's true name unless the assumed name is registered with the department as an alias for the debt collector . . .
2. Fail to clearly disclose the name and full business address of the person to whom the claim has been assigned or is owed at the time of making any demand for money.

N.D. Admin. Code §§ 13-04-02-08(1), (4) (WESTLAW through Supplement 279 (September 1, 2002)).

Restrictions on Communication with Debtors

No collection agency or debt collector shall:

3. In collection letters or publications, or in any communication, oral or written, threaten wage garnishment or legal suit without an objective intention to engage a lawyer and commence legal action upon the debtor's failure to comply with the request or demand made.

N.D. Admin. Code § 13-04-02-02(5) (WESTLAW through Supplement 279 (September 1, 2002)).

OREGON

It shall be an unlawful collection practice for a debt collector, while collecting or attempting to collect a debt to do any of the following: (h) Communicate with the debtor in writing without clearly identifying the name of the debt collector, the name of the person, if any, for whom the debt collector is attempting to collect the debt and the debt collector's business address, on all initial communications. In subsequent communications involving multiple accounts, the debt collector may eliminate the name of the person, if any, for whom the debt collector is attempting to collect the debt, and the term "various" may be substituted in its place. Or. Rev. Stat. § 646.639(2)(h) (WESTLAW through End of 2001 Reg. Sess. and 2001 Cumulative Supplement).

PUERTO RICO

Special Text or Address Requirements

Puerto Rico does not have a special text requirement, however, a 1984 FTC Consent Decree required a consumer finance company to provide notices in Spanish when collecting debts from consumers in Puerto Rico. (*AVCO Financial Services, Inc.*, 104 F.T.C. 485 (1984)).

TENNESSEE

Special Text or Address Requirements

No collection service, or manager or solicitor hereof, shall (b) use any contract or business-inducing form containing type less then ten (10) points in size. Tenn. Comp. R. & Regs. 0320-2-.02 (1)(b) (WESTLAW through Oct. 28, 2002).

In order to protect the rights of creditors, all letters of collection or notices of collection from a collection agency shall contain language stating that the collection agency is licensed by the collection service board of the department of commerce and insurance.

Tenn. Code. Ann § 62-20-111(b) (West, WESTLAW through End of 2002 Second Reg. Session).

Restrictions on Communication with Debtors

(1) No collection service, or manager or solicitor hereof, shall:

- (a) misrepresent the terms of its listing contract or the commission chargeable thereunder;
- (b) use any contract or business-inducing form containing type less then ten (10) points in size;
- (c) solicit claims for collection under any ambiguous or deceptive contract, or one that provides for a docket, listing, filing, or tracing fee, or similar charges;
- (d) state or imply that the collection service has a legal "department" or "affiliation"; or
- (e) use on its stationery or otherwise language which is any way deceptive as to services offered or performed.

Tenn. Comp. R. & Regs. 0320-2-.02 (WESTLAW through Oct. 28, 2002).

TEXAS

Special Text or Address Requirements

Except as otherwise provided by this section, in debt collection or obtaining information concerning a consumer, a debt collector may not use a fraudulent, deceptive, or misleading representation that employs the following practices:

(1) using a name other than the:

(A) true business or professional name or the true personal or legal name of the debt collector while engaged in debt collection; or

(B) name appearing on the face of the credit card while engaged in the collection of a credit card debt.

(4) failing to disclose in any communication with the debtor the name of the person to whom the debt has been assigned or is owed when making a demand for money;

(5) failing to disclose, except in a formal pleading made in connection with a legal action:

(A) that the debt collector is attempting to collect a debt and that any information obtained will be used for that purpose, if the communication is the initial written or oral communication with the debtor; or

(B) that the communication is from a debt collector, if the communication is a subsequent written or oral communication with the debtor;

(6) using a written communication that fails to indicate clearly the name of the debt collector and the debt collector's street address or post office box and telephone number if the written notice refers to a delinquent consumer debt;

(7) using a written communication that demands a response to a place other than the debt collector's or creditor's street address or post office box.

Tex. Fin. Code Ann. § 392.304(a)(1), (4)-(7) (West, WESTLAW through end of 2003 Second Called Sess.).

UTAH

Special Text or Address Requirements

(1) As used in this section:

(b) "Creditor," in addition to its definition under Section 70C-1-302, includes an agent of a creditor engaged in administering or collecting the creditor's accounts.

A creditor may submit a negative credit report to a credit reporting agency, only if the creditor notifies the party whose credit record is the subject of the negative report. After providing this notice, a creditor may submit additional information to a credit reporting agency respecting the same transaction or extension of credit that gave rise to the original negative credit report without providing any additional notice.

(2) (a) Notice shall be in writing and shall be delivered in person or mailed first class, postage prepaid, to the party's last-known address prior to or within 30 days after the transmission of the report.

(b) The notice may be part of any notice of default, billing statement, or other correspondence from the creditor to the party.

(c) The notice is sufficient if it takes substantially the following form: "As required by Utah law, you are hereby notified that a negative credit report reflecting on your credit record may be submitted to a credit reporting agency if you fail to fulfill the terms of your credit obligations."

(d) The notice may, in the creditor's discretion, be more specific than the form given in Subsection (c). For example, the notice may provide particular information regarding an account or list the approximate date on which the creditor submitted or intends to submit a negative credit report.

Utah Code Ann. § 70c-7-107 (LEXIS, WESTLAW through the 2002 5th Special Session).

VERMONT

Use Licensed Agency Name Only

The use of any false, fraudulent, deceptive, or misleading representation or means to collect or attempt to collect any debt arising out of a consumer transaction or to obtain information concerning debtors constitutes an unfair and deceptive trade act and practice in commerce under Vermont Statute title 9, section 2453(a).

Such unfair and deceptive acts include (but shall not be limited to) the following:

(a) The use of any business, company, or organization name while engaged in the collection of claims, other than the true name of the debt collector's business, company, or organization.

Vt. Code R. 104.04(a) (Weil, WESTLAW through August 2002 (Issue no. 154)).

Special Text or Address Requirements

The use of any false, fraudulent, deceptive, or misleading representation or means to collect or attempt to collect any debt arising out of a consumer transaction or to obtain information concerning debtors constitutes an unfair and deceptive trade act and practice in commerce under Vermont Statute title 9, section 2453(a).

Such unfair and deceptive acts include (but shall not be limited to) the following:

(b) The failure to clearly disclose in all written communications made to the debtor or to members of the debtor's family in order to collect or attempt to collect a claim or to obtain information about a debtor that the debt collector is attempting to collect a claim and any information obtained will be used for that purpose;

(d) The failure to clearly disclose the name and full business address of the person to whom the claim has been assigned at the time of communicating the first demand for money after the date of assignment.

Vt. Code R. 104.04(b), (d) (Weil, WESTLAW through August 2002 (Issue no. 154)).

Unfair and deceptive acts include (but shall not be limited to) the following:

(b) Any communication with a debtor in the name of an attorney or upon stationery or other written matter bearing an attorney's name.

Vt. Code R. 104.06(b) (Weil, WESTLAW through August 2002 (Issue no. 154)).

WASHINGTON

Itemized Debt and Other Charges

No licensee or employee of a licensee shall give or send to any debtor or cause to be given or sent to any debtor, any notice, letter, message, or form which represents or implies that a claim exists unless it shall indicate in clear and legible type: the name of the licensee and the city, street, and number at which he is licensed to do business; the name of the original creditor to whom the debtor owed the claim if such name is known to the licensee or employee: PROVIDED, That upon written request of the debtor, the licensee shall make a reasonable effort to obtain the name of such person and provide this name to the debtor; . . . Wash. Rev. Code Ann. § 19.16.250(8)(a)-(b) (West, WESTLAW through Chap. 3 of 2002 Reg. Session).

If the notice, letter, message, or form is the first notice to the debtor or if the licensee is attempting to collect a different amount than indicated in his or its first notice to the debtor, an itemization must be made including:

(i) Amount owing on the original obligation at the time it was received by the licensee for collection or by assignment;
(ii) Interest or service charge, collection costs, or late payment charges, if any, added to the original obligation by the original creditor, customer or assignor before it was received by the licensee for collection, if the such information is known by the licensee or employee: PROVIDED, That upon written request of the debtor, the licensee shall make a reasonable effort to obtain information on such items and provide this information to the debtor;
(iii) Interest or service charge, if any, added by the licensee or customer or assignor after the obligation was received by the licensee for collection;
(iv) Collection costs, if any, that the licensee is attempting to collect;
(v) Attorneys' fees, if any, that the licensee is attempting to collect on his or its own behalf or on the behalf of a customer or assignor;
(vi) Any other charge or fee the licensee is attempting to collect on his or its own behalf or on behalf of a customer or assignor.

Wash. Rev. Code Ann. § 19.16.250(8)(c) (West, WESTLAW through Chap. 3 of 2002 Reg. Session).

Disclosure of rate of interest:

Whenever a collection agency is required pursuant to RCW 19.16.250 (8)(c) to disclose to the debtor that interest charges are being added to the original obligation, the collection agency must also disclose to the debtor the rate of interest. The rate of interest cannot exceed the legal maximum rate established in chapter 19.52 RCW. Wash. Admin. Code § 308-29-070 (WESTLAW through Jan. 2, 2002).

Use Licensed Agency Name Only

No licensee or employee of a licensee shall use any name while engaged in the making of a demand for any claim other than the name set forth on his or its current license issued hereunder. Wash. Rev. Code. Ann. § 19.16.250 (7) (West, WESTLAW through Chap. 3 of 2002 Reg. Session).

WEST VIRGINIA

No debt collector shall use, distribute, sell or prepare for use any written communication which violates or fails to conform to United States postal laws and regulations. W. Va. Code Ann. § 46A-2-129 (West, WESTLAW through 2002 First Ex. Session).

Use Licensed Agency Name Only

No debt collector shall use any fraudulent, deceptive or misleading representation or means to collect or attempt to collect claims or to obtain information concerning consumers. Without limiting the general application of the foregoing, the following conduct is deemed to violate this section:

(2) The use of any business, company, or organization name while engaged in the collection of claims, other than the true name of the debt collector's business, company, or organization. W. Va. Code Ann. § 46A-2-127(a) (West, WESTLAW through 2002 First Ex. Session).

Editor's note: Those collecting debt arising from the rental of consumer goods under rent-to-own agreements must provide a mini-Miranda warning in all communications:

No debt collector shall use any fraudulent, deceptive or misleading representation or means to collect or attempt to collect claims or to obtain information concerning consumers. Without limiting the general application of the foregoing, the following conduct is deemed to violate this section:

(2) The failure to clearly disclose in all communications made to collect or attempt to collect a claim or to obtain or attempt to obtain information about a consumer, that the debt collector is attempting to collect a claim and that any information obtained will be used for that purpose. W. Va. Code Ann. § 46B-4-7(2) (West, WESTLAW through 2002 First Ex. Session).

WISCONSIN

Special Text or Address Requirements

Within five days after the initial communication with a debtor, the licensed collection agency shall, unless the initial communication is written and contains the following notice or the debtor has paid the debt, send the following notice in not less than eight-point, boldface type:

"This collection agency is licensed by the Office of the Administrator of the Division of Banking, P.O. Box 7876, Madison, Wisconsin 53707."

This notice shall be typed or printed on either a collection notice or on the validation of any debt directed to the debtor by the licensee pursuant to Section 809 of the Federal Fair Debt Collection Practices Act.

Where the notice required by sub. (1) is printed on the reverse side of any collection notice or validation sent by the licensee, the front of such notice shall bear the following statement in not less than 8 point boldface type:

Notice: See Reverse Side for Important Information.

Wis. Admin. Code DFI-Bkg § 74.11 (2) (WESTLAW through 2001 Act 15, published 8/31/01).

Use of Alias—Registration or Forbidden

In any oral or written communication with a debtor, any collector, solicitor, licensee, person, employee or agent of a collection agency may use a separate alias. However, any alias shall be registered with and approved by the office of administrator of the division of banking prior to use. The real name of a person using an alias will be available from the office of administrator of the division of banking. No collector, solicitor, licensee, person, employee or agent may have more than one alias. No change of alias may be authorized unless good cause is shown. When using an alias, persons shall also identify the agency which they represent using the name under which it is licensed to do business. A licensee may forward printed collection notices to a debtor which are unsigned. Wis. Admin. Code DFI-Bkg § 74.12 (WESTLAW through 2001 Act 15, published 8/31/01).

WYOMING

Itemized Debt and Other Charges

At the consumer's written or verbal request, licensees shall furnish to the consumer a complete written accounting of matters pertaining to him. Such an accounting should itemize his debts turned over for collection and, in each instance, the name of the creditor, amount claimed to be owed, added charges if any, date and payment received and the amount still owing. Such requests from any one consumer should be reasonable in number, and in no instance will be required more often than payments are made.

Wyo. R. & Regs. Ch. 3 § 2 (WESTLAW with amendments received through November 21, 2001).

(a) Within five days after the initial communication with a consumer in connection with the collection of any debt, a debt collector shall, unless the following information is contained in the initial communication or the consumer has paid the debt, send the consumer a written notice containing:

(i) The amount of the debt;

(ii) The name of the creditor to whom the debt is owed;

(iii) A statement that unless the consumer, within thirty days after receipt of the notice, disputes the validity of the debt, or any portion thereof, the debt will be assumed to be valid by the debt collector;

(iv) A statement that if the consumer notifies the debt collector in writing within the thirty-day period that the debt, or any portion thereof, is disputed, the debt collector will obtain the verification of the debt or a copy of a judgment against the consumer and a copy of such verification or judgment will be mailed to the consumer by the debt collector; and

(v) A statement that, upon the consumer's written request within the thirty-day period, the debt collector will provide the consumer with the name and address of the original creditor, if different from the current creditor.

(b) If the consumer notifies the debt collector in writing within the thirty-day period described in subsection (a) that the debt, or any portion thereof, is disputed, or that the consumer requests the name and address of the original creditor, the debt collector shall cease collection of the debt, or any disputed portion thereof, until the debt collector obtains verification of the debt or a copy of a judgment, or the name and address of the original creditor, and a copy of such verification or judgment, or name and address of the original creditor, is mailed to the consumer by the debt collector.

(c) The failure of a consumer to dispute the validity of a debt under this section may not be construed by any court as an admission of liability by the consumer.

Wyo. R. & Regs. Ch. 4, § 12(a-c) (WESTLAW with amendments received through November 21, 2001).

Use Licensed Agency Name Only

A debt collector shall not use any business, company, or organization name other than the true name of the collector's business, company, or organization.

Wyo. R. & Regs. Ch. 4, § 10(m) (WESTLAW with amendments received through November 21, 2001).

Special Text or Address Requirements

A collector must disclose clearly in all communications made to collect a debt or to obtain information about a consumer, that the debt collector is attempting to collect a debt and that any information obtained will be used for that purpose, except as otherwise provided for communications to acquire location information.

Who. R. & Regs. Ch. 4 § 10(k) (WESTLAW with amendments received through November 21, 2001).

P.O. BOX 390106, MINNEAPOLIS, MN 55439-0106
TEL (952) 926-6547 FAX (952) 926-1624
E-MAIL COMPLIANCE@ACAINTERNATIONAL.ORG
WWW.ACAINTERNATIONAL.ORG

THIS INFORMATION IS NOT INTENDED TO BE, NOR IS IT, LEGAL ADVICE. IT IS INTENDED FOR INFORMATIONAL PURPOSES ONLY. WE MAKE NO WARRANTY, EXPRESS OR IMPLIED, AS TO THE ACCURACY OR RELIABILITY OF THE INFORMATION CONTAINED IN THIS DOCUMENT. THESE COMMUNICATIONS DO NOT ESTABLISH AN ATTORNEY-CLIENT RELATIONSHIP BETWEEN US. YOU MUST RETAIN YOUR OWN ATTORNEY TO RECEIVE LEGAL ADVICE.

APPENDIX IV

CLASS ACTION FAIRNESS ACT OF 2005

One Hundred Ninth Congress of the United States of America

AT THE FIRST SESSION

Begun and held at the City of Washington on Tuesday, The fourth day of January, two thousand and five

AN ACT

To amend the procedures that apply to consideration of interstate class actions to assure fairer outcomes for class members and defendants, and for other purposes.

Be it enacted by the Senate and House of Representatives of the United States of America in Congress assembled,

SECTION 1. SHORT TITLE; REFERENCE; TABLE OF CONTENTS.

(a) SHORT TITLE.—This Act may be cited as the "Class Action Fairness Act of 2005."

(b) REFERENCE.—Whenever in this Act reference is made to an amendment to, or repeal of, a section or other provision, the reference shall be considered to be made to a section or other provision of title 28, United States Code.

(c) TABLE OF CONTENTS.—The table of contents for this Act is as follows:

SEC. 2. FINDINGS AND PURPOSES.

(a) FINDINGS.—Congress finds the following:

(1) Class action lawsuits are an important and valuable part of the legal system when they permit the fair and efficient resolution of legitimate claims of numerous parties by allowing the claims to be aggregated into a single action against a defendant that has allegedly caused harm.

(2) Over the past decade, there have been abuses of the class action device that have—

(A) harmed class members with legitimate claims and defendants that have acted responsibly;

(B) adversely affected interstate commerce; and

(C) undermined public respect for our judicial system.

(3) Class members often receive little or no benefit from class actions, and are sometimes harmed, such as where—

(A) counsel are awarded large fees, while leaving class members with coupons or other awards of little or no value;

(B) unjustified awards are made to certain plaintiffs at the expense of other class members; and

(C) confusing notices are published that prevent class members from being able to fully understand and effectively exercise their rights.

(4) Abuses in class actions undermine the national judicial system, the free flow of interstate commerce, and the concept of diversity jurisdiction as intended by the framers of the United States Constitution, in that State and local courts are—

(A) keeping cases of national importance out of Federal court;

(B) sometimes acting in ways that demonstrate bias against out-of-State defendants; and

(C) making judgments that impose their view of the law on other States and bind the rights of the residents of those States.

(b) PURPOSES.—The purposes of this Act are to—

(1) assure fair and prompt recoveries for class members with legitimate claims;

(2) restore the intent of the framers of the United States Constitution by providing for Federal court consideration of interstate cases of national importance under diversity jurisdiction; and

(3) benefit society by encouraging innovation and lowering consumer prices.

SEC. 3. CONSUMER CLASS ACTION BILL OF RIGHTS AND IMPROVED PROCEDURES FOR INTERSTATE CLASS ACTIONS.

(a) IN GENERAL.—Part V is amended by inserting after chapter 113 the following:

"CHAPTER 114—CLASS ACTIONS

"Sec.
"1711. Definitions.
"1712. Coupon settlements.
"1713. Protection against loss by class members.

"1714. Protection against discrimination based on geographic location.
"1715. Notifications to appropriate Federal and State officials.

§ 1711. Definitions

"In this chapter:

"(1) CLASS.—The term 'class' means all of the class members in a class action.

"(2) CLASS ACTION.—The term 'class action' means any civil action filed in a district court of the United States under rule 23 of the Federal Rules of Civil Procedure or any civil action that is removed to a district court of the United States that was originally filed under a State statute or rule of judicial procedure authorizing an action to be brought by 1 or more representatives as a class action.

"(3) CLASS COUNSEL.—The term 'class counsel' means the persons who serve as the attorneys for the class members in a proposed or certified class action.

"(4) CLASS MEMBERS.—The term 'class members' means the persons (named or unnamed) who fall within the definition of the proposed or certified class in a class action.

"(5) PLAINTIFF CLASS ACTION.—The term 'plaintiff class action' means a class action in which class members are plaintiffs.

"(6) PROPOSED SETTLEMENT.—The term 'proposed settlement' means an agreement regarding a class action that is subject to court approval and that, if approved, would be binding on some or all class members.

"§ 1712. Coupon settlements

"(a) CONTINGENT FEES IN COUPON SETTLEMENTS.—If a proposed settlement in a class action provides for a recovery of coupons to a class member, the portion of any attorney's fee award to class counsel that is attributable to the award of the coupons shall be based on the value to class members of the coupons that are redeemed.

"(b) OTHER ATTORNEY'S FEE AWARDS IN COUPON SETTLEMENTS.—

"(1) IN GENERAL.—If a proposed settlement in a class action provides for a recovery of coupons to class members, and a portion of the recovery of the coupons is not used to determine the attorney's fee to be paid to class counsel, any attorney's fee award shall be based upon the amount of time class counsel reasonably expended working on the action.

"(2) COURT APPROVAL.—Any attorney's fee under this subsection shall be subject to approval by the court and shall include an appropriate attorney's fee, if any, for obtaining equitable relief, including an injunction, if applicable. Nothing in this sub-section shall be construed to prohibit application of a lodestar with a multiplier method of determining attorney's fees.

"(c) ATTORNEY'S FEE AWARDS CALCULATED ON A MIXED BASIS IN COUPON SETTLEMENTS.—If a proposed settlement in a class action provides for an award of coupons to class members and also provides for equitable relief, including injunctive relief—

"(1) that portion of the attorney's fee to be paid to class counsel that is based upon a portion of the recovery of the coupons shall be calculated in accordance with subsection (a); and

"(2) that portion of the attorney's fee to be paid to class counsel that is not based upon a portion of the recovery of the coupons shall be calculated in accordance with subsection (b).

"(d) SETTLEMENT VALUATION EXPERTISE.—In a class action involving the awarding of coupons, the court may, in its discretion upon the motion of a party, receive expert testimony from a witness qualified to provide information on the actual value to the class members of the coupons that are redeemed.

"(e) JUDICIAL SCRUTINY OF COUPON SETTLEMENTS.—In a proposed settlement under which class members would be awarded coupons, the court may approve the proposed settlement only after a hearing to determine whether, and making a written finding that, the settlement is fair, reasonable, and adequate for class members. The court, in its discretion, may also require that a proposed settlement agreement provide for the distribution of a portion of the value of unclaimed coupons to 1 or more charitable or governmental organizations, as agreed to by the parties. The distribution and redemption of any proceeds under this subsection shall not be used to calculate attorneys' fees under this section.

"§ 1713. Protection against loss by class members

"The court may approve a proposed settlement under which any class member is obligated to pay sums to class counsel that would result in a net loss to the class member only if the court makes a written finding that nonmonetary benefits to the class member substantially outweigh the monetary loss.

"§ 1714. Protection against discrimination based on geographic location

"The court may not approve a proposed settlement that provides for the payment of greater sums to some class members than to others solely on the basis that the class members to whom the greater sums are to be paid are located in closer geographic proximity to the court.

"§ 1715. Notifications to appropriate Federal and State officials

"(a) DEFINITIONS.—

"(1) APPROPRIATE FEDERAL OFFICIAL.—In this section, the term 'appropriate Federal official' means—

"(A) the Attorney General of the United States; or

"(B) in any case in which the defendant is a Federal depository institution, a State depository institution, a depository institution holding company, a foreign bank, or a nondepository institution subsidiary of the foregoing (as such terms are defined in section 3 of the Federal Deposit Insurance Act (12 U.S.C. 1813)), the person who has the primary Federal regulatory or supervisory responsibility with respect to the defendant, if some or all of the matters alleged in the class action are subject to regulation or supervision by that person.

"(2) APPROPRIATE STATE OFFICIAL.—In this section, the term 'appropriate State official' means the person in the State who has the primary regulatory or supervisory responsibility with respect to the defendant, or who licenses or otherwise authorizes the defendant to conduct business in the State, if some or all of the matters alleged in the class action are subject to regulation by that person. If there is no primary regulator, supervisor, or licensing authority, or the matters alleged in the class action are not subject to regulation or supervision by that person, then the appropriate State official shall be the State attorney general.

"(b) IN GENERAL.—Not later than 10 days after a proposed settlement of a class action is filed in court, each defendant that is participating in the proposed settlement shall serve upon the appropriate State official of each State in which a class member resides and the appropriate Federal official, a notice of the proposed settlement consisting of—

"(1) a copy of the complaint and any materials filed with the complaint and any amended complaints (except such materials shall not be required to be served if such materials are made electronically available through the Internet and such service includes notice of how to electronically access such material);

"(2) notice of any scheduled judicial hearing in the class action;

"(3) any proposed or final notification to class members of—

"(A)(i) the members' rights to request exclusion from the class action; or

"(ii) if no right to request exclusion exists, a statement that no such right exists; and

"(B) a proposed settlement of a class action;

"(4) any proposed or final class action settlement;

"(5) any settlement or other agreement contemporaneously made between class counsel and counsel for the defendants;

"(6) any final judgment or notice of dismissal;

"(7)(A) if feasible, the names of class members who reside in each State and the estimated proportionate share of the claims of such members to the entire settlement to that State's appropriate State official; or

"(B) if the provision of information under sub-paragraph (A) is not feasible, a reasonable estimate of the number of class members residing in each State and the estimated proportionate share of the claims of such members to the entire settlement; and

"(8) any written judicial opinion relating to the materials described under subparagraphs (3) through (6).

"(c) DEPOSITORY INSTITUTIONS NOTIFICATION.—

"(1) FEDERAL AND OTHER DEPOSITORY INSTITUTIONS.—In any case in which the defendant is a Federal depository institution, a depository institution holding company, a foreign bank, or a non-depository institution subsidiary of the foregoing, the notice requirements of this section are satisfied by serving the notice required under subsection (b) upon the person who has the primary Federal regulatory or supervisory responsibility with respect to the defendant, if some or all of the matters alleged in the class action are subject to regulation or supervision by that person.

"(2) STATE DEPOSITORY INSTITUTIONS.—In any case in which the defendant is a State depository institution (as that term is defined in section 3 of the Federal Deposit Insurance Act (12 U.S.C. 1813)), the notice requirements of this section are satisfied by serving the notice required under sub-section (b) upon the State bank supervisor (as that term is defined in section 3 of the Federal Deposit Insurance Act (12 U.S.C. 1813)) of the State in which the defendant is incorporated or chartered, if some or all of the matters alleged in the class action are subject to regulation or supervision by that person, and upon the appropriate Federal official.

"(d) FINAL APPROVAL.—An order giving final approval of a proposed settlement may not be issued earlier than 90 days after the later of the dates on which the appropriate Federal official and the appropriate State official are served with the notice required under subsection (b).

"(e) NONCOMPLIANCE IF NOTICE NOT PROVIDED.—

"(1) IN GENERAL.—A class member may refuse to comply with and may choose not to be bound by a settlement agreement or consent decree in a class action if the class member demonstrates that the notice required under subsection (b) has not been provided.

"(2) LIMITATION.—A class member may not refuse to comply with or to be bound by a settlement agreement or consent decree under paragraph (1) if the notice required under subsection (b) was directed to the appropriate Federal official and to either the State attorney general or the person that has primary regulatory, supervisory, or licensing authority over the defendant.

"(3) APPLICATION OF RIGHTS.—The rights created by this subsection shall apply only to class members or any person acting on a class member's behalf, and shall not be construed to limit any other rights affecting a class member's participation in the settlement.

"(f) RULE OF CONSTRUCTION.—Nothing in this section shall be construed to expand the authority of, or impose any obligations, duties, or responsibilities upon, Federal or State officials."

(b) TECHNICAL AND CONFORMING AMENDMENT.—The table of chapters for part V is amended by inserting after the item relating to chapter 113 the following:

"14. Class Actions .... 17".

SEC. 4. FEDERAL DISTRICT COURT JURISDICTION FOR INTERSTATE CLASS ACTIONS.

(a) APPLICATION OF FEDERAL DIVERSITY JURISDICTION.—Section 1332 is amended—

(1) by redesignating subsection (d) as subsection (e); and

(2) by inserting after subsection (c) the following:

"(d)(1) In this subsection—

(A) the term 'class' means all of the class members in a class action;

(B) the term 'class action' means any civil action filed under rule 23 of the Federal Rules of Civil Procedure or similar State statute or rule of judicial procedure authorizing an action to be brought by 1 or more representative persons as a class action;

"(C) the term 'class certification order' means an order issued by a court approving the treatment of some or all aspects of a civil action as a class action; and

"(D) the term 'class members' means the persons (named or unnamed) who fall within the definition of the proposed or certified class in a class action.

"(2) The district courts shall have original jurisdiction of any civil action in which the matter in controversy exceeds the sum or value of $5,000,000, exclusive of interest and costs, and is a class action in which—

"(A) any member of a class of plaintiffs is a citizen of a State different from any defendant;

"(B) any member of a class of plaintiffs is a foreign state or a citizen or subject of a foreign state and any defendant is a citizen of a State; or

"(C) any member of a class of plaintiffs is a citizen of a State and any defendant is a foreign state or a citizen or subject of a foreign state.

"(3) A district court may, in the interests of justice and looking at the totality of the circumstances, decline to exercise jurisdiction under paragraph (2) over a class action in which greater than one-third but less than two-thirds of the members of all proposed plaintiff classes in the aggregate and the primary defendants are citizens of the State in which the action was originally filed based on consideration of—

"(A) whether the claims asserted involve matters of national or interstate interest;

"(B) whether the claims asserted will be governed by laws of the State in which the action was originally filed or by the laws of other States;

"(C) whether the class action has been pleaded in a manner that seeks to avoid Federal jurisdiction;

"(D) whether the action was brought in a forum with a distinct nexus with the class members, the alleged harm, or the defendants;

"(E) whether the number of citizens of the State in which the action was originally filed in all proposed plaintiff classes in the aggregate is substantially larger than the number of citizens from any other State, and the citizenship of the other members of the proposed class is dispersed among a substantial number of States; and

"(F) whether, during the 3-year period preceding the filing of that class action, 1 or more other class actions asserting the same or similar claims on behalf of the same or other persons have been filed.

"(4) A district court shall decline to exercise jurisdiction under paragraph (2)—

"(A)(i) over a class action in which—

"(I) greater than two-thirds of the members of all proposed plaintiff classes in the aggregate are citizens of the State in which the action was originally filed;

"(II) at least 1 defendant is a defendant—

"(aa) from whom significant relief is sought by members of the plaintiff class;

"(bb) whose alleged conduct forms a significant basis for the claims asserted by the proposed plaintiff class; and "(cc) who is a citizen of the State in which the action was originally filed; and

"(III) principal injuries resulting from the alleged conduct or any related conduct of each defendant were incurred in the State in which the action was originally filed; and

"(ii) during the 3-year period preceding the filing of that class action, no other class action has been filed asserting the same or similar factual allegations against any of the defendants on behalf of the same or other persons; or

"(B) two-thirds or more of the members of all proposed plaintiff classes in the aggregate, and the primary defendants, are citizens of the State in which the action was originally filed.

"(5) Paragraphs (2) through (4) shall not apply to any class action in which—

"(A) the primary defendants are States, State officials, or other governmental entities against whom the district court may be foreclosed from ordering relief; or

"(B) the number of members of all proposed plaintiff classes in the aggregate is less than 100.

"(6) In any class action, the claims of the individual class members shall be aggregated to determine whether the matter in controversy exceeds the sum or value of $5,000,000, exclusive of interest and costs.

"(7) Citizenship of the members of the proposed plaintiff classes shall be determined for purposes of paragraphs (2) through (6) as of the date of filing of the complaint or amended complaint, or, if the case stated by the initial pleading is not subject to Federal jurisdiction, as of the date of service by plaintiffs of an amended pleading, motion, or other paper, indicating the existence of Federal jurisdiction.

"(8) This subsection shall apply to any class action before or after the entry of a class certification order by the court with respect to that action.

"(9) Paragraph (2) shall not apply to any class action that solely involves a claim—

"(A) concerning a covered security as defined under 16(f)(3) of the Securities Act of 1933 (15 U.S.C. 78p(f)(3)) and section 28(f)(5)(E) of the Securities Exchange Act of 1934 (15 U.S.C. 78bb(f)(5)(E));

"(B) that relates to the internal affairs or governance of a corporation or other form of business enterprise and that arises under or by virtue of the laws of the State in which such corporation or business enterprise is incorporated or organized; or

"(C) that relates to the rights, duties (including fiduciary duties), and obligations relating to or created by or pursuant to any security (as defined under section 2(a)(1) of the Securities Act of 1933 (15 U.S.C. 77b(a)(1)) and the regulations issued thereunder).

"(10) For purposes of this subsection and section 1453, an unincorporated association shall be deemed to be a citizen of the State where it has its principal place of business and the State under whose laws it is organized.

"(11) (A) For purposes of this subsection and section 1453, a mass action shall be deemed to be a class action removable under paragraphs (2) through (10) if it otherwise meets the provisions of those paragraphs.

"(B)(i) As used in subparagraph (A), the term 'mass action' means any civil action (except a civil action within the scope of section 1711(2)) in which monetary relief claims of 100 or more persons are proposed to be tried jointly on the ground that the plaintiffs' claims involve common questions of law or fact, except that jurisdiction shall exist only over those plaintiffs whose claims in a mass action satisfy the jurisdictional amount requirements under subsection (a).

"(ii) As used in subparagraph (A), the term 'mass action' shall not include any civil action in which—

"(I) all of the claims in the action arise from an event or occurrence in the State in which the action was filed, and that allegedly resulted in injuries in that State or in States contiguous to that State;

"(II) the claims are joined upon motion of a defendant;

"(III) all of the claims in the action are asserted on behalf of the general public (and not on behalf of individual claimants or members of a purported class) pursuant to a State statute specifically authorizing such action; or

"(IV) the claims have been consolidated or coordinated solely for pretrial proceedings.

"(C)(i) Any action(s) removed to Federal court pursuant to this subsection shall not thereafter be transferred to any other court pursuant to section 1407, or the rules promulgated thereunder, unless a majority of the plaintiffs in the action request transfer pursuant to section 1407.

"(ii) This subparagraph will not apply—

"(I) to cases certified pursuant to rule 23 of the Federal Rules of Civil Procedure; or

"(II) if plaintiffs propose that the action proceed as a class action pursuant to rule 23 of the Federal Rules of Civil Procedure.

"(D) The limitations periods on any claims asserted in a mass action that is removed to Federal court pursuant to this subsection shall be deemed tolled during the period that the action is pending in Federal court."

(b) CONFORMING AMENDMENTS.—

(1) Section 1335(a)(1) is amended by inserting "subsection (a) or (d) of" before "section 1332".

(2) Section 1603(b)(3) is amended by striking "(d)" and inserting "(e)".

SEC. 5. REMOVAL OF INTERSTATE CLASS ACTIONS TO FEDERAL DISTRICT COURT.

(a) IN GENERAL.—Chapter 89 is amended by adding after section 1452 the following:

"§ 1453. Removal of class actions

"(a) DEFINITIONS.—In this section, the terms 'class', 'class action', 'class certification order', and 'class member' shall have the meanings given such terms under section 1332(d)(1).

"(b) IN GENERAL.—A class action may be removed to a district court of the United States in accordance with section 1446 (except that the 1-year limitation under section 1446(b) shall not apply), without regard to whether any defendant is a citizen of the State in which the action is brought, except that such action may be removed by any defendant without the consent of all defendants.

"(c) REVIEW OF REMAND ORDERS.—

"(1) IN GENERAL.—Section 1447 shall apply to any removal of a case under this section, except that notwithstanding section 1447(d), a court of appeals may accept an appeal from an order of a district court granting or denying a motion to remand a class action to the State court from which it was removed if application is made to the court of appeals not less than 7 days after entry of the order.

"(2) TIME PERIOD FOR JUDGMENT.—If the court of appeals accepts an appeal under paragraph (1), the court shall complete all action on such appeal, including rendering judgment, not later than 60 days after the date on which such appeal was filed, unless an extension is granted under paragraph (3).

"(3) EXTENSION OF TIME PERIOD.—The court of appeals may grant an extension of the 60-day period described in paragraph (2) if—

"(A) all parties to the proceeding agree to such extension, for any period of time; or

"(B) such extension is for good cause shown and in the interests of justice, for a period not to exceed 10 days.

"(4) DENIAL OF APPEAL.—If a final judgment on the appeal under paragraph (1) is not issued before the end of the period described in paragraph (2), including any extension under paragraph (3), the appeal shall be denied.

"(d) EXCEPTION.—This section shall not apply to any class action that solely involves—

"(1) a claim concerning a covered security as defined under section 16(f)(3) of the Securities Act of 1933 (15 U.S.C. 78p(f)(3)) and section 28(f)(5)(E) of the Securities Exchange Act of 1934 (15 U.S.C. 78bb(f)(5)(E));

"(2) a claim that relates to the internal affairs or governance of a corporation or other form of business enterprise and arises under or by virtue of the laws of the State in which such corporation or business enterprise is incorporated or organized; or

"(3) a claim that relates to the rights, duties (including fiduciary duties), and obligations relating to or created by or pursuant to any security (as defined under section 2(a)(1) of the Securities Act of 1933 (15 U.S.C. 77b(a)(1)) and the regulations issued thereunder)."

(b) TECHNICAL AND CONFORMING AMENDMENTS.—

The table of sections for chapter 89 is amended by adding after the item relating to section 1452 the following:

"1453. Removal of class actions."

SEC. 6. REPORT ON CLASS ACTION SETTLEMENTS.

(a) IN GENERAL.—Not later than 12 months after the date of enactment of this Act, the Judicial Conference of the United States, with the assistance of the Director of the Federal Judicial Center and the Director of the Administrative Office of the United States Courts, shall prepare and transmit to the Committees on the

Judiciary of the Senate and the House of Representatives a report on class action settlements.

(b) CONTENT.—The report under subsection (a) shall contain—

(1) recommendations on the best practices that courts can use to ensure that proposed class action settlements are fair to the class members that the settlements are supposed to benefit;

(2) recommendations on the best practices that courts can use to ensure that—

(A) the fees and expenses awarded to counsel in connection with a class action settlement appropriately reflect the extent to which counsel succeeded in obtaining full redress for the injuries alleged and the time, expense, and risk that counsel devoted to the litigation; and

(B) the class members on whose behalf the settlement is proposed are the primary beneficiaries of the settlement; and

(3) the actions that the Judicial Conference of the United States has taken and intends to take toward having the Federal judiciary implement any or all of the recommendations contained in the report.

(c) AUTHORITY OF FEDERAL COURTS.—Nothing in this section shall be construed to alter the authority of the Federal courts to supervise attorneys' fees.

SEC. 7. ENACTMENT OF JUDICIAL CONFERENCE RECOMMENDATIONS.

Notwithstanding any other provision of law, the amendments to rule 23 of the Federal Rules of Civil Procedure, which are set forth in the order entered by the Supreme Court of the United States on March 27, 2003, shall take effect on the date of enactment of this Act or on December 1, 2003 (as specified in that order), whichever occurs first.

SEC. 8. RULEMAKING AUTHORITY OF SUPREME COURT AND JUDICIAL CONFERENCE.

Nothing in this Act shall restrict in any way the authority of the Judicial Conference and the Supreme Court to propose and prescribe general rules of practice and procedure under chapter 131 of title 28, United States Code.

SEC. 9. EFFECTIVE DATE.

The amendments made by this Act shall apply to any civil action commenced on or after the date of enactment of this Act.

APPENDIX V

MEANINGFUL INVOLVEMENT, MASS MAILINGS AND FDCPA COMPLIANCE

By Jay Winston, Winston & Winston P.C.

Defining the terms

Pursuant to 15 USC 1692(a) the FDCPA was enacted in 1977 "because there [was] abundant evidence of abusive, deceptive, and unfair debt collection practices . . . [that] contribute to the number of personal bankruptcies, to marital instability, to the loss of jobs, and to invasions of individual privacy." 15 USC 1692(c) states "[m]eans other than misrepresentation or other abusive debt collection practices are available for the effective collection of debts." 15 USC 1692(e) states that [it] the purpose of this title is to eliminate "abusive debt collection practices by debt collectors, to insure that those debt collectors who refrain from using abusive debt collection practices are not competitively disadvantaged, and to promote consistent State action to protect consumers against debt collection abuses." The FDCPA, does not define abusive, and does not define deceptive. However, it is clear that Congress intended to deter "abusive" practices because it is mentioned 6 times in section 1692. In connection with the term "abusive," the drafters used terms such as deceptive, unfair or misleading. Judges should be reminded that the statute was designed to prevent "abusive" conduct (i.e., extreme activity, not gray areas).

More importantly 15 USC 1692(e) also added a balancing provision. The goal was "to insure that debt collectors who refrain from using abusive debt collection practices are not competitively disadvantaged." The court should also be reminded that the purpose of the statute was to eliminate acts that "contribute to the number of personal bankruptcies, to marital instability, to the loss of jobs, and to invasions of individual privacy." When dealing with gray areas, remind the court that the challenged activity does not contribute to any of the objectives that the act was intended to prevent. "The act was not intended to shield . . . consumers from the embarrassment and inconvenience which are the natural consequences of debt collection." *Dalton v. FMA Enterprises*, 953 F. Supp. 1525, 1526 (M.D. Fl. 1997), *citing Higgins v. Capital Credit Services, Inc.*, 762 F. Supp. 1128, 1135 (D. Del. 1991).

History and Technology

The FDCPA was enacted in 1977, over 25 years ago. Attorneys were later covered by the act in 1987. The first major court decisions laying the ground work for prohibiting certain practices "by attorneys" occurred in 1993 over 10 years ago. Most law firms were marginally computerized. In as little as ten years technology has made significant strides in enabling law firms to process more claims, more accurately and efficiently. In 1993 only service bureaus and collection agencies could afford the technology to print large numbers of letters. Today, for a few thousand dollars, computer systems and printers are readily available at a local store to enable a solo practitioner with a few paralegals and clerical support staff to accurately and professionally manage over 10,000 accounts per month.

Present Technology

Computerization and technology has now enabled law firms to compete with collection agencies for the placement of claims from large national corporations for the following reason: Economies of scale. Economies of scale is an economic term that stems from our capitalistic society. In layman's terms, similar cases being treated in the same manner based on several common characteristics. The courts should not penalize law firms for adopting technology. Increased efficiency and accuracy should not be equated with engaging in a deceptive trade practice.

Uniformity and Matters involving no legal or professional judgment

When a national creditor engages in the uniform practice of extending credit to millions of individuals based on a "form agreement" or "standard process," it necessarily produces a large number of delinquent accounts that are substantially similar in 99% of the cases. Other types of debts such as "credit cards, bad checks, goods sold and delivered, and services rendered" also produce uniform claims of unpaid debts.

The creditor through technology can separate and segregate accounts based on computer formulas and "coding." Accounts are segregated into several categories such as disputed, undisputed, bankrupt, deceased, pre-legal or legal categories. "Computer coding" by activity or status has enabled this accurate segregation of a large scale of accounts with a high degree of accuracy in a shorter amount of time.

Over the years corporations with the assistance of inside and outside counsel, have developed criteria for their computer programmers to sort and separate accounts by groups into certain categories such as "paying, slow pays, bankruptcy, deceased disputed, undisputed, no-contact, several broken promises or problem accounts. Consequently, a company can forward accounts to a collection agency or a law firm in "batches" of accounts that reliably fall within a pre-set criteria. This pre-set criteria is so accurate that detailed review of the file *becomes unnecessary and merely duplicative, as the review process has already been performed by the client and its computer system based on "uniformly recognized criteria" upon which everyone would agree.*

Only when a law firm, using a reliable system, engaged in their day-to-day duties of managing and supervising their practice, receives responses from debtors refuting this premise does the law firm have an immediate duty to stop the process, and investigate the reliability of the data. The statutory notice states "[u]nless within 30 days after receipt of this letter, the validity of the debt or any portion thereof is disputed, the debt will be assumed valid by our office." *No attorney review is implied by the statutory notice.* Nowhere in the statute is attorney review required. If attorney review is implied, it would overshadow the statutory notice. Based on this interpretation an attorney would be held to a higher standard than a collection agency, which is prohibited by *Heintz v. Jackson.*

In some cases the Judges broadly state in their decision that a letter from an attorney implies that some professional judgment has been made by the attorney with respect to the particular account. The author believes that this phrase has been misused and taken out of context by many consumer attorneys and liberal judges when presiding over extreme cases. <u>All the main cases cited by consumer attorneys involve cases in which the affirmative representation was made in the *text* of the letter.</u> This representation was exhibited through a suit threat, a representation of increased urgency or that the attorney has personally reviewed the file.

The author is unaware of any court decision holding that a plain vanilla letter stating that the file has been referred to the law firm's office with the balance due and the statutory notice violates the FDCPA when used in conjunction with a mass mailing. This type of form letter makes no affirmative misrepresentation as to review, and merely acts as a "notice letter" that the law firm is now representing the creditor. Furthermore, the authors knows of no decision that states omitting the phrase "no review was performed" was a violation.

Several cases have held that an attorney's letterhead is not an implied threat of suit. *Wallace v. Winston & Morrone* (US DC WD 96-C-354-C 1996 Unpublished); *Sturdevant v. Jolas*, 942 F. Supp. 426 (WD Wisc 1996); *Veillard v. Mednick*, 24 F. Supp. 2d 863, (N.D. Ill. 1998). The court must look to the affirmative representations made in the text of the letter. <u>Silence or an omission of what you may do is not a deceptive practice</u>. In *Wallace*, the court noted that a law firm has no other means to identify itself.

Mailing letters in volume is not expressly prohibited by the FDCPA. A law firm letter, sent from the law firm's office by staff of a law firm, is from the law firm and no one else. <u>"The-behind-the-door activities" of the attorney or law firm are protected under the attorney-client privilege and the attorney-work-product rule, trade secret law and are not subject to discovery</u>. The courts must be careful to not destroy statutory and judicial protections that are the mainstay of the judicial system. The courts cannot say, you are entitled to these protections for commercial collections, and for some consumer collection action activity, unless the FDCPA applies. By undertaking to strip these protections, the court is changing its role from judge to legislator.

Attorneys must move the court to the real issue, collecting improper debts. The courts are hesitant in assessing how an attorney should practice law for the reasons set forth above. This practice of law is regulated by the state bar associations and disciplinary committees. However, courts will step in if the practice causes material and substantial damages (i.e., malpractice). The real issue surrounding a mass mailing is: Are you collecting a legally enforceable debt? Can you convince a trier of fact that the debts are more probable than not (51%) due and owing. When defending these suits, defense counsel should stress that the plaintiff cannot show that disputes were not addressed, and that the debtor admits owing the debt. The FDCPA should not be used to penalize accuracy and efficiency.

Permitting consumer attorneys and the courts to subjectively determine if the level of review is unsatisfactory and an FDCPA violation, does not further the goals of the FDCPA and *"contribute to the number of personal bankruptcies, to marital instability, to the loss of jobs, and to invasions of individual privacy."* Furthermore, such review does not "insure that debt collectors who refrain from using abusive debt collection practices are not competitively disadvantaged," as both groups are subject to these lawsuits.

Establishing an efficient process to prove accuracy

Mailing the letter is the last step in the process, not the first. The first step is the initial interview with the client. The second step is a review or implementation of procedures to confirm that the letters are sent to parties who are in default. The third step is verifying the accuracy of the procedures. The fourth step is auditing the procedures. *The final step is the mailing of the non-suit letter. The decision process is made by the law firm in the decision to accept the claim under a pre-set criteria from their ongoing relationship.* Thus, based on experience, a law firm makes a "professional judgment" that it is permissible to mail the collection letters.

The courts must be reminded that some tasks require professional judgment, and other tasks do not. For example, a suit threat or issuing legal papers clearly implies some legal judgment, which is higher than professional judgment. Mailing a statutorily required letter and notifying the debtor of his statutory rights, requires no legal judgment, and no professional judgment as both creditors and collection agencies conduct the same activity without a law license. As no legal judgment or professional judgment is necessary, imposing a higher standard on law firms violates the *Heintz v. Jackson* decision (law firms and collection agencies are to be held to the same standard when performing the same tasks). Attorneys would be at a competitive disadvantage with collection agencies, which would violate 15 U.S.C. 1692(e)'s balancing provision.

The FDCPA was not designed to permit the collection of debts which are unchallengeable or undisputable. In a civil lawsuit, a plaintiff is only required to prove by the preponderance of the evidence (51%) that the debt is owed to win the case. A cause of action to start the lawsuit such as breach of contract (oral or written), unjust enrichment, account stated, goods sold and delivered or services rendered, requires minimal information (i.e., a theory to sue upon, a representation from the client that an amount is due, and damages). The judicial system discourages fact pleading. The discovery process fills this gap. *A court cannot impose a higher standard to mail a letter as opposed to instituting a lawsuit.*

How did the term "meaningful involvement" start?

The term is a misnomer. The term the courts should have used was "no involvement." The term started from collection agencies who falsely implied that they had retained attorneys for the creditor. Attorney review began as dicta in the early "mass mailing cases" because the letters were not from law firms, but from third-party collection agencies who were preparing the letters and making the decision to mail the letters for the law firms. Delegating a task to an employee is far different from delegating the task to an independent third party. Thus, the *text* of these letters were misleading not because the attorney did not provide adequate or nominal review of every letter, but for other reasons—*affirmative misrepresentations*—including (1) falsely implying a sense of urgency, (2) falsely implying, in the text of the letter, that based on personal review of the file by a particular attorney, the attorney made a decision to send the letter, and (3) falsely threatening suit when suit was unlikely. The pertinent sections of the Fair Debt Collection Practices Act are as follows:

> 15 U.S.C. 1692e—A debt collector may not use any false, deceptive, or misleading representation or means in connection with the collection of any debt. Without limiting the general application of the foregoing, the following conduct is a violation of this section:
>
> (3) the false representation or implication that any individual is an attorney or that any communication is from an attorney;
>
> (10) the use of any false representation of deceptive means to collect or attempt to collect any debt or to obtain information concerning a consumer.

The wording of the section states that "affirmative misrepresentations" [the use of] are prohibited; not "passive omissions." This statutory difference should be emphasized to the court. Statutory constructionists identify this distinction in several other areas of the law, most noticeably with real estate law with the duty to disclose (e.g., you cannot hide a defect in your house, but you do not have a duty to disclose the defect.)

Pre Collection Law firm cases prior to *Clomon v. Jackson*

Anthes v. Transworld, 765 F. Supp. 162 (D. Del. 1991) distinguished *Masuda v. Richards*, 759 F. Supp. 1456 (C.D. Cal. 1991). A violation occurred in *Masuda* because the recipient considers the debt more serious because the letter is now coming from an attorney, when in fact it was not. No violation occurred in *Anthes* because the law firm controlled the process. The attorney relied on the information furnished by the client and his office sent the letter directly to the debtor on the attorney's stationary with his name, address, telephone number and signature and from his office. The court concluded that a reasonable trier of fact would have to find that the attorney is an independent attorney retained by the collection agency to send debt collection letters in his own name.

Early cases held that a law firm must maintain a file and be involved in the process of preparing and sending the letter with its own staff. More importantly, this case stood for the proposition that a law firm, with a law license, that prepared the letter on its letterhead, and mailed letters to debtors, did not violate 15 U.S.C.

1692e(3), "[th]e false representation or implication that any individual is an attorney or that the communication is from an attorney." There was no misrepresentation because the term attorney necessarily included the attorney or the firm's clerical staff under their supervision. *Anthes* is still good law.

Clomon v. Jackson

The *Clomon* decision merely followed the same proposition and ruled that when an attorney implies in the text of the letter, attorney review, the attorneys need to be personally involved or need to supervise and control the collection process on a day-to-day basis, and utilize non-legal staff and rely on the recommendation of others.

Clomon, involved a situation in which a collection agency prepared and mailed over 1 million letters a year with the letterhead of a part-time attorney. *The attorney's role was symbolic as he merely lent his name to the collection agency that controlled the entire process.* Preparing the form of the letter was insufficient. The court considered two issues. First, that he "played virtually no role in the debt collection process" 988 F.2d 1314, 1320

> . . . Jackson did not review each debtor's file; he did not determine when particular letters should be sent; he did not approve the sending of particular letters based upon the recommendations of others; and he did not [**17] see particular letters before they were sent-indeed, he did not even know the identities of the persons to whom the letters were issued. [yet claimed to know them in the letters]. In short, the fact that Jackson played virtually no day-to-day role in the debt collection process supports the conclusion that the collection letters were not "from" Jackson in any meaningful sense of that word.

A violation occurred because the attorney affirmatively represented his personal involvement in the text of the letters, when none existed.

> [T]he use of an attorney's signature on a collection letter [in connection with the text] implies that the letter is "from" the attorney who signed it; it implies, in other words, that the attorney directly controlled or supervised the process through which the letter was sent. We have also found here [on these facts] that the use of an attorney's signature implies—at least in the absence of language to the contrary—that the attorney signing the letter formed an opinion about how to manage the case of the debtor to whom the letter was sent. In a mass mailing, these implications are frequently false: the attorney whose [**21] signature is used might play no role either in sending the letters or in determining who should receive them. For this reason, there will be few, if any, cases in which a mass-produced collection letter bearing the facsimile of an attorney's signature will comply with the restrictions imposed by § 1692e.

Clomon did not ban mass mailings! The court held that an attorney cannot affirmatively mislead a debtor into believing that s/he is involved in the process, and then delegate the collection process to a third party, collection agency. The violation was not the mass mailing, but a mass mailing of an affirmatively deceptive letter. Many consumer attorneys allege that the acts stated by the court (i.e., review the file, determine who should be sent letters, etc.) were a specific list of requirements. This conclusion is incorrect. When defending these cases, quote the above paragraph, and include the decision as an exhibit to demonstrate that the judge was showing what was not done, as opposed to what was required to be performed. The court was deeply concerned about the "absent attorney" situation, who delegates his decision making authority to the staff of another corporation.

When *Clomon* was decided in 1993, the reason the court believed that few if any mass mailings by attorneys would be permissible was because the technology was not readily available to permit attorneys to print a large numbers of letters themselves or receive data electronically. The use of paper files was "the way of life." The ability of creditors to summarize the facts of the case electronically and segregate them by codes with a high degree of reliability did not exist, except in rare cases. Due to these technological limitations most law firms, who engaged in mass mailings, would be required to delegate the decision making process, to a non-employee third party (i.e., collection agency). Making any affirmative representations in the letter would be deceptive, because the attorney, law firm, or its staff were not the decision makers as affirmatively represented in the letter. In 2004, the technology exists for the modern law firm to perform these tasks, without the assistance of third parties, (i.e., collection agencies), with a high level of accuracy and professionalism. Since the activity is now performed by the law firm, it is no longer misleading.

Supreme Court's addresses issue tangentially

In *Heintz v. Jenkins*, 514 U.S. 291 (1995), the Supreme Court held that *attorneys were not to be held to a higher standard than collection agencies*. However, several lower courts have ignored this rule. Agencies are permitted to delegate their duties to a third party (client or service bureau) and engage in the same conduct prohibited by *Clomon*: This requirement of involvement has never been applied by the courts to collection agencies. Collection agencies receive the accounts directly from the client, send out letters, do not review the files, do not verify if the debts are valid, or do not even mail the letters (many use service bureaus, or the client to produce the letters), do not respond to mail, or telephone calls; all of which is performed by the client. These services are typically performed at a flat rate of less than $0.50 per account or letter.

Based on *Heintz*, collection agencies, who falsely imply that they are involved in the collection effort, when in fact they have delegated most of their duties to their client (i.e., reading the mail, negotiating settlements, responding to telephone calls, resolving disputes, or printing the letters), violate 15 U.S.C. § 1692e(10) which prohibits "the use of any false representation of deceptive means to collect or attempt to collect any debt or to obtain information concerning a consumer."

Post-*Clomon* decisions of interest

In *Martinez v. Albuquerque*, 867 F. Supp. 1495 (D.C.N.M. 1994), and *Russy v. Rankin*, 911 F. Supp. 1449 (D.C.N.M. 1995), the New Mexico district court similarly followed *Clomon* and *Masuda*, holding it to be a violation for a law firm to delegate their duties to a collection agency. In both New Mexico's cases, a suit threat letter was used. In both cases, the attorney was not involved in the process (absent attorney syndrome).

Avila v. Rubin

Avila v. Rubin, 84 F.3d 222, 227 (7th Cir. 1996) was similar to *Clomon* and a violation was found. The firm sent over 270,000 *suit threat* letters in a year. The attorney owned the collection agency. The law firm possessed no staff. A suit threat letter implies the necessity of attorney review prior to sending the suit threat letter. The attorney admitted that he did not review the debtor's file nor did he approve the sending of the particular letters based on the recommendation of others. The collection agency performed the mailing and all the ministerial acts and was the true source of the letters.

> ***Practice Tip:*** *Attorneys directly representing creditors should attempt to use this distinction to distance themselves from these 2 decisions.*

The *Avila* court relied on *Clomon.*

> [A]n attorney sending dunning letters [with a suit threat] must be directly and personally involved in the mailing of the letters in order to comply with the strictures of FDCPA. This may include reviewing the file of individual debtors to determine if and when a letter should be sent or approving the sending of letters based on the recommendations of others. *See Clomon*, 988 F.2d at 1320.

> ***Practice Tip:*** *Remind the court that attorney involvement MAY include review of the file. Review of the file is not a requirement. Involvement can be shown in different ways, including the recommendation of your staff.*

The *Avila* decision stressed that the attorney made a false affirmative misrepresentation of attorney involvement, raising the stakes, when in fact, they had not.

> An unsophisticated consumer, getting a letter from an "attorney," [after receiving one from a collection agency] knows the price of poker has just gone up. And that clearly is the reason why the dunning campaign [**21] escalates from the collection agency, which might not strike fear in the heart of the consumer, to the attorney, who is better positioned to get the debtor's knees knocking.

Post-*Avila* & *Clomon* Analysis

In both *Avila* and *Clomon* a violation was found not because the attorney was involved in the mass mailing, but because the attorney affirmatively misled the consumer, by the text of the letter, that an attorney had become involved in the case, raising the stakes, when in fact, the collection agency was performing the tasks. After these cases, in both the Second and the Seventh Circuits, the only solution would be to hire an outside counsel who would supervise and control the entire operation and would thereby become meaningfully involved in the processing and prosecution of the claims.

> ***Practice Tip:*** *A suit threat letter should be avoided when engaging in mass mailings. The source of the letter should not be a third-party collection agency.*

Pro-Collection Attorney Cases

Some help came from the case of *Danielson v. Hicks*, 1995 U.S. Dist. LEXIS 22211 (D. Minn. 1995). The letters were generated by employees working for an attorney at the attorney's law firm. The court rejected the analogy to *Clomon* or *Avila*:

> Plaintiffs fail to proffer any legal authority to support their argument that defendants violated § 1692e(3) because the "dunning" letter came from a paralegal rather than an attorney. Their reliance upon *Clomon v. Jackson and Martinez v. Albuquerque Collection Services, Inc.* is misplaced. Both Clomon and Martinez involved letters containing an attorney's signature which were, in fact, generated from a debt [*10] collection agency rather than from an attorney's office. In the present action, however, the letters containing Mr. Hicks' signature were generated by employees working with Mr. Hicks at Mr. Hicks' law firm. The record reflects that Messerli & Kramer had been retained by the FMCC to collect upon debts which were past due. Pursuant to this, Mr. Hicks' office sent letters to the debtors. . . .

The court followed the *Anthes* case. Since the letters were sent by the employees under the explicit direction of the attorney, the act was not violated.

In *Goldberg v. Winston*, 1997 U.S. Dist. LEXIS 3521 (S.D. N.Y.), the district court held that *a non-suit threat* collection letter was created by the attorney, the attorney decided when and which letters were to be sent and the attorney reviewed the hard copies of the data provided on each debtor. The *Goldberg* case also held that legal assistants may review the file to be meaningfully involved, providing that the legal assistants are under the supervision and control of an attorney (relying on the representation of others—client and staff). The court acknowledged that the attorney made a mass mailing and that a facsimile signature was used. In a footnote, the cursory nature of the review, in that it was only a brief look at a computer printout of the debtor's relevant information, was duly noted. Nevertheless, the court felt that such behavior would meet the *Clomon* standard in light of the relatively small size of the debts involved and the fact that the client had "no additional information" on the debtor. The *Goldberg* decision has been cited in many other cases where the attorney was involved in the same way that we were involved.

Other pro-collection attorney cases worth reviewing include *Hohmann v. Winston & Morrone,* (99-2744 N.D. Ill. April 28, 1999 Unpublished) where the court held that our firm designed, directed, controlled and oversaw day to day activities, and no violation occurred. In *Dalton v. FMA Enterprises,* in-house counsel reviewed 10% of files, and the attorney won at Trial. Two other favorable decisions (summary judgment) from the Second Circuit were *Kapeluschnik v. Le Shack & Grodensky, P.C.,* 1999 U.S. Dist. LEXIS 22883, 96 Civ. 1999 (E.D.N.Y. August 25, 1999) and *Mizrahi v. Network Recovery Servs.,* 1999 U.S. Dist. LEXIS 22145 (E.D.N.Y. Nov. 5, 1999) handled by our law firm. A recent case in the Ninth Circuit reiterated *Heinz v. Jenkins,* 514 U.S. 291 (1995) statement that attorneys should not be held to a different standard in collecting debts than other debt collectors nor should they be required to investigate the validity of the claims they prosecute on behalf of their clients. Forgey v. Parker, Bush & Lane, P.C., 2004 U.S. Dist. LEXIS 18076 (D.C. Or. 2004).

Post *Avila: Wexler, Dickerson,* and *Wolpoff* decisions

Prior to 2002, no effort was made by the courts to consider the extent of the review, the amount of time to be devoted to the review of the files, or whether the total amount of time was sufficient for an adequate review. No decision devoted any analysis to the extent of the information that the attorneys should possess to conduct the review. In 2002 and 2003, three Circuit Court of Appeals decisions, two from the Seventh Circuit and one from the Second Circuit, began to consider whether the quality of the review should be considered as a factor.

Consumer attorneys may allege that the *Boyd v. Wexler,* 275 F.3d 642 (7th Cir. 2001), decision is a significant expansion of the concept of meaningful involvement, but it is too early to determine. The appellate court only reviewed the lower court's decision granting the summary judgment because the affidavits contradicted the testimony in the depositions of the three attorneys. In *Wexler,* the three attorneys claimed to have personally reviewed over 439,606 pieces of mail over an eight-and-a-half-month period, despite concentrating a majority of their time on other matters. Furthermore, the affidavit described a complicated review process. The numbers did not add up. "Wexler might think he reviewed the file carefully yet be mistaken." *Id.* at 646.

Judge Posner acknowledged that part of the review process may be delegated to computers

> . . . [t]he Act can be complied with by delegation of part of the review process to a paralegal or even to a computer program, see lawyer. *Avila v. Rubin, supra,* 84 F.3d at 225, 229; *Clomon v. Jackson, supra,* 988 F.2d at 1317, 1321. An attorney's signature implies the attorney has formed a professional judgment about the debtor's case. *Avila v. Rubin, supra,* 84 F.3d at 229; see ABA Model Rule of Professional Conduct Rule 5.5(b) and comment 1 (materially identical to Illinois Rule of Professional Conduct 5.5(b)). In an age of specialization, professionals are not to be criticized for identifying subroutines that paraprofessionals can adequately perform under a professional's supervision.

Judge Posner recognized that mass mailings are permissible. However, he clearly sets forth the fault in Wexler's argument:

> But Wexler does not argue that he has delegated some of the review tasks (for example, ascertaining whether the amount of the claim submitted by the client is the same as the amount that appears on the form letter prepared by the non-lawyer collection agents whom Wexler employs) to non-lawyers; he argues that he performs all these tasks himself, implying that if he is not telling the truth, no one performs them.

Judge Posner refused to set a time value on reviewing a file and did not define "professional judgment."

> We can leave for a future case the determination of the point at which delegation is so extensive or review so perfunctory that the lawyer's supposed authorship of the dunning [**15] letter becomes a deception, not because there was no review but because it was too meager to be meaningful. We are not suggesting a 15-minute minimum; we used that assumption merely to illustrate that a rational jury might find, given the volume of mail, that it was unlikely that Wexler had actually reviewed the plaintiffs' files before authorizing dunning letters to be sent. . . . *Id.* at 645.

The case was appealed, but the Supreme Court would not certify the appeal. The term "review too meager to be meaningful" has been coined and will now be used by the plaintiff's counsel. Defense counsel should work to remind future courts that this issue was never ruled on, merely raised.

It is important to note that the Judge Posner provided Wexler a solution to redeem himself at trial by stating that he relied on his administrative staff, but reserved final professional judgment. The level of professional judgment and level of review is proportional. If several variations of letters, including suit threat letters are used, a higher level of review is required. The attorney has to confirm that the correct letter is used. A simple form letter with no suit threat, and no special language, allows for a lower level of review.

Judge Posner quoted one of the letters used by the defendant and claimed to be amused, but was probably offended. The letter used stated in pertinent part "YOU ARE ABOUT TO BE TREATED IN A MANNER THAT WILL MAKE YOU THINK TWICE BEFORE YOU WRITE ANOTHER WORTHLESS CHECK." *Id.* at 645, 646. The authors strongly discourage anyone from using language of this type in any letter, as the court may deem this letter offensive. The court did not espouse that an attorney must review a file. It merely questioned the credibility of an affidavit, in which an attorney claimed to have reviewed more files than humanly possible, based on the attorney's own review procedures.

Neilson v. Dickerson, 307 F.3d 623 (E.D. Ill. 2002) out of the Seventh Circuit was the second decision in October of 2002. The appellate court upheld the summary judgment in favor of the plaintiff and held the client liable. While this case appears to address attorney review, in dicta, the decision is similar to the earlier *Clomon* type matters, because the client, not the law firm controlled the collection process.

The *Dickerson* law firm did not possess authority to control the collection process in their office. This authority was delegated to the creditor, Household.

Consequently, Household also violated the act for misleading the debtor as to who was actually collecting the debt. Although the firm did receive written and telephone inquiries from cardholders and their attorneys, they did not have authority to resolve the matter. Only the client could resolve the account. Household, not Dickerson, handled any requests for verification of the debt. A telephone number on the letter permitted the debtor to contact the client. An inquiry by a debtor was forwarded immediately to the client for disposition. The court also was upset that the attorney could not negotiate a payment plan, settle or otherwise dispose of the debt and that all responses from the debtors (both telephone and written responses) were sent directly to the client. The client never asked the firm to institute a suit. The court acknowledged that the attorney did take certain steps that rose above the level of involvement in *Avila* and *Clomon*, but reiterated that the attorney was not prepared to institute legal action and had no authority to make decisions.

> ***Practice Tip:*** *While this case dealt with a creditor-attorney relationship, it was exactly like the prior attorney-collection agency cases, in which the attorney delegated control and supervision of the collection process. The issue of attorney review did not prevent the violation. Attorney review without decision making authority is not acceptable.*

In *Miller v. Wolpoff & Abramson*, 321 F.3d 292 (2d Cir. 2003), the law firm also made affirmative representation that the file had been reviewed in the text of the letter. The appellate court reversed the lower court's decision granting summary judgment on the grounds it was premature, as the plaintiff was not provided an opportunity to conduct discovery. The court was unconvinced that the defendant had provided sufficient evidence that the attorney had complied with the *Clomon* standard as a matter of law, nor did the court wish to set a minimum standard.

> While plaintiff asks us to declare a minimum standard requiring attorneys to review a copy of the contract, a credit report, and a full payment history or statement of account to satisfy *Clomon*'s requirement of meaningful attorney involvement, we decline to do so on the record here, in part because there may be circumstances where, following discovery, it becomes clear that the attorney's familiarity with the client's contracts and practices would negate the need to review some if not all of the documents plaintiff seeks to require. For example, an attorney and client could have established a practice whereby the attorney has specified that the entire payment history is to be included in the summary provided by a client. On this undeveloped record, however, it suffices for us to hold that merely being told by a client that a debt is overdue is not enough. *Id.* at 31.

In this case the attorney received significant information. The client furnished the last charge to the account, the date the account was charged off and a synopsis of recent customer service notes regarding their efforts to resolve the account prior to forwarding the matter to the attorneys. However, the appellate court stated on the undeveloped record that mere advice from the client that a debt is overdue is not sufficient for summary judgment (citing the *Dickerson* case in the Seventh Circuit). It is not clear why the court cited *Dickerson* and not *Wexler*, as the attorneys in *Dickerson* violated the FDCPA on other grounds, for delegating the control and supervision to a third party. Also, the affidavits established that the law firm received more than mere advice.

The conclusions of the court may be based on the fact that the law firm received over 55,000 new accounts monthly via electronic transmission and that the attorneys may have mailed over 110,000 letters a month. The sheer volume may have discouraged the court from holding that the quality of review was "nonreviewable" as a matter of law.

The court offered that if after discovery, the attorneys and staff reviewed the information in such a manner as to permit them to arrive at a proper determination to enable them to send the letters, the letters would be in compliance with the FDCPA. The court did not state how the review could be performed. This proposition emphasizes that the court is more concerned with the accuracy of the process, as opposed to the level of review.

While the Second Circuit Court of Appeals is concerned about ultra-large volume mass mailings, the district level courts appear to be not interested in this issue and are willing to grant summary judgment in favor of the defendants. Defense counsel should use this leverage when negotiating, as most consumer attorneys do not wish to invest the amount of time, money, and resources on an issue that may not yield results for several years. In general, consumer attorneys prefer quick settlements, so that they can move on to the next case.

Argument to the courts

A law firm is managed by licensed attorneys who practice law and manage the firm on a daily basis. As a licensed professional, an attorney's expertise permits the attorney to derive new methods to review the files. Review can be performed through eyes or through a program. By analogy, a calculator is used to calculate the numbers at a real estate closing. The math is not performed manually because the calculator is accurate. As an attorney is not required to check the client's math produced by their computers, an attorney is not required to check every file segregated pursuant to an accurate pre-set criteria, when no affirmative legal conclusions are being set forth in the letter. The purpose of technology is to make decisions easier, quicker, and even instantaneous. Embracing technology is not a deceptive practice. The letter is still from a law firm, and the process is controlled by a law firm.

Another analogy is that the controlling partners and law firm are liable for the negligence of their staff. If the actions taken by the staff are treated differently under the FDCPA, will attorneys be able to avoid malpractice liability under this analysis. A similar argument is that only original documentation is acceptable in court. However, courts routinely rely on technology to admit duplicate originals under the Business Record Rule and E-Sign Act (Electronic Signature in Global and National Commerce Act) because the process of reproduction is reliable and accurate. Review is required to establish accuracy, not for the sake of it.

Hypothetical: Supporting the argument

Law firm and new client meet. The law firm is retained for collection work. Attorney receives 10 accounts (credit card) from the client. The accounts are reviewed and the uniform terms and conditions that apply to every account are reviewed. The statements are reviewed. The electronic transmission is compared to the paper statements. The notes are reviewed and indicate broken promises and no answers. The client sends another set of 10 accounts. The accounts are reviewed as before. Other criteria are established. Accounts are to be electronically coded and segregated by additional criteria (i.e.: disputed, bankruptcy, deceased, represented by counsel, accounts past due over 1 year). Twenty more accounts are sent and reviewed. A hundred more accounts are sent and reviewed. A thousand accounts have been reviewed. Over a 1,000 accounts are manually reviewed. Based on experience, a law firm can reasonable conclude that the electronic data matches the paper backup 99% of the time.

The law firm (attorney and staff) is confident in its "professional judgment" that it has an efficient process to segregate files for sending non-suit threat letters. The law firm's judgment is based on the overall reliability and accuracy of the process. Had the firm used clerical staff to review the files, the accuracy may have been actually lower due to human error. Common sense or professional judgment recognizes that an electronic system to maintain the efficiency is superior to a manual system. The firm audits a portion of the accounts periodically and visits and communicates with its client on a regular basis to maintain the level of accuracy.

Common sense and economic efficiency permits you to reduce the necessary documentation because the client always has been able to provide the necessary documentation. Based on the reliability of the data and the accuracy of the process, technology has permitted the firm to process data more efficiently than using employees. To review the data manually would be the same as double-checking your calculator for mistakes. As long as the process is accurate and reliable, the methodology should not be subject to review or attack.

Summary

Based on these two recent decisions, attorneys should be careful in drafting their affidavits. Emphasize the accuracy and benefits of technology as well as the reliance on clerical staff, as done in other sectors of the legal industry.

Interestingly, if the appellate courts continue to hold that "meaningful review" is an issue of fact, then the adequate amount of review of every file becomes an issue of fact, as each case is different, thus no class action. If each case is the same, the review by groups is permissible and no violation. A Catch-22 is created for the consumer attorney. Under this line of reasoning, courts may refuse to grant class action status. One Louisiana court has reached this conclusion in *Moonan v. Barro* (unpublished Oct. 2003 02-3432 East Dist. of Louisiana). If others courts follow this line of reasoning, the consumer bar may lose interest in this theory if class action status is unattainable or uncertain.

It is not clear whether any court has addressed the issue of affirmative misrepresentations versus omissions of facts. If the letters were from a paralegal, would a violation exist versus the unsigned law firm name. Signing a letter establishes that the letter is from the law firm, but it does not imply review, as it is not part of the text. The text of the letter is controlling, not your signature or your letterhead.

Should a law firm merely repeat no review has been performed? The courts are faced with a difficult situation. The authors do not believe that a judge will state that there must be X attorneys for X non-attorneys in a law firm, nor will a court state that you need X, Y, Z in documentation. Where do you draw a line on a mass mailing? (100? 500? 1,000? 10,000? 1,000,000?) per month. This analysis does not consider the intelligence or skill level of the attorney or law firm. Under the consumer attorney's theory, extremely poor professional judgment is not a violation, if the review is performed by a human being; but professional judgment is a violation when performed by systematic procedure. Furthermore, relying on a Math model is flawed. Just because a law firm has the time to perform the review does not mean the review is performed. The math model only penalizes large firms and not small firms with a small client base, which violates the balancing provision of 1692(e). A bizarre result occurs. Firms are penalized for embracing technology, efficiency and accuracy. Instead, the real issue is the degree of involvement of the law firm in the overall collection process, and the accuracy and reliability of the process. The more you look like an "absentee attorney," the more likely a violation will exist.

Practice Tips

Use the special facts of their case to their advantage. Distinguish the text of your letters from the text of the letters in the negative cases, many of which were quite offensive. The Judge in one case implied that had the attorney reviewed the letter, the attorney would not have mailed the unprofessional letter. If no suit threat is used, no legal determination has been made, and the level of participation of an attorney is justifiably lower. Remind the court that an attorney is permitted to start a lawsuit and lose a case.

Our law firm is actively engaged in defense matters and we have a list of approximately 30 cases that are relevant to the issue of meaningful involvement. Although our firm's practice has shifted away from conducting large mass mailings,[1] our experience from the process has provided us significant insight in how to defend these lawsuits. In the event the reader would like a copy of this list of cases involving meaningful involvement, please feel free to contact us.

---

[1] As agencies were not required to be meaningfully involved in the process, they were able to offer their services at a substantially lower cost than our firm when collecting consumer debts. It was no longer cost-effective to provide said services. The firm now primarily provides litigation services to its clients.

APPENDIX VI

ATTORNEY MEANINGFUL INVOLVEMENT UPDATE BY JAY WINSTON

March 2007

Worth Reading: The FDCPA & Attorney Meaningful Involvement—two recent cases and practice points By Jay Winston, Winston & Winston P.C.

Introduction: Attorney Meaningful Involvement: This term is one of the most misunderstood terms in the industry. Many attorneys, both consumer and collection attorneys, incorrectly believe that a general standard exists for adequate attorney involvement. The term was developed as a method to distinguish "no involvement" or [zero involvement] from "some involvement." Every reported case involves a form letter used by a law firm. No Judge has ever set forth in a decision what needs to be done to be involved because all the court is looking for is some involvement. The firm should describe *the process* and to explain the involvement in detail, to establish accuracy and reliability of the process. Bald assertions or conclusions will not persuade the court.

Examine the collection letter and consider whether the letter itself is misleading the consumer as to the involvement of the attorney. In most cases the Judge confines the decision to the letter itself [four-corners rule] and whether it is misleading. Liberal judges consider extrinsic evidence beyond the four-corners rule and consider the firm's practices. The volume of letters mailed by the firm could provide evidence that the letter could be misleading. Make sure this evidence is not advertised on your website.

Below I will discuss two recent decisions reported in the last 60 days which illustrate these points.

1) *Taylor v. Quall*, 471 F. Supp. 2d 1053 (C.D. Cal. 2007)

In this case the plaintiff alleged several violations including that the defendant "failed to fulfill the FDCPA's standard for 'meaningful' attorney involvement."

<u>*Decision:*</u> No FDCPA violation found—No general standard exists under the FDCPA. The letters were not misleading. The Honorable Percy Anderson rejected plaintiff's theory.

> **To the extent that Plaintiff asserts that there is some general standard under the FDCPA for adequate attorney involvement in debt collection actions, he misrepresents the limited holdings of various courts that have addressed specific claims of false or misleading representations under § 1692e, finding violations in circumstances related to the mass mailing of collection letters containing the signatures of attorneys who never reviewed the involved debtors' individual files.**

Judge Anderson stated that the attorney established that he was personally involved in the prosecution of his client's case to an extent far greater than any of the attorneys involved in the cases cited by Plaintiff. More importantly, Judge Anderson noted that an attorney's review does not have to be perfect or complete, as is often alleged by the consumer bar.

> **While Quall's performance may have been less than perfect, the undisputed evidence shows that he at least reviewed Plaintiff's file and personally made every decision related to the [lawsuit].**

As stated above the test is [zero involvement] vs. [some involvement]. The Judge refused to cite specific steps or practices to establish meaningful involvement. The Judge was satisfied that the attorney was supervising and managing the case. It is clearly easier to defend a lawsuit on this theory, because attorney involvement is clearly more apparent when the case enters litigation. Further, the review of the initial letter becomes less important as the judge reviews the attorney's management of the entire case as opposed to the sending of the initial letter.

2) *Kistner v. Law Offices of Michael P. Margelefsky, LLC*, 2007 U.S. Dist. LEXIS 1925 (D. Ohio 1/10/2007)

<u>*Background*</u>

The Defendant was a law firm with its own collection agency which were located at the same location, but with different addresses, telephone numbers, and bank accounts. The firm had one attorney and six staff. The consumer bar believes a case with these facts must be a *Clomon* copy and an easy win—which is not necessarily true as explained below.

The form letter was a basic FDCPA letter, signed "ACCOUNT REPRESENTATIVE," Like many collection letters, it had a detachable stub to enclose with a payment. The letter instructed that checks be made payable to "Michael P. Margelefsky."

The Law firm used a *third party mailing service* located in Michigan to mail these letters. The attorney admitted that his practice was not to review the letters or underlying claims before they were mailed. He admitted that he did not review the plaintiff's letter in this case.

The plaintiff filed a class action alleging that several FDCPA violations including a violation of 15 U.S.C. § 1692e(3) which prohibits debt collectors from "falsely representing or implying that a communication is from an attorney" for the following 5 reasons:

(1) the name of the collection agency is "Law Offices of Michael P. Margelefsky, LLC";

(2) the notice directs the consumer to make checks payable to "Michael P. Margelefsky";

(3) the notice is on "Law Offices of Michael P. Margelefsky, LLC" letterhead;

(4) Margelefsky drafted the notice; and

(5) the law practice and collection business operated out of the same office suite.

<u>Decision:</u> No FDCPA violation found. The letters were not misleading. The Honorable Jack Zouhary limited his analysis to the four corners of the letter.

Judge Zouhary rejected plaintiff's theories with simple arguments. First, he stated that "lawyers can act as debt collectors, and the notice clearly states that it is from a debt collector." Second, he held that directions to make payment to the defendant attorney does not suggest the letter came from an attorney when it is signed by "ACCOUNT REPRESENTATIVE." Third, the Judge properly noted that law firm letterhead alone is not determinative.

Judge Zouhary then cited 2 arguments that have not been followed by some courts. First, he held that "since the consumer is unaware of the author of the notice" it cannot be misleading. Second, he dismissed the issue of "shared office space" because the consumer had no knowledge of this fact.

The Judge emphasized that the letter was signed by "ACCOUNT REPRESENTATIVE," and not the attorney. The source of the letter was not an attorney. The Judge correctly recognized that law firms use clerical staff. The judge dismissed the fact that attorney letterhead was used or that the letter directed the debtor to make the check payable to the attorney. The Judge emphatically stated that plaintiff arguments are " 'blunted' by the specific language used in the notice and the fact that it was signed 'ACCOUNT REPRESENTATIVE.' " In support of its decision, the Judge cited in *Rumpler v. Phillips & Cohen Associates, Ltd.*, 219 F. Supp. 2d 251 (E.D.N.Y. 2002).

In *Rumpler*, "the court found that the use of the title 'Executive Vice President,' coupled with the fact that the notice did not say 'Attorney-at-Law' or 'General Counsel,' made the notice non-deceiving."

It is the author's opinion that the Judge distinguished a "passive omission" from an "affirmative misstatement." As I have argued in the past, courts tend to find violations due to affirmative misstatements, not "passive omissions." Liberal Judges in states such as Connecticut would probably have denied the defendant's motion by relying on plaintiff's arguments, and not the facts.

Practice Tip: *The Judge referred to the letter as a "notice," and stressed that the notices did not make a formal demand for payment. When reviewing letters for our clients, we often recommend the removal of any language demanding payment as it is* *unnecessary and duplicative. Keep the first letter as simple as possible. Remember, the more complicated the letter, the more attorney involvement is required to design and approve the sending of the letter.*

The content of this column is not a substitute for consultation with counsel, nor is it intended for use as a specific response to a set of circumstances. Questions concerning the column may be addressed to Jay Winston at 212/922-9482 or jay@winstonandwinston.com

Article #2

Worth Reading: ***Miller v. Wolpoff & Abramson:* Round 3**

Attorney Meaningful Involvement: By Jay Winston, Winston & Winston P.C.

***Miller v. Wolpoff & Abramson, LLP*, 471 F. Supp. 2d 243 (E.D.N.Y. 2007)**

Procedural History: On November 9, 2001, Wolfpoff & Abramsom (W&A) and Upton, Cohen & Slamowitz (UCS) were granted summary judgment on all issues, including, attorney meaningful involvement by Judge Raggi. Plaintiff appealed and in February, 2003, the Second Circuit affirmed the decision for the defendants, "with respect to allegations of improper fee-sharing and confusing statements, but held that the district court's granting of summary judgment with respect to the plaintiff's 'meaningful attorney involvement' claims against W&A and UCS, in advance of any discovery, was premature."

Following discovery, plaintiff and defendant W&A entered into a consent judgment which substance provided that W&A had not violated the FDCPA in handling his account. UCS remained in the case and renewed its motion for summary judgment which was denied by the Honorable Raymond J. Dearie.

Text of (UCS)(Letter)
"Please be advised that we are the attorneys for [Lord & Taylor]. The above referenced account has been forwarded to us for collection. Please contact this office to arrange for payment."

Key Language from the Judge's Decision
Even a debt collection letter that is literally "from an attorney" may violate Section 1692e(3) if it appears likely to deceive consumers through "overstatement of the degree of [that] attorney's involvement in individual debtors' cases. . . ." Clomon, 988 F.2d at 1319. See also Boyd v. Wexler, 275 F.3d 642, 644 (7th Cir. 2001) ("A lawyer who merely rents his letterhead to a collection agency violates the [FDCPA].").

Clomon also declares that "the use of an attorney's signature on a collection letter implies that the letter is 'from' the attorney who signed it; it implies, in other words, that the ***attorney directly controlled or supervised the process*** through which the letter was sent." 988 F.2d at 1321. Thus in order not to violate Section 1692e(3) a debt collection letter that appears over a lawyer's signature must reflect "meaningful attorney involvement." Miller, 321 F.3d at 305.

The meaningful involvement requirement may be relaxed where a debt collection letter is signed by an attorney but includes a disclaimer about the extent to which attorneys are involved in reviewing individual debtors' cases. Greco,

412 F.3d at 364-65. See also Pujol v. Universal Fidelity Corp., No. 03 CV 5524, 2004 U.S. Dist. LEXIS 10556, at *17-18 (E.D.N.Y. June 9, 2004) (summary judgment for defendants where letter contained disclaimer). But see Sparkman v. Zwicker & Associates, 374 F. Supp. 2d 293, 302 (E.D.N.Y. 2005) (summary judgment for plaintiff where disclaimer was "discursive and confusing").

Elsewhere, however, an attorney who signs a debt collection letter must have some basis for believing that the individual to whom the letter is addressed owes a debt to his client, and that the debt is overdue. "[M]erely being told by a client that a debt is overdue is not enough." Miller, 321 F.3d at 304.

Rulings made by Judge Dearie

"[The] defendant was entitled to reasonable reliance on W&A's review of plaintiff's file, and that reasonable reliance, in this case, would have required that UCS have some knowledge of the procedures W&A followed in conducting its review." Defendant failed to submit evidence that it had sufficient knowledge of W&A's procedures to rely on W&A.

The judge qualified that the reliance cannot be blind. "The attorney's reliance on the other party must be reasonable on the basis of other facts, for example, familiarity with the other party's past reliability or current practices." *Mizrahi v. Network Recovery Services, Inc.*, 1999 U.S. Dist. LEXIS 22145, at *12-13 (E.D.N.Y. Nov. 5, 1999), was cited with approval in which the attorney review process was delegated to a non-attorney since "the review required here is relatively uncomplicated and hardly requires legal training."

The Judge analogized Rule 11 violations to no meaningful involvement and cited several cases to justify the proposition: Several of the cases cited by Judge, involved lawsuits in which the wrong party was sued. The mistakes were obvious because the sanctioned attorneys had blindly relied on others, including other attorneys, and ignored obvious evidence that they were acting incorrectly. While comparing attorney meaningful involvement to Rule 11 sanctions at first blush seems scary, it may actually be helpful to collection law firms, as it is a higher standard to breach.

Based upon my experience, Rule 11 sanctions is an extreme sanction that is rarely awarded in New York state. When sanctions are awarded, they often involve extreme circumstances. Under Federal Rules, you must be warned that the conduct is frivolous and continue said conduct despite said warning. Many sanctions awards are often overruled on appeal. Thus, while the Judge may have not awarded summary judgment on this issue, it appears that the Judge may ultimately rule in favor of the defendants at trial. Clearly, the review was of the non-legal nature and could be delegated. Further, the procedures used (W&A) are arguably common business practices and surely (UCS) was aware of their practices. Unless they engaged in regular practices that blatantly violated the FDCPA in some other manner, it is unlikely the Judge would award sanctions.

4) When arguing reasonable reliance on another party, you must be able to sufficiently describe the process on which you rely, to win at summary judgment. The Judge stated:

> [a]though Slamowitz knew W&A was "thorough," he does not claim to have known anything about the process by which it reviewed plaintiff's

case, other than that it involved an attorney and/or a paralegal. Nor does Slamowitz claim any specific knowledge of the manner in which W&A "covered" Lord & Taylor's "procedures." Finally, his testimony does not indicate what, if anything, he knew about W&A's procedures, or its handling of plaintiff's file, on the day he signed the letter to plaintiff.

> Defendant cites no other evidence to indicate that its reliance on W&A was reasonable, other than the undisputed fact that it was W&A's "affiliate counsel," and received the case only because W&A was not authorized to practice law in New York. . . . But defendant does not claim that it ever made any inquiries of W&A in connection with plaintiff's case. Moreover, the testimony it cites, that of W&A attorney Ronald Abramson, indicates only that W&A understood UCS to have discretion to refuse to pursue the case, if its own review found the facts not to warrant suit—not that there was any dialogue between UCS and W&A about the case.
>
> In sum, although defendant was entitled to rely to some degree on W&A's review of plaintiff's case in sending the July 18, 2000 debt collection letter to plaintiff, it has not adduced facts sufficient to require the finding, as a matter of law, that its reliance in this case was reasonably based on familiarity with W&A's review process. Attorney Slamowitz's testimony indicates that his familiarity with W&A's process was vague, at best. . . .

5) The Judge refused to establish a minimum level of review required to comply with 1692e(3) and noted that no court including the 2d Circuit Court of Appeals had set forth minimum standards. Notwithstanding, Judge Dearie stated that he noticed that the following factors were relevant to other courts and discussed their application in several cases.

the process followed by the attorney who signed the letter;

the information that attorney possessed about the circumstances of the individual debtor to whom the letter was addressed;

the form and substance of the letter itself;

the volume of cases handled by the attorney or firm; and

the attorney's basis for crediting any information about the case that the client provided. The Judge explained this factor in two sentences:

> ***Miller*** . . . suggests that where an attorney has reason to believe that the client is providing reliable information, some degree of reliance is permissible."
>
> [T]here may be circumstances where, following discovery, it becomes clear that the attorney's familiarity with the client's contracts and practices would negate the need to review some if not all of the documents plaintiff seeks to require."

6) To rely on procedures of another requires the attorney or law firm to be familiar with the procedures, to be able to explain the procedures and explain why the procedures are reliable.

Judge Dearie wanted specifics, not conclusions and went to great lengths to explain the differences.

Statements made by the attorney
The judge dismissed answers like: . . . "I rely on my client." . . . "I trust what I get from my client. I rely on the information that they provide to me." Slamowitz also stated that he had particular confidence in Lord & Taylor, which he described as "a very distinguished, very good client." . . . "[T]he information they have provided to us has always been very accurate."

Answers requested by Judge Dearie, but not received
But Slamowitz's reliance on his client does not appear to have been based on knowledge of the client's "contracts and practices." When asked "[w]hat have you done personally to review [Lord & Taylor's] procedures on forwarding accounts?" Slamowitz answered, "I personally have done nothing." Likewise, when asked "do you know how [Lord & Taylor] calculate[s] what's due and owing?" Slamowitz replied, "I don't know their procedures."

For example, attending Attorney-Client meetings at an industry conference would be evidence that UCS was familiar with the client's practices and procedures.

7) The use of the computer system, CLS, in the review process by the defendants is neither affirmative evidence of review alleged or lack of review of the file.

Conclusion

The author recommends that readers review the *Mizrahi v. Network Recovery Services, Inc.*, 1999 U.S. Dist. LEXIS 22145, (E.D.N.Y. Nov. 5, 1999), which was handled by our firm, was heavily cited by Judge Dearie. In winning at Summary Judgment, we went to great lengths to show that the law firm was familiar with the client's procedures, that the attorney and client communicated on a regular basis, and explained how and why the attorneys were familiar with the procedures, and how the process was reliable to prevent errors from occurring.

When prosecuting these cases, the plaintiff's bar, will seek to examine the total number of letters issued for all clients for all purposes, not just the initial demand letter, to convince a Judge that the process is so automated that no attorney involvement exists. To counter this theory, argue that the first letter is a "notice" letter that does not demand payment, and is part of an entire process which you can describe. The letter merely notifies the debtor that the client is represented by counsel, and that it makes the required FDCPA disclosures. Keep the letter as simple as possible and learn your client's procedures for referring claims. These procedures can be received directly from the client or communicated through another law firm or agency.

The content of this column is not a substitute for consultation with counsel, nor is it intended for use as a specific response to a set of circumstances. Questions concerning the column may be addressed to Jay Winston at 212/922-9482 or jay@winstonandwinston.com.

APPENDIX VII

OBLIGATION TO ISSUE INITIAL DEMAND LETTER

By Jay Winston

In a brief decision, the Ninth Circuit Court of Appeals upheld the district court decision that a law firm did not have to send the initial FDPCA letter as it was previously sent by the collection agency, which had referred the case to the law firm for suit. *GARY L. Wiley; Linda P. Wiley, Plaintiffs—Appellants, V. Victor G. Drakulich, Attorney, Defendant—Appellee*, 2008 U.S. App. LEXIS 12233 (9th Cir. Apr. 18, 2008).

The appeals court stated that "[i]t is undisputed that Business & Professional Collection Services sent eight Act-compliant validation letters before Drakulich did anything. In light of the nature of the relationship between Drakulich and Business & Professional Collection Services, Drakulich's actions did not constitute an "initial communication." *See* 15 U.S.C. § 1692g(a). Thus, Drakulich was under no obligation to send additional validation letters. The defendant cited to *Mendus v. Morgan & Assoc., P.C.*, 994 P.2d 84 (Okla. Civ. App. 1999) which held that the notice sent by the collection agency inures to the benefit of the subsequent law firm. The District Court Judge considered the issue only dicta in the *Mendus* decision. Nonetheless, the lower court concluded that there could be only one *initial communication* which warranted a validation notice. The court relied on *Ditty c. Check Rite, LTD*, 973 F Supp. 1320, 1324-25 (D. Utah 1997) and *Senftle v. Landua*, 390 F. Supp. 2d 463 (D. Md. 2005). The court also relied on the direct relationship between the agency and the law firm. The court also cited *Tipping-Lipshie v. Riddle*, 2000 U.S. Dist. LEXIS 2477 *7 (E.D.N.Y. Mar. 1, 2000) which distinguished *Griswold v. J&R Anderson Bus. Servs*, 1983 U.S. Dist. LEXIS 20365 (D. Or. Oct. 21, 1983) because no exception was found where defendant was an assignee of the debt.

The Ninth Circuit Court of Appeals has permitted one debt collector's compliance with the FDCPA to be imputed to another debt collector. To receive this protection, the collection agency/debt buyer and the subsequent debt collector (agency/law firm) would have to have a direct and close relationship. It is the opinion of the author that the direct relationship weakens as more time elapses. This decision should save significant amounts of paper for debt collectors in the

Ninth Circuit. Other circuits may follow this decision since the Ninth Circuit Court of Appeals is a liberal circuit.

The law firm that relies on this decision should institute procedures to obtain and retain a copy of the letter sent by the collection agency/debt buyer; include a copy of the initial letter as part of the lawsuit; and cite this case in the letter as evidence of compliance.[1]

---

[1]This is an excerpt of an article authored by Jay Winston and published in the July 2008 ACA MAP Bulletin.

APPENDIX VIII

RESPONDING TO DEBT PROTESTERS AND STALLING TACTICS

By Jay Winston

Verification. The Fair Debt Collection Practices Act, 15 U.S.C. § 1692g(b) provides that:

> [i]f the consumer notifies the debt collector *in writing within the thirty-day period* after receipt of the initial notification letter from the creditor that the debt, or any portion thereof, is disputed, the debt collector shall cease collection of the debt, or any disputed portion thereof, until the debt collector obtains verification of the debt or a copy of a judgment, or the name and address of the original creditor, and a copy of such verification or judgment, or name and address of the original creditor, is mailed to the consumer by the debt collector.

Many debtors and debtors' counsel have learned that requesting verification of the debt delays the collection and litigation process. However, in many instances, the request is made incorrectly. The statute imposes certain obligations on the debtor. The verification request must be sent in writing and sent to the debt collector within 30 days of receipt of the initial 30-day demand letter. No duty to verify exists if the debtor fails to comply with these two requirements.

Verification does not mean that you must prove the debt. Three decisions state that no evidence must be offered to the debtor of the validity of the debtor.

Chaudhry v. Gallerizzo, 174 F.3d 394, 406 (4th Cir. 1998) states that verification of a debt involves nothing more than the debt collector confirming in writing that the amount being demanded is what the creditor is claiming is owed; The debt collector is not required to keep detailed files of the alleged debt. *See Azar v. Hayter*, 874 F. Supp. 1314, 1317 (N.D. Fla.), *aff'd*, 66 F.3d 342 (11th Cir. 1995), *cert. denied*, 516 U.S. 1048, 133 L. Ed. 2d 666, 116 S. Ct. 712 (1996).

The appeals court further held that consistent with the legislative history, "verification is only intended to eliminate the problem of debt collectors dunning the wrong person or attempting to collect debts which the consumer has already paid." S. Rep. No. 95-382, at 4 (1977), preprinted in 1977 U.S.C.C.A.N., 1695, 1699.

No concomitant obligation exists to forward copies of bills or other detailed evidence of the debt.

We recommend that a debt collector obtain additional proof from the creditor. This proof could be in the form of an affidavit from the client, or additional documentation such as a payment history, statement or a recent computer printout from the client to confirm the balance. When the debtor has a common name, the possibility is present that the wrong party has been contacted, especially if the party was located through skip tracing methods. Do not assume that you have the correct party. Mistakes occur. It may be necessary to check if the debtor's social security number matches, or that the signature on the contract matches the debtor's signature.

Stonehart v. Rosenthal, 2001 U.S. Dist. LEXIS 11566 (S.D.N.Y 2001), followed *Chaudhry* and cited the case in detail. The principle was repeated that verification is only intended to "eliminate the . . . problem of debt collectors dunning the wrong person or attempting to collect debts which the consumer has already paid." *Anderson v. Canyon State, et Al.*, CIV-03-428 PHX JWS; *Transamerica Fin. Serv. v. Sykes* 171 F.3d 553 (7th Cir. 1999). The court in *Stonehart* held that an account statement which consisted of a computer printout was held to be sufficient to verify the debt. The court also held that the referral of the debt gave the collection agency a permissible purpose for obtaining a credit report. The court granted summary judgment against the debtor.

In June of this year, The New York Appellate Division 4th Department also followed the same line of reasoning; *Homeowner's Ass'n of Victoria Woods, III, Inc., v. Incarnato*, 777 N.Y.S.2d 8111 (N.Y. App. Div. 4th Dep't 2004).

Although minimum documentation is necessary to verify the debt, due to the proliferation of debt buyers, who lack documentation, we produce as much documentation as possible as fast as possible in these cases to establish the strength of the case; *Minskoff v. American Express*, 98 F.2d 703 (2d Cir. 1996). Finally, advise the debtor or his/her counsel, that due to the extra work involved, we will ask the court for extra attorneys' fees. By reminding the debtor's counsel that these tactics to stall will ultimately fail and with the risk of sanctions, quicker settlements and fewer summary judgment motions are filed.

Verification only has to be sent to the debtor and receipt need not be proven. *See Mahon v. Credit Bureau of Placer County Inc et al.*, 171 F.3d 1197 (9th Cir. 1999). The Ninth Circuit Court of Appeals held that "1692g(a) requires only that a Notice be 'sent' by a debt collector. A debt collector need not establish actual receipt by the debtor." The court rejected the argument of "that information is not truly sent" until "received." The defendant also sought to focus on the section's reference to "communication" of section 1692g(a) which provides: "Within five days after the initial *communication* with a consumer . . . a debt collector shall, unless the following information is contained in the initial *communication* . . . send the consumer a written notice." The Ninth Circuit rejected the argument, because it misconstrues the section's use of "communication." The court held that

> "[s]ection 1692g(a) uses communication as a noun rather than as a verb. The FDCPA defines communication as "the conveying of information regarding a debt directly or indirectly to any person through any medium." *15 U.S.C. § 1692a*(2). Thus, in section 1692g(a), the word "communication" functions

> [**11] solely as a vehicle of information, whereas the word "sent" operates as the active verb identifying the requisite action."
>
> The language of *15 U.S.C. § 1692g*(a) is plain. Because the language of the statute is plain, we need not consider extrinsic sources to interpret its meaning. *See Pressley v. Capital Credit & Collection Serv., Inc.,* 760 F.2d 922, 924 (9th Cir. 1985). The plain language of section 1692g(a) does not require that a Validation of Debt Notice must be received by a debtor. Instead, the plain language states that such a Notice need only be sent to a debtor.

Tender of Payment. Another tactic used by debt protesters is to offer a promissory note as payment of the debt. However, exchanging a debt for another debt does not eliminate the debt, but acts as a clear admission of liability. *Davis v. Dillard National Bank,* 2003 WL 21297331 (M.D.N.C. 2003). The court held that a tender of payment occurs only when an actual presentment of funds sufficiently extinguishes the entire debt. The court affirmed the principle that merely offering to produce payment or showing a readiness to perform is insufficient to establish tender. Actual production of payment and clearance of funds is necessary to pay a debt.

Disputing Credit Card Charges. Debtors often file answers that they are disputing the credit card charges and demand that the creditor provide copies of the signed charge receipts. However, in today's economy, charge receipts rarely exist. For example, many purchases are made over the internet or over the telephone. Also, even when a cardholder is face to face with the vendor, a signed receipt may not be required, such as in a gas station transaction. To defeat these claims, the use of the Truth In Lending Act is suggested.

Pursuant to the terms and conditions of the credit card agreement, and pursuant to 15 U.S.C. Sec. 1666 and Regulation Z Subsection 226-13(b)(1)-1 of the Truth in Lending Act, a debtor has 60 days from receipt of disputed charges to notify the creditor in writing of billing errors to preserve the debtor's rights. If the defendant fails to object in writing pursuant to their right to dispute the bill, s/he have waived the right to dispute the balance due. *Minskoff v. American Express,* 98 F.2d 703 (2d Cir. 1996).

> [Once a cardholder has established a credit card account, and provided that the card issuer is in compliance with the billing statement disclosure requirements of 15 U.S.C. 1637, [FN4] the cardholder is in a superior position to determine whether the charges reflected on his regular billing statements are legitimate. A cardholder's failure to examine credit card statements that would reveal fraudulent use of the card constitutes a negligent omission that creates apparent authority for charges that would otherwise be *710 considered unauthorized under TILA. *See Transamerica,* 325 N.W.2d at 215.]

This negligent omission to dispute any charges in a timely manner prevents the debtor from disputing the charges at this later date. The defendant's course of performance of using the card and/or making partial payments contradicts the debtor's untimely alleged dispute. In summary, if the debtor was unhappy with the card, s/he could have closed the account, and not continued to use the card until s/he exceeded the credit limit.

APPENDIX IX

VOICE MAIL MESSAGES IN THE WAKE OF *FOTI* DECISION

Fastfax

ACA INTERNATIONAL
The Association of Credit and Collection Professionals

From ACA's Fastfax Service **Page 1 of 7**
Last Updated on April 28, 2009 *Document No. 1146*

Now get immediate access to ACA's compliance expertise. Visit ACA International's Web Site at http://www.acainternational.org to search and access Fastfaxes and other compliance information or to e-mail a compliance officer.

*Updated cited cases (see 2009 WL 909646).

Voice Mail Messages in the Wake of *Foti*

The practice of leaving messages for consumers in the attempt to collect a debt is an important collection method. However, the legal consequences of leaving messages has received significant attention from courts across the country.

At least three provisions of the Fair Debt Collection Practices Act (FDCPA) apply in the context of debt collectors leaving messages for consumers. First, § 807(11) of the FDCPA requires a debt collector to disclose in the initial written communication with the consumer, and if the initial communication is oral, in that oral communication as well, that the debt collector is attempting to collect a debt and any information obtained will be used for that purpose. Additionally, all subsequent communications with the consumer must disclose that the communication is from a debt collector. This requirement is commonly referred to as the mini-Miranda disclosure.

Second, § 806(6) of the FDCPA prohibits debt collectors from engaging in harassing, oppressive, or abusive conduct, including placing a telephone call to a consumer without meaningful disclosure of the caller's identity.

Lastly, § 805(b) prohibits a debt collector from communicating with any person other than the consumer.

Foti Decision

In the past, it was generally a standard practice of the collection industry to omit the mini-Miranda notice from voice mail messages left on a consumer's answering machine. Agencies feared such a disclosure left on a consumer's voice mail could constitute a violation of § 805(b) of the FDCPA, the section of the Act which forbids disclosing the existence of a debt to a third party.

However, federal courts around the nation have recently been addressing this issue. In March 2006, the Southern District of New York found in *Foti v. NCO Fin. Sys., Inc.*, 424 F. Supp. 2d 643 (S.D.N.Y. 2006), that the mini-Miranda disclosure requirement extends to pre-recorded and live messages left on a consumer's answering system. In *Foti*, the court held a pre-recorded message left on a consumer's answering system was a "communication," as defined by the FDCPA. Section 803(2) of the FDCPA defines communication as the "conveying of information regarding a debt directly or indirectly to any person through any medium."

Because the pre-recorded message was left with the consumer after the initial validation notice was sent, the court determined the message was a subsequent communication. To comply with § 807(11), a debt collector must disclose in all communications subsequent to the initial communication with a consumer that the communication is from a debt collector. Numerous courts have held that the disclosure is satisfied if the debt collector states, "This is a communication from a debt collector" or if the name of the debt collection agency [as stated in the written or oral communication] makes clear the communication is from a debt collector.

In *Foti*, the pre-recorded message left by the defendant stated the following: "Good day, we are calling from [Defendant] Financial Systems regarding a personal business matter that requires your immediate attention. Please call back 1-866-701-1275 once again please call back, toll-free, 1-866-701-1275, this is not a solicitation."

The court determined the message contained no other suggestion that the correspondence was from a debt collector other than the agency name. Instead, a consumer would need to recall that she previously received mail from a debt collection agency in order to recognize the call was from a debt collector. The court found that placing such a burden on the consumer was unreasonable. Thus, the court determined the pre-recorded message failed to comply with the requirements of § 807(11) of the FDCPA.

Similar Decisions

Prior to the *Foti* decision, two California district courts addressed the disclosure requirements of the FDCPA and voice messages.[1] One of these courts held both an automated message system and a live caller calling on behalf of a debt collection company must accurately disclose the name of the company and the nature of the

---

[1] *Joseph v. J.J. MacIntyre Cos., L.L.C.*, 281 F. Supp. 2d 1156 (N.D. Cal. 2003); *Hosseinzadeh v. M.R.S. Assocs., Inc.*, 387 F. Supp. 2d 1104 (C.D. Cal. 2005).

company's business when placing telephone calls pursuant to the FDCPA.[2] Similar to *Foti*, the other court held messages left on a consumer's answering machine were communications as defined by the FDCPA.[3] Consequently, the court held the messages must include the mini-Miranda disclosure as required by § 807(11).[4]

A number of other courts have similarly found violations of § 807(11) when the caller did not identify itself as a debt collector in messages left on a consumer's answering machine or voice mail, including courts in California, Florida, Georgia, Massachusetts, and New York.[5] These decisions concluded voice messages left on a consumer's answering machine were communications as defined by § 803(2) of the FDCPA, and as a result had to include the disclosure that the communication is from a debt collector in order to comply with § 807(11).[6] A Minnesota court also concluded voice messages were communications pursuant to the FDCPA, but failed to determine whether compliance with § 807(11) was required.

Third-Party Disclosure

As noted, the obvious concern posed by leaving a message containing the mini-Miranda disclosure is the risk of potential third-party disclosure. Collectors defending cases similar to *Foti* have advanced this argument, stating providing the notice required under § 807(11) could result in a third-party disclosure, a violation of § 805(b) of the FDCPA, if the message was heard by someone other than the consumer.

One district court in California noted this argument may "carry weight" in some circumstances, but the argument was not applicable in the instant case because the consumer lived alone.[7] Similarly, a Minnesota district court held such an argument was not applicable at the current stage in the proceedings as the location where the messages were left was unknown.[8] Yet another court declined to address the third-party disclosure issue, but noted the risk of third-party disclosure is more remote when leaving messages on the consumer's phone than when a collector discloses information about a debt on the face of an envelope or postcard.[9]

---

[2]*Joseph v. J.J. MacIntyre Cos., L.L.C.*, 281 F. Supp. 2d 1156 (N.D. Cal. 2003).

[3]*Hosseinzadeh v. M.R.S. Assocs., Inc.*, 387 F. Supp. 2d 1104 (C.D. Cal. 2005).

[4]*Id.*

[5]*Ostrander v. Accelerated Receivables*, No. 07-CV-827C, 2009 WL 909646 (W.D.N.Y. Mar. 31, 2009); *Edwards v. Niagara Credit Solutions, Inc.*, 586 F. Supp. 2d 1346 (N.D. Ga. 2008); *Valencia v. Affiliated Group, Inc*, No. 07-61381-CIV, 2008 WL 4372895 (S.D. Fla. Sept. 2008); *Masciarelli v. Richard J. Boudreau & Assocs.*, 529 F. Supp. 2d 183 (D. Mass. 2007); *Costa v. Nat'l Action Fin. Servs.*, No. CIV. S-05-2084 FCD/KJM, 2007 WL 4526510 (E.D. Cal. Dec. 19, 2007); *Leyes v. Corporate Collection Services, Inc.*, No. 03 Civ. 8491(DAB), 2007 WL 1225547 (S.D.N.Y. Sept. 18, 2006); *Belin v. Litton Loan Servicing, LP*, No. 8:06-cv-760-T-24 EAJ, 2006 WL 1992410 (M.D. Fla. July 14, 2006).

[6]*Baker v. Allstate Fin. Servs., Inc.*, No. 07-cv-2579 (JNE/JJG), 2008 WL 2042622 (D. Minn. May 3, 2008).

[7]*Costa v. Nat'l Action Fin. Servs.*, No. CIV. S-05-2084 FCD/KJM, 2007 WL 4526510 (E.D. Cal. Dec. 19, 2007).

[8]*Baker v. Allstate Fin. Servs., Inc.*, No. 07-cv-2579 (JNE/JJG), 2008 WL 2042622 (D. Minn. May 3, 2008).

[9]*Joseph v. J.J. MacIntyre Cos., L.L.C.*, 281 F. Supp. 2d 1156 (N.D. Cal. 2003).

Other courts have determined a violation of § 805(b) may occur when a message containing the mini-Miranda disclosure is heard by a third party. In one case, the collector left a message for the consumer on the consumer's assistant's voice mail which included the mini-Miranda disclosure.[10] The court held the voice message in question constituted a "communication" under the FDCPA to a third party which was "in connection with the collection of any debt."[11] Therefore, the court denied the collector's motion for summary judgment, holding the facts demonstrated the voice message violated § 805(b) of the FDCPA.[12] With this holding, the court demonstrated the risk of providing the § 807(11) disclosure when such messages are heard by a third party.

Another court specifically rejected the third-party disclosure argument, asserting the only reason the agency found itself in that predicament was because of the method it chose to use to collect debts (i.e., leaving pre-recorded messages), not because of any contradictory provisions of the FDCPA.[13]

A decision from the Southern District of Florida considered the potential contradiction between leaving the mini-Miranda disclosure and preventing third-party disclosure under the FDCPA. In *Berg v. Merchs. Ass'n Collection Div., Inc.*, No. 08-60660-CIV-DIMITROULEAS (S.D. Fla. Oct. 31, 2008), the court denied the debt collector's motion to dismiss for failure to state a claim, holding that providing the mini-Miranda disclosure in a voice message may violate the third-party disclosure prohibitions of the FDCPA when the message is heard by a third party. In this case, the collector left the consumer a voice message which contained the mini-Miranda disclosure provided in language similar to that suggested by ACA International in response to the *Foti* decision. The consumer subsequently brought suit against the collector for a violation of § 805(b) of the FDCPA.

The relevant question before the court in *Berg* was whether or not the third-party disclosure prohibitions of § 805(b) applied to a voice message left at the consumer's home. The collector argued § 805(b) did not apply to a voice message left at the consumer's home because the collector was not communicating with a third party and a forewarning was included in the message which directed anyone other than the consumer to disconnect. The court disagreed, finding the warning included in the message did not necessarily remove the message from the statutory restriction on third party communications.

The *Berg* court determined a collector may violate § 805(b) if he leaves a message for a consumer when he is aware the message may be heard by others. The court noted the forewarning to disconnect could perhaps persuade other persons from listening to the message, but nothing in the message would alert the consumer to disconnect if he were listening to it in the presence of others. The court also found "prior consent of the consumer given directly to the debt collector" is not provided if a third party, or the consumer in the presence of a third party, continued to listen to the message in spite of the warning. Therefore, the

---

[10] *Niven v. National Action Financial Services, Inc.*, No. 8:07-CV-1326-T-27TBM, 2008 WL 4190961, *1 (M.D. Fla. Sept. 10, 2008).

[11] *Id.* at *2.

[12] *Id.*

[13] *Leyes v. Corporate Collection Services, Inc.*, No. 03 Civ. 8491(DAB), 2007 WL 1225547 (S.D.N.Y. Sept. 18, 2006).

court found the consumer stated a claim under § 805(b) and denied the collector's motion to dismiss.

The court noted its ruling would make it difficult for a collector to comply with §§ 805(b), 806(6), and 807(11) when leaving a message on a consumer's voice mail. However, the court found no reason that a collector is entitled to use voice messages, and noted a collector has other methods to reach consumers including postal mail, in-person contact, and speaking directly via telephone.

Contradictory Opinions

To date, two district courts have found voice messages are not necessarily always "communications" which require the mini-Miranda disclosure. In the first court decision, *Biggs v. Credit Collections, Inc.*, No. CIV-07-0053-F, 2007 WL 4034997 (W.D. Okla. Nov. 15, 2007), the consumers alleged, among other things, the debt collector violated § 807(11) by failing to disclose in an answering machine message that the communication was from a debt collector.

As discussed earlier, § 803(2) of the FDCPA defines communication as the "conveying of information regarding a debt directly or indirectly to any person through any medium." The consumers cited decisions from many of the cases mentioned above which concluded voice mail messages were "communications" for the purpose of § 807. However, the *Biggs* court was not persuaded by such decisions. The court stated, "Words matter—in this instance, the words of the voice mails and the words of the statutory definition of a 'communication.'" The court found the transcript of the voice mail messages demonstrated the messages in question "convey[ed] no information regarding a debt." The court asserted that "no amount of liberal construction can broaden the statutory language to encompass the words recorded in these voice mails." Therefore, the court denied the consumers' motion for summary judgment on the claim that the debt collector's messages violated § 807(11).

However, at least one court declined to follow the reasoning in *Biggs*, concluding the FDCPA requires a broader construction in its terms in favor of the consumer. In *Ramirez v. Apex Fin. Mgmt., LLC*, 567 F. Supp. 2d 1035 (N.D. Ill. 2008), the consumer alleged the collector violated the cease communication provision of the FDCPA by leaving several messages on her answering machine which requested she call the collector as soon as possible, and conveyed other pertinent information, including the fact the consumer should attend to the matter and providing instructions regarding how to do so.

The collector argued the consumer failed to submit sufficient evidence to show the collector "communicated" with the consumer, as the consumer failed to show the phone calls were "regarding the debt" as defined under the FDCPA. In support of its position, the collector argued the court should follow the precedent in *Biggs* and hold the "words" of the voice mail should determine whether it conveyed information regarding the debt. As noted, the court declined to follow *Biggs* and held messages left on an answering machine can be considered indirect communications regarding the debt, which would bring them within the statutory definition of "communication," even if the collector fails to expressly mention the call pertains to collection.

Similarly, one court in the district of Missouri relied on *Foti* to determine whether a conversation with a third party was a "communication" under the FDCPA.[14] Although the facts of the case are distinguished from *Foti* in that no message was left on an answering machine, the court held a communication which did not impart any information regarding the consumer's debt was "in connection with the collection of any debt."[15] In this case, the debt collector called the consumer and ended up speaking with the consumer's girlfriend, who stated she would have the consumer call him back. Subsequently, the collector left his phone number with the consumer's girlfriend.[16] The court determined the call was a "communication," actionable under the FDCPA, because the collector called to inquire about the debt owed by the consumer and the call ultimately ended not with a request for contact information, but with the collector leaving his phone number for the consumer to call him back.[17]

The second court decision, *Reed v. Global Acceptance Credit Co.*, No. C-08-01826 RMW, 2008 WL 3330165 (N.D. Cal. Aug. 12, 2008) created another contradictory opinion when the court held subsequent voice messages may not require literal compliance with § 807(11). In this case, the consumer alleged the collector violated § 807(11) by failing to disclose clearly "the debt collector is attempting to collect a debt and that any information obtained will be used for that purpose" in several voice messages. The voice messages in question provided the name of the collector, the name of the collection agency, the consumer's account number, and requested a return phone call. The court stated the full mini-Miranda was not required, as it was already provided in the initial collection letter and the law only required subsequent communications to convey the communication was from a debt collector. Further, the court noted the Ninth Circuit previously held where the consumer already knows the identity of the debt collector, follow-up notices from the collector are not communications and do not require compliance with § 807(11), so long as they are not false or misleading.[18]

The court determined the messages were not false or misleading, as the collector identified herself and did not make any false representations in the messages. Further, the court held a least sophisticated consumer would have known the collector was a debt collector because its company name suggested it was a collector. The totality of circumstances and prior communications, including the fact the collector provided the consumer with verification of the debt, suggested the consumer would know the nature and identity of the caller in the voice messages. Finally, the court noted § 804(b) prohibits third party disclosure, and considering the collector was required to comply with contradictory obligations and the language of the messages were not false and misleading, the court denied summary judgment for the consumer.

---

[14] *Thomas v. Consumer Adjustment Co.*, Inc., No. 4:07CV01159 AGF, 2008 WL 4412290, F. Supp. 2d (E.D. Mo. Sept. 20, 2008).

[15] *Id.* at *6.

[16] *Id.* at *1.

[17] *Id.* at *6.

[18] *Reed v. Global Acceptance Credit Co.*, No. C-08-01826 RMW, 2008 WL 3330165 (N.D. Cal. Aug. 12, 2008) (citing *Pressley v. Capital Credit & Collection Serv.*, 760 F.2d 922, 925 (9th Cir. 1985)).

Request for FTC Advisory Opinion

In 2005 ACA submitted a Petition for an Advisory Opinion requesting clarification of two provisions of the FDCPA: (1) under § 806(6), must a debt collector identify a corporate name in order to meaningfully disclose the caller's identity; and (2) when leaving a message for a consumer is the collector required to provide the mini-Miranda disclosure under § 807(11).

ACA received a response from the FTC, declining its request. The letter stated that because, at the time, a number of federal courts had ruled consistently on the questions raised, the Commission would not grant the request to issue an advisory opinion.

The letter from the FTC stated "[b]ased on these decisions, there is clear court precedent for the proposition that a debt collector leaving a voice mail message must reveal the name of this employer, even if the name indicates that the message involves a debt."[19]

The FTC further stated that courts have also addressed whether a debt collector must provide the mini-Miranda disclosure when leaving messages for consumers. The FTC concluded "[t]he decisions are uniform in concluding that a collector failing to do so violates Section 807(11)."[20]

Although the letter failed to provide any definitive clarification, it bolsters the viewpoint that to comply with the FDCPA, a debt collector must state the name of their employer and provide the mini-Miranda when leaving messages. The letter did not address how a collector would comply with this requirement without simultaneously violating § 805(b).

The complete text of the FTC letter is available on E-Compliance, Document # 433.

State Advisory Opinion

An ACA member filed a request for an advisory opinion in Maine with regard to *Foti* and similar decisions. Maine's Director of the Consumer Credit Regulation Office provided a written response on June 20, 2006. The response stated, in pertinent part,

> Although I share with others the concern about disclosing information to third parties, on balance I believe that the importance of the "I am a debt collector" disclosure outweighs those concerns. Keep in mind that a spouse is already considered the same as the [consumer] in terms of [third] party communications ... In addition, if a parent authorizes others in a

[19]*Hosseinzadeh v. M.R.S. Assocs., Inc.*, 387 F. Supp. 2d 1104 (C.D. Cal. 2005); *Joseph v. J.J. MacIntyre Cos., L.L.C.*, 281 F. Supp. 2d 1156 (N.D. Cal. 2003); and *Wright v. Credit Bureau of Georgia, Inc.*, 548 F. Supp. 591, *on consideration on other grounds*, 555 F. Supp. 1005 (N.D. Ga. 1982).

[20]*Stinson v. Asset Acceptance, L.L.C.*, No. 1:05CV1026 (JCC), 2006 WL 1647134, (E.D. Va. June 12, 2006); *Foti v. NCO Fin. Sys., Inc.*, 424 F. Supp. 2d 643 (S.D.N.Y. 2006); *Hosseinzadeh v. M.R.S. Assocs., Inc.*, 387 F. Supp. 2d 1104 (C.D. Cal. 2005). *See also Chlanda v. Wymard*, 1995 U.S. Dist. Lexis 14394, *32 n.16 (S.D. Ohio 1995) (voice mail message requesting that the consumer pay a credit card debt violated § 807(11) because it did not include that provision's notice).

> household to listen to telephone answering machine messages, that authorization can be considered akin to permitting others to open and read one's mail.

Although ACA members have commented that such a letter is broad and may not account for all living situations, it may be inferred that the state suggests the mini-Miranda be provided in messages left for the consumer. Debt collectors should consult with their own legal counsel when determining what messages should be left for consumers in light of such opinion.

A Defensive Posture

The above holdings and findings present a dilemma for the debt collection industry. Complying with the § 807(11) requirement to disclose the communication is from a debt collector creates the possibility of an unauthorized third-party disclosure prohibited by § 805(b).

In light of the recent *Berg* case, the most prudent course of action for the collection industry would be to cease leaving messages for consumers. A debt collector cannot be sued under any theory if he does not communicate with the consumer. The next most prudent course of action is to cease leaving messages for consumers in the Eleventh Circuit which includes Florida, Georgia and Alabama. Finally, the next most prudent course of action is to cease leaving messages for consumers located in the Southern District of Florida (as the *Berg* case was decided in this jurisdiction).

For those who choose to continue leaving messages for consumers, ACA has amended its previously recommended message in regards to the *Foti* decision to address the concerns raised by the U.S. District Court for the Southern District of Florida. The proposed message is as follows **(new language in bold):**

> This is a message for Mary Smith. If you are not Mary Smith, please hang up or disconnect. If you are Mary Smith, please continue to listen to this message. There will now be a three second pause in this message. (pause) By continuing to listen to this message, you acknowledge you are Mary Smith. **Ms. Smith, you should not listen to this message so that other people can hear it as it contains personal and private information. There will now be a three second pause in this message to allow you to listen to this message in private. (pause)** This is Bob Jones from ABC Collection Agency. This communication is from a debt collector. This is an attempt to collect a debt and any information obtained will be used for that purpose. Please contact me about an important business matter at [phone #].

ACA does not warrant its legality or your liability should you choose to use it. It is merely the result of balancing risks and the limited options available to collection agencies when leaving a message is imperative to successful collections. Subsequent communications could use the same language or omit "This is an attempt to collect a debt and any information obtained will be used for that purpose."

Some collection agencies have raised concern that if they disclose the voice message is from a debt collector, consumers will never return their phone calls. While this *may* prove to be true, many agencies believe seasoned consumers already know when a voice mail message is from a debt collector even without the disclosure statement. Only time will tell if the disclosure of a debt collector's identity in a phone message will impact the return call rate.

When determining whether to and what message to leave for a consumer, be aware that only certain district courts in California, Florida, Massachusetts, and New York have ruled on this issue. Virginia, Maine, Illinois, and Minnesota have considered this issue, but have not made a final determination. Although complaints have been filed in various districts, ACA is not aware of decisions similar to California, Florida, Massachusetts, and New York in other state or judicial districts. Please note, however, that a letter from the Federal Trade Commission indicated the failure to provide the mini-Miranda when leaving a message for a consumer, would violate § 807(11) of the FDCPA.

At this time, ACA does not have a fail safe course of action for collectors. Please consult with independent legal counsel as you decide whether, and if so how, you will adjust your operations and compliance programs to comply with *Foti* and similar decisions.

ACA International, P.O. Box 390106, Minneapolis, MN 55439-0106
Phone +1(952) 926-6547 Fax (952) 926-1624
E-mail compliance@acainternational.org
Web http://www.acainternational.org

This information is not to be construed as legal advice. Legal advice must be tailored to the specific circumstances of each case. Every effort has been made to assure that this information is up-to-date as of the date of publication. It is not intended to be a full and exhaustive explanation of the law in any area. This information is not intended as legal advice and may not be used as legal advice. It should not be used to replace the advice of your own legal counsel.

APPENDIX X

MODIFICATION OF LICENSING LAW—COLORADO

RULES OF THE ADMINISTRATOR, COLORADO COLLECTION AGENCY BOARD
(effective November 1, 2008)
4 Code of Colorado Regulations 903-1

Scope of Rules

These rules apply to all collection agencies and debt collectors, whether or not exempt from licensing under the Colorado Fair Debt Collection Practices Act, unless the rule is limited to "licensees" or "applicants." The words "client" and "creditor" have the same meaning throughout these rules.

Chapter 1

Licensing and Disciplinary Matters

Rule 1.01 Collections Manager

(1) Whenever an applicant or licensee designates a new collections manager, it shall notify the Administrator by filing a collections manager application form. The collections manager shall meet the qualifications of sections 12-14-119, 12-14-123(2), and the other applicable provisions of the Colorado Fair Debt Collection Practices Act.

(2) Pursuant to section 12-14-122(3)(a), C.R.S., an application filed due to a change of collections manager shall be filed within thirty days of the change. The temporary absence of an approved collections manager does not constitute a change requiring designation of a new manager.

Rule 1.02 Licensure

(1) No license shall issue until all necessary documents and information have been filed, all fees paid, and the designated collection manager's qualifications to collect debts has been determined. No debts may be collected nor creditor accounts solicited until a license has been issued.

(2) Within ninety (90) days after notice from the Administrator that the application is incomplete, the applicant must complete the application for licensure by providing all necessary documents, information, and fees specified. If the licensure application is not completed within that time, the application shall be

null and void and the applicant must then reapply for licensure, including payment of all fees.

Rule 1.03 **Aliases**

(1) Licensees must retain records reflecting the true name of all debt collectors and, if applicable, the one alias used by each debt collector. These records shall be retained for two (2) years after the debt collector leaves the licensee's employment. The Administrator may require a licensee to submit these records at any time.

(2) No debt collector may use more than one alias. The alias must consist of both a first and last name. Debt collectors employed by a licensee may not use the same alias.

Rule 1.04 **Letters of Admonition**

(1) Any letter of admonition issued against a licensee or collections manager shall be mailed by first-class certified mail.

(2) A licensee or collections manager receiving a letter of admonition may appeal the admonishment by filing a written request within forty (40) days after the date of the letter. Upon receipt of a timely appeal, a hearing will be held. While an appeal is pending, the letter of admonition shall be vacated until conclusion of a hearing held pursuant to Rule 1.04(3).

(3) Any hearing held following a request to appeal the issuance of a letter of admonition shall be conducted pursuant to the State Administrative Procedure Act, title 24, article 4, of the Colorado Revised Statutes. If a violation of the Colorado Fair Debt Collection Practices Act, the rules adopted pursuant thereto, or a lawful order has occurred, or the licensee fraudulently obtained a license, the licensee, collections manager, or both, as applicable, may be disciplined as provided in § 12-14-130(10), C.R.S.

(4) If the Administrator determines that a violation is minor or technical, the Administrator has the discretion to issue an advisory letter in lieu of a letter of admonition.

Rule 1.05 **Termination of License**

(1) Upon the termination of a license by revocation, expiration, denial, or surrender, the licensee must immediately cease collection activities. All client accounts must be returned to the clients within thirty (30) days unless the licensee has written authorization from the client to transfer or assign the accounts to another collection agency for collection. No later than the end of the thirty day period, the licensee must file a notarized affidavit with the Administrator of the Collection Agency Board stating its compliance with this rule and providing the names and addresses of all clients for whom it was attempting to collect debts.

(2) The licensee shall not charge or retain any fee or commission for the return or transfer of client accounts made pursuant to Rule 1.05(1).

(3) All consumer payments received after the revocation, expiration, or surrender of a license shall be immediately forwarded in full to the applicable client without the licensee's retention of any fee or commission.

(4) This rule does not prohibit the bulk sale of the licensee's business, assets, and goodwill as a unit, including the provision of information to enable the purchaser to solicit reassignment of client accounts directly from the client after termination of a license. A licensee may not purchase the right to collect client accounts from another licensee but only the right to solicit their reassignment from the client.

(5) This rule does not apply to any license voluntarily surrendered in conjunction with the simultaneous issuance of a new license due to any of the changes listed in § 12-14-122(2)(c), C.R.S.

Rule 1.06 **License Renewals**

Collection agency licenses shall be valid from the date of issuance to the following July 1. In order to renew its license, a licensee must file its completed renewal application and renewal fee on or before July 1 of each year or its license shall automatically expire.

Rule 1.07 **Address Changes**

For purposes of section 12-14-122(1)(a), C.R.S. mandating written notice to the Administrator within thirty days of a change of business address, the business address is the principal place of business printed on the collection agency's license.

Rule 1.08 Abbreviated Applications

(1) A licensee filing an abbreviated license application upon a change of ownership structure pursuant to section 12-14-122(2)(c)(III), C.R.S. is not required to submit the following:
- (a) Investigation fee;
- (b) List of currently employed debt collectors and solicitors;
- (c) License verification forms from other states that license the applicant; and,
- (d) If there has been no change in any of the documentation on file with the administrator:
  - (i) Personal affidavits of owners, officers, members/managers, and partners;
  - (ii) Collections manager application; and
  - (iii) List of branch offices.

Chapter 2

Consumer Protections

Rule 2.01 Notices

(1) The consumer rights information required to be in the initial written communication and the validation of debts notice may be printed on two (2) separate pages provided that the first page contains language referring the consumer to the second page and the two (2) pages are attached together.

(2) Every collection notice mailed or delivered by a licensee must contain the collection agency's name, mailing address, and toll-free telephone number. The collection agency's address may not be printed only on any portion of the collection notice designed to be returned to the agency with the consumer's communication or payment. "Toll-free" means a call made at no cost to the consumer.

Rule 2.02 **Payment Agreements and Schedules**

No collection agency shall engage in unnecessary, additional collection activities on a debt while a consumer is complying with the terms of a payment agreement or schedule agreed to by the collection agency and consumer concerning the debt. "Unnecessary, additional collection activities" shall not include the mailing of payment coupons or reminders, the mailing of receipts, any communications requested by the consumer that do not contain demands for collection, or the filing or notification of post judgment liens.

Rule 2.03 **Costs of Collection**

(1) No collection agency shall add, collect, or attempt to collect a charge for costs of collection unless such costs are expressly authorized by statute or by the contract, agreement, note, or other instrument creating the debt and are not otherwise prohibited by law.

(2) No licensee shall advise, suggest, or request that a client add collection costs to any existing debt unless such costs are specifically authorized by statute.

(3) If a statute, contract, agreement, note, or other instrument specifically authorizes the addition of collection costs and such costs are collected, the licensee may retain only those collection costs exclusive of attorney fees and court costs as its fee or commission for the collection of the debt, unless otherwise agreed to in writing with the assignor.

(4) No collection agency shall add, collect, or attempt to collect costs of collection pursuant to § 13-21-109(1)(b) (II), C.R.S. on any dishonored check, draft, or payment order payable to it unless the check is assigned for collection to another collection agency not owned in whole or in part by the payee collection agency.

Rule 2.04 **Overpayment**

If a collection agency has received final payment of any debt which overpays the debt by more than five dollars ($5.00), it shall issue a refund to the consumer of the amount of the overpayment within thirty (30) days after the end of the month in which the payment was received unless otherwise required by law or as directed by court order.

Rule 2.05 **Cash Payments**

A collection agency shall provide the consumer with a receipt for all payments made in cash or by any other means which does not in and of itself provide evidence of payment. The receipt shall be provided to the consumer within five (5) business days after the payment is received. A "business day" does not include Sundays or legal holidays.

Rule 2.06 **Account Statements**

(1) Subject to the payment record retention requirements of Rule 3.03, a collection agency shall provide the consumer with a written statement of the consumer's payments for as long as the collection agency has had assignment of the debt within ten (10) days after the consumer makes a written request. The statement shall include the consumer's name, the creditor's name, the amounts paid, the dates on which payments were received, the allocation of each payment to, as applicable, principal, interest, court costs, attorney fees, other costs, the interest rate, and the current balance due. Account statements shall be provided upon request without charge once during any twelve (12) month period. If additional statements are requested, they may be provided upon payment of a reasonable fee not to exceed five dollars ($5.00) per statement.

(2) After a debt has been paid or settled in full, a collection agency shall provide a written statement or receipt that the debt has been paid or settled in full within ten (10) business days after request by the consumer. Such a statement shall be provided free of charge. A "business day" does not include Sundays or legal holidays.

Rule 2.07 **Consumer Communication Records**

Collection agencies shall maintain accurate summaries or records of all communication in connection with the collection or attempted collection of a debt with consumers, a consumer's attorney or representative, the consumer's employer, consumer reporting agencies, and persons contacted to obtain location information, for two (2) years following the date of the communication.

Rule 2.08 **Business Cards**

(1) No collection agency shall use a business card in obtaining or attempting to obtain location information about a consumer or in communicating or attempting to communicate with a consumer unless:

(a) The business card does not indicate in any way that the collection agency is in the business of collections or is attempting to collect a debt, or,

(b) The business card is placed in a sealed envelope which contains the consumer's name and does not indicate by means of name, symbol, or any marking, that the envelope is from a collection agency.

Rule 2.09 **Attorney Letters**

(1) During the time that a licensee is in possession of a creditor account, the licensee shall not use or deliver any communication from an attorney unless the creditor has previously provided specific written authorization to commence legal action to collect the debt.

(2) This rule does not prohibit any direct communication from an attorney if the attorney is authorized to collect the debt.

Rule 2.10 **Dual Collections**

No collection agency may knowingly collect a debt that is being collected by another collection agency or attorney.

Rule 2.11 **Office Location**

A collection agency may share an office location with another business as long as all signs, directories, and other business identification information clearly contain the collection agency's name.

Rule 2.12 **Consumer Payments**

(1) All accepted consumer payments must be credited to a consumer's account to reflect payment no later than the next business day following the date payment was received unless the delay will result in any economic harm to the consumer or the payment is by post-dated check. Post-dated checks shall be credited to the consumer's account to reflect payment as of the date of deposit in the collection agency's trust account.

(2) This rule does not prohibit subsequent adjustments to a consumer's account to reflect dishonored checks, drafts, or other payment instruments.

Rule 2.13 Checks Not Paid Upon Presentment

A collection agency collecting a check, draft, or order not paid upon presentment shall send the consumer its validation of debts notice required by § 12-14-109, C.R.S. at least fifteen (15) days prior to the mailing or service of the notice of nonpayment required by § 13-21-109(2)(a) and (3), C.R.S.

Rule 2.14 Payment Authorization by Telephone

(1) If a consumer's authorization for payment of a debt is provided orally, the licensee must also:
   (a) Obtain the consumer's written authorization for the payment prior to the date of payment, or
   (b) If permitted by law, record by audio tape or other digital means the consumer's verbal authorization and retain the recording, or
   (c) Transfer the consumer's telephone call to a manager or another debt collector to verify the amount, means, and verbal authorization for payment.

(2) If a collection agency does not comply with section (1) of this rule and the consumer denies or disputes the purported oral payment authorization within sixty days of the payment, the collection agency must refund the payment amount within five (5) business days of receipt of good funds. A "business day" does not include Sundays or legal holidays.

Rule 2.15 Disclosure of Contact Information

Upon the request of a consumer or person contacted for location information, a licensee shall provide its principal place of business, mailing address, toll-free telephone number, and, if applicable, facsimile number.

Rule 2.16 Debt Collector Obligations

Except as otherwise provided, all references in this Chapter 2 to collection agencies shall apply to debt collectors.

Chapter 3

Creditor Protections

Rule 3.01 **Trust Accounts**

(1) A licensee shall maintain the trust account required by section 12-14-123(1)(c), C.R.S., but need not maintain the account in a Colorado bank or financial institution if the licensee maintains one or more trust accounts in other states for the benefit of its clients, including its Colorado clients, and it executes and files annual written authorization with the Administrator on an approved form acknowledging the account(s) may be attached upon order of a Colorado court.

(2) If any of the trust account information in a licensee's license or renewal application changes, the licensee must file a new bank authorization form within thirty (30) days of the date of the change.

(3) No trust account is required if the licensee does not receive nor have access to any consumer payments because they are made directly to the client according to all of the licensee's contracts or agreements.

(4) A licensee, other than one that only collects debts it owns, shall maintain in its trust account the minimum liquid assets referred to in section 12-14-123(1)(a), C.R.S.

Rule 3.02 **Unidentified Accounts**

(1) If a licensee receives a consumer payment but is unable to identify the client account on whose behalf the payment is made, the licensee shall return the entire payment to the consumer within thirty (30) days after the end of the month in which the payment was received.

(2) No amount may be retained by a licensee as fee or commission from any consumer payment made on an unidentified account.

(3) If a licensee is able to identify, but cannot locate, a client on whose behalf payment is made, the licensee shall comply with applicable state laws on unclaimed property.

Rule 3.03 **Payment Records**

(1) Licensees shall maintain a record of all consumer payments for two (2) years following the date the payment was received.

(2) Records of consumer payments shall include the consumer's name, the client's name, the amounts paid, the dates on which payments were received, the allocation of each payment to, as applicable, principal, interest, court costs, attorney fees, other costs, the interest rate, the current balance due, and the date of deposit of the payment to the trust account.

Rule 3.04 **Bonds**

(1) The bond required of each licensee shall be in the form and manner prescribed by statute, and shall be filed with the Administrator.

(2) As an alternative to the bond, a licensee may present a savings account, deposit, or certificate of deposit.

(a) The savings account, deposit, or certificate of deposit shall be in a federally insured bank or savings and loan association doing business and located in this state or accessible in a branch in this state.

(b) The savings account, deposit, or certificate of deposit shall be assigned to the Attorney General of the State of Colorado for the use of the People of the State of Colorado in the form and manner prescribed by the Administrator. The assignment shall be for a period ending two (2) years after the revocation, expiration, or surrender of a license or on such earlier date as may be determined by the Administrator.

(c) As far as practical, the procedure used to determine claims against a bond shall be used for claims against a savings account, deposit, or certificate of deposit.

Rule 3.05 **Return of Accounts**

(1) If a licensee may retain accounts in the process of collection, as defined in section 12-14-124(6), C.R.S., it must disclose that information to its clients at the time it initially accepts accounts for collection.

(2) This Rule 3.05 takes effect May 1, 2009 and applies to all of the licensee's current and future clients.

Rule 3.06 **Licensee Obligations**

Except as otherwise provided, all references in this Chapter 3 to licensees shall apply to applicants.

CHAPTER 16

Truth in Lending—Regulation Z

After reading the advertisement, the consumer borrowed the sum of $100 for one year with interest at 9 percent. After the loan was made, the consumer learned that the $9 interest was subtracted from the $100 loan and he only received $91. The consumer had to repay the loan in 12 monthly payments over the year. The effective rate of interest on this loan approached 19 percent and not the 9 percent as advertised.

If the loan was secured by a lien on an automobile, the opportunity for the lender to charge expenses in addition to the interest in the printed form contract was only limited by the creativity of the institution. While most major banks attempt to disclose to consumers the cost of borrowing money, some less scrupulous banks and financial institutions are guilty of some form of deceptive and misleading advertising concerning the true cost of borrowing and the accuracy of the annual interest rate.

The Truth in Lending Act (TILA) was originally signed by President Johnson in 1968 and was intended to induce the consumer to shop for the best price for credit in the same way one shops for the best price for an automobile. The creditor is required to make full disclosure of important credit charges so that the consumer may shop for the most favorable credit terms. The Act, amended several times, basically requires creditors to disclose to the consumer the actual cost of the borrowing. The thrust of the Act is to enable the consumer to compare the various credit terms, to require detailed disclosure of the cost of credit, and to protect the consumer against inaccurate and unfair credit billing and credit card practices. The findings and purposes of the TILA are: to assure a meaningful disclosure of credit terms so that the consumer will be able to compare more readily various credit terms available to him and avoid the uninformed use of credit.

Disclosures must be "clear and conspicuous" and are to be presented to the consumer in a "reasonable understandable form." The Act also deals with the practice of leasing automobiles for consumer use as an alternative to installment credit sales since these leases are offered without adequate cost disclosure.

Three basic documents must be considered. The TILA (of which the Fair Credit Billing Act is a part) consists of 40 pages. Regulation Z are the rules and regulations (covering 80 pages) implementing the TILA. The Official Staff Commentary (another 103 pages) to Regulation Z of the TILA is designed to explain and interpret Regulation Z. An in-depth analysis of these 223 pages obviously is beyond the scope of this book, but this chapter will attempt to present an overview of the highlights. The text of the TILA and Regulation Z are included in as appendices to this chapter. The Commentary, not included because of its length, may be ordered from the Board of Governors of the Federal Reserve Board, Washington, D.C.

RECENT ACTIVITY

For four years now the Federal Reserve Board has been working on the revolving credit provisions of Regulation Z. These proposed changes have finally been issued.[1]

The Federal Reserve Board has also issued an update of the "Charm Booklet" dealing with adjustable rate mortgages. The booklet contains new requirements and must be delivered to the debtor with every application for an adjustable rate mortgage loan (ARM). The Home Ownership and Equity Protection Act has been modified with respect to the point and fee thresholds. The HOEPA is effective beginning October 1, 2007. The threshold prior to the change was the greater of 8% of the total amount or $400 on a high cost home loan. The new threshold is $561 which became effective on January 1, 2008.

DEFINITIONS

Creditor. The creditor is the person who has regularly extended credit at least 25 times in the preceding year in connection with the loan, sale of property, services, or otherwise. A creditor who extends loans secured by homes is covered by the Act merely by extending credit five

[1]72 Fed. Reg. 32948; 72 Fed. Reg. 21141.

times in the preceding calendar year providing all the extension of credits were secured by a dwelling.

Extension of Credit. The credit must be repayable by agreement in more than four installments and a finance charge is or may be required. The creditor must also be the person to whom the obligation is initially payable.[2] When a loan is transferred and assigned to another institution, the party to whom the loan is initially payable is still covered by the TILA; and the party and the institution which receive the assignment are still subject to certain disclosure requirements under the Act.

Consumer. The consumer is the party to whom credit is offered. The money, property, or services which are the subject of the transaction must be for personal, family, or household purposes.

Credit Card. A credit card is any card or other credit devised for the purpose of obtaining money, property, labor, or services on credit.

EXEMPTIONS

The creditor must make a determination whether the transaction is a commercial transaction and exempt from the TILA.[3] Commercial, business, agricultural, or organizational credit is exempt from the TILA.[4]

The commentary sets forth factors to consider determining whether a transaction is exempt. With regard to the acquisition of antiques, securities, or art, the following factors are important:

1. The business of the borrower in relation to the property to be acquired.
2. The degree to which the borrower can personally manage the acquisition.
3. The ratio of income from the acquisition to the total income of the borrower.
4. The size of the transaction.
5. The borrower's statement as to the purpose of the loan.

---

[2] 12 CFR § 226.2 (17); *Childs v. Ford Motor Credit Co.*, 470 F. Supp. 708 (N.D. Ala. 1979); *Tom Benson Chevway Rental & Leasing v. Allen*, 571 S.W.2d 346 (Tex. Ct. App.), *cert. denied*, 442 U.S. 930 (1978).

[3] 12 CFR § 226.3; *Smith v. Chapman*, 436 F. Supp. 58 (W.D. Tex. 1977), *aff'd*, 614 F.2d 968 (5th Cir. 1980).

[4] 12 CFR § 226.3.

The commentary also sets forth three examples of exempt transactions involving business purpose credit:

1. A loan to expand a business even if secured by the borrower's residence or personal property.
2. A loan to improve a principal residence by putting in a business office.
3. A business account used occasionally for consumer purposes.

If a firm loans money to employees for personal purposes, the loan is for a consumer purpose and is covered by the Act. A loan for a child's tuition secured by mechanic's tools is considered consumer credit as is a personal account used occasionally for business purposes.[5] Consultation with experienced counsel is recommended for marginal fact situations.

Any credit card issued for the sole purpose of obtaining business credit is exempt under the Act, as well as any credit extension for agricultural purposes. An extension of credit to a corporation or organization is exempt, regardless of the purpose of the credit. Any extension of credit in excess of $25,000 is exempt, except an extension of credit for a residence which is used as the principal dwelling. Such extensions of credit are covered even if they exceed the $25,000 threshold. An extension of credit involving public utility services such as gas, water, electricity, etc. is not covered under the Act. Transactions in securities or commodities accounts in which credit is extended by a broker dealer registered with the Security and Exchange Commission or Commodity Future Trading Commission are not covered.

FINANCE CHARGES

The finance charge is the cost of consumer credit as a dollar amount and includes any charge payable directly or indirectly by the consumer as a result of the extension of credit.[6]

If the charge is made to the consumer in a comparable cash transaction, the charge is not a finance charge. If the charge for the credit transaction exceeds the charge in a cash transaction, the difference is a "finance charge." The burden rests with the creditor to compare a cash transaction and a credit transaction to determine if the difference in price is due to the extension of the credit. The regulation offers concrete examples to illustrate the definition.

---

[5] 12 CFR § 226.3.

[6] *Bates v. Provident Consumer Discount Co.*, 493 F. Supp. 605 (E.D. Penn. 1979); *Meyers v. Clearview Dodge Sales, Inc.*, 539 F.2d 511 (5th Cir. 1976).

Examples follow:

1. Interest is the largest ingredient (sometimes the only ingredient) of the finance charge. The difference between the credit price and the cash price is the interest.
2. If the creditor imposes a charge on the consumer to cover a specific cost of doing business (extending credit), the extra charge becomes a finance charge, since it is incurred by the consumer as a result of the extension of credit.
3. All service, transaction, activity, and carrying charges are considered finance charges.
4. A fee to participate in a credit plan is a finance charge.
5. Loan fees, finders' fees, and similar charges are considered finance charges, as well as fees for an investigation or a credit report.
6. Premiums or any other charge for any insurance protecting the creditor against the consumer's default or other credit loss is a finance charge.
7. Charges for premiums for credit life (insuring the extension of credit), accident, or life insurance are also included in the finance charge with certain exceptions.
8. Premiums for insurance written in connection with a consumer credit transaction against loss or damage to property or liability dealing with property are also included in the finance charges.

   Case law indicates that creditors should include the cost of credit life insurance in the finance charge. If most loans are sold with life insurance, the premium should be included as a finance charge. Court decisions suggest the premium be included as part of the amount when quoting a repayment schedule.[7] If the insurance coverage may be obtained from an insurance company of the consumer's choice and is properly disclosed, the premium need not be included as a finance charge. The consumer must know how much the insurance costs before an election is made, as well as the term of the insurance if the term is less than the term of the transaction. Single interest insurance which protects only the creditor's interest in the property is considered a finance charge.
9. Inspection and handling fees for the disbursement of loan proceeds are considered a finance charge.
10. Fees for preparing a Truth in Lending disclosure statement or charges for a maintenance or service contract are finance charges.
11. Except if imposed in connection with a mortgage on a residence, appraisal, investigation, and credit report fees are finance charges,

[7] *US Life Corp. Credit v. FTC*, 599 F.2d 1387 (5th Cir. 1979).

providing the charge is reasonable in amount and bona fide. They can be excluded as a finance charge in real estate transactions if they are included in the application fee charged to all applicants, even if credit is ultimately denied.

12. Compulsory pre-paid finance charges paid before the consummation of any credit transaction or withheld from the advance are generally a finance charge, although the commentary is not clear on this point and allows exceptions to this general rule.

Finance Charges—Rebates. The TILA was enacted to assure meaningful disclosure of credit terms so that the consumer would be able to compare more readily the various credit terms available. A finance charge is defined as the sum of all charges payable directly or indirectly by the person to whom the credit is extended and imposed by the creditor as an incident to the extension of credit. A finance charge is a charge that is avoidable by paying cash. Finance charges include discounts for the purpose of inducing payment by means other than credit. The debtor claimed the dealer violated the TILA when he purchased the car for cash because he would have paid a cash price for the car $1,500 less than the cash price of his finance transaction. This constitutes a charge that is avoidable by paying cash. The debtor was not offered the rebate. The court held that this constituted a finance charge as defined by TILA and must be disclosed. A higher cash price paid by credit customers is a finance charge and must be disclosed to the consumer. The dealer did not disclose the rebate as a finance charge.

The fact that the rebate was available to some customers, but not available to this particular customer, was considered irrelevant.[8]

Charges not Considered Finance Charges. The regulation leads the lender to believe that if the exemption is not specifically listed, it does not exist. This is not so, since the regulation explicitly states that the creditor must make the decision as to whether the difference in the cost is due to the extension of credit. If the difference in the cost of credit is not due to the extension of credit, it is not a finance charge. The following are examples not considered finance charges:

1. Taxes, license fees, or registration fees paid by both cash or credit customers.
2. Discounts available to both cash and credit customers, such as volume discounts.

[8] *Coelho v. Park Ridge Oldsmobile, Inc.*, 2001 U.S. Dist. LEXIS 14652 (N.D. Ill. 2001).

3. Charges for service policy, auto club membership, or a policy of insurance against latent defects.
4. Application fees may be excluded if designed to recover the cost associated with processing applications for credit and charged to all applicants, not just approved applicants who receive credit.
5. Late payment charges for an unanticipated late payment, exceeding a credit limit, or for delinquency, default, or similar occurrence.
6. Certain fees in transactions secured by real property in residential mortgage transactions, if bona fide and reasonable in amount, including fees for title examination, abstract of title, fees for preparing deeds, mortgages, notary, appraisal, credit reporting fees, and amounts required to be paid into escrow or trust accounts.
7. Discounts offered to induce payment for the purchase by cash, check, or other means.
8. Any charge passed to the buyer imposed by a creditor for providing credit to the buyer or for providing credit on certain terms.
9. "Seller points" (a charge by creditor to the debtor for providing credit), such as those frequently involved in real estate transactions.

COST OF DOING BUSINESS

Charges absorbed by the creditor as a cost of doing business are not finance charges, even though the creditor may take such costs into consideration in determining the interest rate to be charged or the cash price of the property or services sold. However, if the creditor separately imposes a charge on the consumer to cover certain costs, the charge is a finance charge if it otherwise meets the definition.

A discount imposed on a credit obligation when it is assigned by a creditor to another party is not a finance charge as long as the discount is not separately imposed on the consumer. The purpose of the TILA is to assure a meaningful disclosure of credit terms so that the consumer will be able to compare more readily the various credit terms available to the consumer and to protect the consumer against inaccurate and unfair billing in credit card practices. The TILA requires lenders to clearly disclose any finance charges that a consumer would bear under a credit transaction. A finance charge is defined as a sum of all charges payable directly or indirectly by the person to whom the credit is extended and imposed directly or indirectly by the creditor as an incident to the extension of credit.

If the lender did not charge the cash price customers a different price for the same vehicle than credit customers, then the discount is not considered a finance charge. The hidden finance charge does not constitute a finance charge under the TILA since the discount represents a common practice of buying commercial paper at a price less than its face value and such discounts are not finance charges.[9]

CLASS ACTION

Efforts by consumers to avoid mandatory arbitration continue to occupy the legal system. Some consumer attorneys attempted to distinguish claims under the TILA as different from other types of claims and therefore mandatory arbitration clauses in agreements covered by TILA should be unenforceable.

A case in Texas discussed various attacks on the mandatory arbitration clause. The final conclusion was that the TILA contains nothing that indicates Congress intended to create a statutory right to class action relief or preferred a class action as the mechanism by which to affect the remedial purposes of the statute. Citing another case, the Texas court stated as follows:

> So long as the prospective litigant may vindicate his or her statutory cause of action in the arbitral form, the statute will continue to serve both its remedial and deterrent function.

Consumers retain all of their statutory rights under TILA and no language appears in the arbitration provision suggesting a limitation of the substantive rights. The arbitrator may order injunctive relief if allowed to do so under the terms of an arbitration agreement.

The consumer attorney in this instance lost. (*See* Chapter 15.)[10]

The consumer contended that the TILA provided a statutory right to bring class actions. The court upheld the arbitration clause under the Federal Arbitration Act and stated that the amendments to the TILA and its accompanying legislative history indicated that Congress recognized class actions as a useful way to enforce the TILA. The TILA does not provide a basic right to bring the class action, nor does it rely exclusively on class actions as an enforcement mechanism. The consumer failed to demonstrate that Congress intended to override the Federal Arbitration Act's strong presumption in favor of arbitration in cases involving TILA claims.[11]

---

[9] *Balderos v. City Chevrolet, Buick & Geo, Inc.*, No. 97 C 2084, 1998 WL 155912 (N.D. Ill., Mar. 31, 1998), *aff'd in part, rev'd in part*, 214 F.3d 849 (7th Cir. 2000).

[10] *March v. First USA Bank, N.A.*, 103 F. Supp. 2d 909 (N.D. Tex. 2000).

[11] *Sagal v. First USA Bank*, 69 F. Supp. 2d 627 (D. Del. 1999).

ANNUAL PERCENTAGE RATE (APR)

The annual percentage rate (APR) is a measure of credit expressed in a yearly rate.[12] In simple terms, all the finance charges that are included in the definition of finance charges must be translated into a simple interest rate on the outstanding balance for one year.[13] The regulation spends several pages setting forth the appropriate mathematical formulas for translating charges. This process is perhaps the most important contribution of the TILA. The ability of the consumer to understand, in simple terms, the cost of borrowing is the main purpose of the Act, and any effort to evade or circumvent its intent and purpose will expose the lender to liability for violating the provisions of the Act.[14] (*See* Appendix to this chapter.)

If a $100 loan at 6 percent interest is to be repaid in one lump sum at the end of the year with the payment of $106, the annual interest rate is 6 percent. If a $100 loan is repaid monthly, the interest rate almost doubles to 11 to 12 percent. If payments are made quarterly, the interest charge is substantially more than 6 percent, but less than 11 to 12 percent. Labeling a variety of other charges as expenses for a particular procedure or service also misleads the uninformed consumer. The purpose of the Act is to lump together all of these other service and expense charges as interest, since the charge is for the extension of credit. The conversion into an annual simple percentage rate levels the playing field among all the lenders so that the consumer can compare the true rates of interest.

OPEN-END CREDIT

An open-end credit plan is defined under the TILA as one contemplating repeated transactions, such as the Visa or MasterCard credit card or revolving bank credit. Any other plan not contemplating repeated transactions is a closed-end plan. The repeated transaction plan must set forth the terms and conditions of the transaction, including the finance charge or interest charge on the unpaid balance computed in accordance with the terms of the transaction. The open-end credit coverage specifically requires that the creditor have twenty-five open-end accounts in the preceding calendar year, or five open-end accounts if those accounts are secured by a residence. The purpose of identifying an open-end credit plan or a closed-end credit plan is *to determine the extent of the disclosures.* Travel and entertainment cards that do not impose an interest charge are treated as closed-end credit. If the card issuer enters into transactions payable in more

[12] 16 CFR § 226.22.
[13] 12 CFR § 226.4.
[14] 12 CFR § 226.18; TILA 107.

than four installments, the card issuer may be subject to the open-end disclosures if twenty-five accounts were opened in the preceding calendar year.

REQUIRED DISCLOSURES—OPEN-END CREDIT

A General Motors dealership charged a purchaser $2,495 for an extended service contract. The dealer paid General Motors $290 and had an "up charge" or markup of $2,205. The mathematics of this 1,000 percent markup must have made an impression upon the court. The dealer conceded that it did not disclose that it was retaining any portion of the amount listed as paid to General Motors. The court immediately cited Section 128(a)(B)(iii):

Section 128. Consumer Credit Not Under Open-End Credit Plans

(a) For each consumer credit transaction other than an open-end credit plan, the creditor shall disclose each of the following items, to the extent applicable:

(1) . . .

(2) . . . (A) . . .

(i) . . .

(ii) . . .

(iii) . . .

(b) In conjunction with the disclosure of the amount financed, a creditor shall provide a statement of the consumer's right to obtain, upon written request, a written itemization of the amount financed. . . . For the purposes of this subparagraph, "itemization of the amount financed" means a disclosure of the following items, to the extent applicable:

(i) . . .

(ii) . . .

(iii) each amount that is or will be paid to third persons by the creditor on the consumer's behalf, together with an identification of or reference to the third person; and . . .

The defendant argued that the revised commentary to Regulation Z, provided that "the creditor may reflect that the creditor has retained a portion of the amount paid to others." The court pointed out that this revised commentary was issued after the transaction took place in the case. They also pointed out that the revised commentary merely stated that the creditor can include in the "amount paid to others" any amount retained by the creditor without itemizing or noting this fact and that the creditor may reflect that they have retained a portion of the amount paid to others rather than disclosing the specific amount retained.

The revised commentary clarifies that the creditor has the option of disclosing that it retained a portion of the amount paid to others rather than disclosing the specific amount retained. The revised commentary does not offer as an option the failure to disclose completely that an amount was retained. At least in three circuits (Eleventh, Fifth, and Seventh), a dealer will not be able to make a 1,000 percentage markup without disclosure on an extended service warranty. This is considered an up charge. The dealer will be forced to state that it retained an up charge. As a purchaser of an automobile, the debtor is entitled to ask the dealer how much was paid to the other party and who the other party is to whom it paid the monies. The court emphasized the fact that two other circuits agreed with them.[15]

Please note that the statute requires the consumer to submit a *written* request for itemization of the amount financed. Upon receiving this request, the creditor shall provide all other disclosures required to be furnished in response to a written itemization of the amount financed and include any amount paid to third parties or any portion retained by the dealer.

Initial Disclosures. The initial disclosure by the creditor occurs before a credit card is issued and before the consumer pays any fees or charges to the creditor. The disclosure must be clear and conspicuous.[16] The finance charge and the annual percentage rates must be more conspicuous than other disclosures, usually by using bold letters or letters in different colors. The creditor is required to describe an open-end credit "finance charge" and "annual percentage rate." The TILA requires specific disclosures under Section 127A for open-end consumer credit plans, including the following where applicable:

1. The annual percentage rate imposed and a statement that such rate does not include costs other than interest.
2. A full description of any variable rate, including the annual percentage rate, the maximum amount being charged, the maximum annual percentage rate, a table disclosing the repayment options, and other details.
3. An itemization of any fees imposed by the creditor, including annual fees, application fees, transaction fees, and closing costs commonly described as "points," and the time such fees are payable, plus a disclosure as to what is charged by outside third parties, such as

[15]*Jones v. Bill Heard Chevrolet, Inc.*, 212 F.3d 1356 (11th Cir. 2000).
[16]12 CFR § 226.6.

government authorities, appraisers, and attorneys, in addition to a good faith estimate of those fees.

4. If the credit is to be secured by a residence, disclosure that the residence will be forfeited in the event of a default.
5. A clear and conspicuous statement that if a change in rates, terms, or provisions occurs, the consumer may refuse to consummate the agreement and obtain a refund of all fees.
6. A statement of the conditions under which the creditor may terminate the account and require immediate payment of the outstanding balance.
7. The repayment option under the plan.
8. An example of the minimum monthly or periodic payment, and the time needed to repay the entire balance due.
9. A disclosure of the minimum periodic payment, the length of the repayment period, the balloon payment at the end, if any, and whether the repayment covers all interest and charges.
10. Any limitation on the amount of any increase in the minimum payments, resulting in negative amortization.
11. Any limitation contained on the number of extensions of credit.
12. The amount of credit which may be obtained during any month of the defined period.
13. A statement that the consumer should consult a tax advisor regarding the deductibility of interest and charges.
14. The maximum interest rate if a variable rate is used. If the interest rate is set and is unchanged during the entire period of the credit, the maximum rate does not have to be disclosed.

The Official Staff Commentary of the TILA sets forth that payment deferral is not considered a new credit transaction even though the debtor was offered nine one-month payment deferrals, for which he paid each time. The debtor was claiming that the nine deferrals cost him over $1,000 in interest and that he was entitled to a disclosure of this finance charge because of the payment deferrals. The court properly held that the TILA does not create a duty of disclosure when creditors offer payment holidays.[17]

Segregation of Disclosure. The disclosure must be segregated from everything else (such as the advertising copy), and must not contain information that is not related to the disclosure. The purpose is so that the consumer will not be confused and will easily absorb the information.

[17] *Vegal v. P & C Bank*, Ohio Na. No. 97-3915/4147 (6th Cir. Dec. 20, 1998).

The disclosure must be written and copies must be furnished to the consumer who can retain the disclosure. The only specific requirement is that the disclosure is legible. Segregating the disclosure by outlining it in a box, by using bold print or a different color, or by using a different type style is permitted. The disclosure may be placed on the same document as the credit contract, on a separate disclosure statement, on the front and back of the document, or continued to another page.

The creditor must disclose the following information wherever applicable:[18]

1. Identity of the creditor.
2. Amount financed, subtracting any pre-paid finance charge and adding any other amounts to the finance charge.
3. Itemization of the amount financed, including the amount of any proceeds, the amount credited, the amount paid to other persons, and the pre-paid finance charges.
4. Finance charge.
5. Annual percentage rate.
6. Variable rate, where applicable.
7. The payment schedule, which includes the payments and the timing of the payments.
8. The total of the payments.
9. The demand feature, where applicable.
10. The total sale price, if it is a credit sale.
11. Any pre-payment privileges.
12. Any dollar or percentage charge, if applicable, for late payment.
13. Disclosure of security interest if any property is being pledged as security.
14. Any insurance premiums.
15. Security interest charges.
16. Reference to appropriate contract document for information about non-payment default, right to accelerate, or pre-payment privileges.
17. With regard to a residential mortgage, a statement as to whether the mortgage may be assumed.
18. Requirement of a deposit, if applicable.

Timing of Disclosure. A closed-end disclosure must be made before the credit is granted. The phrase used is "before consummation"

[18] 12 CFR § 226.18.

of the transaction.[19] Consummation occurs when the consumer becomes obligated, even if the creditor has the right to disapprove the transaction. With regard to mail or telephone orders for credit sales, the creditor may delay disclosures until the due date of the first payment. Prior to accepting an actual order, the creditor must make available to the consumer the cash price or principal amount, the finance charge, the APR or variable rate information, and repayment terms. Any obligations which are payable on demand at any time after consummation must be disclosed.[20]

Entitled to Disclosure. Only one consumer has primary liability on an obligation and this particular consumer is the only one entitled to disclosure, even though guarantors are involved in the credit extension. Guarantors and endorsers are not considered consumers, but have certain other rights if they are obligated under credit card plans. While the consumer is entitled to disclosure, the Act is not clear as to the extent guarantors and endorsers are entitled to the disclosure provisions. Co-buyers are entitled to disclosure.

The amount of proceeds paid to the consumer, the amount credited to the consumer's account, and any amounts paid to other persons must be itemized. The pre-paid finance charge is usually a part of the finance charge, even though it may be disclosed as part of the amount financed. Often in the instance where one owner or two owners of a house wishes to borrow money, the other owner is required to sign the mortgage even though they have not become obligated under the loan which the mortgage secures. The co-signer is entitled to all disclosure rights at the time of signing as well as any rights of a primary borrower if the property is to be foreclosed.[21]

Disclosure of Fees. The bank contended that they disclosed to the debtor the fax fee and recording charges five weeks prior to the closing. The case fell within the rule that consumer fraud claims may not be predicated upon fully disclosed facts. While full disclosure of the fees was made in advance, no compulsion was exerted upon the debtor to proceed with the transaction and the debtor had the option to reject the entire transaction including the charge for the recording fees and the fax. The court was not impressed.

The court felt that the debtor had no choice but to pay the $23.50 for the fax and recording fee. Any reasonable debtor would conclude that the only sane thing to do was to pay the charges rather than jeopardize the closing and the sale of a condominium. The typical act of consumer fraud involves an individual who falls victim to a commercial entity which enjoys

[19] *Bryson v. Bank of New York*, 584 F. Supp. 1306 (S.D.N.Y. 1984).
[20] 12 CFR § 226.17(b).
[21] *Soto v. PNC Bank*, 221 B.R. 343 (E.D. Pa. 1998).

"disparity of bargaining power." This was a classic example of consumer fraud and an adhesion contract (where one party to the contract has no choice because of the bargaining power of the other party) and the court found that the bank had violated New York General Business Law Section 349, in that the defendant engaged in a consumer-oriented misleading practice injuring the plaintiff.[22]

Whether other courts would follow this decision would probably depend upon whether the judge was consumer friendly or creditor friendly. Cases of this nature often go either way. The prudent lender must understand that using this device to extract a few extra dollars from consumers may expose the lender to liability.

Right of Rescission. The TILA provides that when a loan in a consumer credit transaction is secured by the consumer's principal dwelling, the consumer has the right to rescind the transaction until midnight of the third business day following the consummation of the transactions or delivery of the material disclosures including right of rescission, whichever is later. If the creditor fails to deliver the forms or fails to provide the required information, the consumer's right of rescission is automatically extended for three years after the date of the consummation of the transaction, or until the property is sold, whichever occurs first.[23]

This right of rescission expires in the usual case three years after the loan closes or upon the sale of the secured property, whichever date is earlier. The issue presented is whether a borrower may assert this right to rescind as an affirmative defense in a foreclosure action brought by a lender more than three years after the consummation of the transaction.

This Eleventh Circuit case raises several issues that may be asserted by a borrower in a foreclosure action where transfers were made to the assignee. The court stated that the TILA provides that if a consumer is eligible for rescission under Section 1635, assignees are liable for rescission even if a disclosure violation is not apparent on the face. Consumers are not limited to seeking rescission from creditors, but may seek rescission against any assignee of the obligation.

An important issue is whether a borrower is entitled to rescind a loan transaction due to the failure to make disclosures. The time period is three years or upon sale of the property, whichever is earlier (TILA Section 1685(f)). The United States Supreme Court treated this rule as law in *Beach v. Ocwen Bank*.[24] The consumer alleged rescission and recoupment

---

[22]*Negrin v. Norwest Mortg., Inc.*, 700 N.Y.S.2d 184 (N.Y. App. Div. 2d Dep't 1999); *Gengo v. Target National Bank*, 513 F. Supp. 2d 842 (S. D. Tex. 2007).

[23]12 CFR § 226.15 (2007); 12 CFR § 23.1 (current through April 9, 2009); *Barker v. Potter*, 232 Fed. Appx. 861 (11th Cir. 2007); *Barrett v. Bank One*, N.A. 511 F. Supp. 2d 836 (E.D. Ky. 2007).

[24]523 U.S. 410 (1998). *See Faust v. Deutsche Bank Natl. Trust Co.*, 353 B.R. 94 (Bankr. E.D. Pa. 2006).

after suit was instituted against the consumer. Plaintiff relied on the Supreme Court decision for its proposition that the consumer's rescission claims are time barred due to the three-year period.

The Supreme Court does not often review a section of the TILA and especially one on recoupment. Recoupment has always been allowed in the framework of consumer matters and survives the expiration of the period provided by a statute of limitations that would otherwise bar recoupment as an independent action. The courts usually held that when the plaintiff's action is timely, a defendant may always raise a claim in recoupment even if it can no longer be brought independently. The purpose of the statute of limitations is to keep stale litigation out of the courts, but if the statute would apply and bar an otherwise legitimate defense to a timely lawsuit, the result would be unfair to the consumer. The issue was whether the time limitation was a statute of limitation and whether it operates, with the lapse of time, to extinguish the right, which is the foundation of the claim, or merely to bar the remedy for its enforcement. Normally, a statute of limitations provides that an action may or must be brought within a certain period of time.

The Court held that a statutory right of rescission could cloud a bank's title on a foreclosure and that the three-year time limit on rescission was not in the nature of the statute of limitations, but was a total bar to the claim itself. The court held that the Act permits no right to rescind, defensively or otherwise, after the three-year period has expired. If the creditor has not complied with the TILA, and the consumer had not asserted his right to rescission within the three years under the Act, the consumer forfeits his right to rescind, whether he is being sued for foreclosure or otherwise.

The Supreme Court apparently took this definitive action because the right to rescind was such a powerful weapon of the consumer and a three-year period to assert that right is more than sufficient. Furthermore, no evidence appeared in the Congressional Record indicating the nature of the statute of limitations, as opposed to the fact that the right itself will be taken away at the expiration of the three-year period.[25]

The plaintiff claimed the bank violated the TILA by failing to notify them of their right to rescind for a three-day period. Plaintiff contended the bank's notice was defective because it expired before consummation of the transaction. Section 125 of the TILA provides as follows:

> . . . the obligor (consumer) shall have the right to rescind the transaction until midnight of the third business day following the consummation of the transaction or the delivery of the information and Rescission forms required under this section together with a statement containing the material disclosures required under this chapter whichever is later. . . .

[25]*Fidler v. Central Coop. Bank (In re Fidler)*, 226 B.R. 734 (Bankr. D. Mass. 1998).

If the lender fails to supply the notice of the right to rescind or fails to disclose the regulation, the obligor has three years from the consummation of the loan to rescind.

Consummation. The regulation defines "consummation" as the time that a consumer becomes contractually obligated on credit transactions. The defendants argued that there was no mutual consent until they signed the property improvement agreement and addendum. The court pointed out that the bank offered them a $460,000 loan by the use of a loan commitment letter and that the plaintiffs expressly accepted the essential terms of that offer. The acceptance of the letter of commitment was sufficient consideration under California contract law. The court thereafter held that the loan agreement actually took place when the loan commitment was signed, and not when the property-improvement agreement was signed five days later.

The court defined consummation as the time the consumer becomes contractually obligated in a credit transaction. It certainly can be argued that accepting a commitment letter does obligate the party to perform the terms of the commitment letter and ultimately to execute the improvement agreement. On the other hand, if the loan-commitment letter was breached, the only liability would be the damages for breach of the loan-commitment letter. The lender would have a cause of action for the damages sustained by not granting the loan and having the debtor execute the property-improvement agreements. Executing a loan commitment letter does not make the debtor liable on the credit transaction, but only liable for damages for breaching the loan-commitment letter. Obviously these arguments were not adopted by the Circuit Court of Appeals for the Ninth Circuit in California.[26]

Where a contract expressly states that the buyer becomes contractually obligated upon signing the contract, execution by the buyer constitutes consummation of the contract for the purposes of the TILA.

The issue of the right to rescission in a refinancing reached the Sixth Circuit Court of Appeals and the trial court's decision was reversed.[27] The trial court held that the right of rescission does *not* apply to a refinancing. The Appellate Court for the Sixth Circuit held that no statute prohibits a borrower from exercising the unexpired right to rescind a loan refinancing.

The Eleventh Circuit took the position that even where the agreement contained a condition that neither party was bound until the dealer sold the loan to a lender, the consummation of the contract took place when the contract was signed.[28] To allow the dealer to wait until the contract was

---

[26]*Larson v. California Federal Bank*, 76 F.3d 387 (9th Cir. 1996).

[27]*Barrett v. JP Morgan Chase Bank, N.A.*, 445 F.3d 874 (6th Cir. 2006).

[28]*Bragg et al v. Bill Heard Chevrolet, Inc.*, 374 F.3d 1060 (11th Cir. 2004); *Nigh v. Koons Buick Pontiac GMC, Inc.*, 319 F.3d 119 (4th Cir. 2003); *Cannon v. Metro Ford, Inc.*, 242 F. Supp. 2d 1322 (S.D. Fla. 2002); *Bryson v. Bank of NY*, 584 F. Supp. 1306 (S.D.N.Y. 1984).

sold would not serve the purposes of the TILA to assure meaningful disclosure of credit terms to consumers so they may make an informed choice in obtaining credit. The dealer did not want to disclose the finance terms until such time as he sold the contract to a lender.

In one recent case the plaintiff exercised his statutory 3-day right to cancel a loan subject to the Truth in Lending Act by forwarding a notice that he wishes to rescind the transaction.

Under the TILA the creditor must act on notice of rescission within 20 days of receiving notice. A suit may lie for failure to comply providing it is brought within one year from the date of occurrence of the violation. The debtor alleged that it was a continuing violation because he wrote letters and attempted to contact the lender as to why they did not act on his notice of rescission. The debtor alleged the "continuing violation" theory entitled him to be exempt from the one-year statute.

The failure of the creditor to take corrective measures does not start the limitation period. The court held that the consumer by waiting more than one year after *the date the notice was sent* is barred by the Statute of Limitations.[29]

PERIODIC STATEMENTS

Periodic statements must be sent to the consumer at the end of each billing cycle, if a finance charge has been imposed during the cycle, or if an outstanding debit of more than a dollar remains at the end of the cycle. If no amount is owing, no statement need be sent.[30]

The periodic statement must contain the following:[31]

1. Credit balance.
2. Identification of all transactions.
3. Listing of all credit relating to credit extensions together with other types of credits.
4. Disclosure of any periodic rates that may be used to compute the finance charge, whether or not applied during the cycle.
5. Identification of the balance on which the finance charge is computed.
6. Whether any split rates were charged on the balance.
7. The total finance charge amount for the plan is not required, but each type of finance charge imposed during the cycle must be separately itemized.

---

[29]*Percival v. American Home Mortg. Corp.*, 469 F. Supp. 2d 409 (N.D. Tex. 2007).
[30]12 CFR § 226.7.
[31]12 CFR § 226.7(a).

8. The annual percentage rate.
9. Any other charges actually imposed during the cycle.
10. The closing date of the billing cycle.
11. If applicable, the time within which the new balance shall be paid (a "free ride").
12. The address to send any notice of billing errors.
13. The general purpose address. A telephone number may or may not be included, but the address must be included and must be clear and conspicuous.

The periodic statement must itemize and identify by type the amount of any other finance charges debited to the account and the dollar amount of the finance charge added during the billing cycle. The term "finance charge" must be used. The commentary emphasizes other charges which must be disclosed (not finance charges), such as membership fees, late charges, charges for exceeding credit limit, taxes, and charges in connection with real estate transactions.

SALE CREDIT

Sale credit is defined as using a credit card to buy goods, whereas non-sale credit is defined as using a credit card to obtain cash advances or overdraft checking. The commentary lists separate sale credit rules and non-sale credit rules.

BILLING RIGHTS

At least once a year the creditor must send a statement of the statutory protections for billing errors and disclose to the consumer the claims and defenses available to credit card users.[32]

CHANGE IN TERMS

Any change in terms must be communicated to the consumer at least 15 days before the change or modification takes effect. The commentary sets forth changes that require the 15-day notice as well as those which do not. The 15-day notice does not have to be provided if the consumer's liability or obligation is not affected.[33]

---

[32]12 CFR § 226.9.

[33]*Kurz v. Chase Manhattan Bank USA, N.A.*, 319 F. Supp. 2d 457 (S.D.N.Y. 2004).

CREDIT BALANCES

When a credit balance in excess of $1.00 is created in an open-end transaction, it shall be credited to the consumer's account or any part refunded upon request. A good faith effort to refund to the consumer by cash, check, or money order, or credit to a deposit account of the consumer with respect to any part of the credit balance remaining in the account for more than six months, must be made. If the consumer's current location is not known, no further action is required by the creditor.[34]

DISCLOSURE ON RENEWAL

The creditor must provide the cardholder with notice of renewal at least 30 days, or one billing cycle, before the renewal date.

CLOSED-END CREDIT

All consumer credit is treated as closed-end credit unless it meets the definition of open-end credit. In a typical closed-end credit transaction, credit is advanced for a specific time period and the amount financed, finance charge, and scheduled payments are agreed upon between the lender and the customer. Closed-end credit covers almost all credit transactions, except credit cards and other credit extensions which meet the criteria of open-end credit or revolving credit.

The time of disclosure for a closed-end transaction must be before the consummation of the transaction. The disclosure should reflect the terms of the obligations between the parties. Disclosure statements are to be designed so the consumer can understand any mathematical computation and to provide an easy basis for comparing the cost of credit offered by other competitors. As in open-end credit, finance charges and the APR must be displayed in a clear and conspicuous manner.

PAYMENT SCHEDULE

The number of payments, the amount of each payment, and the timing of the payment schedule to repay the obligation must be disclosed. Usually the due date for the first payment is disclosed, when each subsequent payment is due, and the amount of time between the payments, such as monthly or quarterly payments. The total of all the payments must be set

---

[34] 12 CFR § 226.21.

forth. The provisions for pre-payment must be disclosed in the event of a penalty or other charges.

LATE PAYMENT CHARGES

Late payment charges should include the right to accelerate the debt in favor of the creditor, any fees imposed for collection costs including attorneys' fees or repossession charges and, of course, the charge for making a late payment.[35]

DETRIMENTAL RELIANCE—ACTUAL DAMAGES

To claim actual damages under the TILA, the plaintiff must demonstrate reliance on the inaccurate disclosures and be prevented from obtaining better terms elsewhere—"detrimental reliance." The wording in the statute states that plaintiff is entitled to "any actual damages sustained . . . as a result of a TILA violation." The statute provides for statutory damages, for it may be difficult to prove actual damages. In addition to detrimental reliance, the consumer must show that he or she suffered a loss, because he or she relied on an inaccurate or incomplete disclosure statement. A causal link between the financing institution's non-compliance and the damages sustained must be demonstrated.[36]

LIABILITY OF ASSIGNEE

Section 1641(a) of the TILA states as follows:

> Except as otherwise specifically provided in this title, any civil action for a violation of this title or proceeding under section 108 which may be brought against a creditor may be maintained against any assignee of such creditor only if the violation for which such action or proceeding is brought is apparent on the face of the disclosure statement, except where the assignment was involuntary. For the purpose of this section, a violation apparent on the face of the disclosure statement includes, but is not limited to (1) a disclosure which can be determined to be incomplete or inaccurate from the face of the disclosure statement or other documents assigned, or (2) a disclosure which does not use the terms required to be used by this title.

---

[35]12 CFR § 226.18(e).

[36]*Turner v. Beneficial Corp.*, 242 F.3d 1023 (11th Cir. 2001); *Vikers v. Home Federal Sav. & Loan Ass'n*, 4 N.Y.S.2d 201 (4th Dep't 1978).

Except as provided in Section 125(c), in any action or proceeding by or against any subsequent assignee of the original creditor without knowledge to the contrary by the assignee when he acquires the obligation, written acknowledgment of receipt by a person to whom a statement is required to be given pursuant to this title shall be conclusive proof of the delivery thereof and, except as provided in subsection (a), of compliance with this chapter. This section does not affect the rights of the obligor in any action against the original creditor.

Any consumer who has the right to rescind a transaction under Section 125 may rescind the transaction as against any assignee of the obligation.

"Apparent on the face" means exactly that—for an assignee to be liable under TILA, the violation must be apparent on the face of the assigned disclosure documents. The courts have rejected the concept that even though the violation is not apparent on the face, the assignee owes a duty of diligent inquiry. Even in the situation where there were related loan documents or checks and credits that may have revealed the true cost of the warranty as well as the amount paid to the parties, the violation was not reflected on the face of the documents and required the court to resort to evidence or documents extraneous to the disclosure statement.

A Circuit Court of Appeals also concluded that it would examine only assigned documents to determine liability, even though the additional information to determine the violation was publicly available in the form of state licensing fee tables. Even though the fee tables may be available to the public, those tables do not constitute an "assigned document." In a Court of Appeals decision in the Third Circuit, the court analyzed the prior decisions in other circuits and continued to apply the same strict, narrow interpretation applied to this particular section. The plaintiff conceded at oral argument that liability cannot be created by knowledge. Plaintiff attempted to draw a distinction between constructive knowledge, which she contended would be insufficient, and actual knowledge, which she asserted was sufficient to support assignee liability. The court disagreed. Nothing appeared in the history of the text to support such a premise.

The Federal Trade Commission (FTC) required "holder notice" was included in the retail installment contract and this provided assignee liability with regard to "all claims and defenses which the debtor could assert against the seller." The plaintiff then asserted that the retail installment contract should be enforced as written. But several courts, in addition to this court, have already held that the holder notice language standing alone does not suffice to subject an assignee to liability. The notice could not have such an affect, because inclusion of the required language did not result from bargaining or agreement by the parties to reflect a voluntary and intentional assumption of liability. It cannot be considered voluntarily when the statute requires that a failure to include the holder notice is an unfair and deceptive act. The holder notice is a mandatory clause that must be included because of the actual law.[37]

INSURANCE

If the creditor is attempting to sell credit insurance, disability insurance, or property insurance, the premiums should be properly disclosed to exclude them from the finance charge. If the creditor chooses to include the premium in the finance charge, disclosure is not necessary. If the disclosures are not in compliance with the Act, an incomplete disclosure results and the charge then would have to be included in the finance charge.

ADVERTISEMENT

An advertisement is any commercial method that promotes consumer credit or lease transactions, including newspaper, radio, television, Internet websites, display, point-of-sale literature, price tags, or billboards. Advertising applies to both closed-end credit and open-end credit.[38]

Certain triggering terms (*see* list of examples) and finance rates in advertising copy require disclosure of major terms, including the APR. The rule is intended to insure that all important terms of the credit plan, not just the most attractive terms, appear in an advertisement.

The Act identifies certain words and phrases (the triggering terms) used in advertisement to promote credit which will activate the operation of the TILA with which the creditor must comply.

Examples of triggering terms for closed-end credit are as follows:

a. The amount of down payment:
    1. 10 percent down.
    2. $1,000 down.
    3. 90 percent financing.
    4. Trade-in with $1,000 appraised value.
b. The amount of any payment:
    1. Monthly payments of less than $250 on all our loan plans.

---

[37] *Ramadan v. Chase Manhattan Corp.*, 229 F.3d 194 (3d Cir. 2000); *Green v. Levis Motors, Inc.*, 179 F.3d 286 (5th Cir. 1999); *Ellis v. General Motors Acceptance Corp.*, 160 F.3d 703 (11th Cir. 1998); *Taylor v. Quality Hyundai, Inc.*, 150 F.3d 689 (7th Cir. 1998).

[38] 12 CFR § 226.24.

   2. Pay $30 per $1,000 amount borrowed.
   3. $400 per month.

c. The number of payments or the period of repayment:
   1. Up to four years to pay.
   2. Forty-eight months to pay.
   3. 30-year mortgage available.

d. The amount of any finance charge:
   1. Financing less than $300 per year.
   2. Less than $1,200 interest.
   3. $2 monthly carrying charge.

An advertisement using a triggering term must include the APR, the term of repayment, and the down payment (percentage or amount). The advertisement must state the APR, even if it is the same as the interest rate, and this rate must be identified as the APR, as distinguished from the interest rate.[39] Many consumer groups continually argue that the disclosures are meaningless because a consumer does not have enough time to read the entire disclosure on television.

The APR must be disclosed accurately and must include any finance charges such as points, mortgage insurance premiums, etc. Where variable rates are used or the rates may change in the future, an APR as of a specified date or an estimated APR is permissible.[40]

Advertisements of variable rates should state that the rate may increase or is subject to change. Merely identifying a "graduated payment adjustable mortgage" is insufficient without a statement that the rate itself may increase or is subject to change.

RECORD RETENTION

A creditor shall retain records for at least two years after the date of disclosures.[41]

CONSUMER LEASE

A consumer lease is a lease of personal property, such as an automobile or boat, to a private individual. The lease must be for personal,

[39]TIL Sec. 107.
[40]12 CFR § 226.22.
[41]12 CFR § 226.25.

family, or household purposes and must be for a term of more than four months. Renting a car for a weekend is not a consumer lease. The term excludes leases where the customer pays more than $25,000, but includes leases in which the customer has an option to buy at the end of the lease. A lease in which the payments equal or exceed the value of the property and which allows the consumer to buy the property at the end of the lease for a nominal payment is actually a closed-end credit sale and not a consumer lease. The advertising requirements under consumer leases follow in general the open-end and closed-end credit disclosures.

ARBITRATION

A case in the Ninth Circuit Court (California) reinforces the concept that the use of arbitration provisions in lending agreements is not a violation of the TILA and will be enforced in accordance with federal law. Under federal law an agreement to arbitrate is valid, irrevocable, and enforceable. The Court held that an agreement to arbitrate was not unconscionable despite the fact the terms were not explained to the plaintiffs. The arbitration agreement was not unfair merely because the agreement shields the defendant from class action suits or suits brought on behalf of the general public.[42] (*See* Chapter 5.)

In one particular case,[43] the court stated,

> We know of no case holding that parties dealing at arm's length have a duty to explain to each other the terms of a written contract. We decline to impose such an obligation where the language of the contract clearly and explicitly provides for arbitration of disputes arising out of the contractual relationship.

When the defendants alleged the unconscionability of a contract, the court's response was that an arbitration clause is not "per se" unreasonably favorable to one party over another party. (*See* Chapter 5.)

CRIMINAL LIABILITY

The TILA provides for criminal liability for furnishing false or inaccurate information, for failure to provide information which is required to be disclosed under the provisions of the law, or for using any chart or table

---

[42]*Perry v. Thomas*, 482 U.S. 483, 107 S. Ct. 2520 (1987); *Meyers v. United Home Loan Inc.*, 1993 WL 307747 (N.D. Cal. 1993).

[43]*Perry v. Thomas*, 482 U.S. 483, 107 S. Ct. 2520, 96 L. Ed. 2d 426 (1987); *Meyers v. United Home Loan, Inc.*, No. C-93-1783 MHP, 1993 WL 307747 (N.D. Cal. Aug. 4, 1993).

in such a manner as to consistently understate the APR. The penalty shall be a fine of not more than $5,000, or imprisonment for not more than one year, or both.

STATE LAW

Approximately 30 states have some form of Truth in Lending law which affects interest, usury, credit granting, revolving credit, insurance, banking, or motor vehicle installment credit, etc. The state legislation exempts certain businesses and determines the transactions subject to the TILA.[44]

State law requirements are preempted if they are inconsistent with the federal Act. The federal law prevails if the state law is more lenient. State laws may provide rights, responsibilities, and procedures for consumers and creditors different from those required by the federal law. If the state law adds additional obligations, the creditor must comply with the state law. A careful review of the state law should be performed.

HOME EQUITY

Throughout the regulations specific divisions apply directly to home equity loans and other types of secured mortgage financing. These sections are only applicable to the situation where security is provided by the consumer to the lender, and are not applicable to open-end or closed-end credit transactions.

INTEREST AND COSTS

The cost of liability insurance paid for by a lender and added to the balance of the loan was not considered interest by the Court of Appeals for the Seventh Circuit. There is a distinction between fees which compensate the bank for extending credit and fees which reimburse the bank for the actual costs extended.[45]

The Seventh Circuit also decided that the providers of insurance premium financing are subject to the disclosure requirements of the TILA.[46]

---

[44]12 CFR § 226.29.

[45]*Doe v. Norwest bank Minnesota, N.A.*, 107 F.3d 1297 (8th Cir. 1997); *Richardson v. National City Bank of Evansville*, 141 F.3d 1228 (7th Cir. 1998).

[46]*Autry v. Northwest Premium Services, Inc.*, 144 F.3d 1037 (7th Cir. 1998).

A case confirmed that if you offer credit cards with an introductory interest rate and a higher interest rate for cash advances, and that information is disclosed in a solicitation letter and even referred the reader to the back of letter for a comprehensive list of the terms of the agreement, such a solicitation letter provides adequate disclosure.[47]

STATUTE OF LIMITATIONS

The Real Estate Settlement Procedures Act (RESPA) and the TILA (TILA) contain a one-year statute of limitations; but the courts do allow what they have labeled "equitable tolling." Fraudulent concealment denotes efforts by the defendant to prevent the plaintiff from suing on time and if the defendant lending institution engages in this type of conduct, the courts may allow equitable tolling and permit the debtor to commence suit beyond the statute of limitations of one year.

In the case at hand, the court did not find any of the defendants engaged in the fraudulent conduct beyond the alleged violations themselves.[48] (*See* Disclosure—Right of Rescission.)

PLEADING SUGGESTIONS

We suggest that when a suit is started on a credit card, the complaint contain not only a count for breach of contract but also a count for monies loaned as well as account stated. The reason for the count for monies loaned is that sometimes the original credit card agreement is not available or the debtor never signed a credit card agreement because the debtor merely responded to a solicitation to use a credit card. In those cases, a contract action would not be appropriate and the complaint should be confined to a count for monies loaned and an account stated. Monies loaned alleges that the debtor made purchases on credit or obtained cash advances by using his credit card to be repaid in installments depending upon the terms of the credit card agreement.

In some states, this type of pleading enables a creditor (a lender) to be successful without producing a copy of the signed agreement, because it is not an essential piece of evidence to prove your case. Reliance is placed on the debtor's course of conduct, which is the act of signing for the charges and repaying the monies.

As to the account stated, the creditor must allege that it was their normal business practice to mail itemized monthly billing statements to

---

[47] *Wilson v. First Union Nat'l Bank of Georgia*, No. 2961439, 1998 WL 151646 (Ala. Civ. App. Apr. 3, 1998).

[48] *Thomas v. Ocwen Fed. Bank*, 2002 U.S. Dist. LEXIS 1231 (N.D. Ill. Jan. 23, 2002).

its cardholders and that the debtor retained the statements without objection, in writing, for over 60 days from the date of the disputed statements. The debtor's acceptance of the charges can be inferred from the fact that the debtor continued to use the credit card, made partial payments, and never attempted to cancel the agreement during the period despite having received the statements for several months.

Under Section 15 U.S.C. Section 1666 and Regulation Z Subsection 226-13(b)(1)-1 of the TILA, a debtor has 60 days from receipt of disputed charges to notify the creditor in writing of a billing error to preserve his rights. If the defendant fails to object in writing pursuant to their rights to dispute the bill, the debtor has waived the right to dispute the balance. The case of *Minskoff v. American Express Travel Related Servs. Co.*[49] stated as follows:

> Once a cardholder has established a credit card account, and provided that the card issuer is in compliance with the billing statement disclosure requirements of 15 U.S.C. 1637, the cardholder is in a superior position to determine whether the charges reflected on his regular billing statements are legitimate. A cardholder's failure to examine credit card statement, that would reveal fraudulent use of the card, constitutes a negligent omission that creates apparent authority for charges that would otherwise be considered unauthorized under TILA. (*See TransAmerica*, 325 N.W.2d at 215.)

The negligent omission to dispute any charges in a timely manner prevents the debtor from disputing the charges at a later date. Defendant's course of performance in using the card and/or making partial payments demonstrated a willingness to repay the obligation. This duty to review the terms and conditions are set forth in every credit card agreement. The creditor need not produce signed charge receipts if the debtor did not timely dispute the charge. In today's economy, many charges take place without a signed receipt, such as on-line purchases for airline tickets and telephone purchases.

DEBT PURCHASERS—MONTHLY STATEMENT

A decision from the Seventh Circuit Court of Appeals has made life a little easier for debt purchasers. Under the TILA, only creditors are required to send consumers monthly billing statements. The plaintiff argued that the purchaser of the credit card accounts became subject to the TILA when they purchased the accounts. The debt purchaser did not issue a credit card nor was it an agent of the issuer of the credit card. The Seventh Circuit stated that the Truth in Lending Law applies only to

---

[49] 98 F.3d 703 (2d Cir. 1996); *TransAmerica*, 325 N.W.2d at 215.

creditors and the defendant's had no obligation to send monthly statements to the debtor since no contractual relationship existed between the original card issuer and the debt purchaser.

The assignee stands in the place of the assignor, and should be required to undertake the obligations of the assignor, whether they are contractual or statutory—a surprisingly favorable, but weak decision, by the liberal Seventh Circuit.[50]

COLLECTION OF INTEREST. An interesting case from Minnesota examined an assignment agreement wherein "a debt buyer purchased all right, title and interest of the seller in and to the certain receivables, judgments or evidence of debt described in Exhibit 1" consisting of credit card debt. The debt buyer referred the debt to their attorney and the demand letter routinely added interest to the debt.

The Minnesota court chose to address the "plain meaning" of the wording in the contract and stated that the term "receivable" referred to an amount owed, and does not refer to interest not yet accrued or future attorneys' fees. The amount owed at the time of the assignment was the only amount that the debt buyer could collect. No explicit language was evident that the debt buyer was assigned the rights to collect interest and attorneys' fees. The moral of story is that despite the fact that an assignee stands in the shoes of the assignor and thus can rely on the original contract, the court seemed to feel that specific language should be used covering attorneys fees and interest. While it is questionable whether other courts will follow this particular reasoning, debt buyers should pay more attention to the drafting, especially in Minnesota.[51]

SUPREME COURT DECISIONS—DAMAGE CAPS

The Supreme Court of the United States addressed a decision which removed the damage caps in U.S.C. § 16409(a)(2)(a)(i) and (a)(ii). The amendment to the law created significant confusion because it increased the damage cap to $2,000, but at the same time allowed damages for deception in extending credit to twice the amount of the finance charge in the transaction. Justice Ginsburg commented that "less than the meticulous drafting" of the amendment created confusion, notwithstanding prior to the 1995 amendment, the final clause establishing the $1,000 maximum damage applied to deception in extending credit under 15 U.S.C. § 1640(a)(2)(a)(i) and (a)(ii).

---

[50]*Neff v. Capital Acquisitions and Management Company*, 352 F.3d 1118 (7th Cir. 2003).
[51]*Munoz v. Pipestone Financial, LLC*, 397 F. Supp. 2d 1129 (D.C. Minn. 2005).

The Supreme Court has ruled the multiple of the finance charges will not be applicable for a violation of the TILA under this section.[52]

ADVERSE ACTION NOTICES—FTC MANUAL

The FTC has issued a manual for creditors entitled "How to Write Adverse Action Notices," and it is available free from the FTC. Obtaining a copy of this manual is recommended for any creditor extending credit.

COMPLIANCE OFFICER

Most lending institutions engage a legal compliance officer to be certain that the provisions and the forms of the TILA and Regulation Z are fully complied with and no firm should embark on this form of lending without a careful review of the law and consultation with an experienced attorney.

FAIR CREDIT BILLING

Prior to the "consumer decade" of the 1970s, many major credit grantors ignored debtors' requests regarding billing errors. Frequently, a complaint by the consumer to the credit grantor, department store, credit card issuer, bank, or financial institution would be disregarded, or a form response would be used, stating that the consumer's questions would be reviewed in due course. As a result, consumers never received adequate answers and, in many instances, credit standings were severely impaired by this lack of attention. The creditor continued efforts to collect the debt from the consumer by mailing statements demanding payment. If the consumer failed to pay the erroneous balance due, the collection agency or law firm entered the picture and dunned the consumer with letters and telephone calls. In many cases, the debt was paid despite the fact that the creditor was not entitled to payment. Congress did not overlook this problem when it passed the TILA (*see* Chapter 16), a portion of which has become known as the Fair Credit Billing Act.

The Fair Credit Billing Act prohibits a creditor from engaging in any effort to collect the balance due without first responding to a consumer dispute or request for information by providing a full response and explanation. The Act also addresses other minor abuses. The creditor must treat

---

[52]*Koons Buick Pontiac GMC, Inc. v. Nigh*, 543 U.S. 50 (2004), *rev'g Nigh v. Koons Buick Pontiac GMC Inc.*, 319 F.3d 119 (4th Cir. 2003).

the consumer in a fair and equitable manner when computing billing and balances.

The Act deals with credit card accounts (open-end credits) as to billing errors, the ability of the consumer to correct billing errors, and the prohibition of credit card issuers from ignoring the complaints of the consumer.[53]

Agreements payable in more than four installments or for which the payment of a finance charge is or may be required are covered under the Fair Credit Billing Act.

Consumer Action. To trigger the obligation of the creditor under the Fair Credit Billing Act, the consumer must send a notice "in writing." *An oral notification is insufficient.* The creditor must not mislead or deceive the consumer into believing that a telephone call is sufficient notice. Printing on the monthly statement that all complaints and billing errors will be resolved if the consumer contacts the creditor by using a certain telephone number would constitute a violation of the Act.

Notification. When a creditor, within 60 days after having sent a bill to the purchaser, receives a written notice from the purchaser which sets forth any one or more of the following:

1. information permitting the mailer to identify the name, address and account number,
2. a claim that there is a billing error,
3. the reasons for the billing error,
4. a statement that the charge made to the consumer was not incurred by the consumer,
5. a statement that the consumer requests clarification and documentary evidence to support the clarification,
6. an allegation that goods have not been delivered to the consumer in accordance with the purchase order,
7. a statement that the creditor failed to reflect a payment or credit made by this consumer,
8. a computation error,
9. any other computation, delivery, or billing error,

the creditor shall, unless the debtor has, after giving such written notice, and before the expiration of the time limits set forth herein, agreed that the billing statement was correct:

[53]15 U.S.C. § 1666; *W.T. Grant Company v. C.I.R.*, 483 F.2d 1115 (2d Cir. 1973); 33 Business Lawyer 981 (1978).

1. not later than 30 days after receipt of notice, send a written acknowledgement unless the action in subdivision B is taken within such 30-day period;
2. not later than two complete billing cycles, and in no event later than ninety days after the receipt of the notice:
   a. make the appropriate corrections and notify the debtor of the corrections and explanations thereof, and if the debtor requests, provide copies of documentary evidence of the debtor's indebtedness; and
   b. after an investigation, send a written explanation or clarification setting forth the reasons why the creditor believes the account is correct, and upon request of the debtor, provide copies of the documentary evidence of the debtor's obligation.

The creditor has only two choices: either correct the error and notify the debtor or send a written explanation of why the debtor is wrong. If the creditor resolves the dispute during this procedure, no further notification to the debtor is necessary. During this period of time, the creditor may not impose additional charges, but the creditor may reduce the credit limit by the amount in dispute. If the creditor reports to a credit reporting agency, the matter must be communicated to the agency as a disputed account.

Moratorium on Collection Activity. The law requires the creditor to respond to the consumer complaint before commencing any collection activity. During the period that the creditor does not respond to the consumer, collection activity must be suspended by the creditor and cannot be recommenced until after compliance with the provisions of the Act.[54]

Failure to Comply. A creditor who fails to comply with the above provisions forfeits any right to collect the amount of the error, including any finance charges. The creditor may not directly or indirectly threaten to report any person adversely to a credit reporting agency because of the consumer's failure to pay the amount of the billing error until the creditor has complied with all the conditions of the Act. If, after receiving the explanation from the creditor, the consumer continues to claim that the amount is still in dispute, the creditor may not report the amount as delinquent to any third party, unless the creditor also reports that the amount is in dispute and notifies the consumer of the name and address of the third party or the credit reporting agency. Naturally, a resolution of the dispute must be reported.

---

[54] 15 U.S.C. § 1666.

Consumer Defense. The card issuer is subject to all defenses asserted by the consumer against the seller of the goods or provider of the service. For example, the consumer purchases a toaster for $55. The purchaser uses her credit card. The toaster does not operate properly in that the toast is ejected before it is toasted. The credit card issuer cannot ignore this defense even if the toaster is not returned, and cannot charge the credit card account for the $55 after notification by the consumer of the existence of this defense (15 U.S.C. § 1666i). In order for the consumer to take advantage of these provisions in the Act, the following conditions must be met:

1. The consumer has made a good faith attempt to resolve the dispute with the merchant.
2. The amount of the transaction exceeds $50.
3. The place where the initial transaction occurred was in the same state as the mailing address provided by the cardholder or was within 100 miles from the address.

If the card issuer and merchant are one and the same or the merchant is under the direct control of the card issuer, there is but one creditor and the above requirement of a good faith attempt to resolve the dispute does not apply.

Finance Charges. The consumer is entitled to a window of 14 days to pay before a finance charge is imposed. A statement including the amount upon which the finance charge is based must be mailed at least 14 days prior to the date specified in the statement by which payment must be made.[55] If an open-end consumer credit plan provides a time period within which a debtor may repay any portion of the credit extended without an additional finance charge, such a charge may not be imposed unless a statement is mailed within 14 days prior to the time period specified.

Credit Balance. Credit balances in excess of one dollar should be refunded to the consumer upon written request. Every effort should be made to refund credit balances every six months or upon request. Each state has separate laws concerning credit balances and the creditor should consult with counsel as to specific requirements for its state.[56]

Cash Discounts. The credit card issuer may not enter into any agreement with a merchant to prohibit the merchant from offering a discount to a consumer to pay by cash rather than by credit card. If the

---

[55] 15 U.S.C. § 1666b.
[56] 15 U.S.C. § 1666d.

discount offered by the merchant is less than 5 percent, it shall not be considered a finance charge as determined under the TILA.

UNAUTHORIZED USE OF A CREDIT CARD. A consumer is liable only up to $50 for the "unauthorized use" of a credit card, defined as someone using the credit card with no authority to do so and where the card holder has not received the merchandise or the service offered. To utilize this limited liability, the consumer must notify the credit card issuer.

The credit card issuer initially approving the credit card account must advise the consumer of:

1. the limitation of liability up to $50.
2. the method the consumer should use to notify the creditor as to the loss of the card.

Most credit card accounts provide for oral notification to any employee of the credit card issuer[57] by use of an identified telephone number. The consumer can use someone else authorized by the consumer to notify the credit card issuer.

CONSUMER'S STATEMENTS. Some companies routinely print the entire Fair Credit Billing Act word for word on the back of customers' statements, or the Act may be rephrased.

PROMPT POSTING. All payments must be posted promptly if identifiable.[58]

SELLER OBLIGATION. A seller who accepts a return of merchandise or issues credit for services must notify the credit card issuer promptly so that the consumer's account is credited.[59]

OFFSETS. A card issuer, such as a bank, may not deduct monies from a deposit account (bank account) to make payments on the consumer's credit card account unless previously authorized to do so in writing by the cardholder.[60]

UNMATCHED FUNDS. Unmatched accounts sometimes include credit balances, unclaimed refunds, unclaimed vouchers, or unclaimed bonus certificates. The customer has moved, has left for parts unknown, or, for whatever reason, cannot be located. As a result, the credit balance

---

[57]A debit card or check guarantee card is not covered by this section of the Fair Credit Billing Act.

[58]15 U.S.C. § 1666c.

[59]15 U.S.C. § 1666c.

[60]15 U.S.C. § 1666h.

cannot be refunded. This occurs when companies go out of business and no bankruptcy is filed. Gift certificates and credit vouchers which are never cashed fall into this category.

Most states require the above items to be treated as abandoned property and refunded to the state after a specified period of time. The laws vary from state to state and consultation with counsel is recommended.[61]

> ***Credit & Collection Tip:*** *Have a carefully prepared manual for use by your staff which sets forth the procedures necessary to comply with the Fair Credit Billing Act. An investigation commenced by an administrative agency always begins with a request for records and documents. Furnishing the commission with a procedural manual prepared for use by the staff is a positive step in the right direction. If human error occurred on the part of an employee, you will have shown a good faith intent to comply with the Act.*

---

[61] *American Express Co. v. Koerner,* 452 U.S. 233 (1981); *Mourning v. Family Publications Service, Inc.,* 411 U.S. 356 (1973); *Gary v. American Express Co.,* 743 F.2d 10 (D.C. Cir. 1984); *Lincoln First Bank, N.A. v. Carlson,* 426 N.Y.S.2d 433 (N.Y. Sup. Ct. 1980).

CHAPTER 16
APPENDIX I

TRUTH IN LENDING ACT (TILA)

15 USC 1601-1667f

Sec. 1601.—Congressional findings and declaration of purpose

(a) Informed use of credit
The Congress finds that economic stabilization would be enhanced and the competition among the various financial institutions and other firms engaged in the extension of consumer credit would be strengthened by the informed use of credit. The informed use of credit results from an awareness of the cost thereof by consumers. It is the purpose of this subchapter to assure a meaningful disclosure of credit terms so that the consumer will be able to compare more readily the various credit terms available to him and avoid the uninformed use of credit, and to protect the consumer against inaccurate and unfair credit billing and credit card practices.

(b) Terms of personal property leases
The Congress also finds that there has been a recent trend toward leasing automobiles and other durable goods for consumer use as an alternative to installment credit sales and that these leases have been offered without adequate cost disclosures. It is the purpose of this subchapter to assure a meaningful disclosure of the terms of leases of personal property for personal, family, or household purposes so as to enable the lessee to compare more readily the various lease terms available to him, limit balloon payments in consumer leasing, enable comparison of lease terms with credit terms where appropriate, and to assure meaningful and accurate disclosures of lease terms in advertisements.

Sec. 1602.—Definitions and rules of construction

(a) The definitions and rules of construction set forth in this section are applicable for the purposes of this subchapter.

(b) The term "Board" refers to the Board of Governors of the Federal Reserve System.

(c) The term "organization" means a corporation, government or governmental subdivision or agency, trust, estate, partnership, cooperative, or association.

(d) The term "person" means a natural person or an organization.

(e) The term "credit" means the right granted by a creditor to a debtor to defer payment of debt or to incur debt and defer its payment.

(f) The term "creditor" refers only to a person who both

(1) regularly extends, whether in connection with loans, sales of property or services, or otherwise, consumer credit which is payable by agreement in more than four installments or for which the payment of a finance charge is or may be required, and

(2) is the person to whom the debt arising from the consumer credit transaction is initially payable on the face of the evidence of indebtedness or, if there is no such evidence of indebtedness, by agreement.

Notwithstanding the preceding sentence, in the case of an open-end credit plan involving a credit card, the card issuer and any person who honors the credit card and offers a discount which is a finance charge are creditors. For the purpose of the requirements imposed under part D of this subchapter and sections 1637(a)(5), 1637(a)(6), 1637(a)(7), 1637(b)(1), 1637(b)(2), 1637(b)(3), 1637(b)(8), and 1637(b)(10) of this title, the term "creditor" shall also include card issuers whether or not the amount due is payable by agreement in more than four installments or the payment of a finance charge is or may be required, and the Board shall, by regulation, apply these requirements to such card issuers, to the extent appropriate, even though the requirements are by their terms applicable only to creditors offering open-end credit plans. Any person who originates 2 or more mortgages referred to in subsection (aa) of this section in any 12-month period or any person who originates 1 or more such mortgages through a mortgage broker shall be considered to be a creditor for purposes of this subchapter.

(g) The term "credit sale" refers to any sale in which the seller is a creditor. The term includes any contract in the form of a bailment or lease if the bailee or lessee contracts to pay as compensation for use a sum substantially equivalent to or in excess of the aggregate value of the property and services involved and it is agreed that the bailee or lessee will become, or for no other or a nominal consideration has the option to become, the owner of the property upon full compliance with his obligations under the contract.

(h) The adjective "consumer," used with reference to a credit transaction, characterizes the transaction as one in which the party to whom credit is offered or extended is a natural person, and the money, property, or services which are the subject of the transaction are primarily for personal, family, or household purposes.

(i) The term "open end credit plan" means a plan under which the creditor reasonably contemplates repeated transactions, which prescribes the terms of such transactions, and which provides for a finance charge which may be computed from time to time on the outstanding unpaid balance. A credit plan which is an open end credit plan within the meaning of the preceding sentence is an open end credit plan even if credit information is verified from time to time.

(j) The term "adequate notice," as used in section 1643 of this title, means a printed notice to a cardholder which sets forth the pertinent facts clearly and conspicuously so that a person against whom it is to operate could reasonably be expected to have noticed it and understood its meaning. Such notice may be given to a cardholder by printing the notice on any credit card, or on each periodic statement of account, issued to the cardholder, or by any other means reasonably assuring the receipt thereof by the cardholder.

(k) The term "credit card" means any card, plate, coupon book or other credit device existing for the purpose of obtaining money, property, labor, or services on credit.

(l) The term "accepted credit card" means any credit card which the cardholder has requested and received or has signed or has used, or authorized another to use, for the purpose of obtaining money, property, labor, or services on credit.

(m) The term "cardholder" means any person to whom a credit card is issued or any person who has agreed with the card issuer to pay obligations arising from the issuance of a credit card to another person.

(n) The term "card issuer" means any person who issues a credit card, or the agent of such person with respect to such card.

(o) The term "unauthorized use," as used in section 1643 of this title, means a use of a credit card by a person other than the cardholder who does not have actual, implied, or apparent authority for such use and from which the cardholder receives no benefit.

(p) The term "discount" as used in section 1666f of this title means a reduction made from the regular price. The term "discount" as used in section 1666f of this title shall not mean a surcharge.

(q) The term "surcharge" as used in this section and section 1666f of this title means any means of increasing the regular price to a cardholder which is not imposed upon customers paying by cash, check, or similar means."

(r) The term "State" refers to any State, the Commonwealth of Puerto Rico, the District of Columbia, and any territory or possession of the United States.

(s) The term "agricultural purposes" includes the production, harvest, exhibition, marketing, transportation, processing, or manufacture of agricultural products by a natural person who cultivates, plants, propagates, or nurtures those agricultural products, including but not limited to the acquisition of farmland, real property with a farm residence, and personal property and services used primarily in farming.

(t) The term "agricultural products" includes agricultural, horticultural, viticultural, and dairy products, livestock, wildlife, poultry, bees, forest products, fish and shellfish, and any products thereof, including processed and manufactured products, and any and all products raised or produced on farms and any processed or manufactured products thereof.

(u) The term "material disclosures" means the disclosure, as required by this subchapter, of the annual percentage rate, the method of determining the finance charge and the balance upon which a finance charge will be imposed, the amount of the finance charge, the amount to be financed, the total of payments, the number and amount of payments, the due dates or periods of payments scheduled to repay the indebtedness, and the disclosures required by section 1639(a) of this title.

(v) The term "dwelling" means a residential structure or mobile home which contains one to four family housing units, or individual units of condominiums or cooperatives.

(w) The term "residential mortgage transaction" means a transaction in which a mortgage, deed of trust, purchase money security interest arising under an installment sales contract, or equivalent consensual security interest is created or retained against the consumer's dwelling to finance the acquisition or initial construction of such dwelling.

(x) As used in this section and section 1666f of this title, the term "regular price" means the tag or posted price charged for the property or service if a single price is tagged or posted, or the price charged for the property or service when payment is made by use of an open-end credit plan or a credit card if either

(1) no price is tagged or posted, or

(2) two prices are tagged or posted, one of which is charged when payment is made by use of an open-end credit plan or a credit card and the other when payment is made by use of cash, check, or similar means. For purposes of this definition, payment by check, draft, or other negotiable instrument which may result in the debiting of an open-end credit plan or a credit cardholder's open-end account shall not be considered payment made by use of the plan or the account.

(y) Any reference to any requirement imposed under this subchapter or any provision thereof includes reference to the regulations of the Board under this subchapter or the provision thereof in question.

(z) The disclosure of an amount or percentage which is greater than the amount or percentage required to be disclosed under this subchapter does not in itself constitute a violation of this subchapter.

(aa) (1) A mortgage referred to in this subsection means a consumer credit transaction that is secured by the consumer's principal dwelling, other than a residential mortgage transaction, a reverse mortgage transaction, or a transaction under an open end credit plan, if—

(A) the annual percentage rate at consummation of the transaction will exceed by more than 10 percentage points the yield on Treasury securities having comparable periods of maturity on the fifteenth day of the month immediately preceding the month in which the application for the extension of credit is received by the creditor; or

(B) the total points and fees payable by the consumer at or before closing will exceed the greater of—

(i) 8 percent of the total loan amount; or

(ii) $400.

(2) (A) After the 2-year period beginning on the effective date of the regulations promulgated under section 155 of the Riegle Community Development and Regulatory Improvement Act of 1994, and no more frequently than biennially after the first increase or decrease under this subparagraph, the Board may by regulation increase or decrease the number of percentage points specified in paragraph (1)(A), if the Board determines that the increase or decrease is—

(i) consistent with the consumer protections against abusive lending provided by the amendments made by subtitle B of title I of the Riegle Community Development and Regulatory Improvement Act of 1994; and

(ii) warranted by the need for credit.

(B) An increase or decrease under subparagraph (A) may not result in the number of percentage points referred to in subparagraph (A) being—

(i) less that 8 percentage points; or

(ii) greater than 12 percentage points.

(C) In determining whether to increase or decrease the number of percentage points referred to in subparagraph (A), the Board shall consult with representatives of consumers, including low-income consumers, and lenders.

(3) The amount specified in paragraph (1)(B)(ii) shall be adjusted annually on January 1 by the annual percentage change in the Consumer Price Index, as reported on June 1 of the year preceding such adjustment.

(4) For purposes of paragraph (1)(B), points and fees shall include—

(A) all items included in the finance charge, except interest or the time-price differential;

(B) all compensation paid to mortgage brokers;

(C) each of the charges listed in section 1605(e) of this title (except an escrow for future payment of taxes), unless—

(i) the charge is reasonable;

(ii) the creditor receives no direct or indirect compensation; and

(iii) the charge is paid to a third party unaffiliated with the creditor; and

(D) such other charges as the Board determines to be appropriate.

(5) This subsection shall not be construed to limit the rate of interest or the finance charge that a person may charge a consumer for any extension of credit.

(bb) The term "reverse mortgage transaction" means a nonrecourse transaction in which a mortgage, deed of trust, or equivalent consensual security interest is created against the consumer's principal dwelling—

(1) securing one or more advances; and

(2) with respect to which the payment of any principal, interest, and shared appreciation or equity is due and payable (other than in the case of default) only after—

(A) the transfer of the dwelling;

(B) the consumer ceases to occupy the dwelling as a principal dwelling; or

(C) the death of the consumer

Sec. 1603.—Exempted transactions

This subchapter does not apply to the following:

(1) Credit transactions involving extensions of credit primarily for business, commercial, or agricultural purposes, or to government or governmental agencies or instrumentalities, or to organizations.

(2) Transactions in securities or commodities accounts by a broker-dealer registered with the Securities and Exchange Commission.

(3) Credit transactions, other than those in which a security interest is or will be acquired in real property, or in personal property used or expected to be used as the principal dwelling of the consumer, in which the total amount financed exceeds $25,000.

(4) Transactions under public utility tariffs, if the Board determines that a State regulatory body regulates the charges for the public utility services involved, the charges for delayed payment, and any discount allowed for early payment.

(5) Transactions for which the Board, by rule, determines that coverage under this subchapter is not necessary to carry out the purposes of this subchapter.

(6) Repealed. Pub. L. 96-221, title VI, Sec. 603(c)(3), Mar. 31, 1980, 94 Stat. 169.

(7) Loans made, insured, or guaranteed pursuant to a program authorized by title IV of the Higher Education Act of 1965 (20 U.S.C. 1070 et seq., 42 U.S.C. 2751 et seq.)

Sec. 1604.—Disclosure guidelines

(a) Promulgation, contents, etc., of regulations

The Board shall prescribe regulations to carry out the purposes of this subchapter. Except in the case of a mortgage referred to in section 1602(aa) of this title, these regulations may contain such classifications, differentiations, or other provisions, and may provide for such adjustments and exceptions for any class of transactions, as in the judgment of the Board are necessary or proper to effectuate the purposes of this subchapter, to prevent circumvention or evasion thereof, or to facilitate compliance therewith.

(b) Model disclosure forms and clauses; publication, criteria, compliance, etc. The Board shall publish model disclosure forms and clauses for common transactions to facilitate compliance with the disclosure requirements of this subchapter and to aid the borrower or lessee in understanding the transaction by utilizing readily understandable language to simplify the technical nature of the disclosures. In devising such forms, the Board shall consider the use by creditors or lessors of data processing or similar automated equipment. Nothing in this subchapter may be construed to require a creditor or lessor to use any such model form or clause prescribed by the Board under this section. A creditor or lessor shall be deemed to be in compliance with the disclosure provisions of this subchapter with respect to other than numerical disclosures if the creditor or lessor

(1) uses any appropriate model form or clause as published by the Board, or

(2) uses any such model form or clause and changes it by

(A) deleting any information which is not required by this subchapter, or

(B) rearranging the format, if in making such deletion or rearranging the format, the creditor or lessor does not affect the substance, clarity, or meaningful sequence of the disclosure.

(c) Procedures applicable for adoption of model forms and clauses
Model disclosure forms and clauses shall be adopted by the Board after notice duly given in the Federal Register and an opportunity for public comment in accordance with section 553 of title 5.

(d) Effective dates of regulations containing new disclosure requirements
Any regulation of the Board, or any amendment or interpretation thereof, requiring any disclosure which differs from the disclosures previously required by this part, part D, or part E of this subchapter or by any regulation of the Board promulgated thereunder shall have an effective date of that October 1 which follows by at least six months the date of promulgation, except that the Board may at its discretion take interim action by regulation, amendment, or interpretation to lengthen the period of time permitted for creditors or lessors to adjust their forms to accommodate new requirements or shorten the length of time for creditors or lessors to make such adjustments when it makes a specific finding that such action is necessary to comply with the findings of a court or to prevent unfair or deceptive disclosure practices. Notwithstanding the previous sentence, any creditor or lessor may comply with any such newly promulgated disclosure requirements prior to the effective date of the requirements.

(e) Exemption authority

(1) In general.

The Board may exempt, by regulation, from all or part of this subchapter any class of transactions, other than transactions involving any mortgage described in section 1602(aa) of this title, for which, in the determination of the Board, coverage under all or part of this subchapter does not provide a meaningful benefit to consumers in the form of useful information or protection.

(2) Factors for consideration

In determining which classes of transactions to exempt in whole or in part under paragraph (1), the Board shall consider the following factors and publish its rationale at the time a proposed exemption is published for comment:

(A) The amount of the loan and whether the disclosures, right of rescission, and other provisions provide a benefit to the consumers who are parties to such transactions, as determined by the Board.

(B) The extent to which the requirements of this subchapter complicate, hinder, or make more expensive the credit process for the class of transactions.

(C) The status of the borrower, including—

(i) any related financial arrangements of the borrower, as determined by the Board;

(ii) the financial sophistication of the borrower relative to the type of transaction; and

(iii) the importance to the borrower of the credit, related supporting property, and coverage under this subchapter, as determined by the Board;

(D) whether the loan is secured by the principal residence of the consumer; and

(E) whether the goal of consumer protection would be undermined by such an exemption.

(f) Waiver for certain borrowers

(1) In general

The Board, by regulation, may exempt from the requirements of this subchapter certain credit transactions if—

(A) the transaction involves a consumer—

(i) with an annual earned income of more than $200,000; or

(ii) having net assets in excess of $1,000,000 at the time of the transaction; and

(B) a waiver that is handwritten, signed, and dated by the consumer is first obtained from the consumer.

(2) Adjustments by the Board

The Board, at its discretion, may adjust the annual earned income and net asset requirements of paragraph (1) for inflation.

Sec. 1605.—Determination of finance charge

(a) "Finance charge" defined

Except as otherwise provided in this section, the amount of the finance charge in connection with any consumer credit transaction shall be determined as the sum of all charges, payable directly or indirectly by the person to whom the credit is extended, and imposed directly or indirectly by the creditor as an incident to the extension of credit. The finance charge does not include charges of a type payable in a comparable cash transaction. The finance charge shall not include fees and amounts imposed by third-party closing agents (including settlement agents, attorneys, and escrow and title companies) if the creditor does not require the imposition of the charges or the services provided and does not retain the charges. Examples of charges which are included in the finance charge include any of the following types of charges which are applicable:

1. Interest, time price differential, and any amount payable under a point, discount, or other system or additional charges.
2. Service or carrying charge.
3. Loan fee, finder's fee, or similar charge.
4. Fee for an investigation or credit report.
5. Premium or other charge for any guarantee or insurance protecting the creditor against the obligor's default or other credit loss.
6. Borrower-paid mortgage broker fees, including fees paid directly to the broker or the lender (for delivery to the broker) whether such fees are paid in cash or financed.

(b) Life, accident, or health insurance premiums included in finance charge

Charges or premiums for credit life, accident, or health insurance written in connection with any consumer credit transaction shall be included in the finance charges unless

(1) the coverage of the debtor by the insurance is not a factor in the approval by the creditor of the extension of credit, and this fact is clearly disclosed in writing to the person applying for or obtaining the extension of credit; and

(2) in order to obtain the insurance in connection with the extension of credit, the person to whom the credit is extended must give specific affirmative written indication of his desire to do so after written disclosure to him of the cost thereof.

(c) Property damage and liability insurance premiums included in finance charge

Charges or premiums for insurance, written in connection with any consumer credit transaction, against loss of or damage to property or against liability arising out of the ownership or use of property, shall be included in the finance charge unless a clear and specific statement in writing is furnished by the creditor to the person to whom the credit is extended, setting forth the cost of the insurance if obtained from or through the creditor, and stating that the person to whom the credit is extended may choose the person through which the insurance is to be obtained.

(d) Items exempted from computation of finance charge in all credit transactions

If any of the following items is itemized and disclosed in accordance with the regulations of the Board in connection with any transaction, then the creditor need not include that item in the computation of the finance charge with respect to that transaction:

(1) Fees and charges prescribed by law which actually are or will be paid to public officials for determining the existence of or for perfecting or releasing or satisfying any security related to the credit transaction.

(2) The premium payable for any insurance in lieu of perfecting any security interest otherwise required by the creditor in connection with the transaction, if the premium does not exceed the fees and charges described in paragraph (1) which would otherwise be payable.

(3) Any tax levied on security instruments or on documents evidencing indebtedness if the payment of such taxes is a precondition for recording the instrument securing the evidence of indebtedness.

(e) Items exempted from computation of finance charge in extensions of credit secured by an interest in real property

The following items, when charged in connection with any extension of credit secured by an interest in real property, shall not be included in the computation of the finance charge with respect to that transaction:

(1) Fees or premiums for title examination, title insurance, or similar purposes.

(2) Fees for preparation of loan-related documents.

(3) Escrows for future payments of taxes and insurance.

(4) Fees for notarizing deeds and other documents.

(5) Appraisal fees, including fees related to any pest infestation or flood hazard inspections conducted prior to closing.

(6) Credit reports.

(f) Tolerances for accuracy

In connection with credit transactions not under an open end credit plan that are secured by real property or a dwelling, the disclosure of the finance charge and other disclosures affected by any finance charge—

(1) shall be treated as being accurate for purposes of this subchapter if the amount disclosed as the finance charge—

(A) does not vary from the actual finance charge by more than $100; or

(B) is greater than the amount required to be disclosed under this subchapter; and

(2) shall be treated as being accurate for purposes of section 1635 of this title if—

(A) except as provided in subparagraph (B), the amount disclosed as the finance charge does not vary from the actual finance charge by more than an amount equal to one-half of one percent of the total amount of credit extended; or

(B) in the case of a transaction, other than a mortgage referred to in section 1602(aa) of this title, which—

(i) is a refinancing of the principal balance then due and any accrued and unpaid finance charges of a residential mortgage transaction as defined in section 1602(w) of this title, or is any subsequent refinancing of such a transaction; and

(ii) does not provide any new consolidation or new advance; if the amount disclosed as the finance charge does not vary from the actual finance charge by more than an amount equal to one percent of the total amount of credit extended.

Sec. 1606.—Determination of annual percentage rate

(a) "Annual percentage rate" defined
The annual percentage rate applicable to any extension of consumer credit shall be determined, in accordance with the regulations of the Board,

(1) in the case of any extension of credit other than under an open end credit plan, as

(A) that nominal annual percentage rate which will yield a sum equal to the amount of the finance charge when it is applied to the unpaid balances of the amount financed, calculated according to the actuarial method of allocating payments made on a debt between the amount financed and the amount of the finance charge, pursuant to which a payment is applied first to the accumulated finance charge and the balance is applied to the unpaid amount financed; or

(B) the rate determined by any method prescribed by the Board as a method which materially simplifies computation while retaining reasonable accuracy as compared with the rate determined under subparagraph (A).

(2) in the case of any extension of credit under an open end credit plan, as the quotient (expressed as a percentage) of the total finance charge for the period to which it relates divided by the amount upon which the finance charge for that period is based, multiplied by the number of such periods in a year.

(b) Computation of rate of finance charges for balances within a specified range

Where a creditor imposes the same finance charge for balances within a specified range, the annual percentage rate shall be computed on the median balance within the range, except that if the Board determines that a rate so computed would not be meaningful, or would be materially misleading, the annual percentage rate shall be computed on such other basis as the Board may be regulation require.

(c) Allowable tolerances for purposes of compliance with disclosure requirements
The disclosure of an annual percentage rate is accurate for the purpose of this subchapter if the rate disclosed is within a tolerance not greater than one-eighth of 1 per centum more or less than the actual rate or rounded to the nearest one-fourth of 1 per centum. The Board may allow a greater tolerance to simplify compliance where irregular payments are involved.

(d) Use of rate tables or charts having allowable variance from determined rates
The Board may authorize the use of rate tables or charts which may provide for the disclosure of annual percentage rates which vary from the rate determined in accordance with subsection (a)(1)(A) of this section by not more than such tolerances as the Board may allow. The Board may not allow a tolerance greater than 8 per centum of that rate except to simplify compliance where irregular payments are involved.

(e) Authorization of tolerances in determining annual percentage rates
In the case of creditors determining the annual percentage rate in a manner other than as described in subsection (d) of this section, the Board may authorize other reasonable tolerances.

Sec. 1607.—Administrative enforcement

(a) Enforcing agencies
Compliance with the requirements imposed under this subchapter shall be enforced under
The terms used in paragraph (1) that are not defined in this subchapter or otherwise defined in section 3(s) of the Federal Deposit Insurance Act (12 U.S.C. 1813(s)) shall have the meaning given to them in section 1(b) of the International Banking Act of 1978 (12 U.S.C. 3101).

(1) section 8 of the Federal Deposit Insurance Act (12 U.S.C. 1818), in the case of—

(A) national banks, and Federal branches and Federal agencies of foreign banks, by the Office of the Comptroller of the Currency;

(B) member banks of the Federal Reserve System (other than national banks), branches and agencies of foreign banks (other than Federal branches, Federal agencies, and insured State branches of foreign banks), commercial lending companies owned or controlled by foreign banks, and organizations operating under section 25 or 25(a) of the Federal Reserve Act (12 U.S.C. 601 et seq., 611 et seq.), by the Board; and

(C) banks insured by the Federal Deposit Insurance Corporation (other than members of the Federal Reserve System) and insured State branches of foreign banks, by the Board of Directors of the Federal Deposit Insurance Corporation;

(2) section 8 of the Federal Deposit Insurance Act (12 U.S.C. 1818), by the Director of the Office of Thrift Supervision, in the case of a savings association the deposits of which are insured by the Federal Deposit Insurance Corporation.

(3) the Federal Credit Union Act (12 U.S.C. 1751 et seq.), by the National Credit Union Administration Board with respect to any Federal credit union.

(4) part A of subtitle VII of title 49, by the Secretary of Transportation with respect to any air carrier or foreign air carrier subject to that part.

(5) the Packers and Stockyards Act, 1921 (7 U.S.C. 181 et seq.) (except as provided in section 406 of that Act (7 U.S.C. 226, 227)), by the Secretary of Agriculture with respect to any activities subject to that Act.

(6) the Farm Credit Act of 1971 (12 U.S.C. 2001 et seq.) by the Farm Credit Administration with respect to any Federal land bank, Federal land bank association, Federal intermediate credit bank, or production credit association.

(b) Violations of this subchapter deemed violations of pre-existing statutory requirements; additional agency powers

For the purpose of the exercise by any agency referred to in subsection (a) of this section of its powers under any Act referred to in that subsection, a violation of any requirement imposed under this subchapter shall be deemed to be a violation of a requirement imposed under that Act. In addition to its powers under any provision of law specifically referred to in subsection (a) of this section, each of the agencies referred to in that subsection may exercise, for the purpose of enforcing compliance with any requirement imposed under this subchapter, any other authority conferred on it by law.

(c) Federal Trade Commission as overall enforcing agency

Except to the extent that enforcement of the requirements imposed under this subchapter is specifically committed to some other Government agency under subsection (a) of this section, the Federal Trade Commission shall enforce such requirements. For the purpose of the exercise by the Federal Trade Commission of its functions and powers under the Federal Trade Commission Act (15 U.S.C. 41 et seq.), a violation of any requirement imposed under this subchapter shall be deemed a violation of a requirement imposed under that Act. All of the functions and powers of the Federal Trade Commission under the Federal Trade Commission Act are available to the Commission to enforce compliance by any person with the requirements imposed under this subchapter, irrespective of whether that person is engaged in commerce or meets any other jurisdictional tests in the Federal Trade Commission Act.

(d) Rules and regulations

The authority of the Board to issue regulations under this subchapter does not impair the authority of any other agency designated in this section to make rules respecting its own procedures in enforcing compliance with requirements imposed under this subchapter.

(e) Adjustment of finance charges; procedures applicable, coverage, criteria, etc.

(1) In carrying out its enforcement activities under this section, each agency referred to in subsection (a) or (c) of this section, in cases where an annual percentage rate or finance charge was inaccurately disclosed, shall notify the creditor of such disclosure error and is authorized in accordance with the provisions of this subsection to require the creditor to make an adjustment to the account of the person to whom credit was extended, to assure that such person will not be required to pay a finance charge in excess of the finance charge actually disclosed or the dollar equivalent of the annual percentage rate actually disclosed, whichever is lower. For the purposes of this subsection, except where such disclosure error resulted from a willful violation which was intended to mislead the person to whom credit was extended, in determining whether a disclosure error has occurred and in calculating any adjustment, (A) each agency shall apply (i) with respect to the annual percentage rate, a tolerance of one-quarter of 1 percent more or less than the actual rate, determined without regard to section 1606(c) of this title, and (ii) with respect to the finance charge, a corresponding numerical tolerance as generated by the tolerance provided under this subsection for the annual percentage rate; except that (B) with respect to transactions consummated after two years following March 31, 1980, each agency shall apply (i) for transactions that have a scheduled amortization of ten years or less, with respect to the annual percentage rate, a tolerance not to exceed one-quarter of 1 percent more or less than the actual rate, determined without regard to section 1606(c) of this title, but in no event a tolerance of less than the tolerances allowed under section 1606(c) of this title, (ii) for transactions that have a scheduled amortization of more than ten years, with respect to the annual percentage rate, only such tolerances as are allowed under section 1606(c) of this title, and (iii) for all transactions, with respect to the finance charge, a corresponding numerical tolerance as generated by the tolerances provided under this subsection for the annual percentage rate.

(2) Each agency shall require such an adjustment when it determines that such disclosure error resulted from (A) a clear and consistent pattern or practice of violations, (B) gross negligence, or (C) a willful violation which was intended to mislead the person to whom the credit was extended. Notwithstanding the preceding sentence, except where such disclosure error resulted from a willful violation which was intended to mislead the person to whom credit was extended, an agency need not require such an adjustment if it determines that such disclosure error—

(A) resulted from an error involving the disclosure of a fee or charge that would otherwise be excludable in computing the finance charge, including but not limited to violations involving the disclosures described in sections 1605(b), (c) and (d) of this title, in which event the agency may require such remedial action as it determines to be equitable, except that for transactions consummated after two years after March 31, 1980, such an adjustment shall be ordered for violations of section 1605(b) of this title;

(B) involved a disclosed amount which was 10 per centum or less of the amount that should have been disclosed and

(i) in cases where the error involved a disclosed finance charge, the annual percentage rate was disclosed correctly, and

(ii) in cases where the error involved a disclosed annual percentage rate, the finance charge was disclosed correctly; in which event the agency may require such adjustment as it determines to be equitable;

(C) involved a total failure to disclose either the annual percentage rate or the finance charge, in which event the agency may require such adjustment as it determines to be equitable; or

(D) resulted from any other unique circumstance involving clearly technical and nonsubstantive disclosure violations that do not adversely affect information provided to the consumer and that have not misled or otherwise deceived the consumer. In the case of other such disclosure errors, each agency may require such an adjustment.

(3) Notwithstanding paragraph (2), no adjustment shall be ordered—

(A) if it would have a significantly adverse impact upon the safety or soundness of the creditor, but in any such case, the agency may—

(i) require a partial adjustment in an amount which does not have such an impact; or

(ii) require the full adjustment, but permit the creditor to make the required adjustment in partial payments over an extended period of time which the agency considers to be reasonable, if (in the case of an agency referred to in paragraph (1), (2), or (3) of subsection (a) of this section), the agency determines that a partial adjustment or making partial payments over an extended period is necessary to avoid causing the creditor to become undercapitalized pursuant to section 38 of the Federal Deposit Insurance Act (12 U.S.C. 1831o);

(B) the amount of the adjustment would be less than $1, except that if more than one year has elapsed since the date of the violation, the agency may require that such amount be paid into the Treasury of the United States, or "if"

(C) except where such disclosure error resulted from a willful violation which was intended to mislead the person to whom credit was extended, in the case of an open-end credit plan, more than two years after the violation, or in the case of any other extension of credit, as follows:

(i) with respect to creditors that are subject to examination by the agencies referred to in paragraphs (1) through (3) of subsection (a) of this section, except in connection with violations arising from practices identified in the current examination and only in connection with transactions that are consummated after the date of the immediately preceding examination, except that where practices giving rise to violations identified in earlier examinations have not been corrected, adjustments for those violations shall be required in connection with transactions consummated after the date of examination in which such practices were first identified;

(ii) with respect to creditors that are not subject to examination by such agencies, except in connection with transactions that are consummated after May 10, 1978; and

(iii) in no event after the later of

(I) the expiration of the life of the credit extension, or

(II) two years after the agreement to extend credit was consummated.

(4) (A) Notwithstanding any other provision of this section, an adjustment under this subsection may be required by an agency referred to in subsection (a) or (c) of this section only by an order issued in accordance with cease and desist procedures provided by the provision of law referred to in such subsections.

(B) In case of an agency which is not authorized to conduct cease and desist proceedings, such an order may be issued after an agency hearing on the record conducted at least thirty but not more than sixty days after notice of the alleged violation is served on the creditor. Such a hearing shall be deemed to be a hearing which is subject to the provisions of section 8(h) of the Federal Deposit Insurance Act (12 U.S.C. 1818(h)) and shall be subject to judicial review as provided therein.

(5) Except as otherwise specifically provided in this subsection and notwithstanding any provision of law referred to in subsection (a) or (c) of this section, no agency referred to in subsection (a) or (c) of this section may require a creditor to make dollar adjustments for errors in any requirements under this subchapter, except with regard to the requirements of section 1666d of this title.

(6) A creditor shall not be subject to an order to make an adjustment, if within sixty days after discovering a disclosure error, whether pursuant to a final written examination report or through the creditor's own procedures, the creditor notifies the person concerned of the error and adjusts the account so as to assure that such person will not be required to pay a finance charge in excess of the finance charge actually disclosed or the dollar equivalent of the annual percentage rate actually disclosed, whichever is lower.

(7) Notwithstanding the second sentence of subsection (e)(1), subsection (e)(3)(C)(i), and subsection (e)(3)(C)(ii) of this section, each agency referred to in subsection (a) or (c) of this section shall require an adjustment for an annual percentage rate disclosure error that exceeds a tolerance of one quarter of one percent less than the actual rate, determined without regard to section 1606(c) of this title, with respect to any transaction consummated between January 1, 1977, and March 31, 1980.

Sec. 1608.—Views of other agencies

In the exercise of its functions under this subchapter, the Board may obtain upon requests the views of any other Federal agency which, in the judgment of the Board, exercises regulatory or supervisory functions with respect to any class of creditors subject to this subchapter.

[Sec. 1609—REPEALED]

Sec. 1610.—Effect on other laws

(a) Inconsistent provisions; procedures applicable for determination

(1) Except as provided in subsection (e) of this section, this part and parts B and C of this subchapter, do not annul, alter, or affect the laws of any State relating to the disclosure of information in connection with credit transactions, except to the extent that those laws are inconsistent with the provisions of this subchapter and then only to the extent of the inconsistency. Upon its own motion or upon the request of any creditor, State or other interested party which is submitted in accordance with procedures prescribed in regulations of the Board, the Board shall determine whether any such inconsistency exists. If the Board determines that a State-required disclosure is inconsistent, creditors located in that State may not make disclosures using the inconsistent term or form, and shall incur no liability under the law of that State for failure to use such term or form, notwithstanding that such determination is subsequently amended, rescinded, or determined by judicial or other authority to be invalid for any reason.

(2) Upon its own motion or upon the request of any creditor, State, or other interested party which is submitted in accordance with procedures prescribed in regulations of the Board, the Board shall determine whether any disclosure required under the law of any State is substantially the same in meaning as a disclosure required under this subchapter. If the Board determines that a State-required disclosure is substantially the same in meaning as a disclosure required by this subchapter, then creditors located in that State may make such disclosure in compliance with such State law in lieu of the disclosure required by this subchapter, except that the annual percentage rate and finance charge shall be disclosed as required by section 1632 of this title, and such State-required disclosure may not be made in lieu of the disclosures applicable to certain mortgages under section 1639 of this title.

(b) State credit charge statutes
Except as provided in section 1639 of this title, this subchapter does not otherwise annul, alter or affect in any manner the meaning, scope or applicability of the laws of any State, including, but not limited to, laws relating to the types, amounts or rates of charges, or any element or elements of charges, permissible under such laws in connection with the extension or use of credit, nor does this subchapter extend the applicability of those laws to any class of persons or transactions to which they would not otherwise apply. The provisions of section 1639 of this title do not annul, alter, or affect the applicability of the laws of any State or exempt any person subject to the provisions of section 1639 of this title from complying with the laws of any State, with respect to the requirements for mortgages referred to in section 1602(aa) of this title, except to the extent that those State laws are inconsistent with any provisions of section 1639 of this title, and then only to the extent of the inconsistency.

(c) Disclosure as evidence
In any action or proceeding in any court involving a consumer credit sale, the disclosure of the annual percentage rate as required under this subchapter in connection with that sale may not be received as evidence that the sale was a loan or any type of transaction other than a credit sale.

(d) Contract or other obligations under State or Federal law
Except as specified in sections 1635, 1640, and 1666e of this title, this subchapter and the regulations issued thereunder do not affect the validity or enforceability of any contract or obligation under State or Federal law.

(e) Certain credit and charge card application and solicitation disclosure provisions
The provisions of subsection (c) of section 1632 of this title and subsections (c), (d), (e), and (f) of section 1637 of this title shall supersede any provision of the law of any State relating to the disclosure of information in any credit or charge card application or solicitation which is subject to the requirements of section 1637(c) of this title or any renewal notice which is subject to the requirements of section 1637(d) of this title, except that any State may employ or establish State laws for the purpose of enforcing the requirements of such sections.

Sec. 1611.—Criminal liability for willful and knowing violation

Whoever willfully and knowingly

(1) gives false or inaccurate information or fails to provide information which he is required to disclose under the provisions of this subchapter or any regulation issued thereunder,

(2) uses any chart or table authorized by the Board under section 1606 of this title in such a manner as to consistently understate the annual percentage rate determined under section 1606(a)(1)(A) of this title, or

(3) otherwise fails to comply with any requirement imposed under this subchapter, shall be fined not more than $5,000 or imprisoned not more than one year, or both.

Sec. 1612.—Effect on government agencies

(a) Consultation requirements respecting compliance of credit instruments issued to participating creditor
Any department or agency of the United States which administers a credit program in which it extends, insures, or guarantees consumer credit and in which it provides instruments to a creditor which contain any disclosures required by this subchapter shall, prior to the issuance or continued use of such instruments, consult with the Board to assure that such instruments comply with this subchapter.

(b) Inapplicability of Federal civil or criminal penalties to Federal, State, and local agencies
Federal, State, and local agencies
No civil or criminal penalty provided under this subchapter for any violation thereof may be imposed upon the United States or any department or agency thereof, or upon any State or political subdivision thereof, or any agency of any State of political subdivision.

(c) Inapplicability of Federal civil or criminal penalties to participating creditor where violating instrument issued by United States
A creditor participating in a credit program administered, insured, or guaranteed by any department or agency or the United States shall not be held liable for a civil or criminal penalty under this subchapter in any case in which the violation results from the use of an instrument required by any such department or agency.

(d) Applicability of State penalties to violations by participating creditor
A creditor participating in a credit program administered, insured, or guaranteed by any department or agency of the United States shall not be held liable for a civil or criminal penalty under the laws of any State (other than laws determined under section 1610 of this title to be inconsistent with this subchapter) for any technical or procedural failure, such as a failure to use a specific form, to make information available at a specific place on an instrument, or to use a specific typeface, as required by State law, which is caused by the use of an instrument required to be used by such department or agency.

Sec. 1613.—Annual reports to Congress by Board

Each year the Board shall make a report to the Congress concerning the administration of its functions under this subchapter, including such recommendations as the Board deems necessary or appropriate. In addition, each report of the Board shall include its assessment of the extent to which compliance with the requirements imposed under this subchapter is being achieved.

[Sec. 1614—REPEALED]

APPENDIX II

REGULATION Z TRUTH IN LENDING

12 CFR 226

Subpart A—General

Sec.

226.13 Billing error resolution

226.14 Determination of annual percentage rate

226.15 Right of rescission

226.16 Advertising

Subpart C—Closed-End Credit

226.17 General disclosure requirements

226.18 Content of disclosures

226.19 Certain residential mortgage and variable-rate transactions

226.20 Subsequent disclosure requirements

226.21 Treatment of credit balances

226.22 Determination of annual percentage rate

226.23 Right of rescission

226.24 Advertising

Subpart D—Miscellaneous

226.25 Record retention

226.26 Use of annual percentage rate in oral disclosures

226.27 Language disclosures

226.28 Effect on state laws

226.29 State exemptions

226.30 Limitation on rates

Subpart E—Special Rules for Certain Home Mortgage Transactions

226.31 General rules

226.32 Requirements for certain closed-end home mortgages

226.33 Requirements for reverse mortgages

226.34 Prohibited acts or practices in connection with credit secured by a consumer's Dwelling

226.35 [Reserved]

Subpart F—Electronic Communication

226.36 Requirements for electronic communication

Appendix A—Effect on state laws.*

Appendix B—State exemptions.

Appendix C—Issuance of staff interpretations.

Appendix D—Multiple advance construction loans.

Appendix E—Rules for card issuers that bill on a transaction-by-transaction basis.

Appendix F—Annual percentage rate computations for certain open-end credit plans.

Appendix G—Open-end model forms and clauses.

Appendix H—Closed-end model forms and clauses.

Appendix I—Federal enforcement agencies.

Appendix J—Annual percentage rate computations for closed-end credit transactions.

Appendix K—Total annual loan cost rate computations for reverse mortgage transactions.

Appendix L—Assumed loan periods for computations of total annual loan cost rates.

SUBPART A—GENERAL

Section 226.1—Authority, purpose, coverage, organization, enforcement and liability

(a) *Authority.* This regulation, known as Regulation Z, is issued by the Board of Governors of the Federal Reserve System to implement the federal Truth in Lending Act, which is contained in title I of the Consumer Credit Protection Act, as amended (15 U.S.C. 1601 *et seq.*). This regulation also implements title XII, section 1204 of the Competitive Equality Banking Act of 1987 (Pub. L. 100-86, 101 Stat. 552). Information-collection requirements contained in this regulation have been approved by the Office of Management and Budget under the provisions of 44 U.S.C. 3501 *et seq.* and have been assigned OMB No. 7100-0199.

(b) *Purpose.* The purpose of this regulation is to promote the informed use of consumer credit by requiring disclosures about its terms and cost. The regulation also gives consumers the right to cancel certain credit transactions that involve a

*The appendices A-L have been omitted due to space requirements, but can be obtained from the Federal Trade Commission, Public Reference Branch, 600 Pennsylvania Avenue N.W., Washington, D.C. 20580 or Federal Reserve board, 20th & C Street N.W., Washington D.C. 20551.

lien on a consumer's principal dwelling, regulates certain credit card practices, and provides a means for fair and timely resolution of credit billing disputes. The regulation does not govern charges for consumer credit. The regulation requires a maximum interest rate to be stated in variable-rate contracts secured by the consumer's dwelling. It also imposes limitations on home equity plans that are subject to the requirements of § 226.5b and mortgages that are subject to the requirements of § 226.32. The regulation prohibits certain acts or practices in connection with credit secured by a consumer's principal dwelling.

(c) *Coverage.*

(1) In general, this regulation applies to each individual or business that offers or extends credit when four conditions are met: (i) the credit is offered or extended to consumers; (ii) the offering or extension of credit is done regularly;[1] (iii) the credit is subject to a finance charge or is payable by a written agreement in more than 4 installments; and (iv) the credit is primarily for personal, family, or household purposes.

(2) If a credit card is involved, however, certain provisions apply even if the credit is not subject to a finance charge, or is not payable by a written agreement in more than 4 installments, or if the credit card is to be used for business purposes.

(3) In addition, certain requirements of § 226.5b apply to persons who are not creditors but who provide applications for home equity plans to consumers.

(d) *Organization.* The regulation is divided into subparts and appendices as follows:

(1) Subpart A contains general information. It sets forth: (i) the authority, purpose, coverage, and organization of the regulation; (ii) the definitions of basic terms; (iii) the transactions that are exempt from coverage; and (iv) the method of determining the finance charge.

(2) Subpart B contains the rules for open-end credit. It requires that initial disclosures and periodic statements be provided, as well as additional disclosures for credit and charge card applications and solicitations and for home equity plans subject to the requirements of §§ 226.5a and 226.5b, respectively. It also describes special rules that apply to credit card transactions, treatment of payments and credit balances, procedures for resolving credit billing errors, annual percentage rate calculations, rescission requirements, and advertising rules.

(3) Subpart C relates to closed-end credit. It contains rules on disclosures, treatment of credit balances, annual percentage rate calculations, rescission requirements, and advertising.

(4) Subpart D contains rules on oral disclosures, Spanish language disclosure in Puerto Rico, record retention, effect on state laws, state exemptions, and rate limitations.

---

[1]The meaning of "regularly" is explained in the definition of "creditor" in § 226.2(a).

(5) Subpart E contains special rules for mortgage transactions. Section 226.32 requires certain disclosures and provides limitations for loans that have rates and fees above specified amounts. Section 226.33 requires disclosures, including the total annual loan cost rate, for reverse mortgage transactions. Section 226.34 prohibits specific acts and practices in connection with mortgage transactions.

(6) Several appendices contain information such as the procedures for determinations about state laws, state exemptions and issuance of staff interpretations, special rules for certain kinds of credit plans, a list of enforcement agencies, and the rules for computing annual percentage rates in closed-end credit transactions and total annual loan cost rates for reverse mortgage transactions.

(e) *Enforcement and liability.* Section 108 of the act contains the administrative enforcement provisions. Sections 112, 113, 130, 131, and 134 contain provisions relating to liability for failure to comply with the requirements of the act and the regulation. Section 1204(c) of Title XII of the Competitive Equality Banking Act of 1987, Pub. L. No. 100-86, 101 Stat. 552, incorporates by reference administrative enforcement and civil liability provisions of sections 108 and 130 of the act.

Section 226.2—Definitions and rules of construction

(a) *Definitions.* For purposes of this regulation, the following definitions apply:

(1) *Act* means the Truth in Lending Act (15 U.S.C. 1601 *et seq.*).

(2) *Advertisement* means a commercial message in any medium that promotes, directly or indirectly, a credit transaction.

(3) [Reserved][2]

(4) *Billing cycle* or *cycle* means the interval between the days or dates of regular periodic statements. These intervals shall be equal and no longer than a quarter of a year. An interval will be considered equal if the number of days in the cycle does not vary more than four days from the regular day or date of the periodic statement.

(5) *Board* means the Board of Governors of the Federal Reserve System.

(6) *Business day* means a day on which a creditor's offices are open to the public for carrying on substantially all of its business functions. However, for purposes of rescission under §§ 226.15 and 226.23, and for purposes of § 226.31, the term means all calendar days except Sundays and the legal public holidays specified in 5 U.S.C. 6103(a), such as New Year's Day, the birthday of Martin Luther King, Jr., Washington's Birthday, Memorial Day, Independence Day, Labor Day, Columbus Day, Veterans Day, Thanksgiving Day, and Christmas Day.

---

[2]Footnote reserved.

(7) *Card issuer* means a person that issues a credit card or that person's agent with respect to the card.

(8) *Cardholder* means a natural person to whom a credit card is issued for consumer credit purposes, or a natural person who has agreed with the card issuer to pay consumer credit obligations arising from the issuance of a credit card to another natural person. For purposes of § 226.12(a) and (b), the term includes any person to whom a credit card is issued for any purpose, including business, commercial, or agricultural use, or a person who has agreed with the card issuer to pay obligations arising from the issuance of such a credit card to another person.

(9) *Cash price* means the price at which a creditor, in the ordinary course of business, offers to sell for cash the property or service that is the subject of the transaction. At the creditor's option, the term may include the price of accessories, services related to the sale, service contracts and taxes and fees for license, title, and registration. The term does not include any finance charge.

(10) *Closed-end credit* means consumer credit other than "open-end credit" as defined in this section.

(11) *Consumer* means a cardholder or a natural person to whom consumer credit is offered or extended. However, for purposes of rescission under §§ 226.15 and 226.23, the term also includes a natural person in whose principal dwelling a security interest is or will be retained or acquired, if that person's ownership interest in the dwelling is or will be subject to the security interest.

(12) *Consumer credit* means credit offered or extended to a consumer primarily for personal, family, or household purposes.

(13) *Consummation* means the time that a consumer becomes contractually obligated on a credit transaction.

(14) *Credit* means the right to defer payment of debt or to incur debt and defer its payment.

(15) *Credit card* means any card, plate, coupon book, or other single credit device that may be used from time to time to obtain credit. *Charge card* means a credit card on an account for which no periodic rate is used to compute a finance charge.

(16) *Credit sale* means a sale in which the seller is a creditor. The term includes a bailment or lease (unless terminable without penalty at any time by the consumer) under which the consumer:

(i) Agrees to pay as compensation for use a sum substantially equivalent to, or in excess of, the total value of the property and services involved; and

(ii) Will become (or has the option to become), for no additional consideration or for nominal consideration, the owner of the property upon compliance with the agreement.

(17) *Creditor* means:

(i) A person (A) who regularly extends consumer credit[3] that is subject to a finance charge or is payable by written agreement in more than four installments (not including a downpayment), and (B) to whom the obligation is initially payable, either on the face of the note or contract, or by agreement when there is no note or contract.

(ii) For purposes of §§ 226.4(c)(8) (discounts), 226.9(d) (Finance charge imposed at time of transaction), and 226.12(e) (Prompt notification of returns and crediting of refunds), a person that honors a credit card.

(iii) For purposes of subpart B, any card issuer that extends either open-end credit or credit that is not subject to a finance charge and is not payable by written agreement in more than four installments.

(iv) For purposes of subpart B (except for the credit and charge card disclosures contained in §§ 226.5a and 226.9(e) and (f), the finance charge disclosures contained in §§ 226.6(a) and 226.7(d) through (g) and the right of rescission set forth in § 226.15) and subpart C, any card issuer that extends closed-end credit that is subject to a finance charge or is payable by written agreement in more than four installments.

(18) *Downpayment* means an amount, including the value of any property used as a trade-in, paid to a seller to reduce the cash price of goods or services purchased in a credit sale transaction. A deferred portion of a downpayment may be treated as part of the downpayment if it is payable not later than the due date of the second otherwise regularly scheduled payment and is not subject to a finance charge.

(19) *Dwelling* means a residential structure that contains one to four units, whether or not that structure is attached to real property. The term includes an individual condominium unit, cooperative unit, mobile home, and trailer, if it is used as a residence.

(20) *Open-end credit* means consumer credit extended by a creditor under a plan in which:

(i) The creditor reasonably contemplates repeated transactions;

(ii) The creditor may impose a finance charge from time to time on an outstanding unpaid balance; and

(iii) The amount of credit that may be extended to the consumer during the term of the plan (up to any limit set by the creditor) is generally made available to the extent that any outstanding balance is repaid.

---

[3]A person regularly extends consumer credit only if it extended credit (other than credit subject to the requirements of § 226.32) more than 25 times (or more than five times for transactions secured by a dwelling) in the preceding calendar year. If a person did not meet these numerical standards in the preceding calendar year, the numerical standards shall be applied to the current calendar year. A person regularly extends consumer credit if, in any 12-month period, the person originates more than one credit extension that is subject to the requirements of § 226.32 or one or more such credit extensions through a mortgage broker.

(21) *Periodic rate* means a rate of finance charge that is or may be imposed by a creditor on a balance for a day, week, month, or other subdivision of a year.

(22) *Person* means a natural person or an organization, including a corporation, partnership, proprietorship, association, cooperative, estate, trust, or government unit.

(23) *Prepaid finance charge* means any finance charge paid separately in cash or by check before or at consummation of a transaction, or withheld from the proceeds of the credit at any time.

(24) *Residential mortgage transaction* means a transaction in which a mortgage, deed of trust, purchase money security interest arising under an installment sales contract, or equivalent consensual security interest is created or retained in the consumer's principal dwelling to finance the acquisition or initial construction of that dwelling.

(25) *Security interest* means an interest in property that secures performance of a consumer credit obligation and that is recognized by state or federal law. It does not include incidental interests such as interests in proceeds, accessions, additions, fixtures, insurance proceeds (whether or not the creditor is a loss payee or beneficiary), premium rebates, or interests in after-acquired property. For purposes of disclosure under §§ 226.6 and 226.18, the term does not include an interest that arises solely by operation of law. However, for purposes of the right of rescission under §§ 226.15 and 226.23, the term does include interests that arise solely by operation of law.

(26) *State* means any state, the District of Columbia, the Commonwealth of Puerto Rico, and any territory or possession of the United States.

(b) *Rules of construction.* For purposes of this regulation, the following rules of construction apply:

(1) Where appropriate, the singular form of a word includes the plural form and plural includes singular.

(2) Where the words "obligation" and "transaction" are used in this regulation, they refer to a consumer credit obligation or transaction, depending upon the context. Where the word "credit" is used in this regulation, it means "consumer credit" unless the context clearly indicates otherwise.

(3) Unless defined in this regulation, the words used have the meanings given to them by state law or contract.

(4) Footnotes have the same legal effect as the text of the regulation.

Section 226.3—Exempt transactions

This regulation does not apply to the following:

(a) *Business, commercial, agricultural, or organizational credit.*[4]

---

[4]*The provisions in § 226.12(a) and (b) governing the issurance of credit cards and the liability for their unauthorized use apply to all credit cards, even if the credit cards are issued for use in connection with extensions of credit that otherwise are exempt under this section.*

(1) An extension of credit primarily for a business, commercial or agricultural purpose.

(2) An extension of credit to other than a natural person, including credit to government agencies or instrumentalities.

(b) *Credit over $25,000 not secured by real property or a dwelling.* An extension of credit not secured by real property, or by personal property used or expected to be used as the principal dwelling of the consumer, in which the amount financed exceeds $25,000 or in which there is an express written commitment to extend credit in excess of $25,000.

(c) *Public utility credit.* An extension of credit that involves public utility services provided through pipe, wire, other connected facilities, or radio or similar transmission (including extensions of such facilities), if the charges for service, delayed payment, or any discounts for prompt payment are filed with or regulated by any government unit. The financing of durable goods or home improvements by a public utility is not exempt.

(d) *Securities or commodities accounts.* Transactions in securities or commodities accounts in which credit is extended by a broker-dealer registered with the Securities and Exchange Commission or the Commodity Futures Trading Commission.

(e) *Home fuel budget plans.* An installment agreement for the purchase of home fuels in which no finance charge is imposed.

(f) *Student loan programs.* Loans made, insured, or guaranteed pursuant to a program authorized by title IV of the Higher Education Act of 1965 (20 U.S.C. 1070 *et seq.*).

Section 226.4—Finance charge

(a) *Definition.* The finance charge is the cost of consumer credit as a dollar amount. It includes any charge payable directly or indirectly by the consumer and imposed directly or indirectly by the creditor as an incident to or a condition of the extension of credit. It does not include any charge of a type payable in a comparable cash transaction.

(1) *Charges by third parties.* The finance charge includes fees and amounts charged by someone other than the creditor, unless otherwise excluded under this section, if the creditor:

 (i) Requires the use of a third party as a condition of or an incident to the extension of credit, even if the consumer can choose the third party; or

 (ii) Retains a portion of the third-party charge, to the extent of the portion retained.

(2) *Special rule; closing agent charges.* Fees charged by a third party that conducts the loan closing (such as a settlement agent, attorney, or escrow or title company) are finance charges only if the creditor:

 (i) Requires the particular services for which the consumer is charged;

 (ii) Requires the imposition of the charge; or

 (iii) Retains a portion of the third-party charge, to the extent of the portion retained.

(3) *Special rule; mortgage broker fees.* Fees charged by a mortgage broker (including fees paid by the consumer directly to the broker or to the creditor for delivery to the broker) are finance charges even if the creditor does not require the consumer to use a mortgage broker and even if the creditor does not retain any portion of the charge.

(b) *Example of finance charge.* The finance charge includes the following types of charges, except for charges specifically excluded by paragraphs (c) through (e) of this section:

(1) Interest, time price differential, and any amount payable under an add-on or discount system of additional charges.

(2) Service, transaction, activity, and carrying charges, including any charge imposed on a checking or other transaction account to the extent that the charge exceeds the charge for a similar account without a credit feature.

(3) Points, loan fees, assumption fees, finder's fees, and similar charges.

(4) Appraisal, investigation, and credit report fees.

(5) Premiums or other charges for any guarantee or insurance protecting the creditor against the consumer's default or other credit loss.

(6) Charges imposed on a creditor by another person for purchasing or accepting a consumer's obligation, if the consumer is required to pay the charges in cash, as an addition to the obligation, or as a deduction from the proceeds of the obligation.

(7) Premiums or other charges for credit life, accident, health, or loss-of-income insurance, written in connection with a credit transaction.

(8) Premiums or other charges for insurance against loss of or damage to property, or against liability arising out of the ownership or use of property, written in connection with a credit transaction.

(9) Discounts for the purpose of inducing payment by a means other than the use of credit.

(10) *Debt cancellation fees.* Charges or premiums paid for debt cancellation coverage written in connection with a credit transaction, whether or not the debt cancellation coverage is insurance under applicable law.

(c) *Charges excluded from the finance charge.* The following charges are not finance charges:

(1) Application fees charged to all applicants for credit, whether or not credit is actually extended.

(2) Charges for actual unanticipated late payment, for exceeding a credit limit or for delinquency, default, or a similar occurrence.

(3) Charges imposed by a financial institution for paying items that overdraw an account, unless the payment of such items and the imposition of the charge were previously agreed upon in writing.

(4) Fees charged for participation in a credit plan, whether assessed on an annual or other periodic basis.

(5) Seller's points.

(6) Interest forfeited as a result of an interest reduction required by law on a time deposit used as security for an extension of credit.

(7) *Real-estate related fees.* The following fees in a transaction secured by real property or in a residential mortgage transaction, if the fees are bona fide and reasonable in amount:

(i) Fees for title examination, abstract of title, title insurance, property survey, and similar purposes.

(ii) Fees for preparing loan-related documents, such as deeds, mortgages, and reconveyance or settlement documents.

(iii) Notary, and credit report fees.

(iv) Property appraisal fees or fees for inspections to assess the value or condition of the property if the service is performed prior to closing, including fees related to pest infestation or flood hazard determinations.

(v) Amounts required to be paid into escrow or trustee accounts if the amounts would not otherwise be included in the finance charge.

(8) Discounts offered to induce payment for a purchase by cash, check, or other means, as provided in § 167(b) of the act.

(d) *Insurance and debt cancellation coverage.*

(1) *Voluntary credit.* Premiums for credit life, accident, health, or loss-of-income insurance may be excluded from the finance charge if the following conditions are met:

(i) The insurance coverage is not required by the creditor, and this fact is disclosed in writing.

(ii) The premium for the initial term of insurance coverage is disclosed. If the term of insurance is less than the term of the transaction, the term of insurance also shall be disclosed. The premium may be disclosed on a unit-cost basis only in open-end credit transactions, closed-end credit transactions by mail or telephone under § 226.17(g), and certain closed-end credit transactions involving an insurance plan that limits the total amount of indebtedness subject to coverage.

(iii) The consumer signs or initials an affirmative written request for the insurance after receiving the disclosures specified in this paragraph. Any consumer in the transaction may sign or initial the request.

(2) Premiums for insurance against loss of or damage to property, or against liability arising out of the ownership or use of property,[5] may be excluded from the finance charge if the following conditions are met:

(i) The insurance coverage may be obtained from a person of the consumer's choice,[6] and this fact is disclosed.

---

[5]This includes single interest insurance if the insurer waives all right of subrogation against the consumer.

[6]A creditor may reserve the right to refuse to accept, for reasonable cause, an insurer offered by the consumer.

(ii) If the coverage is obtained from or through the creditor, the premium for the initial term of insurance coverage shall be disclosed. If the term of insurance is less than the term of the transaction, the term of insurance shall also be disclosed. The premium may be disclosed on a unit-cost basis only in open-end credit transactions, closed-end credit transactions by mail or telephone under § 226.17(g), and certain closed-end credit transactions involving an insurance plan that limits the total amount of indebtedness subject to coverage.

(3) *Voluntary debt cancellation fees.*

(i) Charges or premiums paid for debt cancellation coverage of the type specified in paragraph (d)(3)(ii) of this section may be excluded from the finance charge, whether or not the coverage is insurance, if the following conditions are met:

(A) The debt cancellation agreement or coverage is not required by the creditor, and this fact is disclosed in writing;

(B) The fee or premium for the initial term of coverage is disclosed. If the term of coverage is less than the term of the credit transaction, the term of coverage also shall be disclosed. The fee or premium may be disclosed on a unit-cost basis only in open-end credit transactions, closed-end credit transactions by mail or telephone under § 226.17(g), and certain closed-end credit transactions involving a debt cancellation agreement that limits the total amount of indebtedness subject to coverage;

(C) The consumer signs or initials an affirmative written request for coverage after receiving the disclosures specified in this paragraph. Any consumer in the transaction may sign or initial the request.

(ii) Paragraph (d)(3)(i) of this section applies to fees paid for debt cancellation coverage that provides for cancellation of all or part of the debtor's liability for amounts exceeding the value of the collateral securing the obligation, or in the event of the loss of life, health, or income or in case of accident.

(e) *Certain security interest charges.* If itemized and disclosed, the following charges may be excluded from the finance charge:

(1) Taxes and fees prescribed by law that actually are or will be paid to public officials for determining the existence of or for perfecting, releasing, or satisfying a security interest.

(2) The premium for insurance in lieu of perfecting a security interest to the extent that the premium does not exceed the fees described in paragraph (e)(1) of this section that otherwise would be payable.

(3) *Taxes on security instruments.* Any tax levied on security instruments or on documents evidencing indebtedness if the payment of such taxes is a requirement for recording the instrument securing the evidence of indebtedness.

(f) *Prohibited offsets.* Interest, dividends, or other income received or to be received by the consumer on deposits or investments shall not be deducted in computing the finance charge.

SUBPART B—OPEN-END CREDIT

Section 226.5—General disclosure requirements.

(a) *Form of disclosures.*

(1) The creditor shall make the disclosures required by this subpart clearly and conspicuously in writing,[7] in a form that the consumer may keep.[8] The disclosures required by this subpart may be provided to the consumer in electronic form, subject to compliance with the consumer consent and other applicable provisions of the Electronic Signatures in Global and National Commerce Act (E-Sign Act) (15 U.S.C. § 7001 *et seq.*). The disclosures required by §§ 226.5a, 226.5b, and 226.16 may be provided to the consumer in electronic form without regard to the consumer consent or other provisions of the E-Sign Act in the circumstances set forth in those sections.

(2) The terms "finance charge" and "annual percentage rate," when required to be disclosed with a corresponding amount or percentage rate, shall be more conspicuous than any other required disclosure.[9]

(3) Certain disclosures required under § 226.5a for credit and charge card applications and solicitations must be provided in a tabular format or in a prominent location in accordance with the requirements of that section.

(4) For rules governing the form of disclosures for home equity plans, *see* § 226.5b(a).

(b) *Time of disclosures.*

(1) *Initial disclosures.* The creditor shall furnish the initial disclosure statement required by § 226.6 before the first transaction is made under the plan.

---

[7]The disclosure required by section 226.9(d) when a finance charge is imposed at the time of a transaction need not be written.

[8]The disclosures required under Sec. 226.5a for credit and charge card applications and solicitations, the home equity disclosures required under Sec. 226.5b(d), the alternative summary billing rights statement provided for in Sec. 226.9(a)(2s), the credit and charge card renewal disclosures required under Sec. 226.9(e), and the disclosures made under Sec. 226.10(b) about payment requirements need not be in a form that the consumer can keep.

[9]The terms need not be more conspicuous when used under Sec. 226.5a generally for credit and charge card applications and solicitations under Sec. 226.7(d) on periodic statements, under Sec. 226.9(e) in credit and charge card renewal disclosures, and under Sec. 226.16 in advertisements. (But see special rule for annual percentage rate for purchases, Sec. 226.5a(b)(1).)

(2) *Periodic statements.*

(i) The creditor shall mail or deliver a periodic statement as required by § 226.7 for each billing cycle at the end of which an account has a debit or credit balance of more than $1 or on which a finance charge has been imposed. A periodic statement need not be sent for an account if the creditor deems it uncollectible, or if delinquency collection proceedings have been instituted, or if furnishing the statement would violate federal law.

(ii) The creditor shall mail or deliver the periodic statement at least 14 days prior to any date or the end of any time period required to be disclosed under § 226.7(j) in order for the consumer to avoid an additional finance or other charge.[10] A creditor that fails to meet this requirement shall not collect any finance or other charge imposed as a result of such failure.

(3) *Credit and charge card application and solicitation disclosures.* The card issuer shall furnish the disclosures for credit and charge card applications and solicitations in accordance with the timing requirements of § 226.5a.

(4) *Home equity plans.* Disclosures for home equity plans shall be made in accordance with the timing requirements of § 226.5b(b).

(c) *Basis of disclosures and use of estimates.* Disclosures shall reflect the terms of the legal obligation between the parties. If any information necessary for accurate disclosure is unknown to the creditor, it shall make the disclosure based on the best information reasonably available and shall state clearly that the disclosure is an estimate.

(d) *Multiple creditors; multiple consumers.* If the credit plan involves more than one creditor, only one set of disclosures shall be given, and the creditors shall agree among themselves which creditor must comply with the requirements that this regulation imposes on any or all of them. If there is more than one consumer, the disclosures may be made to any consumer who is primarily liable on the account. If the right of rescission under § 226.15 is applicable, however, the disclosures required by §§ 226.6 and 226.15(b) shall be made to each consumer having the right to rescind.

(e) *Effect of subsequent events.* If a disclosure becomes inaccurate because of an event that occurs after the creditor mails or delivers the disclosures, the resulting inaccuracy is not a violation of this regulation, although new disclosures may be required under § 226.9(c).

Section 226.5a—Credit and charge card applications and solicitations.

(a) *General rules.* The card issuer shall provide the disclosures required under this section on or with a solicitation or an application to open a credit or charge card account.

---

[10]This timing requirement does not apply if the creditor is unable to meet the requirement because of an act of God, war, civil disorder, natural disaster, or strike.

(1) *Definition of solicitation.* For purposes of this section, the term "solicitation" means an offer by the card issuer to open a credit or charge card account that does not require the consumer to complete an application.

(2) *Form of disclosures.*

(i) The disclosures in paragraph (b)(1) through (7) of this section shall be provided in a prominent location on or with an application or a solicitation, or other applicable document, and in the form of a table with headings, content, and format substantially similar to any of the applicable tables found in Appendix G.

(ii) The disclosures in paragraphs (b)(8) through (11) of this section shall be provided either in the table containing the disclosures in paragraph (b)(1) through (7), or clearly and conspicuously elsewhere on or with the application or solicitation.

(iii) The disclosure required under paragraph (b)(5) of this section shall contain the term "grace period."

(iv) The terminology in the disclosures under paragraph (b) of this section shall be consistent with that to be used in the disclosures under §§ 226.6 and 226.7.

(v) For an application or a solicitation that is accessed by the consumer in electronic form, the disclosures required under this section may be provided to the consumer in electronic form on or with the application or solicitation.

(3) *Exceptions.* This section does not apply to home-equity plans accessible by a credit or charge card that are of the type subject to the requirements of § 226.5b; overdraft lines of credit tied to asset accounts accessed by check-guarantee cards or by debit cards; or lines of credit accessed by check-guarantee cards or by debit cards that can be used only at automated teller machines.

(4) *Fees based on a percentage.* If the amount of any fee required to be disclosed under this section is determined on the basis of a percentage of another amount, the percentage used and the identification of the amount against which the percentage is applied may be disclosed instead of the amount of the fee.

(5) *Certain fees that vary by state.* If the amount of any fee referred to in paragraphs (b)(8) through (11) of this section varies from state to state, the card issuer may disclose the range of the fees instead of the amount for each state, if the disclosure includes a statement that the amount of the fee varies from state to state.

(b) *Required disclosures.* The card issuer shall disclose the items in this paragraph on or with an application or a solicitation in accordance with the requirements of paragraphs (c), (d) or (e) of this section. A credit card issuer shall disclose all applicable items in this paragraph except for paragraph (b)(7) of this section. A charge card issuer shall disclose the applicable items in paragraphs (b)(2), (4), and (7) through (11) of this section.

(1) *Annual percentage rate.* Each periodic rate that may be used to compute the finance charge on an outstanding balance for purchases, a cash advance,

or a balance transfer, expressed as an annual percentage rate (as determined by § 226.14(b)). When more than one rate applies for a category of transactions, the range of balances to which each rate is applicable shall also be disclosed. The annual percentage rate for purchases disclosed pursuant to this paragraph shall be in at least 18-point type, except for the following: a temporary initial rate that is lower than the rate that will apply after the temporary rate expires, and a penalty rate that will apply upon the occurrence of one or more specific events.

(i) If the account has a variable rate, the card issuer shall also disclose the fact that the rate may vary and how the rate is determined.

(ii) When variable rate disclosures are provided under paragraph (c) of this section, an annual percentage rate disclosure is accurate if the rate was in effect within 60 days before mailing the disclosures. When variable rate disclosures are provided under paragraph (e) of this section, an annual percentage rate disclosure is accurate if the rate was in effect within 30 days before printing the disclosures. Disclosures provided by electronic communication are subject to paragraph (b)(1)(iii) of this section.

(iii) When variable rate disclosures are provided by electronic communication, an annual percentage rate disclosure is accurate if the rate was in effect within 30 days before mailing the disclosures to a consumer's electronic mail address. If disclosures are made available at another location such as the card issuer's Internet website, the annual percentage rate must be one in effect within the last 30 days.

(2) *Fees for issuance or availability.* Any annual or other periodic fee, expressed as an annualized amount, or any other fee that may be imposed for the issuance or availability of a credit or charge card, including any fee based on account activity or inactivity.

(3) *Minimum finance charge.* Any minimum or fixed finance charge that could be imposed during a billing cycle.

(4) *Transaction charges.* Any transaction charge imposed for the use of the card for purchases.

(5) *Grace period.* The date by which or the period within which any credit extended for purchases may be repaid without incurring a finance charge. If no grace period is provided, that fact must be disclosed. If the length of the grace period varies, the card issuer may disclose the range of days, the minimum number of days, or the average number of days in the grace period, if the disclosure is identified as a range, minimum, or average.

(6) *Balance computation method.* The name of the balance computation method listed in paragraph (g) of this section that is used to determine the balance for purchases on which the finance charge is computed, or an explanation of the method used if it is not listed. The explanation may appear outside the table if the table contains a reference to the explanation. In determining which balance computation method to disclose, the card issuer shall

assume that credit extended for purchases will not be repaid within the grace period, if any.

(7) *Statement on charge card payments.* A statement that charges incurred by use of the charge card are due when the periodic statement is received.

(8) *Cash advance fee.* Any fee imposed for an extension of credit in the form of cash.

(9) *Late payment fee.* Any fee imposed for a late payment.

(10) *Over-the-limit fee.* Any fee imposed for exceeding a credit limit.

(11) *Balance transfer fee.* Any fee imposed to transfer an outstanding balance.

(c) *Direct mail and electronic applications and solicitations.* The card issuer shall disclose the applicable items in paragraph (b) of this section on or with an application or solicitation that is mailed to consumers or provided by electronic communication.

(d) *Telephone applications and solicitations*—

(1) *Oral disclosure.* The card issuer shall orally disclose the information in paragraph (b)(1) through (7) of this section, to the extent applicable, in a telephone application or solicitation initiated by the card issuer.

(2) *Alternative disclosure.* The oral disclosure under paragraph (d)(1) of this section need not be given if the card issuer either does not impose a fee described in paragraph (b)(2) of this section or does not impose such a fee unless the consumer uses the card, and the card issuer discloses in writing within 30 days after the consumer requests the card (but in no event later than the delivery of the card) the following:

   (i) The applicable information in paragraph (b) of this section; and

   (ii) The fact that the consumer need not accept the card or pay any fee disclosed unless the consumer uses the card.

(e) *Applications and solicitations made available to general public.* The card issuer shall provide disclosures, to the extent applicable, on or with an application or solicitation that is made available to the general public, including one contained in a catalog, magazine, or other generally available publication. The disclosures shall be provided in accordance with paragraph (e)(1), (2) or (3) of this section.

(1) *Disclosure of required credit information.* The card issuer may disclose in a prominent location on the application or solicitation the following:

   (i) The applicable information in paragraph (b) of this section;

   (ii) The date the required information was printed, including a statement that the required information was accurate as of that date and is subject to change after that date; and

   (iii) A statement that the consumer should contact the card issuer for any change in the required information since it was printed, and a toll-free telephone number or a mailing address for that purpose.

(2) *Inclusion of certain initial disclosures.* The card issuer may disclose on or with the application or solicitation the following:

(i) The disclosures required under § 226.6(a) through (c); and

(ii) A statement that the consumer should contact the card issuer for any change in the required information, and a toll-free telephone number or a mailing address for that purpose.

(3) *No disclosure of credit information.* If none of the items in paragraph (b) of this section is provided on or with the application or solicitation, the card issuer may state in a prominent location on the application or solicitation the following:

(i) There are costs associated with the use of the card; and

(ii) The consumer may contact the card issuer to request specific information about the costs, along with a toll-free telephone number and a mailing address for that purpose.

(4) *Prompt response to requests for information.* Upon receiving a request for any of the information referred to in this paragraph, the card issuer shall promptly and fully disclose the information requested.

(f) *Special charge card rule—card issuer and person extending credit not the same person.* If a cardholder may by use of a charge card access an open-end credit plan that is not maintained by the charge card issuer, the card issuer need not provide the disclosures in paragraphs (c), (d) or (e) of this section for the open-end credit plan if the card issuer states on or with an application or a solicitation the following:

(1) The card issuer will make an independent decision whether to issue the card;

(2) The charge card may arrive before the decision is made about extending credit under the open-end credit plan; and

(3) Approval for the charge card does not constitute approval for the open-end credit plan.

(g) *Balance computation methods defined.* The following methods may be described by name. Methods that differ due to variations such as the allocation of payments, whether the finance charge begins to accrue on the transaction date or the date of posting the transaction, the existence or length of a grace period, and whether the balance is adjusted by charges such as late fees, annual fees and unpaid finance charges do not constitute separate balance computation methods.

(1) (i) *Average daily balance (including new purchases).* This balance is figured by adding the outstanding balance (including new purchases and deducting payments and credits) for each day in the billing cycle, and then dividing by the number of days in the billing cycle.

(ii) *Average daily balance (excluding new purchases).* This balance is figured by adding the outstanding balance (excluding new purchases and deducting payments and credits) for each day in the billing cycle, and then dividing by the number of days in the billing cycle.

(2) (i) *Two-cycle average daily balance (including new purchases).* This balance is the sum of the average daily balances for two billing cycles. The first balance is for the current billing cycle, and is figured by adding the outstanding balance (including new purchases and deducting payments and credits) for each day in the billing cycle, and then dividing by the number of days in the billing cycle. The second balance is for the preceding billing cycle and is figured in the same way as the first balance.

(ii) *Two-cycle average daily balance (excluding new purchases).* This balance is the sum of the average daily balances for two billing cycles. The first balance is for the current billing cycle, and is figured by adding the outstanding balance (excluding new purchases and deducting payments and credits) for each day in the billing cycle, and then dividing by the number of days in the billing cycle. The second balance is for the preceding billing cycle and is figured in the same way as the first balance.

(3) *Adjusted balance.* This balance is figured by deducting payments and credits made during the billing cycle from the outstanding balance at the beginning of the billing cycle.

(4) *Previous balance.* This balance is the outstanding balance at the beginning of the billing cycle.

Section 226.5b—Requirements for home equity plans.

The requirements of this section apply to open-end credit plans secured by the consumer's dwelling. For purposes of this section, an annual percentage rate is the annual percentage rate corresponding to the periodic rate as determined under § 226.14(b).

(a) *Form of disclosures*—

(1) *General.* The disclosures required by paragraph (d) of this section shall be made clearly and conspicuously and shall be grouped together and segregated from all unrelated information. The disclosures may be provided on the application form or on a separate form. The disclosure described in paragraph (d)(4)(iii), the itemization of third-party fees described in paragraph (d)(8), and the variable-rate information described in paragraph (d)(12) of this section may be provided separately from the other required disclosures.

(2) *Precedence of certain disclosures.* The disclosures described in paragraph (d)(1) through (4)(ii) of this section shall precede the other required disclosures.

(3) For an application that is accessed by the consumer in electronic form, the disclosures required under this section may be provided to the consumer in electronic form on or with the application.

(b) *Time of disclosures.* The disclosures and brochure required by paragraphs (d) and (e) of this section shall be provided at the time an application is provided to the consumer.[10a]

[10a]The disclosures and the brochure may be delivered or placed in the mail not later than three business days following receipt of a consumer's application in the case of applications contained in magazines or other publications, or when the application is received by telephone or through an intermediary agent or broker.

(c) *Duties of third parties.* Persons other than the creditor who provide applications to consumers for home equity plans must provide the brochure required under paragraph (e) of this section at the time an application is provided. If such persons have the disclosures required under paragraph (d) of this section for a creditor's home equity plan, they also shall provide the disclosures at such time.[10a]

(d) *Content of disclosures.* The creditor shall provide the following disclosures, as applicable:

(1) *Retention of information.* A statement that the consumer should make or otherwise retain a copy of the disclosures.

(2) *Conditions for disclosed terms.* (i) A statement of the time by which the consumer must submit an application to obtain specific terms disclosed and an identification of any disclosed term that is subject to change prior to opening the plan.

(ii) A statement that, if a disclosed term changes (other than a change due to fluctuations in the index in a variable-rate plan) prior to opening the plan and the consumer therefore elects not to open the plan, the consumer may receive a refund of all fees paid in connection with the application.

(3) *Security interest and risk to home.* A statement that the creditor will acquire a security interest in the consumer's dwelling and that loss of the dwelling may occur in the event of default.

(4) *Possible actions by creditor.* (i) A statement that, under certain conditions, the creditor may terminate the plan and require payment of the outstanding balance in full in a single payment and impose fees upon termination; prohibit additional extensions of credit or reduce the credit limit; and, as specified in the initial agreement, implement certain changes in the plan.

(ii) A statement that the consumer may receive, upon request, information about the conditions under which such actions may occur.

(iii) In lieu of the disclosure required under paragraph (d)(4)(ii) of this section, a statement of such conditions.

(5) *Payment terms.* The payment terms of the plan, including:

(i) The length of the draw period and any repayment period.

(ii) An explanation of how the minimum periodic payment will be determined and the timing of the payments. If paying only the minimum periodic payments may not repay any of the principal or may repay less than the outstanding balance, a statement of this fact, as well as a statement that a balloon payment may result.[10b]

[10b]A balloon payment results if paying the minimum periodic payments does not fully amortize the outstanding balance by a specified date or time, and the consumer must repay the entire outstanding balance at such time.

(iii) An example, based on a $10,000 outstanding balance and a recent annual percentage rate,[10c] showing the minimum periodic payment, any balloon payment, and the time it would take to repay the $10,000 outstanding balance if the consumer made only those payments and obtained no additional extensions of credit.

If different payment terms may apply to the draw and any repayment period, or if different payment terms may apply within either period, the disclosures shall reflect the different payment terms.

(6) *Annual percentage rate.* For fixed-rate plans, a recent annual percentage rate[10c] imposed under the plan and a statement that the rate does not include costs other than interest.

(7) *Fees imposed by creditor.* An itemization of any fees imposed by the creditor to open, use, or maintain the plan, stated as a dollar amount or percentage, and when such fees are payable.

(8) *Fees imposed by third parties to open a plan.* A good faith estimate, stated as a single dollar amount or range, of any fees that may be imposed by persons other than the creditor to open the plan, as well as a statement that the consumer may receive, upon request, a good faith itemization of such fees. In lieu of the statement, the itemization of such fees may be provided.

(9) *Negative amortization.* A statement that negative amortization may occur and that negative amortization increases the principal balance and reduces the consumer's equity in the dwelling.

(10) *Transaction requirements.* Any limitations on the number of extensions of credit and the amount of credit that may be obtained during any time period, as well as any minimum outstanding balance and minimum draw requirements, stated as dollar amounts or percentages.

(11) *Tax implications.* A statement that the consumer should consult a tax advisor regarding the deductibility of interest and charges under the plan.

(12) *Disclosures for variable-rate plans.* For a plan in which the annual percentage rate is variable, the following disclosures, as applicable:

(i) The fact that the annual percentage rate, payment, or term may change due to the variable-rate feature.

(ii) A statement that the annual percentage rate does not include costs other than interest.

(iii) The index used in making rate adjustments and a source of information about the index.

[10c]For fixed-rate plans, a recent annual percentage rate is a rate that has been in effect under the plan within the twelve months preceding the date the disclosures are provided to the consumer. For variable-rate plans, a recent annual percentage rate is the most recent rate provided in the historical example described in paragraph (d)(12)(xi) of this section or a rate that has been in effect under the plan since the date of the most recent rate in the table.

(iv) An explanation of how the annual percentage rate will be determined, including an explanation of how the index is adjusted, such as by the addition of a margin.

(v) A statement that the consumer should ask about the current index value, margin, discount or premium, and annual percentage rate.

(vi) A statement that the initial annual percentage rate is not based on the index and margin used to make later rate adjustments, and the period of time such initial rate will be in effect.

(vii) The frequency of changes in the annual percentage rate.

(viii) Any rules relating to changes in the index value and the annual percentage rate and resulting changes in the payment amount, including, for example, an explanation of payment limitations and rate carryover.

(ix) A statement of any annual or more frequent periodic limitations on changes in the annual percentage rate (or a statement that no annual limitation exists), as well as a statement of the maximum annual percentage rate that may be imposed under each payment option.

(x) The minimum periodic payment required when the maximum annual percentage rate for each payment option is in effect for a $10,000 outstanding balance, and a statement of the earliest date or time the maximum rate may be imposed.

(xi) An historical example, based on a $10,000 extension of credit, illustrating how annual percentage rates and payments would have been affected by index value changes implemented according to the terms of the plan. The historical example shall be based on the most recent 15 years of index values (selected for the same time period each year) and shall reflect all significant plan terms, such as negative amortization, rate carryover, rate discounts, and rate and payment limitations, that would have been affected by the index movement during the period.

(xii) A statement that rate information will be provided on or with each periodic statement.

(e) *Brochure.* The home equity brochure published by the Board or a suitable substitute shall be provided.

(f) *Limitations on home equity plans.* No creditor may, by contract or otherwise:

(1) Change the annual percentage rate unless:

(i) Such change is based on an index that is not under the creditor's control; and

(ii) Such index is available to the general public.

(2) Terminate a plan and demand repayment of the entire outstanding balance in advance of the original term (except for reverse mortgage transactions that are subject to paragraph (f)(4) of this section) unless:

(i) There is fraud or material misrepresentation by the consumer in connection with the plan;

(ii) The consumer fails to meet the repayment terms of the agreement for any outstanding balance;

(iii) Any action or inaction by the consumer adversely affects the creditor's security for the plan, or any right of the creditor in such security; or

(iv) Federal law dealing with credit extended by a depository institution to its executive officers specifically requires that as a condition of the plan the credit shall become due and payable on demand, provided that the creditor includes such a provision in the initial agreement.

(3) Change any term, except that a creditor may:

(i) Provide in the initial agreement that it may prohibit additional extension of credit or reduce the credit limit during any period in which the maximum annual percentage rate is reached. A creditor also may provide in the initial agreement that specified changes will occur if a specified event takes place (for example, that the annual percentage rate will increase a specified amount if the consumer leaves the creditor's employment).

(ii) Change the index and margin used under the plan if the original index is no longer available, the new index has an historical movement substantially similar to that of the original index, and the new index and margin would have resulted in an annual percentage rate substantially similar to the rate in effect at the time the original index became unavailable.

(iii) Make a specified change if the consumer specifically agrees to it in writing at that time.

(iv) Make a change that will unequivocally benefit the consumer throughout the remainder of the plan.

(v) Make an insignificant change to terms.

(vi) Prohibit additional extensions of credit or reduce the credit limit applicable to an agreement during any period in which:

(A) The value of the dwelling that secures the plan declines significantly below the dwelling's appraised value for purposes of the plan;

(B) The creditor reasonably believes that the consumer will be unable to fulfill the repayment obligations under the plan because of a material change in the consumer's financial circumstances;

(C) The consumer is in default of any material obligation under the agreement;

(D) The creditor is precluded by government action from imposing the annual percentage rate provided for in the agreement;

(E) The priority of the creditor's security interest is adversely affected by government action to the extent that the value of the security interest is less than 120 percent of the credit line; or

(F) The creditor is notified by its regulatory agency that continued advances constitute an unsafe and unsound practice.

(4) For reverse mortgage transactions that are subject to § 226.33, terminate a plan and demand repayment of the entire outstanding balance in advance of the original term except:

(i) In the case of default;

(ii) If the consumer transfers title to the property securing the note;

(iii) If the consumer ceases using the property securing the note as the primary dwelling; or

(iv) Upon the consumer's death.

(g) *Refund of fees.* A creditor shall refund all fees paid by the consumer to anyone in connection with an application if any term required to be disclosed under paragraph (d) of this section changes (other than a change due to fluctuations in the index in a variable-rate plan) before the plan is opened and, as a result, the consumer elects not to open the plan.

(h) *Imposition of nonrefundable fees.* Neither a creditor nor any other person may impose a nonrefundable fee in connection with an application until three business days after the consumer receives the disclosures and brochure required under this section.[10d]

Section 226.6—Initial disclosure statement

The creditor shall disclose to the consumer, in terminology consistent with that to be used on the periodic statement, each of the following items, to the extent applicable:

(a) *Finance charge.* The circumstances under which a finance charge will be imposed and an explanation of how it will be determined, as follows:

(1) A statement of when finance charges begin to accrue, including an explanation of whether or not any time period exists within which any credit extended may be repaid without incurring a finance charge. If such a time period is provided, a creditor may, at its option and without disclosure, impose no finance charge when payment is received after the time period's expiration.

(2) A disclosure of each periodic rate that may be used to compute the finance charge, the range of balances to which it is applicable,[11] and the corresponding annual percentage rate.[12] When different periodic rates apply to different types of transactions, the types of transactions to which the periodic rates apply shall also be disclosed.

(3) An explanation of the method used to determine the balance on which the finance charge may be computed.

[10d]If the disclosures and brochure are mailed to the consumer, the consumer is considered to have received them three business days after they are mailed.

[11]A creditor is not required to adjust the range of balances disclosure to reflect the balance below which only a minimum charge applies.

[12]If a creditor is offering a variable rate plan, the creditor shall also disclose: (1) the circumstances under which the rate(s) may increase; (2) any limitations on the increase; and (3) the effect(s) of an increase.

(4) An explanation of how the amount of any finance charge will be determined,[13] including a description of how any finance charge other than the periodic rate will be determined.

(b) *Other charges.* The amount of any charge other than a finance charge that may be imposed as part of the plan, or an explanation of how the charge will be determined.

(c) *Security interests.* The fact that the creditor has or will acquire a security interest in the property purchased under the plan, or in other property identified by item or type.

(d) *Statement of billing rights.* A statement that outlines the consumer's rights and the creditor's responsibilities under §§ 226.12(c) and 226.13 and that is substantially similar to the statement found in appendix G.

(e) *Home equity plan information.* The following disclosures described in § 226.5b(d), as applicable:

(1) A statement of the conditions under which the creditor may take certain action, as described in § 226.5b(d)(4)(i), such as terminating the plan or changing the terms.

(2) The payment information described in § 226.5b(d)(5)(i) and (ii) for both the draw period and any repayment period.

(3) A statement that negative amortization may occur as described in § 226.5b(d)(9).

(4) A statement of any transaction requirements as described in § 226.5b(d)(10).

(5) A statement regarding the tax implications as described in § 226.5b(d)(11).

(6) A statement that the annual percentage rate imposed under the plan does not include costs other than interest as described in §§ 226.5b(d)(6) and 226.5b(d)(12)(ii).

(7) The variable-rate disclosures described in § 226.5b(d)(12)(viii), (x), (xi), and (xii), as well as the disclosure described in § 226.5b(d)(5)(iii), unless the disclosures provided with the application were in a form the consumer could keep and included a representative payment example for the category of payment option chosen by the consumer.

Section 226.7—Periodic statement

The creditor shall furnish the consumer with a periodic statement that discloses the following items, to the extent applicable:

(a) *Previous balance.* The account balance outstanding at the beginning of the billing cycle.

(b) *Identification of transactions.* An identification of each credit transaction in accordance with § 226.8.

(c) *Credits.* Any credit to the account during the billing cycle, including the amount and the date of crediting. The date need not be provided if a delay in crediting does not result in any finance or other charge.

---

[13] If no finance charge is imposed when the outstanding balance is less than a certain amount, no disclosure is required of that fact or of the balance below which no finance charge will be imposed.

(d) *Periodic rates.* Each periodic rate that may be used to compute the finance charge, the range of balances to which it is applicable,[14] and the corresponding annual percentage rate.[15] If different periodic rates apply to different types of transactions, the types of transactions to which the periodic rates apply shall also be disclosed.

(e) *Balance on which finance charge computed.* The amount of the balance to which a periodic rate was applied and an explanation of how that balance was determined. When a balance is determined without first deducting all credits and payments made during the billing cycle, that fact and the amount of the credits and payments shall be disclosed.

(f) *Amount of finance charge.* The amount of any finance charge debited or added to the account during the billing cycle, using the term "finance charge." The components of the finance charge shall be individually itemized and identified to show the amount(s) due to the application of any periodic rates and the amount(s) of any other type of finance charge. If there is more than one periodic rate, the amount of the finance charge attributable to each rate need not be separately itemized and identified.

(g) *Annual percentage rate.* When a finance charge is imposed during the billing cycle, the annual percentage rate(s) determined under § 226.14, using the term "annual percentage rate."

(h) *Other charges.* The amounts, itemized and identified by type, of any charges other than finance charges debited to the account during the billing cycle.

(i) *Closing date of billing cycle; new balance.* The closing date of the billing cycle and the account balance outstanding on that date.

(j) *Free-ride period.* The date by which or the time period within which the new balance or any portion of the new balance must be paid to avoid additional finance charges. If such a time period is provided, a creditor may, at its option and without disclosure, impose no finance charge when payment is received after the time period's expiration.

(k) *Address for notice of billing errors.* The address to be used for notice of billing errors. Alternatively, the address may be provided on the billing rights statement permitted by § 226.9(a)(2).

Section 226.8—Identification of transactions

The creditor shall identify credit transactions on or with the first periodic statement that reflects the transaction by furnishing the following information, as applicable.[16]

---

[14]See footnotes 11 and 13.

[15]If a variable rate plan is involved, the creditor shall disclose the fact that the periodic rate(s) may vary.

[16]Failure to disclose the information required by this section shall not be deemed a failure to comply with the regulation if: (1) the creditor maintains procedures reasonably adapted to obtain and provide the information; and (2) the creditor treats an inquiry for clarification or documentation as a notice of a billing error, including correcting the account in accordance with § 226.13(e). This applies to transactions that take place outside a state, as defined in § 226.2(a), whether or not the creditor maintains procedures reasonably adapted to obtain the required information.

(a) *Sale credit.* For each credit transaction involving the sale of property or services, the following rules shall apply:

(1) *Copy of credit document provided.* When an actual copy of the receipt or other credit document is provided with the first periodic statement reflecting the transaction, the transaction is sufficiently identified if the amount of the transaction and either the date of the transaction or the date of debiting the transaction to the consumer's account are disclosed on the copy or on the periodic statement.

(2) *Copy of credit document not provided—creditor and seller same or related person(s).* When the creditor and the seller are the same person or related persons, and an actual copy of the receipt or other credit document is not provided with the periodic statement, the creditor shall disclose the amount and date of the transaction, and a brief identification[17] of the property or services purchased.[18]

(3) *Copy of credit document not provided—creditor and seller not same or related person(s).* When the creditor and seller are not the same person or related persons, and an actual copy of the receipt or other credit document is not provided with the periodic statement, the creditor shall disclose the amount and date of the transaction; the seller's name; and the city, and state or foreign country where the transaction took place.[19]

(b) *Nonsale credit.* A nonsale credit transaction is sufficiently identified if the first periodic statement reflecting the transaction discloses a brief identification of the transaction;[20] the amount of the transaction; and at least one of the following dates: the date of the transaction, the date of debiting the transaction to the consumer's account, or, if the consumer signed the credit document, the date appearing on the document. If an actual copy of the receipt or other credit document is provided and that copy shows the amount and at least one of the specified dates, the brief identification may be omitted.

---

[17]As an alternative to the brief identification, the creditor may disclose a number or symbol that also appears on the receipt or other credit document given to the consumer, if the number or symbol reasonably identifies that transaction with that creditor, and if the creditor treats an inquiry for clarification or documentation as a notice of a billing error, including correcting the account in accordance with § 226.13(e).

[18]An identification of property or services may be replaced by the seller's name and location of the transaction when: (1) the creditor and the seller are the same person; (2) the creditor's open-end plan has fewer than 15,000 accounts; (3) the creditor provides the consumer with point-of-sale documentation for that transaction; and (4) the creditor treats an inquiry for clarification or documentation as a notice of a billing error, including correcting the account in accordance with § 226.13(e).

[19]The creditor may omit the address or provide any suitable designation that helps the consumer to identify the transaction when the transaction (1) took place at a location that is not fixed; (2) took place in the consumer's home; or (3) was a mail or telephone order.

[20]See footnote 17.

Section 226.9—Subsequent disclosure requirements

(a) *Furnishing statement of billing rights.*

(1) *Annual statement.* The creditor shall mail or deliver the billing rights statement required by § 226.6(d) at least once per calendar year, at intervals of not less than 6 months nor more than 18 months, either to all consumers or to each consumer entitled to receive a periodic statement under § 226.5(b)(2) for any one billing cycle.

(2) *Alternative summary statement.* As an alternative to paragraph (a)(1) of this section, the creditor may mail or deliver, on or with each periodic statement, a statement substantially similar to that in Appendix G.

(b) *Disclosures for supplemental credit devices and additional features.*

(1) If a creditor, within 30 days after mailing or delivering the initial disclosures under § 226.6(a), adds a credit feature to the consumer's account or mails or delivers to the consumer a credit device for which the finance charge terms are the same as those previously disclosed, no additional disclosures are necessary. After 30 days, if the creditor adds a credit feature or furnishes a credit device (other than as a renewal, resupply, or the original issuance of a credit card) on the same finance charge terms, the creditor shall disclose, before the consumer uses the feature or device for the first time, that it is for use in obtaining credit under the terms previously disclosed.

(2) Whenever a credit feature is added or a credit device is mailed or delivered, and the finance charge terms for the feature or device differ from disclosures previously given, the disclosures required by § 226.6(a) that are applicable to the added feature or device shall be given before the consumer uses the feature or device for the first time.

(c) *Change in terms.*

(1) *Written notice required.* Whenever any term required to be disclosed under § 226.6 is changed or the required minimum periodic payment is increased, the creditor shall mail or deliver written notice of the change to each consumer who may be affected. The notice shall be mailed or delivered at least 15 days prior to the effective date of the change. The 15-day timing requirement does not apply if the change has been agreed to by the consumer, or if a periodic rate or other finance charge is increased because of the consumer's delinquency or default; the notice shall be given, however, before the effective date of the change.

(2) *Notice not required.* No notice under this section is required when the change involves late payment charges, charges for documentary evidence, or over-the-limit charges; a reduction of any component of a finance or other charge; suspension of future credit privileges or termination of an account or plan; or when the change results from an agreement involving a court proceeding, or from the consumer's default or delinquency (other than an increase in the periodic rate or other finance charge).

(3) *Notice for home equity plans.* If a creditor prohibits additional extensions of credit or reduces the credit limit applicable to a home equity plan pursuant to § 226.5b(f)(3)(i) or § 226.5b(f)(3)(vi), the creditor shall mail or deliver written notice of the action to each consumer who will be affected. The notice must be provided not later than three business days after the action is taken and shall contain specific reasons for the action. If the creditor requires the consumer to request reinstatement of credit privileges, the notice also shall state that fact.

(d) *Finance charge imposed at time of transaction.*

(1) Any person, other than the card issuer, who imposes a finance charge at the time of honoring a consumer's credit card, shall disclose the amount of that finance charge prior to its imposition.

(2) The card issuer, if other than the person honoring the consumer's credit card, shall have no responsibility for the disclosure required by paragraph (d)(1) of this section, and shall not consider any such charge for purposes of §§ 226.5a, 226.6 and 226.7.

(e) *Disclosures upon renewal of credit or charge card.*

(1) *Notice prior to renewal.* Except as provided in paragraph (e)(2) of this section, a card issuer that imposes any annual or other periodic fee to renew a credit or charge card account subject to § 226.5a, including any fee based on account activity or inactivity, shall mail or deliver written notice of the renewal to the cardholder. The notice shall be provided at least 30 days or one billing cycle, whichever is less, before the mailing or the delivery of the periodic statement on which the renewal fee is initially charged to the account. The notice shall contain the following information:

   (i) The disclosures contained in § 226.5a(b)(1) through (7) that would apply if the account were renewed;[20a] and

   (ii) How and when the cardholder may terminate credit availability under the account to avoid paying the renewal fee.

(2) *Delayed notice.* The disclosures required by paragraph (e)(1) of this section may be provided later than the time in paragraph (e)(1) of this section, but no later than the mailing or the delivery of the periodic statement on which the renewal fee is initially charged to the account, if the card issuer also discloses at that time that:

   (i) The cardholder has 30 days from the time the periodic statement is mailed or delivered to avoid paying the fee or to have the fee recredited if the cardholder terminates credit availability under the account; and

   (ii) The cardholder may use the card during the interim period without having to pay the fee.

[20a]These disclosures need not be provided in tabular format or in a prominent location.

(3) *Notification on periodic statements.* The disclosures required by this paragraph may be made on or with a periodic statement. If any of the disclosures are provided on the back of a periodic statement, the card issuer shall include a reference to those disclosures on the front of the statement.

(f) *Change in credit card account insurance provided*

(1) *Notice prior to change.* If a credit card issuer plans to change the provider of insurance for repayment of all or part of the outstanding balance of an open-end credit card account subject to § 226.5a, the card issuer shall mail or deliver the cardholder written notice of the change not less than 30 days before the change in providers occurs. The notice shall also include the following items, to the extent applicable:
   - (i) Any increase in the rate that will result from the change;
   - (ii) Any substantial decrease in coverage that will result from the change; and
   - (iii) A statement that the cardholder may discontinue the insurance.

(2) *Notice when change in provider occurs.* If a change described in paragraph (f)(1) of this section occurs, the card issuer shall provide the cardholder with a written notice no later than 30 days after the change, including the following items, to the extent applicable:
   - (i) The name and address of the new insurance provider;
   - (ii) A copy of the new policy or group certificate containing the basic terms of the insurance, including the rate to be charged; and
   - (iii) A statement that the cardholder may discontinue the insurance.

(3) *Substantial decrease in coverage.* For purposes of this paragraph, a substantial decrease in coverage is a decrease in a significant term of coverage that might reasonably be expected to affect the cardholder's decision to continue the insurance. Significant terms of coverage include, for example, the following:
   - (i) Type of coverage provided;
   - (ii) Age at which coverage terminates or becomes more restrictive;
   - (iii) Maximum insurable loan balance, maximum periodic benefit payment, maximum number of payments, or other term affecting the dollar amount of coverage or benefits provided;
   - (iv) Eligibility requirements and number and identity of persons covered;
   - (v) Definition of a key term of coverage such as disability;
   - (vi) Exclusions from or limitations on coverage; and
   - (vii) Waiting periods and whether coverage is retroactive.

(4) *Combined notification.* The notices required by paragraphs (f)(1) and (2) of this section may be combined provided the timing requirement of paragraph (f)(1) of this section is met. The notices may be provided on or with a periodic statement.

Section 226.10—Prompt crediting of payments

(a) *General rule.* A creditor shall credit a payment to the consumer's account as of the date of receipt, except when a delay in crediting does not result in a finance or other charge or except as provided in paragraph (b) of this section.

(b) *Specific requirements for payments.* If a creditor specifies, on or with the periodic statement, requirements for the consumer to follow in making payments, but accepts a payment that does not conform to the requirements, the creditor shall credit the payment within 5 days of receipt.

(c) *Adjustment of account.* If a creditor fails to credit a payment, as required by paragraphs (a) and (b) of this section, in time to avoid the imposition of finance or other charges, the creditor shall adjust the consumer's account so that the charges imposed are credited to the consumer's account during the next billing cycle.

Section 226.11—Treatment of credit balances

When a credit balance in excess of $1 is created on a credit account (through transmittal of funds to a creditor in excess of the total balance due on an account, through rebates of unearned finance charges or insurance premiums, or through amounts otherwise owed to or held for the benefit of a consumer), the creditor shall:

(a) Credit the amount of the credit balance to the consumer's account;

(b) Refund any part of the remaining credit balance within 7 business days from receipt of a written request from the consumer; and

(c) Make a good faith effort to refund to the consumer by cash, check, or money order, or credit to a deposit account of the consumer, any part of the credit balance remaining in the account for more than 6 months. No further action is required if the consumer's current location is not known to the creditor and cannot be traced through the consumer's last known address or telephone number.

Section 226.12—Special credit card provisions

(a) *Issuance of credit cards.* Regardless of the purpose for which a credit card is to be used, including business, commercial, or agricultural use, no credit card shall be issued to any person except:

(1) In response to an oral or written request or application for the card; or

(2) As a renewal of, or substitute for, an accepted credit card.[21]

(b) *Liability of cardholder for unauthorized use.* (1) *Limitation on amount.* The liability of a cardholder for unauthorized use[22] of a credit card shall not exceed

---

[21]For purposes of this section, "accepted credit card" means any credit card that a cardholder has requested or applied for and received, or has signed, used, or authorized another person to use to obtain credit. Any credit card issued as a renewal or substitute in accordance with this paragraph becomes an accepted credit card when received by the cardholder.

[22]"Unauthorized use" means the use of a credit card by a person, other than the cardholder, who does not have actual, implied, or apparent authority for such use, and from which the cardholder receives no benefit.

the lesser of $50 or the amount of money, property, labor, or services obtained by the unauthorized use before notification to the card issuer under paragraph (b)(3) of this section.

(2) *Conditions of liability.* A cardholder shall be liable for unauthorized use of a credit card only if:

(i) The credit card is an accepted credit card;

(ii) The card issuer has provided adequate notice[23] of the cardholder's maximum potential liability and of means by which the card issuer may be notified of loss or theft of the card. The notice shall state that the cardholder's liability shall not exceed $50 (or any lesser amount) and that the cardholder may give oral or written notification, and shall describe a means of notification (for example; a telephone number, an address, or both); and

(iii) The card issuer has provided a means to identify the cardholder on the account or the authorized user of the card.

(3) *Notification to card issuer.* Notification to a card issuer is given when steps have been taken as may be reasonably required in the ordinary course of business to provide the card issuer with the pertinent information about the loss, theft, or possible unauthorized use of a credit card, regardless of whether any particular officer, employee, or agent of the card issuer does, in fact, receive the information. Notification may be given, at the option of the person giving it, in person, by telephone, or in writing. Notification in writing is considered given at the time of receipt or, whether or not received, at the expiration of the time ordinarily required for transmission, whichever is earlier.

(4) *Effect of other applicable law or agreement.* If state law or an agreement between a cardholder and the card issuer imposes lesser liability than that provided in this paragraph, the lesser liability shall govern.

(5) *Business use of credit cards.* If 10 or more credit cards are issued by one card issuer for use by the employees of an organization, this section does not prohibit the card issuer and the organization from agreeing to liability for unauthorized use without regard to this section. However, liability for unauthorized use may be imposed on an employee of the organization, by either the card issuer or the organization, only in accordance with this section.

(c) *Right of cardholder to assert claims or defenses against card issuer.*[24]

(1) *General rule.* When a person who honors a credit card fails to resolve satisfactorily a dispute as to property or services purchased with the credit card

---

[23]"Adequate notice" means a printed notice to a cardholder that sets forth clearly the pertinent facts so that the cardholder may reasonably be expected to have noticed it and understood its meaning. The notice may be given by any means reasonably assuring receipt by the cardholder.

[24]This paragraph does not apply to the use of a check guarantee card or a debit card in connection with an overdraft credit plan, or to a check guarantee card used in connection with cash advance checks.

in a consumer credit transaction, the cardholder may assert against the card issuer all claims (other than tort claims) and defenses arising out of the transaction and relating to the failure to resolve the dispute. The cardholder may withhold payment up to the amount of credit outstanding for the property or services that gave rise to the dispute and any finance or other charges imposed on that amount.[25]

(2) *Adverse credit reports prohibited.* If, in accordance with paragraph (c)(1) of this section, the cardholder withholds payment of the amount of credit outstanding for the disputed transaction, the card issuer shall not report that amount as delinquent until the dispute is settled or judgment is rendered.

(3) *Limitations.* The rights stated in paragraphs (c)(1) and (2) of this section apply only if:

(i) The cardholder has made a good faith attempt to resolve the dispute with the person honoring the credit card; and

(ii) The amount of credit extended to obtain the property or services that result in the assertion of the claim or defense by the cardholder exceeds $50, and the disputed transaction occurred in the same state as the cardholder's current designated address or, if not within the same state, within 100 miles from that address.[26]

(d) *Offsets by card issuer prohibited.*

(1) A card issuer may not take any action, either before or after termination of credit card privileges, to offset a cardholder's indebtedness arising from a consumer credit transaction under the relevant credit card plan against funds of the cardholder held on deposit with the card issuer.

(2) This paragraph does not alter or affect the right of a card issuer acting under state or federal law to do any of the following with regard to funds of a

---

[25]The amount of the claim or defense that the cardholder may assert shall not exceed the amount of credit outstanding for the disputed transaction at the time the cardholder first notifies the card issuer or the person honoring the credit card of the existence of the claim or defense. To determine the amount of credit outstanding for purposes of this section, payments and other credits shall be applied to: (1) late charges in the order of entry to the account; then to (2) finance charges in the order of entry to the account; and then to (3) any other debits in the order of entry to the account. If more than one item is included in a single extension of credit, credits are to be distributed pro rata according to prices and applicable taxes.

[26]The limitations stated in paragraph (c)(3)(ii) of this section shall not apply when the person honoring the credit card: (1) is the same person as the card issuer; (2) is controlled by the card issuer directly or indirectly; (3) is under the direct or indirect control of a third person that also directly or indirectly controls the card issuer; (4) controls the card issuer directly or indirectly; (5) is a franchised dealer in the card issuer's products or services; or (6) has obtained the order for the disputed transaction through a mail solicitation made or participated in by the card issuer.

cardholder held on deposit with the card issuer if the same procedure is constitutionally available to creditors generally: obtain or enforce a consensual security interest in the funds; attach or otherwise levy upon the funds; or obtain or enforce a court order relating to the funds.

(3) This paragraph does not prohibit a plan, if authorized in writing by the cardholder, under which the card issuer may periodically deduct all or part of the cardholder's credit card debt from a deposit account held with the card issuer (subject to the limitations in § 226.13(d)(1)).

(e) *Prompt notification of returns and crediting of refunds.*

(1) When a creditor other than the card issuer accepts the return of property or forgives a debt for services that is to be reflected as a credit to the consumer's credit card account, that creditor shall, within 7 business days from accepting the return or forgiving the debt, transmit a credit statement to the card issuer through the card issuer's normal channels for credit statements.

(2) The card issuer shall, within 3 business days from receipt of a credit statement, credit the consumer's account with the amount of the refund.

(3) If a creditor other than a card issuer routinely gives cash refunds to consumers paying in cash, the creditor shall also give credit or cash refunds to consumers using credit cards, unless it discloses at the time the transaction is consummated that credit or cash refunds for returns are not given. This section does not require refunds for returns nor does it prohibit refunds in kind.

(f) *Discounts; tie-in arrangements.* No card issuer may, by contract or otherwise:

(1) Prohibit any person who honors a credit card from offering a discount to a consumer to induce the consumer to pay by cash, check, or similar means rather than by use of a credit card or its underlying account for the purchase of property or services; or

(2) Require any person who honors the card issuer's credit card to open or maintain any account or obtain any other service not essential to the operation of the credit card plan from the card issuer or any other person, as a condition of participation in a credit card plan. If maintenance of an account for clearing purposes is determined to be essential to the operation of the credit card plan, it may be required only if no service charges or minimum balance requirements are imposed.

(g) *Relation to Electronic Fund Transfer Act and Regulation E.* For guidance on whether Regulation Z (12 CFR part 226) or Regulation E (12 CFR part 205) applies in instances involving both credit and electronic fund transfer aspects, refer to Regulation E, 12 CFR 205.12(a) regarding issuance and liability for unauthorized use. On matters other than issuance and liability, this section applies to the credit aspects of combined credit/electronic fund transfer transactions, as applicable.

Section 226.13—Billing error resolution

(a) *Definition of billing error.* For purposes of this section, the term "billing error" means:[27]

(1) A reflection on or with a periodic statement of an extension of credit that is not made to the consumer or to a person who has actual, implied, or apparent authority to use the consumer's credit card or open-end credit plan.

(2) A reflection on or with a periodic statement of an extension of credit that is not identified in accordance with the requirement of §§ 226.7(b) and 226.8.

(3) A reflection on or with a periodic statement of an extension of credit for property or services not accepted by the consumer or the consumer's designee, or not delivered to the consumer or the consumer's designee as agreed.

(4) A reflection on a periodic statement of the creditor's failure to credit properly a payment or other credit issued to the consumer's account.

(5) A reflection on a periodic statement of a computational or similar error of an accounting nature that is made by the creditor.

(6) A reflection on a periodic statement of an extension of credit for which the consumer requests additional clarification, including documentary evidence.

(7) The creditor's failure to mail or deliver a periodic statement to the consumer's last known address if that address was received by the creditor, in writing, at least 20 days before the end of the billing cycle for which the statement was required.

(b) *Billing error notice.*[28] A billing error notice is a written notice[29] from a consumer that:

(1) Is received by a creditor at the address disclosed under § 226.7(k) no later than 60 days after the creditor transmitted the first periodic statement that reflects the alleged billing error;

(2) Enables the creditor to identify the consumer's name and account number; and

(3) To the extent possible, indicates the consumer's belief and the reasons for the belief that a billing error exists, and the type, date, and amount of the error.

---

[27]A creditor shall not accelerate any part of the consumer's indebtedness or restrict or close a consumer's account solely because the consumer has exercised in good faith rights provided by this section. A creditor may be subject to the forfeiture penalty under § 161(e) of the act for failure to comply with any of the requirements of this section.

[28]The creditor need not comply with the requirements of paragraphs (c) through (g) of this section if the consumer concludes that no billing error occurred and voluntarily withdraws the billing error notice.

[29]The creditor may require that the written notice not be made on the payment medium or other material accompanying the periodic statement if the creditor so stipulates in the billing rights statement required by §§ 226.6(d) and 226.9(a).

(c) *Time for resolution; general procedures.*

(1) The creditor shall mail or deliver written acknowledgment to the consumer within 30 days of receiving a billing error notice, unless the creditor has complied with the appropriate resolution procedures of paragraphs (e) and (f) of this section, as applicable, within the 30-day period; and

(2) The creditor shall comply with the appropriate resolution procedures of paragraphs (e) and (f) of this section, as applicable, within two complete billing cycles (but in no event later than 90 days) after receiving a billing error notice.

(d) *Rules pending resolution.* Until a billing error is resolved under paragraph (e) or (f) of this section, the following rules apply:

(1) *Consumer's right to withhold disputed amount; collection action prohibited.* The consumer need not pay (and the creditor may not try to collect) any portion of any required payment that the consumer believes is related to the disputed amount (including related finance or other charges).[30] If the cardholder maintains a deposit account with the card issuer and has agreed to pay the credit card indebtedness by periodic deductions from the cardholder's deposit account, the card issuer shall not deduct any part of the disputed amount or related finance or other charges if a billing error notice is received any time up to three business days before the scheduled payment date.

(2) *Adverse credit reports prohibited.* The creditor or its agent shall not (directly or indirectly) make or threaten to make an adverse report to any person about the consumer's credit standing, or report that an amount or account is delinquent, because the consumer failed to pay the disputed amount or related finance or other charges.

(e) *Procedures if billing error occurred as asserted.* If a creditor determines that a billing error occurred as asserted, it shall within the time limits in paragraph (c)(2) of this section:

(1) Correct the billing error and credit the consumer's account with any disputed amount and related finance or other charges, as applicable; and

(2) Mail or deliver a correction notice to the consumer.

---

[30] A creditor is not prohibited from taking action to collect any undisputed portion of the item or bill; from deducting any disputed amount and related finance or other charges from the consumer's credit limit on the account; or from reflecting a disputed amount and related finance or other charges on a periodic statement, provided that the creditor indicates on or with the periodic statement that payment of any disputed amount and related finance or other charges is not required pending the creditor's compliance with this section.

(f) *Procedures if different billing error or no billing error occurred.* If, after conducting a reasonable investigation,[31] a creditor determines that no billing error occurred or that a different billing error occurred from that asserted, the creditor shall within the time limits in paragraph (c)(2) of this section:

(1) Mail or deliver to the consumer an explanation that sets forth the reasons for the creditor's belief that the billing error alleged by the consumer is incorrect in whole or in part;

(2) Furnish copies of documentary evidence of the consumer's indebtedness, if the consumer so requests; and

(3) If a different billing error occurred, correct the billing error and credit the consumer's account with any disputed amount and related finance or other charges, as applicable.

(g) *Creditor's rights and duties after resolution.* If a creditor, after complying with all of the requirements of this section, determines that a consumer owes all or part of the disputed amount and related finance or other charges, the creditor:

(1) Shall promptly notify the consumer in writing of the time when payment is due and the portion of the disputed amount and related finance or other charges that the consumer still owes;

(2) Shall allow any time period disclosed under §§ 226.6(a)(1) and 226.7(j), during which the consumer can pay the amount due under paragraph (g)(1) of this section without incurring additional finance or other charges;

(3) May report an account or amount as delinquent because the amount due under paragraph (g)(1) of this section remains unpaid after the creditor has allowed any time period disclosed under §§ 226.6(a)(1) and 266.7(j) or 10 days (whichever is longer) during which the consumer can pay the amount; but

(4) May not report that an amount or account is delinquent because the amount due under paragraph (g)(1) of the section remains unpaid, if the creditor receives (within the time allowed for payment in paragraph (g)(3) of this section) further written notice from the consumer that any portion of the billing error is still in dispute, unless the creditor also:

    (i) Promptly reports that the amount or account is in dispute;

    (ii) Mails or delivers to the consumer (at the same time the report is made) a written notice of the name and address of each person to whom the creditor makes a report; and

    (iii) Promptly reports any subsequent resolution of the reported delinquency to all persons to whom the creditor has made a report.

---

[31]If a consumer submits a billing error notice alleging either the nondelivery of property or services under paragraph (a)(3) of this section or that information appearing on a periodic statement is incorrect because a person honoring the consumer's credit card has made an incorrect report to the card issuer, the creditor shall not deny the assertion unless it conducts a reasonable investigation and determines that the property or services were actually delivered, mailed, or sent as agreed or that the information was correct.

(h) *Reassertion of billing error.* A creditor that has fully complied with the requirements of this section has no further responsibilities under this section (other than as provided in paragraph (g)(4) of this section) if a consumer reasserts substantially the same billing error.

(i) *Relation to Electronic Fund Transfer Act and Regulation E.* If an extension of credit is incident to an electronic fund transfer, under an agreement between a consumer and a financial institution to extend credit when the consumer's account is overdrawn or to maintain a specified minimum balance in the consumer's account, the creditor shall comply with the requirements of Regulation E, 12 CFR 205.11 governing error resolution rather than those of paragraphs (a), (b), (c), (e), (f), and (h) of this section.

Section 226.14—Determination of annual percentage rate

(a) *General rule.* The annual percentage rate is a measure of the cost of credit, expressed as a yearly rate. An annual percentage rate shall be considered accurate if it is not more than 1:8 of 1 percentage point above or below the annual percentage rate determined in accordance with this section.[31a]

(b) *Annual percentage rate for sections 226.5a and 226.5b disclosures, for initial disclosures and for advertising purposes.* Where one or more periodic rates may be used to compute the finance charge, the annual percentage rate(s) to be disclosed for purposes of §§ 226.5a, 226.5b, 226.6, and 226.16 shall be computed by multiplying each periodic rate by the number of periods in a year.

(c) *Annual percentage rate for periodic statements.* The annual percentage rate(s) to be disclosed for purposes of § 226.7(d) shall be computed by multiplying each periodic rate by the number of periods in a year and, for purposes of § 226.7(g), shall be determined as follows:

(1) If the finance charge is determined solely by applying one or more periodic rates, at the creditor's option, either:

   (i) By multiplying each periodic rate by the number of periods in a year; or

   (ii) By dividing the total finance charge for the billing cycle by the sum of the balances to which the periodic rates were applied and multiplying the quotient (expressed as a percentage) by the number of billing cycles in a year.

(2) If the finance charge imposed during the billing cycle is or includes a minimum, fixed, or other charge not due to the application of a periodic rate, other than a charge with respect to any specific transaction during the billing cycle, by dividing the total finance charge for the billing cycle by the amount of the balance(s) to which it is applicable[32] and multiplying

[31a]An error in disclosure of the annual percentage rate or finance charge shall not, in itself, be considered a violation of this regulation if: (1) the error resulted from a corresponding error in a calculation tool used in good faith by the creditor; and (2) upon discovery of the error, the creditor promptly discontinues use of that calculation tool for disclosure purposes, and notifies the Board in writing of the error in the calculation tool.

[32]If there is no balance to which the finance charge is applicable, an annual percentage rate cannot be determined under this section.

the quotient (expressed as a percentage) by the number of billing cycles in a year.[33]

(3) If the finance charge imposed during the billing cycle is or includes a charge relating to a specific transaction during the billing cycle (even if the total finance charge also includes any other minimum, fixed, or other charge not due to the application of a periodic rate), by dividing the total finance charge imposed during the billing cycle by the total of all balances and other amounts on which a finance charge was imposed during the billing cycle without duplication, and multiplying the quotient (expressed as a percentage) by the number of billing cycles in a year,[34] except that the annual percentage rate shall not be less than the largest rate determined by multiplying each periodic rate imposed during the billing cycle by the number of periods in a year.[35]

(4) If the finance charge imposed during the billing cycle is or includes a minimum, fixed, or other charge not due to the application of a periodic rate and the total finance charge imposed during the billing cycle does not exceed 50 cents for a monthly or longer billing cycle, or the pro rata part of 50 cents for a billing cycle shorter than monthly, at the creditor's option, by multiplying each applicable periodic rate by the number of periods in a year, notwithstanding the provisions of paragraphs (c)(2) and (3) of this section.

(d) *Calculations where daily periodic rate applied.* If the provisions of paragraphs (c)(1)(ii) or (2) of this section apply and all or a portion of the finance charge is determined by the application of one or more daily periodic rates, the annual percentage rate may be determined either:

(1) By dividing the total finance charge by the average of the daily balances and multiplying the quotient by the number of billing cycles in a year; or

(2) By dividing the total finance charge by the sum of the daily balances and multiplying the quotient by 365.

Section 226.15—Right of rescission

(a) *Consumer's right to rescind.*

(1) (i) Except as provided in paragraph (a)(1)(ii) of this section, in a credit plan in which a security interest is or will be retained or acquired in a consumer's principal dwelling, each consumer whose ownership interest is or will be subject to the security interest shall have the right to rescind: each credit extension made under the plan; the plan when the plan is opened; a security

---

[33]Where the finance charge imposed during the billing cycle is or includes a loan fee, points, or similar charge that relates to the opening of the account, the amount of such charge shall not be included in the calculation of the annual percentage rate.

[34]See Appendix F regarding determination of the denominator for the fraction under this paragraph.

[35]See footnote 33.

interest when added or increased to secure an existing plan; and the increase when a credit limit on the plan is increased.

(ii) As provided in § 125(e) of the act, the consumer does not have the right to rescind each credit extension made under the plan if such extension is made in accordance with a previously established credit limit for the plan.

(2) To exercise the right to rescind, the consumer shall notify the creditor of the rescission by mail, telegram, or other means of written communication. Notice is considered given when mailed, or when filed for telegraphic transmission, or, if sent by other means, when delivered to the creditor's designated place of business.

(3) The consumer may exercise the right to rescind until midnight of the third business day following the occurrence described in paragraph (a)(1) of this section that gave rise to the right of rescission, delivery of the notice required by paragraph (b) of this section, or delivery of all material disclosures,[36] whichever occurs last. If the required notice and material disclosures are not delivered, the right to rescind shall expire three years after the occurrence giving rise to the right of rescission, or upon transfer of all of the consumer's interest in the property, or upon sale of the property, whichever occurs first. In the case of certain administrative proceedings, the rescission period shall be extended in accordance with § 125(f) of the act.

(4) When more than one consumer has the right to rescind, the exercise of the right by one consumer shall be effective as to all consumers.

(b) *Notice of right to rescind.* In any transaction or occurrence subject to rescission, a creditor shall deliver two copies of the notice of the right to rescind to each consumer entitled to rescind (one copy to each if the notice is delivered by electronic communication as provided in § 226.36(b)). The notice shall identify the transaction or occurrence and clearly and conspicuously disclose the following:

1. The retention or acquisition of a security interest in the consumer's principal dwelling.
2. The consumer's right to rescind, as described in paragraph (a)(1) of this section.
3. How to exercise the right to rescind, with a form for that purpose, designating the address of the creditor's place of business.
4. The effects of rescission, as described in paragraph (d) of this section.
5. The date the rescission period expires.

[36]The term "material disclosures" means the information that must be provided to satisfy the requirements in § 226.6 with regard to the method of determining the finance charge and the balance upon which a finance charge will be imposed, the annual percentage rate, the amount or method of determining the amount of any membership or participation fee that may be imposed as part of the plan, and the payment information described in § 226.5b(d)(5)(i) and (ii) that is required under § 226.6(e)(2).

(c) *Delay of creditor's performance.* Unless a consumer waives the right to rescind under paragraph (e) of this section, no money shall be disbursed other than in escrow, no services shall be performed, and no materials delivered until after the rescission period has expired and the creditor is reasonably satisfied that the consumer has not rescinded. A creditor does not violate this section if a third party with no knowledge of the event activating the rescission right does not delay in providing materials or services, as long as the debt incurred for those materials or services is not secured by the property subject to rescission.

(d) *Effects of rescission.*

(1) When a consumer rescinds a transaction, the security interest giving rise to the right of rescission becomes void, and the consumer shall not be liable for any amount, including any finance charge.

(2) Within 20 calendar days after receipt of a notice of rescission, the creditor shall return any money or property that has been given to anyone in connection with the transaction and shall take any action necessary to reflect the termination of the security interest.

(3) If the creditor has delivered any money or property, the consumer may retain possession until the creditor has met its obligation under paragraph (d)(2) of this section. When the creditor has complied with that paragraph, the consumer shall tender the money or property to the creditor or, where the latter would be impracticable or inequitable, tender its reasonable value. At the consumer's option, tender of property may be made at the location of the property or at the consumer's residence. Tender of money must be made at the creditor's designated place of business. If the creditor does not take possession of the money or property within 20 calendar days after the consumer's tender, the consumer may keep it without further obligation.

(4) The procedures outlined in paragraphs (d)(2) and (3) of this section may be modified by court order.

(e) *Consumer's waiver of right to rescind.*

1. The consumer may modify or waive the right to rescind if the consumer determines that the extension of credit is needed to meet a bona fide personal financial emergency. To modify or waive the right, the consumer shall give the creditor a dated written statement that describes the emergency, specifically modifies or waives the right to rescind, and bears the signature of all the consumers entitled to rescind. Printed forms for this purpose are prohibited, except as provided in paragraph (e)(2) of this section.
2. The need of the consumer to obtain funds immediately shall be regarded as a bona fide personal financial emergency provided that the dwelling securing the extension of credit is located in an area declared during June through September 1993, pursuant to 42 U.S.C. 5170, to be a major disaster area because of severe storms and flooding in the Midwest.[36a] In this instance, creditors may use printed forms for the consumer to waive the

[36a] A list of the affected areas will be maintained by the Board.

right to rescind. This exemption to paragraph (e)(1) of this section shall expire one year from the date an area was declared a major disaster.

3. The consumer's need to obtain funds immediately shall be regarded as a bona fide personal financial emergency provided that the dwelling securing the extension of credit is located in an area declared during June through September 1994 to be a major disaster area, pursuant to 42 U.S.C. 5170, because of severe storms and flooding in the South.[36b] In this instance, creditors may use printed forms for the consumer to waive the right to rescind. This exemption to paragraph (e)(1) of this section shall expire one year from the date an area was declared a major disaster.
4. The consumer's need to obtain funds immediately shall be regarded as a bona fide personal financial emergency provided that the dwelling securing the extension of credit is located in an area declared during October 1994 to be a major disaster area, pursuant to 42 U.S.C. 5170, because of severe storms and flooding in Texas.[36c] In this instance, creditors may use printed forms for the consumer to waive the right to rescind. This exemption to paragraph (e)(1) of this section shall expire one year from the date an area was declared a major disaster.

(f) *Exempt transactions.* The right to rescind does not apply to the following:

(1) A residential mortgage transaction.

(2) A credit plan in which a state agency is a creditor.

Section 226.16—Advertising

(a) *Actually available terms.* If an advertisement for credit states specific credit terms, it shall state only those terms that actually are or will be arranged or offered by the creditor.

(b) *Advertisement of terms that require additional disclosures.* If any of the terms required to be disclosed under § 226.6 is set forth in an advertisement, the advertisement shall also clearly and conspicuously set forth the following:[36d]

(1) Any minimum, fixed, transaction, activity or similar charge that could be imposed.

(2) Any periodic rate that may be applied expressed as an annual percentage rate as determined under § 226.14(b). If the plan provides for a variable periodic rate, that fact shall be disclosed.

[36b] A list of the affected areas will be maintained and published by the Board. Such areas now include parts of Alabama, Florida, and Georgia.

[36c] A list of the affected areas will be maintained and published by the Board. Such areas now include the following counties in Texas: Angelina, Austin, Bastrop, Brazos, Brazoria, Burleson, Chambers, Fayette, Fort Bend, Galveston, Grimes, Hardin, Harris, Houston, Jackson, Jasper, Jefferson, Lee, Liberty, Madison, Matagorda, Montgomery, Nacagdoches, Orange, Polk, San Augustine, San Jacinto, Shelby, Trinity, Victoria, Washington, Waller, Walker, and Wharton.

[36d] The disclosures given in accordance with § 226.5a do not constitute advertising terms for purposes of the requirements of this section.

(3) Any membership or participation fee that could be imposed.

(c) *Catalogs or other multiple-page advertisements; electronic advertisements.*

(1) If a catalog or other multiple-page advertisement or an advertisement using electronic communication, gives information in a table or schedule in sufficient detail to permit determination of the disclosures required by paragraph (b) of this section, it shall be considered a single advertisement if:

(i) The table or schedule is clearly and conspicuously set forth; and

(ii) Any statement of terms set forth in § 226.6 appearing anywhere else in the catalog or advertisement clearly refers to the page or location where the table or schedule begins.

(2) A catalog or other mutiple-page advertisement or an advertisement using electronic communication complies with this paragraph if the table or schedule of terms includes all appropriate disclosures for a representative scale of amounts up to the level of the more commonly sold higher-priced property or services offered.

(d) *Additional requirements for home equity plans*

(1) Advertisement of terms that require additional disclosures. If any of the terms required to be disclosed under § 226.6(a) or (b) or the payment terms of the plan are set forth, affirmatively or negatively, in an advertisement for a home equity plan subject to the requirements of § 226.5b, the advertisement also shall clearly and conspicuously set forth the following:

(i) Any loan fee that is a percentage of the credit limit under the plan and an estimate of any other fees imposed for opening the plan, stated as a single dollar amount or a reasonable range.

(ii) Any periodic rate used to compute the finance charge, expressed as an annual percentage rate as determined under section § 226.14(b).

(iii) The maximum annual percentage rate that may be imposed in a variable-rate plan.

(2) *Discounted and premium rates.* If an advertisement states an initial annual percentage rate that is not based on the index and margin used to make later rate adjustments in a variable-rate plan, the advertisement also shall state the period of time such rate will be in effect, and, with equal prominence to the initial rate, a reasonably current annual percentage rate that would have been in effect using the index and margin.

(3) *Balloon payment.* If an advertisement contains a statement about any minimum periodic payment, the advertisement also shall state, if applicable, that a balloon payment may result.[36e]

(4) *Tax implications.* An advertisement that states that any interest expense incurred under the home equity plan is or may be tax deductible may not be misleading in this regard.

[36e]See footnote 10b.

(5) *Misleading terms.* An advertisement may not refer to a home equity plan as "free money" or contain a similarly misleading term.

SUBPART C—CLOSED-END CREDIT

Section 226.17—General disclosure requirements.

(a) *Form of disclosures.*

(1) The creditor shall make the disclosures required by this subpart clearly and conspicuously in writing, in a form that the consumer may keep. The disclosures required by this subpart may be provided to the consumer in electronic form, subject to compliance with the consumer consent and other applicable provisions of the Electronic Signatures in Global and National Commerce Act (E Sign Act) (15 U.S.C. 7001 *et seq.*). The disclosures required by §§ 226.17(g), 226.19(b), and 226.24 may be provided to the consumer in electronic form without regard to the consumer consent or other provisions of the E-Sign Act in the circumstances set forth in those sections. The disclosures shall be grouped together, shall be segregated from everything else, and shall not contain any information not directly related[37] to the disclosures required under § 226.18.[38] The itemization of the amount financed under § 226.18(c)(1) must be separate from the other disclosures under that section.

(2) The terms "finance charge" and "annual percentage rate," when required to be disclosed under § 226.18(d) and (e) together with a corresponding amount or percentage rate, shall be more conspicuous than any other disclosure, except the creditor's identity under § 226.18(a).

(b) *Time of disclosures.* The creditor shall make disclosures before consummation of the transaction. In certain residential mortgage transactions, special timing requirements are set forth in § 226.19(a). In certain variable-rate transactions, special timing requirements for variable-rate disclosures are set forth in § 226.19(b) and § 226.20(c). In certain transactions involving mail or telephone orders or a series of sales, the timing of disclosures may be delayed in accordance with paragraphs (g) and (h) of this section.

(c) *Basis of disclosures and use of estimates.*

(1) The disclosures shall reflect the terms of the legal obligation between the parties.

---

[37]The disclosures may include an acknowledgment of receipt, the date of the transaction, and the consumer's name, address, and account number.

[38]The following disclosures may be made together with or separately from other required disclosures: the creditor's identity under Sec. 226.18(a), the variable rate example under Sec. 226.18(f)(1)(iv), insurance or debt cancellation under Sec. 226.18(n), and certain security interest charges under Sec. 226.18(o).

(2) (i) If any information necessary for an accurate disclosure is unknown to the creditor, the creditor shall make the disclosure based on the best information reasonably available at the time the disclosure is provided to the consumer, and shall state clearly that the disclosure is an estimate.

(ii) For a transaction in which a portion of the interest is determined on a per-diem basis and collected at consummation, any disclosure affected by the per-diem interest shall be considered accurate if the disclosure is based on the information known to the creditor at the time that the disclosure documents are prepared for consummation of the transaction.

(3) The creditor may disregard the effects of the following in making calculations and disclosures.

(i) That payments must be collected in whole cents.

(ii) That dates of scheduled payments and advances may be changed because the scheduled date is not a business day.

(iii) That months have different numbers of days.

(iv) The occurrence of leap year.

(4) In making calculations and disclosures, the creditor may disregard any irregularity in the first period that falls within the limits described below and any payment schedule irregularity that results from the irregular first period:

(i) For transactions in which the term is less than 1 year, a first period not more than 6 days shorter or 13 days longer than a regular period;

(ii) For transactions in which the term is at least 1 year and less than 10 years, a first period not more than 11 days shorter or 21 days longer than a regular period; and

(iii) For transactions in which the term is at least 10 years, a first period shorter than or not more than 32 days longer than a regular period.

(5) If an obligation is payable on demand, the creditor shall make the disclosures based on an assumed maturity of 1 year. If an alternate maturity date is stated in the legal obligation between the parties, the disclosures shall be based on that date.

(6) (i) A series of advances under an agreement to extend credit up to a certain amount may be considered as one transaction.

(ii) When a multiple-advance loan to finance the construction of a dwelling may be permanently financed by the same creditor, the construction phase and the permanent phase may be treated as either one transaction or more than one transaction.

(d) *Multiple creditors; multiple consumers.* If a transaction involves more than one creditor, only one set of disclosures shall be given and the creditors shall agree among themselves which creditor must comply with the requirements that this regulation imposes on any or all of them. If there is more than one consumer, the disclosures may be made to any consumer who is primarily liable on the obligation. If the transaction is rescindable under § 226.23, however, the disclosures shall be made to each consumer who has the right to rescind.

(e) *Effect of subsequent events.* If a disclosure becomes inaccurate because of an event that occurs after the creditor delivers the required disclosures, the inaccuracy is not a violation of this regulation, although new disclosures may be required under paragraph (f) of this section, § 226.19 or § 226.20.

(f) *Early disclosures.* If disclosures are required by this subpart are given before the date of consummation of a transaction and a subsequent event makes them inaccurate, the creditor shall disclose before consummation:[39]

(1) any changed term unless the term was based on an estimate in accordance with § 226.17(c)(2) and was labelled an estimate;

(2) all changed terms, if the annual percentage rate at the time of consummation varies from the annual percentage rate disclosed earlier by more than 1/8 of 1 percentage point in a regular transaction, or more than 1/4 of 1 percentage point in an irregular transaction, as defined in § 226.22(a).

(g) *Mail or telephone orders—delay in disclosures.* If a creditor receives a purchase order or a request for an extension of credit by mail, telephone, or facsimile machine without face-to-face or direct telephone solicitation, the creditor may delay the disclosures until the due date of the first payment, if the following information for representative amounts or ranges of credit is made available in written form or in electronic form to the consumer or to the public before the actual purchase order or request:

(1) The cash price or the principal loan amount.

(2) The total sale price.

(3) The finance charge.

(4) The annual percentage rate, and if the rate may increase after consummation, the following disclosures:

   (i) The circumstances under which the rate may increase.

   (ii) Any limitations on the increase.

   (iii) The effect of an increase.

(5) The terms of repayment.

(h) *Series of sales—delay in disclosures.* If a credit sale is one of a series made under an agreement providing that subsequent sales may be added to an outstanding balance, the creditor may delay the required disclosures until the due date of the first payment for the current sale, if the following two conditions are met:

(1) The consumer has approved in writing the annual percentage rate or rates, the range of balances to which they apply, and the method of treating any unearned finance charge on an existing balance.

---

[39]For certain residential mortgage transactions, Sec. 226.19(a)(2) permits redisclosure no later than consummation or settlement, whichever is later.

(2) The creditor retains no security interest in any property after the creditor has received payments equal to the cash price and any finance charge attributable to the sale of that property. For purposes of this provision, in the case of items purchased on different dates, the first purchased is deemed the first item paid for; in the case of items purchased on the same date, the lowest priced is deemed the first item paid for.

(i) *Interim student credit extensions.* For each transaction involving an interim credit extension under a student credit program, the creditor need not make the following disclosures: the finance charge under § 226.18(d), the payment schedule under § 226.18(g), the total of payments under § 226.18(h), or the total sale price under § 226.18(j).

Section 226.18—Content of disclosures

For each transaction, the creditor shall disclose the following information as applicable:

(a) *Creditor.* The identity of the creditor making the disclosures.

(b) *Amount financed.* The "amount financed," using that term, and a brief description such as "the amount of credit provided to you or on your behalf." The amount financed is calculated by:

(1) Determining the principal loan amount or the cash price (subtracting any downpayment);

(2) Adding any other amounts that are financed by the creditor and are not part of the finance charge; and

(3) Subtracting any prepaid finance charge.

(c) *Itemization of amount financed.*

(1) A separate written itemization of the amount financed, including:[40]

(i) The amount of any proceeds distributed directly to the consumer.

(ii) The amount credited to the consumer's account with the creditor.

(iii) Any amounts paid to other persons by the creditor on the consumer's behalf. The creditor shall identify those persons.[41]

(iv) The prepaid finance charge.

(2) The creditor need not comply with paragraph (c)(1) of this section if the creditor provides a statement that the consumer has the right to receive a written itemization of the amount financed, together with a space for the consumer to indicate whether it is desired, and the consumer does not request it.

---

[40]Good faith estimates of settlement costs provided for transactions subject to the Real Estate Settlement Procedures Act (12 U.S.C. 2601 *et seq.*) may be substituted for the disclosures required by paragraph (c) of this section.

[41]The following payees may be described using generic or other general terms and need not be further identified: public officials or government agencies, credit reporting agencies, appraisers, and insurance companies.

(d) *Finance charge.* The "finance charge", using that term, and a brief description such as "the dollar amount the credit will cost you."

(1) *Mortgage loans.* In a transaction secured by real property or a dwelling, the disclosed finance charge and other disclosures affected by the disclosed finance charge (including the amount financed and the annual percentage rate) shall be treated as accurate if the amount disclosed as the finance charge:

(i) is understated by no more than $100; or

(ii) is greater than the amount required to be disclosed.

(2) *Other credit.* In any other transaction, the amount disclosed as the finance charge shall be treated as accurate if, in a transaction involving an amount financed of $1,000 or less, it is not more than $5 above or below the amount required to be disclosed; or, in a transaction involving an amount financed of more than $1,000, it is not more than $10 above or below the amount required to be disclosed.

(e) *Annual percentage rate.* The "annual percentage rate," using that term, and a brief description such as "the cost of your credit as a yearly rate."[42]

(f) *Variable rate.*

(1) If the annual percentage rate may increase after consummation in a transaction not secured by the consumer's principal dwelling or in a transaction secured by the consumer's principal dwelling with a term of one year or less, the following disclosures:[43]

(i) The circumstances under which the rate may increase.

(ii) Any limitations on the increase

(iii) The effect of an increase.

(iv) An example of the payment terms that would result from an increase.

(2) If the annual percentage rate may increase after consummation in a transaction secured by the consumer's principal dwelling with a term greater than one year, the following disclosures.

(i) The fact that the transaction contains a variable-rate feature.

(ii) A statement that variable-rate disclosures have been provided earlier.

(g) *Payment schedule.* The number, amounts, and timing of payments scheduled to repay the obligation.

(1) In a demand obligation with no alternate maturity date, the creditor may comply with this paragraph by disclosing the due dates or payment periods of any scheduled interest payments for the first year.

---

[42]For any transaction involving a finance charge of $5 or less on an amount financed of $75 or less, or a finance charge of $7.50 or less on an amount financed of more than $75, the creditor need not disclose the annual percentage rate.

[43]Information provided in accordance with §§ 226.18(f)(2) and 226.19(b) may be substituted for the disclosures required by paragraph (f)(1) of this section.

(2) In a transaction in which a series of payments varies because a finance charge is applied to the unpaid principal balance, the creditor may comply with this paragraph by disclosing the following information:

(i) The dollar amounts of the largest and smallest payments in the series.

(ii) A reference to the variations in the other payments in the series.

(h) *Total of payments.* The "total of payments," using that term, and a descriptive explanation such as "the amount you will have paid when you have made all scheduled payments."[44]

(i) *Demand feature.* If the obligation has a demand feature, that fact shall be disclosed. When the disclosures are based on an assumed maturity of 1 year as provided in § 226.17(c)(5), that fact shall also be disclosed.

(j) *Total sale price.* In a credit sale, the "total sale price," using that term, and a descriptive explanation (including the amount of any downpayment) such as "the total price of your purchase on credit, including your downpayment of $." The total sale price is the sum of the cash price, the items described in paragraph (b)(2), and the finance charge disclosed under paragraph (d) of this section.

(k) *Prepayment.*

(1) When an obligation includes a finance charge computed from time to time by application of a rate to the unpaid principal balance, a statement indicating whether or not a penalty may be imposed if the obligation is prepaid in full.

(2) When an obligation includes a finance charge other than the finance charge described in paragraph (k)(1) of this section, a statement indicating whether or not the consumer is entitled to a rebate of any finance charge if the obligation is prepaid in full.

(l) *Late payment.* Any dollar or percentage charge that may be imposed before maturity due to a late payment, other than a deferral or extension charge.

(m) *Security interest.* The fact that the creditor has or will acquire a security interest in the property purchased as part of the transaction, or in other property identified by item or type.

(n) *Insurance and debt cancellation.* The items required by § 226.4(d) in order to exclude certain insurance premiums and debt cancellation fees from the finance charge.

(o) *Certain security interest charges.* The disclosures required by § 226.4(e) in order to exclude from the finance charge certain fees prescribed by law or certain premiums for insurance in lieu of perfecting a security interest.

(p) *Contract reference.* A statement that the consumer should refer to the appropriate contract document for information about nonpayment, default, the right to accelerate the maturity of the obligation, and prepayment rebates and penalties. At the creditor's option, the statement may also include a reference to the contract for further information about security interests and, in a residential mortgage transaction, about the creditor's policy regarding assumption of the obligation.

---

[44]In any transaction involving a single payment, the creditor need not disclose the total of payments.

(q) *Assumption policy*. In a residential mortgage transaction, a statement whether or not a subsequent purchaser of the dwelling from the consumer may be permitted to assume the remaining obligation on its original terms.

(r) *Required deposit*. If the creditor requires the consumer to maintain a deposit as a condition of the specific transaction, a statement that the annual percentage rate does not reflect the effect of the required deposit.[45]

Section 226.19—Certain residential mortgage and variable-rate transactions

(a) *Residential mortgage transactions subject to RESPA.*

(1) *Time of disclosures*. In a residential mortgage transaction subject to the Real Estate Settlement Procedures Act (12 U.S.C. 2601 *et seq.*) the creditor shall make good faith estimates of the disclosures required by § 226.18 before consummation, or shall deliver or place them in the mail not later than three business days after the creditor receives the consumer's written application, whichever is earlier.

(2) *Redisclosure required*. If the annual percentage rate at the time of consummation varies from the annual percentage rate disclosed earlier by more than 1/8 of 1 percentage point in a regular transaction or more than 1/4 of 1 percentage point in an irregular transaction, as defined in § 226.22, the creditor shall disclose all the changed terms no later than consummation or settlement.

(b) *Certain variable-rate transactions*.[45a] If the annual percentage rate may increase after consummation in a transaction secured by the consumer's principal dwelling with a term greater than one year, the following disclosures must be provided at the time an application form is provided or before the consumer pays a nonrefundable fee, whichever is earlier:[45b]

(1) The booklet titled *Consumer Handbook on Adjustable Rate Mortgages* published by the Board and the Federal Home Loan Bank Board, or a suitable substitute.

(2) A loan program disclosure for each variable-rate program in which the consumer expresses an interest. The following disclosures, as applicable, shall be provided:

(i) The fact that the interest rate, payment, or term of the loan can change.

(ii) The index or formula used in making adjustments, and a source of information about the index or formula.

---

[45] A required deposit need not include, for example: (1) an escrow account for items such as taxes, insurance or repairs; (2) a deposit that earns not less than 5 percent per year, or (3) payments under a Morris Plan.

[45a] Information provided in accordance with variable-rate regulations of other federal agencies may be substituted for the disclosures required by paragraph (b) of this section.

[45b] Disclosures may be delivered or placed in the mail not later than three business days following receipt of a consumer's application when the application reaches the creditor by telephone, or through an intermediary agent or broker.

(iii) An explanation of how the interest rate and payment will be determined, including an explanation of how the index is adjusted, such as by the addition of a margin.

(iv) A statement that the consumer should ask about the current margin value and current interest rate.

(v) The fact that the interest rate will be discounted, and a statement that the consumer should ask about the amount of the interest rate discount.

(vi) The frequency of interest rate and payment changes.

(vii) Any rules relating to changes in the index, interest rate, payment amount, and outstanding loan balance including, for example, an explanation of interest rate or payment limitations, negative amortization, and interest rate carryover.

(viii) At the option of the creditor, either of the following:

(A) A historical example, based on a $10,000 loan amount, illustrating how payments and the loan balance would have been affected by interest rate changes implemented according to the terms of the loan program disclosure. The example shall reflect the most recent 15 years of index values. The example shall reflect all significant loan program terms, such as negative amortization, interest rate carryover, interest rate discounts, and interest rate and payment limitations, that would have been affected by the index movement during the period.

(B) The maximum interest rate and payment for a $10,000 loan originated at the initial interest rate (index value plus margin, adjusted by the amount of any discount or premium) in effect as of an identified month and year for the loan program disclosure assuming the maximum periodic increases in rates and payments under the program; and the initial interest rate and payment for that loan and a statement that the periodic payment may increase or decrease substantially depending on changes in the rate.

(ix) An explanation of how the consumer may calculate the payments for the loan amount to be borrowed based on either:

(A) The most recent payment shown in the historical example in paragraph (b)(2)(viii)(A) of this section; or

(B) The initial interest rate used to calculate the maximum interest rate and payment in paragraph (b)(2)(viii)(B) of this section.

(x) The fact that the loan program contains a demand feature.

(xi) The type of information that will be provided in notices of adjustments and the timing of such notices.

(xii) A statement that disclosure forms are available for the creditor's other variable-rate loan programs.

Section 226.20—Subsequent disclosure requirements

(a) *Refinancings.* A refinancing occurs when an existing obligation that was subject to this subpart is satisfied and replaced by a new obligation undertaken by the same consumer. A refinancing is a new transaction requiring new disclosures to the consumer. The new finance charge shall include any unearned portion of the old finance charge that is not credited to the existing obligation. The following shall not be treated as a refinancing:

(1) A renewal of a single payment obligation with no change in the original terms.
(2) A reduction in the annual percentage rate with a corresponding change in the payment schedule.
(3) An agreement involving a court proceeding.
(4) A change in the payment schedule or a change in collateral requirements as a result of the consumer's default or delinquency, unless the rate is increased, or the new amount financed exceeds the unpaid balance plus earned finance charge and premiums for continuation of insurance of the types described in § 226.4(d).
(5) The renewal of optional insurance purchased by the consumer and added to an existing transaction, if disclosures relating to the initial purchase were provided as required by this subpart.

(b) *Assumptions.* An assumption occurs when a creditor expressly agrees in writing with a subsequent consumer to accept that consumer as a primary obligor on an existing residential mortgage transaction. Before the assumption occurs, the creditor shall make new disclosures to the subsequent consumer, based on the remaining obligation. If the finance charge originally imposed on the existing obligation was an add-on or discount finance charge, the creditor need only disclose:

(1) The unpaid balance of the obligation assumed.
(2) The total charges imposed by the creditor in connection with the assumption.
(3) The information required to be disclosed under § 226.18(k), (l), (m), and (n).
(4) The annual percentage rate originally imposed on the obligation.
(5) The payment schedule under § 226.18(g) and the total of payments under § 226.18(h) based on the remaining obligation.

(c) *Variable-rate adjustments.*[45c] An adjustment to the interest rate with or without a corresponding adjustment to the payment in a variable-rate transaction subject to § 226.19(b) is an event requiring new disclosures to the consumer. At least once each year during which an interest rate adjustment is implemented

[45c]Information provided in accordance with variable-rate subsequent disclosure regulations of other federal agencies may be substituted for the disclosure required by paragraph (c) of this section.

without an accompanying payment change, and at least 25, but no more than 120, calendar days before payment at a new level is due, the following disclosures, as applicable, must be delivered or placed in the mail:

(1) The current and prior interest rates.

(2) The index values upon which the current and prior interest rates are based.

(3) The extent to which the creditor has foregone any increase in the interest rate.

(4) The contractual effects of the adjustment, including the payment due after the adjustment is made, and a statement of the loan balance.

(5) The payment, if different from that referred to in paragraph (c)(4) of this section, that would be required to fully amortize the loan at the new interest rate over the remainder of the loan term.

Section 226.21—Treatment of credit balances

When a credit balance in excess of $1 is created in connection with a transaction (through transmittal of funds to a creditor in excess of the total balance due on an account, through rebates of unearned finance charges or insurance premiums, or through amounts otherwise owed to or held for the benefit of a consumer), the creditor shall:

(a) Credit the amount of the credit balance to the consumer's account;

(b) Refund any part of the remaining credit balance, upon the written request of the consumer; and

(c) Make a good faith effort to refund to the consumer by cash, check, or money order, or credit to a deposit account of the consumer, any part of the credit balance remaining in the account for more than six months, except that no further action is required if the consumer's current location is not known to the creditor and cannot be traced through the consumer's last known address or telephone number.

Section 226.22—Determination of annual percentage rate

(a) *Accuracy of annual percentage rate.*

(1) The annual percentage rate is a measure of the cost of credit, expressed as a yearly rate, that relates the amount and timing of value received by the consumer to the amount and timing of payments made. The annual percentage rate shall be determined in accordance with either the actuarial method or the United States Rule method. Explanations, equations and instructions for determining the annual percentage rate in accordance with the actuarial method are set forth in appendix J to this regulation.[45d]

[45d]An error in disclosure of the annual percentage rate or finance charge shall not, in itself, be considered a violation of this regulation if: (1) the error resulted from a corresponding error in a calculation tool used in good faith by the creditor; and (2) upon discovery of the error, the creditor promptly discontinues use of that calculation tool for disclosure purposes and notifies the Board in writing of the error in the calculation tool.

(2) As a general rule, the annual percentage rate shall be considered accurate if it is not more than 1/8 of 1 percentage point above or below the annual percentage rate determined in accordance with paragraph (a)(1) of this section.

(3) In an irregular transaction, the annual percentage rate shall be considered accurate if it is not more than 1/4 of 1 percentage point above or below the annual percentage rate determined in accordance with paragraph (a)(1) of this section.[46]

(4) *Mortgage loans.* If the annual percentage rate disclosed in a transaction secured by real property or a dwelling varies from the actual rate determined in accordance with paragraph (a)(1) of this section, in addition to the tolerance applicable under paragraphs (a)(2) and (3) of this section, the disclosed annual percentage rate shall also be considered accurate if:

(i) The rate results from the disclosed finance charge; and

(ii) (A) The disclosed finance charge would be considered accurate under § 226.18(d)(1); or

(B) For purposes of rescission, if the disclosed finance charge would be considered accurate under § 226.23(g) or (h), whichever applies.

(5) *Additional tolerance for mortgage loans.* In a transaction secured by real property or a dwelling, in addition to the tolerances applicable under paragraphs (a)(2) and (3) of this section, if the disclosed finance charge is calculated incorrectly but is considered accurate under § 226.18(d)(1) or § 226.23(g) or (h), the disclosed annual percentage rate shall be considered accurate:

(i) If the disclosed finance charge is understated, and the disclosed annual percentage rate is also understated but it is closer to the actual annual percentage rate than the rate that would be considered accurate under paragraph (a)(4) of this section;

(ii) If the disclosed finance charge is overstated, and the disclosed annual percentage rate is also overstated but it is closer to the actual annual percentage rate than the rate that would be considered accurate under paragraph (a)(4) of this section.

(b) *Computation tools.*

(1) The Regulation Z Annual Percentage Rate Tables produced by the Board may be used to determine the annual percentage rate, and any rate determined from those tables in accordance with the accompanying instructions complies with the requirements of this section. Volume I of the tables applies to single advance transactions involving up to 480 monthly payments or 104 weekly payments. It may be used for regular transactions and for transactions with any of the following irregularities: an irregular first

[46]For purposes of paragraph (a)(3) of this section, an irregular transaction is one that includes one or more of the following features: multiple advances, irregular payment periods, or irregular payment amounts (other than an irregular first period or an irregular first or final payment).

period, and an irregular first payment, and an irregular final payment. Volume II of the tables applies to transactions involving multiple advances and any type of payment or period irregularity.

(2) Creditors may use any other computation tool in determining the annual percentage rate if the rate so determined equals the rate determined in accordance with appendix J, within the degree of accuracy set forth in paragraph (a) of this section.

(c) *Single add-on rate transactions.* If a single add-on rate is applied to all transactions with maturities up to 60 months and if all payments are equal in amount and period, a single annual percentage rate may be disclosed for all those transactions, so long as it is the highest annual percentage rate for any such transaction.

(d) *Certain transactions involving ranges of balances.* For purposes of disclosing the annual percentage rate referred to in § 226.17(g)(4) (Mail or telephone orders—delay in disclosures) and (h) (Series of sales—delay in disclosures), if the same finance charge is imposed on all balances within a specified range of balances, the annual percentage rate computed for the median balance may be disclosed for all the balances. However, if the annual percentage rate computed for the median balance understates the annual percentage rate computed for the lowest balance by more than 8 percent of the latter rate, the annual percentage rate shall be computed on whatever lower balance will produce an annual percentage rate that does not result in an understatement of more than 8 percent of the rate determined on the lowest balance.

Section 226.23—Right of rescission

(a) *Consumer's right to rescind.*

(1) In a credit transaction in which a security interest is or will be retained or acquired in a consumer's principal dwelling, each consumer whose ownership interest is or will be subject to the security interest shall have the right to rescind the transaction, except for transactions described in paragraph (f) of this section.[47]

(2) To exercise the right to rescind, the consumer shall notify the creditor of the rescission by mail, telegram or other means of written communication. Notice is considered given when mailed, when filed for telegraphic transmission or, if sent by other means, when delivered to the creditor's designated place of business.

(3) The consumer may exercise the right to rescind until midnight of the third business day following consummation, delivery of the notice required by

---

[47]For purposes of this section, the addition to an existing obligation of a security interest in a consumer's principal dwelling is a transaction. The right of rescission applies only to the addition of the security interest and not the existing obligation. The creditor shall deliver the notice required by paragraph (b) of this section but need not deliver new material disclosures. Delivery of the required notice shall begin the rescission period.

paragraph (b) of this section, or delivery of all material disclosures,[48] whichever occurs last. If the required notice or material disclosures are not delivered, the right to rescind shall expire three years after consummation, upon transfer of all of the consumer's interest in the property, or upon sale of the property, whichever occurs first. In the case of certain administrative proceedings, the rescission period shall be extended in accordance with § 125(f) of the act.

(4) When more than one consumer in a transaction has the right to rescind, the exercise of the right by one consumer shall be effective as to all consumers.

(b) (1) *Notice of right to rescind.* In a transaction subject to rescission, a creditor shall deliver two copies of the notice of the right to rescind to each consumer entitled to rescind (one copy to each if the notice is delivered by electronic communication as provided in § 226.36(b)). The notice shall be on a separate document that identifies the transaction and shall clearly and conspicuously disclose the following:

(i) The retention or acquisition of a security interest in the consumer's principal dwelling.
(ii) The consumer's right to rescind the transaction.
(iii) How to exercise the right to rescind, with a form for that purpose, designating the address of the creditor's place of business.
(iv) The effects of rescission, as described in paragraph (d) of this section.
(v) The date the rescission period expires.

(2) *Proper form of notice.* To satisfy the disclosure requirements of paragraph (b)(1) of this section, the creditor shall provide the appropriate model form in appendix H of this part or a substantially similar notice.

(c) *Delay of creditor's performance.* Unless a consumer waives the right of rescission under paragraph (e) of this section, no money shall be disbursed other than in escrow, no services shall be performed and no materials delivered until the rescission period has expired and the creditor is reasonably satisfied that the consumer has not rescinded.

(d) *Effects of rescission.*

(1) When a consumer rescinds a transaction, the security interest giving rise to the right of rescission becomes void and the consumer shall not be liable for any amount, including any finance charge.

(2) Within 20 calendar days after receipt of a notice of rescission, the creditor shall return any money or property that has been given to anyone in connection with the transaction and shall take any action necessary to reflect the termination of the security interest.

---

[48] The term "material disclosures" means the required disclosures of the annual percentage rate, the finance charge, the amount financed, the total payments, the payment schedule, and the disclosures and limitations referred to in § 226.32(c) and (d).

(3) If the creditor has delivered any money or property, the consumer may retain possession until the creditor has met its obligation under paragraph (d)(2) of this section. When the creditor has complied with that paragraph, the consumer shall tender the money or property to the creditor or, where the latter would be impracticable or inequitable, tender its reasonable value. At the consumer's option, tender of property may be made at the location of the property or at the consumer's residence. Tender of money must be made at the creditor's designated place of business. If the creditor does not take possession of the money or property within 20 calendar days after the consumer's tender, the consumer may keep it without further obligation.

(4) The procedures outlined in paragraphs (d)(2) and (3) of this section may be modified by court order.

(e) *Consumer's waiver of right to rescind.*

(1) The consumer may modify or waive the right to rescind if the consumer determines that the extension of credit is needed to meet a bona fide personal financial emergency. To modify or waive the right, the consumer shall give the creditor a dated written statement that describes the emergency, specifically modifies or waives the right to rescind, and bears the signature of all of the consumers entitled to rescind. Printed forms for this purpose are prohibited, except as provided in paragraph (e)(2) of this section.

(2) The need of the consumer to obtain funds immediately shall be regarded as a bona fide personal financial emergency provided that the dwelling securing the extension of credit is located in an area declared during June through September 1993, pursuant to 42 U.S.C. 5170, to be a major disaster area because of severe storms and flooding in the Midwest.[48a] In this instance, creditors may use printed forms for the consumer to waive the right to rescind. This exemption to paragraph (e)(1) of this section shall expire one year from the date an area was declared a major disaster.

(3) The consumer's need to obtain funds immediately shall be regarded as a bona fide personal financial emergency provided that the dwelling securing the extension of credit is located in an area declared during June through September 1994 to be a major disaster area, pursuant to 42 U.S.C. 5170, because of severe storms and flooding in the South.[48b] In this instance, creditors may use printed forms for the consumer to waive the right to rescind. This exemption to paragraph (e)(1) of this section shall expire one year from the date an area was declared a major disaster.

(4) The consumer's need to obtain funds immediately shall be regarded as a bona fide personal financial emergency provided that the dwelling securing the extension of credit is located in an area declared during October 1994 to be a major disaster area, pursuant to 42 U.S.C. 5170, because of severe

---

[48a] A list of the affected areas will be maintained by the Board.

[48b] A list of the affected areas will be maintained and published by the Board. Such areas now include parts of Alabama, Florida, and Georgia.

storms and flooding in Texas.[48c] In this instance, creditors may use printed forms for the consumer to waive the right to rescind. This exemption to paragraph (e)(1) of this section shall expire one year from the date an area was declared a major disaster.

(f) *Exempt transactions.* The right to rescind does not apply to the following:

(1) A residential mortgage transaction.
(2) A refinancing or consolidation by the same creditor of an extension of credit already secured by the consumer's principal dwelling. The right of rescission shall apply, however, to the extent the new amount financed exceeds the unpaid principal balance, any earned unpaid finance charge on the existing debt, and amounts attributed solely to the costs of the refinancing or consolidation.
(3) A transaction in which a state agency is a creditor.
(4) An advance, other than an initial advance, in a series of advances or in a series of single-payment obligations that is treated as a single transaction under § 226.17(c)(6), if the notice required by paragraph (b) of this section and all material disclosures have been given to the consumer.
(5) A renewal of optional insurance premiums that is not considered a refinancing under § 226.20(a)(5).

(g) *Tolerances for accuracy.*

(1) *One-half of 1 percent tolerance.* Except as provided in paragraphs (g)(2) and (h)(2) of this section, the finance charge and other disclosures affected by the finance charge (such as the amount financed and the annual percentage rate) shall be considered accurate for purposes of this section if the disclosed finance charge:
   (i) is understated by no more than 1/2 of 1 percent of the face amount of the note or $100, whichever is greater; or
   (ii) is greater than the amount required to be disclosed.
(2) *One percent tolerance.* In a refinancing of a residential mortgage transaction with a new creditor (other than a transaction covered by § 226.32), if there is no new advance and no consolidation of existing loans, the finance charge and other disclosures affected by the finance charge (such as the amount financed and the annual percentage rate) shall be considered accurate for purposes of this section if the disclosed finance charge:
   (i) is understated by no more than 1 percent of the face amount of the note or $100, whichever is greater; or
   (ii) is greater than the amount required to be disclosed.

[48c] A list of the affected areas will be maintained and published by the Board. Such areas now include the following counties in Texas: Angelina, Austin, Bastrop, Brazos, Brazoria, Burleson, Chambers, Fayette, Fort Bend, Galveston, Grimes, Hardin, Harris, Houston, Jackson, Jasper, Jefferson, Lee, Liberty, Madison, Matagorda, Montgomery, Nacagdoches, Orange, Polk, San Augustine, San Jacinto, Shelby, Trinity, Victoria, Washington, Waller, Walker, and Wharton.

(h) *Special rules for foreclosures.*

(1) *Right to rescind.* After the initiation of foreclosure on the consumer's principal dwelling that secures the credit obligation, the consumer shall have the right to rescind the transaction if:

 (i) A mortgage broker fee that should have been included in the finance charge was not included; or

 (ii) The creditor did not provide the properly completed appropriate model form in appendix H of this part, or a substantially similar notice of rescission.

(2) *Tolerance for disclosures.* After the initiation of foreclosure on the consumer's principal dwelling that secures the credit obligation, the finance charge and other disclosures affected by the finance charge (such as the amount financed and the annual percentage rate) shall be considered accurate for purposes of this section if the disclosed finance charge:

 (i) is understated by no more than $35; or

 (ii) is greater than the amount required to be disclosed.

Section 226.24—Advertising

(a) *Actually available terms.* If an advertisement for credit states specific credit terms, it shall state only those terms that actually are or will be arranged or offered by the creditor.

(b) *Advertisement of rate of finance charge.* If an advertisement states a rate of finance charge, it shall state the rate as an "annual percentage rate," using that term. If the annual percentage rate may be increased after consummation, the advertisement shall state that fact. The advertisement shall not state any other rate, except that a simple annual rate or periodic rate that is applied to an unpaid balance may be stated in conjunction with, but not more conspicuously than, the annual percentage rate.

(c) *Advertisement of terms that require additional disclosures.*

(1) If any of the following terms is set forth in an advertisement, the advertisement shall meet the requirements of paragraph (c)(2) of this section:

 (i) The amount or percentage of any downpayment.

 (ii) The number of payments or period of repayment.

 (iii) The amount of any payment.

 (iv) The amount of any finance charge.

(2) An advertisement stating any of the terms in paragraph (c)(1) of this section shall state the following terms,[49] as applicable:

 (i) The amount or percentage of the downpayment.

 (ii) The terms of repayment.

---

[49]An example of one or more typical extensions of credit with a statement of all the terms applicable to each may be used. An example of one or more typical extensions of credit with a statement of all the terms applicable to each may be used.

(iii) The "annual percentage rate," using that term, and, if the rate may be increased after consummation, that fact.

(d) *Catalogs and multiple-page advertisements; electronic advertisements.*

(1) If a catalog or other multiple-page advertisement, or an advertisement using electronic communication gives information in a table or schedule in sufficient detail to permit determination of the disclosures required by paragraph (c)(2) of this section, it shall be considered a single advertisement if:

(i) The table or schedule is clearly and conspicuously set forth; and

(ii) Any statement of terms of the credit terms in paragraph (c)(1) of this section appearing anywhere else in the catalog or advertisement clearly refers to the page or location where the table or schedule begins.

(2) A catalog or other multiple-page advertisement or an advertisement using electronic communication complies with paragraph (c)(2) of this section if the table or schedule of terms includes all appropriate disclosures for a representative scale of amounts up to the level of the more commonly sold higher-priced property or services offered.

SUBPART D—MISCELLANEOUS

Section 226.25—Record retention

(a) *General rule.* A creditor shall retain evidence of compliance with this regulation (other than advertising requirements under §§ 226.16 and 226.24) for 2 years after the date disclosures are required to be made or action is required to be taken. The administrative agencies responsible for enforcing the regulation may require creditors under their jurisdictions to retain records for a longer period if necessary to carry out their enforcement responsibilities under § 108 of the act.

(b) *Inspection of records.* A creditor shall permit the agency responsible for enforcing this regulation with respect to that creditor to inspect its relevant records for compliance.

Section 226.26—Use of annual percentage rate in oral disclosures

(a) *Open-end credit.* In an oral response to a consumer's inquiry about the cost of open-end credit, only the annual percentage rate or rates shall be stated, except that the periodic rate or rates also may be stated. If the annual percentage rate cannot be determined in advance because there are finance charges other than a periodic rate, the corresponding annual percentage rate shall be stated, and other cost information may be given.

(b) *Closed-end credit.* In an oral response to a consumer's inquiry about the cost of closed-end credit, only the annual percentage rate shall be stated, except that a simple annual rate or periodic rate also may be stated if it is applied to an unpaid balance. If the annual percentage rate cannot be determined in advance, the annual percentage rate for a sample transaction shall be stated, and other cost information for the consumer's specific transaction may be given.

Section 226.27—Language of disclosures

Disclosures required by this regulation may be made in a language other than English, provided that the disclosures are made available in English upon the consumer's request. This requirement for providing English disclosures on request does not apply to advertisements subject to §§ 226.16 and 226.24.

Section 226.28—Effect on state laws

(a) *Inconsistent disclosure requirements.*

(1) Except as provided in paragraph (d) of this section, state law requirements that are inconsistent with the requirements contained in chapter 1 (General provisions), chapter 2 (Credit transactions), or chapter 3 (Credit advertising) of the act and the implementing provisions of this regulation are preempted to the extent of the inconsistency. A state law is inconsistent if it requires a creditor to make disclosures or take actions that contradict the requirements of the federal law. A state law is contradictory if it requires the use of the same term to represent a different amount or a different meaning than the federal law, or if it requires the use of a term different from that required in the federal law to describe the same item. A creditor, state, or other interested party may request the Board to determine whether a state law requirement is inconsistent. After the Board determines that a state law is inconsistent, a creditor may not make disclosures using the inconsistent term or form.

(2) (i) State law requirements are inconsistent with the requirements contained in §§ 161 (Correction of billing errors) or 162 (Regulation of credit reports) of the act and the implementing provisions of this regulation and are preempted if they provide rights, responsibilities, or procedures for consumers or creditors that are different from those required by the federal law. However, a state law that allows a consumer to inquire about an open-end credit account and imposes on the creditor an obligation to respond to such inquiry after the time allowed in the federal law for the consumer to submit written notice of a billing error shall not be preempted in any situation where the time period for making written notice under this regulation has expired. If a creditor gives written notice of a consumer's rights under such state law, the notice shall state that reliance on the longer time period available under state law may result in the loss of important rights that could be preserved by acting more promptly under federal law; it shall also explain that the state law provisions apply only after expiration of the time period for submitting a proper written notice of a billing error under the federal law. If the state disclosures are made on the same side of a page as the required federal disclosures, the state disclosures shall appear under a demarcation line below the federal disclosures, and the federal disclosures shall be identified by a heading indicating that they are made in compliance with federal law.

(ii) State law requirements are inconsistent with the requirements contained in chapter 4 (Credit billing) of the act (other than §§ 161 or 162) and the implementing provisions of this regulation and are preempted if the creditor cannot comply with state law without violating federal law.

(iii) A state may request the Board to determine whether its law is inconsistent with chapter 4 of the act and its implementing provisions.

(b) *Equivalent disclosure requirements.* If the Board determines that a disclosure required by state law (other than a requirement relating to the finance charge, annual percentage rate, or the disclosures required under § 226.32) is substantially the same in meaning as a disclosure required under the act or this regulation, creditors in that state may make the state disclosure in lieu of the federal disclosure. A creditor, state, or other interested party may request the Board to determine whether a state disclosure is substantially the same in meaning as a federal disclosure.

(c) *Request for determination.* The procedures under which a request for a determination may be made under this section are set forth in appendix A.

(d) *Special rule for credit and charge cards.* State law requirements relating to the disclosure of credit information in any credit or charge card application or solicitation that is subject to the requirements of section 127(c) of chapter 2 of the act (§ 226.5a of the regulation) or in any renewal notice for a credit or charge card that is subject to the requirements of section 127(d) of chapter 2 of the act (§ 226.9(e) of the regulation) are preempted. State laws relating to the enforcement of section 127(c) and (d) of the act are not preempted.

Section 226.29—State exemptions

(a) *General rule.* Any state may apply to the Board to exempt a class of transactions within the state from the requirements of chapter 2 (Credit transactions) or chapter 4 (Credit billing) of the act and the corresponding provisions of this regulation. The Board shall grant an exemption if it determines that:

(1) The state law is substantially similar to the federal law or, in the case of chapter 4, affords the consumer greater protection than the federal law; and

(2) There is adequate provision for enforcement.

(b) *Civil liability.*

(1) No exemptions granted under this section shall extend to the civil liability provisions of §§ 130 and 131 of the act.

(2) If an exemption has been granted, the disclosures required by the applicable state law (except any additional requirements not imposed by federal law) shall constitute the disclosures required by this act.

(c) *Applications.* The procedures under which a state may apply for an exemption under this section are set forth in appendix B.

Section 226.30—Limitation on rates

A creditor shall include in any consumer credit contract secured by a dwelling and subject to the act and this regulation the maximum interest rate that may be imposed during the term of the obligation[50] when:

(a) In the case of closed-end credit, the annual percentage rate may increase after consummation, or

(b) In the case of open-end credit, the annual percentage rate may increase during the plan.

SUBPART E—SPECIAL RULES FOR CERTAIN HOME MORTGAGE TRANSACTIONS

Section 226.31—General rules

(a) *Relation to other subparts in this part.* The requirements and limitations of this subpart are in addition to and not in lieu of those contained in other subparts of this part.

(b) *Form of disclosures.*

(1) *General.* The creditor shall make the disclosures required by this subpart clearly and conspicuously in writing, in a form that the consumer may keep.

(2) *Electronic communication.* For rules governing the electronic delivery of disclosures, including a definition of electronic communication, see § 226.36.

(c) *Timing of disclosure.*

(1) *Disclosures for certain closed-end home mortgages.* The creditor shall furnish the disclosures required by § 226.32 at least three business days prior to consummation of a mortgage transaction covered by § 226.32.

  (i) *Change in terms.* After complying with paragraph (c)(1) of this section and prior to consummation, if the creditor changes any term that makes the disclosures inaccurate, new disclosures shall be provided in accordance with the requirements of this subpart.

  (ii) *Telephone disclosures.* A creditor may provide new disclosures by telephone if the consumer initiates the change and if, at consummation:

    (A) The creditor provides new written disclosures; and

    (B) The consumer and creditor sign a statement that the new disclosures were provided by telephone at least three days prior to consummation.

---

[50]Compliance with this section will constitute compliance with the disclosure requirements on limitations on increases in footnote 12 to §§ 226.6(a)(2) and 226.18(f)(2) until October 1, 1988.

(iii) *Consumer's waiver of waiting period before consummation.* The consumer may, after receiving the disclosures required by paragraph (c)(1) of this section, modify or waive the three-day waiting period between delivery of those disclosures and consummation if the consumer determines that the extension of credit is needed to meet a bona fide personal financial emergency. To modify or waive the right, the consumer shall give the creditor a dated written statement that describes the emergency, specifically modifies or waives the waiting period, and bears the signature of all the consumers entitled to the waiting period. Printed forms for this purpose are prohibited, except when creditors are permitted to use printed forms pursuant to § 226.23(e)(2).

(2) *Disclosures for reverse mortgages.* The creditor shall furnish the disclosures required by § 226.33 at least three business days prior to:

(i) Consummation of a closed-end credit transaction; or

(ii) The first transaction under an open-end credit plan.

(d) *Basis of disclosures and use of estimates.*

(1) *Legal Obligation.* Disclosures shall reflect the terms of the legal obligation between the parties.

(2) *Estimates.* If any information necessary for an accurate disclosure is unknown to the creditor, the creditor shall make the disclosure based on the best information reasonably available at the time the disclosure is provided, and shall state clearly that the disclosure is an estimate.

(3) *Pre-diem interest.* For a transaction in which a portion of the interest is determined on a per-diem basis and collected at consummation, any disclosure affected by the per-diem interest shall be considered accurate if the disclosure is based on the information known to the creditor at the time that the disclosure documents are prepared.

(e) *Multiple creditors; multiple consumers.* If a transaction involves more than one creditor, only one set of disclosures shall be given and the creditors shall agree among themselves which creditor must comply with the requirements that this part imposes on any or all of them. If there is more than one consumer, the disclosures may be made to any consumer who is primarily liable on the obligation. If the transaction is rescindable under § 226.15 or § 226.23, however, the disclosures shall be made to each consumer who has the right to rescind.

(f) *Effect of subsequent events.* If a disclosure becomes inaccurate because of an event that occurs after the creditor delivers the required disclosures, the inaccuracy is not a violation of Regulation Z (12 CFR part 226), although new disclosures may be required for mortgages covered by § 226.32 under paragraph (c) of this section, § 226.9(c), § 226.19, or § 226.20.

(g) *Accuracy of annual percentage rate.* For purposes of § 226.32, the annual percentage rate shall be considered accurate, and may be used in determining whether a transaction is covered by § 226.32, if it is accurate according to the requirements and within the tolerances under § 226.22. The finance charge tolerances for rescission under § 226.23(g) or (h) shall not apply for this purpose.

Section 226.32—Requirements for certain closed-end home mortgages

(a) *Coverage.*

(1) Except as provided in paragraph (a)(2) of this section, the requirements of this section apply to a consumer credit transaction that is secured by the consumer's principal dwelling, and in which either:

(i) The annual percentage rate at consummation will exceed by more than 8 percentage points for first-lien loans, or by more than 10 percentage points for subordinate-lien loans, the yield on Treasury securities having comparable periods of maturity to the loan maturity as of the fifteenth day of the month immediately preceding the month in which the application for the extension of credit is received by the creditor; or

(ii) The total points and fees payable by the consumer at or before loan closing will exceed the greater of 8 percent of the total loan amount, or $400; the $400 figure shall be adjusted annually on January 1 by the annual percentage change in the Consumer Price Index that was reported on the preceding June 1.

(2) This section does not apply to the following:

(i) A residential mortgage transaction.

(ii) A reverse mortgage transaction subject to § 226.33.

(iii) An open-end credit plan subject to subpart B of this part.

(b) *Definitions.* For purposes of this subpart, the following definitions apply:

(1) For purposes of paragraph (a)(1)(ii) of this section, *points and fees* mean:

(i) All items required to be disclosed under §§ 226.4(a) and 226.4(b), except interest or the time-price differential;

(ii) All compensation paid to mortgage brokers; and

(iii) All items listed in § 226.4(c)(7) (other than amounts held for future payment of taxes) unless the charge is reasonable, the creditor receives no direct or indirect compensation in connection with the charge, and the charge is not paid to an affiliate of the creditor; and

(iv) Premiums or other charges for credit life, accident, health, or loss-of-income insurance, or debt-cancellation coverage (whether or not the debt-cancellation coverage is insurance under applicable law) that provides for cancellation of all or part of the consumer's liability in the event of the loss of life, health, or income or in the case of accident, written in connection with the credit transaction.

(2) *Affiliate* means any company that controls, is controlled by, or is under common control with another company, as set forth in the Bank Holding Company Act of 1956 (12 U.S.C. 1841 et seq.)

(c) *Disclosures.* In addition to other disclosures required by this part, in a mortgage subject to this section, the creditor shall disclose the following in conspicuous type size:

(1) *Notices.* The following statement: "You are not required to complete this agreement merely because you have received these disclosures or have signed a loan application. If you obtain this loan, the lender will have a mortgage on your home. You could lose your home, and any money you have put into it, if you do no meet your obligations under the loan."

(2) *Annual percentage rate.* The annual percentage rate.

(3) *Regular payment; balloon payment.* The amount of the regular monthly (or other periodic) payment and the amount of any balloon payment. The regular payment disclosed under this paragraph shall be treated as accurate if it is based on an amount borrowed that is deemed accurate and is disclosed under paragraph (c)(5) of this section.

(4) *Variable-rate.* For variable-rate transactions, a statement that the interest rate and monthly payment may increase, and the amount of the single maximum monthly payment, based on the maximum interest rate required to be disclosed under § 226.30.

(5) *Amount borrowed.* For a mortgage refinancing, the total amount the consumer will borrow, as reflected by the face amount of the note; and where the amount borrowed includes premiums or other charges for optional credit insurance or debt-cancellation coverage, that fact shall be stated, grouped together with the disclosure of the amount borrowed. The disclosure of the amount borrowed shall be treated as accurate if it is not more than $100 above or below the amount required to be disclosed.

(d) *Limitations.* A mortgage transaction subject to this section shall not include the following terms:

(1) (i) *Balloon payment.* For a loan with a term of less than five years, a payment schedule with regular periodic payments that when aggregated do not fully amortize the outstanding principal balance.

(ii) *Exception.* The limitations in paragraph (d)(1)(i) of this section do not apply to loans with maturities of less than one year, if the purpose of the loan is a "bridge" loan connected with the acquisition or construction of a dwelling intended to become the consumer's principal dwelling.

(2) *Negative amortization.* A payment schedule with regular periodic payments that cause the principal balance to increase.

(3) *Advance payments.* A payment schedule that consolidates more than two periodic payments and pays them in advance from the proceeds.

(4) *Increased interest rate.* An increase in the interest rate after default.

(5) *Rebates.* A refund calculated by a method less favorable than the actuarial method (as defined by section 933(d) of the Housing and Community Development Act of 1992, 15 U.S.C. 1615(d)), for rebates of interest arising from a loan acceleration due to default.

(6) *Prepayment penalties.* Except as allowed under paragraph (d)(7) of this section, a penalty for paying all or part of the principal before the date on which the principal is due. A prepayment penalty includes computing a refund of unearned interest by a method that is less favorable to the consumer than the actuarial method, as defined by section 933(d) of the Housing and Community Development Act of 1992.

(7) *Prepayment penalty exception.* A mortgage transaction subject to this section may provide for a prepayment penalty otherwise permitted by law (including a refund calculated according to the rule of 78s) if:

(i) The penalty can be exercised only for the first five years following consummation;

(ii) The source of the prepayment funds is not a refinancing by the creditor or an affiliate of the creditor; and

(iii) At consummation, the consumer's total monthly debts (including amounts owed under the mortgage) do not exceed 50 percent of the consumer's monthly gross income, as verified by the consumer's signed financial statement, a credit report, and payment records for employment income.

(8) *Due-on-demand clause.* A demand feature that permits the creditor to terminate the loan in advance of the original maturity date and to demand repayment of the entire outstanding balance, except in the following circumstances:

(i) There is fraud or material misrepresentation by the consumer in connection with the loan;

(ii) The consumer fails to meet the repayment terms of the agreement for any outstanding balance; or

(iii) There is any action or inaction by the consumer that adversely affects the creditor's security for the loan, or any right of the creditor in such security.

Section 226.33—Requirements for reverse mortgages

(a) *Definition.* For purposes of this subpart, *reverse mortgage transaction* means a nonrecourse consumer credit obligation in which:

(1) A mortgage, deed of trust, or equivalent consensual security interest securing one or more advances is created in the consumer's principal dwelling; and

(2) Any principal, interest, or shared appreciation or equity is due and payable (other than in the case of default) only after:

(i) The consumer dies;

(ii) The dwelling is transferred; or

(iii) The consumer ceases to occupy the dwelling as a principal dwelling.

(b) *Content of disclosures.* In addition to other disclosures required by this part, in a reverse mortgage transaction the creditor shall provide the following disclosures in a form substantially similar to the model form found in paragraph (d) of Appendix K of this part:

(1) *Notice.* A statement that the consumer is not obligated to complete the reverse mortgage transaction merely because the consumer has received the disclosures required by this section or has signed an application for a reverse mortgage loan.

(2) *Total annual loan cost rates.* A good-faith projection of the total cost of the credit, determined in accordance with paragraph (c) of this section and expressed as a table of "total annual loan cost rates," using that term, in accordance with Appendix K of this part.

(3) *Itemization of pertinent information.* An itemization of loan terms, charges, the age of the youngest borrower and the appraised property value.

(4) *Explanation of table.* An explanation of the table of total annual loan cost rates as provided in the model form found in paragraph (d) of Appendix K of this part.

(c) *Projected total cost of credit.* The projected total cost of credit shall reflect the following factors, as applicable:

(1) *Costs to consumer.* All costs and charges to the consumer, including the costs of any annuity the consumer purchases as part of the reverse mortgage transaction.

(2) *Payments to consumer.* All advances to and for the benefit of the consumer, including annuity payments that the consumer will receive from an annuity that the consumer purchases as part of the reverse mortgage transaction.

(3) *Additional creditor compensation.* Any shared appreciation or equity in the dwelling that the creditor is entitled by contract to receive.

(4) *Limitations on consumer liability.* Any limitation on the consumer's liability (such as nonrecourse limits and equity conservation agreements).

(5) *Assumed annual appreciation rates.* Each of the following assumed annual appreciation rates for the dwelling:

(i) 0 percent.

(ii) 4 percent.

(iii) 8 percent.

(6) *Assumed loan period.* Each of the following assumed loan periods, as provided in Appendix L of this part:

(i) Two years.

(ii) The actuarial life expectancy of the consumer to become obligated on the reverse mortgage transaction (as of that consumer's most recent birthday). In the case of multiple consumers, the period shall be the actuarial life expectancy of the youngest consumer (as of that consumer's most recent birthday).

(iii) The actuarial life expectancy specified by paragraph (c)(6)(i)(B) of this section, multiplied by a factor of 1.4 and rounded to the nearest full year.

(iv) At the creditor's option, the actuarial life expectancy specified by paragraph (c)(6)(i)(B) of this section, multiplied by a factor of .5 and rounded to the nearest full year.

Section 226.34—Prohibited acts or practices in connection with credit secured by a consumer's dwelling

(a) *Prohibited acts or practices for loans subject to § 226.32.* A creditor extending mortgage credit subject to § 226.32 shall not—

(1) *Home improvement contracts.* Pay a contractor under a home improvement contract from the proceeds of a mortgage covered by § 226.32, other than:

(i) By an instrument payable to the consumer or jointly to the consumer and the contractor; or

(ii) At the election of the consumer, through a third-party escrow agent in accordance with terms established in a written agreement signed by the consumer, the creditor, and the contractor prior to the disbursement.

(2) *Notice to assignee.* Sell or otherwise assign a mortgage subject to § 226.32 without furnishing the following statement to the purchaser or assignee: "Notice: This is a mortgage subject to special rules under the federal Truth in Lending Act. Purchasers or assignees of this mortgage could be liable for all claims and defenses with respect to the mortgage that the borrower could assert against the creditor."

(3) *Refinancings within one-year period.* Within one year of having extended credit subject to § 226.32, refinance any loan subject to § 226.32 to the same borrower into another loan subject to § 226.32, unless the refinancing is in the borrower's interest. An assignee holding or servicing an extension of mortgage credit subject to § 226.32, shall not, for the remainder of the one-year period following the date of origination of the credit, refinance any loan subject to § 226.32 to the same borrower into another loan subject to § 226.32, unless the refinancing is in the borrower's interest. A creditor (or assignee) is prohibited from engaging in acts or practices to evade this provision, including a pattern or practice of arranging for the refinancing of its own loans by affiliated or unaffiliated creditors, or modifying a loan agreement (whether or not the existing loan is satisfied and replaced by the new loan) and charging a fee.

(4) *Repayment ability.* Engage in a pattern or practice of extending credit subject to § 226.32 to a consumer based on the consumer's collateral without regard to the consumer's repayment ability, including the consumer's current and expected income, current obligations, and employment. There is a presumption that a creditor has violated this paragraph (a)(4) if the creditor engages in a pattern or practice of making loans subject to § 226.32 without verifying and documenting consumers' repayment ability.

(b) *Prohibited acts or practices for dwelling-secured loans; open-end credit.* In connection with credit secured by the consumer's dwelling that does not meet the definition in § 226.2(a)(20), a creditor shall not structure a home-secured loan as an open-end plan to evade the requirements of § 226.32.

Section 226.35—[Reserved]

SUBPART F—ELECTRONIC COMMUNICATION

Section 226.36—Requirements for electronic communication

(a) *Definition.* "Electronic communication" means a message transmitted electronically between a creditor and a consumer in a format that allows visual text to be displayed on equipment, for example, a personal computer monitor.

(b) *General rule.* In accordance with the Electronic Signatures in Global and National Commerce Act (the E-Sign Act) (15 U.S.C. 7001 *et seq.*) and the rules of this part, a creditor may provide by electronic communication any disclosure required by this part to be in writing.

(c) *When consent is required.* Under the E-Sign Act, a creditor is required to obtain a consumer's affirmative consent when providing disclosures related to a transaction. For purposes of this requirement, the disclosures required under §§ 226.5a, 226.5b(d) and 226.5b(e), 226.16, 226.17(g)(1) through (5), 226.19(b) and 226.24 are deemed not to be related to a transaction.

(d) *Address or location to receive electronic communication.* A creditor that uses electronic communication to provide disclosures required by this part shall:

(1) Send the disclosure to the consumer's electronic address; or

(2) Make the disclosure available at another location such as an Internet web site; and

  (i) Alert the consumer of the disclosure's availability by sending a notice to the consumer's electronic address (or to a postal address, at the creditor's option). The notice shall identify the account involved and the address of the Internet web site or other location where the disclosure is available; and

  (ii) Make the disclosure available for at least 90 days from the date the disclosure first becomes available or from the date of the notice alerting the consumer of the disclosure, whichever comes later.

(3) *Exceptions.* A creditor need not comply with paragraphs (d)(2)(i) and (ii) of this section for the disclosures required under §§ 226.5a, 226.5b(d) and 226.5b(e), 226.16, 226.17(g)(1) through (5), 226.19(b) and 226.24.

(e) *Redelivery.* When a disclosure provided by electronic communication is returned to a creditor undelivered, the creditor shall take reasonable steps to attempt redelivery using information in its files.

(f) *Electronic signatures.* An electronic signature as defined under the E-Sign satisfies any requirement under this part for a consumer's signature or initials.

Appendix III

FAIR CREDIT BILLING ACT

15 U.S.C. §§ 1666-1666j

TITLE 15—COMMERCE AND TRADE

CHAPTER 41—CONSUMER CREDIT PROTECTION

SUBCHAPTER I—CONSUMER CREDIT COST DISCLOSURE

PART D—CREDIT BILLING

Sec. 1666. Correction of billing errors

(a) Written notice by obligor to creditor; time for and contents of notice; procedure upon receipt of notice by creditor
If a creditor, within sixty days after having transmitted to an obligor a statement of the obligor's account in connection with an extension of consumer credit, receives at the address disclosed under section 1637(b)(10) of this title a written notice (other than notice on a payment stub or other payment medium supplied by the creditor if the creditor so stipulates with the disclosure required under section 1637(a)(7) of this title) from the obligor in which the obligor

(1) sets forth or otherwise enables the creditor to identify the name and account number (if any) of the obligor,

(2) indicates the obligor's belief that the statement contains a billing error and the amount of such billing error, and

(3) sets forth the reasons for the obligor's belief (to the extent applicable) that the statement contains a billing error, the creditor shall, unless the obligor has, after giving such written notice and before the expiration of the time limits herein specified, agreed that the statement was correct

(A) not later than thirty days after the receipt of the notice, send a written acknowledgment thereof to the obligor, unless the action required in subparagraph (B) is taken within such thirty-day period, and

(B) not later than two complete billing cycles of the creditor (in no event later than ninety days) after the receipt of the notice and prior to taking any action to collect the amount, or any part thereof, indicated by the obligor under paragraph (2) either

(i) make appropriate corrections in the account of the obligor, including the crediting of any finance charges on amounts erroneously billed, and transmit to the obligor a notification of such corrections and the creditor's explanation of any change in the amount indicated by the obligor under paragraph (2) and, if any such change is made and the obligor so requests, copies of documentary evidence of the obligor's indebtedness; or

(ii) send a written explanation or clarification to the obligor, after having conducted an investigation, setting forth to the extent applicable the reasons why the creditor believes the account of the obligor was correctly shown in the statement and, upon request of the obligor, provide copies of documentary evidence of the obligor's indebtedness. In the case of a billing error where the obligor alleges that the creditor's billing statement reflects goods not delivered to the obligor or his designee in accordance with the agreement made at the time of the transaction, a creditor may not construe such amount to be correctly shown unless he determines that such goods were actually delivered, mailed, or otherwise sent to the obligor and provides the obligor with a statement of such determination.

After complying with the provisions of this subsection with respect to an alleged billing error, a creditor has no further responsibility under this section if the obligor continues to make substantially the same allegation with respect to such error.

(b) Billing error

For the purpose of this section, a "billing error" consists of any of the following:

(1) A reflection on a statement of an extension of credit which was not made to the obligor or, if made, was not in the amount reflected on such statement.

(2) A reflection on a statement of an extension of credit for which the obligor requests additional clarification including documentary evidence thereof.

(3) A reflection on a statement of goods or services not accepted by the obligor or his designee or not delivered to the obligor or his designee in accordance with the agreement made at the time of a transaction.

(4) The creditor's failure to reflect properly on a statement a payment made by the obligor or a credit issued to the obligor.

(5) A computation error or similar error of an accounting nature of the creditor on a statement.

(6) Failure to transmit the statement required under section 1637(b) of this title to the last address of the obligor which has been disclosed to the creditor, unless that address was furnished less than twenty days before the end of the billing cycle for which the statement is required.

(7) Any other error described in regulations of the Board.

(c) Action by creditor to collect amount or any part thereof regarded by obligor to be a billing error

For the purposes of this section, "action to collect the amount, or any part thereof, indicated by an obligor under paragraph (2)" does not include the sending of statements of account, which may include finance charges on amounts in dispute, to the obligor following written notice from the obligor as specified under subsection (a) of this section, if

(1) the obligor's account is not restricted or closed because of the failure of the obligor to pay the amount indicated under paragraph (2) of subsection (a) of this section, and

(2) the creditor indicates the payment of such amount is not required pending the creditor's compliance with this section.

Nothing in this section shall be construed to prohibit any action by a creditor to collect any amount which has not been indicated by the obligor to contain a billing error.

(d) Restricting or closing by creditor of account regarded by obligor to contain a billing error

Pursuant to regulations of the Board, a creditor operating an open end consumer credit plan may not, prior to the sending of the written explanation or clarification required under paragraph (B)(ii), restrict or close an account with respect to which the obligor has indicated pursuant to subsection (a) of this section that he believes such account to contain a billing error solely because of the obligor's failure to pay the amount indicated to be in error. Nothing in this subsection shall be deemed to prohibit a creditor from applying against the credit limit on the obligor's account the amount indicated to be in error.

(e) Effect of noncompliance with requirements by creditor

Any creditor who fails to comply with the requirements of this section or section 1666a of this title forfeits any right to collect from the obligor the amount indicated by the obligor under paragraph (2) of subsection (a) of this section, and any finance charges thereon, except that the amount required to be forfeited under this subsection may not exceed $50.

Sec. 1666a. Regulation of credit reports

(a) Reports by creditor on obligor's failure to pay amount regarded as billing error

After receiving a notice from an obligor as provided in section 1666(a) of this title, a creditor or his agent may not directly or indirectly threaten to report to any person adversely on the obligor's credit rating or credit standing because of the obligor's failure to pay the amount indicated by the obligor under section 1666(a)(2) of this title, and such amount may not be reported as delinquent to any third party until the creditor has met the requirements of section 1666 of this title and has allowed the obligor the same number of days (not less than ten) thereafter to make payment as is provided under the credit agreement with the obligor for the payment of undisputed amounts.

(b) Reports by creditor on delinquent amounts in dispute; notification of obligor of parties notified of delinquency
If a creditor receives a further written notice from an obligor that an amount is still in dispute within the time allowed for payment under subsection (a) of this section, a creditor may not report to any third party that the amount of the obligor is delinquent because the obligor has failed to pay an amount which he has indicated under section 1666(a)(2) of this title, unless the creditor also reports that the amount is in dispute and, at the same time, notifies the obligor of the name and address of each party to whom the creditor is reporting information concerning the delinquency.

(c) Reports by creditor of subsequent resolution of delinquent amounts
A creditor shall report any subsequent resolution of any delinquencies reported pursuant to subsection (b) of this section to the parties to whom such delinquencies were initially reported.

Sec. 1666b. Length of billing period in credit statement for imposition of finance charge; effect of failure of timely mailing or delivery of statement

(a) Additional finance charge
If an open end consumer credit plan provides a time period within which an obligor may repay any portion of the credit extended without incurring an additional finance charge, such additional finance charge may not be imposed with respect to such portion of the credit extended for the billing cycle of which such period is a part unless a statement which includes the amount upon which the finance charge for that period is based was mailed at least fourteen days prior to the date specified in the statement by which payment must be made in order to avoid imposition of that finance charge.

(b) Excusable cause
Subsection (a) of this section does not apply in any case where a creditor has been prevented, delayed, or hindered in making timely mailing or delivery of such periodic statement within the time period specified in such subsection because of an act of God, war, natural disaster, strike, or other excusable or justifiable cause, as determined under regulations of the Board.

Sec. 1666c. Prompt crediting of payments; imposition of finance charge

Payments received from an obligor under an open end consumer credit plan by the creditor shall be posted promptly to the obligor's account as specified in regulations of the Board. Such regulations shall prevent a finance charge from being imposed on any obligor if the creditor has received the obligor's payment in readily identifiable form in the amount, manner, location, and time indicated by the creditor to avoid the imposition thereof.

Sec. 1666d. Treatment of credit balances

Whenever a credit balance in excess of $1 is created in connection with a consumer credit transaction through

(1) transmittal of funds to a creditor in excess of the total balance due on an account,
(2) rebates of unearned finance charges or insurance premiums, or
(3) amounts otherwise owed to or held for the benefit of an obligor, the creditor shall
   (A) credit the amount of the credit balance to the consumer's account;
   (B) refund any part of the amount of the remaining credit balance, upon request of the consumer; and
   (C) make a good faith effort to refund to the consumer by cash, check, or money order any part of the amount of the credit balance remaining in the account for more than six months, except that no further action is required in any case in which the consumer's current location is not known by the creditor and cannot be traced through the consumer's last known address or telephone number.

Sec. 1666e. Notification of credit card issuer by seller of return of goods, etc., by obligor; credit for account of obligor

With respect to any sales transaction where a credit card has been used to obtain credit, where the seller is a person other than the card issuer, and where the seller accepts or allows a return of the goods or forgiveness of a debit for services which were the subject of such sale, the seller shall promptly transmit to the credit card issuer, a credit statement with respect thereto and the credit card issuer shall credit the account of the obligor for the amount of the transaction.

Sec. 1666f. Inducements to cardholders by sellers of cash discounts for payments by cash, check or similar means; finance charge for sales transactions involving cash discounts

(a) Cash discounts
   With respect to credit card which may be used for extensions of credit in sales transactions in which the seller is a person other than the card issuer, the card issuer may not, by contract, or otherwise, prohibit any such seller from offering a discount to a cardholder to induce the cardholder to pay by cash, check, or similar means rather than use a credit card.

(b) Finance charge

With respect to any sales transaction, any discount from the regular price offered by the seller for the purpose of inducing payment by cash, checks, or other means not involving the use of an open-end credit plan or a credit card shall not constitute a finance charge as determined under section 1605 of this title if such discount is offered to all prospective buyers and its availability is disclosed clearly and conspicuously.

Sec. 1666g. Tie-in services prohibited for issuance of credit card

Notwithstanding any agreement to the contrary, a card issuer may not require a seller, as a condition to participating in a credit card plan, to open an account with or procure any other service from the card issuer or its subsidiary or agent.

Sec. 1666h. Offset of cardholder's indebtedness by issuer of credit card with funds deposited with issuer by cardholder; remedies of creditors under State law not affected

(a) Offset against consumer's funds

A card issuer may not take any action to offset a cardholder's indebtedness arising in connection with a consumer credit transaction under the relevant credit card plan against funds of the cardholder held on deposit with the card issuer unless

(1) such action was previously authorized in writing by the cardholder in accordance with a credit plan whereby the cardholder agrees periodically to pay debts incurred in his open end credit account by permitting the card issuer periodically to deduct all or a portion of such debt from the cardholder's deposit account, and

(2) such action with respect to any outstanding disputed amount not be taken by the card issuer upon request of the cardholder.

In the case of any credit card account in existence on the effective date of this section, the previous written authorization referred to in clause (1) shall not be required until the date (after such effective date) when such account is renewed, but in no case later than one year after such effective date. Such written authorization shall be deemed to exist if the card issuer has previously notified the cardholder that the use of his credit card account will subject any funds which the card issuer holds in deposit accounts of such cardholder to offset against any amounts due and payable on his credit card account which have not been paid in accordance with the terms of the agreement between the card issuer and the cardholder.

(b) Attachments and levies

This section does not alter or affect the right under State law of a card issuer to attach or otherwise levy upon funds of a cardholder held on deposit with the card issuer if that remedy is constitutionally available to creditors generally.

Sec. 1666i. Assertion by cardholder against card issuer of claims and defenses arising out of credit card transaction; prerequisites; limitation on amount of claims or defenses

(a) Claims and defenses assertible

Subject to the limitation contained in subsection (b) of this section, a card issuer who has issued a credit card to a cardholder pursuant to an open end consumer credit plan shall be subject to all claims (other than tort claims) and defenses arising out of any transaction in which the credit card is used as a method of payment or extension of credit if

(1) the obligor has made a good faith attempt to obtain satisfactory resolution of a disagreement or problem relative to the transaction from the person honoring the credit card;

(2) the amount of the initial transaction exceeds $50; and

(3) the place where the initial transaction occurred was in the same State as the mailing address previously provided by the cardholder or was within 100 miles from such address, except that the limitations set forth in clauses (2) and (3) with respect to an obligor's right to assert claims and defenses against a card issuer shall not be applicable to any transaction in which the person honoring the credit card

(A) is the same person as the card issuer,

(B) is controlled by the card issuer,

(C) is under direct or indirect common control with the card issuer,

(D) is a franchised dealer in the card issuer's products or services, or

(E) has obtained the order for such transaction through a mail solicitation made by or participated in by the card issuer in which the cardholder is solicited to enter into such transaction by using the credit card issued by the card issuer.

(b) Amount of claims and defenses assertible

The amount of claims or defenses asserted by the cardholder may not exceed the amount of credit outstanding with respect to such transaction at the time the cardholder first notifies the card issuer or the person honoring the credit card of such claim or defense. For the purpose of determining the amount of credit outstanding in the preceding sentence, payments and credits to the cardholder's account are deemed to have been applied, in the order indicated, to the payment of:

(1) late charges in the order of their entry to the account;

(2) finance charges in order of their entry to the account; and

(3) debits to the account other than those set forth above, in the order in which each debit entry to the account was made.

Sec. 1666j. Applicability of State laws

(a) Consistency of provisions
This part does not annul, alter, or affect, or exempt any person subject to the provisions of this part from complying with, the laws of any State with respect to credit billing practices, except to the extent that those laws are inconsistent with any provision of this part, and then only to the extent of the inconsistency. The Board is authorized to determine whether such inconsistencies exist. The Board may not determine that any State law is inconsistent with any provision of this part if the Board determines that such law gives greater protection to the consumer.

(b) Exemptions by Board from credit billing requirements
The Board shall by regulation exempt from the requirements of this part any class of credit transactions within any State if it determines that under the law of that State that class of transactions is subject to requirements substantially similar to those imposed under this part or that such law gives greater protection to the consumer, and that there is adequate provision for enforcement.

(c) Finance charge or other charge for credit for sales transactions involving cash discounts
Notwithstanding any other provisions of this subchapter, any discount offered under section 1666f(b) of this title shall not be considered a finance charge or other charge for credit under the usury laws of any State or under the laws of any State relating to disclosure of information in connection with credit transactions, or relating to the types, amounts or rates of charges, or to any element or elements of charges permissible under such laws in connection with the extension or use of credit.

CHAPTER 17

E-Commerce Technology

AUTOMATED CLEARING HOUSE NETWORK

The Automated Clearing House (ACH) network is a means to provide electronic payments nationwide. It was originally organized in the late 1960s by a group of bankers and evolved eventually into the National Automated Clearing House Association (NACHA), known as the Electronic Payments Association. NACHA is basically the regulatory body for the ACH network. The ACH offers a wide range of methods of payments to both consumers and corporations including direct deposit, preauthorized bill payment, home banking, point of sale and point of purchase payments, cash concentration and disbursement, corporate trade payments, and re-depositing checks returned for insufficient funds. ACH is fundamentally a batch processing, storing and forwarding system in addition to the fact that everything is done electronically. Transactions received during the day are stored and processed later in batch mode and are sorted and accumulated by destination during a pre-determined time period. No physical handling of checks is involved. The transmission electronically between financial institutions provides significant savings.

The ACH network operates as follows:

1. The originator of the transaction is the one that initiates the entries into the system.
2. The originator can either be a company or a consumer.
3. The originator begins the transaction by debiting the bank account.
4. The originating depository financial institution receives the payment instructions from the originator and this is ultimately transmitted to the ACH operator.

5. The automated clearing house is the clearing facility which may be operated by a private organization or a federal reserve bank. Either the bank or the private organization receives the ACH transactions and these transactions are thereafter routed to the receiving depository financial institution.
6. The receiving depository financial institution receives the ACH entries and posts the entries to the accounts of its depositors.
7. The receiver is a natural person or company which has authorized the originator to initiate the ACH entry to the receiver's account or in simple terms has authorized the originator (consumer) to debit his account and transfer the money to ACH through a financial institution and thereafter have the money credited to the receiver's account through another financial institution.

The ACH network presently includes such applications as payroll, retirement, dividend, interest, and annuity payments in addition to education benefit reimbursements, payments and advances, as well as many other types of credit applications. Debit applications include the collection of insurance premiums, mortgage and rent payments, utility payments, installment payments, membership dues, and a variety of other recurring obligations. The ACH network is also used to operate consumer transactions at automated teller machines and point of sale terminals.

NACHA states in their rule book that the ACH network is a nationwide electronic payment system used by more than 20,000 participating financial institutions, over 3.5 million corporations, and 100 million consumers. NACHA offers several publications, the principal one being the ACH Rules, which is a complete guide to rules and regulations governing the ACH network. NACHA also publishes an ACH compliance manual and a risk management handbook among other publications. Further information can be obtained from NACHA, located at 13665 Dulles Technology Drive, Suite 300, Herndon, VA 20171 (703-561-1100).

The pertinent statutes under which the ACH network operates is Regulation E, which is the Official Staff Interpretation of the Electronic Fund Transfer Act, 31 CFR, Parts 208 and 210 as well as the Federal Reserve Operating Circular #4, 26 CFR, Parts 1-20-25, 31 and 40; 31 CFR, Part 210.

The ACH now allows retail outlets to accept a check instead of a credit card at the point of sale and converts the check immediately into an ACH debit (using back office conversion—BOC).

Arguments have been made that the ability of the ACH process to charge a single debit or continual debits may violate the FDCPA section dealing with postdated checks. Repeated transactions by ACH, or EFT, may be the equivalent of postdated checks and trigger the requirements of the FDCPA.

REGULATION E

Regulation E deals primarily with the Electronic Fund Transfer Act which sets forth the rights and liabilities when using an electronic fund transfer system (EFT).[1]

A commentary has been issued by the Federal Reserve Board with regard to Regulation E.[2]

Basically an electronic fund transfer is any transfer of monies that begins with an electronic terminal, computer, telephone, etc. in order to authorize a financial institution to transfer funds or to debit or credit an account. ATMs, direct deposits or withdrawals of funds, debit card transaction, a check, or acceptance or other paper instrument are not regulated by the EFT system. An electronic check conversion wherein the check is converted to an electronic fund transfer is subject to the Regulation E.

The authorization requirements and receipt requirements are spelled out in Regulation E. A copy of Regulation E is included in the Appendix. An analysis of Regulation E is beyond the scope of this book. For those financial institutions and firms that use EFT, a careful reading of the regulation is recommended with the aid and assistance of counsel.

ELECTRONIC SIGNATURES

The Electronic Signatures in Global and National Commerce Act (E-Sign Act) (*see* Appendix I to this chapter) became effective October 1, 2000.[3] The federal law granted electronic signatures and documents equal standing in interstate commerce with handwritten signatures and written records notwithstanding any state law to the contrary.

In 1999, the National Conference of Commissioners on Uniform State Laws (NCCUSL) adopted the Uniform Electronic Transaction Act (UETA) (*see* Appendix II to this chapter) and proposed it for enactment uniformly throughout the United States. The Act attempted to eliminate the inconsistency of state laws and addressed the validity of electronic contracts and electronic signatures. The declared purpose of UETA is to remove barriers to electronic commerce by validating and effectuating electronic records and signatures. UETA is intended to protect and expand the use of electronic mediums for business at every level.

The Uniform Computer Information Transaction Act (UCITA) was promulgated by the National Conference of Commissioners on Uniform State Laws, also in 1999, and it provides a set of rules for licensing computer information, which may consist of computer software or other identified

---

[1] 15 U.S.C §§ 1693 *et seq.*
[2] 12 C.F.R §§ 205 *et seq.*
[3] Codified at 15 U.S.C. §§ 7001-7031.

forms of computer information. Databases and computerized music also fall under computer information.

The E-Sign Act and UETA both do not require the use of technologies, but help verify either the identity of the signing party or the integrity of the record itself. Furthermore, E-Sign does not afford preferred status to electronic records or signatures by using technologies that verify the identity of the signing party.

INTERSTATE COMMERCE

The E-Sign Act regulates transactions that cross between two states, *interstate commerce,* and the UETA regulates transactions within the state, *intrastate transactions.* Unfortunately, not all of the states have adopted UETA and many states do not have any laws that deal directly with electronic signatures. The use of the Internet affects interstate commerce and the courts lean toward applying the E-Sign Act where no state law has been enacted even though the transaction does not cross state lines.

The federal E-Sign Act is preempted if the state adopts UETA (E-Sign Section 1029(a)(1)). If no law regulates electronic transactions, the E-Sign Act will prevail in those instances where the transaction or the activity has a substantial relation to intrastate commerce or that the activities substantially affect interstate commerce. The E-Sign Act may fall under the substantial relation test, because it bears a substantial relation to interstate commerce notwithstanding those activities are performed within the confines of one state. As UETA is adopted by other states, this problem will disappear. At the moment, the E-Sign Act may or may not apply to an electronic signature transaction if the electronic signature transaction took place within the state in the face of an absence of state law governing electronic signatures. Of course, if the state does have laws governing electronic signatures which are not inconsistent with the E-Sign Act, the state law should prevail.

ELECTRONIC SIGNATURES IN GLOBAL AND NATIONAL COMMERCE ACT (E-SIGN)

The general requirements of E-Sign encompass the following:

1. The specific consent of the consumer must be obtained to receive the information in electronic form.
2. The consumer must understand whether the consent is for a single transmission or for a series of transmissions.

3. The consumer must be advised of the right to withdraw the consent in the future and if consent is withdrawn, whether any fees will be imposed upon him.
4. The consumer must be told exactly the procedure to withdraw the consent.
5. The consumer must be told that a paper record may be obtained when the consumer withdraws his consent and a paper record may be obtained even while the consumer's consent to receive information in electronic form is still in effect.
6. The consumer must be advised whether an option is available to enter the transaction without consenting to receiving the information in electronic form.
7. The consumer must be aware of the fact that information may be accessed electronically and the consumer must be told the information may be received electronically. The consumer must consent electronically.[4]

Paper Record. When using an electronic signature or to receive documents electronically, the record must be provided on paper or in non-electronic form. The right to withdraw the consent to have the record provided in an electronic form must be offered. The user must have the right to withdraw his consent to sign his name electronically, to receive documents electronically and to obtain a paper copy.

Exception. E-Sign does not cover negotiable documents, letters of credit, bulk sales, warehouse receipts, investment securities, or secured transactions under Uniform Commercial Code (UCC) Section 9. Exemptions to E-Sign are UCC Sections 1-107 and 1-207 and Articles 2 and 2a, court orders, notices, and official documents. E-Sign does not apply to wills, family law matters, court orders and some types of legal notices, eviction notices, foreclosure notices, product recalls, and life insurance policies.

Retention. The E-Sign Act provides that an electronic record must be retained, must accurately record and reflect the information set forth in the contract or record and must be accessible to all parties who are entitled to access the records for the period required by law.

Disclosures. E-sign authorizes the use of disclosures required by law, but said disclosures are always subject to all the requirements under

[4]E-Sign Act 101(c).

the Truth in Lending Act and Regulation Z. The consumer must demonstrate the ability to access the information electronically and affirmatively consent to the electronic delivery and the creditor must provide the disclosures in accordance with the specified requirements of the Act.

UNIFORM ELECTRONIC TRANSACTION ACT (UETA)

Electronic Signature. UETA essentially provides that no contract may be denied enforcement or legal effect solely because it is memorialized with an electronic record or authenticated with an electronic signature. Any requirement in the law that a document must be in writing may be satisfied by an electronic record and any requirement for a signature in the law will be satisfied by an electronic signature. UETA will assure that contracts made by e-mail messages or by mere mouse clicks of "I agree" will be legally valid and binding. Although the Act generally sanctions the legality of electronic contracts and an electronic signature, transactions may still be unenforceable for any of the reasons that any other contract is found to be unenforceable, such as failure to deliver services, shortage or failure to make payment.

An electronic signature is defined as "an electronic sound, symbol or process attached to or logically associated with a record and executed or adopted by a person with the intent to sign the record." UETA notes that whether a particular document is "signed" is a question of fact based on the intent of the person who supposedly signed the document. Consequently, a "signature," as we have traditionally thought of it, is not necessary to sign a contract. *Any electronic act that a person intends to use to consummate a transaction or execute a contract may be a signature.*

UETA also provides that an electronic record or signature is attributable to a person if "it was the act of the person," and that such act "may be shown in any manner" including a demonstration of the effectiveness of any security procedure that was used in the electronic transaction. Relevant to the validity of the signature are the circumstances and context at the time of its "creation, execution, or adoption."

With or without a signature, information in electronic form may suffice to attribute an electronic record to a particular person. Such information or evidence of attribution may include the numerical codes, personal identification numbers, or other security procedures.

Electronic Agents. If a line is deployed to accept the terms of an online software license and the user clicks through the "I agree" button, UETA states that the "agent's operations bind the person who deployed the agent for that purpose." The agent is the program which created the "I agree" button and the means with which to implement it.

The term "electronic agents" is defined as a computer program of an electronic or other automated means used independently to initiate an action or respond to electronic records or performance in whole or in part *without review or action by an individual.* (UETA Section 2(6) at 5.) The word "agent" may not be appropriate except to the extent that an electronic agent is an agent in the same manner that a tool is an agent of its user. Because it is an electronic "agent," it is unable to do things without the authorization of the user. In short, the user is involved by utilizing a program which will respond to information.

An individual can avoid an inadvertent error in dealing with an electronic agent providing three steps are taken as outlined in the Act:

1. Notify the other person of the error as promptly as possible.
2. Return the consideration received as a result of the error.
3. Any benefit from the transaction has not been received or used.

Contract Formation. A contract can be formed by the exchange of an e-mail message or using an e-mail message in combination with a paper that is transmitted by fax. An electronic contract can also be formed by "electronic agents," which is a software program to initiate or respond to electronic messages. It is not necessary that the individual be aware or reviewed the actions of the "electronic agents" or the result of the terms of the agreement of the "electronic agent." For example, if two business computers communicated with each other and created a contract by virtue of that communication, this could form a binding contract. A contract also may be created by using forms provided on the Internet, such as filling out an online form which requires you to accept the terms and conditions set forth on the website.

Exceptions. UETA does not apply to the extent that a transaction is governed by the law of wills, codicils or testamentary trusts, any law governing adoption, divorce, or other matters of family law or to the UCC in effect in any state, other than Sections 1-107 and 1-206 and Articles 2 and 2a. UETA does not apply to any court orders or notices involving utility services, the personal residence of an individual, health insurance benefits or any notices regarding products that risk endangering health or safety or any documents required in connection with the handling of hazardous materials, pesticides or other toxic or dangerous materials (15 U.S.C. 7003, Section 103, Subdivision b). Exceptions to the law, such as in notices in utility services, are present in some of the state laws and not present in other states which have adopted UETA.

E-Sign Credit Applications. Credit applications and finance contracts basically could be delivered pursuant to the provisions of E-Sign and UETA. The major concern is that the applications and the finance contracts not only comply with the federal law but also comply with the state law. If the state has adopted UETA, then the contract must comply with UETA.

UNIFORM COMPUTER INFORMATION TRANSACTION ACT (UCITA)

UCITA was created to establish uniformity throughout the 50 states in dealing with computer information transactions. As the statute developed, it became apparent that its contents would depart substantially from traditional contract rules. Whereas originally UCITA was to be incorporated into the UCC, UCITA now stands by itself. The American Law Institute, which initially collaborated with the National Conference of Commissioners on Uniform State Laws, withdrew its support for the statute. A few states adopted the Act while others have taken the statute under consideration. After the Act is reviewed by the state courts, other states may follow suit depending upon the interpretation of the Act by the courts.

The scope of the statute is limited to computer information transactions, which are defined as agreements to create, modify, transfer or license computer information, or informational rights in computer information. Computer information is information in electronic form that is obtained from or through a computer or that is in digital or similar form capable of being processed by a computer. UCITA does not apply to goods like stereos, televisions, and toasters. However, a transaction which includes both goods and computer information may apply the computer information part of the transaction to UCITA, while the UCC will govern the goods portion of the transaction. If the primary subject matter of a non-goods transaction is computer information, UCITA will govern the entire transaction (Section 103(b)).

Exclusions. UCITA expressly excludes financial service transactions, broadcast and cable television, motion pictures, sound recordings, compulsory license, contracts of employment of an individual other than as an independent contractor and a contract that does not require that the information be furnished as computer information. A contract of $5,000 or more is unenforceable unless it is authenticated. Authentication may not be denied legal effect, validity, or enforceability solely on the grounds that it is an electronic authentication. The Act sets forth specific rules to be used when an electronic record or authentication is at issue.

Recognized Warranties. There are certain recognized warranties appropriate for computer information and they are set forth in the Act as follows:

1. Warranty of non-infringement—a licensor will warrant that information shall be delivered free of any claims of any third parties by way of infringement or otherwise.
2. Express warranty—a licensor will expressly warrant that the information to be furnished under the agreement will conform to any description made by the licensor.
3. Merchantability—implied warranty of merchantability of a computer program.
4. Implied warranty—unless disclosed or modified, a merchant that, in a special relationship of reliance with a licensee, collects, compiles, processes, provides or transmits informational context warrants to that licensee that there is no inaccuracy in the informational content caused by the merchant's failure to perform with reasonable care.
5. Intended purpose—if the licensor has reason to know of any particular purpose for which the information is required and the licensee is relying on the licensor for expertise, an implied warranty that the information will be fit for the purpose intended.
6. Third-party beneficiaries—warranties made to licensees extend to persons for whose benefits the licensor intends to supply the information.
7. Disclaimers—disclaimers of warranties must be clear and conspicuous.

Section 401 *et seq.*

Licenses and Contracts. UCITA sets forth in some detail a clarification as to the ownership rights and transfer rights under a license. Another section deals with what is acceptable performance in the context of a computer information transaction, in that a party must perform in a manner that conforms to the contract. Failure to do so allows the other party the right to a remedy subject only to a waiver in the agreement. The remedy structure set forth in UCITA is somewhat modeled on the UCC, but in many respects is much more favorable to the publishers of digital information. The framework for settling disputes is rather unique for determining who owns the information and how it is used.

Shrink-Wrap. Shrink-wrap or click-wrap licenses are considered "mass market licenses" which are different from negotiated licenses. A mass market license is not enforceable against the licensee (consumer) unless the terms to be enforced are readily available to a licensee and the licensee has had an appropriate time to review them. If upon review, the licensee does not like the contract, the computer information may be returned to the vendor for a refund. The right of return may not be waived or disclaimed. *Nowhere else in commercial law is there such a no-fault return policy for rejecting or repudiating a contract.* In the event the contract formation is through shrink-wrap or clickwrap, the Act provides that if a term of the contract violates a fundamental public policy, a court may refuse to enforce the contract or may enforce the remainder without the impermissible clause or it may limit the impermissible clause to avoid a result which would be antagonistic to public policy.

The warranties under UCITA are substantially the same as under the UCC. *A warranty of merchantability and a warranty of fitness for use are present except for the fact that the Act does allow disclaimers of said warranties, which the UCC does not.*

COMPUTER RECORDS

In a New Jersey case, the validity of computer records was at issue.[5] The lender provided a computer printout detailing the loan history from the last renewal date of December 15, 1995. The defendant provided no proof of payments, but alleged since he was a construction worker, he did not maintain a complete set of copies of canceled checks. The lender should be required to provide copies of the canceled checks and at least a loan history from the original date of the loan and not just from the last renewal date.

The court held that the documents provided qualify as business records and that records stored by means of the computer or similar device shown to reflect the data accurately are considered to be originals. The printouts were admissible, because they appeared regular on their face and were issued in the regular course of business prior to the inception of any controversy between the parties. Even though the records did not itemize all the payments made to the bank from the onset of the obligation, the court was satisfied it was enough to establish a *prima facie* case (enough facts to establish plaintiff's claim) of what the bank claims is due on the loan. The court was satisfied that the records were inherently trustworthy.

E-MAIL—COLLECTION OF DELINQUENT ACCOUNTS

At a recent conference, one of my colleagues asked why we cannot collect unpaid accounts by using e-mail. We would immediately save the

[5]*Garden State Bank v. Graef*, 775 A.2d 189 (N.J. Sup. Ct. App. Div. 2001).

cost of preparing a formal letter, and the cost of postage, and the post office could never match the speed within which the e-mail would reach the debtor. Furthermore, the creditor could respond quickly to any complaints of the debtor and why not use technology to improve the collection effort. Unfortunately, sometimes technology and the law come face to face and this time technology may be the loser.

The entire premise presupposes that every debtor owns a computer connected to the Internet, has an e-mail address and knows how to use e-mail. Unfortunately, at this stage such is not the case as to consumers. The company would probably have to maintain two separate and distinct systems for collecting delinquent accounts. While most businesses do use e-mail, a number of retail establishments as well as small individual entrepreneurs do not have a need for the computer. Even if they do have the computer, they may not be connected to the Internet.

When collecting debts from consumers, both creditor and collection agencies are required to comply with both federal and state statutes. The principal federal statute is the Fair Debt Collection Practices Act (FDCPA), which sets a framework as to permissible and prohibited collection practices. Many states have adopted statutes substantially similar to the FDCPA which regulate both creditors and their third-party collectors. Creditors must be careful not to violate a state's Unfair Trade Practice's statute, because a court might consider an activity prohibited by the FDCPA as an unfair trade practice.

Section 805(b) of the Fair Debt Collection Practices Act states in pertinent part that without the prior consent of a consumer, a debt collector may not communicate with any person other than the consumer or the spouse of the consumer in connection with the collection of a debt. The e-mail message is being transmitted through many Internet service providers and in many instances these messages are stored on the Internet service provider's computer as well as on the computer that originated the message. If the message is viewed by anyone other than the recipient, the originator of the message will be exposed to liability under the FDCPA. One might compare this to mailing a letter that falls into the wrong hands and a third party sees the letter. But with a letter, the sender of the letter deposited the letter in the postal box under the care of the United States Postal Service, and the message is enclosed in an envelope. A message by e-mail is a bit different, since e-mail is stored on servers, in your computer and the recipient's computer indefinitely in several places and is available for inspection in several places. The problem might be solved if the consumer consents in writing to the use of e-mail regarding the collection of a debt, but this is unlikely since most debtors are not prone to make it easier for the creditor to communicate with them. In fact, most creditors, collection agencies, and attorneys know many debtors do not return telephone calls or respond to letters.

The Electronic Communications Privacy Act deals with entities providing electronic communication service either to the public or entities providing remote computing service to the public. Some courts have held that this portion of the law does not apply to an employer retrieving a person's e-mail post transmission. The expectation of privacy diminishes once the transmission is complete. Laws are only violated when an e-mail is intercepted from intermediate storage or backup protection storage, both of which automatically occur during the course of transmission, or if the e-mail has been intercepted before the intended recipient has a chance to open it. Once an e-mail has been viewed by the recipient, these laws do not apply to subsequent viewing by the third party accessing the system, either with authorization or without authorization.

If the e-mail message is sent to a debtor at his home address, the debt collector would be protected under the FDCPA if the spouse of the debtor accessed the e-mail message. If the parents of the debtor or the children of the debtor or the brother or sister of the debtor accessed the computer and opened the e-mail message, this is a third-party disclosure and the debt collector may be in violation of the FDCPA. The use of a family computer by children and parents and brothers and even friends is not uncommon, and this risk is evident in utilizing e-mail messages addressed to debtors. An express written consent from the debtor may solve this problem. Obtaining consent from the debtor is not an easy task.

Until this issue is addressed by the court, the recommendation is to delay collection efforts by use of e-mail in favor of the more conventional methods—or else become a case of first impression for the court.

Attorney Privilege. The American Bar Association, in a formal opinion, permits a lawyer to transmit information relating to the representation of a client by unencrypted e-mail sent over the Internet without violating the modern rules of professional conduct. The mode of transmission affords a reasonable expectation of privacy from a technical, logical, and legal standpoint. With regard to highly sensitive information, lawyers should take more exacting measures to preserve the confidentiality of the communication and consider other modes of transmission in these circumstances.

Another case in Kansas addressed the issue of the attorney/client privilege in the event of an inadvertent disclosure of documents.[6] The scholarly court set forth a five part test and devoted some 50 pages to a thorough analysis of the issue.

The various states have set forth in their rules on professional responsibility variations of the above statement. Up to now, we have not had a substantial amount of litigation with regard to e-mail. But as attorneys decide to utilize e-mail for evidence at trials, the issue of privilege, the

---

[6]*Williams v. Sprint/United Mgt. Co.*, 2006 WL 1867478 (D. Kan. July 1, 2006).

extent of the privilege, and the mode of transmission will be before the court. The definition of unusual sensitive matters and routine confidential matters is certainly one that will present problems.

The federal courts have differed as to the legal consequences of a party's inadvertent disclosure of privileged information. The general doctrine usually provides that voluntary disclosure of a communication protected by the attorney/client privilege results in a waiver of a claim or privilege as to those documents.

The court in New York adopted a flexible approach which balances four relevant factors:

1. "The reasonableness of the precautions taken by the producing party to prevent inadvertent disclosure of privileged documents."
2. "The volume of discovery versus the extent of the specific disclosure issue."
3. "The length of time taken by the producing party to rectify the disclosure."
4. "The overarching issue of fairness." [7]

In the instant case, the attorneys failed to use appropriate precautions with regard to the e-mail and failed to properly review the e-mails before producing them.

Discoverable in Litigation. Practically all documents today are in electronic form and a small percentage of the data finds its way to a hard copy. A large percentage of the data is attached to the e-mail. Complex commercial litigation which takes place between large businesses usually involves discovery of electronic data. As a result the cases involving electronic data keep coming and the courts are finally devoting their attention to enforcing the production of electronic data.

The *Morgan Stanley* case[8] and the *Gateway* case[9] both dealt with the imposition of sanctions on the respective defendants. In one case the e-mails were not preserved and in the other case the e-mail was "just plain missing." In both cases the judge applied the adverse inference instruction which advises the jury that the missing e-mail or the destroyed e-mail or the lost e-mail is probably harmful to the party who lost or destroyed the e-mail.

The plaintiff sought discovery of all e-mail communications. The defendant estimated the cost of retrieving these e-mail communications would be astronomical, notwithstanding the claims of the plaintiff that the defendant was somewhat exaggerating. The court stated that

---

[7] *Atronic Intern., GMBH v. SAI Semispecialists of Am., Inc.*, 232 F.R.D. 160 (E.D.N.Y. 2005).

[8] *Coleman (Parent) Holdings, Inc. v. Morgan Stanley & Co., Inc.*, 2005 WL 679071 (Fla. Cir. Ct. Mar. 1, 2005).

[9] *Adams v. Gateway, Inc.*, 2006 WL 2563418 (D. Utah Mar. 22, 2006).

"electronic documents are no less subject to disclosure than paper records" and rejected the fact that it was unlikely that retrieving all this e-mail would produce any evidence that would either be helpful or admissible. The defendant's search not only would include e-mail that is still visible, but would extend to e-mail that has been deleted and e-mail that is stored. Normally, the cost is allocated to the party producing the documents, but where the expenses are significant, the court adopted cost shifting so that plaintiff would bear the cost of the searches and the defendant would bear the cost of reviewing the documents to determine whether any privilege existed.[10]

A decision in the Southern District of New York spent 40 pages discussing the necessary steps to be performed by an attorney so that relevant data will be preserved and produced at the trial.[11] Once litigation is started, the routine document retention policy must be changed and a litigation hold must insure preservation of all relevant documents. Counsel must be familiar with the client's document retention policies as well as the client's data retention architecture. Counsel is under an obligation to communicate directly with information technology personnel who can explain the system-wide back-up procedures and the implementation of the firm's recycling policy. It is not enough to notify the employees that are involved. Counsel must also monitor compliance and must take affirmative steps which are reasonable under the circumstances then and there prevailing. A duty exists that discoverable information is not lost and a duty to preserve is a continuous obligation. New employees must be notified and must be made aware of their obligations. Counsel should communicate with key players in the litigation so that they fully understand what their duty is to put all documents on a litigation hold.

The court went on to say that if the notice to produce only involves a small number of back-up tapes, an obligation rests on counsel to take physical possession of said tapes. In other instances the tapes should be segregated and placed in storage. The court did allow that the attorneys must not necessarily supervise every step of the document production process, but may rely on the client to perform the task. But the attorney is responsible for coordinating the client's discovery efforts.

The court added a significant burden on counsel with regard to the production of information technology. The court spoke with a broad brush, indicating, for example, reasonable steps that could be taken to coordinate client's efforts, all of which are subject to wide interpretations by other courts. The decision is well worth reading to grasp the direction in which the courts are moving. Even if all the parts of this decision are not adopted in other circuits, the thrust of the decision certainly is intended to

---

[10] *Rowe Entertainment Inc. v. William Morris Agency Inc.*, 205 F.R.D. 421, 2002 U.S. Dist. LEXIS 488 (S.D.N.Y. 2002). *See Byers v. Ill. State Police*, 2002 U.S. Dist. LEXIS 9861 (N.D. Ill. May 31, 2002).

[11] *Zubulake v. U.B.S. Warburg*, 217 F.R.D. 309 (S.D.N.Y. 2003).

place a new obligation upon counsel and will have an impact on future decisions.[12]

A federal case in New York held that a party served with discovery concerning a database must produce the database in electronic form and paper form to be sufficient.

Another case has provided that under certain circumstances, direct access to a database may be permissible but that the party seeking direct access must provide sufficient reason and the request must be focused rather than general.[13]

A district court case in the Tenth Circuit covered the application of Rule 34a with regard to the control of the documents. This lengthy decision explores the obligation of the plaintiff to produce e-mail. The case also emphasized the fact that the discovery obligation on the plaintiff cannot be removed merely by asserting that it is burdensome—without offering evidence to substantiate the claim.[14]

In the Southern District of New York, the court in a lengthy decision awarded sanctions for blatantly disregarding the plaintiff's demands for discovery. The defendant contended that everything had been produced, but the court came to a different conclusion.[15]

A case in the Supreme Court has provided that it is "not wrongful for a manager to instruct its employees to comply with a valid document retention policy under ordinary circumstances." Destruction of documents is proper providing the destruction took place before any duty arose to preserve the documents, and providing a valid document retention policy performed in the ordinary course of business is in place.[16]

The development of this area of law progresses each year. Several cases have addressed the issue of the extent of examining the documents to comply with discovery obligations.

In the Southern District of New York, the court stated as follows:

> even in a case involving exclusively hardcopy documents, there is no obligation on the part of a responding party to examine every scrap of paper in its potentially voluminous files in order to comply with its discovery obligations. Rather, it must conduct a diligent search, which involves developing a reasonably comprehensive search strategy. Such a strategy might, for example, include identifying key employees and reviewing any of their files that are likely to be relevant to the claims in the litigation.[17]

---

[12]*Zubulake v. U.B.S. Warburg*, 229 F.R.D. 422, 2004 U.S. Dist. LEXIS 13574 (S.D.N.Y. 2004).

[13]*In re Ford Motor Co.*, 345 F.3d 1315 (11th Cir. 2003); *In re Honeywell International, Inc. Securities Litigation*, 230 F.R.D. 293 (S.D.N.Y. 2003).

[14]*Super Film of America v. UCB Films, Inc.*, 219 F.R.D. 649 (D.C. Kan. 2004).

[15]*Metropolitan Opera Association, Inc. v. Local 100 Hotel Employees and Restaurant Employees International Union*, 212 F.R.D. 178 (S.D.N.Y. 2003).

[16]*Arthur Andersen, LLP v. United States*, 544 U.S. 696 (2005).

[17]*Treppel v. Biovail Corp.*, 233 F.R.D. 363 (S.D.N.Y. 2006). *See Peskoff v. Faber*, 2006 WL 1933483 (D.D.C. July 11, 2006).

The case also stated that the party conducting the electronic discovery must provide the other party with a detailed explanation of the search protocol used.

Several rules directly affect electronically stored information including, but not limited to, Rule 26(a)(1), Rule 26(b)(2), Rule 26(f)(3), Rule 34(b), and Rule 37(f). Rule 26(a)(1) includes electronic information that must be produced, but the electronic information under Rule 26(b)(2) must be reasonably accessible. The court may determine exactly what is reasonable and acceptable upon application by the other party. Rule 26(f)(3) requires discussion at the planning conference as to electronically stored information and Rule 34(b) addresses the format in which the information must be provided. (*See* Appendix.)

METADATA. Metadata is not disclosed or seen when a document is printed in the ordinary course of business, but it does exist. Metadata is the electronic data that tracks and records not only the bibliographic information such as the date and the author, but also tracks the way a document is created, how many edits the document has received and when the edits were made. It contains information such as if a blind copy was sent to a third party and the manner in which the e-mails were received or sent. The courts have uniformly held that metadata is discoverable. If an effort is made to strip out metadata, a litigant may be compelled to produce the metadata. Under certain circumstances metadata can be privileged.

Metadata is the history of the whole file including all that is done to or by the file, how it's done and who does it. Metadata can be scrubbed in such a manner as to remove some of the metadata or with professional help probably almost all of the metadata. A district court decision held that when a party is ordered to produce electronic documents as they are maintained in the ordinary course of business, the producing party should produce the electronic documents with their metadata intact unless:

1. The party timely objects to production of metadata;
2. The parties agree that metadata should not be produced;
3. The producing party requests a protective order.[18]

SERVICE OF PROCESS. At least one judge has recognized that sometimes it is difficult to serve an owner of an offshore website who does not have offices in the United States and conducts the business in one of the lovely Caribbean islands. The owner of the website was operating several gambling websites utilizing a domain name substantially similar to the

[18] *Williams v. Sprint/United Management Co.*, 230 F.R.D. 640 (D. Kan. 2005).

plaintiff. The plaintiff tried to serve an address in the United States, but that address only housed the company's international courier, which could not accept service. The attorney for the defendant refused to accept service. The plaintiff explored the idea of attempting to serve the defendant on the island where the website was allegedly operating, to no avail.

The court bit the bullet and allowed the plaintiff to serve the defendant at his e-mail address since the defendant indicated on the website that all visitors should communicate with them by e-mail. The court relied on the Federal Rules of Civil Procedure for 4(h)(2) and 4(f)(3), which allows the court to direct service by any means providing the method of service is not prohibited by international agreement.[19]

This is the first case of this type that your authors have seen, but this will be just the first step. Other courts will not only follow this Ninth Circuit decision, but may expand its reach.

Voice Mail. As to e-mail and voice mail, once the communications are stored in the system, the employer would have access to these stored communications because they fall under the Stored Wire and Electronic Communication statutes 18 USCA Section 2-701. This access is limited to the employer's use in the ordinary conduct of business. If a stored communication was publicized to co-workers or other third parties for a reason other than to properly conduct the business, the employer might be open to liability. Violations of the Stored Wire and Electronic Communication statute include fines and imprisonment up to one year for a first offense.

When monitoring, it is advisable to provide telephones for personal calls so that personal calls will not be interrupted. Confine the monitoring to the telephones that are used strictly in the ordinary course of business. A detailed manual on monitoring telephone calls should be prepared and each employee should properly acknowledge in writing that the employee has read and understood the manual. A warning label on the telephone is appropriate. Where no warning is placed on the telephone, and somebody walks in and uses the telephone, consent is not implied.[20]

Deleting Data. E-mail is not deleted. When a file is deleted, the entries related to that file are deleted from the file allocation table (FAT) or master file table (MFT) and the space that was used for that particular e-mail is now available for a new use but the e-mail itself has not been deleted or cancelled or even overwritten. The file allocation table may be reproduced and the material itself may be recovered. At some point in time, the computer may utilize this space and overwrite the data that was deleted. Bits and pieces of the deleted data still remains, and to some limited degree, can be reconstructed to be read.

---

[19] *Rio Props. v. Rio Int'l Interlink*, 284 F.3d 1007 (9th Cir. 2002).

[20] *George v. Carusone*, 849 F. Supp. 159 (D. Conn. 1994).

To effectively delete e-mails and other data, overwriting has to take place numerous times to render it non-retrievable. The Department of Defense sets the standard of several overwrites, and many software programs will overwrite anywhere from 20-50 times.

Another disposition of data that is targeted for deletion is to destroy the hard drive itself along with the CDs, disks and DVDs by destroying and crashing them and physically rendering them unusable. The disposal rule that was issued by the Federal Trade Commission and became effective on June 1, 2005 is somewhat vague with regard to the obligations of organizations to dispose of any type of sensitive information. The rule provides many different ways for the destruction or erasing of electronic media containing consumer information. The rule does permit outsourcing the destruction and provides a list of requirements to meet the due diligence standard.

NEW FEDERAL RULES OF CIVIL PROCEDURE REGARDING ELECTRONICALLY STORED INFORMATION

The primary rules that have been affected are Rules 1626, 1633, 1634, and 1637. Under Rule 26(f), parties must discuss issues relating to electronically stored information and preservation and production of ESI. Scheduling orders must address disclosure of ESI. Rule 26(a) for initial disclosures must identify the sources of ESI. Protective orders are available when the discovery is burdensome and the requesting party may now indicate the forms that the producing party wishes to use.

Inadvertent disclosure is also covered in the new rules and a description of the responses to inadvertent disclosure are provided.

INSTANT MESSAGING

Instant messages are normally not stored or monitored by the computer. As a general rule e-mails are saved in the computer of the user until either deleted by the user or some automatic deletion of the e-mail is performed. No place is available where instant messages are stored from which you can respond to a discovery request. Certain service bureaus can install programs to store and maintain instant messages. Absent these programs, the instant messages would end at the servers.

Instant messaging should be monitored and the system should be internal and not for external providers. The problem with using instant messaging with clients or with any third parties is the confidentiality situation, since the other party may be storing the instant messages while the sender may not. One party may have installed the capability of retaining the messages indefinitely whereas the other party may be destroying them on a regular basis after a period of time.

> ***Credit & Collection Tip:*** *The use of instant messaging provides no reasonable expectation of privacy since one party may be storing the instant messages.*

BUSINESS RECORDS

One of the major exceptions to the hearsay rule is the business record exemption. Under this exemption, a document is admissible as a business record if the judge finds that it was:

1. Made in good faith;
2. Made in the regular course of business;
3. Made before the action began;
4. It is the regular course of business to make the record at or about the time of the transaction or occurrences is recorded.

Such a record is presumed to be reliable and, therefore, admissible because entries in those records are routinely made by those charged with the responsibility of making accurate entries and are relied on in the course of doing business. The statute provides that when the preparer has relied on the statement of others, personal knowledge by the witness is a matter affecting the weight rather than the admissibility of the record. Although the preparer's hearsay sources must carry the same indicia of reliability and be shown to have acted in the course of business or a business routine, this can be accomplished by presenting evidence of normal business practice rather than by producing the prime witness who made the entry.

A decision from Massachusetts ruled in favor of the party offering the evidence which in turn was reversed by the appellate court and the final appeal overruled the appellate court.[21] This is an example of how courts in the same state have a totally different perspective. The highest appellate court held that the two computer printouts from the servicing company was sufficient to prove the deficiency in a foreclosure action.

COMPUTER EVIDENCE

Since most of the records of both the collection agencies and law firms involved in collection are contained in computer records, the issue of

[21]*Beal Bank, SSB v. Eurich*, 444 Mass. 813, 831 N.E.2d 909 (Mass. 2005).

admissibility of computer records frequently comes before the court. In one case, the former Vice-President and Supervisor of Federal Deposit Insurance Corporation (FDIC) Operations testified that she personally downloaded information from the computer system onto diskettes at the request of the FDIC. She stated that the day after the firm went into receivership, she tested the data on the diskettes for accuracy and kept them in her exclusive possession. She also testified as to the reliability of the firm's computer system. The court admitted the diskettes as evidence.

The defendants objected on the grounds that they had no method to determine what information was contained on the diskettes or to cross-examine the Vice-President about the information. The FDIC provided the defendants with a computer to visualize the information, but the defendants declined to use the computer. The court stated that even when properly admitted, such records carry no presumption of accuracy and their credibility remains a question for the trier of fact. But the admissibility of business records should be liberally interpreted in favor of admissibility. The witness introducing the document need not have made the entry himself nor even have been employed by the organization during the relevant time. All that is required is that a qualified witness testify that the records were kept in the regular course of business, entries were made of the transaction at the time of the transaction, and the business procedure was to enter the transaction. The liberal application is derived from the recognition that the trustworthiness of such documents come from their being used for business purposes and not used for litigation. The proponent also requires testimony that will establish that the basic elements of the computer system are reliable.

The federal courts generally permit offering electronic evidence. The following are suggestions which an attorney might use in offering said evidence:

1. That the record, report, or document sets forth some transaction, condition, or some analysis.
2. That the particular document or record was entered at the time the transaction or the event took place.
3. That the information entered onto the computer was done by an individual who received this information from a person who had knowledge, preferably personal knowledge, of the event or the transaction.
4. That the particular record or entry was kept in the normal course of business.
5. That it was the normal course of business to make such a record or entry.

The court does not have to identify with precision what status in a particular company's hierarchy a witness must have to be sufficiently knowledgeable to testify about computer records. The witness may be the person who made the writing or record, or had knowledge of the transaction, occurrence or event. Neither the programmer, nor the party who made the entry is necessary, but the knowledge of the basic elements that afford reliability and trustworthiness to computer-generated data is the criteria.[22]

USING FAX MACHINES

Many debt collectors place bold disclaimers on their fax cover sheets in an attempt to avoid any exposure for an unauthorized disclosure to a third party. Using faxes is dangerous not only because of the disclosure to an unauthorized third party, but because that disclosure may be so blatant that the damages the consumer sustains may be substantial. Interestingly, although the debt collector might not have violated Section 803 for an unauthorized disclosure to a third party, under Section 808(5), the debt collector might be liable for causing a charge to the debtor by using the debtor's fax machine. The disclaimer should also be added to any e-mail.

LICENSING

If the automobile dealer or a financial institution is financing over the Internet, which geographically means that they are targeting customers in all 50 states, the website owner will have to comply with the numerous licensing requirements of each state. A website owner referring the work to a finance company is a broker. Licensing for financing consumer motor vehicles is required in 10 states. A website owner who is a broker would have to be licensed in more than 17 states.

INTERNET DOMAIN NAMES—GARNISHMENT

The issue is whether the contractual right to use an Internet domain name can be garnished by a creditor. The court felt that not all contractual rights may be levied upon and were not willing to sanction the garnishment of Network Solutions Incorporated (NSI) services under the terms of the existing garnishment statute. The court treated the domain name in the same way as a telephone number provided by a telephone company. It is merely a right to use the number and therefore a right to use the name.[23]

---

[22]*F.D.I.C. v. Carabetta*, 55 Conn. App. 369, 739 A.2d 301 (Conn. App. Ct. 1999).
[23]*Network Solutions, Inc. v. Umbro Intern. Inc.*, 259 Va. 759, 529 S.E.2d 80 (Va. 2000).

CAN SPAM ACT

The CAN SPAM Act supersedes the anti-spam legislation which had been passed by several dozen states. This anti-spam legislation will supersede the strict and onerous legislation that was recently passed by California.

All the messages must contain a clear and conspicuous identification that the message is an advertisement of solicitation. The recipient must have the ability to opt out and the sender of the message must provide a website address or must be advised of the means to reply to opt out. The sender must also provide a postal address and must identify the name of the sender responsible for sending the message without misleading the recipient. The law has several exceptions which are somewhat similar to the telemarketing sales rule and the opt-out provisions in said rule.

The Act does not provide the most effective weapon against spam—allowing a private action by an individual against the sender of the spam. The Act limits the parties who can enforce the CAN SPAM Act to the Federal Trade Commission.

DIGITAL BASICS—CORPORATE RECORDS

The entrepreneur has arranged his financial affairs in anticipation of his inability to pay his debts and has effectively stripped himself of all his assets that can be attached. He is now in a state of being "judgment proof."

Sometimes the answers may be found in the corporate records and especially in a computer and the digital devices that keep corporate records. Some of the questions that may be proposed to the entrepreneur pursuant to a subpoena served on the corporation might be as follows:

1. Are the books and records kept on a computer?
2. How many computers, laptops, PDAs, and digital devices were used by the corporation and what is the location of each device?
3. Has the debtor sold or disposed of any of these digital devices during the past three years and certainly during the past 90 days?
4. Did the corporation lease all the digital devices or did the corporation own the devices?
5. Does the corporation keep backup records on e-mail, word processing files, or any other records that are being kept by the corporation?

At this stage and depending upon the amount of the judgment, the creditor must make a decision as to what extent he wants to use a digital technologist to examine all these records to determine what disposition was made of the assets of the corporation.

CHAPTER 17
APPENDIX I

ELECTRONIC SIGNATURES IN GLOBAL AND NATIONAL COMMERCE ACT

15 U.S.C. §§ 7001-7031

Sec. 7001. General rule of validity

(a) In general. Notwithstanding any statute, regulation, or other rule of law (other than this subchapter and subchapter II of this chapter), with respect to any transaction in or affecting interstate or foreign commerce

(1) a signature, contract, or other record relating to such transaction may not be denied legal effect, validity, or enforceability solely because it is in electronic form; and

(2) a contract relating to such transaction may not be denied legal effect, validity, or enforceability solely because an electronic signature or electronic record was used in its formation.

(b) Preservation of rights and obligations. This subchapter does not

(1) limit, alter, or otherwise affect any requirement imposed by a statute, regulation, or rule of law relating to the rights and obligations of persons under such statute, regulation, or rule of law other than a requirement that contracts or other records be written, signed, or in nonelectronic form; or

(2) require any person to agree to use or accept electronic records or electronic signatures, other than a governmental agency with respect to a record other than a contract to which it is a party.

(c) Consumer disclosures.

(1) Consent to electronic records. Notwithstanding subsection (a) of this section, if a statute, regulation, or other rule of law requires that information relating to a transaction or transactions in or affecting interstate or foreign commerce be provided or made available to a consumer in writing, the use of an electronic record to provide or make available (whichever is required) such information satisfies the requirement that such information be in writing if

(A) the consumer has affirmatively consented to such use and has not withdrawn such consent;

(B) the consumer, prior to consenting, is provided with a clear and conspicuous statement

(i) informing the consumer of

(I) any right or option of the consumer to have the record provided or made available on paper or in nonelectronic form, and

(II) the right of the consumer to withdraw the consent to have the record provided or made available in an electronic form and of any conditions, consequences (which may include termination of the parties' relationship), or fees in the event of such withdrawal;

(ii) informing the consumer of whether the consent applies

(I) only to the particular transaction which gave rise to the obligation to provide the record, or

(II) to identified categories of records that may be provided or made available during the course of the parties' relationship;

(iii) describing the procedures the consumer must use to withdraw consent as provided in clause (i) and to update information needed to contact the consumer electronically; and

(iv) informing the consumer

(I) how, after the consent, the consumer may, upon request, obtain a paper copy of an electronic record, and

(II) whether any fee will be charged for such copy;

(C) the consumer

(i) prior to consenting, is provided with a statement of the hardware and software requirements for access to and retention of the electronic records; and

(ii) consents electronically, or confirms his or her consent electronically, in a manner that reasonably demonstrates that the consumer can access information in the electronic form that will be used to provide the information that is the subject of the consent; and

(D) after the consent of a consumer in accordance with subparagraph (A), if a change in the hardware or software requirements needed to access or retain electronic records creates a material risk that the consumer will not be able to access or retain a subsequent electronic record that was the subject of the consent, the person providing the electronic record

(i) provides the consumer with a statement of

(I) the revised hardware and software requirements for access to and retention of the electronic records, and

(II) the right to withdraw consent without the imposition of any fees for such withdrawal and without the imposition of any condition or consequence that was not disclosed under subparagraph (B)(i); and

(ii) again complies with subparagraph (C).

(2) Other rights.

(A) Preservation of consumer protections. Nothing in this subchapter affects the content or timing of any disclosure or other record required to be provided or made available to any consumer under any statute, regulation, or other rule of law.

(B) Verification or acknowledgment. If a law that was enacted prior to this chapter expressly requires a record to be provided or made available by a specified method that requires verification or acknowledgment of receipt, the record may be provided or made available electronically only if the method used provides verification or acknowledgment of receipt (whichever is required).

(3) Effect of failure to obtain electronic consent or confirmation of consent. The legal effectiveness, validity, or enforceability of any contract executed by a consumer shall not be denied solely because of the failure to obtain electronic consent or confirmation of consent by that consumer in accordance with paragraph (1)(C)(ii).

(4) Prospective effect. Withdrawal of consent by a consumer shall not affect the legal effectiveness, validity, or enforceability of electronic records provided or made available to that consumer in accordance with paragraph (1) prior to implementation of the consumer's withdrawal of consent. A consumer's withdrawal of consent shall be effective within a reasonable period of time after receipt of the withdrawal by the provider of the record. Failure to comply with paragraph (1)(D) may, at the election of the consumer, be treated as a withdrawal of consent for purposes of this paragraph.

(5) Prior consent. This subsection does not apply to any records that are provided or made available to a consumer who has consented prior to the effective date of this subchapter to receive such records in electronic form as permitted by any statute, regulation, or other rule of law.

(6) Oral communications. An oral communication or a recording of an oral communication shall not qualify as an electronic record for purposes of this subsection except as otherwise provided under applicable law.

(d) Retention of contracts and records.

(1) Accuracy and accessibility. If a statute, regulation, or other rule of law requires that a contract or other record relating to a transaction in or affecting interstate or foreign commerce be retained, that requirement is met by retaining an electronic record of the information in the contract or other record that

(A) accurately reflects the information set forth in the contract or other record; and

(B) remains accessible to all persons who are entitled to access by statute, regulation, or rule of law, for the period required by such statute, regulation, or rule of law, in a form that is capable of being accurately reproduced for later reference, whether by transmission, printing, or otherwise.

(2) Exception. A requirement to retain a contract or other record in accordance with paragraph (1) does not apply to any information whose sole purpose is to enable the contract or other record to be sent, communicated, or received.

(3) Originals. If a statute, regulation, or other rule of law requires a contract or other record relating to a transaction in or affecting interstate or foreign commerce to be provided, available, or retained in its original form, or provides consequences if the contract or other record is not provided, available, or retained in its original form, that statute, regulation, or rule of law is satisfied by an electronic record that complies with paragraph (1).

(4) Checks. If a statute, regulation, or other rule of law requires the retention of a check, that requirement is satisfied by retention of an electronic record of the information on the front and back of the check in accordance with paragraph (1).

(e) Accuracy and ability to retain contracts and other records. Notwithstanding subsection (a) of this section, if a statute, regulation, or other rule of law requires that a contract or other record relating to a transaction in or affecting interstate or foreign commerce be in writing, the legal effect, validity, or enforceability of an electronic record of such contract or other record may be denied if such electronic record is not in a form that is capable of being retained and accurately reproduced for later reference by all parties or persons who are entitled to retain the contract or other record.

(f) Proximity. Nothing in this subchapter affects the proximity required by any statute, regulation, or other rule of law with respect to any warning, notice, disclosure, or other record required to be posted, displayed, or publicly affixed.

(g) Notarization and acknowledgment. If a statute, regulation, or other rule of law requires a signature or record relating to a transaction in or affecting interstate or foreign commerce to be notarized, acknowledged, verified, or made under oath, that requirement is satisfied if the electronic signature of the person authorized to perform those acts, together with all other information required to be included by other applicable statute, regulation, or rule of law, is attached to or logically associated with the signature or record.

(h) Electronic agents. A contract or other record relating to a transaction in or affecting interstate or foreign commerce may not be denied legal effect, validity, or enforceability solely because its formation, creation, or delivery involved the action of one or more electronic agents so long as the action of any such electronic agent is legally attributable to the person to be bound.

(i) Insurance. It is the specific intent of the Congress that this subchapter and subchapter II of this chapter apply to the business of insurance.

(j) Insurance agents and brokers. An insurance agent or broker acting under the direction of a party that enters into a contract by means of an electronic record or electronic signature may not be held liable for any deficiency in the electronic procedures agreed to by the parties under that contract if

(1) the agent or broker has not engaged in negligent, reckless, or intentional tortious conduct;

(2) the agent or broker was not involved in the development or establishment of such electronic procedures; and

(3) the agent or broker did not deviate from such procedures

Sec. 7002. Exemption to preemption

(a) In general. A State statute, regulation, or other rule of law may modify, limit, or supersede the provisions of section 7001 of this title with respect to State law only if such statute, regulation, or rule of law

(1) constitutes an enactment or adoption of the Uniform Electronic Transactions Act as approved and recommended for enactment in all the States by the National Conference of Commissioners on Uniform State Laws in 1999, except that any exception to the scope of such Act enacted by a State under section 3(b)(4) of such Act shall be preempted to the extent such exception is inconsistent with this subchapter or subchapter II of this chapter, or would not be permitted under paragraph (2)(A)(ii) of this subsection; or

(2) (A) specifies the alternative procedures or requirements for the use or acceptance (or both) of electronic records or electronic signatures to establish the legal effect, validity, or enforceability of contracts or other records, if

(i) such alternative procedures or requirements are consistent with this subchapter and subchapter II of this chapter; and

(ii) such alternative procedures or requirements do not require, or accord greater legal status or effect to, the implementation or application of a specific technology or technical specification for performing the functions of creating, storing, generating, receiving, communicating, or authenticating electronic records or electronic signatures; and

(B) if enacted or adopted after June 30, 2000, makes specific reference to this chapter.

(b) Exceptions for actions by States as market participants. Subsection (a)(2)(A)(ii) of this section shall not apply to the statutes, regulations, or other rules of law governing procurement by any State, or any agency or instrumentality thereof.

(c) Prevention of circumvention. Subsection (a) of this section does not permit a State to circumvent this subchapter or subchapter II of this chapter through the imposition of nonelectronic delivery methods under section 8(b)(2) of the Uniform Electronic Transactions Act.

Sec. 7003. Specific exceptions

(a) Excepted requirements. The provisions of section 7001 of this title shall not apply to a contract or other record to the extent it is governed by

(1) a statute, regulation, or other rule of law governing the creation and execution of wills, codicils, or testamentary trusts;

(2) a State statute, regulation, or other rule of law governing adoption, divorce, or other matters of family law; or

(3) the Uniform Commercial Code, as in effect in any State, other than sections 1-107 and 1-206 and Articles 2 and 2A.

(b) Additional exceptions. The provisions of section 7001 of this title shall not apply to

(1) court orders or notices, or official court documents (including briefs, pleadings, and other writings) required to be executed in connection with court proceedings;

(2) any notice of

(A) the cancellation or termination of utility services (including water, heat, and power);

(B) default, acceleration, repossession, foreclosure, or eviction, or the right to cure, under a credit agreement secured by, or a rental agreement for, a primary residence of an individual;

(C) the cancellation or termination of health insurance or benefits or life insurance benefits (excluding annuities); or

(D) recall of a product, or material failure of a product, that risks endangering health or safety; or

(3) any document required to accompany any transportation or handling of hazardous materials, pesticides, or other toxic or dangerous materials.

(c) Review of exceptions.

(1) Evaluation required. The Secretary of Commerce, acting through the Assistant Secretary for Communications and Information, shall review the operation of the exceptions in subsections (a) and (b) of this section to evaluate, over a period of 3 years, whether such exceptions continue to be necessary for the protection of consumers. Within 3 years after June 30, 2000, the Assistant Secretary shall submit a report to the Congress on the results of such evaluation.

(2) Determinations. If a Federal regulatory agency, with respect to matter within its jurisdiction, determines after notice and an opportunity for public comment, and publishes a finding, that one or more such exceptions are no longer necessary for the protection of consumers and eliminating such exceptions will not increase the material risk of

harm to consumers, such agency may extend the application of section 7001 of this title to the exceptions identified in such finding.

Sec. 7004. Applicability to Federal and State governments

(a) Filing and access requirements. Subject to subsection (c)(2) of this section, nothing in this subchapter limits or supersedes any requirement by a Federal regulatory agency, self-regulatory organization, or State regulatory agency that records be filed with such agency or organization in accordance with specified standards or formats.

(b) Preservation of existing rulemaking authority.

(1) Use of authority to interpret. Subject to paragraph (2) and subsection (c) of this section, a Federal regulatory agency or State regulatory agency that is responsible for rulemaking under any other statute may interpret section 7001 of this title with respect to such statute through

(A) the issuance of regulations pursuant to a statute; or

(B) to the extent such agency is authorized by statute to issue orders or guidance, the issuance of orders or guidance of general applicability that are publicly available and published (in the Federal Register in the case of an order or guidance issued by a Federal regulatory agency).

This paragraph does not grant any Federal regulatory agency or State regulatory agency authority to issue regulations, orders, or guidance pursuant to any statute that does not authorize such issuance.

(2) Limitations on interpretation authority. Notwithstanding paragraph (1), a Federal regulatory agency shall not adopt any regulation, order, or guidance described in paragraph (1), and a State regulatory agency is preempted by section 7001 of this title from adopting any regulation, order, or guidance described in paragraph (1), unless

(A) such regulation, order, or guidance is consistent with section 7001 of this title;

(B) such regulation, order, or guidance does not add to the requirements of such section; and

(C) such agency finds, in connection with the issuance of such regulation, order, or guidance, that

(i) there is a substantial justification for the regulation, order, or guidance;

(ii) the methods selected to carry out that purpose

(I) are substantially equivalent to the requirements imposed on records that are not electronic records; and

(II) will not impose unreasonable costs on the acceptance and use of electronic records; and

(iii) the methods selected to carry out that purpose do not require, or accord greater legal status or effect to, the implementation or application of a specific technology or technical specification for performing the functions of creating, storing, generating, receiving, communicating, or authenticating electronic records or electronic signatures.

(3) Performance standards.

(A) Accuracy, record integrity, accessibility. Notwithstanding paragraph (2)(C)(iii), a Federal regulatory agency or State regulatory agency may interpret section 7001(d) of this title to specify performance standards to assure accuracy, record integrity, and accessibility of records that are required to be retained. Such performance standards may be specified in a manner that imposes a requirement in violation of paragraph (2)(C)(iii) if the requirement

(i) serves an important governmental objective; and

(ii) is substantially related to the achievement of that objective. Nothing in this paragraph shall be construed to grant any Federal regulatory agency or State regulatory agency authority to require use of a particular type of software or hardware in order to comply with section 7001(d) of this title.

(B) Paper or printed form. Notwithstanding subsection (c)(1) of this section, a Federal regulatory agency or State regulatory agency may interpret section 7001(d) of this title to require retention of a record in a tangible printed or paper form if

(i) there is a compelling governmental interest relating to law enforcement or national security for imposing such requirement; and

(ii) imposing such requirement is essential to attaining such interest.

(4) Exceptions for actions by government as market participant. Paragraph (2)(C)(iii) shall not apply to the statutes, regulations, or other rules of law governing procurement by the Federal or any State government, or any agency or instrumentality thereof.

(c) Additional limitations.

(1) Reimposing paper prohibited. Nothing in subsection (b) of this section (other than paragraph (3)(B) thereof) shall be construed to grant any Federal regulatory agency or State regulatory agency authority to impose or reimpose any requirement that a record be in a tangible printed or paper form.

(2) Continuing obligation under Government Paperwork Elimination Act. Nothing in subsection (a) or (b) of this section relieves any Federal regulatory agency of its obligations under the Government Paperwork Elimination Act (title XVII of Public Law 105-277).

(d) Authority to exempt from consent provision.

(1) In general. A Federal regulatory agency may, with respect to matter within its jurisdiction, by regulation or order issued after notice and an opportunity for public comment, exempt without condition a specified

category or type of record from the requirements relating to consent in section 7001(c) of this title if such exemption is necessary to eliminate a substantial burden on electronic commerce and will not increase the material risk of harm to consumers.

(2) Prospectuses. Within 30 days after June 30, 2000, the Securities and Exchange Commission shall issue a regulation or order pursuant to paragraph (1) exempting from section 7001(c) of this title any records that are required to be provided in order to allow advertising, sales literature, or other information concerning a security issued by an investment company that is registered under the Investment Company Act of 1940 (15 U.S.C. 80a-1 *et seq.*), or concerning the issuer thereof, to be excluded from the definition of a prospectus under section 77b(a)(10)(A) of this title.

(e) Electronic letters of agency. The Federal Communications Commission shall not hold any contract for telecommunications service or letter of agency for a preferred carrier change, that otherwise complies with the Commission's rules, to be legally ineffective, invalid, or unenforceable solely because an electronic record or electronic signature was used in its formation or authorization.

Sec. 7005. Studies

(a) Delivery. Within 12 months after June 30, 2000, the Secretary of Commerce shall conduct an inquiry regarding the effectiveness of the delivery of electronic records to consumers using electronic mail as compared with delivery of written records via the United States Postal Service and private express mail services. The Secretary shall submit a report to the Congress regarding the results of such inquiry by the conclusion of such 12-month period.

(b) Study of electronic consent. Within 12 months after June 30, 2000, the Secretary of Commerce and the Federal Trade Commission shall submit a report to the Congress evaluating any benefits provided to consumers by the procedure required by section 7001(c)(1)(C)(ii) of this title; any burdens imposed on electronic commerce by that provision; whether the benefits outweigh the burdens; whether the absence of the procedure required by section 7001(c)(1)(C)(ii) of this title would increase the incidence of fraud directed against consumers; and suggesting any revisions to the provision deemed appropriate by the Secretary and the Commission. In conducting this evaluation, the Secretary and the Commission shall solicit comment from the general public, consumer representatives, and electronic commerce businesses.

Sec. 7006. Definitions

For purposes of this subchapter:

(1) Consumer. The term "consumer" means an individual who obtains, through a transaction, products or services which are used primarily

for personal, family, or household purposes, and also means the legal representative of such an individual.

(2) Electronic. The term "electronic" means relating to technology having electrical, digital, magnetic, wireless, optical, electromagnetic, or similar capabilities.

(3) Electronic agent. The term "electronic agent" means a computer program or an electronic or other automated means used independently to initiate an action or respond to electronic records or performances in whole or in part without review or action by an individual at the time of the action or response.

(4) Electronic record. The term "electronic record" means a contract or other record created, generated, sent, communicated, received, or stored by electronic means.

(5) Electronic signature. The term "electronic signature" means an electronic sound, symbol, or process, attached to or logically associated with a contract or other record and executed or adopted by a person with the intent to sign the record.

(6) Federal regulatory agency. The term "Federal regulatory agency" means an agency, as that term is defined in section 552(f) of title 5.

(7) Information. The term "information" means data, text, images, sounds, codes, computer programs, software, databases, or the like.

(8) Person. The term "person" means an individual, corporation, business trust, estate, trust, partnership, limited liability company, association, joint venture, governmental agency, public corporation, or any other legal or commercial entity.

(9) Record. The term "record" means information that is inscribed on a tangible medium or that is stored in an electronic or other medium and is retrievable in perceivable form.

(10) Requirement. The term "requirement" includes a prohibition.

(11) Self-regulatory organization. The term "self-regulatory organization" means an organization or entity that is not a Federal regulatory agency or a State, but that is under the supervision of a Federal regulatory agency and is authorized under Federal law to adopt and administer rules applicable to its members that are enforced by such organization or entity, by a Federal regulatory agency, or by another self-regulatory organization.

(12) State. The term "State" includes the District of Columbia and the territories and possessions of the United States.

(13) Transaction. The term "transaction" means an action or set of actions relating to the conduct of business, consumer, or commercial affairs between two or more persons, including any of the following types of conduct

(A) the sale, lease, exchange, licensing, or other disposition of

(i) personal property, including goods and intangibles;

(ii) services;

(iii) any combination thereof; and

(B) the sale, lease, exchange, or other disposition of any interest in real property, or any combination thereof.

Sec. 7021. Transferable records

(a) Definitions. For purposes of this section:

(1) Transferable record. The term "transferable record" means an electronic record that

(A) would be a note under Article 3 of the Uniform Commercial Code if the electronic record were in writing;

(B) the issuer of the electronic record expressly has agreed is a transferable record; and

(C) relates to a loan secured by real property.

A transferable record may be executed using an electronic signature.

(2) Other definitions. The terms "electronic record," "electronic signature," and "person" have the same meanings provided in section 7006 of this title.

(b) Control. A person has control of a transferable record if a system employed for evidencing the transfer of interests in the transferable record reliably establishes that person as the person to which the transferable record was issued or transferred.

(c) Conditions. A system satisfies subsection (b) of this section, and a person is deemed to have control of a transferable record, if the transferable record is created, stored, and assigned in such a manner that

(1) a single authoritative copy of the transferable record exists which is unique, identifiable, and, except as otherwise provided in paragraphs (4), (5), and (6), unalterable;

(2) the authoritative copy identifies the person asserting control as

(A) the person to whom the transferable record was issued; or

(B) if the authoritative copy indicates that the transferable record has been transferred, the person to whom the transferable record was most recently transferred;

(3) the authoritative copy is communicated to and maintained by the person asserting control or its designated custodian;

(4) copies or revisions that add or change an identified assignee of the authoritative copy can be made only with the consent of the person asserting control;

(5) each copy of the authoritative copy and any copy of a copy is readily identifiable as a copy that is not the authoritative copy; and

(6) any revision of the authoritative copy is readily identifiable as authorized or unauthorized.

(d) Status as holder. Except as otherwise agreed, a person having control of a transferable record is the holder, as defined in section 1-201(20) of the Uniform Commercial Code, of the transferable record and has the same rights and defenses as a holder of an equivalent record or writing under the Uniform Commercial Code, including, if the applicable statutory requirements under section 3-302(a), 9-308, or revised section 9-330 of the Uniform Commercial Code are satisfied, the rights and defenses of a holder in due course or a purchaser, respectively. Delivery, possession, and endorsement are not required to obtain or exercise any of the rights under this subsection.

(e) Obligor rights. Except as otherwise agreed, an obligor under a transferable record has the same rights and defenses as an equivalent obligor under equivalent records or writings under the Uniform Commercial Code.

(f) Proof of control. If requested by a person against which enforcement is sought, the person seeking to enforce the transferable record shall provide reasonable proof that the person is in control of the transferable record. Proof may include access to the authoritative copy of the transferable record and related business records sufficient to review the terms of the transferable record and to establish the identity of the person having control of the transferable record.

(g) UCC references. For purposes of this subsection, all references to the Uniform Commercial Code are to the Uniform Commercial Code as in effect in the jurisdiction the law of which governs the transferable record.

Sec. 7031. Principles governing the use of electronic signatures in international transactions

(a) Promotion of electronic signatures.

(1) Required actions. The Secretary of Commerce shall promote the acceptance and use, on an international basis, of electronic signatures in accordance with the principles specified in paragraph (2) and in a manner consistent with section 7001 of this title. The Secretary of Commerce shall take all actions necessary in a manner consistent with such principles to eliminate or reduce, to the maximum extent possible, the impediments to commerce in electronic signatures, for the purpose of facilitating the development of interstate and foreign commerce.

(2) Principles. The principles specified in this paragraph are the following:

(A) Remove paper-based obstacles to electronic transactions by adopting relevant principles from the Model Law on Electronic Commerce adopted in 1996 by the United Nations Commission on International Trade Law.

(B) Permit parties to a transaction to determine the appropriate authentication technologies and implementation models for their transactions, with assurance that those technologies and implementation models will be recognized and enforced.

(C) Permit parties to a transaction to have the opportunity to prove in court or other proceedings that their authentication approaches and their transactions are valid.

(D) Take a nondiscriminatory approach to electronic signatures and authentication methods from other jurisdictions.

(b) Consultation. In conducting the activities required by this section, the Secretary shall consult with users and providers of electronic signature products and services and other interested persons.

(c) Definitions. As used in this section, the terms "electronic record" and "electronic signature" have the same meanings provided in section 7006 of this title.

Appendix II

UNIFORM ELECTRONIC TRANSACTION ACT—CALIFORNIA

CIVIL CODE §§ 1633.1-1633.17

1633.1. This title may be cited as the Uniform Electronic Transaction Act.

1633.2. In this title the following terms have the following definitions:

(a) "Agreement" means the bargain of the parties in fact, as found in their language or inferred from other circumstances and from rules, regulations, and procedures given the effect of agreements under laws otherwise applicable to a particular transaction.

(b) "Automated transaction" means a transaction conducted or performed, in whole or in part, by electronic means or electronic records, in which the acts or records of one or both parties are not reviewed by an individual in the ordinary course in forming a contract, performing under an existing contract, or fulfilling an obligation required by the transaction.

(c) "Computer program" means a set of statements or instructions to be used directly or indirectly in an information processing system in order to bring about a certain result.

(d) "Contract" means the total legal obligation resulting from the parties' agreement as affected by this title and other applicable law.

(e) "Electronic" means relating to technology having electrical, digital, magnetic, wireless, optical, electromagnetic, or similar capabilities.

(f) "Electronic agent" means a computer program or an electronic or other automated means used independently to initiate an action or respond to electronic records or performances in whole or in part, without review by an individual.

(g) "Electronic record" means a record created, generated, sent, communicated, received, or stored by electronic means.

(h) "Electronic signature" means an electronic sound, symbol, or process attached to or logically associated with an electronic record and executed or adopted by a person with the intent to sign the electronic record.

(i) "Governmental agency" means an executive, legislative, or judicial agency, department, board, commission, authority, institution, or instrumentality of the federal government or of a state or of a county, municipality, or other political subdivision of a state.

(j) "Information" means data, text, images, sounds, codes, computer programs, software, databases, or the like.

(k) "Information processing system" means an electronic system for creating, generating, sending, receiving, storing, displaying, or processing information.

(l) "Person" means an individual, corporation, business trust, estate, trust, partnership, limited liability company, association, joint venture, governmental agency, public corporation, or any other legal or commercial entity.

(m) "Record" means information that is inscribed on a tangible medium or that is stored in an electronic or other medium and is retrievable in perceivable form.

(n) "Security procedure" means a procedure employed for the purpose of verifying that an electronic signature, record, or performance is that of a specific person or for detecting changes or errors in the information in an electronic record. The term includes a procedure that requires the use of algorithms or other codes, identifying words or numbers, encryption, or callback or other acknowledgment procedures.

(o) "Transaction" means an action or set of actions occurring between two or more persons relating to the conduct of business, commercial, or governmental affairs.

1633.3. (a) Except as otherwise provided in subdivisions (b) and (c), this title applies to electronic records and electronic signatures relating to a transaction.

(a) This title does not apply to transactions subject to the following laws:

(1) A law governing the creation and execution of wills, codicils, or testamentary trusts.

(2) Division 1 (commencing with Section 1101) of the Uniform Commercial Code, except Sections 1107 and 1206.

(3) Divisions 3 (commencing with Section 3101), 4 (commencing with Section 4101), 5 (commencing with Section 5101), 8 (commencing with Section 8101), 9 (commencing with Section 9101), and 11 (commencing with Section 11101) of the Uniform Commercial Code.

(4) A law that requires that specifically identifiable text or disclosures in a record or a portion of a record be separately signed, including initialed, from the record. However, this paragraph does not apply to Section 1677 or 1678 of this code or Section 1298 of the Code of Civil Procedure.

(b) This title does not apply to any specific transaction described in Section 17511.5 of the Business and Professions Code, Section 56.11, 56.17, 798.14, 1133, or 1134 of, Sections 1350 to 1376, inclusive, of, Section 1689.6,1689.7, or 1689.13 of, Chapter 2.5 (commencing with Section 1695) of Title 5 of

Part 2 of Division 3 of, Section 1720, 785.15, 1789.14, 1789.16, 1789.33, or 1793.23 of, Chapter 1 (commencing with Section 1801) of Title 2 of Part 4 of Division 3 of, Section 1861.24, 1862.5, 1917.712, 1917.713, 1950.5, 1950.6, 1983, 2924b, 2924c, 2924f, 2924i, 2924j, 2924.3, or 2937 of, Article 1.5 (commencing with Section 2945) of Chapter 2 of Title 14 of Part 4 of Division 3 of, Section 2954.5 or 2963 of, Chapter 2b (commencing with Section 2981) or 2d (commencing with Section 2985.7) of Title 14 of Part 4 of Division 3 of, or Section 3071.5 of, the Civil Code, subdivision (b) of Section 18608 or Section 22328 of the Financial Code, Section 1358.15, 1365, 1368.01, 1368.1, 1371, or 18035.5 of the Health and Safety Code, Section 658, 662, 663, 664, 666, 667.5, 673, 677, 678, 678.1, 786, 10083, 10086, 10087, 10102, 10113.7, 10127.7, 10127.9, 10127.10, 10197, 10199.44, 10199.46, 10235.16, 10235.40, 10509.4, 10509.7, 11624.09, or 11624.1 of the Insurance Code, Section 779.1, 10010.1, or 16482 of the Public Utilities Code, or Section 9975 or 11738 of the Vehicle Code. An electronic record may not be substituted for any notice that is required to be sent pursuant to Section 1162 of the Code of Civil Procedure. Nothing in this subdivision shall be construed to prohibit the recordation of any document with a county recorder by electronic means.

(c) This title applies to an electronic record or electronic signature otherwise excluded from the application of this title under subdivision (b) when used for a transaction subject to a law other than those specified in subdivision (b).

(d) A transaction subject to this title is also subject to other applicable substantive law.

(e) The exclusion of a transaction from the application of this title under subdivision (b) or (c) shall be construed only to exclude the transaction from the application of this title, but shall not be construed to prohibit the transaction from being conducted by electronic means if the transaction may be conducted by electronic means under any other applicable law.

1633.4. This title applies to any electronic record or electronic signature created, generated, sent, communicated, received, or stored on or after January 1, 2000.

1633.5. (a) This title does not require a record or signature to be created, generated, sent, communicated, received, stored, or otherwise processed or used by electronic means or in electronic form.

(a) This title applies only to a transaction between parties each of which has agreed to conduct the transaction by electronic means. Whether the parties agree to conduct a transaction by electronic means is determined from the context and surrounding circumstances, including the parties' conduct. Except for a separate and optional agreement the primary purpose of which is to authorize a transaction to be conducted by electronic means, an agreement to conduct a transaction by electronic means may not be contained in a standard form contract that is not an electronic record. An agreement in such a standard form contract may not be conditioned upon an agreement to conduct transactions by electronic means. An agreement to conduct a transaction by electronic means may not be inferred solely from the fact that a party has used electronic means to pay an account or register a purchase or warranty. This subdivision may not be varied by agreement.

(b) A party that agrees to conduct a transaction by electronic means may refuse to conduct other transactions by electronic means. If a seller sells goods or services by both electronic and nonelectronic means and a buyer purchases the goods or services by conducting the transaction by electronic means, the buyer may refuse to conduct further transactions regarding the goods or services by electronic means. This subdivision may not be varied by agreement.

(c) Except as otherwise provided in this title, the effect of any of its provisions may be varied by agreement. The presence in certain provisions of this title of the words "unless otherwise agreed," or words of similar import, does not imply that the effect of other provisions may not be varied by agreement.

1633.6. This title shall be construed and applied according to all of the following:

(1) To facilitate electronic transactions consistent with other applicable law.

(2) To be consistent with reasonable practices concerning electronic transactions and with the continued expansion of those practices.

(3) To effectuate its general purpose to make uniform the law with respect to the subject of this title among states enacting it.

1633.7. (a) A record or signature may not be denied legal effect or enforceability solely because it is in electronic form.

(a) A contract may not be denied legal effect or enforceability solely because an electronic record was used in its formation.

(b) If a law requires a record to be in writing, an electronic record satisfies the law.

(c) If a law requires a signature, an electronic signature satisfies the law.

1633.8. (a) have agreed to conduct a transaction by electronic means and a law requires a person to provide, send, or deliver information in writing to another person, that requirement is satisfied if the information is provided, sent, or delivered, as the case may be, in an electronic record capable of retention by the recipient at the time of receipt. An electronic record is not capable of retention by the recipient if the sender or its information processing system inhibits the ability of the recipient to print or store the electronic record.

(a) If a law other than this title requires a record to be posted or displayed in a certain manner, to be sent, communicated, or transmitted by a specified method, or to contain information that is formatted in a certain manner, all of the following rules apply:

(1) The record shall be posted or displayed in the manner specified in the other law.

(2) Except as otherwise provided in paragraph (2) of subdivision (d), the record shall be sent, communicated, or transmitted by the method specified in the other law.

(3) The record shall contain the information formatted in the manner specified in the other law.

(b) If a sender inhibits the ability of a recipient to store or print an electronic record, the electronic record is not enforceable against the recipient.

(c) The requirements of this section may not be varied by agreement, except as follows:

(1) To the extent a law other than this title requires information to be provided, sent, or delivered in writing but permits that requirement to be varied by agreement, the requirement under subdivision (a) that the information be in the form of an electronic record capable of retention may also be varied by agreement.

(2) A requirement under a law other than this title to send, communicate, or transmit a record by first-class mail may be varied by agreement to the extent permitted by the other law.

1633.9. (a) An electronic record or electronic signature is attributable to a person if it was the act of the person. The act of the person may be shown in any manner, including a showing of the efficacy of any security procedure applied to determine the person to which the electronic record or electronic signature was attributable.

(a) The effect of an electronic record or electronic signature attributed to a person under subdivision (a) is determined from the context and surrounding circumstances at the time of its creation, execution, or adoption, including the parties' agreement, if any, and otherwise as provided by law.

1633.10. If a change or error in an electronic record occurs in a transmission between parties to a transaction, the following rules apply:

(1) If the parties have agreed to use a security procedure to detect changes or errors and one party has conformed to the procedure, but the other party has not, and the nonconforming party would have detected the change or error had that party also conformed, the conforming party may avoid the effect of the changed or erroneous electronic record.

(2) In an automated transaction involving an individual, the individual may avoid the effect of an electronic record that resulted from an error made by the individual in dealing with the electronic agent of another person if the electronic agent did not provide an opportunity for the prevention or correction of the error and, at the time the individual learns of the error, all of the following conditions are met:

(i) The individual promptly notifies the other person of the error and that the individual did not intend to be bound by the electronic record received by the other person.

(ii) The individual takes reasonable steps, including steps that conform to the other person's reasonable instructions, to return to the other person or, if instructed by the other person, to destroy the consideration received, if any, as a result of the erroneous electronic record.

(iii) The individual has not used or received any benefit or value from the consideration, if any, received from the other person.

(3) If neither paragraph (1) nor (2) applies, the change or error has the effect provided by other law, including the law of mistake, and the parties' contract, if any.

(4) Paragraphs (2) and (3) may not be varied by agreement.

1633.11. (a) If a law requires that a signature be notarized, the requirement is satisfied with respect to an electronic signature if an electronic record includes, in addition to the electronic signature to be notarized, the electronic signature of a notary public together with all other information required to be included in a notarization by other applicable law.

(a) In a transaction, if a law requires that a statement be signed under penalty of perjury, the requirement is satisfied with respect to an electronic signature, if an electronic record includes, in addition to the electronic signature, all of the information as to which the declaration pertains together with a declaration under penalty of perjury by the person who submits the electronic signature that the information is true and correct.

1633.12. (a) If a law requires that a record be retained, the requirement is satisfied by retaining an electronic record of the information in the record, if the electronic record reflects accurately the information set forth in the record at the time it was first generated in its final form as an electronic record or otherwise, and the electronic record remains accessible for later reference.

(a) A requirement to retain a record in accordance with subdivision (a) does not apply to any information the sole purpose of which is to enable the record to be sent, communicated, or received.

(b) A person may satisfy subdivision (a) by using the services of another person if the requirements of subdivision (a) are satisfied.

(c) If a law requires a record to be retained in its original form, or provides consequences if the record is not retained in its original form, that law is satisfied by an electronic record retained in accordance with subdivision (a).

(d) If a law requires retention of a check, that requirement is satisfied by retention of an electronic record of the information on the front and back of the check in accordance with subdivision (a).

(e) A record retained as an electronic record in accordance with subdivision (a) satisfies a law requiring a person to retain a record for evidentiary, audit, or like purposes, unless a law enacted after the effective date of this title specifically prohibits the use of an electronic record for a specified purpose.

(f) This section does not preclude a governmental agency from specifying additional requirements for the retention of a record subject to the agency's jurisdiction.

1633.13. In a proceeding, evidence of a record or signature may not be excluded solely because it is in electronic form.

1633.14. (a) In an automated transaction, the following rules apply:

(1) A contract may be formed by the interaction of electronic agents of the parties, even if no individual was aware of or reviewed the electronic agents' actions or the resulting terms and agreements.

(2) A contract may be formed by the interaction of an electronic agent and an individual, acting on the individual's own behalf or for another person, including by an interaction in which the individual performs actions that the individual is free to refuse to perform and which the individual knows or has reason to know will cause the electronic agent to complete the transaction or performance.

(b) The terms of the contract are determined by the substantive law applicable to it.

1633.15. (a) Unless the sender and the recipient agree to a different method of sending that is reasonable under the circumstances, an electronic record is sent when the information is addressed properly or otherwise directed properly to the recipient and either

(1) enters an information processing system outside the control of the sender or of a person that sent the electronic record on behalf of the sender, or

(2) enters a region of an information processing system that is under the control of the recipient.

(a) Unless the sender and the recipient agree to a different method of receiving that is reasonable under the circumstances, an electronic record is received when the electronic record enters an information processing system that the recipient has designated or uses for the purpose of receiving electronic records or information of the type sent, in a form capable of being processed by that system, and from which the recipient is able to retrieve the electronic record.

(b) Subdivision (b) applies even if the place the information processing system is located is different from the place the electronic record is deemed to be received under subdivision (d).

(c) Unless otherwise expressly provided in the electronic record or agreed between the sender and the recipient, an electronic record is deemed to be sent from the sender's place of business and to be received at the recipient's place of business or, if the recipient is an individual acting on his or her own behalf, at the recipient's place of residence. For purposes of this subdivision, the following rules apply:

(1) If the sender or recipient has more than one place of business, the place of business of that person is the place having the closest relationship to the underlying transaction.

(2) If the sender or the recipient does not have a place of business, the place of business is the sender's or recipient's residence, as the case may be.

(d) An electronic record is received under subdivision (b) even if no individual is aware of its receipt.

(e) Receipt of an electronic acknowledgment from an information processing system described in subdivision (b) establishes that a record was received but, by itself, does not establish that the content sent corresponds to the content received.

(f) If a person is aware that an electronic record purportedly sent under subdivision (a), or purportedly received under subdivision (b), was not actually sent or received, the legal effect of the sending or receipt is determined by other applicable law. Except to the extent permitted by the other law, this subdivision may not be varied by agreement.

1633.16. If a law other than this title requires that a notice of the right to cancel be provided or sent, an electronic record may not substitute for a writing under that other law unless, in addition to satisfying the requirements of that other law and this title, the notice of cancellation may be returned by electronic means. This section may not be varied by agreement.

1633.17. No state agency, board, or commission may require, prohibit, or regulate the use of an electronic signature in a transaction in which the agency, board, or commission is not a party unless a law other than this title expressly authorizes the requirement, prohibition, or regulation.

APPENDIX III

PRACTICAL STRATEGIES FOR CONSTRUCTING ELECTRONIC DISCOVERY AGREEMENTS

By Mark S. Sidoti and Phillip J. Duffy

On the eve of the first anniversary of the effective date of new Federal Rules of Civil Procedure governing discovery of electronically stored information ("ESI"), the challenges of "e-discovery" continue to loom large. The Federal Rules require that parties meet early to formulate specific plans for preservation, collection and disclosure of ESI early in litigation. Often, these E-Discovery Agreements ("EDAs") become part of the Rule 16 Order that emanates from the initial discovery and scheduling conference. EDAs can cover the full range of issues surrounding discovery of ESI, from preservation through forms of production. This article will examine the provisions that are or should be most commonly found in such agreements. Whether working to create a draft agreement, or examining one of the many forms that might be proposed by courts and adversaries, this article will provide some helpful guideposts to ensure that clients' interests are protected.[24]

Preservation

ESI can be evidence and, as such, a party must take reasonable steps to preserve potentially relevant ESI when the party knows or should be aware of a pending or impending lawsuit or investigation. *See, e.g., Zubulake v. UBS Warburg LLC*, 220 F.R.D. 212, 218 (S.D.N.Y., October 22, 2003) ("*Zubulake IV*") (holding if litigation is filed, threatened, or seriously contemplated counsel must immediately initiate litigation hold). For this reason, every EDA should contain a section dealing with preservation of ESI, as well as production of relevant document retention policies. In addition to their stated purpose of "freezing" the status of existing

[24]One important caveat in considering all of the following suggestions: whenever considering the addition of discretionary provisions to an EDA, counsel should be mindful that whatever is being requested of their adversary will likely be requested from their client. In fact, most EDAs contain fully reciprocal obligations. It is critical, therefore, to carefully assess the client's systems, capabilities and practices before suggesting or consenting to obligations in an EDA that one's own client cannot meet.

electronic evidence on each side, these provisions are designed to allow parties to evaluate and test each other's preservation efforts, should the need arise.

First, the agreement should direct parties to maintain, and not destroy or delete, sources of potentially discoverable ESI, including, e-mail back-up tapes, computer hard drives and servers, and network back-up tapes created during a defined "relevant period." This should include the software and hardware necessary to access the data, to the extent it exists (including, if available, so called "legacy" software or systems which are needed to process older data).

It is good practice to take care in selecting the relevant period. The obligation to preserve relevant ESI exists whether or not it has been memorialized in an EDA. Still, the effect of violating a preservation obligation will likely be more serious if the trigger date for the obligation is memorialized in an agreement approved by the parties or incorporated into an order signed by a Judge. Thus, before explicitly agreeing to preserve ESI created during a particular period, counsel must understand their client's computer system well enough to ensure the client it is not agreeing to preserve date it either does not have the capability to preserve, or has already been deleted.

One should also be careful to ensure that the obligation to preserve extends only to sources that may contain potentially discoverable information. Casting too wide a net may have serious implications. Maintenance of back up tapes is expensive and halting tape recycling unnecessarily may prove costly over time. Moreover, unnecessary warehousing of backup tapes creates sources of ESI for future matters that would otherwise not exist.

In addition, all EDA's should provide that, by preserving potentially discoverable information, parties do not waive any objection to the discovery or admissibility of the information. This is most important for sources, such as back up tapes, that the lawyer intends to argue are not "reasonably accessible" under F.R.C.P. 26.

It is also good practice to consider inclusion of a provision that requires the parties to identify appropriate employees who might control or have access to relevant, potentially discoverable ESI. Identifying these "custodians" early could serve to limit the number of employees to whom the preservation obligation is applicable, thereby saving time and costs associated with preservation, and making preservation efforts more manageable.

Finally, an EDA may also require parties to produce document retention policies, any protocols governing retention or destruction of potentially discoverable ESI created during a specified period, and designation of a witness knowledgeable about a party's computer system. (In some jurisdictions, the rules actually require the designation of such a witness at the Rule 26 meet and confer session.) At very least, the EDA should require identification of individuals responsible for maintaining or accessing the party's computer system.

An EDA might address the above preservation issues as follows:

Preservation And Production Of Data

1. *The parties shall (i) produce all document retention policies and protocols for the applicable period from January 1, 2007 to date (the "Relevant Period") that bear upon the retention or destruction of potentially discoverable information created*

by the parties during the Relevant Period and (ii) identify and produce for deposition pursuant to Fed. R. Civ. P. 30(b)(6) a witness or witnesses with knowledge of the document retention policies, protocols and procedures and the computer and electronic data systems maintained by the parties during the Relevant Period, and the parties' efforts relating to the preservation and collection of potentially discoverable information.

2. *The parties shall securely maintain, and not destroy or delete, sources of potentially discoverable information, including, (i) e-mail back-up tapes, computer hard drives and servers, and (ii) network back-up tapes (i.e. tapes or other similar media onto which back-up systems store electronically stored information, or "ESI"), created during the Relevant Period, but only to the extent that these may contain potentially discoverable information. To the extent they exist, the parties shall preserve all such back up tapes and other ESI created during the Relevant Period. By preserving potentially discoverable information in accordance with the terms of this Stipulation and Order, the parties do not waive any objection to the discovery or admissibility of potentially discoverable information.*
3. *All current, legacy or proprietary software and hardware necessary to access, manipulate, print, and otherwise utilize potentially discoverable electronic information shall be securely retained, to the extent that it currently exists, for the remainder of the litigation.*
4. *Understanding the necessity of capturing all relevant data and information on the hard drives or other physical media using forensic methods, the parties shall identify by name, title, or departmental category employees who shall be responsible for maintaining all relevant hard drives and other physical media during the pendency of this litigation.*
5. *To facilitate the identification of the appropriate employees who may possess relevant documents, the parties will provide to each other the identification of the employees that they reasonably believe could have access to, control over or responsibility for potentially discoverable information. The parties will meet and confer in good faith and exchange additional information as may be necessary to facilitate the identification, and limit the number, of employees for whom the provisions of this paragraph shall be applicable.*

Form of Production

Designating the form or forms of production is a critical aspect of any EDA. F.R.C.P. 34 requires parties to produce ESI in its native form or, alternatively, in a "reasonably useable form." Native format is usually considered unwieldy and, as such, parties routinely convert the data into a reasonably useable format such as TIFF (tagged image file format) or PDF (portable document format) before production. Production in one of these formats has distinct advantages. For example, unlike native files, TIFF and PDF documents can be Bates numbered and redacted. These formats allow greater control over production of metadata, as fields can be included or excluded from the "load file" that accompanies the TIFF production. Of course, as discussed below, some of those reasons may inspire parties to ask for ESI in native format under certain circumstances.

A typical EDA will require each party to produce ESI in TIFF format. The agreement should require that each TIFF be created directly from the original electronic document and prohibit a party from creating a TIFF file by printing and scanning paper documents. This process degrades the searchability of the documents, possibly in contravention of the Rule 34.

Moreover, given the potentially significant costs involved in converting documents to TIFF or PDF format, it may be wise to consider including a provision in the EDA that indicates that the parties have not agreed on which party will bear the cost for production of ESI in TIFF. Although parties typically bear their own costs of production in Federal Court cases, this approach allows the parties to reserve their ability to move for cost-shifting, sharing and/or allocation of costs, where appropriate, if production becomes unduly burdensome and costly.

Additionally, many EDAs prescribe the technical requirements for TIFF images and the process that should be undertaken in creating and producing them. These requirements are fairly standard and any reputable vendor will conform to them. An EDA might address all of the above form of production issues as follows:

> ***ESI IN TIFF:*** *EACH PARTY WILL PRODUCE ESI IN TIFF FORMAT. EACH TIFF FILE OF ESI MUST BE CREATED DIRECTLY FROM THE ORIGINAL ELECTRONIC DOCUMENTS; A PARTY MAY NOT CREATE A TIFF FILE OF ESI BY PRINTING OUT PAPER COPIES OF THAT ELECTRONIC DOCUMENT AND THEN SCANNING THAT PAPER COPY OF THE ESI. THE PARTIES HAVE REACHED NO AGREEMENT REGARDING WHICH PARTY WILL BEAR THE COST FOR THE PRODUCTION OF ESI IN TIFF. EACH PARTY RESERVES THE RIGHT TO MOVE FOR SHIFTING, SHARING AND/OR ALLOCATION OF COSTS IF AND WHEN SUCH PRODUCTION BECOMES UNDULY BURDENSOME AND COSTLY.*
>
> ***TECHNICAL SPECIFICATIONS FOR ALL TIFF FILES:*** *ALL TIFF FILES WILL CONFORM TO THE FOLLOWING SPECIFICATIONS:*

1. *All TIFF files will be single page, black and white, dithered (if appropriate), group 4 TIFF at 300 × 300 dpi resolution and 8½ × 11 inch page size, except for documents requiring different resolution or page size.*
2. *A unitization file, in standard format (e.g. Opitcon, Summation Dii, or the like) showing the bates number of each page and the appropriate unitization of the documents, must accompany each TIFF file.*
3. *Regarding spreadsheet and access database files, the parties' technical personnel shall jointly determine, in good faith, a reasonable protocol for producing spreadsheet and access database files.*

Certain types of information may require production in native format. For example, relational data, such as MS Excel spreadsheets, may be incomplete or unusable when simply printed or converted to another static format such as TIFF. Moreover, some parties may wish, for strategic reasons, to have access to the entire universe of metadata available throughout the native document. Because production of ESI in native format will typically be the exception, the EDA may be structured to allow for production of native ESI only upon a special showing of need. A conditional procedure for production of native files may be structured as follows:

> ***SUPPLEMENTAL PRODUCTION OF SPECIFIC NATIVE FORMAT DOCUMENTS:*** *A PARTY MAY REQUEST NATIVE FORMAT FILES OF ELECTRONIC DOCUMENTS FROM A PRODUCING PARTY, IN ACCORDANCE WITH THE PROVISIONS OF THIS PARAGRAPH.*

1. *No requesting party may seek to compel production of native format files of electronic documents on a wholesale or otherwise unreasonable basis.*
2. *Any request for native documents will be carried out under the following protocol:*
    a) *The requesting party will identify in writing those native files sought and the specific basis for the requests.*
    b) *The producing party will respond in writing within fourteen (14) days.*
    c) *If the parties are unable to agree, the parties will submit the matter to the Court.*
    d) *If the requesting party believes the explanation supporting its need to review native files will reveal attorney work-product, the requesting party may, at its discretion, submit such explanation in writing directly to the Court for in camera review.*
    e) *If the Court determines that the explanation does not constitute attorney work-product, a copy of the requesting party's explanation shall thereupon be provided to the producing party.*

The parties have reached no agreement regarding which party will bear the cost for the production of any native files. Each party reserves the right to move for shifting, sharing and/or allocation of costs if and when such production becomes unduly burdensome and costly.

Metadata

Metadata—often described as the hidden "data behind the data" in electronic files—presents certain challenges. E-mail is easiest to deal with, and most parties will agree that some reasonable amount of metadata should be produced. Certain fields of metadata, such as the "bcc" field, are usually considered reasonable and are easily extracted when the data is processed and are part of the normal metadata load file. Still, a lawyer must be clear on the fields selected and speak with a technical expert to be sure the requested fields are readily extracted.

Metadata from MS word documents is more problematic. It is important to clearly delineate which metadata fields, if any, will be produced from non-emails because the selection of fields may have an impact on data collection. This is more of a concern for non-emails because creation dates and similar fields can be unintentionally modified when, for example, individual users attempt to self-collect data. There are, of course, several ways to collect the data without modifying creation dates and, if this is likely to be an issue, it should be discussed with a reputable vendor and an appropriate collection plan developed. Given these difficulties, it is often best not to try and address specific metadata fields for email and non-email documents in the EDA. The better approach may be a conditional procedure for production of metadata similar to that suggested above for native files.

Document Location Protocols

The issue of what steps parties have taken to fulfill their obligations to preserve, collect and produce relevant documents including ESI, has taken center stage in many of the recent decisions in which courts have imposed severe sanctions for spoliation and mismanagement of these procedures. *See, e.g., Doe v. Norwalk Community College*, 2007 WL 2066497 (D. Conn. July 16, 2007) (Rule 37 protection denied where party failed to prevent destruction of e-mail after notice of suit).

The Federal Rules and the weight of decisional law now leave little room for error in these processes, and much of this information has been deemed fully discoverable in most jurisdictions. For these reasons, and particularly where the parties are of relatively equal size and bargaining power, many litigants find it mutually beneficial to agree to disclosure of these procedures and protocols. Such an agreement can be worded as follows:

> ***Document location protocols***: *The parties shall identify with reasonable particularity the methods by which they searched for and collected relevant documents, including ESI. This description shall including a list of custodians (people who may possess relevant documents) whose data was searched, specific search terms and searching conventions utilized, limitations on search terms or conventions, and specific media sources searched (including identification of such sources by custodian and location—e.g., Joe Smith's laptop hard drive; Jane Doe's hardcopy files located in her home office; ABC Co.'s e-mail server back up tapes covering July through December 1996). The parties reserve their right to object to the document location protocols utilized by their respective adversaries, and agree to reconvene to discuss this matter, if necessary, following initial compliance with this paragraph.*

Inaccessible and Unavailable Information

The Federal Rules now require parties to disclose, but not immediately produce, inaccessible data (*e.g.*, backup tapes maintained *solely* for disaster recovery), which may be discoverable for good cause shown (subject to the customary burden vs. expense limitations of Rule 26(b)(2)(C)). Similarly, parties are required to identify ESI that may have become unavailable. These issues present fertile ground for dispute during litigation and thus, it is important to include provisions in the EDA that establish the playing field early. Provisions on these issues might read as follows:

> ***Inaccessible Information***—*Within 60 days from the date of entry of this Stipulation and Order, the parties shall identify potentially discoverable information that each party asserts is inaccessible to the extent that such determination can be made. For all such potentially discoverable information, the parties will indicate whether the data is catalogued, such that the parties can determine more precisely what type of potentially discoverable information might exist, and whether the potentially discoverable information can be selectively searched.*

> ***Unavailable Information***—*Within 60 days from the date of entry of this Stipulation and Order, the parties shall identify, to the extent that they are aware, responsive or potentially responsive data that is no longer available in any form, indicating why the data is no longer available, when it became unavailable and who is responsible for ordering its destruction and destroying it.*

Of course, there are other provisions that should be included in an EDA, including dealing with asserting claims of privilege after production, however, due to space limitations, we will not discuss them here. Moreover, courts, commentators, and adversaries will continue to grapple with the issues presented herein for many years to come and new provisions will be crafted to suit individual needs. Technology will also continue to evolve, perhaps easing some of the burdens of the obligations imposed by the Federal Rules. However, at present, the foregoing provisions should form the backbone of any EDA. With these in place, and the additional issues raised above fully considered, counsel can rest assured that they have laid a strong foundation for ensuring compliance with their discovery obligations, the new rules and the decisional law and minimized the prospect of future e-discovery disputes.

APPENDIX IV

DISCOVERY PROVISIONS—FRCP RULE 26

FEDERAL RULES OF CIVIL PROCEDURE

Rule 26. Duty to Disclose; General Provisions Governing Discovery

(a) Required Disclosures.

(1) Initial Disclosures.

(A) In General. Except as exempted by Rule 26(a)(1)(B) or as otherwise stipulated or ordered by the court, a party must, without awaiting a discovery request, provide to the other parties:

(i) the name and, if known, the address and telephone number of each individual likely to have discoverable information—along with the subjects of that information—that the disclosing party may use to support its claims or defenses, unless the use would be solely for impeachment;

(ii) a copy—or a description by category and location—of all documents, electronically stored information, and tangible things that the disclosing party has in its possession, custody, or control and may use to support its claims or defenses, unless the use would be solely for impeachment;

(iii) a computation of each category of damages claimed by the disclosing party—who must also make available for inspection and copying as under Rule 34 the documents or other evidentiary material, unless privileged or protected from disclosure, on which each computation is based, including materials bearing on the nature and extent of injuries suffered; and

(iv) for inspection and copying as under Rule 34, any insurance agreement under which an insurance business may be liable to satisfy all or part of a possible judgment in the action or to indemnify or reimburse for payments made to satisfy the judgment.

(B) Proceedings Exempt from Initial Disclosure. The following proceedings are exempt from initial disclosure:

(i) an action for review on an administrative record;

(ii) a forfeiture action in rem arising from a federal statute;

(iii) a petition for habeas corpus or any other proceeding to challenge a criminal conviction or sentence;

(iv) an action brought without an attorney by a person in the custody of the United States, a state, or a state subdivision;

(v) an action to enforce or quash an administrative summons or subpoena;

(vi) an action by the United States to recover benefit payments;

(vii) an action by the United States to collect on a student loan guaranteed by the United States;

(viii) a proceeding ancillary to a proceeding in another court; and

(ix) an action to enforce an arbitration award.

(C) Time for Initial Disclosures—In General. A party must make the initial disclosures at or within 14 days after the parties' Rule 26(f) conference unless a different time is set by stipulation or court order, or unless a party objects during the conference that initial disclosures are not appropriate in this action and states the objection in the proposed discovery plan. In ruling on the objection, the court must determine what disclosures, if any, are to be made and must set the time for disclosure.

(D) Time for Initial Disclosures—For Parties Served or Joined Later. A party that is first served or otherwise joined after the Rule 26(f) conference must make the initial disclosures within 30 days after being served or joined, unless a different time is set by stipulation or court order.

(E) Basis for Initial Disclosure; Unacceptable Excuses. A party must make its initial disclosures based on the information then reasonably available to it. A party is not excused from making its disclosures because it has not fully investigated the case or because it challenges the sufficiency of another party's disclosures or because another party has not made its disclosures.

(2) Disclosure of Expert Testimony.

(A) In General. In addition to the disclosures required by Rule 26(a)(1), a party must disclose to the other parties the identity of any witness it may use at trial to present evidence under Federal Rule of Evidence 702, 703, or 705.

(B) Written Report. Unless otherwise stipulated or ordered by the court, this disclosure must be accompanied by a written report—prepared and signed by the witness—if the witness is one retained or specially employed to provide expert testimony in the case or one whose duties as the party's employee regularly involve giving expert testimony. The report must contain:

(i) a complete statement of all opinions the witness will express and the basis and reasons for them;

(ii) the data or other information considered by the witness in forming them;

(iii) any exhibits that will be used to summarize or support them;

(iv) the witness's qualifications, including a list of all publications authored in the previous 10 years;

(v) a list of all other cases in which, during the previous 4 years, the witness testified as an expert at trial or by deposition; and

(vi) a statement of the compensation to be paid for the study and testimony in the case.

(C) Time to Disclose Expert Testimony. A party must make these disclosures at the times and in the sequence that the court orders. Absent a stipulation or a court order, the disclosures must be made:

(i) at least 90 days before the date set for trial or for the case to be ready for trial; or

(ii) if the evidence is intended solely to contradict or rebut evidence on the same subject matter identified by another party under Rule 26(a)(2)(B), within 30 days after the other party's disclosure.

(D) Supplementing the Disclosure. The parties must supplement these disclosures when required under Rule 26(e).

(3) Pretrial Disclosures.

(A) In General. In addition to the disclosures required by Rule 26(a)(1) and (2), a party must provide to the other parties and promptly file the following information about the evidence that it may present at trial other than solely for impeachment:

(i) the name and, if not previously provided, the address and telephone number of each witness—separately identifying those the party expects to present and those it may call if the need arises;

(ii) the designation of those witnesses whose testimony the party expects to present by deposition and, if not taken stenographically, a transcript of the pertinent parts of the deposition; and

(iii) an identification of each document or other exhibit, including summaries of other evidence—separately identifying those items the party expects to offer and those it may offer if the need arises.

(B) Time for Pretrial Disclosures; Objections. Unless the court orders otherwise, these disclosures must be made at least 30 days before trial. Within 14 days after they are made, unless the court sets a different time, a party may serve and promptly file a list of the following objections: any objections to the use under Rule 32(a) of a deposition designated by another party under Rule 26(a)(3)(A)(ii); and any objection, together with the grounds for it, that may be made to the admissibility of materials identified under Rule 26(a)(3)(A)(iii). An objection not so made—except for one under Federal Rule of Evidence 402 or 403—is waived unless excused by the court for good cause.

(4) Form of Disclosures.

Unless the court orders otherwise, all disclosures under Rule 26(a) must be in writing, signed, and served.

(b) Discovery Scope and Limits.

(1) Scope in General.

Unless otherwise limited by court order, the scope of discovery is as follows: Parties may obtain discovery regarding any nonprivileged matter that is relevant to any party's claim or defense—including the existence, description, nature, custody, condition, and location of any documents or other tangible things and the identity and location of persons who know of any discoverable matter. For good cause, the court may order discovery of any matter relevant to the subject matter involved in the action. Relevant information need not be admissible at the trial if the discovery appears reasonably calculated to lead to the discovery of admissible evidence. All discovery is subject to the limitations imposed by Rule 26(b)(2)(C).

(2) Limitations on Frequency and Extent.

(A) When Permitted. By order, the court may alter the limits in these rules on the number of depositions and interrogatories or on the length of depositions under Rule 30. By order or local rule, the court may also limit the number of requests under Rule 36.

(B) Specific Limitations on Electronically Stored Information. A party need not provide discovery of electronically stored information from sources that the party identifies as not reasonably accessible because of undue burden or cost. On motion to compel discovery or for a protective order, the party from whom discovery is sought must show that the information is not reasonably accessible because of undue burden or cost. If that showing is made, the court may nonetheless order discovery from such sources if the requesting party shows good cause, considering the limitations of Rule 26(b)(2)(C). The court may specify conditions for the discovery.

(C) When Required. On motion or on its own, the court must limit the frequency or extent of discovery otherwise allowed by these rules or by local rule if it determines that:

(i) the discovery sought is unreasonably cumulative or duplicative, or can be obtained from some other source that is more convenient, less burdensome, or less expensive;

(ii) the party seeking discovery has had ample opportunity to obtain the information by discovery in the action; or

(iii) the burden or expense of the proposed discovery outweighs its likely benefit, considering the needs of the case, the amount in controversy, the parties' resources, the importance of the issues at stake in the action, and the importance of the discovery in resolving the issues.

(3) Trial Preparation: Materials.

(A) Documents and Tangible Things. Ordinarily, a party may not discover documents and tangible things that are prepared in anticipation of litigation or for trial by or for another party or its representative (including the other party's attorney, consultant, surety, indemnitor, insurer, or agent). But, subject to Rule 26(b)(4), those materials may be discovered if:

(i) they are otherwise discoverable under Rule 26(b)(1); and

(ii) the party shows that it has substantial need for the materials to prepare its case and cannot, without undue hardship, obtain their substantial equivalent by other means.

(B) Protection Against Disclosure. If the court orders discovery of those materials, it must protect against disclosure of the mental impressions, conclusions, opinions, or legal theories of a party's attorney or other representative concerning the litigation.

(C) Previous Statement. Any party or other person may, on request and without the required showing, obtain the person's own previous statement about the action or its subject matter. If the request is refused, the person may move for a court order, and Rule 37(a)(5) applies to the award of expenses. A previous statement is either:

(i) a written statement that the person has signed or otherwise adopted or approved; or

(ii) a contemporaneous stenographic, mechanical, electrical, or other recording—or a transcription of it—that recites substantially verbatim the person's oral statement.

(4) Trial Preparation: Experts.

(A) Expert Who May Testify. A party may depose any person who has been identified as an expert whose opinions may be presented at trial. If Rule 26(a)(2)(B) requires a report from the expert, the deposition may be conducted only after the report is provided.

(B) Expert Employed Only for Trial Preparation. Ordinarily, a party may not, by interrogatories or deposition, discover facts known or opinions held by an expert who has been retained or specially employed by another party in anticipation of litigation or to prepare for trial and who is not expected to be called as a witness at trial. But a party may do so only:

(i) as provided in Rule 35(b); or

(ii) on showing exceptional circumstances under which it is impracticable for the party to obtain facts or opinions on the same subject by other means.

(C) Payment. Unless manifest injustice would result, the court must require that the party seeking discovery:

(i) pay the expert a reasonable fee for time spent in responding to discovery under Rule 26(b)(4)(A) or (B); and

(ii) for discovery under (B), also pay the other party a fair portion of the fees and expenses it reasonably incurred in obtaining the expert's facts and opinions.

(5) Claiming Privilege or Protecting Trial-Preparation Materials.

(A) Information Withheld. When a party withholds information otherwise discoverable by claiming that the information is privileged or subject to protection as trial-preparation material, the party must:

(i) expressly make the claim; and

(ii) describe the nature of the documents, communications, or tangible things not produced or disclosed—and do so in a manner that, without revealing information itself privileged or protected, will enable other parties to assess the claim.

(B) Information Produced. If information produced in discovery is subject to a claim of privilege or of protection as trialpreparation material, the party making the claim may notify any party that received the information of the claim and the basis for it. After being notified, a party must promptly return, sequester, or destroy the specified information and any copies it has; must not use or disclose the information until the claim is resolved; must take reasonable steps to retrieve the information if the party disclosed it before being notified; and may promptly present the information to the court under seal for a determination of the claim. The producing party must preserve the information until the claim is resolved.

(c) Protective Orders.

(1) In General.

A party or any person from whom discovery is sought may move for a protective order in the court where the action is pending—or as an alternative on matters relating to a deposition, in the court for the district where the deposition will be taken. The motion must include a certification that the movant has in good faith conferred or attempted to confer with other affected parties in an effort to resolve the dispute without court action. The court may, for good cause, issue an order to protect a party or person from annoyance, embarrassment, oppression, or undue burden or expense, including one or more of the following:

(A) forbidding the disclosure or discovery;

(B) specifying terms, including time and place, for the disclosure or discovery;

(C) prescribing a discovery method other than the one selected by the party seeking discovery;

(D) forbidding inquiry into certain matters, or limiting the scope of disclosure or discovery to certain matters;

(E) designating the persons who may be present while the discovery is conducted;

(F) requiring that a deposition be sealed and opened only on court order;

(G) requiring that a trade secret or other confidential research, development, or commercial information not be revealed or be revealed only in a specified way; and

(H) requiring that the parties simultaneously file specified documents or information in sealed envelopes, to be opened as the court directs.

(2) Ordering Discovery.

If a motion for a protective order is wholly or partly denied, the court may, on just terms, order that any party or person provide or permit discovery.

(3) Awarding Expenses.

Rule 37(a)(5) applies to the award of expenses.

(d) Timing and Sequence of Discovery.

(1) Timing.

A party may not seek discovery from any source before the parties have conferred as required by Rule 26(f), except in a proceeding exempted from initial disclosure under Rule 26(a)(1)(B), or when authorized by these rules, by stipulation, or by court order.

(2) Sequence.

Unless, on motion, the court orders otherwise for the parties' and witnesses' convenience and in the interests of justice:

(A) methods of discovery may be used in any sequence; and

(B) discovery by one party does not require any other party to delay its discovery.

(e) Supplementation of Disclosures and Responses.

(1) In General.

A party who has made a disclosure under Rule 26(a)—or who has responded to an interrogatory, request for production, or request for admission—must supplement or correct its disclosure or response:

(A) in a timely manner if the party learns that in some material respect the disclosure or response is incomplete or incorrect, and if the additional or corrective information has not otherwise been made known to the other parties during the discovery process or in writing; or

(B) as ordered by the court.

(2) Expert Witness.

For an expert whose report must be disclosed under Rule 26(a)(2)(B), the party's duty to supplement extends both to information included in the report and to information given during the expert's deposition. Any additions or changes to this information must be disclosed by the time the party's pretrial disclosures under Rule 26(a)(3) are due.

(f) Conference of the Parties; Planning for Discovery

(1) Conference Timing.

Except in a proceeding exempted from initial disclosure under Rule 26(a)(1)(B) or when the court orders otherwise, the parties must confer as soon as practicable—and in any event at least 21 days before a scheduling conference is to be held or a scheduling order is due under Rule 16(b).

(2) Conference Content; Parties' Responsibilities.

In conferring, the parties must consider the nature and basis of their claims and defenses and the possibilities for promptly settling or resolving the case; make or arrange for the disclosures required by Rule 26(a)(1); discuss any issues about preserving discoverable information; and develop a proposed discovery plan. The attorneys of record and all unrepresented parties that have appeared in the case are jointly responsible for arranging the conference, for attempting in good faith to agree on the proposed discovery plan, and for submitting to the court within 14 days after the conference a written report outlining the plan. The court may order the parties or attorneys to attend the conference in person.

(3) Discovery Plan.

A discovery plan must state the parties' views and proposals on:

(A) what changes should be made in the timing, form, or requirement for disclosures under Rule 26(a), including a statement of when initial disclosures were made or will be made;

(B) the subjects on which discovery may be needed, when discovery should be completed, and whether discovery should be conducted in phases or be limited to or focused on particular issues;

(C) any issues about disclosure or discovery of electronically stored information, including the form or forms in which it should be produced;

(D) any issues about claims of privilege or of protection as trial-preparation materials, including—if the parties agree on a procedure to assert these claims after production—whether to ask the court to include their agreement in an order;

(E) what changes should be made in the limitations on discovery imposed under these rules or by local rule, and what other limitations should be imposed; and

(F) any other orders that the court should issue under Rule 26(c) or under Rule 16(b) and (c).

(4) Expedited Schedule.

If necessary to comply with its expedited schedule for Rule 16(b) conferences, a court may by local rule:

(A) require the parties' conference to occur less than 21 days before the scheduling conference is held or a scheduling order is due under Rule 16(b); and

(B) require the written report outlining the discovery plan to be filed less than 14 days after the parties' conference, or excuse the parties from submitting a written report and permit them to report orally on their discovery plan at the Rule 16(b) conference.

(g) Signing Disclosures and Discovery Requests, Responses, and Objections.

(1) Signature Required; Effect of Signature.

Every disclosure under Rule 26(a)(1) or (a)(3) and every discovery request, response, or objection must be signed by at least one attorney of record in the attorney's own name—or by the party personally, if unrepresented—and must state the signer's address, e-mail address, and telephone number. By signing, an attorney or party certifies that to the best of the person's knowledge, information, and belief formed after a reasonable inquiry:

(A) with respect to a disclosure, it is complete and correct as of the time it is made; and

(B) with respect to a discovery request, response, or objection, it is:

(i) consistent with these rules and warranted by existing law or by a nonfrivolous argument for extending, modifying, or reversing existing law, or for establishing new law;

(ii) not interposed for any improper purpose, such as to harass, cause unnecessary delay, or needlessly increase the cost of litigation; and

(iii) neither unreasonable nor unduly burdensome or expensive, considering the needs of the case, prior discovery in the case, the amount in controversy, and the importance of the issues at stake in the action.

(2) Failure to Sign.

Other parties have no duty to act on an unsigned disclosure, request, response, or objection until it is signed, and the court must strike it unless a signature is promptly supplied after the omission is called to the attorney's or party's attention.

(3) Sanction for Improper Certification.

If a certification violates this rule without substantial justification, the court, on motion or on its own, must impose an appropriate sanction on the signer, the party on whose behalf the signer was acting, or both. The sanction may include an order to pay the reasonable expenses, including attorney's fees, caused by the violation.

Chapter 18

Equal Credit Opportunity Act

Denying credit because the applicant was a woman or a member of a minority was so prevalent in the 1960s and 1970s that a major segment of the population almost accepted this as a fact of life. The Equal Credit Opportunity Act (ECOA), a part of the Consumer Credit Protection Act, states that if credit is to be extended, the lending institution must consider only the creditworthiness of the applicant and must confine its entire evaluation to whether the applicant has the ability to repay the money. The creditor will not be allowed to evaluate other qualities, characteristics, status, or nature of the particular applicant.

The purpose of the ECOA is to promote the availability of credit to all creditworthy applicants without regard to race, color, religion, national origin, sex, marital status, or age. In addition, an applicant should not be denied credit because income is derived from a public assistance program or due to the fact that the applicant has in good faith exercised any right under the Consumer Credit Protection Act (making a claim or starting a suit against the creditor for a violation of a law). Regulation B prohibits creditor practices which discriminate on the basis of any of these factors.

Regulation B and the commentary to Regulation B are textbook explanations of exactly what the credit grantor is prohibited from considering and evaluating when granting credit. This chapter is designed to provide an overview of the Regulation to apprise the credit grantor of the areas to be considered before extending credit. A thorough reading of both the Regulation and the commentary is recommended.

The Omnibus Consolidated Appropriation Act of 1997 urges lenders to self-correct any violations of the ECOA by granting a privilege to the lender with regard to any programs that involve self-testing to determine whether their compliance programs are effective. If the creditor meets the conditions set forth in these amendments, any reports or results of the self-testing are privileged and may not be obtained or used by any applicant, department, or agency in any proceeding or civil action in which violations of the ECOA are alleged. A copy of the Act and Regulation B, together with the Staff Commentary, is presented in an Appendix to this chapter.

The regulations provide a full set of forms for credit applications including open-end unsecured credit, closed-end unsecured/secured credit, community property, and residential and mortgage loans. The Appendix to Regulation B also provides notification forms and other examples.

RACE, COLOR, RELIGION, AND NATIONAL ORIGIN

A creditor shall not inquire about the race, color, religion, or national origin of an applicant or of any other person in connection with a credit transaction.[1] No questions of this nature may be included in any credit application. A creditor may inquire about the permanent residence or the immigration status of the applicant, and appropriate inquiries may appear on the credit application, since residence and status are germane to a credit decision. Regulation B expressly states that a creditor may request any information in connection with an application for credit except the information prohibited by this law.[2]

Once the product has been offered in a particular area, credit cannot be refused because of race, color, religion, age, sex, marital status, or national origin. The only basis for refusing to extend credit is that the individual does not satisfy credit standards.

The Bank of America found that making the final decision as to whether an applicant is creditworthy and setting a rate for automobile loans as well as setting a maximum markup that a dealer may apply to a customer loan was too much control over the dealer. If the dealer was causing African-Americans to pay a higher finance charge than Caucasian customers in violation of the ECOA, the Bank of America may be liable.[3]

Creditors also cannot deny credit to businesses because of race, color, religion, national origin, sex, marital status or age of the business owners. Credit cannot be denied because the customers of the business are of a certain religion, race, or sex.

---

[1]Sec. 202.1.

[2]Sec. 202.5(b).

[3]*Osborne v. The Bank of America*, 234 F. Supp. 2d 804 (N.D. Tenn. 2002).

SEX

No inquiry as to the sex of an applicant is allowed, although the applicant may designate a title on the application (Ms., Mrs., Mr., and Miss) so long as the form discloses that the designation of title is optional. The application shall use terms that are neutral as to sex.

CHILDBEARING

A creditor may not inquire about birth control practices, intentions concerning the bearing of children, or the ability to bear children. An inquiry may be made concerning the number and ages of applicant's dependents or dependent-related financial obligations, providing the information is requested without regard to sex, marital status, or other prohibited reasons.[4]

AGE AND PUBLIC ASSISTANCE

An applicant's age, unless a minor, or whether applicant is receiving public assistance, shall not be considered except as permitted by the Act. Age may be a variable in an empirically derived (through experience and observation), demonstrably and statistically sound credit scoring system. Age and public assistance may be considered for the purpose of determining a pertinent element of creditworthiness in a judgmental system (*see* subsequent sections of this chapter). The age of an elderly person may be used to favor an elderly applicant in extending credit[5] but the age of an elderly person may not be assigned a negative value in the scoring system.

A creditor may inquire of a consumer whether he/she is over 18 years of age to establish whether he/she has the legal ability to enter into a contract. The creditor also may ask if someone is over the age of 62 to determine retirement age as their income may be reduced or for the purpose of favoring applicants over 62.

CREDIT APPLICATION

The creditor may request any information in connection with an application for credit providing the request is not prohibited under the ECOA or another law. The Act sets forth specific rules as to accepting applications and separate rules for evaluating applications.

---

[4]Sec. 202.6(b)(3).
[5]Sec. 202.6(b)(2).

The Act lists other criteria for considering items in an application for credit:

A. The likelihood that any group will bear or rear children and thus will receive diminished or interrupted income in the future may not be considered.
B. A lack of a telephone listing may not be considered, but having a telephone listing may be considered.
C. Income from a part-time employment annuity or a pension may be considered as well as the continuation of that income.
D. Alimony and child support may be considered to the extent the income is consistently received.
E. Immigration status and a permanent residency may be considered.
F. The creditor may not ask applicants if they are widowed or divorced unless it is a material issue pertinent to the application.
G. The creditor cannot ask about marital status unless their prospective borrower lives in a community property state such as Arizona, California, Idaho, Louisiana, Nevada, New Mexico, Texas, and Washington.

WHAT IS DISCRIMINATION?

In 1973, the Supreme Court stated a complainant in a discrimination case must carry the initial burden under the statute of establishing a *prima facie* case of racial discrimination. They stated that this may be done by showing:

1. that he belongs to a racial minority.
2. that he applied and was qualified for a job for which the employer was seeking applicants.
3. that despite his qualifications, he was rejected.
4. that, after his rejection, the position remained open and the employer continued to seek applicants from persons of complainant's qualifications.

After the complainant offers evidence of these criteria, the employer must offer a legitimate nondiscriminating ground for rejection. Unfortunately, not all the circuits follow this doctrine.[6]

---

[6]*McDonnell Douglas Corp. v. Green*, 411 U.S. 792 (1973).

The courts have limited the Supreme Court decision to the fact situation that was presented to the Supreme Court. The Seventh Circuit has stated that the plaintiff can establish a *prima facie* case either by presenting evidence of having been actually discriminated against on some forbidden ground such as race or by satisfying the *McDonnell Douglas* standard.[7] Under that standard, in a typical case of employment discrimination involving the denial of a promotion to a black employee, the plaintiff would have to show only that he was qualified for the promotion and that a white person was promoted. The burden of proof would move to the employer to come forth with a noninvidious reason why the white person rather than the black person received the promotion. The court stated that the *McDonnell Douglas* standard originated and evolved in cases involving racial discrimination in employment and has been extended to all sorts of other discrimination, not even limited to the employment setting. The case discussed in length the *McDonnell Douglas* standard and it's application by other courts.

SPOUSE

Information concerning a spouse or a former spouse may be requested if:

1. the spouse is permitted to use the account;
2. the spouse is liable on the account;
3. the creditor is relying on the income of the spouse as a basis of repayment, including alimony or child support.

In all other instances, the creditor cannot request information on the application concerning a spouse. At the same time, a creditor cannot inquire whether income is derived from alimony or child support unless the creditor is relying on such income as a basis for repayment of the loan.

SPOUSE—GUARANTOR. *A creditor shall not require the signature of a spouse on any credit instrument if the applicant qualifies under the creditor's standards of creditworthiness for the amount and terms of the credit requested.* Requesting the spouse to sign the application merely because "there is a spouse" may be a violation of the ECOA (Regulation B).[8] If the creditor relies entirely upon the creditworthiness of the applicant and still seeks the spouse's signature, the creditor may fear that the applicant will transfer some of the assets to the spouse and file bankruptcy or leave for parts

[7] *Latimore v. Citibank Federal Savings Bank*, 151 F.3d 712 (7th Cir. 1998).
[8] Sec. 202.7(d).

unknown. The Act prohibits the creditor from requiring the spouse to guarantee a loan under these circumstances.

The law protects the creditor if transfers are made to defraud creditors for the purpose of not repaying the loan. If the borrower does not meet the credit requirements, the creditor can seek an additional guarantor, but may not specify that the spouse be the guarantor. An exception to the rule is where secured credit is offered and the wife's signature is needed to create a valid lien, such as property held by joint tenancy or in community property states.

Spouse—Recoupment. The expiration of the two-year statute of limitations calculated from the execution of said guarantee may bar the institution of such an independent action. No such prohibition exists to the utilization of such grounds as a defense by the spouse. The court stated that whereas the statute of limitations may apply to the institution of the suit against the lender to seek damages or declare the guarantee void, the statute of limitations is of no effect when the spouse uses it as a defense to an action to collect the debt.[9] This is the same concept that applies to situations where we have a usurious contract. The party may declare that the contract is usurious and be subject to the statute of limitations, but where the creditor seeks to collect the money due under the contract, the statute of limitations is not a bar to the use of the defense.

Most spouses do not assert this violation until they are sued by the bank on their guarantee. Some states take the position that the spouse cannot assert the defense of a violation of the ECOA in a civil commercial suit based on the loan or the guarantee. The ECOA sets forth a specific remedy for violation of the Act. A federal civil action may be maintained against the creditor for damages, punitive damages not to exceed $10,000 and attorneys' fees with a two-year statute of limitations. Under these provisions, many courts deny the right of the spouse to assert any claim in a civil suit and state that the spouse is confined to the remedies available under the ECOA to a suit in the federal courts.

The ECOA also provides that a court of competent jurisdiction may issue "equitable and declaratory relief as necessary" to enforce the requirement of the Act. Under this theory, many courts take the position that a spouse may assert a violation as a counterclaim for recoupment in a civil suit, or as an affirmative defense to a collection case, even after the running of the two-year statute of limitations. The courts seem to reason that the statute of limitations is not applicable until such time as the lender decides to institute suit based on the spouse's guarantee—at least in those states that recognize this theory (Iowa, Kansas, New Jersey, Pennsylvania, and Virginia).

---

[9] *Silverman v. Eastrich Multiple Investor Fund, L.P.*, 51 F.3d 28 (3d Cir. 1995).

While these courts may allow the spouse to assert a claim for recoupment or a counterclaim in a civil action by the lender, no authority exists in any of the cases or in any of the statutory language that a violation of the ECOA renders any instrument or contract void because of said violation. The defense is unique and peculiar to the spouse and may be asserted only within the framework of the ECOA. Recoupment tolls the statute of limitations providing the recoupment limits itself to the same transaction upon which the lender is instituting suit. If the counterclaim arises from a different transaction or a transaction that did not deal with the actual basis of the suit of the lender, some courts feel the statute of limitations is tolled. In such cases creditors may be faced with counterclaims based on these violations that occurred with regard to lending transactions that took place years before the one upon which the lending institution is instituting suit.[10]

A case in the Connecticut Superior Court did not allow the invalidation of the entire obligation (consisting of promissory notes) based upon an ECOA violation against some of the individual defendants. The court allowed the creditor to proceed against the husbands. The wives could assert a counterclaim against the creditors, but the court did not allow the violation to stand as a special defense for the husbands who are not the subject of the discrimination.[11]

Authorities are split on the issue of whether a counterclaim for recoupment can be asserted by a spouse guarantee after the statute of limitations has expired. Most of the states support the doctrine of recoupment when it is a matter of defense even after the statute of limitations has run. If the debtor is seeking damages or attorneys' fees, the two-year statute of limitations would apply.

It would be inconsistent with the provisions in the federal statute to allow a violator to enforce its guarantee claim simply because the victim of the violation had not brought an action within the two-year period. The guarantee would not exist in the absence of the violation.[12]

One case was faced with a continuing absolute and unconditional guarantee of payment as well as the guarantors waiving the right to interpose any defense, set-off or counterclaim of any nature or description. A New York appellate court went on to state that the doctrine that a waiver of the right to assert a set-off or counterclaim is not against public policy and will be enforced in the absence of fraud or negligence in the disposition of collateral. The court went on to state "since the defendant's clearly and unequivocably waived their right to interpose any counterclaim in this action, the counterclaim should have been dismissed as a matter of law."[13]

---

[10]*Hammons v. Ehney*, 924 S.W.2d 843 (Mo. 1996).

[11]*Union Trust v. Sirois*, No. CV94-038058S, 1997 WL 600392 (Conn. Super. Ct. Sept. 19, 1997).

[12]*Boone Nat'l S&L Ass'n v. Crouch*, 47 S.W.3d 371 (Mo. 2001).

[13]*Fleet v. Perri Mechanical Company*, 244 A.D.2d 523 (N.Y. App. Div. 2d Dep't 1997).

JOINT APPLICANTS

A joint applicant is someone who applies contemporaneously with the applicant for shared or joint credit and not someone whose signature is required by the creditor as a condition for granting the credit requested. In a case, a wife was the co-owner of the corporation and the financial application detailed the joint ownership of the assets. While the wife did not have a major role in the day-to-day operation of the corporation or any of its subsidiaries, she clearly had an equal stake with her husband in the assets that secured the borrowing. The court held that she was a bona fide joint applicant for the loans and that the ECOA does not protect her from liability upon plaintiff's claim.

The emphasis of the court was on her ownership of the business. The court distinguished other cases where the spouses who were required to sign the notes were not connected to the underlying transactions for which the loans were sought, and played no ownership interest in the business and no role in the negotiations of the loans. In most of the other cases the wives were neither officers nor shareholders in the business and had no material participation in its activities. In this particular case, the husband and wife used the proceeds of the loan to jointly purchase another business and the bank relied on the documents setting forth jointly owned properties in granting the loans.[14]

ADVERSE ACTION

Under Regulation B, a creditor must notify an applicant of any negative action taken with regard to an application for credit[15] within:

1. thirty days after receiving a completed application concerning the creditor's approval of the credit application, the creditor must give notice of or counter offer to the request for credit by the applicant, or adverse action on the credit application.
2. thirty days after taking adverse action on an incomplete application.
3. thirty days after taking adverse action on an existing account.
4. ninety days after notifying the applicant of a counteroffer if the applicant does not expressly accept or use the credit offered.

A notification of adverse action shall be in writing and shall contain a statement of the reasons for the adverse action or of applicant's right to request the reason for the action taken.

---

[14] *Midlantic National Bank v. Hansen*, 48 F.3d 693 (3d Cir. 1995), *cert. dismissed*, 116 S. Ct. 32, 132 L. Ed. 2d 914 (1995).

[15] Sec. 202.9.

Where the lender denied the application but offered the applicant an alternative loan that thereafter was accepted by the debtor, the court concluded that the written notice requirement was not necessary because the debtor had accepted the alternative loan application.[16]

Statements of the adverse action based on the creditor's internal standards or policies, or the fact that the applicant failed to achieve the qualifying score on the creditor's credit scoring system, are insufficient. The notice requirement serves as an adjunct to the anti-discrimination purpose of the legislation. If creditors know they must explain their decision, they will be discouraged from discriminatory practices.

The written notice requirement is triggered only in the event a creditor takes adverse action. No notice is required if any other type of action is taken. Adverse action is the denial or revocation of credit or a change in the terms or refusal to grant credit upon the terms requested. The definition is limited in that it excludes a denial of credit coupled with a counteroffer that thereafter is accepted.

Credit & Collection Tip: *Any denial of credit coupled with a counteroffer is excluded from the written notice requirement when and only when the applicant accepts the counteroffer.*[17]

FURNISHING OF CREDIT INFORMATION

A creditor who furnishes credit information to a credit reporting agency shall designate the participation of both spouses if the applicant's spouse is permitted to use or is contractually liable on the account. With regard to any existing account, the creditor shall designate any such participation 90 days after receiving a written request. If a creditor reports to a credit reporting agency, the participation of both spouses shall be reported where both spouses are participating in the loan. If responding to an inquiry, the creditor must furnish the information to reflect the participation of both spouses.

RETENTION OF RECORDS

The ECOA specifically allows a creditor to retain in its files information that is received from consumer reporting agencies, an applicant, or others without the specific request of the creditor. The creditor must retain

[16]*Diaz v. Virginia Housing Development Authority*, 117 F. Supp. 2d 500 (E.D. Va. 2000).
[17]*See Diaz v. Virginia Housing Development Authority*, 117 F. Supp. 2d 500 (E.D. Va. 2000).

for 25 months applications received and all other information used in evaluating the application that is not returned to the applicant.[18]

ENFORCEMENT AND PENALTIES

The ECOA allows the applicant to sue for civil damages as well as punitive damages, but limits punitive damages to $10,000 in an individual action and the lesser of $500,000 or 1 percent of the creditor's net worth, in a class action.[19]

NEW RULES

Owing to space constraints, we have omitted the final rule promulgated by the Federal Trade Commission for the ECOA, 12 CFR Part 202. A copy can be obtained from the Federal Trade Commission.

---

[18]Sec. 202.12.
[19]Sec. 202.14.

CHAPTER 18
APPENDIX I

PART 202—EQUAL CREDIT OPPORTUNITY ACT (REGULATION B)

Title 12: Banks and Banking

Section **Contents**

Authority: 15 U.S.C. 1691–1691f.

Source: 68 FR 13161, March 18, 2003, unless otherwise noted.

§ 202.1 Authority, scope and purpose.

(a) *Authority and scope.* This regulation is issued by the Board of Governors of the Federal Reserve System pursuant to title VII (Equal Credit Opportunity Act) of the Consumer Credit Protection Act, as amended (15 U.S.C. 1601 *et seq.*). Except as otherwise provided herein, this regulation applies to all persons who are creditors, as defined in § 202.2(1). Information collection requirements contained in this regulation have been approved by the Office of Management and Budget under the provisions of 44 U.S.C. 3501 *et seq.* and have been assigned OMB No. 7100-0201.

(b) *Purpose.* The purpose of this regulation is to promote the availability of credit to all creditworthy applicants without regard to race, color, religion, national origin, sex, marital status, or age (provided the applicant has the capacity to contract); to the fact that all or part of the applicant's income derives from a public assistance program; or to the fact that the applicant has in good faith exercised any right under the Consumer Credit Protection Act. The regulation prohibits creditor practices that discriminate on the basis of any of these factors. The regulation also requires creditors to notify applicants of action taken on their applications; to report credit history in the names of both spouses on an account; to retain records of credit applications; to collect information about the applicant's race and other personal characteristics in applications for certain dwelling-related loans; and to provide applicants with copies of appraisal reports used in connection with credit transactions.

§ 202.2 Definitions.

For the purposes of this regulation, unless the context indicates otherwise, the following definitions apply.

(a) *Account* means an extension of credit. When employed in relation to an account, the word use refers only to open-end credit.

(b) *Act* means the Equal Credit Opportunity Act (title VII of the Consumer Credit Protection Act).

(c) *Adverse action.* (1) The term means:

(i) A refusal to grant credit in substantially the amount or on substantially the terms requested in an application unless the creditor makes a counteroffer (to grant credit in a different amount or on other terms) and the applicant uses or expressly accepts the credit offered;

(ii) A termination of an account or an unfavorable change in the terms of an account that does not affect all or substantially all of a class of the creditor's accounts; or

(iii) A refusal to increase the amount of credit available to an applicant who has made an application for an increase.

(2) The term does not include:

(i) A change in the terms of an account expressly agreed to by an applicant.

(ii) Any action or forbearance relating to an account taken in connection with inactivity, default, or delinquency as to that account;

(iii) A refusal or failure to authorize an account transaction at point of sale or loan, except when the refusal is a termination or an unfavorable change in the terms of an account that does not affect all or substantially all of a class of the creditor's accounts, or when the refusal is a denial of an application for an increase in the amount of credit available under the account;

(iv) A refusal to extend credit because applicable law prohibits the creditor from extending the credit requested; or

(v) A refusal to extend credit because the creditor does not offer the type of credit or credit plan requested.

(3) An action that falls within the definition of both paragraphs (c)(1) and (c) of this section is governed by paragraph (c) of this section.

(d) *Age* refers only to the age of natural persons and means the number of fully elapsed years from the date of an applicant's birth.

(e) *Applicant* means any person who requests or who has received an extension of credit from a creditor, and includes any person who is or may become contractually liable regarding an extension of credit. For purposes of § 202.7(d), the term includes guarantors, sureties, endorsers, and similar parties.

(f) *Application* means an oral or written request for an extension of credit that is made in accordance with procedures used by a creditor for the type of credit requested. The term application does not include the use of an account or line of credit to obtain an amount of credit that is within a previously established credit limit. A *completed application* means an application in connection with which a creditor has received all the information that the creditor regularly obtains and considers in evaluating applications for the amount and type of credit requested (including, but not limited to, credit reports, any additional information requested from the applicant, and any approvals or reports by governmental agencies or other persons that are necessary to guarantee, insure, or provide security for the credit or collateral). The creditor shall exercise reasonable diligence in obtaining such information.

(g) *Business credit* refers to extensions of credit primarily for business or commercial (including agricultural) purposes, but excluding extensions of credit of the types described in § 202.3(a)–(d).

(h) *Consumer credit* means credit extended to a natural person primarily for personal, family, or household purposes.

(i) *Contractually liable* means expressly obligated to repay all debts arising on an account by reason of an agreement to that effect.

(j) *Credit* means the right granted by a creditor to an applicant to defer payment of a debt, incur debt and defer its payment, or purchase property or services and defer payment therefor.

(k) *Credit card* means any card, plate, coupon book, or other single credit device that may be used from time to time to obtain money, property, or services on credit.

(l) *Creditor* means a person who, in the ordinary course of business, regularly participates in a credit decision, including setting the terms of the credit. The term creditor includes a creditor's assignee, transferee, or subrogee who so participates. For purposes of § 202.4(a) and (b), the term creditor also includes a person who, in the ordinary course of business, regularly refers applicants or prospective applicants to creditors, or selects or offers to select creditors to whom requests for credit may be made. A person is not a creditor regarding any violation of the Act or this regulation committed by another creditor unless the person knew or had reasonable notice of the act, policy, or practice that constituted the violation before becoming involved in the credit transaction. The term does not include a person whose only participation in a credit transaction involves honoring a credit card.

(m) *Credit transaction* means every aspect of an applicant's dealings with a creditor regarding an application for credit or an existing extension of credit (including, but not limited to, information requirements; investigation procedures; standards of creditworthiness; terms of credit; furnishing of credit information; revocation, alteration, or termination of credit; and collection procedures).

(n) *Discriminate against an applicant* means to treat an applicant less favorably than other applicants.

(o) *Elderly* means age 62 or older.

(p) *Empirically derived and other credit scoring systems*—(1) *A credit scoring system* is a system that evaluates an applicant's creditworthiness mechanically, based on key attributes of the applicant and aspects of the transaction, and that determines, alone or in conjunction with an evaluation of additional information about the applicant, whether an applicant is deemed creditworthy. To qualify as an *empirically derived, demonstrably and statistically sound, credit scoring system*, the system must be:

(i) Based on data that are derived from an empirical comparison of sample groups or the population of creditworthy and noncreditworthy applicants who applied for credit within a reasonable preceding period of time;

(ii) Developed for the purpose of evaluating the creditworthiness of applicants with respect to the legitimate business interests of the creditor utilizing the system (including, but not limited to, minimizing bad debt losses and operating expenses in accordance with the creditor's business judgment);

(iii) Developed and validated using accepted statistical principles and methodology; and

(iv) Periodically revalidated by the use of appropriate statistical principles and methodology and adjusted as necessary to maintain predictive ability.

A creditor may use an empirically derived, demonstrably and statistically sound, credit scoring system obtained from another person or may obtain credit experience from which to develop such a system. Any such system must satisfy the criteria set forth in paragraph (p)(1)(i) through (iv) of this section; if the creditor is unable during the development process to validate the system based on its own credit experience in accordance with paragraph (p)(1) of this section, the system must be validated when sufficient credit experience becomes available. A system that fails this validity test is no longer an empirically derived, demonstrably and statistically sound, credit scoring system for that creditor.

(q) *Extend credit* and *extension of credit* mean the granting of credit in any form (including, but not limited to, credit granted in addition to any existing credit or credit limit; credit granted pursuant to an open-end credit plan; the refinancing or other renewal of credit, including the issuance of a new credit card in place of an expiring credit card or in substitution for an existing credit card; the consolidation of two or more obligations; or the continuance of existing credit without any special effort to collect at or after maturity).

(r) *Good faith* means honesty in fact in the conduct or transaction.

(s) *Inadvertent error* means a mechanical, electronic, or clerical error that a creditor demonstrates was not intentional and occurred notwithstanding the maintenance of procedures reasonably adapted to avoid such errors.

(t) *Judgmental system of evaluating applicants* means any system for evaluating the creditworthiness of an applicant other than an empirically derived, demonstrably and statistically sound, credit scoring system.

(u) *Marital status* means the state of being unmarried, married, or separated, as defined by applicable state law. The term "unmarried" includes persons who are single, divorced, or widowed.

(v) *Negative factor or value,* in relation to the age of elderly applicants, means utilizing a factor, value, or weight that is less favorable regarding elderly applicants than the creditor's experience warrants or is less favorable than the factor, value, or weight assigned to the class of applicants that are not classified as elderly and are most favored by a creditor on the basis of age.

(w) *Open-end credit* means credit extended under a plan in which a creditor may permit an applicant to make purchases or obtain loans from time to time directly from the creditor or indirectly by use of a credit card, check, or other device.

(x) *Person* means a natural person, corporation, government or governmental subdivision or agency, trust, estate, partnership, cooperative, or association.

(y) *Pertinent element of creditworthiness*, in relation to a judgmental system of evaluating applicants, means any information about applicants that a creditor obtains and considers and that has a demonstrable relationship to a determination of creditworthiness.

(z) *Prohibited basis* means race, color, religion, national origin, sex, marital status, or age (provided that the applicant has the capacity to enter into a binding contract); the fact that all or part of the applicant's income derives from any public assistance program; or the fact that the applicant has in good faith exercised any right under the Consumer Credit Protection Act or any state law upon which an exemption has been granted by the Board.

(aa) *State* means any state, the District of Columbia, the Commonwealth of Puerto Rico, or any territory or possession of the United States.

§ 202.3 Limited exceptions for certain classes of transactions.

(a) *Public utilities credit*—(1) *Definition.* Public utilities credit refers to extensions of credit that involve public utility services provided through pipe, wire, or other connected facilities, or radio or similar transmission (including extensions of such facilities), if the charges for service, delayed payment, and any discount for prompt payment are filed with or regulated by a government unit.

(2) *Exceptions.* The following provisions of this regulation do not apply to public utilities credit:

(i) Section 202.5(d)(1) concerning information about marital status; and

(ii) Section 202.12(b) relating to record retention.

(b) *Securities credit*—(1) *Definition.* Securities credit refers to extensions of credit subject to regulation under section 7 of the Securities Exchange Act of 1934 or extensions of credit by a broker or dealer subject to regulation as a broker or dealer under the Securities Exchange Act of 1934.

(2) *Exceptions.* The following provisions of this regulation do not apply to securities credit:

(i) Section 202.5(b) concerning information about the sex of an applicant;

(ii) Section 202.5(c) concerning information about a spouse or former spouse;

(iii) Section 202.5(d)(1) concerning information about marital status;

(iv) Section 202.7(b) relating to designation of name to the extent necessary to comply with rules regarding an account in which a broker or dealer has an interest, or rules regarding the aggregation of accounts of spouses to determine controlling interests, beneficial interests, beneficial ownership, or purchase limitations and restrictions;

(v) Section 202.7(c) relating to action concerning open-end accounts, to the extent the action taken is on the basis of a change of name or marital status;

(vi) Section 202.7(d) relating to the signature of a spouse or other person;

(vii) Section 202.10 relating to furnishing of credit information; and

(viii) Section 202.12(b) relating to record retention.

(c) *Incidental credit*—(1) *Definition.* Incidental credit refers to extensions of consumer credit other than the types described in paragraphs (a) and (b) of this section:

(i) That are not made pursuant to the terms of a credit card account;

(ii) That are not subject to a finance charge (as defined in Regulation Z, 12 CFR 226.4); and

(iii) That are not payable by agreement in more than four installments.

(2) *Exceptions.* The following provisions of this regulation do not apply to incidental credit:

(i) Section 202.5(b) concerning information about the sex of an applicant, but only to the extent necessary for medical records or similar purposes;

(ii) Section 202.5(c) concerning information about a spouse or former spouse;

(iii) Section 202.5(d)(1) concerning information about marital status;

(iv) Section 202.5(d) concerning information about income derived from alimony, child support, or separate maintenance payments;

(v) Section 202.7(d) relating to the signature of a spouse or other person;

(vi) Section 202.9 relating to notifications;

(vii) Section 202.10 relating to furnishing of credit information; and

(viii) Section 202.12(b) relating to record retention.

(d) *Government credit*—(1) *Definition.* Government credit refers to extensions of credit made to governments or governmental subdivisions, agencies, or instrumentalities.

(2) *Applicability of regulation.* Except for § 202.4(a), the general rule against discrimination on a prohibited basis, the requirements of this regulation do not apply to government credit.

§ 202.4 General rules.

(a) *Discrimination.* A creditor shall not discriminate against an applicant on a prohibited basis regarding any aspect of a credit transaction.

(b) *Discouragement.* A creditor shall not make any oral or written statement, in advertising or otherwise, to applicants or prospective applicants that would discourage on a prohibited basis a reasonable person from making or pursuing an application.

(c) *Written applications.* A creditor shall take written applications for the dwelling-related types of credit covered by § 202.13(a).

(d) *Form of disclosures.* A creditor that provides in writing any disclosures or information required by this regulation must provide the disclosures in a clear and conspicuous manner and, except for the disclosures required by § § 202.5 and 202.13, in a form the applicant may retain.

(e) *Foreign-language disclosures.* Disclosures may be made in languages other than English, provided they are available in English upon request.

§ 202.5 Rules concerning requests for information.

(a) *General rules*—(1) *Requests for information.* Except as provided in paragraphs (b) through (d) of this section, a creditor may request any information in connection with a credit transaction.

(2) *Required collection of information.* Notwithstanding paragraphs (b) through (d) of this section, a creditor shall request information for monitoring purposes as required by § 202.13 for credit secured by the applicant's dwelling. In addition, a creditor may obtain information required by a regulation, order, or agreement issued by, or entered into with, a court or an enforcement agency (including the Attorney General of the United States or a similar state official) to monitor or enforce compliance with the Act, this regulation, or other federal or state statutes or regulations.

(3) *Special-purpose credit.* A creditor may obtain information that is otherwise restricted to determine eligibility for a special purpose credit program, as provided in § 202.8(b), (c), and (d).

(b) *Limitation on information about race, color, religion, national origin, or sex.* A creditor shall not inquire about the race, color, religion, national origin, or sex of an applicant or any other person in connection with a credit transaction, except as provided in paragraphs (b)(1) and (b)(2) of this section.

(1) *Self-test.* A creditor may inquire about the race, color, religion, national origin, or sex of an applicant or any other person in connection with a credit transaction for the purpose of conducting a self-test that meets the requirements of § 202.15. A creditor that makes such an inquiry shall disclose orally or in writing, at the time the information is requested, that:

(i) The applicant will not be required to provide the information;

(ii) The creditor is requesting the information to monitor its compliance with the federal Equal Credit Opportunity Act;

(iii) Federal law prohibits the creditor from discriminating on the basis of this information, or on the basis of an applicant's decision not to furnish the information; and

(iv) If applicable, certain information will be collected based on visual observation or surname if not provided by the applicant or other person.

(2) *Sex.* An applicant may be requested to designate a title on an application form (such as Ms., Miss, Mr., or Mrs.) if the form discloses that the designation of a title is optional. An application form shall otherwise use only terms that are neutral as to sex.

(c) *Information about a spouse or former spouse*—(1) *General rule.* Except as permitted in this paragraph, a creditor may not request any information concerning the spouse or former spouse of an applicant.

(2) *Permissible inquiries.* A creditor may request any information concerning an applicant's spouse (or former spouse under paragraph (c)(2)(v) of this section) that may be requested about the applicant if:

(i) The spouse will be permitted to use the account;

(ii) The spouse will be contractually liable on the account;

(iii) The applicant is relying on the spouse's income as a basis for repayment of the credit requested;

(iv) The applicant resides in a community property state or is relying on property located in such a state as a basis for repayment of the credit requested; or

(v) The applicant is relying on alimony, child support, or separate maintenance payments from a spouse or former spouse as a basis for repayment of the credit requested.

(3) *Other accounts of the applicant.* A creditor may request that an applicant list any account on which the applicant is contractually liable and to provide the name and address of the person in whose name the account is held. A creditor may also ask an applicant to list the names in which the applicant has previously received credit.

(d) *Other limitations on information requests*—(1) *Marital status.* If an applicant applies for individual unsecured credit, a creditor shall not inquire about the applicant's marital status unless the applicant resides in a community property state or is relying on property located in such a state as a basis for repayment of the credit requested. If an application is for other than individual unsecured credit, a creditor may inquire about the applicant's marital status, but shall use only the terms *married, unmarried,* and *separated.* A creditor may explain that the category *unmarried* includes single, divorced, and widowed persons.

(2) *Disclosure about income from alimony, child support, or separate maintenance.* A creditor shall not inquire whether income stated in an application is derived from alimony, child support, or separate maintenance payments unless the creditor discloses to the applicant that such income need not be revealed if the applicant does not want the creditor to consider it in determining the applicant's creditworthiness.

(3) *Childbearing, childrearing.* A creditor shall not inquire about birth control practices, intentions concerning the bearing or rearing of children, or capability to bear children. A creditor may inquire about the number and ages of an applicant's dependents or about dependent-related financial obligations or expenditures, provided such information is requested without regard to sex, marital status, or any other prohibited basis.

(e) *Permanent residency and immigration status.* A creditor may inquire about the permanent residency and immigration status of an applicant or any other person in connection with a credit transaction.

§ 202.6 Rules concerning evaluation of applications.

(a) *General rule concerning use of information.* Except as otherwise provided in the Act and this regulation, a creditor may consider any information obtained, so long as the information is not used to discriminate against an applicant on a prohibited basis.[20]

(b) *Specific rules concerning use of information*—(1) Except as provided in the Act and this regulation, a creditor shall not take a prohibited basis into account in any system of evaluating the creditworthiness of applicants.

---

[20]The legislative history of the Act indicates that the Congress intended an "effects test" concept, as outlined in the employment field by the Supreme Court in the cases of *Griggs* v. *Duke Power Co.*, 401 U.S. 424 (1971), and *Albemarle Paper Co.* v. *Moody*, 422 U.S. 405 (1975), to be applicable to a creditor's determination of creditworthiness.

(2) *Age, receipt of public assistance.* (i) Except as permitted in this paragraph, a creditor shall not take into account an applicant's age (provided that the applicant has the capacity to enter into a binding contract) or whether an applicant's income derives from any public assistance program.

(ii) In an empirically derived, demonstrably and statistically sound, credit scoring system, a creditor may use an applicant's age as a predictive variable, provided that the age of an elderly applicant is not assigned a negative factor or value.

(iii) In a judgmental system of evaluating creditworthiness, a creditor may consider an applicant's age or whether an applicant's income derives from any public assistance program only for the purpose of determining a pertinent element of creditworthiness.

(iv) In any system of evaluating creditworthiness, a creditor may consider the age of an elderly applicant when such age is used to favor the elderly applicant in extending credit.

(3) *Childbearing, childrearing.* In evaluating creditworthiness, a creditor shall not make assumptions or use aggregate statistics relating to the likelihood that any category of persons will bear or rear children or will, for that reason, receive diminished or interrupted income in the future.

(4) *Telephone listing.* A creditor shall not take into account whether there is a telephone listing in the name of an applicant for consumer credit but may take into account whether there is a telephone in the applicant's residence.

(5) *Income.* A creditor shall not discount or exclude from consideration the income of an applicant or the spouse of an applicant because of a prohibited basis or because the income is derived from part-time employment or is an annuity, pension, or other retirement benefit; a creditor may consider the amount and probable continuance of any income in evaluating an applicant's creditworthiness. When an applicant relies on alimony, child support, or separate maintenance payments in applying for credit, the creditor shall consider such payments as income to the extent that they are likely to be consistently made.

(6) *Credit history.* To the extent that a creditor considers credit history in evaluating the creditworthiness of similarly qualified applicants for a similar type and amount of credit, in evaluating an applicant's creditworthiness a creditor shall consider:

(i) The credit history, when available, of accounts designated as accounts that the applicant and the applicant's spouse are permitted to use or for which both are contractually liable;

(ii) On the applicant's request, any information the applicant may present that tends to indicate the credit history being considered by the creditor does not accurately reflect the applicant's creditworthiness; and

(iii) On the applicant's request, the credit history, when available, of any account reported in the name of the applicant's spouse or former spouse that the applicant can demonstrate accurately reflects the applicant's creditworthiness.

(7) *Immigration status.* A creditor may consider the applicant's immigration status or status as a permanent resident of the United States, and any additional information that may be necessary to ascertain the creditor's rights and remedies regarding repayment.

(8) *Marital status.* Except as otherwise permitted or required by law, a creditor shall evaluate married and unmarried applicants by the same standards; and in evaluating joint applicants, a creditor shall not treat applicants differently based on the existence, absence, or likelihood of a marital relationship between the parties.

(9) *Race, color, religion, national origin, sex.* Except as otherwise permitted or required by law, a creditor shall not consider race, color, religion, national origin, or sex (or an applicant's or other person's decision not to provide the information) in any aspect of a credit transaction.

(c) *State property laws.* A creditor's consideration or application of state property laws directly or indirectly affecting creditworthiness does not constitute unlawful discrimination for the purposes of the Act or this regulation.

§ 202.7 Rules concerning extensions of credit.

(a) *Individual accounts.* A creditor shall not refuse to grant an individual account to a creditworthy applicant on the basis of sex, marital status, or any other prohibited basis.

(b) *Designation of name.* A creditor shall not refuse to allow an applicant to open or maintain an account in a birth-given first name and a surname that is the applicant's birth-given surname, the spouse's surname, or a combined surname.

(c) *Action concerning existing open-end accounts*—(1) *Limitations.* In the absence of evidence of the applicant's inability or unwillingness to repay, a creditor shall not take any of the following actions regarding an applicant who is contractually liable on an existing open-end account on the basis of the applicant's reaching a certain age or retiring or on the basis of a change in the applicant's name or marital status:

(i) Require a reapplication, except as provided in paragraph (c)(2) of this section;

(ii) Change the terms of the account; or

(iii) Terminate the account.

(2) *Requiring reapplication.* A creditor may require a reapplication for an open-end account on the basis of a change in the marital status of an applicant who is contractually liable if the credit granted was based in whole or in part on income of the applicant's spouse and if information available to the creditor indicates that the applicant's income may not support the amount of credit currently available.

(d) *Signature of spouse or other person*—(1) *Rule for qualified applicant.* Except as provided in this paragraph, a creditor shall not require the signature of an applicant's spouse or other person, other than a joint applicant, on any credit instrument if the applicant qualifies under the creditor's standards of creditworthiness for the amount and terms of the credit requested. A creditor shall not deem the submission of a joint financial statement or other evidence of jointly held assets as an application for joint credit.

(2) *Unsecured credit.* If an applicant requests unsecured credit and relies in part upon property that the applicant owns jointly with another person to satisfy the creditor's standards of creditworthiness, the creditor may require the signature of the other person only on the instrument(s) necessary, or reasonably believed by the creditor to be necessary, under the law of the state in which the property is located, to enable the creditor to reach the property being relied upon in the event of the death or default of the applicant.

(3) *Unsecured credit—community property states.* If a married applicant requests unsecured credit and resides in a community property state, or if the applicant is relying on property located in such a state, a creditor may require the signature of the spouse on any instrument necessary, or reasonably believed by the creditor to be necessary, under applicable state law to make the community property available to satisfy the debt in the event of default if:

(i) Applicable state law denies the applicant power to manage or control sufficient community property to qualify for the credit requested under the creditor's standards of creditworthiness; and

(ii) The applicant does not have sufficient separate property to qualify for the credit requested without regard to community property.

(4) *Secured credit.* If an applicant requests secured credit, a creditor may require the signature of the applicant's spouse or other person on any instrument necessary, or reasonably believed by the creditor to be necessary, under applicable state law to make the property being offered as security available to satisfy the debt in the event of default, for example, an instrument to create a valid lien, pass clear title, waive inchoate rights, or assign earnings.

(5) *Additional parties.* If, under a creditor's standards of creditworthiness, the personal liability of an additional party is necessary to support the credit requested, a creditor may request a cosigner, guarantor, endorser, or similar party. The applicant's spouse may serve as an additional party, but the creditor shall not require that the spouse be the additional party.

(6) *Rights of additional parties.* A creditor shall not impose requirements upon an additional party that the creditor is prohibited from imposing upon an applicant under this section.

(e) *Insurance.* A creditor shall not refuse to extend credit and shall not terminate an account because credit life, health, accident, disability, or other credit-related insurance is not available on the basis of the applicant's age.

§ 202.8 Special purpose credit programs.

(a) *Standards for programs.* Subject to the provisions of paragraph (b) of this section, the Act and this regulation permit a creditor to extend special purpose credit to applicants who meet eligibility requirements under the following types of credit programs:

(1) Any credit assistance program expressly authorized by federal or state law for the benefit of an economically disadvantaged class of persons;

(2) Any credit assistance program offered by a not-for-profit organization, as defined under section 501(c) of the Internal Revenue Code of 1954, as amended, for the benefit of its members or for the benefit of an economically disadvantaged class of persons; or

(3) Any special purpose credit program offered by a for-profit organization, or in which such an organization participates to meet special social needs, if:

(i) The program is established and administered pursuant to a written plan that identifies the class of persons that the program is designed to benefit and sets forth the procedures and standards for extending credit pursuant to the program; and

(ii) The program is established and administered to extend credit to a class of persons who, under the organization's customary standards of creditworthiness, probably would not receive such credit or would receive it on less favorable terms than are ordinarily available to other applicants applying to the organization for a similar type and amount of credit.

(b) *Rules in other sections*—(1) *General applicability.* All the provisions of this regulation apply to each of the special purpose credit programs described in paragraph (a) of this section except as modified by this section.

(2) *Common characteristics.* A program described in paragraph (a)(2) or (a)(3) of this section qualifies as a special purpose credit program only if it was established and is administered so as not to discriminate against an applicant on any prohibited basis; however, all program participants may be required to share one or more common characteristics (for example, race, national origin, or sex) so long as the program was not established and is not administered with the purpose of evading the requirements of the Act or this regulation.

(c) *Special rule concerning requests and use of information.* If participants in a special purpose credit program described in paragraph (a) of this section are required to possess one or more common characteristics (for example, race, national origin, or sex) and if the program otherwise satisfies the requirements of paragraph (a) of this section, a creditor may request and consider information regarding the common characteristic(s) in determining the applicant's eligibility for the program.

(d) *Special rule in the case of financial need.* If financial need is one of the criteria under a special purpose credit program described in paragraph (a) of this section, the creditor may request and consider, in determining an applicant's eligibility for the program, information regarding the applicant's marital status; alimony, child support, and separate maintenance income; and the spouse's financial resources. In addition, a creditor may obtain the signature of an applicant's spouse or other person on an application or credit instrument relating to a special purpose credit program if the signature is required by federal or state law.

§ 202.9 Notifications.

(a) *Notification of action taken, ECOA notice, and statement of specific reasons*—(1) *When notification is required.* A creditor shall notify an applicant of action taken within:

(i) 30 days after receiving a completed application concerning the creditor's approval of, counteroffer to, or adverse action on the application;

(ii) 30 days after taking adverse action on an incomplete application, unless notice is provided in accordance with paragraph (c) of this section;

(iii) 30 days after taking adverse action on an existing account; or

(iv) 90 days after notifying the applicant of a counteroffer if the applicant does not expressly accept or use the credit offered.

(2) *Content of notification when adverse action is taken.* A notification given to an applicant when adverse action is taken shall be in writing and shall contain a statement of the action taken; the name and address of the creditor; a statement of the provisions of § 701(a) of the Act; the name and address of the federal agency that administers compliance with respect to the creditor; and either:

(i) A statement of specific reasons for the action taken; or

(ii) A disclosure of the applicant's right to a statement of specific reasons within 30 days, if the statement is requested within 60 days of the creditor's notification. The disclosure shall include the name, address, and telephone number of the person or office from which the statement of reasons can be obtained. If the creditor chooses to provide the reasons orally, the creditor shall also disclose the applicant's right to have them confirmed in writing within 30 days of receiving the applicant's written request for confirmation.

(3) *Notification to business credit applicants.* For business credit, a creditor shall comply with the notification requirements of this section in the following manner:

(i) With regard to a business that had gross revenues of $1 million or less in its preceding fiscal year (other than an extension of trade credit, credit incident to a factoring agreement, or other similar types of business credit), a creditor shall comply with paragraphs (a)(1) and (2) of this section, except that:

(A) The statement of the action taken may be given orally or in writing, when adverse action is taken;

(B) Disclosure of an applicant's right to a statement of reasons may be given at the time of application, instead of when adverse action is taken, provided the disclosure contains the information required by paragraph (a)(2)(ii) of this section; and the ECOA notice specified in paragraph (b)(1) of this section;

(C) For an application made entirely by telephone, a creditor satisfies the requirements of paragraph (a)(3)(i) of this section by an oral statement of the action taken and of the applicant's right to a statement of reasons for adverse action.

(ii) With regard to a business that had gross revenues in excess of $1 million in its preceding fiscal year or an extension of trade credit, credit incident to a factoring agreement, or other similar types of business credit, a creditor shall:

(A) Notify the applicant, within a reasonable time, orally or in writing, of the action taken; and

(B) Provide a written statement of the reasons for adverse action and the ECOA notice specified in paragraph (b)(1) of this section if the applicant makes a written request for the reasons within 60 days of the creditor's notification.

(b) *Form of ECOA notice and statement of specific reasons—(1) ECOA notice.* To satisfy the disclosure requirements of paragraph (a)(2) of this section regarding section 701(a) of the Act, the creditor shall provide a notice that is substantially similar to the following:

The federal Equal Credit Opportunity Act prohibits creditors from discriminating against credit applicants on the basis of race, color, religion, national origin, sex, marital status, age (provided the applicant has the capacity to enter into a binding contract); because all or part of the applicant's income derives from any public assistance program; or because the applicant has in good faith exercised any right under the Consumer Credit Protection Act. The federal agency that administers compliance with this law concerning this creditor is [name and address as specified by the appropriate agency listed in appendix A of this regulation].

(2) *Statement of specific reasons.* The statement of reasons for adverse action required by paragraph (a)(2)(i) of this section must be specific and indicate the principal reason(s) for the adverse action. Statements that the adverse action was based on the creditor's internal standards or policies or that the applicant, joint applicant, or similar party failed to achieve the qualifying score on the creditor's credit scoring system are insufficient.

(c) *Incomplete applications*—(1) *Notice alternatives.* Within 30 days after receiving an application that is incomplete regarding matters that an applicant can complete, the creditor shall notify the applicant either:

(i) Of action taken, in accordance with paragraph (a) of this section; or

(ii) Of the incompleteness, in accordance with paragraph (c)(2) of this section.

(2) *Notice of incompleteness.* If additional information is needed from an applicant, the creditor shall send a written notice to the applicant specifying the information needed, designating a reasonable period of time for the applicant to provide the information, and informing the applicant that failure to provide the information requested will result in no further consideration being given to the application. The creditor shall have no further obligation under this section if the applicant fails to respond within the designated time period. If the applicant supplies the requested information within the designated time period, the creditor shall take action on the application and notify the applicant in accordance with paragraph (a) of this section.

(3) *Oral request for information.* At its option, a creditor may inform the applicant orally of the need for additional information. If the application remains incomplete the creditor shall send a notice in accordance with paragraph (c)(1) of this section.

(d) *Oral notifications by small-volume creditors.* In the case of a creditor that did not receive more than 150 applications during the preceding calendar year, the requirements of this section (including statements of specific reasons) are satisfied by oral notifications.

(e) *Withdrawal of approved application.* When an applicant submits an application and the parties contemplate that the applicant will inquire about its status, if the creditor approves the application and the applicant has not inquired within 30 days after applying, the creditor may treat the application as withdrawn and need not comply with paragraph (a)(1) of this section.

(f) *Multiple applicants.* When an application involves more than one applicant, notification need only be given to one of them, but must be given to the primary applicant where one is readily apparent.

(g) *Applications submitted through a third party.* When an application is made on behalf of an applicant to more than one creditor and the applicant expressly accepts or uses credit offered by one of the creditors, notification of action taken by any of the other creditors is not required. If no credit is offered or if the applicant does not expressly accept or use any credit offered, each creditor taking adverse action must comply with this section, directly or through a third party. A notice given by a third party shall disclose the identity of each creditor on whose behalf the notice is given.

§ 202.10 Furnishing of credit information.

(a) *Designation of accounts.* A creditor that furnishes credit information shall designate:

(1) Any new account to reflect the participation of both spouses if the applicant's spouse is permitted to use or is contractually liable on the account (other than as a guarantor, surety, endorser, or similar party); and

(2) Any existing account to reflect such participation, within 90 days after receiving a written request to do so from one of the spouses.

(b) *Routine reports to consumer reporting agency.* If a creditor furnishes credit information to a consumer reporting agency concerning an account designated to reflect the participation of both spouses, the creditor shall furnish the information in a manner that will enable the agency to provide access to the information in the name of each spouse.

(c) *Reporting in response to inquiry.* If a creditor furnishes credit information in response to an inquiry, concerning an account designated to reflect the participation of both spouses, the creditor shall furnish the information in the name of the spouse about whom the information is requested.

§ 202.11 Relation to state law.

(a) *Inconsistent state laws.* Except as otherwise provided in this section, this regulation alters, affects, or preempts only those state laws that are inconsistent with the Act and this regulation and then only to the extent of the inconsistency. A state law is not inconsistent if it is more protective of an applicant.

(b) *Preempted provisions of state law.* (1) A state law is deemed to be inconsistent with the requirements of the Act and this regulation and less protective of an applicant within the meaning of section 705(f) of the Act to the extent that the law:

(i) Requires or permits a practice or act prohibited by the Act or this regulation;

(ii) Prohibits the individual extension of consumer credit to both parties to a marriage if each spouse individually and voluntarily applies for such credit;

(iii) Prohibits inquiries or collection of data required to comply with the Act or this regulation;

(iv) Prohibits asking about or considering age in an empirically derived, demonstrably and statistically sound, credit scoring system to determine a pertinent element of creditworthiness, or to favor an elderly applicant; or

(v) Prohibits inquiries necessary to establish or administer a special purpose credit program as defined by § 202.8.

(2) A creditor, state, or other interested party may request that the Board determine whether a state law is inconsistent with the requirements of the Act and this regulation.

(c) *Laws on finance charges, loan ceilings.* If married applicants voluntarily apply for and obtain individual accounts with the same creditor, the accounts shall not be aggregated or otherwise combined for purposes of determining permissible finance charges or loan ceilings under any federal or state law. Permissible loan ceiling laws shall be construed to permit each spouse to become individually liable up to the amount of the loan ceilings, less the amount for which the applicant is jointly liable.

(d) *State and federal laws not affected.* This section does not alter or annul any provision of state property laws, laws relating to the disposition of decedents' estates, or federal or state banking regulations directed only toward insuring the solvency of financial institutions.

(e) *Exemption for state-regulated transactions*—(1) *Applications.* A state may apply to the Board for an exemption from the requirements of the Act and this regulation for any class of credit transactions within the state. The Board will grant such an exemption if the Board determines that:

(i) The class of credit transactions is subject to state law requirements substantially similar to those of the Act and this regulation or that applicants are afforded greater protection under state law; and

(ii) There is adequate provision for state enforcement.

(2) *Liability and enforcement.* (i) No exemption will extend to the civil liability provisions of section 706 of the Act or the administrative enforcement provisions of section 704 of the Act.

(ii) After an exemption has been granted, the requirements of the applicable state law (except for additional requirements not imposed by federal law) will constitute the requirements of the Act and this regulation.

§ 202.12 Record retention.

(a) *Retention of prohibited information.* A creditor may retain in its files information that is prohibited by the Act or this regulation for use in evaluating applications, without violating the Act or this regulation, if the information was obtained:

(1) From any source prior to March 23, 1977;

(2) From consumer reporting agencies, an applicant, or others without the specific request of the creditor; or

(3) As required to monitor compliance with the Act and this regulation or other federal or state statutes or regulations.

(b) *Preservation of records*—(1) *Applications.* For 25 months (12 months for business credit, except as provided in paragraph (b)(5) of this section) after the date that a creditor notifies an applicant of action taken on an application or of incompleteness, the creditor shall retain in original form or a copy thereof:

(i) Any application that it receives, any information required to be obtained concerning characteristics of the applicant to monitor compliance with the Act and this regulation or other similar law, and any other written or recorded information used in evaluating the application and not returned to the applicant at the applicant's request;

(ii) A copy of the following documents if furnished to the applicant in written form (or, if furnished orally, any notation or memorandum made by the creditor):

(A) The notification of action taken; and

(B) The statement of specific reasons for adverse action; and

(iii) Any written statement submitted by the applicant alleging a violation of the Act or this regulation.

(2) *Existing accounts.* For 25 months (12 months for business credit, except as provided in paragraph (b)(5) of this section) after the date that a creditor notifies an applicant of adverse action regarding an existing account, the creditor shall retain as to that account, in original form or a copy thereof:

(i) Any written or recorded information concerning the adverse action; and

(ii) Any written statement submitted by the applicant alleging a violation of the Act or this regulation.

(3) *Other applications.* For 25 months (12 months for business credit, except as provided in paragraph (b)(5) of this section) after the date that a creditor receives an application for which the creditor is not required to comply with the notification requirements of § 202.9, the creditor shall retain all written or recorded information in its possession concerning the applicant, including any notation of action taken.

(4) *Enforcement proceedings and investigations.* A creditor shall retain the information beyond 25 months (12 months for business credit, except as provided in paragraph (b)(5) of this section) if the creditor has actual notice that it is under

investigation or is subject to an enforcement proceeding for an alleged violation of the Act or this regulation, by the Attorney General of the United States or by an enforcement agency charged with monitoring that creditor's compliance with the Act and this regulation, or if it has been served with notice of an action filed pursuant to section 706 of the Act and § 202.17 of this regulation. The creditor shall retain the information until final disposition of the matter, unless an earlier time is allowed by order of the agency or court.

(5) *Special rule for certain business credit applications.* With regard to a business that had gross revenues in excess of $1 million in its preceding fiscal year, or an extension of trade credit, credit incident to a factoring agreement, or other similar types of business credit, the creditor shall retain records for at least 60 days after notifying the applicant of the action taken. If within that time period the applicant requests in writing the reasons for adverse action or that records be retained, the creditor shall retain records for 12 months.

(6) *Self-tests.* For 25 months after a self-test (as defined in § 202.15) has been completed, the creditor shall retain all written or recorded information about the self-test. A creditor shall retain information beyond 25 months if it has actual notice that it is under investigation or is subject to an enforcement proceeding for an alleged violation, or if it has been served with notice of a civil action. In such cases, the creditor shall retain the information until final disposition of the matter, unless an earlier time is allowed by the appropriate agency or court order.

(7) *Prescreened solicitations.* For 25 months after the date on which an offer of credit is made to potential customers (12 months for business credit, except as provided in paragraph (b)(5) of this section), the creditor shall retain in original form or a copy thereof:

(i) The text of any prescreened solicitation;

(ii) The list of criteria the creditor used to select potential recipients of the solicitation; and

(iii) Any correspondence related to complaints (formal or informal) about the solicitation.

§ 202.13 Information for monitoring purposes.

(a) *Information to be requested.* (1) A creditor that receives an application for credit primarily for the purchase or refinancing of a dwelling occupied or to be occupied by the applicant as a principal residence, where the extension of credit will be secured by the dwelling, shall request as part of the application the following information regarding the applicant(s):

(i) Ethnicity, using the categories Hispanic or Latino, and not Hispanic or Latino; and race, using the categories American Indian or Alaska Native, Asian, Black or African American, Native Hawaiian or Other Pacific Islander, and White;

(ii) Sex;

(iii) Marital status, using the categories married, unmarried, and separated; and

(iv) Age.

(2) *Dwelling* means a residential structure that contains one to four units, whether or not that structure is attached to real property. The term includes, but is not limited to, an individual condominium or cooperative unit and a mobile or other manufactured home.

(b) *Obtaining information.* Questions regarding ethnicity, race, sex, marital status, and age may be listed, at the creditor's option, on the application form or on a separate form that refers to the application. The applicant(s) shall be asked but not required to supply the requested information. If the applicant(s) chooses not to provide the information or any part of it, that fact shall be noted on the form. The creditor shall then also note on the form, to the extent possible, the ethnicity, race, and sex of the applicant(s) on the basis of visual observation or surname.

(c) *Disclosure to applicant(s).* The creditor shall inform the applicant(s) that the information regarding ethnicity, race, sex, marital status, and age is being requested by the federal government for the purpose of monitoring compliance with federal statutes that prohibit creditors from discriminating against applicants on those bases. The creditor shall also inform the applicant(s) that if the applicant(s) chooses not to provide the information, the creditor is required to note the ethnicity, race and sex on the basis of visual observation or surname.

(d) *Substitute monitoring program.* A monitoring program required by an agency charged with administrative enforcement under section 704 of the Act may be substituted for the requirements contained in paragraphs (a), (b), and (c) of this section.

§ 202.14 Rules on providing appraisal reports.

(a) *Providing appraisals.* A creditor shall provide a copy of an appraisal report used in connection with an application for credit that is to be secured by a lien on a dwelling. A creditor shall comply with either paragraph (a)(1) or (a)(2) of this section.

(1) *Routine delivery.* A creditor may routinely provide a copy of an appraisal report to an applicant (whether credit is granted or denied or the application is withdrawn).

(2) *Upon request.* A creditor that does not routinely provide appraisal reports shall provide a copy upon an applicant's written request.

(i) *Notice.* A creditor that provides appraisal reports only upon request shall notify an applicant in writing of the right to receive a copy of an appraisal report. The notice may be given at any time during the application process but no later than when the creditor provides notice of action taken under § 202.9 of this regulation. The notice shall specify that the applicant's request must be in writing, give the creditor's mailing address, and state the time for making the request as provided in paragraph (a)(2)(ii) of this section.

(ii) *Delivery.* A creditor shall mail or deliver a copy of the appraisal report promptly (generally within 30 days) after the creditor receives an applicant's request, receives the report, or receives reimbursement from the applicant for the report, whichever is last to occur. A creditor need not provide a copy when the applicant's request is received more than 90 days after the creditor has provided notice of action taken on the application under § 202.9 of this regulation or 90 days after the application is withdrawn.

(b) *Credit unions.* A creditor that is subject to the regulations of the National Credit Union Administration on making copies of appraisal reports available is not subject to this section.

(c) *Definitions.* For purposes of paragraph (a) of this section, the term dwelling means a residential structure that contains one to four units whether or not that structure is attached to real property. The term includes, but is not limited to, an individual condominium or cooperative unit, and a mobile or other manufactured home. The term *appraisal report* means the document(s) relied upon by a creditor in evaluating the value of the dwelling.

§ 202.15 Incentives for self-testing and self-correction.

(a) *General rules*—(1) *Voluntary self-testing and correction.* The report or results of a self-test that a creditor voluntarily conducts (or authorizes) are privileged as provided in this section. Data collection required by law or by any governmental authority is not a voluntary self-test.

(2) *Corrective action required.* The privilege in this section applies only if the creditor has taken or is taking appropriate corrective action.

(3) *Other privileges.* The privilege created by this section does not preclude the assertion of any other privilege that may also apply.

(b) *Self-test defined*—(1) *Definition.* A self-test is any program, practice, or study that:

(i) Is designed and used specifically to determine the extent or effectiveness of a creditor's compliance with the Act or this regulation; and

(ii) Creates data or factual information that is not available and cannot be derived from loan or application files or other records related to credit transactions.

(2) *Types of information privileged.* The privilege under this section applies to the report or results of the self-test, data or factual information created by the self-test, and any analysis, opinions, and conclusions pertaining to the self-test report or results. The privilege covers work papers or draft documents as well as final documents.

(3) *Types of information not privileged.* The privilege under this section does not apply to:

(i) Information about whether a creditor conducted a self-test, the methodology used or the scope of the self-test, the time period covered by the self-test, or the dates it was conducted; or

(ii) Loan and application files or other business records related to credit transactions, and information derived from such files and records, even if the information has been aggregated, summarized, or reorganized to facilitate analysis.

(c) *Appropriate corrective action*—(1) *General requirement.* For the privilege in this section to apply, appropriate corrective action is required when the self-test shows that it is more likely than not that a violation occurred, even though no violation has been formally adjudicated.

(2) *Determining the scope of appropriate corrective action.* A creditor must take corrective action that is reasonably likely to remedy the cause and effect of a likely violation by:

(i) Identifying the policies or practices that are the likely cause of the violation; and

(ii) Assessing the extent and scope of any violation.

(3) *Types of relief.* Appropriate corrective action may include both prospective and remedial relief, except that to establish a privilege under this section:

(i) A creditor is not required to provide remedial relief to a tester used in a self-test;

(ii) A creditor is only required to provide remedial relief to an applicant identified by the self-test as one whose rights were more likely than not violated; and

(iii) A creditor is not required to provide remedial relief to a particular applicant if the statute of limitations applicable to the violation expired before the creditor obtained the results of the self-test or the applicant is otherwise ineligible for such relief.

(4) *No admission of violation.* Taking corrective action is not an admission that a violation occurred.

(d) *Scope of privilege*—(1) *General rule.* The report or results of a privileged self-test may not be obtained or used:

(i) By a government agency in any examination or investigation relating to compliance with the Act or this regulation; or

(ii) By a government agency or an applicant (including a prospective applicant who alleges a violation of § 202.4(b)) in any proceeding or civil action in which a violation of the Act or this regulation is alleged.

(2) *Loss of privilege.* The report or results of a self-test are not privileged under paragraph (d)(1) of this section if the creditor or a person with lawful access to the report or results:

(i) Voluntarily discloses any part of the report or results, or any other information privileged under this section, to an applicant or government agency or to the public;

(ii) Discloses any part of the report or results, or any other information privileged under this section, as a defense to charges that the creditor has violated the Act or regulation; or

(iii) Fails or is unable to produce written or recorded information about the self-test that is required to be retained under § 202.12(b)(6) when the information is needed to determine whether the privilege applies. This paragraph does not limit any other penalty or remedy that may be available for a violation of § 202.12.

(3) *Limited use of privileged information.* Notwithstanding paragraph (d)(1) of this section, the self-test report or results and any other information privileged under this section may be obtained and used by an applicant or government agency solely to determine a penalty or remedy after a violation of the Act or this regulation has been adjudicated or admitted. Disclosures for this limited purpose may be used only for the particular proceeding in which the adjudication or admission was made. Information disclosed under this paragraph (d)(3) remains privileged under paragraph (d)(1) of this section.

§ 202.16 Enforcement, penalties and liabilities.

(a) *Administrative enforcement*—(1) As set forth more fully in section 704 of the Act, administrative enforcement of the Act and this regulation regarding certain creditors is assigned to the Comptroller of the Currency, Board of Governors of the Federal Reserve System, Board of Directors of the Federal Deposit Insurance Corporation, Office of Thrift Supervision, National Credit Union Administration, Surface Transportation Board, Secretary of Agriculture, Farm Credit Administration, Securities and Exchange Commission, Small Business Administration, and Secretary of Transportation.

(2) Except to the extent that administrative enforcement is specifically assigned to other authorities, compliance with the requirements imposed under the Act and this regulation is enforced by the Federal Trade Commission.

(b) *Penalties and liabilities*—(1) Sections 702(g) and 706(a) and (b) of the Act provide that any creditor that fails to comply with a requirement imposed by the Act or this regulation is subject to civil liability for actual and punitive damages in individual or class actions. Pursuant to sections 702(g) and 704(b), (c), and (d) of the Act, violations of the Act or this regulation also constitute violations of other federal laws. Liability for punitive damages can apply only to nongovernmental entities and is limited to $10,000 in individual actions and the lesser of $500,000 or

1 percent of the creditor's net worth in class actions. Sections 706(c) provides for equitable and declaratory relief and section 706(d) authorizes the awarding of costs and reasonable attorney's fees to an aggrieved applicant in a successful action.

(2) As provided in section 706(f), a civil action under the Act or this regulation may be brought in the appropriate United States district court without regard to the amount in controversy or in any other court of competent jurisdiction within two years after the date of the occurrence of the violation, or within one year after the commencement of an administrative enforcement proceeding or of a civil action brought by the Attorney General of the United States within two years after the alleged violation.

(3) If an agency responsible for administrative enforcement is unable to obtain compliance with the Act or this regulation, it may refer the matter to the Attorney General of the United States. If the Board, the Comptroller of the Currency, the Federal Deposit Insurance Corporation, the Office of Thrift Supervision, or the National Credit Union Administration has reason to believe that one or more creditors have engaged in a pattern or practice of discouraging or denying applications in violation of the Act or this regulation, the agency shall refer the matter to the Attorney General. If the agency has reason to believe that one or more creditors violated section 701(a) of the Act, the agency may refer a matter to the Attorney General.

(4) On referral, or whenever the Attorney General has reason to believe that one or more creditors have engaged in a pattern or practice in violation of the Act or this regulation, the Attorney General may bring a civil action for such relief as may be appropriate, including actual and punitive damages and injunctive relief.

(5) If the Board, the Comptroller of the Currency, the Federal Deposit Insurance Corporation, the Office of Thrift Supervision, or the National Credit Union Administration has reason to believe (as a result of a consumer complaint, a consumer compliance examination, or some other basis) that a violation of the Act or this regulation has occurred which is also a violation of the Fair Housing Act, and the matter is not referred to the Attorney General, the agency shall:

(i) Notify the Secretary of Housing and Urban Development; and

(ii) Inform the applicant that the Secretary of Housing and Urban Development has been notified and that remedies may be available under the Fair Housing Act.

(c) *Failure of compliance.* A creditor's failure to comply with §§ 202.6(b)(6), 202.9, 202.10, 202.12 or 202.13 is not a violation if it results from an inadvertent error. On discovering an error under §§ 202.9 and 202.10, the creditor shall correct it as soon as possible. If a creditor inadvertently obtains the monitoring information regarding the ethnicity, race, and sex of the applicant in a dwelling-related transaction not covered by § 202.13, the creditor may retain information and act on the application without violating the regulation.

[Section 202.17 redesignated as 202.16 at 72 Fed. Reg. 63451, November 9, 2007, effective December 10, 2007, the mandatory compliance date is October 1, 2008]

§ 202.17. [Redesignated]

Appendix A to Part 202—Federal Enforcement Agencies

The following list indicates the federal agencies that enforce Regulation B for particular classes of creditors. Any questions concerning a particular creditor should be directed to its enforcement agency. Terms that are not defined in the Federal Deposit Insurance Act (12 U.S.C. 1813(s)) shall have the meaning given to them in the International Banking Act of 1978 (12 U.S.C. 3101).

National Banks, and federal branches and federal agencies of foreign banks:

Office of the Comptroller of the Currency, Customer Assistance Group, 1301 McKinney Street, Suite 3450, Houston, Texas 77010-9050.

State member banks, branches and agencies of foreign banks (other than federal branches, federal agencies, and insured state branches of foreign banks), commercial lending companies owned or controlled by foreign banks, and organizations operating under section 25 or 25A of the Federal Reserve Act:

Federal Reserve Consumer Help Center, P.O. Box 1200, Minneapolis, MN 55480, toll-free number: (888) 851–1920, fax number: (877) 888–2520, TDD number: (877) 766–8533.

Nonmember Insured Banks and Insured State Branches of Foreign Banks. FDIC Consumer Response Center, 2345 Grand Boulevard, Suite 100, Kansas City, Missouri 64108.

Savings institutions insured under the Savings Association Insurance Fund of the FDIC and federally chartered saving banks insured under the Bank Insurance Fund of the FDIC (but not including state-chartered savings banks insured under the Bank Insurance Fund).

Office of Thrift Supervision Regional Director for the region in which the institution is located.

Federal Credit Unions:

Regional office of the National Credit Union Administration serving the area in which the federal credit union is located.

Air carriers:

Assistant General Counsel for Aviation Enforcement and Proceedings, Department of Transportation, 400 Seventh Street SW., Washington, DC 20590.

Creditors Subject to Surface Transportation Board: Office of Proceedings, Surface Transportation Board, Department of Transportation, 1925 K Street NW., Washington, DC 20423.

Creditors Subject to Packers and Stockyards Act: Nearest Packers and Stockyards Administration area supervisor.

Small Business Investment Companies: Associate Deputy Administrator for Capital Access, United States Small Business Administration, 409 Third Street, SW., 8th Floor, Washington, DC 20416.

Brokers and Dealers: Securities and Exchange Commission, Washington, DC 20549.

Federal Land Banks, Federal Land Bank Associations, Federal Intermediate Credit Banks, and Production Credit Associations:

Farm Credit Administration, 1501 Farm Credit Drive, McLean, VA 22102-5090.

Retailers, Finance Companies, and All Other Creditors Not Listed Above: FTC Regional Office for region in which the creditor operates or Federal Trade Commission, Equal Credit Opportunity, Washington, DC 20580.

[Appendix A amended at 71 Fed. Reg. 28563, May 17, 2006; 72 Fed. Reg. 55020, September 28, 2007, effective October 29, 2007, compliance optional until October 1, 2008]

Appendix B to Part 202—Model Application Forms

1. This appendix contains five model credit application forms, each designated for use in a particular type of consumer credit transaction as indicated by the bracketed caption on each form. The first sample form is intended for use in open-end, unsecured transactions; the second for closed-end, secured transactions; the third for closed-end transactions, whether unsecured or secured; the fourth in transactions involving community property or occurring in community property states; and the fifth in residential mortgage transactions which contains a model disclosure for use in complying with § 202.13 for certain dwelling-related loans. All forms contained in this appendix are models; their use by creditors is optional.

2. The use or modification of these forms is governed by the following instructions. A creditor may change the forms: by asking for additional information not prohibited by § 202.5; by deleting any information request; or by rearranging the format without modifying the substance of the inquiries. In any of these three instances, however, the appropriate notices regarding the optional nature of courtesy titles, the option to disclose alimony, child support, or separate maintenance, and the limitation concerning marital status inquiries must be included in the appropriate places if the items to which they relate appear on the creditor's form.

3. If a creditor uses an appropriate Appendix B model form, or modifies a form in accordance with the above instructions, that creditor shall be deemed to be acting in compliance with the provisions of paragraphs (b), (c), and (d) of § 202.5 of this regulation.

[Open-end, unsecured credit]

CREDIT APPLICATION

IMPORTANT: Read these Directions before completing this Application.

Check Appropriate Box

☐ If you are applying for an individual account in your own name and are relying on your own income or assets and not the income or assets of another person as the basis for repayment of the credit requested, complete only Sections A and D.

☐ If you are applying for a joint account or an account that you and another person will use, complete all Sections, providing information in B about the joint applicant or user.

We intend to apply for joint credit. ______________ ______________
Applicant Co-Applicant

☐ If you are applying for an individual account, but are relying on income from alimony, child support, or separate maintenance or on the income or assets of another person as the basis for repayment of the credit requested, complete all Sections to the extent possible, providing information in B about the person on whose alimony, support, or maintenance payments or income or assets you are relying.

SECTION A—INFORMATION REGARDING APPLICANT

Full Name (Last, First, Middle): ______________ Birthdate: / /

Present Street Address: ______________ Years there: ______

City: ______________ State: ______________ Zip: ______ Telephone: ______________

Social Security No.: ______________ Driver's License No.: ______________

Previous Street Address: ______________ Years there: ______

City: ______________ State: ______________ Zip: ______________

Present Employer: ______________ Years there: ______ Telephone: ______________

Position or title: ______________ Name of supervisor: ______________

Employer's Address: ______________

Previous Employer: ______________ Years there: ______

Previous Employer's Address: ______________

Present net salary or commission: $ ______ per ______ No. Dependents: ______ Ages: ______

Alimony, child support, or separate maintenance income need not be revealed if you do not wish to have it considered as a basis for repaying this obligation.

Alimony, child support, separate maintenance received under: court order ☐ written agreement ☐ oral understanding ☐

Other income: $ ______ per ______ Source(s) of other income: ______________

Is any income listed in this Section likely to be reduced in the next two years?
☐ Yes (Explain in detail on a separate sheet.) No☐

Have you ever received credit from us? ______ When? ______ Office: ______

Checking Account No.: ______________ Institution and Branch: ______________

Savings Account No.: ______________ Institution and Branch: ______________

Name of nearest relative not living with you: ______________ Telephone: ______________

Relationship: ______ Address: ______________

SECTION B—INFORMATION REGARDING JOINT APPLICANT, USER, OR OTHER PARTY (Use separate sheets if necessary.)

Full Name (Last, First, Middle): ______________ Birthdate: / /

Relationship to Applicant (if any): ______________

Present Street Address: ______________ Years there: ______

City: ______________ State: ______________ Zip: ______ Telephone: ______________

Social Security No.: ______________ Driver's License No.: ______________

Present Employer: ______________ Years there: ______ Telephone: ______________

Position or title: ______________ Name of supervisor: ______________

Employer's Address: ______________

Previous Employer: ______________ Years there: ______

Previous Employer's Address: ______________

Present net salary or commission: $ ______ per ______ No. Dependents: ______ Ages: ______

Alimony, child support, or separate maintenance income need not be revealed if you do not wish to have it considered as a basis for repaying this obligation.

Alimony, child support, separate maintenance received under: court order ☐ written agreement ☐ oral understanding ☐

Other income: $ ______ per ______ Source(s) of other income: ______________

Is any income listed in this Section likely to be reduced in the next two years?
☐ Yes (Explain in detail on a separate sheet.) No☐

Checking Account No.: ______________ Institution and Branch: ______________

Savings Account No.: ______________ Institution and Branch: ______________

Name of nearest relative not living with Joint Applicant, User, or Other Party: ______________ Telephone: ______________

Relationship: ______ Address: ______________

SECTION C—MARITAL STATUS
(Do not complete if this is an application for an individual account.)

Applicant: ☐ Married ☐ Separated ☐ Unmarried (including single, divorced, and widowed)
Other Party: ☐ Married ☐ Separated ☐ Unmarried (including single, divorced, and widowed)

[Open-end, unsecured credit]

SECTION D— ASSET AND DEBT INFORMATION (If Section B has been completed, this Section should be completed giving information about both the Applicant and Joint Applicant, User, or Other Person. Please mark Applicant-related information with an "A." If Section B was not completed, only give information about the Applicant in this Section.)

ASSETS OWNED (use separate sheet if necessary.)

Description of Assets	Value	Subject to Debt? Yes/No	Name(s) of Owner(s)
Cash	$		
Automobiles (Make, Model, Year)			
Cash Value of Life Insurance (Issuer, Face Value)			
Real Estate (Location, Date Acquired)			
Marketable Securities (Issuer, Type, No. of Shares)			
Other (List)			
Total Assets	$		

OUTSTANDING DEBTS (Include charge accounts, installment contracts, credit cards, rent, mortgages, etc. Use separate sheet if necessary.)

Creditor	Type of Debt or Acct. No.	Name in Which Acct. Carried	Original Debt	Present Balance	Monthly Payments	Past Due? Yes/No
1. (Landlord or Mortgage Holder)	☐ Rent Payment ☐ Mortgage		$ (Omit rent)	$ (Omit rent)	$	
2.						
3.						
4.						
5.						
6.						
Total Debts			$	$	$	

(Credit References)	Date Paid
1.	
2.	

Are you a co-maker, endorser, or guarantor on any loan or contract? Yes ☐ No ☐ If "yes" for whom? To whom?

Are there any unsatisfied judgments against you? Yes ☐ No ☐ Amount $ If "yes" to whom owed?

Have you been declared bankrupt in the last 14 years? Yes ☐ No ☐ If "yes" where? Year

Other Obligations—(E.g., liability to pay alimony, child support, separate maintenance. Use separate sheet if necessary.)

Everything that I have stated in this application is correct to the best of my knowledge. I understand that you will retain this application whether or not it is approved. You are authorized to check my credit and employment history and to answer questions about your credit experience with me.

Applicant's Signature | Date | Other Signature (Where Applicable) | Date

[Closed-end, secured credit]

CREDIT APPLICATION

IMPORTANT: Read these Directions before completing this Application.

Check Appropriate Box

☐ If you are applying for individual credit in your own name and are relying on your own income or assets and not the income or assets of another person as the basis for repayment of the credit requested, complete Sections A, C, D, and E, omitting B and the second part of C.

☐ If this is an application for joint credit with another person, complete all Sections, providing information in B about the joint applicant.

We intend to apply for joint credit. ________ Applicant ________ Co-Applicant

☐ If you are applying for individual credit, but are relying on income from alimony, child support, or separate maintenance or on the income or assets of another person as the basis for repayment of the credit requested, complete all Sections to the extent possible, providing information in B about the person on whose alimony, support, or maintenance payments or income or assets you are relying.

Amount Requested $ ________ Payment Date Desired ________ Proceeds of Credit To be Used For ________

SECTION A—INFORMATION REGARDING APPLICANT

Full Name (Last, First, Middle): ________ Birthdate: / /

Present Street Address: ________ Years there: ________

City: ________ State: ________ Zip: ________ Telephone: ________

Social Security No.: ________ Driver's License No.: ________

Previous Street Address: ________ Years there: ________

City: ________ State: ________ Zip: ________

Present Employer: ________ Years there: ________ Telephone: ________

Position or title: ________ Name of supervisor: ________

Employer's Address: ________

Previous Employer: ________ Years there: ________

Previous Employer's Address: ________

Present net salary or commission: $ ________ per ________ No. Dependents: ________ Ages: ________

Alimony, child support, or separate maintenance income need not be revealed if you do not wish to have it considered as a basis for repaying this obligation.

Alimony, child support, separate maintenance received under: court order ☐ written agreement ☐ oral understanding ☐

Other income: $ ________ per ________ Source(s) of other income: ________

Is any income listed in this Section likely to be reduced before the credit requested is paid off?
☐ Yes (Explain in detail on a separate sheet.) No ☐

Have you ever received credit from us? ________ When? ________ Office: ________

Checking Account No.: ________ Institution and Branch: ________

Savings Account No.: ________ Institution and Branch: ________

Name of nearest relative not living with you: ________ Telephone: ________

Relationship: ________ Address: ________

SECTION B—INFORMATION REGARDING JOINT APPLICANT, OR OTHER PARTY (Use separate sheets if necessary.)

Full Name (Last, First, Middle): ________ Birthdate: / /

Relationship to Applicant (if any): ________

Present Street Address: ________ Years there: ________

City: ________ State: ________ Zip: ________ Telephone: ________

Social Security No.: ________ Driver's License No.: ________

Present Employer: ________ Years there: ________ Telephone: ________

Position or title: ________ Name of supervisor: ________

Employer's Address: ________

Previous Employer: ________ Years there: ________

Previous Employer's Address: ________

Present net salary or commission: $ ________ per ________ No. Dependents: ________ Ages: ________

Alimony, child support, or separate maintenance income need not be revealed if you do not wish to have it considered as a basis for repaying this obligation.

Alimony, child support, separate maintenance received under: court order ☐ written agreement ☐ oral understanding ☐

Other income: $ ________ per ________ Source(s) of other income: ________

Is any income listed in this Section likely to be reduced before the credit requested is paid off?
☐ Yes (Explain in detail on a separate sheet.) No ☐

Checking Account No.: ________ Institution and Branch: ________

Savings Account No.: ________ Institution and Branch: ________

Name of nearest relative not living with Joint Applicant or Other Party: ________

Relationship: ________ Address: ________

SECTION C—MARITAL STATUS
(Do not complete if this is an application for an individual account.)

Applicant: ☐ Married ☐ Separated ☐ Unmarried (including single, divorced, and widowed)
Other Party: ☐ Married ☐ Separated ☐ Unmarried (including single, divorced, and widowed)

[Closed-end, secured credit]

SECTION D— ASSET AND DEBT INFORMATION (If Section B has been completed, this Section should be completed giving information about both the Applicant and Joint Applicant or Other Person. Please mark Applicant-related information with an "A." If Section B was not completed, only give information about the Applicant in this Section.)

ASSETS OWNED (use separate sheet if necessary.)

Description of Assets	Value	Subject to Debt? Yes/No	Name(s) of Owner(s)
Cash	$		
Automobiles (Make, Model, Year)			
Cash Value of Life Insurance (Issuer, Face Value)			
Real Estate (Location, Date Acquired)			
Marketable Securities (Issuer, Type, No. of Shares)			
Other (List)			
Total Assets	$		

OUTSTANDING DEBTS (Include charge accounts, installment contracts, credit cards, rent, mortgages, etc. Use separate sheet if necessary.)

Creditor	Type of Debt or Acct. No.	Name in Which Acct. Carried	Original Debt	Present Balance	Monthly Payments	Past Due? Yes/No
1. (Landlord or Mortgage Holder)	☐ Rent Payment ☐ Mortgage		$ (Omit rent)	$ (Omit rent)	$	
2.						
3.						
Total Debts			$	$	$	

(Credit References) Date Paid

1.

2.

Are you a co-maker, endorser, or guarantor on any loan or contract?	Yes ☐	No ☐	If "yes" for whom?	To whom?
Are there any unsatisfied judgments against you?	Yes ☐ No ☐	Amount $	If "yes" to whom owed?	
Have you been declared bankrupt in the last 14 years?	Yes ☐ No ☐	If "yes" where?		Year

Other Obligations—(E.g., liability to pay alimony, child support, separate maintenance. Use separate sheet if necessary.)

SECTION E—SECURED CREDIT (Briefly describe the property to be given as security.)

and list names and addresses of all co-owners of the property:

Name Address

If the security is real estate, give the full name of your spouse (if any): ____________

Everything that I have stated in this application is correct to the best of my knowledge. I understand that you will retain this application whether or not it is approved. You are authorized to check my credit and employment history and to answer questions about your credit experience with me.

Applicant's Signature Date Other Signature (Where Applicable) Date

[Closed-end, unsecured/secured credit]

CREDIT APPLICATION

IMPORTANT: Read these Directions before completing this Application.

Check Appropriate Box

☐ If you are applying for individual credit in your own name and are relying on your own income or assets and not the income or assets of another person as the basis for repayment of the credit requested, complete only Sections A and D. If the requested credit is to be secured, also complete the first part of Section C and Section E.

☐ If you are applying for joint credit with another person, complete all Sections except E, providing information in B about the joint applicant. If the requested credit is to be secured, then complete Section E.

We intend to apply for joint credit. ____________ Applicant ____________ Co-Applicant

☐ If you are applying for individual credit, but are relying on income from alimony, child support, or separate maintenance or on the income or assets of another person as the basis for repayment of the credit requested, complete all Sections except E to the extent possible, providing information in B about the person on whose alimony, support, or maintenance payments or income or assets you are relying. If the requested credit is to be secured, then complete Section E.

Amount Requested $ ________ Payment Date Desired ________ Proceeds of Credit To be Used For ________

SECTION A—INFORMATION REGARDING APPLICANT

Full Name (Last, First, Middle): ________ Birthdate: / /

Present Street Address: ________ Years there: ________

City: ________ State: ________ Zip: ________ Telephone: ________

Social Security No.: ________ Driver's License No.: ________

Previous Street Address: ________ Years there: ________

City: ________ State: ________ Zip: ________

Present Employer: ________ Years there: ________ Telephone: ________

Position or title: ________ Name of supervisor: ________

Employer's Address: ________

Previous Employer: ________ Years there: ________

Previous Employer's Address: ________

Present net salary or commission: $ ________ per ________ No. Dependents: ________ Ages: ________

Alimony, child support, or separate maintenance income need not be revealed if you do not wish to have it considered as a basis for repaying this obligation.

Alimony, child support, separate maintenance received under: court order ☐ written agreement ☐ oral understanding ☐

Other income: $ ________ per ________ Source(s) of other income: ________

Is any income listed in this Section likely to be reduced before the credit requested is paid off?
☐ Yes (Explain in detail on a separate sheet.) No☐

Have you ever received credit from us? ________ When? ________ Office: ________

Checking Account No.: ________ Institution and Branch: ________

Savings Account No.: ________ Institution and Branch: ________

Name of nearest relative not living with you: ________ Telephone: ________

Relationship: ________ Address: ________

SECTION B—INFORMATION REGARDING JOINT APPLICANT, OR OTHER PARTY (Use separate sheets if necessary.)

Full Name (Last, First, Middle): ________ Birthdate: / /

Relationship to Applicant (if any): ________

Present Street Address: ________ Years there: ________

City: ________ State: ________ Zip: ________ Telephone: ________

Social Security No.: ________ Driver's License No.: ________

Present Employer: ________ Years there: ________ Telephone: ________

Position or title: ________ Name of supervisor: ________

Employer's Address: ________

Previous Employer: ________ Years there: ________

Previous Employer's Address: ________

Present net salary or commission: $ ________ per ________ No. Dependents: ________ Ages: ________

Alimony, child support, or separate maintenance income need not be revealed if you do not wish to have it considered as a basis for repaying this obligation.

Alimony, child support, separate maintenance received under: court order ☐ written agreement ☐ oral understanding ☐

Other income: $ ________ per ________ Source(s) of other income: ________

Is any income listed in this Section likely to be reduced before the credit requested is paid off?
☐ Yes (Explain in detail on a separate sheet.) No☐

Checking Account No.: ________ Institution and Branch: ________

Savings Account No.: ________ Institution and Branch: ________

Name of nearest relative not living with Joint Applicant or Other Party: ________ Telephone: ________

Relationship: ________ Address: ________

[Closed-end, unsecured/secured credit]

SECTION C—MARITAL STATUS
(Do not complete if this is an application for individual unsecured credit.)

Applicant: ☐ Married ☐ Separated ☐ Unmarried (including single, divorced, and widowed)
Other Party: ☐ Married ☐ Separated ☐ Unmarried (including single, divorced, and widowed)

SECTION D— ASSET AND DEBT INFORMATION (If Section B has been completed, this Section should be completed giving information about both the Applicant and Joint Applicant or Other Person. Please mark Applicant-related information with an "A." If Section B was not completed, only give information about the Applicant in this Section.)

ASSETS OWNED (use separate sheet if necessary.)

Description of Assets	Value	Subject to Debt? Yes/No	Name(s) of Owner(s)
Cash	$		
Automobiles (Make, Model, Year)			
Cash Value of Life Insurance (Issuer, Face Value)			
Real Estate (Location, Date Acquired)			
Marketable Securities (Issuer, Type, No. of Shares)			
Other (List)			
Total Assets	$		

OUTSTANDING DEBTS (Include charge accounts, installment contracts, credit cards, rent, mortgages, etc. Use separate sheet if necessary.)

Creditor	Type of Debt or Acct. No.	Name in Which Acct. Carried	Original Debt	Present Balance	Monthly Payments	Past Due? Yes/No
1. (Landlord or Mortgage Holder)	☐ Rent Payment ☐ Mortgage		$ (Omit rent)	$ (Omit rent)	$	
2.						
3.						
Total Debts			$	$	$	

(Credit References) Date Paid

1.

2.

Are you a co-maker, endorser, or guarantor on any loan or contract? Yes ☐ No ☐ If "yes" for whom? To whom?

Are there any unsatisfied judgments against you? Yes ☐ No ☐ Amount $ If "yes" to whom owed?

Have you been declared bankrupt in the last 14 years? Yes ☐ No ☐ If "yes" where? Year

Other Obligations—(E.g., liability to pay alimony, child support, separate maintenance. Use separate sheet if necessary.)

SECTION E—SECURED CREDIT (Complete only if credit is to be secured.) Briefly describe the property to be given as security.

and list names and addresses of all co-owners of the property:

Name Address

If the security is real estate, give the full name of your spouse (if any): ____________

Everything that I have stated in this application is correct to the best of my knowledge. I understand that you will retain this application whether or not it is approved. You are authorized to check my credit and employment history and to answer questions about your credit experience with me.

Applicant's Signature Date Other Signature (Where Applicable) Date

[Community property]

CREDIT APPLICATION

IMPORTANT: Read these Directions before completing this Application.

Check Appropriate Box

☐ If you are applying for individual credit in your own name, are not married, and are not relying on alimony, child support, or separate maintenance payments or on the income or assets of another person as the basis for repayment of the credit requested, complete only Sections A and D. If the requested credit is to be secured, also complete Section E.

☐ In all other situations, complete all Sections except E, providing information in B about your spouse, a joint applicant or user, or the person on whose alimony, support, or maintenance payments or income or assets you are relying. If the requested credit is to be secured, also complete Section E.

If you intend to apply for joint credit, please initial here. ________ Applicant ________ Co-Applicant

Amount Requested $ ________ Payment Date Desired ________ Proceeds of Credit To be Used For ________

SECTION A—INFORMATION REGARDING APPLICANT

Full Name (Last, First, Middle): ________ Birthdate: / /

Present Street Address: ________ Years there: ____

City: ________ State: ________ Zip: ________ Telephone: ________

Social Security No.: ________ Driver's License No.: ________

Previous Street Address: ________ Years there: ____

City: ________ State: ________ Zip: ________

Present Employer: ________ Years there: ________ Telephone: ________

Position or title: ________ Name of supervisor: ________

Employer's Address: ________

Previous Employer: ________ Years there: ____

Previous Employer's Address: ________

Present net salary or commission: $ ________ per ________ No. Dependents: ________ Ages: ________

Alimony, child support, or separate maintenance income need not be revealed if you do not wish to have it considered as a basis for repaying this obligation.

Alimony, child support, separate maintenance received under: court order ☐ written agreement ☐ oral understanding ☐

Other income: $ ________ per ________ Source(s) of other income: ________

Is any income listed in this Section likely to be reduced in the next two years or before the credit requested is paid off?
☐ Yes (Explain in detail on a separate sheet.) No☐

Have you ever received credit from us? ________ When? ________ Office: ________

Checking Account No.: ________ Institution and Branch: ________

Savings Account No.: ________ Institution and Branch: ________

Name of nearest relative not living with you: ________ Telephone: ________

Relationship: ________ Address: ________

SECTION B—INFORMATION REGARDING SPOUSE, JOINT APPLICANT, USER, OR OTHER PARTY (Use separate sheets if necessary.)

Full Name (Last, First, Middle): ________ Birthdate: / /

Relationship to Applicant (if any): ________

Present Street Address: ________ Years there: ____

City: ________ State: ________ Zip: ________ Telephone: ________

Social Security No.: ________ Driver's License No.: ________

Present Employer: ________ Years there: ________ Telephone: ________

Position or title: ________ Name of supervisor: ________

Employer's Address: ________

Previous Employer: ________ Years there: ____

Previous Employer's Address: ________

Present net salary or commission: $ ________ per ________ No. Dependents: ________ Ages: ________

Alimony, child support, or separate maintenance income need not be revealed if you do not wish to have it considered as a basis for repaying this obligation.

Alimony, child support, separate maintenance received under: court order ☐ written agreement ☐ oral understanding ☐

Other income: $ ________ per ________ Source(s) of other income: ________

Is any income listed in this Section likely to be reduced in the next two years or before the credit requested is paid off?
☐ Yes (Explain in detail on a separate sheet.) No☐

Checking Account No.: ________ Institution and Branch: ________

Savings Account No.: ________ Institution and Branch: ________

Name of nearest relative not living with Spouse, Joint Applicant, User, or Other Party: ________ Telephone: ________

Relationship: ________ Address: ________

[Community property]

SECTION C—MARITAL STATUS

Applicant: ☐ Married ☐ Separated ☐ Unmarried (including single, divorced, and widowed)
Other Party: ☐ Married ☐ Separated ☐ Unmarried (including single, divorced, and widowed)

SECTION D— ASSET AND DEBT INFORMATION (If Section B has been completed, this Section should be completed giving information about both the Applicant and Spouse, Joint Applicant, User, or Other Person. Please mark Applicant-related information with an "A." If Section B was not completed, only give information about the Applicant in this Section.)

ASSETS OWNED (use separate sheet if necessary.)

Description of Assets	Value	Subject to Debt? Yes/No	Name(s) of Owner(s)
Cash	$		
Automobiles (Make, Model, Year)			
Cash Value of Life Insurance (Issuer, Face Value)			
Real Estate (Location, Date Acquired)			
Marketable Securities (Issuer, Type, No. of Shares)			
Other (List)			
Total Assets	$		

OUTSTANDING DEBTS (Include charge accounts, installment contracts, credit cards, rent, mortgages, etc. Use separate sheet if necessary.)

Creditor	Type of Debt or Acct. No.	Name in Which Acct. Carried	Original Debt	Present Balance	Monthly Payments	Past Due? Yes/No
1. (Landlord or Mortgage Holder)	☐ Rent Payment ☐ Mortgage		$ (Omit rent)	$ (Omit rent)	$	
2.						
3.						
Total Debts			$	$	$	

(Credit References) Date Paid

1.

2.

Are you a co-maker, endorser, or guarantor on any loan or contract? Yes ☐ No ☐ If "yes" for whom? To whom?

Are there any unsatisfied judgments against you? Yes ☐ No ☐ Amount $ If "yes" to whom owed?

Have you been declared bankrupt in the last 14 years? Yes ☐ No ☐ If "yes" where? Year

Other Obligations—(E.g., liability to pay alimony, child support, separate maintenance. Use separate sheet if necessary.)

SECTION E—SECURED CREDIT (Complete only if credit is to be secured.) Briefly describe the property to be given as security.

and list names and addresses of all co-owners of the property:

Name Address

Everything that I have stated in this application is correct to the best of my knowledge. I understand that you will retain this application whether or not it is approved. You are authorized to check my credit and employment history and to answer questions about your credit experience with me.

Applicant's Signature Date Other Signature (Where Applicable) Date

Uniform Residential Loan Application

This application is designed to be completed by the applicant(s) with the Lender's assistance. Applicants should complete this form as "Borrower" or "Co-Borrower," as applicable. Co-Borrower information must also be provided (and the appropriate box checked) when ☐ the income or assets of a person other than the "Borrower" (including the Borrower's spouse) will be used as a basis for loan qualification or ☐ the income or assets of the Borrower's spouse will not be used as a basis for loan qualification, but his or her liabilities must be considered because the Borrower resides in a community property state, the security property is located in a community property state, or the Borrower is relying on other property located in a community property state as a basis for repayment of the loan.

I. TYPE OF MORTGAGE AND TERMS OF LOAN

Mortgage Applied for: ☐ VA ☐ FHA	☐ Conventional ☐ USDA/Rural Housing Service	☐ Other (explain):	Agency Case Number	Lender Case Number
Amount $	Interest Rate %	No. of Months	Amortization Type: ☐ Fixed Rate ☐ GPM	☐ Other (explain): ☐ ARM (type):

II. PROPERTY INFORMATION AND PURPOSE OF LOAN

Subject Property Address (street, city, state, & ZIP) | No. of Units

Legal Description of Subject Property (attach description if necessary) | Year Built

Purpose of Loan ☐ Purchase ☐ Construction ☐ Other (explain): ☐ Refinance ☐ Construction-Permanent | Property will be: ☐ Primary Residence ☐ Secondary Residence ☐ Investment

Complete this line if construction or construction-permanent loan.

Year Lot Acquired	Original Cost	Amount Existing Liens	(a) Present Value of Lot	(b) Cost of Improvements	Total (a + b)
	$	$	$	$	$

Complete this line if this is a refinance loan.

Year Acquired	Original Cost	Amount Existing Liens	Purpose of Refinance	Describe Improvements ☐ made ☐ to be made
	$	$		Cost: $

Title will be held in what Name(s) | Manner in which Title will be held | Estate will be held in: ☐ Fee Simple ☐ Leasehold (show expiration date)

Source of Down Payment, Settlement Charges and/or Subordinate Financing (explain)

Borrower — III. BORROWER INFORMATION — Co-Borrower

Borrower	Co-Borrower
Borrower's Name (include Jr. or Sr. if applicable)	Co-Borrower's Name (include Jr. or Sr. if applicable)
Social Security Number / Home Phone (incl. area code) / DOB (MM/DD/YYYY) / Yrs. School	Social Security Number / Home Phone (incl. area code) / DOB (MM/DD/YYYY) / Yrs. School
☐ Married ☐ Unmarried (include single, divorced, widowed) ☐ Separated / Dependents (not listed by Co-Borrower) no. ages	☐ Married ☐ Unmarried (include single, divorced, widowed) ☐ Separated / Dependents (not listed by Borrower) no. ages
Present Address (street, city, state, ZIP) ☐ Own ☐ Rent _____ No. Yrs.	Present Address (street, city, state, ZIP) ☐ Own ☐ Rent _____ No. Yrs.
Mailing Address, if different from Present Address	Mailing Address, if different from Present Address

If residing at present address for less than two years, complete the following:

Borrower	Co-Borrower
Former Address (street, city, state, ZIP) ☐ Own ☐ Rent _____ No. Yrs.	Former Address (street, city, state, ZIP) ☐ Own ☐ Rent _____ No. Yrs.

Borrower — IV. EMPLOYMENT INFORMATION — Co-Borrower

Borrower	Co-Borrower
Name & Address of Employer ☐ Self Employed / Yrs. on this job / Yrs. employed in this line of work/profession	Name & Address of Employer ☐ Self Employed / Yrs. on this job / Yrs. employed in this line of work/profession
Position/Title/Type of Business / Business Phone (incl. area code)	Position/Title/Type of Business / Business Phone (incl. area code)

If employed in current position for less than two years or if currently employed in more than one position, complete the following:

Borrower	Co-Borrower
Name & Address of Employer ☐ Self Employed / Dates (from – to) / Monthly Income $	Name & Address of Employer ☐ Self Employed / Dates (from – to) / Monthly Income $
Position/Title/Type of Business / Business Phone (incl. area code)	Position/Title/Type of Business / Business Phone (incl. area code)
Name & Address of Employer ☐ Self Employed / Dates (from – to) / Monthly Income $	Name & Address of Employer ☐ Self Employed / Dates (from – to) / Monthly Income $
Position/Title/Type of Business / Business Phone (incl. area code)	Position/Title/Type of Business / Business Phone (incl. area code)

Freddie Mac Form 65 01/04 Page 1 of 4 Fannie Mae Form 1003 01/04

V. MONTHLY INCOME AND COMBINED HOUSING EXPENSE INFORMATION

Gross Monthly Income	Borrower	Co-Borrower	Total	Combined Monthly Housing Expense	Present	Proposed
Base Empl. Income*	$	$	$	Rent	$	
Overtime				First Mortgage (P&I)		$
Bonuses				Other Financing (P&I)		
Commissions				Hazard Insurance		
Dividends/Interest				Real Estate Taxes		
Net Rental Income				Mortgage Insurance		
Other (before completing, see the notice in "describe other income," below)				Homeowner Assn. Dues		
				Other:		
Total	$	$	$	Total	$	$

* Self Employed Borrower(s) may be required to provide additional documentation such as tax returns and financial statements.

Describe Other Income **Notice:** Alimony, child support, or separate maintenance income need not be revealed if the Borrower (B) or Co-Borrower (C) does not choose to have it considered for repaying this loan.

B/C		Monthly Amount
		$

VI. ASSETS AND LIABILITIES

This Statement and any applicable supporting schedules may be completed jointly by both married and unmarried Co-Borrowers if their assets and liabilities are sufficiently joined so that the Statement can be meaningfully and fairly presented on a combined basis; otherwise, separate Statements and Schedules are required. If the Co-Borrower section was completed about a spouse, this Statement and supporting schedules must be completed about that spouse also.

Completed ☐ Jointly ☐ Not Jointly

ASSETS Description	Cash or Market Value
Cash deposit toward purchase held by:	$
List checking and savings accounts below	
Name and address of Bank, S&L, or Credit Union	
Acct. no.	$
Name and address of Bank, S&L, or Credit Union	
Acct. no.	$
Name and address of Bank, S&L, or Credit Union	
Acct. no.	$
Name and address of Bank, S&L, or Credit Union	
Acct. no.	$
Stocks & Bonds (Company name/number & description)	$
Life insurance net cash value	$
Face amount: $	
Subtotal Liquid Assets	$
Real estate owned (enter market value from schedule of real estate owned)	$
Vested interest in retirement fund	$
Net worth of business(es) owned (attach financial statement)	$
Automobiles owned (make and year)	$
Other Assets (itemize)	$
Total Assets a.	$

Liabilities and Pledged Assets. List the creditor's name, address and account number for all outstanding debts, including automobile loans, revolving charge accounts, real estate loans, alimony, child support, stock pledges, etc. Use continuation sheet, if necessary. Indicate by (*) those liabilities which will be satisfied upon sale of real estate owned or upon refinancing of the subject property.

LIABILITIES	Monthly Payment & Months Left to Pay	Unpaid Balance
Name and address of Company Acct. no.	$ Payment/Months	$
Name and address of Company Acct. no.	$ Payment/Months	$
Name and address of Company Acct. no.	$ Payment/Months	$
Name and address of Company Acct. no.	$ Payment/Months	$
Name and address of Company Acct. no.	$ Payment/Months	$
Name and address of Company Acct. no.	$ Payment/Months	$
Name and address of Company Acct. no.	$ Payment/Months	$
Alimony/Child Support/Separate Maintenance Payments Owed to:	$	
Job-Related Expense (child care, union dues, etc.)	$	
Total Monthly Payments	$	
Net Worth (a minus b) ➧ $	Total Liabilities b.	$

VI. ASSETS AND LIABILITIES (cont.)

Schedule of Real Estate Owned (If additional properties are owned, use continuation sheet.)

Property Address (enter S if sold, PS if pending sale or R if rental being held for income)	Type of Property	Present Market Value	Amount of Mortgages & Liens	Gross Rental Income	Mortgage Payments	Insurance, Maintenance, Taxes & Misc.	Net Rental Income
		$	$	$	$	$	$
	Totals	$	$	$	$	$	$

List any additional names under which credit has previously been received and indicate appropriate creditor name(s) and account number(s):

Alternate Name	Creditor Name	Account Number

VII. DETAILS OF TRANSACTION

a. Purchase price	$
b. Alterations, improvements, repairs	
c. Land (if acquired separately)	
d. Refinance (incl. debts to be paid off)	
e. Estimated prepaid items	
f. Estimated closing costs	
g. PMI, MIP, Funding Fee	
h. Discount (if Borrower will pay)	
i. **Total costs (add items a through h)**	
j. Subordinate financing	
k. Borrower's closing costs paid by Seller	
l. Other Credits (explain)	
m. Loan amount (exclude PMI, MIP, Funding Fee financed)	
n. PMI, MIP, Funding Fee financed	
o. Loan amount (add m & n)	
p. Cash from/to Borrower (subtract j, k, l & o from i)	

VIII. DECLARATIONS

If you answer "Yes" to any questions a through i, please use continuation sheet for explanation.	Borrower Yes	Borrower No	Co-Borrower Yes	Co-Borrower No
a. Are there any outstanding judgments against you?	☐	☐	☐	☐
b. Have you been declared bankrupt within the past 7 years?	☐	☐	☐	☐
c. Have you had property foreclosed upon or given title or deed in lieu thereof in the last 7 years?	☐	☐	☐	☐
d. Are you a party to a lawsuit?	☐	☐	☐	☐
e. Have you directly or indirectly been obligated on any loan which resulted in foreclosure, transfer of title in lieu of foreclosure, or judgment? (This would include such loans as home mortgage loans, SBA loans, home improvement loans, educational loans, manufactured (mobile) home loans, any mortgage, financial obligation, bond, or loan guarantee. If "Yes," provide details, including date, name and address of Lender, FHA or VA case number, if any, and reasons for the action.)	☐	☐	☐	☐
f. Are you presently delinquent or in default on any Federal debt or any other loan, mortgage, financial obligation, bond, or loan guarantee? If "Yes," give details as described in the preceding question.	☐	☐	☐	☐
g. Are you obligated to pay alimony, child support, or separate maintenance?	☐	☐	☐	☐
h. Is any part of the down payment borrowed?	☐	☐	☐	☐
i. Are you a co-maker or endorser on a note?	☐	☐	☐	☐
j. Are you a U.S. citizen?	☐	☐	☐	☐
k. Are you a permanent resident alien?	☐	☐	☐	☐
l. **Do you intend to occupy the property as your primary residence?** If "Yes," complete question m below.	☐	☐	☐	☐
m. Have you had an ownership interest in a property in the last three years?	☐	☐	☐	☐
(1) What type of property did you own—principal residence (PR), second home (SH), or investment property (IP)?				
(2) How did you hold title to the home—solely by yourself (S), jointly with your spouse (SP), or jointly with another person (O)?				

IX. ACKNOWLEDGMENT AND AGREEMENT

Each of the undersigned specifically represents to Lender and to Lender's actual or potential agents, brokers, processors, attorneys, insurers, servicers, successors and assigns and agrees and acknowledges that: (1) the information provided in this application is true and correct as of the date set forth opposite my signature and that any intentional or negligent misrepresentation of this information contained in this application may result in civil liability, including monetary damages, to any person who may suffer any loss due to reliance upon any misrepresentation that I have made on this application, and/or in criminal penalties including, but not limited to, fine or imprisonment or both under the provisions of Title 18, United States Code, Sec. 1001, et seq.; (2) the loan requested pursuant to this application (the "Loan") will be secured by a mortgage or deed of trust on the property described herein; (3) the property will not be used for any illegal or prohibited purpose or use; (4) all statements made in this application are made for the purpose of obtaining a residential mortgage loan; (5) the property will be occupied as indicated herein; (6) any owner or servicer of the Loan may verify or reverify any information contained in the application from any source named in this application, and Lender, its successors or assigns may retain the original and/or an electronic record of this application, even if the Loan is not approved; (7) the Lender and its agents, brokers, insurers, servicers, successors and assigns may continuously rely on the information contained in the application, and I am obligated to amend and/or supplement the information provided in this application if any of the material facts that I have represented herein should change prior to closing of the Loan; (8) in the event that my payments on the Loan become delinquent, the owner or servicer of the Loan may, in addition to any other rights and remedies that it may have relating to such delinquency, report my name and account information to one or more consumer credit reporting agencies; (9) ownership of the Loan and/or administration of the Loan account may be transferred with such notice as may be required by law; (10) neither Lender nor its agents, brokers, insurers, servicers, successors or assigns has made any representation or warranty, express or implied, to me regarding the property or the condition or value of the property; and (11) my transmission of this application as an "electronic record" containing my "electronic signature," as those terms are defined in applicable federal and/or state laws (excluding audio and video recordings), or my facsimile transmission of this application containing a facsimile of my signature, shall be as effective, enforceable and valid as if a paper version of this application were delivered containing my original written signature.

Borrower's Signature	Date	Co-Borrower's Signature	Date
X		X	

X. INFORMATION FOR GOVERNMENT MONITORING PURPOSES

The following information is requested by the Federal Government for certain types of loans related to a dwelling in order to monitor the lender's compliance with equal credit opportunity, fair housing and home mortgage disclosure laws. You are not required to furnish this information, but are encouraged to do so. The law provides that a lender may discriminate neither on the basis of this information, nor on whether you choose to furnish it. If you furnish the information, please provide both ethnicity and race. For race, you may check more than one designation. If you do not furnish ethnicity, race, or sex, under Federal regulations, this lender is required to note the information on the basis of visual observation or surname. If you do not wish to furnish the information, please check the box below. (Lender must review the above material to assure that the disclosures satisfy all requirements to which the lender is subject under applicable state law for the particular type of loan applied for.)

BORROWER	☐ I do not wish to furnish this information.	**CO-BORROWER**	☐ I do not wish to furnish this information.
Ethnicity:	☐ Hispanic or Latino ☐ Not Hispanic or Latino	**Ethnicity:**	☐ Hispanic or Latino ☐ Not Hispanic or Latino
Race:	☐ American Indian or Alaska Native ☐ Asian ☐ Black or African American ☐ Native Hawaiian or Other Pacific Islander ☐ White	**Race:**	☐ American Indian or Alaska Native ☐ Asian ☐ Black or African American ☐ Native Hawaiian or Other Pacific Islander ☐ White
Sex:	☐ Female ☐ Male	**Sex:**	☐ Female ☐ Male

To be Completed by Interviewer	Interviewer's Name (print or type)	Name and Address of Interviewer's Employer
This application was taken by:	Interviewer's Signature / Date	
☐ Face-to-face interview ☐ Mail ☐ Telephone ☐ Internet	Interviewer's Phone Number (incl. area code)	

Freddie Mac Form 65 01/04 Page 3 of 4 Fannie Mae Form 1003 01/04

Continuation Sheet/Residential Loan Application

Use this continuation sheet if you need more space to complete the Residential Loan Application. Mark B for Borrower or C for Co-Borrower.	Borrower:	Agency Case Number:
	Co-Borrower:	Lender Case Number:

I/We fully understand that it is a Federal crime punishable by fine or imprisonment, or both, to knowingly make any false statements concerning any of the above facts as applicable under the provisions of Title 18, United States Code, Section 1001, et seq.

Borrower's Signature	Date	Co-Borrower's Signature	Date
X		X	

Freddie Mac Form 65 01/04 Page 4 of 4 Fannie Mae Form 1003 01/04

Appendix C to Part 202—Sample Notification Forms

1. This appendix contains ten sample notification forms. Forms C–1 through C–4 are intended for use in notifying an applicant that adverse action has been taken on an application or account under § 202.9(a)(1) and (2)(i) of this regulation. Form C–5 is a notice of disclosure of the right to request specific reasons for adverse action under § § 202.9(a)(1) and (2)(ii). Form C–6 is designed for use in notifying an applicant, under § 202.9(c)(2), that an application is incomplete. Forms C–7 and C–8 are intended for use in connection with applications for business credit under § 202.9(a)(3). Form C–9 is designed for use in notifying an applicant of the right to receive a copy of an appraisal under § 202.14. Form C–10 is designed for use in notifying an applicant for nonmortgage credit that the creditor is requesting applicant characteristic information.

2. Form C–1 contains the Fair Credit Reporting Act disclosure as required by sections 615(a) and (b) of that act. Forms C–2 through C–5 contain only the section 615(a) disclosure (that a creditor obtained information from a consumer reporting agency that played a part in the credit decision). A creditor must provide the 615(a) disclosure when adverse action is taken against a consumer based on information from a consumer reporting agency. A creditor must provide the section 615(b) disclosure when adverse action is taken based on information from an outside source other than a consumer reporting agency. In addition, a creditor must provide the section 615(b) disclosure if the creditor obtained information from an affiliate other than information in a consumer report or other than information concerning the affiliate's own transactions or experiences with the consumer. Creditors may comply with the disclosure requirements for adverse action based on information in a consumer report obtained from an affiliate by providing *either* the section 615(a) or section 615(b) disclosure.

3. The sample forms are illustrative and may not be appropriate for all creditors. They were designed to include some of the factors that creditors most commonly consider. If a creditor chooses to use the checklist of reasons provided in one of the sample forms in this appendix and if reasons commonly used by the creditor are not provided on the form, the creditor should modify the checklist by substituting or adding other reasons. For example, if "inadequate down payment" or "no deposit relationship with us" are common reasons for taking adverse action on an application, the creditor ought to add or substitute such reasons for those presently contained on the sample forms.

4. If the reasons listed on the forms are not the factors actually used, a creditor will not satisfy the notice requirement by simply checking the closest identifiable factor listed. For example, some creditors consider only references from banks or other depository institutions and disregard finance company references altogether; their statement of reasons should disclose "insufficient bank references," not "insufficient credit references." Similarly, a creditor that considers bank references and other credit references as distinct factors should treat the two factors separately and disclose them as appropriate. The creditor should either add such other factors to the form or check "other" and include the appropriate explanation. The creditor need not, however, describe how or why a factor

adversely affected the application. For example, the notice may say "length of residence" rather than "too short a period of residence."

5. A creditor may design its own notification forms or use all or a portion of the forms contained in this appendix. Proper use of Forms C–1 through C–4 will satisfy the requirement of § 202.9(a)(2)(i). Proper use of Forms C–5 and C–6 constitutes full compliance with §§ 202.9(a)(2)(ii) and 202.9(c)(2), respectively. Proper use of Forms C–7 and C–8 will satisfy the requirements of § 202.9(a)(2)(i) and (ii), respectively, for applications for business credit. Proper use of Form C–9 will satisfy the requirements of § 202.14 of this part. Proper use of Form C–10 will satisfy the requirements of § 202.5(b)(1).

Form C-1—Sample Notice of Action Taken and Statement of Reasons

Statement of Credit Denial, Termination, or Change

Date: Applicant's Name: Applicant's Address:

Description of Account, Transaction, or Requested Credit:

Description of Action Taken:

Part I—Principal Reason(s) for Credit Denial, Termination, or Other Action Taken Concerning Credit.

This section must be completed in all instances.

____ Credit application incomplete

____ Insufficient number of credit references provided

____ Unacceptable type of credit references provided

____ Unable to verify credit references

____ Temporary or irregular employment

____ Unable to verify employment

____ Length of employment

____ Income insufficient for amount of credit requested

____ Excessive obligations in relation to income

____ Unable to verify income

____ Length of residence

___ Temporary residence

___ Unable to verify residence

___ No credit file

___ Limited credit experience

___ Poor credit performance with us

___ Delinquent past or present credit obligations with others

___ Collection action or judgment

___ Garnishment or attachment

___ Foreclosure or repossession

___ Bankruptcy

___ Number of recent inquiries on credit bureau report

___ Value or type of collateral not sufficient

___ Other, specify: ___

Part II—Disclosure of Use of Information Obtained From an Outside Source

This section should be completed if the credit decision was based in whole or in part on information that has been obtained from an outside source.

___ Our credit decision was based in whole or in part on information obtained in a report from the consumer reporting agency listed below. You have a right under the Fair Credit Reporting Act to know the information contained in your credit file at the consumer reporting agency. The reporting agency played no part in our decision and is unable to supply specific reasons why we have denied credit to you. You also have a right to a free copy of your report from the reporting agency, if you request it no later than 60 days after you receive this notice. In addition, if you find that any information contained in the report you receive is inaccurate or incomplete, you have the right to dispute the matter with the reporting agency.

Name: Address: [Toll-free] Telephone number:

___ Our credit decision was based in whole or in part on information obtained from an affiliate or from an outside source other than a consumer reporting agency. Under the Fair Credit Reporting Act, you have the right to make a written request, no later than 60 days after you receive this notice, for disclosure of the nature of this information.

If you have any questions regarding this notice, you should contact:

Creditor's name: Creditor's address: Creditor's telephone number:

Notice: The federal Equal Credit Opportunity Act prohibits creditors from discriminating against credit applicants on the basis of race, color, religion, national origin, sex, marital status, age (provided the applicant has the capacity to enter into a binding contract); because all or part of the applicant's income derives from any public assistance program; or because the applicant has in good faith exercised any right under the Consumer Credit Protection Act. The federal agency that administers compliance with this law concerning this creditor is (name and address as specified by the appropriate agency listed in Appendix A).

Form C-2—Sample Notice of Action Taken and Statement of Reasons

Date

Dear Applicant: Thank you for your recent application. Your request for [a loan/a credit card/an increase in your credit limit] was carefully considered, and we regret that we are unable to approve your application at this time, for the following reason(s):

Your Income:

____ is below our minimum requirement.

____ is insufficient to sustain payments on the amount of credit requested.

____ could not be verified.

Your Employment:

____ is not of sufficient length to qualify.

____ could not be verified.

Your Credit History:

____ of making payments on time was not satisfactory.

____ could not be verified.

Your Application:

____ lacks a sufficient number of credit references.

____ lacks acceptable types of credit references.

____ reveals that current obligations are excessive in relation to income.

Other:

The consumer reporting agency contacted that provided information that influenced our decision in whole or in part was [name, address and [toll-free] telephone number of the reporting agency]. The reporting agency played no part in our decision is unable to supply specific reasons why we have denied credit to you. You have a right under the Fair Credit Reporting Act to know the information contained in your credit file at the consumer reporting agency. You also have a right to a free copy of your report from the reporting agency, if you request it no later than 60 days after you receive this notice. In addition, if you find that any information contained in the report you receive is inaccurate or incomplete, you have the right to dispute the matter with the reporting agency. Any questions regarding such information should be directed to [consumer reporting agency]. If you have any questions regarding this letter, you should contact us at [creditor's name, address and telephone number].

Notice: The federal Equal Credit Opportunity Act prohibits creditors from discriminating against credit applicants on the basis of race, color, religion, national origin, sex, marital status, age (provided the applicant has the capacity to enter into a binding contract); because all or part of the applicant's income derives from any public assistance program; or because the applicant has in good faith exercised any right under the Consumer Credit Protection Act. The federal agency that administers compliance with this law concerning this creditor is (name and address as specified by the appropriate agency listed in Appendix A).

Form C-3—Sample Notice of Action Taken and Statement of Reasons (Credit Scoring)

Date

Dear Applicant: Thank you for your recent application for ____. We regret that we are unable to approve your request.

Your application was processed by a credit scoring system that assigns a numerical value to the various items of information we consider in evaluating an application. These numerical values are based upon the results of analyses of repayment histories of large numbers of customers.

The information you provided in your application did not score a sufficient number of points for approval of the application. The reasons why you did not score well compared to other applicants were:

- Insufficient bank references
- Type of occupation
- Insufficient credit experience
- Number of recent inquiries on credit bureau report

In evaluating your application the consumer reporting agency listed below provided us with information that in whole or in part influenced our decision. The consumer reporting agency played no part in our decision and is unable to supply specific reasons why we have denied credit to you. You have a right under the Fair Credit Reporting Act to know the information contained in your credit file at the consumer reporting agency. It can be obtained by contacting: [name, address, and [toll-free] telephone number of the consumer reporting agency]. You also have a right to a free copy of your report from the reporting agency, if you request it no later than 60 days after you receive this notice. In addition, if you find that any information contained in the report you receive is inaccurate or incomplete, you have the right to dispute the matter with the reporting agency.

If you have any questions regarding this letter, you should contact us at

Creditor's Name:

Address:

Telephone:

Sincerely,

Notice: The federal Equal Credit Opportunity Act prohibits creditors from discriminating against credit applicants on the basis of race, color, religion, national origin, sex, marital status, age (with certain limited exceptions); because all or part of the applicant's income derives from any public assistance program; or because the applicant has in good faith exercised any right under the Consumer Credit Protection Act. The federal agency that administers compliance with this law concerning this creditor is (name and address as specified by the appropriate agency listed in appendix A).

Form C-4—Sample Notice of Action Taken, Statement of Reasons and Counteroffer

Date

Dear Applicant: Thank you for your application for ____. We are unable to offer you credit on the terms that you requested for the following reason(s):

We can, however, offer you credit on the following terms: ____.

If this offer is acceptable to you, please notify us within [amount of time] at the following address: ____.

Our credit decision on your application was based in whole or in part on information obtained in a report from [name, address and [toll-free] telephone number of the consumer reporting agency]. You have a right under the Fair Credit Reporting Act to know the information contained in your credit file at the consumer reporting agency. The reporting agency played no part in our decision and is unable to supply specific reasons why we have denied credit to you. You also have a right to a free copy of your report from the reporting agency, if you request it no later than 60 days after you receive this notice. In addition, if you find that any information contained in the report you receive is inaccurate or incomplete, you have the right to dispute the matter with the reporting agency.

You should know that the federal Equal Credit Opportunity Act prohibits creditors, such as ourselves, from discriminating against credit applicants on the basis of their race, color, religion, national origin, sex, marital status, age, (provided the applicant has the capacity to enter into a binding contract), because they receive income from a public assistance program, or because they may have exercised their rights under the Consumer Credit Protection Act. If you believe there has been discrimination in handling your application you should contact the [name and address of the appropriate federal enforcement agency listed in Appendix A].

Sincerely,

Form C–5—Sample Disclosure of Right to Request Specific Reasons for Credit Denial

Date

Dear Applicant: Thank you for applying to us for ____.

After carefully reviewing your application, we are sorry to advise you that we cannot [open an account for you/grant a loan to you/increase your credit limit] at this time. If you would like a statement of specific reasons why your application was denied, please contact [our credit service manager] shown below within 60 days of the date of this letter. We will provide you with the statement of reasons within 30 days after receiving your request.

Creditor's Name

Address

Telephone Number

If we obtained information from a consumer reporting agency as part of our consideration of your application, its name, address, and [toll-free] telephone number is shown below. The reporting agency played no part in our decision and is unable to supply specific reasons why we have denied credit to you. [You have a right under the Fair Credit Reporting Act to know the information contained in your credit file at the consumer reporting agency.] You have a right to a free copy of your report from the reporting agency, if you request it no later than 60 days after you receive this notice. In addition, if you find that any information contained in the report you receive is inaccurate or incomplete, you have the right to dispute the matter with the reporting agency. You can find out about the information contained in your file (if one was used) by contacting:

Consumer reporting agency's name

Address

[Toll-free] Telephone number

Sincerely,

Notice: The federal Equal Credit Opportunity Act prohibits creditors from discriminating against credit applicants on the basis of race, color, religion, national origin, sex, marital status, age (provided the applicant has the capacity to enter into a binding contract); because all or part of the applicant's income derives from any public assistance program; or because the applicant has in good faith exercised any right under the Consumer Credit Protection Act. The federal agency that administers compliance with this law concerning this creditor is (name and address as specified by the appropriate agency listed in appendix A).

Form C-6—Sample Notice of Incomplete Application and Request for Additional Information

Creditor's name

Address

Telephone number

Date

Dear Applicant: Thank you for your application for credit. The following information is needed to make a decision on your application: ____

We need to receive this information by (date). If we do not receive it by that date, we will regrettably be unable to give further consideration to your credit request.

Sincerely,

Form C-7—Sample Notice of Action Taken and Statement of Reasons (Business Credit)

Creditor's name

Creditor's address

Date

Dear Applicant: Thank you for applying to us for credit. We have given your request careful consideration, and regret that we are unable to extend credit to you at this time for the following reasons:

(Insert appropriate reason, such as Value or type of collateral not sufficient; Lack of established earnings record; Slow or past due in trade or loan payments)

Sincerely,

Notice: The federal Equal Credit Opportunity Act prohibits creditors from discriminating against credit applicants on the basis of race, color, religion, national origin, sex, marital status, age (provided the applicant has the capacity to enter into a binding contract); because all or part of the applicant's income derives from any public assistance program; or because the applicant has in good faith exercised any right under the Consumer Credit Protection Act. The federal agency that administers compliance with this law concerning this creditor is (name and address as specified by the appropriate agency listed in appendix A).

Form C-8—Sample Disclosure of Right to Request Specific Reasons for Credit Denial Given at Time of Application (Business Credit)

Creditor's name

Creditor's address

If your application for business credit is denied, you have the right to a written statement of the specific reasons for the denial. To obtain the statement, please contact (name, address and telephone number of the person or office from which the statement of reasons can be obtained) within 60 days from the date you are notified of our decision. We will send you a written statement of reasons for the denial within 30 days of receiving your request for the statement.

Notice: The federal Equal Credit Opportunity Act prohibits creditors from discriminating against credit applicants on the basis of race, color, religion, national origin, sex, marital status, age (provided the applicant has the capacity to enter into a binding contract); because all or part of the applicant's income derives from any public assistance program; or because the applicant has in good faith exercised any right under the Consumer Credit Protection Act. The federal agency that administers compliance with this law concerning this creditor is (name and address as specified by the appropriate agency listed in appendix A).

Form C-9—Sample Disclosure of Right to Receive a Copy of an Appraisal

You have the right to a copy of the appraisal report used in connection with your application for credit. If you wish a copy, please write to us at the mailing address we have provided. We must hear from you no later than 90 days after we notify you about the action taken on your credit application or you withdraw your application.

[In your letter, give us the following information:]

Form C-10—Sample Disclosure About Voluntary Data Notation

We are requesting the following information to monitor our compliance with the federal Equal Credit Opportunity Act, which prohibits unlawful discrimination. You are not required to provide this information. We will not take this information (or your decision not to provide this information) into account in connection with your application or credit transaction. The law provides that a creditor may not discriminate based on this information, or based on whether or not you choose to provide it. [If you choose not to provide the information, we will note it by visual observation or surname].

Appendix D to Part 202—Issuance of Staff Interpretations

1. *Official Staff Interpretations.* Officials in the Board's Division of Consumer and Community Affairs are authorized to issue official staff interpretations of this regulation. These interpretations provide the protection afforded under section 706(e) of the Act. Except in unusual circumstances, such interpretations will not be issued separately but will be incorporated in an official commentary to the regulation, which will be amended periodically.

2. *Requests for Issuance of Official Staff Interpretations.* A request for an official staff interpretation should be in writing and addressed to the Director, Division of Consumer and Community Affairs, Board of Governors of the Federal Reserve System, Washington, DC 20551. The request should contain a complete statement of all relevant facts concerning the issue, including copies of all pertinent documents.

3. *Scope of Interpretations.* No staff interpretations will be issued approving creditors' forms or statements. This restriction does not apply to forms or statements whose use is required or sanctioned by a government agency.

APPENDIX II

TITLE 15—COMMERCE AND TRADE-AMENDMENT-DISCRIMINATION

Title 15, Chapter 41, Subchapter IV

§ 1691. Scope of prohibition

(a) *Activities constituting discrimination.* It shall be unlawful for any creditor to discriminate against any applicant, with respect to any aspect of a credit transaction—

(1) on the basis of race, color, religion, national origin, sex or marital status, or age (provided the applicant has the capacity to contract);

(2) because all or part of the applicant's income derives from any public assistance program; or

(3) because the applicant has in good faith exercised any right under this chapter.

(b) Activities not constituting discrimination. It shall not constitute discrimination for purposes of this subchapter for a creditor—

(1) to make an inquiry of marital status if such inquiry is for the purpose of ascertaining the creditor's rights and remedies applicable to the particular extension of credit and not to discriminate in a determination of credit-worthiness;

(2) to make an inquiry of the applicant's age or of whether the applicant's income derives from any public assistance program if such inquiry is for the purpose of determining the amount and probable continuance of income levels, credit history, or other pertinent element of credit-worthiness as provided in regulations of the Board;

(3) to use any empirically derived credit system which considers age if such system is demonstrably and statistically sound in accordance with regulations of the Board, except that in the operation of such system the age of an elderly applicant may not be assigned a negative factor or value; or

(4) to make an inquiry or to consider the age of an elderly applicant when the age of such applicant is to be used by the creditor in the extension of credit in favor of such applicant.

(c) *Additional activities not constituting discrimination.* It is not a violation of this section for a creditor to refuse to extend credit offered pursuant to—

(1) any credit assistance program expressly authorized by law for an economically disadvantaged class of persons;

(2) any credit assistance program administered by a nonprofit organization for its members or an economically disadvantaged class of persons; or

(3) any special purpose credit program offered by a profit-making organization to meet special social needs which meets standards prescribed in regulations by the Board;

if such refusal is required by or made pursuant to such program.

(d) Reason for adverse action; procedure applicable; "adverse action" defined.

(1) Within thirty days (or such longer reasonable time as specified in regulations of the Board for any class of credit transaction) after receipt of a completed application for credit, a creditor shall notify the applicant of its action on the application.

(2) Each applicant against whom adverse action is taken shall be entitled to a statement of reasons for such action from the creditor. A creditor satisfies this obligation by—

(A) providing statements of reasons in writing as a matter of course to applicants against whom adverse action is taken; or

(B) giving written notification of adverse action which discloses

(i) the applicant's right to a statement of reasons within thirty days after receipt by the creditor of a request made within sixty days after such notification, and

(ii) the identity of the person or office from which such statement may be obtained. Such statement may be given orally if the written notification advises the applicant of his right to have the statement of reasons confirmed in writing on written request.

(3) A statement of reasons meets the requirements of this section only if it contains the specific reasons for the adverse action taken.

(4) Where a creditor has been requested by a third party to make a specific extension of credit directly or indirectly to an applicant, the notification and statement of reasons required by this subsection may be made directly by such creditor, or indirectly through the third party, provided in either case that the identity of the creditor is disclosed.

(5) The requirements of paragraph (2), (3), or (4) may be satisfied by verbal statements or notifications in the case of any creditor who did not act on more than one hundred and fifty applications during the calendar year preceding the calendar year in which the adverse action is taken, as determined under regulations of the Board.

(6) For purposes of this subsection, the term "adverse action" means a denial or revocation of credit, a change in the terms of an existing credit arrangement, or a refusal to grant credit in substantially the amount or on substantially the terms requested. Such term does not include a refusal to extend additional credit under an existing credit arrangement where the applicant is delinquent or otherwise in default, or where such additional credit would exceed a previously established credit limit.

(e) *Appraisals; copies of reports to applicants; costs.* Each creditor shall promptly furnish an applicant, upon written request by the applicant made within a reasonable period of time of the application, a copy of the appraisal report used in connection with the applicant's application for a loan that is or would have been secured by a lien on residential real property. The creditor may require the applicant to reimburse the creditor for the cost of the appraisal.

CHAPTER 19

Skiptracing

A credit and collection manager is often faced with the task of locating a debtor who has left for parts unknown. Some skiptrace firms mislead creditors and promote their services by implying to the creditor that certain information is available to them which is unavailable to others. The creditor incorrectly speculates that the firm is either connected with someone in the social security department or the local utility company, or connected to some state agency which will provide information that is not available to the general public. Since neither may be the case, set forth here are the legal means known to many in the collection industry which enables the creditor to locate a debtor.

APPLICATION

A complete review of the credit application should be made before any skiptracing is done, including a review of credit references, prior addresses, and prior places of employment.

TELEPHONE DIRECTORY

Searching the telephone directory in the county in which the debtor was located is probably the quickest, cheapest, and most efficient method. Several websites provide directories of telephone numbers in all the states, and will locate an address if provided with the telephone number.

CRISSCROSS TELEPHONE DIRECTORY

Directories and websites are available which list telephone numbers by street address. With this type of directory, a call to neighbors in the building in which an individual formerly resided may provide information. Be careful to comply with the Fair Debt Collection Practices Act (*see* Chapter 15). Another type of crisscross directory and website provides a listing of all the telephone numbers in numerical order with an identifying address for each telephone number. If the debtor's telephone number is known, but the address is unknown, the address is available. Some databases provide listings of tenants in the same buildings, or addresses and telephone numbers of nearby residences.

Credit & Collection Tip: *Debt collectors and creditors should comply with the Fair Debt Collection Practices Act when contacting neighbors and follow the procedures for locating debtors prescribed by the Act.*

DATABASES

Many databases have been created for the direct marketing industry to target market the consumer. These databases contain the age, vehicle ownership, house ownership, credit information, buying habits, social security numbers, and other information on wide cross sections of from 75 million to 100 million residents of the United States. The databases of the major credit reporting agencies provide significant information about a prospective borrower or a delinquent debtor and hence are useful in locating people and collecting debts. Some provide programs to assist credit and collection managers. The credit reporting agencies require a "permissible purpose" to order a credit report (*see* Chapter 13), whereas a database providing public information does not require compliance with the Fair Credit Reporting Act. Our office uses four different databases plus three major credit reporting agencies.

The credit reporting agencies are principal purveyors of this information. Most databases are designed to service the creditor attempting to locate the debtor. The three major credit reporting agencies—Experian, Equifax, and TransUnion—all have extensive databases on millions of individuals, and can provide credit reports with detailed information for the creditor attempting to locate a debtor (or extending credit). The database provides valuable credit information from issuers of credit cards, such as banks, whether the individual is current or delinquent and the reason for canceling a credit card.

U.S. POSTAL SERVICE

A letter may be sent by certified mail or registered mail requesting that the Postal Service disclose the delivery address, if it is not the address on the envelope. This information is available for six months after the debtor moves and requests the Post Office to forward the mail to the new address. The letter must be marked "return receipt requested." To be sure that the debtor receives the letter, indicate "restrictive delivery." If the mail is to be forwarded, indicate "forward."

The Postal Service will provide the forwarding address of an individual to an attorney who seeks the information for purposes of instituting suit.

RETURNED MAIL

Mail that is returned to the sender as undeliverable may be marked with various wording which provides useful information.

1. "Refused" may indicate that the debtor is still at the address and the notation on the envelope is usually the handwriting of the mail carrier.
2. "Not there" usually indicates that the debtor is no longer at the address and is probably written by the mail carrier, although the debtor may have written the notation to mislead the creditor. The debtor may be accepting other mail.
3. "Moved, Left No Forwarding Address" means that the debtor has left for parts unknown. This is usually written by the mail carrier or affixed with a rubber stamp, but the mail is probably accumulating at the Post Office and not being picked up.
4. "Moved, Forwarding Expired," written by the mail carrier or an employee at the Post Office, means that when the debtor left, a forwarding address was provided but the retention of said forwarding address has expired. This is usually about six months, and the Postal Service does not forward mail after that time nor does it provide the new address if you request it.

Any other wording on the envelope, such as "not here" or "unknown" or "left," indicates that someone else wrote this on the envelope and returned it to the mail carrier. The party kind enough to write the message could know where the debtor is and some effort might be made to contact that party at the address to which the envelope was delivered. Sometimes cross directories can provide this information, especially if the address is a private or two-family house.

COURT RECORDS

Court records reveal judgments against the debtor, tax liens, and pending litigation. Sometimes these court proceedings may reveal new addresses or other information which may be helpful in locating the debtor. This information may be provided by service bureaus, which are local in nature. To identify these service bureaus, contact a clerk of the court, county clerk, or an attorney located in the state or county familiar with collection. Information is available from bankruptcy petitions, recorded deeds or mortgages, financing statements, and security agreements.

LANDLORD

To know the name of the landlord of the premises where the debtor lives or used to live is helpful. This address information is available from the county clerk or the register where deeds are recorded, or may be obtained from a title company or other local abstract company. An inquiry to an attorney should produce the organization providing this information. Once the name is obtained, an inquiry may be addressed to the landlord to provide information as to where the debtor has relocated. If he or she refuses to cooperate, after a judgment is entered against the debtor an information subpoena may be served on the landlord to provide information such as the name and address of the moving company which moved the debtor's property. A further inquiry to the moving company may produce positive results.

PROPERTY OWNERS

Some states have alphabetical listings of property owners showing the ownership of property statewide. Contact the title company. For those states that do not provide this information, the next best source is the local tax assessor. Verify ownership of property by using local tax assessors to furnish the block and lot of the property, and conduct a search to determine whether the debtor has mortgages, liens, etc. on the property. Service organizations also provide this service.

VOTER REGISTRATION

Usually, the county clerk can tell you where voter registration lists are maintained. The name, address, and telephone number of the registered voters are available.

MOTOR VEHICLE SEARCHES

In most states the Department of Motor Vehicles will furnish information at a cost of a few dollars if provided with a name. Contact the state motor vehicle bureau and obtain the proper form to determine what information must be furnished for a search. Service bureaus provide this type of retrieval service for law firms and financial institutions. Due to the concerns for the privacy of the individual, some states have passed laws which restrict access to this type of information.

LICENSED BUSINESS

If the debtor is a licensed business or the debtor has obtained a license to operate a profession or a business, information can be obtained from the state. Service companies such as plumbers, electricians, barbers, contractors, and home improvement firms all require licensing and information can be obtained from the proper agency. Professions such as attorneys, doctors, architects, accountants, and dentists also are on file with appropriate state agencies and trade associations. Insurance brokers, real estate brokers, and stockbrokers are licensed by the state or an administrative agency of the state or federal government. Searches can be made with the state agencies by furnishing a name and the agency will respond to Freedom of Information requests by furnishing the name and address of the particular debtor or business.

A wide range of businesses require licensing: restaurants and bars, liquor stores, taxi cab drivers, beauticians and barbers, as well as most service businesses involved in health care, care of animals, and the control of insects.

UNION MEMBERSHIPS

If the debtor is practicing a trade, a call to the trade union should provide information, at least as to whether the debtor is a dues-paying member. Any additional information is up to union policy and procedures, but sometimes the extra effort produces results.

SECRETARY OF STATE

All corporations must file with the secretary of state a certificate of incorporation, which provides an address where service of process may be served on the corporation. An inquiry to the state will provide the proper name and address of the corporation, and sometimes the name of the principal owner (who is listed as the person to receive process instead of an agent). The names and addresses of the principals of the corporation appear in the franchise tax returns filed, and usually can be obtained from the proper state office. Sometimes the incorporator of the corporation is a principal but more often the incorporator resigns immediately upon incorporation. Obtaining a copy of the certificate of incorporation will provide the name and address of the incorporators.

GOVERNMENTAL AGENCIES

Agencies such as the Securities and Exchange Commission, the Federal Communications Commission, the Civil Airlines Bureaus, and other types of agencies maintain records on businesses that are involved in their industry, and information may be obtained upon request.

MILITARY SERVICE

Contact can be made with the debtor in military service through one of the following:

- CNC Military Records Bureau, U.S. Marine Corp., Washington, D.C. 20380
- The Navy Locator Service #21, Naval Dept., Washington, D.C. 20350
- Commander U.S. Army Enlisted Records and Evaluation Center, Indianapolis, IN 46249
- Air Force World Wide Locator, Randolph Air Force Base, TX 78150

The best place to start is with the Army, since it has more personnel than the other service branches.

RECORDINGS

The County Clerk's office will indicate whether a debtor is doing business under his/her own name or a partnership name and will show the name and address of the debtor and the partners, as well as the name of the business.

BANKRUPTCY PETITIONS

If the debtor has filed bankruptcy, searching the records of the Bankruptcy Court where the debtor resides will provide information which may assist in locating the debtor. Sometimes relatives listed as creditors may be helpful; even other creditors may help, and may share information. Sometimes a review of the bankruptcy papers will indicate the home state of the debtor to which a debtor may return if financial difficulties are encountered. These documents are available even if the bankruptcy was dismissed.

CENTRAL OFFICE VITAL STATISTICS

This agency provides information as to births, deaths, marriages, divorces, and other special events.

BETTER BUSINESS BUREAU

If complaints have been made against the debtor, the Better Business Bureau will furnish information concerning the firm and the nature of the complaints against the business.

ESTATES

If a relative of the debtor has recently passed away and the estate has been probated, court records may provide information as to residence and also whether the particular debtor will be a beneficiary of any funds of the deceased relative. The probate records may also furnish the names of other relatives of the debtor. If the deceased owed the debtor any monies or the debtor is a beneficiary under the will, and judgment has been obtained against the debtor, consult with counsel since proceedings may be available to execute on any monies that may be paid to the debtor.

MORTGAGES

If a debtor has sold a house and has executed a purchase money mortgage in favor of the buyer, a call to the buyer might produce the address where the payment is being sent. (*See* Chapter 15 as to restrictions on this type of telephone communication.) Consult with counsel since proceedings may be available to attach the payments being made to the debtor if a judgment has been obtained.

CITY RECORDS

Sometimes information can be obtained from Water Department records, utility records, dog and fishing license records, Board of Education records, high school and college records, etc.

CREDIT REPORTING AGENCIES

Inquiry to Equifax, Experian, TransUnion, or Dun & Bradstreet will provide information as to credit inquiries, litigation, and background on businesses and individuals. Be sure you comply with the Fair Credit Reporting Act as to permissible purposes.

SOCIAL SECURITY NUMBER

The first three digits of the social security number indicate the state where it was obtained, which is usually the debtor's home state. Often a debtor returns to his/her family (home state), and efforts to locate the debtor should be targeted there. For more information, *see* Appendix to this chapter.

FORMER EMPLOYERS

If the application lists an employer, contacting the employer may provide the address where the last W-2 form was sent to the debtor. Sometimes a former employer even knows the debtor's new employer.

REMEDIES AFTER JUDGMENT

If the debtor leaves for parts unknown after a judgment is obtained, the number of tracing devices available increases substantially. One of the major devices is the use of the information subpoena, which can be served on a wide variety of third parties to obtain information about the debtor. It can be served on the telephone company, utilities, insurance companies, landlords, banks, security brokers, real estate brokers, and other third parties such as friends, relatives, accountants, and attorneys. The use of this device is limited only by the creativity of the attorney handling the collection case. In addition to this device, the attorney also has available the use of a subpoena to produce books and records which may be addressed not only to the debtor, if service can be effected upon the debtor, but also other third parties listed above. The use of the subpoena by the attorney is often successful. These legal tools are only available after a judgment is obtained and should be in the hands of an experienced collection attorney.

TELEPHONE SKIPTRACING

The use of the telephone by a creditor who is collecting his own debt often will produce better results. A vast difference exists between a creditor doing skiptracing and a debt collector. A debt collector must comply with the Fair Debt Collection Practices Act which sets forth several restrictions and requirements with regard to attempting to locate a debtor. The creditor is not bound by the FDCPA, but must conform to state and local laws and in some instances other federal laws. The creditor also must be certain that it has not become a debt collector by violating certain sections of the Fair Debt Collection Practices Act.

The conversation between a creditor and a third party, such as an employer, may develop as follows:

CR: May I please speak to John Smith?

3P: John Smith hasn't worked here for the past four months.

CR: Thank you very much. Good bye.

Or in the alternative:

CR: May I please speak to John Smith?

3P: John Smith hasn't worked here in four months.

CR: Do you know where he is working now or where he lives?

3P: No, I don't.

CR: Do you know anyone at the firm who would know where he lives or where he works because I do want to get in touch with him.

Contacting the new owner of a residential house or even a commercial property as follows:

CR: May I please speak to Mr. Smith?

3P: Mr. Smith is no longer here.

CR: This is the XYZ Corporation?

3P: No, this the ABC Corporation. We bought the building from the XYZ Corporation about three months ago.

CR: Do you know where XYZ moved?

3P: No, offhand I don't.

CR: Thank you very much.

Or in the alternative:

CR: Do you know where the XYZ Corporation moved?

3P: No, I do not.

CR: Well, did the XYZ Corporation finance your purchase by giving you a mortgage or extending you some kind of credit?

The XYZ Corporation may have taken back a purchase money mortgage at the time that the ABC Corporation purchased the building. ABC would be sending checks to the XYZ Corporation and would certainly know the location of the XYZ Corporation. The same principle would apply to a new owner of a residential home. The creditor also may be able to attach these payments after a judgment has been entered in court.

CHAPTER 19 APPENDIX I

SOCIAL SECURITY NUMBERS BY STATE

The location of where the debtor obtained a social security number (usually before the first job) is indicated in most instances by the first three numbers.

Note: The same areas, when shown more than once, means that certain numbers have been transferred from one state to another, or that an area has been divided for use among certain geographic locations.

New Hampshire	001-003	Idaho	518-519
Maine	004-007	Wyoming	520
Vermont	008-009	Delaware	221-222
Massachusetts	010-034	Virginia	223-231
Rhode Island	035-039	West Virginia	232-236
Connecticut	040-049	North Carolina	237-246
New York	050-134	South Carolina	247-251
New Jersey	135-258	Georgia	252-260
Pennsylvania	259-211	Florida	261-267
Maryland	212-220	Ohio	268-302
North Dakota	501-502	Indiana	303-317
South Dakota	503-504	Illinois	318-361
Nebraska	505-508	Michigan	362-389
Kansas	509-515	Wisconsin	390-399
Montana	516-517	Mississippi (also 587)	425-428

Arkansas	429-432	Washington	531-539
Louisiana	433-439	California	545-57
Colorado	521-524	Oklahoma	440-448
New Mexico (also 585)	525	Texas	449-467
Arizona	526-527	Minnesota	468-477
Utah	528-529	Iowa	478-485
Nevada	530	Missouri	486-500

Table of Cases

(References are to page numbers.)

A

B

C

E

F

H

I

K

L

M

N

O

P

R

S

T

U

V

W

Y

Z

Index

F

T

U